THE HOLY BIBLE

NKJV

NEW KING JAMES VERSION®

AMERICAN BIBLE SOCIETY
NEW YORK

The American Bible Society is a not-for-profit organization which publishes the Scriptures without doctrinal note or comment. Since 1816, its single mission is to make the Bible available to every person in a language and format each can understand and afford. Working toward this goal, the ABS is a member of the United Bible Societies, a worldwide effort that extends to more than 200 countries and territories. You are urged to read the Bible and to share it with others. For a free catalog of other Scripture publications, call the American Bible Society at 1-800-32BIBLE, or write to 1865 Broadway, New York, NY 10023-7505.

Visit the ABS website! **www.americanbible.org.**

ISBN 1-58516-045-8

Printed in the United States of America
Eng. Bible NKJV050-106341
ABS-12/03-50,000-905,000-MW(7)16

PREFACE

Purpose

In the Preface to the 1611 edition, the translators of the King James Version state that it was not their purpose "to make a new translation . . . but to make a good one better." Indebted to the earlier work of William Tyndale and others, they saw their best contribution to consist in revising and enhancing the excellence of the English versions which had sprung from the Reformation of the sixteenth century. In harmony with the purpose of the King James scholars, the translators and editors of the present work have not pursued a goal of innovation. They have perceived the Holy Bible, New King James Version, as a continuation of the labors of the earlier translators, thus unlocking for today's readers the spiritual treasures of the King James tradition.

A Living Legacy

For nearly four hundred years, and throughout several revisions, the King James Bible has been deeply revered among the English-speaking peoples of the world. The quality of translation for which it is historically renowned, and its majesty of style, have enabled that monumental version of the Word of God to make a unique contribution to the religion and language of the English-speaking world.

Although the Elizabethan period and our own era share in zeal for technical advance, the former period was more aggressively devoted to classical learning. Along with this awakened concern for the classics came a flourishing companion interest in the Scriptures as the inspired Word of God. The King James translators were committed to producing an English Bible that would be a precise translation, and by no means a paraphrase or a broadly approximate rendering. On the one hand, the scholars were fully familiar with the original languages of the Bible and were especially gifted in their use of their native English. On the other hand, their reverence for the divine Author and His Word assured a translation of the Scriptures in which only a principle of utmost accuracy could be accepted.

In 1786 the Catholic scholar, Alexander Geddes, said of the King James Bible, "If accuracy and strictest attention to the letter of the text be supposed to constitute an excellent version, this is of all versions the most excellent." George Bernard Shaw became a literary legend in our century because of his severe and often humorous criticisms of our most cherished values. Surprisingly, however, Shaw pays the following tribute to the scholars commissioned by King James: "The translation was extraordinarily well done because to the translators what they were translating was not merely a curious collection of ancient books written by different authors in different stages of culture, but the Word of God divinely revealed through His chosen and expressly inspired scribes. In this conviction they carried out their work with boundless reverence and care and achieved a beautifully artistic result." History agrees with these estimates. Therefore, while seeking to unveil the excellent form of the traditional English Bible, special care has also been taken in the present edition to preserve the work of *precision* which is the legacy of the 1611 translators.

Devotional Quality

The King James scholars readily appreciated the intrinsic beauty of divine revelation. They accordingly disciplined their talents to render well-chosen English words of their time, as well as a graceful, often musical arrangement of language, which has stirred the hearts of Bible readers through the years. The translators, the committees, and the editors of the present edition, while sensitive to the late twentieth-century English idiom, and while adhering faithfully to the Hebrew, Aramaic, and Greek texts, have sought to maintain that lyrical quality which is so highly regarded in the King James Version. This devotional quality is especially apparent in the poetic and prophetic books, although even the relatively plain style of the Gospels and Epistles cannot strictly be likened to modern newspaper style.

The Style

Students of the Bible applaud the timeless devotional character of our historic Bible. Yet it is also universally understood that our language, like all living languages, has undergone profound changes since 1611. Subsequent revisions of the King James Bible have sought to keep abreast of changes in English speech. The present work is a further step toward this objective. Where obsolescence and other reading difficulties exist, present-day vocabulary, punctuation, and grammar have been carefully integrated. Words representing ancient objects, such as *chariot* and *phylactery* have no modern substitutes and are therefore retained.

A special feature of the New King James Version is its conformity to the thought flow of the 1611 Bible. The reader discovers that the sequence and identity of words, phrases, and clauses of the new edition, while much clearer, are so close to the traditional that there is remarkable ease in listening to the reading of either edition while following with the other.

In the discipline of translating biblical and other ancient languages, a standard method of transliteration, that is, the English spelling of untranslated words, such as names of persons and places, has never been commonly adopted. In keeping with the design of the present work, the King James spelling of untranslated words is retained, although made uniform throughout. For example, instead of the spellings of *Isaiah* and *Elijah* in the Old Testament, and *Esaias* and *Elias* in the New Testament, *Isaiah* and *Elijah* now appear in both Testaments.

Standard doctrinal and theological terms used in the King James Version, such as *propitiation, justification,* and *sanctification,* have been retained, except where the original language indicates need for a more precise translation.

Readers of the King James Version will immediately be struck by the absence of several pronouns: *thee, thou,* and *ye* are replaced by the simple *you,* while *your* and *yours* are substituted for *thy* and *thine* as applicable. *Thee, thou, thy,* and *thine* were once forms of address to express a special relationship to human as well as divine persons. These pronouns are no longer part of our language. However, pronouns referring to God in the present work are capitalized. Capitalization of these pronouns benefits the reader by clearly distinguishing divine and human persons referred to in a passage. Without such capitalization the distinction may be obscure, because the antecedent of a pronoun is not always clear from the English.

In addition to the pronoun usages of the seventeenth century, the *-eth* and *-est* verb endings so familiar in the earlier King James editions are now obsolete. Unless a speaker is schooled in these verb endings, there is a common difficulty in selecting the correct form to be used with a given subject of the verb in vocal prayer. That is, should we use *love, loveth,* or *lovest? do, doeth, doest,* or *dost? have, hath,* or *hast?* Therefore, contemporary English usage has been substituted for the previous verb endings.

In older editions of the King James Version, the frequency of the connective *and* far exceeded the limits of present English usage. Also, biblical linguists agree that the Hebrew and Greek original words for this conjunction may commonly be translated otherwise, depending on the immediate context. Therefore, instead of *and,* alternatives such as *also, but, however, now, so, then,* and *thus* are accordingly rendered in the present edition, when the original language permits.

The real character of the King James Version does not reside in its archaic pronouns or verbs or other grammatical forms of the seventeenth century, but rather in the care taken by its scholars to impart the letter and spirit of the original text in a majestic and reverent style.

The Format

The format of the New King James Version is designed to enhance the vividness and devotional quality of the Holy Scriptures:

—Topical page headings assist the reader to identify topics and transitions in the biblical content.
—Words or phrases in *italics* indicate expressions in the original language which require clarification by additional English words.

—Indentions indicate the beginning of a paragraph.

—*Oblique type* in the New Testament indicates a quotation from the Old Testament.

—Poetry is structured as contemporary verse to reflect the poetic form and beauty of the passage in the original language.

—The covenant name of God was usually translated from the Hebrew as "LORD" (using capital letters as shown) in the King James Old Testament. This tradition is maintained. In the present edition the name is so capitalized whenever the covenant name is quoted in the New Testament from a passage in the Old Testament.

—Significant explanatory notes, alternate translations, textual variants and cross references, as well as New Testament citations of Old Testament passages, are supplied in footnotes.

The Old Testament Text

The Hebrew Bible has come down to us through the scrupulous care of ancient scribes who copied the original text in successive generations. By the sixth century A.D. the scribes were succeeded by a group known as the Masoretes, who continued to preserve the sacred Scriptures for another five hundred years in a form known as the Masoretic Text. Babylonia, Palestine, and Tiberias were the main centers of Masoretic activity; but by the tenth century A.D. the Masoretes of Tiberias, led by the family of ben Asher, gained the ascendancy. Through subsequent editions, the ben Asher text became in the twelfth century the only recognized form of the Hebrew Scriptures.

Daniel Bomberg printed the first Rabbinic Bible in 1516-17; that work was followed in 1524-25 by a second edition prepared by Jacob ben Chayyim and also published by Bomberg. The text of ben Chayyim was adopted in most subsequent Hebrew Bibles, including those used by the King James translators. The ben Chayyim text was also used for the first two editions of Rudolph Kittel's *Biblia Hebraica* of 1906 and 1912. In 1937 Paul Kahle published a third edition of *Biblia Hebraica*. This edition was based on the oldest dated manuscript of the ben Asher text, the Leningrad Manuscript B19a (A.D. 1008), which Kahle regarded as superior to that used by ben Chayyim.

For the New King James Version the text used was the 1967/1977 Stuttgart edition of *Biblia Hebraica*, with frequent comparisons being made with the Bomberg edition of 1524-25. The Septuagint (Greek) Version of the Old Testament and the Latin Vulgate were consulted. In addition to referring to a variety of ancient versions of the Hebrew Scriptures, the New King James Version also draws on the resources of relevant manuscripts from the Dead Sea caves. In the few places where the Hebrew is so obscure that the King James followed one of the versions, but where information is now available to resolve these problems, the New King James Version follows the Hebrew text.

The New Testament Text

There is more manuscript support for the New Testament than for any other body of ancient literature. Over five thousand Greek, eight thousand Latin, and many more manuscripts in other languages attest the integrity of the New Testament. There is only one basic New Testament used by Protestants, Roman Catholics, and Orthodox. Minor variations in hand copying have appeared through the centuries, before mechanical printing began about A.D. 1450.

Some variations exist in the spelling of Greek words, in word order, and in similar details. These ordinarily do not show up in translation and do not affect the sense of the text in any way.

Other manuscript differences, regarding the omission or inclusion of a word or a clause, as well as two paragraphs in the Gospels, should not overshadow the overwhelming degree of *agreement* which exists among the ancient records. Bible readers may be assured that the most important differences in the English New Testament of today are due, not to manuscript divergence, but to the way in which translators view the task of translation. The New King James Version follows the historic precedent of the King James Version in maintaining a literal approach to translation, except where the idiom of the original language occasionally cannot be translated directly into our tongue.

The King James New Testament was based on the traditional text of the Greek-speaking churches, first published in 1516, and later called the Textus Receptus or Received Text. Although based on relatively few available manuscripts, these were representative of many more which existed at the time but only became known later. Because the New King James Version is the fifth revision of this historic document translated from specific Greek texts, the editors decided to retain the traditional text in the body of the New Testament.

In closing, let readers be encouraged to approach the Bible "not as the word of men, but as it is in truth, the word of God, which also effectively works in you who believe" (1 Th 2.13). The same Holy Spirit who originated the Scriptures must also make them clear to the reader, for the truths they contain "are spiritually discerned" (1 Co 2.14). It is through the work of the Spirit of life that the Word of life accomplishes its purposes in human hearts and minds. May God teach us His life-giving truth as we submit to Him, that He alone may be glorified.

CONTENTS

OLD TESTAMENT

NEW TESTAMENT

ALPHABETICAL LIST OF
BIBLICAL BOOKS AND ABBREVIATIONS

NAME	ABBREV	PAGE	NAME	ABBREV	PAGE
Acts	Ac	1069	Judges	Jg	234
Amos	Am	899	1 Kings	1 K	326
1 Chronicles	1 Ch	391	2 Kings	2 K	359
2 Chronicles	2 Ch	420	Lamentations	Lm	805
Colossians	Col	1154	Leviticus	Lv	96
1 Corinthians	1 Co	1118	Luke	Lk	1003
2 Corinthians	2 Co	1132	Malachi	Ml	940
Daniel	Dn	867	Mark	Mk	980
Deuteronomy	Dt	171	Matthew	Mt	945
Ecclesiastes	Ec	649	Micah	Mic	911
Ephesians	Eph	1146	Nahum	Nh	918
Esther	Es	483	Nehemiah	Ne	467
Exodus	Ex	53	Numbers	Nu	127
Ezekiel	Ez	813	Obadiah	Ob	907
Ezra	Ezra	456	1 Peter	1 P	1188
Galatians	Ga	1141	2 Peter	2 P	1192
Genesis	Gn	1	Philemon	Phm	1172
Habakkuk	Hb	921	Philippians	Phil	1151
Haggai	Hg	928	Proverbs	Pr	616
Hebrews	He	1173	Psalms	Ps	526
Hosea	Ho	884	Revelation	Rev	1203
Isaiah	Is	666	Romans	Ro	1104
James	Jas	1184	Ruth	Ru	260
Jeremiah	Jr	737	1 Samuel	1 S	264
Job	Job	491	2 Samuel	2 S	297
Joel	Jl	894	Song of Solomon	Sgs	659
John	Jn	1041	1 Thessalonians	1 Th	1158
1 John	1 Jn	1195	2 Thessalonians	2 Th	1161
2 John	2 Jn	1199	1 Timothy	1 Ti	1163
3 John	3 Jn	1200	2 Timothy	2 Ti	1167
Jonah	Jon	909	Titus	Titus	1170
Joshua	Js	209	Zechariah	Zec	930
Jude	Jd	1201	Zephaniah	Zep	924

The
Old Testament

The First Book of Moses Called

GENESIS

The History of Creation

1 In the beginning God created the heavens and the earth. 2The earth was without form, and void; and darkness *was* on the face of the deep. And the Spirit of God was hovering over the face of the waters.

3Then God said, "Let there be light"; and there was light. 4And God saw the light, that *it was* good; and God divided the light from the darkness. 5God called the light Day, and the darkness He called Night. So the evening and the morning were the first day.

6Then God said, "Let there be a firmament in the midst of the waters, and let it divide the waters from the waters." 7Thus God made the firmament, and divided the waters which *were* under the firmament from the waters which *were* above the firmament; and it was so. 8And God called the firmament Heaven. So the evening and the morning were the second day.

9Then God said, "Let the waters under the heavens be gathered together into one place, and let the dry *land* appear"; and it was so. 10And God called the dry *land* Earth, and the gathering together of the waters He called Seas. And God saw that *it was* good.

11Then God said, "Let the earth bring forth grass, the herb *that* yields seed, *and* the fruit tree *that* yields fruit according to its kind, whose seed *is* in itself, on the earth"; and it was so. 12And the earth brought forth grass, the herb *that* yields seed according to its kind, and the tree *that* yields fruit, whose seed *is* in itself according to its kind. And God saw that *it was* good. 13So the evening and the morning were the third day.

14Then God said, "Let there be lights in the firmament of the heavens to divide the day from the night; and let them be for signs and seasons, and for days and years; 15and let them be for lights in the firmament of the heavens to give light on the earth"; and it was so. 16Then God made two great lights: the greater light to rule the day, and the lesser light to rule the night. *He made* the stars also. 17God set them in the firmament of the heavens to give light on the earth, 18and to rule over the day and over the night, and to divide the light from the darkness. And God saw that *it was* good. 19So the evening and the morning were the fourth day.

20Then God said, "Let the waters abound with an abundance of living creatures, and let birds fly above the earth across the face of the firmament of the heavens." 21So God created great sea creatures and every living thing that moves, with which the waters abounded, according to their kind, and every winged bird according to its kind. And God saw that *it was* good. 22And God blessed them, saying, "Be fruitful and multiply, and fill the waters in the seas, and let birds multiply on the earth." 23So the evening and the morning were the fifth day.

24Then God said, "Let the earth bring forth the living creature according to its kind: cattle and creeping thing and beast of the earth, *each* according to its kind"; and it was so. 25And God made the beast of the earth according to its kind, cattle according to its kind, and everything that creeps on the earth according to its kind. And God saw that *it was* good.

26Then God said, "Let Us make man in Our image, according to Our likeness; let them have dominion over the fish of the sea, over the birds of the air, and over the cattle, over all the earth and over every creeping thing that creeps on the earth." 27So God created man in His *own* image; in the image of God He created him; male and female He created them. 28Then God blessed them, and God said to them, "Be fruitful and multiply; fill the earth and subdue it; have dominion over the fish of the sea, over the birds of the air, and over every living thing that moves on the earth."

29And God said, "See, I have given you every herb *that* yields seed which *is* on the face of all the earth, and every tree whose fruit yields seed; to you it shall be for food. 30Also, to every beast of the earth, to every bird of the air, and to everything that creeps on the earth, in which *there is* life, *I have given* every green herb for food"; and it was so. 31Then God saw everything that He had made, and indeed *it was* very good. So the evening and the morning were the sixth day.

2 Thus the heavens and the earth, and all the host of them, were finished. 2And on the seventh day God ended His work which He had done, and He rested on the seventh day from all His work which He had done. 3Then God blessed the seventh day and sanctified it, because in it He rested from all His work which God had created and made.

4This *is* the history of the heavens and the earth when they were created, in the day that the LORD God made the earth and the heavens, 5before any plant of the field was in the earth and before any herb of the field had grown. For the LORD God had not caused it to rain on the earth, and *there was* no man to till the ground; 6but a mist went up from the earth and watered the whole face of the ground.

7And the LORD God formed man *of* the dust of the ground, and breathed into his nostrils the breath of life; and man became a living being.

Life in God's Garden

8The LORD God planted a garden eastward in Eden, and there He put the man whom He had formed. 9And out of the ground the LORD God made every tree grow that is pleasant to the sight and good for food. The tree of life *was* also in the midst of the garden, and the tree of the knowledge of good and evil.

10Now a river went out of Eden to water the garden, and from there it parted and became four riverheads. 11The name of the first *is* Pishon; it *is* the one which skirts the whole land of Havilah, where *there is* gold. 12And the gold of that land *is* good. Bdellium and the onyx stone *are* there. 13The name of the second river *is* Gihon; it *is* the

one which goes around the whole land of Cush. 14The name of the third river *is* Hiddekel;*a* it *is* the one which goes toward the east of Assyria. The fourth river *is* the Euphrates.

15Then the LORD God took the man and put him in the garden of Eden to tend and keep it. 16And the LORD God commanded the man, saying, "Of every tree of the garden you may freely eat; 17but of the tree of the knowledge of good and evil you shall not eat, for in the day that you eat of it you shall surely die."

18And the LORD God said, "*It is* not good that man should be alone; I will make him a helper comparable to him." 19Out of the ground the LORD God formed every beast of the field and every bird of the air, and brought *them* to Adam to see what he would call them. And whatever Adam called each living creature, that *was* its name. 20So Adam gave names to all cattle, to the birds of the air, and to every beast of the field. But for Adam there was not found a helper comparable to him.

21And the LORD God caused a deep sleep to fall on Adam, and he slept; and He took one of his ribs, and closed up the flesh in its place. 22Then the rib which the LORD God had taken from man He made into a woman, and He brought her to the man.

23And Adam said:

"This *is* now bone of my bones
And flesh of my flesh;
She shall be called Woman,
Because she was taken out of
    Man."

24Therefore a man shall leave his father and mother and be joined to his wife, and they shall become one flesh. 25And they were both naked, the man and his wife, and were not ashamed.

The Temptation and Fall of Man

3 Now the serpent was more cunning than any beast of the field which the LORD God had made. And he said to the woman, "Has God indeed said, 'You shall not eat of every tree of the garden'?"

2And the woman said to the serpent, "We may eat the fruit of the trees of

a Or *Tigris*

the garden; 3but of the fruit of the tree which *is* in the midst of the garden, God has said, 'You shall not eat it, nor shall you touch it, lest you die.' "

4Then the serpent said to the woman, "You will not surely die. 5For God knows that in the day you eat of it your eyes will be opened, and you will be like God, knowing good and evil."

6So when the woman saw that the tree *was* good for food, that it *was* pleasant to the eyes, and a tree desirable to make *one* wise, she took of its fruit and ate. She also gave to her husband with her, and he ate. 7Then the eyes of both of them were opened, and they knew that they *were* naked; and they sewed fig leaves together and made themselves coverings.

8And they heard the sound of the Lord God walking in the garden in the cool of the day, and Adam and his wife hid themselves from the presence of the Lord God among the trees of the garden.

9Then the Lord God called to Adam and said to him, "Where *are* you?"

10So he said, "I heard Your voice in the garden, and I was afraid because I was naked; and I hid myself."

11And He said, "Who told you that you *were* naked? Have you eaten from the tree of which I commanded you that you should not eat?"

12Then the man said, "The woman whom You gave *to be* with me, she gave me of the tree, and I ate."

13And the Lord God said to the woman, "What *is* this you have done?"

The woman said, "The serpent deceived me, and I ate."

14So the Lord God said to the serpent:

"Because you have done this,
    You *are* cursed more than all cattle,
    And more than every beast of the field;
    On your belly you shall go,
    And you shall eat dust
    All the days of your life.
15   And I will put enmity
    Between you and the woman,
    And between your seed and her Seed;
    He shall bruise your head,
    And you shall bruise His heel."
16To the woman He said:

"I will greatly multiply your sorrow
    and your conception;
    In pain you shall bring forth children;
    Your desire *shall be* for your husband,
    And he shall rule over you."

17Then to Adam He said, "Because you have heeded the voice of your wife, and have eaten from the tree of which I commanded you, saying, 'You shall not eat of it':

"Cursed *is* the ground for your sake;
    In toil you shall eat *of* it
    All the days of your life.
18   Both thorns and thistles it shall bring forth for you,
    And you shall eat the herb of the field.
19   In the sweat of your face you shall eat bread
    Till you return to the ground,
    For out of it you were taken;
    For dust you *are,*
    And to dust you shall return."

20And Adam called his wife's name Eve, because she was the mother of all living.

21Also for Adam and his wife the Lord God made tunics of skin, and clothed them.

22Then the Lord God said, "Behold, the man has become like one of Us, to know good and evil. And now, lest he put out his hand and take also of the tree of life, and eat, and live forever"— 23therefore the Lord God sent him out of the garden of Eden to till the ground from which he was taken. 24So He drove out the man; and He placed cherubim at the east of the garden of Eden, and a flaming sword which turned every way, to guard the way to the tree of life.

Cain Murders Abel

4 Now Adam knew Eve his wife, and she conceived and bore Cain, and said, "I have acquired a man from the Lord." 2Then she bore again, this time his brother Abel. Now Abel was a keeper of sheep, but Cain was a tiller of the ground. 3And in the process of time it came to pass that Cain brought an offering of the fruit of the ground to the Lord. 4Abel also brought of the firstborn of his flock and of their fat.

And the LORD respected Abel and his offering, 5but He did not respect Cain and his offering. And Cain was very angry, and his countenance fell.

6So the LORD said to Cain, "Why are you angry? And why has your countenance fallen? 7If you do well, will you not be accepted? And if you do not do well, sin lies at the door. And its desire is for you, but you should rule over it."

8Now Cain talked with Abel his brother; and it came to pass, when they were in the field, that Cain rose up against Abel his brother and killed him.

9Then the LORD said to Cain, "Where is Abel your brother?"

He said, "I do not know. Am I my brother's keeper?"

10And He said, "What have you done? The voice of your brother's blood cries out to Me from the ground. 11So now you are cursed from the earth, which has opened its mouth to receive your brother's blood from your hand. 12When you till the ground, it shall no longer yield its strength to you. A fugitive and a vagabond you shall be on the earth."

13And Cain said to the LORD, "My punishment is greater than I can bear! 14Surely You have driven me out this day from the face of the ground; I shall be hidden from Your face; I shall be a fugitive and a vagabond on the earth, and it will happen that anyone who finds me will kill me."

15And the LORD said to him, "Therefore, whoever kills Cain, vengeance shall be taken on him sevenfold." And the LORD set a mark on Cain, lest anyone finding him should kill him.

The Family of Cain

16Then Cain went out from the presence of the LORD and dwelt in the land of Nod on the east of Eden. 17And Cain knew his wife, and she conceived and bore Enoch. And he built a city, and called the name of the city after the name of his son—Enoch. 18To Enoch was born Irad; and Irad begot Mehujael, and Mehujael begot Methushael, and Methushael begot Lamech.

19Then Lamech took for himself two wives: the name of one was Adah, and the name of the second was Zillah. 20And Adah bore Jabal. He was the fa-

ther of those who dwell in tents and have livestock. 21His brother's name was Jubal. He was the father of all those who play the harp and flute. 22And as for Zillah, she also bore Tubal-Cain, an instructor of every craftsman in bronze and iron. And the sister of Tubal-Cain was Naamah.

23Then Lamech said to his wives:

"Adah and Zillah, hear my voice;
  Wives of Lamech, listen to my
    speech!
For I have killed a man for
  wounding me,
Even a young man for hurting me.
24 If Cain shall be avenged sevenfold,
  Then Lamech seventy-sevenfold."

A New Son

25And Adam knew his wife again, and she bore a son and named him Seth, "For God has appointed another seed for me instead of Abel, whom Cain killed." 26And as for Seth, to him also a son was born; and he named him Enosh. Then men began to call on the name of the LORD.

The Family of Adam

5 This is the book of the genealogy of Adam. In the day that God created man, He made him in the likeness of God. 2He created them male and female, and blessed them and called them Mankind in the day they were created. 3And Adam lived one hundred and thirty years, and begot a son in his own likeness, after his image, and named him Seth. 4After he begot Seth, the days of Adam were eight hundred years; and he had sons and daughters. 5So all the days that Adam lived were nine hundred and thirty years; and he died.

6Seth lived one hundred and five years, and begot Enosh. 7After he begot Enosh, Seth lived eight hundred and seven years, and had sons and daughters. 8So all the days of Seth were nine hundred and twelve years; and he died.

9Enosh lived ninety years, and begot Cainan. 10After he begot Cainan, Enosh lived eight hundred and fifteen years, and had sons and daughters. 11So all the days of Enosh were nine hundred and five years; and he died.

12Cainan lived seventy years, and begot Mahalalel. 13After he begot Mahalalel, Cainan lived eight hundred and forty years, and had sons and daughters. 14So all the days of Cainan were nine hundred and ten years; and he died.

15Mahalalel lived sixty-five years, and begot Jared. 16After he begot Jared, Mahalalel lived eight hundred and thirty years, and had sons and daughters. 17So all the days of Mahalalel were eight hundred and ninety-five years; and he died.

18Jared lived one hundred and sixty-two years, and begot Enoch. 19After he begot Enoch, Jared lived eight hundred years, and had sons and daughters. 20So all the days of Jared were nine hundred and sixty-two years; and he died.

21Enoch lived sixty-five years, and begot Methuselah. 22After he begot Methuselah, Enoch walked with God three hundred years, and had sons and daughters. 23So all the days of Enoch were three hundred and sixty-five years. 24And Enoch walked with God; and he *was* not, for God took him.

25Methuselah lived one hundred and eighty-seven years, and begot Lamech. 26After he begot Lamech, Methuselah lived seven hundred and eighty-two years, and had sons and daughters. 27So all the days of Methuselah were nine hundred and sixty-nine years; and he died.

28Lamech lived one hundred and eighty-two years, and had a son. 29And he called his name Noah, saying, "This *one* will comfort us concerning our work and the toil of our hands, because of the ground which the LORD has cursed." 30After he begot Noah, Lamech lived five hundred and ninety-five years, and had sons and daughters. 31So all the days of Lamech were seven hundred and seventy-seven years; and he died.

32And Noah was five hundred years old, and Noah begot Shem, Ham, and Japheth.

The Wickedness and Judgment of Man

6 Now it came to pass, when men began to multiply on the face of the earth, and daughters were born to them, 2that the sons of God saw the daughters of men, that they *were* beautiful; and they took wives for themselves of all whom they chose.

3And the LORD said, "My Spirit shall not strive with man forever, for he *is* indeed flesh; yet his days shall be one hundred and twenty years." 4There were giants on the earth in those days, and also afterward, when the sons of God came in to the daughters of men and they bore *children* to them. Those *were* the mighty men who *were* of old, men of renown.

5Then the LORD saw that the wickedness of man *was* great in the earth, and *that* every intent of the thoughts of his heart *was* only evil continually. 6And the LORD was sorry that He had made man on the earth, and He was grieved in His heart. 7So the LORD said, "I will destroy man whom I have created from the face of the earth, both man and beast, creeping thing and birds of the air, for I am sorry that I have made them." 8But Noah found grace in the eyes of the LORD.

Noah Pleases God

9This is the genealogy of Noah. Noah was a just man, perfect in his generations. Noah walked with God. 10And Noah begot three sons: Shem, Ham, and Japheth.

11The earth also was corrupt before God, and the earth was filled with violence. 12So God looked upon the earth, and indeed it was corrupt; for all flesh had corrupted their way on the earth.

The Ark Prepared

13And God said to Noah, "The end of all flesh has come before Me, for the earth is filled with violence through them; and behold, I will destroy them with the earth. 14Make yourself an ark of gopherwood; make rooms in the ark, and cover it inside and outside with pitch. 15And this is how you shall make it: The length of the ark *shall be* three hundred cubits, its width fifty cubits, and its height thirty cubits. 16You shall make a window for the ark, and you shall finish it to a cubit from above; and set the door of the ark in its side. You shall make it *with* lower, second, and third *decks*. 17And behold, I Myself am bringing floodwaters on the earth, to destroy from under heaven all flesh in which *is* the breath of life; everything that *is* on the earth shall die. 18But I will establish My covenant with you; and you shall go into the ark—you, your sons, your wife, and your sons' wives with you. 19And of every living thing of all flesh you shall bring two of every *sort* into the ark, to keep *them* alive with you; they shall be male and female. 20Of the birds after their kind, of animals after their kind, and of every creeping thing of the earth after its kind, two of every *kind* will come to you to keep *them* alive. 21And you shall take for yourself of all food that is eaten, and you shall gather *it* to yourself; and it shall be food for you and for them."

22Thus Noah did; according to all that God commanded him, so he did.

The Great Flood

7 Then the LORD said to Noah, "Come into the ark, you and all your household, because I have seen *that* you *are* righteous before Me in this generation. 2You shall take with you seven each of every clean animal, a male and his female; two each of animals that *are* unclean, a male and his female; 3also seven each of birds of the air, male and female, to keep the species alive on the face of all the earth. 4For after seven more days I will cause it to rain on the earth forty days and forty nights, and I will destroy from the face of the earth all living things that I have made." 5And Noah did according to all that the LORD commanded him. 6Noah *was* six hundred years old when the floodwaters were on the earth.

7So Noah, with his sons, his wife, and his sons' wives, went into the ark because of the waters of the flood. 8Of clean animals, of animals that *are* unclean, of birds, and of everything that creeps on the earth, 9two by two they went into the ark to Noah, male and female, as God had commanded Noah. 10And it came to pass after seven days that the waters of the flood were on the earth. 11In the six hundredth year of Noah's life, in the second month, the seventeenth day of the month, on that day all the fountains of the great deep were broken up, and the windows of heaven were opened. 12And the rain was on the earth forty days and forty nights.

13On the very same day Noah and Noah's sons, Shem, Ham, and Japheth, and Noah's wife and the three wives of his sons with them, entered the ark— 14they and every beast after its kind, all cattle after their kind, every creeping thing that creeps on the earth after its kind, and every bird after its kind, every bird of every sort. 15And they went into the ark to Noah, two by two, of all flesh in which *is* the breath of life. 16So those that entered, male and female of all flesh, went in as God had commanded him; and the LORD shut him in.

17Now the flood was on the earth forty days. The waters increased and lifted up the ark, and it rose high above the earth. 18The waters prevailed and greatly increased on the earth, and the ark moved about on the surface of the waters. 19And the waters prevailed exceedingly on the earth, and all the high hills under the whole heaven were covered. 20The waters prevailed fifteen cubits upward, and the mountains were covered. 21And all flesh died that moved on the earth: birds and cattle and beasts and every creeping thing that creeps on the earth, and every man. 22All in whose nostrils *was* the breath of the spirit of life, all that *was* on the dry *land,* died. 23So He destroyed all living things which were on the face of the ground: both man and cattle, creeping thing and bird of the air. They were destroyed from the earth. Only Noah and those who *were* with him in the ark remained *alive.* 24And the waters prevailed on the earth one hundred and fifty days.

Noah's Deliverance

8 Then God remembered Noah, and every living thing, and all the animals that *were* with him in the ark. And God made a wind to pass over the earth, and the waters subsided. 2The fountains of the deep and the windows of heaven were also stopped, and the rain from heaven was restrained. 3And the waters receded continually from the earth. At the end of the hundred and fifty days the waters decreased. 4Then the ark rested in the seventh month, the seventeenth day of the month, on the mountains of Ararat. 5And the waters decreased continually until the tenth month. In the tenth *month*, on the first *day* of the month, the tops of the mountains were seen.

6So it came to pass, at the end of forty days, that Noah opened the window of the ark which he had made. 7Then he sent out a raven, which kept going to and fro until the waters had dried up from the earth. 8He also sent out from himself a dove, to see if the waters had receded from the face of the ground. 9But the dove found no resting place for the sole of her foot, and she returned into the ark to him, for the waters *were* on the face of the whole earth. So he put out his hand and took her, and drew her into the ark to himself. 10And he waited yet another seven days, and again he sent the dove out from the ark. 11Then the dove came to him in the evening, and behold, a freshly plucked olive leaf *was* in her mouth; and Noah knew that the waters had receded from the earth. 12So he waited yet another seven days and sent out the dove, which did not return again to him anymore.

13And it came to pass in the six hundred and first year, in the first *month*, the first *day* of the month, that the waters were dried up from the earth; and Noah removed the covering of the ark and looked, and indeed the surface of the ground was dry. 14And in the second month, on the twenty-seventh day of the month, the earth was dried.

15Then God spoke to Noah, saying, 16"Go out of the ark, you and your wife, and your sons and your sons' wives with you. 17Bring out with you every living thing of all flesh that *is* with you: birds and cattle and every creeping thing that creeps on the earth, so that they may abound on the earth, and be fruitful and multiply on the earth." 18So Noah went out, and his sons and his wife and his sons' wives with him. 19Every animal, every creeping thing,

b Compare Genesis 1.28

every bird, *and* whatever creeps on the earth, according to their families, went out of the ark.

God's Covenant with Creation

20Then Noah built an altar to the LORD, and took of every clean animal and of every clean bird, and offered burnt offerings on the altar. 21And the LORD smelled a soothing aroma. Then the LORD said in His heart, "I will never again curse the ground for man's sake, although the imagination of man's heart *is* evil from his youth; nor will I again destroy every living thing as I have done.

22 "While the earth remains,
　　Seedtime and harvest,
　　Cold and heat,
　　Winter and summer,
　　And day and night
　　Shall not cease."

9 So God blessed Noah and his sons, and said to them: "Be fruitful and multiply, and fill the earth.[b] 2And the fear of you and the dread of you shall be on every beast of the earth, on every bird of the air, on all that move *on* the earth, and on all the fish of the sea. They are given into your hand. 3Every moving thing that lives shall be food for you. I have given you all things, even as the green herbs. 4But you shall not eat flesh with its life, *that is,* its blood. 5Surely for your lifeblood I will demand *a reckoning;* from the hand of every beast I will require it, and from the hand of man. From the hand of every man's brother I will require the life of man.

6 "Whoever sheds man's blood,
　　By man his blood shall be shed;
　　For in the image of God
　　He made man.
7 　And as for you, be fruitful and
　　　multiply;
　　Bring forth abundantly in the earth
　　And multiply in it."

8Then God spoke to Noah and to his sons with him, saying: 9"And as for Me, behold, I establish My covenant with you and with your descendants after you, 10and with every living creature that *is* with you: the birds, the cattle, and every beast of the earth with you, of all that go out of the ark, every beast of the earth. 11Thus I establish My covenant with you: Never again shall all flesh be cut off by the waters of the flood; never again shall there be a flood to destroy the earth."

12And God said: "This *is* the sign of the covenant which I make between Me and you, and every living creature that *is* with you, for perpetual generations: 13I set My rainbow in the cloud, and it shall be for the sign of the covenant between Me and the earth. 14It shall be, when I bring a cloud over the earth, that the rainbow shall be seen in the cloud; 15and I will remember My covenant which *is* between Me and you and every living creature of all flesh; the waters shall never again become a flood to destroy all flesh. 16The rainbow shall be in the cloud, and I will look on it to remember the everlasting covenant between God and every living creature of all flesh that *is* on the earth." 17And God said to Noah, "This *is* the sign of the covenant which I have established between Me and all flesh that *is* on the earth."

Noah and His Sons

18Now the sons of Noah who went out of the ark were Shem, Ham, and Japheth. And Ham *was* the father of Canaan. 19These three *were* the sons of Noah, and from these the whole earth was populated.

20And Noah began *to be* a farmer, and he planted a vineyard. 21Then he drank of the wine and was drunk, and became uncovered in his tent. 22And Ham, the father of Canaan, saw the nakedness of his father, and told his two brothers outside. 23But Shem and Japheth took a garment, laid *it* on both their shoulders, and went backward and covered the nakedness of their father. Their faces *were* turned away, and they did not see their father's nakedness.

24So Noah awoke from his wine, and knew what his younger son had done to him. 25Then he said:

"Cursed *be* Canaan;
  A servant of servants
  He shall be to his brethren."
26And he said:

"Blessed *be* the LORD,
  The God of Shem,
  And may Canaan be his servant.
27 May God enlarge Japheth,
  And may he dwell in the tents of
    Shem;
  And may Canaan be his servant."

28And Noah lived after the flood three hundred and fifty years. 29So all the days of Noah were nine hundred and fifty years; and he died.

Nations Descended from Noah

10 Now this *is* the genealogy of the sons of Noah: Shem, Ham, and Japheth. And sons were born to them after the flood.

2The sons of Japheth *were* Gomer, Magog, Madai, Javan, Tubal, Meshech, and Tiras. 3The sons of Gomer *were* Ashkenaz, Riphath, and Togarmah. 4The sons of Javan *were* Elishah, Tarshish, Kittim, and Dodanim. 5From these the coastland *peoples* of the Gentiles were separated into their lands, everyone according to his language, according to their families, into their nations.

6The sons of Ham *were* Cush, Mizraim, Put, and Canaan. 7The sons of Cush *were* Seba, Havilah, Sabtah, Raamah, and Sabtechah; and the sons of Raamah *were* Sheba and Dedan.

8Cush begot Nimrod; he began to be a mighty one on the earth. 9He was a mighty hunter before the LORD; therefore it is said, "Like Nimrod the mighty hunter before the LORD." 10And the beginning of his kingdom was Babel, Erech, Accad, and Calneh, in the land of Shinar. 11From that land he went to Assyria and built Nineveh, Rehoboth Ir, Calah, 12and Resen between Nineveh and Calah (that *is* the principal city).

13Mizraim begot Ludim, Anamim, Lehabim, Naphtuhim, 14Pathrusim, and Casluhim (from whom came the Philistines and Caphtorim).

15Canaan begot Sidon his firstborn, and Heth; 16the Jebusite, the Amorite, and the Girgashite; 17the Hivite, the Arkite, and the Sinite; 18the Arvadite, the Zemarite, and the Hamathite. Afterward the families of the Canaanites were dispersed. 19And the border of the Canaanites was from Sidon as you go toward Gerar, as far as Gaza; then as you go toward Sodom, Gomorrah, Admah, and Zeboiim, as far as Lasha. 20These were the sons of Ham, according to their families, according to their languages, in their lands *and* in their nations.

21And *children* were born also to Shem, the father of all the children of Eber, the brother of Japheth the elder. 22The sons of Shem *were* Elam, Asshur, Arphaxad, Lud, and Aram. 23The sons of Aram *were* Uz, Hul, Gether, and Mash. 24Arphaxad begot Salah, and Salah begot Eber. 25To Eber were born two sons: the name of one *was* Peleg, for in his days the earth was divided; and his brother's name *was* Joktan. 26Joktan begot Almodad, Sheleph, Hazarmaveth, Jerah, 27Hadoram, Uzal, Diklah, 28Obal, Abimael, Sheba, 29Ophir, Havilah, and Jobab. All these *were* the sons of Joktan. 30And their dwelling place was from Mesha as you go toward Sephar, the mountain of the east. 31These *were* the sons of Shem, according to their families, according to their languages, in their lands, according to their nations.

32These *were* the families of the sons of Noah, according to their generations, in their nations; and from these the nations were divided on the earth after the flood.

The Tower of Babel

11 Now the whole earth had one language and one speech. 2And it came to pass, as they journeyed from the east, that they found a plain in the land of Shinar, and they dwelt there. 3Then they said to one another, "Come, let us make bricks and bake *them* thoroughly." They had brick for stone, and they had asphalt for mortar. 4And they said, "Come, let us build ourselves a city, and a tower whose top *is* in the heavens; let us make a name for ourselves, lest we be scattered abroad over the face of the whole earth."

5But the LORD came down to see the city and the tower which the sons of men had built. 6And the LORD said, "Indeed the people *are* one and they all have one language, and this is what they begin to do; now nothing that they propose to do will be withheld from them. 7Come, let Us go down and there confuse their language, that they may not understand one another's speech." 8So the LORD scattered them abroad from there over the face of all the earth, and they ceased building the city. 9Therefore its name is called Babel, because there the LORD confused the language of all the earth; and from there the LORD scattered them abroad over the face of all the earth.

Shem's Descendants

10This *is* the genealogy of Shem: Shem *was* one hundred years old, and begot Arphaxad two years after the flood. 11After he begot Arphaxad, Shem lived five hundred years, and begot sons and daughters.

12Arphaxad lived thirty-five years, and begot Salah. 13After he begot Salah, Arphaxad lived four hundred and three years, and begot sons and daughters.

14Salah lived thirty years, and begot Eber. 15After he begot Eber, Salah lived four hundred and three years, and begot sons and daughters.

16Eber lived thirty-four years, and begot Peleg. 17After he begot Peleg, Eber lived four hundred and thirty years, and begot sons and daughters.

18Peleg lived thirty years, and begot Reu. 19After he begot Reu, Peleg lived two hundred and nine years, and begot sons and daughters.

20Reu lived thirty-two years, and begot Serug. 21After he begot Serug, Reu lived two hundred and seven years, and begot sons and daughters.

22Serug lived thirty years, and begot Nahor. 23After he begot Nahor, Serug lived two hundred years, and begot sons and daughters.

24Nahor lived twenty-nine years, and begot Terah. 25After he begot Terah, Nahor lived one hundred and nineteen years, and begot sons and daughters.

26Now Terah lived seventy years, and begot Abram, Nahor, and Haran.

Terah's Descendants

27This *is* the genealogy of Terah: Terah begot Abram, Nahor, and Haran. Haran begot Lot. 28And Haran died before his father Terah in his native land, in Ur of the Chaldeans. 29Then Abram and Nahor took wives: the name of Abram's wife *was* Sarai, and the name of Nahor's wife, Milcah, the daughter of Haran the father of Milcah and the father of Iscah. 30But Sarai was barren; she had no child.

31And Terah took his son Abram and his grandson Lot, the son of Haran, and his daughter-in-law Sarai, his son Abram's wife, and they went out with them from Ur of the Chaldeans to go to the land of Canaan; and they came to Haran and dwelt there. 32So the days of Terah were two hundred and five years, and Terah died in Haran.

Promises to Abram

12 Now the LORD had said to Abram:

"Get out of your country,
From your family
And from your father's house,
To a land that I will show you.
2   I will make you a great nation;
I will bless you
And make your name great;
And you shall be a blessing.
3   I will bless those who bless you,
And I will curse him who curses you;
And in you all the families of the earth shall be blessed."

4So Abram departed as the LORD had spoken to him, and Lot went with him. And Abram *was* seventy-five years old when he departed from Haran. 5Then Abram took Sarai his wife and Lot his brother's son, and all their possessions that they had gathered, and the people whom they had acquired in Haran, and they departed to go to the land of Canaan. So they came to the land of Canaan. 6Abram passed through the land to the place of Shechem, as far as the terebinth tree of Moreh. And the Canaanites *were* then in the land.

7Then the LORD appeared to Abram and said, "To your descendants I will give this land." And there he built an altar to the LORD, who had appeared to him. 8And he moved from there to the mountain east of Bethel, and he pitched his tent *with* Bethel on the west and Ai on the east; there he built an altar to the LORD and called on the name of the LORD. 9So Abram journeyed, going on still toward the South.

Abram in Egypt

10Now there was a famine in the land, and Abram went down to Egypt to dwell there, for the famine *was* severe in the land. 11And it came to pass, when he was close to entering Egypt, that he said to Sarai his wife, "Indeed I know that you *are* a woman of beautiful countenance. 12Therefore it will happen, when the Egyptians see you, that they will say, 'This *is* his wife'; and they will kill me, but they will let you live. 13Please say you *are* my sister, that it may be well with me for your sake, and that I may live because of you."

14So it was, when Abram came into Egypt, that the Egyptians saw the woman, that she *was* very beautiful. 15The princes of Pharaoh also saw her and commended her to Pharaoh. And the woman was taken to Pharaoh's house. 16He treated Abram well for her sake. He had sheep, oxen, male donkeys, male and female servants, female donkeys, and camels.

17But the LORD plagued Pharaoh and his house with great plagues because of Sarai, Abram's wife. 18And Pharaoh called Abram and said, "What *is* this you have done to me? Why did you not tell me that she *was* your wife? 19Why did you say, 'She *is* my sister'? I might have taken her as my wife. Now therefore, here is your wife; take *her* and go your way." 20So Pharaoh commanded *his* men concerning him; and they sent him away, with his wife and all that he had.

Abram Inherits Canaan

13 Then Abram went up from Egypt, he and his wife and all that he had, and Lot with him, to the South. 2Abram *was* very rich in livestock, in silver, and in gold. 3And he went on his journey from the South as far as Bethel, to the place where his tent had been at the beginning, between Bethel and Ai, 4to the place of the altar which he had made there at first. And there Abram called on the name of the LORD.

5Lot also, who went with Abram, had flocks and herds and tents. 6Now the land was not able to support them, that they might dwell together, for their possessions were so great that they could not dwell together. 7And there was strife between the herdsmen of Abram's livestock and the herdsmen of Lot's livestock. The Canaanites and the Perizzites then dwelt in the land.

8So Abram said to Lot, "Please let there be no strife between you and me, and between my herdsmen and your herdsmen; for we *are* brethren. 9*Is* not the whole land before you? Please separate from me. If *you take* the left, then I will go to the right; or, if *you go* to the right, then I will go to the left."

10And Lot lifted his eyes and saw all the plain of Jordan, that it *was* well watered everywhere (before the LORD destroyed Sodom and Gomorrah) like the garden of the LORD, like the land of Egypt as you go toward Zoar. 11Then Lot chose for himself all the plain of Jordan, and Lot journeyed east. And they separated from each other. 12Abram dwelt in the land of Canaan, and Lot dwelt in the cities of the plain and pitched *his* tent even as far as Sodom. 13But the men of Sodom *were* exceedingly wicked and sinful against the LORD.

14And the LORD said to Abram, after Lot had separated from him: "Lift your eyes now and look from the place where you are—northward, southward, eastward, and westward; 15for all the land which you see I give to you and your descendants[c] forever. 16And I will make your descendants as the dust of the earth; so that if a man could number the dust of the earth, *then* your descendants also could be numbered. 17Arise, walk in the land through its length and its width, for I give it to you."

18Then Abram moved *his* tent, and went and dwelt by the terebinth trees of Mamre, which *are* in Hebron, and built an altar there to the LORD.

Lot's Captivity and Rescue

14 And it came to pass in the days of Amraphel king of Shinar, Arioch king of Ellasar, Chedorlaomer king of Elam, and Tidal king of na-

c Literally *seed,* and so throughout the book

tions, 2*that* they made war with Bera king of Sodom, Birsha king of Gomorrah, Shinab king of Admah, Shemeber king of Zeboiim, and the king of Bela (that is, Zoar). 3All these joined together in the Valley of Siddim (that is, the Salt Sea). 4Twelve years they served Chedorlaomer, and in the thirteenth year they rebelled.

5In the fourteenth year Chedorlaomer and the kings that *were* with him came and attacked the Rephaim in Ashteroth Karnaim, the Zuzim in Ham, the Emim in Shaveh Kiriathaim, 6and the Horites in their mountain of Seir, as far as El Paran, which *is* by the wilderness. 7Then they turned back and came to En Mishpat (that *is,* Kadesh), and attacked all the country of the Amalekites, and also the Amorites who dwelt in Hazezon Tamar.

8And the king of Sodom, the king of Gomorrah, the king of Admah, the king of Zeboiim, and the king of Bela (that *is,* Zoar) went out and joined together in battle in the Valley of Siddim 9against Chedorlaomer king of Elam, Tidal king of nations, Amraphel king of Shinar, and Arioch king of Ellasar— four kings against five. 10Now the Valley of Siddim *was full of* asphalt pits; and the kings of Sodom and Gomorrah fled; *some* fell there, and the remainder fled to the mountains. 11Then they took all the goods of Sodom and Gomorrah, and all their provisions, and went their way. 12They also took Lot, Abram's brother's son who dwelt in Sodom, and his goods, and departed.

13Then one who had escaped came and told Abram the Hebrew, for he dwelt by the terebinth trees of Mamre the Amorite, brother of Eshcol and brother of Aner; and they *were* allies with Abram. 14Now when Abram heard that his brother was taken captive, he armed his three hundred and eighteen trained *servants* who were born in his own house, and went in pursuit as far as Dan. 15He divided his forces against them by night, and he and his servants attacked them and pursued them as far as Hobah, which *is* north of Damascus. 16So he brought back all the goods, and also brought back his brother Lot and his goods, as well as the women and the people.

17And the king of Sodom went out to meet him at the Valley of Shaveh (that is, the King's Valley), after his return from the defeat of Chedorlaomer and the kings who were with him.

Abram and Melchizedek

18Then Melchizedek king of Salem brought out bread and wine; he was the priest of God Most High. 19And he blessed him and said:

"Blessed be Abram of God Most
    High,
Possessor of heaven and earth;
20 And blessed be God Most High,
    Who has delivered your enemies
        into your hand."

And he gave him a tithe of all.

21Now the king of Sodom said to Abram, "Give me the persons, and take the goods for yourself."

22But Abram said to the king of Sodom, "I have raised my hand to the LORD, God Most High, the Possessor of heaven and earth, 23that I will take nothing, from a thread to a sandal strap, and that I will not take anything that is yours, lest you should say, 'I have made Abram rich'— 24except only what the young men have eaten, and the portion of the men who went with me: Aner, Eshcol, and Mamre; let them take their portion."

God's Covenant with Abram

15 After these things the word of the LORD came to Abram in a vision, saying, "Do not be afraid, Abram. I am your shield, your exceedingly great reward."

2But Abram said, "Lord GOD, what will You give me, seeing I go childless, and the heir of my house is Eliezer of Damascus?" 3Then Abram said, "Look, You have given me no offspring; indeed one born in my house is my heir!"

4And behold, the word of the LORD came to him, saying, "This one shall not be your heir, but one who will come from your own body shall be your heir." 5Then He brought him outside and said, "Look now toward heaven, and count the stars if you are able to number them." And He said to him, "So shall your descendants be."

6And he believed in the LORD, and He accounted it to him for righteousness.

7Then He said to him, "I am the LORD, who brought you out of Ur of the Chaldeans, to give you this land to inherit it."

8And he said, "Lord GOD, how shall I know that I will inherit it?"

9So He said to him, "Bring Me a three-year-old heifer, a three-year-old female goat, a three-year-old ram, a turtledove, and a young pigeon." 10Then he brought all these to Him and cut them in two, down the middle, and placed each piece opposite the other; but he did not cut the birds in two. 11And when the vultures came down on the carcasses, Abram drove them away.

12Now when the sun was going down, a deep sleep fell upon Abram; and behold, horror and great darkness fell upon him. 13Then He said to Abram: "Know certainly that your descendants will be strangers in a land that is not theirs, and will serve them, and they will afflict them four hundred years. 14And also the nation whom they serve I will judge; afterward they shall come out with great possessions. 15Now as for you, you shall go to your fathers in peace; you shall be buried at a good old age. 16But in the fourth generation they shall return here, for the iniquity of the Amorites is not yet complete."

17And it came to pass, when the sun went down and it was dark, that behold, there appeared a smoking oven and a burning torch that passed between those pieces. 18On the same day the LORD made a covenant with Abram, saying:

"To your descendants I have given this land, from the river of Egypt to the great river, the River Euphrates— 19the Kenites, the Kenezzites, the Kadmonites, 20the Hittites, the Perizzites, the Rephaim, 21the Amorites, the Canaanites, the Girgashites, and the Jebusites."

Hagar and Ishmael

16 Now Sarai, Abram's wife, had borne him no children. And she had an Egyptian maidservant whose name was Hagar. 2So Sarai said to Abram, "See now, the LORD has restrained me from bearing children.

Please, go in to my maid; perhaps I shall obtain children by her." And Abram heeded the voice of Sarai. 3Then Sarai, Abram's wife, took Hagar her maid, the Egyptian, and gave her to her husband Abram to be his wife, after Abram had dwelt ten years in the land of Canaan. 4So he went in to Hagar, and she conceived. And when she saw that she had conceived, her mistress became despised in her eyes.

5Then Sarai said to Abram, "My wrong be upon you! I gave my maid into your embrace; and when she saw that she had conceived, I became despised in her eyes. The LORD judge between you and me."

6So Abram said to Sarai, "Indeed your maid is in your hand; do to her as you please." And when Sarai dealt harshly with her, she fled from her presence.

7Now the Angel of the LORD found her by a spring of water in the wilderness, by the spring on the way to Shur. 8And He said, "Hagar, Sarai's maid, where have you come from, and where are you going?"

She said, "I am fleeing from the presence of my mistress Sarai."

9The Angel of the LORD said to her, "Return to your mistress, and submit yourself under her hand." 10Then the Angel of the LORD said to her, "I will multiply your descendants exceedingly, so that they shall not be counted for multitude." 11And the Angel of the LORD said to her:

"Behold, you are with child,
And you shall bear a son.
You shall call his name Ishmael,
Because the LORD has heard your
    affliction.
12   He shall be a wild man;
His hand shall be against every
    man,
And every man's hand against him.
And he shall dwell in the presence
    of all his brethren."

13Then she called the name of the LORD who spoke to her, You-Are-the-God-Who-Sees; for she said, "Have I also here seen Him who sees me?" 14Therefore the well was called Beer Lahai Roi; observe, it is between Kadesh and Bered.

15So Hagar bore Abram a son; and Abram named his son, whom Hagar bore, Ishmael. 16Abram was eighty-six years old when Hagar bore Ishmael to Abram.

The Sign of the Covenant

17 When Abram was ninety-nine years old, the LORD appeared to Abram and said to him, "I am Almighty God; walk before Me and be blameless. 2And I will make My covenant between Me and you, and will multiply you exceedingly." 3Then Abram fell on his face, and God talked with him, saying: 4"As for Me, behold, My covenant is with you, and you shall be a father of many nations. 5No longer shall your name be called Abram, but your name shall be Abraham; for I have made you a father of many nations. 6I will make you exceedingly fruitful; and I will make nations of you, and kings shall come from you. 7And I will establish My covenant between Me and you and your descendants after you in their generations, for an everlasting covenant, to be God to you and your descendants after you. 8Also I give to you and your descendants after you the land in which you are a stranger, all the land of Canaan, as an everlasting possession; and I will be their God."

9And God said to Abraham: "As for you, you shall keep My covenant, you and your descendants after you throughout their generations. 10This is My covenant which you shall keep, between Me and you and your descendants after you: Every male child among you shall be circumcised; 11and you shall be circumcised in the flesh of your foreskins, and it shall be a sign of the covenant between Me and you. 12He who is eight days old among you shall be circumcised, every male child in your generations, he who is born in your house or bought with money from any foreigner who is not your descendant. 13He who is born in your house and he who is bought with your money must be circumcised, and My covenant shall be in your flesh for an everlasting covenant. 14And the uncircumcised male child, who is not circumcised in the flesh of his foreskin, that person shall be cut off from his people; he has broken My covenant."

15Then God said to Abraham, "As for Sarai your wife, you shall not call her name Sarai, but Sarah *shall be* her name. 16And I will bless her and also give you a son by her; then I will bless her, and she shall be *a mother of* nations; kings of peoples shall be from her."

17Then Abraham fell on his face and laughed, and said in his heart, "Shall *a child* be born to a man who is one hundred years old? And shall Sarah, who is ninety years old, bear *a child*?" 18And Abraham said to God, "Oh, that Ishmael might live before You!"

19Then God said: "No, Sarah your wife shall bear you a son, and you shall call his name Isaac; I will establish My covenant with him for an everlasting covenant, *and* with his descendants after him. 20And as for Ishmael, I have heard you. Behold, I have blessed him, and will make him fruitful, and will multiply him exceedingly. He shall beget twelve princes, and I will make him a great nation. 21But My covenant I will establish with Isaac, whom Sarah shall bear to you at this set time next year." 22Then He finished talking with him, and God went up from Abraham.

23So Abraham took Ishmael his son, all who were born in his house and all who were bought with his money, every male among the men of Abraham's house, and circumcised the flesh of their foreskins that very same day, as God had said to him. 24Abraham *was* ninety-nine years old when he was circumcised in the flesh of his foreskin. 25And Ishmael his son *was* thirteen years old when he was circumcised in the flesh of his foreskin. 26That very same day Abraham was circumcised, and his son Ishmael; 27and all the men of his house, born in the house or bought with money from a foreigner, were circumcised with him.

The Son of Promise

18 Then the LORD appeared to him by the terebinth trees of Mamre, as he was sitting in the tent door in the heat of the day. 2So he lifted his eyes and looked, and behold, three men were standing by him; and when he saw *them*, he ran from the tent door to meet them, and bowed himself to the ground, 3and said, "My Lord, if I have now found favor in Your sight, do not pass on by Your servant. 4Please let a little water be brought, and wash your feet, and rest yourselves under the tree. 5And I will bring a morsel of bread, that you may refresh your hearts. After that you may pass by, inasmuch as you have come to your servant."

They said, "Do as you have said."

6So Abraham hurried into the tent to Sarah and said, "Quickly, make ready three measures of fine meal; knead *it* and make cakes." 7And Abraham ran to the herd, took a tender and good calf, gave *it* to a young man, and he hastened to prepare it. 8So he took butter and milk and the calf which he had prepared, and set *it* before them; and he stood by them under the tree as they ate.

9Then they said to him, "Where *is* Sarah your wife?"

So he said, "Here, in the tent."

10And He said, "I will certainly return to you according to the time of life, and behold, Sarah your wife shall have a son."

(Sarah was listening in the tent door which *was* behind him.) 11Now Abraham and Sarah were old, well advanced in age; *and* Sarah had passed the age of childbearing. 12Therefore Sarah laughed within herself, saying, "After I have grown old, shall I have pleasure, my lord being old also?"

13And the LORD said to Abraham, "Why did Sarah laugh, saying, 'Shall I surely bear *a child*, since I am old?' 14Is anything too hard for the LORD? At the appointed time I will return to you, according to the time of life, and Sarah shall have a son."

15But Sarah denied *it*, saying, "I did not laugh," for she was afraid.

And He said, "No, but you did laugh!"

Abraham Intercedes for Sodom

16Then the men rose from there and looked toward Sodom, and Abraham went with them to send them on the way. 17And the LORD said, "Shall I hide from Abraham what I am doing,

18since Abraham shall surely become a great and mighty nation, and all the nations of the earth shall be blessed in him? 19For I have known him, in order that he may command his children and his household after him, that they keep the way of the LORD, to do righteousness and justice, that the LORD may bring to Abraham what He has spoken to him." 20And the LORD said, "Because the outcry against Sodom and Gomorrah is great, and because their sin is very grave, 21I will go down now and see whether they have done altogether according to the outcry against it that has come to Me; and if not, I will know."

22Then the men turned away from there and went toward Sodom, but Abraham still stood before the LORD. 23And Abraham came near and said, "Would You also destroy the righteous with the wicked? 24Suppose there were fifty righteous within the city; would You also destroy the place and not spare it for the fifty righteous that were in it? 25Far be it from You to do such a thing as this, to slay the righteous with the wicked, so that the righteous should be as the wicked; far be it from You! Shall not the Judge of all the earth do right?"

26So the LORD said, "If I find in Sodom fifty righteous within the city, then I will spare all the place for their sakes."

27Then Abraham answered and said, "Indeed now, I who am but dust and ashes have taken it upon myself to speak to the Lord: 28Suppose there were five less than the fifty righteous; would You destroy all of the city for lack of five?"

So He said, "If I find there forty-five, I will not destroy it."

29And he spoke to Him yet again and said, "Suppose there should be forty found there?"

So He said, "I will not do it for the sake of forty."

30Then he said, "Let not the Lord be angry, and I will speak: Suppose thirty should be found there?"

So He said, "I will not do it if I find thirty there."

31And he said, "Indeed now, I have taken it upon myself to speak to the Lord: Suppose twenty should be found there?"

So He said, "I will not destroy it for the sake of twenty."

32Then he said, "Let not the Lord be angry, and I will speak but once more: Suppose ten should be found there?"

And He said, "I will not destroy it for the sake of ten." 33So the LORD went His way as soon as He had finished speaking with Abraham; and Abraham returned to his place.

Sodom's Depravity

19 Now the two angels came to Sodom in the evening, and Lot was sitting in the gate of Sodom. When Lot saw them, he rose to meet them, and he bowed himself with his face toward the ground. 2And he said, "Here now, my lords, please turn in to your servant's house and spend the night, and wash your feet; then you may rise early and go on your way."

And they said, "No, but we will spend the night in the open square."

3But he insisted strongly; so they turned in to him and entered his house. Then he made them a feast, and baked unleavened bread, and they ate.

4Now before they lay down, the men of the city, the men of Sodom, both old and young, all the people from every quarter, surrounded the house. 5And they called to Lot and said to him, "Where are the men who came to you tonight? Bring them out to us that we may know them carnally."

6So Lot went out to them through the doorway, shut the door behind him, 7and said, "Please, my brethren, do not do so wickedly! 8See now, I have two daughters who have not known a man; please, let me bring them out to you, and you may do to them as you wish; only do nothing to these men, since this is the reason they have come under the shadow of my roof."

9And they said, "Stand back!" Then they said, "This one came in to stay here, and he keeps acting as a judge; now we will deal worse with you than with them." So they pressed hard against the man Lot, and came near to break down the door. 10But the men reached out their hands and pulled Lot into the house with them, and shut the door. 11And they struck the men who *were* at the doorway of the house with blindness, both small and great, so that they became weary *trying* to find the door.

Sodom and Gomorrah Destroyed

12Then the men said to Lot, "Have you anyone else here? Son-in-law, your sons, your daughters, and whomever you have in the city—take *them* out of this place! 13For we will destroy this place, because the outcry against them has grown great before the face of the LORD, and the LORD has sent us to destroy it."

14So Lot went out and spoke to his sons-in-law, who had married his daughters, and said, "Get up, get out of this place; for the LORD will destroy this city!" But to his sons-in-law he seemed to be joking.

15When the morning dawned, the angels urged Lot to hurry, saying, "Arise, take your wife and your two daughters who are here, lest you be consumed in the punishment of the city." 16And while he lingered, the men took hold of his hand, his wife's hand, and the hands of his two daughters, the LORD being merciful to him, and they brought him out and set him outside the city. 17So it came to pass, when they had brought them outside, that he said, "Escape for your life! Do not look behind you nor stay anywhere in the plain. Escape to the mountains, lest you be destroyed."

18Then Lot said to them, "Please, no, my lords! 19Indeed now, your servant has found favor in your sight, and you have increased your mercy which you have shown me by saving my life; but I cannot escape to the mountains, lest some evil overtake me and I die. 20See now, this city *is* near *enough* to flee to, and it *is* a little one; please let me escape there (*is* it not a little one?) and my soul shall live."

21And he said to him, "See, I have favored you concerning this thing also, in that I will not overthrow this city for which you have spoken. 22Hurry, escape there. For I cannot do anything until you arrive there."

Therefore the name of the city was called Zoar.

23The sun had risen upon the earth when Lot entered Zoar. 24Then the LORD rained brimstone and fire on Sodom and Gomorrah, from the LORD out of the heavens. 25So He overthrew those cities, all the plain, all the inhabitants of the cities, and what grew on the ground.

26But his wife looked back behind him, and she became a pillar of salt.

27And Abraham went early in the morning to the place where he had stood before the LORD. 28Then he looked toward Sodom and Gomorrah, and toward all the land of the plain; and he saw, and behold, the smoke of the land which went up like the smoke of a furnace. 29And it came to pass, when God destroyed the cities of the plain, that God remembered Abraham, and sent Lot out of the midst of the overthrow, when He overthrew the cities in which Lot had dwelt.

The Descendants of Lot

30Then Lot went up out of Zoar and dwelt in the mountains, and his two daughters were with him; for he was afraid to dwell in Zoar. And he and his two daughters dwelt in a cave. 31Now the firstborn said to the younger, "Our father *is* old, and *there is* no man on the earth to come in to us as is the custom of all the earth. 32Come, let us make our father drink wine, and we will lie with him, that we may preserve the lineage of our father." 33So they made their father drink wine that night. And the firstborn went in and lay with her father, and he did not know when she lay down or when she arose.

34It happened on the next day that the firstborn said to the younger, "Indeed I lay with my father last night; let us make him drink wine tonight also, and you go in *and* lie with him, that we may preserve the lineage of our father." 35Then they made their father drink wine that night also. And the younger arose and lay with him, and he did not know when she lay down or when she arose.

36Thus both the daughters of Lot were with child by their father. 37The firstborn bore a son and called his name Moab; he *is* the father of the Moabites to this day. 38And the younger, she also bore a son and called his name Ben-Ammi; he *is* the father of the people of Ammon to this day.

Abraham and Abimelech

20 And Abraham journeyed from there to the South, and dwelt between Kadesh and Shur, and stayed in Gerar. 2Now Abraham said of Sarah his wife, "She *is* my sister." And Abimelech king of Gerar sent and took Sarah.

3But God came to Abimelech in a dream by night, and said to him, "Indeed you *are* a dead man because of the woman whom you have taken, for she *is* a man's wife."

4But Abimelech had not come near her; and he said, "Lord, will You slay a righteous nation also? 5Did he not say to me, 'She *is* my sister'? And she, even she herself said, 'He *is* my brother.' In the integrity of my heart and innocence of my hands I have done this."

6And God said to him in a dream, "Yes, I know that you did this in the integrity of your heart. For I also withheld you from sinning against Me; therefore I did not let you touch her. 7Now therefore, restore the man's wife; for he *is* a prophet, and he will pray for you and you shall live. But if you do not restore *her*, know that you shall surely die, you and all who *are* yours."

8So Abimelech rose early in the morning, called all his servants, and told all these things in their hearing; and the men were very much afraid. 9And Abimelech called Abraham and said to him, "What have you done to us? How have I offended you, that you have brought on me and on my kingdom a great sin? You have done deeds to me that ought not to be done." 10Then Abimelech said to Abraham, "What did you have in view, that you have done this thing?"

11And Abraham said, "Because I thought, surely the fear of God *is* not in this place; and they will kill me on account of my wife. 12But indeed *she* is truly my sister. She *is* the daughter of my father, but not the daughter of my mother; and she became my wife. 13And it came to pass, when God caused me to wander from my father's house, that I said to her, 'This *is* your

kindness that you should do for me: in every place, wherever we go, say of me, "He *is* my brother." ' "

14Then Abimelech took sheep, oxen, and male and female servants, and gave *them* to Abraham; and he restored Sarah his wife to him. 15And Abimelech said, "See, my land *is* before you; dwell where it pleases you." 16Then to Sarah he said, "Behold, I have given your brother a thousand *pieces* of silver; indeed this vindicates you before all who *are* with you and before everybody." Thus she was rebuked.

17So Abraham prayed to God; and God healed Abimelech, his wife, and his female servants. Then they bore *children*; 18for the LORD had closed up all the wombs of the house of Abimelech because of Sarah, Abraham's wife.

Isaac Is Born

21 And the LORD visited Sarah as He had said, and the LORD did for Sarah as He had spoken. 2For Sarah conceived and bore Abraham a son in his old age, at the set time of which God had spoken to him. 3And Abraham called the name of his son who was born to him—whom Sarah bore to him—Isaac. 4Then Abraham circumcised his son Isaac when he was eight days old, as God had commanded him. 5Now Abraham was one hundred years old when his son Isaac was born to him. 6And Sarah said, "God has made me laugh, *and* all who hear will laugh with me." 7She also said, "Who would have said to Abraham that Sarah would nurse children? For I have borne *him* a son in his old age."

Hagar and Ishmael Depart

8So the child grew and was weaned. And Abraham made a great feast on the same day that Isaac was weaned.

9And Sarah saw the son of Hagar the Egyptian, whom she had borne to Abraham, scoffing. 10Therefore she said to Abraham, "Cast out this bondwoman and her son; for the son of this bondwoman shall not be heir with my son, *namely* with Isaac." 11And the matter was very displeasing in Abraham's sight because of his son.

12But God said to Abraham, "Do not

let it be displeasing in your sight because of the lad or because of your bondwoman. Whatever Sarah has said to you, listen to her voice; for in Isaac your seed shall be called. 13Yet I will also make a nation of the son of the bondwoman, because he *is* your seed."

14So Abraham rose early in the morning, and took bread and a skin of water; and putting *it* on her shoulder, he gave *it* and the boy to Hagar, and sent her away. Then she departed and wandered in the Wilderness of Beersheba. 15And the water in the skin was used up, and she placed the boy under one of the shrubs. 16Then she went and sat down across from *him* at a distance of about a bowshot; for she said to herself, "Let me not see the death of the boy." So she sat opposite *him*, and lifted her voice and wept.

17And God heard the voice of the lad. Then the angel of God called to Hagar out of heaven, and said to her, "What ails you, Hagar? Fear not, for God has heard the voice of the lad where he *is*. 18Arise, lift up the lad and hold him with your hand, for I will make him a great nation."

19Then God opened her eyes, and she saw a well of water. And she went and filled the skin with water, and gave the lad a drink. 20So God was with the lad; and he grew and dwelt in the wilderness, and became an archer. 21He dwelt in the Wilderness of Paran; and his mother took a wife for him from the land of Egypt.

A Covenant with Abimelech

22And it came to pass at that time that Abimelech and Phichol, the commander of his army, spoke to Abraham, saying, "God *is* with you in all that you do. 23Now therefore, swear to me by God that you will not deal falsely with me, with my offspring, or with my posterity; but that according to the kindness that I have done to you, you will do to me and to the land in which you have dwelt."

24And Abraham said, "I will swear." 25Then Abraham rebuked Abimelech because of a well of water which Abimelech's servants had seized.

26And Abimelech said, "I do not know who has done this thing; you did not tell me, nor had I heard *of it* until today." 27So Abraham took sheep and oxen and gave them to Abimelech, and the two of them made a covenant. 28And Abraham set seven ewe lambs of the flock by themselves.

29Then Abimelech asked Abraham, "What *is the meaning of* these seven ewe lambs which you have set by themselves?"

30And he said, "You will take *these* seven ewe lambs from my hand, that they may be my witness that I have dug this well." 31Therefore he called that place Beersheba,*d* because the two of them swore an oath there.

32Thus they made a covenant at Beersheba. So Abimelech rose with Phichol, the commander of his army, and they returned to the land of the Philistines. 33Then *Abraham* planted a tamarisk tree in Beersheba, and there called on the name of the LORD, the Everlasting God. 34And Abraham stayed in the land of the Philistines many days.

Abraham's Faith Confirmed

22 Now it came to pass after these things that God tested Abraham, and said to him, "Abraham!"

And he said, "Here I am."

2Then He said, "Take now your son, your only *son* Isaac, whom you love, and go to the land of Moriah, and offer him there as a burnt offering on one of the mountains of which I shall tell you."

3So Abraham rose early in the morning and saddled his donkey, and took two of his young men with him, and Isaac his son; and he split the wood for the burnt offering, and arose and went to the place of which God had told him. 4Then on the third day Abraham lifted his eyes and saw the place afar off. 5And Abraham said to his young men, "Stay here with the donkey; the lad and I will go yonder and worship, and we will come back to you."

6So Abraham took the wood of the burnt offering and laid *it* on Isaac his son; and he took the fire in his hand,

---

d Literally *Well of the Oath* or *Well of the Seven*

and a knife, and the two of them went together. 7But Isaac spoke to Abraham his father and said, "My father!"

And he said, "Here I am, my son."

Then he said, "Look, the fire and the wood, but where *is* the lamb for a burnt offering?"

8And Abraham said, "My son, God will provide for Himself the lamb for a burnt offering." So the two of them went together.

9Then they came to the place of which God had told him. And Abraham built an altar there and placed the wood in order; and he bound Isaac his son and laid him on the altar, upon the wood. 10And Abraham stretched out his hand and took the knife to slay his son.

11But the Angel of the LORD called to him from heaven and said, "Abraham, Abraham!"

So he said, "Here I am."

12And He said, "Do not lay your hand on the lad, or do anything to him; for now I know that you fear God, since you have not withheld your son, your only *son*, from Me."

13Then Abraham lifted his eyes and looked, and there behind *him was* a ram caught in a thicket by its horns. So Abraham went and took the ram, and offered it up for a burnt offering instead of his son. 14And Abraham called the name of the place, The-LORD-Will-Provide; as it is said *to* this day, "In the Mount of the LORD it shall be provided."

15Then the Angel of the LORD called to Abraham a second time out of heaven, 16and said: "By Myself I have sworn, says the LORD, because you have done this thing, and have not withheld your son, your only *son*— 17blessing I will bless you, and multiplying I will multiply your descendants as the stars of the heaven and as the sand which *is* on the seashore; and your descendants shall possess the gate of their enemies. 18In your seed all the nations of the earth shall be blessed, because you have obeyed My voice." 19So Abraham returned to his young men, and they rose and went together to Beersheba; and Abraham dwelt at Beersheba.

The Family of Nahor

20Now it came to pass after these things that it was told Abraham, saying,

"Indeed Milcah also has borne children to your brother Nahor: 21Huz his firstborn, Buz his brother, Kemuel the father of Aram, 22Chesed, Hazo, Pildash, Jidlaph, and Bethuel." 23And Bethuel begot Rebekah. These eight Milcah bore to Nahor, Abraham's brother. 24His concubine, whose name was Reumah, also bore Tebah, Gaham, Thahash, and Maachah.

Sarah's Death and Burial

23 Sarah lived one hundred and twenty-seven years; *these were* the years of the life of Sarah. 2So Sarah died in Kirjath Arba (that *is*, Hebron) in the land of Canaan, and Abraham came to mourn for Sarah and to weep for her.

3Then Abraham stood up from before his dead, and spoke to the sons of Heth, saying, 4"I *am* a foreigner and a visitor among you. Give me property for a burial place among you, that I may bury my dead out of my sight."

5And the sons of Heth answered Abraham, saying to him, 6"Hear us, my lord: You *are* a mighty prince among us; bury your dead in the choicest of our burial places. None of us will withhold from you his burial place, that you may bury your dead."

7Then Abraham stood up and bowed himself to the people of the land, the sons of Heth. 8And he spoke with them, saying, "If it is your wish that I bury my dead out of my sight, hear me, and meet with Ephron the son of Zohar for me, 9that he may give me the cave of Machpelah which he has, which *is* at the end of his field. Let him give it to me at the full price, as property for a burial place among you."

10Now Ephron dwelt among the sons of Heth; and Ephron the Hittite answered Abraham in the presence of the sons of Heth, all who entered at the gate of his city, saying, 11"No, my lord, hear me: I give you the field and the cave that *is* in it; I give it to you in the presence of the sons of my people. I give it to you. Bury your dead!"

12Then Abraham bowed himself down before the people of the land; 13and he spoke to Ephron in the hearing of the people of the land, saying, "If you *will give it,* please hear me. I will give you money for the field; take *it* from me and I will bury my dead there."

14And Ephron answered Abraham, saying to him, 15"My lord, listen to me; the land *is worth* four hundred shekels of silver. What *is* that between you and me? So bury your dead." 16And Abraham listened to Ephron; and Abraham weighed out the silver for Ephron which he had named in the hearing of the sons of Heth, four hundred shekels of silver, currency of the merchants.

17So the field of Ephron which *was* in Machpelah, which *was* before Mamre, the field and the cave which *was* in it, and all the trees that *were* in the field, which *were* within all the surrounding borders, were deeded 18to Abraham as a possession in the presence of the sons of Heth, before all who went in at the gate of his city.

19And after this, Abraham buried Sarah his wife in the cave of the field of Machpelah, before Mamre (that *is*, Hebron) in the land of Canaan. 20So the field and the cave that *is* in it were deeded to Abraham by the sons of Heth as property for a burial place.

A Bride for Isaac

24 Now Abraham was old, well advanced in age; and the LORD had blessed Abraham in all things. 2So Abraham said to the oldest servant of his house, who ruled over all that he had, "Please, put your hand under my thigh, 3and I will make you swear by the LORD, the God of heaven and the God of the earth, that you will not take a wife for my son from the daughters of the Canaanites, among whom I dwell; 4but you shall go to my country and to my family, and take a wife for my son Isaac."

5And the servant said to him, "Perhaps the woman will not be willing to follow me to this land. Must I take your son back to the land from which you came?"

6But Abraham said to him, "Beware that you do not take my son back there. 7The LORD God of heaven, who took me from my father's house and from the land of my family, and who spoke to me and swore to me, saying, 'To your descendants I give this land,' He will send His angel before you, and you shall take a wife for my son from there. 8And if the woman is not willing to follow you, then you will be released from this oath; only do not take my son back there." 9So the servant put his hand under the thigh of Abraham his master, and swore to him concerning this matter.

10Then the servant took ten of his master's camels and departed, for all his master's goods *were in* his hand. And he arose and went to Mesopotamia, to the city of Nahor. 11And he made his camels kneel down outside the city by a well of water at evening time, the time when women go out to draw *water.* 12Then he said, "O LORD God of my master Abraham, please give me success this day, and show kindness to my master Abraham. 13Behold, *here* I stand by the well of water, and the daughters of the men of the city are coming out to draw water. 14Now let it be that the young woman to whom I say, 'Please let down your pitcher that I may drink,' and she says, 'Drink, and I will also give your camels a drink'—*let* her *be the one* You have appointed for Your servant Isaac. And by this I will know that You have shown kindness to my master."

15And it happened, before he had finished speaking, that behold, Rebekah, who was born to Bethuel, son of Milcah, the wife of Nahor, Abraham's brother, came out with her pitcher on her shoulder. 16Now the young woman *was* very beautiful to behold, a virgin; no man had known her. And she went down to the well, filled her pitcher, and came up. 17And the servant ran to meet her and said, "Please let me drink a little water from your pitcher."

18So she said, "Drink, my lord." Then she quickly let her pitcher down to her hand, and gave him a drink. 19And when she had finished giving him a drink, she said, "I will draw *water* for your camels also, until they have finished drinking." 20Then she quickly emptied her pitcher into the trough, ran back to the well to draw *water,* and drew for all his camels. 21And the man, wondering at her, remained silent so as to know whether the LORD had made his journey prosperous or not.

22So it was, when the camels had finished drinking, that the man took a golden nose ring weighing half a shekel, and two bracelets for her wrists weighing ten *shekels* of gold, 23and said, "Whose daughter *are* you? Tell me, please, is there room *in* your father's house for us to lodge?"

24So she said to him, "I *am* the daughter of Bethuel, Milcah's son, whom she bore to Nahor." 25Moreover she said to him, "We have both straw and feed enough, and room to lodge."

26Then the man bowed down his head and worshiped the LORD. 27And he said, "Blessed *be* the LORD God of my master Abraham, who has not forsaken His mercy and His truth toward my master. As for me, being on the way, the LORD led me to the house of my master's brethren." 28So the young woman ran and told her mother's household these things.

29Now Rebekah had a brother whose name *was* Laban, and Laban ran out to the man by the well. 30So it came to pass, when he saw the nose ring, and the bracelets on his sister's wrists, and when he heard the words of his sister Rebekah, saying, "Thus the man spoke to me," that he went to the man. And there he stood by the camels at the well. 31And he said, "Come in, O blessed of the LORD! Why do you stand outside? For I have prepared the house, and a place for the camels."

32Then the man came to the house. And he unloaded the camels, and provided straw and feed for the camels, and water to wash his feet and the feet of the men who *were* with him. 33*Food* was set before him to eat, but he said, "I will not eat until I have told about my errand."

And he said, "Speak on."

34So he said, "I *am* Abraham's servant. 35The LORD has blessed my master greatly, and he has become great; and He has given him flocks and herds, silver and gold, male and female servants, and camels and donkeys. 36And Sarah my master's wife bore a son to my master when she was old; and to him he has given all that he has. 37Now my master made me swear, saying, 'You shall not take a wife for my son from the daughters of the Canaanites, in whose land I dwell; 38but you

shall go to my father's house and to my family, and take a wife for my son.' 39And I said to my master, 'Perhaps the woman will not follow me.' 40But he said to me, 'The LORD, before whom I walk, will send His angel with you and prosper your way; and you shall take a wife for my son from my family and from my father's house. 41You will be clear from this oath when you arrive among my family; for if they will not give *her* to you, then you will be released from my oath.'

42"And this day I came to the well and said, 'O LORD God of my master Abraham, if You will now prosper the way in which I go, 43behold, I stand by the well of water; and it shall come to pass that when the virgin comes out to draw *water*, and I say to her, "Please give me a little water from your pitcher to drink," 44and she says to me, "Drink, and I will draw for your camels also,"— *let* her *be* the woman whom the LORD has appointed for my master's son.'

45"But before I had finished speaking in my heart, there was Rebekah, coming out with her pitcher on her shoulder; and she went down to the well and drew *water*. And I said to her, 'Please let me drink.' 46And she made haste and let her pitcher down from her *shoulder*, and said, 'Drink, and I will give your camels a drink also.' So I drank, and she gave the camels a drink also. 47Then I asked her, and said, 'Whose daughter *are* you?' And she said, 'The daughter of Bethuel, Nahor's son, whom Milcah bore to him.' So I put the nose ring on her nose and the bracelets on her wrists. 48And I bowed my head and worshiped the LORD, and blessed the LORD God of my master Abraham, who had led me in the way of truth to take the daughter of my master's brother for his son. 49Now if you will deal kindly and truly with my master, tell me. And if not, tell me, that I may turn to the right hand or to the left."

50Then Laban and Bethuel answered and said, "The thing comes from the LORD; we cannot speak to you either bad or good. 51Here *is* Rebekah before you; take *her* and go, and let her be your master's son's wife, as the LORD has spoken."

52And it came to pass, when Abraham's servant heard their words, that he worshiped the LORD, *bowing himself* to the earth. 53Then the servant brought out jewelry of silver, jewelry of gold, and clothing, and gave *them* to Rebekah. He also gave precious things to her brother and to her mother.

54And he and the men who *were* with him ate and drank and stayed all night. Then they arose in the morning, and he said, "Send me away to my master."

55But her brother and her mother said, "Let the young woman stay with us *a few* days, at least ten; after that she may go."

56And he said to them, "Do not hinder me, since the LORD has prospered my way; send me away so that I may go to my master."

57So they said, "We will call the young woman and ask her personally." 58Then they called Rebekah and said to her, "Will you go with this man?"

And she said, "I will go."

59So they sent away Rebekah their sister and her nurse, and Abraham's servant and his men. 60And they blessed Rebekah and said to her:

"Our sister, *may* you *become*
  The mother of thousands of ten
    thousands;
And may your descendants possess
  The gates of those who hate them."

61Then Rebekah and her maids arose, and they rode on the camels and followed the man. So the servant took Rebekah and departed.

62Now Isaac came from the way of Beer Lahai Roi, for he dwelt in the South. 63And Isaac went out to meditate in the field in the evening; and he lifted his eyes and looked, and there, the camels *were* coming. 64Then Rebekah lifted her eyes, and when she saw Isaac she dismounted from her camel; 65for she had said to the servant, "Who *is* this man walking in the field to meet us?"

The servant said, "It *is* my master." So she took a veil and covered herself.

66And the servant told Isaac all the things that he had done. 67Then Isaac brought her into his mother Sarah's tent; and he took Rebekah and she became his wife, and he loved her. So Isaac was comforted after his mother's *death.*

Abraham and Keturah

25 Abraham again took a wife, and her name *was* Keturah. 2And she bore him Zimran, Jokshan, Medan, Midian, Ishbak, and Shuah. 3Jokshan begot Sheba and Dedan. And the sons of Dedan were Asshurim, Letushim, and Leummim. 4And the sons of Midian *were* Ephah, Epher, Hanoch, Abidah, and Eldaah. All these *were* the children of Keturah.

5And Abraham gave all that he had to Isaac. 6But Abraham gave gifts to the sons of the concubines which Abraham had; and while he was still living he sent them eastward, away from Isaac his son, to the country of the east.

Abraham's Death and Burial

7This *is* the sum of the years of Abraham's life which he lived: one hundred and seventy-five years. 8Then Abraham breathed his last and died in a good old age, an old man and full *of years,* and was gathered to his people. 9And his sons Isaac and Ishmael buried him in the cave of Machpelah, which *is* before Mamre, in the field of Ephron the son of Zohar the Hittite, 10the field which Abraham purchased from the sons of Heth. There Abraham was buried, and Sarah his wife. 11And it came to pass, after the death of Abraham, that God blessed his son Isaac. And Isaac dwelt at Beer Lahai Roi.

The Families of Ishmael and Isaac

12Now this *is* the genealogy of Ishmael, Abraham's son, whom Hagar the Egyptian, Sarah's maidservant, bore to Abraham. 13And these *were* the names of the sons of Ishmael, by their names, according to their generations: The firstborn of Ishmael, Nebajoth; then Kedar, Adbeel, Mibsam, 14Mishma, Dumah, Massa, 15Hadar, Tema, Jetur, Naphish, and Kedemah. 16These *were* the sons of Ishmael and these *were* their names, by their towns and their settlements, twelve princes according to their nations. 17These *were* the years of the life of Ishmael: one hundred and thirty-seven years; and he breathed his last and died, and was gathered to his people. 18(They dwelt from Havilah as far as Shur, which is east of Egypt as you go toward Assyria.) He died in the presence of all his brethren.

19This is the genealogy of Isaac, Abraham's son. Abraham begot Isaac. 20Isaac was forty years old when he took Rebekah as wife, the daughter of Bethuel the Syrian of Padan Aram, the sister of Laban the Syrian. 21Now Isaac pleaded with the LORD for his wife, because she was barren; and the LORD granted his plea, and Rebekah his wife conceived. 22But the children struggled together within her; and she said, "If all is well, why am I like this?" So she went to inquire of the LORD.

23And the LORD said to her:

"Two nations are in your womb,
Two peoples shall be separated
  from your body;
One people shall be stronger than
  the other,
And the older shall serve the
  younger."

24So when her days were fulfilled for her to give birth, indeed there were twins in her womb. 25And the first came out red. He was like a hairy garment all over; so they called his name Esau.e 26Afterward his brother came out, and his hand took hold of Esau's heel; so his name was called Jacob.f Isaac was sixty years old when she bore them.

27So the boys grew. And Esau was a skillful hunter, a man of the field; but Jacob was a mild man, dwelling in tents. 28And Isaac loved Esau because he ate of his game, but Rebekah loved Jacob.

Esau Sells His Birthright

29Now Jacob cooked a stew; and Esau came in from the field, and he was weary. 30And Esau said to Jacob, "Please feed me with that same red stew, for I am weary." Therefore his name was called Edom.g

31But Jacob said, "Sell me your birthright as of this day."

32And Esau said, "Look, I am about to die; so what is this birthright to me?"

33Then Jacob said, "Swear to me as of this day."

So he swore to him, and sold his birthright to Jacob. 34And Jacob gave

Esau bread and stew of lentils; then he ate and drank, arose, and went his way. Thus Esau despised his birthright.

Isaac and Abimelech

26 There was a famine in the land, besides the first famine that was in the days of Abraham. And Isaac went to Abimelech king of the Philistines, in Gerar.

2Then the LORD appeared to him and said: "Do not go down to Egypt; live in the land of which I shall tell you. 3Dwell in this land, and I will be with you and bless you; for to you and your descendants I give all these lands, and I will perform the oath which I swore to Abraham your father. 4And I will make your descendants multiply as the stars of heaven; I will give to your descendants all these lands; and in your seed all the nations of the earth shall be blessed; 5because Abraham obeyed My voice and kept My charge, My commandments, My statutes, and My laws."

6So Isaac dwelt in Gerar. 7And the men of the place asked about his wife. And he said, "She is my sister"; for he was afraid to say, "She is my wife," because he thought, "lest the men of the place kill me for Rebekah, because she is beautiful to behold." 8Now it came to pass, when he had been there a long time, that Abimelech king of the Philistines looked through a window, and saw, and there was Isaac, showing endearment to Rebekah his wife. 9Then Abimelech called Isaac and said, "Quite obviously she is your wife; so how could you say, 'She is my sister'?"

Isaac said to him, "Because I said, 'Lest I die on account of her.' "

10And Abimelech said, "What is this you have done to us? One of the people might soon have lain with your wife, and you would have brought guilt on us." 11So Abimelech charged all his people, saying, "He who touches this man or his wife shall surely be put to death."

12Then Isaac sowed in that land, and reaped in the same year a hundredfold; and the LORD blessed him. 13The man began to prosper, and continued pros-

---

e Literally Hairy   f Literally Supplanter   g Literally Red pering until he became very prosperous; 14for he had possessions of flocks and possessions of herds and a great number of servants. So the Philistines envied him. 15Now the Philistines had stopped up all the wells which his father's servants had dug in the days of Abraham his father, and they had filled them with earth. 16And Abimelech said to Isaac, "Go away from us, for you are much mightier than we."

17Then Isaac departed from there and pitched his tent in the Valley of Gerar, and dwelt there. 18And Isaac dug again the wells of water which they had dug in the days of Abraham his father, for the Philistines had stopped them up after the death of Abraham. He called them by the names which his father had called them.

19Also Isaac's servants dug in the valley, and found a well of running water there. 20But the herdsmen of Gerar quarreled with Isaac's herdsmen, saying, "The water is ours." So he called the name of the well Esek,h because they quarreled with him. 21Then they dug another well, and they quarreled over that one also. So he called its name Sitnah.i 22And he moved from there and dug another well, and they did not quarrel over it. So he called its name Rehoboth,j because he said, "For now the LORD has made room for us, and we shall be fruitful in the land."

23Then he went up from there to Beersheba. 24And the LORD appeared to him the same night and said, "I am the God of your father Abraham; do not fear, for I am with you. I will bless you and multiply your descendants for My servant Abraham's sake." 25So he built an altar there and called on the name of the LORD, and he pitched his tent there; and there Isaac's servants dug a well.

26Then Abimelech came to him from Gerar with Ahuzzath, one of his friends, and Phichol the commander of his army. 27And Isaac said to them, "Why have you come to me, since you hate me and have sent me away from you?"

28But they said, "We have certainly seen that the LORD is with you. So we said, 'Let there now be an oath between us, between you and us; and let us make a covenant with you, 29that you will do us no harm, since we have not touched you, and since we have done nothing to you but good and have sent you away in peace. You are now the blessed of the LORD.' "

30So he made them a feast, and they ate and drank. 31Then they arose early in the morning and swore an oath with one another; and Isaac sent them away, and they departed from him in peace.

32It came to pass the same day that Isaac's servants came and told him about the well which they had dug, and said to him, "We have found water." 33So he called it Shebah.k Therefore the name of the city is Beershebal to this day.

34When Esau was forty years old, he took as wives Judith the daughter of Beeri the Hittite, and Basemath the daughter of Elon the Hittite. 35And they were a grief of mind to Isaac and Rebekah.

Isaac Blesses Jacob

27 Now it came to pass, when Isaac was old and his eyes were so dim that he could not see, that he called Esau his older son and said to him, "My son."

And he answered him, "Here I am."

2Then he said, "Behold now, I am old. I do not know the day of my death. 3Now therefore, please take your weapons, your quiver and your bow, and go out to the field and hunt game for me. 4And make me savory food, such as I love, and bring it to me that I may eat, that my soul may bless you before I die."

5Now Rebekah was listening when Isaac spoke to Esau his son. And Esau went to the field to hunt game and to bring it. 6So Rebekah spoke to Jacob her son, saying, "Indeed I heard your father speak to Esau your brother, saying, 7'Bring me game and make savory food for me, that I may eat it and bless you in the presence of the LORD before my death.' 8Now therefore, my son,

---

h Literally *Quarrel*   i Literally *Enmity*   j Literally *Spaciousness*   k Literally *Oath* or *Seven*   l Literally *Well of the Oath* or *Well of the Seven* obey my voice according to what I command you. 9Go now to the flock and bring me from there two choice kids of the goats, and I will make savory food from them for your father, such as he loves. 10Then you shall take it to your father, that he may eat it, and that he may bless you before his death."

11And Jacob said to Rebekah his mother, "Look, Esau my brother is a hairy man, and I am a smooth-skinned man. 12Perhaps my father will feel me, and I shall seem to be a deceiver to him; and I shall bring a curse on myself and not a blessing."

13But his mother said to him, "Let your curse be on me, my son; only obey my voice, and go, get them for me." 14And he went and got them and brought them to his mother, and his mother made savory food, such as his father loved. 15Then Rebekah took the choice clothes of her elder son Esau, which were with her in the house, and put them on Jacob her younger son. 16And she put the skins of the kids of the goats on his hands and on the smooth part of his neck. 17Then she gave the savory food and the bread, which she had prepared, into the hand of her son Jacob.

18So he went to his father and said, "My father."

And he said, "Here I am. Who are you, my son?"

19Jacob said to his father, "I am Esau your firstborn; I have done just as you told me; please arise, sit and eat of my game, that your soul may bless me."

20But Isaac said to his son, "How is it that you have found it so quickly, my son?"

And he said, "Because the LORD your God brought it to me."

21Isaac said to Jacob, "Please come near, that I may feel you, my son, whether you are really my son Esau or not." 22So Jacob went near to Isaac his father, and he felt him and said, "The voice is Jacob's voice, but the hands are the hands of Esau." 23And he did not recognize him, because his hands were hairy like his brother Esau's hands; so he blessed him.

24Then he said, "Are you really my son Esau?"

He said, "I am."

25He said, "Bring it near to me, and I will eat of my son's game, so that my soul may bless you." So he brought it near to him, and he ate; and he brought him wine, and he drank. 26Then his father Isaac said to him, "Come near now and kiss me, my son." 27And he came near and kissed him; and he smelled the smell of his clothing, and blessed him and said:

"Surely, the smell of my son
Is like the smell of a field
Which the LORD has blessed.
28 Therefore may God give you
Of the dew of heaven,
Of the fatness of the earth,
And plenty of grain and wine.
29 Let peoples serve you,
And nations bow down to you.
Be master over your brethren,
And let your mother's sons bow
down to you.
Cursed be everyone who curses
you,
And blessed be those who bless
you!"

Esau's Lost Hope

30Now it happened, as soon as Isaac had finished blessing Jacob, and Jacob had scarcely gone out from the presence of Isaac his father, that Esau his brother came in from his hunting. 31He also had made savory food, and brought it to his father, and said to his father, "Let my father arise and eat of his son's game, that your soul may bless me."

32And his father Isaac said to him, "Who are you?"

So he said, "I am your son, your firstborn, Esau."

33Then Isaac trembled exceedingly, and said, "Who? Where is the one who hunted game and brought it to me? I ate all of it before you came, and I have blessed him—and indeed he shall be blessed."

34When Esau heard the words of his father, he cried with an exceedingly great and bitter cry, and said to his father, "Bless me—me also, O my father!"

35But he said, "Your brother came with deceit and has taken away your blessing."

36And Esau said, "Is he not rightly named Jacob? For he has supplanted me these two times. He took away my birthright, and now look, he has taken away my blessing!" And he said, "Have you not reserved a blessing for me?"

37Then Isaac answered and said to Esau, "Indeed I have made him your master, and all his brethren I have given to him as servants; with grain and wine I have sustained him. What shall I do now for you, my son?"

38And Esau said to his father, "Have you only one blessing, my father? Bless me—me also, O my father!" And Esau lifted up his voice and wept.

39Then Isaac his father answered and said to him:

"Behold, your dwelling shall be of
the fatness of the earth,
And of the dew of heaven from
above.
40 By your sword you shall live,
And you shall serve your brother;
And it shall come to pass, when you
become restless,
That you shall break his yoke from
your neck."

Jacob Escapes from Esau

41So Esau hated Jacob because of the blessing with which his father blessed him, and Esau said in his heart, "The days of mourning for my father are at hand; then I will kill my brother Jacob."

42And the words of Esau her older son were told to Rebekah. So she sent and called Jacob her younger son, and said to him, "Surely your brother Esau comforts himself concerning you *by intending* to kill you. 43Now therefore, my son, obey my voice: arise, flee to my brother Laban in Haran. 44And stay with him a few days, until your brother's fury turns away, 45until your brother's anger turns away from you, and he forgets what you have done to him; then I will send and bring you from there. Why should I be bereaved also of you both in one day?"

46And Rebekah said to Isaac, "I am weary of my life because of the daughters of Heth; if Jacob takes a wife of the daughters of Heth, like these *who are* the daughters of the land, what good will my life be to me?"

28 Then Isaac called Jacob and blessed him, and charged him,

and said to him: "You shall not take a wife from the daughters of Canaan. 2Arise, go to Padan Aram, to the house of Bethuel your mother's father; and take yourself a wife from there of the daughters of Laban your mother's brother.

3 "May God Almighty bless you,
And make you fruitful and multiply
you,
That you may be an assembly of
peoples;
4 And give you the blessing of
Abraham,
To you and your descendants with
you,
That you may inherit the land
In which you are a stranger,
Which God gave to Abraham."

5So Isaac sent Jacob away, and he went to Padan Aram, to Laban the son of Bethuel the Syrian, the brother of Rebekah, the mother of Jacob and Esau.

Esau Marries Mahalath

6Esau saw that Isaac had blessed Jacob and sent him away to Padan Aram to take himself a wife from there, *and that* as he blessed him he gave him a charge, saying, "You shall not take a wife from the daughters of Canaan," 7and that Jacob had obeyed his father and his mother and had gone to Padan Aram. 8Also Esau saw that the daughters of Canaan did not please his father Isaac. 9So Esau went to Ishmael and took Mahalath the daughter of Ishmael, Abraham's son, the sister of Nebajoth, to be his wife in addition to the wives he had.

Jacob's Vow at Bethel

10Now Jacob went out from Beersheba and went toward Haran. 11So he came to a certain place and stayed there all night, because the sun had set. And he took one of the stones of that place and put it at his head, and he lay down in that place to sleep. 12Then he dreamed, and behold, a ladder *was* set up on the earth, and its top reached to heaven; and there the angels of God were ascending and descending on it.

13And behold, the LORD stood above it and said: "I *am* the LORD God of Abraham your father and the God of Isaac; the land on which you lie I will give to you and your descendants. 14Also your descendants shall be as the dust of the earth; you shall spread abroad to the west and the east, to the north and the south; and in you and in your seed all the families of the earth shall be blessed. 15Behold, I *am* with you and will keep you wherever you go, and will bring you back to this land; for I will not leave you until I have done what I have spoken to you."

16Then Jacob awoke from his sleep and said, "Surely the LORD is in this place, and I did not know *it*." 17And he was afraid and said, "How awesome *is* this place! This *is* none other than the house of God, and this *is* the gate of heaven!"

18Then Jacob rose early in the morning, and took the stone that he had put at his head, set it up as a pillar, and poured oil on top of it. 19And he called the name of that place Bethel;*m* but the name of that city had been Luz previously. 20Then Jacob made a vow, saying, "If God will be with me, and keep me in this way that I am going, and give me bread to eat and clothing to put on, 21so that I come back to my father's house in peace, then the LORD shall be my God. 22And this stone which I have set as a pillar shall be God's house, and of all that You give me I will surely give a tenth to You."

Jacob Meets Rachel

29 So Jacob went on his journey and came to the land of the people of the East. 2And he looked, and saw a well in the field; and behold, there *were* three flocks of sheep lying by it; for out of that well they watered the flocks. A large stone *was* on the well's mouth. 3Now all the flocks would be gathered there; and they would roll the stone from the well's mouth, water the sheep, and put the stone back in its place on the well's mouth.

4And Jacob said to them, "My brethren, where *are* you from?"

And they said, "We *are* from Haran."

5Then he said to them, "Do you know Laban the son of Nahor?"

And they said, "We know him."

6So he said to them, "Is he well?"

And they said, "*He is* well. And look, his daughter Rachel is coming with the sheep."

7Then he said, "Look, *it is* still high day; *it is* not time for the cattle to be gathered together. Water the sheep, and go and feed *them*."

8But they said, "We cannot until all the flocks are gathered together, and they have rolled the stone from the well's mouth; then we water the sheep."

9Now while he was still speaking with them, Rachel came with her father's sheep, for she was a shepherdess. 10And it came to pass, when Jacob saw Rachel the daughter of Laban his mother's brother, and the sheep of Laban his mother's brother, that Jacob went near and rolled the stone from the well's mouth, and watered the flock of Laban his mother's brother. 11Then Jacob kissed Rachel, and lifted up his voice and wept. 12And Jacob told Rachel that he *was* her father's relative and that he *was* Rebekah's son. So she ran and told her father.

13Then it came to pass, when Laban heard the report about Jacob his sister's son, that he ran to meet him, and embraced him and kissed him, and brought him to his house. So he told Laban all these things. 14And Laban said to him, "Surely you *are* my bone and my flesh." And he stayed with him for a month.

Jacob Marries Leah and Rachel

15Then Laban said to Jacob, "Because you *are* my relative, should you therefore serve me for nothing? Tell me, what *should* your wages *be*?" 16Now Laban had two daughters: the name of the elder *was* Leah, and the name of the younger *was* Rachel. 17Leah's eyes *were* delicate, but Rachel was beautiful of form and appearance.

18Now Jacob loved Rachel; so he said, "I will serve you seven years for Rachel your younger daughter."

19And Laban said, "*It is* better that I give her to you than that I should give her to another man. Stay with me." 20So Jacob served seven years for Rachel, and they seemed *only* a few

---

m Literally *House of God*

days to him because of the love he had for her.

21Then Jacob said to Laban, "Give *me* my wife, for my days are fulfilled, that I may go in to her." 22And Laban gathered together all the men of the place and made a feast. 23Now it came to pass in the evening, that he took Leah his daughter and brought her to Jacob; and he went in to her. 24And Laban gave his maid Zilpah to his daughter Leah *as* a maid. 25So it came to pass in the morning, that behold, it *was* Leah. And he said to Laban, "What is this you have done to me? Was it not for Rachel that I served you? Why then have you deceived me?"

26And Laban said, "It must not be done so in our country, to give the younger before the firstborn. 27Fulfill her week, and we will give you this one also for the service which you will serve with me still another seven years."

28Then Jacob did so and fulfilled her week. So he gave him his daughter Rachel as wife also. 29And Laban gave his maid Bilhah to his daughter Rachel as a maid. 30Then *Jacob* also went in to Rachel, and he also loved Rachel more than Leah. And he served with Laban still another seven years.

The Children of Jacob

31When the LORD saw that Leah *was* unloved, He opened her womb; but Rachel *was* barren. 32So Leah conceived and bore a son, and she called his name Reuben;*n* for she said, "The LORD has surely looked on my affliction. Now therefore, my husband will love me." 33Then she conceived again and bore a son, and said, "Because the LORD has heard that I *am* unloved, He has therefore given me this *son* also." And she called his name Simeon.*o* 34She conceived again and bore a son, and said, "Now this time my husband will become attached to me, because I have borne him three sons." Therefore his name was called Levi.*p* 35And she conceived again and bore a son, and said, "Now I will praise the LORD." Therefore

she called his name Judah.*q* Then she stopped bearing.

30 Now when Rachel saw that she bore Jacob no children, Rachel envied her sister, and said to Jacob, "Give me children, or else I die!"

2And Jacob's anger was aroused against Rachel, and he said, "*Am* I in the place of God, who has withheld from you the fruit of the womb?"

3So she said, "Here is my maid Bilhah; go in to her, and she will bear *a child* on my knees, that I also may have children by her." 4Then she gave him Bilhah her maid as wife, and Jacob went in to her. 5And Bilhah conceived and bore Jacob a son. 6Then Rachel said, "God has judged my case; and He has also heard my voice and given me a son." Therefore she called his name Dan.*r* 7And Rachel's maid Bilhah conceived again and bore Jacob a second son. 8Then Rachel said, "With great wrestlings I have wrestled with my sister, *and* indeed I have prevailed." So she called his name Naphtali.*s*

9When Leah saw that she had stopped bearing, she took Zilpah her maid and gave her to Jacob as wife. 10And Leah's maid Zilpah bore Jacob a son. 11Then Leah said, "A troop comes!"*t* So she called his name Gad.*u* 12And Leah's maid Zilpah bore Jacob a second son. 13Then Leah said, "I am happy, for the daughters will call me blessed." So she called his name Asher.*v*

14Now Reuben went in the days of wheat harvest and found mandrakes in the field, and brought them to his mother Leah. Then Rachel said to Leah, "Please give me *some* of your son's mandrakes."

15But she said to her, "*Is it* a small matter that you have taken away my husband? Would you take away my son's mandrakes also?"

And Rachel said, "Therefore he will lie with you tonight for your son's mandrakes."

16When Jacob came out of the field in the evening, Leah went out to meet him and said, "You must come in to me,

---

n Literally *See, a Son*   *o* Literally *Heard*
r Literally *Judge*   *s* Literally *My Wrestling*
Fortune   *v* Literally *Happy*

p Literally *Attached*   *q* Literally *Praise*
t Or *in fortune*   *u* Literally *Troop* or

for I have surely hired you with my son's mandrakes." And he lay with her that night.

17And God listened to Leah, and she conceived and bore Jacob a fifth son. 18Leah said, "God has given me my wages, because I have given my maid to my husband." So she called his name Issachar.ʷ 19Then Leah conceived again and bore Jacob a sixth son. 20And Leah said, "God has endowed me with a good endowment; now my husband will dwell with me, because I have borne him six sons." So she called his name Zebulun.ˣ 21Afterward she bore a daughter, and called her name Dinah.

22Then God remembered Rachel, and God listened to her and opened her womb. 23And she conceived and bore a son, and said, "God has taken away my reproach." 24So she called his name Joseph,ʸ and said, "The Lord shall add to me another son."

Jacob's Agreement with Laban

25And it came to pass, when Rachel had borne Joseph, that Jacob said to Laban, "Send me away, that I may go to my own place and to my country. 26Give me my wives and my children for whom I have served you, and let me go; for you know my service which I have done for you."

27And Laban said to him, "Please stay, if I have found favor in your eyes, for I have learned by experience that the Lord has blessed me for your sake." 28Then he said, "Name me your wages, and I will give it."

29So Jacob said to him, "You know how I have served you and how your livestock has been with me. 30For what you had before I came was little, and it has increased to a great amount; the Lord has blessed you since my coming. And now, when shall I also provide for my own house?"

31So he said, "What shall I give you?"

And Jacob said, "You shall not give me anything. If you will do this thing for me, I will again feed and keep your flocks: 32Let me pass through all your flock today, removing from there all the speckled and spotted sheep, and

all the brown ones among the lambs, and the spotted and speckled among the goats; and these shall be my wages. 33So my righteousness will answer for me in time to come, when the subject of my wages comes before you: every one that is not speckled and spotted among the goats, and brown among the lambs, will be considered stolen, if it is with me."

34And Laban said, "Oh, that it were according to your word!" 35So he removed that day the male goats that were speckled and spotted, all the female goats that were speckled and spotted, every one that had some white in it, and all the brown ones among the lambs, and gave them into the hand of his sons. 36Then he put three days' journey between himself and Jacob, and Jacob fed the rest of Laban's flocks.

37Now Jacob took for himself rods of green poplar and of the almond and chestnut trees, peeled white strips in them, and exposed the white which was in the rods. 38And the rods which he had peeled, he set before the flocks in the gutters, in the watering troughs where the flocks came to drink, so that they should conceive when they came to drink. 39So the flocks conceived before the rods, and the flocks brought forth streaked, speckled, and spotted. 40Then Jacob separated the lambs, and made the flocks face toward the streaked and all the brown in the flock of Laban; but he put his own flocks by themselves and did not put them with Laban's flock.

41And it came to pass, whenever the stronger livestock conceived, that Jacob placed the rods before the eyes of the livestock in the gutters, that they might conceive among the rods. 42But when the flocks were feeble, he did not put them in; so the feebler were Laban's and the stronger Jacob's. 43Thus the man became exceedingly prosperous, and had large flocks, female and male servants, and camels and donkeys.

Jacob Flees from Laban

31 Now Jacob heard the words of Laban's sons, saying, "Jacob

ʷ Literally *Wages*   ˣ Literally *Dwelling*   ʸ Literally *He Will Add* has taken away all that was our father's, and from what was our father's he has acquired all this wealth." 2And Jacob saw the countenance of Laban, and indeed it *was* not *favorable* toward him as before. 3Then the LORD said to Jacob, "Return to the land of your fathers and to your family, and I will be with you."

4So Jacob sent and called Rachel and Leah to the field, to his flock, 5and said to them, "I see your father's countenance, that it *is* not *favorable* toward me as before; but the God of my father has been with me. 6And you know that with all my might I have served your father. 7Yet your father has deceived me and changed my wages ten times, but God did not allow him to hurt me. 8If he said thus: 'The speckled shall be your wages,' then all the flocks bore speckled. And if he said thus: 'The streaked shall be your wages,' then all the flocks bore streaked. 9So God has taken away the livestock of your father and given *them* to me.

10"And it happened, at the time when the flocks conceived, that I lifted my eyes and saw in a dream, and behold, the rams which leaped upon the flocks *were* streaked, speckled, and gray-spotted. 11Then the Angel of God spoke to me in a dream, saying, 'Jacob.' And I said, 'Here I am.' 12And He said, 'Lift your eyes now and see, all the rams which leap on the flocks *are* streaked, speckled, and gray-spotted; for I have seen all that Laban is doing to you. 13I *am* the God of Bethel, where you anointed the pillar *and* where you made a vow to Me. Now arise, get out of this land, and return to the land of your family.' "

14Then Rachel and Leah answered and said to him, "Is there still any portion or inheritance for us in our father's house? 15Are we not considered strangers by him? For he has sold us, and also completely consumed our money. 16For all these riches which God has taken from our father are *really* ours and our children's; now then, whatever God has said to you, do it."

17Then Jacob rose and set his sons and his wives on camels. 18And he carried away all his livestock and all his possessions which he had gained, his acquired livestock which he had gained in Padan Aram, to go to his father Isaac in the land of Canaan. 19Now Laban had gone to shear his sheep, and Rachel had stolen the household idols that were her father's. 20And Jacob stole away, unknown to Laban the Syrian, in that he did not tell him that he intended to flee. 21So he fled with all that he had. He arose and crossed the river, and headed toward the mountains of Gilead.

Laban Pursues Jacob

22And Laban was told on the third day that Jacob had fled. 23Then he took his brethren with him and pursued him for seven days' journey, and he overtook him in the mountains of Gilead. 24But God had come to Laban the Syrian in a dream by night, and said to him, "Be careful that you speak to Jacob neither good nor bad."

25So Laban overtook Jacob. Now Jacob had pitched his tent in the mountains, and Laban with his brethren pitched in the mountains of Gilead.

26And Laban said to Jacob: "What have you done, that you have stolen away unknown to me, and carried away my daughters like captives *taken* with the sword? 27Why did you flee away secretly, and steal away from me, and not tell me; for I might have sent you away with joy and songs, with timbrel and harp? 28And you did not allow me to kiss my sons and my daughters. Now you have done foolishly in *so* doing. 29It is in my power to do you harm, but the God of your father spoke to me last night, saying, 'Be careful that you speak to Jacob neither good nor bad.' 30And now you have surely gone because you greatly long for your father's house, *but* why did you steal my gods?"

31Then Jacob answered and said to Laban, "Because I was afraid, for I said, 'Perhaps you would take your daughters from me by force.' 32With whomever you find your gods, do not let him live. In the presence of our brethren, identify what I have of yours and take *it* with you." For Jacob did not know that Rachel had stolen them.

33And Laban went into Jacob's tent, into Leah's tent, and into the two maids' tents, but he did not find *them*. Then he went out of Leah's tent and entered Rachel's tent. 34Now Rachel had taken the household idols, put them in the camel's saddle, and sat on them. And Laban searched all about the tent but did not find *them*. 35And she said to her father, "Let it not displease my lord that I cannot rise before you, for the manner of women *is* with me." And he searched but did not find the household idols.

36Then Jacob was angry and rebuked Laban, and Jacob answered and said to Laban: "What *is* my trespass? What *is* my sin, that you have so hotly pursued me? 37Although you have searched all my things, what part of your household things have you found? Set *it* here before my brethren and your brethren, that they may judge between us both! 38These twenty years I *have been* with you; your ewes and your female goats have not miscarried their young, and I have not eaten the rams of your flock. 39That which was torn *by beasts* I did not bring to you; I bore the loss of it. You required it from my hand, *whether* stolen by day or stolen by night. 40*There* I was! In the day the drought consumed me, and the frost by night, and my sleep departed from my eyes. 41Thus I have been in your house twenty years; I served you fourteen years for your two daughters, and six years for your flock, and you have changed my wages ten times. 42Unless the God of my father, the God of Abraham and the Fear of Isaac, had been with me, surely now you would have sent me away empty-handed. God has seen my affliction and the labor of my hands, and rebuked *you* last night."

Laban's Covenant with Jacob

43And Laban answered and said to Jacob, "*These* daughters *are* my daughters, and *these* children *are* my children, and *this* flock *is* my flock; all that you see *is* mine. But what can I do this day to these my daughters or to their children whom they have borne? 44Now therefore, come, let us make a covenant, you and I, and let it be a witness between you and me."

45So Jacob took a stone and set it up *as* a pillar. 46Then Jacob said to his brethren, "Gather stones." And they took stones and made a heap, and they ate there on the heap. 47Laban called it Jegar Sahadutha,*z* but Jacob called it Galeed.*a* 48And Laban said, "This heap *is* a witness between you and me this day." Therefore its name was called Galeed, 49also Mizpah,*b* because he said, "May the LORD watch between you and me when we are absent one from another. 50If you afflict my daughters, or if you take *other* wives besides my daughters, *although* no man *is* with us—see, God *is* witness between you and me!"

51Then Laban said to Jacob, "Here is this heap and here is *this* pillar, which I have placed between you and me. 52This heap *is* a witness, and *this* pillar *is* a witness, that I will not pass beyond this heap to you, and you will not pass beyond this heap and this pillar to me, for harm. 53The God of Abraham, the God of Nahor, and the God of their father judge between us." And Jacob swore by the Fear of his father Isaac. 54Then Jacob offered a sacrifice on the mountain, and called his brethren to eat bread. And they ate bread and stayed all night on the mountain. 55And early in the morning Laban arose, and kissed his sons and daughters and blessed them. Then Laban departed and returned to his place.

Esau Comes to Meet Jacob

32 So Jacob went on his way, and the angels of God met him. 2When Jacob saw them, he said, "This *is* God's camp." And he called the name of that place Mahanaim.*c*

3Then Jacob sent messengers before him to Esau his brother in the land of Seir, the country of Edom. 4And he commanded them, saying, "Speak thus to my lord Esau, 'Thus your servant Jacob says: "I have dwelt with Laban and stayed there until now. 5I have oxen, donkeys, flocks, and male and female servants; and I have sent to tell my lord, that I may find favor in your sight."'" 6Then the messengers returned to Ja-

---

z Literally, in Aramaic, *Heap of Witness*   *a* Literally, in Hebrew, *Heap of Witness*
b Literally *Watch*   *c* Literally *Double Camp*

cob, saying, "We came to your brother Esau, and he also is coming to meet you, and four hundred men *are* with him." 7So Jacob was greatly afraid and distressed; and he divided the people that *were* with him, and the flocks and herds and camels, into two companies. 8And he said, "If Esau comes to the one company and attacks it, then the other company which is left will escape."

9Then Jacob said, "O God of my father Abraham and God of my father Isaac, the LORD who said to me, 'Return to your country and to your family, and I will deal well with you': 10I am not worthy of the least of all the mercies and of all the truth which You have shown Your servant; for I crossed over this Jordan with my staff, and now I have become two companies. 11Deliver me, I pray, from the hand of my brother, from the hand of Esau; for I fear him, lest he come and attack me *and* the mother with the children. 12For You said, 'I will surely treat you well, and make your descendants as the sand of the sea, which cannot be numbered for multitude.' "

13So he lodged there that same night, and took what came to his hand as a present for Esau his brother: 14two hundred female goats and twenty male goats, two hundred ewes and twenty rams, 15thirty milk camels with their colts, forty cows and ten bulls, twenty female donkeys and ten foals. 16Then he delivered *them* to the hand of his servants, every drove by itself, and said to his servants, "Pass over before me, and put some distance between successive droves." 17And he commanded the first one, saying, "When Esau my brother meets you and asks you, saying, 'To whom do you belong, and where are you going? Whose *are* these in front of you?' 18then you shall say, 'They *are* your servant Jacob's. It *is* a present sent to my lord Esau; and behold, he also *is* behind us.' " 19So he commanded the second, the third, and all who followed the droves, saying, "In this manner you shall speak to Esau when you find him; 20and also say, 'Behold, your servant Jacob *is* behind us.' " For he said, "I will appease him with the present that goes before me, and afterward I will see his face; perhaps he will accept me." 21So the present went on over before him, but he himself lodged that night in the camp.

Wrestling with God

22And he arose that night and took his two wives, his two female servants, and his eleven sons, and crossed over the ford of Jabbok. 23He took them, sent them over the brook, and sent over what he had. 24Then Jacob was left alone; and a Man wrestled with him until the breaking of day. 25Now when He saw that He did not prevail against him, He touched the socket of his hip; and the socket of Jacob's hip was out of joint as He wrestled with him. 26And He said, "Let Me go, for the day breaks."

But he said, "I will not let You go unless You bless me!"

27So He said to him, "What *is* your name?"

He said, "Jacob."

28And He said, "Your name shall no longer be called Jacob, but Israel;[d] for you have struggled with God and with men, and have prevailed."

29Then Jacob asked, saying, "Tell *me* Your name, I pray."

And He said, "Why *is* it *that* you ask about My name?" And He blessed him there.

30So Jacob called the name of the place Peniel:[e] "For I have seen God face to face, and my life is preserved." 31Just as he crossed over Penuel[f] the sun rose on him, and he limped on his hip. 32Therefore to this day the children of Israel do not eat the muscle that shrank, which *is* on the hip socket, because He touched the socket of Jacob's hip in the muscle that shrank.

Jacob and Esau Meet

33 Now Jacob lifted his eyes and looked, and there, Esau was coming, and with him were four hundred men. So he divided the children among Leah, Rachel, and the two maidservants. 2And he put the maidservants and their children in front, Leah and her children behind,

---

d Literally *Prince with God*   *e* Literally *Face of God*   *f* Same as *Peniel*, verse 30 and Rachel and Joseph last. 3Then he crossed over before them and bowed himself to the ground seven times, until he came near to his brother.

4But Esau ran to meet him, and embraced him, and fell on his neck and kissed him, and they wept. 5And he lifted his eyes and saw the women and children, and said, "Who *are* these with you?"

So he said, "The children whom God has graciously given your servant." 6Then the maidservants came near, they and their children, and bowed down. 7And Leah also came near with her children, and they bowed down. Afterward Joseph and Rachel came near, and they bowed down.

8Then Esau said, "What *do* you *mean* by all this company which I met?"

And he said, "*These are* to find favor in the sight of my lord."

9But Esau said, "I have enough, my brother; keep what you have for yourself."

10And Jacob said, "No, please, if I have now found favor in your sight, then receive my present from my hand, inasmuch as I have seen your face as though I had seen the face of God, and you were pleased with me. 11Please, take my blessing that is brought to you, because God has dealt graciously with me, and because I have enough." So he urged him, and he took *it*.

12Then Esau said, "Let us take our journey; let us go, and I will go before you."

13But Jacob said to him, "My lord knows that the children *are* weak, and the flocks and herds which are nursing *are* with me. And if the men should drive them hard one day, all the flock will die. 14Please let my lord go on ahead before his servant. I will lead on slowly at a pace which the livestock that go before me, and the children, are able to endure, until I come to my lord in Seir."

15And Esau said, "Now let me leave with you *some* of the people who *are* with me."

But he said, "What need is there? Let me find favor in the sight of my lord." 16So Esau returned that day on his way

to Seir. 17And Jacob journeyed to Succoth, built himself a house, and made booths for his livestock. Therefore the name of the place is called Succoth.g

Jacob Comes to Canaan

18Then Jacob came safely to the city of Shechem, which *is* in the land of Canaan, when he came from Padan Aram; and he pitched his tent before the city. 19And he bought the parcel of land, where he had pitched his tent, from the children of Hamor, Shechem's father, for one hundred pieces of money. 20Then he erected an altar there and called it El Elohe Israel.h

The Dinah Incident

34 Now Dinah the daughter of Leah, whom she had borne to Jacob, went out to see the daughters of the land. 2And when Shechem the son of Hamor the Hivite, prince of the country, saw her, he took her and lay with her, and violated her. 3His soul was strongly attracted to Dinah the daughter of Jacob, and he loved the young woman and spoke kindly to the young woman. 4So Shechem spoke to his father Hamor, saying, "Get me this young woman as a wife."

5And Jacob heard that he had defiled Dinah his daughter. Now his sons were with his livestock in the field; so Jacob held his peace until they came. 6Then Hamor the father of Shechem went out to Jacob to speak with him. 7And the sons of Jacob came in from the field when they heard *it;* and the men were grieved and very angry, because he had done a disgraceful thing in Israel by lying with Jacob's daughter, a thing which ought not to be done. 8But Hamor spoke with them, saying, "The soul of my son Shechem longs for your daughter. Please give her to him as a wife. 9And make marriages with us; give your daughters to us, and take our daughters to yourselves. 10So you shall dwell with us, and the land shall be before you. Dwell and trade in it, and acquire possessions for yourselves in it."

11Then Shechem said to her father

---

g Literally *Booths*   h Literally *God, the God of Israel* and her brothers, "Let me find favor in your eyes, and whatever you say to me I will give. 12Ask me ever so much dowry and gift, and I will give according to what you say to me; but give me the young woman as a wife."

13But the sons of Jacob answered Shechem and Hamor his father, and spoke deceitfully, because he had defiled Dinah their sister. 14And they said to them, "We cannot do this thing, to give our sister to one who is uncircumcised, for that *would be* a reproach to us. 15But on this *condition* we will consent to you: If you will become as we *are*, if every male of you is circumcised, 16then we will give our daughters to you, and we will take your daughters to us; and we will dwell with you, and we will become one people. 17But if you will not heed us and be circumcised, then we will take our daughter and be gone."

18And their words pleased Hamor and Shechem, Hamor's son. 19So the young man did not delay to do the thing, because he was delighted in Jacob's daughter. He *was* more honorable than all the household of his father.

20And Hamor and Shechem his son came to the gate of their city, and spoke with the men of their city, saying: 21"These men *are* at peace with us. Therefore let them dwell in the land and trade in it. For indeed the land *is* large enough for them. Let us take their daughters to us as wives, and let us give them our daughters. 22Only on this *condition* will the men consent to dwell with us, to be one people: if every male among us is circumcised as they *are* circumcised. 23*Will* not their livestock, their property, and every animal of theirs *be* ours? Only let us consent to them, and they will dwell with us." 24And all who went out of the gate of his city heeded Hamor and Shechem his son; every male was circumcised, all who went out of the gate of his city.

25Now it came to pass on the third day, when they were in pain, that two of the sons of Jacob, Simeon and Levi, Dinah's brothers, each took his sword and came boldly upon the city and killed all the males. 26And they killed

Hamor and Shechem his son with the edge of the sword, and took Dinah from Shechem's house, and went out. 27The sons of Jacob came upon the slain, and plundered the city, because their sister had been defiled. 28They took their sheep, their oxen, and their donkeys, what *was* in the city and what *was* in the field, 29and all their wealth. All their little ones and their wives they took captive; and they plundered even all that *was* in the houses.

30Then Jacob said to Simeon and Levi, "You have troubled me by making me obnoxious among the inhabitants of the land, among the Canaanites and the Perizzites; and since I *am* few in number, they will gather themselves together against me and kill me. I shall be destroyed, my household and I."

31But they said, "Should he treat our sister like a harlot?"

Jacob's Return to Bethel

35 Then God said to Jacob, "Arise, go up to Bethel and dwell there; and make an altar there to God, who appeared to you when you fled from the face of Esau your brother."

2And Jacob said to his household and to all who *were* with him, "Put away the foreign gods that *are* among you, purify yourselves, and change your garments. 3Then let us arise and go up to Bethel; and I will make an altar there to God, who answered me in the day of my distress and has been with me in the way which I have gone." 4So they gave Jacob all the foreign gods which *were* in their hands, and the earrings which *were* in their ears; and Jacob hid them under the terebinth tree which *was* by Shechem.

5And they journeyed, and the terror of God was upon the cities that *were* all around them, and they did not pursue the sons of Jacob. 6So Jacob came to Luz (that *is*, Bethel), which *is* in the land of Canaan, he and all the people who *were* with him. 7And he built an altar there and called the place El Bethel,[i] because there God appeared to him when he fled from the face of his brother.

8Now Deborah, Rebekah's nurse,

[i] Literally God of the House of God

died, and she was buried below Bethel under the terebinth tree. So the name of it was called Allon Bachuth.[j]

9Then God appeared to Jacob again, when he came from Padan Aram, and blessed him. 10And God said to him, "Your name is Jacob; your name shall not be called Jacob anymore, but Israel shall be your name." So He called his name Israel. 11Also God said to him: "I am God Almighty. Be fruitful and multiply; a nation and a company of nations shall proceed from you, and kings shall come from your body. 12The land which I gave Abraham and Isaac I give to you; and to your descendants after you I give this land." 13Then God went up from him in the place where He talked with him. 14So Jacob set up a pillar in the place where He talked with him, a pillar of stone; and he poured a drink offering on it, and he poured oil on it. 15And Jacob called the name of the place where God spoke with him, Bethel.

Death of Rachel

16Then they journeyed from Bethel. And where there was but a little distance to go to Ephrath, Rachel labored in childbirth, and she had hard labor. 17Now it came to pass, when she was in hard labor, that the midwife said to her, "Do not fear; you will have this son also." 18And so it was, as her soul was departing (for she died), that she called his name Ben-Oni;[k] but his father called him Benjamin.[l] 19So Rachel died and was buried on the way to Ephrath (that is, Bethlehem). 20And Jacob set a pillar on her grave, which is the pillar of Rachel's grave to this day.

21Then Israel journeyed and pitched his tent beyond the tower of Eder. 22And it happened, when Israel dwelt in that land, that Reuben went and lay with Bilhah his father's concubine; and Israel heard about it.

Jacob's Twelve Sons

Now the sons of Jacob were twelve: 23the sons of Leah were Reuben, Jacob's firstborn, and Simeon, Levi, Judah, Issachar, and Zebulun; 24the sons

of Rachel were Joseph and Benjamin; 25the sons of Bilhah, Rachel's maidservant, were Dan and Naphtali; 26and the sons of Zilpah, Leah's maidservant, were Gad and Asher. These were the sons of Jacob who were born to him in Padan Aram.

Death of Isaac

27Then Jacob came to his father Isaac at Mamre, or Kirjath Arba[m] (that is, Hebron), where Abraham and Isaac had dwelt. 28Now the days of Isaac were one hundred and eighty years. 29So Isaac breathed his last and died, and was gathered to his people, being old and full of days. And his sons Esau and Jacob buried him.

The Family of Esau

36 Now this is the genealogy of Esau, who is Edom. 2Esau took his wives from the daughters of Canaan: Adah the daughter of Elon the Hittite; Aholibamah the daughter of Anah, the daughter of Zibeon the Hivite; 3and Basemath, Ishmael's daughter, sister of Nebajoth. 4Now Adah bore Eliphaz to Esau, and Basemath bore Reuel. 5And Aholibamah bore Jeush, Jaalam, and Korah. These were the sons of Esau who were born to him in the land of Canaan.

6Then Esau took his wives, his sons, his daughters, and all the persons of his household, his cattle and all his animals, and all his goods which he had gained in the land of Canaan, and went to a country away from the presence of his brother Jacob. 7For their possessions were too great for them to dwell together, and the land where they were strangers could not support them because of their livestock. 8So Esau dwelt in Mount Seir. Esau is Edom.

9And this is the genealogy of Esau the father of the Edomites in Mount Seir. 10These were the names of Esau's sons: Eliphaz the son of Adah the wife of Esau, and Reuel the son of Basemath the wife of Esau. 11And the sons of Eliphaz were Teman, Omar, Zepho, Gatam, and Kenaz.

---

j Literally Terebinth of Weeping   k Literally Son of My Sorrow   l Literally Son of the Right
Hand   m Literally Town of Arba

12Now Timna was the concubine of Eliphaz, Esau's son, and she bore Amalek to Eliphaz. These *were* the sons of Adah, Esau's wife.

13These *were* the sons of Reuel: Nahath, Zerah, Shammah, and Mizzah. These were the sons of Basemath, Esau's wife.

14These were the sons of Aholibamah, Esau's wife, the daughter of Anah, the daughter of Zibeon. And she bore to Esau: Jeush, Jaalam, and Korah.

The Chiefs of Edom

15These *were* the chiefs of the sons of Esau. The sons of Eliphaz, the firstborn *son* of Esau, were Chief Teman, Chief Omar, Chief Zepho, Chief Kenaz, 16Chief Korah, Chief Gatam, *and* Chief Amalek. These *were* the chiefs of Eliphaz in the land of Edom. They *were* the sons of Adah.

17These *were* the sons of Reuel, Esau's son: Chief Nahath, Chief Zerah, Chief Shammah, and Chief Mizzah. These *were* the chiefs of Reuel in the land of Edom. These *were* the sons of Basemath, Esau's wife.

18And these *were* the sons of Aholibamah, Esau's wife: Chief Jeush, Chief Jaalam, and Chief Korah. These *were* the chiefs *who descended* from Aholibamah, Esau's wife, the daughter of Anah. 19These *were* the sons of Esau, who is Edom, and these *were* their chiefs.

The Sons of Seir

20These *were* the sons of Seir the Horite who inhabited the land: Lotan, Shobal, Zibeon, Anah, 21Dishon, Ezer, and Dishan. These *were* the chiefs of the Horites, the sons of Seir, in the land of Edom.

22And the sons of Lotan were Hori and Hemam. Lotan's sister *was* Timna.

23These *were* the sons of Shobal: Alvan, Manahath, Ebal, Shepho, and Onam.

24These *were* the sons of Zibeon: both Ajah and Anah. This *was the* Anah who found the water in the wilderness as he pastured the donkeys of his father Zibeon. 25These *were* the children of Anah: Dishon and Aholibamah the daughter of Anah.

26These *were* the sons of Dishon: Hemdan, Eshban, Ithran, and Cheran. 27These *were* the sons of Ezer: Bilhan, Zaavan, and Akan. 28These *were* the sons of Dishan: Uz and Aran.

29These *were* the chiefs of the Horites: Chief Lotan, Chief Shobal, Chief Zibeon, Chief Anah, 30Chief Dishon, Chief Ezer, and Chief Dishan. These *were* the chiefs of the Horites, according to their chiefs in the land of Seir.

The Kings of Edom

31Now these *were* the kings who reigned in the land of Edom before any king reigned over the children of Israel: 32Bela the son of Beor reigned in Edom, and the name of his city *was* Dinhabah. 33And when Bela died, Jobab the son of Zerah of Bozrah reigned in his place. 34When Jobab died, Husham of the land of the Temanites reigned in his place. 35And when Husham died, Hadad the son of Bedad, who attacked Midian in the field of Moab, reigned in his place. And the name of his city *was* Avith. 36When Hadad died, Samlah of Masrekah reigned in his place. 37And when Samlah died, Saul of Rehoboth-*by*-the-River reigned in his place. 38When Saul died, Baal-Hanan the son of Achbor reigned in his place. 39And when Baal-Hanan the son of Achbor died, Hadar reigned in his place; and the name of his city *was* Pau. His wife's name *was* Mehetabel, the daughter of Matred, the daughter of Mezahab.

The Chiefs of Esau

40And these *were* the names of the chiefs of Esau, according to their families and their places, by their names: Chief Timnah, Chief Alvah, Chief Jetheth, 41Chief Aholibamah, Chief Elah, Chief Pinon, 42Chief Kenaz, Chief Teman, Chief Mibzar, 43Chief Magdiel, and Chief Iram. These *were* the chiefs of Edom, according to their dwelling places in the land of their possession. Esau *was* the father of the Edomites.

Joseph Dreams of Greatness

37 Now Jacob dwelt in the land where his father was a stranger, in the land of Canaan. 2This *is* the history of Jacob.

Joseph, *being* seventeen years old, was feeding the flock with his brothers. And the lad *was* with the sons of Bilhah and the sons of Zilpah, his father's wives; and Joseph brought a bad report of them to his father.

3Now Israel loved Joseph more than all his children, because he *was* the son of his old age. Also he made him a tunic of *many* colors. 4But when his brothers saw that their father loved him more than all his brothers, they hated him and could not speak peaceably to him.

5Now Joseph had a dream, and he told *it* to his brothers; and they hated him even more. 6So he said to them, "Please hear this dream which I have dreamed: 7There we were, binding sheaves in the field. Then behold, my sheaf arose and also stood upright; and indeed your sheaves stood all around and bowed down to my sheaf."

8And his brothers said to him, "Shall you indeed reign over us? Or shall you indeed have dominion over us?" So they hated him even more for his dreams and for his words.

9Then he dreamed still another dream and told it to his brothers, and said, "Look, I have dreamed another dream. And this time, the sun, the moon, and the eleven stars bowed down to me."

10So he told *it* to his father and his brothers; and his father rebuked him and said to him, "What *is* this dream that you have dreamed? Shall your mother and I and your brothers indeed come to bow down to the earth before you?" 11And his brothers envied him, but his father kept the matter *in mind.*

Joseph Sold by His Brothers

12Then his brothers went to feed their father's flock in Shechem. 13And Israel said to Joseph, "Are not your brothers feeding *the flock* in Shechem? Come, I will send you to them."

So he said to him, "Here I am."

14Then he said to him, "Please go and see if it is well with your brothers and well with the flocks, and bring back word to me." So he sent him out of the Valley of Hebron, and he went to Shechem.

15Now a certain man found him, and there he was, wandering in the field.

And the man asked him, saying, "What are you seeking?"

16So he said, "I am seeking my brothers. Please tell me where they are feeding *their flocks.*"

17And the man said, "They have departed from here, for I heard them say, 'Let us go to Dothan.' " So Joseph went after his brothers and found them in Dothan.

18Now when they saw him afar off, even before he came near them, they conspired against him to kill him. 19Then they said to one another, "Look, this dreamer is coming! 20Come therefore, let us now kill him and cast him into some pit; and we shall say, 'Some wild beast has devoured him.' We shall see what will become of his dreams!"

21But Reuben heard *it,* and he delivered him out of their hands, and said, "Let us not kill him." 22And Reuben said to them, "Shed no blood, *but* cast him into this pit which *is* in the wilderness, and do not lay a hand on him"— that he might deliver him out of their hands, and bring him back to his father.

23So it came to pass, when Joseph had come to his brothers, that they stripped Joseph *of* his tunic, the tunic of *many* colors that *was* on him. 24Then they took him and cast him into a pit. And the pit *was* empty; *there was* no water in it.

25And they sat down to eat a meal. Then they lifted their eyes and looked, and there was a company of Ishmaelites, coming from Gilead with their camels, bearing spices, balm, and myrrh, on their way to carry *them* down to Egypt. 26So Judah said to his brothers, "What profit *is there* if we kill our brother and conceal his blood? 27Come and let us sell him to the Ishmaelites, and let not our hand be upon him, for he *is* our brother *and* our flesh." And his brothers listened. 28Then Midianite traders passed by; so *the brothers* pulled Joseph up and lifted him out of the pit, and sold him to the Ishmaelites for twenty *shekels* of silver. And they took Joseph to Egypt.

29Then Reuben returned to the pit, and indeed Joseph *was* not in the pit; and he tore his clothes. 30And he returned to his brothers and said, "The lad *is* no *more;* and I, where shall I go?"

31So they took Joseph's tunic, killed a kid of the goats, and dipped the tunic in the blood. **32**Then they sent the tunic of *many* colors, and they brought *it* to their father and said, "We have found this. Do you know whether it *is* your son's tunic or not?"

33And he recognized it and said, "*It is* my son's tunic. A wild beast has devoured him. Without doubt Joseph is torn to pieces." **34**Then Jacob tore his clothes, put sackcloth on his waist, and mourned for his son many days. **35**And all his sons and all his daughters arose to comfort him; but he refused to be comforted, and he said, "For I shall go down into the grave to my son in mourning." Thus his father wept for him.

36Now the Midianites had sold him in Egypt to Potiphar, an officer of Pharaoh *and* captain of the guard.

Judah and Tamar

38 It came to pass at that time that Judah departed from his brothers, and visited a certain Adullamite whose name *was* Hirah. **2**And Judah saw there a daughter of a certain Canaanite whose name *was* Shua, and he married her and went in to her. **3**So she conceived and bore a son, and he called his name Er. **4**She conceived again and bore a son, and she called his name Onan. **5**And she conceived yet again and bore a son, and called his name Shelah. He was at Chezib when she bore him.

6Then Judah took a wife for Er his firstborn, and her name *was* Tamar. **7**But Er, Judah's firstborn, was wicked in the sight of the LORD, and the LORD killed him. **8**And Judah said to Onan, "Go in to your brother's wife and marry her, and raise up an heir to your brother." **9**But Onan knew that the heir would not be his; and it came to pass, when he went in to his brother's wife, that he emitted on the ground, lest he should give an heir to his brother. **10**And the thing which he did displeased the LORD; therefore He killed him also.

11Then Judah said to Tamar his daughter-in-law, "Remain a widow in your father's house till my son Shelah is grown." For he said, "Lest he also die like his brothers." And Tamar went and dwelt in her father's house.

12Now in the process of time the daughter of Shua, Judah's wife, died; and Judah was comforted, and went up to his sheepshearers at Timnah, he and his friend Hirah the Adullamite. **13**And it was told Tamar, saying, "Look, your father-in-law is going up to Timnah to shear his sheep." **14**So she took off her widow's garments, covered *herself* with a veil and wrapped herself, and sat in an open place which *was* on the way to Timnah; for she saw that Shelah was grown, and she was not given to him as a wife. **15**When Judah saw her, he thought she *was* a harlot, because she had covered her face. **16**Then he turned to her by the way, and said, "Please let me come in to you"; for he did not know that she *was* his daughter-in-law.

So she said, "What will you give me, that you may come in to me?"

17And he said, "I will send a young goat from the flock."

So she said, "Will you give *me* a pledge till you send *it?*"

18Then he said, "What pledge shall I give you?"

So she said, "Your signet and cord, and your staff that *is* in your hand." Then he gave *them* to her, and went in to her, and she conceived by him. **19**So she arose and went away, and laid aside her veil and put on the garments of her widowhood.

20And Judah sent the young goat by the hand of his friend the Adullamite, to receive *his* pledge from the woman's hand, but he did not find her. **21**Then he asked the men of that place, saying, "Where is the harlot who *was* openly by the roadside?"

And they said, "There was no harlot in this *place.*"

22So he returned to Judah and said, "I cannot find her. Also, the men of the place said there was no harlot in this *place.*"

23Then Judah said, "Let her take *them* for herself, lest we be shamed; for I sent this young goat and you have not found her."

24And it came to pass, about three months after, that Judah was told, saying, "Tamar your daughter-in-law has played the harlot; furthermore she *is* with child by harlotry."

So Judah said, "Bring her out and let her be burned!"

25When she *was* brought out, she sent to her father-in-law, saying, "By the man to whom these belong, I *am* with child." And she said, "Please determine whose these *are*—the signet and cord, and staff."

26So Judah acknowledged *them* and said, "She has been more righteous than I, because I did not give her to Shelah my son." And he never knew her again.

27Now it came to pass, at the time for giving birth, that behold, twins *were* in her womb. 28And so it was, when she was giving birth, that *the one* put out *his* hand; and the midwife took a scarlet *thread* and bound it on his hand, saying, "This one came out first." 29Then it happened, as he drew back his hand, that his brother came out unexpectedly; and she said, "How did you break through? *This* breach *be* upon you!" Therefore his name was called Perez.[n] 30Afterward his brother came out who had the scarlet *thread* on his hand. And his name was called Zerah.

Joseph a Slave in Egypt

39 Now Joseph had been taken down to Egypt. And Potiphar, an officer of Pharaoh, captain of the guard, an Egyptian, bought him from the Ishmaelites who had taken him down there. 2The LORD was with Joseph, and he was a successful man; and he was in the house of his master the Egyptian. 3And his master saw that the LORD *was* with him and that the LORD made all he did to prosper in his hand. 4So Joseph found favor in his sight, and served him. Then he made him overseer of his house, and all *that* he had he put under his authority. 5So it was, from the time *that* he had made him overseer of his house and all that he had, that the LORD blessed the Egyptian's house for Joseph's sake; and the blessing of the LORD was on all that he had in the house and in the field. 6Thus

he left all that he had in Joseph's hand, and he did not know what he had except for the bread which he ate.

Now Joseph was handsome in form and appearance.

7And it came to pass after these things that his master's wife cast longing eyes on Joseph, and she said, "Lie with me."

8But he refused and said to his master's wife, "Look, my master does not know what *is* with me in the house, and he has committed all that he has to my hand. 9*There is* no one greater in this house than I, nor has he kept back anything from me but you, because you *are* his wife. How then can I do this great wickedness, and sin against God?"

10So it was, as she spoke to Joseph day by day, that he did not heed her, to lie with her *or* to be with her.

11But it happened about this time, when Joseph went into the house to do his work, and none of the men of the house *was* inside, 12that she caught him by his garment, saying, "Lie with me." But he left his garment in her hand, and fled and ran outside. 13And so it was, when she saw that he had left his garment in her hand and fled outside, 14that she called to the men of her house and spoke to them, saying, "See, he has brought in to us a Hebrew to mock us. He came in to me to lie with me, and I cried out with a loud voice. 15And it happened, when he heard that I lifted my voice and cried out, that he left his garment with me, and fled and went outside."

16So she kept his garment with her until his master came home. 17Then she spoke to him with words like these, saying, "The Hebrew servant whom you brought to us came in to me to mock me; 18so it happened, as I lifted my voice and cried out, that he left his garment with me and fled outside."

19So it was, when his master heard the words which his wife spoke to him, saying, "Your servant did to me after this manner," that his anger was aroused. 20Then Joseph's master took him and put him into the prison, a place where the king's prisoners *were* con-

---

n Literally *Breach* or *Breakthrough*

fined. And he was there in the prison. 21But the LORD was with Joseph and showed him mercy, and He gave him favor in the sight of the keeper of the prison. 22And the keeper of the prison committed to Joseph's hand all the prisoners who *were* in the prison; whatever they did there, it was his doing. 23The keeper of the prison did not look into anything *that was* under *Joseph's* authority, because the LORD was with him; and whatever he did, the LORD made *it* prosper.

The Prisoners' Dreams

40 It came to pass after these things *that* the butler and the baker of the king of Egypt offended their lord, the king of Egypt. 2And Pharaoh was angry with his two officers, the chief butler and the chief baker. 3So he put them in custody in the house of the captain of the guard, in the prison, the place where Joseph *was* confined. 4And the captain of the guard charged Joseph with them, and he served them; so they were in custody for a while.

5Then the butler and the baker of the king of Egypt, who *were* confined in the prison, had a dream, both of them, each man's dream in one night *and* each man's dream with its *own* interpretation. 6And Joseph came in to them in the morning and looked at them, and saw that they *were* sad. 7So he asked Pharaoh's officers who *were* with him in the custody of his lord's house, saying, "Why do you look *so* sad today?"

8And they said to him, "We each have had a dream, and *there is* no interpreter of it."

So Joseph said to them, "Do not interpretations belong to God? Tell *them* to me, please."

9Then the chief butler told his dream to Joseph, and said to him, "Behold, in my dream a vine *was* before me, 10and in the vine *were* three branches; it *was* as though it budded, its blossoms shot forth, and its clusters brought forth ripe grapes. 11Then Pharaoh's cup *was* in my hand; and I took the grapes and pressed them into Pharaoh's cup, and placed the cup in Pharaoh's hand."

12And Joseph said to him, "This *is* the interpretation of it: The three branches *are* three days. 13Now within three days Pharaoh will lift up your head and restore you to your place, and you will put Pharaoh's cup in his hand according to the former manner, when you were his butler. 14But remember me when it is well with you, and please show kindness to me; make mention of me to Pharaoh, and get me out of this house. 15For indeed I was stolen away from the land of the Hebrews; and also I have done nothing here that they should put me into the dungeon."

16When the chief baker saw that the interpretation was good, he said to Joseph, "I also *was* in my dream, and there *were* three white baskets on my head. 17In the uppermost basket *were* all kinds of baked goods for Pharaoh, and the birds ate them out of the basket on my head."

18So Joseph answered and said, "This *is* the interpretation of it: The three baskets *are* three days. 19Within three days Pharaoh will lift off your head from you and hang you on a tree; and the birds will eat your flesh from you."

20Now it came to pass on the third day, *which was* Pharaoh's birthday, that he made a feast for all his servants; and he lifted up the head of the chief butler and of the chief baker among his servants. 21Then he restored the chief butler to his butlership again, and he placed the cup in Pharaoh's hand. 22But he hanged the chief baker, as Joseph had interpreted to them. 23Yet the chief butler did not remember Joseph, but forgot him.

Pharaoh's Dreams

41 Then it came to pass, at the end of two full years, that Pharaoh had a dream; and behold, he stood by the river. 2Suddenly there came up out of the river seven cows, fine looking and fat; and they fed in the meadow. 3Then behold, seven other cows came up after them out of the river, ugly and gaunt, and stood by the *other* cows on the bank of the river. 4And the ugly and gaunt cows ate up the seven fine looking and fat cows. So Pharaoh awoke. 5He slept and dreamed a second time; and suddenly seven heads of grain came up on one stalk, plump and good. 6Then behold, seven thin heads, blighted by the east wind, sprang up after them. 7And the seven thin heads devoured the seven plump and full heads. So Pharaoh awoke, and indeed, *it was* a dream. 8Now it came to pass in the morning that his spirit was troubled, and he sent and called for all the magicians of Egypt and all its wise men. And Pharaoh told them his dreams, but *there was* no one who could interpret them for Pharaoh.

9Then the chief butler spoke to Pharaoh, saying: "I remember my faults this day. 10When Pharaoh was angry with his servants, and put me in custody in the house of the captain of the guard, *both* me and the chief baker, 11we each had a dream in one night, he and I. Each of us dreamed according to the interpretation of his *own* dream. 12Now there *was* a young Hebrew man with us there, a servant of the captain of the guard. And we told him, and he interpreted our dreams for us; to each man he interpreted according to his *own* dream. 13And it came to pass, just as he interpreted for us, so it happened. He restored me to my office, and he hanged him."

14Then Pharaoh sent and called Joseph, and they brought him quickly out of the dungeon; and he shaved, changed his clothing, and came to Pharaoh. 15And Pharaoh said to Joseph, "I have had a dream, and *there is* no one who can interpret it. But I have heard it said of you *that* you can understand a dream, to interpret it."

16So Joseph answered Pharaoh, saying, "*It is* not in me; God will give Pharaoh an answer of peace."

17Then Pharaoh said to Joseph: "Behold, in my dream I stood on the bank of the river. 18Suddenly seven cows came up out of the river, fine looking and fat; and they fed in the meadow. 19Then behold, seven other cows came up after them, poor and very ugly and gaunt, such ugliness as I have never seen in all the land of Egypt. 20And the gaunt and ugly cows ate up the first seven, the fat cows. 21When they had eaten them up, no one would have known that they had eaten them, for

they *were* just as ugly as at the beginning. So I awoke. 22Also I saw in my dream, and suddenly seven heads came up on one stalk, full and good. 23Then behold, seven heads, withered, thin, *and* blighted by the east wind, sprang up after them. 24And the thin heads devoured the seven good heads. So I told *this* to the magicians, but *there was* no one who could explain *it* to me."

25Then Joseph said to Pharaoh, "The dreams of Pharaoh *are* one; God has shown Pharaoh what He *is* about to do: 26The seven good cows *are* seven years, and the seven good heads *are* seven years; the dreams *are* one. 27And the seven thin and ugly cows which came up after them *are* seven years, and the seven empty heads blighted by the east wind are seven years of famine. 28This *is* the thing which I have spoken to Pharaoh. God has shown Pharaoh what He *is* about to do. 29Indeed seven years of great plenty will come throughout all the land of Egypt; 30but after them seven years of famine will arise, and all the plenty will be forgotten in the land of Egypt; and the famine will deplete the land. 31So the plenty will not be known in the land because of the famine following, for it *will be* very severe. 32And the dream was repeated to Pharaoh twice because the thing *is* established by God, and God will shortly bring it to pass.

33"Now therefore, let Pharaoh select a discerning and wise man, and set him over the land of Egypt. 34Let Pharaoh do *this*, and let him appoint officers over the land, to collect one-fifth *of the produce* of the land of Egypt in the seven plentiful years. 35And let them gather all the food of those good years that are coming, and store up grain under the authority of Pharaoh, and let them keep food in the cities. 36Then that food shall be as a reserve for the land for the seven years of famine which shall be in the land of Egypt, that the land may not perish during the famine."

Joseph's Rise to Power

37So the advice was good in the eyes of Pharaoh and in the eyes of all his servants. 38And Pharaoh said to his servants, "Can we find *such a one* as this, a man in whom *is* the Spirit of God?"

39Then Pharaoh said to Joseph, "Inasmuch as God has shown you all this, *there is* no one as discerning and wise as you. **40**You shall be over my house, and all my people shall be ruled according to your word; only in regard to the throne will I be greater than you." **41**And Pharaoh said to Joseph, "See, I have set you over all the land of Egypt."

42Then Pharaoh took his signet ring off his hand and put it on Joseph's hand; and he clothed him in garments of fine linen and put a gold chain around his neck. **43**And he had him ride in the second chariot which he had; and they cried out before him, "Bow the knee!" So he set him over all the land of Egypt. **44**Pharaoh also said to Joseph, "I *am* Pharaoh, and without your consent no man may lift his hand or foot in all the land of Egypt." **45**And Pharaoh called Joseph's name Zaphnath-Paaneah. And he gave him as a wife Asenath, the daughter of Poti-Pherah priest of On. So Joseph went out over *all* the land of Egypt.

46Joseph was thirty years old when he stood before Pharaoh king of Egypt. And Joseph went out from the presence of Pharaoh, and went throughout all the land of Egypt. **47**Now in the seven plentiful years the ground brought forth abundantly. **48**So he gathered up all the food of the seven years which were in the land of Egypt, and laid up the food in the cities; he laid up in every city the food of the fields which surrounded them. **49**Joseph gathered very much grain, as the sand of the sea, until he stopped counting, for *it was* immeasurable.

50And to Joseph were born two sons before the years of famine came, whom Asenath, the daughter of Poti-Pherah priest of On, bore to him. **51**Joseph called the name of the firstborn Manasseh:[o] "For God has made me forget all my toil and all my father's house." **52**And the name of the second he called Ephraim:[p] "For God has caused me to be fruitful in the land of my affliction."

53Then the seven years of plenty which were in the land of Egypt ended, **54**and the seven years of famine began to come, as Joseph had said. The famine was in all lands, but in all the land of Egypt there was bread. **55**So when all the land of Egypt was famished, the people cried to Pharaoh for bread. Then Pharaoh said to all the Egyptians, "Go to Joseph; whatever he says to you, do." **56**The famine was over all the face of the earth, and Joseph opened all the storehouses and sold to the Egyptians. And the famine became severe in the land of Egypt. **57**So all countries came to Joseph in Egypt to buy *grain,* because the famine was severe in all lands.

Joseph's Brothers Go to Egypt

42 When Jacob saw that there was grain in Egypt, Jacob said to his sons, "Why do you look at one another?" **2**And he said, "Indeed I have heard that there is grain in Egypt; go down to that place and buy for us there, that we may live and not die."

3So Joseph's ten brothers went down to buy grain in Egypt. **4**But Jacob did not send Joseph's brother Benjamin with his brothers, for he said, "Lest some calamity befall him." **5**And the sons of Israel went to buy *grain* among those who journeyed, for the famine was in the land of Canaan.

6Now Joseph *was* governor over the land; and it was he who sold to all the people of the land. And Joseph's brothers came and bowed down before him with *their* faces to the earth. **7**Joseph saw his brothers and recognized them, but he acted as a stranger to them and spoke roughly to them. Then he said to them, "Where do you come from?"

And they said, "From the land of Canaan to buy food."

8So Joseph recognized his brothers, but they did not recognize him. **9**Then Joseph remembered the dreams which he had dreamed about them, and said to them, "You *are* spies! You have come to see the nakedness of the land!"

10And they said to him, "No, my lord, but your servants have come to buy food. **11**We *are* all one man's sons; we *are* honest *men;* your servants are not spies."

12But he said to them, "No, but you

---

o Literally *Making Forgetful*   p Literally *Fruitfulness* have come to see the nakedness of the land."

13And they said, "Your servants *are* twelve brothers, the sons of one man in the land of Canaan; and in fact, the youngest *is* with our father today, and one *is* no more."

14But Joseph said to them, "It *is* as I spoke to you, saying, 'You *are* spies!' 15In this *manner* you shall be tested: By the life of Pharaoh, you shall not leave this place unless your youngest brother comes here. 16Send one of you, and let him bring your brother; and you shall be kept in prison, that your words may be tested to see whether *there is* any truth in you; or else, by the life of Pharaoh, surely you *are* spies!" 17So he put them all together in prison three days.

18Then Joseph said to them the third day, "Do this and live, *for* I fear God: 19If you *are* honest *men,* let one of your brothers be confined to your prison house; but you, go and carry grain for the famine of your houses. 20And bring your youngest brother to me; so your words will be verified, and you shall not die."

And they did so. 21Then they said to one another, "We *are* truly guilty concerning our brother, for we saw the anguish of his soul when he pleaded with us, and we would not hear; therefore this distress has come upon us."

22And Reuben answered them, saying, "Did I not speak to you, saying, 'Do not sin against the boy'; and you would not listen? Therefore behold, his blood is now required of us." 23But they did not know that Joseph understood *them,* for he spoke to them through an interpreter. 24And he turned himself away from them and wept. Then he returned to them again, and talked with them. And he took Simeon from them and bound him before their eyes.

The Brothers Return to Canaan

25Then Joseph gave a command to fill their sacks with grain, to restore every man's money to his sack, and to give them provisions for the journey. Thus he did for them. 26So they loaded their donkeys with the grain and departed from there. 27But as one *of them* opened his sack to give his donkey feed at the

encampment, he saw his money; and there it was, in the mouth of his sack. 28So he said to his brothers, "My money has been restored, and there it is, in my sack!" Then their hearts failed *them* and they were afraid, saying to one another, "What *is* this *that* God has done to us?"

29Then they went to Jacob their father in the land of Canaan and told him all that had happened to them, saying: 30"The man *who is* lord of the land spoke roughly to us, and took us for spies of the country. 31But we said to him, 'We *are* honest *men;* we are not spies. 32We *are* twelve brothers, sons of our father; one *is* no *more,* and the youngest *is* with our father this day in the land of Canaan.' 33Then the man, the lord of the country, said to us, 'By this I will know that you *are* honest *men:* Leave one of your brothers *here* with me, take *food for* the famine of your households, and be gone. 34And bring your youngest brother to me; so I shall know that you *are* not spies, but *that* you *are* honest *men.* I will grant your brother to you, and you may trade in the land.' "

35Then it happened as they emptied their sacks, that surprisingly each man's bundle of money *was* in his sack; and when they and their father saw the bundles of money, they were afraid. 36And Jacob their father said to them, "You have bereaved me: Joseph is no *more,* Simeon is no *more,* and you want to take Benjamin. All these things are against me."

37Then Reuben spoke to his father, saying, "Kill my two sons if I do not bring him *back* to you; put him in my hands, and I will bring him back to you."

38But he said, "My son shall not go down with you, for his brother is dead, and he is left alone. If any calamity should befall him along the way in which you go, then you would bring down my gray hair with sorrow to the grave."

Joseph's Brothers Return with Benjamin

43 Now the famine *was* severe in the land. 2And it came to pass, when they had eaten up the grain which they had brought from Egypt, that their father said to them, "Go back, buy us a little food."

3But Judah spoke to him, saying, "The man solemnly warned us, saying, 'You shall not see my face unless your brother *is* with you.' 4If you send our brother with us, we will go down and buy you food. 5But if you will not send *him*, we will not go down; for the man said to us, 'You shall not see my face unless your brother *is* with you.' "

6And Israel said, "Why did you deal *so* wrongfully with me *as* to tell the man whether you had still *another* brother?"

7But they said, "The man asked us pointedly about ourselves and our family, saying, '*Is* your father still alive? Have you *another* brother?' And we told him according to these words. Could we possibly have known that he would say, 'Bring your brother down'?"

8Then Judah said to Israel his father, "Send the lad with me, and we will arise and go, that we may live and not die, both we and you *and* also our little ones. 9I myself will be surety for him; from my hand you shall require him. If I do not bring him *back* to you and set him before you, then let me bear the blame forever. 10For if we had not lingered, surely by now we would have returned this second time."

11And their father Israel said to them, "If *it must be* so, then do this: Take some of the best fruits of the land in your vessels and carry down a present for the man—a little balm and a little honey, spices and myrrh, pistachio nuts and almonds. 12Take double money in your hand, and take back in your hand the money that was returned in the mouth of your sacks; perhaps it was an oversight. 13Take your brother also, and arise, go back to the man. 14And may God Almighty give you mercy before the man, that he may release your other brother and Benjamin. If I am bereaved, I am bereaved!"

15So the men took that present and Benjamin, and they took double money in their hand, and arose and went down to Egypt; and they stood before Joseph. 16When Joseph saw Benjamin with them, he said to the steward of his house, "Take *these* men to my home, and slaughter an animal and make ready; for *these* men will dine with me

at noon." 17Then the man did as Joseph ordered, and the man brought the men into Joseph's house.

18Now the men were afraid because they were brought into Joseph's house; and they said, "*It is* because of the money, which was returned in our sacks the first time, that we are brought in, so that he may make a case against us and seize us, to take us as slaves with our donkeys."

19When they drew near to the steward of Joseph's house, they talked with him at the door of the house, 20and said, "O sir, we indeed came down the first time to buy food; 21but it happened, when we came to the encampment, that we opened our sacks, and there, *each* man's money *was* in the mouth of his sack, our money in full weight; so we have brought it back in our hand. 22And we have brought down other money in our hands to buy food. We do not know who put our money in our sacks."

23But he said, "Peace *be* with you, do not be afraid. Your God and the God of your father has given you treasure in your sacks; I had your money." Then he brought Simeon out to them.

24So the man brought the men into Joseph's house and gave *them* water, and they washed their feet; and he gave their donkeys feed. 25Then they made the present ready for Joseph's coming at noon, for they heard that they would eat bread there.

26And when Joseph came home, they brought him the present which *was* in their hand into the house, and bowed down before him to the earth. 27Then he asked them about *their* well-being, and said, "*Is* your father well, the old man of whom you spoke? *Is* he still alive?"

28And they answered, "Your servant our father *is* in good health; he *is* still alive." And they bowed their heads down and prostrated themselves.

29Then he lifted his eyes and saw his brother Benjamin, his mother's son, and said, "*Is* this your younger brother of whom you spoke to me?" And he said, "God be gracious to you, my son." 30Now his heart yearned for his brother; so Joseph made haste and sought *somewhere* to weep. And he

went into *his* chamber and wept there.
31Then he washed his face and came
out; and he restrained himself, and said,
"Serve the bread."

32So they set him a place by himself,
and them by themselves, and the Egyptians who ate with him by themselves;
because the Egyptians could not eat
food with the Hebrews, for that *is* an
abomination to the Egyptians. 33And
they sat before him, the firstborn according to his birthright and the youngest according to his youth; and the men
looked in astonishment at one another.
34Then he took servings to them from
before him, but Benjamin's serving was
five times as much as any of theirs. So
they drank and were merry with him.

Joseph's Cup

44 And he commanded the steward
of his house, saying, "Fill
the men's sacks with food, as much
as they can carry, and put each man's
money in the mouth of his sack.
2Also put my cup, the silver cup, in
the mouth of the sack of the youngest, and his grain money." So he did
according to the word that Joseph
had spoken. 3As soon as the morning
dawned, the men were sent away,
they and their donkeys. 4When they
had gone out of the city, *and* were
not *yet* far off, Joseph said to his
steward, "Get up, follow the men;
and when you overtake them, say to
them, 'Why have you repaid evil for
good? 5*Is* not this *the one* from which
my lord drinks, and with which he indeed practices divination? You have
done evil in so doing.' "
6So he overtook them, and he spoke
to them these same words. 7And they
said to him, "Why does my lord say
these words? Far be it from us that your
servants should do such a thing.
8Look, we brought back to you from the
land of Canaan the money which we
found in the mouth of our sacks. How
then could we steal silver or gold from
your lord's house? 9With whomever of
your servants it is found, let him die,
and we also will be my lord's slaves."
10And he said, "Now also *let* it *be* according to your words; he with whom
it is found shall be my slave, and you
shall be blameless." 11Then each man

speedily let down his sack to the
ground, and each opened his sack.
12So he searched. He began with the
oldest and left off with the youngest;
and the cup was found in Benjamin's
sack. 13Then they tore their clothes, and
each man loaded his donkey and returned to the city.

14So Judah and his brothers came to
Joseph's house, and he *was* still there;
and they fell before him on the ground.
15And Joseph said to them, "What deed
is this you have done? Did you not
know that such a man as I can certainly
practice divination?"
16Then Judah said, "What shall we
say to my lord? What shall we speak?
Or how shall we clear ourselves? God
has found out the iniquity of your
servants; here we are, my lord's slaves,
both we and *he* also with whom the cup
was found."
17But he said, "Far be it from me that
I should do so; the man in whose hand
the cup was found, he shall be my slave.
And as for you, go up in peace to your
father."

Judah Intercedes for Benjamin

18Then Judah came near to him and
said: "O my lord, please let your servant speak a word in my lord's hearing,
and do not let your anger burn against
your servant; for you *are* even like
Pharaoh. 19My lord asked his servants,
saying, 'Have you a father or a
brother?' 20And we said to my lord, 'We
have a father, an old man, and a child
of *his* old age, *who is* young; his brother
is dead, and he alone is left of his mother's children, and his father loves him.'
21Then you said to your servants, 'Bring
him down to me, that I may set my eyes
on him.' 22And we said to my lord, 'The
lad cannot leave his father, for *if* he
should leave his father, *his father* would
die.' 23But you said to your servants,
'Unless your youngest brother comes
down with you, you shall see my face
no more.'
24"So it was, when we went up to
your servant my father, that we told
him the words of my lord. 25And our
father said, 'Go back *and* buy us a little
food.' 26But we said, 'We cannot go
down; if our youngest brother is with
us, then we will go down; for we may

not see the man's face unless our youngest brother *is* with us.' 27Then your servant my father said to us, 'You know that my wife bore me two sons; 28and the one went out from me, and I said, "Surely he is torn to pieces"; and I have not seen him since. 29But if you take this one also from me, and calamity befalls him, you shall bring down my gray hair with sorrow to the grave.'

30"Now therefore, when I come to your servant my father, and the lad *is* not with us, since his life is bound up in the lad's life, 31it will happen, when he sees that the lad *is* not *with us,* that he will die. So your servants will bring down the gray hair of your servant our father with sorrow to the grave. 32For your servant became surety for the lad to my father, saying, 'If I do not bring him *back* to you, then I shall bear the blame before my father forever.' 33Now therefore, please let your servant remain instead of the lad as a slave to my lord, and let the lad go up with his brothers. 34For how shall I go up to my father if the lad *is* not with me, lest perhaps I see the evil that would come upon my father?' "

Joseph Revealed to His Brothers

45 Then Joseph could not restrain himself before all those who stood by him, and he cried out, "Make everyone go out from me!" So no one stood with him while Joseph made himself known to his brothers. 2And he wept aloud, and the Egyptians and the house of Pharaoh heard *it.*

3Then Joseph said to his brothers, "I *am* Joseph; does my father still live?" But his brothers could not answer him, for they were dismayed in his presence. 4And Joseph said to his brothers, "Please come near to me." So they came near. Then he said: "I *am* Joseph your brother, whom you sold into Egypt. 5But now, do not therefore be grieved or angry with yourselves because you sold me here; for God sent me before you to preserve life. 6For these two years the famine *has been* in the land, and *there are* still five years in which *there will be* neither plowing nor harvesting. 7And God sent me before you to preserve a posterity for you

in the earth, and to save your lives by a great deliverance. 8So now *it was* not you *who* sent me here, but God; and He has made me a father to Pharaoh, and lord of all his house, and a ruler throughout all the land of Egypt.

9"Hurry and go up to my father, and say to him, 'Thus says your son Joseph: "God has made me lord of all Egypt; come down to me, do not tarry. 10You shall dwell in the land of Goshen, and you shall be near to me, you and your children, your children's children, your flocks and your herds, and all that you have. 11There I will provide for you, lest you and your household, and all that you have, come to poverty; for *there are* still five years of famine." '

12"And behold, your eyes and the eyes of my brother Benjamin see that *it is* my mouth that speaks to you. 13So you shall tell my father of all my glory in Egypt, and of all that you have seen; and you shall hurry and bring my father down here."

14Then he fell on his brother Benjamin's neck and wept, and Benjamin wept on his neck. 15Moreover he kissed all his brothers and wept over them, and after that his brothers talked with him.

16Now the report of it was heard in Pharaoh's house, saying, "Joseph's brothers have come." So it pleased Pharaoh and his servants well. 17And Pharaoh said to Joseph, "Say to your brothers, 'Do this: Load your animals and depart; go to the land of Canaan. 18Bring your father and your households and come to me; I will give you the best of the land of Egypt, and you will eat the fat of the land. 19Now you are commanded—do this: Take carts out of the land of Egypt for your little ones and your wives; bring your father and come. 20Also do not be concerned about your goods, for the best of all the land of Egypt *is* yours.' "

21Then the sons of Israel did so; and Joseph gave them carts, according to the command of Pharaoh, and he gave them provisions for the journey. 22He gave to all of them, to each man, changes of garments; but to Benjamin he gave three hundred *pieces* of silver and five changes of garments. 23And he sent to his father these *things:* ten donkeys loaded with the good things of Egypt, and ten female donkeys loaded with grain, bread, and food for his father for the journey. 24So he sent his brothers away, and they departed; and he said to them, "See that you do not become troubled along the way."

25Then they went up out of Egypt, and came to the land of Canaan to Jacob their father. 26And they told him, saying, "Joseph is still alive, and he is governor over all the land of Egypt." And Jacob's heart stood still, because he did not believe them. 27But when they told him all the words which Joseph had said to them, and when he saw the carts which Joseph had sent to carry him, the spirit of Jacob their father revived. 28Then Israel said, "It is enough. Joseph my son is still alive. I will go and see him before I die."

Jacob's Journey to Egypt

46 So Israel took his journey with all that he had, and came to Beersheba, and offered sacrifices to the God of his father Isaac. 2Then God spoke to Israel in the visions of the night, and said, "Jacob, Jacob!"

And he said, "Here I am."

3So He said, "I am God, the God of your father; do not fear to go down to Egypt, for I will make of you a great nation there. 4I will go down with you to Egypt, and I will also surely bring you up again; and Joseph will put his hand on your eyes."

5Then Jacob arose from Beersheba; and the sons of Israel carried their father Jacob, their little ones, and their wives, in the carts which Pharaoh had sent to carry him. 6So they took their livestock and their goods, which they had acquired in the land of Canaan, and went to Egypt, Jacob and all his descendants with him. 7His sons and his sons' sons, his daughters and his sons' daughters, and all his descendants he brought with him to Egypt.

8Now these were the names of the children of Israel, Jacob and his sons, who went to Egypt: Reúben was Jacob's firstborn. 9The sons of Reuben were Hanoch, Pallu, Hezron, and Carmi. 10The sons of Simeon were Jemuel, Jamin, Ohad, Jachin, Zohar, and Shaul, the son of a Canaanite woman.

11The sons of Levi were Gershon, Kohath, and Merari. 12The sons of Judah were Er, Onan, Shelah, Perez, and Zerah (but Er and Onan died in the land of Canaan). The sons of Perez were Hezron and Hamul. 13The sons of Issachar were Tola, Puvah, Job, and Shimron. 14The sons of Zebulun were Sered, Elon, and Jahleel. 15These were the sons of Leah, whom she bore to Jacob in Padan Aram, with his daughter Dinah. All the persons, his sons and his daughters, were thirty-three.

16The sons of Gad were Ziphion, Haggi, Shuni, Ezbon, Eri, Arodi, and Areli. 17The sons of Asher were Jimnah, Ishuah, Isui, Beriah, and Serah, their sister. And the sons of Beriah were Heber and Malchiel. 18These were the sons of Zilpah, whom Laban gave to Leah his daughter; and these she bore to Jacob: sixteen persons.

19The sons of Rachel, Jacob's wife, were Joseph and Benjamin. 20And to Joseph in the land of Egypt were born Manasseh and Ephraim, whom Asenath, the daughter of Poti-Pherah priest of On, bore to him. 21The sons of Benjamin were Belah, Becher, Ashbel, Gera, Naaman, Ehi, Rosh, Muppim, Huppim, and Ard. 22These were the sons of Rachel, who were born to Jacob: fourteen persons in all.

23The son of Dan was Hushim. 24The sons of Naphtali were Jahzeel, Guni, Jezer, and Shillem. 25These were the sons of Bilhah, whom Laban gave to Rachel his daughter, and she bore these to Jacob: seven persons in all.

26All the persons who went with Jacob to Egypt, who came from his body, besides Jacob's sons' wives, were sixty-six persons in all. 27And the sons of Joseph who were born to him in Egypt were two persons. All the persons of the house of Jacob who went to Egypt were seventy.

Jacob Settles in Goshen

28Then he sent Judah before him to Joseph, to point out before him the way to Goshen. And they came to the land of Goshen. 29So Joseph made ready his chariot and went up to Goshen to meet his father Israel; and he presented himself to him, and fell on his neck and wept on his neck a good while.

30And Israel said to Joseph, "Now let me die, since I have seen your face, because you *are* still alive."

31Then Joseph said to his brothers and to his father's household, "I will go up and tell Pharaoh, and say to him, 'My brothers and those of my father's house, who *were* in the land of Canaan, have come to me. **32**And the men *are* shepherds, for their occupation has been to feed livestock; and they have brought their flocks, their herds, and all that they have.' **33**So it shall be, when Pharaoh calls you and says, 'What is your occupation?' **34**that you shall say, 'Your servants' occupation has been with livestock from our youth even till now, both we *and* also our fathers,' that you may dwell in the land of Goshen; for every shepherd *is* an abomination to the Egyptians."

47 Then Joseph went and told Pharaoh, and said, "My father and my brothers, their flocks and their herds and all that they possess, have come from the land of Canaan; and indeed they *are* in the land of Goshen." **2**And he took five men from among his brothers and presented them to Pharaoh. **3**Then Pharaoh said to his brothers, "What *is* your occupation?"

And they said to Pharaoh, "Your servants *are* shepherds, both we *and* also our fathers." **4**And they said to Pharaoh, "We have come to dwell in the land, because your servants have no pasture for their flocks, for the famine *is* severe in the land of Canaan. Now therefore, please let your servants dwell in the land of Goshen."

5Then Pharaoh spoke to Joseph, saying, "Your father and your brothers have come to you. **6**The land of Egypt *is* before you. Have your father and brothers dwell in the best of the land; let them dwell in the land of Goshen. And if you know *any* competent men among them, then make them chief herdsmen over my livestock."

7Then Joseph brought in his father Jacob and set him before Pharaoh; and Jacob blessed Pharaoh. **8**Pharaoh said to Jacob, "How old *are* you?"

9And Jacob said to Pharaoh, "The days of the years of my pilgrimage *are* one hundred and thirty years; few and evil have been the days of the years of my life, and they have not attained to the days of the years of the life of my fathers in the days of their pilgrimage." **10**So Jacob blessed Pharaoh, and went out from before Pharaoh.

11And Joseph situated his father and his brothers, and gave them a possession in the land of Egypt, in the best of the land, in the land of Rameses, as Pharaoh had commanded. **12**Then Joseph provided his father, his brothers, and all his father's household with bread, according to the number in *their* families.

Joseph Deals with the Famine

13Now *there was* no bread in all the land; for the famine *was* very severe, so that the land of Egypt and the land of Canaan languished because of the famine. **14**And Joseph gathered up all the money that was found in the land of Egypt and in the land of Canaan, for the grain which they bought; and Joseph brought the money into Pharaoh's house.

15So when the money failed in the land of Egypt and in the land of Canaan, all the Egyptians came to Joseph and said, "Give us bread, for why should we die in your presence? For the money has failed."

16Then Joseph said, "Give your livestock, and I will give you *bread* for your livestock, if the money is gone." **17**So they brought their livestock to Joseph, and Joseph gave them bread *in exchange* for the horses, the flocks, the cattle of the herds, and for the donkeys. Thus he fed them with bread *in exchange* for all their livestock that year.

18When that year had ended, they came to him the next year and said to him, "We will not hide from my lord that our money is gone; my lord also has our herds of livestock. There is nothing left in the sight of my lord but our bodies and our lands. **19**Why should we die before your eyes, both we and our land? Buy us and our land for bread, and we and our land will be servants of Pharaoh; give *us* seed, that we may live and not die, that the land may not be desolate."

20Then Joseph bought all the land

of Egypt for Pharaoh; for every man of the Egyptians sold his field, because the famine was severe upon them. So the land became Pharaoh's. 21And as for the people, he moved them into the cities, from *one* end of the borders of Egypt to the *other* end. 22Only the land of the priests he did not buy; for the priests had rations *allotted to them* by Pharaoh, and they ate their rations which Pharaoh gave them; therefore they did not sell their lands.

23Then Joseph said to the people, "Indeed I have bought you and your land this day for Pharaoh. Look, *here is* seed for you, and you shall sow the land. 24And it shall come to pass in the harvest that you shall give one-fifth to Pharaoh. Four-fifths shall be your own, as seed for the field and for your food, for those of your households and as food for your little ones."

25So they said, "You have saved our lives; let us find favor in the sight of my lord, and we will be Pharaoh's servants." 26And Joseph made it a law over the land of Egypt to this day, *that* Pharaoh should have one-fifth, except for the land of the priests only, *which* did not become Pharaoh's.

Joseph's Vow to Jacob

27So Israel dwelt in the land of Egypt, in the country of Goshen; and they had possessions there and grew and multiplied exceedingly. 28And Jacob lived in the land of Egypt seventeen years. So the length of Jacob's life was one hundred and forty-seven years. 29When the time drew near that Israel must die, he called his son Joseph and said to him, "Now if I have found favor in your sight, please put your hand under my thigh, and deal kindly and truly with me. Please do not bury me in Egypt, 30but let me lie with my fathers; you shall carry me out of Egypt and bury me in their burial place."

And he said, "I will do as you have said."

31Then he said, "Swear to me." And he swore to him. So Israel bowed himself on the head of the bed.

Jacob Blesses Joseph's Sons

48 Now it came to pass after these things that Joseph was told,

"Indeed your father *is* sick"; and he took with him his two sons, Manasseh and Ephraim. 2And Jacob was told, "Look, your son Joseph is coming to you"; and Israel strengthened himself and sat up on the bed. 3Then Jacob said to Joseph: "God Almighty appeared to me at Luz in the land of Canaan and blessed me, 4and said to me, 'Behold, I will make you fruitful and multiply you, and I will make of you a multitude of people, and give this land to your descendants after you *as* an everlasting possession.' 5And now your two sons, Ephraim and Manasseh, who were born to you in the land of Egypt before I came to you in Egypt, *are* mine; as Reuben and Simeon, they shall be mine. 6Your offspring whom you beget after them shall be yours; they will be called by the name of their brothers in their inheritance. 7But as for me, when I came from Padan, Rachel died beside me in the land of Canaan on the way, when *there was* but a little distance to go to Ephrath; and I buried her there on the way to Ephrath (that is, Bethlehem)."

8Then Israel saw Joseph's sons, and said, "Who *are* these?"

9Joseph said to his father, "They *are* my sons, whom God has given me in this *place*."

And he said, "Please bring them to me, and I will bless them." 10Now the eyes of Israel were dim with age, *so that* he could not see. Then Joseph brought them near him, and he kissed them and embraced them. 11And Israel said to Joseph, "I had not thought to see your face; but in fact, God has also shown me your offspring!"

12So Joseph brought them from beside his knees, and he bowed down with his face to the earth. 13And Joseph took them both, Ephraim with his right hand toward Israel's left hand, and Manasseh with his left hand toward Israel's right hand, and brought *them* near him. 14Then Israel stretched out his right hand and laid *it* on Ephraim's head, who *was* the younger, and his left hand on Manasseh's head, guiding his hands knowingly, for Manasseh *was* the firstborn. 15And he blessed Joseph, and said:

"God, before whom my fathers
 Abraham and Isaac walked,
The God who has fed me all my life
 long to this day,
16 The Angel who has redeemed me
 from all evil,
Bless the lads;
Let my name be named upon them,
And the name of my fathers
 Abraham and Isaac;
And let them grow into a multitude
 in the midst of the earth."

17Now when Joseph saw that his father laid his right hand on the head of Ephraim, it displeased him; so he took hold of his father's hand to remove it from Ephraim's head to Manasseh's head. 18And Joseph said to his father, "Not so, my father, for this *one is* the firstborn; put your right hand on his head."

19But his father refused and said, "I know, my son, I know. He also shall become a people, and he also shall be great; but truly his younger brother shall be greater than he, and his descendants shall become a multitude of nations."

20So he blessed them that day, saying, "By you Israel will bless, saying, 'May God make you as Ephraim and as Manasseh!'" And thus he set Ephraim before Manasseh.

21Then Israel said to Joseph, "Behold, I am dying, but God will be with you and bring you back to the land of your fathers. 22Moreover I have given to you one portion above your brothers, which I took from the hand of the Amorite with my sword and my bow."

Jacob's Last Words to His Sons

49 And Jacob called his sons and said, "Gather together, that I may tell you what shall befall you in the last days:
2 "Gather together and hear, you sons
 of Jacob,
And listen to Israel your father.

3 "Reuben, you are my firstborn,
My might and the beginning of my
 strength,
The excellency of dignity and the
 excellency of power.
4 Unstable as water, you shall not
 excel,

Because you went up to your
 father's bed;
Then you defiled *it*—
He went up to my couch.

5 "Simeon and Levi *are* brothers;
Instruments of cruelty *are in* their
 dwelling place.
6 Let not my soul enter their council;
Let not my honor be united to their
 assembly;
For in their anger they slew a man,
And in their self-will they
 hamstrung an ox.
7 Cursed *be* their anger, for *it is*
 fierce;
And their wrath, for it is cruel!
I will divide them in Jacob
And scatter them in Israel.

8 "Judah, you *are he* whom your
 brothers shall praise;
Your hand *shall be* on the neck of
 your enemies;
Your father's children shall bow
 down before you.
9 Judah *is* a lion's whelp;
From the prey, my son, you have
 gone up.
He bows down, he lies down as a
 lion;
And as a lion, who shall rouse him?
10 The scepter shall not depart from
 Judah,
Nor a lawgiver from between his
 feet,
Until Shiloh comes;
And to Him *shall be* the obedience
 of the people.
11 Binding his donkey to the vine,
And his donkey's colt to the choice
 vine,
He washed his garments in wine,
And his clothes in the blood of
 grapes.
12 His eyes *are* darker than wine,
And his teeth whiter than milk.

13 "Zebulun shall dwell by the haven
 of the sea;
He *shall become* a haven for ships,
And his border shall adjoin Sidon.

14 "Issachar is a strong donkey,
Lying down between two burdens;
15 He saw that rest *was* good,
And that the land *was* pleasant;

He bowed his shoulder to bear *a
    burden*,
And became a band of slaves.

16 "Dan shall judge his people
    As one of the tribes of Israel.
17 Dan shall be a serpent by the way,
    A viper by the path,
    That bites the horse's heels
    So that its rider shall fall backward.
18 I have waited for your salvation,
    O Lord!

19 "Gad, a troop shall tramp upon him,
    But he shall triumph at last.

20 "Bread from Asher *shall be* rich,
    And he shall yield royal dainties.

21 "Naphtali *is* a deer let loose;
    He uses beautiful words.

22 "Joseph *is* a fruitful bough,
    A fruitful bough by a well;
    His branches run over the wall.
23 The archers have bitterly grieved
    him,
    Shot *at him* and hated him.
24 But his bow remained in strength,
    And the arms of his hands were
      made strong
    By the hands of the Mighty *God* of
      Jacob
    (From there *is* the Shepherd, the
      Stone of Israel),
25 By the God of your father who will
      help you,
    And by the Almighty who will bless
      you
    With blessings of heaven above,
    Blessings of the deep that lies
      beneath,
    Blessings of the breasts and of the
      womb.
26 The blessings of your father
    Have excelled the blessings of my
      ancestors,
    Up to the utmost bound of the
      everlasting hills.
    They shall be on the head of
      Joseph,
    And on the crown of the head of
      him who was separate from his
      brothers.

27 "Benjamin is a ravenous wolf;
    In the morning he shall devour the
      prey,

And at night he shall divide the
    spoil."
28All these *are* the twelve tribes of Israel, and this *is* what their father spoke to them. And he blessed them; he blessed each one according to his own blessing.

Jacob's Death and Burial

29Then he charged them and said to them: "I am to be gathered to my people; bury me with my fathers in the cave that *is* in the field of Ephron the Hittite, 30in the cave that *is* in the field of Machpelah, which *is* before Mamre in the land of Canaan, which Abraham bought with the field of Ephron the Hittite as a possession for a burial place. 31There they buried Abraham and Sarah his wife, there they buried Isaac and Rebekah his wife, and there I buried Leah. 32The field and the cave that *is* there *were* purchased from the sons of Heth." 33And when Jacob had finished commanding his sons, he drew his feet up into the bed and breathed his last, and was gathered to his people.

50 Then Joseph fell on his father's face and wept over him, and kissed him. 2And Joseph commanded his servants the physicians to embalm his father. So the physicians embalmed Israel. 3Forty days were required for him, for such are the days required for those who are embalmed; and the Egyptians mourned for him seventy days.

4Now when the days of his mourning were past, Joseph spoke to the household of Pharaoh, saying, "If now I have found favor in your eyes, please speak in the hearing of Pharaoh, saying, 5'My father made me swear, saying, "Behold, I am dying; in my grave which I dug for myself in the land of Canaan, there you shall bury me." Now therefore, please let me go up and bury my father, and I will come back.' "

6And Pharaoh said, "Go up and bury your father, as he made you swear."

7So Joseph went up to bury his father; and with him went up all the servants of Pharaoh, the elders of his house, and all the elders of the land of Egypt, 8as well as all the house of Joseph, his brothers, and his father's house. Only their little ones, their flocks, and their herds they left in the land of Goshen. 9And there went up with him both chariots and horsemen, and it was a very great gathering.

10Then they came to the threshing floor of Atad, which is beyond the Jordan, and they mourned there with a great and very solemn lamentation. He observed seven days of mourning for his father. 11And when the inhabitants of the land, the Canaanites, saw the mourning at the threshing floor of Atad, they said, "This is a deep mourning of the Egyptians." Therefore its name was called Abel Mizraim,q which is beyond the Jordan.

12So his sons did for him just as he had commanded them. 13For his sons carried him to the land of Canaan, and buried him in the cave of the field of Machpelah, before Mamre, which Abraham bought with the field from Ephron the Hittite as property for a burial place. 14And after he had buried his father, Joseph returned to Egypt, he and his brothers and all who went up with him to bury his father.

Joseph Reassures His Brothers

15When Joseph's brothers saw that their father was dead, they said, "Perhaps Joseph will hate us, and may actually repay us for all the evil which we did to him." 16So they sent messengers to Joseph, saying, "Before your father died he commanded, saying, 17'Thus you shall say to Joseph: "I beg you, please forgive the trespass of your brothers and their sin; for they did evil to you." ' Now, please, forgive the trespass of the servants of the God of your father." And Joseph wept when they spoke to him.

18Then his brothers also went and fell down before his face, and they said, "Behold, we are your servants."

19Joseph said to them, "Do not be afraid, for am I in the place of God? 20But as for you, you meant evil against me; but God meant it for good, in order to bring it about as it is this day, to save many people alive. 21Now therefore, do not be afraid; I will provide for you and your little ones." And he comforted them and spoke kindly to them.

Death of Joseph

22So Joseph dwelt in Egypt, he and his father's household. And Joseph lived one hundred and ten years. 23Joseph saw Ephraim's children to the third generation. The children of Machir, the son of Manasseh, were also brought up on Joseph's knees.

24And Joseph said to his brethren, "I am dying; but God will surely visit you, and bring you out of this land to the land of which He swore to Abraham, to Isaac, and to Jacob." 25Then Joseph took an oath from the children of Israel, saying, "God will surely visit you, and you shall carry up my bones from here." 26So Joseph died, being one hundred and ten years old; and they embalmed him, and he was put in a coffin in Egypt.

q Literally Mourning of Egypt

EXODUS

Israel's Suffering in Egypt

1 Now these *are* the names of the children of Israel who came to Egypt; each man and his household came with Jacob: 2Reuben, Simeon, Levi, and Judah; 3Issachar, Zebulun, and Benjamin; 4Dan, Naphtali, Gad, and Asher. 5All those who were descendants of Jacob were seventy persons (for Joseph was in Egypt *already*). 6And Joseph died, all his brothers, and all that generation. 7But the children of Israel were fruitful and increased abundantly, multiplied and grew exceedingly mighty; and the land was filled with them.

8Now there arose a new king over Egypt, who did not know Joseph. 9And he said to his people, "Look, the people of the children of Israel *are* more and mightier than we; 10come, let us deal shrewdly with them, lest they multiply, and it happen, in the event of war, that they also join our enemies and fight against us, and *so* go up out of the land." 11Therefore they set taskmasters over them to afflict them with their burdens. And they built for Pharaoh supply cities, Pithom and Raamses. 12But the more they afflicted them, the more they multiplied and grew. And they were in dread of the children of Israel. 13So the Egyptians made the children of Israel serve with rigor. 14And they made their lives bitter with hard bondage—in mortar, in brick, and in all manner of service in the field. All their service in which they made them serve *was* with rigor.

15Then the king of Egypt spoke to the Hebrew midwives, of whom the name of one *was* Shiphrah and the name of the other Puah; 16and he said, "When you do the duties of a midwife for the Hebrew women, and see *them* on the birthstools, if it *is* a son, then you shall kill him; but if it *is* a daughter, then she shall live." 17But the midwives feared God, and did not do as the king of Egypt commanded them, but saved the male children alive. 18So the king of Egypt called for the midwives and said to them, "Why have you done this thing, and saved the male children alive?"

19And the midwives said to Pharaoh, "Because the Hebrew women *are* not like the Egyptian women; for they *are* lively and give birth before the midwives come to them."

20Therefore God dealt well with the midwives, and the people multiplied and grew very mighty. 21And so it was, because the midwives feared God, that He provided households for them.

22So Pharaoh commanded all his people, saying, "Every son who is born you shall cast into the river, and every daughter you shall save alive."

Moses Is Born

2 And a man of the house of Levi went and took *as wife* a daughter of Levi. 2So the woman conceived and bore a son. And when she saw that he *was* a beautiful *child*, she hid him three months. 3But when she could no longer hide him, she took an ark of bulrushes for him, daubed it with asphalt and pitch, put the child in it, and laid *it* in the reeds by the river's bank. 4And his sister stood afar off, to know what would be done to him.

5Then the daughter of Pharaoh came down to bathe at the river. And her maidens walked along the riverside; and when she saw the ark among the reeds, she sent her maid to get it. 6And when she opened *it*, she saw the child, and behold, the baby wept. So she had compassion on him, and said, "This is one of the Hebrews' children."

7Then his sister said to Pharaoh's daughter, "Shall I go and call a nurse for you from the Hebrew women, that she may nurse the child for you?"

8And Pharaoh's daughter said to her, "Go." So the maiden went and called the child's mother. 9Then Pharaoh's daughter said to her, "Take this child away and nurse him for me, and I will give *you* your wages." So the woman took the child and nursed him. 10And the child grew, and she brought him to Pharaoh's daughter, and he became her son. So she called his name Moses,[a] saying, "Because I drew him out of the water."

Moses Flees to Midian

11Now it came to pass in those days, when Moses was grown, that he went out to his brethren and looked at their burdens. And he saw an Egyptian beating a Hebrew, one of his brethren. 12So he looked this way and that way, and when he saw no one, he killed the Egyptian and hid him in the sand. 13And when he went out the second day, behold, two Hebrew men were fighting, and he said to the one who did the wrong, "Why are you striking your companion?"

14Then he said, "Who made you a prince and a judge over us? Do you intend to kill me as you killed the Egyptian?"

So Moses feared and said, "Surely this thing is known!" 15When Pharaoh heard of this matter, he sought to kill Moses. But Moses fled from the face of Pharaoh and dwelt in the land of Midian; and he sat down by a well.

16Now the priest of Midian had seven daughters. And they came and drew water, and they filled the troughs to water their father's flock. 17Then the shepherds came and drove them away; but Moses stood up and helped them, and watered their flock.

18When they came to Reuel their father, he said, "How *is it that* you have come so soon today?"

19And they said, "An Egyptian delivered us from the hand of the shepherds, and he also drew enough water for us and watered the flock."

20So he said to his daughters, "And where *is* he? Why *is it that* you have left the man? Call him, that he may eat bread."

21Then Moses was content to live with the man, and he gave Zipporah his daughter to Moses. 22And she bore *him* a son. He called his name Gershom,[b] for he said, "I have been a stranger in a foreign land."

23Now it happened in the process of time that the king of Egypt died. Then the children of Israel groaned because of the bondage, and they cried out; and their cry came up to God because of the bondage. 24So God heard their groaning, and God remembered His covenant with Abraham, with Isaac, and with Jacob. 25And God looked upon the children of Israel, and God acknowledged *them.*

Moses at the Burning Bush

3 Now Moses was tending the flock of Jethro his father-in-law, the priest of Midian. And he led the flock to the back of the desert, and came to Horeb, the mountain of God. 2And the Angel of the LORD appeared to him in a flame of fire from the midst of a bush. So he looked, and behold, the bush was burning with fire, but the bush *was* not consumed. 3Then Moses said, "I will now turn aside and see this great sight, why the bush does not burn."

4So when the LORD saw that he turned aside to look, God called to him from the midst of the bush and said, "Moses, Moses!"

And he said, "Here I am."

5Then He said, "Do not draw near this place. Take your sandals off your feet, for the place where you stand *is* holy ground." 6Moreover He said, "I *am* the God of your father—the God of Abraham, the God of Isaac, and the God of Jacob." And Moses hid his face, for he was afraid to look upon God.

7And the LORD said: "I have surely seen the oppression of My people who *are* in Egypt, and have heard their cry because of their taskmasters, for I know their sorrows. 8So I have come down to deliver them out of the hand of the Egyptians, and to bring them up from that land to a good and large land, to a land flowing with milk and honey, to the place of the Canaanites and the Hittites and the Amorites and the Perizzites and the Hivites and the Jebusites. 9Now therefore, behold, the cry of the children of Israel has come to Me, and I have also seen the oppression with which the Egyptians oppress them. 10Come now, therefore, and I will send you to Pharaoh that you may bring My people, the children of Israel, out of Egypt."

---

a Literally *Drawn Out*   *b* Literally *Stranger There*

11But Moses said to God, "Who *am* I that I should go to Pharaoh, and that I should bring the children of Israel out of Egypt?"

12So He said, "I will certainly be with you. And this *shall be* a sign to you that I have sent you: When you have brought the people out of Egypt, you shall serve God on this mountain."

13Then Moses said to God, "Indeed, *when* I come to the children of Israel and say to them, 'The God of your fathers has sent me to you,' and they say to me, 'What *is* His name?' what shall I say to them?"

14And God said to Moses, "I AM WHO I AM." And He said, "Thus you shall say to the children of Israel, 'I AM has sent me to you.' " 15Moreover God said to Moses, "Thus you shall say to the children of Israel: 'The LORD God of your fathers, the God of Abraham, the God of Isaac, and the God of Jacob, has sent me to you. This *is* My name forever, and this *is* My memorial to all generations.' 16Go and gather the elders of Israel together, and say to them, 'The LORD God of your fathers, the God of Abraham, of Isaac, and of Jacob, appeared to me, saying, "I have surely visited you and *seen* what is done to you in Egypt; 17and I have said I will bring you up out of the affliction of Egypt to the land of the Canaanites and the Hittites and the Amorites and the Perizzites and the Hivites and the Jebusites, to a land flowing with milk and honey." ' 18Then they will heed your voice; and you shall come, you and the elders of Israel, to the king of Egypt; and you shall say to him, 'The LORD God of the Hebrews has met with us; and now, please, let us go three days' journey into the wilderness, that we may sacrifice to the LORD our God.' 19But I am sure that the king of Egypt will not let you go, no, not even by a mighty hand. 20So I will stretch out My hand and strike Egypt with all My wonders which I will do in its midst; and after that he will let you go. 21And I will give this people favor in the sight of the Egyptians; and it shall be, when you go, that you shall not go empty-handed. 22But every woman shall ask of her neighbor, namely, of her who dwells near her house, articles of silver, articles of gold, and clothing; and you shall put *them* on your sons and on your daughters. So you shall plunder the Egyptians."

Miraculous Signs for Pharaoh

4 Then Moses answered and said, "But suppose they will not believe me or listen to my voice; suppose they say, 'The LORD has not appeared to you.' "

2So the LORD said to him, "What *is* that in your hand?"

He said, "A rod."

3And He said, "Cast it on the ground." So he cast it on the ground, and it became a serpent; and Moses fled from it. 4Then the LORD said to Moses, "Reach out your hand and take *it* by the tail" (and he reached out his hand and caught it, and it became a rod in his hand), 5"that they may believe that the LORD God of their fathers, the God of Abraham, the God of Isaac, and the God of Jacob, has appeared to you."

6Furthermore the LORD said to him, "Now put your hand in your bosom." And he put his hand in his bosom, and when he took it out, behold, his hand *was* leprous, like snow. 7And He said, "Put your hand in your bosom again." So he put his hand in his bosom again, and drew it out of his bosom, and behold, it was restored like his *other* flesh. 8"Then it will be, if they do not believe you, nor heed the message of the first sign, that they may believe the message of the latter sign. 9And it shall be, if they do not believe even these two signs, or listen to your voice, that you shall take water from the river*c* and pour *it* on the dry *land*. The water which you take from the river will become blood on the dry *land*."

10Then Moses said to the LORD, "O my Lord, I *am* not eloquent, neither before nor since You have spoken to Your servant; but I *am* slow of speech and slow of tongue."

11So the LORD said to him, "Who has made man's mouth? Or who makes the mute, the deaf, the seeing, or the blind? *Have* not I, the LORD? 12Now therefore,

c That is, the Nile

go, and I will be with your mouth and teach you what you shall say."

13But he said, "O my Lord, please send by the hand of whomever *else* You may send."

14So the anger of the LORD was kindled against Moses, and He said: "Is not Aaron the Levite your brother? I know that he can speak well. And look, he is also coming out to meet you. When he sees you, he will be glad in his heart. 15Now you shall speak to him and put the words in his mouth. And I will be with your mouth and with his mouth, and I will teach you what you shall do. 16So he shall be your spokesman to the people. And he himself shall be as a mouth for you, and you shall be to him as God. 17And you shall take this rod in your hand, with which you shall do the signs."

Moses Goes to Egypt

18So Moses went and returned to Jethro his father-in-law, and said to him, "Please let me go and return to my brethren who *are* in Egypt, and see whether they are still alive."

And Jethro said to Moses, "Go in peace."

19Now the LORD said to Moses in Midian, "Go, return to Egypt; for all the men who sought your life are dead." 20Then Moses took his wife and his sons and set them on a donkey, and he returned to the land of Egypt. And Moses took the rod of God in his hand.

21And the LORD said to Moses, "When you go back to Egypt, see that you do all those wonders before Pharaoh which I have put in your hand. But I will harden his heart, so that he will not let the people go. 22Then you shall say to Pharaoh, 'Thus says the LORD: "Israel *is* My son, My firstborn. 23So I say to you, let My son go that he may serve Me. But if you refuse to let him go, indeed I will kill your son, your firstborn."'"

24And it came to pass on the way, at the encampment, that the LORD met him and sought to kill him. 25Then Zipporah took a sharp stone and cut off the foreskin of her son and cast *it* at Moses' feet, and said, "Surely you *are* a husband of blood to me!" 26So He let him go. Then she said, "*You are* a husband

of blood!"—because of the circumcision.

27And the LORD said to Aaron, "Go into the wilderness to meet Moses." So he went and met him on the mountain of God, and kissed him. 28So Moses told Aaron all the words of the LORD who had sent him, and all the signs which He had commanded him. 29Then Moses and Aaron went and gathered together all the elders of the children of Israel. 30And Aaron spoke all the words which the LORD had spoken to Moses. Then he did the signs in the sight of the people. 31So the people believed; and when they heard that the LORD had visited the children of Israel and that He had looked on their affliction, then they bowed their heads and worshiped.

First Encounter with Pharaoh

5 Afterward Moses and Aaron went in and told Pharaoh, "Thus says the LORD God of Israel: 'Let My people go, that they may hold a feast to Me in the wilderness.'"

2And Pharaoh said, "Who *is* the LORD, that I should obey His voice to let Israel go? I do not know the LORD, nor will I let Israel go."

3So they said, "The God of the Hebrews has met with us. Please, let us go three days' journey into the desert and sacrifice to the LORD our God, lest He fall upon us with pestilence or with the sword."

4Then the king of Egypt said to them, "Moses and Aaron, why do you take the people from their work? Get *back* to your labor." 5And Pharaoh said, "Look, the people of the land *are* many now, and you make them rest from their labor!"

6So the same day Pharaoh commanded the taskmasters of the people and their officers, saying, 7"You shall no longer give the people straw to make brick as before. Let them go and gather straw for themselves. 8And you shall lay on them the quota of bricks which they made before. You shall not reduce it. For they are idle; therefore they cry out, saying, 'Let us go *and* sacrifice to our God.' 9Let more work be laid on the men, that they may labor in it, and let them not regard false words."

10And the taskmasters of the people

and their officers went out and spoke to the people, saying, "Thus says Pharaoh: 'I will not give you straw. 11Go, get yourselves straw where you can find it; yet none of your work will be reduced.' " 12So the people were scattered abroad throughout all the land of Egypt to gather stubble instead of straw. 13And the taskmasters forced *them* to hurry, saying, "Fulfill your work, *your* daily quota, as when there was straw." 14Also the officers of the children of Israel, whom Pharaoh's taskmasters had set over them, were beaten *and* were asked, "Why have you not fulfilled your task in making brick both yesterday and today, as before?"

15Then the officers of the children of Israel came and cried out to Pharaoh, saying, "Why are you dealing thus with your servants? 16There is no straw given to your servants, and they say to us, 'Make brick!' And indeed your servants *are* beaten, but the fault *is* in your *own* people."

17But he said, "You *are* idle! Idle! Therefore you say, 'Let us go *and* sacrifice to the LORD.' 18Therefore go now *and* work; for no straw shall be given you, yet you shall deliver the quota of bricks." 19And the officers of the children of Israel saw *that* they *were* in trouble after it was said, "You shall not reduce *any* bricks from your daily quota."

20Then, as they came out from Pharaoh, they met Moses and Aaron who stood there to meet them. 21And they said to them, "Let the LORD look on you and judge, because you have made us abhorrent in the sight of Pharaoh and in the sight of his servants, to put a sword in their hand to kill us."

Israel's Deliverance Assured

22So Moses returned to the LORD and said, "Lord, why have You brought trouble on this people? Why *is* it You have sent me? 23For since I came to Pharaoh to speak in Your name, he has done evil to this people; neither have You delivered Your people at all."

6 Then the LORD said to Moses, "Now you shall see what I will do to Pharaoh. For with a strong hand he will let

them go, and with a strong hand he will drive them out of his land."

2And God spoke to Moses and said to him: "I *am* the LORD. 3I appeared to Abraham, to Isaac, and to Jacob, as God Almighty, but *by* My name LORD I was not known to them. 4I have also established My covenant with them, to give them the land of Canaan, the land of their pilgrimage, in which they were strangers. 5And I have also heard the groaning of the children of Israel whom the Egyptians keep in bondage, and I have remembered My covenant. 6Therefore say to the children of Israel: 'I *am* the LORD; I will bring you out from under the burdens of the Egyptians, I will rescue you from their bondage, and I will redeem you with an outstretched arm and with great judgments. 7I will take you as My people, and I will be your God. Then you shall know that I *am* the LORD your God who brings you out from under the burdens of the Egyptians. 8And I will bring you into the land which I swore to give to Abraham, Isaac, and Jacob; and I will give it to you *as* a heritage: I *am* the LORD.' " 9So Moses spoke thus to the children of Israel; but they did not heed Moses, because of anguish of spirit and cruel bondage.

10And the LORD spoke to Moses, saying, 11"Go in, tell Pharaoh king of Egypt to let the children of Israel go out of his land."

12And Moses spoke before the LORD, saying, "The children of Israel have not heeded me. How then shall Pharaoh heed me, for I *am* of uncircumcised lips?"

13Then the LORD spoke to Moses and Aaron, and gave them a command for the children of Israel and for Pharaoh king of Egypt, to bring the children of Israel out of the land of Egypt.

The Family of Moses and Aaron

14These *are* the heads of their fathers' houses: The sons of Reuben, the firstborn of Israel, *were* Hanoch, Pallu, Hezron, and Carmi. These are the families of Reuben. 15And the sons of Simeon *were* Jemuel, Jamin, Ohad, Jachin, Zohar, and Shaul the son of a Canaanite woman. These *are* the families of Simeon. 16These *are* the names of the sons of Levi according to their generations: Gershon, Kohath, and Merari. And the years of the life of Levi *were* one hundred and thirty-seven. 17The sons of Gershon *were* Libni and Shimi according to their families. 18And the sons of Kohath *were* Amram, Izhar, Hebron, and Uzziel. And the years of the life of Kohath *were* one hundred and thirty-three. 19The sons of Merari *were* Mahli and Mushi. These *are* the families of Levi according to their generations.

20Now Amram took for himself Jochebed, his father's sister, as wife; and she bore him Aaron and Moses. And the years of the life of Amram *were* one hundred and thirty-seven. 21The sons of Izhar *were* Korah, Nepheg, and Zichri. 22And the sons of Uzziel *were* Mishael, Elzaphan, and Zithri. 23Aaron took to himself Elisheba, daughter of Amminadab, sister of Nahshon, as wife; and she bore him Nadab, Abihu, Eleazar, and Ithamar. 24And the sons of Korah *were* Assir, Elkanah, and Abiasaph. These are the families of the Korahites. 25Eleazar, Aaron's son, took for himself one of the daughters of Putiel as wife; and she bore him Phinehas. These *are* the heads of the fathers' houses of the Levites according to their families.

26These *are the same* Aaron and Moses to whom the LORD said, "Bring out the children of Israel from the land of Egypt according to their armies." 27These *are* the ones who spoke to Pharaoh king of Egypt, to bring out the children of Israel from Egypt. These *are the same* Moses and Aaron.

Aaron Is Moses' Spokesman

28And it came to pass, on the day the LORD spoke to Moses in the land of Egypt, 29that the LORD spoke to Moses, saying, "I *am* the LORD. Speak to Pharaoh king of Egypt all that I say to you."

30But Moses said before the LORD, "Behold, I *am* of uncircumcised lips, and how shall Pharaoh heed me?"

7 So the LORD said to Moses: "See, I have made you *as* God to Pharaoh, and Aaron your brother shall be your prophet. 2You shall speak all that I command you. And Aaron your brother shall tell Pharaoh to send the children

of Israel out of his land. 3And I will harden Pharaoh's heart, and multiply My signs and My wonders in the land of Egypt. 4But Pharaoh will not heed you, so that I may lay My hand on Egypt and bring My armies *and* My people, the children of Israel, out of the land of Egypt by great judgments. 5And the Egyptians shall know that I *am* the LORD, when I stretch out My hand on Egypt and bring out the children of Israel from among them."

6Then Moses and Aaron did *so;* just as the LORD commanded them, so they did. 7And Moses *was* eighty years old and Aaron eighty-three years old when they spoke to Pharaoh.

Aaron's Miraculous Rod

8Then the LORD spoke to Moses and Aaron, saying, 9"When Pharaoh speaks to you, saying, 'Show a miracle for yourselves,' then you shall say to Aaron, 'Take your rod and cast *it* before Pharaoh, *and* let it become a serpent.' " 10So Moses and Aaron went in to Pharaoh, and they did so, just as the LORD commanded. And Aaron cast down his rod before Pharaoh and before his servants, and it became a serpent. 11But Pharaoh also called the wise men and the sorcerers; so the magicians of Egypt, they also did in like manner with their enchantments. 12For every man threw down his rod, and they became serpents. But Aaron's rod swallowed up their rods. 13And Pharaoh's heart grew hard, and he did not heed them, as the LORD had said.

The First Plague: Waters Become Blood

14So the LORD said to Moses: "Pharaoh's heart *is* hard; he refuses to let the people go. 15Go to Pharaoh in the morning, when he goes out to the water, and you shall stand by the river's bank to meet him; and the rod which was turned to a serpent you shall take in your hand. 16And you shall say to him, 'The LORD God of the Hebrews has sent me to you, saying, "Let My people go, that they may serve Me in the wilderness"; but indeed, until now you would not hear! 17Thus says the LORD: "By this you shall know that I *am* the LORD. Behold, I will strike the waters which *are* in the river with the rod that *is* in my hand, and they shall be turned to blood. 18And the fish that *are* in the river shall die, the river shall stink, and the Egyptians will loathe to drink the water of the river." ' "

19Then the LORD spoke to Moses, "Say to Aaron, 'Take your rod and stretch out your hand over the waters of Egypt, over their streams, over their rivers, over their ponds, and over all their pools of water, that they may become blood. And there shall be blood throughout all the land of Egypt, both in *buckets of* wood and *pitchers of* stone.' " 20And Moses and Aaron did so, just as the LORD commanded. So he lifted up the rod and struck the waters that *were* in the river, in the sight of Pharaoh and in the sight of his servants. And all the waters that *were* in the river were turned to blood. 21The fish that *were* in the river died, the river stank, and the Egyptians could not drink the water of the river. So there was blood throughout all the land of Egypt.

22Then the magicians of Egypt did so with their enchantments; and Pharaoh's heart grew hard, and he did not heed them, as the LORD had said. 23And Pharaoh turned and went into his house. Neither was his heart moved by this. 24So all the Egyptians dug all around the river for water to drink, because they could not drink the water of the river. 25And seven days passed after the LORD had struck the river.

The Second Plague: Frogs

8 And the LORD spoke to Moses, "Go to Pharaoh and say to him, 'Thus says the LORD: "Let My people go, that they may serve Me. 2But if you refuse to let *them* go, behold, I will smite all your territory with frogs. 3So the river shall bring forth frogs abundantly, which shall go up and come into your house, into your bedroom, on your bed, into the houses of your servants, on your people, into your ovens, and into your kneading bowls. 4And the frogs shall come up on you, on your people, and on all your servants." ' "

5Then the LORD spoke to Moses, "Say to Aaron, 'Stretch out your hand with your rod over the streams, over the rivers, and over the ponds, and cause frogs

to come up on the land of Egypt.' " 6So Aaron stretched out his hand over the waters of Egypt, and the frogs came up and covered the land of Egypt. 7And the magicians did so with their enchantments, and brought up frogs on the land of Egypt.

8Then Pharaoh called for Moses and Aaron, and said, "Entreat the LORD that He may take away the frogs from me and from my people; and I will let the people go, that they may sacrifice to the LORD."

9And Moses said to Pharaoh, "Accept the honor of saying when I shall intercede for you, for your servants, and for your people, to destroy the frogs from you and your houses, *that* they may remain in the river only."

10So he said, "Tomorrow." And he said, "*Let it be* according to your word, that you may know that *there is* no one like the LORD our God. 11And the frogs shall depart from you, from your houses, from your servants, and from your people. They shall remain in the river only."

12Then Moses and Aaron went out from Pharaoh. And Moses cried out to the LORD concerning the frogs which He had brought against Pharaoh. 13So the LORD did according to the word of Moses. And the frogs died out of the houses, out of the courtyards, and out of the fields. 14They gathered them together in heaps, and the land stank. 15But when Pharaoh saw that there was relief, he hardened his heart and did not heed them, as the LORD had said.

The Third Plague: Lice

16So the LORD said to Moses, "Say to Aaron, 'Stretch out your rod, and strike the dust of the land, so that it may become lice throughout all the land of Egypt.' " 17And they did so. For Aaron stretched out his hand with his rod and struck the dust of the earth, and it became lice on man and beast. All the dust of the land became lice throughout all the land of Egypt.

18Now the magicians so worked with their enchantments to bring forth lice, but they could not. So there were lice on man and beast. 19Then the magicians said to Pharaoh, "This *is* the finger of God." But Pharaoh's heart grew hard, and he did not heed them, just as the LORD had said.

The Fourth Plague: Flies

20And the LORD said to Moses, "Rise early in the morning and stand before Pharaoh as he comes out to the water. Then say to him, 'Thus says the LORD: "Let My people go, that they may serve Me. 21Or else, if you will not let My people go, behold, I will send swarms *of flies* on you and your servants, on your people and into your houses. The houses of the Egyptians shall be full of swarms *of flies*, and also the ground on which they *stand*. 22And in that day I will set apart the land of Goshen, in which My people dwell, that no swarms *of flies* shall be there, in order that you may know that I *am* the LORD in the midst of the land. 23I will make a difference between My people and your people. Tomorrow this sign shall be."'"
24And the LORD did so. Thick swarms *of flies* came into the house of Pharaoh, *into* his servants' houses, and into all the land of Egypt. The land was corrupted because of the swarms *of flies*.

25Then Pharaoh called for Moses and Aaron, and said, "Go, sacrifice to your God in the land."

26And Moses said, "It is not right to do so, for we would be sacrificing the abomination of the Egyptians to the LORD our God. If we sacrifice the abomination of the Egyptians before their eyes, then will they not stone us? 27We will go three days' journey into the wilderness and sacrifice to the LORD our God as He will command us."

28So Pharaoh said, "I will let you go, that you may sacrifice to the LORD your God in the wilderness; only you shall not go very far away. Intercede for me."

29Then Moses said, "Indeed I am going out from you, and I will entreat the LORD, that the swarms *of flies* may depart tomorrow from Pharaoh, from his servants, and from his people. But let Pharaoh not deal deceitfully anymore in not letting the people go to sacrifice to the LORD."

30So Moses went out from Pharaoh and entreated the LORD. 31And the LORD did according to the word of Moses; He removed the swarms *of flies* from Pharaoh, from his servants, and from his

people. Not one remained. 32But Pharaoh hardened his heart at this time also; neither would he let the people go.

The Fifth Plague: Livestock Diseased

9 Then the LORD said to Moses, "Go in to Pharaoh and tell him, 'Thus says the LORD God of the Hebrews: "Let My people go, that they may serve Me. 2For if you refuse to let *them* go, and still hold them, 3behold, the hand of the LORD will be on your cattle in the field, on the horses, on the donkeys, on the camels, on the oxen, and on the sheep— a very severe pestilence. 4And the LORD will make a difference between the livestock of Israel and the livestock of Egypt. So nothing shall die of all *that* belongs to the children of Israel."'"
5Then the LORD appointed a set time, saying, "Tomorrow the LORD will do this thing in the land."

6So the LORD did this thing on the next day, and all the livestock of Egypt died; but of the livestock of the children of Israel, not one died. 7Then Pharaoh sent, and indeed, not even one of the livestock of the Israelites was dead. But the heart of Pharaoh became hard, and he did not let the people go.

The Sixth Plague: Boils

8So the LORD said to Moses and Aaron, "Take for yourselves handfuls of ashes from a furnace, and let Moses scatter it toward the heavens in the sight of Pharaoh. 9And it will become fine dust in all the land of Egypt, and it will cause boils that break out in sores on man and beast throughout all the land of Egypt." 10Then they took ashes from the furnace and stood before Pharaoh, and Moses scattered *them* toward heaven. And *they* caused boils that break out in sores on man and beast. 11And the magicians could not stand before Moses because of the boils, for the boils were on the magicians and on all the Egyptians. 12But the LORD hardened the heart of Pharaoh; and he did not heed them, just as the LORD had spoken to Moses.

The Seventh Plague: Hail

13Then the LORD said to Moses, "Rise early in the morning and stand before Pharaoh, and say to him, 'Thus says the

L ORD God of the Hebrews: "Let My people go, that they may serve Me, 14for at this time I will send all My plagues to your very heart, and on your servants and on your people, that you may know that *there is* none like Me in all the earth. 15Now if I had stretched out My hand and struck you and your people with pestilence, then you would have been cut off from the earth. 16But indeed for this *purpose* I have raised you up, that I may show My power *in* you, and that My name may be declared in all the earth. 17As yet you exalt yourself against My people in that you will not let them go. 18Behold, tomorrow about this time I will cause very heavy hail to rain down, such as has not been in Egypt since its founding until now. 19Therefore send now *and* gather your livestock and all that you have in the field, for the hail shall come down on every man and every animal which is found in the field and is not brought home; and they shall die." ' "

20He who feared the word of the L ORD among the servants of Pharaoh made his servants and his livestock flee to the houses. 21But he who did not regard the word of the L ORD left his servants and his livestock in the field.

22Then the L ORD said to Moses, "Stretch out your hand toward heaven, that there may be hail in all the land of Egypt—on man, on beast, and on every herb of the field, throughout the land of Egypt." 23And Moses stretched out his rod toward heaven; and the L ORD sent thunder and hail, and fire darted to the ground. And the L ORD rained hail on the land of Egypt. 24So there was hail, and fire mingled with the hail, so very heavy that there was none like it in all the land of Egypt since it became a nation. 25And the hail struck throughout the whole land of Egypt, all that *was* in the field, both man and beast; and the hail struck every herb of the field and broke every tree of the field. 26Only in the land of Goshen, where the children of Israel *were,* there was no hail.

27And Pharaoh sent and called for Moses and Aaron, and said to them, "I have sinned this time. The L ORD *is* righteous, and my people and I *are*

wicked. 28Entreat the L ORD, that there may be no *more* mighty thundering and hail, for *it is* enough. I will let you go, and you shall stay no longer."

29So Moses said to him, "As soon as I have gone out of the city, I will spread out my hands to the L ORD; the thunder will cease, and there will be no more hail, that you may know that the earth *is* the L ORD's. 30But as for you and your servants, I know that you will not yet fear the L ORD God."

31Now the flax and the barley were struck, for the barley *was* in the head and the flax *was* in bud. 32But the wheat and the spelt were not struck, for they *are* late crops.

33So Moses went out of the city from Pharaoh and spread out his hands to the L ORD; then the thunder and the hail ceased, and the rain was not poured on the earth. 34And when Pharaoh saw that the rain, the hail, and the thunder had ceased, he sinned yet more; and he hardened his heart, he and his servants. 35So the heart of Pharaoh was hard; neither would he let the children of Israel go, as the L ORD had spoken by Moses.

The Eighth Plague: Locusts

10 Now the L ORD said to Moses, "Go in to Pharaoh; for I have hardened his heart and the hearts of his servants, that I may show these signs of Mine before him, 2and that you may tell in the hearing of your son and your son's son the mighty things I have done in Egypt, and My signs which I have done among them, that you may know that I *am* the L ORD."

3So Moses and Aaron came in to Pharaoh and said to him, "Thus says the L ORD God of the Hebrews: 'How long will you refuse to humble yourself before Me? Let My people go, that they may serve Me. 4Or else, if you refuse to let My people go, behold, tomorrow I will bring locusts into your territory. 5And they shall cover the face of the earth, so that no one will be able to see the earth; and they shall eat the residue of what is left, which remains to you from the hail, and they shall eat every tree which grows up for you out of the field. 6They shall fill your houses, the houses of all your servants, and the houses of all the Egyptians—which neither your fathers nor your fathers' fathers have seen, since the day that they were on the earth to this day.' " And he turned and went out from Pharaoh.

7Then Pharaoh's servants said to him, "How long shall this man be a snare to us? Let the men go, that they may serve the LORD their God. Do you not yet know that Egypt is destroyed?"

8So Moses and Aaron were brought again to Pharaoh, and he said to them, "Go, serve the LORD your God. Who *are* the ones that are going?"

9And Moses said, "We will go with our young and our old; with our sons and our daughters, with our flocks and our herds we will go, for we must hold a feast to the LORD."

10Then he said to them, "The LORD had better be with you when I let you and your little ones go! Beware, for evil is ahead of you. 11Not so! Go now, you *who are* men, and serve the LORD, for that is what you desired." And they were driven out from Pharaoh's presence.

12Then the LORD said to Moses, "Stretch out your hand over the land of Egypt for the locusts, that they may come upon the land of Egypt, and eat every herb of the land—all that the hail has left." 13So Moses stretched out his rod over the land of Egypt, and the LORD brought an east wind on the land all that day and all *that* night. When it was morning, the east wind brought the locusts. 14And the locusts went up over all the land of Egypt and rested on all the territory of Egypt. *They were* very severe; previously there had been no such locusts as they, nor shall there be such after them. 15For they covered the face of the whole earth, so that the land was darkened; and they ate every herb of the land and all the fruit of the trees which the hail had left. So there remained nothing green on the trees or on the plants of the field throughout all the land of Egypt.

16Then Pharaoh called for Moses and Aaron in haste, and said, "I have sinned against the LORD your God and against you. 17Now therefore, please forgive my sin only this once, and entreat the LORD your God, that He may take away from me this death only." 18So he went out from Pharaoh and entreated the LORD. 19And the LORD turned a very strong west wind, which took the locusts away and blew them into the Red Sea. There remained not one locust in all the territory of Egypt. 20But the LORD hardened Pharaoh's heart, and he did not let the children of Israel go.

The Ninth Plague: Darkness

21Then the LORD said to Moses, "Stretch out your hand toward heaven, that there may be darkness over the land of Egypt, darkness *which* may even be felt." 22So Moses stretched out his hand toward heaven, and there was thick darkness in all the land of Egypt three days. 23They did not see one another; nor did anyone rise from his place for three days. But all the children of Israel had light in their dwellings.

24Then Pharaoh called to Moses and said, "Go, serve the LORD; only let your flocks and your herds be kept back. Let your little ones also go with you."

25But Moses said, "You must also give us sacrifices and burnt offerings, that we may sacrifice to the LORD our God. 26Our livestock also shall go with us; not a hoof shall be left behind. For we must take some of them to serve the LORD our God, and even we do not know with what we must serve the LORD until we arrive there."

27But the LORD hardened Pharaoh's heart, and he would not let them go. 28Then Pharaoh said to him, "Get away from me! Take heed to yourself and see my face no more! For in the day you see my face you shall die!"

29So Moses said, "You have spoken well. I will never see your face again."

Death of the Firstborn Announced

11 And the LORD said to Moses, "I will bring one more plague on Pharaoh and on Egypt. Afterward he will let you go from here. When he lets *you* go, he will surely drive you out of here altogether. 2Speak now in the hearing of the people, and let every man ask from his neighbor and every woman from her neighbor, articles of silver and articles of gold." 3And the LORD gave the people favor in the sight of the Egyptians. Moreover the man Moses *was* very great in the land of

Egypt, in the sight of Pharaoh's servants and in the sight of the people.

4Then Moses said, "Thus says the LORD: 'About midnight I will go out into the midst of Egypt; 5and all the firstborn in the land of Egypt shall die, from the firstborn of Pharaoh who sits on his throne, even to the firstborn of the female servant who is behind the handmill, and all the firstborn of the animals. 6Then there shall be a great cry throughout all the land of Egypt, such as was not like it before, nor shall be like it again. 7But against none of the children of Israel shall a dog move its tongue, against man or beast, that you may know that the LORD does make a difference between the Egyptians and Israel.' 8And all these your servants shall come down to me and bow down to me, saying, 'Get out, and all the people who follow you!' After that I will go out." Then he went out from Pharaoh in great anger.

9But the LORD said to Moses, "Pharaoh will not heed you, so that My wonders may be multiplied in the land of Egypt." 10So Moses and Aaron did all these wonders before Pharaoh; and the LORD hardened Pharaoh's heart, and he did not let the children of Israel go out of his land.

The Passover Instituted

12 Now the LORD spoke to Moses and Aaron in the land of Egypt, saying, 2"This month shall be your beginning of months; it shall be the first month of the year to you. 3Speak to all the congregation of Israel, saying: 'On the tenth of this month every man shall take for himself a lamb, according to the house of his father, a lamb for a household. 4And if the household is too small for the lamb, let him and his neighbor next to his house take it according to the number of the persons; according to each man's need you shall make your count for the lamb. 5Your lamb shall be without blemish, a male of the first year. You may take it from the sheep or from the goats. 6Now you shall keep it until the fourteenth day of the same month. Then the whole assembly of the congregation of Israel shall kill it at twilight. 7And they shall take some of the blood and put it on the two

doorposts and on the lintel of the houses where they eat it. 8Then they shall eat the flesh on that night; roasted in fire, with unleavened bread and with bitter herbs they shall eat it. 9Do not eat it raw, nor boiled at all with water, but roasted in fire—its head with its legs and its entrails. 10You shall let none of it remain until morning, and what remains of it until morning you shall burn with fire. 11And thus you shall eat it: with a belt on your waist, your sandals on your feet, and your staff in your hand. So you shall eat it in haste. It is the LORD's Passover.

12'For I will pass through the land of Egypt on that night, and will strike all the firstborn in the land of Egypt, both man and beast; and against all the gods of Egypt I will execute judgment: I am the LORD. 13Now the blood shall be a sign for you on the houses where you are. And when I see the blood, I will pass over you; and the plague shall not be on you to destroy you when I strike the land of Egypt.

14'So this day shall be to you a memorial; and you shall keep it as a feast to the LORD throughout your generations. You shall keep it as a feast by an everlasting ordinance. 15Seven days you shall eat unleavened bread. On the first day you shall remove leaven from your houses. For whoever eats leavened bread from the first day until the seventh day, that person shall be cut off from Israel. 16On the first day there shall be a holy convocation, and on the seventh day there shall be a holy convocation for you. No manner of work shall be done on them; but that which everyone must eat—that only may be prepared by you. 17So you shall observe the Feast of Unleavened Bread, for on this same day I will have brought your armies out of the land of Egypt. Therefore you shall observe this day throughout your generations as an everlasting ordinance. 18In the first month, on the fourteenth day of the month at evening, you shall eat unleavened bread, until the twenty-first day of the month at evening. 19For seven days no leaven shall be found in your houses, since whoever eats what is leavened, that same person shall be cut off from the congregation of Israel, whether he is a stranger or a native of the land. 20You shall eat nothing leavened; in all your dwellings you shall eat unleavened bread.'"

21Then Moses called for all the elders of Israel and said to them, "Pick out and take lambs for yourselves according to your families, and kill the Passover *lamb*. 22And you shall take a bunch of hyssop, dip *it* in the blood that *is* in the basin, and strike the lintel and the two doorposts with the blood that *is* in the basin. And none of you shall go out of the door of his house until morning. 23For the LORD will pass through to strike the Egyptians; and when He sees the blood on the lintel and on the two doorposts, the LORD will pass over the door and not allow the destroyer to come into your houses to strike *you*. 24And you shall observe this thing as an ordinance for you and your sons forever. 25It will come to pass when you come to the land which the LORD will give you, just as He promised, that you shall keep this service. 26And it shall be, when your children say to you, 'What do you mean by this service?' 27that you shall say, 'It *is* the Passover sacrifice of the LORD, who passed over the houses of the children of Israel in Egypt when He struck the Egyptians and delivered our households.'" So the people bowed their heads and worshiped. 28Then the children of Israel went away and did *so*; just as the LORD had commanded Moses and Aaron, so they did.

The Tenth Plague: Death of the Firstborn

29And it came to pass at midnight that the LORD struck all the firstborn in the land of Egypt, from the firstborn of Pharaoh who sat on his throne to the firstborn of the captive who *was* in the dungeon, and all the firstborn of livestock. 30So Pharaoh rose in the night, he, all his servants, and all the Egyptians; and there was a great cry in Egypt, for *there was* not a house where *there was* not one dead.

The Exodus

31Then he called for Moses and Aaron by night, and said, "Rise, go out from among my people, both you and the children of Israel. And go, serve the LORD as you have said. 32Also take your flocks and your herds, as you have said, and be gone; and bless me also."

33And the Egyptians urged the people, that they might send them out of the land in haste. For they said, "We *shall* all *be* dead." 34So the people took their dough before it was leavened, having their kneading bowls bound up in their clothes on their shoulders. 35Now the children of Israel had done according to the word of Moses, and they had asked from the Egyptians articles of silver, articles of gold, and clothing. 36And the LORD had given the people favor in the sight of the Egyptians, so that they granted them *what they requested*. Thus they plundered the Egyptians.

37Then the children of Israel journeyed from Rameses to Succoth, about six hundred thousand men on foot, besides children. 38A mixed multitude went up with them also, and flocks and herds—a great deal of livestock. 39And they baked unleavened cakes of the dough which they had brought out of Egypt; for it was not leavened, because they were driven out of Egypt and could not wait, nor had they prepared provisions for themselves.

40Now the sojourn of the children of Israel who lived in Egypt *was* four hundred and thirty years. 41And it came to pass at the end of the four hundred and thirty years—on that very same day—it came to pass that all the armies of the LORD went out from the land of Egypt. 42It *is* a night of solemn observance to the LORD for bringing them out of the land of Egypt. This *is* that night of the LORD, a solemn observance for all the children of Israel throughout their generations.

Passover Regulations

43And the LORD said to Moses and Aaron, "This *is* the ordinance of the Passover: No foreigner shall eat it. 44But every man's servant who is bought for money, when you have circumcised him, then he may eat it. 45A sojourner and a hired servant shall not eat it. 46In one house it shall be eaten; you shall not carry any of the flesh outside the house, nor shall you break one of its bones. 47All the congregation of Israel shall keep it. 48And when a stranger dwells with you *and wants* to keep the Passover to the LORD, let all his males be circumcised, and then let him come near and keep it; and he shall be as a native of the land. For no uncircumcised person shall eat it. 49One law shall be for the native-born and for the stranger who dwells among you."

50Thus all the children of Israel did; as the LORD commanded Moses and Aaron, so they did. 51And it came to pass, on that very same day, that the LORD brought the children of Israel out of the land of Egypt according to their armies.

The Firstborn Consecrated

13 Then the LORD spoke to Moses, saying, 2"Consecrate to Me all the firstborn, whatever opens the womb among the children of Israel, *both* of man and beast; it is Mine."

The Feast of Unleavened Bread

3And Moses said to the people: "Remember this day in which you went out of Egypt, out of the house of bondage; for by strength of hand the LORD brought you out of this *place.* No leavened bread shall be eaten. 4On this day you are going out, in the month Abib. 5And it shall be, when the LORD brings you into the land of the Canaanites and the Hittites and the Amorites and the Hivites and the Jebusites, which He swore to your fathers to give you, a land flowing with milk and honey, that you shall keep this service in this month. 6Seven days you shall eat unleavened bread, and on the seventh day *there shall be* a feast to the LORD. 7Unleavened bread shall be eaten seven days. And no leavened bread shall be seen among you, nor shall leaven be seen among you in all your quarters. 8And you shall tell your son in that day, saying, '*This is done* because of what the LORD did for me when I came up from Egypt.' 9It shall be as a sign to you on your hand and as a memorial between your eyes, that the LORD's law may be in your mouth; for with a strong hand the LORD has brought you out of Egypt.

10You shall therefore keep this ordinance in its season from year to year.

The Law of the Firstborn

11"And it shall be, when the LORD brings you into the land of the Canaanites, as He swore to you and your fathers, and gives it to you, 12that you shall set apart to the LORD all that open the womb, that is, every firstborn that comes from an animal which you have; the males *shall be* the LORD's. 13But every firstborn of a donkey you shall redeem with a lamb; and if you will not redeem *it,* then you shall break its neck. And all the firstborn of man among your sons you shall redeem. 14So it shall be, when your son asks you in time to come, saying, 'What *is* this?' that you shall say to him, 'By strength of hand the LORD brought us out of Egypt, out of the house of bondage. 15And it came to pass, when Pharaoh was stubborn about letting us go, that the LORD killed all the firstborn in the land of Egypt, both the firstborn of man and the firstborn of beast. Therefore I sacrifice to the LORD all males that open the womb, but all the firstborn of my sons I redeem.' 16It shall be as a sign on your hand and as frontlets between your eyes, for by strength of hand the LORD brought us out of Egypt."

The Wilderness Way

17Then it came to pass, when Pharaoh had let the people go, that God did not lead them *by* way of the land of the Philistines, although that *was* near; for God said, "Lest perhaps the people change their minds when they see war, and return to Egypt." 18So God led the people around *by* way of the wilderness of the Red Sea. And the children of Israel went up in orderly ranks out of the land of Egypt.

19And Moses took the bones of Joseph with him, for he had placed the children of Israel under solemn oath, saying, "God will surely visit you, and you shall carry up my bones from here with you."[d]

20So they took their journey from Succoth and camped in Etham at the

[d] Compare Genesis 50.25

edge of the wilderness. 21And the LORD went before them by day in a pillar of cloud to lead the way, and by night in a pillar of fire to give them light, so as to go by day and night. 22He did not take away the pillar of cloud by day or the pillar of fire by night *from* before the people.

The Red Sea Crossing

14 Now the LORD spoke to Moses, saying: 2"Speak to the children of Israel, that they turn and camp before Pi Hahiroth, between Migdol and the sea, opposite Baal Zephon; you shall camp before it by the sea. 3For Pharaoh will say of the children of Israel, 'They *are* bewildered by the land; the wilderness has closed them in.' 4Then I will harden Pharaoh's heart, so that he will pursue them; and I will gain honor over Pharaoh and over all his army, that the Egyptians may know that I *am* the LORD." And they did so.

5Now it was told the king of Egypt that the people had fled, and the heart of Pharaoh and his servants was turned against the people; and they said, "Why have we done this, that we have let Israel go from serving us?" 6So he made ready his chariot and took his people with him. 7Also, he took six hundred choice chariots, and all the chariots of Egypt with captains over every one of them. 8And the LORD hardened the heart of Pharaoh king of Egypt, and he pursued the children of Israel; and the children of Israel went out with boldness. 9So the Egyptians pursued them, all the horses *and* chariots of Pharaoh, his horsemen and his army, and overtook them camping by the sea beside Pi Hahiroth, before Baal Zephon.

10And when Pharaoh drew near, the children of Israel lifted their eyes, and behold, the Egyptians marched after them. So they were very afraid, and the children of Israel cried out to the LORD. 11Then they said to Moses, "Because *there were* no graves in Egypt, have you taken us away to die in the wilderness? Why have you so dealt with us, to bring us up out of Egypt? 12Is this not the word that we told you in Egypt, saying, 'Let us alone that we may serve the Egyptians'? For *it would have been* better for us to serve the Egyptians than

that we should die in the wilderness."

13And Moses said to the people, "Do not be afraid. Stand still, and see the salvation of the LORD, which He will accomplish for you today. For the Egyptians whom you see today, you shall see again no more forever. 14The LORD will fight for you, and you shall hold your peace."

15And the LORD said to Moses, "Why do you cry to Me? Tell the children of Israel to go forward. 16But lift up your rod, and stretch out your hand over the sea and divide it. And the children of Israel shall go on dry *ground* through the midst of the sea. 17And I indeed will harden the hearts of the Egyptians, and they shall follow them. So I will gain honor over Pharaoh and over all his army, his chariots, and his horsemen. 18Then the Egyptians shall know that I *am* the LORD, when I have gained honor for Myself over Pharaoh, his chariots, and his horsemen."

19And the Angel of God, who went before the camp of Israel, moved and went behind them; and the pillar of cloud went from before them and stood behind them. 20So it came between the camp of the Egyptians and the camp of Israel. Thus it was a cloud and darkness *to the one*, and it gave light by night *to the other*, so that the one did not come near the other all that night.

21Then Moses stretched out his hand over the sea; and the LORD caused the sea to go *back* by a strong east wind all that night, and made the sea into dry *land*, and the waters were divided. 22So the children of Israel went into the midst of the sea on the dry *ground*, and the waters *were* a wall to them on their right hand and on their left. 23And the Egyptians pursued and went after them into the midst of the sea, all Pharaoh's horses, his chariots, and his horsemen.

24Now it came to pass, in the morning watch, that the LORD looked down upon the army of the Egyptians through the pillar of fire and cloud, and He troubled the army of the Egyptians. 25And He took off their chariot wheels, so that they drove them with difficulty; and the Egyptians said, "Let us flee from the face of Israel, for the LORD fights for them against the Egyptians."

26Then the LORD said to Moses,

"Stretch out your hand over the sea, that the waters may come back upon the Egyptians, on their chariots, and on their horsemen." 27And Moses stretched out his hand over the sea; and when the morning appeared, the sea returned to its full depth, while the Egyptians were fleeing into it. So the LORD overthrew the Egyptians in the midst of the sea. 28Then the waters returned and covered the chariots, the horsemen, *and* all the army of Pharaoh that came into the sea after them. Not so much as one of them remained. 29But the children of Israel had walked on dry *land* in the midst of the sea, and the waters *were* a wall to them on their right hand and on their left.

30So the LORD saved Israel that day out of the hand of the Egyptians, and Israel saw the Egyptians dead on the seashore. 31Thus Israel saw the great work which the LORD had done in Egypt; so the people feared the LORD, and believed the LORD and His servant Moses.

The Song of Moses

15 Then Moses and the children of Israel sang this song to the LORD, and spoke, saying:

"I will sing to the LORD,
For He has triumphed gloriously!
The horse and its rider
He has thrown into the sea!

2 The LORD *is* my strength and song,
And He has become my salvation;
He *is* my God, and I will
praise Him;
My father's God, and I will
exalt Him.

3 The LORD *is* a man of war;
The LORD *is* His name.

4 Pharaoh's chariots and his army He
has cast into the sea;
His chosen captains also are
drowned in the Red Sea.

5 The depths have covered them;
They sank to the bottom like a
stone.

6 "Your right hand, O LORD, has
become glorious in power;
Your right hand, O LORD, has
dashed the enemy in pieces.

7 And in the greatness of Your
excellence

You have overthrown those who
rose against You;
You sent forth Your wrath;
It consumed them like stubble.

8 And with the blast of Your nostrils
The waters were gathered together;
The floods stood upright like a
heap;
The depths congealed in the heart
of the sea.

9 The enemy said, 'I will pursue,
I will overtake,
I will divide the spoil;
My desire shall be satisfied on
them.
I will draw my sword,
My hand shall destroy them.'

10 You blew with Your wind,
The sea covered them;
They sank like lead in the mighty
waters.

11 "Who *is* like You, O LORD, among
the gods?
Who *is* like You, glorious in
holiness,
Fearful in praises, doing wonders?

12 You stretched out Your right hand;
The earth swallowed them.

13 You in Your mercy have led forth
The people whom You have
redeemed;
You have guided *them* in Your
strength
To Your holy habitation.

14 "The people will hear *and* be afraid;
Sorrow will take hold of the
inhabitants of Philistia.

15 Then the chiefs of Edom will be
dismayed;
The mighty men of Moab,
Trembling will take hold of them;
All the inhabitants of Canaan will
melt away.

16 Fear and dread will fall on them;
By the greatness of Your arm
They will be *as* still as a stone,
Till Your people pass over, O LORD,
Till the people pass over
Whom You have purchased.

17 You will bring them in and plant
them
In the mountain of Your
inheritance,
In the place, O LORD, *which* You
have made

For Your own dwelling,
The sanctuary, O LORD, *which* Your
   hands have established.

18 "The LORD shall reign forever and
   ever."

19For the horses of Pharaoh went
with his chariots and his horsemen into
the sea, and the LORD brought back the
waters of the sea upon them. But the
children of Israel went on dry *land* in
the midst of the sea.

The Song of Miriam

20Then Miriam the prophetess, the
sister of Aaron, took the timbrel in her
hand; and all the women went out after
her with timbrels and with dances.
21And Miriam answered them:

   "Sing to the LORD,
   For He has triumphed
      gloriously!
   The horse and its rider
   He has thrown into the sea!"

Bitter Waters Made Sweet

22So Moses brought Israel from the
Red Sea; then they went out into the
Wilderness of Shur. And they went
three days in the wilderness and found
no water. 23Now when they came to
Marah, they could not drink the waters
of Marah, for they *were* bitter. Therefore the name of it was called Marah.*e*
24And the people complained against
Moses, saying, "What shall we drink?"
25So he cried out to the LORD, and the
LORD showed him a tree. When he cast
it into the waters, the waters were made
sweet.

There He made a statute and an ordinance for them, and there He tested
them, 26and said, "If you diligently heed
the voice of the LORD your God and do
what is right in His sight, give ear to
His commandments and keep all His
statutes, I will put none of the diseases
on you which I have brought on the
Egyptians. For I *am* the LORD who
heals you."

27Then they came to Elim, where
there *were* twelve wells of water and
seventy palm trees; so they camped
there by the waters.

e Literally *Bitter*

Bread from Heaven

16 And they journeyed from Elim,
and all the congregation of the
children of Israel came to the Wilderness of Sin, which is between Elim and
Sinai, on the fifteenth day of the second
month after they departed from the
land of Egypt. 2Then the whole congregation of the children of Israel complained against Moses and Aaron in the
wilderness. 3And the children of Israel
said to them, "Oh, that we had died by
the hand of the LORD in the land of
Egypt, when we sat by the pots of meat
and when we ate bread to the full! For
you have brought us out into this wilderness to kill this whole assembly with
hunger."

4Then the LORD said to Moses, "Behold, I will rain bread from heaven for
you. And the people shall go out and
gather a certain quota every day, that
I may test them, whether they will walk
in My law or not. 5And it shall be on
the sixth day that they shall prepare
what they bring in, and it shall be twice
as much as they gather daily."

6Then Moses and Aaron said to all
the children of Israel, "At evening you
shall know that the LORD has brought
you out of the land of Egypt. 7And in
the morning you shall see the glory of
the LORD; for He hears your complaints
against the LORD. But what *are* we, that
you complain against us?" 8Also Moses
said, "*This shall be seen* when the LORD
gives you meat to eat in the evening,
and in the morning bread to the full;
for the LORD hears your complaints
which you make against Him. And
what *are* we? Your complaints *are* not
against us but against the LORD."

9Then Moses spoke to Aaron, "Say
to all the congregation of the children
of Israel, 'Come near before the LORD,
for He has heard your complaints.'"
10Now it came to pass, as Aaron spoke
to the whole congregation of the children of Israel, that they looked toward
the wilderness, and behold, the glory
of the LORD appeared in the cloud.

11And the LORD spoke to Moses, saying, 12"I have heard the complaints of
the children of Israel. Speak to them,
saying, 'At twilight you shall eat meat,

and in the morning you shall be filled with bread. And you shall know that I *am* the LORD your God.' "

13So it was that quails came up at evening and covered the camp, and in the morning the dew lay all around the camp. 14And when the layer of dew lifted, there, on the surface of the wilderness, was a small round substance, *as* fine as frost on the ground. 15So when the children of Israel saw *it,* they said to one another, "What is it?" For they did not know what it *was.*

And Moses said to them, "This *is* the bread which the LORD has given you to eat. 16This is the thing which the LORD has commanded: 'Let every man gather it according to each one's need, one omer for each person, *according to the* number of persons; let every man take for *those* who *are* in his tent.' "

17Then the children of Israel did so and gathered, some more, some less. 18So when they measured *it* by omers, he who gathered much had nothing left over, and he who gathered little had no lack. Every man had gathered according to each one's need. 19And Moses said, "Let no one leave any of it till morning." 20Notwithstanding they did not heed Moses. But some of them left part of it until morning, and it bred worms and stank. And Moses was angry with them. 21So they gathered it every morning, every man according to his need. And when the sun became hot, it melted.

22And so it was, on the sixth day, *that* they gathered twice as much bread, two omers for each one. And all the rulers of the congregation came and told Moses. 23Then he said to them, "This *is* what the LORD has said: 'Tomorrow *is* a Sabbath rest, a holy Sabbath to the LORD. Bake what you will bake *today,* and boil what you will boil; and lay up for yourselves all that remains, to be kept until morning.' " 24So they laid it up till morning, as Moses commanded; and it did not stink, nor were there any worms in it. 25Then Moses said, "Eat that today, for today *is* a Sabbath to the LORD; today you will not find it in the field. 26Six days you shall gather it, but

on the seventh day, the Sabbath, there will be none."

27Now it happened *that some* of the people went out on the seventh day to gather, but they found none. 28And the LORD said to Moses, "How long do you refuse to keep My commandments and My laws? 29See! For the LORD has given you the Sabbath; therefore He gives you on the sixth day bread for two days. Let every man remain in his place; let no man go out of his place on the seventh day." 30So the people rested on the seventh day.

31And the house of Israel called its name Manna.*f* And it *was* like white coriander seed, and the taste of it *was* like wafers *made* with honey.

32Then Moses said, "This *is* the thing which the LORD has commanded: 'Fill an omer with it, to be kept for your generations, that they may see the bread with which I fed you in the wilderness, when I brought you out of the land of Egypt.' " 33And Moses said to Aaron, "Take a pot and put an omer of manna in it, and lay it up before the LORD, to be kept for your generations." 34As the LORD commanded Moses, so Aaron laid it up before the Testimony, to be kept. 35And the children of Israel ate manna forty years, until they came to an inhabited land; they ate manna until they came to the border of the land of Canaan. 36Now an omer *is* one-tenth of an ephah.

Water from the Rock

17 Then all the congregation of the children of Israel set out on their journey from the Wilderness of Sin, according to the commandment of the LORD, and camped in Rephidim; but *there was* no water for the people to drink. 2Therefore the people contended with Moses, and said, "Give us water, that we may drink."

So Moses said to them, "Why do you contend with me? Why do you tempt the LORD?"

3And the people thirsted there for water, and the people complained against Moses, and said, "Why *is* it you have brought us up out of Egypt, to kill us

f Literally *What?* (compare Exodus 16.15)

and our children and our livestock with thirst?"

4So Moses cried out to the LORD, saying, "What shall I do with this people? They are almost ready to stone me!"

5And the LORD said to Moses, "Go on before the people, and take with you some of the elders of Israel. Also take in your hand your rod with which you struck the river, and go. 6Behold, I will stand before you there on the rock in Horeb; and you shall strike the rock, and water will come out of it, that the people may drink."

And Moses did so in the sight of the elders of Israel. 7So he called the name of the place Massah*g* and Meribah,*h* because of the contention of the children of Israel, and because they tempted the LORD, saying, "Is the LORD among us or not?"

Victory over the Amalekites

8Now Amalek came and fought with Israel in Rephidim. 9And Moses said to Joshua, "Choose us some men and go out, fight with Amalek. Tomorrow I will stand on the top of the hill with the rod of God in my hand." 10So Joshua did as Moses said to him, and fought with Amalek. And Moses, Aaron, and Hur went up to the top of the hill. 11And so it was, when Moses held up his hand, that Israel prevailed; and when he let down his hand, Amalek prevailed. 12But Moses' hands *became* heavy; so they took a stone and put *it* under him, and he sat on it. And Aaron and Hur supported his hands, one on one side, and the other on the other side; and his hands were steady until the going down of the sun. 13So Joshua defeated Amalek and his people with the edge of the sword.

14Then the LORD said to Moses, "Write this *for* a memorial in the book and recount *it* in the hearing of Joshua, that I will utterly blot out the remembrance of Amalek from under heaven." 15And Moses built an altar and called its name, The-LORD-Is-My-Banner; 16for he said, "Because the LORD has sworn: the LORD *will have* war with Amalek from generation to generation."

Jethro's Advice

18 And Jethro, the priest of Midian, Moses' father-in-law, heard of all that God had done for Moses and for Israel His people—that the LORD had brought Israel out of Egypt. 2Then Jethro, Moses' father-in-law, took Zipporah, Moses' wife, after he had sent her back, 3with her two sons, of whom the name of one *was* Gershom (for he said, "I have been a stranger in a foreign land")*i* 4and the name of the other *was* Eliezer*j* (for *he said,* "The God of my father *was* my help, and delivered me from the sword of Pharaoh"); 5and Jethro, Moses' father-in-law, came with his sons and his wife to Moses in the wilderness, where he was encamped at the mountain of God. 6Now he had said to Moses, "I, your father-in-law Jethro, am coming to you with your wife and her two sons with her."

7So Moses went out to meet his father-in-law, bowed down, and kissed him. And they asked each other about *their* well-being, and they went into the tent. 8And Moses told his father-in-law all that the LORD had done to Pharaoh and to the Egyptians for Israel's sake, all the hardship that had come upon them on the way, and *how* the LORD had delivered them. 9Then Jethro rejoiced for all the good which the LORD had done for Israel, whom He had delivered out of the hand of the Egyptians. 10And Jethro said, "Blessed *be* the LORD, who has delivered you out of the hand of the Egyptians and out of the hand of Pharaoh, *and* who has delivered the people from under the hand of the Egyptians. 11Now I know that the LORD *is* greater than all the gods; for in the very thing in which they behaved proudly, *He was* above them." 12Then Jethro, Moses' father-in-law, took a burnt offering and *other* sacrifices *to offer* to God. And Aaron came with all the elders of Israel to eat bread with Moses' father-in-law before God.

13And so it was, on the next day, that Moses sat to judge the people; and the people stood before Moses from morn-

---

g Literally *Tempted*   h Literally *Contention*
Is Help

i Compare Exodus 2.22   j Literally *My God*

ing until evening. 14So when Moses' father-in-law saw all that he did for the people, he said, "What *is* this thing that you are doing for the people? Why do you alone sit, and all the people stand before you from morning until evening?"

15And Moses said to his father-in-law, "Because the people come to me to inquire of God. 16When they have a difficulty, they come to me, and I judge between one and another; and I make known the statutes of God, and His laws."

17So Moses' father-in-law said to him, "The thing that you do *is* not good. 18Both you and these people who *are* with you will surely wear yourselves out. For this thing *is* too much for you; you are not able to perform it by yourself. 19Listen now to my voice; I will give you counsel, and God will be with you: Stand before God for the people, so that you may bring the difficulties to God. 20And you shall teach them the statutes and the laws, and show them the way in which they must walk and the work they must do. 21Moreover you shall select from all the people able men, such as fear God, men of truth, hating covetousness; and place *such* over them *to be* rulers of thousands, rulers of hundreds, rulers of fifties, and rulers of tens. 22And let them judge the people at all times. Then it will be *that* every great matter they shall bring to you, but every small matter they themselves shall judge. So it will be easier for you, for they will bear *the burden* with you. 23If you do this thing, and God *so* commands you, then you will be able to endure, and all this people will also go to their place in peace."

24So Moses heeded the voice of his father-in-law and did all that he had said. 25And Moses chose able men out of all Israel, and made them heads over the people: rulers of thousands, rulers of hundreds, rulers of fifties, and rulers of tens. 26So they judged the people at all times; the hard cases they brought to Moses, but they judged every small case themselves.

27Then Moses let his father-in-law depart, and he went his way to his own land.

Israel at Mount Sinai

19 In the third month after the children of Israel had gone out of the land of Egypt, on the same day, they came *to* the Wilderness of Sinai. 2For they had departed from Rephidim, had come *to* the Wilderness of Sinai, and camped in the wilderness. So Israel camped there before the mountain.

3And Moses went up to God, and the LORD called to him from the mountain, saying, "Thus you shall say to the house of Jacob, and tell the children of Israel: 4'You have seen what I did to the Egyptians, and *how* I bore you on eagles' wings and brought you to Myself. 5Now therefore, if you will indeed obey My voice and keep My covenant, then you shall be a special treasure to Me above all people; for all the earth *is* Mine. 6And you shall be to Me a kingdom of priests and a holy nation.' These *are* the words which you shall speak to the children of Israel."

7So Moses came and called for the elders of the people, and laid before them all these words which the LORD commanded him. 8Then all the people answered together and said, "All that the LORD has spoken we will do." So Moses brought back the words of the people to the LORD. 9And the LORD said to Moses, "Behold, I come to you in the thick cloud, that the people may hear when I speak with you, and believe you forever."

So Moses told the words of the people to the LORD.

10Then the LORD said to Moses, "Go to the people and consecrate them today and tomorrow, and let them wash their clothes. 11And let them be ready for the third day. For on the third day the LORD will come down upon Mount Sinai in the sight of all the people. 12You shall set bounds for the people all around, saying, 'Take heed to yourselves *that* you do *not* go up to the mountain or touch its base. Whoever touches the mountain shall surely be put to death. 13Not a hand shall touch him, but he shall surely be stoned or shot *with an arrow;* whether man or beast, he shall not live.' When the trumpet sounds long, they shall come near the mountain."

14So Moses went down from the mountain to the people and sanctified the people, and they washed their clothes. 15And he said to the people, "Be ready for the third day; do not come near your wives."

16Then it came to pass on the third day, in the morning, that there were thunderings and lightnings, and a thick cloud on the mountain; and the sound of the trumpet was very loud, so that all the people who were in the camp trembled. 17And Moses brought the people out of the camp to meet with God, and they stood at the foot of the mountain. 18Now Mount Sinai was completely in smoke, because the LORD descended upon it in fire. Its smoke ascended like the smoke of a furnace, and the whole mountain quaked greatly. 19And when the blast of the trumpet sounded long and became louder and louder, Moses spoke, and God answered him by voice. 20Then the LORD came down upon Mount Sinai, on the top of the mountain. And the LORD called Moses to the top of the mountain, and Moses went up.

21And the LORD said to Moses, "Go down and warn the people, lest they break through to gaze at the LORD, and many of them perish. 22Also let the priests who come near the LORD consecrate themselves, lest the LORD break out against them."

23But Moses said to the LORD, "The people cannot come up to Mount Sinai; for You warned us, saying, 'Set bounds around the mountain and consecrate it.'"

24Then the LORD said to him, "Away! Get down and then come up, you and Aaron with you. But do not let the priests and the people break through to come up to the LORD, lest He break out against them." 25So Moses went down to the people and spoke to them.

The Ten Commandments

20 And God spoke all these words, saying:

2 "I am the LORD your God, who brought you out of the land of Egypt, out of the house of bondage.

3 "You shall have no other gods before Me.

4 "You shall not make for yourself a carved image—any likeness of anything that is in heaven above, or that is in the earth beneath, or that is in the water under the earth; 5you shall not bow down to them nor serve them. For I, the LORD your God, am a jealous God, visiting the iniquity of the fathers upon the children to the third and fourth generations of those who hate Me, 6but showing mercy to thousands, to those who love Me and keep My commandments.

7 "You shall not take the name of the LORD your God in vain, for the LORD will not hold him guiltless who takes His name in vain.

8 "Remember the Sabbath day, to keep it holy. 9Six days you shall labor and do all your work, 10but the seventh day is the Sabbath of the LORD your God. In it you shall do no work: you, nor your son, nor your daughter, nor your male servant, nor your female servant, nor your cattle, nor your stranger who is within your gates. 11For in six days the LORD made the heavens and the earth, the sea, and all that is in them, and rested the seventh day. Therefore the LORD blessed the Sabbath day and hallowed it.

12 "Honor your father and your mother, that your days may be long upon the land which the LORD your God is giving you.

13 "You shall not murder.

14 "You shall not commit adultery.

15 "You shall not steal.

16 "You shall not bear false witness against your neighbor.

17 "You shall not covet your neighbor's house; you shall not covet your neighbor's wife, nor his male servant, nor his female servant, nor his ox, nor his donkey, nor anything that is your neighbor's."

The People Afraid of God's Presence

18Now all the people witnessed the thunderings, the lightning flashes, the sound of the trumpet, and the mountain smoking; and when the people saw *it*, they trembled and stood afar off. 19Then they said to Moses, "You speak with us, and we will hear; but let not God speak with us, lest we die."

20And Moses said to the people, "Do not fear; for God has come to test you, and that His fear may be before you, so that you may not sin." 21So the people stood afar off, but Moses drew near the thick darkness where God *was.*

The Law of the Altar

22Then the LORD said to Moses, "Thus you shall say to the children of Israel: 'You have seen that I have talked with you from heaven. 23You shall not make *anything to be* with Me—gods of silver or gods of gold you shall not make for yourselves. 24An altar of earth you shall make for Me, and you shall sacrifice on it your burnt offerings and your peace offerings, your sheep and your oxen. In every place where I record My name I will come to you, and I will bless you. 25And if you make Me an altar of stone, you shall not build it of hewn stone; for if you use your tool on it, you have profaned it. 26Nor shall you go up by steps to My altar, that your nakedness may not be exposed on it.'

The Law Concerning Servants

21 "Now these *are* the judgments which you shall set before them: 2If you buy a Hebrew servant, he shall serve six years; and in the seventh he shall go out free and pay nothing. 3If he comes in by himself, he shall go out by himself; if he *comes in* married, then his wife shall go out with him. 4If his master has given him a wife, and she has borne him sons or daughters, the wife and her children shall be her master's, and he shall go out by himself. 5But if the servant plainly says, 'I love my master, my wife, and my children; I will not go out free,' 6then his master shall bring him to the judges. He shall also bring him to the door, or to the doorpost, and his master shall pierce his ear with an awl; and he shall serve him forever.

7"And if a man sells his daughter to be a female slave, she shall not go out

as the male slaves do. 8If she does not please her master, who has betrothed her to himself, then he shall let her be redeemed. He shall have no right to sell her to a foreign people, since he has dealt deceitfully with her. 9And if he has betrothed her to his son, he shall deal with her according to the custom of daughters. 10If he takes another *wife,* he shall not diminish her food, her clothing, and her marriage rights. 11And if he does not do these three for her, then she shall go out free, without *paying* money.

The Law Concerning Violence

12"He who strikes a man so that he dies shall surely be put to death. 13However, if he did not lie in wait, but God delivered *him* into his hand, then I will appoint for you a place where he may flee.

14"But if a man acts with premeditation against his neighbor, to kill him by treachery, you shall take him from My altar, that he may die.

15"And he who strikes his father or his mother shall surely be put to death.

16"He who kidnaps a man and sells him, or if he is found in his hand, shall surely be put to death.

17"And he who curses his father or his mother shall surely be put to death.

18"If men contend with each other, and one strikes the other with a stone or with *his* fist, and he does not die but is confined to *his* bed, 19if he rises again and walks about outside with his staff, then he who struck *him* shall be acquitted. He shall only pay *for* the loss of his time, and shall provide *for him* to be thoroughly healed.

20"And if a man beats his male or female servant with a rod, so that he dies under his hand, he shall surely be punished. 21Notwithstanding, if he remains alive a day or two, he shall not be punished; for he *is* his property.

22"If men fight, and hurt a woman with child, so that she gives birth prematurely, yet no harm follows, he shall surely be punished accordingly as the woman's husband imposes on him; and he shall pay as the judges *determine.* 23But if *any* harm follows, then you shall give life for life, 24eye for eye, tooth for tooth, hand for hand, foot for foot, 25burn for burn, wound for wound, stripe for stripe.

26"If a man strikes the eye of his male or female servant, and destroys it, he shall let him go free for the sake of his eye. 27And if he knocks out the tooth of his male or female servant, he shall let him go free for the sake of his tooth.

Animal Control Laws

28"If an ox gores a man or a woman to death, then the ox shall surely be stoned, and its flesh shall not be eaten; but the owner of the ox *shall be* acquitted. 29But if the ox tended to thrust with its horn in times past, and it has been made known to his owner, and he has not kept it confined, so that it has killed a man or a woman, the ox shall be stoned and its owner also shall be put to death. 30If there is imposed on him a sum of money, then he shall pay to redeem his life, whatever is imposed on him. 31Whether it has gored a son or gored a daughter, according to this judgment it shall be done to him. 32If the ox gores a male or female servant, he shall give to their master thirty shekels of silver, and the ox shall be stoned.

33"And if a man opens a pit, or if a man digs a pit and does not cover it, and an ox or a donkey falls in it, 34the owner of the pit shall make *it* good; he shall give money to their owner, but the dead *animal* shall be his.

35"If one man's ox hurts another's, so that it dies, then they shall sell the live ox and divide the money from it; and the dead ox they shall also divide. 36Or if it was known that the ox tended to thrust in time past, and its owner has not kept it confined, he shall surely pay ox for ox, and the dead animal shall be his own.

Responsibility for Property

22 "If a man steals an ox or a sheep, and slaughters it or sells it, he shall restore five oxen for an ox and four sheep for a sheep. 2If the thief is found breaking in, and he is struck so that he dies, *there shall be* no guilt for his bloodshed. 3If the sun has risen on him, *there shall be* guilt for his bloodshed. He should make full restitution; if he has nothing, then he shall be sold for his theft. 4If the theft is certainly found alive in his hand, whether it is an ox or donkey or sheep, he shall restore double.

5"If a man causes a field or vineyard to be grazed, and lets loose his animal, and it feeds in another man's field, he shall make restitution from the best of his own field and the best of his own vineyard.

6"If fire breaks out and catches in thorns, so that stacked grain, standing grain, or the field is consumed, he who kindled the fire shall surely make restitution.

7"If a man delivers to his neighbor money or articles to keep, and it is stolen out of the man's house, if the thief is found, he shall pay double. 8If the thief is not found, then the master of the house shall be brought to the judges *to see* whether he has put his hand into his neighbor's goods.

9"For any kind of trespass, *whether it concerns* an ox, a donkey, a sheep, or clothing, *or* for any kind of lost thing which *another* claims to be his, the cause of both parties shall come before the judges; *and* whomever the judges condemn shall pay double to his neighbor. 10If a man delivers to his neighbor a donkey, an ox, a sheep, or any animal to keep, and it dies, is hurt, or driven away, no one seeing *it*, 11then an oath of the Lord shall be between them both, that he has not put his hand into his neighbor's goods; and the owner of it shall accept *that*, and he shall not make *it* good. 12But if, in fact, it is stolen from him, he shall make restitution to the owner of it. 13If it is torn to pieces *by a beast, then* he shall bring it as evidence, *and* he shall not make good what was torn.

14"And if a man borrows *anything* from his neighbor, and it becomes injured or dies, the owner of it not *being* with it, he shall surely make *it* good. 15If its owner *was* with it, he shall not make *it* good; if it *was* hired, it came for its hire.

Moral and Ceremonial Principles

16"If a man entices a virgin who is not betrothed, and lies with her, he shall surely pay the bride-price for her *to be* his wife. 17If her father utterly refuses to give her to him, he shall pay money according to the bride-price of virgins.

18"You shall not permit a sorceress to live.

19"Whoever lies with an animal shall surely be put to death.

20"He who sacrifices to *any* god, except to the LORD only, he shall be utterly destroyed.

21"You shall neither mistreat a stranger nor oppress him, for you were strangers in the land of Egypt.

22"You shall not afflict any widow or fatherless child. 23If you afflict them in any way, *and* they cry at all to Me, I will surely hear their cry; 24and My wrath will become hot, and I will kill you with the sword; your wives shall be widows, and your children fatherless.

25"If you lend money to *any of* My people *who are* poor among you, you shall not be like a moneylender to him; you shall not charge him interest. 26If you ever take your neighbor's garment as a pledge, you shall return it to him before the sun goes down. 27For that *is* his only covering, it *is* his garment for his skin. What will he sleep in? And it will be that when he cries to Me, I will hear, for I *am* gracious.

28"You shall not revile God, nor curse a ruler of your people.

29"You shall not delay *to offer* the first of your ripe produce and your juices. The firstborn of your sons you shall give to Me. 30Likewise you shall do with your oxen *and* your sheep. It shall be with its mother seven days; on the eighth day you shall give it to Me.

31"And you shall be holy men to Me: you shall not eat meat torn *by beasts* in the field; you shall throw it to the dogs.

Justice for All

23 "You shall not circulate a false report. Do not put your hand with the wicked to be an unrighteous witness. 2You shall not follow a crowd to do evil; nor shall you testify in a dispute so as to turn aside after many to pervert *justice.* 3You shall not show partiality to a poor man in his dispute.

4"If you meet your enemy's ox or his donkey going astray, you shall surely bring it back to him again. 5If you see the donkey of one who hates you lying under its burden, and you would refrain from helping it, you shall surely help him with it.

6"You shall not pervert the judgment of your poor in his dispute. 7Keep yourself far from a false matter; do not kill the innocent and righteous. For I will not justify the wicked. 8And you shall take no bribe, for a bribe blinds the discerning and perverts the words of the righteous.

9"Also you shall not oppress a stranger, for you know the heart of a stranger, because you were strangers in the land of Egypt.

The Law of Sabbaths

10"Six years you shall sow your land and gather in its produce, 11but the seventh *year* you shall let it rest and lie fallow, that the poor of your people may eat; and what they leave, the beasts of the field may eat. In like manner you shall do with your vineyard *and* your olive grove. 12Six days you shall do your work, and on the seventh day you shall rest, that your ox and your donkey may rest, and the son of your female servant and the stranger may be refreshed.

13"And in all that I have said to you, be circumspect and make no mention of the name of other gods, nor let it be heard from your mouth.

Three Annual Feasts

14"Three times you shall keep a feast to Me in the year: 15You shall keep the Feast of Unleavened Bread (you shall eat unleavened bread seven days, as I commanded you, at the time appointed in the month of Abib, for in it you came out of Egypt; none shall appear before Me empty); 16and the Feast of Harvest, the firstfruits of your labors which you have sown in the field; and the Feast of Ingathering at the end of the year, when you have gathered in *the fruit of* your labors from the field.

17"Three times in the year all your males shall appear before the Lord GOD.

18"You shall not offer the blood of My sacrifice with leavened bread; nor shall the fat of My sacrifice remain until morning. 19The first of the firstfruits of your land you shall bring into the house of the LORD your God. You shall not boil a young goat in its mother's milk.

The Angel and the Promises

20"Behold, I send an Angel before you to keep you in the way and to bring you into the place which I have prepared. 21Beware of Him and obey His voice; do not provoke Him, for He will not pardon your transgressions; for My name *is* in Him. 22But if you indeed obey His voice and do all that I speak, then I will be an enemy to your enemies and an adversary to your adversaries. 23For My Angel will go before you and bring you in to the Amorites and the Hittites and the Perizzites and the Canaanites and the Hivites and the Jebusites; and I will cut them off. 24You shall not bow down to their gods, nor serve them, nor do according to their works; but you shall utterly overthrow them and completely break down their *sacred* pillars.

25"So you shall serve the LORD your God, and He will bless your bread and your water. And I will take sickness away from the midst of you. 26No one shall suffer miscarriage or be barren in your land; I will fulfill the number of your days.

27"I will send My fear before you, I will cause confusion among all the people to whom you come, and will make all your enemies turn *their* backs to you. 28And I will send hornets before you, which shall drive out the Hivite, the Canaanite, and the Hittite from before you. 29I will not drive them out from before you in one year, lest the land become desolate and the beasts of the field become too numerous for you. 30Little by little I will drive them out from before you, until you have increased, and you inherit the land. 31And I will set your bounds from the Red Sea to the sea, Philistia, and from the desert to the River. For I will deliver the inhabitants of the land into your hand, and you shall drive them out before you. 32You shall make no covenant with them, nor with their gods. 33They shall not dwell in your land, lest they make you sin against Me. For *if*

you serve their gods, it will surely be a snare to you."

Israel Affirms the Covenant

24 Now He said to Moses, "Come up to the LORD, you and Aaron, Nadab and Abihu, and seventy of the elders of Israel, and worship from afar. 2And Moses alone shall come near the LORD, but they shall not come near; nor shall the people go up with him."

3So Moses came and told the people all the words of the LORD and all the judgments. And all the people answered with one voice and said, "All the words which the LORD has said we will do." 4And Moses wrote all the words of the LORD. And he rose early in the morning, and built an altar at the foot of the mountain, and twelve pillars according to the twelve tribes of Israel. 5Then he sent young men of the children of Israel, who offered burnt offerings and sacrificed peace offerings of oxen to the LORD. 6And Moses took half the blood and put *it* in basins, and half the blood he sprinkled on the altar. 7Then he took the Book of the Covenant and read in the hearing of the people. And they said, "All that the LORD has said we will do, and be obedient." 8And Moses took the blood, sprinkled *it* on the people, and said, "This is the blood of the covenant which the LORD has made with you according to all these words."

On the Mountain with God

9Then Moses went up, also Aaron, Nadab, and Abihu, and seventy of the elders of Israel, 10and they saw the God of Israel. And *there was* under His feet as it were a paved work of sapphire stone, and it was like the very heavens in *its* clarity. 11But on the nobles of the children of Israel He did not lay His hand. So they saw God, and they ate and drank.

12Then the LORD said to Moses, "Come up to Me on the mountain and be there; and I will give you tablets of stone, and the law and commandments which I have written, that you may teach them."

13So Moses arose with his assistant Joshua, and Moses went up to the mountain of God. 14And he said to the elders, "Wait here for us until we come back to you. Indeed, Aaron and Hur *are* with you. If any man has a difficulty, let him go to them." 15Then Moses went up into the mountain, and a cloud covered the mountain.

16Now the glory of the LORD rested on Mount Sinai, and the cloud covered it six days. And on the seventh day He called to Moses out of the midst of the cloud. 17The sight of the glory of the LORD *was* like a consuming fire on the top of the mountain in the eyes of the children of Israel. 18So Moses went into the midst of the cloud and went up into the mountain. And Moses was on the mountain forty days and forty nights.

Offerings for the Sanctuary

25 Then the LORD spoke to Moses, saying: 2"Speak to the children of Israel, that they bring Me an offering. From everyone who gives it willingly with his heart you shall take My offering. 3And this *is* the offering which you shall take from them: gold, silver, and bronze; 4blue, purple, and scarlet *thread,* fine linen, and goats' *hair;* 5ram skins dyed red, badger skins, and acacia wood; 6oil for the light, and spices for the anointing oil and for the sweet incense; 7onyx stones, and stones to be set in the ephod and in the breastplate. 8And let them make Me a sanctuary, that I may dwell among them. 9According to all that I show you, *that is,* the pattern of the tabernacle and the pattern of all its furnishings, just so you shall make *it.*

The Ark of the Testimony

10"And they shall make an ark of acacia wood; two and a half cubits *shall be* its length, a cubit and a half its width, and a cubit and a half its height. 11And you shall overlay it with pure gold, inside and out you shall overlay it, and shall make on it a molding of gold all around. 12You shall cast four rings of gold for it, and put *them* in its four corners; two rings *shall be* on one side, and two rings on the other side. 13And you shall make poles of acacia wood, and overlay them with gold.

14You shall put the poles into the rings on the sides of the ark, that the ark may be carried by them. 15The poles shall be in the rings of the ark; they shall not be taken from it. 16And you shall put into the ark the Testimony which I will give you.

17"You shall make a mercy seat of pure gold; two and a half cubits *shall be* its length and a cubit and a half its width. 18And you shall make two cherubim of gold; of hammered work you shall make them at the two ends of the mercy seat. 19Make one cherub at one end, and the other cherub at the other end; you shall make the cherubim at the two ends of it *of one piece* with the mercy seat. 20And the cherubim shall stretch out *their* wings above, covering the mercy seat with their wings, and they shall face one another; the faces of the cherubim *shall be* toward the mercy seat. 21You shall put the mercy seat on top of the ark, and in the ark you shall put the Testimony that I will give you. 22And there I will meet with you, and I will speak with you from above the mercy seat, from between the two cherubim which *are* on the ark of the Testimony, about everything which I will give you in commandment to the children of Israel.

The Table for the Showbread

23"You shall also make a table of acacia wood; two cubits *shall be* its length, a cubit its width, and a cubit and a half its height. 24And you shall overlay it with pure gold, and make a molding of gold all around. 25You shall make for it a frame of a handbreadth all around, and you shall make a gold molding for the frame all around. 26And you shall make for it four rings of gold, and put the rings on the four corners that *are* at its four legs. 27The rings shall be close to the frame, as holders for the poles to bear the table. 28And you shall make the poles of acacia wood, and overlay them with gold, that the table may be carried with them. 29You shall make its dishes, its pans, its pitchers, and its bowls for pouring. You shall make them of pure gold. 30And you shall set the showbread on the table before Me always.

The Gold Lampstand

31"You shall also make a lampstand of pure gold; the lampstand shall be of hammered work. Its shaft, its branches, its bowls, its *ornamental* knobs, and flowers shall be *of one piece.* 32And six branches shall come out of its sides: three branches of the lampstand out of one side, and three branches of the lampstand out of the other side. 33Three bowls *shall be* made like almond *blossoms* on one branch, *with* an *ornamental* knob and a flower, and three bowls made like almond *blossoms* on the other branch, *with* an *ornamental* knob and a flower—and so for the six branches that come out of the lampstand. 34On the lampstand itself four bowls *shall be* made like almond *blossoms, each with* its *ornamental* knob and flower. 35And *there shall be* a knob under the *first* two branches of the same, a knob under the *second* two branches of the same, and a knob under the *third* two branches of the same, according to the six branches that extend from the lampstand. 36Their knobs and their branches *shall be of one piece;* all of it *shall be* one hammered piece of pure gold. 37You shall make seven lamps for it, and they shall arrange its lamps so that they give light in front of it. 38And its wick-trimmers and their trays *shall be* of pure gold. 39It shall be made of a talent of pure gold, with all these utensils. 40And see to it that you make *them* according to the pattern which was shown you on the mountain.

The Tabernacle

26 "Moreover you shall make the tabernacle *with* ten curtains *of* fine woven linen and blue, purple, and scarlet *thread;* with artistic designs of cherubim you shall weave them. 2The length of each curtain *shall be* twenty-eight cubits, and the width of each curtain four cubits. And every one of the curtains shall have the same measurements. 3Five curtains shall be coupled to one another, and *the other* five curtains *shall be* coupled to one another. 4And you shall make loops of blue *yarn* on the edge of the curtain on the selvedge of *one* set, and likewise you shall do on the outer edge of *the other* curtain of the second set.

5Fifty loops you shall make in the one curtain, and fifty loops you shall make on the edge of the curtain that *is* on the end of the second set, that the loops may be clasped to one another. 6And you shall make fifty clasps of gold, and couple the curtains together with the clasps, so that it may be one tabernacle.

7"You shall also make curtains of goats' *hair,* to be a tent over the tabernacle. You shall make eleven curtains. 8The length of each curtain *shall be* thirty cubits, and the width of each curtain four cubits; and the eleven curtains shall all have the same measurements. 9And you shall couple five curtains by themselves and six curtains by themselves, and you shall double over the sixth curtain at the forefront of the tent. 10You shall make fifty loops on the edge of the curtain that is outermost in *one* set, and fifty loops on the edge of the curtain of the second set. 11And you shall make fifty bronze clasps, put the clasps into the loops, and couple the tent together, that it may be one. 12The remnant that remains of the curtains of the tent, the half curtain that remains, shall hang over the back of the tabernacle. 13And a cubit on one side and a cubit on the other side, of what remains of the length of the curtains of the tent, shall hang over the sides of the tabernacle, on this side and on that side, to cover it.

14"You shall also make a covering of ram skins dyed red for the tent, and a covering of badger skins above that.

15"And for the tabernacle you shall make the boards of acacia wood, standing upright. 16Ten cubits *shall be* the length of a board, and a cubit and a half *shall be* the width of each board. 17Two tenons *shall be* in each board for binding one to another. Thus you shall make for all the boards of the tabernacle. 18And you shall make the boards for the tabernacle, twenty boards for the south side. 19You shall make forty sockets of silver under the twenty boards: two sockets under each of the boards for its two tenons. 20And for the second side of the tabernacle, the north side, *there shall be* twenty boards 21and their forty sockets of silver: two sockets under each of the boards. 22For the far side of the tabernacle, westward, you shall make six boards. 23And you shall also make two boards for the two back corners of the tabernacle. 24They shall be coupled together at the bottom and they shall be coupled together at the top by one ring. Thus it shall be for both of them. They shall be for the two corners. 25So there shall be eight boards with their sockets of silver—sixteen sockets—two sockets under each of the boards.

26"And you shall make bars of acacia wood: five for the boards on one side of the tabernacle, 27five bars for the boards on the other side of the tabernacle, and five bars for the boards of the side of the tabernacle, for the far side westward. 28The middle bar shall pass through the midst of the boards from end to end. 29You shall overlay the boards with gold, make their rings of gold as holders for the bars, and overlay the bars with gold. 30And you shall raise up the tabernacle according to its pattern which you were shown on the mountain.

31"You shall make a veil woven of blue, purple, and scarlet thread, and fine woven linen. It shall be woven with an artistic design of cherubim. 32You shall hang it upon the four pillars of acacia wood overlaid with gold. Their hooks shall be gold, upon four sockets of silver. 33And you shall hang the veil from the clasps. Then you shall bring the ark of the Testimony in there, behind the veil. The veil shall be a divider for you between the holy place and the Most Holy. 34You shall put the mercy seat upon the ark of the Testimony in the Most Holy. 35You shall set the table outside the veil, and the lampstand across from the table on the side of the tabernacle toward the south; and you shall put the table on the north side.

36"You shall make a screen for the door of the tabernacle, woven of blue, purple, and scarlet thread, and fine woven linen, made by a weaver. 37And you shall make for the screen five pillars of acacia wood, and overlay them with gold; their hooks shall be gold, and you shall cast five sockets of bronze for them.

The Altar of Burnt Offering

27 "You shall make an altar of acacia wood, five cubits long and five cubits wide—the altar shall be square—and its height shall be three cubits. 2You shall make its horns on its four corners; its horns shall be of one piece with it. And you shall overlay it with bronze. 3Also you shall make its pans to receive its ashes, and its shovels and its basins and its forks and its firepans; you shall make all its utensils of bronze. 4You shall make a grate for it, a network of bronze; and on the network you shall make four bronze rings at its four corners. 5You shall put it under the rim of the altar beneath, that the network may be midway up the altar. 6And you shall make poles for the altar, poles of acacia wood, and overlay them with bronze. 7The poles shall be put in the rings, and the poles shall be on the two sides of the altar to bear it. 8You shall make it hollow with boards; as it was shown you on the mountain, so shall they make it.

The Court of the Tabernacle

9"You shall also make the court of the tabernacle. For the south side there shall be hangings for the court made of fine woven linen, one hundred cubits long for one side. 10And its twenty pillars and their twenty sockets shall be bronze. The hooks of the pillars and their bands shall be silver. 11Likewise along the length of the north side there shall be hangings one hundred cubits long, with its twenty pillars and their twenty sockets of bronze, and the hooks of the pillars and their bands of silver.

12"And along the width of the court on the west side shall be hangings of fifty cubits, with their ten pillars and their ten sockets. 13The width of the court on the east side shall be fifty cubits. 14The hangings on one side of the gate shall be fifteen cubits, with their three pillars and their three sockets. 15And on the other side shall be hangings of fifteen cubits, with their three pillars and their three sockets.

16"For the gate of the court there shall be a screen twenty cubits long, woven of blue, purple, and scarlet thread, and fine woven linen, made by a weaver. It *shall have* four pillars and four sockets. 17All the pillars around the court shall have bands of silver; their hooks *shall be* of silver and their sockets of bronze. 18The length of the court *shall be* one hundred cubits, the width fifty throughout, and the height five cubits, *made of* fine woven linen, and its sockets of bronze. 19All the utensils of the tabernacle for all its service, all its pegs, and all the pegs of the court, *shall be* of bronze.

The Care of the Lampstand

20"And you shall command the children of Israel that they bring you pure oil of pressed olives for the light, to cause the lamp to burn continually. 21In the tabernacle of meeting, outside the veil which *is* before the Testimony, Aaron and his sons shall tend it from evening until morning before the LORD. *It shall be* a statute forever to their generations on behalf of the children of Israel.

Garments for the Priesthood

28 "Now take Aaron your brother, and his sons with him, from among the children of Israel, that he may minister to Me as priest, Aaron *and* Aaron's sons: Nadab, Abihu, Eleazar, and Ithamar. 2And you shall make holy garments for Aaron your brother, for glory and for beauty. 3So you shall speak to all *who are* gifted artisans, whom I have filled with the spirit of wisdom, that they may make Aaron's garments, to consecrate him, that he may minister to Me as priest. 4And these *are* the garments which they shall make: a breastplate, an ephod,*k* a robe, a skillfully woven tunic, a turban, and a sash. So they shall make holy garments for Aaron your brother and his sons, that he may minister to Me as priest.

The Ephod

5"They shall take the gold, blue, purple, and scarlet *thread,* and the fine linen, 6and they shall make the ephod of gold, blue, purple, *and* scarlet *thread,* and fine woven linen, artistically worked. 7It shall have two shoulder straps joined at its two edges, and *so*

k That is, an ornamented vest

it shall be joined together. 8And the intricately woven band of the ephod, which *is* on it, shall be of the same workmanship, *made of* gold, blue, purple, and scarlet *thread,* and fine woven linen.

9"Then you shall take two onyx stones and engrave on them the names of the sons of Israel: 10six of their names on one stone and six names on the other stone, in order of their birth. 11With the work of an engraver in stone, *like* the engravings of a signet, you shall engrave the two stones with the names of the sons of Israel. You shall set them in settings of gold. 12And you shall put the two stones on the shoulders of the ephod *as* memorial stones for the sons of Israel. So Aaron shall bear their names before the LORD on his two shoulders as a memorial. 13You shall also make settings of gold, 14and you shall make two chains of pure gold like braided cords, and fasten the braided chains to the settings.

The Breastplate

15"You shall make the breastplate of judgment. Artistically woven according to the workmanship of the ephod you shall make it: of gold, blue, purple, and scarlet *thread,* and fine woven linen, you shall make it. 16It shall be doubled into a square: a span *shall be* its length, and a span *shall be* its width. 17And you shall put settings of stones in it, four rows of stones: *The first* row *shall be* a sardius, a topaz, and an emerald; *this shall be* the first row; 18the second row *shall be* a turquoise, a sapphire, and a diamond; 19the third row, a jacinth, an agate, and an amethyst; 20and the fourth row, a beryl, an onyx, and a jasper. They shall be set in gold settings. 21And the stones shall have the names of the sons of Israel, twelve according to their names, *like* the engravings of a signet, each one with its own name; they shall be according to the twelve tribes.

22"You shall make chains for the breastplate at the end, like braided cords of pure gold. 23And you shall make two rings of gold for the breastplate, and put the two rings on the two ends of the breastplate. 24Then you shall put the two braided *chains* of gold in the two rings which are on the ends of the breastplate; 25and the *other* two ends of the two braided *chains* you shall fasten to the two settings, and put them on the shoulder straps of the ephod in the front.

26"You shall make two rings of gold, and put them on the two ends of the breastplate, on the edge of it, which is on the inner side of the ephod. 27And two *other* rings of gold you shall make, and put them on the two shoulder straps, underneath the ephod toward its front, right at the seam above the intricately woven band of the ephod. 28They shall bind the breastplate by means of its rings to the rings of the ephod, using a blue cord, so that it is above the intricately woven band of the ephod, and so that the breastplate does not come loose from the ephod.

29"So Aaron shall bear the names of the sons of Israel on the breastplate of judgment over his heart, when he goes into the holy *place*, as a memorial before the LORD continually. 30And you shall put in the breastplate of judgment the Urim and the Thummim,[l] and they shall be over Aaron's heart when he goes in before the LORD. So Aaron shall bear the judgment of the children of Israel over his heart before the LORD continually.

Other Priestly Garments

31"You shall make the robe of the ephod all of blue. 32There shall be an opening for his head in the middle of it; it shall have a woven binding all around its opening, like the opening in a coat of mail, so that it does not tear. 33And upon its hem you shall make pomegranates of blue, purple, and scarlet, all around its hem, and bells of gold between them all around: 34a golden bell and a pomegranate, a golden bell and a pomegranate, upon the hem of the robe all around. 35And it shall be upon Aaron when he ministers, and its sound will be heard when he goes into the holy *place* before the LORD and when he comes out, that he may not die.

36"You shall also make a plate of pure gold and engrave on it, *like* the engraving of a signet:

HOLINESS TO THE LORD.

37And you shall put it on a blue cord, that it may be on the turban; it shall be on the front of the turban. 38So it shall be on Aaron's forehead, that Aaron may bear the iniquity of the holy things which the children of Israel hallow in all their holy gifts; and it shall always be on his forehead, that they may be accepted before the LORD. 39"You shall skillfully weave the tunic of fine linen *thread,* you shall make the turban of fine linen, and you shall make the sash of woven work.

40"For Aaron's sons you shall make tunics, and you shall make sashes for them. And you shall make hats for them, for glory and beauty. 41So you shall put them on Aaron your brother and on his sons with him. You shall anoint them, consecrate them, and sanctify them, that they may minister to Me as priests. 42And you shall make for them linen trousers to cover their nakedness; they shall reach from the waist to the thighs. 43They shall be on Aaron and on his sons when they come into the tabernacle of meeting, or when they come near the altar to minister in the holy *place*, that they do not incur iniquity and die. *It shall be* a statute forever to him and his descendants after him.

Aaron and His Sons Consecrated

29 "And this is what you shall do to them to hallow them for ministering to Me as priests: Take one young bull and two rams without blemish, 2and unleavened bread, unleavened cakes mixed with oil, and unleavened wafers anointed with oil (you shall make them of wheat flour). 3You shall put them in one basket and bring them in the basket, with the bull and the two rams.

4"And Aaron and his sons you shall bring to the door of the tabernacle of meeting, and you shall wash them with water. 5Then you shall take the garments, put the tunic on Aaron, and the

l Literally *the Lights and the Perfections*

robe of the ephod, the ephod, and the breastplate, and gird him with the intricately woven band of the ephod. 6You shall put the turban on his head, and put the holy crown on the turban. 7And you shall take the anointing oil, pour *it* on his head, and anoint him. 8Then you shall bring his sons and put tunics on them. 9And you shall gird them with sashes, Aaron and his sons, and put the hats on them. The priesthood shall be theirs for a perpetual statute. So you shall consecrate Aaron and his sons.

10"You shall also have the bull brought before the tabernacle of meeting, and Aaron and his sons shall put their hands on the head of the bull. 11Then you shall kill the bull before the LORD, *by* the door of the tabernacle of meeting. 12You shall take *some* of the blood of the bull and put *it* on the horns of the altar with your finger, and pour all the blood beside the base of the altar. 13And you shall take all the fat that covers the entrails, the fatty lobe *attached* to the liver, and the two kidneys and the fat that *is* on them, and burn *them* on the altar. 14But the flesh of the bull, with its skin and its offal, you shall burn with fire outside the camp. It *is* a sin offering.

15"You shall also take one ram, and Aaron and his sons shall put their hands on the head of the ram; 16and you shall kill the ram, and you shall take its blood and sprinkle *it* all around on the altar. 17Then you shall cut the ram in pieces, wash its entrails and its legs, and put *them* with its pieces and with its head. 18And you shall burn the whole ram on the altar. It *is* a burnt offering to the LORD; it *is* a sweet aroma, an offering made by fire to the LORD.

19"You shall also take the other ram, and Aaron and his sons shall put their hands on the head of the ram. 20Then you shall kill the ram, and take some of its blood and put *it* on the tip of the right ear of Aaron and on the tip of the right ear of his sons, on the thumb of their right hand and on the big toe of their right foot, and sprinkle the blood all around on the altar. 21And you shall take some of the blood that is on the altar, and some of the anointing oil, and sprinkle *it* on Aaron and on his gar-

ments, on his sons and on the garments of his sons with him; and he and his garments shall be hallowed, and his sons and his sons' garments with him.

22"Also you shall take the fat of the ram, the fat tail, the fat that covers the entrails, the fatty lobe *attached to* the liver, the two kidneys and the fat on them, the right thigh (for it *is* a ram of consecration), 23one loaf of bread, one cake *made with* oil, and one wafer from the basket of the unleavened bread that *is* before the LORD; 24and you shall put all these in the hands of Aaron and in the hands of his sons, and you shall wave them *as* a wave offering before the LORD. 25You shall receive them back from their hands and burn *them* on the altar as a burnt offering, as a sweet aroma before the LORD. It *is* an offering made by fire to the LORD.

26"Then you shall take the breast of the ram of Aaron's consecration and wave it *as* a wave offering before the LORD; and it shall be your portion. 27And from the ram of the consecration you shall consecrate the breast of the wave offering which is waved, and the thigh of the heave offering which is raised, of *that* which *is* for Aaron and of *that* which is for his sons. 28It shall be from the children of Israel *for* Aaron and his sons by a statute forever. For it is a heave offering; it shall be a heave offering from the children of Israel from the sacrifices of their peace offerings, *that is,* their heave offering to the LORD.

29"And the holy garments of Aaron shall be his sons' after him, to be anointed in them and to be consecrated in them. 30That son who becomes priest in his place shall put them on for seven days, when he enters the tabernacle of meeting to minister in the holy *place.*

31"And you shall take the ram of the consecration and boil its flesh in the holy place. 32Then Aaron and his sons shall eat the flesh of the ram, and the bread that *is* in the basket, *by* the door of the tabernacle of meeting. 33They shall eat those things with which the atonement was made, to consecrate *and* to sanctify them; but an outsider shall not eat *them,* because they *are* holy. 34And if any of the flesh of the consecration offerings, or of the bread, remains until the morning, then you shall burn the remainder with fire. It shall not be eaten, because it *is* holy.

35"Thus you shall do to Aaron and his sons, according to all that I have commanded you. Seven days you shall consecrate them. 36And you shall offer a bull every day *as* a sin offering for atonement. You shall cleanse the altar when you make atonement for it, and you shall anoint it to sanctify it. 37Seven days you shall make atonement for the altar and sanctify it. And the altar shall be most holy. Whatever touches the altar must be holy.

The Daily Offerings

38"Now this *is* what you shall offer on the altar: two lambs of the first year, day by day continually. 39One lamb you shall offer in the morning, and the other lamb you shall offer at twilight. 40With the one lamb shall be one-tenth *of an ephah* of flour mixed with one-fourth of a hin of pressed oil, and one-fourth of a hin of wine *as* a drink offering. 41And the other lamb you shall offer at twilight; and you shall offer with it the grain offering and the drink offering, as in the morning, for a sweet aroma, an offering made by fire to the LORD. 42*This shall be* a continual burnt offering throughout your generations *at* the door of the tabernacle of meeting before the LORD, where I will meet you to speak with you. 43And there I will meet with the children of Israel, and *the tabernacle* shall be sanctified by My glory. 44So I will consecrate the tabernacle of meeting and the altar. I will also consecrate both Aaron and his sons to minister to Me as priests. 45I will dwell among the children of Israel and will be their God. 46And they shall know that I *am* the LORD their God, who brought them up out of the land of Egypt, that I may dwell among them. I *am* the LORD their God.

The Altar of Incense

30 "You shall make an altar to burn incense on; you shall make it of acacia wood. 2A cubit *shall be* its length and a cubit its width—it shall be square—and two cubits *shall be* its height. Its horns *shall be* of one piece with it. 3And you shall overlay its top, its sides all around, and its horns with

pure gold; and you shall make for it a molding of gold all around. 4Two gold rings you shall make for it, under the molding on both its sides. You shall place *them* on its two sides, and they will be holders for the poles with which to bear it. 5You shall make the poles of acacia wood, and overlay them with gold. 6And you shall put it before the veil that *is* before the ark of the Testimony, before the mercy seat that *is* over the Testimony, where I will meet with you.

7"Aaron shall burn on it sweet incense every morning; when he tends the lamps, he shall burn incense on it. 8And when Aaron lights the lamps at twilight, he shall burn incense on it, a perpetual incense before the LORD throughout your generations. 9You shall not offer strange incense on it, or a burnt offering, or a grain offering; nor shall you pour a drink offering on it. 10And Aaron shall make atonement upon its horns once a year with the blood of the sin offering of atonement; once a year he shall make atonement upon it throughout your generations. It *is* most holy to the LORD."

The Ransom Money

11Then the LORD spoke to Moses, saying: 12"When you take the census of the children of Israel for their number, then every man shall give a ransom for himself to the LORD, when you number them, that there may be no plague among them when *you* number them. 13This is what everyone among those who are numbered shall give: half a shekel according to the shekel of the sanctuary (a shekel *is* twenty gerahs). The half-shekel *shall be* an offering to the LORD. 14Everyone included among those who are numbered, from twenty years old and above, shall give an offering to the LORD. 15The rich shall not give more and the poor shall not give less than half a shekel, when *you* give an offering to the LORD, to make atonement for yourselves. 16And you shall take the atonement money of the children of Israel, and shall appoint it for the service of the tabernacle of meeting, that it may be a memorial for the children of Israel before the LORD, to make atonement for yourselves."

The Bronze Laver

17Then the LORD spoke to Moses, saying: 18"You shall also make a laver of bronze, with its base also of bronze, for washing. You shall put it between the tabernacle of meeting and the altar. And you shall put water in it, 19for Aaron and his sons shall wash their hands and their feet in water from it. 20When they go into the tabernacle of meeting, or when they come near the altar to minister, to burn an offering made by fire to the LORD, they shall wash with water, lest they die. 21So they shall wash their hands and their feet, lest they die. And it shall be a statute forever to them—to him and his descendants throughout their generations."

The Holy Anointing Oil

22Moreover the LORD spoke to Moses, saying: 23"Also take for yourself quality spices—five hundred *shekels* of liquid myrrh, half as much sweet-smelling cinnamon (two hundred and fifty *shekels*), two hundred and fifty *shekels* of sweet-smelling cane, 24five hundred *shekels* of cassia, according to the shekel of the sanctuary, and a hin of olive oil. 25And you shall make from these a holy anointing oil, an ointment compounded according to the art of the perfumer. It shall be a holy anointing oil. 26With it you shall anoint the tabernacle of meeting and the ark of the Testimony; 27the table and all its utensils, the lampstand and its utensils, and the altar of incense; 28the altar of burnt offering with all its utensils, and the laver and its base. 29You shall consecrate them, that they may be most holy; whatever touches them must be holy. 30And you shall anoint Aaron and his sons, and consecrate them, that *they* may minister to Me as priests.

31"And you shall speak to the children of Israel, saying: 'This shall be a holy anointing oil to Me throughout your generations. 32It shall not be poured on man's flesh; nor shall you make *any other* like it, according to its composition. It *is* holy, *and* it shall be holy to you. 33Whoever compounds *any* like it, or whoever puts *any* of it on an outsider, shall be cut off from his people.' "

The Incense

34And the LORD said to Moses: "Take sweet spices, stacte and onycha and galbanum, and pure frankincense with *these* sweet spices; there shall be equal amounts of each. 35You shall make of these an incense, a compound according to the art of the perfumer, salted, pure, *and* holy. 36And you shall beat *some* of it very fine, and put some of it before the Testimony in the tabernacle of meeting where I will meet with you. It shall be most holy to you. 37But *as for* the incense which you shall make, you shall not make any for yourselves, according to its composition. It shall be to you holy for the LORD. 38Whoever makes *any* like it, to smell it, he shall be cut off from his people."

Artisans for Building the Tabernacle

31 Then the LORD spoke to Moses, saying: 2"See, I have called by name Bezalel the son of Uri, the son of Hur, of the tribe of Judah. 3And I have filled him with the Spirit of God, in wisdom, in understanding, in knowledge, and in all *manner of* workmanship, 4to design artistic works, to work in gold, in silver, in bronze, 5in cutting jewels for setting, in carving wood, and to work in all *manner of* workmanship.

6"And I, indeed I, have appointed with him Aholiab the son of Ahisamach, of the tribe of Dan; and I have put wisdom in the hearts of all the gifted artisans, that they may make all that I have commanded you: 7the tabernacle of meeting, the ark of the Testimony and the mercy seat that *is* on it, and all the furniture of the tabernacle— 8the table and its utensils, the pure *gold* lampstand with all its utensils, the altar of incense, 9the altar of burnt offering with all its utensils, and the laver and its base— 10the garments of ministry, the holy garments for Aaron the priest and the garments of his sons, to minister as priests, 11and the anointing oil and sweet incense for the holy *place*. According to all that I have commanded you they shall do."

The Sabbath Law

12And the LORD spoke to Moses, saying, 13"Speak also to the children of Israel, saying: 'Surely My Sabbaths you shall keep, for it *is* a sign between Me and you throughout your generations, that *you* may know that I *am* the LORD who sanctifies you. 14You shall keep the Sabbath, therefore, for *it is* holy to you. Everyone who profanes it shall surely be put to death; for whoever does *any* work on it, that person shall be cut off from among his people. 15Work shall be done for six days, but the seventh *is* the Sabbath of rest, holy to the LORD. Whoever does *any* work on the Sabbath day, he shall surely be put to death. 16Therefore the children of Israel shall keep the Sabbath, to observe the Sabbath throughout their generations *as* a perpetual covenant. 17It *is* a sign between Me and the children of Israel forever; for *in* six days the LORD made the heavens and the earth, and on the seventh day He rested and was refreshed.'"

18And when He had made an end of speaking with him on Mount Sinai, He gave Moses two tablets of the Testimony, tablets of stone, written with the finger of God.

The Gold Calf

32 Now when the people saw that Moses delayed coming down from the mountain, the people gathered together to Aaron, and said to him, "Come, make us gods that shall go before us; for *as for* this Moses, the man who brought us up out of the land of Egypt, we do not know what has become of him."

2And Aaron said to them, "Break off the golden earrings which *are* in the ears of your wives, your sons, and your daughters, and bring *them* to me." 3So all the people broke off the golden earrings which *were* in their ears, and brought *them* to Aaron. 4And he received *the* gold from their hand, and he fashioned it with an engraving tool, and made a molded calf.

Then they said, "This *is* your god, O Israel, that brought you out of the land of Egypt!"

5So when Aaron saw *it*, he built an altar before it. And Aaron made a proclamation and said, "Tomorrow *is* a feast to the LORD." 6Then they rose early on the next day, offered burnt offerings, and brought peace offerings; and the people sat down to eat and drink, and rose up to play.

7And the LORD said to Moses, "Go, get down! For your people whom you brought out of the land of Egypt have corrupted *themselves*. 8They have turned aside quickly out of the way which I commanded them. They have made themselves a molded calf, and worshiped it and sacrificed to it, and said, 'This *is* your god, O Israel, that brought you out of the land of Egypt!' " 9And the LORD said to Moses, "I have seen this people, and indeed *is* a stiff-necked people! 10Now therefore, let Me alone, that My wrath may burn hot against them and I may consume them. And I will make of you a great nation."

11Then Moses pleaded with the LORD his God, and said: "LORD, why does Your wrath burn hot against Your people whom You have brought out of the land of Egypt with great power and with a mighty hand? 12Why should the Egyptians speak, and say, 'He brought them out to harm them, to kill them in the mountains, and to consume them from the face of the earth'? Turn from Your fierce wrath, and relent from this harm to Your people. 13Remember Abraham, Isaac, and Israel, Your servants, to whom You swore by Your own self, and said to them, 'I will multiply your descendants as the stars of heaven; and all this land that I have spoken of I give to your descendants, and they shall inherit *it* forever.' "*m* 14So the LORD relented from the harm which He said He would do to His people.

15And Moses turned and went down from the mountain, and the two tablets of the Testimony *were* in his hand. The tablets *were* written on both sides; on the one *side* and on the other they were written. 16Now the tablets *were* the work of God, and the writing *was* the writing of God engraved on the tablets.

17And when Joshua heard the noise of the people as they shouted, he said to Moses, "*There is* a noise of war in the camp."

---

m Compare Genesis 13.15 and 22.17

18But he said:

"*It is* not the noise of the shout of
victory,
Nor the noise of the cry of defeat,
But the sound of singing I hear."

19So it was, as soon as he came near the camp, that he saw the calf *and* the dancing. So Moses' anger became hot, and he cast the tablets out of his hands and broke them at the foot of the mountain. 20Then he took the calf which they had made, burned *it* in the fire, and ground *it* to powder; and he scattered *it* on the water and made the children of Israel drink *it*. 21And Moses said to Aaron, "What did this people do to you that you have brought *so* great a sin upon them?"

22So Aaron said, "Do not let the anger of my lord become hot. You know the people, that they *are set* on evil. 23For they said to me, 'Make us gods that shall go before us; *as for* this Moses, the man who brought us out of the land of Egypt, we do not know what has become of him.' 24And I said to them, 'Whoever has any gold, let them break *it* off.' So they gave *it* to me, and I cast it into the fire, and this calf came out."

25Now when Moses saw that the people *were* unrestrained (for Aaron had not restrained them, to *their* shame among their enemies), 26then Moses stood in the entrance of the camp, and said, "Whoever *is* on the LORD's side— *come* to me!" And all the sons of Levi gathered themselves together to him. 27And he said to them, "Thus says the LORD God of Israel: 'Let every man put his sword on his side, and go in and out from entrance to entrance throughout the camp, and let every man kill his brother, every man his companion, and every man his neighbor.'" 28So the sons of Levi did according to the word of Moses. And about three thousand men of the people fell that day. 29Then Moses said, "Consecrate yourselves today to the LORD, that He may bestow on you a blessing this day, for every man has opposed his son and his brother."

30Now it came to pass on the next day that Moses said to the people, "You have committed a great sin. So now I will go up to the LORD; perhaps I can make atonement for your sin." 31Then Moses returned to the LORD and said, "Oh, these people have committed a great sin, and have made for themselves a god of gold! 32Yet now, if You will forgive their sin—but if not, I pray, blot me out of Your book which You have written."

33And the LORD said to Moses, "Whoever has sinned against Me, I will blot him out of My book. 34Now therefore, go, lead the people to *the place* of which I have spoken to you. Behold, My Angel shall go before you. Nevertheless, in the day when I visit for punishment, I will visit punishment upon them for their sin."

35So the LORD plagued the people because of what they did with the calf which Aaron made.

The Command to Leave Sinai

33 Then the LORD said to Moses, "Depart *and* go up from here, you and the people whom you have brought out of the land of Egypt, to the land of which I swore to Abraham, Isaac, and Jacob, saying, 'To your descendants I will give it.' 2And I will send *My* Angel before you, and I will drive out the Canaanite and the Amorite and the Hittite and the Perizzite and the Hivite and the Jebusite. 3*Go up* to a land flowing with milk and honey; for I will not go up in your midst, lest I consume you on the way, for you *are* a stiff-necked people."

4And when the people heard this bad news, they mourned, and no one put on his ornaments. 5For the LORD had said to Moses, "Say to the children of Israel, 'You *are* a stiff-necked people. I could come up into your midst in one moment and consume you. Now therefore, take off your ornaments, that I may know what to do to you.'" 6So the children of Israel stripped themselves of their ornaments by Mount Horeb.

Moses Meets with the LORD

7Moses took his tent and pitched it outside the camp, far from the camp, and called it the tabernacle of meeting. And it came to pass *that* everyone who sought the LORD went out to the tabernacle of meeting which *was* outside the camp. 8So it was, whenever Moses went out to the tabernacle, *that* all the people rose, and each man stood *at* his tent door and watched Moses until he had gone into the tabernacle. 9And it came to pass, when Moses entered the tabernacle, that the pillar of cloud descended and stood *at* the door of the tabernacle, and *the* LORD talked with Moses. 10All the people saw the pillar of cloud standing *at* the tabernacle door, and all the people rose and worshiped, each man *in* his tent door. 11So the LORD spoke to Moses face to face, as a man speaks to his friend. And he would return to the camp, but his servant Joshua the son of Nun, a young man, did not depart from the tabernacle.

The Promise of God's Presence

12Then Moses said to the LORD, "See, You say to me, 'Bring up this people.' But You have not let me know whom You will send with me. Yet You have said, 'I know you by name, and you have also found grace in My sight.' 13Now therefore, I pray, if I have found grace in Your sight, show me now Your way, that I may know You and that I may find grace in Your sight. And consider that this nation *is* Your people." 14And He said, "My Presence will go *with you*, and I will give you rest." 15Then he said to Him, "If Your Presence does not go *with us*, do not bring us up from here. 16For how then will it be known that Your people and I have found grace in Your sight, except You go with us? So we shall be separate, Your people and I, from all the people who *are* upon the face of the earth." 17So the LORD said to Moses, "I will also do this thing that you have spoken; for you have found grace in My sight, and I know you by name." 18And he said, "Please, show me Your glory." 19Then He said, "I will make all My goodness pass before you, and I will proclaim the name of the LORD before you. I will be gracious to whom I will be gracious, and I will have compassion on whom I will have compassion." 20But He said, "You cannot see My face; for no man shall see Me, and live." 21And the LORD said, "Here is a place by Me, and you shall stand on the rock. 22So it shall be, while My glory passes by, that I will put you in the cleft of the rock, and will cover you with My hand while I pass by. 23Then I will take away My hand, and you shall see My back; but My face shall not be seen."

Moses Makes New Tablets

34 And the LORD said to Moses, "Cut two tablets of stone like the first *ones*, and I will write on *these* tablets the words that were on the first tablets which you broke. 2So be ready in the morning, and come up in the morning to Mount Sinai, and present yourself to Me there on the top of the mountain. 3And no man shall come up with you, and let no man be seen throughout all the mountain; let neither flocks nor herds feed before that mountain."

4So he cut two tablets of stone like the first *ones*. Then Moses rose early in the morning and went up Mount Sinai, as the LORD had commanded him; and he took in his hand the two tablets of stone.

5Now the LORD descended in the cloud and stood with him there, and proclaimed the name of the LORD. 6And the LORD passed before him and proclaimed, "The LORD, the LORD God, merciful and gracious, longsuffering, and abounding in goodness and truth, 7keeping mercy for thousands, forgiving iniquity and transgression and sin, by no means clearing *the guilty*, visiting the iniquity of the fathers upon the children and the children's children to the third and the fourth generation."

8So Moses made haste and bowed his head toward the earth, and worshiped. 9Then he said, "If now I have found grace in Your sight, O Lord, let my Lord, I pray, go among us, even though we *are* a stiff-necked people; and pardon our iniquity and our sin, and take us as Your inheritance."

The Covenant Renewed

10And He said: "Behold, I make a covenant. Before all your people I will do marvels such as have not been done in all the earth, nor in any nation; and all the people among whom you *are* shall see the work of the LORD. For it *is* an awesome thing that I will do with you. 11Observe what I command you this day. Behold, I am driving out from before you the Amorite and the Ca-

naanite and the Hittite and the Perizzite and the Hivite and the Jebusite.
12Take heed to yourself, lest you make
a covenant with the inhabitants of the
land where you are going, lest it be a
snare in your midst. 13But you shall destroy their altars, break their *sacred* pillars, and cut down their wooden images
14(for you shall worship no other god,
for the LORD, whose name *is* Jealous,
is a jealous God), 15lest you make a covenant with the inhabitants of the land,
and they play the harlot with their gods
and make sacrifice to their gods, and
one of them invites you and you eat of
his sacrifice, 16and you take of his
daughters for your sons, and his daughters play the harlot with their gods and
make your sons play the harlot with
their gods.

17"You shall make no molded gods
for yourselves.

18"The Feast of Unleavened Bread
you shall keep. Seven days you shall
eat unleavened bread, as I commanded
you, in the appointed time of the month
of Abib; for in the month of Abib you
came out from Egypt.

19"All that open the womb *are* Mine,
and every male firstborn among your
livestock, *whether* ox or sheep. 20But
the firstborn of a donkey you shall redeem with a lamb. And if you will not
redeem *him*, then you shall break his
neck. All the firstborn of your sons you
shall redeem.

"And none shall appear before Me
empty-handed.

21"Six days you shall work, but on
the seventh day you shall rest; in plowing time and in harvest you shall rest.

22"And you shall observe the Feast
of Weeks, of the firstfruits of wheat harvest, and the Feast of Ingathering at the
year's end.

23"Three times in the year all your
men shall appear before the Lord, the
LORD God of Israel. 24For I will cast out
the nations before you and enlarge your
borders; neither will any man covet
your land when you go up to appear
before the LORD your God three times
in the year.

25"You shall not offer the blood of My
sacrifice with leaven, nor shall the sacrifice of the Feast of the Passover be
left until morning.

26"The first of the firstfruits of your
land you shall bring to the house of the
LORD your God. You shall not boil a
young goat in its mother's milk."

27Then the LORD said to Moses,
"Write these words, for according to
the tenor of these words I have made
a covenant with you and with Israel."
28So he was there with the LORD forty
days and forty nights; he neither ate
bread nor drank water. And He wrote
on the tablets the words of the covenant, the Ten Commandments.

The Shining Face of Moses

29Now it was so, when Moses came
down from Mount Sinai (and the two
tablets of the Testimony *were* in Moses'
hand when he came down from the
mountain), that Moses did not know
that the skin of his face shone while he
talked with Him. 30So when Aaron and
all the children of Israel saw Moses, behold, the skin of his face shone, and
they were afraid to come near him.
31Then Moses called to them, and
Aaron and all the rulers of the congregation returned to him; and Moses
talked with them. 32Afterward all the
children of Israel came near, and he
gave them as commandments all that
the LORD had spoken with him on
Mount Sinai. 33And when Moses had
finished speaking with them, he put a
veil on his face. 34But whenever Moses
went in before the LORD to speak with
Him, he would take the veil off until he
came out; and he would come out and
speak to the children of Israel whatever
he had been commanded. 35And whenever the children of Israel saw the face
of Moses, that the skin of Moses' face
shone, then Moses would put the veil
on his face again, until he went in to
speak with Him.

Sabbath Regulations

35 Then Moses gathered all the congregation of the children of Israel
together, and said to them, "These *are*
the words which the LORD has commanded *you* to do: 2Work shall be done
for six days, but the seventh day shall
be a holy day for you, a Sabbath of rest
to the LORD. Whoever does any work
on it shall be put to death. 3You shall

kindle no fire throughout your dwellings on the Sabbath day."

Offerings for the Tabernacle

4And Moses spoke to all the congregation of the children of Israel, saying, "This is the thing which the LORD commanded, saying: 5'Take from among you an offering to the LORD. Whoever is of a willing heart, let him bring it as an offering to the LORD: gold, silver, and bronze; 6blue, purple, and scarlet thread, fine linen, and goats' hair; 7ram skins dyed red, badger skins, and acacia wood; 8oil for the light, and spices for the anointing oil and for the sweet incense; 9onyx stones, and stones to be set in the ephod and in the breastplate.

Articles of the Tabernacle

10'All who are gifted artisans among you shall come and make all that the LORD has commanded: 11the tabernacle, its tent, its covering, its clasps, its boards, its bars, its pillars, and its sockets; 12the ark and its poles, with the mercy seat, and the veil of the covering; 13the table and its poles, all its utensils, and the showbread; 14also the lampstand for the light, its utensils, its lamps, and the oil for the light; 15the incense altar, its poles, the anointing oil, the sweet incense, and the screen for the door at the entrance of the tabernacle; 16the altar of burnt offering with its bronze grating, its poles, all its utensils, and the laver and its base; 17the hangings of the court, its pillars, their sockets, and the screen for the gate of the court; 18the pegs of the tabernacle, the pegs of the court, and their cords; 19the garments of ministry, for ministering in the holy place—the holy garments for Aaron the priest and the garments of his sons, to minister as priests.' "

The Tabernacle Offerings Presented

20And all the congregation of the children of Israel departed from the presence of Moses. 21Then everyone came whose heart was stirred, and everyone whose spirit was willing, and they brought the LORD's offering for the work of the tabernacle of meeting, for all its service, and for the holy garments. 22They came, both men and women, as many as had a willing heart, and brought earrings and nose rings, rings and necklaces, all jewelry of gold, that is, every man who made an offering of gold to the LORD. 23And every man, with whom was found blue, purple, and scarlet thread, fine linen, goats' hair, red skins of rams, and badger skins, brought them. 24Everyone who offered an offering of silver or bronze brought the LORD's offering. And everyone with whom was found acacia wood for any work of the service, brought it. 25All the women who were gifted artisans spun yarn with their hands, and brought what they had spun, of blue, purple, and scarlet, and fine linen. 26And all the women whose hearts stirred with wisdom spun yarn of goats' hair. 27The rulers brought onyx stones, and the stones to be set in the ephod and in the breastplate, 28and spices and oil for the light, for the anointing oil, and for the sweet incense. 29The children of Israel brought a freewill offering to the LORD, all the men and women whose hearts were willing to bring material for all kinds of work which the LORD, by the hand of Moses, had commanded to be done.

The Artisans Called by God

30And Moses said to the children of Israel, "See, the LORD has called by name Bezalel the son of Uri, the son of Hur, of the tribe of Judah; 31and He has filled him with the Spirit of God, in wisdom and understanding, in knowledge and all manner of workmanship, 32to design artistic works, to work in gold and silver and bronze, 33in cutting jewels for setting, in carving wood, and to work in all manner of artistic workmanship.

34"And He has put in his heart the ability to teach, in him and Aholiab the son of Ahisamach, of the tribe of Dan. 35He has filled them with skill to do all manner of work of the engraver and the designer and the tapestry maker, in blue, purple, and scarlet thread, and fine linen, and of the weaver—those who do every work and those who design artistic works.

36 "And Bezalel and Aholiab, and every gifted artisan in whom the LORD has put wisdom and understanding, to know how to do all manner of work for the service of the sanctuary, shall do according to all that the LORD has commanded."

The People Give More than Enough

2Then Moses called Bezalel and Aholiab, and every gifted artisan in whose heart the LORD had put wisdom, everyone whose heart was stirred, to come and do the work. 3And they received from Moses all the offering which the children of Israel had brought for the work of the service of making the sanctuary. So they continued bringing to him freewill offerings every morning. 4Then all the craftsmen who were doing all the work of the sanctuary came, each from the work he was doing, 5and they spoke to Moses, saying, "The people bring much more than enough for the service of the work which the LORD commanded us to do."

6So Moses gave a commandment, and they caused it to be proclaimed throughout the camp, saying, "Let neither man nor woman do any more work for the offering of the sanctuary." And the people were restrained from bringing, 7for the material they had was sufficient for all the work to be done—indeed too much.

Building the Tabernacle

8Then all the gifted artisans among them who worked on the tabernacle made ten curtains woven of fine linen, and of blue, purple, and scarlet thread; with artistic designs of cherubim they made them. 9The length of each curtain was twenty-eight cubits, and the width of each curtain four cubits; the curtains were all the same size. 10And he coupled five curtains to one another, and the other five curtains he coupled to one another. 11He made loops of blue yarn on the edge of the curtain on the selvedge of one set; likewise he did on the outer edge of the other curtain of the second set. 12Fifty loops he made on one curtain, and fifty loops he made on the edge of the curtain on the end of the second set; the loops held one curtain to another. 13And he made fifty clasps of gold, and coupled the curtains to one another with the clasps, that it might be one tabernacle.

14He made curtains of goats' hair for the tent over the tabernacle; he made eleven curtains. 15The length of each curtain was thirty cubits, and the width of each curtain four cubits; the eleven curtains were the same size. 16He coupled five curtains by themselves and six curtains by themselves. 17And he made fifty loops on the edge of the curtain that is outermost in one set, and fifty loops he made on the edge of the curtain of the second set. 18He also made fifty bronze clasps to couple the tent together, that it might be one. 19Then he made a covering for the tent of ram skins dyed red, and a covering of badger skins above that.

20For the tabernacle he made boards of acacia wood, standing upright. 21The length of each board was ten cubits, and the width of each board a cubit and a half. 22Each board had two tenons for binding one to another. Thus he made for all the boards of the tabernacle. 23And he made boards for the tabernacle, twenty boards for the south side. 24Forty sockets of silver he made to go under the twenty boards: two sockets under each of the boards for its two tenons. 25And for the other side of the tabernacle, the north side, he made twenty boards 26and their forty sockets of silver: two sockets under each of the boards. 27For the west side of the tabernacle he made six boards. 28He also made two boards for the two back corners of the tabernacle. 29And they were coupled at the bottom and coupled together at the top by one ring. Thus he made both of them for the two corners. 30So there were eight boards and their sockets—sixteen sockets of silver—two sockets under each of the boards.

31And he made bars of acacia wood: five for the boards on one side of the tabernacle, 32five bars for the boards on the other side of the tabernacle, and five bars for the boards of the tabernacle on the far side westward. 33And he made the middle bar to pass through the boards from one end to the other. 34He overlaid the boards with gold, made their rings of gold to be holders for the bars, and overlaid the bars with gold.

35And he made a veil of blue, purple, and scarlet *thread*, and fine woven linen; it was worked *with* an artistic design of cherubim. 36He made for it four pillars of acacia *wood*, and overlaid them with gold, with their hooks of gold; and he cast four sockets of silver for them.

37He also made a screen for the tabernacle door, of blue, purple, and scarlet *thread*, and fine woven linen, made by a weaver, 38and its five pillars with their hooks. And he overlaid their capitals and their rings with gold, but their five sockets *were* bronze.

Making the Ark of the Testimony

37 Then Bezalel made the ark of acacia wood; two and a half cubits *was* its length, a cubit and a half its width, and a cubit and a half its height. 2He overlaid it with pure gold inside and outside, and made a molding of gold all around it. 3And he cast for it four rings of gold *to be set* in its four corners: two rings on one side, and two rings on the other side of it. 4He made poles of acacia wood, and overlaid them with gold. 5And he put the poles into the rings at the sides of the ark, to bear the ark. 6He also made the mercy seat of pure gold; two and a half cubits *was* its length and a cubit and a half its width. 7He made two cherubim of beaten gold; he made them of one piece at the two ends of the mercy seat: 8one cherub at one end on this side, and the other cherub at the *other* end on that side. He made the cherubim at the two ends *of one piece* with the mercy seat. 9The cherubim spread out *their* wings above, *and* covered the mercy seat with their wings. They faced one another; the faces of the cherubim were toward the mercy seat.

Making the Table for the Showbread

10He made the table of acacia wood; two cubits *was* its length, a cubit its width, and a cubit and a half its height. 11And he overlaid it with pure gold, and made a molding of gold all around it. 12Also he made a frame of a handbreadth all around it, and made a molding of gold for the frame all around it.

13And he cast for it four rings of gold, and put the rings on the four corners that *were* at its four legs. 14The rings were close to the frame, as holders for the poles to bear the table. 15And he made the poles of acacia wood to bear the table, and overlaid them with gold. 16He made of pure gold the utensils which were on the table: its dishes, its cups, its bowls, and its pitchers for pouring.

Making the Gold Lampstand

17He also made the lampstand of pure gold; of hammered work he made the lampstand. Its shaft, its branches, its bowls, its *ornamental* knobs, and its flowers were of the same piece. 18And six branches came out of its sides: three branches of the lampstand out of one side, and three branches of the lampstand out of the other side. 19There were three bowls made like almond *blossoms* on one branch, with an *ornamental* knob and a flower, and three bowls made like almond *blossoms* on the other branch, with an *ornamental* knob and a flower—and so for the six branches coming out of the lampstand. 20And on the lampstand itself *were* four bowls made like almond *blossoms*, *each with* its *ornamental* knob and flower. 21*There was* a knob under the *first* two branches of the same, a knob under the *second* two branches of the same, and a knob under the *third* two branches of the same, according to the six branches extending from it. 22Their knobs and their branches were of one piece; all of it *was* one hammered piece of pure gold. 23And he made its seven lamps, its wick-trimmers, and its trays of pure gold. 24Of a talent of pure gold he made it, with all its utensils.

Making the Altar of Incense

25He made the incense altar of acacia wood. Its length *was* a cubit and its width a cubit—*it was* square—and two cubits *was* its height. Its horns were *of one piece* with it. 26And he overlaid it with pure gold: its top, its sides all around, and its horns. He also made for it a molding of gold all around it. 27He made two rings of gold for it under its molding, by its two corners on both sides, as holders for the poles with which to bear it. 28And he made the poles of acacia wood, and overlaid them with gold.

Making the Anointing Oil and the Incense

29He also made the holy anointing oil and the pure incense of sweet spices, according to the work of the perfumer.

Making the Altar of Burnt Offering

38 He made the altar of burnt offering of acacia wood; five cubits *was* its length and five cubits its width—*it was* square—and its height *was* three cubits. 2He made its horns on its four corners; the horns were *of one piece* with it. And he overlaid it with bronze. 3He made all the utensils for the altar: the pans, the shovels, the basins, the forks, and the firepans; all its utensils he made of bronze. 4And he made a grate of bronze network for the altar, under its rim, midway from the bottom. 5He cast four rings for the four corners of the bronze grating, *as* holders for the poles. 6And he made the poles of acacia wood, and overlaid them with bronze. 7Then he put the poles into the rings on the sides of the altar, with which to bear it. He made the altar hollow with boards.

Making the Bronze Laver

8He made the laver of bronze and its base of bronze, from the bronze mirrors of the serving women who assembled at the door of the tabernacle of meeting.

Making the Court of the Tabernacle

9Then he made the court on the south side; the hangings of the court *were of* fine woven linen, one hundred cubits long. 10There *were* twenty pillars for them, with twenty bronze sockets. The hooks of the pillars and their bands *were* silver. 11On the north side *the hangings were* one hundred cubits *long*, with twenty pillars and their twenty bronze sockets. The hooks of the pillars and their bands *were* silver. 12And on the west side *there were* hangings of fifty cubits, with ten pillars and their ten sockets. The hooks of the pillars

and their bands *were* silver. 13For the east side *the hangings were* fifty cubits. 14The hangings of one side *of the gate were* fifteen cubits *long, with* their three pillars and their three sockets, 15and the same for the other side of the court gate; on this side and that *were* hangings of fifteen cubits, *with* their three pillars and their three sockets. 16All the hangings of the court all around *were of* fine woven linen. 17The sockets for the pillars *were* bronze, the hooks of the pillars and their bands *were* silver, and the overlay of their capitals *was* silver; and all the pillars of the court had bands of silver. 18The screen for the gate of the court *was* woven of blue, purple, and scarlet *thread*, and of fine woven linen. The length *was* twenty cubits, and the height along its width *was* five cubits, corresponding to the hangings of the court. 19And *there were* four pillars *with* their four sockets of bronze; their hooks *were* silver, and the overlay of their capitals and their bands *was* silver. 20All the pegs of the tabernacle, and of the court all around, *were* bronze.

Materials of the Tabernacle

21This is the inventory of the tabernacle, the tabernacle of the Testimony, which was counted according to the commandment of Moses, for the service of the Levites, by the hand of Ithamar, son of Aaron the priest. 22Bezalel the son of Uri, the son of Hur, of the tribe of Judah, made all that the LORD had commanded Moses. 23And with him *was* Aholiab the son of Ahisamach, of the tribe of Dan, an engraver and designer, a weaver of blue, purple, and scarlet *thread*, and of fine linen.

24All the gold that was used in all the work of the holy *place*, that is, the gold of the offering, was twenty-nine talents and seven hundred and thirty shekels, according to the shekel of the sanctuary. 25And the silver from those who were numbered of the congregation *was* one hundred talents and one thousand seven hundred and seventy-five shekels, according to the shekel of the sanctuary: 26a bekah for each man (*that is*, half a shekel, according to the shekel of the sanctuary), for everyone included in the numbering from twenty years old and above, for six hundred and three thousand, five hundred and fifty *men*. 27And from the hundred talents of silver were cast the sockets of the sanctuary and the bases of the veil: one hundred sockets from the hundred talents, one talent for each socket. 28Then from the one thousand seven hundred and seventy-five *shekels* he made hooks for the pillars, overlaid their capitals, and made bands for them.

29The offering of bronze *was* seventy talents and two thousand four hundred shekels. 30And with it he made the sockets for the door of the tabernacle of meeting, the bronze altar, the bronze grating for it, and all the utensils for the altar, 31the sockets for the court all around, the bases for the court gate, all the pegs for the tabernacle, and all the pegs for the court all around.

Making the Garments of the Priesthood

39 Of the blue, purple, and scarlet *thread* they made garments of ministry, for ministering in the holy *place*, and made the holy garments for Aaron, as the LORD had commanded Moses.

Making the Ephod

2He made the ephod of gold, blue, purple, and scarlet *thread*, and of fine woven linen. 3And they beat the gold into thin sheets and cut *it into* threads, to work *it in with* the blue, purple, and scarlet *thread*, and the fine linen, *into* artistic designs. 4They made shoulder straps for it to couple *it* together; it was coupled together at its two edges. 5And the intricately woven band of his ephod that *was* on it *was* of the same workmanship, *woven of* gold, blue, purple, and scarlet *thread*, and of fine woven linen, as the LORD had commanded Moses.

6And they set onyx stones, enclosed in settings of gold; they were engraved, as signets are engraved, with the names of the sons of Israel. 7He put them on the shoulders of the ephod *as* memorial stones for the sons of Israel, as the LORD had commanded Moses.

Making the Breastplate

8And he made the breastplate, artistically woven like the workmanship of the ephod, of gold, blue, purple, and scarlet *thread*, and of fine woven linen. 9They made the breastplate square by doubling it; a span *was* its length and a span its width when doubled. 10And they set in it four rows of stones: a row with a sardius, a topaz, and an emerald *was* the first row; 11the second row, a turquoise, a sapphire, and a diamond; 12the third row, a jacinth, an agate, and an amethyst; 13the fourth row, a beryl, an onyx, and a jasper. *They were* enclosed in settings of gold in their mountings. 14*There were* twelve stones according to the names of the sons of Israel: according to their names, *engraved like* a signet, each one with its own name according to the twelve tribes. 15And they made chains for the breastplate at the ends, like braided cords of pure gold. 16They also made two settings of gold and two gold rings, and put the two rings on the two ends of the breastplate. 17And they put the two braided *chains* of gold in the two rings on the ends of the breastplate. 18The two ends of the two braided *chains* they fastened in the two settings, and put them on the shoulder straps of the ephod in the front. 19And they made two rings of gold and put *them* on the two ends of the breastplate, on the edge of it, which *was* on the inward side of the ephod. 20They made two *other* gold rings and put them on the two shoulder straps, underneath the ephod toward its front, right at the seam above the intricately woven band of the ephod. 21And they bound the breastplate by means of its rings to the rings of the ephod with a blue cord, so that it would be above the intricately woven band of the ephod, and that the breastplate would not come loose from the ephod, as the LORD had commanded Moses.

Making the Other Priestly Garments

22He made the robe of the ephod of woven work, all of blue. 23And *there was* an opening in the middle of the robe, like the opening in a coat of mail, *with* a woven binding all around the opening, so that it would not tear. 24They made on the hem of the robe pomegranates of blue, purple, and scarlet, and of fine woven *linen*. 25And they made bells of pure gold, and put the bells between the pomegranates on the hem of the robe all around between the pomegranates: 26a bell and a pomegranate, a bell and a pomegranate, all around the hem of the robe to minister in, as the LORD had commanded Moses.

27They made tunics, artistically woven of fine linen, for Aaron and his sons, 28a turban of fine linen, exquisite hats of fine linen, short trousers of fine woven linen, 29and a sash of fine woven linen with blue, purple, and scarlet *thread*, made by a weaver, as the LORD had commanded Moses.

30Then they made the plate of the holy crown of pure gold, and wrote on it an inscription *like* the engraving of a signet:

HOLINESS TO THE LORD.

31And they tied to it a blue cord, to fasten *it* above on the turban, as the LORD had commanded Moses.

The Work Completed

32Thus all the work of the tabernacle of the tent of meeting was finished. And the children of Israel did according to all that the LORD had commanded Moses; so they did. 33And they brought the tabernacle to Moses, the tent and all its furnishings: its clasps, its boards, its bars, its pillars, and its sockets; 34the covering of ram skins dyed red, the covering of badger skins, and the veil of the covering; 35the ark of the Testimony with its poles, and the mercy seat; 36the table, all its utensils, and the showbread; 37the pure *gold* lampstand with its lamps (the lamps set in order), all its utensils, and the oil for light; 38the gold altar, the anointing oil, and the sweet incense; the screen for the tabernacle door; 39the bronze altar, its grate of bronze, its poles, and all its utensils; the laver with its base; 40the hangings of the court, its pillars and its sockets, the screen for the court gate, its cords, and its pegs; all the utensils for the service of the tabernacle, for the tent of meeting; 41and the garments of ministry, to minister in the holy *place:* the holy garments for Aaron the

priest, and his sons' garments, to minister as priests.

42According to all that the LORD had commanded Moses, so the children of Israel did all the work. 43Then Moses looked over all the work, and indeed they had done it; as the LORD had commanded, just so they had done it. And Moses blessed them.

The Tabernacle Erected and Arranged

40 Then the LORD spoke to Moses, saying: 2"On the first day of the first month you shall set up the tabernacle of the tent of meeting. 3You shall put in it the ark of the Testimony, and partition off the ark with the veil. 4You shall bring in the table and arrange the things that are to be set in order on it; and you shall bring in the lampstand and light its lamps. 5You shall also set the altar of gold for the incense before the ark of the Testimony, and put up the screen for the door of the tabernacle. 6Then you shall set the altar of the burnt offering before the door of the tabernacle of the tent of meeting. 7And you shall set the laver between the tabernacle of meeting and the altar, and put water in it. 8You shall set up the court all around, and hang up the screen at the court gate.

9"And you shall take the anointing oil, and anoint the tabernacle and all that *is* in it; and you shall hallow it and all its utensils, and it shall be holy. 10You shall anoint the altar of the burnt offering and all its utensils, and consecrate the altar. The altar shall be most holy. 11And you shall anoint the laver and its base, and consecrate it.

12"Then you shall bring Aaron and his sons to the door of the tabernacle of meeting and wash them with water. 13You shall put the holy garments on Aaron, and anoint him and consecrate him, that he may minister to Me as priest. 14And you shall bring his sons and clothe them with tunics. 15You shall anoint them, as you anointed their father, that they may minister to Me as priests; for their anointing shall surely be an everlasting priesthood throughout their generations."

16Thus Moses did; according to all that the LORD had commanded him, so he did.

17And it came to pass in the first month of the second year, on the first *day* of the month, *that* the tabernacle was raised up. 18So Moses raised up the tabernacle, fastened its sockets, set up its boards, put in its bars, and raised up its pillars. 19And he spread out the tent over the tabernacle and put the covering of the tent on top of it, as the LORD had commanded Moses. 20He took the Testimony and put *it* into the ark, inserted the poles through the rings of the ark, and put the mercy seat on top of the ark. 21And he brought the ark into the tabernacle, hung up the veil of the covering, and partitioned off the ark of the Testimony, as the LORD had commanded Moses.

22He put the table in the tabernacle of meeting, on the north side of the tabernacle, outside the veil; 23and he set the bread in order upon it before the LORD, as the LORD had commanded Moses. 24He put the lampstand in the tabernacle of meeting, across from the table, on the south side of the tabernacle; 25and he lit the lamps before the LORD, as the LORD had commanded Moses. 26He put the gold altar in the tabernacle of meeting in front of the veil; 27and he burned sweet incense on it, as the LORD had commanded Moses. 28He hung up the screen *at* the door of the tabernacle. 29And he put the altar of burnt offering *before* the door of the tabernacle of the tent of meeting, and offered upon it the burnt offering and the grain offering, as the LORD had commanded Moses. 30He set the laver between the tabernacle of meeting and the altar, and put water there for washing; 31and Moses, Aaron, and his sons would wash their hands and their feet *with water* from it. 32Whenever they went into the tabernacle of meeting, and when they came near the altar, they washed, as the LORD had commanded Moses. 33And he raised up the court all around the tabernacle and the altar, and hung up the screen of the court gate. So Moses finished the work.

The Cloud and the Glory

34Then the cloud covered the tabernacle of meeting, and the glory of the LORD filled the tabernacle. 35And Moses was not able to enter the tabernacle of meeting, because the cloud rested above it, and the glory of the LORD filled the tabernacle. 36Whenever the cloud was taken up from above the tabernacle, the children of Israel would go onward in all their journeys. 37But if the cloud was not taken up, then they did not journey till the day that it was taken up. 38For the cloud of the LORD *was* above the tabernacle by day, and fire was over it by night, in the sight of all the house of Israel, throughout all their journeys.

LEVITICUS

The Burnt Offering

1 Now the LORD called to Moses, and spoke to him from the tabernacle of meeting, saying, 2"Speak to the children of Israel, and say to them: 'When any one of you brings an offering to the LORD, you shall bring your offering of the livestock—of the herd and of the flock.

3'If his offering *is* a burnt sacrifice of the herd, let him offer a male without blemish; he shall offer it of his own free will at the door of the tabernacle of meeting before the LORD. 4Then he shall put his hand on the head of the burnt offering, and it will be accepted on his behalf to make atonement for him. 5He shall kill the bull before the LORD; and the priests, Aaron's sons, shall bring the blood and sprinkle the blood all around on the altar that *is by* the door of the tabernacle of meeting. 6And he shall skin the burnt offering and cut it into its pieces. 7The sons of Aaron the priest shall put fire on the altar, and lay the wood in order on the fire. 8Then the priests, Aaron's sons, shall lay the parts, the head, and the fat in order on the wood that *is* on the fire upon the altar; 9but he shall wash its entrails and its legs with water. And the priest shall burn all on the altar as a burnt sacrifice, an offering made by fire, a sweet aroma to the LORD.

10'If his offering *is* of the flocks—of the sheep or of the goats—as a burnt sacrifice, he shall bring a male without blemish. 11He shall kill it on the north side of the altar before the LORD; and the priests, Aaron's sons, shall sprinkle its blood all around on the altar. 12And he shall cut it into its pieces, with its head and its fat; and the priest shall lay them in order on the wood that *is* on the fire upon the altar; 13but he shall wash the entrails and the legs with water. Then the priest shall bring *it* all and burn *it* on the altar; it *is* a burnt sacrifice, an offering made by fire, a sweet aroma to the LORD.

14'And if the burnt sacrifice of his offering to the LORD *is* of birds, then he shall bring his offering of turtledoves or young pigeons. 15The priest shall bring it to the altar, wring off its head, and burn *it* on the altar; its blood shall be drained out at the side of the altar. 16And he shall remove its crop with its feathers and cast it beside the altar on the east side, into the place for ashes. 17Then he shall split it at its wings, *but* shall not divide *it* completely; and the priest shall burn it on the altar, on the wood that *is* on the fire. It *is* a burnt sacrifice, an offering made by fire, a sweet aroma to the LORD.

The Grain Offering

2 'When anyone offers a grain offering to the LORD, his offering shall be *of* fine flour. And he shall pour oil on it, and put frankincense on it. 2He shall bring it to Aaron's sons, the priests, one of whom shall take from it his handful of fine flour and oil with all the frankincense. And the priest shall burn *it as* a memorial on the altar, an offering made by fire, a sweet aroma to the LORD. 3The rest of the grain offering *shall be* Aaron's and his sons'. *It is* most holy of the offerings to the LORD made by fire.

4'And if you bring as an offering a grain offering baked in the oven, *it shall be* unleavened cakes of fine flour mixed with oil, or unleavened wafers anointed with oil. 5But if your offering *is* a grain offering *baked* in a pan, *it shall be of* fine flour, unleavened, mixed with oil. 6You shall break it in pieces and pour oil on it; it *is* a grain offering.

7'If your offering *is* a grain offering *baked* in a covered pan, it shall be made *of* fine flour with oil. 8You shall bring the grain offering that is made of these things to the LORD. And when it is presented to the priest, he shall bring it to the altar. 9Then the priest shall take from the grain offering a memorial portion, and burn *it* on the altar. *It is* an offering made by fire, a sweet aroma to the LORD. 10And what is left of the grain offering *shall be* Aaron's and his sons'. *It is* most holy of the offerings to the LORD made by fire.

11'No grain offering which you bring to the LORD shall be made with leaven, for you shall burn no leaven nor any honey in any offering to the LORD made by fire. 12As for the offering of the first-fruits, you shall offer them to the LORD, but they shall not be burned on the altar for a sweet aroma. 13And every offering of your grain offering you shall season with salt; you shall not allow the salt of the covenant of your God to be lacking from your grain offering. With all your offerings you shall offer salt.

14'If you offer a grain offering of your firstfruits to the LORD, you shall offer for the grain offering of your firstfruits green heads of grain roasted on the fire, grain beaten from full heads. 15And you shall put oil on it, and lay frankincense on it. It *is* a grain offering. 16Then the priest shall burn the memorial portion: *part* of its beaten grain and *part* of its oil, with all the frankincense, as an offering made by fire to the LORD.

The Peace Offering

3 'When his offering *is* a sacrifice of a peace offering, if he offers *it* of the herd, whether male or female, he shall offer it without blemish before the LORD. 2And he shall lay his hand on the head of his offering, and kill it *at* the door of the tabernacle of meeting; and Aaron's sons, the priests, shall sprinkle the blood all around on the altar. 3Then he shall offer from the sacrifice of the peace offering an offering made by fire to the LORD. The fat that covers the entrails and all the fat that *is* on the entrails, 4the two kidneys and the fat that *is* on them by the flanks, and the fatty lobe *attached* to the liver above the kidneys, he shall remove; 5and Aaron's sons shall burn it on the altar upon the burnt sacrifice, which *is* on the wood that *is* on the fire, *as* an offering made by fire, a sweet aroma to the LORD.

6'If his offering as a sacrifice of a peace offering to the LORD *is* of the flock, *whether* male or female, he shall offer it without blemish. 7If he offers a lamb as his offering, then he shall offer it before the LORD. 8And he shall lay his hand on the head of his offering, and kill it before the tabernacle of meet-

ing; and Aaron's sons shall sprinkle its blood all around on the altar.

9'Then he shall offer from the sacrifice of the peace offering, as an offering made by fire to the LORD, its fat *and* the whole fat tail which he shall remove close to the backbone. And the fat that covers the entrails and all the fat that *is* on the entrails, 10the two kidneys and the fat that *is* on them by the flanks, and the fatty lobe *attached* to the liver above the kidneys, he shall remove; 11and the priest shall burn *them* on the altar *as* food, an offering made by fire to the LORD.

12'And if his offering *is* a goat, then he shall offer it before the LORD. 13He shall lay his hand on its head and kill it before the tabernacle of meeting; and the sons of Aaron shall sprinkle its blood all around on the altar. 14Then he shall offer from it his offering, as an offering made by fire to the LORD. The fat that covers the entrails and all the fat that *is* on the entrails, 15the two kidneys and the fat that *is* on them by the flanks, and the fatty lobe *attached* to the liver above the kidneys, he shall remove; 16and the priest shall burn them on the altar *as* food, an offering made by fire for a sweet aroma; all the fat *is* the LORD's.

17'*This shall be* a perpetual statute throughout your generations in all your dwellings: you shall eat neither fat nor blood.' "

The Sin Offering

4 Now the LORD spoke to Moses, saying, 2"Speak to the children of Israel, saying: 'If a person sins unintentionally against any of the commandments of the LORD *in anything* which ought not to be done, and does *any* of them, 3if the anointed priest sins, bringing guilt on the people, then let him offer to the LORD for his sin which he has sinned a young bull without blemish as a sin offering. 4He shall bring the bull to the door of the tabernacle of meeting before the LORD, lay his hand on the bull's head, and kill the bull before the LORD. 5Then the anointed priest shall take some of the bull's blood and bring it to the tabernacle of meeting. 6The priest shall dip his finger in the blood and sprinkle some of the blood seven times before the LORD, in front of the veil of the sanctuary. 7And the priest shall put some of the blood on the horns of the altar of sweet incense before the LORD, which is in the tabernacle of meeting; and he shall pour the remaining blood of the bull at the base of the altar of the burnt offering, which is at the door of the tabernacle of meeting. 8He shall take from it all the fat of the bull as the sin offering. The fat that covers the entrails and all the fat which is on the entrails, 9the two kidneys and the fat that is on them by the flanks, and the fatty lobe *attached* to the liver above the kidneys, he shall remove, 10as it was taken from the bull of the sacrifice of the peace offering; and the priest shall burn them on the altar of the burnt offering. 11But the bull's hide and all its flesh, with its head and legs, its entrails and offal—12the whole bull he shall carry outside the camp to a clean place, where the ashes are poured out, and burn it on wood with fire; where the ashes are poured out it shall be burned.

13'Now if the whole congregation of Israel sins unintentionally, and the thing is hidden from the eyes of the assembly, and they have done *something against* any of the commandments of the LORD *in anything* which should not be done, and are guilty; 14when the sin which they have committed becomes known, then the assembly shall offer a young bull for the sin, and bring it before the tabernacle of meeting. 15And the elders of the congregation shall lay their hands on the head of the bull before the LORD. Then the bull shall be killed before the LORD. 16The anointed priest shall bring some of the bull's blood to the tabernacle of meeting. 17Then the priest shall dip his finger in the blood and sprinkle *it* seven times before the LORD, in front of the veil. 18And he shall put *some* of the blood on the horns of the altar which *is* before the LORD, which *is* in the tabernacle of meeting; and he shall pour the remaining blood at the base of the altar of burnt offering, which is at the door of the tabernacle of meeting. 19He shall take all the fat from it and burn *it* on the altar. 20And he shall do with the bull as he did with the bull as a sin offering;

thus he shall do with it. So the priest shall make atonement for them, and it shall be forgiven them. 21Then he shall carry the bull outside the camp, and burn it as he burned the first bull. It *is* a sin offering for the assembly.

22'When a ruler has sinned, and done *something* unintentionally *against* any of the commandments of the LORD his God *in anything* which should not be done, and is guilty, 23or if his sin which he has committed comes to his knowledge, he shall bring as his offering a kid of the goats, a male without blemish. 24And he shall lay his hand on the head of the goat, and kill it at the place where they kill the burnt offering before the LORD. It *is* a sin offering. 25The priest shall take some of the blood of the sin offering with his finger, put *it* on the horns of the altar of burnt offering, and pour its blood at the base of the altar of burnt offering. 26And he shall burn all its fat on the altar, like the fat of the sacrifice of the peace offering. So the priest shall make atonement for him concerning his sin, and it shall be forgiven him.

27'If anyone of the common people sins unintentionally by doing *something against* any of the commandments of the LORD *in anything* which ought not to be done, and is guilty, 28or if his sin which he has committed comes to his knowledge, then he shall bring as his offering a kid of the goats, a female without blemish, for his sin which he has committed. 29And he shall lay his hand on the head of the sin offering, and kill the sin offering at the place of the burnt offering. 30Then the priest shall take *some* of its blood with his finger, put *it* on the horns of the altar of burnt offering, and pour all *the remaining* blood at the base of the altar. 31He shall remove all its fat, as fat is removed from the sacrifice of the peace offering; and the priest shall burn it on the altar for a sweet aroma to the LORD. So the priest shall make atonement for him, and it shall be forgiven him.

32'If he brings a lamb as his sin offering, he shall bring a female without blemish. 33Then he shall lay his hand on the head of the sin offering, and kill it as a sin offering at the place where they kill the burnt offering. 34The priest shall take *some* of the blood of the sin offering with his finger, put *it* on the horns of the altar of burnt offering, and pour all *the remaining* blood at the base of the altar. 35He shall remove all its fat, as the fat of the lamb is removed from the sacrifice of the peace offering. Then the priest shall burn it on the altar, according to the offerings made by fire to the LORD. So the priest shall make atonement for his sin that he has committed, and it shall be forgiven him.

The Trespass Offering

5 'If a person sins in hearing the utterance of an oath, and *is* a witness, whether he has seen or known *of the matter*—if he does not tell *it*, he bears guilt.

2'Or if a person touches any unclean thing, whether *it is* the carcass of an unclean beast, or the carcass of unclean livestock, or the carcass of unclean creeping things, and he is unaware of it, he also shall be unclean and guilty. 3Or if he touches human uncleanness—whatever uncleanness with which a man may be defiled, and he is unaware of it—when he realizes *it*, then he shall be guilty.

4'Or if a person swears, speaking thoughtlessly with *his* lips to do evil or to do good, whatever *it is* that a man may pronounce by an oath, and he is unaware of it—when he realizes *it*, then he shall be guilty in any of these *matters*.

5'And it shall be, when he is guilty in any of these *matters*, that he shall confess that he has sinned in that *thing*; 6and he shall bring his trespass offering to the LORD for his sin which he has committed, a female from the flock, a lamb or a kid of the goats as a sin offering. So the priest shall make atonement for him concerning his sin.

7'If he is not able to bring a lamb, then he shall bring to the LORD, for his trespass which he has committed, two turtledoves or two young pigeons: one as a sin offering and the other as a burnt offering. 8And he shall bring them to the priest, who shall offer *that* which *is* for the sin offering first, and wring off its head from its neck, but shall not divide *it* completely. 9Then he shall sprinkle *some* of the blood of the sin

offering on the side of the altar, and the rest of the blood shall be drained out at the base of the altar. It *is* a sin offering. 10And he shall offer the second *as* a burnt offering according to the prescribed manner. So the priest shall make atonement on his behalf for his sin which he has committed, and it shall be forgiven him.

11'But if he is not able to bring two turtledoves or two young pigeons, then he who sinned shall bring for his offering one-tenth of an ephah of fine flour as a sin offering. He shall put no oil on it, nor shall he put frankincense on it, for it *is* a sin offering. 12Then he shall bring it to the priest, and the priest shall take his handful of it as a memorial portion, and burn *it* on the altar according to the offerings made by fire to the LORD. It *is* a sin offering. 13The priest shall make atonement for him, for his sin that he has committed in any of these matters; and it shall be forgiven him. *The rest* shall be the priest's as a grain offering.' ''

Offerings with Restitution

14Then the LORD spoke to Moses, saying: 15"If a person commits a trespass, and sins unintentionally in regard to the holy things of the LORD, then he shall bring to the LORD as his trespass offering a ram without blemish from the flocks, with your valuation in shekels of silver according to the shekel of the sanctuary, as a trespass offering. 16And he shall make restitution for the harm that he has done in regard to the holy thing, and shall add one-fifth to it and give it to the priest. So the priest shall make atonement for him with the ram of the trespass offering, and it shall be forgiven him.

17"If a person sins, and commits any of these things which are forbidden to be done by the commandments of the LORD, though he does not know *it*, yet he is guilty and shall bear his iniquity. 18And he shall bring to the priest a ram without blemish from the flock, with your valuation, as a trespass offering. So the priest shall make atonement for him regarding his ignorance in which he erred and did not know *it*, and it shall be forgiven him. 19It is a trespass offering; he has certainly trespassed against the LORD."

6 And the LORD spoke to Moses, saying: 2"If a person sins and commits a trespass against the LORD by lying to his neighbor about what was delivered to him for safekeeping, or about a pledge, or about a robbery, or if he has extorted from his neighbor, 3or if he has found what was lost and lies concerning it, and swears falsely—in any one of these things that a man may do in which he sins: 4then it shall be, because he has sinned and is guilty, that he shall restore what he has stolen, or the thing which he has extorted, or what was delivered to him for safekeeping, or the lost thing which he found, 5or all that about which he has sworn falsely. He shall restore its full value, add one-fifth more to it, *and* give it to whomever it belongs, on the day of his trespass offering. 6And he shall bring his trespass offering to the LORD, a ram without blemish from the flock, with your valuation, as a trespass offering, to the priest. 7So the priest shall make atonement for him before the LORD, and he shall be forgiven for any one of these things that he may have done in which he trespasses."

The Law of the Burnt Offering

8Then the LORD spoke to Moses, saying, 9"Command Aaron and his sons, saying, 'This *is* the law of the burnt offering: The burnt offering *shall be* on the hearth upon the altar all night until morning, and the fire of the altar shall be kept burning on it. 10And the priest shall put on his linen garment, and his linen trousers he shall put on his body, and take up the ashes of the burnt offering which the fire has consumed on the altar, and he shall put them beside the altar. 11Then he shall take off his garments, put on other garments, and carry the ashes outside the camp to a clean place. 12And the fire on the altar shall be kept burning on it; it shall not be put out. And the priest shall burn wood on it every morning, and lay the burnt offering in order on it; and he shall burn on it the fat of the peace offerings. 13A fire shall always be burning on the altar; it shall never go out.

The Law of the Grain Offering

14'This *is* the law of the grain offering: The sons of Aaron shall offer it on the altar before the LORD. 15He shall take from it his handful of the fine flour of the grain offering, with its oil, and all the frankincense which *is* on the grain offering, and shall burn *it* on the altar *for* a sweet aroma, as a memorial to the LORD. 16And the remainder of it Aaron and his sons shall eat; with unleavened bread it shall be eaten in a holy place; in the court of the tabernacle of meeting they shall eat it. 17It shall not be baked with leaven. I have given it *as* their portion of My offerings made by fire; it *is* most holy, like the sin offering and the trespass offering. 18All the males among the children of Aaron may eat it. *It shall be* a statute forever in your generations concerning the offerings made by fire to the LORD. Everyone who touches them must be holy.' "

19And the LORD spoke to Moses, saying, 20"This *is* the offering of Aaron and his sons, which they shall offer to the LORD, *beginning* on the day when he is anointed: one-tenth of an ephah of fine flour as a daily grain offering, half of it in the morning and half of it at night. 21It shall be made in a pan with oil. *When it is* mixed, you shall bring it in. The baked pieces of the grain offering you shall offer *for* a sweet aroma to the LORD. 22The priest from among his sons, who is anointed in his place, shall offer it. *It is* a statute forever to the LORD. It shall be wholly burned. 23For every grain offering for the priest shall be wholly burned. It shall not be eaten."

The Law of the Sin Offering

24Also the LORD spoke to Moses, saying, 25"Speak to Aaron and to his sons, saying, 'This *is* the law of the sin offering: In the place where the burnt offering is killed, the sin offering shall be killed before the LORD. It *is* most holy. 26The priest who offers it for sin shall eat it. In a holy place it shall be eaten, in the court of the tabernacle of meeting. 27Everyone who touches its flesh must be holy. And when its blood is sprinkled on any garment, you shall wash that on which it was sprinkled, in a holy place. 28But the earthen vessel in which it is boiled shall be broken. And if it is boiled in a bronze pot, it shall be both scoured and rinsed in water. 29All the males among the priests may eat it. It *is* most holy. 30But no sin offering from which *any* of the blood is brought into the tabernacle of meeting, to make atonement in the holy place,*a* shall be eaten. It shall be burned in the fire.

The Law of the Trespass Offering

7 'Likewise this *is* the law of the trespass offering (it *is* most holy): 2In the place where they kill the burnt offering they shall kill the trespass offering. And its blood he shall sprinkle all around on the altar. 3And he shall offer from it all its fat. The fat tail and the fat that covers the entrails, 4the two kidneys and the fat that *is* on them by the flanks, and the fatty lobe *attached* to the liver above the kidneys, he shall remove; 5and the priest shall burn them on the altar *as* an offering made by fire to the LORD. It *is* a trespass offering. 6Every male among the priests may eat it. It shall be eaten in a holy place. It *is* most holy. 7The trespass offering *is* like the sin offering; *there is* one law for them both: the priest who makes atonement with it shall have *it*. 8And the priest who offers anyone's burnt offering, that priest shall have for himself the skin of the burnt offering which he has offered. 9Also every grain offering that is baked in the oven and all that is prepared in the covered pan, or in a pan, shall be the priest's who offers it. 10Every grain offering, *whether* mixed with oil or dry, shall belong to all the sons of Aaron, to one *as much* as the other.

The Law of Peace Offerings

11'This *is* the law of the sacrifice of peace offerings which he shall offer to the LORD: 12If he offers it for a thanksgiving, then he shall offer, with the sacrifice of thanksgiving, unleavened cakes mixed with oil, unleavened wafers anointed with oil, or cakes of blended flour mixed with oil. 13Besides

the cakes, *as* his offering he shall offer leavened bread with the sacrifice of thanksgiving of his peace offering. 14And from it he shall offer one cake from each offering *as* a heave offering to the LORD. It shall belong to the priest who sprinkles the blood of the peace offering.

15'The flesh of the sacrifice of his peace offering for thanksgiving shall be eaten the same day it is offered. He shall not leave any of it until morning. 16But if the sacrifice of his offering *is* a vow or a voluntary offering, it shall be eaten the same day that he offers his sacrifice; but on the next day the remainder of it also may be eaten; 17the remainder of the flesh of the sacrifice on the third day must be burned with fire. 18And if *any* of the flesh of the sacrifice of his peace offering is eaten at all on the third day, it shall not be accepted, nor shall it be imputed to him; it shall be an abomination *to* him who offers it, and the person who eats of it shall bear guilt.

19'The flesh that touches any unclean thing shall not be eaten. It shall be burned with fire. And as for the *clean* flesh, all who are clean may eat of it. 20But the person who eats the flesh of the sacrifice of the peace offering that *belongs* to the LORD, while he is unclean, that person shall be cut off from his people. 21Moreover the person who touches any unclean thing, *such as* human uncleanness, *an* unclean animal, or any abominable unclean thing, and who eats the flesh of the sacrifice of the peace offering that *belongs* to the LORD, that person shall be cut off from his people.' "

Fat and Blood May Not Be Eaten

22And the LORD spoke to Moses, saying, 23"Speak to the children of Israel, saying: 'You shall not eat any fat, of ox or sheep or goat. 24And the fat of an animal that dies *naturally*, and the fat of what is torn by wild beasts, may be used in any other way; but you shall by no means eat it. 25For whoever eats the fat of the animal of which men offer an offering made by fire to the LORD, the person who eats *it* shall be cut off

---

a The Most Holy Place when capitalized

from his people. 26Moreover you shall not eat any blood in any of your dwellings, *whether* of bird or beast. 27Whoever eats any blood, that person shall be cut off from his people.' "

The Portion of Aaron and His Sons

28Then the LORD spoke to Moses, saying, 29"Speak to the children of Israel, saying: 'He who offers the sacrifice of his peace offering to the LORD shall bring his offering to the LORD from the sacrifice of his peace offering. 30His own hands shall bring the offerings made by fire to the LORD. The fat with the breast he shall bring, that the breast may be waved *as* a wave offering before the LORD. 31And the priest shall burn the fat on the altar, but the breast shall be Aaron's and his sons'. 32Also the right thigh you shall give to the priest *as* a heave offering from the sacrifices of your peace offerings. 33He among the sons of Aaron, who offers the blood of the peace offering and the fat, shall have the right thigh for *his* part. 34For the breast of the wave offering and the thigh of the heave offering I have taken from the children of Israel, from the sacrifices of their peace offerings, and I have given them to Aaron the priest and to his sons from the children of Israel by a statute forever.' "

35This *is* the consecrated portion for Aaron and his sons, from the offerings made by fire to the LORD, on the day when *Moses* presented them to minister to the LORD as priests. 36The LORD commanded this to be given to them by the children of Israel, on the day that He anointed them, *by* a statute forever throughout their generations.

37This *is* the law of the burnt offering, the grain offering, the sin offering, the trespass offering, the consecrations, and the sacrifice of the peace offering, 38which the LORD commanded Moses on Mount Sinai, on the day when He commanded the children of Israel to offer their offerings to the LORD in the Wilderness of Sinai.

Aaron and His Sons Consecrated

8 And the LORD spoke to Moses, saying: 2"Take Aaron and his sons with him, and the garments, the anointing oil, a bull as the sin offering, two rams, and a basket of unleavened bread; 3and gather all the congregation together at the door of the tabernacle of meeting."

4So Moses did as the LORD commanded him. And the congregation was gathered together at the door of the tabernacle of meeting. 5And Moses said to the congregation, "This *is* what the LORD commanded to be done."

6Then Moses brought Aaron and his sons and washed them with water. 7And he put the tunic on him, girded him with the sash, clothed him with the robe, and put the ephod on him; and he girded him with the intricately woven band of the ephod, and with it tied *the ephod* on him. 8Then he put the breastplate on him, and he put the Urim and the Thummim[b] in the breastplate. 9And he put the turban on his head. Also on the turban, on its front, he put the golden plate, the holy crown, as the LORD had commanded Moses.

10Also Moses took the anointing oil, and anointed the tabernacle and all that *was* in it, and consecrated them. 11He sprinkled some of it on the altar seven times, anointed the altar and all its utensils, and the laver and its base, to consecrate them. 12And he poured some of the anointing oil on Aaron's head and anointed him, to consecrate him.

13Then Moses brought Aaron's sons and put tunics on them, girded them with sashes, and put hats on them, as the LORD had commanded Moses.

14And he brought the bull for the sin offering. Then Aaron and his sons laid their hands on the head of the bull for the sin offering, 15and Moses killed *it*. Then he took the blood, and put *some* on the horns of the altar all around with his finger, and purified the altar. And he poured the blood at the base of the altar, and consecrated it, to make atonement for it. 16Then he took all the fat that *was* on the entrails, the fatty lobe *attached to* the liver, and the two kidneys with their fat, and Moses burned *them* on the altar. 17But the bull, its hide, its flesh, and its offal, he

[b] Literally *the Lights and the Perfections* (compare Exodus 28.30)

burned with fire outside the camp, as the LORD had commanded Moses.

18Then he brought the ram as the burnt offering. And Aaron and his sons laid their hands on the head of the ram, 19and Moses killed it. Then he sprinkled the blood all around on the altar. 20And he cut the ram into pieces; and Moses burned the head, the pieces, and the fat. 21Then he washed the entrails and the legs in water. And Moses burned the whole ram on the altar. It was a burnt sacrifice for a sweet aroma, an offering made by fire to the LORD, as the LORD had commanded Moses.

22And he brought the second ram, the ram of consecration. Then Aaron and his sons laid their hands on the head of the ram, 23and Moses killed it. Also he took some of its blood and put it on the tip of Aaron's right ear, on the thumb of his right hand, and on the big toe of his right foot. 24Then he brought Aaron's sons. And Moses put some of the blood on the tips of their right ears, on the thumbs of their right hands, and on the big toes of their right feet. And Moses sprinkled the blood all around on the altar. 25Then he took the fat and the fat tail, all the fat that was on the entrails, the fatty lobe attached to the liver, the two kidneys and their fat, and the right thigh; 26and from the basket of unleavened bread that was before the LORD he took one unleavened cake, a cake of bread anointed with oil, and one wafer, and put them on the fat and on the right thigh; 27and he put all these in Aaron's hands and in his sons' hands, and waved them as a wave offering before the LORD. 28Then Moses took them from their hands and burned them on the altar, on the burnt offering. They were consecration offerings for a sweet aroma. That was an offering made by fire to the LORD. 29And Moses took the breast and waved it as a wave offering before the LORD. It was Moses' part of the ram of consecration, as the LORD had commanded Moses.

30Then Moses took some of the anointing oil and some of the blood which was on the altar, and sprinkled it on Aaron, on his garments, on his sons, and on the garments of his sons with him; and he consecrated Aaron, his garments, his sons, and the garments of his sons with him.

31And Moses said to Aaron and his sons, "Boil the flesh at the door of the tabernacle of meeting, and eat it there with the bread that is in the basket of consecration offerings, as I commanded, saying, 'Aaron and his sons shall eat it.' 32What remains of the flesh and of the bread you shall burn with fire. 33And you shall not go outside the door of the tabernacle of meeting for seven days, until the days of your consecration are ended. For seven days he shall consecrate you. 34As he has done this day, so the LORD has commanded to do, to make atonement for you. 35Therefore you shall stay at the door of the tabernacle of meeting day and night for seven days, and keep the charge of the LORD, so that you may not die; for so I have been commanded." 36So Aaron and his sons did all the things that the LORD had commanded by the hand of Moses.

The Priestly Ministry Begins

9 It came to pass on the eighth day that Moses called Aaron and his sons and the elders of Israel. 2And he said to Aaron, "Take for yourself a young bull as a sin offering and a ram as a burnt offering, without blemish, and offer them before the LORD. 3And to the children of Israel you shall speak, saying, 'Take a kid of the goats as a sin offering, and a calf and a lamb, both of the first year, without blemish, as a burnt offering, 4also a bull and a ram as peace offerings, to sacrifice before the LORD, and a grain offering mixed with oil; for today the LORD will appear to you.' "

5So they brought what Moses commanded before the tabernacle of meeting. And all the congregation drew near and stood before the LORD. 6Then Moses said, "This is the thing which the LORD commanded you to do, and the glory of the LORD will appear to you." 7And Moses said to Aaron, "Go to the altar, offer your sin offering and your burnt offering, and make atonement for yourself and for the people. Offer the offering of the people, and make atonement for them, as the LORD commanded."

8Aaron therefore went to the altar and killed the calf of the sin offering, which *was* for himself. 9Then the sons of Aaron brought the blood to him. And he dipped his finger in the blood, put *it* on the horns of the altar, and poured the blood at the base of the altar. 10But the fat, the kidneys, and the fatty lobe from the liver of the sin offering he burned on the altar, as the LORD had commanded Moses. 11The flesh and the hide he burned with fire outside the camp.

12And he killed the burnt offering; and Aaron's sons presented to him the blood, which he sprinkled all around on the altar. 13Then they presented the burnt offering to him, with its pieces and head, and he burned *them* on the altar. 14And he washed the entrails and the legs, and burned *them* with the burnt offering on the altar.

15Then he brought the people's offering, and took the goat, which *was* the sin offering for the people, and killed it and offered it for sin, like the first one. 16And he brought the burnt offering and offered it according to the prescribed manner. 17Then he brought the grain offering, took a handful of it, and burned *it* on the altar, besides the burnt sacrifice of the morning.

18He also killed the bull and the ram *as* sacrifices of peace offerings, which *were* for the people. And Aaron's sons presented to him the blood, which he sprinkled all around on the altar, 19and the fat from the bull and the ram—the fatty tail, what covers *the entrails* and the kidneys, and the fatty lobe *attached to* the liver; 20and they put the fat on the breasts. Then he burned the fat on the altar; 21but the breasts and the right thigh Aaron waved *as* a wave offering before the LORD, as Moses had commanded.

22Then Aaron lifted his hand toward the people, blessed them, and came down from offering the sin offering, the burnt offering, and peace offerings. 23And Moses and Aaron went into the tabernacle of meeting, and came out and blessed the people. Then the glory of the LORD appeared to all the people, 24and fire came out from before the LORD and consumed the burnt offering and the fat on the altar. When all the people saw *it*, they shouted and fell on their faces.

The Profane Fire of Nadab and Abihu

10 Then Nadab and Abihu, the sons of Aaron, each took his censer and put fire in it, put incense on it, and offered profane fire before the LORD, which He had not commanded them. 2So fire went out from the LORD and devoured them, and they died before the LORD. 3And Moses said to Aaron, "This is what the LORD spoke, saying:

'By those who come near Me
    I must be regarded as holy;
    And before all the people
    I must be glorified.' "

So Aaron held his peace.

4Then Moses called Mishael and Elzaphan, the sons of Uzziel the uncle of Aaron, and said to them, "Come near, carry your brethren from before the sanctuary out of the camp." 5So they went near and carried them by their tunics out of the camp, as Moses had said.

6And Moses said to Aaron, and to Eleazar and Ithamar, his sons, "Do not uncover your heads nor tear your clothes, lest you die, and wrath come upon all the people. But let your brethren, the whole house of Israel, bewail the burning which the LORD has kindled. 7You shall not go out from the door of the tabernacle of meeting, lest you die, for the anointing oil of the LORD *is* upon you." And they did according to the word of Moses.

Conduct Prescribed for Priests

8Then the LORD spoke to Aaron, saying: 9"Do not drink wine or intoxicating drink, you, nor your sons with you, when you go into the tabernacle of meeting, lest you die. *It shall be* a statute forever throughout your generations, 10that you may distinguish between holy and unholy, and between unclean and clean, 11and that you may teach the children of Israel all the statutes which the LORD has spoken to them by the hand of Moses."

12And Moses spoke to Aaron, and to Eleazar and Ithamar, his sons who were left: "Take the grain offering that remains of the offerings made by fire to the LORD, and eat it without leaven beside the altar; for it *is* most holy. 13You shall eat it in a holy place, because it *is* your due and your sons' due, of the sacrifices made by fire to the LORD; for so I have been commanded. 14The breast of the wave offering and the thigh of the heave offering you shall eat in a clean place, you, your sons, and your daughters with you; for *they are* your due and your sons' due, *which* are given from the sacrifices of peace offerings of the children of Israel. 15The thigh of the heave offering and the breast of the wave offering they shall bring with the offerings of fat made by fire, to offer *as* a wave offering before the LORD. And it shall be yours and your sons' with you, by a statute forever, as the LORD has commanded."

16Then Moses made careful inquiry about the goat of the sin offering, and there it was—burned up. And he was angry with Eleazar and Ithamar, the sons of Aaron *who were* left, saying, 17"Why have you not eaten the sin offering in a holy place, since it *is* most holy, and *God* has given it to you to bear the guilt of the congregation, to make atonement for them before the LORD? 18See! Its blood was not brought inside the holy *place;*[c] indeed you should have eaten it in a holy *place,* as I commanded."

19And Aaron said to Moses, "Look, this day they have offered their sin offering and their burnt offering before the LORD, and such things have befallen me! *If* I had eaten the sin offering today, would it have been accepted in the sight of the LORD?" 20So when Moses heard *that,* he was content.

Foods Permitted and Forbidden

11 Now the LORD spoke to Moses and Aaron, saying to them, 2"Speak to the children of Israel, saying, 'These *are* the animals which you may eat among all the animals that *are* on the earth: 3Among the animals, whatever divides the hoof, having cloven hooves *and* chewing the cud—that you may eat. 4Nevertheless these you shall not eat among those that chew the cud or those that have cloven hooves: the camel, because it chews the cud but

does not have cloven hooves, is unclean to you; 5the rock hyrax, because it chews the cud but does not have cloven hooves, *is* unclean to you; 6the hare, because it chews the cud but does not have cloven hooves, *is* unclean to you; 7and the swine, though it divides the hoof, having cloven hooves, yet does not chew the cud, *is* unclean to you. 8Their flesh you shall not eat, and their carcasses you shall not touch. They *are* unclean to you.

9'These you may eat of all that *are* in the water: whatever in the water has fins and scales, whether in the seas or in the rivers—that you may eat. 10But all in the seas or in the rivers that do not have fins and scales, all that move in the water or any living thing which *is* in the water, they *are* an abomination to you. 11They shall be an abomination to you; you shall not eat their flesh, but you shall regard their carcasses as an abomination. 12Whatever in the water does not have fins or scales—that *shall be* an abomination to you.

13'And these you shall regard as an abomination among the birds; they shall not be eaten, they *are* an abomination: the eagle, the vulture, the buzzard, 14the kite, and the falcon after its kind; 15every raven after its kind, 16the ostrich, the short-eared owl, the sea gull, and the hawk after its kind; 17the little owl, the fisher owl, and the screech owl; 18the white owl, the jackdaw, and the carrion vulture; 19the stork, the heron after its kind, the hoopoe, and the bat.

20'All flying insects that creep on *all* fours *shall be* an abomination to you. 21Yet these you may eat of every flying insect that creeps on *all* fours: those which have jointed legs above their feet with which to leap on the earth. 22These you may eat: the locust after its kind, the destroying locust after its kind, the cricket after its kind, and the grasshopper after its kind. 23But all *other* flying insects which have four feet *shall be* an abomination to you.

Unclean Animals

24'By these you shall become unclean; whoever touches the carcass of

---

c The Most Holy Place when capitalized

any of them shall be unclean until evening; 25whoever carries part of the carcass of any of them shall wash his clothes and be unclean until evening: 26*The carcass* of any animal which divides the foot, but is not cloven-hoofed or does not chew the cud, *is* unclean to you. Everyone who touches it shall be unclean. 27And whatever goes on its paws, among all kinds of animals that go on *all* fours, those *are* unclean to you. Whoever touches any such carcass shall be unclean until evening. 28Whoever carries *any such* carcass shall wash his clothes and be unclean until evening. It *is* unclean to you.

29'These also *shall be* unclean to you among the creeping things that creep on the earth: the mole, the mouse, and the large lizard after its kind; 30the gecko, the monitor lizard, the sand reptile, the sand lizard, and the chameleon. 31These *are* unclean to you among all that creep. Whoever touches them when they are dead shall be unclean until evening. 32Anything on which *any* of them falls, when they are dead shall be unclean, whether *it is* any item of wood or clothing or skin or sack, whatever item *it is,* in which *any* work is done, it must be put in water. And it shall be unclean until evening; then it shall be clean. 33Any earthen vessel into which *any* of them falls you shall break; and whatever *is* in it shall be unclean: 34in such a vessel, any edible food upon which water falls becomes unclean, and any drink that may be drunk from it becomes unclean. 35And everything on which *a part* of *any such* carcass falls shall be unclean; *whether it is* an oven or cooking stove, it shall be broken down; *for they are* unclean, and shall be unclean to you. 36Nevertheless a spring or a cistern, *in* which *there is* plenty of water, shall be clean, but whatever touches any such carcass becomes unclean. 37And if a part of *any such* carcass falls on any planting seed which is to be sown, it *remains* clean. 38But if water is put on the seed, and if *a part* of *any such* carcass falls on it, it *becomes* unclean to you.

39'And if any animal which you may eat dies, he who touches its carcass shall be unclean until evening. 40He who eats of its carcass shall wash his clothes and be unclean until evening. He also who carries its carcass shall wash his clothes and be unclean until evening.

41'And every creeping thing that creeps on the earth *shall be* an abomination. It shall not be eaten. 42Whatever crawls on its belly, whatever goes on *all* fours, or whatever has many feet among all creeping things that creep on the earth—these you shall not eat, for they *are* an abomination. 43You shall not make yourselves abominable with any creeping thing that creeps; nor shall you make yourselves unclean with them, lest you be defiled by them. 44For I *am* the LORD your God. You shall therefore consecrate yourselves, and you shall be holy; for I *am* holy. Neither shall you defile yourselves with any creeping thing that creeps on the earth. 45For I *am* the LORD who brings you up out of the land of Egypt, to be your God. You shall therefore be holy, for I *am* holy.

46'This *is* the law of the animals and the birds and every living creature that moves in the waters, and of every creature that creeps on the earth, 47to distinguish between the unclean and the clean, and between the animal that may be eaten and the animal that may not be eaten.' "

The Ritual After Childbirth

12 Then the LORD spoke to Moses, saying, 2"Speak to the children of Israel, saying: 'If a woman has conceived, and borne a male child, then she shall be unclean seven days; as in the days of her customary impurity she shall be unclean. 3And on the eighth day the flesh of his foreskin shall be circumcised. 4She shall then continue in the blood of *her* purification thirty-three days. She shall not touch any hallowed thing, nor come into the sanctuary until the days of her purification are fulfilled.

5'But if she bears a female child, then she shall be unclean two weeks, as in her customary impurity, and she shall continue in the blood of *her* purification sixty-six days.

6'When the days of her purification are fulfilled, whether for a son or a daughter, she shall bring to the priest a lamb of the first year as a burnt offering, and a young pigeon or a turtledove as a sin offering, to the door of the tabernacle of meeting. 7Then he shall offer it before the LORD, and make atonement for her. And she shall be clean from the flow of her blood. This *is* the law for her who has borne a male or a female.

8'And if she is not able to bring a lamb, then she may bring two turtledoves or two young pigeons—one as a burnt offering and the other as a sin offering. So the priest shall make atonement for her, and she will be clean.' "

The Law Concerning Leprosy

13 And the LORD spoke to Moses and Aaron, saying: 2"When a man has on the skin of his body a swelling, a scab, or a bright spot, and it becomes on the skin of his body *like* a leprous sore, then he shall be brought to Aaron the priest or to one of his sons the priests. 3The priest shall examine the sore on the skin of the body; and if the hair on the sore has turned white, and the sore appears *to be* deeper than the skin of his body, it *is* a leprous sore. Then the priest shall examine him, and pronounce him unclean. 4But if the bright spot *is* white on the skin of his body, and does not appear *to be* deeper than the skin, and its hair has not turned white, then the priest shall isolate *the one who has* the sore seven days. 5And the priest shall examine him on the seventh day; and indeed *if* the sore appears to be as it was, *and* the sore has not spread on the skin, then the priest shall isolate him another seven days. 6Then the priest shall examine him again on the seventh day; and indeed *if* the sore has faded, *and* the sore has not spread on the skin, then the priest shall pronounce him clean; it *is only* a scab, and he shall wash his clothes and be clean. 7But if the scab should at all spread over the skin, after he has been seen by the priest for his cleansing, he shall be seen by the priest again. 8And *if* the priest sees that the scab has indeed spread on the skin, then the priest shall pronounce him unclean. It *is* leprosy.

9"When the leprous sore is on a person, then he shall be brought to the priest. 10And the priest shall examine *him;* and indeed *if* the swelling on the skin *is* white, and it has turned the hair white, and *there is* a spot of raw flesh in the swelling, 11it *is* an old leprosy on the skin of his body. The priest shall pronounce him unclean, and shall not isolate him, for he *is* unclean.

12"And if leprosy breaks out all over the skin, and the leprosy covers all the skin of *the one who has* the sore, from his head to his foot, wherever the priest looks, 13then the priest shall consider; and indeed *if* the leprosy has covered all his body, he shall pronounce *him* clean *who has* the sore. It has all turned white. He *is* clean. 14But when raw flesh appears on him, he shall be unclean. 15And the priest shall examine the raw flesh and pronounce him to be unclean; *for* the raw flesh *is* unclean. It *is* leprosy. 16Or if the raw flesh changes and turns white again, he shall come to the priest. 17And the priest shall examine him; and indeed *if* the sore has turned white, then the priest shall pronounce *him* clean *who has* the sore. He *is* clean.

18"If the body develops a boil in the skin, and it is healed, 19and in the place of the boil there comes a white swelling or a bright spot, reddish-white, then it shall be shown to the priest; 20and *if,* when the priest sees it, it indeed *appears* deeper than the skin, and its hair has turned white, the priest shall pronounce him unclean. It *is* a leprous sore which has broken out of the boil. 21But if the priest examines it, and indeed *there are* no white hairs in it, and it *is* not deeper than the skin, but has faded, then the priest shall isolate him seven days; 22and if it should at all spread over the skin, then the priest shall pronounce him unclean. It *is* a leprous sore. 23But if the bright spot stays in one place, *and* has not spread, it *is* the scar of the boil; and the priest shall pronounce him clean.

24"Or if the body receives a burn on its skin by fire, and the raw *flesh* of the burn becomes a bright spot, reddish-white or white, 25then the priest shall examine it; and indeed *if* the hair of the bright spot has turned white, and it appears deeper than the skin, it *is* leprosy broken out in the burn. Therefore the priest shall pronounce him unclean. It *is* a leprous sore. 26But if the priest examines it, and indeed *there are* no white hairs in the bright spot, and it *is* not deeper than the skin, but has faded, then the priest shall isolate him seven days. 27And the priest shall examine him on the seventh day. If it has at all spread over the skin, then the priest shall pronounce him unclean. It *is* a leprous sore. 28But if the bright spot stays in one place, *and* has not spread on the skin, but has faded, it *is* a swelling from the burn. The priest shall pronounce him clean, for it *is* the scar from the burn.

29"If a man or woman has a sore on the head or the beard, 30then the priest shall examine the sore; and indeed if it appears deeper than the skin, *and there is* in it thin yellow hair, then the priest shall pronounce him unclean. It *is* a scaly leprosy of the head or beard. 31But if the priest examines the scaly sore, and indeed it does not appear deeper than the skin, and *there is* no black hair in it, then the priest shall isolate *the one who has* the scale seven days. 32And on the seventh day the priest shall examine the sore; and indeed *if* the scale has not spread, and there is no yellow hair in it, and the scale does not appear deeper than the skin, 33he shall shave himself, but the scale he shall not shave. And the priest shall isolate *the one who has* the scale another seven days. 34On the seventh day the priest shall examine the scale; and indeed *if* the scale has not spread over the skin, and does not appear deeper than the skin, then the priest shall pronounce him clean. He shall wash his clothes and be clean. 35But if the scale should at all spread over the skin after his cleansing, 36then the priest shall examine him; and indeed *if* the scale has spread over the skin, the priest need not seek for yellow hair. He *is* unclean. 37But if the scale appears to be at a standstill, and there is black hair grown up in it, the scale has healed. He *is* clean, and the priest shall pronounce him clean.

38"If a man or a woman has bright spots on the skin of the body, *specifically* white bright spots, 39then the priest shall look; and indeed *if* the bright spots on the skin of the body *are* dull white, it *is* a white spot *that* grows on the skin. He *is* clean.

40"As for the man whose hair has fallen from his head, he *is* bald, *but* he *is* clean. 41He whose hair has fallen from his forehead, he *is* bald on the forehead, *but* he *is* clean. 42And if there is on the bald head or bald forehead a reddish-white sore, it *is* leprosy breaking out on his bald head or his bald forehead. 43Then the priest shall examine it; and indeed *if* the swelling of the sore *is* reddish-white on his bald head or on his bald forehead, as the appearance of leprosy on the skin of the body, 44he is a leprous man. He *is* unclean. The priest shall surely pronounce him unclean; his sore *is* on his head.

45"Now the leper on whom the sore is, his clothes shall be torn and his head bare; and he shall cover his mustache, and cry, 'Unclean! Unclean!' 46He shall be unclean. All the days he has the sore he shall be unclean. He *is* unclean, and he shall dwell alone; his dwelling *shall be* outside the camp.

The Law Concerning Leprous Garments

47"Also, if a garment has a leprous plague[d] in it, *whether it is* a woolen garment or a linen garment, 48whether *it is* in the warp or woof of linen or wool, whether in leather or in anything made of leather, 49and if the plague is greenish or reddish in the garment or in the leather, whether in the warp or in the woof, or in anything made of leather, it *is* a leprous plague and shall be shown to the priest. 50The priest shall examine the plague and isolate *that which has* the plague seven days. 51And he shall examine the plague on the seventh day. If the plague has spread in the garment, either in the warp or in the woof, in the leather *or* in anything made of leather, the plague *is* an active leprosy. It *is* unclean. 52He shall therefore burn that garment in which is the plague, whether warp or woof, in wool or in linen, or anything of leather, for it *is* an active leprosy; *the garment* shall be burned in the fire.

---

d A mold, fungus, or similar infestation, and so in verses 47-59

53"But if the priest examines *it*, and indeed the plague has not spread in the garment, either in the warp or in the woof, or in anything made of leather, 54then the priest shall command that they wash *the thing* in which *is* the plague; and he shall isolate it another seven days. 55Then the priest shall examine the plague after it has been washed; and indeed *if* the plague has not changed its color, though the plague has not spread, it *is* unclean, and you shall burn it in the fire; it continues eating away, *whether* the damage *is* outside or inside. 56If the priest examines *it*, and indeed the plague has faded after washing it, then he shall tear it out of the garment, whether out of the warp or out of the woof, or out of the leather. 57But if it appears again in the garment, either in the warp or in the woof, or in anything made of leather, it *is* a spreading *plague;* you shall burn with fire that in which is the plague. 58And if you wash the garment, either warp or woof, or whatever is made of leather, if the plague has disappeared from it, then it shall be washed a second time, and shall be clean.

59"This *is* the law of the leprous plague in a garment of wool or linen, either in the warp or woof, or in anything made of leather, to pronounce it clean or to pronounce it unclean."

The Ritual for Cleansing Healed Lepers

14 Then the LORD spoke to Moses, saying, 2"This shall be the law of the leper for the day of his cleansing: He shall be brought to the priest. 3And the priest shall go out of the camp, and the priest shall examine *him;* and indeed, *if* the leprosy is healed in the leper, 4then the priest shall command to take for him who is to be cleansed two living *and* clean birds, cedar wood, scarlet, and hyssop. 5And the priest shall command that one of the birds be killed in an earthen vessel over running water. 6As for the living bird, he shall take it, the cedar wood and the scarlet and the hyssop, and dip them and the living bird in the blood of the bird *that was* killed over the running water. 7And he shall sprinkle it seven times on him who is to be cleansed from the leprosy, and shall pronounce him clean,

and shall let the living bird loose in the open field. 8He who is to be cleansed shall wash his clothes, shave off all his hair, and wash himself in water, that he may be clean. After that he shall come into the camp, and shall stay outside his tent seven days. 9But on the seventh day he shall shave all the hair off his head and his beard and his eyebrows—all his hair he shall shave off. He shall wash his clothes and wash his body in water, and he shall be clean.

10"And on the eighth day he shall take two male lambs without blemish, one ewe lamb of the first year without blemish, three-tenths *of an ephah* of fine flour mixed with oil as a grain offering, and one log of oil. 11Then the priest who makes *him* clean shall present the man who is to be made clean, and those things, before the LORD, *at* the door of the tabernacle of meeting. 12And the priest shall take one male lamb and offer it as a trespass offering, and the log of oil, and wave them *as* a wave offering before the LORD. 13Then he shall kill the lamb in the place where he kills the sin offering and the burnt offering, in a holy place; for as the sin offering *is* the priest's, so *is* the trespass offering. It *is* most holy. 14The priest shall take *some* of the blood of the trespass offering, and the priest shall put *it* on the tip of the right ear of him who is to be cleansed, on the thumb of his right hand, and on the big toe of his right foot. 15And the priest shall take *some* of the log of oil, and pour *it* into the palm of his own left hand. 16Then the priest shall dip his right finger in the oil that *is* in his left hand, and shall sprinkle some of the oil with his finger seven times before the LORD. 17And of the rest of the oil in his hand, the priest shall put *some* on the tip of the right ear of him who is to be cleansed, on the thumb of his right hand, and on the big toe of his right foot, on the blood of the trespass offering. 18The rest of the oil that *is* in the priest's hand he shall put on the head of him who is to be cleansed. So the priest shall make atonement for him before the LORD.

19"Then the priest shall offer the sin offering, and make atonement for him who is to be cleansed from his uncleanness. Afterward he shall kill the burnt offering. 20And the priest shall offer the burnt offering and the grain offering on the altar. So the priest shall make atonement for him, and he shall be clean.

21"But if he *is* poor and cannot afford it, then he shall take one male lamb *as* a trespass offering to be waved, to make atonement for him, one-tenth *of an ephah* of fine flour mixed with oil as a grain offering, a log of oil, 22and two turtledoves or two young pigeons, such as he is able to afford: one shall be a sin offering and the other a burnt offering. 23He shall bring them to the priest on the eighth day for his cleansing, to the door of the tabernacle of meeting, before the LORD. 24And the priest shall take the lamb of the trespass offering and the log of oil, and the priest shall wave them *as* a wave offering before the LORD. 25Then he shall kill the lamb of the trespass offering, and the priest shall take *some* of the blood of the trespass offering and put *it* on the tip of the right ear of him who is to be cleansed, on the thumb of his right hand, and on the big toe of his right foot. 26And the priest shall pour some of the oil into the palm of his own left hand. 27Then the priest shall sprinkle with his right finger *some* of the oil that *is* in his left hand seven times before the LORD. 28And the priest shall put *some* of the oil that *is* in his hand on the tip of the right ear of him who is to be cleansed, on the thumb of the right hand, and on the big toe of his right foot, on the place of the blood of the trespass offering. 29The rest of the oil that *is* in the priest's hand he shall put on the head of him who is to be cleansed, to make atonement for him before the LORD. 30And he shall offer one of the turtledoves or young pigeons, such as he can afford—31such as he is able to afford, the one *as* a sin offering and the other *as* a burnt offering, with the grain offering. So the priest shall make atonement for him who is to be cleansed before the LORD. 32This *is* the law *for one* who had a leprous sore, who cannot afford the usual cleansing."

The Law Concerning Leprous Houses

33And the LORD spoke to Moses and Aaron, saying: 34"When you have come into the land of Canaan, which I give you as a possession, and I put the leprous plague[e] in a house in the land of your possession, 35and he who owns the house comes and tells the priest, saying, 'It seems to me that *there is* some plague in the house,' 36then the priest shall command that they empty the house, before the priest goes *into* it to examine the plague, that all that *is* in the house may not be made unclean; and afterward the priest shall go in to examine the house. 37And he shall examine the plague; and indeed *if* the plague *is* on the walls of the house with ingrained streaks, greenish or reddish, which appear to be deep in the wall, 38then the priest shall go out of the house, to the door of the house, and shut up the house seven days. 39And the priest shall come again on the seventh day and look; and indeed *if* the plague has spread on the walls of the house, 40then the priest shall command that they take away the stones in which *is* the plague, and they shall cast them into an unclean place outside the city. 41And he shall cause the house to be scraped inside, all around, and the dust that they scrape off they shall pour out in an unclean place outside the city. 42Then they shall take other stones and put *them* in the place of *those* stones, and he shall take other mortar and plaster the house.

43"Now if the plague comes back and breaks out in the house, after he has taken away the stones, after he has scraped the house, and after it is plastered, 44then the priest shall come and look; and indeed *if* the plague has spread in the house, it *is* an active leprosy in the house. It *is* unclean. 45And he shall break down the house, its stones, its timber, and all the plaster of the house, and he shall carry *them* outside the city to an unclean place. 46Moreover he who goes into the house at all while it is shut up shall be unclean until evening. 47And he who lies down

---

e Decomposition by mildew, mold, dry rot, etc., and so in verses 34-53 in the house shall wash his clothes, and he who eats in the house shall wash his clothes.

48"But if the priest comes in and examines *it*, and indeed the plague has not spread in the house after the house was plastered, then the priest shall pronounce the house clean, because the plague is healed. 49And he shall take, to cleanse the house, two birds, cedar wood, scarlet, and hyssop. 50Then he shall kill one of the birds in an earthen vessel over running water; 51and he shall take the cedar wood, the hyssop, the scarlet, and the living bird, and dip them in the blood of the slain bird and in the running water, and sprinkle the house seven times. 52And he shall cleanse the house with the blood of the bird and the running water and the living bird, with the cedar wood, the hyssop, and the scarlet. 53Then he shall let the living bird loose outside the city in the open field, and make atonement for the house, and it shall be clean.

54"This *is* the law for any leprous sore and scale, 55for the leprosy of a garment and of a house, 56for a swelling and a scab and a bright spot, 57to teach when *it is* unclean and when *it is* clean. This *is* the law of leprosy."

The Law Concerning Bodily Discharges

15 And the LORD spoke to Moses and Aaron, saying, 2"Speak to the children of Israel, and say to them: 'When any man has a discharge from his body, his discharge *is* unclean. 3And this shall be his uncleanness in regard to his discharge—whether his body runs with his discharge, or his body is stopped up by his discharge, it *is* his uncleanness. 4Every bed is unclean on which he who has the discharge lies, and everything on which he sits shall be unclean. 5And whoever touches his bed shall wash his clothes and bathe in water, and be unclean until evening. 6He who sits on anything on which he who has the discharge sat shall wash his clothes and bathe in water, and be unclean until evening. 7And he who touches the body of him who has the discharge shall wash his clothes and bathe in water, and be unclean until evening. 8If he who has the discharge spits on him who is clean, then he shall wash his clothes and bathe in water, and be unclean until evening. 9Any saddle on which he who has the discharge rides shall be unclean. 10Whoever touches anything that was under him shall be unclean until evening. He who carries *any of* those things shall wash his clothes and bathe in water, and be unclean until evening. 11And whomever the one who has the discharge touches, and has not rinsed his hands in water, he shall wash his clothes and bathe in water, and be unclean until evening. 12The vessel of earth that he who has the discharge touches shall be broken, and every vessel of wood shall be rinsed in water.

13'And when he who has a discharge is cleansed of his discharge, then he shall count for himself seven days for his cleansing, wash his clothes, and bathe his body in running water; then he shall be clean. 14On the eighth day he shall take for himself two turtledoves or two young pigeons, and come before the LORD, to the door of the tabernacle of meeting, and give them to the priest. 15Then the priest shall offer them, the one *as* a sin offering and the other *as* a burnt offering. So the priest shall make atonement for him before the LORD because of his discharge.

16'If any man has an emission of semen, then he shall wash all his body in water, and be unclean until evening. 17And any garment and any leather on which there is semen, it shall be washed with water, and be unclean until evening. 18Also, when a woman lies with a man, and *there is* an emission of semen, they shall bathe in water, and be unclean until evening.

19'If a woman has a discharge, *and* the discharge from her body is blood, she shall be set apart seven days; and whoever touches her shall be unclean until evening. 20Everything that she lies on during her impurity shall be unclean; also everything that she sits on shall be unclean. 21Whoever touches her bed shall wash his clothes and bathe in water, and be unclean until evening. 22And whoever touches anything that she sat on shall wash his clothes and bathe in water, and be unclean until evening. 23If *anything* is on *her* bed or on anything on which she sits, when he touches it, he shall be unclean until evening. 24And if any man lies with her at all, so that her impurity is on him, he shall be unclean seven days; and every bed on which he lies shall be unclean.

25'If a woman has a discharge of blood for many days, other than at the time of her *customary* impurity, or if it runs beyond her *usual time of* impurity, all the days of her unclean discharge shall be as the days of her *customary* impurity. She *shall be* unclean. 26Every bed on which she lies all the days of her discharge shall be to her as the bed of her impurity; and whatever she sits on shall be unclean, as the uncleanness of her impurity. 27Whoever touches those things shall be unclean; he shall wash his clothes and bathe in water, and be unclean until evening.

28'But if she is cleansed of her discharge, then she shall count for herself seven days, and after that she shall be clean. 29And on the eighth day she shall take for herself two turtledoves or two young pigeons, and bring them to the priest, to the door of the tabernacle of meeting. 30Then the priest shall offer the one *as* a sin offering and the other *as* a burnt offering, and the priest shall make atonement for her before the LORD for the discharge of her uncleanness.

31'Thus you shall separate the children of Israel from their uncleanness, lest they die in their uncleanness when they defile My tabernacle that *is* among them. 32This *is* the law for one who has a discharge, and *for him* who emits semen and is unclean thereby, 33and for her who is indisposed because of her *customary* impurity, and for one who has a discharge, either man or woman, and for him who lies with her who is unclean.' "

The Day of Atonement

16 Now the LORD spoke to Moses after the death of the two sons of Aaron, when they offered *profane fire* before the LORD, and died; 2and the LORD said to Moses: "Tell Aaron your brother not to come at *just* any time into the Holy *Place* inside the veil, before the mercy seat which *is* on the ark, lest

he die; for I will appear in the cloud above the mercy seat.

3"Thus Aaron shall come into the Holy *Place:* with *the blood of* a young bull as a sin offering, and *of* a ram as a burnt offering. 4He shall put the holy linen tunic and the linen trousers on his body; he shall be girded with a linen sash, and with the linen turban he shall be attired. These *are* holy garments. Therefore he shall wash his body in water, and put them on. 5And he shall take from the congregation of the children of Israel two kids of the goats as a sin offering, and one ram as a burnt offering.

6"Aaron shall offer the bull as a sin offering, which *is* for himself, and make atonement for himself and for his house. 7He shall take the two goats and present them before the LORD *at* the door of the tabernacle of meeting. 8Then Aaron shall cast lots for the two goats: one lot for the LORD and the other lot for the scapegoat. 9And Aaron shall bring the goat on which the LORD's lot fell, and offer it *as* a sin offering. 10But the goat on which the lot fell to be the scapegoat shall be presented alive before the LORD, to make atonement upon it, *and* to let it go as the scapegoat into the wilderness.

11"And Aaron shall bring the bull of the sin offering, which is for himself, and make atonement for himself and for his house, and shall kill the bull as the sin offering which *is* for himself. 12Then he shall take a censer full of burning coals of fire from the altar before the LORD, with his hands full of sweet incense beaten fine, and bring *it* inside the veil. 13And he shall put the incense on the fire before the LORD, that the cloud of incense may cover the mercy seat that *is* on the Testimony, lest he die. 14He shall take some of the blood of the bull and sprinkle *it* with his finger on the mercy seat on the east *side;* and before the mercy seat he shall sprinkle some of the blood with his finger seven times.

15"Then he shall kill the goat of the sin offering, which *is* for the people, bring its blood inside the veil, do with that blood as he did with the blood of the bull, and sprinkle it on the mercy seat and before the mercy seat.

16So he shall make atonement for the Holy *Place*, because of the uncleanness of the children of Israel, and because of their transgressions, for all their sins; and so he shall do for the tabernacle of meeting which remains among them in the midst of their uncleanness. 17There shall be no man in the tabernacle of meeting when he goes in to make atonement in the Holy *Place*, until he comes out, that he may make atonement for himself, for his household, and for all the assembly of Israel. 18And he shall go out to the altar that *is* before the LORD, and make atonement for it, and shall take some of the blood of the bull and some of the blood of the goat, and put it on the horns of the altar all around. 19Then he shall sprinkle some of the blood on it with his finger seven times, cleanse it, and consecrate it from the uncleanness of the children of Israel.

20"And when he has made an end of atoning for the Holy *Place*, the tabernacle of meeting, and the altar, he shall bring the live goat. 21Aaron shall lay both his hands on the head of the live goat, confess over it all the iniquities of the children of Israel, and all their transgressions, concerning all their sins, putting them on the head of the goat, and shall send *it* away into the wilderness by the hand of a suitable man. 22The goat shall bear on itself all their iniquities to an uninhabited land; and he shall release the goat in the wilderness.

23"Then Aaron shall come into the tabernacle of meeting, shall take off the linen garments which he put on when he went into the Holy *Place*, and shall leave them there. 24And he shall wash his body with water in a holy place, put on his garments, come out and offer his burnt offering and the burnt offering of the people, and make atonement for himself and for the people. 25The fat of the sin offering he shall burn on the altar. 26And he who released the goat as the scapegoat shall wash his clothes and bathe his body in water, and afterward he may come into the camp. 27The bull *for* the sin offering and the goat *for* the sin offering, whose blood

was brought in to make atonement in the Holy *Place*, shall be carried outside the camp. And they shall burn in the fire their skins, their flesh, and their offal. 28Then he who burns them shall wash his clothes and bathe his body in water, and afterward he may come into the camp.

29"*This* shall be a statute forever for you: In the seventh month, on the tenth *day* of the month, you shall afflict your souls, and do no work at all, *whether* a native of your own country or a stranger who dwells among you. 30For on that day *the priest* shall make atonement for you, to cleanse you, *that* you may be clean from all your sins before the LORD. 31It *is* a sabbath of solemn rest for you, and you shall afflict your souls. *It is* a statute forever. 32And the priest, who is anointed and consecrated to minister as priest in his father's place, shall make atonement, and put on the linen clothes, the holy garments; 33then he shall make atonement for the Holy Sanctuary,*f* and he shall make atonement for the tabernacle of meeting and for the altar, and he shall make atonement for the priests and for all the people of the assembly. 34This shall be an everlasting statute for you, to make atonement for the children of Israel, for all their sins, once a year." And he did as the LORD commanded Moses.

The Sanctity of Blood

17 And the LORD spoke to Moses, saying, 2"Speak to Aaron, to his sons, and to all the children of Israel, and say to them, 'This *is* the thing which the LORD has commanded, saying: 3"Whatever man of the house of Israel who kills an ox or lamb or goat in the camp, or who kills *it* outside the camp, 4and does not bring it to the door of the tabernacle of meeting to offer an offering to the LORD before the tabernacle of the LORD, the guilt of bloodshed shall be imputed to that man. He has shed blood; and that man shall be cut off from among his people, 5to the end that the children of Israel may bring their sacrifices which they offer in the open field, that they may bring them to the LORD at the door of the tabernacle of

f That is, the Most Holy Place

meeting, to the priest, and offer them *as* peace offerings to the LORD. 6And the priest shall sprinkle the blood on the altar of the LORD *at* the door of the tabernacle of meeting, and burn the fat for a sweet aroma to the LORD. 7They shall no more offer their sacrifices to demons, after whom they have played the harlot. This shall be a statute forever for them throughout their generations." '

8"Also you shall say to them: 'Whatever man of the house of Israel, or of the strangers who dwell among you, who offers a burnt offering or sacrifice, 9and does not bring it to the door of the tabernacle of meeting, to offer it to the LORD, that man shall be cut off from among his people.

10'And whatever man of the house of Israel, or of the strangers who dwell among you, who eats any blood, I will set My face against that person who eats blood, and will cut him off from among his people. 11For the life of the flesh *is* in the blood, and I have given it to you upon the altar to make atonement for your souls; for it *is* the blood *that* makes atonement for the soul.' 12Therefore I said to the children of Israel, 'No one among you shall eat blood, nor shall any stranger who dwells among you eat blood.'

13"Whatever man of the children of Israel, or of the strangers who dwell among you, who hunts and catches any animal or bird that may be eaten, he shall pour out its blood and cover it with dust; 14for *it is* the life of all flesh. Its blood sustains its life. Therefore I said to the children of Israel, 'You shall not eat the blood of any flesh, for the life of all flesh is its blood. Whoever eats it shall be cut off.'

15"And every person who eats what died *naturally* or what was torn *by beasts*, *whether he is* a native of your own country or a stranger, he shall both wash his clothes and bathe in water, and be unclean until evening. Then he shall be clean. 16But if he does not wash *them* or bathe his body, then he shall bear his guilt."

Laws of Sexual Morality

18 Then the LORD spoke to Moses, saying, 2"Speak to the children of Israel, and say to them: 'I am the LORD your God. 3According to the doings of the land of Egypt, where you dwelt, you shall not do; and according to the doings of the land of Canaan, where I am bringing you, you shall not do; nor shall you walk in their ordinances. 4You shall observe My judgments and keep My ordinances, to walk in them: I *am* the LORD your God. 5You shall therefore keep My statutes and My judgments, which if a man does, he shall live by them: I *am* the LORD.

6'None of you shall approach anyone who is near of kin to him, to uncover his nakedness: I *am* the LORD. 7The nakedness of your father or the nakedness of your mother you shall not uncover. She *is* your mother; you shall not uncover her nakedness. 8The nakedness of your father's wife you shall not uncover; it *is* your father's nakedness. 9The nakedness of your sister, the daughter of your father, or the daughter of your mother, *whether* born at home or elsewhere, their nakedness you shall not uncover. 10The nakedness of your son's daughter or your daughter's daughter, their nakedness you shall not uncover; for theirs *is* your own nakedness. 11The nakedness of your father's wife's daughter, begotten by your father—she *is* your sister—you shall not uncover her nakedness. 12You shall not uncover the nakedness of your father's sister; she *is* near of kin to your father. 13You shall not uncover the nakedness of your mother's sister, for she *is* near of kin to your mother. 14You shall not uncover the nakedness of your father's brother. You shall not approach his wife; she *is* your aunt. 15You shall not uncover the nakedness of your daughter-in-law—she *is* your son's wife—you shall not uncover her nakedness. 16You shall not uncover the nakedness of your brother's wife; it *is* your brother's nakedness. 17You shall not uncover the nakedness of a woman and her daughter, nor shall you take her son's daughter or her daughter's daughter, to uncover her nakedness. They *are* near of kin to her. It *is* wickedness. 18Nor shall you take a woman as a rival to her sister, to uncover her nakedness while the other is alive.

19'Also you shall not approach a

woman to uncover her nakedness as long as she is in her *customary* impurity. 20Moreover you shall not lie carnally with your neighbor's wife, to defile yourself with her. 21And you shall not let any of your descendants pass through *the fire* to Molech, nor shall you profane the name of your God: I *am* the LORD. 22You shall not lie with a male as with a woman. It *is* an abomination. 23Nor shall you mate with any animal, to defile yourself with it. Nor shall any woman stand before an animal to mate with it. It *is* perversion.

24'Do not defile yourselves with any of these things; for by all these the nations are defiled, which I am casting out before you. 25For the land is defiled; therefore I visit the punishment of its iniquity upon it, and the land vomits out its inhabitants. 26You shall therefore keep My statutes and My judgments, and shall not commit *any* of these abominations, *either* any of your own nation or any stranger who dwells among you 27(for all these abominations the men of the land have done, who *were* before you, and thus the land is defiled), 28lest the land vomit you out also when you defile it, as it vomited out the nations that *were* before you. 29For whoever commits any of these abominations, the persons who commit *them* shall be cut off from among their people.

30'Therefore you shall keep My ordinance, so that *you* do not commit *any* of these abominable customs which were committed before you, and that you do not defile yourselves by them: I *am* the LORD your God.'"

Moral and Ceremonial Laws

19 And the LORD spoke to Moses, saying, 2"Speak to all the congregation of the children of Israel, and say to them: 'You shall be holy, for I the LORD your God *am* holy.

3'Every one of you shall revere his mother and his father, and keep My Sabbaths: I *am* the LORD your God.

4'Do not turn to idols, nor make for yourselves molded gods: I *am* the LORD your God.

5'And if you offer a sacrifice of a peace offering to the LORD, you shall offer it of your own free will. 6It shall be eaten the same day you offer *it*, and on the next day. And if any remains until the third day, it shall be burned in the fire. 7And if it is eaten at all on the third day, it *is* an abomination. It shall not be accepted. 8Therefore *everyone* who eats it shall bear his iniquity, because he has profaned the hallowed *offering* of the LORD; and that person shall be cut off from his people.

9'When you reap the harvest of your land, you shall not wholly reap the corners of your field, nor shall you gather the gleanings of your harvest. 10And you shall not glean your vineyard, nor shall you gather *every* grape of your vineyard; you shall leave them for the poor and the stranger: I *am* the LORD your God.

11'You shall not steal, nor deal falsely, nor lie to one another. 12And you shall not swear by My name falsely, nor shall you profane the name of your God: I *am* the LORD.

13'You shall not cheat your neighbor, nor rob *him*. The wages of him who is hired shall not remain with you all night until morning. 14You shall not curse the deaf, nor put a stumbling block before the blind, but shall fear your God: I *am* the LORD.

15'You shall do no injustice in judgment. You shall not be partial to the poor, nor honor the person of the mighty. In righteousness you shall judge your neighbor. 16You shall not go about *as* a talebearer among your people; nor shall you take a stand against the life of your neighbor: I *am* the LORD.

17'You shall not hate your brother in your heart. You shall surely rebuke your neighbor, and not bear sin because of him. 18You shall not take vengeance, nor bear any grudge against the children of your people, but you shall love your neighbor as yourself: I *am* the LORD.

19'You shall keep My statutes. You shall not let your livestock breed with another kind. You shall not sow your field with mixed seed. Nor shall a garment of mixed linen and wool come upon you.

20'Whoever lies carnally with a woman who *is* betrothed to a man as a concubine, and who has not at all been redeemed nor given her freedom, for this there shall be scourging; *but* they shall not be put to death, because she was not free. 21And he shall bring his trespass offering to the LORD, to the door of the tabernacle of meeting, a ram as a trespass offering. 22The priest shall make atonement for him with the ram of the trespass offering before the LORD for his sin which he has committed. And the sin which he has committed shall be forgiven him.

23'When you come into the land, and have planted all kinds of trees for food, then you shall count their fruit as uncircumcised. Three years it shall be as uncircumcised to you. *It* shall not be eaten. 24But in the fourth year all its fruit shall be holy, a praise to the LORD. 25And in the fifth year you may eat its fruit, that it may yield to you its increase: I *am* the LORD your God.

26'You shall not eat *anything* with the blood, nor shall you practice divination or soothsaying. 27You shall not shave around the sides of your head, nor shall you disfigure the edges of your beard. 28You shall not make any cuttings in your flesh for the dead, nor tattoo any marks on you: I *am* the LORD.

29'Do not prostitute your daughter, to cause her to be a harlot, lest the land fall into harlotry, and the land become full of wickedness.

30'You shall keep My Sabbaths and reverence My sanctuary: I *am* the LORD.

31'Give no regard to mediums and familiar spirits; do not seek after them, to be defiled by them: I *am* the LORD your God.

32'You shall rise before the gray headed and honor the presence of an old man, and fear your God: I *am* the LORD.

33'And if a stranger dwells with you in your land, you shall not mistreat him. 34The stranger who dwells among you shall be to you as one born among you, and you shall love him as yourself; for you were strangers in the land of Egypt: I *am* the LORD your God.

35'You shall do no injustice in judgment, in measurement of length, weight, or volume. 36You shall have honest scales, honest weights, an honest ephah, and an honest hin: I *am* the LORD your God, who brought you out of the land of Egypt.

37'Therefore you shall observe all My statutes and all My judgments, and perform them: I *am* the LORD.' "

Penalties for Breaking the Law

20 Then the LORD spoke to Moses, saying, 2"Again, you shall say to the children of Israel: 'Whoever of the children of Israel, or of the strangers who dwell in Israel, who gives *any* of his descendants to Molech, he shall surely be put to death. The people of the land shall stone him with stones. 3I will set My face against that man, and will cut him off from his people, because he has given *some* of his descendants to Molech, to defile My sanctuary and profane My holy name. 4And if the people of the land should in any way hide their eyes from the man, when he gives *some* of his descendants to Molech, and they do not kill him, 5then I will set My face against that man and against his family; and I will cut him off from his people, and all who prostitute themselves with him to commit harlotry with Molech.

6'And the person who turns to mediums and familiar spirits, to prostitute himself with them, I will set My face against that person and cut him off from his people. 7Consecrate yourselves therefore, and be holy, for I *am* the LORD your God. 8And you shall keep My statutes, and perform them: I *am* the LORD who sanctifies you.

9'For everyone who curses his father or his mother shall surely be put to death. He has cursed his father or his mother. His blood *shall be* upon him.

10'The man who commits adultery with *another* man's wife, *he* who commits adultery with his neighbor's wife, the adulterer and the adulteress, shall surely be put to death. 11The man who lies with his father's wife has uncovered his father's nakedness; both of them shall surely be put to death. Their blood *shall be* upon them. 12If a man lies with his daughter-in-law, both of them shall surely be put to death. They have committed perversion. Their blood *shall be* upon them. 13If a man lies with a male as he lies with a woman, both of them have committed an abomination. They shall surely be put to death. Their blood *shall be* upon them. 14If a man marries a woman and her mother, it *is* wickedness. They shall be burned with fire, both he and they, that there may be no wickedness among you. 15If a man mates with an animal, he shall surely be put to death, and you shall kill the animal. 16If a woman approaches any animal and mates with it, you shall kill the woman and the animal. They shall surely be put to death. Their blood *is* upon them.

17'If a man takes his sister, his father's daughter or his mother's daughter, and sees her nakedness and she sees his nakedness, it *is* a wicked thing. And they shall be cut off in the sight of their people. He has uncovered his sister's nakedness. He shall bear his guilt. 18If a man lies with a woman during her sickness and uncovers her nakedness, he has exposed her flow, and she has uncovered the flow of her blood. Both of them shall be cut off from their people.

19'You shall not uncover the nakedness of your mother's sister nor of your father's sister, for that would uncover his near of kin. They shall bear their guilt. 20If a man lies with his uncle's wife, he has uncovered his uncle's nakedness. They shall bear their sin; they shall die childless. 21If a man takes his brother's wife, it *is* an unclean thing. He has uncovered his brother's nakedness. They shall be childless.

22'You shall therefore keep all My statutes and all My judgments, and perform them, that the land where I am bringing you to dwell may not vomit you out. 23And you shall not walk in the statutes of the nation which I am casting out before you; for they commit all these things, and therefore I abhor them. 24But I have said to you, "You shall inherit their land, and I will give it to you to possess, a land flowing with milk and honey." I *am* the Lord your God, who has separated you from the peoples. 25You shall therefore distinguish between clean animals and unclean, between unclean birds and clean, and you shall not make yourselves abominable by beast or by bird, or by any kind of living thing that creeps on the ground, which I have separated from you as unclean. 26And you shall be holy to Me, for I the Lord *am* holy,

and have separated you from the peoples, that you should be Mine.

27'A man or a woman who is a medium, or who has familiar spirits, shall surely be put to death; they shall stone them with stones. Their blood *shall be* upon them.' "

Regulations for Conduct of Priests

21 And the Lord said to Moses, "Speak to the priests, the sons of Aaron, and say to them: 'None shall defile himself for the dead among his people, 2except for his relatives who are nearest to him: his mother, his father, his son, his daughter, and his brother; 3also his virgin sister who is near to him, who has had no husband, for her he may defile himself. 4*Otherwise* he shall not defile himself, *being* a chief man among his people, to profane himself.

5'They shall not make any bald *place* on their heads, nor shall they shave the edges of their beards nor make any cuttings in their flesh. 6They shall be holy to their God and not profane the name of their God, for they offer the offerings of the Lord made by fire, *and* the bread of their God; therefore they shall be holy. 7They shall not take a wife *who is* a harlot or a defiled woman, nor shall they take a woman divorced from her husband; for *the priest* is holy to his God. 8Therefore you shall consecrate him, for he offers the bread of your God. He shall be holy to you, for I the Lord, who sanctify you, *am* holy. 9The daughter of any priest, if she profanes herself by playing the harlot, she profanes her father. She shall be burned with fire.

10'*He who is* the high priest among his brethren, on whose head the anointing oil was poured and who is consecrated to wear the garments, shall not uncover his head nor tear his clothes; 11nor shall he go near any dead body, nor defile himself for his father or his mother; 12nor shall he go out of the sanctuary, nor profane the sanctuary of his God; for the consecration of the anointing oil of his God *is* upon him: I *am* the Lord. 13And he shall take a wife in her virginity. 14A widow or a divorced woman or a defiled woman *or* a harlot—these he shall not marry; but he shall take a virgin of his own people as wife. 15Nor shall he profane his posterity among his people, for I the LORD sanctify him.' "

16And the LORD spoke to Moses, saying, 17"Speak to Aaron, saying: 'No man of your descendants in *succeeding* generations, who has *any* defect, may approach to offer the bread of his God. 18For any man who has a defect shall not approach: a man blind or lame, who has a marred *face* or any *limb* too long, 19a man who has a broken foot or broken hand, 20or is a hunchback or a dwarf, or *a man* who has a defect in his eye, or eczema or scab, or is a eunuch. 21No man of the descendants of Aaron the priest, who has a defect, shall come near to offer the offerings made by fire to the LORD. He has a defect; he shall not come near to offer the bread of his God. 22He may eat the bread of his God, *both* the most holy and the holy; 23only he shall not go near the veil or approach the altar, because he has a defect, lest he profane My sanctuaries; for I the LORD sanctify them.' "

24And Moses told *it* to Aaron and his sons, and to all the children of Israel.

22 Then the LORD spoke to Moses, saying, 2"Speak to Aaron and his sons, that they separate themselves from the holy things of the children of Israel, and that they do not profane My holy name *by* what they dedicate to Me: I *am* the LORD. 3Say to them: 'Whoever of all your descendants throughout your generations, who goes near the holy things which the children of Israel dedicate to the LORD, while he has uncleanness upon him, that person shall be cut off from My presence: I *am* the LORD.

4'Whatever man of the descendants of Aaron, who *is* a leper or has a discharge, shall not eat the holy offerings until he is clean. And whoever touches anything made unclean *by* a corpse, or a man who has had an emission of semen, 5or whoever touches any creeping thing by which he would be made unclean, or any person by whom he would become unclean, whatever his uncleanness may be—6the person who has touched any such thing shall be unclean until evening, and shall not eat the holy

offerings unless he washes his body with water. 7And when the sun goes down he shall be clean; and afterward he may eat the holy *offerings*, because it *is* his food. 8Whatever dies *naturally* or is torn *by beasts* he shall not eat, to defile himself with it: I *am* the LORD.

9'They shall therefore keep My ordinance, lest they bear sin for it and die thereby, if they profane it: I the LORD sanctify them.

10'No outsider shall eat the holy *offering*; one who dwells with the priest, or a hired servant, shall not eat the holy thing. 11But if the priest buys a person with his money, he may eat it; and one who is born in his house may eat his food. 12If the priest's daughter is married to an outsider, she may not eat of the holy offerings. 13But if the priest's daughter is a widow or divorced, and has no child, and has returned to her father's house as in her youth, she may eat her father's food; but no outsider shall eat it.

14'And if a man eats the holy *offering* unintentionally, then he shall restore a holy *offering* to the priest, and add one-fifth to it. 15They shall not profane the holy *offerings* of the children of Israel, which they offer to the LORD, 16or allow them to bear the guilt of trespass when they eat their holy *offerings*; for I the LORD sanctify them.' "

Offerings Accepted and Not Accepted

17And the LORD spoke to Moses, saying, 18"Speak to Aaron and his sons, and to all the children of Israel, and say to them: 'Whatever man of the house of Israel, or of the strangers in Israel, who offers his sacrifice for any of his vows or for any of his freewill offerings, which they offer to the LORD as a burnt offering—19you shall offer of your own free will a male without blemish from the cattle, from the sheep, or from the goats. 20Whatever has a defect, you shall not offer, for it shall not be acceptable on your behalf. 21And whoever offers a sacrifice of a peace offering to the LORD, to fulfill *his* vow, or a freewill offering from the cattle or the sheep, it must be perfect to be accepted; there shall be no defect in it. 22Those *that are* blind or broken or maimed, or have an ulcer or eczema or scabs, you shall not offer to the LORD, nor make an offering by fire of them on the altar to the LORD. 23Either a bull or a lamb that has any limb too long or too short you may offer *as* a freewill offering, but for a vow it shall not be accepted.

24'You shall not offer to the LORD what is bruised or crushed, or torn or cut; nor shall you make *any offering of them* in your land. 25Nor from a foreigner's hand shall you offer any of these as the bread of your God, because their corruption *is* in them, *and* defects *are* in them. They shall not be accepted on your behalf.' "

26And the LORD spoke to Moses, saying: 27"When a bull or a sheep or a goat is born, it shall be seven days with its mother; and from the eighth day and thereafter it shall be accepted as an offering made by fire to the LORD. 28*Whether it is* a cow or ewe, do not kill both her and her young on the same day. 29And when you offer a sacrifice of thanksgiving to the LORD, offer *it* of your own free will. 30On the same day it shall be eaten; you shall leave none of it until morning: I *am* the LORD.

31"Therefore you shall keep My commandments, and perform them: I *am* the LORD. 32You shall not profane My holy name, but I will be hallowed among the children of Israel. I *am* the LORD who sanctifies you, 33who brought you out of the land of Egypt, to be your God: I *am* the LORD."

Feasts of the LORD

23 And the LORD spoke to Moses, saying, 2"Speak to the children of Israel, and say to them: 'The feasts of the LORD, which you shall proclaim *to be* holy convocations, these *are* My feasts.

The Sabbath

3'Six days shall work be done, but the seventh day *is* a Sabbath of solemn rest, a holy convocation. You shall do no work *on it;* it *is* the Sabbath of the LORD in all your dwellings.

The Passover and Unleavened Bread

4'These *are* the feasts of the LORD, holy convocations which you shall proclaim at their appointed times. 5On the fourteenth *day* of the first month at twilight *is* the LORD's Passover. 6And on the fifteenth day of the same month *is* the Feast of Unleavened Bread to the LORD; seven days you must eat unleavened bread. 7On the first day you shall have a holy convocation; you shall do no customary work on it. 8But you shall offer an offering made by fire to the LORD for seven days. The seventh day *shall be* a holy convocation; you shall do no customary work *on it.*' "

The Feast of Firstfruits

9And the LORD spoke to Moses, saying, 10"Speak to the children of Israel, and say to them: 'When you come into the land which I give to you, and reap its harvest, then you shall bring a sheaf of the firstfruits of your harvest to the priest. 11He shall wave the sheaf before the LORD, to be accepted on your behalf; on the day after the Sabbath the priest shall wave it. 12And you shall offer on that day, when you wave the sheaf, a male lamb of the first year, without blemish, as a burnt offering to the LORD. 13Its grain offering *shall be* two-tenths *of an ephah* of fine flour mixed with oil, an offering made by fire to the LORD, for a sweet aroma; and its drink offering *shall be* of wine, one-fourth of a hin. 14You shall eat neither bread nor parched grain nor fresh grain until the same day that you have brought an offering to your God; *it shall be* a statute forever throughout your generations in all your dwellings.

The Feast of Weeks

15'And you shall count for yourselves from the day after the Sabbath, from the day that you brought the sheaf of the wave offering: seven Sabbaths shall be completed. 16Count fifty days to the day after the seventh Sabbath; then you shall offer a new grain offering to the LORD. 17You shall bring from your dwellings two wave *loaves* of two-tenths *of an ephah.* They shall be of fine flour; they shall be baked with leaven. *They are* the firstfruits to the LORD. 18And you shall offer with the bread seven lambs of the first year, without blemish, one young bull, and two rams. They shall be *as* a burnt offering to the LORD, with their grain offering and their drink offerings, an offering made by fire for a sweet aroma to the LORD. 19Then you shall sacrifice one kid of the goats as a sin offering, and two male lambs of the first year as a sacrifice of a peace offering. 20The priest shall wave them with the bread of the first-fruits *as* a wave offering before the LORD, with the two lambs. They shall be holy to the LORD for the priest. 21And you shall proclaim on the same day *that* it is a holy convocation to you. You shall do no customary work *on it.* *It shall be* a statute forever in all your dwellings throughout your generations.

22'When you reap the harvest of your land, you shall not wholly reap the corners of your field when you reap, nor shall you gather any gleaning from your harvest. You shall leave them for the poor and for the stranger: I *am* the LORD your God.' ''

The Feast of Trumpets

23Then the LORD spoke to Moses, saying, 24"Speak to the children of Israel, saying: 'In the seventh month, on the first *day* of the month, you shall have a sabbath-*rest*, a memorial of blowing of trumpets, a holy convocation. 25You shall do no customary work *on it;* and you shall offer an offering made by fire to the LORD.' ''

The Day of Atonement

26And the LORD spoke to Moses, saying; 27"Also the tenth *day* of this seventh month *shall be* the Day of Atonement. It shall be a holy convocation for you; you shall afflict your souls, and offer an offering made by fire to the LORD. 28And you shall do no work on that same day, for it *is* the Day of Atonement, to make atonement for you before the LORD your God. 29For any person who is not afflicted *in soul* on that same day shall be cut off from his people. 30And any person who does any work on that same day, that person I will destroy from among his people. 31You shall do no manner of work; *it shall be* a statute forever throughout your generations in all your dwellings. 32It *shall be* to you a sabbath of *solemn* rest, and you shall afflict your souls; on the ninth *day* of the month at evening, from evening to evening, you shall celebrate your sabbath.''

The Feast of Tabernacles

33Then the LORD spoke to Moses, saying, 34"Speak to the children of Israel, saying: 'The fifteenth day of this seventh month *shall be* the Feast of Tabernacles *for* seven days to the LORD. 35On the first day *there shall be* a holy convocation. You shall do no customary work *on it.* 36For seven days you shall offer an offering made by fire to the LORD. On the eighth day you shall have a holy convocation, and you shall offer an offering made by fire to the LORD. It *is* a sacred assembly, *and* you shall do no customary work *on it.*

37'These *are* the feasts of the LORD which you shall proclaim *to be* holy convocations, to offer an offering made by fire to the LORD, a burnt offering and a grain offering, a sacrifice and drink offerings, everything on its day— 38besides the Sabbaths of the LORD, besides your gifts, besides all your vows, and besides all your freewill offerings which you give to the LORD.

39'Also on the fifteenth day of the seventh month, when you have gathered in the fruit of the land, you shall keep the feast of the LORD *for* seven days; on the first day *there shall be* a sabbath-*rest*, and on the eighth day a sabbath-*rest.* 40And you shall take for yourselves on the first day the fruit of beautiful trees, branches of palm trees, the boughs of leafy trees, and willows of the brook; and you shall rejoice before the LORD your God for seven days. 41You shall keep it as a feast to the LORD for seven days in the year. *It shall be* a statute forever in your generations. You shall celebrate it in the seventh month. 42You shall dwell in booths for seven days. All who are native Israelites shall dwell in booths, 43that your generations may know that I made the children of Israel dwell in booths when I brought them out of the land of Egypt: I *am* the LORD your God.' ''

44So Moses declared to the children of Israel the feasts of the LORD.

Care of the Tabernacle Lamps

24 Then the LORD spoke to Moses, saying: 2"Command the children of Israel that they bring to you pure oil of pressed olives for the light, to make

the lamps burn continually. 3Outside the veil of the Testimony, in the tabernacle of meeting, Aaron shall be in charge of it from evening until morning before the LORD continually; *it shall be* a statute forever in your generations. 4He shall be in charge of the lamps on the pure *gold* lampstand before the LORD continually.

The Bread of the Tabernacle

5"And you shall take fine flour and bake twelve cakes with it. Two-tenths *of an ephah* shall be in each cake. 6You shall set them in two rows, six in a row, on the pure *gold* table before the LORD. 7And you shall put pure frankincense on *each* row, that it may be on the bread for a memorial, an offering made by fire to the LORD. 8Every Sabbath he shall set it in order before the LORD continually, *being taken* from the children of Israel by an everlasting covenant. 9And it shall be for Aaron and his sons, and they shall eat it in a holy place; for it *is* most holy to him from the offerings of the LORD made by fire, by a perpetual statute."

The Penalty for Blasphemy

10Now the son of an Israelite woman, whose father *was* an Egyptian, went out among the children of Israel; and this Israelite *woman's* son and a man of Israel fought each other in the camp. 11And the Israelite woman's son blasphemed the name *of the* LORD and cursed; and so they brought him to Moses. (His mother's name *was* Shelomith the daughter of Dibri, of the tribe of Dan.) 12Then they put him in custody, that the mind of the LORD might be shown to them.

13And the LORD spoke to Moses, saying, 14"Take outside the camp him who has cursed; then let all who heard *him* lay their hands on his head, and let all the congregation stone him. 15"Then you shall speak to the children of Israel, saying: 'Whoever curses his God shall bear his sin. 16And whoever blasphemes the name of the LORD shall surely be put to death. All the congregation shall certainly stone him, the stranger as well as him who is born in the land. When he blasphemes the name *of the* LORD, he shall be put to death.

17'Whoever kills any man shall surely be put to death. 18Whoever kills an animal shall make it good, animal for animal.

19'If a man causes disfigurement of his neighbor, as he has done, so shall it be done to him—20fracture for fracture, eye for eye, tooth for tooth; as he has caused disfigurement of a man, so shall it be done to him. 21And whoever kills an animal shall restore it; but whoever kills a man shall be put to death. 22You shall have the same law for the stranger and for one from your own country; for I *am* the LORD your God.' "

23Then Moses spoke to the children of Israel; and they took outside the camp him who had cursed, and stoned him with stones. So the children of Israel did as the LORD commanded Moses.

The Sabbath of the Seventh Year

25 And the LORD spoke to Moses on Mount Sinai, saying, 2"Speak to the children of Israel, and say to them: 'When you come into the land which I give you, then the land shall keep a sabbath to the LORD. 3Six years you shall sow your field, and six years you shall prune your vineyard, and gather its fruit; 4but in the seventh year there shall be a sabbath of solemn rest for the land, a sabbath to the LORD. You shall neither sow your field nor prune your vineyard. 5What grows of its own accord of your harvest you shall not reap, nor gather the grapes of your untended vine, *for* it is a year of rest for the land. 6And the sabbath *produce* of the land shall be food for you: for you, your male and female servants, your hired man, and the stranger who dwells with you, 7for your livestock and the beasts that *are* in your land—all its produce shall be for food.

The Year of Jubilee

8'And you shall count seven sabbaths of years for yourself, seven times seven years; and the time of the seven sabbaths of years shall be to you forty-nine years. 9Then you shall cause the trumpet of the Jubilee to sound on the tenth *day* of the seventh month; on the Day of Atonement you shall make the trumpet to sound throughout all your land. 10And you shall consecrate the fiftieth year, and proclaim liberty throughout *all* the land to all its inhabitants. It shall be a Jubilee for you; and each of you shall return to his possession, and each of you shall return to his family. 11That fiftieth year shall be a Jubilee to you; in it you shall neither sow nor reap what grows of its own accord, nor gather *the grapes* of your untended vine. 12For it *is* the Jubilee; it shall be holy to you; you shall eat its produce from the field.

13'In this Year of Jubilee, each of you shall return to his possession. 14And if you sell anything to your neighbor or buy from your neighbor's hand, you shall not oppress one another. 15According to the number of years after the Jubilee you shall buy from your neighbor, and according to the number of years of crops he shall sell to you. 16According to the multitude of years you shall increase its price, and according to the fewer number of years you shall diminish its price; for he sells to you *according* to the number *of the years* of the crops. 17Therefore you shall not oppress one another, but you shall fear your God; for I *am* the LORD your God.

Provisions for the Seventh Year

18'So you shall observe My statutes and keep My judgments, and perform them; and you will dwell in the land in safety. 19Then the land will yield its fruit, and you will eat your fill, and dwell there in safety.

20'And if you say, "What shall we eat in the seventh year, since we shall not sow nor gather in our produce?" 21Then I will command My blessing on you in the sixth year, and it will bring forth produce enough for three years. 22And you shall sow in the eighth year, and eat old produce until the ninth year; until its produce comes in, you shall eat *of* the old *harvest.*

Redemption of Property

23'The land shall not be sold permanently, for the land *is* Mine; for you *are* strangers and sojourners with Me. 24And in all the land of your possession you shall grant redemption of the land.

25'If one of your brethren becomes poor, and has sold *some* of his possession, and if his redeeming relative comes to redeem it, then he may redeem what his brother sold. 26Or if the man has no one to redeem it, but he himself becomes able to redeem it, 27then let him count the years since its sale, and restore the remainder to the man to whom he sold it, that he may return to his possession. 28But if he is not able to have *it* restored to himself, then what was sold shall remain in the hand of him who bought it until the Year of Jubilee; and in the Jubilee it shall be released, and he shall return to his possession.

29'If a man sells a house in a walled city, then he may redeem it within a whole year after it is sold; *within* a full year he may redeem it. 30But if it is not redeemed within the space of a full year, then the house in the walled city shall belong permanently to him who bought it, throughout his generations. It shall not be released in the Jubilee. 31However the houses of villages which have no wall around them shall be counted as the fields of the country. They may be redeemed, and they shall be released in the Jubilee. 32Nevertheless the cities of the Levites, *and* the houses in the cities of their possession, the Levites may redeem at any time. 33And if a man purchases a house from the Levites, then the house that was sold in the city of his possession shall be released in the Jubilee; for the houses in the cities of the Levites *are* their possession among the children of Israel. 34But the field of the common-land of their cities may not be sold, for it *is* their perpetual possession.

Lending to the Poor

35'If one of your brethren becomes poor, and falls into poverty among you, then you shall help him, like a stranger or a sojourner, that he may live with you. 36Take no usury or interest from him; but fear your God, that your brother may live with you. 37You shall not lend him your money for usury, nor lend him your food at a profit. 38I *am* the LORD your God, who brought you out of the land of Egypt, to give you the land of Canaan *and* to be your God.

The Law Concerning Slavery

39'And if *one of* your brethren *who dwells* by you becomes poor, and sells himself to you, you shall not compel him to serve as a slave. **40**As a hired servant *and* a sojourner he shall be with you, *and* shall serve you until the Year of Jubilee. **41**And *then* he shall depart from you—he and his children with him—and shall return to his own family. He shall return to the possession of his fathers. **42**For they *are* My servants, whom I brought out of the land of Egypt; they shall not be sold as slaves. **43**You shall not rule over him with rigor, but you shall fear your God. **44**And as for your male and female slaves whom you may have—from the nations that are around you, from them you may buy male and female slaves. **45**Moreover you may buy the children of the strangers who dwell among you, and their families who are with you, which they beget in your land; and they shall become your property. **46**And you may take them as an inheritance for your children after you, to inherit *them as* a possession; they shall be your permanent slaves. But regarding your brethren, the children of Israel, you shall not rule over one another with rigor.

47'Now if a sojourner or stranger close to you becomes rich, and *one of* your brethren *who dwells* by him becomes poor, and sells himself to the stranger *or* sojourner close to you, or to a member of the stranger's family, **48**after he is sold he may be redeemed again. One of his brothers may redeem him; **49**or his uncle or his uncle's son may redeem him; or *anyone* who is near of kin to him in his family may redeem him; or if he is able he may redeem himself. **50**Thus he shall reckon with him who bought him: The price of his release shall be according to the number of years, from the year that he was sold to him until the Year of Jubilee; *it shall be* according to the time of a hired servant for him. **51**If *there are* still many years *remaining*, according to them he shall repay the price of his redemption from the money with which he was bought. **52**And if there remain but a few years until the Year of Jubilee, then he shall reckon with him, *and* according to his years he shall repay him the price of his redemption. **53**He shall be with him as a yearly hired servant, and he shall not rule with rigor over him in your sight. **54**And if he is not redeemed in these *years*, then he shall be released in the Year of Jubilee—he and his children with him. **55**For the children of Israel *are* servants to Me; they *are* My servants whom I brought out of the land of Egypt: I *am* the Lord your God.

Promise of Blessing and Retribution

26 'You shall not make idols for yourselves;
neither a carved image nor a *sacred* pillar shall you rear up for yourselves;
nor shall you set up an engraved stone in your land, to bow down to it;
for I *am* the Lord your God.

2 You shall keep My Sabbaths and reverence My sanctuary:
I *am* the Lord.

3 'If you walk in My statutes and keep My commandments, and perform them,

4 then I will give you rain in its season, and the land shall yield its produce, and the trees of the field shall yield their fruit.

5 Your threshing shall last till the time of vintage, and the vintage shall last till the time of sowing;
you shall eat your bread to the full, and dwell in your land safely.

6 I will give peace in the land, and you shall lie down, and none will make *you* afraid;
I will rid the land of evil beasts, and the sword will not go through your land.

7 You will chase your enemies, and they shall fall by the sword before you.

8 Five of you shall chase a hundred, and a hundred of you shall put ten thousand to flight;
your enemies shall fall by the sword before you.

9 'For I will look on you favorably and make you fruitful, multiply you and confirm My covenant with you.

10 You shall eat the old harvest, and clear out the old because of the new.

11 I will set My tabernacle among you, and My soul shall not abhor you.

12 I will walk among you and be your God, and you shall be My people.

13 I *am* the LORD your God, who brought you out of the land of Egypt, that *you* should not be their slaves;

I have broken the bands of your yoke and made you walk upright.

14 'But if you do not obey Me, and do not observe all these commandments,

15 and if you despise My statutes, or if your soul abhors My judgments, so that you do not perform all My commandments, *but* break My covenant,

16 I also will do this to you:

I will even appoint terror over you, wasting disease and fever which shall consume the eyes and cause sorrow of heart.

And you shall sow your seed in vain, for your enemies shall eat it.

17 I will set My face against you, and you shall be defeated by your enemies.

Those who hate you shall reign over you, and you shall flee when no one pursues you.

18 'And after all this, if you do not obey Me, then I will punish you seven times more for your sins.

19 I will break the pride of your power;

I will make your heavens like iron and your earth like bronze.

20 And your strength shall be spent in vain;

for your land shall not yield its produce, nor shall the trees of the land yield their fruit.

21 'Then, if you walk contrary to Me, and are not willing to obey Me, I will bring on you seven times more plagues, according to your sins.

22 I will also send wild beasts among you, which shall rob you of your children, destroy your livestock, and make you few in number;

and your highways shall be desolate.

23 'And if by these things you are not reformed by Me, but walk contrary to Me,

24 then I also will walk contrary to you, and I will punish you yet seven times for your sins.

25 And I will bring a sword against you that will execute the vengeance of the covenant;

when you are gathered together within your cities I will send pestilence among you;

and you shall be delivered into the hand of the enemy.

26 When I have cut off your supply of bread, ten women shall bake your bread in one oven, and they shall bring back your bread by weight, and you shall eat and not be satisfied.

27 'And after all this, if you do not obey Me, but walk contrary to Me,

28 then I also will walk contrary to you in fury;

and I, even I, will chastise you seven times for your sins.

29 You shall eat the flesh of your sons, and you shall eat the flesh of your daughters.

30 I will destroy your high places, cut down your incense altars, and cast your carcasses on the lifeless forms of your idols;

and My soul shall abhor you.

31 I will lay your cities waste and bring your sanctuaries to desolation, and I will not smell the fragrance of your sweet aromas.

32 I will bring the land to desolation, and your enemies who dwell in it shall be astonished at it.

33 I will scatter you among the nations and draw out a sword after you;

your land shall be desolate and your cities waste.

34 Then the land shall enjoy its sabbaths as long as it lies deso-

late and you *are* in your enemies'
land;

then the land shall rest and enjoy
its sabbaths.

35 As long as *it* lies desolate it shall
rest—

for the time it did not rest on your
sabbaths when you dwelt in it.

36 'And as for those of you who are
left, I will send faintness into
their hearts in the lands of their
enemies;

the sound of a shaken leaf shall
cause them to flee;

they shall flee as though fleeing
from a sword, and they shall fall
when no one pursues.

37 They shall stumble over one
another, as it were before a
sword, when no one pursues;

and you shall have no *power* to
stand before your enemies.

38 You shall perish among the
nations, and the land of your
enemies shall eat you up.

39 And those of you who are left shall
waste away in their iniquity in
your enemies' lands;

also in their fathers' iniquities,
which are with them, they shall
waste away.

40 'But if they confess their iniquity
and the iniquity of their fathers,
with their unfaithfulness in which
they were unfaithful to Me, and
that they also have walked
contrary to Me,

41 and *that* I also have walked
contrary to them and have
brought them into the land of
their enemies;

if their uncircumcised hearts are
humbled, and they accept their
guilt—

42 then I will remember My covenant
with Jacob, and My covenant
with Isaac and My covenant with
Abraham I will remember;

I will remember the land.

43 The land also shall be left empty
by them, and will enjoy its
sabbaths while it lies desolate
without them;

they will accept their guilt, because
they despised My judgments and

because their soul abhorred My
statutes.

44 Yet for all that, when they are in
the land of their enemies, I will
not cast them away, nor shall I
abhor them, to utterly destroy
them and break My covenant
with them;

for I *am* the Lord their God.

45 But for their sake I will remember
the covenant of their ancestors,
whom I brought out of the land
of Egypt in the sight of the
nations, that I might be their God:
I *am* the Lord.' "

46These *are* the statutes and judgments and laws which the Lord made
between Himself and the children of Israel on Mount Sinai by the hand of
Moses.

Redeeming Persons and Property Dedicated to God

27 Now the Lord spoke to Moses,
saying, 2"Speak to the children of
Israel, and say to them: 'When a man
consecrates by a vow certain persons
to the Lord, according to your valuation, 3if your valuation is of a male from
twenty years old up to sixty years old,
then your valuation shall be fifty shekels of silver, according to the shekel of
the sanctuary. 4If it *is* a female, then
your valuation shall be thirty shekels;
5and if from five years old up to twenty
years old, then your valuation for a
male shall be twenty shekels, and for
a female ten shekels; 6and if from a
month old up to five years old, then
your valuation for a male shall be five
shekels of silver, and for a female your
valuation shall be three shekels of silver; 7and if from sixty years old and
above, if *it is* a male, then your valuation shall be fifteen shekels, and for a
female ten shekels.

8'But if he is too poor to pay your valuation, then he shall present himself before the priest, and the priest shall set
a value for him; according to the ability
of him who vowed, the priest shall
value him.

9'If *it is* an animal that men may bring
as an offering to the Lord, all that *anyone* gives to the Lord shall be holy.
10He shall not substitute it or exchange

it, good for bad or bad for good; and if he at all exchanges animal for animal, then both it and the one exchanged for it shall be holy. 11If *it is* an unclean animal which they do not offer as a sacrifice to the LORD, then he shall present the animal before the priest; 12and the priest shall set a value for it, whether it is good or bad; as you, the priest, value it, so it shall be. 13But if he *wants* at all *to* redeem it, then he must add one-fifth to your valuation.

14'And when a man dedicates his house *to be* holy to the LORD, then the priest shall set a value for it, whether it is good or bad; as the priest values it, so it shall stand. 15If he who dedicated it *wants to* redeem his house, then he must add one-fifth of the money of your valuation to it, and it shall be his.

16'If a man dedicates to the LORD *part* of a field of his possession, then your valuation shall be according to the seed for it. A homer of barley seed *shall be valued* at fifty shekels of silver. 17If he dedicates his field from the Year of Jubilee, according to your valuation it shall stand. 18But if he dedicates his field after the Jubilee, then the priest shall reckon to him the money due according to the years that remain till the Year of Jubilee, and it shall be deducted from your valuation. 19And if he who dedicates the field ever wishes to redeem it, then he must add one-fifth of the money of your valuation to it, and it shall belong to him. 20But if he does not want to redeem the field, or if he has sold the field to another man, it shall not be redeemed anymore; 21but the field, when it is released in the Jubilee, shall be holy to the LORD, as a devoted field; it shall be the possession of the priest.

22'And if a man dedicates to the LORD a field which he has bought, which is not the field of his possession, 23then the priest shall reckon to him the worth of your valuation, up to the Year of Jubilee, and he shall give your valuation on that day *as* a holy *offering* to the LORD. 24In the Year of Jubilee the field shall return to him from whom it was bought, to the one who *owned* the land as a possession. 25And all your valuations shall be according to the shekel of the sanctuary: twenty gerahs to the shekel.

26'But the firstborn of the animals, which should be the LORD's firstborn, no man shall dedicate; whether *it is* an ox or sheep, it *is* the LORD's. 27And if *it is* an unclean animal, then he shall redeem *it* according to your valuation, and shall add one-fifth to it; or if it is not redeemed, then it shall be sold according to your valuation.

28'Nevertheless no devoted *offering* that a man may devote to the LORD of all that he has, *both* man and beast, or the field of his possession, shall be sold or redeemed; every devoted *offering is* most holy to the LORD. 29No person under the ban, who may become doomed to destruction among men, shall be redeemed, *but* shall surely be put to death. 30And all the tithe of the land, *whether* of the seed of the land *or* of the fruit of the tree, *is* the LORD's. It *is* holy to the LORD. 31If a man wants at all to redeem *any* of his tithes, he shall add one-fifth to it. 32And concerning the tithe of the herd or the flock, of whatever passes under the rod, the tenth one shall be holy to the LORD. 33He shall not inquire whether it is good or bad, nor shall he exchange it; and if he exchanges it at all, then both it and the one exchanged for it shall be holy; it shall not be redeemed.'"

34These *are* the commandments which the LORD commanded Moses for the children of Israel on Mount Sinai.

The Fourth Book of Moses Called

NUMBERS

The First Census of Israel

1 Now the LORD spoke to Moses in the Wilderness of Sinai, in the tabernacle of meeting, on the first *day* of the second month, in the second year after they had come out of the land of Egypt, saying: 2"Take a census of all the congregation of the children of Israel, by their families, by their fathers' houses, according to the number of names, every male individually, 3from twenty years old and above—all who *are able to* go to war in Israel. You and Aaron shall number them by their armies. 4And with you there shall be a man from every tribe, each one the head of his father's house.

5"These are the names of the men who shall stand with you: from Reuben, Elizur the son of Shedeur; 6from Simeon, Shelumiel the son of Zurishaddai; 7from Judah, Nahshon the son of Amminadab; 8from Issachar, Nethanel the son of Zuar; 9from Zebulun, Eliab the son of Helon; 10from the sons of Joseph: from Ephraim, Elishama the son of Ammihud; from Manasseh, Gamaliel the son of Pedahzur; 11from Benjamin, Abidan the son of Gideoni; 12from Dan, Ahiezer the son of Ammishaddai; 13from Asher, Pagiel the son of Ocran; 14from Gad, Eliasaph the son of Deuel; 15from Naphtali, Ahira the son of Enan." 16These *were* chosen from the congregation, leaders of their fathers' tribes, heads of the divisions in Israel.

17Then Moses and Aaron took these men who had been mentioned by name, 18and they assembled all the congregation together on the first *day* of the second month; and they recited their ancestry by families, by their fathers' houses, according to the number of names, from twenty years old and above, each one individually. 19As the LORD commanded Moses, so he numbered them in the Wilderness of Sinai.

20Now the children of Reuben, Israel's oldest son, their genealogies by their families, by their fathers' house, according to the number of names, every male individually, from twenty years old and above, all who *were able to* go to war: 21those who were numbered of the tribe of Reuben *were* forty-six thousand five hundred.

22From the children of Simeon, their genealogies by their families, by their fathers' house, of those who were numbered, according to the number of names, every male individually, from twenty years old and above, all who *were able to* go to war: 23those who were numbered of the tribe of Simeon *were* fifty-nine thousand three hundred.

24From the children of Gad, their genealogies by their families, by their fathers' house, according to the number of names, from twenty years old and above, all who *were able to* go to war: 25those who were numbered of the tribe of Gad *were* forty-five thousand six hundred and fifty.

26From the children of Judah, their genealogies by their families, by their fathers' house, according to the number of names, from twenty years old and above, all who *were able to* go to war: 27those who were numbered of the tribe of Judah *were* seventy-four thousand six hundred.

28From the children of Issachar, their genealogies by their families, by their fathers' house, according to the number of names, from twenty years old and above, all who *were able to* go to war: 29those who were numbered of the tribe of Issachar *were* fifty-four thousand four hundred.

30From the children of Zebulun, their genealogies by their families, by their fathers' house, according to the number of names, from twenty years old and above, all who *were able to* go to war: 31those who were numbered of the tribe of Zebulun *were* fifty-seven thousand four hundred.

32From the sons of Joseph, the children of Ephraim, their genealogies by their families, by their fathers' house, according to the number of names, from twenty years old and above, all who *were able to* go to war: 33those who were numbered of the tribe of

Ephraim *were* forty thousand five hundred.

34From the children of Manasseh, their genealogies by their families, by their fathers' house, according to the number of names, from twenty years old and above, all who *were able to* go to war: **35**those who were numbered of the tribe of Manasseh *were* thirty-two thousand two hundred.

36From the children of Benjamin, their genealogies by their families, by their fathers' house, according to the number of names, from twenty years old and above, all who *were able to* go to war: **37**those who were numbered of the tribe of Benjamin *were* thirty-five thousand four hundred.

38From the children of Dan, their genealogies by their families, by their fathers' house, according to the number of names, from twenty years old and above, all who *were able to* go to war: **39**those who were numbered of the tribe of Dan *were* sixty-two thousand seven hundred.

40From the children of Asher, their genealogies by their families, by their fathers' house, according to the number of names, from twenty years old and above, all who *were able to* go to war: **41**those who were numbered of the tribe of Asher *were* forty-one thousand five hundred.

42From the children of Naphtali, their genealogies by their families, by their fathers' house, according to the number of names, from twenty years old and above, all who *were able to* go to war: **43**those who were numbered of the tribe of Naphtali *were* fifty-three thousand four hundred.

44These are the ones who were numbered, whom Moses and Aaron numbered, with the leaders of Israel, twelve men, each one representing his father's house. **45**So all who were numbered of the children of Israel, by their fathers' houses, from twenty years old and above, all who *were able to* go to war in Israel—**46**all who were numbered were six hundred and three thousand five hundred and fifty.

47But the Levites were not numbered among them by their fathers' tribe; **48**for the LORD had spoken to Moses, saying: **49**"Only the tribe of Levi you shall not number, nor take a census of them among the children of Israel; **50**but you shall appoint the Levites over the tabernacle of the Testimony, over all its furnishings, and over all things that belong to it; they shall carry the tabernacle and all its furnishings; they shall attend to it and camp around the tabernacle. **51**And when the tabernacle is to go forward, the Levites shall take it down; and when the tabernacle is to be set up, the Levites shall set it up. The outsider who comes near shall be put to death. **52**The children of Israel shall pitch their tents, everyone by his own camp, everyone by his own standard, according to their armies; **53**but the Levites shall camp around the tabernacle of the Testimony, that there may be no wrath on the congregation of the children of Israel; and the Levites shall keep charge of the tabernacle of the Testimony."

54Thus the children of Israel did; according to all that the LORD commanded Moses, so they did.

The Tribes and Leaders by Armies

2 And the LORD spoke to Moses and Aaron, saying: **2**"Everyone of the children of Israel shall camp by his own standard, beside the emblems of his father's house; they shall camp some distance from the tabernacle of meeting. **3**On the east side, toward the rising of the sun, those of the standard of the forces with Judah shall camp according to their armies; and Nahshon the son of Amminadab *shall be* the leader of the children of Judah." **4**And his army was numbered at seventy-four thousand six hundred.

5"Those who camp next to him *shall be* the tribe of Issachar, and Nethanel the son of Zuar *shall be* the leader of the children of Issachar." **6**And his army was numbered at fifty-four thousand four hundred.

7"Then *comes* the tribe of Zebulun, and Eliab the son of Helon *shall be* the leader of the children of Zebulun." **8**And his army was numbered at fifty-seven thousand four hundred. **9**"All who were numbered according to their armies of the forces with Judah, one hundred and eighty-six thousand four hundred—these shall break camp first.

10"On the south side *shall be* the standard of the forces with Reuben according to their armies, and the leader of the children of Reuben *shall be* Elizur the son of Shedeur." 11And his army was numbered at forty-six thousand five hundred.

12"Those who camp next to him *shall be* the tribe of Simeon, and the leader of the children of Simeon *shall be* Shelumiel the son of Zurishaddai." 13And his army was numbered at fifty-nine thousand three hundred.

14"Then *comes* the tribe of Gad, and the leader of the children of Gad *shall be* Eliasaph the son of Reuel." 15And his army was numbered at forty-five thousand six hundred and fifty. 16"All who were numbered according to their armies of the forces with Reuben, one hundred and fifty-one thousand four hundred and fifty—they shall be the second to break camp.

17"And the tabernacle of meeting shall move out with the camp of the Levites in the middle of the camps; as they camp, so they shall move out, everyone in his place, by their standards.

18"On the west side *shall be* the standard of the forces with Ephraim according to their armies, and the leader of the children of Ephraim *shall be* Elishama the son of Ammihud." 19And his army was numbered at forty thousand five hundred.

20"Next to him *comes* the tribe of Manasseh, and the leader of the children of Manasseh *shall be* Gamaliel the son of Pedahzur." 21And his army was numbered at thirty-two thousand two hundred.

22"Then *comes* the tribe of Benjamin, and the leader of the children of Benjamin *shall be* Abidan the son of Gideoni." 23And his army was numbered at thirty-five thousand four hundred. 24"All who were numbered according to their armies of the forces with Ephraim, one hundred and eight thousand one hundred—they shall be the third to break camp.

25"The standard of the forces with Dan *shall be* on the north side according to their armies, and the leader of the children of Dan *shall be* Ahiezer the son of Ammishaddai." 26And his army was numbered at sixty-two thousand seven hundred.

27"Those who camp next to him *shall be* the tribe of Asher, and the leader of the children of Asher *shall be* Pagiel the son of Ocran." 28And his army was numbered at forty-one thousand five hundred.

29"Then *comes* the tribe of Naphtali, and the leader of the children of Naphtali *shall be* Ahira the son of Enan." 30And his army was numbered at fifty-three thousand four hundred. 31"All who were numbered of the forces with Dan, one hundred and fifty-seven thousand six hundred—they shall break camp last, with their standards."

32These *are* the ones who were numbered of the children of Israel by their fathers' houses. All who were numbered according to their armies of the forces *were* six hundred and three thousand five hundred and fifty. 33But the Levites were not numbered among the children of Israel, just as the LORD commanded Moses.

34Thus the children of Israel did according to all that the LORD commanded Moses; so they camped by their standards and so they broke camp, each one by his family, according to their fathers' houses.

The Sons of Aaron

3 Now these *are* the records of Aaron and Moses when the LORD spoke with Moses on Mount Sinai. 2And these *are* the names of the sons of Aaron: Nadab, the firstborn, and Abihu, Eleazar, and Ithamar. 3These *are* the names of the sons of Aaron, the anointed priests, whom he consecrated to minister as priests. 4Nadab and Abihu had died before the LORD when they offered profane fire before the LORD in the Wilderness of Sinai; and they had no children. So Eleazar and Ithamar ministered as priests in the presence of Aaron their father.

The Levites Serve in the Tabernacle

5And the LORD spoke to Moses, saying: 6"Bring the tribe of Levi near, and present them before Aaron the priest, that they may serve him. 7And they shall attend to his needs and the needs of the whole congregation before the tabernacle of meeting, to do the work of the tabernacle. 8Also they shall attend to all the furnishings of the tabernacle of meeting, and to the needs of the children of Israel, to do the work of the tabernacle. 9And you shall give the Levites to Aaron and his sons; they *are* given entirely to him from among the children of Israel. 10So you shall appoint Aaron and his sons, and they shall attend to their priesthood; but the outsider who comes near shall be put to death."

11Then the LORD spoke to Moses, saying: 12"Now behold, I Myself have taken the Levites from among the children of Israel instead of every firstborn who opens the womb among the children of Israel. Therefore the Levites shall be Mine, 13because all the firstborn *are* Mine. On the day that I struck all the firstborn in the land of Egypt, I sanctified to Myself all the firstborn in Israel, both man and beast. They shall be Mine: I *am* the LORD."

Census of the Levites Commanded

14Then the LORD spoke to Moses in the Wilderness of Sinai, saying: 15"Number the children of Levi by their fathers' houses, by their families; you shall number every male from a month old and above."

16So Moses numbered them according to the word of the LORD, as he was commanded. 17These were the sons of Levi by their names: Gershon, Kohath, and Merari. 18And these *are* the names of the sons of Gershon by their families: Libni and Shimei. 19And the sons of Kohath by their families: Amram, Izehar, Hebron, and Uzziel. 20And the sons of Merari by their families: Mahli and Mushi. These *are* the families of the Levites by their fathers' houses.

21From Gershon *came* the family of the Libnites and the family of the Shimites; these *were* the families of the Gershonites. 22Those who were numbered, according to the number of all the males from a month old and above—of those who were numbered *there were* seven thousand five hundred. 23The families of the Gershonites were to camp behind the tabernacle westward. 24And the leader of the father's house of the Gershonites *was* Eliasaph the son

of Lael. 25The duties of the children of Gershon in the tabernacle of meeting *included* the tabernacle, the tent with its covering, the screen for the door of the tabernacle of meeting, 26the screen for the door of the court, the hangings of the court which *are* around the tabernacle and the altar, and their cords, according to all the work relating to them.

27From Kohath *came* the family of the Amramites, the family of the Izharites, the family of the Hebronites, and the family of the Uzzielites; these *were* the families of the Kohathites. 28According to the number of all the males, from a month old and above, *there were* eight thousand six hundred keeping charge of the sanctuary. 29The families of the children of Kohath were to camp on the south side of the tabernacle. 30And the leader of the fathers' house of the families of the Kohathites *was* Elizaphan the son of Uzziel. 31Their duty *included* the ark, the table, the lampstand, the altars, the utensils of the sanctuary with which they ministered, the screen, and all the work relating to them.

32And Eleazar the son of Aaron the priest *was to be* chief over the leaders of the Levites, *with* oversight of those who kept charge of the sanctuary.

33From Merari *came* the family of the Mahlites and the family of the Mushites; these *were* the families of Merari. 34And those who were numbered, according to the number of all the males from a month old and above, *were* six thousand two hundred. 35The leader of the fathers' house of the families of Merari *was* Zuriel the son of Abihail. These *were* to camp on the north side of the tabernacle. 36And the appointed duty of the children of Merari *included* the boards of the tabernacle, its bars, its pillars, its sockets, its utensils, all the work relating to them, 37and the pillars of the court all around, with their sockets, their pegs, and their cords.

38Moreover those who were to camp before the tabernacle on the east, before the tabernacle of meeting, *were* Moses, Aaron, and his sons, keeping charge of the sanctuary, to meet the needs of the children of Israel; but the outsider who came near was to be put to death. 39All who were numbered of the Levites, whom Moses and Aaron numbered at the commandment of the LORD, by their families, all the males from a month old and above, *were* twenty-two thousand.

Levites Dedicated Instead of the Firstborn

40Then the LORD said to Moses: "Number all the firstborn males of the children of Israel from a month old and above, and take the number of their names. 41And you shall take the Levites for Me—I *am* the LORD—instead of all the firstborn among the children of Israel, and the livestock of the Levites instead of all the firstborn among the livestock of the children of Israel." 42So Moses numbered all the firstborn among the children of Israel, as the LORD commanded him. 43And all the firstborn males, according to the number of names from a month old and above, of those who were numbered of them, were twenty-two thousand two hundred and seventy-three.

44Then the LORD spoke to Moses, saying: 45"Take the Levites instead of all the firstborn among the children of Israel, and the livestock of the Levites instead of their livestock. The Levites shall be Mine: I *am* the LORD. 46And for the redemption of the two hundred and seventy-three of the firstborn of the children of Israel, who are more than the number of the Levites, 47you shall take five shekels for each one individually; you shall take *them* in the currency of the shekel of the sanctuary, the shekel of twenty gerahs. 48And you shall give the money, with which the excess number of them is redeemed, to Aaron and his sons."

49So Moses took the redemption money from those who were over and above those who were redeemed by the Levites. 50From the firstborn of the children of Israel he took the money, one thousand three hundred and sixty-five *shekels*, according to the shekel of the sanctuary. 51And Moses gave their redemption money to Aaron and his sons, according to the word of the LORD, as the LORD commanded Moses.

Duties of the Sons of Kohath

4 Then the LORD spoke to Moses and Aaron, saying: 2"Take a census of the sons of Kohath from among the children of Levi, by their families, by their fathers' house, 3from thirty years old and above, even to fifty years old, all who enter the service to do the work in the tabernacle of meeting.

4"This *is* the service of the sons of Kohath in the tabernacle of meeting, *relating to* the most holy things: 5When the camp prepares to journey, Aaron and his sons shall come, and they shall take down the covering veil and cover the ark of the Testimony with it. 6Then they shall put on it a covering of badger skins, and spread over *that* a cloth entirely of blue; and they shall insert its poles.

7"On the table of showbread they shall spread a blue cloth, and put on it the dishes, the pans, the bowls, and the pitchers for pouring; and the showbread shall be on it. 8They shall spread over them a scarlet cloth, and cover the same with a covering of badger skins; and they shall insert its poles. 9And they shall take a blue cloth and cover the lampstand of the light, with its lamps, its wick-trimmers, its trays, and all its oil vessels, with which they service it. 10Then they shall put it with all its utensils in a covering of badger skins, and put *it* on a carrying beam.

11"Over the golden altar they shall spread a blue cloth, and cover it with a covering of badger skins; and they shall insert its poles. 12Then they shall take all the utensils of service with which they minister in the sanctuary, put *them* in a blue cloth, cover them with a covering of badger skins, and put *them* on a carrying beam. 13Also they shall take away the ashes from the altar, and spread a purple cloth over it. 14They shall put on it all its implements with which they minister there—the firepans, the forks, the shovels, the basins, and all the utensils of the altar—and they shall spread on it a covering of badger skins, and insert its poles. 15And when Aaron and his sons have finished covering the sanctuary and all the furnishings of the sanctuary, when the camp is set to go, then the sons of

Kohath shall come to carry *them;* but they shall not touch any holy thing, lest they die.

"These *are* the things in the tabernacle of meeting which the sons of Kohath are to carry.

16"The appointed duty of Eleazar the son of Aaron the priest *is* the oil for the light, the sweet incense, the daily grain offering, the anointing oil, the oversight of all the tabernacle, of all that *is* in it, with the sanctuary and its furnishings."

17Then the LORD spoke to Moses and Aaron, saying: 18"Do not cut off the tribe of the families of the Kohathites from among the Levites; 19but do this in regard to them, that they may live and not die when they approach the most holy things: Aaron and his sons shall go in and appoint each of them to his service and his task. 20But they shall not go in to watch while the holy things are being covered, lest they die."

Duties of the Sons of Gershon

21Then the LORD spoke to Moses, saying: 22"Also take a census of the sons of Gershon, by their fathers' house, by their families. 23From thirty years old and above, even to fifty years old, you shall number them, all who enter to perform the service, to do the work in the tabernacle of meeting. 24This *is* the service of the families of the Gershonites, in serving and carrying: 25They shall carry the curtains of the tabernacle and the tabernacle of meeting *with* its covering, the covering of badger skins that *is* on it, the screen for the door of the tabernacle of meeting, 26the screen for the door of the gate of the court, the hangings of the court which *are* around the tabernacle and altar, and their cords, all the furnishings for their service and all that is made for these things: so shall they serve. 27"Aaron and his sons shall assign all the service of the sons of the Gershonites, all their tasks and all their service. And you shall appoint to them all their tasks as their duty. 28This *is* the service of the families of the sons of Gershon in the tabernacle of meeting. And their duties *shall be* under the authority of Ithamar the son of Aaron the priest.

Duties of the Sons of Merari

29"*As for* the sons of Merari, you shall number them by their families and by their fathers' house. 30From thirty years old and above, even to fifty years old, you shall number them, everyone who enters the service to do the work of the tabernacle of meeting. 31And this *is* what they must carry as all their service for the tabernacle of meeting: the boards of the tabernacle, its bars, its pillars, its sockets, 32and the pillars around the court with their sockets, pegs, and cords, with all their furnishings and all their service; and you shall assign *to each man* by name the items he must carry. 33This *is* the service of the families of the sons of Merari, as all their service for the tabernacle of meeting, under the authority of Ithamar the son of Aaron the priest."

Census of the Levites

34And Moses, Aaron, and the leaders of the congregation numbered the sons of the Kohathites by their families and by their fathers' house, 35from thirty years old and above, even to fifty years old, everyone who entered the service for work in the tabernacle of meeting; 36and those who were numbered by their families were two thousand seven hundred and fifty. 37These *were* the ones who were numbered of the families of the Kohathites, all who might serve in the tabernacle of meeting, whom Moses and Aaron numbered according to the commandment of the LORD by the hand of Moses.

38And those who were numbered of the sons of Gershon, by their families and by their fathers' house, 39from thirty years old and above, even to fifty years old, everyone who entered the service for work in the tabernacle of meeting—40those who were numbered by their families, by their fathers' house, were two thousand six hundred and thirty. 41These *are* the ones who were numbered of the families of the sons of Gershon, of all who might serve in the tabernacle of meeting, whom Moses and Aaron numbered according to the commandment of the LORD.

42Those of the families of the sons of Merari who were numbered, by their families, by their fathers' house, 43from thirty years old and above, even to fifty years old, everyone who entered the service for work in the tabernacle of meeting—44those who were numbered by their families were three thousand two hundred. 45These *are* the ones who were numbered of the families of the sons of Merari, whom Moses and Aaron numbered according to the word of the LORD by the hand of Moses.

46All who were numbered of the Levites, whom Moses, Aaron, and the leaders of Israel numbered, by their families and by their fathers' houses, 47from thirty years old and above, even to fifty years old, everyone who came to do the work of service and the work of bearing burdens in the tabernacle of meeting—48those who were numbered were eight thousand five hundred and eighty.

49According to the commandment of the LORD they were numbered by the hand of Moses, each according to his service and according to his task; thus were they numbered by him, as the LORD commanded Moses.

Ceremonially Unclean Persons Isolated

5 And the LORD spoke to Moses, saying: 2"Command the children of Israel that they put out of the camp every leper, everyone who has a discharge, and whoever becomes defiled by a corpse. 3You shall put out both male and female; you shall put them outside the camp, that they may not defile their camps in the midst of which I dwell." 4And the children of Israel did so, and put them outside the camp; as the LORD spoke to Moses, so the children of Israel did.

Confession and Restitution

5Then the LORD spoke to Moses, saying, 6"Speak to the children of Israel: 'When a man or woman commits any sin that men commit in unfaithfulness against the LORD, and that person is guilty, 7then he shall confess the sin which he has committed. He shall make restitution for his trespass in full, plus one-fifth of it, and give *it* to the one he has wronged. 8But if the man has no relative to whom restitution may be made for the wrong, the restitution for the wrong *must go* to the LORD for the priest, in addition to the ram of the atonement with which atonement is made for him. 9Every offering of all the holy things of the children of Israel, which they bring to the priest, shall be his. 10And every man's holy things shall be his; whatever any man gives the priest shall be his.'"

Concerning Unfaithful Wives

11And the LORD spoke to Moses, saying, 12"Speak to the children of Israel, and say to them: 'If any man's wife goes astray and behaves unfaithfully toward him, 13and a man lies with her carnally, and it is hidden from the eyes of her husband, and it is concealed that she has defiled herself, and *there was* no witness against her, nor was she caught—14if the spirit of jealousy comes upon him and he becomes jealous of his wife, who has defiled herself; or if the spirit of jealousy comes upon him and he becomes jealous of his wife, although she has not defiled herself—15then the man shall bring his wife to the priest. He shall bring the offering required for her, one-tenth of an ephah of barley meal; he shall pour no oil on it and put no frankincense on it, because it *is* a grain offering of jealousy, an offering for remembering, for bringing iniquity to remembrance.

16'And the priest shall bring her near, and set her before the LORD. 17The priest shall take holy water in an earthen vessel, and take some of the dust that is on the floor of the tabernacle and put *it* into the water. 18Then the priest shall stand the woman before the LORD, uncover the woman's head, and put the offering for remembering in her hands, which *is* the grain offering of jealousy. And the priest shall have in his hand the bitter water that brings a curse. 19And the priest shall put her under oath, and say to the woman, "If no man has lain with you, and if you have not gone astray to uncleanness *while* under your husband's *authority,* be free from this bitter water that brings a curse. 20But if you have gone astray *while* under your husband's *authority,* and if you have defiled yourself and some man other than your husband has lain with you"—21then the priest shall put the woman under the oath of the curse, and he shall say to the woman—"the LORD make you a curse and an oath among your people, when the LORD makes your thigh rot and your belly swell; 22and may this water that causes the curse go into your stomach, and make *your* belly swell and *your* thigh rot."

'Then the woman shall say, "Amen, so be it."

23'Then the priest shall write these curses in a book, and he shall scrape *them* off into the bitter water. 24And he shall make the woman drink the bitter water that brings a curse, and the water that brings the curse shall enter her *to become* bitter. 25Then the priest shall take the grain offering of jealousy from the woman's hand, shall wave the offering before the LORD, and bring it to the altar; 26and the priest shall take a handful of the offering, as its memorial portion, burn *it* on the altar, and afterward make the woman drink the water. 27When he has made her drink the water, then it shall be, if she has defiled herself and behaved unfaithfully toward her husband, that the water that brings a curse will enter her *and become* bitter, and her belly will swell, her thigh will rot, and the woman will become a curse among her people. 28But if the woman has not defiled herself, and is clean, then she shall be free and may conceive children.

29'This *is* the law of jealousy, when a wife, *while* under her husband's *authority*, goes astray and defiles herself, 30or when the spirit of jealousy comes upon a man, and he becomes jealous of his wife; then he shall stand the woman before the LORD, and the priest shall execute all this law upon her. 31Then the man shall be free from iniquity, but that woman shall bear her guilt.' "

The Law of the Nazirite

6 Then the LORD spoke to Moses, saying, 2"Speak to the children of Israel, and say to them: 'When either a man or woman consecrates an offering to take the vow of a Nazirite, to separate himself to the LORD, 3he shall separate himself from wine and *similar* drink; he shall drink neither vinegar made from wine nor vinegar made from *similar* drink; neither shall he drink any grape juice, nor eat fresh grapes or raisins. 4All the days of his separation he shall eat nothing that is produced by the grapevine, from seed to skin.

5'All the days of the vow of his separation no razor shall come upon his head; until the days are fulfilled for which he separated himself to the LORD, he shall be holy. *Then* he shall let the locks of the hair of his head grow. 6All the days that he separates himself to the LORD he shall not go near a dead body. 7He shall not make himself unclean even for his father or his mother, for his brother or his sister, when they die, because his separation to God *is* on his head. 8All the days of his separation he shall be holy to the LORD.

9'And if anyone dies very suddenly beside him, and he defiles his consecrated head, then he shall shave his head on the day of his cleansing; on the seventh day he shall shave it. 10Then on the eighth day he shall bring two turtledoves or two young pigeons to the priest, to the door of the tabernacle of meeting; 11and the priest shall offer one as a sin offering and *the* other as a burnt offering, and make atonement for him, because he sinned in regard to the corpse; and he shall sanctify his head that same day. 12He shall consecrate to the LORD the days of his separation, and bring a male lamb in its first year as a trespass offering; but the former days shall be lost, because his separation was defiled.

13'Now this *is* the law of the Nazirite: When the days of his separation are fulfilled, he shall be brought to the door of the tabernacle of meeting. 14And he shall present his offering to the LORD: one male lamb in its first year without blemish as a burnt offering, one ewe lamb in its first year without blemish as a sin offering, one ram without blemish as a peace offering, 15a basket of unleavened bread, cakes of fine flour mixed with oil, unleavened wafers anointed with oil; and their grain offering with their drink offerings.

16'Then the priest shall bring *them* before the LORD and offer his sin offering and his burnt offering; 17and he shall offer the ram as a sacrifice of a peace offering to the LORD, with the basket of unleavened bread; the priest shall also offer its grain offering and its drink offering. 18Then the Nazirite shall shave his consecrated head *at* the door of the tabernacle of meeting, and shall take the hair from his consecrated head and put *it* on the fire which is under the sacrifice of the peace offering.

19'And the priest shall take the boiled shoulder of the ram, one unleavened cake from the basket, and one unleavened wafer, and put *them* upon the hands of the Nazirite after he has shaved his consecrated *hair,* 20and the priest shall wave them as a wave offering before the LORD; they *are* holy for the priest, together with the breast of the wave offering and the thigh of the heave offering. After that the Nazirite may drink wine.'

21"This is the law of the Nazirite who vows to the LORD the offering for his separation, and besides that, whatever else his hand is able to provide; according to the vow which he takes, so he must do according to the law of his separation."

The Priestly Blessing

22And the LORD spoke to Moses, saying: 23"Speak to Aaron and his sons, saying, 'This is the way you shall bless the children of Israel. Say to them:
24 "The LORD bless you and keep you;
25 The LORD make His face shine upon you,
    And be gracious to you;
26 The LORD lift up His countenance upon you,
    And give you peace." '
27"So they shall put My name on the children of Israel, and I will bless them."

Offerings of the Leaders

7 Now it came to pass, when Moses had finished setting up the tabernacle, that he anointed it and consecrated it and all its furnishings, and the altar and all its utensils; so he anointed them and consecrated them. 2Then the leaders of Israel, the heads of their fathers' houses, who *were* the leaders of the tribes and over those who were numbered, made an offering. 3And they brought their offering before the LORD, six covered carts and twelve oxen, a cart for *every* two of the leaders, and for each one an ox; and they presented them before the tabernacle.

4Then the LORD spoke to Moses, saying, 5"Accept *these* from them, that they may be used in doing the work of the tabernacle of meeting; and you shall give them to the Levites, *to* every man according to his service." 6So Moses took the carts and the oxen, and gave them to the Levites. 7Two carts and four oxen he gave to the sons of Gershon, according to their service; 8and four carts and eight oxen he gave to the sons of Merari, according to their service, under the authority of Ithamar the son of Aaron the priest. 9But to the sons of Kohath he gave none, because theirs *was* the service of the holy things, *which* they carried on their shoulders.

10Now the leaders offered the dedication *offering* for the altar when it was anointed; so the leaders offered their offering before the altar. 11For the LORD said to Moses, "They shall offer their offering, one leader each day, for the dedication of the altar."

12And the one who offered his offering on the first day *was* Nahshon the son of Amminadab, from the tribe of Judah. 13His offering *was* one silver platter, the weight of which *was* one hundred and thirty *shekels,* and one silver bowl of seventy shekels, according to the shekel of the sanctuary, both of them full of fine flour mixed with oil as a grain offering; 14one gold pan of ten *shekels,* full of incense; 15one young bull, one ram, and one male lamb in its first year, as a burnt offering; 16one kid of the goats as a sin offering; 17and for the sacrifice of peace offerings: two oxen, five rams, five male goats, and five male lambs in their first year. This *was* the offering of Nahshon the son of Amminadab.

18On the second day Nethanel the son of Zuar, leader of Issachar, presented *an offering.* 19*For* his offering he offered one silver platter, the weight of which *was* one hundred and thirty *shekels,* and one silver bowl of seventy shekels, according to the shekel of the sanctuary, both of them full of fine flour mixed with oil as a grain offering; 20one gold pan of ten *shekels*, full of incense; 21one young bull, one ram, and one male lamb in its first year, as a burnt offering; 22one kid of the goats as a sin offering; 23and as the sacrifice of peace offerings: two oxen, five rams, five male goats, and five male lambs in their first year. This *was* the offering of Nethanel the son of Zuar.

24On the third day Eliab the son of Helon, leader of the children of Zebulun, *presented an offering*. 25His offering *was* one silver platter, the weight of which *was* one hundred and thirty *shekels*, and one silver bowl of seventy shekels, according to the shekel of the sanctuary, both of them full of fine flour mixed with oil as a grain offering; 26one gold pan of ten *shekels*, full of incense; 27one young bull, one ram, and one male lamb in its first year, as a burnt offering; 28one kid of the goats as a sin offering; 29and for the sacrifice of peace offerings: two oxen, five rams, five male goats, and five male lambs in their first year. This *was* the offering of Eliab the son of Helon.

30On the fourth day Elizur the son of Shedeur, leader of the children of Reuben, *presented an offering*. 31His offering *was* one silver platter, the weight of which *was* one hundred and thirty *shekels*, and one silver bowl of seventy shekels, according to the shekel of the sanctuary, both of them full of fine flour mixed with oil as a grain offering; 32one gold pan of ten *shekels*, full of incense; 33one young bull, one ram, and one male lamb in its first year, as a burnt offering; 34one kid of the goats as a sin offering; 35and as the sacrifice of peace offerings: two oxen, five rams, five male goats, and five male lambs in their first year. This *was* the offering of Elizur the son of Shedeur.

36On the fifth day Shelumiel the son of Zurishaddai, leader of the children of Simeon, *presented an offering*. 37His offering *was* one silver platter, the weight of which *was* one hundred and thirty *shekels*, and one silver bowl of seventy shekels, according to the shekel of the sanctuary, both of them full of fine flour mixed with oil as a grain offering; 38one gold pan of ten *shekels*, full of incense; 39one young

bull, one ram, and one male lamb in its first year, as a burnt offering; 40one kid of the goats as a sin offering; 41and as the sacrifice of peace offerings: two oxen, five rams, five male goats, and five male lambs in their first year. This *was* the offering of Shelumiel the son of Zurishaddai.

42On the sixth day Eliasaph the son of Deuel, leader of the children of Gad, *presented an offering*. 43His offering *was* one silver platter, the weight of which *was* one hundred and thirty *shekels*, and one silver bowl of seventy shekels, according to the shekel of the sanctuary, both of them full of fine flour mixed with oil as a grain offering; 44one gold pan of ten *shekels*, full of incense; 45one young bull, one ram, and one male lamb in its first year, as a burnt offering; 46one kid of the goats as a sin offering; 47and as the sacrifice of peace offerings: two oxen, five rams, five male goats, and five male lambs in their first year. This *was* the offering of Eliasaph the son of Deuel.

48On the seventh day Elishama the son of Ammihud, leader of the children of Ephraim, *presented an offering*. 49His offering *was* one silver platter, the weight of which *was* one hundred and thirty *shekels*, and one silver bowl of seventy shekels, according to the shekel of the sanctuary, both of them full of fine flour mixed with oil as a grain offering; 50one gold pan of ten *shekels*, full of incense; 51one young bull, one ram, and one male lamb in its first year, as a burnt offering; 52one kid of the goats as a sin offering; 53and as the sacrifice of peace offerings: two oxen, five rams, five male goats, and five male lambs in their first year. This *was* the offering of Elishama the son of Ammihud.

54On the eighth day Gamaliel the son of Pedahzur, leader of the children of Manasseh, *presented an offering*. 55His offering *was* one silver platter, the weight of which *was* one hundred and thirty *shekels*, and one silver bowl of seventy shekels, according to the shekel of the sanctuary, both of them full of fine flour mixed with oil as a grain offering; 56one gold pan of ten *shekels*, full of incense; 57one young bull, one ram, and one male lamb in its first year, as a burnt offering; 58one kid of the goats as a sin offering; 59and as the sacrifice of peace offerings: two oxen, five rams, five male goats, and five male lambs in their first year. This *was* the offering of Gamaliel the son of Pedahzur.

60On the ninth day Abidan the son of Gideoni, leader of the children of Benjamin, *presented an offering*. 61His offering *was* one silver platter, the weight of which *was* one hundred and thirty *shekels*, and one silver bowl of seventy shekels, according to the shekel of the sanctuary, both of them full of fine flour mixed with oil as a grain offering; 62one gold pan of ten *shekels*, full of incense; 63one young bull, one ram, and one male lamb in its first year, as a burnt offering; 64one kid of the goats as a sin offering; 65and as the sacrifice of peace offerings: two oxen, five rams, five male goats, and five male lambs in their first year. This *was* the offering of Abidan the son of Gideoni.

66On the tenth day Ahiezer the son of Ammishaddai, leader of the children of Dan, *presented an offering*. 67His offering *was* one silver platter, the weight of which *was* one hundred and thirty *shekels*, and one silver bowl of seventy shekels, according to the shekel of the sanctuary, both of them full of fine flour mixed with oil as a grain offering; 68one gold pan of ten *shekels*, full of incense; 69one young bull, one ram, and one male lamb in its first year, as a burnt offering; 70one kid of the goats as a sin offering; 71and as the sacrifice of peace offerings: two oxen, five rams, five male goats, and five male lambs in their first year. This *was* the offering of Ahiezer the son of Ammishaddai.

72On the eleventh day Pagiel the son of Ocran, leader of the children of Asher, *presented an offering*. 73His offering *was* one silver platter, the weight of which *was* one hundred and thirty *shekels*, and one silver bowl of seventy shekels, according to the shekel of the sanctuary, both of them full of fine flour mixed with oil as a grain offering; 74one gold pan of ten *shekels*, full of incense; 75one young bull, one ram, and one male lamb in its first year, as a

burnt offering; 76one kid of the goats as a sin offering; 77and as the sacrifice of peace offerings: two oxen, five rams, five male goats, and five male lambs in their first year. This *was* the offering of Pagiel the son of Ocran.

78On the twelfth day Ahira the son of Enan, leader of the children of Naphtali, *presented an offering*. 79His offering *was* one silver platter, the weight of which *was* one hundred and thirty *shekels*, and one silver bowl of seventy shekels, according to the shekel of the sanctuary, both of them full of fine flour mixed with oil as a grain offering; 80one gold pan of ten *shekels*, full of incense; 81one young bull, one ram, and one male lamb in its first year, as a burnt offering; 82one kid of the goats as a sin offering; 83and as the sacrifice of peace offerings: two oxen, five rams, five male goats, and five male lambs in their first year. This *was* the offering of Ahira the son of Enan.

84This *was* the dedication *offering* for the altar from the leaders of Israel, when it was anointed: twelve silver platters, twelve silver bowls, and twelve gold pans. 85Each silver platter *weighed* one hundred and thirty *shekels* and each bowl seventy *shekels*. All the silver of the vessels *weighed* two thousand four hundred *shekels*, according to the shekel of the sanctuary. 86The twelve gold pans full of incense *weighed* ten *shekels* apiece, according to the shekel of the sanctuary; all the gold of the pans *weighed* one hundred and twenty *shekels*. 87All the oxen for the burnt offering *were* twelve young bulls, the rams twelve, the male lambs in their first year twelve, with their grain offering, and the kids of the goats as a sin offering twelve. 88And all the oxen for the sacrifice of peace offerings were twenty-four bulls, the rams sixty, the male goats sixty, and the lambs in their first year sixty. This *was* the dedication *offering* for the altar after it was anointed.

89Now when Moses went into the tabernacle of meeting to speak with Him, he heard the voice of One speaking to him from above the mercy seat that *was* on the ark of the Testimony, from between the two cherubim; thus He spoke to him.

Arrangement of the Lamps

8 And the LORD spoke to Moses, saying: 2"Speak to Aaron, and say to him, 'When you arrange the lamps, the seven lamps shall give light in front of the lampstand.' " 3And Aaron did so; he arranged the lamps to face toward the front of the lampstand, as the LORD commanded Moses. 4Now this workmanship of the lampstand *was* hammered gold; from its shaft to its flowers it *was* hammered work. According to the pattern which the LORD had shown Moses, so he made the lampstand.

Cleansing and Dedication of the Levites

5Then the LORD spoke to Moses, saying: 6"Take the Levites from among the children of Israel and cleanse them *ceremonially.* 7Thus you shall do to them to cleanse them: Sprinkle water of purification on them, and let them shave all their body, and let them wash their clothes, and *so* make themselves clean. 8Then let them take a young bull with its grain offering of fine flour mixed with oil, and you shall take another young bull as a sin offering. 9And you shall bring the Levites before the tabernacle of meeting, and you shall gather together the whole congregation of the children of Israel. 10So you shall bring the Levites before the LORD, and the children of Israel shall lay their hands on the Levites; 11and Aaron shall offer the Levites before the LORD *like* a wave offering from the children of Israel, that they may perform the work of the LORD. 12Then the Levites shall lay their hands on the heads of the young bulls, and you shall offer one as a sin offering and the other as a burnt offering to the LORD, to make atonement for the Levites. 13"And you shall stand the Levites before Aaron and his sons, and then offer them *like* a wave offering to the LORD. 14Thus you shall separate the Levites from among the children of Israel, and the Levites shall be Mine. 15After that the Levites shall go in to service the tabernacle of meeting. So you shall cleanse them and offer them *like* a wave offering. 16For they *are* wholly given to Me from among the children of Israel; I have taken them for Myself instead of all who open the womb, the firstborn of all the children of Israel. 17For all the firstborn among the children of Israel *are* Mine, *both* man and beast; on the day that I struck all the firstborn in the land of Egypt I sanctified them to Myself. 18I have taken the Levites instead of all the firstborn of the children of Israel. 19And I have given the Levites as a gift to Aaron and his sons from among the children of Israel, to do the work for the children of Israel in the tabernacle of meeting, and to make atonement for the children of Israel, that there be no plague among the children of Israel when the children of Israel come near the sanctuary."

20Thus Moses and Aaron and all the congregation of the children of Israel did to the Levites; according to all that the LORD commanded Moses concerning the Levites, so the children of Israel did to them. 21And the Levites purified themselves and washed their clothes; then Aaron presented them *like* a wave offering before the LORD, and Aaron made atonement for them to cleanse them. 22After that the Levites went in to do their work in the tabernacle of meeting before Aaron and his sons; as the LORD commanded Moses concerning the Levites, so they did to them.

23Then the LORD spoke to Moses, saying, 24"This *is* what *pertains* to the Levites: From twenty-five years old and above one may enter to perform service in the work of the tabernacle of meeting; 25and at the age of fifty years they must cease performing this work, and shall work no more. 26They may minister with their brethren in the tabernacle of meeting, to attend to needs, but they *themselves* shall do no work. Thus you shall do to the Levites regarding their duties."

The Second Passover

9 Now the LORD spoke to Moses in the Wilderness of Sinai, in the first month of the second year after they had come out of the land of Egypt, saying: 2"Let the children of Israel keep the Passover at its appointed time. 3On the fourteenth day of this month, at twilight, you shall keep it at its appointed time. According to all its rites

and ceremonies you shall keep it."
4So Moses told the children of Israel
that they should keep the Passover.
5And they kept the Passover on the
fourteenth day of the first month, at twilight, in the Wilderness of Sinai; according to all that the LORD commanded
Moses, so the children of Israel did.

6Now there were *certain* men who
were defiled by a human corpse, so that
they could not keep the Passover on
that day; and they came before Moses
and Aaron that day. 7And those men
said to him, "We *became* defiled by a
human corpse. Why are we kept from
presenting the offering of the LORD at
its appointed time among the children
of Israel?"

8And Moses said to them, "Stand still,
that I may hear what the LORD will command concerning you."

9Then the LORD spoke to Moses, saying, 10"Speak to the children of Israel,
saying: 'If anyone of you or your posterity is unclean because of a corpse, or
is far away on a journey, he may still
keep the LORD's Passover. 11On the
fourteenth day of the second month, at
twilight, they may keep it. They shall
eat it with unleavened bread and bitter
herbs. 12They shall leave none of it until
morning, nor break one of its bones.
According to all the ordinances of the
Passover they shall keep it. 13But the
man who *is* clean and is not on a journey, and ceases to keep the Passover,
that same person shall be cut off from
among his people, because he did not
bring the offering of the LORD at its
appointed time; that man shall bear
his sin.

14'And if a stranger dwells among
you, and would keep the LORD's Passover, he must do so according to the
rite of the Passover and according to
its ceremony; you shall have one ordinance, both for the stranger and the native of the land.' "

The Cloud and the Fire

15Now on the day that the tabernacle
was raised up, the cloud covered the
tabernacle, the tent of the Testimony;
from evening until morning it was
above the tabernacle like the appearance of fire. 16So it was always: the
cloud covered it *by day*, and the appear-

ance of fire by night. 17Whenever the
cloud was taken up from above the tabernacle, after that the children of Israel
would journey; and in the place where
the cloud settled, there the children of
Israel would pitch their tents. 18At the
command of the LORD the children of
Israel would journey, and at the command of the LORD they would camp; as
long as the cloud stayed above the tabernacle they remained encamped.
19Even when the cloud continued long,
many days above the tabernacle, the
children of Israel kept the charge of the
LORD and did not journey. 20So it was,
when the cloud was above the tabernacle a few days: according to the command of the LORD they would remain
encamped, and according to the command of the LORD they would journey.
21So it was, when the cloud remained
only from evening until morning: when
the cloud was taken up in the morning,
then they would journey; whether by
day or by night, whenever the cloud
was taken up, they would journey.
22*Whether it was* two days, a month,
or a year that the cloud remained above
the tabernacle, the children of Israel
would remain encamped and not journey; but when it was taken up, they
would journey. 23At the command of
the LORD they remained encamped, and
at the command of the LORD they journeyed; they kept the charge of the LORD,
at the command of the LORD by the
hand of Moses.

Two Silver Trumpets

10 And the LORD spoke to Moses,
saying: 2"Make two silver trumpets for yourself; you shall make them
of hammered work; you shall use them
for calling the congregation and for di-
recting the movement of the camps.
3When they blow both of them, all the
congregation shall gather before you at
the door of the tabernacle of meeting.
4But if they blow *only* one, then the
leaders, the heads of the divisions of Israel, shall gather to you. 5When you
sound the advance, the camps that lie
on the east side shall then begin their
journey. 6When you sound the advance
the second time, then the camps that
lie on the south side shall begin their
journey; they shall sound the call for

them to begin their journeys. 7And when the assembly is to be gathered together, you shall blow, but not sound the advance. 8The sons of Aaron, the priests, shall blow the trumpets; and these shall be to you as an ordinance forever throughout your generations.

9"When you go to war in your land against the enemy who oppresses you, then you shall sound an alarm with the trumpets, and you will be remembered before the LORD your God, and you will be saved from your enemies. 10Also in the day of your gladness, in your appointed feasts, and at the beginning of your months, you shall blow the trumpets over your burnt offerings and over the sacrifices of your peace offerings; and they shall be a memorial for you before your God: I *am* the LORD your God."

Departure from Sinai

11Now it came to pass on the twentieth *day* of the second month, in the second year, that the cloud was taken up from above the tabernacle of the Testimony. 12And the children of Israel set out from the Wilderness of Sinai on their journeys; then the cloud settled down in the Wilderness of Paran. 13So they started out for the first time according to the command of the LORD by the hand of Moses.

14The standard of the camp of the children of Judah set out first according to their armies; over their army was Nahshon the son of Amminadab. 15Over the army of the tribe of the children of Issachar *was* Nethanel the son of Zuar. 16And over the army of the tribe of the children of Zebulun *was* Eliab the son of Helon.

17Then the tabernacle was taken down; and the sons of Gershon and the sons of Merari set out, carrying the tabernacle.

18And the standard of the camp of Reuben set out according to their armies; over their army *was* Elizur the son of Shedeur. 19Over the army of the tribe of the children of Simeon *was* Shelumiel the son of Zurishaddai. 20And over the army of the tribe of the children of Gad *was* Eliasaph the son of Deuel.

21Then the Kohathites set out, carrying the holy things. (The tabernacle would be prepared for their arrival.)

22And the standard of the camp of the children of Ephraim set out according to their armies; over their army *was* Elishama the son of Ammihud. 23Over the army of the tribe of the children of Manasseh *was* Gamaliel the son of Pedahzur. 24And over the army of the tribe of the children of Benjamin *was* Abidan the son of Gideoni.

25Then the standard of the camp of the children of Dan (the rear guard of all the camps) set out according to their armies; over their army *was* Ahiezer the son of Ammishaddai. 26Over the army of the tribe of the children of Asher *was* Pagiel the son of Ocran. 27And over the army of the tribe of the children of Naphtali *was* Ahira the son of Enan.

28Thus *was* the order of march of the children of Israel, according to their armies, when they began their journey.

29Now Moses said to Hobab the son of Reuel the Midianite, Moses' father-in-law, "We are setting out for the place of which the LORD said, 'I will give it to you.' Come with us, and we will treat you well; for the LORD has promised good things to Israel."

30And he said to him, "I will not go, but I will depart to my *own* land and to my relatives."

31So *Moses* said, "Please do not leave, inasmuch as you know how we are to camp in the wilderness, and you can be our eyes. 32And it shall be, if you go with us—indeed it shall be—that whatever good the LORD will do to us, the same we will do to you."

33So they departed from the mountain of the LORD on a journey of three days; and the ark of the covenant of the LORD went before them for the three days' journey, to search out a resting place for them. 34And the cloud of the LORD *was* above them by day when they went out from the camp.

35So it was, whenever the ark set out, that Moses said:

"Rise up, O LORD!
Let Your enemies be scattered,
And let those who hate You flee
    before You."

36And when it rested, he said:
"Return, O Lᴏʀᴅ,
To the many thousands of Israel."

The People Complain

11 Now *when* the people complained, it displeased the Lᴏʀᴅ; for the Lᴏʀᴅ heard *it,* and His anger was aroused. So the fire of the Lᴏʀᴅ burned among them, and consumed *some* in the outskirts of the camp. 2Then the people cried out to Moses, and when Moses prayed to the Lᴏʀᴅ, the fire was quenched. 3So he called the name of the place Taberah,ᵃ because the fire of the Lᴏʀᴅ had burned among them.

4Now the mixed multitude who were among them yielded to intense craving; so the children of Israel also wept again and said: "Who will give us meat to eat? 5We remember the fish which we ate freely in Egypt, the cucumbers, the melons, the leeks, the onions, and the garlic; 6but now our whole being *is* dried up; *there is* nothing at all except this manna *before* our eyes!"

7Now the manna *was* like coriander seed, and its color like the color of bdellium. 8The people went about and gathered *it,* ground *it* on millstones or beat *it* in the mortar, cooked *it* in pans, and made cakes of it; and its taste was like the taste of pastry prepared with oil. 9And when the dew fell on the camp in the night, the manna fell on it.

10Then Moses heard the people weeping throughout their families, everyone at the door of his tent; and the anger of the Lᴏʀᴅ was greatly aroused; Moses also was displeased. 11So Moses said to the Lᴏʀᴅ, "Why have You afflicted Your servant? And why have I not found favor in Your sight, that You have laid the burden of all these people on me? 12Did I conceive all these people? Did I beget them, that You should say to me, 'Carry them in your bosom, as a guardian carries a nursing child,' to the land which You swore to their fathers? 13Where am I to get meat to give to all these people? For they weep all over me, saying, 'Give us meat, that we may eat.' 14I am not able to bear all these people alone, because the bur-

den *is* too heavy for me. 15If You treat me like this, please kill me here and now—if I have found favor in Your sight—and do not let me see my wretchedness!"

The Seventy Elders

16So the Lᴏʀᴅ said to Moses: "Gather to Me seventy men of the elders of Israel, whom you know to be the elders of the people and officers over them; bring them to the tabernacle of meeting, that they may stand there with you. 17Then I will come down and talk with you there. I will take of the Spirit that *is* upon you and will put *the same* upon them; and they shall bear the burden of the people with you, that you may not bear *it* yourself alone. 18Then you shall say to the people, 'Consecrate yourselves for tomorrow, and you shall eat meat; for you have wept in the hearing of the Lᴏʀᴅ, saying, "Who will give us meat to eat? For *it was* well with us in Egypt." Therefore the Lᴏʀᴅ will give you meat, and you shall eat. 19You shall eat, not one day, nor two days, nor five days, nor ten days, nor twenty days, 20but *for* a whole month, until it comes out of your nostrils and becomes loathsome to you, because you have despised the Lᴏʀᴅ who is among you, and have wept before Him, saying, "Why did we ever come up out of Egypt?" ' "

21And Moses said, "The people whom I *am* among *are* six hundred thousand men on foot; yet You have said, 'I will give them meat, that they may eat *for* a whole month.' 22Shall flocks and herds be slaughtered for them, to provide enough for them? Or shall all the fish of the sea be gathered together for them, to provide enough for them?"

23And the Lᴏʀᴅ said to Moses, "Has the Lᴏʀᴅ's arm been shortened? Now you shall see whether what I say will happen to you or not."

24So Moses went out and told the people the words of the Lᴏʀᴅ, and he gathered the seventy men of the elders of the people and placed them around the tabernacle. 25Then the Lᴏʀᴅ came down in the cloud, and spoke to him, and took of the Spirit that *was* upon him, and placed *the same* upon the

ᵃ Literally *Burning*

seventy elders; and it happened, when the Spirit rested upon them, that they prophesied, although they never did *so* again.

26But two men had remained in the camp: the name of one *was* Eldad, and the name of the other Medad. And the Spirit rested upon them. Now they *were* among those listed, but who had not gone out to the tabernacle; yet they prophesied in the camp. 27And a young man ran and told Moses, and said, "Eldad and Medad are prophesying in the camp."

28So Joshua the son of Nun, Moses' assistant, *one* of his choice men, answered and said, "Moses my lord, forbid them!"

29Then Moses said to him, "Are you zealous for my sake? Oh, that all the LORD's people were prophets *and* that the LORD would put His Spirit upon them!" 30And Moses returned to the camp, he and the elders of Israel.

The LORD Sends Quail

31Now a wind went out from the LORD, and it brought quail from the sea and left *them* fluttering near the camp, about a day's journey on this side and about a day's journey on the other side, all around the camp, and about two cubits above the surface of the ground. 32And the people stayed up all that day, all night, and all the next day, and gathered the quail (he who gathered least gathered ten homers); and they spread *them* out for themselves all around the camp. 33But while the meat *was* still between their teeth, before it was chewed, the wrath of the LORD was aroused against the people, and the LORD struck the people with a very great plague. 34So he called the name of that place Kibroth Hattaavah,b because there they buried the people who had yielded to craving.

35From Kibroth Hattaavah the people moved to Hazeroth, and camped at Hazeroth.

Dissension of Aaron and Miriam

12 Then Miriam and Aaron spoke against Moses because of the Ethiopian woman whom he had married; for he had married an Ethiopian woman. 2So they said, "Has the LORD indeed spoken only through Moses? Has He not spoken through us also?" And the LORD heard *it*. 3(Now the man Moses *was* very humble, more than all men who *were* on the face of the earth.)

4Suddenly the LORD said to Moses, Aaron, and Miriam, "Come out, you three, to the tabernacle of meeting!" So the three came out. 5Then the LORD came down in the pillar of cloud and stood *in* the door of the tabernacle, and called Aaron and Miriam. And they both went forward. 6Then He said,

"Hear now My words:
If there is a prophet among you,
 I, the LORD, make Myself known to
   him in a vision;
 I speak to him in a dream.
7 Not so with My servant Moses;
 He *is* faithful in all My house.
8 I speak with him face to face,
 Even plainly, and not in dark
   sayings;
 And he sees the form of the LORD.
 Why then were you not afraid
 To speak against My servant
   Moses?"

9So the anger of the LORD was aroused against them, and He departed. 10And when the cloud departed from above the tabernacle, suddenly Miriam *became* leprous, as *white as* snow. Then Aaron turned toward Miriam, and there she was, a leper. 11So Aaron said to Moses, "Oh, my lord! Please do not lay *this* sin on us, in which we have done foolishly and in which we have sinned. 12Please do not let her be as one dead, whose flesh is half consumed when he comes out of his mother's womb!"

13So Moses cried out to the LORD, saying, "Please heal her, O God, I pray!"

14Then the LORD said to Moses, "If her father had but spit in her face, would she not be shamed seven days? Let her be shut out of the camp seven days, and afterward she may be received *again*." 15So Miriam was shut out of the camp seven days, and the people did not journey till Miriam was brought in *again*. 16And afterward the

b Literally *Graves of Craving*

people moved from Hazeroth and camped in the Wilderness of Paran.

Spies Sent into Canaan

13 And the LORD spoke to Moses, saying, 2"Send men to spy out the land of Canaan, which I am giving to the children of Israel; from each tribe of their fathers you shall send a man, every one a leader among them."

3So Moses sent them from the Wilderness of Paran according to the command of the LORD, all of them men who *were* heads of the children of Israel. 4Now these *were* their names: from the tribe of Reuben, Shammua the son of Zaccur; 5from the tribe of Simeon, Shaphat the son of Hori; 6from the tribe of Judah, Caleb the son of Jephunneh; 7from the tribe of Issachar, Igal the son of Joseph; 8from the tribe of Ephraim, Hoshea the son of Nun; 9from the tribe of Benjamin, Palti the son of Raphu; 10from the tribe of Zebulun, Gaddiel the son of Sodi; 11from the tribe of Joseph, *that is*, from the tribe of Manasseh, Gaddi the son of Susi; 12from the tribe of Dan, Ammiel the son of Gemalli; 13from the tribe of Asher, Sethur the son of Michael; 14from the tribe of Naphtali, Nahbi the son of Vophsi; 15from the tribe of Gad, Geuel the son of Machi.

16These *are* the names of the men whom Moses sent to spy out the land. And Moses called Hoshea the son of Nun, Joshua.

17Then Moses sent them to spy out the land of Canaan, and said to them, "Go up this *way* into the South, and go up to the mountains, 18and see what the land is like: whether the people who dwell in it *are* strong or weak, few or many; 19whether the land they dwell in *is* good or bad; whether the cities they inhabit *are* like camps or strongholds; 20whether the land *is* rich or poor; and whether there are forests there or not. Be of good courage. And bring some of the fruit of the land." Now the time *was* the season of the first ripe grapes.

21So they went up and spied out the land from the Wilderness of Zin as far as Rehob, near the entrance of Hamath. 22And they went up through the South

and came to Hebron; Ahiman, Sheshai, and Talmai, the descendants of Anak, *were* there. (Now Hebron was built seven years before Zoan in Egypt.) 23Then they came to the Valley of Eshcol, and there cut down a branch with one cluster of grapes; they carried it between two of them on a pole. *They* also *brought* some of the pomegranates and figs. 24The place was called the Valley of Eshcol,^c because of the cluster which the men of Israel cut down there. 25And they returned from spying out the land after forty days.

26Now they departed and came back to Moses and Aaron and all the congregation of the children of Israel in the Wilderness of Paran, at Kadesh; they brought back word to them and to all the congregation, and showed them the fruit of the land. 27Then they told him, and said: "We went to the land where you sent us. It truly flows with milk and honey, and this *is* its fruit. 28Nevertheless the people who dwell in the land *are* strong; the cities *are* fortified *and* very large; moreover we saw the descendants of Anak there. 29The Amalekites dwell in the land of the South; the Hittites, the Jebusites, and the Amorites dwell in the mountains; and the Canaanites dwell by the sea and along the banks of the Jordan."

30Then Caleb quieted the people before Moses, and said, "Let us go up at once and take possession, for we are well able to overcome it."

31But the men who had gone up with him said, "We are not able to go up against the people, for they *are* stronger than we." 32And they gave the children of Israel a bad report of the land which they had spied out, saying, "The land through which we have gone as spies *is* a land that devours its inhabitants, and all the people whom we saw in it *are* men of *great* stature. 33There we saw the giants (the descendants of Anak came from the giants); and we were like grasshoppers in our own sight, and so we were in their sight."

Israel Refuses to Enter Canaan

14 So all the congregation lifted up their voices and cried, and the

---

c Literally *Cluster*

people wept that night. 2And all the children of Israel complained against Moses and Aaron, and the whole congregation said to them, "If only we had died in the land of Egypt! Or if only we had died in this wilderness! 3Why has the LORD brought us to this land to fall by the sword, that our wives and children should become victims? Would it not be better for us to return to Egypt?" 4So they said to one another, "Let us select a leader and return to Egypt."

5Then Moses and Aaron fell on their faces before all the assembly of the congregation of the children of Israel.

6But Joshua the son of Nun and Caleb the son of Jephunneh, *who were* among those who had spied out the land, tore their clothes; 7and they spoke to all the congregation of the children of Israel, saying: "The land we passed through to spy out *is* an exceedingly good land. 8If the LORD delights in us, then He will bring us into this land and give it to us, 'a land which flows with milk and honey.'*d* 9Only do not rebel against the LORD, nor fear the people of the land, for they *are* our bread; their protection has departed from them, and the LORD *is* with us. Do not fear them."

10And all the congregation said to stone them with stones. Now the glory of the LORD appeared in the tabernacle of meeting before all the children of Israel.

Moses Intercedes for the People

11Then the LORD said to Moses: "How long will these people reject Me? And how long will they not believe Me, with all the signs which I have performed among them? 12I will strike them with the pestilence and disinherit them, and I will make of you a nation greater and mightier than they."

13And Moses said to the LORD: "Then the Egyptians will hear *it,* for by Your might You brought these people up from among them, 14and they will tell *it* to the inhabitants of this land. They have heard that You, LORD, *are* among these people; that You, LORD, are seen face to face and Your cloud stands above them, and You go before them in a pillar of cloud by day and in a pillar

of fire by night. 15Now *if* You kill these people as one man, then the nations which have heard of Your fame will speak, saying, 16'Because the LORD was not able to bring this people to the land which He swore to give them, therefore He killed them in the wilderness.' 17And now, I pray, let the power of my Lord be great, just as You have spoken, saying, 18'The LORD is longsuffering and abundant in mercy, forgiving iniquity and transgression; but He by no means clears *the guilty,* visiting the iniquity of the fathers on the children to the third and fourth *generation.'e* 19Pardon the iniquity of this people, I pray, according to the greatness of Your mercy, just as You have forgiven this people, from Egypt even until now."

20Then the LORD said: "I have pardoned, according to your word; 21but truly, as I live, all the earth shall be filled with the glory of the LORD— 22because all these men who have seen My glory and the signs which I did in Egypt and in the wilderness, and have put Me to the test now these ten times, and have not heeded My voice, 23they certainly shall not see the land of which I swore to their fathers, nor shall any of those who rejected Me see it. 24But My servant Caleb, because he has a different spirit in him and has followed Me fully, I will bring into the land where he went, and his descendants shall inherit it. 25Now the Amalekites and the Canaanites dwell in the valley; tomorrow turn and move out into the wilderness by the Way of the Red Sea."

Death Sentence on the Rebels

26And the LORD spoke to Moses and Aaron, saying, 27"How long *shall I bear with* this evil congregation who complain against Me? I have heard the complaints which the children of Israel make against Me. 28Say to them, 'As I live,' says the LORD, 'just as you have spoken in My hearing, so I will do to you: 29The carcasses of you who have complained against Me shall fall in this wilderness, all of you who were numbered, according to your entire number, from twenty years old and above.

d Compare Exodus 3.8   *e* Compare Exodus 34.6, 7

30Except for Caleb the son of Jephunneh and Joshua the son of Nun, you shall by no means enter the land which I swore I would make you dwell in. 31But your little ones, whom you said would be victims, I will bring in, and they shall know the land which you have despised. 32But *as for* you, your carcasses shall fall in this wilderness. 33And your sons shall be shepherds in the wilderness forty years, and bear the brunt of your infidelity, until your carcasses are consumed in the wilderness. 34According to the number of the days in which you spied out the land, forty days, for each day you shall bear your guilt one year, *namely* forty years, and you shall know My rejection. 35I the LORD have spoken this. I will surely do so to all this evil congregation who are gathered together against Me. In this wilderness they shall be consumed, and there they shall die.' "

36Now the men whom Moses sent to spy out the land, who returned and made all the congregation complain against him by bringing a bad report of the land, 37those very men who brought the evil report about the land, died by the plague before the LORD. 38But Joshua the son of Nun and Caleb the son of Jephunneh remained alive, of the men who went to spy out the land.

A Futile Invasion Attempt

39Then Moses told these words to all the children of Israel, and the people mourned greatly. 40And they rose early in the morning and went up to the top of the mountain, saying, "Here we are, and we will go up to the place which the LORD has promised, for we have sinned!"

41And Moses said, "Now why do you transgress the command of the LORD? For this will not succeed. 42Do not go up, lest you be defeated by your enemies, for the LORD *is* not among you. 43For the Amalekites and the Canaanites *are* there before you, and you shall fall by the sword; because you have turned away from the LORD, the LORD will not be with you."

44But they presumed to go up to the mountaintop. Nevertheless, neither the ark of the covenant of the LORD nor Moses departed from the camp. 45Then the Amalekites and the Canaanites who dwelt in that mountain came down and attacked them, and drove them back as far as Hormah.

Laws of Grain and Drink Offerings

15 And the LORD spoke to Moses, saying, 2"Speak to the children of Israel, and say to them: 'When you have come into the land you are to inhabit, which I am giving to you, 3and you make an offering by fire to the LORD, a burnt offering or a sacrifice, to fulfill a vow or as a freewill offering or in your appointed feasts, to make a sweet aroma to the LORD, from the herd or the flock, 4then he who presents his offering to the LORD shall bring a grain offering of one-tenth *of an ephah* of fine flour mixed with one-fourth of a hin of oil; 5and one-fourth of a hin of wine as a drink offering you shall prepare with the burnt offering or the sacrifice, for each lamb. 6Or for a ram you shall prepare as a grain offering two-tenths *of an ephah* of fine flour mixed with one-third of a hin of oil; 7and as a drink offering you shall offer one-third of a hin of wine as a sweet aroma to the LORD. 8And when you prepare a young bull as a burnt offering, or as a sacrifice to fulfill a vow, or as a peace offering to the LORD, 9then shall be offered with the young bull a grain offering of three-tenths *of an ephah* of fine flour mixed with half a hin of oil; 10and you shall bring as the drink offering half a hin of wine as an offering made by fire, a sweet aroma to the LORD.

11'Thus it shall be done for each young bull, for each ram, or for each lamb or young goat. 12According to the number that you prepare, so you shall do with everyone according to their number. 13All who are native-born shall do these things in this manner, in presenting an offering made by fire, a sweet aroma to the LORD. 14And if a stranger dwells with you, or whoever *is* among you throughout your generations, and would present an offering made by fire, a sweet aroma to the LORD, just as you do, so shall he do. 15One ordinance *shall be* for you of the assembly and for the stranger who dwells *with you*, an ordinance forever throughout your generations; as you are, so shall the stranger be before the LORD. 16One law and one custom shall be for you and for the stranger who dwells with you.' "*f*

17Again the LORD spoke to Moses, saying, 18"Speak to the children of Israel, and say to them: 'When you come into the land to which I bring you, 19then it will be, when you eat of the bread of the land, that you shall offer up a heave offering to the LORD. 20You shall offer up a cake of the first of your ground meal *as* a heave offering; as a heave offering of the threshing floor, so shall you offer it up. 21Of the first of your ground meal you shall give to the LORD a heave offering throughout your generations.

Laws Concerning Unintentional Sin

22'If you sin unintentionally, and do not observe all these commandments which the LORD has spoken to Moses— 23all that the LORD has commanded you by the hand of Moses, from the day the LORD gave commandment and onward throughout your generations—24then it will be, if it is unintentionally committed, without the knowledge of the congregation, that the whole congregation shall offer one young bull as a burnt offering, as a sweet aroma to the LORD, with its grain offering and its drink offering, according to the ordinance, and one kid of the goats as a sin offering. 25So the priest shall make atonement for the whole congregation of the children of Israel, and it shall be forgiven them, for it was unintentional; they shall bring their offering, an offering made by fire to the LORD, and their sin offering before the LORD, for their unintended sin. 26It shall be forgiven the whole congregation of the children of Israel and the stranger who dwells among them, because all the people *did it* unintentionally.

27'And if a person sins unintentionally, then he shall bring a female goat in its first year as a sin offering. 28So the priest shall make atonement for the person who sins unintentionally, when he sins unintentionally before the LORD, to make atonement for him; and

it shall be forgiven him. 29You shall have one law for him who sins unintentionally, *for* him who is native-born among the children of Israel and for the stranger who dwells among them.

Law Concerning Presumptuous Sin

30'But the person who does *anything* presumptuously, *whether he is* native-born or a stranger, that one brings reproach on the LORD, and he shall be cut off from among his people. 31Because he has despised the word of the LORD, and has broken His commandment, that person shall be completely cut off; his guilt *shall be* upon him.' "

Penalty for Violating the Sabbath

32Now while the children of Israel were in the wilderness, they found a man gathering sticks on the Sabbath day. 33And those who found him gathering sticks brought him to Moses and Aaron, and to all the congregation. 34They put him under guard, because it had not been explained what should be done to him.

35Then the LORD said to Moses, "The man must surely be put to death; all the congregation shall stone him with stones outside the camp." 36So, as the LORD commanded Moses, all the congregation brought him outside the camp and stoned him with stones, and he died.

Tassels on Garments

37Again the LORD spoke to Moses, saying, 38"Speak to the children of Israel: Tell them to make tassels on the corners of their garments throughout their generations, and to put a blue thread in the tassels of the corners. 39And you shall have the tassel, that you may look upon it and remember all the commandments of the LORD and do them, and that you *may* not follow the harlotry to which your own heart and your own eyes are inclined, 40and that you may remember and do all My commandments, and be holy for your God. 41I *am* the LORD your God, who brought you out of the land of Egypt, to be your God: I *am* the LORD your God."

---

f Compare Exodus 12.49

Rebellion Against Moses and Aaron

16 Now Korah the son of Izhar, the son of Kohath, the son of Levi, with Dathan and Abiram the sons of Eliab, and On the son of Peleth, sons of Reuben, took *men;* 2and they rose up before Moses with some of the children of Israel, two hundred and fifty leaders of the congregation, representatives of the congregation, men of renown. 3They gathered together against Moses and Aaron, and said to them, "*You take* too much upon yourselves, for all the congregation *is* holy, every one of them, and the LORD *is* among them. Why then do you exalt yourselves above the assembly of the LORD?"

4So when Moses heard *it,* he fell on his face; 5and he spoke to Korah and all his company, saying, "Tomorrow morning the LORD will show who *is* His and *who is* holy, and will cause *him* to come near to Him. That one whom He chooses He will cause to come near to Him. 6Do this: Take censers, Korah and all your company; 7put fire in them and put incense in them before the LORD tomorrow, and it shall be *that* the man whom the LORD chooses *is* the holy one. *You take* too much upon yourselves, you sons of Levi!"

8Then Moses said to Korah, "Hear now, you sons of Levi: 9*Is it* a small thing to you that the God of Israel has separated you from the congregation of Israel, to bring you near to Himself, to do the work of the tabernacle of the LORD, and to stand before the congregation to serve them; 10and that He has brought you near *to Himself,* you and all your brethren, the sons of Levi, with you? And are you seeking the priesthood also? 11Therefore you and all your company *are* gathered together against the LORD. And what *is* Aaron that you complain against him?"

12And Moses sent to call Dathan and Abiram the sons of Eliab, but they said, "We will not come up! 13*Is it* a small thing that you have brought us up out of a land flowing with milk and honey, to kill us in the wilderness, that you should keep acting like a prince over us? 14Moreover you have not brought us into a land flowing with milk and honey, nor given us inheritance of fields and vineyards. Will you put out the eyes of these men? We will not come up!"

15Then Moses was very angry, and said to the LORD, "Do not respect their offering. I have not taken one donkey from them, nor have I hurt one of them."

16And Moses said to Korah, "Tomorrow, you and all your company be present before the LORD—you and they, as well as Aaron. 17Let each take his censer and put incense in it, and each of you bring his censer before the LORD, two hundred and fifty censers; both you and Aaron, each *with* his censer." 18So every man took his censer, put fire in it, laid incense on it, and stood at the door of the tabernacle of meeting with Moses and Aaron. 19And Korah gathered all the congregation against them at the door of the tabernacle of meeting. Then the glory of the LORD appeared to all the congregation.

20And the LORD spoke to Moses and Aaron, saying, 21"Separate yourselves from among this congregation, that I may consume them in a moment."

22Then they fell on their faces, and said, "O God, the God of the spirits of all flesh, shall one man sin, and You be angry with all the congregation?"

23So the LORD spoke to Moses, saying, 24"Speak to the congregation, saying, 'Get away from the tents of Korah, Dathan, and Abiram.' "

25Then Moses rose and went to Dathan and Abiram, and the elders of Israel followed him. 26And he spoke to the congregation, saying, "Depart now from the tents of these wicked men! Touch nothing of theirs, lest you be consumed in all their sins." 27So they got away from around the tents of Korah, Dathan, and Abiram; and Dathan and Abiram came out and stood at the door of their tents, with their wives, their sons, and their little children.

28And Moses said: "By this you shall know that the LORD has sent me to do all these works, for *I have* not *done them* of my own will. 29If these men die naturally like all men, or if they are visited by the common fate of all men, *then* the LORD has not sent me. 30But if the LORD creates a new thing, and the earth opens its mouth and swallows them up with all that belongs to them, and they go down alive into the pit, then you will understand that these men have rejected the LORD."

31Now it came to pass, as he finished speaking all these words, that the ground split apart under them, 32and the earth opened its mouth and swallowed them up, with their households and all the men with Korah, with all *their* goods. 33So they and all those with them went down alive into the pit; the earth closed over them, and they perished from among the assembly. 34Then all Israel who *were* around them fled at their cry, for they said, "Lest the earth swallow us up *also!*"

35And a fire came out from the LORD and consumed the two hundred and fifty men who were offering incense.

36Then the LORD spoke to Moses, saying: 37"Tell Eleazar, the son of Aaron the priest, to pick up the censers out of the blaze, for they are holy, and scatter the fire some distance away. 38The censers of these men who sinned against their own souls, let them be made into hammered plates as a covering for the altar. Because they presented them before the LORD, therefore they are holy; and they shall be a sign to the children of Israel." 39So Eleazar the priest took the bronze censers, which those who were burned up had presented, and they were hammered out as a covering on the altar, 40*to be* a memorial to the children of Israel that no outsider, who *is* not a descendant of Aaron, should come near to offer incense before the LORD, that he might not become like Korah and his companions, just as the LORD had said to him through Moses.

Complaints of the People

41On the next day all the congregation of the children of Israel complained against Moses and Aaron, saying, "You have killed the people of the LORD." 42Now it happened, when the congregation had gathered against Moses and Aaron, that they turned toward the tabernacle of meeting; and suddenly the cloud covered it, and the glory of the LORD appeared. 43Then Moses and Aaron came before the tabernacle of meeting.

44And the LORD spoke to Moses, saying, 45"Get away from among this congregation, that I may consume them in a moment."

And they fell on their faces.

46So Moses said to Aaron, "Take a censer and put fire in it from the altar, put incense *on it*, and take it quickly to the congregation and make atonement for them; for wrath has gone out from the LORD. The plague has begun." 47Then Aaron took *it* as Moses commanded, and ran into the midst of the assembly; and already the plague had begun among the people. So he put in the incense and made atonement for the people. 48And he stood between the dead and the living; so the plague was stopped. 49Now those who died in the plague were fourteen thousand seven hundred, besides those who died in the Korah incident. 50So Aaron returned to Moses at the door of the tabernacle of meeting, for the plague had stopped.

The Budding of Aaron's Rod

17 And the LORD spoke to Moses, saying: 2"Speak to the children of Israel, and get from them a rod from each father's house, all their leaders according to their fathers' houses—twelve rods. Write each man's name on his rod. 3And you shall write Aaron's name on the rod of Levi. For there shall be one rod for the head of *each* father's house. 4Then you shall place them in the tabernacle of meeting before the Testimony, where I meet with you. 5And it shall be *that* the rod of the man whom I choose will blossom; thus I will rid Myself of the complaints of the children of Israel, which they make against you."

6So Moses spoke to the children of Israel, and each of their leaders gave him a rod apiece, for each leader according to their fathers' houses, twelve rods; and the rod of Aaron *was* among their rods. 7And Moses placed the rods before the LORD in the tabernacle of witness.

8Now it came to pass on the next day that Moses went into the tabernacle of witness, and behold, the rod of Aaron, of the house of Levi, had sprouted and put forth buds, had produced blossoms and yielded ripe almonds. 9Then Moses brought out all the rods from before the LORD to all the children of Israel; and they looked, and each man took his rod.

10And the LORD said to Moses, "Bring Aaron's rod back before the Testimony, to be kept as a sign against the rebels, that you may put their complaints away from Me, lest they die." 11Thus did Moses; just as the LORD had commanded him, so he did.

12So the children of Israel spoke to Moses, saying, "Surely we die, we perish, we all perish! 13Whoever even comes near the tabernacle of the LORD must die. Shall we all utterly die?"

Duties of Priests and Levites

18 Then the LORD said to Aaron: "You and your sons and your father's house with you shall bear the iniquity *related to* the sanctuary, and you and your sons with you shall bear the iniquity *associated with* your priesthood. 2Also bring with you your brethren of the tribe of Levi, the tribe of your father, that they may be joined with you and serve you while you and your sons *are* with you before the tabernacle of witness. 3They shall attend to your needs and all the needs of the tabernacle; but they shall not come near the articles of the sanctuary and the altar, lest they die—they and you also. 4They shall be joined with you and attend to the needs of the tabernacle of meeting, for all the work of the tabernacle; but an outsider shall not come near you. 5And you shall attend to the duties of the sanctuary and the duties of the altar, that there *may* be no more wrath on the children of Israel. 6Behold, I Myself have taken your brethren the Levites from among the children of Israel; *they are* a gift to you, given by the LORD, to do the work of the tabernacle of meeting. 7Therefore you and your sons with you shall attend to your priesthood for everything at the altar and behind the veil; and you shall serve. I give your priesthood *to you* as a gift for service, but the outsider who comes near shall be put to death."

Offerings for Support of the Priests

8And the LORD spoke to Aaron: "Here, I Myself have also given you charge of My heave offerings, all the holy gifts of the children of Israel; I have given them as a portion to you and your sons, as an ordinance forever. 9This shall be yours of the most holy things *reserved* from the fire: every offering of theirs, every grain offering and every sin offering and every trespass offering which they render to Me, *shall be* most holy for you and your sons. 10In a most holy *place* you shall eat it; every male shall eat it. It shall be holy to you.

11"This also *is* yours: the heave offering of their gift, with all the wave offerings of the children of Israel; I have given them to you, and your sons and daughters with you, as an ordinance forever. Everyone who is clean in your house may eat it.

12"All the best of the oil, all the best of the new wine and the grain, their firstfruits which they offer to the LORD, I have given them to you. 13Whatever first ripe fruit is in their land, which they bring to the LORD, shall be yours. Everyone who is clean in your house may eat it.

14"Every devoted thing in Israel shall be yours.

15"Everything that first opens the womb of all flesh, which they bring to the LORD, whether man or beast, shall be yours; nevertheless the firstborn of man you shall surely redeem, and the firstborn of unclean animals you shall redeem. 16And those redeemed of the devoted things you shall redeem when one month old, according to your valuation, for five shekels of silver, according to the shekel of the sanctuary, which *is* twenty gerahs. 17But the firstborn of a cow, the firstborn of a sheep, or the firstborn of a goat you shall not redeem; they *are* holy. You shall sprinkle their blood on the altar, and burn their fat *as* an offering made by fire for a sweet aroma to the LORD. 18And their flesh shall be yours, just as the wave breast and the right thigh are yours.

19"All the heave offerings of the holy things, which the children of Israel offer to the LORD, I have given to you and your sons and daughters with you as an ordinance forever; it *is* a covenant of salt forever before the LORD with you and your descendants with you."

20Then the LORD said to Aaron: "You

shall have no inheritance in their land, nor shall you have any portion among them; I *am* your portion and your inheritance among the children of Israel.

Tithes for Support of the Levites

21"Behold, I have given the children of Levi all the tithes in Israel as an inheritance in return for the work which they perform, the work of the tabernacle of meeting. 22Hereafter the children of Israel shall not come near the tabernacle of meeting, lest they bear sin and die. 23But the Levites shall perform the work of the tabernacle of meeting, and they shall bear their iniquity; *it shall be* a statute forever, throughout your generations, that among the children of Israel they shall have no inheritance. 24For the tithes of the children of Israel, which they offer up *as* a heave offering to the LORD, I have given to the Levites as an inheritance; therefore I have said to them, 'Among the children of Israel they shall have no inheritance.' "

The Tithe of the Levites

25Then the LORD spoke to Moses, saying, 26"Speak thus to the Levites, and say to them: 'When you take from the children of Israel the tithes which I have given you from them as your inheritance, then you shall offer up a heave offering of it to the LORD, a tenth of the tithe. 27And your heave offering shall be reckoned to you as though *it were* the grain of the threshing floor and as the fullness of the winepress. 28Thus you shall also offer a heave offering to the LORD from all your tithes which you receive from the children of Israel, and you shall give the LORD's heave offering from it to Aaron the priest. 29Of all your gifts you shall offer up every heave offering due to the LORD, from all the best of them, the consecrated part of them.' 30Therefore you shall say to them: 'When you have lifted up the best of it, then *the rest* shall be accounted to the Levites as the produce of the threshing floor and as the produce of the winepress. 31You may eat it in any place, you and your households, for it *is* your reward for your work in the tabernacle of meeting. 32And you shall bear no sin because of it, when you have lifted up the best of it. But you

shall not profane the holy gifts of the children of Israel, lest you die.' "

Laws of Purification

19 Now the LORD spoke to Moses and Aaron, saying, 2"This *is* the ordinance of the law which the LORD has commanded, saying: 'Speak to the children of Israel, that they bring you a red heifer without blemish, in which there *is* no defect *and* on which a yoke has never come. 3You shall give it to Eleazar the priest, that he may take it outside the camp, and it shall be slaughtered before him; 4and Eleazar the priest shall take some of its blood with his finger, and sprinkle some of its blood seven times directly in front of the tabernacle of meeting. 5Then the heifer shall be burned in his sight: its hide, its flesh, its blood, and its offal shall be burned. 6And the priest shall take cedar wood and hyssop and scarlet, and cast *them* into the midst of the fire burning the heifer. 7Then the priest shall wash his clothes, he shall bathe in water, and afterward he shall come into the camp; the priest shall be unclean until evening. 8And the one who burns it shall wash his clothes in water, bathe in water, and shall be unclean until evening. 9Then a man *who is* clean shall gather up the ashes of the heifer, and store *them* outside the camp in a clean place; and they shall be kept for the congregation of the children of Israel for the water of purification; it *is* for purifying from sin. 10And the one who gathers the ashes of the heifer shall wash his clothes, and be unclean until evening. It shall be a statute forever to the children of Israel and to the stranger who dwells among them.

11'He who touches the dead body of anyone shall be unclean seven days. 12He shall purify himself with the water on the third day and on the seventh day; *then* he will be clean. But if he does not purify himself on the third day and on the seventh day, he will not be clean. 13Whoever touches the body of anyone who has died, and does not purify himself, defiles the tabernacle of the LORD. That person shall be cut off from Israel. He shall be unclean, because the water of purification was not sprinkled on him; his uncleanness *is* still on him.

14'This *is* the law when a man dies in a tent: All who come into the tent and all who *are* in the tent shall be unclean seven days; 15and every open vessel, which has no cover fastened on it, *is* unclean. 16Whoever in the open field touches one who is slain by a sword or who has died, or a bone of a man, or a grave, shall be unclean seven days.

17'And for an unclean *person* they shall take some of the ashes of the heifer burnt for purification from sin, and running water shall be put on them in a vessel. 18A clean person shall take hyssop and dip *it* in the water, sprinkle *it* on the tent, on all the vessels, on the persons who were there, or on the one who touched a bone, the slain, the dead, or a grave. 19The clean *person* shall sprinkle the unclean on the third day and on the seventh day; and on the seventh day he shall purify himself, wash his clothes, and bathe in water; and at evening he shall be clean.

20'But the man who is unclean and does not purify himself, that person shall be cut off from among the assembly, because he has defiled the sanctuary of the LORD. The water of purification has not been sprinkled on him; he *is* unclean. 21It shall be a perpetual statute for them. He who sprinkles the water of purification shall wash his clothes; and he who touches the water of purification shall be unclean until evening. 22Whatever the unclean *person* touches shall be unclean; and the person who touches *it* shall be unclean until evening.' "

Moses' Error at Kadesh

20 Then the children of Israel, the whole congregation, came into the Wilderness of Zin in the first month, and the people stayed in Kadesh; and Miriam died there and was buried there.

2Now there was no water for the congregation; so they gathered together against Moses and Aaron. 3And the people contended with Moses and spoke, saying: "If only we had died when our brethren died before the LORD! 4Why have you brought up the assembly of the LORD into this wilderness, that we and our animals should die here? 5And why have you made us come up out of Egypt, to bring us to this evil place? It *is* not a place of grain or figs or vines or pomegranates; nor *is* there any water to drink." 6So Moses and Aaron went from the presence of the assembly to the door of the tabernacle of meeting, and they fell on their faces. And the glory of the LORD appeared to them.

7Then the LORD spoke to Moses, saying, 8"Take the rod; you and your brother Aaron gather the congregation together. Speak to the rock before their eyes, and it will yield its water; thus you shall bring water for them out of the rock, and give drink to the congregation and their animals." 9So Moses took the rod from before the LORD as He commanded him.

10And Moses and Aaron gathered the assembly together before the rock; and he said to them, "Hear now, you rebels! Must we bring water for you out of this rock?" 11Then Moses lifted his hand and struck the rock twice with his rod; and water came out abundantly, and the congregation and their animals drank.

12Then the LORD spoke to Moses and Aaron, "Because you did not believe Me, to hallow Me in the eyes of the children of Israel, therefore you shall not bring this assembly into the land which I have given them."

13This *was* the water of Meribah,g because the children of Israel contended with the LORD, and He was hallowed among them.

Passage Through Edom Refused

14Now Moses sent messengers from Kadesh to the king of Edom. "Thus says your brother Israel: 'You know all the hardship that has befallen us, 15how our fathers went down to Egypt, and we dwelt in Egypt a long time, and the Egyptians afflicted us and our fathers. 16When we cried out to the LORD, He heard our voice and sent the Angel and brought us up out of Egypt; now here we are in Kadesh, a city on the edge of your border. 17Please let us pass through your country. We will not pass

g Literally *Contention*

through fields or vineyards, nor will we drink water from wells; we will go along the King's Highway; we will not turn aside to the right hand or to the left until we have passed through your territory.' "

18Then Edom said to him, "You shall not pass through my *land,* lest I come out against you with the sword."

19So the children of Israel said to him, "We will go by the Highway, and if I or my livestock drink any of your water, then I will pay for it; let me only pass through on foot, nothing *more.*"

20Then he said, "You shall not pass through." So Edom came out against them with many men and with a strong hand. 21Thus Edom refused to give Israel passage through his territory; so Israel turned away from him.

Death of Aaron

22Now the children of Israel, the whole congregation, journeyed from Kadesh and came to Mount Hor. 23And the LORD spoke to Moses and Aaron in Mount Hor by the border of the land of Edom, saying: 24"Aaron shall be gathered to his people, for he shall not enter the land which I have given to the children of Israel, because you rebelled against My word at the water of Meribah. 25Take Aaron and Eleazar his son, and bring them up to Mount Hor; 26and strip Aaron of his garments and put them on Eleazar his son; for Aaron shall be gathered *to his people* and die there." 27So Moses did just as the LORD commanded, and they went up to Mount Hor in the sight of all the congregation. 28Moses stripped Aaron of his garments and put them on Eleazar his son; and Aaron died there on the top of the mountain. Then Moses and Eleazar came down from the mountain. 29Now when all the congregation saw that Aaron was dead, all the house of Israel mourned for Aaron thirty days.

Canaanites Defeated at Hormah

21 The king of Arad, the Canaanite, who dwelt in the South, heard that Israel was coming on the road to Atharim. Then he fought against Israel and took *some* of them prisoners.

2So Israel made a vow to the LORD, and said, "If You will indeed deliver this people into my hand, then I will utterly destroy their cities." 3And the LORD listened to the voice of Israel and delivered up the Canaanites, and they utterly destroyed them and their cities. So the name of that place was called Hormah.*h*

The Bronze Serpent

4Then they journeyed from Mount Hor by the Way of the Red Sea, to go around the land of Edom; and the soul of the people became very discouraged on the way. 5And the people spoke against God and against Moses: "Why have you brought us up out of Egypt to die in the wilderness? For *there is* no food and no water, and our soul loathes this worthless bread." 6So the LORD sent fiery serpents among the people, and they bit the people; and many of the people of Israel died.

7Therefore the people came to Moses, and said, "We have sinned, for we have spoken against the LORD and against you; pray to the LORD that He take away the serpents from us." So Moses prayed for the people.

8Then the LORD said to Moses, "Make a fiery *serpent,* and set it on a pole; and it shall be that everyone who is bitten, when he looks at it, shall live." 9So Moses made a bronze serpent, and put it on a pole; and so it was, if a serpent had bitten anyone, when he looked at the bronze serpent, he lived.

From Mount Hor to Moab

10Now the children of Israel moved on and camped in Oboth. 11And they journeyed from Oboth and camped at Ije Abarim, in the wilderness which *is* east of Moab, toward the sunrise. 12From there they moved and camped in the Valley of Zered. 13From there they moved and camped on the other side of the Arnon, which *is* in the wilderness that extends from the border of the Amorites; for the Arnon *is* the border of Moab, between Moab and the Amorites. 14Therefore it is said in the Book of the Wars of the LORD:

"Waheb in Suphah,*i*
    The brooks of the Arnon,

---

h Literally *Utter Destruction*   *i* Ancient unknown places; Vulgate reads *What He did in the Red Sea.*

15 And the slope of the brooks
   That reaches to the dwelling of Ar,
   And lies on the border of Moab."
16From there *they went* to Beer,
which *is* the well where the LORD said
to Moses, "Gather the people together,
and I will give them water." 17Then Israel sang this song:

"Spring up, O well!
   All of you sing to it—
18 The well the leaders sank,
   Dug by the nation's nobles,
   By the lawgiver, with their staves."

And from the wilderness *they went*
to Mattanah, 19from Mattanah to Nahaliel, from Nahaliel to Bamoth,
20and from Bamoth, *in* the valley that
is in the country of Moab, to the top of
Pisgah which looks down on the wasteland.

King Sihon Defeated

21Then Israel sent messengers to Sihon king of the Amorites, saying,
22"Let me pass through your land. We
will not turn aside into fields or vineyards; we will not drink water from
wells. We will go by the King's Highway until we have passed through your
territory." 23But Sihon would not allow
Israel to pass through his territory. So
Sihon gathered all his people together
and went out against Israel in the wilderness, and he came to Jahaz and
fought against Israel. 24Then Israel defeated him with the edge of the sword,
and took possession of his land from
the Arnon to the Jabbok, as far as the
people of Ammon; for the border of the
people of Ammon *was* fortified.
25So Israel took all these cities, and Israel dwelt in all the cities of the Amorites, in Heshbon and in all its villages.
26For Heshbon *was* the city of Sihon
king of the Amorites, who had fought
against the former king of Moab, and
had taken all his land from his hand
as far as the Arnon. 27Therefore those
who speak in proverbs say:

"Come to Heshbon, let it be built;
   Let the city of Sihon be repaired.

28 "For fire went out from Heshbon,
   A flame from the city of Sihon;
   It consumed Ar of Moab,

The lords of the heights of the
   Arnon.
29 Woe to you, Moab!
   You have perished, O people of
      Chemosh!
   He has given his sons as fugitives,
   And his daughters into captivity,
   To Sihon king of the Amorites.

30 "But we have shot at them;
   Heshbon has perished as far as
      Dibon.
   Then we laid waste as far as
      Nophah,
   Which *reaches* to Medeba."

31Thus Israel dwelt in the land of the
Amorites. 32Then Moses sent to spy out
Jazer; and they took its villages and
drove out the Amorites who *were* there.

King Og Defeated

33And they turned and went up by the
way to Bashan. So Og king of Bashan
went out against them, he and all his
people, to battle at Edrei. 34Then the
LORD said to Moses, "Do not fear him,
for I have delivered him into your hand,
with all his people and his land; and
you shall do to him as you did to Sihon
king of the Amorites, who dwelt at
Heshbon." 35So they defeated him, his
sons, and all his people, until there was
no survivor left him; and they took possession of his land.

Balak Sends for Balaam

22 Then the children of Israel
moved, and camped in the plains
of Moab on the side of the Jordan
across from Jericho.

2Now Balak the son of Zippor saw
all that Israel had done to the Amorites.
3And Moab was exceedingly afraid of
the people because they *were* many,
and Moab was sick with dread because
of the children of Israel. 4So Moab said
to the elders of Midian, "Now this company will lick up everything around us,
as an ox licks up the grass of the field."
And Balak the son of Zippor *was* king
of the Moabites at that time. 5Then he
sent messengers to Balaam the son of
Beor at Pethor, which *is* near the River[j]
in the land of the sons of his people,
to call him, saying: "Look, a people has

---

j That is, the Euphrates

come from Egypt. See, they cover the face of the earth, and are settling next to me! 6Therefore please come at once, curse this people for me, for they *are* too mighty for me. Perhaps I shall be able to defeat them and drive them out of the land, for I know that he whom you bless *is* blessed, and he whom you curse is cursed."

7So the elders of Moab and the elders of Midian departed with the diviner's fee in their hand, and they came to Balaam and spoke to him the words of Balak. 8And he said to them, "Lodge here tonight, and I will bring back word to you, as the LORD speaks to me." So the princes of Moab stayed with Balaam. 9Then God came to Balaam and said, "Who *are* these men with you?"

10So Balaam said to God, "Balak the son of Zippor, king of Moab, has sent to me, *saying,* 11'Look, a people has come out of Egypt, and they cover the face of the earth. Come now, curse them for me; perhaps I shall be able to overpower them and drive them out.' "

12And God said to Balaam, "You shall not go with them; you shall not curse the people, for they *are* blessed."

13So Balaam rose in the morning and said to the princes of Balak, "Go back to your land, for the LORD has refused to give me permission to go with you."

14And the princes of Moab rose and went to Balak, and said, "Balaam refuses to come with us."

15Then Balak again sent princes, more numerous and more honorable than they. 16And they came to Balaam and said to him, "Thus says Balak the son of Zippor: 'Please let nothing hinder you from coming to me; 17for I will certainly honor you greatly, and I will do whatever you say to me. Therefore please come, curse this people for me.' "

18Then Balaam answered and said to the servants of Balak, "Though Balak were to give me his house full of silver and gold, I could not go beyond the word of the LORD my God, to do less or more. 19Now therefore, please, you also stay here tonight, that I may know what more the LORD will say to me."

20And God came to Balaam at night and said to him, "If the men come to call you, rise *and* go with them; but only the word which I speak to you—that

you shall do." 21So Balaam rose in the morning, saddled his donkey, and went with the princes of Moab.

Balaam, the Donkey, and the Angel

22Then God's anger was aroused because he went, and the Angel of the LORD took His stand in the way as an adversary against him. And he was riding on his donkey, and his two servants *were* with him. 23Now the donkey saw the Angel of the LORD standing in the way with His drawn sword in His hand, and the donkey turned aside out of the way and went into the field. So Balaam struck the donkey to turn her back onto the road. 24Then the Angel of the LORD stood in a narrow path between the vineyards, *with* a wall on this side and a wall on that side. 25And when the donkey saw the Angel of the LORD, she pushed herself against the wall and crushed Balaam's foot against the wall; so he struck her again. 26Then the Angel of the LORD went further, and stood in a narrow place where there *was* no way to turn either to the right hand or to the left. 27And when the donkey saw the Angel of the LORD, she lay down under Balaam; so Balaam's anger was aroused, and he struck the donkey with his staff.

28Then the LORD opened the mouth of the donkey, and she said to Balaam, "What have I done to you, that you have struck me these three times?"

29And Balaam said to the donkey, "Because you have abused me. I wish there were a sword in my hand, for now I would kill you!"

30So the donkey said to Balaam, "*Am* I not your donkey on which you have ridden, ever since *I became* yours, to this day? Was I ever disposed to do this to you?"

And he said, "No."

31Then the LORD opened Balaam's eyes, and he saw the Angel of the LORD standing in the way with His drawn sword in His hand; and he bowed his head and fell flat on his face. 32And the Angel of the LORD said to him, "Why have you struck your donkey these three times? Behold, I have come out to stand against you, because *your* way is perverse before Me. 33The donkey saw Me and turned aside from Me these three times. If she had not turned aside from Me, surely I would also have killed you by now, and let her live."

34And Balaam said to the Angel of the LORD, "I have sinned, for I did not know You stood in the way against me. Now therefore, if it displeases You, I will turn back."

35Then the Angel of the LORD said to Balaam, "Go with the men, but only the word that I speak to you, that you shall speak." So Balaam went with the princes of Balak.

36Now when Balak heard that Balaam was coming, he went out to meet him at the city of Moab, which *is* on the border at the Arnon, the boundary of the territory. **37**Then Balak said to Balaam, "Did I not earnestly send to you, calling for you? Why did you not come to me? Am I not able to honor you?"

38And Balaam said to Balak, "Look, I have come to you! Now, have I any power at all to say anything? The word that God puts in my mouth, that I must speak." **39**So Balaam went with Balak, and they came to Kirjath Huzoth. **40**Then Balak offered oxen and sheep, and he sent *some* to Balaam and to the princes who *were* with him.

Balaam's First Prophecy

41So it was, the next day, that Balak took Balaam and brought him up to the high places of Baal, that from there he might observe the extent of the people.

23 Then Balaam said to Balak, "Build seven altars for me here, and prepare for me here seven bulls and seven rams."

2And Balak did just as Balaam had spoken, and Balak and Balaam offered a bull and a ram on *each* altar. **3**Then Balaam said to Balak, "Stand by your burnt offering, and I will go; perhaps the LORD will come to meet me, and whatever He shows me I will tell you." So he went to a desolate height. **4**And God met Balaam, and he said to Him, "I have prepared the seven altars, and I have offered on *each* altar a bull and a ram."

5Then the LORD put a word in Balaam's mouth, and said, "Return to Balak, and thus you shall speak."

6So he returned to him, and there he was, standing by his burnt offering, he and all the princes of Moab.

7And he took up his oracle and said:
"Balak the king of Moab has
    brought me from Aram,
From the mountains of the east.
'Come, curse Jacob for me,
    And come, denounce Israel!'

8 "How shall I curse whom God has
        not cursed?
    And how shall I denounce *whom*
        the LORD has not denounced?
9   For from the top of the rocks I see
        him,
    And from the hills I behold him;
    There! A people dwelling alone,
    Not reckoning itself among the
        nations.

10 "Who can count the dust of Jacob,
    Or number one-fourth of Israel?
    Let me die the death of the
        righteous,
    And let my end be like his!"

11Then Balak said to Balaam, "What have you done to me? I took you to curse my enemies, and look, you have blessed *them* bountifully!"

12So he answered and said, "Must I not take heed to speak what the LORD has put in my mouth?"

Balaam's Second Prophecy

13Then Balak said to him, "Please come with me to another place from which you may see them; you shall see only the outer part of them, and shall not see them all; curse them for me from there." **14**So he brought him to the field of Zophim, to the top of Pisgah, and built seven altars, and offered a bull and a ram on *each* altar.

15And he said to Balak, "Stand here by your burnt offering while I meet *the* LORD over there."

16Then the LORD met Balaam, and put a word in his mouth, and said, "Go back to Balak, and thus you shall speak." **17**So he came to him, and there he was, standing by his burnt offering, and the princes of Moab were with him. And Balak said to him, "What has the LORD spoken?"

18Then he took up his oracle and said:

"Rise up, Balak, and hear!
Listen to me, son of Zippor!

19 "God *is* not a man, that He
should lie,
Nor a son of man, that He should
repent.
Has He said, and will He not do?
Or has He spoken, and will He not
make it good?
20 Behold, I have received *a command*
to bless;
He has blessed, and I cannot
reverse it.

21 "He has not observed iniquity in
Jacob,
Nor has He seen wickedness in
Israel.
The LORD his God *is* with him,
And the shout of a King *is* among
them.
22 God brings them out of Egypt;
He has strength like a wild ox.

23 "For *there is* no sorcery against
Jacob,
Nor any divination against Israel.
It now must be said of Jacob
And of Israel, 'Oh, what God has
done!'
24 Look, a people rises like a lioness,
And lifts itself up like a lion;
It shall not lie down until it devours
the prey,
And drinks the blood of the slain."

25Then Balak said to Balaam, "Neither curse them at all, nor bless them at all!"

26So Balaam answered and said to Balak, "Did I not tell you, saying, 'All that the LORD speaks, that I must do'?"

Balaam's Third Prophecy

27Then Balak said to Balaam, "Please come, I will take you to another place; perhaps it will please God that you may curse them for me from there."
28So Balak took Balaam to the top of Peor, that overlooks the wasteland.
29Then Balaam said to Balak, "Build for me here seven altars, and prepare for me here seven bulls and seven rams."
30And Balak did as Balaam had said,

and offered a bull and a ram on *every* altar.

24 Now when Balaam saw that it pleased the LORD to bless Israel, he did not go as at other times, to seek to use sorcery, but he set his face toward the wilderness. 2And Balaam raised his eyes, and saw Israel encamped according to their tribes; and the Spirit of God came upon him.
3Then he took up his oracle and said:

"The utterance of Balaam the son of
Beor,
The utterance of the man whose
eyes are opened,
4 The utterance of him who hears the
words of God,
Who sees the vision of the
Almighty,
Who falls down, with eyes wide
open:

5 "How lovely are your tents, O Jacob!
Your dwellings, O Israel!
6 Like valleys that stretch out,
Like gardens by the riverside,
Like aloes planted by the LORD,
Like cedars beside the waters.
7 He shall pour water from his
buckets,
And his seed *shall be* in many
waters.

"His king shall be higher than Agag,
And his kingdom shall be exalted.

8 "God brings him out of Egypt;
He has strength like a wild ox;
He shall consume the nations, his
enemies;
He shall break their bones
And pierce *them* with his arrows.
9 'He bows down, he lies down as a
lion;
And as a lion, who shall
rouse him?'*k*

"Blessed *is* he who blesses you,
And cursed *is* he who curses you."

10Then Balak's anger was aroused against Balaam, and he struck his hands together; and Balak said to Balaam, "I called you to curse my enemies, and look, you have bountifully

---

k Compare Genesis 49.9

blessed *them* these three times!
11Now therefore, flee to your place. I
said I would greatly honor you, but in
fact, the LORD has kept you back from
honor."

12So Balaam said to Balak, "Did I not
also speak to your messengers whom
you sent to me, saying, 13'If Balak were
to give me his house full of silver and
gold, I could not go beyond the word
of the LORD, to do good or bad of my
own will. What the LORD says, that I
must speak'? 14And now, indeed, I am
going to my people. Come, I will advise
you what this people will do to your
people in the latter days."

Balaam's Fourth Prophecy

15So he took up his oracle and said:
"The utterance of Balaam the son of
  Beor,
And the utterance of the man
  whose eyes are opened;
16 The utterance of him who hears the
  words of God,
And has the knowledge of the
  Most High,
Who sees the vision of the
  Almighty,
Who falls down, with eyes wide
  open:

17 "I see Him, but not now;
I behold Him, but not near;
A Star shall come out of Jacob;
A Scepter shall rise out of Israel,
And batter the brow of Moab,
And destroy all the sons of tumult.

18 "And Edom shall be a possession;
Seir also, his enemies, shall be a
  possession,
While Israel does valiantly.
19 Out of Jacob One shall have
  dominion,
And destroy the remains of
  the city."

20Then he looked on Amalek, and he
took up his oracle and said:
"Amalek *was* first among the
  nations,
But *shall be* last until he perishes."
21Then he looked on the Kenites, and
he took up his oracle and said:
"Firm is your dwelling place,
And your nest is set in the rock;
22 Nevertheless Kain shall be burned.

How long until Asshur carries you
  away captive?"
23Then he took up his oracle and said:
"Alas! Who shall live when God
  does this?
24 But ships *shall come* from the
  coasts of Cyprus,
And they shall afflict Asshur and
  afflict Eber,
And so shall *Amalek*, until he
  perishes."
25So Balaam rose and departed and
returned to his place; Balak also went
his way.

Israel's Harlotry in Moab

25 Now Israel remained in Acacia
Grove, and the people began to
commit harlotry with the women of
Moab. 2They invited the people to the
sacrifices of their gods, and the people
ate and bowed down to their gods.
3So Israel was joined to Baal of Peor,
and the anger of the LORD was aroused
against Israel.

4Then the LORD said to Moses, "Take
all the leaders of the people and hang
the offenders before the LORD, out in
the sun, that the fierce anger of the
LORD may turn away from Israel."

5So Moses said to the judges of Israel,
"Every one of you kill his men who
were joined to Baal of Peor."

6And indeed, one of the children of
Israel came and presented to his brethren a Midianite woman in the sight of
Moses and in the sight of all the congregation of the children of Israel, who
were weeping at the door of the tabernacle of meeting. 7Now when Phinehas
the son of Eleazar, the son of Aaron the
priest, saw *it*, he rose from among the
congregation and took a javelin in his
hand; 8and he went after the man of
Israel into the tent and thrust both of
them through, the man of Israel, and
the woman through her body. So the
plague was stopped among the children
of Israel. 9And those who died in the
plague were twenty-four thousand.

10Then the LORD spoke to Moses, saying: 11"Phinehas the son of Eleazar, the
son of Aaron the priest, has turned back
My wrath from the children of Israel,
because he was zealous with My zeal
among them, so that I did not consume
the children of Israel in My zeal.

12Therefore say, 'Behold, I give to him My covenant of peace; 13and it shall be to him and his descendants after him a covenant of an everlasting priesthood, because he was zealous for his God, and made atonement for the children of Israel.'"

14Now the name of the Israelite who was killed, who was killed with the Midianite woman, *was* Zimri the son of Salu, a leader of a father's house among the Simeonites. 15And the name of the Midianite woman who was killed *was* Cozbi the daughter of Zur; he *was* head of the people of a father's house in Midian.

16Then the LORD spoke to Moses, saying: 17"Harass the Midianites, and attack them; 18for they harassed you with their schemes by which they seduced you in the matter of Peor and in the matter of Cozbi, the daughter of a leader of Midian, their sister, who was killed in the day of the plague because of Peor."

The Second Census of Israel

26 And it came to pass, after the plague, that the LORD spoke to Moses and Eleazar the son of Aaron the priest, saying: 2"Take a census of all the congregation of the children of Israel from twenty years old and above, by their fathers' houses, all who are able to go to war in Israel." 3So Moses and Eleazar the priest spoke with them in the plains of Moab by the Jordan, *across from* Jericho, saying: 4"*Take a census of the people* from twenty years old and above, just as the LORD commanded Moses and the children of Israel who came out of the land of Egypt."

5Reuben *was* the firstborn of Israel. The children of Reuben *were: of* Hanoch, the family of the Hanochites; *of* Pallu, the family of the Palluites; 6*of* Hezron, the family of the Hezronites; *of* Carmi, the family of the Carmites. 7These *are* the families of the Reubenites: those who were numbered of them were forty-three thousand seven hundred and thirty. 8And the son of Pallu *was* Eliab. 9The sons of Eliab *were* Nemuel, Dathan, and Abiram. These *are* the Dathan and Abiram, representatives of the congregation, who contended against Moses and Aaron in the company of Korah, when they contended against the LORD; 10and the earth opened its mouth and swallowed them up together with Korah when that company died, when the fire devoured two hundred and fifty men; and they became a sign. 11Nevertheless the children of Korah did not die.

12The sons of Simeon according to their families *were: of* Nemuel, the family of the Nemuelites; *of* Jamin, the family of the Jaminites; *of* Jachin, the family of the Jachinites; 13*of* Zerah, the family of the Zarhites; *of* Shaul, the family of the Shaulites. 14These *are* the families of the Simeonites: twenty-two thousand two hundred.

15The sons of Gad according to their families *were: of* Zephon, the family of the Zephonites; *of* Haggi, the family of the Haggites; *of* Shuni, the family of the Shunites; 16*of* Ozni, the family of the Oznites; *of* Eri, the family of the Erites; 17*of* Arod, the family of the Arodites; *of* Areli, the family of the Arelites. 18These *are* the families of the sons of Gad according to those who were numbered of them: forty thousand five hundred.

19The sons of Judah *were* Er and Onan; and Er and Onan died in the land of Canaan. 20And the sons of Judah according to their families were: *of* Shelah, the family of the Shelanites; *of* Perez, the family of the Parzites; *of* Zerah, the family of the Zarhites. 21And the sons of Perez were: *of* Hezron, the family of the Hezronites; *of* Hamul, the family of the Hamulites. 22These *are* the families of Judah according to those who were numbered of them: seventy-six thousand five hundred.

23The sons of Issachar according to their families *were: of* Tola, the family of the Tolaites; *of* Puah, the family of the Punites; 24*of* Jashub, the family of the Jashubites; *of* Shimron, the family of the Shimronites. 25These *are* the families of Issachar according to those who were numbered of them: sixty-four thousand three hundred.

26The sons of Zebulun according to their families *were:* of Sered, the family of the Sardites; of Elon, the family of the Elonites; of Jahleel, the family of the Jahleelites. 27These *are* the families of the Zebulunites according to those who were numbered of them: sixty thousand five hundred.

28The sons of Joseph according to their families, by Manasseh and Ephraim, *were:* 29The sons of Manasseh: of Machir, the family of the Machirites; and Machir begot Gilead; of Gilead, the family of the Gileadites. 30These *are* the sons of Gilead: *of* Jeezer, the family of the Jeezerites; of Helek, the family of the Helekites; 31*of* Asriel, the family of the Asrielites; *of* Shechem, the family of the Shechemites; 32*of* Shemida, the family of the Shemidaites; *of* Hepher, the family of the Hepherites. 33Now Zelophehad the son of Hepher had no sons, but daughters; and the names of the daughters of Zelophehad *were* Mahlah, Noah, Hoglah, Milcah, and Tirzah. 34These *are* the families of Manasseh; and those who were numbered of them *were* fifty-two thousand seven hundred.

35These *are* the sons of Ephraim according to their families: of Shuthelah, the family of the Shuthalhites; of Becher, the family of the Bachrites; of Tahan, the family of the Tahanites. 36And these *are* the sons of Shuthelah: of Eran, the family of the Eranites. 37These *are* the families of the sons of Ephraim according to those who were numbered of them: thirty-two thousand five hundred.

These *are* the sons of Joseph according to their families.

38The sons of Benjamin according to their families *were:* of Bela, the family of the Belaites; of Ashbel, the family of the Ashbelites; of Ahiram, the family of the Ahiramites; 39of Shupham, the family of the Shuphamites; of Hupham, the family of the Huphamites. 40And the sons of Bela were Ard and Naaman: *of* Ard, the family of the Ardites; of Naaman, the family of the Naamites. 41These *are* the sons of Benjamin according to their families; and those who were numbered of them *were* forty-five thousand six hundred.

42These *are* the sons of Dan according to their families: of Shuham, the family of the Shuhamites. These *are* the families of Dan according to their families. 43All the families of the Shuhamites, according to those who were numbered of them, *were* sixty-four thousand four hundred.

44The sons of Asher according to their families *were:* of Jimna, the family of the Jimnites; of Jesui, the family of the Jesuites; of Beriah, the family of the Beriites. 45Of the sons of Beriah: of Heber, the family of the Heberites; of Malchiel, the family of the Malchielites. 46And the name of the daughter of Asher *was* Serah. 47These *are* the families of the sons of Asher according to those who were numbered of them: fifty-three thousand four hundred.

48The sons of Naphtali according to their families *were:* of Jahzeel, the family of the Jahzeelites; of Guni, the family of the Gunites; 49of Jezer, the family of the Jezerites; of Shillem, the family of the Shillemites. 50These *are* the families of Naphtali according to their families; and those who were numbered of them *were* forty-five thousand four hundred.

51These *are* those who were numbered of the children of Israel: six hundred and one thousand seven hundred and thirty.

52Then the LORD spoke to Moses, saying: 53"To these the land shall be divided as an inheritance, according to the number of names. 54To a large *tribe* you shall give a larger inheritance, and to a small *tribe* you shall give a smaller inheritance. Each shall be given its inheritance according to those who were numbered of them. 55But the land shall be divided by lot; they shall inherit according to the names of the tribes of their fathers. 56According to the lot their inheritance shall be divided between the larger and the smaller."

57And these *are* those who were numbered of the Levites according to their families: of Gershon, the family of the Gershonites; of Kohath, the family of the Kohathites; of Merari, the family of the Merarites. 58These *are* the families of the Levites: the family of the Libnites, the family of the Hebronites, the family of the Mahlites, the family of the Mushites, and the family of the Korathites. And Kohath begot Amram. 59The name of Amram's wife *was* Jochebed the daughter of Levi, who was born to Levi in Egypt; and to

Amram she bore Aaron and Moses and their sister Miriam. 60To Aaron were born Nadab and Abihu, Eleazar and Ithamar. 61And Nadab and Abihu died when they offered profane fire before the LORD.

62Now those who were numbered of them were twenty-three thousand, every male from a month old and above; for they were not numbered among the other children of Israel, because there was no inheritance given to them among the children of Israel.

63These *are* those who were numbered by Moses and Eleazar the priest, who numbered the children of Israel in the plains of Moab by the Jordan, *across from* Jericho. 64But among these there was not a man of those who were numbered by Moses and Aaron the priest when they numbered the children of Israel in the Wilderness of Sinai. 65For the LORD had said of them, "They shall surely die in the wilderness." So there was not left a man of them, except Caleb the son of Jephunneh and Joshua the son of Nun.

Inheritance Laws

27 Then came the daughters of Zelophehad the son of Hepher, the son of Gilead, the son of Machir, the son of Manasseh, from the families of Manasseh the son of Joseph; and these *were* the names of his daughters: Mahlah, Noah, Hoglah, Milcah, and Tirzah. 2And they stood before Moses, before Eleazar the priest, and before the leaders and all the congregation, *by* the doorway of the tabernacle of meeting, saying: 3"Our father died in the wilderness; but he was not in the company of those who gathered together against the LORD, in company with Korah, but he died in his own sin; and he had no sons. 4Why should the name of our father be removed from among his family because he had no son? Give us a possession among our father's brothers."

5So Moses brought their case before the LORD.

6And the LORD spoke to Moses, saying: 7"The daughters of Zelophehad speak *what is* right; you shall surely give them a possession of inheritance among their father's brothers, and cause the inheritance of their father to

pass to them. 8And you shall speak to the children of Israel, saying: 'If a man dies and has no son, then you shall cause his inheritance to pass to his daughter. 9If he has no daughter, then you shall give his inheritance to his brothers. 10If he has no brothers, then you shall give his inheritance to his father's brothers. 11And if his father has no brothers, then you shall give his inheritance to the relative closest to him in his family, and he shall possess it.' " And it shall be to the children of Israel a statute of judgment, just as the LORD commanded Moses.

Joshua the Next Leader of Israel

12Now the LORD said to Moses: "Go up into this Mount Abarim, and see the land which I have given to the children of Israel. 13And when you have seen it, you also shall be gathered to your people, as Aaron your brother was gathered. 14For in the Wilderness of Zin, during the strife of the congregation, you rebelled against My command to hallow Me at the waters before their eyes." (These *are* the waters of Meribah, at Kadesh in the Wilderness of Zin.)

15Then Moses spoke to the LORD, saying: 16"Let the LORD, the God of the spirits of all flesh, set a man over the congregation, 17who may go out before them and go in before them, who may lead them out and bring them in, that the congregation of the LORD may not be like sheep which have no shepherd."

18And the LORD said to Moses: "Take Joshua the son of Nun with you, a man in whom *is* the Spirit, and lay your hand on him; 19set him before Eleazar the priest and before all the congregation, and inaugurate him in their sight. 20And you shall give *some* of your authority to him, that all the congregation of the children of Israel may be obedient. 21He shall stand before Eleazar the priest, who shall inquire before the LORD for him by the judgment of the Urim. At his word they shall go out, and at his word they shall come in, he and all the children of Israel with him— all the congregation."

22So Moses did as the LORD commanded him. He took Joshua and set him before Eleazar the priest and before all the congregation. 23And he laid his hands on him and inaugurated him, just as the LORD commanded by the hand of Moses.

Daily Offerings

28 Now the LORD spoke to Moses, saying, 2"Command the children of Israel, and say to them, 'My offering, My food for My offerings made by fire as a sweet aroma to Me, you shall be careful to offer to Me at their appointed time.'

3"And you shall say to them, 'This *is* the offering made by fire which you shall offer to the LORD: two male lambs in their first year without blemish, day by day, as a regular burnt offering. 4The one lamb you shall offer in the morning, the other lamb you shall offer in the evening, 5and one-tenth of an ephah of fine flour as a grain offering mixed with one-fourth of a hin of pressed oil. 6*It is* a regular burnt offering which was ordained at Mount Sinai for a sweet aroma, an offering made by fire to the LORD. 7And its drink offering *shall be* one-fourth of a hin for each lamb; in a holy *place* you shall pour out the drink to the LORD as an offering. 8The other lamb you shall offer in the evening; as the morning grain offering and its drink offering, you shall offer *it* as an offering made by fire, a sweet aroma to the LORD.

Sabbath Offerings

9'And on the Sabbath day two lambs in their first year, without blemish, and two-tenths *of an ephah* of fine flour as a grain offering, mixed with oil, with its drink offering—10*this is* the burnt offering for every Sabbath, besides the regular burnt offering with its drink offering.

Monthly Offerings

11'At the beginnings of your months you shall present a burnt offering to the LORD: two young bulls, one ram, and seven lambs in their first year, without blemish; 12three-tenths *of an ephah* of fine flour as a grain offering, mixed with oil, for each bull; two-tenths *of an ephah* of fine flour as a grain offering, mixed with oil, for the one ram; 13and one-tenth *of an ephah* of fine

flour, mixed with oil, as a grain offering for each lamb, as a burnt offering of sweet aroma, an offering made by fire to the LORD. 14Their drink offering shall be half a hin of wine for a bull, one-third of a hin for a ram, and one-fourth of a hin for a lamb; this *is* the burnt offering for each month throughout the months of the year. 15Also one kid of the goats as a sin offering to the LORD shall be offered, besides the regular burnt offering and its drink offering.

Offerings at Passover

16'On the fourteenth day of the first month *is* the Passover of the LORD. 17And on the fifteenth day of this month *is* the feast; unleavened bread shall be eaten for seven days. 18On the first day *you shall have* a holy convocation. You shall do no customary work. 19And you shall present an offering made by fire as a burnt offering to the LORD: two young bulls, one ram, and seven lambs in their first year. Be sure they are without blemish. 20Their grain offering shall be of fine flour mixed with oil: three-tenths *of an ephah* you shall offer for a bull, and two-tenths for a ram; 21you shall offer one-tenth *of an ephah* for each of the seven lambs; 22also one goat *as* a sin offering, to make atonement for you. 23You shall offer these besides the burnt offering of the morning, which *is* for a regular burnt offering. 24In this manner you shall offer the food of the offering made by fire daily for seven days, as a sweet aroma to the LORD; it shall be offered besides the regular burnt offering and its drink offering. 25And on the seventh day you shall have a holy convocation. You shall do no customary work.

Offerings at the Feast of Weeks

26'Also on the day of the firstfruits, when you bring a new grain offering to the LORD at your *Feast of* Weeks, you shall have a holy convocation. You shall do no customary work. 27You shall present a burnt offering as a sweet aroma to the LORD: two young bulls, one ram, and seven lambs in their first year, 28with their grain offering of fine flour mixed with oil: three-tenths *of an ephah* for each bull, two-tenths for the one ram, 29and one-tenth for each of the seven lambs; 30also one kid of the goats, to make atonement for you. 31Be sure they are without blemish. You shall present *them* with their drink offerings, besides the regular burnt offering with its grain offering.

Offerings at the Feast of Trumpets

29 'And in the seventh month, on the first *day* of the month, you shall have a holy convocation. You shall do no customary work. For you it is a day of blowing the trumpets. 2You shall offer a burnt offering as a sweet aroma to the LORD: one young bull, one ram, *and* seven lambs in their first year, without blemish. 3Their grain offering *shall be* fine flour mixed with oil: three-tenths *of an ephah* for the bull, two-tenths for the ram, 4and one-tenth for each of the seven lambs; 5also one kid of the goats *as* a sin offering, to make atonement for you; 6besides the burnt offering with its grain offering for the New Moon, the regular burnt offering with its grain offering, and their drink offerings, according to their ordinance, as a sweet aroma, an offering made by fire to the LORD.

Offerings on the Day of Atonement

7'On the tenth *day* of this seventh month you shall have a holy convocation. You shall afflict your souls; you shall not do any work. 8You shall present a burnt offering to the LORD *as* a sweet aroma: one young bull, one ram, *and* seven lambs in their first year. Be sure they are without blemish. 9Their grain offering *shall be of* fine flour mixed with oil: three-tenths *of an ephah* for the bull, two-tenths for the one ram, 10and one-tenth for each of the seven lambs; 11also one kid of the goats *as* a sin offering, besides the sin offering for atonement, the regular burnt offering with its grain offering, and their drink offerings.

Offerings at the Feast of Tabernacles

12'On the fifteenth day of the seventh month you shall have a holy convocation. You shall do no customary work, and you shall keep a feast to the LORD seven days. 13You shall present a burnt offering, an offering made by fire as a sweet aroma to the LORD: thirteen

young bulls, two rams, *and* fourteen lambs in their first year. They shall be without blemish. 14Their grain offering *shall be of* fine flour mixed with oil: three-tenths *of an ephah* for each of the thirteen bulls, two-tenths for each of the two rams, 15and one-tenth for each of the fourteen lambs; 16also one kid of the goats *as* a sin offering, besides the regular burnt offering, its grain offering, and its drink offering.

17'On the second day *present* twelve young bulls, two rams, fourteen lambs in their first year without blemish, 18and their grain offering and their drink offerings for the bulls, for the rams, and for the lambs, by their number, according to the ordinance; 19also one kid of the goats *as* a sin offering, besides the regular burnt offering with its grain offering, and their drink offerings.

20'On the third day *present* eleven bulls, two rams, fourteen lambs in their first year without blemish, 21and their grain offering and their drink offerings for the bulls, for the rams, and for the lambs, by their number, according to the ordinance; 22also one goat *as* a sin offering, besides the regular burnt offering, its grain offering, and its drink offering.

23'On the fourth day *present* ten bulls, two rams, *and* fourteen lambs in their first year, without blemish, 24and their grain offering and their drink offerings for the bulls, for the rams, and for the lambs, by their number, according to the ordinance; 25also one kid of the goats *as* a sin offering, besides the regular burnt offering, its grain offering, and its drink offering.

26'On the fifth day *present* nine bulls, two rams, *and* fourteen lambs in their first year without blemish, 27and their grain offering and their drink offerings for the bulls, for the rams, and for the lambs, by their number, according to the ordinance; 28also one goat *as* a sin offering, besides the regular burnt offering, its grain offering, and its drink offering.

29'On the sixth day *present* eight bulls, two rams, *and* fourteen lambs in their first year without blemish, 30and their grain offering and their drink offerings for the bulls, for the rams, and for the lambs, by their number, according to the ordinance; 31also one goat *as* a sin offering, besides the regular burnt offering, its grain offering, and its drink offering.

32'On the seventh day *present* seven bulls, two rams, *and* fourteen lambs in their first year without blemish, 33and their grain offering and their drink offerings for the bulls, for the rams, and for the lambs, by their number, according to the ordinance; 34also one goat *as* a sin offering, besides the regular burnt offering, its grain offering, and its drink offering.

35'On the eighth day you shall have a sacred assembly. You shall do no customary work. 36You shall present a burnt offering, an offering made by fire as a sweet aroma to the LORD: one bull, one ram, seven lambs in their first year without blemish, 37and their grain offering and their drink offerings for the bull, for the ram, and for the lambs, by their number, according to the ordinance; 38also one goat *as* a sin offering, besides the regular burnt offering, its grain offering, and its drink offering.

39'These you shall present to the LORD at your appointed feasts (besides your vowed offerings and your freewill offerings) as your burnt offerings and your grain offerings, as your drink offerings and your peace offerings.' "

40So Moses told the children of Israel everything, just as the LORD commanded Moses.

The Law Concerning Vows

30 Then Moses spoke to the heads of the tribes concerning the children of Israel, saying, "This *is* the thing which the LORD has commanded: 2If a man makes a vow to the LORD, or swears an oath to bind himself by some agreement, he shall not break his word; he shall do according to all that proceeds out of his mouth.

3"Or if a woman makes a vow to the LORD, and binds *herself* by some agreement while in her father's house in her youth, 4and her father hears her vow and the agreement by which she has bound herself, and her father holds his peace, then all her vows shall stand, and every agreement with which she has bound herself shall stand. 5But if

her father overrules her on the day that he hears, then none of her vows nor her agreements by which she has bound herself shall stand; and the LORD will release her, because her father overruled her.

6"If indeed she takes a husband, while bound by her vows or by a rash utterance from her lips by which she bound herself, 7and her husband hears *it*, and makes no response to her on the day that he hears, then her vows shall stand, and her agreements by which she bound herself shall stand. 8But if her husband overrules her on the day that he hears *it*, he shall make void her vow which she took and what she uttered with her lips, by which she bound herself, and the LORD will release her.

9"Also any vow of a widow or a divorced woman, by which she has bound herself, shall stand against her.

10"If she vowed in her husband's house, or bound herself by an agreement with an oath, 11and her husband heard *it*, and made no response to her *and* did not overrule her, then all her vows shall stand, and every agreement by which she bound herself shall stand. 12But if her husband truly made them void on the day he heard *them*, then whatever proceeded from her lips concerning her vows or concerning the agreement binding her, it shall not stand; her husband has made them void, and the LORD will release her. 13Every vow and every binding oath to afflict her soul, her husband may confirm it, or her husband may make it void. 14Now if her husband makes no response whatever to her from day to day, then he confirms all her vows or all the agreements that bind her; he confirms them, because he made no response to her on the day that he heard *them*. 15But if he does make them void after he has heard *them*, then he shall bear her guilt."

16These *are* the statutes which the LORD commanded Moses, between a man and his wife, and between a father and his daughter in her youth in her father's house.

Vengeance on the Midianites

31 And the LORD spoke to Moses, saying: 2"Take vengeance on the

Midianites for the children of Israel. Afterward you shall be gathered to your people."

3So Moses spoke to the people, saying, "Arm some of yourselves for war, and let them go against the Midianites to take vengeance for the LORD on Midian. 4A thousand from each tribe of all the tribes of Israel you shall send to the war."

5So there were recruited from the divisions of Israel one thousand from *each* tribe, twelve thousand armed for war. 6Then Moses sent them to the war, one thousand from *each* tribe; he sent them to the war with Phinehas the son of Eleazar the priest, with the holy articles and the signal trumpets in his hand. 7And they warred against the Midianites, just as the LORD commanded Moses, and they killed all the males. 8They killed the kings of Midian with *the rest of* those who were killed—Evi, Rekem, Zur, Hur, and Reba, the five kings of Midian. Balaam the son of Beor they also killed with the sword.

9And the children of Israel took the women of Midian captive, with their little ones, and took as spoil all their cattle, all their flocks, and all their goods. 10They also burned with fire all the cities where they dwelt, and all their forts. 11And they took all the spoil and all the booty—of man and beast.

Return from the War

12Then they brought the captives, the booty, and the spoil to Moses, to Eleazar the priest, and to the congregation of the children of Israel, to the camp in the plains of Moab by the Jordan, *across from* Jericho. 13And Moses, Eleazar the priest, and all the leaders of the congregation, went to meet them outside the camp. 14But Moses was angry with the officers of the army, *with* the captains over thousands and captains over hundreds, who had come from the battle.

15And Moses said to them: "Have you kept all the women alive? 16Look, these *women* caused the children of Israel, through the counsel of Balaam, to trespass against the LORD in the incident of Peor, and there was a plague among the congregation of the LORD. 17Now therefore, kill every male among the little ones, and kill every woman who has known a man intimately. 18But keep alive for yourselves all the young girls who have not known a man intimately. 19And as for you, remain outside the camp seven days; whoever has killed any person, and whoever has touched any slain, purify yourselves and your captives on the third day and on the seventh day. 20Purify every garment, everything made of leather, everything woven of goats' *hair*, and everything made of wood."

21Then Eleazar the priest said to the men of war who had gone to the battle, "This *is* the ordinance of the law which the LORD commanded Moses: 22"Only the gold, the silver, the bronze, the iron, the tin, and the lead, 23everything that can endure fire, you shall put through the fire, and it shall be clean; and it shall be purified with the water of purification. But all that cannot endure fire you shall put through water. 24And you shall wash your clothes on the seventh day and be clean, and afterward you may come into the camp."

Division of the Plunder

25Now the LORD spoke to Moses, saying: 26"Count up the plunder that was taken—of man and beast—you and Eleazar the priest and the chief fathers of the congregation; 27and divide the plunder into two parts, between those who took part in the war, who went out to battle, and all the congregation. 28And levy a tribute for the LORD on the men of war who went out to battle: one of every five hundred of the persons, the cattle, the donkeys, and the sheep; 29take *it* from their half, and give *it* to Eleazar the priest as a heave offering to the LORD. 30And from the children of Israel's half you shall take one of every fifty, drawn from the persons, the cattle, the donkeys, and the sheep, from all the livestock, and give them to the Levites who keep charge of the tabernacle of the LORD." 31So Moses and Eleazar the priest did as the LORD commanded Moses.

32The booty remaining from the plunder, which the men of war had taken, was six hundred and seventy-five thousand sheep, 33seventy-two thousand cattle, 34sixty-one thousand donkeys,

35and thirty-two thousand persons in all, of women who had not known a man intimately. 36And the half, the portion for those who had gone out to war, was in number three hundred and thirty-seven thousand five hundred sheep; 37and the LORD's tribute of the sheep was six hundred and seventy-five. 38The cattle *were* thirty-six thousand, of which the LORD's tribute *was* seventy-two. 39The donkeys *were* thirty thousand five hundred, of which the LORD's tribute *was* sixty-one. 40The persons *were* sixteen thousand, of which the LORD's tribute *was* thirty-two persons. 41So Moses gave the tribute *which was* the LORD's heave offering to Eleazar the priest, as the LORD commanded Moses.

42And from the children of Israel's half, which Moses separated from the men who fought—43now the half belonging to the congregation was three hundred and thirty-seven thousand five hundred sheep, 44thirty-six thousand cattle, 45thirty thousand five hundred donkeys, 46and sixteen thousand persons—47and from the children of Israel's half Moses took one of every fifty, drawn from man and beast, and gave them to the Levites, who kept charge of the tabernacle of the LORD, as the LORD commanded Moses.

48Then the officers who *were* over thousands of the army, the captains of thousands and captains of hundreds, came near to Moses; 49and they said to Moses, "Your servants have taken a count of the men of war who *are* under our command, and not a man of us is missing. 50Therefore we have brought an offering for the LORD, what every man found of ornaments of gold: armlets and bracelets and signet rings and earrings and necklaces, to make atonement for ourselves before the LORD." 51So Moses and Eleazar the priest received the gold from them, all the fashioned ornaments. 52And all the gold of the offering that they offered to the LORD, from the captains of thousands and captains of hundreds, was sixteen thousand seven hundred and fifty shekels. 53(The men of war had taken spoil, every man for himself.) 54And Moses and Eleazar the priest received the gold from the captains of thousands and of hundreds, and brought it into the tabernacle of meeting as a memorial for the children of Israel before the LORD.

The Tribes Settling East of the Jordan

32 Now the children of Reuben and the children of Gad had a very great multitude of livestock; and when they saw the land of Jazer and the land of Gilead, that indeed the region *was* a place for livestock, 2the children of Gad and the children of Reuben came and spoke to Moses, to Eleazar the priest, and to the leaders of the congregation, saying, 3"Ataroth, Dibon, Jazer, Nimrah, Heshbon, Elealeh, Shebam, Nebo, and Beon, 4the country which the LORD defeated before the congregation of Israel, *is* a land for livestock, and your servants have livestock." 5Therefore they said, "If we have found favor in your sight, let this land be given to your servants as a possession. Do not take us over the Jordan."

6And Moses said to the children of Gad and to the children of Reuben: "Shall your brethren go to war while you sit here? 7Now why will you discourage the heart of the children of Israel from going over into the land which the LORD has given them? 8Thus your fathers did when I sent them away from Kadesh Barnea to see the land. 9For when they went up to the Valley of Eshcol and saw the land, they discouraged the heart of the children of Israel, so that they did not go into the land which the LORD had given them. 10So the LORD's anger was aroused on that day, and He swore an oath, saying, 11'Surely none of the men who came up from Egypt, from twenty years old and above, shall see the land of which I swore to Abraham, Isaac, and Jacob, because they have not wholly followed Me, 12except Caleb the son of Jephunneh, the Kenizzite, and Joshua the son of Nun, for they have wholly followed the LORD.' 13So the LORD's anger was aroused against Israel, and He made them wander in the wilderness forty years, until all the generation that had done evil in the sight of the LORD was gone. 14And look! You have risen in your fathers' place, a brood of sinful men, to increase still more the fierce anger of the LORD against Israel. 15For if you turn away from following Him, He will once again leave them in the wilderness, and you will destroy all these people."

16Then they came near to him and said: "We will build sheepfolds here for our livestock, and cities for our little ones, 17but we ourselves will be armed, ready *to go* before the children of Israel until we have brought them to their place; and our little ones will dwell in the fortified cities because of the inhabitants of the land. 18We will not return to our homes until every one of the children of Israel has received his inheritance. 19For we will not inherit with them on the other side of the Jordan and beyond, because our inheritance has fallen to us on this eastern side of the Jordan."

20Then Moses said to them: "If you do this thing, if you arm yourselves before the LORD for the war, 21and all your armed men cross over the Jordan before the LORD until He has driven out His enemies from before Him, 22and the land is subdued before the LORD, then afterward you may return and be blameless before the LORD and before Israel; and this land shall be your possession before the LORD. 23But if you do not do so, then take note, you have sinned against the LORD; and be sure your sin will find you out. 24Build cities for your little ones and folds for your sheep, and do what has proceeded out of your mouth."

25And the children of Gad and the children of Reuben spoke to Moses, saying: "Your servants will do as my lord commands. 26Our little ones, our wives, our flocks, and all our livestock will be there in the cities of Gilead; 27but your servants will cross over, every man armed for war, before the LORD to battle, just as my lord says."

28So Moses gave command concerning them to Eleazar the priest, to Joshua the son of Nun, and to the chief fathers of the tribes of the children of Israel. 29And Moses said to them: "If the children of Gad and the children of Reuben cross over the Jordan with you, every man armed for battle before the LORD, and the land is subdued before you,

then you shall give them the land of Gilead as a possession. 30But if they do not cross over armed with you, they shall have possessions among you in the land of Canaan."

31Then the children of Gad and the children of Reuben answered, saying: "As the LORD has said to your servants, so we will do. 32We will cross over armed before the LORD into the land of Canaan, but the possession of our inheritance *shall remain* with us on this side of the Jordan."

33So Moses gave to the children of Gad, to the children of Reuben, and to half the tribe of Manasseh the son of Joseph, the kingdom of Sihon king of the Amorites and the kingdom of Og king of Bashan, the land with its cities within the borders, the cities of the surrounding country. 34And the children of Gad built Dibon and Ataroth and Aroer, 35Atroth and Shophan and Jazer and Jogbehah, 36Beth Nimrah and Beth Haran, fortified cities, and folds for sheep. 37And the children of Reuben built Heshbon and Elealeh and Kirjathaim, 38Nebo and Baal Meon (*their* names being changed) and Shibmah; and they gave *other* names to the cities which they built.

39And the children of Machir the son of Manasseh went to Gilead and took it, and dispossessed the Amorites who *were* in it. 40So Moses gave Gilead to Machir the son of Manasseh, and he dwelt in it. 41Also Jair the son of Manasseh went and took its small towns, and called them Havoth Jair.[l] 42Then Nobah went and took Kenath and its villages, and he called it Nobah, after his own name.

Israel's Journey from Egypt Reviewed

33 These *are* the journeys of the children of Israel, who went out of the land of Egypt by their armies under the hand of Moses and Aaron. 2Now Moses wrote down the starting points of their journeys at the command of the LORD. And these *are* their journeys according to their starting points:

3They departed from Rameses in the first month, on the fifteenth day of the first month; on the day after the Pass-

---

l Literally *Towns of Jair*

over the children of Israel went out with boldness in the sight of all the Egyptians. 4For the Egyptians were burying all *their* firstborn, whom the LORD had killed among them. Also on their gods the LORD had executed judgments.

5Then the children of Israel moved from Rameses and camped at Succoth. 6They departed from Succoth and camped at Etham, which *is* on the edge of the wilderness. 7They moved from Etham and turned back to Pi Hahiroth, which *is* east of Baal Zephon; and they camped near Migdol. 8They departed from before Hahiroth and passed through the midst of the sea into the wilderness, went three days' journey in the Wilderness of Etham, and camped at Marah. 9They moved from Marah and came to Elim. At Elim *were* twelve springs of water and seventy palm trees; so they camped there.

10They moved from Elim and camped by the Red Sea. 11They moved from the Red Sea and camped in the Wilderness of Sin. 12They journeyed from the Wilderness of Sin and camped at Dophkah. 13They departed from Dophkah and camped at Alush. 14They moved from Alush and camped at Rephidim, where there was no water for the people to drink.

15They departed from Rephidim and camped in the Wilderness of Sinai. 16They moved from the Wilderness of Sinai and camped at Kibroth Hattaavah. 17They departed from Kibroth Hattaavah and camped at Hazeroth. 18They departed from Hazeroth and camped at Rithmah. 19They departed from Rithmah and camped at Rimmon Perez. 20They departed from Rimmon Perez and camped at Libnah. 21They moved from Libnah and camped at Rissah. 22They journeyed from Rissah and camped at Kehelathah. 23They went from Kehelathah and camped at Mount Shepher. 24They moved from Mount Shepher and camped at Haradah. 25They moved from Haradah and camped at Makheloth. 26They moved from Makheloth and camped at Tahath. 27They departed from Tahath and camped at Terah. 28They moved from Terah and camped at Mithkah.

29They went from Mithkah and camped at Hashmonah. 30They departed from Hashmonah and camped at Moseroth. 31They departed from Moseroth and camped at Bene Jaakan. 32They moved from Bene Jaakan and camped at Hor Hagidgad. 33They went from Hor Hagidgad and camped at Jotbathah. 34They moved from Jotbathah and camped at Abronah. 35They departed from Abronah and camped at Ezion Geber. 36They moved from Ezion Geber and camped in the Wilderness of Zin, which *is* Kadesh. 37They moved from Kadesh and camped at Mount Hor, on the boundary of the land of Edom.

38Then Aaron the priest went up to Mount Hor at the command of the LORD, and died there in the fortieth year after the children of Israel had come out of the land of Egypt, on the first *day* of the fifth month. 39Aaron *was* one hundred and twenty-three years old when he died on Mount Hor.

40Now the king of Arad, the Canaanite, who dwelt in the South in the land of Canaan, heard of the coming of the children of Israel.

41So they departed from Mount Hor and camped at Zalmonah. 42They departed from Zalmonah and camped at Punon. 43They departed from Punon and camped at Oboth. 44They departed from Oboth and camped at Ije Abarim, at the border of Moab. 45They departed from Ijim[m] and camped at Dibon Gad. 46They moved from Dibon Gad and camped at Almon Diblathaim. 47They moved from Almon Diblathaim and camped in the mountains of Abarim, before Nebo. 48They departed from the mountains of Abarim and camped in the plains of Moab by the Jordan, *across from* Jericho. 49They camped by the Jordan, from Beth Jesimoth as far as the Abel Acacia Grove in the plains of Moab.

Instructions for the Conquest of Canaan

50Now the LORD spoke to Moses in the plains of Moab by the Jordan, *across from* Jericho, saying, 51"Speak to the children of Israel, and say to them: 'When you have crossed the Jor-

---

[m] Same as *Ije Abarim* (compare verse 44)

dan into the land of Canaan, 52then you shall drive out all the inhabitants of the land from before you, destroy all their engraved stones, destroy all their molded images, and demolish all their high places; 53you shall dispossess *the inhabitants of* the land and dwell in it, for I have given you the land to possess. 54And you shall divide the land by lot as an inheritance among your families; to the larger you shall give a larger inheritance, and to the smaller you shall give a smaller inheritance; there everyone's *inheritance* shall be whatever falls to him by lot. You shall inherit according to the tribes of your fathers. 55But if you do not drive out the inhabitants of the land from before you, then it shall be that those whom you let remain *shall be* irritants in your eyes and thorns in your sides, and they shall harass you in the land where you dwell. 56Moreover it shall be *that* I will do to you as I thought to do to them.' "

The Appointed Boundaries of Canaan

34 Then the LORD spoke to Moses, saying, 2"Command the children of Israel, and say to them: 'When you come into the land of Canaan, this *is* the land that shall fall to you as an inheritance—the land of Canaan to its boundaries. 3Your southern border shall be from the Wilderness of Zin along the border of Edom; then your southern border shall extend eastward to the end of the Salt Sea; 4your border shall turn from the southern side of the Ascent of Akrabbim, continue to Zin, and be on the south of Kadesh Barnea; then it shall go on to Hazar Addar, and continue to Azmon; 5the border shall turn from Azmon to the Brook of Egypt, and it shall end at the Sea.

6'As for the western border, you shall have the Great Sea for a border; this shall be your western border.

7'And this shall be your northern border: From the Great Sea you shall mark out your *border* line to Mount Hor; 8from Mount Hor you shall mark out *your border* to the entrance of Hamath; then the direction of the border shall be toward Zedad; 9the border shall proceed to Ziphron, and it shall end at Hazar Enan. This shall be your northern border.

10'You shall mark out your eastern border from Hazar Enan to Shepham; 11the border shall go down from Shepham to Riblah on the east side of Ain; the border shall go down and reach to the eastern side of the Sea of Chinnereth; 12the border shall go down along the Jordan, and it shall end at the Salt Sea. This shall be your land with its surrounding boundaries.' "

13Then Moses commanded the children of Israel, saying: "This *is* the land which you shall inherit by lot, which the LORD has commanded to give to the nine tribes and to the half-tribe. 14For the tribe of the children of Reuben according to the house of their fathers, and the tribe of the children of Gad according to the house of their fathers, have received *their inheritance*; and the half-tribe of Manasseh has received its inheritance. 15The two tribes and the half-tribe have received their inheritance on this side of the Jordan, *across from* Jericho eastward, toward the sunrise."

The Leaders Appointed to Divide the Land

16And the LORD spoke to Moses, saying, 17"These *are* the names of the men who shall divide the land among you as an inheritance: Eleazar the priest and Joshua the son of Nun. 18And you shall take one leader of every tribe to divide the land for the inheritance. 19These *are* the names of the men: from the tribe of Judah, Caleb the son of Jephunneh; 20from the tribe of the children of Simeon, Shemuel the son of Ammihud; 21from the tribe of Benjamin, Elidad the son of Chislon; 22a leader from the tribe of the children of Dan, Bukki the son of Jogli; 23from the sons of Joseph: a leader from the tribe of the children of Manasseh, Hanniel the son of Ephod, 24and a leader from the tribe of the children of Ephraim, Kemuel the son of Shiphtan; 25a leader from the tribe of the children of Zebulun, Elizaphan the son of Parnach; 26a leader from the tribe of the children of Issachar, Paltiel the son of Azzan; 27a leader from the tribe of the children of Asher, Ahihud the son of Shelomi; 28and a leader from the tribe of the children of Naphtali, Pedahel the son of Ammihud."

29These *are* the ones the LORD commanded to divide the inheritance among the children of Israel in the land of Canaan.

Cities for the Levites

35 And the LORD spoke to Moses in the plains of Moab by the Jordan *across from* Jericho, saying: 2"Command the children of Israel that they give the Levites cities to dwell in from the inheritance of their possession, and you shall *also* give the Levites common-land around the cities. 3They shall have the cities to dwell in; and their common-land shall be for their cattle, for their herds, and for all their animals. 4The common-land of the cities which you will give the Levites *shall extend* from the wall of the city outward a thousand cubits all around. 5And you shall measure outside the city on the east side two thousand cubits, on the south side two thousand cubits, on the west side two thousand cubits, and on the north side two thousand cubits. The city *shall be* in the middle. This shall belong to them as common-land for the cities.

6"Now among the cities which you will give to the Levites *you shall appoint* six cities of refuge, to which a manslayer may flee. And to these you shall add forty-two cities. 7So all the cities you will give to the Levites *shall be* forty-eight; these *you shall give* with their common-land. 8And the cities which you will give *shall be* from the possession of the children of Israel; from the larger *tribe* you shall give many, from the smaller you shall give few. Each shall give some of its cities to the Levites, in proportion to the inheritance that each receives."

Cities of Refuge

9Then the LORD spoke to Moses, saying, 10"Speak to the children of Israel, and say to them: 'When you cross the Jordan into the land of Canaan, 11then you shall appoint cities to be cities of refuge for you, that the manslayer who kills any person accidentally may flee there. 12They shall be cities of refuge for you from the avenger, that the manslayer may not die until he stands before the congregation in judgment. 13And of the cities which you give, you shall have six cities of refuge. 14You shall appoint three cities on this side of the Jordan, and three cities you shall appoint in the land of Canaan, *which* will be cities of refuge. 15These six cities shall be for refuge for the children of Israel, for the stranger, and for the sojourner among them, that anyone who kills a person accidentally may flee there.

16'But if he strikes him with an iron implement, so that he dies, he *is* a murderer; the murderer shall surely be put to death. 17And if he strikes him with a stone in the hand, by which one could die, and he does die, he *is* a murderer; the murderer shall surely be put to death. 18Or *if* he strikes him with a wooden hand weapon, by which one could die, and he does die, he *is* a murderer; the murderer shall surely be put to death. 19The avenger of blood himself shall put the murderer to death; when he meets him, he shall put him to death. 20If he pushes him out of hatred or, while lying in wait, hurls something at him so that he dies, 21or in enmity he strikes him with his hand so that he dies, the one who struck *him* shall surely be put to death. He *is* a murderer. The avenger of blood shall put the murderer to death when he meets him.

22'However, if he pushes him suddenly without enmity, or throws anything at him without lying in wait, 23or uses a stone, by which a man could die, throwing *it* at him without seeing *him,* so that he dies, while he was not his enemy or seeking his harm, 24then the congregation shall judge between the manslayer and the avenger of blood according to these judgments. 25So the congregation shall deliver the manslayer from the hand of the avenger of blood, and the congregation shall return him to the city of refuge where he had fled, and he shall remain there until the death of the high priest who was anointed with the holy oil. 26But if the manslayer at any time goes outside the limits of the city of refuge where he fled, 27and the avenger of blood finds him outside the limits of his city of refuge, and the avenger of blood kills the manslayer, he shall not be guilty of blood, 28because he should have remained in his city of refuge until the death of the high priest. But after the death of the high priest the manslayer may return to the land of his possession.

29'And these *things* shall be a statute of judgment to you throughout your generations in all your dwellings. 30Whoever kills a person, the murderer shall be put to death on the testimony of witnesses; but one witness is not *sufficient* testimony against a person for the death *penalty*. 31Moreover you shall take no ransom for the life of a murderer who *is* guilty of death, but he shall surely be put to death. 32And you shall take no ransom for him who has fled to his city of refuge, that he may return to dwell in the land before the death of the priest. 33So you shall not pollute the land where you *are;* for blood defiles the land, and no atonement can be made for the land, for the blood that is shed on it, except by the blood of him who shed it. 34Therefore do not defile the land which you inhabit, in the midst of which I dwell; for I the Lord dwell among the children of Israel.' "

Marriage of Female Heirs

36 Now the chief fathers of the families of the children of Gilead the son of Machir, the son of Manasseh, of the families of the sons of Joseph, came near and spoke before Moses and before the leaders, the chief fathers of the children of Israel. 2And they said: "The Lord commanded my lord *Moses* to give the land as an inheritance by lot to the children of Israel, and my lord was commanded by the Lord to give the inheritance of our brother Zelophehad to his daughters. 3Now if they are married to any of the sons of the *other* tribes of the children of Israel, then their inheritance will be taken from the inheritance of our fathers, and it will be added to the inheritance of the tribe into which they marry; so it will be taken from the lot of our inheritance. 4And when the Jubilee of the children of Israel comes, then their inheritance will be added to the inheritance of the tribe into which they marry; so their inheritance will be taken away from the inheritance of the tribe of our fathers."

5Then Moses commanded the children of Israel according to the word of the Lord, saying: "What the tribe of the sons of Joseph speaks is right. 6This *is* what the Lord commands concerning the daughters of Zelophehad, saying, 'Let them marry whom they think best, but they may marry only within the family of their father's tribe.' 7So the inheritance of the children of Israel shall not change hands from tribe to tribe, for every one of the children of Israel shall keep the inheritance of the tribe of his fathers. 8And every daughter who possesses an inheritance in any tribe of the children of Israel shall be the wife of one of the family of her father's tribe, so that the children of Israel each may possess the inheritance of his fathers. 9Thus no inheritance shall change hands from *one* tribe to another, but every tribe of the children of Israel shall keep its own inheritance."

10Just as the Lord commanded Moses, so did the daughters of Zelophehad; 11for Mahlah, Tirzah, Hoglah, Milcah, and Noah, the daughters of Zelophehad, were married to the sons of their father's brothers. 12They were married into the families of the children of Manasseh the son of Joseph, and their inheritance remained in the tribe of their father's family.

13These *are* the commandments and the judgments which the Lord commanded the children of Israel by the hand of Moses in the plains of Moab by the Jordan, *across from* Jericho.

The Fifth Book of Moses Called

DEUTERONOMY

The Previous Command to Enter Canaan

1 These *are* the words which Moses spoke to all Israel on this side of the Jordan in the wilderness, in the plain opposite Suph, between Paran, Tophel, Laban, Hazeroth, and Dizahab. 2It *is* eleven days' *journey* from Horeb by way of Mount Seir to Kadesh Barnea. 3Now it came to pass in the fortieth year, in the eleventh month, on the first *day* of the month, *that* Moses spoke to the children of Israel according to all that the LORD had given him as commandments to them, 4after he had killed Sihon king of the Amorites, who dwelt in Heshbon, and Og king of Bashan, who dwelt at Ashtaroth in Edrei.

5On this side of the Jordan in the land of Moab, Moses began to explain this law, saying, 6"The LORD our God spoke to us in Horeb, saying: 'You have dwelt long enough at this mountain. 7Turn and take your journey, and go to the mountains of the Amorites, to all the neighboring *places* in the plain, in the mountains and in the lowland, in the South and on the seacoast, to the land of the Canaanites and to Lebanon, as far as the great river, the River Euphrates. 8See, I have set the land before you; go in and possess the land which the LORD swore to your fathers—to Abraham, Isaac, and Jacob—to give to them and their descendants after them.'

Tribal Leaders Appointed

9"And I spoke to you at that time, saying: 'I alone am not able to bear you. 10The LORD your God has multiplied you, and here you *are* today, as the stars of heaven in multitude. 11May the LORD God of your fathers make you a thousand times more numerous than you are, and bless you as He has promised you! 12How can I alone bear your problems and your burdens and your complaints? 13Choose wise, understanding, and knowledgeable men from among your tribes, and I will make them heads over you.' 14And you an-swered me and said, 'The thing which you have told *us* to do *is* good.' 15So I took the heads of your tribes, wise and knowledgeable men, and made them heads over you, leaders of thousands, leaders of hundreds, leaders of fifties, leaders of tens, and officers for your tribes.

16"Then I commanded your judges at that time, saying, 'Hear *the cases* between your brethren, and judge righteously between a man and his brother or the stranger who is with him. 17You shall not show partiality in judgment; you shall hear the small as well as the great; you shall not be afraid in any man's presence, for the judgment *is* God's. The case that is too hard for you, bring to me, and I will hear it.' 18And I commanded you at that time all the things which you should do.

Israel's Refusal to Enter the Land

19"So we departed from Horeb, and went through all that great and terrible wilderness which you saw on the way to the mountains of the Amorites, as the LORD our God had commanded us. Then we came to Kadesh Barnea. 20And I said to you, 'You have come to the mountains of the Amorites, which the LORD our God is giving us. 21Look, the LORD your God has set the land before you; go up *and* possess *it,* as the LORD God of your fathers has spoken to you; do not fear or be discouraged.'

22"And every one of you came near to me and said, 'Let us send men before us, and let them search out the land for us, and bring back word to us of the way by which we should go up, and of the cities into which we shall come.' 23"The plan pleased me well; so I took twelve of your men, one man from *each* tribe. 24And they departed and went up into the mountains, and came to the Valley of Eshcol, and spied it out. 25They also took *some* of the fruit of the land in their hands and brought *it* down to us; and they brought back word to us, saying, '*It is* a good land which the LORD our God is giving us.'

26"Nevertheless you would not go up,

but rebelled against the command of the LORD your God; 27and you complained in your tents, and said, 'Because the LORD hates us, He has brought us out of the land of Egypt to deliver us into the hand of the Amorites, to destroy us. 28Where can we go up? Our brethren have discouraged our hearts, saying, "The people *are* greater and taller than we; the cities *are* great and fortified up to heaven; moreover we have seen the sons of the Anakim there." '

29"Then I said to you, 'Do not be terrified, or afraid of them. 30The LORD your God, who goes before you, He will fight for you, according to all He did for you in Egypt before your eyes, 31and in the wilderness where you saw how the LORD your God carried you, as a man carries his son, in all the way that you went until you came to this place.' 32Yet, for all that, you did not believe the LORD your God, 33who went in the way before you to search out a place for you to pitch your tents, to show you the way you should go, in the fire by night and in the cloud by day.

The Penalty for Israel's Rebellion

34"And the LORD heard the sound of your words, and was angry, and took an oath, saying, 35'Surely not one of these men of this evil generation shall see that good land of which I swore to give to your fathers, 36except Caleb the son of Jephunneh; he shall see it, and to him and his children I am giving the land on which he walked, because he wholly followed the LORD.' 37The LORD was also angry with me for your sakes, saying, 'Even you shall not go in there. 38Joshua the son of Nun, who stands before you, he shall go in there. Encourage him, for he shall cause Israel to inherit it.

39'Moreover your little ones and your children, who you say will be victims, who today have no knowledge of good and evil, they shall go in there; to them I will give it, and they shall possess it. 40But *as for* you, turn and take your journey into the wilderness by the Way of the Red Sea.'

41"Then you answered and said to me, 'We have sinned against the LORD; we will go up and fight, just as the LORD our God commanded us.' And when everyone of you had girded on his weapons of war, you were ready to go up into the mountain.

42"And the LORD said to me, 'Tell them, "Do not go up nor fight, for I *am* not among you; lest you be defeated before your enemies." ' 43So I spoke to you; yet you would not listen, but rebelled against the command of the LORD, and presumptuously went up into the mountain. 44And the Amorites who dwelt in that mountain came out against you and chased you as bees do, and drove you back from Seir to Hormah. 45Then you returned and wept before the LORD, but the LORD would not listen to your voice nor give ear to you.

46"So you remained in Kadesh many days, according to the days that you spent *there.*

The Desert Years

2 "Then we turned and journeyed into the wilderness of the Way of the Red Sea, as the LORD spoke to me, and we skirted Mount Seir for many days.

2"And the LORD spoke to me, saying: 3'You have skirted this mountain long enough; turn northward. 4And command the people, saying, "You *are about to* pass through the territory of your brethren, the descendants of Esau, who live in Seir; and they will be afraid of you. Therefore watch yourselves carefully. 5Do not meddle with them, for I will not give you *any* of their land, no, not so much as one footstep, because I have given Mount Seir to Esau *as* a possession. 6You shall buy food from them with money, that you may eat; and you shall also buy water from them with money, that you may drink.

7"For the LORD your God has blessed you in all the work of your hand. He knows your trudging through this great wilderness. These forty years the LORD your God *has been* with you; you have lacked nothing." '

8"And when we passed beyond our brethren, the descendants of Esau who dwell in Seir, away from the road of the plain, away from Elath and Ezion Geber, we turned and passed by way of the Wilderness of Moab. 9Then the LORD said to me, 'Do not harass Moab, nor contend with them in battle, for I will not give you *any* of their land *as* a possession, because I have given Ar to the descendants of Lot *as* a possession.' "

10(The Emim had dwelt there in times past, a people as great and numerous and tall as the Anakim. 11They were also regarded as giants, like the Anakim, but the Moabites call them Emim. 12The Horites formerly dwelt in Seir, but the descendants of Esau dispossessed them and destroyed them from before them, and dwelt in their place, just as Israel did to the land of their possession which the LORD gave them.)

13" 'Now rise and cross over the Valley of the Zered.' So we crossed over the Valley of the Zered. 14And the time we took to come from Kadesh Barnea until we crossed over the Valley of the Zered *was* thirty-eight years, until all the generation of the men of war was consumed from the midst of the camp, just as the LORD had sworn to them. 15For indeed the hand of the LORD was against them, to destroy them from the midst of the camp until they were consumed.

16"So it was, when all the men of war had finally perished from among the people, 17that the LORD spoke to me, saying: 18'This day you are to cross over at Ar, the boundary of Moab. 19And *when* you come near the people of Ammon, do not harass them or meddle with them, for I will not give you *any* of the land of the people of Ammon *as* a possession, because I have given it to the descendants of Lot *as* a possession.' "

20(That was also regarded as a land of giants; giants formerly dwelt there. But the Ammonites call them Zamzummim, 21a people as great and numerous and tall as the Anakim. But the LORD destroyed them before them, and they dispossessed them and dwelt in their place, 22just as He had done for the descendants of Esau, who dwelt in Seir, when He destroyed the Horites from before them. They dispossessed them and dwelt in their place, even to this day. 23And the Avim, who dwelt in villages as far as Gaza—the Caphtorim, who came from Caphtor, destroyed them and dwelt in their place.)

24" 'Rise, take your journey, and cross over the River Arnon. Look, I have given into your hand Sihon the Amorite, king of Heshbon, and his land. Begin to possess *it*, and engage him in battle. 25This day I will begin to put the dread and fear of you upon the nations under the whole heaven, who shall hear the report of you, and shall tremble and be in anguish because of you.'

King Sihon Defeated

26"And I sent messengers from the Wilderness of Kedemoth to Sihon king of Heshbon, with words of peace, saying, 27'Let me pass through your land; I will keep strictly to the road, and I will turn neither to the right nor to the left. 28You shall sell me food for money, that I may eat, and give me water for money, that I may drink; only let me pass through on foot, 29just as the descendants of Esau who dwell in Seir and the Moabites who dwell in Ar did for me, until I cross the Jordan to the land which the LORD our God is giving us.'

30"But Sihon king of Heshbon would not let us pass through, for the LORD your God hardened his spirit and made his heart obstinate, that He might deliver him into your hand, as *it is* this day.

31"And the LORD said to me, 'See, I have begun to give Sihon and his land over to you. Begin to possess *it*, that you may inherit his land.' 32Then Sihon and all his people came out against us to fight at Jahaz. 33And the LORD our God delivered him over to us; so we defeated him, his sons, and all his people. 34We took all his cities at that time, and we utterly destroyed the men, women, and little ones of every city; we left none remaining. 35We took only the livestock as plunder for ourselves, with the spoil of the cities which we took. 36From Aroer, which *is* on the bank of the River Arnon, and *from* the city that *is* in the ravine, as far as Gilead, there was not one city too strong for us; the LORD our God delivered all to us. 37Only you did not go near the land of the people of Ammon—anywhere along the River Jabbok, or to the cities of the mountains, or wherever the LORD our God had forbidden us.

King Og Defeated

3 "Then we turned and went up the road to Bashan; and Og king of Bashan came out against us, he and all his people, to battle at Edrei. 2And the LORD said to me, 'Do not fear him, for I have delivered him and all his people and his land into your hand; you shall do to him as you did to Sihon king of the Amorites, who dwelt at Heshbon.'

3"So the LORD our God also delivered into our hands Og king of Bashan, with all his people, and we attacked him until he had no survivors remaining. 4And we took all his cities at that time; there was not a city which we did not take from them: sixty cities, all the region of Argob, the kingdom of Og in Bashan. 5All these cities *were* fortified with high walls, gates, and bars, besides a great many rural towns. 6And we utterly destroyed them, as we did to Sihon king of Heshbon, utterly destroying the men, women, and children of every city. 7But all the livestock and the spoil of the cities we took as booty for ourselves.

8"And at that time we took the land from the hand of the two kings of the Amorites who *were* on this side of the Jordan, from the River Arnon to Mount Hermon 9(the Sidonians call Hermon Sirion, and the Amorites call it Senir), 10all the cities of the plain, all Gilead, and all Bashan, as far as Salcah and Edrei, cities of the kingdom of Og in Bashan.

11"For only Og king of Bashan remained of the remnant of the giants. Indeed his bedstead *was* an iron bedstead. (*Is* it not in Rabbah of the people of Ammon?) Nine cubits *is* its length and four cubits its width, according to the standard cubit.

The Land East of the Jordan Divided

12"And this land, *which* we possessed at that time, from Aroer, which *is* by the River Arnon, and half the mountains of Gilead and its cities, I gave to the Reubenites and the Gadites. 13The rest of Gilead, and all Bashan, the kingdom of Og, I gave to half the tribe of Manasseh. (All the region of Argob, with all Bashan, was called the land of the giants. 14Jair the son of Manasseh took all the region of Argob, as far as the border of the Geshurites and the Maachathites, and called Bashan after his own name, Havoth Jair,[a] to this day.)

15"Also I gave Gilead to Machir. 16And to the Reubenites and the Gadites I gave from Gilead as far as the River Arnon, the middle of the river as *the* border, as far as the River Jabbok, the border of the people of Ammon; 17the plain also, with the Jordan as *the* border, from Chinnereth as far as the east side of the Sea of the Arabah (the Salt Sea), below the slopes of Pisgah.

18"Then I commanded you at that time, saying: 'The LORD your God has given you this land to possess. All you men of valor shall cross over armed before your brethren, the children of Israel. 19But your wives, your little ones, and your livestock (I know that you have much livestock) shall stay in your cities which I have given you, 20until the LORD has given rest to your brethren as to you, and they also possess the land which the LORD your God is giving them beyond the Jordan. Then each of you may return to his possession which I have given you.'

21"And I commanded Joshua at that time, saying, 'Your eyes have seen all that the LORD your God has done to these two kings; so will the LORD do to all the kingdoms through which you pass. 22You must not fear them, for the LORD your God Himself fights for you.'

Moses Forbidden to Enter the Land

23"Then I pleaded with the LORD at that time, saying: 24'O Lord GOD, You have begun to show Your servant Your greatness and Your mighty hand, for what god *is there* in heaven or on earth who can do *anything* like Your works and Your mighty *deeds*? 25I pray, let me cross over and see the good land beyond the Jordan, those pleasant mountains, and Lebanon.'

26"But the LORD was angry with me on your account, and would not listen to me. So the LORD said to me: 'Enough

---

a Literally *Towns of Jair*

of that! Speak no more to Me of this matter. 27Go up to the top of Pisgah, and lift your eyes toward the west, the north, the south, and the east; behold *it* with your eyes, for you shall not cross over this Jordan. 28But command Joshua, and encourage him and strengthen him; for he shall go over before this people, and he shall cause them to inherit the land which you will see.'

29"So we stayed in the valley opposite Beth Peor.

Moses Commands Obedience

4 "Now, O Israel, listen to the statutes and the judgments which I teach you to observe, that you may live, and go in and possess the land which the LORD God of your fathers is giving you. 2You shall not add to the word which I command you, nor take from it, that you may keep the commandments of the LORD your God which I command you. 3Your eyes have seen what the LORD did at Baal Peor; for the LORD your God has destroyed from among you all the men who followed Baal of Peor. 4But you who held fast to the LORD your God *are* alive today, every one of you.

5"Surely I have taught you statutes and judgments, just as the LORD my God commanded me, that you should act according *to them* in the land which you go to possess. 6Therefore be careful to observe *them*; for this *is* your wisdom and your understanding in the sight of the peoples who will hear all these statutes, and say, 'Surely this great nation *is* a wise and understanding people.'

7"For what great nation *is there* that has God *so* near to it, as the LORD our God *is* to us, for whatever *reason* we may call upon Him? 8And what great nation *is there* that has *such* statutes and righteous judgments as are in all this law which I set before you this day? 9Only take heed to yourself, and diligently keep yourself, lest you forget the things your eyes have seen, and lest they depart from your heart all the days of your life. And teach them to your children and your grandchildren, 10*especially concerning* the day you stood before the LORD your God in Horeb, when the LORD said to me,

'Gather the people to Me, and I will let them hear My words, that they may learn to fear Me all the days they live on the earth, and *that* they may teach their children.'

11"Then you came near and stood at the foot of the mountain, and the mountain burned with fire to the midst of heaven, with darkness, cloud, and thick darkness. 12And the LORD spoke to you out of the midst of the fire. You heard the sound of the words, but saw no form; *you* only *heard* a voice. 13So He declared to you His covenant which He commanded you to perform, the Ten Commandments; and He wrote them on two tablets of stone. 14And the LORD commanded me at that time to teach you statutes and judgments, that you might observe them in the land which you cross over to possess.

Beware of Idolatry

15"Take careful heed to yourselves, for you saw no form when the LORD spoke to you at Horeb out of the midst of the fire, 16lest you act corruptly and make for yourselves a carved image in the form of any figure: the likeness of male or female, 17the likeness of any animal that *is* on the earth or the likeness of any winged bird that flies in the air, 18the likeness of anything that creeps on the ground or the likeness of any fish that *is* in the water beneath the earth. 19And *take heed*, lest you lift your eyes to heaven, and *when* you see the sun, the moon, and the stars, all the host of heaven, you feel driven to worship them and serve them, which the LORD your God has given to all the peoples under the whole heaven as a heritage. 20But the LORD has taken you and brought you out of the iron furnace, out of Egypt, to be His people, an inheritance, as you are this day. 21Furthermore the LORD was angry with me for your sakes, and swore that I would not cross over the Jordan, and that I would not enter the good land which the LORD your God is giving you as an inheritance. 22But I must die in this land, I must not cross over the Jordan; but you shall cross over and possess that good land. 23Take heed to yourselves, lest you forget the covenant of the LORD your God which He made with you, and make for yourselves a carved image in the form of anything which the LORD your God has forbidden you. 24For the LORD your God *is* a consuming fire, a jealous God.

25"When you beget children and grandchildren and have grown old in the land, and act corruptly and make a carved image in the form of anything, and do evil in the sight of the LORD your God to provoke Him to anger, 26I call heaven and earth to witness against you this day, that you will soon utterly perish from the land which you cross over the Jordan to possess; you will not prolong *your* days in it, but will be utterly destroyed. 27And the LORD will scatter you among the peoples, and you will be left few in number among the nations where the LORD will drive you. 28And there you will serve gods, the work of men's hands, wood and stone, which neither see nor hear nor eat nor smell. 29But from there you will seek the LORD your God, and you will find *Him* if you seek Him with all your heart and with all your soul. 30When you are in distress, and all these things come upon you in the latter days, when you turn to the LORD your God and obey His voice 31(for the LORD your God *is* a merciful God), He will not forsake you nor destroy you, nor forget the covenant of your fathers which He swore to them.

32"For ask now concerning the days that are past, which were before you, since the day that God created man on the earth, and *ask* from one end of heaven to the other, whether *any* great *thing* like this has happened, or *anything* like it has been heard. 33Did *any* people *ever* hear the voice of God speaking out of the midst of the fire, as you have heard, and live? 34Or did God *ever* try to go *and* take for Himself a nation from the midst of *another* nation, by trials, by signs, by wonders, by war, by a mighty hand and an outstretched arm, and by great terrors, according to all that the LORD your God did for you in Egypt before your eyes? 35To you it was shown, that you might know that the LORD Himself *is* God; *there is* none other besides Him. 36Out of heaven He let you hear His voice, that He might instruct you; on earth He showed you His great fire, and

you heard His words out of the midst of the fire. 37And because He loved your fathers, therefore He chose their descendants after them; and He brought you out of Egypt with His Presence, with His mighty power, 38driving out from before you nations greater and mightier than you, to bring you in, to give you their land *as* an inheritance, as *it is* this day. 39Therefore know this day, and consider *it* in your heart, that the LORD Himself *is* God in heaven above and on the earth beneath; *there is* no other. 40You shall therefore keep His statutes and His commandments which I command you today, that it may go well with you and with your children after you, and that you may prolong *your* days in the land which the LORD your God is giving you for all time."

Cities of Refuge East of the Jordan

41Then Moses set apart three cities on this side of the Jordan, toward the rising of the sun, 42that the manslayer might flee there, who kills his neighbor unintentionally, without having hated him in time past, and that by fleeing to one of these cities he might live: 43Bezer in the wilderness on the plateau for the Reubenites, Ramoth in Gilead for the Gadites, and Golan in Bashan for the Manassites.

Introduction to God's Law

44Now this *is* the law which Moses set before the children of Israel. 45These *are* the testimonies, the statutes, and the judgments which Moses spoke to the children of Israel after they came out of Egypt, 46on this side of the Jordan, in the valley opposite Beth Peor, in the land of Sihon king of the Amorites, who dwelt at Heshbon, whom Moses and the children of Israel defeated after they came out of Egypt. 47And they took possession of his land and the land of Og king of Bashan, two kings of the Amorites, who *were* on this side of the Jordan, toward the rising of the sun, 48from Aroer, which *is* on the bank of the River Arnon, even to Mount Sion (that is, Hermon), 49and all the plain on the east side of the Jordan as far as the Sea of the Arabah, below the slopes of Pisgah.

The Ten Commandments Reviewed

5 And Moses called all Israel, and said to them: "Hear, O Israel, the statutes and judgments which I speak in your hearing today, that you may learn them and be careful to observe them. ²The LORD our God made a covenant with us in Horeb. ³The LORD did not make this covenant with our fathers, but with us, those who *are* here today, all of us who *are* alive. ⁴The LORD talked with you face to face on the mountain from the midst of the fire. ⁵I stood between the LORD and you at that time, to declare to you the word of the LORD; for you were afraid because of the fire, and you did not go up the mountain. *He* said:

6   'I *am* the LORD your God who brought you out of the land of Egypt, out of the house of bondage.

7   'You shall have no other gods before Me.

8   'You shall not make for yourself a carved image—any likeness *of anything* that *is* in heaven above, or that *is* in the earth beneath, or that *is* in the water under the earth; ⁹you shall not bow down to them nor serve them. For I, the LORD your God, *am* a jealous God, visiting the iniquity of the fathers upon the children to the third and fourth *generations* of those who hate Me, ¹⁰but showing mercy to thousands, to those who love Me and keep My commandments.

11   'You shall not take the name of the LORD your God in vain, for the LORD will not hold *him* guiltless who takes His name in vain.

12   'Observe the Sabbath day, to keep it holy, as the LORD your God commanded you. ¹³Six days you shall labor and do all your work, ¹⁴but the seventh day *is* the Sabbath of the LORD your God. *In it* you shall do no work: you, nor your son, nor your daughter, nor your male servant, nor your female servant, nor your ox, nor your donkey, nor any

of your cattle, nor your stranger who *is* within your gates, that your male servant and your female servant may rest as well as you. ¹⁵And remember that you were a slave in the land of Egypt, and the LORD your God brought you out from there by a mighty hand and by an outstretched arm; therefore the LORD your God commanded you to keep the Sabbath day.

16   'Honor your father and your mother, as the LORD your God has commanded you, that your days may be long, and that it may be well with you in the land which the LORD your God is giving you.

17   'You shall not murder.

18   'You shall not commit adultery.

19   'You shall not steal.

20   'You shall not bear false witness against your neighbor.

21   'You shall not covet your neighbor's wife; and you shall not desire your neighbor's house, his field, his male servant, his female servant, his ox, his donkey, or anything that *is* your neighbor's.'

²²"These words the LORD spoke to all your assembly, in the mountain from the midst of the fire, the cloud, and the thick darkness, with a loud voice; and He added no more. And He wrote them on two tablets of stone and gave them to me.

The People Afraid of God's Presence

²³"So it was, when you heard the voice from the midst of the darkness, while the mountain was burning with fire, that you came near to me, all the heads of your tribes and your elders. ²⁴And you said: 'Surely the LORD our God has shown us His glory and His greatness, and we have heard His voice from the midst of the fire. We have seen this day that God speaks with man; yet he *still* lives. ²⁵Now therefore, why should we die? For this great fire will consume us; if we hear the voice of the LORD our God anymore, then we shall die. ²⁶For who *is there* of all flesh who has heard the voice of the living God

speaking from the midst of the fire, as we *have*, and lived? 27You go near and hear all that the LORD our God may say, and tell us all that the LORD our God says to you, and we will hear and do *it*.'

28"Then the LORD heard the voice of your words when you spoke to me, and the LORD said to me: 'I have heard the voice of the words of this people which they have spoken to you. They are right *in* all that they have spoken. 29Oh, that they had such a heart in them that they would fear Me and always keep all My commandments, that it might be well with them and with their children forever! 30Go and say to them, "Return to your tents." 31But as for you, stand here by Me, and I will speak to you all the commandments, the statutes, and the judgments which you shall teach them, that they may observe *them* in the land which I am giving them to possess.'

32"Therefore you shall be careful to do as the LORD your God has commanded you; you shall not turn aside to the right hand or to the left. 33You shall walk in all the ways which the LORD your God has commanded you, that you may live and *that it may be* well with you, and *that* you may prolong *your* days in the land which you shall possess.

The Greatest Commandment

6 "Now this *is* the commandment, *and these are* the statutes and judgments which the LORD your God has commanded to teach you, that you may observe *them* in the land which you are crossing over to possess, 2that you may fear the LORD your God, to keep all His statutes and His commandments which I command you, you and your son and your grandson, all the days of your life, and that your days may be prolonged. 3Therefore hear, O Israel, and be careful to observe *it*, that it may be well with you, and that you may multiply greatly as the LORD God of your fathers has promised you—'a land flowing with milk and honey.'[b]

4"Hear, O Israel: The LORD our God,

the LORD *is* one! 5You shall love the LORD your God with all your heart, with all your soul, and with all your strength.

6"And these words which I command you today shall be in your heart. 7You shall teach them diligently to your children, and shall talk of them when you sit in your house, when you walk by the way, when you lie down, and when you rise up. 8You shall bind them as a sign on your hand, and they shall be as frontlets between your eyes. 9You shall write them on the doorposts of your house and on your gates.

Caution Against Disobedience

10"So it shall be, when the LORD your God brings you into the land of which He swore to your fathers, to Abraham, Isaac, and Jacob, to give you large and beautiful cities which you did not build, 11houses full of all good things, which you did not fill, hewn-out wells which you did not dig, vineyards and olive trees which you did not plant—when you have eaten and are full—12*then* beware, lest you forget the LORD who brought you out of the land of Egypt, from the house of bondage. 13You shall fear the LORD your God and serve Him, and shall take oaths in His name. 14You shall not go after other gods, the gods of the peoples who *are* all around you 15(for the LORD your God *is* a jealous God among you), lest the anger of the LORD your God be aroused against you and destroy you from the face of the earth.

16"You shall not tempt the LORD your God as you tempted *Him* in Massah. 17You shall diligently keep the commandments of the LORD your God, His testimonies, and His statutes which He has commanded you. 18And you shall do *what is* right and good in the sight of the LORD, that it may be well with you, and that you may go in and possess the good land of which the LORD swore to your fathers, 19to cast out all your enemies from before you, as the LORD has spoken.

20"When your son asks you in time to come, saying, 'What *is the meaning of* the testimonies, the statutes, and the

---

b Compare Exodus 3.8

judgments which the LORD our God has commanded you?' 21then you shall say to your son: 'We were slaves of Pharaoh in Egypt, and the LORD brought us out of Egypt with a mighty hand; 22and the LORD showed signs and wonders before our eyes, great and severe, against Egypt, Pharaoh, and all his household. 23Then He brought us out from there, that He might bring us in, to give us the land of which He swore to our fathers. 24And the LORD commanded us to observe all these statutes, to fear the LORD our God, for our good always, that He might preserve us alive, as *it is* this day. 25Then it will be righteousness for us, if we are careful to observe all these commandments before the LORD our God, as He has commanded us.'

A Chosen People

7 "When the LORD your God brings you into the land which you go to possess, and has cast out many nations before you, the Hittites and the Girgashites and the Amorites and the Canaanites and the Perizzites and the Hivites and the Jebusites, seven nations greater and mightier than you, 2and when the LORD your God delivers them over to you, you shall conquer them *and* utterly destroy them. You shall make no covenant with them nor show mercy to them. 3Nor shall you make marriages with them. You shall not give your daughter to their son, nor take their daughter for your son. 4For they will turn your sons away from following Me, to serve other gods; so the anger of the LORD will be aroused against you and destroy you suddenly. 5But thus you shall deal with them: you shall destroy their altars, and break down their *sacred* pillars, and cut down their wooden images, and burn their carved images with fire.

6"For you *are* a holy people to the LORD your God; the LORD your God has chosen you to be a people for Himself, a special treasure above all the peoples on the face of the earth. 7The LORD did not set His love on you nor choose you because you were more in number than any other people, for you were the least of all peoples; 8but because the LORD

loves you, and because He would keep the oath which He swore to your fathers, the LORD has brought you out with a mighty hand, and redeemed you from the house of bondage, from the hand of Pharaoh king of Egypt.

9"Therefore know that the LORD your God, He *is* God, the faithful God who keeps covenant and mercy for a thousand generations with those who love Him and keep His commandments; 10and He repays those who hate Him to their face, to destroy them. He will not be slack with him who hates Him; He will repay him to his face. 11Therefore you shall keep the commandment, the statutes, and the judgments which I command you today, to observe them.

Blessings of Obedience

12"Then it shall come to pass, because you listen to these judgments, and keep and do them, that the LORD your God will keep with you the covenant and the mercy which He swore to your fathers. 13And He will love you and bless you and multiply you; He will also bless the fruit of your womb and the fruit of your land, your grain and your new wine and your oil, the increase of your cattle and the offspring of your flock, in the land of which He swore to your fathers to give you. 14You shall be blessed above all peoples; there shall not be a male or female barren among you or among your livestock. 15And the LORD will take away from you all sickness, and will afflict you with none of the terrible diseases of Egypt which you have known, but will lay *them* on all those who hate you. 16Also you shall destroy all the peoples whom the LORD your God delivers over to you; your eye shall have no pity on them; nor shall you serve their gods, for that *will be* a snare to you.

17"If you should say in your heart, 'These nations are greater than I; how can I dispossess them?'—18you shall not be afraid of them, *but* you shall remember well what the LORD your God did to Pharaoh and to all Egypt: 19the great trials which your eyes saw, the signs and the wonders, the mighty hand and the outstretched arm, by which the LORD your God brought you out. So shall the LORD your God do to all the peoples of whom you are afraid. 20Moreover the LORD your God will send the hornet among them until those who are left, who hide themselves from you, are destroyed. 21You shall not be terrified of them; for the LORD your God, the great and awesome God, *is* among you. 22And the LORD your God will drive out those nations before you little by little; you will be unable to destroy them at once, lest the beasts of the field become *too* numerous for you. 23But the LORD your God will deliver them over to you, and will inflict defeat upon them until they are destroyed. 24And He will deliver their kings into your hand, and you will destroy their name from under heaven; no one shall be able to stand against you until you have destroyed them. 25You shall burn the carved images of their gods with fire; you shall not covet the silver or gold *that is* on them, nor take *it* for yourselves, lest you be snared by it; for it *is* an abomination to the LORD your God. 26Nor shall you bring an abomination into your house, lest you be doomed to destruction like it. You shall utterly detest it and utterly abhor it, for it *is* an accursed thing.

Remember the LORD Your God

8 "Every commandment which I command you today you must be careful to observe, that you may live and multiply, and go in and possess the land of which the LORD swore to your fathers. 2And you shall remember that the LORD your God led you all the way these forty years in the wilderness, to humble you *and* test you, to know what *was* in your heart, whether you would keep His commandments or not. 3So He humbled you, allowed you to hunger, and fed you with manna which you did not know nor did your fathers know, that He might make you know that man shall not live by bread alone; but man lives by every *word* that proceeds from the mouth of the LORD. 4Your garments did not wear out on you, nor did your foot swell these forty years. 5You should know in your heart that as a man chastens his son, *so* the LORD your God chastens you.

6"Therefore you shall keep the commandments of the LORD your God, to walk in His ways and to fear Him. 7For the LORD your God is bringing you into a good land, a land of brooks of water, of fountains and springs, that flow out of valleys and hills; 8a land of wheat and barley, of vines and fig trees and pomegranates, a land of olive oil and honey; 9a land in which you will eat bread without scarcity, in which you will lack nothing; a land whose stones *are* iron and out of whose hills you can dig copper. 10When you have eaten and are full, then you shall bless the LORD your God for the good land which He has given you.

11"Beware that you do not forget the LORD your God by not keeping His commandments, His judgments, and His statutes which I command you today, 12lest—*when* you have eaten and are full, and have built beautiful houses and dwell *in them;* 13and *when* your herds and your flocks multiply, and your silver and your gold are multiplied, and all that you have is multiplied; 14when your heart is lifted up, and you forget the LORD your God who brought you out of the land of Egypt, from the house of bondage; 15who led you through that great and terrible wilderness, *in which were* fiery serpents and scorpions and thirsty land where there was no water; who brought water for you out of the flinty rock; 16who fed you in the wilderness with manna, which your fathers did not know, that He might humble you and that He might test you, to do you good in the end—17then you say in your heart, 'My power and the might of my hand have gained me this wealth.'

18"And you shall remember the LORD your God, for *it is* He who gives you power to get wealth, that He may establish His covenant which He swore to your fathers, as *it is* this day. 19Then it shall be, if you by any means forget the LORD your God, and follow other gods, and serve them and worship them, I testify against you this day that you shall surely perish. 20As the nations which the LORD destroys before you, so you shall perish, because you would not be obedient to the voice of the LORD your God.

Israel's Rebellions Reviewed

9 "Hear, O Israel: You *are* to cross over the Jordan today, and go in to dispossess nations greater and mightier than yourself, cities great and fortified up to heaven, 2a people great and tall, the descendants of the Anakim, whom you know, and *of whom* you heard *it said*, 'Who can stand before the descendants of Anak?' 3Therefore understand today that the LORD your God *is* He who goes over before you *as* a consuming fire. He will destroy them and bring them down before you; so you shall drive them out and destroy them quickly, as the LORD has said to you.

4"Do not think in your heart, after the LORD your God has cast them out before you, saying, 'Because of my righteousness the LORD has brought me in to possess this land'; but *it is* because of the wickedness of these nations *that* the LORD is driving them out from before you. 5*It is* not because of your righteousness or the uprightness of your heart *that* you go in to possess their land, but because of the wickedness of these nations *that* the LORD your God drives them out from before you, and that He may fulfill the word which the LORD swore to your fathers, to Abraham, Isaac, and Jacob. 6Therefore understand that the LORD your God is not giving you this good land to possess because of your righteousness, for you *are* a stiff-necked people.

7"Remember! Do not forget how you provoked the LORD your God to wrath in the wilderness. From the day that you departed from the land of Egypt until you came to this place, you have been rebellious against the LORD. 8Also in Horeb you provoked the LORD to wrath, so that the LORD was angry *enough* with you to have destroyed you. 9When I went up into the mountain to receive the tablets of stone, the tablets of the covenant which the LORD made with you, then I stayed on the mountain forty days and forty nights. I neither ate bread nor drank water. 10Then the LORD delivered to me two tablets of stone written with the finger of God, and on them *were* all the words which the LORD had spoken to you on the mountain from the midst of the fire in the day of the assembly. 11And it came to pass, at the end of forty days and forty nights, *that* the LORD gave me the two tablets of stone, the tablets of the covenant.

12"Then the LORD said to me, 'Arise, go down quickly from here, for your people whom you brought out of Egypt have acted corruptly; they have quickly turned aside from the way which I commanded them; they have made themselves a molded image.'

13"Furthermore the LORD spoke to me, saying, 'I have seen this people, and indeed they are a stiff-necked people. 14Let Me alone, that I may destroy them and blot out their name from under heaven; and I will make of you a nation mightier and greater than they.'

15"So I turned and came down from the mountain, and the mountain burned with fire; and the two tablets of the covenant *were* in my two hands. 16And I looked, and behold, you had sinned against the LORD your God—had made for yourselves a molded calf! You had turned aside quickly from the way which the LORD had commanded you. 17Then I took the two tablets and threw them out of my two hands and broke them before your eyes. 18And I fell down before the LORD, as at the first, forty days and forty nights; I neither ate bread nor drank water, because of all your sin which you committed in doing wickedly in the sight of the LORD, to provoke Him to anger. 19For I was afraid of the anger and hot displeasure with which the LORD was angry with you, to destroy you. But the LORD listened to me at that time also. 20And the LORD was very angry with Aaron *and* would have destroyed him; so I prayed for Aaron also at the same time. 21Then I took your sin, the calf which you had made, and burned it with fire and crushed it *and* ground *it* very small, until it was as fine as dust; and I threw its dust into the brook that descended from the mountain.

22"Also at Taberah and Massah and Kibroth Hattaavah you provoked the LORD to wrath. 23Likewise, when the LORD sent you from Kadesh Barnea, saying, 'Go up and possess the land which I have given you,' then you rebelled against the commandment of the

LORD your God, and you did not believe Him nor obey His voice. 24You have been rebellious against the LORD from the day that I knew you.

25"Thus I prostrated myself before the LORD; forty days and forty nights I kept prostrating myself, because the LORD had said He would destroy you. 26Therefore I prayed to the LORD, and said: 'O Lord GOD, do not destroy Your people and Your inheritance whom You have redeemed through Your greatness, whom You have brought out of Egypt with a mighty hand. 27Remember Your servants, Abraham, Isaac, and Jacob; do not look on the stubbornness of this people, or on their wickedness or their sin, 28lest the land from which You brought us should say, "Because the LORD was not able to bring them to the land which He promised them, and because He hated them, He has brought them out to kill them in the wilderness." 29Yet they *are* Your people and Your inheritance, whom You brought out by Your mighty power and by Your outstretched arm.'

The Second Pair of Tablets

10 "At that time the LORD said to me, 'Hew for yourself two tablets of stone like the first, and come up to Me on the mountain and make yourself an ark of wood. 2And I will write on the tablets the words that were on the first tablets, which you broke; and you shall put them in the ark.'

3"So I made an ark of acacia wood, hewed two tablets of stone like the first, and went up the mountain, having the two tablets in my hand. 4And He wrote on the tablets according to the first writing, the Ten Commandments, which the LORD had spoken to you in the mountain from the midst of the fire in the day of the assembly; and the LORD gave them to me. 5Then I turned and came down from the mountain, and put the tablets in the ark which I had made; and there they are, just as the LORD commanded me."

6(Now the children of Israel journeyed from the wells of Bene Jaakan to Moserah, where Aaron died, and where he was buried; and Eleazar his son ministered as priest in his stead. 7From there they journeyed to Gudgo-dah, and from Gudgodah to Jotbathah, a land of rivers of water. 8At that time the LORD separated the tribe of Levi to bear the ark of the covenant of the LORD, to stand before the LORD to minister to Him and to bless in His name, to this day. 9Therefore Levi has no portion nor inheritance with his brethren; the LORD *is* his inheritance, just as the LORD your God promised him.)

10"As at the first time, I stayed in the mountain forty days and forty nights; the LORD also heard me at that time, *and* the LORD chose not to destroy you. 11Then the LORD said to me, 'Arise, begin *your* journey before the people, that they may go in and possess the land which I swore to their fathers to give them.'

The Essence of the Law

12"And now, Israel, what does the LORD your God require of you, but to fear the LORD your God, to walk in all His ways and to love Him, to serve the LORD your God with all your heart and with all your soul, 13*and* to keep the commandments of the LORD and His statutes which I command you today for your good? 14Indeed heaven and the highest heavens belong to the LORD your God, *also* the earth with all that *is* in it. 15The LORD delighted only in your fathers, to love them; and He chose their descendants after them, you above all peoples, as *it is* this day. 16Therefore circumcise the foreskin of your heart, and be stiff-necked no longer. 17For the LORD your God *is* God of gods and Lord of lords, the great God, mighty and awesome, who shows no partiality nor takes a bribe. 18He administers justice for the fatherless and the widow, and loves the stranger, giving him food and clothing. 19Therefore love the stranger, for you were strangers in the land of Egypt. 20You shall fear the LORD your God; you shall serve Him, and to Him you shall hold fast, and take oaths in His name. 21He *is* your praise, and He *is* your God, who has done for you these great and awesome things which your eyes have seen. 22Your fathers went down to Egypt with seventy persons, and now the LORD your God has made you as the stars of heaven in multitude.

Love and Obedience Rewarded

11 "Therefore you shall love the LORD your God, and keep His charge, His statutes, His judgments, and His commandments always. 2Know today that *I do* not *speak* with your children, who have not known and who have not seen the chastening of the LORD your God, His greatness and His mighty hand and His outstretched arm—3His signs and His acts which He did in the midst of Egypt, to Pharaoh king of Egypt, and to all his land; 4what He did to the army of Egypt, to their horses and their chariots: how He made the waters of the Red Sea overflow them as they pursued you, and *how* the LORD has destroyed them to this day; 5what He did for you in the wilderness until you came to this place; 6and what He did to Dathan and Abiram the sons of Eliab, the son of Reuben: how the earth opened its mouth and swallowed them up, their households, their tents, and all the substance that *was* in their possession, in the midst of all Israel—7but your eyes have seen every great act of the LORD which He did.

8"Therefore you shall keep every commandment which I command you today, that you may be strong, and go in and possess the land which you cross over to possess, 9and that you may prolong *your* days in the land which the LORD swore to give your fathers, to them and their descendants, 'a land flowing with milk and honey.'[b] 10For the land which you go to possess *is* not like the land of Egypt from which you have come, where you sowed your seed and watered *it* by foot, as a vegetable garden; 11but the land which you cross over to possess *is* a land of hills and valleys, which drinks water from the rain of heaven, 12a land for which the LORD your God cares; the eyes of the LORD your God *are* always on it, from the beginning of the year to the very end of the year.

13'And it shall be that if you earnestly obey My commandments which I command you today, to love the LORD your God and serve Him with all your heart and with all your soul, 14then I will give *you* the rain for your land in its season, the early rain and the latter rain, that you may gather in your grain, your new wine, and your oil. 15And I will send grass in your fields for your livestock, that you may eat and be filled.' 16Take heed to yourselves, lest your heart be deceived, and you turn aside and serve other gods and worship them, 17lest the LORD's anger be aroused against you, and He shut up the heavens so that there be no rain, and the land yield no produce, and you perish quickly from the good land which the LORD is giving you.

18"Therefore you shall lay up these words of mine in your heart and in your soul, and bind them as a sign on your hand, and they shall be as frontlets between your eyes. 19You shall teach them to your children, speaking of them when you sit in your house, when you walk by the way, when you lie down, and when you rise up. 20And you shall write them on the doorposts of your house and on your gates, 21that your days and the days of your children may be multiplied in the land of which the LORD swore to your fathers to give them, like the days of the heavens above the earth.

22"For if you carefully keep all these commandments which I command you to do—to love the LORD your God, to walk in all His ways, and to hold fast to Him—23then the LORD will drive out all these nations from before you, and you will dispossess greater and mightier nations than yourselves. 24Every place on which the sole of your foot treads shall be yours: from the wilderness and Lebanon, from the river, the River Euphrates, even to the Western Sea,[c] shall be your territory. 25No man shall be able to stand against you; the LORD your God will put the dread of you and the fear of you upon all the land where you tread, just as He has said to you.

26"Behold, I set before you today a blessing and a curse: 27the blessing, if you obey the commandments of the LORD your God which I command you today; 28and the curse, if you do not

---

[b]Compare Exodus 3.8   [c] That is, the Mediterranean

obey the commandments of the LORD your God, but turn aside from the way which I command you today, to go after other gods which you have not known. 29Now it shall be, when the LORD your God has brought you into the land which you go to possess, that you shall put the blessing on Mount Gerizim and the curse on Mount Ebal. 30Are they not on the other side of the Jordan, toward the setting sun, in the land of the Canaanites who dwell in the plain opposite Gilgal, beside the terebinth trees of Moreh? 31For you will cross over the Jordan and go in to possess the land which the LORD your God is giving you, and you will possess it and dwell in it. 32And you shall be careful to observe all the statutes and judgments which I set before you today.

A Prescribed Place of Worship

12 "These *are* the statutes and judgments which you shall be careful to observe in the land which the LORD God of your fathers is giving you to possess, all the days that you live on the earth. 2You shall utterly destroy all the places where the nations which you shall dispossess served their gods, on the high mountains and on the hills and under every green tree. 3And you shall destroy their altars, break their *sacred* pillars, and burn their wooden images with fire; you shall cut down the carved images of their gods and destroy their names from that place. 4You shall not worship the LORD your God *with* such *things.*

5"But you shall seek the place where the LORD your God chooses, out of all your tribes, to put His name for His dwelling place; and there you shall go. 6There you shall take your burnt offerings, your sacrifices, your tithes, the heave offerings of your hand, your vowed offerings, your freewill offerings, and the firstborn of your herds and flocks. 7And there you shall eat before the LORD your God, and you shall rejoice in all to which you have put your hand, you and your households, in which the LORD your God has blessed you.

8"You shall not at all do as we are doing here today—every man doing whatever *is* right in his own eyes— 9for as yet you have not come to the rest and the inheritance which the LORD your God is giving you. 10But *when* you cross over the Jordan and dwell in the land which the LORD your God is giving you to inherit, and He gives you rest from all your enemies round about, so that you dwell in safety, 11then there will be the place where the LORD your God chooses to make His name abide. There you shall bring all that I command you: your burnt offerings, your sacrifices, your tithes, the heave offerings of your hand, and all your choice offerings which you vow to the LORD. 12And you shall rejoice before the LORD your God, you and your sons and your daughters, your male and female servants, and the Levite who *is* within your gates, since he has no portion nor inheritance with you. 13Take heed to yourself that you do not offer your burnt offerings in every place that you see; 14but in the place which the LORD chooses, in one of your tribes, there you shall offer your burnt offerings, and there you shall do all that I command you.

15"However, you may slaughter and eat meat within all your gates, whatever your heart desires, according to the blessing of the LORD your God which He has given you; the unclean and the clean may eat of it, of the gazelle and the deer alike. 16Only you shall not eat the blood; you shall pour it on the earth like water. 17You may not eat within your gates the tithe of your grain or your new wine or your oil, of the firstborn of your herd or your flock, of any of your offerings which you vow, of your freewill offerings, or of the heave offering of your hand. 18But you must eat them before the LORD your God in the place which the LORD your God chooses, you and your son and your daughter, your male servant and your female servant, and the Levite who *is* within your gates; and you shall rejoice before the LORD your God in all to which you put your hands. 19Take heed to yourself that you do not forsake the Levite as long as you live in your land.

20"When the LORD your God enlarges your border as He has promised you, and you say, 'Let me eat meat,' because you long to eat meat, you may eat as much meat as your heart desires. 21If the place where the LORD your God chooses to put His name is too far from you, then you may slaughter from your herd and from your flock which the LORD has given you, just as I have commanded you, and you may eat within your gates as much as your heart desires. 22Just as the gazelle and the deer are eaten, so you may eat them; the unclean and the clean alike may eat them. 23Only be sure that you do not eat the blood, for the blood is the life; you may not eat the life with the meat. 24You shall not eat it; you shall pour it on the earth like water. 25You shall not eat it, that it may go well with you and your children after you, when you do what is right in the sight of the LORD. 26Only the holy things which you have, and your vowed offerings, you shall take and go to the place which the LORD chooses. 27And you shall offer your burnt offerings, the meat and the blood, on the altar of the LORD your God; and the blood of your sacrifices shall be poured out on the altar of the LORD your God, and you shall eat the meat. 28Observe and obey all these words which I command you, that it may go well with you and your children after you forever, when you do what is good and right in the sight of the LORD your God.

Beware of False Gods

29"When the LORD your God cuts off from before you the nations which you go to dispossess, and you displace them and dwell in their land, 30take heed to yourself that you are not ensnared to follow them, after they are destroyed from before you, and that you do not inquire after their gods, saying, 'How did these nations serve their gods? I also will do likewise.' 31You shall not worship the LORD your God in that way; for every abomination to the LORD which He hates they have done to their gods; for they burn even their sons and daughters in the fire to their gods.

32"Whatever I command you, be careful to observe it; you shall not add to it nor take away from it.

Punishment of Apostates

13 "If there arises among you a prophet or a dreamer of dreams, and he gives you a sign or a wonder, 2and the sign or the wonder comes to pass, of which he spoke to you, saying, 'Let us go after other gods'—which you have not known—'and let us serve them,' 3you shall not listen to the words of that prophet or that dreamer of dreams, for the LORD your God is testing you to know whether you love the LORD your God with all your heart and with all your soul. 4You shall walk after the LORD your God and fear Him, and keep His commandments and obey His voice; you shall serve Him and hold fast to Him. 5But that prophet or that dreamer of dreams shall be put to death, because he has spoken in order to turn you away from the LORD your God, who brought you out of the land of Egypt and redeemed you from the house of bondage, to entice you from the way in which the LORD your God commanded you to walk. So you shall put away the evil from your midst.

6"If your brother, the son of your mother, your son or your daughter, the wife of your bosom, or your friend who is as your own soul, secretly entices you, saying, 'Let us go and serve other gods,' which you have not known, neither you nor your fathers, 7of the gods of the people which are all around you, near to you or far off from you, from one end of the earth to the other end of the earth, 8you shall not consent to him or listen to him, nor shall your eye pity him, nor shall you spare him or conceal him; 9but you shall surely kill him; your hand shall be first against him to put him to death, and afterward the hand of all the people. 10And you shall stone him with stones until he dies, because he sought to entice you away from the LORD your God, who brought you out of the land of Egypt, from the house of bondage. 11So all Israel shall hear and fear, and not again do such wickedness as this among you.

12"If you hear someone in one of your cities, which the LORD your God gives you to dwell in, saying, 13'Corrupt men have gone out from among you and enticed the inhabitants of their city, saying, "Let us go and serve other gods" '—which you have not known— 14then you shall inquire, search out, and ask diligently. And *if it is* indeed true *and* certain *that* such an abomination was committed among you, 15you shall surely strike the inhabitants of that city with the edge of the sword, utterly destroying it, all that is in it and its livestock—with the edge of the sword. 16And you shall gather all its plunder into the middle of the street, and completely burn with fire the city and all its plunder, for the LORD your God. It shall be a heap forever; it shall not be built again. 17So none of the accursed things shall remain in your hand, that the LORD may turn from the fierceness of His anger and show you mercy, have compassion on you and multiply you, just as He swore to your fathers, 18because you have listened to the voice of the LORD your God, to keep all His commandments which I command you today, to do *what is* right in the eyes of the LORD your God.

Improper Mourning

14 "You *are* the children of the LORD your God; you shall not cut yourselves nor shave the front of your head for the dead. 2For you *are* a holy people to the LORD your God, and the LORD has chosen you to be a people for Himself, a special treasure above all the peoples who *are* on the face of the earth.

Clean and Unclean Meat

3"You shall not eat any detestable thing. 4These *are* the animals which you may eat: the ox, the sheep, the goat, 5the deer, the gazelle, the roe deer, the wild goat, the mountain goat, the antelope, and the mountain sheep. 6And you may eat every animal with cloven hooves, having the hoof split into two parts, *and that* chews the cud, among the animals. 7Nevertheless, of those that chew the cud or have cloven hooves, you shall not eat, *such as* these: the camel, the hare, and the rock hyrax; for they chew the cud but do not have cloven hooves; they *are* unclean for you. 8Also the swine is unclean for you, because it has cloven hooves, yet *does* not *chew* the cud; you shall not eat their flesh or touch their dead carcasses.

9"These you may eat of all that *are* in the waters: you may eat all that have fins and scales. 10And whatever does not have fins and scales you shall not eat; it *is* unclean for you.

11"All clean birds you may eat. 12But these you shall not eat: the eagle, the vulture, the buzzard, 13the red kite, the falcon, and the kite after their kinds; 14every raven after its kind; 15the ostrich, the short-eared owl, the sea gull, and the hawk after their kinds; 16the little owl, the screech owl, the white owl, 17the jackdaw, the carrion vulture, the fisher owl, 18the stork, the heron after its kind, and the hoopoe and the bat.

19"Also every creeping thing that flies is unclean for you; they shall not be eaten.

20"You may eat all clean birds.

21"You shall not eat anything that dies *of itself;* you may give it to the alien who *is* within your gates, that he may eat it, or you may sell it to a foreigner; for you *are* a holy people to the LORD your God.

"You shall not boil a young goat in its mother's milk.

Tithing Principles

22"You shall truly tithe all the increase of your grain that the field produces year by year. 23And you shall eat before the LORD your God, in the place where He chooses to make His name abide, the tithe of your grain and your new wine and your oil, of the firstborn of your herds and your flocks, that you may learn to fear the LORD your God always. 24But if the journey is too long for you, so that you are not able to carry *the tithe, or* if the place where the LORD your God chooses to put His name is too far from you, when the LORD your God has blessed you, 25then you shall exchange *it* for money, take the money in your hand, and go to the place which the LORD your God chooses. 26And you shall spend that money for whatever your heart desires: for oxen or sheep, for wine or similar drink, for whatever your heart desires; you shall eat there before the LORD your God, and you shall rejoice, you and your household. 27You shall not forsake the Levite who *is* within your gates, for he has no part nor inheritance with you.

28"At the end of *every* third year you shall bring out the tithe of your produce of that year and store *it* up within your gates. 29And the Levite, because he has no portion nor inheritance with you, and the stranger and the fatherless and the widow who *are* within your gates, may come and eat and be satisfied, that the LORD your God may bless you in all the work of your hand which you do.

Debts Canceled Every Seven Years

15 "At the end of *every* seven years you shall grant a release *of debts.* 2And this *is* the form of the release: Every creditor who has lent *anything* to his neighbor shall release *it;* he shall not require *it* of his neighbor or his brother, because it is called the LORD's release. 3Of a foreigner you may require *it;* but you shall give up your claim to what is owed by your brother, 4except when there may be no poor among you; for the LORD will greatly bless you in the land which the LORD your God is giving you to possess *as* an inheritance—5only if you carefully obey the voice of the LORD your God, to observe with care all these commandments which I command you today. 6For the LORD your God will bless you just as He promised you; you shall lend to many nations, but you shall not borrow; you shall reign over many nations, but they shall not reign over you.

Generosity to the Poor

7"If there is among you a poor man of your brethren, within any of the gates in your land which the LORD your God is giving you, you shall not harden your heart nor shut your hand from your poor brother, 8but you shall open your hand wide to him and willingly lend him sufficient for his need, whatever he needs. 9Beware lest there be a wicked thought in your heart, saying, 'The seventh year, the year of release, is at hand,' and your eye be evil against your poor brother and you give him nothing, and he cry out to the LORD against you, and it become sin among you. 10You shall surely give to him, and your heart should not be grieved when

you give to him, because for this thing the LORD your God will bless you in all your works and in all to which you put your hand. 11For the poor will never cease from the land; therefore I command you, saying, 'You shall open your hand wide to your brother, to your poor and your needy, in your land. '

The Law Concerning Bondservants

12"If your brother, a Hebrew man, or a Hebrew woman, is sold to you and serves you six years, then in the seventh year you shall let him go free from you. 13And when you send him away free from you, you shall not let him go away empty-handed; 14you shall supply him liberally from your flock, from your threshing floor, and from your winepress. *From what* the LORD has blessed you with, you shall give to him. 15You shall remember that you were a slave in the land of Egypt, and the LORD your God redeemed you; therefore I command you this thing today. 16And if it happens that he says to you, 'I will not go away from you,' because he loves you and your house, since he prospers with you, 17then you shall take an awl and thrust *it* through his ear to the door, and he shall be your servant forever. Also to your female servant you shall do likewise. 18It shall not seem hard to you when you send him away free from you; for he has been worth a double hired servant in serving you six years. Then the LORD your God will bless you in all that you do.

The Law Concerning Firstborn Animals

19"All the firstborn males that come from your herd and your flock you shall sanctify to the LORD your God; you shall do no work with the firstborn of your herd, nor shear the firstborn of your flock. 20You and your household shall eat *it* before the LORD your God year by year in the place which the LORD chooses. 21But if there is a defect in it, *if it is* lame or blind *or has* any serious defect, you shall not sacrifice it to the LORD your God. 22You may eat it within your gates; the unclean and the clean *person* alike *may eat it,* as *if it were* a gazelle or a deer. 23Only you shall not eat its blood; you shall pour it on the ground like water.

The Passover Reviewed

16 "Observe the month of Abib, and keep the Passover to the LORD your God, for in the month of Abib the LORD your God brought you out of Egypt by night. 2Therefore you shall sacrifice the Passover to the LORD your God, from the flock and the herd, in the place where the LORD chooses to put His name. 3You shall eat no leavened bread with it; seven days you shall eat unleavened bread with it, *that is,* the bread of affliction (for you came out of the land of Egypt in haste), that you may remember the day in which you came out of the land of Egypt all the days of your life. 4And no leaven shall be seen among you in all your territory for seven days, nor shall *any* of the meat which you sacrifice the first day at twilight remain overnight until morning.

5"You may not sacrifice the Passover within any of your gates which the LORD your God gives you; 6but at the place where the LORD your God chooses to make His name abide, there you shall sacrifice the Passover at twilight, at the going down of the sun, at the time you came out of Egypt. 7And you shall roast and eat *it* in the place which the LORD your God chooses, and in the morning you shall turn and go to your tents. 8Six days you shall eat unleavened bread, and on the seventh day there *shall be* a sacred assembly to the LORD your God. You shall do no work *on it.*

The Feast of Weeks Reviewed

9"You shall count seven weeks for yourself; begin to count the seven weeks from *the time* you begin *to put* the sickle to the grain. 10Then you shall keep the Feast of Weeks to the LORD your God with the tribute of a freewill offering from your hand, which you shall give as the LORD your God blesses you. 11You shall rejoice before the LORD your God, you and your son and your daughter, your male servant and your female servant, the Levite who *is* within your gates, the stranger and the fatherless and the widow who *are* among you, at the place where the LORD your God chooses to make His name abide. 12And you shall remember that you were a slave in Egypt, and you shall be careful to observe these statutes.

The Feast of Tabernacles Reviewed

13"You shall observe the Feast of Tabernacles seven days, when you have gathered from your threshing floor and from your winepress. 14And you shall rejoice in your feast, you and your son and your daughter, your male servant and your female servant and the Levite, the stranger and the fatherless and the widow, who *are* within your gates. 15Seven days you shall keep a sacred feast to the LORD your God in the place which the LORD chooses, because the LORD your God will bless you in all your produce and in all the work of your hands, so that you surely rejoice.

16"Three times a year all your males shall appear before the LORD your God in the place which He chooses: at the Feast of Unleavened Bread, at the Feast of Weeks, and at the Feast of Tabernacles; and they shall not appear before the LORD empty-handed. 17Every man *shall give* as he is able, according to the blessing of the LORD your God which He has given you.

Justice Must Be Administered

18"You shall appoint judges and officers in all your gates, which the LORD your God gives you, according to your tribes, and they shall judge the people with just judgment. 19You shall not pervert justice; you shall not show partiality, nor take a bribe, for a bribe blinds the eyes of the wise and twists the words of the righteous. 20You shall follow what is altogether just, that you may live and inherit the land which the LORD your God is giving you.

21"You shall not plant for yourself any tree, as a wooden image, near the altar which you build for yourself to the LORD your God. 22You shall not set up a sacred pillar, which the LORD your God hates.

17 "You shall not sacrifice to the LORD your God a bull or sheep which has any blemish *or* defect, for that *is* an abomination to the LORD your God.

2"If there is found among you, within any of your gates which the LORD your God gives you, a man or a woman who has been wicked in the sight of the LORD your God, in transgressing His covenant, 3who has gone and served other gods and worshiped them, either the sun or moon or any of the host of heaven, which I have not commanded, 4and it is told you, and you hear *of it*, then you shall inquire diligently. And if *it is* indeed true *and* certain that such an abomination has been committed in Israel, 5then you shall bring out to your gates that man or woman who has committed that wicked thing, and shall stone to death that man or woman with stones. 6Whoever is deserving of death shall be put to death on the testimony of two or three witnesses; he shall not be put to death on the testimony of one witness. 7The hands of the witnesses shall be the first against him to put him to death, and afterward the hands of all the people. So you shall put away the evil from among you.

8"If a matter arises which is too hard for you to judge, between degrees of guilt for bloodshed, between one judgment or another, or between one punishment or another, matters of controversy within your gates, then you shall arise and go up to the place which the LORD your God chooses. 9And you shall come to the priests, the Levites, and to the judge *there* in those days, and inquire *of them;* they shall pronounce upon you the sentence of judgment. 10You shall do according to the sentence which they pronounce upon you in that place which the LORD chooses. And you shall be careful to do according to all that they order you. 11According to the sentence of the law in which they instruct you, according to the judgment which they tell you, you shall do; you shall not turn aside *to* the right hand or *to* the left from the sentence which they pronounce upon you. 12Now the man who acts presumptuously and will not heed the priest who stands to minister there before the LORD your God, or the judge, that man shall die. So you shall put away the evil from Israel. 13And all the people shall hear and fear, and no longer act presumptuously.

Principles Governing Kings

14"When you come to the land which the LORD your God is giving you, and possess it and dwell in it, and say, 'I will set a king over me like all the nations that *are* around me,' 15you shall surely set a king over you whom the LORD your God chooses; *one* from among your brethren you shall set as king over you; you may not set a foreigner over you, who *is* not your brother. 16But he shall not multiply horses for himself, nor cause the people to return to Egypt to multiply horses, for the LORD has said to you, 'You shall not return that way again.' 17Neither shall he multiply wives for himself, lest his heart turn away; nor shall he greatly multiply silver and gold for himself.

18"Also it shall be, when he sits on the throne of his kingdom, that he shall write for himself a copy of this law in a book, from *the one* before the priests, the Levites. 19And it shall be with him, and he shall read it all the days of his life, that he may learn to fear the LORD his God and be careful to observe all the words of this law and these statutes, 20that his heart may not be lifted above his brethren, that he may not turn aside from the commandment *to* the right hand or *to* the left, and that he may prolong *his* days in his kingdom, he and his children in the midst of Israel.

The Portion of the Priests and Levites

18 "The priests, the Levites—all the tribe of Levi—shall have no part nor inheritance with Israel; they shall eat the offerings of the LORD made by fire, and His portion. 2Therefore they shall have no inheritance among their brethren; the LORD is their inheritance, as He said to them.

3"And this shall be the priest's due from the people, from those who offer a sacrifice, whether *it is* bull or sheep: they shall give to the priest the shoulder, the cheeks, and the stomach. 4The firstfruits of your grain and your new wine and your oil, and the first of the fleece of your sheep, you shall give him. 5For the LORD your God has chosen him out of all your tribes to stand to minister in the name of the LORD, him and his sons forever.

6"So if a Levite comes from any of your gates, from where he dwells among all Israel, and comes with all the desire of his mind to the place which the LORD chooses, 7then he may serve in the name of the LORD his God as all his brethren the Levites *do,* who stand there before the LORD. 8They shall have equal portions to eat, besides what comes from the sale of his inheritance.

Avoid Wicked Customs

9"When you come into the land which the LORD your God is giving you, you shall not learn to follow the abominations of those nations. 10There shall not be found among you *anyone* who makes his son or his daughter pass through the fire, *or one* who practices witchcraft, *or* a soothsayer, or one who interprets omens, or a sorcerer, 11or one who conjures spells, or a medium, or a spiritist, or one who calls up the dead. 12For all who do these things *are* an abomination to the LORD, and because of these abominations the LORD your God drives them out from before you. 13You shall be blameless before the LORD your God. 14For these nations which you will dispossess listened to soothsayers and diviners; but as for you, the LORD your God has not appointed such for you.

A New Prophet Like Moses

15"The LORD your God will raise up for you a Prophet like me from your midst, from your brethren. Him you shall hear, 16according to all you desired of the LORD your God in Horeb in the day of the assembly, saying, 'Let me not hear again the voice of the LORD my God, nor let me see this great fire anymore, lest I die.'

17"And the LORD said to me: 'What they have spoken is good. 18I will raise up for them a Prophet like you from among their brethren, and will put My words in His mouth, and He shall speak to them all that I command Him. 19And it shall be *that* whoever will not hear My words, which He speaks in My name, I will require *it* of him. 20But the prophet who presumes to speak a word in My name, which I have not commanded him to speak, or who speaks in the name of other gods, that prophet

shall die.' 21And if you say in your heart, 'How shall we know the word which the LORD has not spoken?'— 22when a prophet speaks in the name of the LORD, if the thing does not happen or come to pass, that *is* the thing which the LORD has not spoken; the prophet has spoken it presumptuously; you shall not be afraid of him.

Three Cities of Refuge

19 "When the LORD your God has cut off the nations whose land the LORD your God is giving you, and you dispossess them and dwell in their cities and in their houses, 2you shall separate three cities for yourself in the midst of your land which the LORD your God is giving you to possess. 3You shall prepare roads for yourself, and divide into three parts the territory of your land which the LORD your God is giving you to inherit, that any manslayer may flee there.

4"And this *is* the case of the manslayer who flees there, that he may live: Whoever kills his neighbor unintentionally, not having hated him in time past—5as when *a man* goes to the woods with his neighbor to cut timber, and his hand swings a stroke with the ax to cut down the tree, and the head slips from the handle and strikes his neighbor so that he dies—he shall flee to one of these cities and live; 6lest the avenger of blood, while his anger is hot, pursue the manslayer and overtake him, because the way is long, and kill him, though he *was* not deserving of death, since he had not hated the victim in time past. 7Therefore I command you, saying, 'You shall separate three cities for yourself.'

8"Now if the LORD your God enlarges your territory, as He swore to your fathers, and gives you the land which He promised to give to your fathers, 9and if you keep all these commandments and do them, which I command you today, to love the LORD your God and to walk always in His ways, then you shall add three more cities for yourself besides these three, 10lest innocent blood be shed in the midst of your land which the LORD your God is giving you *as* an inheritance, and *thus* guilt of bloodshed be upon you.

11"But if anyone hates his neighbor, lies in wait for him, rises against him and strikes him mortally, so that he dies, and he flees to one of these cities, 12then the elders of his city shall send and bring him from there, and deliver him over to the hand of the avenger of blood, that he may die. 13Your eye shall not pity him, but you shall put away *the guilt of* innocent blood from Israel, that it may go well with you.

Property Boundaries

14"You shall not remove your neighbor's landmark, which the men of old have set, in your inheritance which you will inherit in the land that the LORD your God is giving you to possess.

The Law Concerning Witnesses

15"One witness shall not rise against a man concerning any iniquity or any sin that he commits; by the mouth of two or three witnesses the matter shall be established. 16If a false witness rises against any man to testify against him of wrongdoing, 17then both men in the controversy shall stand before the LORD, before the priests and the judges who serve in those days. 18And the judges shall make careful inquiry, and indeed, *if* the witness *is* a false witness, who has testified falsely against his brother, 19then you shall do to him as he thought to have done to his brother; so you shall put away the evil from among you. 20And those who remain shall hear and fear, and hereafter they shall not again commit such evil among you. 21Your eye shall not pity: life *shall be* for life, eye for eye, tooth for tooth, hand for hand, foot for foot.

Principles Governing Warfare

20 "When you go out to battle against your enemies, and see horses and chariots *and* people more numerous than you, do not be afraid of them; for the LORD your God *is* with you, who brought you up from the land of Egypt. 2So it shall be, when you are on the verge of battle, that the priest shall approach and speak to the people. 3And he shall say to them, 'Hear, O Israel: Today you are on the verge of battle with your enemies. Do not let your heart faint, do not be afraid, and do not tremble or be terrified because of them; 4for the LORD your God *is* He who goes with you, to fight for you against your enemies, to save you.'

5"Then the officers shall speak to the people, saying: 'What man *is there* who has built a new house and has not dedicated it? Let him go and return to his house, lest he die in the battle and another man dedicate it. 6Also what man *is there* who has planted a vineyard and has not eaten of it? Let him go and return to his house, lest he die in the battle and another man eat of it. 7And what man *is there* who is betrothed to a woman and has not married her? Let him go and return to his house, lest he die in the battle and another man marry her.'

8"The officers shall speak further to the people, and say, 'What man *is there who is* fearful and fainthearted? Let him go and return to his house, lest the heart of his brethren faint like his heart.' 9And so it shall be, when the officers have finished speaking to the people, that they shall make captains of the armies to lead the people.

10"When you go near a city to fight against it, then proclaim an offer of peace to it. 11And it shall be that if they accept your offer of peace, and open to you, then all the people *who are* found in it shall be placed under tribute to you, and serve you. 12Now if *the city* will not make peace with you, but war against you, then you shall besiege it. 13And when the LORD your God delivers it into your hands, you shall strike every male in it with the edge of the sword. 14But the women, the little ones, the livestock, and all that is in the city, all its spoil, you shall plunder for yourself; and you shall eat the enemies' plunder which the LORD your God gives you. 15Thus you shall do to all the cities *which are* very far from you, which *are* not of the cities of these nations.

16"But of the cities of these peoples which the LORD your God gives you *as* an inheritance, you shall let nothing that breathes remain alive, 17but you shall utterly destroy them: the Hittite and the Amorite and the Canaanite and the Perizzite and the Hivite and the

Jebusite, just as the LORD your God has commanded you, 18lest they teach you to do according to all their abominations which they have done for their gods, and you sin against the LORD your God.

19"When you besiege a city for a long time, while making war against it to take it, you shall not destroy its trees by wielding an ax against them; if you can eat of them, do not cut them down to use in the siege, for the tree of the field is man's food. 20Only the trees which you know are not trees for food you may destroy and cut down, to build siegeworks against the city that makes war with you, until it is subdued.

The Law Concerning Unsolved Murder

21 "If anyone is found slain, lying in the field in the land which the LORD your God is giving you to possess, and it is not known who killed him, 2then your elders and your judges shall go out and measure the distance from the slain man to the surrounding cities. 3And it shall be that the elders of the city nearest to the slain man will take a heifer which has not been worked and which has not pulled with a yoke. 4The elders of that city shall bring the heifer down to a valley with flowing water, which is neither plowed nor sown, and they shall break the heifer's neck there in the valley. 5Then the priests, the sons of Levi, shall come near, for the LORD your God has chosen them to minister to Him and to bless in the name of the LORD; by their word every controversy and every assault shall be settled. 6And all the elders of that city nearest to the slain man shall wash their hands over the heifer whose neck is broken in the valley. 7Then they shall answer and say, 'Our hands have not shed this blood, nor have our eyes seen it. 8Provide atonement, O LORD, for Your people Israel, whom You have redeemed, and do not lay innocent blood to the charge of Your people Israel.' And atonement shall be provided on their behalf for the blood. 9So you shall put away the guilt of innocent blood from among you when you do what is right in the sight of the LORD.

Female Captives

10"When you go out to war against your enemies, and the LORD your God delivers them into your hand, and you take them captive, 11and you see among the captives a beautiful woman, and desire her and would take her for your wife, 12then you shall bring her home to your house, and she shall shave her head and trim her nails. 13She shall put off the clothes of her captivity, remain in your house, and mourn her father and her mother a full month; after that you may go in to her and be her husband, and she shall be your wife. 14And it shall be, if you have no delight in her, then you shall set her free, but you certainly shall not sell her for money; you shall not treat her brutally, because you have humbled her.

Firstborn Inheritance Rights

15"If a man has two wives, one loved and the other unloved, and they have borne him children, both the loved and the unloved, and if the firstborn son is of her who is unloved, 16then it shall be, on the day he bequeaths his possessions to his sons, that he must not bestow firstborn status on the son of the loved wife in preference to the son of the unloved, the true firstborn. 17But he shall acknowledge the son of the unloved wife as the firstborn by giving him a double portion of all that he has, for he is the beginning of his strength; the right of the firstborn is his.

The Rebellious Son

18"If a man has a stubborn and rebellious son who will not obey the voice of his father or the voice of his mother, and who, when they have chastened him, will not heed them, 19then his father and his mother shall take hold of him and bring him out to the elders of his city, to the gate of his city. 20And they shall say to the elders of his city, 'This son of ours is stubborn and rebellious; he will not obey our voice; he is a glutton and a drunkard.' 21Then all the men of his city shall stone him to death with stones; so you shall put away the evil from among you, and all Israel shall hear and fear.

Miscellaneous Laws

22"If a man has committed a sin deserving of death, and he is put to death, and you hang him on a tree, 23his body shall not remain overnight on the tree, but you shall surely bury him that day, so that you do not defile the land which the LORD your God is giving you *as* an inheritance; for he who is hanged *is* accursed of God.

22 "You shall not see your brother's ox or his sheep going astray, and hide yourself from them; you shall certainly bring them back to your brother. 2And if your brother *is* not near you, or if you do not know him, then you shall bring it to your own house, and it shall remain with you until your brother seeks it; then you shall restore it to him. 3You shall do the same with his donkey, and so shall you do with his garment; with any lost thing of your brother's, which he has lost and you have found, you shall do likewise; you must not hide yourself.

4"You shall not see your brother's donkey or his ox fall down along the road, and hide yourself from them; you shall surely help him lift *them* up again.

5"A woman shall not wear anything that pertains to a man, nor shall a man put on a woman's garment, for all who do so *are* an abomination to the LORD your God.

6"If a bird's nest happens to be before you along the way, in any tree or on the ground, with young ones or eggs, with the mother sitting on the young or on the eggs, you shall not take the mother with the young; 7you shall surely let the mother go, and take the young for yourself, that it may be well with you and *that* you may prolong *your* days.

8"When you build a new house, then you shall make a parapet for your roof, that you may not bring guilt of bloodshed on your household if anyone falls from it.

9"You shall not sow your vineyard with different kinds of seed, lest the yield of the seed which you have sown and the fruit of your vineyard be defiled.

10"You shall not plow with an ox and a donkey together.

11"You shall not wear a garment of different sorts, *such as* wool and linen mixed together.

12"You shall make tassels on the four corners of the clothing with which you cover *yourself.*

Laws of Sexual Morality

13"If any man takes a wife, and goes in to her, and detests her, 14and charges her with shameful conduct, and brings a bad name on her, and says, 'I took this woman, and when I came to her I found she *was* not a virgin,' 15then the father and mother of the young woman shall take and bring out *the evidence of* the young woman's virginity to the elders of the city at the gate. 16And the young woman's father shall say to the elders, 'I gave my daughter to this man as wife, and he detests her. 17Now he has charged her with shameful conduct, saying, "I found your daughter *was* not a virgin," and yet these *are the evidences of* my daughter's virginity.' And they shall spread the cloth before the elders of the city. 18Then the elders of that city shall take that man and punish him; 19and they shall fine him one hundred *shekels* of silver and give *them* to the father of the young woman, because he has brought a bad name on a virgin of Israel. And she shall be his wife; he cannot divorce her all his days.

20"But if the thing is true, *and evidences of* virginity are not found for the young woman, 21then they shall bring out the young woman to the door of her father's house, and the men of her city shall stone her to death with stones, because she has done a disgraceful thing in Israel, to play the harlot in her father's house. So you shall put away the evil from among you.

22"If a man is found lying with a woman married to a husband, then both of them shall die—the man that lay with the woman, and the woman; so you shall put away the evil from Israel.

23"If a young woman *who is* a virgin is betrothed to a husband, and a man finds her in the city and lies with her, 24then you shall bring them both out to the gate of that city, and you shall stone them to death with stones, the young woman because she did not cry out in the city, and the man because he humbled his neighbor's wife; so you shall put away the evil from among you.

25"But if a man finds a betrothed young woman in the countryside, and the man forces her and lies with her, then only the man who lay with her shall die. 26But you shall do nothing to the young woman; *there is* in the young woman no sin *deserving* of death, for just as when a man rises against his neighbor and kills him, even so *is* this matter. 27For he found her in the countryside, *and* the betrothed young woman cried out, but *there was* no one to save her.

28"If a man finds a young woman *who is* a virgin, who is not betrothed, and he seizes her and lies with her, and they are found out, 29then the man who lay with her shall give to the young woman's father fifty *shekels* of silver, and she shall be his wife because he has humbled her; he shall not be permitted to divorce her all his days.

30"A man shall not take his father's wife, nor uncover his father's bed.

Those Excluded from the Congregation

23 "He who is emasculated by crushing or mutilation shall not enter the assembly of the LORD.

2"One of illegitimate birth shall not enter the assembly of the LORD; even to the tenth generation none of his *descendants* shall enter the assembly of the LORD.

3"An Ammonite or Moabite shall not enter the assembly of the LORD; even to the tenth generation none of his *descendants* shall enter the assembly of the LORD forever, 4because they did not meet you with bread and water on the road when you came out of Egypt, and because they hired against you Balaam the son of Beor from Pethor of Mesopotamia, to curse you. 5Nevertheless the LORD your God would not listen to Balaam, but the LORD your God turned the curse into a blessing for you, because the LORD your God loves you. 6You shall not seek their peace nor their prosperity all your days forever.

7"You shall not abhor an Edomite, for he *is* your brother. You shall not abhor

an Egyptian, because you were an alien in his land. 8The children of the third generation born to them may enter the assembly of the LORD.

Cleanliness of the Camp Site

9"When the army goes out against your enemies, then keep yourself from every wicked thing. 10If there is any man among you who becomes unclean by some occurrence in the night, then he shall go outside the camp; he shall not come inside the camp. 11But it shall be, when evening comes, that he shall wash with water; and when the sun sets, he may come into the camp.

12"Also you shall have a place outside the camp, where you may go out; 13and you shall have an implement among your equipment, and when you sit down outside, you shall dig with it and turn and cover your refuse. 14For the LORD your God walks in the midst of your camp, to deliver you and give your enemies over to you; therefore your camp shall be holy, that He may see no unclean thing among you, and turn away from you.

Miscellaneous Laws

15"You shall not give back to his master the slave who has escaped from his master to you. 16He may dwell with you in your midst, in the place which he chooses within one of your gates, where it seems best to him; you shall not oppress him.

17"There shall be no *ritual* harlot of the daughters of Israel, or a perverted[d] one of the sons of Israel. 18You shall not bring the wages of a harlot or the price of a dog to the house of the LORD your God for any vowed offering, for both of these *are* an abomination to the LORD your God.

19"You shall not charge interest to your brother—interest on money *or* food *or* anything that is lent out at interest. 20To a foreigner you may charge interest, but to your brother you shall not charge interest, that the LORD your God may bless you in all to which you set your hand in the land which you are entering to possess.

21"When you make a vow to the LORD

---

[d] One practicing sodomy and prostitution in religious rituals

your God, you shall not delay to pay it; for the LORD your God will surely require it of you, and it would be sin to you. 22But if you abstain from vowing, it shall not be sin to you. 23That which has gone from your lips you shall keep and perform, for you voluntarily vowed to the LORD your God what you have promised with your mouth.

24"When you come into your neighbor's vineyard, you may eat your fill of grapes at your pleasure, but you shall not put *any* in your container. 25When you come into your neighbor's standing grain, you may pluck the heads with your hand, but you shall not use a sickle on your neighbor's standing grain.

Law Concerning Divorce

24 "When a man takes a wife and marries her, and it happens that she finds no favor in his eyes because he has found some uncleanness in her, and he writes her a certificate of divorce, puts *it* in her hand, and sends her out of his house, 2when she has departed from his house, and goes and becomes another man's *wife,* 3if the latter husband detests her and writes her a certificate of divorce, puts *it* in her hand, and sends her out of his house, or if the latter husband dies who took her as his wife, 4then her former husband who divorced her must not take her back to be his wife after she has been defiled; for that *is* an abomination before the LORD, and you shall not bring sin on the land which the LORD your God is giving you *as* an inheritance.

Miscellaneous Laws

5"When a man has taken a new wife, he shall not go out to war or be charged with any business; he shall be free at home one year, and bring happiness to his wife whom he has taken.

6"No man shall take the lower or the upper millstone in pledge, for he takes *one's* living in pledge.

7"If a man is found kidnapping any of his brethren of the children of Israel, and mistreats him or sells him, then that kidnapper shall die; and you shall put away the evil from among you.

8"Take heed in an outbreak of leprosy, that you carefully observe and do according to all that the priests, the Levites, shall teach you; just as I commanded them, *so* you shall be careful to do. 9Remember what the LORD your God did to Miriam on the way when you came out of Egypt!

10"When you lend your brother anything, you shall not go into his house to get his pledge. 11You shall stand outside, and the man to whom you lend shall bring the pledge out to you. 12And if the man *is* poor, you shall not keep his pledge overnight. 13You shall in any case return the pledge to him again when the sun goes down, that he may sleep in his own garment and bless you; and it shall be righteousness to you before the LORD your God.

14"You shall not oppress a hired servant *who is* poor and needy, *whether* one of your brethren or one of the aliens who *is* in your land within your gates. 15Each day you shall give *him* his wages, and not let the sun go down on it, for he *is* poor and has set his heart on it; lest he cry out against you to the LORD, and it be sin to you.

16"Fathers shall not be put to death for *their* children, nor shall children be put to death for *their* fathers; a person shall be put to death for his own sin.

17"You shall not pervert justice due the stranger or the fatherless, nor take a widow's garment as a pledge. 18But you shall remember that you were a slave in Egypt, and the LORD your God redeemed you from there; therefore I command you to do this thing.

19"When you reap your harvest in your field, and forget a sheaf in the field, you shall not go back to get it; it shall be for the stranger, the fatherless, and the widow, that the LORD your God may bless you in all the work of your hands. 20When you beat your olive trees, you shall not go over the boughs again; it shall be for the stranger, the fatherless, and the widow. 21When you gather the grapes of your vineyard, you shall not glean *it* afterward; it shall be for the stranger, the fatherless, and the widow. 22And you shall remember that you were a slave in the land of Egypt; therefore I command you to do this thing.

25

"If there is a dispute between men, and they come to court, that *the judges* may judge them, and they justify the righteous and condemn the wicked, 2then it shall be, if the wicked man deserves to be beaten, that the judge will cause him to lie down and be beaten in his presence, according to his guilt, with a certain number of blows. 3Forty blows he may give him *and* no more, lest he should exceed this and beat him with many blows above these, and your brother be humiliated in your sight.

4"You shall not muzzle an ox while it treads out *the grain.*

Marriage Duty of the Surviving Brother

5"If brothers dwell together, and one of them dies and has no son, the widow of the dead man shall not be *married* to a stranger outside *the family;* her husband's brother shall go in to her, take her as his wife, and perform the duty of a husband's brother to her. 6And it shall be *that* the firstborn son which she bears will succeed to the name of his dead brother, that his name may not be blotted out of Israel. 7But if the man does not want to take his brother's wife, then let his brother's wife go up to the gate to the elders, and say, 'My husband's brother refuses to raise up a name to his brother in Israel; he will not perform the duty of my husband's brother.' 8Then the elders of his city shall call him and speak to him. But *if* he stands firm and says, 'I do not want to take her,' 9then his brother's wife shall come to him in the presence of the elders, remove his sandal from his foot, spit in his face, and answer and say, 'So shall it be done to the man who will not build up his brother's house.' 10And his name shall be called in Israel, 'The house of him who had his sandal removed.'

Miscellaneous Laws

11"If *two* men fight together, and the wife of one draws near to rescue her husband from the hand of the one attacking him, and puts out her hand and seizes him by the genitals, 12then you shall cut off her hand; your eye shall not pity *her.*

13"You shall not have in your bag differing weights, a heavy and a light. 14You shall not have in your house differing measures, a large and a small. 15You shall have a perfect and just weight, a perfect and just measure, that your days may be lengthened in the land which the LORD your God is giving you. 16For all who do such things, all who behave unrighteously, *are* an abomination to the LORD your God.

Destroy the Amalekites

17"Remember what Amalek did to you on the way as you were coming out of Egypt, 18how he met you on the way and attacked your rear ranks, all the stragglers at your rear, when you *were* tired and weary; and he did not fear God. 19Therefore it shall be, when the LORD your God has given you rest from your enemies all around, in the land which the LORD your God is giving you to possess *as* an inheritance, *that* you will blot out the remembrance of Amalek from under heaven. You shall not forget.

Offerings of Firstfruits and Tithes

26

"And it shall be, when you come into the land which the LORD your God is giving you *as* an inheritance, and you possess it and dwell in it, 2that you shall take some of the first of all the produce of the ground, which you shall bring from your land that the LORD your God is giving you, and put *it* in a basket and go to the place where the LORD your God chooses to make His name abide. 3And you shall go to the one who is priest in those days, and say to him, 'I declare today to the LORD your God that I have come to the country which the LORD swore to our fathers to give us.' 4"Then the priest shall take the basket out of your hand and set it down before the altar of the LORD your God. 5And you shall answer and say before the LORD your God: 'My father *was* a Syrian, about to perish, and he went down to Egypt and dwelt there, few in number; and there he became a nation, great, mighty, and populous. 6But the Egyptians mistreated us, afflicted us, and laid hard bondage on us. 7Then we cried out to the LORD God of our fathers, and the LORD heard our voice and looked on our affliction and our labor and our oppression. 8So the LORD brought us out of Egypt with a mighty hand and with an outstretched arm, with great terror and with signs and wonders. 9He has brought us to this place and has given us this land, "a land flowing with milk and honey";*e* 10and now, behold, I have brought the firstfruits of the land which you, O LORD, have given me.'

"Then you shall set it before the LORD your God, and worship before the LORD your God. 11So you shall rejoice in every good *thing* which the LORD your God has given to you and your house, you and the Levite and the stranger who *is* among you.

12"When you have finished laying aside all the tithe of your increase in the third year—the year of tithing—and have given *it* to the Levite, the stranger, the fatherless, and the widow, so that they may eat within your gates and be filled, 13then you shall say before the LORD your God: 'I have removed the holy *tithe* from *my* house, and also have given them to the Levite, the stranger, the fatherless, and the widow, according to all Your commandments which You have commanded me; I have not transgressed Your commandments, nor have I forgotten *them*. 14I have not eaten any of it when in mourning, nor have I removed *any* of it for an unclean *use,* nor given *any* of it for the dead. I have obeyed the voice of the LORD my God, and have done according to all that You have commanded me. 15Look down from Your holy habitation, from heaven, and bless Your people Israel and the land which You have given us, just as You swore to our fathers, "a land flowing with milk and honey." '*e*

A Special People of God

16"This day the LORD your God commands you to observe these statutes and judgments; therefore you shall be careful to observe them with all your heart and with all your soul. 17Today you have proclaimed the LORD to be your God, and that you will walk in His ways and keep His statutes, His commandments, and His judgments, and

that you will obey His voice. 18Also today the LORD has proclaimed you to be His special people, just as He promised you, that *you* should keep all His commandments, 19and that He will set you high above all nations which He has made, in praise, in name, and in honor, and that you may be a holy people to the LORD your God, just as He has spoken."

The Law Inscribed on Stones

27 Now Moses, with the elders of Israel, commanded the people, saying: "Keep all the commandments which I command you today. 2And it shall be, on the day when you cross over the Jordan to the land which the LORD your God is giving you, that you shall set up for yourselves large stones, and whitewash them with lime. 3You shall write on them all the words of this law, when you have crossed over, that you may enter the land which the LORD your God is giving you, 'a land flowing with milk and honey,'*e* just as the LORD God of your fathers promised you. 4Therefore it shall be, when you have crossed over the Jordan, *that* on Mount Ebal you shall set up these stones, which I command you today, and you shall whitewash them with lime. 5And there you shall build an altar to the LORD your God, an altar of stones; you shall not use an iron *tool* on them. 6You shall build with whole stones the altar of the LORD your God, and offer burnt offerings on it to the LORD your God. 7You shall offer peace offerings, and shall eat there, and rejoice before the LORD your God. 8And you shall write very plainly on the stones all the words of this law."

9Then Moses and the priests, the Levites, spoke to all Israel, saying, "Take heed and listen, O Israel: This day you have become the people of the LORD your God. 10Therefore you shall obey the voice of the LORD your God, and observe His commandments and His statutes which I command you today."

Curses Pronounced from Mount Ebal

11And Moses commanded the people on the same day, saying, 12"These shall

e Compare Exodus 3.8

stand on Mount Gerizim to bless the people, when you have crossed over the Jordan: Simeon, Levi, Judah, Issachar, Joseph, and Benjamin; 13and these shall stand on Mount Ebal to curse: Reuben, Gad, Asher, Zebulun, Dan, and Naphtali.

14"And the Levites shall speak with a loud voice and say to all the men of Israel: 15'Cursed *is* the one who makes a carved or molded image, an abomination to the LORD, the work of the hands of the craftsman, and sets *it* up in secret.'

"And all the people shall answer and say, 'Amen!'

16'Cursed *is* the one who treats his father or his mother with contempt.'

"And all the people shall say, 'Amen!'

17'Cursed *is* the one who moves his neighbor's landmark.'

"And all the people shall say, 'Amen!'

18'Cursed *is* the one who makes the blind to wander off the road.'

"And all the people shall say, 'Amen!'

19'Cursed *is* the one who perverts the justice due the stranger, the fatherless, and widow.'

"And all the people shall say, 'Amen!'

20'Cursed *is* the one who lies with his father's wife, because he has uncovered his father's bed.'

"And all the people shall say, 'Amen!'

21'Cursed *is* the one who lies with any kind of animal.'

"And all the people shall say, 'Amen!'

22'Cursed *is* the one who lies with his sister, the daughter of his father or the daughter of his mother.'

"And all the people shall say, 'Amen!'

23'Cursed *is* the one who lies with his mother-in-law.'

"And all the people shall say, 'Amen!'

24'Cursed *is* the one who attacks his neighbor secretly.'

"And all the people shall say, 'Amen!'

.25'Cursed *is* the one who takes a bribe to slay an innocent person.'

"And all the people shall say, 'Amen!'

26'Cursed *is* the one who does not confirm *all* the words of this law.'

"And all the people shall say, 'Amen!' "

Blessings on Obedience

28 "Now it shall come to pass, if you diligently obey the voice of the LORD your God, to observe carefully all His commandments which I command you today, that the LORD your God will set you high above all nations of the earth. 2And all these blessings shall come upon you and overtake you, because you obey the voice of the LORD your God:

3"Blessed *shall* you *be* in the city, and blessed *shall* you *be* in the country.

4"Blessed *shall be* the fruit of your body, the produce of your ground and the increase of your herds, the increase of your cattle and the offspring of your flocks.

5"Blessed *shall be* your basket and your kneading bowl.

6"Blessed *shall* you *be* when you come in, and blessed *shall* you *be* when you go out.

7"The LORD will cause your enemies who rise against you to be defeated before your face; they shall come out against you one way and flee before you seven ways.

8"The LORD will command the blessing on you in your storehouses and in all to which you set your hand, and He will bless you in the land which the LORD your God is giving you.

9"The LORD will establish you as a holy people to Himself, just as He has sworn to you, if you keep the commandments of the LORD your God and walk in His ways. 10Then all peoples of the earth shall see that you are called by the name of the LORD, and they shall be afraid of you. 11And the LORD will grant you plenty of goods, in the fruit of your body, in the increase of your livestock, and in the produce of your ground, in the land of which the LORD swore to your fathers to give you. 12The LORD will open to you His good treasure, the heavens, to give the rain to your land in its season, and to bless all the work of your hand. You shall lend to many nations, but you shall not borrow. 13And the LORD will make you the head and not the tail; you shall be above only, and not be beneath, if you heed the commandments of the LORD your God, which I command you today, and are careful to observe *them.* 14So you shall not turn aside from any of the words which I command you this day, *to* the right or the left, to go after other gods to serve them.

Curses on Disobedience

15"But it shall come to pass, if you do not obey the voice of the Lord your God, to observe carefully all His commandments and His statutes which I command you today, that all these curses will come upon you and overtake you:

16"Cursed *shall* you *be* in the city, and cursed *shall* you *be* in the country.

17"Cursed *shall be* your basket and your kneading bowl.

18"Cursed *shall be* the fruit of your body and the produce of your land, the increase of your cattle and the offspring of your flocks.

19"Cursed *shall* you *be* when you come in, and cursed *shall* you *be* when you go out.

20"The Lord will send on you cursing, confusion, and rebuke in all that you set your hand to do, until you are destroyed and until you perish quickly, because of the wickedness of your doings in which you have forsaken Me. 21The Lord will make the plague cling to you until He has consumed you from the land which you are going to possess. 22The Lord will strike you with consumption, with fever, with inflammation, with severe burning fever, with the sword, with scorching, and with mildew; they shall pursue you until you perish. 23And your heavens which *are* over your head shall be bronze, and the earth which is under you *shall be* iron. 24The Lord will change the rain of your land to powder and dust; from the heaven it shall come down on you until you are destroyed.

25"The Lord will cause you to be defeated before your enemies; you shall go out one way against them and flee seven ways before them; and you shall become troublesome to all the kingdoms of the earth. 26Your carcasses shall be food for all the birds of the air and the beasts of the earth, and no one shall frighten *them* away. 27The Lord will strike you with the boils of Egypt, with tumors, with the scab, and with the itch, from which you cannot be healed. 28The Lord will strike you with madness and blindness and confusion

of heart. 29And you shall grope at noonday, as a blind man gropes in darkness; you shall not prosper in your ways; you shall be only oppressed and plundered continually, and no one shall save *you*.

30"You shall betroth a wife, but another man shall lie with her; you shall build a house, but you shall not dwell in it; you shall plant a vineyard, but shall not gather its grapes. 31Your ox *shall be* slaughtered before your eyes, but you shall not eat of it; your donkey *shall be* violently taken away from before you, and shall not be restored to you; your sheep *shall be* given to your enemies, and you shall have no one to rescue *them*. 32Your sons and your daughters *shall be* given to another people, and your eyes shall look and fail *with longing* for them all day long; and *there shall be* no strength in your hand. 33A nation whom you have not known shall eat the fruit of your land and the produce of your labor, and you shall be only oppressed and crushed continually. 34So you shall be driven mad because of the sight which your eyes see. 35The Lord will strike you in the knees and on the legs with severe boils which cannot be healed, and from the sole of your foot to the top of your head.

36"The Lord will bring you and the king whom you set over you to a nation which neither you nor your fathers have known, and there you shall serve other gods—wood and stone. 37And you shall become an astonishment, a proverb, and a byword among all nations where the Lord will drive you.

38"You shall carry much seed out to the field but gather little in, for the locust shall consume it. 39You shall plant vineyards and tend *them,* but you shall neither drink *of* the wine nor gather the *grapes;* for the worms shall eat them. 40You shall have olive trees throughout all your territory, but you shall not anoint *yourself* with the oil; for your olives shall drop off. 41You shall beget sons and daughters, but they shall not be yours; for they shall go into captivity. 42Locusts shall consume all your trees and the produce of your land.

43"The alien who *is* among you shall rise higher and higher above you, and you shall come down lower and lower. 44He shall lend to you, but you shall not lend to him; he shall be the head, and you shall be the tail.

45"Moreover all these curses shall come upon you and pursue and overtake you, until you are destroyed, because you did not obey the voice of the LORD your God, to keep His commandments and His statutes which He commanded you. 46And they shall be upon you for a sign and a wonder, and on your descendants forever.

47"Because you did not serve the LORD your God with joy and gladness of heart, for the abundance of everything, 48therefore you shall serve your enemies, whom the LORD will send against you, in hunger, in thirst, in nakedness, and in need of everything; and He will put a yoke of iron on your neck until He has destroyed you. 49The LORD will bring a nation against you from afar, from the end of the earth, *as swift* as the eagle flies, a nation whose language you will not understand, 50a nation of fierce countenance, which does not respect the elderly nor show favor to the young. 51And they shall eat the increase of your livestock and the produce of your land, until you are destroyed; they shall not leave you grain or new wine or oil, *or* the increase of your cattle or the offspring of your flocks, until they have destroyed you.

52"They shall besiege you at all your gates until your high and fortified walls, in which you trust, come down throughout all your land; and they shall besiege you at all your gates throughout all your land which the LORD your God has given you. 53You shall eat the fruit of your own body, the flesh of your sons and your daughters whom the LORD your God has given you, in the siege and desperate straits in which your enemy shall distress you. 54The sensitive and very refined man among you will be hostile toward his brother, toward the wife of his bosom, and toward the rest of his children whom he leaves behind, 55so that he will not give any of them the flesh of his children whom he will eat, because he has nothing left in the siege and desperate straits in which your enemy shall distress you at all your gates. 56The tender and delicate woman among you, who would not venture to set the sole of her foot on the ground because of her delicateness and sensitivity, will refuse to the husband of her bosom, and to her son and her daughter, 57her placenta which comes out from between her feet and her children whom she bears; for she will eat them secretly for lack of everything in the siege and desperate straits in which your enemy shall distress you at all your gates.

58"If you do not carefully observe all the words of this law that are written in this book, that you may fear this glorious and awesome name, THE LORD YOUR GOD, 59then the LORD will bring upon you and your descendants extraordinary plagues—great and prolonged plagues—and serious and prolonged sicknesses. 60Moreover He will bring back on you all the diseases of Egypt, of which you were afraid, and they shall cling to you. 61Also every sickness and every plague, which *is* not written in this Book of the Law, will the LORD bring upon you until you are destroyed. 62You shall be left few in number, whereas you were as the stars of heaven in multitude, because you would not obey the voice of the LORD your God. 63And it shall be, *that* just as the LORD rejoiced over you to do you good and multiply you, so the LORD will rejoice over you to destroy you and bring you to nothing; and you shall be plucked from off the land which you go to possess.

64"Then the LORD will scatter you among all peoples, from one end of the earth to the other, and there you shall serve other gods, which neither you nor your fathers have known—wood and stone. 65And among those nations you shall find no rest, nor shall the sole of your foot have a resting place; but there the LORD will give you a trembling heart, failing eyes, and anguish of soul. 66Your life shall hang in doubt before you; you shall fear day and night, and have no assurance of life. 67In the morning you shall say, 'Oh, that it were evening!' And at evening you shall say, 'Oh, that it were morning!' because of the fear which terrifies your heart, and because of the sight which your eyes see.

68"And the LORD will take you back

to Egypt in ships, by the way of which I said to you, 'You shall never see it again.' And there you shall be offered for sale to your enemies as male and female slaves, but no one will buy you."

The Covenant Renewed in Moab

29 These *are* the words of the covenant which the LORD commanded Moses to make with the children of Israel in the land of Moab, besides the covenant which He made with them in Horeb.

2Now Moses called all Israel and said to them: "You have seen all that the LORD did before your eyes in the land of Egypt, to Pharaoh and to all his servants and to all his land—3the great trials which your eyes have seen, the signs, and those great wonders. 4Yet the LORD has not given you a heart to perceive and eyes to see and ears to hear, to this *very* day. 5And I have led you forty years in the wilderness. Your clothes have not worn out on you, and your sandals have not worn out on your feet. 6You have not eaten bread, nor have you drunk wine or *similar* drink, that you may know that I *am* the LORD your God. 7And when you came to this place, Sihon king of Heshbon and Og king of Bashan came out against us to battle, and we conquered them. 8We took their land and gave it as an inheritance to the Reubenites, to the Gadites, and to half the tribe of Manasseh. 9Therefore keep the words of this covenant, and do them, that you may prosper in all that you do.

10"All of you stand today before the LORD your God: your leaders and your tribes and your elders and your officers, all the men of Israel, 11your little ones and your wives—also the stranger who *is* in your camp, from the one who cuts your wood to the one who draws your water—12that you may enter into covenant with the LORD your God, and into His oath, which the LORD your God makes with you today, 13that He may establish you today as a people for Himself, and *that* He may be God to you, just as He has spoken to you, and just as He has sworn to your fathers, to Abraham, Isaac, and Jacob.

14"I make this covenant and this oath, not with you alone, 15but with *him* who stands here with us today before the LORD our God, as well as with *him* who *is* not here with us today 16(for you know that we dwelt in the land of Egypt and that we came through the nations which you passed by, 17and you saw their abominations and their idols which *were* among them—wood and stone and silver and gold); 18so that there may not be among you man or woman or family or tribe, whose heart turns away today from the LORD our God, to go *and* serve the gods of these nations, and that there may not be among you a root bearing bitterness or wormwood; 19and so it may not happen, when he hears the words of this curse, that he blesses himself in his heart, saying, 'I shall have peace, even though I follow the dictates of my heart'—as though the drunkard could be included with the sober.

20"The LORD would not spare him; for then the anger of the LORD and His jealousy would burn against that man, and every curse that is written in this book would settle on him, and the LORD would blot out his name from under heaven. 21And the LORD would separate him from all the tribes of Israel for adversity, according to all the curses of the covenant that are written in this Book of the Law, 22so that the coming generation of your children who rise up after you, and the foreigner who comes from a far land, would say, when they see the plagues of that land and the sicknesses which the LORD has laid on it:

23'The whole land *is* brimstone, salt, and burning; it is not sown, nor does it bear, nor does any grass grow there, like the overthrow of Sodom and Gomorrah, Admah, and Zeboiim, which the LORD overthrew in His anger and His wrath.' 24All nations would say, 'Why has the LORD done so to this land? What does the heat of this great anger mean?' 25Then *people* would say: 'Because they have forsaken the covenant of the LORD God of their fathers, which He made with them when He brought them out of the land of Egypt; 26for they went and served other gods and worshiped them, gods that they did not know and that He had not given to them. 27Then the anger of the LORD was aroused against this land, to bring on it every curse that is written in this book. 28And the LORD uprooted them from their land in anger, in wrath, and in great indignation, and cast them into another land, as *it is* this day.'

29"The secret *things belong* to the LORD our God, but those *things which are* revealed *belong* to us and to our children forever, that *we* may do all the words of this law.

The Blessing of Returning to God

30 "Now it shall come to pass, when all these things come upon you, the blessing and the curse which I have set before you, and you call *them* to mind among all the nations where the LORD your God drives you, 2and you return to the LORD your God and obey His voice, according to all that I command you today, you and your children, with all your heart and with all your soul, 3that the LORD your God will bring you back from captivity, and have compassion on you, and gather you again from all the nations where the LORD your God has scattered you. 4If *any* of you are driven out to the farthest *parts* under heaven, from there the LORD your God will gather you, and from there He will bring you. 5Then the LORD your God will bring you to the land which your fathers possessed, and you shall possess it. He will prosper you and multiply you more than your fathers. 6And the LORD your God will circumcise your heart and the heart of your descendants, to love the LORD your God with all your heart and with all your soul, that you may live.

7"Also the LORD your God will put all these curses on your enemies and on those who hate you, who persecuted you. 8And you will again obey the voice of the LORD and do all His commandments which I command you today. 9The LORD your God will make you abound in all the work of your hand, in the fruit of your body, in the increase of your livestock, and in the produce of your land for good. For the LORD will again rejoice over you for good as He rejoiced over your fathers, 10if you obey the voice of the LORD your God, to keep His commandments and His statutes which are written in this Book of the Law, *and* if you turn to the LORD your God with all your heart and with all your soul.

The Choice of Life or Death

11"For this commandment which I command you today *is* not *too* mysterious for you, nor *is* it far off. 12It *is* not in heaven, that you should say, 'Who will ascend into heaven for us and bring it to us, that we may hear it and do it?' 13Nor *is* it beyond the sea, that you should say, 'Who will go over the sea for us and bring it to us, that we may hear it and do it?' 14But the word *is* very near you, in your mouth and in your heart, that you may do it.

15"See, I have set before you today life and good, death and evil, 16in that I command you today to love the LORD your God, to walk in His ways, and to keep His commandments, His statutes, and His judgments, that you may live and multiply; and the LORD your God will bless you in the land which you go to possess. 17But if your heart turns away so that you do not hear, and are drawn away, and worship other gods and serve them, 18I announce to you today that you shall surely perish; you shall not prolong *your* days in the land which you cross over the Jordan to go in and possess. 19I call heaven and earth as witnesses today against you, *that* I have set before you life and death, blessing and cursing; therefore choose life, that both you and your descendants may live; 20that you may love the LORD your God, that you may obey His voice, and that you may cling to Him, for He *is* your life and the length of your days; and that you may dwell in the land which the LORD swore to your fathers, to Abraham, Isaac, and Jacob, to give them."

Joshua the New Leader of Israel

31 Then Moses went and spoke these words to all Israel. 2And he said to them: "I *am* one hundred and twenty years old today. I can no longer go out and come in. Also the LORD has said to me, 'You shall not cross over this Jordan.' 3The LORD your God Himself crosses over before you; He will destroy these nations from before you, and you shall dispossess them. Joshua himself crosses over before you, just as the LORD has said. 4And the LORD will do to them as He did to Sihon and Og, the kings of the Amorites and their land, when He destroyed them. 5The LORD will give them over to you, that you may do to them according to every commandment which I have commanded you. 6Be strong and of good courage, do not fear nor be afraid of them; for the LORD your God, He *is* the One who goes with you. He will not leave you nor forsake you."

7Then Moses called Joshua and said to him in the sight of all Israel, "Be strong and of good courage, for you must go with this people to the land which the LORD has sworn to their fathers to give them, and you shall cause them to inherit it. 8And the LORD, He *is* the One who goes before you. He will be with you, He will not leave you nor forsake you; do not fear nor be dismayed."

The Law to Be Read Every Seven Years

9So Moses wrote this law and delivered it to the priests, the sons of Levi, who bore the ark of the covenant of the LORD, and to all the elders of Israel. 10And Moses commanded them, saying: "At the end of *every* seven years, at the appointed time in the year of release, at the Feast of Tabernacles, 11when all Israel comes to appear before the LORD your God in the place which He chooses, you shall read this law before all Israel in their hearing. 12Gather the people together, men and women and little ones, and the stranger who *is* within your gates, that they may hear and that they may learn to fear the LORD your God and carefully observe all the words of this law, 13and *that* their children, who have not known it, may hear and learn to fear the LORD your God as long as you live in the land which you cross the Jordan to possess."

Prediction of Israel's Rebellion

14Then the LORD said to Moses, "Behold, the days approach when you must die; call Joshua, and present yourselves in the tabernacle of meeting, that I may inaugurate him."

So Moses and Joshua went and presented themselves in the tabernacle of meeting. 15Now the LORD appeared at the tabernacle in a pillar of cloud, and the pillar of cloud stood above the door of the tabernacle.

16And the LORD said to Moses: "Behold, you will rest with your fathers; and this people will rise and play the harlot with the gods of the foreigners of the land, where they go *to be* among them, and they will forsake Me and break My covenant which I have made with them. 17Then My anger shall be aroused against them in that day, and I will forsake them, and I will hide My face from them, and they shall be devoured. And many evils and troubles shall befall them, so that they will say in that day, 'Have not these evils come upon us because our God *is* not among us?' 18And I will surely hide My face in that day because of all the evil which they have done, in that they have turned to other gods.

19"Now therefore, write down this song for yourselves, and teach it to the children of Israel; put it in their mouths, that this song may be a witness for Me against the children of Israel. 20When I have brought them to the land flowing with milk and honey, of which I swore to their fathers, and they have eaten and filled themselves and grown fat, then they will turn to other gods and serve them; and they will provoke Me and break My covenant. 21Then it shall be, when many evils and troubles have come upon them, that this song will testify against them as a witness; for it will not be forgotten in the mouths of their descendants, for I know the inclination of their behavior today, even before I have brought them to the land of which I swore *to give them*."

22Therefore Moses wrote this song the same day, and taught it to the children of Israel. 23Then He inaugurated Joshua the son of Nun, and said, "Be strong and of good courage; for you shall bring the children of Israel into the land of which I swore to them, and I will be with you."

24So it was, when Moses had completed writing the words of this law in a book, when they were finished, 25that Moses commanded the Levites, who bore the ark of the covenant of the

LORD, saying: 26"Take this Book of the Law, and put it beside the ark of the covenant of the LORD your God, that it may be there as a witness against you; 27for I know your rebellion and your stiff neck. *If* today, while I am yet alive with you, you have been rebellious against the LORD, then how much more after my death? 28Gather to me all the elders of your tribes, and your officers, that I may speak these words in their hearing and call heaven and earth to witness against them. 29For I know that after my death you will become utterly corrupt, and turn aside from the way which I have commanded you. And evil will befall you in the latter days, because you will do evil in the sight of the LORD, to provoke Him to anger through the work of your hands."

The Song of Moses

30Then Moses spoke in the hearing of all the assembly of Israel the words of this song until they were ended:

32 "Give ear, O heavens, and I will speak;
And hear, O earth, the words of my mouth.
2   Let my teaching drop as the rain,
My speech distill as the dew,
As raindrops on the tender herb,
And as showers on the grass.
3   For I proclaim the name of the LORD:
Ascribe greatness to our God.
4   *He is* the Rock, His work *is* perfect;
For all His ways *are* justice,
A God of truth and without injustice;
Righteous and upright *is* He.

5   "They have corrupted themselves;
They are not His children,
Because of their blemish:
A perverse and crooked generation.
6   Do you thus deal with the LORD,
O foolish and unwise people?
Is He not your Father, *who* bought you?
Has He not made you and established you?

7   "Remember the days of old,
Consider the years of many generations.
Ask your father, and he will show you;
Your elders, and they will tell you:
8   When the Most High divided their inheritance to the nations,
When He separated the sons of Adam,
He set the boundaries of the peoples
According to the number of the children of Israel.
9   For the LORD's portion *is* His people;
Jacob *is* the place of His inheritance.

10   "He found him in a desert land
And in the wasteland, a howling wilderness;
He encircled him, He instructed him,
He kept him as the apple of His eye.
11   As an eagle stirs up its nest,
Hovers over its young,
Spreading out its wings, taking them up,
Carrying them on its wings,
12   *So* the LORD alone led him,
And *there was* no foreign god with him.

13   "He made him ride in the heights of the earth,
That he might eat the produce of the fields;
He made him draw honey from the rock,
And oil from the flinty rock;
14   Curds from the cattle, and milk of the flock,
With fat of lambs;
And rams of the breed of Bashan, and goats,
With the choicest wheat;
And you drank wine, the blood of the grapes.

15   "But Jeshurun grew fat and kicked;
You grew fat, you grew thick,
You are obese!
Then he forsook God *who* made him,
And scornfully esteemed the Rock of his salvation.
16   They provoked Him to jealousy with foreign *gods*;

With abominations they provoked
  Him to anger.
17 They sacrificed to demons, not
      to God,
   To gods they did not know,
   To new *gods*, new arrivals
   That your fathers did not fear.
18 Of the Rock *who* begot you, you are
      unmindful,
   And have forgotten the God who
      fathered you.

19 "And when the LORD saw *it*, He
      spurned *them*,
   Because of the provocation of His
      sons and His daughters.
20 And He said: 'I will hide My face
      from them,
   I will see what their end *will be*,
   For they *are* a perverse generation,
   Children in whom *is* no faith.
21 They have provoked Me to jealousy
      by *what* is not God;
   They have moved Me to anger by
      their foolish idols.
   But I will provoke them to jealousy
      by *those who are* not a nation;
   I will move them to anger by a
      foolish nation.
22 For a fire is kindled in My anger,
   And shall burn to the lowest hell;
   It shall consume the earth with her
      increase,
   And set on fire the foundations of
      the mountains.

23 'I will heap disasters on them;
   I will spend My arrows on them.
24 *They shall be* wasted with hunger,
   Devoured by pestilence and bitter
      destruction;
   I will also send against them the
      teeth of beasts,
   With the poison of serpents of the
      dust.
25 The sword shall destroy outside;
   There shall be terror within
   For the young man and virgin,
   The nursing child with the man of
      gray hairs.
26 I would have said, "I will dash them
      in pieces,
   I will make the memory of them to
      cease from among men,"
27 Had I not feared the wrath of the
      enemy,

Lest their adversaries should
   misunderstand,
Lest they should say, "Our hand *is*
   high;
And it is not the LORD who has done
   all this." '

28 "For they *are* a nation void of
      counsel,
   Nor *is there any* understanding in
      them.
29 Oh, that they were wise, *that* they
      understood this,
   That they would consider their
      latter end!
30 How could one chase a thousand,
   And two put ten thousand to flight,
   Unless their Rock had sold them,
   And the LORD had surrendered
      them?
31 For their rock *is* not like our Rock,
   Even our enemies themselves *being*
      judges.
32 For their vine *is* of the vine of
      Sodom
   And of the fields of Gomorrah;
   Their grapes *are* grapes of gall,
   Their clusters *are* bitter.
33 Their wine *is* the poison of
      serpents,
   And the cruel venom of cobras.

34 'Is this not laid up in store with Me,
   Sealed up among My treasures?
35 Vengeance is Mine, and
      recompense;
   Their foot shall slip in *due* time;
   For the day of their calamity *is* at
      hand,
   And the things to come hasten
      upon them.'

36 "For the LORD will judge His people
   And have compassion on His
      servants,
   When He sees that *their* power is
      gone,
   And *there is* no one *remaining*,
      bond or free.
37 He will say: 'Where *are* their gods,
   The rock in which they sought
      refuge?
38 Who ate the fat of their sacrifices,
   And drank the wine of their drink
      offering?
   Let them rise and help you,
   And be your refuge.

39 'Now see that I, *even* I, *am* He,
   And *there is* no God besides Me;
   I kill and I make alive;
   I wound and I heal;
   Nor *is there any* who can deliver
      from My hand.
40 For I raise My hand to heaven,
   And say, "*As* I live forever,
41 If I whet My glittering sword,
   And My hand takes hold on
      judgment,
   I will render vengeance to My
      enemies,
   And repay those who hate Me.
42 I will make My arrows drunk with
      blood,
   And My sword shall devour flesh,
   With the blood of the slain and the
      captives,
   From the heads of the leaders of the
      enemy." '

43 "Rejoice, O Gentiles, *with* His
      people;
   For He will avenge the blood of His
      servants,
   And render vengeance to His
      adversaries;
   He will provide atonement for His
      land *and* His people."

44So Moses came with Joshua the son
of Nun and spoke all the words of this
song in the hearing of the people.
45Moses finished speaking all these
words to all Israel, 46and he said to
them: "Set your hearts on all the words
which I testify among you today, which
you shall command your children to be
careful to observe—all the words of this
law. 47For it *is* not a futile thing for you,
because it *is* your life, and by this word
you shall prolong *your* days in the land
which you cross over the Jordan to possess."

Moses to Die on Mount Nebo

48Then the LORD spoke to Moses that
very same day, saying: 49"Go up this
mountain of the Abarim, Mount Nebo,
which *is* in the land of Moab, across
from Jericho; view the land of Canaan,
which I give to the children of Israel
as a possession; 50and die on the mountain which you ascend, and be gathered
to your people, just as Aaron your
brother died on Mount Hor and was
gathered to his people; 51because you

trespassed against Me among the children of Israel at the waters of Meribah
Kadesh, in the Wilderness of Zin, because you did not hallow Me in the
midst of the children of Israel. 52Yet
you shall see the land before *you*,
though you shall not go there, into the
land which I am giving to the children
of Israel."

Moses' Final Blessing on Israel

33 Now this *is* the blessing with
which Moses the man of God
blessed the children of Israel before his
death. 2And he said:
   "The LORD came from Sinai,
      And dawned on them from Seir;
      He shone forth from Mount Paran,
      And He came with ten thousands
         of saints;
      From His right hand
      Came a fiery law for them.
3 Yes, He loves the people;
      All His saints *are* in Your hand;
      They sit down at Your feet;
      Everyone receives Your words.
4 Moses commanded a law for us,
      A heritage of the congregation of
         Jacob.
5 And He was King in Jeshurun,
      When the leaders of the people
         were gathered,
      All the tribes of Israel together.

6 "Let Reuben live, and not die,
      Nor let his men be few."

7And this he said of Judah:
   "Hear, LORD, the voice of Judah,
   And bring him to his people;
   Let his hands be sufficient for him,
   And may You be a help against his
      enemies."

8And of Levi he said:
   "*Let* Your Thummim and Your Urim
      be with Your holy one,
   Whom You tested at Massah,
   And with whom You contended at
      the waters of Meribah,
9 Who says of his father and mother,
   'I have not seen them';
   Nor did he acknowledge his
      brothers,
   Or know his own children;
   For they have observed Your word
   And kept Your covenant.

10 They shall teach Jacob Your
   judgments,
   And Israel Your law.
   They shall put incense before You,
   And a whole burnt sacrifice on
   Your altar.
11 Bless his substance, LORD,
   And accept the work of his hands;
   Strike the loins of those who rise
   against him,
   And of those who hate him, that
   they rise not again."

12 Of Benjamin he said:
   "The beloved of the LORD shall dwell
   in safety by Him,
   Who shelters him all the day
   long;
   And he shall dwell between His
   shoulders."

13 And of Joseph he said:
   "Blessed of the LORD *is* his land,
   With the precious things of heaven,
   with the dew,
   And the deep lying beneath,
14 With the precious fruits of the sun,
   With the precious produce of the
   months,
15 With the best things of the ancient
   mountains,
   With the precious things of the
   everlasting hills,
16 With the precious things of the
   earth and its fullness,
   And the favor of Him who dwelt
   in the bush.
   Let *the blessing* come 'on the head
   of Joseph,
   And on the crown of the head of
   him *who was* separate from his
   brothers.'*f*
17 His glory *is like* a firstborn bull,
   And his horns *like* the horns of the
   wild ox;
   Together with them
   He shall push the peoples
   To the ends of the earth;
   They *are* the ten thousands of
   Ephraim,
   And they *are* the thousands of
   Manasseh."

18 And of Zebulun he said:
   "Rejoice, Zebulun, in your going out,
   And Issachar in your tents!

19 They shall call the peoples *to* the
   mountain;
   There they shall offer sacrifices of
   righteousness;
   For they shall partake *of* the
   abundance of the seas
   And *of* treasures hidden in the
   sand."

20 And of Gad he said:
   "Blessed *is* he who enlarges Gad;
   He dwells as a lion,
   And tears the arm and the crown
   of his head.
21 He provided the first *part* for
   himself,
   Because a lawgiver's portion was
   reserved there.
   He came *with* the heads of the
   people;
   He administered the justice of the
   LORD,
   And His judgments with Israel."

22 And of Dan he said:
   "Dan *is* a lion's whelp;
   He shall leap from Bashan."

23 And of Naphtali he said:
   "O Naphtali, satisfied with favor,
   And full of the blessing of the LORD,
   Possess the west and the south."

24 And of Asher he said:
   "Asher *is* most blessed of sons;
   Let him be favored by his brothers,
   And let him dip his foot in oil.
25 Your sandals *shall be* iron and
   bronze;
   As your days, *so shall* your
   strength *be*.

26 "*There is* no one like the God of
   Jeshurun,
   Who rides the heavens to help you,
   And in His excellency on the
   clouds.
27 The eternal God *is your* refuge,
   And underneath *are* the everlasting
   arms;
   He will thrust out the enemy from
   before you,
   And will say, 'Destroy!'
28 Then Israel shall dwell in safety,
   The fountain of Jacob alone,

f Compare Genesis 49.26

In a land of grain and new wine;
His heavens shall also drop dew.
29 Happy *are* you, O Israel!
Who *is* like you, a people saved by
    the LORD,
The shield of your help
And the sword of your majesty!
Your enemies shall submit to you,
And you shall tread down their
    high places."

Moses Dies on Mount Nebo

34 Then Moses went up from the plains of Moab to Mount Nebo, to the top of Pisgah, which is across from Jericho. And the LORD showed him all the land of Gilead as far as Dan, 2all Naphtali and the land of Ephraim and Manasseh, all the land of Judah as far as the Western Sea,g 3the South, and the plain of the Valley of Jericho, the city of palm trees, as far as Zoar. 4Then the LORD said to him, "This *is* the land of which I swore to give Abraham, Isaac, and Jacob, saying, 'I will give it to your descendants.' I have caused you to see *it* with your eyes, but you shall not cross over there."

5So Moses the servant of the LORD died there in the land of Moab, according to the word of the LORD. 6And He buried him in a valley in the land of Moab, opposite Beth Peor; but no one knows his grave to this day. 7Moses *was* one hundred and twenty years old when he died. His eyes were not dim nor his natural vigor diminished. 8And the children of Israel wept for Moses in the plains of Moab thirty days. So the days of weeping *and* mourning for Moses ended.

9Now Joshua the son of Nun was full of the spirit of wisdom, for Moses had laid his hands on him; so the children of Israel heeded him, and did as the LORD had commanded Moses.

10But since then there has not arisen in Israel a prophet like Moses, whom the LORD knew face to face, 11in all the signs and wonders which the LORD sent him to do in the land of Egypt, before Pharaoh, before all his servants, and in all his land, 12and by all that mighty power and all the great terror which Moses performed in the sight of all Israel.

g That is, the Mediterranean

The Book of

JOSHUA

God's Commission to Joshua

1 After the death of Moses the servant of the LORD, it came to pass that the LORD spoke to Joshua the son of Nun, Moses' assistant, saying: 2"Moses My servant is dead. Now therefore, arise, go over this Jordan, you and all this people, to the land which I am giving to them—the children of Israel. 3Every place that the sole of your foot will tread upon I have given you, as I said to Moses. 4From the wilderness and this Lebanon as far as the great river, the River Euphrates, all the land of the Hittites, and to the Great Sea toward the going down of the sun, shall be your territory. 5No man shall *be able to* stand before you all the days of your life; as I was with Moses, *so* I will be with you. I will not leave you nor forsake you. 6Be strong and of good courage, for to this people you shall divide as an inheritance the land which I swore to their fathers to give them. 7Only be strong and very courageous, that you may observe to do according to all the law which Moses My servant commanded you; do not turn from it to the right hand or to the left, that you may prosper wherever you go. 8This Book of the Law shall not depart from your mouth, but you shall meditate in it day and night, that you may observe to do according to all that is written in it. For then you will make your way prosperous, and then you will have good success. 9Have I not commanded you? Be strong and of good courage; do not be afraid, nor be dismayed, for the LORD your God *is* with you wherever you go."

The Order to Cross the Jordan

10Then Joshua commanded the officers of the people, saying, 11"Pass through the camp and command the people, saying, 'Prepare provisions for yourselves, for within three days you will cross over this Jordan, to go in to possess the land which the LORD your God is giving you to possess.'"

12And to the Reubenites, the Gadites, and half the tribe of Manasseh Joshua spoke, saying, 13"Remember the word which Moses the servant of the LORD commanded you, saying, 'The LORD your God is giving you rest and is giving you this land.' 14Your wives, your little ones, and your livestock shall remain in the land which Moses gave you on this side of the Jordan. But you shall pass before your brethren armed, all your mighty men of valor, and help them, 15until the LORD has given your brethren rest, as He *gave* you, and they also have taken possession of the land which the LORD your God is giving them. Then you shall return to the land of your possession and enjoy it, which Moses the LORD's servant gave you on this side of the Jordan toward the sunrise."

16So they answered Joshua, saying, "All that you command us we will do, and wherever you send us we will go. 17Just as we heeded Moses in all things, so we will heed you. Only the LORD your God be with you, as He was with Moses. 18Whoever rebels against your command and does not heed your words, in all that you command him, shall be put to death. Only be strong and of good courage."

Rahab Hides the Spies

2 Now Joshua the son of Nun sent out two men from Acacia Grove to spy secretly, saying, "Go, view the land, especially Jericho."

So they went, and came to the house of a harlot named Rahab, and lodged there. 2And it was told the king of Jericho, saying, "Behold, men have come here tonight from the children of Israel to search out the country."

3So the king of Jericho sent to Rahab, saying, "Bring out the men who have come to you, who have entered your house, for they have come to search out all the country."

4Then the woman took the two men and hid them. So she said, "Yes, the men came to me, but I did not know where they *were* from. 5And it happened as the gate was being shut, when it was dark, that the men went out. Where the men went I do not know; pursue them quickly, for you may overtake them." 6(But she had brought them up to the roof and hidden them with the stalks of flax, which she had laid in order on the roof.) 7Then the men pursued them by the road to the Jordan, to the fords. And as soon as those who pursued them had gone out, they shut the gate.

8Now before they lay down, she came up to them on the roof, 9and said to the men: "I know that the LORD has given you the land, that the terror of you has fallen on us, and that all the inhabitants of the land are fainthearted because of you. 10For we have heard how the LORD dried up the water of the Red Sea for you when you came out of Egypt, and what you did to the two kings of the Amorites who *were* on the other side of the Jordan, Sihon and Og, whom you utterly destroyed. 11And as soon as we heard *these things*, our hearts melted; neither did there remain any more courage in anyone because of you, for the LORD your God, He *is* God in heaven above and on earth beneath. 12Now therefore, I beg you, swear to me by the LORD, since I have shown you kindness, that you also will show kindness to my father's house, and give me a true token, 13and spare my father, my mother, my brothers, my sisters, and all that they have, and deliver our lives from death."

14So the men answered her, "Our lives for yours, if none of you tell this business of ours. And it shall be, when the LORD has given us the land, that we will deal kindly and truly with you."

15Then she let them down by a rope through the window, for her house *was* on the city wall; she dwelt on the wall. 16And she said to them, "Get to the mountain, lest the pursuers meet you. Hide there three days, until the pursuers have returned. Afterward you may go your way."

17So the men said to her: "We *will be* blameless of this oath of yours which you have made us swear, 18unless, *when* we come into the land, you bind this line of scarlet cord in the window through which you let us down, and un-

less you bring your father, your mother, your brothers, and all your father's household to your own home. 19So it shall be *that* whoever goes outside the doors of your house into the street, his blood *shall be* on his own head, and we *will be* guiltless. And whoever is with you in the house, his blood *shall be* on our head if a hand is laid on him. 20And if you tell this business of ours, then we will be free from your oath which you made us swear."

21Then she said, "According to your words, so *be* it." And she sent them away, and they departed. And she bound the scarlet cord in the window.

22They departed and went to the mountain, and stayed there three days until the pursuers returned. The pursuers sought *them* all along the way, but did not find *them*. 23So the two men returned, descended from the mountain, and crossed over; and they came to Joshua the son of Nun, and told him all that had befallen them. 24And they said to Joshua, "Truly the LORD has delivered all the land into our hands, for indeed all the inhabitants of the country are fainthearted because of us."

Israel Crosses the Jordan

3 Then Joshua rose early in the morning; and they set out from Acacia Grove and came to the Jordan, he and all the children of Israel, and lodged there before they crossed over. 2So it was, after three days, that the officers went through the camp; 3and they commanded the people, saying, "When you see the ark of the covenant of the LORD your God, and the priests, the Levites, bearing it, then you shall set out from your place and go after it. 4Yet there shall be a space between you and it, about two thousand cubits by measure. Do not come near it, that you may know the way by which you must go, for you have not passed *this* way before."

5And Joshua said to the people, "Sanctify yourselves, for tomorrow the LORD will do wonders among you." 6Then Joshua spoke to the priests, saying, "Take up the ark of the covenant and cross over before the people."

So they took up the ark of the covenant and went before the people.

7And the LORD said to Joshua, "This day I will begin to exalt you in the sight of all Israel, that they may know that, as I was with Moses, so I will be with you. 8You shall command the priests who bear the ark of the covenant, saying, 'When you have come to the edge of the water of the Jordan, you shall stand in the Jordan.' "

9So Joshua said to the children of Israel, "Come here, and hear the words of the LORD your God." 10And Joshua said, "By this you shall know that the living God is among you, and that He will without fail drive out from before you the Canaanites and the Hittites and the Hivites and the Perizzites and the Girgashites and the Amorites and the Jebusites: 11Behold, the ark of the covenant of the Lord of all the earth is crossing over before you into the Jordan. 12Now therefore, take for yourselves twelve men from the tribes of Israel, one man from every tribe. 13And it shall come to pass, as soon as the soles of the feet of the priests who bear the ark of the LORD, the Lord of all the earth, shall rest in the waters of the Jordan, that the waters of the Jordan shall be cut off, the waters that come down from upstream, and they shall stand as a heap."

14So it was, when the people set out from their camp to cross over the Jordan, with the priests bearing the ark of the covenant before the people, 15and as those who bore the ark came to the Jordan, and the feet of the priests who bore the ark dipped in the edge of the water (for the Jordan overflows all its banks during the whole time of harvest), 16that the waters which came down from upstream stood still, and rose in a heap very far away at Adam, the city that is beside Zaretan. So the waters that went down into the Sea of the Arabah, the Salt Sea, failed, and were cut off; and the people crossed over opposite Jericho. 17Then the priests who bore the ark of the covenant of the LORD stood firm on dry ground in the midst of the Jordan; and all Israel crossed over on dry ground, until all the people had crossed completely over the Jordan.

The Memorial Stones

4 And it came to pass, when all the people had completely crossed over the Jordan, that the LORD spoke to Joshua, saying: 2"Take for yourselves twelve men from the people, one man from every tribe, 3and command them, saying, 'Take for yourselves twelve stones from here, out of the midst of the Jordan, from the place where the priests' feet stood firm. You shall carry them over with you and leave them in the lodging place where you lodge tonight.' "

4Then Joshua called the twelve men whom he had appointed from the children of Israel, one man from every tribe; 5and Joshua said to them: "Cross over before the ark of the LORD your God into the midst of the Jordan, and each one of you take up a stone on his shoulder, according to the number of the tribes of the children of Israel, 6that this may be a sign among you when your children ask in time to come, saying, 'What do these stones mean to you?' 7Then you shall answer them that the waters of the Jordan were cut off before the ark of the covenant of the LORD; when it crossed over the Jordan, the waters of the Jordan were cut off. And these stones shall be for a memorial to the children of Israel forever."

8And the children of Israel did so, just as Joshua commanded, and took up twelve stones from the midst of the Jordan, as the LORD had spoken to Joshua, according to the number of the tribes of the children of Israel, and carried them over with them to the place where they lodged, and laid them down there. 9Then Joshua set up twelve stones in the midst of the Jordan, in the place where the feet of the priests who bore the ark of the covenant stood; and they are there to this day.

10So the priests who bore the ark stood in the midst of the Jordan until everything was finished that the LORD had commanded Joshua to speak to the people, according to all that Moses had commanded Joshua; and the people hurried and crossed over. 11Then it came to pass, when all the people had completely crossed over, that the ark of the LORD and the priests crossed over in the presence of the people. 12And the men of Reuben, the men of Gad, and half the tribe of Manasseh crossed over armed before the children of Israel, as Moses had spoken to them. 13About forty thousand prepared for war crossed over before the LORD for battle, to the plains of Jericho. 14On that day the LORD exalted Joshua in the sight of all Israel; and they feared him, as they had feared Moses, all the days of his life.

15Then the LORD spoke to Joshua, saying, 16"Command the priests who bear the ark of the Testimony to come up from the Jordan." 17Joshua therefore commanded the priests, saying, "Come up from the Jordan." 18And it came to pass, when the priests who bore the ark of the covenant of the LORD had come from the midst of the Jordan, and the soles of the priests' feet touched the dry land, that the waters of the Jordan returned to their place and overflowed all its banks as before.

19Now the people came up from the Jordan on the tenth day of the first month, and they camped in Gilgal on the east border of Jericho. 20And those twelve stones which they took out of the Jordan, Joshua set up in Gilgal. 21Then he spoke to the children of Israel, saying: "When your children ask their fathers in time to come, saying, 'What are these stones?' 22then you shall let your children know, saying, 'Israel crossed over this Jordan on dry land'; 23for the LORD your God dried up the waters of the Jordan before you until you had crossed over, as the LORD your God did to the Red Sea, which He dried up before us until we had crossed over, 24that all the peoples of the earth may know the hand of the LORD, that it is mighty, that you may fear the LORD your God forever."

The Second Generation Circumcised

5 So it was, when all the kings of the Amorites who were on the west side of the Jordan, and all the kings of the Canaanites who were by the sea, heard that the LORD had dried up the waters of the Jordan from before the children of Israel until we had crossed over, that their heart melted; and there was no spirit in them any longer because of the children of Israel.

2At that time the LORD said to Joshua, "Make flint knives for yourself, and circumcise the sons of Israel again the second time." 3So Joshua made flint knives for himself, and circumcised the sons of Israel at the hill of the foreskins. 4And this is the reason why Joshua circumcised them: All the people who came out of Egypt who were males, all the men of war, had died in the wilderness on the way, after they had come out of Egypt. 5For all the people who came out had been circumcised, but all the people born in the wilderness, on the way as they came out of Egypt, had not been circumcised. 6For the children of Israel walked forty years in the wilderness, till all the people who were men of war, who came out of Egypt, were consumed, because they did not obey the voice of the LORD—to whom the LORD swore that He would not show them the land which the LORD had sworn to their fathers that He would give us, "a land flowing with milk and honey."a 7Then Joshua circumcised their sons whom He raised up in their place; for they were uncircumcised, because they had not been circumcised on the way.

8So it was, when they had finished circumcising all the people, that they stayed in their places in the camp till they were healed. 9Then the LORD said to Joshua, "This day I have rolled away the reproach of Egypt from you." Therefore the name of the place is called Gilgalb to this day.

10Now the children of Israel camped in Gilgal, and kept the Passover on the fourteenth day of the month at twilight on the plains of Jericho. 11And they ate of the produce of the land on the day after the Passover, unleavened bread and parched grain, on the very same day. 12Then the manna ceased on the day after they had eaten the produce of the land; and the children of Israel no longer had manna, but they ate the food of the land of Canaan that year.

a Compare Exodus 3.8   b Literally Rolling

The Commander of the Army of the LORD

13And it came to pass, when Joshua was by Jericho, that he lifted his eyes and looked, and behold, a Man stood opposite him with His sword drawn in His hand. And Joshua went to Him and said to Him, "*Are* You for us or for our adversaries?"

14So He said, "No, but *as* Commander of the army of the LORD I have now come."

And Joshua fell on his face to the earth and worshiped, and said to Him, "What does my Lord say to His servant?"

15Then the Commander of the LORD's army said to Joshua, "Take your sandal off your foot, for the place where you stand *is* holy." And Joshua did so.

The Destruction of Jericho

6 Now Jericho was securely shut up because of the children of Israel; none went out, and none came in. 2And the LORD said to Joshua: "See! I have given Jericho into your hand, its king, *and* the mighty men of valor. 3You shall march around the city, all *you* men of war; you shall go all around the city once. This you shall do six days. 4And seven priests shall bear seven trumpets of rams' horns before the ark. But the seventh day you shall march around the city seven times, and the priests shall blow the trumpets. 5It shall come to pass, when they make a long *blast* with the ram's horn, *and* when you hear the sound of the trumpet, that all the people shall shout with a great shout; then the wall of the city will fall down flat. And the people shall go up every man straight before him."

6Then Joshua the son of Nun called the priests and said to them, "Take up the ark of the covenant, and let seven priests bear seven trumpets of rams' horns before the ark of the LORD." 7And he said to the people, "Proceed, and march around the city, and let him who is armed advance before the ark of the LORD."

8So it was, when Joshua had spoken to the people, that the seven priests bearing the seven trumpets of rams' horns before the LORD advanced and blew the trumpets, and the ark of the covenant of the LORD followed them. 9The armed men went before the priests who blew the trumpets, and the rear guard came after the ark, while *the priests* continued blowing the trumpets. 10Now Joshua had commanded the people, saying, "You shall not shout or make any noise with your voice, nor shall a word proceed out of your mouth, until the day I say to you, 'Shout!' Then you shall shout." 11So he had the ark of the LORD circle the city, going around *it* once. Then they came into the camp and lodged in the camp.

12And Joshua rose early in the morning, and the priests took up the ark of the LORD. 13Then seven priests bearing seven trumpets of rams' horns before the ark of the LORD went on continually and blew with the trumpets. And the armed men went before them. But the rear guard came after the ark of the LORD, while *the priests* continued blowing the trumpets. 14And the second day they marched around the city once and returned to the camp. So they did six days.

15But it came to pass on the seventh day that they rose early, about the dawning of the day, and marched around the city seven times in the same manner. On that day only they marched around the city seven times. 16And the seventh time it happened, when the priests blew the trumpets, that Joshua said to the people: "Shout, for the LORD has given you the city! 17Now the city shall be doomed by the LORD to destruction, it and all who *are* in it. Only Rahab the harlot shall live, she and all who *are* with her in the house, because she hid the messengers that we sent. 18And you, by all means abstain from the accursed things, lest you become accursed when you take of the accursed things, and make the camp of Israel a curse, and trouble it. 19But all the silver and gold, and vessels of bronze and iron, *are* consecrated to the LORD; they shall come into the treasury of the LORD."

20So the people shouted when *the priests* blew the trumpets. And it happened when the people heard the sound of the trumpet, and the people shouted with a great shout, that the wall fell down flat. Then the people went up into the city, every man straight before him, and they took the city. 21And they utterly destroyed all that *was* in the city, both man and woman, young and old, ox and sheep and donkey, with the edge of the sword.

22But Joshua had said to the two men who had spied out the country, "Go into the harlot's house, and from there bring out the woman and all that she has, as you swore to her." 23And the young men who had been spies went in and brought out Rahab, her father, her mother, her brothers, and all that she had. So they brought out all her relatives and left them outside the camp of Israel. 24But they burned the city and all that *was* in it with fire. Only the silver and gold, and the vessels of bronze and iron, they put into the treasury of the house of the LORD. 25And Joshua spared Rahab the harlot, her father's household, and all that she had. So she dwells in Israel to this day, because she hid the messengers whom Joshua sent to spy out Jericho.

26Then Joshua charged *them* at that time, saying, "Cursed *be* the man before the LORD who rises up and builds this city Jericho; he shall lay its foundation with his firstborn, and with his youngest he shall set up its gates."

27So the LORD was with Joshua, and his fame spread throughout all the country.

Defeat at Ai

7 But the children of Israel committed a trespass regarding the accursed things, for Achan the son of Carmi, the son of Zabdi, the son of Zerah, of the tribe of Judah, took of the accursed things; so the anger of the LORD burned against the children of Israel.

2Now Joshua sent men from Jericho to Ai, which *is* beside Beth Aven, on the east side of Bethel, and spoke to them, saying, "Go up and spy out the country." So the men went up and spied out Ai. 3And they returned to Joshua and said to him, "Do not let all the people go up, but let about two or three thousand men go up and attack Ai. Do not weary all the people there, for *the people of Ai are* few." 4So about three thousand men went up there from the

people, but they fled before the men of Ai. 5And the men of Ai struck down about thirty-six men, for they chased them *from* before the gate as far as Shebarim, and struck them down on the descent; therefore the hearts of the people melted and became like water.

6Then Joshua tore his clothes, and fell to the earth on his face before the ark of the LORD until evening, he and the elders of Israel; and they put dust on their heads. 7And Joshua said, "Alas, Lord GOD, why have You brought this people over the Jordan at all—to deliver us into the hand of the Amorites, to destroy us? Oh, that we had been content, and dwelt on the other side of the Jordan! 8O Lord, what shall I say when Israel turns its back before its enemies? 9For the Canaanites and all the inhabitants of the land will hear *it*, and surround us, and cut off our name from the earth. Then what will You do for Your great name?"

The Sin of Achan

10So the LORD said to Joshua: "Get up! Why do you lie thus on your face? 11Israel has sinned, and they have also transgressed My covenant which I commanded them. For they have even taken some of the accursed things, and have both stolen and deceived; and they have also put *it* among their own stuff. 12Therefore the children of Israel could not stand before their enemies, *but* turned *their* backs before their enemies, because they have become doomed to destruction. Neither will I be with you anymore, unless you destroy the accursed from among you. 13Get up, sanctify the people, and say, 'Sanctify yourselves for tomorrow, because thus says the LORD God of Israel: "*There is* an accursed thing in your midst, O Israel; you cannot stand before your enemies until you take away the accursed thing from among you." 14In the morning therefore you shall be brought according to your tribes. And it shall be *that* the tribe which the LORD takes shall come according to families; and the family which the LORD takes shall come by households; and the household which the LORD takes shall come man by man. 15Then it shall be *that* he who is taken with the accursed thing shall be burned with fire, he and all that he has, because he has transgressed the covenant of the LORD, and because he has done a disgraceful thing in Israel.' "

16So Joshua rose early in the morning and brought Israel by their tribes, and the tribe of Judah was taken. 17He brought the clan of Judah, and he took the family of the Zarhites; and he brought the family of the Zarhites man by man, and Zabdi was taken. 18Then he brought his household man by man, and Achan the son of Carmi, the son of Zabdi, the son of Zerah, of the tribe of Judah, was taken.

19Now Joshua said to Achan, "My son, I beg you, give glory to the LORD God of Israel, and make confession to Him, and tell me now what you have done; do not hide it from me."

20And Achan answered Joshua and said, "Indeed I have sinned against the LORD God of Israel, and this is what I have done: 21When I saw among the spoils a beautiful Babylonian garment, two hundred shekels of silver, and a wedge of gold weighing fifty shekels, I coveted them and took them. And there they are, hidden in the earth in the midst of my tent, with the silver under it."

22So Joshua sent messengers, and they ran to the tent; and there it was, hidden in his tent, with the silver under it. 23And they took them from the midst of the tent, brought them to Joshua and to all the children of Israel, and laid them out before the LORD. 24Then Joshua, and all Israel with him, took Achan the son of Zerah, the silver, the garment, the wedge of gold, his sons, his daughters, his oxen, his donkeys, his sheep, his tent, and all that he had, and they brought them to the Valley of Achor. 25And Joshua said, "Why have you troubled us? The LORD will trouble you this day." So all Israel stoned him with stones; and they burned them with fire after they had stoned them with stones.

26Then they raised over him a great heap of stones, still there to this day. So the LORD turned from the fierceness of His anger. Therefore the name of that place has been called the Valley of Achorc to this day.

The Fall of Ai

8 Now the LORD said to Joshua: "Do not be afraid, nor be dismayed; take all the people of war with you, and arise, go up to Ai. See, I have given into your hand the king of Ai, his people, his city, and his land. 2And you shall do to Ai and its king as you did to Jericho and its king. Only its spoil and its cattle you shall take as booty for yourselves. Lay an ambush for the city behind it."

3So Joshua arose, and all the people of war, to go up against Ai; and Joshua chose thirty thousand mighty men of valor and sent them away by night. 4And he commanded them, saying: "Behold, you shall lie in ambush against the city, behind the city. Do not go very far from the city, but all of you be ready. 5Then I and all the people who are with me will approach the city; and it will come about, when they come out against us as at the first, that we shall flee before them. 6For they will come out after us till we have drawn them from the city, for they will say, 'They are fleeing before us as at the first.' Therefore we will flee before them. 7Then you shall rise from the ambush and seize the city, for the LORD your God will deliver it into your hand. 8And it will be, when you have taken the city, that you shall set the city on fire. According to the commandment of the LORD you shall do. See, I have commanded you. "

9Joshua therefore sent them out; and they went to lie in ambush, and stayed between Bethel and Ai, on the west side of Ai; but Joshua lodged that night among the people. 10Then Joshua rose up early in the morning and mustered the people, and went up, he and the elders of Israel, before the people to Ai. 11And all the people of war who were with him went up and drew near; and they came before the city and camped on the north side of Ai. Now a valley lay between them and Ai. 12So he took about five thousand men and set them

c Literally Trouble

in ambush between Bethel and Ai, on the west side of the city. 13And when they had set the people, all the army that *was* on the north of the city, and its rear guard on the west of the city, Joshua went that night into the midst of the valley.

14Now it happened, when the king of Ai saw *it*, that the men of the city hurried and rose early and went out against Israel to battle, he and all his people, at an appointed place before the plain. But he did not know that *there was* an ambush against him behind the city. 15And Joshua and all Israel made as if they were beaten before them, and fled by the way of the wilderness. 16So all the people who *were* in Ai were called together to pursue them. And they pursued Joshua and were drawn away from the city. 17There was not a man left in Ai or Bethel who did not go out after Israel. So they left the city open and pursued Israel.

18Then the LORD said to Joshua, "Stretch out the spear that *is* in your hand toward Ai, for I will give it into your hand." And Joshua stretched out the spear that *was* in his hand toward the city. 19So *those in* ambush arose quickly out of their place; they ran as soon as he had stretched out his hand, and they entered the city and took it, and hurried to set the city on fire. 20And when the men of Ai looked behind them, they saw, and behold, the smoke of the city ascended to heaven. So they had no power to flee this way or that way, and the people who had fled to the wilderness turned back on the pursuers.

21Now when Joshua and all Israel saw that the ambush had taken the city and that the smoke of the city ascended, they turned back and struck down the men of Ai. 22Then the others came out of the city against them; so they were *caught* in the midst of Israel, some on this side and some on that side. And they struck them down, so that they let none of them remain or escape. 23But the king of Ai they took alive, and brought him to Joshua.

24And it came to pass when Israel had made an end of slaying all the inhabit-

ants of Ai in the field, in the wilderness where they pursued them, and when they all had fallen by the edge of the sword until they were consumed, that all the Israelites returned to Ai and struck it with the edge of the sword. 25So it was *that* all who fell that day, both men and women, *were* twelve thousand—all the people of Ai. 26For Joshua did not draw back his hand, with which he stretched out the spear, until he had utterly destroyed all the inhabitants of Ai. 27Only the livestock and the spoil of that city Israel took as booty for themselves, according to the word of the LORD which He had commanded Joshua. 28So Joshua burned Ai and made it a heap forever, a desolation to this day. 29And the king of Ai he hanged on a tree until evening. And as soon as the sun was down, Joshua commanded that they should take his corpse down from the tree, cast it at the entrance of the gate of the city, and raise over it a great heap of stones *that remains* to this day.

Joshua Renews the Covenant

30Now Joshua built an altar to the LORD God of Israel in Mount Ebal, 31as Moses the servant of the LORD had commanded the children of Israel, as it is written in the Book of the Law of Moses: "an altar of whole stones over which no man has wielded an iron tool."[d] And they offered on it burnt offerings to the LORD, and sacrificed peace offerings. 32And there, in the presence of the children of Israel, he wrote on the stones a copy of the law of Moses, which he had written. 33Then all Israel, with their elders and officers and judges, stood on either side of the ark before the priests, the Levites, who bore the ark of the covenant of the LORD, the stranger as well as he who was born among them. Half of them *were* in front of Mount Gerizim and half of them in front of Mount Ebal, as Moses the servant of the LORD had commanded before, that they should bless the people of Israel. 34And afterward he read all the words of the law, the blessings and the cursings, according to all that is written in the Book of

d Compare Deuteronomy 27.5, 6

the Law. 35There was not a word of all that Moses had commanded which Joshua did not read before all the assembly of Israel, with the women, the little ones, and the strangers who were living among them.

The Treaty with the Gibeonites

9 And it came to pass when all the kings who *were* on this side of the Jordan, in the hills and in the lowland and in all the coasts of the Great Sea toward Lebanon—the Hittite, the Amorite, the Canaanite, the Perizzite, the Hivite, and the Jebusite—heard *about it*, 2that they gathered together to fight with Joshua and Israel with one accord.

3But when the inhabitants of Gibeon heard what Joshua had done to Jericho and Ai, 4they worked craftily, and went and pretended to be ambassadors. And they took old sacks on their donkeys, old wineskins torn and mended, 5old and patched sandals on their feet, and old garments on themselves; and all the bread of their provision was dry *and* moldy. 6And they went to Joshua, to the camp at Gilgal, and said to him and to the men of Israel, "We have come from a far country; now therefore, make a covenant with us."

7Then the men of Israel said to the Hivites, "Perhaps you dwell among us; so how can we make a covenant with you?"

8But they said to Joshua, "We *are* your servants."

And Joshua said to them, "Who *are* you, and where do you come from?"

9So they said to him: "From a very far country your servants have come, because of the name of the LORD your God; for we have heard of His fame, and all that He did in Egypt, 10and all that He did to the two kings of the Amorites who *were* beyond the Jordan—to Sihon king of Heshbon, and Og king of Bashan, who was at Ashtaroth. 11Therefore our elders and all the inhabitants of our country spoke to us, saying, 'Take provisions with you for the journey, and go to meet them, and say to them, "We *are* your servants; now therefore, make a covenant with us." ' 12This bread of ours we took hot *for* our provision from our houses on the day we departed to come to you.

But now look, it is dry and moldy. 13And these wineskins which we filled *were* new, and see, they are torn; and these our garments and our sandals have become old because of the very long journey."

14Then the men of Israel took some of their provisions; but they did not ask counsel of the LORD. 15So Joshua made peace with them, and made a covenant with them to let them live; and the rulers of the congregation swore to them.

16And it happened at the end of three days, after they had made a covenant with them, that they heard that they *were* their neighbors who dwelt near them. 17Then the children of Israel journeyed and came to their cities on the third day. Now their cities *were* Gibeon, Chephirah, Beeroth, and Kirjath Jearim. 18But the children of Israel did not attack them, because the rulers of the congregation had sworn to them by the LORD God of Israel. And all the congregation complained against the rulers.

19Then all the rulers said to all the congregation, "We have sworn to them by the LORD God of Israel; now therefore, we may not touch them. 20This we will do to them: We will let them live, lest wrath be upon us because of the oath which we swore to them." 21And the rulers said to them, "Let them live, but let them be woodcutters and water carriers for all the congregation, as the rulers had promised them."

22Then Joshua called for them, and he spoke to them, saying, "Why have you deceived us, saying, 'We *are* very far from you,' when you dwell near us? 23Now therefore, you *are* cursed, and none of you shall be freed from being slaves—woodcutters and water carriers for the house of my God."

24So they answered Joshua and said, "Because your servants were clearly told that the LORD your God commanded His servant Moses to give you all the land, and to destroy all the inhabitants of the land from before you; therefore we were very much afraid for our lives because of you, and have done this thing. 25And now, here we are, in your hands; do with us as it seems good and right to do to us." 26So he did to them, and delivered them out of the hand of the children of Israel, so that they did not kill them. 27And that day Joshua made them woodcutters and water carriers for the congregation and for the altar of the LORD, in the place which He would choose, even to this day.

The Sun Stands Still

10 Now it came to pass when Adoni-Zedek king of Jerusalem heard how Joshua had taken Ai and had utterly destroyed it—as he had done to Jericho and its king, so he had done to Ai and its king—and how the inhabitants of Gibeon had made peace with Israel and were among them, 2that they feared greatly, because Gibeon *was* a great city, like one of the royal cities, and because it *was* greater than Ai, and all its men *were* mighty. 3Therefore Adoni-Zedek king of Jerusalem sent to Hoham king of Hebron, Piram king of Jarmuth, Japhia king of Lachish, and Debir king of Eglon, saying, 4"Come up to me and help me, that we may attack Gibeon, for it has made peace with Joshua and with the children of Israel."

5Therefore the five kings of the Amorites, the king of Jerusalem, the king of Hebron, the king of Jarmuth, the king of Lachish, *and* the king of Eglon, gathered together and went up, they and all their armies, and camped before Gibeon and made war against it.

6And the men of Gibeon sent to Joshua at the camp at Gilgal, saying, "Do not forsake your servants; come up to us quickly, save us and help us, for all the kings of the Amorites who dwell in the mountains have gathered together against us."

7So Joshua ascended from Gilgal, he and all the people of war with him, and all the mighty men of valor. 8And the LORD said to Joshua, "Do not fear them, for I have delivered them into your hand; not a man of them shall stand before you." 9Joshua therefore came upon them suddenly, having marched all night from Gilgal. 10So the LORD routed them before Israel, killed them with a great slaughter at Gibeon, chased them along the road that goes to Beth Horon, and struck them down as far as Azekah and Makkedah. 11And it happened, as they fled before Israel *and* were on the descent of Beth Horon, that the LORD cast down large hailstones from heaven on them as far as Azekah, and they died. *There were* more who died from the hailstones than the children of Israel killed with the sword.

12Then Joshua spoke to the LORD in the day when the LORD delivered up the Amorites before the children of Israel, and he said in the sight of Israel:

"Sun, stand still over Gibeon;
    And Moon, in the Valley of
        Aijalon."
13 So the sun stood still,
    And the moon stopped,
    Till the people had revenge
    Upon their enemies.

Is this not written in the Book of Jasher? So the sun stood still in the midst of heaven, and did not hasten to go *down* for about a whole day. 14And there has been no day like that, before it or after it, that the LORD heeded the voice of a man; for the LORD fought for Israel.

15Then Joshua returned, and all Israel with him, to the camp at Gilgal.

The Amorite Kings Executed

16But these five kings had fled and hidden themselves in a cave at Makkedah. 17And it was told Joshua, saying, "The five kings have been found hidden in the cave at Makkedah."

18So Joshua said, "Roll large stones against the mouth of the cave, and set men by it to guard them. 19And do not stay *there* yourselves, *but* pursue your enemies, and attack their rear *guard*. Do not allow them to enter their cities, for the LORD your God has delivered them into your hand." 20Then it happened, while Joshua and the children of Israel made an end of slaying them with a very great slaughter, till they had finished, that those who escaped entered fortified cities. 21And all the people returned to the camp, to Joshua at Makkedah, in peace.

No one moved his tongue against any of the children of Israel.

22Then Joshua said, "Open the mouth of the cave, and bring out those five kings to me from the cave." 23And they did so, and brought out those five kings to him from the cave: the king of Jerusalem, the king of Hebron, the king of Jarmuth, the king of Lachish, *and* the king of Eglon.

24So it was, when they brought out those kings to Joshua, that Joshua called for all the men of Israel, and said to the captains of the men of war who went with him, "Come near, put your feet on the necks of these kings." And they drew near and put their feet on their necks. 25Then Joshua said to them, "Do not be afraid, nor be dismayed; be strong and of good courage, for thus the LORD will do to all your enemies against whom you fight." 26And afterward Joshua struck them and killed them, and hanged them on five trees; and they were hanging on the trees until evening. 27So it was at the time of the going down of the sun *that* Joshua commanded, and they took them down from the trees, cast them into the cave where they had been hidden, and laid large stones against the cave's mouth, *which remain* until this very day.

Conquest of the Southland

28On that day Joshua took Makkedah, and struck it and its king with the edge of the sword. He utterly destroyed them—all the people who *were* in it. He let none remain. He also did to the king of Makkedah as he had done to the king of Jericho.

29Then Joshua passed from Makkedah, and all Israel with him, to Libnah; and they fought against Libnah. 30And the LORD also delivered it and its king into the hand of Israel; he struck it and all the people who *were* in it with the edge of the sword. He let none remain in it, but did to its king as he had done to the king of Jericho.

31Then Joshua passed from Libnah, and all Israel with him, to Lachish; and they encamped against it and fought against it. 32And the LORD delivered Lachish into the hand of Israel, who took it on the second day, and struck it and all the people who *were* in it with the edge of the sword, according to all that he had done to Libnah. 33Then Horam king of Gezer came up to help Lachish; and Joshua struck him and his people, until he left him none remaining.

34From Lachish Joshua passed to Eglon, and all Israel with him; and they encamped against it and fought against it. 35They took it on that day and struck it with the edge of the sword; all the people who *were* in it he utterly destroyed that day, according to all that he had done to Lachish.

36So Joshua went up from Eglon, and all Israel with him, to Hebron; and they fought against it. 37And they took it and struck it with the edge of the sword— its king, all its cities, and all the people who *were* in it; he left none remaining, according to all that he had done to Eglon, but utterly destroyed it and all the people who *were* in it.

38Then Joshua returned, and all Israel with him, to Debir; and they fought against it. 39And he took it and its king and all its cities; they struck them with the edge of the sword and utterly destroyed all the people who *were* in it. He left none remaining; as he had done to Hebron, so he did to Debir and its king, as he had done also to Libnah and its king.

40So Joshua conquered all the land: the mountain country and the South and the lowland and the wilderness slopes, and all their kings; he left none remaining, but utterly destroyed all that breathed, as the LORD God of Israel had commanded. 41And Joshua conquered them from Kadesh Barnea as far as Gaza, and all the country of Goshen, even as far as Gibeon. 42All these kings and their land Joshua took at one time, because the LORD God of Israel fought for Israel. 43Then Joshua returned, and all Israel with him, to the camp at Gilgal.

The Northern Conquest

11 And it came to pass, when Jabin king of Hazor heard *these things*, that he sent to Jobab king of Madon, to the king of Shimron, to the king of Achshaph, 2and to the kings who *were* from the north, in the mountains, in the plain south of Chinneroth, in the lowland, and in the heights of Dor on the west, 3to the Canaanites in the east and in the west, the Amorite, the Hittite, the Perizzite, the Jebusite in the mountains, and the Hivite below Hermon in the

land of Mizpah. 4So they went out, they and all their armies with them, *as* many people *as* the sand that *is* on the seashore in multitude, with very many horses and chariots. 5And when all these kings had met together, they came and camped together at the waters of Merom to fight against Israel.

6But the LORD said to Joshua, "Do not be afraid because of them, for tomorrow about this time I will deliver all of them slain before Israel. You shall hamstring their horses and burn their chariots with fire." 7So Joshua and all the people of war with him came against them suddenly by the waters of Merom, and they attacked them. 8And the LORD delivered them into the hand of Israel, who defeated them and chased them to Greater Sidon, to the Brook Misrephoth, and to the Valley of Mizpah eastward; they attacked them until they left none of them remaining. 9So Joshua did to them as the LORD had told him: he hamstrung their horses and burned their chariots with fire.

10Joshua turned back at that time and took Hazor, and struck its king with the sword; for Hazor was formerly the head of all those kingdoms. 11And they struck all the people who *were* in it with the edge of the sword, utterly destroying *them*. There was none left breathing. Then he burned Hazor with fire.

12So all the cities of those kings, and all their kings, Joshua took and struck with the edge of the sword. He utterly destroyed them, as Moses the servant of the LORD had commanded. 13But *as for* the cities that stood on their mounds,e Israel burned none of them, except Hazor only, *which* Joshua burned. 14And all the spoil of these cities and the livestock, the children of Israel took as booty for themselves; but they struck every man with the edge of the sword until they had destroyed them, and they left none breathing. 15As the LORD had commanded Moses his servant, so Moses commanded Joshua, and so Joshua did. He left nothing undone of all that the LORD had commanded Moses.

Summary of Joshua's Conquests

16Thus Joshua took all this land: the mountain country, all the South, all the land of Goshen, the lowland, and the Jordan plain—the mountains of Israel and its lowlands, 17from Mount Halak and the ascent to Seir, even as far as Baal Gad in the Valley of Lebanon below Mount Hermon. He captured all their kings, and struck them down and killed them. 18Joshua made war a long time with all those kings. 19There was not a city that made peace with the children of Israel, except the Hivites, the inhabitants of Gibeon. All *the others* they took in battle. 20For it was of the LORD to harden their hearts, that they should come against Israel in battle, that He might utterly destroy them, *and* that they might receive no mercy, but that He might destroy them, as the LORD had commanded Moses.

21And at that time Joshua came and cut off the Anakim from the mountains: from Hebron, from Debir, from Anab, from all the mountains of Judah, and from all the mountains of Israel; Joshua utterly destroyed them with their cities. 22None of the Anakim were left in the land of the children of Israel; they remained only in Gaza, in Gath, and in Ashdod.

23So Joshua took the whole land, according to all that the LORD had said to Moses; and Joshua gave it as an inheritance to Israel according to their divisions by their tribes. Then the land rested from war.

The Kings Conquered by Moses

12 These *are* the kings of the land whom the children of Israel defeated, and whose land they possessed on the other side of the Jordan toward the rising of the sun, from the River Arnon to Mount Hermon, and all the eastern Jordan plain: 2One king was Sihon king of the Amorites, who dwelt in Heshbon *and* ruled half of Gilead, from Aroer, which is on the bank of the River Arnon, from the middle of that river, even as far as the River Jabbok, *which is* the border of the Ammonites, 3and the eastern Jordan plain from the

---

e Heaps of successive city ruins

Sea of Chinneroth as far as the Sea of the Arabah (the Salt Sea), the road to Beth Jeshimoth, and southward below the slopes of Pisgah. 4*The other king was* Og king of Bashan and his territory, *who was* of the remnant of the giants, who dwelt at Ashtaroth and at Edrei, 5and reigned over Mount Hermon, over Salcah, over all Bashan, as far as the border of the Geshurites and the Maachathites, and over half of Gilead *to* the border of Sihon king of Heshbon.

6These Moses the servant of the LORD and the children of Israel had conquered; and Moses the servant of the LORD had given it *as* a possession to the Reubenites, the Gadites, and half the tribe of Manasseh.

The Kings Conquered by Joshua

7And these *are* the kings of the country which Joshua and the children of Israel conquered on this side of the Jordan, on the west, from Baal Gad in the Valley of Lebanon as far as Mount Halak and the ascent to Seir, which Joshua gave to the tribes of Israel *as* a possession according to their divisions, 8in the mountain country, in the lowlands, in the *Jordan* plain, in the slopes, in the wilderness, and in the South— the Hittites, the Amorites, the Canaanites, the Perizzites, the Hivites, and the Jebusites: 9the king of Jericho, one; the king of Ai, which *is* beside Bethel, one; 10the king of Jerusalem, one; the king of Hebron, one; 11the king of Jarmuth, one; the king of Lachish, one; 12the king of Eglon, one; the king of Gezer, one; 13the king of Debir, one; the king of Geder, one; 14the king of Hormah, one; the king of Arad, one; 15the king of Libnah, one; the king of Adullam, one; 16the king of Makkedah, one; the king of Bethel, one; 17the king of Tappuah, one; the king of Hepher, one; 18the king of Aphek, one; the king of Lasharon, one; 19the king of Madon, one; the king of Hazor, one; 20the king of Shimron Meron, one; the king of Achshaph, one; 21the king of Taanach, one; the king of Megiddo, one; 22the king of Kedesh, one; the king of Jokneam in Carmel, one; 23the king of Dor in the heights of Dor, one; the king

of the people of Gilgal, one; 24the king of Tirzah, one—all the kings, thirty-one.

Remaining Land to Be Conquered

13 Now Joshua was old, advanced in years. And the LORD said to him: "You are old, advanced in years, and there remains very much land yet to be possessed. 2This is the land that yet remains: all the territory of the Philistines and all *that of* the Geshurites, 3from Sihor, which *is* east of Egypt, as far as the border of Ekron northward (*which* is counted as Canaanite): the five lords of the Philistines—the Gazites, the Ashdodites, the Ashkelonites, the Gittites, and the Ekronites; also the Avites; 4from the south, all the land of the Canaanites, and Mearah that belongs to the Sidonians as far as Aphek, to the border of the Amorites; 5the land of the Gebalites, and all Lebanon, toward the sunrise, from Baal Gad below Mount Hermon as far as the entrance to Hamath; 6all the inhabitants of the mountains from Lebanon as far as the Brook Misrephoth, *and* all the Sidonians— them I will drive out from before the children of Israel; only divide it by lot to Israel as an inheritance, as I have commanded you. 7Now therefore, divide this land as an inheritance to the nine tribes and half the tribe of Manasseh."

The Land Divided East of the Jordan

8With the other half-tribe the Reubenites and the Gadites received their inheritance, which Moses had given them, beyond the Jordan eastward, as Moses the servant of the LORD had given them: 9from Aroer which *is* on the bank of the River Arnon, and the town that *is* in the midst of the ravine, and all the plain of Medeba as far as Dibon; 10all the cities of Sihon king of the Amorites, who reigned in Heshbon, as far as the border of the children of Ammon; 11Gilead, and the border of the Geshurites and Maachathites, all Mount Hermon, and all Bashan as far as Salcah; 12all the kingdom of Og in Bashan, who reigned in Ashtaroth and Edrei, who remained of the remnant of the giants; for Moses had defeated and cast out these.

13Nevertheless the children of Israel

did not drive out the Geshurites or the Maachathites, but the Geshurites and the Maachathites dwell among the Israelites until this day.

14Only to the tribe of Levi he had given no inheritance; the sacrifices of the LORD God of Israel made by fire *are* their inheritance, as He said to them.

The Land of Reuben

15And Moses had given to the tribe of the children of Reuben *an inheritance* according to their families. 16Their territory was from Aroer, which *is* on the bank of the River Arnon, and the city that *is* in the midst of the ravine, and all the plain by Medeba; 17Heshbon and all its cities that *are* in the plain: Dibon, Bamoth Baal, Beth Baal Meon, 18Jahaza, Kedemoth, Mephaath, 19Kirjathaim, Sibmah, Zereth Shahar on the mountain of the valley, 20Beth Peor, the slopes of Pisgah, and Beth Jeshimoth—21all the cities of the plain and all the kingdom of Sihon king of the Amorites, who reigned in Heshbon, whom Moses had struck with the princes of Midian: Evi, Rekem, Zur, Hur, and Reba, who *were* princes of Sihon dwelling in the country. 22The children of Israel also killed with the sword Balaam the son of Beor, the soothsayer, among those who were killed by them. 23And the border of the children of Reuben was the bank of the Jordan. This *was* the inheritance of the children of Reuben according to their families, the cities and their villages.

The Land of Gad

24Moses also had given *an inheritance* to the tribe of Gad, to the children of Gad according to their families. 25Their territory was Jazer, and all the cities of Gilead, and half the land of the Ammonites as far as Aroer, which *is* before Rabbah, 26and from Heshbon to Ramath Mizpah and Betonim, and from Mahanaim to the border of Debir, 27and in the valley Beth Haram, Beth Nimrah, Succoth, and Zaphon, the rest of the kingdom of Sihon king of Heshbon, with the Jordan as *its* border, as far as the edge of the Sea of Chinnereth, on the other side of the Jordan eastward. 28This *is* the inheritance of the children of Gad according to their families, the cities and their villages.

Half the Tribe of Manasseh (East)

29Moses also had given *an inheritance* to half the tribe of Manasseh; it was for half the tribe of the children of Manasseh according to their families: 30Their territory was from Mahanaim, all Bashan, all the kingdom of Og king of Bashan, and all the towns of Jair which are in Bashan, sixty cities; 31half of Gilead, and Ashtaroth and Edrei, cities of the kingdom of Og in Bashan, *were* for the children of Machir the son of Manasseh, for half of the children of Machir according to their families.

32These *are the areas* which Moses had distributed as an inheritance in the plains of Moab on the other side of the Jordan, by Jericho eastward. 33But to the tribe of Levi Moses had given no inheritance; the LORD God of Israel *was* their inheritance, as He had said to them.

The Land Divided West of the Jordan

14 These *are the areas* which the children of Israel inherited in the land of Canaan, which Eleazar the priest, Joshua the son of Nun, and the heads of the fathers of the tribes of the children of Israel distributed as an inheritance to them. 2Their inheritance *was* by lot, as the LORD had commanded by the hand of Moses, for the nine tribes and the half-tribe. 3For Moses had given the inheritance of the two tribes and the half-tribe on the other side of the Jordan; but to the Levites he had given no inheritance among them. 4For the children of Joseph were two tribes: Manasseh and Ephraim. And they gave no part to the Levites in the land, except cities to dwell *in*, with their common-lands for their livestock and their property. 5As the LORD had commanded Moses, so the children of Israel did; and they divided the land.

Caleb Inherits Hebron

6Then the children of Judah came to Joshua in Gilgal. And Caleb the son of Jephunneh the Kenizzite said to him: "You know the word which the LORD said to Moses the man of God concerning you and me in Kadesh Barnea. 7I *was* forty years old when Moses the servant of the LORD sent me from Kadesh Barnea to spy out the land, and I brought back word to him as *it was* in my heart. 8Nevertheless my brethren who went up with me made the heart of the people melt, but I wholly followed the LORD my God. 9So Moses swore on that day, saying, 'Surely the land where your foot has trodden shall be your inheritance and your children's forever, because you have wholly followed the LORD my God.' 10And now, behold, the LORD has kept me alive, as He said, these forty-five years, ever since the LORD spoke this word to Moses while Israel wandered in the wilderness; and now, here I am this day, eighty-five years old. 11As yet I *am as* strong this day as on the day that Moses sent me; just as my strength *was* then, so now *is* my strength for war, both for going out and for coming in. 12Now therefore, give me this mountain of which the LORD spoke in that day; for you heard in that day how the Anakim *were* there, and *that* the cities *were* great *and* fortified. It may be that the LORD *will be* with me, and I shall be able to drive them out as the LORD said.''

13And Joshua blessed him, and gave Hebron to Caleb the son of Jephunneh as an inheritance. 14Hebron therefore became the inheritance of Caleb the son of Jephunneh the Kenizzite to this day, because he wholly followed the LORD God of Israel. 15And the name of Hebron formerly was Kirjath Arba (*Arba was* the greatest man among the Anakim).

Then the land had rest from war.

The Land of Judah

15 So *this* was the lot of the tribe of the children of Judah according to their families:

The border of Edom at the Wilderness of Zin southward *was* the extreme southern boundary. 2And their southern border began at the shore of the Salt Sea, from the bay that faces southward. 3Then it went out to the southern side of the Ascent of Akrabbim, passed along to Zin, ascended on the south side of Kadesh Barnea, passed along to Hezron, went up to Adar, and went around to Karkaa. 4*From there* it passed toward Azmon and went out to the Brook of Egypt; and the border ended at the sea. This shall be your southern border.

5The east border *was* the Salt Sea as far as the mouth of the Jordan.

And the border on the northern quarter *began* at the bay of the sea at the mouth of the Jordan. 6The border went up to Beth Hoglah and passed north of Beth Arabah; and the border went up to the stone of Bohan the son of Reuben. 7Then the border went up toward Debir from the Valley of Achor, and it turned northward toward Gilgal, which *is* before the Ascent of Adummim, which *is* on the south side of the valley. The border continued toward the waters of En Shemesh and ended at En Rogel. 8And the border went up by the Valley of the Son of Hinnom to the southern slope of the Jebusite *city* (which *is* Jerusalem). The border went up to the top of the mountain that *lies* before the Valley of Hinnom westward, which *is* at the end of the Valley of Rephaim northward. 9Then the border went around from the top of the hill to the fountain of the water of Nephtoah, and extended to the cities of Mount Ephron. And the border went around to Baalah (which *is* Kirjath Jearim). 10Then the border turned westward from Baalah to Mount Seir, passed along to the side of Mount Jearim on the north (which *is* Chesalon), went down to Beth Shemesh, and passed on to Timnah. 11And the border went out to the side of Ekron northward. Then the border went around to Shicron, passed along to Mount Baalah, and extended to Jabneel; and the border ended at the sea.

12The west border *was* the coastline of the Great Sea. This *is* the boundary of the children of Judah all around according to their families.

Caleb Occupies Hebron and Debir

13Now to Caleb the son of Jephunneh he gave a share among the children of Judah, according to the commandment of the LORD to Joshua, *namely,* Kirjath Arba, which *is* Hebron (*Arba was* the father of Anak). 14Caleb drove out the three sons of Anak from there: Sheshai, Ahiman, and Talmai, the children of Anak. 15Then he went up from there to the inhabitants of Debir (formerly the name of Debir *was* Kirjath Sepher).

16And Caleb said, "He who attacks Kirjath Sepher and takes it, to him I will give Achsah my daughter as wife." 17So Othniel the son of Kenaz, the brother of Caleb, took it; and he gave him Achsah his daughter as wife. 18Now it was so, when she came *to him,* that she persuaded him to ask her father for a field. So she dismounted from *her* donkey, and Caleb said to her, "What do you wish?" 19She answered, "Give me a blessing; since you have given me land in the South, give me also springs of water." So he gave her the upper springs and the lower springs.

The Cities of Judah

20This *was* the inheritance of the tribe of the children of Judah according to their families:

21The cities at the limits of the tribe of the children of Judah, toward the border of Edom in the South, were Kabzeel, Eder, Jagur, 22Kinah, Dimonah, Adadah, 23Kedesh, Hazor, Ithnan, 24Ziph, Telem, Bealoth, 25Hazor, Hadattah, Kerioth, Hezron (which *is* Hazor), 26Amam, Shema, Moladah, 27Hazar Gaddah, Heshmon, Beth Pelet, 28Hazar Shual, Beersheba, Bizjothjah, 29Baalah, Ijim, Ezem, 30Eltolad, Chesil, Hormah, 31Ziklag, Madmannah, Sansannah, 32Lebaoth, Shilhim, Ain, and Rimmon: all the cities *are* twenty-nine, with their villages.

33In the lowland: Eshtaol, Zorah, Ashnah, 34Zanoah, En Gannim, Tappuah, Enam, 35Jarmuth, Adullam, Socoh, Azekah, 36Sharaim, Adithaim, Gederah, and Gederothaim: fourteen cities with their villages; 37Zenan, Hadashah, Migdal Gad, 38Dilean, Mizpah, Joktheel, 39Lachish, Bozkath, Eglon, 40Cabbon, Lahmas, Kithlish, 41Gederoth, Beth Dagon, Naamah, and Makkedah: sixteen cities with their villages; 42Libnah, Ether, Ashan, 43Jiphtah, Ashnah, Nezib, 44Keilah, Achzib, and Mareshah: nine cities with their villages; 45Ekron, with its towns and villages; 46from Ekron to the sea, all that *lay* near Ashdod, with their villages;

47Ashdod with its towns and villages, Gaza with its towns and villages—as far as the Brook of Egypt and the Great Sea with *its* coastline.

48And in the mountain country: Shamir, Jattir, Sochoh, 49Dannah, Kirjath Sannah (which *is* Debir), 50Anab, Eshtemoh, Anim, 51Goshen, Holon, and Giloh: eleven cities with their villages; 52Arab, Dumah, Eshean, 53Janum, Beth Tappuah, Aphekah, 54Humtah, Kirjath Arba (which *is* Hebron), and Zior: nine cities with their villages; 55Maon, Carmel, Ziph, Juttah, 56Jezreel, Jokdeam, Zanoah, 57Kain, Gibeah, and Timnah: ten cities with their villages; 58Halhul, Beth Zur, Gedor, 59Maarath, Beth Anoth, and Eltekon: six cities with their villages; 60Kirjath Baal (which *is* Kirjath Jearim) and Rabbah: two cities with their villages.

61In the wilderness: Beth Arabah, Middin, Secacah, 62Nibshan, the City of Salt, and En Gedi: six cities with their villages.

63As for the Jebusites, the inhabitants of Jerusalem, the children of Judah could not drive them out; but the Jebusites dwell with the children of Judah at Jerusalem to this day.

Ephraim and West Manasseh

16 The lot fell to the children of Joseph from the Jordan, by Jericho, to the waters of Jericho on the east, to the wilderness that goes up from Jericho through the mountains to Bethel, 2then went out from Bethel to Luz, passed along to the border of the Archites at Ataroth, 3and went down westward to the boundary of the Japhletites, as far as the boundary of Lower Beth Horon to Gezer; and it ended at the sea.

4So the children of Joseph, Manasseh and Ephraim, took their inheritance.

The Land of Ephraim

5The border of the children of Ephraim, according to their families, was *thus:* The border of their inheritance on the east side was Ataroth Addar as far as Upper Beth Horon.

6And the border went out toward the sea on the north side of Michmethath; then the border went around eastward to Taanath Shiloh, and passed by it on the east of Janohah. 7Then it went down from Janohah to Ataroth and Naarah, reached to Jericho, and came out at the Jordan.

8The border went out from Tappuah westward to the Brook Kanah, and it ended at the sea. This *was* the inheritance of the tribe of the children of Ephraim according to their families. 9The separate cities for the children of Ephraim *were* among the inheritance of the children of Manasseh, all the cities with their villages.

10And they did not drive out the Canaanites who dwelt in Gezer; but the Canaanites dwell among the Ephraimites to this day and have become forced laborers.

The Other Half-Tribe of Manasseh (West)

17 There was also a lot for the tribe of Manasseh, for he *was* the firstborn of Joseph: *namely* for Machir the firstborn of Manasseh, the father of Gilead, because he was a man of war; therefore he was given Gilead and Bashan. 2And there was *a lot* for the rest of the children of Manasseh according to their families: for the children of Abiezer, the children of Helek, the children of Asriel, the children of Shechem, the children of Hepher, and the children of Shemida; these *were* the male children of Manasseh the son of Joseph according to their families.

3But Zelophehad the son of Hepher, the son of Gilead, the son of Machir, the son of Manasseh, had no sons, but only daughters. And these *are* the names of his daughters: Mahlah, Noah, Hoglah, Milcah, and Tirzah. 4And they came near before Eleazar the priest, before Joshua the son of Nun, and before the rulers, saying, "The LORD commanded Moses to give us an inheritance among our brothers." Therefore, according to the commandment of the LORD, he gave them an inheritance among their father's brothers. 5Ten shares fell to Manasseh, besides the land of Gilead and Bashan, which *were* on the other side of the Jordan, 6because the daughters of Manasseh received an inheritance among his sons; and the rest of Manasseh's sons had the land of Gilead.

7And the territory of Manasseh was from Asher to Michmethath, that *lies* east of Shechem; and the border went along south to the inhabitants of En Tappuah. 8Manasseh had the land of Tappuah, but Tappuah on the border of Manasseh *belonged* to the children of Ephraim. 9And the border descended to the Brook Kanah, southward to the brook. These cities of Ephraim *are* among the cities of Manasseh. The border of Manasseh *was* on the north side of the brook; and it ended at the sea.

10Southward *it was* Ephraim's, northward *it was* Manasseh's, and the sea was its border. Manasseh's territory was adjoining Asher on the north and Issachar on the east. 11And in Issachar and in Asher, Manasseh had Beth Shean and its towns, Ibleam and its towns, the inhabitants of Dor and its towns, the inhabitants of En Dor and its towns, the inhabitants of Taanach and its towns, and the inhabitants of Megiddo and its towns—three hilly regions. 12Yet the children of Manasseh could not drive out *the inhabitants of* those cities, but the Canaanites were determined to dwell in that land. 13And it happened, when the children of Israel grew strong, that they put the Canaanites to forced labor, but did not utterly drive them out.

More Land for Ephraim and Manasseh

14Then the children of Joseph spoke to Joshua, saying, "Why have you given us *only* one lot and one share to inherit, since we *are* a great people, inasmuch as the LORD has blessed us until now?"

15So Joshua answered them, "If you *are* a great people, *then* go up to the forest *country* and clear a place for yourself there in the land of the Perizzites and the giants, since the mountains of Ephraim are too confined for you."

16But the children of Joseph said, "The mountain country is not enough for us; and all the Canaanites who dwell in the land of the valley have chariots of iron, *both those* who *are* of Beth Shean and its towns and *those* who *are* of the Valley of Jezreel."

17And Joshua spoke to the house of Joseph—to Ephraim and Manasseh—

saying, "You *are* a great people and have great power; you shall not have only one lot, 18but the mountain country shall be yours. Although it *is* wooded, you shall cut it down, and its farthest extent shall be yours; for you shall drive out the Canaanites, though they have iron chariots *and* are strong."

The Remainder of the Land Divided

18 Now the whole congregation of the children of Israel assembled together at Shiloh, and set up the tabernacle of meeting there. And the land was subdued before them. 2But there remained among the children of Israel seven tribes which had not yet received their inheritance.

3Then Joshua said to the children of Israel: "How long will you neglect to go and possess the land which the LORD God of your fathers has given you? 4Pick out from among you three men for *each* tribe, and I will send them; they shall rise and go through the land, survey it according to their inheritance, and come *back* to me. 5And they shall divide it into seven parts. Judah shall remain in their territory on the south, and the house of Joseph shall remain in their territory on the north. 6You shall therefore survey the land in seven parts and bring *the survey* here to me, that I may cast lots for you here before the LORD our God. 7But the Levites have no part among you, for the priesthood of the LORD *is* their inheritance. And Gad, Reuben, and half the tribe of Manasseh have received their inheritance beyond the Jordan on the east, which Moses the servant of the LORD gave them."

8Then the men arose to go away; and Joshua charged those who went to survey the land, saying, "Go, walk through the land, survey it, and come back to me, that I may cast lots for you here before the LORD in Shiloh." 9So the men went, passed through the land, and wrote the survey in a book in seven parts by cities; and they came to Joshua at the camp in Shiloh. 10Then Joshua cast lots for them in Shiloh before the LORD, and there Joshua divided the land to the children of Israel according to their divisions.

The Land of Benjamin

11Now the lot of the tribe of the children of Benjamin came up according to their families, and the territory of their lot came out between the children of Judah and the children of Joseph. 12Their border on the north side began at the Jordan, and the border went up to the side of Jericho on the north, and went up through the mountains westward; it ended at the Wilderness of Beth Aven. 13The border went over from there toward Luz, to the side of Luz (which *is* Bethel) southward; and the border descended to Ataroth Addar, near the hill that *lies* on the south side of Lower Beth Horon.

14Then the border extended around the west side to the south, from the hill that *lies* before Beth Horon southward; and it ended at Kirjath Baal (which *is* Kirjath Jearim), a city of the children of Judah. This *was* the west side.

15The south side *began* at the end of Kirjath Jearim, and the border extended on the west and went out to the spring of the waters of Nephtoah. 16Then the border came down to the end of the mountain that *lies* before the Valley of the Son of Hinnom, which *is* in the Valley of the Rephaim on the north, descended to the Valley of Hinnom, to the side of the Jebusite *city* on the south, and descended to En Rogel. 17And it went around from the north, went out to En Shemesh, and extended toward Geliloth, which is before the Ascent of Adummim, and descended to the stone of Bohan the son of Reuben. 18Then it passed along toward the north side of Arabah, and went down to Arabah. 19And the border passed along to the north side of Beth Hoglah; then the border ended at the north bay at the Salt Sea, at the south end of the Jordan. This *was* the southern boundary.

20The Jordan was its border on the east side. This *was* the inheritance of the children of Benjamin, according to its boundaries all around, according to their families.

21Now the cities of the tribe of the children of Benjamin, according to their families, were Jericho, Beth Hoglah, Emek Keziz, 22Beth Arabah, Zemaraim, Bethel, 23Avim, Parah, Ophrah,

24Chephar Haammoni, Ophni, and Gaba: twelve cities with their villages; 25Gibeon, Ramah, Beeroth, 26Mizpah, Chephirah, Mozah, 27Rekem, Irpeel, Taralah, 28Zelah, Eleph, Jebus (which *is* Jerusalem), Gibeath, *and* Kirjath: fourteen cities with their villages. This was the inheritance of the children of Benjamin according to their families.

Simeon's Inheritance with Judah

19 The second lot came out for Simeon, for the tribe of the children of Simeon according to their families. And their inheritance was within the inheritance of the children of Judah. 2They had in their inheritance Beersheba (Sheba), Moladah, 3Hazar Shual, Balah, Ezem, 4Eltolad, Bethul, Hormah, 5Ziklag, Beth Marcaboth, Hazar Susah, 6Beth Lebaoth, and Sharuhen: thirteen cities and their villages; 7Ain, Rimmon, Ether, and Ashan: four cities and their villages; 8and all the villages that *were* all around these cities as far as Baalath Beer, Ramah of the South. This *was* the inheritance of the tribe of the children of Simeon according to their families.

9The inheritance of the children of Simeon *was included* in the share of the children of Judah, for the share of the children of Judah was too much for them. Therefore the children of Simeon had *their* inheritance within the inheritance of that people.

The Land of Zebulun

10The third lot came out for the children of Zebulun according to their families, and the border of their inheritance was as far as Sarid. 11Their border went toward the west and to Maralah, went to Dabbasheth, and extended along the brook that is east of Jokneam. 12Then from Sarid it went eastward toward the sunrise along the border of Chisloth Tabor, and went out toward Daberath, bypassing Japhia. 13And from there it passed along on the east of Gath Hepher, toward Eth Kazin, and extended to Rimmon, which borders on Neah. 14Then the border went around it on the north side of Hannathon, and it ended in the Valley of Jiphthah El. 15Included were Kattath, Nahallal, Shimron, Idalah, and Bethlehem: twelve cities with their villages. 16This *was* the inheritance of the children of Zebulun according to their families, these cities with their villages.

The Land of Issachar

17The fourth lot came out to Issachar, for the children of Issachar according to their families. 18And their territory went to Jezreel, and *included* Chesulloth, Shunem, 19Haphraim, Shion, Anaharath, 20Rabbith, Kishion, Abez, 21Remeth, En Gannim, En Haddah, and Beth Pazzez. 22And the border reached to Tabor, Shahazimah, and Beth Shemesh; their border ended at the Jordan: sixteen cities with their villages. 23This *was* the inheritance of the tribe of the children of Issachar according to their families, the cities and their villages.

The Land of Asher

24The fifth lot came out for the tribe of the children of Asher according to their families. 25And their territory included Helkath, Hali, Beten, Achshaph, 26Alammelech, Amad, and Mishal; it reached to Mount Carmel westward, along *the Brook* Shihor Libnath. 27It turned toward the sunrise to Beth Dagon; and it reached to Zebulun and to the Valley of Jiphthah El, then northward beyond Beth Emek and Neiel, bypassing Cabul *which was* on the left, 28including Ebron, Rehob, Hammon, and Kanah, as far as Greater Sidon. 29And the border turned to Ramah and to the fortified city of Tyre; then the border turned to Hosah, and ended at the sea by the region of Achzib. 30Also Ummah, Aphek, and Rehob *were included:* twenty-two cities with their villages. 31This *was* the inheritance of the tribe of the children of Asher according to their families, these cities with their villages.

The Land of Naphtali

32The sixth lot came out to the children of Naphtali, for the children of Naphtali according to their families. 33And their border began at Heleph, enclosing the territory from the terebinth tree in Zaanannim, Adami Nekeb, and Jabneel, as far as Lakkum; it ended at the Jordan. 34From Heleph the border extended westward to Aznoth Tabor, and went out from there toward Hukkok; it adjoined Zebulun on the south side and Asher on the west side, and ended at Judah by the Jordan toward the sunrise. 35And the fortified cities *are* Ziddim, Zer, Hammath, Rakkath, Chinnereth, 36Adamah, Ramah, Hazor, 37Kedesh, Edrei, En Hazor, 38Iron, Migdal El, Horem, Beth Anath, and Beth Shemesh: nineteen cities with their villages. 39This *was* the inheritance of the tribe of the children of Naphtali according to their families, the cities and their villages.

The Land of Dan

40The seventh lot came out for the tribe of the children of Dan according to their families. 41And the territory of their inheritance was Zorah, Eshtaol, Ir Shemesh, 42Shaalabbin, Aijalon, Jethlah, 43Elon, Timnah, Ekron, 44Eltekeh, Gibbethon, Baalath, 45Jehud, Bene Berak, Gath Rimmon, 46Me Jarkon, and Rakkon, with the region near Joppa. 47And the border of the children of Dan went beyond these, because the children of Dan went up to fight against Leshem and took it; and they struck it with the edge of the sword, took possession of it, and dwelt in it. They called Leshem, Dan, after the name of Dan their father. 48This *is* the inheritance of the tribe of the children of Dan according to their families, these cities with their villages.

Joshua's Inheritance

49When they had made an end of dividing the land as an inheritance according to their borders, the children of Israel gave an inheritance among them to Joshua the son of Nun. 50According to the word of the LORD they gave him the city which he asked for, Timnath Serah in the mountains of Ephraim; and he built the city and dwelt in it.

51These *were* the inheritances which Eleazar the priest, Joshua the son of Nun, and the heads of the fathers of the tribes of the children of Israel divided as an inheritance by lot in Shiloh before the LORD, at the door of the tabernacle of meeting. So they made an end of dividing the country.

The Cities of Refuge

20 The LORD also spoke to Joshua, saying, 2"Speak to the children of Israel, saying: 'Appoint for yourselves cities of refuge, of which I spoke to you through Moses, 3that the slayer who kills a person accidentally or unintentionally may flee there; and they shall be your refuge from the avenger of blood. 4And when he flees to one of those cities, and stands at the entrance of the gate of the city, and declares his case in the hearing of the elders of that city, they shall take him into the city as one of them, and give him a place, that he may dwell among them. 5Then if the avenger of blood pursues him, they shall not deliver the slayer into his hand, because he struck his neighbor unintentionally, but did not hate him beforehand. 6And he shall dwell in that city until he stands before the congregation for judgment, *and* until the death of the one who is high priest in those days. Then the slayer may return and come to his own city and his own house, to the city from which he fled.' "

7So they appointed Kedesh in Galilee, in the mountains of Naphtali, Shechem in the mountains of Ephraim, and Kirjath Arba (which *is* Hebron) in the mountains of Judah. 8And on the other side of the Jordan, by Jericho eastward, they assigned Bezer in the wilderness on the plain, from the tribe of Reuben, Ramoth in Gilead, from the tribe of Gad, and Golan in Bashan, from the tribe of Manasseh. 9These were the cities appointed for all the children of Israel and for the stranger who dwelt among them, that whoever killed a person accidentally might flee there, and not die by the hand of the avenger of blood until he stood before the congregation.

Cities of the Levites

21 Then the heads of the fathers' *houses* of the Levites came near to Eleazar the priest, to Joshua the son of Nun, and to the heads of the fathers' *houses* of the tribes of the children of Israel. 2And they spoke to them at Shiloh in the land of Canaan, saying, "The LORD commanded through Moses to give us cities to dwell in, with their common-lands for our livestock." 3So the children of Israel gave to the Levites from their inheritance, at the commandment of the LORD, these cities and their common-lands:

4Now the lot came out for the families of the Kohathites. And the children of Aaron the priest, *who were* of the Levites, had thirteen cities by lot from the tribe of Judah, from the tribe of Simeon, and from the tribe of Benjamin. 5The rest of the children of Kohath had ten cities by lot from the families of the tribe of Ephraim, from the tribe of Dan, and from the half-tribe of Manasseh.

6And the children of Gershon had thirteen cities by lot from the families of the tribe of Issachar, from the tribe of Asher, from the tribe of Naphtali, and from the half-tribe of Manasseh in Bashan.

7The children of Merari according to their families had twelve cities from the tribe of Reuben, from the tribe of Gad, and from the tribe of Zebulun.

8And the children of Israel gave these cities with their common-lands by lot to the Levites, as the LORD had commanded by the hand of Moses.

9So they gave from the tribe of the children of Judah and from the tribe of the children of Simeon these cities which are designated by name, 10which were for the children of Aaron, one of the families of the Kohathites, *who were* of the children of Levi; for the lot was theirs first. 11And they gave them Kirjath Arba (*Arba was* the father of Anak), which *is* Hebron, in the mountains of Judah, with the common-land surrounding it. 12But the fields of the city and its villages they gave to Caleb the son of Jephunneh as his possession.

13Thus to the children of Aaron the priest they gave Hebron with its common-land (a city of refuge for the slayer), Libnah with its common-land, 14Jattir with its common-land, Eshtemoa with its common-land, 15Holon with its common-land, Debir with its common-land, 16Ain with its common-land, Juttah with its common-land, and Beth Shemesh with its common-land: nine cities from those two tribes; 17and from the tribe of Benjamin, Gibeon with its common-land, Geba with

its common-land, 18Anathoth with its common-land, and Almon with its common-land: four cities. 19All the cities of the children of Aaron, the priests, *were* thirteen cities with their common-lands.

20And the families of the children of Kohath, the Levites, the rest of the children of Kohath, even they had the cities of their lot from the tribe of Ephraim. 21For they gave them Shechem with its common-land in the mountains of Ephraim (a city of refuge for the slayer), Gezer with its common-land, 22Kibzaim with its common-land, and Beth Horon with its common-land: four cities; 23and from the tribe of Dan, Eltekeh with its common-land, Gibbethon with its common-land, 24Aijalon with its common-land, *and* Gath Rimmon with its common-land: four cities; 25and from the half-tribe of Manasseh, Tanach with its common-land and Gath Rimmon with its common-land: two cities. 26All the ten cities with their common-lands were for the rest of the families of the children of Kohath.

27Also to the children of Gershon, of the families of the Levites, from the *other* half-tribe of Manasseh, *they gave* Golan in Bashan with its common-land (a city of refuge for the slayer), and Be Eshterah with its common-land: two cities; 28and from the tribe of Issachar, Kishion with its common-land, Daberath with its common-land, 29Jarmuth with its common-land, *and* En Gannim with its common-land: four cities; 30and from the tribe of Asher, Mishal with its common-land, Abdon with its common-land, 31Helkath with its common-land, and Rehob with its common-land: four cities; 32and from the tribe of Naphtali, Kedesh in Galilee with its common-land (a city of refuge for the slayer), Hammoth Dor with its common-land, and Kartan with its common-land: three cities. 33All the cities of the Gershonites according to their families *were* thirteen cities with their common-lands.

34And to the families of the children of Merari, the rest of the Levites, from the tribe of Zebulun, Jokneam with its common-land, Kartah with its common-land, 35Dimnah with its common-land, *and* Nahalal with its common-land: four cities; 36and from the tribe of Reuben,

Bezer with its common-land, Jahaz with its common-land, 37Kedemoth with its common-land, and Mephaath with its common-land: four cities; 38and from the tribe of Gad, Ramoth in Gilead with its common-land (a city of refuge for the slayer), Mahanaim with its common-land, 39Heshbon with its common-land, *and* Jazer with its common-land: four cities in all. 40So all the cities for the children of Merari according to their families, the rest of the families of the Levites, were *by* their lot twelve cities.

41All the cities of the Levites within the possession of the children of Israel *were* forty-eight cities with their common-lands. 42Every one of these cities had its common-land surrounding it; thus *were* all these cities.

The Promise Fulfilled

43So the Lord gave to Israel all the land of which He had sworn to give to their fathers, and they took possession of it and dwelt in it. 44The Lord gave them rest all around, according to all that He had sworn to their fathers. And not a man of all their enemies stood against them; the Lord delivered all their enemies into their hand. 45Not a word failed of any good thing which the Lord had spoken to the house of Israel. All came to pass.

Eastern Tribes Return to Their Lands

22 Then Joshua called the Reubenites, the Gadites, and half the tribe of Manasseh, 2and said to them: "You have kept all that Moses the servant of the Lord commanded you, and have obeyed my voice in all that I commanded you. 3You have not left your brethren these many days, up to this day, but have kept the charge of the commandment of the Lord your God. 4And now the Lord your God has given rest to your brethren, as He promised them; now therefore, return and go to your tents *and* to the land of your possession, which Moses the servant of the Lord gave you on the other side of the Jordan. 5But take careful heed to do the commandment and the law which Moses the servant of the Lord commanded you, to love the Lord your God, to walk in all His ways, to keep His

commandments, to hold fast to Him, and to serve Him with all your heart and with all your soul." 6So Joshua blessed them and sent them away, and they went to their tents.

7Now to half the tribe of Manasseh Moses had given a possession in Bashan, but to the *other* half of it Joshua gave *a possession* among their brethren on this side of the Jordan, westward. And indeed, when Joshua sent them away to their tents, he blessed them, 8and spoke to them, saying, "Return with much riches to your tents, with very much livestock, with silver, with gold, with bronze, with iron, and with very much clothing. Divide the spoil of your enemies with your brethren."

9So the children of Reuben, the children of Gad, and half the tribe of Manasseh returned, and departed from the children of Israel at Shiloh, which *is* in the land of Canaan, to go to the country of Gilead, to the land of their possession, which they had obtained according to the word of the Lord by the hand of Moses.

An Altar by the Jordan

10And when they came to the region of the Jordan which *is* in the land of Canaan, the children of Reuben, the children of Gad, and half the tribe of Manasseh built an altar there by the Jordan—a great, impressive altar. 11Now the children of Israel heard *someone* say, "Behold, the children of Reuben, the children of Gad, and half the tribe of Manasseh have built an altar on the frontier of the land of Canaan, in the region of the Jordan—on the children of Israel's side." 12And when the children of Israel heard *of it*, the whole congregation of the children of Israel gathered together at Shiloh to go to war against them.

13Then the children of Israel sent Phinehas the son of Eleazar the priest to the children of Reuben, to the children of Gad, and to half the tribe of Manasseh, into the land of Gilead, 14and with him ten rulers, one ruler each from the chief house of every tribe of Israel; and each one *was* the head of the house of his father among the divisions of Israel. 15Then they came to the children of Reuben, to the children of Gad, and to half the tribe of Manasseh, to the land of Gilead, and they spoke with them, saying, 16"Thus says the whole congregation of the LORD: 'What treachery is this that you have committed against the God of Israel, to turn away this day from following the LORD, in that you have built for yourselves an altar, that you might rebel this day against the LORD? 17Is the iniquity of Peor not enough for us, from which we are not cleansed till this day, although there was a plague in the congregation of the LORD, 18but that you must turn away this day from following the LORD? And it shall be, if you rebel today against the LORD, that tomorrow He will be angry with the whole congregation of Israel. 19Nevertheless, if the land of your possession is unclean, then cross over to the land of the possession of the LORD, where the LORD's tabernacle stands, and take possession among us; but do not rebel against the LORD, nor rebel against us, by building yourselves an altar besides the altar of the LORD our God. 20Did not Achan the son of Zerah commit a trespass in the accursed thing, and wrath fell on all the congregation of Israel? And that man did not perish alone in his iniquity.'"

21Then the children of Reuben, the children of Gad, and half the tribe of Manasseh answered and said to the heads of the divisions of Israel: 22"The LORD God of gods, the LORD God of gods, He knows, and let Israel itself know—if it is in rebellion, or if in treachery against the LORD, do not save us this day. 23If we have built ourselves an altar to turn from following the LORD, or if to offer on it burnt offerings or grain offerings, or if to offer peace offerings on it, let the LORD Himself require an account. 24But in fact we have done it for fear, for a reason, saying, 'In time to come your descendants may speak to our descendants, saying, "What have you to do with the LORD God of Israel? 25For the LORD has made the Jordan a border between you and us, you children of Reuben and children of Gad. You have no part in the LORD." So your descendants would make our descendants cease fearing the LORD.' 26Therefore we said, 'Let us now pre-pare to build ourselves an altar, not for burnt offering nor for sacrifice, 27but that it may be a witness between you and us and our generations after us, that we may perform the service of the LORD before Him with our burnt offerings, with our sacrifices, and with our peace offerings; that your descendants may not say to our descendants in time to come, "You have no part in the LORD."' 28Therefore we said that it will be, when they say this to us or to our generations in time to come, that we may say, 'Here is the replica of the altar of the LORD which our fathers made, though not for burnt offerings nor for sacrifices; but it is a witness between you and us.' 29Far be it from us that we should rebel against the LORD, and turn from following the LORD this day, to build an altar for burnt offerings, for grain offer ings, or for sacrifices, besides the altar of the LORD our God which is before His tabernacle."

30Now when Phinehas the priest and the rulers of the congregation, the heads of the divisions of Israel who were with him, heard the words that the children of Reuben, the children of Gad, and the children of Manasseh spoke, it pleased them. 31Then Phinehas the son of Eleazar the priest said to the children of Reuben, the children of Gad, and the children of Manasseh, "This day we perceive that the LORD is among us, because you have not committed this treachery against the LORD. Now you have delivered the children of Israel out of the hand of the LORD."

32And Phinehas the son of Eleazar the priest, and the rulers, returned from the children of Reuben and the children of Gad, from the land of Gilead to the land of Canaan, to the children of Israel, and brought back word to them. 33So the thing pleased the children of Israel, and the children of Israel blessed God; they spoke no more of going against them in battle, to destroy the land where the children of Reuben and Gad dwelt.

34The children of Reuben and the children of Gad called the altar, Witness, "For it is a witness between us that the LORD is God."

Joshua's Farewell Address

23 Now it came to pass, a long time after the LORD had given rest to Israel from all their enemies round about, that Joshua was old, advanced in age. 2And Joshua called for all Israel, for their elders, for their heads, for their judges, and for their officers, and said to them:

"I am old, advanced in age. 3You have seen all that the LORD your God has done to all these nations because of you, for the LORD your God *is* He who has fought for you. 4See, I have divided to you by lot these nations that remain, to be an inheritance for your tribes, from the Jordan, with all the nations that I have cut off, as far as the Great Sea westward. 5And the LORD your God will expel them from before you and drive them out of your sight. So you shall possess their land, as the LORD your God promised you. 6Therefore be very courageous to keep and to do all that is written in the Book of the Law of Moses, lest you turn aside from it to the right hand or to the left, 7*and* lest you go among these nations, these who remain among you. You shall not make mention of the name of their gods, nor cause *anyone* to swear *by them;* you shall not serve them nor bow down to them, 8but you shall hold fast to the LORD your God, as you have done to this day. 9For the LORD has driven out from before you great and strong nations; but *as for* you, no one has been able to stand against you to this day. 10One man of you shall chase a thousand, for the LORD your God *is* He who fights for you, as He promised you. 11Therefore take careful heed to yourselves, that you love the LORD your God. 12Or else, if indeed you do go back, and cling to the remnant of these nations— these that remain among you—and make marriages with them, and go in to them and they to you, 13know for certain that the LORD your God will no longer drive out these nations from before you. But they shall be snares and traps to you, and scourges on your sides and thorns in your eyes, until you perish from this good land which the LORD your God has given you.

14"Behold, this day I *am* going the way of all the earth. And you know in all your hearts and in all your souls that not one thing has failed of all the good things which the LORD your God spoke concerning you. All have come to pass for you; not one word of them has failed. 15Therefore it shall come to pass, that as all the good things have come upon you which the LORD your God promised you, so the LORD will bring upon you all harmful things, until He has destroyed you from this good land which the LORD your God has given you. 16When you have transgressed the covenant of the LORD your God, which He commanded you, and have gone and served other gods, and bowed down to them, then the anger of the LORD will burn against you, and you shall perish quickly from the good land which He has given you."

The Covenant at Shechem

24 Then Joshua gathered all the tribes of Israel to Shechem and called for the elders of Israel, for their heads, for their judges, and for their officers; and they presented themselves before God. 2And Joshua said to all the people, "Thus says the LORD God of Israel: 'Your fathers, *including* Terah, the father of Abraham and the father of Nahor, dwelt on the other side of the River*f* in old times; and they served other gods. 3Then I took your father Abraham from the other side of the River, led him throughout all the land of Canaan, and multiplied his descendants and gave him Isaac. 4To Isaac I gave Jacob and Esau. To Esau I gave the mountains of Seir to possess, but Jacob and his children went down to Egypt. 5Also I sent Moses and Aaron, and I plagued Egypt, according to what I did among them. Afterward I brought you out.

6'Then I brought your fathers out of Egypt, and you came to the sea; and the Egyptians pursued your fathers with chariots and horsemen to the Red Sea. 7So they cried out to the LORD; and He put darkness between you and the Egyptians, brought the sea upon them,

f The Euphrates (so also verses 3, 14, and 15)

and covered them. And your eyes saw what I did in Egypt. Then you dwelt in the wilderness a long time. 8And I brought you into the land of the Amorites, who dwelt on the other side of the Jordan, and they fought with you. But I gave them into your hand, that you might possess their land, and I destroyed them from before you. 9Then Balak the son of Zippor, king of Moab, arose to make war against Israel, and sent and called Balaam the son of Beor to curse you. 10But I would not listen to Balaam; therefore he continued to bless you. So I delivered you out of his hand. 11Then you went over the Jordan and came to Jericho. And the men of Jericho fought against you—*also* the Amorites, the Perizzites, the Canaanites, the Hittites, the Girgashites, the Hivites, and the Jebusites. But I delivered them into your hand. 12I sent the hornet before you which drove them out from before you, *also* the two kings of the Amorites, *but* not with your sword or with your bow. 13I have given you a land for which you did not labor, and cities which you did not build, and you dwell in them; you eat of the vineyards and olive groves which you did not plant.'

14"Now therefore, fear the LORD, serve Him in sincerity and in truth, and put away the gods which your fathers served on the other side of the River and in Egypt. Serve the LORD! 15And if it seems evil to you to serve the LORD, choose for yourselves this day whom you will serve, whether the gods which your fathers served that *were* on the other side of the River, or the gods of the Amorites, in whose land you dwell. But as for me and my house, we will serve the LORD."

16So the people answered and said: "Far be it from us that we should forsake the LORD to serve other gods; 17for the LORD our God *is* He who brought us and our fathers up out of the land of Egypt, from the house of bondage, who did those great signs in our sight, and preserved us in all the way that we went and among all the people through whom we passed. 18And the LORD drove out from before us all the people, including the Amorites who dwelt in the land. We

also will serve the LORD, for He *is* our God."

19But Joshua said to the people, "You cannot serve the LORD, for He *is* a holy God. He *is* a jealous God; He will not forgive your transgressions nor your sins. 20If you forsake the LORD and serve foreign gods, then He will turn and do you harm and consume you, after He has done you good."

21And the people said to Joshua, "No, but we will serve the LORD!"

22So Joshua said to the people, "You *are* witnesses against yourselves that you have chosen the LORD for yourselves, to serve Him."

And they said, "*We are* witnesses!"

23"Now therefore," *he said*, "put away the foreign gods which *are* among you, and incline your heart to the LORD God of Israel."

24And the people said to Joshua, "The LORD our God we will serve, and His voice we will obey!"

25So Joshua made a covenant with the people that day, and made for them a statute and an ordinance in Shechem.

26Then Joshua wrote these words in the Book of the Law of God. And he took a large stone, and set it up there under the oak that *was* by the sanctuary of the LORD. 27And Joshua said to all the people, "Behold, this stone shall be a witness to us, for it has heard all the words of the LORD which He spoke to us. It shall therefore be a witness to you, lest you deny your God." 28So Joshua let the people depart, each to his own inheritance.

Death of Joshua and Eleazar

29Now it came to pass after these things that Joshua the son of Nun, the servant of the LORD, died, *being* one hundred and ten years old. 30And they buried him within the border of his inheritance at Timnath Serah, which *is* in the mountains of Ephraim, on the north side of Mount Gaash.

31Israel served the LORD all the days of Joshua, and all the days of the elders who outlived Joshua, who had known all the works of the LORD which He had done for Israel.

32The bones of Joseph, which the

children of Israel had brought up out of Egypt, they buried at Shechem, in the plot of ground which Jacob had bought from the sons of Hamor the father of Shechem for one hundred pieces of silver, and which had become an inheritance of the children of Joseph.

33And Eleazar the son of Aaron died. They buried him in a hill *belonging to* Phinehas his son, which was given to him in the mountains of Ephraim.

The Book of

JUDGES

The Continuing Conquest of Canaan

1 Now after the death of Joshua it came to pass that the children of Israel asked the LORD, saying, "Who shall be first to go up for us against the Canaanites to fight against them?"

2And the LORD said, "Judah shall go up. Indeed I have delivered the land into his hand."

3So Judah said to Simeon his brother, "Come up with me to my allotted territory, that we may fight against the Canaanites; and I will likewise go with you to your allotted territory." And Simeon went with him. 4Then Judah went up, and the LORD delivered the Canaanites and the Perizzites into their hand; and they killed ten thousand men at Bezek. 5And they found Adoni-Bezek in Bezek, and fought against him; and they defeated the Canaanites and the Perizzites. 6Then Adoni-Bezek fled, and they pursued him and caught him and cut off his thumbs and big toes. 7And Adoni-Bezek said, "Seventy kings with their thumbs and big toes cut off used to gather *scraps* under my table; as I have done, so God has repaid me." Then they brought him to Jerusalem, and there he died.

8Now the children of Judah fought against Jerusalem and took it; they struck it with the edge of the sword and set the city on fire. 9And afterward the children of Judah went down to fight against the Canaanites who dwelt in the mountains, in the South, and in the low-land. 10Then Judah went against the Canaanites who dwelt in Hebron. (Now the name of Hebron *was* formerly Kirjath Arba.) And they killed Sheshai, Ahiman, and Talmai.

11From there they went against the inhabitants of Debir. (The name of Debir *was* formerly Kirjath Sepher.)

12Then Caleb said, "Whoever attacks Kirjath Sepher and takes it, to him I will give my daughter Achsah as wife." 13And Othniel the son of Kenaz, Caleb's younger brother, took it; so he gave him his daughter Achsah as wife. 14Now it happened, when she came *to him,* that she urged him to ask her father for a field. And she dismounted from *her* donkey, and Caleb said to her, "What do you wish?" 15So she said to him, "Give me a blessing; since you have given me land in the South, give me also springs of water."

And Caleb gave her the upper springs and the lower springs.

16Now the children of the Kenite, Moses' father-in-law, went up from the City of Palms with the children of Judah into the Wilderness of Judah, which *lies* in the South *near* Arad; and they went and dwelt among the people. 17And Judah went with his brother Simeon, and they attacked the Canaanites who inhabited Zephath, and utterly destroyed it. So the name of the city was called Hormah. 18Also Judah took Gaza with its territory, Ashkelon with its territory, and Ekron with its territory. 19So the LORD was with Judah.

And they drove out the mountaineers, but they could not drive out the inhabitants of the lowland, because they had chariots of iron. 20And they gave Hebron to Caleb, as Moses had said. Then he expelled from there the three sons of Anak. 21But the children of Benjamin did not drive out the Jebusites who inhabited Jerusalem; so the Jebusites dwell with the children of Benjamin in Jeru salem to this day.

22And the house of Joseph also went up against Bethel, and the LORD was with them. 23So the house of Joseph sent men to spy out Bethel. (The name of the city was formerly Luz.) 24And when the spies saw a man coming out of the city, they said to him, "Please show us the entrance to the city, and we will show you mercy." 25So he showed them the entrance to the city, and they struck the city with the edge of the sword; but they let the man and all his family go. 26And the man went to the land of the Hittites, built a city, and called its name Luz, which is its name to this day.

Incomplete Conquest of the Land

27However, Manasseh did not drive out the inhabitants of Beth Shean and its villages, or Taanach and its villages, or the inhabitants of Dor and its villages, or the inhabitants of Ibleam and its villages, or the inhabitants of Megiddo and its villages; for the Canaanites were determined to dwell in that land. 28And it came to pass, when Israel was strong, that they put the Canaanites under tribute, but did not completely drive them out.

29Nor did Ephraim drive out the Canaanites who dwelt in Gezer; so the Canaanites dwelt in Gezer among them.

30Nor did Zebulun drive out the inhabitants of Kitron or the inhabitants of Nahalol; so the Canaanites dwelt among them, and were put under tribute.

31Nor did Asher drive out the inhabitants of Acco or the inhabitants of Sidon, or of Ahlab, Achzib, Helbah, Aphik, or Rehob. 32So the Asherites dwelt among the Canaanites, the inhab-

itants of the land; for they did not drive them out.

33Nor did Naphtali drive out the inhabitants of Beth Shemesh or the inhabitants of Beth Anath; but they dwelt among the Canaanites, the inhabitants of the land. Nevertheless the inhabitants of Beth Shemesh and Beth Anath were put under tribute to them.

34And the Amorites forced the children of Dan into the mountains, for they would not allow them to come down to the valley; 35and the Amorites were determined to dwell in Mount Heres, in Aijalon, and in Shaalbim; yet when the strength of the house of Joseph became greater, they were put under tribute.

36Now the boundary of the Amorites was from the Ascent of Akrabbim, from Sela, and upward.

Israel's Disobedience

2 Then the Angel of the LORD came up from Gilgal to Bochim, and said: "I led you up from Egypt and brought you to the land of which I swore to your fathers; and I said, 'I will never break My covenant with you. 2And you shall make no covenant with the inhabitants of this land; you shall tear down their altars.' But you have not obeyed My voice. Why have you done this? 3Therefore I also said, 'I will not drive them out before you; but they shall be thorns in your side, and their gods shall be a snare to you.'" 4So it was, when the Angel of the LORD spoke these words to all the children of Israel, that the people lifted up their voices and wept.

5Then they called the name of that place Bochim;a and they sacrificed there to the LORD. 6And when Joshua had dismissed the people, the children of Israel went each to his own inheritance to possess the land.

Death of Joshua

7So the people served the LORD all the days of Joshua, and all the days of the elders who outlived Joshua, who had seen all the great works of the LORD which He had done for Israel. 8Now Joshua the son of Nun, the servant of

a Literally Weeping

the LORD, died *when he was* one hundred and ten years old. 9And they buried him within the border of his inheritance at Timnath Heres, in the mountains of Ephraim, on the north side of Mount Gaash. 10When all that generation had been gathered to their fathers, another generation arose after them who did not know the LORD nor the work which He had done for Israel.

Israel's Unfaithfulness

11Then the children of Israel did evil in the sight of the LORD, and served the Baals; 12and they forsook the LORD God of their fathers, who had brought them out of the land of Egypt; and they followed other gods from *among* the gods of the people who *were* all around them, and they bowed down to them; and they provoked the LORD to anger. 13They forsook the LORD and served Baal and the Ashtoreths.[b] 14And the anger of the LORD was hot against Israel. So He delivered them into the hands of plunderers who despoiled them; and He sold them into the hands of their enemies all around, so that they could no longer stand before their enemies. 15Wherever they went out, the hand of the LORD was against them for calamity, as the LORD had said, and as the LORD had sworn to them. And they were greatly distressed.

16Nevertheless, the LORD raised up judges who delivered them out of the hand of those who plundered them. 17Yet they would not listen to their judges, but they played the harlot with other gods, and bowed down to them. They turned quickly from the way in which their fathers walked, in obeying the commandments of the LORD; they did not do so. 18And when the LORD raised up judges for them, the LORD was with the judge and delivered them out of the hand of their enemies all the days of the judge; for the LORD was moved to pity by their groaning because of those who oppressed them and harassed them. 19And it came to pass, when the judge was dead, that they reverted and behaved more corruptly than their fathers, by following other gods, to serve them and bow down to

them. They did not cease from their own doings nor from their stubborn way.

20Then the anger of the LORD was hot against Israel; and He said, "Because this nation has transgressed My covenant which I commanded their fathers, and has not heeded My voice, 21I also will no longer drive out before them any of the nations which Joshua left when he died, 22so that through them I may test Israel, whether they will keep the ways of the LORD, to walk in them as their fathers kept *them,* or not." 23Therefore the LORD left those nations, without driving them out immediately; nor did He deliver them into the hand of Joshua.

The Nations Remaining in the Land

3 Now these *are* the nations which the LORD left, that He might test Israel by them, *that is,* all who had not known any of the wars in Canaan 2(*this was* only so that the generations of the children of Israel might be taught to know war, at least those who had not formerly known it), 3*namely,* five lords of the Philistines, all the Canaanites, the Sidonians, and the Hivites who dwelt in Mount Lebanon, from Mount Baal Hermon to the entrance of Hamath. 4And they were *left, that He might* test Israel by them, to know whether they would obey the commandments of the LORD, which He had commanded their fathers by the hand of Moses.

5Thus the children of Israel dwelt among the Canaanites, the Hittites, the Amorites, the Perizzites, the Hivites, and the Jebusites. 6And they took their daughters to be their wives, and gave their daughters to their sons; and they served their gods.

Othniel

7So the children of Israel did evil in the sight of the LORD. They forgot the LORD their God, and served the Baals and Asherahs.[c] 8Therefore the anger of the LORD was hot against Israel, and He sold them into the hand of Cushan-Rishathaim king of Mesopotamia; and the children of Israel served Cushan-Rishathaim eight years. 9When the chil-

---

b Canaanite goddesses   c Name or symbol for Canaanite goddesses dren of Israel cried out to the LORD, the LORD raised up a deliverer for the children of Israel, who delivered them: Othniel the son of Kenaz, Caleb's younger brother. 10The Spirit of the LORD came upon him, and he judged Israel. He went out to war, and the LORD delivered Cushan-Rishathaim king of Mesopotamia into his hand; and his hand prevailed over Cushan-Rishathaim. 11So the land had rest for forty years. Then Othniel the son of Kenaz died.

Ehud

12And the children of Israel again did evil in the sight of the LORD. So the LORD strengthened Eglon king of Moab against Israel, because they had done evil in the sight of the LORD. 13Then he gathered to himself the people of Ammon and Amalek, went and defeated Israel, and took possession of the City of Palms. 14So the children of Israel served Eglon king of Moab eighteen years.

15But when the children of Israel cried out to the LORD, the LORD raised up a deliverer for them: Ehud the son of Gera, the Benjamite, a left-handed man. By him the children of Israel sent tribute to Eglon king of Moab. 16Now Ehud made himself a dagger (it was double-edged and a cubit in length) and fastened it under his clothes on his right thigh. 17So he brought the tribute to Eglon king of Moab. (Now Eglon *was* a very fat man.) 18And when he had finished presenting the tribute, he sent away the people who had carried the tribute. 19But he himself turned back from the stone images that *were* at Gilgal, and said, "I have a secret message for you, O king."

He said, "Keep silence!" And all who attended him went out from him.

20So Ehud came to him (now he was sitting upstairs in his cool private chamber). Then Ehud said, "I have a message from God for you." So he arose from *his* seat. 21Then Ehud reached with his left hand, took the dagger from his right thigh, and thrust it into his belly. 22Even the hilt went in after the blade, and the fat closed over the blade, for he did not draw the dagger out of his belly; and his entrails came out. 23Then Ehud went out through the porch and shut the doors of the upper room behind him and locked them.

24When he had gone out, *Eglon's* servants came to look, and *to their* surprise, the doors of the upper room were locked. So they said, "He is probably attending to his needs in the cool chamber." 25So they waited till they were embarrassed, and still he had not opened the doors of the upper room. Therefore they took the key and opened *them.* And there was their master, fallen dead on the floor.

26But Ehud had escaped while they delayed, and passed beyond the stone images and escaped to Seirah. 27And it happened, when he arrived, that he blew the trumpet in the mountains of Ephraim, and the children of Israel went down with him from the mountains; and he led them. 28Then he said to them, "Follow *me,* for the LORD has delivered your enemies the Moabites into your hand." So they went down after him, seized the fords of the Jordan leading to Moab, and did not allow anyone to cross over. 29And at that time they killed about ten thousand men of Moab, all stout men of valor; not a man escaped. 30So Moab was subdued that day under the hand of Israel. And the land had rest for eighty years.

Shamgar

31After him was Shamgar the son of Anath, who killed six hundred men of the Philistines with an ox goad; and he also delivered Israel.

Deborah

4 When Ehud was dead, the children of Israel again did evil in the sight of the LORD. 2So the LORD sold them into the hand of Jabin king of Canaan, who reigned in Hazor. The commander of his army *was* Sisera, who dwelt in Harosheth Hagoyim. 3And the children of Israel cried out to the LORD; for Jabin had nine hundred chariots of iron, and for twenty years he had harshly oppressed the children of Israel.

4Now Deborah, a prophetess, the wife of Lapidoth, was judging Israel at that time. 5And she would sit under the palm tree of Deborah between Ramah and Bethel in the mountains of Ephraim. And the children of Israel came up to her for judgment. 6Then she sent and called for Barak the son of Abinoam from Kedesh in Naphtali, and said to him, "Has not the LORD God of Israel commanded, 'Go and deploy *troops* at Mount Tabor; take with you ten thousand men of the sons of Naphtali and of the sons of Zebulun; 7and against you I will deploy Sisera, the commander of Jabin's army, with his chariots and his multitude at the River Kishon; and I will deliver him into your hand'?"

8And Barak said to her, "If you will go with me, then I will go; but if you will not go with me, I will not go!"

9So she said, "I will surely go with you; nevertheless there will be no glory for you in the journey you are taking, for the LORD will sell Sisera into the hand of a woman." Then Deborah arose and went with Barak to Kedesh. 10And Barak called Zebulun and Naphtali to Kedesh; he went up with ten thousand men under his command, and Deborah went up with him.

11Now Heber the Kenite, of the children of Hobab the father-in-law of Moses, had separated himself from the Kenites and pitched his tent near the terebinth tree at Zaanaim, which *is* beside Kedesh.

12And they reported to Sisera that Barak the son of Abinoam had gone up to Mount Tabor. 13So Sisera gathered together all his chariots, nine hundred chariots of iron, and all the people who *were* with him, from Harosheth Hagoyim to the River Kishon.

14Then Deborah said to Barak, "Up! For this *is* the day in which the LORD has delivered Sisera into your hand. Has not the LORD gone out before you?" So Barak went down from Mount Tabor with ten thousand men following him. 15And the LORD routed Sisera and all *his* chariots and all *his* army with the edge of the sword before Barak; and Sisera alighted from *his* chariot and fled away on foot. 16But Barak pursued the chariots and the army as far as Harosheth Hagoyim, and all the army of Sisera fell by the edge of the sword; not a man was left.

17However, Sisera had fled away on foot to the tent of Jael, the wife of Heber the Kenite; for *there was* peace between Jabin king of Hazor and the house of Heber the Kenite. 18And Jael went out to meet Sisera, and said to him, "Turn aside, my lord, turn aside to me; do not fear." And when he had turned aside with her into the tent, she covered him with a blanket.

19Then he said to her, "Please give me a little water to drink, for I am thirsty." So she opened a jug of milk, gave him a drink, and covered him. 20And he said to her, "Stand at the door of the tent, and if any man comes and inquires of you, and says, 'Is there any man here?' you shall say, 'No.'"

21Then Jael, Heber's wife, took a tent peg and took a hammer in her hand, and went softly to him and drove the peg into his temple, and it went down into the ground; for he was fast asleep and weary. So he died. 22And then, as Barak pursued Sisera, Jael came out to meet him, and said to him, "Come, I will show you the man whom you seek." And when he went into her *tent*, there lay Sisera, dead with the peg in his temple.

23So on that day God subdued Jabin king of Canaan in the presence of the children of Israel. 24And the hand of the children of Israel grew stronger and stronger against Jabin king of Canaan, until they had destroyed Jabin king of Canaan.

The Song of Deborah

5 Then Deborah and Barak the son of Abinoam sang on that day, saying:
2 "When leaders lead in Israel,
    When the people willingly offer
       themselves,
    Bless the LORD!

3 "Hear, O kings! Give ear, O princes!
    I, *even* I, will sing to the LORD;
    I will sing praise to the LORD God
       of Israel.

4 "LORD, when You went out from
       Seir,
    When You marched from the field
       of Edom,
    The earth trembled and the
       heavens poured,
    The clouds also poured water;

5   The mountains gushed before the
     Lord,
    This Sinai, before the Lord God of
    Israel.

6 "In the days of Shamgar, son of
     Anath,
    In the days of Jael,
    The highways were deserted,
    And the travelers walked along the
     byways.
7 Village life ceased, it ceased in
     Israel,
    Until I, Deborah, arose,
    Arose a mother in Israel.
8 They chose new gods;
    Then *there was* war in the gates;
    Not a shield or spear was seen
     among forty thousand in Israel.
9 My heart *is* with the rulers of Israel
    Who offered themselves willingly
     with the people.
    Bless the Lord!

10 "Speak, you who ride on white
     donkeys,
    Who sit in judges' attire,
    And who walk along the road.
11 Far from the noise of the archers,
     among the watering places,
    There they shall recount the
     righteous acts of the Lord,
    The righteous acts *for* His villagers
     in Israel;
    Then the people of the Lord shall
     go down to the gates.

12 "Awake, awake, Deborah!
    Awake, awake, sing a song!
    Arise, Barak, and lead your
     captives away,
    O son of Abinoam!

13 "Then the survivors came down, the
     people against the nobles;
    The Lord came down for me
     against the mighty.
14 From Ephraim *were* those whose
     roots were in Amalek.
    After you, Benjamin, with your
     peoples,
    From Machir rulers came down,
    And from Zebulun those who bear
     the recruiter's staff.
15 And the princes of Issachar *were*
    with Deborah;

As Issachar, so *was* Barak
Sent into the valley under his
  command;
Among the divisions of Reuben
There were great resolves of heart.
16 Why did you sit among the
     sheepfolds,
    To hear the pipings for the flocks?
    The divisions of Reuben have great
     searchings of heart.
17 Gilead stayed beyond the Jordan,
    And why did Dan remain on ships?
    Asher continued at the seashore,
    And stayed by his inlets.
18 Zebulun *is* a people *who*
     jeopardized their lives to the
     point of death,
    Naphtali also, on the heights of the
     battlefield.

19 "The kings came *and* fought,
    Then the kings of Canaan fought
    In Taanach, by the waters of
     Megiddo;
    They took no spoils of silver.
20 They fought from the heavens;
    The stars from their courses fought
     against Sisera.
21 The torrent of Kishon swept them
     away,
    That ancient torrent, the torrent of
     Kishon.
    O my soul, march on in strength!
22 Then the horses' hooves pounded,
    The galloping, galloping of his
     steeds.
23 'Curse Meroz,' said the angel[d] of the
     Lord,
    'Curse its inhabitants bitterly,
    Because they did not come to the
     help of the Lord,
    To the help of the Lord against the
     mighty.'

24 "Most blessed among women is Jael,
    The wife of Heber the Kenite;
    Blessed is she among women in
     tents.
25 He asked for water, she gave milk;
    She brought out cream in a lordly
     bowl.
26 She stretched her hand to the tent
     peg,
    Her right hand to the workmen's
     hammer;

d Or *Angel*

She pounded Sisera, she pierced
   his head,
She split and struck through his
   temple.
27 At her feet he sank, he fell, he lay
       still;
    At her feet he sank, he fell;
    Where he sank, there he fell dead.

28 "The mother of Sisera looked
       through the window,
    And cried out through the lattice,
    'Why is his chariot *so* long in
       coming?
    Why tarries the clatter of his
       chariots?'
29 Her wisest ladies answered her,
    Yes, she answered herself,
30 'Are they not finding and dividing
       the spoil:
    To every man a girl *or* two;
    For Sisera, plunder of dyed
       garments,
    Plunder of garments embroidered
       and dyed,
    Two pieces of dyed embroidery for
       the neck of the looter?'

31 "Thus let all Your enemies perish,
       O LORD!
    But *let* those who love Him *be* like
       the sun
    When it comes out in full strength."
So the land had rest for forty years.

Midianites Oppress Israel

6 Then the children of Israel did evil
in the sight of the LORD. So the LORD
delivered them into the hand of Midian
for seven years, 2and the hand of Midian prevailed against Israel. Because of
the Midianites, the children of Israel
made for themselves the dens, the
caves, and the strongholds which *are*
in the mountains. 3So it was, whenever
Israel had sown, Midianites would
come up; also Amalekites and the people of the East would come up against
them. 4Then they would encamp
against them and destroy the produce
of the earth as far as Gaza, and leave
no sustenance for Israel, neither sheep
nor ox nor donkey. 5For they would
come up with their livestock and their
tents, coming in as numerous as locusts; both they and their camels were
without number; and they would enter
the land to destroy it. 6So Israel was

greatly impoverished because of the
Midianites, and the children of Israel
cried out to the LORD.

7And it came to pass, when the children of Israel cried out to the LORD because of the Midianites, 8that the LORD
sent a prophet to the children of Israel,
who said to them, "Thus says the LORD
God of Israel: 'I brought you up from
Egypt and brought you out of the house
of bondage; 9and I delivered you out
of the hand of the Egyptians and out of
the hand of all who oppressed you,
and drove them out before you and
gave you their land. 10Also I said to you,
"I *am* the LORD your God; do not fear
the gods of the Amorites, in whose land
you dwell." But you have not obeyed
My voice.' "

Gideon

11Now the Angel of the LORD came
and sat under the terebinth tree which
was in Ophrah, which *belonged* to
Joash the Abiezrite, while his son Gideon threshed wheat in the winepress,
in order to hide *it* from the Midianites.
12And the Angel of the LORD appeared
to him, and said to him, "The LORD *is*
with you, you mighty man of valor!"

13Gideon said to Him, "O my lord, if
the LORD is with us, why then has all
this happened to us? And where *are* all
His miracles which our fathers told us
about, saying, 'Did not the LORD bring
us up from Egypt?' But now the LORD
has forsaken us and delivered us into
the hands of the Midianites."

14Then the LORD turned to him and
said, "Go in this might of yours, and
you shall save Israel from the hand of
the Midianites. Have I not sent you?"

15So he said to Him, "O my Lord, how
can I save Israel? Indeed my clan *is* the
weakest in Manasseh, and I *am* the
least in my father's house."

16And the LORD said to him, "Surely
I will be with you, and you shall defeat
the Midianites as one man."

17Then he said to Him, "If now I have
found favor in Your sight, then show
me a sign that it is You who talk with
me. 18Do not depart from here, I pray,
until I come to You and bring out my
offering and set *it* before You."

And He said, "I will wait until you
come back."

19So Gideon went in and prepared a young goat, and unleavened bread from an ephah of flour. The meat he put in a basket, and he put the broth in a pot; and he brought *them* out to Him under the terebinth tree and presented *them*. **20**The Angel of God said to him, "Take the meat and the unleavened bread and lay *them* on this rock, and pour out the broth." And he did so.

21Then the Angel of the LORD put out the end of the staff that *was* in His hand, and touched the meat and the unleavened bread; and fire rose out of the rock and consumed the meat and the unleavened bread. And the Angel of the LORD departed out of his sight.

22Now Gideon perceived that He *was* the Angel of the LORD. So Gideon said, "Alas, O Lord GOD! For I have seen the Angel of the LORD face to face."

23Then the LORD said to him, "Peace *be* with you; do not fear, you shall not die." **24**So Gideon built an altar there to the LORD, and called it The-LORD-*Is*-Peace. To this day it *is* still in Ophrah of the Abiezrites.

25Now it came to pass the same night that the LORD said to him, "Take your father's young bull, the second bull of seven years old, and tear down the altar of Baal that your father has, and cut down the wooden image that *is* beside it; **26**and build an altar to the LORD your God on top of this rock in the proper arrangement, and take the second bull and offer a burnt sacrifice with the wood of the image which you shall cut down." **27**So Gideon took ten men from among his servants and did as the LORD had said to him. But because he feared his father's household and the men of the city too much to do *it* by day, he did *it* by night.

Gideon Destroys the Altar of Baal

28And when the men of the city arose early in the morning, there was the altar of Baal, torn down; and the wooden image that *was* beside it was cut down, and the second bull was being offered on the altar *which had been* built. **29**So they said to one another, "Who has done this thing?" And when they had inquired and asked, they said,

"Gideon the son of Joash has done this thing." **30**Then the men of the city said to Joash, "Bring out your son, that he may die, because he has torn down the altar of Baal, and because he has cut down the wooden image that *was* beside it."

31But Joash said to all who stood against him, "Would you plead for Baal? Would you save him? Let the one who would plead for him be put to death by morning! If he *is* a god, let him plead for himself, because his altar has been torn down!" **32**Therefore on that day he called him Jerubbaal,[e] saying, "Let Baal plead against him, because he has torn down his altar."

33Then all the Midianites and Amalekites, the people of the East, gathered together; and they crossed over and encamped in the Valley of Jezreel. **34**But the Spirit of the LORD came upon Gideon; then he blew the trumpet, and the Abiezrites gathered behind him. **35**And he sent messengers throughout all Manasseh, who also gathered behind him. He also sent messengers to Asher, Zebulun, and Naphtali; and they came up to meet them.

The Sign of the Fleece

36So Gideon said to God, "If You will save Israel by my hand as You have said—**37**look, I shall put a fleece of wool on the threshing floor; if there is dew on the fleece only, and *it is* dry on all the ground, then I shall know that You will save Israel by my hand, as You have said." **38**And it was so. When he rose early the next morning and squeezed the fleece together, he wrung the dew out of the fleece, a bowlful of water. **39**Then Gideon said to God, "Do not be angry with me, but let me speak just once more: Let me test, I pray, just once more with the fleece; let it now be dry only on the fleece, but on all the ground let there be dew." **40**And God did so that night. It was dry on the fleece only, but there was dew on all the ground.

Gideon's Valiant Three Hundred

7 Then Jerubbaal (that *is*, Gideon) and all the people who *were* with him

---

e Literally *Let Baal Plead*

rose early and encamped beside the well of Harod, so that the camp of the Midianites was on the north side of them by the hill of Moreh in the valley.

2And the LORD said to Gideon, "The people who *are* with you *are* too many for Me to give the Midianites into their hands, lest Israel claim glory for itself against Me, saying, 'My own hand has saved me.' 3Now therefore, proclaim in the hearing of the people, saying, 'Whoever *is* fearful and afraid, let him turn and depart at once from Mount Gilead.' " And twenty-two thousand of the people returned, and ten thousand remained.

4But the LORD said to Gideon, "The people *are* still *too* many; bring them down to the water, and I will test them for you there. Then it will be, *that* of whom I say to you, 'This one shall go with you,' the same shall go with you; and of whomever I say to you, 'This one shall not go with you,' the same shall not go." 5So he brought the people down to the water. And the LORD said to Gideon, "Everyone who laps from the water with his tongue, as a dog laps, you shall set apart by himself; likewise everyone who gets down on his knees to drink." 6And the number of those who lapped, *putting* their hand to their mouth, was three hundred men; but all the rest of the people got down on their knees to drink water. 7Then the LORD said to Gideon, "By the three hundred men who lapped I will save you, and deliver the Midianites into your hand. Let all the *other* people go, every man to his place." 8So t he people took provisions and their trumpets in their hands. And he sent away all *the rest of* Israel, every man to his tent, and retained those three hundred men. Now the camp of Midian was below him in the valley.

9It happened on the same night that the LORD said to him, "Arise, go down against the camp, for I have delivered it into your hand. 10But if you are afraid to go down, go down to the camp with Purah your servant, 11and you shall hear what they say; and afterward your hands shall be strengthened to go down against the camp." Then he went down with Purah his servant to the outpost of the armed men who *were* in the camp. 12Now the Midianites and Amalekites, all the people of the East, were lying in the valley as numerous as locusts; and their camels *were* without number, as the sand by the seashore in multitude.

13And when Gideon had come, there was a man telling a dream to his companion. He said, "I have had a dream: *To my* surprise, a loaf of barley bread tumbled into the camp of Midian; it came to a tent and struck it so that it fell and overturned, and the tent collapsed."

14Then his companion answered and said, "This *is* nothing else but the sword of Gideon the son of Joash, a man of Israel! Into his hand God has delivered Midian and the whole camp."

15And so it was, when Gideon heard the telling of the dream and its interpretation, that he worshiped. He returned to the camp of Israel, and said, "Arise, for the LORD has delivered the camp of Midian into your hand." 16Then he divided the three hundred men *into* three companies, and he put a trumpet into every man's hand, with empty pitchers, and torches inside the pitchers. 17And he said to them, "Look at me and do likewise; watch, and when I come to the edge of the camp you shall do as I do: 18When I blow the trumpet, I and all who *are* with me, then you also blow the trumpets on every side of the whole camp, and say, '*The sword of* the LORD and of Gideon!' "

19So Gideon and the hundred men who *were* with him came to the outpost of the camp at the beginning of the middle watch, just as they had posted the watch; and they blew the trumpets and broke the pitchers that *were* in their hands. 20Then the three companies blew the trumpets and broke the pitchers—they held the torches in their left hands and the trumpets in their right hands for blowing—and they cried, "The sword of the LORD and of Gideon!" 21And every man stood in his place all around the camp; and the whole army ran and cried out and fled. 22When the three hundred blew the trumpets, the LORD set every man's sword against his companion throughout the whole camp; and the army fled to Beth Acacia, toward Zererah, as far as the border of Abel Meholah, by Tabbath.

23And the men of Israel gathered together from Naphtali, Asher, and all Manasseh, and pursued the Midianites. 24Then Gideon sent messengers throughout all the mountains of Ephraim, saying, "Come down against the Midianites, and seize from them the watering places as far as Beth Barah and the Jordan." Then all the men of Ephraim gathered together and seized the watering places as far as Beth Barah and the Jordan. 25And they captured two princes of the Midianites, Oreb and Zeeb. They killed Oreb at the rock of Oreb, and Zeeb they killed at the winepress of Zeeb. They pursued Midian and brought the heads of Oreb and Zeeb to Gideon on the other side of the Jordan.

Gideon Subdues the Midianites

8 Now the men of Ephraim said to him, "Why have you done this to us by not calling us when you went to fight with the Midianites?" And they reprimanded him sharply.

2So he said to them, "What have I done now in comparison with you? *Is* not the gleaning *of the grapes* of Ephraim better than the vintage of Abiezer? 3God has delivered into your hands the princes of Midian, Oreb and Zeeb. And what was I able to do in comparison with you?" Then their anger toward him subsided when he said that.

4When Gideon came to the Jordan, he and the three hundred men who *were* with him crossed over, exhausted but still in pursuit. 5Then he said to the men of Succoth, "Please give loaves of bread to the people who follow me, for they are exhausted, and I am pursuing Zebah and Zalmunna, kings of Midian."

6And the leaders of Succoth said, "*Are* the hands of Zebah and Zalmunna now in your hand, that we should give bread to your army?"

7So Gideon said, "For this cause, when the LORD has delivered Zebah and Zalmunna into my hand, then I will tear your flesh with the thorns of the wilderness and with briers!" 8Then he went up from there to Penuel and spoke to them in the same way. And the men of Penuel answered him as the men of Succoth had answered. 9So he also spoke to the men of Penuel, saying, "When I come back in peace, I will tear down this tower!"

10Now Zebah and Zalmunna *were* at Karkor, and their armies with them, about fifteen thousand, all who were left of all the army of the people of the East; for one hundred and twenty thousand men who drew the sword had fallen. 11Then Gideon went up by the road of those who dwell in tents on the east of Nobah and Jogbehah; and he attacked the army while the camp felt secure. 12When Zebah and Zalmunna fled, he pursued them; and he took the two kings of Midian, Zebah and Zalmunna, and routed the whole army.

13Then Gideon the son of Joash returned from battle, from the Ascent of Heres. 14And he caught a young man of the men of Succoth and interrogated him; and he wrote down for him the leaders of Succoth and its elders, seventy-seven men. 15Then he came to the men of Succoth and said, "Here are Zebah and Zalmunna, about whom you ridiculed me, saying, '*Are* the hands of Zebah and Zalmunna now in your hand, that we should give bread to your weary men?' " 16And he took the elders of the city, and thorns of the wilderness and briers, and with them he taught the men of Succoth. 17Then he tore down the tower of Penuel and killed the men of the city.

18And he said to Zebah and Zalmunna, "What kind of men *were they* whom you killed at Tabor?"

So they answered, "As you *are*, so *were* they; each one resembled the son of a king."

19Then he said, "They *were* my brothers, the sons of my mother. *As* the LORD lives, if you had let them live, I would not kill you." 20And he said to Jether his firstborn, "Rise, kill them!" But the youth would not draw his sword; for he was afraid, because he *was* still a youth.

21So Zebah and Zalmunna said, "Rise yourself, and kill us; for as a man *is, so is* his strength." So Gideon arose and killed Zebah and Zalmunna, and took the crescent ornaments that *were* on their camels' necks.

Gideon's Ephod

22Then the men of Israel said to Gideon, "Rule over us, both you and your son, and your grandson also; for you have delivered us from the hand of Midian."

23But Gideon said to them, "I will not rule over you, nor shall my son rule over you; the LORD shall rule over you." 24Then Gideon said to them, "I would like to make a request of you, that each of you would give me the earrings from his plunder." For they had golden earrings, because they *were* Ishmaelites. 25So they answered, "We will gladly give *them*." And they spread out a garment, and each man threw into it the earrings from his plunder. 26Now the weight of the gold earrings that he requested was one thousand seven hundred *shekels* of gold, besides the crescent ornaments, pendants, and purple robes which *were* on the kings of Midian, and besides the chains that *were* around their camels' necks. 27Then Gideon made it into an ephod and set it up in his city, Ophrah. And all Israel played the harlot with it there. It became a snare to Gideon and to his house.

28Thus Midian was subdued before the children of Israel, so that they lifted their heads no more. And the country was quiet for forty years in the days of Gideon.

Death of Gideon

29Then Jerubbaal the son of Joash went and dwelt in his own house. 30Gideon had seventy sons who were his own offspring, for he had many wives. 31And his concubine who *was* in Shechem also bore him a son, whose name he called Abimelech. 32Now Gideon the son of Joash died at a good old age, and was buried in the tomb of Joash his father, in Ophrah of the Abiezrites.

33So it was, as soon as Gideon was dead, that the children of Israel again played the harlot with the Baals, and made Baal-Berith their god. 34Thus the children of Israel did not remember the LORD their God, who had delivered them from the hands of all their enemies on every side; 35nor did they show kindness to the house of Jerubbaal (Gideon) in accordance with the good he had done for Israel.

Abimelech's Conspiracy

9 Then Abimelech the son of Jerubbaal went to Shechem, to his mother's brothers, and spoke with them and with all the family of the house of his mother's father, saying, 2"Please speak in the hearing of all the men of Shechem: 'Which is better for you, that all seventy of the sons of Jerubbaal reign over you, or that one reign over you?' Remember that I *am* your own flesh and bone."

3And his mother's brothers spoke all these words concerning him in the hearing of all the men of Shechem; and their heart was inclined to follow Abimelech, for they said, "He is our brother." 4So they gave him seventy *shekels* of silver from the temple of Baal-Berith, with which Abimelech hired worthless and reckless men; and they followed him. 5Then he went to his father's house at Ophrah and killed his brothers, the seventy sons of Jerubbaal, on one stone. But Jotham the youngest son of Jerubbaal was left, because he hid himself. 6And all the men of Shechem gathered together, all of Beth Millo, and they went and made Abimelech king beside the terebinth tree at the pillar that *was* in Shechem.

The Parable of the Trees

7Now when they told Jotham, he went and stood on top of Mount Gerizim, and lifted his voice and cried out. And he said to them:

"Listen to me, you men of Shechem,
That God may listen to you!

8 "The trees once went forth to anoint
a king over them.
And they said to the olive tree,
'Reign over us!'
9 But the olive tree said to them,
'Should I cease giving my oil,
With which they honor God
and men,
And go to sway over trees?'

10 "Then the trees said to the fig tree,
'You come *and* reign over us!'
11 But the fig tree said to them,

'Should I cease my sweetness and
    my good fruit,
And go to sway over trees?'

12 "Then the trees said to the vine,
    'You come *and* reign over us!'
13 But the vine said to them,
    'Should I cease my new wine,
    Which cheers *both* God and men,
    And go to sway over trees?'

14 "Then all the trees said to the
    bramble,
    'You come *and* reign over us!'
15 And the bramble said to the trees,
    'If in truth you anoint me as king
        over you,
    Then come *and* take shelter in my
        shade;
    But if not, let fire come out of the
        bramble
    And devour the cedars of Lebanon!'

16"Now therefore, if you have acted
in truth and sincerity in making Abimelech king, and if you have dealt well
with Jerubbaal and his house, and have
done to him as he deserves—17for my
father fought for you, risked his life,
and delivered you out of the hand of
Midian; 18but you have risen up against
my father's house this day, and killed
his seventy sons on one stone, and
made Abimelech, the son of his female
servant, king over the men of Shechem,
because he is your brother—19if then
you have acted in truth and sincerity
with Jerubbaal and with his house this
day, *then* rejoice in Abimelech, and let
him also rejoice in you. 20But if not, let
fire come from Abimelech and devour
the men of Shechem and Beth Millo;
and let fire come from the men of Shechem and from Beth Millo and devour
Abimelech!" 21And Jotham ran away
and fled; and he went to Beer and dwelt
there, for fear of Abimelech his brother.

Downfall of Abimelech

22After Abimelech had reigned over
Israel three years, 23God sent a spirit
of ill will between Abimelech and the
men of Shechem; and the men of Shechem dealt treacherously with Abimelech, 24that the crime *done* to the seventy sons of Jerubbaal might be settled
and their blood be laid on Abimelech
their brother, who killed them, and on

the men of Shechem, who aided him in
the killing of his brothers. 25And the
men of Shechem set men in ambush
against him on the tops of the mountains, and they robbed all who passed
by them along that way; and it was told
Abimelech.

26Now Gaal the son of Ebed came
with his brothers and went over to Shechem; and the men of Shechem put
their confidence in him. 27So they went
out into the fields, and gathered *grapes*
from their vineyards and trod *them*,
and made merry. And they went into
the house of their god, and ate and
drank, and cursed Abimelech. 28Then
Gaal the son of Ebed said, "Who *is*
Abimelech, and who *is* Shechem, that
we should serve him? *Is he* not the son
of Jerubbaal, and *is not* Zebul his officer? Serve the men of Hamor the father of Shechem; but why should we
serve him? 29If only this people were under my authority! Then I would remove
Abimelech." So he said to Abimelech,
"Increase your army and come out!"

30When Zebul, the ruler of the city,
heard the words of Gaal the son of
Ebed, his anger was aroused. 31And he
sent messengers to Abimelech secretly,
saying, "Take note! Gaal the son of
Ebed and his brothers have come to
Shechem; and here they are, fortifying
the city against you. 32Now therefore,
get up by night, you and the people who
are with you, and lie in wait in the field.
33And it shall be, as soon as the sun is
up in the morning, *that* you shall rise
early and rush upon the city; and *when*
he and the people who are with him
come out against you, you may then do
to them as you find opportunity."

34So Abimelech and all the people
who *were* with him rose by night, and
lay in wait against Shechem in four
companies. 35When Gaal the son of
Ebed went out and stood in the entrance to the city gate, Abimelech and
the people who *were* with him rose
from lying in wait. 36And when Gaal
saw the people, he said to Zebul, "Look,
people are coming down from the tops
of the mountains!"

But Zebul said to him, "You see the
shadows of the mountains as *if they
were* men."

37So Gaal spoke again and said, "See,

people are coming down from the center of the land, and another company is coming from the Diviners' Terebinth Tree."

38Then Zebul said to him, "Where indeed is your mouth now, with which you said, 'Who is Abimelech, that we should serve him?' Are not these the people whom you despised? Go out, if you will, and fight with them now."

39So Gaal went out, leading the men of Shechem, and fought with Abimelech. 40And Abimelech chased him, and he fled from him; and many fell wounded, to the very entrance of the gate. 41Then Abimelech dwelt at Arumah, and Zebul drove out Gaal and his brothers, so that they would not dwell in Shechem.

42And it came about on the next day that the people went out into the field, and they told Abimelech. 43So he took his people, divided them into three companies, and lay in wait in the field. And he looked, and there were the people, coming out of the city; and he rose against them and attacked them. 44Then Abimelech and the company that was with him rushed forward and stood at the entrance of the gate of the city; and the other two companies rushed upon all who were in the fields and killed them. 45So Abimelech fought against the city all that day; he took the city and killed the people who were in it; and he demolished the city and sowed it with salt.

46Now when all the men of the tower of Shechem had heard that, they entered the stronghold of the temple of the god Berith. 47And it was told Abimelech that all the men of the tower of Shechem were gathered together. 48Then Abimelech went up to Mount Zalmon, he and all the people who were with him. And Abimelech took an ax in his hand and cut down a bough from the trees, and took it and laid it on his shoulder; then he said to the people who were with him, "What you have seen me do, make haste and do as I have done." 49So each of the people likewise cut down his own bough and followed Abimelech, put them against the stronghold, and

set the stronghold on fire above them, so that all the people of the tower of Shechem died, about a thousand men and women.

50Then Abimelech went to Thebez, and he encamped against Thebez and took it. 51But there was a strong tower in the city, and all the men and women—all the people of the city—fled there and shut themselves in; then they went up to the top of the tower. 52So Abimelech came as far as the tower and fought against it; and he drew near the door of the tower to burn it with fire. 53But a certain woman dropped an upper millstone on Abimelech's head and crushed his skull. 54Then he called quickly to the young man, his armorbearer, and said to him, "Draw your sword and kill me, lest men say of me, 'A woman killed him.'" So his young man thrust him through, and he died. 55And when the men of Israel saw that Abimelech was dead, they departed, every man to his place.

56Thus God repaid the wickedness of Abimelech, which he had done to his father by killing his seventy brothers. 57And all the evil of the men of Shechem God returned on their own heads, and on them came the curse of Jotham the son of Jerubbaal.

Tola

10 After Abimelech there arose to save Israel Tola the son of Puah, the son of Dodo, a man of Issachar; and he dwelt in Shamir in the mountains of Ephraim. 2He judged Israel twenty-three years; and he died and was buried in Shamir.

Jair

3After him arose Jair, a Gileadite; and he judged Israel twenty-two years. 4Now he had thirty sons who rode on thirty donkeys; they also had thirty towns, which are called "Havoth Jair"*f* to this day, which are in the land of Gilead. 5And Jair died and was buried in Camon.

Israel Oppressed Again

6Then the children of Israel again did evil in the sight of the LORD, and served

---

f Literally Towns of Jair (compare Numbers 32.41 and Deuteronomy 3.14) the Baals and the Ashtoreths, the gods of Syria, the gods of Sidon, the gods of Moab, the gods of the people of Ammon, and the gods of the Philistines; and they forsook the LORD and did not serve Him. 7So the anger of the LORD was hot against Israel; and He sold them into the hands of the Philistines and into the hands of the people of Ammon. 8From that year they harassed and oppressed the children of Israel for eighteen years—all the children of Israel who *were* on the other side of the Jordan in the land of the Amorites, in Gilead. 9Moreover the people of Ammon crossed over the Jordan to fight against Judah also, against Benjamin, and against the house of Ephraim, so that Israel was severely distressed.

10And the children of Israel cried out to the LORD, saying, "We have sinned against You, because we have both forsaken our God and served the Baals!"

11So the LORD said to the children of Israel, "*Did I* not *deliver you* from the Egyptians and from the Amorites and from the people of Ammon and from the Philistines? 12Also the Sidonians and Amalekites and Maonites oppressed you; and you cried out to Me, and I delivered you from their hand. 13Yet you have forsaken Me and served other gods. Therefore I will deliver you no more. 14Go and cry out to the gods which you have chosen; let them deliver you in your time of distress."

15And the children of Israel said to the LORD, "We have sinned! Do to us whatever seems best to You; only deliver us this day, we pray." 16So they put away the foreign gods from among them and served the LORD. And His soul could no longer endure the misery of Israel.

17Then the people of Ammon gathered together and encamped in Gilead. And the children of Israel assembled together and encamped in Mizpah. 18And the people, the leaders of Gilead, said to one another, "Who *is* the man who will begin the fight against the people of Ammon? He shall be head over all the inhabitants of Gilead."

Jephthah

11 Now Jephthah the Gileadite was a mighty man of valor, but he *was* the son of a harlot; and Gilead begot Jephthah. 2Gilead's wife bore sons; and when his wife's sons grew up, they drove Jephthah out, and said to him, "You shall have no inheritance in our father's house, for you *are* the son of another woman." 3Then Jephthah fled from his brothers and dwelt in the land of Tob; and worthless men banded together with Jephthah and went out *raiding* with him.

4It came to pass after a time that the people of Ammon made war against Israel. 5And so it was, when the people of Ammon made war against Israel, that the elders of Gilead went to get Jephthah from the land of Tob. 6Then they said to Jephthah, "Come and be our commander, that we may fight against the people of Ammon."

7So Jephthah said to the elders of Gilead, "Did you not hate me, and expel me from my father's house? Why have you come to me now when you are in distress?"

8And the elders of Gilead said to Jephthah, "That is why we have turned again to you now, that you may go with us and fight against the people of Ammon, and be our head over all the inhabitants of Gilead."

9So Jephthah said to the elders of Gilead, "If you take me back home to fight against the people of Ammon, and the LORD delivers them to me, shall I be your head?"

10And the elders of Gilead said to Jephthah, "The LORD will be a witness between us, if we do not do according to your words." 11Then Jephthah went with the elders of Gilead, and the people made him head and commander over them; and Jephthah spoke all his words before the LORD in Mizpah.

12Now Jephthah sent messengers to the king of the people of Ammon, saying, "What do you have against me, that you have come to fight against me in my land?"

13And the king of the people of Ammon answered the messengers of Jephthah, "Because Israel took away my land when they came up out of Egypt, from the Arnon as far as the Jabbok, and to the Jordan. Now therefore, restore those *lands* peaceably."

14So Jephthah again sent messengers to the king of the people of Ammon, 15and said to him, "Thus says Jephthah: 'Israel did not take away the land of Moab, nor the land of the people of Ammon; 16for when Israel came up from Egypt, they walked through the wilderness as far as the Red Sea and came to Kadesh. 17Then Israel sent messengers to the king of Edom, saying, "Please let me pass through your land." But the king of Edom would not heed. And in like manner they sent to the king of Moab, but he would not *consent*. So Israel remained in Kadesh. 18And they went along through the wilderness and bypassed the land of Edom and the land of Moab, came to the east side of the land of Moab, and encamped on the other side of the Arnon. But they did not enter the border of Moab, for the Arnon *was* the border of Moab. 19Then Israel sent messengers to Sihon king of the Amorites, king of Heshbon; and Israel said to him, "Please let us pass through your land into our place." 20But Sihon did not trust Israel to pass through his territory. So Sihon gathered all his people together, encamped in Jahaz, and fought against Israel. 21And the LORD God of Israel delivered Sihon and all his people into the hand of Israel, and they defeated them. Thus Israel gained possession of all the land of the Amorites, who inhabited that country. 22They took possession of all the territory of the Amorites, from the Arnon to the Jabbok and from the wilderness to the Jordan.

23'And now the LORD God of Israel has dispossessed the Amorites from before His people Israel; should you then possess it? 24Will you not possess whatever Chemosh your god gives you to possess? So whatever the LORD our God takes possession of before us, we will possess. 25And now, *are* you any better than Balak the son of Zippor, king of Moab? Did he ever strive against Israel? Did he ever fight against them? 26While Israel dwelt in Heshbon and its villages, in Aroer and its villages, and in all the cities along the banks of the Arnon, for three hundred years, why did you not recover *them* within that time? 27Therefore I have not sinned against you, but you wronged me by fighting against me. May the LORD, the Judge, render judgment this day between the children of Israel and the people of Ammon.'" 28However, the king of the people of Ammon did not heed the words which Jephthah sent him.

Jephthah's Vow and Victory

29Then the Spirit of the LORD came upon Jephthah, and he passed through Gilead and Manasseh, and passed through Mizpah of Gilead; and from Mizpah of Gilead he advanced *toward* the people of Ammon. 30And Jephthah made a vow to the LORD, and said, "If You will indeed deliver the people of Ammon into my hands, 31then it will be that whatever comes out of the doors of my house to meet me, when I return in peace from the people of Ammon, shall surely be the LORD's, and I will offer it up as a burnt offering."

32So Jephthah advanced toward the people of Ammon to fight against them, and the LORD delivered them into his hands. 33And he defeated them from Aroer as far as Minnith—twenty cities—and to Abel Keramim, with a very great slaughter. Thus the people of Ammon were subdued before the children of Israel.

Jephthah's Daughter

34When Jephthah came to his house at Mizpah, there was his daughter, coming out to meet him with timbrels and dancing; and she *was his* only child. Besides her he had neither son nor daughter. 35And it came to pass, when he saw her, that he tore his clothes, and said, "Alas, my daughter! You have brought me very low! You are among those who trouble me! For I have given my word to the LORD, and I cannot go back on it."

36So she said to him, "My father, *if* you have given your word to the LORD, do to me according to what has gone out of your mouth, because the LORD has avenged you of your enemies, the people of Ammon." 37Then she said to her father, "Let this thing be done for me: let me alone for two months, that I may go and wander on the mountains and bewail my virginity, my friends and I."

38So he said, "Go." And he sent her away *for* two months; and she went with her friends, and bewailed her virginity on the mountains. 39And it was so at the end of two months that she returned to her father, and he carried out his vow with her which he had vowed. She knew no man.

And it became a custom in Israel 40*that* the daughters of Israel went four days each year to lament the daughter of Jephthah the Gileadite.

Jephthah's Conflict with Ephraim

12 Then the men of Ephraim gathered together, crossed over toward Zaphon, and said to Jephthah, "Why did you cross over to fight against the people of Ammon, and did not call us to go with you? We will burn your house down on you with fire!"

2And Jephthah said to them, "My people and I were in a great struggle with the people of Ammon; and when I called you, you did not deliver me out of their hands. 3So when I saw that you would not deliver *me,* I took my life in my hands and crossed over against the people of Ammon; and the LORD delivered them into my hand. Why then have you come up to me this day to fight against me?" 4Now Jephthah gathered together all the men of Gilead and fought against Ephraim. And the men of Gilead defeated Ephraim, because they said, "You Gileadites *are* fugitives of Ephraim among the Ephraimites *and* among the Manassites." 5The Gileadites seized the fords of the Jordan before the Ephraimites *arrived.* And when *any* Ephraimite who escaped said, "Let me cross over," the men of Gilead would say to him, "*Are* you an Ephraimite?" If he said, "No," 6then they would say to him, "Then say, 'Shibboleth'!" And he would say, "Sibboleth," for he could not pronounce *it* right. Then they would take him and kill him at the fords of the Jordan. There fell at that time forty-two thousand Ephraimites.

7And Jephthah judged Israel six years. Then Jephthah the Gileadite died and was buried among the cities of Gilead.

Ibzan, Elon, and Abdon

8After him, Ibzan of Bethlehem judged Israel. 9He had thirty sons. And he gave away thirty daughters in marriage, and brought in thirty daughters from elsewhere for his sons. He judged Israel seven years. 10Then Ibzan died and was buried at Bethlehem.

11After him, Elon the Zebulunite judged Israel. He judged Israel ten years. 12And Elon the Zebulunite died and was buried at Aijalon in the country of Zebulun.

13After him, Abdon the son of Hillel the Pirathonite judged Israel. 14He had forty sons and thirty grandsons, who rode on seventy young donkeys. He judged Israel eight years. 15Then Abdon the son of Hillel the Pirathonite died and was buried in Pirathon in the land of Ephraim, in the mountains of the Amalekites.

The Birth of Samson

13 Again the children of Israel did evil in the sight of the LORD, and the LORD delivered them into the hand of the Philistines for forty years.

2Now there was a certain man from Zorah, of the family of the Danites, whose name *was* Manoah; and his wife *was* barren and had no children. 3And the Angel of the LORD appeared to the woman and said to her, "Indeed now, you are barren and have borne no children, but you shall conceive and bear a son. 4Now therefore, please be careful not to drink wine or *similar* drink, and not to eat anything unclean. 5For behold, you shall conceive and bear a son. And no razor shall come upon his head, for the child shall be a Nazirite to God from the womb; and he shall begin to deliver Israel out of the hand of the Philistines."

6So the woman came and told her husband, saying, "A Man of God came to me, and His countenance *was* like the countenance of the Angel of God, very awesome; but I did not ask Him where He *was* from, and He did not tell me His name. 7And He said to me, 'Behold, you shall conceive and bear a son. Now drink no wine or *similar* drink, nor eat anything unclean, for the child shall be a Nazirite to God from the womb to the day of his death.' "

8Then Manoah prayed to the LORD, and said, "O my Lord, please let the Man of God whom You sent come to us again and teach us what we shall do for the child who will be born."

9And God listened to the voice of Manoah, and the Angel of God came to the woman again as she was sitting in the field; but Manoah her husband *was* not with her. 10Then the woman ran in haste and told her husband, and said to him, "Look, the Man who came to me the *other* day has just now appeared to me!"

11So Manoah arose and followed his wife. When he came to the Man, he said to Him, "Are You the Man who spoke to this woman?"

And He said, "I *am*."

12Manoah said, "Now let Your words come *to pass!* What will be the boy's rule of life, and his work?"

13So the Angel of the LORD said to Manoah, "Of all that I said to the woman let her be careful. 14She may not eat anything that comes from the vine, nor may she drink wine or *similar* drink, nor eat anything unclean. All that I commanded her let her observe."

15Then Manoah said to the Angel of the LORD, "Please let us detain You, and we will prepare a young goat for You."

16And the Angel of the LORD said to Manoah, "Though you detain Me, I will not eat your food. But if you offer a burnt offering, you must offer it to the LORD." (For Manoah did not know He *was* the Angel of the LORD.)

17Then Manoah said to the Angel of the LORD, "What *is* Your name, that when Your words come *to pass* we may honor You?"

18And the Angel of the LORD said to him, "Why do you ask My name, seeing it *is* wonderful?"

19So Manoah took the young goat with the grain offering, and offered it upon the rock to the LORD. And He did a wondrous thing while Manoah and his wife looked on—20it happened as the flame went up toward heaven from the altar—the Angel of the LORD ascended in the flame of the altar! When Manoah and his wife saw *this*, they fell on their faces to the ground. 21When the Angel of the LORD appeared no more to Manoah and his wife, then Manoah knew that He *was* the Angel of the LORD.

22And Manoah said to his wife, "We shall surely die, because we have seen God!"

23But his wife said to him, "If the LORD had desired to kill us, He would not have accepted a burnt offering and a grain offering from our hands, nor would He have shown us all these *things*, nor would He have told us *such things* as these at this time."

24So the woman bore a son and called his name Samson; and the child grew, and the LORD blessed him. 25And the Spirit of the LORD began to move upon him at Mahaneh Dan�g between Zorah and Eshtaol.

Samson's Philistine Wife

14 Now Samson went down to Timnah, and saw a woman in Timnah of the daughters of the Philistines. 2So he went up and told his father and mother, saying, "I have seen a woman in Timnah of the daughters of the Philistines; now therefore, get her for me as a wife."

3Then his father and mother said to him, "*Is there* no woman among the daughters of your brethren, or among all my people, that you must go and get a wife from the uncircumcised Philistines?"

And Samson said to his father, "Get her for me, for she pleases me well."

4But his father and mother did not know that it was of the LORD—that He was seeking an occasion to move against the Philistines. For at that time the Philistines had dominion over Israel.

5So Samson went down to Timnah with his father and mother, and came to the vineyards of Timnah.

Now *to his* surprise, a young lion *came* roaring against him. 6And the Spirit of the LORD came mightily upon him, and he tore the lion apart as one would have torn apart a young goat, though *he had* nothing in his hand. But

g Literally *Camp of Dan* (compare 18.12)

he did not tell his father or his mother what he had done.

7Then he went down and talked with the woman; and she pleased Samson well. 8After some time, when he returned to get her, he turned aside to see the carcass of the lion. And behold, a swarm of bees and honey *were* in the carcass of the lion. 9He took some of it in his hands and went along, eating. When he came to his father and mother, he gave *some* to them, and they also ate. But he did not tell them that he had taken the honey out of the carcass of the lion.

10So his father went down to the woman. And Samson gave a feast there, for young men used to do so. 11And it happened, when they saw him, that they brought thirty companions to be with him.

12Then Samson said to them, "Let me pose a riddle to you. If you can correctly solve and explain it to me within the seven days of the feast, then I will give you thirty linen garments and thirty changes of clothing. 13But if you cannot explain *it* to me, then you shall give me thirty linen garments and thirty changes of clothing."

And they said to him, "Pose your riddle, that we may hear it."

14So he said to them:

"Out of the eater came something to eat,
And out of the strong came something sweet."

Now for three days they could not explain the riddle.

15But it came to pass on the seventh day that they said to Samson's wife, "Entice your husband, that he may explain the riddle to us, or else we will burn you and your father's house with fire. Have you invited us in order to take what is ours? *Is that* not *so?*"

16Then Samson's wife wept on him, and said, "You only hate me! You do not love me! You have posed a riddle to the sons of my people, but you have not explained *it* to me."

And he said to her, "Look, I have not explained *it* to my father or my mother; so should I explain *it* to you?" 17Now she had wept on him the seven days while their feast lasted. And it happened on the seventh day that he told

her, because she pressed him so much. Then she explained the riddle to the sons of her people. 18So the men of the city said to him on the seventh day before the sun went down:

"What *is* sweeter than honey?
And what *is* stronger than a lion?"

And he said to them:

"If you had not plowed with my heifer,
You would not have solved my riddle!"

19Then the Spirit of the LORD came upon him mightily, and he went down to Ashkelon and killed thirty of their men, took their apparel, and gave the changes *of clothing* to those who had explained the riddle. So his anger was aroused, and he went back up to his father's house. 20And Samson's wife was *given* to his companion, who had been his best man.

Samson Defeats the Philistines

15 After a while, in the time of wheat harvest, it happened that Samson visited his wife with a young goat. And he said, "Let me go in to my wife, into *her* room." But her father would not permit him to go in.

2Her father said, "I really thought that you thoroughly hated her; therefore I gave her to your companion. *Is* not her younger sister better than she? Please, take her instead."

3And Samson said to them, "This time I shall be blameless regarding the Philistines if I harm them!" 4Then Samson went and caught three hundred foxes; and he took torches, turned *the foxes* tail to tail, and put a torch between each pair of tails. 5When he had set the torches on fire, he let *the foxes* go into the standing grain of the Philistines, and burned up both the shocks and the standing grain, as well as the vineyards *and* olive groves.

6Then the Philistines said, "Who has done this?"

And they answered, "Samson, the son-in-law of the Timnite, because he has taken his wife and given her to his companion." So the Philistines came up and burned her and her father with fire.

7Samson said to them, "Since you would do a thing like this, I will surely take revenge on you, and after that I will cease." 8So he attacked them hip and thigh with a great slaughter; then he went down and dwelt in the cleft of the rock of Etam.

9Now the Philistines went up, encamped in Judah, and deployed themselves against Lehi. 10And the men of Judah said, "Why have you come up against us?"

So they answered, "We have come up to arrest Samson, to do to him as he has done to us."

11Then three thousand men of Judah went down to the cleft of the rock of Etam, and said to Samson, "Do you not know that the Philistines rule over us? What is this you have done to us?"

And he said to them, "As they did to me, so I have done to them."

12But they said to him, "We have come down to arrest you, that we may deliver you into the hand of the Philistines."

Then Samson said to them, "Swear to me that you will not kill me yourselves."

13So they spoke to him, saying, "No, but we will tie you securely and deliver you into their hand; but we will surely not kill you." And they bound him with two new ropes and brought him up from the rock.

14When he came to Lehi, the Philistines came shouting against him. Then the Spirit of the LORD came mightily upon him; and the ropes that were on his arms became like flax that is burned with fire, and his bonds broke loose from his hands. 15He found a fresh jawbone of a donkey, reached out his hand and took it, and killed a thousand men with it. 16Then Samson said:

"With the jawbone of a donkey,
Heaps upon heaps,
With the jawbone of a donkey
I have slain a thousand men!"

17And so it was, when he had finished speaking, that he threw the jawbone from his hand, and called that place Ramath Lehi.h

18Then he became very thirsty; so he cried out to the LORD and said, "You have given this great deliverance by the hand of Your servant; and now shall I die of thirst and fall into the hand of the uncircumcised?" 19So God split the hollow place that is in Lehi,i and water came out, and he drank; and his spirit returned, and he revived. Therefore he called its name En Hakkore,j which is in Lehi to this day. 20And he judged Israel twenty years in the days of the Philistines.

Samson and Delilah

16 Now Samson went to Gaza and saw a harlot there, and went in to her. 2When the Gazites were told, "Samson has come here!" they surrounded the place and lay in wait for him all night at the gate of the city. They were quiet all night, saying, "In the morning, when it is daylight, we will kill him." 3And Samson lay low till midnight; then he arose at midnight, took hold of the doors of the gate of the city and the two gateposts, pulled them up, bar and all, put them on his shoulders, and carried them to the top of the hill that faces Hebron.

4Afterward it happened that he loved a woman in the Valley of Sorek, whose name was Delilah. 5And the lords of the Philistines came up to her and said to her, "Entice him, and find out where his great strength lies, and by what means we may overpower him, that we may bind him to afflict him; and every one of us will give you eleven hundred pieces of silver."

6So Delilah said to Samson, "Please tell me where your great strength lies, and with what you may be bound to afflict you."

7And Samson said to her, "If they bind me with seven fresh bowstrings, not yet dried, then I shall become weak, and be like any other man."

8So the lords of the Philistines brought up to her seven fresh bowstrings, not yet dried, and she bound him with them. 9Now men were lying in wait, staying with her in the room. And she said to him, "The Philistines are upon you, Samson!" But he broke the bowstrings as a strand of yarn breaks when it touches fire. So the secret of his strength was not known.

h Literally *Jawbone Height*   i Literally *Jawbone* (compare verse 14)   j Literally *Spring of*
the Caller

10Then Delilah said to Samson, "Look, you have mocked me and told me lies. Now, please tell me what you may be bound with."

11So he said to her, "If they bind me securely with new ropes that have never been used, then I shall become weak, and be like any *other* man."

12Therefore Delilah took new ropes and bound him with them, and said to him, "The Philistines *are* upon you, Samson!" And *men were* lying in wait, staying in the room. But he broke them off his arms like a thread.

13Delilah said to Samson, "Until now you have mocked me and told me lies. Tell me what you may be bound with." And he said to her, "If you weave the seven locks of my head into the web of the loom"—

14So she wove *it* tightly with the batten of the loom, and said to him, "The Philistines *are* upon you, Samson!" But he awoke from his sleep, and pulled out the batten and the web from the loom.

15Then she said to him, "How can you say, 'I love you,' when your heart *is* not with me? You have mocked me these three times, and have not told me where your great strength *lies*." 16And it came to pass, when she pestered him daily with her words and pressed him, *so* that his soul was vexed to death, 17that he told her all his heart, and said to her, "No razor has ever come upon my head, for I *have been* a Nazirite to God from my mother's womb. If I am shaven, then my strength will leave me, and I shall become weak, and be like any *other* man."

18When Delilah saw that he had told her all his heart, she sent and called for the lords of the Philistines, saying, "Come up once more, for he has told me all his heart." So the lords of the Philistines came up to her and brought the money in their hand. 19Then she lulled him to sleep on her knees, and called for a man and had him shave off the seven locks of his head. Then she began to torment him, and his strength left him. 20And she said, "The Philistines *are* upon you, Samson!" So he awoke from his sleep, and said, "I will go out as before, at other times, and shake myself free!" But he did not

know that the LORD had departed from him.

21Then the Philistines took him and put out his eyes, and brought him down to Gaza. They bound him with bronze fetters, and he became a grinder in the prison. 22However, the hair of his head began to grow again after it had been shaven.

Samson Dies with the Philistines

23Now the lords of the Philistines gathered together to offer a great sacrifice to Dagon their god, and to rejoice. And they said:

"Our god has delivered into our hands
Samson our enemy!"

24When the people saw him, they praised their god; for they said:

"Our god has delivered into our hands our enemy,
The destroyer of our land,
And the one who multiplied our dead."

25So it happened, when their hearts were merry, that they said, "Call for Samson, that he may perform for us." So they called for Samson from the prison, and he performed for them. And they stationed him between the pillars. 26Then Samson said to the lad who held him by the hand, "Let me feel the pillars which support the temple, so that I can lean on them." 27Now the temple was full of men and women. All the lords of the Philistines *were* there—about three thousand men and women on the roof watching while Samson performed.

28Then Samson called to the LORD, saying, "O Lord GOD, remember me, I pray! Strengthen me, I pray, just this once, O God, that I may with one *blow* take vengeance on the Philistines for my two eyes!" 29And Samson took hold of the two middle pillars which supported the temple, and he braced himself against them, one on his right and the other on his left. 30Then Samson said, "Let me die with the Philistines!" And he pushed with *all his* might, and the temple fell on the lords and all the people who *were* in it. So the dead that he killed at his death were more than he had killed in his life.

31And his brothers and all his father's

household came down and took him, and brought *him* up and buried him between Zorah and Eshtaol in the tomb of his father Manoah. He had judged Israel twenty years.

Micah's Idolatry

17 Now there was a man from the mountains of Ephraim, whose name *was* Micah. 2And he said to his mother, "The eleven hundred *shekels* of silver that were taken from you, and on which you put a curse, even saying it in my ears—here *is* the silver with me; I took it."

And his mother said, "*May you be* blessed by the LORD, my son!" 3So when he had returned the eleven hundred *shekels* of silver to his mother, his mother said, "I had wholly dedicated the silver from my hand to the LORD for my son, to make a carved image and a molded image; now therefore, I will return it to you." 4Thus he returned the silver to his mother. Then his mother took two hundred *shekels* of silver and gave them to the silversmith, and he made it into a carved image and a molded image; and they were in the house of Micah.

5The man Micah had a shrine, and made an ephod and household idols; and he consecrated one of his sons, who became his priest. 6In those days *there was* no king in Israel; everyone did *what was* right in his own eyes.

7Now there was a young man from Bethlehem in Judah, of the family of Judah; he *was* a Levite, and was staying there. 8The man departed from the city of Bethlehem in Judah to stay wherever he could find *a place*. Then he came to the mountains of Ephraim, to the house of Micah, as he journeyed. 9And Micah said to him, "Where do you come from?"

So he said to him, "I *am* a Levite from Bethlehem in Judah, and I am on my way to find *a place* to stay."

10Micah said to him, "Dwell with me, and be a father and a priest to me, and I will give you ten *shekels* of silver per year, a suit of clothes, and your sustenance." So the Levite went in. 11Then the Levite was content to dwell with the man; and the young man became like one of his sons to him. 12So Micah con-

secrated the Levite, and the young man became his priest, and lived in the house of Micah. 13Then Micah said, "Now I know that the LORD will be good to me, since I have a Levite as priest!"

The Danites Adopt Micah's Idolatry

18 In those days *there was* no king in Israel. And in those days the tribe of the Danites was seeking an inheritance for itself to dwell in; for until that day *their* inheritance among the tribes of Israel had not fallen to them. 2So the children of Dan sent five men of their family from their territory, men of valor from Zorah and Eshtaol, to spy out the land and search it. They said to them, "Go, search the land." So they went to the mountains of Ephraim, to the house of Micah, and lodged there. 3While they *were* at the house of Micah, they recognized the voice of the young Levite. They turned aside and said to him, "Who brought you here? What are you doing in this *place*? What do you have here?"

4He said to them, "Thus and so Micah did for me. He has hired me, and I have become his priest."

5So they said to him, "Please inquire of God, that we may know whether the journey on which we go will be prosperous."

6And the priest said to them, "Go in peace. The presence of the LORD *be* with you on your way."

7So the five men departed and went to Laish. They saw the people who *were* there, how they dwelt safely, in the manner of the Sidonians, quiet and secure. *There were* no rulers in the land who might put *them* to shame for anything. They *were* far from the Sidonians, and they had no ties with anyone.

8Then *the spies* came back to their brethren at Zorah and Eshtaol, and their brethren said to them, "What *is* your *report*?"

9So they said, "Arise, let us go up against them. For we have seen the land, and indeed it *is* very good. *Would* you *do* nothing? Do not hesitate to go, *and* enter to possess the land. 10When you go, you will come to a secure people and a large land. For God has given it into your hands, a place where *there is* no lack of anything that *is* on the earth."

11And six hundred men of the family of the Danites went from there, from Zorah and Eshtaol, armed with weapons of war. 12Then they went up and encamped in Kirjath Jearim in Judah. (Therefore they call that place Mahaneh Dan[k] to this day. There *it is,* west of Kirjath Jearim.) 13And they passed from there to the mountains of Ephraim, and came to the house of Micah.

14Then the five men who had gone to spy out the country of Laish answered and said to their brethren, "Do you know that there are in these houses an ephod, household idols, a carved image, and a molded image? Now therefore, consider what you should do." 15So they turned aside there, and came to the house of the young Levite man—to the house of Micah—and greeted him. 16The six hundred men armed with their weapons of war, who *were* of the children of Dan, stood by the entrance of the gate. 17Then the five men who had gone to spy out the land went up. Entering there, they took the carved image, the ephod, the household idols, and the molded image. The priest stood at the entrance of the gate with the six hundred men *who were* armed with weapons of war.

18When these went into Micah's house and took the carved image, the ephod, the household idols, and the molded image, the priest said to them, "What are you doing?"

19And they said to him, "Be quiet, put your hand over your mouth, and come with us; be a father and a priest to us. *Is it* better for you to be a priest to the household of one man, or that you be a priest to a tribe and a family in Israel?" 20So the priest's heart was glad; and he took the ephod, the household idols, and the carved image, and took his place among the people.

21Then they turned and departed, and put the little ones, the livestock, and the goods in front of them. 22When they were a good way from the house of Micah, the men who *were* in the houses near Micah's house gathered together

and overtook the children of Dan. 23And they called out to the children of Dan. So they turned around and said to Micah, "What ails you, that you have gathered such a company?"

24So he said, "You have taken away my gods which I made, and the priest, and you have gone away. Now what more do I have? How can you say to me, 'What ails you?'"

25And the children of Dan said to him, "Do not let your voice be heard among us, lest angry men fall upon you, and you lose your life, with the lives of your household!" 26Then the children of Dan went their way. And when Micah saw that they *were* too strong for him, he turned and went back to his house.

Danites Settle in Laish

27So they took *the things* Micah had made, and the priest who had belonged to him, and went to Laish, to a people quiet and secure; and they struck them with the edge of the sword and burned the city with fire. 28*There was* no deliverer, because it *was* far from Sidon, and they had no ties with anyone. It was in the valley that belongs to Beth Rehob. So they rebuilt the city and dwelt there. 29And they called the name of the city Dan, after the name of Dan their father, who was born to Israel. However, the name of the city formerly *was* Laish.

30Then the children of Dan set up for themselves the carved image; and Jonathan the son of Gershom, the son of Manasseh, and his sons were priests to the tribe of Dan until the day of the captivity of the land. 31So they set up for themselves Micah's carved image which he made, all the time that the house of God was in Shiloh.

The Levite's Concubine

19 And it came to pass in those days, when *there was* no king in Israel, that there was a certain Levite staying in the remote mountains of Ephraim. He took for himself a concubine from Bethlehem in Judah. 2But his concubine played the harlot against him, and went away from him to her father's house at Bethlehem in Judah, and was there four

___
[k] Literally *Camp of Dan*

whole months. 3Then her husband arose and went after her, to speak kindly to her *and* bring her back, having his servant and a couple of donkeys with him. So she brought him into her father's house; and when the father of the young woman saw him, he was glad to meet him. 4Now his father-in-law, the young woman's father, detained him; and he stayed with him three days. So they ate and drank and lodged there.

5Then it came to pass on the fourth day that they arose early in the morning, and he stood to depart; but the young woman's father said to his son-in-law, "Refresh your heart with a morsel of bread, and afterward go your way."

6So they sat down, and the two of them ate and drank together. Then the young woman's father said to the man, "Please be content to stay all night, and let your heart be merry." 7And when the man stood to depart, his father-in-law urged him; so he lodged there again. 8Then he arose early in the morning on the fifth day to depart, but the young woman's father said, "Please refresh your heart." So they delayed until afternoon; and both of them ate.

9And when the man stood to depart— he and his concubine and his servant— his father-in-law, the young woman's father, said to him, "Look, the day is now drawing toward evening; please spend the night. See, the day is coming to an end; lodge here, that your heart may be merry. Tomorrow go your way early, so that you may get home."

10However, the man was not willing to spend that night; so he rose and departed, and came opposite Jebus (that is, Jerusalem). With him were the two saddled donkeys; his concubine *was* also with him. 11They *were* near Jebus, and the day was far spent; and the servant said to his master, "Come, please, and let us turn aside into this city of the Jebusites and lodge in it."

12But his master said to him, "We will not turn aside here into a city of foreigners, who *are* not of the children of Israel; we will go on to Gibeah." 13So he said to his servant, "Come, let us draw near to one of these places, and spend the night in Gibeah or in Ramah." 14And they passed by and went

their way; and the sun went down on them near Gibeah, which belongs to Benjamin. 15They turned aside there to go in to lodge in Gibeah. And when he went in, he sat down in the open square of the city, for no one would take them into *his* house to spend the night.

16Just then an old man came in from his work in the field at evening, who also *was* from the mountains of Ephraim; he was staying in Gibeah, whereas the men of the place *were* Benjamites. 17And when he raised his eyes, he saw the traveler in the open square of the city; and the old man said, "Where are you going, and where do you come from?"

18So he said to him, "We *are* passing from Bethlehem in Judah toward the remote mountains of Ephraim; I *am* from there. I went to Bethlehem in Judah; *now* I am going to the house of the LORD. But there *is* no one who will take me into his house, 19although we have both straw and fodder for our donkeys, and bread and wine for myself, for your female servant, and for the young man *who is* with your servant; *there is* no lack of anything."

20And the old man said, "Peace *be* with you! However, *let* all your needs *be* my responsibility; only do not spend the night in the open square." 21So he brought him into his house, and gave fodder to the donkeys. And they washed their feet, and ate and drank.

Gibeah's Crime

22As they were enjoying themselves, suddenly certain men of the city, perverted men, surrounded the house *and* beat on the door. They spoke to the master of the house, the old man, saying, "Bring out the man who came to your house, that we may know him *carnally!*"

23But the man, the master of the house, went out to them and said to them, "No, my brethren! I beg you, do not act *so* wickedly! Seeing this man has come into my house, do not commit this outrage. 24Look, *here is* my virgin daughter and *the man's* concubine; let me bring them out now. Humble them, and do with them as you please; but to this man do not do such a vile thing!" 25But the men would not heed him. So the man took his concubine and brought *her* out to them. And they knew her and abused her all night until morning; and when the day began to break, they let her go.

26Then the woman came as the day was dawning, and fell down at the door of the man's house where her master *was*, till it was light.

27When her master arose in the morning, and opened the doors of the house and went out to go his way, there was his concubine, fallen *at* the door of the house with her hands on the threshold. 28And he said to her, "Get up and let us be going." But there was no answer. So the man lifted her onto the donkey; and the man got up and went to his place.

29When he entered his house he took a knife, laid hold of his concubine, and divided her into twelve pieces, limb by limb, and sent her throughout all the territory of Israel. 30And so it was that all who saw it said, "No such deed has been done or seen from the day that the children of Israel came up from the land of Egypt until this day. Consider it, confer, and speak up!"

Israel's War with the Benjamites

20 So all the children of Israel came out, from Dan to Beersheba, as well as from the land of Gilead, and the congregation gathered together as one man before the LORD at Mizpah. 2And the leaders of all the people, all the tribes of Israel, presented themselves in the assembly of the people of God, four hundred thousand foot soldiers who drew the sword. 3(Now the children of Benjamin heard that the children of Israel had gone up to Mizpah.)

Then the children of Israel said, "Tell *us*, how did this wicked deed happen?"

4So the Levite, the husband of the woman who was murdered, answered and said, "My concubine and I went into Gibeah, which belongs to Benjamin, to spend the night. 5And the men of Gibeah rose against me, and surrounded the house at night because of me. They intended to kill me, but instead they ravished my concubine so that she died. 6So I took hold of my concubine, cut her in pieces, and sent her

throughout all the territory of the inheritance of Israel, because they committed lewdness and outrage in Israel. 7Look! All of you *are* children of Israel; give your advice and counsel here and now!"

8So all the people arose as one man, saying, "None *of us* will go to his tent, nor will any turn back to his house; 9but now this *is* the thing which we will do to Gibeah: *We will go up* against it by lot. 10We will take ten men out of *every* hundred throughout all the tribes of Israel, a hundred out of *every* thousand, and a thousand out of *every* ten thousand, to make provisions for the people, that when they come to Gibeah in Benjamin, they may repay all the vileness that they have done in Israel." 11So all the men of Israel were gathered against the city, united together as one man.

12Then the tribes of Israel sent men through all the tribe of Benjamin, saying, "What *is* this wickedness that has occurred among you? 13Now therefore, deliver up the men, the perverted men who *are* in Gibeah, that we may put them to death and remove the evil from Israel!" But the children of Benjamin would not listen to the voice of their brethren, the children of Israel. 14Instead, the children of Benjamin gathered together from their cities to Gibeah, to go to battle against the children of Israel. 15And from their cities at that time the children of Benjamin numbered twenty-six thousand men who drew the sword, besides the inhabitants of Gibeah, who numbered seven hundred select men. 16Among all this people *were* seven hundred select men *who were* left-handed; every one could sling a stone at a hair's *breadth* and not miss. 17Now besides Benjamin, the men of Israel numbered four hundred thousand men who drew the sword; all of these *were* men of war.

18Then the children of Israel arose and went up to the house of God to inquire of God. They said, "Which of us shall go up first to battle against the children of Benjamin?"

The LORD said, "Judah first!"

19So the children of Israel rose in the morning and encamped against Gibeah. 20And the men of Israel went out to bat-

tle against Benjamin, and the men of
Israel put themselves in battle array to
fight against them at Gibeah. 21Then
the children of Benjamin came out of
Gibeah, and on that day cut down to
the ground twenty-two thousand men
of the Israelites. 22And the people, that
is, the men of Israel, encouraged themselves and again formed the battle line
at the place where they had put themselves in array on the first day.
23Then the children of Israel went up
and wept before the LORD until evening,
and asked counsel of the LORD, saying,
"Shall I again draw near for battle
against the children of my brother Benjamin?"

And the LORD said, "Go up against
him."

24So the children of Israel approached the children of Benjamin on
the second day. 25And Benjamin went
out against them from Gibeah on the
second day, and cut down to the ground
eighteen thousand more of the children
of Israel; all these drew the sword.

26Then all the children of Israel, that
is, all the people, went up and came to
the house of God and wept. They sat
there before the LORD and fasted that
day until evening; and they offered
burnt offerings and peace offerings
before the LORD. 27So the children of
Israel inquired of the LORD (the ark
of the covenant of God was there in
those days, 28and Phinehas the son of
Eleazar, the son of Aaron, stood before it in those days), saying, "Shall I yet
again go out to battle against the children of my brother Benjamin, or shall I
cease?"

And the LORD said, "Go up, for tomorrow I will deliver them into your hand."

29Then Israel set men in ambush all
around Gibeah. 30And the children of
Israel went up against the children of
Benjamin on the third day, and put
themselves in battle array against Gibeah as at the other times. 31So the children of Benjamin went out against the
people, and were drawn away from the
city. They began to strike down and kill
some of the people, as at the other
times, in the highways (one of which
goes up to Bethel and the other to Gibeah) and in the field, about thirty men
of Israel. 32And the children of Benjamin said, "They are defeated before us,
as at first."

But the children of Israel said, "Let
us flee and draw them away from the
city to the highways." 33So all the men
of Israel rose from their place and put
themselves in battle array at Baal Tamar. Then Israel's men in ambush burst
forth from their position in the plain of
Geba. 34And ten thousand select men
from all Israel came against Gibeah,
and the battle was fierce. But the Benjamites did not know that disaster was
upon them. 35The LORD defeated Benjamin before Israel. And the children of
Israel destroyed that day twenty-five
thousand one hundred Benjamites; all
these drew the sword.

36So the children of Benjamin saw
that they were defeated. The men of Israel had given ground to the Benjamites, because they relied on the men in
ambush whom they had set against Gibeah. 37And the men in ambush quickly
rushed upon Gibeah; the men in ambush spread out and struck the whole
city with the edge of the sword.
38Now the appointed signal between
the men of Israel and the men in ambush was that they would make a great
cloud of smoke rise up from the city,
39whereupon the men of Israel would
turn in battle. Now Benjamin had begun
to strike and kill about thirty of the men
of Israel. For they said, "Surely they are
defeated before us, as in the first battle." 40But when the cloud began to rise
from the city in a column of smoke, the
Benjamites looked behind them, and
there was the whole city going up in
smoke to heaven. 41And when the men
of Israel turned back, the men of Benjamin panicked, for they saw that disaster had come upon them. 42Therefore
they turned their backs before the men
of Israel in the direction of the wilderness; but the battle overtook them, and
whoever came out of the cities they destroyed in their midst. 43They surrounded the Benjamites, chased them,
and easily trampled them down as far
as the front of Gibeah toward the east.
44And eighteen thousand men of Benjamin fell; all these were men of valor.
45Then they turned and fled toward the
wilderness to the rock of Rimmon; and
they cut down five thousand of them

on the highways. Then they pursued them relentlessly up to Gidom, and killed two thousand of them. 46So all who fell of Benjamin that day were twenty-five thousand men who drew the sword; all these *were* men of valor.

47But six hundred men turned and fled toward the wilderness to the rock of Rimmon, and they stayed at the rock of Rimmon for four months. 48And the men of Israel turned back against the children of Benjamin, and struck them down with the edge of the sword—from *every* city, men and beasts, all who were found. They also set fire to all the cities they came to.

Wives Provided for the Benjamites

21 Now the men of Israel had sworn an oath at Mizpah, saying, "None of us shall give his daughter to Benjamin as a wife." 2Then the people came to the house of God, and remained there before God till evening. They lifted up their voices and wept bitterly, 3and said, "O LORD God of Israel, why has this come to pass in Israel, that today there should be one tribe *missing* in Israel?"

4So it was, on the next morning, that the people rose early and built an altar there, and offered burnt offerings and peace offerings. 5The children of Israel said, "Who *is there* among all the tribes of Israel who did not come up with the assembly to the LORD?" For they had made a great oath concerning anyone who had not come up to the LORD at Mizpah, saying, "He shall surely be put to death." 6And the children of Israel grieved for Benjamin their brother, and said, "One tribe is cut off from Israel today. 7What shall we do for wives for those who remain, seeing we have sworn by the LORD that we will not give them our daughters as wives?"

8And they said, "What one *is there* from the tribes of Israel who did not come up to Mizpah to the LORD?" And, in fact, no one had come to the camp from Jabesh Gilead to the assembly. 9For when the people were counted, indeed, not one of the inhabitants of Jabesh Gilead *was* there. 10So the congregation sent out there twelve thousand of their most valiant men, and com-

manded them, saying, "Go and strike the inhabitants of Jabesh Gilead with the edge of the sword, including the women and children. 11And this *is* the thing that you shall do: You shall utterly destroy every male, and every woman who has known a man intimately." 12So they found among the inhabitants of Jabesh Gilead four hundred young virgins who had not known a man intimately; and they brought them to the camp at Shiloh, which is in the land of Canaan.

13Then the whole congregation sent *word* to the children of Benjamin who *were* at the rock of Rimmon, and announced peace to them. 14So Benjamin came back at that time, and they gave them the women whom they had saved alive of the women of Jabesh Gilead; and yet they had not found enough for them.

15And the people grieved for Benjamin, because the LORD had made a void in the tribes of Israel.

16Then the elders of the congregation said, "What shall we do for wives for those who remain, since the women of Benjamin have been destroyed?" 17And they said, "*There must be* an inheritance for the survivors of Benjamin, that a tribe may not be destroyed from Israel. 18However, we cannot give them wives from our daughters, for the children of Israel have sworn an oath, saying, 'Cursed *be* the one who gives a wife to Benjamin.' " 19Then they said, "In fact, *there is* a yearly feast of the LORD in Shiloh, which *is* north of Bethel, on the east side of the highway that goes up from Bethel to Shechem, and south of Lebonah."

20Therefore they instructed the children of Benjamin, saying, "Go, lie in wait in the vineyards, 21and watch; and just when the daughters of Shiloh come out to perform their dances, then come out from the vineyards, and every man catch a wife for himself from the daughters of Shiloh; then go to the land of Benjamin. 22Then it shall be, when their fathers or their brothers come to us to complain, that we will say to them, 'Be kind to them for our sakes, because we did not take a wife for any of them in the war; for *it is* not *as though* you have given the *women* to them at this time, making yourselves guilty of your oath.'"

23And the children of Benjamin did so; they took enough wives for their number from those who danced, whom they caught. Then they went and returned to their inheritance, and they rebuilt the cities and dwelt in them.

24So the children of Israel departed from there at that time, every man to his tribe and family; they went out from there, every man to his inheritance.

25In those days *there was* no king in Israel; everyone did *what was* right in his own eyes.

The Book of
RUTH

Elimelech's Family Goes to Moab

1 Now it came to pass, in the days when the judges ruled, that there was a famine in the land. And a certain man of Bethlehem, Judah, went to dwell in the country of Moab, he and his wife and his two sons. 2The name of the man *was* Elimelech, the name of his wife *was* Naomi, and the names of his two sons *were* Mahlon and Chilion—Ephrathites of Bethlehem, Judah. And they went to the country of Moab and remained there. 3Then Elimelech, Naomi's husband, died; and she was left, and her two sons. 4Now they took wives of the women of Moab: the name of the one *was* Orpah, and the name of the other Ruth. And they dwelt there about ten years. 5Then both Mahlon and Chilion also died; so the woman survived her two sons and her husband.

Naomi Returns with Ruth

6Then she arose with her daughters-in-law that she might return from the country of Moab, for she had heard in the country of Moab that the LORD had visited His people by giving them bread. 7Therefore she went out from the place where she was, and her two daughters-in-law with her; and they went on the way to return to the land of Judah. 8And Naomi said to her two daughters-in-law, "Go, return each to her mother's house. The LORD deal kindly with you, as you have dealt with the dead and with me. 9The LORD grant that you may find rest, each in the house of her husband."

So she kissed them, and they lifted up their voices and wept. 10And they said to her, "Surely we will return with you to your people."

11But Naomi said, "Turn back, my daughters; why will you go with me? *Are* there still sons in my womb, that they may be your husbands? 12Turn back, my daughters, go—for I am too old to have a husband. If I should say I have hope, *if* I should have a husband tonight and should also bear sons, 13would you wait for them till they were grown? Would you restrain yourselves from having husbands? No, my daughters; for it grieves me very much for your sakes that the hand of the LORD has gone out against me!"

14Then they lifted up their voices and wept again; and Orpah kissed her mother-in-law, but Ruth clung to her.

15And she said, "Look, your sister-in-law has gone back to her people and to her gods; return after your sister-in-law."

16But Ruth said:

"Entreat me not to leave you,
    Or *to* turn back from following
        after you;
    For wherever you go, I will go;
    And wherever you lodge, I will
        lodge;

Your people *shall be* my people,
And your God, my God.
17 Where you die, I will die,
And there will I be buried.
The LORD do so to me, and more
also,
If *anything but* death parts you
and me."
18When she saw that she was determined to go with her, she stopped
speaking to her.

19Now the two of them went until
they came to Bethlehem. And it happened, when they had come to Bethlehem, that all the city was excited because of them; and the women said, "*Is*
this Naomi?"

20But she said to them, "Do not call
me Naomi;*a* call me Mara,*b* for the
Almighty has dealt very bitterly with
me. 21I went out full, and the LORD
has brought me home again empty.
Why do you call me Naomi, since the
LORD has testified against me, and the
Almighty has afflicted me?"

22So Naomi returned, and Ruth the
Moabitess her daughter-in-law with
her, who returned from the country of
Moab. Now they came to Bethlehem at
the beginning of barley harvest.

Ruth Meets Boaz

2 There was a relative of Naomi's husband, a man of great wealth, of the
family of Elimelech. His name *was*
Boaz. 2So Ruth the Moabitess said to
Naomi, "Please let me go to the field,
and glean heads of grain after *him* in
whose sight I may find favor."
And she said to her, "Go, my
daughter."

3Then she left, and went and gleaned
in the field after the reapers. And she
happened to come to the part of the
field *belonging* to Boaz, who *was* of the
family of Elimelech.

4Now behold, Boaz came from Bethlehem, and said to the reapers, "The
LORD *be* with you!"
And they answered him, "The LORD
bless you!"

5Then Boaz said to his servant who
was in charge of the reapers, "Whose
young woman *is* this?"

6So the servant who was in charge

of the reapers answered and said, "It
is the young Moabite woman who came
back with Naomi from the country of
Moab. 7And she said, 'Please let me
glean and gather after the reapers
among the sheaves.' So she came and
has continued from morning until now,
though she rested a little in the house."

8Then Boaz said to Ruth, "You will
listen, my daughter, will you not? Do
not go to glean in another field, nor go
from here, but stay close by my young
women. 9*Let* your eyes *be* on the field
which they reap, and go after them.
Have I not commanded the young men
not to touch you? And when you are
thirsty, go to the vessels and drink from
what the young men have drawn."

10So she fell on her face, bowed down
to the ground, and said to him, "Why
have I found favor in your eyes, that
you should take notice of me, since I
am a foreigner?"

11And Boaz answered and said to her,
"It has been fully reported to me, all
that you have done for your mother-in-
law since the death of your husband,
and *how* you have left your father and
your mother and the land of your birth,
and have come to a people whom you
did not know before. 12The LORD repay your work, and a full reward be
given you by the LORD God of Israel,
under whose wings you have come for
refuge."

13Then she said, "Let me find favor
in your sight, my lord; for you have
comforted me, and have spoken kindly
to your maidservant, though I am not
like one of your maidservants."

14Now Boaz said to her at mealtime,
"Come here, and eat of the bread, and
dip your piece of bread in the vinegar."
So she sat beside the reapers, and he
passed parched *grain* to her; and she
ate and was satisfied, and kept some
back. 15And when she rose up to glean,
Boaz commanded his young men, saying, "Let her glean even among the
sheaves, and do not reproach her.
16Also let *grain* from the bundles fall
purposely for her; leave *it* that she may
glean, and do not rebuke her."

17So she gleaned in the field until evening, and beat out what she had

---

a Literally *Pleasant*   *b* Literally *Bitter*

gleaned, and it was about an ephah of barley. 18Then she took *it* up and went into the city, and her mother-in-law saw what she had gleaned. So she brought out and gave to her what she had kept back after she had been satisfied.

19And her mother-in-law said to her, "Where have you gleaned today? And where did you work? Blessed be the one who took notice of you."

So she told her mother-in-law with whom she had worked, and said, "The man's name with whom I worked today *is* Boaz."

20Then Naomi said to her daughter-in-law, "Blessed *be* he of the Lord, who has not forsaken His kindness to the living and the dead!" And Naomi said to her, "This man *is* a relation of ours, one of our close relatives."

21Ruth the Moabitess said, "He also said to me, 'You shall stay close by my young men until they have finished all my harvest.' "

22And Naomi said to Ruth her daughter-in-law, "*It is* good, my daughter, that you go out with his young women, and that people do not meet you in any other field." 23So she stayed close by the young women of Boaz, to glean until the end of barley harvest and wheat harvest; and she dwelt with her mother-in-law.

Ruth's Redemption Assured

3 Then Naomi her mother-in-law said to her, "My daughter, shall I not seek security for you, that it may be well with you? 2Now Boaz, whose young women you were with, *is he* not our relative? In fact, he is winnowing barley tonight at the threshing floor. 3Therefore wash yourself and anoint yourself, put on your *best* garment and go down to the threshing floor; *but* do not make yourself known to the man until he has finished eating and drinking. 4Then it shall be, when he lies down, that you shall notice the place where he lies; and you shall go in, uncover his feet, and lie down; and he will tell you what you should do."

5And she said to her, "All that you say to me I will do."

6So she went down to the threshing floor and did according to all that her mother-in-law instructed her. 7And af-

ter Boaz had eaten and drunk, and his heart was cheerful, he went to lie down at the end of the heap of grain; and she came softly, uncovered his feet, and lay down.

8Now it happened at midnight that the man was startled, and turned himself; and there, a woman was lying at his feet. 9And he said, "Who *are* you?"

So she answered, "I *am* Ruth, your maidservant. Take your maidservant under your wing, for you are a close relative."

10Then he said, "Blessed *are* you of the Lord, my daughter! For you have shown more kindness at the end than at the beginning, in that you did not go after young men, whether poor or rich. 11And now, my daughter, do not fear. I will do for you all that you request, for all the people of my town know that you *are* a virtuous woman. 12Now it is true that I *am* a close relative; however, there is a relative closer than I. 13Stay this night, and in the morning it shall be *that* if he will perform the duty of a close relative for you—good; let him do it. But if he does not want to perform the duty for you, then I will perform the duty for you, *as* the Lord lives! Lie down until morning."

14So she lay at his feet until morning, and she arose before one could recognize another. Then he said, "Do not let it be known that the woman came to the threshing floor." 15Also he said, "Bring the shawl that *is* on you and hold it." And when she held it, he measured six *ephahs* of barley, and laid *it* on her. Then she went into the city.

16When she came to her mother-in-law, she said, "*Is* that you, my daughter?"

Then she told her all that the man had done for her. 17And she said, "These six *ephahs* of barley he gave me; for he said to me, 'Do not go empty-handed to your mother-in-law.' "

18Then she said, "Sit still, my daughter, until you know how the matter will turn out; for the man will not rest until he has concluded the matter this day."

Boaz Redeems Ruth

4 Now Boaz went up to the gate and sat down there; and behold, the close relative of whom Boaz had spoken came by. So Boaz said, "Come aside, friend, sit down here." So he came aside and sat down. 2And he took ten men of the elders of the city, and said, "Sit down here." So they sat down. 3Then he said to the close relative, "Naomi, who has come back from the country of Moab, sold the piece of land which *belonged* to our brother Elimelech. 4And I thought to inform you, saying, 'Buy *it* back in the presence of the inhabitants and the elders of my people. If you will redeem *it*, redeem *it;* but if you will not redeem *it, then* tell me, that I may know; for *there is* no one but you to redeem *it,* and I *am* next after you.' "

And he said, "I will redeem *it.*"

5Then Boaz said, "On the day you buy the field from the hand of Naomi, you must also buy *it* from Ruth the Moabitess, the wife of the dead, to perpetuate the name of the dead through his inheritance."

6And the close relative said, "I cannot redeem *it* for myself, lest I ruin my own inheritance. You redeem my right of redemption for yourself, for I cannot redeem *it.*"

7Now this *was the custom* in former times in Israel concerning redeeming and exchanging, to confirm anything: one man took off his sandal and gave *it* to the other, and this *was* a confirmation in Israel.

8Therefore the close relative said to Boaz, "Buy *it* for yourself." So he took off his sandal. 9And Boaz said to the elders and all the people, "You *are* witnesses this day that I have bought all that was Elimelech's, and all that *was* Chilion's and Mahlon's, from the hand of Naomi. 10Moreover, Ruth the Moabitess, the widow of Mahlon, I have acquired as my wife, to perpetuate the name of the dead through his inheritance, that the name of the dead may not be cut off from among his brethren and from his position at the gate. You *are* witnesses this day."

11And all the people who *were* at the gate, and the elders, said, "*We are* witnesses. The LORD make the woman who is coming to your house like Rachel and Leah, the two who built the house of Israel; and may you prosper in Ephrathah and be famous in Bethlehem. 12May your house be like the house of Perez, whom Tamar bore to Judah, because of the offspring which the LORD will give you from this young woman."

Descendants of Boaz and Ruth

13So Boaz took Ruth and she became his wife; and when he went in to her, the LORD gave her conception, and she bore a son. 14Then the women said to Naomi, "Blessed *be* the LORD, who has not left you this day without a close relative; and may his name be famous in Israel! 15And may he be to you a restorer of life and a nourisher of your old age; for your daughter-in-law, who loves you, who is better to you than seven sons, has borne him." 16Then Naomi took the child and laid him on her bosom, and became a nurse to him. 17Also the neighbor women gave him a name, saying, "There is a son born to Naomi." And they called his name Obed. He *is* the father of Jesse, the father of David.

18Now this *is* the genealogy of Perez: Perez begot Hezron; 19Hezron begot Ram, and Ram begot Amminadab; 20Amminadab begot Nahshon, and Nahshon begot Salmon; 21Salmon begot Boaz, and Boaz begot Obed; 22Obed begot Jesse, and Jesse begot David.

The First Book of

SAMUEL

The Family of Elkanah

1 Now there was a certain man of Ramathaim Zophim, of the mountains of Ephraim, and his name *was* Elkanah the son of Jeroham, the son of Elihu, the son of Tohu, the son of Zuph, an Ephraimite. 2And he had two wives: the name of one *was* Hannah, and the name of the other Peninnah. Peninnah had children, but Hannah had no children. 3This man went up from his city yearly to worship and sacrifice to the LORD of hosts in Shiloh. Also the two sons of Eli, Hophni and Phinehas, the priests of the LORD, *were* there. 4And whenever the time came for Elkanah to make an offering, he would give portions to Peninnah his wife and to all her sons and daughters. 5But to Hannah he would give a double portion, for he loved Hannah, although the LORD had closed her womb. 6And her rival also provoked her severely, to make her miserable, because the LORD had closed her womb. 7So it was, year by year, when she went up to the house of the LORD, that she provoked her; therefore she wept and did not eat.

Hannah's Vow

8Then Elkanah her husband said to her, "Hannah, why do you weep? Why do you not eat? And why is your heart grieved? *Am* I not better to you than ten sons?"

9So Hannah arose after they had finished eating and drinking in Shiloh. Now Eli the priest was sitting on the seat by the doorpost of the tabernacle of the LORD. 10And she *was* in bitterness of soul, and prayed to the LORD and wept in anguish. 11Then she made a vow and said, "O LORD of hosts, if You will indeed look on the affliction of Your maidservant and remember me, and not forget Your maidservant, but will give Your maidservant a male child, then I will give him to the LORD all the days of his life, and no razor shall come upon his head."

12And it happened, as she continued praying before the LORD, that Eli watched her mouth. 13Now Hannah spoke in her heart; only her lips moved, but her voice was not heard. Therefore Eli thought she was drunk. 14So Eli said to her, "How long will you be drunk? Put your wine away from you!"

15But Hannah answered and said, "No, my lord, I *am* a woman of sorrowful spirit. I have drunk neither wine nor intoxicating drink, but have poured out my soul before the LORD. 16Do not consider your maidservant a wicked woman, for out of the abundance of my complaint and grief I have spoken until now."

17Then Eli answered and said, "Go in peace, and the God of Israel grant your petition which you have asked of Him."

18And she said, "Let your maidservant find favor in your sight." So the woman went her way and ate, and her face was no longer *sad*.

Samuel Is Born and Dedicated

19Then they rose early in the morning and worshiped before the LORD, and returned and came to their house at Ramah. And Elkanah knew Hannah his wife, and the LORD remembered her. 20So it came to pass in the process of time that Hannah conceived and bore a son, and called his name Samuel,*a* saying, "Because I have asked for him from the LORD."

21Now the man Elkanah and all his house went up to offer to the LORD the yearly sacrifice and his vow. 22But Hannah did not go up, for she said to her husband, "*Not* until the child is weaned; then I will take him, that he may appear before the LORD and remain there forever."

23So Elkanah her husband said to her, "Do what seems best to you; wait until you have weaned him. Only let the LORD establish His word." Then the woman stayed and nursed her son until she had weaned him.

a Literally *Heard by God*

24Now when she had weaned him, she took him up with her, with three bulls, one ephah of flour, and a skin of wine, and brought him to the house of the LORD in Shiloh. And the child *was* young. 25Then they slaughtered a bull, and brought the child to Eli. 26And she said, "O my lord! As your soul lives, my lord, I *am* the woman who stood by you here, praying to the LORD. 27For this child I prayed, and the LORD has granted me my petition which I asked of Him. 28Therefore I also have lent him to the LORD; as long as he lives he shall be lent to the LORD." So they worshiped the LORD there.

Hannah's Prayer

2 And Hannah prayed and said:
"My heart rejoices in the LORD;
My horn[b] is exalted in the LORD.
I smile at my enemies,
Because I rejoice in Your salvation.

2   "No one is holy like the LORD,
For *there is* none besides You,
Nor *is there* any rock like our God.

3   "Talk no more so very proudly;
Let no arrogance come from your mouth,
For the LORD *is* the God of knowledge;
And by Him actions are weighed.

4   "The bows of the mighty men *are* broken,
And those who stumbled are girded with strength.
5   *Those who were* full have hired themselves out for bread,
And the hungry have ceased *to hunger.*
Even the barren has borne seven,
And she who has many children has become feeble.

6   "The LORD kills and makes alive;
He brings down to the grave and brings up.
7   The LORD makes poor and makes rich;
He brings low and lifts up.
8   He raises the poor from the dust

And lifts the beggar from the ash heap,
To set *them* among princes
And make them inherit the throne of glory.

"For the pillars of the earth *are* the LORD's,
And He has set the world upon them.
9   He will guard the feet of His saints,
But the wicked shall be silent in darkness.

"For by strength no man shall prevail.
10 The adversaries of the LORD shall be broken in pieces;
From heaven He will thunder against them.
The LORD will judge the ends of the earth.

"He will give strength to His king,
And exalt the horn of His anointed."

11Then Elkanah went to his house at Ramah. But the child ministered to the LORD before Eli the priest.

The Wicked Sons of Eli

12Now the sons of Eli *were* corrupt; they did not know the LORD. 13And the priests' custom with the people *was that* when any man offered a sacrifice, the priest's servant would come with a three-pronged fleshhook in his hand while the meat was boiling. 14Then he would thrust *it* into the pan, or kettle, or caldron, or pot; and the priest would take for himself all that the fleshhook brought up. So they did in Shiloh to all the Israelites who came there. 15Also, before they burned the fat, the priest's servant would come and say to the man who sacrificed, "Give meat for roasting to the priest, for he will not take boiled meat from you, but raw."

16And *if* the man said to him, "They should really burn the fat first; *then* you may take *as much* as your heart desires," he would then answer him, "*No,* but you must give *it* now; and if not, I will take *it* by force."

17Therefore the sin of the young men

b That is, strength

was very great before the LORD, for men abhorred the offering of the LORD.

Samuel's Childhood Ministry

18But Samuel ministered before the LORD, *even as* a child, wearing a linen ephod. 19Moreover his mother used to make him a little robe, and bring *it* to him year by year when she came up with her husband to offer the yearly sacrifice. 20And Eli would bless Elkanah and his wife, and say, "The LORD give you descendants from this woman for the loan that was given to the LORD." Then they would go to their own home.

21And the LORD visited Hannah, so that she conceived and bore three sons and two daughters. Meanwhile the child Samuel grew before the LORD.

Prophecy Against Eli's Household

22Now Eli was very old; and he heard everything his sons did to all Israel, and how they lay with the women who assembled at the door of the tabernacle of meeting. 23So he said to them, "Why do you do such things? For I hear of your evil dealings from all the people. 24No, my sons! For *it is* not a good report that I hear. You make the LORD's people transgress. 25If one man sins against another, God will judge him. But if a man sins against the LORD, who will intercede for him?" Nevertheless they did not heed the voice of their father, because the LORD desired to kill them.

26And the child Samuel grew in stature, and in favor both with the LORD and men.

27Then a man of God came to Eli and said to him, "Thus says the LORD: 'Did I not clearly reveal Myself to the house of your father when they were in Egypt in Pharaoh's house? 28Did I not choose him out of all the tribes of Israel *to be* My priest, to offer upon My altar, to burn incense, and to wear an ephod before Me? And did I not give to the house of your father all the offerings of the children of Israel made by fire? 29Why do you kick at My sacrifice and My offering which I have commanded *in My* dwelling place, and honor your sons more than Me, to make yourselves fat with the best of all the offerings of Israel My people?' 30Therefore the LORD God of Israel says: 'I said indeed *that* your house and the house of your father would walk before Me forever.' But now the LORD says: 'Far be it from Me; for those who honor Me I will honor, and those who despise Me shall be lightly esteemed. 31Behold, the days are coming that I will cut off your arm and the arm of your father's house, so that there will not be an old man in your house. 32And you will see an enemy *in* My dwelling place, *despite* all the good which God does for Israel. And there shall not be an old man in your house forever. 33But any of your men *whom* I do not cut off from My altar shall consume your eyes and grieve your heart. And all the descendants of your house shall die in the flower of their age. 34Now this *shall be* a sign to you that will come upon your two sons, on Hophni and Phinehas: in one day they shall die, both of them. 35Then I will raise up for Myself a faithful priest *who* shall do according to what *is* in My heart and in My mind. I will build him a sure house, and he shall walk before My anointed forever. 36And it shall come to pass that everyone who is left in your house will come *and* bow down to him for a piece of silver and a morsel of bread, and say, "Please, put me in one of the priestly positions, that I may eat a piece of bread." ' "

Samuel's First Prophecy

3 Now the boy Samuel ministered to the LORD before Eli. And the word of the LORD was rare in those days; *there was* no widespread revelation. 2And it came to pass at that time, while Eli *was* lying down in his place, and when his eyes had begun to grow so dim that he could not see, 3and before the lamp of God went out in the tabernacle of the LORD where the ark of God *was*, and while Samuel was lying down, 4that the LORD called Samuel. And he answered, "Here I am!" 5So he ran to Eli and said, "Here I am, for you called me."

And he said, "I did not call; lie down again." And he went and lay down.

6Then the LORD called yet again, "Samuel!"

So Samuel arose and went to Eli, and said, "Here I am, for you called me."

He answered, "I did not call, my son; lie down again." 7(Now Samuel did not yet know the LORD, nor was the word of the LORD yet revealed to him.)

8And the LORD called Samuel again the third time. So he arose and went to Eli, and said, "Here I am, for you did call me."

Then Eli perceived that the LORD had called the boy. 9Therefore Eli said to Samuel, "Go, lie down; and it shall be, if He calls you, that you must say, 'Speak, LORD, for Your servant hears.'" So Samuel went and lay down in his place.

10Now the LORD came and stood and called as at other times, "Samuel! Samuel!"

And Samuel answered, "Speak, for Your servant hears."

11Then the LORD said to Samuel: "Behold, I will do something in Israel at which both ears of everyone who hears it will tingle. 12In that day I will perform against Eli all that I have spoken concerning his house, from beginning to end. 13For I have told him that I will judge his house forever for the iniquity which he knows, because his sons made themselves vile, and he did not restrain them. 14And therefore I have sworn to the house of Eli that the iniquity of Eli's house shall not be atoned for by sacrifice or offering forever."

15So Samuel lay down until morning, and opened the doors of the house of the LORD. And Samuel was afraid to tell Eli the vision. 16Then Eli called Samuel and said, "Samuel, my son!"

He answered, "Here I am."

17And he said, "What is the word that the LORD spoke to you? Please do not hide it from me. God do so to you, and more also, if you hide anything from me of all the things that He said to you." 18Then Samuel told him everything, and hid nothing from him. And he said, "It is the LORD. Let Him do what seems good to Him."

19So Samuel grew, and the LORD was with him and let none of his words fall to the ground. 20And all Israel from Dan to Beersheba knew that Samuel had been established as a prophet of the LORD. 21Then the LORD appeared again in Shiloh. For the LORD revealed Himself to Samuel in Shiloh by the word of the LORD.

4 And the word of Samuel came to all Israel.

The Ark of God Captured

Now Israel went out to battle against the Philistines, and encamped beside Ebenezer; and the Philistines encamped in Aphek. 2Then the Philistines put themselves in battle array against Israel. And when they joined battle, Israel was defeated by the Philistines, who killed about four thousand men of the army in the field. 3And when the people had come into the camp, the elders of Israel said, "Why has the LORD defeated us today before the Philistines? Let us bring the ark of the covenant of the LORD from Shiloh to us, that when it comes among us it may save us from the hand of our enemies." 4So the people sent to Shiloh, that they might bring from there the ark of the covenant of the LORD of hosts, who dwells *between* the cherubim. And the two sons of Eli, Hophni and Phinehas, *were* there with the ark of the covenant of God.

5And when the ark of the covenant of the LORD came into the camp, all Israel shouted so loudly that the earth shook. 6Now when the Philistines heard the noise of the shout, they said, "What *does* the sound of this great shout in the camp of the Hebrews *mean*?" Then they understood that the ark of the LORD had come into the camp. 7So the Philistines were afraid, for they said, "God has come into the camp!" And they said, "Woe to us! For such a thing has never happened before. 8Woe to us! Who will deliver us from the hand of these mighty gods? These *are* the gods who struck the Egyptians with all the plagues in the wilderness. 9Be strong and conduct yourselves like men, you Philistines, that you do not become servants of the Hebrews, as they have been to you. Conduct yourselves like men, and fight!"

10So the Philistines fought, and Israel was defeated, and every man fled to his tent. There was a very great slaughter, and there fell of Israel thirty thousand foot soldiers. 11Also the ark of God was captured; and the two sons of Eli, Hophni and Phinehas, died.

Death of Eli

12Then a man of Benjamin ran from the battle line the same day, and came to Shiloh with his clothes torn and dirt on his head. 13Now when he came, there was Eli, sitting on a seat by the wayside watching, for his heart trembled for the ark of God. And when the man came into the city and told *it*, all the city cried out. 14When Eli heard the noise of the outcry, he said, "What *does* the sound of this tumult *mean*?" And the man came quickly and told Eli. 15Eli was ninety-eight years old, and his eyes were so dim that he could not see.

16Then the man said to Eli, "I *am* he who came from the battle. And I fled today from the battle line."

And he said, "What happened, my son?"

17So the messenger answered and said, "Israel has fled before the Philistines, and there has been a great slaughter among the people. Also your two sons, Hophni and Phinehas, are dead; and the ark of God has been captured."

18Then it happened, when he made mention of the ark of God, that Eli fell off the seat backward by the side of the gate; and his neck was broken and he died, for the man was old and heavy. And he had judged Israel forty years.

Ichabod

19Now his daughter-in-law, Phinehas' wife, was with child, *due* to be delivered; and when she heard the news that the ark of God was captured, and that her father-in-law and her husband were dead, she bowed herself and gave birth, for her labor pains came upon her. 20And about the time of her death the women who stood by her said to her, "Do not fear, for you have borne a son." But she did not answer, nor did she regard *it*. 21Then she named the child Ichabod,c saying, "The glory has departed from Israel!" because the ark of God had been captured and because of her father-in-law and her husband. 22And she said, "The glory has de-

parted from Israel, for the ark of God has been captured."

The Philistines and the Ark

5 Then the Philistines took the ark of God and brought it from Ebenezer to Ashdod. 2When the Philistines took the ark of God, they brought it into the house of Dagond and set it by Dagon. 3And when the people of Ashdod arose early in the morning, there was Dagon, fallen on its face to the earth before the ark of the LORD. So they took Dagon and set it in its place again. 4And when they arose early the next morning, there was Dagon, fallen on its face to the ground before the ark of the LORD. The head of Dagon and both the palms of its hands *were* broken off on the threshold; only Dagon's torso was left of it. 5Therefore neither the priests of Dagon nor any who come into Dagon's house tread on the threshold of Dagon in Ashdod to this day.

6But the hand of the LORD was heavy on the people of Ashdod, and He ravaged them and struck them with tumors,e *both* Ashdod and its territory. 7And when the men of Ashdod saw how *it was*, they said, "The ark of the God of Israel must not remain with us, for His hand is harsh toward us and Dagon our god." 8Therefore they sent and gathered to themselves all the lords of the Philistines, and said, "What shall we do with the ark of the God of Israel?"

And they answered, "Let the ark of the God of Israel be carried away to Gath." So they carried the ark of the God of Israel away. 9So it was, after they had carried it away, that the hand of the LORD was against the city with a very great destruction; and He struck the men of the city, both small and great, and tumors broke out on them.

10Therefore they sent the ark of God to Ekron. So it was, as the ark of God came to Ekron, that the Ekronites cried out, saying, "They have brought the ark of the God of Israel to us, to kill us and our people!" 11So they sent and gathered together all the lords of the Philistines, and said, "Send away the ark of the God of Israel, and let it go back to

---

c Literally *Inglorious*   d A Philistine idol   e Probably bubonic plague its own place, so that it does not kill us and our people." For there was a deadly destruction throughout all the city; the hand of God was very heavy there. 12And the men who did not die were stricken with the tumors, and the cry of the city went up to heaven.

The Ark Returned to Israel

6 Now the ark of the LORD was in the country of the Philistines seven months. 2And the Philistines called for the priests and the diviners, saying, "What shall we do with the ark of the LORD? Tell us how we should send it to its place."

3So they said, "If you send away the ark of the God of Israel, do not send it empty; but by all means return *it* to Him *with* a trespass offering. Then you will be healed, and it will be known to you why His hand is not removed from you."

4Then they said, "What *is* the trespass offering which we shall return to Him?"

They answered, "Five golden tumors and five golden rats, *according to* the number of the lords of the Philistines. For the same plague *was* on all of you and on your lords. 5Therefore you shall make images of your tumors and images of your rats that ravage the land, and you shall give glory to the God of Israel; perhaps He will lighten His hand from you, from your gods, and from your land. 6Why then do you harden your hearts as the Egyptians and Pharaoh hardened their hearts? When He did mighty things among them, did they not let the people go, that they might depart? 7Now therefore, make a new cart, take two milk cows which have never been yoked, and hitch the cows to the cart; and take their calves home, away from them. 8Then take the ark of the LORD and set it on the cart; and put the articles of gold which you are returning to Him *as* a trespass offering in a chest by its side. Then send it away, and let it go. 9And watch: if it goes up the road to its own territory, to Beth Shemesh, *then* He has done us this great evil. But if not, then we shall know that *it is* not His hand *that* struck us—it happened to us by chance."

10Then the men did so; they took two milk cows and hitched them to the cart, and shut up their calves at home. 11And they set the ark of the LORD on the cart, and the chest with the gold rats and the images of their tumors. 12Then the cows headed straight for the road to Beth Shemesh, *and* went along the highway, lowing as they went, and did not turn aside to the right hand or the left. And the lords of the Philistines went after them to the border of Beth Shemesh.

13Now *the people of* Beth Shemesh *were* reaping their wheat harvest in the valley; and they lifted their eyes and saw the ark, and rejoiced to see *it*. 14Then the cart came into the field of Joshua of Beth Shemesh, and stood there; a large stone *was* there. So they split the wood of the cart and offered the cows as a burnt offering to the LORD. 15The Levites took down the ark of the LORD and the chest that *was* with it, in which *were* the articles of gold, and put *them* on the large stone. Then the men of Beth Shemesh offered burnt offerings and made sacrifices the same day to the LORD. 16So when the five lords of the Philistines had seen *it*, they returned to Ekron the same day.

17These *are* the golden tumors which the Philistines returned *as* a trespass offering to the LORD: one for Ashdod, one for Gaza, one for Ashkelon, one for Gath, one for Ekron; 18and the golden rats, *according to* the number of all the cities of the Philistines *belonging* to the five lords, *both* fortified cities and country villages, even as far as the large *stone of* Abel on which they set the ark of the LORD, *which stone remains* to this day in the field of Joshua of Beth Shemesh.

19Then He struck the men of Beth Shemesh, because they had looked into the ark of the LORD. He struck fifty thousand and seventy men of the people, and the people lamented because the LORD had struck the people with a great slaughter.

The Ark at Kirjath Jearim

20And the men of Beth Shemesh said, "Who is able to stand before this holy LORD God? And to whom shall it go up from us?" 21So they sent messengers to the inhabitants of Kirjath Jearim, saying, "The Philistines have brought back the ark of the LORD; come down *and* take it up with you."

7 Then the men of Kirjath Jearim came and took the ark of the LORD, and brought it into the house of Abinadab on the hill, and consecrated Eleazar his son to keep the ark of the LORD.

Samuel Judges Israel

2So it was that the ark remained in Kirjath Jearim a long time; it was there twenty years. And all the house of Israel lamented after the LORD.

3Then Samuel spoke to all the house of Israel, saying, "If you return to the LORD with all your hearts, *then* put away the foreign gods and the Ashtoreths*f* from among you, and prepare your hearts for the LORD, and serve Him only; and He will deliver you from the hand of the Philistines." 4So the children of Israel put away the Baals and the Ashtoreths,*f* and served the LORD only.

5And Samuel said, "Gather all Israel to Mizpah, and I will pray to the LORD for you." 6So they gathered together at Mizpah, drew water, and poured *it* out before the LORD. And they fasted that day, and said there, "We have sinned against the LORD." And Samuel judged the children of Israel at Mizpah.

7Now when the Philistines heard that the children of Israel had gathered together at Mizpah, the lords of the Philistines went up against Israel. And when the children of Israel heard *of it,* they were afraid of the Philistines. 8So the children of Israel said to Samuel, "Do not cease to cry out to the LORD our God for us, that He may save us from the hand of the Philistines."

9And Samuel took a suckling lamb and offered *it as* a whole burnt offering to the LORD. Then Samuel cried out to the LORD for Israel, and the LORD answered him. 10Now as Samuel was offering up the burnt offering, the Philistines drew near to battle against Israel. But the LORD thundered with a loud thunder upon the Philistines that day, and so confused them that they were overcome before Israel. 11And the men

of Israel went out of Mizpah and pursued the Philistines, and drove them back as far as below Beth Car. 12Then Samuel took a stone and set *it* up between Mizpah and Shen, and called its name Ebenezer,*g* saying, "Thus far the LORD has helped us."

13So the Philistines were subdued, and they did not come anymore into the territory of Israel. And the hand of the LORD was against the Philistines all the days of Samuel. 14Then the cities which the Philistines had taken from Israel were restored to Israel, from Ekron to Gath; and Israel recovered its territory from the hands of the Philistines. Also there was peace between Israel and the Amorites.

15And Samuel judged Israel all the days of his life. 16He went from year to year on a circuit to Bethel, Gilgal, and Mizpah, and judged Israel in all those places. 17But he always returned to Ramah, for his home *was* there. There he judged Israel, and there he built an altar to the LORD.

Israel Demands a King

8 Now it came to pass when Samuel was old that he made his sons judges over Israel. 2The name of his firstborn was Joel, and the name of his second, Abijah; *they were* judges in Beersheba. 3But his sons did not walk in his ways; they turned aside after dishonest gain, took bribes, and perverted justice.

4Then all the elders of Israel gathered together and came to Samuel at Ramah, 5and said to him, "Look, you are old, and your sons do not walk in your ways. Now make us a king to judge us like all the nations."

6But the thing displeased Samuel when they said, "Give us a king to judge us." So Samuel prayed to the LORD. 7And the LORD said to Samuel, "Heed the voice of the people in all that they say to you; for they have not rejected you, but they have rejected Me, that I should not reign over them. 8According to all the works which they have done since the day that I brought them up out of Egypt, even to this day—with which they have forsaken Me and

---

f Canaanite goddesses   *g* Literally *Stone of Help*

served other gods—so they are doing to you also. 9Now therefore, heed their voice. However, you shall solemnly forewarn them, and show them the behavior of the king who will reign over them."

10So Samuel told all the words of the LORD to the people who asked him for a king. 11And he said, "This will be the behavior of the king who will reign over you: He will take your sons and appoint *them* for his own chariots and *to be* his horsemen, and *some* will run before his chariots. 12He will appoint captains over his thousands and captains over his fifties, *will set some* to plow his ground and reap his harvest, and *some* to make his weapons of war and equipment for his chariots. 13He will take your daughters *to be* perfumers, cooks, and bakers. 14And he will take the best of your fields, your vineyards, and your olive groves, and give *them* to his servants. 15He will take a tenth of your grain and your vintage, and give it to his officers and servants. 16And he will take your male servants, your female servants, your finest young men, and your donkeys, and put *them* to his work. 17He will take a tenth of your sheep. And you will be his servants. 18And you will cry out in that day because of your king whom you have chosen for yourselves, and the LORD will not hear you in that day."

19Nevertheless the people refused to obey the voice of Samuel; and they said, "No, but we will have a king over us, 20that we also may be like all the nations, and that our king may judge us and go out before us and fight our battles."

21And Samuel heard all the words of the people, and he repeated them in the hearing of the LORD. 22So the LORD said to Samuel, "Heed their voice, and make them a king."

And Samuel said to the men of Israel, "Every man go to his city."

Saul Chosen to Be King

9 There was a man of Benjamin whose name *was* Kish the son of Abiel, the son of Zeror, the son of Bechorath, the son of Aphiah, a Benjamite, a mighty man of power. 2And he had a choice and handsome son whose name *was* Saul. *There was* not a more handsome person than he among the children of Israel. From his shoulders upward *he was* taller than any of the people.

3Now the donkeys of Kish, Saul's father, were lost. And Kish said to his son Saul, "Please take one of the servants with you, and arise, go and look for the donkeys." 4So he passed through the mountains of Ephraim and through the land of Shalisha, but they did not find *them*. Then they passed through the land of Shaalim, and *they were* not *there*. Then he passed through the land of the Benjamites, but they did not find *them*.

5When they had come to the land of Zuph, Saul said to his servant who *was* with him, "Come, let us return, lest my father cease *caring* about the donkeys and become worried about us."

6And he said to him, "Look now, *there is* in this city a man of God, and *he is* an honorable man; all that he says surely comes to pass. So let us go there; perhaps he can show us the way that we should go."

7Then Saul said to his servant, "But look, *if* we go, what shall we bring the man? For the bread in our vessels is all gone, and *there is* no present to bring to the man of God. What do we have?"

8And the servant answered Saul again and said, "Look, I have here at hand one-fourth of a shekel of silver. I will give *that* to the man of God, to tell us our way." 9(Formerly in Israel, when a man went to inquire of God, he spoke thus: "Come, let us go to the seer"; for *he who is* now *called* a prophet was formerly called a seer.)

10Then Saul said to his servant, "Well said; come, let us go." So they went to the city where the man of God *was*.

11As they went up the hill to the city, they met some young women going out to draw water, and said to them, "Is the seer here?"

12And they answered them and said, "Yes, there he is, just ahead of you. Hurry now; for today he came to this city, because there is a sacrifice of the people today on the high place. 13As soon as you come into the city, you will surely find him before he goes up to the high place to eat. For the people will not eat until he comes, because he must bless the sacrifice; afterward those who are invited will eat. Now therefore, go up, for about this time you will find him." 14So they went up to the city. As they were coming into the city, there was Samuel, coming out toward them on his way up to the high place.

15Now the LORD had told Samuel in his ear the day before Saul came, saying, 16"Tomorrow about this time I will send you a man from the land of Benjamin, and you shall anoint him commander over My people Israel, that he may save My people from the hand of the Philistines; for I have looked upon My people, because their cry has come to Me."

17So when Samuel saw Saul, the LORD said to him, "There he is, the man of whom I spoke to you. This one shall reign over My people." 18Then Saul drew near to Samuel in the gate, and said, "Please tell me, where *is* the seer's house?"

19Samuel answered Saul and said, "I *am* the seer. Go up before me to the high place, for you shall eat with me today; and tomorrow I will let you go and will tell you all that *is* in your heart. 20But as for your donkeys that were lost three days ago, do not be anxious about them, for they have been found. And on whom *is* all the desire of Israel? *Is it* not on you and on all your father's house?"

21And Saul answered and said, "*Am* I not a Benjamite, of the smallest of the tribes of Israel, and my family the least of all the families of the tribe of Benjamin? Why then do you speak like this to me?"

22Now Samuel took Saul and his servant and brought them into the hall, and had them sit in the place of honor among those who were invited; there *were* about thirty persons. 23And Samuel said to the cook, "Bring the portion which I gave you, of which I said to you, 'Set it apart.' " 24So the cook took up the thigh with its upper part and set *it* before Saul. And *Samuel* said, "Here it is, what was kept back. *It* was set apart for you. Eat; for until this time it has been kept for you, since I said I invited the people." So Saul ate with Samuel that day.

25When they had come down from the high place into the city, *Samuel* spoke with Saul on the top of the house. 26They arose early; and it was about the dawning of the day that Samuel called to Saul on the top of the house, saying, "Get up, that I may send you on your way." And Saul arose, and both of them went outside, he and Samuel.

Saul Anointed King

27As they were going down to the outskirts of the city, Samuel said to Saul, "Tell the servant to go on ahead of us." And he went on. "But you stand here awhile, that I may announce to you the word of God."

10 Then Samuel took a flask of oil and poured *it* on his head, and kissed him and said: "*Is it* not because the LORD has anointed you commander over His inheritance? 2When you have departed from me today, you will find two men by Rachel's tomb in the territory of Benjamin at Zelzah; and they will say to you, 'The donkeys which you went to look for have been found. And now your father has ceased caring about the donkeys and is worrying about you, saying, "What shall I do about my son?" ' 3Then you shall go on forward from there and come to the terebinth tree of Tabor. There three men going up to God at Bethel will meet you, one carrying three young goats, another carrying three loaves of bread, and another carrying a skin of wine. 4And they will greet you and give you two *loaves* of bread, which you shall receive from their hands. 5After that you shall come to the hill of God where the Philistine garrison *is*. And it will happen, when you have come there to the city, that you will meet a group of prophets coming down from the high place with a stringed instrument, a tambourine, a flute, and a harp before them; and they will be prophesying. 6Then the Spirit of the LORD will come upon you, and you will prophesy with them and be turned into another man. 7And let it be, when these signs come to you, *that* you do as the occasion demands; for God *is* with you. 8You shall go down before me to Gilgal; and surely I will come down to you to offer burnt offerings *and* make sacrifices of peace offerings. Seven days you shall wait, till I come to you and show you what you should do."

9So it was, when he had turned his back to go from Samuel, that God gave him another heart; and all those signs came to pass that day. 10When they came there to the hill, there was a group of prophets to meet him; then the Spirit of God came upon him, and he prophesied among them. 11And it happened, when all who knew him formerly saw that he ˮindeed prophesied among the prophets, that the people said to one another, "What *is* this *that* has come upon the son of Kish? *Is* Saul also among the prophets?" 12Then a man from there answered and said, "But who *is* their father?" Therefore it became a proverb: "*Is* Saul also among the prophets?" 13And when he had finished prophesying, he went to the high place.

14Then Saul's uncle said to him and his servant, "Where did you go?"

So he said, "To look for the donkeys. When we saw that *they were* nowhere *to be found,* we went to Samuel."

15And Saul's uncle said, "Tell me, please, what Samuel said to you."

16So Saul said to his uncle, "He told us plainly that the donkeys had been found." But about the matter of the kingdom, he did not tell him what Samuel had said.

Saul Proclaimed King

17Then Samuel called the people together to the LORD at Mizpah, 18and said to the children of Israel, "Thus says the LORD God of Israel: 'I brought up Israel out of Egypt, and delivered you from the hand of the Egyptians *and* from the hand of all kingdoms and from those who oppressed you.' 19But you have today rejected your God, who Himself saved you from all your adversities and your tribulations; and you have said to Him, 'No, set a king over us!' Now therefore, present yourselves before the LORD by your tribes and by your clans."

20And when Samuel had caused all the tribes of Israel to come near, the tribe of Benjamin was chosen. 21When he had caused the tribe of Benjamin to come near by their families, the family of Matri was chosen. And Saul the son of Kish was chosen. But when they sought him, he could not be found. 22Therefore they inquired of the LORD further, "Has the man come here yet?"

And the LORD answered, "There he is, hidden among the equipment."

23So they ran and brought him from there; and when he stood among the people, he was taller than any of the people from his shoulders upward. 24And Samuel said to all the people, "Do you see him whom the LORD has chosen, that *there is* no one like him among all the people?"

So all the people shouted and said, "Long live the king!"

25Then Samuel explained to the people the behavior of royalty, and wrote *it* in a book and laid *it* up before the LORD. And Samuel sent all the people away, every man to his house. 26And Saul also went home to Gibeah; and valiant *men* went with him, whose hearts God had touched. 27But some rebels said, "How can this man save us?" So they despised him, and brought him no presents. But he held his peace.

Saul Saves Jabesh Gilead

11 Then Nahash the Ammonite came up and encamped against Jabesh Gilead; and all the men of Jabesh said to Nahash, "Make a covenant with us, and we will serve you."

2And Nahash the Ammonite answered them, "On this *condition* I will make *a covenant* with you, that I may put out all your right eyes, and bring reproach on all Israel."

3Then the elders of Jabesh said to him, "Hold off for seven days, that we may send messengers to all the territory of Israel. And then, if *there is* no one to save us, we will come out to you."

4So the messengers came to Gibeah of Saul and told the news in the hearing of the people. And all the people lifted up their voices and wept. 5Now there was Saul, coming behind the herd from the field; and Saul said, "What *troubles* the people, that they weep?" And they told him the words of the men of Jabesh. 6Then the Spirit of God came upon Saul when he heard this news, and his anger was greatly aroused.

7So he took a yoke of oxen and cut them in pieces, and sent *them* throughout all the territory of Israel by the hands of messengers, saying, "Whoever does not go out with Saul and Samuel to battle, so it shall be done to his oxen."

And the fear of the LORD fell on the people, and they came out with one consent. 8When he numbered them in Bezek, the children of Israel were three hundred thousand, and the men of Judah thirty thousand. 9And they said to the messengers who came, "Thus you shall say to the men of Jabesh Gilead: 'Tomorrow, by *the time* the sun is hot, you shall have help.'" Then the messengers came and reported *it* to the men of Jabesh, and they were glad. 10Therefore the men of Jabesh said, "Tomorrow we will come out to you, and you may do with us whatever seems good to you."

11So it was, on the next day, that Saul put the people in three companies; and they came into the midst of the camp in the morning watch, and killed Ammonites until the heat of the day. And it happened that those who survived were scattered, so that no two of them were left together.

12Then the people said to Samuel, "Who *is* he who said, 'Shall Saul reign over us?' Bring the men, that we may put them to death."

13But Saul said, "Not a man shall be put to death this day, for today the LORD has accomplished salvation in Israel."

14Then Samuel said to the people, "Come, let us go to Gilgal and renew the kingdom there." 15So all the people went to Gilgal, and there they made Saul king before the LORD in Gilgal. There they made sacrifices of peace offerings before the LORD, and there Saul and all the men of Israel rejoiced greatly.

Samuel's Address at Saul's Coronation

12 Now Samuel said to all Israel: "Indeed I have heeded your voice in all that you said to me, and have made a king over you. 2And now here is the king, walking before you; and I am old and grayheaded, and look, my sons *are* with you. I have walked before you from my childhood to this day. 3Here I am. Witness against me before the LORD and before His anointed: Whose ox have I taken, or whose donkey have I taken, or whom have I cheated? Whom have I oppressed, or from whose hand have I received *any* bribe with which to blind my eyes? I will restore *it* to you."

4And they said, "You have not cheated us or oppressed us, nor have you taken anything from any man's hand."

5Then he said to them, "The LORD *is* witness against you, and His anointed *is* witness this day, that you have not found anything in my hand."

And they answered, "*He is* witness."

6Then Samuel said to the people, "*It is* the LORD who raised up Moses and Aaron, and who brought your fathers up from the land of Egypt. 7Now therefore, stand still, that I may reason with you before the LORD concerning all the righteous acts of the LORD which He did to you and your fathers: 8When Jacob had gone into Egypt, and your fathers cried out to the LORD, then the LORD sent Moses and Aaron, who brought your fathers out of Egypt and made them dwell in this place. 9And when they forgot the LORD their God, He sold them into the hand of Sisera, commander of the army of Hazor, into the hand of the Philistines, and into the hand of the king of Moab; and they fought against them. 10Then they cried out to the LORD, and said, 'We have sinned, because we have forsaken the LORD and served the Baals and Ashtoreths;[h] but now deliver us from the hand of our enemies, and we will serve You.' 11And the LORD sent Jerubbaal, Bedan, Jephthah, and Samuel, and delivered you out of the hand of your enemies on every side; and you dwelt in safety. 12And when you saw that Nahash king of the Ammonites came against you, you said to me, 'No, but a king shall reign over us,' when the LORD your God *was* your king.

13"Now therefore, here is the king whom you have chosen *and* whom you have desired. And take note, the LORD has set a king over you. 14If you fear

---

h Canaanite goddesses

the LORD and serve Him and obey His voice, and do not rebel against the commandment of the LORD, then both you and the king who reigns over you will continue following the LORD your God. 15However, if you do not obey the voice of the LORD, but rebel against the commandment of the LORD, then the hand of the LORD will be against you, as *it was* against your fathers.

16"Now therefore, stand and see this great thing which the LORD will do before your eyes: 17*Is* today not the wheat harvest? I will call to the LORD, and He will send thunder and rain, that you may perceive and see that your wickedness *is* great, which you have done in the sight of the LORD, in asking a king for yourselves."

18So Samuel called to the LORD, and the LORD sent thunder and rain that day; and all the people greatly feared the LORD and Samuel.

19And all the people said to Samuel, "Pray for your servants to the LORD your God, that we may not die; for we have added to all our sins the evil of asking a king for ourselves."

20Then Samuel said to the people, "Do not fear. You have done all this wickedness; yet do not turn aside from following the LORD, but serve the LORD with all your heart. 21And do not turn aside; for *then you would go* after empty things which cannot profit or deliver, for they *are* nothing. 22For the LORD will not forsake His people, for His great name's sake, because it has pleased the LORD to make you His people. 23Moreover, as for me, far be it from me that I should sin against the LORD in ceasing to pray for you; but I will teach you the good and the right way. 24Only fear the LORD, and serve Him in truth with all your heart; for consider what great things He has done for you. 25But if you still do wickedly, you shall be swept away, both you and your king."

Saul's Unlawful Sacrifice

13 Saul reigned one year; and when he had reigned two years over Israel,*ⁱ* 2Saul chose for himself three thousand *men* of Israel. Two thousand were with Saul in Michmash and in the mountains of Bethel, and a thousand were with Jonathan in Gibeah of Benjamin. The rest of the people he sent away, every man to his tent.

3And Jonathan attacked the garrison of the Philistines that *was* in Geba, and the Philistines heard *of it*. Then Saul blew the trumpet throughout all the land, saying, "Let the Hebrews hear!" 4Now all Israel heard it said *that* Saul had attacked a garrison of the Philistines, and *that* Israel had also become an abomination to the Philistines. And the people were called together to Saul at Gilgal.

5Then the Philistines gathered together to fight with Israel, thirty thousand chariots and six thousand horsemen, and people as the sand which *is* on the seashore in multitude. And they came up and encamped in Michmash, to the east of Beth Aven. 6When the men of Israel saw that they were in danger (for the people were distressed), then the people hid in caves, in thickets, in rocks, in holes, and in pits. 7And *some of* the Hebrews crossed over the Jordan to the land of Gad and Gilead.

As for Saul, he *was* still in Gilgal, and all the people followed him trembling. 8Then he waited seven days, according to the time set by Samuel. But Samuel did not come to Gilgal; and the people were scattered from him. 9So Saul said, "Bring a burnt offering and peace offerings here to me." And he offered the burnt offering. 10Now it happened, as soon as he had finished presenting the burnt offering, that Samuel came; and Saul went out to meet him, that he might greet him.

11And Samuel said, "What have you done?"

Saul said, "When I saw that the people were scattered from me, and *that* you did not come within the days appointed, and *that* the Philistines gathered together at Michmash, 12then I said, 'The Philistines will now come down on me at Gilgal, and I have not made supplication to the LORD.' Therefore I felt com-

---

ⁱ The Hebrew is difficult (compare 2 Samuel 5.4; 2 Kings 14.2; see also 2 Samuel 2.10; Acts 13.21).

pelled, and offered a burnt offering."

13And Samuel said to Saul, "You have done foolishly. You have not kept the commandment of the LORD your God, which He commanded you. For now the LORD would have established your kingdom over Israel forever. 14But now your kingdom shall not continue. The LORD has sought for Himself a man after His own heart, and the LORD has commanded him *to be* commander over His people, because you have not kept what the LORD commanded you."

15Then Samuel arose and went up from Gilgal to Gibeah of Benjamin. And Saul numbered the people present with him, about six hundred men.

No Weapons for the Army

16Saul, Jonathan his son, and the people present with them remained in Gibeah of Benjamin. But the Philistines encamped in Michmash. 17Then raiders came out of the camp of the Philistines in three companies. One company turned onto the road to Ophrah, to the land of Shual, 18another company turned to the road *to* Beth Horon, and another company turned *to* the road of the border that overlooks the Valley of Zeboim toward the wilderness.

19Now there was no blacksmith to be found throughout all the land of Israel, for the Philistines said, "Lest the Hebrews make swords or spears." 20But all the Israelites would go down to the Philistines to sharpen each man's plowshare, his mattock, his ax, and his sickle; 21and the charge for a sharpening was a pim*ʲ* for the plowshares, the mattocks, the forks, and the axes, and to set the points of the goads. 22So it came about, on the day of battle, that there was neither sword nor spear found in the hand of any of the people who *were* with Saul and Jonathan. But they were found with Saul and Jonathan his son.

23And the garrison of the Philistines went out to the pass of Michmash.

Jonathan Defeats the Philistines

14 Now it happened one day that Jonathan the son of Saul said to the young man who bore his armor, "Come, let us go over to the Philistines' garrison that *is* on the other side." But he did not tell his father. 2And Saul was sitting in the outskirts of Gibeah under a pomegranate tree which *is* in Migron. The people who *were* with him *were* about six hundred men. 3Ahijah the son of Ahitub, Ichabod's brother, the son of Phinehas, the son of Eli, the LORD's priest in Shiloh, was wearing an ephod. But the people did not know that Jonathan had gone.

4Between the passes, by which Jonathan sought to go over to the Philistines' garrison, *there was* a sharp rock on one side and a sharp rock on the other side. And the name of one *was* Bozez, and the name of the other Seneh. 5The front of one faced northward opposite Michmash, and the other southward opposite Gibeah.

6Then Jonathan said to the young man who bore his armor, "Come, let us go over to the garrison of these uncircumcised; it may be that the LORD will work for us. For nothing restrains the LORD from saving by many or by few."

7So his armorbearer said to him, "Do all that is in your heart. Go then; here I am with you, according to your heart."

8Then Jonathan said, "Very well, let us cross over to *these* men, and we will show ourselves to them. 9If they say thus to us, 'Wait until we come to you,' then we will stand still in our place and not go up to them. 10But if they say thus, 'Come up to us,' then we will go up. For the LORD has delivered them into our hand, and this *will be* a sign to us."

11So both of them showed themselves to the garrison of the Philistines. And the Philistines said, "Look, the Hebrews are coming out of the holes where they have hidden." 12Then the men of the garrison called to Jonathan and his armorbearer, and said, "Come up to us, and we will show you something."

Jonathan said to his armorbearer, "Come up after me, for the LORD has delivered them into the hand of Israel." 13And Jonathan climbed up on his hands and knees with his armorbearer after him; and they fell before Jona-

ʲ About two-thirds shekel weight

than. And as he came after him, his armorbearer killed them. 14That first slaughter which Jonathan and his armorbearer made was about twenty men within about half an acre of land.

15And there was trembling in the camp, in the field, and among all the people. The garrison and the raiders also trembled; and the earth quaked, so that it was a very great trembling. 16Now the watchmen of Saul in Gibeah of Benjamin looked, and there was the multitude, melting away; and they went here and there. 17Then Saul said to the people who were with him, "Now call the roll and see who has gone from us." And when they had called the roll, surprisingly, Jonathan and his armorbearer were not there. 18And Saul said to Ahijah, "Bring the ark of God here" (for at that time the ark of God was with the children of Israel). 19Now it happened, while Saul talked to the priest, that the noise which was in the camp of the Philistines continued to increase; so Saul said to the priest, "Withdraw your hand." 20Then Saul and all the people who were with him assembled, and they went to the battle; and indeed every man's sword was against his neighbor, and there was very great confusion. 21Moreover the Hebrews who were with the Philistines before that time, who went up with them into the camp from the surrounding country, they also joined the Israelites who were with Saul and Jonathan. 22Likewise all the men of Israel who had hidden in the mountains of Ephraim, when they heard that the Philistines fled, they also followed hard after them in the battle. 23So the LORD saved Israel that day, and the battle shifted to Beth Aven.

Saul's Rash Oath

24And the men of Israel were distressed that day, for Saul had placed the people under oath, saying, "Cursed is the man who eats any food until evening, before I have taken vengeance on my enemies." So none of the people tasted food. 25Now all the people of the land came to a forest; and there was honey on the ground. 26And when the people had come into the woods, there was the honey, dripping; but no one put his hand to his mouth, for the people feared the oath. 27But Jonathan had not heard his father charge the people with the oath; therefore he stretched out the end of the rod that was in his hand and dipped it in a honeycomb, and put his hand to his mouth; and his countenance brightened. 28Then one of the people said, "Your father strictly charged the people with an oath, saying, 'Cursed is the man who eats food this day.' " And the people were faint.

29But Jonathan said, "My father has troubled the land. Look now, how my countenance has brightened because I tasted a little of this honey. 30How much better if the people had eaten freely today of the spoil of their enemies which they found! For now would there not have been a much greater slaughter among the Philistines?"

31Now they had driven back the Philistines that day from Michmash to Aijalon. So the people were very faint. 32And the people rushed on the spoil, and took sheep, oxen, and calves, and slaughtered them on the ground; and the people ate them with the blood. 33Then they told Saul, saying, "Look, the people are sinning against the LORD by eating with the blood!"

So he said, "You have dealt treacherously; roll a large stone to me this day." 34Then Saul said, "Disperse yourselves among the people, and say to them, 'Bring me here every man's ox and every man's sheep, slaughter them here, and eat; and do not sin against the LORD by eating with the blood.' " So every one of the people brought his ox with him that night, and slaughtered it there. 35Then Saul built an altar to the LORD. This was the first altar that he built to the LORD.

36Now Saul said, "Let us go down after the Philistines by night, and plunder them until the morning light; and let us not leave a man of them."

And they said, "Do whatever seems good to you."

Then the priest said, "Let us draw near to God here."

37So Saul asked counsel of God, "Shall I go down after the Philistines? Will You deliver them into the hand of Israel?" But He did not answer him that day. 38And Saul said, "Come over here, all you chiefs of the people, and know

and see what this sin was today.
39For *as* the LORD lives, who saves Israel, though it be in Jonathan my son,
he shall surely die." But not a man
among all the people answered him.
40Then he said to all Israel, "You be
on one side, and my son Jonathan and
I will be on the other side."

And the people said to Saul, "Do
what seems good to you."
41Therefore Saul said to the LORD
God of Israel, "Give a perfect *lot*." So
Saul and Jonathan were taken, but the
people escaped. 42And Saul said, "Cast
lots between my son Jonathan and me."
So Jonathan was taken. 43Then Saul
said to Jonathan, "Tell me what you
have done."

And Jonathan told him, and said, "I
only tasted a little honey with the end
of the rod that *was* in my hand. So now
I must die!"
44Saul answered, "God do so and
more also; for you shall surely die, Jonathan."
45But the people said to Saul, "Shall
Jonathan die, who has accomplished
this great deliverance in Israel? Certainly not! *As* the LORD lives, not one
hair of his head shall fall to the ground,
for he has worked with God this day."
So the people rescued Jonathan, and he
did not die.
46Then Saul returned from pursuing
the Philistines, and the Philistines went
to their own place.

Saul's Continuing Wars

47So Saul established his sovereignty
over Israel, and fought against all his
enemies on every side, against Moab,
against the people of Ammon, against
Edom, against the kings of Zobah, and
against the Philistines. Wherever he
turned, he harassed *them.* 48And he
gathered an army and attacked the Amalekites, and delivered Israel from the
hands of those who plundered them.
49The sons of Saul were Jonathan,
Jishui, and Malchishua. And the names
of his two daughters *were these:* the
name of the firstborn Merab, and the
name of the younger Michal. 50The
name of Saul's wife *was* Ahinoam the
daughter of Ahimaaz. And the name of
the commander of his army *was* Abner
the son of Ner, Saul's uncle. 51Kish *was*

the father of Saul, and Ner the father
of Abner *was* the son of Abiel.
52Now there was fierce war with the
Philistines all the days of Saul. And
when Saul saw any strong man or any
valiant man, he took him for himself.

Saul Spares King Agag

15 Samuel also said to Saul, "The
LORD sent me to anoint you king
over His people, over Israel. Now therefore, heed the voice of the words of the
LORD. 2Thus says the LORD of hosts: 'I
will punish Amalek *for* what he did to
Israel, how he ambushed him on the
way when he came up from Egypt.
3Now go and attack Amalek, and utterly destroy all that they have, and do
not spare them. But kill both man and
woman, infant and nursing child, ox
and sheep, camel and donkey.' "
4So Saul gathered the people together
and numbered them in Telaim, two
hundred thousand foot soldiers and ten
thousand men of Judah. 5And Saul
came to a city of Amalek, and lay in
wait in the valley.
6Then Saul said to the Kenites, "Go,
depart, get down from among the Amalekites, lest I destroy you with them. For
you showed kindness to all the children
of Israel when they came up out of
Egypt." So the Kenites departed from
among the Amalekites. 7And Saul attacked the Amalekites, from Havilah all
the way to Shur, which is east of Egypt.
8He also took Agag king of the Amalekites alive, and utterly destroyed all the
people with the edge of the sword.
9But Saul and the people spared Agag
and the best of the sheep, the oxen, the
fatlings, the lambs, and all *that was*
good, and were unwilling to utterly destroy them. But everything despised
and worthless, that they utterly destroyed.

Saul Rejected as King

10Now the word of the LORD came to
Samuel, saying, 11"I greatly regret that
I have set up Saul *as* king, for he has
turned back from following Me, and has
not performed My commandments."
And it grieved Samuel, and he cried out
to the LORD all night. 12So when Samuel
rose early in the morning to meet Saul,
it was told Samuel, saying, "Saul went

to Carmel, and indeed, he set up a monument for himself; and he has gone on around, passed by, and gone down to Gilgal." 13Then Samuel went to Saul, and Saul said to him, "Blessed *are* you of the LORD! I have performed the commandment of the LORD."

14But Samuel said, "What then *is* this bleating of the sheep in my ears, and the lowing of the oxen which I hear?"

15And Saul said, "They have brought them from the Amalekites; for the people spared the best of the sheep and the oxen, to sacrifice to the LORD your God; and the rest we have utterly destroyed."

16Then Samuel said to Saul, "Be quiet! And I will tell you what the LORD said to me last night."

And he said to him, "Speak on."

17So Samuel said, "When you *were* little in your own eyes, *were* you not head of the tribes of Israel? And did not the LORD anoint you king over Israel? 18Now the LORD sent you on a mission, and said, 'Go, and utterly destroy the sinners, the Amalekites, and fight against them until they are consumed.' 19Why then did you not obey the voice of the LORD? Why did you swoop down on the spoil, and do evil in the sight of the LORD?"

20And Saul said to Samuel, "But I have obeyed the voice of the LORD, and gone on the mission on which the LORD sent me, and brought back Agag king of Amalek; I have utterly destroyed the Amalekites. 21But the people took of the plunder, sheep and oxen, the best of the things which should have been utterly destroyed, to sacrifice to the LORD your God in Gilgal."

22So Samuel said:

"Has the LORD *as great* delight in
    burnt offerings and sacrifices,
As in obeying the voice of the
    LORD?
Behold, to obey is better than
    sacrifice,
And to heed than the fat of rams.
23 For rebellion *is as* the sin of
    witchcraft,
And stubbornness *is as* iniquity and
    idolatry.
Because you have rejected the
    word of the LORD,
He also has rejected you from *being*
    king."

24Then Saul said to Samuel, "I have sinned, for I have transgressed the commandment of the LORD and your words, because I feared the people and obeyed their voice. 25Now therefore, please pardon my sin, and return with me, that I may worship the LORD."

26But Samuel said to Saul, "I will not return with you, for you have rejected the word of the LORD, and the LORD has rejected you from being king over Israel."

27And as Samuel turned around to go away, *Saul* seized the edge of his robe, and it tore. 28So Samuel said to him, "The LORD has torn the kingdom of Israel from you today, and has given it to a neighbor of yours, *who is* better than you. 29And also the Strength of Israel will not lie nor relent. For He *is* not a man, that He should relent."

30Then he said, "I have sinned; *yet* honor me now, please, before the elders of my people and before Israel, and return with me, that I may worship the LORD your God." 31So Samuel turned back after Saul, and Saul worshiped the LORD.

32Then Samuel said, "Bring Agag king of the Amalekites here to me." So Agag came to him cautiously.

And Agag said, "Surely the bitterness of death is past."

33But Samuel said, "As your sword has made women childless, so shall your mother be childless among women." And Samuel hacked Agag in pieces before the LORD in Gilgal.

34Then Samuel went to Ramah, and Saul went up to his house at Gibeah of Saul. 35And Samuel went no more to see Saul until the day of his death. Nevertheless Samuel mourned for Saul, and the LORD regretted that He had made Saul king over Israel.

David Anointed King

16 Now the LORD said to Samuel, "How long will you mourn for Saul, seeing I have rejected him from reigning over Israel? Fill your horn with oil, and go; I am sending you to Jesse the Bethlehemite. For I have provided Myself a king among his sons."

2And Samuel said, "How can I go? If Saul hears *it*, he will kill me."

But the LORD said, "Take a heifer with

you, and say, 'I have come to sacrifice to the LORD.' 3Then invite Jesse to the sacrifice, and I will show you what you shall do; you shall anoint for Me the one I name to you."

4So Samuel did what the LORD said, and went to Bethlehem. And the elders of the town trembled at his coming, and said, "Do you come peaceably?"

5And he said, "Peaceably; I have come to sacrifice to the LORD. Sanctify yourselves, and come with me to the sacrifice." Then he consecrated Jesse and his sons, and invited them to the sacrifice.

6So it was, when they came, that he looked at Eliab and said, "Surely the LORD's anointed is before Him!"

7But the LORD said to Samuel, "Do not look at his appearance or at his physical stature, because I have refused him. For the LORD does not see as man sees; for man looks at the outward appearance, but the LORD looks at the heart."

8So Jesse called Abinadab, and made him pass before Samuel. And he said, "Neither has the LORD chosen this one." 9Then Jesse made Shammah pass by. And he said, "Neither has the LORD chosen this one." 10Thus Jesse made seven of his sons pass before Samuel. And Samuel said to Jesse, "The LORD has not chosen these." 11And Samuel said to Jesse, "Are all the young men here?" Then he said, "There remains yet the youngest, and there he is, keeping the sheep."

And Samuel said to Jesse, "Send and bring him. For we will not sit down till he comes here." 12So he sent and brought him in. Now he was ruddy, with bright eyes, and good-looking. And the LORD said, "Arise, anoint him; for this is the one!" 13Then Samuel took the horn of oil and anointed him in the midst of his brothers; and the Spirit of the LORD came upon David from that day forward. So Samuel arose and went to Ramah.

A Distressing Spirit Troubles Saul

14But the Spirit of the LORD departed from Saul, and a distressing spirit from the LORD troubled him. 15And Saul's servants said to him, "Surely, a distressing spirit from God is troubling you. 16Let our master now command your servants, who are before you, to seek out a man who is a skillful player on the harp. And it shall be that he will play it with his hand when the distressing spirit from God is upon you, and you shall be well."

17So Saul said to his servants, "Provide me now a man who can play well, and bring him to me."

18Then one of the servants answered and said, "Look, I have seen a son of Jesse the Bethlehemite, who is skillful in playing, a mighty man of valor, a man of war, prudent in speech, and a handsome person; and the LORD is with him."

19Therefore Saul sent messengers to Jesse, and said, "Send me your son David, who is with the sheep." 20And Jesse took a donkey loaded with bread, a skin of wine, and a young goat, and sent them by his son David to Saul. 21So David came to Saul and stood before him. And he loved him greatly, and he became his armorbearer. 22Then Saul sent to Jesse, saying, "Please let David stand before me, for he has found favor in my sight." 23And so it was, whenever the spirit from God was upon Saul, that David would take a harp and play it with his hand. Then Saul would become refreshed and well, and the distressing spirit would depart from him.

David and Goliath

17 Now the Philistines gathered their armies together to battle, and were gathered at Sochoh, which belongs to Judah; they encamped between Sochoh and Azekah, in Ephes Dammim. 2And Saul and the men of Israel were gathered together, and they encamped in the Valley of Elah, and drew up in battle array against the Philistines. 3The Philistines stood on a mountain on one side, and Israel stood on a mountain on the other side, with a valley between them.

4And a champion went out from the camp of the Philistines, named Goliath, from Gath, whose height was six cubits and a span. 5He had a bronze helmet on his head, and he was armed with a coat of mail, and the weight of the coat was five thousand shekels of bronze. 6And he had bronze armor on his legs and a bronze javelin between his shoulders. 7Now the staff of his spear *was* like a weaver's beam, and his iron spearhead *weighed* six hundred shekels; and a shield-bearer went before him. 8Then he stood and cried out to the armies of Israel, and said to them, "Why have you come out to line up for battle? *Am* I not a Philistine, and you the servants of Saul? Choose a man for yourselves, and let him come down to me. 9If he is able to fight with me and kill me, then we will be your servants. But if I prevail against him and kill him, then you shall be our servants and serve us." 10And the Philistine said, "I defy the armies of Israel this day; give me a man, that we may fight together." 11When Saul and all Israel heard these words of the Philistine, they were dismayed and greatly afraid.

12Now David *was* the son of that Ephrathite of Bethlehem Judah, whose name *was* Jesse, and who had eight sons. And the man was old, advanced *in years*, in the days of Saul. 13The three oldest sons of Jesse had gone to follow Saul to the battle. The names of his three sons who went to the battle *were* Eliab the firstborn, next to him Abinadab, and the third Shammah. 14David *was* the youngest. And the three oldest followed Saul. 15But David occasionally went and returned from Saul to feed his father's sheep at Bethlehem.

16And the Philistine drew near and presented himself forty days, morning and evening.

17Then Jesse said to his son David, "Take now for your brothers an ephah of this dried *grain* and these ten loaves, and run to your brothers at the camp. 18And carry these ten cheeses to the captain of *their* thousand, and see how your brothers fare, and bring back news of them." 19Now Saul and they and all the men of Israel *were* in the Valley of Elah, fighting with the Philistines.

20So David rose early in the morning, left the sheep with a keeper, and took *the things* and went as Jesse had commanded him. And he came to the camp as the army was going out to the fight and shouting for the battle. 21For Israel and the Philistines had drawn up in battle array, army against army. 22And

David left his supplies in the hand of the supply keeper, ran to the army, and came and greeted his brothers. 23Then as he talked with them, there was the champion, the Philistine of Gath, Goliath by name, coming up from the armies of the Philistines; and he spoke according to the same words. So David heard *them*. 24And all the men of Israel, when they saw the man, fled from him and were dreadfully afraid. 25So the men of Israel said, "Have you seen this man who has come up? Surely he has come up to defy Israel; and it shall be *that* the man who kills him the king will enrich with great riches, will give him his daughter, and give his father's house exemption *from taxes* in Israel."

26Then David spoke to the men who stood by him, saying, "What shall be done for the man who kills this Philistine and takes away the reproach from Israel? For who *is* this uncircumcised Philistine, that he should defy the armies of the living God?"

27And the people answered him in this manner, saying, "So shall it be done for the man who kills him."

28Now Eliab his oldest brother heard when he spoke to the men; and Eliab's anger was aroused against David, and he said, "Why did you come down here? And with whom have you left those few sheep in the wilderness? I know your pride and the insolence of your heart, for you have come down to see the battle."

29And David said, "What have I done now? *Is there* not a cause?" 30Then he turned from him toward another and said the same thing; and these people answered him as the first ones *did*.

31Now when the words which David spoke were heard, they reported *them* to Saul; and he sent for him. 32Then David said to Saul, "Let no man's heart fail because of him; your servant will go and fight with this Philistine."

33And Saul said to David, "You are not able to go against this Philistine to fight with him; for you *are* a youth, and he a man of war from his youth."

34But David said to Saul, "Your servant used to keep his father's sheep, and when a lion or a bear came and took a lamb out of the flock, 35I went out after it and struck it, and delivered *the lamb* from its mouth; and when it arose against me, I caught *it* by its beard, and struck and killed it. 36Your servant has killed both lion and bear; and this uncircumcised Philistine will be like one of them, seeing he has defied the armies of the living God." 37Moreover David said, "The LORD, who delivered me from the paw of the lion and from the paw of the bear, He will deliver me from the hand of this Philistine."

And Saul said to David, "Go, and the LORD be with you!"

38So Saul clothed David with his armor, and he put a bronze helmet on his head; he also clothed him with a coat of mail. 39David fastened his sword to his armor and tried to walk, for he had not tested *them*. And David said to Saul, "I cannot walk with these, for I have not tested *them*." So David took them off.

40Then he took his staff in his hand; and he chose for himself five smooth stones from the brook, and put them in a shepherd's bag, in a pouch which he had, and his sling was in his hand. And he drew near to the Philistine. 41So the Philistine came, and began drawing near to David, and the man who bore the shield *went* before him. 42And when the Philistine looked about and saw David, he disdained him; for he was *only* a youth, ruddy and good-looking. 43So the Philistine said to David, "*Am* I a dog, that you come to me with sticks?" And the Philistine cursed David by his gods. 44And the Philistine said to David, "Come to me, and I will give your flesh to the birds of the air and the beasts of the field!"

45Then David said to the Philistine, "You come to me with a sword, with a spear, and with a javelin. But I come to you in the name of the LORD of hosts, the God of the armies of Israel, whom you have defied. 46This day the LORD will deliver you into my hand, and I will strike you and take your head from you. And this day I will give the carcasses of the camp of the Philistines to the birds of the air and the wild beasts of the earth, that all the earth may know that there is a God in Israel. 47Then all this assembly shall know that the LORD

does not save with sword and spear; for the battle *is* the LORD's, and He will give you into our hands."

48So it was, when the Philistine arose and came and drew near to meet David, that David hurried and ran toward the army to meet the Philistine. 49Then David put his hand in his bag and took out a stone; and he slung *it* and struck the Philistine in his forehead, so that the stone sank into his forehead, and he fell on his face to the earth. 50So David prevailed over the Philistine with a sling and a stone, and struck the Philistine and killed him. But *there was* no sword in the hand of David. 51Therefore David ran and stood over the Philistine, took his sword and drew it out of its sheath and killed him, and cut off his head with it.

And when the Philistines saw that their champion was dead, they fled. 52Now the men of Israel and Judah arose and shouted, and pursued the Philistines as far as the entrance of the valley and to the gates of Ekron. And the wounded of the Philistines fell along the road to Shaaraim, even as far as Gath and Ekron. 53Then the children of Israel returned from chasing the Philistines, and they plundered their tents. 54And David took the head of the Philistine and brought it to Jerusalem, but he put his armor in his tent.

55When Saul saw David going out against the Philistine, he said to Abner, the commander of the army, "Abner, whose son *is* this youth?"

And Abner said, "As your soul lives, O king, I do not know."

56So the king said, "Inquire whose son this young man *is*."

57Then, as David returned from the slaughter of the Philistine, Abner took him and brought him before Saul with the head of the Philistine in his hand. 58And Saul said to him, "Whose son *are* you, young man?"

So David answered, "*I am* the son of your servant Jesse the Bethlehemite."

Saul Resents David

18 Now when he had finished speaking to Saul, the soul of Jonathan was knit to the soul of David, and Jonathan loved him as his own soul. 2Saul took him that day, and would not

let him go home to his father's house anymore. 3Then Jonathan and David made a covenant, because he loved him as his own soul. 4And Jonathan took off the robe that *was* on him and gave it to David, with his armor, even to his sword and his bow and his belt.

5So David went out wherever Saul sent him, *and* behaved wisely. And Saul set him over the men of war, and he was accepted in the sight of all the people and also in the sight of Saul's servants. 6Now it had happened as they were coming *home,* when David was returning from the slaughter of the Philistine, that the women had come out of all the cities of Israel, singing and dancing, to meet King Saul, with tambourines, with joy, and with musical instruments. 7So the women sang as they danced, and said:

"Saul has slain his thousands,
And David his ten thousands."

8Then Saul was very angry, and the saying displeased him; and he said, "They have ascribed to David ten thousands, and to me they have ascribed *only* thousands. Now *what* more can he have but the kingdom?" 9So Saul eyed David from that day forward.

10And it happened on the next day that the distressing spirit from God came upon Saul, and he prophesied inside the house. So David played *music* with his hand, as at other times; but *there was* a spear in Saul's hand. 11And Saul cast the spear, for he said, "I will pin David to the wall!" But David escaped his presence twice.

12Now Saul was afraid of David, because the LORD was with him, but had departed from Saul. 13Therefore Saul removed him from his presence, and made him his captain over a thousand; and he went out and came in before the people. 14And David behaved wisely in all his ways, and the LORD *was* with him. 15Therefore, when Saul saw that he behaved very wisely, he was afraid of him. 16But all Israel and Judah loved David, because he went out and came in before them.

David Marries Michal

17Then Saul said to David, "Here is my older daughter Merab; I will give her to you as a wife. Only be valiant

for me, and fight the LORD's battles." For Saul thought, "Let my hand not be against him, but let the hand of the Philistines be against him."

18So David said to Saul, "Who *am* I, and what *is* my life *or* my father's family in Israel, that I should be son-in-law to the king?" 19But it happened at the time when Merab, Saul's daughter, should have been given to David, that she was given to Adriel the Meholathite as a wife.

20Now Michal, Saul's daughter, loved David. And they told Saul, and the thing pleased him. 21So Saul said, "I will give her to him, that she may be a snare to him, and that the hand of the Philistines may be against him." Therefore Saul said to David a second time, "You shall be my son-in-law today."

22And Saul commanded his servants, "Communicate with David secretly, and say, 'Look, the king has delight in you, and all his servants love you. Now therefore, become the king's son-in-law.' "

23So Saul's servants spoke those words in the hearing of David. And David said, "Does it seem to you *a* light *thing* to be a king's son-in-law, seeing I *am* a poor and lightly esteemed man?" 24And the servants of Saul told him, saying, "In this manner David spoke."

25Then Saul said, "Thus you shall say to David: 'The king does not desire any dowry but one hundred foreskins of the Philistines, to take vengeance on the king's enemies.' " But Saul thought to make David fall by the hand of the Philistines. 26So when his servants told David these words, it pleased David well to become the king's son-in-law. Now the days had not expired; 27therefore David arose and went, he and his men, and killed two hundred men of the Philistines. And David brought their foreskins, and they gave them in full count to the king, that he might become the king's son-in-law. Then Saul gave him Michal his daughter as a wife.

28Thus Saul saw and knew that the LORD *was* with David, and *that* Michal, Saul's daughter, loved him; 29and Saul was still more afraid of David. So Saul became David's enemy continually. 30Then the princes of the Philistines went out *to war.* And so it was, whenever they went out, *that* David behaved more wisely than all the servants of Saul, so that his name became highly esteemed.

Saul Persecutes David

19 Now Saul spoke to Jonathan his son and to all his servants, that they should kill David; but Jonathan, Saul's son, delighted greatly in David. 2So Jonathan told David, saying, "My father Saul seeks to kill you. Therefore please be on your guard until morning, and stay in a secret *place* and hide. 3And I will go out and stand beside my father in the field where you *are,* and I will speak with my father about you. Then what I observe, I will tell you."

4Thus Jonathan spoke well of David to Saul his father, and said to him, "Let not the king sin against his servant, against David, because he has not sinned against you, and because his works *have been* very good toward you. 5For he took his life in his hands and killed the Philistine, and the LORD brought about a great deliverance for all Israel. You saw *it* and rejoiced. Why then will you sin against innocent blood, to kill David without a cause?"

6So Saul heeded the voice of Jonathan, and Saul swore, "*As* the LORD lives, he shall not be killed." 7Then Jonathan called David, and Jonathan told him all these things. So Jonathan brought David to Saul, and he was in his presence as in times past.

8And there was war again; and David went out and fought with the Philistines, and struck them with a mighty blow, and they fled from him.

9Now the distressing spirit from the LORD came upon Saul as he sat in his house with his spear in his hand. And David was playing *music* with *his* hand. 10Then Saul sought to pin David to the wall with the spear, but he slipped away from Saul's presence; and he drove the spear into the wall. So David fled and escaped that night.

11Saul also sent messengers to David's house to watch him and to kill him in the morning. And Michal, David's wife, told him, saying, "If you do not save your life tonight, tomorrow you

will be killed." 12So Michal let David down through a window. And he went and fled and escaped. 13And Michal took an image and laid *it* in the bed, put a cover of goats' *hair* for his head, and covered *it* with clothes. 14So when Saul sent messengers to take David, she said, "He *is* sick."

15Then Saul sent the messengers *back* to see David, saying, "Bring him up to me in the bed, that I may kill him." 16And when the messengers had come in, there was the image in the bed, with a cover of goats' *hair* for his head. 17Then Saul said to Michal, "Why have you deceived me like this, and sent my enemy away, so that he has escaped?"

And Michal answered Saul, "He said to me, 'Let me go! Why should I kill you?' "

18So David fled and escaped, and went to Samuel at Ramah, and told him all that Saul had done to him. And he and Samuel went and stayed in Naioth. 19Now it was told Saul, saying, "Take note, David *is* at Naioth in Ramah!" 20Then Saul sent messengers to take David. And when they saw the group of prophets prophesying, and Samuel standing *as* leader over them, the Spirit of God came upon the messengers of Saul, and they also prophesied. 21And when Saul was told, he sent other messengers, and they prophesied likewise. Then Saul sent messengers again the third time, and they prophesied also. 22Then he also went to Ramah, and came to the great well that *is* at Sechu. So he asked, and said, "Where *are* Samuel and David?"

And *someone* said, "Indeed *they are* at Naioth in Ramah." 23So he went there to Naioth in Ramah. Then the Spirit of God was upon him also, and he went on and prophesied until he came to Naioth in Ramah. 24And he also stripped off his clothes and prophesied before Samuel in like manner, and lay down naked all that day and all that night. Therefore they say, "*Is* Saul also among the prophets?"*k*

Jonathan's Loyalty to David

20 Then David fled from Naioth in Ramah, and went and said to Jon-

k Compare 1 Samuel 10.12

athan, "What have I done? What *is* my iniquity, and what *is* my sin before your father, that he seeks my life?"

2So Jonathan said to him, "By no means! You shall not die! Indeed, my father will do nothing either great or small without first telling me. And why should my father hide this thing from me? It *is* not *so!*"

3Then David took an oath again, and said, "Your father certainly knows that I have found favor in your eyes, and he has said, 'Do not let Jonathan know this, lest he be grieved.' But truly, *as* the LORD lives and *as* your soul lives, *there is* but a step between me and death."

4So Jonathan said to David, "Whatever you yourself desire, I will do *it* for you."

5And David said to Jonathan, "Indeed tomorrow *is* the New Moon, and I should not fail to sit with the king to eat. But let me go, that I may hide in the field until the third *day* at evening. 6If your father misses me at all, then say, 'David earnestly asked *permission* of me that he might run over to Bethlehem, his city, for *there is* a yearly sacrifice there for all the family.' 7If he says thus: '*It is* well,' your servant will be safe. But if he is very angry, be sure that evil is determined by him. 8Therefore you shall deal kindly with your servant, for you have brought your servant into a covenant of the LORD with you. Nevertheless, if there is iniquity in me, kill me yourself, for why should you bring me to your father?"

9But Jonathan said, "Far be it from you! For if I knew certainly that evil was determined by my father to come upon you, then would I not tell you?"

10Then David said to Jonathan, "Who will tell me, or what *if* your father answers you roughly?"

11And Jonathan said to David, "Come, let us go out into the field." So both of them went out into the field. 12Then Jonathan said to David: "The LORD God of Israel *is witness!* When I have sounded out my father sometime tomorrow, *or* the third *day*, and indeed *there is* good toward David, and I do not send to you and tell you, 13may the LORD do so and much more to Jonathan. But if it pleases my father *to do* you

evil, then I will report it to you and send you away, that you may go in safety. And the LORD be with you as He has been with my father. 14And you shall not only show me the kindness of the LORD while I still live, that I may not die; 15but you shall not cut off your kindness from my house forever, no, not when the LORD has cut off every one of the enemies of David from the face of the earth." 16So Jonathan made *a covenant* with the house of David, *saying,* "Let the LORD require *it* at the hand of David's enemies."

17Now Jonathan again caused David to vow, because he loved him; for he loved him as he loved his own soul. 18Then Jonathan said to David, "Tomorrow *is* the New Moon; and you will be missed, because your seat will be empty. 19And *when* you have stayed three days, go down quickly and come to the place where you hid on the day of the deed; and remain by the stone Ezel. 20Then I will shoot three arrows to the side, as though I shot at a target; 21and there I will send a lad, *saying,* 'Go, find the arrows.' If I expressly say to the lad, 'Look, the arrows *are* on this side of you; get them and come'—then, as the LORD lives, *there is* safety for you and no harm. 22But if I say thus to the young man, 'Look, the arrows *are* beyond you'—go your way, for the LORD has sent you away. 23And as for the matter which you and I have spoken of, indeed the LORD *be* between you and me forever."

24Then David hid in the field. And when the New Moon had come, the king sat down to eat the feast. 25Now the king sat on his seat, as at other times, on a seat by the wall. And Jonathan arose, and Abner sat by Saul's side, but David's place was empty. 26Nevertheless Saul did not say anything that day, for he thought, "Something has happened to him; he *is* unclean, surely he *is* unclean." 27And it happened the next day, the second *day* of the month, that David's place was empty. And Saul said to Jonathan his son, "Why has the son of Jesse not come to eat, either yesterday or today?"

28So Jonathan answered Saul, "David earnestly asked *permission* of me *to go* to Bethlehem. 29And he said,

'Please let me go, for our family has a sacrifice in the city, and my brother has commanded me *to be there*. And now, if I have found favor in your eyes, please let me get away and see my brothers.' Therefore he has not come to the king's table."

30Then Saul's anger was aroused against Jonathan, and he said to him, "You son of a perverse, rebellious *woman!* Do I not know that you have chosen the son of Jesse to your own shame and to the shame of your mother's nakedness? 31For as long as the son of Jesse lives on the earth, you shall not be established, nor your kingdom. Now therefore, send and bring him to me, for he shall surely die."

32And Jonathan answered Saul his father, and said to him, "Why should he be killed? What has he done?" 33Then Saul cast a spear at him to kill him, by which Jonathan knew that it was determined by his father to kill David.

34So Jonathan arose from the table in fierce anger, and ate no food the second day of the month, for he was grieved for David, because his father had treated him shamefully.

35And so it was, in the morning, that Jonathan went out into the field at the time appointed with David, and a little lad *was* with him. 36Then he said to his lad, "Now run, find the arrows which I shoot." As the lad ran, he shot an arrow beyond him. 37When the lad had come to the place where the arrow was which Jonathan had shot, Jonathan cried out after the lad and said, "*Is* not the arrow beyond you?" 38And Jonathan cried out after the lad, "Make haste, hurry, do not delay!" So Jonathan's lad gathered up the arrows and came back to his master. 39But the lad did not know anything. Only Jonathan and David knew of the matter. 40Then Jonathan gave his weapons to his lad, and said to him, "Go, carry *them* to the city."

41As soon as the lad had gone, David arose from *a place* toward the south, fell on his face to the ground, and bowed down three times. And they kissed one another; and they wept together, but David more so. 42Then Jonathan said to David, "Go in peace, since we have both sworn in the name of the LORD, saying, 'May the LORD be between you and me, and between your descendants and my descendants, forever.'" So he arose and departed, and Jonathan went into the city.

David and the Holy Bread

21 Now David came to Nob, to Ahimelech the priest. And Ahimelech was afraid when he met David, and said to him, "Why *are* you alone, and no one is with you?"

2So David said to Ahimelech the priest, "The king has ordered me on some business, and said to me, 'Do not let anyone know anything about the business on which I send you, or what I have commanded you.' And I have directed *my* young men to such and such a place. 3Now therefore, what have you on hand? Give *me* five *loaves of* bread in my hand, or whatever can be found."

4And the priest answered David and said, "*There is* no common bread on hand; but there is holy bread, if the young men have at least kept themselves from women."

5Then David answered the priest, and said to him, "Truly, women *have been* kept from us about three days since I came out. And the vessels of the young men are holy, and *the bread is* in effect common, even though it was consecrated in the vessel this day."

6So the priest gave him holy *bread;* for there was no bread there but the showbread which had been taken from before the LORD, in order to put hot bread *in its place* on the day when it was taken away.

7Now a certain man of the servants of Saul *was* there that day, detained before the LORD. And his name *was* Doeg, an Edomite, the chief of the herdsmen who *belonged* to Saul.

8And David said to Ahimelech, "Is there not here on hand a spear or a sword? For I have brought neither my sword nor my weapons with me, because the king's business required haste."

9So the priest said, "The sword of Goliath the Philistine, whom you killed in the Valley of Elah, there it is, wrapped in a cloth behind the ephod. If you will take that, take *it.* For *there is* no other except that one here."

And David said, "There is none like it; give it to me."

David Flees to Gath

10Then David arose and fled that day from before Saul, and went to Achish the king of Gath. 11And the servants of Achish said to him, "Is this not David the king of the land? Did they not sing of him to one another in dances, saying:

'Saul has slain his thousands,
And David his ten thousands'?"[1]

12Now David took these words to heart, and was very much afraid of Achish the king of Gath. 13So he changed his behavior before them, pretended madness in their hands, scratched on the doors of the gate, and let his saliva fall down on his beard. 14Then Achish said to his servants, "Look, you see the man is insane. Why have you brought him to me? 15Have I need of madmen, that you have brought this *fellow* to play the madman in my presence? Shall this *fellow* come into my house?"

David's Four Hundred Men

22 David therefore departed from there and escaped to the cave of Adullam. So when his brothers and all his father's house heard *it*, they went down there to him. 2And everyone *who was* in distress, everyone who *was* in debt, and everyone *who was* discontented gathered to him. So he became captain over them. And there were about four hundred men with him.

3Then David went from there to Mizpah of Moab; and he said to the king of Moab, "Please let my father and mother come here with you, till I know what God will do for me." 4So he brought them before the king of Moab, and they dwelt with him all the time that David was in the stronghold.

5Now the prophet Gad said to David, "Do not stay in the stronghold; depart, and go to the land of Judah." So David departed and went into the forest of Hereth.

Saul Murders the Priests

6When Saul heard that David and the men who *were* with him had been discovered—now Saul was staying in Gibeah under a tamarisk tree in Ramah, with his spear in his hand, and all his servants standing about him— 7then Saul said to his servants who stood about him, "Hear now, you Benjamites! Will the son of Jesse give every one of you fields and vineyards, *and* make you all captains of thousands and captains of hundreds? 8All of you have conspired against me, and *there is* no one who reveals to me that my son has made a covenant with the son of Jesse; and *there is* not one of you who is sorry for me or reveals to me that my son has stirred up my servant against me, to lie in wait, as *it is* this day."

9Then answered Doeg the Edomite, who was set over the servants of Saul, and said, "I saw the son of Jesse going to Nob, to Ahimelech the son of Ahitub. 10And he inquired of the LORD for him, gave him provisions, and gave him the sword of Goliath the Philistine."

11So the king sent to call Ahimelech the priest, the son of Ahitub, and all his father's house, the priests who *were* in Nob. And they all came to the king. 12And Saul said, "Hear now, son of Ahitub!"

He answered, "Here I am, my lord."

13Then Saul said to him, "Why have you conspired against me, you and the son of Jesse, in that you have given him bread and a sword, and have inquired of God for him, that he should rise against me, to lie in wait, as it is this day?"

14So Ahimelech answered the king and said, "And who among all your servants *is as* faithful as David, who is the king's son-in-law, who goes at your bidding, and is honorable in your house? 15Did I then begin to inquire of God for him? Far be it from me! Let not the king impute anything to his servant, *or* to any in the house of my father. For your servant knew nothing of all this, little or much."

16And the king said, "You shall surely die, Ahimelech, you and all your father's house!" 17Then the king said to the guards who stood about him, "Turn and kill the priests of the LORD, because their hand also *is* with David,

[1] Compare 1 Samuel 18.7

and because they knew when he fled and did not tell it to me." But the servants of the king would not lift their hands to strike the priests of the LORD. 18And the king said to Doeg, "You turn and kill the priests!" So Doeg the Edomite turned and struck the priests, and killed on that day eighty-five men who wore a linen ephod. 19Also Nob, the city of the priests, he struck with the edge of the sword, both men and women, children and nursing infants, oxen and donkeys and sheep—with the edge of the sword.

20Now one of the sons of Ahimelech the son of Ahitub, named Abiathar, escaped and fled after David. 21And Abiathar told David that Saul had killed the LORD's priests. 22So David said to Abiathar, "I knew that day, when Doeg the Edomite *was* there, that he would surely tell Saul. I have caused *the death* of all the persons of your father's house. 23Stay with me; do not fear. For he who seeks my life seeks your life, but with me you *shall be* safe."

David Saves the City of Keilah

23 Then they told David, saying, "Look, the Philistines are fighting against Keilah, and they are robbing the threshing floors."

2Therefore David inquired of the LORD, saying, "Shall I go and attack these Philistines?"

And the LORD said to David, "Go and attack the Philistines, and save Keilah."

3But David's men said to him, "Look, we are afraid here in Judah. How much more then if we go to Keilah against the armies of the Philistines?" 4Then David inquired of the LORD once again.

And the LORD answered him and said, "Arise, go down to Keilah. For I will deliver the Philistines into your hand." 5And David and his men went to Keilah and fought with the Philistines, struck them with a mighty blow, and took away their livestock. So David saved the inhabitants of Keilah.

6Now it happened, when Abiathar the son of Ahimelech fled to David at Keilah, *that* he went down *with* an ephod in his hand.

7And Saul was told that David had gone to Keilah. So Saul said, "God has delivered him into my hand, for he has shut himself in by entering a town that has gates and bars." 8Then Saul called all the people together for war, to go down to Keilah to besiege David and his men.

9When David knew that Saul plotted evil against him, he said to Abiathar the priest, "Bring the ephod here." 10Then David said, "O LORD God of Israel, Your servant has certainly heard that Saul seeks to come to Keilah to destroy the city for my sake. 11Will the men of Keilah deliver me into his hand? Will Saul come down, as Your servant has heard? O LORD God of Israel, I pray, tell Your servant."

And the LORD said, "He will come down."

12Then David said, "Will the men of Keilah deliver me and my men into the hand of Saul?"

And the LORD said, "They will deliver *you*."

13So David and his men, about six hundred, arose and departed from Keilah and went wherever they could go. Then it was told Saul that David had escaped from Keilah; so he halted the expedition.

David in Wilderness Strongholds

14And David stayed in strongholds in the wilderness, and remained in the mountains in the Wilderness of Ziph. Saul sought him every day, but God did not deliver him into his hand. 15So David saw that Saul had come out to seek his life. And David *was* in the Wilderness of Ziph in a forest. 16Then Jonathan, Saul's son, arose and went to David in the woods and strengthened his hand in God. 17And he said to him, "Do not fear, for the hand of Saul my father shall not find you. You shall be king over Israel, and I shall be next to you. Even my father Saul knows that." 18So the two of them made a covenant before the LORD. And David stayed in the woods, and Jonathan went to his own house.

19Then the Ziphites came up to Saul at Gibeah, saying, "Is David not hiding with us in strongholds in the woods, in the hill of Hachilah, which *is* on the south of Jeshimon? 20Now therefore, O king, come down according to all the desire of your soul to come down; and our part *shall be* to deliver him into the king's hand."

21And Saul said, "Blessed *are* you of the LORD, for you have compassion on me. 22Please go and find out for sure, and see the place where his hideout is, *and* who has seen him there. For I am told he is very crafty. 23See therefore, and take knowledge of all the lurking places where he hides; and come back to me with certainty, and I will go with you. And it shall be, if he is in the land, that I will search for him throughout all the clans of Judah."

24So they arose and went to Ziph before Saul. But David and his men *were* in the Wilderness of Maon, in the plain on the south of Jeshimon. 25When Saul and his men went to seek *him*, they told David. Therefore he went down to the rock, and stayed in the Wilderness of Maon. And when Saul heard *that*, he pursued David in the Wilderness of Maon. 26Then Saul went on one side of the mountain, and David and his men on the other side of the mountain. So David made haste to get away from Saul, for Saul and his men were encircling David and his men to take them. 27But a messenger came to Saul, saying, "Hurry and come, for the Philistines have invaded the land!" 28Therefore Saul returned from pursuing David, and went against the Philistines; so they called that place the Rock of Escape. 29Then David went up from there and dwelt in strongholds at En Gedi.

David Spares Saul

24 Now it happened, when Saul had returned from following the Philistines, that it was told him, saying, "Take note! David *is* in the Wilderness of En Gedi." 2Then Saul took three thousand chosen men from all Israel, and went to seek David and his men on the Rocks of the Wild Goats. 3So he came to the sheepfolds by the road, where there *was* a cave; and Saul went in to attend to his needs. (David and his men were staying in the recesses of the cave.) 4Then the men of David said to him, "This is the day of which the LORD said to you, 'Behold, I will deliver your enemy into your hand, that you may do to him as it seems good

to you.' " And David arose and secretly cut off a corner of Saul's robe. 5Now it happened afterward that David's heart troubled him because he had cut Saul's *robe.* 6And he said to his men, "The LORD forbid that I should do this thing to my master, the LORD's anointed, to stretch out my hand against him, seeing he *is* the anointed of the LORD." 7So David restrained his servants with *these* words, and did not allow them to rise against Saul. And Saul got up from the cave and went on *his* way.

8David also arose afterward, went out of the cave, and called out to Saul, saying, "My lord the king!" And when Saul looked behind him, David stooped with his face to the earth, and bowed down. 9And David said to Saul: "Why do you listen to the words of men who say, 'Indeed David seeks your harm'? 10Look, this day your eyes have seen that the LORD delivered you today into my hand in the cave, and *someone* urged *me* to kill you. But *my eye* spared you, and I said, 'I will not stretch out my hand against my lord, for he *is* the LORD's anointed.' 11Moreover, my father, see! Yes, see the corner of your robe in my hand! For in that I cut off the corner of your robe, and did not kill you, know and see that *there is* neither evil nor rebellion in my hand, and I have not sinned against you. Yet you hunt my life to take it. 12Let the LORD judge between you and me, and let the LORD avenge me on you. But my hand shall not be against you. 13As the proverb of the ancients says, 'Wickedness proceeds from the wicked.' But my hand shall not be against you. 14After whom has the king of Israel come out? Whom do you pursue? A dead dog? A flea? 15Therefore let the LORD be judge, and judge between you and me, and see and plead my case, and deliver me out of your hand."

16So it was, when David had finished speaking these words to Saul, that Saul said, "*Is* this your voice, my son David?" And Saul lifted up his voice and wept. 17Then he said to David: "You *are* more righteous than I; for you have rewarded me with good, whereas I have rewarded you with evil. 18And you have shown this day how you have dealt well with me; for when the LORD delivered me into your hand, you did not kill me. 19For if a man finds his enemy, will he let him get away safely? Therefore may the LORD reward you with good for what you have done to me this day. 20And now I know indeed that you shall surely be king, and that the kingdom of Israel shall be established in your hand. 21Therefore swear now to me by the LORD that you will not cut off my descendants after me, and that you will not destroy my name from my father's house."

22So David swore to Saul. And Saul went home, but David and his men went up to the stronghold.

Death of Samuel

25 Then Samuel died; and the Israelites gathered together and lamented for him, and buried him at his home in Ramah. And David arose and went down to the Wilderness of Paran.

David and the Wife of Nabal

2Now *there was* a man in Maon whose business *was* in Carmel, and the man *was* very rich. He had three thousand sheep and a thousand goats. And he was shearing his sheep in Carmel. 3The name of the man *was* Nabal, and the name of his wife Abigail. And *she was* a woman of good understanding and beautiful appearance; but the man *was* harsh and evil in *his* doings. He *was of the house of* Caleb.

4When David heard in the wilderness that Nabal was shearing his sheep, 5David sent ten young men; and David said to the young men, "Go up to Carmel, go to Nabal, and greet him in my name. 6And thus you shall say to him who lives *in prosperity:* 'Peace *be* to you, peace to your house, and peace to all that you have! 7Now I have heard that you have shearers. Your shepherds were with us, and we did not hurt them, nor was there anything missing from them all the while they were in Carmel. 8Ask your young men, and they will tell you. Therefore let *my* young men find favor in your eyes, for we come on a feast day. Please give whatever comes to your hand to your servants and to your son David.' "

9So when David's young men came, they spoke to Nabal according to all these words in the name of David, and waited.

10Then Nabal answered David's servants, and said, "Who *is* David, and who *is* the son of Jesse? There are many servants nowadays who break away each one from his master. 11Shall I then take my bread and my water and my meat that I have killed for my shearers, and give *it* to men when I do not know where they *are* from?"

12So David's young men turned on their heels and went back; and they came and told him all these words. 13Then David said to his men, "Every man gird on his sword." So every man girded on his sword, and David also girded on his sword. And about four hundred men went with David, and two hundred stayed with the supplies.

14Now one of the young men told Abigail, Nabal's wife, saying, "Look, David sent messengers from the wilderness to greet our master; and he reviled them. 15But the men *were* very good to us, and we were not hurt, nor did we miss anything as long as we accompanied them, when we were in the fields. 16They were a wall to us both by night and day, all the time we were with them keeping the sheep. 17Now therefore, know and consider what you will do, for harm is determined against our master and against all his household. For he *is such* a scoundrel that *one* cannot speak to him."

18Then Abigail made haste and took two hundred *loaves* of bread, two skins of wine, five sheep already dressed, five seahs of roasted *grain,* one hundred clusters of raisins, and two hundred cakes of figs, and loaded *them* on donkeys. 19And she said to her servants, "Go on before me; see, I am coming after you." But she did not tell her husband Nabal.

20So it was, *as* she rode on the donkey, that she went down under cover of the hill; and there were David and his men, coming down toward her, and she met them. 21Now David had said, "Surely in vain I have protected all that this *fellow* has in the wilderness, so that nothing was missed of all that *belongs* to him. And he has repaid me evil for good. 22May God do so, and more also, to the enemies of David, if I leave one male of all who *belong* to him by morning light."

23Now when Abigail saw David, she dismounted quickly from the donkey, fell on her face before David, and bowed down to the ground. 24So she fell at his feet and said: "On me, my lord, *on* me *let* this iniquity *be!* And please let your maidservant speak in your ears, and hear the words of your maidservant. 25Please, let not my lord regard this scoundrel Nabal. For as his name *is,* so *is* he: Nabal*m* *is* his name, and folly *is* with him! But I, your maidservant, did not see the young men of my lord whom you sent. 26Now therefore, my lord, *as* the LORD lives and *as* your soul lives, since the LORD has held you back from coming to bloodshed and from avenging yourself with your own hand, now then, let your enemies and those who seek harm for my lord be as Nabal. 27And now this present which your maidservant has brought to my lord, let it be given to the young men who follow my lord. 28Please forgive the trespass of your maidservant. For the LORD will certainly make for my lord an enduring house, because my lord fights the battles of the LORD, and evil is not found in you throughout your days. 29Yet a man has risen to pursue you and seek your life, but the life of my lord shall be bound in the bundle of the living with the LORD your God; and the lives of your enemies He shall sling out, *as from* the pocket of a sling. 30And it shall come to pass, when the LORD has done for my lord according to all the good that He has spoken concerning you, and has appointed you ruler over Israel, 31that this will be no grief to you, nor offense of heart to my lord, either that you have shed blood without cause, or that my lord has avenged himself. But when the LORD has dealt well with my lord, then remember your maidservant."

32Then David said to Abigail: "Blessed *is* the LORD God of Israel, who sent you this day to meet me! 33And blessed *is* your advice and blessed *are* you, because you have kept me this day from coming to bloodshed and from

avenging myself with my own hand. 34For indeed, *as* the LORD God of Israel lives, who has kept me back from hurting you, unless you had hurried and come to meet me, surely by morning light no males would have been left to Nabal!" 35So David received from her hand what she had brought him, and said to her, "Go up in peace to your house. See, I have heeded your voice and respected your person."

36Now Abigail went to Nabal, and there he was, holding a feast in his house, like the feast of a king. And Nabal's heart *was* merry within him, for he *was* very drunk; therefore she told him nothing, little or much, until morning light. 37So it was, in the morning, when the wine had gone from Nabal, and his wife had told him these things, that his heart died within him, and he became *like* a stone. 38Then it happened, *after* about ten days, that the LORD struck Nabal, and he died.

39So when David heard that Nabal was dead, he said, "Blessed *be* the LORD, who has pleaded the cause of my reproach from the hand of Nabal, and has kept His servant from evil! For the LORD has returned the wickedness of Nabal on his own head."

And David sent and proposed to Abigail, to take her as his wife. 40When the servants of David had come to Abigail at Carmel, they spoke to her saying, "David sent us to you, to ask you to become his wife."

41Then she arose, bowed her face to the earth, and said, "Here is your maidservant, a servant to wash the feet of the servants of my lord." 42So Abigail rose in haste and rode on a donkey, attended by five of her maidens; and she followed the messengers of David, and became his wife. 43David also took Ahinoam of Jezreel, and so both of them were his wives.

44But Saul had given Michal his daughter, David's wife, to Palti the son of Laish, who *was* from Gallim.

David Spares Saul a Second Time

26 Now the Ziphites came to Saul at Gibeah, saying, "Is David not hiding in the hill of Hachilah, opposite

m Literally *Fool*

Jeshimon?" 2Then Saul arose and went down to the Wilderness of Ziph, having three thousand chosen men of Israel with him, to seek David in the Wilderness of Ziph. 3And Saul encamped in the hill of Hachilah, which *is* opposite Jeshimon, by the road. But David stayed in the wilderness, and he saw that Saul came after him into the wilderness. 4David therefore sent out spies, and understood that Saul had indeed come.

5So David arose and came to the place where Saul had encamped. And David saw the place where Saul lay, and Abner the son of Ner, the commander of his army. Now Saul lay within the camp, with the people encamped all around him. 6Then David answered, and said to Ahimelech the Hittite and to Abishai the son of Zeruiah, brother of Joab, saying, "Who will go down with me to Saul in the camp?"

And Abishai said, "I will go down with you."

7So David and Abishai came to the people by night; and there Saul lay sleeping within the camp, with his spear stuck in the ground by his head. And Abner and the people lay all around him. 8Then Abishai said to David, "God has delivered your enemy into your hand this day. Now therefore, please, let me strike him at once with the spear, right to the earth; and I will not *have to strike* him a second time!"

9But David said to Abishai, "Do not destroy him; for who can stretch out his hand against the LORD's anointed, and be guiltless?" 10David said furthermore, "As the LORD lives, the LORD shall strike him, or his day shall come to die, or he shall go out to battle and perish. 11The LORD forbid that I should stretch out my hand against the LORD's anointed. But please, take now the spear and the jug of water that *are* by his head, and let us go." 12So David took the spear and the jug of water *by* Saul's head, and they got away; and no man saw or knew *it* or awoke. For they *were* all asleep, because a deep sleep from the LORD had fallen on them.

13Now David went over to the other side, and stood on the top of a hill afar off, a great distance *being* between

them. 14And David called out to the people and to Abner the son of Ner, saying, "Do you not answer, Abner?"

Then Abner answered and said, "Who *are* you, calling out to the king?"

15So David said to Abner, "*Are* you not a man? And who *is* like you in Israel? Why then have you not guarded your lord the king? For one of the people came in to destroy your lord the king. 16This thing that you have done *is* not good. *As* the LORD lives, you deserve to die, because you have not guarded your master, the LORD's anointed. And now see where the king's spear *is*, and the jug of water that *was* by his head."

17Then Saul knew David's voice, and said, "*Is* that your voice, my son David?"

David said, "*It is* my voice, my lord, O king." 18And he said, "Why does my lord thus pursue his servant? For what have I done, or what evil *is* in my hand? 19Now therefore, please, let my lord the king hear the words of his servant: If the LORD has stirred you up against me, let Him accept an offering. But if *it is* the children of men, *may* they *be* cursed before the LORD, for they have driven me out this day from sharing in the inheritance of the LORD, saying, 'Go, serve other gods.' 20So now, do not let my blood fall to the earth before the face of the LORD. For the king of Israel has come out to seek a flea, as when one hunts a partridge in the mountains."

21Then Saul said, "I have sinned. Return, my son David. For I will harm you no more, because my life was precious in your eyes this day. Indeed I have played the fool and erred exceedingly."

22And David answered and said, "Here is the king's spear. Let one of the young men come over and get it. 23May the LORD repay every man *for* his righteousness and his faithfulness; for the LORD delivered you into *my* hand today, but I would not stretch out my hand against the LORD's anointed. 24And indeed, as your life was valued much this day in my eyes, so let my life be valued much in the eyes of the LORD, and let Him deliver me out of all tribulation."

25Then Saul said to David, "*May* you

be blessed, my son David! You shall both do great things and also still prevail."

So David went on his way, and Saul returned to his place.

David Allied with the Philistines

27 And David said in his heart, "Now I shall perish someday by the hand of Saul. *There is* nothing better for me than that I should speedily escape to the land of the Philistines; and Saul will despair of me, to seek me anymore in any part of Israel. So I shall escape out of his hand." 2Then David arose and went over with the six hundred men who *were* with him to Achish the son of Maoch, king of Gath. 3So David dwelt with Achish at Gath, he and his men, each man with his household, *and* David with his two wives, Ahinoam the Jezreelitess, and Abigail the Carmelitess, Nabal's widow. 4And it was told Saul that David had fled to Gath; so he sought him no more.

5Then David said to Achish, "If I have now found favor in your eyes, let them give me a place in some town in the country, that I may dwell there. For why should your servant dwell in the royal city with you?" 6So Achish gave him Ziklag that day. Therefore Ziklag has belonged to the kings of Judah to this day. 7Now the time that David dwelt in the country of the Philistines was one full year and four months.

8And David and his men went up and raided the Geshurites, the Girzites, and the Amalekites. For those nations were the inhabitants of the land from of old, as you go to Shur, even as far as the land of Egypt. 9Whenever David attacked the land, he left neither man nor woman alive, but took away the sheep, the oxen, the donkeys, the camels, and the apparel, and returned and came to Achish. 10Then Achish would say, "Where have you made a raid today?" And David would say, "Against the southern *area* of Judah, or against the southern *area* of the Jerahmeelites, or against the southern *area* of the Kenites." 11David would save neither man nor woman alive, to bring *news* to Gath, saying, "Lest they should inform on us, saying, 'Thus David did.'" And thus

was his behavior all the time he dwelt in the country of the Philistines. 12So Achish believed David, saying, "He has made his people Israel utterly abhor him; therefore he will be my servant forever."

28 Now it happened in those days that the Philistines gathered their armies together for war, to fight with Israel. And Achish said to David, "You assuredly know that you will go out with me to battle, you and your men." 2So David said to Achish, "Surely you know what your servant can do." And Achish said to David, "Therefore I will make you one of my chief guardians forever."

Saul Consults a Medium

3Now Samuel had died, and all Israel had lamented for him and buried him in Ramah, in his own city. And Saul had put the mediums and the spiritists out of the land.

4Then the Philistines gathered together, and came and encamped at Shunem. So Saul gathered all Israel together, and they encamped at Gilboa. 5When Saul saw the army of the Philistines, he was afraid, and his heart trembled greatly. 6And when Saul inquired of the LORD, the LORD did not answer him, either by dreams or by Urim or by the prophets.

7Then Saul said to his servants, "Find me a woman who is a medium, that I may go to her and inquire of her." And his servants said to him, "In fact, *there is* a woman who is a medium at En Dor."

8So Saul disguised himself and put on other clothes, and he went, and two men with him; and they came to the woman by night. And he said, "Please conduct a seance for me, and bring up for me the one I shall name to you."

9Then the woman said to him, "Look, you know what Saul has done, how he has cut off the mediums and the spiritists from the land. Why then do you lay a snare for my life, to cause me to die?"

10And Saul swore to her by the LORD, saying, "*As* the LORD lives, no punishment shall come upon you for this thing."

11Then the woman said, "Whom shall I bring up for you?"

And he said, "Bring up Samuel for me."

12When the woman saw Samuel, she cried out with a loud voice. And the woman spoke to Saul, saying, "Why have you deceived me? For you *are* Saul!"

13And the king said to her, "Do not be afraid. What did you see?"

And the woman said to Saul, "I saw a spirit ascending out of the earth."

14So he said to her, "What *is* his form?"

And she said, "An old man is coming up, and he *is* covered with a mantle." And Saul perceived that it *was* Samuel, and he stooped with *his* face to the ground and bowed down.

15Now Samuel said to Saul, "Why have you disturbed me by bringing me up?"

And Saul answered, "I am deeply distressed; for the Philistines make war against me, and God has departed from me and does not answer me anymore, neither by prophets nor by dreams. Therefore I have called you, that you may reveal to me what I should do."

16Then Samuel said: "So why do you ask me, seeing the Lord has departed from you and has become your enemy? 17And the Lord has done for Himself[n] as He spoke by me. For the Lord has torn the kingdom out of your hand and given it to your neighbor, David. 18Because you did not obey the voice of the Lord nor execute His fierce wrath upon Amalek, therefore the Lord has done this thing to you this day. 19Moreover the Lord will also deliver Israel with you into the hand of the Philistines. And tomorrow you and your sons *will be* with me. The Lord will also deliver the army of Israel into the hand of the Philistines."

20Immediately Saul fell full length on the ground, and was dreadfully afraid because of the words of Samuel. And there was no strength in him, for he had eaten no food all day or all night.

21And the woman came to Saul and saw that he was severely troubled, and said to him, "Look, your maidservant has obeyed your voice, and I have put my life in my hands and heeded the words which you spoke to me. 22Now therefore, please, heed also the voice of your maidservant, and let me set a piece of bread before you; and eat, that you may have strength when you go on *your* way."

23But he refused and said, "I will not eat."

So his servants, together with the woman, urged him; and he heeded their voice. Then he arose from the ground and sat on the bed. 24Now the woman had a fatted calf in the house, and she hastened to kill it. And she took flour and kneaded *it,* and baked unleavened bread from it. 25So she brought *it* before Saul and his servants, and they ate. Then they rose and went away that night.

The Philistines Reject David

29 Then the Philistines gathered together all their armies at Aphek, and the Israelites encamped by a fountain which *is* in Jezreel. 2And the lords of the Philistines passed in review by hundreds and by thousands, but David and his men passed in review at the rear with Achish. 3Then the princes of the Philistines said, "What *are* these Hebrews *doing here?*"

And Achish said to the princes of the Philistines, "*Is* this not David, the servant of Saul king of Israel, who has been with me these days, or these years? And to this day I have found no fault in him since he defected *to me.*"

4But the princes of the Philistines were angry with him; so the princes of the Philistines said to him, "Make this fellow return, that he may go back to the place which you have appointed for him, and do not let him go down with us to battle, lest in the battle he become our adversary. For with what could he reconcile himself to his master, if not with the heads of these men? 5*Is* this not David, of whom they sang to one another in dances, saying:

'Saul has slain his thousands,
    And David his ten thousands'?"[o]

6Then Achish called David and said

---

[n] Or *him,* that is, David   [o] Compare 1 Samuel 18.7

to him, "Surely, *as* the LORD lives, you have been upright, and your going out and your coming in with me in the army *is* good in my sight. For to this day I have not found evil in you since the day of your coming to me. Nevertheless the lords do not favor you. 7Therefore return now, and go in peace, that you may not displease the lords of the Philistines."

8So David said to Achish, "But what have I done? And to this day what have you found in your servant as long as I have been with you, that I may not go and fight against the enemies of my lord the king?"

9Then Achish answered and said to David, "I know that you *are* as good in my sight as an angel of God; nevertheless the princes of the Philistines have said, 'He shall not go up with us to the battle.' 10Now therefore, rise early in the morning with your master's servants who have come with you. And as soon as you are up early in the morning and have light, depart."

11So David and his men rose early to depart in the morning, to return to the land of the Philistines. And the Philistines went up to Jezreel.

David's Conflict with the Amalekites

30 Now it happened, when David and his men came to Ziklag, on the third day, that the Amalekites had invaded the South and Ziklag, attacked Ziklag and burned it with fire, 2and had taken captive the women and those who *were* there, from small to great; they did not kill anyone, but carried *them* away and went their way. 3So David and his men came to the city, and there it was, burned with fire; and their wives, their sons, and their daughters had been taken captive. 4Then David and the people who *were* with him lifted up their voices and wept, until they had no more power to weep. 5And David's two wives, Ahinoam the Jezreelitess, and Abigail the widow of Nabal the Carmelite, had been taken captive. 6Now David was greatly distressed, for the people spoke of stoning him, because the soul of all the people was grieved, every man for his sons and his daughters. But David strengthened himself in the LORD his God.

7Then David said to Abiathar the priest, Ahimelech's son, "Please bring the ephod here to me." And Abiathar brought the ephod to David. 8So David inquired of the LORD, saying, "Shall I pursue this troop? Shall I overtake them?"

And He answered him, "Pursue, for you shall surely overtake *them* and without fail recover *all*."

9So David went, he and the six hundred men who *were* with him, and came to the Brook Besor, where those stayed who were left behind. 10But David pursued, he and four hundred men; for two hundred stayed *behind*, who were so weary that they could not cross the Brook Besor.

11Then they found an Egyptian in the field, and brought him to David; and they gave him bread and he ate, and they let him drink water. 12And they gave him a piece of a cake of figs and two clusters of raisins. So when he had eaten, his strength came back to him; for he had eaten no bread nor drunk water for three days and three nights. 13Then David said to him, "To whom do you *belong,* and where *are* you from?"

And he said, "I *am* a young man from Egypt, servant of an Amalekite; and my master left me behind, because three days ago I fell sick. 14We made an invasion of the southern *area* of the Cherethites, in the *territory* which *belongs* to Judah, and of the southern *area* of Caleb; and we burned Ziklag with fire."

15And David said to him, "Can you take me down to this troop?"

So he said, "Swear to me by God that you will neither kill me nor deliver me into the hands of my master, and I will take you down to this troop."

16And when he had brought him down, there they were, spread out over all the land, eating and drinking and dancing, because of all the great spoil which they had taken from the land of the Philistines and from the land of Judah. 17Then David attacked them from twilight until the evening of the next day. Not a man of them escaped, except four hundred young men who rode on camels and fled. 18So David recovered all that the Amalekites had carried away, and David rescued his two wives. 19And nothing of theirs was lacking, either small or great, sons or daughters, spoil or anything which they had taken from them; David recovered all. 20Then David took all the flocks and herds they had driven before those *other* livestock, and said, "This *is* David's spoil."

21Now David came to the two hundred men who had been so weary that they could not follow David, whom they also had made to stay at the Brook Besor. So they went out to meet David and to meet the people who *were* with him. And when David came near the people, he greeted them. 22Then all the wicked and worthless men of those who went with David answered and said, "Because they did not go with us, we will not give them *any* of the spoil that we have recovered, except for every man's wife and children, that they may lead *them* away and depart."

23But David said, "My brethren, you shall not do so with what the LORD has given us, who has preserved us and delivered into our hand the troop that came against us. 24For who will heed you in this matter? But as his part *is* who goes down to the battle, so *shall* his part *be* who stays by the supplies; they shall share alike." 25So it was, from that day forward; he made it a statute and an ordinance for Israel to this day.

26Now when David came to Ziklag, he sent *some* of the spoil to the elders of Judah, to his friends, saying, "Here is a present for you from the spoil of the enemies of the LORD"— 27to *those* who *were* in Bethel, *those* who *were* in Ramoth of the South, *those* who *were* in Jattir, 28*those* who *were* in Aroer, *those* who *were* in Siphmoth, *those* who *were* in Eshtemoa, 29*those* who *were* in Rachal, *those* who *were* in the cities of the Jerahmeelites, *those* who *were* in the cities of the Kenites, 30*those* who *were* in Hormah, *those* who *were* in Chorashan, *those* who *were* in Athach, 31*those* who *were* in Hebron, and to all the places where David himself and his men were accustomed to rove.

The Tragic End of Saul and His Sons

31 Now the Philistines fought against Israel; and the men of Israel fled from before the Philistines, and fell slain on Mount Gilboa. 2Then the Philistines followed hard after Saul and his sons. And the Philistines killed Jonathan, Abinadab, and Malchishua, Saul's sons. 3The battle became fierce against Saul. The archers hit him, and he was severely wounded by the archers.

4Then Saul said to his armorbearer, "Draw your sword, and thrust me through with it, lest these uncircumcised men come and thrust me through and abuse me."

But his armorbearer would not, for he was greatly afraid. Therefore Saul took a sword and fell on it. 5And when his armorbearer saw that Saul was dead, he also fell on his sword, and died with him. 6So Saul, his three sons, his armorbearer, and all his men died together that same day.

7And when the men of Israel who *were* on the other side of the valley, and *those* who *were* on the other side of the Jordan, saw that the men of Israel had fled and that Saul and his sons were dead, they forsook the cities and fled; and the Philistines came and dwelt in them. 8So it happened the next day, when the Philistines came to strip the slain, that they found Saul and his three sons fallen on Mount Gilboa. 9And they cut off his head and stripped off his armor, and sent *word* throughout the land of the Philistines, to proclaim *it in* the temple of their idols and among the people. 10Then they put his armor in the temple of the Ashtoreths, and they fastened his body to the wall of Beth Shan.

11Now when the inhabitants of Jabesh Gilead heard what the Philistines had done to Saul, 12all the valiant men arose and traveled all night, and took the body of Saul and the bodies of his sons from the wall of Beth Shan; and they came to Jabesh and burned them there. 13Then they took their bones and buried *them* under the tamarisk tree at Jabesh, and fasted seven days.

The Second Book of
SAMUEL

The Report of Saul's Death

1 Now it came to pass after the death of Saul, when David had returned from the slaughter of the Amalekites, and David had stayed two days in Ziklag, 2on the third day, behold, it happened that a man came from Saul's camp with his clothes torn and dust on his head. So it was, when he came to David, that he fell to the ground and prostrated himself.

3And David said to him, "Where have you come from?"

So he said to him, "I have escaped from the camp of Israel."

4Then David said to him, "How did the matter go? Please tell me."

And he answered, "The people have fled from the battle, many of the people are fallen and dead, and Saul and Jonathan his son are dead also."

5So David said to the young man who told him, "How do you know that Saul and Jonathan his son are dead?"

6Then the young man who told him said, "As I happened by chance to be on Mount Gilboa, there was Saul, leaning on his spear; and indeed the chariots and horsemen followed hard after him. 7Now when he looked behind him, he saw me and called to me. And I answered, 'Here I am.' 8And he said to me, 'Who are you?' So I answered him, 'I am an Amalekite.' 9He said to me again, 'Please stand over me and kill me, for anguish has come upon me, but my life still remains in me.' 10So I stood over him and killed him, because I was sure that he could not live after he had fallen. And I took the crown that was on his head and the bracelet that was on his arm, and have brought them here to my lord."

11Therefore David took hold of his own clothes and tore them, and so did all the men who were with him. 12And they mourned and wept and fasted until evening for Saul and for Jonathan his son, for the people of the LORD and for the house of Israel, because they had fallen by the sword.

13Then David said to the young man who told him, "Where are you from?"

And he answered, "I am the son of an alien, an Amalekite."

14So David said to him, "How was it you were not afraid to put forth your hand to destroy the LORD's anointed?" 15Then David called one of the young men and said, "Go near, and execute him!" And he struck him so that he died. 16So David said to him, "Your blood is on your own head, for your own mouth has testified against you, saying, 'I have killed the LORD's anointed.' "

The Song of the Bow

17Then David lamented with this lamentation over Saul and over Jonathan his son, 18and he told them to teach the children of Judah the Song of the Bow; indeed it is written in the Book of Jasher:

19 "The beauty of Israel is slain on your
high places!
How the mighty have fallen!
20 Tell it not in Gath,
Proclaim it not in the streets of
Ashkelon—
Lest the daughters of the Philistines
rejoice,
Lest the daughters of the
uncircumcised triumph.

21 "O mountains of Gilboa,
Let there be no dew nor rain
upon you,
Nor fields of offerings.
For the shield of the mighty is cast
away there!
The shield of Saul, not anointed
with oil.
22 From the blood of the slain,
From the fat of the mighty,
The bow of Jonathan did not turn
back,
And the sword of Saul did not
return empty.

23 "Saul and Jonathan were beloved
and pleasant in their lives,
And in their death they were not
divided;

They were swifter than eagles,
They were stronger than lions.

24 "O daughters of Israel, weep over
   Saul,
   Who clothed you in scarlet, with
      luxury;
   Who put ornaments of gold on your
      apparel.

25 "How the mighty have fallen in the
      midst of the battle!
   Jonathan *was* slain in your high
      places.
26   I am distressed for you, my brother
      Jonathan;
   You have been very pleasant to me;
   Your love to me was wonderful,
   Surpassing the love of women.

27 "How the mighty have fallen,
   And the weapons of war perished!"

David Anointed King of Judah

2 It happened after this that David inquired of the LORD, saying, "Shall I
go up to any of the cities of Judah?"
   And the LORD said to him, "Go up."
David said, "Where shall I go up?"
And He said, "To Hebron."
   2So David went up there, and his two
wives also, Ahinoam the Jezreelitess,
and Abigail the widow of Nabal the
Carmelite. 3And David brought up the
men who *were* with him, every man
with his household. So they dwelt in the
cities of Hebron.
   4Then the men of Judah came, and
there they anointed David king over the
house of Judah. And they told David,
saying, "The men of Jabesh Gilead
were the ones who buried Saul."
5So David sent messengers to the men
of Jabesh Gilead, and said to them,
"You *are* blessed of the LORD, for you
have shown this kindness to your lord,
to Saul, and have buried him. 6And now
may the LORD show kindness and truth
to you. I also will repay you this kindness, because you have done this thing.
7Now therefore, let your hands be
strengthened, and be valiant; for your
master Saul is dead, and also the house
of Judah has anointed me king over
them."

Ishbosheth Made King of Israel

8But Abner the son of Ner, commander of Saul's army, took Ishbosheth
the son of Saul and brought him over
to Mahanaim; 9and he made him king
over Gilead, over the Ashurites, over
Jezreel, over Ephraim, over Benjamin,
and over all Israel. 10Ishbosheth, Saul's
son, *was* forty years old when he began to reign over Israel, and he reigned
two years. Only the house of Judah followed David. 11And the time that David was king in Hebron over the house
of Judah was seven years and six
months.

Israel and Judah at War

12Now Abner the son of Ner, and the
servants of Ishbosheth the son of Saul,
went out from Mahanaim to Gibeon.
13And Joab the son of Zeruiah, and the
servants of David, went out and met
them by the pool of Gibeon. So they sat
down, one on one side of the pool and
the other on the other side of the pool.
14Then Abner said to Joab, "Let the
young men now arise and compete before us."
   And Joab said, "Let them arise."
   15So they arose and went over by
number, twelve from Benjamin, *followers* of Ishbosheth the son of Saul,
and twelve from the servants of David.
16And each one grasped his opponent
by the head and *thrust* his sword in his
opponent's side; so they fell down together. Therefore that place was called
the Field of Sharp Swords, which *is* in
Gibeon. 17So there was a very fierce
battle that day, and Abner and the men
of Israel were beaten before the servants of David.
   18Now the three sons of Zeruiah were
there: Joab and Abishai and Asahel.
And Asahel *was as* fleet of foot as a
wild gazelle. 19So Asahel pursued Abner, and in going he did not turn to the
right hand or to the left from following
Abner.
   20Then Abner looked behind him and
said, "*Are* you Asahel?"
   He answered, "I *am*."
   21And Abner said to him, "Turn aside
to your right hand or to your left, and
lay hold on one of the young men and
take his armor for yourself." But Asahel

would not turn aside from following him. 22So Abner said again to Asahel, "Turn aside from following me. Why should I strike you to the ground? How then could I face your brother Joab?" 23However, he refused to turn aside. Therefore Abner struck him in the stomach with the blunt end of the spear, so that the spear came out of his back; and he fell down there and died on the spot. So it was *that* as many as came to the place where Asahel fell down and died, stood still.

24Joab and Abishai also pursued Abner. And the sun was going down when they came to the hill of Ammah, which *is* before Giah by the road to the Wilderness of Gibeon. 25Now the children of Benjamin gathered together behind Abner and became a unit, and took their stand on top of a hill. 26Then Abner called to Joab and said, "Shall the sword devour forever? Do you not know that it will be bitter in the latter end? How long will it be then until you tell the people to return from pursuing their brethren?"

27And Joab said, "*As* God lives, unless you had spoken, surely then by morning all the people would have given up pursuing their brethren." 28So Joab blew a trumpet; and all the people stood still and did not pursue Israel anymore, nor did they fight anymore. 29Then Abner and his men went on all that night through the plain, crossed over the Jordan, and went through all Bithron; and they came to Mahanaim.

30So Joab returned from pursuing Abner. And when he had gathered all the people together, there were missing of David's servants nineteen men and Asahel. 31But the servants of David had struck down, of Benjamin and Abner's men, three hundred and sixty men who died. 32Then they took up Asahel and buried him in his father's tomb, which *was in* Bethlehem. And Joab and his men went all night, and they came to Hebron at daybreak.

3 Now there was a long war between the house of Saul and the house of David. But David grew stronger and stronger, and the house of Saul grew weaker and weaker.

Sons of David

2Sons were born to David in Hebron: His firstborn was Amnon by Ahinoam the Jezreelitess; 3his second, Chileab, by Abigail the widow of Nabal the Carmelite; the third, Absalom the son of Maacah, the daughter of Talmai, king of Geshur; 4the fourth, Adonijah the son of Haggith; the fifth, Shephatiah the son of Abital; 5and the sixth, Ithream, by David's wife Eglah. These were born to David in Hebron.

Abner Joins Forces with David

6Now it was so, while there was war between the house of Saul and the house of David, that Abner was strengthening *his hold* on the house of Saul.

7And Saul had a concubine, whose name *was* Rizpah, the daughter of Aiah. So *Ishbosheth* said to Abner, "Why have you gone in to my father's concubine?"

8Then Abner became very angry at the words of Ishbosheth, and said, "*Am* I a dog's head that belongs to Judah? Today I show loyalty to the house of Saul your father, to his brothers, and to his friends, and have not delivered you into the hand of David; and you charge me today with a fault concerning this woman? 9May God do so to Abner, and more also, if I do not do for David as the Lord has sworn to him— 10to transfer the kingdom from the house of Saul, and set up the throne of David over Israel and over Judah, from Dan to Beersheba." 11And he could not answer Abner another word, because he feared him.

12Then Abner sent messengers on his behalf to David, saying, "Whose *is* the land?" saying *also*, "Make your covenant with me, and indeed my hand *shall be* with you to bring all Israel to you."

13And *David* said, "Good, I will make a covenant with you. But one thing I require of you: you shall not see my face unless you first bring Michal, Saul's daughter, when you come to see my face." 14So David sent messengers to Ishbosheth, Saul's son, saying, "Give *me* my wife Michal, whom I betrothed to myself for a hundred foreskins of the Philistines." 15And Ishbosheth sent and took her from *her* husband, from Paltiel the son of Laish. 16Then her husband went along with her to Bahurim, weeping behind her. So Abner said to him, "Go, return!" And he returned.

17Now Abner had communicated with the elders of Israel, saying, "In time past you were seeking for David *to be* king over you. 18Now then, do *it!* For the LORD has spoken of David, saying, 'By the hand of My servant David, I will save My people Israel from the hand of the Philistines and the hand of all their enemies.' " 19And Abner also spoke in the hearing of Benjamin. Then Abner also went to speak in the hearing of David in Hebron all that seemed good to Israel and the whole house of Benjamin.

20So Abner and twenty men with him came to David at Hebron. And David made a feast for Abner and the men who *were* with him. 21Then Abner said to David, "I will arise and go, and gather all Israel to my lord the king, that they may make a covenant with you, and that you may reign over all that your heart desires." So David sent Abner away, and he went in peace.

Joab Murders Abner

22At that moment the servants of David and Joab came from a raid and brought much spoil with them. But Abner *was* not with David in Hebron, for he had sent him away, and he had gone in peace. 23When Joab and all the troops that *were* with him had come, they told Joab, saying, "Abner the son of Ner came to the king, and he sent him away, and he has gone in peace." 24Then Joab came to the king and said, "What have you done? Look, Abner came to you; why *is* it *that* you sent him away, and he has already gone? 25Surely you realize that Abner the son of Ner came to deceive you, to know your going out and your coming in, and to know all that you are doing."

26And when Joab had gone from David's presence, he sent messengers after Abner, who brought him back from the well of Sirah. But David did not know *it*. 27Now when Abner had returned to Hebron, Joab took him aside in the gate to speak with him privately, and there stabbed him in the stomach, so that he died for the blood of Asahel his brother.

28Afterward, when David heard *it,* he said, "My kingdom and I *are* guiltless before the LORD forever of the blood of Abner the son of Ner. 29Let it rest on the head of Joab and on all his father's house; and let there never fail to be in the house of Joab one who has a discharge or is a leper, who leans on a staff or falls by the sword, or who lacks bread." 30So Joab and Abishai his brother killed Abner, because he had killed their brother Asahel at Gibeon in the battle.

David's Mourning for Abner

31Then David said to Joab and to all the people who were with him, "Tear your clothes, gird yourselves with sackcloth, and mourn for Abner." And King David followed the coffin. 32So they buried Abner in Hebron; and the king lifted up his voice and wept at the grave of Abner, and all the people wept. 33And the king sang *a lament* over Abner and said:

"Should Abner die as a fool dies?
34   Your hands were not bound
     Nor your feet put into fetters;
     As a man falls before wicked men,
     so you fell."

Then all the people wept over him again.

35And when all the people came to persuade David to eat food while it was still day, David took an oath, saying, "God do so to me, and more also, if I taste bread or anything else till the sun goes down!" 36Now all the people took note *of it*, and it pleased them, since whatever the king did pleased all the people. 37For all the people and all Israel understood that day that it had not been the king's *intent* to kill Abner the son of Ner. 38Then the king said to his servants, "Do you not know that a prince and a great man has fallen this day in Israel? 39And I *am* weak today, though anointed king; and these men, the sons of Zeruiah, *are* too harsh for me. The LORD shall repay the evildoer according to his wickedness."

Ishbosheth Is Murdered

4 When Saul's son[a] heard that Abner had died in Hebron, he lost heart, and all Israel was troubled. 2Now Saul's son *had* two men *who were* captains of troops. The name of one *was* Baanah and the name of the other Rechab, the sons of Rimmon the Beerothite, of the children of Benjamin. (For Beeroth also was *part* of Benjamin, 3because the Beerothites fled to Gittaim and have been sojourners there until this day.)

4Jonathan, Saul's son, had a son *who was* lame in *his* feet. He was five years old when the news about Saul and Jonathan came from Jezreel; and his nurse took him up and fled. And it happened, as she made haste to flee, that he fell and became lame. His name *was* Mephibosheth.

5Then the sons of Rimmon the Beerothite, Rechab and Baanah, set out and came at about the heat of the day to the house of Ishbosheth, who was lying on his bed at noon. 6And they came there, all the way into the house, *as though* to get wheat, and they stabbed him in the stomach. Then Rechab and Baanah his brother escaped. 7For when they came into the house, he was lying on his bed in his bedroom; then they struck him and killed him, beheaded him and took his head, and were all night escaping through the plain. 8And they brought the head of Ishbosheth to David at Hebron, and said to the king, "Here is the head of Ishbosheth, the son of Saul your enemy, who sought your life; and the LORD has avenged my lord the king this day of Saul and his descendants."

9But David answered Rechab and Baanah his brother, the sons of Rimmon the Beerothite, and said to them, "*As* the LORD lives, who has redeemed my life from all adversity, 10when someone told me, saying, 'Look, Saul is dead,' thinking to have brought good news, I arrested him and had him executed in Ziklag—the one who *thought* I would give him a reward for *his* news. 11How much more, when wicked men have killed a righteous person in his own house on his bed? Therefore, shall I not now require his blood at your hand and remove you from the earth?" 12So David commanded his young men, and they executed them, cut off their hands and feet, and hanged *them* by the pool in Hebron. But they took the head of Ishbosheth and buried *it* in the tomb of Abner in Hebron.

David Reigns over All Israel

5 Then all the tribes of Israel came to David at Hebron and spoke, saying, "Indeed we *are* your bone and your flesh. 2Also, in time past, when Saul was king over us, you were the one who led Israel out and brought them in; and the LORD said to you, 'You shall shepherd My people Israel, and be ruler over Israel.'" 3Therefore all the elders of Israel came to the king at Hebron, and King David made a covenant with them at Hebron before the LORD. And they anointed David king over Israel. 4David *was* thirty years old when he began to reign, *and* he reigned forty years. 5In Hebron he reigned over Judah seven years and six months, and in Jerusalem he reigned thirty-three years over all Israel and Judah.

The Conquest of Jerusalem

6And the king and his men went to Jerusalem against the Jebusites, the inhabitants of the land, who spoke to David, saying, "You shall not come in here; but the blind and the lame will repel you," thinking, "David cannot come in here." 7Nevertheless David took the stronghold of Zion (that *is*, the City of David).

8Now David said on that day, "Whoever climbs up by way of the water shaft and defeats the Jebusites (the lame and the blind, *who are* hated by David's soul), *he shall be chief and captain.*"[b] Therefore they say, "The blind and the lame shall not come into the house."

9Then David dwelt in the stronghold, and called it the City of David. And David built all around from the Millo and inward. 10So David went on and became great, and the LORD God of hosts *was* with him.

11Then Hiram king of Tyre sent mes-

a That is, Ishbosheth   b Compare 1 Chronicles 11.6

sengers to David, and cedar trees, and carpenters and masons. And they built David a house. 12So David knew that the LORD had established him as king over Israel, and that He had exalted His kingdom for the sake of His people Israel.

13And David took more concubines and wives from Jerusalem, after he had come from Hebron. Also more sons and daughters were born to David. 14Now these *are* the names of those who were born to him in Jerusalem: Shammua, Shobab, Nathan, Solomon, 15Ibhar, Elishua, Nepheg, Japhia, 16Elishama, Eliada, and Eliphelet.

The Philistines Defeated

17Now when the Philistines heard that they had anointed David king over Israel, all the Philistines went up to search for David. And David heard *of it* and went down to the stronghold. 18The Philistines also went and deployed themselves in the Valley of Rephaim. 19So David inquired of the LORD, saying, "Shall I go up against the Philistines? Will You deliver them into my hand?"

And the LORD said to David, "Go up, for I will doubtless deliver the Philistines into your hand."

20So David went to Baal Perazim, and David defeated them there; and he said, "The LORD has broken through my enemies before me, like a breakthrough of water." Therefore he called the name of that place Baal Perazim.c 21And they left their images there, and David and his men carried them away.

22Then the Philistines went up once again and deployed themselves in the Valley of Rephaim. 23Therefore David inquired of the LORD, and He said, "You shall not go up; circle around behind them, and come upon them in front of the mulberry trees. 24And it shall be, when you hear the sound of marching in the tops of the mulberry trees, then you shall advance quickly. For then the LORD will go out before you to strike the camp of the Philistines." 25And David did so, as the LORD commanded him; and he drove back the Philistines from Geba as far as Gezer.

The Ark Brought to Jerusalem

6 Again David gathered all *the* choice men of Israel, thirty thousand. 2And David arose and went with all the people who *were* with him from Baale Judah to bring up from there the ark of God, whose name is called by the Name, the LORD of Hosts, who dwells *between* the cherubim. 3So they set the ark of God on a new cart, and brought it out of the house of Abinadab, which *was* on the hill; and Uzzah and Ahio, the sons of Abinadab, drove the new cart. 4And they brought it out of the house of Abinadab, which *was* on the hill, accompanying the ark of God; and Ahio went before the ark. 5Then David and all the house of Israel played *music* before the LORD on all kinds of *instruments of* fir wood, on harps, on stringed instruments, on tambourines, on sistrums, and on cymbals.

6And when they came to Nachon's threshing floor, Uzzah put out *his hand* to the ark of God and took hold of it, for the oxen stumbled. 7Then the anger of the LORD was aroused against Uzzah, and God struck him there for *his* error; and he died there by the ark of God. 8And David became angry because of the LORD's outbreak against Uzzah; and he called the name of the place Perez Uzzahd to this day.

9David was afraid of the LORD that day; and he said, "How can the ark of the LORD come to me?" 10So David would not move the ark of the LORD with him into the City of David; but David took it aside into the house of Obed-Edom the Gittite. 11The ark of the LORD remained in the house of Obed-Edom the Gittite three months. And the LORD blessed Obed-Edom and all his household.

12Now it was told King David, saying, "The LORD has blessed the house of Obed-Edom and all that *belongs* to him, because of the ark of God." So David went and brought up the ark of God from the house of Obed-Edom to the City of David with gladness. 13And so it was, when those bearing the ark of the LORD had gone six paces, that he sacrificed oxen and fatted sheep.

---

c Literally *Master of Breakthroughs*   d Literally *Outburst Against Uzzah*

14Then David danced before the LORD with all *his* might; and David *was* wearing a linen ephod. 15So David and all the house of Israel brought up the ark of the LORD with shouting and with the sound of the trumpet.

16Now as the ark of the LORD came into the City of David, Michal, Saul's daughter, looked through a window and saw King David leaping and whirling before the LORD; and she despised him in her heart. 17So they brought the ark of the LORD, and set it in its place in the midst of the tabernacle that David had erected for it. Then David offered burnt offerings and peace offerings before the LORD. 18And when David had finished offering burnt offerings and peace offerings, he blessed the people in the name of the LORD of hosts. 19Then he distributed among all the people, among the whole multitude of Israel, both the women and the men, to everyone a loaf of bread, a piece *of* *meat*, and a cake of raisins. So all the people departed, everyone to his house.

20Then David returned to bless his household. And Michal the daughter of Saul came out to meet David, and said, "How glorious was the king of Israel today, uncovering himself today in the eyes of the maids of his servants, as one of the base fellows shamelessly uncovers himself!"

21So David said to Michal, "*It was* before the LORD, who chose me instead of your father and all his house, to appoint me ruler over the people of the LORD, over Israel. Therefore I will play *music* before the LORD. 22And I will be even more undignified than this, and will be humble in my own sight. But as for the maidservants of whom you have spoken, by them I will be held in honor."

23Therefore Michal the daughter of Saul had no children to the day of her death.

God's Covenant with David

7 Now it came to pass when the king was dwelling in his house, and the LORD had given him rest from all his enemies all around, 2that the king said to Nathan the prophet, "See now, I dwell in a house of cedar, but the ark of God dwells inside tent curtains."

3Then Nathan said to the king, "Go, do all that *is* in your heart, for the LORD *is* with you."

4But it happened that night that the word of the LORD came to Nathan, saying, 5"Go and tell My servant David, 'Thus says the LORD: "Would you build a house for Me to dwell in? 6For I have not dwelt in a house since the time that I brought the children of Israel up from Egypt, even to this day, but have moved about in a tent and in a tabernacle. 7Wherever I have moved about with all the children of Israel, have I ever spoken a word to anyone from the tribes of Israel, whom I commanded to shepherd My people Israel, saying, 'Why have you not built Me a house of cedar?' " ' 8Now therefore, thus shall you say to My servant David, 'Thus says the LORD of hosts: "I took you from the sheepfold, from following the sheep, to be ruler over My people, over Israel. 9And I have been with you wherever you have gone, and have cut off all your enemies from before you, and have made you a great name, like the name of the great men who *are* on the earth. 10Moreover I will appoint a place for My people Israel, and will plant them, that they may dwell in a place of their own and move no more; nor shall the sons of wickedness oppress them anymore, as previously, 11since the time that I commanded judges *to be* over My people Israel, and have caused you to rest from all your enemies. Also the LORD tells you that He will make you a house.

12"When your days are fulfilled and you rest with your fathers, I will set up your seed after you, who will come from your body, and I will establish his kingdom. 13He shall build a house for My name, and I will establish the throne of his kingdom forever. 14I will be his Father, and he shall be My son. If he commits iniquity, I will chasten him with the rod of men and with the blows of the sons of men. 15But My mercy shall not depart from him, as I took *it* from Saul, whom I removed from before you. 16And your house and your kingdom shall be established forever before you. Your throne shall be established forever." ' "

17According to all these words and

according to all this vision, so Nathan spoke to David.

David's Thanksgiving to God

18Then King David went in and sat before the Lord; and he said: "Who *am* I, O Lord God? And what is my house, that You have brought me this far? 19And yet this was a small thing in Your sight, O Lord God; and You have also spoken of Your servant's house for a great while to come. *Is* this the manner of man, O Lord God? 20Now what more can David say to You? For You, Lord God, know Your servant. 21For Your word's sake, and according to Your own heart, You have done all these great things, to make Your servant know *them.* 22Therefore You are great, O Lord God. For *there is* none like You, nor *is there any* God besides You, according to all that we have heard with our ears. 23And who *is* like Your people, like Israel, the one nation on the earth whom God went to redeem for Himself as a people, to make for Himself a name—and to do for Yourself great and awesome deeds for Your land—before Your people whom You redeemed for Yourself from Egypt, the nations, and their gods? 24For You have made Your people Israel Your very own people forever; and You, Lord, have become their God.

25"Now, O Lord God, the word which You have spoken concerning Your servant and concerning his house, establish *it* forever and do as You have said. 26So let Your name be magnified forever, saying, 'The Lord of hosts *is* the God over Israel.' And let the house of Your servant David be established before You. 27For You, O Lord of hosts, God of Israel, have revealed *this* to Your servant, saying, 'I will build you a house.' Therefore Your servant has found it in his heart to pray this prayer to You.

28"And now, O Lord God, You are God, and Your words are true, and You have promised this goodness to Your servant. 29Now therefore, let it please You to bless the house of Your servant, that it may continue before You forever; for You, O Lord God, have spoken

it, and with Your blessing let the house of Your servant be blessed forever."

David's Further Conquests

8 After this it came to pass that David attacked the Philistines and subdued them. And David took Metheg Ammah from the hand of the Philistines.

2Then he defeated Moab. Forcing them down to the ground, he measured them off with a line. With two lines he measured off those to be put to death, and with one full line those to be kept alive. So the Moabites became David's servants, *and* brought tribute.

3David also defeated Hadadezer the son of Rehob, king of Zobah, as he went to recover his territory at the River Euphrates. 4David took from him one thousand *chariots,* seven hundred[e] horsemen, and twenty thousand foot soldiers. Also David hamstrung all the chariot horses, except that he spared *enough* of them for one hundred chariots.

5When the Syrians of Damascus came to help Hadadezer king of Zobah, David killed twenty-two thousand of the Syrians. 6Then David put garrisons in Syria of Damascus; and the Syrians became David's servants, *and* brought tribute. So the Lord preserved David wherever he went. 7And David took the shields of gold that had belonged to the servants of Hadadezer, and brought them to Jerusalem. 8Also from Betah and from Berothai, cities of Hadadezer, King David took a large amount of bronze.

9When Toi king of Hamath heard that David had defeated all the army of Hadadezer, 10then Toi sent Joram his son to King David, to greet him and bless him, because he had fought against Hadadezer and defeated him (for Hadadezer had been at war with Toi); and *Joram* brought with him articles of silver, articles of gold, and articles of bronze. 11King David also dedicated these to the Lord, along with the silver and gold that he had dedicated from all the nations which he had subdued—12from Syria, from Moab, from the people of Ammon, from the

---

e Or *seven thousand* (compare 1 Chronicles 18.4)

Philistines, from Amalek, and from the spoil of Hadadezer the son of Rehob, king of Zobah.

13And David made *himself* a name when he returned from killing eighteen thousand Syrians in the Valley of Salt. 14He also put garrisons in Edom; throughout all Edom he put garrisons, and all the Edomites became David's servants. And the LORD preserved David wherever he went.

David's Administration

15So David reigned over all Israel; and David administered judgment and justice to all his people. 16Joab the son of Zeruiah *was* over the army; Jehoshaphat the son of Ahilud *was* recorder; 17Zadok the son of Ahitub and Ahimelech the son of Abiathar *were* the priests; Seraiah *was* the scribe; 18Benaiah the son of Jehoiada *was over* both the Cherethites and the Pelethites; and David's sons were chief ministers.

David's Kindness to Mephibosheth

9 Now David said, "Is there still anyone who is left of the house of Saul, that I may show him kindness for Jonathan's sake?"

2And *there was* a servant of the house of Saul whose name *was* Ziba. So when they had called him to David, the king said to him, "*Are* you Ziba?"

He said, "At your service!"

3Then the king said, "*Is* there not still someone of the house of Saul, to whom I may show the kindness of God?"

And Ziba said to the king, "There is still a son of Jonathan *who is* lame in *his* feet."

4So the king said to him, "Where *is* he?"

And Ziba said to the king, "Indeed he *is* in the house of Machir the son of Ammiel, in Lo Debar."

5Then King David sent and brought him out of the house of Machir the son of Ammiel, from Lo Debar.

6Now when Mephibosheth the son of Jonathan, the son of Saul, had come to David, he fell on his face and prostrated himself. Then David said, "Mephibosheth?"

And he answered, "Here is your servant!"

7So David said to him, "Do not fear, for I will surely show you kindness for Jonathan your father's sake, and will restore to you all the land of Saul your grandfather; and you shall eat bread at my table continually."

8Then he bowed himself, and said, "What *is* your servant, that you should look upon such a dead dog as I?"

9And the king called to Ziba, Saul's servant, and said to him, "I have given to your master's son all that belonged to Saul and to all his house. 10You therefore, and your sons and your servants, shall work the land for him, and you shall bring in *the harvest*, that your master's son may have food to eat. But Mephibosheth your master's son shall eat bread at my table always." Now Ziba had fifteen sons and twenty servants.

11Then Ziba said to the king, "According to all that my lord the king has commanded his servant, so will your servant do."

"As for Mephibosheth," *said the king*, "he shall eat at my table like one of the king's sons." 12Mephibosheth had a young son whose name *was* Micha. And all who dwelt in the house of Ziba *were* servants of Mephibosheth. 13So Mephibosheth dwelt in Jerusalem, for he ate continually at the king's table. And he was lame in both his feet.

The Ammonites and Syrians Defeated

10 It happened after this that the king of the people of Ammon died, and Hanun his son reigned in his place. 2Then David said, "I will show kindness to Hanun the son of Nahash, as his father showed kindness to me."

So David sent by the hand of his servants to comfort him concerning his father. And David's servants came into the land of the people of Ammon. 3And the princes of the people of Ammon said to Hanun their lord, "Do you think that David really honors your father because he has sent comforters to you? Has David not *rather* sent his servants to you to search the city, to spy it out, and to overthrow it?"

4Therefore Hanun took David's servants, shaved off half of their beards, cut off their garments in the middle, at their buttocks, and sent them away. 5When they told David, he sent to meet them, because the men were greatly ashamed. And the king said, "Wait at Jericho until your beards have grown, and *then* return."

6When the people of Ammon saw that they had made themselves repulsive to David, the people of Ammon sent and hired the Syrians of Beth Rehob and the Syrians of Zoba, twenty thousand foot soldiers; and from the king of Maacah one thousand men, and from Ish-Tob twelve thousand men. 7Now when David heard *of it*, he sent Joab and all the army of the mighty men. 8Then the people of Ammon came out and put themselves in battle array at the entrance of the gate. And the Syrians of Zoba, Beth Rehob, Ish-Tob, and Maacah *were* by themselves in the field.

9When Joab saw that the battle line was against him before and behind, he chose some of Israel's best and put *them* in battle array against the Syrians. 10And the rest of the people he put under the command of Abishai his brother, that he might set *them* in battle array against the people of Ammon. 11Then he said, "If the Syrians are too strong for me, then you shall help me; but if the people of Ammon are too strong for you, then I will come and help you. 12Be of good courage, and let us be strong for our people and for the cities of our God. And may the LORD do *what is* good in His sight."

13So Joab and the people who *were* with him drew near for the battle against the Syrians, and they fled before him. 14When the people of Ammon saw that the Syrians were fleeing, they also fled before Abishai, and entered the city. So Joab returned from the people of Ammon and went to Jerusalem.

15When the Syrians saw that they had been defeated by Israel, they gathered together. 16Then Hadadezer sent and brought out the Syrians who *were* beyond the River,*f* and they came to Helam. And Shobach the commander of Hadadezer's army *went* before them. 17When it was told David, he gathered all Israel, crossed over the Jordan, and came to Helam. And the Syrians set themselves in battle array against David and fought with him. 18Then the Syrians fled before Israel; and David killed seven hundred charioteers and forty thousand horsemen of the Syrians, and struck Shobach the commander of their army, who died there. 19And when all the kings *who were* servants to Hadadezer saw that they were defeated by Israel, they made peace with Israel and served them. So the Syrians were afraid to help the people of Ammon anymore.

David, Bathsheba, and Uriah

11 It happened in the spring of the year, at the time when kings go out *to battle*, that David sent Joab and his servants with him, and all Israel; and they destroyed the people of Ammon and besieged Rabbah. But David remained at Jerusalem.

2Then it happened one evening that David arose from his bed and walked on the roof of the king's house. And from the roof he saw a woman bathing, and the woman *was* very beautiful to behold. 3So David sent and inquired about the woman. And *someone* said, "*Is* this not Bathsheba, the daughter of Eliam, the wife of Uriah the Hittite?" 4Then David sent messengers, and took her; and she came to him, and he lay with her, for she was cleansed from her impurity; and she returned to her house. 5And the woman conceived; so she sent and told David, and said, "I *am* with child."

6Then David sent to Joab, *saying*, "Send me Uriah the Hittite." And Joab sent Uriah to David. 7When Uriah had come to him, David asked how Joab was doing, and how the people were doing, and how the war prospered. 8And David said to Uriah, "Go down to your house and wash your feet." So Uriah departed from the king's house, and a gift *of food* from the king followed him. 9But Uriah slept at the door of the king's house with all the servants of his lord, and did not go down to his house. 10So when they told David, saying, "Uriah did not go down to his house," David said to Uriah, "Did you not come from a journey? Why did you not go down to your house?"

11And Uriah said to David, "The ark

f That is, the Euphrates

and Israel and Judah are dwelling in tents, and my lord Joab and the servants of my lord are encamped in the open fields. Shall I then go to my house to eat and drink, and to lie with my wife? *As* you live, and *as* your soul lives, I will not do this thing."

12Then David said to Uriah, "Wait here today also, and tomorrow I will let you depart." So Uriah remained in Jerusalem that day and the next. 13Now when David called him, he ate and drank before him; and he made him drunk. And at evening he went out to lie on his bed with the servants of his lord, but he did not go down to his house.

14In the morning it happened that David wrote a letter to Joab and sent *it* by the hand of Uriah. 15And he wrote in the letter, saying, "Set Uriah in the forefront of the hottest battle, and retreat from him, that he may be struck down and die." 16So it was, while Joab besieged the city, that he assigned Uriah to a place where he knew there *were* valiant men. 17Then the men of the city came out and fought with Joab. And *some* of the people of the servants of David fell; and Uriah the Hittite died also.

18Then Joab sent and told David all the things concerning the war, 19and charged the messenger, saying, "When you have finished telling the matters of the war to the king, 20if it happens that the king's wrath rises, and he says to you: 'Why did you approach so near to the city when you fought? Did you not know that they would shoot from the wall? 21Who struck Abimelech the son of Jerubbesheth? Was it not a woman who cast a piece of a millstone on him from the wall, so that he died in Thebez? Why did you go near the wall?'—then you shall say, 'Your servant Uriah the Hittite is dead also.'

22So the messenger went, and came and told David all that Joab had sent by him. 23And the messenger said to David, "Surely the men prevailed against us and came out to us in the field; then we drove them back as far as the entrance of the gate. 24The archers shot from the wall at your servants; and *some* of the king's servants are

dead, and your servant Uriah the Hittite is dead also."

25Then David said to the messenger, "Thus you shall say to Joab: 'Do not let this thing displease you, for the sword devours one as well as another. Strengthen your attack against the city, and overthrow it.' So encourage him."

26When the wife of Uriah heard that Uriah her husband was dead, she mourned for her husband. 27And when her mourning was over, David sent and brought her to his house, and she became his wife and bore him a son. But the thing that David had done displeased the LORD.

Nathan's Parable and David's Confession

12 Then the LORD sent Nathan to David. And he came to him, and said to him: "There were two men in one city, one rich and the other poor. 2The rich *man* had exceedingly many flocks and herds. 3But the poor *man* had nothing, except one little ewe lamb which he had bought and nourished; and it grew up together with him and with his children. It ate of his own food and drank from his own cup and lay in his bosom; and it was like a daughter to him. 4And a traveler came to the rich man, who refused to take from his own flock and from his own herd to prepare one for the wayfaring man who had come to him; but he took the poor man's lamb and prepared it for the man who had come to him."

5So David's anger was greatly aroused against the man, and he said to Nathan, "*As* the LORD lives, the man who has done this shall surely die! 6And he shall restore fourfold for the lamb, because he did this thing and because he had no pity."

7Then Nathan said to David, "You *are* the man! Thus says the LORD God of Israel: 'I anointed you king over Israel, and I delivered you from the hand of Saul. 8I gave you your master's house and your master's wives into your keeping, and gave you the house of Israel and Judah. And if *that had been* too little, I also would have given you much more! 9Why have you despised the commandment of the LORD, to do evil in His sight? You have killed Uriah the

Hittite with the sword; you have taken his wife *to be* your wife, and have killed him with the sword of the people of Ammon. 10Now therefore, the sword shall never depart from your house, because you have despised Me, and have taken the wife of Uriah the Hittite to be your wife.' 11Thus says the Lord: 'Behold, I will raise up adversity against you from your own house; and I will take your wives before your eyes and give *them* to your neighbor, and he shall lie with your wives in the sight of this sun. 12For you did *it* secretly, but I will do this thing before all Israel, before the sun.' "

13So David said to Nathan, "I have sinned against the Lord."

And Nathan said to David, "The Lord also has put away your sin; you shall not die. 14However, because by this deed you have given great occasion to the enemies of the Lord to blaspheme, the child also *who is* born to you shall surely die." 15Then Nathan departed to his house.

The Death of David's Son

And the Lord struck the child that Uriah's wife bore to David, and it became ill. 16David therefore pleaded with God for the child, and David fasted and went in and lay all night on the ground. 17So the elders of his house arose *and went* to him, to raise him up from the ground. But he would not, nor did he eat food with them. 18Then on the seventh day it came to pass that the child died. And the servants of David were afraid to tell him that the child was dead. For they said, "Indeed, while the child was alive, we spoke to him, and he would not heed our voice. How can we tell him that the child is dead? He may do some harm!"

19When David saw that his servants were whispering, David perceived that the child was dead. Therefore David said to his servants, "Is the child dead?"

And they said, "He is dead."

20So David arose from the ground, washed and anointed himself, and changed his clothes; and he went into the house of the Lord and worshiped. Then he went to his own house; and

when he requested, they set food before him, and he ate. 21Then his servants said to him, "What *is* this that you have done? You fasted and wept for the child *while he was* alive, but when the child died, you arose and ate food."

22And he said, "While the child was alive, I fasted and wept; for I said, 'Who can tell *whether* the Lord will be gracious to me, that the child may live?' 23But now he is dead; why should I fast? Can I bring him back again? I shall go to him, but he shall not return to me."

Solomon Is Born

24Then David comforted Bathsheba his wife, and went in to her and lay with her. So she bore a son, and he called his name Solomon. Now the Lord loved him, 25and He sent *word* by the hand of Nathan the prophet: So he called his name Jedidiah,g because of the Lord.

Rabbah Is Captured

26Now Joab fought against Rabbah of the people of Ammon, and took the royal city. 27And Joab sent messengers to David, and said, "I have fought against Rabbah, and I have taken the city's water *supply*. 28Now therefore, gather the rest of the people together and encamp against the city and take it, lest I take the city and it be called after my name." 29So David gathered all the people together and went to Rabbah, fought against it, and took it. 30Then he took their king's crown from his head. Its weight *was* a talent of gold, with precious stones. And it was *set* on David's head. Also he brought out the spoil of the city in great abundance. 31And he brought out the people who *were* in it, and put *them to work* with saws and iron picks and iron axes, and made them cross over to the brick works. So he did to all the cities of the people of Ammon. Then David and all the people returned to Jerusalem.

Amnon and Tamar

13 After this Absalom the son of David had a lovely sister, whose name *was* Tamar; and Amnon the son of David loved her. 2Amnon was so dis-

g Literally *Beloved of the Lord*

tressed over his sister Tamar that he became sick; for she *was* a virgin. And it was improper for Amnon to do anything to her. 3But Amnon had a friend whose name *was* Jonadab the son of Shimeah, David's brother. Now Jonadab *was* a very crafty man. 4And he said to him, "Why *are* you, the king's son, becoming thinner day after day? Will you not tell me?"

Amnon said to him, "I love Tamar, my brother Absalom's sister."

5So Jonadab said to him, "Lie down on your bed and pretend to be ill. And when your father comes to see you, say to him, 'Please let my sister Tamar come and give me food, and prepare the food in my sight, that I may see *it* and eat it from her hand.'" 6Then Amnon lay down and pretended to be ill; and when the king came to see him, Amnon said to the king, "Please let Tamar my sister come and make a couple of cakes for me in my sight, that I may eat from her hand."

7And David sent home to Tamar, saying, "Now go to your brother Amnon's house, and prepare food for him." 8So Tamar went to her brother Amnon's house; and he was lying down. Then she took flour and kneaded *it*, made cakes in his sight, and baked the cakes. 9And she took the pan and placed *them* out before him, but he refused to eat. Then Amnon said, "Have everyone go out from me." And they all went out from him. 10Then Amnon said to Tamar, "Bring the food into the bedroom, that I may eat from your hand." And Tamar took the cakes which she had made, and brought *them* to Amnon her brother in the bedroom. 11Now when she had brought *them* to him to eat, he took hold of her and said to her, "Come, lie with me, my sister."

12But she answered him, "No, my brother, do not force me, for no such thing should be done in Israel. Do not do this disgraceful thing! 13And I, where could I take my shame? And as for you, you would be like one of the fools in Israel. Now therefore, please speak to the king; for he will not withhold me from you." 14However, he would not heed her voice; and being stronger than she, he forced her and lay with her.

15Then Amnon hated her exceedingly, so that the hatred with which he hated her *was* greater than the love with which he had loved her. And Amnon said to her, "Arise, be gone!"

16So she said to him, "No, indeed! This evil of sending me away is worse than the other that you did to me."

But he would not listen to her. 17Then he called his servant who attended him, and said, "Here! Put this *woman* out, away from me, and bolt the door behind her." 18Now she had on a robe of many colors, for the king's virgin daughters wore such apparel. And his servant put her out and bolted the door behind her.

19Then Tamar put ashes on her head, and tore her robe of many colors that *was* on her, and laid her hand on her head and went away crying bitterly. 20And Absalom her brother said to her, "Has Amnon your brother been with you? But now hold your peace, my sister. He *is* your brother; do not take this thing to heart." So Tamar remained desolate in her brother Absalom's house.

21But when King David heard of all these things, he was very angry. 22And Absalom spoke to his brother Amnon neither good nor bad. For Absalom hated Amnon, because he had forced his sister Tamar.

Absalom Murders Amnon

23And it came to pass, after two full years, that Absalom had sheepshearers in Baal Hazor, which *is* near Ephraim; so Absalom invited all the king's sons. 24Then Absalom came to the king and said, "Kindly note, your servant has sheepshearers; please, let the king and his servants go with your servant."

25But the king said to Absalom, "No, my son, let us not all go now, lest we be a burden to you." Then he urged him, but he would not go; and he blessed him.

26Then Absalom said, "If not, please let my brother Amnon go with us."

And the king said to him, "Why should he go with you?" 27But Absalom urged him; so he let Amnon and all the king's sons go with him.

28Now Absalom had commanded his servants, saying, "Watch now, when

Amnon's heart is merry with wine, and when I say to you, 'Strike Amnon!' then kill him. Do not be afraid. Have I not commanded you? Be courageous and valiant." 29So the servants of Absalom did to Amnon as Absalom had commanded. Then all the king's sons arose, and each one got on his mule and fled.

30And it came to pass, while they were on the way, that news came to David, saying, "Absalom has killed all the king's sons, and not one of them is left!" 31So the king arose and tore his garments and lay on the ground, and all his servants stood by with their clothes torn. 32Then Jonadab the son of Shimeah, David's brother, answered and said, "Let not my lord suppose they have killed all the young men, the king's sons, for only Amnon is dead. For by the command of Absalom this has been determined from the day that he forced his sister Tamar. 33Now therefore, let not my lord the king take the thing to his heart, to think that all the king's sons are dead. For only Amnon is dead."

Absalom Flees to Geshur

34Then Absalom fled. And the young man who was keeping watch lifted his eyes and looked, and there, many people were coming from the road on the hillside behind him. 35And Jonadab said to the king, "Look, the king's sons are coming; as your servant said, so it is." 36So it was, as soon as he had finished speaking, that the king's sons indeed came, and they lifted up their voice and wept. Also the king and all his servants wept very bitterly.

37But Absalom fled and went to Talmai the son of Ammihud, king of Geshur. And *David* mourned for his son every day. 38So Absalom fled and went to Geshur, and was there three years. 39And King David longed to go to Absalom. For he had been comforted concerning Amnon, because he was dead.

Absalom Returns to Jerusalem

14 So Joab the son of Zeruiah perceived that the king's heart *was* concerned about Absalom. 2And Joab sent to Tekoa and brought from there a wise woman, and said to her, "Please pretend to be a mourner, and put on mourning apparel; do not anoint yourself with oil, but act like a woman who has been mourning a long time for the dead. 3Go to the king and speak to him in this manner." So Joab put the words in her mouth.

4And when the woman of Tekoa spoke to the king, she fell on her face to the ground and prostrated herself, and said, "Help, O king!"

5Then the king said to her, "What troubles you?"

And she answered, "Indeed I *am* a widow, my husband is dead. 6Now your maidservant had two sons; and the two fought with each other in the field, and *there was* no one to part them, but the one struck the other and killed him. 7And now the whole family has risen up against your maidservant, and they said, 'Deliver him who struck his brother, that we may execute him for the life of his brother whom he killed; and we will destroy the heir also.' So they would extinguish my ember that is left, and leave to my husband *neither* name nor remnant on the earth."

8Then the king said to the woman, "Go to your house, and I will give orders concerning you."

9And the woman of Tekoa said to the king, "My lord, O king, *let* the iniquity *be* on me and on my father's house, and the king and his throne *be* guiltless."

10So the king said, "Whoever says *anything* to you, bring him to me, and he shall not touch you anymore."

11Then she said, "Please let the king remember the LORD your God, and do not permit the avenger of blood to destroy anymore, lest they destroy my son."

And he said, "*As* the LORD lives, not one hair of your son shall fall to the ground."

12Therefore the woman said, "Please, let your maidservant speak *another* word to my lord the king."

And he said, "Say on."

13So the woman said: "Why then have you schemed such a thing against the people of God? For the king speaks this thing as one who is guilty, *in that* the king does not bring his banished one home again. 14For we will surely die and *become* like water spilled on the ground, which cannot be gathered up again. Yet God does not take away a life; but He devises means, so that His banished ones are not expelled from Him. 15Now therefore, I have come to speak of this thing to my lord the king because the people have made me afraid. And your maidservant said, 'I will now speak to the king; it may be that the king will perform the request of his maidservant. 16For the king will hear and deliver his maidservant from the hand of the man *who would* destroy me and my son together from the inheritance of God.' 17Your maidservant said, 'The word of my lord the king will now be comforting; for as the angel of God, so *is* my lord the king in discerning good and evil. And may the LORD your God be with you.' "

18Then the king answered and said to the woman, "Please do not hide from me anything that I ask you."

And the woman said, "Please, let my lord the king speak."

19So the king said, "*Is* the hand of Joab with you in all this?" And the woman answered and said, "*As* you live, my lord the king, no one can turn to the right hand or to the left from anything that my lord the king has spoken. For your servant Joab commanded me, and he put all these words in the mouth of your maidservant. 20To bring about this change of affairs your servant Joab has done this thing; but my lord *is* wise, according to the wisdom of the angel of God, to know everything that *is* in the earth."

21And the king said to Joab, "All right, I have granted this thing. Go therefore, bring back the young man Absalom."

22Then Joab fell to the ground on his face and bowed himself, and thanked the king. And Joab said, "Today your servant knows that I have found favor in your sight, my lord, O king, in that the king has fulfilled the request of his servant." 23So Joab arose and went to Geshur, and brought Absalom to Jerusalem. 24And the king said, "Let him return to his own house, but do not let him see my face." So Absalom returned to his own house, but did not see the king's face.

David Forgives Absalom

25Now in all Israel there was no one who was praised as much as Absalom for his good looks. From the sole of his foot to the crown of his head there was no blemish in him. 26And when he cut the hair of his head—at the end of every year he cut *it* because it was heavy on him—when he cut it, he weighed the hair of his head at two hundred shekels according to the king's standard. 27To Absalom were born three sons, and one daughter whose name *was* Tamar. She was a woman of beautiful appearance.

28And Absalom dwelt two full years in Jerusalem, but did not see the king's face. 29Therefore Absalom sent for Joab, to send him to the king, but he would not come to him. And when he sent again the second time, he would not come. 30So he said to his servants, "See, Joab's field is near mine, and he has barley there; go and set it on fire." And Absalom's servants set the field on fire.

31Then Joab arose and came to Absalom's house, and said to him, "Why have your servants set my field on fire?"

32And Absalom answered Joab, "Look, I sent to you, saying, 'Come here, so that I may send you to the king, to say, "Why have I come from Geshur? *It would be* better for me *to be* there still." ' Now therefore, let me see the king's face; but if there is iniquity in me, let him execute me."

33So Joab went to the king and told him. And when he had called for Absalom, he came to the king and bowed himself on his face to the ground before the king. Then the king kissed Absalom.

Absalom's Treason

15 After this it happened that Absalom provided himself with chariots and horses, and fifty men to run before him. 2Now Absalom would rise early and stand beside the way to the gate. *So* it was, whenever anyone who had a lawsuit came to the king for a decision, that Absalom would call to him and say, "What city *are* you from?" And he would say, "Your servant *is*

from such and such a tribe of Israel."
3Then Absalom would say to him,
"Look, your case *is* good and right; but
there is no deputy of the king to hear
you." 4Moreover Absalom would say,
"Oh, that I were made judge in the land,
and everyone who has any suit or cause
would come to me; then I would give
him justice." 5And *so* it was, whenever
anyone came near to bow down to him,
that he would put out his hand and take
him and kiss him. 6In this manner Absalom acted toward all Israel who came
to the king for judgment. So Absalom
stole the hearts of the men of Israel.

7Now it came to pass after forty years
that Absalom said to the king, "Please,
let me go to Hebron and pay the vow
which I made to the LORD. 8For your
servant took a vow while I dwelt at Geshur in Syria, saying, 'If the LORD indeed brings me back to Jerusalem, then
I will serve the LORD.' "

9And the king said to him, "Go in
peace." So he arose and went to Hebron.

10Then Absalom sent spies throughout all the tribes of Israel, saying, "As
soon as you hear the sound of the trumpet, then you shall say, 'Absalom reigns
in Hebron!' " 11And with Absalom went
two hundred men invited from Jerusalem, and they went along innocently
and did not know anything. 12Then Absalom sent for Ahithophel the Gilonite,
David's counselor, from his city—from
Giloh—while he offered sacrifices. And
the conspiracy grew strong, for the people with Absalom continually increased
in number.

David Escapes from Jerusalem

13Now a messenger came to David,
saying, "The hearts of the men of Israel
are with Absalom."

14So David said to all his servants
who *were* with him at Jerusalem,
"Arise, and let us flee, or we shall not
escape from Absalom. Make haste to
depart, lest he overtake us suddenly
and bring disaster upon us, and strike
the city with the edge of the sword."
15And the king's servants said to the
king, "We *are* your servants, *ready to
do* whatever my lord the king commands." 16Then the king went out with
all his household after him. But the king

left ten women, concubines, to keep the
house. 17And the king went out with all
the people after him, and stopped at the
outskirts. 18Then all his servants passed
before him; and all the Cherethites, all
the Pelethites, and all the Gittites, six
hundred men who had followed him
from Gath, passed before the king.

19Then the king said to Ittai the Gittite, "Why are you also going with us?
Return and remain with the king. For
you *are* a foreigner and also an exile
from your own place. 20In fact, you
came *only* yesterday. Should I make
you wander up and down with us today,
since I go I know not where? Return,
and take your brethren back. Mercy
and truth *be* with you."

21But Ittai answered the king and
said, "*As* the LORD lives, and *as* my lord
the king lives, surely in whatever place
my lord the king shall be, whether in
death or life, even there also your servant will be."

22So David said to Ittai, "Go, and
cross over." Then Ittai the Gittite and
all his men and all the little ones who
were with him crossed over. 23And all
the country wept with a loud voice, and
all the people crossed over. The king
himself also crossed over the Brook
Kidron, and all the people crossed over
toward the way of the wilderness.

24There was Zadok also, and all the
Levites with him, bearing the ark of the
covenant of God. And they set down
the ark of God, and Abiathar went up
until all the people had finished crossing over from the city. 25Then the king
said to Zadok, "Carry the ark of God
back into the city. If I find favor in the
eyes of the LORD, He will bring me back
and show me *both* it and His dwelling
place. 26But if He says thus: 'I have no
delight in you,' here I am, let Him do
to me as seems good to Him." 27The
king also said to Zadok the priest, "*Are
you not* a seer? Return to the city in
peace, and your two sons with you,
Ahimaaz your son, and Jonathan the
son of Abiathar. 28See, I will wait in the
plains of the wilderness until word
comes from you to inform me."
29Therefore Zadok and Abiathar carried the ark of God back to Jerusalem.
And they remained there.

30So David went up by the Ascent of

the *Mount of* Olives, and wept as he went up; and he had his head covered and went barefoot. And all the people who *were* with him covered their heads and went up, weeping as they went up. 31Then *someone* told David, saying, "Ahithophel *is* among the conspirators with Absalom." And David said, "O LORD, I pray, turn the counsel of Ahithophel into foolishness!"

32Now it happened when David had come to the top *of the mountain,* where he worshiped God—there was Hushai the Archite coming to meet him with his robe torn and dust on his head. 33David said to him, "If you go on with me, then you will become a burden to me. 34But if you return to the city, and say to Absalom, 'I will be your servant, O king; *as* I *was* your father's servant previously, so I *will* now also *be* your servant,' then you may defeat the counsel of Ahithophel for me. 35And *do* you not *have* Zadok and Abiathar the priests with you there? Therefore it will be *that* whatever you hear from the king's house, you shall tell to Zadok and Abiathar the priests. 36Indeed *they have* there with them their two sons, Ahimaaz, Zadok's *son,* and Jonathan, Abiathar's *son;* and by them you shall send me everything you hear."

37So Hushai, David's friend, went into the city. And Absalom came into Jerusalem.

Mephibosheth's Servant

16 When David was a little past the top *of the mountain,* there was Ziba the servant of Mephibosheth, who met him with a couple of saddled donkeys, and on them two hundred *loaves* of bread, one hundred clusters of raisins, one hundred summer fruits, and a skin of wine. 2And the king said to Ziba, "What do you mean to do with these?"

So Ziba said, "The donkeys *are* for the king's household to ride on, the bread and summer fruit for the young men to eat, and the wine for those who are faint in the wilderness to drink."

3Then the king said, "And where *is* your master's son?"

And Ziba said to the king, "Indeed he is staying in Jerusalem, for he said, 'Today the house of Israel will restore the kingdom of my father to me.'"

4So the king said to Ziba, "Here, all that *belongs* to Mephibosheth *is* yours."

And Ziba said, "I humbly bow before you, *that* I may find favor in your sight, my lord, O king!"

Shimei Curses David

5Now when King David came to Bahurim, there was a man from the family of the house of Saul, whose name *was* Shimei the son of Gera, coming from there. He came out, cursing continuously as he came. 6And he threw stones at David and at all the servants of King David. And all the people and all the mighty men *were* on his right hand and on his left. 7Also Shimei said thus when he cursed: "Come out! Come out! You bloodthirsty man, you rogue! 8The LORD has brought upon you all the blood of the house of Saul, in whose place you have reigned; and the LORD has delivered the kingdom into the hand of Absalom your son. So now you *are caught* in your own evil, because you are a bloodthirsty man!"

9Then Abishai the son of Zeruiah said to the king, "Why should this dead dog curse my lord the king? Please, let me go over and take off his head!"

10But the king said, "What have I to do with you, you sons of Zeruiah? So let him curse, because the LORD has said to him, 'Curse David.' Who then shall say, 'Why have you done so?'"

11And David said to Abishai and all his servants, "See how my son who came from my own body seeks my life. How much more now *may this* Benjamite? Let him alone, and let him curse; for so the LORD has ordered him. 12It may be that the LORD will look on my affliction, and that the LORD will repay me with good for his cursing this day." 13And as David and his men went along the road, Shimei went along the hillside opposite him and cursed as he went, threw stones at him and kicked up dust. 14Now the king and all the people who *were* with him became weary; so they refreshed themselves there.

The Advice of Ahithophel

15Meanwhile Absalom and all the people, the men of Israel, came to Jerusalem; and Ahithophel *was* with him. 16And so it was, when Hushai the Archite, David's friend, came to Absalom, that Hushai said to Absalom, "*Long* live the king! *Long* live the king!"

17So Absalom said to Hushai, "*Is* this your loyalty to your friend? Why did you not go with your friend?"

18And Hushai said to Absalom, "No, but whom the LORD and this people and all the men of Israel choose, his I will be, and with him I will remain. 19"Furthermore, whom should I serve? *Should I* not *serve* in the presence of his son? As I have served in your father's presence, so will I be in your presence."

20Then Absalom said to Ahithophel, "Give advice as to what we should do."

21And Ahithophel said to Absalom, "Go in to your father's concubines, whom he has left to keep the house; and all Israel will hear that you are abhorred by your father. Then the hands of all who are with you will be strong." 22So they pitched a tent for Absalom on the top of the house, and Absalom went in to his father's concubines in the sight of all Israel.

23Now the advice of Ahithophel, which he gave in those days, *was* as if one had inquired at the oracle of God. So *was* all the advice of Ahithophel both with David and with Absalom.

17 Moreover Ahithophel said to Absalom, "Now let me choose twelve thousand men, and I will arise and pursue David tonight. 2I will come upon him while he *is* weary and weak, and make him afraid. And all the people who *are* with him will flee, and I will strike only the king. 3Then I will bring back all the people to you. When all return except the man whom you seek, all the people will be at peace."

4And the saying pleased Absalom and all the elders of Israel.

The Advice of Hushai

5Then Absalom said, "Now call Hushai the Archite also, and let us hear what he says too." 6And when Hushai came to Absalom, Absalom spoke to him, saying, "Ahithophel has spoken in this manner. Shall we do as he says? If not, speak up."

7So Hushai said to Absalom: "The advice that Ahithophel has given *is* not good at this time. 8For," said Hushai, "you know your father and his men, that they *are* mighty men, and they *are* enraged in their minds, like a bear robbed of her cubs in the field; and your father *is* a man of war, and will not camp with the people. 9Surely by now he is hidden in some pit, or in some *other* place. And it will be, when some of them are overthrown at the first, that whoever hears *it* will say, 'There is a slaughter among the people who follow Absalom.' 10And even he *who is* valiant, whose heart *is* like the heart of a lion, will melt completely. For all Israel knows that your father *is* a mighty man, and *those* who *are* with him *are* valiant men. 11Therefore I advise that all Israel be fully gathered to you, from Dan to Beersheba, like the sand that *is* by the sea for multitude, and that you go to battle in person. 12So we will come upon him in some place where he may be found, and we will fall on him as the dew falls on the ground. And of him and all the men who *are* with him there shall not be left so much as one. 13Moreover, if he has withdrawn into a city, then all Israel shall bring ropes to that city; and we will pull it into the river, until there is not one small stone found there."

14So Absalom and all the men of Israel said, "The advice of Hushai the Archite *is* better than the advice of Ahithophel." For the LORD had purposed to defeat the good advice of Ahithophel, to the intent that the LORD might bring disaster on Absalom.

Hushai Warns David to Escape

15Then Hushai said to Zadok and Abiathar the priests, "Thus and so Ahithophel advised Absalom and the elders of Israel, and thus and so I have advised. 16Now therefore, send quickly and tell David, saying, 'Do not spend this night in the plains of the wilderness, but speedily cross over, lest the king and all the people who *are* with him be swallowed up.' " 17Now Jonathan and Ahimaaz stayed at En Rogel, for they dared not be seen coming into the city; so a female servant would come and tell them, and they would go and tell King David. 18Nevertheless a lad saw them, and told Absalom. But both of them went away quickly and came to a man's house in Bahurim, who had a well in his court; and they went down into it. 19Then the woman took and spread a covering over the well's mouth, and spread ground grain on it; and the thing was not known. 20And when Absalom's servants came to the woman at the house, they said, "Where *are* Ahimaaz and Jonathan?"

So the woman said to them, "They have gone over the water brook."

And when they had searched and could not find *them,* they returned to Jerusalem. 21Now it came to pass, after they had departed, that they came up out of the well and went and told King David, and said to David, "Arise and cross over the water quickly. For thus has Ahithophel advised against you."

22So David and all the people who *were* with him arose and crossed over the Jordan. By morning light not one of them was left who had not gone over the Jordan.

23Now when Ahithophel saw that his advice was not followed, he saddled a donkey, and arose and went home to his house, to his city. Then he put his household in order, and hanged himself, and died; and he was buried in his father's tomb.

24Then David went to Mahanaim. And Absalom crossed over the Jordan, he and all the men of Israel with him. 25And Absalom made Amasa captain of the army instead of Joab. This Amasa *was* the son of a man whose name *was* Jithra, an Israelite, who had gone in to Abigail the daughter of Nahash, sister of Zeruiah, Joab's mother. 26So Israel and Absalom encamped in the land of Gilead.

27Now it happened, when David had come to Mahanaim, that Shobi the son of Nahash from Rabbah of the people of Ammon, Machir the son of Ammiel from Lo Debar, and Barzillai the Gileadite from Rogelim, 28brought beds and basins, earthen vessels and wheat, barley and flour, parched *grain* and beans, lentils and parched *seeds,* 29honey and curds, sheep and cheese of the herd, for David and the people who *were* with him to eat. For they said,

"The people are hungry and weary and thirsty in the wilderness."

Absalom's Defeat and Death

18 And David numbered the people who *were* with him, and set captains of thousands and captains of hundreds over them. 2Then David sent out one third of the people under the hand of Joab, one third under the hand of Abishai the son of Zeruiah, Joab's brother, and one third under the hand of Ittai the Gittite. And the king said to the people, "I also will surely go out with you myself."

3But the people answered, "You shall not go out! For if we flee away, they will not care about us; nor if half of us die, will they care about us. But *you are* worth ten thousand of us now. For you are now more help to us in the city."

4Then the king said to them, "Whatever seems best to you I will do." So the king stood beside the gate, and all the people went out by hundreds and by thousands. 5Now the king had commanded Joab, Abishai, and Ittai, saying, "*Deal* gently for my sake with the young man Absalom." And all the people heard when the king gave all the captains orders concerning Absalom.

6So the people went out into the field of battle against Israel. And the battle was in the woods of Ephraim. 7The people of Israel were overthrown there before the servants of David, and a great slaughter of twenty thousand took place there that day. 8For the battle there was scattered over the face of the whole countryside, and the woods devoured more people that day than the sword devoured.

9Then Absalom met the servants of David. Absalom rode on a mule. The mule went under the thick boughs of a great terebinth tree, and his head caught in the terebinth; so he was left hanging between heaven and earth. And the mule which *was* under him went on. 10Now a certain man saw *it* and told Joab, and said, "I just saw Absalom hanging in a terebinth tree!"

11So Joab said to the man who told him, "You just saw *him!* And why did you not strike him there to the ground? I would have given you ten *shekels* of silver and a belt."

12But the man said to Joab, "Though I were to receive a thousand *shekels* of silver in my hand, I would not raise my hand against the king's son. For in our hearing the king commanded you and Abishai and Ittai, saying, 'Beware lest anyone *touch* the young man Absalom!' 13Otherwise I would have dealt falsely against my own life. For there is nothing hidden from the king, and you yourself would have set yourself against *me.*"

14Then Joab said, "I cannot linger with you." And he took three spears in his hand and thrust them through Absalom's heart, while he was *still* alive in the midst of the terebinth tree. 15And ten young men who bore Joab's armor surrounded Absalom, and struck and killed him.

16So Joab blew the trumpet, and the people returned from pursuing Israel. For Joab held back the people. 17And they took Absalom and cast him into a large pit in the woods, and laid a very large heap of stones over him. Then all Israel fled, everyone to his tent.

18Now Absalom in his lifetime had taken and set up a pillar for himself, which *is* in the King's Valley. For he said, "I have no son to keep my name in remembrance." He called the pillar after his own name. And to this day it is called Absalom's Monument.

David Hears of Absalom's Death

19Then Ahimaaz the son of Zadok said, "Let me run now and take the news to the king, how the LORD has avenged him of his enemies."

20And Joab said to him, "You shall not take the news this day, for you shall take the news another day. But today you shall take no news, because the king's son is dead." 21Then Joab said to the Cushite, "Go, tell the king what you have seen." So the Cushite bowed himself to Joab and ran.

22And Ahimaaz the son of Zadok said again to Joab, "But whatever happens, please let me also run after the Cushite."

So Joab said, "Why will you run, my son, since you have no news ready?"

23"But whatever happens," *he said,* "let me run."

So he said to him, "Run." Then Ahimaaz ran by way of the plain, and outran the Cushite.

24Now David was sitting between the two gates. And the watchman went up to the roof over the gate, to the wall, lifted his eyes and looked, and there was a man, running alone. 25Then the watchman cried out and told the king. And the king said, "If he *is* alone, *there is* news in his mouth." And he came rapidly and drew near.

26Then the watchman saw *another* man running, and the watchman called to the gatekeeper and said, "There is *another* man, running alone!"

And the king said, "He also brings news."

27So the watchman said, "I think the running of the first is like the running of Ahimaaz the son of Zadok."

And the king said, "He *is* a good man, and comes with good news."

28So Ahimaaz called out and said to the king, "All is well!" Then he bowed down with his face to the earth before the king, and said, "Blessed *be* the LORD your God, who has delivered up the men who raised their hand against my lord the king!"

29The king said, "Is the young man Absalom safe?"

Ahimaaz answered, "When Joab sent the king's servant and *me* your servant, I saw a great tumult, but I did not know what *it was* about."

30And the king said, "Turn aside *and* stand here." So he turned aside and stood still.

31Just then the Cushite came, and the Cushite said, "There is good news, my lord the king! For the LORD has avenged you this day of all those who rose against you."

32And the king said to the Cushite, "Is the young man Absalom safe?"

So the Cushite answered, "May the enemies of my lord the king, and all who rise against you to do harm, be like *that* young man!"

David's Mourning for Absalom

33Then the king was deeply moved, and went up to the chamber over the gate, and wept. And as he went, he said thus: "O my son Absalom—my son, my son Absalom—if only I had died in your place! O Absalom my son, my son!"

19 And Joab was told, "Behold, the king is weeping and mourning for Absalom." 2So the victory that day was *turned* into mourning for all the people. For the people heard it said that day, "The king is grieved for his son." 3And the people stole back into the city that day, as people who are ashamed steal away when they flee in battle. 4But the king covered his face, and the king cried out with a loud voice, "O my son Absalom! O Absalom, my son, my son!"

5Then Joab came into the house to the king, and said, "Today you have disgraced all your servants who today have saved your life, the lives of your sons and daughters, the lives of your wives and the lives of your concubines, 6in that you love your enemies and hate your friends. For you have declared today that you regard neither princes nor servants; for today I perceive that if Absalom had lived and all of us had died today, then it would have pleased you well. 7Now therefore, arise, go out and speak comfort to your servants. For I swear by the LORD, if you do not go out, not one will stay with you this night. And that will be worse for you than all the evil that has befallen you from your youth until now." 8Then the king arose and sat in the gate. And they told all the people, saying, "There is the king, sitting in the gate." So all the people came before the king.

For everyone of Israel had fled to his tent.

David Returns to Jerusalem

9Now all the people were in a dispute throughout all the tribes of Israel, saying, "The king saved us from the hand of our enemies, he delivered us from the hand of the Philistines, and now he has fled from the land because of Absalom. 10But Absalom, whom we anointed over us, has died in battle. Now therefore, why do you say nothing about bringing back the king?"

11So King David sent to Zadok and Abiathar the priests, saying, "Speak to the elders of Judah, saying, 'Why are you the last to bring the king back to his house, since the words of all Israel have come to the king, to his *very* house? 12You *are* my brethren, you *are* my bone and my flesh. Why then are you the last to bring back the king?' 13And say to Amasa, '*Are* you not my bone and my flesh? God do so to me, and more also, if you are not commander of the army before me continually in place of Joab.' " 14So he swayed the hearts of all the men of Judah, just as *the heart of* one man, so that they sent *this word* to the king: "Return, you and all your servants!"

15Then the king returned and came to the Jordan. And Judah came to Gilgal, to go to meet the king, to escort the king across the Jordan. 16And Shimei the son of Gera, a Benjamite, who *was* from Bahurim, hurried and came down with the men of Judah to meet King David. 17*There were* a thousand men of Benjamin with him, and Ziba the servant of the house of Saul, and his fifteen sons and his twenty servants with him; and they went over the Jordan before the king. 18Then a ferryboat went across to carry over the king's household, and to do what he thought good.

David's Mercy to Shimei

Now Shimei the son of Gera fell down before the king when he had crossed the Jordan. 19Then he said to the king, "Do not let my lord impute iniquity to me, or remember what wrong your servant did on the day that my lord the king left Jerusalem, that the king should take *it* to heart. 20For I, your servant, know that I have sinned. Therefore here I am, the first to come today of all the house of Joseph to go down to meet my lord the king."

21But Abishai the son of Zeruiah answered and said, "Shall not Shimei be put to death for this, because he cursed the LORD's anointed?"

22And David said, "What have I to do with you, you sons of Zeruiah, that you should be adversaries to me today? Shall any man be put to death today in Israel? For do I not know that today I *am* king over Israel?" 23Therefore the king said to Shimei, "You shall not die." And the king swore to him.

David and Mephibosheth Meet

24Now Mephibosheth the son of Saul came down to meet the king. And he had not cared for his feet, nor trimmed his mustache, nor washed his clothes, from the day the king departed until the day he returned in peace. 25So it was, when he had come to Jerusalem to meet the king, that the king said to him, "Why did you not go with me, Mephibosheth?"

26And he answered, "My lord, O king, my servant deceived me. For your servant said, 'I will saddle a donkey for myself, that I may ride on it and go to the king,' because your servant is lame. 27And he has slandered your servant to my lord the king, but my lord the king is like the angel of God. Therefore do what is good in your eyes. 28For all my father's house were but dead men before my lord the king. Yet you set your servant among those who eat at your own table. Therefore what right have I still to cry out anymore to the king?"

29So the king said to him, "Why do you speak anymore of your matters? I have said, 'You and Ziba divide the land.' "

30Then Mephibosheth said to the king, "Rather, let him take it all, inasmuch as my lord the king has come back in peace to his own house."

David's Kindness to Barzillai

31And Barzillai the Gileadite came down from Rogelim and went across the Jordan with the king, to escort him across the Jordan. 32Now Barzillai was a very aged man, eighty years old. And he had provided the king with supplies while he stayed at Mahanaim, for he was a very rich man. 33And the king said to Barzillai, "Come across with me, and I will provide for you while you are with me in Jerusalem."

34But Barzillai said to the king, "How long have I to live, that I should go up with the king to Jerusalem? 35I am today eighty years old. Can I discern between the good and bad? Can your servant taste what I eat or what I drink? Can I hear any longer the voice of singing men and singing women? Why then should your servant be a further burden to my lord the king? 36Your servant will go a little way across the Jordan with the king. And why should the king repay me with such a reward? 37Please

let your servant turn back again, that I may die in my own city, near the grave of my father and mother. But here is your servant Chimham; let him cross over with my lord the king, and do for him what seems good to you."

38And the king answered, "Chimham shall cross over with me, and I will do for him what seems good to you. Now whatever you request of me, I will do for you." 39Then all the people went over the Jordan. And when the king had crossed over, the king kissed Barzillai and blessed him, and he returned to his own place.

The Quarrel About the King

40Now the king went on to Gilgal, and Chimham went on with him. And all the people of Judah escorted the king, and also half the people of Israel. 41Just then all the men of Israel came to the king, and said to the king, "Why have our brethren, the men of Judah, stolen you away and brought the king, his household, and all David's men with him across the Jordan?"

42So all the men of Judah answered the men of Israel, "Because the king is a close relative of ours. Why then are you angry over this matter? Have we ever eaten at the king's expense? Or has he given us any gift?"

43And the men of Israel answered the men of Judah, and said, "We have ten shares in the king; therefore we also have more right to David than you. Why then do you despise us—were we not the first to advise bringing back our king?"

Yet the words of the men of Judah were fiercer than the words of the men of Israel.

The Rebellion of Sheba

20 And there happened to be there a rebel, whose name was Sheba the son of Bichri, a Benjamite. And he blew a trumpet, and said:

"We have no share in David,
    Nor do we have inheritance in the
        son of Jesse;
    Every man to his tents, O Israel!"
2So every man of Israel deserted David, and followed Sheba the son of Bichri. But the men of Judah, from the Jordan

as far as Jerusalem, remained loyal to their king.

3Now David came to his house at Jerusalem. And the king took the ten women, his concubines whom he had left to keep the house, and put them in seclusion and supported them, but did not go in to them. So they were shut up to the day of their death, living in widowhood.

4And the king said to Amasa, "Assemble the men of Judah for me within three days, and be present here yourself." 5So Amasa went to assemble *the men of* Judah. But he delayed longer than the set time which David had appointed him. 6And David said to Abishai, "Now Sheba the son of Bichri will do us more harm than Absalom. Take your lord's servants and pursue him, lest he find for himself fortified cities, and escape us." 7So Joab's men, with the Cherethites, the Pelethites, and all the mighty men, went out after him. And they went out of Jerusalem to pursue Sheba the son of Bichri. 8When they *were* at the large stone which *is* in Gibeon, Amasa came before them. Now Joab was dressed in battle armor; on it was a belt *with* a sword fastened in its sheath at his hips; and as he was going forward, it fell out. 9Then Joab said to Amasa, "*Are* you in health, my brother?" And Joab took Amasa by the beard with his right hand to kiss him. 10But Amasa did not notice the sword that *was* in Joab's hand. And he struck him with it in the stomach, and his entrails poured out on the ground; and he did not *strike* him again. Thus he died.

Then Joab and Abishai his brother pursued Sheba the son of Bichri. 11Meanwhile one of Joab's men stood near Amasa, and said, "Whoever favors Joab and whoever *is* for David—follow Joab!" 12But Amasa wallowed in *his* blood in the middle of the highway. And when the man saw that all the people stood still, he moved Amasa from the highway to the field and threw a garment over him, when he saw that everyone who came upon him halted. 13When he was removed from the highway, all the people went on after Joab to pursue Sheba the son of Bichri.

14And he went through all the tribes of Israel to Abel and Beth Maachah and all the Berites. So they were gathered together and also went after *Sheba*. 15Then they came and besieged him in Abel of Beth Maachah; and they cast up a siege mound against the city, and it stood by the rampart. And all the people who *were* with Joab battered the wall to throw it down.

16Then a wise woman cried out from the city, "Hear, hear! Please say to Joab, 'Come nearby, that I may speak with you.'" 17When he had come near to her, the woman said, "*Are* you Joab?"

He answered, "I *am*."

Then she said to him, "Hear the words of your maidservant."

And he answered, "I am listening."

18So she spoke, saying, "They used to talk in former times, saying, 'They shall surely seek *guidance* at Abel,' and so they would end *disputes*. 19I *am among the* peaceable *and* faithful in Israel. You seek to destroy a city and a mother in Israel. Why would you swallow up the inheritance of the Lord?"

20And Joab answered and said, "Far be it, far be it from me, that I should swallow up or destroy! 21That *is* not so. But a man from the mountains of Ephraim, Sheba the son of Bichri by name, has raised his hand against the king, against David. Deliver him only, and I will depart from the city."

So the woman said to Joab, "Watch, his head will be thrown to you over the wall." 22Then the woman in her wisdom went to all the people. And they cut off the head of Sheba the son of Bichri, and threw *it* out to Joab. Then he blew a trumpet, and they withdrew from the city, every man to his tent. So Joab returned to the king at Jerusalem.

David's Government Officers

23And Joab *was* over all the army of Israel; Benaiah the son of Jehoiada *was* over the Cherethites and the Pelethites; 24Adoram *was* in charge of revenue; Jehoshaphat the son of Ahilud *was* recorder; 25Sheva *was* scribe; Zadok and Abiathar *were* the priests; 26and Ira the Jairite was a chief minister under David.

David Avenges the Gibeonites

21 Now there was a famine in the days of David for three years, year after year; and David inquired of the LORD. And the LORD answered, "*It is* because of Saul and *his* bloodthirsty house, because he killed the Gibeonites." 2So the king called the Gibeonites and spoke to them. Now the Gibeonites *were* not of the children of Israel, but of the remnant of the Amorites; the children of Israel had sworn protection to them, but Saul had sought to kill them in his zeal for the children of Israel and Judah.

3Therefore David said to the Gibeonites, "What shall I do for you? And with what shall I make atonement, that you may bless the inheritance of the LORD?"

4And the Gibeonites said to him, "We will have no silver or gold from Saul or from his house, nor shall you kill any man in Israel for us."

So he said, "Whatever you say, I will do for you."

5Then they answered the king, "As for the man who consumed us and plotted against us, *that* we should be destroyed from remaining in any of the territories of Israel, 6let seven men of his descendants be delivered to us, and we will hang them before the LORD in Gibeah of Saul, *whom* the LORD chose."

And the king said, "I will give *them*."

7But the king spared Mephibosheth the son of Jonathan, the son of Saul, because of the LORD's oath that *was* between them, between David and Jonathan the son of Saul. 8So the king took Armoni and Mephibosheth, the two sons of Rizpah the daughter of Aiah, whom she bore to Saul, and the five sons of Michal^h the daughter of Saul, whom she brought up for Adriel the son of Barzillai the Meholathite; 9and he delivered them into the hands of the Gibeonites, and they hanged them on the hill before the LORD. So they fell, *all* seven together, and were put to death in the days of harvest, in the first *days*, in the beginning of barley harvest.

10Now Rizpah the daughter of Aiah took sackcloth and spread it for herself on the rock, from the beginning of harvest until the late rains poured on them from heaven. And she did not allow the birds of the air to rest on them by day nor the beasts of the field by night.

11And David was told what Rizpah the daughter of Aiah, the concubine of Saul, had done. 12Then David went and took the bones of Saul, and the bones of Jonathan his son, from the men of Jabesh Gilead who had stolen them from the street of Beth Shan, where the Philistines had hung them up, after the Philistines had struck down Saul in Gilboa. 13So he brought up the bones of Saul and the bones of Jonathan his son from there; and they gathered the bones of those who had been hanged. 14They buried the bones of Saul and Jonathan his son in the country of Benjamin in Zelah, in the tomb of Kish his father. So they performed all that the king commanded. And after that God heeded the prayer for the land.

Philistine Giants Destroyed

15When the Philistines were at war again with Israel, David and his servants with him went down and fought against the Philistines; and David grew faint. 16Then Ishbi-Benob, who *was* one of the sons of the giant, the weight of whose bronze spear *was* three hundred *shekels*, who was bearing a new *sword*, thought he could kill David. 17But Abishai the son of Zeruiah came to his aid, and struck the Philistine and killed him. Then the men of David swore to him, saying, "You shall go out no more with us to battle, lest you quench the lamp of Israel."

18Now it happened afterward that there was again a battle with the Philistines at Gob. Then Sibbechai the Hushathite killed Saph, who *was* one of the sons of the giant. 19Again there was war at Gob with the Philistines, where Elhanan the son of Jaare-Oregim the Bethlehemite killed *the brother of* Goliath the Gittite, the shaft of whose spear *was* like a weaver's beam.

20Yet again there was war at Gath, where there was a man of *great* stature, who had six fingers on each hand and six toes on each foot, twenty-four in number; and he also was born to the

h Or *Merab* (compare 1 Samuel 18.19 and 25.44; 2 Samuel 3.14 and 6.23) giant. 21So when he defied Israel, Jonathan the son of Shimea, David's brother, killed him.

22These four were born to the giant in Gath, and fell by the hand of David and by the hand of his servants.

Praise for God's Deliverance

22 Then David spoke to the LORD the words of this song, on the day when the LORD had delivered him from the hand of all his enemies, and from the hand of Saul. 2And he said:*i*

> "The LORD *is* my rock and my
>   fortress and my deliverer;
> 3 The God of my strength, in whom
>   I will trust;
> My shield and the horn of my
>   salvation,
> My stronghold and my refuge;
> My Savior, You save me from
>   violence.
> 4 I will call upon the LORD, *who is*
>   *worthy* to be praised;
> So shall I be saved from my
>   enemies.

> 5 "When the waves of death
>   surrounded me,
> The floods of ungodliness made me
>   afraid.
> 6 The sorrows of Sheol
>   surrounded me;
> The snares of death confronted me.
> 7 In my distress I called upon the
>   LORD,
> And cried out to my God;
> He heard my voice from His
>   temple,
> And my cry *entered* His ears.

> 8 "Then the earth shook and trembled;
> The foundations of heaven quaked
>   and were shaken,
> Because He was angry.
> 9 Smoke went up from His nostrils,
> And devouring fire from His
>   mouth;
> Coals were kindled by it.
> 10 He bowed the heavens also, and
>   came down
> With darkness under His feet.
> 11 He rode upon a cherub, and flew;
> And He was seen upon the wings
>   of the wind.

> 12 He made darkness canopies
>   around Him,
> Dark waters *and* thick clouds of the
>   skies.
> 13 From the brightness before Him
> Coals of fire were kindled.

> 14 "The LORD thundered from heaven,
> And the Most High uttered His
>   voice.
> 15 He sent out arrows and scattered
>   them;
> Lightning bolts, and He vanquished
>   them.
> 16 Then the channels of the sea were
>   seen,
> The foundations of the world were
>   uncovered,
> At the rebuke of the LORD,
> At the blast of the breath of His
>   nostrils.

> 17 "He sent from above, He took me,
> He drew me out of many waters.
> 18 He delivered me from my strong
>   enemy,
> From those who hated me;
> For they were too strong for me.
> 19 They confronted me in the day of
>   my calamity,
> But the LORD was my support.
> 20 He also brought me out into a broad
>   place;
> He delivered me because He
>   delighted in me.

> 21 "The LORD rewarded me according
>   to my righteousness;
> According to the cleanness of my
>   hands
> He has recompensed me.
> 22 For I have kept the ways of the
>   LORD,
> And have not wickedly departed
>   from my God.
> 23 For all His judgments *were*
>   before me;
> And *as for* His statutes, I did not
>   depart from them.
> 24 I was also blameless before Him,
> And I kept myself from my iniquity.
> 25 Therefore the LORD has
>   recompensed me according to my
>   righteousness,

i Compare Psalm 18

According to my cleanness in His
    eyes.

26 "With the merciful You will show
    Yourself merciful;
    With a blameless man You will
      show Yourself blameless;
27 With the pure You will show
    Yourself pure;
    And with the devious You will
      show Yourself shrewd.
28 You will save the humble people;
    But Your eyes *are* on the haughty,
      that You may bring *them* down.

29 "For You *are* my lamp, O LORD;
    The LORD shall enlighten my
      darkness.
30 For by You I can run against a
    troop;
    By my God I can leap over a wall.
31 *As for* God, His way *is* perfect;
    The word of the LORD *is* proven;
    He *is* a shield to all who trust
      in Him.

32 "For who *is* God, except the LORD?
    And who *is* a rock, except our God?
33 God *is* my strength *and* power,
    And He makes my way perfect.
34 He makes my feet like the *feet* of
    deer,
    And sets me on my high places.
35 He teaches my hands to make war,
    So that my arms can bend a bow
      of bronze.

36 "You have also given me the shield
    of Your salvation;
    Your gentleness has made me
      great.
37 You enlarged my path under me;
    So my feet did not slip.

38 "I have pursued my enemies and
    destroyed them;
    Neither did I turn back again till
      they were destroyed.
39 And I have destroyed them and
    wounded them,
    So that they could not rise;
    They have fallen under my feet.
40 For You have armed me with
    strength for the battle;
    You have subdued under me those
      who rose against me.

41 You have also given me the necks
    of my enemies,
    So that I destroyed those who hated
      me.
42 They looked, but *there was* none
    to save;
    Even to the LORD, but He did not
      answer them.
43 Then I beat them as fine as the dust
    of the earth;
    I trod them like dirt in the streets,
    And I spread them out.

44 "You have also delivered me from
    the strivings of my people;
    You have kept me as the head of
      the nations.
    A people I have not known shall
      serve me.
45 The foreigners submit to me;
    As soon as they hear, they obey me.
46 The foreigners fade away,
    And come frightened from their
      hideouts.

47 "The LORD lives!
    Blessed *be* my Rock!
    Let God be exalted,
    The Rock of my salvation!
48 *It is* God who avenges me,
    And subdues the peoples under me;
49 He delivers me from my enemies.
    You also lift me up above those
      who rise against me;
    You have delivered me from the
      violent man.
50 Therefore I will give thanks to You,
    O LORD, among the Gentiles,
    And sing praises to Your name.

51 *He is* the tower of salvation to His
    king,
    And shows mercy to His anointed,
    To David and his descendants
      forevermore."

David's Last Words

23 Now these *are* the last words of
David.
    Thus says David the son of Jesse;
    Thus says the man raised up on
      high,
    The anointed of the God of Jacob,
    And the sweet psalmist of Israel:

2 "The Spirit of the LORD spoke by me,
    And His word *was* on my tongue.

3 The God of Israel said,
  The Rock of Israel spoke to me:
  'He who rules over men *must be*
      just,
  Ruling in the fear of God.
4 And *he shall be* like the light of
      the morning *when* the sun rises,
  A morning without clouds,
  Like the tender grass *springing* out
      of the earth,
  By clear shining after rain.'

5 "Although my house *is* not so
      with God,
  Yet He has made with me an
      everlasting covenant,
  Ordered in all *things* and secure.
  For *this is* all my salvation and all
      my desire;
  Will He not make *it* increase?
6 But *the* sons of rebellion *shall* all
      be as thorns thrust away,
  Because they cannot be taken with
      hands.
7 But the man *who* touches them
  Must be armed with iron and the
      shaft of a spear,
  And they shall be utterly burned
      with fire in *their* place."

David's Mighty Men

8These *are* the names of the mighty men whom David had: Josheb-Basshebeth*ⁱ* the Tachmonite, chief among the captains. He was called Adino the Eznite, because he had killed eight hundred men at one time. 9And after him *was* Eleazar the son of Dodo, the Ahohite, *one* of the three mighty men with David when they defied the Philistines *who* were gathered there for battle, and the men of Israel had retreated. 10He arose and attacked the Philistines until his hand was weary, and his hand stuck to the sword. The LORD brought about a great victory that day; and the people returned after him only to plunder. 11And after him *was* Shammah the son of Agee the Hararite. The Philistines had gathered together into a troop where there was a piece of ground full of lentils. So the people fled from the Philistines. 12But he stationed himself in the middle of the field, defended it, and killed the Philistines. So the LORD br ought about a great victory.

13Then three of the thirty chief men went down at harvest time and came to David at the cave of Adullam. And the troop of Philistines encamped in the Valley of Rephaim. 14David *was* then in the stronghold, and the garrison of the Philistines *was* then *in* Bethlehem. 15And David said with longing, "Oh, that someone would give me a drink of the water from the well of Bethlehem, which *is* by the gate!" 16So the three mighty men broke through the camp of the Philistines, drew water from the well of Bethlehem that *was* by the gate, and took it and brought *it* to David. Nevertheless he would not drink it, but poured it out to the LORD. 17And he said, "Far be it from me, O LORD, that I should do this! Is *this not* the blood of the men who went in *jeopardy of* their lives?" Therefore he would not drink it.

These things were done by the three mighty men.

18Now Abishai the brother of Joab, the son of Zeruiah, was chief of *another* three. He lifted his spear against three hundred *men*, killed *them*, and won a name among *these* three. 19Was he not the most honored of three? Therefore he became their captain. However, he did not attain to the *first* three.

20Benaiah *was* the son of Jehoiada, the son of a valiant man from Kabzeel, who had done many deeds. He had killed two lion-like heroes of Moab. He also had gone down and killed a lion in the midst of a pit on a snowy day. 21And he killed an Egyptian, a spectacular man. The Egyptian *had* a spear in his hand; so he went down to him with a staff, wrested the spear out of the Egyptian's hand, and killed him with his own spear. 22These *things* Benaiah the son of Jehoiada did, and won a name among three mighty men. 23He was more honored than the thirty, but he did not attain to the *first* three. And David appointed him over his guard.

24Asahel the brother of Joab *was* one of the thirty; Elhanan the son of Dodo of Bethlehem, 25Shammah the Harodite, Elika the Harodite, 26Helez the

---

ⁱ Literally *One Who Sits in the Seat* (compare 1 Chronicles 11.11)

Paltite, Ira the son of Ikkesh the Te-koite, 27Abiezer the Anathothite, Me-bunnai the Hushathite, 28Zalmon the Ahohite, Maharai the Netophathite, 29Heleb the son of Baanah (the Ne-tophathite), Ittai the son of Ribai from Gibeah of the children of Benjamin, 30Benaiah a Pirathonite, Hiddai from the brooks of Gaash, 31Abi-Albon the Arbathite, Azmaveth the Barhumite, 32Eliahba the Shaalbonite (of the sons of Jashen), Jonathan, 33Shammah the Hararite, Ahiam the son of Sharar the Hararite, 34Eliphelet the son of Ahas-bai, the son of the Maachathite, Eliam the son of Ahithophel the Gilonite, 35Hezrai the Carmelite, Paarai the Ar-bite, 36Igal the son of Nathan of Zobah, Bani the Gadite, 37Zelek the Ammonite, Naharai the Beerothite (armorbearer of Joab the son of Zeruiah), 38Ira the Ith-rite, Gareb the Ithrite, 39*and* Uriah the Hittite: thirty-seven in all.

David's Census of Israel and Judah

24 Again the anger of the LORD was aroused against Israel, and He moved David against them to say, "Go, number Israel and Judah."

2So the king said to Joab the com-mander of the army who *was* with him, "Now go throughout all the tribes of Is-rael, from Dan to Beersheba, and count the people, that I may know the number of the people."

3And Joab said to the king, "Now may the LORD your God add to the peo-ple a hundred times more than there are, and may the eyes of my lord the king see *it.* But why does my lord the king desire this thing?" 4Nevertheless the king's word prevailed against Joab and against the captains of the army. Therefore Joab and the captains of the army went out from the presence of the king to count the people of Israel.

5And they crossed over the Jordan and camped in Aroer, on the right side of the town which *is* in the midst of the ravine of Gad, and toward Jazer. 6Then they came to Gilead and to the land of Tahtim Hodshi; they came to Dan Jaan and around to Sidon; 7and they came to the stronghold of Tyre and to all the cities of the Hivites

and the Canaanites. Then they went out to South Judah *as far as* Beersheba. 8So when they had gone through all the land, they came to Jerusalem at the end of nine months and twenty days. 9Then Joab gave the sum of the number of the people to the king. And there were in Israel eight hundred thousand valiant men who drew the sword, and the men of Judah were five hundred thousand men.

The Judgment on David's Sin

10And David's heart condemned him after he had numbered the people. So David said to the LORD, "I have sinned greatly in what I have done; but now, I pray, O LORD, take away the iniquity of Your servant, for I have done very foolishly."

11Now when David arose in the morning, the word of the LORD came to the prophet Gad, David's seer, say-ing, 12"Go and tell David, 'Thus says the LORD: "I offer you three *things;* choose one of them for yourself, that I may do *it* to you." ' " 13So Gad came to David and told him; and he said to him, "Shall seven[k] years of famine come to you in your land? Or shall you flee three months before your enemies, while they pursue you? Or shall there be three days' plague in your land? Now consider and see what answer I should take back to Him who sent me."

14And David said to Gad, "I am in great distress. Please let us fall into the hand of the LORD, for His mercies *are* great; but do not let me fall into the hand of man."

15So the LORD sent a plague upon Is-rael from the morning till the appointed time. From Dan to Beersheba seventy thousand men of the people died. 16And when the angel[l] stretched out His hand over Jerusalem to destroy it, the LORD relented from the destruction, and said to the angel who was destroying the people, "It is enough; now restrain your hand." And the angel of the LORD was by the threshing floor of Araunah the Jebusite.

17Then David spoke to the LORD when he saw the angel who was strik-ing the people, and said, "Surely I have

---

k Or *three* in 1 Chronicles 21.12   l Or *Angel*

sinned, and I have done wickedly; but these sheep, what have they done? Let Your hand, I pray, be against me and against my father's house."

The Altar on the Threshing Floor

18And Gad came that day to David and said to him, "Go up, erect an altar to the LORD on the threshing floor of Araunah the Jebusite." 19So David, according to the word of Gad, went up as the LORD commanded. 20Now Araunah looked, and saw the king and his servants coming toward him. So Araunah went out and bowed before the king with his face to the ground.

21Then Araunah said, "Why has my lord the king come to his servant?"

And David said, "To buy the threshing floor from you, to build an altar to the LORD, that the plague may be withdrawn from the people."

22Now Araunah said to David, "Let my lord the king take and offer up whatever *seems* good to him. Look, *here are* oxen for burnt sacrifice, and threshing implements and the yokes of the oxen for wood. 23All these, O king, Araunah has given to the king."

And Araunah said to the king, "May the LORD your God accept you."

24Then the king said to Araunah, "No, but I will surely buy *it* from you for a price; nor will I offer burnt offerings to the LORD my God with that which costs me nothing." So David bought the threshing floor and the oxen for fifty shekels of silver. 25And David built there an altar to the LORD, and offered burnt offerings and peace offerings. So the LORD heeded the prayers for the land, and the plague was withdrawn from Israel.

KINGS

Adonijah Presumes to Be King

1 Now King David was old, advanced in years; and they put covers on him, but he could not get warm. 2Therefore his servants said to him, "Let a young woman, a virgin, be sought for our lord the king, and let her stand before the king, and let her care for him; and let her lie in your bosom, that our lord the king may be warm." 3So they sought for a lovely young woman throughout all the territory of Israel, and found Abishag the Shunammite, and brought her to the king. 4The young woman *was* very lovely; and she cared for the king, and served him; but the king did not know her.

5Then Adonijah the son of Haggith exalted himself, saying, "I will be king"; and he prepared for himself chariots and horsemen, and fifty men to run before him. 6(And his father had not rebuked him at any time by saying, "Why have you done so?" He *was* also very good-looking. *His mother* had borne him after Absalom.) 7Then he conferred with Joab the son of Zeruiah and with Abiathar the priest, and they followed and helped Adonijah. 8But Zadok the priest, Benaiah the son of Jehoiada, Nathan the prophet, Shimei, Rei, and the mighty men who *belonged* to David were not with Adonijah.

9And Adonijah sacrificed sheep and oxen and fattened cattle by the stone of Zoheleth, which *is* by En Rogel; he also invited all his brothers, the king's sons, and all the men of Judah, the king's servants. 10But he did not invite Nathan the prophet, Benaiah, the mighty men, or Solomon his brother.

11So Nathan spoke to Bathsheba the mother of Solomon, saying, "Have you not heard that Adonijah the son of Haggith has become king, and David our lord does not know *it?* 12Come, please, let me now give you advice, that you may save your own life and the life of your son Solomon. 13Go immediately to King David and say to him, 'Did you not, my lord, O king, swear to your maidservant, saying, "Assuredly your son Solomon shall reign after me, and he shall sit on my throne"? Why then has Adonijah become king?' 14Then, while you are still talking there with the king, I also will come in after you and confirm your words."

15So Bathsheba went into the chamber to the king. (Now the king was very old, and Abishag the Shunammite was serving the king.) 16And Bathsheba bowed and did homage to the king. Then the king said, "What is your wish?"

17Then she said to him, "My lord, you swore by the LORD your God to your maidservant, *saying,* 'Assuredly Solomon your son shall reign after me, and he shall sit on my throne.' 18So now, look! Adonijah has become king; and now, my lord the king, you do not know about *it.* 19He has sacrificed oxen and fattened cattle and sheep in abundance, and has invited all the sons of the king, Abiathar the priest, and Joab the commander of the army; but Solomon your servant he has not invited. 20And as for you, my lord, O king, the eyes of all Israel *are* on you, that you should tell them who will sit on the throne of my lord the king after him. 21Otherwise it will happen, when my lord the king rests with his fathers, that I and my son Solomon will be counted as offenders."

22And just then, while she was still talking with the king, Nathan the prophet also came in. 23So they told the king, saying, "Here is Nathan the prophet." And when he came in before the king, he bowed down before the king with his face to the ground. 24And Nathan said, "My lord, O king, have you said, 'Adonijah shall reign after me, and he shall sit on my throne'? 25For he has gone down today, and has sacrificed oxen and fattened cattle and sheep in abundance, and has invited all the king's sons, and the commanders of the army, and Abiathar the priest; and look! They are eating and drinking before him; and they say, '*Long* live King Adonijah!' 26But he has not invited me—me your servant—nor Zadok the priest, nor Benaiah the son of Jehoiada, nor your servant Solomon. 27Has this thing been done by my lord the king, and you have not told your servant who should sit on the throne of my lord the king after him?"

David Proclaims Solomon King

28Then King David answered and said, "Call Bathsheba to me." So she came into the king's presence and stood before the king. 29And the king took an oath and said, "As the LORD lives, who has redeemed my life from every distress, 30just as I swore to you by the LORD God of Israel, saying, 'Assuredly Solomon your son shall be king after me, and he shall sit on my throne in my place,' so I certainly will do this day."

31Then Bathsheba bowed with her face to the earth, and paid homage to the king, and said, "Let my lord King David live forever!"

32And King David said, "Call to me Zadok the priest, Nathan the prophet, and Benaiah the son of Jehoiada." So they came before the king. 33The king also said to them, "Take with you the servants of your lord, and have Solomon my son ride on my own mule, and take him down to Gihon. 34There let Zadok the priest and Nathan the prophet anoint him king over Israel; and blow the horn, and say, 'Long live King Solomon!' 35Then you shall come up after him, and he shall come and sit on my throne, and he shall be king in my place. For I have appointed him to be ruler over Israel and Judah."

36Benaiah the son of Jehoiada answered the king and said, "Amen! May the LORD God of my lord the king say so too. 37As the LORD has been with my lord the king, even so may He be with Solomon, and make his throne greater than the throne of my lord King David."

38So Zadok the priest, Nathan the prophet, Benaiah the son of Jehoiada, the Cherethites, and the Pelethites went down and had Solomon ride on King David's mule, and took him to Gihon. 39Then Zadok the priest took a horn of oil from the tabernacle and anointed Solomon. And they blew the horn, and all the people said, "Long live King Solomon!" 40And all the people went up

after him; and the people played the flutes and rejoiced with great joy, so that the earth seemed to split with their sound.

41Now Adonijah and all the guests who were with him heard it as they finished eating. And when Joab heard the sound of the horn, he said, "Why is the city in such a noisy uproar?" 42While he was still speaking, there came Jonathan, the son of Abiathar the priest. And Adonijah said to him, "Come in, for you are a prominent man, and bring good news."

43Then Jonathan answered and said to Adonijah, "No! Our lord King David has made Solomon king. 44The king has sent with him Zadok the priest, Nathan the prophet, Benaiah the son of Jehoiada, the Cherethites, and the Pelethites; and they have made him ride on the king's mule. 45So Zadok the priest and Nathan the prophet have anointed him king at Gihon; and they have gone up from there rejoicing, so that the city is in an uproar. This is the noise that you have heard. 46Also Solomon sits on the throne of the kingdom. 47And moreover the king's servants have gone to bless our lord King David, saying, 'May God make the name of Solomon better than your name, and may He make his throne greater than your throne.' Then the king bowed himself on the bed. 48Also the king said thus, 'Blessed be the LORD God of Israel, who has given one to sit on my throne this day, while my eyes see it!' "

49So all the guests who were with Adonijah were afraid, and arose, and each one went his way.

50Now Adonijah was afraid of Solomon; so he arose, and went and took hold of the horns of the altar. 51And it was told Solomon, saying, "Indeed Adonijah is afraid of King Solomon; for look, he has taken hold of the horns of the altar, saying, 'Let King Solomon swear to me today that he will not put his servant to death with the sword.' "

52Then Solomon said, "If he proves himself a worthy man, not one hair of him shall fall to the earth; but if wickedness is found in him, he shall die." 53So King Solomon sent them to bring him down from the altar. And he came and fell down before King Solomon;

and Solomon said to him, "Go to your house."

David's Instructions to Solomon

2 Now the days of David drew near that he should die, and he charged Solomon his son, saying: 2"I go the way of all the earth; be strong, therefore, and prove yourself a man. 3And keep the charge of the LORD your God: to walk in His ways, to keep His statutes, His commandments, His judgments, and His testimonies, as it is written in the Law of Moses, that you may prosper in all that you do and wherever you turn; 4that the LORD may fulfill His word which He spoke concerning me, saying, 'If your sons take heed to their way, to walk before Me in truth with all their heart and with all their soul,' He said, 'you shall not lack a man on the throne of Israel.'

5"Moreover you know also what Joab the son of Zeruiah did to me, and what he did to the two commanders of the armies of Israel, to Abner the son of Ner and Amasa the son of Jether, whom he killed. And he shed the blood of war in peacetime, and put the blood of war on his belt that was around his waist, and on his sandals that were on his feet. 6Therefore do according to your wisdom, and do not let his gray hair go down to the grave in peace.

7"But show kindness to the sons of Barzillai the Gileadite, and let them be among those who eat at your table, for so they came to me when I fled from Absalom your brother.

8"And see, you have with you Shimei the son of Gera, a Benjamite from Bahurim, who cursed me with a malicious curse in the day when I went to Mahanaim. But he came down to meet me at the Jordan, and I swore to him by the LORD, saying, 'I will not put you to death with the sword.' 9Now therefore, do not hold him guiltless, for you are a wise man and know what you ought to do to him; but bring his gray hair down to the grave with blood."

Death of David

10So David rested with his fathers, and was buried in the City of David. 11The period that David reigned over Israel was forty years; seven years he reigned in Hebron, and in Jerusalem he reigned thirty-three years. 12Then Solomon sat on the throne of his father David; and his kingdom was firmly established.

Solomon Executes Adonijah

13Now Adonijah the son of Haggith came to Bathsheba the mother of Solomon. So she said, "Do you come peaceably?"

And he said, "Peaceably." 14Moreover he said, "I have something to say to you."

And she said, "Say it."

15Then he said, "You know that the kingdom was mine, and all Israel had set their expectations on me, that I should reign. However, the kingdom has been turned over, and has become my brother's; for it was his from the LORD. 16Now I ask one petition of you; do not deny me."

And she said to him, "Say it."

17Then he said, "Please speak to King Solomon, for he will not refuse you, that he may give me Abishag the Shunammite as wife."

18So Bathsheba said, "Very well, I will speak for you to the king."

19Bathsheba therefore went to King Solomon, to speak to him for Adonijah. And the king rose up to meet her and bowed down to her, and sat down on his throne and had a throne set for the king's mother; so she sat at his right hand. 20Then she said, "I desire one small petition of you; do not refuse me."

And the king said to her, "Ask it, my mother, for I will not refuse you."

21So she said, "Let Abishag the Shunammite be given to Adonijah your brother as wife."

22And King Solomon answered and said to his mother, "Now why do you ask Abishag the Shunammite for Adonijah? Ask for him the kingdom also—for he is my older brother—for him, and for Abiathar the priest, and for Joab the son of Zeruiah." 23Then King Solomon swore by the LORD, saying, "May God do so to me, and more also, if Adonijah has not spoken this word against his own life! 24Now therefore, as the LORD lives, who has confirmed me and set me on the throne of David my father, and who has established a house for me, as

He promised, Adonijah shall be put to death today!"

25So King Solomon sent by the hand of Benaiah the son of Jehoiada; and he struck him down, and he died.

Abiathar Exiled, Joab Executed

26And to Abiathar the priest the king said, "Go to Anathoth, to your own fields, for you *are* deserving of death; but I will not put you to death at this time, because you carried the ark of the Lord GOD before my father David, and because you were afflicted every time my father was afflicted." 27So Solomon removed Abiathar from being priest to the LORD, that he might fulfill the word of the LORD which He spoke concerning the house of Eli at Shiloh.

28Then news came to Joab, for Joab had defected to Adonijah, though he had not defected to Absalom. So Joab fled to the tabernacle of the LORD, and took hold of the horns of the altar. 29And King Solomon was told, "Joab has fled to the tabernacle of the LORD; there *he is*, by the altar." Then Solomon sent Benaiah the son of Jehoiada, saying, "Go, strike him down." 30So Benaiah went to the tabernacle of the LORD, and said to him, "Thus says the king, 'Come out!' "

And he said, "No, but I will die here." And Benaiah brought back word to the king, saying, "Thus said Joab, and thus he answered me."

31Then the king said to him, "Do as he has said, and strike him down and bury him, that you may take away from me and from the house of my father the innocent blood which Joab shed. 32So the LORD will return his blood on his head, because he struck down two men more righteous and better than he, and killed them with the sword—Abner the son of Ner, the commander of the army of Israel, and Amasa the son of Jether, the commander of the army of Judah—though my father David did not know *it*. 33Their blood shall therefore return upon the head of Joab and upon the head of his descendants forever. But upon David and his descendants, upon his house and his throne, there shall be peace forever from the LORD."

34So Benaiah the son of Jehoiada went up and struck and killed him; and

he was buried in his own house in the wilderness. 35The king put Benaiah the son of Jehoiada in his place over the army, and the king put Zadok the priest in the place of Abiathar.

Shimei Executed

36Then the king sent and called for Shimei, and said to him, "Build yourself a house in Jerusalem and dwell there, and do not go out from there anywhere. 37For it shall be, on the day you go out and cross the Brook Kidron, know for certain you shall surely die; your blood shall be on your own head."

38And Shimei said to the king, "The saying *is* good. As my lord the king has said, so your servant will do." So Shimei dwelt in Jerusalem many days.

39Now it happened at the end of three years, that two slaves of Shimei ran away to Achish the son of Maachah, king of Gath. And they told Shimei, saying, "Look, your slaves *are* in Gath!" 40So Shimei arose, saddled his donkey, and went to Achish at Gath to seek his slaves. And Shimei went and brought his slaves from Gath. 41And Solomon was told that Shimei had gone from Jerusalem to Gath and had come back. 42Then the king sent and called for Shimei, and said to him, "Did I not make you swear by the LORD, and warn you, saying, 'Know for certain that on the day you go out and travel anywhere, you shall surely die'? And you said to me, 'The word I have heard *is* good.' 43Why then have you not kept the oath of the LORD and the commandment that I gave you?" 44The king said moreover to Shimei, "You know, as your heart acknowledges, all the wickedness that you did to my father David; therefore the LORD will return your wickedness on your own head. 45But King Solomon *shall be* blessed, and the throne of David shall be established before the LORD forever."

46So the king commanded Benaiah the son of Jehoiada; and he went out and struck him down, and he died. Thus the kingdom was established in the hand of Solomon.

Solomon Requests Wisdom

3 Now Solomon made a treaty with Pharaoh king of Egypt, and married

Pharaoh's daughter; then he brought her to the City of David until he had finished building his own house, and the house of the LORD, and the wall all around Jerusalem. 2Meanwhile the people sacrificed at the high places, because there was no house built for the name of the LORD until those days. 3And Solomon loved the LORD, walking in the statutes of his father David, except that he sacrificed and burned incense at the high places.

4Now the king went to Gibeon to sacrifice there, for that was the great high place: Solomon offered a thousand burnt offerings on that altar. 5At Gibeon the LORD appeared to Solomon in a dream by night; and God said, "Ask! What shall I give you?"

6And Solomon said: "You have shown great mercy to Your servant David my father, because he walked before You in truth, in righteousness, and in uprightness of heart with You; You have continued this great kindness for him, and You have given him a son to sit on his throne, as it is this day. 7Now, O LORD my God, You have made Your servant king instead of my father David, but I am a little child; I do not know how to go out or come in. 8And Your servant is in the midst of Your people whom You have chosen, a great people, too numerous to be numbered or counted. 9Therefore give to Your servant an understanding heart to judge Your people, that I may discern between good and evil. For who is able to judge this great people of Yours?"

10The speech pleased the LORD, that Solomon had asked this thing. 11Then God said to him: "Because you have asked this thing, and have not asked long life for yourself, nor have asked riches for yourself, nor have asked the life of your enemies, but have asked for yourself understanding to discern justice, 12behold, I have done according to your words; see, I have given you a wise and understanding heart, so that there has not been anyone like you before you, nor shall any like you arise after you. 13And I have also given you what you have not asked: both riches and honor, so that there shall not be anyone like you among the kings all your days. 14So if you walk in My ways, to keep

My statutes and My commandments, as your father David walked, then I will lengthen your days."

15Then Solomon awoke; and indeed it had been a dream. And he came to Jerusalem and stood before the ark of the covenant of the LORD, offered up burnt offerings, offered peace offerings, and made a feast for all his servants.

Solomon's Wise Judgment

16Now two women who were harlots came to the king, and stood before him. 17And one woman said, "O my lord, this woman and I dwell in the same house; and I gave birth while she was in the house. 18Then it happened, the third day after I had given birth, that this woman also gave birth. And we were together; no one was with us in the house, except the two of us in the house. 19And this woman's son died in the night, because she lay on him. 20So she arose in the middle of the night and took my son from my side, while your maidservant slept, and laid him in her bosom, and laid her dead child in my bosom. 21And when I rose in the morning to nurse my son, there he was, dead. But when I had examined him in the morning, indeed, he was not my son whom I had borne."

22Then the other woman said, "No! But the living one is my son, and the dead one is your son."

And the first woman said, "No! But the dead one is your son, and the living one is my son."

Thus they spoke before the king.

23And the king said, "The one says, 'This is my son, who lives, and your son is the dead one'; and the other says, 'No! But your son is the dead one, and my son is the living one.'" 24Then the king said, "Bring me a sword." So they brought a sword before the king. 25And the king said, "Divide the living child in two, and give half to one, and half to the other."

26Then the woman whose son was living spoke to the king, for she yearned with compassion for her son; and she said, "O my lord, give her the living child, and by no means kill him!"

But the other said, "Let him be neither mine nor yours, but divide him."

27So the king answered and said,

"Give the first woman the living child, and by no means kill him; she *is* his mother."

28And all Israel heard of the judgment which the king had rendered; and they feared the king, for they saw that the wisdom of God *was* in him to administer justice.

Solomon's Administration

4 So King Solomon was king over all Israel. 2And these *were* his officials: Azariah the son of Zadok, the priest; 3Elihoreph and Ahijah, the sons of Shisha, scribes; Jehoshaphat the son of Ahilud, the recorder; 4Benaiah the son of Jehoiada, over the army; Zadok and Abiathar, the priests; 5Azariah the son of Nathan, over the officers; Zabud the son of Nathan, a priest *and* the king's friend; 6Ahishar, over the household; and Adoniram the son of Abda, over the labor force.

7And Solomon had twelve governors over all Israel, who provided food for the king and his household; each one made provision for one month of the year. 8These *are* their names: Ben-Hur, in the mountains of Ephraim; 9Ben-Deker, in Makaz, Shaalbim, Beth Shemesh, and Elon Beth Hanan; 10Ben-Hesed, in Arubboth; to him *belonged* Sochoh and all the land of Hepher; 11Ben-Abinadab, *in* all the regions of Dor; he had Taphath the daughter of Solomon as wife; 12Baana the son of Ahilud, *in* Taanach, Megiddo, and all Beth Shean, which *is* beside Zaretan below Jezreel, from Beth Shean to Abel Meholah, as far as the other side of Jokneam; 13Ben-Geber, in Ramoth Gilead; to him *belonged* the towns of Jair the son of Manasseh, in Gilead; to him *also belonged* the region of Argob in Bashan—sixty large cities with walls and bronze gate-bars; 14Ahinadab the son of Iddo, *in* Mahanaim; 15Ahimaaz, in Naphtali; he also took Basemath the daughter of Solomon as wife; 16Baanah the son of Hushai, in Asher and Aloth; 17Jehoshaphat the son of Paruah, in Issachar; 18Shimei the son of Elah, in Benjamin; 19Geber the son of Uri, in the land of Gilead, *in* the country of Sihon king of the Amorites, and of Og king of Bashan. *He was* the only governor who *was* in the land.

Prosperity and Wisdom of Solomon's Reign

20Judah and Israel *were* as numerous as the sand by the sea in multitude, eating and drinking and rejoicing. 21So Solomon reigned over all kingdoms from the River*a to* the land of the Philistines, as far as the border of Egypt. *They* brought tribute and served Solomon all the days of his life.

22Now Solomon's provision for one day was thirty kors of fine flour, sixty kors of meal, 23ten fatted oxen, twenty oxen from the pastures, and one hundred sheep, besides deer, gazelles, roebucks, and fatted fowl.

24For he had dominion over all *the region* on this side of the River*a* from Tiphsah even to Gaza, namely over all the kings on this side of the River; and he had peace on every side all around him. 25And Judah and Israel dwelt safely, each man under his vine and his fig tree, from Dan as far as Beersheba, all the days of Solomon.

26Solomon had forty thousand stalls of horses for his chariots, and twelve thousand horsemen. 27And these governors, each man in his month, provided food for King Solomon and for all who came to King Solomon's table. There was no lack in their supply. 28They also brought barley and straw to the proper place, for the horses and steeds, each man according to his charge.

29And God gave Solomon wisdom and exceedingly great understanding, and largeness of heart like the sand on the seashore. 30Thus Solomon's wisdom excelled the wisdom of all the men of the East and all the wisdom of Egypt. 31For he was wiser than all men—than Ethan the Ezrahite, and Heman, Chalcol, and Darda, the sons of Mahol; and his fame was in all the surrounding nations. 32He spoke three thousand proverbs, and his songs were one thousand and five. 33Also he spoke of trees, from the cedar tree of Lebanon even to the hyssop that springs out of the wall; he spoke also of animals, of birds, of creeping things, and of fish. 34And men

---

a That is, the Euphrates

of all nations, from all the kings of the earth who had heard of his wisdom, came to hear the wisdom of Solomon.

Solomon Prepares to Build the Temple

5 Now Hiram king of Tyre sent his servants to Solomon, because he heard that they had anointed him king in place of his father, for Hiram had always loved David. ²Then Solomon sent to Hiram, saying:

3 You know how my father David could not build a house for the name of the LORD his God because of the wars which were fought against him on every side, until the LORD put *his foes* under the soles of his feet.

4 But now the LORD my God has given me rest on every side; *there is* neither adversary nor evil occurrence.

5 And behold, I propose to build a house for the name of the LORD my God, as the LORD spoke to my father David, saying, "Your son, whom I will set on your throne in your place, he shall build the house for My name."

6 Now therefore, command that they cut down cedars for me from Lebanon; and my servants will be with your servants, and I will pay you wages for your servants according to whatever you say. For you know *there is* none among us who has skill to cut timber like the Sidonians.

7So it was, when Hiram heard the words of Solomon, that he rejoiced greatly and said,

Blessed *be* the LORD this day, for He has given David a wise son over this great people!

8Then Hiram sent to Solomon, saying: I have considered *the message* which you sent me, *and* I will do all you desire concerning the cedar and cypress logs.

9 My servants shall bring *them* down from Lebanon to the sea; I will float them in rafts by sea to the place you indicate to me, and will have them broken apart

there; then you can take *them* away. And you shall fulfill my desire by giving food for my household.

10Then Hiram gave Solomon cedar and cypress logs *according to* all his desire. ¹¹And Solomon gave Hiram twenty thousand kors of wheat *as* food for his household, and twenty kors of pressed oil. Thus Solomon gave to Hiram year by year.

¹²So the LORD gave Solomon wisdom, as He had promised him; and there was peace between Hiram and Solomon, and the two of them made a treaty together.

¹³Then King Solomon raised up a labor force out of all Israel; and the labor force was thirty thousand men. ¹⁴And he sent them to Lebanon, ten thousand a month in shifts: they were one month in Lebanon *and* two months at home; Adoniram *was* in charge of the labor force. ¹⁵Solomon had seventy thousand who carried burdens, and eighty thousand who quarried *stone* in the mountains, ¹⁶besides three thousand three hundred from the chiefs of Solomon's deputies, who supervised the people who labored in the work. ¹⁷And the king commanded them to quarry large stones, costly stones, *and* hewn stones, to lay the foundation of the temple. ¹⁸So Solomon's builders, Hiram's builders, and the Gebalites quarried *them;* and they prepared timber and stones to build the temple.

Solomon Builds the Temple

6 And it came to pass in the four hundred and eightieth year after the children of Israel had come out of the land of Egypt, in the fourth year of Solomon's reign over Israel, in the month of Ziv, which *is* the second month, that he began to build the house of the LORD. ²Now the house which King Solomon built for the LORD, its length *was* sixty cubits, its width twenty, and its height thirty cubits. ³The vestibule in front of the sanctuary[b] of the house *was* twenty cubits long across the width of the house, *and* the width of *the vestibule extended* ten cubits from the front of

---

b Here the main room of the temple; elsewhere called the holy place (compare Exodus 26.33 and Ezekiel 41.1) the house. 4And he made for the house windows with beveled frames.

5Against the wall of the temple he built chambers all around, *against* the walls of the temple, all around the sanctuary and the inner sanctuary.c Thus he made side chambers all around it. 6The lowest chamber *was* five cubits wide, the middle *was* six cubits wide, and the third *was* seven cubits wide; for he made narrow ledges around the outside of the temple, so that *the support beams* would not be fastened into the walls of the temple. 7And the temple, when it was being built, was built with stone finished at the quarry, so that no hammer or chisel *or* any iron tool was heard in the temple while it was being built. 8The doorway for the middle story *was* on the right side of the temple. They went up by stairs to the middle *story,* and from the middle to the third.

9So he built the temple and finished it, and he paneled the temple with beams and boards of cedar. 10And he built side chambers against the entire temple, each five cubits high; they were attached to the temple with cedar beams.

11Then the word of the LORD came to Solomon, saying: 12"Concerning this temple which you are building, if you walk in My statutes, execute My judgments, keep all My commandments, and walk in them, then I will perform My word with you, which I spoke to your father David. 13And I will dwell among the children of Israel, and will not forsake My people Israel."

14So Solomon built the temple and finished it. 15And he built the inside walls of the temple with cedar boards; from the floor of the temple to the ceiling he paneled the inside with wood; and he covered the floor of the temple with planks of cypress. 16Then he built the twenty-cubit room at the rear of the temple, from floor to ceiling, with cedar boards; he built *it* inside as the inner sanctuary, as the Most Holy *Place.* 17And in front of it the temple sanctuary was forty cubits *long.* 18The inside of the temple was cedar, carved with ornamental buds and open flowers. All

was cedar; there was no stone *to be* seen.

19And he prepared the inner sanctuary inside the temple, to set the ark of the covenant of the LORD there. 20The inner sanctuary *was* twenty cubits long, twenty cubits wide, and twenty cubits high. He overlaid it with pure gold, and overlaid the altar of cedar. 21So Solomon overlaid the inside of the temple with pure gold. He stretched gold chains across the front of the inner sanctuary, and overlaid it with gold. 22The whole temple he overlaid with gold, until he had finished all the temple; also he overlaid with gold the entire altar that *was* by the inner sanctuary.

23Inside the inner sanctuary he made two cherubim *of* olive wood, *each* ten cubits high. 24One wing of the cherub *was* five cubits, and the other wing of the cherub five cubits: ten cubits from the tip of one wing to the tip of the other. 25And the other cherub *was* ten cubits; both cherubim *were* of the same size and shape. 26The height of one cherub *was* ten cubits, and so *was* the other cherub. 27Then he set the cherubim inside the inner room; and they stretched out the wings of the cherubim so that the wing of the one touched *one* wall, and the wing of the other cherub touched the other wall. And their wings touched each other in the middle of the room. 28Also he overlaid the cherubim with gold.

29Then he carved all the walls of the temple all around, both the inner and outer *sanctuaries,* with carved figures of cherubim, palm trees, and open flowers. 30And the floor of the temple he overlaid with gold, both the inner and outer *sanctuaries.*

31For the entrance of the inner sanctuary he made doors *of* olive wood; the lintel *and* doorposts *were* one-fifth *of the wall.* 32The two doors *were* of olive wood; and he carved on them figures of cherubim, palm trees, and open flowers, and overlaid *them* with gold; and he spread gold on the cherubim and on the palm trees. 33So for the door of the sanctuary he also made doorposts *of* olive wood, one-fourth *of the wall.*

---

c Here the inner room of the temple; elsewhere called the Most Holy Place (compare verse 16)

34And the two doors *were of* cypress wood; two panels *comprised* one folding door, and two panels *comprised* the other folding door. 35Then he carved cherubim, palm trees, and open flowers *on them*, and overlaid *them* with gold applied evenly on the carved work.

36And he built the inner court with three rows of hewn stone and a row of cedar beams.

37In the fourth year the foundation of the house of the LORD was laid, in the month of Ziv. 38And in the eleventh year, in the month of Bul, which is the eighth month, the house was finished in all its details and according to all its plans. So he was seven years in building it.

Solomon's Other Buildings

7 But Solomon took thirteen years to build his own house; so he finished all his house.

2He also built the House of the Forest of Lebanon; its length *was* one hundred cubits, its width fifty cubits, and its height thirty cubits, with four rows of cedar pillars, and cedar beams on the pillars. 3And *it was* paneled with cedar above the beams that *were* on forty-five pillars, fifteen *to* a row. 4*There were* windows *with beveled frames in* three rows, and window *was* opposite window *in* three tiers. 5And all the doorways and doorposts *had* rectangular frames; and window *was* opposite window *in* three tiers.

6He also made the Hall of Pillars: its length *was* fifty cubits, and its width thirty cubits; and in front of them *was* a portico with pillars, and a canopy *was* in front of them.

7Then he made a hall for the throne, the Hall of Judgment, where he might judge; and *it was* paneled with cedar from floor to ceiling.

8And the house where he dwelt *had* another court inside the hall, of like workmanship. Solomon also made a house like this hall for Pharaoh's daughter, whom he had taken *as wife.*

9All these *were of* costly stones cut to size, trimmed with saws, inside and out, from the foundation to the eaves, and also on the outside to the great court. 10The foundation *was of* costly stones, large stones, some ten cubits and some eight cubits. 11And above *were* costly stones, hewn to size, and cedar wood. 12The great court *was* enclosed with three rows of hewn stones and a row of cedar beams. So were the inner court of the house of the LORD and the vestibule of the temple.

Hiram the Craftsman

13Now King Solomon sent and brought Huram from Tyre. 14He *was* the son of a widow from the tribe of Naphtali, and his father *was* a man of Tyre, a bronze worker; he was filled with wisdom and understanding and skill in working with all kinds of bronze work. So he came to King Solomon and did all his work.

The Bronze Pillars for the Temple

15And he cast two pillars of bronze, each one eighteen cubits high, and a line of twelve cubits measured the circumference of each. 16Then he made two capitals *of* cast bronze, to set on the tops of the pillars. The height of one capital *was* five cubits, and the height of the other capital *was* five cubits. 17*He* made a lattice network, with wreaths of chainwork, for the capitals which *were* on top of the pillars: seven chains for one capital and seven for the other capital. 18So he made the pillars, and two rows of pomegranates above the network all around to cover the capitals that *were* on top; and thus he did for the other capital.

19The capitals which *were* on top of the pillars in the hall *were* in the shape of lilies, four cubits. 20The capitals on the two pillars also *had pomegranates* above, by the convex surface which *was* next to the network; and there *were* two hundred such pomegranates in rows on each of the capitals all around.

21Then he set up the pillars by the vestibule of the temple; he set up the pillar on the right and called its name Jachin, and he set up the pillar on the left and called its name Boaz. 22The tops of the pillars were in the shape of lilies. So the work of the pillars was finished.

The Sea and the Oxen

23And he made the Sea of cast bronze, ten cubits from one brim to the other; *it was* completely round. Its height *was* five cubits, and a line of thirty cubits measured its circumference.

24Below its brim *were* ornamental buds encircling it all around, ten to a cubit, all the way around the Sea. The ornamental buds *were* cast in two rows when it was cast. **25**It stood on twelve oxen: three looking toward the north, three looking toward the west, and three looking toward the south, and three looking toward the east; the Sea *was set* upon them, and all their back parts *pointed* inward. **26**It *was* a handbreadth thick; and its brim was shaped like the brim of a cup, *like* a lily blossom. It contained two thousand baths.

The Carts and the Lavers

27He also made ten carts of bronze; four cubits *was* the length of each cart, four cubits its width, and three cubits its height. **28**And this *was* the design of the carts: They had panels, and the panels *were* between frames; **29**on the panels that *were* between the frames *were* lions, oxen, and cherubim. And on the frames *was* a pedestal on top. Below the lions and oxen *were* wreaths of plaited work. **30**Every cart had four bronze wheels and axles of bronze, and its four feet had supports. Under the laver *were* supports of cast *bronze* beside each wreath. **31**Its opening inside the crown at the top *was* one cubit in diameter; and the opening *was* round, shaped *like* a pedestal, one and a half cubits in outside diameter; and also on the opening *were* engravings, but the panels were square, not round. **32**Under the panels *were* the four wheels, and the axles of the wheels *were joined* to the cart. The height of a wheel *was* one and a half cubits. **33**The workmanship of the wheels *was* like the workmanship of a chariot wheel; their axle pins, their rims, their spokes, and their hubs *were* all of cast *bronze*. **34**And *there were* four supports at the four corners of each cart; its supports *were* part of the cart itself. **35**On the top of the cart, at the height

of half a cubit, *it was* perfectly round. And on the top of the cart, its flanges and its panels *were* of the same casting. **36**On the plates of its flanges and on its panels he engraved cherubim, lions, and palm trees, wherever there was a clear space on each, with wreaths all around. **37**Thus he made the ten carts. All of them were of the same mold, one measure, *and* one shape.

38Then he made ten lavers of bronze; each laver contained forty baths, *and* each laver *was* four cubits. On each of the ten carts *was* a laver. **39**And he put five carts on the right side of the house, and five on the left side of the house. He set the Sea on the right side of the house, toward the southeast.

Furnishings of the Temple

40Huram made the lavers and the shovels and the bowls. So Huram finished doing all the work that he was to do for King Solomon *for* the house of the LORD: **41**the two pillars, the *two* bowl-shaped capitals that *were* on top of the two pillars; the two networks covering the two bowl-shaped capitals which *were* on top of the pillars; **42**four hundred pomegranates for the two networks (two rows of pomegranates for each network, to cover the two bowl-shaped capitals that *were* on top of the pillars); **43**the ten carts, and ten lavers on the carts; **44**one Sea, and twelve oxen under the Sea; **45**the pots, the shovels, and the bowls.

All these articles which Huram made for King Solomon *for* the house of the LORD *were of* burnished bronze. **46**In the plain of Jordan the king had them cast in clay molds, between Succoth and Zaretan. **47**And Solomon did not weigh all the articles, because *there were* so many; the weight of the bronze was not determined.

48Thus Solomon had all the furnishings made for the house of the LORD: the altar of gold, and the table of gold on which *was* the showbread; **49**the lampstands of pure gold, five on the right *side* and five on the left in front of the inner sanctuary, with the flowers and the lamps and the wick-trimmers of gold; **50**the basins, the trimmers, the bowls, the ladles, and the censers of pure gold; and the hinges of gold, *both* for the doors of the inner room (the Most Holy *Place*) *and* for the doors of the main hall of the temple.

51So all the work that King Solomon had done for the house of the LORD was finished; and Solomon brought in the things which his father David had dedicated: the silver and the gold and the furnishings. He put them in the treasuries of the house of the LORD.

The Ark Brought into the Temple

8 Now Solomon assembled the elders of Israel and all the heads of the tribes, the chief fathers of the children of Israel, to King Solomon in Jerusalem, that they might bring up the ark of the covenant of the LORD from the City of David, which *is* Zion. 2Therefore all the men of Israel assembled with King Solomon at the feast in the month of Ethanim, which *is* the seventh month. 3So all the elders of Israel came, and the priests took up the ark. 4Then they brought up the ark of the LORD, the tabernacle of meeting, and all the holy furnishings that *were* in the tabernacle. The priests and the Levites brought them up. 5Also King Solomon, and all the congregation of Israel who were assembled with him, *were* with him before the ark, sacrificing sheep and oxen that could not be counted or numbered for multitude. 6Then the priests brought in the ark of the covenant of the LORD to its place, into the inner sanctuary of the temple, to the Most Holy *Place*, under the wings of the cherubim. 7For the cherubim spread *their* two wings over the place of the ark, and the cherubim overshadowed the ark and its poles. 8The poles extended so that the ends of the poles could be seen from the holy *place*, in front of the inner sanctuary; but they could not be seen from outside. And they are there to this day. 9Nothing *was* in the ark except the two tablets of stone which Moses put there at Horeb, when the LORD made *a covenant* with the children of Israel, when they came out of the land of Egypt.

10And it came to pass, when the priests came out of the holy *place*, that the cloud filled the house of the LORD, 11so that the priests could not continue ministering because of the cloud; for the glory of the LORD filled the house of the LORD.

12Then Solomon spoke:

"The LORD said He would dwell in the dark cloud.

13 I have surely built You an exalted house,
    And a place for You to dwell in forever."

Solomon's Speech at Completion of the Work

14Then the king turned around and blessed the whole assembly of Israel, while all the assembly of Israel was standing. 15And he said: "Blessed *be* the LORD God of Israel, who spoke with His mouth to my father David, and with His hand has fulfilled *it*, saying, 16'Since the day that I brought My people Israel out of Egypt, I have chosen no city from any tribe of Israel *in which* to build a house, that My name might be there; but I chose David to be over My people Israel.' 17Now it was in the heart of my father David to build a temple for the name of the LORD God of Israel. 18But the LORD said to my father David, 'Whereas it was in your heart to build a temple for My name, you did well that it was in your heart. 19Nevertheless you shall not build the temple, but your son who will come from your body, he shall build the temple for My name.' 20So the LORD has fulfilled His word which He spoke; and I have filled the position of my father David, and sit on the throne of Israel, as the LORD promised; and I have built a temple for the name of the LORD God of Israel. 21And there I have made a place for the ark, in which *is* the covenant of the LORD which He made with our fathers, when He brought them out of the land of Egypt."

Solomon's Prayer of Dedication

22Then Solomon stood before the altar of the LORD in the presence of all the assembly of Israel, and spread out his hands toward heaven; 23and he said: "LORD God of Israel, *there is* no God in heaven above or on earth below like You, who keep *Your* covenant and mercy with Your servants who walk before You with all their hearts. 24You have kept what You promised Your servant David my father; You have both spoken with Your mouth and fulfilled *it* with Your hand, as *it is* this day. 25Therefore, LORD God of Israel, now keep what You promised Your servant David my father, saying, 'You shall not fail to have a man sit before Me on the throne of Israel, only if your sons take heed to their way, that they walk before Me as you have walked before Me.' 26And now I pray, O God of Israel, let Your word come true, which You have spoken to Your servant David my father.

27"But will God indeed dwell on the earth? Behold, heaven and the heaven of heavens cannot contain You. How much less this temple which I have built! 28Yet regard the prayer of Your servant and his supplication, O LORD my God, and listen to the cry and the prayer which Your servant is praying before You today: 29that Your eyes may be open toward this temple night and day, toward the place of which You said, 'My name shall be there,' that You may hear the prayer which Your servant makes toward this place. 30And may You hear the supplication of Your servant and of Your people Israel, when they pray toward this place. Hear in heaven Your dwelling place; and when You hear, forgive.

31"When anyone sins against his neighbor, and is forced to take an oath, and comes *and* takes an oath before Your altar in this temple, 32then hear in heaven, and act, and judge Your servants, condemning the wicked, bringing his way on his head, and justifying the righteous by giving him according to his righteousness.

33"When Your people Israel are defeated before an enemy because they have sinned against You, and when they turn back to You and confess Your name, and pray and make supplication to You in this temple, 34then hear in heaven, and forgive the sin of Your people Israel, and bring them back to the land which You gave to their fathers.

35"When the heavens are shut up and there is no rain because they have sinned against You, when they pray toward this place and confess Your name, and turn from their sin because You afflict them, 36then hear in heaven, and

forgive the sin of Your servants, Your people Israel, that You may teach them the good way in which they should walk; and send rain on Your land which You have given to Your people as an inheritance.

37"When there is famine in the land, pestilence *or* blight *or* mildew, locusts *or* grasshoppers; when their enemy besieges them in the land of their cities; whatever plague or whatever sickness *there is;* 38whatever prayer, whatever supplication is made by anyone, *or* by all Your people Israel, when each one knows the plague of his own heart, and spreads out his hands toward this temple: 39then hear in heaven Your dwelling place, and forgive, and act, and give to everyone according to all his ways, whose heart You know (for You alone know the hearts of all the sons of men), 40that they may fear You all the days that they live in the land which You gave to our fathers.

41"Moreover, concerning a foreigner, who *is* not of Your people Israel, but has come from a far country for Your name's sake 42(for they will hear of Your great name and Your strong hand and Your outstretched arm), when he comes and prays toward this temple, 43hear in heaven Your dwelling place, and do according to all for which the foreigner calls to You, that all peoples of the earth may know Your name and fear You, as *do* Your people Israel, and that they may know that this temple which I have built is called by Your name.

44"When Your people go out to battle against their enemy, wherever You send them, and when they pray to the LORD toward the city which You have chosen and the temple which I have built for Your name, 45then hear in heaven their prayer and their supplication, and maintain their cause.

46"When they sin against You (for *there is* no one who does not sin), and You become angry with them and deliver them to the enemy, and they take them captive to the land of the enemy, far or near; 47yet when they come to themselves in the land where they were carried captive, and repent, and make supplication to You in the land of those who took them captive, saying, 'We have sinned and done wrong, we have committed wickedness'; 48and *when* they return to You with all their heart and with all their soul in the land of their enemies who led them away captive, and pray to You toward their land which You gave to their fathers, the city which You have chosen and the temple which I have built for Your name: 49then hear in heaven Your dwelling place their prayer and their supplication, and maintain their cause, 50and forgive Your people who have sinned against You, and all their transgressions which they have transgressed against You; and grant them compassion before those who took them captive, that they may have compassion on them 51(for they *are* Your people and Your inheritance, whom You brought out of Egypt, out of the iron furnace), 52that Your eyes may be open to the supplication of Your servant and the supplication of Your people Israel, to listen to them whenever they call to You. 53For You separated them from among all the peoples of the earth *to be* Your inheritance, as You spoke by Your servant Moses, when You brought our fathers out of Egypt, O Lord God."

Solomon Blesses the Assembly

54And so it was, when Solomon had finished praying all this prayer and supplication to the LORD, that he arose from before the altar of the LORD, from kneeling on his knees with his hands spread up to heaven. 55Then he stood and blessed all the assembly of Israel with a loud voice, saying: 56"Blessed *be* the LORD, who has given rest to His people Israel, according to all that He promised. There has not failed one word of all His good promise, which He promised through His servant Moses. 57May the LORD our God be with us, as He was with our fathers. May He not leave us nor forsake us, 58that He may incline our hearts to Himself, to walk in all His ways, and to keep His commandments and His statutes and His judgments, which He commanded our fathers. 59And may these words of mine, with which I have made supplication before the LORD, be near the LORD our God day and night, that He may maintain the cause of His servant and

the cause of His people Israel, as each day may require, 60that all the peoples of the earth may know that the LORD is God; *there is* no other. 61Let your heart therefore be loyal to the LORD our God, to walk in His statutes and keep His commandments, as at this day."

Solomon Dedicates the Temple

62Then the king and all Israel with him offered sacrifices before the LORD. 63And Solomon offered a sacrifice of peace offerings, which he offered to the LORD, twenty-two thousand bulls and one hundred and twenty thousand sheep. So the king and all the children of Israel dedicated the house of the LORD. 64On the same day the king consecrated the middle of the court that *was* in front of the house of the LORD; for there he offered burnt offerings, grain offerings, and the fat of the peace offerings, because the bronze altar that *was* before the LORD *was* too small to receive the burnt offerings, the grain offerings, and the fat of the peace offerings.

65At that time Solomon held a feast, and all Israel with him, a great assembly from the entrance of Hamath to the Brook of Egypt, before the LORD our God, seven days and seven *more* days—fourteen days. 66On the eighth day he sent the people away; and they blessed the king, and went to their tents joyful and glad of heart for all the good that the LORD had done for His servant David, and for Israel His people.

God's Second Appearance to Solomon

9 And it came to pass, when Solomon had finished building the house of the LORD and the king's house, and all Solomon's desire which he wanted to do, 2that the LORD appeared to Solomon the second time, as He had appeared to him at Gibeon. 3And the LORD said to him: "I have heard your prayer and your supplication that you have made before Me; I have consecrated this house which you have built to put My name there forever, and My eyes and My heart will be there perpetually. 4Now if you walk before Me as your father David walked, in integrity of heart and in uprightness, to do according to all that I have commanded you, and if you keep My statutes and My judgments, 5then I will establish the throne of your kingdom over Israel forever, as I promised David your father, saying, 'You shall not fail to have a man on the throne of Israel.' 6*But* if you or your sons at all turn from following Me, and do not keep My comm andments *and* My statutes which I have set before you, but go and serve other gods and worship them, 7then I will cut off Israel from the land which I have given them; and this house which I have consecrated for My name I will cast out of My sight. Israel will be a proverb and a byword among all peoples. 8And *as for* this house, *which* is exalted, everyone who passes by it will be astonished and will hiss, and say, 'Why has the LORD done thus to this land and to this house?' 9Then they will answer, 'Because they forsook the LORD their God, who brought their fathers out of the land of Egypt, and have embraced other gods, and worshiped them and served them; therefore the LORD has brought all this calamity on them.' "

Solomon and Hiram Exchange Gifts

10Now it happened at the end of twenty years, when Solomon had built the two houses, the house of the LORD and the king's house 11(Hiram the king of Tyre had supplied Solomon with cedar and cypress and gold, as much as he desired), *that* King Solomon then gave Hiram twenty cities in the land of Galilee. 12Then Hiram went from Tyre to see the cities which Solomon had given him, but they did not please him. 13So he said, "What *kind of* cities *are* these which you have given me, my brother?" And he called them the land of Cabul,d as they are to this day. 14Then Hiram sent the king one hundred and twenty talents of gold.

Solomon's Additional Achievements

15And this *is* the reason for the labor force which King Solomon raised: to build the house of the LORD, his own house, the Millo, the wall of Jerusalem, Hazor, Megiddo, and Gezer. 16(Pharaoh king of Egypt had gone up and taken

Gezer and burned it with fire, had killed the Canaanites who dwelt in the city, and had given it *as* a dowry to his daughter, Solomon's wife.) 17And Solomon built Gezer, Lower Beth Horon, 18Baalath, and Tadmor in the wilderness, in the land *of Judah,* 19all the storage cities that Solomon had, cities for his chariots and cities for his cavalry, and whatever Solomon desired to build in Jerusalem, in Lebanon, and in all the land of his dominion.

20All the people *who were* left of the Amorites, Hittites, Perizzites, Hivites, and Jebusites, who *were* not of the children of Israel—21that is, their descendants who were left in the land after them, whom the children of Israel had not been able to destroy completely—from these Solomon raised forced labor, as it is to this day. 22But of the children of Israel Solomon made no forced laborers, because they *were* men of war and his servants: his officers, his captains, commanders of his chariots, and his cavalry.

23Others *were* chiefs of the officials who *were* over Solomon's work: five hundred and fifty, who ruled over the people who did the work.

24But Pharaoh's daughter came up from the City of David to her house which *Solomon* had built for her. Then he built the Millo.

25Now three times a year Solomon offered burnt offerings and peace offerings on the altar which he had built for the LORD, and he burned incense with them *on the altar* that *was* before the LORD. So he finished the temple.

26King Solomon also built a fleet of ships at Ezion Geber, which *is* near Elath on the shore of the Red Sea, in the land of Edom. 27Then Hiram sent his servants with the fleet, seamen who knew the sea, to work with the servants of Solomon. 28And they went to Ophir, and acquired four hundred and twenty talents of gold from there, and brought *it* to King Solomon.

The Queen of Sheba's Praise of Solomon

10 Now when the queen of Sheba heard of the fame of Solomon

d Literally *Good for Nothing*

concerning the name of the LORD, she came to test him with hard questions. 2She came to Jerusalem with a very great retinue, with camels that bore spices, very much gold, and precious stones; and when she came to Solomon, she spoke with him about all that was in her heart. 3So Solomon answered all her questions; there was nothing so difficult for the king that he could not explain it to her. 4And when the queen of Sheba had seen all the wisdom of Solomon, the house that he had built, 5the food on his table, the seating of his servants, the service of his waiters and their apparel, his cupbearers, and his entryway by which he went up to the house of the LORD, there was no more spirit in her. 6Then she said to the king: "It was a true report which I heard in my own land about your words and your wisdom. 7However I did not believe the words until I came and saw with my own eyes; and indeed the half was not told me. Your wisdom and prosperity exceed the fame of which I heard. 8Happy *are* your men and happy *are* these your servants, who stand continually before you *and* hear your wisdom! 9Blessed be the LORD your God, who delighted in you, setting you on the throne of Israel! Because the LORD has loved Israel forever, therefore He made you king, to do justice and righteousness."

10Then she gave the king one hundred and twenty talents of gold, spices in great quantity, and precious stones. There never again came such abundance of spices as the queen of Sheba gave to King Solomon. 11Also, the ships of Hiram, which brought gold from Ophir, brought great *quantities* of almug wood and precious stones from Ophir. 12And the king made steps of the almug wood for the house of the LORD and for the king's house, also harps and stringed instruments for singers. There never again came such almug wood, nor has the like been seen to this day.

13Now King Solomon gave the queen of Sheba all she desired, whatever she asked, besides what Solomon had given her according to the royal generosity. So she turned and went to her own country, she and her servants.

Solomon's Great Wealth

14The weight of gold that came to Solomon yearly was six hundred and sixty-six talents of gold, 15besides *that* from the traveling merchants, from the income of traders, from all the kings of Arabia, and from the governors of the country.

16And King Solomon made two hundred large shields *of* hammered gold; six hundred *shekels* of gold went into each shield. 17He also *made* three hundred shields *of* hammered gold; three minas of gold went into each shield. The king put them in the House of the Forest of Lebanon.

18Moreover the king made a great throne of ivory, and overlaid it with pure gold. 19The throne had six steps, and the top of the throne *was* round at the back; *there were* armrests on either side of the place of the seat, and two lions stood beside the armrests. 20Twelve lions stood there, one on each side of the six steps; nothing like *this* had been made for any *other* kingdom.

21All King Solomon's drinking vessels *were* gold, and all the vessels of the House of the Forest of Lebanon *were* pure gold. Not *one was* silver, for this was accounted as nothing in the days of Solomon. 22For the king had merchant ships at sea with the fleet of Hiram. Once every three years the merchant ships came bringing gold, silver, ivory, apes, and monkeys. 23So King Solomon surpassed all the kings of the earth in riches and wisdom.

24Now all the earth sought the presence of Solomon to hear his wisdom, which God had put in his heart. 25Each man brought his present: articles of silver and gold, garments, armor, spices, horses, and mules, at a set rate year by year.

26And Solomon gathered chariots and horsemen; he had one thousand four hundred chariots and twelve thousand horsemen, whom he stationed in the chariot cities and with the king at Jerusalem. 27The king made silver *as common* in Jerusalem as stones, and he made cedar trees as abundant as the sycamores which *are* in the lowland.

28Also Solomon had horses imported from Egypt and Keveh; the king's merchants bought them in Keveh at the *current* price. 29Now a chariot that was imported from Egypt cost six hundred *shekels* of silver, and a horse one hundred and fifty; and thus, through their agents, they exported *them* to all the kings of the Hittites and the kings of Syria.

Solomon's Heart Turns from the Lord

11 But King Solomon loved many foreign women, as well as the daughter of Pharaoh: women of the Moabites, Ammonites, Edomites, Sidonians, *and* Hittites—2from the nations of whom the Lord had said to the children of Israel, "You shall not intermarry with them, nor they with you. Surely they will turn away your hearts after their gods." Solomon clung to these in love. 3And he had seven hundred wives, princesses, and three hundred concubines; and his wives turned away his heart. 4For it was so, when Solomon was old, that his wives turned his heart after other gods; and his heart was not loyal to the Lord his God, as *was* the heart of his father David. 5For Solomon went after Ashtoreth the goddess of the Sidonians, and after Milcom the abomination of the Ammonites. 6Solomon did evil in the sight of the Lord, and did not fully follow the Lord, as *did* his father David. 7Then Solomon built a high place for Chemosh the abomination of Moab, on the hill that *is* east of Jerusalem, and for Molech the abomination of the people of Ammon. 8And he did likewise for all his foreign wives, who burned incense and sacrificed to their gods.

9So the Lord became angry with Solomon, because his heart had turned from the Lord God of Israel, who had appeared to him twice, 10and had commanded him concerning this thing, that he should not go after other gods; but he did not keep what the Lord had commanded. 11Therefore the Lord said to Solomon, "Because you have done this, and have not kept My covenant and My statutes, which I have commanded you, I will surely tear the kingdom away from you and give it to your servant. 12Nevertheless I will not do it in your days, for the sake of your father David; I will tear it out of the hand of your son. 13However I will not tear away the whole kingdom; I will give one tribe to your son for the sake of my servant David, and for the sake of Jerusalem which I have chosen."

Adversaries of Solomon

14Now the Lord raised up an adversary against Solomon, Hadad the Edomite; he *was* a descendant of the king in Edom. 15For it happened, when David was in Edom, and Joab the commander of the army had gone up to bury the slain, after he had killed every male in Edom 16(because for six months Joab remained there with all Israel, until he had cut down every male in Edom), 17that Hadad fled to go to Egypt, he and certain Edomites of his father's servants with him. Hadad *was* still a little child. 18Then they arose from Midian and came to Paran; and they took men with them from Paran and came to Egypt, to Pharaoh king of Egypt, who gave him a house, apportioned food for him, and gave him land. 19And Hadad found great favor in the sight of Pharaoh, so that he gave him as wife the sister of his own wife, that is, the sister of Queen Tahpenes. 20Then the sister of Tahpenes bore him Genubath his son, whom Tahpenes weaned in Pharaoh's house. And Genubath was in Pharaoh's household among the sons of Pharaoh.

21So when Hadad heard in Egypt that David rested with his fathers, and that Joab the commander of the army was dead, Hadad said to Pharaoh, "Let me depart, that I may go to my own country."

22Then Pharaoh said to him, "But what have you lacked with me, that suddenly you seek to go to your own country?"

So he answered, "Nothing, but do let me go anyway."

23And God raised up *another* adversary against him, Rezon the son of Eliadah, who had fled from his lord, Hadadezer king of Zobah. 24So he gathered men to him and became captain over a band *of raiders*, when David killed those *of Zobah*. And they went to Damascus and dwelt there, and reigned in Damascus. 25He was an adversary of Israel all the days of Solomon (besides the trouble that Hadad *caused*); and he abhorred Israel, and reigned over Syria.

Jeroboam's Rebellion

26Then Solomon's servant, Jeroboam the son of Nebat, an Ephraimite from Zereda, whose mother's name *was* Zeruah, a widow, also rebelled against the king.
27And this *is* what caused him to rebel against the king: Solomon had built the Millo *and* repaired the damages to the City of David his father. 28The man Jeroboam *was* a mighty man of valor; and Solomon, seeing that the young man was industrious, made him the officer over all the labor force of the house of Joseph.
29Now it happened at that time, when Jeroboam went out of Jerusalem, that the prophet Ahijah the Shilonite met him on the way; and he had clothed himself with a new garment, and the two *were* alone in the field. 30Then Ahijah took hold of the new garment that *was* on him, and tore it *into* twelve pieces. 31And he said to Jeroboam, "Take for yourself ten pieces, for thus says the LORD, the God of Israel: 'Behold, I will tear the kingdom out of the hand of Solomon and will give ten tribes to you 32(but he shall have one tribe for the sake of My servant David, and for the sake of Jerusalem, the city which I have chosen out of all the tribes of Israel), 33because they have forsaken Me, and worshiped Ashtoreth the goddess of the Sidonians, Chemosh the god of the Moabites, and Milcom the god of the people of Ammon, and have not walked in My ways to do *what is* right in My eyes and *keep* My statutes and My judgments, as *did* his father David. 34However I will not take the whole kingdom out of his hand, because I have made him ruler all the days of his life for the sake of My servant David, whom I chose because he kept My commandments and My statutes. 35But I will take the kingdom out of his son's hand and give it to you—ten tribes. 36And to his son I will give one tribe, that My servant David may always have a lamp before Me in Jerusalem, the city which I have chosen for Myself, to put My name there. 37So I will take you, and you shall reign over all your

heart desires, and you shall be king over Israel. 38Then it shall be, if you heed all that I command you, walk in My ways, and do *what is* right in My sight, to keep My statutes and My commandments, as My servant David did, then I will be with you and build for you an enduring house, as I built for David, and will give Israel to you. 39And I will afflict the descendants of David because of this, but not forever.' "
40Solomon therefore sought to kill Jeroboam. But Jeroboam arose and fled to Egypt, to Shishak king of Egypt, and was in Egypt until the death of Solomon.

Death of Solomon

41Now the rest of the acts of Solomon, all that he did, and his wisdom, *are* they not written in the book of the acts of Solomon? 42And the period that Solomon reigned in Jerusalem over all Israel *was* forty years. 43Then Solomon rested with his fathers, and was buried in the City of David his father. And Rehoboam his son reigned in his place.

The Revolt Against Rehoboam

12 And Rehoboam went to Shechem, for all Israel had gone to Shechem to make him king. 2So it happened, when Jeroboam the son of Nebat heard *it* (he was still in Egypt, for he had fled from the presence of King Solomon and had been dwelling in Egypt), 3that they sent and called him. Then Jeroboam and the whole assembly of Israel came and spoke to Rehoboam, saying, 4"Your father made our yoke heavy; now therefore, lighten the burdensome service of your father, and his heavy yoke which he put on us, and we will serve you."
5So he said to them, "Depart *for* three days, then come back to me." And the people departed.
6Then King Rehoboam consulted the elders who stood before his father Solomon while he still lived, and he said, "How do you advise *me* to answer these people?"
7And they spoke to him, saying, "If you will be a servant to these people today, and serve them, and answer them, and speak good words to them,

then they will be your servants forever."

8But he rejected the advice which the elders had given him, and consulted the young men who had grown up with him, who stood before him. 9And he said to them, "What advice do you give? How should we answer this people who have spoken to me, saying, 'Lighten the yoke which your father put on us'?"

10Then the young men who had grown up with him spoke to him, saying, "Thus you should speak to this people who have spoken to you, saying, 'Your father made our yoke heavy, but you make *it* lighter on us'—thus you shall say to them: 'My little *finger* shall be thicker than my father's waist! 11And now, whereas my father put a heavy yoke on you, I will add to your yoke; my father chastised you with whips, but I will chastise you with scourges!' "

12So Jeroboam and all the people came to Rehoboam the third day, as the king had directed, saying, "Come back to me the third day." 13Then the king answered the people roughly, and rejected the advice which the elders had given him; 14and he spoke to them according to the advice of the young men, saying, "My father made your yoke heavy, but I will add to your yoke; my father chastised you with whips, but I will chastise you with scourges!" 15So the king did not listen to the people; for the turn *of events* was from the LORD, that He might fulfill His word, which the LORD had spoken by Ahijah the Shilonite to Jeroboam the son of Nebat.

16Now when all Israel saw that the king did not listen to them, the people answered the king, saying:

"What share have we in David?
We have no inheritance in the son of Jesse.
To your tents, O Israel!
Now, see to your own house,
    O David!"

So Israel departed to their tents. 17But Rehoboam reigned over the children of Israel who dwelt in the cities of Judah.

18Then King Rehoboam sent Adoram, who *was* in charge of the revenue; but all Israel stoned him with stones,

and he died. Therefore King Rehoboam mounted his chariot in haste to flee to Jerusalem. 19So Israel has been in rebellion against the house of David to this day.

20Now it came to pass when all Israel heard that Jeroboam had come back, they sent for him and called him to the congregation, and made him king over all Israel. There was none who followed the house of David, but the tribe of Judah only.

21And when Rehoboam came to Jerusalem, he assembled all the house of Judah with the tribe of Benjamin, one hundred and eighty thousand chosen *men* who were warriors, to fight against the house of Israel, that he might restore the kingdom to Rehoboam the son of Solomon. 22But the word of God came to Shemaiah the man of God, saying, 23"Speak to Rehoboam the son of Solomon, king of Judah, to all the house of Judah and Benjamin, and to the rest of the people, saying, 24'Thus says the LORD: "You shall not go up nor fight against your brethren the children of Israel. Let every man return to his house, for this thing is from Me." ' " Therefore they obeyed the word of the LORD, and turned back, according to the word of the LORD.

Jeroboam's Gold Calves

25Then Jeroboam built Shechem in the mountains of Ephraim, and dwelt there. Also he went out from there and built Penuel. 26And Jeroboam said in his heart, "Now the kingdom may return to the house of David: 27If these people go up to offer sacrifices in the house of the LORD at Jerusalem, then the heart of this people will turn back to their lord, Rehoboam king of Judah, and they will kill me and go back to Rehoboam king of Judah."

28Therefore the king asked advice, made two calves of gold, and said to the people, "It is too much for you to go up to Jerusalem. Here are your gods, O Israel, which brought you up from the land of Egypt!" 29And he set up one in Bethel, and the other he put in Dan. 30Now this thing became a sin, for the people went *to worship* before the one as far as Dan. 31He made shrines on the high places, and made priests from every class of people, who were not of the sons of Levi.

32Jeroboam ordained a feast on the fifteenth day of the eighth month, like the feast that *was* in Judah, and offered sacrifices on the altar. So he did at Bethel, sacrificing to the calves that he had made. And at Bethel he installed the priests of the high places which he had made. 33So he made offerings on the altar which he had made at Bethel on the fifteenth day of the eighth month, in the month which he had devised in his own heart. And he ordained a feast for the children of Israel, and offered sacrifices on the altar and burned incense.

The Message of the Man of God

13 And behold, a man of God went from Judah to Bethel by the word of the LORD, and Jeroboam stood by the altar to burn incense. 2Then he cried out against the altar by the word of the LORD, and said, "O altar, altar! Thus says the LORD: 'Behold, a child, Josiah by name, shall be born to the house of David; and on you he shall sacrifice the priests of the high places who burn incense on you, and men's bones shall be burned on you.' " 3And he gave a sign the same day, saying, "This *is* the sign which the LORD has spoken: Surely the altar shall split apart, and the ashes on it shall be poured out."

4So it came to pass when King Jeroboam heard the saying of the man of God, who cried out against the altar in Bethel, that he stretched out his hand from the altar, saying, "Arrest him!" Then his hand, which he stretched out toward him, withered, so that he could not pull it back to himself. 5The altar also was split apart, and the ashes poured out from the altar, according to the sign which the man of God had given by the word of the LORD. 6Then the king answered and said to the man of God, "Please entreat the favor of the LORD your God, and pray for me, that my hand may be restored to me."

So the man of God entreated the LORD, and the king's hand was restored to him, and became as before. 7Then the king said to the man of God, "Come home with me and refresh yourself, and I will give you a reward."

8But the man of God said to the king, "If you were to give me half your house, I would not go in with you; nor would I eat bread nor drink water in this place. 9For so it was commanded me by the word of the LORD, saying, 'You shall not eat bread, nor drink water, nor return by the same way you came.' " 10So he went another way and did not return by the way he came to Bethel.

Death of the Man of God

11Now an old prophet dwelt in Bethel, and his sons came and told him all the works that the man of God had done that day in Bethel; they also told their father the words which he had spoken to the king. 12And their father said to them, "Which way did he go?" For his sons had seen which way the man of God went who came from Judah. 13Then he said to his sons, "Saddle the donkey for me." So they saddled the donkey for him; and he rode on it, 14and went after the man of God, and found him sitting under an oak. Then he said to him, "*Are* you the man of God who came from Judah?"

And he said, "I *am.*"

15Then he said to him, "Come home with me and eat bread."

16And he said, "I cannot return with you nor go in with you; neither can I eat bread nor drink water with you in this place. 17For I have been told by the word of the LORD, 'You shall not eat bread nor drink water there, nor return by going the way you came.' "

18He said to him, "I too *am* a prophet as you *are,* and an angel spoke to me by the word of the LORD, saying, 'Bring him back with you to your house, that he may eat bread and drink water.' " (He was lying to him.)

19So he went back with him, and ate bread in his house, and drank water.

20Now it happened, as they sat at the table, that the word of the LORD came to the prophet who had brought him back; 21and he cried out to the man of God who came from Judah, saying, "Thus says the LORD: 'Because you have disobeyed the word of the LORD, and have not kept the commandment which the LORD your God commanded you, 22but you came back, ate bread, and drank water in the place of which *the* LORD said to you, "Eat no bread and drink no water," your corpse shall not come to the tomb of your fathers.' "

23So it was, after he had eaten bread and after he had drunk, that he saddled the donkey for him, the prophet whom he had brought back. 24When he was gone, a lion met him on the road and killed him. And his corpse was thrown on the road, and the donkey stood by it. The lion also stood by the corpse. 25And there, men passed by and saw the corpse thrown on the road, and the lion standing by the corpse. Then they went and told *it* in the city where the old prophet dwelt.

26Now when the prophet who had brought him back from the way heard *it*, he said, "It *is* the man of God who was disobedient to the word of the LORD. Therefore the LORD has delivered him to the lion, which has torn him and killed him, according to the word of the LORD which He spoke to him." 27And he spoke to his sons, saying, "Saddle the donkey for me." So they saddled *it*. 28Then he went and found his corpse thrown on the road, and the donkey and the lion standing by the corpse. The lion had not eaten the corpse nor torn the donkey. 29And the prophet took up the corpse of the man of God, laid it on the donkey, and brought it back. So the old prophet came to the city to mourn, and to bury him. 30Then he laid the corpse in his own tomb; and they mourned over him, *saying*, "Alas, my brother!" 31So it was, after he had buried him, that he spoke to his sons, saying, "When I am dead, then bury me in the tomb where the man of God *is* buried; lay my bones beside his bones. 32For the saying which he cried out by the word of the LORD against the altar in Bethel, and against all the shrines on the high places which *are* in the cities of Samaria, will surely come to pass."

33After this event Jeroboam did not turn from his evil way, but again he made priests from every class of people for the high places; whoever wished, he consecrated him, and he became *one* of the priests of the high places. 34And this thing was the sin of the house of Jeroboam, so as to exterminate and destroy *it* from the face of the earth.

Judgment on the House of Jeroboam

14 At that time Abijah the son of Jeroboam became sick. 2And Jeroboam said to his wife, "Please arise, and disguise yourself, that they may not recognize you as the wife of Jeroboam, and go to Shiloh. Indeed, Ahijah the prophet *is* there, who told me that *I would be* king over this people. 3Also take with you ten loaves, *some* cakes, and a jar of honey, and go to him; he will tell you what will become of the child." 4And Jeroboam's wife did so; she arose and went to Shiloh, and came to the house of Ahijah. But Ahijah could not see, for his eyes were glazed by reason of his age.

5Now the LORD had said to Ahijah, "Here is the wife of Jeroboam, coming to ask you something about her son, for he *is* sick. Thus and thus you shall say to her; for it will be, when she comes in, that she will pretend *to be* another *woman.*"

6And so it was, when Ahijah heard the sound of her footsteps as she came through the door, he said, "Come in, wife of Jeroboam. Why do you pretend *to be* another *person?* For I *have been* sent to you *with* bad *news.* 7Go, tell Jeroboam, 'Thus says the LORD God of Israel: "Because I exalted you from among the people, and made you ruler over My people Israel, 8and tore the kingdom away from the house of David, and gave it to you; and *yet* you have not been as My servant David, who kept My commandments and who followed Me with all his heart, to do only *what was* right in My eyes; 9but you have done more evil than all who were before you, for you have gone and made for yourself other gods and molded images to provoke Me to anger, and have cast Me behind your back—10therefore behold! I will bring disaster on the house of Jeroboam, and will cut off from Jeroboam every male in Israel, bond and free; I will take away the remnant of the house of Jeroboam, as one takes away refuse until it is all gone. 11The dogs shall eat whoever belongs to Jeroboam and dies in the city, and the birds of the air shall eat whoever dies in the field; for the LORD has spoken!" ' 12Arise therefore, go to your own house. When your feet enter the city, the child shall die. 13And all Israel shall mourn for him and bury him, for he is the only one of Jeroboam who shall come to the grave, because in him there is found something good toward the LORD God of Israel in the house of Jeroboam.

14"Moreover the LORD will raise up for Himself a king over Israel who shall cut off the house of Jeroboam; this is the day. What? Even now! 15For the LORD will strike Israel, as a reed is shaken in the water. He will uproot Israel from this good land which He gave to their fathers, and will scatter them beyond the River,*e* because they have made their wooden images,*f* provoking the LORD to anger. 16And He will give Israel up because of the sins of Jeroboam, who sinned and who made Israel sin."

17Then Jeroboam's wife arose and departed, and came to Tirzah. When she came to the threshold of the house, the child died. 18And they buried him; and all Israel mourned for him, according to the word of the LORD which He spoke through His servant Ahijah the prophet.

Death of Jeroboam

19Now the rest of the acts of Jeroboam, how he made war and how he reigned, indeed they *are* written in the book of the chronicles of the kings of Israel. 20The period that Jeroboam reigned *was* twenty-two years. So he rested with his fathers. Then Nadab his son reigned in his place.

Rehoboam Reigns in Judah

21And Rehoboam the son of Solomon reigned in Judah. Rehoboam *was* forty-one years old when he became king. He reigned seventeen years in Jerusalem, the city which the LORD had chosen out of all the tribes of Israel, to put His name there. His mother's name *was* Naamah, an Ammonitess. 22Now Judah did evil in the sight of the LORD, and they provoked Him to jealousy with their sins which they committed, more than all that their fathers had done. 23For they also built for themselves high places, *sacred* pillars, and wooden images on every high hill and under every green tree. 24And there were also perverted persons*g* in the land. They did according to all the abominations of the nations which the LORD had cast out before the children of Israel.

25It happened in the fifth year of King Rehoboam *that* Shishak king of Egypt came up against Jerusalem. 26And he took away the treasures of the house of the LORD and the treasures of the king's house; he took away everything. He also took away all the gold shields which Solomon had made. 27Then King Rehoboam made bronze shields in their place, and committed *them* to the hands of the captains of the guard, who guarded the doorway of the king's house. 28And whenever the king entered the house of the LORD, the guards carried them, then brought them back into the guardroom.

29Now the rest of the acts of Rehoboam, and all that he did, *are* they not written in the book of the chronicles of the kings of Judah? 30And there was war between Rehoboam and Jeroboam all *their* days. 31So Rehoboam rested with his fathers, and was buried with his fathers in the City of David. His mother's name *was* Naamah, an Ammonitess. Then Abijam his son reigned in his place.

Abijam Reigns in Judah

15 In the eighteenth year of King Jeroboam the son of Nebat, Abijam became king over Judah. 2He reigned three years in Jerusalem. His mother's name *was* Maachah the granddaughter of Abishalom. 3And he walked in all the sins of his father, which he had done before him; his heart was not loyal to the LORD his God, as was the heart of his father David. 4Nevertheless for David's sake the LORD his God gave him a lamp in Jerusalem, by setting up his son after him and by establishing Jerusalem; 5because David did *what was* right in

---

e That is, the Euphrates   *f* Canaanite deities prostitution in religious rituals

g That is, those practicing sodomy and

the eyes of the LORD, and had not turned aside from anything that He commanded him all the days of his life, except in the matter of Uriah the Hittite. 6And there was war between Rehoboam and Jeroboam all the days of his life. 7Now the rest of the acts of Abijam, and all that he did, *are* they not written in the book of the chronicles of the kings of Judah? And there was war between Abijam and Jeroboam.

8So Abijam rested with his fathers, and they buried him in the City of David. Then Asa his son reigned in his place.

Asa Reigns in Judah

9In the twentieth year of Jeroboam king of Israel, Asa became king over Judah. 10And he reigned forty-one years in Jerusalem. His grandmother's name *was* Maachah the granddaughter of Abishalom. 11Asa did *what was* right in the eyes of the LORD, as *did* his father David. 12And he banished the perverted persons from the land, and removed all the idols that his fathers had made. 13Also he removed Maachah his grandmother from *being* queen mother, because she had made an obscene image of Asherah.*h* And Asa cut down her obscene image and burned *it* by the Brook Kidron. 14But the high places were not removed. Nevertheless Asa's heart was loyal to the LORD all his days. 15He also brought into the house of the LORD the things which his father had dedicated, and the things which he himself had dedicated: silver and gold and utensils.

16Now there was war between Asa and Baasha king of Israel all their days. 17And Baasha king of Israel came up against Judah, and built Ramah, that he might let none go out or come in to Asa king of Judah. 18Then Asa took all the silver and gold *that was* left in the treasuries of the house of the LORD and the treasuries of the king's house, and delivered them into the hand of his servants. And King Asa sent them to Ben-Hadad the son of Tabrimmon, the son of Hezion, king of Syria, who dwelt in Damascus, saying, 19"*Let there be* a treaty between you and me, as there was between my father and your father.

See, I have sent you a present of silver and gold. Come and break your treaty with Baasha king of Israel, so that he will withdraw from me."

20So Ben-Hadad heeded King Asa, and sent the captains of his armies against the cities of Israel. He attacked Ijon, Dan, Abel Beth Maachah, and all Chinneroth, with all the land of Naphtali. 21Now it happened, when Baasha heard *it*, that he stopped building Ramah, and remained in Tirzah.

22Then King Asa made a proclamation throughout all Judah; none *was* exempted. And they took away the stones and timber of Ramah, which Baasha had used for building; and with them King Asa built Geba of Benjamin, and Mizpah.

23The rest of all the acts of Asa, all his might, all that he did, and the cities which he built, *are* they not written in the book of the chronicles of the kings of Judah? But in the time of his old age he was diseased in his feet. 24So Asa rested with his fathers, and was buried with his fathers in the City of David his father. Then Jehoshaphat his son reigned in his place.

Nadab Reigns in Israel

25Now Nadab the son of Jeroboam became king over Israel in the second year of Asa king of Judah, and he reigned over Israel two years. 26And he did evil in the sight of the LORD, and walked in the way of his father, and in his sin by which he had made Israel sin.

27Then Baasha the son of Ahijah, of the house of Issachar, conspired against him. And Baasha killed him at Gibbethon, which *belonged* to the Philistines, while Nadab and all Israel laid siege to Gibbethon. 28Baasha killed him in the third year of Asa king of Judah, and reigned in his place. 29And it was so, when he became king, *that* he killed all the house of Jeroboam. He did not leave to Jeroboam anyone that breathed, until he had destroyed him, according to the word of the LORD which He had spoken by His servant Ahijah the Shilonite, 30because of the sins of Jeroboam, which he had sinned and by which he had made Israel sin,

h A Canaanite goddess

because of his provocation with which he had provoked the LORD God of Israel to anger.

31Now the rest of the acts of Nadab, and all that he did, *are* they not written in the book of the chronicles of the kings of Israel? 32And there was war between Asa and Baasha king of Israel all their days.

Baasha Reigns in Israel

33In the third year of Asa king of Judah, Baasha the son of Ahijah became king over all Israel in Tirzah, and *reigned* twenty-four years. 34He did evil in the sight of the LORD, and walked in the way of Jeroboam, and in his sin by which he had made Israel sin.

16 Then the word of the LORD came to Jehu the son of Hanani, against Baasha, saying: 2"Inasmuch as I lifted you out of the dust and made you ruler over My people Israel, and you have walked in the way of Jeroboam, and have made My people Israel sin, to provoke Me to anger with their sins, 3surely I will take away the posterity of Baasha and the posterity of his house, and I will make your house like the house of Jeroboam the son of Nebat. 4The dogs shall eat whoever belongs to Baasha and dies in the city, and the birds of the air shall eat whoever dies in the fields."

5Now the rest of the acts of Baasha, what he did, and his might, *are* they not written in the book of the chronicles of the kings of Israel? 6So Baasha rested with his fathers and was buried in Tirzah. Then Elah his son reigned in his place.

7And also the word of the LORD came by the prophet Jehu the son of Hanani against Baasha and his house, because of all the evil that he did in the sight of the LORD in provoking Him to anger with the work of his hands, in being like the house of Jeroboam, and because he killed them.

Elah Reigns in Israel

8In the twenty-sixth year of Asa king of Judah, Elah the son of Baasha became king over Israel, *and reigned* two years in Tirzah. 9Now his servant Zimri, commander of half *his* chariots, conspired against him as he was in Tirzah drinking himself drunk in the house of Arza, steward of *his* house in Tirzah. 10And Zimri went in and struck him and killed him in the twenty-seventh year of Asa king of Judah, and reigned in his place.

11Then it came to pass, when he began to reign, as soon as he was seated on his throne, *that* he killed all the household of Baasha; he did not leave him one male, neither of his relatives nor of his friends. 12Thus Zimri destroyed all the household of Baasha, according to the word of the LORD, which He spoke against Baasha by Jehu the prophet, 13for all the sins of Baasha and the sins of Elah his son, by which they had sinned and by which they had made Israel sin, in provoking the LORD God of Israel to anger with their idols.

14Now the rest of the acts of Elah, and all that he did, *are* they not written in the book of the chronicles of the kings of Israel?

Zimri Reigns in Israel

15In the twenty-seventh year of Asa king of Judah, Zimri had reigned in Tirzah seven days. And the people *were* encamped against Gibbethon, which *belonged* to the Philistines. 16Now the people *who were* encamped heard it said, "Zimri has conspired and also has killed the king." So all Israel made Omri, the commander of the army, king over Israel that day in the camp. 17Then Omri and all Israel with him went up from Gibbethon, and they besieged Tirzah. 18And it happened, when Zimri saw that the city was taken, that he went into the citadel of the king's house and burned the king's house down upon himself with fire, and died, 19because of the sins which he had committed in doing evil in the sight of the LORD, in walking in the way of Jeroboam, and in his sin which he had committed to make Israel sin.

20Now the rest of the acts of Zimri, and the treason he committed, *are* they not written in the book of the chronicles of the kings of Israel?

Omri Reigns in Israel

21Then the people of Israel were divided into two parts: half of the people followed Tibni the son of Ginath, to make him king, and half followed Omri. 22But the people who followed Omri prevailed over the people who followed Tibni the son of Ginath. So Tibni died and Omri reigned. 23In the thirty-first year of Asa king of Judah, Omri became king over Israel, *and reigned* twelve years. Six years he reigned in Tirzah. 24And he bought the hill of Samaria from Shemer for two talents of silver; then he built on the hill, and called the name of the city which he built, Samaria, after the name of Shemer, owner of the hill. 25Omri did evil in the eyes of the LORD, and did worse than all who *were* before him. 26For he walked in all the ways of Jeroboam the son of Nebat, and in his sin by which he had made Israel sin, provoking the LORD God of Israel to anger with their idols.

27Now the rest of the acts of Omri which he did, and the might that he showed, *are* they not written in the book of the chronicles of the kings of Israel?

28So Omri rested with his fathers and was buried in Samaria. Then Ahab his son reigned in his place.

Ahab Reigns in Israel

29In the thirty-eighth year of Asa king of Judah, Ahab the son of Omri became king over Israel; and Ahab the son of Omri reigned over Israel in Samaria twenty-two years. 30Now Ahab the son of Omri did evil in the sight of the LORD, more than all who *were* before him. 31And it came to pass, as though it had been a trivial thing for him to walk in the sins of Jeroboam the son of Nebat, that he took as wife Jezebel the daughter of Ethbaal, king of the Sidonians; and he went and served Baal and worshiped him. 32Then he set up an altar for Baal in the temple of Baal, which he had built in Samaria. 33And Ahab made a wooden image.[i] Ahab did more to provoke the LORD God of Israel to anger than all the kings of Israel who were before him. 34In his days Hiel of Bethel built Jericho. He laid its foundation with Abiram his firstborn, and with his youngest *son* Segub he set up its

gates, according to the word of the LORD, which He had spoken through Joshua the son of Nun.[j]

Elijah Proclaims a Drought

17 And Elijah the Tishbite, of the inhabitants of Gilead, said to Ahab, "*As* the LORD God of Israel lives, before whom I stand, there shall not be dew nor rain these years, except at my word."

2Then the word of the LORD came to him, saying, 3"Get away from here and turn eastward, and hide by the Brook Cherith, which flows into the Jordan. 4And it will be *that* you shall drink from the brook, and I have commanded the ravens to feed you there."

5So he went and did according to the word of the LORD, for he went and stayed by the Brook Cherith, which flows into the Jordan. 6The ravens brought him bread and meat in the morning, and bread and meat in the evening; and he drank from the brook. 7And it happened after a while that the brook dried up, because there had been no rain in the land.

Elijah and the Widow

8Then the word of the LORD came to him, saying, 9"Arise, go to Zarephath, which *belongs* to Sidon, and dwell there. See, I have commanded a widow there to provide for you." 10So he arose and went to Zarephath. And when he came to the gate of the city, indeed a widow *was* there gathering sticks. And he called to her and said, "Please bring me a little water in a cup, that I may drink." 11And as she was going to get *it,* he called to her and said, "Please bring me a morsel of bread in your hand."

12So she said, "As the LORD your God lives, I do not have bread, only a handful of flour in a bin, and a little oil in a jar; and see, I *am* gathering a couple of sticks that I may go in and prepare it for myself and my son, that we may eat it, and die."

13And Elijah said to her, "Do not fear; go *and* do as you have said, but make me a small cake from it first, and bring *it* to me; and afterward make *some* for

---

i A Canaanite goddess   j Compare Joshua 6.26

yourself and your son. 14For thus says the LORD God of Israel: 'The bin of flour shall not be used up, nor shall the jar of oil run dry, until the day the LORD sends rain on the earth.' "

15So she went away and did according to the word of Elijah; and she and he and her household ate for *many* days. 16The bin of flour was not used up, nor did the jar of oil run dry, according to the word of the LORD which He spoke by Elijah.

Elijah Revives the Widow's Son

17Now it happened after these things *that* the son of the woman who owned the house became sick. And his sickness was so serious that there was no breath left in him. 18So she said to Elijah, "What have I to do with you, O man of God? Have you come to me to bring my sin to remembrance, and to kill my son?"

19And he said to her, "Give me your son." So he took him out of her arms and carried him to the upper room where he was staying, and laid him on his own bed. 20Then he cried out to the LORD and said, "O LORD my God, have You also brought tragedy on the widow with whom I lodge, by killing her son?" 21And he stretched himself out on the child three times, and cried out to the LORD and said, "O LORD my God, I pray, let this child's soul come back to him." 22Then the LORD heard the voice of Elijah; and the soul of the child came back to him, and he revived.

23And Elijah took the child and brought him down from the upper room into the house, and gave him to his mother. And Elijah said, "See, your son lives!"

24Then the woman said to Elijah, "Now by this I know that you *are* a man of God, *and* that the word of the LORD in your mouth *is* the truth."

Elijah's Message to Ahab

18 And it came to pass *after* many days that the word of the LORD came to Elijah, in the third year, saying, "Go, present yourself to Ahab, and I will send rain on the earth."

2So Elijah went to present himself to Ahab; and *there was* a severe famine in Samaria. 3And Ahab had called Oba-

diah, who *was* in charge of *his* house. (Now Obadiah feared the LORD greatly. 4For so it was, while Jezebel massacred the prophets of the LORD, that Obadiah had taken one hundred prophets and hidden them, fifty to a cave, and had fed them with bread and water.) 5And Ahab had said to Obadiah, "Go into the land to all the springs of water and to all the brooks; perhaps we may find grass to keep the horses and mules alive, so that we will not have to kill any livestock." 6So they divided the land between them to explore it; Ahab went one way by himself, and Obadiah went another way by himself.

7Now as Obadiah was on his way, suddenly Elijah met him; and he recognized him, and fell on his face, and said, "*Is* that you, my lord Elijah?"

8And he answered him, "*It is* I. Go, tell your master, 'Elijah *is here.'* "

9So he said, "How have I sinned, that you are delivering your servant into the hand of Ahab, to kill me? 10*As* the LORD your God lives, there is no nation or kingdom where my master has not sent someone to hunt for you; and when they said, '*He is* not *here,'* he took an oath from the kingdom or nation that they could not find you. 11And now you say, 'Go, tell your master, "Elijah *is here*"*!* 12And it shall come to pass, *as soon as* I am gone from you, that the Spirit of the LORD will carry you to a place I do not know; so when I go and tell Ahab, and he cannot find you, he will kill me. But I your servant have feared the LORD from my youth. 13Was it not reported to my lord what I did when Jezebel killed the prophets of the LORD, how I hid one hundred men of the LORD's prophets, fifty to a cave, and fed them with bread and water? 14And now you say, 'Go, tell your master, "Elijah *is here.*" ' He will kill me!"

15Then Elijah said, "*As* the LORD of hosts lives, before whom I stand, I will surely present myself to him today."

16So Obadiah went to meet Ahab, and told him; and Ahab went to meet Elijah.

17Then it happened, when Ahab saw Elijah, that Ahab said to him, "*Is that* you, O troubler of Israel?"

18And he answered, "I have not troubled Israel, but you and your father's house *have*, in that you have forsaken the commandments of the LORD and have followed the Baals. 19Now therefore, send *and* gather all Israel to me on Mount Carmel, the four hundred and fifty prophets of Baal, and the four hundred prophets of Asherah,ᵏ who eat at Jezebel's table."

Elijah's Mount Carmel Victory

20So Ahab sent for all the children of Israel, and gathered the prophets together on Mount Carmel. 21And Elijah came to all the people, and said, "How long will you falter between two opinions? If the LORD *is* God, follow Him; but if Baal, follow him." But the people answered him not a word. 22Then Elijah said to the people, "I alone am left a prophet of the LORD; but Baal's prophets *are* four hundred and fifty men. 23Therefore let them give us two bulls; and let them choose one bull for themselves, cut it in pieces, and lay *it* on the wood, but put no fire *under it;* and I will prepare the other bull, and lay *it* on the wood, but put no fire *under it.* 24Then you call on the name of your gods, and I will call on the name of the LORD; and the God who answers by fire, He is God."

So all the people answered and said, "It is well spoken."

25Now Elijah said to the prophets of Baal, "Choose one bull for yourselves and prepare *it* first, for you *are* many; and call on the name of your god, but put no fire *under it.*"

26So they took the bull which was given them, and they prepared *it,* and called on the name of Baal from morning even till noon, saying, "O Baal, hear us!" But *there was* no voice; no one answered. Then they leaped about the altar which they had made. 27And so it was, at noon, that Elijah mocked them and said, "Cry aloud, for he *is* a god; either he is meditating, or he is busy, or he is on a journey, *or* perhaps he is sleeping and must be awakened." 28So they cried aloud, and cut themselves, as was their custom, with knives and lances, until the blood gushed out on them. 29And when midday was past, they prophesied until the *time* of the offering of the *evening* sacrifice. But *there was* no voice; no one answered, no one paid attention.

30Then Elijah said to all the people, "Come near to me." So all the people came near to him. And he repaired the altar of the LORD *that was* broken down. 31And Elijah took twelve stones, according to the number of the tribes of the sons of Jacob, to whom the word of the LORD had come, saying, "Israel shall be your name."ˡ 32Then with the stones he built an altar in the name of the LORD; and he made a trench around the altar large enough to hold two seahs of seed. 33And he put the wood in order, cut the bull in pieces, and laid *it* on the wood, and said, "Fill four waterpots with water, and pour *it* on the burnt sacrifice and on the wood." 34Then he said, "Do *it* a second time," and they did *it* a second time; and he said, "Do *it* a third time," and they did *it* a third time. 35So the water ran all around the altar; and he also filled the trench with water.

36And it came to pass, at *the time of* the offering of the *evening* sacrifice, that Elijah the prophet came near and said, "LORD God of Abraham, Isaac, and Israel, let it be known this day that You *are* God in Israel and I *am* Your servant, and *that* I have done all these things at Your word. 37Hear me, O LORD, hear me, that this people may know that You *are* the LORD God, and *that* You have turned their hearts back *to* You again."

38Then the fire of the LORD fell and consumed the burnt sacrifice, and the wood and the stones and the dust, and it licked up the water that *was* in the trench. 39Now when all the people saw *it,* they fell on their faces; and they said, "The LORD, He *is* God! The LORD, He *is* God!"

40And Elijah said to them, "Seize the prophets of Baal! Do not let one of them escape!" So they seized them; and Elijah brought them down to the Brook Kishon and executed them there.

The Drought Ends

41Then Elijah said to Ahab, "Go up, eat and drink; for *there is* the sound of abundance of rain." 42So Ahab went up to eat and drink. And Elijah went up

ᵏ A Canaanite goddess   ˡ Compare Genesis 32.28

to the top of Carmel; then he bowed down on the ground, and put his face between his knees, 43and said to his servant, "Go up now, look toward the sea."

So he went up and looked, and said, "*There is* nothing." And seven times he said, "Go again."

44Then it came to pass the seventh *time,* that he said, "There is a cloud, as small as a man's hand, rising out of the sea!" So he said, "Go up, say to Ahab, 'Prepare *your chariot,* and go down before the rain stops you.' "

45Now it happened in the meantime that the sky became black with clouds and wind, and there was a heavy rain. So Ahab rode away and went to Jezreel. 46Then the hand of the LORD came upon Elijah; and he girded up his loins and ran ahead of Ahab to the entrance of Jezreel.

Elijah Escapes from Jezebel

19 And Ahab told Jezebel all that Elijah had done, also how he had executed all the prophets with the sword. 2Then Jezebel sent a messenger to Elijah, saying, "So let the gods do *to me,* and more also, if I do not make your life as the life of one of them by tomorrow about this time." 3And when he saw *that,* he arose and ran for his life, and went to Beersheba, which *belongs* to Judah, and left his servant there.

4But he himself went a day's journey into the wilderness, and came and sat down under a broom tree. And he prayed that he might die, and said, "It is enough! Now, LORD, take my life, for I *am* no better than my fathers!"

5Then as he lay and slept under a broom tree, suddenly an angel[m] touched him, and said to him, "Arise *and* eat." 6Then he looked, and there by his head *was* a cake baked on coals, and a jar of water. So he ate and drank, and lay down again. 7And the angel[m] of the LORD came back the second time, and touched him, and said, "Arise *and* eat, because the journey *is* too great for you." 8So he arose, and ate and drank; and he went in the strength of that food

forty days and forty nights as far as Horeb, the mountain of God.

9And there he went into a cave, and spent the night in that place; and behold, the word of the LORD *came* to him, and He said to him, "What are you doing here, Elijah?"

10So he said, "I have been very zealous for the LORD God of hosts; for the children of Israel have forsaken Your covenant, torn down Your altars, and killed Your prophets with the sword. I alone am left; and they seek to take my life."

God's Revelation to Elijah

11Then He said, "Go out, and stand on the mountain before the LORD." And behold, the LORD passed by, and a great and strong wind tore into the mountains and broke the rocks in pieces before the LORD, *but* the LORD *was* not in the wind; and after the wind an earthquake, *but* the LORD *was* not in the earthquake; 12and after the earthquake a fire, *but* the LORD *was* not in the fire; and after the fire a still small voice.

13So it was, when Elijah heard *it,* that he wrapped his face in his mantle and went out and stood in the entrance of the cave. Suddenly a voice *came* to him, and said, "What are you doing here, Elijah?"

14And he said, "I have been very zealous for the LORD God of hosts; because the children of Israel have forsaken Your covenant, torn down Your altars, and killed Your prophets with the sword. I alone am left; and they seek to take my life."

15Then the LORD said to him: "Go, return on your way to the Wilderness of Damascus; and when you arrive, anoint Hazael *as* king over Syria. 16Also you shall anoint Jehu the son of Nimshi *as* king over Israel. And Elisha the son of Shaphat of Abel Meholah you shall anoint *as* prophet in your place. 17It shall be *that* whoever escapes the sword of Hazael, Jehu will kill; and whoever escapes the sword of Jehu, Elisha will kill. 18Yet I have reserved seven thousand in Israel, all whose knees have not bowed to Baal, and every mouth that has not kissed him."

m Or *Angel*

Elisha Follows Elijah

19So he departed from there, and found Elisha the son of Shaphat, who *was* plowing *with* twelve yoke *of oxen* before him, and he was with the twelfth. Then Elijah passed by him and threw his mantle on him. 20And he left the oxen and ran after Elijah, and said, "Please let me kiss my father and my mother, and *then* I will follow you."

And he said to him, "Go back again, for what have I done to you?"

21So *Elisha* turned back from him, and took a yoke of oxen and slaughtered them and boiled their flesh, using the oxen's equipment, and gave it to the people, and they ate. Then he arose and followed Elijah, and became his servant.

Ahab Defeats the Syrians

20 Now Ben-Hadad the king of Syria gathered all his forces together; thirty-two kings *were* with him, with horses and chariots. And he went up and besieged Samaria, and made war against it. 2Then he sent messengers into the city to Ahab king of Israel, and said to him, "Thus says Ben-Hadad: 3'Your silver and your gold *are* mine; your loveliest wives and children are mine.' "

4And the king of Israel answered and said, "My lord, O king, just as you say, I and all that I have *are* yours."

5Then the messengers came back and said, "Thus speaks Ben-Hadad, saying, 'Indeed I have sent to you, saying, "You shall deliver to me your silver and your gold, your wives and your children"; 6but I will send my servants to you tomorrow about this time, and they shall search your house and the houses of your servants. And it shall be, *that* whatever is pleasant in your eyes, they will put *it* in their hands and take *it.*' "

7So the king of Israel called all the elders of the land, and said, "Notice, please, and see how this *man* seeks trouble, for he sent to me for my wives, my children, my silver, and my gold; and I did not deny him."

8And all the elders and all the people said to him, "Do not listen or consent."

9Therefore he said to the messengers of Ben-Hadad, "Tell my lord the king, 'All that you sent for to your servant the first time I will do, but this thing I cannot do.' "

And the messengers departed and brought back word to him.

10Then Ben-Hadad sent to him and said, "The gods do so to me, and more also, if enough dust is left of Samaria for a handful for each of the people who follow me."

11So the king of Israel answered and said, "Tell *him,* 'Let not the one who puts on *his armor* boast like the one who takes *it off.*' "

12And it happened when *Ben-Hadad* heard this message, as he and the kings *were* drinking at the command post, that he said to his servants, "Get ready." And they got ready to attack the city.

13Suddenly a prophet approached Ahab king of Israel, saying, "Thus says the LORD: 'Have you seen all this great multitude? Behold, I will deliver it into your hand today, and you shall know that I *am* the LORD.' "

14So Ahab said, "By whom?"

And he said, "Thus says the LORD: 'By the young leaders of the provinces.' "

Then he said, "Who will set the battle in order?"

And he answered, "You."

15Then he mustered the young leaders of the provinces, and there were two hundred and thirty-two; and after them he mustered all the people, all the children of Israel—seven thousand.

16So they went out at noon. Meanwhile Ben-Hadad and the thirty-two kings helping him were getting drunk at the command post. 17The young leaders of the provinces went out first. And Ben-Hadad sent out *a patrol,* and they told him, saying, "Men are coming out of Samaria!" 18So he said, "If they have come out for peace, take them alive; and if they have come out for war, take them alive."

19Then these young leaders of the provinces went out of the city with the army which followed them. 20And each one killed his man; so the Syrians fled, and Israel pursued them; and Ben-Hadad the king of Syria escaped on a horse with the cavalry. 21Then the king of Israel went out and attacked the horses and chariots, and killed the Syrians with a great slaughter.

22And the prophet came to the king of Israel and said to him, "Go, strengthen yourself; take note, and see what you should do, for in the spring of the year the king of Syria will come up against you."

The Syrians Again Defeated

23Then the servants of the king of Syria said to him, "Their gods *are* gods of the hills. Therefore they were stronger than we; but if we fight against them in the plain, surely we will be stronger than they. 24So do this thing: Dismiss the kings, each from his position, and put captains in their places; 25and you shall muster an army like the army that you have lost, horse for horse and chariot for chariot. Then we will fight against them in the plain; surely we will be stronger than they."

And he listened to their voice and did so.

26So it was, in the spring of the year, that Ben-Hadad mustered the Syrians and went up to Aphek to fight against Israel. 27And the children of Israel were mustered and given provisions, and they went against them. Now the children of Israel encamped before them like two little flocks of goats, while the Syrians filled the countryside.

28Then a man of God came and spoke to the king of Israel, and said, "Thus says the LORD: 'Because the Syrians have said, "The LORD *is* God of the hills, but He *is* not God of the valleys," therefore I will deliver all this great multitude into your hand, and you shall know that I *am* the LORD.' " 29And they encamped opposite each other for seven days. So it was that on the seventh day the battle was joined; and the children of Israel killed one hundred thousand foot soldiers *of* the Syrians in one day. 30But the rest fled to Aphek, into the city; then a wall fell on twenty-seven thousand of the men *who were* left.

And Ben-Hadad fled and went into the city, into an inner chamber.

Ahab's Treaty with Ben-Hadad

31Then his servants said to him, "Look now, we have heard that the kings of the house of Israel *are* merciful kings. Please, let us put sackcloth around our waists and ropes around our heads, and go out to the king of Israel; perhaps he will spare your life." 32So they wore sackcloth around their waists and *put* ropes around their heads, and came to the king of Israel and said, "Your servant Ben-Hadad says, 'Please let me live.' "

And he said, "*Is* he still alive? He *is* my brother."

33Now the men were watching closely to see whether *any sign of mercy would come* from him; and they quickly grasped *at this word* and said, "Your brother Ben-Hadad."

So he said, "Go, bring him." Then Ben-Hadad came out to him; and he had him come up into the chariot.

34So *Ben-Hadad* said to him, "The cities which my father took from your father I will restore; and you may set up marketplaces for yourself in Damascus, as my father did in Samaria."

Then *Ahab said,* "I will send you away with this treaty." So he made a treaty with him and sent him away.

Ahab Condemned

35Now a certain man of the sons of the prophets said to his neighbor by the word of the LORD, "Strike me, please." And the man refused to strike him. 36Then he said to him, "Because you have not obeyed the voice of the LORD, surely, as soon as you depart from me, a lion shall kill you." And as soon as he left him, a lion found him and killed him.

37And he found another man, and said, "Strike me, please." So the man struck him, inflicting a wound. 38Then the prophet departed and waited for the king by the road, and disguised himself with a bandage over his eyes. 39Now as the king passed by, he cried out to the king and said, "Your servant went out into the midst of the battle; and there, a man came over and brought a man to me, and said, 'Guard this man; if by any means he is missing, your life shall be for his life, or else you shall pay a talent of silver.' 40While your servant was busy here and there, he was gone."

Then the king of Israel said to him,

"So *shall* your judgment *be;* you yourself have decided *it.*"

41And he hastened to take the bandage away from his eyes; and the king of Israel recognized him as one of the prophets. 42Then he said to him, "Thus says the LORD: 'Because you have let slip out of *your* hand a man whom I appointed to utter destruction, therefore your life shall go for his life, and your people for his people.'"

43So the king of Israel went to his house sullen and displeased, and came to Samaria.

Naboth Is Murdered for His Vineyard

21 And it came to pass after these things *that* Naboth the Jezreelite had a vineyard which *was* in Jezreel, next to the palace of Ahab king of Samaria. 2So Ahab spoke to Naboth, saying, "Give me your vineyard, that I may have it for a vegetable garden, because it *is* near, next to my house; and for it I will give you a vineyard better than it. *Or,* if it seems good to you, I will give you its worth in money."

3But Naboth said to Ahab, "The LORD forbid that I should give the inheritance of my fathers to you!"

4So Ahab went into his house sullen and displeased because of the word which Naboth the Jezreelite had spoken to him; for he had said, "I will not give you the inheritance of my fathers." And he lay down on his bed, and turned away his face, and would eat no food.

5But Jezebel his wife came to him, and said to him, "Why is your spirit so sullen that you eat no food?"

6He said to her, "Because I spoke to Naboth the Jezreelite, and said to him, 'Give me your vineyard for money; or else, if it pleases you, I will give you *another* vineyard for it.' And he answered, 'I will not give you my vineyard.'"

7Then Jezebel his wife said to him, "You now exercise authority over Israel! Arise, eat food, and let your heart be cheerful; I will give you the vineyard of Naboth the Jezreelite."

8And she wrote letters in Ahab's name, sealed *them* with his seal, and sent the letters to the elders and the nobles who *were* dwelling in the city with Naboth. 9She wrote in the letters, saying,

Proclaim a fast, and seat Naboth with high honor among the people; 10and seat two men, scoundrels, before him to bear witness against him, saying, You have blasphemed God and the king. *Then* take him out, and stone him, that he may die.

11So the men of his city, the elders and nobles who were inhabitants of his city, did as Jezebel had sent to them, as it *was* written in the letters which she had sent to them. 12They proclaimed a fast, and seated Naboth with high honor among the people. 13And two men, scoundrels, came in and sat before him; and the scoundrels witnessed against him, against Naboth, in the presence of the people, saying, "Naboth has blasphemed God and the king!" Then they took him outside the city and stoned him with stones, so that he died. 14Then they sent to Jezebel, saying, "Naboth has been stoned and is dead."

15And it came to pass, when Jezebel heard that Naboth had been stoned and was dead, that Jezebel said to Ahab, "Arise, take possession of the vineyard of Naboth the Jezreelite, which he refused to give you for money; for Naboth is not alive, but dead." 16So it was, when Ahab heard that Naboth was dead, that Ahab got up and went down to take possession of the vineyard of Naboth the Jezreelite.

The LORD Condemns Ahab

17Then the word of the LORD came to Elijah the Tishbite, saying, 18"Arise, go down to meet Ahab king of Israel, who *lives* in Samaria. There *he is,* in the vineyard of Naboth, where he has gone down to take possession of it. 19You shall speak to him, saying, 'Thus says the LORD: "Have you murdered and also taken possession?"' And you shall speak to him, saying, 'Thus says the LORD: "In the place where dogs licked the blood of Naboth, dogs shall lick your blood, even yours."'"

20So Ahab said to Elijah, "Have you found me, O my enemy?"

And he answered, "I have found *you,*

because you have sold yourself to do evil in the sight of the LORD: 21'Behold, I will bring calamity on you. I will take away your posterity, and will cut off from Ahab every male in Israel, both bond and free. 22I will make your house like the house of Jeroboam the son of Nebat, and like the house of Baasha the son of Ahijah, because of the provocation with which you have provoked *Me* to anger, and made Israel sin.' 23And concerning Jezebel the LORD also spoke, saying, 'The dogs shall eat Jezebel by the wall of Jezreel.' 24The dogs shall eat whoever belongs to Ahab and dies in the city, and the birds of the air shall eat whoever dies in the field."

25But there was no one like Ahab who sold himself to do wickedness in the sight of the LORD, because Jezebel his wife stirred him up. 26And he behaved very abominably in following idols, according to all *that* the Amorites had done, whom the LORD had cast out before the children of Israel.

27So it was, when Ahab heard those words, that he tore his clothes and put sackcloth on his body, and fasted and lay in sackcloth, and went about mourning.

28And the word of the LORD came to Elijah the Tishbite, saying, 29"See how Ahab has humbled himself before Me? Because he has humbled himself before Me, I will not bring the calamity in his days. In the days of his son I will bring the calamity on his house."

Micaiah Warns Ahab

22 Now three years passed without war between Syria and Israel. 2Then it came to pass, in the third year, that Jehoshaphat the king of Judah went down to *visit* the king of Israel.

3And the king of Israel said to his servants, "Do you know that Ramoth in Gilead *is* ours, but we hesitate to take it out of the hand of the king of Syria?" 4So he said to Jehoshaphat, "Will you go with me to fight at Ramoth Gilead?"

Jehoshaphat said to the king of Israel, "I *am* as you *are*, my people as your people, my horses as your horses." 5Also Jehoshaphat said to the king of Israel, "Please inquire for the word of the LORD today."

6Then the king of Israel gathered the prophets together, about four hundred men, and said to them, "Shall I go against Ramoth Gilead to fight, or shall I refrain?"

So they said, "Go up, for the Lord will deliver *it* into the hand of the king."

7And Jehoshaphat said, "*Is there* not still a prophet of the LORD here, that we may inquire of Him?"[n]

8So the king of Israel said to Jehoshaphat, "*There is* still one man, Micaiah the son of Imlah, by whom we may inquire of the LORD; but I hate him, because he does not prophesy good concerning me, but evil."

And Jehoshaphat said, "Let not the king say such things!"

9Then the king of Israel called an officer and said, "Bring Micaiah the son of Imlah quickly!"

10The king of Israel and Jehoshaphat the king of Judah, having put on *their* robes, sat each on his throne, at a threshing floor at the entrance of the gate of Samaria; and all the prophets prophesied before them. 11Now Zedekiah the son of Chenaanah had made horns of iron for himself; and he said, "Thus says the LORD: 'With these you shall gore the Syrians until they are destroyed.' " 12And all the prophets prophesied so, saying, "Go up to Ramoth Gilead and prosper, for the LORD will deliver *it* into the king's hand."

13Then the messenger who had gone to call Micaiah spoke to him, saying, "Now listen, the words of the prophets with one accord encourage the king. Please, let your word be like the word of one of them, and speak encouragement."

14And Micaiah said, "*As* the LORD lives, whatever the LORD says to me, that I will speak."

15Then he came to the king; and the king said to him, "Micaiah, shall we go to war against Ramoth Gilead, or shall we refrain?"

And he answered him, "Go and prosper, for the LORD will deliver *it* into the hand of the king!"

16So the king said to him, "How many

[n] Or *him*

times shall I make you swear that you tell me nothing but the truth in the name of the Lord?"

17Then he said, "I saw all Israel scattered on the mountains, as sheep that have no shepherd. And the Lord said, 'These have no master. Let each return to his house in peace.' "

18And the king of Israel said to Jehoshaphat, "Did I not tell you he would not prophesy good concerning me, but evil?"

19Then *Micaiah* said, "Therefore hear the word of the Lord: I saw the Lord sitting on His throne, and all the host of heaven standing by, on His right hand and on His left. 20And the Lord said, 'Who will persuade Ahab to go up, that he may fall at Ramoth Gilead?' So one spoke in this manner, and another spoke in that manner. 21Then a spirit came forward and stood before the Lord, and said, 'I will persuade him.' 22The Lord said to him, 'In what way?' So he said, 'I will go out and be a lying spirit in the mouth of all his prophets.' And the Lord said, 'You shall persuade *him*, and also prevail. Go out and do so.' 23Therefore look! The Lord has put a lying spirit in the mouth of all these prophets of yours, and the Lord has declared disaster against you."

24Now Zedekiah the son of Chenaanah went near and struck Micaiah on the cheek, and said, "Which way did the spirit from the Lord go from me to speak to you?"

25And Micaiah said, "Indeed, you shall see on that day when you go into an inner chamber to hide!"

26So the king of Israel said, "Take Micaiah, and return him to Amon the governor of the city and to Joash the king's son; 27and say, 'Thus says the king: "Put this *fellow* in prison, and feed him with bread of affliction and water of affliction, until I come in peace." ' "

28But Micaiah said, "If you ever return in peace, the Lord has not spoken by me." And he said, "Take heed, all you people!"

Ahab Dies in Battle

29So the king of Israel and Jehoshaphat the king of Judah went up to Ramoth Gilead. 30And the king of Israel said to Jehoshaphat, "I will disguise myself and go into battle; but you put on your robes." So the king of Israel disguised himself and went into battle.

31Now the king of Syria had commanded the thirty-two captains of his chariots, saying, "Fight with no one small or great, but only with the king of Israel." 32So it was, when the captains of the chariots saw Jehoshaphat, that they said, "Surely it *is* the king of Israel!" Therefore they turned aside to fight against him, and Jehoshaphat cried out. 33And it happened, when the captains of the chariots saw that it *was* not the king of Israel, that they turned back from pursuing him. 34Now a *certain* man drew a bow at random, and struck the king of Israel between the joints of his armor. So he said to the driver of his chariot, "Turn around and take me out of the battle, for I am wounded."

35The battle increased that day; and the king was propped up in his chariot, facing the Syrians, and died at evening. The blood ran out from the wound onto the floor of the chariot. 36Then, as the sun was going down, a shout went throughout the army, saying, "Every man to his city, and every man to his own country!"

37So the king died, and was brought to Samaria. And they buried the king in Samaria. 38Then *someone* washed the chariot at a pool in Samaria, and the dogs licked up his blood while the harlots bathed, according to the word of the Lord which He had spoken.

39Now the rest of the acts of Ahab, and all that he did, the ivory house which he built and all the cities that he built, *are* they not written in the book of the chronicles of the kings of Israel? 40So Ahab rested with his fathers. Then Ahaziah his son reigned in his place.

Jehoshaphat Reigns in Judah

41Jehoshaphat the son of Asa had become king over Judah in the fourth year of Ahab king of Israel. 42Jehoshaphat *was* thirty-five years old when he became king, and he reigned twenty-five years in Jerusalem. His mother's name *was* Azubah the daughter of Shilhi. 43And he walked in all the ways of his father Asa. He did not turn aside from them, doing *what was* right in the eyes of the LORD. Nevertheless the high places were not taken away, *for* the people offered sacrifices and burned incense on the high places. 44Also Jehoshaphat made peace with the king of Israel.

45Now the rest of the acts of Jehoshaphat, the might that he showed, and how he made war, *are* they not written in the book of the chronicles of the kings of Judah? 46And the rest of the perverted persons,ᵒ who remained in the days of his father Asa, he banished from the land. 47*There was* then no king in Edom, only a deputy of the king.

48Jehoshaphat made merchant ships to go to Ophir for gold; but they never sailed, for the ships were wrecked at Ezion Geber. 49Then Ahaziah the son of Ahab said to Jehoshaphat, "Let my servants go with your servants in the ships." But Jehoshaphat would not.

50And Jehoshaphat rested with his fathers, and was buried with his fathers in the City of David his father. Then Jehoram his son reigned in his place.

Ahaziah Reigns in Israel

51Ahaziah the son of Ahab became king over Israel in Samaria in the seventeenth year of Jehoshaphat king of Judah, and reigned two years over Israel. 52He did evil in the sight of the LORD, and walked in the way of his father and in the way of his mother and in the way of Jeroboam the son of Nebat, who had made Israel sin; 53for he served Baal and worshiped him, and provoked the LORD God of Israel to anger, according to all that his father had done.

ᵒ That is, those practicing sodomy and prostitution in religious rituals

KINGS

God Judges Ahaziah

1 Moab rebelled against Israel after the death of Ahab.

2Now Ahaziah fell through the lattice of his upper room in Samaria, and was injured; so he sent messengers and said to them, "Go, inquire of Baal-Zebub, the god of Ekron, whether I shall recover from this injury." 3But the angel*a* of the LORD said to Elijah the Tishbite, "Arise, go up to meet the messengers of the king of Samaria, and say to them, '*Is it* because *there is* no God in Israel *that* you are going to inquire of Baal-Zebub, the god of Ekron?' 4Now therefore, thus says the LORD: 'You shall not come down from the bed to which you have gone up, but you shall surely die.' " So Elijah departed.

5And when the messengers returned to him, he said to them, "Why have you come back?"

6So they said to him, "A man came up to meet us, and said to us, 'Go, return to the king who sent you, and say to him, "Thus says the LORD: '*Is it* because *there is* no God in Israel *that* you are sending to inquire of Baal-Zebub, the god of Ekron? Therefore you shall not come down from the bed to which you have gone up, but you shall surely die.' " ' "

7Then he said to them, "What kind of man *was it* who came up to meet you and told you these words?"

8So they answered him, "A hairy man wearing a leather belt around his waist."

And he said, "It *is* Elijah the Tishbite."

9Then the king sent to him a captain of fifty with his fifty men. So he went up to him; and there he was, sitting on the top of a hill. And he spoke to him: "Man of God, the king has said, 'Come down!' "

10So Elijah answered and said to the captain of fifty, "If I *am* a man of God, then let fire come down from heaven and consume you and your fifty men."

And fire came down from heaven and consumed him and his fifty. 11Then he sent to him another captain of fifty with his fifty men.

And he answered and said to him: "Man of God, thus has the king said, 'Come down quickly!' "

12So Elijah answered and said to them, "If I *am* a man of God, let fire come down from heaven and consume you and your fifty men." And the fire of God came down from heaven and consumed him and his fifty.

13Again, he sent a third captain of fifty with his fifty men. And the third captain of fifty went up, and came and fell on his knees before Elijah, and pleaded with him, and said to him: "Man of God, please let my life and the life of these fifty servants of yours be precious in your sight. 14Look, fire has come down from heaven and burned up the first two captains of fifties with their fifties. But let my life now be precious in your sight."

15And the angel*a* of the LORD said to Elijah, "Go down with him; do not be afraid of him." So he arose and went down with him to the king. 16Then he said to him, "Thus says the LORD: 'Because you have sent messengers to inquire of Baal-Zebub, the god of Ekron, *is it* because *there is* no God in Israel to inquire of His word? Therefore you shall not come down from the bed to which you have gone up, but you shall surely die.' "

17So *Ahaziah* died according to the word of the LORD which Elijah had spoken. Because he had no son, Jehoram*b* became king in his place, in the second year of Jehoram the son of Jehoshaphat, king of Judah.

18Now the rest of the acts of Ahaziah which he did, *are* they not written in the book of the chronicles of the kings of Israel?

Elijah Ascends to Heaven

2 And it came to pass, when the LORD was about to take up Elijah into

---

a Or *Angel*   *b* The son of Ahab king of Israel (compare 3.1) heaven by a whirlwind, that Elijah went with Elisha from Gilgal. 2Then Elijah said to Elisha, "Stay here, please, for the LORD has sent me on to Bethel."

But Elisha said, "As the LORD lives, and as your soul lives, I will not leave you!" So they went down to Bethel.

3Now the sons of the prophets who were at Bethel came out to Elisha, and said to him, "Do you know that the LORD will take away your master from over you today?"

And he said, "Yes, I know; keep silent!"

4Then Elijah said to him, "Elisha, stay here, please, for the LORD has sent me on to Jericho."

But he said, "As the LORD lives, and as your soul lives, I will not leave you!" So they came to Jericho.

5Now the sons of the prophets who were at Jericho came to Elisha and said to him, "Do you know that the LORD will take away your master from over you today?"

So he answered, "Yes, I know; keep silent!"

6Then Elijah said to him, "Stay here, please, for the LORD has sent me on to the Jordan."

But he said, "As the LORD lives, and as your soul lives, I will not leave you!" So the two of them went on. 7And fifty men of the sons of the prophets went and stood facing them at a distance, while the two of them stood by the Jordan. 8Now Elijah took his mantle, rolled it up, and struck the water; and it was divided this way and that, so that the two of them crossed over on dry ground.

9And so it was, when they had crossed over, that Elijah said to Elisha, "Ask! What may I do for you, before I am taken away from you?"

Elisha said, "Please let a double portion of your spirit be upon me."

10So he said, "You have asked a hard thing. Nevertheless, if you see me when I am taken from you, it shall be so for you; but if not, it shall not be so." 11Then it happened, as they continued on and talked, that suddenly a chariot of fire appeared with horses of fire, and separated the two of them; and Elijah went up by a whirlwind into heaven.

12And Elisha saw it, and he cried out, "My father, my father, the chariot of Israel and its horsemen!" So he saw him no more. And he took hold of his own clothes and tore them into two pieces. 13He also took up the mantle of Elijah that had fallen from him, and went back and stood by the bank of the Jordan. 14Then he took the mantle of Elijah that had fallen from him, and struck the water, and said, "Where is the LORD God of Elijah?" And when he also had struck the water, it was divided this way and that; and Elisha crossed over.

15Now when the sons of the prophets who were from Jericho saw him, they said, "The spirit of Elijah rests on Elisha." And they came to meet him, and bowed to the ground before him. 16Then they said to him, "Look now, there are fifty strong men with your servants. Please let them go and search for your master, lest perhaps the Spirit of the LORD has taken him up and cast him upon some mountain or into some valley."

And he said, "You shall not send anyone."

17But when they urged him till he was ashamed, he said, "Send them!" Therefore they sent fifty men, and they searched for three days but did not find him. 18And when they came back to him, for he had stayed in Jericho, he said to them, "Did I not say to you, 'Do not go'?"

Elisha Performs Miracles

19Then the men of the city said to Elisha, "Please notice, the situation of this city is pleasant, as my lord sees; but the water is bad, and the ground barren." 20And he said, "Bring me a new bowl, and put salt in it." So they brought it to him. 21Then he went out to the source of the water, and cast in the salt there, and said, "Thus says the LORD: 'I have healed this water; from it there shall be no more death or barrenness.' " 22So the water remains healed to this day, according to the word of Elisha which he spoke.

23Then he went up from there to Bethel; and as he was going up the road, some youths came from the city and mocked him, and said to him, "Go up, you baldhead! Go up, you baldhead!"

24So he turned around and looked at them, and pronounced a curse on them in the name of the LORD. And two female bears came out of the woods and mauled forty-two of the youths.

25Then he went from there to Mount Carmel, and from there he returned to Samaria.

Moab Rebels Against Israel

3 Now Jehoram the son of Ahab became king over Israel at Samaria in the eighteenth year of Jehoshaphat king of Judah, and reigned twelve years. 2And he did evil in the sight of the LORD, but not like his father and mother; for he put away the *sacred* pillar of Baal that his father had made. 3Nevertheless he persisted in the sins of Jeroboam the son of Nebat, who had made Israel sin; he did not depart from them.

4Now Mesha king of Moab was a sheepbreeder, and he regularly paid the king of Israel one hundred thousand lambs and the wool of one hundred thousand rams. 5But it happened, when Ahab died, that the king of Moab rebelled against the king of Israel.

6So King Jehoram went out of Samaria at that time and mustered all Israel. 7Then he went and sent to Jehoshaphat king of Judah, saying, "The king of Moab has rebelled against me. Will you go with me to fight against Moab?"

And he said, "I will go up; I *am* as you *are,* my people as your people, my horses as your horses." 8Then he said, "Which way shall we go up?"

And he answered, "By way of the Wilderness of Edom."

9So the king of Israel went with the king of Judah and the king of Edom, and they marched on that roundabout route seven days; and there was no water for the army, nor for the animals that followed them. 10And the king of Israel said, "Alas! For the LORD has called these three kings together to deliver them into the hand of Moab."

11But Jehoshaphat said, "*Is there* no prophet of the LORD here, that we may inquire of the LORD by him?"

So one of the servants of the king of Israel answered and said, "Elisha the son of Shaphat *is* here, who poured water on the hands of Elijah."

12And Jehoshaphat said, "The word of the LORD is with him." So the king of Israel and Jehoshaphat and the king of Edom went down to him.

13Then Elisha said to the king of Israel, "What have I to do with you? Go to the prophets of your father and the prophets of your mother."

But the king of Israel said to him, "No, for the LORD has called these three kings *together* to deliver them into the hand of Moab."

14And Elisha said, "*As* the LORD of hosts lives, before whom I stand, surely were it not that I regard the presence of Jehoshaphat king of Judah, I would not look at you, nor see you. 15But now bring me a musician."

Then it happened, when the musician played, that the hand of the LORD came upon him. 16And he said, "Thus says the LORD: 'Make this valley full of ditches.' 17For thus says the LORD: 'You shall not see wind, nor shall you see rain; yet that valley shall be filled with water, so that you, your cattle, and your animals may drink.' 18And this is a simple matter in the sight of the LORD; He will also deliver the Moabites into your hand. 19Also you shall attack every fortified city and every choice city, and shall cut down every good tree, and stop up every spring of water, and ruin every good piece of land with stones."

20Now it happened in the morning, when the grain offering was offered, that suddenly water came by way of Edom, and the land was filled with water.

21And when all the Moabites heard that the kings had come up to fight against them, all who were able to bear arms and older were gathered; and they stood at the border. 22Then they rose up early in the morning, and the sun was shining on the water; and the Moabites saw the water on the other side *as* red as blood. 23And they said, "This is blood; the kings have surely struck swords and have killed one another; now therefore, Moab, to the spoil!"

24So when they came to the camp of Israel, Israel rose up and attacked the Moabites, so that they fled before them; and they entered *their* land, killing the

Moabites. 25Then they destroyed the cities, and each man threw a stone on every good piece of land and filled it; and they stopped up all the springs of water and cut down all the good trees. But they left the stones of Kir Haraseth *intact.* However the slingers surrounded and attacked it.

26And when the king of Moab saw that the battle was too fierce for him, he took with him seven hundred men who drew swords, to break through to the king of Edom, but they could not. 27Then he took his eldest son who would have reigned in his place, and offered him *as* a burnt offering upon the wall; and there was great indignation against Israel. So they departed from him and returned to *their own* land.

Elisha and the Widow's Oil

4 A certain woman of the wives of the sons of the prophets cried out to Elisha, saying, "Your servant my husband is dead, and you know that your servant feared the LORD. And the creditor is coming to take my two sons to be his slaves."

2So Elisha said to her, "What shall I do for you? Tell me, what do you have in the house?" And she said, "Your maidservant has nothing in the house but a jar of oil."

3Then he said, "Go, borrow vessels from everywhere, from all your neighbors—empty vessels; do not gather just a few. 4And when you have come in, you shall shut the door behind you and your sons; then pour it into all those vessels, and set aside the full ones."

5So she went from him and shut the door behind her and her sons, who brought *the vessels* to her; and she poured *it* out. 6Now it came to pass, when the vessels were full, that she said to her son, "Bring me another vessel." And he said to her, "*There is* not another vessel." So the oil ceased. 7Then she came and told the man of God. And he said, "Go, sell the oil and pay your debt; and you *and* your sons live on the rest."

Elisha Raises the Shunammite's Son

8Now it happened one day that Elisha went to Shunem, where there *was* a notable woman, and she persuaded him to eat some food. So it was, as often as he passed by, he would turn in there to eat some food. 9And she said to her husband, "Look now, I know that this *is* a holy man of God, who passes by us regularly. 10Please, let us make a small upper room on the wall; and let us put a bed for him there, and a table and a chair and a lampstand; so it will be, whenever he comes to us, he can turn in there."

11And it happened one day that he came there, and he turned in to the upper room and lay down there. 12Then he said to Gehazi his servant, "Call this Shunammite woman." When he had called her, she stood before him. 13And he said to him, "Say now to her, 'Look, you have been concerned for us with all this care. What *can I* do for you? Do you want me to speak on your behalf to the king or to the commander of the army?' "

She answered, "I dwell among my own people."

14So he said, "What then *is* to be done for her?"

And Gehazi answered, "Actually, she has no son, and her husband is old."

15So he said, "Call her." When he had called her, she stood in the doorway. 16Then he said, "About this time next year you shall embrace a son."

And she said, "No, my lord. Man of God, do not lie to your maidservant!"

17But the woman conceived, and bore a son when the appointed time had come, of which Elisha had told her.

18And the child grew. Now it happened one day that he went out to his father, to the reapers. 19And he said to his father, "My head, my head!"

So he said to a servant, "Carry him to his mother." 20When he had taken him and brought him to his mother, he sat on her knees till noon, and *then* died. 21And she went up and laid him on the bed of the man of God, shut *the door* upon him, and went out. 22Then she called to her husband, and said, "Please send me one of the young men and one of the donkeys, that I may run to the man of God and come back."

23So he said, "Why are you going to him today? *It is* neither the New Moon nor the Sabbath."

And she said, "*It is* well." 24Then she

saddled a donkey, and said to her servant, "Drive, and go forward; do not
slacken the pace for me unless I tell
you." 25And so she departed, and went
to the man of God at Mount Carmel.

So it was, when the man of God saw
her afar off, that he said to his servant
Gehazi, "Look, the Shunammite
woman! 26Please run now to meet her,
and say to her, 'Is it well with you? Is
it well with your husband? Is it well
with the child?' "

And she answered, "It is well."
27Now when she came to the man of
God at the hill, she caught him by the
feet, but Gehazi came near to push her
away. But the man of God said, "Let
her alone; for her soul is in deep distress, and the LORD has hidden it from
me, and has not told me."

28So she said, "Did I ask a son of
my lord? Did I not say, 'Do not deceive me'?"

29Then he said to Gehazi, "Get yourself ready, and take my staff in your
hand, and be on your way. If you meet
anyone, do not greet him; and if anyone
greets you, do not answer him; but lay
my staff on the face of the child."

30And the mother of the child said,
"As the LORD lives, and as your soul
lives, I will not leave you." So he arose
and followed her. 31Now Gehazi went
on ahead of them, and laid the staff on
the face of the child; but there was neither voice nor hearing. Therefore he
went back to meet him, and told him,
saying, "The child has not awakened."

32When Elisha came into the house,
there was the child, lying dead on his
bed. 33He went in therefore, shut the
door behind the two of them, and
prayed to the LORD. 34And he went up
and lay on the child, and put his mouth
on his mouth, his eyes on his eyes, and
his hands on his hands; and he
stretched himself out on the child, and
the flesh of the child became warm.
35He returned and walked back and
forth in the house, and again went up
and stretched himself out on him; then
the child sneezed seven times, and the
child opened his eyes. 36And he called
Gehazi and said, "Call this Shunammite
woman." So he called her. And when
she came in to him, he said, "Pick up
your son." 37So she went in, fell at his

feet, and bowed to the ground; then she
picked up her son and went out.

Elisha Purifies the Pot of Stew

38And Elisha returned to Gilgal, and
there was a famine in the land. Now
the sons of the prophets were sitting before him; and he said to his servant,
"Put on the large pot, and boil stew for
the sons of the prophets." 39So one
went out into the field to gather herbs,
and found a wild vine, and gathered
from it a lapful of wild gourds, and
came and sliced them into the pot of
stew, though they did not know what
they were. 40Then they served it to the
men to eat. Now it happened, as they
were eating the stew, that they cried out
and said, "Man of God, there is death
in the pot!" And they could not eat it.
41So he said, "Then bring some
flour." And he put it into the pot, and
said, "Serve it to the people, that they
may eat." And there was nothing harmful in the pot.

Elisha Feeds One Hundred Men

42Then a man came from Baal Shalisha, and brought the man of God bread
of the firstfruits, twenty loaves of barley
bread, and newly ripened grain in his
knapsack. And he said, "Give it to the
people, that they may eat."

43But his servant said, "What? Shall
I set this before one hundred men?"

He said again, "Give it to the people,
that they may eat; for thus says the
LORD: 'They shall eat and have some
left over.' " 44So he set it before them;
and they ate and had some left over,
according to the word of the LORD.

Naaman's Leprosy Healed

5 Now Naaman, commander of the
army of the king of Syria, was a
great and honorable man in the eyes
of his master, because by him the LORD
had given victory to Syria. He was also
a mighty man of valor, but a leper.
2And the Syrians had gone out on raids,
and had brought back captive a young
girl from the land of Israel. She waited
on Naaman's wife. 3Then she said to
her mistress, "If only my master were
with the prophet who is in Samaria! For
he would heal him of his leprosy."
4And Naaman went in and told his

master, saying, "Thus and thus said the girl who *is* from the land of Israel."

5Then the king of Syria said, "Go now, and I will send a letter to the king of Israel."

So he departed and took with him ten talents of silver, six thousand *shekels* of gold, and ten changes of clothing. 6Then he brought the letter to the king of Israel, which said,

Now be advised, when this letter comes to you, that I have sent Naaman my servant to you, that you may heal him of his leprosy.

7And it happened, when the king of Israel read the letter, that he tore his clothes and said, "*Am* I God, to kill and make alive, that this man sends a man to me to heal him of his leprosy? Therefore please consider, and see how he seeks a quarrel with me."

8So it was, when Elisha the man of God heard that the king of Israel had torn his clothes, that he sent to the king, saying, "Why have you torn your clothes? Please let him come to me, and he shall know that there is a prophet in Israel."

9Then Naaman went with his horses and chariot, and he stood at the door of Elisha's house. 10And Elisha sent a messenger to him, saying, "Go and wash in the Jordan seven times, and your flesh shall be restored to you, and *you shall* be clean." 11But Naaman became furious, and went away and said, "Indeed, I said to myself, 'He will surely come out *to me*, and stand and call on the name of the LORD his God, and wave his hand over the place, and heal the leprosy.' 12*Are* not the Abanah and the Pharpar, the rivers of Damascus, better than all the waters of Israel? Could I not wash in them and be clean?" So he turned and went away in a rage. 13And his servants came near and spoke to him, and said, "My father, *if* the prophet had told you *to do* something great, would you not have done *it*? How much more then, when he says to you, 'Wash, and be clean'?" 14So he went down and dipped seven times in the Jordan, according to the saying of the man of God; and his flesh was restored like the flesh of a little child, and he was clean.

15And he returned to the man of God, he and all his aides, and came and stood before him; and he said, "Indeed, now I know that *there is* no God in all the earth, except in Israel; now therefore, please take a gift from your servant."

16But he said, "*As* the LORD lives, before whom I stand, I will receive nothing." And he urged him to take *it*, but he refused.

17So Naaman said, "Then, if not, please let your servant be given two mule-loads of earth; for your servant will no longer offer either burnt offering or sacrifice to other gods, but to the LORD. 18Yet in this thing may the LORD pardon your servant: when my master goes into the temple of Rimmon to worship there, and he leans on my hand, and I bow down in the temple of Rimmon—when I bow down in the temple of Rimmon, may the LORD please pardon your servant in this thing."

19Then he said to him, "Go in peace." So he departed from him a short distance.

Gehazi's Greed

20But Gehazi, the servant of Elisha the man of God, said, "Look, my master has spared Naaman this Syrian, while not receiving from his hands what he brought; but *as* the LORD lives, I will run after him and take something from him." 21So Gehazi pursued Naaman. When Naaman saw *him* running after him, he got down from the chariot to meet him, and said, "*Is* all well?"

22And he said, "All *is* well. My master has sent me, saying, 'Indeed, just now two young men of the sons of the prophets have come to me from the mountains of Ephraim. Please give them a talent of silver and two changes of garments.' "

23So Naaman said, "Please, take two talents." And he urged him, and bound two talents of silver in two bags, with two changes of garments, and handed *them* to two of his servants; and they carried *them* on ahead of him. 24When he came to the citadel, he took *them* from their hand, and stored *them* away in the house; then he let the men go, and they departed. 25Now he went in and stood before his master. Elisha said to him, "Where *did you go*, Gehazi?"

And he said, "Your servant did not go anywhere."

26Then he said to him, "Did not my heart go *with you* when the man turned back from his chariot to meet you? *Is it* time to receive money and to receive clothing, olive groves and vineyards, sheep and oxen, male and female servants? 27Therefore the leprosy of Naaman shall cling to you and your descendants forever." And he went out from his presence leprous, *as white* as snow.

The Floating Ax Head

6 And the sons of the prophets said to Elisha, "See now, the place where we dwell with you is too small for us. 2Please, let us go to the Jordan, and let every man take a beam from there, and let us make there a place where we may dwell."

So he answered, "Go."

3Then one said, "Please consent to go with your servants."

And he answered, "I will go." 4So he went with them. And when they came to the Jordan, they cut down trees. 5But as one was cutting down a tree, the iron *ax head* fell into the water; and he cried out and said, "Alas, master! For it was borrowed."

6So the man of God said, "Where did it fall?" And he showed him the place. So he cut off a stick, and threw *it* in there; and he made the iron float. 7Therefore he said, "Pick *it* up for yourself." So he reached out his hand and took it.

The Blinded Syrians Captured

8Now the king of Syria was making war against Israel; and he consulted with his servants, saying, "My camp *will be* in such and such a place." 9And the man of God sent to the king of Israel, saying, "Beware that you do not pass this place, for the Syrians are coming down there." 10Then the king of Israel sent *someone* to the place of which the man of God had told him. Thus he warned him, and he was watchful there, not just once or twice.

11Therefore the heart of the king of Syria was greatly troubled by this thing; and he called his servants and said to them, "Will you not show me which of us *is* for the king of Israel?"

12And one of his servants said, "None, my lord, O king; but Elisha, the prophet who *is* in Israel, tells the king of Israel the words that you speak in your bedroom."

13So he said, "Go and see where he *is,* that I may send and get him."

And it was told him, saying, "Surely *he is* in Dothan."

14Therefore he sent horses and chariots and a great army there, and they came by night and surrounded the city. 15And when the servant of the man of God arose early and went out, there was an army, surrounding the city with horses and chariots. And his servant said to him, "Alas, my master! What shall we do?"

16So he answered, "Do not fear, for those who *are* with us *are* more than those who *are* with them." 17And Elisha prayed, and said, "LORD, I pray, open his eyes that he may see." Then the LORD opened the eyes of the young man, and he saw. And behold, the mountain *was* full of horses and chariots of fire all around Elisha. 18So when *the Syrians* came down to him, Elisha prayed to the LORD, and said, "Strike this people, I pray, with blindness." And He struck them with blindness according to the word of Elisha.

19Now Elisha said to them, "This *is* not the way, nor *is* this the city. Follow me, and I will bring you to the man whom you seek." But he led them to Samaria.

20So it was, when they had come to Samaria, that Elisha said, "LORD, open the eyes of these *men,* that they may see." And the LORD opened their eyes, and they saw; and there *they were,* inside Samaria!

21Now when the king of Israel saw them, he said to Elisha, "My father, shall I kill *them?* Shall I kill *them?*"

22But he answered, "You shall not kill *them.* Would you kill those whom you have taken captive with your sword and your bow? Set food and water before them, that they may eat and drink and go to their master." 23Then he prepared a great feast for them; and after they ate and drank, he sent them away and they went to their master. So the bands of Syrian *raiders* came no more into the land of Israel.

Syria Besieges Samaria in Famine

24And it happened after this that Ben-Hadad king of Syria gathered all his army, and went up and besieged Samaria. 25And there was a great famine in Samaria; and indeed they besieged it until a donkey's head was *sold* for eighty *shekels* of silver, and one-fourth of a kab of dove droppings for five *shekels* of silver.

26Then, as the king of Israel was passing by on the wall, a woman cried out to him, saying, "Help, my lord, O king!"

27And he said, "If the LORD does not help you, where can I find help for you? From the threshing floor or from the winepress?" 28Then the king said to her, "What is troubling you?"

And she answered, "This woman said to me, 'Give your son, that we may eat him today, and we will eat my son tomorrow.' 29So we boiled my son, and ate him. And I said to her on the next day, 'Give your son, that we may eat him'; but she has hidden her son."

30Now it happened, when the king heard the words of the woman, that he tore his clothes; and as he passed by on the wall, the people looked, and there underneath *he had* sackcloth on his body. 31Then he said, "God do so to me and more also, if the head of Elisha the son of Shaphat remains on him today!"

32But Elisha was sitting in his house, and the elders were sitting with him. And *the king* sent a man ahead of him, but before the messenger came to him, he said to the elders, "Do you see how this son of a murderer has sent someone to take away my head? Look, when the messenger comes, shut the door, and hold him fast at the door. *Is* not the sound of his master's feet behind him?" 33And while he was still talking with them, there was the messenger, coming down to him; and then *the king* said, "Surely this calamity *is* from the LORD; why should I wait for the LORD any longer?"

7 Then Elisha said, "Hear the word of the LORD. Thus says the LORD: 'Tomorrow about this time a seah of fine flour *shall be sold* for a shekel, and two seahs of barley for a shekel, at the gate of Samaria.'"

2So an officer on whose hand the king leaned answered the man of God and said, "Look, *if* the LORD would make windows in heaven, could this thing be?"

And he said, "In fact, you shall see *it* with your eyes, but you shall not eat of it."

The Syrians Flee

3Now there were four leprous men at the entrance of the gate; and they said to one another, "Why are we sitting here until we die? 4If we say, 'We will enter the city,' the famine *is* in the city, and we shall die there. And if we sit here, we die also. Now therefore, come, let us surrender to the army of the Syrians. If they keep us alive, we shall live; and if they kill us, we shall only die." 5And they rose at twilight to go to the camp of the Syrians; and when they had come to the outskirts of the Syrian camp, to their surprise no one *was* there. 6For the LORD had caused the army of the Syrians to hear the noise of chariots and the noise of horses—the noise of a great army; so they said to one another, "Look, the king of Israel has hired against us the kings of the Hittites and the kings of the Egyptians to attack us!" 7Therefore they arose and fled at twilight, and left the camp intact—their tents, their horses, and their donkeys—and they fled for their lives. 8And when these lepers came to the outskirts of the camp, they went into one tent and ate and drank, and carried from it silver and gold and clothing, and went and hid *them;* then they came back and entered another tent, and carried *some* from there *also,* and went and hid *it.*

9Then they said to one another, "We are not doing right. This day *is* a day of good news, and we remain silent. If we wait until morning light, some punishment will come upon us. Now therefore, come, let us go and tell the king's household." 10So they went and called to the gatekeepers of the city, and told them, saying, "We went to the Syrian camp, and surprisingly no one *was* there, not a human sound—only horses and donkeys tied, and the tents intact." 11And the gatekeepers called out, and they told *it* to the king's household inside.

12So the king arose in the night and said to his servants, "Let me now tell you what the Syrians have done to us. They know that we *are* hungry; therefore they have gone out of the camp to hide themselves in the field, saying, 'When they come out of the city, we shall catch them alive, and get into the city.' "

13And one of his servants answered and said, "Please, let several *men* take five of the remaining horses which are left in the city. Look, they *may either become* like all the multitude of Israel that are left in it; or indeed, *I say*, they *may become* like all the multitude of Israel left from those who are consumed; so let us send them and see." 14Therefore they took two chariots with horses; and the king sent them in the direction of the Syrian army, saying, "Go and see." 15And they went after them to the Jordan; and indeed all the road *was* full of garments and weapons which the Syrians had thrown away in their haste. So the messengers returned and told the king. 16Then the people went out and plundered the tents of the Syrians. So a seah of fine flour was *sold* for a shekel, and two seahs of barley for a shekel, according to the word of the LORD.

17Now the king had appointed the officer on whose hand he leaned to have charge of the gate. But the people trampled him in the gate, and he died, just as the man of God had said, who spoke when the king came down to him. 18So it happened just as the man of God had spoken to the king, saying, "Two seahs of barley for a shekel, and a seah of fine flour for a shekel, shall be *sold* tomorrow about this time in the gate of Samaria."

19Then that officer had answered the man of God and said, "Now look, *if* the LORD would make windows in heaven, could such a thing be?"

And he had said, "In fact, you shall see *it* with your eyes, but you shall not eat of it." 20And so it happened to him,

for the people trampled him in the gate, and he died.

The King Restores the Shunammite's Land

8 Then Elisha spoke to the woman whose son he had restored to life, saying, "Arise and go, you and your household, and stay wherever you can; for the LORD has called for a famine, and furthermore, it will come upon the land for seven years." 2So the woman arose and did according to the saying of the man of God, and she went with her household and dwelt in the land of the Philistines seven years.

3It came to pass, at the end of seven years, that the woman returned from the land of the Philistines; and she went to make an appeal to the king for her house and for her land. 4Then the king talked with Gehazi, the servant of the man of God, saying, "Tell me, please, all the great things Elisha has done." 5Now it happened, as he was telling the king how he had restored the dead to life, that there was the woman whose son he had restored to life, appealing to the king for her house and for her land. And Gehazi said, "My lord, O king, this *is* the woman, and this *is* her son whom Elisha restored to life." 6And when the king asked the woman, she told him.

So the king appointed a certain officer for her, saying, "Restore all that *was* hers, and all the proceeds of the field from the day that she left the land until now."

Death of Ben-Hadad

7Then Elisha went to Damascus, and Ben-Hadad king of Syria was sick; and it was told him, saying, "The man of God has come here." 8And the king said to Hazael, "Take a present in your hand, and go to meet the man of God, and inquire of the LORD by him, saying, 'Shall I recover from this disease?' " 9So Hazael went to meet him and took a present with him, of every good thing of Damascus, forty camel-loads; and he came and stood before him, and said, "Your son Ben-Hadad king of Syria has sent me to you, saying, 'Shall I recover from this disease?' "

10And Elisha said to him, "Go, say

to him, 'You shall certainly recover.' However the LORD has shown me that he will really die.'' 11Then he set his countenance in a stare until he was ashamed; and the man of God wept. 12And Hazael said, "Why is my lord weeping?''

He answered, "Because I know the evil that you will do to the children of Israel: Their strongholds you will set on fire, and their young men you will kill with the sword; and you will dash their children, and rip open their women with child.''

13So Hazael said, "But what *is* your servant—a dog, that he should do this gross thing?''

And Elisha answered, "The LORD has shown me that you *will become* king over Syria.''

14Then he departed from Elisha, and came to his master, who said to him, "What did Elisha say to you?'' And he answered, "He told me you would surely recover.'' 15But it happened on the next day that he took a thick cloth and dipped *it* in water, and spread *it* over his face so that he died; and Hazael reigned in his place.

Jehoram Reigns in Judah

16Now in the fifth year of Joram the son of Ahab, king of Israel, Jehoshaphat *having been* king of Judah, Jehoram the son of Jehoshaphat began to reign as king of Judah. 17He was thirty-two years old when he became king, and he reigned eight years in Jerusalem. 18And he walked in the way of the kings of Israel, just as the house of Ahab had done, for the daughter of Ahab was his wife; and he did evil in the sight of the LORD. 19Yet the LORD would not destroy Judah, for the sake of his servant David, as He promised him to give a lamp to him *and* his sons forever.

20In his days Edom revolted against Judah's authority, and made a king over themselves. 21So Joram went to Zair, and all his chariots with him. Then he rose by night and attacked the Edomites who had surrounded him and the captains of the chariots; and the troops fled to their tents. 22Thus Edom has been in revolt against Judah's au-

thority to this day. And Libnah revolted at that time.

23Now the rest of the acts of Joram, and all that he did, *are* they not written in the book of the chronicles of the kings of Judah? 24So Joram rested with his fathers, and was buried with his fathers in the City of David. Then Ahaziah his son reigned in his place.

Ahaziah Reigns in Judah

25In the twelfth year of Joram the son of Ahab, king of Israel, Ahaziah the son of Jehoram, king of Judah, began to reign. 26Ahaziah *was* twenty-two years old when he became king, and he reigned one year in Jerusalem. His mother's name *was* Athaliah the granddaughter of Omri, king of Israel. 27And he walked in the way of the house of Ahab, and did evil in the sight of the LORD, like the house of Ahab, for he *was* the son-in-law of the house of Ahab.

28Now he went with Joram the son of Ahab to war against Hazael king of Syria at Ramoth Gilead; and the Syrians wounded Joram. 29Then King Joram went back to Jezreel to recover from the wounds which the Syrians had inflicted on him at Ramah, when he fought against Hazael king of Syria. And Ahaziah the son of Jehoram, king of Judah, went down to see Joram the son of Ahab in Jezreel, because he was sick.

Jehu Anointed King of Israel

9 And Elisha the prophet called one of the sons of the prophets, and said to him, "Get yourself ready, take this flask of oil in your hand, and go to Ramoth Gilead. 2Now when you arrive at that place, look there for Jehu the son of Jehoshaphat, the son of Nimshi, and go in and make him rise up from among his associates, and take him to an inner room. 3Then take the flask of oil, and pour *it* on his head, and say, 'Thus says the LORD: "I have anointed you king over Israel." ' Then open the door and flee, and do not delay.''

4So the young man, the servant of the prophet, went to Ramoth Gilead. 5And when he arrived, there *were* the captains of the army sitting; and he said, "I have a message for you, Commander."

Jehu said, "For which *one* of us?"

And he said, "For you, Commander." 6Then he arose and went into the house. And he poured the oil on his head, and said to him, "Thus says the LORD God of Israel: 'I have anointed you king over the people of the LORD, over Israel. 7You shall strike down the house of Ahab your master, that I may avenge the blood of My servants the prophets, and the blood of all the servants of the LORD, at the hand of Jezebel. 8For the whole house of Ahab shall perish; and I will cut off from Ahab all the males in Israel, both bond and free. 9So I will make the house of Ahab like the house of Jeroboam the son of Nebat, and like the house of Baasha the son of Ahijah. 10The dogs shall eat Jezebel on the plot *of ground* at Jezreel, and *there shall be* none to bury *her.*' " And he opened the door and fled.

11Then Jehu came out to the servants of his master, and *one* said to him, "*Is* all well? Why did this madman come to you?"

And he said to them, "You know the man and his babble."

12And they said, "A lie! Tell us now."

So he said, "Thus and thus he spoke to me, saying, 'Thus says the LORD: "I have anointed you king over Israel." ' "

13Then each man hastened to take his garment and put *it* under him on the top of the steps; and they blew trumpets, saying, "Jehu is king!"

Joram of Israel Killed

14So Jehu the son of Jehoshaphat, the son of Nimshi, conspired against Joram. (Now Joram had been defending Ramoth Gilead, he and all Israel, against Hazael king of Syria. 15But King Joram had returned to Jezreel to recover from the wounds which the Syrians had inflicted on him when he fought with Hazael king of Syria.) And Jehu said, "If you are so minded, let no one leave *or* escape from the city to go and tell *it* in Jezreel." 16So Jehu rode in a chariot and went to Jezreel, for Joram was laid up there; and Ahaziah king of Judah had come down to see Joram.

17Now a watchman stood on the tower in Jezreel, and he saw the company of Jehu as he came, and said, "I see a company of men."

And Joram said, "Get a horseman and send him to meet them, and let him say, '*Is it* peace?' "

18So the horseman went to meet him, and said, "Thus says the king: '*Is it* peace?' "

And Jehu said, "What have you to do with peace? Turn around and follow me."

So the watchman reported, saying, "The messenger went to them, but is not coming back."

19Then he sent out a second horseman who came to them, and said, "Thus says the king: '*Is it* peace?' "

And Jehu answered, "What have you to do with peace? Turn around and follow me."

20So the watchman reported, saying, "He went up to them and is not coming back; and the driving *is* like the driving of Jehu the son of Nimshi, for he drives furiously!"

21Then Joram said, "Make ready." And his chariot was made ready. Then Joram king of Israel and Ahaziah king of Judah went out, each in his chariot; and they went out to meet Jehu, and met him on the property of Naboth the Jezreelite. 22Now it happened, when Joram saw Jehu, that he said, "*Is it* peace, Jehu?"

So he answered, "What peace, as long as the harlotries of your mother Jezebel and her witchcraft *are so* many?"

23Then Joram turned around and fled, and said to Ahaziah, "Treachery, Ahaziah!" 24Now Jehu drew his bow with full strength and shot Jehoram between his arms; and the arrow came out at his heart, and he sank down in his chariot. 25Then *Jehu* said to Bidkar his captain, "Pick *him* up, *and* throw him into the tract of the field of Naboth the Jezreelite; for remember, when you and I were riding together behind Ahab his father, that the LORD laid this burden upon him: 26'Surely I saw yesterday the blood of Naboth and the blood of his sons,' says the LORD, 'and I will repay you in this plot,' says the LORD. Now therefore, take *and* throw him on the plot *of ground,* according to the word of the LORD."

Ahaziah of Judah Killed

27But when Ahaziah king of Judah saw *this,* he fled by the road to Beth Haggan. So Jehu pursued him, and said, "Shoot him also in the chariot." *And they shot him* at the Ascent of Gur, which is by Ibleam. Then he fled to Megiddo, and died there. 28And his servants carried him in the chariot to Jerusalem, and buried him in his tomb with his fathers in the City of David. 29In the eleventh year of Joram the son of Ahab, Ahaziah had become king over Judah.

Jezebel's Violent Death

30Now when Jehu had come to Jezreel, Jezebel heard *of it;* and she put paint on her eyes and adorned her head, and looked through a window. 31Then, as Jehu entered at the gate, she said, "*Is it* peace, Zimri, murderer of your master?"

32And he looked up at the window, and said, "Who *is* on my side? Who?" So two *or* three eunuchs looked out at him. 33Then he said, "Throw her down." So they threw her down, and *some* of her blood spattered on the wall and on the horses; and he trampled her underfoot. 34And when he had gone in, he ate and drank. Then he said, "Go now, see to this accursed *woman,* and bury her, for she was a king's daughter." 35So they went to bury her, but they found no more of her than the skull and the feet and the palms of *her* hands. 36Therefore they came back and told him. And he said, "This *is* the word of the LORD, which He spoke by His servant Elijah the Tishbite, saying, 'On the plot *of ground* at Jezreel dogs shall eat the flesh of Jezebel;[c] 37and the corpse of Jezebel shall be as refuse on the surface of the field, in the plot at Jezreel, so that they shall not say, "Here *lies* Jezebel." ' "

Ahab's Seventy Sons Killed

10 Now Ahab had seventy sons in Samaria. And Jehu wrote and sent letters to Samaria, to the rulers of Jezreel, to the elders, and to those who reared Ahab's *sons,* saying:
2   Now as soon as this letter comes to you, since your master's sons *are* with you, and you have chariots and horses, a fortified city also, and weapons, 3choose the best qualified of your master's sons, set *him* on his father's throne, and fight for your master's house.

4But they were exceedingly afraid, and said, "Look, two kings could not stand up to him; how then can we stand?" 5And he who *was* in charge of the house, and he who *was* in charge of the city, the elders also, and those who reared *the sons,* sent to Jehu, saying, "We *are* your servants, we will do all you tell us; but we will not make anyone king. Do *what is* good in your sight." 6Then he wrote a second letter to them, saying:

If you *are* for me and will obey my voice, take the heads of the men, your master's sons, and come to me at Jezreel by this time tomorrow.

Now the king's sons, seventy persons, *were* with the great men of the city, *who* were rearing them. 7So it was, when the letter came to them, that they took the king's sons and slaughtered seventy persons, put their heads in baskets and sent *them* to him at Jezreel.

8Then a messenger came and told him, saying, "They have brought the heads of the king's sons."

And he said, "Lay them in two heaps at the entrance of the gate until morning."

9So it was, in the morning, that he went out and stood, and said to all the people, "You *are* righteous. Indeed I conspired against my master and killed him; but who killed all these? 10Know now that nothing shall fall to the earth of the word of the LORD which the LORD spoke concerning the house of Ahab; for the LORD has done what He spoke by His servant Elijah." 11So Jehu killed all who remained of the house of Ahab in Jezreel, and all his great men and his close acquaintances and his priests, until he left him none remaining.

---

c Compare 1 Kings 21.23

Ahaziah's Forty-two Brothers Killed

12And he arose and departed and went to Samaria. On the way, at Beth Eked of the Shepherds, 13Jehu met with the brothers of Ahaziah king of Judah, and said, "Who *are* you?"

So they answered, "We *are* the brothers of Ahaziah; we have come down to greet the sons of the king and the sons of the queen mother."

14And he said, "Take them alive!" So they took them alive, and killed them at the well of Beth Eked, forty-two men; and he left none of them.

The Rest of Ahab's Family Killed

15Now when he departed from there, he met Jehonadab the son of Rechab, *coming* to meet him; and he greeted him and said to him, "Is your heart right, as my heart *is* toward your heart?"

And Jehonadab answered, "It is."

Jehu said, "If it is, give *me* your hand." So he gave *him* his hand, and he took him up to him into the chariot. 16Then he said, "Come with me, and see my zeal for the Lord." So they had him ride in his chariot. 17And when he came to Samaria, he killed all who remained to Ahab in Samaria, till he had destroyed them, according to the word of the Lord which He spoke to Elijah.

Worshipers of Baal Killed

18Then Jehu gathered all the people together, and said to them, "Ahab served Baal a little, Jehu will serve him much. 19Now therefore, call to me all the prophets of Baal, all his servants, and all his priests. Let no one be missing, for I have a great sacrifice for Baal. Whoever is missing shall not live." But Jehu acted deceptively, with the intent of destroying the worshipers of Baal. 20And Jehu said, "Proclaim a solemn assembly for Baal." So they proclaimed it. 21Then Jehu sent throughout all Israel; and all the worshipers of Baal came, so that there was not a man left who did not come. So they came into the temple of Baal, and the temple of Baal was full from one end to the other. 22And he said to the one in charge of the wardrobe, "Bring out vestments for all the worshipers of Baal." So he brought out vestments for them. 23Then Jehu and Jehonadab the son of Rechab went into the temple of Baal, and said to the worshipers of Baal, "Search and see that no servants of the Lord are here with you, but only the worshipers of Baal." 24So they went in to offer sacrifices and burnt offerings. Now Jehu had appointed for himself eighty men on the outside, and had said, "If any of the men whom I have brought into your hands escapes, *whoever lets him escape, it shall be* his life for the life of the other."

25Now it happened, as soon as he had made an end of offering the burnt offering, that Jehu said to the guard and to the captains, "Go in *and* kill them; let no one come out!" And they killed them with the edge of the sword; then the guards and the officers threw *them* out, and went into the inner room of the temple of Baal. 26And they brought the *sacred* pillars out of the temple of Baal and burned them. 27Then they broke down the *sacred* pillar of Baal, and tore down the temple of Baal and made it a refuse dump to this day. 28Thus Jehu destroyed Baal from Israel.

29However Jehu did not turn away from the sins of Jeroboam the son of Nebat, who had made Israel sin, *that is*, from the golden calves that *were* at Bethel and Dan. 30And the Lord said to Jehu, "Because you have done well in doing *what is* right in My sight, *and* have done to the house of Ahab all that *was* in My heart, your sons shall sit on the throne of Israel to the fourth *generation*." 31But Jehu took no heed to walk in the law of the Lord God of Israel with all his heart; for he did not depart from the sins of Jeroboam, who had made Israel sin.

Death of Jehu

32In those days the Lord began to cut off *parts* of Israel; and Hazael conquered them in all the territory of Israel 33from the Jordan eastward: all the land of Gilead—Gad, Reuben, and Manasseh—from Aroer, which *is* by the River Arnon, including Gilead and Bashan.

34Now the rest of the acts of Jehu, all that he did, and all his might, *are* they not written in the book of the chronicles of the kings of Israel? 35So Jehu rested with his fathers, and they buried him in Samaria. Then Jehoahaz his son reigned in his place. 36And the period that Jehu reigned over Israel in Samaria *was* twenty-eight years.

Athaliah Reigns in Judah

11 When Athaliah the mother of Ahaziah saw that her son was dead, she arose and destroyed all the royal heirs. 2But Jehosheba, the daughter of King Joram, sister of Ahaziah, took Joash the son of Ahaziah, and stole him away from among the king's sons *who were* being murdered; and they hid him and his nurse in the bedroom, from Athaliah, so that he was not killed. 3So he was hidden with her in the house of the LORD for six years, while Athaliah reigned over the land.

Joash Crowned King of Judah

4In the seventh year Jehoiada sent and brought the captains of hundreds—of the bodyguards and the escorts—and brought them into the house of the LORD to him. And he made a covenant with them and took an oath from them in the house of the LORD, and showed them the king's son. 5Then he commanded them, saying, "This *is* what you shall do: One-third of you who come on duty on the Sabbath shall be keeping watch over the king's house, 6one-third *shall be* at the gate of Sur, and one-third at the gate behind the escorts. You shall keep the watch of the house, lest it be broken down. 7The two contingents of you who go off duty on the Sabbath shall keep the watch of the house of the LORD for the king. 8But you shall surround the king on all sides, every man with his weapons in his hand; and whoever comes within range, let him be put to death. You are to be with the king as he goes out and as he comes in."

9So the captains of the hundreds did according to all that Jehoiada the priest commanded. Each of them took his men who were to be on duty on the Sabbath, with those who were going off duty on the Sabbath, and came to Jehoiada the priest. 10And the priest gave the captains of hundreds the spears and shields which *had belonged* to King David, that were in the temple of the LORD. 11Then the escorts stood, every man with his weapons in his hand, all around the king, from the right side of the temple to the left side of the temple, by the altar and the house. 12And he brought out the king's son, put the crown on him, and *gave him* the Testimony;d they made him king and anointed him, and they clapped their hands and said, "Long live the king!"

Death of Athaliah

13Now when Athaliah heard the noise of the escorts *and* the people, she came to the people *in* the temple of the LORD. 14When she looked, there was the king standing by a pillar according to custom; and the leaders and the trumpeters were by the king. All the people of the land were rejoicing and blowing trumpets. So Athaliah tore her clothes and cried out, "Treason! Treason!"

15And Jehoiada the priest commanded the captains of the hundreds, the officers of the army, and said to them, "Take her outside under guard, and slay with the sword whoever follows her." For the priest had said, "Do not let her be killed in the house of the LORD." 16So they seized her; and she went by way of the horses' entrance *into* the king's house, and there she was killed.

17Then Jehoiada made a covenant between the LORD, the king, and the people, that they should be the LORD's people, and *also* between the king and the people. 18And all the people of the land went to the temple of Baal, and tore it down. They thoroughly broke in pieces its altars and images, and killed Mattan the priest of Baal before the altars. And the priest appointed officers over the house of the LORD. 19Then he took the captains of hundreds, the bodyguards, the escorts, and all the people of the land; and they brought the king down from the house of the LORD, and went by way of the gate of the escorts to the king's house. Then he sat on the throne

d That is, the Law (compare Exodus 25.16, 21 and Deuteronomy 31.9) of the kings. 20So all the people of the land rejoiced; and the city was quiet, for they had slain Athaliah with the sword in the king's house. 21Jehoash was seven years old when he became king.

Jehoash Repairs the Temple

12 In the seventh year of Jehu, Jehoash became king, and he reigned forty years in Jerusalem. His mother's name was Zibiah of Beersheba. 2Jehoash did what was right in the sight of the LORD all the days in which Jehoiada the priest instructed him. 3But the high places were not taken away; the people still sacrificed and burned incense on the high places.

4And Jehoash said to the priests, "All the money of the dedicated gifts that are brought into the house of the LORD—each man's census money, each man's assessment money*e*—and all the money that a man purposes in his heart to bring into the house of the LORD, 5let the priests take it themselves, each from his constituency; and let them repair the damages of the temple, wherever any dilapidation is found."

6Now it was so, by the twenty-third year of King Jehoash, that the priests had not repaired the damages of the temple. 7So King Jehoash called Jehoiada the priest and the other priests, and said to them, "Why have you not repaired the damages of the temple? Now therefore, do not take more money from your constituency, but deliver it for repairing the damages of the temple." 8And the priests agreed that they would neither receive more money from the people, nor repair the damages of the temple.

9Then Jehoiada the priest took a chest, bored a hole in its lid, and set it beside the altar, on the right side as one comes into the house of the LORD; and the priests who kept the door put there all the money brought into the house of the LORD. 10So it was, whenever they saw that there was much money in the chest, that the king's scribe and the high priest came up and put it in bags, and counted the money that was found in the house of the LORD. 11Then they gave the money, which had been apportioned, into the hands of those who did the work, who had the oversight of the house of the LORD; and they paid it out to the carpenters and builders who worked on the house of the LORD, 12and to masons and stonecutters, and for buying timber and hewn stone, to repair the damage of the house of the LORD, and for all that was paid out to repair the temple. 13However there were not made for the house of the LORD basins of silver, trimmers, sprinkling-bowls, trumpets, any articles of gold or articles of silver, from the money brought into the house of the LORD. 14But they gave that to the workmen, and they repaired the house of the LORD with it. 15Moreover they did not require an account from the men into whose hand they delivered the money to be paid to workmen, for they dealt faithfully. 16The money from the trespass offerings and the money from the sin offerings was not brought into the house of the LORD. It belonged to the priests.

Hazael Threatens Jerusalem

17Hazael king of Syria went up and fought against Gath, and took it; then Hazael set his face to go up to Jerusalem. 18And Jehoash king of Judah took all the sacred things that his fathers, Jehoshaphat and Jehoram and Ahaziah, kings of Judah, had dedicated, and his own sacred things, and all the gold found in the treasuries of the house of the LORD and in the king's house, and sent them to Hazael king of Syria. Then he went away from Jerusalem.

Death of Joash

19Now the rest of the acts of Joash, and all that he did, are they not written in the book of the chronicles of the kings of Judah?

20And his servants arose and formed a conspiracy, and killed Joash in the house of the Millo, which goes down to Silla. 21For Jozachar the son of Shimeath and Jehozabad the son of Shomer, his servants, struck him. So he died, and they buried him with his

---

e Compare Leviticus 27.2ff

fathers in the City of David. Then Amaziah his son reigned in his place.

Jehoahaz Reigns in Israel

13 In the twenty-third year of Joash the son of Ahaziah, king of Judah, Jehoahaz the son of Jehu became king over Israel in Samaria, *and reigned* seventeen years. 2And he did evil in the sight of the LORD, and followed the sins of Jeroboam the son of Nebat, who had made Israel sin. He did not depart from them.

3Then the anger of the LORD was aroused against Israel, and He delivered them into the hand of Hazael king of Syria, and into the hand of Ben-Hadad the son of Hazael, all *their* days. 4So Jehoahaz pleaded with the LORD, and the LORD listened to him; for He saw the oppression of Israel, because the king of Syria oppressed them. 5Then the LORD gave Israel a deliverer, so that they escaped from under the hand of the Syrians; and the children of Israel dwelt in their tents as before. 6Nevertheless they did not depart from the sins of the house of Jeroboam, who had made Israel sin, *but* walked in them; and the wooden image*ƒ* also remained in Samaria. 7For He left of the army of Jehoahaz only fifty horsemen, ten chariots, and ten thousand foot soldiers; for the king of Syria had destroyed them and made them like the dust at threshing.

8Now the rest of the acts of Jehoahaz, all that he did, and his might, *are* they not written in the book of the chronicles of the kings of Israel? 9So Jehoahaz rested with his fathers, and they buried him in Samaria. Then Joash his son reigned in his place.

Jehoash Reigns in Israel

10In the thirty-seventh year of Joash king of Judah, Jehoash the son of Jehoahaz became king over Israel in Samaria, *and reigned* sixteen years. 11And he did evil in the sight of the LORD. He did not depart from all the sins of Jeroboam the son of Nebat, who made Israel sin, *but* walked in them.

12Now the rest of the acts of Joash, all that he did, and his might with which

he fought against Amaziah king of Judah, *are* they not written in the book of the chronicles of the kings of Israel? 13So Joash rested with his fathers. Then Jeroboam sat on his throne. And Joash was buried in Samaria with the kings of Israel.

Death of Elisha

14Elisha had become sick with the illness of which he would die. Then Joash the king of Israel came down to him, and wept over his face, and said, "O my father, my father, the chariots of Israel and their horsemen!"

15And Elisha said to him, "Take a bow and some arrows." So he took himself a bow and some arrows. 16Then he said to the king of Israel, "Put your hand on the bow." So he put his hand *on it,* and Elisha put his hands on the king's hands. 17And he said, "Open the east window"; and he opened *it.* Then Elisha said, "Shoot"; and he shot. And he said, "The arrow of the LORD's deliverance and the arrow of deliverance from Syria; for you must strike the Syrians at Aphek till you have destroyed *them.*" 18Then he said, "Take the arrows"; so he took *them.* And he said to the king of Israel, "Strike the ground"; so he struck three times, and stopped. 19And the man of God was angry with him, and said, "You should have struck five or six times; then you would have struck Syria till you had destroyed *it!* But now you will strike Syria *only* three times."

20Then Elisha died, and they buried him. And the *raiding* bands from Moab invaded the land in the spring of the year. 21So it was, as they were burying a man, that suddenly they spied a band *of raiders;* and they put the man in the tomb of Elisha; and when the man was let down and touched the bones of Elisha, he revived and stood on his feet.

Israel Recaptures Cities from Syria

22And Hazael king of Syria oppressed Israel all the days of Jehoahaz. 23But the LORD was gracious to them, had compassion on them, and regarded them, because of His covenant with Abraham, Isaac, and Jacob, and would

ƒ A Canaanite goddess

not yet destroy them or cast them from His presence.

24Now Hazael king of Syria died. Then Ben-Hadad his son reigned in his place. 25And Jehoash the son of Jehoahaz recaptured from the hand of Ben-Hadad, the son of Hazael, the cities which he had taken out of the hand of Jehoahaz his father by war. Three times Joash defeated him and recaptured the cities of Israel.

Amaziah Reigns in Judah

14 In the second year of Joash the son of Jehoahaz, king of Israel, Amaziah the son of Joash, king of Judah, became king. 2He was twenty-five years old when he became king, and he reigned twenty-nine years in Jerusalem. His mother's name was Jehoaddan of Jerusalem. 3And he did *what was* right in the sight of the LORD, yet not like his father David; he did everything as his father Joash had done. 4However the high places were not taken away, and the people still sacrificed and burned incense on the high places.

5Now it happened, as soon as the kingdom was established in his hand, that he executed his servants who had murdered his father the king. 6But the children of the murderers he did not execute, according to what is written in the Book of the Law of Moses, in which the LORD commanded, saying, "Fathers shall not be put to death for their children, nor shall children be put to death for their fathers; but a person shall be put to death for his own sin."[g]

7He killed ten thousand Edomites in the Valley of Salt, and took Sela by war, and called its name Joktheel to this day.

8Then Amaziah sent messengers to Jehoash the son of Jehoahaz, the son of Jehu, king of Israel, saying, "Come, let us face one another *in battle.*" 9And Jehoash king of Israel sent to Amaziah king of Judah, saying, "The thistle that *was* in Lebanon sent to the cedar that *was* in Lebanon, saying, 'Give your daughter to my son as wife'; and a wild beast that *was* in Lebanon passed by and trampled the thistle. 10You have indeed defeated Edom, and your heart has lifted you up. Glory *in*

that, and stay at home; for why should you meddle with trouble so that you fall—you and Judah with you?"

11But Amaziah would not heed. Therefore Jehoash king of Israel went out; so he and Amaziah king of Judah faced one another at Beth Shemesh, which *belongs* to Judah. 12And Judah was defeated by Israel, and every man fled to his tent. 13Then Jehoash king of Israel captured Amaziah king of Judah, the son of Jehoash, the son of Ahaziah, at Beth Shemesh; and he went to Jerusalem; and broke down the wall of Jerusalem from the Gate of Ephraim to the Corner Gate—four hundred cubits. 14And he took all the gold and silver, all the articles that were found in the house of the LORD and in the treasuries of the king's house, and hostages, and returned to Samaria.

15Now the rest of the acts of Jehoash which he did—his might, and how he fought with Amaziah king of Judah— *are* they not written in the book of the chronicles of the kings of Israel? 16So Jehoash rested with his fathers, and was buried in Samaria with the kings of Israel. Then Jeroboam his son reigned in his place.

17Amaziah the son of Joash, king of Judah, lived fifteen years after the death of Jehoash the son of Jehoahaz, king of Israel. 18Now the rest of the acts of Amaziah, *are* they not written in the book of the chronicles of the kings of Judah? 19And they formed a conspiracy against him in Jerusalem, and he fled to Lachish; but they sent after him to Lachish and killed him there. 20Then they brought him on horses, and he was buried at Jerusalem with his fathers in the City of David.

21And all the people of Judah took Azariah, who *was* sixteen years old, and made him king instead of his father Amaziah. 22He built Elath and restored it to Judah, after the king rested with his fathers.

Jeroboam II Reigns in Israel

23In the fifteenth year of Amaziah the son of Joash, king of Judah, Jeroboam the son of Joash, king of Israel, became king in Samaria, *and reigned* forty-one

---

[g] Deuteronomy 24.16

years. 24And he did evil in the sight of the LORD; he did not depart from all the sins of Jeroboam the son of Nebat, who had made Israel sin. 25He restored the territory of Israel from the entrance of Hamath to the Sea of the Arabah, according to the word of the LORD God of Israel, which He had spoken through His servant Jonah the son of Amittai, the prophet who *was* from Gath He-pher. 26For the LORD saw *that* the affliction of Israel *was* very bitter; and whether bond or free, there was no helper for Israel. 27And the LORD did not say that He would blot out the name of Israel from under heaven; but He saved them by the hand of Jeroboam the son of Joash.

28Now the rest of the acts of Jeroboam, and all that he did—his might, how he made war, and how he recaptured for Israel, from Damascus and Hamath, *what belonged* to Judah—are they not written in the book of the chronicles of the kings of Israel? 29So Jeroboam rested with his fathers, the kings of Israel. Then Zechariah his son reigned in his place.

Azariah Reigns in Judah

15 In the twenty-seventh year of Jeroboam king of Israel, Azariah the son of Amaziah, king of Judah, became king. 2He was sixteen years old when he became king, and he reigned fifty-two years in Jerusalem. His mother's name *was* Jecholiah of Jerusalem. 3And he did *what was* right in the sight of the LORD, according to all that his father Amaziah had done, 4except that the high places were not removed; the people still sacrificed and burned incense on the high places. 5Then the LORD struck the king, so that he was a leper until the day of his death; so he dwelt in an isolated house. And Jotham the king's son *was* over the *royal* house, judging the people of the land.

6Now the rest of the acts of Azariah, and all that he did, *are* they not written in the book of the chronicles of the kings of Judah? 7So Azariah rested with his fathers, and they buried him with his fathers in the City of David.

Then Jotham his son reigned in his place.

Zechariah Reigns in Israel

8In the thirty-eighth year of Azariah king of Judah, Zechariah the son of Jeroboam reigned over Israel in Samaria six months. 9And he did evil in the sight of the LORD, as his fathers had done; he did not depart from the sins of Jeroboam the son of Nebat, who had made Israel sin. 10Then Shallum the son of Jabesh conspired against him, and struck and killed him in front of the people; and he reigned in his place.

11Now the rest of the acts of Zechariah, indeed they *are* written in the book of the chronicles of the kings of Israel.

12This *was* the word of the LORD which He spoke to Jehu, saying, "Your sons shall sit on the throne of Israel to the fourth *generation*."[h] And so it was.

Shallum Reigns in Israel

13Shallum the son of Jabesh became king in the thirty-ninth year of Uzziah king of Judah; and he reigned a full month in Samaria. 14For Menahem the son of Gadi went up from Tirzah, came to Samaria, and struck Shallum the son of Jabesh in Samaria and killed him; and he reigned in his place.

15Now the rest of the acts of Shallum, and the conspiracy which he led, indeed they *are* written in the book of the chronicles of the kings of Israel. 16Then from Tirzah, Menahem attacked Tiphsah, all who *were* there, and its territory. Because they did not surrender, therefore he attacked *it*. All the women there who were with child he ripped open.

Menahem Reigns in Israel

17In the thirty-ninth year of Azariah king of Judah, Menahem the son of Gadi became king over Israel, *and reigned* ten years in Samaria. 18And he did evil in the sight of the LORD; he did not depart all his days from the sins of Jeroboam the son of Nebat, who had made Israel sin. 19Pul[i] king of Assyria came against the land; and Menahem

h 2 Kings 10.30   i That is, Tiglath-Pileser III (compare verse 29) gave Pul a thousand talents of silver, that his hand might be with him to strengthen the kingdom under his control. 20And Menahem exacted the money from Israel, from all the very wealthy, from each man fifty shekels of silver, to give to the king of Assyria. So the king of Assyria turned back, and did not stay there in the land.

21Now the rest of the acts of Menahem, and all that he did, *are* they not written in the book of the chronicles of the kings of Israel? 22So Menahem rested with his fathers. Then Pekahiah his son reigned in his place.

Pekahiah Reigns in Israel

23In the fiftieth year of Azariah king of Judah, Pekahiah the son of Menahem became king over Israel in Samaria, *and reigned* two years. 24And he did evil in the sight of the LORD; he did not depart from the sins of Jeroboam the son of Nebat, who had made Israel sin. 25Then Pekah the son of Remaliah, an officer of his, conspired against him and killed him in Samaria, in the citadel of the king's house, along with Argob and Arieh; and with him were fifty men of Gilead. He killed him and reigned in his place.

26Now the rest of the acts of Pekahiah, and all that he did, indeed they *are* written in the book of the chronicles of the kings of Israel.

Pekah Reigns in Israel

27In the fifty-second year of Azariah king of Judah, Pekah the son of Remaliah became king over Israel in Samaria, *and reigned* twenty years. 28And he did evil in the sight of the LORD; he did not depart from the sins of Jeroboam the son of Nebat, who had made Israel sin. 29In the days of Pekah king of Israel, Tiglath-Pileser king of Assyria came and took Ijon, Abel Beth Maachah, Janoah, Kedesh, Hazor, Gilead, and Galilee, all the land of Naphtali; and he carried them captive to Assyria. 30Then Hoshea the son of Elah led a conspiracy against Pekah the son of Remaliah, and struck and killed him; so he reigned in his place in the twentieth year of Jotham the son of Uzziah.

31Now the rest of the acts of Pekah, and all that he did, indeed they *are* written in the book of the chronicles of the kings of Israel.

Jotham Reigns in Judah

32In the second year of Pekah the son of Remaliah, king of Israel, Jotham the son of Uzziah, king of Judah, began to reign. 33He was twenty-five years old when he became king, and he reigned sixteen years in Jerusalem. His mother's name *was* Jerusha the daughter of Zadok. 34And he did *what was* right in the sight of the LORD; he did according to all that his father Uzziah had done. 35However the high places were not removed; the people still sacrificed and burned incense on the high places. He built the Upper Gate of the house of the LORD.

36Now the rest of the acts of Jotham, and all that he did, *are* they not written in the book of the chronicles of the kings of Judah? 37In those days the LORD began to send Rezin king of Syria and Pekah the son of Remaliah against Judah. 38So Jotham rested with his fathers, and was buried with his fathers in the City of David his father. Then Ahaz his son reigned in his place.

Ahaz Reigns in Judah

16 In the seventeenth year of Pekah the son of Remaliah, Ahaz the son of Jotham, king of Judah, began to reign. 2Ahaz *was* twenty years old when he became king, and he reigned sixteen years in Jerusalem; and he did not do *what was* right in the sight of the LORD his God, as his father David *had done.* 3But he walked in the way of the kings of Israel; indeed he made his son pass through the fire, according to the abominations of the nations whom the LORD had cast out from before the children of Israel. 4And he sacrificed and burned incense on the high places, on the hills, and under every green tree.

5Then Rezin king of Syria and Pekah the son of Remaliah, king of Israel, came up to Jerusalem to *make* war; and they besieged Ahaz but could not overcome *him.* 6At that time Rezin king of Syria captured Elath for Syria, and drove the men of Judah from Elath. Then the Edomites went to Elath, and dwell there to this day.

7So Ahaz sent messengers to Tiglath-Pileser king of Assyria, saying, "I *am* your servant and your son. Come up and save me from the hand of the king of Syria and from the hand of the king of Israel, who rise up against me." 8And Ahaz took the silver and gold that was found in the house of the LORD, and in the treasuries of the king's house, and sent *it as* a present to the king of Assyria. 9So the king of Assyria heeded him; for the king of Assyria went up against Damascus and took it, carried *its people* captive to Kir, and killed Rezin.

10Now King Ahaz went to Damascus to meet Tiglath-Pileser king of Assyria, and saw an altar that *was* at Damascus; and King Ahaz sent to Urijah the priest the design of the altar and its pattern, according to all its workmanship. 11Then Urijah the priest built an altar according to all that King Ahaz had sent from Damascus. So Urijah the priest made *it* before King Ahaz came back from Damascus. 12And when the king came back from Damascus, the king saw the altar; and the king approached the altar and made offerings on it. 13So he burned his burnt offering and his grain offering; and he poured his drink offering and sprinkled the blood of his peace offerings on the altar. 14He also brought the bronze altar which *was* before the LORD, from the front of the temple—from between the *new* altar and the house of the LORD— and put it on the north side of the *new* altar. 15Then King Ahaz commanded Urijah the priest, saying, "On the great *new* altar burn the morning burnt offering, the evening grain offering, the king's burnt sacrifice, and his grain offering, with the burnt offering of all the people of the land, their grain offering, and their drink offerings; and sprinkle on it all the blood of the burnt offering and all the blood of the sacrifice. And the bronze altar shall be for me to inquire *by*." 16Thus did Urijah the priest, according to all that King Ahaz commanded.

17And King Ahaz cut off the panels of the carts, and removed the lavers from them; and he took down the Sea from the bronze oxen that *were* under it, and put it on a pavement of stones.

18Also he removed the Sabbath pavilion which they had built in the temple, and he removed the king's outer entrance from the house of the LORD, on account of the king of Assyria. 19Now the rest of the acts of Ahaz which he did, *are* they not written in the book of the chronicles of the kings of Judah? 20So Ahaz rested with his fathers, and was buried with his fathers in the City of David. Then Hezekiah his son reigned in his place.

Hoshea Reigns in Israel

17 In the twelfth year of Ahaz king of Judah, Hoshea the son of Elah became king of Israel in Samaria, *and he reigned* nine years. 2And he did evil in the sight of the LORD, but not as the kings of Israel who were before him. 3Shalmaneser king of Assyria came up against him; and Hoshea became his vassal, and paid him tribute money. 4And the king of Assyria uncovered a conspiracy by Hoshea; for he had sent messengers to So, king of Egypt, and brought no tribute to the king of Assyria, as *he had done* year by year. Therefore the king of Assyria shut him up, and bound him in prison.

Israel Carried Captive to Assyria

5Now the king of Assyria went throughout all the land, and went up to Samaria and besieged it for three years. 6In the ninth year of Hoshea, the king of Assyria took Samaria and carried Israel away to Assyria, and placed them in Halah and by the Habor, the River of Gozan, and in the cities of the Medes.

7For so it was that the children of Israel had sinned against the LORD their God, who had brought them up out of the land of Egypt, from under the hand of Pharaoh king of Egypt; and they had feared other gods, 8and had walked in the statutes of the nations whom the LORD had cast out from before the children of Israel, and of the kings of Israel, which they had made. 9Also the children of Israel secretly did against the LORD their God things that *were* not right, and they built for themselves high places in all their cities, from watchtower to fortified city. 10They set up for themselves *sacred* pillars and wooden images[j] on every high hill and under every green tree. 11There they burned incense on all the high places, like the nations whom the LORD had carried away before them; and they did wicked things to provoke the LORD to anger, 12for they served idols, of which the LORD had said to them, "You shall not do this thing."

13Yet the LORD testified against Israel and against Judah, by all of His prophets, every seer, saying, "Turn from your evil ways, and keep My commandments and My statutes, according to all the law which I commanded your fathers, and which I sent to you by My servants the prophets." 14Nevertheless they would not hear, but stiffened their necks, like the necks of their fathers, who did not believe in the LORD their God. 15And they rejected His statutes and His covenant that He had made with their fathers, and His testimonies which He had testified against them; they followed idols, became idolaters, and went after the nations who were all around them, concerning whom the LORD had charged them that they should not do like them. 16So they left all the commandments of the LORD their God, made for themselves a molded image and two calves, made a wooden image and worshiped all the host of heaven, and served Baal. 17And they caused their sons and daughters to pass through the fire, practiced witchcraft and soothsaying, and sold themselves to do evil in the sight of the LORD, to provoke Him to anger. 18Therefore the LORD was very angry with Israel, and removed them from His sight; there was none left but the tribe of Judah alone.

19Also Judah did not keep the commandments of the LORD their God, but walked in the statutes of Israel which they made. 20And the LORD rejected all the descendants of Israel, afflicted them, and delivered them into the hand of plunderers, until He had cast them from His sight. 21For He tore Israel from the house of David, and they made Jeroboam the son of Nebat king. Then Jeroboam drove Israel from following the LORD, and made them commit a great sin. 22For the children of Israel walked in all the sins of Jeroboam which he did; they did not depart from them, 23until the LORD removed Israel out of His sight, as He had said by all His servants the prophets. So Israel was carried away from their own land to Assyria, as it is to this day.

Assyria Resettles Samaria

24Then the king of Assyria brought people from Babylon, Cuthah, Ava, Hamath, and from Sepharvaim, and placed them in the cities of Samaria instead of the children of Israel; and they took possession of Samaria and dwelt in its cities. 25And it was so, at the beginning of their dwelling there, that they did not fear the LORD; therefore the LORD sent lions among them, which killed some of them. 26So they spoke to the king of Assyria, saying, "The nations whom you have removed and placed in the cities of Samaria do not know the rituals of the God of the land; therefore He has sent lions among them, and indeed, they are killing them because they do not know the rituals of the God of the land." 27Then the king of Assyria commanded, saying, "Send there one of the priests whom you brought from there; let him go and dwell there, and let him teach them the rituals of the God of the land." 28Then one of the priests whom they had carried away from Samaria came and dwelt in Bethel, and taught them how they should fear the LORD.

29However every nation continued to make gods of its own, and put them in the shrines on the high places which the Samaritans had made, every nation in the cities where they dwelt. 30The men of Babylon made Succoth Benoth, the men of Cuth made Nergal, the men of Hamath made Ashima, 31and the Avites made Nibhaz and Tartak; and the Sepharvites burned their children in fire to Adrammelech and Anammelech, the gods of Sepharvaim. 32So they feared the LORD, and from every class they appointed for themselves priests of the high places, who sacrificed for

j Canaanite deities

them in the shrines of the high places. 33They feared the LORD, yet served their own gods—according to the rituals of the nations from among whom they were carried away.

34To this day they continue practicing the former rituals; they do not fear the LORD, nor do they follow their statutes or their ordinances, or the law and commandment which the LORD had commanded the children of Jacob, whom He named Israel, 35with whom the LORD had made a covenant and charged them, saying: "You shall not fear other gods, nor bow down to them nor serve them nor sacrifice to them; 36but the LORD, who brought you up from the land of Egypt with great power and an outstretched arm, Him you shall fear, Him you shall worship, and to Him you shall offer sacrifice. 37And the statutes, the ordinances, the law, and the commandment which He wrote for you, you shall be careful to observe forever; you shall not fear other gods. 38And the covenant that I have made with you, you shall not forget, nor shall you fear other gods. 39But the LORD your God you shall fear; and He will deliver you from the hand of all your enemies." 40However they did not obey, but they followed their former rituals. 41So these nations feared the LORD, yet served their carved images; also their children and their children's children have continued doing as their fathers did, even to this day.

Hezekiah Reigns in Judah

18 Now it came to pass in the third year of Hoshea the son of Elah, king of Israel, *that* Hezekiah the son of Ahaz, king of Judah, began to reign. 2He was twenty-five years old when he became king, and he reigned twenty-nine years in Jerusalem. His mother's name *was* Abi the daughter of Zechariah. 3And he did *what was* right in the sight of the LORD, according to all that his father David had done.

4He removed the high places and broke the *sacred* pillars, cut down the wooden image[k] and broke in pieces the bronze serpent that Moses had made;

for until those days the children of Israel burned incense to it, and called it Nehushtan.[l] 5He trusted in the LORD God of Israel, so that after him was none like him among all the kings of Judah, nor who were before him. 6For he held fast to the LORD; he did not depart from following Him, but kept His commandments, which the LORD had commanded Moses. 7The LORD was with him; he prospered wherever he went. And he rebelled against the king of Assyria and did not serve him. 8He subdued the Philistines, as far as Gaza and its territory, from watchtower to fortified city.

9Now it came to pass in the fourth year of King Hezekiah, which *was* the seventh year of Hoshea the son of Elah, king of Israel, *that* Shalmaneser king of Assyria came up against Samaria and besieged it. 10And at the end of three years they took it. In the sixth year of Hezekiah, that *is*, the ninth year of Hoshea king of Israel, Samaria was taken. 11Then the king of Assyria carried Israel away captive to Assyria, and put them in Halah and by the Habor, the River of Gozan, and in the cities of the Medes, 12because they did not obey the voice of the LORD their God, but transgressed His covenant *and* all that Moses the servant of the LORD had commanded; and they would neither hear nor do *them*.

13And in the fourteenth year of King Hezekiah, Sennacherib king of Assyria came up against all the fortified cities of Judah and took them. 14Then Hezekiah king of Judah sent to the king of Assyria at Lachish, saying, "I have done wrong; turn away from me; whatever you impose on me I will pay." And the king of Assyria assessed Hezekiah king of Judah three hundred talents of silver and thirty talents of gold. 15So Hezekiah gave *him* all the silver that was found in the house of the LORD and in the treasuries of the king's house. 16At that time Hezekiah stripped *the gold from* the doors of the temple of the LORD, and *from* the pillars which Hezekiah king of Judah had overlaid, and gave it to the king of Assyria.

---

k A Canaanite goddess   l Literally *Bronze Thing*

Sennacherib Boasts Against the Lord

17Then the king of Assyria sent *the* Tartan,*m* *the* Rabsaris,*n* *and the* Rabshakeh*o* from Lachish, with a great army against Jerusalem, to King Hezekiah. And they went up and came to Jerusalem. When they had come up, they went and stood by the aqueduct from the upper pool, which *was* on the highway to the Fuller's Field. 18And when they had called to the king, Eliakim the son of Hilkiah, who *was* over the household, Shebna the scribe, and Joah the son of Asaph, the recorder, came out to them. 19Then *the* Rabshakeh said to them, "Say now to Hezekiah, 'Thus says the great king, the king of Assyria: "What confidence *is* this in which you trust? 20You speak of *having* plans and power for war; but *they are* mere words. And in whom do you trust, that you rebel against me? 21Now look! You are trusting in the staff of this broken reed, Egypt, on which if a man leans, it will go into his hand and pierce it. So *is* Pharaoh king of Egypt to all who trust in him. 22But if you say to me, 'We trust in the Lord our God,' *is* it not He whose high places and whose altars Hezekiah has taken away, and said to Judah and Jerusalem, 'You shall worship before this altar in Jerusalem'?" ' 23Now therefore, I urge you, give a pledge to my master the king of Assyria, and I will give you two thousand horses—if you are able on your part to put riders on them! 24How then will you repel one captain of the least of my master's servants, and put your trust in Egypt for chariots and horsemen? 25Have I now come up without the Lord against this place to destroy it? The Lord said to me, 'Go up against this land, and destroy it.' "

26Then Eliakim the son of Hilkiah, Shebna, and Joah said to *the* Rabshakeh, "Please speak to your servants in Aramaic, for we understand *it;* and do not speak to us in Hebrew in the hearing of the people who *are* on the wall."

27But *the* Rabshakeh said to them, "Has my master sent me to your master and to you to speak these words, and not to the men who sit on the wall, who will eat and drink their own waste with you?"

28Then *the* Rabshakeh stood and called out with a loud voice in Hebrew, and spoke, saying, "Hear the word of the great king, the king of Assyria! 29Thus says the king: 'Do not let Hezekiah deceive you, for he shall not be able to deliver you from his hand; 30nor let Hezekiah make you trust in the Lord, saying, "The Lord will surely deliver us; this city shall not be given into the hand of the king of Assyria." ' 31Do not listen to Hezekiah; for thus says the king of Assyria: 'Make *peace* with me by a present and come out to me; and every one of you eat from his own vine and every one from his own fig tree, and every one of you drink the waters of his own cistern; 32until I come and take you away to a land like your own land, a land of grain and new wine, a land of bread and vineyards, a land of olive groves and honey, that you may live and not die. But do not listen to Hezekiah, lest he persuade you, saying, "The Lord will deliver us." 33Has any of the gods of the nations at all delivered its land from the hand of the king of Assyria? 34Where *are* the gods of Hamath and Arpad? Where *are* the gods of Sepharvaim and Hena and Ivah? Indeed, have they delivered Samaria from my hand? 35Who among all the gods of the lands have delivered their countries from my hand, that the Lord should deliver Jerusalem from my hand?' "

36But the people held their peace and answered him not a word; for the king's commandment was, "Do not answer him." 37Then Eliakim the son of Hilkiah, who *was* over the household, Shebna the scribe, and Joah the son of Asaph, the recorder, came to Hezekiah with *their* clothes torn, and told him the words of *the* Rabshakeh.

Isaiah Assures Deliverance

19 And so it was, when King Hezekiah heard *it,* that he tore his clothes, covered himself with sackcloth, and went into the house of the Lord.

---

m A title, probably *Commander in Chief*   *n* A title, probably *Chief Officer*   *o* A title, probably
Chief of Staff or *Governor*

2Then he sent Eliakim, who *was* over the household, Shebna the scribe, and the elders of the priests, covered with sackcloth, to Isaiah the prophet, the son of Amoz. 3And they said to him, "Thus says Hezekiah: 'This day *is* a day of trouble, and rebuke, and blasphemy; for the children have come to birth, but *there is* no strength to bring them forth. 4It may be that the LORD your God will hear all the words of *the* Rabshakeh, whom his master the king of Assyria has sent to reproach the living God, and will rebuke the words which the LORD your God has heard. Therefore lift up *your* prayer for the remnant that is left.' "

5So the servants of King Hezekiah came to Isaiah. 6And Isaiah said to them, "Thus you shall say to your master, 'Thus says the LORD: "Do not be afraid of the words which you have heard, with which the servants of the king of Assyria have blasphemed Me. 7Surely I will send a spirit upon him, and he shall hear a rumor and return to his own land; and I will cause him to fall by the sword in his own land." ' "

Sennacherib's Threat and Hezekiah's Prayer

8Then *the* Rabshakeh returned and found the king of Assyria warring against Libnah, for he heard that he had departed from Lachish. 9And the king heard concerning Tirhakah king of Ethiopia, "Look, he has come out to make war with you." So he again sent messengers to Hezekiah, saying, 10"Thus you shall speak to Hezekiah king of Judah, saying: 'Do not let your God in whom you trust deceive you, saying, "Jerusalem shall not be given into the hand of the king of Assyria." 11Look! You have heard what the kings of Assyria have done to all lands by utterly destroying them; and shall you be delivered? 12Have the gods of the nations delivered those whom my fathers have destroyed, Gozan and Haran and Rezeph, and the people of Eden who *were* in Telassar? 13Where *is* the king of Hamath, the king of Arpad, and the king of the city of Sepharvaim, Hena, and Ivah?' "

14And Hezekiah received the letter from the hand of the messengers, and read it; and Hezekiah went up to the house of the LORD, and spread it before the LORD. 15Then Hezekiah prayed before the LORD, and said: "O LORD God of Israel, *the One* who dwells *between* the cherubim, You are God, You alone, of all the kingdoms of the earth. You have made heaven and earth. 16Incline Your ear, O LORD, and hear; open Your eyes, O LORD, and see; and hear the words of Sennacherib, which he has sent to reproach the living God. 17Truly, LORD, the kings of Assyria have laid waste the nations and their lands, 18and have cast their gods into the fire; for they *were* not gods, but the work of men's hands—wood and stone. Therefore they destroyed them. 19Now therefore, O LORD our God, I pray, save us from his hand, that all the kingdoms of the earth may know that You *are* the LORD God, You alone."

The Word of the LORD Concerning Sennacherib

20Then Isaiah the son of Amoz sent to Hezekiah, saying, "Thus says the LORD God of Israel: 'Because you have prayed to Me against Sennacherib king of Assyria, I have heard.' 21This *is* the word which the LORD has spoken concerning him:

    'The virgin, the daughter of Zion,
      Has despised you, laughed you to scorn;
      The daughter of Jerusalem
      Has shaken *her* head behind your back!

22 'Whom have you reproached and blasphemed?
      Against whom have you raised *your* voice,
      And lifted up your eyes on high?
      Against the Holy *One* of Israel.
23 By your messengers you have reproached the Lord,
      And said: "By the multitude of my chariots
      I have come up to the height of the mountains,
      To the limits of Lebanon;
      I will cut down its tall cedars
      And its choice cypress trees;
      I will enter the extremity of its borders,
      To its fruitful forest.

24 I have dug and drunk strange
        water,
      And with the soles of my feet I have
        dried up
      All the brooks of defense."

25 'Did you not hear long ago
      How I made it,
      From ancient times that I
        formed it?
      Now I have brought it to pass,
      That you should be
      For crushing fortified cities *into*
        heaps of ruins.
26 Therefore their inhabitants had
        little power;
      They were dismayed and
        confounded;
      They were *as* the grass of the field
      And the green herb,
      As the grass on the housetops
      And *grain* blighted before it is
        grown.

27 'But I know your dwelling place,
      Your going out and your coming in,
      And your rage against Me.
28 Because your rage against Me and
        your tumult
      Have come up to My ears,
      Therefore I will put My hook in
        your nose
      And My bridle in your lips,
      And I will turn you back
      By the way which you came.
29 'This *shall be* a sign to you:
      You shall eat this year such as
        grows of itself,
      And in the second year what
        springs from the same;
      Also in the third year sow and reap,
      Plant vineyards and eat the fruit of
        them.
30 And the remnant who have escaped
        of the house of Judah
      Shall again take root downward,
      And bear fruit upward.
31 For out of Jerusalem shall go a
        remnant,
      And those who escape from Mount
        Zion.
      The zeal of the LORD of hosts will
        do this.'
32 "Therefore thus says the LORD concerning the king of Assyria:

      'He shall not come into this city,
      Nor shoot an arrow there,
      Nor come before it with shield,
      Nor build a siege mound against it.
33 By the way that he came,
      By the same shall he return;
      And he shall not come into this
        city,'
      Says the LORD.
34 'For I will defend this city, to
        save it
      For My own sake and for My
        servant David's sake.' "

Sennacherib's Defeat and Death

35And it came to pass on a certain
night that the angel[p] of the LORD went
out, and killed in the camp of the Assyrians one hundred and eighty-five thousand; and when *people* arose early in
the morning, there were the corpses—
all dead. 36So Sennacherib king of Assyria departed and went away, returned
home, and remained at Nineveh.
37Now it came to pass, as he was worshiping in the temple of Nisroch his
god, that his sons Adrammelech and
Sharezer struck him down with the
sword; and they escaped into the land
of Ararat. Then Esarhaddon his son
reigned in his place.

Hezekiah's Life Extended

20 In those days Hezekiah was sick
      and near death. And Isaiah the
prophet, the son of Amoz, went to him
and said to him, "Thus says the LORD:
'Set your house in order, for you shall
die, and not live.' "
2Then he turned his face toward the
wall, and prayed to the LORD, saying,
3"Remember now, O LORD, I pray, how
I have walked before You in truth and
with a loyal heart, and have done *what
was* good in Your sight." And Hezekiah
wept bitterly.
4And it happened, before Isaiah had
gone out into the middle court, that the
word of the LORD came to him, saying,
5"Return and tell Hezekiah the leader
of My people, 'Thus says the LORD, the
God of David your father: "I have heard
your prayer, I have seen your tears;
surely I will heal you. On the third day

p Or *Angel*

you shall go up to the house of the LORD. 6And I will add to your days fifteen years. I will deliver you and this city from the hand of the king of Assyria; and I will defend this city for My own sake, and for the sake of My servant David." ' "

7Then Isaiah said, "Take a lump of figs." So they took and laid it on the boil, and he recovered.

8And Hezekiah said to Isaiah, "What is the sign that the LORD will heal me, and that I shall go up to the house of the LORD the third day?"

9Then Isaiah said, "This is the sign to you from the LORD, that the LORD will do the thing which He has spoken: shall the shadow go forward ten degrees or go backward ten degrees?"

10And Hezekiah answered, "It is an easy thing for the shadow to go down ten degrees; no, but let the shadow go backward ten degrees."

11So Isaiah the prophet cried out to the LORD, and He brought the shadow ten degrees backward, by which it had gone down on the sundial of Ahaz.

The Babylonian Envoys

12At that time Berodach-Baladan the son of Baladan, king of Babylon, sent letters and a present to Hezekiah, for he heard that Hezekiah had been sick. 13And Hezekiah was attentive to them, and showed them all the house of his treasures—the silver and gold, the spices and precious ointment, and all his armory—all that was found among his treasures. There was nothing in his house or in all his dominion that Hezekiah did not show them.

14Then Isaiah the prophet went to King Hezekiah, and said to him, "What did these men say, and from where did they come to you?"

So Hezekiah said, "They came from a far country, from Babylon."

15And he said, "What have they seen in your house?"

So Hezekiah answered, "They have seen all that is in my house; there is nothing among my treasures that I have not shown them."

16Then Isaiah said to Hezekiah, "Hear the word of the LORD: 17'Behold, the days are coming when all that is in your house, and what your fathers have accumulated until this day, shall be carried to Babylon; nothing shall be left,' says the LORD. 18'And they shall take away some of your sons who will descend from you, whom you will beget; and they shall be eunuchs in the palace of the king of Babylon.' "

19So Hezekiah said to Isaiah, "The word of the LORD which you have spoken is good!" For he said, "Will there not be peace and truth at least in my days?"

Death of Hezekiah

20Now the rest of the acts of Hezekiah—all his might, and how he made a pool and a tunnel and brought water into the city—are they not written in the book of the chronicles of the kings of Judah? 21So Hezekiah rested with his fathers. Then Manasseh his son reigned in his place.

Manasseh Reigns in Judah

21 Manasseh was twelve years old when he became king, and he reigned fifty-five years in Jerusalem. His mother's name was Hephzibah. 2And he did evil in the sight of the LORD, according to the abominations of the nations whom the LORD had cast out before the children of Israel. 3For he rebuilt the high places which Hezekiah his father had destroyed; he raised up altars for Baal, and made a wooden image,q as Ahab king of Israel had done; and he worshiped all the host of heavenr and served them. 4He also built altars in the house of the LORD, of which the LORD had said, "In Jerusalem I will put My name." 5And he built altars for all the host of heaven in the two courts of the house of the LORD. 6Also he made his son pass through the fire, practiced soothsaying, used witchcraft, and consulted spiritists and mediums. He did much evil in the sight of the LORD, to provoke Him to anger. 7He even set a carved image of Asherahs that he had made, in the house of which the LORD had said to David and to Solomon his son, "In this house and in Jerusalem, which I have chosen out of all the tribes

q A Canaanite goddess   r The gods of the Assyrians   s A Canaanite goddess of Israel, I will put My name forever; 8and I will not make the feet of Israel wander anymore from the land which I gave their fathers—only if they are careful to do according to all that I have commanded them, and according to all the law that My servant Moses commanded them." 9But they paid no attention, and Manasseh seduced them to do more evil than the nations whom the LORD had destroyed before the children of Israel.

10And the LORD spoke by His servants the prophets, saying, 11"Because Manasseh king of Judah has done these abominations (he has acted more wickedly than all the Amorites who *were* before him, and has also made Judah sin with his idols), 12therefore thus says the LORD God of Israel: 'Behold, *I* am bringing *such* calamity upon Jerusalem and Judah, that whoever hears of it, both his ears will tingle. 13And I will stretch over Jerusalem the measuring line of Samaria and the plummet of the house of Ahab; I will wipe Jerusalem as *one* wipes a dish, wiping *it* and turning *it* upside down. 14So I will forsake the remnant of My inheritance and deliver them into the hand of their enemies; and they shall become victims of plunder to all their enemies, 15because they have done evil in My sight, and have provoked Me to anger since the day their fathers came out of Egypt, even to this day.' "

16Moreover Manasseh shed very much innocent blood, till he had filled Jerusalem from one end to another, besides his sin by which he made Judah sin, in doing evil in the sight of the LORD.

17Now the rest of the acts of Manasseh—all that he did, and the sin that he committed—*are* they not written in the book of the chronicles of the kings of Judah? 18So Manasseh rested with his fathers, and was buried in the garden of his own house, in the garden of Uzza. Then his son Amon reigned in his place.

Amon's Reign and Death

19Amon *was* twenty-two years old when he became king, and he reigned two years in Jerusalem. His mother's name *was* Meshullemeth the daughter of Haruz of Jotbah. 20And he did evil in the sight of the LORD, as his father Manasseh had done. 21So he walked in all the ways that his father had walked; and he served the idols that his father had served, and worshiped them. 22He forsook the LORD God of his fathers, and did not walk in the way of the LORD.

23Then the servants of Amon conspired against him, and killed the king in his own house. 24But the people of the land executed all those who had conspired against King Amon. Then the people of the land made his son Josiah king in his place.

25Now the rest of the acts of Amon which he did, *are* they not written in the book of the chronicles of the kings of Judah? 26And he was buried in his tomb in the garden of Uzza. Then Josiah his son reigned in his place.

Josiah Reigns in Judah

22 Josiah *was* eight years old when he became king, and he reigned thirty-one years in Jerusalem. His mother's name *was* Jedidah the daughter of Adaiah of Bozkath. 2And he did *what was* right in the sight of the LORD, and walked in all the ways of his father David; he did not turn aside to the right hand or to the left.

Hilkiah Finds the Book of the Law

3Now it came to pass, in the eighteenth year of King Josiah, *that* the king sent Shaphan the scribe, the son of Azaliah, the son of Meshullam, to the house of the LORD, saying: 4"Go up to Hilkiah the high priest, that he may count the money which has been brought into the house of the LORD, which the doorkeepers have gathered from the people. 5And let them deliver it into the hand of those doing the work, who are the overseers in the house of the LORD; let them give it to those who *are* in the house of the LORD doing the work, to repair the damages of the house—6to carpenters and builders and masons—and to buy timber and hewn stone to repair the house. 7However there need be no accounting made with them of the money delivered into their hand, because they deal faithfully."

8Then Hilkiah the high priest said to

Shaphan the scribe, "I have found the Book of the Law in the house of the LORD." And Hilkiah gave the book to Shaphan, and he read it. 9So Shaphan the scribe went to the king, bringing the king word, saying, "Your servants have gathered the money that was found in the house, and have delivered it into the hand of those who do the work, who oversee the house of the LORD." 10Then Shaphan the scribe showed the king, saying, "Hilkiah the priest has given me a book." And Shaphan read it before the king.

11Now it happened, when the king heard the words of the Book of the Law, that he tore his clothes. 12Then the king commanded Hilkiah the priest, Ahikam the son of Shaphan, Achbor the son of Michaiah, Shaphan the scribe, and Asaiah a servant of the king, saying, 13"Go, inquire of the LORD for me, for the people and for all Judah, concerning the words of this book that has been found; for great *is* the wrath of the LORD that is aroused against us, because our fathers have not obeyed the words of this book, to do according to all that is written concerning us."

14So Hilkiah the priest, Ahikam, Achbor, Shaphan, and Asaiah went to Huldah the prophetess, the wife of Shallum the son of Tikvah, the son of Harhas, keeper of the wardrobe. (She dwelt in Jerusalem in the Second Quarter.) And they spoke with her. 15Then she said to them, "Thus says the LORD God of Israel, 'Tell the man who sent you to Me, 16"Thus says the LORD: 'Behold, I will bring calamity on this place and on its inhabitants—all the words of the book which the king of Judah has read—17because they have forsaken Me and burned incense to other gods, that they might provoke Me to anger with all the works of their hands. Therefore My wrath shall be aroused against this place and shall not be quenched.' " ' 18But as for the king of Judah, who sent you to inquire of the LORD, in this manner you shall speak to him, 'Thus says the LORD God of Israel: "*Concerning* the words which you have heard—19because your heart was tender, and you humbled yourself be-

fore the LORD when you heard what I spoke against this place and against its inhabitants, that they would become a desolation and a curse, and you tore your clothes and wept before Me, I also have heard *you*," says the LORD. 20Surely, therefore, I will gather you to your fathers, and you shall be gathered to your grave in peace; and your eyes shall not see all the calamity which I will bring on this place." ' " So they brought back word to the king.

Josiah Restores True Worship

23 Now the king sent them to gather all the elders of Judah and Jerusalem to him. 2The king went up to the house of the LORD with all the men of Judah, and with him all the inhabitants of Jerusalem—the priests and the prophets and all the people, both small and great. And he read in their hearing all the words of the Book of the Covenant which had been found in the house of the LORD.

3Then the king stood by a pillar and made a covenant before the LORD, to follow the LORD and to keep His commandments and His testimonies and His statutes, with all *his* heart and all *his* soul, to perform the words of this covenant that were written in this book. And all the people took a stand for the covenant. 4And the king commanded Hilkiah the high priest, the priests of the second order, and the doorkeepers, to bring out of the temple of the LORD all the articles that were made for Baal, for Asherah,ˢ and for all the host of heaven;ᵗ and he burned them outside Jerusalem in the fields of Kidron, and carried their ashes to Bethel. 5Then he removed the idolatrous priests whom the kings of Judah had ordained to burn incense on the high places in the cities of Judah and in the places all around Jerusalem, and those who burned incense to Baal, to the sun, to the moon, to the constellations, and to all the host of heaven. 6And he brought out the wooden imageᵘ from the house of the LORD, to the Brook Kidron outside Jerusalem, burned it at the Brook Kidron and ground *it* to ashes, and threw its ashes on the graves of the common peo-

---

ˢ A Canaanite goddess   ᵗ The gods of the Assyrians   ᵘ A Canaanite goddess ple. 7Then he tore down the *ritual booths* of the perverted persons[v] that *were* in the house of the LORD, where the women wove hangings for the wooden image. 8And he brought all the priests from the cities of Judah, and defiled the high places where the priests had burned incense, from Geba to Beersheba; also he broke down the high places at the gates which *were* at the entrance of the Gate of Joshua the governor of the city, which *were* to the left of the city gate. 9Nevertheless the priests of the high places did not come up to the altar of the LORD in Jerusalem, but they ate unleavened bread among their brethren.

10And he defiled Topheth, which *is* in the Valley of the Son of Hinnom, that no man might make his son or his daughter pass through the fire to Molech. 11Then he removed the horses that the kings of Judah had dedicated to the sun, at the entrance to the house of the LORD, by the chamber of Nathan-Melech, the officer who *was* in the court; and he burned the chariots of the sun with fire. 12The altars that *were* on the roof, the upper chamber of Ahaz, which the kings of Judah had made, and the altars which Manasseh had made in the two courts of the house of the LORD, the king broke down and pulverized there, and threw their dust into the Brook Kidron. 13Then the king defiled the high places that *were* east of Jerusalem, which *were* on the south of the Mount of Corruption, which Solomon king of Israel had built for Ashtoreth the abomination of the Sidonians, for Chemosh the abomination of the Moabites, and for Milcom the abomination of the people of Ammon. 14And he broke in pieces the *sacred* pillars and cut down the wooden images, and filled their places with the bones of men.

15Moreover the altar that *was* at Bethel, *and* the high place which Jeroboam the son of Nebat, who made Israel sin, had made, both that altar and the high place he broke down; and he burned the high place *and* crushed *it* to powder, and burned the wooden image. 16As Josiah turned, he saw the tombs that *were* there on the mountain.

And he sent and took the bones out of the tombs and burned *them* on the altar, and defiled it according to the word of the LORD which the man of God proclaimed, who proclaimed these words. 17Then he said, "What gravestone *is* this that I see?"

So the men of the city told him, "*It is* the tomb of the man of God who came from Judah and proclaimed these things which you have done against the altar of Bethel."

18And he said, "Let him alone; let no one move his bones." So they let his bones alone, with the bones of the prophet who came from Samaria.

19Now Josiah also took away all the shrines of the high places that *were* in the cities of Samaria, which the kings of Israel had made to provoke the LORD to anger; and he did to them according to all the deeds he had done in Bethel. 20He executed all the priests of the high places who *were* there, on the altars, and burned men's bones on them; and he returned to Jerusalem.

21Then the king commanded all the people, saying, "Keep the Passover to the LORD your God, as *it is* written in this Book of the Covenant." 22Such a Passover surely had never been held since the days of the judges who judged Israel, nor in all the days of the kings of Israel and the kings of Judah. 23But in the eighteenth year of King Josiah this Passover was held before the LORD in Jerusalem. 24Moreover Josiah put away those who consulted mediums and spiritists, the household gods and idols, all the abominations that were seen in the land of Judah and in Jerusalem, that he might perform the words of the law which were written in the book that Hilkiah the priest found in the house of the LORD. 25Now before him there was no king like him, who turned to the LORD with all his heart, with all his soul, and with all his might, according to all the Law of Moses; nor after him did *any* arise like him.

Impending Judgment on Judah

26Nevertheless the LORD did not turn from the fierceness of His great wrath, with which His anger was aroused

---

v That is, those practicing sodomy and prostitution in religious rituals against Judah, because of all the provocations with which Manasseh had provoked Him. 27And the LORD said, "I will also remove Judah from My sight, as I have removed Israel, and will cast off this city Jerusalem which I have chosen, and the house of which I said, 'My name shall be there.' "w

Josiah Dies in Battle

28Now the rest of the acts of Josiah, and all that he did, *are* they not written in the book of the chronicles of the kings of Judah? 29In his days Pharaoh Necho king of Egypt went to the aid of the king of Assyria, to the River Euphrates; and King Josiah went against him. And *Pharaoh Necho* killed him at Megiddo when he confronted him. 30Then his servants moved his body in a chariot from Megiddo, brought him to Jerusalem, and buried him in his own tomb. And the people of the land took Jehoahaz the son of Josiah, anointed him, and made him king in his father's place.

The Reign and Captivity of Jehoahaz

31Jehoahaz *was* twenty-three years old when he became king, and he reigned three months in Jerusalem. His mother's name *was* Hamutal the daughter of Jeremiah of Libnah. 32And he did evil in the sight of the LORD, according to all that his fathers had done. 33Now Pharaoh Necho put him in prison at Riblah in the land of Hamath, that he might not reign in Jerusalem; and he imposed on the land a tribute of one hundred talents of silver and a talent of gold. 34Then Pharaoh Necho made Eliakim the son of Josiah king in place of his father Josiah, and changed his name to Jehoiakim. And *Pharaoh* took Jehoahaz and went to Egypt, and hex died there.

Jehoiakim Reigns in Judah

35So Jehoiakim gave the silver and gold to Pharaoh; but he taxed the land to give money according to the command of Pharaoh; he exacted the silver and gold from the people of the land, from every one according to his assessment, to give *it* to Pharaoh Necho.

36Jehoiakim *was* twenty-five years old when he became king, and he reigned eleven years in Jerusalem. His mother's name *was* Zebudah the daughter of Pedaiah of Rumah. 37And he did evil in the sight of the LORD, according to all that his fathers had done.

Judah Overrun by Enemies

24 In his days Nebuchadnezzar king of Babylon came up, and Jehoiakim became his vassal *for* three years. Then he turned and rebelled against him. 2And the LORD sent against him *raiding* bands of Chaldeans, bands of Syrians, bands of Moabites, and bands of the people of Ammon; He sent them against Judah to destroy it, according to the word of the LORD which He had spoken by His servants the prophets. 3Surely at the commandment of the LORD *this* came upon Judah, to remove *them* from His sight because of the sins of Manasseh, according to all that he had done, 4and also because of the innocent blood that he had shed; for he had filled Jerusalem with innocent blood, which the LORD would not pardon.

5Now the rest of the acts of Jehoiakim, and all that he did, *are* they not written in the book of the chronicles of the kings of Judah? 6So Jehoiakim rested with his fathers. Then Jehoiachin his son reigned in his place.

7And the king of Egypt did not come out of his land anymore, for the king of Babylon had taken all that belonged to the king of Egypt from the Brook of Egypt to the River Euphrates.

The Reign and Captivity of Jehoiachin

8Jehoiachin *was* eighteen years old when he became king, and he reigned in Jerusalem three months. His mother's name *was* Nehushta the daughter of Elnathan of Jerusalem. 9And he did evil in the sight of the LORD, according to all that his father had done.

10At that time the servants of Nebuchadnezzar king of Babylon came up against Jerusalem, and the city was besieged. 11And Nebuchadnezzar king of Babylon came against the city, as his

w 1 Kings 8.29   x That is, Jehoahaz

servants were besieging it. 12Then Jehoiachin king of Judah, his mother, his
servants, his princes, and his officers
went out to the king of Babylon; and
the king of Babylon, in the eighth year
of his reign, took him prisoner.

The Captivity of Jerusalem

13And he carried out from there all
the treasures of the house of the Lord
and the treasures of the king's house,
and he cut in pieces all the articles of
gold which Solomon king of Israel had
made in the temple of the Lord, as the
Lord had said. 14Also he carried into
captivity all Jerusalem: all the captains
and all the mighty men of valor, ten
thousand captives, and all the craftsmen and smiths. None remained except
the poorest people of the land. 15And
he carried Jehoiachin captive to Babylon. The king's mother, the king's
wives, his officers, and the mighty of
the land he carried into captivity from
Jerusalem to Babylon. 16All the valiant
men, seven thousand, and craftsmen
and smiths, one thousand, all *who were*
strong *and* fit for war, these the king
of Babylon brought captive to Babylon.

Zedekiah Reigns in Judah

17Then the king of Babylon made
Mattaniah, *Jehoiachin's* uncle, king in
his place, and changed his name to
Zedekiah.

18Zedekiah *was* twenty-one years old
when he became king, and he reigned
eleven years in Jerusalem. His mother's
name *was* Hamutal the daughter of
Jeremiah of Libnah. 19He also did evil
in the sight of the Lord, according to
all that Jehoiakim had done. 20For because of the anger of the Lord *this* happened in Jerusalem and Judah, that He
finally cast them out from His presence.
Then Zedekiah rebelled against the
king of Babylon.

The Fall and Captivity of Judah

25 Now it came to pass in the ninth
year of his reign, in the tenth
month, on the tenth *day* of the month,
that Nebuchadnezzar king of Babylon
and all his army came against Jerusalem and encamped against it; and they

built a siege wall against it all around.
2So the city was besieged until the eleventh year of King Zedekiah. 3By the
ninth *day* of the *fourth* month the famine had become so severe in the city
that there was no food for the people
of the land.

4Then the city wall was broken
through, and all the men of war *fled* at
night by way of the gate between two
walls, which was by the king's garden,
even though the Chaldeans *were* still
encamped all around against the city.
And *the king* went by way of the plain.y
5But the army of the Chaldeans pursued
the king, and they overtook him in the
plains of Jericho. All his army was scattered from him. 6So they took the king
and brought him up to the king of Babylon at Riblah, and they pronounced
judgment on him. 7Then they killed the
sons of Zedekiah before his eyes, put
out the eyes of Zedekiah, bound him
with bronze fetters, and took him to
Babylon.

8And in the fifth month, on the seventh *day* of the month (which *was* the
nineteenth year of King Nebuchadnezzar king of Babylon), Nebuzaradan the
captain of the guard, a servant of the
king of Babylon, came to Jerusalem.
9He burned the house of the Lord and
the king's house; all the houses of Jerusalem, that is, all the houses of the
great, he burned with fire. 10And all the
army of the Chaldeans who *were with*
the captain of the guard broke down
the walls of Jerusalem all around.

11Then Nebuzaradan the captain of
the guard carried away captive the rest
of the people *who* remained in the city
and the defectors who had deserted to
the king of Babylon, with the rest of
the multitude. 12But the captain of the
guard left *some* of the poor of the land
as vinedressers and farmers. 13The
bronze pillars that *were* in the house
of the Lord, and the carts and the
bronze Sea that *were* in the house of
the Lord, the Chaldeans broke in
pieces, and carried their bronze to
Babylon. 14They also took away the
pots, the shovels, the trimmers, the
spoons, and all the bronze utensils
with which the priests ministered. 15The

y That is, the Jordan Valley

firepans and the basins, the things of solid gold and solid silver, the captain of the guard took away. 16The two pillars, one Sea, and the carts, which Solomon had made for the house of the LORD, the bronze of all these articles was beyond measure. 17The height of one pil lar *was* eighteen cubits, and the capital on it *was* of bronze. The height of the capital was three cubits, and the network and pomegranates all around the capital were all of bronze. The second pillar was the same, with a network.

18And the captain of the guard took Seraiah the chief priest, Zephaniah the second priest, and the three doorkeepers. 19He also took out of the city an officer who had charge of the men of war, five men of the king's close associates who were found in the city, the chief recruiting officer of the army, who mustered the people of the land, and sixty men of the people of the land *who were* found in the city. 20So Nebuzaradan, captain of the guard, took these and brought them to the king of Babylon at Riblah. 21Then the king of Babylon struck them and put them to death at Riblah in the land of Hamath. Thus Judah was carried away captive from its own land.

Gedaliah Made Governor of Judah

22Then he made Gedaliah the son of Ahikam, the son of Shaphan, governor over the people who remained in the land of Judah, whom Nebuchadnezzar king of Babylon had left. 23Now when all the captains of the armies, they and *their* men, heard that the king of Baby-

lon had made Gedaliah governor, they came to Gedaliah at Mizpah—Ishmael the son of Nethaniah, Johanan the son of Careah, Seraiah the son of Tanhumeth the Netophathite, and Jaazaniah the son of a Maachathite, they and their men. 24And Gedaliah took an oath before them and their men, and said to them, "Do not be afraid of the servants of the Chaldeans. Dwell in the land and serve the king of Babylon, and it shall be well with you."

25But it happened in the seventh month that Ishmael the son of Nethaniah, the son of Elishama, of the royal family, came with ten men and struck and killed Gedaliah, the Jews, as well as the Chaldeans who were with him at Mizpah. 26And all the people, small and great, and the captains of the armies, arose and went to Egypt; for they were afraid of the Chaldeans.

Jehoiachin Released from Prison

27Now it came to pass in the thirty-seventh year of the captivity of Jehoiachin king of Judah, in the twelfth month, on the twenty-seventh *day* of the month, *that* Evil-Merodach king of Babylon, in the year that he began to reign, released Jehoiachin king of Judah from prison. 28He spoke kindly to him, and gave him a more prominent seat than those of the kings who *were* with him in Babylon. 29So Jehoiachin changed from his prison garments, and he ate bread regularly before the king all the days of his life. 30And as for his provisions, *there was* a regular ration given him by the king, a portion for each day, all the days of his life.

The First Book of the
CHRONICLES

The Family of Adam—Seth to Abraham

1 Adam, Seth, Enosh, 2Cainan, Mahalalel, Jared, 3Enoch, Methuselah, Lamech, 4Noah, Shem, Ham, and Japheth.

5The sons of Japheth *were* Gomer, Magog, Madai, Javan, Tubal, Meshech, and Tiras. 6The sons of Gomer *were* Ashkenaz, Diphath, and Togarmah. 7The sons of Javan *were* Elishah, Tarshishah, Kittim, and Rodanim.

8The sons of Ham *were* Cush, Mizraim, Put, and Canaan. 9The sons of Cush *were* Seba, Havilah, Sabta, Raama, and Sabtecha. The sons of Raama *were* Sheba and Dedan. 10Cush begot Nimrod; he began to be a mighty one on the earth. 11Mizraim begot Ludim, Anamim, Lehabim, Naphtuhim, 12Pathrusim, Casluhim (from whom came the Philistines and the Caphtorim). 13Canaan begot Sidon, his firstborn, and Heth; 14the Jebusite, the Amorite, and the Girgashite; 15the Hivite, the Arkite, and the Sinite; 16the Arvadite, the Zemarite, and the Hamathite.

17The sons of Shem *were* Elam, Asshur, Arphaxad, Lud, Aram, Uz, Hul, Gether, and Meshech. 18Arphaxad begot Shelah, and Shelah begot Eber. 19To Eber were born two sons: the name of one *was* Peleg,*a* for in his days the earth was divided; and his brother's name *was* Joktan. 20Joktan begot Almodad, Sheleph, Hazarmaveth, Jerah, 21Hadoram, Uzal, Diklah, 22Ebal, Abimael, Sheba, 23Ophir, Havilah, and Jobab. All these *were* the sons of Joktan.

24Shem, Arphaxad, Shelah, 25Eber, Peleg, Reu, 26Serug, Nahor, Terah, 27and Abram, who is Abraham. 28The sons of Abraham *were* Isaac and Ishmael.

The Family of Ishmael

29These *are* their genealogies: The firstborn of Ishmael *was* Nebajoth; then Kedar, Adbeel, Mibsam, 30Mishma, Dumah, Massa, Hadad, Tema, 31Jetur, Naphish, and Kedemah. These *were* the sons of Ishmael.

The Family of Keturah

32Now the sons born to Keturah, Abraham's concubine, *were* Zimran, Jokshan, Medan, Midian, Ishbak, and Shuah. The sons of Jokshan *were* Sheba and Dedan. 33The sons of Midian *were* Ephah, Epher, Hanoch, Abida, and Eldaah. All these were the children of Keturah.

The Family of Isaac

34And Abraham begot Isaac. The sons of Isaac *were* Esau and Israel. 35The sons of Esau *were* Eliphaz, Reuel, Jeush, Jaalam, and Korah. 36And the sons of Eliphaz *were* Teman, Omar, Zephi, Gatam, *and* Kenaz; and *by* Timna,*b* Amalek. 37The sons of Reuel *were* Nahath, Zerah, Shammah, and Mizzah.

The Family of Seir

38The sons of Seir *were* Lotan, Shobal, Zibeon, Anah, Dishon, Ezer, and Dishan. 39And the sons of Lotan *were* Hori and Homam; Lotan's sister *was* Timna. 40The sons of Shobal *were* Alian, Manahath, Ebal, Shephi, and Onam. The sons of Zibeon *were* Ajah and Anah. 41The son of Anah *was* Dishon. The sons of Dishon *were* Hamran, Eshban, Ithran, and Cheran. 42The sons of Ezer *were* Bilhan, Zaavan, *and* Jaakan. The sons of Dishan *were* Uz and Aran.

The Kings of Edom

43Now these *were* the kings who reigned in the land of Edom before a king reigned over the children of Israel: Bela the son of Beor, and the name of his city was Dinhabah. 44And when Bela died, Jobab the son of Zerah of Bozrah reigned in his place. 45When Jobab died, Husham of the land of the Temanites reigned in his place. 46And when Husham died, Hadad the son of Bedad, who attacked Midian in the field of Moab, reigned in his place.

---

a Literally *Division*   *b* Compare Genesis 36.12

The name of his city *was* Avith. 47When Hadad died, Samlah of Masrekah reigned in his place. 48And when Samlah died, Saul of Rehoboth-by-the-River reigned in his place. 49When Saul died, Baal-Hanan the son of Achbor reigned in his place. 50And when Baal-Hanan died, Hadad reigned in his place; and the name of his city was Pai. His wife's name was Mehetabel the daughter of Matred, the daughter of Mezahab. 51Hadad died also. And the chiefs of Edom were Chief Timnah, Chief Aliah, Chief Je theth, 52Chief Aholibamah, Chief Elah, Chief Pinon, 53Chief Kenaz, Chief Teman, Chief Mibzar, 54Chief Magdiel, and Chief Iram. These *were* the chiefs of Edom.

The Family of Israel

2 These *were* the sons of Israel: Reuben, Simeon, Levi, Judah, Issachar, Zebulun, 2Dan, Joseph, Benjamin, Naphtali, Gad, and Asher.

From Judah to David

3The sons of Judah *were* Er, Onan, and Shelah. *These* three were born to him by the daughter of Shua, the Canaanitess. Er, the firstborn of Judah, was wicked in the sight of the LORD; so He killed him. 4And Tamar, his daughter-in-law, bore him Perez and Zerah. All the sons of Judah *were* five. 5The sons of Perez *were* Hezron and Hamul. 6The sons of Zerah *were* Zimri, Ethan, Heman, Calcol, and Dara—five of them in all.

7The son of Carmi *was* Achar, the troubler of Israel, who transgressed in the accursed thing.

8The son of Ethan *was* Azariah.

9Also the sons of Hezron who were born to him were Jerahmeel, Ram, and Chelubai. 10Ram begot Amminadab, and Amminadab begot Nahshon, leader of the children of Judah; 11Nahshon begot Salma, and Salma begot Boaz; 12Boaz begot Obed, and Obed begot Jesse; 13Jesse begot Eliab his firstborn, Abinadab the second, Shimea the third, 14Nethanel the fourth, Raddai the fifth, 15Ozem the sixth, *and* David the seventh.

16Now their sisters *were* Zeruiah and Abigail. And the sons of Zeruiah *were* Abishai, Joab, and Asahel—three. 17Abigail bore Amasa; and the father of Amasa *was* Jether the Ishmaelite.[c]

The Family of Hezron

18Caleb the son of Hezron had children by Azubah, *his* wife, and by Jerioth. Now these were her sons: Jesher, Shobab, and Ardon. 19When Azubah died, Caleb took Ephrath as his wife, who bore him Hur. 20And Hur begot Uri, and Uri begot Bezalel.

21Now afterward Hezron went in to the daughter of Machir the father of Gilead, whom he married when he *was* sixty years old; and she bore him Segub. 22Segub begot Jair, who had twenty-three cities in the land of Gilead. 23(Geshur and Syria took from them the towns of Jair, with Kenath and its towns—sixty towns.) All these *belonged* to the sons of Machir the father of Gilead. 24After Hezron died in Caleb Ephrathah, Hezron's wife Abijah bore him Ashhur the father of Tekoa.

The Family of Jerahmeel

25The sons of Jerahmeel, the firstborn of Hezron, *were* Ram, the firstborn, and Bunah, Oren, Ozem, *and* Ahijah. 26Jerahmeel had another wife, whose name was Atarah; she was the mother of Onam. 27The sons of Ram, the firstborn of Jerahmeel, were Maaz, Jamin, and Eker. 28The sons of Onam were Shammai and Jada. The sons of Shammai *were* Nadab and Abishur.

29And the name of the wife of Abishur *was* Abihail, and she bore him Ahban and Molid. 30The sons of Nadab *were* Seled and Appaim; Seled died without children. 31The son of Appaim *was* Ishi, the son of Ishi *was* Sheshan, and Sheshan's son *was* Ahlai. 32The sons of Jada, the brother of Shammai, *were* Jether and Jonathan; Jether died without children. 33The sons of Jonathan *were* Peleth and Zaza. These were the sons of Jerahmeel.

34Now Sheshan had no sons, only daughters. And Sheshan had an Egyptian servant whose name *was* Jarha. 35Sheshan gave his daughter to Jarha his servant as wife, and she bore him

c Compare 2 Samuel 17.25

Attai. 36Attai begot Nathan, and Nathan begot Zabad; 37Zabad begot Ephlal, and Ephlal begot Obed; 38Obed begot Jehu, and Jehu begot Azariah; 39Azariah begot Helez, and Helez begot Eleasah; 40Eleasah begot Sismai, and Sismai begot Shallum; 41Shallum begot Jekamiah, and Jekamiah begot Elishama.

The Family of Caleb

42The descendants of Caleb the brother of Jerahmeel were Mesha, his firstborn, who was the father of Ziph, and the sons of Mareshah the father of Hebron. 43The sons of Hebron were Korah, Tappuah, Rekem, and Shema. 44Shema begot Raham the father of Jorkoam, and Rekem begot Shammai. 45And the son of Shammai was Maon, and Maon was the father of Beth Zur.

46Ephah, Caleb's concubine, bore Haran, Moza, and Gazez; and Haran begot Gazez. 47And the sons of Jahdai were Regem, Jotham, Geshan, Pelet, Ephah, and Shaaph.

48Maachah, Caleb's concubine, bore Sheber and Tirhanah. 49She also bore Shaaph the father of Madmannah, Sheva the father of Machbenah and the father of Gibea. And the daughter of Caleb was Achsah.

50These were the descendants of Caleb: The sons of Hur, the firstborn of Ephrathah, were Shobal the father of Kirjath Jearim, 51Salma the father of Bethlehem, and Hareph the father of Beth Gader.

52And Shobal the father of Kirjath Jearim had descendants: Haroeh, and half of the families of Manuhoth. 53The families of Kirjath Jearim were the Ithrites, the Puthites, the Shumathites, and the Mishraites. From these came the Zorathites and the Eshtaolites.

54The sons of Salma were Bethlehem, the Netophathites, Atroth Beth Joab, half of the Manahethites, and the Zorites. 55And the families of the scribes who dwelt at Jabez were the Tirathites, the Shimeathites, and the Suchathites. These were the Kenites who came from Hammath, the father of the house of Rechab.

The Family of David

3 Now these were the sons of David who were born to him in Hebron: The firstborn was Amnon, by Ahinoam the Jezreelitess; the second, Daniel, by Abigail the Carmelitess; 2the third, Absalom the son of Maacah, the daughter of Talmai, king of Geshur; the fourth, Adonijah the son of Haggith; 3the fifth, Shephatiah, by Abital; the sixth, Ithream, by his wife Eglah.

4These six were born to him in Hebron. There he reigned seven years and six months, and in Jerusalem he reigned thirty-three years. 5And these were born to him in Jerusalem: Shimea, Shobab, Nathan, and Solomon—four by Bathshua the daughter of Ammiel. 6Also there were Ibhar, Elishama, Eliphelet, 7Nogah, Nepheg, Japhia, 8Elishama, Eliada, and Eliphelet—nine in all. 9These were all the sons of David, besides the sons of the concubines, and Tamar their sister.

The Family of Solomon

10Solomon's son was Rehoboam; Abijah was his son, Asa his son, Jehoshaphat his son, 11Joram his son, Ahaziah his son, Joash his son, 12Amaziah his son, Azariah his son, Jotham his son, 13Ahaz his son, Hezekiah his son, Manasseh his son, 14Amon his son, and Josiah his son. 15The sons of Josiah were Johanan the firstborn, the second Jehoiakim, the third Zedekiah, and the fourth Shallum. 16The sons of Jehoiakim were Jeconiah his son and Zedekiahd his son.

The Family of Jeconiah

17And the sons of Jeconiah were Assir, Shealtiel his son, 18and Malchiram, Pedaiah, Shenazzar, Jecamiah, Hoshama, and Nedabiah. 19The sons of Pedaiah were Zerubbabel and Shimei. The sons of Zerubbabel were Meshullam, Hananiah, Shelomith their sister, 20and Hashubah, Ohel, Berechiah, Hasadiah, and Jushab-Hesed—five in all. 21The sons of Hananiah were Pelatiah and Jeshaiah, the sons of Re-

d Compare 2 Kings 24.17

phaiah, the sons of Arnan, the sons of Obadiah, and the sons of Shechaniah. 22The son of Shechaniah was Shemaiah. The sons of Shemaiah were Hattush, Igal, Bariah, Neariah, and Shaphat—six in all. 23The sons of Neariah were Elioenai, Hezekiah, and Azrikam—three in all. 24The sons of Elioenai were Hodaviah, Eliashib, Pelaiah, Akkub, Johanan, Delaiah, and Anani—seven in all.

The Family of Judah

4 The sons of Judah were Perez, Hezron, Carmi, Hur, and Shobal. 2And Reaiah the son of Shobal begot Jahath, and Jahath begot Ahumai and Lahad. These were the families of the Zorathites. 3These were the sons of the father of Etam: Jezreel, Ishma, and Idbash; and the name of their sister was Hazelelponi; 4and Penuel was the father of Gedor, and Ezer was the father of Hushah.

These were the sons of Hur, the firstborn of Ephrathah the father of Bethlehem.

5And Ashhur the father of Tekoa had two wives, Helah and Naarah. 6Naarah bore him Ahuzzam, Hepher, Temeni, and Haahashtari. These were the sons of Naarah. 7The sons of Helah were Zereth, Zohar, and Ethnan; 8and Koz begot Anub, Zobebah, and the families of Aharhel the son of Harum.

9Now Jabez was more honorable than his brothers, and his mother called his name Jabez,[e] saying, "Because I bore him in pain." 10And Jabez called on the God of Israel saying, "Oh, that You would bless me indeed, and enlarge my territory, that Your hand would be with me, and that You would keep me from evil, that I may not cause pain!" So God granted him what he requested.

11Chelub the brother of Shuhah begot Mehir, who was the father of Eshton. 12And Eshton begot Beth-Rapha, Paseah, and Tehinnah the father of Ir-Nahash. These were the men of Rechah. 13The sons of Kenaz were Othniel and Seraiah. The sons of Othniel were Hathath, 14and Meonothai who begot Ophrah. Seraiah begot Joab the father

of Ge Harashim,[f] for they were craftsmen. 15The sons of Caleb the son of Jephunneh were Iru, Elah, and Naam. The son of Elah was Kenaz. 16The sons of Jehallelel were Ziph, Ziphah, Tiria, and Asarel. 17The sons of Ezrah were Jether, Mered, Epher, and Jalon. And Mered's wife bore Miriam, Shammai, and Ishbah the father of Eshtemoa. 18(His wife Jehudijah bore Jered the father of Gedor, Heber the father of Sochoh, and Jekuthiel the father of Zanoah.) And these were the sons of Bithiah the daughter of Pharaoh, whom Mered took.

19The sons of Hodiah's wife, the sister of Naham, were the fathers of Keilah the Garmite and of Eshtemoa the Maachathite. 20And the sons of Shimon were Amnon, Rinnah, Ben-Hanan, and Tilon. And the sons of Ishi were Zoheth and Ben-Zoheth.

21The sons of Shelah the son of Judah were Er the father of Lecah, Laadah the father of Mareshah, and the families of the house of the linen workers of the house of Ashbea; 22also Jokim, the men of Chozeba, and Joash; Saraph, who ruled in Moab, and Jashubi-Lehem. Now the records are ancient. 23These were the potters and those who dwell at Netaim and Gederah; there they dwelt with the king for his work.

The Family of Simeon

24The sons of Simeon were Nemuel, Jamin, Jarib, Zerah, and Shaul, 25Shallum his son, Mibsam his son, and Mishma his son. 26And the sons of Mishma were Hamuel his son, Zacchur his son, and Shimei his son. 27Shimei had sixteen sons and six daughters; but his brothers did not have many children, nor did any of their families multiply as much as the children of Judah.

28They dwelt at Beersheba, Moladah, Hazar Shual, 29Bilhah, Ezem, Tolad, 30Bethuel, Hormah, Ziklag, 31Beth Marcaboth, Hazar Susim, Beth Biri, and at Shaaraim. These were their cities until the reign of David. 32And their villages were Etam, Ain, Rimmon, Tochen, and Ashan—five cities—33and all the villages that were around these cities as far as Baal. These were their dwelling

---

e Literally *He Will Cause Pain*   f Literally *Valley of Craftsmen* places, and they maintained their genealogy: 34Meshobab, Jamlech, and Joshah the son of Amaziah; 35Joel, and Jehu the son of Joshibiah, the son of Seraiah, the son of Asiel; 36Elioenai, Jaakobah, Jeshohaiah, Asaiah, Adiel, Jesimiel, and Benaiah; 37Ziza the son of Shiphi, the son of Allon, the son of Jedaiah, the son of Shimri, the son of Shemaiah— 38these mentioned by name *were* leaders in their families, and their father's house increased greatly.

39So they went to the entrance of Gedor, as far as the east side of the valley, to seek pasture for their flocks. 40And they found rich, good pasture, and the land *was* broad, quiet, and peaceful; for some Hamites formerly lived there.

41These recorded by name came in the days of Hezekiah king of Judah; and they attacked their tents and the Meunites who were found there, and utterly destroyed them, as it is to this day. So they dwelt in their place, because *there was* pasture for their flocks there. 42Now *some* of them, five hundred men of the sons of Simeon, went to Mount Seir, having as their captains Pelatiah, Neariah, Rephaiah, and Uzziel, the sons of Ishi. 43And they defeated the rest of the Amalekites who had escaped. They have dwelt there to this day.

The Family of Reuben

5 Now the sons of Reuben the firstborn of Israel—he *was* indeed the firstborn, but because he defiled his father's bed, his birthright was given to the sons of Joseph, the son of Israel, so that the genealogy is not listed according to the birthright; 2yet Judah prevailed over his brothers, and from him *came* a ruler, although the birthright was Joseph's—3the sons of Reuben the firstborn of Israel were Hanoch, Pallu, Hezron, and Carmi.

4The sons of Joel *were* Shemaiah his son, Gog his son, Shimei his son, 5Micah his son, Reaiah his son, Baal his son, 6and Beerah his son, whom Tiglath-Pileser king of Assyria carried into captivity. He *was* leader of the Reubenites. 7And his brethren by their families, when the genealogy of their generations was registered: the chief, Jeiel, and Zechariah, 8and Bela the son of

Azaz, the son of Shema, the son of Joel, who dwelt in Aroer, as far as Nebo and Baal Meon. 9Eastward they settled as far as the entrance of the wilderness this side of the River Euphrates, because their cattle had multiplied in the land of Gilead.

10Now in the days of Saul they made war with the Hagrites, who fell by their hand; and they dwelt in their tents throughout the entire *area* east of Gilead.

The Family of Gad

11And the children of Gad dwelt next to them in the land of Bashan as far as Salcah: 12Joel *was* the chief, Shapham the next, then Jaanai and Shaphat in Bashan, 13and their brethren of their father's house: Michael, Meshullam, Sheba, Jorai, Jachan, Zia, and Eber— seven *in all.* 14These *were* the children of Abihail the son of Huri, the son of Jaroah, the son of Gilead, the son of Michael, the son of Jeshishai, the son of Jahdo, the son of Buz; 15Ahi the son of Abdiel, the son of Guni, *was* chief of their father's house. 16And *the Gadites* dwelt in Gilead, in Bashan and in its villages, and in all the commonlands of Sharon within their borders. 17All these were registered by genealogies in the days of Jotham king of Judah, and in the days of Jeroboam king of Israel.

18The sons of Reuben, the Gadites, and half the tribe of Manasseh *had* forty-four thousand seven hundred and sixty valiant men, men able to bear shield and sword, to shoot with the bow, and skillful in war, who went to war. 19They made war with the Hagrites, Jetur, Naphish, and Nodab. 20And they were helped against them, and the Hagrites were delivered into their hand, and all who *were* with them, for they cried out to God in the battle. He heeded their prayer, because they put their trust in Him. 21Then they took away their livestock—fifty thousand of their camels, two hundred and fifty thousand of their sheep, and two thousand of their donkeys—also one hundred thousand of their men; 22for many fell dead, because the war *was* God's. And they dwelt in their place until the captivity.

The Family of Manasseh (East)

23So the children of the half-tribe of Manasseh dwelt in the land. Their *numbers* increased from Bashan to Baal Hermon, that is, to Senir, or Mount Hermon. 24These *were* the heads of their fathers' houses: Epher, Ishi, Eliel, Azriel, Jeremiah, Hodaviah, and Jahdiel. They were mighty men of valor, famous men, *and* heads of their fathers' houses.

25And they were unfaithful to the God of their fathers, and played the harlot after the gods of the peoples of the land, whom God had destroyed before them. 26So the God of Israel stirred up the spirit of Pul king of Assyria, that is, Tiglath-Pileser king of Assyria. He carried the Reubenites, the Gadites, and the half-tribe of Manasseh into captivity. He took them to Halah, Habor, Hara, and the river of Gozan to this day.

The Family of Levi

6 The sons of Levi *were* Gershon, Kohath, and Merari. 2The sons of Kohath *were* Amram, Izhar, Hebron, and Uzziel. 3The children of Amram *were* Aaron, Moses, and Miriam. And the sons of Aaron *were* Nadab, Abihu, Eleazar, and Ithamar. 4Eleazar begot Phinehas, *and* Phinehas begot Abishua; 5Abishua begot Bukki, and Bukki begot Uzzi; 6Uzzi begot Zerahiah, and Zerahiah begot Meraioth; 7Meraioth begot Amariah, and Amariah begot Ahitub; 8Ahitub begot Zadok, and Zadok begot Ahimaaz; 9Ahimaaz begot Azariah, and Azariah begot Johanan; 10Johanan begot Azariah (it was he who ministered as priest in the temple that Solomon built in Jerusalem); 11Azariah begot Amariah, and Amariah begot Ahitub; 12Ahitub begot Zadok, and Zadok begot Shallum; 13Shallum begot Hilkiah, and Hilkiah begot Azariah; 14Azariah begot Seraiah, and Seraiah begot Jehozadak. 15Jehozadak went *into captivity* when the LORD carried Judah and Jerusalem into captivity by the hand of Nebuchadnezzar.

16The sons of Levi *were* Gershon, Kohath, and Merari. 17These are the names of the sons of Gershon: Libni and Shimei. 18The sons of Kohath *were* Amram, Izhar, Hebron, and Uzziel. 19The sons of Merari *were* Mahli and Mushi. Now these *are* the families of the Levites according to their fathers: 20Of Gershon *were* Libni his son, Jahath his son, Zimmah his son, 21Joah his son, Iddo his son, Zerah his son, *and* Jeatherai his son. 22The sons of Kohath *were* Amminadab his son, Korah his son, Assir his son, 23Elkanah his son, Ebiasaph his son, Assir his son, 24Tahath his son, Uriel his son, Uzziah his son, and Shaul his son. 25The sons of Elkanah *were* Amasai and Ahimoth. 26As for Elkanah,g the sons of Elkanah *were* Zophai his son, Nahathh his son, 27Eliabh his son, Jeroham his son, *and* Elkanah his son. 28The sons of Samuel *were Joel* the firstborn, and Abijah the second. 29The sons of Merari *were* Mahli, Libni his son, Shimei his son, Uzzah his son, 30Shimea his son, Haggiah his son, *and* Asaiah his son.

Musicians in the House of the LORD

31Now these are the men whom David appointed over the service of song in the house of the LORD, after the ark came to rest. 32They were ministering with music before the dwelling place of the tabernacle of meeting, until Solomon had built the house of the LORD in Jerusalem, and they served in their office according to their order.

33And these *are* the ones who ministered with their sons: Of the sons of the Kohathites *were* Heman the singer, the son of Joel, the son of Samuel, 34the son of Elkanah, the son of Jeroham, the son of Eliel, the son of Toah, 35the son of Zuph, the son of Elkanah, the son of Mahath, the son of Amasai, 36the son of Elkanah, the son of Joel, the son of Azariah, the son of Zephaniah, 37the son of Tahath, the son of Assir, the son of Ebiasaph, the son of Korah, 38the son of Izhar, the son of Kohath, the son of Levi, the son of Israel. 39And his brother Asaph, who stood at his right hand, *was* Asaph the son of Berachiah, the son of Shimea, 40the son of Michael, the son of Baaseiah, the son of Malchijah, 41the son of Ethni, the son of Zerah, the son of Adaiah, 42the son of Ethan, the son of

---

g Compare verse 35   h Compare verse 34

Zimmah, the son of Shimei, 43the son of Jahath, the son of Gershon, the son of Levi.

44Their brethren, the sons of Merari, on the left hand, *were* Ethan the son of Kishi, the son of Abdi, the son of Malluch, 45the son of Hashabiah, the son of Amaziah, the son of Hilkiah, 46the son of Amzi, the son of Bani, the son of Shamer, 47the son of Mahli, the son of Mushi, the son of Merari, the son of Levi.

48And their brethren, the Levites, *were* appointed to every kind of service of the tabernacle of the house of God.

The Family of Aaron

49But Aaron and his sons offered sacrifices on the altar of burnt offering and on the altar of incense, for all the work of the Most Holy *Place,* and to make atonement for Israel, according to all that Moses the servant of God had commanded. 50Now these *are* the sons of Aaron: Eleazar his son, Phinehas his son, Abishua his son, 51Bukki his son, Uzzi his son, Zerahiah his son, 52Meraioth his son, Amariah his son, Ahitub his son, 53Zadok his son, *and* Ahimaaz his son.

Dwelling Places of the Levites

54Now these *are* their dwelling places throughout their settlements in their territory, for they were *given* by lot to the sons of Aaron, of the family of the Kohathites: 55They gave them Hebron in the land of Judah, with its surrounding common-lands. 56But the fields of the city and its villages they gave to Caleb the son of Jephunneh. 57And to the sons of Aaron they gave *one of* the cities of refuge, Hebron; also Libnah with its common-lands, Jattir, Eshtemoa with its common-lands, 58Hilen with its common-lands, Debir with its common-lands, 59Ashan with its common-lands, and Beth Shemesh with its common-lands. 60And from the tribe of Benjamin: Geba with its common-lands, Alemeth with its common-lands, and Anathoth with its common-lands. All their cities among their families *were* thirteen.

61To the rest of the family of the tribe of the Kohathites *they gave* by lot ten cities from half the tribe of Manasseh.

62And to the sons of Gershon, throughout their families, *they gave* thirteen cities from the tribe of Issachar, from the tribe of Asher, from the tribe of Naphtali, and from the tribe of Manasseh in Bashan. 63To the sons of Merari, throughout their families, *they gave* twelve cities from the tribe of Reuben, from the tribe of Gad, and from the tribe of Zebulun. 64So the children of Israel gave *these* cities with their common-lands to the Levites. 65And they gave by lot from the tribe of the children of Judah, from the tribe of the children of Simeon, and from the tribe of the children of Benjamin these cities which are called by *their* names.

66Now some of the families of the sons of Kohath *were given* cities as their territory from the tribe of Ephraim. 67And they gave them *one of* the cities of refuge, Shechem with its common-lands, in the mountains of Ephraim, also Gezer with its common-lands, 68Jokmeam with its common-lands, Beth Horon with its common-lands, 69Aijalon with its common-lands, and Gath Rimmon with its common-lands. 70And from the half-tribe of Manasseh: Aner with its common-lands and Bileam with its common-lands, for the rest of the family of the sons of Kohath.

71From the family of the half-tribe of Manasseh the sons of Gershon *were given* Golan in Bashan with its common-lands and Ashtaroth with its common-lands. 72And from the tribe of Issachar: Kedesh with its common-lands, Daberath with its common-lands, 73Ramoth with its common-lands, and Anem with its common-lands. 74And from the tribe of Asher: Mashal with its common-lands, Abdon with its common-lands, 75Hukok with its common-lands, and Rehob with its common-lands. 76And from the tribe of Naphtali: Kedesh in Galilee with its common-lands, Hammon with its common-lands, and Kirjathaim with its common-lands.

77From the tribe of Zebulun the rest of the children of Merari *were given* Rimmon with its common-lands and Tabor with its common-lands. 78And on the other side of the Jordan, across from Jericho, on the east side of the Jordan, *they were given* from the tribe of

Reuben: Bezer in the wilderness with its common-lands, Jahzah with its common-lands, 79Kedemoth with its common-lands, and Mephaath with its common-lands. 80And from the tribe of Gad: Ramoth in Gilead with its common-lands, Mahanaim with its common-lands, 81Heshbon with its common-lands, and Jazer with its common-lands.

The Family of Issachar

7 The sons of Issachar were Tola, Puah, Jashub, and Shimron—four in all. 2The sons of Tola were Uzzi, Rephaiah, Jeriel, Jahmai, Jibsam, and Shemuel, heads of their father's house. The sons of Tola were mighty men of valor in their generations; their number in the days of David was twenty-two thousand six hundred. 3The son of Uzzi was Izrahiah, and the sons of Izrahiah were Michael, Obadiah, Joel, and Ishiah. All five of them were chief men. 4And with them, by their generations, according to their fathers' houses, were thirty-six thousand troops ready for war; for they had many wives and sons. 5Now their brethren among all the families of Issachar were mighty men of valor, listed by their genealogies, eighty-seven thousand in all.

The Family of Benjamin

6The sons of Benjamin were Bela, Becher, and Jediael—three in all. 7The sons of Bela were Ezbon, Uzzi, Uzziel, Jerimoth, and Iri—five in all. They were heads of their fathers' houses, and they were listed by their genealogies, twenty-two thousand and thirty-four mighty men of valor. 8The sons of Becher were Zemirah, Joash, Eliezer, Elioenai, Omri, Jerimoth, Abijah, Anathoth, and Alemeth. All these are the sons of Becher. 9And they were recorded by genealogy according to their generations, heads of their fathers' houses, twenty thousand two hundred mighty men of valor. 10The son of Jediael was Bilhan, and the sons of Bilhan were Jeush, Benjamin, Ehud, Chenaanah, Zethan, Tharshish, and Ahishahar.

11All these sons of Jediael were heads of their fathers' houses; there were seventeen thousand two hundred mighty men of valor fit to go out for war and battle. 12Shuppim and Huppim were the sons of Ir, and Hushim was the son of Aher.

The Family of Naphtali

13The sons of Naphtali were Jahziel, Guni, Jezer, and Shallum, the sons of Bilhah.

The Family of Manasseh (West)

14The descendants of Manasseh: his Syrian concubine bore him Machir the father of Gilead, the father of Asriel.[i] 15Machir took as his wife the sister of Huppim and Shuppim,[j] whose name was Maachah. The name of Gilead's grandson was Zelophehad,[k] but Zelophehad begot only daughters. 16(Maachah the wife of Machir bore a son, and she called his name Peresh. The name of his brother was Sheresh, and his sons were Ulam and Rakem. 17The son of Ulam was Bedan.) These were the descendants of Gilead the son of Machir, the son of Manasseh. 18His sister Hammoleketh bore Ishhod, Abiezer, and Mahlah. 19And the sons of Shemida were Ahian, Shechem, Likhi, and Aniam.

The Family of Ephraim

20The sons of Ephraim were Shuthelah, Bered his son, Tahath his son, Eladah his son, Tahath his son, 21Zabad his son, Shuthelah his son, and Ezer and Elead. The men of Gath who were born in that land killed them because they came down to take away their cattle. 22Then Ephraim their father mourned many days, and his brethren came to comfort him. 23And when he went in to his wife, she conceived and bore a son; and he called his name Beriah,[l] because tragedy had come upon his house. 24Now his daughter was Sheerah, who built Lower and Upper Beth Horon and Uzzen Sheerah; 25and Rephah was his son, as well as Resheph, and Telah his son, Tahan his son, 26Laadan his son,

---

i The son of Gilead (compare Numbers 26.30, 31) 26.30–33   l Literally In Tragedy   j Compare verse 12   k Compare Numbers

Ammihud his son, Elishama his son, 27Nun his son, and Joshua his son.

28Now their possessions and dwelling places were Bethel and its towns: to the east Naaran, to the west Gezer and its towns, and Shechem and its towns, as far as Ayyah and its towns; 29and by the borders of the children of Manasseh were Beth Shean and its towns, Taanach and its towns, Megiddo and its towns, Dor and its towns. In these dwelt the children of Joseph, the son of Israel.

The Family of Asher

30The sons of Asher were Imnah, Ishvah, Ishvi, Beriah, and their sister Serah. 31The sons of Beriah were Heber and Malchiel, who was the father of Birzaith. 32And Heber begot Japhlet, Shomer, Hotham, and their sister Shua. 33The sons of Japhlet were Pasach, Bimhal, and Ashvath. These were the children of Japhlet. 34The sons of Shemer were Ahi, Rohgah, Jehubbah, and Aram. 35And the sons of his brother Helem were Zophah, Imna, Shelesh, and Amal. 36The sons of Zophah were Suah, Harnepher, Shual, Beri, Imrah, 37Bezer, Hod, Shamma, Shilshah, Jithran, and Beera. 38The sons of Jether were Jephunneh, Pispah, and Ara. 39The sons of Ulla were Arah, Haniel, and Rizia.

40All these were the children of Asher, heads of their fathers' houses, choice men, mighty men of valor, chief leaders. And they were recorded by genealogies among the army fit for battle; their number was twenty-six thousand.

The Family Tree of King Saul of Benjamin

8 Now Benjamin begot Bela his firstborn, Ashbel the second, Aharah the third, 2Nohah the fourth, and Rapha the fifth. 3The sons of Bela were Addar, Gera, Abihud, 4Abishua, Naaman, Ahoah, 5Gera, Shephuphan, and Huram.

6These are the sons of Ehud, who were the heads of the fathers' houses of the inhabitants of Geba, and who forced them to move to Manahath: 7Naaman, Ahijah, and Gera who forced them to move. He begot Uzza and Ahihud.

8Also Shaharaim had children in the country of Moab, after he had sent away Hushim and Baara his wives. 9By Hodesh his wife he begot Jobab, Zibia, Mesha, Malcam, 10Jeuz, Sachiah, and Mirmah. These were his sons, heads of their fathers' houses.

11And by Hushim he begot Abitub and Elpaal. 12The sons of Elpaal were Eber, Misham, and Shemed, who built Ono and Lod with its towns; 13and Beriah and Shema, who were heads of their fathers' houses of the inhabitants of Aijalon, who drove out the inhabitants of Gath. 14Ahio, Shashak, Jeremoth, 15Zebadiah, Arad, Eder, 16Michael, Ispah, and Joha were the sons of Beriah. 17Zebadiah, Meshullam, Hizki, Heber, 18Ishmerai, Jizliah, and Jobab were the sons of Elpaal. 19Jakim, Zichri, Zabdi, 20Elienai, Zillethai, Eliel, 21Adaiah, Beraiah, and Shimrath were the sons of Shimei. 22Ishpan, Eber, Eliel, 23Abdon, Zichri, Hanan, 24Hananiah, Elam, Antothijah, 25Iphdeiah, and Penuel were the sons of Shashak. 26Shamsherai, Shehariah, Athaliah, 27Jaareshiah, Elijah, and Zichri were the sons of Jeroham.

28These were heads of the fathers' houses by their generations, chief men. These dwelt in Jerusalem.

29Now the father of Gibeon, whose wife's name was Maacah, dwelt at Gibeon. 30And his firstborn son was Abdon, then Zur, Kish, Baal, Nadab, 31Gedor, Ahio, Zecher, 32and Mikloth, who begot Shimeah. They also dwelt alongside their relatives in Jerusalem, with their brethren. 33Ner[m] begot Kish, Kish begot Saul, and Saul begot Jonathan, Malchishua, Abinadab, and Esh-Baal. 34The son of Jonathan was Merib-Baal, and Merib-Baal begot Micah. 35The sons of Micah were Pithon, Melech, Tarea, and Ahaz. 36And Ahaz begot Jehoaddah; Jehoaddah begot Alemeth, Azmaveth, and Zimri; and Zimri begot Moza. 37Moza begot Binea, Raphah his son, Eleasah his son, and Azel his son.

38Azel had six sons whose names were these: Azrikam, Bocheru, Ishmael,

m Also the son of Gibeon (compare 9.36, 39)

Sheariah, Obadiah, and Hanan. All these *were* the sons of Azel. 39And the sons of Eshek his brother *were* Ulam his firstborn, Jeush the second, and Eliphelet the third.

40The sons of Ulam were mighty men of valor—archers. *They* had many sons and grandsons, one hundred and fifty *in all*. These *were* all sons of Benjamin.

9 So all Israel was recorded by genealogies, and indeed, they *were* inscribed in the book of the kings of Israel. But Judah was carried away captive to Babylon because of their unfaithfulness. 2And the first inhabitants who *dwelt* in their possessions in their cities *were* Israelites, priests, Levites, and the Nethinim.

Dwellers in Jerusalem

3Now in Jerusalem the children of Judah dwelt, and some of the children of Benjamin, and of the children of Ephraim and Manasseh: 4Uthai the son of Ammihud, the son of Omri, the son of Imri, the son of Bani, of the descendants of Perez, the son of Judah. 5Of the Shilonites: Asaiah the firstborn and his sons. 6Of the sons of Zerah: Jeuel, and their brethren—six hundred and ninety. 7Of the sons of Benjamin: Sallu the son of Meshullam, the son of Hodaviah, the son of Hassenuah; 8Ibneiah the son of Jeroham; Elah the son of Uzzi, the son of Michri; Meshullam the son of Shephatiah, the son of Reuel, the son of Ibnijah; 9and their brethren, according to their generations—nine hundred and fifty-six. All these men *were* heads of a father's *house* in their fathers' houses.

The Priests at Jerusalem

10Of the priests: Jedaiah, Jehoiarib, and Jachin; 11Azariah the son of Hilkiah, the son of Meshullam, the son of Zadok, the son of Meraioth, the son of Ahitub, the officer over the house of God; 12Adaiah the son of Jeroham, the son of Pashur, the son of Malchijah; Maasai the son of Adiel, the son of Jahzerah, the son of Meshullam, the son of Meshillemith, the son of Immer; 13and their brethren, heads of their fathers' *houses*—one thousand seven hundred and sixty. *They were* very able

men for the work of the service of the house of God.

The Levites at Jerusalem

14Of the Levites: Shemaiah the son of Hasshub, the son of Azrikam, the son of Hashabiah, of the sons of Merari; 15Bakbakkar, Heresh, Galal, and Mattaniah the son of Micah, the son of Zichri, the son of Asaph; 16Obadiah the son of Shemaiah, the son of Galal, the son of Jeduthun; and Berechiah the son of Asa, the son of Elkanah, who lived in the villages of the Netophathites.

The Levite Gatekeepers

17And the gatekeepers *were* Shallum, Akkub, Talmon, Ahiman, and their brethren. Shallum *was* the chief. 18Until then *they had been* gatekeepers for the camps of the children of Levi at the King's Gate on the east.

19Shallum the son of Kore, the son of Ebiasaph, the son of Korah, and his brethren, from his father's house, the Korahites, *were* in charge of the work of the service, gatekeepers of the tabernacle. Their fathers had been keepers of the entrance to the camp of the LORD. 20And Phinehas the son of Eleazar had been the officer over them in time past; the LORD *was* with him. 21Zechariah the son of Meshelemiah *was* keeper of the door of the tabernacle of meeting.

22All those chosen as gatekeepers *were* two hundred and twelve. They were recorded by their genealogy, in their villages. David and Samuel the seer had appointed them to their trusted office. 23So they and their children *were* in charge of the gates of the house of the LORD, the house of the tabernacle, by assignment. 24The gatekeepers were assigned to the four directions: the east, west, north, and south. 25And their brethren in their villages *had* to come with them from time to time for seven days. 26For in this trusted office *were* four chief gatekeepers; they were Levites. And they had charge over the chambers and treasuries of the house of God. 27And they lodged *all* around the house of God because they *had* the responsibility, and they *were* in charge of opening *it* every morning.

Other Levite Responsibilities

28Now *some* of them were in charge of the serving vessels, for they brought them in and took them out by count. 29*Some* of them *were* appointed over the furnishings and over all the implements of the sanctuary, and over the fine flour and the wine and the oil and the incense and the spices. 30And *some* of the sons of the priests made the ointment of the spices.

31Mattithiah of the Levites, the firstborn of Shallum the Korahite, had the trusted office over the things that were baked in the pans. 32And some of their brethren of the sons of the Kohathites *were* in charge of preparing the showbread for every Sabbath.

33These are the singers, heads of the fathers' *houses* of the Levites, *who* lodged in the chambers, *and were* free *from other duties;* for they were employed in *that* work day and night. 34These heads of the fathers' *houses* of the Levites *were* heads throughout their generations. They dwelt at Jerusalem.

The Family of King Saul

35Jeiel the father of Gibeon, whose wife's name *was* Maacah, dwelt at Gibeon. 36His firstborn son *was* Abdon, then Zur, Kish, Baal, Ner, Nadab, 37Gedor, Ahio, Zechariah, and Mikloth. 38And Mikloth begot Shimeam. They also dwelt alongside their relatives in Jerusalem, with their brethren. 39Ner begot Kish, Kish begot Saul, and Saul begot Jonathan, Malchishua, Abinadab, and Esh-Baal. 40The son of Jonathan *was* Merib-Baal, and Merib-Baal begot Micah. 41The sons of Micah *were* Pithon, Melech, Tahrea, *and* Ahaz. 42And Ahaz begot Jarah; Jarah begot Alemeth, Azmaveth, and Zimri; and Zimri begot Moza; 43Moza begot Binea, Rephaiah his son, Eleasah his son, and Azel his son.

44And Azel had six sons whose names *were* these: Azrikam, Bocheru, Ishmael, Sheariah, Obadiah, and Hanan; these *were* the sons of Azel.

Tragic End of Saul and His Sons

10 Now the Philistines fought against Israel; and the men of Israel fled from before the Philistines, and fell slain on Mount Gilboa. 2Then the Philistines followed hard after Saul and his sons. And the Philistines killed Jonathan, Abinadab, and Malchishua, Saul's sons. 3The battle became fierce against Saul. The archers hit him, and he was wounded by the archers. 4Then Saul said to his armorbearer, "Draw your sword, and thrust me through with it, lest these uncircumcised men come and abuse me." But his armorbearer would not, for he was greatly afraid. Therefore Saul took a sword and fell on it. 5And when his armorbearer saw that Saul was dead, he also fell on his sword and died. 6So Saul and his three sons died, and all his house died together. 7And when all the men of Israel who *were* in the valley saw that they had fled and that Saul and his sons were dead, they forsook their cities and fled; then the Philistines came and dwelt in them.

8So it happened the next day, when the Philistines came to strip the slain, that they found Saul and his sons fallen on Mount Gilboa. 9And they stripped him and took his head and his armor, and sent word *throughout* the land of the Philistines to proclaim the news *in the temple* of their idols and among the people. 10Then they put his armor in the temple of their gods, and fastened his head in the temple of Dagon.

11And when all Jabesh Gilead heard all that the Philistines had done to Saul, 12all the valiant men arose and took the body of Saul and the bodies of his sons; and they brought them to Jabesh, and buried their bones under the tamarisk tree at Jabesh, and fasted seven days.

13So Saul died for his unfaithfulness which he had committed against the LORD, because he did not keep the word of the LORD, and also because he consulted a medium for guidance. 14But *he* did not inquire of the LORD; therefore He killed him, and turned the kingdom over to David the son of Jesse.

David Made King over All Israel

11 Then all Israel came together to David at Hebron, saying, "Indeed we *are* your bone and your flesh. 2Also, in time past, even when Saul was king, you *were* the one who led Israel out and brought them in; and the LORD your God said to you, 'You shall shepherd My people Israel, and be ruler over My people Israel.' " 3Therefore all the elders of Israel came to the king at Hebron, and David made a covenant with them at Hebron before the LORD. And they anointed David king over Israel, according to the word of the LORD by Samuel.

The City of David

4And David and all Israel went to Jerusalem, which is Jebus, where the Jebusites were, the inhabitants of the land. 5But the inhabitants of Jebus said to David, "You shall not come in here!" Nevertheless David took the stronghold of Zion (that is, the City of David). 6Now David said, "Whoever attacks the Jebusites first shall be chief and captain." And Joab the son of Zeruiah went up first, and became chief. 7Then David dwelt in the stronghold; therefore they called it the City of David. 8And he built the city around it, from the Millo to the surrounding area. Joab repaired the rest of the city. 9So David went on and became great, and the LORD of hosts was with him.

The Mighty Men of David

10Now these were the heads of the mighty men whom David had, who strengthened themselves with him in his kingdom, with all Israel, to make him king, according to the word of the LORD concerning Israel.

11And this is the number of the mighty men whom David had: Jashobeam the son of a Hachmonite, chief of the captains; he had lifted up his spear against three hundred, killed by him at one time.

12After him was Eleazar the son of Dodo, the Ahohite, who was one of the three mighty men. 13He was with David at Pasdammim. Now there the Philistines were gathered for battle, and there was a piece of ground full of barley. So the people fled from the Philistines. 14But they stationed themselves in the middle of that field, defended it, and killed the Philistines. So the LORD brought about a great victory.

15Now three of the thirty chief men went down to the rock to David, into the cave of Adullam; and the army of the Philistines encamped in the Valley of Rephaim. 16David was then in the stronghold, and the garrison of the Philistines was then in Bethlehem. 17And David said with longing, "Oh, that someone would give me a drink of water from the well of Bethlehem, which is by the gate!" 18So the three broke through the camp of the Philistines, drew water from the well of Bethlehem that was by the gate, and took it and brought it to David. Nevertheless David would not drink it, but poured it out to the LORD. 19And he said, "Far be it from me, O my God, that I should do this! Shall I drink the blood of these men who have put their lives in jeopardy? For at the risk of their lives they brought it." Therefore he would not drink it. These things were done by the three mighty men.

20Abishai the brother of Joab was chief of another three. He had lifted up his spear against three hundred men, killed them, and won a name among these three. 21Of the three he was more honored than the other two men. Therefore he became their captain. However he did not attain to the first three.

22Benaiah was the son of Jehoiada, the son of a valiant man from Kabzeel, who had done many deeds. He had killed two lion-like heroes of Moab. He also had gone down and killed a lion in the midst of a pit on a snowy day. 23And he killed an Egyptian, a man of great height, five cubits tall. In the Egyptian's hand there was a spear like a weaver's beam; and he went down to him with a staff, wrested the spear out of the Egyptian's hand, and killed him with his own spear. 24These things Benaiah the son of Jehoiada did, and won a name among three mighty men. 25Indeed he was more honored than the thirty, but he did not attain to the first three. And David appointed him over his guard.

26Also the mighty warriors were Asahel the brother of Joab, Elhanan the son of Dodo of Bethlehem, 27Shammoth the Harorite, Helez the Pelonite, 28Ira the son of Ikkesh the Tekoite, Abiezer the Anathothite, 29Sibbechai the Hushathite, Ilai the Ahohite, 30Maharai the

Netophathite, Heled the son of Baanah the Netophathite, 31Ithai the son of Ribai of Gibeah, of the sons of Benjamin, Benaiah the Pirathonite, 32Hurai of the brooks of Gaash, Abiel the Arbathite, 33Azmaveth the Baharumite, Eliahba the Shaalbonite, 34the sons of Hashem the Gizonite, Jonathan the son of Shageh the Hararite, 35Ahiam the son of Sacar the Hararite, Eliphal the son of Ur, 36Hepher the Mecherathite, Ahijah the Pelonite, 37Hezro the Carmelite, Naarai the son of Ezbai, 38Joel the brother of Nathan, Mibhar the son of Hagri, 39Zelek the Ammonite, Naharai the Berothite (the armorbearer of Joab the son of Zeruiah), 40Ira the Ithrite, Gareb the Ithrite, 41Uriah the Hittite, Zabad the son of Ahlai, 42Adina the son of Shiza the Reubenite (a chief of the Reubenites) and thirty with him, 43Hanan the son of Maachah, Joshaphat the Mithnite, 44Uzzia the Ashterathite, Shama and Jeiel the sons of Hotham the Aroerite, 45Jediael the son of Shimri, and Joha his brother, the Tizite, 46Eliel the Mahavite, Jeribai and Joshaviah the sons of Elnaam, Ithmah the Moabite, 47Eliel, Obed, and Jaasiel the Mezobaite.

The Growth of David's Army

12 Now these *were* the men who came to David at Ziklag while he was still a fugitive from Saul the son of Kish; and they *were* among the mighty men, helpers in the war, 2armed with bows, using both the right hand and the left in *hurling* stones and *shooting* arrows with the bow. *They were* of Benjamin, Saul's brethren.

3The chief *was* Ahiezer, then Joash, the sons of Shemaah the Gibeathite; Jeziel and Pelet the sons of Azmaveth; Berachah, and Jehu the Anathothite; 4Ishmaiah the Gibeonite, a mighty man among the thirty, and over the thirty; Jeremiah, Jahaziel, Johanan, and Jozabad the Gederathite; 5Eluzai, Jerimoth, Bealiah, Shemariah, and Shephatiah the Haruphite; 6Elkanah, Jisshiah, Azarel, Joezer, and Jashobeam, the Korahites; 7and Joelah and Zebadiah the sons of Jeroham of Gedor.

8*Some* Gadites joined David at the stronghold in the wilderness, mighty men of valor, men trained for battle, who could handle shield and spear, whose faces *were like* the faces of lions, and *were* as swift as gazelles on the mountains: 9Ezer the first, Obadiah the second, Eliab the third, 10Mishmannah the fourth, Jeremiah the fifth, 11Attai the sixth, Eliel the seventh, 12Johanan the eighth, Elzabad the ninth, 13Jeremiah the tenth, and Machbanai the eleventh. 14These *were* from the sons of Gad, captains of the army; the least was over a hundred, and the greatest was over a thousand. 15These *are* the ones who crossed the Jordan in the first month, when it had overflowed all its banks; and they put to flight all *those* in the valleys, to the east and to the west.

16Then some of the sons of Benjamin and Judah came to David at the stronghold. 17And David went out to meet them, and answered and said to them, "If you have come peaceably to me to help me, my heart will be united with you; but if to betray me to my enemies, since *there is* no wrong in my hands, may the God of our fathers look and bring judgment." 18Then the Spirit came upon Amasai, chief of the captains, *and he said:*

"*We are* yours, O David;
We *are* on your side, O son of Jesse!
Peace, peace to you,
And peace to your helpers!
For your God helps you."

So David received them, and made them captains of the troop.

19And *some* from Manasseh defected to David when he was going with the Philistines to battle against Saul; but they did not help them, for the lords of the Philistines sent him away by agreement, saying, "He may defect to his master Saul *and endanger* our heads." 20When he went to Ziklag, those of Manasseh who defected to him were Adnah, Jozabad, Jediael, Michael, Jozabad, Elihu, and Zillethai, captains of the thousands who *were* from Manasseh. 21And they helped David against the bands *of raiders*, for they *were* all mighty men of valor, and they were captains in the army. 22For at *that* time they came to David day by day to help him, until *it was* a great army, like the army of God.

David's Army at Hebron

23Now these *were* the numbers of the divisions *that were* equipped for war, *and* came to David at Hebron to turn *over* the kingdom of Saul to him, according to the word of the LORD: 24of the sons of Judah bearing shield and spear, six thousand eight hundred armed for war; 25of the sons of Simeon, mighty men of valor fit for war, seven thousand one hundred; 26of the sons of Levi four thousand six hundred; 27Jehoiada, the leader of the Aaronites, and with him three thousand seven hundred; 28Zadok, a young man, a valiant warrior, and from his father's house twenty-two captains; 29of the sons of Benjamin, relatives of Saul, three thousand (until then the greatest part of them had remained loyal to the house of Saul); 30of the sons of Ephraim twenty thousand eight hundred, mighty men of valor, famous men throughout their father's house; 31of the half-tribe of Manasseh eighteen thousand, who were designated by name to come and make David king; 32of the sons of Issachar who had understanding of the times, to know what Israel ought to do, their chiefs were two hundred; and all their brethren were at their command; 33of Zebulun there were fifty thousand who went out to battle, expert in war with all weapons of war, stouthearted men who could keep ranks; 34of Naphtali one thousand captains, and with them thirty-seven thousand with shield and spear; 35of the Danites who could keep battle formation, twenty-eight thousand six hundred; 36of Asher, those who could go out to war, able to keep battle formation, forty thousand; 37of the Reubenites and the Gadites and the half-tribe of Manasseh, from the other side of the Jordan, one hundred and twenty thousand armed for battle with every *kind* of weapon of war.

38All these men of war, who could keep ranks, came to Hebron with a loyal heart, to make David king over all Israel; and all the rest of Israel *were* of one mind to make David king. 39And they were there with David three days, eating and drinking, for their brethren had prepared for them. 40Moreover those who were near to them, from as far away as Issachar and Zebulun and Naphtali, were bringing food on donkeys and camels, on mules and oxen—provisions of flour and cakes of figs and cakes of raisins, wine and oil and oxen and sheep abundantly, for *there was* joy in Israel.

The Ark Brought from Kirjath Jearim

13 Then David consulted with the captains of thousands and hundreds, *and* with every leader. 2And David said to all the assembly of Israel, "If *it seems* good to you, and if it is of the LORD our God, let us send out to our brethren everywhere *who are* left in all the land of Israel, and with them to the priests and Levites *who are* in their cities *and* their common-lands, that they may gather together to us; 3and let us bring the ark of our God back to us, for we have not inquired at it since the days of Saul." 4Then all the assembly said that they would do so, for the thing was right in the eyes of all the people.

5So David gathered all Israel together, from Shihor in Egypt to as far as the entrance of Hamath, to bring the ark of God from Kirjath Jearim. 6And David and all Israel went up to Baalah, to Kirjath Jearim, which belonged to Judah, to bring up from there the ark of God the LORD, who dwells *between* the cherubim, where *His* name is proclaimed. 7So they carried the ark of God on a new cart from the house of Abinadab, and Uzza and Ahio drove the cart. 8Then David and all Israel played *music* before God with all *their* might, with singing, on harps, on stringed instruments, on tambourines, on cymbals, and with trumpets.

9And when they came to Chidon's threshing floor, Uzza put out his hand to hold the ark, for the oxen stumbled. 10Then the anger of the LORD was aroused against Uzza, and He struck him because he put his hand to the ark; and he died there before God. 11And David became angry because of the LORD's outbreak against Uzza; therefore that place is called Perez Uzza[n] to

n Literally *Outburst Against Uzza*

this day. 12David was afraid of God that day, saying, "How can I bring the ark of God to me?"

13So David would not move the ark with him into the City of David, but took it aside into the house of Obed-Edom the Gittite. 14The ark of God remained with the family of Obed-Edom in his house three months. And the LORD blessed the house of Obed-Edom and all that he had.

David Established at Jerusalem

14 Now Hiram king of Tyre sent messengers to David, and cedar trees, with masons and carpenters, to build him a house. 2So David knew that the LORD had established him as king over Israel, for his kingdom was highly exalted for the sake of His people Israel.

3Then David took more wives in Jerusalem, and David begot more sons and daughters. 4And these are the names of his children whom he had in Jerusalem: Shammua, Shobab, Nathan, Solomon, 5Ibhar, Elishua, Elpelet, 6Nogah, Nepheg, Japhia, 7Elishama, Beeliada, and Eliphelet.

The Philistines Defeated

8Now when the Philistines heard that David had been anointed king over all Israel, all the Philistines went up to search for David. And David heard *of it* and went out against them. 9Then the Philistines went and made a raid on the Valley of Rephaim. 10And David inquired of God, saying, "Shall I go up against the Philistines? Will You deliver them into my hand?"

The LORD said to him, "Go up, for I will deliver them into your hand."

11So they went up to Baal Perazim, and David defeated them there. Then David said, "God has broken through my enemies by my hand like a breakthrough of water." Therefore they called the name of that place Baal Perazim.º 12And when they left their gods there, David gave a commandment, and they were burned with fire.

13Then the Philistines once again made a raid on the valley. 14Therefore David inquired again of God, and God said to him, "You shall not go up after them; circle around them, and come upon them in front of the mulberry trees. 15And it shall be, when you hear a sound of marching in the tops of the mulberry trees, then you shall go out to battle, for God has gone out before you to strike the camp of the Philistines." 16So David did as God commanded him, and they drove back the army of the Philistines from Gibeon as far as Gezer. 17Then the fame of David went out into all lands, and the LORD brought the fear of him upon all nations.

The Ark Brought to Jerusalem

15 David built houses for himself in the City of David; and he prepared a place for the ark of God, and pitched a tent for it. 2Then David said, "No one may carry the ark of God but the Levites, for the LORD has chosen them to carry the ark of God and to minister before Him forever." 3And David gathered all Israel together at Jerusalem, to bring up the ark of the LORD to its place, which he had prepared for it. 4Then David assembled the children of Aaron and the Levites: 5of the sons of Kohath, Uriel the chief, and one hundred and twenty of his brethren; 6of the sons of Merari, Asaiah the chief, and two hundred and twenty of his brethren; 7of the sons of Gershom, Joel the chief, and one hundred and thirty of his brethren; 8of the sons of Elizaphan, Shemaiah the chief, and two hundred of his brethren; 9of the sons of Hebron, Eliel the chief, and eighty of his brethren; 10of the sons of Uzziel, Amminadab the chief, and one hundred and twelve of his brethren.

11And David called for Zadok and Abiathar the priests, and for the Levites: for Uriel, Asaiah, Joel, Shemaiah, Eliel, and Amminadab. 12He said to them, "You *are* the heads of the fathers' *houses* of the Levites; sanctify yourselves, you and your brethren, that you may bring up the ark of the LORD God of Israel to *the place* I have prepared for it. 13For because you *did* not *do it* the first *time*, the LORD our God broke out against us, because we did not consult Him about the proper order."

º Literally *Master of Breakthroughs*

14So the priests and the Levites sanctified themselves to bring up the ark of the LORD God of Israel. 15And the children of the Levites bore the ark of God on their shoulders, by its poles, as Moses had commanded according to the word of the LORD.

16Then David spoke to the leaders of the Levites to appoint their brethren *to be* the singers accompanied by instruments of music, stringed instruments, harps, and cymbals, by raising the voice with resounding joy. 17So the Levites appointed Heman the son of Joel; and of his brethren, Asaph the son of Berechiah; and of their brethren, the sons of Merari, Ethan the son of Kushaiah; 18and with them their brethren of the second *rank:* Zechariah, Ben, Jaaziel, Shemiramoth, Jehiel, Unni, Eliab, Benaiah, Maaseiah, Mattithiah, Elipheleh, Mikneiah, Obed-Edom, and Jeiel, the gatekeepers; 19the singers, Heman, Asaph, and Ethan, *were* to sound the cymbals of bronze; 20Zechariah, Aziel, Shemiramoth, Jehiel, Unni, Eliab, Maaseiah, and Benaiah, with strings according to Alamoth; 21Mattithiah, Elipheleh, Mikneiah, Obed-Edom, Jeiel, and Azaziah, to direct with harps on the Sheminith; 22Chenaniah, leader of the Levites, was instructor *in charge of* the music, because he *was* skillful; 23Berechiah and Elkanah *were* doorkeepers for the ark; 24Shebaniah, Joshaphat, Nethanel, Amasai, Zechariah, Benaiah, and Eliezer, the priests, were to blow the trumpets before the ark of God; and Obed-Edom and Jehiah, doorkeepers for the ark.

25So David, the elders of Israel, and the captains over thousands went to bring up the ark of the covenant of the LORD from the house of Obed-Edom with joy. 26And so it was, when God helped the Levites who bore the ark of the covenant of the LORD, that they offered seven bulls and seven rams. 27David was clothed with a robe of fine linen, as were all the Levites who bore the ark, the singers, and Chenaniah the music master *with* the singers. David also wore a linen ephod. 28Thus all Israel brought up the ark of the covenant of the LORD with shouting and with the sound of the horn, with trumpets and with cymbals, making music with stringed instruments and harps. 29And it happened, *as* the ark of the covenant of the LORD came to the City of David, that Michal, Saul's daughter, looked through a window and saw King David whirling and playing music; and she despised him in her heart.

The Ark Placed in the Tabernacle

16 So they brought the ark of God, and set it in the midst of the tabernacle that David had erected for it. Then they offered burnt offerings and peace offerings before God. 2And when David had finished offering the burnt offerings and the peace offerings, he blessed the people in the name of the LORD. 3Then he distributed to everyone of Israel, both man and woman, to everyone a loaf of bread, a piece *of meat,* and a cake of raisins.

4And he appointed some of the Levites to minister before the ark of the LORD, to commemorate, to thank, and to praise the LORD God of Israel: 5Asaph the chief, and next to him Zechariah, *then* Jeiel, Shemiramoth, Jehiel, Mattithiah, Eliab, Benaiah, and Obed-Edom: Jeiel with stringed instruments and harps, but Asaph made music with cymbals; 6Benaiah and Jahaziel the priests regularly *blew* the trumpets before the ark of the covenant of God.

David's Song of Thanksgiving

7On that day David first delivered *this psalm* into the hand of Asaph and his brethren, to thank the LORD:

8   Oh, give thanks to the LORD!
    Call upon His name;
    Make known His deeds among the
      peoples!
9   Sing to Him, sing psalms to Him;
    Talk of all His wondrous works!
10 Glory in His holy name;
    Let the hearts of those rejoice who
      seek the LORD!
11 Seek the LORD and His strength;
    Seek His face evermore!
12 Remember His marvelous works
      which He has done,
    His wonders, and the judgments of
      His mouth,
13   O seed of Israel His servant,
    You children of Jacob, His chosen
      ones!

14 He *is* the LORD our God;
    His judgments *are* in all the earth.
15 Remember His covenant forever,
    The word which He commanded,
      for a thousand generations,
16 *The covenant which* He made with
      Abraham,
    And His oath to Isaac,
17 And confirmed it to Jacob for a
      statute,
    To Israel *for* an everlasting
      covenant,
18 Saying, "To you I will give the land
      of Canaan
    As the allotment of your
      inheritance,"
19 When you were few in number,
    Indeed very few, and strangers
      in it.

20 When they went from one nation
      to another,
    And from *one* kingdom to another
      people,
21 He permitted no man to do them
      wrong;
    Yes, He rebuked kings for their
      sakes,
22 *Saying,* "Do not touch My anointed
      ones,
    And do My prophets no harm." *p*

23 Sing to the LORD, all the earth;
    Proclaim the good news of His
      salvation from day to day.
24 Declare His glory among the
      nations,
    His wonders among all peoples.

25 For the LORD *is* great and greatly
      to be praised;
    He *is* also to be feared above all
      gods.
26 For all the gods of the peoples *are*
      idols,
    But the LORD made the heavens.
27 Honor and majesty *are* before Him;
    Strength and gladness are in His
      place.

28 Give to the LORD, O families of the
      peoples,
    Give to the LORD glory and
      strength.

29 Give to the LORD the glory *due* His
      name;
    Bring an offering, and come before
      Him.
    Oh, worship the LORD in the beauty
      of holiness!
30 Tremble before Him, all the earth.
    The world also is firmly
      established,
    It shall not be moved.

31 Let the heavens rejoice, and let the
      earth be glad;
    And let them say among the
      nations, "The LORD reigns."
32 Let the sea roar, and all its fullness;
    Let the field rejoice, and all that *is*
      in it.
33 Then the trees of the woods shall
      rejoice before the LORD,
    For He is coming to judge the
      earth.*q*

34 Oh, give thanks to the LORD, for *He
      is* good!
    For His mercy *endures* forever.*r*
35 And say, "Save us, O God of our
      salvation;
    Gather us together, and deliver us
      from the Gentiles,
    To give thanks to Your holy name,
    To triumph in Your praise."

36 Blessed *be* the LORD God of Israel
    From everlasting to everlasting!*s*
And all the people said, "Amen!" and
praised the LORD.

Regular Worship Maintained

37So he left Asaph and his brothers
there before the ark of the covenant of
the LORD to minister before the ark regularly, as every day's work required;
38and Obed-Edom with his sixty-eight
brethren, including Obed-Edom the son
of Jeduthun, and Hosah, *to be* gatekeepers; 39and Zadok the priest and his
brethren the priests, before the tabernacle of the LORD at the high place that
was at Gibeon, 40to offer burnt offerings
to the LORD on the altar of burnt offering regularly morning and evening, and
to do according to all that is written in
the Law of the LORD which He com-

---

p Compare verses 8–22 with Psalm 105.1–15   *q* Compare verses 23–33 with Psalm 96.1–13
r Compare verse 34 with Psalm 106.1   *s* Compare verses 35, 36 with Psalm 106.47, 48

manded Israel; 41and with them Heman and Jeduthun and the rest who were chosen, who were designated by name, to give thanks to the LORD, because His mercy *endures* forever; 42and with them Heman and Jeduthun, to sound aloud with trumpets and cymbals and the musical instruments of God. Now the sons of Jeduthun *were* gatekeepers.

43Then all the people departed, every man to his house; and David returned to bless his house.

God's Covenant with David

17 Now it came to pass, when David was dwelling in his house, that David said to Nathan the prophet, "See now, I dwell in a house of cedar, but the ark of the covenant of the LORD *is* under tent curtains."

2Then Nathan said to David, "Do all that *is* in your heart, for God *is* with you."

3But it happened that night that the word of God came to Nathan, saying, 4"Go and tell My servant David, 'Thus says the LORD: "You shall not build Me a house to dwell in. 5For I have not dwelt in a house since the time that I brought up Israel, even to this day, but have gone from tent to tent, and from *one* tabernacle *to another*. 6Wherever I have moved about with all Israel, have I ever spoken a word to any of the judges of Israel, whom I commanded to shepherd My people, saying, 'Why have you not built Me a house of cedar?' " ' 7Now therefore, thus shall you say to My servant David, 'Thus says the LORD of hosts: "I took you from the sheepfold, from following the sheep, to be ruler over My people Israel. 8And I have been with you wherever you have gone, and have cut off all your enemies from before you, and have made you a name like the name of the great men who *are* on the earth. 9More over I will appoint a place for My people Israel, and will plant them, that they may dwell in a place of their own and move no more; nor shall the sons of wickedness oppress them anymore, as previously, 10since the time that I commanded judges *to be* over My people Israel. Also I will subdue all your enemies. Furthermore I tell you that the LORD will build you a house. 11And it

shall be, when your days are fulfilled, when you must go *to be* with your fathers, that I will set up your seed after you, who will be of your sons; and I will establish his kingdom. 12He shall build Me a house, and I will establish his throne forever. 13I will be his Father, and he shall be My son; and I will not take My mercy away from him, as I took *it* from *him* who was before you. 14And I will establish him in My house and in My kingdom forever; and his throne shall be established forever." ' "

15According to all these words and according to all this vision, so Nathan spoke to David.

16Then King David went in and sat before the LORD; and he said: "Who *am* I, O LORD God? And what is my house, that You have brought me this far? 17And *yet* this was a small thing in Your sight, O God; and You have *also* spoken of Your servant's house for a great while to come, and have regarded me according to the rank of a man of high degree, O LORD God. 18What more can David *say* to You for the honor of Your servant? For You know Your servant. 19O LORD, for Your servant's sake, and according to Your own heart, You have done all this greatness, in making known all these great things. 20O LORD, *there is* none like You, nor *is there any* God besides You, according to all that we have heard with our ears. 21And who *is* like Your people Israel, the one nation on the earth whom God went to redeem for Himself *as* a people—to make for Yourself a name by great and awesome deeds, by driving out nations from before Your people whom You redeemed from Egypt? 22For You have made Your people Israel Your very own people forever; and You, LORD, have become their God.

23"And now, O LORD, the word which You have spoken concerning Your servant and concerning his house, *let it* be established forever, and do as You have said. 24So let it be established, that Your name may be magnified forever, saying, 'The LORD of hosts, the God of Israel, *is* Israel's God.' And let the house of Your servant David be established before You. 25For You, O my God, have revealed to Your servant that You will build him a house. Therefore Your servant has found it *in his heart* to pray before You. 26And now, LORD, You are God, and have promised this goodness to Your servant. 27Now You have been pleased to bless the house of Your servant, that it may continue before You forever; for You have blessed it, O LORD, and *it shall be* blessed forever."

David's Further Conquests

18 After this it came to pass that David attacked the Philistines, subdued them, and took Gath and its towns from the hand of the Philistines. 2Then he defeated Moab, and the Moabites became David's servants, *and* brought tribute.

3And David defeated Hadadezer king of Zobah *as far as* Hamath, as he went to establish his power by the River Euphrates. 4David took from him one thousand chariots, seven thousand*t* horsemen, and twenty thousand foot soldiers. Also David hamstrung all the chariot *horses*, except that he spared enough of them for one hundred chariots. 5When the Syrians of Damascus came to help Hadadezer king of Zobah, David killed twenty-two thousand of the Syrians. 6Then David put *garrisons* in Syria of Damascus; and the Syrians became David's servants, *and* brought tribute. So the LORD preserved David wherever he went. 7And David took the shields of gold that were on the servants of Hadadezer, and brought them to Jerusalem. 8Also from Tibhath and from Chun, cities of Hadadezer, David brought a large amount of bronze, with which Solomon made the bronze Sea, the pillars, and the articles of bronze.

9Now when Tou king of Hamath heard that David had defeated all the army of Hadadezer king of Zobah, 10he sent Hadoram his son to King David, to greet him and bless him, because he had fought against Hadadezer and defeated him (for Hadadezer had been at war with Tou); and *Hadoram brought with him* all kinds of articles of gold, silver, and bronze. 11King David also dedicated these to the LORD, along with the silver and gold that he had brought from all *these* nations—

from Edom, from Moab, from the people of Ammon, from the Philistines, and from Amalek.

12Moreover Abishai the son of Zeruiah killed eighteen thousand Edomites in the Valley of Salt. 13He also put garrisons in Edom, and all the Edomites became David's servants. And the LORD preserved David wherever he went.

David's Administration

14So David reigned over all Israel, and administered judgment and justice to all his people. 15Joab the son of Zeruiah *was* over the army; Jehoshaphat the son of Ahilud *was* recorder; 16Zadok the son of Ahitub and Abimelech the son of Abiathar *were* the priests; Shavsha *was* the scribe; 17Benaiah the son of Jehoiada *was* over the Cherethites and the Pelethites; and David's sons *were* chief ministers at the king's side.

The Ammonites and Syrians Defeated

19 It happened after this that Nahash the king of the people of Ammon died, and his son reigned in his place. 2Then David said, "I will show kindness to Hanun the son of Nahash, because his father showed kindness to me." So David sent messengers to comfort him concerning his father. And David's servants came to Hanun in the land of the people of Ammon to comfort him.

3And the princes of the people of Ammon said to Hanun, "Do you think that David really honors your father because he has sent comforters to you? Did his servants not come to you to search and to overthrow and to spy out the land?"

4Therefore Hanun took David's servants, shaved them, and cut off their garments in the middle, at their buttocks, and sent them away. 5Then *some* went and told David about the men; and he sent to meet them, because the men were greatly ashamed. And the king said, "Wait at Jericho until your beards have grown, and *then* return."

6When the people of Ammon saw that they had made themselves repulsive to David, Hanun and the people of

---

t Or *seven hundred* (compare 2 Samuel 8.4)

Ammon sent a thousand talents of silver to hire for themselves chariots and horsemen from Mesopotamia, from Syrian Maacah, and from Zobah. 7So they hired for themselves thirty-two thousand chariots, with the king of Maacah and his people, who came and encamped before Medeba. Also the people of Ammon gathered together from their cities, and came to battle.

8Now when David heard *of it*, he sent Joab and all the army of the mighty men. 9Then the people of Ammon came out and put themselves in battle array before the gate of the city, and the kings who had come *were* by themselves in the field.

10When Joab saw that the battle line was against him before and behind, he chose some of Israel's best, and put *them* in battle array against the Syrians. 11And the rest of the people he put under the command of Abishai his brother, and they set *themselves* in battle array against the people of Ammon. 12Then he said, "If the Syrians are too strong for me, then you shall help me; but if the people of Ammon are too strong for you, then I will help you. 13Be of good courage, and let us be strong for our people and for the cities of our God. And may the LORD do *what is* good in His sight."

14So Joab and the people who *were* with him drew near for the battle against the Syrians, and they fled before him. 15When the people of Ammon saw that the Syrians were fleeing, they also fled before Abishai his brother, and entered the city. So Joab went to Jerusalem.

16Now when the Syrians saw that they had been defeated by Israel, they sent messengers and brought the Syrians who were beyond the River,ᵘ and Shophach the commander of Hadadezer's army *went* before them. 17When it was told David, he gathered all Israel, crossed over the Jordan and came upon them, and set up in battle array against them. So when David had set up in *battle* array against the Syrians, they fought with him. 18Then the Syrians fled before Israel; and David killed

seven thousandᵛ charioteers and forty thousand foot soldiersʷ of the Syrians, and killed Shophach the commander of the army. 19And when the servants of Hadadezer saw that they were defeated by Israel, they made peace with David and became his servants. So the Syrians were not willing to help the people of Ammon anymore.

Rabbah Is Conquered

20 It happened in the spring of the year, at the time kings go out *to battle,* that Joab led out the armed forces and ravaged the country of the people of Ammon, and came and besieged Rabbah. But David stayed at Jerusalem. And Joab defeated Rabbah and overthrew it. 2Then David took their king's crown from his head, and found it to weigh a talent of gold, and *there were* precious stones in it. And it was set on David's head. Also he brought out the spoil of the city in great abundance. 3And he brought out the people who *were* in it, and put *them* to work with saws, with iron picks, and with axes. So David did to all the cities of the people of Ammon. Then David and all the people returned *to* Jerusalem.

Philistine Giants Destroyed

4Now it happened afterward that war broke out at Gezer with the Philistines, at which time Sibbechai the Hushathite killed Sippai, *who was one* of the sons of the giant. And they were subdued.

5Again there was war with the Philistines, and Elhanan the son of Jair killed Lahmi the brother of Goliath the Gittite, the shaft of whose spear *was* like a weaver's beam.

6Yet again there was war at Gath, where there was a man of *great* stature, with twenty-four fingers and toes, six *on each hand* and six *on each foot;* and he also was born to the giant. 7So when he defied Israel, Jonathan the son of Shimea, David's brother, killed him.

8These were born to the giant in Gath, and they fell by the hand of David and by the hand of his servants.

ᵘ That is, the Euphrates ᵛ Or *seven hundred* (compare 2 Samuel 10.18) ʷ Or *horsemen* (compare 2 Samuel 10.18)

The Census of Israel and Judah

21 Now Satan stood up against Israel, and moved David to number Israel. 2So David said to Joab and to the leaders of the people, "Go, number Israel from Beersheba to Dan, and bring the number of them to me that I may know *it*."

3And Joab answered, "May the LORD make His people a hundred times more than they are. But, my lord the king, *are* they not all my lord's servants? Why then does my lord require this thing? Why should he be a cause of guilt in Israel?"

· 4Nevertheless the king's word prevailed against Joab. Therefore Joab departed and went throughout all Israel and came to Jerusalem. 5Then Joab gave the sum of the number of the people to David. All Israel *had* one million one hundred thousand men who drew the sword, and Judah *had* four hundred and seventy thousand men who drew the sword. 6But he did not count Levi and Benjamin among them, for the king's word was abominable to Joab.

7And God was displeased with this thing; therefore He struck Israel. 8So David said to God, "I have sinned greatly, because I have done this thing; but now, I pray, take away the iniquity of Your servant, for I have done very foolishly."

9Then the LORD spoke to Gad, David's seer, saying, 10"Go and tell David, saying, 'Thus says the LORD: "I offer you three *things;* choose one of them for yourself, that I may do *it* to you." ' "

11So Gad came to David and said to him, "Thus says the LORD: 'Choose for yourself, 12either three^x years of famine, or three months to be defeated by your foes with the sword of your enemies overtaking *you,* or else for three days the sword of the LORD—the plague in the land, with the angel^y of the LORD destroying throughout all the territory of Israel.' Now consider what answer I should take back to Him who sent me."

13And David said to Gad, "I am in great distress. Please let me fall into the hand of the LORD, for His mercies *are* very great; but do not let me fall into the hand of man."

14So the LORD sent a plague upon Israel, and seventy thousand men of Israel fell. 15And God sent an angel to Jerusalem to destroy it. As he^z was destroying, the LORD looked and relented of the disaster, and said to the angel who was destroying, "It is enough; now restrain your^a hand." And the angel of the LORD stood by the threshing floor of Ornan the Jebusite.

16Then David lifted his eyes and saw the angel of the LORD standing between earth and heaven, having in his hand a drawn sword stretched out over Jerusalem. So David and the elders, clothed in sackcloth, fell on their faces. 17And David said to God, "Was it not I who commanded the people to be numbered? I am the one who has sinned and done evil indeed; but these sheep, what have they done? Let Your hand, I pray, O LORD my God, be against me and my father's house, but not against Your people that they should be plagued."

18Therefore, the angel of the LORD commanded Gad to say to David that David should go and erect an altar to the LORD on the threshing floor of Ornan the Jebusite. 19So David went up at the word of Gad, which he had spoken in the name of the LORD. 20Now Ornan turned and saw the angel; and his four sons *who were* with him hid themselves, but Ornan continued threshing wheat. 21So David came to Ornan, and Ornan looked and saw David. And he went out from the threshing floor, and bowed before David with *his* face to the ground. 22Then David said to Ornan, "Grant me the place of *this* threshing floor, that I may build an altar on it to the LORD. You shall grant it to me at the full price, that the plague may be withdrawn from the people."

23But Ornan said to David, "Take *it* to yourself, and let my lord the king do *what is* good in his eyes. Look, I *also* give *you* the oxen for burnt offerings, the threshing implements for wood, and the wheat for the grain offering; I give *it* all."

---

^{x} Or *seven* (compare 2 Samuel 24.13)　　^{y} Or *Angel,* and so elsewhere in this chapter
^{z} Or *He*　　^{a} Or *Your*

24Then King David said to Ornan, "No, but I will surely buy *it* for the full price, for I will not take what is yours for the LORD, nor offer burnt offerings with *that which* costs *me* nothing." 25So David gave Ornan six hundred shekels of gold by weight for the place. 26And David built there an altar to the LORD, and offered burnt offerings and peace offerings, and called on the LORD; and He answered him from heaven by fire on the altar of burnt offering.

27So the LORD commanded the angel, and he returned his sword to its sheath.

28At that time, when David saw that the LORD had answered him on the threshing floor of Ornan the Jebusite, he sacrificed there. 29For the tabernacle of the LORD and the altar of the burnt offering, which Moses had made in the wilderness, *were* at that time at the high place in Gibeon. 30But David could not go before it to inquire of God, for he was afraid of the sword of the angel of the LORD.

David Prepares to Build the Temple

22 Then David said, "This *is* the house of the LORD God, and this *is* the altar of burnt offering for Israel." 2So David commanded to gather the aliens who *were* in the land of Israel; and he appointed masons to cut hewn stones to build the house of God. 3And David prepared iron in abundance for the nails of the doors of the gates and for the joints, and bronze in abundance beyond measure, 4and cedar trees in abundance; for the Sidonians and those from Tyre brought much cedar wood to David.

5Now David said, "Solomon my son *is* young and inexperienced, and the house to be built for the LORD *must be* exceedingly magnificent, famous and glorious throughout all countries. I will now make preparation for it." So David made abundant preparations before his death.

6Then he called for his son Solomon, and charged him to build a house for the LORD God of Israel. 7And David said to Solomon: "My son, as for me, it was in my mind to build a house to the name of the LORD my God; 8but the word of the LORD came to me, saying, 'You have shed much blood and have made great wars; you shall not build a house for My name, because you have shed much blood on the earth in My sight. 9Behold, a son shall be born to you, who shall be a man of rest; and I will give him rest from all his enemies all around. His name shall be Solomon,[b] for I will give peace and quietness to Israel in his days. 10He shall build a house for My name, and he shall be My son, and I *will be* his Father; and I will establish the throne of his kingdom over Israel forever.' 11Now, my son, may the LORD be with you; and may you prosper, and build the house of the LORD your God, as He has said to you. 12Only may the LORD give you wisdom and understanding, and give you charge concerning Israel, that you may keep the law of the LORD your God. 13Then you will prosper, if you take care to fulfill the statutes and judgments with which the LORD charged Moses concerning Israel. Be strong and of good courage; do not fear nor be dismayed. 14Indeed I have taken much trouble to prepare for the house of the LORD one hundred thousand talents of gold and one million talents of silver, and bronze and iron beyond measure, for it is so abundant. I have prepared timber and stone also, and you may add to them. 15Moreover *there are* workmen with you in abundance: woodsmen and stonecutters, and all types of skillful men for every kind of work. 16Of gold and silver and bronze and iron *there is* no limit. Arise and begin working, and the LORD be with you."

17David also commanded all the leaders of Israel to help Solomon his son, *saying,* 18"*Is* not the LORD your God with you? And has He *not* given you rest on every side? For He has given the inhabitants of the land into my hand, and the land is subdued before the LORD and before His people. 19Now set your heart and your soul to seek the LORD your God. Therefore arise and build the sanctuary of the LORD God, to bring the ark of the covenant of the LORD and the holy articles

b Literally *Peaceful*

of God into the house that is to be built for the name of the LORD."

The Divisions of the Levites

23 So when David was old and full of days, he made his son Solomon king over Israel.

2And he gathered together all the leaders of Israel, with the priests and the Levites. 3Now the Levites were numbered from the age of thirty years and above; and the number of individual males was thirty-eight thousand. 4Of these, twenty-four thousand were to look after the work of the house of the LORD, six thousand were officers and judges, 5four thousand were gatekeepers, and four thousand praised the LORD with *musical* instruments, "which I made," *said David,* "for giving praise."

6Also David separated them into divisions among the sons of Levi: Gershon, Kohath, and Merari.

7Of the Gershonites: Laadan and Shimei. 8The sons of Laadan: the first Jehiel, then Zetham and Joel—three *in all.* 9The sons of Shimei: Shelomith, Haziel, and Haran—three *in all.* These were the heads of the fathers' *houses* of Laadan. 10And the sons of Shimei: Jahath, Zina, Jeush, and Beriah. These *were* the four sons of Shimei. 11Jahath was the first and Zizah the second. But Jeush and Beriah did not have many sons; therefore they were assigned as one father's house.

12The sons of Kohath: Amram, Izhar, Hebron, and Uzziel—four *in all.* 13The sons of Amram: Aaron and Moses; and Aaron was set apart, he and his sons forever, that he should sanctify the most holy things, to burn incense before the LORD, to minister to Him, and to give the blessing in His name forever. 14Now the sons of Moses the man of God were reckoned to the tribe of Levi. 15The sons of Moses *were* Gershon and Eliezer. 16Of the sons of Gershon, Shebuel *was* the first. 17Of the descendants of Eliezer, Rehabiah was the first. And Eliezer had no other sons, but the sons of Rehabiah were very many. 18Of the sons of Izhar, Shelomith *was* the first. 19Of the sons of Hebron, Jeriah *was* the first, Amariah the second, Jahaziel the third, and Jekameam the fourth.

20Of the sons of Uzziel, Michah *was* the first and Jesshiah the second.

21The sons of Merari *were* Mahli and Mushi. The sons of Mahli *were* Eleazar and Kish. 22And Eleazar died, and had no sons, but only daughters; and their brethren, the sons of Kish, took them *as wives.* 23The sons of Mushi *were* Mahli, Eder, and Jeremoth—three *in all.*

24These *were* the sons of Levi by their fathers' houses—the heads of the fathers' *houses* as they were counted individually by the number of their names, who did the work for the service of the house of the LORD, from the age of twenty years and above.

25For David said, "The LORD God of Israel has given rest to His people, that they may dwell in Jerusalem forever"; 26and also to the Levites, "They shall no longer carry the tabernacle, or any of the articles for its service." 27For by the last words of David the Levites *were* numbered from twenty years old and above; 28because their duty *was* to help the sons of Aaron in the service of the house of the LORD, in the courts and in the chambers, in the purifying of all holy things and the work of the service of the house of God, 29both with the showbread and the fine flour for the grain offering, with the unleavened cakes and *what is baked in* the pan, with what is mixed and with all kinds of measures and sizes; 30to stand every morning to thank and praise the LORD, and likewise at evening; 31and at every presentation of a burnt offering to the LORD on the Sabbaths and on the New Moons and on the set feasts, by number according to the ordinance governing them, regularly before the LORD; 32and that they should attend to the needs of the tabernacle of meeting, the needs of the holy *place,* and the needs of the sons of Aaron their brethren in the work of the house of the LORD.

The Divisions of the Priests

24 Now *these are* the divisions of the sons of Aaron. The sons of Aaron *were* Nadab, Abihu, Eleazar, and Ithamar. 2And Nadab and Abihu died before their father, and had no children; therefore Eleazar and Ithamar ministered as priests. 3Then David with Zadok of the sons of Eleazar, and Ahimelech of the sons of Ithamar, divided them according to the schedule of their service.

4There were more leaders found of the sons of Eleazar than of the sons of Ithamar, and *thus* they were divided. Among the sons of Eleazar *were* sixteen heads of *their* fathers' houses, and eight heads of their fathers' houses among the sons of Ithamar. 5Thus they were divided by lot, one group as another, for there were officials of the sanctuary and officials *of the house* of God, from the sons of Eleazar and from the sons of Ithamar. 6And the scribe, Shemaiah the son of Nethanel, *one of* the Levites, wrote them down before the king, the leaders, Zadok the priest, Ahimelech the son of Abiathar, and the heads of the fathers' *houses* of the priests and Levites, one father's house taken for Eleazar and *one* for Ithamar.

7Now the first lot fell to Jehoiarib, the second to Jedaiah, 8the third to Harim, the fourth to Seorim, 9the fifth to Malchijah, the sixth to Mijamin, 10the seventh to Hakkoz, the eighth to Abijah, 11the ninth to Jeshua, the tenth to Shecaniah, 12the eleventh to Eliashib, the twelfth to Jakim, 13the thirteenth to Huppah, the fourteenth to Jeshebeab, 14the fifteenth to Bilgah, the sixteenth to Immer, 15the seventeenth to Hezir, the eighteenth to Happizzez, 16the nineteenth to Pethahiah, the twentieth to Jehezekel, 17the twenty-first to Jachin, the twenty-second to Gamul, 18the twenty-third to Delaiah, the twenty-fourth to Maaziah.

19This *was* the schedule of their service for coming into the house of the LORD according to their ordinance by the hand of Aaron their father, as the LORD God of Israel had commanded him.

Other Levites

20And the rest of the sons of Levi: of the sons of Amram, Shubael; of the sons of Shubael, Jehdeiah. 21Concerning Rehabiah, of the sons of Rehabiah, the first *was* Isshiah. 22Of the Izharites, Shelomoth; of the sons of Shelomoth, Jahath. 23Of the sons *of Hebron,* Jeriah

was the first, Amariah the second, Jahaziel the third, *and* Jekameam the fourth. 24Of the sons of Uzziel, Michah; of the sons of Michah, Shamir. 25The brother of Michah, Isshiah; of the sons of Isshiah, Zechariah. 26The sons of Merari *were* Mahli and Mushi; the son of Jaaziah, Beno. 27The sons of Merari by Jaaziah *were* Beno, Shoham, Zaccur, and Ibri. 28Of Mahli: Eleazar, who had no sons. 29Of Kish: the son of Kish, Jerahmeel.

30Also the sons of Mushi *were* Mahli, Eder, and Jerimoth. These *were* the sons of the Levites according to their fathers' houses.

31These also cast lots just as their brothers the sons of Aaron did, in the presence of King David, Zadok, Ahimelech, and the heads of the fathers' *houses* of the priests and Levites. The chief fathers *did* just as their younger brethren.

The Musicians

25 Moreover David and the captains of the army separated for the service *some* of the sons of Asaph, of Heman, and of Jeduthun, who *should* prophesy with harps, stringed instruments, and cymbals. And the number of the skilled men performing their service was: 2Of the sons of Asaph: Zaccur, Joseph, Nethaniah, and Asharelah; the sons of Asaph *were* under the direction of Asaph, who prophesied according to the order of the king. 3Of Jeduthun, the sons of Jeduthun: Gedaliah, Zeri, Jeshaiah, Shimei, Hashabiah, and Mattithiah, six, under the direction of their father Jeduthun, who prophesied with a harp to give thanks and to praise the LORD. 4Of Heman, the sons of Heman: Bukkiah, Mattaniah, Uzziel, Shebuel, Jerimoth, Hananiah, Hanani, Eliathah, Giddalti, Romamti-Ezer, Joshbekashah, Mallothi, Hothir, *and* Mahazioth. 5All these *were* the sons of Heman the king's seer in the words of God, to exalt his horn.c For God gave Heman fourteen sons and three daughters.

6All these *were* under the direction of their father for the music *in* the house of the LORD, with cymbals, stringed in-

---

c That is, to increase his power or influence

struments, and harps, for the service of the house of God. Asaph, Jeduthun, and Heman *were* under the authority of the king. 7So the number of them, with their brethren who were instructed in the songs of the LORD, all who were skillful, *was* two hundred and eighty-eight.

8And they cast lots for their duty, the small as well as the great, the teacher with the student.

9Now the first lot for Asaph came out for Joseph; the second for Gedaliah, him with his brethren and sons, twelve; 10the third for Zaccur, his sons and his brethren, twelve; 11the fourth for Jizri, his sons and his brethren, twelve; 12the fifth for Nethaniah, his sons and his brethren, twelve; 13the sixth for Bukkiah, his sons and his brethren, twelve; 14the seventh for Jesharelah, his sons and his brethren, twelve; 15the eighth for Jeshaiah, his sons and his brethren, twelve; 16the ninth for Mattaniah, his sons and his brethren, twelve; 17the tenth for Shimei, his sons and his brethren, twelve; 18the eleventh for Azarel, his sons and his brethren, twelve; 19the twelfth for Hashabiah, his sons and his brethren, twelve; 20the thirteenth for Shubael, his sons and his brethren, twelve; 21the fourteenth for Mattithiah, his sons and his brethren, twelve; 22the fifteenth for Jeremoth, his sons and his brethren, twelve; 23the sixteenth for Hananiah, his sons and his brethren, twelve; 24the seventeenth for Joshbekashah, his sons and his brethren, twelve; 25the eighteenth for Hanani, his sons and his brethren, twelve; 26the nineteenth for Mallothi, his sons and his brethren, twelve; 27the twentieth for Eliathah, his sons and his brethren, twelve; 28the twenty-first for Hothir, his sons and his brethren, twelve; 29the twenty-second for Giddalti, his sons and his brethren, twelve; 30the twenty-third for Mahazioth, his sons and his brethren, twelve; 31the twenty-fourth for Romamti-Ezer, his sons and his brethren, twelve.

The Gatekeepers

26 Concerning the divisions of the gatekeepers: of the Korahites, Meshelemiah the son of Kore, of the sons of Asaph. 2And the sons of Meshelemiah *were* Zechariah the firstborn, Jediael the second, Zebadiah the third, Jathniel the fourth, 3Elam the fifth, Jehohanan the sixth, Eliehoenai the seventh.

4Moreover the sons of Obed-Edom *were* Shemaiah the firstborn, Jehozabad the second, Joah the third, Sacar the fourth, Nethanel the fifth, 5Ammiel the sixth, Issachar the seventh, Peulthai the eighth; for God blessed him.

6Also to Shemaiah his son were sons born who governed their fathers' houses, because they *were* men of great ability. 7The sons of Shemaiah *were* Othni, Rephael, Obed, and Elzabad, whose brothers Elihu and Semachiah *were* able men.

8All these *were* of the sons of Obed-Edom, they and their sons and their brethren, able men with strength for the work: sixty-two of Obed-Edom.

9And Meshelemiah had sons and brethren, eighteen able men.

10Also Hosah, of the children of Merari, had sons: Shimri the first (for *though* he was not the firstborn, his father made him the first), 11Hilkiah the second, Tebaliah the third, Zechariah the fourth; all the sons and brethren of Hosah *were* thirteen.

12Among these *were* the divisions of the gatekeepers, among the chief men, *having* duties just like their brethren, to serve in the house of the LORD. 13And they cast lots for each gate, the small as well as the great, according to their father's house. 14The lot for the East *Gate* fell to Shelemiah. Then they cast lots *for* his son Zechariah, a wise counselor, and his lot came out for the North Gate; 15to Obed-Edom the South Gate, and to his sons the storehouse. 16To Shuppim and Hosah *the lot came out* for the West Gate, with the Shallecheth Gate on the ascending highway—watchman opposite watchman. 17On the east were *six* Levites, on the north four each day, on the south four each day, and for the storehouse two by two. 18As for the Parbar on the west, *there were* four on the highway *and* two at the Parbar. 19These were the divisions of the gatekeepers among the sons of Korah and among the sons of Merari.

The Treasuries and Other Duties

20Of the Levites, Ahijah *was* over the treasuries of the house of God and over the treasuries of the dedicated things. 21The sons of Laadan, the descendants of the Gershonites of Laadan, heads of their fathers' *houses*, of Laadan the Gershonite: Jehieli. 22The sons of Jehieli, Zetham and Joel his brother, *were* over the treasuries of the house of the Lord. 23Of the Amramites, the Izharites, the Hebronites, and the Uzzielites: 24Shebuel the son of Gershom, the son of Moses, *was* overseer of the treasuries. 25And his brethren by Eliezer *were* Rehabiah his son, Jeshaiah his son, Joram his son, Zichri his son, and Shelomith his son.

26This Shelomith and his brethren *were* over all the treasuries of the dedicated things which King David and the heads of fathers' *houses*, the captains over thousands and hundreds, and the captains of the army, had dedicated. 27Some of the spoils won in battles they dedicated to maintain the house of the Lord. 28And all that Samuel the seer, Saul the son of Kish, Abner the son of Ner, and Joab the son of Zeruiah had dedicated, every dedicated *thing*, was under the hand of Shelomith and his brethren.

29Of the Izharites, Chenaniah and his sons *performed* duties as officials and judges over Israel outside Jerusalem.

30Of the Hebronites, Hashabiah and his brethren, one thousand seven hundred able men, had the oversight of Israel on the west side of the Jordan for all the business of the Lord, and in the service of the king. 31Among the Hebronites, Jerijah *was* head of the Hebronites according to his genealogy of the fathers. In the fortieth year of the reign of David they were sought, and there were found among them capable men at Jazer of Gilead. 32And his brethren *were* two thousand seven hundred able men, heads of fathers' *houses*, whom King David made officials over the Reubenites, the Gadites, and the half-tribe of Manasseh, for every matter pertaining to God and the affairs of the king.

The Military Divisions

27 And the children of Israel, according to their number, the heads of fathers' *houses*, the captains of thousands and hundreds and their officers, served the king in every matter of the *military* divisions. *These divisions* came in and went out month by month throughout all the months of the year, each division *having* twenty-four thousand.

2Over the first division for the first month *was* Jashobeam the son of Zabdiel, and in his division *were* twenty-four thousand; 3he *was* of the children of Perez, and the chief of all the captains of the army for the first month. 4Over the division of the second month *was* Dodai an Ahohite, and of his division Mikloth also *was* the leader; in his division *were* twenty-four thousand. 5The third captain of the army for the third month *was* Benaiah, the son of Jehoiada the priest, who was chief; in his division *were* twenty-four thousand. 6This was the Benaiah who *was* mighty among the thirty, and was over the thirty; in his division *was* Ammizabad his son. 7The fourth *captain* for the fourth month *was* Asahel the brother of Joab, and Zebadiah his son after him; in his division *were* twenty-four thousand. 8The fifth *captain* for the fifth month *was* Shamhuth the Izrahite; in his division were twenty-four thousand. 9The sixth *captain* for the sixth month *was* Ira the son of Ikkesh the Tekoite; in his division *were* twenty-four thousand. 10The seventh *captain* for the seventh month *was* Helez the Pelonite, of the children of Ephraim; in his division *were* twenty-four thousand. 11The eighth *captain* for the eighth month *was* Sibbechai the Hushathite, of the Zarhites; in his division *were* twenty-four thousand. 12The ninth *captain* for the ninth month *was* Abiezer the Anathothite, of the Benjamites; in his division *were* twenty-four thousand. 13The tenth *captain* for the tenth month *was* Maharai the Netophathite, of the Zarhites; in his division *were* twenty-four thousand. 14The eleventh *captain* for the eleventh month *was* Benaiah the Pirathonite, of the children of Ephraim; in his division *were* twenty-four thousand. 15The twelfth *captain* for the twelfth month *was* Heldai the Netophathite, of Othniel; in his division *were* twenty-four thousand.

Leaders of Tribes

16Furthermore, over the tribes of Israel: the officer over the Reubenites *was* Eliezer the son of Zichri; over the Simeonites, Shephatiah the son of Maachah; 17over the Levites, Hashabiah the son of Kemuel; over the Aaronites, Zadok; 18over Judah, Elihu, *one* of David's brothers; *over* Issachar, Omri the son of Michael; 19over Zebulun, Ishmaiah the son of Obadiah; *over* Naphtali, Jerimoth the son of Azriel; 20over the children of Ephraim, Hoshea the son of Azaziah; *over* the half-tribe of Manasseh, Joel the son of Pedaiah; 21over the half-*tribe* of Manasseh in Gilead, Iddo the son of Zechariah; *over* Benjamin, Jaasiel the son of Abner; 22over Dan, Azarel the son of Jeroham. These *were* the leaders of the tribes of Israel.

23But David did not take the number of those twenty years old and under, because the LORD had said He would multiply Israel like the stars of the heavens. 24Joab the son of Zeruiah began a census, but he did not finish, for wrath came upon Israel because of this census; nor was the number recorded in the account of the chronicles of King David.

Other State Officials

25And Azmaveth the son of Adiel *was* over the king's treasuries; and Jehonathan the son of Uzziah was over the storehouses in the field, in the cities, in the villages, and in the fortresses. 26Ezri the son of Chelub was over those who did the work of the field for tilling the ground. 27And Shimei the Ramathite *was* over the vineyards, and Zabdi the Shiphmite was over the produce of the vineyards for the supply of wine. 28Baal-Hanan the Gederite was over the olive trees and the sycamore trees that *were* in the lowlands, and Joash *was* over the store of oil. 29And Shitrai the Sharonite *was* over the herds that fed in Sharon, and Shaphat the son of Adlai was over the herds *that were* in the valleys. 30Obil the Ishmaelite *was* over the camels, Jehdeiah the Meronothite *was*

over the donkeys, 31and Jaziz the Hagrite *was* over the flocks. All these *were* the officials over King David's property.

32Also Jehonathan, David's uncle, *was* a counselor, a wise man, and a scribe; and Jehiel the son of Hachmoni *was* with the king's sons. 33Ahithophel *was* the king's counselor, and Hushai the Archite *was* the king's companion. 34After Ahithophel *was* Jehoiada the son of Benaiah, then Abiathar. And the general of the king's army *was* Joab.

Solomon Instructed to Build the Temple

28 Now David assembled at Jerusalem all the leaders of Israel: the officers of the tribes and the captains of the divisions who served the king, the captains over thousands and captains over hundreds, and the stewards over all the substance and possessions of the king and of his sons, with the officials, the valiant men, and all the mighty men of valor.

2Then King David rose to his feet and said, "Hear me, my brethren and my people: I *had* it in my heart to build a house of rest for the ark of the covenant of the LORD, and for the footstool of our God, and had made preparations to build it. 3But God said to me, 'You shall not build a house for My name, because you *have been* a man of war and have shed blood.' 4However the LORD God of Israel chose me above all the house of my father to be king over Israel forever, for He has chosen Judah *to be* the ruler. And of the house of Judah, the house of my father, and among the sons of my father, He was pleased with me to make *me* king over all Israel. 5And of all my sons (for the LORD has given me many sons) He has chosen my son Solomon to sit on the throne of the kingdom of the LORD over Israel. 6Now He said to me, 'It is your son Solomon *who* shall build My house and My courts; for I have chosen him *to be* My son, and I will be his Father. 7Moreover I will establish his kingdom forever, if he is steadfast to observe My commandments and My judgments, as it is this day.' 8Now therefore, in the sight of all Israel, the assembly of the LORD, and in the hearing of our God, be careful to seek out all the commandments of the LORD your God, that you may possess this good land, and leave *it* as an inheritance for your children after you forever.

9"As for you, my son Solomon, know the God of your father, and serve Him with a loyal heart and with a willing mind; for the LORD searches all hearts and understands all the intent of the thoughts. If you seek Him, He will be found by you; but if you forsake Him, He will cast you off forever. 10Consider now, for the LORD has chosen you to build a house for the sanctuary; be strong, and do it."

11Then David gave his son Solomon the plans for the vestibule, its houses, its treasuries, its upper chambers, its inner chambers, and the place of the mercy seat; 12and the plans for all that he had by the Spirit, of the courts of the house of the LORD, of all the chambers all around, of the treasuries of the house of God, and of the treasuries for the dedicated things; 13also for the division of the priests and the Levites, for all the work of the service of the house of the LORD, and for all the articles of service in the house of the LORD. 14*He gave* gold by weight for *things* of gold, for all articles used in every kind of service; also *silver* for all articles of silver by weight, for all articles used in every kind of service; 15the weight for the lampstands of gold, and their lamps of gold, by weight for each lampstand and its lamps; for the lampstands of silver by weight, for the lampstand and its lamps, according to the use of each lampstand. 16And by weight *he gave* gold for the tables of the showbread, for each table, and silver for the tables of silver; 17also pure gold for the forks, the basins, the pitchers of pure gold, and the golden bowls—*he gave gold* by weight for every bowl; and for the silver bowls, *silver* by weight for every bowl; 18and refined gold by weight for the altar of incense, and for the construction of the chariot, that is, the gold cherubim that spread *their wings* and overshadowed the ark of the covenant of the LORD. 19"All *this*," *said David,* "the LORD made me understand in writing, by *His* hand upon me, all the works of these plans."

20And David said to his son Solomon, "Be strong and of good courage, and do *it;* do not fear nor be dismayed, for the LORD God—my God—*will be* with you. He will not leave you nor forsake you, until you have finished all the work for the service of the house of the LORD. 21*Here are* the divisions of the priests and the Levites for all the service of the house of God; and every willing craftsman *will be* with you for all manner of workmanship, for every kind of service; also the leaders and all the people *will be* completely at your command."

Offerings for Building the Temple

29 Furthermore King David said to all the assembly: "My son Solomon, whom alone God has chosen, *is* young and inexperienced; and the work *is* great, because the temple *is* not for man but for the LORD God. 2Now for the house of my God I have prepared with all my might: gold for *things to be made of* gold, silver for *things of* silver, bronze for *things of* bronze, iron for *things of* iron, wood for *things of* wood, onyx stones, *stones* to be set, glistening stones of various colors, all kinds of precious stones, and marble slabs in abundance. 3Moreover, because I have set my affection on the house of my God, I have given to the house of my God, over and above all that I have prepared for the holy house, my own special treasure of gold and silver: 4three thousand talents of gold, of the gold of Ophir, and seven thousand talents of refined silver, to overlay the walls of the houses; 5the gold for *things of* gold and the silver for *things of* silver, and for all kinds of work *to be done* by the hands of craftsmen. Who *then* is willing to consecrate himself this day to the LORD?"

6Then the leaders of the fathers' *houses,* leaders of the tribes of Israel, the captains of thousands and of hundreds, with the officers over the king's work, offered willingly. 7They gave for the work of the house of God five thousand talents and ten thousand darics of gold, ten thousand talents of silver, eighteen thousand talents of bronze, and one hundred thousand talents of iron. 8And whoever had *precious* stones gave *them* to the treasury of the house of the LORD, into the hand of Jehiel the

Gershonite. 9Then the people rejoiced, for they had offered willingly, because with a loyal heart they had offered willingly to the LORD; and King David also rejoiced greatly.

David's Praise to God

10Therefore David blessed the LORD before all the assembly; and David said: "Blessed are You, LORD God of Israel, our Father, forever and ever.

11 Yours, O LORD, *is* the greatness,
    The power and the glory,
    The victory and the majesty;
    For all *that is* in heaven and in earth *is Yours;*
    Yours *is* the kingdom, O LORD,
    And You are exalted as head over all.

12 Both riches and honor *come* from You,
    And You reign over all.
    In Your hand *is* power and might;
    In Your hand *it is* to make great
    And to give strength to all.

13 "Now therefore, our God,
    We thank You
    And praise Your glorious name.

14 But who *am* I, and who *are* my people,
    That we should be able to offer so willingly as this?
    For all things *come* from You,
    And of Your own we have given You.

15 For we *are* aliens and pilgrims before You,
    As *were* all our fathers;
    Our days on earth *are* as a shadow,
    And without hope.

16"O LORD our God, all this abundance that we have prepared to build You a house for Your holy name is from Your hand, and *is* all Your own. 17I know also, my God, that You test the heart and have pleasure in uprightness. As for me, in the uprightness of my heart I have willingly offered all these *things;* and now with joy I have seen Your people, who are present here to offer willingly to You. 18O LORD God of Abraham, Isaac, and Israel, our fathers, keep this forever in the intent of the thoughts of the heart of Your peo-

ple, and fix their heart toward You. 19And give my son Solomon a loyal heart to keep Your commandments and Your testimonies and Your statutes, to do all *these things,* and to build the temple for which I have made provision."

20Then David said to all the assembly, "Now bless the LORD your God." So all the assembly blessed the LORD God of their fathers, and bowed their heads and prostrated themselves before the LORD and the king.

Solomon Anointed King

21And they made sacrifices to the LORD and offered burnt offerings to the LORD on the next day: a thousand bulls, a thousand rams, a thousand lambs, with their drink offerings, and sacrifices in abundance for all Israel. 22So they ate and drank before the LORD with great gladness on that day. And they made Solomon the son of David king the second time, and anointed *him* before the LORD *to be* the leader, and Zadok *to be* priest. 23Then Solomon sat on the throne of the LORD as king instead of David his father, and prospered; and all Israel obeyed him. 24All the leaders and the mighty men, and also all the sons of King David, submitted themselves to King Solomon. 25So the LORD exalted Solomon exceedingly in the sight of all Israel, and bestowed on him *such* royal majesty as had not been on any king before him in Israel.

The Close of David's Reign

26Thus David the son of Jesse reigned over all Israel. 27And the period that he reigned over Israel *was* forty years; seven years he reigned in Hebron, and thirty-three *years* he reigned in Jerusalem. 28So he died in a good old age, full of days and riches and honor; and Solomon his son reigned in his place. 29Now the acts of King David, first and last, indeed they *are* written in the book of Samuel the seer, in the book of Nathan the prophet, and in the book of Gad the seer, 30with all his reign and his might, and the events that happened to him, to Israel, and to all the kingdoms of the lands.

The Second Book of the
CHRONICLES

Solomon Requests Wisdom

1 Now Solomon the son of David was strengthened in his kingdom, and the LORD his God *was* with him and exalted him exceedingly.

2And Solomon spoke to all Israel, to the captains of thousands and of hundreds, to the judges, and to every leader in all Israel, the heads of the fathers' *houses.* 3Then Solomon, and all the assembly with him, went to the high place that *was* at Gibeon; for the tabernacle of meeting with God was there, which Moses the servant of the LORD had made in the wilderness. 4But David had brought up the ark of God from Kirjath Jearim to *the place* David had prepared for it, for he had pitched a tent for it at Jerusalem. 5Now the bronze altar that Bezalel the son of Uri, the son of Hur, had made, he put before the tabernacle of the LORD; Solomon and the assembly sought Him *there.* 6And Solomon went up there to the bronze altar before the LORD, which *was* at the tabernacle of meeting, and offered a thousand burnt offerings on it.

7On that night God appeared to Solomon, and said to him, "Ask! What shall I give you?"

8And Solomon said to God: "You have shown great mercy to David my father, and have made me king in his place. 9Now, O LORD God, let Your promise to David my father be established, for You have made me king over a people like the dust of the earth in multitude. 10Now give me wisdom and knowledge, that I may go out and come in before this people; for who can judge this great people of Yours?"

11Then God said to Solomon: "Because this was in your heart, and you have not asked riches or wealth or honor or the life of your enemies, nor have you asked long life—but have asked wisdom and knowledge for yourself, that you may judge My people over whom I have made you king— 12wisdom and knowledge *are* granted to you; and I will give you riches and wealth and honor, such as none of the kings have had who *were* before you, nor shall any after you have the like."

Solomon's Military and Economic Power

13So Solomon came to Jerusalem from the high place that *was* at Gibeon, from before the tabernacle of meeting, and reigned over Israel. 14And Solomon gathered chariots and horsemen; he had one thousand four hundred chariots and twelve thousand horsemen, whom he stationed in the chariot cities and with the king in Jerusalem. 15Also the king made silver and gold as common in Jerusalem as stones, and he made cedars as abundant as the sycamores which *are* in the lowland. 16And Solomon had horses imported from Egypt and Keveh; the king's merchants bought them in Keveh at the *current* price. 17They also acquired and imported from Egypt a chariot for six hundred *shekels* of silver, and a horse for one hundred and fifty; thus, through their agents, they exported them to all the kings of the Hittites and the kings of Syria.

Solomon Prepares to Build the Temple

2 Then Solomon determined to build a temple for the name of the LORD, and a royal house for himself. 2Solomon selected seventy thousand men to bear burdens, eighty thousand to quarry *stone* in the mountains, and three thousand six hundred to oversee them.

3Then Solomon sent to Hiram king of Tyre, saying:

As you have dealt with David my father, and sent him cedars to build himself a house to dwell in, *so deal with me.* 4Behold, I am building a temple for the name of the LORD my God, to dedicate *it* to Him, to burn before Him sweet incense, for the continual showbread, for the burnt offerings morning and evening, on the Sabbaths, on the New Moons, and on the set feasts of the LORD our God. This *is an ordinance* forever to Israel.

5 And the temple which I build *will be* great, for our God is greater than all gods. 6But who is able to build Him a temple, since heaven and the heaven of heavens cannot contain Him? Who *am* I then, that I should build Him a temple, except to burn sacrifice before Him?

7 Therefore send me at once a man skillful to work in gold and silver, in bronze and iron, in purple and crimson and blue, who has skill to engrave with the skillful men who are with me in Judah and Jerusalem, whom David my father provided. 8Also send me cedar and cypress and algum logs from Lebanon, for I know that your servants have skill to cut timber in Lebanon; and indeed my servants *will be* with your servants, 9to prepare timber for me in abundance, for the temple which I am about to build *shall be* great and wonderful.

10 And indeed I will give to your servants, the woodsmen who cut timber, twenty thousand kors of ground wheat, twenty thousand kors of barley, twenty thousand baths of wine, and twenty thousand baths of oil.

11Then Hiram king of Tyre answered in writing, which he sent to Solomon:

Because the LORD loves His people, He has made you king over them.

12Hiram also said:

Blessed *be* the LORD God of Israel, who made heaven and earth, for He has given King David a wise son, endowed with prudence and understanding, who will build a temple for the LORD and a royal house for himself!

13 And now I have sent a skillful man, endowed with understanding, Huram my master *craftsman* 14(the son of a woman of the daughters of Dan, and his father was a man of Tyre), skilled to work in gold and silver, bronze and iron, stone and wood, purple and blue, fine linen and crimson, and to make any engraving and to accomplish any plan which may be given to him, with your skillful men and with the skillful men of my lord David your father.

15 Now therefore, the wheat, the barley, the oil, and the wine which my lord has spoken of, let him send to his servants. 16And we will cut wood from Lebanon, as much as you need; we will bring it to you in rafts by sea to Joppa, and you will carry it up to Jerusalem.

17Then Solomon numbered all the aliens who *were* in the land of Israel, after the census in which David his father had numbered them; and there were found to be one hundred and fifty-three thousand six hundred. 18And he made seventy thousand of them bearers of burdens, eighty thousand stonecutters in the mountain, and three thousand six hundred overseers to make the people work.

Solomon Builds the Temple

3 Now Solomon began to build the house of the LORD at Jerusalem on Mount Moriah, where *the LORD* had appeared to his father David, at the place that David had prepared on the threshing floor of Ornan the Jebusite. 2And he began to build on the second *day* of the second month in the fourth year of his reign.

3This is the foundation which Solomon laid for building the house of God: The length *was* sixty cubits (by cubits according to the former measure) and the width twenty cubits. 4And the vestibule that *was* in front *of the sanc-*

tuary[a] was twenty cubits long across the width of the house, and the height *was* one hundred and twenty. He overlaid the inside with pure gold. 5The larger room he paneled with cypress which he overlaid with fine gold, and he carved palm trees and chainwork on it. 6And he decorated the house with precious stones for beauty, and the gold *was* gold from Parvaim. 7He also overlaid the house—the beams and doorposts, its walls and doors—with gold; and he carved cherubim on the walls.

8And he made the Most Holy Place. Its length was according to the width of the house, twenty cubits, and its width twenty cubits. He overlaid it with six hundred talents of fine gold. 9The weight of the nails *was* fifty shekels of gold; and he overlaid the upper area with gold. 10In the Most Holy Place he made two cherubim, fashioned by carving, and overlaid them with gold. 11The wings of the cherubim *were* twenty cubits in *overall* length: one wing *of the one cherub was* five cubits, touching the wall of the room, and the other wing *was* five cubits, touching the wing of the other cherub; 12*one* wing of the other cherub *was* five cubits, touching the wall of the room, and the other wing *also was* five cubits, touching the wing of the other cherub. 13The wings of these cherubim spanned twenty cubits overall. They stood on their feet, and they faced inward. 14And he made the veil of blue, purple, crimson, and fine linen, and wove cherubim into it.

15Also he made in front of the temple two pillars thirty-five[b] cubits high, and the capital that *was* on the top of each of *them* was five cubits. 16He made wreaths of chainwork, as in the inner sanctuary, and put *them* on top of the pillars; and he made one hundred pomegranates, and put *them* on the wreaths of chainwork. 17Then he set up the pillars before the temple, one on the right hand and the other on the left; he called the name of the one on the right hand Jachin, and the name of the one on the left Boaz.

Furnishings of the Temple

4 Moreover he made a bronze altar: twenty cubits was its length, twenty cubits its width, and ten cubits its height.

2Then he made the Sea of cast *bronze,* ten cubits from one brim to the other; *it was* completely round. Its height *was* five cubits, and a line of thirty cubits measured its circumference. 3And under it *was* the likeness of oxen encircling it all around, ten to a cubit, all the way around the Sea. The oxen *were* cast in two rows, when it was cast. 4It stood on twelve oxen: three looking toward the north, three looking toward the west, three looking toward the south, and three looking toward the east; the Sea *was set* upon them, and all their back parts *pointed* inward. 5It *was* a handbreadth thick; and its brim was shaped like the brim of a cup, *like* a lily blossom. It contained three thousand baths.

6He also made ten lavers, and put five on the right side and five on the left, to wash in them; such things as they offered for the burnt offering they would wash in them, but the Sea *was* for the priests to wash in. 7And he made ten lampstands of gold according to their design, and set *them* in the temple, five on the right side and five on the left. 8He also made ten tables, and placed *them* in the temple, five on the right side and five on the left. And he made one hundred bowls of gold.

9Furthermore he made the court of the priests, and the great court and doors for the court; and he overlaid these doors with bronze. 10He set the Sea on the right side, toward the southeast.

11Then Huram made the pots and the shovels and the bowls. So Huram finished doing the work that he was to do for King Solomon for the house of God: 12the two pillars and the bowl-shaped capitals *that were* on top of the two pillars; the two networks covering the two bowl-shaped capitals which *were* on top of the pillars; 13four hundred pomegranates for the two networks (two rows of pomegranates for each net-

---

[a] The main room of the temple; elsewhere called the holy place (compare 1 Kings 6.3)
[b] Or *eighteen* (compare 1 Kings 7.15; 2 Kings 25.17; and Jeremiah 52.21)

work, to cover the two bowl-shaped capitals that *were* on the pillars); 14he also made carts and the lavers on the carts; 15one Sea and twelve oxen under it; 16also the pots, the shovels, the forks—and all their articles Huram his master *craftsman* made of burnished bronze for King Solomon for the house of the LORD.

17In the plain of Jordan the king had them cast in clay molds, between Succoth and Zeredah. 18And Solomon had all these articles made in such great abundance that the weight of the bronze was not determined.

19Thus Solomon had all the furnishings made for the house of God: the altar of gold and the tables on which *was* the showbread; 20the lampstands with their lamps of pure gold, to burn in the prescribed manner in front of the inner sanctuary, 21with the flowers and the lamps and the wick-trimmers of gold, of purest gold; 22the trimmers, the bowls, the ladles, and the censers of pure gold. As for the entry of the sanctuary, its inner doors to the Most Holy *Place*, and the doors of the main hall of the temple, *were* gold.

5 So all the work that Solomon had done for the house of the LORD was finished; and Solomon brought in the things which his father David had dedicated: the silver and the gold and all the furnishings. And he put *them* in the treasuries of the house of God.

The Ark Brought into the Temple

2Now Solomon assembled the elders of Israel and all the heads of the tribes, the chief fathers of the children of Israel, in Jerusalem, that they might bring the ark of the covenant of the LORD up from the City of David, which *is* Zion. 3Therefore all the men of Israel assembled with the king at the feast, which *was* in the seventh month. 4So all the elders of Israel came, and the Levites took up the ark. 5Then they brought up the ark, the tabernacle of meeting, and all the holy furnishings that *were* in the tabernacle. The priests and the Levites brought them up. 6Also King Solomon, and all the congregation of Israel who were assembled with him before the ark, were sacrificing sheep and oxen that could not be counted or numbered for multitude. 7Then the priests brought in the ark of the covenant of the LORD to its place, into the inner sanctuary of the temple, to the Most Holy *Place*, under the wings of the cherubim. 8For the cherubim spread *their* wings over the place of the ark, and the cherubim overshadowed the ark and its poles. 9The poles extended so that the ends of the poles of the ark could be seen from *the holy place*, in front of the inner sanctuary; but they could not be seen from outside. And they are there to this day. 10Nothing was in the ark except the two tablets which Moses put *there* at Horeb, when the LORD made *a covenant* with the children of Israel, when they had come out of Egypt.

11And it came to pass when the priests came out of the *Most* Holy *Place* (for all the priests who *were* present had sanctified themselves, without keeping to their divisions), 12and the Levites *who were* the singers, all those of Asaph and Heman and Jeduthun, with their sons and their brethren, stood at the east end of the altar, clothed in white linen, having cymbals, stringed instruments and harps, and with them one hundred and twenty priests sounding with trumpets—13indeed it came to pass, when the trumpeters and singers *were* as one, to make one sound to be heard in praising and thanking the LORD, and when they lifted up their voice with the trumpets and cymbals and instruments of music, and praised the LORD, *saying*:

"For He is good,
For His mercy *endures* forever,"c
that the house, the house of the LORD, was filled with a cloud, 14so that the priests could not continue ministering because of the cloud; for the glory of the LORD filled the house of God.

6 Then Solomon spoke:
"The LORD said
He would dwell in the dark cloud.
2 I have surely built You an exalted house,

---

c Compare Psalm 106.1

And a place for You to dwell in forever."

Solomon's Speech upon Completion of the Work

3Then the king turned around and blessed the whole assembly of Israel, while all the assembly of Israel was standing. 4And he said: "Blessed *be* the LORD God of Israel, who has fulfilled with His hands *what* He spoke with His mouth to my father David, saying, 5'Since the day that I brought My people out of the land of Egypt, I have chosen no city from any tribe of Israel *in which* to build a house, that My name might be there, nor did I choose any man to be a ruler over My people Israel. 6Yet I have chosen Jerusalem, that My name may be there, and I have chosen David to be over My people Israel.' 7Now it was in the heart of my father David to build a temple for the name of the LORD God of Israel. 8But the LORD said to my father David, 'Whereas it was in your heart to build a temple for My name, you did well in that it was in your heart. 9Nevertheless you shall not build the temple, but your son who will come from your body, he shall build the temple for My name.' 10So the LORD has fulfilled His word which He spoke, and I have filled the position of my father David, and sit on the throne of Israel, as the LORD promised; and I have built the temple for the name of the LORD God of Israel. 11And there I have put the ark, in which *is* the covenant of the LORD which He made with the children of Israel."

Solomon's Prayer of Dedication

12Then *Solomon* stood before the altar of the LORD in the presence of all the assembly of Israel, and spread out his hands 13(for Solomon had made a bronze platform five cubits long, five cubits wide, and three cubits high, and had set it in the midst of the court; and he stood on it, knelt down on his knees before all the assembly of Israel, and spread out his hands toward heaven); 14and he said: "LORD God of Israel, *there is* no God in heaven or on earth like You, who keep *Your* covenant and mercy with Your servants who walk before You with all their hearts. 15You

have kept what You promised Your servant David my father; You have both spoken with Your mouth and fulfilled *it* with Your hand, as *it is* this day. 16Therefore, LORD God of Israel, now keep what You promised Your servant David my father, saying, 'You shall not fail to have a man sit before Me on the throne of Israel, only if your sons take heed to their way, that they walk in My law as you have walked before Me.' 17And now, O LORD God of Israel, let Your word come true, which You have spoken to Your servant David.

18"But will God indeed dwell with men on the earth? Behold, heaven and the heaven of heavens cannot contain You. How much less this temple which I have built! 19Yet regard the prayer of Your servant and his supplication, O LORD my God, and listen to the cry and the prayer which Your servant is praying before You: 20that Your eyes may be open toward this temple day and night, toward the place where *You* said *You would* put Your name, that You may hear the prayer which Your servant makes toward this place. 21And may You hear the supplications of Your servant and of Your people Israel, when they pray toward this place. Hear from heaven Your dwelling place, and when You hear, forgive.

22"If anyone sins against his neighbor, and is forced to take an oath, and comes *and* takes an oath before Your altar in this temple, 23then hear from heaven, and act, and judge Your servants, bringing retribution on the wicked by bringing his way on his own head, and justifying the righteous by giving him according to his righteousness.

24"Or if Your people Israel are defeated before an enemy because they have sinned against You, and return and confess Your name, and pray and make supplication before You in this temple, 25then hear from heaven and forgive the sin of Your people Israel, and bring them back to the land which You gave to them and their fathers.

26"When the heavens are shut up and there is no rain because they have sinned against You, when they pray toward this place and confess Your name, and turn from their sin because You afflict them, 27then hear *in* heaven, and forgive the sin of Your servants, Your people Israel, that You may teach them the good way in which they should walk; and send rain on Your land which You have given to Your people as an inheritance.

28"When there is famine in the land, pestilence or blight or mildew, locusts or grasshoppers; when their enemies besiege them in the land of their cities; whatever plague or whatever sickness *there is;* 29whatever prayer, whatever supplication is *made* by anyone, or by all Your people Israel, when each one knows his own burden and his own grief, and spreads out his hands to this temple: 30then hear from heaven Your dwelling place, and forgive, and give to everyone according to all his ways, whose heart You know (for You alone know the hearts of the sons of men), 31that they may fear You, to walk in Your ways as long as they live in the land which You gave to our fathers.

32"Moreover, concerning a foreigner, who is not of Your people Israel, but has come from a far country for the sake of Your great name and Your mighty hand and Your outstretched arm, when they come and pray in this temple: 33then hear from heaven Your dwelling place, and do according to all for which the foreigner calls to You, that all peoples of the earth may know Your name and fear You, as *do* Your people Israel, and that they may know that this temple which I have built is called by Your name.

34"When Your people go out to battle against their enemies, wherever You send them, and when they pray to You toward this city which You have chosen and the temple which I have built for Your name, 35then hear from heaven their prayer and their supplication, and maintain their cause.

36"When they sin against You (for *there is* no one who does not sin), and You become angry with them and deliver them to the enemy, and they take them captive to a land far or near; 37yet when they come to themselves in the land where they were carried captive, and repent, and make supplication to You in the land of their captivity, saying, 'We have sinned, we have done wrong, and have committed wickedness'; 38and *when* they return to You with all their heart and with all their soul in the land of their captivity, where they have been carried captive, and pray toward their land which You gave to their fathers, the city which You have chosen, and toward the temple which I have built for Your name: 39then hear from heaven Your dwelling place their prayer and their supplications, and maintain their cause, and forgive Your people who have sinned against You. 40Now, my God, I pray, let Your eyes be open and *let* Your ears *be* attentive to the prayer *made* in this place.

41 "Now therefore,
Arise, O LORD God, to Your resting place,
You and the ark of Your strength.
Let Your priests, O LORD God, be clothed with salvation,
And let Your saints rejoice in goodness.

42 "O LORD God, do not turn away the face of Your Anointed;
Remember the mercies of Your servant David."*d*

Solomon Dedicates the Temple

7 When Solomon had finished praying, fire came down from heaven and consumed the burnt offering and the sacrifices; and the glory of the LORD filled the temple. 2And the priests could not enter the house of the LORD, because the glory of the LORD had filled the LORD's house. 3When all the children of Israel saw how the fire came down, and the glory of the LORD on the temple, they bowed their faces to the ground on the pavement, and worshiped and praised the LORD, *saying:*

"For *He is* good,
For His mercy *endures* forever."*e*

4Then the king and all the people offered sacrifices before the LORD. 5King Solomon offered a sacrifice of twenty-two thousand bulls and one hundred and twenty thousand sheep. So the king and all the people dedicated the house of God. 6And the priests at-

d Compare Psalm 132.8–10   *e* Compare Psalm 106.1

tended to their services; the Levites also with instruments of the music of the LORD, which King David had made to praise the LORD, saying, "For His mercy *endures* forever,"[e] whenever David offered praise by their ministry. The priests sounded trumpets opposite them, while all Israel stood.

7Furthermore Solomon consecrated the middle of the court that *was* in front of the house of the LORD; for there he offered burnt offerings and the fat of the peace offerings, because the bronze altar which Solomon had made was not able to receive the burnt offerings, the grain offerings, and the fat.

8At that time Solomon kept the feast seven days, and all Israel with him, a very great assembly from the entrance of Hamath to the Brook of Egypt.[f] 9And on the eighth day they held a sacred assembly, for they observed the dedication of the altar seven days, and the feast seven days. 10On the twenty-third day of the seventh month he sent the people away to their tents, joyful and glad of heart for the good that the LORD had done for David, for Solomon, and for His people Israel. 11Thus Solomon finished the house of the LORD and the king's house; and Solomon successfully accomplished all that came into his heart to make in the house of the LORD and in his own house.

God's Second Appearance to Solomon

12Then the LORD appeared to Solomon by night, and said to him: "I have heard your prayer, and have chosen this place for Myself as a house of sacrifice. 13When I shut up heaven and there is no rain, or command the locusts to devour the land, or send pestilence among My people, 14if My people who are called by My name will humble themselves, and pray and seek My face, and turn from their wicked ways, then I will hear from heaven, and will forgive their sin and heal their land. 15Now My eyes will be open and My ears attentive to prayer *made* in this place. 16For now I have chosen and sanctified this house, that My name may be there forever; and My eyes and My heart will be there perpetually. 17As for you, if you walk

before Me as your father David walked, and do according to all that I have commanded you, and if you keep My statutes and My judgments, 18then I will establish the throne of your kingdom, as I covenanted with David your father, saying, 'You shall not fail *to have* a man as ruler in Israel.'

19"But if you turn away and forsake My statutes and My commandments which I have set before you, and go and serve other gods, and worship them, 20then I will uproot them from My land which I have given them; and this house which I have sanctified for My name I will cast out of My sight, and will make it a proverb and a byword among all peoples.

21"And *as for* this house, which is exalted, everyone who passes by it will be astonished and say, 'Why has the LORD done thus to this land and this house?' 22Then they will answer, 'Because they forsook the LORD God of their fathers, who brought them out of the land of Egypt, and embraced other gods, and worshiped them and served them; therefore He has brought all this calamity on them.'"

Solomon's Additional Achievements

8 It came to pass at the end of twenty years, when Solomon had built the house of the LORD and his own house, 2that the cities which Hiram had given to Solomon, Solomon built them; and he settled the children of Israel there. 3And Solomon went to Hamath Zobah and seized it. 4He also built Tadmor in the wilderness, and all the storage cities which he built in Hamath. 5He built Upper Beth Horon and Lower Beth Horon, fortified cities *with* walls, gates, and bars, 6also Baalath and all the storage cities that Solomon had, and all the chariot cities and the cities of the cavalry, and all that Solomon desired to build in Jerusalem, in Lebanon, and in all the land of his dominion.

7All the people *who were* left of the Hittites, Amorites, Perizzites, Hivites, and Jebusites, who *were* not of Israel—8that is, their descendants who were left in the land after them, whom the children of Israel did not destroy—from

---

[e]*Compare Psalm 106.1*   [f] That is, the Shihor (compare 1 Chronicles 13.5)

these Solomon raised forced labor, as it is to this day. 9But Solomon did not make the children of Israel servants for his work. Some *were* men of war, captains of his officers, captains of his chariots, and his cavalry. 10And others *were* chiefs of the officials of King Solomon: two hundred and fifty, who ruled over the people.

11Now Solomon brought the daughter of Pharaoh up from the City of David to the house he had built for her, for he said, "My wife shall not dwell in the house of David king of Israel, because *the places* to which the ark of the LORD has come are holy."

12Then Solomon offered burnt offerings to the LORD on the altar of the LORD which he had built before the vestibule, 13according to the daily rate, offering according to the commandment of Moses, for the Sabbaths, the New Moons, and the three appointed yearly feasts—the Feast of Unleavened Bread, the Feast of Weeks, and the Feast of Tabernacles. 14And, according to the order of David his father, he appointed the divisions of the priests for their service, the Levites for their duties (to praise and serve before the priests) as the duty of each day required, and the gatekeepers by their divisions at each gate; for so David the man of God had commanded. 15They did not depart from the command of the king to the priests and Levites concerning any matter or concerning the treasuries.

16Now all the work of Solomon was well-ordered from the day of the foundation of the house of the LORD until it was finished. So the house of the LORD was completed.

17Then Solomon went to Ezion Geber and Elath on the seacoast, in the land of Edom. 18And Hiram sent him ships by the hand of his servants, and servants who knew the sea. They went with the servants of Solomon to Ophir, and acquired four hundred and fifty talents of gold from there, and brought it to King Solomon.

The Queen of Sheba's Praise of Solomon

9 Now when the queen of Sheba heard of the fame of Solomon, she came to Jerusalem to test Solomon with hard questions, *having* a very great retinue, camels that bore spices, gold in abundance, and precious stones; and when she came to Solomon, she spoke with him about all that was in her heart. 2So Solomon answered all her questions; there was nothing so difficult for Solomon that he could not explain it to her. 3And when the queen of Sheba had seen the wisdom of Solomon, the house that he had built, 4the food on his table, the seating of his servants, the service of his waiters and their apparel, his cupbearers and their apparel, and his entryway by which he went up to the house of the LORD, there was no more spirit in her.

5Then she said to the king: "*It was* a true report which I heard in my own land about your words and your wisdom. 6However I did not believe their words until I came and saw with my own eyes; and indeed the half of the greatness of your wisdom was not told me. You exceed the fame of which I heard. 7Happy *are* your men and happy *are* these your servants, who stand continually before you and hear your wisdom! 8Blessed be the LORD your God, who delighted in you, setting you on His throne *to be* king for the LORD your God! Because your God has loved Israel, to establish them forever, therefore He made you king over them, to do justice and righteousness."

9And she gave the king one hundred and twenty talents of gold, spices in great abundance, and precious stones; there never were any spices such as those the queen of Sheba gave to King Solomon.

10Also, the servants of Hiram and the servants of Solomon, who brought gold from Ophir, brought algum wood and precious stones. 11And the king made walkways *of* the algum wood for the house of the LORD and for the king's house, also harps and stringed instruments for singers; and there were none such *as these* seen before in the land of Judah.

12Now King Solomon gave to the queen of Sheba all she desired, whatever she asked, *much more* than she had brought to the king. So she turned and went to her own country, she and her servants.

Solomon's Great Wealth

13The weight of gold that came to Solomon yearly was six hundred and sixty-six talents of gold, 14besides *what* the traveling merchants and traders brought. And all the kings of Arabia and governors of the country brought gold and silver to Solomon. 15And King Solomon made two hundred large shields of hammered gold; six hundred *shekels* of hammered gold went into each shield. 16*He* also *made* three hundred shields of hammered gold; three hundred *shekels* of gold went into each shield. The king put them in the House of the Forest of Lebanon.

17Moreover the king made a great throne of ivory, and overlaid it with pure gold. 18The throne *had* six steps, with a footstool of gold, *which were* fastened to the throne; there were armrests on either side of the place of the seat, and two lions stood beside the armrests. 19Twelve lions stood there, one on each side of the six steps; nothing like *this* had been made for any *other* kingdom.

20All King Solomon's drinking vessels *were* gold, and all the vessels of the House of the Forest of Lebanon *were* pure gold. Not *one was* silver, for this was accounted as nothing in the days of Solomon. 21For the king's ships went to Tarshish with the servants of Hiram. Once every three years the merchant ships came, bringing gold, silver, ivory, apes, and monkeys.

22So King Solomon surpassed all the kings of the earth in riches and wisdom. 23And all the kings of the earth sought the presence of Solomon to hear his wisdom, which God had put in his heart. 24Each man brought his present: articles of silver and gold, garments, armor, spices, horses, and mules, at a set rate year by year.

25Solomon had four thousand stalls for horses and chariots, and twelve thousand horsemen whom he stationed in the chariot cities and with the king at Jerusalem.

26So he reigned over all the kings from the River^g to the land of the Philistines, as far as the border of Egypt.

27The king made silver *as common* in Jerusalem as stones, and he made cedar trees as abundant as the sycamores which *are* in the lowland. 28And they brought horses to Solomon from Egypt and from all lands.

Death of Solomon

29Now the rest of the acts of Solomon, first and last, *are* they not written in the book of Nathan the prophet, in the prophecy of Ahijah the Shilonite, and in the visions of Iddo the seer concerning Jeroboam the son of Nebat? 30Solomon reigned in Jerusalem over all Israel forty years. 31Then Solomon rested with his fathers, and was buried in the City of David his father. And Rehoboam his son reigned in his place.

The Revolt Against Rehoboam

10 And Rehoboam went to Shechem, for all Israel had gone to Shechem to make him king. 2So it happened, when Jeroboam the son of Nebat heard *it* (he was in Egypt, where he had fled from the presence of King Solomon), that Jeroboam returned from Egypt. 3Then they sent for him and called him. And Jeroboam and all Israel came and spoke to Rehoboam, saying, 4"Your father made our yoke heavy; now therefore, lighten the burdensome service of your father and his heavy yoke which he put on us, and we will serve you."

5So he said to them, "Come back to me after three days." And the people departed.

6Then King Rehoboam consulted the elders who stood before his father Solomon while he still lived, saying, "How do you advise *me* to answer these people?"

7And they spoke to him, saying, "If you are kind to these people, and please them, and speak good words to them, they will be your servants forever."

8But he rejected the advice which the elders had given him, and consulted the young men who had grown up with him, who stood before him. 9And he said to them, "What advice do you give? How should we answer this people who have spoken to me, saying, 'Lighten the

g That is, the Euphrates

yoke which your father put on us'?"

10Then the young men who had grown up with him spoke to him, saying, "Thus you should speak to the people who have spoken to you, saying, 'Your father made our yoke heavy, but you make it lighter on us'—thus you shall say to them: 'My little finger shall be thicker than my father's waist! 11And now, whereas my father put a heavy yoke on you, I will add to your yoke; my father chastised you with whips, but I will chastise you with scourges!' "

12So Jeroboam and all the people came to Rehoboam on the third day, as the king had directed, saying, "Come back to me the third day." 13Then the king answered them roughly. King Rehoboam rejected the advice of the elders, 14and he spoke to them according to the advice of the young men, saying, "My father made your yoke heavy, but I will add to it; my father chastised you with whips, but I will chastise you with scourges!" 15So the king did not listen to the people; for the turn of events was from God, that the LORD might fulfill His word, which He had spoken by the hand of Ahijah the Shilonite to Jeroboam the son of Nebat.

16Now when all Israel saw that the king did not listen to them, the people answered the king, saying:

"What share have we in David?
We have no inheritance in the son
    of Jesse.
Every man to your tents, O Israel!
Now see to your own house,
    O David!"

So all Israel departed to their tents. 17But Rehoboam reigned over the children of Israel who dwelt in the cities of Judah.

18Then King Rehoboam sent Hadoram, who was in charge of revenue; but the children of Israel stoned him with stones, and he died. Therefore King Rehoboam mounted his chariot in haste to flee to Jerusalem. 19So Israel has been in rebellion against the house of David to this day.

11 Now when Rehoboam came to Jerusalem, he assembled from the house of Judah and Benjamin one hundred and eighty thousand chosen men who were warriors, to fight against Israel, that he might restore the kingdom to Rehoboam.

2But the word of the LORD came to Shemaiah the man of God, saying, 3"Speak to Rehoboam the son of Solomon, king of Judah, and to all Israel in Judah and Benjamin, saying, 4'Thus says the LORD: "You shall not go up or fight against your brethren! Let every man return to his house, for this thing is from Me." ' " Therefore they obeyed the words of the LORD, and turned back from attacking Jeroboam.

Rehoboam Fortifies the Cities

5So Rehoboam dwelt in Jerusalem, and built cities for defense in Judah. 6And he built Bethlehem, Etam, Tekoa, 7Beth Zur, Sochoh, Adullam, 8Gath, Mareshah, Ziph, 9Adoraim, Lachish, Azekah, 10Zorah, Aijalon, and Hebron, which are in Judah and Benjamin, fortified cities. 11And he fortified the strongholds, and put captains in them, and stores of food, oil, and wine. 12Also in every city he put shields and spears, and made them very strong, having Judah and Benjamin on his side.

Priests and Levites Move to Judah

13And from all their territories the priests and the Levites who were in all Israel took their stand with him. 14For the Levites left their common-lands and their possessions and came to Judah and Jerusalem, for Jeroboam and his sons had rejected them from serving as priests to the LORD. 15Then he appointed for himself priests for the high places, for the demons, and the calf idols which he had made. 16And after the Levites left, those from all the tribes of Israel, such as set their heart to seek the LORD God of Israel, came to Jerusalem to sacrifice to the LORD God of their fathers. 17So they strengthened the kingdom of Judah, and made Rehoboam the son of Solomon strong for three years, because they walked in the way of David and Solomon for three years.

The Family of Rehoboam

18Then Rehoboam took for himself as wife Mahalath the daughter of Jerimoth the son of David, and of Abihail the daughter of Eliah the son of Jesse. 19And she bore him children: Jeush, Shamariah, and Zaham. 20After her he took Maachah the granddaughter[h] of Absalom; and she bore him Abijah, Attai, Ziza, and Shelomith. 21Now Rehoboam loved Maachah the granddaughter of Absalom more than all his wives and his concubines; for he took eighteen wives and sixty concubines, and begot twenty-eight sons and sixty daughters. 22And Rehoboam appointed Abijah the son of Maachah as chief, *to be* leader among his brothers; for he *intended* to make him king. 23He dealt wisely, and dispersed some of his sons throughout all the territories of Judah and Benjamin, to every fortified city; and he gave them provisions in abundance. He also sought many wives *for them.*

Egypt Attacks Judah

12 Now it came to pass, when Rehoboam had established the kingdom and had strengthened himself, that he forsook the law of the LORD, and all Israel along with him. 2And it happened in the fifth year of King Rehoboam *that* Shishak king of Egypt came up against Jerusalem, because they had transgressed against the LORD, 3with twelve hundred chariots, sixty thousand horsemen, and people without number who came with him out of Egypt—the Lubim and the Sukkiim and the Ethiopians. 4And he took the fortified cities of Judah and came to Jerusalem.

5Then Shemaiah the prophet came to Rehoboam and the leaders of Judah, who were gathered together in Jerusalem because of Shishak, and said to them, "Thus says the LORD: 'You have forsaken Me, and therefore I also have left you in the hand of Shishak.'"

6So the leaders of Israel and the king humbled themselves; and they said, "The LORD *is* righteous."

7Now when the LORD saw that they humbled themselves, the word of the LORD came to Shemaiah, saying, "They have humbled themselves; *therefore* I will not destroy them, but I will grant them some deliverance. My wrath shall not be poured out on Jerusalem by the hand of Shishak. 8Nevertheless they will be his servants, that they may distinguish My service from the service of the kingdoms of the nations."

9So Shishak king of Egypt came up against Jerusalem, and took away the treasures of the house of the LORD and the treasures of the king's house; he took everything. He also carried away the gold shields which Solomon had made. 10Then King Rehoboam made bronze shields in their place, and committed *them* to the hands of the captains of the guard, who guarded the doorway of the king's house. 11And whenever the king entered the house of the LORD, the guard would go and bring them out; then they would take them back into the guardroom. 12When he humbled himself, the wrath of the LORD turned from him, so as not to destroy *him* completely; and things also went well in Judah.

The End of Rehoboam's Reign

13Thus King Rehoboam strengthened himself in Jerusalem and reigned. Now Rehoboam *was* forty-one years old when he became king; and he reigned seventeen years in Jerusalem, the city which the LORD had chosen out of all the tribes of Israel, to put His name there. His mother's name *was* Naamah, an Ammonitess. 14And he did evil, because he did not prepare his heart to seek the LORD.

15The acts of Rehoboam, first and last, *are* they not written in the book of Shemaiah the prophet, and of Iddo the seer concerning genealogies? And *there were* wars between Rehoboam and Jeroboam all their days. 16So Rehoboam rested with his fathers, and was buried in the City of David. Then Abijah his son reigned in his place.

Abijah Reigns in Judah

13 In the eighteenth year of King Jeroboam, Abijah became king over Judah. 2He reigned three years in Jerusalem. His mother's name *was* Michaiah the daughter of Uriel of Gibeah.

And there was war between Abijah and Jeroboam. 3Abijah set the battle in

---

h Literally *daughter,* but in the broader sense of granddaughter (compare 2 Chronicles 13.2) order with an army of valiant warriors, four hundred thousand choice men. Jeroboam also drew up in battle formation against him with eight hundred thousand choice men, mighty men of valor.

4Then Abijah stood on Mount Zemaraim, which *is* in the mountains of Ephraim, and said, "Hear me, Jeroboam and all Israel: 5Should you not know that the LORD God of Israel gave the dominion over Israel to David forever, to him and his sons, by a covenant of salt? 6Yet Jeroboam the son of Nebat, the servant of Solomon the son of David, rose up and rebelled against his lord. 7Then worthless rogues gathered to him, and strengthened themselves against Rehoboam the son of Solomon, when Rehoboam was young and inexperienced and could not withstand them. 8And now you think to withstand the kingdom of the LORD, which is in the hand of the sons of David; and you *are* a great multitude, and with you are the gold calves which Jeroboam made for you as gods. 9Have you not cast out the priests of the LORD, the sons of Aaron, and the Levites, and made for yourselves priests, like the peoples of *other* lands, so that whoever comes to consecrate himself with a young bull and seven rams may be a priest of *things that are* not gods? 10But as for us, the LORD *is* our God, and we have not forsaken Him; and the priests who minister to the LORD *are* the sons of Aaron, and the Levites *attend to their* duties. 11And they burn to the LORD every morning and every evening burnt sacrifices and sweet incense; *they* also *set* the showbread *in order on* the pure *gold* table, and the lampstand of gold with its lamps to burn every evening; for we keep the command of the LORD our God, but you have forsaken Him. 12Now look, God Himself is with us as *our* head, and His priests with sounding trumpets to sound the alarm against you. O children of Israel, do not fight against the LORD God of your fathers, for you shall not prosper!"

13But Jeroboam caused an ambush to go around behind them; so they were in front of Judah, and the ambush *was* behind them. 14And when Judah looked around, to their surprise the battle line *was* at both front and rear; and they cried out to the LORD, and the priests sounded the trumpets. 15Then the men of Judah gave a shout; and as the men of Judah shouted, it happened that God struck Jeroboam and all Israel before Abijah and Judah. 16And the children of Israel fled before Judah, and God delivered them into their hand. 17Then Abijah and his people struck them with a great slaughter; so five hundred thousand choice men of Israel fell slain. 18Thus the children of Israel were subdued at that time; and the children of Judah prevailed, because they relied on the LORD God of their fathers.

19And Abijah pursued Jeroboam and took cities from him: Bethel with its villages, Jeshanah with its villages, and Ephrain with its villages. 20So Jeroboam did not recover strength again in the days of Abijah; and the LORD struck him, and he died.

21But Abijah grew mighty, married fourteen wives, and begot twenty-two sons and sixteen daughters. 22Now the rest of the acts of Abijah, his ways, and his sayings *are* written in the annals of the prophet Iddo.

14 So Abijah rested with his fathers, and they buried him in the City of David. Then Asa his son reigned in his place. In his days the land was quiet for ten years.

Asa Reigns in Judah

2Asa did *what was* good and right in the eyes of the LORD his God, 3for he removed the altars of the foreign *gods* and the high places, and broke down the *sacred* pillars and cut down the wooden images. 4He commanded Judah to seek the LORD God of their fathers, and to observe the law and the commandment. 5He also removed the high places and the incense altars from all the cities of Judah, and the kingdom was quiet under him. 6And he built fortified cities in Judah, for the land had rest; he had no war in those years, because the LORD had given him rest. 7Therefore he said to Judah, "Let us build these cities and make walls around *them*, and towers, gates, and bars, *while* the land *is* yet before us, because we have sought the LORD our God; we have sought *Him*, and He has given us rest on every side." So they built and prospered. 8And Asa had an army of three hundred thousand from Judah who carried shields and spears, and from Benjamin two hundred and eighty thousand men who carried shields and drew bows; all these *were* mighty men of valor.

9Then Zerah the Ethiopian came out against them with an army of a million men and three hundred chariots, and he came to Mareshah. 10So Asa went out against him, and they set the troops in battle array in the Valley of Zephathah at Mareshah. 11And Asa cried out to the LORD his God, and said, "LORD, *it is* nothing for You to help, whether with many or with those who have no power; help us, O LORD our God, for we rest on You, and in Your name we go against this multitude. O LORD, You *are* our God; do not let man prevail against You!"

12So the LORD struck the Ethiopians before Asa and Judah, and the Ethiopians fled. 13And Asa and the people who *were* with him pursued them to Gerar. So the Ethiopians were overthrown, and they could not recover, for they were broken before the LORD and His army. And they carried away very much spoil. 14Then they defeated all the cities around Gerar, for the fear of the LORD came upon them; and they plundered all the cities, for there was exceedingly much spoil in them. 15They also attacked the livestock enclosures, and carried off sheep and camels in abundance, and returned to Jerusalem.

The Reforms of Asa

15 Now the Spirit of God came upon Azariah the son of Oded. 2And he went out to meet Asa, and said to him: "Hear me, Asa, and all Judah and Benjamin. The LORD *is* with you while you are with Him. If you seek Him, He will be found by you; but if you forsake Him, He will forsake you. 3For a long time Israel *has been* without the true God, without a teaching priest, and without law; 4but when in their trouble they turned to the LORD God of Israel, and sought Him, He was found by them. 5And in those times *there was*

no peace to the one who went out, nor to the one who came in, but great turmoil *was* on all the inhabitants of the lands. 6So nation was destroyed by nation, and city by city, for God troubled them with every adversity. 7But you, be strong and do not let your hands be weak, for your work shall be rewarded!"

8And when Asa heard these words and the prophecy of Oded the prophet, he took courage, and removed the abominable idols from all the land of Judah and Benjamin and from the cities which he had taken in the mountains of Ephraim; and he restored the altar of the LORD that *was* before the vestibule of the LORD. 9Then he gathered all Judah and Benjamin, and those who dwelt with them from Ephraim, Manasseh, and Simeon, for they came over to him in great numbers from Israel when they saw that the LORD his God was with him.

10So they gathered together at Jerusalem in the third month, in the fifteenth year of the reign of Asa. 11And they offered to the LORD at that time seven hundred bulls and seven thousand sheep from the spoil they had brought. 12Then they entered into a covenant to seek the LORD God of their fathers with all their heart and with all their soul; 13and whoever would not seek the LORD God of Israel was to be put to death, whether small or great, whether man or woman. 14Then they took an oath before the LORD with a loud voice, with shouting and trumpets and rams' horns. 15And all Judah rejoiced at the oath, for they had sworn with all their heart and sought Him with all their soul; and He was found by them, and the LORD gave them rest all around.

16Also he removed Maachah, the mother of Asa the king, from *being* queen mother, because she had made an obscene image of Asherah;*i* and Asa cut down her obscene image, then crushed and burned *it* by the Brook Kidron. 17But the high places were not removed from Israel. Nevertheless the heart of Asa was loyal all his days.

18He also brought into the house of

i A Canaanite deity

God the things that his father had dedicated and that he himself had dedicated: silver and gold and utensils. 19And there was no war until the thirty-fifth year of the reign of Asa.

Asa's Treaty with Syria

16 In the thirty-sixth year of the reign of Asa, Baasha king of Israel came up against Judah and built Ramah, that he might let none go out or come in to Asa king of Judah. 2Then Asa brought silver and gold from the treasuries of the house of the LORD and of the king's house, and sent to Ben-Hadad king of Syria, who dwelt in Damascus, saying, 3"Let there be a treaty between you and me, as there was between my father and your father. See, I have sent you silver and gold; come, break your treaty with Baasha king of Israel, so that he will withdraw from me."

4So Ben-Hadad heeded King Asa, and sent the captains of his armies against the cities of Israel. They attacked Ijon, Dan, Abel Maim, and all the storage cities of Naphtali. 5Now it happened, when Baasha heard it, that he stopped building Ramah and ceased his work. 6Then King Asa took all Judah, and they carried away the stones and timber of Ramah, which Baasha had used for building; and with them he built Geba and Mizpah.

Hanani's Message to Asa

7And at that time Hanani the seer came to Asa king of Judah, and said to him: "Because you have relied on the king of Syria, and have not relied on the LORD your God, therefore the army of the king of Syria has escaped from your hand. 8Were the Ethiopians and the Lubim not a huge army with very many chariots and horsemen? Yet, because you relied on the LORD, He delivered them into your hand. 9For the eyes of the LORD run to and fro throughout the whole earth, to show Himself strong on behalf of those whose heart is loyal to Him. In this you have done foolishly; therefore from now on you shall have wars." 10Then Asa was angry with the seer, and put him in prison, for he was enraged at him because of this. And Asa oppressed some of the people at that time.

Illness and Death of Asa

11Note that the acts of Asa, first and last, are indeed written in the book of the kings of Judah and Israel. 12And in the thirty-ninth year of his reign, Asa became diseased in his feet, and his malady was severe; yet in his disease he did not seek the LORD, but the physicians. 13So Asa rested with his fathers; he died in the forty-first year of his reign. 14They buried him in his own tomb, which he had made for himself in the City of David; and they laid him in the bed which was filled with spices and various ingredients prepared in a mixture of ointments. They made a very great burning for him.

Jehoshaphat Reigns in Judah

17 Then Jehoshaphat his son reigned in his place, and strengthened himself against Israel. 2And he placed troops in all the fortified cities of Judah, and set garrisons in the land of Judah and in the cities of Ephraim which Asa his father had taken. 3Now the LORD was with Jehoshaphat, because he walked in the former ways of his father David; he did not seek the Baals, 4but sought the God of his father, and walked in His commandments and not according to the acts of Israel. 5Therefore the LORD established the kingdom in his hand; and all Judah gave presents to Jehoshaphat, and he had riches and honor in abundance. 6And his heart took delight in the ways of the LORD; moreover he removed the high places and wooden images from Judah.

7Also in the third year of his reign he sent his leaders, Ben-Hail, Obadiah, Zechariah, Nethanel, and Michaiah, to teach in the cities of Judah. 8And with them he sent Levites: Shemaiah, Nethaniah, Zebadiah, Asahel, Shemiramoth, Jehonathan, Adonijah, Tobijah, and Tobadonijah—the Levites; and with them Elishama and Jehoram, the priests. 9So they taught in Judah, and had the Book of the Law of the LORD with them; they went throughout all the cities of Judah and taught the people.

10And the fear of the LORD fell on all the kingdoms of the lands that *were* around Judah, so that they did not make war against Jehoshaphat. 11Also *some* of the Philistines brought Jehoshaphat presents and silver as tribute; and the Arabians brought him flocks, seven thousand seven hundred rams and seven thousand seven hundred male goats.

12So Jehoshaphat became increasingly powerful, and he built fortresses and storage cities in Judah. 13He had much property in the cities of Judah; and the men of war, mighty men of valor, *were* in Jerusalem.

14These *are* their numbers, according to their fathers' houses. Of Judah, the captains of thousands: Adnah the captain, and with him three hundred thousand mighty men of valor; 15and next to him *was* Jehohanan the captain, and with him two hundred and eighty thousand; 16and next to him *was* Amasiah the son of Zichri, who willingly offered himself to the LORD, and with him two hundred thousand mighty men of valor. 17Of Benjamin: Eliada a mighty man of valor, and with him two hundred thousand men armed with bow and shield; 18and next to him *was* Jehozabad, and with him one hundred and eighty thousand prepared for war. 19These served the king, besides those the king put in the fortified cities throughout all Judah.

Micaiah Warns Ahab

18 Jehoshaphat had riches and honor in abundance; and by marriage he allied himself with Ahab. 2After some years he went down to *visit* Ahab in Samaria; and Ahab killed sheep and oxen in abundance for him and the people who were with him, and persuaded him to go up *with him* to Ramoth Gilead. 3So Ahab king of Israel said to Jehoshaphat king of Judah, "Will you go with me *against* Ramoth Gilead?"

And he answered him, "I *am* as you *are*, and my people as your people; *we will be* with you in the war."

4Also Jehoshaphat said to the king of Israel, "Please inquire for the word of the LORD today."

5Then the king of Israel gathered the prophets together, four hundred men, and said to them, "Shall we go to war against Ramoth Gilead, or shall I refrain?"

So they said, "Go up, for God will deliver it into the king's hand."

6But Jehoshaphat said, "*Is there* not still a prophet of the LORD here, that we may inquire of Him?"*i*

7So the king of Israel said to Jehoshaphat, "*There is* still one man by whom we may inquire of the LORD; but I hate him, because he never prophesies good concerning me, but always evil. He *is* Micaiah the son of Imla."

And Jehoshaphat said, "Let not the king say such things!"

8Then the king of Israel called one *of his* officers and said, "Bring Micaiah the son of Imla quickly!"

9The king of Israel and Jehoshaphat king of Judah, clothed in *their* robes, sat each on his throne; and they sat at a threshing floor at the entrance of the gate of Samaria; and all the prophets prophesied before them. 10Now Zedekiah the son of Chenaanah had made horns of iron for himself; and he said, "Thus says the LORD: 'With these you shall gore the Syrians until they are destroyed.' "

11And all the prophets prophesied so, saying, "Go up to Ramoth Gilead and prosper, for the LORD will deliver *it* into the king's hand."

12Then the messenger who had gone to call Micaiah spoke to him, saying, "Now listen, the words of the prophets with one accord encourage the king. Therefore please let your word be like *the word of* one of them, and speak encouragement."

13And Micaiah said, "*As the* LORD lives, whatever my God says, that I will speak."

14Then he came to the king; and the king said to him, "Micaiah, shall we go to war against Ramoth Gilead, or shall I refrain?"

And he said, "Go and prosper, and they shall be delivered into your hand!"

15So the king said to him, "How many

i Or *him*

times shall I make you swear that you tell me nothing but the truth in the name of the LORD?"

16Then he said, "I saw all Israel scattered on the mountains, as sheep that have no shepherd. And the LORD said, 'These have no master. Let each return to his house in peace.' "

17And the king of Israel said to Jehoshaphat, "Did I not tell you he would not prophesy good concerning me, but evil?"

18Then Micaiah said, "Therefore hear the word of the LORD: I saw the LORD sitting on His throne, and all the host of heaven standing on His right hand and His left. 19And the LORD said, 'Who will persuade Ahab king of Israel to go up, that he may fall at Ramoth Gilead?' So one spoke in this manner, and another spoke in that manner. 20Then a spirit came forward and stood before the LORD, and said, 'I will persuade him.' The LORD said to him, 'In what way?' 21So he said, 'I will go out and be a lying spirit in the mouth of all his prophets.' And the LORD said, 'You shall persuade him and also prevail; go out and do so.' 22Therefore look! The LORD has put a lying spirit in the mouth of these prophets of yours, and the LORD has declared disaster against you."

23Then Zedekiah the son of Chenaanah went near and struck Micaiah on the cheek, and said, "Which way did the spirit from the LORD go from me to speak to you?"

24And Micaiah said, "Indeed you shall see on that day when you go into an inner chamber to hide!"

25Then the king of Israel said, "Take Micaiah, and return him to Amon the governor of the city and to Joash the king's son; 26and say, 'Thus says the king: "Put this fellow in prison, and feed him with bread of affliction and water of affliction, until I return in peace." ' "

27But Micaiah said, "If you ever return in peace, the LORD has not spoken by me." And he said, "Take heed, all you people!"

Ahab Dies in Battle

28So the king of Israel and Jehoshaphat the king of Judah went up to Ra-

moth Gilead. 29And the king of Israel said to Jehoshaphat, "I will disguise myself and go into battle; but you put on your robes." So the king of Israel disguised himself, and they went into battle.

30Now the king of Syria had commanded the captains of the chariots who were with him, saying, "Fight with no one small or great, but only with the king of Israel."

31So it was, when the captains of the chariots saw Jehoshaphat, that they said, "It is the king of Israel!" Therefore they surrounded him to attack; but Jehoshaphat cried out, and the LORD helped him, and God diverted them from him. 32For so it was, when the captains of the chariots saw that it was not the king of Israel, that they turned back from pursuing him. 33Now a certain man drew a bow at random, and struck the king of Israel between the joints of his armor. So he said to the driver of his chariot, "Turn around and take me out of the battle, for I am wounded." 34The battle increased that day, and the king of Israel propped himself up in his chariot facing the Syrians until evening; and about the time of sunset he died.

19 Then Jehoshaphat the king of Judah returned safely to his house in Jerusalem. 2And Jehu the son of Hanani the seer went out to meet him, and said to King Jehoshaphat, "Should you help the wicked and love those who hate the LORD? Therefore the wrath of the LORD is upon you. 3Nevertheless good things are found in you, in that you have removed the wooden images from the land, and have prepared your heart to seek God."

The Reforms of Jehoshaphat

4So Jehoshaphat dwelt at Jerusalem; and he went out again among the people from Beersheba to the mountains of Ephraim, and brought them back to the LORD God of their fathers. 5Then he set judges in the land throughout all the fortified cities of Judah, city by city, 6and said to the judges, "Take heed to what you are doing, for you do not judge for man but for the LORD, who is with you in the judgment. 7Now therefore, let the fear of the LORD be upon you; take care and do *it*, for *there is* no iniquity with the LORD our God, no partiality, nor taking of bribes.''

8Moreover in Jerusalem, for the judgment of the LORD and for controversies, Jehoshaphat appointed some of the Levites and priests, and some of the chief fathers of Israel, when they returned to Jerusalem. 9And he commanded them, saying, ''Thus you shall act in the fear of the LORD, faithfully and with a loyal heart: 10Whatever case comes to you from your brethren who dwell in their cities, whether of bloodshed or offenses against law or commandment, against statutes or ordinances, you shall warn them, lest they trespass against the LORD and wrath come upon you and your brethren. Do this, and you will not be guilty. 11And take notice: Amariah the chief priest *is* over you in all matters of the LORD; and Zebadiah the son of Ishmael, the ruler of the house of Judah, for all the king's matters; also the Levites *will be* officials before you. Behave courageously, and the LORD will be with the good.''

Ammon, Moab, and Mount Seir Defeated

20 It happened after this *that* the people of Moab with the people of Ammon, and *others* with them besides the Ammonites, came to battle against Jehoshaphat. 2Then some came and told Jehoshaphat, saying, ''A great multitude is coming against you from beyond the sea, from Syria; and they are in Hazazon Tamar'' (which *is* En Gedi). 3And Jehoshaphat feared, and set himself to seek the LORD, and proclaimed a fast throughout all Judah. 4So Judah gathered together to ask *help* from the LORD; and from all the cities of Judah they came to seek the LORD.

5Then Jehoshaphat stood in the assembly of Judah and Jerusalem, in the house of the LORD, before the new court, 6and said: ''O LORD God of our fathers, *are* You not God in heaven, and do You *not* rule over all the kingdoms of the nations, and in Your hand *is there not* power and might, so that no one is able to withstand You? 7*Are* You not our God, *who* drove out the inhabitants of this land before Your people Israel, and

gave it to the descendants of Abraham Your friend forever? 8And they dwell in it, and have built You a sanctuary in it for Your name, saying, 9'If disaster comes upon us—sword, judgment, pestilence, or famine—we will stand before this temple and in Your presence (for Your name *is* in this temple), and cry out to You in our affliction, and You will hear and save.' 10And now, here are the people of Ammon, Moab, and Mount Seir—whom You would not let Israel invade when they came out of the land of Egypt, but they turned from them and did not destroy them— 11here they are, rewarding us by coming to throw us out of Your possession which You have given us to inherit. 12O our God, will You not judge them? For we have no power against this great multitude that is coming against us; nor do we know what to do, but our eyes *are* upon You.''

13Now all Judah, with their little ones, their wives, and their children, stood before the LORD.

14Then the Spirit of the LORD came upon Jahaziel the son of Zechariah, the son of Benaiah, the son of Jeiel, the son of Mattaniah, a Levite of the sons of Asaph, in the midst of the assembly. 15And he said, ''Listen, all you of Judah and you inhabitants of Jerusalem, and you, King Jehoshaphat! Thus says the LORD to you: 'Do not be afraid nor dismayed because of this great multitude, for the battle *is* not yours, but God's. 16Tomorrow go down against them. They will surely come up by the Ascent of Ziz, and you will find them at the end of the brook before the Wilderness of Jeruel. 17You will not *need* to fight in this *battle*. Position yourselves, stand still and see the salvation of the LORD, who is with you, O Judah and Jerusalem!' Do not fear or be dismayed; tomorrow go out against them, for the LORD *is* with you.''

18And Jehoshaphat bowed his head with *his* face to the ground, and all Judah and the inhabitants of Jerusalem bowed before the LORD, worshiping the LORD. 19Then the Levites of the children of the Kohathites and of the children of the Korahites stood up to praise the LORD God of Israel with voices loud and high.

20So they rose early in the morning and went out into the Wilderness of Tekoa; and as they went out, Jehoshaphat stood and said, "Hear me, O Judah and you inhabitants of Jerusalem: Believe in the LORD your God, and you shall be established; believe His prophets, and you shall prosper." 21And when he had consulted with the people, he appointed those who should sing to the LORD, and who should praise the beauty of holiness, as they went out before the army and were saying:

"Praise the LORD,
    For His mercy *endures* forever."*k*

22Now when they began to sing and to praise, the LORD set ambushes against the people of Ammon, Moab, and Mount Seir, who had come against Judah; and they were defeated. 23For the people of Ammon and Moab stood up against the inhabitants of Mount Seir to utterly kill and destroy *them*. And when they had made an end of the inhabitants of Seir, they helped to destroy one another.

24So when Judah came to a place overlooking the wilderness, they looked toward the multitude; and there *were* their dead bodies, fallen on the earth. No one had escaped. 25When Jehoshaphat and his people came to take away their spoil, they found among them an abundance of valuables on the dead bodies, and precious jewelry, which they stripped off for themselves, more than they could carry away; and they were three days gathering the spoil because there was so much. 26And on the fourth day they assembled in the Valley of Berachah, for there they blessed the LORD; therefore the name of that place was called The Valley of Berachah*l* until this day. 27Then they returned, every man of Judah and Jerusalem, with Jehoshaphat in front of them, to go back to Jerusalem with joy, for the LORD had made them rejoice over their enemies. 28So they came to Jerusalem, with stringed instruments and harps and trumpets, to the house of the LORD. 29And the fear of God was on all the kingdoms of *those* countries when they heard that the LORD had fought against the enemies of Israel. 30Then the realm of Jehoshaphat was quiet, for his God gave him rest all around.

The End of Jehoshaphat's Reign

31So Jehoshaphat was king over Judah. *He was* thirty-five years old when he became king, and he reigned twenty-five years in Jerusalem. His mother's name *was* Azubah the daughter of Shilhi. 32And he walked in the way of his father Asa, and did not turn aside from it, doing *what was* right in the sight of the LORD. 33Nevertheless the high places were not taken away, for as yet the people had not directed their hearts to the God of their fathers.

34Now the rest of the acts of Jehoshaphat, first and last, indeed they *are* written in the book of Jehu the son of Hanani, which *is* mentioned in the book of the kings of Israel.

35After this Jehoshaphat king of Judah allied himself with Ahaziah king of Israel, who acted very wickedly. 36And he allied himself with him to make ships to go to Tarshish, and they made the ships in Ezion Geber. 37But Eliezer the son of Dodavah of Mareshah prophesied against Jehoshaphat, saying, "Because you have allied yourself with Ahaziah, the LORD has destroyed your works." Then the ships were wrecked, so that they were not able to go to Tarshish.

Jehoram Reigns in Judah

21 And Jehoshaphat rested with his fathers, and was buried with his fathers in the City of David. Then Jehoram his son reigned in his place. 2He had brothers, the sons of Jehoshaphat: Azariah, Jehiel, Zechariah, Azaryahu, Michael, and Shephatiah; all these *were* the sons of Jehoshaphat king of Israel. 3Their father gave them great gifts of silver and gold and precious things, with fortified cities in Judah; but he gave the kingdom to Jehoram, because he *was* the firstborn.

4Now when Jehoram was established over the kingdom of his father, he strengthened himself and killed all his brothers with the sword, and also *others* of the princes of Israel.

---

k Compare Psalm 106.1   *l* Literally *Blessing*

5Jehoram *was* thirty-two years old when he became king, and he reigned eight years in Jerusalem. 6And he walked in the way of the kings of Israel, just as the house of Ahab had done, for he had the daughter of Ahab as a wife; and he did evil in the sight of the LORD. 7Yet the LORD would not destroy the house of David, because of the covenant that He had made with David, and since He had promised to give a lamp to him and to his sons forever.

8In his days Edom revolted against Judah's authority, and made a king over themselves. 9So Jehoram went out with his officers, and all his chariots with him. And he rose by night and attacked the Edomites who had surrounded him and the captains of the chariots. 10Thus Edom has been in revolt against Judah's authority to this day. At that time Libnah revolted against his rule, because he had forsaken the LORD God of his fathers. 11Moreover he made high places in the mountains of Judah, and caused the inhabitants of Jerusalem to commit harlotry, and led Judah astray.

12And a letter came to him from Elijah the prophet, saying,

> Thus says the LORD God of your father David:
> Because you have not walked in the ways of Jehoshaphat your father, or in the ways of Asa king of Judah, 13but have walked in the way of the kings of Israel, and have made Judah and the inhabitants of Jerusalem to play the harlot like the harlotry of the house of Ahab, and also have killed your brothers, those of your father's household, *who were* better than yourself, 14behold, the LORD will strike your people with a serious affliction— your children, your wives, and all your possessions; 15and you *will become* very sick with a disease of your intestines, until your intestines come out by reason of the sickness, day by day.

16Moreover the LORD stirred up against Jehoram the spirit of the Philis-

tines and the Arabians who *were* near the Ethiopians. 17And they came up into Judah and invaded it, and carried away all the possessions that were found in the king's house, and also his sons and his wives, so that there was not a son left to him except Jehoahaz, the youngest of his sons.

18After all this the LORD struck him in his intestines with an incurable disease. 19Then it happened in the course of time, after the end of two years, that his intestines came out because of his sickness; so he died in severe pain. And his people made no burning for him, like the burning for his fathers.

20He was thirty-two years old when he became king. He reigned in Jerusalem eight years and, to no one's sorrow, departed. However they buried him in the City of David, but not in the tombs of the kings.

Ahaziah Reigns in Judah

22 Then the inhabitants of Jerusalem made Ahaziah his youngest son king in his place, for the raiders who came with the Arabians into the camp had killed all the older *sons.* So Ahaziah the son of Jehoram, king of Judah, reigned. 2Ahaziah *was* forty-two[m] years old when he became king, and he reigned one year in Jerusalem. His mother's name *was* Athaliah the granddaughter of Omri. 3He also walked in the ways of the house of Ahab, for his mother advised him to do wickedly. 4Therefore he did evil in the sight of the LORD, like the house of Ahab; for they were his counselors after the death of his father, to his destruction. 5He also followed their advice, and went with Jehoram the son of Ahab king of Israel to war against Hazael king of Syria at Ramoth Gilead; and the Syrians wounded Joram. 6Then he returned to Jezreel to recover from the wounds which he had received at Ramah, when he fought against Hazael king of Syria. And Azariah the son of Jehoram, king of Judah, went down to see Jehoram the son of Ahab in Jezreel, because he was sick.

7His going to Joram was God's occasion for Ahaziah's downfall; for when

m Or *twenty-two* (compare 2 Kings 8.26)

he arrived, he went out with Jehoram against Jehu the son of Nimshi, whom the LORD had anointed to cut off the house of Ahab. 8And it happened, when Jehu was executing judgment on the house of Ahab, and found the princes of Judah and the sons of Ahaziah's brothers who served Ahaziah, that he killed them. 9Then he searched for Ahaziah; and they caught him (he was hiding in Samaria), and brought him to Jehu. When they had killed him, they buried him, "because," they said, "he is the son of Jehoshaphat, who sought the LORD with all his heart."

So the house of Ahaziah had no one to assume power over the kingdom.

Athaliah Reigns in Judah

10Now when Athaliah the mother of Ahaziah saw that her son was dead, she arose and destroyed all the royal heirs of the house of Judah. 11But Jehoshabeath, the daughter of the king, took Joash the son of Ahaziah, and stole him away from among the king's sons who were being murdered, and put him and his nurse in a bedroom. So Jehoshabeath, the daughter of King Jehoram, the wife of Jehoiada the priest (for she was the sister of Ahaziah), hid him from Athaliah so that she did not kill him. 12And he was hidden with them in the house of God for six years, while Athaliah reigned over the land.

Joash Crowned King of Judah

23 In the seventh year Jehoiada strengthened himself, *and made a* covenant with the captains of hundreds: Azariah the son of Jeroham, Ishmael the son of Jehohanan, Azariah the son of Obed, Maaseiah the son of Adaiah, and Elishaphat the son of Zichri. 2And they went throughout Judah and gathered the Levites from all the cities of Judah, and the chief fathers of Israel, and they came to Jerusalem.

3Then all the assembly made a covenant with the king in the house of God. And he said to them, "Behold, the king's son shall reign, as the LORD has said of the sons of David. 4This *is* what you shall do: One-third of you entering on the Sabbath, of the priests and the Levites, *shall be* keeping watch over the doors; 5one-third *shall be* at the king's house; and one-third at the Gate of the Foundation. All the people *shall be* in the courts of the house of the LORD. 6But let no one come into the house of the LORD except the priests and those of the Levites who serve. They may go in, for they *are* holy; but all the people shall keep the watch of the LORD. 7And the Levites shall surround the king on all sides, every man with his weapons in his hand; and whoever comes into the house, let him be put to death. You are to be with the king when he comes in and when he goes out."

8So the Levites and all Judah did according to all that Jehoiada the priest commanded. And each man took his men who were to be on duty on the Sabbath, with those who were going *off duty* on the Sabbath; for Jehoiada the priest had not dismissed the divisions. 9And Jehoiada the priest gave to the captains of hundreds the spears and the large and small shields which *had belonged* to King David, that *were* in the temple of God. 10Then he set all the people, every man with his weapon in his hand, from the right side of the temple to the left side of the temple, along by the altar and by the temple, all around the king. 11And they brought out the king's son, put the crown on him, *gave him* the Testimony,ⁿ and made him king. Then Jehoiada and his sons anointed him, and said, "*Long* live the king!"

Death of Athaliah

12Now when Athaliah heard the noise of the people running and praising the king, she came to the people *in* the temple of the LORD. 13*When* she looked, there was the king standing by his pillar at the entrance; and the leaders and the trumpeters *were* by the king. All the people of the land were rejoicing and blowing trumpets, also the singers with musical instruments, and those who led in praise. So Athaliah tore her clothes and said, "Treason! Treason!"

14And Jehoiada the priest brought out the captains of hundreds who were set over the army, and said to them,

ⁿ That is, the Law (compare Exodus 25.16, 21; 31.18)

"Take her outside under guard, and slay with the sword whoever follows her." For the priest had said, "Do not kill her in the house of the LORD."

15So they seized her; and she went by way of the entrance of the Horse Gate *into* the king's house, and they killed her there.

16Then Jehoiada made a covenant between himself, the people, and the king, that they should be the LORD's people. 17And all the people went to the temple of Baal, and tore it down. They broke in pieces its altars and images, and killed Mattan the priest of Baal before the altars. 18Also Jehoiada appointed the oversight of the house of the LORD to the hand of the priests, the Levites, whom David had assigned in the house of the LORD, to offer the burnt offerings of the LORD, as *it is* written in the Law of Moses, with rejoicing and with singing, *as it was established* by David. 19And he set the gatekeepers at the gates of the house of the LORD, so that no one *who was* in any way unclean should enter.

20Then he took the captains of hundreds, the nobles, the governors of the people, and all the people of the land, and brought the king down from the house of the LORD; and they went through the Upper Gate to the king's house, and set the king on the throne of the kingdom. 21So all the people of the land rejoiced; and the city was quiet, for they had slain Athaliah with the sword.

Joash Repairs the Temple

24 Joash *was* seven years old when he became king, and he reigned forty years in Jerusalem. His mother's name *was* Zibiah of Beersheba. 2Joash did *what was* right in the sight of the LORD all the days of Jehoiada the priest. 3And Jehoiada took two wives for him, and he had sons and daughters.

4Now it happened after this *that* Joash set his heart on repairing the house of the LORD. 5Then he gathered the priests and the Levites, and said to them, "Go out to the cities of Judah, and gather from all Israel money to repair the house of your God from year to year, and see that you do it quickly." However the Levites did not do it

quickly. 6So the king called Jehoiada the chief *priest*, and said to him, "Why have you not required the Levites to bring in from Judah and from Jerusalem the collection, *according to the commandment* of Moses the servant of the LORD and of the assembly of Israel, for the tabernacle of witness?" 7For the sons of Athaliah, that wicked woman, had broken into the house of God, and had also presented all the dedicated things of the house of the LORD to the Baals.

8Then at the king's command they made a chest, and set it outside at the gate of the house of the LORD. 9And they made a proclamation throughout Judah and Jerusalem to bring to the LORD the collection *that* Moses the servant of God *had imposed* on Israel in the wilderness. 10Then all the leaders and all the people rejoiced, brought their contributions, and put *them* into the chest until all had given. 11So it was, at that time, when the chest was brought to the king's official by the hand of the Levites, and when they saw that *there was* much money, that the king's scribe and the high priest's officer came and emptied the chest, and took it and returned it to its place. Thus they did day by day, and gathered money in abundance.

12The king and Jehoiada gave it to those who did the work of the service of the house of the LORD; and they hired masons and carpenters to repair the house of the LORD, and also those who worked in iron and bronze to restore the house of the LORD. 13So the workmen labored, and the work was completed by them; they restored the house of God to its original condition and reinforced it. 14When they had finished, they brought the rest of the money before the king and Jehoiada; they made from it articles for the house of the LORD, articles for serving and offering, spoons and vessels of gold and silver. And they offered burnt offerings in the house of the LORD continually all the days of Jehoiada.

Apostasy of Joash

15But Jehoiada grew old and was full of days, and he died; *he was* one hundred and thirty years old when he died. 16And they buried him in the City of

David among the kings, because he had done good in Israel, both toward God and His house.

17Now after the death of Jehoiada the leaders of Judah came and bowed down to the king. And the king listened to them. 18Therefore they left the house of the LORD God of their fathers, and served wooden images and idols; and wrath came upon Judah and Jerusalem because of their trespass. 19Yet He sent prophets to them, to bring them back to the LORD; and they testified against them, but they would not listen.

20Then the Spirit of God came upon Zechariah the son of Jehoiada the priest, who stood above the people, and said to them, "Thus says God: 'Why do you transgress the commandments of the LORD, so that you cannot prosper? Because you have forsaken the LORD, He also has forsaken you.' " 21So they conspired against him, and at the command of the king they stoned him with stones in the court of the house of the LORD. 22Thus Joash the king did not remember the kindness which Jehoiada his father had done to him, but killed his son; and as he died, he said, "The LORD look on it, and repay!"

Death of Joash

23So it happened in the spring of the year that the army of Syria came up against him; and they came to Judah and Jerusalem, and destroyed all the leaders of the people from among the people, and sent all their spoil to the king of Damascus. 24For the army of the Syrians came with a small company of men; but the LORD delivered a very great army into their hand, because they had forsaken the LORD God of their fathers. So they executed judgment against Joash. 25And when they had withdrawn from him (for they left him severely wounded), his own servants conspired against him because of the blood of the sons of Jehoiada the priest, and killed him on his bed. So he died. And they buried him in the City of David, but they did not bury him in the tombs of the kings.

26These are the ones who conspired against him: Zabad the son of Shimeath

the Ammonitess, and Jehozabad the son of Shimrith the Moabitess. 27Now concerning his sons, and the many oracles about him, and the repairing of the house of God, indeed they are written in the annals of the book of the kings. Then Amaziah his son reigned in his place.

Amaziah Reigns in Judah

25 Amaziah was twenty-five years old when he became king, and he reigned twenty-nine years in Jerusalem. His mother's name was Jehoaddan of Jerusalem. 2And he did what was right in the sight of the LORD, but not with a loyal heart.

3Now it happened, as soon as the kingdom was established for him, that he executed his servants who had murdered his father the king. 4However he did not execute their children, but did as it is written in the Law in the Book of Moses, where the LORD commanded, saying, "The fathers shall not be put to death for their children, nor shall the children be put to death for their fathers; but a person shall die for his own sin."o

The War Against Edom

5Moreover Amaziah gathered Judah together and set over them captains of thousands and captains of hundreds, according to their fathers' houses, throughout all Judah and Benjamin; and he numbered them from twenty years old and above, and found them to be three hundred thousand choice men, able to go to war, who could handle spear and shield. 6He also hired one hundred thousand mighty men of valor from Israel for one hundred talents of silver. 7But a man of God came to him, saying, "O king, do not let the army of Israel go with you, for the LORD is not with Israel—not with any of the children of Ephraim. 8But if you go, be gone! Be strong in battle! Even so, God shall make you fall before the enemy; for God has power to help and to overthrow."

9Then Amaziah said to the man of God, "But what shall we do about the

o Compare Deuteronomy 24.16

hundred talents which I have given to the troops of Israel?"

And the man of God answered, "The LORD is able to give you much more than this." 10So Amaziah discharged the troops that had come to him from Ephraim, to go back home. Therefore their anger was greatly aroused against Judah, and they returned home in great anger.

11Then Amaziah strengthened himself, and leading his people, he went to the Valley of Salt and killed ten thousand of the people of Seir. 12Also the children of Judah took captive ten thousand alive, brought them to the top of the rock, and cast them down from the top of the rock, so that they all were dashed in pieces.

13But as for the soldiers of the army which Amaziah had discharged, so that they would not go with him to battle, they raided the cities of Judah from Samaria to Beth Horon, killed three thousand in them, and took much spoil.

14Now it was so, after Amaziah came from the slaughter of the Edomites, that he brought the gods of the people of Seir, set them up *to be* his gods, and bowed down before them and burned incense to them. 15Therefore the anger of the LORD was aroused against Amaziah, and He sent him a prophet who said to him, "Why have you sought the gods of the people, which could not rescue their own people from your hand?"

16So it was, as he talked with him, that *the king* said to him, "Have we made you the king's counselor? Cease! Why should you be killed?"

Then the prophet ceased, and said, "I know that God has determined to destroy you, because you have done this and have not heeded my advice."

Israel Defeats Judah

17Now Amaziah king of Judah asked advice and sent to Joash the son of Jehoahaz, the son of Jehu, king of Israel, saying, "Come, let us face one another *in battle.*"

18And Joash king of Israel sent to Amaziah king of Judah, saying, "The thistle that *was* in Lebanon sent to the cedar that was in Lebanon, saying, 'Give your daughter to my son as wife'; and a wild beast that *was* in Lebanon passed by and trampled the thistle. 19Indeed you say that you have defeated the Edomites, and your heart is lifted up to boast. Stay at home now; why should you meddle with trouble, that you should fall—you and Judah with you?"

20But Amaziah would not heed, for it *came* from God, that He might give them into the hand *of their enemies,* because they sought the gods of Edom. 21So Joash king of Israel went out; and he and Amaziah king of Judah faced one another at Beth Shemesh, which *belongs* to Judah. 22And Judah was defeated by Israel, and every man fled to his tent. 23Then Joash the king of Israel captured Amaziah king of Judah, the son of Joash, the son of Jehoahaz, at Beth Shemesh; and he brought him to Jerusalem, and broke down the wall of Jerusalem from the Gate of Ephraim to the Corner Gate—four hundred cubits. 24And *he took* all the gold and silver, all the articles that were found in the house of God with Obed-Edom, the treasures of the king's house, and hostages, and returned to Samaria.

Death of Amaziah

25Amaziah the son of Joash, king of Judah, lived fifteen years after the death of Joash the son of Jehoahaz, king of Israel. 26Now the rest of the acts of Amaziah, from first to last, indeed *are* they not written in the book of the kings of Judah and Israel? 27After the time that Amaziah turned away from following the LORD, they made a conspiracy against him in Jerusalem, and he fled to Lachish; but they sent after him to Lachish and killed him there. 28Then they brought him on horses and buried him with his fathers in the City of Judah.

Uzziah Reigns in Judah

26 Now all the people of Judah took Uzziah, who *was* sixteen years old, and made him king instead of his father Amaziah. 2He built Elath and restored it to Judah, after the king rested with his fathers.

3Uzziah *was* sixteen years old when he became king, and he reigned fifty-two years in Jerusalem. His mother's name was Jecholiah of Jerusalem.

4And he did *what was* right in the sight of the LORD, according to all that his father Amaziah had done. 5He sought God in the days of Zechariah, who had understanding in the visions of God; and as long as he sought the LORD, God made him prosper.

6Now he went out and made war against the Philistines, and broke down the wall of Gath, the wall of Jabneh, and the wall of Ashdod; and he built cities *around* Ashdod and among the Philistines. 7God helped him against the Philistines, against the Arabians who lived in Gur Baal, and against the Meunites. 8Also the Ammonites brought tribute to Uzziah. His fame spread as far as the entrance of Egypt, for he became exceedingly strong.

9And Uzziah built towers in Jerusalem at the Corner Gate, at the Valley Gate, and at the corner buttress of the wall; then he fortified them. 10Also he built towers in the desert. He dug many wells, for he had much livestock, both in the lowlands and in the plains; *he also had* farmers and vinedressers in the mountains and in Carmel, for he loved the soil.

11Moreover Uzziah had an army of fighting men who went out to war by companies, according to the number on their roll as prepared by Jeiel the scribe and Maaseiah the officer, under the hand of Hananiah, *one* of the king's captains. 12The total number of chief officers of the mighty men of valor *was* two thousand six hundred. 13And under their authority *was* an army of three hundred and seven thousand five hundred, that made war with mighty power, to help the king against the enemy. 14Then Uzziah prepared for them, for the entire army, shields, spears, helmets, body armor, bows, and slings *to cast* stones. 15And he made devices in Jerusalem, invented by skillful men, to be on the towers and the corners, to shoot arrows and large stones. So his fame spread far and wide, for he was marvelously helped till he became strong.

The Penalty for Uzziah's Pride

16But when he was strong his heart was lifted up, to *his* destruction, for he transgressed against the LORD his God by entering the temple of the LORD to burn incense on the altar of incense. 17So Azariah the priest went in after him, and with him were eighty priests of the LORD—valiant men. 18And they withstood King Uzziah, and said to him, "*It is* not for you, Uzziah, to burn incense to the LORD, but for the priests, the sons of Aaron, who are consecrated to burn incense. Get out of the sanctuary, for you have trespassed! You *shall have* no honor from the LORD God."

19Then Uzziah became furious; and he *had* a censer in his hand to burn incense. And while he was angry with the priests, leprosy broke out on his forehead, before the priests in the house of the LORD, beside the incense altar. 20And Azariah the chief priest and all the priests looked at him, and there, on his forehead, he *was* leprous; so they thrust him out of that place. Indeed he also hurried to get out, because the LORD had struck him.

21King Uzziah was a leper until the day of his death. He dwelt in an isolated house, because he was a leper; for he was cut off from the house of the LORD. Then Jotham his son *was* over the king's house, judging the people of the land.

22Now the rest of the acts of Uzziah, from first to last, the prophet Isaiah the son of Amoz wrote. 23So Uzziah rested with his fathers, and they buried him with his fathers in the field of burial which *belonged* to the kings, for they said, "He is a leper." Then Jotham his son reigned in his place.

Jotham Reigns in Judah

27 Jotham *was* twenty-five years old when he became king, and he reigned sixteen years in Jerusalem. His mother's name *was* Jerushah the daughter of Zadok. 2And he did *what was* right in the sight of the LORD, according to all that his father Uzziah had done (although he did not enter the temple of the LORD). But still the people acted corruptly.

3He built the Upper Gate of the house of the LORD, and he built extensively on the wall of Ophel. 4Moreover he built cities in the mountains of Judah, and in the forests he built fortresses and towers. 5He also fought with the king of the Ammonites and defeated them. And the people of Ammon gave him in that year one hundred talents of silver, ten thousand kors of wheat, and ten thousand of barley. The people of Ammon paid this to him in the second and third years also. 6So Jotham became mighty, because he prepared his ways before the LORD his God.

7Now the rest of the acts of Jotham, and all his wars and his ways, indeed they *are* written in the book of the kings of Israel and Judah. 8He was twenty-five years old when he became king, and he reigned sixteen years in Jerusalem. 9So Jotham rested with his fathers, and they buried him in the City of David. Then Ahaz his son reigned in his place.

Ahaz Reigns in Judah

28 Ahaz *was* twenty years old when he became king, and he reigned sixteen years in Jerusalem; and he did not do *what was* right in the sight of the LORD, as his father David *had done.* 2For he walked in the ways of the kings of Israel, and made molded images for the Baals. 3He burned incense in the Valley of the Son of Hinnom, and burned his children in the fire, according to the abominations of the nations whom the LORD had cast out before the children of Israel. 4And he sacrificed and burned incense on the high places, on the hills, and under every green tree.

Syria and Israel Defeat Judah

5Therefore the LORD his God delivered him into the hand of the king of Syria. They defeated him, and carried away a great multitude of them as captives, and brought *them* to Damascus. Then he was also delivered into the hand of the king of Israel, who defeated him with a great slaughter. 6For Pekah the son of Remaliah killed one hundred and twenty thousand in Judah in one day, all valiant men, because they had forsaken the LORD God of their fathers. 7Zichri, a mighty man of Ephraim, killed Maaseiah the king's son, Azrikam the officer over the house, and Elkanah *who was* second to the king. 8And the children of Israel carried away captive of their brethren two hundred thousand women, sons, and

daughters; and they also took away much spoil from them, and brought the spoil to Samaria.

Israel Returns the Captives

9But a prophet of the LORD was there, whose name *was* Oded; and he went out before the army that came to Samaria, and said to them: "Look, because the LORD God of your fathers was angry with Judah, He has delivered them into your hand; but you have killed them in a rage *that* reaches up to heaven. 10And now you propose to force the children of Judah and Jerusalem to be your male and female slaves; *but are* you not also guilty before the LORD your God? 11Now hear me, therefore, and return the captives, whom you have taken captive from your brethren, for the fierce wrath of the LORD *is* upon you."

12Then some of the heads of the children of Ephraim, Azariah the son of Johanan, Berechiah the son of Meshillemoth, Jehizkiah the son of Shallum, and Amasa the son of Hadlai, stood up against those who came from the war, 13and said to them, "You shall not bring the captives here, for we *already* have offended the LORD. You intend to add to our sins and to our guilt; for our guilt is great, and *there is* fierce wrath against Israel." 14So the armed men left the captives and the spoil before the leaders and all the assembly. 15Then the men who were designated by name rose up and took the captives, and from the spoil they clothed all who were naked among them, dressed them and gave them sandals, gave them food and drink, and anointed them; and they let all the feeble ones ride on donkeys. So they brought them to their brethren at Jericho, the city of palm trees. Then they returned to Samaria.

Assyria Refuses to Help Judah

16At the same time King Ahaz sent to the kings of Assyria to help him. 17For again the Edomites had come, attacked Judah, and carried away captives. 18The Philistines also had invaded the cities of the lowland and of the South of Judah, and had taken Beth Shemesh, Aijalon, Gederoth, Sochoh with its villages, Timnah with its villages, and Gimzo with its villages; and they dwelt there. 19For the LORD brought Judah low because of Ahaz king of Israel, for he had encouraged moral decline in Judah and had been continually unfaithful to the LORD. 20Also Tiglath-Pileser king of Assyria came to him and distressed him, and did not assist him. 21For Ahaz took part *of the treasures* from the house of the LORD, from the house of the king, and from the leaders, and he gave *it* to the king of Assyria; but he did not help him.

Apostasy and Death of Ahaz

22Now in the time of his distress King Ahaz became increasingly unfaithful to the LORD. This *is that* King Ahaz. 23For he sacrificed to the gods of Damascus which had defeated him, saying, "Because the gods of the kings of Syria help them, I will sacrifice to them that they may help me." But they were the ruin of him and of all Israel. 24So Ahaz gathered the articles of the house of God, cut in pieces the articles of the house of God, shut up the doors of the house of the LORD, and made for himself altars in every corner of Jerusalem. 25And in every single city of Judah he made high places to burn incense to other gods, and provoked to anger the LORD God of his fathers.

26Now the rest of his acts and all his ways, from first to last, indeed they *are* written in the book of the kings of Judah and Israel. 27So Ahaz rested with his fathers, and they buried him in the city, in Jerusalem; but they did not bring him into the tombs of the kings of Israel. Then Hezekiah his son reigned in his place.

Hezekiah Reigns in Judah

29 Hezekiah became king *when he was* twenty-five years old, and he reigned twenty-nine years in Jerusalem. His mother's name *was* Abijah the daughter of Zechariah. 2And he did *what was* right in the sight of the LORD, according to all that his father David had done.

Hezekiah Cleanses the Temple

3In the first year of his reign, in the first month, he opened the doors of the house of the LORD and repaired them.

4Then he brought in the priests and the Levites, and gathered them in the East Square, 5and said to them: "Hear me, Levites! Now sanctify yourselves, sanctify the house of the LORD God of your fathers, and carry out the rubbish from the holy *place.* 6For our fathers have trespassed and done evil in the eyes of the LORD our God; they have forsaken Him, have turned their faces away from the dwelling place of the LORD, and turned *their* backs *on Him.* 7They have also shut up the doors of the vestibule, put out the lamps, and have not burned incense or offered burnt offerings in the holy *place* to the God of Israel. 8Therefore the wrath of the LORD fell upon Judah and Jerusalem, and He has given them up to trouble, to desolation, and to jeering, as you see with your eyes. 9For indeed, because of this our fathers have fallen by the sword; and our sons, our daughters, and our wives *are* in captivity.

10"Now *it is* in my heart to make a covenant with the LORD God of Israel, that His fierce wrath may turn away from us. 11My sons, do not be negligent now, for the LORD has chosen you to stand before Him, to serve Him, and that you should minister to Him and burn incense."

12Then these Levites arose: Mahath the son of Amasai and Joel the son of Azariah, of the sons of the Kohathites; of the sons of Merari, Kish the son of Abdi and Azariah the son of Jehallelel; of the Gershonites, Joah the son of Zimmah and Eden the son of Joah; 13of the sons of Elizaphan, Shimri and Jeiel; of the sons of Asaph, Zechariah and Mattaniah; 14of the sons of Heman, Jehiel and Shimei; and of the sons of Jeduthun, Shemaiah and Uzziel.

15And they gathered their brethren, sanctified themselves, and went according to the commandment of the king, at the words of the LORD, to cleanse the house of the LORD. 16Then the priests went into the inner part of the house of the LORD to cleanse *it,* and brought out all the debris that they found in the temple of the LORD to the court of the house of the LORD. And the Levites took *it* out and carried *it* to the Brook Kidron.

17Now they began to sanctify on the

first *day* of the first month, and on the eighth day of the month they came to the vestibule of the LORD. So they sanctified the house of the LORD in eight days, and on the sixteenth day of the first month they finished.

18Then they went in to King Hezekiah and said, "We have cleansed all the house of the LORD, the altar of burnt offerings with all its articles, and the table of the showbread with all its articles. 19Moreover all the articles which King Ahaz in his reign had cast aside in his transgression we have prepared and sanctified; and there they *are*, before the altar of the LORD."

Hezekiah Restores Temple Worship

20Then King Hezekiah rose early, gathered the rulers of the city, and went up to the house of the LORD. 21And they brought seven bulls, seven rams, seven lambs, and seven male goats for a sin offering for the kingdom, for the sanctuary, and for Judah. Then he commanded the priests, the sons of Aaron, to offer *them* on the altar of the LORD. 22So they killed the bulls, and the priests received the blood and sprinkled *it* on the altar. Likewise they killed the rams and sprinkled the blood on the altar. They also killed the lambs and sprinkled the blood on the altar. 23Then they brought out the male goats *for* the sin offering before the king and the assembly, and they laid their hands on them. 24And the priests killed them; and they presented their blood on the altar as a sin offering to make an atonement for all Israel, for the king commanded *that* the burnt offering and the sin offering *be made* for all Isr ael.

25And he stationed the Levites in the house of the LORD with cymbals, with stringed instruments, and with harps, according to the commandment of David, of Gad the king's seer, and of Nathan the prophet; for thus *was* the commandment of the LORD by his prophets. 26The Levites stood with the instruments of David, and the priests with the trumpets. 27Then Hezekiah commanded *them* to offer the burnt offering on the altar. And when the burnt offering began, the song of the LORD *also* began, with the trumpets and with the instruments of David king of Israel.

28So all the assembly worshiped, the singers sang, and the trumpeters sounded; all *this* continued until the burnt offering was finished. 29And when they had finished offering, the king and all who were present with him bowed and worshiped. 30Moreover King Hezekiah and the leaders commanded the Levites to sing praise to the LORD with the words of David and of Asaph the seer. So they sang praises with gladness, and they bowed their heads and worshiped.

31Then Hezekiah answered and said, "Now *that* you have consecrated yourselves to the LORD, come near, and bring sacrifices and thank offerings into the house of the LORD." So the assembly brought in sacrifices and thank offerings, and as many as were of a willing heart *brought* burnt offerings. 32And the number of the burnt offerings which the assembly brought was seventy bulls, one hundred rams, *and* two hundred lambs; all these *were* for a burnt offering to the LORD. 33The consecrated things *were* six hundred bulls and three thousand sheep. 34But the priests were too few, so that they could not skin all the burnt offerings; therefore their brethren the Levites helped them until the work was ended and until the *other* priests had sanctified themselves, for the Levites were more diligent in sanctifying themselves than the priests. 35Also the burnt offerings *were* in abundance, with the fat of the peace offerings and *with* the drink offerings for *every* burnt offering.

So the service of the house of the LORD was set in order. 36Then Hezekiah and all the people rejoiced that God had prepared the people, since the events took place so suddenly.

Hezekiah Keeps the Passover

30 And Hezekiah sent to all Israel and Judah, and also wrote letters to Ephraim and Manasseh, that they should come to the house of the LORD at Jerusalem, to keep the Passover to the LORD God of Israel. 2For the king and his leaders and all the assembly in Jerusalem had agreed to keep the Passover in the second month. 3For they could not keep it at the regular time, because a sufficient number of priests had not consecrated themselves, nor had the people gathered together at Jerusalem. 4And the matter pleased the king and all the assembly. 5So they resolved to make a proclamation throughout all Israel, from Beersheba to Dan, that they should come to keep the Passover to the LORD God of Israel at Jerusalem, since they had not done *it* for a long *time* in the *prescribed* manner.

6Then the runners went throughout all Israel and Judah with the letters from the king and his leaders, and spoke according to the command of the king: "Children of Israel, return to the LORD God of Abraham, Isaac, and Israel; then He will return to the remnant of you who have escaped from the hand of the kings of Assyria. 7And do not be like your fathers and your brethren, who trespassed against the LORD God of their fathers, so that He gave them up to desolation, as you see. 8Now do not be stiff-necked, as your fathers *were, but* yield yourselves to the LORD; and enter His sanctuary, which He has sanctified forever, and serve the LORD your God, that the fierceness of His wrath may turn away from you. 9For if you return to the LORD, your brethren and your children *will be treated* with compassion by those who lead them captive, so that they may come back to this land; for the LORD your God *is* gracious and merciful, and will not turn *His* face from you if you return to Him."

10So the runners passed from city to city through the country of Ephraim and Manasseh, as far as Zebulun; but they laughed at them and mocked them. 11Nevertheless some from Asher, Manasseh, and Zebulun humbled themselves and came to Jerusalem. 12Also the hand of God was on Judah to give them singleness of heart to obey the command of the king and the leaders, at the word of the LORD.

13Now many people, a very great assembly, gathered at Jerusalem to keep the Feast of Unleavened Bread in the second month. 14They arose and took away the altars that *were* in Jerusalem, and they took away all the incense altars and cast *them* into the Brook Kidron. 15Then they slaughtered the Passover *lambs* on the fourteenth *day*

of the second month. The priests and the Levites were ashamed, and sanctified themselves, and brought the burnt offerings to the house of the LORD. 16They stood in their place according to their custom, according to the Law of Moses the man of God; the priests sprinkled the blood *received* from the hand of the Levites. 17For *there were* many in the assembly who had not sanctified themselves; therefore the Levites had charge of the slaughter of the Passover *lambs* for everyone *who was* not clean, to sanctify *them* to the LORD. 18For a multitude of the people, many from Ephraim, Manasseh, Issachar, and Zebulun, had not cleansed themselves, yet they ate the Passover contrary to what was written. But Hezekiah prayed for them, saying, "May the good LORD provide atonement for everyone 19*who* prepares his heart to seek God, the LORD God of his fathers, though *he is* not *cleansed* according to the purification of the sanctuary." 20And the LORD listened to Hezekiah and healed the people.

21So the children of Israel who were present at Jerusalem kept the Feast of Unleavened Bread seven days with great gladness; and the Levites and the priests praised the LORD day by day, *singing* to the LORD, accompanied by loud instruments. 22And Hezekiah gave encouragement to all the Levites who taught the good knowledge of the LORD; and they ate throughout the feast seven days, offering peace offerings and making confession to the LORD God of their fathers.

23Then the whole assembly agreed to keep *the feast* another seven days, and they kept it *another* seven days with gladness. 24For Hezekiah king of Judah gave to the assembly a thousand bulls and seven thousand sheep, and the leaders gave to the assembly a thousand bulls and ten thousand sheep; and a great number of priests sanctified themselves. 25The whole assembly of Judah rejoiced, also the priests and Levites, all the assembly that came from Israel, the sojourners who came from the land of Israel, and those who dwelt in Judah. 26So there was great joy in Jerusalem, for since the time of Solomon the son of David, king of Israel, *there had* been nothing like this in Jerusalem. 27Then the priests, the Levites, arose and blessed the people, and their voice was heard; and their prayer came *up* to His holy dwelling place, to heaven.

The Reforms of Hezekiah

31 Now when all this was finished, all Israel who were present went out to the cities of Judah and broke the sacred pillars in pieces, cut down the wooden images, and threw down the high places and the altars—from all Judah, Benjamin, Ephraim, and Manasseh—until they had utterly destroyed them all. Then all the children of Israel returned to their own cities, every man to his possession.

2And Hezekiah appointed the divisions of the priests and the Levites according to their divisions, each man according to his service, the priests and Levites for burnt offerings and peace offerings, to serve, to give thanks, and to praise in the gates of the camp*p* of the LORD. 3The king also *appointed* a portion of his possessions for the burnt offerings: for the morning and evening burnt offerings, the burnt offerings for the Sabbaths and the New Moons and the set feasts, as *it is* written in the Law of the LORD.

4Moreover he commanded the people who dwelt in Jerusalem to contribute support for the priests and the Levites, that they might devote themselves to the Law of the LORD.

5As soon as the commandment was circulated, the children of Israel brought in abundance the firstfruits of grain and wine, oil and honey, and of all the produce of the field; and they brought in abundantly the tithe of everything. 6And the children of Israel and Judah, who dwelt in the cities of Judah, brought the tithe of oxen and sheep; also the tithe of holy things which were consecrated to the LORD their God they laid in heaps.

7In the third month they began laying them in heaps, and they finished in the seventh month. 8And when Hezekiah and the leaders came and saw the heaps, they blessed the LORD and His

people Israel. 9Then Hezekiah questioned the priests and the Levites concerning the heaps. 10And Azariah the chief priest, from the house of Zadok, answered him and said, "Since *the people* began to bring the offerings into the house of the LORD, we have had enough to eat and have plenty left, for the LORD has blessed His people; and what is left *is* this great abundance."

11Now Hezekiah commanded *them* to prepare rooms in the house of the LORD, and they prepared them. 12Then they faithfully brought in the offerings, the tithes, and the dedicated things; Cononiah the Levite had charge of them, and Shimei his brother *was* the next. 13Jehiel, Azaziah, Nahath, Asahel, Jerimoth, Jozabad, Eliel, Ismachiah, Mahath, and Benaiah *were* overseers under the hand of Cononiah and Shimei his brother, at the commandment of Hezekiah the king and Azariah the ruler of the house of God. 14Kore the son of Imnah the Levite, the keeper of the East Gate, *was* over the freewill offerings to God, to distribute the offerings of the LORD and the most holy things. 15And under him *were* Eden, Miniamin, Jeshua, Shemaiah, Amariah, and Shecaniah, *his* faithful assistants in the cities of the priests, to distribute allotments to their brethren by divisions, to the great as well as the small.

16Besides those males from three years old and up who were written in the genealogy, they distributed to everyone who entered the house of the LORD his daily portion for the work of his service, by his division, 17and to the priests who were written in the genealogy according to their father's house, and to the Levites from twenty years old and up according to their work, by their divisions, 18and to all who were written in the genealogy—their little ones and their wives, their sons and daughters, the whole company of them—for in their faithfulness they sanctified themselves in holiness.

19Also for the sons of Aaron the priests, *who were* in the fields of the common-lands of their cities, in every single city, *there were* men who were designated by name to distribute por-

---

p That is, the temple

tions to all the males among the priests and to all who were listed by genealogies among the Levites.

20Thus Hezekiah did throughout all Judah, and he did what *was* good and right and true before the LORD his God. 21And in every work that he began in the service of the house of God, in the law and in the commandment, to seek his God, he did *it* with all his heart. So he prospered.

Sennacherib Boasts Against the LORD

32 After these deeds of faithfulness, Sennacherib king of Assyria came and entered Judah; he encamped against the fortified cities, thinking to win them over to himself. 2And when Hezekiah saw that Sennacherib had come, and that his purpose was to make war against Jerusalem, 3he consulted with his leaders and commanders to stop the water from the springs which *were* outside the city; and they helped him. 4Thus many people gathered together who stopped all the springs and the brook that ran through the land, saying, "Why should the kings of Assyria come and find much water?" 5And he strengthened himself, built up all the wall that was broken, raised *it* up to the towers, and *built* another wall outside; also he repaired the Millo *in* the City of David, and made weapons and shields in abundance. 6Then he set military captains over the people, gathered them together to him in the open square of the city gate, and gave them encouragement, saying, 7"Be strong and courageous; do not be afraid nor dismayed before the king of Assyria, nor before all the multitude that *is* with him; for *there are* more with us than with him. 8With him *is* an arm of flesh; but with us *is* the LORD our God, to help us and to fight our battles." And the people were strengthened by the words of Hezekiah king of Judah.

9After this Sennacherib king of Assyria sent his servants to Jerusalem (but he and all the forces with him *laid siege* against Lachish), to Hezekiah king of Judah, and to all Judah who *were* in Jerusalem, saying, 10"Thus says Sennacherib king of Assyria: 'In what do you trust, that you remain under siege in Jerusalem? 11Does not Hezekiah persuade you to give yourselves over to die by famine and by thirst, saying, "The LORD our God will deliver us from the hand of the king of Assyria"? 12Has not the same Hezekiah taken away His high places and His altars, and commanded Judah and Jerusalem, saying, "You shall worship before one altar and burn incense on it"? 13Do you not know what I and my fathers have done to all the peoples of *other* lands? Were the gods of the nations of those lands in any way able to deliver their lands out of my hand? 14Who *was there* among all the gods of those nations that my fathers utterly destroyed that could deliver his people from my hand, that your God should be able to deliver you from my hand? 15Now therefore, do not let Hezekiah deceive you or persuade you like this, and do not believe him; for no god of any nation or kingdom was able to deliver his people from my hand or the hand of my fathers. How much less will your God deliver you from my hand?' "

16Furthermore, his servants spoke against the LORD God and against His servant Hezekiah.

17He also wrote letters to revile the LORD God of Israel, and to speak against Him, saying, "As the gods of the nations of *other* lands have not delivered their people from my hand, so the God of Hezekiah will not deliver His people from my hand." 18Then they called out with a loud voice in Hebrew to the people of Jerusalem who *were* on the wall, to frighten them and trouble them, that they might take the city. 19And they spoke against the God of Jerusalem, as against the gods of the people of the earth—the work of men's hands.

Sennacherib's Defeat and Death

20Now because of this King Hezekiah and the prophet Isaiah, the son of Amoz, prayed and cried out to heaven. 21Then the LORD sent an angel who cut down every mighty man of valor, leader, and captain in the camp of the king of Assyria. So he returned shamefaced to his own land. And when he had gone into the temple of his god, some of his own offspring struck him down with the sword there.

22Thus the LORD saved Hezekiah and the inhabitants of Jerusalem from the hand of Sennacherib the king of Assyria, and from the hand of all *others*, and guided them on every side. 23And many brought gifts to the LORD at Jerusalem, and presents to Hezekiah king of Judah, so that he was exalted in the sight of all nations thereafter.

Hezekiah Humbles Himself

24In those days Hezekiah was sick and near death, and he prayed to the LORD; and He spoke to him and gave him a sign. 25But Hezekiah did not repay according to the favor *shown* him, for his heart was lifted up; therefore wrath was looming over him and over Judah and Jerusalem. 26Then Hezekiah humbled himself for the pride of his heart, he and the inhabitants of Jerusalem, so that the wrath of the LORD did not come upon them in the days of Hezekiah.

Hezekiah's Wealth and Honor

27Hezekiah had very great riches and honor. And he made himself treasuries for silver, for gold, for precious stones, for spices, for shields, and for all kinds of desirable items; 28storehouses for the harvest of grain, wine, and oil; and stalls for all kinds of livestock, and folds for flocks. 29Moreover he provided cities for himself, and possessions of flocks and herds in abundance; for God had given him very much property. 30This same Hezekiah also stopped the water outlet of Upper Gihon, and brought the water by tunnel to the west side of the City of David. Hezekiah prospered in all his works.

31However, *regarding* the ambassadors of the princes of Babylon, whom they sent to him to inquire about the wonder that was *done* in the land, God withdrew from him, in order to test him, that He might know all *that was* in his heart.

Death of Hezekiah

32Now the rest of the acts of Hezekiah, and his goodness, indeed they *are* written in the vision of Isaiah the prophet, the son of Amoz, *and* in the book of the kings of Judah and Israel. 33So Hezekiah rested with his fathers, and they buried him in the upper tombs of the sons of David; and all Judah and the inhabitants of Jerusalem honored him at his death. Then Manasseh his son reigned in his place.

Manasseh Reigns in Judah

33 Manasseh *was* twelve years old when he became king, and he reigned fifty-five years in Jerusalem. 2But he did evil in the sight of the LORD, according to the abominations of the nations whom the LORD had cast out before the children of Israel. 3For he rebuilt the high places which Hezekiah his father had broken down; he raised up altars for the Baals, and made wooden images; and he worshiped all the host of heavenq and served them. 4He also built altars in the house of the LORD, of which the LORD had said, "In Jerusalem shall My name be forever." 5And he built altars for all the host of heaven in the two courts of the house of the LORD. 6Also he caused his sons to pass through the fire in the Valley of the Son of Hinnom; he practiced soothsaying, used witchcraft and sorcery, and consulted mediums and spiritists. He did much evil in the sight of the LORD, to provoke Him to anger. 7He even set a carved image, the idol which he had made, in the house of God, of which God had said to David and to Solomon his son, "In this house and in Jerusalem, which I have chosen out of all the tribes of Israel, I will put My name forever; 8and I will not again remove the foot of Israel from the land which I have appointed for your fathers—only if they are careful to do all that I have commanded them, according to the whole law and the statutes and the ordinances by the hand of Moses." 9So Manasseh seduced Judah and the inhabitants of Jerusalem to do more evil than the nations whom the LORD had destroyed before the children of Israel.

Manasseh Restored After Repentance

10And the LORD spoke to Manasseh and his people, but they would not lis-

q The gods of the Assyrians

ten. 11Therefore the LORD brought upon them the captains of the army of the king of Assyria, who took Manasseh with hooks,[r] bound him with bronze *fetters*, and carried him off to Babylon. 12Now when he was in affliction, he implored the LORD his God, and humbled himself greatly before the God of his fathers, 13and prayed to Him; and He received his entreaty, heard his supplication, and brought him back to Jerusalem into his kingdom. Then Manasseh knew that the LORD *was* God.

14After this he built a wall outside the City of David on the west side of Gihon, in the valley, as far as the entrance of the Fish Gate; and *it* enclosed Ophel, and he raised it to a very great height. Then he put military captains in all the fortified cities of Judah. 15He took away the foreign gods and the idol from the house of the LORD, and all the altars that he had built in the mount of the house of the LORD and in Jerusalem; and he cast *them* out of the city. 16He also repaired the altar of the LORD, sacrificed peace offerings and thank offerings on it, and commanded Judah to serve the LORD God of Israel. 17Nevertheless the people still sacrificed on the high places, *but* only to the LORD their God.

Death of Manasseh

18Now the rest of the acts of Manasseh, his prayer to his God, and the words of the seers who spoke to him in the name of the LORD God of Israel, indeed they *are written* in the book of the kings of Israel. 19Also his prayer and *how God* received his entreaty, and all his sin and trespass, and the sites where he built high places and set up wooden images and carved images, before he was humbled, indeed they *are* written among the sayings of Hozai. 20So Manasseh rested with his fathers, and they buried him in his own house. Then his son Amon reigned in his place.

Amon's Reign and Death

21Amon *was* twenty-two years old when he became king, and he reigned two years in Jerusalem. 22But he did evil in the sight of the LORD, as his father Manasseh had done; for Amon sacrificed to all the carved images which his father Manasseh had made, and served them. 23And he did not humble himself before the LORD, as his father Manasseh had humbled himself; but Amon trespassed more and more.

24Then his servants conspired against him, and killed him in his own house. 25But the people of the land executed all those who had conspired against King Amon. Then the people of the land made his son Josiah king in his place.

Josiah Reigns in Judah

34 Josiah *was* eight years old when he became king, and he reigned thirty-one years in Jerusalem. 2And he did *what was* right in the sight of the LORD, and walked in the ways of his father David; *he* did *not* turn aside to the right hand or to the left.

3For in the eighth year of his reign, while he was still young, he began to seek the God of his father David; and in the twelfth year he began to purge Judah and Jerusalem of the high places, the wooden images, the carved images, and the molded images. 4They broke down the altars of the Baals in his presence, and the incense altars which *were* above them he cut down; and the wooden images, the carved images, and the molded images he broke in pieces, and made dust of them and scattered *it* on the graves of those who had sacrificed to them. 5He also burned the bones of the priests on their altars, and cleansed Judah and Jerusalem. 6And *so he did* in the cities of Manasseh, Ephraim, and Simeon, as far as Naphtali and all around, with axes. 7When he had broken down the altars and the wooden images, had beaten the carved images into powder, and cut down all the incense altars throughout all the land of Israel, he returned to Jerusalem.

Hilkiah Finds the Book of the Law

8In the eighteenth year of his reign, when he had purged the land and the temple, he sent Shaphan the son of Azaliah, Maaseiah the governor of the city, and Joah the son of Joahaz the recorder, to repair the house of the LORD

---

r That is, nose hooks (compare 2 Kings 19.28)

his God. 9When they came to Hilkiah the high priest, they delivered the money that was brought into the house of God, which the Levites who kept the doors had gathered from the hand of Manasseh and Ephraim, from all the remnant of Israel, from all Judah and Benjamin, and *which* they had brought back to Jerusalem. 10Then they put *it* in the hand of the foremen who had the oversight of the house of the LORD; and they gave it to the workmen who worked in the house of the LORD, to repair and restore the house. 11They gave *it* to the craftsmen and builders to buy hewn stone and timber for beams, and to floor the houses which the kings of Judah had destroyed. 12And the men did the work faithfully. Their overseers *were* Jahath and Obadiah the Levites, of the sons of Merari, and Zechariah and Meshullam, of the sons of the Kohathites, to supervise. *Others of* the Levites, all of whom were skillful with instruments of music, 13*were* over the burden bearers and *were* overseers of all who did work in any kind of service. And *some* of the Levites *were* scribes, officers, and gatekeepers.

14Now when they brought out the money that was brought into the house of the LORD, Hilkiah the priest found the Book of the Law of the LORD *given* by Moses. 15Then Hilkiah answered and said to Shaphan the scribe, "I have found the Book of the Law in the house of the LORD." And Hilkiah gave the book to Shaphan. 16So Shaphan carried the book to the king, bringing the king word, saying, "All that was committed to your servants they are doing. 17And they have gathered the money that was found in the house of the LORD, and have delivered it into the hand of the overseers and the workmen." 18Then Shaphan the scribe told the king, saying, "Hilkiah the priest has given me a book." And Shaphan read it before the king.

19Thus it happened, when the king heard the words of the Law, that he tore his clothes. 20Then the king commanded Hilkiah, Ahikam the son of Shaphan, Abdon the son of Micah, Shaphan the scribe, and Asaiah a servant of the king, saying, 21"Go, inquire of the LORD for me, and for those who are left in Israel and Judah, concerning the words of the book that is found; for great *is* the wrath of the LORD that is poured out on us, because our fathers have not kept the word of the LORD, to do according to all that is written in this book."

22So Hilkiah and those the king *had appointed* went to Huldah the prophetess, the wife of Shallum the son of Tokhath, the son of Hasrah, keeper of the wardrobe. (She dwelt in Jerusalem in the Second Quarter.) And they spoke to her to that *effect.*

23Then she answered them, "Thus says the LORD God of Israel, 'Tell the man who sent you to Me, 24"Thus says the LORD: 'Behold, I will bring calamity on this place and on its inhabitants, all the curses that are written in the book which they have read before the king of Judah, 25because they have forsaken Me and burned incense to other gods, that they might provoke Me to anger with all the works of their hands. Therefore My wrath will be poured out on this place, and not be quenched.' "' 26But as for the king of Judah, who sent you to inquire of the LORD, in this manner you shall speak to him, 'Thus says the LORD God of Israel: "*Concerning* the words which you have heard— 27because your heart was tender, and you humbled yourself before God when you heard His words against this place and against its inhabitants, and you humbled yourself before Me, and you tore your clothes and wept before Me, I also have heard *you,*" says the LORD. 28"Surely I will gather you to your fathers, and you shall be gathered to your grave in peace; and your eyes shall not see all the calamity which I will bring on this place and its inhabitants." ' " So they brought back word to the king.

Josiah Restores True Worship

29Then the king sent and gathered all the elders of Judah and Jerusalem. 30The king went up to the house of the LORD, with all the men of Judah and the inhabitants of Jerusalem—the priests and the Levites, and all the people, great and small. And he read in their hearing all the words of the Book of the Covenant which had been found in the house of the LORD. 31Then the king stood in his place and made a covenant before the LORD, to follow the LORD, and to keep His commandments and His testimonies and His statutes with all his heart and all his soul, to perform the words of the covenant that were written in this book. 32And he made all who were present in Jerusalem and Benjamin take a stand. So the inhabitants of Jerusalem did according to the covenant of God, the God of their fathers. 33Thus Josiah removed all the abominations from all the country that *belonged* to the children of Israel, and made all who were present in Israel diligently serve the LORD their God. All his days they did not depart from following the LORD God of their fathers.

Josiah Keeps the Passover

35 Now Josiah kept a Passover to the LORD in Jerusalem, and they slaughtered the Passover *lambs* on the fourteenth *day* of the first month. 2And he set the priests in their duties and encouraged them for the service of the house of the LORD. 3Then he said to the Levites who taught all Israel, who were holy to the LORD: "Put the holy ark in the house which Solomon the son of David, king of Israel, built. *It shall* no longer *be* a burden on *your* shoulders. Now serve the LORD your God and His people Israel. 4Prepare *yourselves* according to your fathers' houses, according to your divisions, following the written instruction of David king of Israel and the written instruction of Solomon his son. 5And stand in the holy *place* according to the divisions of the fathers' houses of your brethren the *lay* people, and *according to* the division of the father's house of the Levites. 6So slaughter the Passover *offerings*, consecrate yourselves, and prepare *them* for your brethren, that *they* may do according to the word of the LORD by the hand of Moses."

7Then Josiah gave the *lay* people lambs and young goats from the flock, all for Passover *offerings* for all who were present, to the number of thirty thousand, as well as three thousand cattle; these *were* from the king's possessions. 8And his leaders gave willingly to the people, to the priests, and to the Levites. Hilkiah, Zechariah, and Jehiel,

rulers of the house of God, gave to the priests for the Passover *offerings* two thousand six hundred *from the flock,* and three hundred cattle. 9Also Conaniah, his brothers Shemaiah and Nethanel, and Hashabiah and Jeiel and Jozabad, chief of the Levites, gave to the Levites for Passover *offerings* five thousand *from the flock* and five hundred cattle.

10So the service was prepared, and the priests stood in their places, and the Levites in their divisions, according to the king's command. 11And they slaughtered the Passover *offerings;* and the priests sprinkled *the blood* with their hands, while the Levites skinned *the animals.* 12Then they removed the burnt offerings that *they* might give them to the divisions of the fathers' houses of the *lay* people, to offer to the LORD, as *it is* written in the Book of Moses. And so *they did* with the cattle. 13Also they roasted the Passover *offerings* with fire according to the ordinance; but the *other* holy *offerings* they boiled in pots, in caldrons, and in pans, and divided *them* quickly among all the *lay* people. 14Then afterward they prepared portions for themselves and for the priests, because the priests, the sons of Aaron, *were busy* in offering burnt offerings and fat until night; therefore the Levites prepared portions for themselves and for the priests, the sons of Aaron. 15And the singers, the sons of Asaph, *were* in their places, according to the command of David, Asaph, Heman, and Jeduthun the king's seer. Also the gatekeepers were at each gate; they did not have to leave their position, because their brethren the Levites prepared portions for them.

16So all the service of the LORD was prepared the same day, to keep the Passover and to offer burnt offerings on the altar of the LORD, according to the command of King Josiah. 17And the children of Israel who were present kept the Passover at that time, and the Feast of Unleavened Bread for seven days. 18There had been no Passover kept in Israel like that since the days of Samuel the prophet; and none of the kings of Israel had kept such a Passover as Josiah kept, with the priests and the Levites, all Judah and Israel who were present, and the inhabitants of Jerusalem. 19In the eighteenth year of the reign of Josiah this Passover was kept.

Josiah Dies in Battle

20After all this, when Josiah had prepared the temple, Necho king of Egypt came up to fight against Carchemish by the Euphrates; and Josiah went out against him. 21But he sent messengers to him, saying, "What have I to do with you, king of Judah? *I have* not *come* against you this day, but against the house with which I have war; for God commanded me to make haste. Refrain *from meddling with* God, who *is* with me, lest He destroy you." 22Nevertheless Josiah would not turn his face from him, but disguised himself so that he might fight with him, and did not heed the words of Necho from the mouth of God. So he came to fight in the Valley of Megiddo.

23And the archers shot King Josiah; and the king said to his servants, "Take me away, for I am severely wounded." 24His servants therefore took him out of that chariot and put him in the second chariot that he had, and they brought him to Jerusalem. So he died, and was buried in *one of* the tombs of his fathers. And all Judah and Jerusalem mourned for Josiah.

25Jeremiah also lamented for Josiah. And to this day all the singing men and the singing women speak of Josiah in their lamentations. They made it a custom in Israel; and indeed they *are* written in the Laments.

26Now the rest of the acts of Josiah and his goodness, according to *what was* written in the Law of the LORD, 27and his deeds from first to last, indeed they *are* written in the book of the kings of Israel and Judah.

The Reign and Captivity of Jehoahaz

36 Then the people of the land took Jehoahaz the son of Josiah, and made him king in his father's place in Jerusalem. 2Jehoahaz *was* twenty-three years old when he became king, and he reigned three months in Jerusalem. 3Now the king of Egypt deposed him at Jerusalem; and he imposed on the land a tribute of one hundred talents of silver and a talent of gold. 4Then the king of Egypt made *Jehoahaz's* brother Eliakim king over Judah and Jerusalem, and changed his name to Jehoiakim. And Necho took Jehoahaz his brother and carried him off to Egypt.

The Reign and Captivity of Jehoiakim

5Jehoiakim *was* twenty-five years old when he became king, and he reigned eleven years in Jerusalem. And he did evil in the sight of the LORD his God. 6Nebuchadnezzar king of Babylon came up against him, and bound him in bronze *fetters* to carry him off to Babylon. 7Nebuchadnezzar also carried off *some* of the articles from the house of the LORD to Babylon, and put them in his temple at Babylon. 8Now the rest of the acts of Jehoiakim, the abominations which he did, and what was found against him, indeed they *are* written in the book of the kings of Israel and Judah. Then Jehoiachin his son reigned in his place.

The Reign and Captivity of Jehoiachin

9Jehoiachin *was* eight years old when he became king, and he reigned in Jerusalem three months and ten days. And he did evil in the sight of the LORD. 10At the turn of the year King Nebuchadnezzar summoned *him* and took him to Babylon, with the costly articles from the house of the LORD, and made Zedekiah, *Jehoiakim's* brother, king over Judah and Jerusalem.

Zedekiah Reigns in Judah

11Zedekiah *was* twenty-one years old when he became king, and he reigned eleven years in Jerusalem. 12He did evil in the sight of the LORD his God, *and* did not humble himself before Jeremiah the prophet, *who spoke* from the mouth of the LORD. 13And he also rebelled against King Nebuchadnezzar, who had made him swear *an oath* by God; but he stiffened his neck and hardened his heart against turning to the LORD God of Israel. 14Moreover all the leaders of the priests and the people transgressed more and more, *according* to all the abominations of the nations, and defiled the house of the LORD which He had consecrated in Jerusalem.

The Fall of Jerusalem

15And the LORD God of their fathers sent *warnings* to them by His messengers, rising up early and sending *them*, because He had compassion on His people and on His dwelling place. 16But they mocked the messengers of God, despised His words, and scoffed at His prophets, until the wrath of the LORD arose against His people, till *there was* no remedy.

17Therefore He brought against them the king of the Chaldeans, who killed their young men with the sword in the house of their sanctuary, and had no compassion on young man or virgin, on the aged or the weak; He gave *them* all into his hand. 18And all the articles from the house of God, great and small, the treasures of the house of the LORD, and the treasures of the king and of his leaders, all *these* he took to Babylon. 19Then they burned the house of God, broke down the wall of Jerusalem, burned all its palaces with fire, and destroyed all its precious possessions.

20And those who escaped from the sword he carried away to Babylon, where they became servants to him and his sons until the rule of the kingdom of Persia, 21to fulfill the word of the LORD by the mouth of Jeremiah, until the land had enjoyed her Sabbaths. As long as she lay desolate she kept Sabbath, to fulfill seventy years.

The Proclamation of Cyrus

22Now in the first year of Cyrus king of Persia, that the word of the LORD by the mouth of Jeremiah might be fulfilled, the LORD stirred up the spirit of Cyrus king of Persia, so that he made a proclamation throughout all his kingdom, and also *put it* in writing, saying,

23 Thus says Cyrus king of Persia:
All the kingdoms of the earth the LORD God of heaven has given me. And He has commanded me to build Him a house at Jerusalem which is in Judah. Who *is* among you of all His people? May the LORD his God *be* with him, and let him go up!

The Book of
EZRA

End of the Babylonian Captivity

1 Now in the first year of Cyrus king of Persia, that the word of the LORD by the mouth of Jeremiah might be fulfilled, the LORD stirred up the spirit of Cyrus king of Persia, so that he made a proclamation throughout all his kingdom, and also *put it* in writing, saying,

2 Thus says Cyrus king of Persia: All the kingdoms of the earth the LORD God of heaven has given me. And He has commanded me to build Him a house at Jerusalem which *is* in Judah. 3Who *is* among you of all His people? May his God be with him, and let him go up to Jerusalem which *is* in Judah, and build the house of the LORD God of Israel (He *is* God), which *is* in Jerusalem. 4And whoever is left in any place where he dwells, let the men of his place help him with silver and gold, with goods and livestock, besides the freewill offerings for the house of God which *is* in Jerusalem.

5Then the heads of the fathers' *houses* of Judah and Benjamin, and the priests and the Levites, with all whose spirits God had moved, arose to go up and build the house of the LORD which *is* in Jerusalem. 6And all those who *were* around them encouraged them with articles of silver and gold, with goods and livestock, and with precious things, besides all *that* was willingly offered.

7King Cyrus also brought out the articles of the house of the LORD, which Nebuchadnezzar had taken from Jerusalem and put in the temple of his gods; 8and Cyrus king of Persia brought them out by the hand of Mithredath the treasurer, and counted them out to Sheshbazzar the prince of Judah. 9This *is* the number of them: thirty gold platters, one thousand silver platters, twenty-nine knives, 10thirty gold basins, four hundred and ten silver basins

of a similar *kind, and* one thousand other articles. 11All the articles of gold and silver *were* five thousand four hundred. All *these* Sheshbazzar took with the captives who were brought from Babylon to Jerusalem.

The Captives Who Returned to Jerusalem

2 Now*a* these *are* the people of the province who came back from the captivity, of those who had been carried away, whom Nebuchadnezzar the king of Babylon had carried away to Babylon, and who returned to Jerusalem and Judah, everyone to his *own* city.

2*Those* who came with Zerubbabel *were* Jeshua, Nehemiah, Seraiah, Reelaiah, Mordecai, Bilshan, Mispar, Bigvai, Rehum, *and* Baanah. The number of the men of the people of Israel: 3the people of Parosh, two thousand one hundred and seventy-two; 4the people of Shephatiah, three hundred and seventy-two; 5the people of Arah, seven hundred and seventy-five; 6the people of Pahath-Moab, of the people of Jeshua *and* Joab, two thousand eight hundred and twelve; 7the people of Elam, one thousand two hundred and fifty-four; 8the people of Zattu, nine hundred and forty-five; 9the people of Zaccai, seven hundred and sixty; 10the people of Bani, six hundred and forty-two; 11the people of Bebai, six hundred and twenty-three; 12the people of Azgad, one thousand two hundred and twenty-two; 13the people of Adonikam, six hundred and sixty-six; 14the people of Bigvai, two thousand and fifty-six; 15the people of Adin, four hundred and fifty-four; 16the people of Ater of Hezekiah, ninety-eight; 17the people of Bezai, three hundred and twenty-three; 18the people of Jorah, one hundred and twelve; 19the people of Hashum, two hundred and twenty-three; 20the people of Gibbar, ninety-five; 21the people of Bethlehem, one hundred and twenty-three; 22the men

a Compare this chapter with Nehemiah 7.6–73.

of Netophah, fifty-six; 23the men of Anathoth, one hundred and twenty-eight; 24the people of Azmaveth, forty-two; 25the people of Kirjath Arim, Chephirah, and Beeroth, seven hundred and forty-three; 26the people of Ramah and Geba, six hundred and twenty-one; 27the men of Michmas, one hundred and twenty-two; 28the men of Bethel and Ai, two hundred and twenty-three; 29the people of Nebo, fifty-two; 30the people of Magbish, one hundred and fifty-six; 31the people of the other Elam, one thousand two hundred and fifty-four; 32the people of Harim, three hundred and twenty; 33the people of Lod, Hadid, and Ono, seven hundred and twenty-five; 34the people of Jericho, three hundred and forty-five; 35the people of Senaah, three thousand six hundred and thirty.

36The priests: the sons of Jedaiah, of the house of Jeshua, nine hundred and seventy-three; 37the sons of Immer, one thousand and fifty-two; 38the sons of Pashhur, one thousand two hundred and forty-seven; 39the sons of Harim, one thousand and seventeen.

40The Levites: the sons of Jeshua and Kadmiel, of the sons of Hodaviah, seventy-four.

41The singers: the sons of Asaph, one hundred and twenty-eight.

42The sons of the gatekeepers: the sons of Shallum, the sons of Ater, the sons of Talmon, the sons of Akkub, the sons of Hatita, and the sons of Shobai, one hundred and thirty-nine in all.

43The Nethinim: the sons of Ziha, the sons of Hasupha, the sons of Tabbaoth, 44the sons of Keros, the sons of Siaha, the sons of Padon, 45the sons of Lebanah, the sons of Hagabah, the sons of Akkub, 46the sons of Hagab, the sons of Shalmai, the sons of Hanan, 47the sons of Giddel, the sons of Gahar, the sons of Reaiah, 48the sons of Rezin, the sons of Nekoda, the sons of Gazzam, 49the sons of Uzza, the sons of Paseah, the sons of Besai, 50the sons of Asnah, the sons of Meunim, the sons of Nephusim, 51the sons of Bakbuk, the sons of Hakupha, the sons of Harhur, 52the sons of Bazluth, the sons of Mehida, the sons of Harsha, 53the sons of Barkos, the sons of Sisera, the sons of

Tamah, 54the sons of Neziah, and the sons of Hatipha.

55The sons of Solomon's servants: the sons of Sotai, the sons of Sophereth, the sons of Peruda, 56the sons of Jaala, the sons of Darkon, the sons of Giddel, 57the sons of Shephatiah, the sons of Hattil, the sons of Pochereth of Zebaim, and the sons of Ami. 58All the Nethinim and the children of Solomon's servants were three hundred and ninety-two.

59And these were the ones who came up from Tel Melah, Tel Harsha, Cherub, Addan, and Immer; but they could not identify their father's house or their genealogy, whether they were of Israel: 60the sons of Delaiah, the sons of Tobiah, and the sons of Nekoda, six hundred and fifty-two; 61and of the sons of the priests: the sons of Habaiah, the sons of Koz, and the sons of Barzillai, who took a wife of the daughters of Barzillai the Gileadite, and was called by their name. 62These sought their listing among those who were registered by genealogy, but they were not found; therefore they were excluded from the priesthood as defiled. 63And the governor said to them that they should not eat of the most holy things till a priest could consult with the Urim and Thummim.

64The whole assembly together was forty-two thousand three hundred and sixty, 65besides their male and female servants, of whom there were seven thousand three hundred and thirty-seven; and they had two hundred men and women singers. 66Their horses were seven hundred and thirty-six, their mules two hundred and forty-five, 67their camels four hundred and thirty-five, and their donkeys six thousand seven hundred and twenty.

68Some of the heads of the fathers' houses, when they came to the house of the LORD which is in Jerusalem, offered freely for the house of God, to erect it in its place: 69According to their ability, they gave to the treasury for the work sixty-one thousand gold drachmas, five thousand minas of silver, and one hundred priestly garments.

70So the priests and the Levites, some of the people, the singers, the gatekeepers, and the Nethinim, dwelt in their cities, and all Israel in their cities.

Worship Restored at Jerusalem

3 And when the seventh month had come, and the children of Israel *were* in the cities, the people gathered together as one man to Jerusalem. 2Then Jeshua the son of Jozadak and his brethren the priests, and Zerubbabel the son of Shealtiel and his brethren, arose and built the altar of the God of Israel, to offer burnt offerings on it, as *it is* written in the Law of Moses the man of God. 3Though fear *had come* upon them because of the people of those countries, they set the altar on its bases; and they offered burnt offerings on it to the LORD, *both* the morning and evening burnt offerings. 4They also kept the Feast of Tabernacles, as *it is* written, and *offered* the daily burnt offerings in the number required by ordinance for each day. 5Afterwards *they offered* the regular burnt offering, and *those* for New Moons and for all the appointed feasts of the LORD that were consecrated, and *those* of everyone who willingly offered a freewill offering to the LORD. 6From the first day of the seventh month they began to offer burnt offerings to the LORD, although the foundation of the temple of the LORD had not been laid. 7They also gave money to the masons and the carpenters, and food, drink, and oil to the people of Sidon and Tyre to bring cedar logs from Lebanon to the sea, to Joppa, according to the permission which they had from Cyrus king of Persia.

Restoration of the Temple Begins

8Now in the second month of the second year of their coming to the house of God at Jerusalem, Zerubbabel the son of Shealtiel, Jeshua the son of Jozadak, and the rest of their brethren the priests and the Levites, and all those who had come out of the captivity to Jerusalem, began *work* and appointed the Levites from twenty years old and above to oversee the work of the house of the LORD. 9Then Jeshua *with* his sons and brothers, Kadmiel *with* his sons, and the sons of Judah, arose as one to oversee those working on the house of God: the sons of Henadad *with* their sons and their brethren the Levites.

10When the builders laid the foundation of the temple of the LORD, the priests stood in their apparel with trumpets, and the Levites, the sons of Asaph, with cymbals, to praise the LORD, according to the ordinance of David king of Israel. 11And they sang responsively, praising and giving thanks to the LORD:

> "For *He is* good,
> For His mercy *endures* forever
>   toward Israel."*b*

Then all the people shouted with a great shout, when they praised the LORD, because the foundation of the house of the LORD was laid.

12But many of the priests and Levites and heads of the fathers' *houses*, old men who had seen the first temple, wept with a loud voice when the foundation of this temple was laid before their eyes. Yet many shouted aloud for joy, 13so that the people could not discern the noise of the shout of joy from the noise of the weeping of the people, for the people shouted with a loud shout, and the sound was heard afar off.

Resistance to Rebuilding the Temple

4 Now when the adversaries of Judah and Benjamin heard that the descendants of the captivity were building the temple of the LORD God of Israel, 2they came to Zerubbabel and the heads of the fathers' *houses*, and said to them, "Let us build with you, for we seek your God as you *do;* and we have sacrificed to Him since the days of Esarhaddon king of Assyria, who brought us here." 3But Zerubbabel and Jeshua and the rest of the heads of the fathers' *houses* of Israel said to them, "You may do nothing with us to build a house for our God; but we alone will build to the LORD God of Israel, as King Cyrus the king of Persia has commanded us." 4Then the people of the land tried to discourage the people of Judah. They troubled them in building, 5and hired counselors against them to frustrate their purpose all the days of Cyrus king of Persia, even until the reign of Darius king of Persia.

b Compare Psalm 136.1

Rebuilding of Jerusalem Opposed

6In the reign of Ahasuerus, in the beginning of his reign, they wrote an accusation against the inhabitants of Judah and Jerusalem.

7In the days of Artaxerxes also, Bishlam, Mithredath, Tabel, and the rest of their companions wrote to Artaxerxes king of Persia; and the letter *was* written in Aramaic script, and translated into the Aramaic language. 8Rehum the commander and Shimshai the scribe wrote a letter against Jerusalem to King Artaxerxes in this fashion:

9   From Rehum the commander, Shimshai the scribe, and the rest of their companions—*representatives* of the Dinaites, the Apharsathchites, the Tarpelites, the people of Persia and Erech and Babylon and Shushan, the Dehavites, the Elamites, 10and the rest of the nations whom the great and noble Osnapper took captive and settled in the cities of Samaria and the remainder beyond the River^c—and so forth.

11(This *is* a copy of the letter that they sent him)

To King Artaxerxes from your servants, the men *of the region* beyond the River, and so forth:

12   Let it be known to the king that the Jews who came up from you have come to us at Jerusalem, and are building the rebellious and evil city, and are finishing *its* walls and repairing the foundations. 13Let it now be known to the king that, if this city is built and the walls completed, they will not pay tax, tribute, or custom, and the king's treasury will be diminished. 14Now because we receive support from the palace, it was not proper for us to see the king's dishonor; therefore we have sent and informed the king, 15that search may be made in the book of the records of your fathers. And you will find in the book of the records and know that this city *is* a rebellious city, harmful to kings

and provinces, and that they have incited sedition within the city in former times, for which cause this city was destroyed.

16   We inform the king that if this city is rebuilt and its walls are completed, the result will be that you will have no dominion beyond the River.

17The king sent an answer:

To Rehum the commander, *to* Shimshai the scribe, *to* the rest of their companions who dwell in Samaria, and *to* the remainder beyond the River:

Peace, and so forth.

18   The letter which you sent to us has been clearly read before me. 19And I gave the command, and a search has been made, and it was found that this city in former times has revolted against kings, and rebellion and sedition have been fostered in it. 20There have also been mighty kings over Jerusalem, who have ruled over all *the region* beyond the River; and tax, tribute, and custom were paid to them. 21Now give the command to make these men cease, that this city may not be built until the command is given by me.

22   Take heed now that you do not fail to do this. Why should damage increase to the hurt of the kings?

23Now when the copy of King Artaxerxes' letter *was* read before Rehum, Shimshai the scribe, and their companions, they went up in haste to Jerusalem against the Jews, and by force of arms made them cease. 24Thus the work of the house of God which *is* at Jerusalem ceased, and it was discontinued until the second year of the reign of Darius king of Persia.

Restoration of the Temple Resumed

5 Then the prophet Haggai and Zechariah the son of Iddo, prophets, prophesied to the Jews who *were* in Judah and Jerusalem, in the name of the

---

c That is, the Euphrates

God of Israel, *who was* over them. 2So Zerubbabel the son of Shealtiel and Jeshua the son of Jozadak rose up and began to build the house of God which *is* in Jerusalem; and the prophets of God *were* with them, helping them.

3At the same time Tattenai the governor of *the region* beyond the River[c] and Shethar-Boznai and their companions came to them and spoke thus to them: "Who has commanded you to build this temple and finish this wall?" 4Then, accordingly, we told them the names of the men who were constructing this building. 5But the eye of their God was upon the elders of the Jews, so that they could not make them cease till a report could go to Darius. Then a written answer was returned concerning this *matter*. 6This is a copy of the letter that Tattenai sent:

The governor of *the region* beyond the River, and Shethar-Boznai, and his companions, the Persians who *were in the region* beyond the River, to Darius the king.

7(They sent a letter to him, in which was written thus)

To Darius the king:

All peace.

8   Let it be known to the king that we went into the province of Judea, to the temple of the great God, which is being built with heavy stones, and timber is being laid in the walls; and this work goes on diligently and prospers in their hands.

9   Then we asked those elders, *and* spoke thus to them: "Who commanded you to build this temple and to finish these walls?" 10We also asked them their names to inform you, that we might write the names of the men who *were* chief among them.

11   And thus they returned us an answer, saying: "We are the servants of the God of heaven and earth, and we are rebuilding the temple that was built many years ago, which a great king of Israel built and completed. 12But because our fathers provoked the God of heaven to wrath, He gave them into the hand of Nebuchadnezzar king of Babylon, the Chaldean, *who* destroyed this temple and carried the people away to Babylon. 13However, in the first year of Cyrus king of Babylon, King Cyrus issued a decree to build this house of God. 14Also, the gold and silver articles of the house of God, which Nebuchadnezzar had taken from the temple that *was* in Jerusalem and carried into the temple of Babylon—those King Cyrus took from the temple of Babylon, and they were given to one named Sheshbazzar, whom he had made governor. 15And he said to him, 'Take these articles; go, carry them to the temple *site* that *is* in Jerusalem, and let the house of God be rebuilt on its former site.' 16Then the same Sheshbazzar came *and* laid the foundation of the house of God which *is* in Jerusalem; but from that time even until now it has been under construction, and it is not finished."

17   Now therefore, if *it seems* good to the king, let a search be made in the king's treasure house, which *is* there in Babylon, whether it is *so* that a decree was issued by King Cyrus to build this house of God at Jerusalem, and let the king send us his pleasure concerning this *matter*.

The Decree of Darius

6 Then King Darius issued a decree, and a search was made in the archives, where the treasures were stored in Babylon. 2And at Achmetha,[d] in the palace that *is* in the province of Media, a scroll was found, and in it a record *was* written thus:

3   In the first year of King Cyrus, King Cyrus issued a decree *concerning* the house of God at Jerusalem: "Let the house be rebuilt, the place

---

[c]That is, the Euphrates   [d] Probably *Ecbatana*, the ancient capital of Media

where they offered sacrifices; and let the foundations of it be firmly laid, its height sixty cubits *and* its width sixty cubits, [4]*with* three rows of heavy stones and one row of new timber. Let the expenses be paid from the king's treasury. [5]Also let the gold and silver articles of the house of God, which Nebuchadnezzar took from the temple which *is* in Jerusalem and brought to Babylon, be restored and taken back to the temple which *is* in Jerusalem, *each* to its place; and deposit *them* in the house of God"—

6   Now *therefore*, Tattenai, governor of *the region* beyond the River, and Shethar-Boznai, and your companions the Persians who *are* beyond the River, keep yourselves far from there. [7]Let the work of this house of God alone; let the governor of the Jews and the elders of the Jews build this house of God on its site.

8   Moreover I issue a decree *as to* what you shall do for the elders of these Jews, for the building of this house of God: Let the cost be paid at the king's expense from taxes *on the region* beyond the River; this is to be given immediately to these men, so that they are not hindered. [9]And whatever they need—young bulls, rams, and lambs for the burnt offerings of the God of heaven, wheat, salt, wine, and oil, according to the request of the priests who *are* in Jerusalem—let it be given them day by day without fail, [10]that they may offer sacrifices of sweet aroma to the God of heaven, and pray for the life of the king and his sons.

11   Also I issue a decree that whoever alters this edict, let a timber be pulled from his house and erected, and let him be hanged on it; and let his house be made a refuse heap because of this. [12]And may the God who causes His name to dwell there destroy any king or people who put their hand to alter it, or to destroy this house of God which is in

Jerusalem. I Darius issue a decree; let it be done diligently.

The Temple Completed and Dedicated

[13]Then Tattenai, governor of *the region* beyond the River, Shethar-Boznai, and their companions diligently did according to what King Darius had sent. [14]So the elders of the Jews built, and they prospered through the prophesying of Haggai the prophet and Zechariah the son of Iddo. And they built and finished *it*, according to the commandment of the God of Israel, and according to the command of Cyrus, Darius, and Artaxerxes king of Persia. [15]Now the temple was finished on the third day of the month of Adar, which was in the sixth year of the reign of King Darius. [16]Then the children of Israel, the priests and the Levites and the rest of the descendants of the captivity, celebrated the dedication of this house of God with joy. [17]And they offered sacrifices at the dedication of this house of God, one hundred bulls, two hundred rams, four hundred lambs, and as a sin offering for all Israel twelve male goats, according to the number of the tribes of Israel. [18]They assigned the priests to their divisions and the Levites to their divisions, over the service of God in Jerusalem, as it is written in the Book of Moses.

The Passover Celebrated

[19]And the descendants of the captivity kept the Passover on the fourteenth *day* of the first month. [20]For the priests and the Levites had purified themselves; all of them *were ritually* clean. And they slaughtered the Passover *lambs* for all the descendants of the captivity, for their brethren the priests, and for themselves. [21]Then the children of Israel who had returned from the captivity ate together with all who had separated themselves from the filth of the nations of the land in order to seek the LORD God of Israel. [22]And they kept the Feast of Unleavened Bread seven days with joy; for the LORD made them joyful, and turned the heart of the king of Assyria toward them, to strengthen their hands in the work of the house of God, the God of Israel.

The Arrival of Ezra

7 Now after these things, in the reign of Artaxerxes king of Persia, Ezra the son of Seraiah, the son of Azariah, the son of Hilkiah, 2the son of Shallum, the son of Zadok, the son of Ahitub, 3the son of Amariah, the son of Azariah, the son of Meraioth, 4the son of Zerahiah, the son of Uzzi, the son of Bukki, 5the son of Abishua, the son of Phinehas, the son of Eleazar, the son of Aaron the chief priest—6this Ezra came up from Babylon; and he *was* a skilled scribe in the Law of Moses, which the LORD God of Israel had given. The king granted him all his request, according to the hand of the LORD his God upon him. 7*Some* of the children of Israel, the priests, the Levites, the singers, the gatekeepers, and the Nethinim came up to Jerusalem in the seventh year of King Artaxerxes. 8And Ezra came to Jerusalem in the fifth month, which *was* in the seventh year of the king. 9On the first *day* of the first month he began *his* journey from Babylon, and on the first *day* of the fifth month he came to Jerusalem, according to the good hand of his God upon him. 10For Ezra had prepared his heart to seek the Law of the LORD, and to do *it,* and to teach statutes and ordinances in Israel.

The Letter of Artaxerxes to Ezra

11This *is* a copy of the letter that King Artaxerxes gave Ezra the priest, the scribe, expert in the words of the commandments of the LORD, and of His statutes to Israel:

12 Artaxerxes, king of kings,

To Ezra the priest, a scribe of the Law of the God of heaven:

Perfect *peace,* and so forth.

13 I issue a decree that all those of the people of Israel and the priests and Levites in my realm, who volunteer to go up to Jerusalem, may go with you. 14And whereas you are being sent by the king and his seven counselors to inquire concerning Judah and Jerusalem, with regard to the Law of your God which *is* in your hand; 15and *whereas you are* to carry the silver and gold which the king and his counselors have freely offered to the God of Israel, whose dwelling *is* in Jerusalem; 16and *whereas* all the silver and gold that you may find in all the province of Babylon, along with the freewill offering of the people and the priests, *are to be* freely offered for the house of their God in Jerusalem—17now therefore, be careful to buy with this money bulls, rams, and lambs, with their grain offerings and their drink offerings, and offer them on the altar of the house of your God in Jerusalem.

18 And whatever seems good to you and your brethren to do with the rest of the silver and the gold, do it according to the will of your God. 19Also the articles that are given to you for the service of the house of your God, deliver in full before the God of Jerusalem. 20And whatever more may be needed for the house of your God, which you may have occasion to provide, pay *for it* from the king's treasury.

21 And I, *even* I, Artaxerxes the king, issue a decree to all the treasurers who *are in the region* beyond the River, that whatever Ezra the priest, the scribe of the Law of the God of heaven, may require of you, let it be done diligently, 22up to one hundred talents of silver, one hundred kors of wheat, one hundred baths of wine, one hundred baths of oil, and salt without prescribed limit. 23Whatever is commanded by the God of heaven, let it diligently be done for the house of the God of heaven. For why should there be wrath against the realm of the king and his sons?

24 Also we inform you that it shall not be lawful to impose tax, tribute, or custom *on* any of the priests, Levites, singers, gatekeepers, Nethinim, or servants of this house of God. 25And you, Ezra, according to your God-given wisdom, set

magistrates and judges who may judge all the people who *are in the region* beyond the River, all such as know the laws of your God; and teach those who do not know *them.* 26Whoever will not observe the law of your God and the law of the king, let judgment be executed speedily on him, whether *it be* death, or banishment, or confiscation of goods, or imprisonment.

27Blessed *be* the Lord God of our fathers, who has put *such a thing as* this in the king's heart, to beautify the house of the Lord which *is* in Jerusalem, 28and has extended mercy to me before the king and his counselors, and before all the king's mighty princes.

So I was encouraged, as the hand of the Lord my God *was* upon me; and I gathered leading men of Israel to go up with me.

Heads of Families Who Returned with Ezra

8 These *are* the heads of their fathers' *houses,* and *this is* the genealogy of those who went up with me from Babylon, in the reign of King Artaxerxes: 2of the sons of Phinehas, Gershom; of the sons of Ithamar, Daniel; of the sons of David, Hattush; 3of the sons of Shecaniah, of the sons of Parosh, Zechariah; and registered with him *were* one hundred and fifty males; 4of the sons of Pahath-Moab, Eliehoenai the son of Zerahiah, and with him two hundred males; 5of the sons of Shechaniah, Ben-Jahaziel, and with him three hundred males; 6of the sons of Adin, Ebed the son of Jonathan, and with him fifty males; 7of the sons of Elam, Jeshaiah the son of Athaliah, and with him seventy males; 8of the sons of Shephatiah, Zebadiah the son of Michael, and with him eighty males; 9of the sons of Joab, Obadiah the son of Jehiel, and with him two hundred and eighteen males; 10of the sons of Shelomith, Ben-Josiphiah, and with him one hundred and sixty males; 11of the sons of Bebai, Zechariah the son of Bebai, and with him twenty-eight males; 12of the sons of Azgad, Johanan the son of Hakkatan, and with him one hundred and ten males; 13of the last sons of Adonikam, whose names *are* these—Eliphelet,

Jeiel, and Shemaiah—and with them sixty males; 14also of the sons of Bigvai, Uthai and Zabbud, and with them seventy males.

Servants for the Temple

15Now I gathered them by the river that flows to Ahava, and we camped there three days. And I looked among the people and the priests, and found none of the sons of Levi there. 16Then I sent for Eliezer, Ariel, Shemaiah, Elnathan, Jarib, Elnathan, Nathan, Zechariah, and Meshullam, leaders; also for Joiarib and Elnathan, men of understanding. 17And I gave them a command for Iddo the chief man at the place Casiphia, and I told them what they should say to Iddo *and* his brethren the Nethinim at the place Casiphia—that they should bring us servants for the house of our God. 18Then, by the good hand of our God upon us, they brought us a man of understanding, of the sons of Mahli the son of Levi, the son of Israel, namely Sherebiah, with his sons and brothers, eighteen men; 19and Hashabiah, and with him Jeshaiah of the sons of Merari, his brothers and their sons, twenty men; 20also of the Nethinim, whom David and the leaders had appointed for the service of the Levites, two hundred and twenty Nethinim. All of them were designated by name.

Fasting and Prayer for Protection

21Then I proclaimed a fast there at the river of Ahava, that we might humble ourselves before our God, to seek from Him the right way for us and our little ones and all our possessions. 22For I was ashamed to request of the king an escort of soldiers and horsemen to help us against the enemy on the road, because we had spoken to the king, saying, "The hand of our God *is* upon all those for good who seek Him, but His power and His wrath *are* against all those who forsake Him." 23So we fasted and entreated our God for this, and He answered our prayer.

Gifts for the Temple

24And I separated twelve of the leaders of the priests—Sherebiah, Hashabiah, and ten of their brethren with them—25and weighed out to them the silver, the gold, and the articles, the offering for the house of our God which the king and his counselors and his princes, and all Israel *who were* present, had offered. 26I weighed into their hand six hundred and fifty talents of silver, silver articles *weighing* one hundred talents, one hundred talents of gold, 27twenty gold basins *worth* a thousand drachmas, and two vessels of fine polished bronze, precious as gold. 28And I said to them, "You *are* holy to the LORD; the articles *are* holy also; and the silver and the gold *are* a freewill offering to the LORD God of your fathers. 29Watch and keep *them* until you weigh *them* before the leaders of the priests and the Levites and heads of the fathers' *houses* of Israel in Jerusalem, *in* the chambers of the house of the LORD." 30So the priests and the Levites received the silver and the gold and the articles by weight, to bring *them* to Jerusalem to the house of our God.

The Return to Jerusalem

31Then we departed from the river of Ahava on the twelfth *day* of the first month, to go to Jerusalem. And the hand of our God was upon us, and He delivered us from the hand of the enemy and from ambush along the road. 32So we came to Jerusalem, and stayed there three days.

33Now on the fourth day the silver and the gold and the articles were weighed in the house of our God by the hand of Meremoth the son of Uriah the priest, and with him *was* Eleazar the son of Phinehas; with them *were* the Levites, Jozabad the son of Jeshua and Noadiah the son of Binnui, 34with the number *and* weight of everything. All the weight was written down at that time.

35The children of those who had been carried away captive, who had come from the captivity, offered burnt offerings to the God of Israel: twelve bulls for all Israel, ninety-six rams, seventy-seven lambs, and twelve male goats *as* a sin offering. All *this was* a burnt offering to the LORD.

36And they delivered the king's orders to the king's satraps and the governors *in the region* beyond the River. So they gave support to the people and the house of God.

Intermarriage with Pagans

9 When these things were done, the leaders came to me, saying, "The people of Israel and the priests and the Levites have not separated themselves from the peoples of the lands, with respect to the abominations of the Canaanites, the Hittites, the Perizzites, the Jebusites, the Ammonites, the Moabites, the Egyptians, and the Amorites. 2For they have taken some of their daughters *as wives* for themselves and their sons, so that the holy seed is mixed with the peoples of *those* lands. Indeed, the hand of the leaders and rulers has been foremost in this trespass." 3So when I heard this thing, I tore my garment and my robe, and plucked out some of the hair of my head and beard, and sat down astonished. 4Then everyone who trembled at the words of the God of Israel assembled to me, because of the transgression of those who had been carried away captive, and I sat astonished until the evening sacrifice.

5At the evening sacrifice I arose from my fasting; and having torn my garment and my robe, I fell on my knees and spread out my hands to the LORD my God. 6And I said: "O my God, I am too ashamed and humiliated to lift up my face to You, my God; for our iniquities have risen higher than *our* heads, and our guilt has grown up to the heavens. 7Since the days of our fathers to this day we *have been* very guilty, and for our iniquities we, our kings, *and* our priests have been delivered into the hand of the kings of the lands, to the sword, to captivity, to plunder, and to humiliation, as *it is* this day. 8And now for a little while grace has been *shown* from the LORD our God, to leave us a remnant to escape, and to give us a peg in His holy place, that our God may enlighten our eyes and give us a measure of revival in our bondage. 9For we *were* slaves. Yet our God did not forsake us in our bondage; but He extended mercy to us in the sight of the kings of Persia, to revive us, to repair the house of our God, to rebuild its ruins, and to give us a wall in Judah and Jerusalem. 10And now, O our God, what shall we say after this? For we have forsaken Your commandments, 11which You commanded by Your servants the prophets, saying, 'The land which you are entering to possess is an unclean land, with the uncleanness of the peoples of the lands, with their abominations which have filled it from one end to another with their impurity. 12Now therefore, do not give your daughters as wives for their sons, nor take their daughters to your sons; and never seek their peace or prosperity, that you may be strong and eat the good of the land, and leave *it* as an inheritance to your children forever.' 13And after all that has come upon us for our evil deeds and for our great guilt, since You our God have punished us less than our iniquities *deserve,* and have given us *such* deliverance as this, 14should we again break Your commandments, and join in marriage with the people *committing* these abominations? Would You not be angry with us until You had consumed *us,* so that *there would be* no remnant or survivor? 15O LORD God of Israel, You *are* righteous, for we are left as a remnant, as *it is* this day. Here we *are* before You, in our guilt, though no one can stand before You because of this!"

Confession of Improper Marriages

10 Now while Ezra was praying, and while he was confessing, weeping, and bowing down before the house of God, a very large assembly of men, women, and children gathered to him from Israel; for the people wept very bitterly. 2And Shechaniah the son of Jehiel, *one* of the sons of Elam, spoke up and said to Ezra, "We have trespassed against our God, and have taken pagan wives from the peoples of the land; yet now there is hope in Israel in spite of this. 3Now therefore, let us make a covenant with our God to put away all these wives and those who have been born to them, according to the advice of my master and of those who tremble at the commandment of our God; and let it be done according to the law. 4Arise, for *this* matter *is* your *responsibility.* We also *are* with you. Be of good courage, and do *it.*"

5Then Ezra arose, and made the leaders of the priests, the Levites, and all Israel swear an oath that they would do according to this word. So they swore an oath. 6Then Ezra rose up from before the house of God, and went into the chamber of Jehohanan the son of Eliashib; and *when* he came there, he ate no bread and drank no water, for he mourned because of the guilt of those from the captivity.

7And they issued a proclamation throughout Judah and Jerusalem to all the descendants of the captivity, that they must gather at Jerusalem, 8and that whoever would not come within three days, according to the instructions of the leaders and elders, all his property would be confiscated, and he himself would be separated from the assembly of those from the captivity.

9So all the men of Judah and Benjamin gathered at Jerusalem within three days. It *was* the ninth month, on the twentieth of the month; and all the people sat in the open square of the house of God, trembling because of *this* matter and because of heavy rain. 10Then Ezra the priest stood up and said to them, "You have transgressed and have taken pagan wives, adding to the guilt of Israel. 11Now therefore, make confession to the LORD God of your fathers, and do His will; separate yourselves from the peoples of the land, and from the pagan wives."

12Then all the assembly answered and said with a loud voice, "Yes! As you have said, so we must do. 13But *there are* many people; *it is* the season for heavy rain, and we are not able to stand outside. Nor *is this* the work of one or two days, for *there are* many of us who have transgressed in this matter. 14Please, let the leaders of our entire assembly stand; and let all those in our cities who have taken pagan wives come at appointed times, together with the elders and judges of their cities, until the fierce wrath of our God is turned away from us in this matter." 15Only Jonathan the son of Asahel and Jahaziah the son of Tikvah opposed this, and Meshullam and Shabbethai the Levite gave them support.

16Then the descendants of the captivity did so. And Ezra the priest, *with* certain heads of the fathers' *households,* were set apart by the fathers' *house-*

holds, each of them by name; and they sat down on the first day of the tenth month to examine the matter. 17By the first day of the first month they finished *questioning* all the men who had taken pagan wives.

Pagan Wives Put Away

18And among the sons of the priests who had taken pagan wives *the following* were found of the sons of Jeshua the son of Jozadak, and his brothers: Maaseiah, Eliezer, Jarib, and Gedaliah. 19And they gave their promise that they would put away their wives; and *being* guilty, *they presented* a ram of the flock as their trespass offering.

20Also of the sons of Immer: Hanani and Zebadiah; 21of the sons of Harim: Maaseiah, Elijah, Shemaiah, Jehiel, and Uzziah; 22of the sons of Pashhur: Elioenai, Maaseiah, Ishmael, Nethanel, Jozabad, and Elasah.

23Also of the Levites: Jozabad, Shimei, Kelaiah (the same *is* Kelita), Pethahiah, Judah, and Eliezer.

24Also of the singers: Eliashib; and of the gatekeepers: Shallum, Telem, and Uri.

25And others of Israel: of the sons of Parosh: Ramiah, Jeziah, Malchiah, Mijamin, Eleazar, Malchijah, and Benaiah; 26of the sons of Elam: Mattaniah, Zechariah, Jehiel, Abdi, Jeremoth, and Eliah; 27of the sons of Zattu: Elioenai, Eliashib, Mattaniah, Jeremoth, Zabad, and Aziza; 28of the sons of Bebai: Jehohanan, Hananiah, Zabbai, *and* Athlai; 29of the sons of Bani: Meshullam, Malluch, Adaiah, Jashub, Sheal, *and* Ramoth; 30of the sons of Pahath-Moab: Adna, Chelal, Benaiah, Maaseiah, Mattaniah, Bezalel, Binnui, and Manasseh; 31of the sons of Harim: Eliezer, Ishijah, Malchijah, Shemaiah, Shimeon, 32Benjamin, Malluch, *and* Shemariah; 33of the sons of Hashum: Mattenai, Mattattah, Zabad, Eliphelet, Jeremai, Manasseh, *and* Shimei; 34of the sons of Bani: Maadai, Amram, Uel, 35Benaiah, Bedeiah, Cheluh, 36Vaniah, Meremoth, Eliashib, 37Mattaniah, Mattenai, Jaasai, 38Bani, Binnui, Shimei, 39Shelemiah, Nathan, Adaiah, 40Machnadebai, Shashai, Sharai, 41Azarel, Shelemiah, Shemariah, 42Shallum, Amariah, *and* Joseph; 43of the sons of Nebo: Jeiel, Mattithiah, Zabad, Zebina, Jaddai, Joel, *and* Benaiah.

44All these had taken pagan wives, and *some* of them had wives *by whom* they had children.

The Book of
NEHEMIAH

Nehemiah Prays for His People

1 The words of Nehemiah the son of Hachaliah.

It came to pass in the month of Chislev, *in* the twentieth year, as I was in Shushan the citadel, 2that Hanani one of my brethren came with men from Judah; and I asked them concerning the Jews who had escaped, who had survived the captivity, and concerning Jerusalem. 3And they said to me, "The survivors who are left from the captivity in the province *are* there in great distress and reproach. The wall of Jerusalem *is* also broken down, and its gates *are* burned with fire."

4So it was, when I heard these words, that I sat down and wept, and mourned *for many* days; I was fasting and praying before the God of heaven.

5And I said: "I pray, LORD God of heaven, O great and awesome God, *You* who keep *Your* covenant and mercy with those who love You[a] and observe Your[b] commandments, 6please let Your ear be attentive and Your eyes open, that You may hear the prayer of Your servant which I pray before You now, day and night, for the children of Israel Your servants, and confess the sins of the children of Israel which we have sinned against You. Both my father's house and I have sinned. 7We have acted very corruptly against You, and have not kept the commandments, the statutes, nor the ordinances which You commanded Your servant Moses. 8Remember, I pray, the word that You commanded Your servant Moses, saying, 'If you are unfaithful, I will scatter you among the nations;[c] 9but *if* you return to Me, and keep My commandments and do them, though some of you were cast out to the farthest part of the heavens, *yet* I will gather them from there, and bring them to the place which I have chosen as a dwelling for My name.'[d] 10Now these *are* Your servants and Your people, whom You have redeemed by Your great power, and by Your strong hand. 11O Lord, I pray, please let Your ear be attentive to the prayer of Your servant, and to the prayer of Your servants who desire to fear Your name; and let Your servant prosper this day, I pray, and grant him mercy in the sight of this man."

For I was the king's cupbearer.

Nehemiah Sent to Judah

2 And it came to pass in the month of Nisan, in the twentieth year of King Artaxerxes, *when* wine *was* before him, that I took the wine and gave it to the king. Now I had never been sad in his presence before. 2Therefore the king said to me, "Why *is* your face sad, since you *are* not sick? This *is* nothing but sorrow of heart."

So I became dreadfully afraid, 3and said to the king, "May the king live forever! Why should my face not be sad, when the city, the place of my fathers' tombs, *lies* waste, and its gates are burned with fire?"

4Then the king said to me, "What do you request?"

So I prayed to the God of heaven. 5And I said to the king, "If it pleases the king, and if your servant has found favor in your sight, I ask that you send me to Judah, to the city of my fathers' tombs, that I may rebuild it."

6Then the king said to me (the queen also sitting beside him), "How long will your journey be? And when will you return?" So it pleased the king to send me; and I set him a time.

7Furthermore I said to the king, "If it pleases the king, let letters be given to me for the governors *of the region* beyond the River,[e] that they must permit me to pass through till I come to Judah, 8and a letter to Asaph the keeper of the king's forest, that he must give me timber to make beams for the gates of the citadel which *pertains* to the temple, for the city wall, and for the house that I will occupy." And the king

---

a Or *Him*   *b* Or *His*   *c* Compare Leviticus 26.33   *d* Compare Deuteronomy 30.2–5
e That is, the Euphrates, and so elsewhere in this book

granted *them* to me according to the good hand of my God upon me.

9Then I went to the governors *in the region* beyond the River, and gave them the king's letters. Now the king had sent captains of the army and horsemen with me. 10When Sanballat the Horonite and Tobiah the Ammonite official heard *of it,* they were deeply disturbed that a man had come to seek the well-being of the children of Israel.

Nehemiah Views the Wall of Jerusalem

11So I came to Jerusalem and was there three days. 12Then I arose in the night, I and a few men with me; I told no one what my God had put in my heart to do at Jerusalem; nor was there any animal with me, except the one on which I rode. 13And I went out by night through the Valley Gate to the Serpent Well and the Refuse Gate, and viewed the walls of Jerusalem which were broken down and its gates which were burned with fire. 14Then I went on to the Fountain Gate and to the King's Pool, but *there was* no room for the animal under me to pass. 15So I went up in the night by the valley, and viewed the wall; then I turned back and entered by the Valley Gate, and so returned. 16And the officials did not know where I had gone or what I had done; I had not yet told the Jews, the priests, the nobles, the officials, or the others who did the work.

17Then I said to them, "You see the distress that we *are* in, how Jerusalem *lies* waste, and its gates are burned with fire. Come and let us build the wall of Jerusalem, that we may no longer be a reproach." 18And I told them of the hand of my God which had been good upon me, and also of the king's words that he had spoken to me.

So they said, "Let us rise up and build." Then they set their hands to *this* good *work.*

19But when Sanballat the Horonite, Tobiah the Ammonite official, and Geshem the Arab heard *of it,* they laughed at us and despised us, and said, "What *is* this thing that you are doing? Will you rebel against the king?"

20So I answered them, and said to them, "The God of heaven Himself will prosper us; therefore we His servants will arise and build, but you have no heritage or right or memorial in Jerusalem."

Rebuilding the Wall

3 Then Eliashib the high priest rose up with his brethren the priests and built the Sheep Gate; they consecrated it and hung its doors. They built as far as the Tower of the Hundred, *and* consecrated it, then as far as the Tower of Hananel. 2Next to *Eliashib* the men of Jericho built. And next to them Zaccur the son of Imri built.

3Also the sons of Hassenaah built the Fish Gate; they laid its beams and hung its doors with its bolts and bars. 4And next to them Meremoth the son of Urijah, the son of Koz, made repairs. Next to them Meshullam the son of Berechiah, the son of Meshezabel, made repairs. Next to them Zadok the son of Baana made repairs. 5Next to them the Tekoites made repairs; but their nobles did not put their shoulders to the work of their Lord.

6Moreover Jehoiada the son of Paseah and Meshullam the son of Besodeiah repaired the Old Gate; they laid its beams and hung its doors, with its bolts and bars. 7And next to them Melatiah the Gibeonite, Jadon the Meronothite, the men of Gibeon and Mizpah, repaired the residence of the governor *of the region* beyond the River. 8Next to him Uzziel the son of Harhaiah, one of the goldsmiths, made repairs. Also next to him Hananiah, one of the perfumers, made repairs; and they fortified Jerusalem as far as the Broad Wall. 9And next to them Rephaiah the son of Hur, leader of half the district of Jerusalem, made repairs. 10Next to them Jedaiah the son of Harumaph made repairs in front of his house. And next to him Hattush the son of Hashabniah made repairs.

11Malchijah the son of Harim and Hashub the son of Pahath-Moab repaired another section, as well as the Tower of the Ovens. 12And next to him was Shallum the son of Hallohesh, leader of half the district of Jerusalem; he and his daughters made repairs.

13Hanun and the inhabitants of Zanoah repaired the Valley Gate. They built it, hung its doors with its bolts and bars, and *repaired* a thousand cubits of the wall as far as the Refuse Gate.

14Malchijah the son of Rechab, leader of the district of Beth Haccerem, repaired the Refuse Gate; he built it and hung its doors with its bolts and bars.

15Shallun the son of Col-Hozeh, leader of the district of Mizpah, repaired the Fountain Gate; he built it, covered it, hung its doors with its bolts and bars, and repaired the wall of the Pool of Shelah by the King's Garden, as far as the stairs that go down from the City of David. 16After him Nehemiah the son of Azbuk, leader of half the district of Beth Zur, made repairs as far as *the place* in front of the tombs of David, to the man-made pool, and as far as the House of the Mighty.

17After him the Levites, *under* Rehum the son of Bani, made repairs. Next to him Hashabiah, leader of half the district of Keilah, made repairs for his district. 18After him their brethren, *under* Bavai the son of Henadad, leader of the *other* half of the district of Keilah, made repairs. 19And next to him Ezer the son of Jeshua, the leader of Mizpah, repaired another section in front of the Ascent to the Armory at the buttress. 20After him Baruch the son of Zabbai carefully repaired the other section, from the buttress to the door of the house of Eliashib the high priest. 21After him Meremoth the son of Urijah, the son of Koz, repaired another section, from the door of the house of Eliashib to the end of the house of Eliashib.

22And after him the priests, the men of the plain, made repairs. 23After him Benjamin and Hasshub made repairs opposite their house. After them Azariah the son of Maaseiah, the son of Ananiah, made repairs by his house. 24After him Binnui the son of Henadad repaired another section, from the house of Azariah to the buttress, even as far as the corner. 25Palal the son of Uzai *made repairs* opposite the buttress, and on the tower which projects from the king's upper house that *was* by the court of the prison. After him Pedaiah the son of Parosh *made repairs.*

26Moreover the Nethinim who dwelt in Ophel *made repairs* as far as *the place* in front of the Water Gate toward the east, and on the projecting tower. 27After them the Tekoites repaired another section, next to the great projecting tower, and as far as the wall of Ophel.

28Beyond the Horse Gate the priests made repairs, each in front of his *own* house. 29After them Zadok the son of Immer made repairs in front of his *own* house. After him Shemaiah the son of Shechaniah, the keeper of the East Gate, made repairs. 30After him Hananiah the son of Shelemiah, and Hanun, the sixth son of Zalaph, repaired another section. After him Meshullam the son of Berechiah made repairs in front of his dwelling. 31After him Malchijah, one of the goldsmiths, made repairs as far as the house of the Nethinim and of the merchants, in front of the Miphkad Gate, and as far as the upper room at the corner. 32And between the upper room at the corner, as far as the Sheep Gate, the goldsmiths and the merchants made repairs.

The Wall Defended Against Enemies

4 But it so happened, when Sanballat heard that we were rebuilding the wall, that he was furious and very indignant, and mocked the Jews. 2And he spoke before his brethren and the army of Samaria, and said, "What are these feeble Jews doing? Will they fortify themselves? Will they offer sacrifices? Will they complete it in a day? Will they revive the stones from the heaps of rubbish—*stones* that are burned?"

3Now Tobiah the Ammonite *was* beside him, and he said, "Whatever they build, if even a fox goes up *on it,* he will break down their stone wall."

4Hear, O our God, for we are despised; turn their reproach on their own heads, and give them as plunder to a land of captivity! 5Do not cover their iniquity, and do not let their sin be blotted out from before You; for they have provoked *You* to anger before the builders.

6So we built the wall, and the entire wall was joined together up to half its *height,* for the people had a mind to work.

7Now it happened, when Sanballat,

Tobiah, the Arabs, the Ammonites, and the Ashdodites heard that the walls of Jerusalem were being restored and the gaps were beginning to be closed, that they became very angry, 8and all of them conspired together to come *and* attack Jerusalem and create confusion. 9Nevertheless we made our prayer to our God, and because of them we set a watch against them day and night.

10Then Judah said, "The strength of the laborers is failing, and *there is* so much rubbish that we are not able to build the wall."

11And our adversaries said, "They will neither know nor see anything, till we come into their midst and kill them and cause the work to cease."

12So it was, when the Jews who dwelt near them came, that they told us ten times, "From whatever place you turn, *they will be* upon us."

13Therefore I positioned *men* behind the lower parts of the wall, at the openings; and I set the people according to their families, with their swords, their spears, and their bows. 14And I looked, and arose and said to the nobles, to the leaders, and to the rest of the people, "Do not be afraid of them. Remember the Lord, great and awesome, and fight for your brethren, your sons, your daughters, your wives, and your houses."

15And it happened, when our enemies heard that it was known to us, and *that* God had brought their plot to nothing, that all of us returned to the wall, everyone to his work. 16So it was, from that time on, *that* half of my servants worked at construction, while the other half held the spears, the shields, the bows, and *wore* armor; and the leaders *were* behind all the house of Judah. 17Those who built on the wall, and those who carried burdens, loaded themselves so that with one hand they worked at construction, and with the other held a weapon. 18Every one of the builders had his sword girded at his side as he built. And the one who sounded the trumpet *was* beside me. 19Then I said to the nobles, the rulers, and the rest of the people, "The work *is* great and extensive, and we are separated far from one another on the wall. 20Wherever you hear the sound of the trumpet, rally to us there. Our God will fight for us."

21So we labored in the work, and half of *the men* held the spears from daybreak until the stars appeared. 22At the same time I also said to the people, "Let each man and his servant stay at night in Jerusalem, that they may be our guard by night and a working party by day." 23So neither I, my brethren, my servants, nor the men of the guard who followed me took off our clothes, *except* that everyone took them off for washing.

Nehemiah Deals with Oppression

5 And there was a great outcry of the people and their wives against their Jewish brethren. 2For there were those who said, "We, our sons, and our daughters *are* many; therefore let us get grain, that we may eat and live."

3There were also *some* who said, "We have mortgaged our lands and vineyards and houses, that we might buy grain because of the famine."

4There were also those who said, "We have borrowed money for the king's tax *on* our lands and vineyards. 5Yet now our flesh *is* as the flesh of our brethren, our children as their children; and indeed we are forcing our sons and our daughters to be slaves, and *some* of our daughters have been brought into slavery. *It is* not in our power *to* redeem them, for other men have our lands and vineyards."

6And I became very angry when I heard their outcry and these words. 7After serious thought, I rebuked the nobles and rulers, and said to them, "Each of you is exacting usury from his brother." So I called a great assembly against them. 8And I said to them, "According to our ability we have redeemed our Jewish brethren who were sold to the nations. Now indeed, will you even sell your brethren? Or should they be sold to us?"

Then they were silenced and found nothing *to say.* 9Then I said, "What you are doing *is* not good. Should you not walk in the fear of our God because of the reproach of the nations, our enemies? 10I also, *with* my brethren and my servants, am lending them money and grain. Please, let us stop this usury!

11Restore now to them, even this day, their lands, their vineyards, their olive groves, and their houses, also a hundredth of the money and the grain, the new wine and the oil, that you have charged them."

12So they said, "We will restore *it*, and will require nothing from them; we will do as you say."

Then I called the priests, and required an oath from them that they would do according to this promise. 13Then I shook out the fold of my garment and said, "So may God shake out each man from his house, and from his property, who does not perform this promise. Even thus may he be shaken out and emptied."

And all the assembly said, "Amen!" and praised the LORD. Then the people did according to this promise.

The Generosity of Nehemiah

14Moreover, from the time that I was appointed to be their governor in the land of Judah, from the twentieth year until the thirty-second year of King Artaxerxes, twelve years, neither I nor my brothers ate the governor's provisions. 15But the former governors who *were* before me laid burdens on the people, and took from them bread and wine, besides forty shekels of silver. Yes, even their servants bore rule over the people, but I did not do so, because of the fear of God. 16Indeed, I also continued the work on this wall, and we did not buy any land. All my servants *were* gathered there for the work.

17And at my table *were* one hundred and fifty Jews and rulers, besides those who came to us from the nations around us. 18Now *that* which was prepared daily *was* one ox *and* six choice sheep. Also fowl were prepared for me, and once every ten days an abundance of all kinds of wine. Yet in spite of this I did not demand the governor's provisions, because the bondage was heavy on this people.

19Remember me, my God, for good, *according to* all that I have done for this people.

Conspiracy Against Nehemiah

6 Now it happened when Sanballat, Tobiah, Geshem the Arab, and the rest of our enemies heard that I had rebuilt the wall, and *that* there were no breaks left in it (though at that time I had not hung the doors in the gates), 2that Sanballat and Geshem sent to me, saying, "Come, let us meet together among the villages in the plain of Ono." But they thought to do me harm.

3So I sent messengers to them, saying, "I *am* doing a great work, so that I cannot come down. Why should the work cease while I leave it and go down to you?"

4But they sent me this message four times, and I answered them in the same manner.

5Then Sanballat sent his servant to me as before, the fifth time, with an open letter in his hand. 6In it *was* written:

It is reported among the nations, and Geshem says, *that* you and the Jews plan to rebel; therefore, according to these rumors, you are rebuilding the wall, that you may be their king. 7And you have also appointed prophets to proclaim concerning you at Jerusalem, saying, "*There is* a king in Judah!" Now these matters will be reported to the king. So come, therefore, and let us consult together.

8Then I sent to him, saying, "No such things as you say are being done, but you invent them in your own heart."

9For they all *were trying to* make us afraid, saying, "Their hands will be weakened in the work, and it will not be done."

Now therefore, O God, strengthen my hands.

10Afterward I came to the house of Shemaiah the son of Delaiah, the son of Mehetabel, who *was* a secret informer; and he said, "Let us meet together in the house of God, within the temple, and let us close the doors of the temple, for they are coming to kill you; indeed, at night they will come to kill you."

11And I said, "Should such a man as I flee? And who *is there* such as I who would go into the temple to save his life? I will not go in!" 12Then I perceived that God had not sent him at all, but that he pronounced *this* prophecy against me because Tobiah and Sanballat had hired him. 13For this reason he *was* hired, that I should be afraid and act that way and sin, so *that* they might have *cause* for an evil report, that they might reproach me.

14My God, remember Tobiah and Sanballat, according to these their works, and the prophetess Noadiah and the rest of the prophets who would have made me afraid.

The Wall Completed

15So the wall was finished on the twenty-fifth *day* of Elul, in fifty-two days. 16And it happened, when all our enemies heard *of it*, and all the nations around us saw *these things*, that they were very disheartened in their own eyes; for they perceived that this work was done by our God.

17Also in those days the nobles of Judah sent many letters to Tobiah, and *the letters of* Tobiah came to them. 18For many in Judah were pledged to him, because he was the son-in-law of Shechaniah the son of Arah, and his son Jehohanan had married the daughter of Meshullam the son of Berechiah. 19Also they reported his good deeds before me, and reported my words to him. Tobiah sent letters to frighten me.

7 Then it was, when the wall was built and I had hung the doors, when the gatekeepers, the singers, and the Levites had been appointed, 2that I gave the charge of Jerusalem to my brother Hanani, and Hananiah the leader of the citadel, for he *was* a faithful man and feared God more than many.

3And I said to them, "Do not let the gates of Jerusalem be opened until the sun is hot; and while they stand *guard*, let them shut and bar the doors; and appoint guards from among the inhabitants of Jerusalem, one at his watch station and another in front of his own house."

The Captives Who Returned to Jerusalem

4Now the city *was* large and spacious, but the people in it *were* few, and the houses *were* not rebuilt. 5Then my God put it into my heart to gather the nobles, the rulers, and the people, that they might be registered by genealogy. And I found a register of the genealogy of those who had come up in the first *return,* and found written in it:

6 These*f are* the people of the province who came back from the captivity, of those who had been carried away, whom Nebuchadnezzar the king of Babylon had carried away, and who returned to Jerusalem and Judah, everyone to his city.

7 Those who came with Zerubbabel *were* Jeshua, Nehemiah, Azariah, Raamiah, Nahamani, Mordecai, Bilshan, Mispereth, Bigvai, Nehum, and Baanah.

The number of the men of the people of Israel: 8the sons of Parosh, two thousand one hundred and seventy-two;
9the sons of Shephatiah, three hundred and seventy-two;
10the sons of Arah, six hundred and fifty-two;
11the sons of Pahath-Moab, of the sons of Jeshua and Joab, two thousand eight hundred and eighteen;
12the sons of Elam, one thousand two hundred and fifty-four;
13the sons of Zattu, eight hundred and forty-five;
14the sons of Zaccai, seven hundred and sixty;
15the sons of Binnui, six hundred and forty-eight;
16the sons of Bebai, six hundred and twenty-eight;
17the sons of Azgad, two thousand three hundred and twenty-two;
18the sons of Adonikam, six hundred and sixty-seven;
19the sons of Bigvai, two thousand and sixty-seven;
20the sons of Adin, six hundred and fifty-five;
21the sons of Ater of Hezekiah, ninety-eight;
22the sons of Hashum, three hundred and twenty-eight;

f Compare verses 6–72 with Ezra 2.1–70

23the sons of Bezai, three hundred and twenty-four;

24the sons of Hariph, one hundred and twelve;

25the sons of Gibeon, ninety-five;

26the men of Bethlehem and Netophah, one hundred and eighty-eight;

27the men of Anathoth, one hundred and twenty-eight;

28the men of Beth Azmaveth, forty-two;

29the men of Kirjath Jearim, Chephirah, and Beeroth, seven hundred and forty-three;

30the men of Ramah and Geba, six hundred and twenty-one;

31the men of Michmas, one hundred and twenty-two;

32the men of Bethel and Ai, one hundred and twenty-three;

33the men of the other Nebo, fifty-two;

34the sons of the other Elam, one thousand two hundred and fifty-four;

35the sons of Harim, three hundred and twenty;

36the sons of Jericho, three hundred and forty-five;

37the sons of Lod, Hadid, and Ono, seven hundred and twenty-one;

38the sons of Senaah, three thousand nine hundred and thirty.

39 The priests: the sons of Jedaiah, of the house of Jeshua, nine hundred and seventy-three;

40the sons of Immer, one thousand and fifty-two;

41the sons of Pashhur, one thousand two hundred and forty-seven;

42the sons of Harim, one thousand and seventeen.

43 The Levites: the sons of Jeshua, of Kadmiel,
and of the sons of Hodevah, seventy-four.

44 The singers: the sons of Asaph, one hundred and forty-eight.

45 The gatekeepers: the sons of Shallum,
the sons of Ater,

the sons of Talmon,
the sons of Akkub,
the sons of Hatita,
the sons of Shobai, one hundred and thirty-eight.

46 The Nethinim: the sons of Ziha,
the sons of Hasupha,
the sons of Tabbaoth,
47the sons of Keros,
the sons of Sia,
the sons of Padon,
48the sons of Lebana,
the sons of Hagaba,
the sons of Salmai,
49the sons of Hanan,
the sons of Giddel,
the sons of Gahar,
50the sons of Reaiah,
the sons of Rezin,
the sons of Nekoda,
51the sons of Gazzam,
the sons of Uzza,
the sons of Paseah,
52the sons of Besai,
the sons of Meunim,
the sons of Nephishesim,
53the sons of Bakbuk,
the sons of Hakupha,
the sons of Harhur,
54the sons of Bazlith,
the sons of Mehida,
the sons of Harsha,
55the sons of Barkos,
the sons of Sisera,
the sons of Tamah,
56the sons of Neziah,
and the sons of Hatipha.

57 The sons of Solomon's servants:
the sons of Sotai,
the sons of Sophereth,
the sons of Perida,
58the sons of Jaala,
the sons of Darkon,
the sons of Giddel,
59the sons of Shephatiah,
the sons of Hattil,
the sons of Pochereth of Zebaim,
and the children of Amon.
60All the Nethinim, and the sons of Solomon's servants, *were* three hundred and ninety-two.

61 And these *were* the ones who came up from Tel Melah, Tel Harsha, Cherub, Addon, and Immer, but

they could not identify their father's house nor their lineage, whether they *were* of Israel: 62the sons of Delaiah,
the sons of Tobiah,
the sons of Nekoda, six hundred and forty-two;
63and of the priests: the sons of Habaiah,
the sons of Koz,
the sons of Barzillai, who took a wife of the daughters of Barzillai the Gileadite, and was called by their name.
64These sought their listing *among* those who were registered by genealogy, but it was not found; therefore they were excluded from the priesthood as defiled. 65And the governor said to them that they should not eat of the most holy things till a priest could consult with the Urim and Thummim.

66   Altogether the whole assembly *was* forty-two thousand three hundred and sixty, 67besides their male and female servants, of whom *there were* seven thousand three hundred and thirty-seven; and they had two hundred and forty-five men and women singers. 68Their horses were seven hundred and thirty-six, their mules two hundred and forty-five, 69*their* camels four hundred and thirty-five, *and* donkeys six thousand seven hundred and twenty.

70   And some of the heads of the fathers' houses gave to the work. The governor gave to the treasury one thousand gold drachmas, fifty basins, and five hundred and thirty priestly garments. 71Some of the heads of the fathers' *houses* gave to the treasury of the work twenty thousand gold drachmas, and two thousand two hundred silver minas. 72And that which the rest of the people gave *was* twenty thousand gold drachmas, two thousand silver minas, and sixty-seven priestly garments.
73So the priests, the Levites, the gatekeepers, the singers, *some* of the people, the Nethinim, and all Israel dwelt in their cities.

Ezra Reads the Law

When the seventh month came, the children of Israel *were* in their cities.

8 Now all the people gathered together as one man in the open square that *was* in front of the Water Gate; and they told Ezra the scribe to bring the Book of the Law of Moses, which the LORD had commanded Israel. 2So Ezra the priest brought the Law before the assembly of men and women and all who *could* hear with understanding on the first day of the seventh month. 3Then he read from it in the open square that *was* in front of the Water Gate from morning until midday, before the men and women and those who could understand; and the ears of all the people *were attentive* to the Book of the Law.

4So Ezra the scribe stood on a platform of wood which they had made for the purpose; and beside him, at his right hand, stood Mattithiah, Shema, Anaiah, Urijah, Hilkiah, and Maaseiah; and at his left hand Pedaiah, Mishael, Malchijah, Hashum, Hashbadana, Zechariah, *and* Meshullam. 5And Ezra opened the book in the sight of all the people, for he was *standing* above all the people; and when he opened it, all the people stood up. 6And Ezra blessed the LORD, the great God.

Then all the people answered, "Amen, Amen!" while lifting up their hands. And they bowed their heads and worshiped the LORD with *their* faces to the ground.

7Also Jeshua, Bani, Sherebiah, Jamin, Akkub, Shabbethai, Hodijah, Maaseiah, Kelita, Azariah, Jozabad, Hanan, Pelaiah, and the Levites, helped the people to understand the Law; and the people *stood* in their place. 8So they read distinctly from the book, in the Law of God; and they gave the sense, and helped *them* to understand the reading.

9And Nehemiah, who *was* the governor, Ezra the priest *and* scribe, and the Levites who taught the people said to all the people, "This day *is* holy to the LORD your God; do not mourn nor weep." For all the people wept, when they heard the words of the Law.

10Then he said to them, "Go your way, eat the fat, drink the sweet, and send portions to those for whom nothing is prepared; for *this* day *is* holy to our Lord. Do not sorrow, for the joy of the LORD is your strength."

11So the Levites quieted all the people, saying, "Be still, for the day *is* holy; do not be grieved." 12And all the people went their way to eat and drink, to send portions and rejoice greatly, because they understood the words that were declared to them.

The Feast of Tabernacles

13Now on the second day the heads of the fathers' *houses* of all the people, with the priests and Levites, were gathered to Ezra the scribe, in order to understand the words of the Law. 14And they found written in the Law, which the LORD had commanded by Moses, that the children of Israel should dwell in booths during the feast of the seventh month, 15and that they should announce and proclaim in all their cities and in Jerusalem, saying, "Go out to the mountain, and bring olive branches, branches of oil trees, myrtle branches, palm branches, and branches of leafy trees, to make booths, as *it is* written."

16Then the people went out and brought *them* and made themselves booths, each one on the roof of his house, or in their courtyards or the courts of the house of God, and in the open square of the Water Gate and in the open square of the Gate of Ephraim. 17So the whole assembly of those who had returned from the captivity made booths and sat under the booths; for since the days of Joshua the son of Nun until that day the children of Israel had not done so. And there was very great gladness. 18Also day by day, from the first day until the last day, he read from the Book of the Law of God. And they kept the feast seven days; and on the eighth day *there was* a sacred assembly, according to the *prescribed* manner.

The People Confess Their Sins

9 Now on the twenty-fourth day of this month the children of Israel were assembled with fasting, in sackcloth, and with dust on their heads. 2Then those of Israelite lineage separated themselves from all foreigners; and they stood and confessed their sins and the iniquities of their fathers. 3And they stood up in their place and read from the Book of the Law of the LORD their God *for one*-fourth of the day; and *for another* fourth they confessed and worshiped the LORD their God.

4Then Jeshua, Bani, Kadmiel, Shebaniah, Bunni, Sherebiah, Bani, *and* Chenani stood on the stairs of the Levites and cried out with a loud voice to the LORD their God. 5And the Levites, Jeshua, Kadmiel, Bani, Hashabniah, Sherebiah, Hodijah, Shebaniah, *and* Pethahiah, said:

"Stand up *and* bless the LORD
   your God
Forever and ever!

"Blessed be Your glorious name,
  Which is exalted above all blessing
   and praise!
6 You alone *are* the LORD;
  You have made heaven,
  The heaven of heavens, with all
   their host,
  The earth and everything on it,
  The seas and all that is in them,
  And You preserve them all.
  The host of heaven worships You.

7 "You *are* the LORD God,
  Who chose Abram,
  And brought him out of Ur of the
   Chaldeans,
  And gave him the name Abraham;
8 You found his heart faithful
   before You,
  And made a covenant with him
  To give the land of the Canaanites,
  The Hittites, the Amorites,
  The Perizzites, the Jebusites,
  And the Girgashites—
  To give *it* to his descendants.
  You have performed Your words,
  For You *are* righteous.

9 "You saw the affliction of our fathers
   in Egypt,
  And heard their cry by the Red Sea.
10 You showed signs and wonders
   against Pharaoh,

Against all his servants,
And against all the people of his
land.
For You knew that they acted
proudly against them.
So You made a name for Yourself,
as *it is* this day.
11 And You divided the sea before
them,
So that they went through the midst
of the sea on the dry land;
And their persecutors You threw
into the deep,
As a stone into the mighty waters.
12 Moreover You led them by day
with a cloudy pillar,
And by night with a pillar of fire,
To give them light on the road
Which they should travel.

13 "You came down also on Mount
Sinai,
And spoke with them from heaven,
And gave them just ordinances and
true laws,
Good statutes and commandments.
14 You made known to them Your
holy Sabbath,
And commanded them precepts,
statutes and laws,
By the hand of Moses Your servant.
15 You gave them bread from heaven
for their hunger,
And brought them water out of the
rock for their thirst,
And told them to go in to possess
the land
Which You had sworn to give them.

16 "But they and our fathers acted
proudly,
Hardened their necks,
And did not heed Your
commandments.
17 They refused to obey,
And they were not mindful of Your
wonders
That You did among them.
But they hardened their necks,
And in their rebellion
They appointed a leader
To return to their bondage.
But You *are* God,
Ready to pardon,
Gracious and merciful,

Slow to anger,
Abundant in kindness,
And did not forsake them.

18 "Even when they made a molded
calf for themselves,
And said, 'This *is* your god
That brought you up out of Egypt,'
And worked great provocations,
19 Yet in Your manifold mercies
You did not forsake them in the
wilderness.
The pillar of the cloud did not
depart from them by day,
To lead them on the road;
Nor the pillar of fire by night,
To show them light,
And the way they should go.
20 You also gave Your good Spirit to
instruct them,
And did not withhold Your manna
from their mouth,
And gave them water for their
thirst.
21 Forty years You sustained them in
the wilderness;
They lacked nothing;
Their clothes did not wear out[g]
And their feet did not swell.

22 "Moreover You gave them
kingdoms and nations,
And divided them into districts.
So they took possession of the land
of Sihon,
The land of the king of Heshbon,
And the land of Og king of Bashan.
23 You also multiplied their children
as the stars of heaven,
And brought them into the land
Which You had told their fathers
To go in and possess.
24 So the people went in
And possessed the land;
You subdued before them the
inhabitants of the land,
The Canaanites,
And gave them into their hands,
With their kings
And the people of the land,
That they might do with them as
they wished.
25 And they took strong cities and a
rich land,

g Compare Deuteronomy 29.5

And possessed houses full of all
goods,
Cisterns *already* dug, vineyards,
olive groves,
And fruit trees in abundance.
So they ate and were filled and
grew fat,
And delighted themselves in Your
great goodness.

26 "Nevertheless they were disobedient
And rebelled against You,
Cast Your law behind their backs
And killed Your prophets, who
testified against them
To turn them to Yourself;
And they worked great
provocations.
27 Therefore You delivered them into
the hand of their enemies,
Who oppressed them;
And in the time of their trouble,
When they cried to You,
You heard from heaven;
And according to Your abundant
mercies
You gave them deliverers who
saved them
From the hand of their enemies.

28 "But after they had rest,
They again did evil before You.
Therefore You left them in the hand
of their enemies,
So that they had dominion over
them;
Yet when they returned and cried
out to You,
You heard from heaven;
And many times You delivered
them according to Your mercies,
29 And testified against them,
That You might bring them back
to Your law.
Yet they acted proudly,
And did not heed Your
commandments,
But sinned against Your
judgments,
'Which if a man does, he shall live
by them.'[h]
And they shrugged their shoulders,
Stiffened their necks,
And would not hear.
30 Yet for many years You had
patience with them,

And testified against them by Your
Spirit in Your prophets.
Yet they would not listen;
Therefore You gave them into the
hand of the peoples of the lands.
31 Nevertheless in Your great mercy
You did not utterly consume them
nor forsake them;
For You *are* God, gracious and
merciful.

32 "Now therefore, our God,
The great, the mighty, and
awesome God,
Who keeps covenant and mercy:
Do not let all the trouble seem small
before You
That has come upon us,
Our kings and our princes,
Our priests and our prophets,
Our fathers and on all Your people,
From the days of the kings of
Assyria until this day.
33 However You *are* just in all that has
befallen us;
For You have dealt faithfully,
But we have done wickedly.
34 Neither our kings nor our princes,
Our priests nor our fathers,
Have kept Your law,
Nor heeded Your commandments
and Your testimonies,
With which You testified against
them.
35 For they have not served You in
their kingdom,
Or in the many good *things* that
You gave them,
Or in the large and rich land which
You set before them;
Nor did they turn from their wicked
works.

36 "Here we *are*, servants today!
And the land that You gave to our
fathers,
To eat its fruit and its bounty,
Here we *are*, servants in it!
37 And it yields much increase to the
kings
You have set over us,
Because of our sins;
Also they have dominion over our
bodies and our cattle
At their pleasure;
And we *are* in great distress.

h Compare Leviticus 18.5

38 "And because of all this,
We make a sure *covenant* and
   write *it;*
Our leaders, our Levites, *and* our
   priests seal *it.*"

The People Who Sealed the Covenant

10 Now those who placed *their* seal on *the document were:*
Nehemiah the governor, the son of Hacaliah, and Zedekiah, 2Seraiah, Azariah, Jeremiah, 3Pashhur, Amariah, Malchijah, 4Hattush, Shebaniah, Malluch, 5Harim, Meremoth, Obadiah, 6Daniel, Ginnethon, Baruch, 7Meshullam, Abijah, Mijamin, 8Maaziah, Bilgai, *and* Shemaiah. These *were* the priests.

9   The Levites: Jeshua the son
    of Azaniah, Binnui of the sons
    of Henadad, *and* Kadmiel.

10 Their brethren: Shebaniah,
    Hodijah, Kelita, Pelaiah, Hanan,
    11Micha, Rehob, Hashabiah,
    12Zaccur, Sherebiah, Shebaniah,
    13Hodijah, Bani, *and* Beninu.

14 The leaders of the people: Parosh,
    Pahath-Moab, Elam, Zattu, Bani,
    15Bunni, Azgad, Bebai, 16Adonijah,
    Bigvai, Adin, 17Ater, Hezekiah,
    Azzur, 18Hodijah, Hashum, Bezai,
    19Hariph, Anathoth, Nebai,
    20Magpiash, Meshullam, Hezir,
    21Meshezabel, Zadok, Jaddua,
    22Pelatiah, Hanan, Anaiah,
    23Hoshea, Hananiah, Hasshub,
    24Hallohesh, Pilha, Shobek,
    25Rehum, Hashabnah, Maaseiah,
    26Ahijah, Hanan, Anan, 27Malluch,
    Harim, *and* Baanah.

The Covenant That Was Sealed

28Now the rest of the people—the priests, the Levites, the gatekeepers, the singers, the Nethinim, and all those who had separated themselves from the peoples of the lands to the Law of God, their wives, their sons, and their daughters, everyone who had knowledge and understanding—29these joined with their brethren, their nobles, and entered into a curse and an oath to walk in God's Law, which was given by Moses the servant of God, and to observe and do all the commandments of the LORD our Lord, and His ordinances and His statutes: 30We would not give our daughters as wives to the peoples of the land, nor take their daughters for our sons; 31if the peoples of the land brought wares or any grain to sell on the Sabbath day, we would not buy it from them on the Sabbath, or on a holy day; and we would forego the seventh year's *produce* and the exacting of every debt.

32Also we made ordinances for ourselves, to exact from ourselves yearly one-third of a shekel for the service of the house of our God: 33for the showbread, for the regular grain offering, for the regular burnt offering of the Sabbaths, the New Moons, and the set feasts; for the holy things, for the sin offerings to make atonement for Israel, and all the work of the house of our God. 34We cast lots among the priests, the Levites, and the people, for *bringing* the wood offering into the house of our God, according to our fathers' houses, at the appointed times year by year, to burn on the altar of the LORD our God as *it is* written in the Law.

35And *we made ordinances* to bring the firstfruits of our ground and the firstfruits of all fruit of all trees, year by year, to the house of the LORD; 36to bring the firstborn of our sons and our cattle, as *it is* written in the Law, and the firstborn of our herds and our flocks, to the house of our God, to the priests who minister in the house of our God; 37to bring the firstfruits of our dough, our offerings, the fruit from all kinds of trees, *the* new wine and oil, to the priests, to the storerooms of the house of our God; and to bring the tithes of our land to the Levites, for the Levites should receive the tithes in all our farming communities. 38And the priest, the descendant of Aaron, shall be with the Levites when the Levites receive tithes; and the Levites shall bring up a tenth of the tithes to the house of our God, to the rooms of the storehouse.

39For the children of Israel and the children of Levi shall bring the offering of the grain, of the new wine and the oil, to the storerooms where the articles of the sanctuary *are, where* the priests who minister and the gatekeepers and the singers *are;* and we will not neglect the house of our God.

The People Dwelling in Jerusalem

11 Now the leaders of the people dwelt at Jerusalem; the rest of the people cast lots to bring one out of ten to dwell in Jerusalem, the holy city, and nine-tenths *were to dwell* in *other* cities. 2And the people blessed all the men who willingly offered themselves to dwell at Jerusalem.

3These *are* the heads of the province who dwelt in Jerusalem. (But in the cities of Judah everyone dwelt in his own possession in their cities—Israelites, priests, Levites, Nethinim, and descendants of Solomon's servants.) 4Also in Jerusalem dwelt *some* of the children of Judah and of the children of Benjamin.

The children of Judah: Athaiah the son of Uzziah, the son of Zechariah, the son of Amariah, the son of Shephatiah, the son of Mahalalel, of the children of Perez; 5and Maaseiah the son of Baruch, the son of Col-Hozeh, the son of Hazaiah, the son of Adaiah, the son of Joiarib, the son of Zechariah, the son of Shiloni. 6All the sons of Perez who dwelt at Jerusalem *were* four hundred and sixty-eight valiant men.

7And these are the sons of Benjamin: Sallu the son of Meshullam, the son of Joed, the son of Pedaiah, the son of Kolaiah, the son of Maaseiah, the son of Ithiel, the son of Jeshaiah; 8and after him Gabbai *and* Sallai, nine hundred and twenty-eight. 9Joel the son of Zichri *was* their overseer, and Judah the son of Senuah *was* second over the city.

10Of the priests: Jedaiah the son of Joiarib, and Jachin; 11Seraiah the son of Hilkiah, the son of Meshullam, the son of Zadok, the son of Meraioth, the son of Ahitub, *was* the leader of the house of God. 12Their brethren who did the work of the house *were* eight hundred and twenty-two; and Adaiah the son of Jeroham, the son of Pelaliah, the son of Amzi, the son of Zechariah, the son of Pashhur, the son of Malchijah, 13and his brethren, heads of the fathers' *houses,* were two hundred and forty-two; and Amashai the son of Azarel, the son of Ahzai, the son of

Meshillemoth, the son of Immer, 14and their brethren, mighty men of valor, *were* one hundred and twenty-eight. Their overseer *was* Zabdiel the son of *one of* the great men.

15Also of the Levites: Shemaiah the son of Hasshub, the son of Azrikam, the son of Hashabiah, the son of Bunni; 16Shabbethai and Jozabad, of the heads of the Levites, *had* the oversight of the business outside of the house of God; 17Mattaniah the son of Micha, the son of Zabdi, the son of Asaph, the leader *who* began the thanksgiving with prayer; Bakbukiah, the second among his brethren; and Abda the son of Shammua, the son of Galal, the son of Jeduthun. 18All the Levites in the holy city *were* two hundred and eighty-four.

19Moreover the gatekeepers, Akkub, Talmon, and their brethren who kept the gates, *were* one hundred and seventy-two.

20And the rest of Israel, of the priests *and* Levites, *were* in all the cities of Judah, everyone in his inheritance. 21But the Nethinim dwelt in Ophel. And Ziha and Gishpa *were* over the Nethinim.

22Also the overseer of the Levites at Jerusalem *was* Uzzi the son of Bani, the son of Hashabiah, the son of Mattaniah, the son of Micha, of the sons of Asaph, the singers in charge of the service of the house of God. 23For *it was* the king's command concerning them that a certain portion should be for the singers, a quota day by day. 24Pethahiah the son of Meshezabel, of the children of Zerah the son of Judah, *was* the king's deputy in all matters concerning the people.

The People Dwelling Outside Jerusalem

25And as for the villages with their fields, *some* of the children of Judah dwelt in Kirjath Arba and its villages, Dibon and its villages, Jekabzeel and its villages; 26in Jeshua, Moladah, Beth Pelet, 27Hazar Shual, and Beersheba and its villages; 28in Ziklag and Meconah and its villages; 29in En Rimmon, Zorah, Jarmuth, 30Zanoah, Adullam, and their villages; in Lachish and its fields; in Azekah and its villages. They dwelt from Beersheba to the Valley of Hinnom.

31Also the children of Benjamin from Geba *dwelt* in Michmash, Aija, and Bethel, and their villages; 32in Anathoth, Nob, Ananiah; 33in Hazor, Ramah, Gittaim; 34in Hadid, Zeboim, Neballat; 35in Lod, Ono, *and* the Valley of Craftsmen. 36Some of the Judean divisions of Levites *were* in Benjamin.

The Priests and Levites

12 Now these *are* the priests and the Levites who came up with Zerubbabel the son of Shealtiel, and Jeshua: Seraiah, Jeremiah, Ezra, 2Amariah, Malluch, Hattush, 3Shechaniah, Rehum, Meremoth, 4Iddo, Ginnethoi, Abijah, 5Mijamin, Maadiah, Bilgah, 6Shemaiah, Joiarib, Jedaiah, 7Sallu, Amok, Hilkiah, *and* Jedaiah. These *were* the heads of the priests and their brethren in the days of Jeshua.

8Moreover the Levites *were* Jeshua, Binnui, Kadmiel, Sherebiah, Judah, *and* Mattaniah *who* led the thanksgiving *psalms*, he and his brethren. 9Also Bakbukiah and Unni, their brethren, *stood* across from them in *their* duties.

10Jeshua begot Joiakim, Joiakim begot Eliashib, Eliashib begot Joiada, 11Joiada begot Jonathan, and Jonathan begot Jaddua.

12Now in the days of Joiakim, the priests, the heads of the fathers' *houses were:* of Seraiah, Meraiah; of Jeremiah, Hananiah; 13of Ezra, Meshullam; of Amariah, Jehohanan; 14of Melichu, Jonathan; of Shebaniah, Joseph; 15of Harim, Adna; of Meraioth, Helkai; 16of Iddo, Zechariah; of Ginnethon, Meshullam; 17of Abijah, Zichri; *the son* of Minjamin; of Moadiah, Piltai; 18of Bilgah, Shammua; of Shemaiah, Jehonathan; 19of Joiarib, Mattenai; of Jedaiah, Uzzi; 20of Sallai, Kallai; of Amok, Eber; 21of Hilkiah, Hashabiah; *and* of Jedaiah, Nethanel.

22During the reign of Darius the Persian, a record *was also* kept of the Levites and priests *who had been* heads of their fathers' *houses* in the days of Eliashib, Joiada, Johanan, and Jaddua. 23The sons of Levi, the heads of the fathers' *houses* until the days of Johanan

the son of Eliashib, *were* written in the book of the chronicles.

24And the heads of the Levites *were* Hashabiah, Sherebiah, and Jeshua the son of Kadmiel, with their brothers across from them, to praise *and* give thanks, group alternating with group, according to the command of David the man of God. 25Mattaniah, Bakbukiah, Obadiah, Meshullam, Talmon, and Akkub *were* gatekeepers keeping the watch at the storerooms of the gates. 26These *lived* in the days of Joiakim the son of Jeshua, the son of Jozadak, and in the days of Nehemiah the governor, and of Ezra the priest, the scribe.

Nehemiah Dedicates the Wall

27Now at the dedication of the wall of Jerusalem they sought out the Levites in all their places, to bring them to Jerusalem to celebrate the dedication with gladness, both with thanksgivings and singing, *with* cymbals and stringed instruments and harps. 28And the sons of the singers gathered together from the countryside around Jerusalem, from the villages of the Netophathites, 29from the house of Gilgal, and from the fields of Geba and Azmaveth; for the singers had built themselves villages all around Jerusalem. 30Then the priests and Levites purified themselves, and purified the people, the gates, and the wall.

31So I brought the leaders of Judah up on the wall, and appointed two large thanksgiving choirs. *One* went to the right hand on the wall toward the Refuse Gate. 32After them went Hoshaiah and half of the leaders of Judah, 33and Azariah, Ezra, Meshullam, 34Judah, Benjamin, Shemaiah, Jeremiah, 35and some of the priests' sons with trumpets—Zechariah the son of Jonathan, the son of Shemaiah, the son of Mattaniah, the son of Michaiah, the son of Zaccur, the son of Asaph, 36and his brethren, Shemaiah, Azarel, Milalai, Gilalai, Maai, Nethanel, Judah, *and* Hanani, with the musical instruments of David the man of God. And Ezra the scribe *went* before them. 37By the Fountain Gate, in front of them, they went up the stairs of the City of David, on the stairway of the wall, beyond the house of David, as far as the Water Gate eastward.

38The other thanksgiving choir went the opposite *way,* and I *was* behind them with half of the people on the wall, going past the Tower of the Ovens as far as the Broad Wall, 39and above the Gate of Ephraim, above the Old Gate, above the Fish Gate, the Tower of Hananel, the Tower of the Hundred, as far as the Sheep Gate; and they stopped by the Gate of the Prison.

40So the two thanksgiving choirs stood in the house of God, likewise I and the half of the rulers with me; 41and the priests, Eliakim, Maaseiah, Minjamin, Michaiah, Elioenai, Zechariah, *and* Hananiah, with trumpets; 42also Maaseiah, Shemaiah, Eleazar, Uzzi, Jehohanan, Malchijah, Elam, and Ezer. The singers sang loudly with Jezrahiah the director.

43Also that day they offered great sacrifices, and rejoiced, for God had made them rejoice with great joy; the women and the children also rejoiced, so that the joy of Jerusalem was heard afar off.

Temple Responsibilities

44And at the same time some were appointed over the rooms of the storehouse for the offerings, the firstfruits, and the tithes, to gather into them from the fields of the cities the portions specified by the Law for the priests and Levites; for Judah rejoiced over the priests and Levites who ministered. 45Both the singers and the gatekeepers kept the charge of their God and the charge of the purification, according to the command of David *and* Solomon his son. 46For in the days of David and Asaph of old *there were* chiefs of the singers, and songs of praise and thanksgiving to God. 47In the days of Zerubbabel and in the days of Nehemiah all Israel gave the portions for the singers and the gatekeepers, a portion for each day. They also consecrated *holy things* for the Levites, and the Levites consecrated *them* for the children of Aaron.

Principles of Separation

13 On that day they read from the Book of Moses in the hearing of the people, and in it was found written that no Ammonite or Moabite should ever come into the assembly of God, 2because they had not met the children of Israel with bread and water, but hired Balaam against them to curse them. However, our God turned the curse into a blessing. 3So it was, when they had heard the Law, that they separated all the mixed multitude from Israel.

The Reforms of Nehemiah

4Now before this, Eliashib the priest, having authority over the storerooms of the house of our God, *was* allied with Tobiah. 5And he had prepared for him a large room, where previously they had stored the grain offerings, the frankincense, the articles, the tithes of grain, the new wine and oil, which were commanded *to be given* to the Levites and singers and gatekeepers, and the offerings for the priests. 6But during all this I was not in Jerusalem, for in the thirty-second year of Artaxerxes king of Babylon I had returned to the king. Then after certain days I obtained leave from the king, 7and I came to Jerusalem and discovered the evil that Eliashib had done for Tobiah, in preparing a room for him in the courts of the house of God. 8And it grieved me bitterly; therefore I threw all the household goods of Tobiah out of the room. 9Then I commanded them to cleanse the rooms; and I brought back into them the articles of the house of God, with the grain offering and the frankincense.

10I also realized that the portions for the Levites had not been given *them;* for each of the Levites and the singers who did the work had gone back to his field. 11So I contended with the rulers, and said, "Why is the house of God forsaken?" And I gathered them together and set them in their place. 12Then all Judah brought the tithe of the grain and the new wine and the oil to the storehouse. 13And I appointed as treasurers over the storehouse Shelemiah the priest and Zadok the scribe, and of the Levites, Pedaiah; and next to them *was* Hanan the son of Zaccur, the son of Mattaniah; for they were considered faithful, and their task *was* to distribute to their brethren.

14Remember me, O my God, concerning this, and do not wipe out my good deeds that I have done for the house of my God, and for its services!

15In those days I saw *people* in Judah treading wine presses on the Sabbath, and bringing in sheaves, and loading donkeys with wine, grapes, figs, and all *kinds of* burdens, which they brought into Jerusalem on the Sabbath day. And I warned *them* about the day on which they were selling provisions. 16Men of Tyre dwelt there also, who brought in fish and all kinds of goods, and sold *them* on the Sabbath to the children of Judah, and in Jerusalem.

17Then I contended with the nobles of Judah, and said to them, "What evil thing *is* this that you do, by which you profane the Sabbath day? 18Did not your fathers do thus, and did not our God bring all this disaster on us and on this city? Yet you bring added wrath on Israel by profaning the Sabbath."

19So it was, at the gates of Jerusalem, as it began to be dark before the Sabbath, that I commanded the gates to be shut, and charged that they must not be opened till after the Sabbath. Then I posted *some* of my servants at the gates, *so that* no burdens would be brought in on the Sabbath day. 20Now the merchants and sellers of all kinds of wares lodged outside Jerusalem once or twice. 21Then I warned them, and said to them, "Why do you spend the night around the wall? If you do *so* again, I will lay hands on you!" From that time on they came no *more* on the Sabbath. 22And I commanded the Levites that they should cleanse themselves, and

that they should go and guard the gates, to sanctify the Sabbath day.

Remember me, O my God, *concerning* this also, and spare me according to the greatness of Your mercy!

23In those days I also saw Jews *who* had married women of Ashdod, Ammon, *and* Moab. 24And half of their children spoke the language of Ashdod, and could not speak the language of Judah, but spoke according to the language of one or the other people.

25So I contended with them and cursed them, struck some of them and pulled out their hair, and made them swear by God, *saying,* "You shall not give your daughters as wives to their sons, nor take their daughters for your sons or yourselves. 26Did not Solomon king of Israel sin by these things? Yet among many nations there was no king like him, who was beloved of his God; and God made him king over all Israel. Nevertheless pagan women caused even him to sin. 27Should we then hear of your doing all this great evil, transgressing against our God by marrying pagan women?"

28And *one* of the sons of Joiada, the son of Eliashib the high priest, *was* a son-in-law of Sanballat the Horonite; therefore I drove him from me.

29Remember them, O my God, because they have defiled the priesthood and the covenant of the priesthood and the Levites.

30Thus I cleansed them of everything pagan. I also assigned duties to the priests and the Levites, each to his service, 31and *to bringing* the wood offering and the firstfruits at appointed times.

Remember me, O my God, for good!

The Book of
ESTHER

The King Dethrones Queen Vashti

1 Now it came to pass in the days of Ahasuerus[a] (this *was* the Ahasuerus who reigned over one hundred and twenty-seven provinces, from India to Ethiopia), 2in those days when King Ahasuerus sat on the throne of his kingdom, which *was* in Shushan the citadel, 3*that* in the third year of his reign he made a feast for all his officials and servants—the powers of Persia and Media, the nobles, and the princes of the provinces *being* before him— 4when he showed the riches of his glorious kingdom and the splendor of his excellent majesty for many days, one hundred and eighty days *in all.*

5And when these days were completed, the king made a feast lasting seven days for all the people who were present in Shushan the citadel, from great to small, in the court of the garden of the king's palace. 6*There were* white and blue linen *curtains* fastened with cords of fine linen and purple on silver rods and marble pillars; *and the* couches *were* of gold and silver on a *mosaic* pavement of alabaster, turquoise, and white and black marble. 7And they served drinks in golden vessels, each vessel being different from the other, with royal wine in abundance, according to the generosity of the king. 8In accordance with the law, the drinking was not compulsory; for so the king had ordered all the officers of his household, that they should do according to each man's pleasure.

9Queen Vashti also made a feast for the women *in* the royal palace which *belonged* to King Ahasuerus.

10On the seventh day, when the heart of the king was merry with wine, he commanded Mehuman, Biztha, Harbona, Bigtha, Abagtha, Zethar, and Carcas, seven eunuchs who served in the presence of King Ahasuerus, 11to bring Queen Vashti before the king, *wearing* her royal crown, in order to show her beauty to the people and the officials, for she *was* beautiful to behold. 12But Queen Vashti refused to come at the king's command *brought* by *his* eunuchs; therefore the king was furious, and his anger burned within him.

13Then the king said to the wise men who understood the times (for this *was* the king's manner toward all who knew law and justice, 14those closest to him *being* Carshena, Shethar, Admatha, Tarshish, Meres, Marsena, and Memucan, the seven princes of Persia and Media, who had access to the king's presence, *and* who ranked highest in the kingdom): 15"What *shall we* do to Queen Vashti, according to law, because she did not obey the command of King Ahasuerus *brought to her* by the eunuchs?"

16And Memucan answered before the king and the princes: "Queen Vashti has not only wronged the king, but also all the princes, and all the people who *are* in all the provinces of King Ahasuerus. 17For the queen's behavior will become known to all women, so that they will despise their husbands in their eyes, when they report, 'King Ahasuerus commanded Queen Vashti to be brought in before him, but she did not come.' 18This very day the *noble* ladies of Persia and Media will say to all the king's officials that they have heard of the behavior of the queen. Thus *there will be* excessive contempt and wrath. 19If it pleases the king, let a royal decree go out from him, and let it be recorded in the laws of the Persians and the Medes, so that it will not be altered, that Vashti shall come no more before King Ahasuerus; and let the king give her royal position to another who is better than she. 20When the king's decree which he will make is proclaimed throughout all his empire (for it is great), all wives will honor their husbands, both great and small."

21And the reply pleased the king and

---

[a] Generally identified with Xerxes I (485–464 B.C.)

the princes, and the king did according to the word of Memucan. 22Then he sent letters to all the king's provinces, to each province in its own script, and to every people in their own language, that each man should be master in his own house, and speak in the language of his own people.

Esther Becomes Queen

2 After these things, when the wrath of King Ahasuerus subsided, he remembered Vashti, what she had done, and what had been decreed against her. 2Then the king's servants who attended him said: "Let beautiful young virgins be sought for the king; 3and let the king appoint officers in all the provinces of his kingdom, that they may gather all the beautiful young virgins to Shushan the citadel, into the women's quarters, under the custody of Hegai the king's eunuch, custodian of the women. And let beauty preparations be given *them*. 4Then let the young woman who pleases the king be queen instead of Vashti."

This thing pleased the king, and he did so.

5In Shushan the citadel there was a certain Jew whose name *was* Mordecai the son of Jair, the son of Shimei, the son of Kish, a Benjamite. 6*Kish* had been carried away from Jerusalem with the captives who had been captured with Jeconiah king of Judah, whom Nebuchadnezzar the king of Babylon had carried away. 7And *Mordecai* had brought up Hadassah, that *is*, Esther, his uncle's daughter, for she had neither father nor mother. The young woman *was* lovely and beautiful. When her father and mother died, Mordecai took her as his own daughter.

8So it was, when the king's command and decree were heard, and when many young women were gathered at Shushan the citadel, *under* the custody of Hegai, that Esther also was taken to the king's palace, into the care of Hegai the custodian of the women. 9Now the young woman pleased him, and she obtained his favor; so he readily gave beauty preparations to her, besides her allowance. Then seven choice maidservants were provided for her from the king's palace, and he moved her and

her maidservants to the best *place* in the house of the women.

10Esther had not revealed her people or family, for Mordecai had charged her not to reveal *it*. 11And every day Mordecai paced in front of the court of the women's quarters, to learn of Esther's welfare and what was happening to her.

12Each young woman's turn came to go in to King Ahasuerus after she had completed twelve months' preparation, according to the regulations for the women, for thus were the days of their preparation apportioned: six months with oil of myrrh, and six months with perfumes and preparations for beautifying women. 13Thus *prepared, each* young woman went to the king, and she was given whatever she desired to take with her from the women's quarters to the king's palace. 14In the evening she went, and in the morning she returned to the second house of the women, to the custody of Shaashgaz, the king's eunuch who kept the concubines. She would not go in to the king again unless the king delighted in her and called for her by name.

15Now when the turn came for Esther the daughter of Abihail the uncle of Mordecai, who had taken her as his daughter, to go in to the king, she requested nothing but what Hegai the king's eunuch, the custodian of the women, advised. And Esther obtained favor in the sight of all who saw her. 16So Esther was taken to King Ahasuerus, into his royal palace, in the tenth month, which *is* the month of Tebeth, in the seventh year of his reign. 17The king loved Esther more than all the *other* women, and she obtained grace and favor in his sight more than all the virgins; so he set the royal crown upon her head and made her queen instead of Vashti. 18Then the king made a great feast, the Feast of Esther, for all his officials and servants; and he proclaimed a holiday in the provinces and gave gifts according to the generosity of a king.

Mordecai Discovers a Plot

19When virgins were gathered together a second time, Mordecai sat within the king's gate. 20Now Esther had not revealed her family and her people, just as Mordecai had charged her, for Esther obeyed the command of Mordecai as when she was brought up by him.

21In those days, while Mordecai sat within the king's gate, two of the king's eunuchs, Bigthan and Teresh, door-keepers, became furious and sought to lay hands on King Ahasuerus. 22So the matter became known to Mordecai, who told Queen Esther, and Esther informed the king in Mordecai's name. 23And when an inquiry was made into the matter, it was confirmed, and both were hanged on a gallows; and it was written in the book of the chronicles in the presence of the king.

Haman's Conspiracy Against the Jews

3 After these things King Ahasuerus promoted Haman, the son of Hammedatha the Agagite, and advanced him and set his seat above all the princes who *were* with him. 2And all the king's servants who *were* within the king's gate bowed and paid homage to Haman, for so the king had commanded concerning him. But Mordecai would not bow or pay homage. 3Then the king's servants who *were* within the king's gate said to Mordecai, "Why do you transgress the king's command?" 4Now it happened, when they spoke to him daily and he would not listen to them, that they told *it* to Haman, to see whether Mordecai's words would stand; for *Mordecai* had told them that he *was* a Jew. 5When Haman saw that Mordecai did not bow or pay him homage, Haman was filled with wrath. 6But he disdained to lay hands on Mordecai alone, for they had told him of the people of Mordecai. Instead, Haman sought to destroy all the Jews who *were* throughout the whole kingdom of Ahasuerus—the people of Mordecai.

7In the first month, which is the month of Nisan, in the twelfth year of King Ahasuerus, they cast Pur (that *is*, the lot), before Haman to determine the day and the month, until *it fell on the* twelfth *month*, which *is* the month of Adar.

8Then Haman said to King Ahasuerus, "There is a certain people scattered and dispersed among the people in all the provinces of your kingdom;

their laws *are* different from all *other* people's, and they do not keep the king's laws. Therefore it *is* not fitting for the king to let them remain. 9If it pleases the king, let *a decree* be written that they be destroyed, and I will pay ten thousand talents of silver into the hands of those who do the work, to bring *it* into the king's treasuries."

10So the king took his signet ring from his hand and gave it to Haman, the son of Hammedatha the Agagite, the enemy of the Jews. 11And the king said to Haman, "The money and the people *are* given to you, to do with them as seems good to you."

12Then the king's scribes were called on the thirteenth day of the first month, and *a decree* was written according to all that Haman commanded—to the king's satraps, to the governors who *were* over each province, to the officials of all people, to every province according to its script, and to every people in their language. In the name of King Ahasuerus it was written, and sealed with the king's signet ring. 13And the letters were sent by couriers into all the king's provinces, to destroy, to kill, and to annihilate all the Jews, both young and old, little children and women, in one day, on the thirteenth *day* of the twelfth *month*, which *is* the month of Adar, and to plunder their possessions. 14A copy of the document was to be issued as law in every province, being published for all people, that they should be ready for that day. 15The couriers went out, hastened by the king's command; and the decree was proclaimed in Shushan the citadel. So the king and Haman sat down to drink, but the city of Shushan was perplexed.

Esther Agrees to Help the Jews

4 When Mordecai learned all that had happened, he tore his clothes and put on sackcloth and ashes, and went out into the midst of the city. He cried out with a loud and bitter cry. 2He went as far as the front of the king's gate, for no one *might* enter the king's gate clothed with sackcloth. 3And in every province where the king's command and decree arrived, *there was* great mourning among the Jews, with fasting, weeping, and wailing; and many lay in sackcloth and ashes.

4So Esther's maids and eunuchs came and told her, and the queen was deeply distressed. Then she sent garments to clothe Mordecai and take his sackcloth away from him, but he would not accept *them*. 5Then Esther called Hathach, *one* of the king's eunuchs whom he had appointed to attend her, and she gave him a command concerning Mordecai, to learn what and why this *was*. 6So Hathach went out to Mordecai in the city square that *was* in front of the king's gate. 7And Mordecai told him all that had happened to him, and the sum of money that Haman had promised to pay into the king's treasuries to destroy the Jews. 8He also gave him a copy of the written decree for their destruction, which was given at Shushan, that he might show it to Esther and explain it to her, and that he might command her to go in to the king to make supplication to him and plead before him for her people. 9So Hathach returned and told Esther the words of Mordecai.

10Then Esther spoke to Hathach, and gave him a command for Mordecai: 11"All the king's servants and the people of the king's provinces know that any man or woman who goes into the inner court to the king, who has not been called, *he has* but one law: put *all* to death, except the one to whom the king holds out the golden scepter, that he may live. Yet I myself have not been called to go in to the king these thirty days." 12So they told Mordecai Esther's words.

13And Mordecai told *them* to answer Esther: "Do not think in your heart that you will escape in the king's palace any more than all the other Jews. 14For if you remain completely silent at this time, relief and deliverance will arise for the Jews from another place, but you and your father's house will perish. Yet who knows whether you have come to the kingdom for *such* a time as this?"

15Then Esther told *them* to reply to Mordecai: 16"Go, gather all the Jews who are present in Shushan, and fast for me; neither eat nor drink for three days, night or day. My maids and I will fast likewise. And so I will go to the king, which *is* against the law; and if I perish, I perish!"

17So Mordecai went his way and did according to all that Esther commanded him.

Esther's Banquet

5 Now it happened on the third day that Esther put on *her* royal *robes* and stood in the inner court of the king's palace, across from the king's house, while the king sat on his royal throne in the royal house, facing the entrance of the house. 2So it was, when the king saw Queen Esther standing in the court, *that* she found favor in his sight, and the king held out to Esther the golden scepter that *was* in his hand. Then Esther went near and touched the top of the scepter.

3And the king said to her, "What do you wish, Queen Esther? What *is* your request? It shall be given to you—up to half the kingdom!"

4So Esther answered, "If it pleases the king, let the king and Haman come today to the banquet that I have prepared for him."

5Then the king said, "Bring Haman quickly, that he may do as Esther has said." So the king and Haman went to the banquet that Esther had prepared.

6At the banquet of wine the king said to Esther, "What *is* your petition? It shall be granted you. What *is* your request, up to half the kingdom? It shall be done!"

7Then Esther answered and said, "My petition and request *is this*: 8If I have found favor in the sight of the king, and if it pleases the king to grant my petition and fulfill my request, then let the king and Haman come to the banquet which I will prepare for them, and tomorrow I will do as the king has said."

Haman's Plot Against Mordecai

9So Haman went out that day joyful and with a glad heart; but when Haman saw Mordecai in the king's gate, and that he did not stand or tremble before him, he was filled with indignation against Mordecai. 10Nevertheless Haman restrained himself and went home, and he sent and called for his friends and his wife Zeresh. 11Then Haman told them of his great riches, the multitude of his children, everything in which the king had promoted him, and how he had advanced him above the officials and servants of the king.

12Moreover Haman said, "Besides, Queen Esther invited no one but me to come in with the king to the banquet that she prepared; and tomorrow I am again invited by her, along with the king. 13Yet all this avails me nothing, so long as I see Mordecai the Jew sitting at the king's gate."

14Then his wife Zeresh and all his friends said to him, "Let a gallows be made, fifty cubits high, and in the morning suggest to the king that Mordecai be hanged on it; then go merrily with the king to the banquet."

And the thing pleased Haman; so he had the gallows made.

The King Honors Mordecai

6 That night the king could not sleep. So one was commanded to bring the book of the records of the chronicles; and they were read before the king. 2And it was found written that Mordecai had told of Bigthana and Teresh, two of the king's eunuchs, the doorkeepers who had sought to lay hands on King Ahasuerus. 3Then the king said, "What honor or dignity has been bestowed on Mordecai for this?"

And the king's servants who attended him said, "Nothing has been done for him."

4So the king said, "Who *is* in the court?" Now Haman had *just* entered the outer court of the king's palace to suggest that the king hang Mordecai on the gallows that he had prepared for him.

5The king's servants said to him, "Haman is there, standing in the court."

And the king said, "Let him come in."

6So Haman came in, and the king asked him, "What shall be done for the man whom the king delights to honor?"

Now Haman thought in his heart, "Whom would the king delight to honor more than me?" 7And Haman answered the king, "*For* the man whom the king delights to honor, 8let a royal robe be brought which the king has worn, and a horse on which the king has ridden, which has a royal crest placed on its head. 9Then let this robe and horse be delivered to the hand of one of the king's most noble princes, that he may array the man whom the king delights to honor. Then parade him on horseback through the city square, and proclaim before him: 'Thus shall it be done to the man whom the king delights to honor!' "

10Then the king said to Haman, "Hurry, take the robe and the horse, as you have suggested, and do so for Mordecai the Jew who sits within the king's gate! Leave nothing undone of all that you have spoken."

11So Haman took the robe and the horse, arrayed Mordecai and led him on horseback through the city square, and proclaimed before him, "Thus shall it be done to the man whom the king delights to honor!"

12Afterward Mordecai went back to the king's gate. But Haman hurried to his house, mourning and with his head covered. 13When Haman told his wife Zeresh and all his friends everything that had happened to him, his wise men and his wife Zeresh said to him, "If Mordecai, before whom you have begun to fall, is of Jewish descent, you will not prevail against him but will surely fall before him."

14While they *were* still talking with him, the king's eunuchs came, and hastened to bring Haman to the banquet which Esther had prepared.

Haman Hanged Instead of Mordecai

7 So the king and Haman went to dine with Queen Esther. 2And on the second day, at the banquet of wine, the king again said to Esther, "What *is* your petition, Queen Esther? It shall be granted you. And what *is* your request, up to half the kingdom? It shall be done!"

3Then Queen Esther answered and said, "If I have found favor in your sight, O king, and if it pleases the king, let my life be given me at my petition, and my people at my request. 4For we have been sold, my people and I, to be destroyed, to be killed, and to be annihilated. Had we been sold as male and female slaves, I would have held my tongue, although the enemy could never compensate for the king's loss."

5So King Ahasuerus answered and said to Queen Esther, "Who is he, and where is he, who would dare presume in his heart to do such a thing?"

6And Esther said, "The adversary and enemy *is* this wicked Haman!"

So Haman was terrified before the king and queen.

7Then the king arose in his wrath from the banquet of wine *and went* into the palace garden; but Haman stood before Queen Esther, pleading for his life, for he saw that evil was determined against him by the king. 8When the king returned from the palace garden to the place of the banquet of wine, Haman had fallen across the couch where Esther *was*. Then the king said, "Will he also assault the queen while I *am* in the house?"

As the word left the king's mouth, they covered Haman's face. 9Now Harbonah, one of the eunuchs, said to the king, "Look! The gallows, fifty cubits high, which Haman made for Mordecai, who spoke good on the king's behalf, is standing at the house of Haman."

Then the king said, "Hang him on it!"

10So they hanged Haman on the gallows that he had prepared for Mordecai. Then the king's wrath subsided.

Esther Saves the Jews

8 On that day King Ahasuerus gave Queen Esther the house of Haman, the enemy of the Jews. And Mordecai came before the king, for Esther had told how he *was related* to her. 2So the king took off his signet ring, which he had taken from Haman, and gave it to Mordecai; and Esther appointed Mordecai over the house of Haman.

3Now Esther spoke again to the king, fell down at his feet, and implored him with tears to counteract the evil of Haman the Agagite, and the scheme which he had devised against the Jews. 4And the king held out the golden scepter toward Esther. So Esther arose and stood before the king, 5and said, "If it pleases the king, and if I have found favor in his sight, and the thing *seems* right to the king and I am pleasing in his eyes, let it be written to revoke the letters devised by Haman, the son of Hammedatha the Agagite, which he

wrote to annihilate the Jews who *are* in all the king's provinces. 6For how can I endure to see the evil that will come to my people? Or how can I endure to see the destruction of my countrymen?"

7Then King Ahasuerus said to Queen Esther and Mordecai the Jew, "Indeed, I have given Esther the house of Haman, and they have hanged him on the gallows because he *tried to* lay his hand on the Jews. 8You yourselves write *a decree* concerning the Jews, as you please, in the king's name, and seal *it* with the king's signet ring; for whatever is written in the king's name and sealed with the king's signet ring no one can revoke."

9So the king's scribes were called at that time, in the third month, which *is* the month of Sivan, on the twenty-third *day;* and it was written, according to all that Mordecai commanded, to the Jews, the satraps, the governors, and the princes of the provinces from India to Ethiopia, one hundred and twenty-seven provinces *in all,* to every province in its own script, to every people in their own language, and to the Jews in their own script and language. 10And he wrote in the name of King Ahasuerus, sealed *it* with the king's signet ring, and sent letters by couriers on horseback, riding on royal horses bred from swift steeds.

11By these letters the king permitted the Jews who *were* in every city to gather together and protect their lives— to destroy, kill, and annihilate all the forces of any people or province that would assault them, *both* little children and women, and to plunder their possessions, 12on one day in all the provinces of King Ahasuerus, on the thirteenth *day* of the twelfth month, which *is* the month of Adar. 13A copy of the document was to be issued as a decree in every province and published for all people, so that the Jews would be ready on that day to avenge themselves on their enemies. 14The couriers who rode on royal horses went out, hastened and pressed on by the king's command. And the decree was issued in Shushan the citadel.

15So Mordecai went out from the presence of the king in royal apparel of blue and white, with a great crown of gold and a garment of fine linen and purple; and the city of Shushan rejoiced and was glad. 16The Jews had light and gladness, joy and honor. 17And in every province and city, wherever the king's command and decree came, the Jews had joy and gladness, a feast and a holiday. Then many of the people of the land became Jews, because fear of the Jews fell upon them.

The Jews Destroy Their Tormentors

9 Now in the twelfth month, that *is,* the month of Adar, on the thirteenth day, *the time* came for the king's command and his decree to be executed. On the day that the enemies of the Jews had hoped to overpower them, the opposite occurred, in that the Jews themselves overpowered those who hated them. 2The Jews gathered together in their cities throughout all the provinces of King Ahasuerus to lay hands on those who sought their harm. And no one could withstand them, because fear of them fell upon all people. 3And all the officials of the provinces, the satraps, the governors, and all those doing the king's work, helped the Jews, because the fear of Mordecai fell upon them. 4For Mordecai *was* great in the king's palace, and his fame spread throughout all the provinces; for this man Mordecai became increasingly prominent. 5Thus the Jews defeated all their enemies with the stroke of the sword, with slaughter and destruction, and did what they pleased with those who hated them.

6And in Shushan the citadel the Jews killed and destroyed five hundred men. 7Also Parshandatha, Dalphon, Aspatha, 8Poratha, Adalia, Aridatha, 9Parmashta, Arisai, Aridai, and Vajezatha—10the ten sons of Haman the son of Hammedatha, the enemy of the Jews—they killed; but they did not lay a hand on the plunder.

11On that day the number of those who were killed in Shushan the citadel was brought to the king. 12And the king said to Queen Esther, "The Jews have killed and destroyed five hundred men in Shushan the citadel, and the ten sons of Haman. What have they done in the rest of the king's provinces? Now what *is* your petition? It shall be granted to

you. Or what *is* your further request? It shall be done."

13Then Esther said, "If it pleases the king, let it be granted to the Jews who *are* in Shushan to do again tomorrow according to today's decree, and let Haman's ten sons be hanged on the gallows."

14So the king commanded this to be done; the decree was issued in Shushan, and they hanged Haman's ten sons.

15And the Jews who *were* in Shushan gathered together again on the fourteenth day of the month of Adar and killed three hundred men at Shushan; but they did not lay a hand on the plunder.

16The remainder of the Jews in the king's provinces gathered together and protected their lives, had rest from their enemies, and killed seventy-five thousand of their enemies; but they did not lay a hand on the plunder. 17This *was* on the thirteenth day of the month of Adar. And on the fourteenth of *the month* they rested and made it a day of feasting and gladness.

The Feast of Purim

18But the Jews who *were* at Shushan assembled together on the thirteenth *day,* as well as on the fourteenth; and on the fifteenth of *the month* they rested, and made it a day of feasting and gladness. 19Therefore the Jews of the villages who dwelt in the unwalled towns celebrated the fourteenth day of the month of Adar *with* gladness and feasting, as a holiday, and for sending presents to one another.

20And Mordecai wrote these things and sent letters to all the Jews, near and far, who *were* in all the provinces of King Ahasuerus, 21to establish among them that they should celebrate yearly the fourteenth and fifteenth days of the month of Adar, 22as the days on which the Jews had rest from their enemies, as the month which was turned from sorrow to joy for them, and from mourning to a holiday; that they should make them days of feasting and joy, of sending presents to one another and gifts to the poor. 23So the Jews accepted the custom which they had begun, as Mordecai had written to them, 24because Haman, the son of Hammedatha the Agagite, the enemy of all the Jews, had plotted against the Jews to annihilate them, and had cast Pur (that *is,* the lot), to consume them and destroy them; 25but when *Esther* came before the king, he commanded by letter that this wicked plot which *Haman* had devised against the Jews should return on his own head, and that he and his sons should be hanged on the gallows.

26So they called these days Purim, after the name Pur. Therefore, because of all the words of this letter, what they had seen concerning this matter, and what had happened to them, 27the Jews established and imposed it upon themselves and their descendants and all who would join them, that without fail they should celebrate these two days every year, according to the written *instructions* and according to the *prescribed* time, 28*that* these days *should be* remembered and kept throughout every generation, every family, every province, and every city, that these days of Purim should not fail *to be observed* among the Jews, and *that* the memory of them should not perish among their descendants.

29Then Queen Esther, the daughter of Abihail, with Mordecai the Jew, wrote

with full authority to confirm this second letter about Purim. 30And *Mordecai* sent letters to all the Jews, to the one hundred and twenty-seven provinces of the kingdom of Ahasuerus, *with* words of peace and truth, 31to confirm these days of Purim at their *appointed* time, as Mordecai the Jew and Queen Esther had prescribed for them, and as they had decreed for themselves and their descendants concerning matters of their fasting and lamenting. 32So the decree of Esther confirmed these matters of Purim, and it was written in the book.

Mordecai's Advancement

10 And King Ahasuerus imposed tribute on the land and *on* the islands of the sea. 2Now all the acts of his power and his might, and the account of the greatness of Mordecai, to which the king advanced him, *are* they not written in the book of the chronicles of the kings of Media and Persia? 3For Mordecai the Jew *was* second to King Ahasuerus, and was great among the Jews and well received by the multitude of his brethren, seeking the good of his people and speaking peace to all his countrymen.

The Book of
JOB

Job and His Family in Uz

1 There was a man in the land of Uz, whose name *was* Job; and that man was blameless and upright, and one who feared God and shunned evil. 2And seven sons and three daughters were born to him. 3Also, his possessions were seven thousand sheep, three thousand camels, five hundred yoke of oxen, five hundred female donkeys, and a very large household, so that this man was the greatest of all the people of the East.

4And his sons would go and feast *in their* houses, each on his *appointed* day, and would send and invite their three sisters to eat and drink with them. 5So it was, when the days of feasting had run their course, that Job would send and sanctify them, and he would rise early in the morning and offer burnt offerings *according to* the number of them all. For Job said, "It may be that my sons have sinned and cursed God in their hearts." Thus Job did regularly.

Satan Attacks Job's Character

6Now there was a day when the sons of God came to present themselves before the LORD, and Satan also came among them. 7And the LORD said to Satan, "From where do you come?"

So Satan answered the LORD and said, "From going to and fro on the earth, and from walking back and forth on it."

8Then the LORD said to Satan, "Have you considered My servant Job, that *there is* none like him on the earth, a blameless and upright man, one who fears God and shuns evil?"

9So Satan answered the LORD and said, "Does Job fear God for nothing? 10Have You not made a hedge around him, around his household, and around all that he has on every side? You have blessed the work of his hands, and his possessions have increased in the land. 11But now, stretch out Your hand and touch all that he has, and he will surely curse You to Your face!"

12And the LORD said to Satan, "Be-

hold, all that he has *is* in your power; only do not lay a hand on his *person*."

So Satan went out from the presence of the LORD.

Job Loses His Property and Children

13Now there was a day when his sons and daughters *were* eating and drinking wine in their oldest brother's house; 14and a messenger came to Job and said, "The oxen were plowing and the donkeys feeding beside them, 15when the Sabeans raided *them* and took them away—indeed they have killed the servants with the edge of the sword; and I alone have escaped to tell you!"

16While he *was* still speaking, another also came and said, "The fire of God fell from heaven and burned up the sheep and the servants, and consumed them; and I alone have escaped to tell you!"

17While he *was* still speaking, another also came and said, "The Chaldeans formed three bands, raided the camels and took them away, yes, and killed the servants with the edge of the sword; and I alone have escaped to tell you!"

18While he *was* still speaking, another also came and said, "Your sons and daughters *were* eating and drinking wine in their oldest brother's house, 19and suddenly a great wind came from across the wilderness and struck the four corners of the house, and it fell on the young people, and they are dead; and I alone have escaped to tell you!"

20Then Job arose, tore his robe, and shaved his head; and he fell to the ground and worshiped. 21And he said:

"Naked I came from my mother's
    womb,
And naked shall I return there.
The LORD gave, and the LORD has
    taken away;
Blessed be the name of the LORD."

22In all this Job did not sin nor charge God with wrong.

Satan Attacks Job's Health

2 Again there was a day when the sons of God came to present them-

491

selves before the LORD, and Satan came also among them to present himself before the LORD. 2And the LORD said to Satan, "From where do you come?"

Satan answered the LORD and said, "From going to and fro on the earth, and from walking back and forth on it."

3Then the LORD said to Satan, "Have you considered My servant Job, that *there is* none like him on the earth, a blameless and upright man, one who fears God and shuns evil? And still he holds fast to his integrity, although you incited Me against him, to destroy him without cause."

4So Satan answered the LORD and said, "Skin for skin! Yes, all that a man has he will give for his life. 5But stretch out Your hand now, and touch his bone and his flesh, and he will surely curse You to Your face!"

6And the LORD said to Satan, "Behold, he *is* in your hand, but spare his life."

7So Satan went out from the presence of the LORD, and struck Job with painful boils from the sole of his foot to the crown of his head. 8And he took for himself a potsherd with which to scrape himself while he sat in the midst of the ashes.

9Then his wife said to him, "Do you still hold fast to your integrity? Curse God and die!"

10But he said to her, "You speak as one of the foolish women speaks. Shall we indeed accept good from God, and shall we not accept adversity?" In all this Job did not sin with his lips.

Job's Three Friends

11Now when Job's three friends heard of all this adversity that had come upon him, each one came from his own place—Eliphaz the Temanite, Bildad the Shuhite, and Zophar the Naamathite. For they had made an appointment together to come and mourn with him, and to comfort him. 12And when they raised their eyes from afar, and did not recognize him, they lifted their voices and wept; and each one tore his robe and sprinkled dust on his head toward heaven. 13So they sat down with him on the ground seven days and seven nights, and no one

spoke a word to him, for they saw that *his* grief was very great.

Job Deplores His Birth

3 After this Job opened his mouth and cursed the day of his *birth.* 2And Job spoke, and said:

3 "May the day perish on which I was born,
　And the night *in which* it was said,
　'A male child is conceived.'
4 May that day be darkness;
　May God above not seek it,
　Nor the light shine upon it.
5 May darkness and the shadow of death claim it;
　May a cloud settle on it;
　May the blackness of the day terrify it.
6 *As for* that night, may darkness seize it;
　May it not rejoice among the days of the year,
　May it not come into the number of the months.
7 Oh, may that night be barren!
　May no joyful shout come into it!
8 May those curse it who curse the day,
　Those who are ready to arouse Leviathan.
9 May the stars of its morning be dark;
　May it look for light, but *have* none,
　And not see the dawning of the day;
10 Because it did not shut up the doors of my *mother's* womb,
　Nor hide sorrow from my eyes.

11 "Why did I not die at birth?
　Why did I *not* perish when I came from the womb?
12 Why did the knees receive me?
　Or why the breasts, that I should nurse?
13 For now I would have lain still and been quiet,
　I would have been asleep;
　Then I would have been at rest
14 With kings and counselors of the earth,
　Who built ruins for themselves,
15 Or with princes who had gold,
　Who filled their houses *with* silver;
16 Or *why* was I not hidden like a stillborn child,

Like infants who never saw light?
17 There the wicked cease *from* troubling,
And there the weary are at rest.
18 *There* the prisoners rest together;
They do not hear the voice of the oppressor.
19 The small and great are there,
And the servant *is* free from his master.

20 "Why is light given to him who is in misery,
And life to the bitter of soul,
21 Who long for death, but it does not *come*,
And search for it more than hidden treasures;
22 Who rejoice exceedingly,
And are glad when they can find the grave?
23 *Why is light given* to a man whose way is hidden,
And whom God has hedged in?
24 For my sighing comes before I eat,
And my groanings pour out like water.
25 For the thing I greatly feared has come upon me,
And what I dreaded has happened to me.
26 I am not at ease, nor am I quiet;
I have no rest, for trouble comes."

Eliphaz: Job Has Sinned

4 Then Eliphaz the Temanite answered and said:

2 "*If* one attempts a word with you, will you become weary?
But who can withhold himself from speaking?
3 Surely you have instructed many,
And you have strengthened weak hands.
4 Your words have upheld him who was stumbling,
And you have strengthened the feeble knees;
5 But now it comes upon you, and you are weary;
It touches you, and you are troubled.
6 *Is* not your reverence your confidence?

And the integrity of your ways your hope?

7 "Remember now, who *ever* perished being innocent?
Or where were the upright *ever* cut off?
8 Even as I have seen,
Those who plow iniquity
And sow trouble reap the same.
9 By the blast of God they perish,
And by the breath of His anger they are consumed.
10 The roaring of the lion,
The voice of the fierce lion,
And the teeth of the young lions are broken.
11 The old lion perishes for lack of prey,
And the cubs of the lioness are scattered.

12 "Now a word was secretly brought to me,
And my ear received a whisper of it.
13 In disquieting thoughts from the visions of the night,
When deep sleep falls on men,
14 Fear came upon me, and trembling,
Which made all my bones shake.
15 Then a spirit passed before my face;
The hair on my body stood up.
16 It stood still,
But I could not discern its appearance.
A form *was* before my eyes;
There was silence;
Then I heard a voice *saying*:
17 'Can a mortal be more righteous than God?
Can a man be more pure than his Maker?
18 If He puts no trust in His servants,
If He charges His angels with error,
19 How much more those who dwell in houses of clay,
Whose foundation is in the dust,
Who are crushed before a moth?
20 They are broken in pieces from morning till evening;
They perish forever, with no one regarding.
21 Does not their own excellence go away?
They die, even without wisdom.'

Eliphaz: Job Is Chastened by God

5 "Call out now;
Is there anyone who will answer you?
And to which of the holy ones will you turn?

2 For wrath kills a foolish man,
And envy slays a simple one.

3 I have seen the foolish taking root,
But suddenly I cursed his dwelling place.

4 His sons are far from safety,
They are crushed in the gate,
And *there is* no deliverer.

5 Because the hungry eat up his harvest,
Taking it even from the thorns,
And a snare snatches their substance.

6 For affliction does not come from the dust,
Nor does trouble spring from the ground;

7 Yet man is born to trouble,
As the sparks fly upward.

8 "But as for me, I would seek God,
And to God I would commit my cause—

9 Who does great things, and unsearchable,
Marvelous things without number.

10 He gives rain on the earth,
And sends waters on the fields.

11 He sets on high those who are lowly,
And those who mourn are lifted to safety.

12 He frustrates the devices of the crafty,
So that their hands cannot carry out their plans.

13 He catches the wise in their own craftiness,
And the counsel of the cunning comes quickly upon them.

14 They meet with darkness in the daytime,
And grope at noontime as in the night.

15 But He saves the needy from the sword,
From the mouth of the mighty,
And from their hand.

16 So the poor have hope,
And injustice shuts her mouth.

17 "Behold, happy *is* the man whom God corrects;
Therefore do not despise the chastening of the Almighty.

18 For He bruises, but He binds up;
He wounds, but His hands make whole.

19 He shall deliver you in six troubles,
Yes, in seven no evil shall touch you.

20 In famine He shall redeem you from death,
And in war from the power of the sword.

21 You shall be hidden from the scourge of the tongue,
And you shall not be afraid of destruction when it comes.

22 You shall laugh at destruction and famine,
And you shall not be afraid of the beasts of the earth.

23 For you shall have a covenant with the stones of the field,
And the beasts of the field shall be at peace with you.

24 You shall know that your tent *is* in peace;
You shall visit your dwelling and find nothing amiss.

25 You shall also know that your descendants *shall be* many,
And your offspring like the grass of the earth.

26 You shall come to the grave at a full age,
As a sheaf of grain ripens in its season.

27 Behold, this we have searched out;
It *is* true.
Hear it, and know for yourself."

Job: My Complaint Is Just

6 Then Job answered and said:

2 "Oh, that my grief were fully weighed,
And my calamity laid with it on the scales!

3 For then it would be heavier than the sand of the sea—
Therefore my words have been rash.

4 For the arrows of the Almighty *are* within me;
My spirit drinks in their poison;

The terrors of God are arrayed
against me.
5 Does the wild donkey bray when
it has grass,
Or does the ox low over its fodder?
6 Can flavorless food be eaten
without salt?
Or is there *any* taste in the white
of an egg?
7 My soul refuses to touch them;
They *are* as loathsome food to me.

8 "Oh, that I might have my request,
That God would grant *me* the thing
that I long for!
9 That it would please God to
crush me,
That He would loose His hand and
cut me off!
10 Then I would still have comfort;
Though in anguish I would exult,
He will not spare;
For I have not concealed the words
of the Holy One.

11 "What strength do I have, that I
should hope?
And what *is* my end, that I should
prolong my life?
12 *Is* my strength the strength of
stones?
Or is my flesh bronze?
13 *Is* my help not within me?
And is success driven from me?

14 "To him who is afflicted, kindness
should be shown by his friend,
Even though he forsakes the fear
of the Almighty.
15 My brothers have dealt deceitfully
like a brook,
Like the streams of the brooks that
pass away,
16 Which are dark because of the ice,
And into which the snow vanishes.
17 When it is warm, they cease to
flow;
When it is hot, they vanish from
their place.
18 The paths of their way turn aside,
They go nowhere and perish.
19 The caravans of Tema look,
The travelers of Sheba hope for
them.
20 They are disappointed because
they were confident;
They come there and are confused.

21 For now you are nothing,
You see terror and are afraid.
22 Did I ever say, 'Bring *something*
to me'?
Or, 'Offer a bribe for me from your
wealth'?
23 Or, 'Deliver me from the enemy's
hand'?
Or, 'Redeem me from the hand of
oppressors'?

24 "Teach me, and I will hold my
tongue;
Cause me to understand wherein I
have erred.
25 How forceful are right words!
But what does your arguing prove?
26 Do you intend to rebuke *my* words,
And the speeches of a desperate
one, *which are* as wind?
27 Yes, you overwhelm the fatherless,
And you undermine your friend.
28 Now therefore, be pleased to look
at me;
For I would never lie to your face.
29 Yield now, let there be no injustice!
Yes, concede, my righteousness
still stands!
30 Is there injustice on my tongue?
Cannot my taste discern the
unsavory?

Job: My Suffering Is Comfortless

7 "*Is there* not a time of hard service
for man on earth?
Are not his days also like the days
of a hired man?
2 Like a servant who earnestly
desires the shade,
And like a hired man who eagerly
looks for his wages,
3 So I have been allotted months of
futility,
And wearisome nights have been
appointed to me.
4 When I lie down, I say, 'When shall
I arise,
And the night be ended?'
For I have had my fill of tossing till
dawn.
5 My flesh is caked with worms and
dust,
My skin is cracked and breaks out
afresh.

6 "My days are swifter than a
weaver's shuttle,

And are spent without hope.
7 Oh, remember that my life *is* a
breath!
My eye will never again see good.
8 The eye of him who sees me will
see me no *more;*
While your *eyes* are upon me, I
shall no longer *be.*
9 *As* the cloud disappears and
vanishes away,
So he who goes down to the grave
does not come up.
10 He shall never return to his house,
Nor shall his place know him
anymore.

11 "Therefore I will not restrain my
mouth;
I will speak in the anguish of my
spirit;
I will complain in the bitterness of
my soul.
12 *Am* I a sea, or a sea serpent,
That You set a guard over me?
13 When I say, 'My bed will
comfort me,
My couch will ease my complaint,'
14 Then You scare me with dreams
And terrify me with visions,
15 So that my soul chooses strangling
And death rather than my body.
16 I loathe *my life;*
I would not live forever.
Let me alone,
For my days *are but* a breath.

17 "What *is* man, that You should
exalt him,
That You should set Your heart
on him,
18 That You should visit him every
morning,
And test him every moment?
19 How long?
Will You not look away from me,
And let me alone till I swallow my
saliva?
20 Have I sinned?
What have I done to You,
O watcher of men?
Why have You set me as Your
target,
So that I am a burden to myself?
21 Why then do You not pardon my
transgression,
And take away my iniquity?
For now I will lie down in the dust,

And You will seek me diligently,
But I *will* no longer *be."*

Bildad: Job Should Repent

8 Then Bildad the Shuhite answered
and said:

2 "How long will you speak these
things,
And the words of your mouth *be*
like a strong wind?
3 Does God subvert judgment?
Or does the Almighty pervert
justice?
4 If your sons have sinned
against Him,
He has cast them away for their
transgression.
5 If you would earnestly seek God
And make your supplication to the
Almighty,
6 If you *were* pure and upright,
Surely now He would awake
for you,
And prosper your rightful dwelling
place.
7 Though your beginning was small,
Yet your latter end would increase
abundantly.

8 "For inquire, please, of the
former age,
And consider the things discovered
by their fathers;
9 For we *were born* yesterday, and
know nothing,
Because our days on earth *are* a
shadow.
10 Will they not teach you and tell
you,
And utter words from their heart?

11 "Can the papyrus grow up without
a marsh?
Can the reeds flourish without
water?
12 While it *is* yet green *and* not cut
down,
It withers before any *other* plant.
13 So *are* the paths of all who
forget God;
And the hope of the hypocrite shall
perish,
14 Whose confidence shall be cut off,
And whose trust *is* a spider's web.
15 He leans on his house, but it does
not stand.

He holds it fast, but it does not
endure.

16 He grows green in the sun,
And his branches spread out in his
garden.

17 His roots wrap around the rock
heap,
And look for a place in the stones.

18 If he is destroyed from his place,
Then *it* will deny him, *saying*, 'I
have not seen you.'

19 "Behold, this is the joy of His way,
And out of the earth others will
grow.

20 Behold, God will not cast away the
blameless,
Nor will He uphold the evildoers.

21 He will yet fill your mouth with
laughing,
And your lips with rejoicing.

22 Those who hate you will be clothed
with shame,
And the dwelling place of the
wicked will come to nothing."

Job: There Is No Mediator

9 Then Job answered and said:

2 "Truly I know *it is* so,
But how can a man be righteous
before God?

3 If one wished to contend with Him,
He could not answer Him one time
out of a thousand.

4 *God is* wise in heart and mighty in
strength.
Who has hardened *himself* against
Him and prospered?

5 He removes the mountains, and
they do not know
When He overturns them in His
anger;

6 He shakes the earth out of its place,
And its pillars tremble;

7 He commands the sun, and it does
not rise;
He seals off the stars;

8 He alone spreads out the heavens,
And treads on the waves of the sea;

9 He made the Bear, Orion, and the
Pleiades,
And the chambers of the south;

10 He does great things past
finding out,
Yes, wonders without number.

11 If He goes by me, I do not see *Him*;

If He moves past, I do not
perceive Him;

12 If He takes away, who can
hinder Him?
Who can say to Him, 'What are You
doing?'

13 God will not withdraw His anger,
The allies of the proud lie prostrate
beneath Him.

14 "How then can I answer Him,
And choose my words *to reason*
with Him?

15 For though I were righteous, I could
not answer Him;
I would beg mercy of my Judge.

16 If I called and He answered me,
I would not believe that He was
listening to my voice.

17 For He crushes me with a tempest,
And multiplies my wounds without
cause.

18 He will not allow me to catch my
breath,
But fills me with bitterness.

19 If *it is a matter* of strength, indeed
He is strong;
And if of justice, who will appoint
my day *in court?*

20 Though I were righteous, my own
mouth would condemn me;
Though I *were* blameless, it would
prove me perverse.

21 "I am blameless, yet I do not know
myself;
I despise my life.

22 It *is* all one *thing;*
Therefore I say, 'He destroys the
blameless and the wicked.'

23 If the scourge slays suddenly,
He laughs at the plight of the
innocent.

24 The earth is given into the hand of
the wicked.
He covers the faces of its judges.
If it is not *He*, who else could it be?

25 "Now my days are swifter than a
runner;
They flee away, they see no good.

26 They pass by like swift ships,
Like an eagle swooping on its prey.

27 If I say, 'I will forget my complaint,
I will put off my sad face and wear
a smile,'

28 I am afraid of all my sufferings;

I know that You will not hold me
  innocent.
29 *If* I am condemned,
  Why then do I labor in vain?
30 If I wash myself with snow water,
  And cleanse my hands with soap,
31 Yet You will plunge me into the pit,
  And my own clothes will abhor me.

32 "For *He is* not a man, as I *am,*
  That I may answer Him,
  And that we should go to court
    together.
33 Nor is there any mediator
    between us,
  Who may lay his hand on us both.
34 Let Him take His rod away
    from me,
  And do not let dread of Him
    terrify me.
35 *Then* I would speak and not
    fear Him,
  But it is not so with me.

Job: I Would Plead with God

10 "My soul loathes my life;
  I will give free course to my com-
    plaint,
  I will speak in the bitterness of my
    soul.
2 I will say to God, 'Do not
    condemn me;
  Show me why You contend
    with me.
3 *Does it* seem good to You that You
    should oppress,
  That You should despise the work
    of Your hands,
  And smile on the counsel of the
    wicked?
4 Do You have eyes of flesh?
  Or do You see as man sees?
5 *Are* Your days like the days of a
    mortal man?
  Are Your years like the days of a
    mighty man,
6 That You should seek for my
    iniquity
  And search out my sin,
7 Although You know that I am not
    wicked,
  And *there is* no one who can deliver
    from Your hand?

8 'Your hands have made me and
    fashioned me,
  An intricate unity;

Yet You would destroy me.
9 Remember, I pray, that You have
    made me like clay.
  And will You turn me into dust
    again?
10 Did You not pour me out like
    milk,
  And curdle me like cheese,
11 Clothe me with skin and flesh,
  And knit me together with bones
    and sinews?
12 You have granted me life and favor,
  And Your care has preserved my
    spirit.

13 'And these *things* You have hidden
    in Your heart;
  I know that this *was* with You:
14 If I sin, then You mark me,
  And will not acquit me of my
    iniquity.
15 If I am wicked, woe to me;
  Even *if* I am righteous, I cannot lift
    up my head.
  I am full of disgrace;
  See my misery!
16 If *my head* is exalted,
  You hunt me like a fierce lion,
  And again You show Yourself
    awesome against me.
17 You renew Your witnesses
    against me,
  And increase Your indignation
    toward me;
  Changes and war are *ever* with
    me.

18 'Why then have You brought me out
    of the womb?
  Oh, that I had perished and no eye
    had seen me!
19 I would have been as though I had
    not been.
  I would have been carried from the
    womb to the grave.
20 Are not my days few?
  Cease! Leave me alone, that I may
    take a little comfort,
21 Before I go *to the place from which*
    I shall not return,
  To the land of darkness and the
    shadow of death,
22 A land as dark as darkness *itself,*
  As the shadow of death, without
    any order,
  Where even the light *is* like
    darkness.'"

Zophar Urges Job to Repent

11 Then Zophar the Naamathite answered and said:

2 "Should not the multitude of words
be answered?
And should a man full of talk be
vindicated?
3 Should your empty talk make men
hold their peace?
And when you mock, should no one
rebuke you?
4 For you have said,
'My doctrine *is* pure,
And I am clean in your eyes.'
5 But oh, that God would speak,
And open His lips against you,
6 That He would show you the
secrets of wisdom!
For *they would* double *your*
prudence.
Know therefore that God exacts
from you
Less than your iniquity *deserves.*

7 "Can you search out the deep things
of God?
Can you find out the limits of the
Almighty?
8 *They are* higher than heaven—
what can you do?
Deeper than Sheol— what can you
know?
9 Their measure *is* longer than the
earth
And broader than the sea.

10 "If He passes by, imprisons, and
gathers *to judgment,*
Then who can hinder Him?
11 For He knows deceitful men;
He sees wickedness also.
Will He not then consider *it?*
12 For an empty-headed man will be
wise,
When a wild donkey's colt is born
a man.

13 "If you would prepare your heart,
And stretch out your hands
toward Him;
14 If iniquity *were* in your hand, *and
you* put it far away,
And would not let wickedness
dwell in your tents;
15 Then surely you could lift up your
face without spot;

Yes, you could be steadfast, and not
fear;
16 Because you would forget *your*
misery,
And remember *it* as waters *that
have* passed away,
17 And *your* life would be brighter
than noonday.
Though you were dark, you would
be like the morning.
18 And you would be secure, because
there is hope;
Yes, you would dig *around you, and*
take your rest in safety.
19 You would also lie down, and no
one would make *you* afraid;
Yes, many would court your favor.
20 But the eyes of the wicked will fail,
And they shall not escape,
And their hope—loss of life!"

Job Answers His Critics

12 Then Job answered and said:

2 "No doubt you *are* the people,
And wisdom will die with you!
3 But I have understanding as well
as you;
I *am* not inferior to you.
Indeed, who does not *know* such
things as these?

4 "I am one mocked by his friends,
Who called on God, and He
answered him,
The just and blameless *who is*
ridiculed.
5 A lamp is despised in the thought
of one who is at ease;
It is made ready for those whose
feet slip.
6 The tents of robbers prosper,
And those who provoke God are
secure—
In what God provides by His hand.

7 "But now ask the beasts, and they
will teach you;
And the birds of the air, and they
will tell you;
8 Or speak to the earth, and it will
teach you;
And the fish of the sea will explain
to you.
9 Who among all these does not
know

That the hand of the Lord has done this,

10 In whose hand *is* the life of every living thing,
And the breath of all mankind?

11 Does not the ear test words
And the mouth taste its food?

12 Wisdom *is* with aged men,
And with length of days, understanding.

13 "With Him *are* wisdom and strength,
He has counsel and understanding.

14 If He breaks *a thing* down, it cannot be rebuilt;
If He imprisons a man, there can be no release.

15 If He withholds the waters, they dry up;
If He sends them out, they overwhelm the earth.

16 With Him *are* strength and prudence.
The deceived and the deceiver *are* His.

17 He leads counselors away plundered,
And makes fools of the judges.

18 He loosens the bonds of kings,
And binds their waist with a belt.

19 He leads princes away plundered,
And overthrows the mighty.

20 He deprives the trusted ones of speech,
And takes away the discernment of the elders.

21 He pours contempt on princes,
And disarms the mighty.

22 He uncovers deep things out of darkness,
And brings the shadow of death to light.

23 He makes nations great, and destroys them;
He enlarges nations, and guides them.

24 He takes away the understanding of the chiefs of the people of the earth,
And makes them wander in a pathless wilderness.

25 They grope in the dark without light,
And He makes them stagger like a drunken *man.*

13 "Behold, my eye has seen all *this,*
My ear has heard and understood it.

2 What you know, I also know;
I *am* not inferior to you.

3 But I would speak to the Almighty,
And I desire to reason with God.

4 But you forgers of lies,
You *are* all worthless physicians.

5 Oh, that you would be silent,
And it would be your wisdom!

6 Now hear my reasoning,
And heed the pleadings of my lips.

7 Will you speak wickedly for God,
And talk deceitfully for Him?

8 Will you show partiality for Him?
Will you contend for God?

9 Will it be well when He searches you out?
Or can you mock Him as one mocks a man?

10 He will surely rebuke you
If you secretly show partiality.

11 Will not His excellence make you afraid,
And the dread of Him fall upon you?

12 Your platitudes *are* proverbs of ashes,
Your defenses are defenses of clay.

13 "Hold your peace with me, and let me speak,
Then let come on me what *may!*

14 Why do I take my flesh in my teeth,
And put my life in my hands?

15 Though He slay me, yet will I trust Him.
Even so, I will defend my own ways before Him.

16 He also *shall* be my salvation,
For a hypocrite could not come before Him.

17 Listen carefully to my speech,
And to my declaration with your ears.

18 See now, I have prepared *my* case,
I know that I shall be vindicated.

19 Who *is* he *who* will contend with me?
If now I hold my tongue, I perish.

Job's Despondent Prayer

20 "Only two *things* do not do to me,
Then I will not hide myself from You:

21 Withdraw Your hand far from me,

And let not the dread of You make
me afraid.
22 Then call, and I will answer;
Or let me speak, then You respond
to me.
23 How many *are* my iniquities and
sins?
Make me know my transgression
and my sin.
24 Why do You hide Your face,
And regard me as Your enemy?
25 Will You frighten a leaf driven to
and fro?
And will You pursue dry stubble?
26 For You write bitter things
against me,
And make me inherit the iniquities
of my youth.
27 You put my feet in the stocks,
And watch closely all my paths.
You set a limit for the soles of my
feet.

28 "*Man* decays like a rotten thing,
Like a garment that is moth-eaten.

14 "Man *who is* born of woman
Is of few days and full of trouble.
2 He comes forth like a flower and
fades away;
He flees like a shadow and does not
continue.
3 And do You open Your eyes on
such a one,
And bring me to judgment with
Yourself?
4 Who can bring a clean *thing* out of
an unclean?
No one!
5 Since his days *are* determined,
The number of his months *is*
with You;
You have appointed his limits, so
that he cannot pass.
6 Look away from him that he may
rest,
Till like a hired man he finishes
his day.

7 "For there is hope for a tree,
If it is cut down, that it will sprout
again,
And that its tender shoots will not
cease.
8 Though its root may grow old in
the earth,

And its stump may die in the
ground,
9 *Yet* at the scent of water it will
bud
And bring forth branches like a
plant.
10 But man dies and is laid away;
Indeed he breathes his last
And where *is* he?
11 *As* water disappears from the
sea,
And a river becomes parched and
dries up,
12 So man lies down and does not rise.
Till the heavens *are* no more,
They will not awake
Nor be roused from their sleep.

13 "Oh, that You would hide me in the
grave,
That You would conceal me until
Your wrath is past,
That You would appoint me a set
time, and remember me!
14 If a man dies, shall he live *again*?
All the days of my hard service I
will wait,
Till my change comes.
15 You shall call, and I will
answer You;
You shall desire the work of Your
hands.
16 For now You number my steps,
But do not watch over my sin.
17 My transgression *is* sealed up in
a bag,
And You cover my iniquity.

18 "But *as* a mountain falls *and*
crumbles away,
And *as* a rock is moved from its
place;
19 *As* water wears away stones,
And as torrents wash away the soil
of the earth;
So You destroy the hope of man.
20 You prevail forever against him,
and he passes on;
You change his countenance and
send him away.
21 His sons come to honor, and he
does not know *it;*
They are brought low, and he does
not perceive *it.*
22 But his flesh will be in pain
over it,
And his soul will mourn over it."

Eliphaz Accuses Job of Folly

15 Then Eliphaz the Temanite answered and said:

2 "Should a wise man answer with
　　empty knowledge,
　And fill himself with the east wind?
3 Should he reason with unprofitable
　　talk,
　Or by speeches with which he can
　　do no good?
4 Yes, you cast off fear,
　And restrain prayer before God.
5 For your iniquity teaches your
　　mouth,
　And you choose the tongue of the
　　crafty.
6 Your own mouth condemns you,
　　and not I;
　Yes, your own lips testify
　　against you.

7 "Are you the first man who was
　　born?
　Or were you made before the hills?
8 Have you heard the counsel
　　of God?
　Do you limit wisdom to yourself?
9 What do you know that we do not
　　know?
　What do you understand that is not
　　in us?
10 Both the gray-haired and the aged
　　are among us,
　Much older than your father.
11 Are the consolations of God too
　　small for you,
　And the word spoken gently
　　with you?
12 Why does your heart carry you
　　away,
　And what do your eyes wink at,
13 That you turn your spirit
　　against God,
　And let such words go out of your
　　mouth?

14 "What is man, that he could be pure?
　And he who is born of a woman,
　　that he could be righteous?
15 If God puts no trust in His saints,
　And the heavens are not pure in His
　　sight,
16 How much less man, who is
　　abominable and filthy,
　Who drinks iniquity like water!

17 "I will tell you, hear me;
　What I have seen I will declare,
18 What wise men have told,
　Not hiding anything received from
　　their fathers,
19 To whom alone the land was given,
　And no alien passed among them:
20 The wicked man writhes with pain
　　all his days,
　And the number of years is hidden
　　from the oppressor.
21 Dreadful sounds are in his ears;
　In prosperity the destroyer comes
　　upon him.
22 He does not believe that he will
　　return from darkness,
　For a sword is waiting for him.
23 He wanders about for bread,
　　saying, 'Where is it?'
　He knows that a day of darkness
　　is ready at his hand.
24 Trouble and anguish make him
　　afraid;
　They overpower him, like a king
　　ready for battle.
25 For he stretches out his hand
　　against God,
　And acts defiantly against the
　　Almighty,
26 Running stubbornly against Him
　With his strong, embossed shield.

27 "Though he has covered his face
　　with his fatness,
　And made his waist heavy with fat,
28 He dwells in desolate cities,
　In houses which no one inhabits,
　Which are destined to become
　　ruins.
29 He will not be rich,
　Nor will his wealth continue,
　Nor will his possessions
　　overspread the earth.
30 He will not depart from darkness;
　The flame will dry out his branches,
　And by the breath of His mouth he
　　will go away.
31 Let him not trust in futile things,
　　deceiving himself,
　For futility will be his reward.
32 It will be accomplished before his
　　time,
　And his branch will not be green.
33 He will shake off his unripe grape
　　like a vine,
　And cast off his blossom like an
　　olive tree.

34 For the company of hypocrites *will
    be* barren,
    And fire will consume the tents of
    bribery.
35 They conceive trouble and bring
    forth futility;
    Their womb prepares deceit."

Job Reproaches His Pitiless Friends

16 Then Job answered and said:

2 "I have heard many such things;
    Miserable comforters *are* you all!
3 Shall words of wind have an end?
    Or what provokes you that you
    answer?
4 I also could speak as you *do,*
    If your soul were in my soul's place.
    I could heap up words against you,
    And shake my head at you;
5 *But* I would strengthen you with
    my mouth,
    And the comfort of my lips would
    relieve *your grief.*

6 "Though I speak, my grief is not
    relieved;
    And *if* I remain silent, how am I
    eased?
7 But now He has worn me out;
    You have made desolate all my
    company.
8 You have shriveled me up,
    And it is a witness *against me;*
    My leanness rises up against me
    And bears witness to my face.
9 He tears *me* in His wrath, and
    hates me;
    He gnashes at me with His teeth;
    My adversary sharpens His gaze
    on me.
10 They gape at me with their mouth,
    They strike me reproachfully on
    the cheek,
    They gather together against me.
11 God has delivered me to the
    ungodly,
    And turned me over to the hands
    of the wicked.
12 I was at ease, but He has
    shattered me;
    He also has taken *me* by my neck,
    and shaken me to pieces;
    He has set me up for His target,
13 His archers surround me.
    He pierces my heart and does not
    pity;

He pours out my gall on the ground.
14 He breaks me with wound upon
    wound;
    He runs at me like a warrior.

15 "I have sewn sackcloth over my
    skin,
    And laid my head in the dust.
16 My face is flushed from weeping,
    And on my eyelids *is* the shadow
    of death;
17 Although no violence *is* in my
    hands,
    And my prayer *is* pure.

18 "O earth, do not cover my blood,
    And let my cry have no *resting*
    place!
19 Surely even now my witness *is* in
    heaven,
    And my evidence *is* on high.
20 My friends scorn me;
    My eyes pour out *tears* to God.
21 Oh, that one might plead for a man
    with God,
    As a man *pleads* for his neighbor!
22 For when a few years are finished,
    I shall go the way of no return.

Job Prays for Relief

17 "My spirit is broken,
        My days are extinguished,
    The grave *is ready* for me.
2 *Are* not mockers with me?
    And does not my eye dwell on their
    provocation?

3 "Now put down a pledge for me with
    Yourself.
    Who *is* he *who* will shake hands
    with me?
4 For You have hidden their heart
    from understanding;
    Therefore You will not exalt *them.*
5 He who speaks flattery to *his*
    friends,
    Even the eyes of his children will
    fail.

6 "But He has made me a byword of
    the people,
    And I have become one in whose
    face men spit.
7 My eye has also grown dim because
    of sorrow,
    And all my members *are* like
    shadows.

8   Upright *men* are astonished at this,
    And the innocent stirs himself up
    against the hypocrite.
9   Yet the righteous will hold to
    his way,
    And he who has clean hands will
    be stronger and stronger.

10 "But please, come back again, all
    of you,
    For I shall not find *one* wise *man*
    among you.
11 My days are past,
    My purposes are broken off,
    Even the thoughts of my heart.
12 They change the night into day;
    'The light *is* near,' *they say*, in the
    face of darkness.
13 If I wait *for* the grave *as* my house,
    If I make my bed in the darkness,
14 If I say to corruption, 'You *are* my
    father,'
    And to the worm, 'You *are* my
    mother and my sister,'
15 Where then *is* my hope?
    As for my hope, who can see it?
16 *Will* they go down to the gates of
    Sheol?
    Shall *we have* rest together in the
    dust?"

Bildad: The Wicked Are Punished

18 Then Bildad the Shuhite an-
      swered and said:

2   "How long *till* you put an end to
    words?
    Gain understanding, and afterward
    we will speak.
3   Why are we counted as beasts,
    And regarded as stupid in your
    sight?
4   You who tear yourself in anger,
    Shall the earth be forsaken for you?
    Or shall the rock be removed from
    its place?

5   "The light of the wicked indeed
    goes out,
    And the flame of his fire does not
    shine.
6   The light is dark in his tent,
    And his lamp beside him is put out.
7   The steps of his strength are
    shortened,
    And his own counsel casts him
    down.

8   For he is cast into a net by his own
    feet,
    And he walks into a snare.
9   The net takes *him* by the heel,
    And a snare lays hold of him.
10 A noose *is* hidden for him on the
    ground,
    And a trap for him in the road.
11 Terrors frighten him on every side,
    And drive him to his feet.
12 His strength is starved,
    And destruction *is* ready at his side.
13 It devours patches of his skin;
    The firstborn of death devours his
    limbs.
14 He is uprooted from the shelter of
    his tent,
    And they parade him before the
    king of terrors.
15 They dwell in his tent *who are* none
    of his;
    Brimstone is scattered on his
    dwelling.
16 His roots are dried out below,
    And his branch withers above.
17 The memory of him perishes from
    the earth,
    And he has no name among the
    renowned.
18 He is driven from light into
    darkness,
    And chased out of the world.
19 He has neither son nor posterity
    among his people,
    Nor any remaining in his dwellings.
20 Those in the west are astonished at
    his day,
    As those in the east are frightened.
21 Surely such *are* the dwellings of the
    wicked,
    And this *is* the place *of him who*
    does not know God."

Job Trusts in His Redeemer

19 Then Job answered and said:

2   "How long will you torment my soul,
    And break me in pieces with
    words?
3   These ten times you have
    reproached me;
    You are not ashamed *that* you have
    wronged me.
4   And if indeed I have erred,
    My error remains with me.
5   If indeed you exalt *yourselves*
    against me,

And plead my disgrace against me,

6 Know then that God has
       wronged me,
   And has surrounded me with
       His net.

7 "If I cry out concerning wrong, I am
       not heard.
   If I cry aloud, *there is* no justice.
8 He has fenced up my way, so that
       I cannot pass;
   And He has set darkness in my
       paths.
9 He has stripped me of my glory,
   And taken the crown *from* my
       head.
10 He breaks me down on every side,
       And I am gone;
   My hope He has uprooted like a
       tree.
11 He has also kindled His wrath
       against me,
   And He counts me as *one of* His
       enemies.
12 His troops come together
   And build up their road against me;
   They encamp all around my tent.

13 "He has removed my brothers far
       from me,
   And my acquaintances are
       completely estranged from me.
14 My relatives have failed,
   And my close friends have
       forgotten me.
15 Those who dwell in my house, and
       my maidservants,
   Count me as a stranger;
   I am an alien in their sight.
16 I call my servant, but he gives no
       answer;
   I beg him with my mouth.
17 My breath is offensive to my wife,
   And I am repulsive to the children
       of my own body.
18 Even young children despise me;
   I arise, and they speak against me.
19 All my close friends abhor me,
   And those whom I love have turned
       against me.
20 My bone clings to my skin and to
       my flesh,
   And I have escaped by the skin of
       my teeth.

21 "Have pity on me, have pity on me,
       O you my friends,

For the hand of God has struck me!
22 Why do you persecute me as God
       does,
   And are not satisfied with my flesh?

23 "Oh, that my words were written!
   Oh, that they were inscribed in a
       book!
24 That they were engraved on a rock
   With an iron pen and lead, forever!
25 For I know *that* my Redeemer lives,
   And He shall stand at last on the
       earth;
26 And after my skin is destroyed, this
       I know,
   That in my flesh I shall see God,
27 Whom I shall see for myself,
   And my eyes shall behold, and not
       another.
   How my heart yearns within me!
28 If you should say, 'How shall we
       persecute him?'—
   Since the root of the matter is found
       in me,
29 Be afraid of the sword for
       yourselves;
   For wrath *brings* the punishment of
       the sword,
   That you may know *there is* a
       judgment."

Zophar's Sermon on the Wicked Man

20 Then Zophar the Naamathite an-
       swered and said:

2 "Therefore my anxious thoughts
       make me answer,
   Because of the turmoil within me.
3 I have heard the rebuke that
       reproaches me,
   And the spirit of my understanding
       causes me to answer.

4 "Do you *not* know this of old,
   Since man was placed on earth,
5 That the triumphing of the wicked
       is short,
   And the joy of the hypocrite is *but*
       for a moment?
6 Though his haughtiness mounts up
       to the heavens,
   And his head reaches to the clouds,
7 *Yet* he will perish forever like his
       own refuse;
   Those who have seen him will say,
       'Where is he?'

8 He will fly away like a dream, and
  not be found;
  Yes, he will be chased away like a
  vision of the night.
9 The eye *that* saw him will *see him*
  no more,
  Nor will his place behold him
  anymore.
10 His children will seek the favor of
  the poor,
  And his hands will restore his
  wealth.
11 His bones are full of his youthful
  vigor,
  But it will lie down with him in the
  dust.

12 "Though evil is sweet in his mouth,
   And he hides it under his tongue,
13 *Though* he spares it and does not
   forsake it,
   But still keeps it in his mouth,
14 *Yet* his food in his stomach turns
   sour;
   It becomes cobra venom
   within him.
15 He swallows down riches
   And vomits them up again;
   God casts them out of his belly.
16 He will suck the poison of cobras;
   The viper's tongue will slay him.
17 He will not see the streams,
   The rivers flowing with honey and
   cream.
18 He will restore that for which he
   labored,
   And will not swallow *it* down;
   From the proceeds of business
   He will get no enjoyment.
19 For he has oppressed *and* forsaken
   the poor,
   He has violently seized a house
   which he did not build.

20 "Because he knows no quietness in
   his heart,
   He will not save anything he
   desires.
21 Nothing is left for him to eat;
   Therefore his well-being will not
   last.
22 In his self-sufficiency he will be in
   distress;
   Every hand of misery will come
   against him.
23 *When* he is about to fill his
   stomach,

   God will cast on him the fury of His
   wrath,
   And will rain *it* on him while he is
   eating.
24 He will flee from the iron weapon;
   A bronze bow will pierce him
   through.
25 It is drawn, and comes out of the
   body;
   Yes, the glittering *point comes* out
   of his gall.
   Terrors *come* upon him;
26 Total darkness *is* reserved for his
   treasures.
   An unfanned fire will
   consume him;
   It shall go ill with him who is left
   in his tent.
27 The heavens will reveal his
   iniquity,
   And the earth will rise up
   against him.
28 The increase of his house will
   depart,
   And his goods will flow away in the
   day of His wrath.
29 This *is* the portion from God for a
   wicked man,
   The heritage appointed to him
   by God."

Job's Discourse on the Wicked

21 Then Job answered and said:

2 "Listen carefully to my speech,
   And let this be your consolation.
3 Bear with me that I may speak,
   And after I have spoken, keep
   mocking.

4 "As for me, *is* my complaint
   against man?
   And if *it were*, why should I not be
   impatient?
5 Look at me and be astonished;
   Put *your* hand over *your* mouth.
6 Even when I remember I am
   terrified,
   And trembling takes hold of my
   flesh.
7 Why do the wicked live *and*
   become old,
   Yes, become mighty in power?
8 Their descendants are established
   with them in their sight,
   And their offspring before
   their eyes.

9   Their houses *are* safe from fear,
    Neither *is* the rod of God upon
    them.
10 Their bull breeds without failure;
    Their cow calves without
    miscarriage.
11 They send forth their little ones like
    a flock,
    And their children dance.
12 They sing to the tambourine and
    harp,
    And rejoice to the sound of the
    flute.
13 They spend their days in wealth,
    And in a moment go down to the
    grave.
14 Yet they say to God, 'Depart
    from us,
    For we do not desire the knowledge
    of Your ways.
15 Who *is* the Almighty, that we
    should serve Him?
    And what profit do we have if we
    pray to Him?'
16 Indeed their prosperity *is* not in
    their hand;
    The counsel of the wicked is far
    from me.

17 "How often is the lamp of the wicked
    put out?
    How often does their destruction
    come upon them,
    The sorrows *God* distributes in His
    anger?
18 They are like straw before the
    wind,
    And like chaff that a storm carries
    away.
19 *They say*, 'God lays up one's
    iniquity for his children';
    Let Him recompense him, that he
    may know *it*.
20 Let his eyes see his destruction,
    And let him drink of the wrath of
    the Almighty.
21 For what does he care about his
    household after him,
    When the number of his months is
    cut in half?

22 "Can *anyone* teach God knowledge,
    Since He judges those on high?
23 One dies in his full strength,
    Being wholly at ease and secure;
24 His pails are full of milk,
    And the marrow of his bones is
    moist.
25 Another man dies in the bitterness
    of his soul,
    Never having eaten with pleasure.
26 They lie down alike in the dust,
    And worms cover them.

27 "Look, I know your thoughts,
    And the schemes *with which* you
    would wrong me.
28 For you say,
    'Where *is* the house of the prince?
    And where *is* the tent,
    The dwelling place of the wicked?'
29 Have you not asked those who
    travel the road?
    And do you not know their signs?
30 For the wicked are reserved for the
    day of doom;
    They shall be brought out on the
    day of wrath.
31 Who condemns his way to his face?
    And who repays him *for what* he
    has done?
32 Yet he shall be brought to the
    grave,
    And a vigil kept over the tomb.
33 The clods of the valley shall be
    sweet to him;
    Everyone shall follow him,
    As countless *have gone* before him.
34 How then can you comfort me with
    empty words,
    Since falsehood remains in your
    answers?"

Eliphaz Accuses Job of Wickedness

22 Then Eliphaz the Temanite an-
    swered and said:

2   "Can a man be profitable to God,
    Though he who is wise may be
    profitable to himself?
3   *Is it* any pleasure to the Almighty
    that you are righteous?
    Or *is it* gain *to Him* that you make
    your ways blameless?

4   "Is it because of your fear of Him
    that He corrects you,
    And enters into judgment with you?
5   *Is* not your wickedness great,
    And your iniquity without end?
6   For you have taken pledges from
    your brother for no reason,

And stripped the naked of their
clothing.

7 You have not given the weary
water to drink,
And you have withheld bread from
the hungry.

8 But the mighty man possessed the
land,
And the honorable man dwelt in it.

9 You have sent widows away empty,
And the strength of the fatherless
was crushed.

10 Therefore snares *are* all
around you,
And sudden fear troubles you,

11 Or darkness *so that* you
cannot see;
And an abundance of water
covers you.

12 "Is not God in the height of heaven?
And see the highest stars, how lofty
they are!

13 And you say, 'What does God
know?
Can He judge through the deep
darkness?

14 Thick clouds cover Him, so that He
cannot see,
And He walks above the circle of
heaven.'

15 Will you keep to the old way
Which wicked men have trod,

16 Who were cut down before their
time,
Whose foundations were swept
away by a flood?

17 They said to God, 'Depart from us!
What can the Almighty do to
them?'

18 Yet He filled their houses with good
things;
But the counsel of the wicked is far
from me.

19 "The righteous see *it* and are glad,
And the innocent laugh at them:

20 'Surely our adversaries are cut
down,
And the fire consumes their
remnant.'

21 "Now acquaint yourself with Him,
and be at peace;
Thereby good will come to you.

22 Receive, please, instruction from
His mouth,
And lay up His words in your heart.

23 If you return to the Almighty, you
will be built up;
You will remove iniquity far from
your tents.

24 Then you will lay your gold in the
dust,
And the *gold* of Ophir among the
stones of the brooks.

25 Yes, the Almighty will be your gold
And your precious silver;

26 For then you will have your delight
in the Almighty,
And lift up your face to God.

27 You will make your prayer to Him,
He will hear you,
And you will pay your vows.

28 You will also declare a thing,
And it will be established for you;
So light will shine on your ways.

29 When they cast *you* down, and you
say, 'Exaltation *will come!'*
Then He will save the humble
person.

30 He will *even* deliver one who is not
innocent;
Yes, he will be delivered by the
purity of your hands.''

Job Proclaims God's Righteous Judgments

23 Then Job answered and said:

2 "Even today my complaint is
bitter;
My hand is listless because of my
groaning.

3 Oh, that I knew where I might
find Him,
That I might come to His seat!

4 I would present *my* case
before Him,
And fill my mouth with arguments.

5 I would know the words *which* He
would answer me,
And understand what He would say
to me.

6 Would He contend with me in His
great power?
No! But He would take *note* of me.

7 There the upright could reason
with Him,
And I would be delivered forever
from my Judge.

8 "Look, I go forward, but He is not
there,

And backward, but I cannot
   perceive Him;
9 When He works on the left hand, I
   cannot behold *Him;*
   When He turns to the right hand, I
   cannot see *Him.*
10 But He knows the way that I
   take;
   When He has tested me, I shall
   come forth as gold.
11 My foot has held fast to His steps;
   I have kept His way and not turned
   aside.
12 I have not departed from the
   commandment of His lips;
   I have treasured the words of His
   mouth
   More than my necessary *food.*

13 "But He *is* unique, and who can
   make Him change?
   And *whatever* His soul desires,
   that He does.
14 For He performs *what is* appointed
   for me,
   And many such *things are*
   with Him.
15 Therefore I am terrified at His
   presence;
   When I consider *this,* I am afraid
   of Him.
16 For God made my heart weak,
   And the Almighty terrifies me;
17 Because I was not cut off from the
   presence of darkness,
   And He did *not* hide deep darkness
   from my face.

Job Complains of Violence on the Earth

24 "*Since* times are not hidden from
   the Almighty,
   Why do those who know Him see
   not His days?

2 "*Some* remove landmarks;
   They seize flocks violently and feed
   on *them;*
3 They drive away the donkey of the
   fatherless;
   They take the widow's ox as a
   pledge.
4 They push the needy off the road;
   All the poor of the land are forced
   to hide.
5 Indeed, *like* wild donkeys in the
   desert,
   They go out to their work,
   searching for food.

The wilderness *yields* food for them
   and for *their* children.
6 They gather their fodder in the field
   And glean in the vineyard of the
   wicked.
7 They spend the night naked,
   without clothing,
   And have no covering in the cold.
8 They are wet with the showers of
   the mountains,
   And huddle around the rock for
   want of shelter.

9 "*Some* snatch the fatherless from
   the breast,
   And take a pledge from the poor.
10 They cause *the poor* to go naked,
   without clothing;
   And they take away the sheaves
   from the hungry.
11 They press out oil within their
   walls,
   And tread winepresses, yet suffer
   thirst.
12 The dying groan in the city,
   And the souls of the wounded
   cry out;
   Yet God does not charge *them* with
   wrong.

13 "There are those who rebel against
   the light;
   They do not know its ways
   Nor abide in its paths.
14 The murderer rises with the light;
   He kills the poor and needy;
   And in the night he is like a thief.
15 The eye of the adulterer waits for
   the twilight,
   Saying, 'No eye will see me';
   And he disguises *his* face.
16 In the dark they break into houses
   Which they marked for themselves
   in the daytime;
   They do not know the light.
17 For the morning is the same to
   them as the shadow of death;
   If *someone* recognizes *them,*
   They are in the terrors of the
   shadow of death.

18 "They *should be* swift on the face of
   the waters,
   Their portion *should be* cursed in
   the earth,
   So that no *one would* turn into the
   way of their vineyards.

19 As drought and heat consume the
   snow waters,
   So the grave *consumes those who*
   have sinned.
20 The womb *should* forget him,
   The worm *should* feed sweetly
   on him;
   He *should* be remembered no more,
   And wickedness *should* be broken
   like a tree.
21 For he preys on the barren *who* do
   not bear,
   And does no good for the widow.

22 "But *God* draws the mighty away
   with His power;
   He rises up, but no *man* is sure of
   life.
23 He gives them security, and they
   rely *on it;*
   Yet His eyes *are* on their ways.
24 They are exalted for a little while,
   Then they are gone.
   They are brought low;
   They are taken out of the way like
   all *others;*
   They dry out like the heads of
   grain.

25 "Now if *it is* not *so,* who will prove
   me a liar,
   And make my speech worth
   nothing?"

Bildad: How Can Man Be Righteous?

25 Then Bildad the Shuhite an-
      swered and said:

2 "Dominion and fear *belong* to Him;
   He makes peace in His high places.
3 Is there any number to His armies?
   Upon whom does His light not rise?
4 How then can man be righteous
   before God?
   Or how can he be pure *who is* born
   of a woman?
5 If even the moon does not shine,
   And the stars are not pure in His
   sight,
6 How much less man, *who is* a
   maggot,
   And a son of man, *who is* a worm?"

Job: Man's Frailty and God's Majesty

26 But Job answered and said:

2 "How have you helped *him who is*
   without power?

How have you saved the arm *that
   has* no strength?
3 How have you counseled *one who
   has* no wisdom?
   And *how* have you declared sound
   advice to many?
4 To whom have you uttered words?
   And whose spirit came from you?

5 "The dead tremble,
   Those under the waters and those
   inhabiting them.
6 Sheol *is* naked before Him,
   And Destruction has no covering.
7 He stretches out the north over
   empty space;
   He hangs the earth on nothing.
8 He binds up the water in His thick
   clouds,
   Yet the clouds are not broken
   under it.
9 He covers the face of *His* throne,
   And spreads His cloud over it.
10 He drew a circular horizon on the
   face of the waters,
   At the boundary of light and
   darkness.
11 The pillars of heaven tremble,
   And are astonished at His rebuke.
12 He stirs up the sea with His power,
   And by His understanding He
   breaks up the storm.
13 By His Spirit He adorned the
   heavens;
   His hand pierced the fleeing
   serpent.
14 Indeed these *are* the mere edges of
   His ways,
   And how small a whisper we hear
   of Him!
   But the thunder of His power who
   can understand?"

Job Maintains His Integrity

27 Moreover Job continued his dis-
      course, and said:

2 "*As* God lives, *who* has taken away
   my justice,
   And the Almighty, *who* has made
   my soul bitter,
3 As long as my breath *is* in me,
   And the breath of God in my
   nostrils,
4 My lips will not speak wickedness,
   Nor my tongue utter deceit.
5 Far be it from me

That I should say you are right;
Till I die I will not put away my
    integrity from me.
6 My righteousness I hold fast, and
    will not let it go;
My heart shall not reproach *me* as
    long as I live.

7 "May my enemy be like the wicked,
And he who rises up against me
    like the unrighteous.
8 For what is the hope of the
    hypocrite,
Though he may gain *much*,
If God takes away his life?
9 Will God hear his cry
When trouble comes upon him?
10 Will he delight himself in the
    Almighty?
Will he always call on God?

11 "I will teach you about the hand
    of God;
What *is* with the Almighty I will not
    conceal.
12 Surely all of you have seen *it*;
Why then do you behave with
    complete nonsense?

13 "This is the portion of a wicked man
    with God,
And the heritage of oppressors,
    received from the Almighty:
14 If his children are multiplied, *it is*
    for the sword;
And his offspring shall not be
    satisfied with bread.
15 Those who survive him shall be
    buried in death,
And their widows shall not weep,
16 Though he heaps up silver like
    dust,
And piles up clothing like clay—
17 He may pile *it* up, but the just will
    wear *it*,
And the innocent will divide the
    silver.
18 He builds his house like a moth,
Like a booth *which* a watchman
    makes.
19 The rich man will lie down,
But not be gathered *up*;
He opens his eyes,
And he *is* no more.
20 Terrors overtake him like a flood;
A tempest steals him away in the
    night.

21 The east wind carries him away,
    and he is gone;
It sweeps him out of his place.
22 It hurls against him and does not
    spare;
He flees desperately from its
    power.
23 *Men* shall clap their hands at him,
And shall hiss him out of his place.

Job's Discourse on Wisdom

28 "Surely there is a mine for silver,
And a place *where* gold is
    refined.
2 Iron is taken from the earth,
And copper *is* smelted *from* ore.
3 *Man* puts an end to darkness,
And searches every recess
For ore in the darkness and the
    shadow of death.
4 He breaks open a shaft away from
    people;
In places forgotten by feet
They hang far away from men;
They swing to and fro.
5 *As for* the earth, from it comes
    bread,
But underneath it is turned up as
    by fire;
6 Its stones *are* the source of
    sapphires,
And it contains gold dust.
7 *That* path no bird knows,
Nor has the falcon's eye seen it.
8 The proud lions have not
    trodden it,
Nor has the fierce lion passed
    over it.
9 He puts his hand on the flint;
He overturns the mountains at the
    roots.
10 He cuts out channels in the rocks,
And his eye sees every precious
    thing.
11 He dams up the streams from
    trickling;
What is hidden he brings forth to
    light.

12 "But where can wisdom be found?
And where *is* the place of
    understanding?
13 Man does not know its value,
Nor is it found in the land of the
    living.
14 The deep says, '*It is* not in me';
And the sea says, '*It is* not with me.'

15 It cannot be purchased for gold,
    Nor can silver be weighed *for* its
        price.
16 It cannot be valued in the gold of
        Ophir,
    In precious onyx or sapphire.
17 Neither gold nor crystal can
        equal it,
    Nor can it be exchanged for jewelry
        of fine gold.
18 No mention shall be made of coral
        or quartz,
    For the price of wisdom *is* above
        rubies.
19 The topaz of Ethiopia cannot
        equal it,
    Nor can it be valued in pure gold.

20 "From where then does wisdom
        come?
    And where *is* the place of
        understanding?
21 It is hidden from the eyes of all
        living,
    And concealed from the birds of
        the air.
22 Destruction and Death say,
    'We have heard a report about it
        with our ears.'
23 God understands its way,
    And He knows its place.
24 For He looks to the ends of the
        earth,
    And sees under the whole heavens,
25 To establish a weight for the wind,
    And apportion the waters by
        measure.
26 When He made a law for the rain,
    And a path for the thunderbolt,
27 Then He saw *wisdom* and
        declared it;
    He prepared it, indeed, He searched
        it out.
28 And to man He said,
    'Behold, the fear of the Lord, that
        is wisdom,
    And to depart from evil *is*
        understanding.' "

Job's Summary Defense

29 Job further continued his dis-
course, and said:

2 "Oh, that I were as *in* months past,
    As *in* the days *when* God watched
        over me;

3 When His lamp shone upon my
        head,
    And when by His light I walked
        through darkness;
4 Just as I was in the days of my
        prime,
    When the friendly counsel of God
        was over my tent;
5 When the Almighty *was* yet
        with me,
    When my children *were*
        around me;
6 When my steps were bathed with
        cream,
    And the rock poured out rivers of
        oil for me!

7 "When I went out to the gate by the
        city,
    When I took my seat in the open
        square,
8 The young men saw me and hid,
    And the aged arose *and* stood;
9 The princes refrained from talking,
    And put *their* hand on their mouth;
10 The voice of nobles was hushed,
    And their tongue stuck to the roof
        of their mouth.
11 When the ear heard, then it
        blessed me,
    And when the eye saw, then it
        approved me;
12 Because I delivered the poor who
        cried out,
    The fatherless and *the one who* had
        no helper.
13 The blessing of a perishing *man*
        came upon me,
    And I caused the widow's heart to
        sing for joy.
14 I put on righteousness, and it
        clothed me;
    My justice *was* like a robe and a
        turban.
15 I *was* eyes to the blind,
    And I *was* feet to the lame.
16 I *was* a father to the poor,
    And I searched out the case *that* I
        did not know.
17 I broke the fangs of the wicked,
    And plucked the victim from his
        teeth.

18 "Then I said, 'I shall die in my nest,
    And multiply *my* days as the sand.
19 My root *is* spread out to the waters,
    And the dew lies all night on my
        branch.

20 My glory *is* fresh within me,
   And my bow is renewed in my
      hand.'

21 "*Men* listened to me and waited,
   And kept silence for my counsel.
22 After my words they did not speak
      again,
   And my speech settled on them
      as dew.
23 They waited for me *as* for the rain,
   And they opened their mouth wide
      as for the spring rain.
24 *If* I mocked at them, they did not
      believe *it,*
   And the light of my countenance
      they did not cast down.
25 I chose the way for them, and sat
      as chief;
   So I dwelt as a king in the army,
   As one *who* comforts mourners.

30 "But now they mock at me, *men*
      younger than I,
   Whose fathers I disdained to put
      with the dogs of my flock.
2 Indeed, what *profit* is the strength
      of their hands to me?
   Their vigor has perished.
3 *They are* gaunt from want and
      famine,
   Fleeing late to the wilderness,
      desolate and waste,
4 Who pluck mallow by the bushes,
   And broom tree roots *for* their food.
5 They were driven out from
      among *men,*
   They shouted at them as *at* a thief.
6 *They had* to live in the clefts of the
      valleys,
   In caves of the earth and the rocks.
7 Among the bushes they brayed,
   Under the nettles they nestled.
8 *They were* sons of fools,
   Yes, sons of vile men;
   They were scourged from the land.

9 "And now I am their taunting song;
   Yes, I am their byword.
10 They abhor me, they keep far
      from me;
   They do not hesitate to spit in my
      face.
11 Because He has loosed my
      bowstring and afflicted me,
   They have cast off restraint
      before me.

12 At *my* right *hand* the rabble arises;
   They push away my feet,
   And they raise against me their
      ways of destruction.
13 They break up my path,
   They promote my calamity;
   They have no helper.
14 They come as broad breakers;
   Under the ruinous storm they roll
      along.
15 Terrors are turned upon me;
   They pursue my honor as the wind,
   And my prosperity has passed like
      a cloud.

16 "And now my soul is poured out
      because of my *plight;*
   The days of affliction take hold
      of me.
17 My bones are pierced in me at
      night,
   And my gnawing pains take no
      rest.
18 By great force my garment is
      disfigured;
   It binds me about as the collar of
      my coat.
19 He has cast me into the mire,
   And I have become like dust and
      ashes.

20 "I cry out to You, but You do not
      answer me;
   I stand up, and You regard me.
21 *But* You have become cruel to me;
   With the strength of Your hand
      You oppose me.
22 You lift me up to the wind and
      cause me to ride *on it;*
   You spoil my success.
23 For I know *that* You will bring me
      to death,
   And *to* the house appointed for all
      living.

24 "Surely He would not stretch out *His*
      hand against a heap of ruins,
   If they cry out when He
      destroys *it.*
25 Have I not wept for him who was
      in trouble?
   Has *not* my soul grieved for the
      poor?
26 But when I looked for good, evil
      came *to me;*
   And when I waited for light, then
      came darkness.

27 My heart is in turmoil and cannot
　　rest;
　　Days of affliction confront me.
28 I go about mourning, but not in
　　the sun;
　　I stand up in the assembly *and* cry
　　out for help.
29 I am a brother of jackals,
　　And a companion of ostriches.
30 My skin grows black and falls
　　from me;
　　My bones burn with fever.
31 My harp is *turned* to mourning,
　　And my flute to the voice of those
　　who weep.

31 "I have made a covenant with my
　　eyes;
　　Why then should I look upon a
　　young woman?
2 For what *is* the allotment of God
　　from above,
　　And the inheritance of the
　　Almighty from on high?
3 *Is* it not destruction for the wicked,
　　And disaster for the workers of
　　iniquity?
4 Does He not see my ways,
　　And count all my steps?

5 "If I have walked with falsehood,
　　Or if my foot has hastened to deceit,
6 Let me be weighed on honest
　　scales,
　　That God may know my integrity.
7 If my step has turned from the way,
　　Or my heart walked after my eyes,
　　Or if any spot adheres to my hands,
8 *Then* let me sow, and another eat;
　　Yes, let my harvest be rooted out.

9 "If my heart has been enticed by a
　　woman,
　　Or *if* I have lurked at my neighbor's
　　door,
10 *Then* let my wife grind for another,
　　And let others bow down over her.
11 For that *would be* wickedness;
　　Yes, it *would be* iniquity *deserving
　　of* judgment.
12 For that *would be* a fire *that*
　　consumes to destruction,
　　And would root out all my increase.

13 "If I have despised the cause of my
　　male or female servant
　　When they complained against me,

14 What then shall I do when God
　　rises up?
　　When He punishes, how shall I
　　answer Him?
15 Did not He who made me in the
　　womb make them?
　　Did not the same One fashion us
　　in the womb?

16 "If I have kept the poor from *their*
　　desire,
　　Or caused the eyes of the widow
　　to fail,
17 Or eaten my morsel by myself,
　　So that the fatherless could not eat
　　of it
18 (But from my youth I reared him
　　as a father,
　　And from my mother's womb I
　　guided *the widow*);
19 If I have seen anyone perish for
　　lack of clothing,
　　Or any poor *man* without covering;
20 If his heart has not blessed me,
　　And *if* he was *not* warmed with the
　　fleece of my sheep;
21 If I have raised my hand against the
　　fatherless,
　　When I saw I had help in the gate;
22 *Then* let my arm fall from my
　　shoulder,
　　Let my arm be torn from the socket.
23 For destruction *from* God *is* a terror
　　to me,
　　And because of His magnificence I
　　cannot endure.

24 "If I have made gold my hope,
　　Or said to fine gold, '*You are* my
　　confidence';
25 If I have rejoiced because my
　　wealth *was* great,
　　And because my hand had gained
　　much;
26 If I have observed the sun when it
　　shines,
　　Or the moon moving *in* brightness,
27 So that my heart has been secretly
　　enticed,
　　And my mouth has kissed my hand;
28 This also *would be* an iniquity
　　deserving of judgment,
　　For I would have denied God *who
　　is* above.

29 "If I have rejoiced at the destruction
　　of him who hated me,

Or lifted myself up when evil
   found him
30 (Indeed I have not allowed my
    mouth to sin
    By asking for a curse on his soul);
31 If the men of my tent have not
    said;
    'Who is there that has not been
    satisfied with his meat?'
32 (*But* no sojourner had to lodge in
    the street,
    For I have opened my doors to the
    traveler);
33 If I have covered my transgressions
    as Adam,
    By hiding my iniquity in my bosom,
34 Because I feared the great
    multitude,
    And dreaded the contempt of
    families,
    So that I kept silence
    And did not go out of the door—
35 Oh, that I had one to hear me!
    Here is my mark.
    Oh, that the Almighty would
    answer me,
    That my Prosecutor had written a
    book!
36 Surely I would carry it on my
    shoulder,
    And bind it on me *like* a crown;
37 I would declare to Him the number
    of my steps;
    Like a prince I would
    approach Him.

38 "If my land cries out against me,
    And its furrows weep together;
39   If I have eaten its fruit without
     money,
     Or caused its owners to lose their
     lives;
40   *Then* let thistles grow instead of
     wheat,
     And weeds instead of barley."
The words of Job are ended.

Elihu Contradicts Job's Friends

32 So these three men ceased answering Job, because he *was*
righteous in his own eyes. 2Then the
wrath of Elihu, the son of Barachel the
Buzite, of the family of Ram, was
aroused against Job; his wrath was
aroused because he justified himself
rather than God. 3Also against his three
friends his wrath was aroused, because

they had found no answer, and *yet* had
condemned Job.
4Now because they *were* years older
than he, Elihu had waited to speak to
Job. 5When Elihu saw that *there was*
no answer in the mouth of these three
men, his wrath was aroused.
6So Elihu, the son of Barachel the
Buzite, answered and said:
   "I *am* young in years, and you *are*
      very old;
    Therefore I was afraid,
    And dared not declare my opinion
      to you.
7   I said, 'Age should speak,
    And multitude of years should
      teach wisdom.'
8   But *there is* a spirit in man,
    And the breath of the Almighty
      gives him understanding.
9   Great men are not *always* wise,
    Nor do the aged *always* understand
      justice.

10 "Therefore I say, 'Listen to me,
    I also will declare my opinion.'
11 Indeed I waited for your words,
    I listened to your reasonings, while
      you searched out what to say.
12 I paid close attention to you;
    And surely not one of you
      convinced Job,
    Or answered his words—
13 Lest you say,
    'We have found wisdom';
    God will vanquish him, not man.
14 Now he has not directed *his* words
      against me;
    So I will not answer him with your
      words.

15 "They are dismayed and answer no
      more;
    Words escape them.
16 And I have waited, because they
      did not speak,
    Because they stood still *and*
      answered no more.
17 I also will answer my part,
    I too will declare my opinion.
18 For I am full of words;
    The spirit within me compels me.
19 Indeed my belly *is* like wine *that*
      has no vent;
    It is ready to burst like new
      wineskins.
20 I will speak, that I may find relief;

I must open my lips and answer.
21 Let me not, I pray, show partiality
to anyone;
Nor let me flatter any man.
22 For I do not know how to flatter,
Else my Maker would soon take me
away.

Elihu Contradicts Job

33 "But please, Job, hear my speech,
And listen to all my words.
2 Now, I open my mouth;
My tongue speaks in my mouth.
3 My words *come* from my upright
heart;
My lips utter pure knowledge.
4 The Spirit of God has made me,
And the breath of the Almighty
gives me life.
5 If you can answer me,
Set *your words* in order before me;
Take your stand.
6 Truly I *am* as your spokesman
before God;
I also have been formed out of clay.
7 Surely no fear of me will
terrify you,
Nor will my hand be heavy on you.

8 "Surely you have spoken in my
hearing,
And I have heard the sound of *your*
words, *saying,*
9 'I *am* pure, without transgression;
I *am* innocent, and *there is* no
iniquity in me.
10 Yet He finds occasions against me,
He counts me as His enemy;
11 He puts my feet in the stocks,
He watches all my paths.'

12 "Look, *in* this you are not righteous.
I will answer you,
For God is greater than man.
13 Why do you contend with Him?
For He does not give an accounting
of any of His words.
14 For God may speak in one way, or
in another,
Yet man does not perceive it.
15 In a dream, in a vision of the night,
When deep sleep falls upon men,
While slumbering on their beds,
16 Then He opens the ears of men,
And seals their instruction.
17 In order to turn man *from his* deed,
And conceal pride from man,

18 He keeps back his soul from the
Pit,
And his life from perishing by the
sword.

19 "*Man* is also chastened with pain on
his bed,
And with strong *pain* in many of
his bones,
20 So that his life abhors bread,
And his soul succulent food.
21 His flesh wastes away from sight,
And his bones stick out *which once*
were not seen.
22 Yes, his soul draws near the Pit,
And his life to the executioners.

23 "If there is a messenger for him,
A mediator, one among a thousand,
To show man His uprightness,
24 Then He is gracious to him, and
says,
'Deliver him from going down to
the Pit;
I have found a ransom';
25 His flesh shall be young like a
child's,
He shall return to the days of his
youth.
26 He shall pray to God, and He will
delight in him,
He shall see His face with joy,
For He restores to man His
righteousness.
27 Then he looks at men and says,
'I have sinned, and perverted *what
was* right,
And it did not profit me.'
28 He will redeem his soul from going
down to the Pit,
And his life shall see the light.

29 "Behold, God works all these *things,*
Twice, *in fact,* three *times* with
a man,
30 To bring back his soul from the Pit,
That he may be enlightened with
the light of life.

31 "Give ear, Job, listen to me;
Hold your peace, and I will speak.
32 If you have anything to say,
answer me;
Speak, for I desire to justify you.
33 If not, listen to me;
Hold your peace, and I will teach
you wisdom."

Elihu Proclaims God's Justice

34 Elihu further answered and said:

2 "Hear my words, you wise *men*;
Give ear to me, you who have knowledge.
3 For the ear tests words
As the palate tastes food.
4 Let us choose justice for ourselves;
Let us know among ourselves what *is* good.

5 "For Job has said, 'I am righteous,
But God has taken away my justice;
6 Should I lie concerning my right?
My wound *is* incurable, *though I am* without transgression.'
7 What man *is* like Job,
Who drinks scorn like water,
8 Who goes in company with the workers of iniquity,
And walks with wicked men?
9 For he has said, 'It profits a man nothing
That he should delight in God.'

10 "Therefore listen to me, you men of understanding:
Far be it from God *to do* wickedness,
And *from* the Almighty to *commit* iniquity.
11 For He repays man *according to* his work,
And makes man to find a reward according to *his* way.
12 Surely God will never do wickedly,
Nor will the Almighty pervert justice.
13 Who gave Him charge over the earth?
Or who appointed *Him over* the whole world?
14 If He should set His heart on it,
If He should gather to Himself His Spirit and His breath,
15 All flesh would perish together,
And man would return to dust.

16 "If *you have* understanding, hear this;
Listen to the sound of my words:
17 Should one who hates justice govern?
Will you condemn *Him who is* most just?

18 *Is it fitting* to say to a king, 'You *are* worthless,'
And to nobles, 'You *are* wicked'?
19 Yet He is not partial to princes,
Nor does He regard the rich more than the poor;
For they *are* all the work of His hands.
20 In a moment they die, in the middle of the night;
The people are shaken and pass away;
The mighty are taken away without a hand.

21 "For His eyes *are* on the ways of man,
And He sees all his steps.
22 There is no darkness nor shadow of death
Where the workers of iniquity may hide themselves.
23 For He need not further consider a man,
That he should go before God in judgment.
24 He breaks in pieces mighty men without inquiry,
And sets others in their place.
25 Therefore He knows their works;
He overthrows *them* in the night,
And they are crushed.
26 He strikes them as wicked *men*
In the open sight of others,
27 Because they turned back from Him,
And would not consider any of His ways,
28 So that they caused the cry of the poor to come to Him;
For He hears the cry of the afflicted.
29 When He gives quietness, who then can make trouble?
And when He hides *His* face, who then can see Him,
Whether *it is* against a nation or a man alone?—
30 That the hypocrite should not reign,
Lest the people be ensnared.

31 "For has *anyone* said to God,
'I have borne *chastening;*
I will offend no more;
32 Teach me *what* I do not see;
If I have done iniquity, I will do no more'?

33 Should He repay *it* according to
    your *terms,*
    Just because you disavow it?
    You must choose, and not I;
    Therefore speak what you know.

34 "Men of understanding say to me,
    Wise men who listen to me:
35 'Job speaks without knowledge,
    His words *are* without wisdom.'
36 Oh, that Job were tried to the
    utmost,
    Because *his* answers *are like* those
    of wicked men!
37 For he adds rebellion to his sin;
    He claps *his hands* among us,
    And multiplies his words
    against God."

Elihu Condemns Self-Righteousness

35 Moreover Elihu answered and
said:

2 "Do you think this is right?
    Do you say,
    'My righteousness is more than
    God's'?
3 For you say,
    'What advantage will it be to You?
    What profit shall I have, more than
    if I had sinned?'

4 "I will answer you,
    And your companions with you.
5 Look to the heavens and see;
    And behold the clouds—
    They are higher than you.
6 If you sin, what do you accomplish
    against Him?
    Or, *if* your transgressions are
    multiplied, what do you do
    to Him?
7 If you are righteous, what do you
    give Him?
    Or what does He receive from your
    hand?
8 Your wickedness affects a man
    such as you,
    And your righteousness a son
    of man.

9 "Because of the multitude of
    oppressions they cry out;
    They cry out for help because of the
    arm of the mighty.
10 But no one says, 'Where *is* God my
    Maker,

    Who gives songs in the night,
11 Who teaches us more than the
    beasts of the earth,
    And makes us wiser than the birds
    of heaven?'
12 There they cry out, but He does not
    answer,
    Because of the pride of evil men.
13 Surely God will not listen to empty
    talk,
    Nor will the Almighty regard it.
14 Although you say you do not
    see Him,
    Yet justice *is* before Him, and you
    must wait for Him.
15 And now, because He has not
    punished in His anger,
    Nor taken much notice of folly,
16 Therefore Job opens his mouth in
    vain;
    He multiplies words without
    knowledge."

Elihu Proclaims God's Goodness

36 Elihu also proceeded and said:

2 "Bear with me a little, and I will
    show you
    That *there are* yet words to speak
    on God's behalf.
3 I will fetch my knowledge from
    afar;
    I will ascribe righteousness to my
    Maker.
4 For truly my words *are* not
    false;
    One who is perfect in knowledge
    is with you.

5 "Behold, God *is* mighty, but despises
    no one;
    He is mighty in strength of
    understanding.
6 He does not preserve the life of the
    wicked,
    But gives justice to the oppressed.
7 He does not withdraw His eyes
    from the righteous;
    But *they are* on the throne with
    kings,
    For He has seated them forever,
    And they are exalted.
8 And if *they are* bound in fetters,
    Held in the cords of affliction,
9 Then He tells them their work and
    their transgressions—
    That they have acted defiantly.

10   He also opens their ear to
        instruction,
        And commands that they turn from
        iniquity.
11   If they obey and serve *Him,*
        They shall spend their days in
        prosperity,
        And their years in pleasures.
12   But if they do not obey,
        They shall perish by the sword,
        And they shall die without
        knowledge.

13   "But the hypocrites in heart store up
        wrath;
        They do not cry for help when He
        binds them.
14   They die in youth,
        And their life *ends* among the
        perverted persons.ᵃ
15   He delivers the poor in their
        affliction,
        And opens their ears in oppression.

16   "Indeed He would have brought you
        out of dire distress,
        Into a broad place where *there is*
        no restraint;
        And what is set on your table *would
        be* full of richness.
17   But you are filled with the judgment
        due the wicked;
        Judgment and justice take hold
        of you.
18   Because *there is* wrath, *beware* lest
        He take you away with *one*
        blow;
        For a large ransom would not help
        you avoid *it.*
19   Will your riches,
        Or all the mighty forces,
        Keep you from distress?
20   Do not desire the night,
        When people are cut off in their
        place.
21   Take heed, do not turn to iniquity,
        For you have chosen this rather
        than affliction.

22   "Behold, God is exalted by His
        power;
        Who teaches like Him?
23   Who has assigned Him His way,
        Or who has said, 'You have done
        wrong'?

Elihu Proclaims God's Majesty

24   "Remember to magnify His work,
        Of which men have sung.
25   Everyone has seen it;
        Man looks on *it* from afar.

26   "Behold, God *is* great, and we do not
            know *Him;*
        Nor can the number of His years
            be discovered.
27   For He draws up drops of water,
        Which distill as rain from the mist,
28   Which the clouds drop down
        And pour abundantly on man.
29   Indeed, can *anyone* understand the
            spreading of clouds,
        The thunder from His canopy?
30   Look, He scatters His light upon it,
        And covers the depths of the sea.
31   For by these He judges the peoples;
        He gives food in abundance.
32   He covers *His* hands with lightning,
        And commands it to strike.
33   His thunder declares it,
        The cattle also, concerning the
            rising *storm.*

37   "At this also my heart trembles,
            And leaps from its place.
2   Hear attentively the thunder of His
            voice,
        And the rumbling *that* comes from
            His mouth.
3   He sends it forth under the whole
            heaven,
        His lightning to the ends of the
            earth.
4   After it a voice roars;
        He thunders with His majestic
            voice,
        And He does not restrain them
            when His voice is heard.
5   God thunders marvelously with His
            voice;
        He does great things which we
            cannot comprehend.
6   For He says to the snow, 'Fall *on*
            the earth';
        Likewise to the gentle rain and the
            heavy rain of His strength.
7   He seals the hand of every man,
        That all men may know His work.
8   The beasts go into dens,
        And remain in their lairs.

ᵃ That is, those practicing sodomy and prostitution in religious rituals

9 From the chamber *of the south*
   comes the whirlwind,
   And cold from the scattering winds
   of the north.
10 By the breath of God ice is given,
   And the broad waters are frozen.
11 Also with moisture He saturates the
   thick clouds;
   He scatters His bright clouds.
12 And they swirl about, being turned
   by His guidance,
   That they may do whatever He
   commands them
   On the face of the whole earth.
13 He causes it to come,
   Whether for correction,
   Or for His land,
   Or for mercy.

14 "Listen to this, O Job;
   Stand still and consider the
   wondrous works of God.
15 Do you know when God dispatches
   them,
   And causes the light of His cloud
   to shine?
16 Do you know how the clouds are
   balanced,
   Those wondrous works of Him who
   is perfect in knowledge?
17 Why *are* your garments hot,
   When He quiets the earth by the
   south *wind*?
18 With Him, have you spread out the
   skies,
   Strong as a cast metal mirror?

19 "Teach us what we should say
   to Him,
   For we can prepare nothing
   because of the darkness.
20 Should He be told that I *wish to*
   speak?
   If a man were to speak, surely he
   would be swallowed up.
21 Even now *men* cannot look at the
   light *when it is* bright in the skies,
   When the wind has passed and
   cleared them.
22 He comes from the north *as* golden
   splendor;
   With God *is* awesome majesty.
23 *As for* the Almighty, we cannot
   find Him;
   He is excellent in power,
   In judgment and abundant justice;
   He does not oppress.

24 Therefore men fear Him;
   He shows no partiality to any *who
   are* wise of heart.' "

The LORD Reveals His Omnipotence to Job

38 Then the LORD answered Job out
of the whirlwind, and said:

2 "Who *is* this who darkens counsel
   By words without knowledge?
3 Now prepare yourself like a man;
   I will question you, and you shall
   answer Me.

4 "Where were you when I laid the
   foundations of the earth?
   Tell *Me*, if you have understanding.
5 Who determined its
   measurements?
   Surely you know!
   Or who stretched the line upon it?
6 To what were its foundations
   fastened?
   Or who laid its cornerstone,
7 When the morning stars sang
   together,
   And all the sons of God shouted
   for joy?

8 "Or *who* shut in the sea with doors,
   When it burst forth *and* issued from
   the womb;
9 When I made the clouds its
   garment,
   And thick darkness its swaddling
   band;
10 When I fixed My limit for it,
   And set bars and doors;
11 When I said,
   'This far you may come, but no
   farther,
   And here your proud waves must
   stop!'

12 "Have you commanded the morning
   since your days *began*,
   And caused the dawn to know its
   place,
13 That it might take hold of the ends
   of the earth,
   And the wicked be shaken out
   of it?
14 It takes on form like clay *under* a
   seal,
   And stands out like a garment.

15 From the wicked their light is
 withheld,
 And the upraised arm is broken.

16 "Have you entered the springs of
 the sea?
 Or have you walked in search of
 the depths?

17 Have the gates of death been
 revealed to you?
 Or have you seen the doors of the
 shadow of death?

18 Have you comprehended the
 breadth of the earth?
 Tell *Me*, if you know all this.

19 "Where *is* the way *to* the dwelling
 of light?
 And darkness, where *is* its place,

20 That you may take it to its territory,
 That you may know the paths *to*
 its home?

21 Do you know *it*, because you were
 born then,
 Or *because* the number of your
 days *is* great?

22 "Have you entered the treasury of
 snow,
 Or have you seen the treasury of
 hail,

23 Which I have reserved for the time
 of trouble,
 For the day of battle and war?

24 By what way is light diffused,
 Or the east wind scattered over the
 earth?

25 "Who has divided a channel for the
 overflowing *water*,
 Or a path for the thunderbolt,

26 To cause it to rain on a land *where*
 there is no one,
 A wilderness in which *there is*
 no man;

27 To satisfy the desolate waste,
 And cause to spring forth the
 growth of tender grass?

28 Has the rain a father?
 Or who has begotten the drops
 of dew?

29 From whose womb comes the ice?
 And the frost of heaven, who gives
 it birth?

30 The waters harden like stone,
 And the surface of the deep is
 frozen.

31 "Can you bind the cluster of the
 Pleiades,
 Or loose the belt of Orion?

32 Can you bring out Mazzaroth in its
 season?
 Or can you guide the Great Bear
 with its cubs?

33 Do you know the ordinances of the
 heavens?
 Can you set their dominion over the
 earth?

34 "Can you lift up your voice to the
 clouds,
 That an abundance of water may
 cover you?

35 Can you send out lightnings, that
 they may go,
 And say to you, 'Here we *are!*'?

36 Who has put wisdom in the mind?
 Or who has given understanding to
 the heart?

37 Who can number the clouds by
 wisdom?
 Or who can pour out the bottles of
 heaven,

38 When the dust hardens in clumps,
 And the clods cling together?

39 "Can you hunt the prey for the lion,
 Or satisfy the appetite of the young
 lions,

40 When they crouch in *their* dens,
 Or lurk in their lairs to lie in wait?

41 Who provides food for the raven,
 When its young ones cry to God,
 And wander about for lack of food?

39 "Do you know the time when the
 wild mountain goats bear
 young?
 Or can you mark when the deer
 gives birth?

2 Can you number the months *that*
 they fulfill?
 Or do you know the time when they
 bear young?

3 They bow down,
 They bring forth their young,
 They deliver their offspring.

4 Their young ones are healthy,
 They grow strong with grain;
 They depart and do not return to
 them.

5 "Who set the wild donkey free?
 Who loosed the bonds of the
 onager,

6   Whose home I have made the
        wilderness,
    And the barren land his dwelling?
7   He scorns the tumult of the city;
    He does not heed the shouts of the
        driver.
8   The range of the mountains *is* his
        pasture,
    And he searches after every green
        thing.

9   "Will the wild ox be willing to
        serve you?
    Will he bed by your manger?
10 Can you bind the wild ox in the
        furrow with ropes?
    Or will he plow the valleys
        behind you?
11 Will you trust him because his
        strength *is* great?
    Or will you leave your labor to
        him?
12 Will you trust him to bring home
        your grain,
    And gather it to your threshing
        floor?

13 "The wings of the ostrich wave
        proudly,
    But are her wings and pinions *like*
        the kindly stork's?
14 For she leaves her eggs on the
        ground,
    And warms them in the dust;
15 She forgets that a foot may crush
        them,
    Or that a wild beast may break
        them.
16 She treats her young harshly, as
        though *they were* not hers;
    Her labor is in vain, without
        concern,
17 Because God deprived her of
        wisdom,
    And did not endow her with
        understanding.
18 When she lifts herself on high,
    She scorns the horse and its rider.

19 "Have you given the horse strength?
    Have you clothed his neck with
        thunder?
20 Can you frighten him like a locust?
    His majestic snorting strikes terror.
21 He paws in the valley, and rejoices
        in *his* strength;
    He gallops into the clash of arms.

22 He mocks at fear, and is not
        frightened;
    Nor does he turn back from the
        sword.
23 The quiver rattles against him,
    The glittering spear and javelin.
24 He devours the distance with
        fierceness and rage;
    Nor does he come to a halt because
        the trumpet *has* sounded.
25 At *the blast of* the trumpet he
        says, 'Aha!'
    He smells the battle from afar,
    The thunder of captains and
        shouting.

26 "Does the hawk fly by your wisdom,
    And spread its wings toward the
        south?
27 Does the eagle mount up at your
        command,
    And make its nest on high?
28 On the rock it dwells and resides,
    On the crag of the rock and the
        stronghold.
29 From there it spies out the prey;
    Its eyes observe from afar.
30 Its young ones suck up blood;
    And where the slain *are*, there it *is*."

40 Moreover the Lord answered
     Job, and said:

2   "Shall the one who contends with
        the Almighty correct *Him*?
    He who rebukes God, let him
        answer it."

Job's Response to God

3Then Job answered the Lord and
said:

4   "Behold, I am vile;
    What shall I answer You?
    I lay my hand over my mouth.
5   Once I have spoken, but I will not
        answer;
    Yes, twice, but I will proceed no
        further."

God's Challenge to Job

6Then the Lord answered Job out of
the whirlwind, and said:

7   "Now prepare yourself like a man;
    I will question you, and you shall
        answer Me:

8 "Would you indeed annul My
      judgment?
   Would you condemn Me that you
      may be justified?
9 Have you an arm like God?
   Or can you thunder with a voice
      like His?
10 Then adorn yourself *with* majesty
      and splendor,
   And array yourself with glory and
      beauty.
11 Disperse the rage of your wrath;
   Look on everyone *who is* proud,
      and humble him.
12 Look on everyone *who is* proud,
      and bring him low;
   Tread down the wicked in their
      place.
13 Hide them in the dust together,
   Bind their faces in hidden
      darkness.
14 Then I will also confess to you
   That your own right hand can
      save you.

15 "Look now at the behemoth,[b] which
      I made *along* with you;
   He eats grass like an ox.
16 See now, his strength *is* in his hips,
   And his power *is* in his stomach
      muscles.
17 He moves his tail like a cedar;
   The sinews of his thighs are tightly
      knit.
18 His bones *are like* beams of bronze,
   His ribs like bars of iron.
19 He *is* the first of the ways of God;
   Only He who made him can bring
      near His sword.
20 Surely the mountains yield food
      for him,
   And all the beasts of the field play
      there.
21 He lies under the lotus trees,
   In a covert of reeds and marsh.
22 The lotus trees cover him *with* their
      shade;
   The willows by the brook
      surround him.
23 Indeed the river may rage,
   Yet he is not disturbed;
   He is confident, though the Jordan
      gushes into his mouth,
24 *Though* he takes it in his eyes,

   Or one pierces *his* nose with a
      snare.

41 "Can you draw out Leviathan[c]
      with a hook,
   Or *snare* his tongue with a line
      which you lower?
2 Can you put a reed through his
      nose,
   Or pierce his jaw with a hook?
3 Will he make many supplications
      to you?
   Will he speak softly to you?
4 Will he make a covenant with
      you?
   Will you take him as a servant
      forever?
5 Will you play with him as *with* a
      bird,
   Or will you leash him for your
      maidens?
6 Will *your* companions make a
      banquet of him?
   Will they apportion him among the
      merchants?
7 Can you fill his skin with harpoons,
   Or his head with fishing spears?
8 Lay your hand on him;
   Remember the battle—
   Never do it again!
9 Indeed, *any* hope of *overcoming*
      him is false;
   Shall *one not* be overwhelmed at
      the sight of him?
10 No one *is so* fierce that he would
      dare stir him up.
   Who then is able to stand
      against Me?
11 Who has preceded Me, that I should
      pay *him?*
   Everything under heaven is Mine.

12 "I will not conceal his limbs,
   His mighty power, or his graceful
      proportions.
13 Who can remove his outer coat?
   Who can approach *him* with a
      double bridle?
14 Who can open the doors of his face,
   With his terrible teeth all around?
15 *His* rows of scales are *his* pride,
   Shut up tightly *as with* a seal;
16 One is so near another
   That no air can come between
      them;

---

b A large animal, exact identity unknown   c A large sea creature, exact identity unknown

17 They are joined one to another,
   They stick together and cannot be
     parted.
18 His sneezings flash forth light,
   And his eyes *are* like the eyelids of
     the morning.
19 Out of his mouth go burning lights;
   Sparks of fire shoot out.
20 Smoke goes out of his nostrils,
   As *from* a boiling pot and burning
     rushes.
21 His breath kindles coals,
   And a flame goes out of his mouth.
22 Strength dwells in his neck,
   And sorrow dances before him.
23 The folds of his flesh are joined
     together;
   They are firm on him and cannot
     be moved.
24 His heart is as hard as stone,
   Even as hard as the lower
     millstone.
25 When he raises himself up, the
     mighty are afraid;
   Because of his crashings they are
     beside themselves.
26 *Though* the sword reaches him, it
     cannot avail;
   Nor does spear, dart, or javelin.
27 He regards iron as straw,
   And bronze as rotten wood.
28 The arrow cannot make him flee;
   Slingstones become like stubble
     to him.
29 Darts are regarded as straw;
   He laughs at the threat of javelins.
30 His undersides *are* like sharp
     potsherds;
   He spreads pointed *marks* in the
     mire.
31 He makes the deep boil like a pot;
   He makes the sea like a pot of
     ointment.
32 He leaves a shining wake
     behind him;
   One would think the deep had
     white hair.
33 On earth there is nothing like him,
   Which is made without fear.
34 He beholds every high *thing*;
   He *is* king over all the children of
     pride.''

Job's Repentance and Restoration

42 Then Job answered the Lord and
     said:

2 ''I know that You can do everything,
   And that no purpose *of Yours* can
     be withheld from You.
3 *You asked,* 'Who *is* this who hides
     counsel without knowledge?'
   Therefore I have uttered what I did
     not understand,
   Things too wonderful for me, which
     I did not know.
4 Listen, please, and let me speak;
   You said, 'I will question you, and
     you shall answer Me.'

5 ''I have heard of You by the hearing
     of the ear,
   But now my eye sees You.
6 Therefore I abhor *myself,*
   And repent in dust and ashes.''

7And so it was, after the Lord had
spoken these words to Job, that the
Lord said to Eliphaz the Temanite, ''My
wrath is aroused against you and your
two friends, for you have not spoken
of Me *what is* right, as My servant Job
has. 8Now therefore, take for yourselves seven bulls and seven rams, go
to My servant Job, and offer up for
yourselves a burnt offering; and My
servant Job shall pray for you. For I will
accept him, lest I deal with you *according to your* folly; because you have not
spoken of Me *what is* right, as My
servant Job *has.''*

9So Eliphaz the Temanite and Bildad
the Shuhite *and* Zophar the Naamathite
went and did as the Lord commanded
them; for the Lord had accepted Job.
10And the Lord restored Job's losses
when he prayed for his friends. Indeed
the Lord gave Job twice as much as he
had before. 11Then all his brothers, all
his sisters, and all those who had been
his acquaintances before, came to him
and ate food with him in his house; and
they consoled him and comforted him
for all the adversity that the Lord had
brought upon him. Each one gave him
a piece of silver and each a ring of gold.
12Now the Lord blessed the latter
days of Job more than his beginning;
for he had fourteen thousand sheep, six
thousand camels, one thousand yoke of
oxen, and one thousand female donkeys. 13He also had seven sons and
three daughters. 14And he called the
name of the first Jemimah, the name
of the second Keziah, and the name of

the third Keren-Happuch. 15In all the land were found no women *so* beautiful as the daughters of Job; and their father gave them an inheritance among their brothers.

16After this Job lived one hundred and forty years, and saw his children and grandchildren *for* four generations. 17So Job died, old and full of days.

The Book of
PSALMS

BOOK ONE: PSALMS 1—41

PSALM 1

The Way of the Righteous and the End of the Ungodly

1 Blessed *is* the man
  Who walks not in the counsel of the
    ungodly,
    Nor stands in the path of sinners,
    Nor sits in the seat of the scornful;
2 But his delight *is* in the law of the
    LORD,
    And in His law he meditates day
    and night.
3 He shall be like a tree
    Planted by the rivers of water,
    That brings forth its fruit in its
    season,
    Whose leaf also shall not wither;
    And whatever he does shall prosper.

4 The ungodly *are* not so,
    But *are* like the chaff which the wind
    drives away.
5 Therefore the ungodly shall not
    stand in the judgment,
    Nor sinners in the congregation of
    the righteous.

6 For the LORD knows the way of the
    righteous,
    But the way of the ungodly shall
    perish.

PSALM 2

The Messiah's Triumph and Kingdom

1 Why do the nations rage,
    And the people plot a vain thing?
2 The kings of the earth set
    themselves,
    And the rulers take counsel
    together,
    Against the LORD and against His
    Anointed, *saying,*
3 "Let us break Their bonds in pieces
    And cast away Their cords from us."

4 He who sits in the heavens shall
    laugh;
    The LORD shall hold them in
    derision.

5 Then He shall speak to them in His
    wrath,
    And distress them in His deep
    displeasure:
6 "Yet I have set My King
    On My holy hill of Zion."

7 "I will declare the decree:
    The LORD has said to Me,
    'You *are* My Son,
    Today I have begotten You.
8 Ask of Me, and I will give *You*
    The nations *for* Your inheritance,
    And the ends of the earth *for* Your
    possession.
9 You shall break them with a rod of
    iron;
    You shall dash them to pieces like
    a potter's vessel.' "

10 Now therefore, be wise, O kings;
    Be instructed, you judges of the
    earth.
11 Serve the LORD with fear,
    And rejoice with trembling.
12 Kiss the Son, lest He be angry,
    And you perish *in* the way,
    When His wrath is kindled but a
    little.
    Blessed *are* all those who put their
    trust in Him.

PSALM 3

The LORD Helps His Troubled People

A Psalm of David when he fled from Absalom
his son.

1 LORD, how they have increased who
    trouble me!
    Many *are* they who rise up
    against me.
2 Many *are* they who say of me,
    "*There is* no help for him in God."
    Selah

3 But You, O LORD, *are* a shield
    for me,
    My glory and the One who lifts up
    my head.
4 I cried to the LORD with my voice,
    And He heard me from His holy hill.
    Selah

5 I lay down and slept;
  I awoke, for the LORD sustained me.
6 I will not be afraid of ten thousands
    of people
  Who have set *themselves* against me
    all around.

7 Arise, O LORD;
  Save me, O my God!
  For You have struck all my enemies
    on the cheekbone;
  You have broken the teeth of the
    ungodly.
8 Salvation *belongs* to the LORD.
  Your blessing *is* upon Your people.
                                    Selah

PSALM 4

The Safety of the Faithful

To the Chief Musician. With stringed instruments. A Psalm of David.

1 Hear me when I call, O God of my
    righteousness!
  You have relieved me in *my* distress;
  Have mercy on me, and hear my
    prayer.

2 How long, O you sons of men,
  Will you turn my glory to shame?
  How long will you love
    worthlessness
  And seek falsehood?   Selah
3 But know that the LORD has set apart
    for Himself him who is godly;
  The LORD will hear when I call
    to Him.

4 Be angry, and do not sin.
  Meditate within your heart on your
    bed, and be still.   Selah
5 Offer the sacrifices of righteousness,
  And put your trust in the LORD.

6 *There are* many who say,
  "Who will show us *any* good?"
  LORD, lift up the light of Your
    countenance upon us.
7 You have put gladness in my heart,
  More than in the season that their
    grain and wine increased.
8 I will both lie down in peace, and
    sleep;
  For You alone, O LORD, make me
    dwell in safety.

PSALM 5

A Prayer for Guidance

To the Chief Musician. With flutes.
A Psalm of David.

1 Give ear to my words, O LORD,
  Consider my meditation.
2 Give heed to the voice of my cry,
  My King and my God,
  For to You I will pray.
3 My voice You shall hear in the
    morning, O LORD;
  In the morning I will direct *it* to You,
  And I will look up.

4 For You *are* not a God who takes
    pleasure in wickedness,
  Nor shall evil dwell with You.
5 The boastful shall not stand in Your
    sight;
  You hate all workers of iniquity.
6 You shall destroy those who speak
    falsehood;
  The LORD abhors the bloodthirsty
    and deceitful man.

7 But as for me, I will come into Your
    house in the multitude of Your
    mercy;
  In fear of You I will worship toward
    Your holy temple.
8 Lead me, O LORD, in Your
    righteousness because of my
    enemies;
  Make Your way straight before my
    face.
9 For *there is* no faithfulness in their
    mouth;
  Their inward part *is* destruction;
  Their throat *is* an open tomb;
  They flatter with their tongue.
10 Pronounce them guilty, O God!
  Let them fall by their own counsels;
  Cast them out in the multitude of
    their transgressions,
  For they have rebelled against You.

11 But let all those rejoice who put their
    trust in You;
  Let them ever shout for joy, because
    You defend them;
  Let those also who love Your name
  Be joyful in You.
12 For You, O LORD, will bless the
    righteous;
  With favor You will surround him
    as *with* a shield.

PSALM 6

A Prayer of Faith in Time of Distress

To the Chief Musician. With stringed instruments. On an eight-stringed harp.
A Psalm of David.

1 O Lord, do not rebuke me in Your
anger,
Nor chasten me in Your hot
displeasure.
2 Have mercy on me, O Lord, for I *am*
weak;
O Lord, heal me, for my bones are
troubled.
3 My soul also is greatly troubled;
But You, O Lord—how long?

4 Return, O Lord, deliver me!
Oh, save me for Your mercies' sake!
5 For in death *there is* no
remembrance of You;
In the grave who will give You
thanks?

6 I am weary with my groaning;
All night I make my bed swim;
I drench my couch with my tears.
7 My eye wastes away because of
grief;
It grows old because of all my
enemies.

8 Depart from me, all you workers of
iniquity;
For the Lord has heard the voice of
my weeping.
9 The Lord has heard my
supplication;
The Lord will receive my prayer.
10 Let all my enemies be ashamed and
greatly troubled;
Let them turn back *and* be ashamed
suddenly.

PSALM 7

Prayer and Praise for Deliverance from Enemies

A Meditation of David, which he sang to the
Lord concerning the words of Cush,
a Benjamite.

1 O Lord my God, in You I put my
trust;
Save me from all those who
persecute me;
And deliver me,
2 Lest they tear me like a lion,

Rending *me* in pieces, while *there
is* none to deliver.

3 O Lord my God, if I have done this:
If there is iniquity in my hands,
4 If I have repaid evil to him who was
at peace with me,
Or have plundered my enemy
without cause,
5 Let the enemy pursue me and
overtake *me;*
Yes, let him trample my life to the
earth,
And lay my honor in the dust.
      Selah

6 Arise, O Lord, in Your anger;
Lift Yourself up because of the rage
of my enemies;
Rise up for me *to* the judgment You
have commanded!
7 So the congregation of the peoples
shall surround You;
For their sakes, therefore, return on
high.
8 The Lord shall judge the peoples;
Judge me, O Lord, according to my
righteousness,
And according to my integrity
within me.

9 Oh, let the wickedness of the wicked
come to an end,
But establish the just;
For the righteous God tests the
hearts and minds.
10 My defense *is* of God,
Who saves the upright in heart.

11 God *is* a just judge,
And God is angry *with the wicked*
every day.
12 If he does not turn back,
He will sharpen His sword;
He bends His bow and makes it
ready.
13 He also prepares for Himself
instruments of death;
He makes His arrows into fiery
shafts.

14 Behold, *the wicked* brings forth
iniquity;
Yes, he conceives trouble and brings
forth falsehood.
15 He made a pit and dug it out,

And has fallen into the ditch *which*
  he made.
16 His trouble shall return upon his
  own head,
  And his violent dealing shall come
  down on his own crown.

17 I will praise the LORD according to
  His righteousness,
  And will sing praise to the name of
  the LORD Most High.

PSALM 8

The Glory of the LORD in Creation

To the Chief Musician. On the instrument of
Gath. A Psalm of David.

1 O LORD, our Lord,
  How excellent *is* Your name in all
  the earth,
  Who have set Your glory above the
  heavens!

2 Out of the mouth of babes and
  nursing infants
  You have ordained strength,
  Because of Your enemies,
  That You may silence the enemy
  and the avenger.

3 When I consider Your heavens, the
  work of Your fingers,
  The moon and the stars, which You
  have ordained,
4 What is man that You are mindful
  of him,
  And the son of man that You
  visit him?
5 For You have made him a little
  lower than the angels,
  And You have crowned him with
  glory and honor.

6 You have made him to have
  dominion over the works of Your
  hands;
  You have put all *things* under his
  feet,
7 All sheep and oxen—
  Even the beasts of the field,
8 The birds of the air,
  And the fish of the sea
  That pass through the paths of the
  seas.

9 O LORD, our Lord,
  How excellent *is* Your name in all
  the earth!

PSALM 9

Prayer and Thanksgiving for the LORD's Righteous Judgments

To the Chief Musician. To *the tune of* "Death
of the Son." A Psalm of David.

1 I will praise *You,* O LORD, with my
  whole heart;
  I will tell of all Your marvelous
  works.
2 I will be glad and rejoice in You;
  I will sing praise to Your name,
  O Most High.

3 When my enemies turn back,
  They shall fall and perish at Your
  presence.
4 For You have maintained my right
  and my cause;
  You sat on the throne judging in
  righteousness.
5 You have rebuked the nations,
  You have destroyed the wicked;
  You have blotted out their name
  forever and ever.

6 O enemy, destructions are finished
  forever!
  And you have destroyed cities;
  Even their memory has perished.
7 But the LORD shall endure forever;
  He has prepared His throne for
  judgment.
8 He shall judge the world in
  righteousness,
  And He shall administer judgment
  for the peoples in uprightness.

9 The LORD also will be a refuge for
  the oppressed,
  A refuge in times of trouble.
10 And those who know Your name
  will put their trust in You;
  For You, LORD, have not forsaken
  those who seek You.

11 Sing praises to the LORD, who dwells
  in Zion!
  Declare His deeds among the
  people.
12 When He avenges blood, He
  remembers them;
  He does not forget the cry of the
  humble.

13 Have mercy on me, O LORD!
  Consider my trouble from those who
  hate me,

You who lift me up from the gates
of death,
14 That I may tell of all Your praise
In the gates of the daughter of Zion.
I will rejoice in Your salvation.

15 The nations have sunk down in the
pit *which* they made;
In the net which they hid, their own
foot is caught.
16 The LORD is known *by* the judgment
He executes;
The wicked is snared in the work
of his own hands.
                    Meditation.   Selah

17 The wicked shall be turned into hell,
And all the nations that forget God.
18 For the needy shall not always be
forgotten;
The expectation of the poor shall *not*
perish forever.

19 Arise, O LORD,
Do not let man prevail;
Let the nations be judged in Your
sight.
20 Put them in fear, O LORD,
That the nations may know
themselves *to be but* men.
                                        Selah

PSALM 10

A Song of Confidence in God's Triumph over Evil

1 Why do You stand afar off, O LORD?
Why do You hide in times of
trouble?
2 The wicked in *his* pride persecutes
the poor;
Let them be caught in the plots
which they have devised.

3 For the wicked boasts of his heart's
desire;
He blesses the greedy *and*
renounces the LORD.
4 The wicked in his proud
countenance does not seek God;
God *is* in none of his thoughts.

5 His ways are always prospering;
Your judgments *are* far above, out
of his sight;
As for all his enemies, he sneers at
them.

6 He has said in his heart, "I shall not
be moved;
I shall never be in adversity."
7 His mouth is full of cursing and
deceit and oppression;
Under his tongue *is* trouble and
iniquity.

8 He sits in the lurking places of the
villages;
In the secret places he murders the
innocent;
His eyes are secretly fixed on the
helpless.
9 He lies in wait secretly, as a lion in
his den;
He lies in wait to catch the poor;
He catches the poor when he draws
him into his net.
10 So he crouches, he lies low,
That the helpless may fall by his
strength.
11 He has said in his heart,
"God has forgotten;
He hides His face;
He will never see."

12 Arise, O LORD!
O God, lift up Your hand!
Do not forget the humble.
13 Why do the wicked renounce God?
He has said in his heart,
"You will not require *an account.*"

14 But You have seen, for You observe
trouble and grief,
To repay *it* by Your hand.
The helpless commits himself
to You;
You are the helper of the fatherless.
15 Break the arm of the wicked and the
evil *man;*
Seek out his wickedness *until* You
find none.

16 The LORD *is* King forever and ever;
The nations have perished out of His
land.
17 LORD, You have heard the desire of
the humble;
You will prepare their heart;
You will cause Your ear to hear,
18 To do justice to the fatherless and
the oppressed,
That the man of the earth may
oppress no more.

PSALM 11

Faith in the Lord's Righteousness

To the Chief Musician. A Psalm of David.

1　In the Lord I put my trust;
　　How can you say to my soul,
　"Flee *as* a bird to your mountain"?
2　For look! The wicked bend
　　　their bow,
　　They make ready their arrow on the
　　　string,
　　That they may shoot secretly at the
　　　upright in heart.
3　If the foundations are destroyed,
　　What can the righteous do?

4　The Lord *is* in His holy temple,
　　The Lord's throne *is* in heaven;
　　His eyes behold,
　　His eyelids test the sons of men.
5　The Lord tests the righteous,
　　But the wicked and the one who
　　　loves violence His soul hates.
6　Upon the wicked He will rain coals;
　　Fire and brimstone and a burning
　　　wind
　　Shall be the portion of their cup.

7　For the Lord *is* righteous,
　　He loves righteousness;
　　His countenance beholds the
　　　upright.[a]

PSALM 12

Man's Treachery and God's Constancy

To the Chief Musician. On an eight-stringed
harp. A Psalm of David.

1　Help, Lord, for the godly man
　　　ceases!
　　For the faithful disappear from
　　　among the sons of men.
2　They speak idly everyone with his
　　　neighbor;
　　With flattering lips *and* a double
　　　heart they speak.

3　May the Lord cut off all flattering
　　　lips,
　　And the tongue that speaks proud
　　　things,
4　Who have said,
　　"With our tongue we will prevail;
　　Our lips *are* our own;
　　Who *is* lord over us?"

5　"For the oppression of the poor, for
　　　the sighing of the needy,

a Or *The upright beholds His countenance*

Now I will arise," says the Lord;
"I will set *him* in the safety for which
　he yearns."

6　The words of the Lord *are* pure
　　　words,
　　Like silver tried in a furnace of
　　　earth,
　　Purified seven times.
7　You shall keep them, O Lord,
　　You shall preserve them from this
　　　generation forever.

8　The wicked prowl on every side,
　　When vileness is exalted among the
　　　sons of men.

PSALM 13

Trust in the Salvation of the Lord

To the Chief Musician. A Psalm of David.

1　How long, O Lord? Will You forget
　　　me forever?
　　How long will You hide Your face
　　　from me?
2　How long shall I take counsel in my
　　　soul,
　　Having sorrow in my heart daily?
　　How long will my enemy be exalted
　　　over me?

3　Consider *and* hear me, O Lord
　　　my God;
　　Enlighten my eyes,
　　Lest I sleep the *sleep of* death;
4　Lest my enemy say,
　　"I have prevailed against him";
　　Lest those who trouble me rejoice
　　　when I am moved.

5　But I have trusted in Your mercy;
　　My heart shall rejoice in Your
　　　salvation.
6　I will sing to the Lord,
　　Because He has dealt bountifully
　　　with me.

PSALM 14

Folly of the Godless, and God's Final Triumph

To the Chief Musician. A Psalm of David.

1　The fool has said in his heart,
　"*There is* no God."
　　They are corrupt,
　　They have done abominable works,
　　There is none who does good.

2 The Lord looks down from heaven
     upon the children of men,
     To see if there are any who
     understand, who seek God.
3 They have all turned aside,
     They have together become corrupt;
     There is none who does good,
     No, not one.

4 Have all the workers of iniquity no
     knowledge,
     Who eat up my people *as* they eat
     bread,
     And do not call on the Lord?
5 There they are in great fear,
     For God *is* with the generation of the
     righteous.
6 You shame the counsel of the poor,
     But the Lord *is* his refuge.

7 Oh, that the salvation of Israel *would
     come* out of Zion!
     When the Lord brings back the
     captivity of His people,
     Let Jacob rejoice *and* Israel be glad.

PSALM 15

The Character of Those Who May Dwell with the Lord

A Psalm of David.

1 Lord, who may abide in Your
     tabernacle?
     Who may dwell in Your holy hill?

2 He who walks uprightly,
     And works righteousness,
     And speaks the truth in his heart;
3 He *who* does not backbite with his
     tongue,
     Nor does evil to his neighbor,
     Nor does he take up a reproach
     against his friend;
4 In whose eyes a vile person is
     despised,
     But he honors those who fear the
     Lord;
     He *who* swears to his own hurt and
     does not change;
5 He *who* does not put out his money
     at usury,
     Nor does he take a bribe against
     the innocent.

He who does these *things* shall
     never be moved.

PSALM 16

The Hope of the Faithful, and the Messiah's Victory

A Michtam of David.

1 Preserve me, O God, for in You I put
     my trust.

2 *O my soul,* you have said to the
     Lord,
     "You *are* my Lord,
     My goodness is nothing apart
     from You."
3 As for the saints who *are* on the
     earth,
     "They are the excellent ones, in
     whom is all my delight."

4 Their sorrows shall be multiplied
     who hasten *after* another *god;*
     Their drink offerings of blood I will
     not offer,
     Nor take up their names on my lips.

5 O Lord, *You are* the portion of my
     inheritance and my cup;
     You maintain my lot.
6 The lines have fallen to me in
     pleasant *places;*
     Yes, I have a good inheritance.

7 I will bless the Lord who has given
     me counsel;
     My heart also instructs me in the
     night seasons.
8 I have set the Lord always
     before me;
     Because *He is* at my right hand I
     shall not be moved.

9 Therefore my heart is glad, and my
     glory rejoices;
     My flesh also will rest in hope.
10 For You will not leave my soul in
     Sheol,
     Nor will You allow Your Holy One
     to see corruption.
11 You will show me the path of life;
     In Your presence *is* fullness of joy;
     At Your right hand *are* pleasures
     forevermore.

PSALM 17

Prayer with Confidence in Final Salvation

A Prayer of David.

1 Hear a just cause, O Lord,
     Attend to my cry;

Give ear to my prayer *which is* not
from deceitful lips.
2 Let my vindication come from Your
presence;
Let Your eyes look on the things that
are upright.

3 You have tested my heart;
You have visited *me* in the night;
You have tried me and have found
nothing;
I have purposed that my mouth shall
not transgress.
4 Concerning the works of men,
By the word of Your lips,
I have kept away from the paths of
the destroyer.
5 Uphold my steps in Your paths,
That my footsteps may not slip.

6 I have called upon You, for You will
hear me, O God;
Incline Your ear to me, *and* hear my
speech.
7 Show Your marvelous
lovingkindness by Your right
hand,
O You who save those who trust
in You
From those who rise up *against
them.*
8 Keep me as the apple of Your eye;
Hide me under the shadow of Your
wings,
9 From the wicked who oppress me,
From my deadly enemies who
surround me.

10 They have closed up their fat *hearts*;
With their mouths they speak
proudly.
11 They have now surrounded us in our
steps;
They have set their eyes, crouching
down to the earth,
12 As a lion is eager to tear his prey,
And like a young lion lurking in
secret places.

13 Arise, O LORD,
Confront him, cast him down;
Deliver my life from the wicked with
Your sword,
14 With Your hand from men, O LORD,
From men of the world *who have*
their portion in *this* life,
And whose belly You fill with Your
hidden treasure.

They are satisfied with children,
And leave the rest of their
possession for their babes.

15 As for me, I will see Your face in
righteousness;
I shall be satisfied when I awake in
Your likeness.

PSALM 18

God the Sovereign Savior

To the Chief Musician. A Psalm of David the
servant of the LORD, who spoke to the LORD the
words of this song on the day that the LORD delivered him from the hand of all his enemies
and from the hand of Saul. And he said:

1 I will love You, O LORD, my strength.
2 The LORD is my rock and my fortress
and my deliverer;
My God, my strength, in whom I will
trust;
My shield and the horn of my
salvation, my stronghold.
3 I will call upon the LORD, *who is
worthy* to be praised;
So shall I be saved from my enemies.

4 The pangs of death surrounded me,
And the floods of ungodliness made
me afraid.
5 The sorrows of Sheol
surrounded me;
The snares of death confronted me.
6 In my distress I called upon the
LORD,
And cried out to my God;
He heard my voice from His temple,
And my cry came before Him, *even*
to His ears.

7 Then the earth shook and trembled;
The foundations of the hills also
quaked and were shaken,
Because He was angry.
8 Smoke went up from His nostrils,
And devouring fire from His mouth;
Coals were kindled by it.
9 He bowed the heavens also, and
came down
With darkness under His feet.
10 And He rode upon a cherub, and
flew;
He flew upon the wings of the wind.
11 He made darkness His secret place;
His canopy around Him *was* dark
waters
And thick clouds of the skies.

12 From the brightness before Him,
His thick clouds passed with
hailstones and coals of fire.

13 The LORD thundered from heaven,
And the Most High uttered His
voice,
Hailstones and coals of fire.

14 He sent out His arrows and scattered
the foe,
Lightnings in abundance, and He
vanquished them.

15 Then the channels of the sea were
seen,
The foundations of the world were
uncovered
At Your rebuke, O LORD,
At the blast of the breath of Your
nostrils.

16 He sent from above, He took me;
He drew me out of many waters.

17 He delivered me from my strong
enemy,
From those who hated me,
For they were too strong for me.

18 They confronted me in the day of
my calamity,
But the LORD was my support.

19 He also brought me out into a broad
place;
He delivered me because He
delighted in me.

20 The LORD rewarded me according to
my righteousness;
According to the cleanness of my
hands
He has recompensed me.

21 For I have kept the ways of the LORD,
And have not wickedly departed
from my God.

22 For all His judgments *were* before
me,
And I did not put away His statutes
from me.

23 I was also blameless before Him,
And I kept myself from my iniquity.

24 Therefore the LORD has
recompensed me according to my
righteousness,
According to the cleanness of my
hands in His sight.

25 With the merciful You will show
Yourself merciful;
With a blameless man You will
show Yourself blameless;

26 With the pure You will show
Yourself pure;
And with the devious You will show
Yourself shrewd.

27 For You will save the humble
people,
But will bring down haughty looks.

28 For You will light my lamp;
The LORD my God will enlighten my
darkness.

29 For by You I can run against a troop,
By my God I can leap over a wall.

30 *As for* God, His way *is* perfect;
The word of the LORD is proven;
He *is* a shield to all who trust in Him.

31 For who *is* God, except the LORD?
And who *is* a rock, except our God?

32 *It is* God who arms me with
strength,
And makes my way perfect.

33 He makes my feet like the *feet of*
deer,
And sets me on my high places.

34 He teaches my hands to make war,
So that my arms can bend a bow of
bronze.

35 You have also given me the shield
of Your salvation;
Your right hand has held me up,
Your gentleness has made me great.

36 You enlarged my path under me,
So my feet did not slip.

37 I have pursued my enemies and
overtaken them;
Neither did I turn back again till
they were destroyed.

38 I have wounded them,
So that they could not rise;
They have fallen under my feet.

39 For You have armed me with
strength for the battle;
You have subdued under me those
who rose up against me.

40 You have also given me the necks
of my enemies,
So that I destroyed those who
hated me.

41 They cried out, but *there was* none
to save;
Even to the LORD, but He did not
answer them.

42 Then I beat them as fine as the dust
before the wind;
I cast them out like dirt in the streets.

43 You have delivered me from the
   strivings of the people;
   You have made me the head of the
   nations;
   A people I have not known shall
   serve me.
44 As soon as they hear of me they
   obey me;
   The foreigners submit to me.
45 The foreigners fade away,
   And come frightened from their
   hideouts.

46 The LORD lives!
   Blessed *be* my Rock!
   Let the God of my salvation be
   exalted.
47 *It is* God who avenges me,
   And subdues the peoples under me;
48 He delivers me from my enemies.
   You also lift me up above those who
   rise against me;
   You have delivered me from the
   violent man.
49 Therefore I will give thanks to You,
   O LORD, among the Gentiles,
   And sing praises to Your name.

50 Great deliverance He gives to His
   king,
   And shows mercy to His anointed,
   To David and his descendants
   forevermore.

PSALM 19

The Perfect Revelation of the LORD

To the Chief Musician. A Psalm of David.

1 The heavens declare the glory
   of God;
   And the firmament shows His
   handiwork.
2 Day unto day utters speech,
   And night unto night reveals
   knowledge.
3 *There is* no speech nor language
   Where their voice is not heard.
4 Their line has gone out through all
   the earth,
   And their words to the end of the
   world.

   In them He has set a tabernacle for
   the sun,
5 Which *is* like a bridegroom coming
   out of his chamber,
   And rejoices like a strong man to
   run its race.

6 Its rising *is* from one end of heaven,
   And its circuit to the other end;
   And there is nothing hidden from its
   heat.

7 The law of the LORD *is* perfect,
   converting the soul;
   The testimony of the LORD *is* sure,
   making wise the simple;
8 The statutes of the LORD *are* right,
   rejoicing the heart;
   The commandment of the LORD *is*
   pure, enlightening the eyes;
9 The fear of the LORD *is* clean,
   enduring forever;
   The judgments of the LORD *are* true
   and righteous altogether.
10 More to be desired *are they* than
   gold,
   Yea, than much fine gold;
   Sweeter also than honey and the
   honeycomb.
11 Moreover by them Your servant is
   warned,
   And in keeping them *there is* great
   reward.

12 Who can understand *his* errors?
   Cleanse me from secret *faults.*
13 Keep back Your servant also from
   presumptuous *sins;*
   Let them not have dominion
   over me.
   Then I shall be blameless,
   And I shall be innocent of great
   transgression.

14 Let the words of my mouth and the
   meditation of my heart
   Be acceptable in Your sight,
   O LORD, my strength and my
   Redeemer.

PSALM 20

The Assurance of God's Saving Work

To the Chief Musician. A Psalm of David.

1 May the LORD answer you in the day
   of trouble;
   May the name of the God of Jacob
   defend you;
2 May He send you help from the
   sanctuary,
   And strengthen you out of Zion;
3 May He remember all your
   offerings,
   And accept your burnt sacrifice.
                                        Selah

4 May He grant you according to your
    heart's *desire*,
  And fulfill all your purpose.
5 We will rejoice in your salvation,
  And in the name of our God we will
    set up *our* banners!
  May the LORD fulfill all your
    petitions.

6 Now I know that the LORD saves His
    anointed;
  He will answer him from His holy
    heaven
  With the saving strength of His right
    hand.

7 Some *trust* in chariots, and some in
    horses;
  But we will remember the name of
    the LORD our God.
8 They have bowed down and fallen;
  But we have risen and stand upright.

9 Save, LORD!
  May the King answer us when we
    call.

PSALM 21

Joy in the Salvation of the LORD

To the Chief Musician. A Psalm of David.

1 The king shall have joy in Your
    strength, O LORD;
  And in Your salvation how greatly
    shall he rejoice!
2 You have given him his heart's
    desire,
  And have not withheld the request
    of his lips.   Selah

3 For You meet him with the blessings
    of goodness;
  You set a crown of pure gold upon
    his head.
4 He asked life from You, *and* You
    gave *it* to him—
  Length of days forever and ever.
5 His glory *is* great in Your salvation;
  Honor and majesty You have placed
    upon him.
6 For You have made him most
    blessed forever;
  You have made him exceedingly
    glad with Your presence.
7 For the king trusts in the LORD,
  And through the mercy of the Most
    High he shall not be moved.

8 Your hand will find all Your
    enemies;
  Your right hand will find those who
    hate You.
9 You shall make them as a fiery oven
    in the time of Your anger;
  The LORD shall swallow them up in
    His wrath,
  And the fire shall devour them.
10 Their offspring You shall destroy
    from the earth,
  And their descendants from among
    the sons of men.
11 For they intended evil against You;
  They devised a plot *which* they are
    not able *to perform*.
12 Therefore You will make them turn
    their back;
  You will make ready *Your arrows*
    on Your string toward their faces.

13 Be exalted, O LORD, in Your own
    strength!
  We will sing and praise Your power.

PSALM 22

The Suffering, Praise, and Posterity of the Messiah

To the Chief Musician. Set to "The Deer of the
    Dawn." A Psalm of David.

1 My God, My God, why have You
    forsaken Me?
  Why are You so far from helping Me,
  And from the words of My groaning?
2 O My God, I cry in the daytime, but
    You do not hear;
  And in the night season, and am not
    silent.

3 But You *are* holy,
  Enthroned in the praises of Israel.
4 Our fathers trusted in You;
  They trusted, and You delivered
    them.
5 They cried to You, and were
    delivered;
  They trusted in You, and were not
    ashamed.

6 But I *am* a worm, and no man;
  A reproach of men, and despised by
    the people.
7 All those who see Me ridicule Me;
  They shoot out the lip, they shake
    the head, *saying*,

8 "He trusted in the LORD, let Him
   rescue Him;
   Let Him deliver Him, since He
   delights in Him!"

9 But You *are* He who took Me out
   of the womb;
   You made Me trust *while* on My
   mother's breasts.
10 I was cast upon You from birth.
   From My mother's womb
   You *have been* My God.
11 Be not far from Me,
   For trouble *is* near;
   For *there is* none to help.

12 Many bulls have surrounded Me;
   Strong *bulls* of Bashan have
   encircled Me.
13 They gape at Me *with* their mouths,
   Like a raging and roaring lion.

14 I am poured out like water,
   And all My bones are out of joint;
   My heart is like wax;
   It has melted within Me.
15 My strength is dried up like a
   potsherd,
   And My tongue clings to My jaws;
   You have brought Me to the dust of
   death.

16 For dogs have surrounded Me;
   The congregation of the wicked has
   enclosed Me.
   They pierced My hands and My feet;
17 I can count all My bones.
   They look *and* stare at Me.
18 They divide My garments among
   them,
   And for My clothing they cast lots.

19 But You, O LORD, do not be far
   from Me;
   O My Strength, hasten to help Me!
20 Deliver Me from the sword,
   My precious *life* from the power of
   the dog.
21 Save Me from the lion's mouth
   And from the horns of the wild oxen!

   You have answered Me.

22 I will declare Your name to My
   brethren;
   In the midst of the assembly I will
   praise You.

23 You who fear the LORD, praise Him!
   All you descendants of Jacob,
   glorify Him,
   And fear Him, all you offspring of
   Israel!
24 For He has not despised nor
   abhorred the affliction of the
   afflicted;
   Nor has He hidden His face
   from Him;
   But when He cried to Him, He heard.

25 My praise *shall be* of You in the
   great assembly;
   I will pay My vows before those who
   fear Him.
26 The poor shall eat and be satisfied;
   Those who seek Him will praise the
   LORD.
   Let your heart live forever!

27 All the ends of the world
   Shall remember and turn to the
   LORD,
   And all the families of the nations
   Shall worship before You.
28 For the kingdom *is* the LORD's,
   And He rules over the nations.

29 All the prosperous of the earth
   Shall eat and worship;
   All those who go down to the dust
   Shall bow before Him,
   Even he who cannot keep himself
   alive.

30 A posterity shall serve Him.
   It will be recounted of the Lord to
   the *next* generation,
31 They will come and declare His
   righteousness to a people who
   will be born,
   That He has done *this.*

PSALM 23

The LORD the Shepherd of His People

A Psalm of David.

1 The LORD *is* my shepherd;
   I shall not want.
2 He makes me to lie down in green
   pastures;
   He leads me beside the still waters.
3 He restores my soul;
   He leads me in the paths of
   righteousness
   For His name's sake.

4 Yea, though I walk through the
      valley of the shadow of death,
   I will fear no evil;
   For You *are* with me;
   Your rod and Your staff, they
      comfort me.

5 You prepare a table before me in the
      presence of my enemies;
   You anoint my head with oil;
   My cup runs over.
6 Surely goodness and mercy shall
      follow me
   All the days of my life;
   And I will dwell in the house of the
      LORD
   Forever.

PSALM 24

The King of Glory and His Kingdom

A Psalm of David.

1 The earth *is* the LORD's, and all its
      fullness,
   The world and those who dwell
      therein.
2 For He has founded it upon the seas,
   And established it upon the waters.

3 Who may ascend into the hill of the
      LORD?
   Or who may stand in His holy place?
4 He who has clean hands and a pure
      heart,
   Who has not lifted up his soul to an
      idol,
   Nor sworn deceitfully.
5 He shall receive blessing from the
      LORD,
   And righteousness from the God of
      his salvation.
6 This *is* Jacob, the generation of
      those who seek Him,
   Who seek Your face.   Selah

7 Lift up your heads, O you gates!
   And be lifted up, you everlasting
      doors!
   And the King of glory shall come in.
8 Who *is* this King of glory?
   The LORD strong and mighty,
   The LORD mighty in battle.
9 Lift up your heads, O you gates!
   Lift up, you everlasting doors!
   And the King of glory shall come in.

10 Who is this King of glory?
   The LORD of hosts,
   He *is* the King of glory.   Selah

PSALM 25

A Plea for Deliverance and Forgiveness

A Psalm of David.

1 To You, O LORD, I lift up my soul.
2 O my God, I trust in You;
   Let me not be ashamed;
   Let not my enemies triumph
      over me.
3 Indeed, let no one who waits on You
      be ashamed;
   Let those be ashamed who deal
      treacherously without cause.

4 Show me Your ways, O LORD;
   Teach me Your paths.
5 Lead me in Your truth and teach me,
   For You *are* the God of my salvation;
   On You I wait all the day.

6 Remember, O LORD, Your tender
      mercies and Your
      lovingkindnesses,
   For they *are* from of old.
7 Do not remember the sins of my
      youth, nor my transgressions;
   According to Your mercy
      remember me,
   For Your goodness' sake, O LORD.

8 Good and upright *is* the LORD;
   Therefore He teaches sinners in
      the way.
9 The humble He guides in justice,
   And the humble He teaches His way.
10 All the paths of the LORD *are* mercy
      and truth,
   To such as keep His covenant and
      His testimonies.
11 For Your name's sake, O LORD,
   Pardon my iniquity, for it *is* great.

12 Who *is* the man that fears the LORD?
   Him shall He[b] teach in the way He[b]
      chooses.
13 He himself shall dwell in prosperity,
   And his descendants shall inherit
      the earth.
14 The secret of the LORD *is* with those
      who fear Him,

b Or *he*

And He will show them His
covenant.
15 My eyes *are* ever toward the LORD,
For He shall pluck my feet out of
the net.

16 Turn Yourself to me, and have
mercy on me,
For I *am* desolate and afflicted.
17 The troubles of my heart have
enlarged;
Bring me out of my distresses!
18 Look on my affliction and my pain,
And forgive all my sins.
19 Consider my enemies, for they are
many;
And they hate me with cruel hatred.
20 Keep my soul, and deliver me;
Let me not be ashamed, for I put my
trust in You.
21 Let integrity and uprightness
preserve me,
For I wait for You.

22 Redeem Israel, O God,
Out of all their troubles!

PSALM 26

A Prayer for Divine Scrutiny and Redemption

A Psalm of David.

1 Vindicate me, O LORD,
For I have walked in my integrity.
I have also trusted in the LORD;
I shall not slip.
2 Examine me, O LORD, and prove me;
Try my mind and my heart.
3 For Your lovingkindness *is* before
my eyes,
And I have walked in Your truth.
4 I have not sat with idolatrous
mortals,
Nor will I go in with hypocrites.
5 I have hated the assembly of
evildoers,
And will not sit with the wicked.

6 I will wash my hands in innocence;
So I will go about Your altar,
O LORD,
7 That I may proclaim with the voice
of thanksgiving,
And tell of all Your wondrous works.
8 LORD, I have loved the habitation of
Your house,
And the place where Your glory
dwells.

9 Do not gather my soul with sinners,
Nor my life with bloodthirsty men,
10 In whose hands *is* a sinister scheme,
And whose right hand is full of
bribes.
11 But as for me, I will walk in my
integrity;
Redeem me and be merciful to me.
12 My foot stands in an even place;
In the congregations I will bless the
LORD.

PSALM 27

An Exuberant Declaration of Faith

A Psalm of David.

1 The LORD *is* my light and my
salvation;
Whom shall I fear?
The LORD *is* the strength of my life;
Of whom shall I be afraid?
2 When the wicked came against me
To eat up my flesh,
My enemies and foes,
They stumbled and fell.
3 Though an army may encamp
against me,
My heart shall not fear;
Though war may rise against me,
In this I *will be* confident.

4 One *thing* I have desired of the LORD,
That will I seek:
That I may dwell in the house of the
LORD
All the days of my life,
To behold the beauty of the LORD,
And to inquire in His temple.
5 For in the time of trouble
He shall hide me in His pavilion;
In the secret place of His tabernacle
He shall hide me;
He shall set me high upon a rock.

6 And now my head shall be lifted up
above my enemies all around me;
Therefore I will offer sacrifices of
joy in His tabernacle;
I will sing, yes, I will sing praises
to the LORD.

7 Hear, O LORD, *when* I cry with my
voice!
Have mercy also upon me, and
answer me.
8 *When You said,* "Seek My face,"
My heart said to You, "Your face,
LORD, I will seek."

9 Do not hide Your face from me;
   Do not turn Your servant away in
      anger;
   You have been my help;
   Do not leave me nor forsake me,
   O God of my salvation.
10 When my father and my mother
      forsake me,
   Then the LORD will take care of me.

11 Teach me Your way, O LORD,
   And lead me in a smooth path,
      because of my enemies.
12 Do not deliver me to the will of my
      adversaries;
   For false witnesses have risen
      against me,
   And such as breathe out violence.
13 *I would have lost heart,* unless I had
      believed
   That I would see the goodness of the
      LORD
   In the land of the living.

14 Wait on the LORD;
   Be of good courage,
   And He shall strengthen your heart;
   Wait, I say, on the LORD!

PSALM 28

Rejoicing in Answered Prayer

A Psalm of David.

1 To You I will cry, O LORD my Rock:
   Do not be silent to me,
   Lest, if You *are* silent to me,
   I become like those who go down
      to the pit.
2 Hear the voice of my supplications
   When I cry to You,
   When I lift up my hands toward
      Your holy sanctuary.

3 Do not take me away with the
      wicked
   And with the workers of iniquity,
   Who speak peace to their neighbors,
   But evil *is* in their hearts.
4 Give them according to their deeds,
   And according to the wickedness of
      their endeavors;
   Give them according to the work of
      their hands;
   Render to them what they deserve.
5 Because they do not regard the
      works of the LORD,
   Nor the operation of His hands,

He shall destroy them
And not build them up.

6 Blessed *be* the LORD,
   Because He has heard the voice of
      my supplications!
7 The LORD *is* my strength and my
      shield;
   My heart trusted in Him, and I am
      helped;
   Therefore my heart greatly rejoices,
   And with my song I will praise Him.

8 The LORD *is* their strength,
   And He *is* the saving refuge of His
      anointed.
9 Save Your people,
   And bless Your inheritance;
   Shepherd them also,
   And bear them up forever.

PSALM 29

Praise to God in His Holiness and Majesty

A Psalm of David.

1 Give unto the LORD, O you mighty
      ones,
   Give unto the LORD glory and
      strength.
2 Give unto the LORD the glory due to
      His name;
   Worship the LORD in the beauty of
      holiness.

3 The voice of the LORD *is* over the
      waters;
   The God of glory thunders;
   The LORD *is* over many waters.
4 The voice of the LORD *is* powerful;
   The voice of the LORD *is* full of
      majesty.

5 The voice of the LORD breaks the
      cedars,
   Yes, the LORD splinters the cedars
      of Lebanon.
6 He makes them also skip like a calf,
   Lebanon and Sirion like a young
      wild ox.
7 The voice of the LORD divides the
      flames of fire.

8 The voice of the LORD shakes the
      wilderness;
   The LORD shakes the Wilderness of
      Kadesh.

9 The voice of the LORD makes the
      deer give birth,
   And strips the forests bare;
   And in His temple everyone says,
      "Glory!"

10 The LORD sat *enthroned* at the Flood,
   And the LORD sits as King forever.
11 The LORD will give strength to His
      people;
   The LORD will bless His people with
      peace.

PSALM 30

The Blessedness of Answered Prayer

A Psalm. A Song at the dedication of the house
of David.

1 I will extol You, O LORD, for You
      have lifted me up,
   And have not let my foes rejoice
      over me.
2 O LORD my God, I cried out to You,
   And You healed me.
3 O LORD, You brought my soul up
      from the grave;
   You have kept me alive, that I
      should not go down to the pit.

4 Sing praise to the LORD, you saints
      of His,
   And give thanks at the
      remembrance of His holy name.
5 For His anger *is but for* a moment,
   His favor *is for* life;
   Weeping may endure for a night,
   But joy *comes* in the morning.

6 Now in my prosperity I said,
   "I shall never be moved."
7 LORD, by Your favor You have made
      my mountain stand strong;
   You hid Your face, *and* I was
      troubled.

8 I cried out to You, O LORD;
   And to the LORD I made supplication:
9 "What profit *is there* in my blood,
   When I go down to the pit?
   Will the dust praise You?
   Will it declare Your truth?
10 Hear, O LORD, and have mercy
      on me;
   LORD, be my helper!"

11 You have turned for me my
      mourning into dancing;

You have put off my sackcloth and
   clothed me with gladness,
12 To the end that *my* glory may sing
      praise to You and not be silent.
   O LORD my God, I will give thanks
      to You forever.

PSALM 31

The LORD a Fortress in Adversity

To the Chief Musician. A Psalm of David.

1 In You, O LORD, I put my trust;
   Let me never be ashamed;
   Deliver me in Your righteousness.
2 Bow down Your ear to me,
   Deliver me speedily;
   Be my rock of refuge,
   A fortress of defense to save me.

3 For You *are* my rock and my
      fortress;
   Therefore, for Your name's sake,
   Lead me and guide me.
4 Pull me out of the net which they
      have secretly laid for me,
   For You *are* my strength.
5 Into Your hand I commit my spirit;
   You have redeemed me, O LORD God
      of truth.

6 I have hated those who regard
      useless idols;
   But I trust in the LORD.
7 I will be glad and rejoice in Your
      mercy,
   For You have considered my
      trouble;
   You have known my soul in
      adversities,
8 And have not shut me up into the
      hand of the enemy;
   You have set my feet in a wide place.

9 Have mercy on me, O LORD, for I am
      in trouble;
   My eye wastes away with grief,
   Yes, my soul and my body!
10 For my life is spent with grief,
   And my years with sighing;
   My strength fails because of my
      iniquity,
   And my bones waste away.
11 I am a reproach among all my
      enemies,
   But especially among my neighbors,
   And *am* repulsive to my
      acquaintances;

Those who see me outside flee
    from me.
12 I am forgotten like a dead man, out
    of mind;
  I am like a broken vessel.
13 For I hear the slander of many;
  Fear *is* on every side;
  While they take counsel together
    against me,
  They scheme to take away my life.

14 But as for me, I trust in You, O LORD;
  I say, "You *are* my God."
15 My times *are* in Your hand;
  Deliver me from the hand of my
    enemies,
  And from those who persecute me.
16 Make Your face shine upon Your
    servant;
  Save me for Your mercies' sake.
17 Do not let me be ashamed, O LORD,
    for I have called upon You;
  Let the wicked be ashamed;
  Let them be silent in the grave.
18 Let the lying lips be put to silence,
  Which speak insolent things
    proudly and contemptuously
    against the righteous.

19 Oh, how great *is* Your goodness,
  Which You have laid up for those
    who fear You,
  Which You have prepared for those
    who trust in You
  In the presence of the sons of men!
20 You shall hide them in the secret
    place of Your presence
  From the plots of man;
  You shall keep them secretly in a
    pavilion
  From the strife of tongues.

21 Blessed *be* the LORD,
  For He has shown me His marvelous
    kindness in a strong city!
22 For I said in my haste,
  "I am cut off from before Your eyes";
  Nevertheless You heard the voice of
    my supplications
  When I cried out to You.

23 Oh, love the LORD, all you His saints!
  For the LORD preserves the faithful,
  And fully repays the proud person.
24 Be of good courage,
  And He shall strengthen your heart,
  All you who hope in the LORD.

PSALM 32

The Joy of Forgiveness

A Psalm of David. A Contemplation.

1 Blessed *is he whose* transgression *is*
    forgiven,
  Whose sin *is* covered.
2 Blessed *is* the man to whom the
    LORD does not impute iniquity,
  And in whose spirit *there is* no
    deceit.

3 When I kept silent, my bones
    grew old
  Through my groaning all the day
    long.
4 For day and night Your hand was
    heavy upon me;
  My vitality was turned into the
    drought of summer.   Selah
5 I acknowledged my sin to You,
  And my iniquity I have not hidden.
  I said, "I will confess my
    transgressions to the LORD,"
  And You forgave the iniquity of
    my sin.   Selah

6 For this cause everyone who is godly
    shall pray to You
  In a time when You may be found;
  Surely in a flood of great waters
  They shall not come near him.
7 You *are* my hiding place;
  You shall preserve me from trouble;
  You shall surround me with songs
    of deliverance.   Selah

8 I will instruct you and teach you in
    the way you should go;
  I will guide you with My eye.
9 Do not be like the horse *or* like the
    mule,
  Which have no understanding,
  Which must be harnessed with bit
    and bridle,
  Else they will not come near you.

10 Many sorrows *shall be* to the
    wicked;
  But he who trusts in the LORD, mercy
    shall surround him.
11 Be glad in the LORD and rejoice, you
    righteous;
  And shout for joy, all *you* upright
    in heart!

PSALM 33

The Sovereignty of the Lord in Creation and History

1 Rejoice in the Lord, O you
    righteous!
    For praise from the upright is
    beautiful.
2 Praise the Lord with the harp;
    Make melody to Him with an
    instrument of ten strings.
3 Sing to Him a new song;
    Play skillfully with a shout of joy.

4 For the word of the Lord *is* right,
    And all His work *is done* in truth.
5 He loves righteousness and justice;
    The earth is full of the goodness of
    the Lord.

6 By the word of the Lord the heavens
    were made,
    And all the host of them by the
    breath of His mouth.
7 He gathers the waters of the sea
    together as a heap;
    He lays up the deep in storehouses.

8 Let all the earth fear the Lord;
    Let all the inhabitants of the world
    stand in awe of Him.
9 For He spoke, and it was *done;*
    He commanded, and it stood fast.

10 The Lord brings the counsel of the
    nations to nothing;
    He makes the plans of the peoples
    of no effect.
11 The counsel of the Lord stands
    forever,
    The plans of His heart to all
    generations.
12 Blessed *is* the nation whose God *is*
    the Lord,
    The people He has chosen as His
    own inheritance.

13 The Lord looks from heaven;
    He sees all the sons of men.
14 From the place of His dwelling He
    looks
    On all the inhabitants of the earth;
15 He fashions their hearts
    individually;
    He considers all their works.

16 No king *is* saved by the multitude
    of an army;
    A mighty man is not delivered by
    great strength.
17 A horse *is* a vain hope for safety;
    Neither shall it deliver *any* by its
    great strength.

18 Behold, the eye of the Lord *is* on
    those who fear Him,
    On those who hope in His mercy,
19 To deliver their soul from death,
    And to keep them alive in famine.

20 Our soul waits for the Lord;
    He *is* our help and our shield.
21 For our heart shall rejoice in Him,
    Because we have trusted in His holy
    name.
22 Let Your mercy, O Lord, be upon us,
    Just as we hope in You.

PSALM 34

The Happiness of Those Who Trust in God

A Psalm of David when he pretended madness
before Abimelech, who drove him away,
and he departed.

1 I will bless the Lord at all times;
    His praise *shall* continually *be* in my
    mouth.
2 My soul shall make its boast in the
    Lord;
    The humble shall hear *of it* and be
    glad.
3 Oh, magnify the Lord with me,
    And let us exalt His name together.

4 I sought the Lord, and He heard me,
    And delivered me from all my fears.
5 They looked to Him and were
    radiant,
    And their faces were not ashamed.
6 This poor man cried out, and the
    Lord heard *him,*
    And saved him out of all his troubles.
7 The angel[c] of the Lord encamps all
    around those who fear Him,
    And delivers them.

8 Oh, taste and see that the Lord *is*
    good;
    Blessed *is* the man *who* trusts
    in Him!

c Or *Angel*

9 Oh, fear the LORD, you His saints!
There is no want to those who
fear Him.
10 The young lions lack and suffer
hunger;
But those who seek the LORD shall
not lack any good *thing.*

11 Come, you children, listen to me;
I will teach you the fear of the LORD.
12 Who *is* the man *who* desires life,
And loves *many* days, that he may
see good?
13 Keep your tongue from evil,
And your lips from speaking deceit.
14 Depart from evil and do good;
Seek peace and pursue it.

15 The eyes of the LORD *are* on the
righteous,
And His ears *are open* to their cry.
16 The face of the LORD *is* against those
who do evil,
To cut off the remembrance of them
from the earth.

17 *The righteous* cry out, and the LORD
hears,
And delivers them out of all their
troubles.
18 The LORD *is* near to those who have
a broken heart,
And saves such as have a contrite
spirit.

19 Many *are* the afflictions of the
righteous,
But the LORD delivers him out of
them all.
20 He guards all his bones;
Not one of them is broken.
21 Evil shall slay the wicked,
And those who hate the righteous
shall be condemned.
22 The LORD redeems the soul of His
servants,
And none of those who trust in Him
shall be condemned.

PSALM 35

The LORD the Avenger of His People

A Psalm of David.

1 Plead *my cause,* O LORD, with those
who strive with me;

Fight against those who fight
against me.
2 Take hold of shield and buckler,
And stand up for my help.
3 Also draw out the spear,
And stop those who pursue me.
Say to my soul,
"I *am* your salvation."

4 Let those be put to shame and
brought to dishonor
Who seek after my life;
Let those be turned back and
brought to confusion
Who plot my hurt.
5 Let them be like chaff before the
wind,
And let the angel[c] of the LORD chase
them.
6 Let their way be dark and slippery,
And let the angel of the LORD pursue
them.
7 For without cause they have hidden
their net for me *in* a pit,
Which they have dug without cause
for my life.
8 Let destruction come upon him
unexpectedly,
And let his net that he has hidden
catch himself;
Into that very destruction let him
fall.

9 And my soul shall be joyful in the
LORD;
It shall rejoice in His salvation.
10 All my bones shall say,
"LORD, who *is* like You,
Delivering the poor from him who
is too strong for him,
Yes, the poor and the needy from
him who plunders him?"

11 Fierce witnesses rise up;
They ask me *things* that I do not
know.
12 They reward me evil for good,
To the sorrow of my soul.
13 But as for me, when they were sick,
My clothing *was* sackcloth;
I humbled myself with fasting;
And my prayer would return to my
own heart.
14 I paced about as though *he were* my
friend *or* brother;

c Or *Angel*

I bowed down heavily, as one who
  mourns *for his* mother.

15 But in my adversity they rejoiced
   And gathered together;
   Attackers gathered against me,
   And I did not know *it;*
   They tore *at me* and did not cease;
16 With ungodly mockers at feasts
   They gnashed at me with their teeth.

17 Lord, how long will You look on?
   Rescue me from their destructions,
   My precious *life* from the lions.
18 I will give You thanks in the great
     assembly;
   I will praise You among many
     people.

19 Let them not rejoice over me who
     are wrongfully my enemies;
   Nor let them wink with the eye who
     hate me without a cause.
20 For they do not speak peace,
   But they devise deceitful matters
   Against *the* quiet ones in the land.
21 They also opened their mouth wide
     against me,
   And said, "Aha, aha!
   Our eyes have seen *it."*

22 *This* You have seen, O LORD;
   Do not keep silence.
   O Lord, do not be far from me.
23 Stir up Yourself, and awake to my
     vindication,
   To my cause, my God and my Lord.
24 Vindicate me, O LORD my God,
     according to Your righteousness;
   And let them not rejoice over me.
25 Let them not say in their hearts,
     "Ah, so we would have it!"
   Let them not say, "We have
     swallowed him up."

26 Let them be ashamed and brought
     to mutual confusion
   Who rejoice at my hurt;
   Let them be clothed with shame and
     dishonor
   Who exalt themselves against me.

27 Let them shout for joy and be glad,
   Who favor my righteous cause;
   And let them say continually,
   "Let the LORD be magnified,
   Who has pleasure in the prosperity
     of His servant."

28 And my tongue shall speak of Your
     righteousness
   And of Your praise all the day long.

PSALM 36

Man's Wickedness and God's Perfections

To the Chief Musician. A Psalm of David the
servant of the LORD.

1 An oracle within my heart
   concerning the transgression of
   the wicked:
   There is no fear of God before his
     eyes.
2 For he flatters himself in his own
     eyes,
   When he finds out his iniquity *and*
     when he hates.
3 The words of his mouth *are*
   wickedness and deceit;
   He has ceased to be wise *and* to do
     good.
4 He devises wickedness on his bed;
   He sets himself in a way *that is* not
     good;
   He does not abhor evil.

5 Your mercy, O LORD, *is* in the
     heavens;
   Your faithfulness *reaches* to the
     clouds.
6 Your righteousness *is* like the great
     mountains;
   Your judgments *are* a great deep;
   O LORD, You preserve man and
     beast.

7 How precious *is* Your
     lovingkindness, O God!
   Therefore the children of men put
     their trust under the shadow of
     Your wings.
8 They are abundantly satisfied with
     the fullness of Your house,
   And You give them drink from the
     river of Your pleasures.
9 For with You *is* the fountain of life;
   In Your light we see light.

10 Oh, continue Your lovingkindness to
     those who know You,
   And Your righteousness to the
     upright in heart.
11 Let not the foot of pride come
     against me,
   And let not the hand of the wicked
     drive me away.

12 There the workers of iniquity have
   fallen;
   They have been cast down and are
   not able to rise.

PSALM 37

The Heritage of the Righteous and the Calamity of the Wicked

A Psalm of David.

1 Do not fret because of evildoers,
   Nor be envious of the workers of
   iniquity.
2 For they shall soon be cut down like
   the grass,
   And wither as the green herb.

3 Trust in the LORD, and do good;
   Dwell in the land, and feed on His
   faithfulness.
4 Delight yourself also in the LORD,
   And He shall give you the desires
   of your heart.

5 Commit your way to the LORD,
   Trust also in Him,
   And He shall bring it to pass.
6 He shall bring forth your
   righteousness as the light,
   And your justice as the noonday.

7 Rest in the LORD, and wait patiently
   for Him;
   Do not fret because of him who
   prospers in his way,
   Because of the man who brings
   wicked schemes to pass.
8 Cease from anger, and forsake
   wrath;
   Do not fret—it only causes harm.

9 For evildoers shall be cut off;
   But those who wait on the LORD,
   They shall inherit the earth.
10 For yet a little while and the wicked
   shall be no more;
   Indeed, you will look carefully for
   his place,
   But it shall be no more.
11 But the meek shall inherit the earth,
   And shall delight themselves in the
   abundance of peace.

12 The wicked plots against the just,
   And gnashes at him with his teeth.
13 The Lord laughs at him,
   For He sees that his day is coming.
14 The wicked have drawn the sword

And have bent their bow,
To cast down the poor and needy,
To slay those who are of upright
conduct.
15 Their sword shall enter their own
   heart,
   And their bows shall be broken.

16 A little that a righteous man has
   Is better than the riches of many
   wicked.
17 For the arms of the wicked shall be
   broken,
   But the LORD upholds the righteous.

18 The LORD knows the days of the
   upright,
   And their inheritance shall be
   forever.
19 They shall not be ashamed in the
   evil time,
   And in the days of famine they shall
   be satisfied.
20 But the wicked shall perish;
   And the enemies of the LORD,
   Like the splendor of the meadows,
   shall vanish.
   Into smoke they shall vanish away.

21 The wicked borrows and does not
   repay,
   But the righteous shows mercy and
   gives.
22 For those blessed by Him shall
   inherit the earth,
   But those cursed by Him shall be
   cut off.

23 The steps of a good man are ordered
   by the LORD,
   And He delights in his way.
24 Though he fall, he shall not be
   utterly cast down;
   For the LORD upholds him with His
   hand.

25 I have been young, and now am old;
   Yet I have not seen the righteous
   forsaken,
   Nor his descendants begging bread.
26 He is ever merciful, and lends;
   And his descendants are blessed.

27 Depart from evil, and do good;
   And dwell forevermore.
28 For the LORD loves justice,
   And does not forsake His saints;
   They are preserved forever,

But the descendants of the wicked
  shall be cut off.
29 The righteous shall inherit the land,
  And dwell in it forever.

30 The mouth of the righteous speaks
  wisdom,
  And his tongue talks of justice.
31 The law of his God *is* in his heart;
  None of his steps shall slide.

32 The wicked watches the righteous,
  And seeks to slay him.
33 The LORD will not leave him in his
  hand,
  Nor condemn him when he is
  judged.

34 Wait on the LORD,
  And keep His way,
  And He shall exalt you to inherit the
  land;
  When the wicked are cut off, you
  shall see *it*.
35 I have seen the wicked in great
  power,
  And spreading himself like a native
  green tree.
36 Yet he passed away, and behold, he
  was no *more;*
  Indeed I sought him, but he could
  not be found.

37 Mark the blameless *man*, and
  observe the upright;
  For the future of *that* man *is* peace.
38 But the transgressors shall be
  destroyed together;
  The future of the wicked shall be
  cut off.

39 But the salvation of the righteous *is*
  from the LORD;
  He is their strength in the time of
  trouble.
40 And the LORD shall help them and
  deliver them;
  He shall deliver them from the
  wicked,
  And save them,
  Because they trust in Him.

PSALM 38

Prayer in Time of Chastening

A Psalm of David. To bring to remembrance.
1 O LORD, do not rebuke me in Your
  wrath,

Nor chasten me in Your hot
  displeasure!
2 For Your arrows pierce me deeply,
  And Your hand presses me down.

3 *There is* no soundness in my flesh
  Because of Your anger,
  Nor *any* health in my bones
  Because of my sin.
4 For my iniquities have gone over my
  head;
  Like a heavy burden they are too
  heavy for me.
5 My wounds are foul *and* festering
  Because of my foolishness.

6 I am troubled, I am bowed down
  greatly;
  I go mourning all the day long.
7 For my loins are full of
  inflammation,
  And *there is* no soundness in my
  flesh.
8 I am feeble and severely broken;
  I groan because of the turmoil of my
  heart.

9 Lord, all my desire *is* before You;
  And my sighing is not hidden
  from You.
10 My heart pants, my strength
  fails me;
  As for the light of my eyes, it also
  has gone from me.

11 My loved ones and my friends stand
  aloof from my plague,
  And my relatives stand afar off.
12 Those also who seek my life lay
  snares *for me;*
  Those who seek my hurt speak of
  destruction,
  And plan deception all the day long.

13 But I, like a deaf *man*, do not hear;
  And *I am* like a mute *who* does not
  open his mouth.
14 Thus I am like a man who does not
  hear,
  And in whose mouth *is* no response.

15 For in You, O LORD, I hope;
  You will hear, O Lord my God.
16 For I said, *"Hear me,* lest they
  rejoice over me,
  Lest, when my foot slips, they exalt
  themselves against me."

17 For I *am* ready to fall,
  And my sorrow *is* continually
   before me.
18 For I will declare my iniquity;
  I will be in anguish over my sin.
19 But my enemies *are* vigorous, *and*
   they are strong;
  And those who hate me wrongfully
   have multiplied.
20 Those also who render evil for good,
  They are my adversaries, because I
   follow *what is* good.

21 Do not forsake me, O LORD;
  O my God, be not far from me!
22 Make haste to help me,
  O Lord, my salvation!

PSALM 39

Prayer for Wisdom and Forgiveness

To the Chief Musician. To Jeduthun.
A Psalm of David.

1 I said, "I will guard my ways,
  Lest I sin with my tongue;
  I will restrain my mouth with a
   muzzle,
  While the wicked are before me."
2 I was mute with silence,
  I held my peace *even* from good;
  And my sorrow was stirred up.
3 My heart was hot within me;
  While I was musing, the fire burned.
  Then I spoke with my tongue:

4 "LORD, make me to know my end,
  And what *is* the measure of my days,
  That I may know how frail I *am*.
5 Indeed, You have made my days *as*
   handbreadths,
  And my age *is* as nothing
   before You;
  Certainly every man at his best state
  is but vapor.   Selah
6 Surely every man walks about like
   a shadow;
  Surely they busy themselves in vain;
  He heaps up *riches*,
  And does not know who will gather
   them.

7 "And now, Lord, what do I wait for?
  My hope *is* in You.
8 Deliver me from all my
   transgressions;
  Do not make me the reproach of the
   foolish.

9 I was mute, I did not open my mouth,
  Because it was You who did *it*.
10 Remove Your plague from me;
  I am consumed by the blow of Your
   hand.
11 When with rebukes You correct
   man for iniquity,
  You make his beauty melt away like
   a moth;
  Surely every man *is* vapor.   Selah

12 "Hear my prayer, O LORD,
  And give ear to my cry;
  Do not be silent at my tears;
  For I *am* a stranger with You,
  A sojourner, as all my fathers *were*.
13 Remove Your gaze from me, that I
   may regain strength,
  Before I go away and am no more."

PSALM 40

Faith Persevering in Trial

To the Chief Musician. A Psalm of David.

1 I waited patiently for the LORD;
  And He inclined to me,
  And heard my cry.
2 He also brought me up out of a
   horrible pit,
  Out of the miry clay,
  And set my feet upon a rock,
  And established my steps.
3 He has put a new song in my
   mouth—
  Praise to our God;
  Many will see *it* and fear,
  And will trust in the LORD.

4 Blessed *is* that man who makes the
   LORD his trust,
  And does not respect the proud, nor
   such as turn aside to lies.
5 Many, O LORD my God, *are* Your
   wonderful works
  Which You have done;
  And Your thoughts toward us
  Cannot be recounted to You in
   order;
  If I would declare and speak *of them*,
  They are more than can be
   numbered.

6 Sacrifice and offering You did not
   desire;
  My ears You have opened.
  Burnt offering and sin offering You
   did not require.
7 Then I said, "Behold, I come;

In the scroll of the book *it is* written
of me.

8 I delight to do Your will, O my God,
And Your law *is* within my heart."

9 I have proclaimed the good news of
righteousness
In the great assembly;
Indeed, I do not restrain my lips,
O LORD, You Yourself know.

10 I have not hidden Your
righteousness within my heart;
I have declared Your faithfulness
and Your salvation;
I have not concealed Your
lovingkindness and Your truth
From the great assembly.

11 Do not withhold Your tender
mercies from me, O LORD;
Let Your lovingkindness and Your
truth continually preserve me.

12 For innumerable evils have
surrounded me;
My iniquities have overtaken me, so
that I am not able to look up;
They are more than the hairs of my
head;
Therefore my heart fails me.

13 Be pleased, O LORD, to deliver me;
O LORD, make haste to help me!

14 Let them be ashamed and brought
to mutual confusion
Who seek to destroy my life;
Let them be driven backward and
brought to dishonor
Who wish me evil.

15 Let them be confounded because of
their shame,
Who say to me, "Aha, aha!"

16 Let all those who seek You rejoice
and be glad in You;
Let such as love Your salvation say
continually,
"The LORD be magnified!"

17 But I *am* poor and needy;
Yet the LORD thinks upon me.
You *are* my help and my deliverer;
Do not delay, O my God.

PSALM 41

The Blessing and Suffering of the Godly

To the Chief Musician. A Psalm of David.

1 Blessed *is* he who considers the
poor;

The LORD will deliver him in time
of trouble.

2 The LORD will preserve him and
keep him alive,
And he will be blessed on the earth;
You will not deliver him to the will
of his enemies.

3 The LORD will strengthen him on his
bed of illness;
You will sustain him on his sickbed.

4 I said, "LORD, be merciful to me;
Heal my soul, for I have sinned
against You."

5 My enemies speak evil of me:
"When will he die, and his name
perish?"

6 And if he comes to see *me,* he speaks
lies;
His heart gathers iniquity to itself;
When he goes out, he tells *it.*

7 All who hate me whisper together
against me;
Against me they devise my hurt.

8 "An evil disease," *they say,* "clings
to him.
And *now* that he lies down, he will
rise up no more."

9 Even my own familiar friend in
whom I trusted,
Who ate my bread,
Has lifted up *his* heel against me.

10 But You, O LORD, be merciful to me,
and raise me up,
That I may repay them.

11 By this I know that You are well
pleased with me,
Because my enemy does not triumph
over me.

12 As for me, You uphold me in my
integrity,
And set me before Your face forever.

13 Blessed *be* the LORD God of Israel
From everlasting to everlasting!
Amen and Amen.

BOOK TWO: PSALMS 42—72

PSALM 42

Yearning for God in the Midst of Distresses

To the Chief Musician. A Contemplation of the
sons of Korah.

1 As the deer pants for the water
brooks,

So pants my soul for You, O God.
2 My soul thirsts for God, for the
    living God.
When shall I come and appear
    before God?
3 My tears have been my food day and
    night,
While they continually say to me,
"Where *is* your God?"

4 When I remember these *things*,
I pour out my soul within me.
For I used to go with the multitude;
I went with them to the house
    of God,
With the voice of joy and praise,
With a multitude that kept a pilgrim
    feast.

5 Why are you cast down, O my soul?
And *why* are you disquieted
    within me?
Hope in God, for I shall yet
    praise Him
For the help of His countenance.

6 O my God, my soul is cast down
    within me;
Therefore I will remember You from
    the land of the Jordan,
And from the heights of Hermon,
From the Hill Mizar.
7 Deep calls unto deep at the noise of
    Your waterfalls;
All Your waves and billows have
    gone over me.
8 The Lord will command His
    lovingkindness in the daytime,
And in the night His song *shall be*
    with me—
A prayer to the God of my life.

9 I will say to God my Rock,
"Why have You forgotten me?
Why do I go mourning because of
    the oppression of the enemy?"
10 *As* with a breaking of my bones,
My enemies reproach me,
While they say to me all day long,
"Where *is* your God?"

11 Why are you cast down, O my soul?
And why are you disquieted
    within me?
Hope in God;
For I shall yet praise Him,
The help of my countenance and
    my God.

PSALM 43

Prayer to God in Time of Trouble

1 Vindicate me, O God,
And plead my cause against an
    ungodly nation;
Oh, deliver me from the deceitful
    and unjust man!
2 For You *are* the God of my strength;
Why do You cast me off?
Why do I go mourning because of
    the oppression of the enemy?

3 Oh, send out Your light and Your
    truth!
Let them lead me;
Let them bring me to Your holy hill
And to Your tabernacle.
4 Then I will go to the altar of God,
To God my exceeding joy;
And on the harp I will praise You,
O God, my God.

5 Why are you cast down, O my soul?
And why are you disquieted
    within me?
Hope in God;
For I shall yet praise Him,
The help of my countenance and
    my God.

PSALM 44

Redemption Remembered in Present Dishonor

To the Chief Musician. A Contemplation of the
sons of Korah.

1 We have heard with our ears, O God,
Our fathers have told us,
The deeds You did in their days,
In days of old:
2 You drove out the nations with Your
    hand,
But them You planted;
You afflicted the peoples, and cast
    them out.
3 For they did not gain possession of
    the land by their own sword,
Nor did their own arm save them;
But it was Your right hand, Your
    arm, and the light of Your
    countenance,
Because You favored them.

4 You are my King, O God;
Command victories for Jacob.
5 Through You we will push down our
    enemies;

Through Your name we will trample
   those who rise up against us.
6 For I will not trust in my bow,
   Nor shall my sword save me.
7 But You have saved us from our
   enemies,
   And have put to shame those who
   hated us.
8 In God we boast all day long,
   And praise Your name forever.
                      Selah

9 But You have cast *us* off and put us
   to shame,
   And You do not go out with our
   armies.
10 You make us turn back from the
   enemy,
   And those who hate us have taken
   spoil for themselves.
11 You have given us up like sheep
   intended for food,
   And have scattered us among the
   nations.
12 You sell Your people for *next to*
   nothing,
   And are not enriched by selling
   them.

13 You make us a reproach to our
   neighbors,
   A scorn and a derision to those all
   around us.
14 You make us a byword among the
   nations,
   A shaking of the head among the
   peoples.
15 My dishonor *is* continually
   before me,
   And the shame of my face has
   covered me,
16 Because of the voice of him who
   reproaches and reviles,
   Because of the enemy and the
   avenger.

17 All this has come upon us;
   But we have not forgotten You,
   Nor have we dealt falsely with Your
   covenant.
18 Our heart has not turned back,
   Nor have our steps departed from
   Your way;
19 But You have severely broken us in
   the place of jackals,
   And covered us with the shadow of
   death.

20 If we had forgotten the name of
   our God,
   Or stretched out our hands to a
   foreign god,
21 Would not God search this out?
   For He knows the secrets of the
   heart.
22 Yet for Your sake we are killed all
   day long;
   We are accounted as sheep for the
   slaughter.

23 Awake! Why do You sleep, O Lord?
   Arise! Do not cast *us* off forever.
24 Why do You hide Your face,
   And forget our affliction and our
   oppression?
25 For our soul is bowed down to the
   dust;
   Our body clings to the ground.
26 Arise for our help,
   And redeem us for Your mercies'
   sake.

PSALM 45

The Glories of the Messiah and His Bride

To the Chief Musician. Set to "The Lilies."
A Contemplation of the sons of Korah.
A Song of Love.

1 My heart is overflowing with a good
   theme;
   I recite my composition concerning
   the King;
   My tongue *is* the pen of a ready
   writer.

2 You are fairer than the sons of men;
   Grace is poured upon Your lips;
   Therefore God has blessed You
   forever.
3 Gird Your sword upon *Your* thigh,
   O Mighty One,
   With Your glory and Your majesty.
4 And in Your majesty ride
   prosperously because of truth,
   humility, *and* righteousness;
   And Your right hand shall teach
   You awesome things.
5 Your arrows *are* sharp in the heart
   of the King's enemies;
   The peoples fall under You.

6 Your throne, O God, *is* forever and
   ever;
   A scepter of righteousness *is* the
   scepter of Your kingdom.

7 You love righteousness and hate
  wickedness;
  Therefore God, Your God, has
    anointed You
  With the oil of gladness more than
    Your companions.
8 All Your garments are scented with
    myrrh and aloes *and* cassia,
  Out of the ivory palaces, by which
    they have made You glad.
9 Kings' daughters *are* among Your
    honorable women;
  At Your right hand stands the queen
    in gold from Ophir.

10 Listen, O daughter,
  Consider and incline your ear;
  Forget your own people also, and
    your father's house;
11 So the King will greatly desire your
    beauty;
  Because He *is* your Lord,
    worship Him.
12 And the daughter of Tyre *will come*
    with a gift;
  The rich among the people will seek
    your favor.

13 The royal daughter *is* all glorious
    within *the palace;*
  Her clothing *is* woven with gold.
14 She shall be brought to the King in
    robes of many colors;
  The virgins, her companions who
    follow her, shall be brought to
    You.
15 With gladness and rejoicing they
    shall be brought;
  They shall enter the King's palace.

16 Instead of Your fathers shall be
    Your sons,
  Whom You shall make princes in all
    the earth.
17 I will make Your name to be
    remembered in all generations;
  Therefore the people shall praise
    You forever and ever.

PSALM 46

God the Refuge of His People and
Conqueror of the Nations

To the Chief Musician. A Psalm of the sons of
Korah. A Song for Alamoth.

1 God *is* our refuge and strength,
  A very present help in trouble.
2 Therefore we will not fear,

Even though the earth be removed,
And though the mountains be
  carried into the midst of the sea;
3 *Though* its waters roar *and* be
    troubled,
  Though the mountains shake with
    its swelling. Selah

4 *There is* a river whose streams shall
    make glad the city of God,
  The holy *place* of the tabernacle of
    the Most High.
5 God *is* in the midst of her, she shall
    not be moved;
  God shall help her, just at the break
    of dawn.
6 The nations raged, the kingdoms
    were moved;
  He uttered His voice, the earth
    melted.

7 The LORD of hosts *is* with us;
  The God of Jacob *is* our refuge.
                                Selah

8 Come, behold the works of the LORD,
  Who has made desolations in the
    earth.
9 He makes wars cease to the end of
    the earth;
  He breaks the bow and cuts the
    spear in two;
  He burns the chariot in the fire.

10 Be still, and know that I *am* God;
  I will be exalted among the nations,
  I will be exalted in the earth!

11 The LORD of hosts *is* with us;
  The God of Jacob *is* our refuge.
                                Selah

PSALM 47

Praise to God, the Ruler of the Earth

To the Chief Musician. A Psalm of the sons
of Korah.

1 Oh, clap your hands, all you
    peoples!
  Shout to God with the voice of
    triumph!
2 For the LORD Most High *is* awesome;
  He is a great King over all the earth.
3 He will subdue the peoples under us,
  And the nations under our feet.
4 He will choose our inheritance
    for us,
  The excellence of Jacob whom He
    loves. Selah

5 God has gone up with a shout,
The LORD with the sound of a
    trumpet.
6 Sing praises to God, sing praises!
Sing praises to our King, sing
    praises!
7 For God *is* the King of all the earth;
Sing praises with understanding.

8 God reigns over the nations;
God sits on His holy throne.
9 The princes of the people have
    gathered together,
The people of the God of Abraham.
For the shields of the earth *belong*
    to God;
He is greatly exalted.

PSALM 48

The Glory of God in Zion

A Song. A Psalm of the sons of Korah.

1 Great *is* the LORD, and greatly to be
    praised
In the city of our God,
In His holy mountain.
2 Beautiful in elevation,
The joy of the whole earth,
Is Mount Zion *on* the sides of the
    north,
The city of the great King.
3 God *is* in her palaces;
He is known as her refuge.

4 For behold, the kings assembled,
They passed by together.
5 They saw *it, and* so they marveled;
They were troubled, they hastened
    away.
6 Fear took hold of them there,
And pain, as of a woman in birth
    pangs,
7 *As when* You break the ships of
    Tarshish
With an east wind.

8 As we have heard,
So we have seen
In the city of the LORD of hosts,
In the city of our God:
God will establish it forever.
                                    Selah

9 We have thought, O God, on Your
    lovingkindness,
In the midst of Your temple.
10 According to Your name, O God,

So *is* Your praise to the ends of the
    earth;
Your right hand is full of
    righteousness.
11 Let Mount Zion rejoice,
Let the daughters of Judah be glad,
Because of Your judgments.

12 Walk about Zion,
And go all around her.
Count her towers;
13 Mark well her bulwarks;
Consider her palaces;
That you may tell *it* to the
    generation following.
14 For this *is* God,
Our God forever and ever;
He will be our guide
Even to death.

PSALM 49

The Confidence of the Foolish

To the Chief Musician. A Psalm of the sons
of Korah.

1 Hear this, all peoples;
Give ear, all inhabitants of the
    world,
2 Both low and high,
Rich and poor together.
3 My mouth shall speak wisdom,
And the meditation of my heart *shall
    give* understanding.
4 I will incline my ear to a proverb;
I will disclose my dark saying on the
    harp.

5 Why should I fear in the days of evil,
When the iniquity at my heels
    surrounds me?
6 Those who trust in their wealth
And boast in the multitude of their
    riches,
7 None *of them* can by any means
    redeem *his* brother,
Nor give to God a ransom for him—
8 For the redemption of their souls *is*
    costly,
And it shall cease forever—
9 That he should continue to live
    eternally,
And not see the Pit.

10 For he sees wise men die;
Likewise the fool and the senseless
    person perish,
And leave their wealth to others.

11 Their inner thought *is that* their
   houses *will last* forever,
   Their dwelling places to all
   generations;
   They call *their* lands after their own
   names.
12 Nevertheless man, *though* in honor,
   does not remain;
   He is like the beasts *that* perish.

13 This is the way of those who *are*
   foolish,
   And of their posterity who approve
   their sayings.   Selah
14 Like sheep they are laid in the grave;
   Death shall feed on them;
   The upright shall have dominion
   over them in the morning;
   And their beauty shall be consumed
   in the grave, far from their
   dwelling.
15 But God will redeem my soul from
   the power of the grave,
   For He shall receive me.   Selah

16 Do not be afraid when one becomes
   rich,
   When the glory of his house is
   increased;
17 For when he dies he shall carry
   nothing away;
   His glory shall not descend
   after him.
18 Though while he lives he blesses
   himself
   (For *men* will praise you when you
   do well for yourself),
19 He shall go to the generation of his
   fathers;
   They shall never see light.
20 A man *who is* in honor, yet does not
   understand,
   Is like the beasts *that* perish.

PSALM 50

God the Righteous Judge

A Psalm of Asaph.

1 The Mighty One, God the LORD,
  Has spoken and called the earth
  From the rising of the sun to its
  going down.
2 Out of Zion, the perfection of beauty,
  God will shine forth.
3 Our God shall come, and shall not
  keep silent;
  A fire shall devour before Him,

And it shall be very tempestuous all
   around Him.

4 He shall call to the heavens from
  above,
  And to the earth, that He may judge
  His people:
5 "Gather My saints together to Me,
  Those who have made a covenant
  with Me by sacrifice."
6 Let the heavens declare His
  righteousness,
  For God Himself *is* Judge.   Selah

7 "Hear, O My people, and I will speak,
  O Israel, and I will testify
  against you;
  I *am* God, your God!
8 I will not rebuke you for your
  sacrifices
  Or your burnt offerings,
  Which are continually before Me.
9 I will not take a bull from your
  house,
  Nor goats out of your folds.
10 For every beast of the forest *is* Mine,
   And the cattle on a thousand hills.
11 I know all the birds of the
   mountains,
   And the wild beasts of the field *are*
   Mine.

12 "If I were hungry, I would not tell
   you;
   For the world *is* Mine, and all its
   fullness.
13 Will I eat the flesh of bulls,
   Or drink the blood of goats?
14 Offer to God thanksgiving,
   And pay your vows to the Most
   High.
15 Call upon Me in the day of trouble;
   I will deliver you, and you shall
   glorify Me."

16 But to the wicked God says:
   "What *right* have you to declare My
   statutes,
   Or take My covenant in your mouth,
17 Seeing you hate instruction
   And cast My words behind you?
18 When you saw a thief, you
   consented with him,
   And have been a partaker with
   adulterers.
19 You give your mouth to evil,
   And your tongue frames deceit.

20 You sit *and* speak against your
      brother;
   You slander your own mother's son.
21 These *things* you have done, and I
      kept silent;
   You thought that I was altogether
      like you;
   But I will rebuke you,
   And set *them* in order before your
      eyes.

22 "Now consider this, you who
      forget God,
   Lest I tear *you* in pieces,
   And *there be* none to deliver:
23 Whoever offers praise glorifies Me;
   And to him who orders *his* conduct
      aright
   I will show the salvation of God."

PSALM 51

A Prayer of Repentance

To the Chief Musician. A Psalm of David when
Nathan the prophet went to him, after he had
gone in to Bathsheba.

1 Have mercy upon me, O God,
   According to Your lovingkindness;
   According to the multitude of Your
      tender mercies,
   Blot out my transgressions.
2 Wash me thoroughly from my
      iniquity,
   And cleanse me from my sin.

3 For I acknowledge my
      transgressions,
   And my sin *is* always before me.
4 Against You, You only, have I
      sinned,
   And done *this* evil in Your sight—
   That You may be found just when
      You speak,
   And blameless when You judge.

5 Behold, I was brought forth in
      iniquity,
   And in sin my mother conceived me.
6 Behold, You desire truth in the
      inward parts,
   And in the hidden *part* You will
      make me to know wisdom.

7 Purge me with hyssop, and I shall
      be clean;
   Wash me, and I shall be whiter than
      snow.

8 Make me hear joy and gladness,
   That the bones You have broken
      may rejoice.
9 Hide Your face from my sins,
   And blot out all my iniquities.

10 Create in me a clean heart, O God,
   And renew a steadfast spirit
      within me.
11 Do not cast me away from Your
      presence,
   And do not take Your Holy Spirit
      from me.

12 Restore to me the joy of Your
      salvation,
   And uphold me *by Your* generous
      Spirit.
13 *Then* I will teach transgressors Your
      ways,
   And sinners shall be converted
      to You.

14 Deliver me from the guilt of
      bloodshed, O God,
   The God of my salvation,
   And my tongue shall sing aloud of
      Your righteousness.
15 O Lord, open my lips,
   And my mouth shall show forth
      Your praise.
16 For You do not desire sacrifice, or
      else I would give *it;*
   You do not delight in burnt offering.
17 The sacrifices of God *are* a broken
      spirit,
   A broken and a contrite heart—
   These, O God, You will not despise.

18 Do good in Your good pleasure to
      Zion;
   Build the walls of Jerusalem.
19 Then You shall be pleased with the
      sacrifices of righteousness,
   With burnt offering and whole burnt
      offering;
   Then they shall offer bulls on Your
      altar.

PSALM 52

The End of the Wicked and the Peace of the Godly

To the Chief Musician. A Contemplation of David when Doeg the Edomite went and told Saul,
and said to him, "David has gone to the house
of Ahimelech."

1 Why do you boast in evil,
   O mighty man?

The goodness of God *endures*
continually.
2 Your tongue devises destruction,
Like a sharp razor, working
deceitfully.
3 You love evil more than good,
Lying rather than speaking
righteousness. Selah
4 You love all devouring words,
You deceitful tongue.

5 God shall likewise destroy you
forever;
He shall take you away, and pluck
you out of *your* dwelling place,
And uproot you from the land of the
living. Selah
6 The righteous also shall see and fear,
And shall laugh at him, *saying,*
7 "Here is the man *who* did not make
God his strength,
But trusted in the abundance of his
riches,
And strengthened himself in his
wickedness."

8 But I *am* like a green olive tree in
the house of God;
I trust in the mercy of God forever
and ever.
9 I will praise You forever,
Because You have done *it;*
And in the presence of Your saints
I will wait on Your name, for *it is*
good.

PSALM 53

Folly of the Godless, and the Restoration of Israel

To the Chief Musician. Set to "Mahalath."
A Contemplation of David.

1 The fool has said in his heart,
"*There is* no God."
They are corrupt, and have done
abominable iniquity;
There is none who does good.

2 God looks down from heaven upon
the children of men,
To see if there are *any* who
understand, who seek God.
3 Every one of them has turned aside;
They have together become corrupt;
There is none who does good,
No, not one.

4 Have the workers of iniquity no
knowledge,
Who eat up my people *as* they eat
bread,
And do not call upon God?
5 There they are in great fear
Where no fear was,
For God has scattered the bones of
him who encamps against you;
You have put *them* to shame,
Because God has despised them.

6 Oh, that the salvation of Israel
would come out of Zion!
When God brings back the captivity
of His people,
Let Jacob rejoice *and* Israel be glad.

PSALM 54

Answered Prayer for Deliverance from Adversaries

To the Chief Musician. With stringed instruments. A Contemplation of David when the
Ziphites went and said to Saul, "Is David not
hiding with us?"

1 Save me, O God, by Your name,
And vindicate me by Your strength.
2 Hear my prayer, O God;
Give ear to the words of my mouth.
3 For strangers have risen up
against me,
And oppressors have sought after
my life;
They have not set God before them.
Selah

4 Behold, God *is* my helper;
The Lord *is* with those who uphold
my life.
5 He will repay my enemies for their
evil.
Cut them off in Your truth.

6 I will freely sacrifice to You;
I will praise Your name, O LORD, for
it is good.
7 For He has delivered me out of all
trouble;
And my eye has seen *its desire* upon
my enemies.

PSALM 55

Trust in God Concerning the Treachery of Friends

To the Chief Musician. With stringed instruments. A Contemplation of David.

1 Give ear to my prayer, O God,
And do not hide Yourself from my
supplication.

2 Attend to me, and hear me;
I am restless in my complaint, and
moan noisily,
3 Because of the voice of the enemy,
Because of the oppression of the
wicked;
For they bring down trouble
upon me,
And in wrath they hate me.
4 My heart is severely pained
within me,
And the terrors of death have fallen
upon me.
5 Fearfulness and trembling have
come upon me,
And horror has overwhelmed me.
6 So I said, "Oh, that I had wings like
a dove!
I would fly away and be at rest.
7 Indeed, I would wander far off,
And remain in the wilderness.
                                        Selah
8 I would hasten my escape
From the windy storm *and* tempest."

9 Destroy, O Lord, *and* divide their
tongues,
For I have seen violence and strife
in the city.
10 Day and night they go around it on
its walls;
Iniquity and trouble *are* also in the
midst of it.
11 Destruction *is* in its midst;
Oppression and deceit do not depart
from its streets.

12 For *it is* not an enemy *who*
reproaches me;
Then I could bear *it.*
Nor *is it* one *who* hates me who has
exalted *himself* against me;
Then I could hide from him.
13 But *it was* you, a man my equal,
My companion and my
acquaintance.
14 We took sweet counsel together,
And walked to the house of God in
the throng.

15 Let death seize them;
Let them go down alive into hell,
For wickedness *is* in their dwellings
and among them.

16 As for me, I will call upon God,
And the LORD shall save me.

17 Evening and morning and at noon
I will pray, and cry aloud,
And He shall hear my voice.
18 He has redeemed my soul in peace
from the battle *that was*
against me,
For there were many against me.
19 God will hear, and afflict them,
Even He who abides from of old.
                                        Selah
Because they do not change,
Therefore they do not fear God.

20 He has put forth his hands against
those who were at peace with
him;
He has broken his covenant.
21 *The words* of his mouth were
smoother than butter,
But war *was* in his heart;
His words were softer than oil,
Yet they *were* drawn swords.

22 Cast your burden on the LORD,
And He shall sustain you;
He shall never permit the righteous
to be moved.

23 But You, O God, shall bring them
down to the pit of destruction;
Bloodthirsty and deceitful men shall
not live out half their days;
But I will trust in You.

PSALM 56

Prayer for Relief from Tormentors

To the Chief Musician. Set to "The Silent Dove
in Distant Lands." A Michtam of David when
the Philistines captured him in Gath.

1 Be merciful to me, O God, for man
would swallow me up;
Fighting all day he oppresses me.
2 My enemies would hound *me*
all day,
For *there are* many who fight
against me, O Most High.

3 Whenever I am afraid,
I will trust in You.
4 In God (I will praise His word),
In God I have put my trust;
I will not fear.
What can flesh do to me?

5 All day they twist my words;
All their thoughts *are* against me for
evil.
6 They gather together,

They hide, they mark my steps,
When they lie in wait for my life.
7 Shall they escape by iniquity?
In anger cast down the peoples,
　O God!

8 You number my wanderings;
Put my tears into Your bottle;
Are they not in Your book?
9 When I cry out *to You,*
Then my enemies will turn back;
This I know, because God *is* for me.
10 In God (I will praise *His* word),
In the LORD (I will praise *His* word),
11 In God I have put my trust;
I will not be afraid.
What can man do to me?

12 Vows *made* to You *are binding* upon
　me, O God;
I will render praises to You,
13 For You have delivered my soul
　from death.
Have You not *kept* my feet from
　falling,
That I may walk before God
In the light of the living?

PSALM 57

Prayer for Safety from Enemies

To the Chief Musician. Set to "Do Not Destroy."
A Michtam of David when he fled from Saul
into the cave.

1 Be merciful to me, O God, be
　merciful to me!
For my soul trusts in You;
And in the shadow of Your wings I
　will make my refuge,
Until *these* calamities have
　passed by.

2 I will cry out to God Most High,
To God who performs *all things*
　for me.
3 He shall send from heaven and
　save me;
He reproaches the one who would
　swallow me up.　　Selah
God shall send forth His mercy and
　His truth.

4 My soul *is* among lions;
I lie *among* the sons of men
Who are set on fire,
Whose teeth *are* spears and arrows,
And their tongue a sharp sword.

5 Be exalted, O God, above the
　heavens;
Let Your glory *be* above all the
　earth.

6 They have prepared a net for my
　steps;
My soul is bowed down;
They have dug a pit before me;
Into the midst of it they *themselves*
　have fallen.　　Selah

7 My heart is steadfast, O God, my
　heart is steadfast;
I will sing and give praise.
8 Awake, my glory!
Awake, lute and harp!
I will awaken the dawn.

9 I will praise You, O Lord, among the
　peoples;
I will sing to You among the nations.
10 For Your mercy reaches unto the
　heavens,
And Your truth unto the clouds.

11 Be exalted, O God, above the
　heavens;
Let Your glory *be* above all the
　earth.

PSALM 58

The Just Judgment of the Wicked

To the Chief Musician. Set to "Do Not Destroy."
A Michtam of David.

1 Do you indeed speak righteousness,
　you silent ones?
Do you judge uprightly, you sons
　of men?
2 No, in heart you work wickedness;
You weigh out the violence of your
　hands in the earth.

3 The wicked are estranged from the
　womb;
They go astray as soon as they are
　born, speaking lies.
4 Their poison *is* like the poison of a
　serpent;
They are like the deaf cobra *that*
　stops its ear,
5 Which will not heed the voice of
　charmers,
Charming ever so skillfully.

6 Break their teeth in their mouth,
　O God!

Break out the fangs of the young
  lions, O Lord!
7 Let them flow away as waters *which*
  run continually;
  When he bends *his bow*,
  Let his arrows be as if cut in pieces.
8 *Let them be* like a snail which melts
  away as it goes,
  Like a stillborn child of a woman,
  that they may not see the sun.

9 Before your pots can feel *the*
  burning thorns,
  He shall take them away as with a
  whirlwind,
  As in His living and burning wrath.
10 The righteous shall rejoice when he
  sees the vengeance;
  He shall wash his feet in the blood
  of the wicked,
11 So that men will say,
  "Surely *there is* a reward for the
  righteous;
  Surely He is God who judges in the
  earth."

PSALM 59

The Assured Judgment of the Wicked

To the Chief Musician. Set to "Do Not Destroy."
A Michtam of David when Saul sent men, and
they watched the house in order to kill him.

1 Deliver me from my enemies, O my
  God;
  Defend me from those who rise up
  against me.
2 Deliver me from the workers of
  iniquity,
  And save me from bloodthirsty men.

3 For look, they lie in wait for my life;
  The mighty gather against me,
  Not *for* my transgression nor *for* my
  sin, O Lord.
4 They run and prepare themselves
  through no fault *of mine*.

  Awake to help me, and behold!
5 You therefore, O Lord God of hosts,
  the God of Israel,
  Awake to punish all the nations;
  Do not be merciful to any wicked
  transgressors.   Selah

6 At evening they return,
  They growl like a dog,
  And go all around the city.
7 Indeed, they belch with their mouth;

Swords *are* in their lips;
  For *they say*, "Who hears?"

8 But You, O Lord, shall laugh at
  them;
  You shall have all the nations in
  derision.
9 I will wait for You, O You his
  Strength;
  For God *is* my defense.
10 My God of mercy shall come to
  meet me;
  God shall let me see *my desire* on
  my enemies.

11 Do not slay them, lest my people
  forget;
  Scatter them by Your power,
  And bring them down,
  O Lord our shield.
12 *For* the sin of their mouth *and* the
  words of their lips,
  Let them even be taken in their
  pride,
  And for the cursing and lying *which*
  they speak.
13 Consume *them* in wrath, consume
  them,
  That they *may* not *be*;
  And let them know that God rules
  in Jacob
  To the ends of the earth.   Selah

14 And at evening they return,
  They growl like a dog,
  And go all around the city.
15 They wander up and down for food,
  And howl if they are not satisfied.

16 But I will sing of Your power;
  Yes, I will sing aloud of Your mercy
  in the morning;
  For You have been my defense
  And refuge in the day of my trouble.
17 To You, O my Strength, I will sing
  praises;
  For God *is* my defense,
  My God of mercy.

PSALM 60

Urgent Prayer for the Restored Favor of God

To the Chief Musician. Set to "Lily of the Testimony." A Michtam of David. For teaching.
When he fought against Mesopotamia and Syria
of Zobah, and Joab returned and killed twelve
thousand Edomites in the Valley of Salt.

1 O God, You have cast us off;
  You have broken us down;

You have been displeased;
Oh, restore us again!
2 You have made the earth tremble;
You have broken it;
Heal its breaches, for it is shaking.
3 You have shown Your people hard
things;
You have made us drink the wine
of confusion.

4 You have given a banner to those
who fear You,
That it may be displayed because of
the truth.   Selah
5 That Your beloved may be
delivered,
Save *with* Your right hand, and
hear me.

6 God has spoken in His holiness:
"I will rejoice;
I will divide Shechem
And measure out the Valley of
Succoth.
7 Gilead *is* Mine, and Manasseh *is*
Mine;
Ephraim also *is* the helmet for My
head;
Judah *is* My lawgiver.
8 Moab *is* My washpot;
Over Edom I will cast My shoe;
Philistia, shout in triumph because
of Me."

9 Who will bring me *to* the strong city?
Who will lead me to Edom?
10 *Is it* not You, O God, *who* cast
us off?
And You, O God, *who* did not go out
with our armies?
11 Give us help from trouble,
For the help of man *is* useless.
12 Through God we will do valiantly,
For *it is* He *who* shall tread down
our enemies.[d]

PSALM 61

Assurance of God's Eternal Protection

To the Chief Musician. On a stringed instrument. A Psalm of David.

1 Hear my cry, O God;
Attend to my prayer.
2 From the end of the earth I will cry
to You,
When my heart is overwhelmed;

---

d Compare verses 5-12 with 108.6-13

Lead me to the rock that is higher
than I.
3 For You have been a shelter for me,
A strong tower from the enemy.
4 I will abide in Your tabernacle
forever;
I will trust in the shelter of Your
wings.   Selah
5 For You, O God, have heard my
vows;
You have given *me* the heritage of
those who fear Your name.
6 You will prolong the king's life,
His years as many generations.
7 He shall abide before God forever.
Oh, prepare mercy and truth, *which*
may preserve him!

8 So I will sing praise to Your name
forever,
That I may daily perform my vows.

PSALM 62

A Calm Resolve to Wait for the Salvation of God

To the Chief Musician. To Jeduthun. A Psalm
of David.

1 Truly my soul silently *waits* for God;
From Him *comes* my salvation.
2 He only *is* my rock and my
salvation;
He is my defense;
I shall not be greatly moved.

3 How long will you attack a man?
You shall be slain, all of you,
Like a leaning wall and a tottering
fence.
4 They only consult to cast *him* down
from his high position;
They delight in lies;
They bless with their mouth,
But they curse inwardly.   Selah

5 My soul, wait silently for God alone,
For my expectation *is* from Him.
6 He only *is* my rock and my
salvation;
He is my defense;
I shall not be moved.
7 In God *is* my salvation and my glory;
The rock of my strength,
And my refuge, *is* in God.

8 Trust in Him at all times, you people;
  Pour out your heart before Him;
  God *is* a refuge for us.   Selah

9 Surely men of low degree *are* a
      vapor,
  Men of high degree *are* a lie;
  If they are weighed on the scales,
  They *are* altogether *lighter* than
      vapor.
10 Do not trust in oppression,
  Nor vainly hope in robbery;
  If riches increase,
  Do not set *your* heart *on them.*

11 God has spoken once,
  Twice I have heard this:
  That power *belongs* to God.
12 Also to You, O Lord, *belongs* mercy;
  For You render to each one
      according to his work.

PSALM 63

Joy in the Fellowship of God

A Psalm of David when he was in the wilderness
of Judah.

1 O God, You *are* my God;
  Early will I seek You;
  My soul thirsts for You;
  My flesh longs for You
  In a dry and thirsty land
  Where there is no water.
2 So I have looked for You in the
      sanctuary,
  To see Your power and Your glory.

3 Because Your lovingkindness *is*
      better than life,
  My lips shall praise You.
4 Thus I will bless You while I live;
  I will lift up my hands in Your name.
5 My soul shall be satisfied as with
      marrow and fatness,
  And my mouth shall praise You with
      joyful lips.

6 When I remember You on my bed,
  I meditate on You in the *night*
      watches.
7 Because You have been my help,
  Therefore in the shadow of Your
      wings I will rejoice.
8 My soul follows close behind You;
  Your right hand upholds me.

9 But those *who* seek my life, to
      destroy *it,*

Shall go into the lower parts of the
    earth.
10 They shall fall by the sword;
  They shall be a portion for jackals.

11 But the king shall rejoice in God;
  Everyone who swears by Him shall
      glory;
  But the mouth of those who speak
      lies shall be stopped.

PSALM 64

Oppressed by the Wicked but Rejoicing in the LORD

To the Chief Musician. A Psalm of David.

1 Hear my voice, O God, in my
      meditation;
  Preserve my life from fear of the
      enemy.
2 Hide me from the secret plots of the
      wicked,
  From the rebellion of the workers of
      iniquity,
3 Who sharpen their tongue like a
      sword,
  And bend *their bows to shoot* their
      arrows—bitter words,
4 That they may shoot in secret at the
      blameless;
  Suddenly they shoot at him and do
      not fear.

5 They encourage themselves *in* an
      evil matter;
  They talk of laying snares secretly;
  They say, "Who will see them?"
6 They devise iniquities:
  "We have perfected a shrewd
      scheme."
  Both the inward thought and the
      heart of man are deep.

7 But God shall shoot at them *with* an
      arrow;
  Suddenly they shall be wounded.
8 So He will make them stumble over
      their own tongue;
  All who see them shall flee away.
9 All men shall fear,
  And shall declare the work of God;
  For they shall wisely consider His
      doing.

10 The righteous shall be glad in the
      LORD, and trust in Him.
  And all the upright in heart shall
      glory.

PSALM 65

Praise to God for His Salvation and Providence

To the Chief Musician. A Psalm of David.
A Song.

1 Praise is awaiting You, O God, in
  Zion;
  And to You the vow shall be
  performed.
2 O You who hear prayer,
  To You all flesh will come.
3 Iniquities prevail against me;
  As for our transgressions,
  You will provide atonement for
  them.

4 Blessed *is the man* You choose,
  And cause to approach *You,*
  That he may dwell in Your courts.
  We shall be satisfied with the
  goodness of Your house,
  Of Your holy temple.

5 *By* awesome deeds in righteousness
  You will answer us,
  O God of our salvation,
  You who are the confidence of all
  the ends of the earth,
  And of the far-off seas;
6 Who established the mountains by
  His strength,
  Being clothed with power;
7 You who still the noise of the seas,
  The noise of their waves,
  And the tumult of the peoples.
8 They also who dwell in the farthest
  parts are afraid of Your signs;
  You make the outgoings of the
  morning and evening rejoice.

9 You visit the earth and water it,
  You greatly enrich it;
  The river of God is full of water;
  You provide their grain,
  For so You have prepared it.
10 You water its ridges abundantly,
  You settle its furrows;
  You make it soft with showers,
  You bless its growth.

11 You crown the year with Your
  goodness,
  And Your paths drip *with*
  abundance.
12 They drop *on* the pastures of the
  wilderness,

And the little hills rejoice on every
  side.
13 The pastures are clothed with flocks;
  The valleys also are covered with
  grain;
  They shout for joy, they also sing.

PSALM 66

Praise to God for His Awesome Works

To the Chief Musician. A Song. A Psalm.

1 Make a joyful shout to God, all the
  earth!
2 Sing out the honor of His name;
  Make His praise glorious.
3 Say to God,
  "How awesome are Your works!
  Through the greatness of Your
  power
  Your enemies shall submit
  themselves to You.
4 All the earth shall worship You
  And sing praises to You;
  They shall sing praises *to* Your
  name."   Selah

5 Come and see the works of God;
  He is awesome *in His* doing toward
  the sons of men.
6 He turned the sea into dry *land;*
  They went through the river on foot.
  There we will rejoice in Him.
7 He rules by His power forever;
  His eyes observe the nations;
  Do not let the rebellious exalt
  themselves.   Selah

8 Oh, bless our God, you peoples!
  And make the voice of His praise to
  be heard,
9 Who keeps our soul among the
  living,
  And does not allow our feet to be
  moved.
10 For You, O God, have tested us;
  You have refined us as silver is
  refined.
11 You brought us into the net;
  You laid affliction on our backs.
12 You have caused men to ride over
  our heads;
  We went through fire and through
  water;
  But You brought us out to rich
  fulfillment.

13 I will go into Your house with burnt
  offerings;

I will pay You my vows,
14 Which my lips have uttered
And my mouth has spoken when I
was in trouble.
15 I will offer You burnt sacrifices of
fat animals,
With the sweet aroma of rams;
I will offer bulls with goats.   Selah

16 Come *and* hear, all you who
fear God,
And I will declare what He has done
for my soul.
17 I cried to Him with my mouth,
And He was extolled with my
tongue.
18 If I regard iniquity in my heart,
The Lord will not hear.
19 *But* certainly God has heard *me;*
He has attended to the voice of my
prayer.

20 Blessed *be* God,
Who has not turned away my
prayer,
Nor His mercy from me!

PSALM 67

An Invocation and a Doxology

To the Chief Musician. On stringed instruments.
A Psalm. A Song.

1 God be merciful to us and bless us,
And cause His face to shine upon us,
Selah
2 That Your way may be known on
earth,
Your salvation among all nations.

3 Let the peoples praise You, O God;
Let all the peoples praise You.
4 Oh, let the nations be glad and sing
for joy!
For You shall judge the people
righteously,
And govern the nations on earth.
Selah

5 Let the peoples praise You,
O God;
Let all the peoples praise You.
6 *Then* the earth shall yield her
increase;
God, our own God, shall bless us.
7 God shall bless us,
And all the ends of the earth shall
fear Him.

PSALM 68

The Glory of God in His Goodness to Israel

To the Chief Musician. A Psalm of David.
A Song.

1 Let God arise,
Let His enemies be scattered;
Let those also who hate Him flee
before Him.
2 As smoke is driven away,
So drive *them* away;
As wax melts before the fire,
So let the wicked perish at the
presence of God.
3 But let the righteous be glad;
Let them rejoice before God;
Yes, let them rejoice exceedingly.

4 Sing to God, sing praises to His
name;
Extol Him who rides on the clouds,
By His name Yah,
And rejoice before Him.

5 A father of the fatherless, a defender
of widows,
Is God in His holy habitation.
6 God sets the solitary in families;
He brings out those who are bound
into prosperity;
But the rebellious dwell in a dry
land.

7 O God, when You went out before
Your people,
When You marched through the
wilderness,   Selah
8 The earth shook;
The heavens also dropped *rain* at the
presence of God;
Sinai itself *was moved* at the
presence of God, the God of
Israel.
9 You, O God, sent a plentiful rain,
Whereby You confirmed Your
inheritance,
When it was weary.
10 Your congregation dwelt in it;
You, O God, provided from Your
goodness for the poor.

11 The Lord gave the word;
Great *was* the company of those
who proclaimed *it:*
12 "Kings of armies flee, they flee,
And she who remains at home
divides the spoil.

13 Though you lie down among the
      sheepfolds,
   You will be like the wings of a dove
      covered with silver,
   And her feathers with yellow gold."
14 When the Almighty scattered kings
      in it,
   It was *white* as snow in Zalmon.

15 A mountain of God *is* the mountain
      of Bashan;
   A mountain *of many* peaks *is* the
      mountain of Bashan.
16 Why do you fume with envy, you
      mountains of *many* peaks?
   This is the mountain *which* God
      desires to dwell in;
   Yes, the LORD will dwell *in it* forever.

17 The chariots of God *are* twenty
      thousand,
   Even thousands of thousands;
   The Lord is among them *as in* Sinai,
      in the Holy *Place.*
18 You have ascended on high,
   You have led captivity captive;
   You have received gifts among men,
   Even *from* the rebellious,
   That the LORD God might dwell
      there.

19 Blessed *be* the Lord,
   Who daily loads us *with benefits,*
   The God of our salvation!   Selah
20 Our God *is* the God of salvation;
   And to GOD the Lord *belong* escapes
      from death.

21 But God will wound the head of His
      enemies,
   The hairy scalp of the one who still
      goes on in his trespasses.
22 The Lord said, "I will bring back
      from Bashan,
   I will bring *them* back from the
      depths of the sea,
23 That your foot may crush *them* in
      blood,
   And the tongues of your dogs *may
      have* their portion from *your*
      enemies."

24 They have seen Your procession,
      O God,
   The procession of my God, my King,
      into the sanctuary.
25 The singers went before, the players

on instruments *followed* after;
   Among *them were* the maidens
      playing timbrels.
26 Bless God in the congregations,
   The Lord, from the fountain of
      Israel.
27 There *is* little Benjamin, their leader,
   The princes of Judah *and* their
      company,
   The princes of Zebulun *and* the
      princes of Naphtali.

28 Your God has commanded your
      strength;
   Strengthen, O God, what You have
      done for us.
29 Because of Your temple at
      Jerusalem,
   Kings will bring presents to You.
30 Rebuke the beasts of the reeds,
   The herd of bulls with the calves of
      the peoples,
   Till everyone submits himself with
      pieces of silver.
   Scatter the peoples *who* delight
      in war.
31 Envoys will come out of Egypt;
   Ethiopia will quickly stretch out her
      hands to God.

32 Sing to God, you kingdoms of the
      earth;
   Oh, sing praises to the Lord,   Selah
33 To Him who rides on the heaven of
      heavens, *which were* of old!
   Indeed, He sends out His voice, a
      mighty voice.
34 Ascribe strength to God;
   His excellence *is* over Israel,
   And His strength *is* in the clouds.
35 O God, *You are* more awesome than
      Your holy places.
   The God of Israel *is* He who gives
      strength and power to *His* people.

   Blessed *be* God!

PSALM 69

An Urgent Plea for Help in Trouble

To the Chief Musician. Set to "The Lilies."
A Psalm of David.
1 Save me, O God!
   For the waters have come up to *my*
      neck.
2 I sink in deep mire,

Where *there is* no standing;
I have come into deep waters,
Where the floods overflow me.

3 I am weary with my crying;
My throat is dry;
My eyes fail while I wait for my God.

4 Those who hate me without a cause
Are more than the hairs of my head;
They are mighty who would
      destroy me,
Being my enemies wrongfully;
Though I have stolen nothing,
I *still* must restore *it.*

5 O God, You know my foolishness;
And my sins are not hidden
      from You.
6 Let not those who wait for You,
      O Lord God of hosts, be ashamed
      because of me;
Let not those who seek You be
      confounded because of me,
      O God of Israel.
7 Because for Your sake I have borne
      reproach;
Shame has covered my face.
8 I have become a stranger to my
      brothers,
And an alien to my mother's
      children;
9 Because zeal for Your house has
      eaten me up,
And the reproaches of those who
      reproach You have fallen on me.
10 When I wept *and chastened* my soul
      with fasting,
That became my reproach.
11 I also made sackcloth my garment;
I became a byword to them.
12 Those who sit in the gate speak
      against me,
And I *am* the song of the drunkards.

13 But as for me, my prayer *is* to You,
      O Lord, *in* the acceptable time;
O God, in the multitude of Your
      mercy,
Hear me in the truth of Your
      salvation.
14 Deliver me out of the mire,
And let me not sink;
Let me be delivered from those who
      hate me,
And out of the deep waters.
15 Let not the floodwater overflow me,
Nor let the deep swallow me up;

And let not the pit shut its mouth
      on me.

16 Hear me, O Lord, for Your
      lovingkindness *is* good;
Turn to me according to the
      multitude of Your tender mercies.
17 And do not hide Your face from
      Your servant,
For I am in trouble;
Hear me speedily.
18 Draw near to my soul, *and*
      redeem it;
Deliver me because of my enemies.

19 You know my reproach, my shame,
      and my dishonor;
My adversaries *are* all before You.
20 Reproach has broken my heart,
And I am full of heaviness;
I looked *for someone* to take pity,
      but *there was* none;
And for comforters, but I found
      none.
21 They also gave me gall for my food,
And for my thirst they gave me
      vinegar to drink.

22 Let their table become a snare
      before them,
And their well-being a trap.
23 Let their eyes be darkened, so that
      they do not see;
And make their loins shake
      continually.
24 Pour out Your indignation upon
      them,
And let Your wrathful anger take
      hold of them.
25 Let their dwelling place be desolate;
Let no one live in their tents.
26 For they persecute the *ones* You
      have struck,
And talk of the grief of those You
      have wounded.
27 Add iniquity to their iniquity,
And let them not come into Your
      righteousness.
28 Let them be blotted out of the book
      of the living,
And not be written with the
      righteous.

29 But I *am* poor and sorrowful;
Let Your salvation, O God, set me
      up on high.
30 I will praise the name of God with
      a song,

And will magnify Him with
    thanksgiving.
31 *This* also shall please the LORD
    better than an ox *or* bull,
Which has horns and hooves.
32 The humble shall see *this and* be
    glad;
And you who seek God, your hearts
    shall live.
33 For the LORD hears the poor,
And does not despise His prisoners.

34 Let heaven and earth praise Him,
The seas and everything that moves
    in them.
35 For God will save Zion
And build the cities of Judah,
That they may dwell there and
    possess it.
36 Also, the descendants of His
    servants shall inherit it,
And those who love His name shall
    dwell in it.

PSALM 70

Prayer for Relief from Adversaries

To the Chief Musician. *A Psalm* of David. To
bring to remembrance.

1 *Make haste,* O God, to deliver me!
Make haste to help me, O LORD!

2 Let them be ashamed and
    confounded
Who seek my life;
Let them be turned back and
    confused
Who desire my hurt.
3 Let them be turned back because of
    their shame,
Who say, "Aha, aha!"

4 Let all those who seek You rejoice
    and be glad in You;
And let those who love Your
    salvation say continually,
"Let God be magnified!"

5 But I *am* poor and needy;
Make haste to me, O God!
You *are* my help and my deliverer;
O LORD, do not delay.

PSALM 71

God the Rock of Salvation

1 In You, O LORD, I put my trust;
Let me never be put to shame.

2 Deliver me in Your righteousness,
    and cause me to escape;
Incline Your ear to me, and save me.
3 Be my strong refuge,
To which I may resort continually;
You have given the commandment
    to save me,
For You *are* my rock and my
    fortress.

4 Deliver me, O my God, out of the
    hand of the wicked,
Out of the hand of the unrighteous
    and cruel man.
5 For You are my hope, O Lord GOD;
You are my trust from my youth.
6 By You I have been upheld from
    birth;
You are He who took me out of my
    mother's womb.
My praise *shall be* continually
    of You.

7 I have become as a wonder to many,
But You *are* my strong refuge.
8 Let my mouth be filled *with* Your
    praise
And with Your glory all the day.

9 Do not cast me off in the time of
    old age;
Do not forsake me when my
    strength fails.
10 For my enemies speak against me;
And those who lie in wait for my life
    take counsel together,
11 Saying, "God has forsaken him;
Pursue and take him, for *there is*
    none to deliver *him.*"

12 O God, do not be far from me;
O my God, make haste to help me!
13 Let them be confounded *and*
    consumed
Who are adversaries of my life;
Let them be covered *with* reproach
    and dishonor
Who seek my hurt.

14 But I will hope continually,
And will praise You yet more and
    more.
15 My mouth shall tell of Your
    righteousness
And Your salvation all the day,
For I do not know *their* limits.

16 I will go in the strength of the
    Lord God;
   I will make mention of Your
    righteousness, of Yours only.

17 O God, You have taught me from my
    youth;
   And to this *day* I declare Your
    wondrous works.

18 Now also when *I am* old and
    grayheaded,
   O God, do not forsake me,
   Until I declare Your strength to *this*
    generation,
   Your power to everyone *who* is to
    come.

19 Also Your righteousness, O God, *is*
    very high,
   You who have done great things;
   O God, who *is* like You?

20 *You,* who have shown me great and
    severe troubles,
   Shall revive me again,
   And bring me up again from the
    depths of the earth.

21 You shall increase my greatness,
   And comfort me on every side.

22 Also with the lute I will praise You—
   And Your faithfulness, O my God!
   To You I will sing with the harp,
   O Holy One of Israel.

23 My lips shall greatly rejoice when I
    sing to You,
   And my soul, which You have
    redeemed.

24 My tongue also shall talk of Your
    righteousness all the day long;
   For they are confounded,
   For they are brought to shame
   Who seek my hurt.

PSALM 72

Glory and Universality of the Messiah's Reign

A Psalm of Solomon.

1 Give the king Your judgments,
    O God,
   And Your righteousness to the
    king's Son.

2 He will judge Your people with
    righteousness,
   And Your poor with justice.

3 The mountains will bring peace to
    the people,
   And the little hills, by righteousness.

4 He will bring justice to the poor of
    the people;
   He will save the children of the
    needy,
   And will break in pieces the
    oppressor.

5 They shall fear You
   As long as the sun and moon endure,
   Throughout all generations.

6 He shall come down like rain upon
    the grass before mowing,
   Like showers *that* water the earth.

7 In His days the righteous shall
    flourish,
   And abundance of peace,
   Until the moon is no more.

8 He shall have dominion also from
    sea to sea,
   And from the River to the ends of
    the earth.

9 Those who dwell in the wilderness
    will bow before Him,
   And His enemies will lick the dust.

10 The kings of Tarshish and of the
    isles
   Will bring presents;
   The kings of Sheba and Seba
   Will offer gifts.

11 Yes, all kings shall fall down
    before Him;
   All nations shall serve Him.

12 For He will deliver the needy when
    he cries,
   The poor also, and *him* who has no
    helper.

13 He will spare the poor and needy,
   And will save the souls of the needy.

14 He will redeem their life from
    oppression and violence;
   And precious shall be their blood in
    His sight.

15 And He shall live;
   And the gold of Sheba will be given
    to Him;
   Prayer also will be made for Him
    continually,
   And daily He shall be praised.

16 There will be an abundance of grain
    in the earth,
   On the top of the mountains;
   Its fruit shall wave like Lebanon;
   And *those* of the city shall flourish
    like grass of the earth.

17 His name shall endure forever;
   His name shall continue as long as
      the sun.
   And *men* shall be blessed in Him;
   All nations shall call Him blessed.

18 Blessed *be* the Lord God, the God
      of Israel,
   Who only does wondrous things!
19 And blessed *be* His glorious name
      forever!
   And let the whole earth be filled
      with His glory.
   Amen and Amen.

20 The prayers of David the son of
      Jesse are ended.

BOOK THREE: PSALMS 73—89

PSALM 73

The Tragedy of the Wicked, and the Blessedness of Trust in God

A Psalm of Asaph.

1 Truly God *is* good to Israel,
   To such as are pure in heart.
2 But as for me, my feet had almost
      stumbled;
   My steps had nearly slipped.
3 For I *was* envious of the boastful,
   When I saw the prosperity of the
      wicked.

4 For *there are* no pangs in their
      death,
   But their strength *is* firm.
5 They *are* not in trouble *as other* men,
   Nor are they plagued like *other* men.
6 Therefore pride serves as their
      necklace;
   Violence covers them *like* a garment.
7 Their eyes bulge with abundance;
   They have more than heart could
      wish.
8 They scoff and speak wickedly
      concerning oppression;
   They speak loftily.
9 They set their mouth against the
      heavens,
   And their tongue walks through the
      earth.

10 Therefore his people return here,
   And waters of a full *cup* are drained
      by them.
11 And they say, "How does God
      know?

And is there knowledge in the Most
   High?"
12 Behold, these *are* the ungodly,
   Who are always at ease;
   They increase *in* riches.
13 Surely I have cleansed my heart *in*
      vain,
   And washed my hands in innocence.
14 For all day long I have been plagued,
   And chastened every morning.

15 If I had said, "I will speak thus,"
   Behold, I would have been untrue to
      the generation of Your children.
16 When I thought *how* to understand
      this,
   It *was* too painful for me—
17 Until I went into the sanctuary
      of God;
   Then I understood their end.

18 Surely You set them in slippery
      places;
   You cast them down to destruction.
19 Oh, how they are *brought* to
      desolation, as in a moment!
   They are utterly consumed with
      terrors.
20 As a dream when *one* awakes,
   So, Lord, when You awake,
   You shall despise their image.

21 Thus my heart was grieved,
   And I was vexed in my mind.
22 I *was* so foolish and ignorant;
   I was *like* a beast before You.
23 Nevertheless I *am* continually
      with You;
   You hold *me* by my right hand.
24 You will guide me with Your
      counsel,
   And afterward receive me *to* glory.

25 Whom have I in heaven *but You*?
   And *there is* none upon earth *that*
      I desire besides You.
26 My flesh and my heart fail;
   But God *is* the strength of my heart
      and my portion forever.

27 For indeed, those who are far from
      You shall perish;
   You have destroyed all those who
      desert You for harlotry.
28 But *it is* good for me to draw near
      to God;

I have put my trust in the Lord GOD,
That I may declare all Your works.

PSALM 74

A Plea for Relief from Oppressors

A Contemplation of Asaph.

1 O God, why have You cast *us* off
        forever?
    Why does Your anger smoke against
        the sheep of Your pasture?
2 Remember Your congregation,
        which You have purchased of old,
    The tribe of Your inheritance, *which*
        You have redeemed—
    This Mount Zion where You have
        dwelt.
3 Lift up Your feet to the perpetual
        desolations.
    The enemy has damaged everything
        in the sanctuary.
4 Your enemies roar in the midst of
        Your meeting place;
    They set up their banners *for* signs.
5 They seem like men who lift up
    Axes among the thick trees.
6 And now they break down its carved
        work, all at once,
    With axes and hammers.
7 They have set fire to Your
        sanctuary;
    They have defiled the dwelling place
        of Your name to the ground.
8 They said in their hearts,
    "Let us destroy them altogether."
    They have burned up all the meeting
        places of God in the land.

9 We do not see our signs;
    There is no longer any prophet;
    Nor *is there* any among us who
        knows how long.
10 O God, how long will the adversary
        reproach?
    Will the enemy blaspheme Your
        name forever?
11 Why do You withdraw Your hand,
        even Your right hand?
    Take it out of Your bosom and
        destroy *them.*
12 For God *is* my King from of old,
    Working salvation in the midst of
        the earth.
13 You divided the sea by Your
        strength;
    You broke the heads of the sea
        serpents in the waters.

14 You broke the heads of Leviathan
        in pieces,
    And gave him *as* food to the people
        inhabiting the wilderness.
15 You broke open the fountain and the
        flood;
    You dried up mighty rivers.
16 The day *is* Yours, the night also *is*
        Yours;
    You have prepared the light and
        the sun.
17 You have set all the borders of the
        earth;
    You have made summer and winter.

18 Remember this, *that* the enemy has
        reproached, O LORD,
    And *that* a foolish people has
        blasphemed Your name.
19 Oh, do not deliver the life of Your
        turtledove to the wild beast!
    Do not forget the life of Your poor
        forever.
20 Have respect to the covenant;
    For the dark places of the earth are
        full of the haunts of cruelty.
21 Oh, do not let the oppressed return
        ashamed!
    Let the poor and needy praise Your
        name.

22 Arise, O God, plead Your own cause;
    Remember how the foolish man
        reproaches You daily.
23 Do not forget the voice of Your
        enemies;
    The tumult of those who rise up
        against You increases
        continually.

PSALM 75

Thanksgiving for God's Righteous Judgment

To the Chief Musician. Set to "Do Not Destroy."
A Psalm of Asaph. A Song.

1 We give thanks to You, O God, we
        give thanks!
    For Your wondrous works declare
        that Your name is near.

2 "When I choose the proper time,
    I will judge uprightly.
3 The earth and all its inhabitants are
        dissolved;
    I set up its pillars firmly.   Selah

4 "I said to the boastful, 'Do not deal
        boastfully,'

And to the wicked, 'Do not lift up
the horn.
5 Do not lift up your horn on high;
Do *not* speak with a stiff neck.' "

6 For exaltation *comes* neither from
the east
Nor from the west nor from the
south.
7 But God *is* the Judge:
He puts down one,
And exalts another.
8 For in the hand of the LORD *there is*
a cup,
And the wine is red;
It is fully mixed, and He pours it out;
Surely its dregs shall all the wicked
of the earth
Drain *and* drink down.

9 But I will declare forever,
I will sing praises to the God of
Jacob.

10 "All the horns of the wicked I will
also cut off,
But the horns of the righteous shall
be exalted."

PSALM 76

The Majesty of God in Judgment

To the Chief Musician. On stringed instruments.
A Psalm of Asaph. A Song.

1 In Judah God *is* known;
His name *is* great in Israel.
2 In Salem*e* also is His tabernacle,
And His dwelling place in Zion.
3 There He broke the arrows of
the bow,
The shield and sword of battle.
Selah

4 You *are* more glorious and excellent
Than the mountains of prey.
5 The stouthearted were plundered;
They have sunk into their sleep;
And none of the mighty men have
found the use of their hands.
6 At Your rebuke, O God of Jacob,
Both the chariot and horse were cast
into a dead sleep.

7 You, Yourself, *are* to be feared;
And who may stand in Your
presence

e That is, Jerusalem

When once You are angry?
8 You caused judgment to be heard
from heaven;
The earth feared and was still,
9 When God arose to judgment,
To deliver all the oppressed of the
earth.   Selah

10 Surely the wrath of man shall
praise You;
With the remainder of wrath You
shall gird Yourself.

11 Make vows to the LORD your God,
and pay *them*;
Let all who are around Him bring
presents to Him who ought to be
feared.
12 He shall cut off the spirit of princes;
He is awesome to the kings of the
earth.

PSALM 77

The Consoling Memory of God's Redemptive Works

To the Chief Musician. To Jeduthun. A Psalm
of Asaph.

1 I cried out to God with my voice—
To God with my voice;
And He gave ear to me.
2 In the day of my trouble I sought
the Lord;
My hand was stretched out in the
night without ceasing;
My soul refused to be comforted.
3 I remembered God, and was
troubled;
I complained, and my spirit was
overwhelmed.   Selah

4 You hold my eyelids *open*;
I am so troubled that I cannot speak.
5 I have considered the days of old,
The years of ancient times.
6 I call to remembrance my song in
the night;
I meditate within my heart,
And my spirit makes diligent search.

7 Will the Lord cast off forever?
And will He be favorable no more?
8 Has His mercy ceased forever?
Has *His* promise failed forevermore?
9 Has God forgotten to be gracious?

Has He in anger shut up His tender
mercies?   Selah

10 And I said, "This *is* my anguish;
But I will remember the years of the
right hand of the Most High."
11 I will remember the works of the
LORD;
Surely I will remember Your
wonders of old.
12 I will also meditate on all Your work,
And talk of Your deeds.
13 Your way, O God, *is* in the
sanctuary;
Who *is* so great a God as *our* God?
14 You *are* the God who does wonders;
You have declared Your strength
among the peoples.
15 You have with *Your* arm redeemed
Your people,
The sons of Jacob and Joseph.
Selah

16 The waters saw You, O God;
The waters saw You, they were
afraid;
The depths also trembled.
17 The clouds poured out water;
The skies sent out a sound;
Your arrows also flashed about.
18 The voice of Your thunder *was* in
the whirlwind;
The lightnings lit up the world;
The earth trembled and shook.
19 Your way *was* in the sea,
Your path in the great waters,
And Your footsteps were not
known.
20 You led Your people like a flock
By the hand of Moses and Aaron.

PSALM 78

God's Kindness to Rebellious Israel

A Contemplation of Asaph.

1 Give ear, O my people, *to* my law;
Incline your ears to the words of my
mouth.
2 I will open my mouth in a parable;
I will utter dark sayings of old,
3 Which we have heard and known,
And our fathers have told us.
4 We will not hide *them* from their
children,
Telling to the generation to come the
praises of the LORD,
And His strength and His wonderful
works that He has done.

5 For He established a testimony in
Jacob,
And appointed a law in Israel,
Which He commanded our fathers,
That they should make them known
to their children;
6 That the generation to come might
know *them*,
The children *who* would be born,
That they may arise and declare
them to their children,
7 That they may set their hope in God,
And not forget the works of God,
But keep His commandments;
8 And may not be like their fathers,
A stubborn and rebellious
generation,
A generation *that* did not set its
heart aright,
And whose spirit was not faithful
to God.

9 The children of Ephraim, *being*
armed *and* carrying bows,
Turned back in the day of battle.
10 They did not keep the covenant
of God;
They refused to walk in His law,
11 And forgot His works
And His wonders that He had shown
them.

12 Marvelous things He did in the sight
of their fathers,
In the land of Egypt, *in* the field of
Zoan.
13 He divided the sea and caused them
to pass through;
And He made the waters stand up
like a heap.
14 In the daytime also He led them with
the cloud,
And all the night with a light of fire.
15 He split the rocks in the wilderness,
And gave *them* drink in abundance
like the depths.
16 He also brought streams out of the
rock,
And caused waters to run down like
rivers.

17 But they sinned even more
against Him
By rebelling against the Most High
in the wilderness.
18 And they tested God in their heart
By asking for the food of their fancy.

19 Yes, they spoke against God:
They said, "Can God prepare a table
in the wilderness?
20 Behold, He struck the rock,
So that the waters gushed out,
And the streams overflowed.
Can He give bread also?
Can He provide meat for His
people?"

21 Therefore the LORD heard *this* and
was furious;
So a fire was kindled against Jacob,
And anger also came up against
Israel,
22 Because they did not believe in God,
And did not trust in His salvation.
23 Yet He had commanded the clouds
above,
And opened the doors of heaven,
24 Had rained down manna on them
to eat,
And given them of the bread of
heaven.
25 Men ate angels' food;
He sent them food to the full.

26 He caused an east wind to blow in
the heavens;
And by His power He brought in the
south wind.
27 He also rained meat on them like the
dust,
Feathered fowl like the sand of the
seas;
28 And He let *them* fall in the midst of
their camp,
All around their dwellings.
29 So they ate and were well filled,
For He gave them their own desire.
30 They were not deprived of their
craving;
But while their food *was* still in their
mouths,
31 The wrath of God came against
them,
And slew the stoutest of them,
And struck down the choice *men* of
Israel.

32 In spite of this they still sinned,
And did not believe in His wondrous
works.
33 Therefore their days He consumed
in futility,
And their years in fear.

34 When He slew them, then they
sought Him;
And they returned and sought
earnestly for God.
35 Then they remembered that God
was their rock,
And the Most High God their
Redeemer.
36 Nevertheless they flattered Him
with their mouth,
And they lied to Him with their
tongue;
37 For their heart was not steadfast
with Him,
Nor were they faithful in His
covenant.
38 But He, *being* full of compassion,
forgave *their* iniquity,
And did not destroy *them*.
Yes, many a time He turned His
anger away,
And did not stir up all His wrath;
39 For He remembered that they *were
but* flesh,
A breath that passes away and does
not come again.

40 How often they provoked Him in the
wilderness,
And grieved Him in the desert!
41 Yes, again and again they
tempted God,
And limited the Holy One of Israel.
42 They did not remember His power:
The day when He redeemed them
from the enemy,
43 When He worked His signs in Egypt,
And His wonders in the field of
Zoan;
44 Turned their rivers into blood,
And their streams, that they could
not drink.
45 He sent swarms of flies among them,
which devoured them,
And frogs, which destroyed them.
46 He also gave their crops to the
caterpillar,
And their labor to the locust.
47 He destroyed their vines with hail,
And their sycamore trees with
frost.
48 He also gave up their cattle to the
hail,
And their flocks to fiery lightning.
49 He cast on them the fierceness of His
anger,
Wrath, indignation, and trouble,

By sending angels of destruction
among them.
50 He made a path for His anger;
He did not spare their soul from
death,
But gave their life over to the plague,
51 And destroyed all the firstborn in
Egypt,
The first of *their* strength in the tents
of Ham.
52 But He made His own people go
forth like sheep,
And guided them in the wilderness
like a flock;
53 And He led them on safely, so that
they did not fear;
But the sea overwhelmed their
enemies.
54 And He brought them to His holy
border,
This mountain *which* His right hand
had acquired.
55 He also drove out the nations before
them,
Allotted them an inheritance by
survey,
And made the tribes of Israel dwell
in their tents.

56 Yet they tested and provoked the
Most High God,
And did not keep His testimonies,
57 But turned back and acted
unfaithfully like their fathers;
They were turned aside like a
deceitful bow.
58 For they provoked Him to anger
with their high places,
And moved Him to jealousy with
their carved images.
59 When God heard *this,* He was
furious,
And greatly abhorred Israel,
60 So that He forsook the tabernacle of
Shiloh,
The tent He had placed among men,
61 And delivered His strength into
captivity,
And His glory into the enemy's
hand.
62 He also gave His people over to the
sword,
And was furious with His
inheritance.
63 The fire consumed their young men,
And their maidens were not given
in marriage.

64 Their priests fell by the sword,
And their widows made no
lamentation.

65 Then the Lord awoke as *from* sleep,
Like a mighty man who shouts
because of wine.
66 And He beat back His enemies;
He put them to a perpetual reproach.

67 Moreover He rejected the tent of
Joseph,
And did not choose the tribe of
Ephraim,
68 But chose the tribe of Judah,
Mount Zion which He loved.
69 And He built His sanctuary like the
heights,
Like the earth which He has
established forever.
70 He also chose David His servant,
And took him from the sheepfolds;
71 From following the ewes that had
young He brought him,
To shepherd Jacob His people,
And Israel His inheritance.
72 So he shepherded them according to
the integrity of his heart,
And guided them by the skillfulness
of his hands.

PSALM 79

*A Dirge and a Prayer for Israel,
Destroyed by Enemies*

A Psalm of Asaph.

1 O God, the nations have come into
Your inheritance;
Your holy temple they have defiled;
They have laid Jerusalem in heaps.
2 The dead bodies of Your servants
They have given *as* food for the
birds of the heavens,
The flesh of Your saints to the beasts
of the earth.
3 Their blood they have shed like
water all around Jerusalem,
And *there was* no one to bury *them.*
4 We have become a reproach to our
neighbors,
A scorn and derision to those who
are around us.

5 How long, Lord?
Will You be angry forever?
Will Your jealousy burn like fire?
6 Pour out Your wrath on the nations
that do not know You,

And on the kingdoms that do not
    call on Your name.
7 For they have devoured Jacob,
    And laid waste his dwelling place.

8 Oh, do not remember former
    iniquities against us!
    Let Your tender mercies come
        speedily to meet us,
    For we have been brought very low.
9 Help us, O God of our salvation,
    For the glory of Your name;
    And deliver us, and provide
        atonement for our sins,
    For Your name's sake!
10 Why should the nations say,
 "Where *is* their God?"
    Let there be known among the
        nations in our sight
    The avenging of the blood of Your
        servants *which has been* shed.

11 Let the groaning of the prisoner
    come before You;
    According to the greatness of Your
        power
    Preserve those who are appointed
        to die;
12 And return to our neighbors
    sevenfold into their bosom
    Their reproach with which they
        have reproached You, O Lord.

13 So we, Your people and sheep of
    Your pasture,
    Will give You thanks forever;
    We will show forth Your praise to
        all generations.

PSALM 80

Prayer for Israel's Restoration

To the Chief Musician. Set to "The Lilies."
A Testimony of Asaph. A Psalm.

1 Give ear, O Shepherd of Israel,
    You who lead Joseph like a flock;
    You who dwell *between* the
        cherubim, shine forth!
2 Before Ephraim, Benjamin, and
    Manasseh,
    Stir up Your strength,
    And come *and* save us!

3 Restore us, O God;
    Cause Your face to shine,
    And we shall be saved!

4 O Lord God of hosts,
    How long will You be angry
    Against the prayer of Your people?
5 You have fed them with the bread
    of tears,
    And given them tears to drink in
        great measure.
6 You have made us a strife to our
    neighbors,
    And our enemies laugh among
        themselves.

7 Restore us, O God of hosts;
    Cause Your face to shine,
    And we shall be saved!

8 You have brought a vine out of
    Egypt;
    You have cast out the nations, and
        planted it.
9 You prepared *room* for it,
    And caused it to take deep root,
    And it filled the land.
10 The hills were covered with its
    shadow,
    And the mighty cedars with its
        boughs.
11 She sent out her boughs to the
    Sea,[f]
    And her branches to the River.[g]

12 Why have You broken down her
    hedges,
    So that all who pass by the way
        pluck her *fruit*?
13 The boar out of the woods
    uproots it,
    And the wild beast of the field
        devours it.

14 Return, we beseech You, O God of
    hosts;
    Look down from heaven and see,
    And visit this vine
15 And the vineyard which Your right
    hand has planted,
    And the branch *that* You made
        strong for Yourself.
16 *It is* burned with fire, *it is* cut down;
    They perish at the rebuke of Your
        countenance.
17 Let Your hand be upon the man of
    Your right hand,
    Upon the son of man *whom* You
        made strong for Yourself.

f That is, the Mediterranean   *g* That is, the Euphrates

18 Then we will not turn back
   from You;
   Revive us, and we will call upon
   Your name.

19 Restore us, O Lord God of hosts;
   Cause Your face to shine,
   And we shall be saved!

PSALM 81

An Appeal for Israel's Repentance

To the Chief Musician. On an instrument of
Gath. A Psalm of Asaph.

1 Sing aloud to God our strength;
   Make a joyful shout to the God of
   Jacob.
2 Raise a song and strike the
   timbrel,
   The pleasant harp with the lute.

3 Blow the trumpet at the time of the
   New Moon,
   At the full moon, on our solemn
   feast day.
4 For this *is* a statute for Israel,
   A law of the God of Jacob.
5 This He established in Joseph *as* a
   testimony,
   When He went throughout the land
   of Egypt,
   Where I heard a language I did not
   understand.

6 "I removed his shoulder from the
   burden;
   His hands were freed from the
   baskets.
7 You called in trouble, and I
   delivered you;
   I answered you in the secret place
   of thunder;
   I tested you at the waters of
   Meribah.   Selah

8 "Hear, O My people, and I will
   admonish you!
   O Israel, if you will listen to Me!
9 There shall be no foreign god
   among you;
   Nor shall you worship any
   foreign god.
10 I *am* the Lord your God,
   Who brought you out of the land of
   Egypt;

Open your mouth wide, and I will
   fill it.

11 "But My people would not heed My
   voice,
   And Israel would *have* none of Me.
12 So I gave them over to their own
   stubborn heart,
   To walk in their own counsels.

13 "Oh, that My people would listen
   to Me,
   That Israel would walk in My
   ways!
14 I would soon subdue their enemies,
   And turn My hand against their
   adversaries.
15 The haters of the Lord would
   pretend submission to Him,
   But their fate would endure forever.
16 He would have fed them also with
   the finest of wheat;
   And with honey from the rock I
   would have satisfied you."

PSALM 82

A Plea for Justice

A Psalm of Asaph.

1 God stands in the congregation of
   the mighty;
   He judges among the gods.[h]
2 How long will you judge unjustly,
   And show partiality to the wicked?
                           Selah
3 Defend the poor and fatherless;
   Do justice to the afflicted and needy.
4 Deliver the poor and needy;
   Free *them* from the hand of the
   wicked.

5 They do not know, nor do they
   understand;
   They walk about in darkness;
   All the foundations of the earth are
   unstable.

6 I said, "You *are* gods,[h]
   And all of you *are* children of the
   Most High.
7 But you shall die like men,
   And fall like one of the princes."

8 Arise, O God, judge the earth;
   For You shall inherit all nations.

[h] That is, the judges

PSALM 83

Prayer to Frustrate Conspiracy Against Israel

A Song. A Psalm of Asaph.

1 Do not keep silent, O God!
   Do not hold Your peace,
   And do not be still, O God!
2 For behold, Your enemies make a
      tumult;
   And those who hate You have lifted
      up their head.
3 They have taken crafty counsel
      against Your people,
   And consulted together against
      Your sheltered ones.
4 They have said, "Come, and let us
      cut them off from *being* a nation,
   That the name of Israel may be
      remembered no more."

5 For they have consulted together
      with one consent;
   They form a confederacy
      against You:
6 The tents of Edom and the
      Ishmaelites;
   Moab and the Hagrites;
7 Gebal, Ammon, and Amalek;
   Philistia with the inhabitants of
      Tyre;
8 Assyria also has joined with them;
   They have helped the children
      of Lot.   Selah

9 Deal with them as *with* Midian,
   As *with* Sisera,
   As *with* Jabin at the Brook Kishon,
10 Who perished at En Dor,
   Who became *as* refuse on the earth.
11 Make their nobles like Oreb and like
      Zeeb,
   Yes, all their princes like Zebah and
      Zalmunna,
12 Who said, "Let us take for ourselves
   The pastures of God for a
      possession."

13 O my God, make them like the
      whirling dust,
   Like the chaff before the wind!
14 As the fire burns the woods,
   And as the flame sets the mountains
      on fire,
15 So pursue them with Your tempest,
   And frighten them with Your storm.
16 Fill their faces with shame,
   That they may seek Your name,
      O Lord.
17 Let them be confounded and
      dismayed forever;
   Yes, let them be put to shame and
      perish,
18 That they may know that You,
      whose name alone *is* the Lord,
   Are the Most High over all the earth.

PSALM 84

The Blessedness of Dwelling in the House of God

To the Chief Musician. On an instrument of
   Gath. A Psalm of the sons of Korah.

1 How lovely *is* Your tabernacle,
   O Lord of hosts!
2 My soul longs, yes, even faints
   For the courts of the Lord;
   My heart and my flesh cry out for
      the living God.

3 Even the sparrow has found a home,
   And the swallow a nest for herself,
   Where she may lay her young—
   Even Your altars, O Lord of hosts,
   My King and my God.
4 Blessed *are* those who dwell in Your
      house;
   They will still be praising You.
                              Selah

5 Blessed *is* the man whose strength
      is in You,
   Whose heart *is* set on pilgrimage.
6 *As they* pass through the Valley of
      Baca,
   They make it a spring;
   The rain also covers it with pools.
7 They go from strength to strength;
   Each one appears before God in
      Zion.

8 O Lord God of hosts, hear my
      prayer;
   Give ear, O God of Jacob!   Selah
9 O God, behold our shield,
   And look upon the face of Your
      anointed.

10 For a day in Your courts *is* better
      than a thousand.
   I would rather be a doorkeeper in
      the house of my God
   Than dwell in the tents of
      wickedness.
11 For the Lord God *is* a sun and shield;

The LORD will give grace and glory;
No good *thing* will He withhold
From those who walk uprightly.

12 O LORD of hosts,
Blessed *is* the man who trusts
    in You!

PSALM 85

Prayer that the LORD Will Restore Favor to the Land

To the Chief Musician. A Psalm of the sons
of Korah.

1 LORD, You have been favorable to
    Your land;
You have brought back the captivity
    of Jacob.
2 You have forgiven the iniquity of
    Your people;
You have covered all their sin.
                                          Selah
3 You have taken away all Your
    wrath;
You have turned from the fierceness
    of Your anger.

4 Restore us, O God of our salvation,
And cause Your anger toward us to
    cease.
5 Will You be angry with us forever?
Will You prolong Your anger to all
    generations?
6 Will You not revive us again,
That Your people may rejoice
    in You?
7 Show us Your mercy, LORD,
And grant us Your salvation.

8 I will hear what God the LORD will
    speak,
For He will speak peace
To His people and to His saints;
But let them not turn back to folly.
9 Surely His salvation *is* near to those
    who fear Him,
That glory may dwell in our land.

10 Mercy and truth have met together;
Righteousness and peace have
    kissed.
11 Truth shall spring out of the earth,
And righteousness shall look down
    from heaven.
12 Yes, the LORD will give *what is* good;
And our land will yield its increase.
13 Righteousness will go before Him,

And shall make His footsteps *our*
    pathway.

PSALM 86

Prayer for Mercy, with Meditation on the Excellencies of the LORD

A Prayer of David.

1 Bow down Your ear, O LORD, hear
    me;
For I *am* poor and needy.
2 Preserve my life, for I *am* holy;
You are my God;
Save Your servant who trusts
    in You!
3 Be merciful to me, O Lord,
For I cry to You all day long.
4 Rejoice the soul of Your servant,
For to You, O Lord, I lift up my soul.
5 For You, Lord, *are* good, and ready
    to forgive,
And abundant in mercy to all those
    who call upon You.

6 Give ear, O LORD, to my prayer;
And attend to the voice of my
    supplications.
7 In the day of my trouble I will call
    upon You,
For You will answer me.

8 Among the gods *there is* none like
    You, O Lord;
Nor *are there any works* like Your
    works.
9 All nations whom You have made
Shall come and worship before You,
    O Lord,
And shall glorify Your name.
10 For You *are* great, and do wondrous
    things;
You alone *are* God.

11 Teach me Your way, O LORD;
I will walk in Your truth;
Unite my heart to fear Your name.
12 I will praise You, O Lord my God,
    with all my heart,
And I will glorify Your name
    forevermore.
13 For great *is* Your mercy toward me,
And You have delivered my soul
    from the depths of Sheol.

14 O God, the proud have risen
    against me,
And a mob of violent *men* have
    sought my life,

And have not set You before them.
15 But You, O Lord, *are* a God full of
       compassion, and gracious,
   Longsuffering and abundant in
       mercy and truth.

16 Oh, turn to me, and have mercy on
       me!
   Give Your strength to Your servant,
   And save the son of Your
       maidservant.
17 Show me a sign for good,
   That those who hate me may see *it*
       and be ashamed,
   Because You, Lord, have helped me
       and comforted me.

PSALM 87

The Glories of the City of God

A Psalm of the sons of Korah. A Song.

1 His foundation *is* in the holy
       mountains.
2 The Lord loves the gates of Zion
   More than all the dwellings of Jacob.
3 Glorious things are spoken of you,
   O city of God!   Selah

4 "I will make mention of Rahab and
       Babylon to those who know Me;
   Behold, O Philistia and Tyre, with
       Ethiopia:
   'This *one* was born there.' "

5 And of Zion it will be said,
   "This *one* and that *one* were born
       in her;
   And the Most High Himself shall
       establish her."
6 The Lord will record,
   When He registers the peoples:
   "This *one* was born there."   Selah

7 Both the singers and the players on
       instruments *say,*
   "All my springs *are* in you."

PSALM 88

A Prayer for Help in Despondency

A Song. A Psalm of the sons of Korah. To the
Chief Musician. Set to "Mahalath Leannoth." A
Contemplation of Heman the Ezrahite.

1 O Lord, God of my salvation,
   I have cried out day and night before
       You.
2 Let my prayer come before You;
   Incline Your ear to my cry.

3 For my soul is full of troubles,
   And my life draws near to the grave.
4 I am counted with those who go
       down to the pit;
   I am like a man *who has* no strength,
5 Adrift among the dead,
   Like the slain who lie in the grave,
   Whom You remember no more,
   And who are cut off from Your hand.

6 You have laid me in the lowest pit,
   In darkness, in the depths.
7 Your wrath lies heavy upon me,
   And You have afflicted *me* with all
       Your waves.   Selah
8 You have put away my
       acquaintances far from me;
   You have made me an abomination
       to them;
   I am shut up, and I cannot get out;
9 My eye wastes away because of
       affliction.

   Lord, I have called daily upon You;
   I have stretched out my hands
       to You.
10 Will You work wonders for the
       dead?
   Shall the dead arise *and* praise You?
                                   Selah
11 Shall Your lovingkindness be
       declared in the grave?
   Or Your faithfulness in the place of
       destruction?
12 Shall Your wonders be known in the
       dark?
   And Your righteousness in the land
       of forgetfulness?

13 But to You I have cried out, O Lord,
   And in the morning my prayer
       comes before You.
14 Lord, why do You cast off my soul?
   Why do You hide Your face
       from me?
15 I *have been* afflicted and ready to
       die from *my* youth;
   I suffer Your terrors;
   I am distraught.
16 Your fierce wrath has gone over me;
   Your terrors have cut me off.
17 They came around me all day long
       like water;
   They engulfed me altogether.
18 Loved one and friend You have put
       far from me,

And my acquaintances into
  darkness.

PSALM 89

Remembering the Covenant with David, and Sorrow for Lost Blessings

A Contemplation of Ethan the Ezrahite.

1 I will sing of the mercies of the LORD
    forever;
  With my mouth will I make known
    Your faithfulness to all
    generations.
2 For I have said, "Mercy shall be built
    up forever;
  Your faithfulness You shall
    establish in the very heavens."

3 "I have made a covenant with My
    chosen,
  I have sworn to My servant David:
4 'Your seed I will establish forever,
  And build up your throne to all
    generations.'"   Selah

5 And the heavens will praise Your
    wonders, O LORD;
  Your faithfulness also in the
    assembly of the saints.
6 For who in the heavens can be
    compared to the LORD?
  Who among the sons of the mighty
    can be likened to the LORD?
7 God is greatly to be feared in the
    assembly of the saints,
  And to be held in reverence by all
    those around Him.
8 O LORD God of hosts,
  Who *is* mighty like You, O LORD?
  Your faithfulness also
    surrounds You.
9 You rule the raging of the sea;
  When its waves rise, You still them.
10 You have broken Rahab in pieces,
    as one who is slain;
  You have scattered Your enemies
    with Your mighty arm.

11 The heavens *are* Yours, the earth
    also *is* Yours;
  The world and all its fullness, You
    have founded them.
12 The north and the south, You have
    created them;
  Tabor and Hermon rejoice in Your
    name.
13 You have a mighty arm;

Strong is Your hand, *and* high is
    Your right hand.
14 Righteousness and justice *are* the
    foundation of Your throne;
  Mercy and truth go before Your
    face.
15 Blessed *are* the people who know
    the joyful sound!
  They walk, O LORD, in the light of
    Your countenance.
16 In Your name they rejoice all day
    long,
  And in Your righteousness they are
    exalted.
17 For You *are* the glory of their
    strength,
  And in Your favor our horn is
    exalted.
18 For our shield *belongs* to the LORD,
  And our king to the Holy One of
    Israel.

19 Then You spoke in a vision to Your
    holy one,
  And said: "I have given help to *one*
    who is mighty;
  I have exalted one chosen from the
    people.
20 I have found My servant David;
  With My holy oil I have
    anointed him,
21 With whom My hand shall be
    established;
  Also My arm shall strengthen him.
22 The enemy shall not outwit him,
  Nor the son of wickedness
    afflict him.
23 I will beat down his foes before his
    face,
  And plague those who hate him.

24 "But My faithfulness and My mercy
    shall be with him,
  And in My name his horn shall be
    exalted.
25 Also I will set his hand over the sea,
  And his right hand over the rivers.
26 He shall cry to Me, 'You *are* my
    Father,
  My God, and the rock of my
    salvation.'
27 Also I will make him My firstborn,
  The highest of the kings of the earth.
28 My mercy I will keep for him
    forever,
  And My covenant shall stand firm
    with him.

29 His seed also I will make *to endure*
     forever,
   And his throne as the days of
     heaven.

30 "If his sons forsake My law
   And do not walk in My judgments,
31 If they break My statutes
   And do not keep My
     commandments,
32 Then I will punish their
     transgression with the rod,
   And their iniquity with stripes.
33 Nevertheless My lovingkindness I
     will not utterly take from him,
   Nor allow My faithfulness to fail.
34 My covenant I will not break,
   Nor alter the word that has gone out
     of My lips.
35 Once I have sworn by My holiness;
   I will not lie to David:
36 His seed shall endure forever,
   And his throne as the sun before Me;
37 It shall be established forever like
     the moon,
   Even *like* the faithful witness in
     the sky."   Selah

38 But You have cast off and abhorred,
   You have been furious with Your
     anointed.
39 You have renounced the covenant of
     Your servant;
   You have profaned his crown *by
     casting it* to the ground.
40 You have broken down all his
     hedges;
   You have brought his strongholds to
     ruin.
41 All who pass by the way
     plunder him;
   He is a reproach to his neighbors.
42 You have exalted the right hand of
     his adversaries;
   You have made all his enemies
     rejoice.
43 You have also turned back the edge
     of his sword,
   And have not sustained him in the
     battle.
44 You have made his glory cease,
   And cast his throne down to the
     ground.
45 The days of his youth You have
     shortened;
   You have covered him with shame.
                                      Selah

46 How long, LORD?
   Will You hide Yourself forever?
   Will Your wrath burn like fire?
47 Remember how short my time is;
   For what futility have You created
     all the children of men?
48 What man can live and not see
     death?
   Can he deliver his life from the
     power of the grave?   Selah

49 Lord, where *are* Your former
     lovingkindnesses,
   Which You swore to David in Your
     truth?
50 Remember, Lord, the reproach of
     Your servants—
   How I bear in my bosom *the
     reproach of* all the many peoples,
51 With which Your enemies have
     reproached, O LORD,
   With which they have reproached
     the footsteps of Your anointed.

52 Blessed *be* the LORD forevermore!
   Amen and Amen.

   BOOK FOUR: PSALMS 90—106

   ## PSALM 90

   ### The Eternity of God, and Man's Frailty

   A Prayer of Moses the man of God.

1 LORD, You have been our dwelling
     place in all generations.
2 Before the mountains were brought
     forth,
   Or ever You had formed the earth
     and the world,
   Even from everlasting to
     everlasting, You *are* God.

3 You turn man to destruction,
   And say, "Return, O children
     of men."
4 For a thousand years in Your sight
   Are like yesterday when it is past,
   And *like* a watch in the night.
5 You carry them away *like* a flood;
   They are like a sleep.
   In the morning they are like grass
     which grows up:
6 In the morning it flourishes and
     grows up;
   In the evening it is cut down and
     withers.

7 For we have been consumed by
     Your anger,

And by Your wrath we are terrified.
8 You have set our iniquities
     before You,
  Our secret *sins* in the light of Your
     countenance.
9 For all our days have passed away
     in Your wrath;
  We finish our years like a sigh.
10 The days of our lives *are* seventy
     years;
  And if by reason of strength *they are*
     eighty years,
  Yet their boast *is* only labor and
     sorrow;
  For it is soon cut off, and we fly
     away.
11 Who knows the power of Your
     anger?
  For as the fear of You, *so is* Your
     wrath.

12 So teach *us* to number our days,
  That we may gain a heart of wisdom.

13 Return, O LORD!
  How long?
  And have compassion on Your
     servants.
14 Oh, satisfy us early with Your
     mercy,
  That we may rejoice and be glad all
     our days!
15 Make us glad according to the days
     in which You have afflicted us,
  The years *in which* we have seen
     evil.
16 Let Your work appear to Your
     servants,
  And Your glory to their children.
17 And let the beauty of the LORD our
     God be upon us,
  And establish the work of our hands
     for us;
  Yes, establish the work of our hands.

PSALM 91

Safety of Abiding in the Presence of God

1 He who dwells in the secret place
     of the Most High
  Shall abide under the shadow of the
     Almighty.
2 I will say of the LORD, "*He is* my
     refuge and my fortress;
  My God, in Him I will trust."

3 Surely He shall deliver you from the
     snare of the fowler

And from the perilous pestilence.
4 He shall cover you with His feathers,
  And under His wings you shall take
     refuge;
  His truth *shall be your* shield and
     buckler.
5 You shall not be afraid of the terror
     by night,
  Nor of the arrow *that* flies by day,
6 *Nor* of the pestilence *that* walks in
     darkness,
  Nor of the destruction *that* lays
     waste at noonday.

7 A thousand may fall at your side,
  And ten thousand at your right
     hand;
  But it shall not come near you.
8 Only with your eyes shall you look,
  And see the reward of the wicked.

9 Because you have made the LORD,
     who is my refuge,
  Even the Most High, your dwelling
     place,
10 No evil shall befall you,
  Nor shall any plague come near
     your dwelling;
11 For He shall give His angels charge
     over you,
  To keep you in all your ways.
12 In *their* hands they shall bear
     you up,
  Lest you dash your foot against a
     stone.
13 You shall tread upon the lion and
     the cobra,
  The young lion and the serpent you
     shall trample underfoot.

14 "Because he has set his love upon Me,
     therefore I will deliver him;
  I will set him on high, because he
     has known My name.
15 He shall call upon Me, and I will
     answer him;
  I *will be* with him in trouble;
  I will deliver him and honor him.
16 With long life I will satisfy him,
  And show him My salvation."

PSALM 92

Praise to the LORD for His Love and Faithfulness

A Psalm. A Song for the Sabbath day.

1 *It is* good to give thanks to the LORD,
  And to sing praises to Your name,
     O Most High;

2 To declare Your lovingkindness in
      the morning,
   And Your faithfulness every night,
3 On an instrument of ten strings,
   On the lute,
   And on the harp,
   With harmonious sound.
4 For You, LORD, have made me glad
      through Your work;
   I will triumph in the works of Your
      hands.

5 O LORD, how great are Your works!
   Your thoughts are very deep.
6 A senseless man does not know,
   Nor does a fool understand this.
7 When the wicked spring up like
      grass,
   And when all the workers of iniquity
      flourish,
   It is that they may be destroyed
      forever.

8 But You, LORD, are on high
      forevermore.
9 For behold, Your enemies, O LORD,
   For behold, Your enemies shall
      perish;
   All the workers of iniquity shall be
      scattered.

10 But my horn You have exalted like
      a wild ox;
   I have been anointed with fresh oil.
11 My eye also has seen my desire on
      my enemies;
   My ears hear my desire on the
      wicked
   Who rise up against me.

12 The righteous shall flourish like a
      palm tree,
   He shall grow like a cedar in
      Lebanon.
13 Those who are planted in the house
      of the LORD
   Shall flourish in the courts of
      our God.
14 They shall still bear fruit in old age;
   They shall be fresh and flourishing,
15 To declare that the LORD is upright;
   He is my rock, and there is no
      unrighteousness in Him.

PSALM 93

The Eternal Reign of the LORD

1 The LORD reigns, He is clothed with
      majesty;

The LORD is clothed,
He has girded Himself with strength.
Surely the world is established, so
   that it cannot be moved.
2 Your throne is established from
      of old;
   You are from everlasting.

3 The floods have lifted up, O LORD,
   The floods have lifted up their voice;
   The floods lift up their waves.
4 The LORD on high is mightier
   Than the noise of many waters,
   Than the mighty waves of the sea.

5 Your testimonies are very sure;
   Holiness adorns Your house,
   O LORD, forever.

PSALM 94

God the Refuge of the Righteous

1 O LORD God, to whom vengeance
      belongs—
   O God, to whom vengeance belongs,
      shine forth!
2 Rise up, O Judge of the earth;
   Render punishment to the proud.
3 LORD, how long will the wicked,
   How long will the wicked triumph?

4 They utter speech, and speak
      insolent things;
   All the workers of iniquity boast in
      themselves.
5 They break in pieces Your people,
      O LORD,
   And afflict Your heritage.
6 They slay the widow and the
      stranger,
   And murder the fatherless.
7 Yet they say, "The LORD does
      not see,
   Nor does the God of Jacob
      understand."

8 Understand, you senseless among
      the people;
   And you fools, when will you be
      wise?
9 He who planted the ear, shall He not
      hear?
   He who formed the eye, shall He
      not see?
10 He who instructs the nations, shall
      He not correct,
   He who teaches man knowledge?

11 The Lord knows the thoughts
      of man,
   That they *are* futile.

12 Blessed *is* the man whom You
      instruct, O Lord,
   And teach out of Your law,
13 That You may give him rest from
      the days of adversity,
   Until the pit is dug for the wicked.
14 For the Lord will not cast off His
      people,
   Nor will He forsake His inheritance.
15 But judgment will return to
      righteousness,
   And all the upright in heart will
      follow it.

16 Who will rise up for me against the
      evildoers?
   Who will stand up for me against
      the workers of iniquity?
17 Unless the Lord *had been* my help,
   My soul would soon have settled in
      silence.
18 If I say, "My foot slips,"
   Your mercy, O Lord, will hold
      me up.
19 In the multitude of my anxieties
      within me,
   Your comforts delight my soul.

20 Shall the throne of iniquity, which
      devises evil by law,
   Have fellowship with You?
21 They gather together against the life
      of the righteous,
   And condemn innocent blood.
22 But the Lord has been my defense,
   And my God the rock of my refuge.
23 He has brought on them their own
      iniquity,
   And shall cut them off in their own
      wickedness;
   The Lord our God shall cut them off.

PSALM 95

A Call to Worship and Obedience

1 Oh come, let us sing to the Lord!
   Let us shout joyfully to the Rock of
      our salvation.
2 Let us come before His presence
      with thanksgiving;
   Let us shout joyfully to Him with
      psalms.
3 For the Lord *is* the great God,
   And the great King above all gods.

4 In His hand *are* the deep places of
      the earth;
   The heights of the hills *are* His also.
5 The sea *is* His, for He made it;
   And His hands formed the dry *land*.

6 Oh come, let us worship and bow
      down;
   Let us kneel before the Lord our
      Maker.
7 For He *is* our God,
   And we *are* the people of His
      pasture,
   And the sheep of His hand.

   Today, if you will hear His voice:
8 "Do not harden your hearts, as in the
      rebellion,
   As *in* the day of trial in the
      wilderness,
9 When your fathers tested Me;
   They tried Me, though they saw My
      work.
10 For forty years I was grieved with
      that generation,
   And said, 'It *is* a people who go
      astray in their hearts,
   And they do not know My ways.'
11 So I swore in My wrath,
   'They shall not enter My rest.' "

PSALM 96

A Song of Praise to God Coming
in Judgment

1 Oh, sing to the Lord a new song!
   Sing to the Lord, all the earth.
2 Sing to the Lord, bless His name;
   Proclaim the good news of His
      salvation from day to day.
3 Declare His glory among the
      nations,
   His wonders among all peoples.

4 For the Lord *is* great and greatly to
      be praised;
   He *is* to be feared above all gods.
5 For all the gods of the peoples *are*
      idols,
   But the Lord made the heavens.
6 Honor and majesty *are* before Him;
   Strength and beauty *are* in His
      sanctuary.

7 Give to the Lord, O families of the
      peoples,
   Give to the Lord glory and strength.

8 Give to the LORD the glory *due* His
  name;
  Bring an offering, and come into His
  courts.
9 Oh, worship the LORD in the beauty
  of holiness!
  Tremble before Him, all the earth.

10 Say among the nations, "The LORD
   reigns;
   The world also is firmly established,
   It shall not be moved;
   He shall judge the peoples
   righteously."

11 Let the heavens rejoice, and let the
   earth be glad;
   Let the sea roar, and all its fullness;
12 Let the field be joyful, and all that
   is in it.
   Then all the trees of the woods will
   rejoice before the LORD.
13 For He is coming, for He is coming
   to judge the earth.
   He shall judge the world with
   righteousness,
   And the peoples with His truth.

PSALM 97

A Song of Praise to the Sovereign LORD

1 The LORD reigns;
  Let the earth rejoice;
  Let the multitude of isles be glad!

2 Clouds and darkness surround Him;
  Righteousness and justice *are* the
  foundation of His throne.
3 A fire goes before Him,
  And burns up His enemies round
  about.
4 His lightnings light the world;
  The earth sees and trembles.
5 The mountains melt like wax at the
  presence of the LORD,
  At the presence of the Lord of the
  whole earth.
6 The heavens declare His
  righteousness,
  And all the peoples see His glory.

7 Let all be put to shame who serve
  carved images,
  Who boast of idols.
  Worship Him, all *you* gods.
8 Zion hears and is glad,
  And the daughters of Judah rejoice

Because of Your judgments, O LORD.
9 For You, LORD, *are* most high above
  all the earth;
  You are exalted far above all gods.

10 You who love the LORD, hate evil!
   He preserves the souls of His saints;
   He delivers them out of the hand of
   the wicked.
11 Light is sown for the righteous,
   And gladness for the upright in
   heart.
12 Rejoice in the LORD, you righteous,
   And give thanks at the
   remembrance of His holy name.

PSALM 98

A Song of Praise to the LORD for His Salvation and Judgment

A Psalm.

1 Oh, sing to the LORD a new song!
  For He has done marvelous things;
  His right hand and His holy arm
  have gained Him the victory.
2 The LORD has made known His
  salvation;
  His righteousness He has revealed
  in the sight of the nations.
3 He has remembered His mercy and
  His faithfulness to the house of
  Israel;
  All the ends of the earth have seen
  the salvation of our God.

4 Shout joyfully to the LORD, all the
  earth;
  Break forth in song, rejoice, and sing
  praises.
5 Sing to the LORD with the harp,
  With the harp and the sound of a
  psalm,
6 With trumpets and the sound of a
  horn;
  Shout joyfully before the LORD, the
  King.

7 Let the sea roar, and all its fullness,
  The world and those who dwell
  in it;
8 Let the rivers clap *their* hands;
  Let the hills be joyful together
  before the LORD,
9 For He is coming to judge the earth.
  With righteousness He shall judge
  the world,
  And the peoples with equity.

PSALM 99

Praise to the Lord for His Holiness

1 The Lord reigns;
  Let the peoples tremble!
  He dwells *between* the cherubim;
  Let the earth be moved!
2 The Lord *is* great in Zion,
  And He *is* high above all the peoples.
3 Let them praise Your great and
      awesome name—
  He *is* holy.

4 The King's strength also loves
      justice;
  You have established equity;
  You have executed justice and
      righteousness in Jacob.
5 Exalt the Lord our God,
  And worship at His footstool—
  He *is* holy.

6 Moses and Aaron were among His
      priests,
  And Samuel was among those who
      called upon His name;
  They called upon the Lord, and He
      answered them.
7 He spoke to them in the cloudy
      pillar;
  They kept His testimonies and the
      ordinance He gave them.

8 You answered them, O Lord
      our God;
  You were to them God-Who-
      Forgives,
  Though You took vengeance on
      their deeds.
9 Exalt the Lord our God,
  And worship at His holy hill;
  For the Lord our God *is* holy.

PSALM 100

A Song of Praise for the Lord's Faithfulness to His People

A Psalm of Thanksgiving.

1 Make a joyful shout to the Lord, all
      you lands!
2 Serve the Lord with gladness;
  Come before His presence with
      singing.
3 Know that the Lord, He *is* God;
  It is He *who* has made us, and not
      we ourselves;
  We are His people and the sheep of
      His pasture.

4 Enter into His gates with
      thanksgiving,
  And into His courts with praise.
  Be thankful to Him, *and* bless His
      name.
5 For the Lord *is* good;
  His mercy *is* everlasting,
  And His truth *endures* to all
      generations.

PSALM 101

Promised Faithfulness to the Lord

A Psalm of David.

1 I will sing of mercy and justice;
  To You, O Lord, I will sing praises.

2 I will behave wisely in a perfect way.
  Oh, when will You come to me?
  I will walk within my house with a
      perfect heart.

3 I will set nothing wicked before my
      eyes;
  I hate the work of those who fall
      away;
  It shall not cling to me.
4 A perverse heart shall depart
      from me;
  I will not know wickedness.

5 Whoever secretly slanders his
      neighbor,
  Him I will destroy;
  The one who has a haughty look and
      a proud heart,
  Him I will not endure.

6 My eyes *shall be* on the faithful of
      the land,
  That they may dwell with me;
  He who walks in a perfect way,
  He shall serve me.
7 He who works deceit shall not dwell
      within my house;
  He who tells lies shall not continue
      in my presence.
8 Early I will destroy all the wicked
      of the land,
  That I may cut off all the evildoers
      from the city of the Lord.

PSALM 102

The Lord's Eternal Love

A Prayer of the afflicted, when he is overwhelmed and pours out his complaint before
the Lord.

1 Hear my prayer, O Lord,
  And let my cry come to You.

2 Do not hide Your face from me in
the day of my trouble;
Incline Your ear to me;
In the day that I call, answer me
speedily.

3 For my days are consumed like
smoke,
And my bones are burned like a
hearth.
4 My heart is stricken and withered
like grass,
So that I forget to eat my bread.
5 Because of the sound of my
groaning
My bones cling to my skin.
6 I am like a pelican of the wilderness;
I am like an owl of the desert.
7 I lie awake,
And am like a sparrow alone on the
housetop.

8 My enemies reproach me all day
long;
Those who deride me swear an oath
against me.
9 For I have eaten ashes like bread,
And mingled my drink with
weeping,
10 Because of Your indignation and
Your wrath;
For You have lifted me up and cast
me away.
11 My days are like a shadow that
lengthens,
And I wither away like grass.

12 But You, O Lord, shall endure
forever,
And the remembrance of Your name
to all generations.
13 You will arise and have mercy on
Zion;
For the time to favor her,
Yes, the set time, has come.
14 For Your servants take pleasure in
her stones,
And show favor to her dust.
15 So the nations shall fear the name
of the Lord,
And all the kings of the earth Your
glory.
16 For the Lord shall build up Zion;
He shall appear in His glory.
17 He shall regard the prayer of the
destitute,
And shall not despise their prayer.

18 This will be written for the
generation to come,
That a people yet to be created may
praise the Lord.
19 For He looked down from the height
of His sanctuary;
From heaven the Lord viewed the
earth,
20 To hear the groaning of the prisoner,
To release those appointed to death,
21 To declare the name of the Lord in
Zion,
And His praise in Jerusalem,
22 When the peoples are gathered
together,
And the kingdoms, to serve the
Lord.

23 He weakened my strength in
the way;
He shortened my days.
24 I said, "O my God,
Do not take me away in the midst
of my days;
Your years are throughout all
generations.
25 Of old You laid the foundation of the
earth,
And the heavens are the work of
Your hands.
26 They will perish, but You will
endure;
Yes, they will all grow old like a
garment;
Like a cloak You will change
them,
And they will be changed.
27 But You are the same,
And Your years will have no end.
28 The children of Your servants will
continue,
And their descendants will be
established before You."

PSALM 103

Praise for the Lord's Mercies

A Psalm of David.

1 Bless the Lord, O my soul;
And all that is within me, bless His
holy name!
2 Bless the Lord, O my soul,
And forget not all His benefits:
3 Who forgives all your iniquities,
Who heals all your diseases,
4 Who redeems your life from
destruction,

Who crowns you with
lovingkindness and tender
mercies,
5 Who satisfies your mouth with good
things,
So that your youth is renewed like
the eagle's.

6 The LORD executes righteousness
And justice for all who are
oppressed.
7 He made known His ways to Moses,
His acts to the children of Israel.
8 The LORD *is* merciful and gracious,
Slow to anger, and abounding in
mercy.
9 He will not always strive *with us,*
Nor will He keep *His anger* forever.
10 He has not dealt with us according
to our sins,
Nor punished us according to our
iniquities.

11 For as the heavens are high above
the earth,
So great is His mercy toward those
who fear Him;
12 As far as the east is from the west,
So far has He removed our
transgressions from us.
13 As a father pities *his* children,
So the LORD pities those who
fear Him.
14 For He knows our frame;
He remembers that we *are* dust.

15 *As for* man, his days *are* like grass;
As a flower of the field, so he
flourishes.
16 For the wind passes over it, and it
is gone,
And its place remembers it no
more.[i]
17 But the mercy of the LORD *is* from
everlasting to everlasting
On those who fear Him,
And His righteousness to children's
children,
18 To such as keep His covenant,
And to those who remember His
commandments to do them.

19 The LORD has established His throne
in heaven,
And His kingdom rules over all.

20 Bless the LORD, you His angels,
Who excel in strength, who do His
word,
Heeding the voice of His word.
21 Bless the LORD, all y*o*u His hosts,
You ministers of His, who do His
pleasure.
22 Bless the LORD, all His works,
In all places of His dominion.

Bless the LORD, O my soul!

PSALM 104

Praise to the Sovereign LORD for His Creation and Providence

1 Bless the LORD, O my soul!

O LORD my God, You are very great:
You are clothed with honor and
majesty,
2 Who cover *Yourself* with light as
with a garment,
Who stretch out the heavens like a
curtain.

3 He lays the beams of His upper
chambers in the waters,
Who makes the clouds His chariot,
Who walks on the wings of the wind,
4 Who makes His angels spirits,
His ministers a flame of fire.

5 *You who* laid the foundations of the
earth,
So *that* it should not be moved
forever,
6 You covered it with the deep as *with*
a garment;
The waters stood above the
mountains.
7 At Your rebuke they fled;
At the voice of Your thunder they
hastened away.
8 They went up over the mountains;
They went down into the valleys,
To the place which You founded for
them.
9 You have set a boundary that they
may not pass over,
That they may not return to cover
the earth.

10 He sends the springs into the
valleys;
They flow among the hills.

i Compare Job 7.10

11 They give drink to every beast of the
    field;
   The wild donkeys quench their
    thirst.
12 By them the birds of the heavens
    have their home;
   They sing among the branches.
13 He waters the hills from His upper
    chambers;
   The earth is satisfied with the fruit
    of Your works.

14 He causes the grass to grow for the
    cattle,
   And vegetation for the service
    of man,
   That he may bring forth food from
    the earth,
15 And wine *that* makes glad the heart
    of man,
   Oil to make *his* face shine,
   And bread *which* strengthens man's
    heart.
16 The trees of the LORD are full *of sap*,
   The cedars of Lebanon which He
    planted,
17 Where the birds make their nests;
   The stork has her home in the fir
    trees.
18 The high hills *are* for the wild goats;
   The cliffs are a refuge for the rock
    badgers.*j*

19 He appointed the moon for seasons;
   The sun knows its going down.
20 You make darkness, and it is night,
   In which all the beasts of the forest
    creep about.
21 The young lions roar after their prey,
   And seek their food from God.
22 *When* the sun rises, they gather
    together
   And lie down in their dens.
23 Man goes out to his work
   And to his labor until the evening.

24 O LORD, how manifold are Your
    works!
   In wisdom You have made them all.
   The earth is full of Your
    possessions—
25 This great and wide sea,
   In which *are* innumerable teeming
    things,
   Living things both small and great.

26 There the ships sail about;
   There is that Leviathan
   Which You have made to play there.
27 These all wait for You,
   That You may give *them* their food
    in due season.
28 *What* You give them they gather in;
   You open Your hand, they are filled
    with good.
29 You hide Your face, they are
    troubled;
   You take away their breath, they die
    and return to their dust.
30 You send forth Your Spirit, they are
    created;
   And You renew the face of the earth.

31 May the glory of the LORD endure
    forever;
   May the LORD rejoice in His works.
32 He looks on the earth, and it
    trembles;
   He touches the hills, and they
    smoke.

33 I will sing to the LORD as long as I
    live;
   I will sing praise to my God while I
    have my being.
34 May my meditation be sweet to Him;
   I will be glad in the LORD.
35 May sinners be consumed from the
    earth,
   And the wicked be no more.

   Bless the LORD, O my soul!
   Praise the LORD!

PSALM 105

The Eternal Faithfulness of the LORD

1 Oh, give thanks to the LORD!
   Call upon His name;
   Make known His deeds among the
    peoples!
2 Sing to Him, sing psalms to Him;
   Talk of all His wondrous works!
3 Glory in His holy name;
   Let the hearts of those rejoice who
    seek the LORD!
4 Seek the LORD and His strength;
   Seek His face evermore!
5 Remember His marvelous works
    which He has done,

---

j Or *rock hyrax* (compare Leviticus 11.5)

His wonders, and the judgments of
  His mouth,
6 O seed of Abraham His servant,
  You children of Jacob, His chosen
    ones!

7 He *is* the LORD our God;
  His judgments *are* in all the earth.
8 He remembers His covenant forever,
  The word *which* He commanded, for
    a thousand generations,
9 *The covenant* which He made with
    Abraham,
  And His oath to Isaac,
10 And confirmed it to Jacob for a
     statute,
   To Israel *as* an everlasting covenant,
11 Saying, "To you I will give the land
     of Canaan
   As the allotment of your
     inheritance,"
12 When they were few in number,
   Indeed very few, and strangers in it.

13 When they went from one nation to
     another,
   From *one* kingdom to another
     people,
14 He permitted no one to do them
     wrong;
   Yes, He rebuked kings for their
     sakes,
15 *Saying*, "Do not touch My anointed
     ones,
   And do My prophets no harm."

16 Moreover He called for a famine in
     the land;
   He destroyed all the provision of
     bread.
17 He sent a man before them—
   Joseph—*who* was sold as a slave.
18 They hurt his feet with fetters,
   He was laid in irons.
19 Until the time that his word came
     to pass,
   The word of the LORD tested him.
20 The king sent and released him,
   The ruler of the people let him go
     free.
21 He made him lord of his house,
   And ruler of all his possessions,
22 To bind his princes at his pleasure,
   And teach his elders wisdom.

23 Israel also came into Egypt,
   And Jacob dwelt in the land of Ham.

24 He increased His people greatly,
   And made them stronger than their
     enemies.
25 He turned their heart to hate His
     people,
   To deal craftily with His servants.

26 He sent Moses His servant,
   And Aaron whom He had chosen.
27 They performed His signs among
     them,
   And wonders in the land of Ham.
28 He sent darkness, and made *it* dark;
   And they did not rebel against His
     word.
29 He turned their waters into blood,
   And killed their fish.
30 Their land abounded with frogs,
   Even in the chambers of their kings.
31 He spoke, and there came swarms
     of flies,
   And lice in all their territory.
32 He gave them hail for rain,
   And flaming fire in their land.
33 He struck their vines also, and their
     fig trees,
   And splintered the trees of their
     territory.
34 He spoke, and locusts came,
   Young locusts without number,
35 And ate up all the vegetation in their
     land,
   And devoured the fruit of their
     ground.
36 He also destroyed all the firstborn
     in their land,
   The first of all their strength.

37 He also brought them out with silver
     and gold,
   And *there was* none feeble among
     His tribes.
38 Egypt was glad when they departed,
   For the fear of them had fallen upon
     them.
39 He spread a cloud for a covering,
   And fire to give light in the night.
40 *The people* asked, and He brought
     quail,
   And satisfied them with the bread
     of heaven.
41 He opened the rock, and water
     gushed out;
   It ran in the dry places *like* a river.

42 For He remembered His holy
     promise,

And Abraham His servant.
43 He brought out His people with joy,
His chosen ones with gladness.
44 He gave them the lands of the
Gentiles,
And they inherited the labor of the
nations,
45 That they might observe His statutes
And keep His laws.

Praise the LORD!

PSALM 106

Joy in Forgiveness of Israel's Sins

1 Praise the LORD!

Oh, give thanks to the LORD, for *He
is* good!
For His mercy *endures* forever.

2 Who can utter the mighty acts of the
LORD?
Who can declare all His praise?
3 Blessed *are* those who keep justice,
And he who does righteousness at
all times!

4 Remember me, O LORD, with the
favor *You have toward* Your
people.
Oh, visit me with Your salvation,
5 That I may see the benefit of Your
chosen ones,
That I may rejoice in the gladness
of Your nation,
That I may glory with Your
inheritance.

6 We have sinned with our fathers,
We have committed iniquity,
We have done wickedly.
7 Our fathers in Egypt did not
understand Your wonders;
They did not remember the
multitude of Your mercies,
But rebelled by the sea—the
Red Sea.

8 Nevertheless He saved them for His
name's sake,
That He might make His mighty
power known.
9 He rebuked the Red Sea also, and
it dried up;
So He led them through the depths,
As through the wilderness.

10 He saved them from the hand of him
who hated *them*,
And redeemed them from the hand
of the enemy.
11 The waters covered their enemies;
There was not one of them left.
12 Then they believed His words;
They sang His praise.

13 They soon forgot His works;
They did not wait for His counsel,
14 But lusted exceedingly in the
wilderness,
And tested God in the desert.
15 And He gave them their request,
But sent leanness into their soul.

16 When they envied Moses in the
camp,
And Aaron the saint of the LORD,
17 The earth opened up and swallowed
Dathan,
And covered the faction of Abiram.
18 A fire was kindled in their company;
The flame burned up the wicked.

19 They made a calf in Horeb,
And worshiped the molded image.
20 Thus they changed their glory
Into the image of an ox that eats
grass.
21 They forgot God their Savior,
Who had done great things in Egypt,
22 Wondrous works in the land of Ham,
Awesome things by the Red Sea.
23 Therefore He said that He would
destroy them,
Had not Moses His chosen one stood
before Him in the breach,
To turn away His wrath, lest He
destroy *them*.

24 Then they despised the pleasant
land;
They did not believe His word,
25 But complained in their tents,
And did not heed the voice of the
LORD.
26 Therefore He raised His hand *in an
oath* against them,
To overthrow them in the
wilderness,
27 To overthrow their descendants
among the nations,
And to scatter them in the lands.

28 They joined themselves also to Baal
of Peor,

And ate sacrifices made to the dead.
29 Thus they provoked *Him* to anger
     with their deeds,
     And the plague broke out among
     them.
30 Then Phinehas stood up and
     intervened,
     And the plague was stopped.
31 And that was accounted to him for
     righteousness
     To all generations forevermore.

32 They angered *Him* also at the waters
     of strife,
     So that it went ill with Moses on
     account of them;
33 Because they rebelled against His
     Spirit,
     So that he spoke rashly with his lips.

34 They did not destroy the peoples,
     Concerning whom the LORD had
     commanded them,
35 But they mingled with the Gentiles
     And learned their works;
36 They served their idols,
     Which became a snare to them.
37 They even sacrificed their sons
     And their daughters to demons,
38 And shed innocent blood,
     The blood of their sons and
     daughters,
     Whom they sacrificed to the idols of
     Canaan;
     And the land was polluted with
     blood.
39 Thus they were defiled by their own
     works,
     And played the harlot by their own
     deeds.

40 Therefore the wrath of the LORD was
     kindled against His people,
     So that He abhorred His own
     inheritance.
41 And He gave them into the hand of
     the Gentiles,
     And those who hated them ruled
     over them.
42 Their enemies also oppressed them,
     And they were brought into
     subjection under their hand.
43 Many times He delivered them;
     But they rebelled in their counsel,
     And were brought low for their
     iniquity.

44 Nevertheless He regarded their
     affliction,
     When He heard their cry;
45 And for their sake He remembered
     His covenant,
     And relented according to the
     multitude of His mercies.
46 He also made them to be pitied
     By all those who carried them away
     captive.

47 Save us, O LORD our God,
     And gather us from among the
     Gentiles,
     To give thanks to Your holy name,
     To triumph in Your praise.

48 Blessed *be* the LORD God of Israel
     From everlasting to everlasting!
     And let all the people say, "Amen!"

Praise the LORD!

BOOK FIVE: PSALMS 107—150

PSALM 107

Thanksgiving to the LORD for His Great Works of Deliverance

1 Oh, give thanks to the LORD, for *He
     is* good!
     For His mercy *endures* forever.
2 Let the redeemed of the LORD say *so,*
     Whom He has redeemed from the
     hand of the enemy,
3 And gathered out of the lands,
     From the east and from the west,
     From the north and from the south.

4 They wandered in the wilderness in
     a desolate way;
     They found no city to dwell in.
5 Hungry and thirsty,
     Their soul fainted in them.
6 Then they cried out to the LORD in
     their trouble,
     And He delivered them out of their
     distresses.
7 And He led them forth by the
     right way,
     That they might go to a city for a
     dwelling place.
8 Oh, that *men* would give thanks to
     the LORD *for* His goodness,
     And *for* His wonderful works to the
     children of men!
9 For He satisfies the longing soul,

And fills the hungry soul with
   goodness.

10 Those who sat in darkness and in
   the shadow of death,
   Bound in affliction and irons—
11 Because they rebelled against the
   words of God,
   And despised the counsel of the
   Most High,
12 Therefore He brought down their
   heart with labor;
   They fell down, and *there was* none
   to help.
13 Then they cried out to the LORD in
   their trouble,
   And He saved them out of their
   distresses.
14 He brought them out of darkness
   and the shadow of death,
   And broke their chains in pieces.
15 Oh, that *men* would give thanks to
   the LORD *for* His goodness,
   And *for* His wonderful works to the
   children of men!
16 For He has broken the gates of
   bronze,
   And cut the bars of iron in two.

17 Fools, because of their
   transgression,
   And because of their iniquities, were
   afflicted.
18 Their soul abhorred all manner of
   food,
   And they drew near to the gates of
   death.
19 Then they cried out to the LORD in
   their trouble,
   And He saved them out of their
   distresses.
20 He sent His word and healed them,
   And delivered *them* from their
   destructions.
21 Oh, that *men* would give thanks to
   the LORD *for* His goodness,
   And *for* His wonderful works to the
   children of men!
22 Let them sacrifice the sacrifices of
   thanksgiving,
   And declare His works with
   rejoicing.

23 Those who go down to the sea in
   ships,
   Who do business on great waters,
24 They see the works of the LORD,

And His wonders in the deep.
25 For He commands and raises the
   stormy wind,
   Which lifts up the waves of the sea.
26 They mount up to the heavens,
   They go down again to the depths;
   Their soul melts because of trouble.
27 They reel to and fro, and stagger like
   a drunken man,
   And are at their wits' end.
28 Then they cry out to the LORD in
   their trouble,
   And He brings them out of their
   distresses.
29 He calms the storm,
   So that its waves are still.
30 Then they are glad because they are
   quiet;
   So He guides them to their desired
   haven.
31 Oh, that *men* would give thanks to
   the LORD *for* His goodness,
   And *for* His wonderful works to the
   children of men!
32 Let them exalt Him also in the
   assembly of the people,
   And praise Him in the company of
   the elders.

33 He turns rivers into a wilderness,
   And the watersprings into dry
   ground;
34 A fruitful land into barrenness,
   For the wickedness of those who
   dwell in it.
35 He turns a wilderness into pools of
   water,
   And dry land into watersprings.
36 There He makes the hungry dwell,
   That they may establish a city for a
   dwelling place,
37 And sow fields and plant vineyards,
   That they may yield a fruitful
   harvest.
38 He also blesses them, and they
   multiply greatly;
   And He does not let their cattle
   decrease.

39 When they are diminished and
   brought low
   Through oppression, affliction and
   sorrow,
40 He pours contempt on princes,
   And causes them to wander in the
   wilderness *where there is* no
   way;

41 Yet He sets the poor on high, far
   from affliction,
   And makes *their* families like a
   flock.
42 The righteous see *it* and rejoice,
   And all iniquity stops its mouth.

43 Whoever *is* wise will observe these
   things,
   And they will understand the
   lovingkindness of the LORD.

PSALM 108

Assurance of God's Victory over Enemies

A Song. A Psalm of David.

1 O God, my heart is steadfast;
   I will sing and give praise, even with
   my glory.
2 Awake, lute and harp!
   I will awaken the dawn.
3 I will praise You, O LORD, among the
   peoples,
   And I will sing praises to You among
   the nations.
4 For Your mercy *is* great above the
   heavens,
   And Your truth *reaches* to the
   clouds.

5 Be exalted, O God, above the
   heavens,
   And Your glory above all the earth;
6 That Your beloved may be
   delivered,
   Save *with* Your right hand, and
   hear me.

7 God has spoken in His holiness:
   "I will rejoice;
   I will divide Shechem
   And measure out the Valley of
   Succoth.
8 Gilead *is* Mine; Manasseh *is* Mine;
   Ephraim also *is* the helmet for My
   head;
   Judah *is* My lawgiver.
9 Moab *is* My washpot;
   Over Edom I will cast My shoe;
   Over Philistia I will triumph."

10 Who will bring me *into* the strong
   city?
   Who will lead me to Edom?

11 *Is it* not *You*, O God, *who* cast
   us off?
   And *You*, O God, *who* did not go out
   with our armies?
12 Give us help from trouble,
   For the help of man is useless.
13 Through God we will do valiantly,
   For *it is* He *who* shall tread down
   our enemies.[k]

PSALM 109

Plea for Judgment of False Accusers

To the Chief Musician. A Psalm of David.

1 Do not keep silent,
   O God of my praise!
2 For the mouth of the wicked and the
   mouth of the deceitful
   Have opened against me;
   They have spoken against me with
   a lying tongue.
3 They have also surrounded me with
   words of hatred,
   And fought against me without a
   cause.
4 In return for my love they are my
   accusers,
   But I *give myself to* prayer.
5 Thus they have rewarded me evil for
   good,
   And hatred for my love.

6 Set a wicked man over him,
   And let an accuser stand at his right
   hand.
7 When he is judged, let him be found
   guilty,
   And let his prayer become sin.
8 Let his days be few,
   And let another take his office.
9 Let his children be fatherless,
   And his wife a widow.
10 Let his children continually be
   vagabonds, and beg;
   Let them seek *their bread* also from
   their desolate places.
11 Let the creditor seize all that he has,
   And let strangers plunder his labor.
12 Let there be none to extend mercy
   to him,
   Nor let there be any to favor his
   fatherless children.
13 Let his posterity be cut off,
   And in the generation following let
   their name be blotted out.

k Compare verses 6-13 with 60.5-12

14 Let the iniquity of his fathers be
     remembered before the LORD,
     And let not the sin of his mother be
     blotted out.
15 Let them be continually before the
     LORD,
     That He may cut off the memory of
     them from the earth;
16 Because he did not remember to
     show mercy,
     But persecuted the poor and needy
     man,
     That he might even slay the broken
     in heart.
17 As he loved cursing, so let it come
     to him;
     As he did not delight in blessing, so
     let it be far from him.
18 As he clothed himself with cursing
     as with his garment,
     So let it enter his body like water,
     And like oil into his bones.
19 Let it be to him like the garment
     which covers him,
     And for a belt with which he girds
     himself continually.
20 *Let* this *be* the LORD's reward to my
     accusers,
     And to those who speak evil against
     my person.

21 But You, O GOD the Lord,
     Deal with me for Your name's sake;
     Because Your mercy *is* good,
     deliver me.
22 For I *am* poor and needy,
     And my heart is wounded within me.
23 I am gone like a shadow when it
     lengthens;
     I am shaken off like a locust.
24 My knees are weak through fasting,
     And my flesh is feeble from lack of
     fatness.
25 I also have become a reproach to
     them;
     When they look at me, they shake
     their heads.

26 Help me, O LORD my God!
     Oh, save me according to Your
     mercy,
27 That they may know that this *is*
     Your hand—
     That You, LORD, have done it!
28 Let them curse, but You bless;
     When they arise, let them be
     ashamed,

     But let Your servant rejoice.
29 Let my accusers be clothed with
     shame,
     And let them cover themselves with
     their own disgrace as with a
     mantle.

30 I will greatly praise the LORD with
     my mouth;
     Yes, I will praise Him among the
     multitude.
31 For He shall stand at the right hand
     of the poor,
     To save *him* from those who
     condemn him.

PSALM 110

Announcement of the Messiah's Reign

A Psalm of David.

1   The LORD said to my Lord,
     "Sit at My right hand,
     Till I make Your enemies Your
     footstool."
2   The LORD shall send the rod of Your
     strength out of Zion.
     Rule in the midst of Your enemies!

3   Your people *shall be* volunteers
     In the day of Your power;
     In the beauties of holiness, from the
     womb of the morning,
     You have the dew of Your youth.
4   The LORD has sworn
     And will not relent,
     "You *are* a priest forever
     According to the order of
     Melchizedek."

5   The Lord *is* at Your right hand;
     He shall execute kings in the day of
     His wrath.
6   He shall judge among the nations,
     He shall fill *the places* with dead
     bodies,
     He shall execute the heads of many
     countries.
7   He shall drink of the brook by the
     wayside;
     Therefore He shall lift up the head.

PSALM 111

Praise to God for His Faithfulness and Justice

1   Praise the LORD!

     I will praise the LORD with *my* whole
     heart,

In the assembly of the upright and
in the congregation.

2 The works of the LORD *are* great,
Studied by all who have pleasure in
them.
3 His work *is* honorable and glorious,
And His righteousness endures
forever.
4 He has made His wonderful works
to be remembered;
The LORD *is* gracious and full of
compassion.
5 He has given food to those who
fear Him;
He will ever be mindful of His
covenant.
6 He has declared to His people the
power of His works,
In giving them the heritage of the
nations.

7 The works of His hands *are* verity
and justice;
All His precepts *are* sure.
8 They stand fast forever and ever,
And are done in truth and
uprightness.
9 He has sent redemption to His
people;
He has commanded His covenant
forever:
Holy and awesome *is* His name.

10 The fear of the LORD *is* the beginning
of wisdom;
A good understanding have all those
who do *His commandments.*
His praise endures forever.

PSALM 112
The Blessed State of the Righteous

1 Praise the LORD!

Blessed *is* the man *who* fears the
LORD,
Who delights greatly in His
commandments.

2 His descendants will be mighty on
earth;
The generation of the upright will
be blessed.
3 Wealth and riches *will be* in his
house,
And his righteousness endures
forever.

4 Unto the upright there arises light
in the darkness;
He is gracious, and full of
compassion, and righteous.
5 A good man deals graciously and
lends;
He will guide his affairs with
discretion.
6 Surely he will never be shaken;
The righteous will be in everlasting
remembrance.
7 He will not be afraid of evil tidings;
His heart is steadfast, trusting in the
LORD.
8 His heart *is* established;
He will not be afraid,
Until he sees *his desire* upon his
enemies.

9 He has dispersed abroad,
He has given to the poor;
His righteousness endures forever;
His horn will be exalted with honor.
10 The wicked will see *it* and be
grieved;
He will gnash his teeth and melt
away;
The desire of the wicked shall
perish.

PSALM 113
The Majesty and Condescension of God

1 Praise the LORD!

Praise, O servants of the LORD,
Praise the name of the LORD!
2 Blessed be the name of the LORD
From this time forth and
forevermore!
3 From the rising of the sun to its
going down
The LORD's name *is* to be praised.

4 The LORD *is* high above all nations,
His glory above the heavens.
5 Who *is* like the LORD our God,
Who dwells on high,
6 Who humbles Himself to behold
The things that are in the heavens
and in the earth?

7 He raises the poor out of the dust,
And lifts the needy out of the ash
heap,
8 That He may seat *him* with princes—
With the princes of His people.

9 He grants the barren woman a
      home,
    Like a joyful mother of children.

    Praise the LORD!

PSALM 114

The Power of God in His Deliverance of Israel

1 When Israel went out of Egypt,
    The house of Jacob from a people
      of strange language,
2 Judah became His sanctuary,
    And Israel His dominion.

3 The sea saw *it* and fled;
    Jordan turned back.
4 The mountains skipped like rams,
    The little hills like lambs.
5 What ails you, O sea, that you fled?
    O Jordan, *that* you turned back?
6 O mountains, *that* you skipped like
      rams?
    O little hills, like lambs?

7 Tremble, O earth, at the presence of
      the Lord,
    At the presence of the God of Jacob,
8 Who turned the rock *into* a pool of
      water,
    The flint into a fountain of waters.

PSALM 115

The Futility of Idols and the Trustworthiness of God

1 Not unto us, O LORD, not unto us,
    But to Your name give glory,
    Because of Your mercy,
    Because of Your truth.
2 Why should the Gentiles say,
    "So where *is* their God?"

3 But our God *is* in heaven;
    He does whatever He pleases.
4 Their idols *are* silver and gold,
    The work of men's hands.
5 They have mouths, but they do not
      speak;
    Eyes they have, but they do not see;
6 They have ears, but they do not
      hear;
    Noses they have, but they do not
      smell;
7 They have hands, but they do not
      handle;
    Feet they have, but they do not walk;

Nor do they mutter through their
      throat.
8 Those who make them are like
      them;
    So is everyone who trusts in them.

9 O Israel, trust in the LORD;
    He *is* their help and their shield.
10 O house of Aaron, trust in the LORD;
    He *is* their help and their shield.
11 You who fear the LORD, trust in the
      LORD;
    He *is* their help and their shield.

12 The LORD has been mindful of *us;*
    He will bless us;
    He will bless the house of Israel;
    He will bless the house of Aaron.
13 He will bless those who fear the
      LORD,
    Both small and great.

14 May the LORD give you increase
      more and more,
    You and your children.
15 *May* you *be* blessed by the LORD,
    Who made heaven and earth.

16 The heaven, *even* the heavens, *are*
      the LORD's;
    But the earth He has given to the
      children of men.
17 The dead do not praise the LORD,
    Nor any who go down into silence.
18 But we will bless the LORD
    From this time forth and
      forevermore.

    Praise the LORD!

PSALM 116

Thanksgiving for Deliverance from Death

1 I love the LORD, because He has
      heard
    My voice *and* my supplications.
2 Because He has inclined His ear
      to me,
    Therefore I will call *upon Him* as
      long as I live.

3 The pains of death surrounded me,
    And the pangs of Sheol laid hold
      of me;
    I found trouble and sorrow.
4 Then I called upon the name of the
      LORD:

"O LORD, I implore You, deliver my
    soul!"

5 Gracious *is* the LORD, and righteous;
    Yes, our God *is* merciful.
6 The LORD preserves the simple;
    I was brought low, and He saved me.
7 Return to your rest, O my soul,
    For the LORD has dealt bountifully
        with you.

8 For You have delivered my soul
        from death,
    My eyes from tears,
    And my feet from falling.
9 I will walk before the LORD
    In the land of the living.
10 I believed, therefore I spoke,
    "I am greatly afflicted."
11 I said in my haste,
    "All men *are* liars."

12 What shall I render to the LORD
    For all His benefits toward me?
13 I will take up the cup of salvation,
    And call upon the name of the LORD.
14 I will pay my vows to the LORD
    Now in the presence of all His
        people.

15 Precious in the sight of the LORD
    Is the death of His saints.

16 O LORD, truly I *am* Your servant;
    I *am* Your servant, the son of Your
        maidservant;
    You have loosed my bonds.
17 I will offer to You the sacrifice of
        thanksgiving,
    And will call upon the name of the
        LORD.

18 I will pay my vows to the LORD
    Now in the presence of all His
        people,
19 In the courts of the LORD's house,
    In the midst of you, O Jerusalem.

Praise the LORD!

PSALM 117

Let All Peoples Praise the LORD

1 Praise the LORD, all you Gentiles!
    Laud Him, all you peoples!
2 For His merciful kindness is great
    toward us,

And the truth of the LORD *endures*
    forever.

Praise the LORD!

PSALM 118

Praise to God for His Everlasting Mercy

1 Oh, give thanks to the LORD, for *He
    is* good!
    For His mercy *endures* forever.

2 Let Israel now say,
    "His mercy *endures* forever."
3 Let the house of Aaron now say,
    "His mercy *endures* forever."
4 Let those who fear the LORD
        now say,
    "His mercy *endures* forever."

5 I called on the LORD in distress;
    The LORD answered me *and set me
    in a broad place.
6 The LORD *is* on my side;
    I will not fear.
    What can man do to me?
7 The LORD is for me among those who
        help me;
    Therefore I shall see *my desire* on
        those who hate me.
8 *It is* better to trust in the LORD
    Than to put confidence in man.
9 *It is* better to trust in the LORD
    Than to put confidence in princes.

10 All nations surrounded me,
    But in the name of the LORD I will
        destroy them.
11 They surrounded me,
    Yes, they surrounded me;
    But in the name of the LORD I will
        destroy them.
12 They surrounded me like bees;
    They were quenched like a fire of
        thorns;
    For in the name of the LORD I will
        destroy them.
13 You pushed me violently, that I
        might fall,
    But the LORD helped me.
14 The LORD *is* my strength and song,
    And He has become my salvation.[l]
15 The voice of rejoicing and salvation
    Is in the tents of the righteous;

---

[l] Compare Exodus 15.2

The right hand of the LORD does valiantly.

16 The right hand of the LORD is exalted;
The right hand of the LORD does valiantly.

17 I shall not die, but live,
And declare the works of the LORD.

18 The LORD has chastened me severely,
But He has not given me over to death.

19 Open to me the gates of righteousness;
I will go through them,
And I will praise the LORD.

20 This is the gate of the LORD,
Through which the righteous shall enter.

21 I will praise You,
For You have answered me,
And have become my salvation.

22 The stone *which* the builders rejected
Has become the chief cornerstone.

23 This was the LORD's doing;
It *is* marvelous in our eyes.

24 This *is* the day the LORD has made;
We will rejoice and be glad in it.

25 Save now, I pray, O LORD;
O LORD, I pray, send now prosperity.

26 Blessed *is* he who comes in the name of the LORD!
We have blessed you from the house of the LORD.

27 God *is* the LORD,
And He has given us light;
Bind the sacrifice with cords to the horns of the altar.

28 You *are* my God, and I will praise You;
You are my God, I will exalt You.

29 Oh, give thanks to the LORD, for *He is* good!
For His mercy *endures* forever.

PSALM 119

Meditations on the Excellencies of the Word of God

א ALEPH

1 Blessed *are* the undefiled in the way,
Who walk in the law of the LORD!

2 Blessed *are* those who keep His testimonies,
Who seek Him with the whole heart!

3 They also do no iniquity;
They walk in His ways.

4 You have commanded *us*
To keep Your precepts diligently.

5 Oh, that my ways were directed
To keep Your statutes!

6 Then I would not be ashamed,
When I look into all Your commandments.

7 I will praise You with uprightness of heart,
When I learn Your righteous judgments.

8 I will keep Your statutes;
Oh, do not forsake me utterly!

ב BETH

9 How can a young man cleanse his way?
By taking heed according to Your word.

10 With my whole heart I have sought You;
Oh, let me not wander from Your commandments!

11 Your word I have hidden in my heart,
That I might not sin against You.

12 Blessed *are* You, O LORD!
Teach me Your statutes.

13 With my lips I have declared
All the judgments of Your mouth.

14 I have rejoiced in the way of Your testimonies,
As *much as* in all riches.

15 I will meditate on Your precepts,
And contemplate Your ways.

16 I will delight myself in Your statutes;
I will not forget Your word.

ג GIMEL

17 Deal bountifully with Your servant,
That I may live and keep Your word.

18 Open my eyes, that I may see
Wondrous things from Your law.

19 I *am* a stranger in the earth;
Do not hide Your commandments from me.

20 My soul breaks with longing
For Your judgments at all times.

21 You rebuke the proud—the cursed,
Who stray from Your commandments.

22 Remove from me reproach and
      contempt,
   For I have kept Your testimonies.
23 Princes also sit *and* speak
      against me,
   But Your servant meditates on Your
      statutes.
24 Your testimonies also *are* my
      delight
   And my counselors.

ד DALETH

25 My soul clings to the dust;
   Revive me according to Your word.
26 I have declared my ways, and You
      answered me;
   Teach me Your statutes.
27 Make me understand the way of
      Your precepts;
   So shall I meditate on Your
      wonderful works.
28 My soul melts from heaviness;
   Strengthen me according to Your
      word.
29 Remove from me the way of lying,
   And grant me Your law graciously.
30 I have chosen the way of truth;
   Your judgments I have laid
      before me.
31 I cling to Your testimonies;
   O LORD, do not put me to shame!
32 I will run the course of Your
      commandments,
   For You shall enlarge my heart.

ה HE

33 Teach me, O LORD, the way of Your
      statutes,
   And I shall keep it *to* the end.
34 Give me understanding, and I shall
      keep Your law;
   Indeed, I shall observe it with *my*
      whole heart.
35 Make me walk in the path of Your
      commandments,
   For I delight in it.
36 Incline my heart to Your
      testimonies,
   And not to covetousness.
37 Turn away my eyes from looking at
      worthless things,
   And revive me in Your way.
38 Establish Your word to Your
      servant,
   Who *is devoted* to fearing You.
39 Turn away my reproach which I
      dread,

For Your judgments *are* good.
40 Behold, I long for Your precepts;
   Revive me in Your righteousness.

ו WAW

41 Let Your mercies come also to me,
      O LORD—
   Your salvation according to Your
      word.
42 So shall I have an answer for him
      who reproaches me,
   For I trust in Your word.
43 And take not the word of truth
      utterly out of my mouth,
   For I have hoped in Your
      ordinances.
44 So shall I keep Your law
      continually,
   Forever and ever.
45 And I will walk at liberty,
   For I seek Your precepts.
46 I will speak of Your testimonies also
      before kings,
   And will not be ashamed.
47 And I will delight myself in Your
      commandments,
   Which I love.
48 My hands also I will lift up to Your
      commandments,
   Which I love,
   And I will meditate on Your
      statutes.

ז ZAYIN

49 Remember the word to Your
      servant,
   Upon which You have caused me to
      hope.
50 This *is* my comfort in my affliction,
   For Your word has given me life.
51 The proud have me in great derision,
   Yet I do not turn aside from
      Your law.
52 I remembered Your judgments of
      old, O LORD,
   And have comforted myself.
53 Indignation has taken hold of me
   Because of the wicked, who forsake
      Your law.
54 Your statutes have been my songs
   In the house of my pilgrimage.
55 I remember Your name in the night,
      O LORD,
   And I keep Your law.
56 This has become mine,
   Because I kept Your precepts.

ח HETH

57 *You are* my portion, O LORD;
  I have said that I would keep Your
    words.
58 I entreated Your favor with *my*
    whole heart;
  Be merciful to me according to Your
    word.
59 I thought about my ways,
  And turned my feet to Your
    testimonies.
60 I made haste, and did not delay
  To keep Your commandments.
61 The cords of the wicked have
    bound me,
  But I have not forgotten Your law.
62 At midnight I will rise to give thanks
    to You,
  Because of Your righteous
    judgments.
63 I *am* a companion of all who
    fear You,
  And of those who keep Your
    precepts.
64 The earth, O LORD, is full of Your
    mercy;
  Teach me Your statutes.

ט TETH

65 You have dealt well with Your
    servant,
  O LORD, according to Your word.
66 Teach me good judgment and
    knowledge,
  For I believe Your commandments.
67 Before I was afflicted I went astray,
  But now I keep Your word.
68 You *are* good, and do good;
  Teach me Your statutes.
69 The proud have forged a lie
    against me,
  But I will keep Your precepts with
    my whole heart.
70 Their heart is as fat as grease,
  But I delight in Your law.
71 *It is* good for me that I have been
    afflicted,
  That I may learn Your statutes.
72 The law of Your mouth *is* better
    to me
  Than thousands of *coins of* gold and
    silver.

י YOD

73 Your hands have made me and
    fashioned me;

  Give me understanding, that I may
    learn Your commandments.
74 Those who fear You will be glad
    when they see me,
  Because I have hoped in Your
    word.
75 I know, O LORD, that Your
    judgments *are* right,
  And *that* in faithfulness You have
    afflicted me.
76 Let, I pray, Your merciful kindness
    be for my comfort,
  According to Your word to Your
    servant.
77 Let Your tender mercies come to me,
    that I may live;
  For Your law *is* my delight.
78 Let the proud be ashamed,
  For they treated me wrongfully with
    falsehood;
  But I will meditate on Your
    precepts.
79 Let those who fear You turn to me,
  Those who know Your testimonies.
80 Let my heart be blameless regarding
    Your statutes,
  That I may not be ashamed.

כ KAPH

81 My soul faints for Your salvation,
  But I hope in Your word.
82 My eyes fail *from searching* Your
    word,
  Saying, "When will You
    comfort me?"
83 For I have become like a wineskin
    in smoke,
  Yet I do not forget Your statutes.
84 How many *are* the days of Your
    servant?
  When will You execute judgment on
    those who persecute me?
85 The proud have dug pits for me,
  Which *is* not according to Your law.
86 All Your commandments *are*
    faithful;
  They persecute me wrongfully;
  Help me!
87 They almost made an end of me on
    earth,
  But I did not forsake Your
    precepts.
88 Revive me according to Your
    lovingkindness,
  So that I may keep the testimony of
    Your mouth.

ל LAMED

89 Forever, O LORD,
Your word is settled in heaven.
90 Your faithfulness *endures* to all
generations;
You established the earth, and it
abides.
91 They continue this day according to
Your ordinances,
For all *are* Your servants.
92 Unless Your law *had been* my
delight,
I would then have perished in my
affliction.
93 I will never forget Your precepts,
For by them You have given me life.
94 I *am* Yours, save me;
For I have sought Your precepts.
95 The wicked wait for me to
destroy me,
But I will consider Your testimonies.
96 I have seen the consummation of all
perfection,
But Your commandment *is*
exceedingly broad.

מ MEM

97 Oh, how I love Your law!
It *is* my meditation all the day.
98 You, through Your commandments,
make me wiser than my enemies;
For they *are* ever with me.
99 I have more understanding than all
my teachers,
For Your testimonies *are* my
meditation.
100 I understand more than the ancients,
Because I keep Your precepts.
101 I have restrained my feet from every
evil way,
That I may keep Your word.
102 I have not departed from Your
judgments,
For You Yourself have taught me.
103 How sweet are Your words to my
taste,
Sweeter than honey to my mouth!
104 Through Your precepts I get
understanding;
Therefore I hate every false way.

נ NUN

105 Your word *is* a lamp to my feet
And a light to my path.
106 I have sworn and confirmed

That I will keep Your righteous
judgments.
107 I am afflicted very much;
Revive me, O LORD, according to
Your word.
108 Accept, I pray, the freewill offerings
of my mouth, O LORD,
And teach me Your judgments.
109 My life *is* continually in my hand,
Yet I do not forget Your law.
110 The wicked have laid a snare
for me,
Yet I have not strayed from Your
precepts.
111 Your testimonies I have taken as a
heritage forever,
For they *are* the rejoicing of my
heart.
112 I have inclined my heart to perform
Your statutes
Forever, to the very end.

ס SAMEK

113 I hate the double-minded,
But I love Your law.
114 You *are* my hiding place and my
shield;
I hope in Your word.
115 Depart from me, you evildoers,
For I will keep the commandments
of my God!
116 Uphold me according to Your word,
that I may live;
And do not let me be ashamed of
my hope.
117 Hold me up, and I shall be safe,
And I shall observe Your statutes
continually.
118 You reject all those who stray from
Your statutes,
For their deceit *is* falsehood.
119 You put away all the wicked of the
earth *like* dross;
Therefore I love Your testimonies.
120 My flesh trembles for fear of You,
And I am afraid of Your judgments.

ע AYIN

121 I have done justice and
righteousness;
Do not leave me to my oppressors.
122 Be surety for Your servant for good;
Do not let the proud oppress me.
123 My eyes fail *from seeking* Your
salvation
And Your righteous word.

124 Deal with Your servant according to
      Your mercy,
      And teach me Your statutes.
125 I *am* Your servant;
      Give me understanding,
      That I may know Your testimonies.
126 *It is* time for *You* to act, O LORD,
      For they have regarded Your law as
      void.
127 Therefore I love Your
      commandments
      More than gold, yes, than fine gold!
128 Therefore all *Your* precepts
      concerning all *things*
      I consider *to be* right;
      I hate every false way.

ﬦ PE

129 Your testimonies are wonderful;
      Therefore my soul keeps them.
130 The entrance of Your words gives
      light;
      It gives understanding to the simple.
131 I opened my mouth and panted,
      For I longed for Your
      commandments.
132 Look upon me and be merciful
      to me,
      As Your custom *is* toward those who
      love Your name.
133 Direct my steps by Your word,
      And let no iniquity have dominion
      over me.
134 Redeem me from the oppression
      of man,
      That I may keep Your precepts.
135 Make Your face shine upon Your
      servant,
      And teach me Your statutes.
136 Rivers of water run down from my
      eyes,
      Because *men* do not keep Your law.

ﬧ TSADDE

137 Righteous *are* You, O LORD,
      And upright *are* Your judgments.
138 Your testimonies, *which* You have
      commanded,
      Are righteous and very faithful.
139 My zeal has consumed me,
      Because my enemies have forgotten
      Your words.
140 Your word *is* very pure;
      Therefore Your servant loves it.
141 I *am* small and despised,
      Yet I do not forget Your precepts.

142 Your righteousness *is* an everlasting
      righteousness,
      And Your law *is* truth.
143 Trouble and anguish have
      overtaken me,
      Yet Your commandments *are* my
      delights.
144 The righteousness of Your
      testimonies *is* everlasting;
      Give me understanding, and I shall
      live.

﬩ QOPH

145 I cry out with *my* whole heart;
      Hear me, O LORD!
      I will keep Your statutes.
146 I cry out to You;
      Save me, and I will keep Your
      testimonies.
147 I rise before the dawning of the
      morning,
      And cry for help;
      I hope in Your word.
148 My eyes are awake through the
      night watches,
      That I may meditate on Your word.
149 Hear my voice according to Your
      lovingkindness;
      O LORD, revive me according to Your
      justice.
150 They draw near who follow after
      wickedness;
      They are far from Your law.
151 You *are* near, O LORD,
      And all Your commandments *are*
      truth.
152 Concerning Your testimonies,
      I have known of old that You have
      founded them forever.

ﬧ RESH

153 Consider my affliction and
      deliver me,
      For I do not forget Your law.
154 Plead my cause and redeem me;
      Revive me according to Your word.
155 Salvation *is* far from the wicked,
      For they do not seek Your statutes.
156 Great *are* Your tender mercies,
      O LORD;
      Revive me according to Your
      judgments.
157 Many *are* my persecutors and my
      enemies,
      Yet I do not turn from Your
      testimonies.

158 I see the treacherous, and am
    disgusted,
    Because they do not keep Your
    word.
159 Consider how I love Your precepts;
    Revive me, O LORD, according to
    Your lovingkindness.
160 The entirety of Your word *is* truth,
    And every one of Your righteous
    judgments *endures* forever.

ש SHIN

161 Princes persecute me without a
    cause,
    But my heart stands in awe of Your
    word.
162 I rejoice at Your word
    As one who finds great treasure.
163 I hate and abhor lying,
    But I love Your law.
164 Seven times a day I praise You,
    Because of Your righteous
    judgments.
165 Great peace have those who love
    Your law,
    And nothing causes them to
    stumble.
166 LORD, I hope for Your salvation,
    And I do Your commandments.
167 My soul keeps Your testimonies,
    And I love them exceedingly.
168 I keep Your precepts and Your
    testimonies,
    For all my ways *are* before You.

ת TAU

169 Let my cry come before You,
    O LORD;
    Give me understanding according to
    Your word.
170 Let my supplication come
    before You;
    Deliver me according to Your word.
171 My lips shall utter praise,
    For You teach me Your statutes.
172 My tongue shall speak of Your
    word,
    For all Your commandments *are*
    righteousness.
173 Let Your hand become my help,
    For I have chosen Your precepts.
174 I long for Your salvation, O LORD,
    And Your law *is* my delight.
175 Let my soul live, and it shall
    praise You;
    And let Your judgments help me.
176 I have gone astray like a lost sheep;

Seek Your servant,
For I do not forget Your
commandments.

PSALM 120

Plea for Relief from Bitter Foes

A Song of Ascents.

1 In my distress I cried to the LORD,
   And He heard me.
2 Deliver my soul, O LORD, from lying
   lips
   And from a deceitful tongue.

3 What shall be given to you,
   Or what shall be done to you,
   You false tongue?
4 Sharp arrows of the warrior,
   With coals of the broom tree!

5 Woe is me, that I dwell in Meshech,
   That I dwell among the tents of
   Kedar!
6 My soul has dwelt too long
   With one who hates peace.
7 I *am for* peace;
   But when I speak, they *are* for war.

PSALM 121

God the Help of Those Who Seek Him

A Song of Ascents.

1 I will lift up my eyes to the hills—
   From whence comes my help?
2 My help *comes* from the LORD,
   Who made heaven and earth.

3 He will not allow your foot to be
   moved;
   He who keeps you will not slumber.
4 Behold, He who keeps Israel
   Shall neither slumber nor sleep.

5 The LORD *is* your keeper;
   The LORD *is* your shade at your right
   hand.
6 The sun shall not strike you by day,
   Nor the moon by night.

7 The LORD shall preserve you from
   all evil;
   He shall preserve your soul.
8 The LORD shall preserve your going
   out and your coming in
   From this time forth, and even
   forevermore.

PSALM 122

The Joy of Going to the House of the LORD

A Song of Ascents. Of David.

1 I was glad when they said to me,
"Let us go into the house of the
LORD."
2 Our feet have been standing
Within your gates, O Jerusalem!

3 Jerusalem is built
As a city that is compact together,
4 Where the tribes go up,
The tribes of the LORD,
To the Testimony of Israel,
To give thanks to the name of the
LORD.
5 For thrones are set there for
judgment,
The thrones of the house of David.

6 Pray for the peace of Jerusalem:
"May they prosper who love you.
7 Peace be within your walls,
Prosperity within your palaces."
8 For the sake of my brethren and
companions,
I will now say, "Peace be
within you."
9 Because of the house of the LORD
our God
I will seek your good.

PSALM 123

Prayer for Relief from Contempt

A Song of Ascents.

1 Unto You I lift up my eyes,
O You who dwell in the heavens.
2 Behold, as the eyes of servants look
to the hand of their masters,
As the eyes of a maid to the hand
of her mistress,
So our eyes look to the LORD
our God,
Until He has mercy on us.

3 Have mercy on us, O LORD, have
mercy on us!
For we are exceedingly filled with
contempt.
4 Our soul is exceedingly filled
With the scorn of those who are at
ease,
With the contempt of the proud.

PSALM 124

The LORD the Defense of His People

A Song of Ascents. Of David.

1 "If it had not been the LORD who was
on our side,"
Let Israel now say—
2 "If it had not been the LORD who was
on our side,
When men rose up against us,
3 Then they would have swallowed us
alive,
When their wrath was kindled
against us;
4 Then the waters would have
overwhelmed us,
The stream would have gone over
our soul;
5 Then the swollen waters
Would have gone over our soul."

6 Blessed be the LORD,
Who has not given us as prey to
their teeth.
7 Our soul has escaped as a bird from
the snare of the fowlers;
The snare is broken, and we have
escaped.
8 Our help is in the name of the LORD,
Who made heaven and earth.

PSALM 125

The LORD the Strength of His People

A Song of Ascents.

1 Those who trust in the LORD
Are like Mount Zion,
Which cannot be moved, but abides
forever.
2 As the mountains surround
Jerusalem,
So the LORD surrounds His people
From this time forth and forever.

3 For the scepter of wickedness shall
not rest
On the land allotted to the righteous,
Lest the righteous reach out their
hands to iniquity.

4 Do good, O LORD, to those who are
good,
And to those who are upright in
their hearts.

5 As for such as turn aside to their
crooked ways,

The Lord shall lead them away
With the workers of iniquity.

Peace *be* upon Israel!

PSALM 126

A Joyful Return to Zion

A Song of Ascents.

1 When the Lord brought back the
captivity of Zion,
We were like those who dream.
2 Then our mouth was filled with
laughter,
And our tongue with singing.
Then they said among the nations,
"The Lord has done great things for
them."
3 The Lord has done great things
for us,
And we are glad.

4 Bring back our captivity, O Lord,
As the streams in the South.

5 Those who sow in tears
Shall reap in joy.
6 He who continually goes forth
weeping,
Bearing seed for sowing,
Shall doubtless come again with
rejoicing,
Bringing his sheaves *with him.*

PSALM 127

Laboring and Prospering with the Lord

A Song of Ascents. Of Solomon.

1 Unless the Lord builds the house,
They labor in vain who build it;
Unless the Lord guards the city,
The watchman stays awake in vain.
2 *It is* vain for you to rise up early,
To sit up late,
To eat the bread of sorrows;
For so He gives His beloved sleep.

3 Behold, children *are* a heritage from
the Lord,
The fruit of the womb *is* a reward.
4 Like arrows in the hand of a warrior,
So *are* the children of one's youth.
5 Happy *is* the man who has his quiver
full of them;
They shall not be ashamed,
But shall speak with their enemies
in the gate.

PSALM 128

Blessings of Those Who Fear the Lord

A Song of Ascents.

1 Blessed *is* every one who fears the
Lord,
Who walks in His ways.
2 When you eat the labor of your
hands,
You *shall be* happy, and *it shall be*
well with you.
3 Your wife *shall be* like a fruitful vine
In the very heart of your house,
Your children like olive plants
All around your table.
4 Behold, thus shall the man be
blessed
Who fears the Lord.

5 The Lord bless you out of Zion,
And may you see the good of
Jerusalem
All the days of your life.
6 Yes, may you see your children's
children.

Peace *be* upon Israel!

PSALM 129

Song of Victory over Zion's Enemies

A Song of Ascents.

1 "Many a time they have afflicted me
from my youth,"
Let Israel now say—
2 "Many a time they have afflicted me
from my youth;
Yet they have not prevailed
against me.
3 The plowers plowed on my back;
They made their furrows long."
4 The Lord *is* righteous;
He has cut in pieces the cords of the
wicked.

5 Let all those who hate Zion
Be put to shame and turned back.
6 Let them be as the grass *on* the
housetops,
Which withers before it grows up,
7 With which the reaper does not fill
his hand,
Nor he who binds sheaves, his arms.
8 Neither let those who pass by
them say,
"The blessing of the Lord *be*
upon you;

We bless you in the name of the
LORD!''

PSALM 130

Waiting for the Redemption of the LORD

A Song of Ascents.

1 Out of the depths I have cried to
You, O LORD;
2 Lord, hear my voice!
Let Your ears be attentive
To the voice of my supplications.

3 If You, LORD, should mark iniquities,
O Lord, who could stand?
4 But *there is* forgiveness with You,
That You may be feared.

5 I wait for the LORD, my soul waits,
And in His word I do hope.
6 My soul *waits* for the Lord
More than those who watch for the
morning—
Yes, more than those who watch for
the morning.

7 O Israel, hope in the LORD;
For with the LORD *there is* mercy,
And with Him *is* abundant
redemption.
8 And He shall redeem Israel
From all his iniquities.

PSALM 131

Simple Trust in the LORD

A Song of Ascents. Of David.

1 LORD, my heart is not haughty,
Nor my eyes lofty.
Neither do I concern myself with
great matters,
Nor with things too profound for me.

2 Surely I have calmed and quieted
my soul,
Like a weaned child with his
mother;
Like a weaned child *is* my soul
within me.

3 O Israel, hope in the LORD
From this time forth and forever.

PSALM 132

The Eternal Dwelling of God in Zion

A Song of Ascents.

1 LORD, remember David
And all his afflictions;

2 How he swore to the LORD,
And vowed to the Mighty One of
Jacob:
3 "Surely I will not go into the chamber
of my house,
Or go up to the comfort of my bed;
4 I will not give sleep to my eyes
Or slumber to my eyelids,
5 Until I find a place for the LORD,
A dwelling place for the Mighty One
of Jacob.''

6 Behold, we heard of it in Ephrathah;
We found it in the fields of the
woods.
7 Let us go into His tabernacle;
Let us worship at His footstool.
8 Arise, O LORD, to Your resting place,
You and the ark of Your strength.
9 Let Your priests be clothed with
righteousness,
And let Your saints shout for joy.

10 For Your servant David's sake,
Do not turn away the face of Your
Anointed.

11 The LORD has sworn *in* truth to
David;
He will not turn from it:
"I will set upon your throne the fruit
of your body.
12 If your sons will keep My covenant
And My testimony which I shall
teach them,
Their sons also shall sit upon your
throne forevermore.''

13 For the LORD has chosen Zion;
He has desired *it* for His dwelling
place:
14 "This *is* My resting place forever;
Here I will dwell, for I have
desired it.
15 I will abundantly bless her
provision;
I will satisfy her poor with bread.
16 I will also clothe her priests with
salvation,
And her saints shall shout aloud
for joy.
17 There I will make the horn of David
grow;
I will prepare a lamp for My
Anointed.
18 His enemies I will clothe with
shame,

But upon Himself His crown shall
flourish."

PSALM 133

Blessed Unity of the People of God

A Song of Ascents. Of David.

1 Behold, how good and how pleasant
   it is
   For brethren to dwell together in
   unity!

2 *It is* like the precious oil upon the
   head,
   Running down on the beard,
   The beard of Aaron,
   Running down on the edge of his
   garments.
3 *It is* like the dew of Hermon,
   Descending upon the mountains of
   Zion;
   For there the LORD commanded the
   blessing—
   Life forevermore.

PSALM 134

Praising the LORD in His House at Night

A Song of Ascents.

1 Behold, bless the LORD,
   All *you* servants of the LORD,
   Who by night stand in the house of
   the LORD!
2 Lift up your hands *in* the sanctuary,
   And bless the LORD.

3 The LORD who made heaven and
   earth
   Bless you from Zion!

PSALM 135

Praise to God in Creation and Redemption

1 Praise the LORD!

   Praise the name of the LORD;
   Praise *Him*, O you servants of the
   LORD!
2 You who stand in the house of the
   LORD,
   In the courts of the house of our
   God,
3 Praise the LORD, for the LORD *is*
   good;

Sing praises to His name, for *it is*
pleasant.
4 For the LORD has chosen Jacob for
   Himself,
   Israel for His special treasure.

5 For I know that the LORD *is* great,
   And our Lord *is* above all gods.
6 Whatever the LORD pleases He does,
   In heaven and in earth,
   In the seas and in all deep places.
7 He causes the vapors to ascend from
   the ends of the earth;
   He makes lightning for the rain;
   He brings the wind out of His
   treasuries.

8 He destroyed the firstborn of Egypt,
   Both of man and beast.
9 He sent signs and wonders into the
   midst of you, O Egypt,
   Upon Pharaoh and all his servants.
10 He defeated many nations
   And slew mighty kings—
11 Sihon king of the Amorites,
   Og king of Bashan,
   And all the kingdoms of Canaan—
12 And gave their land *as* a heritage,
   A heritage to Israel His people.

13 Your name, O LORD, *endures*
   forever,
   Your fame, O LORD, throughout all
   generations.
14 For the LORD will judge His people,
   And He will have compassion on His
   servants.

15 The idols of the nations *are* silver
   and gold,
   The work of men's hands.
16 They have mouths, but they do not
   speak;
   Eyes they have, but they do not see;
17 They have ears, but they do not
   hear;
   Nor is there *any* breath in their
   mouths.
18 Those who make them are like
   them;
   So is everyone who trusts in them.

19 Bless the LORD, O house of Israel!
   Bless the LORD, O house of Aaron!
20 Bless the LORD, O house of Levi!
   You who fear the LORD, bless the
   LORD!

21 Blessed be the Lord out of Zion,
Who dwells in Jerusalem!

Praise the Lord!

PSALM 136

Thanksgiving to God for His Enduring Mercy

1 Oh, give thanks to the Lord, for *He is* good!
For His mercy *endures* forever.
2 Oh, give thanks to the God of gods!
For His mercy *endures* forever.
3 Oh, give thanks to the Lord of lords!
For His mercy *endures* forever:

4 To Him who alone does great wonders,
For His mercy *endures* forever;
5 To Him who by wisdom made the heavens,
For His mercy *endures* forever;
6 To Him who laid out the earth above the waters,
For His mercy *endures* forever;
7 To Him who made great lights,
For His mercy *endures* forever—
8 The sun to rule by day,
For His mercy *endures* forever;
9 The moon and stars to rule by night,
For His mercy *endures* forever.

10 To Him who struck Egypt in their firstborn,
For His mercy *endures* forever;
11 And brought out Israel from among them,
For His mercy *endures* forever;
12 With a strong hand, and with an outstretched arm,
For His mercy *endures* forever;
13 To Him who divided the Red Sea in two,
For His mercy *endures* forever;
14 And made Israel pass through the midst of it,
For His mercy *endures* forever;
15 But overthrew Pharaoh and his army in the Red Sea,
For His mercy *endures* forever;
16 To Him who led His people through the wilderness,
For His mercy *endures* forever;
17 To Him who struck down great kings,
For His mercy *endures* forever;

18 And slew famous kings,
For His mercy *endures* forever—
19 Sihon king of the Amorites,
For His mercy *endures* forever;
20 And Og king of Bashan,
For His mercy *endures* forever—
21 And gave their land as a heritage,
For His mercy *endures* forever;
22 A heritage to Israel His servant,
For His mercy *endures* forever.

23 Who remembered us in our lowly state,
For His mercy *endures* forever;
24 And rescued us from our enemies,
For His mercy *endures* forever;
25 Who gives food to all flesh,
For His mercy *endures* forever.

26 Oh, give thanks to the God of heaven!
For His mercy *endures* forever.

PSALM 137

Longing for Zion in a Foreign Land

1 By the rivers of Babylon,
There we sat down, yea, we wept
When we remembered Zion.
2 We hung our harps
Upon the willows in the midst of it.
3 For there those who carried us away captive asked of us a song,
And those who plundered us *requested* mirth,
Saying, "Sing us *one* of the songs of Zion!"

4 How shall we sing the Lord's song
In a foreign land?
5 If I forget you, O Jerusalem,
Let my right hand forget *its skill!*
6 If I do not remember you,
Let my tongue cling to the roof of my mouth—
If I do not exalt Jerusalem
Above my chief joy.

7 Remember, O Lord, against the sons of Edom
The day of Jerusalem,
Who said, "Raze *it,* raze *it,*
To its very foundation!"

8 O daughter of Babylon, who are to be destroyed,

Happy the one who repays you as
you have served us!

9 Happy the one who takes and
dashes
Your little ones against the rock!

PSALM 138

The LORD's Goodness to the Faithful

A Psalm of David.

1 I will praise You with my whole
heart;
Before the gods I will sing praises
to You.

2 I will worship toward Your holy
temple,
And praise Your name
For Your lovingkindness and Your
truth;
For You have magnified Your word
above all Your Name.

3 In the day when I cried out, You
answered me,
And made me bold *with* strength in
my soul.

4 All the kings of the earth shall praise
You, O LORD,
When they hear the words of Your
mouth.

5 Yes, they shall sing of the ways of
the LORD,
For great *is* the glory of the LORD.

6 Though the LORD *is* on high,
Yet He regards the lowly;
But the proud He knows from afar.

7 Though I walk in the midst of
trouble, You will revive me;
You will stretch out Your hand
Against the wrath of my enemies,
And Your right hand will save me.

8 The LORD will perfect *that which*
concerns me;
Your mercy, O LORD, *endures*
forever;
Do not forsake the works of Your
hands.

PSALM 139

God's Perfect Knowledge of Man

For the Chief Musician. A Psalm of David.

1 O LORD, You have searched me and
known *me.*

2 You know my sitting down and my
rising up;

You understand my thought afar off.

3 You comprehend my path and my
lying down,
And are acquainted with all my
ways.

4 For *there is* not a word on my
tongue,
But behold, O LORD, You know it
altogether.

5 You have hedged me behind and
before,
And laid Your hand upon me.

6 *Such* knowledge *is* too wonderful
for me;
It is high, I cannot *attain* it.

7 Where can I go from Your Spirit?
Or where can I flee from Your
presence?

8 If I ascend into heaven, You *are*
there;
If I make my bed in hell, behold, You
are there.

9 *If* I take the wings of the morning,
And dwell in the uttermost parts of
the sea,

10 Even there Your hand shall lead me,
And Your right hand shall hold me.

11 If I say, "Surely the darkness shall
fall on me,"
Even the night shall be light
about me;

12 Indeed, the darkness shall not hide
from You,
But the night shines as the day;
The darkness and the light *are* both
alike *to You.*

13 For You formed my inward parts;
You covered me in my mother's
womb.

14 I will praise You, for I am fearfully
and wonderfully made;
Marvelous are Your works,
And *that* my soul knows very well.

15 My frame was not hidden from You,
When I was made in secret,
And skillfully wrought in the lowest
parts of the earth.

16 Your eyes saw my substance, being
yet unformed.
And in Your book they all were
written,
The days fashioned for me,
When *as yet there were* none of
them.

17 How precious also are Your
    thoughts to me, O God!
    How great is the sum of them!
18 *If* I should count them, they would
    be more in number than the sand;
    When I awake, I am still with You.

19 Oh, that You would slay the wicked,
    O God!
    Depart from me, therefore, you
    bloodthirsty men.
20 For they speak against You
    wickedly;
    Your enemies take *Your name* in
    vain.
21 Do I not hate them, O Lord, who
    hate You?
    And do I not loathe those who rise
    up against You?
22 I hate them with perfect hatred;
    I count them my enemies.

23 Search me, O God, and know my
    heart;
    Try me, and know my anxieties;
24 And see if *there is any* wicked way
    in me,
    And lead me in the way everlasting.

PSALM 140

Prayer for Deliverance from Evil Men

To the Chief Musician. A Psalm of David.

1 Deliver me, O Lord, from evil men;
    Preserve me from violent men,
2 Who plan evil things in *their* hearts;
    They continually gather together
    for war.
3 They sharpen their tongues like a
    serpent;
    The poison of asps *is* under their
    lips.   Selah

4 Keep me, O Lord, from the hands
    of the wicked;
    Preserve me from violent men,
    Who have purposed to make my
    steps stumble.
5 The proud have hidden a snare for
    me, and cords;
    They have spread a net by the
    wayside;
    They have set traps for me.   Selah

6 I said to the Lord: "You *are* my God;
    Hear the voice of my supplications,
    O Lord.

7 O God the Lord, the strength of my
    salvation,
    You have covered my head in the
    day of battle.
8 Do not grant, O Lord, the desires of
    the wicked;
    Do not further his *wicked* scheme,
    Lest they be exalted.   Selah

9 "*As for* the head of those who
    surround me,
    Let the evil of their lips cover them;
10 Let burning coals fall upon them;
    Let them be cast into the fire,
    Into deep pits, that they rise not up
    again.
11 Let not a slanderer be established
    in the earth;
    Let evil hunt the violent man to
    overthrow *him*."

12 I know that the Lord will maintain
    The cause of the afflicted,
    And justice for the poor.
13 Surely the righteous shall give
    thanks to Your name;
    The upright shall dwell in Your
    presence.

PSALM 141

Prayer for Safekeeping from Wickedness

A Psalm of David.

1 Lord, I cry out to You;
    Make haste to me!
    Give ear to my voice when I cry out
    to You.
2 Let my prayer be set before You *as*
    incense,
    The lifting up of my hands *as* the
    evening sacrifice.

3 Set a guard, O Lord, over my
    mouth;
    Keep watch over the door of my lips.
4 Do not incline my heart to any evil
    thing,
    To practice wicked works
    With men who work iniquity;
    And do not let me eat of their
    delicacies.

5 Let the righteous strike me;
    It shall be a kindness.
    And let him rebuke me;
    It shall be as excellent oil;
    Let my head not refuse it.

For still my prayer *is* against the
deeds of the wicked.

6 Their judges are overthrown by the
sides of the cliff,
And they hear my words, for they
are sweet.

7 Our bones are scattered at the
mouth of the grave,
As when one plows and breaks up
the earth.

8 But my eyes *are* upon You, O God
the Lord;
In You I take refuge;
Do not leave my soul destitute.

9 Keep me from the snares they have
laid for me,
And from the traps of the workers
of iniquity.

10 Let the wicked fall into their own
nets,
While I escape safely.

PSALM 142

A Plea for Relief from Persecutors

A Contemplation of David. A Prayer when he
was in the cave.

1 I cry out to the Lord with my voice;
With my voice to the Lord I make
my supplication.

2 I pour out my complaint before Him;
I declare before Him my trouble.

3 When my spirit was overwhelmed
within me,
Then You knew my path.
In the way in which I walk
They have secretly set a snare
for me.

4 Look on *my* right hand and see,
For *there is* no one who
acknowledges me;
Refuge has failed me;
No one cares for my soul.

5 I cried out to You, O Lord:
I said, "You *are* my refuge,
My portion in the land of the living.

6 Attend to my cry,
For I am brought very low;
Deliver me from my persecutors,
For they are stronger than I.

7 Bring my soul out of prison,
That I may praise Your name;
The righteous shall surround me,

For You shall deal bountifully
with me."

PSALM 143

An Earnest Appeal for Guidance and Deliverance

A Psalm of David.

1 Hear my prayer, O Lord,
Give ear to my supplications!
In Your faithfulness answer me,
And in Your righteousness.

2 Do not enter into judgment with
Your servant,
For in Your sight no one living is
righteous.

3 For the enemy has persecuted my
soul;
He has crushed my life to the
ground;
He has made me dwell in darkness,
Like those who have long been
dead.

4 Therefore my spirit is overwhelmed
within me;
My heart within me is distressed.

5 I remember the days of old;
I meditate on all Your works;
I muse on the work of Your hands.

6 I spread out my hands to You;
My soul *longs* for You like a thirsty
land.   Selah

7 Answer me speedily, O Lord;
My spirit fails!
Do not hide Your face from me,
Lest I be like those who go down
into the pit.

8 Cause me to hear Your
lovingkindness in the morning,
For in You do I trust;
Cause me to know the way in which
I should walk,
For I lift up my soul to You.

9 Deliver me, O Lord, from my
enemies;
In You I take shelter.

10 Teach me to do Your will,
For You *are* my God;
Your Spirit *is* good.
Lead me in the land of uprightness.

11 Revive me, O Lord, for Your name's
sake!

For Your righteousness' sake bring
my soul out of trouble.
12 In Your mercy cut off my enemies,
And destroy all those who afflict my
soul;
For I *am* Your servant.

PSALM 144

A Song to the LORD Who Preserves and Prospers His People

A Psalm of David.

1 Blessed *be* the LORD my Rock,
Who trains my hands for war,
And my fingers for battle—
2 My lovingkindness and my fortress,
My high tower and my deliverer,
My shield and *the One* in whom I
take refuge,
Who subdues my people under me.

3 LORD, what *is* man, that You take
knowledge of him?
Or the son of man, that You are
mindful of him?
4 Man is like a breath;
His days *are* like a passing shadow.

5 Bow down Your heavens, O LORD,
and come down;
Touch the mountains, and they shall
smoke.
6 Flash forth lightning and scatter
them;
Shoot out Your arrows and destroy
them.
7 Stretch out Your hand from above;
Rescue me and deliver me out of
great waters,
From the hand of foreigners,
8 Whose mouth speaks lying words,
And whose right hand *is* a right
hand of falsehood.

9 I will sing a new song to You, O God;
On a harp of ten strings I will sing
praises to You,
10 *The One* who gives salvation to
kings,
Who delivers David His servant
From the deadly sword.

11 Rescue me and deliver me from the
hand of foreigners,
Whose mouth speaks lying words,
And whose right hand *is* a right
hand of falsehood—

12 That our sons *may be* as plants
grown up in their youth;
That our daughters *may be* as
pillars,
Sculptured in palace style;
13 *That* our barns *may be* full,
Supplying all kinds of produce;
That our sheep may bring forth
thousands
And ten thousands in our fields;
14 *That* our oxen *may be* well laden;
That there be no breaking in or
going out;
That there be no outcry in our
streets.
15 Happy *are* the people who are in
such a state;
Happy *are* the people whose God *is*
the LORD!

PSALM 145

A Song of God's Majesty and Love

A Praise of David.

1 I will extol You, my God, O King;
And I will bless Your name forever
and ever.
2 Every day I will bless You,
And I will praise Your name forever
and ever.
3 Great *is* the LORD, and greatly to be
praised;
And His greatness *is* unsearchable.

4 One generation shall praise Your
works to another,
And shall declare Your mighty acts.
5 I will meditate on the glorious
splendor of Your majesty,
And on Your wondrous works.
6 *Men* shall speak of the might of
Your awesome acts,
And I will declare Your greatness.
7 They shall utter the memory of Your
great goodness,
And shall sing of Your
righteousness.

8 The LORD *is* gracious and full of
compassion,
Slow to anger and great in mercy.
9 The LORD *is* good to all,
And His tender mercies *are* over all
His works.

10 All Your works shall praise You,
O LORD,

And Your saints shall bless You.
11 They shall speak of the glory of
Your kingdom,
And talk of Your power,
12 To make known to the sons of men
His mighty acts,
And the glorious majesty of His
kingdom.
13 Your kingdom *is* an everlasting
kingdom,
And Your dominion *endures*
throughout all generations.

14 The LORD upholds all who fall,
And raises up all *who are* bowed
down.
15 The eyes of all look expectantly
to You,
And You give them their food in due
season.
16 You open Your hand
And satisfy the desire of every living
thing.

17 The LORD *is* righteous in all His
ways,
Gracious in all His works.
18 The LORD *is* near to all who call upon
Him,
To all who call upon Him in truth.
19 He will fulfill the desire of those who
fear Him;
He also will hear their cry and save
them.
20 The LORD preserves all who
love Him,
But all the wicked He will destroy.
21 My mouth shall speak the praise of
the LORD,
And all flesh shall bless His holy
name
Forever and ever.

PSALM 146

The Happiness of Those Whose Help Is the LORD

1 Praise the LORD!

Praise the LORD, O my soul!
2 While I live I will praise the LORD;
I will sing praises to my God while
I have my being.

3 Do not put your trust in princes,
Nor in a son of man, in whom *there
is* no help.

4 His spirit departs, he returns to his
earth;
In that very day his plans perish.

5 Happy *is he* who *has* the God of
Jacob for his help,
Whose hope *is* in the LORD his God,
6 Who made heaven and earth,
The sea, and all that *is* in them;
Who keeps truth forever,
7 Who executes justice for the
oppressed,
Who gives food to the hungry.
The LORD gives freedom to the
prisoners.

8 The LORD opens *the eyes of* the
blind;
The LORD raises those who are
bowed down;
The LORD loves the righteous.
9 The LORD watches over the
strangers;
He relieves the fatherless and
widow;
But the way of the wicked He turns
upside down.

10 The LORD shall reign forever—
Your God, O Zion, to all
generations.

Praise the LORD!

PSALM 147

Praise to God for His Word and Providence

1 Praise the LORD!
For *it is* good to sing praises to
our God;
For *it is* pleasant, *and* praise is
beautiful.

2 The LORD builds up Jerusalem;
He gathers together the outcasts of
Israel.
3 He heals the brokenhearted
And binds up their wounds.
4 He counts the number of the stars;
He calls them all by name.
5 Great *is* our Lord, and mighty in
power;
His understanding *is* infinite.
6 The LORD lifts up the humble;
He casts the wicked down to the
ground.

7 Sing to the LORD with thanksgiving;
  Sing praises on the harp to our God,
8 Who covers the heavens with
    clouds,
  Who prepares rain for the earth,
  Who makes grass to grow on the
    mountains.
9 He gives to the beast its food,
  And to the young ravens that cry.

10 He does not delight in the strength
    of the horse;
   He takes no pleasure in the legs of
    a man.
11 The LORD takes pleasure in those
    who fear Him,
   In those who hope in His mercy.

12 Praise the LORD, O Jerusalem!
   Praise your God, O Zion!
13 For He has strengthened the bars of
    your gates;
   He has blessed your children
    within you.
14 He makes peace *in* your borders,
   And fills you with the finest wheat.

15 He sends out His command *to the*
    earth;
   His word runs very swiftly.
16 He gives snow like wool;
   He scatters the frost like ashes;
17 He casts out His hail like morsels;
   Who can stand before His cold?
18 He sends out His word and melts
    them;
   He causes His wind to blow, *and* the
    waters flow.

19 He declares His word to Jacob,
   His statutes and His judgments to
    Israel.
20 He has not dealt thus with any
    nation;
   And *as for His* judgments, they have
    not known them.

   Praise the LORD!

PSALM 148

Praise to the LORD from Creation

1 Praise the LORD!

  Praise the LORD from the heavens;
  Praise Him in the heights!
2 Praise Him, all His angels;

Praise Him, all His hosts!
3 Praise Him, sun and moon;
  Praise Him, all you stars of light!
4 Praise Him, you heavens of
    heavens,
  And you waters above the
    heavens!

5 Let them praise the name of the
    LORD,
  For He commanded and they were
    created.
6 He also established them forever
    and ever;
  He made a decree which shall not
    pass away.

7 Praise the LORD from the earth,
  You great sea creatures and all the
    depths;
8 Fire and hail, snow and clouds;
  Stormy wind, fulfilling His word;
9 Mountains and all hills;
  Fruitful trees and all cedars;
10 Beasts and all cattle;
   Creeping things and flying fowl;
11 Kings of the earth and all peoples;
   Princes and all judges of the earth;
12 Both young men and maidens;
   Old men and children.

13 Let them praise the name of the
    LORD,
   For His name alone is exalted;
   His glory *is* above the earth and
    heaven.
14 And He has exalted the horn of His
    people,
   The praise of all His saints—
   Of the children of Israel,
   A people near to Him.

   Praise the LORD!

PSALM 149

Praise to God for His Salvation and Judgment

1 Praise the LORD!

  Sing to the LORD a new song,
  And His praise in the assembly of
    saints.

2 Let Israel rejoice in their Maker;
  Let the children of Zion be joyful in
    their King.

3 Let them praise His name with the
dance;
Let them sing praises to Him with
the timbrel and harp.
4 For the LORD takes pleasure in His
people;
He will beautify the humble with
salvation.

5 Let the saints be joyful in glory;
Let them sing aloud on their beds.
6 *Let* the high praises of God *be* in
their mouth,
And a two-edged sword in their
hand,
7 To execute vengeance on the
nations,
And punishments on the peoples;
8 To bind their kings with chains,
And their nobles with fetters of
iron;
9 To execute on them the written
judgment—
This honor have all His saints.

Praise the LORD!

PSALM 150

Let All Things Praise the LORD

1 Praise the LORD!

Praise God in His sanctuary;
Praise Him in His mighty
firmament!

2 Praise Him for His mighty acts;
Praise Him according to His
excellent greatness!

3 Praise Him with the sound of the
trumpet;
Praise Him with the lute and harp!
4 Praise Him with the timbrel and
dance;
Praise Him with stringed
instruments and flutes!
5 Praise Him with loud cymbals;
Praise Him with clashing cymbals!

6 Let everything that has breath
praise the LORD.

Praise the LORD!

The Book of
PROVERBS

The Beginning of Knowledge

1 The proverbs of Solomon the son of David, king of Israel:

2 To know wisdom and instruction,
To perceive the words of understanding,

3 To receive the instruction of wisdom,
Justice, judgment, and equity;

4 To give prudence to the simple,
To the young man knowledge and discretion—

5 A wise *man* will hear and increase learning,
And a man of understanding will attain wise counsel,

6 To understand a proverb and an enigma,
The words of the wise and their riddles.

7 The fear of the LORD *is* the beginning of knowledge,
But fools despise wisdom and instruction.

Shun Evil Counsel

8 My son, hear the instruction of your father,
And do not forsake the law of your mother;

9 For they *will be* a graceful ornament on your head,
And chains about your neck.

10 My son, if sinners entice you,
Do not consent.

11 If they say, "Come with us,
Let us lie in wait to *shed* blood;
Let us lurk secretly for the innocent without cause;

12 Let us swallow them alive like Sheol,
And whole, like those who go down to the Pit;

13 We shall find all *kinds* of precious possessions,
We shall fill our houses with spoil;

14 Cast in your lot among us,
Let us all have one purse"—

15 My son, do not walk in the way with them,
Keep your foot from their path;

16 For their feet run to evil,
And they make haste to shed blood.

17 Surely, in vain the net is spread
In the sight of any bird;

18 But they lie in wait for their *own* blood,
They lurk secretly for their *own* lives.

19 So *are* the ways of everyone who is greedy for gain;
It takes away the life of its owners.

The Call of Wisdom

20 Wisdom calls aloud outside;
She raises her voice in the open squares.

21 She cries out in the chief concourses,
At the openings of the gates in the city
She speaks her words:

22 "How long, you simple ones, will you love simplicity?
For scorners delight in their scorning,
And fools hate knowledge.

23 Turn at my rebuke;
Surely I will pour out my spirit on you;
I will make my words known to you.

24 Because I have called and you refused,
I have stretched out my hand and no one regarded,

25 Because you disdained all my counsel,
And would have none of my rebuke,

26 I also will laugh at your calamity;
I will mock when your terror comes,

27 When your terror comes like a storm,
And your destruction comes like a whirlwind,
When distress and anguish come upon you.

616

28 "Then they will call on me, but I will
     not answer;
   They will seek me diligently, but
     they will not find me.
29 Because they hated knowledge
   And did not choose the fear of the
     LORD,
30 They would have none of my
     counsel
   And despised my every rebuke.
31 Therefore they shall eat the fruit of
     their own way,
   And be filled to the full with their
     own fancies.
32 For the turning away of the simple
     will slay them,
   And the complacency of fools will
     destroy them;
33 But whoever listens to me will
     dwell safely,
   And will be secure, without fear of
     evil."

The Value of Wisdom

2 My son, if you receive my words,
   And treasure my commands within
     you,
2   So that you incline your ear to
       wisdom,
     And apply your heart to
       understanding;
3   Yes, if you cry out for discernment,
     And lift up your voice for
       understanding,
4   If you seek her as silver,
     And search for her as *for* hidden
       treasures;
5   Then you will understand the fear
       of the LORD,
     And find the knowledge of God.
6   For the LORD gives wisdom;
     From His mouth *come* knowledge
       and understanding;
7   He stores up sound wisdom for the
       upright;
     He is a shield to those who walk
       uprightly;
8   He guards the paths of justice,
     And preserves the way of His
       saints.
9   Then you will understand
       righteousness and justice,
     Equity *and* every good path.

10   When wisdom enters your heart,
     And knowledge is pleasant to your
       soul,

11   Discretion will preserve you;
     Understanding will keep you,
12   To deliver you from the way of evil,
     From the man who speaks perverse
       things,
13   From those who leave the paths of
       uprightness
     To walk in the ways of darkness;
14   Who rejoice in doing evil,
     And delight in the perversity of the
       wicked;
15   Whose ways *are* crooked,
     And *who are* devious in their paths;
16   To deliver you from the immoral
       woman,
     From the seductress *who* flatters
       with her words,
17   Who forsakes the companion of her
       youth,
     And forgets the covenant of
       her God.
18   For her house leads down to death,
     And her paths to the dead;
19   None who go to her return,
     Nor do they regain the paths of
       life—
20   So you may walk in the way of
       goodness,
     And keep *to* the paths of
       righteousness.
21   For the upright will dwell in the
       land,
     And the blameless will remain
       in it;
22   But the wicked will be cut off from
       the earth,
     And the unfaithful will be uprooted
       from it.

Guidance for the Young

3 My son, do not forget my law,
   But let your heart keep my
     commands;
2   For length of days and long life
     And peace they will add to you.

3   Let not mercy and truth
       forsake you;
     Bind them around your neck,
     Write them on the tablet of your
       heart,
4   *And* so find favor and high esteem
     In the sight of God and man.

5   Trust in the LORD with all your
       heart,

And lean not on your own
understanding;
6 In all your ways acknowledge Him,
And He shall direct your paths.

7 Do not be wise in your own eyes;
Fear the LORD and depart from evil.
8 It will be health to your flesh,
And strength to your bones.

9 Honor the LORD with your
possessions,
And with the firstfruits of all your
increase;
10 So your barns will be filled with
plenty,
And your vats will overflow with
new wine.

11 My son, do not despise the
chastening of the LORD,
Nor detest His correction;
12 For whom the LORD loves He
corrects,
Just as a father the son *in whom*
he delights.

13 Happy *is* the man *who* finds
wisdom,
And the man *who* gains
understanding;
14 For her proceeds *are* better than the
profits of silver,
And her gain than fine gold.
15 She *is* more precious than rubies,
And all the things you may desire
cannot compare with her.
16 Length of days *is* in her right hand,
In her left hand riches and honor.
17 Her ways *are* ways of pleasantness,
And all her paths *are* peace.
18 She *is* a tree of life to those who
take hold of her,
And happy *are all* who retain her.

19 The LORD by wisdom founded the
earth;
By understanding He established
the heavens;
20 By His knowledge the depths were
broken up,
And clouds drop down the dew.

21 My son, let them not depart from
your eyes—
Keep sound wisdom and discretion;

22 So they will be life to your soul
And grace to your neck.
23 Then you will walk safely in your
way,
And your foot will not stumble.
24 When you lie down, you will not
be afraid;
Yes, you will lie down and your
sleep will be sweet.
25 Do not be afraid of sudden terror,
Nor of trouble from the wicked
when it comes;
26 For the LORD will be your
confidence,
And will keep your foot from being
caught.

27 Do not withhold good from those
to whom it is due,
When it is in the power of your
hand to do *so.*
28 Do not say to your neighbor,
"Go, and come back,
And tomorrow I will give *it,*"
When *you have* it with you.
29 Do not devise evil against your
neighbor,
For he dwells by you for safety's
sake.
30 Do not strive with a man without
cause,
If he has done you no harm.

31 Do not envy the oppressor,
And choose none of his ways;
32 For the perverse *person is* an
abomination to the LORD,
But His secret counsel *is* with the
upright.
33 The curse of the LORD *is* on the
house of the wicked,
But He blesses the home of the just.
34 Surely He scorns the scornful,
But gives grace to the humble.
35 The wise shall inherit glory,
But shame shall be the legacy of
fools.

Security in Wisdom

4 Hear, *my* children, the instruction
of a father,
And give attention to know
understanding;
2 For I give you good doctrine:
Do not forsake my law.
3 When I was my father's son,

Tender and the only one in the sight
of my mother,

4 He also taught me, and said to me:
"Let your heart retain my words;
Keep my commands, and live.

5 Get wisdom! Get understanding!
Do not forget, nor turn away from
the words of my mouth.

6 Do not forsake her, and she will
preserve you;
Love her, and she will keep you.

7 Wisdom *is* the principal thing;
Therefore get wisdom.
And in all your getting, get
understanding.

8 Exalt her, and she will
promote you;
She will bring you honor, when you
embrace her.

9 She will place on your head an
ornament of grace;
A crown of glory she will deliver
to you."

10 Hear, my son, and receive my
sayings,
And the years of your life will be
many.

11 I have taught you in the way of
wisdom;
I have led you in right paths.

12 When you walk, your steps will not
be hindered,
And when you run, you will not
stumble.

13 Take firm hold of instruction, do
not let go;
Keep her, for she *is* your life.

14 Do not enter the path of the wicked,
And do not walk in the way of evil.

15 Avoid it, do not travel on it;
Turn away from it and pass on.

16 For they do not sleep unless they
have done evil;
And their sleep is taken away
unless they make *someone* fall.

17 For they eat the bread of
wickedness,
And drink the wine of violence.

18 But the path of the just *is* like the
shining sun,
That shines ever brighter unto the
perfect day.

19 The way of the wicked *is* like
darkness;

They do not know what makes
them stumble.

20 My son, give attention to my words;
Incline your ear to my sayings.

21 Do not let them depart from your
eyes;
Keep them in the midst of your
heart;

22 For they *are* life to those who find
them,
And health to all their flesh.

23 Keep your heart with all diligence,
For out of it *spring* the issues of life.

24 Put away from you a deceitful
mouth,
And put perverse lips far from you.

25 Let your eyes look straight ahead,
And your eyelids look right
before you.

26 Ponder the path of your feet,
And let all your ways be
established.

27 Do not turn to the right or the left;
Remove your foot from evil.

The Peril of Adultery

5 My son, pay attention to my
wisdom;
Lend your ear to my
understanding,

2 That you may preserve discretion,
And your lips may keep
knowledge.

3 For the lips of an immoral woman
drip honey,
And her mouth *is* smoother
than oil;

4 But in the end she is bitter as
wormwood,
Sharp as a two-edged sword.

5 Her feet go down to death,
Her steps lay hold of hell.

6 Lest you ponder *her* path of life—
Her ways are unstable;
You do not know *them.*

7 Therefore hear me now, *my*
children,
And do not depart from the words
of my mouth.

8 Remove your way far from her,
And do not go near the door of her
house,

9 Lest you give your honor to others,
And your years to the cruel *one;*

10　Lest aliens be filled with your
　　　wealth,
　　And your labors go to the house of
　　　a foreigner;
11　And you mourn at last,
　　When your flesh and your body are
　　　consumed,
12　And say:
　"How I have hated instruction,
　　And my heart despised correction!
13　I have not obeyed the voice of my
　　　teachers,
　　Nor inclined my ear to those who
　　　instructed me!
14　I was on the verge of total ruin,
　　In the midst of the assembly and
　　　congregation."

15　Drink water from your own cistern,
　　And running water from your own
　　　well.
16　Should your fountains be dispersed
　　　abroad,
　　Streams of water in the streets?
17　Let them be only your own,
　　And not for strangers with you.
18　Let your fountain be blessed,
　　And rejoice with the wife of your
　　　youth.
19　As a loving deer and a graceful doe,
　　Let her breasts satisfy you at all
　　　times;
　　And always be enraptured with her
　　　love.
20　For why should you, my son, be
　　　enraptured by an immoral
　　　woman,
　　And be embraced in the arms of a
　　　seductress?

21　For the ways of man are before the
　　　eyes of the LORD,
　　And He ponders all his paths.
22　His own iniquities entrap the
　　　wicked man,
　　And he is caught in the cords of
　　　his sin.
23　He shall die for lack of instruction,
　　And in the greatness of his folly he
　　　shall go astray.

Dangerous Promises

6 My son, if you become surety for
　　　your friend,
　　If you have shaken hands in pledge
　　　for a stranger,

2　You are snared by the words of
　　　your mouth;
　　You are taken by the words of your
　　　mouth.
3　So do this, my son, and deliver
　　　yourself;
　　For you have come into the hand
　　　of your friend:
　　Go and humble yourself;
　　Plead with your friend.
4　Give no sleep to your eyes,
　　Nor slumber to your eyelids.
5　Deliver yourself like a gazelle from
　　　the hand of the hunter,
　　And like a bird from the hand of
　　　the fowler.

The Folly of Indolence

6　Go to the ant, you sluggard!
　　Consider her ways and be wise,
7　Which, having no captain,
　　Overseer or ruler,
8　Provides her supplies in the
　　　summer,
　　And gathers her food in the
　　　harvest.
9　How long will you slumber,
　　　O sluggard?
　　When will you rise from your
　　　sleep?
10　A little sleep, a little slumber,
　　A little folding of the hands to
　　　sleep—
11　So shall your poverty come on you
　　　like a prowler,
　　And your need like an armed man.

The Wicked Man

12　A worthless person, a wicked man,
　　Walks with a perverse mouth;
13　He winks with his eyes,
　　He shuffles his feet,
　　He points with his fingers;
14　Perversity is in his heart,
　　He devises evil continually,
　　He sows discord.
15　Therefore his calamity shall come
　　　suddenly;
　　Suddenly he shall be broken
　　　without remedy.

16　These six things the LORD hates,
　　Yes, seven are an abomination to
　　　Him:
17　A proud look,
　　A lying tongue,
　　Hands that shed innocent blood,

18 A heart that devises wicked plans,
    Feet that are swift in running to
       evil,
19 A false witness *who* speaks lies,
    And one who sows discord among
       brethren.

Beware of Adultery

20 My son, keep your father's
       command,
    And do not forsake the law of your
       mother.
21 Bind them continually upon your
       heart;
    Tie them around your neck.
22 When you roam, they will lead you;
    When you sleep, they will
       keep you;
    And *when* you awake, they will
       speak with you.
23 For the commandment *is* a lamp,
    And the law a light;
    Reproofs of instruction *are* the way
       of life,
24 To keep you from the evil woman,
    From the flattering tongue of a
       seductress.
25 Do not lust after her beauty in your
       heart,
    Nor let her allure you with her
       eyelids.
26 For by means of a harlot
    A *man is reduced* to a crust of
       bread;
    And an adulteress will prey upon
       his precious life.
27 Can a man take fire to his bosom,
    And his clothes not be burned?
28 Can one walk on hot coals,
    And his feet not be seared?
29 So *is* he who goes in to his
       neighbor's wife;
    Whoever touches her shall not be
       innocent.

30 *People* do not despise a thief
    If he steals to satisfy himself when
       he is starving.
31 Yet *when* he is found, he must
       restore sevenfold;
    He may have to give up all the
       substance of his house.
32 Whoever commits adultery with a
       woman lacks understanding;
    He *who* does so destroys his own
       soul.
33 Wounds and dishonor he will get,

    And his reproach will not be wiped
       away.
34 For jealousy *is* a husband's fury;
    Therefore he will not spare in the
       day of vengeance.
35 He will accept no recompense,
    Nor will he be appeased though you
       give many gifts.

7 My son, keep my words,
   And treasure my commands within
      you.
2 Keep my commands and live,
   And my law as the apple of
      your eye.
3 Bind them on your fingers;
   Write them on the tablet of your
      heart.
4 Say to wisdom, "You *are* my
      sister,"
   And call understanding *your*
      nearest kin,
5 That they may keep you from the
      immoral woman,
   From the seductress *who* flatters
      with her words.

The Crafty Harlot

6 For at the window of my house
   I looked through my lattice,
7 And saw among the simple,
   I perceived among the youths,
   A young man devoid of
      understanding,
8 Passing along the street near her
      corner;
   And he took the path to her house
9 In the twilight, in the evening,
   In the black and dark night.

10 And there a woman met him,
    With the attire of a harlot, and a
       crafty heart.
11 She *was* loud and rebellious,
    Her feet would not stay at home.
12 At times *she was* outside, at times
       in the open square,
    Lurking at every corner.
13 So she caught him and kissed him;
    With an impudent face she said
       to him:
14 "*I have* peace offerings with me;
    Today I have paid my vows.
15 So I came out to meet you,
    Diligently to seek your face,
    And I have found you.
16 I have spread my bed with tapestry,

Colored coverings of Egyptian
linen.
17 I have perfumed my bed
With myrrh, aloes, and cinnamon.
18 Come, let us take our fill of love
until morning;
Let us delight ourselves with love.
19 For my husband *is* not at home;
He has gone on a long journey;
20 He has taken a bag of money
with him,
And will come home on the
. appointed day.''

21 With her enticing speech she
caused him to yield,
With her flattering lips she
seduced him.
22 Immediately he went after her, as
an ox goes to the slaughter,
Or as a fool to the correction of the
stocks,
23 Till an arrow struck his liver.
As a bird hastens to the snare,
He did not know it *would cost* his
life.

24 Now therefore, listen to me, *my*
children;
Pay attention to the words of my
mouth:
25 Do not let your heart turn aside to
her ways,
Do not stray into her paths;
26 For she has cast down many
wounded,
And all who were slain by her were
strong *men*.
27 Her house *is* the way to hell,
Descending to the chambers of
death.

The Excellence of Wisdom

8 Does not wisdom cry out,
And understanding lift up her
voice?
2 She takes her stand on the top of
the high hill,
Beside the way, where the paths
meet.
3 She cries out by the gates, at the
entry of the city,
At the entrance of the doors:
4 "To you, O men, I call,
And my voice *is* to the sons of men.
5 O you simple ones, understand
prudence,

And you fools, be of an
understanding heart.
6 Listen, for I will speak of excellent
things,
And from the opening of my lips
will come right things;
7 For my mouth will speak truth;
Wickedness *is* an abomination to
my lips.
8 All the words of my mouth *are* with
righteousness;
Nothing crooked or perverse *is* in
them.
9 They *are* all plain to him who
understands,
And right to those who find
knowledge.
10 Receive my instruction, and not
silver,
And knowledge rather than choice
gold;
11 For wisdom *is* better than rubies,
And all the things one may desire
cannot be compared with her.

12 "I, wisdom, dwell with prudence,
And find out knowledge *and*
discretion.
13 The fear of the Lord *is* to hate evil;
Pride and arrogance and the
evil way
And the perverse mouth I hate.
14 Counsel *is* mine, and sound
wisdom;
I *am* understanding, I have
strength.
15 By me kings reign,
And rulers decree justice.
16 By me princes rule, and nobles,
All the judges of the earth.
17 I love those who love me,
And those who seek me diligently
will find me.
18 Riches and honor *are* with me,
Enduring riches and righteousness.
19 My fruit *is* better than gold, yes,
than fine gold,
And my revenue than choice silver.
20 I traverse the way of righteousness,
In the midst of the paths of justice,
21 That I may cause those who love
me to inherit wealth,
That I may fill their treasuries.

22 "The Lord possessed me at the
beginning of His way,
Before His works of old.

23 I have been established from
   everlasting,
   From the beginning, before there
   was ever an earth.
24 When *there were* no depths I was
   brought forth,
   When *there were* no fountains
   abounding with water.
25 Before the mountains were settled,
   Before the hills, I was brought
   forth;
26 While as yet He had not made the
   earth or the fields,
   Or the primal dust of the world.
27 When He prepared the heavens, I
   was there,
   When He drew a circle on the face
   of the deep,
28 When He established the clouds
   above,
   When He strengthened the
   fountains of the deep,
29 When He assigned to the sea its
   limit,
   So that the waters would not
   transgress His command,
   When He marked out the
   foundations of the earth,
30 Then I was beside Him *as* a master
   craftsman;
   And I was daily *His* delight,
   Rejoicing always before Him,
31 Rejoicing in His inhabited world,
   And my delight *was* with the sons
   of men.

32 "Now therefore, listen to me, *my*
   children,
   For blessed *are those who* keep my
   ways.
33 Hear instruction and be wise,
   And do not disdain *it.*
34 Blessed is the man who listens to
   me,
   Watching daily at my gates,
   Waiting at the posts of my doors.
35 For whoever finds me finds life,
   And obtains favor from the LORD;
36 But he who sins against me wrongs
   his own soul;
   All those who hate me love death."

The Way of Wisdom

9 Wisdom has built her house,
   She has hewn out her seven pillars;
2 She has slaughtered her meat,
   She has mixed her wine,

She has also furnished her table.
3 She has sent out her maidens,
   She cries out from the highest
   places of the city,
4 "Whoever *is* simple, let him turn in
   here!"
   As for him who lacks
   understanding, she says to him,
5 "Come, eat of my bread
   And drink of the wine I have mixed.
6 Forsake foolishness and live,
   And go in the way of
   understanding.

7 "He who corrects a scoffer gets
   shame for himself,
   And he who rebukes a wicked *man*
   only harms himself.
8 Do not correct a scoffer, lest he
   hate you;
   Rebuke a wise *man,* and he will
   love you.
9 Give *instruction* to a wise *man,* and
   he will be still wiser;
   Teach a just *man,* and he will
   increase in learning.

10 "The fear of the LORD *is* the
   beginning of wisdom,
   And the knowledge of the Holy One
   is understanding.
11 For by me your days will be
   multiplied,
   And years of life will be added
   to you.
12 If you are wise, you are wise for
   yourself,
   And *if* you scoff, you will bear *it*
   alone."

The Way of Folly

13 A foolish woman is clamorous;
   She is simple, and knows nothing.
14 For she sits at the door of her
   house,
   On a seat *by* the highest places of
   the city,
15 To call to those who pass by,
   Who go straight on their way:
16 "Whoever *is* simple, let him turn in
   here";
   And *as for* him who lacks
   understanding, she says to him,
17 "Stolen water is sweet,
   And bread *eaten* in secret is
   pleasant."

18 But he does not know that the dead
    are there,
    That her guests *are* in the depths
    of hell.

Wise Sayings of Solomon

10 The proverbs of Solomon:

A wise son makes a glad father,
But a foolish son *is* the grief of his
mother.

2 Treasures of wickedness profit
    nothing,
    But righteousness delivers from
    death.

3 The LORD will not allow the
    righteous soul to famish,
    But He casts away the desire of the
    wicked.

4 He who has a slack hand becomes
    poor,
    But the hand of the diligent makes
    rich.

5 He who gathers in summer *is* a wise
    son;
    He who sleeps in harvest *is* a son
    who causes shame.

6 Blessings *are* on the head of the
    righteous,
    But violence covers the mouth of
    the wicked.

7 The memory of the righteous *is*
    blessed,
    But the name of the wicked will rot.

8 The wise in heart will receive
    commands,
    But a prating fool will fall.

9 He who walks with integrity walks
    securely,
    But he who perverts his ways will
    become known.

10 He who winks with the eye causes
    trouble,
    But a prating fool will fall.

11 The mouth of the righteous *is* a well
    of life,
    But violence covers the mouth of
    the wicked.

12 Hatred stirs up strife,
    But love covers all sins.

13 Wisdom is found on the lips of him
    who has understanding,
    But a rod *is* for the back of him who
    is devoid of understanding.

14 Wise *people* store up knowledge,
    But the mouth of the foolish *is* near
    destruction.

15 The rich man's wealth *is* his strong
    city;
    The destruction of the poor *is* their
    poverty.

16 The labor of the righteous *leads* to
    life,
    The wages of the wicked to sin.

17 He who keeps instruction *is in* the
    way of life,
    But he who refuses correction goes
    astray.

18 Whoever hides hatred *has* lying
    lips,
    And whoever spreads slander *is* a
    fool.

19 In the multitude of words sin is not
    lacking,
    But he who restrains his lips *is*
    wise.

20 The tongue of the righteous *is*
    choice silver;
    The heart of the wicked *is worth*
    little.

21 The lips of the righteous feed many,
    But fools die for lack of wisdom.

22 The blessing of the LORD makes *one*
    rich,
    And He adds no sorrow with it.

23 To do evil *is* like sport to a fool,
    But a man of understanding has
    wisdom.

24 The fear of the wicked will come
    upon him,
    And the desire of the righteous will
    be granted.

25 When the whirlwind passes by, the
    wicked *is* no *more*,
    But the righteous *has* an
    everlasting foundation.

26 As vinegar to the teeth and smoke
    to the eyes,

So *is* the lazy *man* to those who
send him.

27 The fear of the Lord prolongs days,
But the years of the wicked will be
shortened.
28 The hope of the righteous *will be*
gladness,
But the expectation of the wicked
will perish.
29 The way of the Lord *is* strength for
the upright,
But destruction *will come* to the
workers of iniquity.

30 The righteous will never be
removed,
But the wicked will not inhabit the
earth.
31 The mouth of the righteous brings
forth wisdom,
But the perverse tongue will be
cut out.
32 The lips of the righteous know what
is acceptable,
But the mouth of the wicked *what
is* perverse.

11 Dishonest scales *are* an
abomination to the Lord,
But a just weight *is* His delight.

2 When pride comes, then comes
shame;
But with the humble *is* wisdom.

3 The integrity of the upright will
guide them,
But the perversity of the unfaithful
will destroy them.
4 Riches do not profit in the day of
wrath,
But righteousness delivers from
death.
5 The righteousness of the blameless
will direct his way aright,
But the wicked will fall by his own
wickedness.
6 The righteousness of the upright
will deliver them,
But the unfaithful will be caught by
their lust.

7 When a wicked man dies, *his*
expectation will perish,
And the hope of the unjust
perishes.

8 The righteous is delivered from
trouble,
And it comes to the wicked instead.
9 The hypocrite with *his* mouth
destroys his neighbor,
But through knowledge the
righteous will be delivered.
10 When it goes well with the
righteous, the city rejoices;
And when the wicked perish, *there
is* jubilation.
11 By the blessing of the upright the
city is exalted,
But it is overthrown by the mouth
of the wicked.

12 He who is devoid of wisdom
despises his neighbor,
But a man of understanding holds
his peace.

13 A talebearer reveals secrets,
But he who is of a faithful spirit
conceals a matter.

14 Where *there is* no counsel, the
people fall;
But in the multitude of counselors
there is safety.

15 He who is surety for a stranger will
suffer,
But one who hates being surety is
secure.

16 A gracious woman retains honor,
But ruthless *men* retain riches.
17 The merciful man does good for his
own soul,
But *he who is* cruel troubles his
own flesh.
18 The wicked *man* does deceptive
work,
But he who sows righteousness *will*
have a sure reward.
19 As righteousness *leads* to life,
So he who pursues evil *pursues it*
to his own death.
20 Those who are of a perverse heart
are an abomination to the Lord,
But *the* blameless in their ways *are*
His delight.
21 *Though they join* forces, the wicked
will not go unpunished;
But the posterity of the righteous
will be delivered.

22 As a ring of gold in a swine's snout,
So is a lovely woman who lacks
discretion.

23 The desire of the righteous is only
good,
But the expectation of the wicked
is wrath.

24 There is one who scatters, yet
increases more;
And there is one who withholds
more than is right,
But it leads to poverty.

25 The generous soul will be made
rich,
And he who waters will also be
watered himself.

26 The people will curse him who
withholds grain,
But blessing will be on the head of
him who sells it.

27 He who earnestly seeks good finds
favor,
But trouble will come to him who
seeks evil.

28 He who trusts in his riches will fall,
But the righteous will flourish like
foliage.

29 He who troubles his own house will
inherit the wind,
And the fool will be servant to the
wise of heart.

30 The fruit of the righteous is a tree
of life,
And he who wins souls is wise.

31 If the righteous will be
recompensed on the earth,
How much more the ungodly and
the sinner.

12 Whoever loves instruction loves
knowledge,
But he who hates correction is
stupid.

2 A good man obtains favor from the
LORD,
But a man of wicked intentions He
will condemn.

3 A man is not established by
wickedness,
But the root of the righteous cannot
be moved.

4 An excellent wife is the crown of
her husband,
But she who causes shame is like
rottenness in his bones.

5 The thoughts of the righteous are
right,
But the counsels of the wicked are
deceitful.

6 The words of the wicked are, "Lie
in wait for blood,"
But the mouth of the upright will
deliver them.

7 The wicked are overthrown and are
no more,
But the house of the righteous will
stand.

8 A man will be commended
according to his wisdom,
But he who is of a perverse heart
will be despised.

9 Better is the one who is slighted but
has a servant,
Than he who honors himself but
lacks bread.

10 A righteous man regards the life of
his animal,
But the tender mercies of the
wicked are cruel.

11 He who tills his land will be
satisfied with bread,
But he who follows frivolity is
devoid of understanding.

12 The wicked covet the catch of evil
men,
But the root of the righteous yields
fruit.

13 The wicked is ensnared by the
transgression of his lips,
But the righteous will come
through trouble.

14 A man will be satisfied with good
by the fruit of his mouth,
And the recompense of a man's
hands will be rendered to him.

15 The way of a fool is right in his own
eyes,

But he who heeds counsel *is* wise.

16 A fool's wrath is known at once,
But a prudent *man* covers shame.

17 He *who* speaks truth declares
righteousness,
But a false witness, deceit.

18 There is one who speaks like the
piercings of a sword,
But the tongue of the wise
promotes health.

19 The truthful lip shall be established
forever,
But a lying tongue *is* but for a
moment.

20 Deceit is in the heart of those who
devise evil,
But counselors of peace have joy.

21 No grave trouble will overtake the
righteous,
But the wicked shall be filled with
evil.

22 Lying lips *are* an abomination to
the LORD,
But those who deal truthfully *are*
His delight.

23 A prudent man conceals
knowledge,
But the heart of fools proclaims
foolishness.

24 The hand of the diligent will rule,
But the lazy *man* will be put to
forced labor.

25 Anxiety in the heart of man causes
depression,
But a good word makes it glad.

26 The righteous should choose his
friends carefully,
For the way of the wicked leads
them astray.

27 The lazy *man* does not roast what
he took in hunting,
But diligence *is* man's precious
possession.

28 In the way of righteousness *is* life,
And in *its* pathway *there is* no
death.

13 A wise son *heeds* his father's
instruction,
But a scoffer does not listen to
rebuke.

2 A man shall eat well by the fruit
of *his* mouth,
But the soul of the unfaithful feeds
on violence.

3 He who guards his mouth preserves
his life,
But he who opens wide his lips
shall have destruction.

4 The soul of a lazy *man* desires, and
has nothing;
But the soul of the diligent shall be
made rich.

5 A righteous *man* hates lying,
But a wicked *man* is loathsome and
comes to shame.

6 Righteousness guards *him whose*
way is blameless,
But wickedness overthrows the
sinner.

7 There is one who makes himself
rich, yet *has* nothing;
And one who makes himself poor,
yet *has* great riches.

8 The ransom of a man's life *is* his
riches,
But the poor does not hear rebuke.

9 The light of the righteous rejoices,
But the lamp of the wicked will be
put out.

10 By pride comes nothing but strife,
But with the well-advised *is*
wisdom.

11 Wealth *gained by* dishonesty will
be diminished,
But he who gathers by labor will
increase.

12 Hope deferred makes the heart
sick,
But *when* the desire comes, *it is* a
tree of life.

13 He who despises the word will be
destroyed,
But he who fears the
commandment will be rewarded.

14 The law of the wise *is* a fountain
of life,
To turn *one* away from the snares
of death.

15 Good understanding gains favor,
But the way of the unfaithful *is*
hard.

16 Every prudent *man* acts with
knowledge,
But a fool lays open *his* folly.

17 A wicked messenger falls into
trouble,
But a faithful ambassador *brings*
health.

18 Poverty and shame *will come* to
him who disdains correction,
But he who regards a rebuke will
be honored.

19 A desire accomplished is sweet to
the soul,
But *it is* an abomination to fools to
depart from evil.

20 He who walks with wise *men* will
be wise,
But the companion of fools will be
destroyed.

21 Evil pursues sinners,
But to the righteous, good shall be
repaid.

22 A good *man* leaves an inheritance
to his children's children,
But the wealth of the sinner is
stored up for the righteous.

23 Much food *is in* the fallow *ground*
of the poor,
And for lack of justice there is
waste.

24 He who spares his rod hates
his son,
But he who loves him disciplines
him promptly.

25 The righteous eats to the satisfying
of his soul,
But the stomach of the wicked shall
be in want.

14 The wise woman builds her
house,
But the foolish pulls it down with
her hands.

2 He who walks in his uprightness
fears the LORD,

But *he who is* perverse in his ways
despises Him.

3 In the mouth of a fool *is* a rod of
pride,
But the lips of the wise will
preserve them.

4 Where no oxen *are*, the trough *is*
clean;
But much increase *comes* by the
strength of an ox.

5 A faithful witness does not lie,
But a false witness will utter lies.

6 A scoffer seeks wisdom and does
not *find it*,
But knowledge *is* easy to him who
understands.

7 Go from the presence of a
foolish man,
When you do not perceive *in him*
the lips of knowledge.

8 The wisdom of the prudent *is* to
understand his way,
But the folly of fools *is* deceit.

9 Fools mock at sin,
But among the upright *there is*
favor.

10 The heart knows its own bitterness,
And a stranger does not share
its joy.

11 The house of the wicked will be
overthrown,
But the tent of the upright will
flourish.

12 There is a way *that seems* right to
a man,
But its end *is* the way of death.

13 Even in laughter the heart may
sorrow,
And the end of mirth *may be* grief.

14 The backslider in heart will be
filled with his own ways,
But a good man *will be satisfied*
from above.

15 The simple believes every word,
But the prudent considers well his
steps.

16 A wise *man* fears and departs from
     evil,
   But a fool rages and is self-
     confident.
17 A quick-tempered *man* acts
     foolishly,
   And a man of wicked intentions is
     hated.
18 The simple inherit folly,
   But the prudent are crowned with
     knowledge.
19 The evil will bow before the good,
   And the wicked at the gates of the
     righteous.

20 The poor *man* is hated even by his
     own neighbor,
   But the rich *has* many friends.
21 He who despises his neighbor sins;
   But he who has mercy on the poor,
     happy *is* he.

22 Do they not go astray who devise
     evil?
   But mercy and truth *belong* to those
     who devise good.

23 In all labor there is profit,
   But idle chatter *leads* only to
     poverty.

24 The crown of the wise is their
     riches,
   But the foolishness of fools *is* folly.

25 A true witness delivers souls,
   But a deceitful *witness* speaks lies.

26 In the fear of the LORD *there is*
     strong confidence,
   And His children will have a place
     of refuge.
27 The fear of the LORD *is* a fountain
     of life,
   To turn *one* away from the snares
     of death.

28 In a multitude of people *is* a king's
     honor,
   But in the lack of people *is* the
     downfall of a prince.

29 *He who is* slow to wrath has great
     understanding,
   But *he who is* impulsive exalts folly.

30 A sound heart *is* life to the body,
   But envy *is* rottenness to the bones.

31 He who oppresses the poor
     reproaches his Maker,
   But he who honors Him has mercy
     on the needy.

32 The wicked is banished in his
     wickedness,
   But the righteous has a refuge in
     his death.

33 Wisdom rests in the heart of him
     who has understanding,
   But *what is* in the heart of fools is
     made known.

34 Righteousness exalts a nation,
   But sin *is* a reproach to *any* people.

35 The king's favor *is* toward a wise
     servant,
   But his wrath *is against* him who
     causes shame.

15 A soft answer turns away
          wrath,
   But a harsh word stirs up anger.
2 The tongue of the wise uses
     knowledge rightly,
   But the mouth of fools pours forth
     foolishness.

3 The eyes of the LORD *are* in every
     place,
   Keeping watch on the evil and the
     good.

4 A wholesome tongue *is* a tree of
     life,
   But perverseness in it breaks the
     spirit.

5 A fool despises his father's
     instruction,
   But he who receives correction is
     prudent.

6 *In* the house of the righteous *there
     is* much treasure,
   But in the revenue of the wicked
     is trouble.

7 The lips of the wise disperse
     knowledge,
   But the heart of the fool *does* not
     do so.

8 The sacrifice of the wicked *is* an
     abomination to the LORD,

But the prayer of the upright *is* His delight.

9 The way of the wicked *is* an abomination to the LORD,
But He loves him who follows righteousness.

10 Harsh discipline *is* for him who forsakes the way,
And he who hates correction will die.

11 Hell and Destruction *are* before the LORD;
So how much more the hearts of the sons of men.

12 A scoffer does not love one who corrects him,
Nor will he go to the wise.

13 A merry heart makes a cheerful countenance,
But by sorrow of the heart the spirit is broken.

14 The heart of him who has understanding seeks knowledge,
But the mouth of fools feeds on foolishness.

15 All the days of the afflicted *are* evil,
But he who is of a merry heart *has* a continual feast.

16 Better *is* a little with the fear of the LORD,
Than great treasure with trouble.

17 Better *is* a dinner of herbs*ᵃ* where love is,
Than a fatted calf with hatred.

18 A wrathful man stirs up strife,
But *he who is* slow to anger allays contention.

19 The way of the lazy *man is* like a hedge of thorns,
But the way of the upright *is* a highway.

20 A wise son makes a father glad,
But a foolish man despises his mother.

21 Folly *is* joy *to him who is* destitute of discernment,
But a man of understanding walks uprightly.

22 Without counsel, plans go awry,
But in the multitude of counselors they are established.

23 A man has joy by the answer of his mouth,
And a word *spoken* in due season, how good *it is!*

24 The way of life *winds* upward for the wise,
That he may turn away from hell below.

25 The LORD will destroy the house of the proud,
But He will establish the boundary of the widow.

26 The thoughts of the wicked *are* an abomination to the LORD,
But *the words* of the pure *are* pleasant.

27 He who is greedy for gain troubles his own house,
But he who hates bribes will live.

28 The heart of the righteous studies how to answer,
But the mouth of the wicked pours forth evil.

29 The LORD *is* far from the wicked,
But He hears the prayer of the righteous.

30 The light of the eyes rejoices the heart,
And a good report makes the bones healthy.

31 The ear that hears the rebukes of life
Will abide among the wise.

32 He who disdains instruction despises his own soul,
But he who heeds rebuke gets understanding.

ᵃ Or *vegetables*

33 The fear of the Lord *is* the
    instruction of wisdom,
    And before honor *is* humility.

16 The preparations of the heart
    belong to man,
    But the answer of the tongue *is*
    from the Lord.

2   All the ways of a man *are* pure in
    his own eyes,
    But the Lord weighs the spirits.

3   Commit your works to the Lord,
    And your thoughts will be
    established.

4   The Lord has made all for Himself,
    Yes, even the wicked for the day
    of doom.

5   Everyone proud in heart *is* an
    abomination to the Lord;
    Though they join forces, none will
    go unpunished.

6   In mercy and truth
    Atonement is provided for iniquity;
    And by the fear of the Lord *one*
    departs from evil.

7   When a man's ways please the
    Lord,
    He makes even his enemies to be
    at peace with him.

8   Better *is* a little with righteousness,
    Than vast revenues without justice.

9   A man's heart plans his way,
    But the Lord directs his steps.

10 Divination *is* on the lips of the king;
    His mouth must not transgress in
    judgment.

11 Honest weights and scales *are* the
    Lord's;
    All the weights in the bag *are* His
    work.

12 *It is* an abomination for kings to
    commit wickedness,
    For a throne is established by
    righteousness.

13 Righteous lips *are* the delight of
    kings,
    And they love him who speaks
    what is right.

14 As messengers of death *is* the
    king's wrath,
    But a wise man will appease it.

15 In the light of the king's face *is*
    life,
    And his favor *is* like a cloud of the
    latter rain.

16 How much better to get wisdom
    than gold!
    And to get understanding is to be
    chosen rather than silver.

17 The highway of the upright *is* to
    depart from evil;
    He who keeps his way preserves
    his soul.

18 Pride *goes* before destruction,
    And a haughty spirit before a fall.

19 Better *to be* of a humble spirit with
    the lowly,
    Than to divide the spoil with the
    proud.

20 He who heeds the word wisely will
    find good,
    And whoever trusts in the Lord,
    happy *is* he.

21 The wise in heart will be called
    prudent,
    And sweetness of the lips increases
    learning.

22 Understanding *is* a wellspring of
    life to him who has it.
    But the correction of fools *is* folly.

23 The heart of the wise teaches his
    mouth,
    And adds learning to his lips.

24 Pleasant words *are like* a
    honeycomb,
    Sweetness to the soul and health to
    the bones.

25 There is a way *that seems* right to
    a man,
    But its end *is* the way of death.

26 The person who labors, labors for
    himself,
    For his *hungry* mouth drives
    him *on.*

27 An ungodly man digs up evil,
   And *it is* on his lips like a burning
   fire.
28 A perverse man sows strife,
   And a whisperer separates the best
   of friends.
29 A violent man entices his neighbor,
   And leads him in a way *that is* not
   good.
30 He winks his eye to devise perverse
   things;
   He purses his lips *and* brings about
   evil.

31 The silver-haired head *is* a crown
   of glory,
   If it is found in the way of
   righteousness.

32 *He who is* slow to anger *is* better
   than the mighty,
   And he who rules his spirit than he
   who takes a city.

33 The lot is cast into the lap,
   But its every decision *is* from the
   Lord.

17 Better *is* a dry morsel with
   quietness,
   Than a house full of feasting *with*
   strife.

2 A wise servant will rule over a son
   who causes shame,
   And will share an inheritance
   among the brothers.

3 The refining pot *is* for silver and the
   furnace for gold,
   But the Lord tests the hearts.

4 An evildoer gives heed to false
   lips;
   A liar listens eagerly to a spiteful
   tongue.

5 He who mocks the poor reproaches
   his Maker;
   He who is glad at calamity will not
   go unpunished.

6 Children's children *are* the crown
   of old men,
   And the glory of children *is* their
   father.

7 Excellent speech is not becoming
   to a fool,
   Much less lying lips to a prince.

8 A present *is* a precious stone in the
   eyes of its possessor;
   Wherever he turns, he prospers.

9 He who covers a transgression
   seeks love,
   But he who repeats a matter
   separates friends.

10 Rebuke is more effective for a wise
   man
   Than a hundred blows on a fool.

11 An evil *man* seeks only rebellion;
   Therefore a cruel messenger will be
   sent against him.

12 Let a man meet a bear robbed of
   her cubs,
   Rather than a fool in his folly.

13 Whoever rewards evil for good,
   Evil will not depart from his house.

14 The beginning of strife *is like*
   releasing water;
   Therefore stop contention before a
   quarrel starts.

15 He who justifies the wicked, and he
   who condemns the just,
   Both of them alike *are* an
   abomination to the Lord.

16 Why *is there* in the hand of a fool
   the purchase price of wisdom,
   Since *he has* no heart *for it?*

17 A friend loves at all times,
   And a brother is born for adversity.

18 A man devoid of understanding
   shakes hands in a pledge,
   And becomes surety for his friend.

19 He who loves transgression loves
   strife,
   And he who exalts his gate seeks
   destruction.

20 He who has a deceitful heart finds
   no good,
   And he who has a perverse tongue
   falls into evil.

21 He who begets a scoffer *does so* to
      his sorrow,
      And the father of a fool has no joy.

22 A merry heart does good, *like*
      medicine,
      But a broken spirit dries the bones.

23 A wicked *man* accepts a bribe
      behind the back
      To pervert the ways of justice.

24 Wisdom *is* in the sight of him who
      has understanding,
      But the eyes of a fool *are* on the
      ends of the earth.

25 A foolish son *is* a grief to his father,
      And bitterness to her who
      bore him.

26 Also, to punish the righteous *is* not
      good,
      Nor to strike princes for *their*
      uprightness.

27 He who has knowledge spares his
      words,
      And a man of understanding is of
      a calm spirit.
28 Even a fool is counted wise when
      he holds his peace;
      When he shuts his lips, *he is*
      considered perceptive.

18 A man who isolates himself
      seeks his own desire;
      He rages against all wise judgment.

2 A fool has no delight in
      understanding,
      But in expressing his own heart.

3 When the wicked comes, contempt
      comes also;
      And with dishonor *comes*
      reproach.

4 The words of a man's mouth *are*
      deep waters;
      The wellspring of wisdom *is* a
      flowing brook.

5 *It is* not good to show partiality to
      the wicked,
      Or to overthrow the righteous in
      judgment.

6 A fool's lips enter into contention,
      And his mouth calls for blows.
7 A fool's mouth *is* his destruction,
      And his lips *are* the snare of his
      soul.
8 The words of a talebearer *are* like
      tasty trifles,
      And they go down into the inmost
      body.

9 He who is slothful in his work
      Is a brother to him who is a great
      destroyer.

10 The name of the LORD *is* a strong
      tower;
      The righteous run to it and are safe.
11 The rich man's wealth *is* his strong
      city,
      And like a high wall in his own
      esteem.

12 Before destruction the heart of a
      man is haughty,
      And before honor *is* humility.

13 He who answers a matter before he
      hears *it*,
      It *is* folly and shame to him.

14 The spirit of a man will sustain him
      in sickness,
      But who can bear a broken spirit?

15 The heart of the prudent acquires
      knowledge,
      And the ear of the wise seeks
      knowledge.

16 A man's gift makes room for him,
      And brings him before great men.

17 The first *one* to plead his cause
      seems right,
      Until his neighbor comes and
      examines him.

18 Casting lots causes contentions to
      cease,
      And keeps the mighty apart.

19 A brother offended *is harder to win*
      than a strong city,
      And contentions *are* like the bars
      of a castle.

20 A man's stomach shall be satisfied
      from the fruit of his mouth;

From the produce of his lips he
shall be filled.

21 Death and life *are* in the power of
the tongue,
And those who love it will eat its
fruit.

22 *He who* finds a wife finds a good
thing,
And obtains favor from the Lord.

23 The poor *man* uses entreaties,
But the rich answers roughly.

24 A man *who has* friends must
himself be friendly,[b]
But there is a friend *who* sticks
closer than a brother.

19 Better *is* the poor who walks in
his integrity
Than *one who is* perverse in his
lips, and is a fool.

2 Also it is not good *for* a soul *to be*
without knowledge,
And he sins who hastens with *his*
feet.

3 The foolishness of a man twists
his way,
And his heart frets against the
Lord.

4 Wealth makes many friends,
But the poor is separated from his
friend.

5 A false witness will not go
unpunished,
And *he who* speaks lies will not
escape.

6 Many entreat the favor of the
nobility,
And every man *is* a friend to one
who gives gifts.

7 All the brothers of the poor
hate him;
How much more do his friends go
far from him!
He may pursue *them with* words,
yet they abandon *him.*

8 He who gets wisdom loves his own
soul;
He who keeps understanding will
find good.

9 A false witness will not go
unpunished,
And *he who* speaks lies shall
perish.

10 Luxury is not fitting for a fool,
Much less for a servant to rule over
princes.

11 The discretion of a man makes him
slow to anger,
And his glory *is* to overlook a
transgression.

12 The king's wrath *is* like the roaring
of a lion,
But his favor *is* like dew on the
grass.

13 A foolish son *is* the ruin of his
father,
And the contentions of a wife *are*
a continual dripping.

14 Houses and riches *are* an
inheritance from fathers,
But a prudent wife *is* from the Lord.

15 Laziness casts *one* into a deep
sleep,
And an idle person will suffer
hunger.

16 He who keeps the commandment
keeps his soul,
But he who is careless of his ways
will die.

17 He who has pity on the poor lends
to the Lord,
And He will pay back what he has
given.

18 Chasten your son while there is
hope,
And do not set your heart on his
destruction.

19 *A man of* great wrath will suffer
punishment;

---

[b] Or *may come to ruin*

For if you rescue *him*, you will have to do it again.

20 Listen to counsel and receive instruction,
That you may be wise in your latter days.

21 There are many plans in a man's heart,
Nevertheless the LORD's counsel—that will stand.

22 What is desired in a man is kindness,
And a poor man is better than a liar.

23 The fear of the LORD *leads* to life,
And *he who has it* will abide in satisfaction;
He will not be visited with evil.

24 A lazy *man* buries his hand in the bowl,
And will not so much as bring it to his mouth again.

25 Strike a scoffer, and the simple will become wary;
Rebuke one who has understanding, *and* he will discern knowledge.

26 He who mistreats *his* father *and* chases away *his* mother
Is a son who causes shame and brings reproach.

27 Cease listening to instruction, my son,
And you will stray from the words of knowledge.

28 A disreputable witness scorns justice,
And the mouth of the wicked devours iniquity.

29 Judgments are prepared for scoffers,
And beatings for the backs of fools.

20 Wine *is* a mocker,
Strong drink *is* a brawler,
And whoever is led astray by it is not wise.

2 The wrath of a king *is* like the roaring of a lion;
Whoever provokes him to anger sins *against* his own life.

3 *It is* honorable for a man to stop striving,
Since any fool can start a quarrel.

4 The lazy *man* will not plow because of winter;
He will beg during harvest and *have* nothing.

5 Counsel in the heart of man *is like* deep water,
But a man of understanding will draw it out.

6 Most men will proclaim each his own goodness,
But who can find a faithful man?

7 The righteous *man* walks in his integrity;
His children *are* blessed after him.

8 A king who sits on the throne of judgment
Scatters all evil with his eyes.

9 Who can say, "I have made my heart clean,
I am pure from my sin"?

10 Diverse weights *and* diverse measures,
They *are* both alike, an abomination to the LORD.

11 Even a child is known by his deeds,
Whether what he does *is* pure and right.

12 The hearing ear and the seeing eye,
The LORD has made them both.

13 Do not love sleep, lest you come to poverty;
Open your eyes, *and* you will be satisfied with bread.

14 "*It is* good for nothing," cries the buyer;
But when he has gone his way, then he boasts.

15 There is gold and a multitude of
   rubies,
   But the lips of knowledge *are* a
   precious jewel.

16 Take the garment of one who is
   surety *for* a stranger,
   And hold it as a pledge *when it* is
   for a seductress.

17 Bread gained by deceit *is* sweet to
   a man,
   But afterward his mouth will be
   filled with gravel.

18 Plans are established by counsel;
   By wise counsel wage war.

19 He who goes about *as* a talebearer
   reveals secrets;
   Therefore do not associate with one
   who flatters with his lips.

20 Whoever curses his father or his
   mother,
   His lamp will be put out in deep
   darkness.

21 An inheritance gained hastily at the
   beginning
   Will not be blessed at the end.

22 Do not say, "I will recompense
   evil";
   Wait for the LORD, and He will
   save you.

23 Diverse weights *are* an
   abomination to the LORD,
   And dishonest scales *are* not good.

24 A man's steps *are* of the LORD;
   How then can a man understand
   his own way?

25 *It is* a snare for a man to devote
   rashly *something* as holy,
   And afterward to reconsider *his*
   vows.

26 A wise king sifts out the wicked,
   And brings the threshing wheel
   over them.

27 The spirit of a man *is* the lamp of
   the LORD,
   Searching all the inner depths of
   his heart.

28 Mercy and truth preserve the king,
   And by lovingkindness he upholds
   his throne.

29 The glory of young men *is* their
   strength,
   And the splendor of old men *is* their
   gray head.

30 Blows that hurt cleanse away evil,
   As *do* stripes the inner depths of
   the heart.

21 The king's heart *is* in the hand
   of the LORD,
   Like the rivers of water; He turns
   it wherever He wishes.

2 Every way of a man *is* right in his
   own eyes,
   But the LORD weighs the hearts.

3 To do righteousness and justice
   Is more acceptable to the LORD than
   sacrifice.

4 A haughty look, a proud heart,
   And the plowing of the wicked *are*
   sin.

5 The plans of the diligent *lead* surely
   to plenty,
   But *those of* everyone *who is* hasty,
   surely to poverty.

6 Getting treasures by a lying tongue
   Is the fleeting fantasy of those who
   seek death.

7 The violence of the wicked will
   destroy them,
   Because they refuse to do justice.

8 The way of a guilty man *is*
   perverse;
   But *as for* the pure, his work *is*
   right.

9 Better to dwell in a corner of a
   housetop,
   Than in a house shared with a
   contentious woman.

10 The soul of the wicked desires
    evil;
    His neighbor finds no favor in his
    eyes.

11 When the scoffer is punished, the
simple is made wise;
But when the wise is instructed, he
receives knowledge.

12 The righteous *God* wisely considers
the house of the wicked,
Overthrowing the wicked for *their*
wickedness.

13 Whoever shuts his ears to the cry
of the poor
Will also cry himself and not be
heard.

14 A gift in secret pacifies anger,
And a bribe behind the back, strong
wrath.

15 *It is* a joy for the just to do justice,
But destruction *will come* to the
workers of iniquity.

16 A man who wanders from the way
of understanding
Will rest in the assembly of the
dead.

17 He who loves pleasure *will be* a
poor man;
He who loves wine and oil will not
be rich.

18 The wicked *shall be* a ransom for
the righteous,
And the unfaithful for the upright.

19 Better to dwell in the wilderness,
Than with a contentious and angry
woman.

20 *There is* desirable treasure,
And oil in the dwelling of the wise,
But a foolish man squanders it.

21 He who follows righteousness and
mercy
Finds life, righteousness and honor.

22 A wise *man* scales the city of the
mighty,
And brings down the trusted
stronghold.

23 Whoever guards his mouth and
tongue
Keeps his soul from troubles.

24 A proud *and* haughty *man*—
"Scoffer" *is* his name;
He acts with arrogant pride.

25 The desire of the lazy *man*
kills him,
For his hands refuse to labor.

26 He covets greedily all day long,
But the righteous gives and does
not spare.

27 The sacrifice of the wicked *is* an
abomination;
How much more *when* he brings it
with wicked intent!

28 A false witness shall perish,
But the man who hears *him* will
speak endlessly.

29 A wicked man hardens his face,
But *as for* the upright, he
establishes his way.

30 *There is* no wisdom or
understanding
Or counsel against the Lord.

31 The horse *is* prepared for the day
of battle,
But deliverance *is* of the Lord.

22 A *good* name is to be chosen
rather than great riches,
Loving favor rather than silver and
gold.

2 The rich and the poor have this in
common,
The Lord *is* the maker of them all.

3 A prudent *man* foresees evil and
hides himself,
But the simple pass on and are
punished.

4 By humility *and* the fear of the
Lord
Are riches and honor and life.

5 Thorns *and* snares *are* in the way
of the perverse;
He who guards his soul will be far
from them.

6 Train up a child in the way he
should go,

And when he is old he will not
depart from it.

7 The rich rules over the poor,
And the borrower *is* servant to the
lender.

8 He who sows iniquity will reap
sorrow,
And the rod of his anger will fail.

9 He who has a generous eye will be
blessed,
For he gives of his bread to the
poor.

10 Cast out the scoffer, and contention
will leave;
Yes, strife and reproach will cease.

11 He who loves purity of heart
And has grace on his lips,
The king *will be* his friend.

12 The eyes of the LORD preserve
knowledge,
But He overthrows the words of the
faithless.

13 The lazy *man* says, "*There is* a lion
outside!
I shall be slain in the streets!"

14 The mouth of an immoral woman
is a deep pit;
He who is abhorred by the LORD
will fall there.

15 Foolishness *is* bound up in the heart
of a child;
The rod of correction will drive it
far from him.

16 He who oppresses the poor to
increase his *riches,*
And he who gives to the rich, *will*
surely *come* to poverty.

Sayings of the Wise

17 Incline your ear and hear the words
of the wise,
And apply your heart to my
knowledge;

18 For *it is* a pleasant thing if you keep
them within you;
Let them all be fixed upon your lips,

19 So that your trust may be in the
LORD;
I have instructed you today,
even you.

20 Have I not written to you excellent
things
Of counsels and knowledge,

21 That I may make you know the
certainty of the words of truth,
That you may answer words of
truth
To those who send to you?

22 Do not rob the poor because he *is*
poor,
Nor oppress the afflicted at the
gate;

23 For the LORD will plead their cause,
And plunder the soul of those who
plunder them.

24 Make no friendship with an angry
man,
And with a furious man do not go,

25 Lest you learn his ways
And set a snare for your soul.

26 Do not be one of those who shakes
hands in a pledge,
One of those who is surety for
debts;

27 If you have nothing *with which* to
pay,
Why should he take away your bed
from under you?

28 Do not remove the ancient
landmark
Which your fathers have set.

29 Do you see a man *who* excels in
his work?
He will stand before kings;
He will not stand before
unknown *men.*

23 When you sit down to eat with
a ruler,
Consider carefully what *is*
before you;

2 And put a knife to your throat
If you *are* a man given to appetite.

3 Do not desire his delicacies,
For they *are* deceptive food.

4 Do not overwork to be rich;
Because of your own
understanding, cease!

5   Will you set your eyes on that
        which is not?
    For *riches* certainly make
        themselves wings;
    They fly away like an eagle *toward*
        heaven.

6   Do not eat the bread of a miser,
    Nor desire his delicacies;
7   For as he thinks in his heart, so
        is he.
    "Eat and drink!" he says to you,
    But his heart is not with you.
8   The morsel you have eaten, you
        will vomit up,
    And waste your pleasant words.

9   Do not speak in the hearing of a
        fool,
    For he will despise the wisdom of
        your words.

10 Do not remove the ancient
        landmark,
    Nor enter the fields of the
        fatherless;
11 For their Redeemer *is* mighty;
    He will plead their cause
        against you.

12 Apply your heart to instruction,
    And your ears to words of
        knowledge.

13 Do not withhold correction from a
        child,
    For *if* you beat him with a rod, he
        will not die.
14 You shall beat him with a rod,
    And deliver his soul from hell.

15 My son, if your heart is wise,
    My heart will rejoice—indeed, I
        myself;
16 Yes, my inmost being will rejoice
    When your lips speak right things.

17 Do not let your heart envy sinners,
    But *be zealous* for the fear of the
        LORD all the day;
18 For surely there is a hereafter,
    And your hope will not be cut off.

19 Hear, my son, and be wise;
    And guide your heart in the way.
20 Do not mix with winebibbers,
    Or with gluttonous eaters of meat;

21 For the drunkard and the glutton
        will come to poverty,
    And drowsiness will clothe *a man*
        with rags.

22 Listen to your father who
        begot you,
    And do not despise your mother
        when she is old.

23 Buy the truth, and do not sell *it,*
    Also wisdom and instruction and
        understanding.

24 The father of the righteous will
        greatly rejoice,
    And he who begets a wise *child* will
        delight in him.
25 Let your father and your mother be
        glad,
    And let her who bore you rejoice.

26 My son, give me your heart,
    And let your eyes observe my ways.
27 For a harlot *is* a deep pit,
    And a seductress *is* a narrow well.
28 She also lies in wait as *for* a victim,
    And increases the unfaithful
        among men.

29 Who has woe?
    Who has sorrow?
    Who has contentions?
    Who has complaints?
    Who has wounds without cause?
    Who has redness of eyes?
30 Those who linger long at the wine,
    Those who go in search of mixed
        wine.
31 Do not look on the wine when it
        is red,
    When it sparkles in the cup,
    When it swirls around smoothly;
32 At the last it bites like a serpent,
    And stings like a viper.
33 Your eyes will see strange things,
    And your heart will utter perverse
        things.
34 Yes, you will be like one who lies
        down in the midst of the sea,
    Or like one who lies at the top of
        the mast, *saying:*
35 "They have struck me, *but* I was not
        hurt;
    They have beaten me, but I did not
        feel *it.*
    When shall I awake, that I may
        seek another *drink?*"

24 Do not be envious of evil men,
Nor desire to be with them;

2 For their heart devises violence,
And their lips talk of
troublemaking.

3 Through wisdom a house is built,
And by understanding it is
established;

4 By knowledge the rooms are filled
With all precious and pleasant
riches.

5 A wise man *is* strong,
Yes, a man of knowledge increases
strength;

6 For by wise counsel you will wage
your own war,
And in a multitude of counselors
there is safety.

7 Wisdom *is* too lofty for a fool;
He does not open his mouth in the
gate.

8 He who plots to do evil
Will be called a schemer.

9 The devising of foolishness *is* sin,
And the scoffer *is* an abomination
to men.

10 *If* you faint in the day of adversity,
Your strength *is* small.

11 Deliver *those who* are drawn
toward death,
And hold back *those* stumbling to
the slaughter.

12 If you say, "Surely we did not know
this,"
Does not He who weighs the hearts
consider *it?*
He who keeps your soul, does He
not know *it?*
And will He *not* render to *each* man
according to his deeds?

13 My son, eat honey because *it is*
good,
And the honeycomb *which is* sweet
to your taste;

14 So *shall* the knowledge of wisdom
be to your soul;
If you have found *it*, there is a
prospect,
And your hope will not be cut off.

15 Do not lie in wait, O wicked *man,*
against the dwelling of the
righteous;
Do not plunder his resting place;

16 For a righteous *man* may fall seven
times
And rise again,
But the wicked shall fall by
calamity.

17 Do not rejoice when your enemy
falls,
And do not let your heart be glad
when he stumbles;

18 Lest the LORD see *it,* and it
displease Him,
And He turn away His wrath
from him.

19 Do not fret because of evildoers,
Nor be envious of the wicked;

20 For there will be no prospect for the
evil *man;*
The lamp of the wicked will be
put out.

21 My son, fear the LORD and the king;
Do not associate with those given
to change;

22 For their calamity will rise
suddenly,
And who knows the ruin those two
can bring?

Further Sayings of the Wise

23 These *things* also *belong* to the
wise:
It is not good to show partiality in
judgment.

24 He who says to the wicked, "You
are righteous,"
Him the people will curse;
Nations will abhor him.

25 But those who rebuke *the wicked*
will have delight,
And a good blessing will come
upon them.

26 He who gives a right answer kisses
the lips.

27 Prepare your outside work,
Make it fit for yourself in the field;
And afterward build your house.

28 Do not be a witness against your
neighbor without cause,

For would you deceive with your lips?

29 Do not say, "I will do to him just as he has done to me;
I will render to the man according to his work."

30 I went by the field of the lazy *man*,
And by the vineyard of the man devoid of understanding;
31 And there it was, all overgrown with thorns;
Its surface was covered with nettles;
Its stone wall was broken down.
32 When I saw *it*, I considered *it* well;
I looked on *it and* received instruction:
33 A little sleep, a little slumber,
A little folding of the hands to rest;
34 So shall your poverty come *like* a prowler,
And your need like an armed man.

Further Wise Sayings of Solomon

25 These also *are* proverbs of Solomon which the men of Hezekiah king of Judah copied:
2 *It is* the glory of God to conceal a matter,
But the glory of kings *is* to search out a matter.

3 *As* the heavens for height and the earth for depth,
So the heart of kings *is* unsearchable.

4 Take away the dross from silver,
And it will go to the silversmith *for* jewelry.
5 Take away the wicked from before the king,
And his throne will be established in righteousness.

6 Do not exalt yourself in the presence of the king,
And do not stand in the place of the great;
7 For *it is* better that he say to you, "Come up here,"
Than that you should be put lower in the presence of the prince,
Whom your eyes have seen.

8 Do not go hastily to court;
For what will you do in the end,
When your neighbor has put you to shame?
9 Debate your case with your neighbor,
And do not disclose the secret to another;
10 Lest he who hears *it* expose your shame,
And your reputation be ruined.

11 A word fitly spoken *is like* apples of gold
In settings of silver.
12 *Like* an earring of gold and an ornament of fine gold
Is a wise rebuker to an obedient ear.

13 Like the cold of snow in time of harvest
Is a faithful messenger to those who send him,
For he refreshes the soul of his masters.

14 Whoever falsely boasts of giving
Is like clouds and wind without rain.

15 By long forbearance a ruler is persuaded,
And a gentle tongue breaks a bone.

16 Have you found honey?
Eat only as much as you need,
Lest you be filled with it and vomit.

17 Seldom set foot in your neighbor's house,
Lest he become weary of you and hate you.

18 A man who bears false witness against his neighbor
Is like a club, a sword, and a sharp arrow.

19 Confidence in an unfaithful *man* in time of trouble
Is like a bad tooth and a foot out of joint.

20 *Like* one who takes away a garment in cold weather,
And like vinegar on soda,

Is one who sings songs to a heavy
heart.

21 If your enemy is hungry, give him
bread to eat;
And if he is thirsty, give him water
to drink;

22 For *so* you will heap coals of fire
on his head,
And the Lord will reward you.

23 The north wind brings forth rain,
And a backbiting tongue an angry
countenance.

24 *It is* better to dwell in a corner of
a housetop,
Than in a house shared with a
contentious woman.

25 *As* cold water to a weary soul,
So *is* good news from a far country.

26 A righteous *man* who falters before
the wicked
Is like a murky spring and a
polluted well.

27 *It is* not good to eat much honey;
So to seek one's own glory *is not*
glory.

28 Whoever *has* no rule over his own
spirit
Is like a city broken down, without
walls.

26

As snow in summer and rain in
harvest,
So honor is not fitting for a fool.

2 Like a flitting sparrow, like a flying
swallow,
So a curse without cause shall not
alight.

3 A whip for the horse,
A bridle for the donkey,
And a rod for the fool's back.

4 Do not answer a fool according to
his folly,
Lest you also be like him.

5 Answer a fool according to his
folly,
Lest he be wise in his own eyes.

6 He who sends a message by the
hand of a fool
Cuts off *his own* feet *and* drinks
violence.

7 *Like* the legs of the lame that hang
limp
Is a proverb in the mouth of fools.

8 Like one who binds a stone in a
sling
Is he who gives honor to a fool.

9 *Like* a thorn *that* goes into the hand
of a drunkard
Is a proverb in the mouth of fools.

10 The great *God* who formed
everything
Gives the fool *his* hire and the
transgressor *his* wages.

11 As a dog returns to his own vomit,
So a fool repeats his folly.

12 Do you see a man wise in his own
eyes?
There is more hope for a fool than
for him.

13 The lazy *man* says, "*There is* a lion
in the road!
A fierce lion *is* in the streets!"

14 *As* a door turns on its hinges,
So *does* the lazy *man* on his bed.

15 The lazy *man* buries his hand in the
bowl;[c]
It wearies him to bring it back to
his mouth.

16 The lazy *man is* wiser in his own
eyes
Than seven men who can answer
sensibly.

17 He who passes by *and* meddles in
a quarrel not his own
Is like one who takes a dog by the
ears.

18 Like a madman who throws
firebrands, arrows, and death,

19 *Is* the man *who* deceives his
neighbor,
And says, "I was only joking!"

20 Where *there is* no wood, the fire
goes out;
And where *there is* no talebearer,
strife ceases.

21 *As* charcoal *is* to burning coals, and
wood to fire,

c Compare 19.24

So *is* a contentious man to kindle strife.

22 The words of a talebearer *are* like tasty trifles,
And they go down into the inmost body.

23 Fervent lips with a wicked heart
Are like earthenware covered with silver dross.

24 He who hates, disguises *it* with his lips,
And lays up deceit within himself;

25 When he speaks kindly, do not believe him,
For *there are* seven abominations in his heart;

26 *Though his* hatred is covered by deceit,
His wickedness will be revealed before the assembly.

27 Whoever digs a pit will fall into it,
And he who rolls a stone will have it roll back on him.

28 A lying tongue hates *those who are* crushed by it,
And a flattering mouth works ruin.

27 Do not boast about tomorrow,
For you do not know what a day may bring forth.

2 Let another man praise you, and not your own mouth;
A stranger, and not your own lips.

3 A stone *is* heavy and sand *is* weighty,
But a fool's wrath *is* heavier than both of them.

4 Wrath *is* cruel and anger a torrent,
But who *is* able to stand before jealousy?

5 Open rebuke *is* better
Than love carefully concealed.

6 Faithful *are* the wounds of a friend,
But the kisses of an enemy *are* deceitful.

7 A satisfied soul loathes the honeycomb,
But to a hungry soul every bitter thing *is* sweet.

8 Like a bird that wanders from its nest
Is a man who wanders from his place.

9 Ointment and perfume delight the heart,
And the sweetness of a man's friend *gives delight* by hearty counsel.

10 Do not forsake your own friend or your father's friend,
Nor go to your brother's house in the day of your calamity;
Better *is* a neighbor nearby than a brother far away.

11 My son, be wise, and make my heart glad,
That I may answer him who reproaches me.

12 A prudent *man* foresees evil *and* hides himself;
The simple pass on *and* are punished.

13 Take the garment of him who is surety for a stranger,
And hold it in pledge *when* he is surety for a seductress.

14 He who blesses his friend with a loud voice, rising early in the morning,
It will be counted a curse to him.

15 A continual dripping on a very rainy day
And a contentious woman are alike;

16 Whoever restrains her restrains the wind,
And grasps oil with his right hand.

17 *As* iron sharpens iron,
So a man sharpens the countenance of his friend.

18 Whoever keeps the fig tree will eat its fruit;
So he who waits on his master will be honored.

19 As in water face *reflects* face,
So a man's heart *reveals* the man.

20 Hell and Destruction are never full;
So the eyes of man are never satisfied.

21 The refining pot *is* for silver and the furnace for gold,
And a man *is valued* by what others say of him.

22 Though you grind a fool in a mortar with a pestle along with crushed grain,
Y*et* his foolishness will not depart from him.

23 Be diligent to know the state of your flocks,
And attend to your herds;
24 For riches *are* not forever,
Nor does a crown *endure* to all generations.
25 *When* the hay is removed, and the tender grass shows itself,
And the herbs of the mountains are gathered in,
26 The lambs *will provide* your clothing,
And the goats the price of a field;
27 *You shall have* enough goats' milk for your food,
For the food of your household,
And the nourishment of your maidservants.

28 The wicked flee when no one pursues,
But the righteous are bold as a lion.

2 Because of the transgression of a land, many *are* its princes;
But by a man of understanding *and* knowledge
Right will be prolonged.

3 A poor man who oppresses the poor
Is like a driving rain which leaves no food.

4 Those who forsake the law praise the wicked,
But such as keep the law contend with them.

5 Evil men do not understand justice,
But those who seek the LORD understand all.

6 Better *is* the poor who walks in his integrity
Than one perverse *in his* ways, though he *be* rich.

7 Whoever keeps the law *is* a discerning son,
But a companion of gluttons shames his father.

8 One who increases his possessions by usury and extortion
Gathers it for him who will pity the poor.

9 One who turns away his ear from hearing the law,
Even his prayer *is* an abomination.

10 Whoever causes the upright to go astray in an evil way,
He himself will fall into his own pit;
But the blameless will inherit good.

11 The rich man *is* wise in his own eyes,
But the poor who has understanding searches him out.

12 When the righteous rejoice, *there is* great glory;
But when the wicked arise, men hide themselves.

13 He who covers his sins will not prosper,
But whoever confesses and forsakes *them* will have mercy.

14 Happy *is* the man who is always reverent,
But he who hardens his heart will fall into calamity.

15 *Like* a roaring lion and a charging bear
Is a wicked ruler over poor people.

16 A ruler who lacks understanding *is* a great oppressor,
But he who hates covetousness will prolong *his* days.

17 A man burdened with bloodshed
   will flee into a pit;
   Let no one help him.

18 Whoever walks blamelessly will be
   saved,
   But *he who is* perverse *in his* ways
   will suddenly fall.

19 He who tills his land will have
   plenty of bread,
   But he who follows frivolity will
   have poverty enough!

20 A faithful man will abound with
   blessings,
   But he who hastens to be rich will
   not go unpunished.

21 To show partiality *is* not good,
   Because for a piece of bread a man
   will transgress.

22 A man with an evil eye hastens
   after riches,
   And does not consider that poverty
   will come upon him.

23 He who rebukes a man will find
   more favor afterward
   Than he who flatters with the
   tongue.

24 Whoever robs his father or his
   mother,
   And says, "*It is* no transgression,"
   The same *is* companion to a
   destroyer.

25 He who is of a proud heart stirs up
   strife,
   But he who trusts in the Lord will
   be prospered.

26 He who trusts in his own heart is
   a fool,
   But whoever walks wisely will be
   delivered.

27 He who gives to the poor will not
   lack,
   But he who hides his eyes will have
   many curses.

28 When the wicked arise, men hide
   themselves;
   But when they perish, the righteous
   increase.

29 He who is often rebuked, *and*
   hardens *his* neck,
   Will suddenly be destroyed, and
   that without remedy.

2 When the righteous are in
   authority, the people rejoice;
   But when a wicked *man* rules, the
   people groan.

3 Whoever loves wisdom makes his
   father rejoice,
   But a companion of harlots wastes
   his wealth.

4 The king establishes the land by
   justice,
   But he who receives bribes
   overthrows it.

5 A man who flatters his neighbor
   Spreads a net for his feet.

6 By transgression an evil man is
   snared,
   But the righteous sings and
   rejoices.

7 The righteous considers the cause
   of the poor,
   But the wicked does not
   understand *such* knowledge.

8 Scoffers set a city aflame,
   But wise *men* turn away wrath.

9 *If* a wise man contends with a
   foolish man,
   Whether *the fool* rages or laughs,
   there is no peace.

10 The bloodthirsty hate the
   blameless,
   But the upright seek his well-being.

11 A fool vents all his feelings,
   But a wise *man* holds them back.

12 If a ruler pays attention to lies,
   All his servants *become* wicked.

13 The poor *man* and the oppressor
   have this in common:
   The Lord gives light to the eyes of
   both.

14 The king who judges the poor with
   truth,

His throne will be established
forever.

15 The rod and rebuke give wisdom,
But a child left *to himself* brings
shame to his mother.

16 When the wicked are multiplied,
transgression increases;
But the righteous will see their fall.

17 Correct your son, and he will give
you rest;
Yes, he will give delight to your
soul.

18 Where *there is* no revelation, the
people cast off restraint;
But happy *is* he who keeps the law.

19 A servant will not be corrected by
mere words;
For though he understands, he will
not respond.

20 Do you see a man hasty in his
words?
There is more hope for a fool than
for him.

21 He who pampers his servant from
childhood
Will have him as a son in the end.

22 An angry man stirs up strife,
And a furious man abounds in
transgression.

23 A man's pride will bring him low,
But the humble in spirit will retain
honor.

24 Whoever is a partner with a thief
hates his own life;
He swears to tell the truth, but
reveals nothing.

25 The fear of man brings a snare,
But whoever trusts in the LORD
shall be safe.

26 Many seek the ruler's favor,
But justice for man *comes* from the
LORD.

27 An unjust man *is* an abomination
to the righteous,

And *he who is* upright in the way
is an abomination to the wicked.

The Wisdom of Agur

30 The words of Agur the son of Ja-
keh, *his* utterance. This man declared to Ithiel—to Ithiel and Ucal:

2 Surely I *am* more stupid than *any*
man,
And do not have the understanding
of a man.

3 I neither learned wisdom
Nor have knowledge of the
Holy One.

4 Who has ascended into heaven, or
descended?
Who has gathered the wind in His
fists?
Who has bound the waters in a
garment?
Who has established all the ends
of the earth?
What *is* His name, and what *is* His
Son's name,
If you know?

5 Every word of God *is* pure;
He *is* a shield to those who put their
trust in Him.

6 Do not add to His words,
Lest He rebuke you, and you be
found a liar.

7 Two *things* I request of You
(Deprive me not before I die):

8 Remove falsehood and lies far from
me;
Give me neither poverty nor
riches—
Feed me with the food allotted
to me;

9 Lest I be full and deny *You*,
And say, "Who *is* the LORD?"
Or lest I be poor and steal,
And profane the name of my God.

10 Do not malign a servant to his
master,
Lest he curse you, and you be found
guilty.

11 *There is* a generation *that* curses
its father,
And does not bless its mother.

12 *There is* a generation *that is* pure
in its own eyes,

Yet is not washed from its
filthiness.

13 *There is* a generation—oh, how
lofty are their eyes!
And their eyelids are lifted up.
14 *There is* a generation whose teeth
are like swords,
And whose fangs *are like* knives,
To devour the poor from off the
earth,
And the needy from *among* men.

15 The leech has two daughters—
Give *and* Give!

There are three *things that* are
never satisfied,
Four never say, "Enough!":
16 The grave,
The barren womb,
The earth *that* is not satisfied with
water—
And the fire never says, "Enough!"

17 The eye *that* mocks *his* father,
And scorns obedience to *his*
mother,
The ravens of the valley will pick
it out,
And the young eagles will eat it.

18 There are three *things which* are
too wonderful for me,
Yes, four *which* I do not
understand:
19 The way of an eagle in the air,
The way of a serpent on a rock,
The way of a ship in the midst of
the sea,
And the way of a man with a
virgin.

20 This *is* the way of an adulterous
woman:
She eats and wipes her mouth,
And says, "I have done no
wickedness."

21 For three *things* the earth is
perturbed,
Yes, for four it cannot bear up:
22 For a servant when he reigns,
A fool when he is filled with food,
23 A hateful *woman* when she is
married,

And a maidservant who succeeds
her mistress.

24 There are four *things which* are
little on the earth,
But they *are* exceedingly wise:
25 The ants *are* a people not strong,
Yet they prepare their food in the
summer;
26 The rock badgers[d] are a feeble folk,
Yet they make their homes in the
crags;
27 The locusts have no king,
Yet they all advance in ranks;
28 The spider[e] skillfully grasps with
its hands,
And it is in kings' palaces.

29 There are three *things which* are
majestic in pace,
Yes, four *which* are stately in walk:
30 A lion, *which is* mighty among
beasts
And does not turn away from any;
31 A greyhound,[f]
A male goat also,
And a king *whose* troops *are*
with him.

32 If you have been foolish in exalting
yourself,
Or if you have devised evil, *put
your* hand on *your* mouth.
33 For *as* the churning of milk
produces butter,
And wringing the nose produces
blood,
So the forcing of wrath produces
strife.

The Words of King Lemuel's Mother

31 The words of King Lemuel, the utterance which his mother taught
him:
2 What, my son?
And what, son of my womb?
And what, son of my vows?
3 Do not give your strength to
women,
Nor your ways to that which
destroys kings.

4 *It is* not for kings, O Lemuel,
It is not for kings to drink wine,

---

d Or *hyraxes*   e Or *lizard*   f Exact identity unknown

Nor for princes intoxicating drink;
5 Lest they drink and forget the law,
And pervert the justice of all the afflicted.
6 Give strong drink to him who is perishing,
And wine to those who are bitter of heart.
7 Let him drink and forget his poverty,
And remember his misery no more.

8 Open your mouth for the speechless,
In the cause of all *who are* appointed to die.
9 Open your mouth, judge righteously,
And plead the cause of the poor and needy.

The Virtuous Wife

10 Who can find a virtuous[g] wife?
For her worth *is* far above rubies.
11 The heart of her husband safely trusts her;
So he will have no lack of gain.
12 She does him good and not evil
All the days of her life.
13 She seeks wool and flax,
And willingly works with her hands.
14 She is like the merchant ships,
She brings her food from afar.
15 She also rises while it is yet night,
And provides food for her household,
And a portion for her maidservants.
16 She considers a field and buys it;
From her profits she plants a vineyard.
17 She girds herself with strength,
And strengthens her arms.
18 She perceives that her merchandise *is* good,

And her lamp does not go out by night.
19 She stretches out her hands to the distaff,
And her hand holds the spindle.
20 She extends her hand to the poor,
Yes, she reaches out her hands to the needy.
21 She is not afraid of snow for her household,
For all her household *is* clothed with scarlet.
22 She makes tapestry for herself;
Her clothing *is* fine linen and purple.
23 Her husband is known in the gates,
When he sits among the elders of the land.
24 She makes linen garments and sells *them*,
And supplies sashes for the merchants.
25 Strength and honor *are* her clothing;
She shall rejoice in time to come.
26 She opens her mouth with wisdom,
And on her tongue *is* the law of kindness.
27 She watches over the ways of her household,
And does not eat the bread of idleness.
28 Her children rise up and call her blessed;
Her husband *also*, and he praises her:
29 "Many daughters have done well,
But you excel them all."
30 Charm *is* deceitful and beauty *is* passing,
But a woman *who* fears the LORD, she shall be praised.
31 Give her of the fruit of her hands,
And let her own works praise her in the gates.

g Literally *a wife of valor*, in the sense of all forms of excellence

The Book of
ECCLESIASTES

The Vanity of Life

1 The words of the Preacher, the son of David, king in Jerusalem.
2 "Vanity[a] of vanities," says the Preacher;
"Vanity of vanities, all *is* vanity."

3 What profit has a man from all his labor
In which he toils under the sun?
4 *One* generation passes away, and *another* generation comes;
But the earth abides forever.
5 The sun also rises, and the sun goes down,
And hastens to the place where it arose.
6 The wind goes toward the south,
And turns around to the north;
The wind whirls about continually,
And comes again on its circuit.
7 All the rivers run into the sea,
Yet the sea *is* not full;
To the place from which the rivers come,
There they return again.
8 All things *are* full of labor;
Man cannot express *it*.
The eye is not satisfied with seeing,
Nor the ear filled with hearing.

9 That which has been *is* what will be,
That which *is* done is what will be done,
And *there is* nothing new under the sun.
10 Is there anything of which it may be said,
"See, this *is* new"?
It has already been in ancient times before us.
11 *There is* no remembrance of former *things*,
Nor will there be any remembrance of *things* that are to come
By *those* who will come after.

The Grief of Wisdom

12 I, the Preacher, was king over Israel in Jerusalem. 13 And I set my heart to seek and search out by wisdom concerning all that is done under heaven; this burdensome task God has given to the sons of man, by which they may be exercised. 14 I have seen all the works that are done under the sun; and indeed, all *is* vanity and grasping for the wind.
15 *What is* crooked cannot be made straight,
And what is lacking cannot be numbered.

16 I communed with my heart, saying, "Look, I have attained greatness, and have gained more wisdom than all who were before me in Jerusalem. My heart has understood great wisdom and knowledge." 17 And I set my heart to know wisdom and to know madness and folly. I perceived that this also is grasping for the wind.
18 For in much wisdom *is* much grief,
And he who increases knowledge increases sorrow.

The Vanity of Pleasure

2 I said in my heart, "Come now, I will test you with mirth; therefore enjoy pleasure"; but surely, this also *was* vanity. 2 I said of laughter—"Madness!"; and of mirth, "What does it accomplish?" 3 I searched in my heart *how* to gratify my flesh with wine, while guiding my heart with wisdom, and how to lay hold on folly, till I might see what *was* good for the sons of men to do under heaven all the days of their lives.

4 I made my works great, I built myself houses, and planted myself vineyards. 5 I made myself gardens and orchards, and I planted all *kinds* of fruit trees in them. 6 I made myself water pools from which to water the growing trees of the grove. 7 I acquired male and

---

a Or *Absurdity, Frustration, Futility, Nonsense;* and so throughout the book female servants, and had servants born in my house. Yes, I had greater possessions of herds and flocks than all who were in Jerusalem before me. 8I also gathered for myself silver and gold and the special treasures of kings and of the provinces. I acquired male and female singers, the delights of the sons of men, *and* musical instruments[b] of all kinds.

9So I became great and excelled more than all who were before me in Jerusalem. Also my wisdom remained with me.

10 Whatever my eyes desired I did not
      keep from them.
    I did not withhold my heart from
      any pleasure,
    For my heart rejoiced in all my
      labor;
    And this was my reward from all
      my labor.
11 Then I looked on all the works that
      my hands had done
    And on the labor in which I had
      toiled;
    And indeed all *was* vanity and
      grasping for the wind.
    There was no profit under the sun.

The End of the Wise and the Fool

12 Then I turned myself to consider
      wisdom and madness and folly;
    For what *can* the man *do* who
      succeeds the king?—
    Only what he has already done.
13 Then I saw that wisdom excels
      folly
    As light excels darkness.
14 The wise man's eyes *are* in his
      head,
    But the fool walks in darkness.
    Yet I myself perceived
    That the same event happens to
      them all.

15 So I said in my heart,
    "As it happens to the fool,
    It also happens to me,
    And why was I then more wise?"
    Then I said in my heart,
    "This also *is* vanity."
16 For *there is* no more remembrance
      of the wise than of the fool
      forever,

b Exact meaning unknown

    Since all that now *is* will be
      forgotten in the days to come.
    And how does a wise *man*
      die?
    As the fool!
17Therefore I hated life because the work that was done under the sun *was* distressing to me, for all *is* vanity and grasping for the wind.

18Then I hated all my labor in which I had toiled under the sun, because I must leave it to the man who will come after me. 19And who knows whether he will be wise or a fool? Yet he will rule over all my labor in which I toiled and in which I have shown myself wise under the sun. This also *is* vanity. 20Therefore I turned my heart and despaired of all the labor in which I had toiled under the sun. 21For there is a man whose labor *is* with wisdom, knowledge, and skill; yet he must leave his heritage to a man who has not labored for it. This also *is* vanity and a great evil. 22For what has man for all his labor, and for the striving of his heart with which he has toiled under the sun? 23For all his days *are* sorrowful, and his work burdensome; even in the night his heart takes no rest. This also is vanity.

24Nothing *is* better for a man *than* that he should eat and drink, and *that* his soul should enjoy good in his labor. This also, I saw, was from the hand of God. 25For who can eat, or who can have enjoyment, more than I? 26For *God* gives wisdom and knowledge and joy to a man who *is* good in His sight; but to the sinner He gives the work of gathering and collecting, that he may give to *him who is* good before God. This also *is* vanity and grasping for the wind.

Everything Has Its Time

3 To everything *there is* a season,
   A time for every purpose under
     heaven:
   2A time to be born,
     And a time to die;
   A time to plant,
     And a time to pluck *what is*
       planted;

3A time to kill,
  And a time to heal;
 A time to break down,
  And a time to build up;
4A time to weep,
  And a time to laugh;
 A time to mourn,
  And a time to dance;
5A time to cast away stones,
  And a time to gather stones;
 A time to embrace,
  And a time to refrain from
    embracing;
6A time to gain,
  And a time to lose;
 A time to keep,
  And a time to throw away;
7A time to tear,
  And a time to sew;
 A time to keep silence,
  And a time to speak;
8A time to love,
  And a time to hate;
 A time of war,
  And a time of peace.

The God-Given Task

9What profit has the worker from that
in which he labors? 10I have seen the
God-given task with which the sons of
men are to be occupied. 11He has made
everything beautiful in its time. Also He
has put eternity in their hearts, except
that no one can find out the work that
God does from beginning to end.

12I know that nothing *is* better for
them than to rejoice, and to do good
in their lives, 13and also that every man
should eat and drink and enjoy the
good of all his labor—it *is* the gift
of God.
14 I know that whatever God does,
  It shall be forever.
  Nothing can be added to it,
  And nothing taken from it.
  God does *it*, that men should fear
    before Him.
15 That which is has already been,
  And what is to be has already been;
  And God requires an account of
    what is past.

Injustice Seems to Prevail

16Moreover I saw under the sun:
 In the place of judgment,
 Wickedness *was* there;

And *in* the place of righteousness,
 Iniquity *was* there.
17I said in my heart,
 "God shall judge the righteous and
    the wicked,
 For *there is* a time there for every
    purpose and for every work."
18I said in my heart, "Concerning the
condition of the sons of men, God tests
them, that they may see that they themselves are *like* animals." 19For what
happens to the sons of men also happens to animals; one thing befalls them:
as one dies, so dies the other. Surely,
they all have one breath; man has no
advantage over animals, for all *is* vanity. 20All go to one place: all are from
the dust, and all return to dust.
21Who knows the spirit of the sons of
men, which goes upward, and the spirit
of the animal, which goes down to the
earth? 22So I perceived that nothing *is*
better than that a man should rejoice
in his own works, for that *is* his heritage. For who can bring him to see what
will happen after him?

4 Then I returned and considered all
  the oppression that is done under
the sun:
  And look! The tears of the
    oppressed,
  But they have no comforter—
  On the side of their oppressors
    there is power,
  But they have no comforter.
2 Therefore I praised the dead who
    were already dead,
  More than the living who are still
    alive.
3 Yet, better than both *is he* who has
    never existed,
  Who has not seen the evil work that
    is done under the sun.

The Vanity of Selfish Toil

4Again, I saw that for all toil and
every skillful work a man is envied by
his neighbor. This also *is* vanity and
grasping for the wind.
5 The fool folds his hands
  And consumes his own flesh.
6 Better a handful *with* quietness
  Than both hands full, *together with*
    toil and grasping for the wind.

7Then I returned, and I saw vanity under the sun:

8 There is one alone, without companion:
He has neither son nor brother.
Yet *there is* no end to all his labors,
Nor is his eye satisfied with riches.
But he never asks,
"For whom do I toil and deprive myself of good?"
This also *is* vanity and a grave misfortune.

The Value of a Friend

9 Two *are* better than one,
Because they have a good reward for their labor.

10 For if they fall, one will lift up his companion.
But woe to him *who is* alone when he falls,
For *he has* no one to help him up.

11 Again, if two lie down together, they will keep warm;
But how can one be warm *alone?*

12 Though one may be overpowered by another, two can withstand him.
And a threefold cord is not quickly broken.

Popularity Passes Away

13 Better a poor and wise youth
Than an old and foolish king who will be admonished no more.

14 For he comes out of prison to be king,
Although he was born poor in his kingdom.

15 I saw all the living who walk under the sun;
They were with the second youth who stands in his place.

16 *There was* no end of all the people over whom he was made king;
Yet those who come afterward will not rejoice in him.
Surely this also *is* vanity and grasping for the wind.

Fear God, Keep Your Vows

5 Walk prudently when you go to the house of God; and draw near to hear rather than to give the sacrifice of fools, for they do not know that they do evil.

2 Do not be rash with your mouth,
And let not your heart utter anything hastily before God.
For God *is* in heaven, and you on earth;
Therefore let your words be few.

3 For a dream comes through much activity,
And a fool's voice *is known* by *his* many words.

4 When you make a vow to God, do not delay to pay it;
For *He has* no pleasure in fools.
Pay what you have vowed—

5 Better not to vow than to vow and not pay.

6Do not let your mouth cause your flesh to sin, nor say before the messenger *of* God that it *was* an error. Why should God be angry at your excuse and destroy the work of your hands? 7For in the multitude of dreams and many words *there is* also vanity. But fear God.

The Vanity of Gain and Honor

8If you see the oppression of the poor, and the violent perversion of justice and righteousness in a province, do not marvel at the matter; for high official watches over high official, and higher officials are over them. 9Moreover the profit of the land is for all; *even* the king is served from the field.

10 He who loves silver will not be satisfied with silver;
Nor he who loves abundance, with increase.
This also *is* vanity.

11 When goods increase,
They increase who eat them;
So what profit have the owners
Except to see *them* with their eyes?

12 The sleep of a laboring man *is* sweet,
Whether he eats little or much;
But the abundance of the rich will not permit him to sleep.

13 There is a severe evil *which* I have seen under the sun:
Riches kept for their owner to his hurt.

14 But those riches perish through misfortune;
When he begets a son, *there is* nothing in his hand.

15 As he came from his mother's womb, naked shall he return,
To go as he came;
And he shall take nothing from his labor
Which he may carry away in his hand.

16 And this also *is* a severe evil—
Just exactly as he came, so shall he go.
And what profit has he who has labored for the wind?

17 All his days he also eats in darkness,
And *he has* much sorrow and sickness and anger.

18Here is what I have seen: *It is* good and fitting *for one* to eat and drink, and to enjoy the good of all his labor in which he toils under the sun all the days of his life which God gives him; for it *is* his heritage. 19As for every man to whom God has given riches and wealth, and given him power to eat of it, to receive his heritage and rejoice in his labor—this *is* the gift of God. 20For he will not dwell unduly on the days of his life, because God keeps *him* busy with the joy of his heart.

6 There is an evil which I have seen under the sun, and it *is* common among men: 2A man to whom God has given riches and wealth and honor, so that he lacks nothing for himself of all he desires; yet God does not give him power to eat of it, but a foreigner consumes it. This *is* vanity, and it *is* an evil affliction.

3If a man begets a hundred *children* and lives many years, so that the days of his years are many, but his soul is not satisfied with goodness, or indeed he has no burial, I say *that* a stillborn child *is* better than he—4for it comes in vanity and departs in darkness, and its name is covered with darkness. 5Though it has not seen the sun or known *anything*, this has more rest than that man, 6even if he lives a thousand years twice—but has not seen goodness. Do not all go to one place?

7 All the labor of man *is* for his mouth,
And yet the soul is not satisfied.

8 For what more has the wise *man* than the fool?
What does the poor man have,
Who knows *how* to walk before the living?

9 Better *is* the sight of the eyes than the wandering of desire.
This also *is* vanity and grasping for the wind.

10 Whatever one is, he has been named already,
For it is known that he *is* man;
And he cannot contend with Him who is mightier than he.

11 Since there are many things that increase vanity,
How *is* man the better?

12For who knows what *is* good for man in life, all the days of his vain life which he passes like a shadow? Who can tell a man what will happen after him under the sun?

The Value of Practical Wisdom

7 A good name *is* better than precious ointment,
And the day of death than the day of one's birth;

2 Better to go to the house of mourning
Than to go to the house of feasting,
For that *is* the end of all men;
And the living will take *it* to heart.

3 Sorrow *is* better than laughter,
For by a sad countenance the heart is made better.

4 The heart of the wise *is* in the house of mourning,
But the heart of fools *is* in the house of mirth.

5 *It is* better to hear the rebuke of the wise
Than for a man to hear the song of fools.

6 For like the crackling of thorns under a pot,
So *is* the laughter of the fool.
This also is vanity.

7 Surely oppression destroys a wise *man's* reason,
And a bribe debases the heart.

8 The end of a thing *is* better than
its beginning;
The patient in spirit *is* better than
the proud in spirit.
9 Do not hasten in your spirit to be
angry,
For anger rests in the bosom of
fools.
10 Do not say,
"Why were the former days better
than these?"
For you do not inquire wisely
concerning this.

11 Wisdom *is* good with an
inheritance,
And profitable to those who see the
sun.
12 For wisdom *is* a defense *as* money
is a defense,
But the excellence of knowledge *is*
that wisdom gives life to those
who have it.

13 Consider the work of God;
For who can make straight what He
has made crooked?
14 In the day of prosperity be joyful,
But in the day of adversity
consider:
Surely God has appointed the one
as well as the other,
So that man can find out nothing
that will come after him.
15 I have seen everything in my days
of vanity:
There is a just *man* who perishes
in his righteousness,
And there is a wicked *man* who
prolongs *life* in his wickedness.

16 Do not be overly righteous,
Nor be overly wise:
Why should you destroy yourself?
17 Do not be overly wicked,
Nor be foolish:
Why should you die before your
time?
18 *It is* good that you grasp this,
And also not remove your hand
from the other;
For he who fears God will escape
them all.

19 Wisdom strengthens the wise
More than ten rulers of the city.

20 For *there is* not a just man on earth
who does good
And does not sin.
21 Also do not take to heart
everything people say,
Lest you hear your servant cursing
you.
22 For many times, also, your own
heart has known
That even you have cursed others.

23 All this I have proved by wisdom.
I said, "I will be wise";
But it *was* far from me.
24 As for that which is far off and
exceedingly deep,
Who can find it out?
25 I applied my heart to know,
To search and seek out wisdom and
the reason *of things*,
To know the wickedness of folly,
Even of foolishness *and* madness.
26 And I find more bitter than death
The woman whose heart *is* snares
and nets,
Whose hands *are* fetters.
He who pleases God shall escape
from her,
But the sinner shall be trapped
by her.

27 "Here is what I have found," says
the Preacher,
"*Adding* one thing to the other to
find out the reason,
28 Which my soul still seeks but I
cannot find:
One man among a thousand I have
found,
But a woman among all these I
have not found.
29 Truly, this only I have found:
That God made man upright,
But they have sought out many
schemes."

8 Who *is* like a wise *man*?
And who knows the interpretation
of a thing?
A man's wisdom makes his face
shine,
And the sternness of his face is
changed.

Obey Authorities for God's Sake

2 I *say*, "Keep the king's commandment for the sake of your oath to God.

3Do not be hasty to go from his presence. Do not take your stand for an evil thing, for he does whatever pleases him."

4   Where the word of a king *is, there is* power;
     And who may say to him, "What are you doing?"
5   He who keeps his command will experience nothing harmful;
     And a wise man's heart discerns both time and judgment,
6   Because for every matter there is a time and judgment,
     Though the misery of man increases greatly.
7   For he does not know what will happen;
     So who can tell him when it will occur?
8   No one has power over the spirit to retain the spirit,
     And no one has power in the day of death.
     There is no release from that war,
     And wickedness will not deliver those who are given to it.

9All this I have seen, and applied my heart to every work that is done under the sun: *There is* a time in which one man rules over another to his own hurt.

Death Comes to All

10Then I saw the wicked buried, who had come and gone from the place of holiness, and they were forgotten in the city where they had so done. This also *is* vanity. 11Because the sentence against an evil work is not executed speedily, therefore the heart of the sons of men is fully set in them to do evil. 12Though a sinner does evil a hundred *times,* and his *days* are prolonged, yet I surely know that it will be well with those who fear God, who fear before Him. 13But it will not be well with the wicked; nor will he prolong *his* days, *which are* as a shadow, because he does not fear before God.

14There is a vanity which occurs on earth, that there are just *men* to whom it happens according to the work of the wicked; again, there are wicked *men* to whom it happens according to the work of the righteous. I said that this also *is* vanity.

15So I commended enjoyment, because a man has nothing better under the sun than to eat, drink, and be merry; for this will remain with him in his labor *all* the days of his life which God gives him under the sun.

16When I applied my heart to know wisdom and to see the business that is done on earth, even though one sees no sleep day or night, 17then I saw all the work of God, that a man cannot find out the work that is done under the sun. For though a man labors to discover *it,* yet he will not find *it;* moreover, though a wise *man* attempts to know *it,* he will not be able to find *it.*

9 For I considered all this in my heart, so that I could declare it all: that the righteous and the wise and their works *are* in the hand of God. People know neither love nor hatred *by* anything *they see* before them. 2All things *come* alike to all:
     One event *happens* to the righteous and the wicked;
     To the good, the clean, and the unclean;
     To him who sacrifices and him who does not sacrifice.
     As is the good, so *is* the sinner;
     He who takes an oath as *he* who fears an oath.

3This *is* an evil in all that is done under the sun: that one thing *happens* to all. Truly the hearts of the sons of men are full of evil; madness *is* in their hearts while they live, and after that *they go* to the dead. 4But for him who is joined to all the living there is hope, for a living dog is better than a dead lion.

5   For the living know that they will die;
     But the dead know nothing,
     And they have no more reward,
     For the memory of them is forgotten.
6   Also their love, their hatred, and their envy have now perished;
     Nevermore will they have a share
     In anything done under the sun.

7   Go, eat your bread with joy,
     And drink your wine with a merry heart;
     For God has already accepted your works.

8 Let your garments always be white,
And let your head lack no oil.

9Live joyfully with the wife whom you love all the days of your vain life which He has given you under the sun, all your days of vanity; for that *is* your portion in life, and in the labor which you perform under the sun.

10Whatever your hand finds to do, do *it* with your might; for *there is* no work or device or knowledge or wisdom in the grave where you are going.

11I returned and saw under the sun that—

The race *is* not to the swift,
Nor the battle to the strong,
Nor bread to the wise,
Nor riches to men of
understanding,
Nor favor to men of skill;
But time and chance happen to
them all.

12 For man also does not know his
time:
Like fish taken in a cruel net,
Like birds caught in a snare,
So the sons of men *are* snared in
an evil time,
When it falls suddenly upon them.

Wisdom Superior to Folly

13This wisdom I have also seen under the sun, and it *seemed* great to me: 14*There was* a little city with few men in it; and a great king came against it, besieged it, and built great snares around it. 15Now there was found in it a poor wise man, and he by his wisdom delivered the city. Yet no one remembered that same poor man.

16Then I said:

"Wisdom *is* better than strength.
Nevertheless the poor man's
wisdom *is* despised,
And his words are not heard.
17 Words of the wise, *spoken* quietly,
should be heard
Rather than the shout of a ruler of
fools.
18 Wisdom *is* better than weapons
of war;
But one sinner destroys much
good."

10 Dead flies putrefy the
perfumer's ointment,
And cause it to give off a foul odor;

So does a little folly to one
respected for wisdom *and* honor.
2 A wise man's heart *is* at his right
hand,
But a fool's heart at his left.
3 Even when a fool walks along
the way,
He lacks wisdom,
And he shows everyone *that* he *is*
a fool.
4 If the spirit of the ruler rises
against you,
Do not leave your post;
For conciliation pacifies great
offenses.

5 There is an evil I have seen under
the sun,
As an error proceeding from the
ruler:
6 Folly is set in great dignity,
While the rich sit in a lowly place.
7 I have seen servants on horses,
While princes walk on the ground
like servants.

8 He who digs a pit will fall into it,
And whoever breaks through a
wall will be bitten by a serpent.
9 He who quarries stones may be
hurt by them,
And he who splits wood may be
endangered by it.
10 If the ax is dull,
And one does not sharpen the edge,
Then he must use more strength;
But wisdom brings success.

11 A serpent may bite when *it is* not
charmed;
The babbler is no different.
12 The words of a wise man's mouth
are gracious,
But the lips of a fool shall swallow
him up;
13 The words of his mouth begin with
foolishness,
And the end of his talk *is* raving
madness.
14 A fool also multiplies words.
No man knows what is to be;
Who can tell him what will be after
him?
15 The labor of fools wearies them,
For they do not even know how to
go to the city!

16 Woe to you, O land, when your
      king *is* a child,
   And your princes feast in the
      morning!
17 Blessed *are* you, O land, when your
      king *is* the son of nobles,
   And your princes feast at the
      proper time—
   For strength and not for
      drunkenness!
18 Because of laziness the building
      decays,
   And through idleness of hands the
      house leaks.
19 A feast is made for laughter,
   And wine makes merry;
   But money answers everything.

20 Do not curse the king, even in your
      thought;
   Do not curse the rich, even in your
      bedroom;
   For a bird of the air may carry your
      voice,
   And a bird in flight may tell the
      matter.

The Value of Diligence

11 Cast your bread upon the
         waters,
   For you will find it after many days.
2 Give a serving to seven, and also
      to eight,
   For you do not know what evil will
      be on the earth.

3 If the clouds are full of rain,
   They empty *themselves* upon the
      earth;
   And if a tree falls to the south or
      the north,
   In the place where the tree falls,
      there it shall lie.
4 He who observes the wind will not
      sow,
   And he who regards the clouds will
      not reap.

5 As you do not know what *is* the
      way of the wind,[c]
   Or how the bones *grow* in the
      womb of her who is with child,
   So you do not know the works of
      God who makes everything.
6 In the morning sow your seed,

And in the evening do not withhold
   your hand;
For you do not know which will
   prosper,
Either this or that,
Or whether both alike *will be* good.

7 Truly the light is sweet,
   And *it is* pleasant for the eyes to
      behold the sun;
8 But if a man lives many years
   And rejoices in them all,
   Yet let him remember the days of
      darkness,
   For they will be many.
   All that is coming *is* vanity.

Seek God in Early Life

9 Rejoice, O young man, in your
      youth,
   And let your heart cheer you in the
      days of your youth;
   Walk in the ways of your heart,
   And in the sight of your eyes;
   But know that for all these
   God will bring you into judgment.
10 Therefore remove sorrow from
      your heart,
   And put away evil from your
      flesh,
   For childhood and youth *are* vanity.

12 Remember now your Creator in
         the days of your youth,
   Before the difficult days come,
   And the years draw near when
      you say,
   "I have no pleasure in them":
2 While the sun and the light,
   The moon and the stars,
   Are not darkened,
   And the clouds do not return after
      the rain;
3 In the day when the keepers of the
      house tremble,
   And the strong men bow down;
   When the grinders cease because
      they are few,
   And those that look through the
      windows grow dim;
4 When the doors are shut in the
      streets,
   And the sound of grinding is low;
   When one rises up at the sound of
      a bird,

c Or *spirit*

And all the daughters of music are
 brought low.
5 Also they are afraid of height,
 And of terrors in the way;
 When the almond tree blossoms,
 The grasshopper is a burden,
 And desire fails.
 For man goes to his eternal home,
 And the mourners go about the
  streets.

6 *Remember your Creator* before the
  silver cord is loosed,
 Or the golden bowl is broken,
 Or the pitcher shattered at the
  fountain,
 Or the wheel broken at the well.
7 Then the dust will return to the
  earth as it was,
 And the spirit will return to God
  who gave it.

8 "Vanity of vanities," says the
  Preacher,
 "All *is* vanity."

The Whole Duty of Man

9And moreover, because the Preacher was wise, he still taught the people knowledge; yes, he pondered and sought out *and* set in order many proverbs. 10The Preacher sought to find acceptable words; and *what was* written *was* upright—words of truth. 11The words of the wise are like goads, and the words of scholars are like well-driven nails, given by one Shepherd. 12And further, my son, be admonished by these. Of making many books *there is* no end, and much study *is* wearisome to the flesh.

13Let us hear the conclusion of the whole matter:

 Fear God and keep His
  commandments,
 For this is man's all.
14 For God will bring every work into
  judgment,
 Including every secret thing,
 Whether good or evil.

SONG OF SOLOMON

1 The song of songs, which *is* Solomon's.

The Banquet

THE SHULAMITE[a]

2 Let him kiss me with the kisses of
his mouth—
For your[b] love *is* better than wine.

3 Because of the fragrance of your
good ointments,
Your name *is* ointment poured
forth;
Therefore the virgins love you.

4 Draw me away!

THE DAUGHTERS OF JERUSALEM

We will run after you.[b]

THE SHULAMITE

The king has brought me into his
chambers.

THE DAUGHTERS OF JERUSALEM

We will be glad and rejoice in you.[c]

We will remember your[d] love more
than wine.

THE SHULAMITE

Rightly do they love you.[d]

5 I *am* dark, but lovely,
O daughters of Jerusalem,
Like the tents of Kedar,
Like the curtains of Solomon.

6 Do not look upon me, because I *am*
dark,
Because the sun has tanned me.
My mother's sons were angry
with me;
They made me the keeper of the
vineyards,
But my own vineyard I have not
kept.

(TO HER BELOVED)

7 Tell me, O you whom I love,
Where you feed *your flock,*

Where you make *it* rest at noon.
For why should I be as one who
veils herself
By the flocks of your companions?

THE BELOVED

8 If you do not know, O fairest among
women,
Follow in the footsteps of the flock,
And feed your little goats
Beside the shepherds' tents.

9 I have compared you, my love,
To my filly among Pharaoh's
chariots.

10 Your cheeks are lovely with
ornaments,
Your neck with chains *of gold.*

THE DAUGHTERS OF JERUSALEM

11 We will make you[e] ornaments of
gold
With studs of silver.

THE SHULAMITE

12 While the king *is* at his table,
My spikenard sends forth its
fragrance.

13 A bundle of myrrh *is* my beloved
to me,
That lies all night between my
breasts.

14 My beloved *is* to me a cluster of
henna *blooms*
In the vineyards of En Gedi.

THE BELOVED

15 Behold, you *are* fair, my love!
Behold, you *are* fair!
You *have* dove's eyes. ·

THE SHULAMITE

16 Behold, you *are* handsome, my
beloved!
Yes, pleasant!
Also our bed *is* green.

17 The beams of our houses *are* cedar,
And our rafters of fir.

---

a A Palestinian young woman (compare 6.13). The speaker and audience are identified according
to the number, gender, and person of the Hebrew words. Occasionally the identity is not certain.
b Masculine singular, that is, the Beloved   c Feminine singular, that is, the Shulamite
d Masculine singular, that is, the Beloved   e Feminine singular, that is, the Shulamite

2 I *am* the rose of Sharon,
And the lily of the valleys.

THE BELOVED

2   Like a lily among thorns,
So is my love among the daughters.

THE SHULAMITE

3   Like an apple tree among the trees
of the woods,
So *is* my beloved among the sons.
I sat down in his shade with great
delight,
And his fruit *was* sweet to my taste.

THE SHULAMITE TO THE DAUGHTERS OF
JERUSALEM

4   He brought me to the banqueting
house,
And his banner over me *was* love.
5   Sustain me with cakes of raisins,
Refresh me with apples,
For I *am* lovesick.

6   His left hand *is* under my head,
And his right hand embraces me.
7   I charge you, O daughters of
Jerusalem,
By the gazelles or by the does of
the field,
Do not stir up nor awaken love
Until it pleases.

The Beloved's Request

THE SHULAMITE

8   The voice of my beloved!
Behold, he comes
Leaping upon the mountains,
Skipping upon the hills.
9   My beloved is like a gazelle or a
young stag.
Behold, he stands behind our wall;
He is looking through the windows,
Gazing through the lattice.

10   My beloved spoke, and said to me:
"Rise up, my love, my fair one,
And come away.
11   For lo, the winter is past,
The rain is over *and* gone.
12   The flowers appear on the earth;
The time of singing has come,
And the voice of the turtledove
Is heard in our land.
13   The fig tree puts forth her green
figs,

And the vines *with* the tender
grapes
Give a good smell.
Rise up, my love, my fair one,
And come away!

14   "O my dove, in the clefts of the rock,
In the secret *places* of the cliff,
Let me see your face,
Let me hear your voice;
For your voice *is* sweet,
And your face *is* lovely."

HER BROTHERS

15   Catch us the foxes,
The little foxes that spoil the vines,
For our vines *have* tender grapes.

THE SHULAMITE

16   My beloved *is* mine, and I *am* his.
He feeds *his flock* among the lilies.

(TO HER BELOVED)

17   Until the day breaks
And the shadows flee away,
Turn, my beloved,
And be like a gazelle
Or a young stag
Upon the mountains of Bether.

A Troubled Night

THE SHULAMITE

3 By night on my bed I sought the
one I love;
I sought him, but I did not find him.
2   "I will rise now," *I said,*
"And go about the city;
In the streets and in the squares
I will seek the one I love."
I sought him, but I did not find him.
3   The watchmen who go about the
city found me;
I said,
"Have you seen the one I love?"

4   Scarcely had I passed by them,
When I found the one I love.
I held him and would not let
him go,
Until I had brought him to the
house of my mother,
And into the chamber of her who
conceived me.
5   I charge you, O daughters of
Jerusalem,

By the gazelles or by the does of
    the field,
Do not stir up nor awaken love
Until it pleases.

The Coming of Solomon

THE SHULAMITE

6 Who *is* this coming out of the
    wilderness
Like pillars of smoke,
Perfumed with myrrh and
    frankincense,
With all the merchant's fragrant
    powders?
7 Behold, it *is* Solomon's couch,
With sixty valiant men around it,
Of the valiant of Israel.
8 They all hold swords,
Being expert in war.
Every man *has* his sword on his
    thigh
Because of fear in the night.

9 Of the wood of Lebanon
Solomon the King
Made himself a palanquin:*f*
10 He made its pillars *of* silver,
Its support *of* gold,
Its seat *of* purple,
Its interior paved *with* love
By the daughters of Jerusalem.
11 Go forth, O daughters of Zion,
And see King Solomon with the
    crown
With which his mother crowned
    him
On the day of his wedding,
The day of the gladness of his
    heart.

THE BELOVED

4 Behold, you *are* fair, my love!
Behold, you *are* fair!
You *have* dove's eyes behind your
    veil.
Your hair *is* like a flock of goats,
Going down from Mount Gilead.
2 Your teeth *are* like a flock of shorn
    sheep
Which have come up from the
    washing,
Every one of which bears twins,
And none *is* barren among them.

3 Your lips *are* like a strand of
    scarlet,
And your mouth is lovely.
Your temples behind your veil
Are like a piece of pomegranate.
4 Your neck *is* like the tower of
    David,
Built for an armory,
On which hang a thousand
    bucklers,
All shields of mighty men.
5 Your two breasts *are* like two
    fawns,
Twins of a gazelle,
Which feed among the lilies.

6 Until the day breaks
And the shadows flee away,
I will go my way to the mountain
    of myrrh
And to the hill of frankincense.

7 You *are* all fair, my love,
And *there is* no spot in you.
8 Come with me from Lebanon, *my*
    spouse,
With me from Lebanon.
Look from the top of Amana,
From the top of Senir and Hermon,
From the lions' dens,
From the mountains of the
    leopards.

9 You have ravished my heart,
My sister, *my* spouse;
You have ravished my heart
With one *look* of your eyes,
With one link of your necklace.
10 How fair is your love,
My sister, *my* spouse!
How much better than wine is your
    love,
And the scent of your perfumes
Than all spices!
11 Your lips, O *my* spouse,
Drip as the honeycomb;
Honey and milk *are* under your
    tongue;
And the fragrance of your
    garments
Is like the fragrance of Lebanon.

12 A garden enclosed
Is my sister, *my* spouse,
A spring shut up,

f A portable enclosed chair

A fountain sealed.
13 Your plants *are* an orchard of
       pomegranates
    With pleasant fruits,
    Fragrant henna with spikenard,
14 Spikenard and saffron,
    Calamus and cinnamon,
    With all trees of frankincense,
    Myrrh and aloes,
    With all the chief spices—
15 A fountain of gardens,
    A well of living waters,
    And streams from Lebanon.

THE SHULAMITE

16 Awake, O north *wind,*
    And come, O south!
    Blow upon my garden,
    That its spices may flow out.
    Let my beloved come to his garden
    And eat its pleasant fruits.

THE BELOVED

5 I have come to my garden, my
       sister, *my* spouse;
    I have gathered my myrrh with my
       spice;
    I have eaten my honeycomb with
       my honey;
    I have drunk my wine with my
       milk.

(TO HIS FRIENDS)

    Eat, O friends!
    Drink, yes, drink deeply,
    O beloved ones!

The Shulamite's Troubled Evening

THE SHULAMITE

2 I sleep, but my heart is awake;
    It is the voice of my beloved!
    He knocks, *saying,*
    "Open for me, my sister, my love,
    My dove, my perfect one;
    For my head is covered with dew,
    My locks with the drops of the
       night."

3 I have taken off my robe;
    How can I put it on *again?*
    I have washed my feet;
    How can I defile them?
4 My beloved put his hand
    By the latch *of the door,*
    And my heart yearned for him.
5 I arose to open for my beloved,

And my hands dripped *with* myrrh,
My fingers with liquid myrrh,
On the handles of the lock.

6 I opened for my beloved,
    But my beloved had turned away
       and was gone.
    My heart leaped up when he spoke.
    I sought him, but I could not
       find him;
    I called him, but he gave me no
       answer.
7 The watchmen who went about the
       city found me.
    They struck me, they wounded me;
    The keepers of the walls
    Took my veil away from me.
8 I charge you, O daughters of
       Jerusalem,
    If you find my beloved,
    That you tell him I *am* lovesick!

THE DAUGHTERS OF JERUSALEM

9 What *is* your beloved
    More than *another* beloved,
    O fairest among women?
    What *is* your beloved
    More than *another* beloved,
    That you so charge us?

THE SHULAMITE

10 My beloved *is* white and ruddy,
    Chief among ten thousand.
11 His head *is like* the finest gold;
    His locks *are* wavy,
    And black as a raven.
12 His eyes *are* like doves
    By the rivers of waters,
    Washed with milk,
    And fitly set.
13 His cheeks *are* like a bed of spices,
    Banks of scented herbs.
    His lips *are* lilies,
    Dripping liquid myrrh.

14 His hands *are* rods of gold
    Set with beryl.
    His body *is* carved ivory
    Inlaid *with* sapphires.
15 His legs *are* pillars of marble
    Set on bases of fine gold.
    His countenance *is* like Lebanon,
    Excellent as the cedars.
16 His mouth *is* most sweet,
    Yes, he *is* altogether lovely.
    This *is* my beloved,

And this *is* my friend,
O daughters of Jerusalem!

THE DAUGHTERS OF JERUSALEM

6 Where has your beloved gone,
O fairest among women?
Where has your beloved turned
aside,
That we may seek him with you?

THE SHULAMITE

2 My beloved has gone to his garden,
To the beds of spices,
To feed *his flock* in the gardens,
And to gather lilies.
3 I *am* my beloved's,
And my beloved *is* mine.
He feeds *his flock* among the lilies.

Praise of the Shulamite's Beauty

THE BELOVED

4 O my love, you *are as* beautiful as
Tirzah,
Lovely as Jerusalem,
Awesome as *an army* with banners!
5 Turn your eyes away from me,
For they have overcome me.
Your hair *is* like a flock of goats
Going down from Gilead.
6 Your teeth *are* like a flock of sheep
Which have come up from the
washing;
Every one bears twins,
And none *is* barren among them.
7 Like a piece of pomegranate
Are your temples behind your
veil.

8 There are sixty queens
And eighty concubines,
And virgins without number.
9 My dove, my perfect one,
Is the only one,
The only one of her mother,
The favorite of the one who bore
her.
The daughters saw her
And called her blessed,
The queens and the concubines,
And they praised her.

10 Who is she who looks forth as the
morning,
Fair as the moon,
Clear as the sun,

Awesome as *an army* with
banners?

THE SHULAMITE

11 I went down to the garden of nuts
To see the verdure of the valley,
To see whether the vine had
budded
And the pomegranates had
bloomed.
12 Before I was even aware,
My soul had made me
As the chariots of my noble people.

THE BELOVED AND HIS FRIENDS

13 Return, return, O Shulamite;
Return, return, that we may look
upon you!

THE SHULAMITE

What would you see in the
Shulamite—
As it were, the dance of the two
camps?

Expressions of Praise

THE BELOVED

7 How beautiful are your feet in
sandals,
O prince's daughter!
The curves of your thighs *are* like
jewels,
The work of the hands of a skillful
workman.
2 Your navel *is* a rounded goblet;
It lacks no blended beverage.
Your waist *is* a heap of wheat
Set about with lilies.
3 Your two breasts *are* like two
fawns,
Twins of a gazelle.
4 Your neck *is* like an ivory tower,
Your eyes *like* the pools in Heshbon
By the gate of Bath Rabbim.
Your nose *is* like the tower of
Lebanon
Which looks toward Damascus.
5 Your head *crowns* you like *Mount*
Carmel,
And the hair of your head *is* like
purple;
A king *is* held captive by *your*
tresses.

6 How fair and how pleasant you are,
O love, with your delights!

7   This stature of yours is like a palm
    tree,
    And your breasts *like* its clusters.
8   I said, "I will go up to the palm tree,
    I will take hold of its branches."
    Let now your breasts be like
    clusters of the vine,
    The fragrance of your breath like
    apples,
9   And the roof of your mouth like the
    best wine.

THE SHULAMITE

    The wine goes *down* smoothly for
    my beloved,
    Moving gently the lips of sleepers.
10 I *am* my beloved's,
    And his desire *is* toward me.

11 Come, my beloved,
    Let us go forth to the field;
    Let us lodge in the villages.
12 Let us get up early to the vineyards;
    Let us see if the vine has budded,
    Whether the grape blossoms are
    open,
    And the pomegranates are in
    bloom.
    There I will give you my love.
13 The mandrakes give off a
    fragrance,
    And at our gates *are* pleasant *fruits*,
    All manner, new and old,
    Which I have laid up for you, my
    beloved.

8   Oh, that you were like my brother,
    Who nursed at my mother's breasts!
    If I should find you outside,
    I would kiss you;
    I would not be despised.
2   I would lead you *and* bring you
    Into the house of my mother,
    She *who* used to instruct me.
    I would cause you to drink of spiced
    wine,
    Of the juice of my pomegranate.

(TO THE DAUGHTERS OF JERUSALEM)

3   His left hand *is* under my head,
    And his right hand embraces me.
4   I charge you, O daughters of
    Jerusalem,
    Do not stir up nor awaken love
    Until it pleases.

Love Renewed in Lebanon

A RELATIVE

5   Who *is* this coming up from the
    wilderness,
    Leaning upon her beloved?

    I awakened you under the apple
    tree.
    There your mother brought you
    forth;
    There she *who* bore you brought
    you forth.

THE SHULAMITE TO HER BELOVED

6   Set me as a seal upon your heart,
    As a seal upon your arm;
    For love *is as* strong as death,
    Jealousy *as* cruel as the grave;
    Its flames *are* flames of fire,
    A most vehement flame.

7   Many waters cannot quench love,
    Nor can the floods drown it.
    If a man would give for love
    All the wealth of his house,
    It would be utterly despised.

THE SHULAMITE'S BROTHERS

8   We have a little sister,
    And she has no breasts.
    What shall we do for our sister
    In the day when she is spoken for?
9   If she *is* a wall,
    We will build upon her
    A battlement of silver;
    And if she *is* a door,
    We will enclose her
    With boards of cedar.

THE SHULAMITE

10 I *am* a wall,
    And my breasts like towers;
    Then I became in his eyes
    As one who found peace.
11 Solomon had a vineyard at Baal
    Hamon;
    He leased the vineyard to keepers;
    Everyone was to bring for its fruit
    A thousand silver coins.

(TO SOLOMON)

12 My own vineyard *is* before me.
    You, O Solomon, *may have* a
    thousand,
    And those who tend its fruit two
    hundred.

THE BELOVED

13 You who dwell in the gardens,
    The companions listen for your
        voice—
    Let me hear it!

THE SHULAMITE

14 Make haste, my beloved,
    And be like a gazelle
    Or a young stag
    On the mountains of spices.

The Book of

ISAIAH

1 The vision of Isaiah the son of Amoz, which he saw concerning Judah and Jerusalem in the days of Uzziah, Jotham, Ahaz, *and* Hezekiah, kings of Judah.

The Wickedness of Judah

2 Hear, O heavens, and give ear,
  O earth!
 For the LORD has spoken:
 "I have nourished and brought up
  children,
 And they have rebelled against Me;
3 The ox knows its owner
 And the donkey its master's crib;
 But Israel does not know,
 My people do not consider."

4 Alas, sinful nation,
 A people laden with iniquity,
 A brood of evildoers,
 Children who are corrupters!
 They have forsaken the LORD,
 They have provoked to anger
 The Holy One of Israel,
 They have turned away backward.

5 Why should you be stricken again?
 You will revolt more and more.
 The whole head is sick,
 And the whole heart faints.
6 From the sole of the foot even to
  the head,
 There is no soundness in it,
 But wounds and bruises and
  putrefying sores;
 They have not been closed or
  bound up,
 Or soothed with ointment.

7 Your country *is* desolate,
 Your cities *are* burned with fire;
 Strangers devour your land in your
  presence;
 And *it is* desolate, as overthrown
  by strangers.
8 So the daughter of Zion is left as a
  booth in a vineyard,
 As a hut in a garden of cucumbers,
 As a besieged city.
9 Unless the LORD of hosts
 Had left to us a very small remnant,

We would have become like
 Sodom,
We would have been made like
 Gomorrah.

10 Hear the word of the LORD,
 You rulers of Sodom;
 Give ear to the law of our God,
 You people of Gomorrah:
11 "To what purpose *is* the multitude
  of your sacrifices to Me?"
 Says the LORD.
 "I have had enough of burnt
  offerings of rams
 And the fat of fed cattle.
 I do not delight in the blood of bulls,
 Or of lambs or goats.

12 "When you come to appear
  before Me,
 Who has required this from your
  hand,
 To trample My courts?
13 Bring no more futile sacrifices;
 Incense is an abomination to Me.
 The New Moons, the Sabbaths, and
  the calling of assemblies—
 I cannot endure iniquity and the
  sacred meeting.
14 Your New Moons and your
  appointed feasts
 My soul hates;
 They are a trouble to Me,
 I am weary of bearing *them*.
15 When you spread out your hands,
 I will hide My eyes from you;
 Even though you make many
  prayers,
 I will not hear.
 Your hands are full of blood.

16 "Wash yourselves, make yourselves
  clean;
 Put away the evil of your doings
  from before My eyes.
 Cease to do evil,
17 Learn to do good;
 Seek justice,
 Rebuke the oppressor;
 Defend the fatherless,
 Plead for the widow.

18 "Come now, and let us reason
    together,"
   Says the Lord,
   "Though your sins are like scarlet,
   They shall be as white as snow;
   Though they are red like crimson,
   They shall be as wool.
19 If you are willing and obedient,
   You shall eat the good of the land;
20 But if you refuse and rebel,
   You shall be devoured by the
    sword";
   For the mouth of the Lord has
    spoken.

The Degenerate City

21 How the faithful city has become
    a harlot!
   It was full of justice;
   Righteousness lodged in it,
   But now murderers.
22 Your silver has become dross,
   Your wine mixed with water.
23 Your princes *are* rebellious,
   And companions of thieves;
   Everyone loves bribes,
   And follows after rewards.
   They do not defend the fatherless,
   Nor does the cause of the widow
    come before them.

24 Therefore the Lord says,
   The Lord of hosts, the Mighty One
    of Israel,
   "Ah, I will rid Myself of My
    adversaries,
   And take vengeance on My
    enemies.
25 I will turn My hand against you,
   And thoroughly purge away your
    dross,
   And take away all your alloy.
26 I will restore your judges as at the
    first,
   And your counselors as at the
    beginning.
   Afterward you shall be called the
    city of righteousness, the faithful
    city."

27 Zion shall be redeemed with
    justice,
   And her penitents with
    righteousness.
28 The destruction of transgressors
    and of sinners *shall be* together,
   And those who forsake the Lord
    shall be consumed.
29 For they shall be ashamed of the
    terebinth trees
   Which you have desired;
   And you shall be embarrassed
    because of the gardens
   Which you have chosen.
30 For you shall be as a terebinth
    whose leaf fades,
   And as a garden that has no
    water.
31 The strong shall be as tinder,
   And the work of it as a spark;
   Both will burn together,
   And no one shall quench *them*.

The Future House of God

2 The word that Isaiah the son of
  Amoz saw concerning Judah and
Jerusalem.
2 Now it shall come to pass in the
    latter days
   That the mountain of the Lord's
    house
   Shall be established on the top of
    the mountains,
   And shall be exalted above the
    hills;
   And all nations shall flow to it.
3 Many people shall come and say,
   "Come, and let us go up to the
    mountain of the Lord,
   To the house of the God of Jacob;
   He will teach us His ways,
   And we shall walk in His paths."
   For out of Zion shall go forth
    the law,
   And the word of the Lord from
    Jerusalem.
4 He shall judge between the nations,
   And rebuke many people;
   They shall beat their swords into
    plowshares,
   And their spears into pruning
    hooks;
   Nation shall not lift up sword
    against nation,
   Neither shall they learn war
    anymore.

The Day of the Lord

5 O house of Jacob, come and let us
    walk
   In the light of the Lord.

6 For You have forsaken Your
   people, the house of Jacob,
Because they are filled with eastern
   ways;
They *are* soothsayers like the
   Philistines,
And they are pleased with the
   children of foreigners.
7 Their land is also full of silver and
   gold,
And there is no end to their
   treasures;
Their land is also full of horses,
And there is no end to their
   chariots.
8 Their land is also full of idols;
They worship the work of their own
   hands,
That which their own fingers have
   made.
9 People bow down,
And each man humbles himself;
Therefore do not forgive them.

10 Enter into the rock, and hide in the
   dust,
From the terror of the Lord
And the glory of His majesty.
11 The lofty looks of man shall be
   humbled,
The haughtiness of men shall be
   bowed down,
And the Lord alone shall be exalted
   in that day.

12 For the day of the Lord of hosts
Shall come upon everything proud
   and lofty,
Upon everything lifted up—
And it shall be brought low—
13 Upon all the cedars of Lebanon
   that are high and lifted up,
And upon all the oaks of Bashan;
14 Upon all the high mountains,
And upon all the hills *that are*
   lifted up;
15 Upon every high tower,
And upon every fortified wall;
16 Upon all the ships of Tarshish,
And upon all the beautiful sloops.
17 The loftiness of man shall be bowed
   down,
And the haughtiness of men shall
   be brought low;
The Lord alone will be exalted in
   that day,

18 But the idols He shall utterly
   abolish.

19 They shall go into the holes of the
   rocks,
And into the caves of the earth,
From the terror of the Lord
And the glory of His majesty,
When He arises to shake the earth
   mightily.

20 In that day a man will cast away
   his idols of silver
And his idols of gold,
Which they made, *each* for himself
   to worship,
To the moles and bats,
21 To go into the clefts of the rocks,
And into the crags of the rugged
   rocks,
From the terror of the Lord
And the glory of His majesty,
When He arises to shake the earth
   mightily.

22 Sever yourselves from such a man,
Whose breath *is* in his nostrils;
For of what account is he?

Judgment on Judah and Jerusalem

3 For behold, the Lord, the Lord of
   hosts,
Takes away from Jerusalem and
   from Judah
The stock and the store,
The whole supply of bread and the
   whole supply of water;
2 The mighty man and the man
   of war,
The judge and the prophet,
And the diviner and the elder;
3 The captain of fifty and the
   honorable man,
The counselor and the skillful
   artisan,
And the expert enchanter.

4 "I will give children *to be* their
   princes,
And babes shall rule over them.
5 The people will be oppressed,
Every one by another and every
   one by his neighbor;
The child will be insolent toward
   the elder,
And the base toward the
   honorable."

6   When a man takes hold of his
    brother
    In the house of his father, *saying*,
    "You have clothing;
    You be our ruler,
    And *let* these ruins *be* under your
    power,"
7   In that day he will protest, saying,
    "I cannot cure *your* ills,
    For in my house *is* neither food nor
    clothing;
    Do not make me a ruler of the
    people."

8   For Jerusalem stumbled,
    And Judah is fallen,
    Because their tongue and their
    doings
    Are against the LORD,
    To provoke the eyes of His glory.
9   The look on their countenance
    witnesses against them,
    And they declare their sin as
    Sodom;
    They do not hide *it*.
    Woe to their soul!
    For they have brought evil upon
    themselves.

10 "Say to the righteous that *it shall be*
    well *with them*,
    For they shall eat the fruit of their
    doings.
11 Woe to the wicked! *It shall be* ill
    with him,
    For the reward of his hands shall
    be given him.
12 *As for* My people, children *are* their
    oppressors,
    And women rule over them.
    O My people! Those who lead you
    cause *you* to err,
    And destroy the way of your
    paths."

Oppression and Luxury Condemned

13 The LORD stands up to plead,
    And stands to judge the people.
14 The LORD will enter into judgment
    With the elders of His people
    And His princes:
    "For you have eaten up the vineyard;
    The plunder of the poor *is* in your
    houses.
15 What do you mean by crushing My
    people

And grinding the faces of the
    poor?"
    Says the Lord GOD of hosts.
16 Moreover the LORD says:
    "Because the daughters of Zion are
    haughty,
    And walk with outstretched necks
    And wanton eyes,
    Walking and mincing *as* they go,
    Making a jingling with their feet,
17 Therefore the Lord will strike with
    a scab
    The crown of the head of the
    daughters of Zion,
    And the LORD will uncover their
    secret parts."

18 In that day the Lord will take away
    the finery:
    The jingling anklets, the scarves,
    and the crescents;
19 The pendants, the bracelets, and
    the veils;
20 The headdresses, the leg
    ornaments, and the headbands;
    The perfume boxes, the charms,
21 and the rings;
    The nose jewels,
22 the festal apparel, and the
    mantles;
    The outer garments, the purses,
23 and the mirrors;
    The fine linen, the turbans, and the
    robes.
24 And so it shall be:
    Instead of a sweet smell there will
    be a stench;
    Instead of a sash, a rope;
    Instead of well-set hair, baldness;
    Instead of a rich robe, a girding of
    sackcloth;
    And branding instead of beauty.
25 Your men shall fall by the sword,
    And your mighty in the war.

26 Her gates shall lament and
    mourn,
    And she *being* desolate shall sit on
    the ground.

4 And in that day seven women shall
    take hold of one man, saying,
    "We will eat our own food and wear
    our own apparel;
    Only let us be called by your name,
    To take away our reproach."

The Renewal of Zion

2 In that day the Branch of the LORD
shall be beautiful and glorious;
And the fruit of the earth *shall be*
excellent and appealing
For those of Israel who have
escaped.

3And it shall come to pass that *he who
is* left in Zion and remains in Jerusalem
will be called holy—everyone who is recorded among the living in Jerusalem.
4When the Lord has washed away the
filth of the daughters of Zion, and
purged the blood of Jerusalem from her
midst, by the spirit of judgment and by
the spirit of burning, 5then the LORD will
create above every dwelling place of
Mount Zion, and above her assemblies,
a cloud and smoke by day and the shining of a flaming fire by night. For over
all the glory there *will be* a covering.
6And there will be a tabernacle for
shade in the daytime from the heat, for
a place of refuge, and for a shelter from
storm and rain.

God's Disappointing Vineyard

5 Now let me sing to my Well-
beloved
A song of my Beloved regarding
His vineyard:

My Well-beloved has a vineyard
On a very fruitful hill.
2 He dug it up and cleared out its
stones,
And planted it with the choicest
vine.
He built a tower in its midst,
And also made a winepress in it;
So He expected *it* to bring forth
good grapes,
But it brought forth wild grapes.

3 "And now, O inhabitants of
Jerusalem and men of Judah,
Judge, please, between Me and My
vineyard.
4 What more could have been done
to My vineyard
That I have not done in it?
Why then, when I expected *it* to
bring forth *good* grapes,
Did it bring forth wild grapes?
5 And now, please let Me tell you
what I will do to My vineyard:

I will take away its hedge, and it
shall be burned;
And break down its wall, and it
shall be trampled down.
6 I will lay it waste;
It shall not be pruned or dug,
But there shall come up briers and
thorns.
I will also command the clouds
That they rain no rain on it."

7 For the vineyard of the LORD of
hosts *is* the house of Israel,
And the men of Judah are His
pleasant plant.
He looked for justice, but behold,
oppression;
For righteousness, but behold, a cry
for help.

Impending Judgment on Excesses

8 Woe to those who join house to
house;
They add field to field,
Till *there is* no place
Where they may dwell alone in the
midst of the land!
9 In my hearing the LORD of hosts
said,
"Truly, many houses shall be
desolate,
Great and beautiful ones, without
inhabitant.
10 For ten acres of vineyard shall yield
one bath,
And a homer of seed shall yield one
ephah."

11 Woe to those who rise early in the
morning,
That they may follow intoxicating
drink;
Who continue until night, *till* wine
inflames them!
12 The harp and the strings,
The tambourine and flute,
And wine are in their feasts;
But they do not regard the work of
the LORD,
Nor consider the operation of His
hands.

13 Therefore my people have gone
into captivity,
Because *they have* no knowledge;
Their honorable men *are* famished,

And their multitude dried up with
thirst.
14 Therefore Sheol has enlarged itself
And opened its mouth beyond
measure;
Their glory and their multitude and
their pomp,
And he who is jubilant, shall
descend into it.
15 People shall be brought down,
Each man shall be humbled,
And the eyes of the lofty shall be
humbled.
16 But the LORD of hosts shall be
exalted in judgment,
And God who is holy shall be
hallowed in righteousness.
17 Then the lambs shall feed in their
pasture,
And in the waste places of the fat
ones strangers shall eat.

18 Woe to those who draw iniquity
with cords of vanity,
And sin as if with a cart rope;
19 That say, "Let Him make speed *and*
hasten His work,
That we may see *it;*
And let the counsel of the Holy One
of Israel draw near and come,
That we may know *it.*"

20 Woe to those who call evil good,
and good evil;
Who put darkness for light, and
light for darkness;
Who put bitter for sweet, and sweet
for bitter!

21 Woe to *those who are* wise in their
own eyes,
And prudent in their own sight!

22 Woe to men mighty at drinking
wine,
Woe to men valiant for mixing
intoxicating drink,
23 Who justify the wicked for a bribe,
And take away justice from the
righteous man!

24 Therefore, as the fire devours the
stubble,
And the flame consumes the chaff,
So their root will be as rottenness,
And their blossom will ascend like
dust;

Because they have rejected the law
of the LORD of hosts,
And despised the word of the Holy
One of Israel.
25 Therefore the anger of the LORD is
aroused against His people;
He has stretched out His hand
against them
And stricken them,
And the hills trembled.
Their carcasses *were* as refuse in
the midst of the streets.

For all this His anger is not turned
away,
But His hand *is* stretched out still.

26 He will lift up a banner to the
nations from afar,
And will whistle to them from the
end of the earth;
Surely they shall come with speed,
swiftly.
27 No one will be weary or stumble
among them,
No one will slumber or sleep;
Nor will the belt on their loins be
loosed,
Nor the strap of their sandals be
broken;
28 Whose arrows *are* sharp,
And all their bows bent;
Their horses' hooves will seem like
flint,
And their wheels like a whirlwind.
29 Their roaring *will be* like a lion,
They will roar like young lions;
Yes, they will roar
And lay hold of the prey;
They will carry *it* away safely,
And no one will deliver.
30 In that day they will roar against
them
Like the roaring of the sea.
And if *one* looks to the land,
Behold, darkness *and* sorrow;
And the light is darkened by the
clouds.

Isaiah Called to Be a Prophet

6 In the year that King Uzziah died, I
saw the Lord sitting on a throne,
high and lifted up, and the train of His
robe filled the temple. 2Above it stood
seraphim; each one had six wings: with
two he covered his face, with two he
covered his feet, and with two he flew.

3And one cried to another and said:
  "Holy, holy, holy *is* the LORD of
    hosts;
  The whole earth *is* full of His
    glory!"
4And the posts of the door were shaken
by the voice of him who cried out, and
the house was filled with smoke.
  5So I said:
  "Woe *is* me, for I am undone!
  Because I *am* a man of unclean
    lips,
  And I dwell in the midst of a people
    of unclean lips;
  For my eyes have seen the King,
  The LORD of hosts."
6Then one of the seraphim flew to me,
having in his hand a live coal *which* he
had taken with the tongs from the altar.
7And he touched my mouth *with it*, and
said:
  "Behold, this has touched your lips;
  Your iniquity is taken away,
  And your sin purged."
8Also I heard the voice of the Lord,
saying:
  "Whom shall I send,
  And who will go for Us?"
Then I said, "Here *am* I! Send me."
9And He said, "Go, and tell this
people:
  'Keep on hearing, but do not
    understand;
  Keep on seeing, but do not
    perceive.'

10 "Make the heart of this people dull,
  And their ears heavy,
  And shut their eyes;
  Lest they see with their eyes,
  And hear with their ears,
  And understand with their heart,
  And return and be healed."
11Then I said, "Lord, how long?"
And He answered:
  "Until the cities are laid waste and
    without inhabitant,
  The houses are without a man,
  The land is utterly desolate,
12 The LORD has removed men far
    away,
  And the forsaken places *are* many
    in the midst of the land.
13 But yet a tenth *will be* in it,
  And will return and be for
    consuming,
  As a terebinth tree or as an oak,

  Whose stump *remains* when it is
    cut down.
  So the holy seed *shall be* its stump."

Isaiah Sent to King Ahaz

7 Now it came to pass in the days of
Ahaz the son of Jotham, the son of
Uzziah, king of Judah, *that* Rezin king
of Syria and Pekah the son of Remaliah,
king of Israel, went up to Jerusalem to
make war against it, but could not prevail against it. 2And it was told to the
house of David, saying, "Syria's forces
are deployed in Ephraim." So his heart
and the heart of his people were moved
as the trees of the woods are moved
with the wind.
  3Then the LORD said to Isaiah, "Go
out now to meet Ahaz, you and Shear-
Jashub your son, at the end of the aqueduct from the upper pool, on the highway to the Fuller's Field, 4and say to
him: 'Take heed, and be quiet; do not
fear or be fainthearted for these two
stubs of smoking firebrands, for the
fierce anger of Rezin and Syria, and the
son of Remaliah. 5Because Syria,
Ephraim, and the son of Remaliah have
plotted evil against you, saying,
6"Let us go up against Judah and trouble it, and let us make a gap in its wall
for ourselves, and set a king over them,
the son of Tabel"—7thus says the
Lord GOD:
  "It shall not stand,
  Nor shall it come to pass.
8 For the head of Syria *is* Damascus,
  And the head of Damascus *is*
    Rezin.
  Within sixty-five years Ephraim
    will be broken,
  So that it will not *be* a people.
9 The head of Ephraim *is* Samaria,
  And the head of Samaria *is*
    Remaliah's son.
  If you will not believe,
  Surely you shall not be
    established."' "

The Immanuel Prophecy

  10Moreover the LORD spoke again to
Ahaz, saying, 11"Ask a sign for yourself
from the LORD your God; ask it either
in the depth or in the height above."
12But Ahaz said, "I will not ask, nor
will I test the LORD!"
  13Then he said, "Hear now, O house

of David! *Is it* a small thing for you to weary men, but will you weary my God also? 14Therefore the Lord Himself will give you a sign: Behold, the virgin shall conceive and bear a Son, and shall call His name Immanuel.*a* 15Curds and honey He shall eat, that He may know to refuse the evil and choose the good. 16For before the Child shall know to refuse the evil and choose the good, the land that you dread will be forsaken by both her kings. 17The LORD will bring the king of Assyria upon you and your people and your father's house—days that have not come since the day that Ephraim departed from Judah."

18 And it shall come to pass in
       that day
     That the LORD will whistle for
       the fly
     That *is* in the farthest part of the
       rivers of Egypt,
     And for the bee that *is* in the land
       of Assyria.
19 They will come, and all of them will
       rest
     In the desolate valleys and in the
       clefts of the rocks,
     And on all thorns and in all
       pastures.

20 In the same day the Lord will shave
       with a hired razor,
     With those from beyond the River,*b*
       with the king of Assyria,
     The head and the hair of the legs,
     And will also remove the beard.

21 It shall be in that day
     That a man will keep alive a young
       cow and two sheep;
22 So it shall be, from the abundance
       of milk they give,
     That he will eat curds;
     For curds and honey everyone will
       eat who is left in the land.

23 It shall happen in that day,
     That wherever there could be a
       thousand vines
     Worth a thousand *shekels* of silver,
     It will be for briers and thorns.
24 With arrows and bows men will
       come there,

Because all the land will become
  briers and thorns.

25 And to any hill which could be dug
       with the hoe,
     You will not go there for fear of
       briers and thorns;
     But it will become a range for oxen
     And a place for sheep to roam.

Assyria Will Invade the Land

8 Moreover the LORD said to me, "Take a large scroll, and write on it with a man's pen concerning Maher-Shalal-Hash-Baz.*c* 2And I will take for Myself faithful witnesses to record, Uriah the priest and Zechariah the son of Jeberechiah."

3Then I went to the prophetess, and she conceived and bore a son. Then the LORD said to me, "Call his name Maher-Shalal-Hash-Baz; 4for before the child shall have knowledge to cry 'My father' and 'My mother,' the riches of Damascus and the spoil of Samaria will be taken away before the king of Assyria."

5The LORD also spoke to me again, saying:
6 "Inasmuch as these people refused
     The waters of Shiloah that flow
       softly,
     And rejoice in Rezin and in
       Remaliah's son;
7 Now therefore, behold, the Lord
     brings up over them
     The waters of the River,*d* strong
       and mighty—
     The king of Assyria and all his
       glory;
     He will go up over all his channels
     And go over all his banks.
8 He will pass through Judah,
     He will overflow and pass over,
     He will reach up to the neck;
     And the stretching out of his wings
     Will fill the breadth of Your land,
       O Immanuel.*e*

9 "Be shattered, O you peoples, and
     be broken in pieces!
     Give ear, all you from far countries.
     Gird yourselves, but be broken in
       pieces;

---

a Literally *God-With-Us*   *b* That is, the Euphrates   *c* Literally *Speed the Spoil, Hasten the Booty*   *d* That is, the Euphrates   *e* Literally *God-With-Us*

Gird yourselves, but be broken in
pieces.

10 Take counsel together, but it will
come to nothing;
Speak the word, but it will not
stand,
For God *is* with us."

Fear God, Heed His Word

11For the LORD spoke thus to me with
a strong hand, and instructed me that
I should not walk in the way of this people, saying:

12 "Do not say, 'A conspiracy,'
Concerning all that this people call
a conspiracy,
Nor be afraid of their threats, nor
be troubled.

13 The LORD of hosts, Him you shall
hallow;
Let Him *be* your fear,
And *let* Him *be* your dread.

14 He will be as a sanctuary,
But a stone of stumbling and a rock
of offense
To both the houses of Israel,
As a trap and a snare to the
inhabitants of Jerusalem.

15 And many among them shall
stumble;
They shall fall and be broken,
Be snared and taken."

16 Bind up the testimony,
Seal the law among my disciples.

17 And I will wait on the LORD,
Who hides His face from the house
of Jacob;
And I will hope in Him.

18 Here am I and the children whom
the LORD has given me!
We are for signs and wonders in
Israel
From the LORD of hosts,
Who dwells in Mount Zion.

19And when they say to you, "Seek
those who are mediums and wizards,
who whisper and mutter," should not
a people seek their God? *Should they
seek* the dead on behalf of the living?
20To the law and to the testimony! If
they do not speak according to this
word, *it is* because *there is* no light in
them.

21They will pass through it hard-
pressed and hungry; and it shall happen, when they are hungry, that they
will be enraged and curse their king
and their God, and look upward.
22Then they will look to the earth, and
see trouble and darkness, gloom of anguish; and *they will be* driven into darkness.

The Government of the Promised Son

9 Nevertheless the gloom *will* not *be*
upon her who *is* distressed,
As when at first He lightly
esteemed
The land of Zebulun and the land
of Naphtali,
And afterward more heavily
oppressed *her,*
By the way of the sea, beyond the
Jordan,
In Galilee of the Gentiles.

2 The people who walked in
darkness
Have seen a great light;
Those who dwelt in the land of the
shadow of death,
Upon them a light has shined.

3 You have multiplied the nation
And increased its joy;
They rejoice before You
According to the joy of harvest,
As *men* rejoice when they divide
the spoil.

4 For You have broken the yoke of
his burden
And the staff of his shoulder,
The rod of his oppressor,
As in the day of Midian.

5 For every warrior's sandal from the
noisy battle,
And garments rolled in blood,
Will be used for burning *and* fuel
of fire.

6 For unto us a Child is born,
Unto us a Son is given;
And the government will be upon
His shoulder.
And His name will be called
Wonderful, Counselor,
Mighty God,
Everlasting Father, Prince of Peace.

7 Of the increase of *His* government
and peace
There will be no end,
Upon the throne of David and over
His kingdom,

To order it and establish it with
judgment and justice
From that time forward, even
forever.
The zeal of the Lord of hosts will
perform this.

The Punishment of Samaria

8 The LORD sent a word against
Jacob,
And it has fallen on Israel.
9 All the people will know—
Ephraim and the inhabitant of
Samaria—
Who say in pride and arrogance of
heart:
10 "The bricks have fallen down,
But we will rebuild with hewn
stones;
The sycamores are cut down,
But we will replace them with
cedars."
11 Therefore the LORD shall set up
The adversaries of Rezin
against him,
And spur his enemies on,
12 The Syrians before and the
Philistines behind;
And they shall devour Israel with
an open mouth.

For all this His anger is not turned
away,
But His hand is stretched out still.

13 For the people do not turn to Him
who strikes them,
Nor do they seek the LORD of hosts.
14 Therefore the LORD will cut off head
and tail from Israel,
Palm branch and bulrush in
one day.
15 The elder and honorable, he is the
head;
The prophet who teaches lies, he
is the tail.
16 For the leaders of this people cause
them to err,
And those who are led by them are
destroyed.
17 Therefore the Lord will have no joy
in their young men,
Nor have mercy on their fatherless
and widows;
For everyone is a hypocrite and an
evildoer,
And every mouth speaks folly.

For all this His anger is not turned
away,
But His hand is stretched out still.

18 For wickedness burns as the fire;
It shall devour the briers and
thorns,
And kindle in the thickets of the
forest;
They shall mount up like rising
smoke.
19 Through the wrath of the LORD of
hosts
The land is burned up,
And the people shall be as fuel for
the fire;
No man shall spare his brother.
20 And he shall snatch on the right
hand
And be hungry;
He shall devour on the left hand
And not be satisfied;
Every man shall eat the flesh of his
own arm.
21 Manasseh shall devour Ephraim,
and Ephraim Manasseh;
Together they shall be against
Judah.

For all this His anger is not turned
away,
But His hand is stretched out still.

10 "Woe to those who decree
unrighteous decrees,
Who write misfortune,
Which they have prescribed
2 To rob the needy of justice,
And to take what is right from the
poor of My people,
That widows may be their prey,
And that they may rob the
fatherless.
3 What will you do in the day of
punishment,
And in the desolation which will
come from afar?
To whom will you flee for help?
And where will you leave your
glory?
4 Without Me they shall bow down
among the prisoners,
And they shall fall among the
slain."

For all this His anger is not turned
away,
But His hand is stretched out still.

Arrogant Assyria Also Judged

5 "Woe to Assyria, the rod of My
      anger
      And the staff in whose hand is My
      indignation.
6 I will send him against an ungodly
      nation,
      And against the people of My wrath
      I will give him charge,
      To seize the spoil, to take the prey,
      And to tread them down like the
      mire of the streets.
7 Yet he does not mean so,
      Nor does his heart think so;
      But *it is* in his heart to destroy,
      And cut off not a few nations.
8 For he says,
      '*Are* not my princes altogether
      kings?
9 *Is* not Calno like Carchemish?
      Is not Hamath like Arpad?
      Is not Samaria like Damascus?
10 As my hand has found the
      kingdoms of the idols,
      Whose carved images excelled
      those of Jerusalem and Samaria,
11 As I have done to Samaria and her
      idols,
      Shall I not do also to Jerusalem and
      her idols?' "

12Therefore it shall come to pass,
when the Lord has performed all His
work on Mount Zion and on Jerusalem,
that He will say, "I will punish the fruit
of the arrogant heart of the king of Assyria, and the glory of his haughty
looks."

13For he says:
"By the strength of my hand I have
      done *it,*
      And by my wisdom, for I am
      prudent;
      Also I have removed the
      boundaries of the people,
      And have robbed their treasuries;
      So I have put down the inhabitants
      like a valiant *man.*
14 My hand has found like a nest the
      riches of the people,
      And as one gathers eggs *that are*
      left,
      I have gathered all the earth;
      And there was no one who moved
      his wing,
      Nor opened *his* mouth with even a
      peep."

15 Shall the ax boast itself against him
      who chops with it?
      Or shall the saw exalt itself against
      him who saws with it?
      As if a rod could wield *itself* against
      those who lift it up,
      Or as if a staff could lift up, *as if it
      were* not wood!
16 Therefore the Lord, the Lord of
      hosts,
      Will send leanness among his fat
      ones;
      And under his glory
      He will kindle a burning
      Like the burning of a fire.
17 So the Light of Israel will be for a
      fire,
      And his Holy One for a flame;
      It will burn and devour
      His thorns and his briers in
      one day.
18 And it will consume the glory of his
      forest and of his fruitful field,
      Both soul and body;
      And they will be as when a sick
      man wastes away.
19 Then the rest of the trees of his
      forest
      Will be so few in number
      That a child may write them.

The Returning Remnant of Israel

20 And it shall come to pass in
      that day
      That the remnant of Israel,
      And such as have escaped of the
      house of Jacob,
      Will never again depend on him
      who defeated them,
      But will depend on the Lord, the
      Holy One of Israel, in truth.
21 The remnant will return, the
      remnant of Jacob,
      To the Mighty God.
22 For though your people, O Israel,
      be as the sand of the sea,
      A remnant of them will return;
      The destruction decreed shall
      overflow with righteousness.
23 For the Lord God of hosts
      Will make a determined end
      In the midst of all the land.

24Therefore thus says the Lord God
of hosts: "O My people, who dwell in
Zion, do not be afraid of the Assyrian.
He shall strike you with a rod and lift
up his staff against you, in the manner

of Egypt. 25For yet a very little while and the indignation will cease, as will My anger in their destruction.'' 26And the LORD of hosts will stir up a scourge for him like the slaughter of Midian at the rock of Oreb; *as* His rod was on the sea, so will He lift it up in the manner of Egypt.

27 It shall come to pass in that day
That his burden will be taken away
from your shoulder,
And his yoke from your neck,
And the yoke will be destroyed
because of the anointing oil.

28 He has come to Aiath,
He has passed Migron;
At Michmash he has attended to his
equipment.

29 They have gone along the ridge,
They have taken up lodging at
Geba.
Ramah is afraid,
Gibeah of Saul has fled.

30 Lift up your voice,
O daughter of Gallim!
Cause it to be heard as far as
Laish—
O poor Anathoth!

31 Madmenah has fled,
The inhabitants of Gebim seek
refuge.

32 As yet he will remain at Nob that
day;
He will shake his fist at the mount
of the daughter of Zion,
The hill of Jerusalem.

33 Behold, the Lord,
The LORD of hosts,
Will lop off the bough with terror;
Those of high stature *will be* hewn
down,
And the haughty will be humbled.

34 He will cut down the thickets of the
forest with iron,
And Lebanon will fall by the
Mighty One.

The Reign of Jesse's Offspring

11 There shall come forth a Rod
from the stem of Jesse,
And a Branch shall grow out of his
roots.

2 The Spirit of the LORD shall rest
upon Him,
The Spirit of wisdom and
understanding,
The Spirit of counsel and might,
The Spirit of knowledge and of the
fear of the LORD.

3 His delight *is* in the fear of the
LORD,
And He shall not judge by the sight
of His eyes,
Nor decide by the hearing of His
ears;

4 But with righteousness He shall
judge the poor,
And decide with equity for the
meek of the earth;
He shall strike the earth with the
rod of His mouth,
And with the breath of His lips He
shall slay the wicked.

5 Righteousness shall be the belt of
His loins,
And faithfulness the belt of His
waist.

6 "The wolf also shall dwell with the
lamb,
The leopard shall lie down with the
young goat,
The calf and the young lion and the
fatling together;
And a little child shall lead them.

7 The cow and the bear shall graze;
Their young ones shall lie down
together;
And the lion shall eat straw like
the ox.

8 The nursing child shall play by the
cobra's hole,
And the weaned child shall put his
hand in the viper's den.

9 They shall not hurt nor destroy in
all My holy mountain,
For the earth shall be full of the
knowledge of the LORD
As the waters cover the sea.

10 "And in that day there shall be a
Root of Jesse,
Who shall stand as a banner to the
people;
For the Gentiles shall seek Him,
And His resting place shall be
glorious."

11 It shall come to pass in that day
That the Lord shall set His hand
again the second time

To recover the remnant of His
   people who are left,
From Assyria and Egypt,
From Pathros and Cush,
From Elam and Shinar,
From Hamath and the islands of
   the sea.

12 He will set up a banner for the
   nations,
And will assemble the outcasts of
   Israel,
And gather together the dispersed
   of Judah
From the four corners of the earth.
13 Also the envy of Ephraim shall
   depart,
And the adversaries of Judah shall
   be cut off;
Ephraim shall not envy Judah,
And Judah shall not harass
   Ephraim.
14 But they shall fly down upon the
   shoulder of the Philistines toward
   the west;
Together they shall plunder the
   people of the East;
They shall lay their hand on Edom
   and Moab;
And the people of Ammon shall
   obey them.
15 The LORD will utterly destroy the
   tongue of the Sea of Egypt;
With His mighty wind He will
   shake His fist over the River,*f*
And strike it in the seven streams,
And make *men* cross over dryshod.
16 There will be a highway for the
   remnant of His people
Who will be left from Assyria,
As it was for Israel
In the day that he came up from
   the land of Egypt.

A Hymn of Praise

12 And in that day you will say:

"O LORD, I will praise You;
Though You were angry with me,
Your anger is turned away, and
   You comfort me.
2 Behold, God *is* my salvation,
I will trust and not be afraid;
'For YAH, the LORD, *is* my strength
   and song;

He also has become my
   salvation.' "*g*

3 Therefore with joy you will draw
   water
From the wells of salvation.
4 And in that day you will say:
"Praise the LORD, call upon His
   name;
Declare His deeds among the
   peoples,
Make mention that His name is
   exalted.
5 Sing to the LORD,
For He has done excellent things;
This *is* known in all the earth.
6 Cry out and shout, O inhabitant of
   Zion,
For great *is* the Holy One of Israel
   in your midst!"

Proclamation Against Babylon

13 The burden against Babylon
which Isaiah the son of Amoz
saw.
2 "Lift up a banner on the high
   mountain,
Raise your voice to them;
Wave your hand, that they may
   enter the gates of the nobles.
3 I have commanded My sanctified
   ones;
I have also called My mighty ones
   for My anger—
Those who rejoice in My
   exaltation."

4 The noise of a multitude in the
   mountains,
Like that of many people!
A tumultuous noise of the
   kingdoms of nations gathered
   together!
The LORD of hosts musters
The army for battle.
5 They come from a far country,
From the end of heaven—
The LORD and His weapons of
   indignation,
To destroy the whole land.

6 Wail, for the day of the LORD *is* at
   hand!
It will come as destruction from the
   Almighty.

---

f That is, the Euphrates   *g* Compare Exodus 15.2

7 Therefore all hands will be
       limp,
   Every man's heart will melt,
8 And they will be afraid.
   Pangs and sorrows will take hold
       of *them;*
   They will be in pain as a woman
       in childbirth;
   They will be amazed at one
       another;
   Their faces *will be like* flames.

9 Behold, the day of the LORD comes,
   Cruel, with both wrath and fierce
       anger,
   To lay the land desolate;
   And He will destroy its sinners
       from it.
10 For the stars of heaven and their
       constellations
   Will not give their light;
   The sun will be darkened in its
       going forth,
   And the moon will not cause its
       light to shine.

11 "I will punish the world for *its*
       evil,
   And the wicked for their iniquity;
   I will halt the arrogance of the
       proud,
   And will lay low the haughtiness
       of the terrible.
12 I will make a mortal more rare than
       fine gold,
   A man more than the golden wedge
       of Ophir.
13 Therefore I will shake the heavens,
   And the earth will move out of her
       place,
   In the wrath of the LORD of hosts
   And in the day of His fierce anger.
14 It shall be as the hunted gazelle,
   And as a sheep that no man
       takes up;
   Every man will turn to his own
       people,
   And everyone will flee to his own
       land.
15 Everyone who is found will be
       thrust through,
   And everyone who is captured will
       fall by the sword.
16 Their children also will be dashed
       to pieces before their eyes;
   Their houses will be plundered
   And their wives ravished.

17 "Behold, I will stir up the Medes
       against them,
   Who will not regard silver;
   And *as for* gold, they will not
       delight in it.
18 Also *their* bows will dash the young
       men to pieces,
   And they will have no pity on the
       fruit of the womb;
   Their eye will not spare children.
19 And Babylon, the glory of
       kingdoms,
   The beauty of the Chaldeans' pride,
   Will be as when God overthrew
       Sodom and Gomorrah.
20 It will never be inhabited,
   Nor will it be settled from
       generation to generation;
   Nor will the Arabian pitch tents
       there,
   Nor will the shepherds make their
       sheepfolds there.
21 But wild beasts of the desert will
       lie there,
   And their houses will be full of
       owls;
   Ostriches will dwell there,
   And wild goats will caper there.
22 The hyenas will howl in their
       citadels,
   And jackals in their pleasant
       palaces.
   Her time *is* near to come,
   And her days will not be
       prolonged."

Mercy on Jacob

14 For the LORD will have mercy on
Jacob, and will still choose Israel,
and settle them in their own land. The
strangers will be joined with them, and
they will cling to the house of Jacob.
2Then people will take them and bring
them to their place, and the house of
Israel will possess them for servants
and maids in the land of the LORD; they
will take them captive whose captives
they were, and rule over their oppressors.

Fall of the King of Babylon

3It shall come to pass in the day the
LORD gives you rest from your sorrow,
and from your fear and the hard bondage in which you were made to serve,
4that you will take up this proverb
against the king of Babylon, and say:

"How the oppressor has ceased,
The golden city ceased!
5 The LORD has broken the staff of
the wicked,
The scepter of the rulers;
6 He who struck the people in wrath
with a continual stroke,
He who ruled the nations in anger,
Is persecuted *and* no one hinders.
7 The whole earth is at rest *and* quiet;
They break forth into singing.
8 Indeed the cypress trees rejoice
over you,
And the cedars of Lebanon,
Saying, 'Since you were cut down,
No woodsman has come up
against us.'

9 "Hell from beneath is excited
about you,
To meet *you* at your coming;
It stirs up the dead for you,
All the chief ones of the earth;
It has raised up from their thrones
All the kings of the nations.
10 They all shall speak and say to you:
'Have you also become as weak
as we?
Have you become like us?
11 Your pomp is brought down to
Sheol,
And the sound of your stringed
instruments;
The maggot is spread under you,
And worms cover you.'

The Fall of Lucifer

12 "How you are fallen from heaven,
O Lucifer,[h] son of the morning!
How you are cut down to the
ground,
You who weakened the nations!
13 For you have said in your heart:
'I will ascend into heaven,
I will exalt my throne above the
stars of God;
I will also sit on the mount of the
congregation
On the farthest sides of the north;
14 I will ascend above the heights of
the clouds,
I will be like the Most High.'
15 Yet you shall be brought down to
Sheol,
To the lowest depths of the Pit.

16 "Those who see you will gaze at you,
And consider you, *saying:*
'*Is* this the man who made the earth
tremble,
Who shook kingdoms,
17 Who made the world as a
wilderness
And destroyed its cities,
Who did not open the house of his
prisoners?'

18 "All the kings of the nations,
All of them, sleep in glory,
Everyone in his own house;
19 But you are cast out of your grave
Like an abominable branch,
Like the garment of those who are
slain,
Thrust through with a sword,
Who go down to the stones of
the pit,
Like a corpse trodden underfoot.
20 You will not be joined with them
in burial,
Because you have destroyed your
land
And slain your people.
The brood of evildoers shall never
be named.
21 Prepare slaughter for his children
Because of the iniquity of their
fathers,
Lest they rise up and possess the
land,
And fill the face of the world with
cities."

Babylon Destroyed

22 "For I will rise up against them,"
says the LORD of hosts,
"And cut off from Babylon the name
and remnant,
And offspring and posterity," says
the LORD.
23 "I will also make it a possession for
the porcupine,
And marshes of muddy water;
I will sweep it with the broom of
destruction," says the LORD of
hosts.

Assyria Destroyed

24 The LORD of hosts has sworn,
saying,
"Surely, as I have thought, so it shall
come to pass,

[h] Literally *Day Star*

And as I have purposed, *so* it shall
   stand:

25 That I will break the Assyrian in
   My land,
   And on My mountains tread him
   underfoot.
   Then his yoke shall be removed
   from them,
   And his burden removed from their
   shoulders.

26 This *is* the purpose that is purposed
   against the whole earth,
   And this *is* the hand that is
   stretched out over all the nations.

27 For the Lord of hosts has purposed,
   And who will annul *it?*
   His hand *is* stretched out,
   And who will turn it back?"

Philistia Destroyed

28This is the burden which came in
the year that King Ahaz died.

29 "Do not rejoice, all you of Philistia,
   Because the rod that struck you is
   broken;
   For out of the serpent's roots will
   come forth a viper,
   And its offspring *will be* a fiery
   flying serpent.

30 The firstborn of the poor will feed,
   And the needy will lie down in
   safety;
   I will kill your roots with famine,
   And it will slay your remnant.

31 Wail, O gate! Cry, O city!
   All you of Philistia *are* dissolved;
   For smoke will come from the
   north,
   And no one *will be* alone in his
   appointed times."

32 What will they answer the
   messengers of the nation?
   That the Lord has founded Zion,
   And the poor of His people shall
   take refuge in it.

Proclamation Against Moab

15 The burden against Moab.

Because in the night Ar of Moab
   is laid waste
And destroyed,
Because in the night Kir of
   Moab is laid waste
And destroyed,

2 He has gone up to the temple and
   Dibon,
   To the high places to weep.
   Moab will wail over Nebo and over
   Medeba;
   On all their heads *will be* baldness,
   And every beard cut off.

3 In their streets they will clothe
   themselves with sackcloth;
   On the tops of their houses
   And in their streets
   Everyone will wail, weeping
   bitterly.

4 Heshbon and Elealeh will cry out,
   Their voice shall be heard as far as
   Jahaz;
   Therefore the armed soldiers of
   Moab will cry out;
   His life will be burdensome to him.

5 "My heart will cry out for Moab;
   His fugitives *shall flee* to Zoar,
   Like a three-year-old heifer.
   For by the Ascent of Luhith
   They will go up with weeping;
   For in the way of Horonaim
   They will raise up a cry of
   destruction,

6 For the waters of Nimrim will be
   desolate,
   For the green grass has withered
   away;
   The grass fails, there is nothing
   green.

7 Therefore the abundance they have
   gained,
   And what they have laid up,
   They will carry away to the Brook
   of the Willows.

8 For the cry has gone all around the
   borders of Moab,
   Its wailing to Eglaim
   And its wailing to Beer Elim.

9 For the waters of Dimon will be full
   of blood;
   Because I will bring more upon
   Dimon,
   Lions upon him who escapes from
   Moab,
   And on the remnant of the land."

Moab Destroyed

16 Send the lamb to the ruler of
   the land,
   From Sela to the wilderness,
   To the mount of the daughter of
   Zion.

2 For it shall be as a wandering bird
　　thrown out of the nest;
　　So shall be the daughters of Moab
　　　at the fords of the Arnon.

3 "Take counsel, execute judgment;
　　Make your shadow like the night
　　　in the middle of the day;
　　Hide the outcasts,
　　Do not betray him who escapes.
4 Let My outcasts dwell with you,
　　O Moab;
　　Be a shelter to them from the face
　　　of the spoiler.
　　For the extortioner is at an end,
　　Devastation ceases,
　　The oppressors are consumed out
　　　of the land.
5 In mercy the throne will be
　　established;
　　And One will sit on it in truth, in
　　　the tabernacle of David,
　　Judging and seeking justice and
　　　hastening righteousness."

6 We have heard of the pride of
　　Moab—
　　He is very proud—
　　Of his haughtiness and his pride
　　　and his wrath;
　　But his lies *shall* not *be* so.
7 Therefore Moab shall wail for
　　Moab;
　　Everyone shall wail.
　　For the foundations of Kir Hareseth
　　　you shall mourn;
　　Surely *they are* stricken.

8 For the fields of Heshbon languish,
　　And the vine of Sibmah;
　　The lords of the nations have
　　　broken down its choice plants,
　　Which have reached to Jazer
　　And wandered through the
　　　wilderness.
　　Her branches are stretched out,
　　They are gone over the sea.
9 Therefore I will bewail the vine of
　　Sibmah,
　　With the weeping of Jazer;
　　I will drench you with my tears,
　　O Heshbon and Elealeh;
　　For battle cries have fallen
　　Over your summer fruits and your
　　　harvest.

10 Gladness is taken away,
　　And joy from the plentiful field;

In the vineyards there will be no
　　singing,
　　Nor will there be shouting;
　　No treaders will tread out wine in
　　　the presses;
　　I have made their shouting cease.
11 Therefore my heart shall resound
　　like a harp for Moab,
　　And my inner being for Kir Heres.

12 And it shall come to pass,
　　When it is seen that Moab is weary
　　　on the high place,
　　That he will come to his sanctuary
　　　to pray;
　　But he will not prevail.
13 This *is* the word which the LORD has
spoken concerning Moab since that
time. 14 But now the LORD has spoken,
saying, "Within three years, as the
years of a hired man, the glory of Moab
will be despised with all that great multitude, and the remnant *will be* very
small *and* feeble."

Proclamation Against Syria and Israel

17 The burden against Damascus.

"Behold, Damascus will cease from
　　being a city,
　　And it will be a ruinous heap.
2 The cities of Aroer *are* forsaken;
　　They will be for flocks
　　Which lie down, and no one will
　　　make *them* afraid.
3 The fortress also will cease from
　　Ephraim,
　　The kingdom from Damascus,
　　And the remnant of Syria;
　　They will be as the glory of the
　　　children of Israel,"
　　Says the LORD of hosts.

4 "In that day it shall come to pass
　　That the glory of Jacob will wane,
　　And the fatness of his flesh grow
　　　lean.
5 It shall be as when the harvester
　　gathers the grain,
　　And reaps the heads with his arm;
　　It shall be as he who gathers heads
　　　of grain
　　In the Valley of Rephaim.
6 Yet gleaning grapes will be left
　　in it,
　　Like the shaking of an olive tree,

Two *or* three olives at the top of
   the uppermost bough,
Four *or* five in its most fruitful
   branches,"
Says the LORD God of Israel.

7 In that day a man will look to his
   Maker,
And his eyes will have respect for
   the Holy One of Israel.
8 He will not look to the altars,
The work of his hands;
He will not respect what his fingers
   have made,
Nor the wooden images[i] nor the
   incense altars.

9 In that day his strong cities will be
   as a forsaken bough
And an uppermost branch,
Which they left because of the
   children of Israel;
And there will be desolation.

10 Because you have forgotten the
   God of your salvation,
And have not been mindful of the
   Rock of your stronghold,
Therefore you will plant pleasant
   plants
And set out foreign seedlings;
11 In the day you will make your plant
   to grow,
And in the morning you will make
   your seed to flourish;
But the harvest *will be* a heap of
   ruins
In the day of grief and desperate
   sorrow.

12 Woe to the multitude of many
   people
Who make a noise like the roar of
   the seas,
And to the rushing of nations
That make a rushing like the
   rushing of mighty waters!
13 The nations will rush like the
   rushing of many waters;
But *God* will rebuke them and they
   will flee far away,
And be chased like the chaff of the
   mountains before the wind,
Like a rolling thing before the
   whirlwind.

14 Then behold, at eventide,
   trouble!
And before the morning, he *is* no
   more.
This *is* the portion of those who
   plunder us,
And the lot of those who rob us.

Proclamation Against Ethiopia

18 Woe to the land shadowed with
   buzzing wings,
Which *is* beyond the rivers of
   Ethiopia,
2 Which sends ambassadors by sea,
Even in vessels of reed on the
   waters, *saying,*
"Go, swift messengers, to a nation
   tall and smooth *of skin,*
To a people terrible from their
   beginning onward,
A nation powerful and treading
   down,
Whose land the rivers divide."

3 All inhabitants of the world and
   dwellers on the earth:
When he lifts up a banner on the
   mountains, you see *it;*
And when he blows a trumpet, you
   hear *it.*
4 For so the LORD said to me,
"I will take My rest,
And I will look from My dwelling
   place
Like clear heat in sunshine,
Like a cloud of dew in the heat of
   harvest."
5 For before the harvest, when the
   bud is perfect
And the sour grape is ripening in
   the flower,
He will both cut off the sprigs with
   pruning hooks
And take away *and* cut down the
   branches.
6 They will be left together for the
   mountain birds of prey
And for the beasts of the earth;
The birds of prey will summer on
   them,
And all the beasts of the earth will
   winter on them.

7 In that time a present will be
   brought to the LORD of hosts

---

[i] Canaanite deities

From a people tall and smooth *of
    skin,*
And from a people terrible from
    their beginning onward,
A nation powerful and treading
    down,
Whose land the rivers divide—
To the place of the name of the
    LORD of hosts,
To Mount Zion.

Proclamation Against Egypt

19 The burden against Egypt.

Behold, the LORD rides on a swift
    cloud,
And will come into Egypt;
The idols of Egypt will totter at His
    presence,
And the heart of Egypt will melt in
    its midst.

2 "I will set Egyptians against
    Egyptians;
Everyone will fight against his
    brother,
And everyone against his
    neighbor,
City against city, kingdom against
    kingdom.

3 The spirit of Egypt will fail in its
    midst;
I will destroy their counsel,
And they will consult the idols and
    the charmers,
The mediums and the sorcerers.

4 And the Egyptians I will give
Into the hand of a cruel master,
And a fierce king will rule over
    them,"
Says the Lord, the LORD of hosts.

5 The waters will fail from the sea,
And the river will be wasted and
    dried up.

6 The rivers will turn foul;
The brooks of defense will be
    emptied and dried up;
The reeds and rushes will wither.

7 The papyrus reeds by the River,*j* by
    the mouth of the River,
And everything sown by the River,
Will wither, be driven away, and be
    no more.

8 The fishermen also will mourn;

All those will lament who cast
    hooks into the River,
And they will languish who spread
    nets on the waters.

9 Moreover those who work in fine
    flax
And those who weave fine fabric
    will be ashamed;

10 And its foundations will be broken.
All who make wages *will be*
    troubled of soul.

11 Surely the princes of Zoan *are*
    fools;
Pharaoh's wise counselors give
    foolish counsel.
How do you say to Pharaoh, "I *am*
    the son of the wise,
The son of ancient kings?"

12 Where *are* they?
Where are your wise men?
Let them tell you now,
And let them know what the LORD
    of hosts has purposed against
    Egypt.

13 The princes of Zoan have become
    fools;
The princes of Noph*k* are deceived;
They have also deluded Egypt,
Those who are the mainstay of its
    tribes.

14 The LORD has mingled a perverse
    spirit in her midst;
And they have caused Egypt to err
    in all her work,
As a drunken man staggers in his
    vomit.

15 Neither will there be *any* work for
    Egypt,
Which the head or tail,
Palm branch or bulrush, may do.*l*

16In that day Egypt will be like
women, and will be afraid and fear because of the waving of the hand of the
LORD of hosts, which He waves over it.
17And the land of Judah will be a terror
to Egypt; everyone who makes mention
of it will be afraid in himself, because
of the counsel of the LORD of hosts
which He has determined against it.

Egypt, Assyria, and Israel Blessed

18In that day five cities in the land
of Egypt will speak the language of Canaan and swear by the LORD of hosts;

---

j That is, the Nile   *k* That is, ancient Memphis   *l* Compare Isaiah 9.14–16 one will be called the City of Destruction.

19In that day there will be an altar to the LORD in the midst of the land of Egypt, and a pillar to the LORD at its border. 20And it will be for a sign and for a witness to the LORD of hosts in the land of Egypt; for they will cry to the LORD because of the oppressors, and He will send them a Savior and a Mighty One, and He will deliver them. 21Then the LORD will be known to Egypt, and the Egyptians will know the LORD in that day, and will make sacrifice and offering; yes, they will make a vow to the LORD and perform *it.* 22And the LORD will strike Egypt, He will strike and heal *it;* they will return to the LORD, and He will be entreated by them and heal them.

23In that day there will be a highway from Egypt to Assyria, and the Assyrian will come into Egypt and the Egyptian into Assyria, and the Egyptians will serve with the Assyrians. 24In that day Israel will be one of three with Egypt and Assyria—a blessing in the midst of the land, 25whom the LORD of hosts shall bless, saying, "Blessed *is* Egypt My people, and Assyria the work of My hands, and Israel My inheritance."

The Sign Against Egypt and Ethiopia

20 In the year that Tartan*m* came to Ashdod, when Sargon the king of Assyria sent him, and he fought against Ashdod and took it, 2at the same time the LORD spoke by Isaiah the son of Amoz, saying, "Go, and remove the sackcloth from your body, and take your sandals off your feet." And he did so, walking naked and barefoot.

3Then the LORD said, "Just as My servant Isaiah has walked naked and barefoot three years *for* a sign and a wonder against Egypt and Ethiopia, 4so shall the king of Assyria lead away the Egyptians as prisoners and the Ethiopians as captives, young and old, naked and barefoot, with their buttocks uncovered, to the shame of Egypt. 5Then they shall be afraid and ashamed of Ethiopia their expectation and Egypt their glory. 6And the inhabitant of this

territory will say in that day, 'Surely such *is* our expectation, wherever we flee for help to be delivered from the king of Assyria; and how shall we escape?' "

The Fall of Babylon Proclaimed

21 The burden against the Wilderness of the Sea.

As whirlwinds in the South pass through,
So it comes from the desert, from a terrible land.

2 A distressing vision is declared to me;
The treacherous dealer deals treacherously,
And the plunderer plunders.
Go up, O Elam!
Besiege, O Media!
All its sighing I have made to cease.

3 Therefore my loins are filled with pain;
Pangs have taken hold of me, like the pangs of a woman in labor.
I was distressed when *I* heard *it;*
I was dismayed when *I* saw *it.*

4 My heart wavered, fearfulness frightened me;
The night for which I longed He turned into fear for me.

5 Prepare the table,
Set a watchman in the tower,
Eat and drink.
Arise, you princes,
Anoint the shield!

6 For thus has the Lord said to me:
"Go, set a watchman,
Let him declare what he sees."

7 And he saw a chariot *with* a pair of horsemen,
A chariot of donkeys, *and* a chariot of camels,
And he listened earnestly with great care.

8 Then he cried, "A lion, my Lord!
I stand continually on the watchtower in the daytime;
I have sat at my post every night.

9 And look, here comes a chariot of men *with* a pair of horsemen!"
Then he answered and said,

m Or *the Commander in Chief*

"Babylon is fallen, is fallen!
And all the carved images of her
     gods
He has broken to the ground.' "

10 Oh, my threshing and the grain of
     my floor!
That which I have heard from the
     LORD of hosts,
The God of Israel,
I have declared to you.

Proclamation Against Edom

11The burden against Dumah.
He calls to me out of Seir,
"Watchman, what of the night?
Watchman, what of the night?"
12 The watchman said,
"The morning comes, and also the
     night.
If you will inquire, inquire;
Return! Come back!"

Proclamation Against Arabia

13The burden against Arabia.
In the forest in Arabia you will
     lodge,
O you traveling companies of
     Dedanites.
14 O inhabitants of the land of Tema,
Bring water to him who is thirsty;
With their bread they met him who
     fled.
15 For they fled from the swords, from
     the drawn sword,
From the bent bow, and from the
     distress of war.

16For thus the LORD has said to me:
"Within a year, according to the year
of a hired man, all the glory of Kedar
will fail; 17and the remainder of the
number of archers, the mighty men of
the people of Kedar, will be diminished;
for the LORD God of Israel has spoken it."

Proclamation Against Jerusalem

22 The burden against the Valley of
        Vision.
What ails you now, that you have
     all gone up to the housetops,
2 You who are full of noise,
A tumultuous city, a joyous city?
Your slain men are not slain with
     the sword,
Nor dead in battle.

3 All your rulers have fled together;
They are captured by the archers.
All who are found in you are bound
     together;
They have fled from afar.
4 Therefore I said, "Look away
     from me,
I will weep bitterly;
Do not labor to comfort me
Because of the plundering of the
     daughter of my people."

5 For it is a day of trouble and
     treading down and perplexity
By the Lord GOD of hosts
In the Valley of Vision—
Breaking down the walls
And of crying to the mountain.
6 Elam bore the quiver
With chariots of men and
     horsemen,
And Kir uncovered the shield.
7 It shall come to pass that your
     choicest valleys
Shall be full of chariots,
And the horsemen shall set
     themselves in array at the gate.

8 He removed the protection of
     Judah.
You looked in that day to the armor
     of the House of the Forest;
9 You also saw the damage to the city
     of David,
That it was great;
And you gathered together the
     waters of the lower pool.
10 You numbered the houses of
     Jerusalem,
And the houses you broke down
To fortify the wall.
11 You also made a reservoir between
     the two walls
For the water of the old pool.
But you did not look to its Maker,
Nor did you have respect for Him
     who fashioned it long ago.

12 And in that day the Lord GOD of
     hosts
Called for weeping and for
     mourning,
For baldness and for girding with
     sackcloth.
13 But instead, joy and gladness,
Slaying oxen and killing sheep,
Eating meat and drinking wine:

"Let us eat and drink, for tomorrow
we die!"

14 Then it was revealed in my hearing
by the LORD of hosts,
"Surely for this iniquity there will be
no atonement for you,
Even to your death," says the Lord
GOD of hosts.

The Judgment on Shebna

15Thus says the Lord GOD of hosts:
"Go, proceed to this steward,
To Shebna, who is over the house,
and say:

16 'What have you here, and whom
have you here,
That you have hewn a sepulcher
here,
As he who hews himself a
sepulcher on high,
Who carves a tomb for himself in
a rock?

17 Indeed, the LORD will throw you
away violently,
O mighty man,
And will surely seize you.

18 He will surely turn violently and
toss you like a ball
Into a large country;
There you shall die, and there your
glorious chariots
Shall be the shame of your master's
house.

19 So I will drive you out of your
office,
And from your position he will pull
you down.

20 'Then it shall be in that day,
That I will call My servant Eliakim
the son of Hilkiah;

21 I will clothe him with your robe
And strengthen him with your belt;
I will commit your responsibility
into his hand.
He shall be a father to the
inhabitants of Jerusalem
And to the house of Judah.

22 The key of the house of David
I will lay on his shoulder;
So he shall open, and no one shall
shut;
And he shall shut, and no one shall
open.

23 I will fasten him as a peg in a secure
place,
And he will become a glorious
throne to his father's house.

24'They will hang on him all the glory
of his father's house, the offspring and
the posterity, all vessels of small quantity, from the cups to all the pitchers.
25In that day,' says the LORD of hosts,
'the peg that is fastened in the secure
place will be removed and be cut down
and fall, and the burden that was on
it will be cut off; for the LORD has
spoken.' "

Proclamation Against Tyre

23 The burden against Tyre.

Wail, you ships of Tarshish!
For it is laid waste,
So that there is no house, no
harbor;
From the land of Cyprus[n] it is
revealed to them.

2 Be still, you inhabitants of the
coastland,
You merchants of Sidon,
Whom those who cross the sea
have filled.

3 And on great waters the grain of
Shihor,
The harvest of the River,[o] is her
revenue;
And she is a marketplace for the
nations.

4 Be ashamed, O Sidon;
For the sea has spoken,
The strength of the sea, saying,
"I do not labor, nor bring forth
children;
Neither do I rear young men,
Nor bring up virgins."

5 When the report reaches Egypt,
They also will be in agony at the
report of Tyre.

6 Cross over to Tarshish;
Wail, you inhabitants of the
coastland!

7 Is this your joyous city,
Whose antiquity is from ancient
days,

---

n Western lands, especially Cyprus   o That is, the Nile

Whose feet carried her far off to
   dwell?
8 Who has taken this counsel against
   Tyre, the crowning *city*,
   Whose merchants *are* princes,
   Whose traders *are* the honorable of
   the earth?
9 The LORD of hosts has purposed it,
   To bring to dishonor the pride of
   all glory,
   To bring into contempt all the
   honorable of the earth.

10 Overflow through your land like
   the River,[o]
   O daughter of Tarshish;
   There is no more strength.
11 He stretched out His hand over
   the sea,
   He shook the kingdoms;
   The LORD has given a
   commandment against Canaan
   To destroy its strongholds.
12 And He said, "You will rejoice no
   more,
   O you oppressed virgin daughter of
   Sidon.
   Arise, cross over to Cyprus;
   There also you will have no rest."

13 Behold, the land of the Chaldeans,
   This people *which* was not;
   Assyria founded it for wild beasts
   of the desert.
   They set up its towers,
   They raised up its palaces,
   And brought it to ruin.

14 Wail, you ships of Tarshish!
   For your strength is laid waste.
15Now it shall come to pass in that
day that Tyre will be forgotten seventy
years, according to the days of one
king. At the end of seventy years it will
happen to Tyre as *in* the song of the
harlot:
16 "Take a harp, go about the city,
   You forgotten harlot;
   Make sweet melody, sing many
   songs,
   That you may be remembered."
17And it shall be, at the end of seventy
years, that the LORD will deal with Tyre.
She will return to her hire, and commit
fornication with all the kingdoms of the

world on the face of the earth. 18Her
gain and her pay will be set apart for
the LORD; it will not be treasured nor
laid up, for her gain will be for those
who dwell before the LORD, to eat suffi-
ciently, and for fine clothing.

Impending Judgment on the Earth

24 Behold, the LORD makes the
   earth empty and makes it
   waste,
   Distorts its surface
   And scatters abroad its inhabitants.
2 And it shall be:
   As with the people, so with the
   priest;
   As with the servant, so with his
   master;
   As with the maid, so with her
   mistress;
   As with the buyer, so with the
   seller;
   As with the lender, so with the
   borrower;
   As with the creditor, so with the
   debtor.
3 The land shall be entirely emptied
   and utterly plundered,
   For the LORD has spoken this word.

4 The earth mourns *and* fades away,
   The world languishes *and* fades
   away;
   The haughty people of the earth
   languish.
5 The earth is also defiled under its
   inhabitants,
   Because they have transgressed the
   laws,
   Changed the ordinance,
   Broken the everlasting covenant.
6 Therefore the curse has devoured
   the earth,
   And those who dwell in it are
   desolate.
   Therefore the inhabitants of the
   earth are burned,
   And few men *are* left.

7 The new wine fails, the vine
   languishes,
   All the merry-hearted sigh.
8 The mirth of the tambourine
   ceases,
   The noise of the jubilant ends,

[o]That is, the Nile

The joy of the harp ceases.
9 They shall not drink wine with a
  song;
  Strong drink is bitter to those who
  drink it.
10 The city of confusion is broken
   down;
   Every house is shut up, so that none
   may go in.
11 *There is* a cry for wine in the
   streets,
   All joy is darkened,
   The mirth of the land is gone.
12 In the city desolation is left,
   And the gate is stricken with
   destruction.
13 When it shall be thus in the midst
   of the land among the people,
   It shall be like the shaking of an
   olive tree,
   Like the gleaning of grapes when
   the vintage is done.

14 They shall lift up their voice, they
   shall sing;
   For the majesty of the LORD
   They shall cry aloud from the sea.
15 Therefore glorify the LORD in the
   dawning light,
   The name of the LORD God of
   Israel in the coastlands of the sea.
16 From the ends of the earth we have
   heard songs:
   "Glory to the righteous!"
   But I said, "I am ruined, ruined!
   Woe to me!
   The treacherous dealers have dealt
   treacherously,
   Indeed, the treacherous dealers
   have dealt very
   treacherously."

17 Fear and the pit and the snare
   Are upon you, O inhabitant of the
   earth.
18 And it shall be
   That he who flees from the noise
   of the fear
   Shall fall into the pit,
   And he who comes up from the
   midst of the pit
   Shall be caught in the snare;
   For the windows from on high are
   open,
   And the foundations of the earth
   are shaken.

19 The earth is violently broken,
   The earth is split open,
   The earth is shaken exceedingly.
20 The earth shall reel to and fro like
   a drunkard,
   And shall totter like a hut;
   Its transgression shall be heavy
   upon it,
   And it will fall, and not rise again.

21 It shall come to pass in that day
   That the LORD will punish on high
   the host of exalted ones,
   And on the earth the kings of the
   earth.
22 They will be gathered together,
   As prisoners are gathered in the
   pit,
   And will be shut up in the prison;
   After many days they will be
   punished.
23 Then the moon will be disgraced
   And the sun ashamed;
   For the LORD of hosts will reign
   On Mount Zion and in Jerusalem
   And before His elders, gloriously.

Praise to God

25 O LORD, You *are* my God.
   I will exalt You,
   I will praise Your name,
   For You have done wonderful
   things;
   Your counsels of old *are*
   faithfulness *and* truth.
2 For You have made a city a ruin,
  A fortified city a ruin,
  A palace of foreigners to be a city
  no more;
  It will never be rebuilt.
3 Therefore the strong people will
  glorify You;
  The city of the terrible nations will
  fear You.
4 For You have been a strength to the
  poor,
  A strength to the needy in his
  distress,
  A refuge from the storm,
  A shade from the heat;
  For the blast of the terrible ones *is*
  as a storm *against* the wall.
5 You will reduce the noise of aliens,
  As heat in a dry place;
  As heat in the shadow of a cloud,
  The song of the terrible ones will
  be diminished.

6 And in this mountain
The LORD of hosts will make for all
    people
A feast of choice pieces,
A feast of wines on the lees,
Of fat things full of marrow,
Of well-refined wines on the lees.
7 And He will destroy on this
    mountain
The surface of the covering cast
    over all people,
And the veil that is spread over all
    nations.
8 He will swallow up death forever,
And the Lord GOD will wipe away
    tears from all faces;
The rebuke of His people
He will take away from all the
    earth;
For the LORD has spoken.

9 And it will be said in that day:
"Behold, this *is* our God;
We have waited for Him, and He
    will save us.
This *is* the LORD;
We have waited for Him;
We will be glad and rejoice in His
    salvation."

10 For on this mountain the hand of
    the LORD will rest,
And Moab shall be trampled down
    under Him,
As straw is trampled down for the
    refuse heap.
11 And He will spread out His hands
    in their midst
As a swimmer reaches out to swim,
And He will bring down their
    pride
Together with the trickery of their
    hands.
12 The fortress of the high fort of your
    walls
He will bring down, lay low,
And bring to the ground, down to
    the dust.

A Song of Salvation

26 In that day this song will be sung
in the land of Judah:
"We have a strong city;
God will appoint salvation *for* walls
    and bulwarks.
2 Open the gates,
That the righteous nation which
    keeps the truth may enter in.
3 You will keep *him* in perfect peace,
Whose mind *is* stayed *on You,*
Because he trusts in You.
4 Trust in the LORD forever,
For in Yah, the LORD, *is* everlasting
    strength.
5 For He brings down those who
    dwell on high,
The lofty city;
He lays it low,
He lays it low to the ground,
He brings it down to the dust.
6 The foot shall tread it down—
The feet of the poor
And the steps of the needy."

7 The way of the just *is* uprightness;
O Most Upright,
You weigh the path of the just.
8 Yes, in the way of Your judgments,
O LORD, we have waited for You;
The desire of *our* soul *is* for Your
    name
And for the remembrance of You.
9 With my soul I have desired You
    in the night,
Yes, by my spirit within me I will
    seek You early;
For when Your judgments *are* in
    the earth,
The inhabitants of the world will
    learn righteousness.

10 Let grace be shown to the wicked,
Yet he will not learn righteousness;
In the land of uprightness he will
    deal unjustly,
And will not behold the majesty of
    the LORD.
11 LORD, *when* Your hand is lifted up,
    they will not see.
But they will see and be ashamed
For *their* envy of people;
Yes, the fire of Your enemies shall
    devour them.

12 LORD, You will establish peace
    for us,
For You have also done all our
    works in us.
13 O LORD our God, masters
    besides You
Have had dominion over us;
But by You only we make mention
    of Your name.

14 *They are* dead, they will not live;
   They are deceased, they will not
     rise.
   Therefore You have punished and
     destroyed them,
   And made all their memory to
     perish.
15 You have increased the nation,
     O LORD,
   You have increased the nation;
   You are glorified;
   You have expanded all the borders
     of the land.

16 LORD, in trouble they have
     visited You,
   They poured out a prayer *when*
     Your chastening *was* upon
     them.
17 As a woman with child
   Is in pain and cries out in her
     pangs,
   When she draws near the time of
     her delivery,
   So have we been in Your sight,
     O LORD.
18 We have been with child, we have
     been in pain;
   We have, as it were, brought forth
     wind;
   We have not accomplished any
     deliverance in the earth,
   Nor have the inhabitants of the
     world fallen.

19 Your dead shall live;
   Together with my dead body they
     shall arise.
   Awake and sing, you who dwell in
     dust;
   For your dew *is like* the dew of
     herbs,
   And the earth shall cast out the
     dead.

Take Refuge from the Coming Judgment

20 Come, my people, enter your
     chambers,
   And shut your doors behind you;
   Hide yourself, as it were, for a little
     moment,
   Until the indignation is past.
21 For behold, the LORD comes out of
     His place

To punish the inhabitants of the
     earth for their iniquity;
   The earth will also disclose her
     blood,
   And will no more cover her slain.

27 In that day the LORD with His
     severe sword, great and strong,
   Will punish Leviathan the fleeing
     serpent,
   Leviathan that twisted serpent;
   And He will slay the reptile that *is*
     in the sea.

The Restoration of Israel

2 In that day sing to her,
   "A vineyard of red wine!
3 I, the LORD, keep it,
   I water it every moment;
   Lest any hurt it,
   I keep it night and day.
4 Fury *is* not in Me.
   Who would set briers *and* thorns
   Against Me in battle?
   I would go through them,
   I would burn them together.
5 Or let him take hold of My strength,
   That he may make peace with Me;
   And he shall make peace with Me."

6 Those who come He shall cause to
     take root in Jacob;
   Israel shall blossom and bud,
   And fill the face of the world with
     fruit.

7 Has He struck Israel as He struck
     those who struck him?
   Or has He been slain according to
     the slaughter of those who were
     slain by Him?
8 In measure, by sending it away,
   You contended with it.
   He removes *it* by His rough wind
   In the day of the east wind.
9 Therefore by this the iniquity of
     Jacob will be covered;
   And this *is* all the fruit of taking
     away his sin:
   When he makes all the stones of
     the altar
   Like chalkstones that are beaten to
     dust,
   Wooden images[p] and incense
     altars shall not stand.

p Canaanite deities

10 Yet the fortified city *will be*
desolate,
The habitation forsaken and left
like a wilderness;
There the calf will feed, and there
it will lie down
And consume its branches.
11 When its boughs are withered, they
will be broken off;
The women come *and* set them on
fire.
For it *is* a people of no
understanding;
Therefore He who made them will
not have mercy on them,
And He who formed them will
show them no favor.

12 And it shall come to pass in
that day
That the LORD will thresh,
From the channel of the River^q to
the Brook of Egypt;
And you will be gathered one
by one,
O you children of Israel.

13 So it shall be in that day:
The great trumpet will be blown;
They will come, who are about to
perish in the land of Assyria,
And they who are outcasts in the
land of Egypt,
And shall worship the LORD in the
holy mount at Jerusalem.

Woe to Ephraim and Jerusalem

28 Woe to the crown of pride, to the
drunkards of Ephraim,
Whose glorious beauty *is* a fading
flower
Which *is* at the head of the verdant
valleys,
To those who are overcome with
wine!
2 Behold, the Lord has a mighty and
strong one,
Like a tempest of hail and a
destroying storm,
Like a flood of mighty waters
overflowing,
Who will bring *them* down to the
earth with *His* hand.
3 The crown of pride, the drunkards
of Ephraim,

Will be trampled underfoot;
4 And the glorious beauty is a fading
flower
Which *is* at the head of the verdant
valley,
Like the first fruit before the
summer,
Which an observer sees;
He eats it up while it is still in his
hand.

5 In that day the LORD of hosts
will be
For a crown of glory and a diadem
of beauty
To the remnant of His people,
6 For a spirit of justice to him who
sits in judgment,
And for strength to those who turn
back the battle at the gate.

7 But they also have erred through
wine,
And through intoxicating drink are
out of the way;
The priest and the prophet have
erred through intoxicating drink,
They are swallowed up by wine,
They are out of the way through
intoxicating drink;
They err in vision, they stumble *in*
judgment.
8 For all tables are full of vomit *and*
filth;
No place *is* clean.

9 "Whom will he teach knowledge?
And whom will he make to
understand the message?
Those *just* weaned from milk?
Those *just* drawn from the breasts?
10 For precept *must be* upon precept,
precept upon precept,
Line upon line, line upon line,
Here a little, there a little."

11 For with stammering lips and
another tongue
He will speak to this people,
12 To whom He said, "This *is* the rest
with which
You may cause the weary to rest,"
And, "This *is* the refreshing";
Yet they would not hear.

^q That is, the Euphrates

13 But the word of the LORD was to
    them,
      "Precept upon precept, precept upon
        precept,
      Line upon line, line upon line,
      Here a little, there a little,"
      That they might go and fall
        backward, and be broken
      And snared and caught.

14 Therefore hear the word of the
      LORD, you scornful men,
      Who rule this people who *are* in
        Jerusalem,
15 Because you have said, "We have
      made a covenant with death,
      And with Sheol we are in
        agreement.
      When the overflowing scourge
        passes through,
      It will not come to us,
      For we have made lies our refuge,
      And under falsehood we have
        hidden ourselves."

A Cornerstone in Zion

16 Therefore thus says the Lord GOD:
      "Behold, I lay in Zion a stone for a
        foundation,
      A tried stone, a precious
        cornerstone, a sure foundation;
      Whoever believes will not act
        hastily.
17 Also I will make justice the
      measuring line,
      And righteousness the plummet;
      The hail will sweep away the refuge
        of lies,
      And the waters will overflow the
        hiding place.
18 Your covenant with death will be
      annulled,
      And your agreement with Sheol
        will not stand;
      When the overflowing scourge
        passes through,
      Then you will be trampled down
        by it.
19 As often as it goes out it will
        take you;
      For morning by morning it will pass
        over,
      And by day and by night;
      It will be a terror just to understand
        the report."

20 For the bed is too short to stretch
        out *on,*
      And the covering so narrow that
        one cannot wrap himself *in it.*
21 For the LORD will rise up as *at*
      Mount Perazim,
      He will be angry as in the Valley
        of Gibeon—
      That He may do His work, His
        awesome work,
      And bring to pass His act, His
        unusual act.
22 Now therefore, do not be mockers,
      Lest your bonds be made strong;
      For I have heard from the Lord GOD
        of hosts,
      A destruction determined even
        upon the whole earth.

Listen to the Teaching of God

23 Give ear and hear my voice,
      Listen and hear my speech.
24 Does the plowman keep plowing all
        day to sow?
      Does he keep turning his soil and
        breaking the clods?
25 When he has leveled its surface,
      Does he not sow the black cummin
      And scatter the cummin,
      Plant the wheat in rows,
      The barley in the appointed place,
      And the spelt in its place?
26 For He instructs him in right
        judgment,
      His God teaches him.

27 For the black cummin is not
        threshed with a threshing sledge,
      Nor is a cartwheel rolled over the
        cummin;
      But the black cummin is beaten out
        with a stick,
      And the cummin with a rod.
28 Bread *flour* must be ground;
      Therefore he does not thresh it
        forever,
      Break *it with* his cartwheel,
      Or crush it *with* his horsemen.
29 This also comes from the LORD of
        hosts,
      Who is wonderful in counsel *and*
        excellent in guidance.

Woe to Jerusalem

29 "Woe to Ariel,[r] to Ariel, the city
        where David dwelt!

---

r That is, Jerusalem

Add year to year;
Let feasts come around.
2 Yet I will distress Ariel;
There shall be heaviness and
sorrow,
And it shall be to Me as Ariel.
3 I will encamp against you all
around,
I will lay siege against you with a
mound,
And I will raise siegeworks
against you.
4 You shall be brought down,
You shall speak out of the
ground;
Your speech shall be low, out of the
dust;
Your voice shall be like a
medium's, out of the ground;
And your speech shall whisper out
of the dust.

5 "Moreover the multitude of your
foes
Shall be like fine dust,
And the multitude of the terrible
ones
Like chaff that passes away;
Yes, it shall be in an instant,
suddenly.
6 You will be punished by the LORD
of hosts
With thunder and earthquake and
great noise,
With storm and tempest
And the flame of devouring fire.
7 The multitude of all the nations
who fight against Ariel,
Even all who fight against her and
her fortress,
And distress her,
Shall be as a dream of a night
vision.
8 It shall even be as when a hungry
man dreams,
And look—he eats;
But he awakes, and his soul is still
empty;
Or as when a thirsty man
dreams,
And look—he drinks;
But he awakes, and indeed *he is*
faint,
And his soul still craves:
So the multitude of all the nations
shall be,
Who fight against Mount Zion."

The Blindness of Disobedience

9 Pause and wonder!
Blind yourselves and be blind!
They are drunk, but not with
wine;
They stagger, but not with
intoxicating drink.
10 For the LORD has poured out on you
The spirit of deep sleep,
And has closed your eyes, namely,
the prophets;
And He has covered your heads,
namely, the seers.
11The whole vision has become to
you like the words of a book that is
sealed, which *men* deliver to one who
is literate, saying, "Read this, please."
And he says, "I cannot, for it *is*
sealed."
12Then the book is delivered to one
who is illiterate, saying, "Read this,
please."
And he says, "I am not literate."
13Therefore the Lord said:
"Inasmuch as these people draw
near with their mouths
And honor Me with their lips,
But have removed their hearts far
from Me,
And their fear toward Me is taught
by the commandment of men,
14 Therefore, behold, I will again do
a marvelous work
Among this people,
A marvelous work and a wonder;
For the wisdom of their wise *men*
shall perish,
And the understanding of their
prudent *men* shall be hidden."

15 Woe to those who seek deep to
hide their counsel far from the
LORD,
And their works are in the dark;
They say, "Who sees us?" and,
"Who knows us?"
16 Surely you have things turned
around!
Shall the potter be esteemed as the
clay;
For shall the thing made say of him
who made it,
"He did not make me"?
Or shall the thing formed say of
him who formed it,
"He has no understanding"?

Future Recovery of Wisdom

17 *Is* it not yet a very little while
    Till Lebanon shall be turned into a
    fruitful field,
    And the fruitful field be esteemed
    as a forest?
18 In that day the deaf shall hear the
    words of the book,
    And the eyes of the blind shall see
    out of obscurity and out of
    darkness.
19 The humble also shall increase
    their joy in the LORD,
    And the poor among men shall
    rejoice
    In the Holy One of Israel.
20 For the terrible one is brought to
    nothing,
    The scornful one is consumed,
    And all who watch for iniquity are
    cut off—
21 Who make a man an offender by a
    word,
    And lay a snare for him who
    reproves in the gate,
    And turn aside the just by empty
    words.
22 Therefore thus says the LORD, who
redeemed Abraham, concerning the
house of Jacob:
    "Jacob shall not now be ashamed,
    Nor shall his face now grow pale;
23 But when he sees his children,
    The work of My hands, in his
    midst,
    They will hallow My name,
    And hallow the Holy One of Jacob,
    And fear the God of Israel.
24 These also who erred in spirit will
    come to understanding,
    And those who complained will
    learn doctrine."

Futile Confidence in Egypt

30 "Woe to the rebellious children,"
        says the LORD,
    "Who take counsel, but not of Me,
    And who devise plans, but not of
    My Spirit,
    That they may add sin to sin;
2   Who walk to go down to Egypt,
    And have not asked My advice,
    To strengthen themselves in the
    strength of Pharaoh,
    And to trust in the shadow of
    Egypt!
3   Therefore the strength of Pharaoh
    Shall be your shame,
    And trust in the shadow of Egypt
    Shall be *your* humiliation.
4   For his princes were at Zoan,
    And his ambassadors came to
    Hanes.
5   They were all ashamed of a people
    who could not benefit them,
    Or be help or benefit,
    But a shame and also a reproach."
6 The burden against the beasts of the
South.
    Through a land of trouble and
    anguish,
    From which *came* the lioness and
    lion,
    The viper and fiery flying serpent,
    They will carry their riches on the
    backs of young donkeys,
    And their treasures on the humps
    of camels,
    To a people *who* shall not profit;
7   For the Egyptians shall help in vain
    and to no purpose.
    Therefore I have called her
    Rahab-Hem-Shebeth.^{s}

A Rebellious People

8   Now go, write it before them on a
    tablet,
    And note it on a scroll,
    That it may be for time to come,
    Forever and ever:
9   That this *is* a rebellious people,
    Lying children,
    Children *who* will not hear the law
    of the LORD;
10 Who say to the seers, "Do not see,"
    And to the prophets, "Do not
    prophesy to us right things;
    Speak to us smooth things,
    prophesy deceits.
11 Get out of the way,
    Turn aside from the path,
    Cause the Holy One of Israel
    To cease from before us."
12 Therefore thus says the Holy One
of Israel:
    "Because you despise this word,
    And trust in oppression and
    perversity,
    And rely on them,

^{s} Literally *Rahab Sits Idle*

13 Therefore this iniquity shall be
        to you
    Like a breach ready to fall,
    A bulge in a high wall,
    Whose breaking comes suddenly,
        in an instant.
14 And He shall break it like the
        breaking of the potter's vessel,
    Which is broken in pieces;
    He shall not spare.
    So there shall not be found among
        its fragments
    A shard to take fire from the
        hearth,
    Or to take water from the cistern."
15 For thus says the Lord GOD, the
Holy One of Israel:
    "In returning and rest you shall be
        saved;
    In quietness and confidence shall
        be your strength."
    But you would not,
16 And you said, "No, for we will flee
        on horses"—
    Therefore you shall flee!
    And, "We will ride on swift
        horses"—
    Therefore those who pursue you
        shall be swift!

17 One thousand *shall flee* at the
        threat of one,
    At the threat of five you shall flee,
    Till you are left as a pole on top of
        a mountain
    And as a banner on a hill.

God Will Be Gracious

18 Therefore the LORD will wait, that
        He may be gracious to you;
    And therefore He will be exalted,
        that He may have mercy on you.
    For the LORD *is* a God of justice;
    Blessed *are* all those who wait
        for Him.

19 For the people shall dwell in Zion
        at Jerusalem;
    You shall weep no more.
    He will be very gracious to you at
        the sound of your cry;
    When He hears it, He will
        answer you.
20 And *though* the Lord gives you
    The bread of adversity and the
        water of affliction,

Yet your teachers will not be
        moved into a corner anymore,
    But your eyes shall see your
        teachers.
21 Your ears shall hear a word behind
        you, saying,
    "This *is* the way, walk in it,"
    Whenever you turn to the right
        hand
    Or whenever you turn to the left.
22 You will also defile the covering of
        your images of silver,
    And the ornament of your molded
        images of gold.
    You will throw them away as an
        unclean thing;
    You will say to them, "Get away!"

23 Then He will give the rain for your
        seed
    With which you sow the ground,
    And bread of the increase of the
        earth;
    It will be fat and plentiful.
    In that day your cattle will feed
    In large pastures.
24 Likewise the oxen and the young
        donkeys that work the ground
    Will eat cured fodder,
    Which has been winnowed with the
        shovel and fan.
25 There will be on every high
        mountain
    And on every high hill
    Rivers *and* streams of waters,
    In the day of the great slaughter,
    When the towers fall.
26 Moreover the light of the moon will
        be as the light of the sun,
    And the light of the sun will be
        sevenfold,
    As the light of seven days,
    In the day that the LORD binds up
        the bruise of His people
    And heals the stroke of their
        wound.

Judgment on Assyria

27 Behold, the name of the LORD
        comes from afar,
    Burning *with* His anger,
    And *His* burden *is* heavy;
    His lips are full of indignation,
    And His tongue like a devouring
        fire.
28 His breath is like an overflowing
        stream,

Which reaches up to the neck,
To sift the nations with the sieve
    of futility;
And *there shall be* a bridle in the
    jaws of the people,
Causing *them* to err.

29 You shall have a song
    As in the night *when* a holy festival
        is kept,
    And gladness of heart as when one
        goes with a flute,
    To come into the mountain of the
        LORD,
    To the Mighty One of Israel.
30 The LORD will cause His glorious
        voice to be heard,
    And show the descent of His arm,
    With the indignation of *His* anger
    And the flame of a devouring fire,
    With scattering, tempest, and
        hailstones.
31 For through the voice of the LORD
    Assyria will be beaten down,
    As He strikes with the rod.
32 And *in* every place where the staff
        of punishment passes,
    Which the LORD lays on him,
    It will be with tambourines and
        harps;
    And in battles of brandishing He
        will fight with it.
33 For Tophet *was* established of old,
    Yes, for the king it is prepared.
    He has made *it* deep and large;
    Its pyre *is* fire with much wood;
    The breath of the LORD, like a
        stream of brimstone,
    Kindles it.

The Folly of Not Trusting God

31 Woe to those who go down to
        Egypt for help,
And rely on horses,
Who trust in chariots because *they
    are* many,
And in horsemen because they are
    very strong,
But who do not look to the Holy
    One of Israel,
Nor seek the LORD!
2   Yet He also *is* wise and will bring
        disaster,
    And will not call back His words,
    But will arise against the house of
        evildoers,

And against the help of those who
    work iniquity.
3   Now the Egyptians *are* men, and
        not God;
    And their horses are flesh, and not
        spirit.
    When the LORD stretches out His
        hand,
    Both he who helps will fall,
    And he who is helped will fall
        down;
    They all will perish together.

God Will Deliver Jerusalem

4For thus the LORD has spoken to me:
    "As a lion roars,
    And a young lion over his prey
    (When a multitude of shepherds is
        summoned against him,
    He will not be afraid of their voice
    Nor be disturbed by their noise),
    So the LORD of hosts will come
        down
    To fight for Mount Zion and for its
        hill.
5   Like birds flying about,
    So will the LORD of hosts defend
        Jerusalem.
    Defending, He will also deliver *it;*
    Passing over, He will preserve *it.*"
6Return *to Him* against whom the
children of Israel have deeply revolted.
7For in that day every man shall throw
away his idols of silver and his idols
of gold—sin, which your own hands
have made for yourselves.
8   "Then Assyria shall fall by a sword
        not of man,
    And a sword not of mankind shall
        devour him.
    But he shall flee from the sword,
    And his young men shall become
        forced labor.
9   He shall cross over to his
        stronghold for fear,
    And his princes shall be afraid of
        the banner,"
    Says the LORD,
    Whose fire *is* in Zion
    And whose furnace *is* in Jerusalem.

A Reign of Righteousness

32 Behold, a king will reign in
        righteousness,
    And princes will rule with justice.
2   A man will be as a hiding place
        from the wind,

And a cover from the tempest,
As rivers of water in a dry place,
As the shadow of a great rock in a
    weary land.
3 The eyes of those who see will not
    be dim,
And the ears of those who hear will
    listen.
4 Also the heart of the rash will
    understand knowledge,
And the tongue of the stammerers
    will be ready to speak plainly.

5 The foolish person will no longer
    be called generous,
Nor the miser said *to be* bountiful;
6 For the foolish person will speak
    foolishness,
And his heart will work iniquity:
To practice ungodliness,
To utter error against the LORD,
To keep the hungry unsatisfied,
And he will cause the drink of the
    thirsty to fail.
7 Also the schemes of the schemer
    are evil;
He devises wicked plans
To destroy the poor with lying
    words,
Even when the needy speaks
    justice.
8 But a generous man devises
    generous things,
And by generosity he shall stand.

Consequences of Complacency

9 Rise up, you women who are at
    ease,
Hear my voice;
You complacent daughters,
Give ear to my speech.
10 In a year and *some* days
You will be troubled, you
    complacent women;
For the vintage will fail,
The gathering will not come.
11 Tremble, you *women* who are at
    ease;
Be troubled, you complacent ones;
Strip yourselves, make yourselves
    bare,
And gird *sackcloth* on *your* waists.

12 People shall mourn upon their
    breasts
For the pleasant fields, for the
    fruitful vine.

13 On the land of my people will come
    up thorns *and* briers,
Yes, on all the happy homes *in* the
    joyous city;
14 Because the palaces will be
    forsaken,
The bustling city will be deserted.
The forts and towers will become
    lairs forever,
A joy of wild donkeys, a pasture
    of flocks—
15 Until the Spirit is poured upon us
    from on high,
And the wilderness becomes a
    fruitful field,
And the fruitful field is counted as
    a forest.

The Peace of God's Reign

16 Then justice will dwell in the
    wilderness,
And righteousness remain in the
    fruitful field.
17 The work of righteousness will be
    peace,
And the effect of righteousness,
    quietness and assurance forever.
18 My people will dwell in a peaceful
    habitation,
In secure dwellings, and in quiet
    resting places,
19 Though hail comes down on the
    forest,
And the city is brought low in
    humiliation.

20 Blessed *are* you who sow beside all
    waters,
Who send out freely the feet of the
    ox and the donkey.

A Prayer in Deep Distress

33 Woe to you who plunder, though
    you *have* not *been* plundered;
And you who deal treacherously,
    though they have not dealt
    treacherously with you!
When you cease plundering,
You will be plundered;
When you make an end of dealing
    treacherously,
They will deal treacherously
    with you.

2 O LORD, be gracious to us;
We have waited for You.
Be their arm every morning,

Our salvation also in the time of
    trouble.
3 At the noise of the tumult the
    people shall flee;
When You lift Yourself up, the
    nations shall be scattered;
4 And Your plunder shall be
    gathered
Like the gathering of the
    caterpillar;
As the running to and fro of locusts,
He shall run upon them.

5 The Lord is exalted, for He dwells
    on high;
He has filled Zion with justice and
    righteousness.
6 Wisdom and knowledge will be the
    stability of your times,
And the strength of salvation;
The fear of the Lord *is* His treasure.

7 Surely their valiant ones shall cry
    outside,
The ambassadors of peace shall
    weep bitterly.
8 The highways lie waste,
The traveling man ceases.
He has broken the covenant,
He has despised the cities,
He regards no man.
9 The earth mourns *and* languishes,
Lebanon is shamed *and* shriveled;
Sharon is like a wilderness,
And Bashan and Carmel shake off
    their fruits.

Impending Judgment on Zion

10 "Now I will rise," says the Lord;
"Now I will be exalted,
Now I will lift Myself up.
11 You shall conceive chaff,
You shall bring forth stubble;
Your breath, *as* fire, shall
    devour you.
12 And the people shall be *like* the
    burnings of lime;
Like thorns cut up they shall be
    burned in the fire.
13 Hear, you *who are* afar off, what I
    have done;
And you *who are* near,
    acknowledge My might."

14 The sinners in Zion are afraid;
Fearfulness has seized the
    hypocrites:

"Who among us shall dwell with the
    devouring fire?
Who among us shall dwell with
    everlasting burnings?"
15 He who walks righteously and
    speaks uprightly,
He who despises the gain of
    oppressions,
Who gestures with his hands,
    refusing bribes,
Who stops his ears from hearing of
    bloodshed,
And shuts his eyes from seeing evil:
16 He will dwell on high;
His place of defense *will be* the
    fortress of rocks;
Bread will be given him,
His water *will be* sure.

The Land of the Majestic King

17 Your eyes will see the King in His
    beauty;
They will see the land that is very
    far off.
18 Your heart will meditate on terror:
"Where *is* the scribe?
Where *is* he who weighs?
Where *is* he who counts the
    towers?"
19 You will not see a fierce people,
A people of obscure speech, beyond
    perception,
Of a stammering tongue *that you*
    cannot understand.

20 Look upon Zion, the city of our
    appointed feasts;
Your eyes will see Jerusalem, a
    quiet home,
A tabernacle *that* will not be taken
    down;
Not one of its stakes will ever be
    removed,
Nor will any of its cords be
    broken.
21 But there the majestic Lord *will be*
    for us
A place of broad rivers *and*
    streams,
In which no galley with oars will
    sail,
Nor majestic ships pass by
22 (For the Lord *is* our Judge,
The Lord *is* our Lawgiver,
The Lord *is* our King;
He will save us);
23 Your tackle is loosed,

They could not strengthen their
mast,
They could not spread the sail.

Then the prey of great plunder is
divided;
The lame take the prey.
24 And the inhabitant will not say, "I
am sick";
The people who dwell in it *will be*
forgiven *their* iniquity.

Judgment on the Nations

34 Come near, you nations, to hear;
And heed, you people!
Let the earth hear, and all that is
in it,
The world and all things that come
forth from it.
2 For the indignation of the LORD *is*
against all nations,
And *His* fury against all their
armies;
He has utterly destroyed them,
He has given them over to the
slaughter.
3 Also their slain shall be thrown out;
Their stench shall rise from their
corpses,
And the mountains shall be melted
with their blood.
4 All the host of heaven shall be
dissolved,
And the heavens shall be rolled up
like a scroll;
All their host shall fall down
As the leaf falls from the vine,
And as *fruit* falling from a fig tree.

5 "For My sword shall be bathed in
heaven;
Indeed it shall come down on
Edom,
And on the people of My curse, for
judgment.
6 The sword of the LORD is filled with
blood,
It is made overflowing with fatness,
With the blood of lambs and goats,
With the fat of the kidneys of rams.
For the LORD has a sacrifice in
Bozrah,
And a great slaughter in the land
of Edom.
7 The wild oxen shall come down
with them,

And the young bulls with the
mighty bulls;
Their land shall be soaked with
blood,
And their dust saturated with
fatness."

8 For *it is* the day of the LORD's
vengeance,
The year of recompense for the
cause of Zion.
9 Its streams shall be turned into
pitch,
And its dust into brimstone;
Its land shall become burning pitch.
10 It shall not be quenched night
or day;
Its smoke shall ascend forever.
From generation to generation it
shall lie waste;
No one shall pass through it forever
and ever.
11 But the pelican and the porcupine
shall possess it,
Also the owl and the raven shall
dwell in it.
And He shall stretch out over it
The line of confusion and the
stones of emptiness.
12 They shall call its nobles to the
kingdom,
But none *shall be* there, and all its
princes shall be nothing.

13 And thorns shall come up in its
palaces,
Nettles and brambles in its
fortresses;
It shall be a habitation of jackals,
A courtyard for ostriches.
14 The wild beasts of the desert shall
also meet with the jackals,
And the wild goat shall bleat to its
companion;
Also the night creature shall rest
there,
And find for herself a place of rest.
15 There the arrow snake shall make
her nest and lay *eggs*
And hatch, and gather *them* under
her shadow;
There also shall the hawks be
gathered,
Every one with her mate.

16 "Search from the book of the LORD,
and read:

Not one of these shall fail;
Not one shall lack her mate.
For My mouth has commanded it,
     and His Spirit has gathered them.
17 He has cast the lot for them,
And His hand has divided it among
     them with a measuring line.
They shall possess it forever;
From generation to generation they
     shall dwell in it."

The Future Glory of Zion

35 The wilderness and the wasteland
     shall be glad for them,
And the desert shall rejoice and
     blossom as the rose;
2 It shall blossom abundantly and
     rejoice,
Even with joy and singing.
The glory of Lebanon shall be given
     to it,
The excellence of Carmel and
     Sharon.
They shall see the glory of the
     LORD,
The excellency of our God.

3   Strengthen the weak hands,
And make firm the feeble knees.
4   Say to those who are fearful-
     hearted,
"Be strong, do not fear!
Behold, your God will come with
     vengeance,
With the recompense of God;
He will come and save you."

5   Then the eyes of the blind shall be
     opened,
And the ears of the deaf shall be
     unstopped.
6   Then the lame shall leap like a deer,
And the tongue of the dumb sing.
For waters shall burst forth in the
     wilderness,
And streams in the desert.
7   The parched ground shall become
     a pool,
And the thirsty land springs of
     water;
In the habitation of jackals, where
     each lay,
There shall be grass with reeds and
     rushes.

8 A highway shall be there, and a
     road,
And it shall be called the Highway
     of Holiness.
The unclean shall not pass over it,
But it shall be for others.
Whoever walks the road, although
     a fool,
Shall not go astray.
9 No lion shall be there,
Nor shall any ravenous beast go up
     on it;
It shall not be found there.
But the redeemed shall walk there,
10 And the ransomed of the LORD shall
     return,
And come to Zion with singing,
With everlasting joy on their heads.
They shall obtain joy and gladness,
And sorrow and sighing shall flee
     away.

Sennacherib Boasts Against the LORD

36 Now it came to pass in the four-
     teenth year of King Hezekiah
that Sennacherib king of Assyria came
up against all the fortified cities of Judah and took them. 2Then the king of
Assyria sent the Rabshakeh[t] with a
great army from Lachish to King Hezekiah at Jerusalem. And he stood by the
aqueduct from the upper pool, on the
highway to the Fuller's Field. 3And
Eliakim the son of Hilkiah, who was
over the household, Shebna the scribe,
and Joah the son of Asaph, the recorder, came out to him.

4Then the Rabshakeh said to them,
"Say now to Hezekiah, 'Thus says the
great king, the king of Assyria: "What
confidence is this in which you trust?
5I say you speak of having plans and
power for war; but they are mere
words. Now in whom do you trust, that
you rebel against me? 6Look! You are
trusting in the staff of this broken reed,
Egypt, on which if a man leans, it will
go into his hand and pierce it. So is
Pharaoh king of Egypt to all who trust
in him.

7"But if you say to me, 'We trust in
the LORD our God,' is it not He whose
high places and whose altars Hezekiah
has taken away, and said to Judah and

---

t A title, probably Chief of Staff or Governor

Jerusalem, 'You shall worship before this altar'?'' 8Now therefore, I urge you, give a pledge to my master the king of Assyria, and I will give you two thousand horses—if you are able on your part to put riders on them! 9How then will you repel one captain of the least of my master's servants, and put your trust in Egypt for chariots and horsemen? 10Have I now come up without the LORD against this land to destroy it? The LORD said to me, 'Go up against this land, and destroy it.' ''

11Then Eliakim, Shebna, and Joah said to the Rabshakeh, "Please speak to your servants in Aramaic, for we understand it; and do not speak to us in Hebrew in the hearing of the people who are on the wall."

12But the Rabshakeh said, "Has my master sent me to your master and to you to speak these words, and not to the men who sit on the wall, who will eat and drink their own waste with you?"

13Then the Rabshakeh stood and called out with a loud voice in Hebrew, and said, "Hear the words of the great king, the king of Assyria! 14Thus says the king: 'Do not let Hezekiah deceive you, for he will not be able to deliver you; 15nor let Hezekiah make you trust in the LORD, saying, "The LORD will surely deliver us; this city will not be given into the hand of the king of Assyria." ' 16Do not listen to Hezekiah; for thus says the king of Assyria: 'Make peace with me by a present and come out to me; and every one of you eat from his own vine and every one from his own fig tree, and every one of you drink the waters of his own cistern; 17until I come and take you away to a land like your own land, a land of grain and new wine, a land of bread and vineyards. 18Beware lest Hezekiah persuade you, saying, "The LORD will deliver us." Has any one of the gods of the nations delivered its land from the hand of the king of Assyria? 19Where are the gods of Hamath and Arpad? Where are the gods of Sepharvaim? Indeed, have they delivered Samaria from my hand? 20Who among all the gods of these lands have delivered their countries from my hand, that the LORD

should deliver Jerusalem from my hand?' ''

21But they held their peace and answered him not a word; for the king's commandment was, "Do not answer him." 22Then Eliakim the son of Hilkiah, who was over the household, Shebna the scribe, and Joah the son of Asaph, the recorder, came to Hezekiah with their clothes torn, and told him the words of the Rabshakeh.

Isaiah Assures Deliverance

37 And so it was, when King Hezekiah heard it, that he tore his clothes, covered himself with sackcloth, and went into the house of the LORD. 2Then he sent Eliakim, who was over the household, Shebna the scribe, and the elders of the priests, covered with sackcloth, to Isaiah the prophet, the son of Amoz. 3And they said to him, "Thus says Hezekiah: 'This day is a day of trouble and rebuke and blasphemy; for the children have come to birth, but there is no strength to bring them forth. 4It may be that the LORD your God will hear the words of the Rabshakeh, whom his master the king of Assyria has sent to reproach the living God, and will rebuke the words which the LORD your God has heard. Therefore lift up your prayer for the remnant that is left.' ''

5So the servants of King Hezekiah came to Isaiah. 6And Isaiah said to them, "Thus you shall say to your master, 'Thus says the LORD: "Do not be afraid of the words which you have heard, with which the servants of the king of Assyria have blasphemed Me. 7Surely I will send a spirit upon him, and he shall hear a rumor and return to his own land; and I will cause him to fall by the sword in his own land." ' ''

Sennacherib's Threat and Hezekiah's Prayer

8Then the Rabshakeh returned, and found the king of Assyria warring against Libnah, for he heard that he had departed from Lachish. 9And the king heard concerning Tirhakah king of Ethiopia, "He has come out to make war with you." So when he heard it, he sent messengers to Hezekiah, saying, 10"Thus you shall speak to Hezekiah king of Judah, saying: 'Do not let your God in whom you trust deceive you, saying, "Jerusalem shall not be given into the hand of the king of Assyria." 11Look! You have heard what the kings of Assyria have done to all lands by utterly destroying them; and shall you be delivered? 12Have the gods of the nations delivered those whom my fathers have destroyed, Gozan and Haran and Rezeph, and the people of Eden who *were* in Telassar? 13Where *is* the king of Hamath, the king of Arpad, and the king of the city of Sepharvaim, Hena, and Ivah?' "

14And Hezekiah received the letter from the hand of the messengers, and read it; and Hezekiah went up to the house of the LORD, and spread it before the LORD. 15Then Hezekiah prayed to the LORD, saying: 16"O LORD of hosts, God of Israel, *the One* who dwells *between* the cherubim, You *are* God, You alone, of all the kingdoms of the earth. You have made heaven and earth. 17Incline Your ear, O LORD, and hear; open Your eyes, O LORD, and see; and hear all the words of Sennacherib, which he has sent to reproach the living God. 18Truly, LORD, the kings of Assyria have laid waste all the nations and their lands, 19and have cast their gods into the fire; for they *were* not gods, but the work of men's hands—wood and stone. Therefore they destroyed them. 20Now therefore, O LORD our God, save us from his hand, that all the kingdoms of the earth may know that You *are* the LORD, You alone."

The Word of the LORD Concerning Sennacherib

21Then Isaiah the son of Amoz sent to Hezekiah, saying, "Thus says the LORD God of Israel, 'Because you have prayed to Me against Sennacherib king of Assyria, 22this *is* the word which the LORD has spoken concerning him:

"The virgin, the daughter of Zion,
  Has despised you, laughed you to
    scorn;
  The daughter of Jerusalem
  Has shaken *her* head behind your
    back!

23 "Whom have you reproached and
    blasphemed?

Against whom have you raised
  your voice,
And lifted up your eyes on high?
Against the Holy One of Israel.
24 By your servants you have
    reproached the Lord,
And said, 'By the multitude of my
    chariots
I have come up to the height of the
    mountains,
To the limits of Lebanon;
I will cut down its tall cedars
And its choice cypress trees;
I will enter its farthest height,
To its fruitful forest.
25 I have dug and drunk water,
And with the soles of my feet I have
    dried up
All the brooks of defense.'

26 "Did you not hear long ago
How I made it,
From ancient times that I
    formed it?
Now I have brought it to pass,
That you should be
For crushing fortified cities *into*
    heaps of ruins.
27 Therefore their inhabitants *had*
    little power;
They were dismayed and
    confounded;
They were *as* the grass of the field
And the green herb,
As the grass on the housetops
And grain blighted before it is
    grown.

28 "But I know your dwelling place,
Your going out and your coming in,
And your rage against Me.
29 Because your rage against Me and
    your tumult
Have come up to My ears,
Therefore I will put My hook in
    your nose
And My bridle in your lips,
And I will turn you back
By the way which you came." '
30"This *shall be* a sign to you:
You shall eat this year such as
    grows of itself,
And the second year what springs
    from the same;
Also in the third year sow and reap,
Plant vineyards and eat the fruit of
    them.

31 And the remnant who have escaped
    of the house of Judah
    Shall again take root downward,
    And bear fruit upward.
32 For out of Jerusalem shall go a
    remnant,
    And those who escape from Mount
    Zion.
    The zeal of the LORD of hosts will
    do this.
33"Therefore thus says the LORD concerning the king of Assyria:
    'He shall not come into this city,
    Nor shoot an arrow there,
    Nor come before it with shield,
    Nor build a siege mound against it.
34 By the way that he came,
    By the same shall he return;
    And he shall not come into this
    city,'
    Says the LORD.
35 'For I will defend this city, to
    save it
    For My own sake and for My
    servant David's sake.' "

Sennacherib's Defeat and Death

36Then the angel[u] of the LORD went out, and killed in the camp of the Assyrians one hundred and eighty-five thousand; and when *people* arose early in the morning, there were the corpses—all dead. **37**So Sennacherib king of Assyria departed and went away, returned *home*, and remained at Nineveh. **38**Now it came to pass, as he was worshiping in the house of Nisroch his god, that his sons Adrammelech and Sharezer struck him down with the sword; and they escaped into the land of Ararat. Then Esarhaddon his son reigned in his place.

Hezekiah's Life Extended

38 In those days Hezekiah was sick and near death. And Isaiah the prophet, the son of Amoz, went to him and said to him, "Thus says the LORD: 'Set your house in order, for you shall die and not live.' "

2Then Hezekiah turned his face toward the wall, and prayed to the LORD, **3**and said, "Remember now, O LORD, I pray, how I have walked before You in truth and with a loyal heart, and have done *what is* good in Your sight." And Hezekiah wept bitterly.

4And the word of the LORD came to Isaiah, saying, **5**"Go and tell Hezekiah, 'Thus says the LORD, the God of David your father: "I have heard your prayer, I have seen your tears; surely I will add to your days fifteen years. **6**I will deliver you and this city from the hand of the king of Assyria, and I will defend this city." ' **7**And this *is* the sign to you from the LORD, that the LORD will do this thing which He has spoken: **8**Behold, I will bring the shadow on the sundial, which has gone down with the sun on the sundial of Ahaz, ten degrees backward." So the sun returned ten degrees on the dial by which it had gone down.

9This is the writing of Hezekiah king of Judah, when he had been sick and had recovered from his sickness:

10   I said,
    "In the prime of my life
    I shall go to the gates of Sheol;
    I am deprived of the remainder of
      my years."
11   I said,
    "I shall not see Yah,
    The LORD in the land of the living;
    I shall observe man no more among
      the inhabitants of the world.
12   My life span is gone,
    Taken from me like a shepherd's
      tent;
    I have cut off my life like a weaver.
    He cuts me off from the loom;
    From day until night You make an
      end of me.
13   I have considered until morning—
    Like a lion,
    So He breaks all my bones;
    From day until night You make an
      end of me.
14   Like a crane *or* a swallow, so I
      chattered;
    I mourned like a dove;
    My eyes fail *from looking* upward.
    O LORD, I am oppressed;
    Undertake for me!

15   "What shall I say?
    He has both spoken to me,
    And He Himself has done *it*.
    I shall walk carefully all my years
    In the bitterness of my soul.

u Or *Angel*

16 O Lord, by these *things men* live;
    And in all these *things is* the life
       of my spirit;
    So You will restore me and make
       me live.
17 Indeed *it was* for *my own* peace
    That I had great bitterness;
    But You have lovingly *delivered* my
       soul from the pit of corruption,
    For You have cast all my sins
       behind Your back.
18 For Sheol cannot thank You,
    Death cannot praise You;
    Those who go down to the pit
       cannot hope for Your truth.
19 The living, the living man, he shall
       praise You,
    As I *do* this day;
    The father shall make known Your
       truth to the children.

20 "The LORD *was read*y to save me;
    Therefore we will sing my songs
       with stringed instruments
    All the days of our life, in the house
       of the LORD."
21Now Isaiah had said, "Let them
take a lump of figs, and apply *it* as a
poultice on the boil, and he shall recover."
22And Hezekiah had said, "What *is*
the sign that I shall go up to the house
of the LORD?"

The Babylonian Envoys

39 At that time Merodach-Baladan
the son of Baladan, king of Babylon, sent letters and a present to Hezekiah, for he heard that he had been sick
and had recovered. 2And Hezekiah was
pleased with them, and showed them
the house of his treasures—the silver
and gold, the spices and precious ointment, and all his armory—all that was
found among his treasures. There was
nothing in his house or in all his dominion that Hezekiah did not show them.
3Then Isaiah the prophet went to
King Hezekiah, and said to him, "What
did these men say, and from where did
they come to you?"
So Hezekiah said, "They came to me
from a far country, from Babylon."
4And he said, "What have they seen
in your house?"
So Hezekiah answered, "They have
seen all that *is* in my house; there is

nothing among my treasures that I have
not shown them."
5Then Isaiah said to Hezekiah, "Hear
the word of the LORD of hosts: 6'Behold,
the days are coming when all that *is* in
your house, and what your fathers have
accumulated until this day, shall be carried to Babylon; nothing shall be left,'
says the LORD. 7'And they shall take
away *some* of your sons who will descend from you, whom you will beget;
and they shall be eunuchs in the palace
of the king of Babylon.' "
8So Hezekiah said to Isaiah, "The
word of the LORD which you have spoken *is* good!" For he said, "At least
there will be peace and truth in my
days."

God's People Are Comforted

40 "Comfort, yes, comfort My
people!"
    Says your God.
2   "Speak comfort to Jerusalem, and
       cry out to her,
    That her warfare is ended,
    That her iniquity is pardoned;
    For she has received from the
       LORD's hand
    Double for all her sins."

3   The voice of one crying in the
       wilderness:
    "Prepare the way of the LORD;
    Make straight in the desert
    A highway for our God.
4   Every valley shall be exalted
    And every mountain and hill
       brought low;
    The crooked places shall be made
       straight
    And the rough places smooth;
5   The glory of the LORD shall be
       revealed,
    And all flesh shall see *it* together;
    For the mouth of the LORD has
       spoken."

6   The voice said, "Cry out!"
    And he said, "What shall I cry?"

    "All flesh *is* grass,
    And all its loveliness *is* like the
       flower of the field.
7   The grass withers, the flower fades,
    Because the breath of the LORD
       blows upon it;

Surely the people *are* grass.
8 The grass withers, the flower fades,
But the word of our God stands
forever."

9 O Zion,
You who bring good tidings,
Get up into the high mountain;
O Jerusalem,
You who bring good tidings,
Lift up your voice with strength,
Lift *it* up, be not afraid;
Say to the cities of Judah, "Behold
your God!"

10 Behold, the Lord GOD shall come
with a strong *hand,*
And His arm shall rule for Him;
Behold, His reward *is* with Him,
And His work before Him.
11 He will feed His flock like a
shepherd;
He will gather the lambs with
His arm,
And carry *them* in His bosom,
And gently lead those who are with
young.

12 Who has measured the waters in
the hollow of His hand,
Measured heaven with a span
And calculated the dust of the earth
in a measure?
Weighed the mountains in scales
And the hills in a balance?
13 Who has directed the Spirit of the
LORD,
Or *as* His counselor has taught
Him?
14 With whom did He take counsel,
and *who* instructed Him,
And taught Him in the path of
justice?
Who taught Him knowledge,
And showed Him the way of
understanding?

15 Behold, the nations *are* as a drop
in a bucket,
And are counted as the small dust
on the scales;
Look, He lifts up the isles as a very
little thing.
16 And Lebanon *is* not sufficient to
burn,
Nor its beasts sufficient for a burnt
offering.

17 All nations before Him *are* as
nothing,
And they are counted by Him less
than nothing and worthless.

18 To whom then will you liken God?
Or what likeness will you compare
to Him?
19 The workman molds an image,
The goldsmith overspreads it with
gold,
And the silversmith casts silver
chains.
20 Whoever *is* too impoverished for
such a contribution
Chooses a tree *that* will not rot;
He seeks for himself a skillful
workman
To prepare a carved image *that* will
not totter.

21 Have you not known?
Have you not heard?
Has it not been told you from the
beginning?
Have you not understood from the
foundations of the earth?
22 *It is* He who sits above the circle
of the earth,
And its inhabitants *are* like
grasshoppers,
Who stretches out the heavens like
a curtain,
And spreads them out like a tent
to dwell in.
23 He brings the princes to nothing;
He makes the judges of the earth
useless.

24 Scarcely shall they be planted,
Scarcely shall they be sown,
Scarcely shall their stock take root
in the earth,
When He will also blow on them,
And they will wither,
And the whirlwind will take them
away like stubble.

25 "To whom then will you liken Me,
Or *to whom* shall I be equal?" says
the Holy One.
26 Lift up your eyes on high,
And see who has created these
things,
Who brings out their host by
number;
He calls them all by name,

By the greatness of His might
And the strength of *His* power;
Not one is missing.

27 Why do you say, O Jacob,
And speak, O Israel:
"My way is hidden from the LORD,
And my just claim is passed over
by my God"?
28 Have you not known?
Have you not heard?
The everlasting God, the LORD,
The Creator of the ends of the
earth,
Neither faints nor is weary.
His understanding is unsearchable.
29 He gives power to the weak,
And to *those who have* no might
He increases strength.
30 Even the youths shall faint and be
weary,
And the young men shall utterly
fall,
31 But those who wait on the LORD
Shall renew *their* strength;
They shall mount up with wings
like eagles,
They shall run and not be weary,
They shall walk and not faint.

Israel Assured of God's Help

41 "Keep silence before Me,
O coastlands,
And let the people renew *their*
strength!
Let them come near, then let them
speak;
Let us come near together for
judgment.

2 "Who raised up one from the east?
Who in righteousness called him to
His feet?
Who gave the nations before him,
And made *him* rule over kings?
Who gave *them* as the dust *to* his
sword,
As driven stubble to his bow?
3 Who pursued them, *and* passed
safely
By the way *that* he had not gone
with his feet?
4 Who has performed and done *it,*
Calling the generations from the
beginning?
'I, the LORD, am the first;
And with the last I *am* He.' "

5 The coastlands saw *it* and feared,
The ends of the earth were afraid;
They drew near and came.
6 Everyone helped his neighbor,
And said to his brother,
"Be of good courage!"
7 So the craftsman encouraged the
goldsmith;
He who smooths *with* the hammer
inspired him who strikes the
anvil,
Saying, "It *is* ready for the
soldering";
Then he fastened it with pegs,
That it might not totter.

8 "But you, Israel, *are* My servant,
Jacob whom I have chosen,
The descendants of Abraham My
friend.
9 *You* whom I have taken from the
ends of the earth,
And called from its farthest
regions,
And said to you,
'You *are* My servant,
I have chosen you and have not cast
you away:
10 Fear not, for I *am* with you;
Be not dismayed, for I *am*
your God.
I will strengthen you,
Yes, I will help you,
I will uphold you with My righteous
right hand.'

11 "Behold, all those who were
incensed against you
Shall be ashamed and disgraced;
They shall be as nothing,
And those who strive with you shall
perish.
12 You shall seek them and not find
them—
Those who contended with you.
Those who war against you
Shall be as nothing,
As a nonexistent thing.
13 For I, the LORD your God, will hold
your right hand,
Saying to you, 'Fear not, I will
help you.'

14 "Fear not, you worm Jacob,
You men of Israel!
I will help you," says the LORD

And your Redeemer, the Holy One
    of Israel.
15 "Behold, I will make you into a new
    threshing sledge with sharp
    teeth;
    You shall thresh the mountains and
    beat *them* small,
    And make the hills like chaff.
16 You shall winnow them, the wind
    shall carry them away,
    And the whirlwind shall scatter
    them;
    You shall rejoice in the LORD,
    And glory in the Holy One of Israel.

17 "The poor and needy seek water, but
    there is none,
    Their tongues fail for thirst.
    I, the LORD, will hear them;
    I, the God of Israel, will not forsake
    them.
18 I will open rivers in desolate
    heights,
    And fountains in the midst of the
    valleys;
    I will make the wilderness a pool
    of water,
    And the dry land springs of water.
19 I will plant in the wilderness the
    cedar and the acacia tree,
    The myrtle and the oil tree;
    I will set in the desert the cypress
    tree *and* the pine
    And the box tree together,
20 That they may see and know,
    And consider and understand
    together,
    That the hand of the LORD has done
    this,
    And the Holy One of Israel has
    created it.

The Futility of Idols

21 "Present your case," says the LORD.
    "Bring forth your strong *reasons,*"
    says the King of Jacob.
22 "Let them bring forth and show us
    what will happen;
    Let them show the former things,
    what they *were,*
    That we may consider them,
    And know the latter end of them;
    Or declare to us things to come.
23 Show the things that are to come
    hereafter,
    That we may know that you *are*
    gods;

Yes, do good or do evil,
    That we may be dismayed and see
    it together.
24 Indeed you *are* nothing,
    And your work *is* nothing;
    He who chooses you *is* an
    abomination.

25 "I have raised up one from the north,
    And he shall come;
    From the rising of the sun he shall
    call on My name;
    And he shall come against princes
    as *though* mortar,
    As the potter treads clay.
26 Who has declared from the
    beginning, that we may know?
    And former times, that we may say,
    '*He is* righteous'?
    Surely *there is* no one who shows,
    Surely *there is* no one who
    declares,
    Surely *there is* no one who hears
    your words.
27 The first time *I said* to Zion,
    'Look, there they are!'
    And I will give to Jerusalem one
    who brings good tidings.
28 For I looked, and *there was*
    no man;
    I looked among them, but *there
    was* no counselor,
    Who, when I asked of them, could
    answer a word.
29 Indeed they *are* all worthless;
    Their works *are* nothing;
    Their molded images *are* wind and
    confusion.

The Servant of the LORD

42 "Behold! My Servant whom I
    uphold,
    My Elect One *in whom* My soul
    delights!
    I have put My Spirit upon Him;
    He will bring forth justice to the
    Gentiles.
2 He will not cry out, nor raise *His
    voice,*
    Nor cause His voice to be heard in
    the street.
3 A bruised reed He will not break,
    And smoking flax He will not
    quench;
    He will bring forth justice for truth.
4 He will not fail nor be discouraged,

Till He has established justice in the
earth;
And the coastlands shall wait for
His law."

5 Thus says God the LORD,
Who created the heavens and
stretched them out,
Who spread forth the earth and
that which comes from it,
Who gives breath to the people
on it,
And spirit to those who walk on it:
6 "I, the LORD, have called You in
righteousness,
And will hold Your hand;
I will keep You and give You as a
covenant to the people,
As a light to the Gentiles,
7 To open blind eyes,
To bring out prisoners from the
prison,
Those who sit in darkness from the
prison house.
8 I *am* the LORD, that *is* My name;
And My glory I will not give to
another,
Nor My praise to carved images.
9 Behold, the former things have
come to pass,
And new things I declare;
Before they spring forth I tell you
of them."

Praise to the LORD

10 Sing to the LORD a new song,
And His praise from the ends of the
earth,
You who go down to the sea, and
all that is in it,
You coastlands and you
inhabitants of them!
11 Let the wilderness and its cities lift
up *their voice*,
The villages *that* Kedar inhabits.
Let the inhabitants of Sela sing,
Let them shout from the top of the
mountains.
12 Let them give glory to the LORD,
And declare His praise in the
coastlands.
13 The LORD shall go forth like a
mighty man;
He shall stir up *His* zeal like a man
of war.
He shall cry out, yes, shout aloud;

He shall prevail against His
enemies.

Promise of the LORD's Help

14 "I have held My peace a long time,
I have been still and restrained
Myself.
Now I will cry like a woman in
labor,
I will pant and gasp at once.
15 I will lay waste the mountains and
hills,
And dry up all their vegetation;
I will make the rivers coastlands,
And I will dry up the pools.
16 I will bring the blind by a way they
did not know;
I will lead them in paths they have
not known.
I will make darkness light before
them,
And crooked places straight.
These things I will do for them,
And not forsake them.
17 They shall be turned back,
They shall be greatly ashamed,
Who trust in carved images,
Who say to the molded images,
'You *are* our gods.'

18 "Hear, you deaf;
And look, you blind, that you
may see.
19 Who *is* blind but My servant,
Or deaf as My messenger *whom* I
send?
Who *is* blind as *he who is* perfect,
And blind as the LORD's servant?
20 Seeing many things, but you do not
observe;
Opening the ears, but he does not
hear."

Israel's Obstinate Disobedience

21 The LORD is well pleased for His
righteousness' sake;
He will exalt the law and make *it*
honorable.
22 But this *is* a people robbed and
plundered;
All of them are snared in holes,
And they are hidden in prison
houses;
They are for prey, and no one
delivers;
For plunder, and no one says,
"Restore!"

23 Who among you will give ear to
     this?
     Who will listen and hear for the
       time to come?
24 Who gave Jacob for plunder, and
       Israel to the robbers?
     Was it not the LORD,
     He against whom we have sinned?
     For they would not walk in His
       ways,
     Nor were they obedient to His law.
25 Therefore He has poured on him
       the fury of His anger
     And the strength of battle;
     It has set him on fire all around,
     Yet he did not know;
     And it burned him,
     Yet he did not take *it* to heart.

The Redeemer of Israel

43 But now, thus says the LORD, who
       created you, O Jacob,
     And He who formed you, O Israel:
     "Fear not, for I have redeemed you;
     I have called *you* by your name;
     You *are* Mine.
2 When you pass through the waters,
     I *will be* with you;
     And through the rivers, they shall
       not overflow you.
     When you walk through the fire,
       you shall not be burned,
     Nor shall the flame scorch you.
3 For I *am* the LORD your God,
     The Holy One of Israel, your
       Savior;
     I gave Egypt for your ransom,
     Ethiopia and Seba in your place.
4 Since you were precious in My
       sight,
     You have been honored,
     And I have loved you;
     Therefore I will give men for you,
     And people for your life.
5 Fear not, for I *am* with you;
     I will bring your descendants from
       the east,
     And gather you from the west;
6 I will say to the north, 'Give
       them up!'
     And to the south, 'Do not keep them
       back!'
     Bring My sons from afar,
     And My daughters from the ends
       of the earth—
7 Everyone who is called by My
       name,

Whom I have created for My
       glory;
I have formed him, yes, I have
       made him."

8 Bring out the blind people who
       have eyes,
     And the deaf who have ears.
9 Let all the nations be gathered
       together,
     And let the people be assembled.
     Who among them can declare this,
     And show us former things?
     Let them bring out their
       witnesses, that they may be
       justified;
     Or let them hear and say, "*It is*
       truth."
10 "You *are* My witnesses," says the
       LORD,
     "And My servant whom I have
       chosen,
     That you may know and
       believe Me,
     And understand that I *am* He.
     Before Me there was no God
       formed,
     Nor shall there be after Me.
11 I, *even* I, *am* the LORD,
     And besides Me *there is* no savior.
12 I have declared and saved,
     I have proclaimed,
     And *there was* no foreign *god*
       among you;
     Therefore you *are* My witnesses,"
     Says the LORD, "that I *am* God.
13 Indeed before the day *was*, I *am* He;
     And *there is* no one who can deliver
       out of My hand;
     I work, and who will reverse it?"

14 Thus says the LORD, your
       Redeemer,
     The Holy One of Israel:
     "For your sake I will send to
       Babylon,
     And bring them all down as
       fugitives—
     The Chaldeans, who rejoice in their
       ships.
15 I *am* the LORD, your Holy One,
     The Creator of Israel, your King."

16 Thus says the LORD, who makes a
       way in the sea
     And a path through the mighty
       waters,

17 Who brings forth the chariot and
    horse,
    The army and the power
    (They shall lie down together, they
       shall not rise;
    They are extinguished, they are
       quenched like a wick):
18 "Do not remember the former
    things,
    Nor consider the things of old.
19 Behold, I will do a new thing,
    Now it shall spring forth;
    Shall you not know it?
    I will even make a road in the
      wilderness
    And rivers in the desert.
20 The beast of the field will honor Me,
    The jackals and the ostriches,
    Because I give waters in the
      wilderness
    And rivers in the desert,
    To give drink to My people, My
      chosen.
21 This people I have formed for
    Myself;
    They shall declare My praise.

Pleading with Unfaithful Israel

22 "But you have not called upon Me,
    O Jacob;
    And you have been weary of Me,
    O Israel.
23 You have not brought Me the sheep
    for your burnt offerings,
    Nor have you honored Me with
      your sacrifices.
    I have not caused you to serve with
      grain offerings,
    Nor wearied you with incense.
24 You have bought Me no sweet cane
    with money,
    Nor have you satisfied Me with the
      fat of your sacrifices;
    But you have burdened Me with
      your sins,
    You have wearied Me with your
      iniquities.

25 "I, *even* I, *am* He who blots out
    your transgressions for My own
    sake;
    And I will not remember your sins.
26 Put Me in remembrance;
    Let us contend together;
    State your *case,* that you may be
      acquitted.
27 Your first father sinned,

    And your mediators have
      transgressed against Me.
28 Therefore I will profane the princes
    of the sanctuary;
    I will give Jacob to the curse,
    And Israel to reproaches.

God's Blessing on Israel

44 "Yet hear me now, O Jacob My
    servant,
    And Israel whom I have chosen.
2 Thus says the LORD who made you
    And formed you from the womb,
    who will help you:
    'Fear not, O Jacob My servant;
    And you, Jeshurun, whom I have
      chosen.
3 For I will pour water on him who
    is thirsty,
    And floods on the dry ground;
    I will pour My Spirit on your
      descendants,
    And My blessing on your offspring;
4 They will spring up among the
    grass
    Like willows by the
      watercourses.'
5 One will say, 'I *am* the LORD's';
    Another will call *himself* by the
      name of Jacob;
    Another will write *with* his hand,
    'The LORD's,'
    And name *himself* by the name of
      Israel.

There Is No Other God

6 "Thus says the LORD, the King of
    Israel,
    And his Redeemer, the LORD of
      hosts:
    'I *am* the First and I *am* the Last;
    Besides Me *there is* no God.
7 And who can proclaim as I do?
    Then let him declare it and set it
      in order for Me,
    Since I appointed the ancient
      people.
    And the things that are coming and
      shall come,
    Let them show these to them.
8 Do not fear, nor be afraid;
    Have I not told you from that time,
      and declared *it?*
    You *are* My witnesses.
    Is there a God besides Me?
    Indeed *there is* no other Rock;
    I know not *one.*' "

Idolatry Is Foolishness

9 Those who make an image, all of
  them *are* useless,
  And their precious things shall not
  profit;
  They *are* their own witnesses;
  They neither see nor know, that
  they may be ashamed.
10 Who would form a god or mold an
  image
  That profits him nothing?
11 Surely all his companions would be
  ashamed;
  And the workmen, they *are*
  mere men.
  Let them all be gathered together,
  Let them stand up;
  Yet they shall fear,
  They shall be ashamed together.

12 The blacksmith with the tongs
  works one in the coals,
  Fashions it with hammers,
  And works it with the strength of
  his arms.
  Even so, he is hungry, and his
  strength fails;
  He drinks no water and is faint.

13 The craftsman stretches out *his*
  rule,
  He marks one out with chalk;
  He fashions it with a plane,
  He marks it out with the compass,
  And makes it like the figure of
  a man,
  According to the beauty of a man,
  that it may remain in the house.
14 He cuts down cedars for himself,
  And takes the cypress and the oak;
  He secures *it* for himself among the
  trees of the forest.
  He plants a pine, and the rain
  nourishes *it*.

15 Then it shall be for a man to burn,
  For he will take some of it and
  warm himself;
  Yes, he kindles *it* and bakes bread;
  Indeed he makes a god and
  worships *it*;
  He makes it a carved image, and
  falls down to it.
16 He burns half of it in the fire;
  With this half he eats meat;
  He roasts a roast, and is satisfied.

He even warms *himself* and says,
"Ah! I am warm,
I have seen the fire."
17 And the rest of it he makes into
  a god,
  His carved image.
  He falls down before it and
  worships *it*,
  Prays to it and says,
  "Deliver me, for you *are* my god!"

18 They do not know nor
  understand;
  For He has shut their eyes, so that
  they cannot see,
  And their hearts, so that they
  cannot understand.
19 And no one considers in his heart,
  Nor *is there* knowledge nor
  understanding to say,
  "I have burned half of it in the fire,
  Yes, I have also baked bread on its
  coals;
  I have roasted meat and eaten *it*;
  And shall I make the rest of it an
  abomination?
  Shall I fall down before a block of
  wood?"
20 He feeds on ashes;
  A deceived heart has turned him
  aside;
  And he cannot deliver his soul,
  Nor say, "*Is there* not a lie in my
  right hand?"

Israel Is Not Forgotten

21 "Remember these, O Jacob,
  And Israel, for you *are* My
  servant;
  I have formed you, you *are* My
  servant;
  O Israel, you will not be forgotten
  by Me!
22 I have blotted out, like a thick
  cloud, your transgressions,
  And like a cloud, your sins.
  Return to Me, for I have
  redeemed you."

23 Sing, O heavens, for the LORD has
  done *it*!
  Shout, you lower parts of the earth;
  Break forth into singing, you
  mountains,
  O forest, and every tree in it!
  For the LORD has redeemed Jacob,
  And glorified Himself in Israel.

Judah Will Be Restored

24 Thus says the LORD, your
     Redeemer,
     And He who formed you from the
       womb:
     "I *am* the LORD, who makes all
       things,
     Who stretches out the heavens all
       alone,
     Who spreads abroad the earth by
       Myself;
25 Who frustrates the signs of the
     babblers,
     And drives diviners mad;
     Who turns wise men backward,
     And makes their knowledge
       foolishness;
26 Who confirms the word of His
     servant,
     And performs the counsel of His
       messengers;
     Who says to Jerusalem, 'You shall
       be inhabited,'
     To the cities of Judah, 'You shall
       be built,'
     And I will raise up her waste
       places;
27 Who says to the deep, 'Be dry!
     And I will dry up your rivers';
28 Who says of Cyrus, '*He is* My
     shepherd,
     And he shall perform all My
       pleasure,
     Saying to Jerusalem, "You shall be
       built,"
     And to the temple, "Your
       foundation shall be laid." ' '

Cyrus, God's Instrument

45 "Thus says the LORD to His
         anointed,
     To Cyrus, whose right hand I have
       held—
     To subdue nations before him
     And loose the armor of kings,
     To open before him the double
       doors,
     So that the gates will not be
       shut:
2 'I will go before you
     And make the crooked places
       straight;
     I will break in pieces the gates of
       bronze
     And cut the bars of iron.
3 I will give you the treasures of
     darkness

And hidden riches of secret places,
     That you may know that I, the
       LORD,
     Who call *you* by your name,
     Am the God of Israel.
4 For Jacob My servant's sake,
     And Israel My elect,
     I have even called you by your
       name;
     I have named you, though you have
       not known Me.
5 I *am* the LORD, and *there is* no
     other;
     There is no God besides Me.
     I will gird you, though you have not
       known Me,
6 That they may know from the
     rising of the sun to its setting
     That *there is* none besides Me.
     I *am* the LORD, and *there is* no
       other;
7 I form the light and create
     darkness,
     I make peace and create calamity;
     I, the LORD, do all these *things.*'

8 "Rain down, you heavens, from
     above,
     And let the skies pour down
       righteousness;
     Let the earth open, let them bring
       forth salvation,
     And let righteousness spring up
       together.
     I, the LORD, have created it.

9 "Woe to him who strives with his
     Maker!
     Let the potsherd *strive* with the
       potsherds of the earth!
     Shall the clay say to him who forms
       it, 'What are you making?'
     Or shall your handiwork *say,* 'He
       has no hands'?
10 Woe to him who says to *his* father,
     'What are you begetting?'
     Or to the woman, 'What have you
       brought forth?' "

11 Thus says the LORD,
     The Holy One of Israel, and his
       Maker:
     "Ask Me of things to come
       concerning My sons;
     And concerning the work of My
       hands, you command Me.

12 I have made the earth,
And created man on it.
I—My hands—stretched out the
    heavens,
And all their host I have
    commanded.
13 I have raised him up in
    righteousness,
And I will direct all his ways;
He shall build My city
And let My exiles go free,
Not for price nor reward,"
Says the LORD of hosts.

The LORD, the Only Savior

14Thus says the LORD:
"The labor of Egypt and
    merchandise of Cush
And of the Sabeans, men of stature,
Shall come over to you, and they
    shall be yours;
They shall walk behind you,
They shall come over in chains;
And they shall bow down to you.
They will make supplication to you,
    saying, 'Surely God *is* in you,
And *there is* no other;
There is no other God.' "

15 Truly You *are* God, who hide
    Yourself,
O God of Israel, the Savior!
16 They shall be ashamed
And also disgraced, all of them;
They shall go in confusion together,
Who are makers of idols.
17 *But* Israel shall be saved by the
    LORD
With an everlasting salvation;
You shall not be ashamed or
    disgraced
Forever and ever.

18 For thus says the LORD,
Who created the heavens,
Who is God,
Who formed the earth and made it,
Who has established it,
Who did not create it in vain,
Who formed it to be inhabited:
"I *am* the LORD, and *there is* no
    other.
19 I have not spoken in secret,
In a dark place of the earth;
I did not say to the seed of Jacob,
'Seek Me in vain';

I, the LORD, speak righteousness,
I declare things that are right.

20 "Assemble yourselves and come;
Draw near together,
You *who have* escaped from the
    nations.
They have no knowledge,
Who carry the wood of their carved
    image,
And pray to a god *that* cannot save.
21 Tell and bring forth *your case;*
Yes, let them take counsel together.
Who has declared this from ancient
    time?
Who has told it from that time?
Have not I, the LORD?
And *there is* no other God
    besides Me,
A just God and a Savior;
There is none besides Me.

22 "Look to Me, and be saved,
All you ends of the earth!
For I *am* God, and *there is* no other.
23 I have sworn by Myself;
The word has gone out of My
    mouth *in* righteousness,
And shall not return,
That to Me every knee shall bow,
Every tongue shall take an oath.
24 He shall say,
'Surely in the LORD I have
    righteousness and strength.
To Him *men* shall come,
And all shall be ashamed
Who are incensed against Him.
25 In the LORD all the descendants of
    Israel
Shall be justified, and shall glory.' "

Dead Idols and the Living God

46 Bel bows down, Nebo stoops;
Their idols were on the beasts and
    on the cattle.
Your carriages *were* heavily
    loaded,
A burden to the weary *beast.*
2 They stoop, they bow down
    together;
They could not deliver the burden,
But have themselves gone into
    captivity.

3 "Listen to Me, O house of Jacob,
And all the remnant of the house
    of Israel,

Who have been upheld *by Me* from birth,
Who have been carried from the womb:
4 Even to *your* old age, I *am* He,
And *even* to gray hairs I will carry *you!*
I have made, and I will bear;
Even I will carry, and will deliver *you.*

5 "To whom will you liken Me, and make *Me* equal
And compare Me, that we should be alike?
6 They lavish gold out of the bag,
And weigh silver on the scales;
They hire a goldsmith, and he makes it a god;
They prostrate themselves, yes, they worship.
7 They bear it on the shoulder, they carry it
And set it in its place, and it stands;
From its place it shall not move.
Though *one* cries out to it, yet it cannot answer
Nor save him out of his trouble.

8 "Remember this, and show yourselves men;
Recall to mind, O you transgressors.
9 Remember the former things of old,
For I *am* God, and *there is* no other;
I *am* God, and *there is* none like Me,
10 Declaring the end from the beginning,
And from ancient times *things* that are not *yet* done,
Saying, 'My counsel shall stand,
And I will do all My pleasure,'
11 Calling a bird of prey from the east,
The man who executes My counsel, from a far country.
Indeed I have spoken *it;*
I will also bring it to pass.
I have purposed *it;*
I will also do it.

12 "Listen to Me, you stubborn-hearted,
Who *are* far from righteousness:
13 I bring My righteousness near, it shall not be far off;
My salvation shall not linger.

And I will place salvation in Zion,
For Israel My glory.

The Humiliation of Babylon

47 "Come down and sit in the dust,
O virgin daughter of Babylon;
Sit on the ground without a throne,
O daughter of the Chaldeans!
For you shall no more be called
Tender and delicate.
2 Take the millstones and grind meal.
Remove your veil,
Take off the skirt,
Uncover the thigh,
Pass through the rivers.
3 Your nakedness shall be uncovered,
Yes, your shame will be seen;
I will take vengeance,
And I will not arbitrate with a man."

4 *As for* our Redeemer, the LORD of hosts *is* His name,
The Holy One of Israel.

5 "Sit in silence, and go into darkness,
O daughter of the Chaldeans;
For you shall no longer be called
The Lady of Kingdoms.
6 I was angry with My people;
I have profaned My inheritance,
And given them into your hand.
You showed them no mercy;
On the elderly you laid your yoke very heavily.
7 And you said, 'I shall be a lady forever,'
So that you did not take these *things* to heart,
Nor remember the latter end of them.

8 "Therefore hear this now, *you who are* given to pleasures,
Who dwell securely,
Who say in your heart, 'I *am,* and *there is* no one else besides me;
I shall not sit *as* a widow,
Nor shall I know the loss of children';
9 But these two *things* shall come to you
In a moment, in one day:
The loss of children, and widowhood.

They shall come upon you in their
   fullness
Because of the multitude of your
   sorceries,
For the great abundance of your
   enchantments.

10 "For you have trusted in your
    wickedness;
   You have said, 'No one sees me';
   Your wisdom and your knowledge
    have warped you;
   And you have said in your heart,
   'I *am*, and *there is* no one else
    besides me.'
11 Therefore evil shall come
    upon you;
   You shall not know from where it
    arises.
   And trouble shall fall upon you;
   You will not be able to put it off.
   And desolation shall come upon
    you suddenly,
   Which you shall not know.

12 "Stand now with your enchantments
   And the multitude of your
    sorceries,
   In which you have labored from
    your youth—
   Perhaps you will be able to profit,
   Perhaps you will prevail.
13 You are wearied in the multitude
    of your counsels;
   Let now the astrologers, the
    stargazers,
   And the monthly prognosticators
   Stand up and save you
   From what shall come upon you.
14 Behold, they shall be as stubble,
   The fire shall burn them;
   They shall not deliver themselves
   From the power of the flame;
   It shall not *be* a coal to be
    warmed by,
   Nor a fire to sit before!
15 Thus shall they be to you
   With whom you have labored,
   Your merchants from your youth;
   They shall wander each one to his
    quarter.
   No one shall save you.

Israel Refined for God's Glory

48 "Hear this, O house of Jacob,
   Who are called by the name of
    Israel,

And have come forth from the
   wellsprings of Judah;
Who swear by the name of the
   LORD,
And make mention of the God of
   Israel,
But not in truth or in righteousness;
2 For they call themselves after the
   holy city,
   And lean on the God of Israel;
   The LORD of hosts *is* His name:

3 "I have declared the former things
    from the beginning;
   They went forth from My mouth,
    and I caused them to hear it.
   Suddenly I did *them*, and they
    came to pass.
4 Because I knew that you *were*
    obstinate,
   And your neck *was* an iron sinew,
   And your brow bronze,
5 Even from the beginning I have
    declared *it* to you;
   Before it came to pass I proclaimed
    it to you,
   Lest you should say, 'My idol has
    done them,
   And my carved image and my
    molded image
   Have commanded them.'

6 "You have heard;
   See all this.
   And will you not declare *it*?
   I have made you hear new things
    from this time,
   Even hidden things, and you did
    not know them.
7 They are created now and not from
    the beginning;
   And before this day you have not
    heard them,
   Lest you should say, 'Of course I
    knew them.'
8 Surely you did not hear,
   Surely you did not know;
   Surely from long ago your ear was
    not opened.
   For I knew that you would deal
    very treacherously,
   And were called a transgressor
    from the womb.

9 "For My name's sake I will defer My
    anger,

And *for* My praise I will restrain it
from you,
So that I do not cut you off.
10 Behold, I have refined you, but not
as silver;
I have tested you in the furnace of
affliction.
11 For My own sake, for My own sake,
I will do *it*;
For how should *My name* be
profaned?
And I will not give My glory to
another.

God's Ancient Plan to Redeem Israel

12 "Listen to Me, O Jacob,
And Israel, My called:
I *am* He, I *am* the First,
I *am* also the Last.
13 Indeed My hand has laid the
foundation of the earth,
And My right hand has stretched
out the heavens;
When I call to them,
They stand up together.

14 "All of you, assemble yourselves,
and hear!
Who among them has declared
these *things*?
The LORD loves him;
He shall do His pleasure on
Babylon,
And His arm *shall be against* the
Chaldeans.
15 I, *even* I, have spoken;
Yes, I have called him,
I have brought him, and his way
will prosper.

16 "Come near to Me, hear this:
I have not spoken in secret from the
beginning;
From the time that it was, I *was*
there.
And now the Lord GOD and His
Spirit
Have[v] sent Me."

17 Thus says the LORD, your
Redeemer,
The Holy One of Israel:
"I *am* the LORD your God,
Who teaches you to profit,
Who leads you by the way you
should go.
18 Oh, that you had heeded My
commandments!
Then your peace would have been
like a river,
And your righteousness like the
waves of the sea.
19 Your descendants also would have
been like the sand,
And the offspring of your body like
the grains of sand;
His name would not have been
cut off
Nor destroyed from before Me."

20 Go forth from Babylon!
Flee from the Chaldeans!
With a voice of singing,
Declare, proclaim this,
Utter it to the end of the earth;
Say, "The LORD has redeemed
His servant Jacob!"
21 And they did not thirst
When He led them through the
deserts;
He caused the waters to flow from
the rock for them;
He also split the rock, and the
waters gushed out.

22 "*There is* no peace," says the LORD,
"for the wicked."

The Servant, the Light to the Gentiles

49 "Listen, O coastlands, to Me,
And take heed, you peoples
from afar!
The LORD has called Me from the
womb;
From the matrix of My mother He
has made mention of My name.
2 And He has made My mouth like
a sharp sword;
In the shadow of His hand He has
hidden Me,
And made Me a polished shaft;
In His quiver He has hidden Me."

3 "And He said to me,
'You *are* My servant, O Israel,
In whom I will be glorified.'
4 Then I said, 'I have labored in vain,
I have spent my strength for
nothing and in vain;

v The Hebrew verb is singular.

Yet surely my just reward *is* with
the Lord,
And my work with my God.' "

5 "And now the Lord says,
Who formed Me from the womb *to
be* His Servant,
To bring Jacob back to Him,
So that Israel is gathered to Him
(For I shall be glorious in the eyes
of the Lord,
And My God shall be My strength),
6 Indeed He says,
'It is too small a thing that You
should be My Servant
To raise up the tribes of Jacob,
And to restore the preserved ones
of Israel;
I will also give You as a light to
the Gentiles,
That You should be My salvation
to the ends of the earth.' "

7 Thus says the Lord,
The Redeemer of Israel, their
Holy One,
To Him whom man despises,
To Him whom the nation abhors,
To the Servant of rulers:
"Kings shall see and arise,
Princes also shall worship,
Because of the Lord who is faithful,
The Holy One of Israel;
And He has chosen You."
8 Thus says the Lord:
"In an acceptable time I have
heard You,
And in the day of salvation I have
helped You;
I will preserve You and give You
As a covenant to the people,
To restore the earth,
To cause them to inherit the
desolate heritages;
9 That You may say to the prisoners,
'Go forth,'
To those who *are* in darkness,
'Show yourselves.'

"They shall feed along the roads,
And their pastures *shall be* on all
desolate heights.
10 They shall neither hunger nor
thirst,
Neither heat nor sun shall strike
them;

For He who has mercy on them will
lead them,
Even by the springs of water He
will guide them.
11 I will make each of My mountains
a road,
And My highways shall be
elevated.
12 Surely these shall come from afar;
Look! Those from the north and the
west,
And these from the land of Sinim."

13 Sing, O heavens!
Be joyful, O earth!
And break out in singing,
O mountains!
For the Lord has comforted His
people,
And will have mercy on His
afflicted.

God Will Remember Zion

14 But Zion said, "The Lord has
forsaken me,
And my Lord has forgotten me."

15 "Can a woman forget her nursing
child,
And not have compassion on the
son of her womb?
Surely they may forget,
Yet I will not forget you.
16 See, I have inscribed you on the
palms *of My hands;*
Your walls *are* continually
before Me.
17 Your sons shall make haste;
Your destroyers and those who laid
you waste
Shall go away from you.
18 Lift up your eyes, look around
and see;
All these gather together *and* come
to you.
As I live," says the Lord,
"You shall surely clothe yourselves
with them all as an ornament,
And bind them *on you* as a bride
does.

19 "For your waste and desolate places,
And the land of your destruction,
Will even now be too small for the
inhabitants;

And those who swallowed you up
will be far away.
20 The children you will have,
After you have lost the others,
Will say again in your ears,
'The place *is* too small for me;
Give me a place where I may
dwell.'
21 Then you will say in your heart,
'Who has begotten these for me,
Since I have lost my children and
am desolate,
A captive, and wandering to
and fro?
And who has brought these up?
There I was, left alone;
But these, where *were* they?' "
22 Thus says the Lord GOD:
"Behold, I will lift My hand in an
oath to the nations,
And set up My standard for the
peoples;
They shall bring your sons in *their*
arms,
And your daughters shall be
carried on *their* shoulders;
23 Kings shall be your foster fathers,
And their queens your nursing
mothers;
They shall bow down to you with
their faces to the earth,
And lick up the dust of your feet.
Then you will know that I *am* the
LORD,
For they shall not be ashamed who
wait for Me."

24 Shall the prey be taken from the
mighty,
Or the captives of the righteous be
delivered?
25 But thus says the LORD:
"Even the captives of the mighty
shall be taken away,
And the prey of the terrible be
delivered;
For I will contend with him who
contends with you,
And I will save your children.
26 I will feed those who oppress you
with their own flesh,
And they shall be drunk with their
own blood as with sweet wine.
All flesh shall know
That I, the LORD, *am* your Savior,
And your Redeemer, the Mighty
One of Jacob."

The Servant, Israel's Hope

50 Thus says the LORD:

"Where *is* the certificate of your
mother's divorce,
Whom I have put away?
Or which of My creditors *is it* to
whom I have sold you?
For your iniquities you have sold
yourselves,
And for your transgressions your
mother has been put away.
2 Why, when I came, *was there*
no man?
Why, when I called, *was there* none
to answer?
Is My hand shortened at all that it
cannot redeem?
Or have I no power to deliver?
Indeed with My rebuke I dry up
the sea,
I make the rivers a wilderness;
Their fish stink because *there is* no
water,
And die of thirst.
3 I clothe the heavens with
blackness,
And I make sackcloth their
covering."

4 "The Lord GOD has given Me
The tongue of the learned,
That I should know how to speak
A word in season to *him who is*
weary.
He awakens Me morning by
morning,
He awakens My ear
To hear as the learned.
5 The Lord GOD has opened My ear;
And I was not rebellious,
Nor did I turn away.
6 I gave My back to those who
struck *Me,*
And My cheeks to those who
plucked out the beard;
I did not hide My face from shame
and spitting.

7 "For the Lord GOD will help Me;
Therefore I will not be disgraced;
Therefore I have set My face like
a flint,
And I know that I will not be
ashamed.
8 *He is* near who justifies Me;

Who will contend with Me?
Let us stand together.
Who *is* My adversary?
Let him come near Me.
9 Surely the Lord God will help Me;
Who *is* he *who* will condemn Me?
Indeed they will all grow old like
a garment;
The moth will eat them up.

10 "Who among you fears the Lord?
Who obeys the voice of His
Servant?
Who walks in darkness
And has no light?
Let him trust in the name of the
Lord
And rely upon his God.
11 Look, all you who kindle a fire,
Who encircle *yourselves* with
sparks:
Walk in the light of your fire and
in the sparks you have kindled—
This you shall have from My hand:
You shall lie down in torment.

The Lord Comforts Zion

51 "Listen to Me, you who follow
after righteousness,
You who seek the Lord:
Look to the rock *from which* you
were hewn,
And to the hole of the pit *from
which* you were dug.
2 Look to Abraham your father,
And to Sarah *who* bore you;
For I called him alone,
And blessed him and
increased him."

3 For the Lord will comfort Zion,
He will comfort all her waste
places;
He will make her wilderness like
Eden,
And her desert like the garden of
the Lord;
Joy and gladness will be found
in it,
Thanksgiving and the voice of
melody.

4 "Listen to Me, My people;
And give ear to Me, O My nation:
For law will proceed from Me,
And I will make My justice rest
As a light of the peoples.

5 My righteousness *is* near,
My salvation has gone forth,
And My arms will judge the
peoples;
The coastlands will wait upon Me,
And on My arm they will trust.
6 Lift up your eyes to the heavens,
And look on the earth beneath.
For the heavens will vanish away
like smoke,
The earth will grow old like a
garment,
And those who dwell in it will die
in like manner;
But My salvation will be forever,
And My righteousness will not be
abolished.

7 "Listen to Me, you who know
righteousness,
You people in whose heart *is*
My law:
Do not fear the reproach of men,
Nor be afraid of their insults.
8 For the moth will eat them up like
a garment,
And the worm will eat them like
wool;
But My righteousness will be
forever,
And My salvation from generation
to generation."

9 Awake, awake, put on strength,
O arm of the Lord!
Awake as in the ancient days,
In the generations of old.
Are You not *the arm* that cut Rahab
apart,
And wounded the serpent?

10 *Are* You not *the One* who dried up
the sea,
The waters of the great deep;
That made the depths of the sea a
road
For the redeemed to cross over?
11 So the ransomed of the Lord shall
return,
And come to Zion with singing,
With everlasting joy on their heads.
They shall obtain joy and gladness;
Sorrow and sighing shall flee away.

12 "I, *even* I, *am* He who comforts you.
Who *are* you that you should be
afraid

Of a man *who* will die,
And of the son of a man *who* will
be made like grass?
13 And you forget the LORD your
Maker,
Who stretched out the heavens
And laid the foundations of the
earth;
You have feared continually
every day
Because of the fury of the
oppressor,
When *he has* prepared to destroy.
And where *is* the fury of the
oppressor?
14 The captive exile hastens, that he
may be loosed,
That he should not die in the pit,
And that his bread should not fail.
15 But I *am* the LORD your God,
Who divided the sea whose waves
roared—
The LORD of hosts *is* His name.
16 And I have put My words in your
mouth;
I have covered you with the shadow
of My hand,
That I may plant the heavens,
Lay the foundations of the earth,
And say to Zion, 'You *are* My
people.' "

God's Fury Removed

17 Awake, awake!
Stand up, O Jerusalem,
You who have drunk at the hand
of the LORD
The cup of His fury;
You have drunk the dregs of the
cup of trembling,
And drained *it* out.
18 *There is* no one to guide her
Among all the sons she has brought
forth;
Nor *is there any* who takes her by
the hand
Among all the sons she has
brought up.
19 These two *things* have come to you;
Who will be sorry for you?—
Desolation and destruction, famine
and sword—
By whom will I comfort you?
20 Your sons have fainted,
They lie at the head of all the
streets,
Like an antelope in a net;

They are full of the fury of the
LORD,
The rebuke of your God.

21 Therefore please hear this, you
afflicted,
And drunk but not with wine.
22 Thus says your Lord,
The LORD and your God,
Who pleads the cause of His
people:
"See, I have taken out of your hand
The cup of trembling,
The dregs of the cup of My fury;
You shall no longer drink it.
23 But I will put it into the hand of
those who afflict you,
Who have said to you,
'Lie down, that we may walk
over you.'
And you have laid your body like
the ground,
And as the street, for those who
walk over."

God Redeems Jerusalem

52 Awake, awake!
Put on your strength, O Zion;
Put on your beautiful garments,
O Jerusalem, the holy city!
For the uncircumcised and the
unclean
Shall no longer come to you.
2 Shake yourself from the dust,
arise;
Sit down, O Jerusalem!
Loose yourself from the bonds of
your neck,
O captive daughter of Zion!
3For thus says the LORD:
"You have sold yourselves for
nothing,
And you shall be redeemed without
money."
4For thus says the Lord GOD:
"My people went down at first
Into Egypt to dwell there;
Then the Assyrian oppressed them
without cause.
5 Now therefore, what have I here,"
says the LORD,
"That My people are taken away for
nothing?
Those who rule over them
Make them wail," says the LORD,
"And My name *is* blasphemed
continually every day.

6   Therefore My people shall know
        My name;
    Therefore *they shall know* in
        that day
    That I *am* He who speaks:
    'Behold, *it is* I.' "

7   How beautiful upon the mountains
    Are the feet of him who brings good
        news,
    Who proclaims peace,
    Who brings glad tidings of good
        things,
    Who proclaims salvation,
    Who says to Zion,
    "Your God reigns!"
8   Your watchmen shall lift up *their*
        voices,
    With their voices they shall sing
        together;
    For they shall see eye to eye
    When the Lord brings back Zion.
9   Break forth into joy, sing together,
    You waste places of Jerusalem!
    For the Lord has comforted His
        people,
    He has redeemed Jerusalem.
10 The Lord has made bare His
        holy arm
    In the eyes of all the nations;
    And all the ends of the earth
        shall see
    The salvation of our God.

11 Depart! Depart! Go out from there,
    Touch no unclean *thing;*
    Go out from the midst of her,
    Be clean,
    You who bear the vessels of the
        Lord.
12 For you shall not go out with haste,
    Nor go by flight;
    For the Lord will go before you,
    And the God of Israel *will be* your
        rear guard.

The Sin-Bearing Servant

13 Behold, My Servant shall deal
        prudently;
    He shall be exalted and extolled
        and be very high.
14 Just as many were astonished
        at you,
    So His visage was marred more
        than any man,

And His form more than the sons
    of men;
15 So shall He sprinkle[w] many
        nations.
    Kings shall shut their mouths
        at Him;
    For what had not been told them
        they shall see,
    And what they had not heard they
        shall consider.

53 Who has believed our report?
    And to whom has the arm of the
        Lord been revealed?
2   For He shall grow up before Him
        as a tender plant,
    And as a root out of dry ground.
    He has no form or comeliness;
    And when we see Him,
    There is no beauty that we should
        desire Him.
3   He is despised and rejected by men,
    A Man of sorrows and acquainted
        with grief.
    And we hid, as it were, *our* faces
        from Him;
    He was despised, and we did not
        esteem Him.

4   Surely He has borne our griefs
    And carried our sorrows;
    Yet we esteemed Him stricken,
    Smitten by God, and afflicted.
5   But He *was* wounded for our
        transgressions,
    He was bruised for our iniquities;
    The chastisement for our peace *was*
        upon Him,
    And by His stripes we are healed.
6   All we like sheep have gone astray;
    We have turned, every one, to his
        own way;
    And the Lord has laid on Him the
        iniquity of us all.

7   He was oppressed and He was
        afflicted,
    Yet He opened not His mouth;
    He was led as a lamb to the
        slaughter,
    And as a sheep before its shearers
        is silent,
    So He opened not His mouth.
8   He was taken from prison and from
        judgment,

---

w Or *startle*

And who will declare His
generation?
For He was cut off from the land
of the living;
For the transgressions of My people
He was stricken.
9 And they made His grave with the
wicked—
But with the rich at His death,
Because He had done no violence,
Nor *was any* deceit in His mouth.

10 Yet it pleased the LORD to
bruise Him;
He has put *Him* to grief.
When You make His soul an
offering for sin,
He shall see *His* seed, He shall
prolong *His* days,
And the pleasure of the LORD shall
prosper in His hand.
11 He shall see the labor of His soul,
and be satisfied.
By His knowledge My righteous
Servant shall justify many,
For He shall bear their iniquities.
12 Therefore I will divide Him a
portion with the great,
And He shall divide the spoil with
the strong,
Because He poured out His soul
unto death,
And He was numbered with the
transgressors,
And He bore the sin of many,
And made intercession for the
transgressors.

A Perpetual Covenant of Peace

54 "Sing, O barren,
You *who* have not borne!
Break forth into singing, and cry
aloud,
You *who* have not labored with
child!
For more *are* the children of the
desolate
Than the children of the married
woman," says the LORD.
2 "Enlarge the place of your tent,
And let them stretch out the
curtains of your dwellings;
Do not spare;
Lengthen your cords,
And strengthen your stakes.
3 For you shall expand to the right
and to the left,

And your descendants will inherit
the nations,
And make the desolate cities
inhabited.

4 "Do not fear, for you will not be
ashamed;
Neither be disgraced, for you will
not be put to shame;
For you will forget the shame of
your youth,
And will not remember the
reproach of your widowhood
anymore.
5 For your Maker *is* your husband,
The LORD of hosts *is* His name;
And your Redeemer *is* the Holy
One of Israel;
He is called the God of the whole
earth.
6 For the LORD has called you
Like a woman forsaken and
grieved in spirit,
Like a youthful wife when you were
refused,"
Says your God.
7 "For a mere moment I have
forsaken you,
But with great mercies I will
gather you.
8 With a little wrath I hid My face
from you for a moment;
But with everlasting kindness I will
have mercy on you,"
Says the LORD, your Redeemer.

9 "For this *is* like the waters of Noah
to Me;
For as I have sworn
That the waters of Noah would no
longer cover the earth,
So have I sworn
That I would not be angry with you,
nor rebuke you.
10 For the mountains shall depart
And the hills be removed,
But My kindness shall not depart
from you,
Nor shall My covenant of peace be
removed,"
Says the LORD, who has mercy
on you.

11 "O you afflicted one,
Tossed with tempest, *and* not
comforted,

Behold, I will lay your stones with
colorful gems,
And lay your foundations with
sapphires.
12 I will make your pinnacles of
rubies,
Your gates of crystal,
And all your walls of precious
stones.
13 All your children *shall be* taught by
the Lord,
And great *shall be* the peace of your
children.
14 In righteousness you shall be
established;
You shall be far from oppression,
for you shall not fear;
And from terror, for it shall not
come near you.
15 Indeed they shall surely assemble,
but not because of Me.
Whoever assembles against you
shall fall for your sake.

16 "Behold, I have created the
blacksmith
Who blows the coals in the fire,
Who brings forth an instrument for
his work;
And I have created the spoiler to
destroy.
17 No weapon formed against you
shall prosper,
And every tongue *which* rises
against you in judgment
You shall condemn.
This *is* the heritage of the servants
of the Lord,
And their righteousness *is*
from Me,"
Says the Lord.

An Invitation to Abundant Life

55 "Ho! Everyone who thirsts,
Come to the waters;
And you who have no money,
Come, buy and eat.
Yes, come, buy wine and milk
Without money and without price.
2 Why do you spend money for *what*
is not bread,
And your wages for *what* does not
satisfy?
Listen carefully to Me, and eat
what is good,
And let your soul delight itself in
abundance.

3 Incline your ear, and come to Me.
Hear, and your soul shall live;
And I will make an everlasting
covenant with you—
The sure mercies of David.
4 Indeed I have given him *as* a
witness to the people,
A leader and commander for the
people.
5 Surely you shall call a nation you
do not know,
And nations *who* do not know you
shall run to you,
Because of the Lord your God,
And the Holy One of Israel;
For He has glorified you."

6 Seek the Lord while He may be
found,
Call upon Him while He is near.
7 Let the wicked forsake his way,
And the unrighteous man his
thoughts;
Let him return to the Lord,
And He will have mercy on him;
And to our God,
For He will abundantly pardon.

8 "For My thoughts *are* not your
thoughts,
Nor *are* your ways My ways," says
the Lord.
9 "For *as* the heavens are higher than
the earth,
So are My ways higher than your
ways,
And My thoughts than your
thoughts.

10 "For as the rain comes down, and
the snow from heaven,
And do not return there,
But water the earth,
And make it bring forth and bud,
That it may give seed to the sower
And bread to the eater,
11 So shall My word be that goes forth
from My mouth;
It shall not return to Me void,
But it shall accomplish what I
please,
And it shall prosper *in the thing* for
which I sent it.

12 "For you shall go out with joy,
And be led out with peace;
The mountains and the hills

Shall break forth into singing
before you,
And all the trees of the field shall
clap *their* hands.
13 Instead of the thorn shall come up
the cypress tree,
And instead of the brier shall come
up the myrtle tree;
And it shall be to the LORD for a
name,
For an everlasting sign *that* shall
not be cut off."

Salvation for the Gentiles

56 Thus says the LORD:

"Keep justice, and do righteousness,
For My salvation *is* about to come,
And My righteousness to be
revealed.
2 Blessed *is* the man *who* does this,
And the son of man *who* lays hold
on it;
Who keeps from defiling the
Sabbath,
And keeps his hand from doing any
evil."

3 Do not let the son of the foreigner
Who has joined himself to the LORD
Speak, saying,
"The LORD has utterly separated me
from His people";
Nor let the eunuch say,
"Here I am, a dry tree."
4 For thus says the LORD:
"To the eunuchs who keep My
Sabbaths,
And choose what pleases Me,
And hold fast My covenant,
5 Even to them I will give in My
house
And within My walls a place and
a name
Better than that of sons and
daughters;
I will give them an everlasting
name
That shall not be cut off.

6 "Also the sons of the foreigner
Who join themselves to the LORD,
to serve Him,
And to love the name of the LORD,
to be His servants—
Everyone who keeps from defiling
the Sabbath,

And holds fast My covenant—
7 Even them I will bring to My holy
mountain,
And make them joyful in My house
of prayer.
Their burnt offerings and their
sacrifices
Will be accepted on My altar;
For My house shall be called a
house of prayer for all nations."
8 The Lord GOD, who gathers the
outcasts of Israel, says,
"Yet I will gather to him
Others besides those who are
gathered to him."

Israel's Irresponsible Leaders

9 All you beasts of the field, come to
devour,
All you beasts in the forest.
10 His watchmen *are* blind,
They are all ignorant;
They *are* all dumb dogs,
They cannot bark;
Sleeping, lying down, loving to
slumber.
11 Yes, *they are* greedy dogs
Which never have enough.
And they *are* shepherds
Who cannot understand;
They all look to their own way,
Every one for his own gain,
From his *own* territory.
12 "Come," *one says,* "I will bring wine,
And we will fill ourselves with
intoxicating drink;
Tomorrow will be as today,
And much more abundant."

Israel's Futile Idolatry

57 The righteous perishes,
And no man takes *it* to heart;
Merciful men *are* taken away,
While no one considers
That the righteous is taken away
from evil.
2 He shall enter into peace;
They shall rest in their beds,
Each one walking *in* his
uprightness.

3 "But come here,
You sons of the sorceress,
You offspring of the adulterer and
the harlot!
4 Whom do you ridicule?

Against whom do you make a wide
    mouth
And stick out the tongue?
Are you not children of
    transgression,
Offspring of falsehood,
5   Inflaming yourselves with gods
    under every green tree,
Slaying the children in the valleys,
Under the clefts of the rocks?
6   Among the smooth *stones* of the
    stream
Is your portion;
They, they, *are* your lot!
Even to them you have poured a
    drink offering,
You have offered a grain offering.
Should I receive comfort in these?

7   "On a lofty and high mountain
    You have set your bed;
Even there you went up
To offer sacrifice.
8   Also behind the doors and their
    posts
You have set up your
    remembrance;
For you have uncovered yourself *to
    those other* than Me,
And have gone up to them;
You have enlarged your bed
And made *a covenant* with them;
You have loved their bed,
Where you saw *their* nudity.
9   You went to the king with
    ointment,
And increased your perfumes;
You sent your messengers far off,
And *even* descended to Sheol.
10 You are wearied in the length of
    your way;
Yet you did not say, 'There is no
    hope.'
You have found the life of your
    hand;
Therefore you were not grieved.

11 "And of whom have you been afraid,
    or feared,
That you have lied
And not remembered Me,
Nor taken *it* to your heart?
Is it not because I have held My
    peace from of old
That you do not fear Me?
12 I will declare your righteousness
And your works,

For they will not profit you.
13 When you cry out,
Let your collection *of idols*
    deliver you.
But the wind will carry them all
    away,
A breath will take *them*.
But he who puts his trust in Me
    shall possess the land,
And shall inherit My holy
    mountain."

Healing for the Backslider

14 And one shall say,
"Heap it up! Heap it up!
Prepare the way,
Take the stumbling block out of the
    way of My people."

15 For thus says the High and
    Lofty One
Who inhabits eternity, whose name
    is Holy:
"I dwell in the high and holy *place*,
With him *who* has a contrite and
    humble spirit,
To revive the spirit of the humble,
And to revive the heart of the
    contrite ones.
16 For I will not contend forever,
Nor will I always be angry;
For the spirit would fail before Me,
And the souls *which* I have made.
17 For the iniquity of his covetousness
I was angry and struck him;
I hid and was angry,
And he went on backsliding in the
    way of his heart.
18 I have seen his ways, and will
    heal him;
I will also lead him,
And restore comforts to him
And to his mourners.

19 "I create the fruit of the lips:
Peace, peace to *him who is* far off
    and to *him who is* near,"
Says the Lord,
"And I will heal him."
20 But the wicked *are* like the
    troubled sea,
When it cannot rest,
Whose waters cast up mire and
    dirt.

21 "*There is* no peace,"
Says my God, "for the wicked."

Fasting that Pleases God

58 "Cry aloud, spare not;
  Lift up your voice like a
    trumpet;
  Tell My people their transgression,
  And the house of Jacob their sins.
2 Yet they seek Me daily,
  And delight to know My ways,
  As a nation that did righteousness,
  And did not forsake the ordinance
    of their God.
  They ask of Me the ordinances of
    justice;
  They take delight in
    approaching God.
3 'Why have we fasted,' *they say,* 'and
    You have not seen?
  Why have we afflicted our souls,
    and You take no notice?'

  "In fact, in the day of your fast you
    find pleasure,
  And exploit all your laborers.
4 Indeed you fast for strife and
    debate,
  And to strike with the fist of
    wickedness.
  You will not fast as *you do* this day,
  To make your voice heard on high.
5 Is it a fast that I have chosen,
  A day for a man to afflict his soul?
  Is it to bow down his head like a
    bulrush,
  And to spread out sackcloth and
    ashes?
  Would you call this a fast,
  And an acceptable day to the LORD?

6 "*Is* this not the fast that I have
    chosen:
  To loose the bonds of wickedness,
  To undo the heavy burdens,
  To let the oppressed go free,
  And that you break every yoke?
7 *Is it* not to share your bread with
    the hungry,
  And that you bring to your house
    the poor who are cast out;
  When you see the naked, that you
    cover him,
  And not hide yourself from your
    own flesh?
8 Then your light shall break forth
    like the morning,
  Your healing shall spring forth
    speedily,
  And your righteousness shall go
    before you;

  The glory of the LORD shall be your
    rear guard.
9 Then you shall call, and the LORD
    will answer;
  You shall cry, and He will say,
    'Here I *am.*'

  "If you take away the yoke from
    your midst,
  The pointing of the finger, and
    speaking wickedness,
10 *If* you extend your soul to the
    hungry
  And satisfy the afflicted soul,
  Then your light shall dawn in the
    darkness,
  And your darkness shall *be* as the
    noonday.
11 The LORD will guide you
    continually,
  And satisfy your soul in drought,
  And strengthen your bones;
  You shall be like a watered garden,
  And like a spring of water, whose
    waters do not fail.
12 Those from among you
  Shall build the old waste places;
  You shall raise up the foundations
    of many generations;
  And you shall be called the
    Repairer of the Breach,
  The Restorer of Streets to Dwell In.

13 "If you turn away your foot from the
    Sabbath,
  From doing your pleasure on My
    holy day,
  And call the Sabbath a delight,
  The holy *day* of the LORD
    honorable,
  And shall honor Him, not doing
    your own ways,
  Nor finding your own pleasure,
  Nor speaking *your own* words,
14 Then you shall delight yourself in
    the LORD;
  And I will cause you to ride on the
    high hills of the earth,
  And feed you with the heritage of
    Jacob your father.
  The mouth of the LORD has
    spoken."

Separated from God

59 Behold, the LORD's hand is not
    shortened,
  That it cannot save;

Nor His ear heavy,
That it cannot hear.
2 But your iniquities have separated
you from your God;
And your sins have hidden *His* face
from you,
So that He will not hear.
3 For your hands are defiled with
blood,
And your fingers with iniquity;
Your lips have spoken lies,
Your tongue has muttered
perversity.

4 No one calls for justice,
Nor does *any* plead for truth.
They trust in empty words and
speak lies;
They conceive evil and bring forth
iniquity.
5 They hatch vipers' eggs and weave
the spider's web;
He who eats of their eggs dies,
And *from* that which is crushed a
viper breaks out.

6 Their webs will not become
garments,
Nor will they cover themselves
with their works;
Their works *are* works of iniquity,
And the act of violence *is* in their
hands.
7 Their feet run to evil,
And they make haste to shed
innocent blood;
Their thoughts *are* thoughts of
iniquity;
Wasting and destruction *are* in
their paths.
8 The way of peace they have not
known,
And *there is* no justice in their
ways;
They have made themselves
crooked paths;
Whoever takes that way shall not
know peace.

Sin Confessed

9 Therefore justice is far from us,
Nor does righteousness
overtake us;
We look for light, but there is
darkness!
For brightness, *but* we walk in
blackness!

10 We grope for the wall like the blind,
And we grope as if *we had* no eyes;
We stumble at noonday as at
twilight;
We are as dead *men* in desolate
places.
11 We all growl like bears,
And moan sadly like doves;
We look for justice, but *there is*
none;
For salvation, *but* it is far from us.
12 For our transgressions are
multiplied before You,
And our sins testify against us;
For our transgressions *are* with us,
And *as for* our iniquities, we know
them:
13 In transgressing and lying against
the LORD,
And departing from our God,
Speaking oppression and revolt,
Conceiving and uttering from the
heart words of falsehood.
14 Justice is turned back,
And righteousness stands afar off;
For truth is fallen in the street,
And equity cannot enter.
15 So truth fails,
And he *who* departs from evil
makes himself a prey.

The Redeemer of Zion

Then the LORD saw *it*, and it
displeased Him
That *there was* no justice.
16 He saw that *there was* no man,
And wondered that *there was* no
intercessor;
Therefore His own arm brought
salvation for Him;
And His own righteousness, it
sustained Him.
17 For He put on righteousness as a
breastplate,
And a helmet of salvation on His
head;
He put on the garments of
vengeance for clothing,
And was clad with zeal as a cloak.
18 According to *their* deeds,
accordingly He will repay,
Fury to His adversaries,
Recompense to His enemies;
The coastlands He will fully repay.
19 So shall they fear
The name of the LORD from the
west,

And His glory from the rising of
the sun;
When the enemy comes in like a
flood,
The Spirit of the LORD will lift up
a standard against him.

20 "The Redeemer will come to Zion,
And to those who turn from
transgression in Jacob,"
Says the LORD.
21 "As for Me," says the LORD, "this
is My covenant with them: My Spirit
who is upon you, and My words which
I have put in your mouth, shall not depart from your mouth, nor from the
mouth of your descendants, nor from
the mouth of your descendants' descendants," says the LORD, "from this
time and forevermore."

The Gentiles Bless Zion

60 Arise, shine;
For your light has come!
And the glory of the LORD is risen
upon you.
2 For behold, the darkness shall
cover the earth,
And deep darkness the people;
But the LORD will arise over you,
And His glory will be seen
upon you.
3 The Gentiles shall come to your
light,
And kings to the brightness of your
rising.

4 "Lift up your eyes all around,
and see:
They all gather together, they come
to you;
Your sons shall come from afar,
And your daughters shall be nursed
at your side.
5 Then you shall see and become
radiant,
And your heart shall swell with joy;
Because the abundance of the sea
shall be turned to you,
The wealth of the Gentiles shall
come to you.
6 The multitude of camels shall cover
your land,
The dromedaries of Midian and
Ephah;
All those from Sheba shall come;
They shall bring gold and incense,

And they shall proclaim the praises
of the LORD.
7 All the flocks of Kedar shall be
gathered together to you,
The rams of Nebaioth shall
minister to you;
They shall ascend with acceptance
on My altar,
And I will glorify the house of My
glory.

8 "Who are these who fly like a cloud,
And like doves to their roosts?
9 Surely the coastlands shall wait
for Me;
And the ships of Tarshish will come
first,
To bring your sons from afar,
Their silver and their gold with
them,
To the name of the LORD your God,
And to the Holy One of Israel,
Because He has glorified you.

10 "The sons of foreigners shall build
up your walls,
And their kings shall minister
to you;
For in My wrath I struck you,
But in My favor I have had mercy
on you.
11 Therefore your gates shall be open
continually;
They shall not be shut day or night,
That men may bring to you the
wealth of the Gentiles,
And their kings in procession.
12 For the nation and kingdom which
will not serve you shall perish,
And those nations shall be utterly
ruined.

13 "The glory of Lebanon shall come
to you,
The cypress, the pine, and the box
tree together,
To beautify the place of My
sanctuary;
And I will make the place of My
feet glorious.
14 Also the sons of those who
afflicted you
Shall come bowing to you,
And all those who despised you
shall fall prostrate at the soles of
your feet;

And they shall call you The City of
the LORD,
Zion of the Holy One of Israel.

15 "Whereas you have been forsaken
and hated,
So that no one went through *you,*
I will make you an eternal
excellence,
A joy of many generations.
16 You shall drink the milk of the
Gentiles,
And milk the breast of kings;
You shall know that I, the LORD, *am*
your Savior
And your Redeemer, the Mighty
One of Jacob.

17 "Instead of bronze I will bring gold,
Instead of iron I will bring silver,
Instead of wood, bronze,
And instead of stones, iron.
I will also make your officers peace,
And your magistrates
righteousness.
18 Violence shall no longer be heard
in your land,
Neither wasting nor destruction
within your borders;
But you shall call your walls
Salvation,
And your gates Praise.

God the Glory of His People

19 "The sun shall no longer be your
light by day,
Nor for brightness shall the moon
give light to you;
But the LORD will be to you an
everlasting light,
And your God your glory.
20 Your sun shall no longer go down,
Nor shall your moon withdraw
itself;
For the LORD will be your
everlasting light,
And the days of your mourning
shall be ended.
21 Also your people *shall* all *be*
righteous;
They shall inherit the land forever,
The branch of My planting,
The work of My hands,
That I may be glorified.
22 A little one shall become a
thousand,
And a small one a strong nation.

I, the LORD, will hasten it in its
time."

The Good News of Salvation

61 "The Spirit of the Lord GOD *is*
upon Me,
Because the LORD has anointed Me
To preach good tidings to the
poor;
He has sent Me to heal the
brokenhearted,
To proclaim liberty to the captives,
And the opening of the prison to
those who are bound;
2 To proclaim the acceptable year of
the LORD,
And the day of vengeance of
our God;
To comfort all who mourn,
3 To console those who mourn in
Zion,
To give them beauty for ashes,
The oil of joy for mourning,
The garment of praise for the spirit
of heaviness;
That they may be called trees of
righteousness,
The planting of the LORD, that He
may be glorified."

4 And they shall rebuild the old
ruins,
They shall raise up the former
desolations,
And they shall repair the ruined
cities,
The desolations of many
generations.
5 Strangers shall stand and feed your
flocks,
And the sons of the foreigner
Shall be your plowmen and your
vinedressers.
6 But you shall be named the priests
of the LORD,
They shall call you the servants of
our God.
You shall eat the riches of the
Gentiles,
And in their glory you shall boast.
7 Instead of your shame *you shall
have* double *honor,*
And *instead of* confusion they shall
rejoice in their portion.
Therefore in their land they shall
possess double;
Everlasting joy shall be theirs.

8 "For I, the LORD, love justice;
I hate robbery for burnt offering;
I will direct their work in truth,
And will make with them an
everlasting covenant.
9 Their descendants shall be known
among the Gentiles,
And their offspring among the
people.
All who see them shall
acknowledge them,
That they *are* the posterity *whom*
the LORD has blessed."

10 I will greatly rejoice in the LORD,
My soul shall be joyful in my God;
For He has clothed me with the
garments of salvation,
He has covered me with the robe
of righteousness,
As a bridegroom decks *himself* with
ornaments,
And as a bride adorns *herself* with
her jewels.
11 For as the earth brings forth its bud,
As the garden causes the things
that are sown in it to spring forth,
So the Lord GOD will cause
righteousness and praise to
spring forth before all the
nations.

Assurance of Zion's Salvation

62 For Zion's sake I will not hold My
peace,
And for Jerusalem's sake I will not
rest,
Until her righteousness goes forth
as brightness,
And her salvation as a lamp *that*
burns.
2 The Gentiles shall see your
righteousness,
And all kings your glory.
You shall be called by a new name,
Which the mouth of the LORD will
name.
3 You shall also be a crown of glory
In the hand of the LORD,
And a royal diadem
In the hand of your God.
4 You shall no longer be termed
Forsaken,
Nor shall your land any more be
termed Desolate;

But you shall be called Hephzibah,[x]
and your land Beulah;[y]
For the LORD delights in you,
And your land shall be married.
5 For *as* a young man marries a
virgin,
So shall your sons marry you;
And *as* the bridegroom rejoices
over the bride,
So shall your God rejoice over you.

6 I have set watchmen on your walls,
O Jerusalem;
They shall never hold their peace
day or night.
You who make mention of the
LORD, do not keep silent,
7 And give Him no rest till He
establishes
And till He makes Jerusalem a
praise in the earth.

8 The LORD has sworn by His right
hand
And by the arm of His strength:
"Surely I will no longer give your
grain
As food for your enemies;
And the sons of the foreigner shall
not drink your new wine,
For which you have labored.
9 But those who have gathered it
shall eat it,
And praise the LORD;
Those who have brought it
together shall drink it in My holy
courts."

10 Go through,
Go through the gates!
Prepare the way for the people;
Build up,
Build up the highway!
Take out the stones,
Lift up a banner for the peoples!

11 Indeed the LORD has proclaimed
To the end of the world:
"Say to the daughter of Zion,
'Surely your salvation is coming;
Behold, His reward *is* with Him,
And His work before Him.'"
12 And they shall call them The Holy
People,
The Redeemed of the LORD;

---

x Literally *My Delight Is in Her*   y Literally *Married*

And you shall be called Sought Out,
A City Not Forsaken.

The LORD in Judgment and Salvation

63 Who *is* this who comes from
Edom,
With dyed garments from Bozrah,
This *One who is* glorious in His
apparel,
Traveling in the greatness of His
strength?—

"I who speak in righteousness,
mighty to save."

2 Why *is* Your apparel red,
And Your garments like one who
treads in the winepress?

3 "I have trodden the winepress alone,
And from the peoples no one *was*
with Me.
For I have trodden them in My
anger,
And trampled them in My fury;
Their blood is sprinkled upon My
garments,
And I have stained all My robes.
4 For the day of vengeance *is* in My
heart,
And the year of My redeemed has
come.
5 I looked, but *there was* no one to
help,
And I wondered
That *there was* no one to uphold;
Therefore My own arm brought
salvation for Me;
And My own fury, it sustained Me.
6 I have trodden down the peoples in
My anger,
Made them drunk in My fury,
And brought down their strength to
the earth."

God's Mercy Remembered

7 I will mention the lovingkindnesses
of the LORD
And the praises of the LORD,
According to all that the LORD has
bestowed on us,
And the great goodness toward the
house of Israel,
Which He has bestowed on them
according to His mercies,
According to the multitude of His
lovingkindnesses.

8 For He said, "Surely they *are* My
people,
Children *who* will not lie."
So He became their Savior.
9 In all their affliction He was
afflicted,
And the Angel of His Presence
saved them;
In His love and in His pity He
redeemed them;
And He bore them and carried
them
All the days of old.
10 But they rebelled and grieved His
Holy Spirit;
So He turned Himself against them
as an enemy,
And He fought against them.

11 Then he remembered the days
of old,
Moses *and* his people, *saying:*
"Where *is* He who brought them up
out of the sea
With the shepherd of His flock?
Where *is* He who put His Holy
Spirit within them,
12 Who led *them* by the right hand of
Moses,
With His glorious arm,
Dividing the water before them
To make for Himself an everlasting
name,
13 Who led them through the deep,
As a horse in the wilderness,
That they might not stumble?"

14 As a beast goes down into the
valley,
And the Spirit of the LORD causes
him to rest,
So You lead Your people,
To make Yourself a glorious name.

A Prayer of Penitence

15 Look down from heaven,
And see from Your habitation, holy
and glorious.
Where *are* Your zeal and Your
strength,
The yearning of Your heart and
Your mercies toward me?
Are they restrained?
16 Doubtless You *are* our Father,
Though Abraham was ignorant
of us,

And Israel does not
   acknowledge us.
You, O Lᴏʀᴅ, *are* our Father;
Our Redeemer from Everlasting *is*
   Your name.
17 O Lᴏʀᴅ, why have You made us
   stray from Your ways,
And hardened our heart from Your
   fear?
Return for Your servants' sake,
The tribes of Your inheritance.
18 Your holy people have possessed
   it but a little while;
Our adversaries have trodden
   down Your sanctuary.
19 We have become *like* those of old,
   over whom You never ruled,
Those who were never called by
   Your name.

64 Oh, that You would rend the
   heavens!
That You would come down!
That the mountains might shake at
   Your presence—
2 As fire burns brushwood,
As fire causes water to boil—
To make Your name known to
   Your adversaries,
That the nations may tremble at
   Your presence!
3 When You did awesome things *for*
   which we did not look,
You came down,
The mountains shook at Your
   presence.
4 For since the beginning of the
   world
Men have not heard nor perceived
   by the ear,
Nor has the eye seen any God
   besides You,
Who acts for the one who waits
   for Him.
5 You meet him who rejoices and
   does righteousness,
Who remembers You in Your ways.
You are indeed angry, for we have
   sinned—
In these ways we continue;
And we need to be saved.

6 But we are all like an unclean *thing*,
And all our righteousnesses *are*
   like filthy rags;
We all fade as a leaf,
And our iniquities, like the wind,

Have taken us away.
7 And *there is* no one who calls on
   Your name,
Who stirs himself up to take hold
   of You;
For You have hidden Your face
   from us,
And have consumed us because of
   our iniquities.

8 But now, O Lᴏʀᴅ,
You *are* our Father;
We *are* the clay, and You our
   potter;
And all we *are* the work of Your
   hand.
9 Do not be furious, O Lᴏʀᴅ,
Nor remember iniquity forever;
Indeed, please look—we all *are*
   Your people!
10 Your holy cities are a wilderness,
Zion is a wilderness,
Jerusalem a desolation.
11 Our holy and beautiful temple,
Where our fathers praised You,
Is burned up with fire;
And all our pleasant things are laid
   waste.
12 Will You restrain Yourself because
   of these *things*, O Lᴏʀᴅ?
Will You hold Your peace, and
   afflict us very severely?

The Righteousness of God's Judgment

65 "I was sought by *those who* did
   not ask *for Me*;
I was found by *those who* did not
   seek Me.
I said, 'Here I am, here I am,'
To a nation *that* was not called by
   My name.
2 I have stretched out My hands all
   day long to a rebellious people,
Who walk in a way *that is* not
   good,
According to their own thoughts;
3 A people who provoke Me to anger
   continually to My face;
Who sacrifice in gardens,
And burn incense on altars of
   brick;
4 Who sit among the graves,
And spend the night in the tombs;
Who eat swine's flesh,
And the broth of abominable things
   is *in* their vessels;
5 Who say, 'Keep to yourself,

Do not come near me,
For I am holier than you!'
These *are* smoke in My nostrils,
A fire that burns all the day.

6 "Behold, *it is* written before Me:
I will not keep silence, but will
repay—
Even repay into their bosom—
7 Your iniquities and the iniquities of
your fathers together,"
Says the LORD,
"Who have burned incense on the
mountains
And blasphemed Me on the hills;
Therefore I will measure their
former work into their bosom."
8Thus says the LORD:
"As the new wine is found in the
cluster,
And *one* says, 'Do not destroy it,
For a blessing *is* in it,'
So will I do for My servants' sake,
That I may not destroy them all.
9 I will bring forth descendants from
Jacob,
And from Judah an heir of My
mountains;
My elect shall inherit it,
And My servants shall dwell there.
10 Sharon shall be a fold of flocks,
And the Valley of Achor a place for
herds to lie down,
For My people who have
sought Me.

11 "But you *are* those who forsake the
LORD,
Who forget My holy mountain,
Who prepare a table for Gad,[z]
And who furnish a drink offering
for Meni.[a]
12 Therefore I will number you for the
sword,
And you shall all bow down to the
slaughter;
Because, when I called, you did not
answer;
When I spoke, you did not hear,
But did evil before My eyes,
And chose *that* in which I do not
delight."
13Therefore thus says the Lord
GOD:
"Behold, My servants shall eat,

But you shall be hungry;
Behold, My servants shall drink,
But you shall be thirsty;
Behold, My servants shall
rejoice,
But you shall be ashamed;
14 Behold, My servants shall sing for
joy of heart,
But you shall cry for sorrow of
heart,
And wail for grief of spirit.
15 You shall leave your name as a
curse to My chosen;
For the Lord GOD will slay you,
And call His servants by another
name;
16 So that he who blesses himself in
the earth
Shall bless himself in the God of
truth;
And he who swears in the earth
Shall swear by the God of truth;
Because the former troubles are
forgotten,
And because they are hidden from
My eyes.

The Glorious New Creation

17 "For behold, I create new heavens
and a new earth;
And the former shall not be
remembered or come to mind.
18 But be glad and rejoice forever in
what I create;
For behold, I create Jerusalem *as*
a rejoicing,
And her people a joy.
19 I will rejoice in Jerusalem,
And joy in My people;
The voice of weeping shall no
longer be heard in her,
Nor the voice of crying.

20 "No more shall an infant from there
live but a few days,
Nor an old man who has not
fulfilled his days;
For the child shall die one hundred
years old,
But the sinner *being* one hundred
years old shall be accursed.
21 They shall build houses and inhabit
them;
They shall plant vineyards and eat
their fruit.

---

z Literally *Troop* or *Fortune*, a pagan deity   a Literally *Number* or *Destiny*, a pagan deity

22 They shall not build and another
    inhabit;
    They shall not plant and
    another eat;
    For as the days of a tree, *so shall
    be* the days of My people,
    And My elect shall long enjoy the
    work of their hands.
23 They shall not labor in vain,
    Nor bring forth children for
    trouble;
    For they *shall be* the descendants
    of the blessed of the LORD,
    And their offspring with them.

24 "It shall come to pass
    That before they call, I will answer;
    And while they are still speaking,
    I will hear.
25 The wolf and the lamb shall feed
    together,
    The lion shall eat straw like the ox,
    And dust *shall be* the serpent's
    food.
    They shall not hurt nor destroy in
    all My holy mountain,"
    Says the LORD.

True Worship and False

66 Thus says the LORD:

    "Heaven *is* My throne,
    And earth *is* My footstool.
    Where *is* the house that you will
    build Me?
    And where *is* the place of My rest?
2   For all those *things* My hand has
    made,
    And all those *things* exist,"
    Says the LORD.
    "But on this *one* will I look:
    On *him who is* poor and of a
    contrite spirit,
    And who trembles at My word.

3   "He who kills a bull *is as if* he slays
    a man;
    He who sacrifices a lamb, *as if* he
    breaks a dog's neck;
    He who offers a grain offering, *as
    if he offers* swine's blood;
    He who burns incense, *as if* he
    blesses an idol.
    Just as they have chosen their own
    ways,
    And their soul delights in their
    abominations,

4   So will I choose their delusions,
    And bring their fears on them;
    Because, when I called, no one
    answered,
    When I spoke they did not hear;
    But they did evil before My eyes,
    And chose *that* in which I do not
    delight."

The LORD Vindicates Zion

5   Hear the word of the LORD,
    You who tremble at His word:
    "Your brethren who hated you,
    Who cast you out for My name's
    sake, said,
    'Let the LORD be glorified,
    That we may see your joy.'
    But they shall be ashamed."

6   The sound of noise from the city!
    A voice from the temple!
    The voice of the LORD,
    Who fully repays His enemies!

7   "Before she was in labor, she gave
    birth;
    Before her pain came,
    She delivered a male child.
8   Who has heard such a thing?
    Who has seen such things?
    Shall the earth be made to give
    birth in one day?
    Or shall a nation be born at once?
    For as soon as Zion was in labor,
    She gave birth to her children.
9   Shall I bring to the time of birth,
    and not cause delivery?" says the
    LORD.
    "Shall I who cause delivery shut up
    the womb?" says your God.
10 "Rejoice with Jerusalem,
    And be glad with her, all you who
    love her;
    Rejoice for joy with her, all you
    who mourn for her;
11 That you may feed and be satisfied
    With the consolation of her bosom,
    That you may drink deeply and be
    delighted
    With the abundance of her glory."
12 For thus says the LORD:
    "Behold, I will extend peace to her
    like a river,
    And the glory of the Gentiles like
    a flowing stream.
    Then you shall feed;
    On *her* sides shall you be carried,

And be dandled on *her* knees.
13 As one whom his mother comforts,
So I will comfort you;
And you shall be comforted in
Jerusalem."

The Reign and Indignation of God

14 When you see *this*, your heart shall
rejoice,
And your bones shall flourish like
grass;
The hand of the LORD shall be
known to His servants,
And *His* indignation to His
enemies.
15 For behold, the LORD will come with
fire
And with His chariots, like a
whirlwind,
To render His anger with fury,
And His rebuke with flames of fire.
16 For by fire and by His sword
The LORD will judge all flesh;
And the slain of the LORD shall be
many.

17 "Those who sanctify themselves and
purify themselves,
To go to the gardens
After an *idol* in the midst,
Eating swine's flesh and the
abomination and the mouse,
Shall be consumed together," says
the LORD.
18"For I *know* their works and their
thoughts. It shall be that I will gather
all nations and tongues; and they shall
come and see My glory. 19I will set a
sign among them; and those among
them who escape I will send to the nations: *to* Tarshish and Pul and Lud, who
draw the bow, and Tubal and Javan,
to the coastlands afar off who have not
heard My fame nor seen My glory. And
they shall declare My glory among the
Gentiles. 20Then they shall bring all
your brethren for an offering to the
LORD out of all nations, on horses and
in chariots and in litters, on mules and
on camels, to My holy mountain Jerusalem," says the LORD, "as the children
of Israel bring an offering in a clean
vessel into the house of the LORD.
21And I will also take some of them for
priests *and* Levites," says the LORD.
22 "For as the new heavens and the
new earth
Which I will make shall remain
before Me," says the LORD,
"So shall your descendants and your
name remain.
23 And it shall come to pass
That from one New Moon to
another,
And from one Sabbath to
another,
All flesh shall come to worship
before Me," says the LORD.

24 "And they shall go forth and look
Upon the corpses of the men
Who have transgressed against Me.
For their worm does not die,
And their fire is not quenched.
They shall be an abhorrence to all
flesh."

The Book of
JEREMIAH

1 The words of Jeremiah the son of Hilkiah, of the priests who *were* in Anathoth in the land of Benjamin, 2to whom the word of the LORD came in the days of Josiah the son of Amon, king of Judah, in the thirteenth year of his reign. 3It came also in the days of Jehoiakim the son of Josiah, king of Judah, until the end of the eleventh year of Zedekiah the son of Josiah, king of Judah, until the carrying away of Jerusalem captive in the fifth month.

The Prophet Is Called

4Then the word of the LORD came to me, saying:

5   "Before I formed you in the womb I knew you;
    Before you were born I sanctified you;
    I ordained you a prophet to the nations."

6Then said I:
  "Ah, Lord GOD!
    Behold, I cannot speak, for I *am* a youth."

7But the LORD said to me:
  "Do not say, 'I *am* a youth,'
    For you shall go to all to whom I send you,
    And whatever I command you, you shall speak.

8   Do not be afraid of their faces,
    For I *am* with you to deliver you," says the LORD.

9Then the LORD put forth His hand and touched my mouth, and the LORD said to me:

  "Behold, I have put My words in your mouth.

10   See, I have this day set you over the nations and over the kingdoms,
    To root out and to pull down,
    To destroy and to throw down,
    To build and to plant."

11Moreover the word of the LORD came to me, saying, "Jeremiah, what do you see?"

And I said, "I see a branch of an almond tree."

12Then the LORD said to me, "You have seen well, for I am ready to perform My word."

13And the word of the LORD came to me the second time, saying, "What do you see?"

And I said, "I see a boiling pot, and it is facing away from the north."

14Then the LORD said to me:

  "Out of the north calamity shall break forth
    On all the inhabitants of the land.

15   For behold, I am calling
    All the families of the kingdoms of the north," says the LORD;
  "They shall come and each one set his throne
    At the entrance of the gates of Jerusalem,
    Against all its walls all around,
    And against all the cities of Judah.

16   I will utter My judgments
    Against them concerning all their wickedness,
    Because they have forsaken Me,
    Burned incense to other gods,
    And worshiped the works of their own hands.

17   "Therefore prepare yourself and arise,
    And speak to them all that I command you.
    Do not be dismayed before their faces,
    Lest I dismay you before them.

18   For behold, I have made you this day
    A fortified city and an iron pillar,
    And bronze walls against the whole land—
    Against the kings of Judah,
    Against its princes,
    Against its priests,
    And against the people of the land.

19   They will fight against you,
    But they shall not prevail against you.
    For I *am* with you," says the LORD, "to deliver you."

God's Case Against Israel

2 Moreover the word of the LORD came to me, saying, 2"Go and cry

in the hearing of Jerusalem, saying,
'Thus says the LORD:
　"I remember you,
　　The kindness of your youth,
　　The love of your betrothal,
　　When you went after Me in the
　　　wilderness,
　　In a land not sown.
3　Israel *was* holiness to the LORD,
　　The firstfruits of His increase.
　　All that devour him will offend;
　　Disaster will come upon them,"
　　　says the LORD.' "

4 Hear the word of the LORD, O house
of Jacob and all the families of the
house of Israel. 5 Thus says the LORD:
　"What injustice have your fathers
　　found in Me,
　　That they have gone far from Me,
　　Have followed idols,
　　And have become idolaters?
6　Neither did they say, 'Where *is* the
　　　LORD,
　　Who brought us up out of the land
　　　of Egypt,
　　Who led us through the wilderness,
　　Through a land of deserts and
　　　pits,
　　Through a land of drought and the
　　　shadow of death,
　　Through a land that no one crossed
　　And where no one dwelt?'
7　I brought you into a bountiful
　　　country,
　　To eat its fruit and its goodness.
　　But when you entered, you defiled
　　　My land
　　And made My heritage an
　　　abomination.
8　The priests did not say, 'Where *is*
　　　the LORD?'
　　And those who handle the law did
　　　not know Me;
　　The rulers also transgressed
　　　against Me;
　　The prophets prophesied by
　　　Baal,
　　And walked after *things that* do
　　　not profit.

9　"Therefore I will yet bring charges
　　　against you," says the LORD,
　"And against your children's
　　children I will bring charges.

10　For pass beyond the coasts of
　　　Cyprus^a and see,
　　Send to Kedar^b and consider
　　　diligently,
　　And see if there has been such *a*
　　　thing.
11　Has a nation changed *its* gods,
　　Which *are* not gods?
　　But My people have changed their
　　　Glory
　　For *what* does not profit.
12　Be astonished, O heavens, at this,
　　And be horribly afraid;
　　Be very desolate," says the LORD.

13　"For My people have committed two
　　　evils:
　　They have forsaken Me, the
　　　fountain of living waters,
　　And hewn themselves cisterns—
　　　broken cisterns that can hold
　　　no water.

14　"*Is* Israel a servant?
　　Is he a homeborn *slave?*
　　Why is he plundered?
15　The young lions roared at him, *and*
　　　growled;
　　They made his land waste;
　　His cities are burned, without
　　　inhabitant.
16　Also the people of Noph^c and
　　　Tahpanhes
　　Have broken the crown of your
　　　head.
17　Have you not brought this on
　　　yourself,
　　In that you have forsaken the LORD
　　　your God
　　When He led you in the way?
18　And now why take the road to
　　　Egypt,
　　To drink the waters of Sihor?
　　Or why take the road to Assyria,
　　To drink the waters of the River?^d
19　Your own wickedness will
　　　correct you,
　　And your backslidings will
　　　rebuke you.
　　Know therefore and see that *it is*
　　　an evil and bitter *thing*
　　That you have forsaken the LORD
　　　your God,
　　And the fear of Me *is* not in you,"
　　Says the Lord GOD of hosts.

<hr>

^a Western lands, especially Cyprus　　^b In the northern Arabian desert, representative of the
eastern cultures　　^c That is, Memphis in ancient Egypt　　^d That is, the Euphrates

20 "For of old I have broken your yoke
  and burst your bonds;
   And you said, 'I will not transgress,'
   When on every high hill and under
      every green tree
   You lay down, playing the harlot.
21 Yet I had planted you a noble vine,
      a seed of highest quality.
   How then have you turned
      before Me
   Into the degenerate plant of an
      alien vine?
22 For though you wash yourself with
      lye, and use much soap,
   Yet your iniquity is marked before
      Me," says the Lord GOD.

23 "How can you say, 'I am not
      polluted,
   I have not gone after the Baals'?
   See your way in the valley;
   Know what you have done:
   You are a swift dromedary
      breaking loose in her ways,
24 A wild donkey used to the
      wilderness,
   That sniffs at the wind in her
      desire;
   In her time of mating, who can turn
      her away?
   All those who seek her will not
      weary themselves;
   In her month they will find her.
25 Withhold your foot from being
      unshod, and your throat from
      thirst.
   But you said, 'There is no hope.
   No! For I have loved aliens, and
      after them I will go.'

26 "As the thief is ashamed when he
      is found out,
   So is the house of Israel ashamed;
   They and their kings and their
      princes, and their priests and
      their prophets,
27 Saying to a tree, 'You *are* my
      father,'
   And to a stone, 'You gave birth
      to me.'
   For they have turned *their* back to
      Me, and not *their* face.
   But in the time of their trouble
   They will say, 'Arise and save us.'
28 But where *are* your gods that you
      have made for yourselves?
   Let them arise,

If they can save you in the time of
   your trouble;
For *according to* the number of
   your cities
Are your gods, O Judah.

29 "Why will you plead with Me?
   You all have transgressed against
      Me," says the LORD.
30 "In vain I have chastened your
      children;
   They received no correction.
   Your sword has devoured your
      prophets
   Like a destroying lion.

31 "O generation, see the word of the
      LORD!
   Have I been a wilderness to Israel,
   Or a land of darkness?
   Why do My people say, 'We are
      lords;
   We will come no more to You'?
32 Can a virgin forget her ornaments,
   Or a bride her attire?
   Yet My people have forgotten Me
      days without number.

33 "Why do you beautify your way to
      seek love?
   Therefore you have also taught
   The wicked women your ways.
34 Also on your skirts is found
   The blood of the lives of the poor
      innocents.
   I have not found it by secret search,
   But plainly on all these things.
35 Yet you say, 'Because I am
      innocent,
   Surely His anger shall turn
      from me.'
   Behold, I will plead My case
      against you,
   Because you say, 'I have not
      sinned.'
36 Why do you gad about so much to
      change your way?
   Also you shall be ashamed of Egypt
      as you were ashamed of Assyria.
37 Indeed you will go forth from him
   With your hands on your head;
   For the LORD has rejected your
      trusted allies,
   And you will not prosper by them.

Israel Is Shameless

3 "They say, 'If a man divorces his
      wife,

And she goes from him
And becomes another man's,
May he return to her again?'
Would not that land be greatly
polluted?
But you have played the harlot with
many lovers;
Yet return to Me," says the LORD.

2 "Lift up your eyes to the desolate
heights and see:
Where have you not lain *with men*?
By the road you have sat for them
Like an Arabian in the wilderness;
And you have polluted the land
With your harlotries and your
wickedness.
3 Therefore the showers have been
withheld,
And there has been no latter rain.
You have had a harlot's forehead;
You refuse to be ashamed.
4 Will you not from this time cry
to Me,
'My Father, You *are* the guide of my
youth?
5 Will He remain angry forever?
Will He keep it to the end?'
Behold, you have spoken and done
evil things,
As you were able."

A Call to Repentance

6The LORD said also to me in the days
of Josiah the king: "Have you seen
what backsliding Israel has done? She
has gone up on every high mountain and under every green tree, and
there played the harlot. 7And I said, after she had done all these *things*, 'Return to Me.' But she did not return.
And her treacherous sister Judah
saw it. 8Then I saw that for all the
causes for which backsliding Israel had
committed adultery, I had put her
away and given her a certificate of divorce; yet her treacherous sister Judah
did not fear, but went and played
the harlot also. 9So it came to pass,
through her casual harlotry, that she
defiled the land and committed
adultery with stones and trees. 10And
yet for all this her treacherous sister
Judah has not turned to Me with her
whole heart, but in pretense," says the
LORD.

11Then the LORD said to me, "Backsliding Israel has shown herself more
righteous than treacherous Judah.
12Go and proclaim these words toward
the north, and say:
'Return, backsliding Israel,' says the
LORD;
'I will not cause My anger to fall
on you.
For I *am* merciful,' says the LORD;
'I will not remain angry forever.
13 Only acknowledge your iniquity,
That you have transgressed against
the LORD your God,
And have scattered your charms
To alien deities under every green
tree,
And you have not obeyed My
voice,' says the LORD.
14"Return, O backsliding children,"
says the LORD; "for I am married to you.
I will take you, one from a city and
two from a family, and I will bring
you to Zion. 15And I will give you shepherds according to My heart, who will
feed you with knowledge and understanding.
16"Then it shall come to pass, when
you are multiplied and increased in the
land in those days," says the LORD,
"that they will say no more, 'The ark
of the covenant of the LORD.' It shall
not come to mind, nor shall they remember it, nor shall they visit *it*, nor
shall it be made anymore.
17"At that time Jerusalem shall be
called The Throne of the LORD, and all
the nations shall be gathered to it, to
the name of the LORD, to Jerusalem. No
more shall they follow the dictates of
their evil hearts.
18"In those days the house of Judah
shall walk with the house of Israel, and
they shall come together out of the land
of the north to the land that I have given
as an inheritance to your fathers.
19"But I said:
'How can I put you among the
children
And give you a pleasant land,
A beautiful heritage of the hosts of
nations?'
"And I said:
'You shall call Me, "My Father,"
And not turn away from Me.'
20 Surely, *as* a wife treacherously
departs from her husband,

So have you dealt treacherously
   with Me,
O house of Israel," says the LORD.

21 A voice was heard on the desolate
    heights,
   Weeping *and* supplications of the
    children of Israel.
   For they have perverted their way;
   They have forgotten the LORD
    their God.

22 "Return, you backsliding children,
   And I will heal your backslidings."

   "Indeed we do come to You,
   For You are the LORD our God.
23 Truly, in vain *is salvation hoped for*
    from the hills,
   And from the multitude of
    mountains;
   Truly, in the LORD our God
   Is the salvation of Israel.
24 For shame has devoured
   The labor of our fathers from our
    youth—
   Their flocks and their herds,
   Their sons and their daughters.
25 We lie down in our shame,
   And our reproach covers us.
   For we have sinned against the
    LORD our God,
   We and our fathers,
   From our youth even to this day,
   And have not obeyed the voice of
    the LORD our God."

4 "If you will return, O Israel," says
    the LORD,
   "Return to Me;
   And if you will put away your
    abominations out of My sight,
   Then you shall not be moved.
2 And you shall swear, 'The LORD
    lives,'
   In truth, in judgment, and in
    righteousness;
   The nations shall bless themselves
    in Him,
   And in Him they shall glory."
3For thus says the LORD to the men
of Judah and Jerusalem:
   "Break up your fallow ground,
   And do not sow among thorns.
4 Circumcise yourselves to the LORD,
   And take away the foreskins of
    your hearts,

You men of Judah and inhabitants
   of Jerusalem,
Lest My fury come forth like fire,
And burn so that no one can
   quench *it*,
Because of the evil of your doings."

An Imminent Invasion

5Declare in Judah and proclaim in Je-
rusalem, and say:
   "Blow the trumpet in the land;
   Cry, 'Gather together,'
   And say, 'Assemble yourselves,
   And let us go into the fortified
    cities.'
6 Set up the standard toward Zion.
   Take refuge! Do not delay!
   For I will bring disaster from the
    north,
   And great destruction."

7 The lion has come up from his
    thicket,
   And the destroyer of nations is on
    his way.
   He has gone forth from his place
   To make your land desolate.
   Your cities will be laid waste,
   Without inhabitant.
8 For this, clothe yourself with
    sackcloth,
   Lament and wail.
   For the fierce anger of the LORD
   Has not turned back from us.

9 "And it shall come to pass in that
    day," says the LORD,
   "*That* the heart of the king shall
    perish,
   And the heart of the princes;
   The priests shall be astonished,
   And the prophets shall wonder."

10 Then I said, "Ah, Lord GOD!
   Surely You have greatly deceived
    this people and Jerusalem,
   Saying, 'You shall have peace,'
   Whereas the sword reaches to the
    heart."

11 At that time it will be said
   To this people and to Jerusalem,
   "A dry wind of the desolate heights
    blows in the wilderness
   Toward the daughter of My
    people—

Not to fan or to cleanse—
12 A wind too strong for these will
 come for Me;
 Now I will also speak judgment
 against them."

13 "Behold, he shall come up like
 clouds,
 And his chariots like a whirlwind.
 His horses are swifter than eagles.
 Woe to us, for we are plundered!"

14 O Jerusalem, wash your heart from
 wickedness,
 That you may be saved.
 How long shall your evil thoughts
 lodge within you?
15 For a voice declares from Dan
 And proclaims affliction from
 Mount Ephraim:
16 "Make mention to the nations,
 Yes, proclaim against Jerusalem,
 That watchers come from a far
 country
 And raise their voice against the
 cities of Judah.
17 Like keepers of a field they are
 against her all around,
 Because she has been rebellious
 against Me," says the LORD.
18 "Your ways and your doings
 Have procured these things for you.
 This is your wickedness,
 Because it is bitter,
 Because it reaches to your heart."

Sorrow for the Doomed Nation

19 O my soul, my soul!
 I am pained in my very heart!
 My heart makes a noise in me;
 I cannot hold my peace,
 Because you have heard, O my
 soul,
 The sound of the trumpet,
 The alarm of war.
20 Destruction upon destruction is
 cried,
 For the whole land is plundered.
 Suddenly my tents are plundered,
 And my curtains in a moment.
21 How long will I see the standard,
 And hear the sound of the trumpet?

22 "For My people are foolish,
 They have not known Me.
 They are silly children,
 And they have no understanding.

They are wise to do evil,
 But to do good they have no
 knowledge."

23 I beheld the earth, and indeed it
 was without form, and void;
 And the heavens, they had no light.
24 I beheld the mountains, and indeed
 they trembled,
 And all the hills moved back and
 forth.
25 I beheld, and indeed there was
 no man,
 And all the birds of the heavens had
 fled.
26 I beheld, and indeed the fruitful
 land was a wilderness,
 And all its cities were broken down
 At the presence of the LORD,
 By His fierce anger.

27 For thus says the LORD:
 "The whole land shall be desolate;
 Yet I will not make a full end.
28 For this shall the earth mourn,
 And the heavens above be black,
 Because I have spoken.
 I have purposed and will not relent,
 Nor will I turn back from it.
29 The whole city shall flee from the
 noise of the horsemen and
 bowmen.
 They shall go into thickets and
 climb up on the rocks.
 Every city shall be forsaken,
 And not a man shall dwell in it.

30 "And when you are plundered,
 What will you do?
 Though you clothe yourself with
 crimson,
 Though you adorn yourself with
 ornaments of gold,
 Though you enlarge your eyes with
 paint,
 In vain you will make yourself fair;
 Your lovers will despise you;
 They will seek your life.

31 "For I have heard a voice as of a
 woman in labor,
 The anguish as of her who brings
 forth her first child,
 The voice of the daughter of Zion
 bewailing herself;
 She spreads her hands, saying,
 'Woe is me now, for my soul is
 weary
 Because of murderers!'

The Justice of God's Judgment

5 "Run to and fro through the streets
  of Jerusalem;
See now and know;
And seek in her open places
If you can find a man,
If there is *anyone* who executes
  judgment,
Who seeks the truth,
And I will pardon her.

2 Though they say, 'As the LORD
  lives,'
Surely they swear falsely."

3 O LORD, *are* not Your eyes on the
  truth?
You have stricken them,
But they have not grieved;
You have consumed them,
But they have refused to receive
  correction.
They have made their faces harder
  than rock;
They have refused to return.

4 Therefore I said, "Surely these *are*
  poor.
They are foolish;
For they do not know the way of
  the LORD,
The judgment of their God.

5 I will go to the great men and speak
  to them,
For they have known the way of
  the LORD,
The judgment of their God."

But these have altogether broken
  the yoke
And burst the bonds.

6 Therefore a lion from the forest
  shall slay them,
A wolf of the deserts shall destroy
  them;
A leopard will watch over their
  cities.
Everyone who goes out from there
  shall be torn in pieces,
Because their transgressions are
  many;
Their backslidings have increased.

7 "How shall I pardon you for this?
Your children have forsaken Me
And sworn by *those that are* not
  gods.

When I had fed them to the full,
Then they committed adultery
And assembled themselves by
  troops in the harlots' houses.

8 They were *like* well-fed lusty
  stallions;
Every one neighed after his
  neighbor's wife.

9 Shall I not punish *them* for these
  things?" says the LORD.
"And shall I not avenge Myself on
  such a nation as this?

10 "Go up on her walls and destroy,
But do not make a complete end.
Take away her branches,
For they *are* not the LORD's.

11 For the house of Israel and the
  house of Judah
Have dealt very treacherously with
  Me," says the LORD.

12 They have lied about the LORD,
And said, "*It is* not He.
Neither will evil come upon us,
Nor shall we see sword or famine.

13 And the prophets become wind,
For the word *is* not in them.
Thus shall it be done to them."

14 Therefore thus says the LORD God
of hosts:
"Because you speak this word,
Behold, I will make My words in
  your mouth fire,
And this people wood,
And it shall devour them.

15 Behold, I will bring a nation against
  you from afar,
O house of Israel," says the LORD.
"It *is* a mighty nation,
It *is* an ancient nation,
A nation whose language you do
  not know,
Nor can you understand what they
  say.

16 Their quiver *is* like an open tomb;
They *are* all mighty men.

17 And they shall eat up your harvest
  and your bread,
Which your sons and daughters
  should eat.
They shall eat up your flocks and
  your herds;
They shall eat up your vines and
  your fig trees;
They shall destroy your fortified
  cities,

In which you trust, with the sword.
18"Nevertheless in those days," says the LORD, "I will not make a complete end of you. 19And it will be when you say, 'Why does the LORD our God do all these *things* to us?' then you shall answer them, 'Just as you have forsaken Me and served foreign gods in your land, so you shall serve aliens in a land *that is* not yours.'

20 "Declare this in the house of Jacob
And proclaim it in Judah, saying,
21 'Hear this now, O foolish people,
Without understanding,
Who have eyes and see not,
And who have ears and hear not:
22 Do you not fear Me?' says the LORD.
'Will you not tremble at My
presence,
Who have placed the sand as the
bound of the sea,
By a perpetual decree, that it
cannot pass beyond it?
And though its waves toss to
and fro,
Yet they cannot prevail;
Though they roar, yet they cannot
pass over it.
23 But this people has a defiant and
rebellious heart;
They have revolted and departed.
24 They do not say in their heart,
"Let us now fear the LORD our God,
Who gives rain, both the former
and the latter, in its season.
He reserves for us the appointed
weeks of the harvest."
25 Your iniquities have turned these
things away,
And your sins have withheld good
from you.

26 'For among My people are found
wicked *men;*
They lie in wait as one who sets
snares;
They set a trap;
They catch men.
27 As a cage is full of birds,
So their houses *are* full of deceit.
Therefore they have become great
and grown rich.
28 They have grown fat, they are
sleek;
Yes, they surpass the deeds of the
wicked;
They do not plead the cause,

The cause of the fatherless;
Yet they prosper,
And the right of the needy they do
not defend.
29 Shall I not punish *them* for these
things?' says the LORD.
'Shall I not avenge Myself on such
a nation as this?'

30 "An astonishing and horrible thing
Has been committed in the land:
31 The prophets prophesy falsely,
And the priests rule by their *own*
power;
And My people love *to have it* so.
But what will you do in the end?

Impending Destruction from the North

6 "O you children of Benjamin,
Gather yourselves to flee from the
midst of Jerusalem!
Blow the trumpet in Tekoa,
And set up a signal-fire in Beth
Haccerem;
For disaster appears out of the
north,
And great destruction.
2 I have likened the daughter of Zion
To a lovely and delicate woman.
3 The shepherds with their flocks
shall come to her.
They shall pitch *their* tents against
her all around.
Each one shall pasture in his own
place."

4 "Prepare war against her;
Arise, and let us go up at noon.
Woe to us, for the day goes away,
For the shadows of the evening are
lengthening.
5 Arise, and let us go by night,
And let us destroy her palaces."
6For thus has the LORD of hosts said:
"Cut down trees,
And build a mound against
Jerusalem.
This *is* the city to be punished.
She *is* full of oppression in her
midst.
7 As a fountain wells up with water,
So she wells up with her
wickedness.
Violence and plundering are heard
in her.
Before Me continually *are* grief and
wounds.

8 Be instructed, O Jerusalem,
Lest My soul depart from you;
Lest I make you desolate,
A land not inhabited."
9 Thus says the LORD of hosts:
"They shall thoroughly glean as a
vine the remnant of Israel;
As a grape-gatherer, put your hand
back into the branches."

10 To whom shall I speak and give
warning,
That they may hear?
Indeed their ear is uncircumcised,
And they cannot give heed.
Behold, the word of the LORD is a
reproach to them;
They have no delight in it.
11 Therefore I am full of the fury of
the LORD.
I am weary of holding it in.
"I will pour it out on the children
outside,
And on the assembly of young men
together;
For even the husband shall be
taken with the wife,
The aged with him who is full of
days.
12 And their houses shall be turned
over to others,
Fields and wives together;
For I will stretch out My hand
Against the inhabitants of the
land," says the LORD.
13 "Because from the least of them
even to the greatest of them,
Everyone is given to covetousness;
And from the prophet even to the
priest,
Everyone deals falsely.
14 They have also healed the hurt of
My people slightly,
Saying, 'Peace, peace!'
When there is no peace.
15 Were they ashamed when they had
committed abomination?
No! They were not at all ashamed;
Nor did they know how to blush.
Therefore they shall fall among
those who fall;
At the time I punish them,
They shall be cast down," says the
LORD.
16 Thus says the LORD:
"Stand in the ways and see,

And ask for the old paths, where
the good way is,
And walk in it;
Then you will find rest for your
souls.
But they said, 'We will not walk
in it.'
17 Also, I set watchmen over you,
saying,
'Listen to the sound of the trumpet!'
But they said, 'We will not listen.'
18 Therefore hear, you nations,
And know, O congregation, what
is among them.
19 Hear, O earth!
Behold, I will certainly bring
calamity on this people—
The fruit of their thoughts,
Because they have not heeded My
words
Nor My law, but rejected it.
20 For what purpose to Me
Comes frankincense from Sheba,
And sweet cane from a far country?
Your burnt offerings are not
acceptable,
Nor your sacrifices sweet to Me."
21 Therefore thus says the LORD:
"Behold, I will lay stumbling blocks
before this people,
And the fathers and the sons
together shall fall on them.
The neighbor and his friend shall
perish."
22 Thus says the LORD:
"Behold, a people comes from the
north country,
And a great nation will be raised
from the farthest parts of the
earth.
23 They will lay hold on bow and
spear;
They are cruel and have no mercy;
Their voice roars like the sea;
And they ride on horses,
As men of war set in array against
you, O daughter of Zion."

24 We have heard the report of it;
Our hands grow feeble.
Anguish has taken hold of us,
Pain as of a woman in labor.
25 Do not go out into the field,
Nor walk by the way.
Because of the sword of the enemy,
Fear is on every side.
26 O daughter of my people,

Dress in sackcloth
And roll about in ashes!
Make mourning *as for* an only son,
   most bitter lamentation;
For the plunderer will suddenly
   come upon us.

27 "I have set you *as* an assayer *and* a
      fortress among My people,
   That you may know and test their
      way.
28 They *are* all stubborn rebels,
      walking as slanderers.
   They are bronze and iron,
   They *are* all corrupters;
29 The bellows blow fiercely,
   The lead is consumed by the fire;
   The smelter refines in vain,
   For the wicked are not drawn off.
30 *People* will call them rejected
      silver,
   Because the LORD has rejected
      them."

Trusting in Lying Words

7 The word that came to Jeremiah
from the LORD, saying, 2"Stand in
the gate of the LORD's house, and proclaim there this word, and say, 'Hear
the word of the LORD, all *you of* Judah
who enter in at these gates to worship
the LORD!' " 3Thus says the LORD of
hosts, the God of Israel: "Amend your
ways and your doings, and I will cause
you to dwell in this place. 4Do not trust
in these lying words, saying, 'The temple of the LORD, the temple of the LORD,
the temple of the LORD *are* these.'

5"For if you thoroughly amend your
ways and your doings, if you thoroughly execute judgment between a
man and his neighbor, 6*if* you do not
oppress the stranger, the fatherless, and
the widow, and do not shed innocent
blood in this place, or walk after other
gods to your hurt, 7then I will cause you
to dwell in this place, in the land that I
gave to your fathers forever and ever.

8"Behold, you trust in lying words
that cannot profit. 9Will you steal, murder, commit adultery, swear falsely,
burn incense to Baal, and walk after
other gods whom you do not know,
10and *then* come and stand before Me
in this house which is called by My
name, and say, 'We are delivered to do
all these abominations'? 11Has this

house, which is called by My name, become a den of thieves in your eyes? Behold, I, even I, have seen *it*," says the
LORD.

12"But go now to My place which *was*
in Shiloh, where I set My name at the
first, and see what I did to it because
of the wickedness of My people Israel.
13And now, because you have done all
these works," says the LORD, "and I
spoke to you, rising up early and speaking, but you did not hear, and I called
you, but you did not answer, 14therefore
I will do to the house which is called
by My name, in which you trust, and
to this place which I gave to you and
your fathers, as I have done to Shiloh.
15And I will cast you out of My sight,
as I have cast out all your brethren—
the whole posterity of Ephraim.

16"Therefore do not pray for this people, nor lift up a cry or prayer for them,
nor make intercession to Me; for I will
not hear you. 17Do you not see what
they do in the cities of Judah and in
the streets of Jerusalem? 18The children
gather wood, the fathers kindle the fire,
and the women knead dough, to make
cakes for the queen of heaven; and *they*
pour out drink offerings to other gods,
that they may provoke Me to anger.
19Do they provoke Me to anger?" says
the LORD. "*Do they* not *provoke* themselves, to the shame of their own
faces?"

20Therefore thus says the Lord GOD:
"Behold, My anger and My fury will be
poured out on this place—on man and
on beast, on the trees of the field and
on the fruit of the ground. And it will
burn and not be quenched."

21Thus says the LORD of hosts, the
God of Israel: "Add your burnt offerings to your sacrifices and eat meat.
22For I did not speak to your fathers,
or command them in the day that I
brought them out of the land of Egypt,
concerning burnt offerings or sacrifices. 23But this is what I commanded
them, saying, 'Obey My voice, and I will
be your God, and you shall be My people. And walk in all the ways that I have
commanded you, that it may be well
with you.' 24Yet they did not obey or
incline their ear, but followed the counsels *and* the dictates of their evil hearts,
and went backward and not forward.

25Since the day that your fathers came out of the land of Egypt until this day, I have even sent to you all My servants the prophets, daily rising up early and sending *them.* 26Yet they did not obey Me or incline their ear, but stiffened their neck. They did worse than their fathers.

27"Therefore you shall speak all these words to them, but they will not obey you. You shall also call to them, but they will not answer you.

Judgment on Obscene Religion

28"So you shall say to them, 'This *is* a nation that does not obey the voice of the LORD their God nor receive correction. Truth has perished and has been cut off from their mouth. 29Cut off your hair and cast *it* away, and take up a lamentation on the desolate heights; for the LORD has rejected and forsaken the generation of His wrath.' 30For the children of Judah have done evil in My sight," says the LORD. "They have set their abominations in the house which is called by My name, to pollute it. 31And they have built the high places of Tophet, which *is* in the Valley of the Son of Hinnom, to burn their sons and their daughters in the fire, which I did not command, nor did it come into My heart.

32"Therefore behold, the days are coming," says the LORD, "when it will no more be called Tophet, or the Valley of the Son of Hinnom, but the Valley of Slaughter; for they will bury in Tophet until there is no room. 33The corpses of this people will be food for the birds of the heaven and for the beasts of the earth. And no one will frighten *them away.* 34Then I will cause to cease from the cities of Judah and from the streets of Jerusalem the voice of mirth and the voice of gladness, the voice of the bridegroom and the voice of the bride. For the land shall be desolate.

8 "At that time," says the LORD, "they shall bring out the bones of the kings of Judah, and the bones of its princes, and the bones of the priests, and the bones of the prophets, and the bones of the inhabitants of Jerusalem, out of their graves. 2They shall spread them before the sun and the moon and all the host of heaven, which they have loved and which they have served and after which they have walked, which they have sought and which they have worshiped. They shall not be gathered nor buried; they shall be like refuse on the face of the earth. 3Then death shall be chosen rather than life by all the residue of those who remain of this evil family, who remain in all the places where I have driven them," says the LORD of hosts.

The Peril of False Teaching

4"Moreover you shall say to them, 'Thus says the LORD:

"Will they fall and not rise?
Will one turn away and not return?
5 Why has this people slidden back,
Jerusalem, in a perpetual
backsliding?
They hold fast to deceit,
They refuse to return.
6 I listened and heard,
But they do not speak aright.
No man repented of his
wickedness,
Saying, 'What have I done?'
Everyone turned to his own course,
As the horse rushes into the battle.

7 "Even the stork in the heavens
Knows her appointed times;
And the turtledove, the swift, and
the swallow
Observe the time of their coming.
But My people do not know the
judgment of the LORD.

8 "How can you say, 'We *are* wise,
And the law of the LORD *is* with us'?
Look, the false pen of the scribe
certainly works falsehood.
9 The wise men are ashamed,
They are dismayed and taken.
Behold, they have rejected the
word of the LORD;
So what wisdom do they have?
10 Therefore I will give their wives to
others,
And their fields to those who will
inherit *them;*
Because from the least even to the
greatest
Everyone is given to covetousness;
From the prophet even to the priest

Everyone deals falsely.
11 For they have healed the hurt of the
daughter of My people slightly,
Saying, 'Peace, peace!'
When *there is* no peace.
12 Were they ashamed when they had
committed abomination?
No! They were not at all ashamed,
Nor did they know how to blush.
Therefore they shall fall among
those who fall;
In the time of their punishment
They shall be cast down," says the
LORD.

13 "I will surely consume them," says
the LORD.
"No grapes *shall be* on the vine,
Nor figs on the fig tree,
And the leaf shall fade;
And *the things* I have given them
shall pass away from them." ' "

14 "Why do we sit still?
Assemble yourselves,
And let us enter the fortified cities,
And let us be silent there.
For the LORD our God has put us
to silence
And given us water of gall to drink,
Because we have sinned against the
LORD.

15 "*We* looked for peace, but no good
came;
And for a time of health, and there
was trouble!
16 The snorting of His horses was
heard from Dan.
The whole land trembled at the
sound of the neighing of His
strong ones;
For they have come and devoured
the land and all that is in it,
The city and those who dwell in it."

17 "For behold, I will send serpents
among you,
Vipers which cannot be charmed,
And they shall bite you," says the
LORD.

The Prophet Mourns for the People

18 I would comfort myself in sorrow;
My heart *is* faint in me.
19 Listen! The voice,

The cry of the daughter of my
people
From a far country:
"*Is* not the LORD in Zion?
Is not her King in her?"

"Why have they provoked Me to
anger
With their carved images—
With foreign idols?"

20 "The harvest is past,
The summer is ended,
And we are not saved!"

21 For the hurt of the daughter of my
people I am hurt.
I am mourning;
Astonishment has taken hold
of me.
22 *Is there* no balm in Gilead,
Is there no physician there?
Why then is there no recovery
For the health of the daughter of
my people?

9 Oh, that my head were waters,
And my eyes a fountain of tears,
That I might weep day and night
For the slain of the daughter of my
people!
2 Oh, that I had in the wilderness
A lodging place for travelers;
That I might leave my people,
And go from them!
For they *are* all adulterers,
An assembly of treacherous men.

3 "And *like* their bow they have bent
their tongues *for* lies.
They are not valiant for the truth
on the earth.
For they proceed from evil to evil,
And they do not know Me," says
the LORD.
4 "Everyone take heed to his
neighbor,
And do not trust any brother;
For every brother will utterly
supplant,
And every neighbor will walk with
slanderers.
5 Everyone will deceive his neighbor,
And will not speak the truth;
They have taught their tongue to
speak lies;

They weary themselves to commit
iniquity.
6   Your dwelling place *is* in the midst
of deceit;
Through deceit they refuse to know
Me," says the LORD.
7Therefore thus says the LORD of
hosts:
"Behold, I will refine them and try
them;
For how shall I deal with the
daughter of My people?
8   Their tongue *is* an arrow shot out;
It speaks deceit;
One speaks peaceably to his
neighbor with his mouth,
But in his heart he lies in wait.
9   Shall I not punish them for these
things?" says the LORD.
"Shall I not avenge Myself on such
a nation as this?"

10 I will take up a weeping and
wailing for the mountains,
And for the dwelling places of the
wilderness a lamentation,
Because they are burned up,
So that no one can pass through;
Nor can *men* hear the voice of the
cattle.
Both the birds of the heavens and
the beasts have fled;
They are gone.

11 "I will make Jerusalem a heap of
ruins, a den of jackals.
I will make the cities of Judah
desolate, without an inhabitant."
12Who *is* the wise man who may understand this? And *who is he* to whom
the mouth of the LORD has spoken, that
he may declare it? Why does the land
perish *and* burn up like a wilderness,
so that no one can pass through?
13And the LORD said, "Because they
have forsaken My law which I set before them, and have not obeyed My
voice, nor walked according to it,
14but they have walked according to the
dictates of their own hearts and after
the Baals, which their fathers taught
them," 15therefore thus says the LORD
of hosts, the God of Israel: "Behold, I
will feed them, this people, with wormwood, and give them water of gall to
drink. 16I will scatter them also among
the Gentiles, whom neither they nor

their fathers have known. And I will
send a sword after them until I have
consumed them."

The People Mourn in Judgment

17Thus says the LORD of hosts:
"Consider and call for the mourning
women,
That they may come;
And send for skillful wailing
women,
That they may come.
18 Let them make haste
And take up a wailing for us,
That our eyes may run with tears,
And our eyelids gush with water.
19 For a voice of wailing is heard from
Zion:
'How we are plundered!
We are greatly ashamed,
Because we have forsaken the land,
Because we have been cast out of
our dwellings.' "

20 Yet hear the word of the LORD,
O women,
And let your ear receive the word
of His mouth;
Teach your daughters wailing,
And everyone her neighbor a
lamentation.
21 For death has come through our
windows,
Has entered our palaces,
To kill off the children—*no longer
to be* outside!
And the young men—*no longer* on
the streets!

22 Speak, "Thus says the LORD:

'Even the carcasses of men shall fall
as refuse on the open field,
Like cuttings after the harvester,
And no one shall gather *them.*' "
23Thus says the LORD:
"Let not the wise *man* glory in his
wisdom,
Let not the mighty *man* glory in his
might,
Nor let the rich *man* glory in his
riches;
24 But let him who glories glory in
this,
That he understands and
knows Me,

That I *am* the LORD, exercising
lovingkindness, judgment, and
righteousness in the earth.
For in these I delight," says the
LORD.

25"Behold, the days are coming,"
says the LORD, "that I will punish all
who are circumcised with the uncircumcised—26Egypt, Judah, Edom, the
people of Ammon, Moab, and all *who
are* in the farthest corners, who dwell
in the wilderness. For all *these* nations
are uncircumcised, and all the house of
Israel *are* uncircumcised in the heart."

Idols and the True God

10 Hear the word which the LORD
speaks to you, O house of Israel.
2Thus says the LORD:
"Do not learn the way of the
Gentiles;
Do not be dismayed at the signs of
heaven,
For the Gentiles are dismayed at
them.
3   For the customs of the peoples *are*
futile;
For *one* cuts a tree from the forest,
The work of the hands of the
workman, with the ax.
4   They decorate it with silver and
gold;
They fasten it with nails and
hammers
So that it will not topple.
5   They *are* upright, like a palm
tree,
And they cannot speak;
They must be carried,
Because they cannot go *by
themselves.*
Do not be afraid of them,
For they cannot do evil,
Nor can they do any good."

6   Inasmuch as *there is* none like You,
O LORD
(You *are* great, and Your name *is*
great in might),
7   Who would not fear You, O King
of the nations?
For this is Your rightful due.
For among all the wise *men* of the
nations,

And in all their kingdoms,
There is none like You.
8   But they are altogether dull-hearted
and foolish;
A wooden idol *is* a worthless
doctrine.
9   Silver is beaten into plates;
It is brought from Tarshish,
And gold from Uphaz,
The work of the craftsman
And of the hands of the metalsmith;
Blue and purple *are* their clothing;
They *are* all the work of skillful
men.
10   But the LORD *is* the true God;
He *is* the living God and the
everlasting King.
At His wrath the earth will tremble,
And the nations will not be able to
endure His indignation.

11Thus you shall say to them: "The
gods that have not made the heavens
and the earth shall perish from the
earth and from under these heavens."
12   He has made the earth by His
power,
He has established the world by His
wisdom,
And has stretched out the heavens
at His discretion.
13   When He utters His voice,
There is a multitude of waters in
the heavens:
"And He causes the vapors to ascend
from the ends of the earth.
He makes lightning for the rain,
He brings the wind out of His
treasuries."*e*

14   Everyone is dull-hearted, without
knowledge;
Every metalsmith is put to shame
by an image;
For his molded image *is*
falsehood,
And *there is* no breath in them.
15   They *are* futile, a work of errors;
In the time of their punishment they
shall perish.
16   The Portion of Jacob *is* not like
them,
For He *is* the Maker of all *things,*
And Israel *is* the tribe of His
inheritance;
The LORD of hosts *is* His name.

e Compare Psalm 135.7

The Coming Captivity of Judah

17 Gather up your wares from the
    land,
    O inhabitant of the fortress!
18For thus says the LORD:
    "Behold, I will throw out at this time
    The inhabitants of the land,
    And will distress them,
    That they may find it so."

19 Woe is me for my hurt!
    My wound is severe.
    But I say, "Truly this is an infirmity,
    And I must bear it."
20 My tent is plundered,
    And all my cords are broken;
    My children have gone from me,
    And they are no more.
    There is no one to pitch my tent
    anymore,
    Or set up my curtains.

21 For the shepherds have become
    dull-hearted,
    And have not sought the LORD;
    Therefore they shall not prosper,
    And all their flocks shall be
    scattered.
22 Behold, the noise of the report has
    come,
    And a great commotion out of the
    north country,
    To make the cities of Judah
    desolate, a den of jackals.

23 O LORD, I know the way of man is
    not in himself;
    It is not in man who walks to direct
    his own steps.
24 O LORD, correct me, but with
    justice;
    Not in Your anger, lest You bring
    me to nothing.
25 Pour out Your fury on the Gentiles,
    who do not know You,
    And on the families who do not call
    on Your name;
    For they have eaten up Jacob,
    Devoured him and consumed him,
    And made his dwelling place
    desolate.

The Broken Covenant

11 The word that came to Jeremiah
from the LORD, saying, 2"Hear the
words of this covenant, and speak to
the men of Judah and to the inhabitants
of Jerusalem; 3and say to them, 'Thus
says the LORD God of Israel: "Cursed
is the man who does not obey the words
of this covenant 4which I commanded
your fathers in the day I brought them
out of the land of Egypt, from the iron
furnace, saying, 'Obey My voice, and
do according to all that I command you;
so shall you be My people, and I will
be your God,' 5that I may establish the
oath which I have sworn to your fathers, to give them 'a land flowing with
milk and honey,' as it is this day."'"
And I answered and said, "So be it,
LORD."

6Then the LORD said to me, "Proclaim
all these words in the cities of Judah
and in the streets of Jerusalem, saying:
'Hear the words of this covenant and
do them. 7For I earnestly exhorted your
fathers in the day I brought them up
out of the land of Egypt, until this day,
rising early and exhorting, saying,
"Obey My voice." 8Yet they did not
obey or incline their ear, but everyone
followed the dictates of his evil heart;
therefore I will bring upon them all the
words of this covenant, which I commanded them to do, but which they
have not done.'"

9And the LORD said to me, "A conspiracy has been found among the men of
Judah and among the inhabitants of Jerusalem. 10They have turned back to
the iniquities of their forefathers who
refused to hear My words, and they
have gone after other gods to serve
them; the house of Israel and the house
of Judah have broken My covenant
which I made with their fathers."

11Therefore thus says the LORD: "Behold, I will surely bring calamity on
them which they will not be able to escape; and though they cry out to Me, I
will not listen to them. 12Then the cities
of Judah and the inhabitants of Jerusalem will go and cry out to the gods to
whom they offer incense, but they will
not save them at all in the time of their
trouble. 13For according to the number
of your cities were your gods, O Judah;
and according to the number of the
streets of Jerusalem you have set up altars to that shameful thing, altars to
burn incense to Baal.

14"So do not pray for this people, or

lift up a cry or prayer for them; for I will not hear *them* in the time that they cry out to Me because of their trouble. 15 "What has My beloved to do in My house,

Having done lewd deeds with many?

And the holy flesh has passed from you.

When you do evil, then you rejoice.

16 The LORD called your name,

Green Olive Tree, Lovely *and* of Good Fruit.

With the noise of a great tumult

He has kindled fire on it,

And its branches are broken.

17"For the LORD of hosts, who planted you, has pronounced doom against you for the evil of the house of Israel and of the house of Judah, which they have done against themselves to provoke Me to anger in offering incense to Baal."

Jeremiah's Life Threatened

18Now the LORD gave me knowledge *of it,* and I know *it;* for You showed me their doings. 19But I *was* like a docile lamb brought to the slaughter; and I did not know that they had devised schemes against me, *saying,* "Let us destroy the tree with its fruit, and let us cut him off from the land of the living, that his name may be remembered no more."

20 But, O LORD of hosts,

You who judge righteously,

Testing the mind and the heart,

Let me see Your vengeance on them,

For to You I have revealed my cause.

21"Therefore thus says the LORD concerning the men of Anathoth who seek your life, saying, 'Do not prophesy in the name of the LORD, lest you die by our hand'—22therefore thus says the LORD of hosts: 'Behold, I will punish them. The young men shall die by the sword, their sons and their daughters shall die by famine; 23and there shall be no remnant of them, for I will bring catastrophe on the men of Anathoth, *even* the year of their punishment.' "

Jeremiah's Question

12 Righteous *are* You, O LORD, when I plead with You;

Yet let me talk with You about *Your* judgments.

Why does the way of the wicked prosper?

Why are those happy who deal so treacherously?

2 You have planted them, yes, they have taken root;

They grow, yes, they bear fruit.

You *are* near in their mouth

But far from their mind.

3 But You, O LORD, know me;

You have seen me,

And You have tested my heart toward You.

Pull them out like sheep for the slaughter,

And prepare them for the day of slaughter.

4 How long will the land mourn,

And the herbs of every field wither?

The beasts and birds are consumed,

For the wickedness of those who dwell there,

Because they said, "He will not see our final end."

The LORD Answers Jeremiah

5 "If you have run with the footmen, and they have wearied you,

Then how can you contend with horses?

And *if* in the land of peace,

In which you trusted, *they wearied you,*

Then how will you do in the floodplain of the Jordan?

6 For even your brothers, the house of your father,

Even they have dealt treacherously with you;

Yes, they have called a multitude after you.

Do not believe them,

Even though they speak smooth words to you.

7 "I have forsaken My house, I have left My heritage;

I have given the dearly beloved of My soul into the hand of her enemies.

8 My heritage is to Me like a lion in the forest;

It cries out against Me;

Therefore I have hated it.

9 My heritage *is* to Me *like* a speckled
     vulture;
   The vultures all around *are*
     against her.
   Come, assemble all the beasts of
     the field,
   Bring them to devour!

10 "Many rulers have destroyed My
     vineyard,
   They have trodden My portion
     underfoot;
   They have made My pleasant
     portion a desolate wilderness.
11 They have made it desolate;
   Desolate, it mourns to Me;
   The whole land is made desolate,
   Because no one takes *it* to heart.
12 The plunderers have come
   On all the desolate heights in the
     wilderness,
   For the sword of the LORD shall
     devour
   From *one* end of the land to the
     other end of the land;
   No flesh shall have peace.
13 They have sown wheat but reaped
     thorns;
   They have put themselves to pain
     but do not profit.
   But be ashamed of your harvest
   Because of the fierce anger of the
     LORD."

14Thus says the LORD: "Against all
My evil neighbors who touch the inheritance which I have caused My people
Israel to inherit—behold, I will pluck
them out of their land and pluck out
the house of Judah from among them.
15Then it shall be, after I have plucked
them out, that I will return and have
compassion on them and bring them
back, everyone to his heritage and
everyone to his land. 16And it shall be,
if they will learn carefully the ways of
My people, to swear by My name, 'As
the LORD lives,' as they taught My people to swear by Baal, then they shall
be established in the midst of My people. 17But if they do not obey, I will utterly pluck up and destroy that nation,"
says the LORD.

Symbol of the Linen Sash

13 Thus the LORD said to me: "Go
and get yourself a linen sash, and
put it around your waist, but do not put

it in water." 2So I got a sash according
to the word of the LORD, and put *it*
around my waist.

3And the word of the LORD came
to me the second time, saying, 4"Take
the sash that you acquired, which *is*
around your waist, and arise, go to the
Euphrates, and hide it there in a
hole in the rock." 5So I went and hid
it by the Euphrates, as the LORD commanded me.

6Now it came to pass after many days
that the LORD said to me, "Arise, go to
the Euphrates, and take from there the
sash which I commanded you to hide
there." 7Then I went to the Euphrates
and dug, and I took the sash from the
place where I had hidden it; and there
was the sash, ruined. It was profitable
for nothing.

8Then the word of the LORD came to
me, saying, 9"Thus says the LORD: 'In
this manner I will ruin the pride of Judah and the great pride of Jerusalem.
10This evil people, who refuse to hear
My words, who follow the dictates of
their hearts, and walk after other gods
to serve them and worship them, shall
be just like this sash which is profitable
for nothing. 11For as the sash clings to
the waist of a man, so I have caused
the whole house of Israel and the whole
house of Judah to cling to Me,' says the
LORD, 'that they may become My people, for renown, for praise, and for
glory; but they would not hear.'

Symbol of the Wine Bottles

12"Therefore you shall speak to them
this word: 'Thus says the LORD God of
Israel: "Every bottle shall be filled with
wine." '

"And they will say to you, 'Do we not
certainly know that every bottle will be
filled with wine?'

13"Then you shall say to them, 'Thus
says the LORD: "Behold, I will fill all the
inhabitants of this land—even the kings
who sit on David's throne, the priests,
the prophets, and all the inhabitants of
Jerusalem—with drunkenness! 14And
I will dash them one against another,
even the fathers and the sons together,"
says the LORD. "I will not pity nor spare
nor have mercy, but will destroy
them." ' "

Pride Precedes Captivity

15 Hear and give ear:
Do not be proud,
For the LORD has spoken.
16 Give glory to the LORD your God
Before He causes darkness,
And before your feet stumble
On the dark mountains,
And while you are looking for
light,
He turns it into the shadow of death
And makes *it* dense darkness.
17 But if you will not hear it,
My soul will weep in secret for *your*
pride;
My eyes will weep bitterly
And run down with tears,
Because the LORD's flock has been
taken captive.

18 Say to the king and to the queen
mother,
"Humble yourselves;
Sit down,
For your rule shall collapse, the
crown of your glory."
19 The cities of the South shall be
shut up,
And no one shall open *them;*
Judah shall be carried away
captive, all of it;
It shall be wholly carried away
captive.

20 Lift up your eyes and see
Those who come from the north.
Where *is* the flock *that* was given
to you,
Your beautiful sheep?
21 What will you say when He
punishes you?
For you have taught them
To be chieftains, to be head
over you.
Will not pangs seize you,
Like a woman in labor?
22 And if you say in your heart,
"Why have these things come
upon me?"
For the greatness of your iniquity
Your skirts have been uncovered,
Your heels made bare.
23 Can the Ethiopian change his skin
or the leopard its spots?
Then may you also do good who
are accustomed to do evil.

24 "Therefore I will scatter them like
stubble
That passes away by the wind of
the wilderness.
25 This is your lot,
The portion of your measures from
Me," says the LORD,
"Because you have forgotten Me
And trusted in falsehood.
26 Therefore I will uncover your skirts
over your face,
That your shame may appear.
27 I have seen your adulteries
And your *lustful* neighings,
The lewdness of your harlotry,
Your abominations on the hills in
the fields.
Woe to you, O Jerusalem!
Will you still not be made clean?"

Sword, Famine, and Pestilence

14 The word of the LORD that came
to Jeremiah concerning the
droughts.
2 "Judah mourns,
And her gates languish;
They mourn for the land,
And the cry of Jerusalem has
gone up.
3 Their nobles have sent their lads
for water;
They went to the cisterns *and* found
no water.
They returned with their vessels
empty;
They were ashamed and
confounded
And covered their heads.
4 Because the ground is parched,
For there was no rain in the land,
The plowmen were ashamed;
They covered their heads.
5 Yes, the deer also gave birth in the
field,
But left because there was no
grass.
6 And the wild donkeys stood in the
desolate heights;
They sniffed at the wind like
jackals;
Their eyes failed because *there was*
no grass."

7 O LORD, though our iniquities
testify against us,
Do it for Your name's sake;
For our backslidings are many,

We have sinned against You.

8 O the Hope of Israel, his Savior in
time of trouble,
Why should You be like a stranger
in the land,
And like a traveler *who* turns aside
to tarry for a night?

9 Why should You be like a man
astonished,
Like a mighty one *who* cannot
save?
Yet You, O LORD, *are* in our midst,
And we are called by Your name;
Do not leave us!

10Thus says the LORD to this people:
"Thus they have loved to wander;
They have not restrained their
feet.
Therefore the LORD does not accept
them;
He will remember their iniquity
now,
And punish their sins."

11Then the LORD said to me, "Do not
pray for this people, for *their* good.
12When they fast, I will not hear their
cry; and when they offer burnt offering
and grain offering, I will not accept
them. But I will consume them by the
sword, by the famine, and by the pestilence."

13Then I said, "Ah, Lord GOD! Behold,
the prophets say to them, 'You shall not
see the sword, nor shall you have famine, but I will give you assured peace
in this place.' "

14And the LORD said to me, "The
prophets prophesy lies in My name. I
have not sent them, commanded them,
nor spoken to them; they prophesy to
you a false vision, divination, a worthless thing, and the deceit of their heart.
15Therefore thus says the LORD concerning the prophets who prophesy in
My name, whom I did not send, and
who say, 'Sword and famine shall not
be in this land'—'By sword and famine
those prophets shall be consumed!
16And the people to whom they prophesy shall be cast out in the streets
of Jerusalem because of the famine and
the sword; they will have no one to bury
them—them nor their wives, their sons
nor their daughters—for I will pour
their wickedness on them.'

17"Therefore you shall say this word
to them:

'Let my eyes flow with tears night
and day,
And let them not cease;
For the virgin daughter of my
people
Has been broken with a mighty
stroke, with a very severe blow.

18 If I go out to the field,
Then behold, those slain with the
sword!
And if I enter the city,
Then behold, those sick from
famine!
Yes, both prophet and priest go
about in a land they do not
know.' "

The People Plead for Mercy

19 Have You utterly rejected Judah?
Has Your soul loathed Zion?
Why have You stricken us so that
there is no healing for us?
We looked for peace, but *there was*
no good;
And for the time of healing, and
there was trouble.

20 We acknowledge, O LORD, our
wickedness
And the iniquity of our fathers,
For we have sinned against You.

21 Do not abhor *us,* for Your name's
sake;
Do not disgrace the throne of Your
glory.
Remember, do not break Your
covenant with us.

22 Are there any among the idols of
the nations that can cause rain?
Or can the heavens give showers?
Are You not He, O LORD our God?
Therefore we will wait for You,
Since You have made all these.

The LORD Will Not Relent

15 Then the LORD said to me, "*Even*
if Moses and Samuel stood before
Me, My mind *would* not *be* favorable
toward this people. Cast *them* out of My
sight, and let them go forth. 2And it
shall be, if they say to you, 'Where
should we go?' then you shall tell them,
'Thus says the LORD:

"Such as *are* for death, to death;
And such as *are* for the sword, to
the sword;
And such as *are* for the famine, to
the famine;

And such as *are* for the captivity,
to the captivity." '

3"And I will appoint over them four
forms *of destruction*," says the LORD:
"the sword to slay, the dogs to drag,
the birds of the heavens and the beasts
of the earth to devour and destroy.
4I will hand them over to trouble, to all
kingdoms of the earth, because of Manasseh the son of Hezekiah, king of Judah, for what he did in Jerusalem.

5   "For who will have pity on you,
      O Jerusalem?
      Or who will bemoan you?
      Or who will turn aside to ask how
         you are doing?
6   You have forsaken Me," says the
         LORD,
      "You have gone backward.
      Therefore I will stretch out My
         hand against you and
         destroy you;
      I am weary of relenting!
7   And I will winnow them with a
         winnowing fan in the gates of
         the land;
      I will bereave *them* of children;
      I will destroy My people,
      Since they do not return from their
         ways.
8   Their widows will be increased to
         Me more than the sand of the
         seas;
      I will bring against them,
      Against the mother of the
         young men,
      A plunderer at noonday;
      I will cause anguish and terror to
         fall on them suddenly.

9   "She languishes who has borne
         seven;
      She has breathed her last;
      Her sun has gone down
      While *it was* yet day;
      She has been ashamed and
         confounded.
      And the remnant of them I will
         deliver to the sword
      Before their enemies," says the
         LORD.

Jeremiah's Dejection

10   Woe is me, my mother,
      That you have borne me,
      A man of strife and a man of
         contention to the whole earth!

      I have neither lent for interest,
      Nor have men lent to me for
         interest.
      Every one of them curses me.
11The LORD said:
      "Surely it will be well with your
         remnant;
      Surely I will cause the enemy to
         intercede with you
      In the time of adversity and in the
         time of affliction.
12   Can anyone break iron,
      The northern iron and the bronze?
13   Your wealth and your treasures
      I will give as plunder without price,
      Because of all your sins,
      Throughout your territories.
14   And I will make *you* cross over with
         your enemies
      Into a land *which* you do not know;
      For a fire is kindled in My anger,
      Which shall burn upon you."

15   O LORD, You know;
      Remember me and visit me,
      And take vengeance for me on my
         persecutors.
      In Your enduring patience, do not
         take me away.
      Know that for Your sake I have
         suffered rebuke.
16   Your words were found, and I ate
         them,
      And Your word was to me the joy
         and rejoicing of my heart;
      For I am called by Your name,
      O LORD God of hosts.
17   I did not sit in the assembly of the
         mockers,
      Nor did I rejoice;
      I sat alone because of Your hand,
      For You have filled me with
         indignation.
18   Why is my pain perpetual
      And my wound incurable,
      Which refuses to be healed?
      Will You surely be to me like an
         unreliable stream,
      As waters *that* fail?

The LORD Reassures Jeremiah

19Therefore thus says the LORD:
   "If you return,
      Then I will bring you back;
      You shall stand before Me;
      If you take out the precious from
         the vile,

You shall be as My mouth.
Let them return to you,
But you must not return to them.
20 And I will make you to this people
a fortified bronze wall;
And they will fight against you,
But they shall not prevail against
you;
For I *am* with you to save you
And deliver you," says the LORD.
21 "I will deliver you from the hand of
the wicked,
And I will redeem you from the grip
of the terrible."

Jeremiah's Life-Style and Message

16 The word of the LORD also came
to me, saying, 2"You shall not
take a wife, nor shall you have sons or
daughters in this place." 3For thus says
the LORD concerning the sons and
daughters who are born in this place,
and concerning their mothers who bore
them and their fathers who begot them
in this land: 4"They shall die gruesome
deaths; they shall not be lamented nor
shall they be buried, *but* they shall be
like refuse on the face of the earth. They
shall be consumed by the sword and by
famine, and their corpses shall be meat
for the birds of heaven and for the
beasts of the earth."

5For thus says the LORD: "Do not enter the house of mourning, nor go to
lament or bemoan them; for I have
taken away My peace from this people," says the LORD, "lovingkindness
and mercies. 6Both the great and the
small shall die in this land. They shall
not be buried; neither shall men lament
for them, cut themselves, nor make
themselves bald for them. 7Nor shall
men break *bread* in mourning for them,
to comfort them for the dead; nor shall
men give them the cup of consolation
to drink for their father or their mother.
8Also you shall not go into the house
of feasting to sit with them, to eat and
drink."

9For thus says the LORD of hosts, the
God of Israel: "Behold, I will cause to
cease from this place, before your eyes
and in your days, the voice of mirth
and the voice of gladness, the voice of the
bridegroom and the voice of the bride.
10"And it shall be, when you show
this people all these words, and they

say to you, 'Why has the LORD pronounced all this great disaster against
us? Or what *is* our iniquity? Or what *is*
our sin that we have committed against
the LORD our God?' 11then you shall say
to them, 'Because your fathers have forsaken Me,' says the LORD; 'they have
walked after other gods and have
served them and worshiped them, and
have forsaken Me and not kept My law.
12And you have done worse than your
fathers, for behold, each one follows the
dictates of his own evil heart, so that
no one listens to Me. 13Therefore I will
cast you out of this land into a land that
you do not know, neither you nor your
fathers; and there you shall serve other
gods day and night, where I will not
show you favor.'

God Will Restore Israel

14"Therefore behold, the days are
coming," says the LORD, "that it shall
no more be said, 'The LORD lives who
brought up the children of Israel from
the land of Egypt,' 15but, 'The LORD
lives who brought up the children of Israel from the land of the north and from
all the lands where He had driven
them.' For I will bring them back into
their land which I gave to their fathers.

16"Behold, I will send for many fishermen," says the LORD, "and they shall
fish them; and afterward I will send for
many hunters, and they shall hunt them
from every mountain and every hill,
and out of the holes of the rocks.
17For My eyes *are* on all their ways;
they are not hidden from My face, nor
is their iniquity hidden from My eyes.
18And first I will repay double for their
iniquity and their sin, because they
have defiled My land; they have filled
My inheritance with the carcasses of
their detestable and abominable idols."
19   O LORD, my strength and my
fortress,
My refuge in the day of affliction,
The Gentiles shall come to You
From the ends of the earth and say,
"Surely our fathers have inherited
lies,
Worthlessness and unprofitable
things."
20   Will a man make gods for himself,
Which *are* not gods?

21 "Therefore behold, I will this once
cause them to know,
I will cause them to know
My hand and My might;
And they shall know that My name
is the LORD.

Judah's Sin and Punishment

17 "The sin of Judah *is* written with
a pen of iron;
With the point of a diamond *it is*
engraved
On the tablet of their heart,
And on the horns of your altars,
2 While their children remember
Their altars and their wooden
images*f*
By the green trees on the high
hills.
3 O My mountain in the field,
I will give as plunder your wealth,
all your treasures,
And your high places of sin within
all your borders.
4 And you, even yourself,
Shall let go of your heritage which
I gave you;
And I will cause you to serve your
enemies
In the land which you do not
know;
For you have kindled a fire in My
anger *which* shall burn forever."
5Thus says the LORD:
"Cursed *is* the man who trusts in
man
And makes flesh his strength,
Whose heart departs from the
LORD.
6 For he shall be like a shrub in the
desert,
And shall not see when good
comes,
But shall inhabit the parched places
in the wilderness,
In a salt land *which is* not
inhabited.

7 "Blessed *is* the man who trusts in the
LORD,
And whose hope is the LORD.
8 For he shall be like a tree planted
by the waters,
Which spreads out its roots by the
river,

And will not fear when heat comes;
But its leaf will be green,
And will not be anxious in the year
of drought,
Nor will cease from yielding fruit.

9 "The heart *is* deceitful above all
things,
And desperately wicked;
Who can know it?
10 I, the LORD, search the heart,
I test the mind,
Even to give every man according
to his ways,
According to the fruit of his doings.

11 "*As* a partridge that broods but does
not hatch,
So is he who gets riches, but not
by right;
It will leave him in the midst of his
days,
And at his end he will be a fool."

12 A glorious high throne from the
beginning
Is the place of our sanctuary.
13 O LORD, the hope of Israel,
All who forsake You shall be
ashamed.

"Those who depart from Me
Shall be written in the earth,
Because they have forsaken the
LORD,
The fountain of living waters."

Jeremiah Prays for Deliverance

14 Heal me, O LORD, and I shall be
healed;
Save me, and I shall be saved,
For You *are* my praise.
15 Indeed they say to me,
"Where *is* the word of the LORD?
Let it come now!"
16 As for me, I have not hurried away
from *being* a shepherd *who*
follows You,
Nor have I desired the woeful day;
You know what came out of my
lips;
It was right there before You.
17 Do not be a terror to me;
You *are* my hope in the day of
doom.

---

f Canaanite deities

18 Let them be ashamed who
 persecute me,
 But do not let me be put to shame;
 Let them be dismayed,
 But do not let me be dismayed.
 Bring on them the day of doom,
 And destroy them with double
 destruction!

Hallow the Sabbath Day

19Thus the LORD said to me: "Go and
stand in the gate of the children of the
people, by which the kings of Judah
come in and by which they go out, and
in all the gates of Jerusalem; 20and say
to them, 'Hear the word of the LORD,
you kings of Judah, and all Judah, and
all the inhabitants of Jerusalem, who
enter by these gates. 21Thus says the
LORD: "Take heed to yourselves, and
bear no burden on the Sabbath day, nor
bring it in by the gates of Jerusalem;
22nor carry a burden out of your houses
on the Sabbath day, nor do any work,
but hallow the Sabbath day, as I commanded your fathers. 23But they did not
obey nor incline their ear, but made
their neck stiff, that they might not hear
nor receive instruction.

24"And it shall be, if you heed Me
carefully," says the LORD, "to bring no
burden through the gates of this city on
the Sabbath day, but hallow the Sabbath day, to do no work in it, 25then
shall enter the gates of this city kings
and princes sitting on the throne of David, riding in chariots and on horses,
they and their princes, accompanied by
the men of Judah and the inhabitants
of Jerusalem; and this city shall remain
forever. 26And they shall come from the
cities of Judah and from the places
around Jerusalem, from the land of
Benjamin and from the lowland, from
the mountains and from the South,
bringing burnt offerings and sacrifices,
grain offerings and incense, bringing
sacrifices of praise to the house of the
LORD.

27"But if you will not heed Me to hallow the Sabbath day, such as not carrying a burden when entering the gates
of Jerusalem on the Sabbath day, then
I will kindle a fire in its gates, and it
shall devour the palaces of Jerusalem,
and it shall not be quenched."'"

The Potter and the Clay

18 The word which came to Jeremiah from the LORD, saying:
2"Arise and go down to the potter's
house, and there I will cause you to hear
My words." 3Then I went down to the
potter's house, and there he was, making something at the wheel. 4And
the vessel that he made of clay was
marred in the hand of the potter; so
he made it again into another vessel, as it seemed good to the potter to
make.

5Then the word of the LORD came to
me, saying: 6"O house of Israel, can I
not do with you as this potter?" says
the LORD. "Look, as the clay is in the
potter's hand, so are you in My hand,
O house of Israel! 7The instant I speak
concerning a nation and concerning a
kingdom, to pluck up, to pull down, and
to destroy it, 8if that nation against
whom I have spoken turns from its evil,
I will relent of the disaster that I
thought to bring upon it. 9And the instant I speak concerning a nation and
concerning a kingdom, to build and to
plant it, 10if it does evil in My sight so
that it does not obey My voice, then I
will relent concerning the good with
which I said I would benefit it.

11"Now therefore, speak to the men
of Judah and to the inhabitants of Jerusalem, saying, 'Thus says the LORD:
"Behold, I am fashioning a disaster and
devising a plan against you. Return
now every one from his evil way, and
make your ways and your doings
good."'"

God's Warning Rejected

12And they said, "That is hopeless!
So we will walk according to our own
plans, and we will every one obey the
dictates of his evil heart."

13Therefore thus says the LORD:
 "Ask now among the Gentiles,
 Who has heard such things?
 The virgin of Israel has done a very
 horrible thing.
14 Will a man leave the snow water
 of Lebanon,
 Which comes from the rock of the
 field?
 Will the cold flowing waters be
 forsaken for strange waters?

15 "Because My people have
     forgotten Me,
    They have burned incense to
     worthless idols.
    And they have caused themselves
     to stumble in their ways,
    From the ancient paths,
    To walk in pathways and not on a
     highway,
16   To make their land desolate *and* a
     perpetual hissing;
    Everyone who passes by it will be
     astonished
    And shake his head.
17   I will scatter them as with an east
     wind before the enemy;
    I will show them the back and not
     the face
    In the day of their calamity."

Jeremiah Persecuted

18Then they said, "Come and let us
devise plans against Jeremiah; for the
law shall not perish from the priest, nor
counsel from the wise, nor the word
from the prophet. Come and let us attack him with the tongue, and let us not
give heed to any of his words."
19   Give heed to me, O LORD,
    And listen to the voice of those who
     contend with me!
20   Shall evil be repaid for good?
    For they have dug a pit for my life.
    Remember that I stood before You
    To speak good for them,
    To turn away Your wrath from
     them.
21   Therefore deliver up their children
     to the famine,
    And pour out their *blood*
    By the force of the sword;
    Let their wives *become* widows
    And bereaved of their children.
    Let their men be put to death,
    Their young men *be* slain
    By the sword in battle.
22   Let a cry be heard from their
     houses,
    When You bring a troop suddenly
     upon them;
    For they have dug a pit to take me,
    And hidden snares for my feet.
23   Yet, LORD, You know all their
     counsel
    Which is against me, to slay *me*.
    Provide no atonement for their
     iniquity,

    Nor blot out their sin from Your
     sight;
    But let them be overthrown
     before You.
    Deal *thus* with them
    In the time of Your anger.

The Sign of the Broken Flask

19 Thus says the LORD: "Go and get
a potter's earthen flask, and *take*
some of the elders of the people and
some of the elders of the priests.
2And go out to the Valley of the Son
of Hinnom, which *is* by the entry of the
Potsherd Gate; and proclaim there the
words that I will tell you, 3and say,
'Hear the word of the LORD, O kings of
Judah and inhabitants of Jerusalem.
Thus says the LORD of hosts, the God
of Israel: "Behold, I will bring such a
catastrophe on this place, that whoever
hears of it, his ears will tingle.

4"Because they have forsaken Me
and made this an alien place, because
they have burned incense in it to other
gods whom neither they, their fathers,
nor the kings of Judah have known, and
have filled this place with the blood of
the innocents 5(they have also built the
high places of Baal, to burn their sons
with fire *for* burnt offerings to Baal,
which I did not command or speak, nor
did it come into My mind), 6therefore
behold, the days are coming," says the
LORD, "that this place shall no more be
called Tophet or the Valley of the Son
of Hinnom, but the Valley of Slaughter.
7And I will make void the counsel of
Judah and Jerusalem in this place, and
I will cause them to fall by the sword
before their enemies and by the hands
of those who seek their lives; their
corpses I will give as meat for the birds
of the heaven and for the beasts of the
earth. 8I will make this city desolate and
a hissing; everyone who passes by it
will be astonished and hiss because of
all its plagues. 9And I will cause them
to eat the flesh of their sons and the
flesh of their daughters, and everyone
shall eat the flesh of his friend in the
siege and in the desperation with which
their enemies and those who seek their
lives shall drive them to despair." '

10"Then you shall break the flask in
the sight of the men who go with you,
11and say to them, 'Thus says the LORD

of hosts: "Even so I will break this people and this city, as *one* breaks a potter's vessel, which cannot be made whole again; and they shall bury *them* in Tophet till *there is* no place to bury. 12Thus I will do to this place," says the LORD, "and to its inhabitants, and make this city like Tophet. 13And the houses of Jerusalem and the houses of the kings of Judah shall be defiled like the place of Tophet, because of all the houses on whose roofs they have burned incense to all the host of heaven, and poured out drink offerings to other gods." ' "

14Then Jeremiah came from Tophet, where the LORD had sent him to prophesy; and he stood in the court of the Lord's house and said to all the people, 15"Thus says the LORD of hosts, the God of Israel: 'Behold, I will bring on this city and on all her towns all the doom that I have pronounced against it, because they have stiffened their necks that they might not hear My words.' "

The Word of God to Pashhur

20 Now Pashhur the son of Immer, the priest who *was* also chief governor in the house of the LORD, heard that Jeremiah prophesied these things. 2Then Pashhur struck Jeremiah the prophet, and put him in the stocks that *were* in the high gate of Benjamin, which *was* by the house of the LORD.

3And it happened on the next day that Pashhur brought Jeremiah out of the stocks. Then Jeremiah said to him, "The LORD has not called your name Pashhur, but Magor-Missabib.g 4For thus says the LORD: 'Behold, I will make you a terror to yourself and to all your friends; and they shall fall by the sword of their enemies, and your eyes shall see *it*. I will give all Judah into the hand of the king of Babylon, and he shall carry them captive to Babylon and slay them with the sword. 5Moreover I will deliver all the wealth of this city, all its produce, and all its precious things; all the treasures of the kings of Judah I will give into the hand of their enemies, who will plunder them, seize them, and carry them to Babylon. 6And you,

Pashhur, and all who dwell in your house, shall go into captivity. You shall go to Babylon, and there you shall die, and be buried there, you and all your friends, to whom you have prophesied lies.' "

Jeremiah's Unpopular Ministry

7   O LORD, You induced me, and I was
         persuaded;
     You are stronger than I, and have
         prevailed.
     I am in derision daily;
     Everyone mocks me.
8   For when I spoke, I cried out;
     I shouted, "Violence and plunder!"
     Because the word of the LORD was
         made to me
     A reproach and a derision daily.
9   Then I said, "I will not make
         mention of Him,
     Nor speak anymore in His
         name."
     But *His word* was in my heart like
         a burning fire
     Shut up in my bones;
     I was weary of holding *it* back,
     And I could not.
10   For I heard many mocking:
     "Fear on every side!"
     "Report," *they say,* "and we will
         report it!"
     All my acquaintances watched for
         my stumbling, *saying,*
     "Perhaps he can be induced;
     Then we will prevail against him,
     And we will take our revenge
         on him."

11   But the LORD *is* with me as a
         mighty, awesome One.
     Therefore my persecutors will
         stumble, and will not prevail.
     They will be greatly ashamed, for
         they will not prosper.
     Their everlasting confusion will
         never be forgotten.
12   But, O LORD of hosts,
     You who test the righteous,
     And see the mind and heart,
     Let me see Your vengeance on
         them;
     For I have pleaded my cause before
         You.

g Literally *Fear on Every Side*

13 Sing to the Lord! Praise the Lord!
  For He has delivered the life of the
     poor
  From the hand of evildoers.

14 Cursed *be* the day in which I was
     born!
  Let the day not be blessed in which
     my mother bore me!
15 Let the man *be* cursed
  Who brought news to my father,
     saying,
  "A male child has been born to you!"
  Making him very glad.
16 And let that man be like the cities
  Which the Lord overthrew, and did
     not relent;
  Let him hear the cry in the morning
  And the shouting at noon,
17 Because he did not kill me from the
     womb,
  That my mother might have been
     my grave,
  And her womb always enlarged
     with me.
18 Why did I come forth from the
     womb to see labor and sorrow,
  That my days should be consumed
     with shame?

Jerusalem's Doom Is Sealed

21 The word which came to Jeremiah from the Lord when King
Zedekiah sent to him Pashhur the son
of Melchiah, and Zephaniah the son of
Maaseiah, the priest, saying, 2"Please
inquire of the Lord for us, for Nebuchadnezzar king of Babylon makes war
against us. Perhaps the Lord will deal
with us according to all His wonderful works, that *the king* may go away
from us."

3Then Jeremiah said to them, "Thus
you shall say to Zedekiah, 4'Thus says
the Lord God of Israel: "Behold, I will
turn back the weapons of war that *are*
in your hands, with which you fight
against the king of Babylon and the
Chaldeans who besiege you outside the
walls; and I will assemble them in
the midst of this city. 5I Myself will fight
against you with an outstretched hand
and with a strong arm, even in anger
and fury and great wrath. 6I will strike
the inhabitants of this city, both man
and beast; they shall die of a great pestilence. 7And afterward," says the Lord,

"I will deliver Zedekiah king of Judah,
his servants and the people, and such
as are left in this city from the pestilence and the sword and the famine,
into the hand of Nebuchadnezzar king
of Babylon, into the hand of their enemies, and into the hand of those who
seek their life; and he shall strike
them with the edge of the sword. He
shall not spare them, or have pity or
mercy." '

8"Now you shall say to this people,
'Thus says the Lord: "Behold, I set before you the way of life and the way
of death. 9He who remains in this city
shall die by the sword, by famine, and
by pestilence; but he who goes out and
defects to the Chaldeans who besiege
you, he shall live, and his life shall be
as a prize to him. 10For I have set My
face against this city for adversity and
not for good," says the Lord. "It shall
be given into the hand of the king of
Babylon, and he shall burn it with
fire." '

Message to the House of David

11"And concerning the house of the
king of Judah, *say,* 'Hear the word of
the Lord, 12O house of David! Thus
says the Lord:
  "Execute judgment in the morning;
     And deliver *him who is* plundered
  Out of the hand of the oppressor,
  Lest My fury go forth like fire
  And burn so that no one can
     quench *it,*
  Because of the evil of your doings.

13 "Behold, I *am* against you,
     O inhabitant of the valley,
  And rock of the plain," says the
     Lord,
  "Who say, 'Who shall come down
     against us?
  Or who shall enter our dwellings?'
14 But I will punish you according to
     the fruit of your doings," says
     the Lord;
  "I will kindle a fire in its forest,
     And it shall devour all things
     around it." ' "

22 Thus says the Lord: "Go down to
the house of the king of Judah,
and there speak this word, 2and say,
'Hear the word of the Lord, O king of

Judah, you who sit on the throne of David, you and your servants and your people who enter these gates! 3Thus says the LORD: "Execute judgment and righteousness, and deliver the plundered out of the hand of the oppressor. Do no wrong and do no violence to the stranger, the fatherless, or the widow, nor shed innocent blood in this place. 4For if you indeed do this thing, then shall enter the gates of this house, riding on horses and in chariots, accompanied by servants and people, kings who sit on the throne of David. 5But if you will not hear these words, I swear by Myself," says the LORD, "that this house shall become a desolation." ' "

6For thus says the LORD to the house of the king of Judah:

"You *are* Gilead to Me,
The head of Lebanon;
Yet I surely will make you a
    wilderness,
Cities *which* are not inhabited.
7   I will prepare destroyers against
        you,
    Everyone with his weapons;
    They shall cut down your choice
        cedars
    And cast *them* into the fire.

8And many nations will pass by this city; and everyone will say to his neighbor, 'Why has the LORD done so to this great city?' 9Then they will answer, 'Because they have forsaken the covenant of the LORD their God, and worshiped other gods and served them.' "

10   Weep not for the dead, nor
        bemoan him;
    Weep bitterly for him who goes
        away,
    For he shall return no more,
    Nor see his native country.

Message to the Sons of Josiah

11For thus says the LORD concerning Shallum the son of Josiah, king of Judah, who reigned instead of Josiah his father, who went from this place: "He shall not return here anymore, 12but he shall die in the place where they have led him captive, and shall see this land no more.
13   "Woe to him who builds his house
        by unrighteousness
    And his chambers by injustice,

    Who uses his neighbor's service
        without wages
    And gives him nothing for his
        work,
14   Who says, 'I will build myself a
        wide house with spacious
        chambers,
    And cut out windows for it,
    Paneling *it* with cedar
    And painting *it* with vermilion.'

15   "Shall you reign because you
        enclose *yourself* in cedar?
    Did not your father eat and drink,
    And do justice and righteousness?
    Then *it was* well with him.
16   He judged the cause of the poor and
        needy;
    Then *it was* well.
    Was not this knowing Me?" says
        the LORD.
17   "Yet your eyes and your heart *are*
        for nothing but your
        covetousness,
    For shedding innocent blood,
    And practicing oppression and
        violence."

18Therefore thus says the LORD concerning Jehoiakim the son of Josiah, king of Judah:

    "They shall not lament for him,
    Saying, 'Alas, my brother!' or 'Alas,
        my sister!'
    They shall not lament for him,
    Saying, 'Alas, master!' or 'Alas, his
        glory!'
19   He shall be buried with the burial
        of a donkey,
    Dragged and cast out beyond the
        gates of Jerusalem.

20   "Go up to Lebanon, and cry out,
    And lift up your voice in Bashan;
    Cry from Abarim,
    For all your lovers are destroyed.
21   I spoke to you in your prosperity,
    But you said, 'I will not hear.'
    This *has been* your manner from
        your youth,
    That you did not obey My voice.
22   The wind shall eat up all your
        rulers,
    And your lovers shall go into
        captivity;
    Surely then you will be ashamed
        and humiliated
    For all your wickedness.

23 O inhabitant of Lebanon,
Making your nest in the cedars,
How gracious will you be when
    pangs come upon you,
Like the pain of a woman in labor?

Message to Coniah

24"As I live," says the LORD, "though
Coniah the son of Jehoiakim, king of
Judah, were the signet on My right
hand, yet I would pluck you off;
25and I will give you into the hand of
those who seek your life, and into the
hand of those whose face you fear—
the hand of Nebuchadnezzar king of
Babylon and the hand of the Chaldeans. 26So I will cast you out, and your
mother who bore you, into another
country where you were not born; and
there you shall die. 27But to the land
to which they desire to return, there
they shall not return.

28 "Is this man Coniah a despised,
    broken idol—
A vessel in which is no pleasure?
Why are they cast out, he and his
    descendants,
And cast into a land which they do
    not know?
29 O earth, earth, earth,
Hear the word of the LORD!
30 Thus says the LORD:
'Write this man down as childless,
A man who shall not prosper in his
    days;
For none of his descendants shall
    prosper,
Sitting on the throne of David,
And ruling anymore in Judah.' "

The Branch of Righteousness

23 "Woe to the shepherds who destroy and scatter the sheep of My
pasture!" says the LORD. 2Therefore
thus says the LORD God of Israel against
the shepherds who feed My people:
"You have scattered My flock, driven
them away, and not attended to them.
Behold, I will attend to you for the evil
of your doings," says the LORD. 3"But
I will gather the remnant of My flock
out of all countries where I have driven
them, and bring them back to their
folds; and they shall be fruitful and
increase. 4I will set up shepherds over
them who will feed them; and they
shall fear no more, nor be dismayed,

nor shall they be lacking," says the
LORD.
5 "Behold, the days are coming," says
    the LORD,
"That I will raise to David a Branch
    of righteousness;
A King shall reign and prosper,
And execute judgment and
    righteousness in the earth.
6 In His days Judah will be saved,
And Israel will dwell safely;
Now this is His name by which He
    will be called:

THE LORD OUR RIGHTEOUSNESS.

7"Therefore, behold, the days are
coming," says the LORD, "that they shall
no longer say, 'As the LORD lives who
brought up the children of Israel from
the land of Egypt,' 8but, 'As the LORD
lives who brought up and led the descendants of the house of Israel from
the north country and from all the countries where I had driven them.' And
they shall dwell in their own land."

False Prophets and Empty Oracles

9 My heart within me is broken
Because of the prophets;
All my bones shake.
I am like a drunken man,
And like a man whom wine has
    overcome,
Because of the LORD,
And because of His holy words.
10 For the land is full of adulterers;
For because of a curse the land
    mourns.
The pleasant places of the
    wilderness are dried up.
Their course of life is evil,
And their might is not right.

11 "For both prophet and priest are
    profane;
Yes, in My house I have found their
    wickedness," says the LORD.
12 "Therefore their way shall be to
    them
Like slippery ways;
In the darkness they shall be
    driven on
And fall in them;
For I will bring disaster on them,
The year of their punishment," says
    the LORD.

13 "And I have seen folly in the
   prophets of Samaria:
   They prophesied by Baal
   And caused My people Israel to err.
14 Also I have seen a horrible thing
   in the prophets of Jerusalem:
   They commit adultery and walk in
   lies;
   They also strengthen the hands of
   evildoers,
   So that no one turns back from his
   wickedness.
   All of them are like Sodom to Me,
   And her inhabitants like
   Gomorrah.
15"Therefore thus says the LORD of
hosts concerning the prophets:
   'Behold, I will feed them with
   wormwood,
   And make them drink the water of
   gall;
   For from the prophets of Jerusalem
   Profaneness has gone out into all
   the land.' "
16Thus says the LORD of hosts:
   "Do not listen to the words of the
   prophets who prophesy to you.
   They make you worthless;
   They speak a vision of their own
   heart,
   Not from the mouth of the LORD.
17 They continually say to those who
   despise Me,
   'The LORD has said, "You shall have
   peace" ';
   And to everyone who walks
   according to the dictates of his
   own heart, they say,
   'No evil shall come upon you.' "

18 For who has stood in the counsel
   of the LORD,
   And has perceived and heard His
   word?
   Who has marked His word and
   heard it?
19 Behold, a whirlwind of the LORD
   has gone forth in fury—
   A violent whirlwind!
   It will fall violently on the head of
   the wicked.
20 The anger of the LORD will not turn
   back
   Until He has executed and
   performed the thoughts of His
   heart.

   In the latter days you will
   understand it perfectly.

21 "I have not sent these prophets, yet
   they ran.
   I have not spoken to them, yet they
   prophesied.
22 But if they had stood in My counsel,
   And had caused My people to hear
   My words,
   Then they would have turned them
   from their evil way
   And from the evil of their doings.

23 "Am I a God near at hand," says the
   LORD,
   "And not a God afar off?
24 Can anyone hide himself in secret
   places,
   So I shall not see him?" says the
   LORD;
   "Do I not fill heaven and earth?"
   says the LORD.
25"I have heard what the prophets
have said who prophesy lies in My
name, saying, 'I have dreamed, I have
dreamed!' 26How long will this be in
the heart of the prophets who prophesy
lies? Indeed they are prophets of the deceit of their own heart, 27who try to
make My people forget My name by
their dreams which everyone tells his
neighbor, as their fathers forgot My
name for Baal.
28 "The prophet who has a dream, let
   him tell a dream;
   And he who has My word, let him
   speak My word faithfully.
   What is the chaff to the wheat?"
   says the LORD.
29 "Is not My word like a fire?" says
   the LORD,
   "And like a hammer that breaks the
   rock in pieces?
30"Therefore behold, I am against the
prophets," says the LORD, "who steal
My words every one from his neighbor.
31Behold, I am against the prophets,"
says the LORD, "who use their tongues
and say, 'He says.' 32Behold, I am
against those who prophesy false
dreams," says the LORD, "and tell them,
and cause My people to err by their lies
and by their recklessness. Yet I did not
send them or command them; therefore
they shall not profit this people at all,"
says the LORD.

33"So when these people or the prophet or the priest ask you, saying, 'What is the oracle of the LORD?' you shall then say to them, 'What oracle?' I will even forsake you," says the LORD. 34"And *as for* the prophet and the priest and the people who say, 'The oracle of the LORD!' I will even punish that man and his house. 35Thus every one of you shall say to his neighbor, and every one to his brother, 'What has the LORD answered?' and, 'What has the LORD spoken?' 36And the oracle of the LORD you shall mention no more. For every man's word will be his oracle, for you have perverted the words of the living God, the LORD of hosts, our God. 37Thus you shall say to the prophet, 'What has the LORD answered you?' and, 'What has the LORD spoken?' 38But since you say, 'The oracle of the LORD!' therefore thus says the LORD: 'Because you say this word, "The oracle of the LORD!" and I have sent to you, saying, "Do not say, 'The oracle of the LORD!'" 39therefore behold, I, even I, will utterly forget you and forsake you, and the city that I gave you and your fathers, and *will cast you* out of My presence. 40And I will bring an everlasting reproach upon you, and a perpetual shame, which shall not be forgotten.' "

The Sign of Two Baskets of Figs

24 The LORD showed me, and there were two baskets of figs set before the temple of the LORD, after Nebuchadnezzar king of Babylon had carried away captive Jeconiah the son of Jehoiakim, king of Judah, and the princes of Judah with the craftsmen and smiths, from Jerusalem, and had brought them to Babylon. 2One basket *had* very good figs, like the figs *that are* first ripe; and the other basket *had* very bad figs which could not be eaten, they were so bad. 3Then the LORD said to me, "What do you see, Jeremiah?"

And I said, "Figs, the good figs, very good; and the bad, very bad, which cannot be eaten, they are so bad."

4Again the word of the LORD came to me, saying, 5"Thus says the LORD, the God of Israel: 'Like these good figs, so will I acknowledge those who are carried away captive from Judah, whom I have sent out of this place for

their own good, into the land of the Chaldeans. 6For I will set My eyes on them for good, and I will bring them back to this land; I will build them and not pull *them* down, and I will plant them and not pluck *them* up. 7Then I will give them a heart to know Me, that I *am* the LORD; and they shall be My people, and I will be their God, for they shall return to Me with their whole heart.

8'And as the bad figs which cannot be eaten, they are so bad'—surely thus says the LORD—'so will I give up Zedekiah the king of Judah, his princes, the residue of Jerusalem who remain in this land, and those who dwell in the land of Egypt. 9I will deliver them to trouble into all the kingdoms of the earth, for *their* harm, *to be* a reproach and a byword, a taunt and a curse, in all places where I shall drive them. 10And I will send the sword, the famine, and the pestilence among them, till they are consumed from the land that I gave to them and their fathers.' "

Seventy Years of Desolation

25 The word that came to Jeremiah concerning all the people of Judah, in the fourth year of Jehoiakim the son of Josiah, king of Judah (which *was* the first year of Nebuchadnezzar king of Babylon), 2which Jeremiah the prophet spoke to all the people of Judah and to all the inhabitants of Jerusalem, saying: 3"From the thirteenth year of Josiah the son of Amon, king of Judah, even to this day, this *is* the twenty-third year in which the word of the LORD has come to me; and I have spoken to you, rising early and speaking, but you have not listened. 4And the LORD has sent to you all His servants the prophets, rising early and sending *them,* but you have not listened nor inclined your ear to hear. 5They said, 'Repent now everyone of his evil way and his evil doings, and dwell in the land that the LORD has given to you and your fathers forever and ever. 6Do not go after other gods to serve them and worship them, and do not provoke Me to anger with the works of your hands; and I will not harm you.' 7Yet you have not listened to Me," says the LORD, "that you might provoke Me to anger with the works of your hands to your own hurt.

8"Therefore thus says the LORD of hosts: 'Because you have not heard My words, 9behold, I will send and take all the families of the north,' says the LORD, 'and Nebuchadnezzar the king of Babylon, My servant, and will bring them against this land, against its inhabitants, and against these nations all around, and will utterly destroy them, and make them an astonishment, a hissing, and perpetual desolations. 10Moreover I will take from them the voice of mirth and the voice of gladness, the voice of the bridegroom and the voice of the bride, the sound of the millstones and the light of the lamp. 11And this whole land shall be a desolation *and* an astonishment, and these nations shall serve the king of Babylon seventy years.

12'Then it will come to pass, when seventy years are completed, *that* I will punish the king of Babylon and that nation, the land of the Chaldeans, for their iniquity,' says the LORD; 'and I will make it a perpetual desolation. 13So I will bring on that land all My words which I have pronounced against it, all that is written in this book, which Jeremiah has prophesied concerning all the nations. 14(For many nations and great kings shall be served by them also; and I will repay them according to their deeds and according to the works of their own hands.)' "

Judgment on the Nations

15For thus says the LORD God of Israel to me: "Take this wine cup of fury from My hand, and cause all the nations, to whom I send you, to drink it. 16And they will drink and stagger and go mad because of the sword that I will send among them."

17Then I took the cup from the LORD's hand, and made all the nations drink, to whom the LORD had sent me: 18Jerusalem and the cities of Judah, its kings and its princes, to make them a desolation, an astonishment, a hissing, and a curse, as *it is* this day; 19Pharaoh king of Egypt, his servants, his princes, and all his people; 20all the mixed multi-

tude, all the kings of the land of Uz, all the kings of the land of the Philistines (namely, Ashkelon, Gaza, Ekron, and the remnant of Ashdod); 21Edom, Moab, and the people of Ammon; 22all the kings of Tyre, all the kings of Sidon, and the kings of the coastlands which *are* across the sea; 23Dedan, Tema, Buz, and all *who are* in the farthest corners; 24all the kings of Arabia and all the kings of the mixed multitude who dwell in the desert; 25all the kings of Zimri, all the kings of Elam, and all the kings of the Medes; 26all the kings of the north, far and near, one with another; and all the kingdoms of the world which *are* on the face of the earth. Also the king of Sheshach[h] shall drink after them.

27"Therefore you shall say to them, 'Thus says the LORD of hosts, the God of Israel: "Drink, be drunk, and vomit! Fall and rise no more, because of the sword which I will send among you." ' 28And it shall be, if they refuse to take the cup from your hand to drink, then you shall say to them, 'Thus says the LORD of hosts: "You shall certainly drink! 29For behold, I begin to bring calamity on the city which is called by My name, and should you be utterly unpunished? You shall not be unpunished, for I will call for a sword on all the inhabitants of the earth," says the LORD of hosts.'

30"Therefore prophesy against them all these words, and say to them:

'The LORD will roar from on high,
And utter His voice from His holy habitation;
He will roar mightily against His fold.
He will give a shout, as those who tread *the grapes*,
Against all the inhabitants of the earth.
31   A noise will come to the ends of the earth—
For the LORD has a controversy with the nations;
He will plead His case with all flesh.
He will give those *who are* wicked to the sword,' says the LORD."
32Thus says the LORD of hosts:
"Behold, disaster shall go forth

[h] A code word for *Babylon* (compare 51.41)

From nation to nation,
And a great whirlwind shall be
    raised up
From the farthest parts of the earth.
33"And at that day the slain of the LORD
shall be from *one* end of the earth even
to the *other* end of the earth. They shall
not be lamented, or gathered, or buried;
they shall become refuse on the ground.
34 "Wail, shepherds, and cry!
    Roll about *in the ashes,*
    You leaders of the flock!
    For the days of your slaughter and
        your dispersions are fulfilled;
    You shall fall like a precious vessel.
35 And the shepherds will have no
        way to flee,
    Nor the leaders of the flock to
        escape.
36 A voice of the cry of the shepherds,
    And a wailing of the leaders to the
        flock *will be heard.*
    For the LORD has plundered their
        pasture.
37 And the peaceful dwellings are cut
        down
    Because of the fierce anger of the
        LORD.
38 He has left His lair like the lion;
    For their land is desolate
    Because of the fierceness of the
        Oppressor,
    And because of His fierce anger."

Jeremiah Saved from Death

26 In the beginning of the reign of
Jehoiakim the son of Josiah, king
of Judah, this word came from the
LORD, saying, 2"Thus says the LORD:
'Stand in the court of the LORD's house,
and speak to all the cities of Judah,
which come to worship *in* the LORD's
house, all the words that I command
you to speak to them. Do not diminish
a word. 3Perhaps everyone will listen
and turn from his evil way, that I may
relent concerning the calamity which I
purpose to bring on them because of
the evil of their doings.' 4And you shall
say to them, 'Thus says the LORD: "If
you will not listen to Me, to walk in My
law which I have set before you,
5to heed the words of My servants the
prophets whom I sent to you, both rising up early and sending *them* (but you
have not heeded), 6then I will make this
house like Shiloh, and will make this
city a curse to all the nations of the
earth." ' "
7So the priests and the prophets and
all the people heard Jeremiah speaking
these words in the house of the LORD.
8Now it happened, when Jeremiah had
made an end of speaking all that the
LORD had commanded *him* to speak to
all the people, that the priests and the
prophets and all the people seized him,
saying, "You will surely die! 9Why have
you prophesied in the name of the
LORD, saying, 'This house shall be like
Shiloh, and this city shall be desolate,
without an inhabitant'?" And all the
people were gathered against Jeremiah
in the house of the LORD.
10When the princes of Judah heard
these things, they came up from the
king's house to the house of the LORD
and sat down in the entry of the New
Gate of the LORD's *house.* 11And the
priests and the prophets spoke to the
princes and all the people, saying, "This
man deserves to die! For he has prophesied against this city, as you have heard
with your ears."
12Then Jeremiah spoke to all the
princes and all the people, saying: "The
LORD sent me to prophesy against this
house and against this city with all the
words that you have heard. 13Now
therefore, amend your ways and your
doings, and obey the voice of the LORD
your God; then the LORD will relent concerning the doom that He has pronounced against you. 14As for me, here
I am, in your hand; do with me as seems
good and proper to you. 15But know for
certain that if you put me to death, you
will surely bring innocent blood on
yourselves, on this city, and on its inhabitants; for truly the LORD has sent
me to you to speak all these words in
your hearing."
16So the princes and all the people
said to the priests and the prophets,
"This man does not deserve to die. For
he has spoken to us in the name of the
LORD our God."
17Then certain of the elders of the
land rose up and spoke to all the assembly of the people, saying: 18"Micah of
Moresheth prophesied in the days of
Hezekiah king of Judah, and spoke to
all the people of Judah, saying, 'Thus
says the LORD of hosts:

"Zion shall be plowed *like* a field,
Jerusalem shall become heaps of
  ruins,
And the mountain of the temple
Like the bare hills of the forest." '[i]

19Did Hezekiah king of Judah and all Judah ever put him to death? Did he not fear the LORD and seek the LORD's favor? And the LORD relented concerning the doom which He had pronounced against them. But we are doing great evil against ourselves."

20Now there was also a man who prophesied in the name of the LORD, Urijah the son of Shemaiah of Kirjath Jearim, who prophesied against this city and against this land according to all the words of Jeremiah. 21And when Jehoiakim the king, with all his mighty men and all the princes, heard his words, the king sought to put him to death; but when Urijah heard *it,* he was afraid and fled, and went to Egypt. 22Then Jehoiakim the king sent men to Egypt: Elnathan the son of Achbor, and *other* men *who went* with him to Egypt. 23And they brought Urijah from Egypt and brought him to Jehoiakim the king, who killed him with the sword and cast his dead body into the graves of the common people.

24Nevertheless the hand of Ahikam the son of Shaphan was with Jeremiah, so that they should not give him into the hand of the people to put him to death.

Symbol of the Bonds and Yokes

27 In the beginning of the reign of Jehoiakim the son of Josiah, king of Judah, this word came to Jeremiah from the LORD, saying, 2"Thus says the LORD to me: 'Make for yourselves bonds and yokes, and put them on your neck, 3and send them to the king of Edom, the king of Moab, the king of the Ammonites, the king of Tyre, and the king of Sidon, by the hand of the messengers who come to Jerusalem to Zedekiah king of Judah. 4And command them to say to their masters, "Thus says the LORD of hosts, the God of Israel—thus you shall say to your masters: 5'I have made the earth, the man and the beast that *are* on the ground, by My great power and by My outstretched arm, and have given it to whom it seemed proper to Me. 6And now I have given all these lands into the hand of Nebuchadnezzar the king of Babylon, My servant; and the beasts of the field I have also given him to serve him. 7So all nations shall serve him and his son and his son's son, until the time of his land comes; and then many nations and great kings shall make him serve them. 8And it shall be, *that* the nation and kingdom which will not serve Nebuchadnezzar the king of Babylon, and which will not put its neck under the yoke of the king of Babylon, that nation I will punish,' says the LORD, 'with the sword, the famine, and the pestilence, until I have consumed them by his hand. 9Therefore do not listen to your prophets, your diviners, your dreamers, your soothsayers, or your sorcerers, who speak to you, saying, "You shall not serve the king of Babylon." 10For they prophesy a lie to you, to remove you far from your land; and I will drive you out, and you will perish. 11But the nations that bring their necks under the yoke of the king of Babylon and serve him, I will let them remain in their own land,' says the LORD, 'and they shall till it and dwell in it.' " ' "

12I also spoke to Zedekiah king of Judah according to all these words, saying, "Bring your necks under the yoke of the king of Babylon, and serve him and his people, and live! 13Why will you die, you and your people, by the sword, by the famine, and by the pestilence, as the LORD has spoken against the nation that will not serve the king of Babylon? 14Therefore do not listen to the words of the prophets who speak to you, saying, 'You shall not serve the king of Babylon,' for they prophesy a lie to you; 15for I have not sent them," says the LORD, "yet they prophesy a lie in My name, that I may drive you out, and that you may perish, you and the prophets who prophesy to you."

16Also I spoke to the priests and to all this people, saying, "Thus says the LORD: 'Do not listen to the words of your prophets who prophesy to you, saying, "Behold, the vessels of the LORD's house will now shortly be

[i] Compare Micah 3.12

brought back from Babylon"; for they prophesy a lie to you. 17Do not listen to them; serve the king of Babylon, and live! Why should this city be laid waste? 18But if they *are* prophets, and if the word of the LORD is with them, let them now make intercession to the LORD of hosts, that the vessels which are left in the house of the LORD, *in* the house of the king of Judah, and at Jerusalem, do not go to Babylon.'

19"For thus says the LORD of hosts concerning the pillars, concerning the Sea, concerning the carts, and concerning the remainder of the vessels that remain in this city, 20which Nebuchadnezzar king of Babylon did not take, when he carried away captive Jeconiah the son of Jehoiakim, king of Judah, from Jerusalem to Babylon, and all the nobles of Judah and Jerusalem—21yes, thus says the LORD of hosts, the God of Israel, concerning the vessels that remain in the house of the LORD, and in the house of the king of Judah and of Jerusalem: 22'They shall be carried to Babylon, and there they shall be until the day that I visit them,' says the LORD. 'Then I will bring them up and restore them to this place.' "

Hananiah's Falsehood and Doom

28 And it happened in the same year, at the beginning of the reign of Zedekiah king of Judah, in the fourth year *and* in the fifth month, *that* Hananiah the son of Azur the prophet, who *was* from Gibeon, spoke to me in the house of the LORD in the presence of the priests and of all the people, saying, 2"Thus speaks the LORD of hosts, the God of Israel, saying: 'I have broken the yoke of the king of Babylon. 3Within two full years I will bring back to this place all the vessels of the LORD's house, that Nebuchadnezzar king of Babylon took away from this place and carried to Babylon. 4And I will bring back to this place Jeconiah the son of Jehoiakim, king of Judah, with all the captives of Judah who went to Babylon,' says the LORD, 'for I will break the yoke of the king of Babylon.' "

5Then the prophet Jeremiah spoke to the prophet Hananiah in the presence of the priests and in the presence of all the people who stood in the house of the LORD, 6and the prophet Jeremiah said, "Amen! The LORD do so; the LORD perform your words which you have prophesied, to bring back the vessels of the LORD's house and all who were carried away captive, from Babylon to this place. 7Nevertheless hear now this word that I speak in your hearing and in the hearing of all the people: 8The prophets who have been before me and before you of old prophesied against many countries and great kingdoms—of war and disaster and pestilence. 9As for the prophet who prophesies of peace, when the word of the prophet comes to pass, the prophet will be known *as* one whom the LORD has truly sent."

10Then Hananiah the prophet took the yoke off the prophet Jeremiah's neck and broke it. 11And Hananiah spoke in the presence of all the people, saying, "Thus says the LORD: 'Even so I will break the yoke of Nebuchadnezzar king of Babylon from the neck of all nations within the space of two full years.' " And the prophet Jeremiah went his way.

12Now the word of the LORD came to Jeremiah, after Hananiah the prophet had broken the yoke from the neck of the prophet Jeremiah, saying, 13"Go and tell Hananiah, saying, 'Thus says the LORD: "You have broken the yokes of wood, but you have made in their place yokes of iron." 14For thus says the LORD of hosts, the God of Israel: "I have put a yoke of iron on the neck of all these nations, that they may serve Nebuchadnezzar king of Babylon; and they shall serve him. I have given him the beasts of the field also." ' "

15Then the prophet Jeremiah said to Hananiah the prophet, "Hear now, Hananiah, the LORD has not sent you, but you make this people trust in a lie. 16Therefore thus says the LORD: 'Behold, I will cast you from the face of the earth. This year you shall die, because you have taught rebellion against the LORD.' "

17So Hananiah the prophet died the same year in the seventh month.

Jeremiah's Letter to the Captives

29 Now these *are* the words of the letter that Jeremiah the prophet sent from Jerusalem to the remainder of the elders who were carried away captive—to the priests, the prophets, and all the people whom Nebuchadnezzar had carried away captive from Jerusalem to Babylon. 2(This happened after Jeconiah the king, the queen mother, the eunuchs, the princes of Judah and Jerusalem, the craftsmen, and the smiths had departed from Jerusalem.) 3*The letter was sent* by the hand of Elasah the son of Shaphan, and Gemariah the son of Hilkiah, whom Zedekiah king of Judah sent to Babylon, to Nebuchadnezzar king of Babylon, saying,

4   Thus says the LORD of hosts, the God of Israel, to all who were carried away captive, whom I have caused to be carried away from Jerusalem to Babylon:

5   Build houses and dwell *in them;* plant gardens and eat their fruit. 6Take wives and beget sons and daughters; and take wives for your sons and give your daughters to husbands, so that they may bear sons and daughters—that you may be increased there, and not diminished. 7And seek the peace of the city where I have caused you to be carried away captive, and pray to the LORD for it; for in its peace you will have peace.

8   For thus says the LORD of hosts, the God of Israel: Do not let your prophets and your diviners who are in your midst deceive you, nor listen to your dreams which you cause to be dreamed. 9For they prophesy falsely to you in My name; I have not sent them, says the LORD.

10   For thus says the LORD: After seventy years are completed at Babylon, I will visit you and perform My good word toward you, and cause you to return to this place. 11For I know the thoughts that I think toward you, says the LORD, thoughts of peace and not of evil, to give you a future and a hope. 12Then you will call upon Me and go and pray to Me, and I will

listen to you. 13And you will seek Me and find *Me,* when you search for Me with all your heart.
14I will be found by you, says the LORD, and I will bring you back from your captivity; I will gather you from all the nations and from all the places where I have driven you, says the LORD, and I will bring you to the place from which I cause you to be carried away captive.

15   Because you have said, "The LORD has raised up prophets for us in Babylon"—16therefore thus says the LORD concerning the king who sits on the throne of David, concerning all the people who dwell in this city, and concerning your brethren who have not gone out with you into captivity—17thus says the LORD of hosts: Behold, I will send on them the sword, the famine, and the pestilence, and will make them like rotten figs that cannot be eaten, they are so bad. 18And I will pursue them with the sword, with famine, and with pestilence; and I will deliver them to trouble among all the kingdoms of the earth—to be a curse, an astonishment, a hissing, and a reproach among all the nations where I have driven them, 19because they have not heeded My words, says the LORD, which I sent to them by My servants the prophets, rising up early and sending *them;* neither would you heed, says the LORD. 20Therefore hear the word of the LORD, all you of the captivity, whom I have sent from Jerusalem to Babylon.

21   Thus says the LORD of hosts, the God of Israel, concerning Ahab the son of Kolaiah, and Zedekiah the son of Maaseiah, who prophesy a lie to you in My name: Behold, I will deliver them into the hand of Nebuchadnezzar king of Babylon, and he shall slay them before your eyes. 22And because of them a curse shall be taken up by all the captivity of Judah who *are* in Babylon, saying, "The LORD make you like Zedekiah and Ahab, whom

the king of Babylon roasted in the fire"; 23because they have done disgraceful things in Israel, have committed adultery with their neighbors' wives, and have spoken lying words in My name, which I have not commanded them. Indeed I know, and *am* a witness, says the LORD.

24 You shall also speak to Shemaiah the Nehelamite, saying, 25Thus speaks the LORD of hosts, the God of Israel, saying: You have sent letters in your name to all the people who *are* at Jerusalem, to Zephaniah the son of Maaseiah the priest, and to all the priests, saying, 26"The LORD has made you priest instead of Jehoiada the priest, so that there should be officers *in* the house of the LORD over every man *who* is demented and considers himself a prophet, that you should put him in prison and in the stocks. 27Now therefore, why have you not rebuked Jeremiah of Anathoth who makes himself a prophet to you? 28For he has sent to us *in* Babylon, saying, 'This *captivity is* long; build houses and dwell *in them,* and plant gardens and eat their fruit.' "

29 Now Zephaniah the priest read this letter in the hearing of Jeremiah the prophet. 30Then the word of the LORD came to Jeremiah, saying: 31Send to all those in captivity, saying, Thus says the LORD concerning Shemaiah the Nehelamite: Because Shemaiah has prophesied to you, and I have not sent him, and he has caused you to trust in a lie—32therefore thus says the LORD: Behold, I will punish Shemaiah the Nehelamite and his family: he shall not have anyone to dwell among this people, nor shall he see the good that I will do for My people, says the LORD, because he has taught rebellion against the LORD.

Restoration of Israel and Judah

30 The word that came to Jeremiah from the LORD, saying, 2"Thus speaks the LORD God of Israel, saying:

'Write in a book for yourself all the words that I have spoken to you. 3For behold, the days are coming,' says the LORD, 'that I will bring back from captivity My people Israel and Judah,' says the LORD. 'And I will cause them to return to the land that I gave to their fathers, and they shall possess it.' "

4Now these *are* the words that the LORD spoke concerning Israel and Judah.

5"For thus says the LORD:
  'We have heard a voice of trembling,
  Of fear, and not of peace.
6 Ask now, and see,
  Whether a man is ever in labor with child?
  So why do I see every man *with* his hands on his loins
  Like a woman in labor,
  And all faces turned pale?
7 Alas! For that day *is* great,
  So that none *is* like it;
  And it *is* the time of Jacob's trouble,
  But he shall be saved out of it.

8 'For it shall come to pass in that day,'
  Says the LORD of hosts,
  '*That* I will break his yoke from your neck,
  And will burst your bonds;
  Foreigners shall no more enslave them.
9 But they shall serve the LORD their God,
  And David their king,
  Whom I will raise up for them.

10 'Therefore do not fear, O My servant Jacob,' says the LORD,
  'Nor be dismayed, O Israel;
  For behold, I will save you from afar,
  And your seed from the land of their captivity.
  Jacob shall return, have rest and be quiet,
  And no one shall make *him* afraid.
11 For I *am* with you,' says the LORD,
  'to save you;
  Though I make a full end of all nations where I have scattered you,

Yet I will not make a complete end
 of you.
But I will correct you in justice,
And will not let you go altogether
 unpunished.'
 12"For thus says the LORD:
 'Your affliction *is* incurable,
 Your wound *is* severe.
13 *There is* no one to plead your cause,
 That you may be bound up;
 You have no healing medicines.
14 All your lovers have forgotten you;
 They do not seek you;
 For I have wounded you with the
  wound of an enemy,
 With the chastisement of a
  cruel one,
 For the multitude of your iniquities,
 Because your sins have increased.
15 Why do you cry about your
  affliction?
 Your sorrow *is* incurable.
 Because of the multitude of your
  iniquities,
 Because your sins have increased,
 I have done these things to you.
16 'Therefore all those who devour you
  shall be devoured;
 And all your adversaries, every
  one of them, shall go into
  captivity;
 Those who plunder you shall
  become plunder,
 And all who prey upon you I will
  make a prey.
17 For I will restore health to you
 And heal you of your wounds,' says
  the LORD,
 'Because they called you an outcast
  saying:
  "This *is* Zion;
  No one seeks her."'
 18"Thus says the LORD:
 'Behold, I will bring back the
  captivity of Jacob's tents,
 And have mercy on his dwelling
  places;
 The city shall be built upon its own
  mound,
 And the palace shall remain
  according to its own plan.
19 Then out of them shall proceed
  thanksgiving
 And the voice of those who make
  merry;
 I will multiply them, and they shall
  not diminish;

I will also glorify them, and they
 shall not be small.
20 Their children also shall be as
  before,
 And their congregation shall be
  established before Me;
 And I will punish all who oppress
  them.
21 Their nobles shall be from among
  them,
 And their governor shall come
  from their midst;
 Then I will cause him to draw near,
 And he shall approach Me;
 For who *is* this who pledged his
  heart to approach Me?' says the
  LORD.
22 'You shall be My people,
 And I will be your God.'"

23 Behold, the whirlwind of the LORD
 Goes forth with fury,
 A continuing whirlwind;
 It will fall violently on the head of
  the wicked.
24 The fierce anger of the LORD will
  not return until He has done it,
 And until He has performed the
  intents of His heart.

In the latter days you will
 consider it.

The Remnant of Israel Saved

31 "At the same time," says the
LORD, "I will be the God of all the
families of Israel, and they shall be My
people."
 2Thus says the LORD:
 "The people who survived the sword
 Found grace in the wilderness—
 Israel, when I went to give him
  rest."

3 The LORD has appeared of old to
  me, *saying:*
 "Yes, I have loved you with an
  everlasting love;
 Therefore with lovingkindness I
  have drawn you.
4 Again I will build you, and you
  shall be rebuilt,
 O virgin of Israel!
 You shall again be adorned with
  your tambourines,
 And shall go forth in the dances of
  those who rejoice.

5   You shall yet plant vines on the
     mountains of Samaria;
  The planters shall plant and eat
    them as ordinary food.
6   For there shall be a day
  When the watchmen will cry on
    Mount Ephraim,
  'Arise, and let us go up *to* Zion,
  To the LORD our God.' "
  7For thus says the LORD:
  "Sing with gladness for Jacob,
  And shout among the chief of the
    nations;
  Proclaim, give praise, and say,
  'O LORD, save Your people,
  The remnant of Israel!'
8   Behold, I will bring them from the
    north country,
  And gather them from the ends of
    the earth,
  Among them the blind and the
    lame,
  The woman with child
  And the one who labors with child,
    together;
  A great throng shall return there.
9   They shall come with weeping,
  And with supplications I will lead
    them.
  I will cause them to walk by the
    rivers of waters,
  In a straight way in which they
    shall not stumble;
  For I am a Father to Israel,
  And Ephraim *is* My firstborn.

10   "Hear the word of the LORD,
    O nations,
  And declare *it* in the isles afar off,
    and say,
  'He who scattered Israel will gather
    him,
  And keep him as a shepherd *does*
    his flock.'
11   For the LORD has redeemed Jacob,
  And ransomed him from the hand
    of one stronger than he.
12   Therefore they shall come and sing
    in the height of Zion,
  Streaming to the goodness of the
    LORD—
  For wheat and new wine and oil,
  For the young of the flock and the
    herd;
  Their souls shall be like a well-
    watered garden,

  And they shall sorrow no more
    at all.
13   "Then shall the virgin rejoice in the
    dance,
  And the young men and the old,
    together;
  For I will turn their mourning
    to joy,
  Will comfort them,
  And make them rejoice rather than
    sorrow.
14   I will satiate the soul of the priests
    with abundance,
  And My people shall be satisfied
    with My goodness, says the
    LORD."

Mercy on Ephraim

  15Thus says the LORD:
  "A voice was heard in Ramah,
  Lamentation *and* bitter weeping,
  Rachel weeping for her children,
  Refusing to be comforted for her
    children,
  Because they *are* no more."
  16Thus says the LORD:
  "Refrain your voice from weeping,
  And your eyes from tears;
  For your work shall be rewarded,
    says the LORD,
  And they shall come back from the
    land of the enemy.
17   There is hope in your future, says
    the LORD,
  That *your* children shall come back
    to their own border.

18   "I have surely heard Ephraim
    bemoaning himself:
  'You have chastised me, and I was
    chastised,
  Like an untrained bull;
  Restore me, and I will return,
  For You *are* the LORD my God.
19   Surely, after my turning, I
    repented;
  And after I was instructed, I struck
    myself on the thigh;
  I was ashamed, yes, even
    humiliated,
  Because I bore the reproach of my
    youth.'
20   *Is* Ephraim My dear son?
  Is he a pleasant child?
  For though I spoke against him,
  I earnestly remember him still;

Therefore My heart yearns for him;
I will surely have mercy on him,
    says the Lord.

21 "Set up signposts,
    Make landmarks;
    Set your heart toward the highway,
    The way in *which* you went.
    Turn back, O virgin of Israel,
    Turn back to these your cities.
22 How long will you gad about,
    O you backsliding daughter?
    For the Lord has created a new
        thing in the earth—
    A woman shall encompass a man."

Future Prosperity of Judah

23Thus says the Lord of hosts, the
God of Israel: "They shall again use this
speech in the land of Judah and in its
cities, when I bring back their captivity:
'The Lord bless you, O home of justice,
and mountain of holiness!' 24And there
shall dwell in Judah itself, and in all
its cities together, farmers and those going out with flocks. 25For I have satiated
the weary soul, and I have replenished
every sorrowful soul."

26After this I awoke and looked
around, and my sleep was sweet to me.
27"Behold, the days are coming, says
the Lord, that I will sow the house of
Israel and the house of Judah with the
seed of man and the seed of beast.
28And it shall come to pass, *that* as I
have watched over them to pluck up,
to break down, to throw down, to destroy, and to afflict, so I will watch over
them to build and to plant, says the
Lord. 29In those days they shall say no
more:

    'The fathers have eaten sour grapes,
      And the children's teeth are set on
        edge.'

30But every one shall die for his own
iniquity; every man who eats the sour
grapes, his teeth shall be set on edge.

A New Covenant

31"Behold, the days are coming, says
the Lord, when I will make a new covenant with the house of Israel and with
the house of Judah—32not according to
the covenant that I made with their fathers in the day *that* I took them by
the hand to lead them out of the land
of Egypt, My covenant which they

broke, though I was a husband to them,
says the Lord. 33But this *is* the covenant
that I will make with the house of Israel
after those days, says the Lord: I will
put My law in their minds, and write it
on their hearts; and I will be their God,
and they shall be My people. 34No more
shall every man teach his neighbor, and
every man his brother, saying, 'Know
the Lord,' for they all shall know Me,
from the least of them to the greatest
of them, says the Lord. For I will forgive their iniquity, and their sin I will
remember no more."

35 Thus says the Lord,
    Who gives the sun for a light
      by day,
    The ordinances of the moon and
      the stars for a light by night,
    Who disturbs the sea,
    And its waves roar
    (The Lord of hosts *is* His name):

36 "If those ordinances depart
    From before Me, says the Lord,
    Then the seed of Israel shall also
      cease
    From being a nation before Me
      forever."
37Thus says the Lord:
    "If heaven above can be measured,
    And the foundations of the earth
      searched out beneath,
    I will also cast off all the seed of
      Israel
    For all that they have done, says
      the Lord.
38"Behold, the days are coming, says
the Lord, that the city shall be built for
the Lord from the Tower of Hananel
to the Corner Gate. 39The surveyor's
line shall again extend straight forward
over the hill Gareb; then it shall turn
toward Goath. 40And the whole valley
of the dead bodies and of the ashes, and
all the fields as far as the Brook Kidron,
to the corner of the Horse Gate toward
the east, *shall be* holy to the Lord. It
shall not be plucked up or thrown down
anymore forever."

Jeremiah Buys a Field

32 The word that came to Jeremiah
from the Lord in the tenth year
of Zedekiah king of Judah, which was
the eighteenth year of Nebuchadnezzar. 2For then the king of Babylon's

army besieged Jerusalem, and Jeremiah the prophet was shut up in the court of the prison, which *was in* the king of Judah's house. 3For Zedekiah king of Judah had shut him up, saying, "Why do you prophesy and say, 'Thus says the LORD: "Behold, I will give this city into the hand of the king of Babylon, and he shall take it; 4and Zedekiah king of Judah shall not escape from the hand of the Chaldeans, but shall surely be delivered into the hand of the king of Babylon, and shall speak with him face to face, and see him eye to eye; 5then he shall lead Zedekiah to Babylon, and there he shall be until I visit him," says the LORD; "though you fight with the Chaldeans, you shall not succeed" '?"

6And Jeremiah said, "The word of the LORD came to me, saying, 7'Behold, Hanamel the son of Shallum your uncle will come to you, saying, "Buy my field which *is* in Anathoth, for the right of redemption *is* yours to buy *it*." ' 8Then Hanamel my uncle's son came to me in the court of the prison according to the word of the LORD, and said to me, 'Please buy my field that *is* in Anathoth, which *is* in the country of Benjamin; for the right of inheritance *is* yours, and the redemption yours; buy *it* for yourself.' Then I knew that this was the word of the LORD. 9So I bought the field from Hanamel, the son of my uncle who *was* in Anathoth, and weighed *out to* him the money—seventeen shekels of silver. 10And I signed the deed and sealed *it*, took witnesses, and weighed the money on the scales. 11So I took the purchase deed, *both* that which was sealed *according* to the law and custom, and that which was open; 12and I gave the purchase deed to Baruch the son of Neriah, son of Mahseiah, in the presence of Hanamel my uncle's *son*, and in the presence of the witnesses who signed the purchase deed, before all the Jews who sat in the court of the prison.

13"Then I charged Baruch before them, saying, 14'Thus says the LORD of hosts, the God of Israel: "Take these deeds, both this purchase deed which is sealed and this deed which is open, and put them in an earthen vessel, that they may last many days." 15For thus says the LORD of hosts, the God of Israel: "Houses and fields and vineyards shall be possessed again in this land." '

Jeremiah Prays for Understanding

16"Now when I had delivered the purchase deed to Baruch the son of Neriah, I prayed to the LORD, saying: 17'Ah, Lord GOD! Behold, You have made the heavens and the earth by Your great power and outstretched arm. There is nothing too hard for You. 18You show lovingkindness to thousands, and repay the iniquity of the fathers into the bosom of their children after them—the Great, the Mighty God, whose name *is* the LORD of hosts. 19You are great in counsel and mighty in work, for your eyes *are* open to all the ways of the sons of men, to give everyone according to his ways and according to the fruit of his doings. 20You have set signs and wonders in the land of Egypt, to this day, and in Israel and among *other* men; and You have made Yourself a name, as it is this day. 21You have brought Your people Israel out of the land of Egypt with signs and wonders, with a strong hand and an outstretched arm, and with great terror; 22You have given them this land, of which You swore to their fathers to give them—"a land flowing with milk and honey."*i* 23And they came in and took possession of it, but they have not obeyed Your voice or walked in Your law. They have done nothing of all that You commanded them to do; therefore You have caused all this calamity to come upon them.

24'Look, the siege mounds! They have come to the city to take it; and the city has been given into the hand of the Chaldeans who fight against it, because of the sword and famine and pestilence. What You have spoken has happened; there You see *it!* 25And You have said to me, O Lord GOD, "Buy the field for money, and take witnesses"!—yet the city has been given into the hand of the Chaldeans.' "

i Exodus 3.8

God's Assurance of the People's Return

26Then the word of the LORD came to Jeremiah, saying, 27"Behold, I *am* the LORD, the God of all flesh. Is there anything too hard for Me? 28Therefore thus says the LORD: 'Behold, I will give this city into the hand of the Chaldeans, into the hand of Nebuchadnezzar king of Babylon, and he shall take it. 29And the Chaldeans who fight against this city shall come and set fire to this city and burn it, with the houses on whose roofs they have offered incense to Baal and poured out drink offerings to other gods, to provoke Me to anger; 30because the children of Israel and the children of Judah have done only evil before Me from their youth. For the children of Israel have provoked Me only to anger with the work of their hands,' says the LORD. 31'For this city has been to Me *a provocation of* My anger and My fury from the day that they built it, even to this day; so I will remove it from before My face 32because of all the evil of the children of Israel and the children of Judah, which they have done to provoke Me to anger—they, their kings, their princes, their priests, their prophets, the men of Judah, and the inhabitants of Jerusalem. 33And they have turned to Me the back, and not the face; though I taught them, rising up early and teaching *them,* yet they have not listened to receive instruction. 34But they set their abominations in the house which is called by My name, to defile it. 35And they built the high places of Baal which *are* in the Valley of the Son of Hinnom, to cause their sons and their daughters to pass through *the fire* to Molech, which I did not command them, nor did it come into My mind that they should do this abomination, to cause Judah to sin.'

36"Now therefore, thus says the LORD, the God of Israel, concerning this city of which you say, 'It shall be delivered into the hand of the king of Babylon by the sword, by the famine, and by the pestilence: 37Behold, I will gather them out of all countries where I have driven them in My anger, in My fury, and in great wrath; I will bring them back to this place, and I will cause them to dwell safely. 38They shall be My people, and I will be their God; 39then I will give them one heart and one way, that they may fear Me forever, for the good of them and their children after them. 40And I will make an everlasting covenant with them, that I will not turn away from doing them good; but I will put My fear in their hearts so that they will not depart from Me. 41Yes, I will rejoice over them to do them good, and I will assuredly plant them in this land, with all My heart and with all My soul.'

42"For thus says the LORD: 'Just as I have brought all this great calamity on this people, so I will bring on them all the good that I have promised them. 43And fields will be bought in this land of which you say, "*It is* desolate, without man or beast; it has been given into the hand of the Chaldeans." 44Men will buy fields for money, sign deeds and seal *them,* and take witnesses, in the land of Benjamin, in the places around Jerusalem, in the cities of Judah, in the cities of the mountains, in the cities of the lowland, and in the cities of the South; for I will cause their captives to return,' says the LORD."

Excellence of the Restored Nation

33 Moreover the word of the LORD came to Jeremiah a second time, while he was still shut up in the court of the prison, saying, 2"Thus says the LORD who made it, the LORD who formed it to establish it (the LORD *is* His name): 3'Call to Me, and I will answer you, and show you great and mighty things, which you do not know.'

4"For thus says the LORD, the God of Israel, concerning the houses of this city and the houses of the kings of Judah, which have been pulled down *to fortify*ᵏ against the siege mounds and the sword: 5'They come to fight with the Chaldeans, but *only* to fill their placesˡ with the dead bodies of men whom I will slay in My anger and My fury, all for whose wickedness I have hidden My face from this city. 6Behold, I will bring it health and healing; I will

---

ᵏ Compare Isaiah 22.10   ˡ Compare 2 Kings 23.14

heal them and reveal to them the abundance of peace and truth. 7And I will cause the captives of Judah and the captives of Israel to return, and will rebuild those places as at the first. 8I will cleanse them from all their iniquity by which they have sinned against Me, and I will pardon all their iniquities by which they have sinned and by which they have transgressed against Me. 9Then it shall be to Me a name of joy, a praise, and an honor before all nations of the earth, who shall hear all the good that I do to them; they shall fear and tremble for all the goodness and all the prosperity that I provide for it.'

10"Thus says the LORD: 'Again there shall be heard in this place—of which you say, "It is desolate, without man and without beast"—in the cities of Judah, in the streets of Jerusalem that are desolate, without man and without inhabitant and without beast, 11the voice of joy and the voice of gladness, the voice of the bridegroom and the voice of the bride, the voice of those who will say:

"Praise the LORD of hosts,
   For the LORD is good,
   For His mercy endures forever"—
and of those who will bring the sacrifice of praise into the house of the LORD. For I will cause the captives of the land to return as at the first,' says the LORD.

12"Thus says the LORD of hosts: 'In this place which is desolate, without man and without beast, and in all its cities, there shall again be a dwelling place of shepherds causing their flocks to lie down. 13In the cities of the mountains, in the cities of the lowland, in the cities of the South, in the land of Benjamin, in the places around Jerusalem, and in the cities of Judah, the flocks shall again pass under the hands of him who counts them,' says the LORD.

14'Behold, the days are coming,' says the LORD, 'that I will perform that good thing which I have promised to the house of Israel and to the house of Judah:

15 'In those days and at that time
   I will cause to grow up to David
   A Branch of righteousness;

   He shall execute judgment and
     righteousness in the earth.
16 In those days Judah will be saved,
   And Jerusalem will dwell safely.
   And this is the name by which she
     will be called:

THE LORD OUR RIGHTEOUSNESS.'m

17"For thus says the LORD: 'David shall never lack a man to sit on the throne of the house of Israel; 18nor shall the priests, the Levites, lack a man to offer burnt offerings before Me, to kindle grain offerings, and to sacrifice continually.' "

The Permanence of God's Covenant

19And the word of the LORD came to Jeremiah, saying, 20"Thus says the LORD: 'If you can break My covenant with the day and My covenant with the night, so that there will not be day and night in their season, 21then My covenant may also be broken with David My servant, so that he shall not have a son to reign on his throne, and with the Levites, the priests, My ministers. 22As the host of heaven cannot be numbered, nor the sand of the sea measured, so will I multiply the descendants of David My servant and the Levites who minister to Me.' "

23Moreover the word of the LORD came to Jeremiah, saying, 24"Have you not considered what these people have spoken, saying, 'The two families which the LORD has chosen, He has also cast them off'? Thus they have despised My people, as if they should no more be a nation before them.

25"Thus says the LORD: 'If My covenant is not with day and night, and if I have not appointed the ordinances of heaven and earth, 26then I will cast away the descendants of Jacob and David My servant, so that I will not take any of his descendants to be rulers over the descendants of Abraham, Isaac, and Jacob. For I will cause their captives to return, and will have mercy on them.' "

Zedekiah Warned by God

34 The word which came to Jeremiah from the LORD, when Nebuchadnezzar king of Babylon and all his

m Compare 23.5, 6

army, all the kingdoms of the earth under his dominion, and all the people, fought against Jerusalem and all its cities, saying, 2"Thus says the LORD, the God of Israel: 'Go and speak to Zedekiah king of Judah and tell him, "Thus says the LORD: 'Behold, I will give this city into the hand of the king of Babylon, and he shall burn it with fire. 3And you shall not escape from his hand, but shall surely be taken and delivered into his hand; your eyes shall see the eyes of the king of Babylon, he shall speak with you face to face, and you shall go to Babylon.' " ' 4Yet hear the word of the LORD, O Zedekiah king of Judah! Thus says the LORD concerning you: 'You shall not die by the sword. 5You shall die in peace; as in the ceremonies of your fathers, the former kings who were before you, so they shall burn incense for you and lament for you, *saying,* "Alas, lord!" For I have pronounced the word, says the LORD.' "

6Then Jeremiah the prophet spoke all these words to Zedekiah king of Judah in Jerusalem, 7when the king of Babylon's army fought against Jerusalem and all the cities of Judah that were left, against Lachish and Azekah; for *only* these fortified cities remained of the cities of Judah.

Treacherous Treatment of Slaves

8*This is* the word that came to Jeremiah from the LORD, after King Zedekiah had made a covenant with all the people who *were* at Jerusalem to proclaim liberty to them: 9that every man should set free his male and female slave—a Hebrew man or woman—that no one should keep a Jewish brother in bondage. 10Now when all the princes and all the people, who had entered into the covenant, heard that everyone should set free his male and female slaves, that no one should keep them in bondage anymore, they obeyed and let *them* go. 11But afterward they changed their minds and made the male and female slaves return, whom they had set free, and brought them into subjection as male and female slaves. 12Therefore the word of the LORD came to Jeremiah from the LORD, say-

ing, 13"Thus says the LORD, the God of Israel: 'I made a covenant with your fathers in the day that I brought them out of the land of Egypt, out of the house of bondage, saying, 14"At the end of seven years let every man set free his Hebrew brother, who has been sold to him; and when he has served you six years, you shall let him go free from you." But your fathers did not obey Me nor incline their ear. 15Then you recently turned and did what was right in My sight—every man proclaiming liberty to his neighbor; and you made a covenant before Me in the house which is called by My name. 16Then you turned around and profaned My name, and every one of you brought back his male and female slaves, whom he had set at liberty, at their pleasure, and brought them back into subjection, to be your male and female slaves.'

17"Therefore thus says the LORD: 'You have not obeyed Me in proclaiming liberty, every one to his brother and every one to his neighbor. Behold, I proclaim liberty to you,' says the LORD—'to the sword, to pestilence, and to famine! And I will deliver you to trouble among all the kingdoms of the earth. 18And I will give the men who have transgressed My covenant, who have not performed the words of the covenant which they made before Me, when they cut the calf in two and passed between the parts of it— 19the princes of Judah, the princes of Jerusalem, the eunuchs, the priests, and all the people of the land who passed between the parts of the calf—20I will give them into the hand of their enemies and into the hand of those who seek their life. Their dead bodies shall be for meat for the birds of the heaven and the beasts of the earth. 21And I will give Zedekiah king of Judah and his princes into the hand of their enemies, into the hand of those who seek their life, and into the hand of the king of Babylon's army which has gone back from you. 22Behold, I will command,' says the LORD, 'and cause them to return to this city. They will fight against it and take it and burn it with fire; and I will make the cities of Judah a desolation without inhabitant.' "

The Obedient Rechabites

35 The word which came to Jeremiah from the LORD in the days of Jehoiakim the son of Josiah, king of Judah, saying, 2"Go to the house of the Rechabites, speak to them, and bring them into the house of the LORD, into one of the chambers, and give them wine to drink."

3Then I took Jaazaniah the son of Jeremiah, the son of Habazziniah, his brothers and all his sons, and the whole house of the Rechabites, 4and I brought them into the house of the LORD, into the chamber of the sons of Hanan the son of Igdaliah, a man of God, which *was* by the chamber of the princes, above the chamber of Maaseiah the son of Shallum, the keeper of the door. 5Then I set before the sons of the house of the Rechabites bowls full of wine, and cups; and I said to them, "Drink wine."

6But they said, "We will drink no wine, for Jonadab the son of Rechab, our father, commanded us, saying, 'You shall drink no wine, you nor your sons, forever. 7You shall not build a house, sow seed, plant a vineyard, nor have *any of these*; but all your days you shall dwell in tents, that you may live many days in the land where you are sojourners.' 8Thus we have obeyed the voice of Jonadab the son of Rechab, our father, in all that he charged us, to drink no wine all our days, we, our wives, our sons, or our daughters, 9nor to build ourselves houses to dwell in; nor do we have vineyard, field, or seed. 10But we have dwelt in tents, and have obeyed and done according to all that Jonadab our father commanded us. 11But it came to pass, when Nebuchadnezzar king of Babylon came up into the land, that we said, 'Come, let us go to Jerusalem for fear of the army of the Chaldeans and for fear of the army of the Syrians.' So we dwell at Jerusalem."

12Then came the word of the LORD to Jeremiah, saying, 13"Thus says the LORD of hosts, the God of Israel: 'Go and tell the men of Judah and the inhabitants of Jerusalem, "Will you not receive instruction to obey My words?" says the LORD. 14"The words of Jonadab the son of Rechab, which he commanded his sons, not to drink wine, are performed; for to this day they drink none, and obey their father's commandment. But although I have spoken to you, rising early and speaking, you did not obey Me. 15I have also sent to you all My servants the prophets, rising up early and sending *them*, saying, 'Turn now everyone from his evil way, amend your doings, and do not go after other gods to serve them; then you will dwell in the land which I have given you and your fathers.' But you have not inclined your ear, nor obeyed Me. 16Surely the sons of Jonadab the son of Rechab have performed the commandment of their father, which he commanded them, but this people has not obeyed Me." '

17"Therefore thus says the LORD God of hosts, the God of Israel: 'Behold, I will bring on Judah and on all the inhabitants of Jerusalem all the doom that I have pronounced against them; because I have spoken to them but they have not heard, and I have called to them but they have not answered.' "

18And Jeremiah said to the house of the Rechabites, "Thus says the LORD of hosts, the God of Israel: 'Because you have obeyed the commandment of Jonadab your father, and kept all his precepts and done according to all that he commanded you, 19therefore thus says the LORD of hosts, the God of Israel: "Jonadab the son of Rechab shall not lack a man to stand before Me forever." ' "

The Scroll Read in the Temple

36 Now it came to pass in the fourth year of Jehoiakim the son of Josiah, king of Judah, *that* this word came to Jeremiah from the LORD, saying: 2"Take a scroll of a book and write on it all the words that I have spoken to you against Israel, against Judah, and against all the nations, from the day I spoke to you, from the days of Josiah even to this day. 3It may be that the house of Judah will hear all the adversities which I purpose to bring upon them, that everyone may turn from his evil way, that I may forgive their iniquity and their sin."

4Then Jeremiah called Baruch the son of Neriah; and Baruch wrote on a scroll of a book, at the instruction of

Jeremiah, all the words of the LORD which He had spoken to him. 5And Jeremiah commanded Baruch, saying, "I *am* confined, I cannot go into the house of the LORD. 6You go, therefore, and read from the scroll which you have written at my instruction, the words of the LORD, in the hearing of the people in the LORD's house on the day of fasting. And you shall also read them in the hearing of all Judah who come from their cities. 7It may be that they will present their supplication before the LORD, and everyone will turn from his evil way. For great *is* the anger and the fury that the LORD has pronounced against this people." 8And Baruch the son of Neriah did according to all that Jeremiah the prophet commanded him, reading from the book the words of the LORD in the LORD's house.

9Now it came to pass in the fifth year of Jehoiakim the son of Josiah, king of Judah, in the ninth month, *that* they proclaimed a fast before the LORD to all the people in Jerusalem, and to all the people who came from the cities of Judah to Jerusalem. 10Then Baruch read from the book the words of Jeremiah in the house of the LORD, in the chamber of Gemariah the son of Shaphan the scribe, in the upper court at the entry of the New Gate of the LORD's house, in the hearing of all the people.

The Scroll Read in the Palace

11When Michaiah the son of Gemariah, the son of Shaphan, heard all the words of the LORD from the book, 12he then went down to the king's house, into the scribe's chamber; and there all the princes were sitting— Elishama the scribe, Delaiah the son of Shemaiah, Elnathan the son of Achbor, Gemariah the son of Shaphan, Zedekiah the son of Hananiah, and all the princes. 13Then Michaiah declared to them all the words that he had heard when Baruch read the book in the hearing of the people. 14Therefore all the princes sent Jehudi the son of Nethaniah, the son of Shelemiah, the son of Cushi, to Baruch, saying, "Take in your hand the scroll from which you have read in the hearing of the people, and come." So Baruch the son of Neriah took the scroll in his hand and came

to them. 15And they said to him, "Sit down now, and read it in our hearing." So Baruch read *it* in their hearing.

16Now it happened, when they had heard all the words, that they looked in fear from one to another, and said to Baruch, "We will surely tell the king of all these words." 17And they asked Baruch, saying, "Tell us now, how did you write all these words—at his instruction?"

18So Baruch answered them, "He proclaimed with his mouth all these words to me, and I wrote *them* with ink in the book."

19Then the princes said to Baruch, "Go and hide, you and Jeremiah; and let no one know where you are."

The King Destroys Jeremiah's Scroll

20And they went to the king, into the court; but they stored the scroll in the chamber of Elishama the scribe, and told all the words in the hearing of the king. 21So the king sent Jehudi to bring the scroll, and he took it from Elishama the scribe's chamber. And Jehudi read it in the hearing of the king and in the hearing of all the princes who stood beside the king. 22Now the king was sitting in the winter house in the ninth month, with *a fire* burning on the hearth before him. 23And it happened, when Jehudi had read three or four columns, *that the king* cut it with the scribe's knife and cast *it* into the fire that *was* on the hearth, until all the scroll was consumed in the fire that *was* on the hearth. 24Yet they were not afraid, nor did they tear their garments, the king nor any of his servants who heard all these words. 25Nevertheless Elnathan, Delaiah, and Gemariah implored the king not to burn the scroll; but he would not listen to them. 26And the king commanded Jerahmeel the king's son, Seraiah the son of Azriel, and Shelemiah the son of Abdeel, to seize Baruch the scribe and Jeremiah the prophet, but the LORD hid them.

Jeremiah Rewrites the Scroll

27Now after the king had burned the scroll with the words which Baruch had written at the instruction of Jeremiah, the word of the LORD came to Jeremiah, saying: 28"Take yet another scroll, and write on it all the former words that were in the first scroll which Jehoiakim the king of Judah has burned. 29And you shall say to Jehoiakim king of Judah, 'Thus says the LORD: "You have burned this scroll, saying, 'Why have you written in it that the king of Babylon will certainly come and destroy this land, and cause man and beast to cease from here?' " 30Therefore thus says the LORD concerning Jehoiakim king of Judah: "He shall have no one to sit on the throne of David, and his dead body shall be cast out to the heat of the day and the frost of the night. 31I will punish him, his family, and his servants for their iniquity; and I will bring on them, on the inhabitants of Jerusalem, and on the men of Judah all the doom that I have pronounced against them; but they did not heed." ' "

32Then Jeremiah took another scroll and gave it to Baruch the scribe, the son of Neriah, who wrote on it at the instruction of Jeremiah all the words of the book which Jehoiakim king of Judah had burned in the fire. And besides, there were added to them many similar words.

Zedekiah's Vain Hope

37 Now King Zedekiah the son of Josiah reigned instead of Coniah the son of Jehoiakim, whom Nebuchadnezzar king of Babylon made king in the land of Judah. 2But neither he nor his servants nor the people of the land gave heed to the words of the LORD which He spoke by the prophet Jeremiah.

3And Zedekiah the king sent Jehucal the son of Shelemiah, and Zephaniah the son of Maaseiah, the priest, to the prophet Jeremiah, saying, "Pray now to the LORD our God for us." 4Now Jeremiah was coming and going among the people, for they had not yet put him in prison. 5Then Pharaoh's army came up from Egypt; and when the Chaldeans who were besieging Jerusalem heard news of them, they departed from Jerusalem.

6Then the word of the LORD came to the prophet Jeremiah, saying, 7"Thus says the LORD, the God of Israel, 'Thus you shall say to the king of Judah, who sent you to Me to inquire of Me: "Behold, Pharaoh's army which has come up to help you will return to Egypt, to their own land. 8And the Chaldeans shall come back and fight against this city, and take it and burn it with fire." ' 9Thus says the LORD: 'Do not deceive yourselves, saying, "The Chaldeans will surely depart from us," for they will not depart. 10For though you had defeated the whole army of the Chaldeans who fight against you, and there remained only wounded men among them, they would rise up, every man in his tent, and burn the city with fire.' "

Jeremiah Imprisoned

11And it happened, when the army of the Chaldeans left the siege of Jerusalem for fear of Pharaoh's army, 12that Jeremiah went out of Jerusalem to go into the land of Benjamin to claim his property there among the people. 13And when he was in the Gate of Benjamin, a captain of the guard was there whose name was Irijah the son of Shelemiah, the son of Hananiah; and he seized Jeremiah the prophet, saying, "You are defecting to the Chaldeans!"

14Then Jeremiah said, "False! I am not defecting to the Chaldeans." But he did not listen to him.

So Irijah seized Jeremiah and brought him to the princes. 15Therefore the princes were angry with Jeremiah, and they struck him and put him in prison in the house of Jonathan the scribe. For they had made that the prison.

16When Jeremiah entered the dungeon and the cells, and Jeremiah had remained there many days, 17then Zedekiah the king sent and took him out. The king asked him secretly in his house, and said, "Is there any word from the LORD?"

And Jeremiah said, "There is." Then he said, "You shall be delivered into the hand of the king of Babylon!"

18Moreover Jeremiah said to King Zedekiah, "What offense have I committed against you, against your servants, or against this people, that you have put me in prison? 19Where now are your prophets who prophesied to you, saying, 'The king of Babylon will not come against you or against this land?' 20Therefore please hear now, O my lord the king. Please, let my petition be accepted before you, and do not make me return to the house of Jonathan the scribe, lest I die there."

21Then Zedekiah the king commanded that they should commit Jeremiah to the court of the prison, and that they should give him daily a piece of bread from the bakers' street, until all the bread in the city was gone. Thus Jeremiah remained in the court of the prison.

Jeremiah in the Dungeon

38 Now Shephatiah the son of Mattan, Gedaliah the son of Pashhur, Jucal the son of Shelemiah, and Pashhur the son of Malchiah heard the words that Jeremiah had spoken to all the people, saying, 2"Thus says the LORD: 'He who remains in this city shall die by the sword, by famine, and by pestilence; but he who goes over to the Chaldeans shall live; his life shall be as a prize to him, and he shall live.'*n* 3Thus says the LORD: 'This city shall surely be given into the hand of the king of Babylon's army, which shall take it.'"

4Therefore the princes said to the king, "Please, let this man be put to death, for thus he weakens the hands of the men of war who remain in this city, and the hands of all the people, by speaking such words to them. For this man does not seek the welfare of this people, but their harm."

5Then Zedekiah the king said, "Look, he *is* in your hand. For the king can *do* nothing against you." 6So they took Jeremiah and cast him into the dungeon of Malchiah the king's son, which *was* in the court of the prison, and they let Jeremiah down with ropes. And in the dungeon *there was* no water, but mire. So Jeremiah sank in the mire.

7Now Ebed-Melech the Ethiopian, one of the eunuchs, who was in the king's house, heard that they had put Jeremiah in the dungeon. When the king was sitting at the Gate of Benjamin, 8Ebed-Melech went out of the king's house and spoke to the king, saying: 9"My lord the king, these men have done evil in all that they have done to Jeremiah the prophet, whom they have cast into the dungeon, and he is likely to die from hunger in the place where he is. For *there is* no more bread in the city." 10Then the king commanded Ebed-Melech the Ethiopian, saying, "Take from here thirty men with you, and lift Jeremiah the prophet out of the dungeon before he dies." 11So Ebed-Melech took the men with him and went into the house of the king under the treasury, and took from there old clothes and old rags, and let them down by ropes into the dungeon to Jeremiah. 12Then Ebed-Melech the Ethiopian said to Jeremiah, "Please put these old clothes and rags under your armpits, under the ropes." And Jeremiah did so. 13So they pulled Jeremiah up with ropes and lifted him out of the dungeon. And Jeremiah remained in the court of the prison.

Zedekiah's Fears and Jeremiah's Advice

14Then Zedekiah the king sent and had Jeremiah the prophet brought to him at the third entrance of the house of the LORD. And the king said to Jeremiah, "I will ask you something. Hide nothing from me."

15Jeremiah said to Zedekiah, "If I declare *it* to you, will you not surely put me to death? And if I give you advice, you will not listen to me."

16So Zedekiah the king swore secretly to Jeremiah, saying, "*As* the LORD lives, who made our very souls, I will not put you to death, nor will I give you into the hand of these men who seek your life."

17Then Jeremiah said to Zedekiah, "Thus says the LORD, the God of hosts, the God of Israel: 'If you surely surrender to the king of Babylon's princes, then your soul shall live; this city shall not be burned with fire, and you and your house shall live. 18But if you do not surrender to the king of Babylon's princes, then this city shall be given into the hand of the Chaldeans; they shall burn it with fire, and you shall not escape from their hand.'"

19And Zedekiah the king said to Jeremiah, "I am afraid of the Jews who

n Compare 21.9

have defected to the Chaldeans, lest they deliver me into their hand, and they abuse me."

20But Jeremiah said, "They shall not deliver you. Please, obey the voice of the LORD which I speak to you. So it shall be well with you, and your soul shall live. 21But if you refuse to surrender, this is the word that the LORD has shown me: 22'Now behold, all the women who are left in the king of Judah's house *shall be* surrendered to the king of Babylon's princes, and those *women* shall say:

"Your close friends have set upon
   you
And prevailed against you;
Your feet have sunk in the mire,
And they have turned away again."

23'So they shall surrender all your wives and children to the Chaldeans. You shall not escape from their hand, but shall be taken by the hand of the king of Babylon. And you shall cause this city to be burned with fire.' "

24Then Zedekiah said to Jeremiah, "Let no one know of these words, and you shall not die. 25But if the princes hear that I have talked with you, and they come to you and say to you, 'Declare to us now what you have said to the king, and also what the king said to you; do not hide *it* from us, and we will not put you to death,' 26then you shall say to them, 'I presented my request before the king, that he would not make me return to Jonathan's house to die there.' "

27Then all the princes came to Jeremiah and asked him. And he told them according to all these words that the king had commanded. So they stopped speaking with him, for the conversation had not been heard. 28Now Jeremiah remained in the court of the prison until the day that Jerusalem was taken. And he was *there* when Jerusalem was taken.

The Fall of Jerusalem

39 In the ninth year of Zedekiah king of Judah, in the tenth month, Nebuchadnezzar king of Babylon and all his army came against Jerusalem,

and besieged it. 2In the eleventh year of Zedekiah, in the fourth month, on the ninth *day* of the month, the city was penetrated.

3Then all the princes of the king of Babylon came in and sat in the Middle Gate: Nergal-Sharezer, Samgar-Nebo, Sarsechim, Rabsaris,o Nergal-Sarezer, Rabmag,p with the rest of the princes of the king of Babylon.

4So it was, when Zedekiah the king of Judah and all the men of war saw them, that they fled and went out of the city by night, by way of the king's garden, by the gate between the two walls. And he went out by way of the plain.q 5But the Chaldean army pursued them and overtook Zedekiah in the plains of Jericho. And when they had captured him, they brought him up to Nebuchadnezzar king of Babylon, to Riblah in the land of Hamath, where he pronounced judgment on him. 6Then the king of Babylon killed the sons of Zedekiah before his eyes in Riblah; the king of Babylon also killed all the nobles of Judah. 7Moreover he put out Zedekiah's eyes, and bound him with bronze fetters to carry him off to Babylon. 8And the Chaldeans burned the king's house and the houses of the people with fire, and broke down the walls of Jerusalem. 9Then Nebuzaradan the captain of the guard carried away captive to Babylon the remnant of the people who remained in the city and those who defected to him, with the rest of the people who remained. 10But Nebuzaradan the captain of the guard left in the land of Judah the poor people, who had nothing, and gave them vineyards and fields at the same time.

Jeremiah Goes Free

11Now Nebuchadnezzar king of Babylon gave charge concerning Jeremiah to Nebuzaradan the captain of the guard, saying, 12"Take him and look after him, and do him no harm; but do to him just as he says to you." 13So Nebuzaradan the captain of the guard sent Nebushasban, Rabsaris, Nergal-Sharezer, Rabmag, and all the king of Babylon's chief officers; 14then they

---

o A title, probably *Chief Officer;* also verse 13
verse 13   q That is, the Jordan Valley

p A title, probably *Troop Commander;* also

sent *someone* to take Jeremiah from the court of the prison, and committed him to Gedaliah the son of Ahikam, the son of Shaphan, that he should take him home. So he dwelt among the people.

15Meanwhile the word of the LORD had come to Jeremiah while he was shut up in the court of the prison, saying, 16"Go and speak to Ebed-Melech the Ethiopian, saying, 'Thus says the LORD of hosts, the God of Israel: "Behold, I will bring My words upon this city for adversity and not for good, and they shall be *performed* in that day before you. 17But I will deliver you in that day," says the LORD, "and you shall not be given into the hand of the men of whom you *are* afraid. 18For I will surely deliver you, and you shall not fall by the sword; but your life shall be as a prize to you, because you have put your trust in Me," says the LORD.' "

Jeremiah with Gedaliah the Governor

40 The word that came to Jeremiah from the LORD after Nebuzaradan the captain of the guard had let him go from Ramah, when he had taken him bound in chains among all who were carried away captive from Jerusalem and Judah, who were carried away captive to Babylon.

2And the captain of the guard took Jeremiah and said to him: "The LORD your God has pronounced this doom on this place. 3Now the LORD has brought *it*, and has done just as He said. Because you *people* have sinned against the LORD, and not obeyed His voice, therefore this thing has come upon you. 4And now look, I free you this day from the chains that *were* on your hand. If it seems good to you to come with me to Babylon, come, and I will look after you. But if it seems wrong for you to come with me to Babylon, remain here. See, all the land *is* before you; wherever it seems good and convenient for you to go, go there."

5Now while Jeremiah had not yet gone back, *Nebuzaradan said,* "Go back to Gedaliah the son of Ahikam, the son of Shaphan, whom the king of Babylon has made governor over the cities of Judah, and dwell with him among the people. Or go wherever it seems convenient for you to go." So the

captain of the guard gave him rations and a gift and let him go. 6Then Jeremiah went to Gedaliah the son of Ahikam, to Mizpah, and dwelt with him among the people who were left in the land.

7And when all the captains of the armies who *were* in the fields, they and their men, heard that the king of Babylon had made Gedaliah the son of Ahikam governor in the land, and had committed to him men, women, children, and the poorest of the land who had not been carried away captive to Babylon, 8then they came to Gedaliah at Mizpah—Ishmael the son of Nethaniah, Johanan and Jonathan the sons of Kareah, Seraiah the son of Tanhumeth, the sons of Ephai the Netophathite, and Jezaniah the son of a Maachathite, they and their men. 9And Gedaliah the son of Ahikam, the son of Shaphan, took an oath before them and their men, saying, "Do not be afraid to serve the Chaldeans. Dwell in the land and serve the king of Babylon, and it shall be well with you. 10As for me, I will indeed dwell at Mizpah and serve the Chaldeans who come to us. But you, gather wine and summer fruit and oil, put *them* in your vessels, and dwell in your cities that you have taken." 11Likewise, when all the Jews who *were* in Moab, among the Ammonites, in Edom, and who *were* in all the countries, heard that the king of Babylon had left a remnant of Judah, and that he had set over them Gedaliah the son of Ahikam, the son of Shaphan, 12then all the Jews returned out of all places where they had been driven, and came to the land of Judah, to Gedaliah at Mizpah, and gathered wine and summer fruit in abundance.

13Moreover Johanan the son of Kareah and all the captains of the forces that *were* in the fields came to Gedaliah at Mizpah, 14and said to him, "Do you certainly know that Baalis the king of the Ammonites has sent Ishmael the son of Nethaniah to murder you?" But Gedaliah the son of Ahikam did not believe them.

15Then Johanan the son of Kareah spoke secretly to Gedaliah in Mizpah, saying, "Let me go, please, and I will kill Ishmael the son of Nethaniah, and no one will know *it*. Why should he murder you, so that all the Jews who are gathered to you would be scattered, and the remnant in Judah perish?''

16But Gedaliah the son of Ahikam said to Johanan the son of Kareah, "You shall not do this thing, for you speak falsely concerning Ishmael."

Insurrection Against Gedaliah

41 Now it came to pass in the seventh month *that* Ishmael the son of Nethaniah, the son of Elishama, of the royal family and of the officers of the king, came with ten men to Gedaliah the son of Ahikam, at Mizpah. And there they ate bread together in Mizpah. 2Then Ishmael the son of Nethaniah, and the ten men who were with him, arose and struck Gedaliah the son of Ahikam, the son of Shaphan, with the sword, and killed him whom the king of Babylon had made governor over the land. 3Ishmael also struck down all the Jews who were with him, *that is,* with Gedaliah at Mizpah, and the Chaldeans who were found there, the men of war.

4And it happened, on the second day after he had killed Gedaliah, when as yet no one knew *it*, 5that certain men came from Shechem, from Shiloh, and from Samaria, eighty men with their beards shaved and their clothes torn, having cut themselves, with offerings and incense in their hand, to bring *them* to the house of the LORD. 6Now Ishmael the son of Nethaniah went out from Mizpah to meet them, weeping as he went along; and it happened as he met them that he said to them, "Come to Gedaliah the son of Ahikam!" 7So it was, when they came into the midst of the city, that Ishmael the son of Nethaniah killed them *and cast them* into the midst of a pit, he and the men who were with him. 8But ten men were found among them who said to Ishmael, "Do not kill us, for we have treasures of wheat, barley, oil, and honey in the field." So he desisted and did not kill them among their brethren. 9Now the pit into which Ishmael had cast all the dead bodies of the men whom he had slain, because of Gedaliah, *was* the same one Asa the king had made for fear of Baasha king of Israel. Ishmael

the son of Nethaniah filled it with *the* slain. 10Then Ishmael carried away captive all the rest of the people who *were* in Mizpah, the king's daughters and all the people who remained in Mizpah, whom Nebuzaradan the captain of the guard had committed to Gedaliah the son of Ahikam. And Ishmael the son of Nethaniah carried them away captive and departed to go over to the Ammonites.

11But when Johanan the son of Kareah and all the captains of the forces that *were* with him heard of all the evil that Ishmael the son of Nethaniah had done, 12they took all the men and went to fight with Ishmael the son of Nethaniah; and they found him by the great pool that *is* in Gibeon. 13So it was, when all the people who *were* with Ishmael saw Johanan the son of Kareah, and all the captains of the forces who *were* with him, that they were glad. 14Then all the people whom Ishmael had carried away captive from Mizpah turned around and came back, and went to Johanan the son of Kareah. 15But Ishmael the son of Nethaniah escaped from Johanan with eight men and went to the Ammonites.

16Then Johanan the son of Kareah, and all the captains of the forces that were with him, took from Mizpah all the rest of the people whom he had recovered from Ishmael the son of Nethaniah after he had murdered Gedaliah the son of Ahikam—the mighty men of war and the women and the children and the eunuchs, whom he had brought back from Gibeon. 17And they departed and dwelt in the habitation of Chimham, which is near Bethlehem, as they went on their way to Egypt, 18because of the Chaldeans; for they were afraid of them, because Ishmael the son of Nethaniah had murdered Gedaliah the son of Ahikam, whom the king of Babylon had made governor in the land.

The Flight to Egypt Forbidden

42 Now all the captains of the forces, Johanan the son of Kareah, Jezaniah the son of Hoshaiah, and all the people, from the least to the greatest, came near 2and said to Jeremiah the prophet, "Please, let our petition be acceptable to you, and pray for us to the Lord your God, for all this remnant (since we are left *but* a few of many, as you can see), 3that the Lord your God may show us the way in which we should walk and the thing we should do."

4Then Jeremiah the prophet said to them, "I have heard. Indeed, I will pray to the Lord your God according to your words, and it shall be, *that* whatever the Lord answers you, I will declare *it* to you. I will keep nothing back from you."

5So they said to Jeremiah, "Let the Lord be a true and faithful witness between us, if we do not do according to everything which the Lord your God sends us by you. 6Whether *it is* pleasing or displeasing, we will obey the voice of the Lord our God to whom we send you, that it may be well with us when we obey the voice of the Lord our God."

7And it happened after ten days that the word of the Lord came to Jeremiah. 8Then he called Johanan the son of Kareah, all the captains of the forces which *were* with him, and all the people from the least even to the greatest, 9and said to them, "Thus says the Lord, the God of Israel, to whom you sent me to present your petition before Him: 10'If you will still remain in this land, then I will build you and not pull *you* down, and I will plant you and not pluck *you* up. For I relent concerning the disaster that I have brought upon you. 11Do not be afraid of the king of Babylon, of whom you are afraid; do not be afraid of him,' says the Lord, 'for I *am* with you, to save you and deliver you from his hand. 12And I will show you mercy, that he may have mercy on you and cause you to return to your own land.'

13"But if you say, 'We will not dwell in this land,' disobeying the voice of the Lord your God, 14saying, 'No, but we will go to the land of Egypt where we shall see no war, nor hear the sound of the trumpet, nor be hungry for bread, and there we will dwell'—15Then hear now the word of the Lord, O remnant of Judah! Thus says the Lord of hosts, the God of Israel: 'If you wholly set your faces to enter Egypt, and go to dwell there, 16then it shall be *that* the sword

which you feared shall overtake you there in the land of Egypt; the famine of which you were afraid shall follow close after you there *in* Egypt; and there you shall die. 17So shall it be with all the men who set their faces to go to Egypt to dwell there. They shall die by the sword, by famine, and by pestilence. And none of them shall remain or escape from the disaster that I will bring upon them.'

18"For thus says the Lord of hosts, the God of Israel: 'As My anger and My fury have been poured out on the inhabitants of Jerusalem, so will My fury be poured out on you when you enter Egypt. And you shall be an oath, an astonishment, a curse, and a reproach; and you shall see this place no more.'

19"The Lord has said concerning you, O remnant of Judah, 'Do not go to Egypt!' Know certainly that I have admonished you this day. 20For you were hypocrites in your hearts when you sent me to the Lord your God, saying, 'Pray for us to the Lord our God, and according to all that the Lord your God says, so declare to us and we will do *it*.' 21And I have this day declared *it* to you, but you have not obeyed the voice of the Lord your God, or anything which He has sent you by me. 22Now therefore, know certainly that you shall die by the sword, by famine, and by pestilence in the place where you desire to go to dwell."

Jeremiah Taken to Egypt

43 Now it happened, when Jeremiah had stopped speaking to all the people all the words of the Lord their God, for which the Lord their God had sent him to them, all these words, 2that Azariah the son of Hoshaiah, Johanan the son of Kareah, and all the proud men spoke, saying to Jeremiah, "You speak falsely! The Lord our God has not sent you to say, 'Do not go to Egypt to dwell there.' 3But Baruch the son of Neriah has set you against us, to deliver us into the hand of the Chaldeans, that they may put us to death or carry us away captive to Babylon." 4So Johanan the son of Kareah, all the captains of the forces, and all the people would not obey the voice of the Lord, to remain in the land of Judah. 5But

Johanan the son of Kareah and all the captains of the forces took all the remnant of Judah who had returned to dwell in the land of Judah, from all nations where they had been driven— 6men, women, children, the king's daughters, and every person whom Nebuzaradan the captain of the guard had left with Gedaliah the son of Ahikam, the son of Shaphan, and Jeremiah the prophet and Baruch the son of Neriah. 7So they went to the land of Egypt, for they did not obey the voice of the LORD. And they went as far as Tahpanhes.

8Then the word of the LORD came to Jeremiah in Tahpanhes, saying, 9"Take large stones in your hand, and hide them in the sight of the men of Judah, in the clay in the brick courtyard which *is* at the entrance to Pharaoh's house in Tahpanhes; 10and say to them, 'Thus says the LORD of hosts, the God of Israel: "Behold, I will send and bring Nebuchadnezzar the king of Babylon, My servant, and will set his throne above these stones that I have hidden. And he will spread his royal pavilion over them. 11When he comes, he shall strike the land of Egypt *and deliver* to death *those appointed* for death, and to captivity *those appointed* for captivity, and to the sword *those appointed* for the sword. 12I will kindle a fire in the houses of the gods of Egypt, and he shall burn them and carry them away captive. And he shall array himself with the land of Egypt, as a shepherd puts on his garment, and he shall go out from there in peace. 13He shall also break the sacred pillars of Beth Shemesh that *are* in the land of Egypt; and the houses of the gods of the Egyptians he shall burn with fire." ' "

Israelites Will Be Punished in Egypt

44 The word that came to Jeremiah concerning all the Jews who dwell in the land of Egypt, who dwell at Migdol, at Tahpanhes, at Noph,r and in the country of Pathros, saying, 2"Thus says the LORD of hosts, the God of Israel: 'You have seen all the calamity that I have brought on Jerusalem and on all the cities of Judah; and be-

hold, this day they *are* a desolation, and no one dwells in them, 3because of their wickedness which they have committed to provoke Me to anger, in that they went to burn incense *and* to serve other gods whom they did not know, they nor you nor your fathers. 4However I have sent to you all My servants the prophets, rising early and sending *them*, saying, "Oh, do not do this abominable thing that I hate!" 5But they did not listen or incline their ear to turn from their wickedness, to burn no incense to other gods. 6So My fury and My anger were poured out and kindled in the cities of Judah and in the streets of Jerusalem; and they are wasted *and* desolate, as it is this day.'

7"Now therefore, thus says the LORD, the God of hosts, the God of Israel: 'Why do you commit *this* great evil against yourselves, to cut off from you man and woman, child and infant, out of Judah, leaving none to remain, 8in that you provoke Me to wrath with the works of your hands, burning incense to other gods in the land of Egypt where you have gone to dwell, that you may cut yourselves off and be a curse and a reproach among all the nations of the earth? 9Have you forgotten the wickedness of your fathers, the wickedness of the kings of Judah, the wickedness of their wives, your own wickedness, and the wickedness of your wives, which they committed in the land of Judah and in the streets of Jerusalem? 10They have not been humbled, to this day, nor have they feared; they have not walked in My law or in My statutes that I set before you and your fathers.'

11"Therefore thus says the LORD of hosts, the God of Israel: 'Behold, I will set My face against you for catastrophe and for cutting off all Judah. 12And I will take the remnant of Judah who have set their faces to go into the land of Egypt to dwell there, and they shall all be consumed *and* fall in the land of Egypt. They shall be consumed by the sword *and* by famine. They shall die, from the least to the greatest, by the sword and by famine; and they shall be an oath, an astonishment, a curse

r That is, ancient Memphis

and a reproach! 13For I will punish those who dwell in the land of Egypt, as I have punished Jerusalem, by the sword, by famine, and by pestilence, 14so that none of the remnant of Judah who have gone into the land of Egypt to dwell there shall escape or survive, lest they return to the land of Judah, to which they desire to return and dwell. For none shall return except those who escape.' "

15Then all the men who knew that their wives had burned incense to other gods, with all the women who stood by, a great multitude, and all the people who dwelt in the land of Egypt, in Pathros, answered Jeremiah, saying: 16"As for the word that you have spoken to us in the name of the LORD, we will not listen to you! 17But we will certainly do whatever has gone out of our own mouth, to burn incense to the queen of heaven and pour out drink offerings to her, as we have done, we and our fathers, our kings and our princes, in the cities of Judah and in the streets of Jerusalem. For then we had plenty of food, were well-off, and saw no trouble. 18But since we stopped burning incense to the queen of heaven and pouring out drink offerings to her, we have lacked everything and have been consumed by the sword and by famine."

19The women also said, "And when we burned incense to the queen of heaven and poured out drink offerings to her, did we make cakes for her, to worship her, and pour out drink offerings to her without our husbands' permission?"

20Then Jeremiah spoke to all the people—the men, the women, and all the people who had given him that answer—saying: 21"The incense that you burned in the cities of Judah and in the streets of Jerusalem, you and your fathers, your kings and your princes, and the people of the land, did not the LORD remember them, and did it not come into His mind? 22So the LORD could no longer bear it, because of the evil of your doings and because of the abominations which you committed. Therefore your land is a desolation, an astonishment, a curse, and without an inhabitant, as it is this day. 23Because you have burned incense and because

you have sinned against the LORD, and have not obeyed the voice of the LORD or walked in His law, in His statutes or in His testimonies, therefore this calamity has happened to you, as at this day."

24Moreover Jeremiah said to all the people and to all the women, "Hear the word of the LORD, all Judah who are in the land of Egypt! 25Thus says the LORD of hosts, the God of Israel, saying: 'You and your wives have spoken with your mouths and fulfilled with your hands, saying, "We will surely keep our vows that we have made, to burn incense to the queen of heaven and pour out drink offerings to her." You will surely keep your vows and perform your vows!' 26Therefore hear the word of the LORD, all Judah who dwell in the land of Egypt: 'Behold, I have sworn by My great name,' says the LORD, 'that My name shall no more be named in the mouth of any man of Judah in all the land of Egypt, saying, "The Lord GOD lives." 27Behold, I will watch over them for adversity and not for good. And all the men of Judah who are in the land of Egypt shall be consumed by the sword and by famine, until there is an end to them. 28Yet a small number who escape the sword shall return from the land of Egypt to the land of Judah; and all the remnant of Judah, who have gone to the land of Egypt to dwell there, shall know whose words will stand, Mine or theirs. 29And this shall be a sign to you,' says the LORD, 'that I will punish you in this place, that you may know that My words will surely stand against you for adversity.'

30"Thus says the LORD: 'Behold, I will give Pharaoh Hophra king of Egypt into the hand of his enemies and into the hand of those who seek his life, as I gave Zedekiah king of Judah into the hand of Nebuchadnezzar king of Babylon, his enemy who sought his life.' "

Assurance to Baruch

45 The word that Jeremiah the prophet spoke to Baruch the son of Neriah, when he had written these words in a book at the instruction of Jeremiah, in the fourth year of Jehoiakim the son of Josiah, king of Judah, saying, 2"Thus says the LORD, the

God of Israel, to you, O Baruch: 3'You said, "Woe is me now! For the LORD has added grief to my sorrow. I fainted in my sighing, and I find no rest." '

4"Thus you shall say to him, 'Thus says the LORD: "Behold, what I have built I will break down, and what I have planted I will pluck up, that is, this whole land. 5And do you seek great things for yourself? Do not seek *them;* for behold, I will bring adversity on all flesh," says the LORD. "But I will give your life to you as a prize in all places, wherever you go." ' "

Judgment on Egypt

46 The word of the LORD which came to Jeremiah the prophet against the nations. 2Against Egypt.

Concerning the army of Pharaoh Necho, king of Egypt, which was by the River Euphrates in Carchemish, and which Nebuchadnezzar king of Babylon defeated in the fourth year of Jehoiakim the son of Josiah, king of Judah:

3   "Order the buckler and shield,
    And draw near to battle!
4   Harness the horses,
    And mount up, you horsemen!
    Stand forth with *your* helmets,
    Polish the spears,
    Put on the armor!
5   Why have I seen them dismayed
    and turned back?
    Their mighty ones are beaten
      down;
    They have speedily fled,
    And did not look back,
    For fear *was* all around," says the
      LORD.
6   "Do not let the swift flee away,
    Nor the mighty man escape;
    They will stumble and fall
    Toward the north, by the River
      Euphrates.

7   "Who *is* this coming up like a
      flood,
    Whose waters move like the rivers?
8   Egypt rises up like a flood,
    And *its* waters move like the rivers;
    And he says, 'I will go up *and* cover
      the earth,

    I will destroy the city and its
      inhabitants.'
9   Come up, O horses, and rage,
    O chariots!
    And let the mighty men come forth:
    The Ethiopians and the Libyans
      who handle the shield,
    And the Lydians who handle *and*
      bend the bow.
10   For this *is* the day of the Lord GOD
      of hosts,
    A day of vengeance,
    That He may avenge Himself on
      His adversaries.
    The sword shall devour;
    It shall be satiated and made drunk
      with their blood;
    For the Lord GOD of hosts has a
      sacrifice
    In the north country by the River
      Euphrates.

11   "Go up to Gilead and take balm,
    O virgin, the daughter of Egypt;
    In vain you will use many
      medicines;
    You shall not be cured.
12   The nations have heard of your
      shame,
    And your cry has filled the land;
    For the mighty man has stumbled
      against the mighty;
    They both have fallen together."

Babylonia Will Strike Egypt

13The word that the LORD spoke to Jeremiah the prophet, how Nebuchadnezzar king of Babylon would come *and* strike the land of Egypt.

14   "Declare in Egypt, and proclaim in
      Migdol;
    Proclaim in Noph[r] and in
      Tahpanhes;
    Say, 'Stand fast and prepare
      yourselves,
    For the sword devours all
      around you.'
15   Why are your valiant *men* swept
      away?
    They did not stand
    Because the LORD drove them
      away.
16   He made many fall;
    Yes, one fell upon another.
    And they said, 'Arise!

r That is, ancient Memphis

Let us go back to our own people
And to the land of our nativity
From the oppressing sword.'
17 They cried there,
'Pharaoh, king of Egypt, *is but* a
noise.
He has passed by the appointed
time!'

18 "*As* I live," says the King,
Whose name *is* the LORD of
hosts,
"Surely as Tabor *is* among the
mountains
And as Carmel by the sea, *so* he
shall come.
19 O you daughter dwelling in Egypt,
Prepare yourself to go into
captivity!
For Noph[r] shall be waste and
desolate, without inhabitant.

20 "Egypt *is* a very pretty heifer,
But destruction comes, it comes
from the north.
21 Also her mercenaries are in her
midst like fat bulls,
For they also are turned back,
They have fled away together.
They did not stand,
For the day of their calamity had
come upon them,
The time of their punishment.
22 Her noise shall go like a serpent,
For they shall march with an army
And come against her with axes,
Like those who chop wood.

23 "They shall cut down her forest,"
says the LORD,
"Though it cannot be searched,
Because they *are* innumerable,
And more numerous than
grasshoppers.
24 The daughter of Egypt shall be
ashamed;
She shall be delivered into the hand
Of the people of the north."
25The LORD of hosts, the God of Israel, says: "Behold, I will bring punishment on Amon[s] of No,[t] and Pharaoh
and Egypt, with their gods and their
kings—Pharaoh and those who trust in
him. 26And I will deliver them into the
hand of those who seek their lives, into

the hand of Nebuchadnezzar king of
Babylon and the hand of his servants.
Afterward it shall be inhabited as in the
days of old," says the LORD.

God Will Preserve Israel

27 "But do not fear, O My servant
Jacob,
And do not be dismayed, O Israel!
For behold, I will save you from
afar,
And your offspring from the land
of their captivity;
Jacob shall return, have rest and be
at ease;
No one shall make *him* afraid.
28 Do not fear, O Jacob My servant,"
says the LORD,
"For I *am* with you;
For I will make a complete end of
all the nations
To which I have driven you,
But I will not make a complete end
of you.
I will rightly correct you,
For I will not leave you wholly
unpunished."

Judgment on Philistia

47 The word of the LORD that came
to Jeremiah the prophet against
the Philistines, before Pharaoh attacked Gaza.
2Thus says the LORD:
"Behold, waters rise out of the
north,
And shall be an overflowing flood;
They shall overflow the land and
all that is in it,
The city and those who dwell
within;
Then the men shall cry,
And all the inhabitants of the land
shall wail.
3 At the noise of the stamping hooves
of his strong horses,
At the rushing of his chariots,
At the rumbling of his wheels,
The fathers will not look back for
their children,
Lacking courage,
4 Because of the day that comes to
plunder all the Philistines,
To cut off from Tyre and Sidon
every helper who remains;

---

r That is, ancient Memphis   s A sun god   t That is, ancient Thebes

For the LORD shall plunder the
 Philistines,
The remnant of the country of
 Caphtor.
5 Baldness has come upon Gaza,
Ashkelon is cut off
With the remnant of their
 valley.
How long will you cut yourself?

6 "O you sword of the LORD,
How long until you are quiet?
Put yourself up into your
 scabbard,
Rest and be still!
7 How can it be quiet,
Seeing the LORD has given it a
 charge
Against Ashkelon and against the
 seashore?
There He has appointed it."

Judgment on Moab

48 Against Moab.
Thus says the LORD of hosts, the
God of Israel:
 "Woe to Nebo!
For it is plundered,
Kirjathaim is shamed *and* taken;
The high stronghold is shamed and
 dismayed—
2 No more praise of Moab.
In Heshbon they have devised evil
 against her:
'Come, and let us cut her off as a
 nation.'
You also shall be cut down,
 O Madmen!*u*
The sword shall pursue you;
3 A voice of crying *shall be* from
 Horonaim:
'Plundering and great destruction!'

4 "Moab is destroyed;
Her little ones have caused a cry
 to be heard;
5 For in the Ascent of Luhith they
 ascend with continual weeping;
For in the descent of Horonaim the
 enemies have heard a cry of
 destruction.

6 "Flee, save your lives!
And be like the juniper in the
 wilderness.

u A city of Moab

7 For because you have trusted in
 your works and your treasures,
You also shall be taken.
And Chemosh shall go forth into
 captivity,
His priests and his princes together.
8 And the plunderer shall come
 against every city;
No one shall escape.
The valley also shall perish,
And the plain shall be destroyed,
As the LORD has spoken.

9 "Give wings to Moab,
That she may flee and get away;
For her cities shall be desolate,
Without any to dwell in them.
10 Cursed *is* he who does the work of
 the LORD deceitfully,
And cursed *is* he who keeps back
 his sword from blood.

11 "Moab has been at ease from his
 youth;
He has settled on his dregs,
And has not been emptied from
 vessel to vessel,
Nor has he gone into captivity.
Therefore his taste remained
 in him,
And his scent has not changed.

12 "Therefore behold, the days are
 coming," says the LORD,
"That I shall send him wine-workers
Who will tip him over
And empty his vessels
And break the bottles.
13 Moab shall be ashamed of
 Chemosh,
As the house of Israel was ashamed
 of Bethel, their confidence.

14 "How can you say, 'We *are* mighty
And strong men for the war'?
15 Moab is plundered and gone up
 from her cities;
Her chosen young men have gone
 down to the slaughter," says
 the King,
Whose name *is* the LORD of hosts.

16 "The calamity of Moab *is* near at
 hand,
And his affliction comes quickly.

17 Bemoan him, all you who are
        around him;
    And all you who know his name,
    Say, 'How the strong staff is
        broken,
    The beautiful rod!'

18 "O daughter inhabiting Dibon,
    Come down from *your* glory,
    And sit in thirst;
    For the plunderer of Moab has
        come against you,
    He has destroyed your strongholds.
19 O inhabitant of Aroer,
    Stand by the way and watch;
    Ask him who flees
    And her who escapes;
    Say, 'What has happened?'
20 Moab is shamed, for he is broken
        down.
    Wail and cry!
    Tell it in Arnon, that Moab is
        plundered.

21 "And judgment has come on the
        plain country:
    On Holon and Jahzah and
        Mephaath,
22 On Dibon and Nebo and Beth
        Diblathaim,
23 On Kirjathaim and Beth Gamul and
        Beth Meon,
24 On Kerioth and Bozrah,
    On all the cities of the land of
        Moab,
    Far or near.
25 The horn of Moab is cut off,
    And his arm is broken," says the
        LORD.

26 "Make him drunk,
    Because he exalted *himself* against
        the LORD.
    Moab shall wallow in his vomit,
    And he shall also be in derision.
27 For was not Israel a derision
        to you?
    Was he found among thieves?
    For whenever you speak of him,
    You shake *your head in scorn.*
28 You who dwell in Moab,
    Leave the cities and dwell in the
        rock,
    And be like the dove *which* makes
        her nest
    In the sides of the cave's mouth.

29 "We have heard the pride of Moab
    (He *is* exceedingly proud),
    Of his loftiness and arrogance and
        pride,
    And of the haughtiness of his
        heart."

30 "I know his wrath," says the LORD,
    "But it *is* not right;
    His lies have made nothing right.
31 Therefore I will wail for Moab,
    And I will cry out for all Moab;
    I will mourn for the men of
        Kir Heres.
32 O vine of Sibmah! I will weep for
        you with the weeping of Jazer.
    Your plants have gone over the sea,
    They reach to the sea of Jazer.
    The plunderer has fallen on your
        summer fruit and your vintage.
33 Joy and gladness are taken
    From the plentiful field
    And from the land of Moab;
    I have caused wine to fail from the
        winepresses;
    No one will tread with joyous
        shouting—
    Not joyous shouting!

34 "From the cry of Heshbon to Elealeh
        and to Jahaz
    They have uttered their voice,
    From Zoar to Horonaim,
    Like a three-year-old heifer;
    For the waters of Nimrim also shall
        be desolate.

35 "Moreover," says the LORD,
    "I will cause to cease in Moab
    The one who offers *sacrifices* in the
        high places
    And burns incense to his gods.
36 Therefore My heart shall wail like
        flutes for Moab,
    And like flutes My heart shall wail
    For the men of Kir Heres.
    Therefore the riches they have
        acquired have perished.

37 "For every head *shall be* bald, and
        every beard clipped;
    On all the hands *shall be* cuts, and
        on the loins sackcloth—
38 A general lamentation
    On all the housetops of Moab,
    And in its streets;
    For I have broken Moab like a

vessel in which *is* no pleasure,"
says the LORD.

39 "They shall wail:
'How she is broken down!
How Moab has turned her back
with shame!'
So Moab shall be a derision
And a dismay to all those
about her."

40 For thus says the LORD:
"Behold, one shall fly like an
eagle,
And spread his wings over Moab.

41 Kerioth is taken,
And the strongholds are surprised;
The mighty men's hearts in Moab
on that day shall be
Like the heart of a woman in birth
pangs.

42 And Moab shall be destroyed as a
people,
Because he exalted *himself* against
the LORD.

43 Fear and the pit and the snare *shall
be* upon you,
O inhabitant of Moab," says the
LORD.

44 "He who flees from the fear shall fall
into the pit,
And he who gets out of the pit shall
be caught in the snare.
For upon Moab, upon it I will bring
The year of their punishment," says
the LORD.

45 "Those who fled stood under the
shadow of Heshbon
Because of exhaustion.
But a fire shall come out of
Heshbon,
A flame from the midst of Sihon,
And shall devour the brow of
Moab,
The crown of the head of the sons
of tumult.

46 Woe to you, O Moab!
The people of Chemosh perish;
For your sons have been taken
captive,
And your daughters captive.

47 "Yet I will bring back the captives
of Moab
In the latter days," says the LORD.
Thus far *is* the judgment of Moab.

Judgment on Ammon

49 Against the Ammonites.
Thus says the LORD:
"Has Israel no sons?
Has he no heir?
Why *then* does Milcom[v] inherit
Gad,
And his people dwell in its cities?

2 Therefore behold, the days are
coming," says the LORD,
"That I will cause to be heard an
alarm of war
In Rabbah of the Ammonites;
It shall be a desolate mound,
And her villages shall be burned
with fire.
Then Israel shall take possession of
his inheritance," says the LORD.

3 "Wail, O Heshbon, for Ai is
plundered!
Cry, you daughters of Rabbah,
Gird yourselves with sackcloth!
Lament and run to and fro by the
walls;
For Milcom shall go into captivity
With his priests and his princes
together.

4 Why do you boast in the valleys,
Your flowing valley, O backsliding
daughter?
Who trusted in her treasures,
saying,
'Who will come against me?'

5 Behold, I will bring fear upon you,"
Says the Lord GOD of hosts,
"From all those who are around you;
You shall be driven out, everyone
headlong,
And no one will gather those who
wander off.

6 But afterward I will bring back
The captives of the people of
Ammon," says the LORD.

Judgment on Edom

7 Against Edom.
Thus says the LORD of hosts:
"*Is* wisdom no more in Teman?
Has counsel perished from the
prudent?
Has their wisdom vanished?

8 Flee, turn back, dwell in the depths,
O inhabitants of Dedan!

---

[v] Literally *their king*, a god of the Ammonites; also called *Molech* (compare verse 3)

For I will bring the calamity of Esau
    upon him,
The time *that* I will punish him.
9 If grape-gatherers came to you,
    Would they not leave *some*
       gleaning grapes?
    If thieves by night,
    Would they not destroy until they
       have enough?
10 But I have made Esau bare;
    I have uncovered his secret
       places,^w
    And he shall not be able to hide
       himself.
    His descendants are plundered,
    His brethren and his neighbors,
    And he *is* no more.
11 Leave your fatherless children,
    I will preserve *them* alive;
    And let your widows trust in Me."

12For thus says the LORD: "Behold, those whose judgment *was* not to drink of the cup have assuredly drunk. And *are* you the one who will altogether go unpunished? You shall not go unpunished, but you shall surely drink *of it.* 13For I have sworn by Myself," says the LORD, "that Bozrah shall become a desolation, a reproach, a waste, and a curse. And all its cities shall be perpetual wastes."

14 I have heard a message from the
    LORD,
    And an ambassador has been sent
      to the nations:
    "Gather together, come against her,
    And rise up to battle!

15 "For indeed, I will make you small
      among nations,
    Despised among men.
16 Your fierceness has deceived you,
    The pride of your heart,
    O you who dwell in the clefts of the
      rock,
    Who hold the height of the hill!
    Though you make your nest as high
      as the eagle,
    I will bring you down from there,"
    says the LORD.^x

17 "Edom also shall be an
      astonishment;
    Everyone who goes by it will be
      astonished

    And will hiss at all its plagues.
18 As in the overthrow of Sodom and
      Gomorrah
    And their neighbors," says the
      LORD,
   "No one shall remain there,
    Nor shall a son of man dwell in it.

19 "Behold, he shall come up like a lion
      from the floodplain of the Jordan
    Against the dwelling place of the
      strong;
    But I will suddenly make him run
      away from her.
    And who *is* a chosen *man that* I
      may appoint over her?
    For who *is* like Me?
    Who will arraign Me?
    And who *is* that shepherd
    Who will withstand Me?"

20 Therefore hear the counsel of the
      LORD that He has taken against
      Edom,
    And His purposes that He has
      proposed against the inhabitants
      of Teman:
    Surely the least of the flock shall
      draw them out;
    Surely He shall make their
      dwelling places desolate with
      them.
21 The earth shakes at the noise of
      their fall;
    At the cry its noise is heard at the
      Red Sea.
22 Behold, He shall come up and fly
      like the eagle,
    And spread His wings over Bozrah;
    The heart of the mighty men of
      Edom in that day shall be
    Like the heart of a woman in birth
      pangs.

Judgment on Damascus

23Against Damascus.
  "Hamath and Arpad are shamed,
    For they have heard bad news.
    They are fainthearted;
    There is trouble on the sea;
    It cannot be quiet.
24 Damascus has grown feeble;
    She turns to flee,
    And fear has seized *her.*

---

^w Compare Obadiah 5, 6   ^x Compare Obadiah 3, 4

Anguish and sorrows have taken
    her like a woman in labor.
25 Why is the city of praise not
    deserted, the city of My joy?
26 Therefore her young men shall fall
    in her streets,
    And all the men of war shall be cut
    off in that day," says the LORD
    of hosts.
27 "I will kindle a fire in the wall of
    Damascus,
    And it shall consume the palaces
    of Ben-Hadad."y

Judgment on Kedar and Hazor

28Against Kedar and against the
kingdoms of Hazor, which Nebuchad-
nezzar king of Babylon shall strike.
  Thus says the LORD:
  "Arise, go up to Kedar,
  And devastate the men of the East!
29 Their tents and their flocks they
    shall take away.
  They shall take for themselves their
    curtains,
  All their vessels and their camels;
  And they shall cry out to them,
  'Fear is on every side!'

30 "Flee, get far away! Dwell in the
    depths,
  O inhabitants of Hazor!" says the
    LORD.
  "For Nebuchadnezzar king of
    Babylon has taken counsel
    against you,
  And has conceived a plan
    against you.

31 "Arise, go up to the wealthy nation
    that dwells securely," says the
    LORD,
  "Which has neither gates nor bars,
    Dwelling alone.
32 Their camels shall be for booty,
  And the multitude of their cattle for
    plunder.
  I will scatter to all winds those in
    the farthest corners,
  And I will bring their calamity from
    all its sides," says the LORD.
33 "Hazor shall be a dwelling for
    jackals, a desolation forever;
  No one shall reside there,
  Nor son of man dwell in it."

Judgment on Elam

34The word of the LORD that came to
Jeremiah the prophet against Elam, in
the beginning of the reign of Zedekiah
king of Judah, saying, 35"Thus says the
LORD of hosts:
  'Behold, I will break the bow of
    Elam,
  The foremost of their might.
36 Against Elam I will bring the four
    winds
  From the four quarters of heaven,
  And scatter them toward all those
    winds;
  There shall be no nations where the
    outcasts of Elam will not go.
37 For I will cause Elam to be
    dismayed before their enemies
  And before those who seek their
    life.
  I will bring disaster upon them,
  My fierce anger,' says the LORD;
  'And I will send the sword after
    them
  Until I have consumed them.
38 I will set My throne in Elam,
  And will destroy from there the
    king and the princes,' says
    the LORD.

39 'But it shall come to pass in the
    latter days:
  I will bring back the captives of
    Elam,' says the LORD."

Judgment on Babylon and Babylonia

50 The word that the LORD spoke
against Babylon and against the
land of the Chaldeans by Jeremiah the
prophet.
2 "Declare among the nations,
  Proclaim, and set up a standard;
  Proclaim—do not conceal it—
  Say, 'Babylon is taken, Bel is
    shamed.
  Merodachz is broken in pieces;
  Her idols are humiliated,
  Her images are broken in
    pieces.'
3 For out of the north a nation comes
    up against her,
  Which shall make her land
    desolate,
  And no one shall dwell therein.

---

y Compare Amos 1.4   z A Babylonian god; sometimes spelled *Marduk*

They shall move, they shall depart,
Both man and beast.

4 "In those days and in that time,"
      says the LORD,
   "The children of Israel shall come,
   They and the children of Judah
      together;
   With continual weeping they shall
      come,
   And seek the LORD their God.
5 They shall ask the way to Zion,
   With their faces toward it, *saying*,
   'Come and let us join ourselves to
      the LORD
   In a perpetual covenant
   That will not be forgotten.'

6 "My people have been lost sheep.
   Their shepherds have led them
      astray;
   They have turned them away *on* the
      mountains.
   They have gone from mountain to
      hill;
   They have forgotten their resting
      place.
7 All who found them have devoured
      them;
   And their adversaries said, 'We
      have not offended,
   Because they have sinned against
      the LORD, the habitation of
      justice,
   The LORD, the hope of their fathers.'

8 "Move from the midst of Babylon,
   Go out of the land of the Chaldeans;
   And be like the rams before the
      flocks.
9 For behold, I will raise and cause
      to come up against Babylon
   An assembly of great nations from
      the north country,
   And they shall array themselves
      against her;
   From there she shall be captured.
   Their arrows *shall be* like *those* of
      an expert warrior;
   None shall return in vain.
10 And Chaldea shall become plunder;
    All who plunder her shall be
      satisfied," says the LORD.

11 "Because you were glad, because
      you rejoiced,
    You destroyers of My heritage,
    Because you have grown fat like a
      heifer threshing grain,
    And you bellow like bulls,
12 Your mother shall be deeply
      ashamed;
    She who bore you shall be
      ashamed.
    Behold, the least of the nations
      shall be a wilderness,
    A dry land and a desert.
13 Because of the wrath of the LORD
    She shall not be inhabited,
    But she shall be wholly desolate.
    Everyone who goes by Babylon
      shall be horrified
    And hiss at all her plagues.

14 "Put yourselves in array against
      Babylon all around,
    All you who bend the bow;
    Shoot at her, spare no arrows,
    For she has sinned against the
      LORD.
15 Shout against her all around;
    She has given her hand,
    Her foundations have fallen,
    Her walls are thrown down;
    For it *is* the vengeance of the LORD.
    Take vengeance on her.
    As she has done, so do to her.
16 Cut off the sower from Babylon,
    And him who handles the sickle at
      harvest time.
    For fear of the oppressing sword
    Everyone shall turn to his own
      people,
    And everyone shall flee to his own
      land.

17 "Israel *is* like scattered sheep;
    The lions have driven *him* away.
    First the king of Assyria devoured
      him;
    Now at last this Nebuchadnezzar
      king of Babylon has broken
      his bones."
18 Therefore thus says the LORD of
hosts, the God of Israel:
    "Behold, I will punish the king of
      Babylon and his land,
    As I have punished the king of
      Assyria.
19 But I will bring back Israel to his
      home,
    And he shall feed on Carmel and
      Bashan;

His soul shall be satisfied on Mount
  Ephraim and Gilead.
20 In those days and in that time,"
  says the LORD,
  "The iniquity of Israel shall be
    sought, but *there shall be* none;
  And the sins of Judah, but they
    shall not be found;
  For I will pardon those whom I
    preserve.

21 "Go up against the land of
    Merathaim, against it,
  And against the inhabitants of
    Pekod.
  Waste and utterly destroy them,"
    says the LORD,
  "And do according to all that I have
    commanded you.
22 A sound of battle *is* in the land,
  And of great destruction.
23 How the hammer of the whole
    earth has been cut apart
    and broken!
  How Babylon has become a
    desolation among the nations!
  I have laid a snare for you;
24 You have indeed been trapped,
    O Babylon,
  And you were not aware;
  You have been found and also
    caught,
  Because you have contended
    against the LORD.
25 The LORD has opened His
    armory,
  And has brought out the weapons
    of His indignation;
  For this *is* the work of the Lord GOD
    of hosts
  In the land of the Chaldeans.
26 Come against her from the farthest
    border;
  Open her storehouses;
  Cast her up as heaps of ruins,
  And destroy her utterly;
  Let nothing of her be left.
27 Slay all her bulls,
  Let them go down to the slaughter.
  Woe to them!
  For their day has come, the time of
    their punishment.
28 The voice of those who flee and
    escape from the land of Babylon
  Declares in Zion the vengeance of
    the LORD our God,
  The vengeance of His temple.

29 "Call together the archers against
    Babylon.
  All you who bend the bow, encamp
    against it all around;
  Let none of them escape.
  Repay her according to her work;
  According to all she has done, do
    to her;
  For she has been proud against the
    LORD,
  Against the Holy One of Israel.
30 Therefore her young men shall fall
    in the streets,
  And all her men of war shall be cut
    off in that day," says the LORD.
31 "Behold, I *am* against you,
  O most haughty one!" says the
    Lord GOD of hosts;
  "For your day has come,
  The time *that* I will punish you.
32 The most proud shall stumble and
    fall,
  And no one will raise him up;
  I will kindle a fire in his cities,
  And it will devour all around him."
33 Thus says the LORD of hosts:
  "The children of Israel *were*
    oppressed,
  Along with the children of Judah;
  All who took them captive have
    held them fast;
  They have refused to let them go.
34 Their Redeemer *is* strong;
  The LORD of hosts *is* His name.
  He will thoroughly plead their
    case,
  That He may give rest to the land,
  And disquiet the inhabitants of
    Babylon.

35 "A sword *is* against the Chaldeans,"
    says the LORD,
  "Against the inhabitants of Babylon,
  And against her princes and her
    wise men.
36 A sword *is* against the soothsayers,
    and they will be fools.
  A sword *is* against her mighty men,
    and they will be dismayed.
37 A sword *is* against their horses,
  Against their chariots,
  And against all the mixed peoples
    who *are* in her midst;
  And they will become like
    women.
  A sword *is* against her treasures,
    and they will be robbed.

38 A drought *is* against her waters,
  and they will be dried up.
  For it *is* the land of carved images,
  And they are insane with *their*
    idols.

39 "Therefore the wild desert beasts
    shall dwell *there* with the jackals,
  And the ostriches shall dwell in it.
  It shall be inhabited no more
    forever,
  Nor shall it be dwelt in from
    generation to generation.

40 As God overthrew Sodom and
    Gomorrah
  And their neighbors," says the
    LORD,
  "So no one shall reside there,
  Nor son of man dwell in it.

41 "Behold, a people shall come from
    the north,
  And a great nation and many kings
  Shall be raised up from the ends
    of the earth.

42 They shall hold the bow and the
    lance;
  They *are* cruel and shall not show
    mercy.
  Their voice shall roar like the sea;
  They shall ride on horses,
  Set in array, like a man for the
    battle,
  Against you, O daughter of
    Babylon.

43 "The king of Babylon has heard the
    report about them,
  And his hands grow feeble;
  Anguish has taken hold of him,
  Pangs as of a woman in childbirth.

44 "Behold, he shall come up like a lion
    from the floodplain of the Jordan
  Against the dwelling place of the
    strong;
  But I will make them suddenly run
    away from her.
  And who *is* a chosen *man that* I
    may appoint over her?
  For who *is* like Me?
  Who will arraign Me?
  And who *is* that shepherd
  Who will withstand Me?"

45 Therefore hear the counsel of the
    LORD that He has taken against
    Babylon,
  And His purposes that He has
    proposed against the land of
    the Chaldeans:
  Surely the least of the flock shall
    draw them out;
  Surely He will make their dwelling
    place desolate with them.

46 At the noise of the taking of
    Babylon
  The earth trembles,
  And the cry is heard among the
    nations.

The Utter Destruction of Babylon

51 Thus says the LORD:

"Behold, I will raise up against
    Babylon,
  Against those who dwell in
    Leb Kamai,[a]
  A destroying wind.

2 And I will send winnowers to
    Babylon,
  Who shall winnow her and empty
    her land.
  For in the day of doom
  They shall be against her all
    around.

3 Against *her* let the archer bend his
    bow,
  And lift himself up against *her* in
    his armor.
  Do not spare her young men;
  Utterly destroy all her army.

4 Thus the slain shall fall in the land
    of the Chaldeans,
  And *those* thrust through in her
    streets.

5 For Israel is not forsaken, nor
    Judah,
  By his God, the LORD of hosts,
  Though their land was filled with
    sin against the Holy One of
    Israel."

6 Flee from the midst of Babylon,
  And every one save his life!
  Do not be cut off in her iniquity,
  For this *is* the time of the LORD's
    vengeance;

a Code word for Chaldea (Babylonia); may be translated *The Midst of Those Who Rise Up Against Me*

He shall recompense her.
7 Babylon *was* a golden cup in the
    Lord's hand,
  That made all the earth drunk.
  The nations drank her wine;
  Therefore the nations are
    deranged.
8 Babylon has suddenly fallen and
    been destroyed.
  Wail for her!
  Take balm for her pain;
  Perhaps she may be healed.

9 We would have healed Babylon,
  But she is not healed.
  Forsake her, and let us go everyone
    to his own country;
  For her judgment reaches to
    heaven and is lifted up to
    the skies.
10 The Lord has revealed our
    righteousness.
  Come and let us declare in Zion the
    work of the Lord our God.

11 Make the arrows bright!
  Gather the shields!
  The Lord has raised up the spirit
    of the kings of the Medes.
  For His plan *is* against Babylon to
    destroy it,
  Because it *is* the vengeance of the
    Lord,
  The vengeance for His temple.
12 Set up the standard on the walls of
    Babylon;
  Make the guard strong,
  Set up the watchmen,
  Prepare the ambushes.
  For the Lord has both devised and
    done
  What He spoke against the
    inhabitants of Babylon.
13 O you who dwell by many waters,
  Abundant in treasures,
  Your end has come,
  The measure of your covetousness.
14 The Lord of hosts has sworn by
    Himself:
  "Surely I will fill you with men, as
    with locusts,
  And they shall lift up a shout
    against you."

15 He has made the earth by His
    power;

He has established the world by His
  wisdom,
And stretched out the heaven by
  His understanding.
16 When He utters *His* voice—
  There is a multitude of waters in
    the heavens:
  "He causes the vapors to ascend
    from the ends of the earth;
  He makes lightnings for the rain;
  He brings the wind out of His
    treasuries."[b]

17 Everyone is dull-hearted, without
    knowledge;
  Every metalsmith is put to shame
    by the carved image;
  For his molded image *is* falsehood,
  And *there is* no breath in them.
18 They *are* futile, a work of errors;
  In the time of their punishment they
    shall perish.
19 The Portion of Jacob *is* not like
    them,
  For He *is* the Maker of all things;
  And *Israel is* the tribe of His
    inheritance.
  The Lord of hosts *is* His name.

20 "You *are* My battle-ax *and* weapons
    of war:
  For with you I will break the nation
    in pieces;
  With you I will destroy kingdoms;
21 With you I will break in pieces the
    horse and its rider;
  With you I will break in pieces the
    chariot and its rider;
22 With you also I will break in pieces
    man and woman;
  With you I will break in pieces old
    and young;
  With you I will break in pieces the
    young man and the maiden;
23 With you also I will break in pieces
    the shepherd and his flock;
  With you I will break in pieces the
    farmer and his yoke of oxen;
  And with you I will break in pieces
    governors and rulers.

24 "And I will repay Babylon
  And all the inhabitants of Chaldea
  For all the evil they have done

b Compare Psalm 135.7

In Zion in your sight," says the
LORD.

25 "Behold, I *am* against you,
O destroying mountain,
Who destroys all the earth," says
the LORD.
"And I will stretch out My hand
against you,
Roll you down from the rocks,
And make you a burnt mountain.
26 They shall not take from you a
stone for a corner
Nor a stone for a foundation,
But you shall be desolate forever,"
says the LORD.

27 Set up a banner in the land,
Blow the trumpet among the
nations!
Prepare the nations against her,
Call the kingdoms together
against her:
Ararat, Minni, and Ashkenaz.
Appoint a general against her;
Cause the horses to come up like
the bristling locusts.
28 Prepare against her the nations,
With the kings of the Medes,
Its governors and all its rulers,
All the land of his dominion.
29 And the land will tremble and
sorrow;
For every purpose of the LORD shall
be performed against Babylon,
To make the land of Babylon a
desolation without inhabitant.
30 The mighty men of Babylon have
ceased fighting,
They have remained in their
strongholds;
Their might has failed,
They became *like* women;
They have burned her dwelling
places,
The bars of her *gate* are broken.
31 One runner will run to meet
another,
And one messenger to meet
another,
To show the king of Babylon that
his city is taken on *all* sides;
32 The passages are blocked,
The reeds they have burned with
fire,
And the men of war are terrified.
33For thus says the LORD of hosts, the
God of Israel:
"The daughter of Babylon *is* like a
threshing floor
When it is time to thresh her;
Yet a little while
And the time of her harvest will
come."

34 "Nebuchadnezzar the king of
Babylon
Has devoured me, he has crushed
me;
He has made me an empty vessel,
He has swallowed me up like a
monster;
He has filled his stomach with my
delicacies,
He has spit me out.
35 Let the violence *done* to me and my
flesh *be* upon Babylon,"
The inhabitant of Zion will say;
"And my blood be upon the
inhabitants of Chaldea!"
Jerusalem will say.
36Therefore thus says the LORD:
"Behold, I will plead your case and
take vengeance for you.
I will dry up her sea and make her
springs dry.
37 Babylon shall become a heap,
A dwelling place for jackals,
An astonishment and a hissing,
Without an inhabitant.
38 They shall roar together like lions,
They shall growl like lions' whelps.
39 In their excitement I will prepare
their feasts;
I will make them drunk,
That they may rejoice,
And sleep a perpetual sleep
And not awake," says the LORD.
40 "I will bring them down
Like lambs to the slaughter,
Like rams with male goats.

41 "Oh, how Sheshach[c] is taken!
Oh, how the praise of the whole
earth is seized!
How Babylon has become desolate
among the nations!
42 The sea has come up over Babylon;
She is covered with the multitude
of its waves.

c A code word for Babylon (compare Jeremiah 25.26)

43 Her cities are a desolation,
A dry land and a wilderness,
A land where no one dwells,
Through which no son of man
passes.
44 I will punish Bel in Babylon,
And I will bring out of his mouth
what he has swallowed;
And the nations shall not stream to
him anymore.
Yes, the wall of Babylon shall fall.

45 "My people, go out of the midst
of her!
And let everyone deliver himself
from the fierce anger of the LORD.
46 And lest your heart faint,
And you fear for the rumor that *will
be* heard in the land
(A rumor will come *one* year,
And after that, in *another* year
A rumor *will come*,
And violence in the land,
Ruler against ruler),
47 Therefore behold, the days are
coming
That I will bring judgment on the
carved images of Babylon;
Her whole land shall be ashamed,
And all her slain shall fall in her
midst.
48 Then the heavens and the earth and
all that *is* in them
Shall sing joyously over Babylon;
For the plunderers shall come to
her from the north," says the
LORD.

49 As Babylon *has caused* the slain of
Israel to fall,
So at Babylon the slain of all the
earth shall fall.
50 You who have escaped the sword,
Get away! Do not stand still!
Remember the LORD afar off,
And let Jerusalem come to your
mind.

51 We are ashamed because we have
heard reproach.
Shame has covered our faces,
For strangers have come into the
sanctuaries of the LORD's house.

52 "Therefore behold, the days are
coming," says the LORD,

"That I will bring judgment on her
carved images,
And throughout all her land the
wounded shall groan.
53 Though Babylon were to mount up
to heaven,
And though she were to fortify the
height of her strength,
Yet from Me plunderers would
come to her," says the LORD.

54 The sound of a cry *comes* from
Babylon,
And great destruction from the
land of the Chaldeans,
55 Because the LORD is plundering
Babylon
And silencing her loud voice,
Though her waves roar like great
waters,
And the noise of their voice is
uttered,
56 Because the plunderer comes
against her, against Babylon,
And her mighty men are taken.
Every one of their bows is broken;
For the LORD *is* the God of
recompense,
He will surely repay.

57 "And I will make drunk
Her princes and wise men,
Her governors, her deputies, and
her mighty men.
And they shall sleep a perpetual
sleep
And not awake," says the King,
Whose name *is* the LORD of hosts.
58 Thus says the LORD of hosts:
"The broad walls of Babylon shall
be utterly broken,
And her high gates shall be burned
with fire;
The people will labor in vain,
And the nations, because of the
fire;
And they shall be weary."

Jeremiah's Command to Seraiah

59 The word which Jeremiah the
prophet commanded Seraiah the son of
Neriah, the son of Mahseiah, when he
went with Zedekiah the king of Judah
to Babylon in the fourth year of his
reign. And Seraiah *was* the quartermas-
ter. 60 So Jeremiah wrote in a book all
the evil that would come upon Babylon,

all these words that are written against Babylon. 61And Jeremiah said to Seraiah, "When you arrive in Babylon and see it, and read all these words, 62then you shall say, 'O Lord, You have spoken against this place to cut it off, so that none shall remain in it, neither man nor beast, but it shall be desolate forever.' 63Now it shall be, when you have finished reading this book, *that* you shall tie a stone to it and throw it out into the Euphrates. 64Then you shall say, 'Thus Babylon shall sink and not rise from the catastrophe that I will bring upon her. And they shall be weary.' "

Thus far *are* the words of Jeremiah.

The Fall of Jerusalem Reviewed

52 Zedekiah *was* twenty-one years old when he became king, and he reigned eleven years in Jerusalem. His mother's name *was* Hamutal the daughter of Jeremiah of Libnah. 2He also did evil in the sight of the Lord, according to all that Jehoiakim had done. 3For because of the anger of the Lord *this* happened in Jerusalem and Judah, till He finally cast them out from His presence. Then Zedekiah rebelled against the king of Babylon.

4Now it came to pass in the ninth year of his reign, in the tenth month, on the tenth *day* of the month, *that* Nebuchadnezzar king of Babylon and all his army came against Jerusalem and encamped against it; and *they* built a siege wall against it all around. 5So the city was besieged until the eleventh year of King Zedekiah. 6By the fourth month, on the ninth day of the month, the famine had become so severe in the city that there was no food for the people of the land. 7Then the city wall was broken through, and all the men of war fled and went out of the city at night by way of the gate between the two walls, which *was* by the king's garden, even though the Chaldeans *were* near the city all around. And they went by way of the plain.^d

8But the army of the Chaldeans pursued the king, and they overtook Zedekiah in the plains of Jericho. All his army was scattered from him. 9So they took the king and brought him up to the king of Babylon at Riblah in the land of Hamath, and he pronounced judgment on him. 10Then the king of Babylon killed the sons of Zedekiah before his eyes. And he killed all the princes of Judah in Riblah. 11He also put out the eyes of Zedekiah; and the king of Babylon bound him in bronze fetters, took him to Babylon, and put him in prison till the day of his death.

The Temple and City Plundered and Burned

12Now in the fifth month, on the tenth *day* of the month (which *was* the nineteenth year of King Nebuchadnezzar king of Babylon), Nebuzaradan, the captain of the guard, *who* served the king of Babylon, came to Jerusalem. 13He burned the house of the Lord and the king's house; all the houses of Jerusalem, that is, all the houses of the great, he burned with fire. 14And all the army of the Chaldeans who *were* with the captain of the guard broke down all the walls of Jerusalem all around. 15Then Nebuzaradan the captain of the guard carried away captive *some* of the poor people, the rest of the people who remained in the city, the defectors who had deserted to the king of Babylon, and the rest of the craftsmen. 16But Nebuzaradan the captain of the guard left *some* of the poor of the land as vinedressers and farmers.

17The bronze pillars that *were* in the house of the Lord, and the carts and the bronze Sea that *were* in the house of the Lord, the Chaldeans broke in pieces, and carried all their bronze to Babylon. 18They also took away the pots, the shovels, the trimmers, the bowls, the spoons, and all the bronze utensils with which the priests ministered. 19The basins, the firepans, the bowls, the pots, the lampstands, the spoons, and the cups, whatever *was* solid gold and whatever *was* solid silver, the captain of the guard took away. 20The two pillars, one Sea, the twelve bronze bulls which *were* under *it, and* the carts, which King Solomon had made for the house of the Lord—the bronze of all these articles was beyond

^d That is, the Jordan Valley

measure. 21Now *concerning* the pillars: the height of one pillar *was* eighteen cubits, a measuring line of twelve cubits could measure its circumference, and its thickness *was* four fingers; *it was* hollow. 22A capital of bronze *was* on it; and the height of one capital *was* five cubits, with a network and pomegranates all around the capital, all of bronze. The second pillar, with pomegranates was the same. 23There were ninety-six pomegranates on the sides; all the pomegranates, all around on the network, *were* one hundred.

The People Taken Captive to Babylonia

24The captain of the guard took Seraiah the chief priest, Zephaniah the second priest, and the three doorkeepers. 25He also took out of the city an officer who had charge of the men of war, seven men of the king's close associates who were found in the city, the principal scribe of the army who mustered the people of the land, and sixty men of the people of the land who were found in the midst of the city. 26And Nebuzaradan the captain of the guard took these and brought them to the king of Babylon at Riblah. 27Then the king of Babylon struck them and put them to death at Riblah in the land of Hamath. Thus Judah was carried away captive from its own land.

28These *are* the people whom Nebuchadnezzar carried away captive: in the seventh year, three thousand and twenty-three Jews; 29in the eighteenth year of Nebuchadnezzar he carried away captive from Jerusalem eight hundred and thirty-two persons; 30in the twenty-third year of Nebuchadnezzar, Nebuzaradan the captain of the guard carried away captive of the Jews seven hundred and forty-five persons. All the persons *were* four thousand six hundred.

Jehoiachin Released from Prison

31Now it came to pass in the thirty-seventh year of the captivity of Jehoiachin king of Judah, in the twelfth month, on the twenty-fifth *day* of the month, *that* Evil-Merodach king of Babylon, in the first *year* of his reign, lifted up the head of Jehoiachin king of Judah and brought him out of prison. 32And he spoke kindly to him and gave him a more prominent seat than those of the kings who *were* with him in Babylon. 33So Jehoiachin changed from his prison garments, and he ate bread regularly before the king all the days of his life. 34And as for his provisions, there was a regular ration given him by the king of Babylon, a portion for each day until the day of his death, all the days of his life.

The Book of
LAMENTATIONS

Jerusalem in Affliction

1 How lonely sits the city
That was full of people!
How like a widow is she,
Who *was* great among the nations!
The princess among the provinces
Has become a slave!

2 She weeps bitterly in the night,
Her tears *are* on her cheeks;
Among all her lovers
She has none to comfort *her.*
All her friends have dealt
treacherously with her;
They have become her enemies.

3 Judah has gone into captivity,
Under affliction and hard
servitude;
She dwells among the nations,
She finds no rest;
All her persecutors overtake her in
dire straits.

4 The roads to Zion mourn
Because no one comes to the set
feasts.
All her gates are desolate;
Her priests sigh,
Her virgins are afflicted,
And she *is* in bitterness.

5 Her adversaries have become the
master,
Her enemies prosper;
For the LORD has afflicted her
Because of the multitude of her
transgressions.
Her children have gone into
captivity before the enemy.

6 And from the daughter of Zion
All her splendor has departed.
Her princes have become like deer
That find no pasture,
That flee without strength
Before the pursuer.

7 In the days of her affliction and
roaming,
Jerusalem remembers all her
pleasant things

That she had in the days of old.
When her people fell into the hand
of the enemy,
With no one to help her,
The adversaries saw her
And mocked at her downfall.

8 Jerusalem has sinned gravely,
Therefore she has become vile.
All who honored her despise her
Because they have seen her
nakedness;
Yes, she sighs and turns away.

9 Her uncleanness *is* in her skirts;
She did not consider her destiny;
Therefore her collapse was
awesome;
She had no comforter.
"O LORD, behold my affliction,
For *the* enemy is exalted!"

10 The adversary has spread his hand
Over all her pleasant things;
For she has seen the nations enter
her sanctuary,
Those whom You commanded
Not to enter Your assembly.

11 All her people sigh,
They seek bread;
They have given their valuables for
food to restore life.
"See, O LORD, and consider,
For I am scorned."

12 "*Is it* nothing to you, all you who
pass by?
Behold and see
If there is any sorrow like my
sorrow,
Which has been brought on me,
Which the LORD has inflicted
In the day of His fierce anger.

13 "From above He has sent fire into
my bones,
And it overpowered them;
He has spread a net for my feet
And turned me back;
He has made me desolate
And faint all the day.

14 "The yoke of my transgressions was
      bound;
   They were woven together by His
      hands,
   And thrust upon my neck.
   He made my strength fail;
   The Lord delivered me into the
      hands of *those whom* I am not
      able to withstand.

15 "The Lord has trampled underfoot
      all my mighty *men* in my midst;
   He has called an assembly
      against me
   To crush my young men;
   The Lord trampled *as* in a
      winepress
   The virgin daughter of Judah.

16 "For these *things* I weep;
   My eye, my eye overflows with
      water;
   Because the comforter, who should
      restore my life,
   Is far from me.
   My children are desolate
   Because the enemy prevailed."

17 Zion spreads out her hands,
   But no one comforts her;
   The LORD has commanded
      concerning Jacob
   That those around him *become* his
      adversaries;
   Jerusalem has become an unclean
      thing among them.

18 "The LORD is righteous,
   For I rebelled against His
      commandment.
   Hear now, all peoples,
   And behold my sorrow;
   My virgins and my young men
   Have gone into captivity.

19 "I called for my lovers,
   But they deceived me;
   My priests and my elders
   Breathed their last in the city,
   While they sought food
   To restore their life.

20 "See, O LORD, that I *am* in distress;
   My soul is troubled;
   My heart is overturned within me,
   For I have been very rebellious.
   Outside the sword bereaves,

At home *it is* like death.

21 "They have heard that I sigh,
   But no one comforts me.
   All my enemies have heard of my
      trouble;
   They are glad that You have
      done *it.*
   Bring on the day You have
      announced,
   That they may become like me.

22 "Let all their wickedness come
      before You,
   And do to them as You have done
      to me
   For all my transgressions;
   For my sighs *are* many,
   And my heart *is* faint."

God's Anger with Jerusalem

2 How the Lord has covered the
   daughter of Zion
   With a cloud in His anger!
   He cast down from heaven to the
      earth
   The beauty of Israel,
   And did not remember His
      footstool
   In the day of His anger.

2 The Lord has swallowed up and has
      not pitied
   All the dwelling places of Jacob.
   He has thrown down in His wrath
   The strongholds of the daughter of
      Judah;
   He has brought *them* down to the
      ground;
   He has profaned the kingdom and
      its princes.

3 He has cut off in fierce anger
   Every horn of Israel;
   He has drawn back His right hand
   From before the enemy.
   He has blazed against Jacob like a
      flaming fire
   Devouring all around.

4 Standing like an enemy, He has
      bent His bow;
   With His right hand, like an
      adversary,
   He has slain all *who were* pleasing
      to His eye;
   On the tent of the daughter of Zion,
   He has poured out His fury like fire.

5 The Lord was like an enemy.
   He has swallowed up Israel,
   He has swallowed up all her
      palaces;
   He has destroyed her strongholds,
   And has increased mourning and
      lamentation
   In the daughter of Judah.

6 He has done violence to His
      tabernacle,
   As if it were a garden;
   He has destroyed His place of
      assembly;
   The LORD has caused
   The appointed feasts and Sabbaths
      to be forgotten in Zion.
   In His burning indignation He has
      spurned the king and the priest.

7 The Lord has spurned His altar,
   He has abandoned His sanctuary;
   He has given up the walls of her
      palaces
   Into the hand of the enemy.
   They have made a noise in the
      house of the LORD
   As on the day of a set feast.

8 The LORD has purposed to destroy
   The wall of the daughter of Zion.
   He has stretched out a line;
   He has not withdrawn His hand
      from destroying;
   Therefore He has caused the
      rampart and wall to lament;
   They languished together.

9 Her gates have sunk into the
      ground;
   He has destroyed and broken her
      bars.
   Her king and her princes are
      among the nations;
   The Law is no more,
   And her prophets find no vision
      from the LORD.

10 The elders of the daughter of Zion
   Sit on the ground and keep silence;
   They throw dust on their heads
   And gird themselves with
      sackcloth.
   The virgins of Jerusalem
   Bow their heads to the ground.

11 My eyes fail with tears,
   My heart is troubled;
   My bile is poured on the ground
   Because of the destruction of the
      daughter of my people,
   Because the children and the
      infants
   Faint in the streets of the city.

12 They say to their mothers,
   "Where is grain and wine?"
   As they swoon like the wounded
   In the streets of the city,
   As their life is poured out
   In their mothers' bosom.

13 How shall I console you?
   To what shall I liken you,
   O daughter of Jerusalem?
   What shall I compare with you, that
      I may comfort you,
   O virgin daughter of Zion?
   For your ruin is spread wide as
      the sea;
   Who can heal you?

14 Your prophets have seen for you
   False and deceptive visions;
   They have not uncovered your
      iniquity,
   To bring back your captives,
   But have envisioned for you false
      prophecies and delusions.

15 All who pass by clap their hands
      at you;
   They hiss and shake their heads
   At the daughter of Jerusalem:
   "Is this the city that is called
   'The perfection of beauty,
   The joy of the whole earth'?"

16 All your enemies have opened their
      mouth against you;
   They hiss and gnash their teeth.
   They say, "We have swallowed
      her up!
   Surely this is the day we have
      waited for;
   We have found it, we have
      seen it!"

17 The LORD has done what He
      purposed;
   He has fulfilled His word
   Which He commanded in days
      of old.
   He has thrown down and has not
      pitied,

And He has caused an enemy to
   rejoice over you;
He has exalted the horn of your
   adversaries.

18 Their heart cried out to the Lord,
  "O wall of the daughter of Zion,
   Let tears run down like a river day
     and night;
   Give yourself no relief;
   Give your eyes no rest.

19 "Arise, cry out in the night,
   At the beginning of the watches;
   Pour out your heart like water
     before the face of the Lord.
   Lift your hands toward Him
   For the life of your young children,
   Who faint from hunger at the head
     of every street."

20 "See, O Lord, and consider!
   To whom have You done this?
   Should the women eat their
     offspring,
   The children they have cuddled?
   Should the priest and prophet be
     slain
   In the sanctuary of the Lord?

21 "Young and old lie
   On the ground in the streets;
   My virgins and my young men
   Have fallen by the sword;
   You have slain *them* in the day of
     Your anger,
   You have slaughtered *and* not
     pitied.

22 "You have invited as to a feast day
   The terrors that surround me.
   In the day of the Lord's anger
   There was no refugee or survivor.
   Those whom I have borne and
     brought up
   My enemies have destroyed."

The Prophet's Anguish and Hope

3 I *am* the man *who* has seen
   affliction by the rod of
   His wrath.
2 He has led me and made *me* walk
   In darkness and not *in* light.
3 Surely He has turned His hand
   against me
   Time and time again throughout
     the day.

4 He has aged my flesh and my skin,
   And broken my bones.
5 He has besieged me
   And surrounded *me* with bitterness
     and woe.
6 He has set me in dark places
   Like the dead of long ago.

7 He has hedged me in so that I
   cannot get out;
   He has made my chain heavy.
8 Even when I cry and shout,
   He shuts out my prayer.
9 He has blocked my ways with hewn
   stone;
   He has made my paths crooked.

10 He *has been* to me a bear lying in
   wait,
   Like a lion in ambush.
11 He has turned aside my ways and
   torn me in pieces;
   He has made me desolate.
12 He has bent His bow
   And set me up as a target for the
     arrow.

13 He has caused the arrows of His
   quiver
   To pierce my loins.
14 I have become the ridicule of all my
   people—
   Their taunting song all the day.
15 He has filled me with bitterness,
   He has made me drink wormwood.
16 He has also broken my teeth with
   gravel,
   And covered me with ashes.
17 You have moved my soul far from
   peace;
   I have forgotten prosperity.
18 And I said, "My strength and my
   hope
   Have perished from the Lord."

19 Remember my affliction and
   roaming,
   The wormwood and the gall.
20 My soul still remembers
   And sinks within me.
21 This I recall to my mind,
   Therefore I have hope.

22 *Through* the Lord's mercies we are
   not consumed,
   Because His compassions fail not.

23 *They are* new every morning;
Great *is* Your faithfulness.
24 "The Lord *is* my portion," says my
soul,
"Therefore I hope in Him!"

25 The Lord *is* good to those who wait
for Him,
To the soul *who* seeks Him.
26 *It is* good that *one* should hope and
wait quietly
For the salvation of the Lord.
27 *It is* good for a man to bear
The yoke in his youth.

28 Let him sit alone and keep silent,
Because *God* has laid *it* on him;
29 Let him put his mouth in the dust—
There may yet be hope.
30 Let him give *his* cheek to the one
who strikes him,
And be full of reproach.

31 For the Lord will not cast off
forever.
32 Though He causes grief,
Yet He will show compassion
According to the multitude of His
mercies.
33 For He does not afflict willingly,
Nor grieve the children of men.

34 To crush under one's feet
All the prisoners of the earth,
35 To turn aside the justice *due* a man
Before the face of the Most High,
36 Or subvert a man in his cause—
The Lord does not approve.

37 Who *is* he *who* speaks and it
comes to pass,
When the Lord has not
commanded *it?*
38 *Is it* not from the mouth of the
Most High
That woe and well-being proceed?
39 Why should a living man complain,
A man for the punishment of his
sins?

40 Let us search out and examine our
ways,
And turn back to the Lord;
41 Let us lift our hearts and hands
To God in heaven.
42 We have transgressed and rebelled;
You have not pardoned.

43 You have covered *Yourself* with
anger
And pursued us;
You have slain *and* not pitied.
44 You have covered Yourself with a
cloud,
That prayer should not pass
through.
45 You have made us an offscouring
and refuse
In the midst of the peoples.

46 All our enemies
Have opened their mouths
against us.
47 Fear and a snare have come
upon us,
Desolation and destruction.
48 My eyes overflow with rivers of
water
For the destruction of the daughter
of my people.

49 My eyes flow and do not cease,
Without interruption,
50 Till the Lord from heaven
Looks down and sees.
51 My eyes bring suffering to my soul
Because of all the daughters of my
city.

52 My enemies without cause
Hunted me down like a bird.
53 They silenced my life in the pit
And threw stones at me.
54 The waters flowed over my head;
I said, "I am cut off!"

55 I called on Your name, O Lord,
From the lowest pit.
56 You have heard my voice:
"Do not hide Your ear
From my sighing, from my cry for
help."
57 You drew near on the day I called
on You,
And said, "Do not fear!"

58 O Lord, You have pleaded the case
for my soul;
You have redeemed my life.
59 O Lord, You have seen *how* I am
wronged;
Judge my case.
60 You have seen all their vengeance,
All their schemes against me.

61 You have heard their reproach,
    O LORD,
   All their schemes against me,
62 The lips of my enemies
   And their whispering against me all
    the day.
63 Look at their sitting down and their
    rising up;
   I *am* their taunting song.

64 Repay them, O LORD,
   According to the work of their
    hands.
65 Give them a veiled heart;
   Your curse *be* upon them!
66 In Your anger,
   Pursue and destroy them
   From under the heavens of the
    LORD.

The Degradation of Zion

4 How the gold has become dim!
   How changed the fine gold!
   The stones of the sanctuary are
    scattered
   At the head of every street.

2 The precious sons of Zion,
   Valuable as fine gold,
   How they are regarded as clay pots,
   The work of the hands of the potter!

3 Even the jackals present their
    breasts
   To nurse their young;
   But the daughter of my people *is*
    cruel,
   Like ostriches in the wilderness.

4 The tongue of the infant clings
   To the roof of its mouth for thirst;
   The young children ask for bread,
   But no one breaks *it* for them.

5 Those who ate delicacies
   Are desolate in the streets;
   Those who were brought up in
    scarlet
   Embrace ash heaps.

6 The punishment of the iniquity of
    the daughter of my people
   Is greater than the punishment of
    the sin of Sodom,

Which was overthrown in a
    moment,
With no hand to help her!

7 Her Nazirites*ᵃ* were brighter than
    snow
   And whiter than milk;
   They were more ruddy in body than
    rubies,
   Like sapphire in their appearance.

8 *Now* their appearance is blacker
    than soot;
   They go unrecognized in the
    streets;
   Their skin clings to their bones,
   It has become as dry as wood.

9 *Those* slain by the sword are
    better off
   Than *those* who die of hunger;
   For these pine away,
   Stricken *for lack* of the fruits of the
    field.

10 The hands of the compassionate
    women
   Have cooked their own children;
   They became food for them
   In the destruction of the daughter
    of my people.

11 The LORD has fulfilled His fury,
   He has poured out His fierce
    anger.
   He kindled a fire in Zion,
   And it has devoured its
    foundations.

12 The kings of the earth,
   And all inhabitants of the world,
   Would not have believed
   That the adversary and the enemy
   Could enter the gates of
    Jerusalem—

13 Because of the sins of her prophets
   And the iniquities of her priests,
   Who shed in her midst
   The blood of the just.

14 They wandered blind in the streets;
   They have defiled themselves with
    blood,

ᵃ Or *nobles*

So that no one would touch their
garments.

15 They cried out to them,
"Go away, unclean!
Go away, go away,
Do not touch us!"
When they fled and wandered,
Those among the nations said,
"They shall no longer dwell *here.*"

16 The face of the LORD scattered
them;
He no longer regards them.
The people do not respect the
priests
Nor show favor to the elders.

17 Still our eyes failed us,
Watching vainly for our help;
In our watching we watched
For a nation *that* could not save *us.*

18 They tracked our steps
So that we could not walk in our
streets.
Our end was near;
Our days were over,
For our end had come.

19 Our pursuers were swifter
Than the eagles of the heavens.
They pursued us on the mountains
And lay in wait for us in the
wilderness.

20 The breath of our nostrils, the
anointed of the LORD,
Was caught in their pits,
Of whom we said, "Under his
shadow
We shall live among the nations."

21 Rejoice and be glad, O daughter of
Edom,
You who dwell in the land of Uz!
The cup shall also pass over to you
And you shall become drunk and
make yourself naked.

22 *The punishment of* your iniquity is
accomplished,
O daughter of Zion;
He will no longer send you into
captivity.
He will punish your iniquity,
O daughter of Edom;
He will uncover your sins!

A Prayer for Restoration

5 Remember, O LORD, what has come
upon us;
Look, and behold our reproach!

2 Our inheritance has been turned
over to aliens,
And our houses to foreigners.

3 We have become orphans and
waifs,
Our mothers *are* like widows.

4 We pay for the water we drink,
And our wood comes at a price.

5 *They* pursue at our heels;
We labor *and* have no rest.

6 We have given our hand *to* the
Egyptians
And the Assyrians, to be satisfied
with bread.

7 Our fathers sinned *and are* no
more,
But we bear their iniquities.

8 Servants rule over us;
There is none to deliver *us* from
their hand.

9 We get our bread *at the risk* of our
lives,
Because of the sword in the
wilderness.

10 Our skin is hot as an oven,
Because of the fever of famine.

11 They ravished the women in Zion,
The maidens in the cities of Judah.

12 Princes were hung up by their
hands,
And elders were not respected.

13 Young men ground at the
millstones;
Boys staggered under *loads of*
wood.

14 The elders have ceased *gathering*
at the gate,
And the young men from their
music.

15 The joy of our heart has ceased;
Our dance has turned into
mourning.

16 The crown has fallen *from* our
head.
Woe to us, for we have sinned!

17 Because of this our heart is faint;
Because of these *things* our eyes
grow dim;

18 Because of Mount Zion which is
      desolate,
   With foxes walking about on it.

19 You, O LORD, remain
      forever;
   Your throne from generation to
      generation.

20 Why do You forget us forever,
   And forsake us for so long a time?
21 Turn us back to You, O LORD, and
      we will be restored;
   Renew our days as of old,
22 Unless You have utterly
      rejected us,
   And are very angry with us!

The Book of

EZEKIEL

Ezekiel's Vision of God

1 Now it came to pass in the thirtieth year, in the fourth *month*, on the fifth *day* of the month, as I *was* among the captives by the River Chebar, *that* the heavens were opened and I saw visions of God. 2On the fifth *day* of the month, which *was* in the fifth year of King Jehoiachin's captivity, 3the word of the LORD came expressly to Ezekiel the priest, the son of Buzi, in the land of the Chaldeans by the River Chebar; and the hand of the LORD was upon him there.

4Then I looked, and behold, a whirlwind was coming out of the north, a great cloud with raging fire engulfing itself; and brightness *was* all around it and radiating out of its midst like the color of amber, out of the midst of the fire. 5Also from within it *came* the likeness of four living creatures. And this *was* their appearance: they had the likeness of a man. 6Each one had four faces, and each one had four wings. 7Their legs *were* straight, and the soles of their feet *were* like the soles of calves' feet. They sparkled like the color of burnished bronze. 8The hands of a man *were* under their wings on their four sides; and each of the four had faces and wings. 9Their wings touched one another. *The creatures* did not turn when they went, but each one went straight forward.

10As for the likeness of their faces, *each* had the face of a man; each of the four had the face of a lion on the right side, each of the four had the face of an ox on the left side, and each of the four had the face of an eagle. 11Thus *were* their faces. Their wings stretched upward; two *wings* of each one touched one another, and two covered their bodies. 12And each one went straight forward; they went wherever the spirit wanted to go, and they did not turn when they went.

13As for the likeness of the living creatures, their appearance *was* like burning coals of fire, like the appearance of torches going back and forth among the living creatures. The fire was bright, and out of the fire went lightning. 14And the living creatures ran back and forth, in appearance like a flash of lightning.

15Now as I looked at the living creatures, behold, a wheel *was* on the earth beside each living creature with its four faces. 16The appearance of the wheels and their workings *was* like the color of beryl, and all four had the same likeness. The appearance of their workings *was*, as it were, a wheel in the middle of a wheel. 17When they moved, they went toward any one of four directions; they did not turn aside when they went. 18As for their rims, they were so high they were awesome; and their rims *were* full of eyes, all around the four of them. 19When the living creatures went, the wheels went beside them; and when the living creatures were lifted up from the earth, the wheels were lifted up. 20Wherever the spirit wanted to go, they went, *because* there the spirit went; and the wheels were lifted together with them, for the spirit of the living creatures *was* in the wheels. 21When those went, *these* went; when those stood, *these* stood; and when those were lifted up from the earth, the wheels were lifted up together with them, for the spirit of the living creatures *was* in the wheels.

22The likeness of the firmament above the heads of the living creatures *was* like the color of an awesome crystal, stretched out over their heads. 23And under the firmament their wings *spread out* straight, one toward another. Each one had two which covered one side, and each one had two which covered the other side of the body. 24When they went, I heard the noise of their wings, like the noise of many waters, like the voice of the Almighty, a tumult like the noise of an army; and when they stood still, they let down their wings. 25A voice came from above the firmament that *was* over their heads; whenever they stood, they let down their wings.

26And above the firmament over their

heads *was* the likeness of a throne, in appearance like a sapphire stone; on the likeness of the throne *was* a likeness with the appearance of a man high above it. 27Also from the appearance of His waist and upward I saw, as it were, the color of amber with the appearance of fire all around within it; and from the appearance of His waist and downward I saw, as it were, the appearance of fire with brightness all around. 28Like the appearance of a rainbow in a cloud on a rainy day, so *was* the appearance of the brightness all around it. This *was* the appearance of the likeness of the glory of the LORD.

Ezekiel Sent to Rebellious Israel

So when I saw *it*, I fell on my face, and I heard a voice of One speaking.

2 And He said to me, "Son of man, stand on your feet, and I will speak to you." 2Then the Spirit entered me when He spoke to me, and set me on my feet; and I heard Him who spoke to me. 3And He said to me: "Son of man, I am sending you to the children of Israel, to a rebellious nation that has rebelled against Me; they and their fathers have transgressed against Me to this very day. 4For *they are* impudent and stubborn children. I am sending you to them, and you shall say to them, 'Thus says the Lord GOD.' 5As for them, whether they hear or whether they refuse—for they *are* a rebellious house—yet they will know that a prophet has been among them.

6"And you, son of man, do not be afraid of them nor be afraid of their words, though briers and thorns *are* with you and you dwell among scorpions; do not be afraid of their words or dismayed by their looks, though they *are* a rebellious house. 7You shall speak My words to them, whether they hear or whether they refuse, for they *are* rebellious. 8But you, son of man, hear what I say to you. Do not be rebellious like that rebellious house; open your mouth and eat what I give you."

9Now when I looked, there was a hand stretched out to me; and behold, a scroll of a book *was* in it. 10Then He spread it before me; and *there was* writing on the inside and on the outside, and written on it *were* lamentations and mourning and woe.

3 Moreover He said to me, "Son of man, eat what you find; eat this scroll, and go, speak to the house of Israel." 2So I opened my mouth, and He caused me to eat that scroll.

3And He said to me, "Son of man, feed your belly, and fill your stomach with this scroll that I give you." So I ate, and it was in my mouth like honey in sweetness.

4Then He said to me: "Son of man, go to the house of Israel and speak with My words to them. 5For you *are* not sent to a people of unfamiliar speech and of hard language, *but* to the house of Israel, 6not to many people of unfamiliar speech and of hard language, whose words you cannot understand. Surely, had I sent you to them, they would have listened to you. 7But the house of Israel will not listen to you, because they will not listen to Me; for all the house of Israel *are* impudent and hard-hearted. 8Behold, I have made your face strong against their faces, and your forehead strong against their foreheads. 9Like adamant stone, harder than flint, I have made your forehead; do not be afraid of them, nor be dismayed at their looks, though they *are* a rebellious house."

10Moreover He said to me: "Son of man, receive into your heart all My words that I speak to you, and hear with your ears. 11And go, get to the captives, to the children of your people, and speak to them and tell them, 'Thus says the Lord GOD,' whether they hear, or whether they refuse."

12Then the Spirit lifted me up, and I heard behind me a great thunderous voice: "Blessed *is* the glory of the LORD from His place!" 13*I* also *heard* the noise of the wings of the living creatures that touched one another, and the noise of the wheels beside them, and a great thunderous noise. 14So the Spirit lifted me up and took me away, and I went in bitterness, in the heat of my spirit; but the hand of the LORD was strong upon me. 15Then I came to the captives at Tel Abib, who dwelt by the River Chebar; and I sat where they sat, and remained there astonished among them seven days.

Ezekiel Is a Watchman

16Now it came to pass at the end of seven days that the word of the LORD came to me, saying, 17"Son of man, I have made you a watchman for the house of Israel; therefore hear a word from My mouth, and give them warning from Me: 18When I say to the wicked, 'You shall surely die,' and you give him no warning, nor speak to warn the wicked from his wicked way, to save his life, that same wicked *man* shall die in his iniquity; but his blood I will require at your hand. 19Yet, if you warn the wicked, and he does not turn from his wickedness, nor from his wicked way, he shall die in his iniquity; but you have delivered your soul.

20"Again, when a righteous *man* turns from his righteousness and commits iniquity, and I lay a stumbling block before him, he shall die; because you did not give him warning, he shall die in his sin, and his righteousness which he has done shall not be remembered; but his blood I will require at your hand. 21Nevertheless if you warn the righteous *man* that the righteous should not sin, and he does not sin, he shall surely live because he took warning; also you will have delivered your soul."

22Then the hand of the LORD was upon me there, and He said to me, "Arise, go out into the plain, and there I shall talk with you."

23So I arose and went out into the plain, and behold, the glory of the LORD stood there, like the glory which I saw by the River Chebar; and I fell on my face. 24Then the Spirit entered me and set me on my feet, and spoke with me and said to me: "Go, shut yourself inside your house. 25And you, O son of man, surely they will put ropes on you and bind you with them, so that you cannot go out among them. 26I will make your tongue cling to the roof of your mouth, so that you shall be mute and not be one to rebuke them, for they *are* a rebellious house. 27But when I speak with you, I will open your mouth, and you shall say to them, 'Thus says the Lord GOD.' He who hears, let him hear; and he who refuses, let him refuse; for they *are* a rebellious house.

The Siege of Jerusalem Portrayed

4 "You also, son of man, take a clay tablet and lay it before you, and portray on it a city, Jerusalem. 2Lay siege against it, build a siege wall against it, and heap up a mound against it; set camps against it also, and place battering rams against it all around. 3Moreover take for yourself an iron plate, and set it *as* an iron wall between you and the city. Set your face against it, and it shall be besieged, and you shall lay siege against it. This *will be* a sign to the house of Israel.

4"Lie also on your left side, and lay the iniquity of the house of Israel upon it. *According* to the number of the days that you lie on it, you shall bear their iniquity. 5For I have laid on you the years of their iniquity, according to the number of the days, three hundred and ninety days; so you shall bear the iniquity of the house of Israel. 6And when you have completed them, lie again on your right side; then you shall bear the iniquity of the house of Judah forty days. I have laid on you a day for each year.

7"Therefore you shall set your face toward the siege of Jerusalem; your arm *shall be* uncovered, and you shall prophesy against it. 8And surely I will restrain you so that you cannot turn from one side to another till you have ended the days of your siege.

9"Also take for yourself wheat, barley, beans, lentils, millet, and spelt; put them into one vessel, and make bread of them for yourself. *During* the number of days that you lie on your side, three hundred and ninety days, you shall eat it. 10And your food which you eat *shall be* by weight, twenty shekels a day; from time to time you shall eat it. 11You shall also drink water by measure, one-sixth of a hin; from time to time you shall drink. 12And you shall eat it *as* barley cakes; and bake it using fuel of human waste in their sight."

13Then the LORD said, "So shall the children of Israel eat their defiled bread among the Gentiles, where I will drive them."

14So I said, "Ah, Lord GOD! Indeed I have never defiled myself from my youth till now; I have never eaten what died of itself or was torn by beasts, nor has abominable flesh ever come into my mouth."

15Then He said to me, "See, I am giving you cow dung instead of human waste, and you shall prepare your bread over it."

16Moreover He said to me, "Son of man, surely I will cut off the supply of bread in Jerusalem; they shall eat bread by weight and with anxiety, and shall drink water by measure and with dread, 17that they may lack bread and water, and be dismayed with one another, and waste away because of their iniquity.

A Sword Against Jerusalem

5 "And you, son of man, take a sharp sword, take it as a barber's razor, and pass *it* over your head and your beard; then take scales to weigh and divide the hair. 2You shall burn with fire one-third in the midst of the city, when the days of the siege are finished; then you shall take one-third and strike around *it* with the sword, and one-third you shall scatter in the wind: I will draw out a sword after them. 3You shall also take a small number of them and bind them in the edge of your *garment.* 4Then take some of them again and throw them into the midst of the fire, and burn them in the fire. From there a fire will go out into all the house of Israel.

5"Thus says the Lord God: 'This *is* Jerusalem; I have set her in the midst of the nations and the countries all around her. 6She has rebelled against My judgments by doing wickedness more than the nations, and against My statutes more than the countries that *are* all around her; for they have refused My judgments, and they have not walked in My statutes.' 7Therefore thus says the Lord God: 'Because you have multiplied *disobedience* more than the nations that *are* all around you, have not walked in My statutes nor kept My judgments, nor even done according to the judgments of the nations that *are* all around you'—8therefore thus says the Lord God: 'Indeed I, even I, *am* against you and will execute judgments in your midst in the sight of the nations. 9And I will do among you what I have

never done, and the like of which I will never do again, because of all your abominations. 10Therefore fathers shall eat *their* sons in your midst, and sons shall eat their fathers; and I will execute judgments among you, and all of you who remain I will scatter to all the winds.

11'Therefore, *as* I live,' says the Lord God, 'surely, because you have defiled My sanctuary with all your detestable things and with all your abominations, therefore I will also diminish *you;* My eye will not spare, nor will I have any pity. 12One-third of you shall die of the pestilence, and be consumed with famine in your midst; and one-third shall fall by the sword all around you; and I will scatter another third to all the winds, and I will draw out a sword after them.

13'Thus shall My anger be spent, and I will cause My fury to rest upon them, and I will be avenged; and they shall know that I, the Lord, have spoken *it* in My zeal, when I have spent My fury upon them. 14Moreover I will make you a waste and a reproach among the nations that *are* all around you, in the sight of all who pass by.

15'So it shall be a reproach, a taunt, a lesson, and an astonishment to the nations that *are* all around you, when I execute judgments among you in anger and in fury and in furious rebukes. I, the Lord, have spoken. 16When I send against them the terrible arrows of famine which shall be for destruction, which I will send to destroy you, I will increase the famine upon you and cut off your supply of bread. 17So I will send against you famine and wild beasts, and they will bereave you. Pestilence and blood shall pass through you, and I will bring the sword against you. I, the Lord, have spoken.' "

Judgment on Idolatrous Israel

6 Now the word of the Lord came to me, saying: 2"Son of man, set your face toward the mountains of Israel, and prophesy against them, 3and say, 'O mountains of Israel, hear the word of the Lord God! Thus says the Lord God to the mountains, to the hills, to the ravines, and to the valleys: "Indeed

I, *even* I, will bring a sword against you, and I will destroy your high places. 4Then your altars shall be desolate, your incense altars shall be broken, and I will cast down your slain *men* before your idols. 5And I will lay the corpses of the children of Israel before their idols, and I will scatter your bones all around your altars. 6In all your dwelling places the cities shall be laid waste, and the high places shall be desolate, so that your altars may be laid waste and made desolate, your idols may be broken and made to cease, your incense altars may be cut down, and your works may be abolished. 7The slain shall fall in your midst, and you shall know that I *am* the LORD.

8"Yet I will leave a remnant, so that you may have *some* who escape the sword among the nations, when you are scattered through the countries. 9Then those of you who escape will remember Me among the nations where they are carried captive, because I was crushed by their adulterous heart which has departed from Me, and by their eyes which play the harlot after their idols; they will loathe themselves for the evils which they committed in all their abominations. 10And they shall know that I *am* the LORD; I have not said in vain that I would bring this calamity upon them."

11'Thus says the Lord GOD: "Pound your fists and stamp your feet, and say, 'Alas, for all the evil abominations of the house of Israel! For they shall fall by the sword, by famine, and by pestilence. 12He who is far off shall die by the pestilence, he who is near shall fall by the sword, and he who remains and is besieged shall die by the famine. Thus will I spend My fury upon them. 13Then you shall know that I *am* the LORD, when their slain are among their idols all around their altars, on every high hill, on all the mountaintops, under every green tree, and under every thick oak, wherever they offered sweet incense to all their idols. 14So I will stretch out My hand against them and make the land desolate, yes, more desolate than the wilderness toward Diblah, in all their dwelling places. Then they shall know that I *am* the LORD.' " ' "

Judgment on Israel Is Near

7 Moreover the word of the LORD came to me, saying, 2"And you, son of man, thus says the Lord GOD to the land of Israel:

'An end! The end has come upon the four corners of the land.

3   Now the end *has come* upon you,
     And I will send My anger against you;
     I will judge you according to your ways,
     And I will repay you for all your abominations.

4   My eye will not spare you,
     Nor will I have pity;
     But I will repay your ways,
     And your abominations will be in your midst;
     Then you shall know that I *am* the LORD!'

5"Thus says the Lord GOD:

'A disaster, a singular disaster;
Behold, it has come!

6   An end has come,
     The end has come;
     It has dawned for you;
     Behold, it has come!

7   Doom has come to you, you who dwell in the land;
     The time has come,
     A day of trouble *is* near,
     And not of rejoicing in the mountains.

8   Now upon you I will soon pour out My fury,
     And spend My anger upon you;
     I will judge you according to your ways,
     And I will repay you for all your abominations.

9   'My eye will not spare,
     Nor will I have pity;
     I will repay you according to your ways,
     And your abominations will be in your midst.
     Then you shall know that I *am* the LORD who strikes.

10   'Behold, the day!
     Behold, it has come!
     Doom has gone out;

The rod has blossomed,
Pride has budded.
11 Violence has risen up into a rod of
    wickedness;
None of them *shall remain*,
None of their multitude,
None of them;
Nor *shall there be* wailing for them.
12 The time has come,
The day draws near.

  'Let not the buyer rejoice,
Nor the seller mourn,
For wrath *is* on their whole
    multitude.
13 For the seller shall not return to
    what has been sold,
Though he may still be alive;
For the vision concerns the whole
    multitude,
And it shall not turn back;
No one will strengthen himself
Who lives in iniquity.

14 'They have blown the trumpet and
    made everyone ready,
But no one goes to battle;
For My wrath *is* on all their
    multitude.
15 The sword *is* outside,
And the pestilence and famine
    within.
Whoever *is* in the field
Will die by the sword;
And whoever *is* in the city,
Famine and pestilence will
    devour him.

16 'Those who survive will escape and
    be on the mountains
Like doves of the valleys,
All of them mourning,
Each for his iniquity.
17 Every hand will be feeble,
And every knee will be *as* weak *as*
    water.
18 They will also be girded with
    sackcloth;
Horror will cover them;
Shame *will be* on every face,
Baldness on all their heads.

19 'They will throw their silver into the
    streets,
And their gold will be like refuse;
Their silver and their gold will not
    be able to deliver them

In the day of the wrath of the Lord;
They will not satisfy their souls,
Nor fill their stomachs,
Because it became their stumbling
    block of iniquity.

20 'As for the beauty of his ornaments,
He set it in majesty;
But they made from it
The images of their abominations—
Their detestable things;
Therefore I have made it
Like refuse to them.
21 I will give it as plunder
Into the hands of strangers,
And to the wicked of the earth as
    spoil;
And they shall defile it.
22 I will turn My face from them,
And they will defile My secret
    place;
For robbers shall enter it and
    defile it.

23 'Make a chain,
For the land is filled with crimes
    of blood,
And the city is full of violence.
24 Therefore I will bring the worst of
    the Gentiles,
And they will possess their houses;
I will cause the pomp of the strong
    to cease,
And their holy places shall be
    defiled.
25 Destruction comes;
They will seek peace, but *there
    shall be* none.
26 Disaster will come upon disaster,
And rumor will be upon rumor.
Then they will seek a vision from
    a prophet;
But the law will perish from the
    priest,
And counsel from the elders.

27 'The king will mourn,
The prince will be clothed with
    desolation,
And the hands of the common
    people will tremble.
I will do to them according to
    their way,
And according to what they
    deserve I will judge them;
Then they shall know that I *am* the
    Lord!' "

Abominations in the Temple

8 And it came to pass in the sixth year, in the sixth *month*, on the fifth *day* of the month, as I sat in my house with the elders of Judah sitting before me, that the hand of the Lord GOD fell upon me there. 2Then I looked, and there was a likeness, like the appearance of fire—from the appearance of His waist and downward, fire; and from His waist and upward, like the appearance of brightness, like the color of amber. 3He stretched out the form of a hand, and took me by a lock of my hair; and the Spirit lifted me up between earth and heaven, and brought me in visions of God to Jerusalem, to the door of the north gate of the inner *court*, where the seat of the image of jealousy *was*, which provokes to jealousy. 4And behold, the glory of the God of Israel *was* there, like the vision that I saw in the plain.

5Then He said to me, "Son of man, lift your eyes now toward the north." So I lifted my eyes toward the north, and there, north of the altar gate, was this image of jealousy in the entrance.

6Furthermore He said to me, "Son of man, do you see what they are doing, the great abominations that the house of Israel commits here, to make Me go far away from My sanctuary? Now turn again, you will see greater abominations." 7So He brought me to the door of the court; and when I looked, there was a hole in the wall. 8Then He said to me, "Son of man, dig into the wall"; and when I dug into the wall, there was a door.

9And He said to me, "Go in, and see the wicked abominations which they are doing there." 10So I went in and saw, and there—every sort of creeping thing, abominable beasts, and all the idols of the house of Israel, portrayed all around on the walls. 11And there stood before them seventy men of the elders of the house of Israel, and in their midst stood Jaazaniah the son of Shaphan. Each man had a censer in his hand, and a thick cloud of incense went up. 12Then He said to me, "Son of man, have you seen what the elders of the house of Israel do in the dark, every man in the room of his idols? For they

say, 'The LORD does not see us, the LORD has forsaken the land.' "

13And He said to me, "Turn again, *and* you will see greater abominations that they are doing." 14So He brought me to the door of the north gate of the LORD's house; and to my dismay, women were sitting there weeping for Tammuz.

15Then He said to me, "Have you seen *this*, O son of man? Turn again, you will see greater abominations than these." 16So He brought me into the inner court of the LORD's house; and there, at the door of the temple of the LORD, between the porch and the altar, *were* about twenty-five men with their backs toward the temple of the LORD and their faces toward the east, and they were worshiping the sun toward the east.

17And He said to me, "Have you seen *this*, O son of man? Is it a trivial thing to the house of Judah to commit the abominations which they commit here? For they have filled the land with violence; then they have returned to provoke Me to anger. Indeed they put the branch to their nose. 18Therefore I also will act in fury. My eye will not spare nor will I have pity; and though they cry in My ears with a loud voice, I will not hear them."

The Wicked Are Slain

9 Then He called out in my hearing with a loud voice, saying, "Let those who have charge over the city draw near, each *with* a deadly weapon in his hand." 2And suddenly six men came from the direction of the upper gate, which faces north, each with his battle-ax in his hand. One man among them *was* clothed with linen and had a writer's inkhorn at his side. They went in and stood beside the bronze altar.

3Now the glory of the God of Israel had gone up from the cherub, where it had been, to the threshold of the temple. And He called to the man clothed with linen, who *had* the writer's inkhorn at his side; 4and the LORD said to him, "Go through the midst of the city, through the midst of Jerusalem, and put a mark on the foreheads of the men who sigh and cry over all the abominations that are done within it."

5To the others He said in my hearing,

"Go after him through the city and kill; do not let your eye spare, nor have any pity. 6Utterly slay old *and* young men, maidens and little children and women; but do not come near anyone on whom is the mark; and begin at My sanctuary." So they began with the elders who *were* before the temple. 7Then He said to them, "Defile the temple, and fill the courts with the slain. Go out!" And they went out and killed in the city.

8So it was, that while they were killing them, I was left *alone;* and I fell on my face and cried out, and said, "Ah, Lord God! Will You destroy all the remnant of Israel in pouring out Your fury on Jerusalem?"

9Then He said to me, "The iniquity of the house of Israel and Judah *is* exceedingly great, and the land is full of bloodshed, and the city full of perversity; for they say, 'The Lord has forsaken the land, and the Lord does not see!' 10And as for Me also, My eye will neither spare, nor will I have pity, *but* I will recompense their deeds on their own head."

11Just then, the man clothed with linen, who *had* the inkhorn at his side, reported back and said, "I have done as You commanded me."

The Glory Departs from the Temple

10 And I looked, and there in the firmament that was above the head of the cherubim, there appeared something like a sapphire stone, having the appearance of the likeness of a throne. 2Then He spoke to the man clothed with linen, and said, "Go in among the wheels, under the cherub, fill your hands with coals of fire from among the cherubim, and scatter *them* over the city." And he went in as I watched.

3Now the cherubim were standing on the south side of the temple when the man went in, and the cloud filled the inner court. 4Then the glory of the Lord went up from the cherub, *and* paused over the threshold of the temple; and the house was filled with the cloud, and the court was full of the brightness of the Lord's glory. 5And the sound of the wings of the cherubim was heard *even* in the outer court, like the voice of Almighty God when He speaks.

6Then it happened, when He commanded the man clothed in linen, saying, "Take fire from among the wheels, from among the cherubim," that he went in and stood beside the wheels. 7And the cherub stretched out his hand from among the cherubim to the fire that *was* among the cherubim, and took *some of it* and put *it* into the hands of the *man* clothed with linen, who took *it* and went out. 8The cherubim appeared to have the form of a man's hand under their wings.

9And when I looked, there were four wheels by the cherubim, one wheel by one cherub and another wheel by each other cherub; the wheels appeared *to have* the color of a beryl stone. 10*As for* their appearance, all four looked alike—as it were, a wheel in the middle of a wheel. 11When they went, they went toward *any of* their four directions; they did not turn aside when they went, but followed in the direction the head was facing. They did not turn aside when they went. 12And their whole body, with their back, their hands, their wings, and the wheels that the four had, *were* full of eyes all around. 13As for the wheels, they were called in my hearing, "Wheel."

14Each one had four faces: the first face *was* the face of a cherub, the second face the face of a man, the third the face of a lion, and the fourth the face of an eagle. 15And the cherubim were lifted up. This *was* the living creature I saw by the River Chebar. 16When the cherubim went, the wheels went beside them; and when the cherubim lifted their wings to mount up from the earth, the same wheels also did not turn from beside them. 17When *the cherubim* stood still, *the wheels* stood still, and when *one* was lifted up, *the other* lifted itself up, for the spirit of the living creature *was* in them.

18Then the glory of the Lord departed from the threshold of the temple and stood over the cherubim. 19And the cherubim lifted their wings and mounted up from the earth in my sight. When they went out, the wheels *were* beside them; and they stood at the door of the east gate of the Lord's house, and the glory of the God of Israel *was* above them.

20This *is* the living creature I saw under the God of Israel by the River Chebar, and I knew they *were* cherubim. 21Each one had four faces and each one four wings, and the likeness of the hands of a man *was* under their wings. 22And the likeness of their faces *was* the same *as* the faces which I had seen by the River Chebar, their appearance and their persons. They each went straight forward.

Judgment on Wicked Counselors

11 Then the Spirit lifted me up and brought me to the East Gate of the LORD's house, which faces eastward; and there at the door of the gate were twenty-five men, among whom I saw Jaazaniah the son of Azzur, and Pelatiah the son of Benaiah, princes of the people. 2And He said to me: "Son of man, these *are* the men who devise iniquity and give wicked counsel in this city, 3who say, '*The time is* not near to build houses; this *city is* the caldron, and we *are* the meat.' 4Therefore prophesy against them, prophesy, O son of man!' "

5Then the Spirit of the LORD fell upon me, and said to me, "Speak! 'Thus says the LORD: "Thus you have said, O house of Israel; for I know the things that come into your mind. 6You have multiplied your slain in this city, and you have filled its streets with the slain." 7Therefore thus says the Lord GOD: "Your slain whom you have laid in its midst, they *are* the meat, and this *city is* the caldron; but I shall bring you out of the midst of it. 8You have feared the sword; and I will bring a sword upon you," says the Lord GOD. 9"And I will bring you out of its midst, and deliver you into the hands of strangers, and execute judgments on you. 10You shall fall by the sword. I will judge you at the border of Israel. Then you shall know that I *am* the LORD. 11This *city* shall not be your caldron, nor shall you be the meat in its midst. I will judge you at the border of Israel. 12And you shall know that I *am* the LORD; for you have not walked in My statutes nor executed My judgments, but have done according to the customs of the Gentiles which *are* all around you." ' "

13Now it happened, while I was prophesying, that Pelatiah the son of Benaiah died. Then I fell on my face and cried with a loud voice, and said, "Ah, Lord GOD! Will You make a complete end of the remnant of Israel?"

God Will Restore Israel

14Again the word of the LORD came to me, saying, 15"Son of man, your brethren, your relatives, your countrymen, and all the house of Israel in its entirety, *are* those about whom the inhabitants of Jerusalem have said, 'Get far away from the LORD; this land has been given to us as a possession.' 16Therefore say, 'Thus says the Lord GOD: "Although I have cast them far off among the Gentiles, and although I have scattered them among the countries, yet I shall be a little sanctuary for them in the countries where they have gone." ' 17Therefore say, 'Thus says the Lord GOD: "I will gather you from the peoples, assemble you from the countries where you have been scattered, and I will give you the land of Israel." ' 18And they will go there, and they will take away all its detestable things and all its abominations from there. 19Then I will give them one heart, and I will put a new spirit within them, and take the stony heart out of their flesh, and give them a heart of flesh, 20that they may walk in My statutes and keep My judgments and do them; and they shall be My people, and I will be their God. 21But *as for those* whose hearts follow the desire for their detestable things and their abominations, I will recompense their deeds on their own heads," says the Lord GOD.

22So the cherubim lifted up their wings, with the wheels beside them, and the glory of the God of Israel *was* high above them. 23And the glory of the LORD went up from the midst of the city and stood on the mountain, which *is* on the east side of the city. 24Then the Spirit took me up and brought me in a vision by the Spirit of God into Chaldea, to those in captivity. And the vision that I had seen went up from me. 25So I spoke to those in captivity of all the things the LORD had shown me.

Judah's Captivity Portrayed

12 Now the word of the LORD came to me, saying: 2"Son of man, you dwell in the midst of a rebellious house, which has eyes to see but does not see, and ears to hear but does not hear; for they *are* a rebellious house.

3"Therefore, son of man, prepare your belongings for captivity, and go into captivity by day in their sight. You shall go from your place into captivity to another place in their sight. It may be that they will consider, though they *are* a rebellious house. 4By day you shall bring out your belongings in their sight, as though going into captivity; and at evening you shall go in their sight, like those who go into captivity. 5Dig through the wall in their sight, and carry your belongings out through it. 6In their sight you shall bear *them* on *your* shoulders *and* carry *them* out at twilight; you shall cover your face, so that you cannot see the ground, for I have made you a sign to the house of Israel."

7So I did as I was commanded. I brought out my belongings by day, as though going into captivity, and at evening I dug through the wall with my hand. I brought *them* out at twilight, *and* I bore *them* on *my* shoulder in their sight.

8And in the morning the word of the LORD came to me, saying, 9"Son of man, has not the house of Israel, the rebellious house, said to you, 'What are you doing?' 10Say to them, 'Thus says the Lord GOD: "This burden *concerns* the prince in Jerusalem and all the house of Israel who are among them."' 11Say, 'I *am* a sign to you. As I have done, so shall it be done to them; they shall be carried away into captivity.' 12And the prince who *is* among them shall bear *his belongings* on *his* shoulder at twilight and go out. They shall dig through the wall to carry *them* out through it. He shall cover his face, so that he cannot see the ground with *his* eyes. 13I will also spread My net over him, and he shall be caught in My snare. I will bring him to Babylon, *to* the land of the Chaldeans; yet he shall not see it, though he shall die there. 14I will scatter to every wind all who *are* around him to help him, and all his troops; and I will draw out the sword after them.

15"Then they shall know that I *am* the LORD, when I scatter them among the nations and disperse them throughout the countries. 16But I will spare a few of their men from the sword, from famine, and from pestilence, that they may declare all their abominations among the Gentiles wherever they go. Then they shall know that I *am* the LORD."

Judgment Not Postponed

17Moreover the word of the LORD came to me, saying, 18"Son of man, eat your bread with quaking, and drink your water with trembling and anxiety. 19And say to the people of the land, 'Thus says the Lord GOD to the inhabitants of Jerusalem *and* to the land of Israel: "They shall eat their bread with anxiety, and drink their water with dread, so that her land may be emptied of all who are in it, because of the violence of all those who dwell in it. 20Then the cities that are inhabited shall be laid waste, and the land shall become desolate; and you shall know that I *am* the LORD."'"

21And the word of the LORD came to me, saying, 22"Son of man, what *is* this proverb *that* you *people* have about the land of Israel, which says, 'The days are prolonged, and every vision fails'? 23Tell them therefore, 'Thus says the Lord GOD: "I will lay this proverb to rest, and they shall no more use it as a proverb in Israel."' But say to them, "The days are at hand, and the fulfillment of every vision. 24For no more shall there be any false vision or flattering divination within the house of Israel. 25For I *am* the LORD. I speak, and the word which I speak will come to pass; it will no more be postponed; for in your days, O rebellious house, I will say the word and perform it," says the Lord GOD.'"

26Again the word of the LORD came to me, saying, 27"Son of man, look, the house of Israel is saying, 'The vision that he sees *is* for many days *from now*, and he prophesies of times far off.' 28Therefore say to them, 'Thus says the Lord GOD: "None of My words will be postponed any more, but the word which I speak will be done," says the Lord GOD.' "

Woe to Foolish Prophets

13 And the word of the LORD came to me, saying, 2"Son of man, prophesy against the prophets of Israel who prophesy, and say to those who prophesy out of their own heart, 'Hear the word of the LORD!' "

3Thus says the Lord GOD: "Woe to the foolish prophets, who follow their own spirit and have seen nothing! 4O Israel, your prophets are like foxes in the deserts. 5You have not gone up into the gaps to build a wall for the house of Israel to stand in battle on the day of the LORD. 6They have envisioned futility and false divination, saying, 'Thus says the LORD!' But the LORD has not sent them; yet they hope that the word may be confirmed. 7Have you not seen a futile vision, and have you not spoken false divination? You say, 'The LORD says,' but I have not spoken."

8Therefore thus says the Lord GOD: "Because you have spoken nonsense and envisioned lies, therefore I *am* indeed against you," says the Lord GOD. 9"My hand will be against the prophets who envision futility and who divine lies; they shall not be in the assembly of My people, nor be written in the record of the house of Israel, nor shall they enter into the land of Israel. Then you shall know that I *am* the Lord GOD.

10"Because, indeed, because they have seduced My people, saying, 'Peace!' when *there is* no peace—and one builds a wall, and they plaster it with untempered *mortar*—11say to those who plaster *it* with untempered *mortar*, that it will fall. There will be flooding rain, and you, O great hailstones, shall fall; and a stormy wind shall tear *it* down. 12Surely, when the wall has fallen, will it not be said to you, 'Where *is* the mortar with which you plastered *it?*' "

13Therefore thus says the Lord GOD: "I will cause a stormy wind to break forth in My fury; and there shall be a flooding rain in My anger, and great hailstones in fury to consume *it*. 14So I will break down the wall you have plastered with untempered *mortar*, and bring it down to the ground,

so that its foundation will be uncovered; it will fall, and you shall be consumed in the midst of it. Then you shall know that I *am* the LORD.

15"Thus will I accomplish My wrath on the wall and on those who have plastered it with untempered *mortar;* and I will say to you, 'The wall *is* no *more*, nor those who plastered it, 16*that is,* the prophets of Israel who prophesy concerning Jerusalem, and who see visions of peace for her when *there is* no peace,' " says the Lord GOD.

17"Likewise, son of man, set your face against the daughters of your people, who prophesy out of their own heart; prophesy against them, 18and say, 'Thus says the Lord GOD: "Woe to the *women* who sew *magic* charms on their sleeves and make veils for the heads of people of every height to hunt souls! Will you hunt the souls of My people, and keep yourselves alive? 19And will you profane Me among My people for handfuls of barley and for pieces of bread, killing people who should not die, and keeping people alive who should not live, by your lying to My people who listen to lies?"

20'Therefore thus says the Lord GOD: "Behold, I *am* against your *magic* charms by which you hunt souls there like birds. I will tear them from your arms, and let the souls go, the souls you hunt like birds. 21I will also tear off your veils and deliver My people out of your hand, and they shall no longer be as prey in your hand. Then you shall know that I *am* the LORD.

22"Because with lies you have made the heart of the righteous sad, whom I have not made sad; and you have strengthened the hands of the wicked, so that he does not turn from his wicked way to save his life. 23Therefore you shall no longer envision futility nor practice divination; for I will deliver My people out of your hand, and you shall know that I *am* the LORD." ' "

Idolatry Will Be Punished

14 Now some of the elders of Israel came to me and sat before me. 2And the word of the LORD came to me, saying, 3"Son of man, these men have set up their idols in their hearts, and put before them that which causes them to stumble into iniquity. Should I let Myself be inquired of at all by them?

4"Therefore speak to them, and say to them, 'Thus says the Lord GOD: "Everyone of the house of Israel who sets up his idols in his heart, and puts before him what causes him to stumble into iniquity, and then comes to the prophet, I the LORD will answer him who comes, according to the multitude of his idols, 5that I may seize the house of Israel by their heart, because they are all estranged from Me by their idols." '

6"Therefore say to the house of Israel, 'Thus says the Lord GOD: "Repent, turn away from your idols, and turn your faces away from all your abominations. 7For anyone of the house of Israel, or of the strangers who dwell in Israel, who separates himself from Me and sets up his idols in his heart and puts before him what causes him to stumble into iniquity, then comes to a prophet to inquire of him concerning Me, I the LORD will answer him by Myself. 8I will set My face against that man and make him a sign and a proverb, and I will cut him off from the midst of My people. Then you shall know that I am the LORD.

9"And if the prophet is induced to speak anything, I the LORD have induced that prophet, and I will stretch out My hand against him and destroy him from among My people Israel. 10And they shall bear their iniquity; the punishment of the prophet shall be the same as the punishment of the one who inquired, 11that the house of Israel may no longer stray from Me, nor be profaned anymore with all their transgressions, but that they may be My people and I may be their God," says the Lord GOD.' "

Judgment on Persistent Unfaithfulness

12The word of the LORD came again to me, saying: 13"Son of man, when a land sins against Me by persistent unfaithfulness, I will stretch out My hand against it; I will cut off its supply of bread, send famine on it, and cut off man and beast from it. 14Even if these three men, Noah, Daniel, and Job, were in it, they would deliver only themselves by their righteousness," says the Lord GOD.

15"If I cause wild beasts to pass through the land, and they empty it, and make it so desolate that no man may pass through because of the beasts, 16even though these three men were in it, as I live," says the Lord GOD, "they would deliver neither sons nor daughters; only they would be delivered, and the land would be desolate.

17"Or if I bring a sword on that land, and say, 'Sword, go through the land,' and I cut off man and beast from it, 18even though these three men were in it, as I live," says the Lord GOD, "they would deliver neither sons nor daughters, but only they themselves would be delivered.

19"Or if I send a pestilence into that land and pour out My fury on it in blood, and cut off from it man and beast, 20even though Noah, Daniel, and Job were in it, as I live," says the Lord GOD, "they would deliver neither son nor daughter; they would deliver only themselves by their righteousness."

21For thus says the Lord GOD: "How much more it shall be when I send My four severe judgments on Jerusalem—the sword and famine and wild beasts and pestilence—to cut off man and beast from it? 22Yet behold, there shall be left in it a remnant who will be brought out, both sons and daughters; surely they will come out to you, and you will see their ways and their doings. Then you will be comforted concerning the disaster that I have brought upon Jerusalem, all that I have brought upon it. 23And they will comfort you, when you see their ways and their doings; and you shall know that I have done nothing without cause that I have done in it," says the Lord GOD.

The Outcast Vine

15 Then the word of the LORD came to me, saying: 2"Son of man, how is the wood of the vine better than any other wood, the vine branch which is among the trees of the forest? 3Is wood taken from it to make any object? Or can men make a peg from it to hang any vessel on? 4Instead, it is thrown into the fire for fuel; the fire devours both ends of it, and its middle is burned. Is it useful for any work? 5Indeed, when it was whole, no object could be made

from it. How much less will it be useful for *any* work when the fire has devoured it, and it is burned?

6"Therefore thus says the Lord GOD: 'Like the wood of the vine among the trees of the forest, which I have given to the fire for fuel, so I will give up the inhabitants of Jerusalem; 7and I will set My face against them. They will go out from *one* fire, but *another* fire shall devour them. Then you shall know that I *am* the LORD, when I set My face against them. 8Thus I will make the land desolate, because they have persisted in unfaithfulness,' says the Lord GOD."

God's Love for Jerusalem

16 Again the word of the LORD came to me, saying, 2"Son of man, cause Jerusalem to know her abominations, 3and say, 'Thus says the Lord GOD to Jerusalem: "Your birth and your nativity *are* from the land of Canaan; your father *was* an Amorite and your mother a Hittite. 4*As for* your nativity, on the day you were born your navel cord was not cut, nor were you washed in water to cleanse *you;* you were not rubbed with salt nor wrapped in swaddling cloths. 5No eye pitied you, to do any of these things for you, to have compassion on you; but you were thrown out into the open field, when you yourself were loathed on the day you were born.

6"And when I passed by you and saw you struggling in your own blood, I said to you in your blood, 'Live!' Yes, I said to you in your blood, 'Live!' 7I made you thrive like a plant in the field; and you grew, matured, and became very beautiful. *Your* breasts were formed, your hair grew, but you *were* naked and bare.

8"When I passed by you again and looked upon you, indeed your time *was* the time of love; so I spread My wing over you and covered your nakedness. Yes, I swore an oath to you and entered into a covenant with you, and you became Mine," says the Lord GOD.

9"Then I washed you in water; yes, I thoroughly washed off your blood, and I anointed you with oil. 10I clothed you in embroidered cloth and gave you sandals of badger skin; I clothed you with fine linen and covered you with silk.

11I adorned you with ornaments, put bracelets on your wrists, and a chain on your neck. 12And I put a jewel in your nose, earrings in your ears, and a beautiful crown on your head. 13Thus you were adorned with gold and silver, and your clothing *was of* fine linen, silk, and embroidered cloth. You ate *pastry of* fine flour, honey, and oil. You were exceedingly beautiful, and succeeded to royalty. 14Your fame went out among the nations because of your beauty, for it *was* perfect through My splendor which I had bestowed on you," says the Lord GOD.

Jerusalem's Harlotry

15"But you trusted in your own beauty, played the harlot because of your fame, and poured out your harlotry on everyone passing by who *would have* it. 16You took some of your garments and adorned multicolored high places for yourself, and played the harlot on them. *Such* things should not happen, nor be. 17You have also taken your beautiful jewelry from My gold and My silver, which I had given you, and made for yourself male images and played the harlot with them. 18You took your embroidered garments and covered them, and you set My oil and My incense before them. 19Also My food which I gave you—the pastry of fine flour, oil, and honey *which* I fed you— you set it before them as sweet incense; and *so* it was," says the Lord GOD.

20"Moreover you took your sons and your daughters, whom you bore to Me, and these you sacrificed to them to be devoured. *Were* your *acts* of harlotry a small matter, 21that you have slain My children and offered them up to them by causing them to pass through *the fire?* 22And in all your abominations and acts of harlotry you did not remember the days of your youth, when you were naked and bare, struggling in your blood.

23"Then it was so, after all your wickedness—'Woe, woe to you!' says the Lord GOD—24*that* you also built for yourself a shrine, and made a high place for yourself in every street. 25You built your high places at the head of every road, and made your beauty to be abhorred. You offered yourself to everyone who passed by, and multiplied your acts of harlotry. 26You also committed harlotry with the Egyptians, your very fleshly neighbors, and increased your acts of harlotry to provoke Me to anger.

27"Behold, therefore, I stretched out My hand against you, diminished your allotment, and gave you up to the will of those who hate you, the daughters of the Philistines, who were ashamed of your lewd behavior. 28You also played the harlot with the Assyrians, because you were insatiable; indeed you played the harlot with them and still were not satisfied. 29Moreover you multiplied your acts of harlotry as far as the land of the trader, Chaldea; and even then you were not satisfied.

30"How degenerate is your heart!" says the Lord GOD, "seeing you do all these *things*, the deeds of a brazen harlot.

Jerusalem's Adultery

31"You erected your shrine at the head of every road, and built your high place in every street. Yet you were not like a harlot, because you scorned payment. 32*You are* an adulterous wife, *who* takes strangers instead of her husband. 33Men make payment to all harlots, but you made your payments to all your lovers, and hired them to come to you from all around for your harlotry. 34You are the opposite of *other* women in your harlotry, because no one solicited you to be a harlot. In that you gave payment but no payment was given you, therefore you are the opposite."

Jerusalem's Lovers Will Abuse Her

35'Now then, O harlot, hear the word of the LORD! 36Thus says the Lord GOD: "Because your filthiness was poured out and your nakedness uncovered in your harlotry with your lovers, and with all your abominable idols, and because of the blood of your children which you gave to them, 37surely, therefore, I will gather all your lovers with whom you took pleasure, all those you loved, *and* all those you hated; I will gather them from all around against you and will uncover your nakedness to them, that they may see all your

nakedness. 38And I will judge you as women who break wedlock or shed blood are judged; I will bring blood upon you in fury and jealousy. 39I will also give you into their hand, and they shall throw down your shrines and break down your high places. They shall also strip you of your clothes, take your beautiful jewelry, and leave you naked and bare.

40"They shall also bring up an assembly against you, and they shall stone you with stones and thrust you through with their swords. 41They shall burn your houses with fire, and execute judgments on you in the sight of many women; and I will make you cease playing the harlot, and you shall no longer hire lovers. 42So I will lay to rest My fury toward you, and My jealousy shall depart from you. I will be quiet, and be angry no more. 43Because you did not remember the days of your youth, but agitated Me with all these *things*, surely I will also recompense your deeds on *your own* head," says the Lord GOD. "And you shall not commit lewdness in addition to all your abominations.

More Wicked than Samaria and Sodom

44"Indeed everyone who quotes proverbs will use *this* proverb against you: 'Like mother, like daughter!' 45You *are* your mother's daughter, loathing husband and children; and you *are* the sister of your sisters, who loathed their husbands and children; your mother *was* a Hittite and your father an Amorite.

46"Your elder sister *is* Samaria, who dwells with her daughters to the north of you; and your younger sister, who dwells to the south of you, *is* Sodom and her daughters. 47You did not walk in their ways nor act according to their abominations; but, as *if that were* too little, you became more corrupt than they in all your ways.

48"*As* I live," says the Lord GOD, "neither your sister Sodom nor her daughters have done as you and your daughters have done. 49Look, this was the iniquity of your sister Sodom: She and her daughter had pride, fullness of food, and abundance of idleness; neither did she strengthen the hand of the poor and needy. 50And they were haughty and committed abomination before Me; therefore I took them away as I saw *fit*.

51"Samaria did not commit half of your sins; but you have multiplied your abominations more than they, and have justified your sisters by all the abominations which you have done. 52You who judged your sisters, bear your own shame also, because the sins which you committed were more abominable than theirs; they are more righteous than you. Yes, be disgraced also, and bear your own shame, because you justified your sisters.

53"When I bring back their captives, the captives of Sodom and her daughters, and the captives of Samaria and her daughters, then *I will also bring back* the captives of your captivity among them, 54that you may bear your own shame and be disgraced by all that you did when you comforted them. 55When your sisters, Sodom and her daughters, return to their former state, and Samaria and her daughters return to their former state, then you and your daughters will return to your former state. 56For your sister Sodom was not a byword in your mouth in the days of your pride, 57before your wickedness was uncovered. It was like the time of the reproach of the daughters of Syria and all *those* around her, and of the daughters of the Philistines, who despise you everywhere. 58You have paid for your lewdness and your abominations," says the LORD. 59For thus says the Lord GOD: "I will deal with you as you have done, who despised the oath by breaking the covenant.

An Everlasting Covenant

60"Nevertheless I will remember My covenant with you in the days of your youth, and I will establish an everlasting covenant with you. 61Then you will remember your ways and be ashamed, when you receive your older and your younger sisters; for I will give them to you for daughters, but not because of My covenant with you. 62And I will establish My covenant with you. Then you shall know that I *am* the LORD, 63that you may remember and be ashamed, and never open your mouth anymore because of your shame, when

I provide you an atonement for all you have done," says the Lord GOD.' "

The Eagles and the Vine

17 And the word of the LORD came to me, saying, 2"Son of man, pose a riddle, and speak a parable to the house of Israel, 3and say, 'Thus says the Lord GOD:

"A great eagle with large wings and
        long pinions,
Full of feathers of various colors,
Came to Lebanon
And took from the cedar the
        highest branch.
4   He cropped off its topmost young
        twig
And carried it to a land of trade;
He set it in a city of merchants.
5   Then he took some of the seed of
        the land
And planted it in a fertile field;
He placed *it* by abundant waters
And set it like a willow tree.
6   And it grew and became a
        spreading vine of low stature;
Its branches turned toward him,
But its roots were under it.
So it became a vine,
Brought forth branches,
And put forth shoots.

7   "But there was another great eagle
        with large wings and many
        feathers;
And behold, this vine bent its roots
        toward him,
And stretched its branches toward
        him,
From the garden terrace where it
        had been planted,
That he might water it.
8   It was planted in good soil by many
        waters,
To bring forth branches, bear fruit,
And become a majestic vine." '
9"Say, 'Thus says the Lord GOD:
"Will it thrive?
Will he not pull up its roots,
Cut off its fruit,
And leave it to wither?
All of its spring leaves will wither,
And no great power or many
        people
Will be needed to pluck it up by its
        roots.
10   Behold, *it is* planted,

Will it thrive?
Will it not utterly wither when the
  east wind touches it?
It will wither in the garden terrace
  where it grew.'''"

11Moreover the word of the LORD
came to me, saying, 12"Say now to the
rebellious house: 'Do you not know
what these *things mean?*' Tell *them,* 'Indeed the king of Babylon went to Jerusalem and took its king and princes,
and led them with him to Babylon.
13And he took the king's offspring,
made a covenant with him, and put him
under oath. He also took away the
mighty of the land, 14that the kingdom
might be brought low and not lift itself
up, *but* that by keeping his covenant it
might stand. 15But he rebelled against
him by sending his ambassadors to
Egypt, that they might give him horses
and many people. Will he prosper? Will
he who does such *things* escape? Can
he break a covenant and still be delivered?

16'*As* I live,' says the Lord GOD,
'surely in the place *where* the king
dwells who made him king, whose oath
he despised and whose covenant he
broke—with him in the midst of Babylon he shall die. 17Nor will Pharaoh
with *his* mighty army and great company do anything in the war, when they
heap up a siege mound and build a wall
to cut off many persons. 18Since he despised the oath by breaking the covenant, and in fact gave his hand and still
did all these *things,* he shall not escape.'"

19Therefore thus says the Lord GOD:
"*As* I live, surely My oath which he despised, and My covenant which he
broke, I will recompense on his own
head. 20I will spread My net over him,
and he shall be taken in My snare. I
will bring him to Babylon and try him
there for the treason which he committed against Me. 21All his fugitives with
all his troops shall fall by the sword,
and those who remain shall be scattered to every wind; and you shall know
that I, the LORD, have spoken."

Israel Exalted at Last

22Thus says the Lord GOD: "I will take
also *one* of the highest branches of the
high cedar and set *it* out. I will crop

off from the topmost of its young twigs
a tender one, and will plant *it* on a high
and prominent mountain. 23On the
mountain height of Israel I will plant
it; and it will bring forth boughs, and
bear fruit, and be a majestic cedar. Under it will dwell birds of every sort; in
the shadow of its branches they will
dwell. 24And all the trees of the field
shall know that I, the LORD, have
brought down the high tree and exalted
the low tree, dried up the green tree and
made the dry tree flourish; I, the LORD,
have spoken and have done *it.*"

A False Proverb Refuted

18 The word of the LORD came to me
again, saying, 2"What do you
mean when you use this proverb concerning the land of Israel, saying:

'The fathers have eaten sour
  grapes,
And the children's teeth are set on
  edge'?

3"*As* I live," says the Lord GOD, "you
shall no longer use this proverb in
Israel.
4   "Behold, all souls are Mine;
    The soul of the father
    As well as the soul of the son is
      Mine;
    The soul who sins shall die.
5   But if a man is just
    And does what is lawful and
      right;
6   If he has not eaten on the
      mountains,
    Nor lifted up his eyes to the idols
      of the house of Israel,
    Nor defiled his neighbor's wife,
    Nor approached a woman during
      her impurity;
7   If he has not oppressed anyone,
    But has restored to the debtor his
      pledge;
    Has robbed no one by violence,
    But has given his bread to the
      hungry
    And covered the naked with
      clothing;
8   If he has not exacted usury
    Nor taken any increase,
    But has withdrawn his hand from
      iniquity
    And executed true judgment
      between man and man;
9   *If* he has walked in My statutes

And kept My judgments
  faithfully—
He *is* just;
He shall surely live!"
Says the Lord GOD.

10 "If he begets a son *who is* a robber
  Or a shedder of blood,
  Who does any of these *things*
11   And does none of those *duties,*
  But has eaten on the mountains
  Or defiled his neighbor's wife;
12   If he has oppressed the poor and
    needy,
  Robbed by violence,
  Not restored the pledge,
  Lifted his eyes to the idols,
  Or committed abomination;
13   If he has exacted usury
  Or taken increase—
  Shall he then live?
  He shall not live!
  If he has done any of these
    abominations,
  He shall surely die;
  His blood shall be upon him.

14 "*If*, however, he begets a son
  Who sees all the sins which his
    father has done,
  And considers but does not do
    likewise;
15   *Who* has not eaten on the
    mountains,
  Nor lifted his eyes to the idols of
    the house of Israel,
  Nor defiled his neighbor's wife;
16   Has not oppressed anyone,
  Nor withheld a pledge,
  Nor robbed by violence,
  But has given his bread to the
    hungry
  And covered the naked with
    clothing;
17   *Who* has withdrawn his hand from
    the poor
  And not received usury or increase,
  But has executed My judgments
  And walked in My statutes—
  He shall not die for the iniquity of
    his father;
  He shall surely live!

18 "*As for* his father,
  Because he cruelly oppressed,
  Robbed his brother by violence,

And did what *is* not good among
  his people,
Behold, he shall die for his
  iniquity.

Turn and Live

19"Yet you say, 'Why should the son not bear the guilt of the father?' Because the son has done what is lawful and right, and has kept all My statutes and observed them, he shall surely live. 20The soul who sins shall die. The son shall not bear the guilt of the father, nor the father bear the guilt of the son. The righteousness of the righteous shall be upon himself, and the wickedness of the wicked shall be upon himself.

21"But if a wicked man turns from all his sins which he has committed, keeps all My statutes, and does what is lawful and right, he shall surely live; he shall not die. 22None of the transgressions which he has committed shall be remembered against him; because of the righteousness which he has done, he shall live. 23Do I have any pleasure at all that the wicked should die?" says the Lord GOD, "*and* not that he should turn from his ways and live?

24"But when a righteous man turns away from his righteousness and commits iniquity, and does according to all the abominations that the wicked *man* does, shall he live? All the righteousness which he has done shall not be remembered; because of the unfaithfulness of which he is guilty and the sin which he has committed, because of them he shall die.

25"Yet you say, 'The way of the Lord is not fair.' Hear now, O house of Israel, is it not My way which is fair, and your ways which are not fair? 26When a righteous *man* turns away from his righteousness, commits iniquity, and dies in it, it is because of the iniquity which he has done that he dies. 27Again, when a wicked *man* turns away from the wickedness which he committed, and does what is lawful and right, he preserves himself alive. 28Because he considers and turns away from all the transgressions which he committed, he shall surely live; he shall not die. 29Yet the house of Israel says, 'The way of the Lord is not fair.' O house of Israel, is it not My ways which are fair, and your ways which are not fair?

30"Therefore I will judge you, O house of Israel, every one according to his ways," says the Lord GOD. "Repent, and turn from all your transgressions, so that iniquity will not be your ruin. **31**Cast away from you all the transgressions which you have committed, and get yourselves a new heart and a new spirit. For why should you die, O house of Israel? **32**For I have no pleasure in the death of one who dies," says the Lord GOD. "Therefore turn and live!"

Israel Degraded

19 "Moreover take up a lamentation for the princes of Israel, ²and say:
'What *is* your mother? A lioness:
She lay down among the lions;
Among the young lions she
    nourished her cubs.

3   She brought up one of her cubs,
    And he became a young lion;
    He learned to catch prey,
    And he devoured men.
4   The nations also heard of him;
    He was trapped in their pit,
    And they brought him with chains
      to the land of Egypt.

5   'When she saw that she waited, *that*
      her hope was lost,
    She took another of her cubs *and*
      made him a young lion.
6   He roved among the lions,
    And became a young lion;
    He learned to catch prey;
    He devoured men.
7   He knew their desolate places,
    And laid waste their cities;
    The land with its fullness was
      desolated
    By the noise of his roaring.
8   Then the nations set against him
      from the provinces on every side,
    And spread their net over him;
    He was trapped in their pit.
9   They put him in a cage with chains,
    And brought him to the king of
      Babylon;
    They brought him in nets,
    That his voice should no longer be
      heard on the mountains of Israel.

10 'Your mother *was* like a vine in your
      bloodline,

    Planted by the waters,
    Fruitful and full of branches
    Because of many waters.
11 She had strong branches for
      scepters of rulers.
    She towered in stature above the
      thick branches,
    And was seen in her height amid
      the dense foliage.
12 But she was plucked up in fury,
    She was cast down to the ground,
    And the east wind dried her fruit.
    Her strong branches were broken
      and withered;
    The fire consumed them.
13 And now she *is* planted in the
      wilderness,
    In a dry and thirsty land.
14 Fire has come out from a rod of her
      branches
    And devoured her fruit,
    So that she has no strong branch—
      a scepter for ruling.' "

This *is* a lamentation, and has become a lamentation.

The Rebellions of Israel

20 It came to pass in the seventh year, in the fifth *month*, on the tenth *day* of the month, *that* certain of the elders of Israel came to inquire of the LORD, and sat before me. ²Then the word of the LORD came to me, saying, ³"Son of man, speak to the elders of Israel, and say to them, 'Thus says the Lord GOD: "Have you come to inquire of Me? *As* I live," says the Lord GOD, "I will not be inquired of by you." ' ⁴Will you judge them, son of man, will you judge *them*? Then make known to them the abominations of their fathers. ⁵"Say to them, 'Thus says the Lord GOD: "On the day when I chose Israel and raised My hand in an oath to the descendants of the house of Jacob, and made Myself known to them in the land of Egypt, I raised My hand in an oath to them, saying, 'I *am* the LORD your God.' ⁶On that day I raised My hand in an oath to them, to bring them out of the land of Egypt into a land that I had searched out for them, 'flowing with milk and honey,' the glory of all lands. ⁷Then I said to them, 'Each of you, throw away the abominations which are before his eyes, and do not defile yourselves with the idols of

Egypt. I *am* the Lord your God.' 8But they rebelled against Me and would not obey Me. They did not all cast away the abominations which were before their eyes, nor did they forsake the idols of Egypt. Then I said, 'I will pour out My fury on them and fulfill My anger against them in the midst of the land of Egypt.' 9But I acted for My name's sake, that it should not be profaned before the Gentiles among whom they *were,* in whose sight I had made Myself known to them, to bring them out of the land of Egypt.

10"Therefore I made them go out of the land of Egypt and brought them into the wilderness. 11And I gave them My statutes and showed them My judgments, 'which, *if* a man does, he shall live by them.'*a* 12Moreover I also gave them My Sabbaths, to be a sign between them and Me, that they might know that I *am* the Lord who sanctifies them. 13Yet the house of Israel rebelled against Me in the wilderness; they did not walk in My statutes; they despised My judgments, 'which, *if* a man does, he shall live by them'; and they greatly defiled My Sabbaths. Then I said I would pour out My fury on them in the wilderness, to consume them. 14But I acted for My name's sake, that it should not be profaned before the Gentiles, in whose sight I had brought them out. 15So I also raised My hand in an oath to them in the wilderness, that I would not bring them into the land which I had given *them,* 'flowing with milk and honey,' the glory of all lands, 16because they despised My judgments and did not walk in My statutes, but profaned My Sabbaths; for their heart went after their idols. 17Nevertheless My eye spared them from destruction. I did not make an end of them in the wilderness.

18"But I said to their children in the wilderness, 'Do not walk in the statutes of your fathers, nor observe their judgments, nor defile yourselves with their idols. 19I *am* the Lord your God: Walk in My statutes, keep My judgments, and do them; 20hallow My Sabbaths, and they will be a sign between Me and you, that you may know that I *am* the Lord your God.'

21"Notwithstanding, the children rebelled against Me; they did not walk in My statutes, and were not careful to observe My judgments, 'which, *if* a man does, he shall live by them';*a* but they profaned My Sabbaths. Then I said I would pour out My fury on them and fulfill My anger against them in the wilderness. 22Nevertheless I withdrew My hand and acted for My name's sake, that it should not be profaned in the sight of the Gentiles, in whose sight I had brought them out. 23Also I raised My hand in an oath to those in the wilderness, that I would scatter them among the Gentiles and disperse them throughout the countries, 24because they had not executed My judgments, but had despised My statutes, profaned My Sabbaths, and their eyes were fixed on their fathers' idols.

25"Therefore I also gave them up to statutes *that were* not good, and judgments by which they could not live; 26and I pronounced them unclean because of their ritual gifts, in that they caused all their firstborn to pass through *the fire,* that I might make them desolate and that they might know that I am the Lord."'

27"Therefore, son of man, speak to the house of Israel, and say to them, 'Thus says the Lord God: "In this too your fathers have blasphemed Me, by being unfaithful to Me. 28When I brought them into the land *concerning* which I had raised My hand in an oath to give them, and they saw all the high hills and all the thick trees, there they offered their sacrifices and provoked Me with their offerings. There they also sent up their sweet aroma and poured out their drink offerings. 29Then I said to them, 'What *is* this high place to which you go?' So its name is called Bamah*b* to this day."' 30Therefore say to the house of Israel, 'Thus says the Lord God: "Are you defiling yourselves in the manner of your fathers, and committing harlotry according to their abominations? 31For when you offer your gifts and make your sons pass through the fire, you defile yourselves with all your idols, even to this day. So shall I be inquired of by you, O house

---

a Leviticus 18.5   *b* Literally *High Place*

of Israel? *As* I live," says the Lord GOD, "I will not be inquired of by you. 32What you have in your mind shall never be, when you say, 'We will be like the Gentiles, like the families in other countries, serving wood and stone.'

God Will Restore Israel

33"*As* I live," says the Lord GOD, "surely with a mighty hand, with an outstretched arm, and with fury poured out, I will rule over you. 34I will bring you out from the peoples and gather you out of the countries where you are scattered, with a mighty hand, with an outstretched arm, and with fury poured out. 35And I will bring you into the wilderness of the peoples, and there I will plead My case with you face to face. 36Just as I pleaded My case with your fathers in the wilderness of the land of Egypt, so I will plead My case with you," says the Lord GOD.

37"I will make you pass under the rod, and I will bring you into the bond of the covenant; 38I will purge the rebels from among you, and those who transgress against Me; I will bring them out of the country where they dwell, but they shall not enter the land of Israel. Then you will know that I *am* the LORD.

39"As for you, O house of Israel," thus says the Lord GOD: "Go, serve every one of you his idols—and hereafter—if you will not obey Me; but profane My holy name no more with your gifts and your idols. 40For on My holy mountain, on the mountain height of Israel," says the Lord GOD, "there all the house of Israel, all of them in the land, shall serve Me; there I will accept them, and there I will require your offerings and the firstfruits of your sacrifices, together with all your holy things. 41I will accept you as a sweet aroma when I bring you out from the peoples and gather you out of the countries where you have been scattered; and I will be hallowed in you before the Gentiles. 42Then you shall know that I *am* the LORD, when I bring you into the land of Israel, into the country *for* which I raised My hand in an oath to give to your fathers. 43And there you shall remember your ways and all your doings with which you were defiled; and you shall loathe yourselves in your own

sight because of all the evils that you have committed. 44Then you shall know that I *am* the LORD, when I have dealt with you for My name's sake, not according to your wicked ways nor according to your corrupt doings, O house of Israel," says the Lord GOD.' "

Fire in the Forest

45Furthermore the word of the LORD came to me, saying, 46"Son of man, set your face toward the south; preach against the south and prophesy against the forest land, the South, 47and say to the forest of the South, 'Hear the word of the LORD! Thus says the Lord GOD: "Behold, I will kindle a fire in you, and it shall devour every green tree and every dry tree in you; the blazing flame shall not be quenched, and all faces from the south to the north shall be scorched by it. 48All flesh shall see that I, the LORD, have kindled it; it shall not be quenched." ' "

49Then I said, "Ah, Lord GOD! They say of me, 'Does he not speak parables?' "

Babylon, the Sword of God

21 And the word of the LORD came to me, saying, 2"Son of man, set your face toward Jerusalem, preach against the holy places, and prophesy against the land of Israel; 3and say to the land of Israel, 'Thus says the LORD: "Behold, I *am* against you, and I will draw My sword out of its sheath and cut off both righteous and wicked from you. 4Because I will cut off both righteous and wicked from you, therefore My sword shall go out of its sheath against all flesh from south *to* north, 5that all flesh may know that I, the LORD, have drawn My sword out of its sheath; it shall not return anymore." ' 6Sigh therefore, son of man, with a breaking heart, and sigh with bitterness before their eyes. 7And it shall be when they say to you, 'Why are you sighing?' that you shall answer, 'Because of the news; when it comes, every heart will melt, all hands will be feeble, every spirit will faint, and all knees will be weak *as* water. Behold, it is coming and shall be brought to pass,' says the Lord GOD."

8Again the word of the LORD came

to me, saying, [9]"Son of man, prophesy and say, 'Thus says the LORD!' Say:

'A sword, a sword is sharpened
And also polished!
10   Sharpened to make a dreadful
      slaughter,
   Polished to flash like lightning!
   Should we then make mirth?
   It despises the scepter of My son,
   As it does all wood.
11   And He has given it to be polished,
   That it may be handled;
   This sword is sharpened, and it is
      polished
   To be given into the hand of the
      slayer.'

12 "Cry and wail, son of man;
   For it will be against My people,
   Against all the princes of Israel.
   Terrors including the sword will be
      against My people;
   Therefore strike *your* thigh.

13 "Because *it is* a testing,
   And what if *the sword* despises
      even the scepter?
   The scepter shall be no *more*,"
says the Lord GOD.
14 "You therefore, son of man,
      prophesy,
   And strike *your* hands together.
   The third time let the sword do
      double *damage.*
   It *is* the sword *that* slays,
   The sword that slays the great *men,*
   That enters their private chambers.
15 I have set the point of the sword
      against all their gates,
   That the heart may melt and many
      may stumble.
   Ah! *It is* made bright;
   It is grasped for slaughter:

16 "Swords at the ready!
   Thrust right!
   Set your blade!
   Thrust left—
   Wherever your edge is ordered!

17 "I also will beat My fists together,
   And I will cause My fury to rest;
   I, the LORD, have spoken."

18The word of the LORD came to me again, saying: [19]"And son of man, appoint for yourself two ways for the sword of the king of Babylon to go; both of them shall go from the same land. Make a sign; put *it* at the head of the road to the city. [20]Appoint a road for the sword to go to Rabbah of the Ammonites, and to Judah, into fortified Jerusalem. [21]For the king of Babylon stands at the parting of the road, at the fork of the two roads, to use divination: he shakes the arrows, he consults the images, he looks at the liver. [22]In his right hand is the divination for Jerusalem: to set up battering rams, to call for a slaughter, to lift the voice with shouting, to set battering rams against the gates, to heap up a *siege* mound, and to build a wall. [23]And it will be to them like a false divination in the eyes of those who have sworn oaths with them; but he will bring their iniquity to remembrance, that they may be taken.

[24]"Therefore thus says the Lord GOD: 'Because you have made your iniquity to be remembered, in that your transgressions are uncovered, so that in all your doings your sins appear—because you have come to remembrance, you shall be taken in hand.

[25]'Now to you, O profane, wicked prince of Israel, whose day has come, whose iniquity *shall* end, [26]thus says the Lord GOD:

"Remove the turban, and take off the
   crown;
   Nothing *shall remain* the same.
   Exalt the humble, and humble the
      exalted.
27 Overthrown, overthrown,
   I will make it overthrown!
   It shall be no *longer*,
   Until He comes whose right it is,
   And I will give it *to Him.*"'

A Sword Against the Ammonites

[28]"And you, son of man, prophesy and say, 'Thus says the Lord GOD concerning the Ammonites and concerning their reproach,' and say:

'A sword, a sword *is* drawn,
   Polished for slaughter,
   For consuming, for flashing—
29 While they see false visions for you,
   While they divine a lie to you,
   To bring you on the necks of the
      wicked, the slain

Whose day has come,
Whose iniquity *shall* end.

30 'Return *it* to its sheath.
I will judge you
In the place where you were
   created,
In the land of your nativity.
31 I will pour out My indignation
      on you;
I will blow against you with the fire
   of My wrath,
And deliver you into the hands of
   brutal men *who are* skillful to
   destroy.
32 You shall be fuel for the fire;
Your blood shall be in the midst of
   the land.
You shall not be remembered,
For I the LORD have spoken.' "

Sins of Jerusalem

22 Moreover the word of the LORD came to me, saying, 2"Now, son of man, will you judge, will you judge the bloody city? Yes, show her all her abominations! 3Then say, 'Thus says the Lord GOD: "The city sheds blood in her own midst, that her time may come; and she makes idols within herself to defile herself. 4You have become guilty by the blood which you have shed, and have defiled yourself with the idols which you have made. You have caused your days to draw near, and have come to *the end of* your years; therefore I have made you a reproach to the nations, and a mockery to all countries. 5*Those* near and *those* far from you will mock you as infamous *and* full of tumult.

6"Look, the princes of Israel: each one has used his power to shed blood in you. 7In you they have made light of father and mother; in your midst they have oppressed the stranger; in you they have mistreated the fatherless and the widow. 8You have despised My holy things and profaned My Sabbaths. 9In you are men who slander to cause bloodshed; in you are those who eat on the mountains; in your midst they commit lewdness. 10In you men uncover their fathers' nakedness; in you they violate women who are set apart during their impurity. 11One commits abomination with his neighbor's wife; another

lewdly defiles his daughter-in-law; and another in you violates his sister, his father's daughter. 12In you they take bribes to shed blood; you take usury and increase; you have made profit from your neighbors by extortion, and have forgotten Me," says the Lord GOD.

13"Behold, therefore, I beat My fists at the dishonest profit which you have made, and at the bloodshed which has been in your midst. 14Can your heart endure, or can your hands remain strong, in the days when I shall deal with you? I, the LORD, have spoken, and will do *it*. 15I will scatter you among the nations, disperse you throughout the countries, and remove your filthiness completely from you. 16You shall defile yourself in the sight of the nations; then you shall know that I *am* the LORD." ' "

Israel in the Furnace

17The word of the LORD came to me, saying, 18"Son of man, the house of Israel has become dross to Me; they *are* all bronze, tin, iron, and lead, in the midst of a furnace; they have become dross from silver. 19Therefore thus says the Lord GOD: 'Because you have all become dross, therefore behold, I will gather you into the midst of Jerusalem. 20*As men* gather silver, bronze, iron, lead, and tin into the midst of a furnace, to blow fire on it, to melt *it;* so I will gather *you* in My anger and in My fury, and I will leave *you there* and melt you. 21Yes, I will gather you and blow on you with the fire of My wrath, and you shall be melted in its midst. 22As silver is melted in the midst of a furnace, so shall you be melted in its midst; then you shall know that I, the LORD, have poured out My fury on you.' "

Israel's Wicked Leaders

23And the word of the LORD came to me, saying, 24"Son of man, say to her: 'You *are* a land that is not cleansed or rained on in the day of indignation.' 25The conspiracy of her prophets in her midst is like a roaring lion tearing the prey; they have devoured people; they have taken treasure and precious things; they have made many widows in her midst. 26Her priests have violated

My law and profaned My holy things; they have not distinguished between the holy and unholy, nor have they made known *the difference* between the unclean and the clean; and they have hidden their eyes from My Sabbaths, so that I am profaned among them. 27Her princes in her midst *are* like wolves tearing the prey, to shed blood, to destroy people, and to get dishonest gain. 28Her prophets plastered them with untempered *mortar*, seeing false visions, and divining lies for them, saying, 'Thus says the Lord GOD,' when the LORD had not spoken. 29The people of the land have used oppressions, committed robbery, and mistreated the poor and needy; and they wrongfully oppress the stranger. 30So I sought for a man among them who would make a wall, and stand in the gap before Me on behalf of the land, that I should not destroy it; but I found no one. 31Therefore I have poured out My indignation on them; I have consumed them with the fire of My wrath; and I have recompensed their deeds on their own heads," says the Lord GOD.

Two Harlot Sisters

23 The word of the LORD came again to me, saying:
2 "Son of man, there were two women,
   The daughters of one mother.
3 They committed harlotry in Egypt,
   They committed harlotry in their youth;
   Their breasts were there embraced,
   Their virgin bosom was there pressed.
4 Their names: Oholah the elder and Oholibah her sister;
   They were Mine,
   And they bore sons and daughters.
   As for their names,
   Samaria *is* Oholah, and Jerusalem *is* Oholibah.

The Older Sister, Samaria

5 "Oholah played the harlot even though she was Mine;
   And she lusted for her lovers, the neighboring Assyrians,
6 *Who were* clothed in purple,
   Captains and rulers,

All of them desirable young men,
   Horsemen riding on horses.
7 Thus she committed her harlotry with them,
   All of them choice men of Assyria;
   And with all for whom she lusted,
   With all their idols, she defiled herself.
8 She has never given up her harlotry *brought* from Egypt,
   For in her youth they had lain with her,
   Pressed her virgin bosom,
   And poured out their immorality upon her.

9 "Therefore I have delivered her
   Into the hand of her lovers,
   Into the hand of the Assyrians,
   For whom she lusted.
10 They uncovered her nakedness,
   Took away her sons and daughters,
   And slew her with the sword;
   She became a byword among women,
   For they had executed judgment on her.

The Younger Sister, Jerusalem

11"Now although her sister Oholibah saw *this*, she became more corrupt in her lust than she, and in her harlotry more corrupt than her sister's harlotry.
12 "She lusted for the neighboring Assyrians,
   Captains and rulers,
   Clothed most gorgeously,
   Horsemen riding on horses,
   All of them desirable young men.
13 Then I saw that she was defiled;
   Both *took* the same way.
14 But she increased her harlotry;
   She looked at men portrayed on the wall,
   Images of Chaldeans portrayed in vermilion,
15 Girded with belts around their waists,
   Flowing turbans on their heads,
   All of them looking like captains,
   In the manner of the Babylonians of Chaldea,
   The land of their nativity.
16 As soon as her eyes saw them,
   She lusted for them
   And sent messengers to them in Chaldea.

17 "Then the Babylonians came to her,
  into the bed of love,
  And they defiled her with their
  immorality;
  So she was defiled by them, and
  alienated herself from them.
18 She revealed her harlotry and
  uncovered her nakedness.
  Then I alienated Myself from her,
  As I had alienated Myself from her
  sister.

19 "Yet she multiplied her harlotry
  In calling to remembrance the days
  of her youth,
  When she had played the harlot in
  the land of Egypt.
20 For she lusted for her paramours,
  Whose flesh *is like* the flesh of
  donkeys,
  And whose issue *is like* the issue
  of horses.
21 Thus you called to remembrance
  the lewdness of your youth,
  When the Egyptians pressed your
  bosom
  Because of your youthful breasts.

Judgment on Jerusalem

22 "Therefore, Oholibah, thus says the
Lord GOD:
  'Behold, I will stir up your lovers
  against you,
  From whom you have alienated
  yourself,
  And I will bring them against you
  from every side:
23 The Babylonians,
  All the Chaldeans,
  Pekod, Shoa, Koa,
  All the Assyrians with them,
  All of them desirable young men,
  Governors and rulers,
  Captains and men of renown,
  All of them riding on horses.
24 And they shall come against you
  With chariots, wagons, and war-
  horses,
  With a horde of people.
  They shall array against you
  Buckler, shield, and helmet all
  around.

  'I will delegate judgment to them,
  And they shall judge you according
  to their judgments.
25 I will set My jealousy against you,

And they shall deal furiously
  with you;
They shall remove your nose and
  your ears,
And your remnant shall fall by the
  sword;
They shall take your sons and your
  daughters,
And your remnant shall be
  devoured by fire.
26 They shall also strip you of your
  clothes
  And take away your beautiful
  jewelry.

27 'Thus I will make you cease your
  lewdness and your harlotry
  Brought from the land of Egypt,
  So that you will not lift your eyes
  to them,
  Nor remember Egypt anymore.'
28 "For thus says the Lord GOD:
'Surely I will deliver you into the hand
of those you hate, into the hand *of those*
from whom you alienated yourself.
29They will deal hatefully with you,
take away all you have worked for, and
leave you naked and bare. The nakedness of your harlotry shall be uncovered, both your lewdness and your harlotry. 30I will do these *things* to you
because you have gone as a harlot after
the Gentiles, because you have become
defiled by their idols. 31You have
walked in the way of your sister; therefore I will put her cup in your hand.'
32"Thus says the Lord GOD:
  'You shall drink of your sister's cup,
  The deep and wide one;
  You shall be laughed to scorn
  And held in derision;
  It contains much.
33 You will be filled with drunkenness
  and sorrow,
  The cup of horror and desolation,
  The cup of your sister Samaria.
34 You shall drink and drain it,
  You shall break its shards,
  And tear at your own breasts;
  For I have spoken,'
  Says the Lord GOD.
35"Therefore thus says the Lord GOD:
  'Because you have forgotten Me and
  cast Me behind your back,
  Therefore you shall bear the
  penalty

Of your lewdness and your
   harlotry.' "

Both Sisters Judged

36The LORD also said to me: "Son of
man, will you judge Oholah and Oholibah? Then declare to them their
abominations. 37For they have committed adultery, and blood *is* on their
hands. They have committed adultery
with their idols, and even sacrificed
their sons whom they bore to Me, passing them through *the fire,* to devour
them. 38Moreover they have done this
to Me: They have defiled My sanctuary
on the same day and profaned My Sabbaths. 39For after they had slain their
children for their idols, on the same day
they came into My sanctuary to profane
it; and indeed thus they have done in
the midst of My house.

40"Furthermore you sent for men to
come from afar, to whom a messenger
was sent; and there they came. And you
washed yourself for them, painted your
eyes, and adorned yourself with ornaments. 41You sat on a stately couch,
with a table prepared before it, on
which you had set My incense and My
oil. 42The sound of a carefree multitude
was with her, and Sabeans *were*
brought from the wilderness with men
of the common sort, who put bracelets
on their wrists and beautiful crowns on
their heads. 43Then I said concerning
her who had grown old in adulteries,
'Will they commit harlotry with her
now, and she *with them?*' 44Yet they
went in to her, as men go in to a woman
who plays the harlot; thus they went
in to Oholah and Oholibah, the lewd
women. 45But righteous men will judge
them after the manner of adulteresses,
and after the manner of women who
shed blood, because they *are* adulteresses, and blood *is* on their hands.

46"For thus says the Lord GOD: 'Bring
up an assembly against them, give them
up to trouble and plunder. 47The assembly shall stone them with stones and
execute them with their swords; they
shall slay their sons and their daughters, and burn their houses with fire.
48Thus I will cause lewdness to cease
from the land, that all women may be
taught not to practice your lewdness.
49They shall repay you for your lewd-

ness, and you shall pay for your idolatrous sins. Then you shall know that I
am the Lord GOD.' "

Symbol of the Cooking Pot

24 Again, in the ninth year, in the
tenth month, on the tenth *day* of
the month, the word of the LORD came
to me, saying, 2"Son of man, write
down the name of the day, this very
day—the king of Babylon started his
siege against Jerusalem this very day.
3And utter a parable to the rebellious
house, and say to them, 'Thus says the
Lord GOD:

"Put on a pot, set *it* on,
   And also pour water into it.
4   Gather pieces *of meat* in it,
   Every good piece,
   The thigh and the shoulder.
   Fill *it* with choice cuts;
5   Take the choice of the flock.
   Also pile *fuel* bones under it,
   Make it boil well,
   And let the cuts simmer in it."
6'Therefore thus says the Lord GOD:
"Woe to the bloody city,
   To the pot whose scum *is* in it,
   And whose scum is not gone
      from it!
   Bring it out piece by piece,
   On which no lot has fallen.
7   For her blood is in her midst;
   She set it on top of a rock;
   She did not pour it on the ground,
   To cover it with dust.
8   That it may raise up fury and take
      vengeance,
   I have set her blood on top of a
      rock,
   That it may not be covered."
9'Therefore thus says the Lord GOD:
"Woe to the bloody city!
   I too will make the pyre great.
10   Heap on the wood,
   Kindle the fire;
   Cook the meat well,
   Mix in the spices,
   And let the cuts be burned up.

11   "Then set the pot empty on the coals,
   That it may become hot and its
      bronze may burn,
   That its filthiness may be melted
      in it,
   That its scum may be consumed.
12   She has grown weary with lies,

And her great scum has not gone
from her.
Let her scum *be* in the fire!
13 In your filthiness *is* lewdness.
Because I have cleansed you, and
you were not cleansed,
You will not be cleansed of your
filthiness anymore,
Till I have caused My fury to rest
upon you.
14 I, the LORD, have spoken *it;*
It shall come to pass, and I will
do *it;*
I will not hold back,
Nor will I spare,
Nor will I relent;
According to your ways
And according to your deeds
They will judge you,"
Says the Lord GOD.' "

The Prophet's Wife Dies

15Also the word of the LORD came to
me, saying, 16"Son of man, behold, I
take away from you the desire of your
eyes with one stroke; yet you shall neither mourn nor weep, nor shall your
tears run down. 17Sigh in silence, make
no mourning for the dead; bind your
turban on your head, and put your sandals on your feet; do not cover *your* lips,
and do not eat man's bread *of sorrow.*"

18So I spoke to the people in the
morning, and at evening my wife died;
and the next morning I did as I was
commanded.

19And the people said to me, "Will
you not tell us what these *things signify*
to us, that you behave so?"

20Then I answered them, "The word
of the LORD came to me, saying,
21'Speak to the house of Israel, "Thus
says the Lord GOD: 'Behold, I will profane My sanctuary, your arrogant
boast, the desire of your eyes, the delight of your soul; and your sons and
daughters whom you left behind shall
fall by the sword. 22And you shall do
as I have done; you shall not cover *your*
lips nor eat man's bread *of sorrow.*
23Your turbans shall be on your heads
and your sandals on your feet; you shall
neither mourn nor weep, but you shall
pine away in your iniquities and mourn
with one another. 24Thus Ezekiel is a
sign to you; according to all that he has
done you shall do; and when this

comes, you shall know that I *am* the
Lord GOD.' "

25'And you, son of man—*will it* not
be in the day when I take from them
their stronghold, their joy and their
glory, the desire of their eyes, and that
on which they set their minds, their
sons and their daughters: 26on that day
one who escapes will come to you to
let *you* hear *it* with *your* ears; 27on that
day your mouth will be opened to him
who has escaped; you shall speak and
no longer be mute. Thus you will be a
sign to them; and they shall know that
I *am* the LORD.' "

Proclamation Against Ammon

25 The word of the LORD came to me,
saying, 2"Son of man, set your
face against the Ammonites, and
prophesy against them. 3Say to the
Ammonites, 'Hear the word of the Lord
GOD! Thus says the Lord GOD: "Because
you said, 'Aha!' against My sanctuary
when it was profaned, and against the
land of Israel when it was desolate, and
against the house of Judah when they
went into captivity, 4indeed, therefore,
I will deliver you as a possession to the
men of the East, and they shall set their
encampments among you and make
their dwellings among you; they shall
eat your fruit, and they shall drink your
milk. 5And I will make Rabbah a stable
for camels and Ammon a resting place
for flocks. Then you shall know that I
am the LORD."

6'For thus says the Lord GOD: "Because you clapped *your* hands, stamped
your feet, and rejoiced in heart with all
your disdain for the land of Israel,
7indeed, therefore, I will stretch out My
hand against you, and give you as plunder to the nations; I will cut you off from
the peoples, and I will cause you to perish from the countries; I will destroy
you, and you shall know that I *am* the
LORD."

Proclamation Against Moab

8'Thus says the Lord GOD: "Because
Moab and Seir say, 'Look! The house
of Judah *is* like all the nations,'
9therefore, behold, I will clear the territory of Moab of cities, of the cities on
its frontier, the glory of the country,
Beth Jeshimoth, Baal Meon, and Kirja-

thaim. 10To the men of the East I will give it as a possession, together with the Ammonites, that the Ammonites may not be remembered among the nations. 11And I will execute judgments upon Moab, and they shall know that I *am* the LORD."

Proclamation Against Edom

12"Thus says the Lord GOD: "Because of what Edom did against the house of Judah by taking vengeance, and has greatly offended by avenging itself on them," 13therefore thus says the Lord GOD: "I will also stretch out My hand against Edom, cut off man and beast from it, and make it desolate from Teman; Dedan shall fall by the sword. 14I will lay My vengeance on Edom by the hand of My people Israel, that they may do in Edom according to My anger and according to My fury; and they shall know My vengeance," says the Lord GOD.

Proclamation Against Philistia

15"Thus says the Lord GOD: "Because the Philistines dealt vengefully and took vengeance with a spiteful heart, to destroy because of the old hatred," 16therefore thus says the Lord GOD: "I will stretch out My hand against the Philistines, and I will cut off the Cherethites and destroy the remnant of the seacoast. 17I will execute great vengeance on them with furious rebukes; and they shall know that I *am* the LORD, when I lay My vengeance upon them." ' "

Proclamation Against Tyre

26 And it came to pass in the eleventh year, on the first *day* of the month, *that* the word of the LORD came to me, saying, 2"Son of man, because Tyre has said against Jerusalem, 'Aha! She is broken who *was* the gateway of the peoples; now she is turned over to me; I shall be filled; she is laid waste.' 3"Therefore thus says the Lord GOD: 'Behold, I *am* against you, O Tyre, and will cause many nations to come up against you, as the sea causes its waves to come up. 4And they shall destroy the walls of Tyre and break down her towers; I will also scrape her dust from her, and make her like the top of a rock.

5It shall be *a place for* spreading nets in the midst of the sea, for I have spoken,' says the Lord GOD; 'it shall become plunder for the nations. 6Also her daughter *villages* which *are* in the fields shall be slain by the sword. Then they shall know that I am the LORD.'

7"For thus says the Lord GOD: 'Behold, I will bring against Tyre from the north Nebuchadnezzar king of Babylon, king of kings, with horses, with chariots, and with horsemen, and an army with many people. 8He will slay with the sword your daughter *villages* in the fields; he will heap up a siege mound against you, build a wall against you, and raise a defense against you. 9He will direct his battering rams against your walls, and with his axes he will break down your towers. 10Because of the abundance of his horses, their dust will cover you; your walls will shake at the noise of the horsemen, the wagons, and the chariots, when he enters your gates, as men enter a city that has been breached. 11With the hooves of his horses he will trample all your streets; he will slay your people by the sword, and your strong pillars will fall to the ground. 12They will plunder your riches and pillage your merchandise; they will break down your walls and destroy your pleasant houses; they will lay your stones, your timber, and your soil in the midst of the water. 13I will put an end to the sound of your songs, and the sound of your harps shall be heard no more. 14I will make you like the top of a rock; you shall be *a place for* spreading nets, and you shall never be rebuilt, for I the LORD have spoken,' says the Lord GOD.

15"Thus says the Lord GOD to Tyre: 'Will the coastlands not shake at the sound of your fall, when the wounded cry, when slaughter is made in the midst of you? 16Then all the princes of the sea will come down from their thrones, lay aside their robes, and take off their embroidered garments; they will clothe themselves with trembling; they will sit on the ground, tremble *every* moment, and be astonished at you. 17And they will take up a lamentation for you, and say to you:

"How you have perished,

O one inhabited by seafaring
men,
O renowned city,
Who was strong at sea,
She and her inhabitants,
Who caused their terror *to be* on
all her inhabitants!
18 Now the coastlands tremble on the
day of your fall;
Yes, the coastlands by the sea are
troubled at your departure." '

19"For thus says the Lord GOD: 'When I make you a desolate city, like cities that are not inhabited, when I bring the deep upon you, and great waters cover you, 20then I will bring you down with those who descend into the Pit, to the people of old, and I will make you dwell in the lowest part of the earth, in places desolate from antiquity, with those who go down to the Pit, so that you may never be inhabited; and I shall establish glory in the land of the living. 21I will make you a terror, and you *shall be* no *more;* though you are sought for, you will never be found again,' says the Lord GOD."

Lamentation for Tyre

27 The word of the LORD came again to me, saying, 2"Now, son of man, take up a lamentation for Tyre, 3and say to Tyre, 'You who are situated at the entrance of the sea, merchant of the peoples on many coastlands, thus says the Lord GOD:
"O Tyre, you have said,
'I *am* perfect in beauty.'
4 Your borders *are* in the midst of the
seas.
Your builders have perfected your
beauty.
5 They made all *your* planks of fir
trees from Senir;
They took a cedar from Lebanon
to make you a mast.
6 *Of* oaks from Bashan they made
your oars;
The company of Ashurites have
inlaid your planks
With ivory from the coasts of
Cyprus.c
7 Fine embroidered linen from Egypt
was what you spread for your
sail;

Blue and purple from the coasts of
Elishah was what covered you.
8 "Inhabitants of Sidon and Arvad
were your oarsmen;
Your wise men, O Tyre, were
in you;
They became your pilots.
9 Elders of Gebal and its wise men
Were in you to caulk your seams;
All the ships of the sea
And their oarsmen were in you
To market your merchandise.

10 "Those from Persia, Lydia, and
Libya
Were in your army as men of war;
They hung shield and helmet
in you;
They gave splendor to you.
11 Men of Arvad with your army *were*
on your walls *all* around,
And the men of Gammad were in
your towers;
They hung their shields on your
walls *all* around;
They made your beauty perfect.

12"Tarshish *was* your merchant because of your many luxury goods. They gave you silver, iron, tin, and lead for your goods. 13Javan, Tubal, and Meshech *were* your traders. They bartered human lives and vessels of bronze for your merchandise. 14Those from the house of Togarmah traded for your wares with horses, steeds, and mules. 15The men of Dedan *were* your traders; many isles *were* the market of your hand. They brought you ivory tusks and ebony as payment. 16Syria *was* your merchant because of the abundance of goods you made. They gave you for your wares emeralds, purple, embroidery, fine linen, corals, and rubies. 17Judah and the land of Israel *were* your traders. They traded for your merchandise wheat of Minnith, millet, honey, oil, and balm. 18Damascus *was* your merchant because of the abundance of goods you made, because of your many luxury items, with the wine of Helbon and with white wool. 19Dan and Javan paid for your wares, traversing back and forth. Wrought iron, cassia, and cane were among your

c Western lands, especially Cyprus

merchandise. 20Dedan *was* your merchant in saddlecloths for riding. 21Arabia and all the princes of Kedar *were* your regular merchants. They traded with you in lambs, rams, and goats. 22The merchants of Sheba and Raamah *were* your merchants. They traded for your wares the choicest spices, all kinds of precious stones, and gold. 23Haran, Canneh, Eden, the merchants of Sheba, Assyria, *and* Chilmad *were* your merchants. 24These *were* your merchants in choice items—in purple clothes, in embroidered garments, in chests of multicolored apparel, in sturdy woven cords, which were in your marketplace.

25 "The ships of Tarshish were carriers
    of your merchandise.
    You were filled and very glorious
    in the midst of the seas.
26 Your oarsmen brought you into
    many waters,
    But the east wind broke you in the
    midst of the seas.

27 "Your riches, wares, and
    merchandise,
    Your mariners and pilots,
    Your caulkers and merchandisers,
    All your men of war who *are* in you,
    And the entire company which *is*
    in your midst,
    Will fall into the midst of the seas
    on the day of your ruin.
28 The common-land will shake at the
    sound of the cry of your pilots.

29 "All who handle the oar,
    The mariners,
    All the pilots of the sea
    Will come down from their ships
    and stand on the shore.
30 They will make their voice heard
    because of you;
    They will cry bitterly and cast dust
    on their heads;
    They will roll about in ashes;
31 They will shave themselves
    completely bald because of you,
    Gird themselves with sackcloth,
    And weep for you
    With bitterness of heart *and* bitter
    wailing.
32 In their wailing for you
    They will take up a lamentation,
    And lament for you:

'What *city is* like Tyre,
Destroyed in the midst of the sea?

33 'When your wares went out by sea,
    You satisfied many people;
    You enriched the kings of the earth
    With your many luxury goods and
    your merchandise.
34 But you are broken by the seas in
    the depths of the waters;
    Your merchandise and the entire
    company will fall in your midst.
35 All the inhabitants of the isles will
    be astonished at you;
    Their kings will be greatly afraid,
    And *their* countenance will be
    troubled.
36 The merchants among the peoples
    will hiss at you;
    You will become a horror, and *be*
    no more forever.' " ' "

Proclamation Against the King of Tyre

28 The word of the LORD came to me again, saying, 2"Son of man, say to the prince of Tyre, 'Thus says the Lord GOD:
    "Because your heart *is* lifted up,
    And you say, 'I *am* a god,
    I sit *in* the seat of gods,
    In the midst of the seas,'
    Yet you *are* a man, and not a god,
    Though you set your heart as the
    heart of a god
3   (Behold, you *are* wiser than Daniel!
    There is no secret that can be
    hidden from you!
4   With your wisdom and your
    understanding
    You have gained riches for
    yourself,
    And gathered gold and silver into
    your treasuries;
5   By your great wisdom in trade you
    have increased your riches,
    And your heart is lifted up because
    of your riches),"
6'Therefore thus says the Lord GOD:
    "Because you have set your heart as
    the heart of a god,
7   Behold, therefore, I will bring
    strangers against you,
    The most terrible of the nations;
    And they shall draw their swords
    against the beauty of your
    wisdom,
    And defile your splendor.

8   They shall throw you down into
       the Pit,
    And you shall die the death of the
       slain
    In the midst of the seas.

9   "Will you still say before him who
       slays you,
    'I *am* a god'?
    But you *shall be* a man, and not
       a god,
    In the hand of him who slays you.
10 You shall die the death of the
       uncircumcised
    By the hand of aliens;
    For I have spoken," says the
       Lord God.' "

Lamentation for the King of Tyre

11Moreover the word of the Lord
came to me, saying, 12"Son of man,
take up a lamentation for the king of
Tyre, and say to him, 'Thus says the
Lord God:

    "You *were* the seal of perfection,
    Full of wisdom and perfect in
       beauty.
13 You were in Eden, the garden
       of God;
    Every precious stone *was* your
       covering:
    The sardius, topaz, and diamond,
    Beryl, onyx, and jasper,
    Sapphire, turquoise, and emerald
       with gold.
    The workmanship of your timbrels
       and pipes
    Was prepared for you on the day
       you were created.

14 "You *were* the anointed cherub who
       covers;
    I established you;
    You were on the holy mountain
       of God;
    You walked back and forth in the
       midst of fiery stones.
15 You *were* perfect in your ways
       from the day you were created,
    Till iniquity was found in you.

16 "By the abundance of your trading
    You became filled with violence
       within,
    And you sinned;
    Therefore I cast you as a profane
       thing

    Out of the mountain of God;
    And I destroyed you, O covering
       cherub,
    From the midst of the fiery stones.

17 "Your heart was lifted up because
       of your beauty;
    You corrupted your wisdom for the
       sake of your splendor;
    I cast you to the ground,
    I laid you before kings,
    That they might gaze at you.

18 "You defiled your sanctuaries
    By the multitude of your iniquities,
    By the iniquity of your trading;
    Therefore I brought fire from your
       midst;
    It devoured you,
    And I turned you to ashes upon the
       earth
    In the sight of all who saw you.
19 All who knew you among the
       peoples are astonished at you;
    You have become a horror,
    And *shall be* no more forever." ' "

Proclamation Against Sidon

20Then the word of the Lord came
to me, saying, 21"Son of man, set your
face toward Sidon, and prophesy
against her, 22and say, 'Thus says the
Lord God:

    "Behold, I *am* against you, O Sidon;
    I will be glorified in your midst;
    And they shall know that I *am* the
       Lord,
    When I execute judgments in her
       and am hallowed in her.
23 For I will send pestilence upon her,
    And blood in her streets;
    The wounded shall be judged in her
       midst
    By the sword against her on every
       side;
    Then they shall know that I *am* the
       Lord.

24"And there shall no longer be a
pricking brier or a painful thorn for the
house of Israel from among all *who
are* around them, who despise them.
Then they shall know that I *am* the
Lord God."

Israel's Future Blessing

25'Thus says the Lord God: "When I
have gathered the house of Israel from

the peoples among whom they are scattered, and am hallowed in them in the sight of the Gentiles, then they will dwell in their own land which I gave to My servant Jacob. 26And they will dwell safely there, build houses, and plant vineyards; yes, they will dwell securely, when I execute judgments on all those around them who despise them. Then they shall know that I *am* the LORD their God." ' "

Proclamation Against Egypt

29 In the tenth year, in the tenth *month,* on the twelfth *day* of the month, the word of the LORD came to me, saying, 2"Son of man, set your face against Pharaoh king of Egypt, and prophesy against him, and against all Egypt. 3Speak, and say, 'Thus says the Lord GOD:

"Behold, I *am* against you,
  O Pharaoh king of Egypt,
  O great monster who lies in the
    midst of his rivers,
Who has said, 'My River[d] *is*
    my own;
I have made *it* for myself.'
4 But I will put hooks in your jaws,
  And cause the fish of your rivers
    to stick to your scales;
  I will bring you up out of the midst
    of your rivers,
  And all the fish in your rivers will
    stick to your scales.
5 I will leave you in the wilderness,
  You and all the fish of your rivers;
  You shall fall on the open field;
  You shall not be picked up or
    gathered.
  I have given you as food
  To the beasts of the field
  And to the birds of the heavens.

6 "Then all the inhabitants of Egypt
  Shall know that I *am* the LORD,
  Because they have been a staff of
    reed to the house of Israel.
7 When they took hold of you with
    the hand,
  You broke and tore all their
    shoulders;
  When they leaned on you,
  You broke and made all their backs
    quiver."

8'Therefore thus says the Lord GOD: "Surely I will bring a sword upon you and cut off from you man and beast. 9And the land of Egypt shall become desolate and waste; then they will know that I *am* the LORD, because he said, 'The River *is* mine, and I have made *it.*' 10Indeed, therefore, I *am* against you and against your rivers, and I will make the land of Egypt utterly waste and desolate, from Migdol *to* Syene, as far as the border of Ethiopia. 11Neither foot of man shall pass through it nor foot of beast pass through it, and it shall be uninhabited forty years. 12I will make the land of Egypt desolate in the midst of the countries *that are* desolate; and among the cities *that are* laid waste, her cities shall be desolate forty years; and I will scatter the Egyptians among the nations and disperse them throughout the countries."

13'Yet, thus says the Lord GOD: "At the end of forty years I will gather the Egyptians from the peoples among whom they were scattered. 14I will bring back the captives of Egypt and cause them to return to the land of Pathros, to the land of their origin, and there they shall be a lowly kingdom. 15It shall be the lowliest of kingdoms; it shall never again exalt itself above the nations, for I will diminish them so that they will not rule over the nations anymore. 16No longer shall it be the confidence of the house of Israel, but will remind them of *their* iniquity when they turned to follow them. Then they shall know that I *am* the Lord GOD." ' "

Babylonia Will Plunder Egypt

17And it came to pass in the twenty-seventh year, in the first *month,* on the first *day* of the month, *that* the word of the LORD came to me, saying, 18"Son of man, Nebuchadnezzar king of Babylon caused his army to labor strenuously against Tyre; every head *was* made bald, and every shoulder rubbed raw; yet neither he nor his army received wages from Tyre, for the labor which they expended on it. 19Therefore thus says the Lord GOD: 'Surely I will give the land of Egypt to Nebuchadnezzar king of Babylon; he shall take away

---

d That is, the Nile

her wealth, carry off her spoil, and remove her pillage; and that will be the wages for his army. 20I have given him the land of Egypt *for* his labor, because they worked for Me,' says the Lord GOD.

21'In that day I will cause the horn of the house of Israel to spring forth, and I will open your mouth to speak in their midst. Then they shall know that I *am* the LORD.' "

Egypt and Her Allies Will Fall

30 The word of the LORD came to me again, saying, 2"Son of man, prophesy and say, 'Thus says the Lord GOD:

"Wail, 'Woe to the day!'
3 For the day *is* near,
Even the day of the LORD *is* near;
It will be a day of clouds, the time of the Gentiles.
4 The sword shall come upon Egypt,
And great anguish shall be in Ethiopia,
When the slain fall in Egypt,
And they take away her wealth,
And her foundations are broken down.
5"Ethiopia, Libya, Lydia, all the mingled people, Chub, and the men of the lands who are allied, shall fall with them by the sword."
6'Thus says the LORD:

"Those who uphold Egypt shall fall,
And the pride of her power shall come down.
From Migdol *to* Syene
Those within her shall fall by the sword,"
Says the Lord GOD.

7 "They shall be desolate in the midst of the desolate countries,
And her cities shall be in the midst of the cities *that are* laid waste.
8 Then they will know that I *am* the LORD,
When I have set a fire in Egypt
And all her helpers are destroyed.
9 On that day messengers shall go forth from Me in ships
To make the careless Ethiopians afraid,

And great anguish shall come upon them,
As on the day of Egypt;
For indeed it is coming!"
10'Thus says the Lord GOD:
"I will also make a multitude of Egypt to cease
By the hand of Nebuchadnezzar king of Babylon.
11 He and his people with him, the most terrible of the nations,
Shall be brought to destroy the land;
They shall draw their swords against Egypt,
And fill the land with the slain.
12 I will make the rivers dry,
And sell the land into the hand of the wicked;
I will make the land waste, and all that is in it,
By the hand of aliens.
I, the LORD, have spoken."
13'Thus says the Lord GOD:
"I will also destroy the idols,
And cause the images to cease from Noph;*e*
There shall no longer be princes from the land of Egypt;
I will put fear in the land of Egypt.
14 I will make Pathros desolate,
Set fire to Zoan,
And execute judgments in No.*f*
15 I will pour My fury on Sin,*g* the strength of Egypt;
I will cut off the multitude of No,
16 And set a fire in Egypt;
Sin shall have great pain,
No shall be split open,
And Noph *shall be in* distress daily.
17 The young men of Aven*h* and Pi Beseth shall fall by the sword,
And these *cities* shall go into captivity.
18 At Tehaphnehes the day shall also be darkened,
When I break the yokes of Egypt there.
And her arrogant strength shall cease in her;
As for her, a cloud shall cover her,
And her daughters shall go into captivity.

---

e That is, ancient Memphis   *f* That is, ancient Thebes   *g* That is, ancient Pelusium
h That is, ancient On (Heliopolis)

19   Thus I will execute judgments on
      Egypt,
      Then they shall know that I *am* the
      LORD.' ' "

Proclamation Against Pharaoh

20And it came to pass in the eleventh
year, in the first *month,* on the seventh
day of the month, *that* the word of the
LORD came to me, saying, 21"Son of
man, I have broken the arm of Pharaoh
king of Egypt; and see, it has not been
bandaged for healing, nor a splint put
on to bind it, to make it strong enough
to hold a sword. 22Therefore thus says
the Lord GOD: 'Surely I *am* against
Pharaoh king of Egypt, and will break
his arms, both the strong one and the
one that was broken; and I will make
the sword fall out of his hand. 23I will
scatter the Egyptians among the nations, and disperse them throughout the
countries. 24I will strengthen the arms
of the king of Babylon and put My
sword in his hand; but I will break
Pharaoh's arms, and he will groan before him with the groanings of a mortally wounded *man.* 25Thus I will
strengthen the arms of the king of
Babylon, but the arms of Pharaoh shall
fall down; they shall know that I *am*
the LORD, when I put My sword into the
hand of the king of Babylon and he
stretches it out against the land of
Egypt. 26I will scatter the Egyptians
among the nations and disperse them
throughout the countries. Then they
shall know that I *am* the LORD.' "

Egypt Cut Down Like a Great Tree

31 Now it came to pass in the eleventh year, in the third *month,* on
the first *day* of the month, *that* the word
of the LORD came to me, saying,
2"Son of man, say to Pharaoh king of
Egypt and to his multitude:

      'Whom are you like in your
         greatness?
3   Indeed Assyria *was* a cedar in
         Lebanon,
      With fine branches that shaded the
         forest,
      And of high stature;
      And its top was among the thick
         boughs.
4   The waters made it grow;
      Underground waters gave it height,

      With their rivers running around
         the place where it was planted,
      And sent out rivulets to all the trees
         of the field.

5   'Therefore its height was exalted
         above all the trees of the field;
      Its boughs were multiplied,
      And its branches became long
         because of the abundance
         of water,
      As it sent them out.
6   All the birds of the heavens made
         their nests in its boughs;
      Under its branches all the beasts of
         the field brought forth their
         young;
      And in its shadow all great nations
         made their home.

7   'Thus it was beautiful in greatness
         and in the length of its branches,
      Because its roots reached to
         abundant waters.
8   The cedars in the garden of God
         could not hide it;
      The fir trees were not like its
         boughs,
      And the chestnut trees were not
         like its branches;
      No tree in the garden of God was
         like it in beauty.
9   I made it beautiful with a multitude
         of branches,
      So that all the trees of Eden
         envied it,
      That *were* in the garden of God.'

10"Therefore thus says the Lord GOD:
'Because you have increased in height,
and it set its top among the thick
boughs, and its heart was lifted up in
its height, 11therefore I will deliver it
into the hand of the mighty one of the
nations, and he shall surely deal with
it; I have driven it out for its wickedness. 12And aliens, the most terrible
of the nations, have cut it down and
left it; its branches have fallen on the
mountains and in all the valleys; its
boughs lie broken by all the rivers of
the land; and all the peoples of the
earth have gone from under its shadow
and left it.
13   'On its ruin will remain
         all the birds of the heavens,
      And all the beasts of the field will
         come to its branches—

14'So that no trees by the waters may ever again exalt themselves for their height, nor set their tops among the thick boughs, that no tree which drinks water may ever be high enough to reach up to them.

'For they have all been delivered to death,
To the depths of the earth,
Among the children of men who go down to the Pit.'

15"Thus says the Lord GOD: 'In the day when it went down to hell, I caused mourning. I covered the deep because of it. I restrained its rivers, and the great waters were held back. I caused Lebanon to mourn for it, and all the trees of the field wilted because of it. 16I made the nations shake at the sound of its fall, when I cast it down to hell together with those who descend into the Pit; and all the trees of Eden, the choice and best of Lebanon, all that drink water, were comforted in the depths of the earth. 17They also went down to hell with it, with those *slain* by the sword; and *those who were* its *strong* arm dwelt in its shadows among the nations.

18'To which of the trees in Eden will you then be likened in glory and greatness? Yet you shall be brought down with the trees of Eden to the depths of the earth; you shall lie in the midst of the uncircumcised, with *those* slain by the sword. This *is* Pharaoh and all his multitude,' says the Lord GOD."

Lamentation for Pharaoh and Egypt

32 And it came to pass in the twelfth year, in the twelfth *month*, on the first *day* of the month, *that* the word of the LORD came to me, saying, 2"Son of man, take up a lamentation for Pharaoh king of Egypt, and say to him:

'You are like a young lion among the nations,
And you *are* like a monster in the seas,
Bursting forth in your rivers,
Troubling the waters with your feet,
And fouling their rivers.'

3"Thus says the Lord GOD:
'I will therefore spread My net over you with a company of many people,
And they will draw you up in My net.
4 Then I will leave you on the land;
I will cast you out on the open fields,
And cause to settle on you all the birds of the heavens.
And with you I will fill the beasts of the whole earth.
5 I will lay your flesh on the mountains,
And fill the valleys with your carcass.
6 'I will also water the land with the flow of your blood,
Even to the mountains;
And the riverbeds will be full of you.
7 When *I* put out your light,
I will cover the heavens, and make its stars dark;
I will cover the sun with a cloud,
And the moon shall not give her light.
8 All the bright lights of the heavens I will make dark over you,
And bring darkness upon your land,'

Says the Lord GOD.

9'I will also trouble the hearts of many peoples, when I bring your destruction among the nations, into the countries which you have not known. 10Yes, I will make many peoples astonished at you, and their kings shall be horribly afraid of you when I brandish My sword before them; and they shall tremble *every* moment, every man for his own life, in the day of your fall.'

11"For thus says the Lord GOD: 'The sword of the king of Babylon shall come upon you. 12By the swords of the mighty warriors, all of them the most terrible of the nations, I will cause your multitude to fall.

'They shall plunder the pomp of Egypt,
And all its multitude shall be destroyed.
13 Also I will destroy all its animals
From beside its great waters;
The foot of man shall muddy them no more,

Nor shall the hooves of animals
  muddy them.
14 Then I will make their waters clear,
  And make their rivers run like oil,'
  Says the Lord God.

15 'When I make the land of Egypt
    desolate,
  And the country is destitute of all
    that once filled it,
  When I strike all who dwell in it,
  Then they shall know that I *am* the
    Lord.

16 'This *is* the lamentation
  With which they shall lament her;
  The daughters of the nations shall
    lament her;
  They shall lament for her, for
    Egypt,
  And for all her multitude,'
  Says the Lord God."

Egypt and Others Consigned to the Pit

17It came to pass also in the twelfth
year, on the fifteenth *day* of the month,
that the word of the Lord came to me,
saying:
18 "Son of man, wail over the multitude
    of Egypt,
  And cast them down to the depths
    of the earth,
  Her and the daughters of the
    famous nations,
  With those who go down to the Pit:
19 'Whom do you surpass in beauty?
  Go down, be placed with the
    uncircumcised.'

20 "They shall fall in the midst of *those*
    slain by the sword;
  She is delivered to the sword,
  Drawing her and all her multitudes.
21 The strong among the mighty
  Shall speak to him out of the midst
    of hell
  With those who help him:
  'They have gone down,
  They lie with the uncircumcised,
    slain by the sword.'

22 "Assyria *is* there, and all her
    company,
  With their graves all around her,
  All of them slain, fallen by the
    sword.

23 Her graves are set in the recesses
    of the Pit,
  And her company is all around her
    grave,
  All of them slain, fallen by the
    sword,
  Who caused terror in the land of
    the living.

24 "There *is* Elam and all her multitude,
  All around her grave,
  All of them slain, fallen by the
    sword,
  Who have gone down
    uncircumcised to the lower parts
    of the earth,
  Who caused their terror in the land
    of the living;
  Now they bear their shame with
    those who go down to the Pit.
25 They have set her bed in the midst
    of the slain,
  With all her multitude,
  With her graves all around it,
  All of them uncircumcised, slain by
    the sword;
  Though their terror was caused
  In the land of the living,
  Yet they bear their shame
  With those who go down to the Pit;
  It was put in the midst of the slain.

26 "There *are* Meshech and Tubal and
    all their multitudes,
  With all their graves around it,
  All of them uncircumcised, slain by
    the sword,
  Though they caused their terror in
    the land of the living.
27 They do not lie with the mighty
  Who are fallen of the
    uncircumcised,
  Who have gone down to hell with
    their weapons of war;
  They have laid their swords under
    their heads,
  But their iniquities will be on their
    bones,
  Because of the terror of the mighty
    in the land of the living.
28 Yes, you shall be broken in the
    midst of the uncircumcised,
  And lie with *those* slain by the
    sword.

29 "There *is* Edom,
  Her kings and all her princes,
  Who despite their might

Are laid beside *those* slain by the
    sword;
They shall lie with the
    uncircumcised,
And with those who go down to
    the Pit.
30 There *are* the princes of the north,
All of them, and all the Sidonians,
Who have gone down with the slain
In shame at the terror which they
    caused by their might;
They lie uncircumcised with *those*
    slain by the sword,
And bear their shame with those
    who go down to the Pit.

31 "Pharaoh will see them
And be comforted over all his
    multitude,
Pharaoh and all his army,
Slain by the sword,"
Says the Lord GOD.

32 "For I have caused My terror in the
    land of the living;
And he shall be placed in the midst
    of the uncircumcised
With *those* slain by the sword,
Pharaoh and all his multitude,"
Says the Lord GOD.

The Watchman and His Message

33 Again the word of the LORD came
to me, saying, 2"Son of man,
speak to the children of your people,
and say to them: 'When I bring the
sword upon a land, and the people of
the land take a man from their territory
and make him their watchman, 3when
he sees the sword coming upon the
land, if he blows the trumpet and warns
the people, 4then whoever hears the
sound of the trumpet and does not
take warning, if the sword comes and
takes him away, his blood shall be on
his *own* head. 5He heard the sound of
the trumpet, but did not take warning;
his blood shall be upon himself. But he
who takes warning will save his life.
6But if the watchman sees the sword
coming and does not blow the trumpet,
and the people are not warned, and the
sword comes and takes *any* person
from among them, he is taken away in
his iniquity; but his blood I will require
at the watchman's hand.'

7"So you, son of man: I have made
you a watchman for the house of Israel;
therefore you shall hear a word from
My mouth and warn them for Me.
8When I say to the wicked, 'O wicked
man, you shall surely die!' and you do
not speak to warn the wicked from his
way, that wicked *man* shall die in his
iniquity; but his blood I will require at
your hand. 9Nevertheless if you warn
the wicked to turn from his way, and
he does not turn from his way, he shall
die in his iniquity; but you have delivered your soul.

10"Therefore you, O son of man, say
to the house of Israel: 'Thus you say,
"If our transgressions and our sins *lie*
upon us, and we pine away in them,
how can we then live?" ' 11Say to them:
'*As* I live,' says the Lord GOD, 'I have
no pleasure in the death of the wicked,
but that the wicked turn from his way
and live. Turn, turn from your evil
ways! For why should you die, O house
of Israel?'

The Fairness of God's Judgment

12"Therefore you, O son of man, say
to the children of your people: 'The
righteousness of the righteous man
shall not deliver him in the day of his
transgression; as for the wickedness of
the wicked, he shall not fall because of
it in the day that he turns from his wickedness; nor shall the righteous be able
to live because of *his righteousness* in
the day that he sins.' 13When I say to
the righteous *that* he shall surely live,
but he trusts in his own righteousness
and commits iniquity, none of his righteous works shall be remembered; but
because of the iniquity that he has committed, he shall die. 14Again, when I say
to the wicked, 'You shall surely die,' if
he turns from his sin and does what is
lawful and right, 15if the wicked restores the pledge, gives back what he
has stolen, and walks in the statutes of
life without committing iniquity, he
shall surely live; he shall not die.
16None of his sins which he has committed shall be remembered against
him; he has done what is lawful and
right; he shall surely live.
17"Yet the children of your people
say, 'The way of the LORD is not fair.'

But it is their way which is not fair! 18When the righteous turns from his righteousness and commits iniquity, he shall die because of it. 19But when the wicked turns from his wickedness and does what is lawful and right, he shall live because of it. 20Yet you say, 'The way of the LORD is not fair.' O house of Israel, I will judge every one of you according to his own ways."

The Fall of Jerusalem

21And it came to pass in the twelfth year of our captivity, in the tenth *month*, on the fifth *day* of the month, *that* one who had escaped from Jerusalem came to me and said, "The city has been captured!"
22Now the hand of the LORD had been upon me the evening before the man came who had escaped. And He had opened my mouth; so when he came to me in the morning, my mouth was opened, and I was no longer mute.

The Cause of Judah's Ruin

23Then the word of the LORD came to me, saying: 24"Son of man, they who inhabit those ruins in the land of Israel are saying, 'Abraham was only one, and he inherited the land. But we *are* many; the land has been given to us as a possession.'
25"Therefore say to them, 'Thus says the Lord GOD: "You eat *meat* with blood, you lift up your eyes toward your idols, and shed blood. Should you then possess the land? 26You rely on your sword, you commit abominations, and you defile one another's wives. Should you then possess the land?" '
27"Say thus to them, 'Thus says the Lord GOD: "*As* I live, surely those who *are* in the ruins shall fall by the sword, and the one who *is* in the open field I will give to the beasts to be devoured, and those who *are* in the strongholds and caves shall die of the pestilence. 28For I will make the land most desolate, her arrogant strength shall cease, and the mountains of Israel shall be so desolate that no one will pass through. 29Then they shall know that I *am* the LORD, when I have made the land most desolate because of all their abominations which they have committed." '

Hearing and Not Doing

30"As for you, son of man, the children of your people are talking about you beside the walls and in the doors of the houses; and they speak to one another, everyone saying to his brother, 'Please come and hear what the word is that comes from the LORD.' 31So they come to you as people do, they sit before you *as* My people, and they hear your words, but they do not do them; for with their mouth they show much love, *but* their hearts pursue their *own* gain. 32Indeed you *are* to them as a very lovely song of one who has a pleasant voice and can play well on an instrument; for they hear your words, but they do not do them. 33And when this comes to pass—surely it will come—then they will know that a prophet has been among them."

Irresponsible Shepherds

34 And the word of the LORD came to me, saying, 2"Son of man, prophesy against the shepherds of Israel, prophesy and say to them, 'Thus says the Lord GOD to the shepherds: "Woe to the shepherds of Israel who feed themselves! Should not the shepherds feed the flocks? 3You eat the fat and clothe yourselves with the wool; you slaughter the fatlings, *but* you do not feed the flock. 4The weak you have not strengthened, nor have you healed those who were sick, nor bound up the broken, nor brought back what was driven away, nor sought what was lost; but with force and cruelty you have ruled them. 5So they were scattered because *there was* no shepherd; and they became food for all the beasts of the field when they were scattered. 6My sheep wandered through all the mountains, and on every high hill; yes, My flock was scattered over the whole face of the earth, and no one was seeking or searching *for them*."
7'Therefore, you shepherds, hear the word of the LORD: 8"*As* I live," says the Lord GOD, "surely because My flock became a prey, and My flock became food for every beast of the field, because *there was* no shepherd, nor did My shepherds search for My flock, but the shepherds fed themselves and did not

feed My flock"—9therefore, O shepherds, hear the word of the LORD! 10Thus says the Lord GOD: "Behold, I *am* against the shepherds, and I will require My flock at their hand; I will cause them to cease feeding the sheep, and the shepherds shall feed themselves no more; for I will deliver My flock from their mouths, that they may no longer be food for them."

God, the True Shepherd

11'For thus says the Lord GOD: "Indeed I Myself will search for My sheep and seek them out. 12As a shepherd seeks out his flock on the day he is among his scattered sheep, so will I seek out My sheep and deliver them from all the places where they were scattered on a cloudy and dark day. 13And I will bring them out from the peoples and gather them from the countries, and will bring them to their own land; I will feed them on the mountains of Israel, in the valleys and in all the inhabited places of the country. 14I will feed them in good pasture, and their fold shall be on the high mountains of Israel. There they shall lie down in a good fold and feed in rich pasture on the mountains of Israel. 15I will feed My flock, and I will make them lie down," says the Lord GOD. 16"I will seek what was lost and bring back what was driven away, bind up the broken and strengthen what was sick; but I will destroy the fat and the strong, and feed them in judgment."

17'And *as for* you, O My flock, thus says the Lord GOD: "Behold, I shall judge between sheep and sheep, between rams and goats. 18*Is it* too little for you to have eaten up the good pasture, that you must tread down with your feet the residue of your pasture—and to have drunk of the clear waters, that you must foul the residue with your feet? 19And *as for* My flock, they eat what you have trampled with your feet, and they drink what you have fouled with your feet."

20'Therefore thus says the Lord GOD to them: "Behold, I Myself will judge between the fat and the lean sheep. 21Because you have pushed with side and shoulder, butted all the weak ones with your horns, and scattered them abroad, 22therefore I will save My flock, and they shall no longer be a prey; and I will judge between sheep and sheep. 23I will establish one shepherd over them, and he shall feed them—My servant David. He shall feed them and be their shepherd. 24And I, the LORD, will be their God, and My servant David a prince among them; I, the LORD, have spoken.

25"I will make a covenant of peace with them, and cause wild beasts to cease from the land; and they will dwell safely in the wilderness and sleep in the woods. 26I will make them and the places all around My hill a blessing; and I will cause showers to come down in their season; there shall be showers of blessing. 27Then the trees of the field shall yield their fruit, and the earth shall yield her increase. They shall be safe in their land; and they shall know that I *am* the LORD, when I have broken the bands of their yoke and delivered them from the hand of those who enslaved them. 28And they shall no longer be a prey for the nations, nor shall beasts of the land devour them; but they shall dwell safely, and no one shall make *them* afraid. 29I will raise up for them a garden of renown, and they shall no longer be consumed with hunger in the land, nor bear the shame of the Gentiles anymore. 30Thus they shall know that I, the LORD their God, *am* with them, and they, the house of Israel, *are* My people," says the Lord GOD.' "

31"You are My flock, the flock of My pasture; you *are* men, *and* I *am* your God," says the Lord GOD.

Judgment on Mount Seir

35 Moreover the word of the LORD came to me, saying, 2"Son of man, set your face against Mount Seir and prophesy against it, 3and say to it, 'Thus says the Lord GOD:

"Behold, O Mount Seir, I *am*
  against you;
I will stretch out My hand
  against you,
And make you most desolate;
4 I shall lay your cities waste,
And you shall be desolate.
Then you shall know that I *am* the
  LORD.

5"Because you have had an ancient

hatred, and have shed *the blood of* the children of Israel by the power of the sword at the time of their calamity, *when* their iniquity *came to an* end, 6therefore, *as* I live," says the Lord GOD, "I will prepare you for blood, and blood shall pursue you; since you have not hated blood, therefore blood shall pursue you. 7Thus I will make Mount Seir most desolate, and cut off from it the one who leaves and the one who returns. 8And I will fill its mountains with the slain; on your hills and in your valleys and in all your ravines those who are slain by the sword shall fall. 9I will make you perpetually desolate, and your cities shall be uninhabited; then you shall know that I *am* the LORD.

10"Because you have said, 'These two nations and these two countries shall be mine, and we will possess them,' although the LORD was there, 11therefore, *as* I live," says the Lord GOD, "I will do according to your anger and according to the envy which you showed in your hatred against them; and I will make Myself known among them when I judge you. 12Then you shall know that I *am* the LORD. I have heard all your blasphemies which you have spoken against the mountains of Israel, saying, 'They are desolate; they are given to us to consume.' 13Thus with your mouth you have boasted against Me and multiplied your words against Me; I have heard *them.*"

14'Thus says the Lord GOD: "The whole earth will rejoice when I make you desolate. 15As you rejoiced because the inheritance of the house of Israel was desolate, so I will do to you; you shall be desolate, O Mount Seir, as well as all of Edom—all of it! Then they shall know that I *am* the LORD." '

Blessing on Israel

36 "And you, son of man, prophesy to the mountains of Israel, and say, 'O mountains of Israel, hear the word of the LORD! 2Thus says the Lord GOD: "Because the enemy has said of you, 'Aha! The ancient heights have become our possession,' " ' 3therefore prophesy, and say, 'Thus says the Lord GOD: "Because they made you desolate and swallowed you up on every side, so that you became the possession of the rest of the nations, and you are taken up by the lips of talkers and slandered by the people"—4therefore, O mountains of Israel, hear the word of the Lord GOD! Thus says the Lord GOD to the mountains, the hills, the rivers, the valleys, the desolate wastes, and the cities that have been forsaken, which became plunder and mockery to the rest of the nations all around—5therefore thus says the Lord GOD: "Surely I have spoken in My burning jealousy against the rest of the nations and against all Edom, who gave My land to themselves as a possession, with wholehearted joy *and* spiteful minds, in order to plunder its open country." '

6"Therefore prophesy concerning the land of Israel, and say to the mountains, the hills, the rivers, and the valleys, 'Thus says the Lord GOD: "Behold, I have spoken in My jealousy and My fury, because you have borne the shame of the nations." 7Therefore thus says the Lord GOD: "I have raised My hand in an oath that surely the nations that *are* around you shall bear their own shame. 8But you, O mountains of Israel, you shall shoot forth your branches and yield your fruit to My people Israel, for they are about to come. 9For indeed I *am* for you, and I will turn to you, and you shall be tilled and sown. 10I will multiply men upon you, all the house of Israel, all of it; and the cities shall be inhabited and the ruins rebuilt. 11I will multiply upon you man and beast; and they shall increase and bear young; I will make you inhabited as in former times, and do better *for you* than at your beginnings. Then you shall know that I *am* the LORD. 12Yes, I will cause men to walk on you, My people Israel; they shall take possession of you, and you shall be their inheritance; no more shall you bereave them *of children.*"

13'Thus says the Lord GOD: "Because they say to you, 'You devour men and bereave your nation *of children,*' 14therefore you shall devour men no more, nor bereave your nation anymore," says the Lord GOD. 15Nor will I let you hear the taunts of the nations anymore, nor bear the reproach of the peoples anymore, nor shall you cause your nation to stumble anymore," says the Lord GOD.' "

The Renewal of Israel

16Moreover the word of the LORD came to me, saying: 17"Son of man, when the house of Israel dwelt in their own land, they defiled it by their own ways and deeds; to Me their way was like the uncleanness of a woman in her customary impurity. 18Therefore I poured out My fury on them for the blood they had shed on the land, and for their idols *with which* they had defiled it. 19So I scattered them among the nations, and they were dispersed throughout the countries; I judged them according to their ways and their deeds. 20When they came to the nations, wherever they went, they profaned My holy name—when they said of them, 'These *are* the people of the LORD, *and* yet they have gone out of His land.' 21But I had concern for My holy name, which the house of Israel had profaned among the nations wherever they went.

22"Therefore say to the house of Israel, 'Thus says the Lord GOD: "I do not do *this* for your sake, O house of Israel, but for My holy name's sake, which you have profaned among the nations wherever you went. 23And I will sanctify My great name, which has been profaned among the nations, which you have profaned in their midst; and the nations shall know that I *am* the LORD," says the Lord GOD, "when I am hallowed in you before their eyes. 24For I will take you from among the nations, gather you out of all countries, and bring you into your own land. 25Then I will sprinkle clean water on you, and you shall be clean; I will cleanse you from all your filthiness and from all your idols. 26I will give you a new heart and put a new spirit within you; I will take the heart of stone out of your flesh and give you a heart of flesh. 27I will put My Spirit within you and cause you to walk in My statutes, and you will keep My judgments and do *them*. 28Then you shall dwell in the land that I gave to your fathers; you shall be My people, and I will be your God. 29I will deliver you from all your uncleannesses. I will call for the grain and multiply it, and bring no famine upon you. 30And I will

multiply the fruit of your trees and the increase of your fields, so that you need never again bear the reproach of famine among the nations. 31Then you will remember your evil ways and your deeds that *were* not good; and you will loathe yourselves in your own sight, for your iniquities and your abominations. 32Not for your sake do I do *this*," says the Lord GOD, "let it be known to you. Be ashamed and confounded for your own ways, O house of Israel!"

33'Thus says the Lord GOD: "On the day that I cleanse you from all your iniquities, I will also enable *you* to dwell in the cities, and the ruins shall be rebuilt. 34The desolate land shall be tilled instead of lying desolate in the sight of all who pass by. 35So they will say, 'This land that was desolate has become like the garden of Eden; and the wasted, desolate, and ruined cities *are now* fortified *and* inhabited.' 36Then the nations which are left all around you shall know that I, the LORD, have rebuilt the ruined places *and* planted what was desolate. I, the LORD, have spoken *it*, and I will do *it*."

37'Thus says the Lord GOD: "I will also let the house of Israel inquire of Me to do this for them: I will increase their men like a flock. 38Like a flock *offered as* holy *sacrifices*, like the flock at Jerusalem on its feast days, so shall the ruined cities be filled with flocks of men. Then they shall know that I *am* the LORD." ' "

The Dry Bones Live

37 The hand of the LORD came upon me and brought me out in the Spirit of the LORD, and set me down in the midst of the valley; and it *was* full of bones. 2Then He caused me to pass by them all around, and behold, *there were* very many in the open valley; and indeed *they were* very dry. 3And He said to me, "Son of man, can these bones live?"

So I answered, "O Lord GOD, You know."

4Again He said to me, "Prophesy to these bones, and say to them, 'O dry bones, hear the word of the LORD! 5Thus says the Lord GOD to these bones: "Surely I will cause breath to enter into you, and you shall live. 6I will put sinews on you and bring flesh upon you, cover you with skin and put breath in you; and you shall live. Then you shall know that I *am* the LORD." ' "

7So I prophesied as I was commanded; and as I prophesied, there was a noise, and suddenly a rattling; and the bones came together, bone to bone. 8Indeed, as I looked, the sinews and the flesh came upon them, and the skin covered them over; but *there was* no breath in them.

9Also He said to me, "Prophesy to the breath, prophesy, son of man, and say to the breath, 'Thus says the Lord GOD: "Come from the four winds, O breath, and breathe on these slain, that they may live." ' " 10So I prophesied as He commanded me, and breath came into them, and they lived, and stood upon their feet, an exceedingly great army.

11Then He said to me, "Son of man, these bones are the whole house of Israel. They indeed say, 'Our bones are dry, our hope is lost, and we ourselves are cut off!' 12Therefore prophesy and say to them, 'Thus says the Lord GOD: "Behold, O My people, I will open your graves and cause you to come up from your graves, and bring you into the land of Israel. 13Then you shall know that I *am* the LORD, when I have opened your graves, O My people, and brought you up from your graves. 14I will put My Spirit in you, and you shall live, and I will place you in your own land. Then you shall know that I, the LORD, have spoken *it* and performed *it*," says the LORD.' "

One Kingdom, One King

15Again the word of the LORD came to me, saying, 16"As for you, son of man, take a stick for yourself and write on it: 'For Judah and for the children of Israel, his companions.' Then take another stick and write on it, 'For Joseph, the stick of Ephraim, and *for* all the house of Israel, his companions.' 17Then join them one to another for yourself into one stick, and they will become one in your hand.

18"And when the children of your people speak to you, saying, 'Will you not show us what you *mean* by these?'—19say to them, 'Thus says the Lord GOD: "Surely I will take the stick

of Joseph, which *is* in the hand of Ephraim, and the tribes of Israel, his companions; and I will join them with it, with the stick of Judah, and make them one stick, and they will be one in My hand." ' 20And the sticks on which you write will be in your hand before their eyes.

21"Then say to them, 'Thus says the Lord GOD: "Surely I will take the children of Israel from among the nations, wherever they have gone, and will gather them from every side and bring them into their own land; 22and I will make them one nation in the land, on the mountains of Israel; and one king shall be king over them all; they shall no longer be two nations, nor shall they ever be divided into two kingdoms again. 23They shall not defile themselves anymore with their idols, nor with their detestable things, nor with any of their transgressions; but I will deliver them from all their dwelling places in which they have sinned, and will cleanse them. Then they shall be My people, and I will be their God.

24"David My servant *shall be* king over them, and they shall all have one shepherd; they shall also walk in My judgments and observe My statutes, and do them. 25Then they shall dwell in the land that I have given to Jacob My servant, where your fathers dwelt; and they shall dwell there, they, their children, and their children's children, forever; and My servant David *shall be* their prince forever. 26Moreover I will make a covenant of peace with them, and it shall be an everlasting covenant with them; I will establish them and multiply them, and I will set My sanctuary in their midst forevermore. 27My tabernacle also shall be with them; indeed I will be their God, and they shall be My people. 28The nations also will know that I, the LORD, sanctify Israel, when My sanctuary is in their midst forevermore." ' "

Gog and Allies Attack Israel

38 Now the word of the LORD came to me, saying, 2"Son of man, set your face against Gog, of the land of Magog, the prince of Rosh, Meshech, and Tubal, and prophesy against him, 3and say, 'Thus says the Lord GOD:

"Behold, I *am* against you, O Gog, the prince of Rosh, Meshech, and Tubal. 4I will turn you around, put hooks into your jaws, and lead you out, with all your army, horses, and horsemen, all splendidly clothed, a great company *with* bucklers and shields, all of them handling swords. 5Persia, Ethiopia, and Libya are with them, all of them *with* shield and helmet; 6Gomer and all its troops; the house of Togarmah *from* the far north and all its troops—many people *are* with you.

7"Prepare yourself and be ready, you and all your companies that are gathered about you; and be a guard for them. 8After many days you will be visited. In the latter years you will come into the land of those brought back from the sword *and* gathered from many people on the mountains of Israel, which had long been desolate; they were brought out of the nations, and now all of them dwell safely. 9You will ascend, coming like a storm, covering the land like a cloud, you and all your troops and many peoples with you."

10Thus says the Lord GOD: "On that day it shall come to pass *that* thoughts will arise in your mind, and you will make an evil plan: 11You will say, 'I will go up against a land of unwalled villages; I will go to a peaceful people, who dwell safely, all of them dwelling without walls, and having neither bars nor gates'—12to take plunder and to take booty, to stretch out your hand against the waste places *that are again* inhabited, and against a people gathered from the nations, who have acquired livestock and goods, who dwell in the midst of the land. 13Sheba, Dedan, the merchants of Tarshish, and all their young lions will say to you, 'Have you come to take plunder? Have you gathered your army to take booty, to carry away silver and gold, to take away livestock and goods, to take great plunder?' "'

14"Therefore, son of man, prophesy and say to Gog, 'Thus says the Lord GOD: "On that day when My people Israel dwell safely, will you not know *it*? 15Then you will come from your place out of the far north, you and many peoples with you, all of them riding on horses, a great company and a mighty army. 16You will come up against My people Israel like a cloud, to cover the land. It will be in the latter days that I will bring you against My land, so that the nations may know Me, when I am hallowed in you, O Gog, before their eyes." 17Thus says the Lord GOD: "Are *you* he of whom I have spoken in former days by My servants the prophets of Israel, who prophesied for years in those days that I would bring you against them?

Judgment on Gog

18"And it will come to pass at the same time, when Gog comes against the land of Israel," says the Lord GOD, "*that* My fury will show in My face. 19For in My jealousy *and* in the fire of My wrath I have spoken: 'Surely in that day there shall be a great earthquake in the land of Israel, 20so that the fish of the sea, the birds of the heavens, the beasts of the field, all creeping things that creep on the earth, and all men who *are* on the face of the earth shall shake at My presence. The mountains shall be thrown down, the steep places shall fall, and every wall shall fall to the ground.' 21I will call for a sword against Gog throughout all My mountains," says the Lord GOD. "Every man's sword will be against his brother. 22And I will bring him to judgment with pestilence and bloodshed; I will rain down on him, on his troops, and on the many peoples who *are* with him, flooding rain, great hailstones, fire, and brimstone. 23Thus I will magnify Myself and sanctify Myself, and I will be known in the eyes of many nations. Then they shall know that I *am* the LORD." '

Gog's Armies Destroyed

39 "And you, son of man, prophesy against Gog, and say, 'Thus says the Lord GOD: "Behold, I *am* against you, O Gog, the prince of Rosh, Meshech, and Tubal; 2and I will turn you around and lead you on, bringing you up from the far north, and bring you against the mountains of Israel. 3Then I will knock the bow out of your left hand, and cause the arrows to fall out of your right hand. 4You shall fall upon the mountains of Israel, you and all your troops and the peoples who *are* with you; I will give you to birds of prey of every sort and *to* the beasts of the field to be devoured. 5You shall fall on the open field; for I have spoken," says the Lord GOD. 6"And I will send fire on Magog and on those who live in security in the coastlands. Then they shall know that I *am* the LORD. 7So I will make My holy name known in the midst of My people Israel, and I will not *let them* profane My holy name anymore. Then the nations shall know that *I am* the LORD, the Holy One in Israel. 8Surely it is coming, and it shall be done," says the Lord GOD. "This *is* the day of which I have spoken.

9"Then those who dwell in the cities of Israel will go out and set on fire and burn the weapons, both the shields and bucklers, the bows and arrows, the javelins and spears; and they will make fires with them for seven years. 10They will not take wood from the field nor cut down *any* from the forests, because they will make fires with the weapons; and they will plunder those who plundered them, and pillage those who pillaged them," says the Lord GOD.

The Burial of Gog

11"It will come to pass in that day *that* I will give Gog a burial place there in Israel, the valley of those who pass by east of the sea; and it will obstruct travelers, because there they will bury Gog and all his multitude. Therefore they will call *it* the Valley of Hamon Gog.*i* 12For seven months the house of Israel will be burying them, in order to cleanse the land. 13Indeed all the people of the land will be burying, and they will gain renown for it on the day that I am glorified," says the Lord GOD. 14"They will set apart men regularly employed, with the help of a search party, to pass through the land and bury those bodies remaining on the ground, in order to cleanse it. At the end of seven months they will make a search. 15The search party will pass through the land; and *when anyone* sees a man's bone, he shall set up a marker by it, till the buriers have buried

it in the Valley of Hamon Gog. 16*The* name of *the* city *will* also *be* Hamonah. Thus they shall cleanse the land." '

A Triumphant Festival

17"And as for you, son of man, thus says the Lord GOD, 'Speak to every sort of bird and to every beast of the field:
"Assemble yourselves and come;
  Gather together from all sides to
    My sacrificial meal
  Which I am sacrificing for you,
  A great sacrificial meal on the
    mountains of Israel,
  That you may eat flesh and drink
    blood.
18 You shall eat the flesh of the
    mighty,
  Drink the blood of the princes of
    the earth,
  Of rams and lambs,
  Of goats and bulls,
  All of them fatlings of Bashan.
19 You shall eat fat till you are full,
  And drink blood till you are drunk,
  At My sacrificial meal
  Which I am sacrificing for you.
20 You shall be filled at My table
  With horses and riders,
  With mighty men
  And with all the men of war," says
    the Lord GOD.

Israel Restored to the Land

21"I will set My glory among the nations; all the nations shall see My judgment which I have executed, and My hand which I have laid on them. 22So the house of Israel shall know that I *am* the LORD their God from that day forward. 23The Gentiles shall know that the house of Israel went into captivity for their iniquity; because they were unfaithful to Me, therefore I hid My face from them. I gave them into the hand of their enemies, and they all fell by the sword. 24According to their uncleanness and according to their transgressions I have dealt with them, and hidden My face from them." '

25"Therefore thus says the Lord GOD: 'Now I will bring back the captives of Jacob, and have mercy on the whole house of Israel; and I will be jealous for My holy name—26after they have

i Literally *The Multitude of Gog*

borne their shame, and all their unfaithfulness in which they were unfaithful to Me, when they dwelt safely in their own land and no one made them afraid. 27When I have brought them back from the peoples and gathered them out of their enemies' lands, and I am hallowed in them in the sight of many nations, 28then they shall know that I am the LORD their God, who sent them into captivity among the nations, but also brought them back to their land, and left none of them captive any longer. 29And I will not hide My face from them anymore; for I shall have poured out My Spirit on the house of Israel,' says the Lord GOD."

A New City, a New Temple

40 In the twenty-fifth year of our captivity, at the beginning of the year, on the tenth day of the month, in the fourteenth year after the city was captured, on the very same day the hand of the LORD was upon me; and He took me there. 2In the visions of God He took me into the land of Israel and set me on a very high mountain; on it toward the south was something like the structure of a city. 3He took me there, and behold, there was a man whose appearance was like the appearance of bronze. He had a line of flax and a measuring rod in his hand, and he stood in the gateway.

4And the man said to me, "Son of man, look with your eyes and hear with your ears, and fix your mind on everything I show you; for you were brought here so that I might show them to you. Declare to the house of Israel everything you see." 5Now there was a wall all around the outside of the temple. In the man's hand was a measuring rod six cubits long, each being a cubit and a handbreadth; and he measured the width of the wall structure, one rod; and the height, one rod.

The Eastern Gateway of the Temple

6Then he went to the gateway which faced east; and he went up its stairs and measured the threshold of the gateway, which was one rod wide, and the other threshold was one rod wide. 7Each gate chamber was one rod long and one rod wide; between the gate chambers was

a space of five cubits; and the threshold of the gateway by the vestibule of the inside gate was one rod. 8He also measured the vestibule of the inside gate, one rod. 9Then he measured the vestibule of the gateway, eight cubits; and the gateposts, two cubits. The vestibule of the gate was on the inside. 10In the eastern gateway were three gate chambers on one side and three on the other; the three were all the same size; also the gateposts were of the same size on this side and that side.

11He measured the width of the entrance to the gateway, ten cubits; and the length of the gate, thirteen cubits. 12There was a space in front of the gate chambers, one cubit on this side and one cubit on that side; the gate chambers were six cubits on this side and six cubits on that side. 13Then he measured the gateway from the roof of one gate chamber to the roof of the other; the width was twenty-five cubits, as door faces door. 14He measured the gateposts, sixty cubits high, and the court all around the gateway extended to the gatepost. 15From the front of the entrance gate to the front of the vestibule of the inner gate was fifty cubits. 16There were beveled window frames in the gate chambers and in their intervening archways on the inside of the gateway all around, and likewise in the vestibules. There were windows all around on the inside. And on each gatepost were palm trees.

The Outer Court

17Then he brought me into the outer court; and there were chambers and a pavement made all around the court; thirty chambers faced the pavement. 18The pavement was by the side of the gateways, corresponding to the length of the gateways; this was the lower pavement. 19Then he measured the width from the front of the lower gateway to the front of the inner court exterior, one hundred cubits toward the east and the north.

The Northern Gateway

20On the outer court was also a gateway facing north, and he measured its length and its width. 21Its gate chambers, three on this side and three on that side, its gateposts and its archways, had the same measurements as the first gate; its length *was* fifty cubits and its width twenty-five cubits. 22Its windows and those of its archways, and also its palm trees, *had* the same measurements as the gateway facing east; it was ascended by seven steps, and its archway *was* in front of it. 23A gate of the inner court was opposite the northern gateway, just as the eastern *gateway;* and he measured from gateway to gateway, one hundred cubits.

The Southern Gateway

24After that he brought me toward the south, and there a gateway was facing south; and he measured its gateposts and archways according to these same measurements. 25*There were* windows in it and in its archways all around like those windows; its length *was* fifty cubits and its width twenty-five cubits. 26Seven steps led up to it, and its archway *was* in front of them; and it had palm trees on its gateposts, one on this side and one on that side. 27*There was* also a gateway on the inner court, facing south; and he measured from gateway to gateway toward the south, one hundred cubits.

Gateways of the Inner Court

28Then he brought me to the inner court through the southern gateway; he measured the southern gateway according to these same measurements. 29Also its gate chambers, its gateposts, and its archways *were* according to these same measurements; *there were* windows in it and in its archways all around; *it was* fifty cubits long and twenty-five cubits wide. 30*There were* archways all around, twenty-five cubits long and five cubits wide. 31Its archways faced the outer court, palm trees *were* on its gateposts, and going up to it *were* eight steps.

32And he brought me into the inner court facing east; he measured the gateway according to these same measurements. 33Also its gate chambers, its gateposts, and its archways *were* according to these same measurements; and *there were* windows in it and in its archways all around; *it was* fifty cubits long and twenty-five cubits wide.

34Its archways faced the outer court, and palm trees *were* on its gateposts on this side and on that side; and going up to it *were* eight steps.

35Then he brought me to the north gateway and measured *it* according to these same measurements—36also its gate chambers, its gateposts, and its archways. It had windows all around; its length *was* fifty cubits and its width twenty-five cubits. 37Its gateposts faced the outer court, palm trees *were* on its gateposts on this side and on that side, and going up to it *were* eight steps.

Where Sacrifices Were Prepared

38*There was* a chamber and its entrance by the gateposts of the gateway, where they washed the burnt offering. 39In the vestibule of the gateway *were* two tables on this side and two tables on that side, on which to slay the burnt offering, the sin offering, and the trespass offering. 40At the outer side of the vestibule, as one goes up to the entrance of the northern gateway, *were* two tables; and on the other side of the vestibule of the gateway *were* two tables. 41Four tables *were* on this side and four tables on that side, by the side of the gateway, eight tables on which they slaughtered *the sacrifices.* 42*There were* also four tables of hewn stone for the burnt offering, one cubit and a half long, one cubit and a half wide, and one cubit high; on these they laid the instruments with which they slaughtered the burnt offering and the sacrifice. 43Inside *were* hooks, a handbreadth wide, fastened all around; and the flesh of the sacrifices *was* on the tables.

Chambers for Singers and Priests

44Outside the inner gate *were* the chambers for the singers in the inner court, one facing south at the side of the northern gateway, and the other facing north at the side of the southern gateway. 45Then he said to me, "This chamber which faces south *is* for the priests who have charge of the temple. 46The chamber which faces north *is* for the priests who have charge of the altar; these *are* the sons of Zadok, from the sons of Levi, who come near the LORD to minister to Him."

Dimensions of the Inner Court and Vestibule

47And he measured the court, one hundred cubits long and one hundred cubits wide, foursquare. The altar *was* in front of the temple. 48Then he brought me to the vestibule of the temple and measured the doorposts of the vestibule, five cubits on this side and five cubits on that side; and the width of the gateway was three cubits on this side and three cubits on that side. 49The length of the vestibule *was* twenty cubits, and the width eleven cubits; and by the steps which led up to it *there were* pillars by the doorposts, one on this side and another on that side.

Dimensions of the Sanctuary

41 Then he brought me into the sanctuary[j] and measured the doorposts, six cubits wide on one side and six cubits wide on the other side— the width of the tabernacle. 2The width of the entryway *was* ten cubits, and the side walls of the entrance *were* five cubits on this side and five cubits on the other side; and he measured its length, forty cubits, and its width, twenty cubits.

3Also he went inside and measured the doorposts, two cubits; and the entrance, six cubits *high;* and the width of the entrance, seven cubits. 4He measured the length, twenty cubits; and the width, twenty cubits, beyond the sanctuary; and he said to me, "This *is* the Most Holy Place."

The Side Chambers on the Wall

5Next, he measured the wall of the temple, six cubits. The width of each side chamber all around the temple *was* four cubits on every side. 6The side chambers *were* in three stories, one above the other, thirty chambers in each story; they rested on ledges which *were* for the side chambers all around, that they might be supported, but not fastened to the wall of the temple. 7As one went up from story to story, the side chambers became wider all around, because their supporting ledges in the wall of the temple ascended like steps; therefore the width of the structure increased as one went up *from* the lowest *story* to the highest by way of the middle one. 8I also saw an elevation all around the temple; it was the foundation of the side chambers, a full rod, *that is,* six cubits *high.* 9The thickness of the outer wall of the side chambers *was* five cubits, and so also the remaining terrace by the place of the side chambers of the temple. 10And between *it and* the *wall* chambers was a width of twenty cubits all around the temple on every side. 11The doors of the side chambers opened on the terrace, one door toward the north and another toward the south; and the width of the terrace *was* five cubits all around.

The Building at the Western End

12The building that faced the separating courtyard at its western end *was* seventy cubits wide; the wall of the building *was* five cubits thick all around, and its length ninety cubits.

Dimensions and Design of the Temple Area

13So he measured the temple, one hundred cubits long; and the separating courtyard with the building and its walls *was* one hundred cubits long; 14also the width of the eastern face of the temple, including the separating courtyard, *was* one hundred cubits. 15He measured the length of the building behind it, facing the separating courtyard, with its galleries on the one side and on the other side, one hundred cubits, as well as the inner temple and the porches of the court, 16their doorposts and the beveled window frames. And the galleries all around their three stories opposite the threshold were paneled with wood from the ground to the windows—the windows were covered— 17from the space above the door, even to the inner room, as well as outside, and on every wall all around, inside and outside, by measure.

18And *it was* made with cherubim and palm trees, a palm tree between cherub and cherub. *Each* cherub had

---

j Here the main room of the temple; sometimes called the *holy place* (compare Exodus 26.33) two faces, 19so that the face of a man *was* toward a palm tree on one side, and the face of a young lion toward a palm tree on the other side; thus *it was* made throughout the temple all around. 20From the floor to the space above the door, and on the wall of the sanctuary, cherubim and palm trees *were* carved.

21The doorposts of the temple *were* square, *as was* the front of the sanctuary; their appearance was similar. 22The altar *was* of wood, three cubits high, and its length two cubits. Its corners, its length, and its sides *were* of wood; and he said to me, "This *is* the table that *is* before the LORD."

23The temple and the sanctuary had two doors. 24The doors had two panels *apiece*, two folding panels: two *panels* for one door and two panels for the other *door*. 25Cherubim and palm trees *were* carved on the doors of the temple just as they *were* carved on the walls. A wooden canopy *was* on the front of the vestibule outside. 26*There were* beveled window *frames* and palm trees on one side and on the other, on the sides of the vestibule—also on the side chambers of the temple and on the canopies.

The Chambers for the Priests

42 Then he brought me out into the outer court, by the way toward the north; and he brought me into the chamber which *was* opposite the separating courtyard, and which *was* opposite the building toward the north. 2Facing the length, *which was* one hundred cubits (the width was fifty cubits), was the north door. 3Opposite the inner court of twenty *cubits*, and opposite the pavement of the outer court, *was* gallery against gallery in three *stories*. 4In front of the chambers, toward the inside, *was* a walk ten cubits wide, at a distance of one cubit; and their doors faced north. 5Now the upper chambers *were* shorter, because the galleries took away *space* from them more than from the lower and middle stories of the building. 6For they *were* in three *stories* and did not have pillars like the pillars of the courts; therefore *the upper level* was shortened more than the lower and middle levels from the ground up.

7And a wall which *was* outside ran parallel to the chambers, at the front of the chambers, toward the outer court; its length *was* fifty cubits. 8The length of the chambers toward the outer court *was* fifty cubits, whereas that facing the temple *was* one hundred cubits. 9At the lower chambers *was* the entrance on the east side, as one goes into them from the outer court.

10Also *there were* chambers in the thickness of the wall of the court toward the east, opposite the separating courtyard and opposite the building. 11*There was* a walk in front of them also, and their appearance *was* like the chambers which *were* toward the north; they *were* as long and as wide as the others, and all their exits and entrances *were* according to plan. 12And corresponding to the doors of the chambers that *were* facing south, as one enters them, *there was* a door in front of the walk, the way directly in front of the wall toward the east.

13Then he said to me, "The north chambers *and* the south chambers, which *are* opposite the separating courtyard, *are* the holy chambers where the priests who approach the LORD shall eat the most holy offerings. There they shall lay the most holy offerings—the grain offering, the sin offering, and the trespass offering—for the place *is* holy. 14When the priests enter them, they shall not go out of the holy *chamber* into the outer court; but there they shall leave their garments in which they minister, for they *are* holy. They shall put on other garments; then they may approach *that* which *is* for the people."

Outer Dimensions of the Temple

15Now when he had finished measuring the inner temple, he brought me out through the gateway that faces toward the east, and measured it all around. 16He measured the east side with the measuring rod,[k] five hundred rods by the measuring rod all around. 17He measured the north side, five hundred rods by the measuring rod all around. 18He measured the south side, five hundred rods by the measuring rod. 19He came around to the west side *and* measured five hundred rods by the measuring rod. 20He measured it on the four sides; it had a wall all around, five hundred cubits long and five hundred wide, to separate the holy areas from the common.

The Temple, the LORD's Dwelling Place

43 Afterward he brought me to the gate, the gate that faces toward the east. 2And behold, the glory of the God of Israel came from the way of the east. His voice was like the sound of many waters; and the earth shone with His glory. 3It was like the appearance of the vision which I saw—like the vision which I saw when I came to destroy the city. The visions were like the vision which I saw by the River Chebar; and I fell on my face. 4And the glory of the LORD came into the temple by way of the gate which faces toward the east. 5The Spirit lifted me up and brought me into the inner court; and behold, the glory of the LORD filled the temple.

6Then I heard Him speaking to me from the temple, while a man stood beside me. 7And He said to me, "Son of man, this is the place of My throne and the place of the soles of My feet, where I will dwell in the midst of the children of Israel forever. No more shall the house of Israel defile My holy name, they nor their kings, by their harlotry or with the carcasses of their kings on their high places. 8When they set their threshold by My threshold, and their doorpost by My doorpost, with a wall between them and Me, they defiled My holy name by the abominations which they committed; therefore I have consumed them in My anger. 9Now let them put their harlotry and the carcasses of their kings far away from Me, and I will dwell in their midst forever.

10"Son of man, describe the temple to the house of Israel, that they may be ashamed of their iniquities; and let them measure the pattern. 11And if they are ashamed of all that they have done, make known to them the design of the temple and its arrangement, its exits and its entrances, its entire design and all its ordinances, all its forms and all its laws. Write it down in their sight, so that they may keep its whole design

and all its ordinances, and perform them. 12This is the law of the temple: The whole area surrounding the mountaintop is most holy. Behold, this is the law of the temple.

Dimensions of the Altar

13"These are the measurements of the altar in cubits (the cubit is one cubit and a handbreadth): the base one cubit high and one cubit wide, with a rim all around its edge of one span. This is the height of the altar: 14from the base on the ground to the lower ledge, two cubits; the width of the ledge, one cubit; from the smaller ledge to the larger ledge, four cubits; and the width of the ledge, one cubit. 15The altar hearth is four cubits high, with four horns extending upward from the hearth. 16The altar hearth is twelve cubits long, twelve wide, square at its four corners; 17the ledge, fourteen cubits long and fourteen wide on its four sides, with a rim of half a cubit around it; its base, one cubit all around; and its steps face toward the east."

Consecrating the Altar

18And He said to me, "Son of man, thus says the Lord GOD: 'These are the ordinances for the altar on the day when it is made, for sacrificing burnt offerings on it, and for sprinkling blood on it. 19You shall give a young bull for a sin offering to the priests, the Levites, who are of the seed of Zadok, who approach Me to minister to Me,' says the Lord GOD. 20You shall take some of its blood and put it on the four horns of the altar, on the four corners of the ledge, and on the rim around it; thus you shall cleanse it and make atonement for it. 21Then you shall also take the bull of the sin offering, and burn it in the appointed place of the temple, outside the sanctuary. 22On the second day you shall offer a kid of the goats without blemish for a sin offering; and they shall cleanse the altar, as they cleansed it with the bull. 23When you have finished cleansing it, you shall offer a young bull without blemish, and a ram from the flock without blemish. 24When you offer them before the LORD, the priests shall throw salt on them, and they will offer them up as a burnt offering to the LORD. 25Every day for seven days you shall prepare a goat *for* a sin offering; they shall also prepare a young bull and a ram from the flock, both without blemish. 26Seven days they shall make atonement for the altar and purify it, and so consecrate *it*. 27When these days are over it shall be, on the eighth day and thereafter, that the priests shall offer your burnt offerings and your peace offerings on the altar; and I will accept you,' says the Lord GOD."

The East Gate and the Prince

44 Then He brought me back to the outer gate of the sanctuary which faces toward the east, but it *was* shut. 2And the LORD said to me, "This gate shall be shut; it shall not be opened, and no man shall enter by it, because the LORD God of Israel has entered by it; therefore it shall be shut. 3*As for* the prince, *because* he *is* the prince, he may sit in it to eat bread before the LORD; he shall enter by way of the vestibule of the gateway, and go out the same way."

Those Admitted to the Temple

4Also He brought me by way of the north gate to the front of the temple; so I looked, and behold, the glory of the LORD filled the house of the LORD; and I fell on my face. 5And the LORD said to me, "Son of man, mark well, see with your eyes and hear with your ears, all that I say to you concerning all the ordinances of the house of the LORD and all its laws. Mark well who may enter the house and all who go out from the sanctuary.

6"Now say to the rebellious, to the house of Israel, 'Thus says the Lord GOD: "O house of Israel, let Us have no more of all your abominations. 7When you brought in foreigners, uncircumcised in heart and uncircumcised in flesh, to be in My sanctuary to defile it—My house—and when you offered My food, the fat and the blood, then they broke My covenant because of all your abominations. 8And you have not kept charge of My holy things, but you have set *others* to keep charge of My sanctuary for you." 9Thus says the Lord GOD: "No foreigner, uncircum-

cised in heart or uncircumcised in flesh, shall enter My sanctuary, including any foreigner who *is* among the children of Israel.

Laws Governing Priests

10"And the Levites who went far from Me, when Israel went astray, who strayed away from Me after their idols, they shall bear their iniquity. 11Yet they shall be ministers in My sanctuary, *as* gatekeepers of the house and ministers of the house; they shall slay the burnt offering and the sacrifice for the people, and they shall stand before them to minister to them. 12Because they ministered to them before their idols and caused the house of Israel to fall into iniquity, therefore I have raised My hand in an oath against them," says the Lord GOD, "that they shall bear their iniquity. 13And they shall not come near Me to minister to Me as priest, nor come near any of My holy things, nor into the Most Holy *Place;* but they shall bear their shame and their abominations which they have committed. 14Nevertheless I will make them keep charge of the temple, for all its work, and for all that has to be done in it.

15"But the priests, the Levites, the sons of Zadok, who kept charge of My sanctuary when the children of Israel went astray from Me, they shall come near Me to minister to Me; and they shall stand before Me to offer to Me the fat and the blood," says the Lord GOD. 16"They shall enter My sanctuary, and they shall come near My table to minister to Me, and they shall keep My charge. 17And it shall be, whenever they enter the gates of the inner court, that they shall put on linen garments; no wool shall come upon them while they minister within the gates of the inner court or within the house. 18They shall have linen turbans on their heads and linen trousers on their bodies; they shall not clothe themselves with *anything that causes* sweat. 19When they go out to the outer court, to the *outer* court to the people, they shall take off their garments in which they have ministered, leave them in the holy chambers, and put on other garments; and in their holy garments they shall not sanctify the people.

20"They shall neither shave their heads, nor let their hair grow long, but they shall keep their hair well trimmed. 21No priest shall drink wine when he enters the inner court. 22They shall not take as wife a widow or a divorced woman, but take virgins of the descendants of the house of Israel, or widows of priests.

23"And they shall teach My people *the difference* between the holy and the unholy, and cause them to discern between the unclean and the clean. 24In controversy they shall stand as judges, *and* judge it according to My judgments. They shall keep My laws and My statutes in all My appointed meetings, and they shall hallow My Sabbaths.

25"They shall not defile *themselves* by coming near a dead person. Only for father or mother, for son or daughter, for brother or unmarried sister may they defile themselves. 26After he is cleansed, they shall count seven days for him. 27And on the day that he goes to the sanctuary to minister in the sanctuary, he must offer his sin offering in the inner court," says the Lord GOD.

28"It shall be, in regard to their inheritance, *that* I *am* their inheritance. You shall give them no possession in Israel, for I *am* their possession. 29They shall eat the grain offering, the sin offering, and the trespass offering; every dedicated thing in Israel shall be theirs. 30The best of all firstfruits of any kind, and every sacrifice of any kind from all your sacrifices, shall be the priest's; also you shall give to the priest the first of your ground meal, to cause a blessing to rest on your house. 31The priests shall not eat anything, bird or beast, that died naturally or was torn *by wild beasts.*

The Holy District

45 "Moreover, when you divide the land by lot into inheritance, you shall set apart a district for the LORD, a holy section of the land; its length *shall be* twenty-five thousand *cubits,* and the width ten thousand. It *shall be* holy throughout its territory all around. 2Of this there shall be a square plot for the sanctuary, five hundred by five hundred *rods,* with fifty cubits around it for an open space. 3So this is the district

you shall measure: twenty-five thousand *cubits* long and ten thousand wide; in it shall be the sanctuary, the Most Holy *Place.* 4It shall be a holy *section* of the land, belonging to the priests, the ministers of the sanctuary, who come near to minister to the LORD; it shall be a place for their houses and a holy place for the sanctuary. 5An area twenty-five thousand *cubits* long and ten thousand wide shall belong to the Levites, the ministers of the temple; they shall have twenty chambers as a possession.

Properties of the City and the Prince

6"You shall appoint as the property of the city *an area* five thousand *cubits* wide and twenty-five thousand long, adjacent to the district of the holy *section;* it shall belong to the whole house of Israel.

7"The prince shall have *a section* on one side and the other of the holy district and the city's property; and bordering on the holy district and the city's property, extending westward on the west side and eastward on the east side, the length *shall be* side by side with one of the *tribal* portions, from the west border to the east border. 8The land shall be his possession in Israel; and My princes shall no more oppress My people, but they shall give *the rest of* the land to the house of Israel, according to their tribes."

Laws Governing the Prince

9'Thus says the Lord GOD: "Enough, O princes of Israel! Remove violence and plundering, execute justice and righteousness, and stop dispossessing My people," says the Lord GOD. 10"You shall have honest scales, an honest ephah, and an honest bath. 11The ephah and the bath shall be of the same measure, so that the bath contains one-tenth of a homer, and the ephah one-tenth of a homer; their measure shall be according to the homer. 12The shekel *shall be* twenty gerahs; twenty shekels, twenty-five shekels, *and* fifteen shekels shall be your mina.

13"This *is* the offering which you shall offer: you shall give one-sixth of an ephah from a homer of wheat, and one-sixth of an ephah from a homer of barley. 14The ordinance concerning oil, the bath of oil, *is* one-tenth of a bath from a kor. A kor *is* a homer or ten baths, for ten baths *are* a homer. 15And one lamb shall be given from a flock of two hundred, from the rich pastures of Israel. These shall be for grain offerings, burnt offerings, and peace offerings, to make atonement for them," says the Lord GOD. 16"All the people of the land shall give this offering for the prince in Israel. 17Then it shall be the prince's part *to give* burnt offerings, grain offerings, and drink offerings, at the feasts, the New Moons, the Sabbaths, and at all the appointed seasons of the house of Israel. He shall prepare the sin offering, the grain offering, the burnt offering, and the peace offerings to make atonement for the house of Israel."

Keeping the Feasts

18'Thus says the Lord GOD: "In the first *month*, on the first *day* of the month, you shall take a young bull without blemish and cleanse the sanctuary. 19The priest shall take some of the blood of the sin offering and put *it* on the doorposts of the temple, on the four corners of the ledge of the altar, and on the gateposts of the gate of the inner court. 20And so you shall do on the seventh *day* of the month for everyone who has sinned unintentionally or in ignorance. Thus you shall make atonement for the temple.

21"In the first *month*, on the fourteenth day of the month, you shall observe the Passover, a feast of seven days; unleavened bread shall be eaten. 22And on that day the prince shall prepare for himself and for all the people of the land a bull *for* a sin offering. 23On the seven days of the feast he shall prepare a burnt offering to the LORD, seven bulls and seven rams without blemish, daily for seven days, and a kid of the goats daily *for* a sin offering. 24And he shall prepare a grain offering of one ephah for each bull and one ephah for each ram, together with a hin of oil for each ephah.

25"In the seventh *month*, on the fifteenth day of the month, at the feast, he shall do likewise for seven days, according to the sin offering, the burnt offering, the grain offering, and the oil."

The Manner of Worship

46 'Thus says the Lord GOD: "The gateway of the inner court that faces toward the east shall be shut the six working days; but on the Sabbath it shall be opened, and on the day of the New Moon it shall be opened. 2The prince shall enter by way of the vestibule of the gateway from the outside, and stand by the gatepost. The priests shall prepare his burnt offering and his peace offerings. He shall worship at the threshold of the gate. Then he shall go out, but the gate shall not be shut until evening. 3Likewise the people of the land shall worship at the entrance to this gateway before the LORD on the Sabbaths and the New Moons. 4The burnt offering that the prince offers to the LORD on the Sabbath day *shall be* six lambs without blemish, and a ram without blemish; 5and the grain offering *shall be one* ephah for a ram, and the grain offering for the lambs, as much as he wants to give, as well as a hin of oil with every ephah. 6On the day of the New Moon *it shall be* a young bull without blemish, six lambs, and a ram; they shall be without blemish. 7He shall prepare a grain offering of an ephah for a bull, an ephah for a ram, as much as he wants to give for the lambs, and a hin of oil with every ephah. 8When the prince enters, he shall go in by way of the vestibule of the gateway, and go out the same way.

9"But when the people of the land come before the LORD on the appointed feast days, whoever enters by way of the north gate to worship shall go out by way of the south gate; and whoever enters by way of the south gate shall go out by way of the north gate. He shall not return by way of the gate through which he came, but shall go out through the opposite gate. 10The prince shall then be in their midst. When they go in, he shall go in; and when they go out, he shall go out. 11At the festivals and the appointed feast days the grain offering shall be an ephah for a bull, an ephah for a ram, as much as he wants to give for the lambs, and a hin of oil with every ephah.

12"Now when the prince makes a voluntary burnt offering or voluntary peace offering to the LORD, the gate that faces toward the east shall then be opened for him; and he shall prepare his burnt offering and his peace offerings as he did on the Sabbath day. Then he shall go out, and after he goes out the gate shall be shut.

13"You shall daily make a burnt offering to the LORD *of* a lamb of the first year without blemish; you shall prepare it every morning. 14And you shall prepare a grain offering with it every morning, a sixth of an ephah, and a third of a hin of oil to moisten the fine flour. This grain offering is a perpetual ordinance, to be made regularly to the LORD. 15Thus they shall prepare the lamb, the grain offering, and the oil, *as* a regular burnt offering every morning."

The Prince and Inheritance Laws

16'Thus says the Lord GOD: "If the prince gives a gift *of some* of his inheritance to any of his sons, it shall belong to his sons; it is their possession by inheritance. 17But if he gives a gift of some of his inheritance to one of his servants, it shall be his until the year of liberty, after which it shall return to the prince. But his inheritance shall belong to his sons; it shall become theirs. 18Moreover the prince shall not take any of the people's inheritance by evicting them from their property; he shall provide an inheritance for his sons from his own property, so that none of My people may be scattered from his property." ' "

How the Offerings Were Prepared

19Now he brought me through the entrance, which *was* at the side of the gate, into the holy chambers of the priests which face toward the north; and there a place *was* situated at their extreme western end. 20And he said to me, "This *is* the place where the priests shall boil the trespass offering and the sin offering, *and* where they shall bake the grain offering, so that they do not bring *them* out into the outer court to sanctify the people."

21Then he brought me out into the outer court and caused me to pass by the four corners of the court; and in fact, in every corner of the court *there was another* court. 22In the four corners of the court *were* enclosed courts, forty *cubits* long and thirty wide; all four corners *were* the same size. 23*There was* a row *of building stones* all around in them, all around the four of them; and cooking hearths were made under the rows of stones all around. 24And he said to me, "These *are* the kitchens where the ministers of the temple shall boil the sacrifices of the people."

The Healing Waters and Trees

47 Then he brought me back to the door of the temple; and there was water, flowing from under the threshold of the temple toward the east, for the front of the temple faced east; the water was flowing from under the right side of the temple, south of the altar. 2He brought me out by way of the north gate, and led me around on the outside to the outer gateway that faces east; and there was water, running out on the right side.

3And when the man went out to the east with the line in his hand, he measured one thousand cubits, and he brought me through the waters; the water *came up to my* ankles. 4Again he measured one thousand and brought me through the waters; the water *came up to my* knees. Again he measured one thousand and brought me through; the water *came up to my* waist. 5Again he measured one thousand, *and it was* a river that I could not cross; for the water was too deep, water in which one must swim, a river that could not be crossed. 6He said to me, "Son of man, have you seen *this*?" Then he brought me and returned me to the bank of the river.

7When I returned, there, along the bank of the river, *were* very many trees on one side and the other. 8Then he said to me: "This water flows toward the eastern region, goes down into the valley, and enters the sea. When it reaches the sea, *its* waters are healed. 9And it shall be *that* every living thing that moves, wherever the rivers go, will live. There will be a very great multitude of fish, because these waters go there; for they will be healed, and everything will live wherever the river goes. 10It shall be *that* fishermen will stand by it from En Gedi to En Eglaim; they will be *places* for spreading their nets. Their fish will be of the same kinds as the fish of the Great Sea, exceedingly many. 11But its swamps and marshes will not be healed; they will be given over to salt. 12Along the bank of the river, on this side and that, will grow all *kinds of* trees used for food; their leaves will not wither, and their fruit will not fail. They will bear fruit every month, because their water flows from the sanctuary. Their fruit will be for food, and their leaves for medicine."

Borders of the Land

13Thus says the Lord GOD: "These *are* the borders by which you shall divide the land as an inheritance among the twelve tribes of Israel. Joseph *shall have two* portions. 14You shall inherit it equally with one another; for I raised My hand in an oath to give it to your fathers, and this land shall fall to you as your inheritance.

15"This *shall be* the border of the land on the north: from the Great Sea, *by* the road to Hethlon, as one goes to Zedad, 16Hamath, Berothah, Sibraim (which *is* between the border of Damascus and the border of Hamath), to Hazar Hatticon (which *is* on the border of Hauran). 17Thus the boundary shall be from the Sea to Hazar Enan, the border of Damascus; and as for the north, northward, it is the border of Hamath. *This is* the north side.

18"On the east side you shall mark out the border from between Hauran and Damascus, and between Gilead and the land of Israel, along the Jordan, and along the eastern side of the sea. *This is* the east side.

19"The south side, toward the South, *shall be* from Tamar to the waters of Meribah by Kadesh, along the brook to the Great Sea. *This is* the south side, toward the South.

20"The west side *shall be* the Great Sea, from the *southern* boundary until one comes to a point opposite Hamath. This *is* the west side.

21"Thus you shall divide this land among yourselves according to the tribes of Israel. 22It shall be that you

will divide it by lot as an inheritance for yourselves, and for the strangers who dwell among you and who bear children among you. They shall be to you as native-born among the children of Israel; they shall have an inheritance with you among the tribes of Israel. 23And it shall be *that* in whatever tribe the stranger dwells, there you shall give *him* his inheritance," says the Lord GOD.

Division of the Land

48 "Now these *are* the names of the tribes: From the northern border along the road to Hethlon at the entrance of Hamath, to Hazar Enan, the border of Damascus northward, in the direction of Hamath, *there shall be* one *section for* Dan from its east to its west side; 2by the border of Dan, from the east side to the west, one *section for* Asher; 3by the border of Asher, from the east side to the west, one *section for* Naphtali; 4by the border of Naphtali, from the east side to the west, one *section for* Manasseh; 5by the border of Manasseh, from the east side to the west, one *section for* Ephraim; 6by the border of Ephraim, from the east side to the west, one *section for* Reuben; 7by the border of Reuben, from the east side to the west, one *section for* Judah; 8by the border of Judah, from the east side to the west, shall be the district which you shall set apart, twenty-five thousand *cubits* in width, and *in* length the same as one of the *other* portions, from the east side to the west, with the sanctuary in the center.

9"The district that you shall set apart for the LORD *shall be* twenty-five thousand *cubits* in length and ten thousand in width. 10To these—to the priests—the holy district shall belong: on the north twenty-five thousand *cubits in length*, on the west ten thousand in width, on the east ten thousand in width, and on the south twenty-five thousand in length. The sanctuary of the LORD shall be in the center. 11*It shall be* for the priests of the sons of Zadok, who are sanctified, who have kept My charge, who did not go astray when the children of Israel went astray, as the Levites went astray. 12And *this* district of land that is set apart shall be to them a thing most holy by the border of the Levites.

13"Opposite the border of the priests, the Levites *shall have an area* twenty-five thousand *cubits* in length and ten thousand in width; its entire length *shall be* twenty-five thousand and its width ten thousand. 14And they shall not sell or exchange any of it; they may not alienate this best *part* of the land, for *it is* holy to the LORD.

15"The five thousand *cubits* in width that remain, along the edge of the twenty-five thousand, shall be for general use by the city, for dwellings and common-land; and the city shall be in the center. 16These *shall be* its measurements: the north side four thousand five hundred *cubits*, the south side four thousand five hundred, the east side four thousand five hundred, and the west side four thousand five hundred. 17The common-land of the city shall be: to the north two hundred and fifty *cubits*, to the south two hundred and fifty, to the east two hundred and fifty, and to the west two hundred and fifty. 18The rest of the length, alongside the district of the holy *section, shall be* ten thousand *cubits* to the east and ten thousand to the west. It shall be adjacent to the district of the holy *section,* and its produce shall be food for the workers of the city. 19The workers of the city, from all the tribes of Israel, shall cultivate it. 20The entire district *shall be* twenty-five thousand *cubits* by twenty-five thousand *cubits,* foursquare. You shall set apart the holy district with the property of the city.

21"The rest *shall belong* to the prince, on one side and on the other of the holy district and of the city's property, next to the twenty-five thousand *cubits* of the *holy* district as far as the eastern border, and westward next to the twenty-five thousand as far as the western border, adjacent to the *tribal* portions; *it shall belong* to the prince. It shall be the holy district, and the sanctuary of the temple *shall be* in the cen-

ter. 22Moreover, apart from the possession of the Levites and the possession of the city *which are* in the midst of what *belongs* to the prince, *the area* between the border of Judah and the border of Benjamin shall belong to the prince.

23"As for the rest of the tribes, from the east side to the west, Benjamin *shall have* one *section;* 24by the border of Benjamin, from the east side to the west, Simeon *shall have* one *section;* 25by the border of Simeon, from the east side to the west, Issachar *shall have* one *section;* 26by the border of Issachar, from the east side to the west, Zebulun *shall have* one *section;* 27by the border of Zebulun, from the east side to the west, Gad *shall have* one *section;* 28by the border of Gad, on the south side, toward the South, the border shall be from Tamar *to* the waters of Meribah *by* Kadesh, along the brook to the Great Sea. 29This *is* the land which you shall divide by lot as an inheritance among the tribes of Israel, and these *are* their portions," says the Lord GOD.

The Gates of the City and Its Name

30"These *are* the exits of the city. On the north side, measuring four thousand five hundred *cubits* 31(the gates of the city *shall be* named after the tribes of Israel), the three gates northward: one gate for Reuben, one gate for Judah, and one gate for Levi; 32on the east side, four thousand five hundred *cubits,* three gates: one gate for Joseph, one gate for Benjamin, and one gate for Dan; 33on the south side, measuring four thousand five hundred *cubits,* three gates: one gate for Simeon, one gate for Issachar, and one gate for Zebulun; 34on the west side, four thousand five hundred *cubits* with their three gates: one gate for Gad, one gate for Asher, and one gate for Naphtali. 35All the way around *shall be* eighteen thousand *cubits;* and the name of the city from *that* day *shall be:* THE LORD IS THERE."

DANIEL

Daniel and His Friends Obey God

1 In the third year of the reign of Jehoiakim king of Judah, Nebuchadnezzar king of Babylon came to Jerusalem and besieged it. 2And the Lord gave Jehoiakim king of Judah into his hand, with some of the articles of the house of God, which he carried into the land of Shinar to the house of his god; and he brought the articles into the treasure house of his god.

3Then the king instructed Ashpenaz, the master of his eunuchs, to bring some of the children of Israel and some of the king's descendants and some of the nobles, 4young men in whom *there was* no blemish, but good-looking, gifted in all wisdom, possessing knowledge and quick to understand, who *had* ability to serve in the king's palace, and whom they might teach the language and literature of the Chaldeans. 5And the king appointed for them a daily provision of the king's delicacies and of the wine which he drank, and three years of training for them, so that at the end of *that time* they might serve before the king. 6Now from among those of the sons of Judah were Daniel, Hananiah, Mishael, and Azariah. 7To them the chief of the eunuchs gave names: he gave Daniel *the name* Belteshazzar; to Hananiah, Shadrach; to Mishael, Meshach; and to Azariah, Abed-Nego.

8But Daniel purposed in his heart that he would not defile himself with the portion of the king's delicacies, nor with the wine which he drank; therefore he requested of the chief of the eunuchs that he might not defile himself. 9Now God had brought Daniel into the favor and goodwill of the chief of the eunuchs. 10And the chief of the eunuchs said to Daniel, "I fear my lord the king, who has appointed your food and drink. For why should he see your faces looking worse than the young men who *are* your age? Then you would endanger my head before the king."

11So Daniel said to the steward whom the chief of the eunuchs had set over

Daniel, Hananiah, Mishael, and Azariah, 12"Please test your servants for ten days, and let them give us vegetables to eat and water to drink. 13Then let our appearance be examined before you, and the appearance of the young men who eat the portion of the king's delicacies; and as you see fit, *so* deal with your servants." 14So he consented with them in this matter, and tested them ten days.

15And at the end of ten days their features appeared better and fatter in flesh than all the young men who ate the portion of the king's delicacies. 16Thus the steward took away their portion of delicacies and the wine that they were to drink, and gave them vegetables.

17As for these four young men, God gave them knowledge and skill in all literature and wisdom; and Daniel had understanding in all visions and dreams.

18Now at the end of the days, when the king had said that they should be brought in, the chief of the eunuchs brought them in before Nebuchadnezzar. 19Then the king interviewed them, and among them all none was found like Daniel, Hananiah, Mishael, and Azariah; therefore they served before the king. 20And in all matters of wisdom *and* understanding about which the king examined them, he found them ten times better than all the magicians *and* astrologers who *were* in all his realm. 21Thus Daniel continued until the first year of King Cyrus.

Nebuchadnezzar's Dream

2 Now in the second year of Nebuchadnezzar's reign, Nebuchadnezzar had dreams; and his spirit was *so* troubled that his sleep left him. 2Then the king gave the command to call the magicians, the astrologers, the sorcerers, and the Chaldeans to tell the king his dreams. So they came and stood before the king. 3And the king said to them, "I have had a dream, and my spirit is anxious to know the dream."

4Then the Chaldeans spoke to the

king in Aramaic, "O king, live forever! Tell your servants the dream, and we will give the interpretation."

5The king answered and said to the Chaldeans, "My decision is firm: if you do not make known the dream to me, and its interpretation, you shall be cut in pieces, and your houses shall be made an ash heap. 6However, if you tell the dream and its interpretation, you shall receive from me gifts, rewards, and great honor. Therefore tell me the dream and its interpretation."

7They answered again and said, "Let the king tell his servants the dream, and we will give its interpretation."

8The king answered and said, "I know for certain that you would gain time, because you see that my decision is firm: 9if you do not make known the dream to me, *there is only* one decree for you! For you have agreed to speak lying and corrupt words before me till the time has changed. Therefore tell me the dream, and I shall know that you can give me its interpretation."

10The Chaldeans answered the king, and said, "There is not a man on earth who can tell the king's matter; therefore no king, lord, or ruler has *ever* asked such things of any magician, astrologer, or Chaldean. 11*It is* a difficult thing that the king requests, and there is no other who can tell it to the king except the gods, whose dwelling is not with flesh."

12For this reason the king was angry and very furious, and gave the command to destroy all the wise *men* of Babylon. 13So the decree went out, and they began killing the wise *men;* and they sought Daniel and his companions, to kill *them.*

God Reveals Nebuchadnezzar's Dream

14Then with counsel and wisdom Daniel answered Arioch, the captain of the king's guard, who had gone out to kill the wise *men* of Babylon; 15he answered and said to Arioch the king's captain, "Why is the decree from the king so urgent?" Then Arioch made the decision known to Daniel.

16So Daniel went in and asked the king to give him time, that he might tell the king the interpretation. 17Then Daniel went to his house, and made the decision known to Hananiah, Mishael, and Azariah, his companions, 18that they might seek mercies from the God of heaven concerning this secret, so that Daniel and his companions might not perish with the rest of the wise *men* of Babylon. 19Then the secret was revealed to Daniel in a night vision. So Daniel blessed the God of heaven.

20Daniel answered and said:

"Blessed be the name of God forever
    and ever,
  For wisdom and might are His.
21 And He changes the times and the
    seasons;
  He removes kings and raises up
    kings;
  He gives wisdom to the wise
  And knowledge to those who have
    understanding.
22 He reveals deep and secret things;
  He knows what *is* in the darkness,
  And light dwells with Him.

23 "I thank You and praise You,
    O God of my fathers;
  You have given me wisdom and
    might,
  And have now made known to me
    what we asked of You,
  For You have made known to us
    the king's demand."

Daniel Explains the Dream

24Therefore Daniel went to Arioch, whom the king had appointed to destroy the wise *men* of Babylon. He went and said thus to him: "Do not destroy the wise *men* of Babylon; take me before the king, and I will tell the king the interpretation."

25Then Arioch quickly brought Daniel before the king, and said thus to him, "I have found a man of the captives of Judah, who will make known to the king the interpretation."

26The king answered and said to Daniel, whose name *was* Belteshazzar, "Are you able to make known to me the dream which I have seen, and its interpretation?"

27Daniel answered in the presence of the king, and said, "The secret which the king has demanded, the wise *men*, the astrologers, the magicians, and the soothsayers cannot declare to the king. 28But there is a God in heaven who reveals secrets, and He has made known to King Nebuchadnezzar what will be in the latter days. Your dream, and the visions of your head upon your bed, were these: 29As for you, O king, thoughts came *to* your *mind while* on your bed, *about* what would come to pass after this; and He who reveals secrets has made known to you what will be. 30But as for me, this secret has not been revealed to me because I have more wisdom than anyone living, but for *our* sakes who make known the interpretation to the king, and that you may know the thoughts of your heart.

31"You, O king, were watching; and behold, a great image! This great image, whose splendor *was* excellent, stood before you; and its form *was* awesome. 32This image's head *was* of fine gold, its chest and arms of silver, its belly and thighs of bronze, 33its legs of iron, its feet partly of iron and partly of clay. 34You watched while a stone was cut out without hands, which struck the image on its feet of iron and clay, and broke them in pieces. 35Then the iron, the clay, the bronze, the silver, and the gold were crushed together, and became like chaff from the summer threshing floors; the wind carried them away so that no trace of them was found. And the stone that struck the image became a great mountain and filled the whole earth.

36"This *is* the dream. Now we will tell the interpretation of it before the king. 37You, O king, *are* a king of kings. For the God of heaven has given you a kingdom, power, strength, and glory; 38and wherever the children of men dwell, or the beasts of the field and the birds of the heaven, He has given *them* into your hand, and has made you ruler over them all—you *are* this head of gold. 39But after you shall arise another kingdom inferior to yours; then another, a third kingdom of bronze, which shall rule over all the earth. 40And the fourth kingdom shall be as strong as iron, inasmuch as iron breaks in pieces and shatters everything; and like iron that crushes, *that kingdom* will break in pieces and crush all the others. 41Whereas you saw the feet and toes, partly of potter's clay and partly of iron, the kingdom shall be divided; yet the strength of the iron shall be in it, just as you saw the iron mixed with ceramic clay. 42And *as* the toes of the feet *were* partly of iron and partly of clay, *so* the kingdom shall be partly strong and partly fragile. 43As you saw iron mixed with ceramic clay, they will mingle with the seed of men; but they will not adhere to one another, just as iron does not mix with clay. 44And in the days of these kings the God of heaven will set up a kingdom which shall never be destroyed; and the kingdom shall not be left to other people; it shall break in pieces and consume all these kingdoms, and it shall stand forever. 45Inasmuch as you saw that the stone was cut out of the mountain without hands, and that it broke in pieces the iron, the bronze, the clay, the silver, and the gold—the great God has made known to the king what will come to pass after this. The dream is certain, and its interpretation is sure."

Daniel and His Friends Promoted

46Then King Nebuchadnezzar fell on his face, prostrate before Daniel, and commanded that they should present an offering and incense to him. 47The king answered Daniel, and said, "Truly your God *is* the God of gods, the Lord of kings, and a revealer of secrets, since you could reveal this secret." 48Then the king promoted Daniel and gave him many great gifts; and he made him ruler over the whole province of Babylon, and chief administrator over all the wise *men* of Babylon. 49Also Daniel petitioned the king, and he set Shadrach, Meshach, and Abed-Nego over the affairs of the province of Babylon; but Daniel *sat* in the gate*a* of the king.

The Image of Gold

3 Nebuchadnezzar the king made an image of gold, whose height *was* sixty cubits *and* its width six cubits. He set it up in the plain of Dura, in the province of Babylon. 2And King Nebuchadnezzar sent *word* to gather together the satraps, the administrators,

a That is, the king's court

the governors, the counselors, the treasurers, the judges, the magistrates, and
all the officials of the provinces, to come
to the dedication of the image which
King Nebuchadnezzar had set up.
3So the satraps, the administrators, the
governors, the counselors, the treasurers, the judges, the magistrates, and all
the officials of the provinces gathered
together for the dedication of the image
that King Nebuchadnezzar had set up;
and they stood before the image that
Nebuchadnezzar had set up. 4Then a
herald cried aloud: "To you it is commanded, O peoples, nations, and languages, 5that at the time you hear the
sound of the horn, flute, harp, lyre, and
psaltery, in symphony with all kinds
of music, you shall fall down and worship the gold image that King Nebuchadnezzar has set up; 6and whoever
does not fall down and worship shall
be cast immediately into the midst of a
burning fiery furnace."

7So at that time, when all the people
heard the sound of the horn, flute, harp,
and lyre, in symphony with all kinds
of music, all the people, nations, and
languages fell down and worshiped the
gold image which King Nebuchadnezzar had set up.

Daniel's Friends Disobey the King

8Therefore at that time certain Chaldeans came forward and accused the
Jews. 9They spoke and said to King
Nebuchadnezzar, "O king, live forever!
10You, O king, have made a decree that
everyone who hears the sound of the
horn, flute, harp, lyre, and psaltery, in
symphony with all kinds of music, shall
fall down and worship the gold image;
11and whoever does not fall down and
worship shall be cast into the midst of
a burning fiery furnace. 12There are
certain Jews whom you have set over
the affairs of the province of Babylon:
Shadrach, Meshach, and Abed-Nego;
these men, O king, have not paid due
regard to you. They do not serve your
gods or worship the gold image which
you have set up."

13Then Nebuchadnezzar, in rage and
fury, gave the command to bring Shadrach, Meshach, and Abed-Nego. So
they brought these men before the king.
14Nebuchadnezzar spoke, saying to

them, "Is it true, Shadrach, Meshach,
and Abed-Nego, that you do not serve
my gods or worship the gold image
which I have set up? 15Now if you are
ready at the time you hear the sound
of the horn, flute, harp, lyre, and psaltery, in symphony with all kinds of music, and you fall down and worship the
image which I have made, good! But if
you do not worship, you shall be cast
immediately into the midst of a burning
fiery furnace. And who is the god who
will deliver you from my hands?"

16Shadrach, Meshach, and Abed-
Nego answered and said to the king,
"O Nebuchadnezzar, we have no need
to answer you in this matter. 17If that
is the case, our God whom we serve is
able to deliver us from the burning fiery
furnace, and He will deliver us from
your hand, O king. 18But if not, let it
be known to you, O king, that we do
not serve your gods, nor will we worship the gold image which you have
set up."

Saved in Fiery Trial

19Then Nebuchadnezzar was full of
fury, and the expression on his face
changed toward Shadrach, Meshach,
and Abed-Nego. He spoke and commanded that they heat the furnace
seven times more than it was usually
heated. 20And he commanded certain
mighty men of valor who were in his
army to bind Shadrach, Meshach, and
Abed-Nego, and cast them into the
burning fiery furnace. 21Then these
men were bound in their coats, their
trousers, their turbans, and their other
garments, and were cast into the midst
of the burning fiery furnace. 22There-
fore, because the king's command was
urgent, and the furnace exceedingly
hot, the flame of the fire killed those
men who took up Shadrach, Meshach,
and Abed-Nego. 23And these three
men, Shadrach, Meshach, and Abed-
Nego, fell down bound into the midst
of the burning fiery furnace.

24Then King Nebuchadnezzar was
astonished; and he rose in haste and
spoke, saying to his counselors, "Did
we not cast three men bound into the
midst of the fire?"

They answered and said to the king,
"True, O king."

25"Look!" he answered, "I see four men loose, walking in the midst of the fire; and they are not hurt, and the form of the fourth is like the Son of God."[b]

Nebuchadnezzar Praises God

26Then Nebuchadnezzar went near the mouth of the burning fiery furnace *and* spoke, saying, "Shadrach, Meshach, and Abed-Nego, servants of the Most High God, come out, and come *here*." Then Shadrach, Meshach, and Abed-Nego came from the midst of the fire. 27And the satraps, administrators, governors, and the king's counselors gathered together, and they saw these men on whose bodies the fire had no power; the hair of their head was not singed nor were their garments affected, and the smell of fire was not on them.

28Nebuchadnezzar spoke, saying, "Blessed be the God of Shadrach, Meshach, and Abed-Nego, who sent His Angel[c] and delivered His servants who trusted in Him, and they have frustrated the king's word, and yielded their bodies, that they should not serve nor worship any god except their own God! 29Therefore I make a decree that any people, nation, or language which speaks anything amiss against the God of Shadrach, Meshach, and Abed-Nego shall be cut in pieces, and their houses shall be made an ash heap; because there is no other God who can deliver like this."

30Then the king promoted Shadrach, Meshach, and Abed-Nego in the province of Babylon.

Nebuchadnezzar's Second Dream

4 Nebuchadnezzar the king,
To all peoples, nations, and languages that dwell in all the earth:

Peace be multiplied to you.

2 I thought it good to declare the signs and wonders that the Most High God has worked for me.

3 How great *are* His signs,
And how mighty His wonders!
His kingdom *is* an everlasting kingdom,
And His dominion *is* from generation to generation.

4 I, Nebuchadnezzar, was at rest in my house, and flourishing in my palace. 5I saw a dream which made me afraid, and the thoughts on my bed and the visions of my head troubled me. 6Therefore I issued a decree to bring in all the wise *men* of Babylon before me, that they might make known to me the interpretation of the dream. 7Then the magicians, the astrologers, the Chaldeans, and the soothsayers came in, and I told them the dream; but they did not make known to me its interpretation. 8But at last Daniel came before me (his name *is* Belteshazzar, according to the name of my god; in him *is* the Spirit of the Holy God), and I told the dream before him, *saying:* 9"Belteshazzar, chief of the magicians, because I know that the Spirit of the Holy God *is* in you, and no secret troubles you, explain to me the visions of my dream that I have seen, and its interpretation.

10 "These *were* the visions of my head *while* on my bed:
I was looking, and behold,
A tree in the midst of the earth,
And its height was great.

11 The tree grew and became strong;
Its height reached to the heavens,
And it could be seen to the ends of all the earth.

12 Its leaves *were* lovely,
Its fruit abundant,
And in it *was* food for all.
The beasts of the field found shade under it,
The birds of the heavens dwelt in its branches,
And all flesh was fed from it.

---

[b] Or *a son of the gods*   [c] Or *angel*

13 "I saw in the visions of my head
while on my bed, and there was a
watcher, a holy one, coming down
from heaven. 14He cried aloud and
said thus:
'Chop down the tree and cut off its
   branches,
Strip off its leaves and scatter its
   fruit.
Let the beasts get out from
   under it,
And the birds from its branches.
15 Nevertheless leave the stump and
   roots in the earth,
Bound with a band of iron and
   bronze,
In the tender grass of the field.
Let it be wet with the dew of
   heaven,
And *let* him graze with the beasts
On the grass of the earth.
16 Let his heart be changed from *that*
   of a man,
Let him be given the heart of a
   beast,
And let seven times*d* pass over
   him.

17 'This decision *is* by the decree of the
   watchers,
And the sentence by the word of
   the holy ones,
In order that the living may know
That the Most High rules in the
   kingdom of men,
Gives it to whomever He will,
And sets over it the lowest of men.'
18 "This dream I, King
Nebuchadnezzar, have seen. Now
you, Belteshazzar, declare its
interpretation, since all the wise
men of my kingdom are not able
to make known to me the
interpretation; but you *are* able, for
the Spirit of the Holy God *is* in
you."

Daniel Explains the Second Dream

19 Then Daniel, whose name was
Belteshazzar, was astonished for a
time, and his thoughts troubled
him. *So* the king spoke, and said,
"Belteshazzar, do not let the dream
or its interpretation trouble you."

Belteshazzar answered and said,
"My lord, *may* the dream concern
those who hate you, and its
interpretation concern your
enemies!

20 "The tree that you saw, which grew
and became strong, whose height
reached to the heavens and which
could be seen by all the earth,
21whose leaves *were* lovely and its
fruit abundant, in which *was* food
for all, under which the beasts of
the field dwelt, and in whose
branches the birds of the heaven
had their home—22it *is* you, O king,
who have grown and become
strong; for your greatness has
grown and reaches to the heavens,
and your dominion to the end of the
earth.

23 "And inasmuch as the king saw a
watcher, a holy one, coming down
from heaven and saying, 'Chop
down the tree and destroy it, but
leave its stump and roots in the
earth, *bound* with a band of iron
and bronze in the tender grass of
the field; let it be wet with the dew
of heaven, and let him graze with
the beasts of the field, till seven
times pass over him'; 24this is the
interpretation, O king, and this is
the decree of the Most High, which
has come upon my lord the king:
25They shall drive you from men,
your dwelling shall be with the
beasts of the field, and they shall
make you eat grass like oxen. They
shall wet you with the dew of
heaven, and seven times shall pass
over you, till you know that the
Most High rules in the kingdom of
men, and gives it to whomever He
chooses.

26 "And inasmuch as they gave the
command to leave the stump *and*
roots of the tree, your kingdom
shall be assured to you, after you
come to know that Heaven rules.
27Therefore, O king, let my advice
be acceptable to you; break off your

---

d Possibly *seven years*, also in verses 23, 25, and 32

sins by *being* righteous, and your iniquities by showing mercy to *the* poor. Perhaps there may be a lengthening of your prosperity."

Nebuchadnezzar's Humiliation

28 All *this* came upon King Nebuchadnezzar. 29At the end of the twelve months he was walking about the royal palace of Babylon. 30The king spoke, saying, "Is not this great Babylon, that I have built for a royal dwelling by my mighty power and for the honor of my majesty?"

31 While the word *was still* in the king's mouth, a voice fell from heaven: "King Nebuchadnezzar, to you it is spoken: the kingdom has departed from you! 32And they shall drive you from men, and your dwelling *shall be* with the beasts of the field. They shall make you eat grass like oxen; and seven times shall pass over you, until you know that the Most High rules in the kingdom of men, and gives it to whomever He chooses."

33 That very hour the word was fulfilled concerning Nebuchadnezzar; he was driven from men and ate grass like oxen; his body was wet with the dew of heaven till his hair had grown like eagles' *feathers* and his nails like birds' *claws*.

Nebuchadnezzar Praises God

34 And at the end of the time I, Nebuchadnezzar, lifted my eyes to heaven, and my understanding returned to me; and I blessed the Most High and praised and honored Him who lives forever:
For His dominion *is* an everlasting dominion,
And His kingdom *is* from generation to generation.
35 All the inhabitants of the earth *are* reputed as nothing;
He does according to His will in the army of heaven

And *among* the inhabitants of the earth.
No one can restrain His hand
Or say to Him, "What have You done?"
36 At the same time my reason returned to me, and for the glory of my kingdom, my honor and splendor returned to me. My counselors and nobles resorted to me, I was restored to my kingdom, and excellent majesty was added to me. 37Now I, Nebuchadnezzar, praise and extol and honor the King of heaven, all of whose works *are* truth, and His ways justice. And those who walk in pride He is able to put down.

Belshazzar's Feast

5 Belshazzar the king made a great feast for a thousand of his lords, and drank wine in the presence of the thousand. 2While he tasted the wine, Belshazzar gave the command to bring the gold and silver vessels which his father Nebuchadnezzar had taken from the temple which *had been* in Jerusalem, that the king and his lords, his wives, and his concubines might drink from them. 3Then they brought the gold vessels that had been taken from the temple of the house of God which *had been* in Jerusalem; and the king and his lords, his wives, and his concubines drank from them. 4They drank wine, and praised the gods of gold and silver, bronze and iron, wood and stone.

5In the same hour the fingers of a man's hand appeared and wrote opposite the lampstand on the plaster of the wall of the king's palace; and the king saw the part of the hand that wrote. 6Then the king's countenance changed, and his thoughts troubled him, so that the joints of his hips were loosened and his knees knocked against each other. 7The king cried aloud to bring in the astrologers, the Chaldeans, and the soothsayers. The king spoke, saying to the wise *men* of Babylon, "Whoever reads this writing, and tells me its interpretation, shall be clothed with purple and *have* a chain of gold around his neck; and he shall be the third ruler in the kingdom." 8Now all the king's wise *men* came, but they could not read the writing, or make known to the king its interpretation. 9Then King Belshazzar was greatly troubled, his countenance was changed, and his lords were astonished.

10The queen, because of the words of the king and his lords, came to the banquet hall. The queen spoke, saying, "O king, live forever! Do not let your thoughts trouble you, nor let your countenance change. 11There is a man in your kingdom in whom *is* the Spirit of the Holy God. And in the days of your father, light and understanding and wisdom, like the wisdom of the gods, were found in him; and King Nebuchadnezzar your father—your father the king—made him chief of the magicians, astrologers, Chaldeans, *and* soothsayers. 12Inasmuch as an excellent spirit, knowledge, understanding, interpreting dreams, solving riddles, and explaining enigmas were found in this Daniel, whom the king named Belteshazzar, now let Daniel be called, and he will give the interpretation."

The Writing on the Wall Explained

13Then Daniel was brought in before the king. The king spoke, and said to Daniel, "*Are* you that Daniel who is one of the captives from Judah, whom my father the king brought from Judah? 14I have heard of you, that the Spirit of God *is* in you, and *that* light and understanding and excellent wisdom are found in you. 15Now the wise *men,* the astrologers, have been brought in before me, that they should read this writing and make known to me its interpretation, but they could not give the interpretation of the thing. 16And I have heard of you, that you can give interpretations and explain enigmas. Now if you can read the writing and make known to me its interpretation, you shall be clothed with purple and *have* a chain of gold around your neck, and shall be the third ruler in the kingdom."

17Then Daniel answered, and said before the king, "Let your gifts be for yourself, and give your rewards to another; yet I will read the writing to the king, and make known to him the inter-

pretation. 18O king, the Most High God gave Nebuchadnezzar your father a kingdom and majesty, glory and honor. 19And because of the majesty that He gave him, all peoples, nations, and languages trembled and feared before him. Whomever he wished, he executed; whomever he wished, he kept alive; whomever he wished, he set up; and whomever he wished, he put down. 20But when his heart was lifted up, and his spirit was hardened in pride, he was deposed from his kingly throne, and they took his glory from him. 21Then he was driven from the sons of men, his heart was made like the beasts, and his dwelling *was* with the wild donkeys. They fed him with grass like oxen, and his body was wet with the dew of heaven, till he knew that the Most High God rules in the kingdom of men, and appoints over it whomever He chooses.

22"But you his son, Belshazzar, have not humbled your heart, although you knew all this. 23And you have lifted yourself up against the Lord of heaven. They have brought the vessels of His house before you, and you and your lords, your wives and your concubines, have drunk wine from them. And you have praised the gods of silver and gold, bronze and iron, wood and stone, which do not see or hear or know; and the God who *holds* your breath in His hand and owns all your ways, you have not glorified. 24Then the fingers of the hand were sent from Him, and this writing was written.

25"And this is the inscription that was written:

MENE,*e* MENE, TEKEL,*f* UPHARSIN.*g*

26This *is* the interpretation of *each* word. MENE: God has numbered your kingdom, and finished it; 27TEKEL: You have been weighed in the balances, and found wanting; 28PERES: Your kingdom has been divided, and given to the Medes and Persians." 29Then Belshazzar gave the command, and they clothed Daniel with purple and *put* a chain of gold around his neck, and made a proclamation concerning him

---

e Literally *a mina* (50 shekels) from the verb "to number"   *f* Literally *a shekel* from the verb "to weigh"   *g* Literally *and half-shekels* from the verb "to divide" that he should be the third ruler in the kingdom.

Belshazzar's Fall

30That very night Belshazzar, king of the Chaldeans, was slain. 31And Darius the Mede received the kingdom, *being* about sixty-two years old.

The Plot Against Daniel

6 It pleased Darius to set over the kingdom one hundred and twenty satraps, to be over the whole kingdom; 2and over these, three governors, of whom Daniel *was* one, that the satraps might give account to them, so that the king would suffer no loss. 3Then this Daniel distinguished himself above the governors and satraps, because an excellent spirit *was* in him; and the king gave thought to setting him over the whole realm. 4So the governors and satraps sought to find *some* charge against Daniel concerning the kingdom; but they could find no charge or fault, because he *was* faithful; nor was there any error or fault found in him. 5Then these men said, "We shall not find any charge against this Daniel unless we find *it* against him concerning the law of his God."

6So these governors and satraps thronged before the king, and said thus to him: "King Darius, live forever! 7All the governors of the kingdom, the administrators and satraps, the counselors and advisors, have consulted together to establish a royal statute and to make a firm decree, that whoever petitions any god or man for thirty days, except you, O king, shall be cast into the den of lions. 8Now, O king, establish the decree and sign the writing, so that it cannot be changed, according to the law of the Medes and Persians, which does not alter." 9Therefore King Darius signed the written decree.

Daniel in the Lions' Den

10Now when Daniel knew that the writing was signed, he went home. And in his upper room, with his windows open toward Jerusalem, he knelt down on his knees three times that day, and prayed and gave thanks before his God, as was his custom since early days. 11Then these men assembled and found Daniel praying and making supplication before his God. 12And they went before the king, and spoke concerning the king's decree: "Have you not signed a decree that every man who petitions any god or man within thirty days, except you, O king, shall be cast into the den of lions?"

The king answered and said, "The thing *is* true, according to the law of the Medes and Persians, which does not alter."

13So they answered and said before the king, "That Daniel, who is one of the captives from Judah, does not show due regard for you, O king, or for the decree that you have signed, but makes his petition three times a day."

14And the king, when he heard *these* words, was greatly displeased with himself, and set *his* heart on Daniel to deliver him; and he labored till the going down of the sun to deliver him. 15Then these men approached the king, and said to the king, "Know, O king, that *it is* the law of the Medes and Persians that no decree or statute which the king establishes may be changed."

16So the king gave the command, and they brought Daniel and cast *him* into the den of lions. *But* the king spoke, saying to Daniel, "Your God, whom you serve continually, He will deliver you." 17Then a stone was brought and laid on the mouth of the den, and the king sealed it with his own signet ring and with the signets of his lords, that the purpose concerning Daniel might not be changed.

Daniel Saved from the Lions

18Now the king went to his palace and spent the night fasting; and no musicians[h] were brought before him. Also his sleep went from him. 19Then the king arose very early in the morning and went in haste to the den of lions. 20And when he came to the den, he cried out with a lamenting voice to Daniel. The king spoke, saying to Daniel, "Daniel, servant of the living God, has your God, whom you serve continually,

[h] Exact meaning unknown

been able to deliver you from the lions?"

21Then Daniel said to the king, "O king, live forever! 22My God sent His angel and shut the lions' mouths, so that they have not hurt me, because I was found innocent before Him; and also, O king, I have done no wrong before you."

23Now the king was exceedingly glad for him, and commanded that they should take Daniel up out of the den. So Daniel was taken up out of the den, and no injury whatever was found on him, because he believed in his God.

Darius Honors God

24And the king gave the command, and they brought those men who had accused Daniel, and they cast *them* into the den of lions—them, their children, and their wives; and the lions overpowered them, and broke all their bones in pieces before they ever came to the bottom of the den.

25Then King Darius wrote:

To all peoples, nations, and languages that dwell in all the earth:

Peace be multiplied to you.

26 I make a decree that in every dominion of my kingdom *men must* tremble and fear before the God of Daniel.

For He *is* the living God,
And steadfast forever;
His kingdom *is the one* which shall not be destroyed,
And His dominion *shall endure* to the end.
27 He delivers and rescues,
And He works signs and wonders
In heaven and on earth,
Who has delivered Daniel from the power of the lions.

28So this Daniel prospered in the reign of Darius and in the reign of Cyrus the Persian.

Vision of the Four Beasts

7 In the first year of Belshazzar king of Babylon, Daniel had a dream and visions of his head *while* on his bed. Then he wrote down the dream, telling the main facts.

2Daniel spoke, saying, "I saw in my vision by night, and behold, the four winds of heaven were stirring up the Great Sea. 3And four great beasts came up from the sea, each different from the other. 4The first *was* like a lion, and had eagle's wings. I watched till its wings were plucked off; and it was lifted up from the earth and made to stand on two feet like a man, and a man's heart was given to it.

5"And suddenly another beast, a second, like a bear. It was raised up on one side, and *had* three ribs in its mouth between its teeth. And they said thus to it: 'Arise, devour much flesh!'

6"After this I looked, and there was another, like a leopard, which had on its back four wings of a bird. The beast also had four heads, and dominion was given to it.

7"After this I saw in the night visions, and behold, a fourth beast, dreadful and terrible, exceedingly strong. It had huge iron teeth; it was devouring, breaking in pieces, and trampling the residue with its feet. It *was* different from all the beasts that *were* before it, and it had ten horns. 8I was considering the horns, and there was another horn, a little one, coming up among them, before whom three of the first horns were plucked out by the roots. And there, in this horn, *were* eyes like the eyes of a man, and a mouth speaking pompous words.

Vision of the Ancient of Days

9 "I watched till thrones were put in place,
And the Ancient of Days was seated;
His garment *was* white as snow,
And the hair of His head *was* like pure wool.
His throne *was* a fiery flame,
Its wheels a burning fire;
10 A fiery stream issued
And came forth from before Him.
A thousand thousands ministered to Him;
Ten thousand times ten thousand stood before Him.
The court was seated,
And the books were opened.

11"I watched then because of the sound of the pompous words which the horn was speaking; I watched till the beast was slain, and its body destroyed and given to the burning flame. 12As for the rest of the beasts, they had their dominion taken away, yet their lives were prolonged for a season and a time.

13 "I was watching in the night visions,
   And behold, *One* like the Son
      of Man,
   Coming with the clouds of heaven!
   He came to the Ancient of Days,
   And they brought Him near
      before Him.
14 Then to Him was given dominion
      and glory and a kingdom,
   That all peoples, nations, and
      languages should serve Him.
   His dominion *is* an everlasting
      dominion,
   Which shall not pass away,
   And His kingdom *the one*
   Which shall not be destroyed.

Daniel's Visions Interpreted

15"I, Daniel, was grieved in my spirit within *my* body, and the visions of my head troubled me. 16I came near to one of those who stood by, and asked him the truth of all this. So he told me and made known to me the interpretation of these things: 17'Those great beasts, which are four, *are* four kings[i] *which* arise out of the earth. 18But the saints of the Most High shall receive the kingdom, and possess the kingdom forever, even forever and ever.'

19"Then I wished to know the truth about the fourth beast, which was different from all the others, exceedingly dreadful, *with* its teeth of iron and its nails of bronze, *which* devoured, broke in pieces, and trampled the residue with its feet; 20and the ten horns that *were* on its head, and the other *horn* which came up, before which three fell, namely, that horn which had eyes and a mouth which spoke pompous words, whose appearance *was* greater than his fellows.

21"I was watching; and the same horn was making war against the saints, and prevailing against them, 22until the Ancient of Days came, and a judgment was made *in favor* of the saints of the Most

High, and the time came for the saints to possess the kingdom.

23"Thus he said:
   'The fourth beast shall be
   A fourth kingdom on earth,
   Which shall be different from all
      other kingdoms,
   And shall devour the whole earth,
   Trample it and break it in pieces.
24 The ten horns *are* ten kings
   Who shall arise from this kingdom.
   And another shall rise after them;
   He shall be different from the first
      ones,
   And shall subdue three kings.
25 He shall speak *pompous* words
      against the Most High,
   Shall persecute the saints of the
      Most High,
   And shall intend to change times
      and law.
   Then *the saints* shall be given into
      his hand
   For a time and times and half a
      time.

26 'But the court shall be seated,
   And they shall take away his
      dominion,
   To consume and destroy *it* forever.
27 Then the kingdom and dominion,
   And the greatness of the kingdoms
      under the whole heaven,
   Shall be given to the people, the
      saints of the Most High.
   His kingdom *is* an everlasting
      kingdom,
   And all dominions shall serve and
      obey Him.'

28"This *is* the end of the account. As for me, Daniel, my thoughts greatly troubled me, and my countenance changed; but I kept the matter in my heart."

Vision of a Ram and a Goat

8 In the third year of the reign of King Belshazzar a vision appeared *to* me—to me, Daniel—after the one that appeared to me the first time. 2I saw in the vision, and it so happened while I was looking, that I *was* in Shushan, the citadel, which *is* in the province of Elam; and I saw in the vision that I was

---

[i] Representing their kingdoms (compare verse 23)

by the River Ulai. 3Then I lifted my eyes and saw, and there, standing beside the river, was a ram which had two horns, and the two horns *were* high; but one *was* higher than the other, and the higher *one* came up last. 4I saw the ram pushing westward, northward, and southward, so that no animal could withstand him; nor *was there any* that could deliver from his hand, but he did according to his will and became great.

5And as I was considering, suddenly a male goat came from the west, across the surface of the whole earth, without touching the ground; and the goat *had* a notable horn between his eyes. 6Then he came to the ram that had two horns, which I had seen standing beside the river, and ran at him with furious power. 7And I saw him confronting the ram; he was moved with rage against him, attacked the ram, and broke his two horns. There was no power in the ram to withstand him, but he cast him down to the ground and trampled him; and there was no one that could deliver the ram from his hand.

8Therefore the male goat grew very great; but when he became strong, the large horn was broken, and in place of it four notable ones came up toward the four winds of heaven. 9And out of one of them came a little horn which grew exceedingly great toward the south, toward the east, and toward the Glorious *Land.* 10And it grew up to the host of heaven; and it cast down *some* of the host and *some* of the stars to the ground, and trampled them. 11He even exalted *himself* as high as the Prince of the host; and by him the daily *sacrifices* were taken away, and the place of His sanctuary was cast down. 12Because of transgression, an army was given over to *the* horn to oppose the daily *sacrifices;* and he cast truth down to the ground. He did *all this* and prospered.

13Then I heard a holy one speaking; and *another* holy one said to that certain *one* who was speaking, "How long *will* the vision *be, concerning* the daily *sacrifices* and the transgression of desolation, the giving of both the sanctuary and the host to be trampled underfoot?"

14And he said to me, "For two thousand three hundred days; then the sanctuary shall be cleansed."

Gabriel Interprets the Vision

15Then it happened, when I, Daniel, had seen the vision and was seeking the meaning, that suddenly there stood before me one having the appearance of a man. 16And I heard a man's voice between *the banks of* the Ulai, who called, and said, "Gabriel, make this *man* understand the vision." 17So he came near where I stood, and when he came I was afraid and fell on my face; but he said to me, "Understand, son of man, that the vision *refers* to the time of the end."

18Now, as he was speaking with me, I was in a deep sleep with my face to the ground; but he touched me, and stood me upright. 19And he said, "Look, I am making known to you what shall happen in the latter time of the indignation; for at the appointed time the end *shall be.* 20The ram which you saw, having the two horns—*they are* the kings of Media and Persia. 21And the male goat *is* the kingdom[j] of Greece. The large horn that *is* between its eyes *is* the first king. 22As for the broken *horn* and the four that stood up in its place, four kingdoms shall arise out of that nation, but not with its power.

23 "And in the latter time of their
    kingdom,
    When the transgressors have
    reached their fullness,
    A king shall arise,
    Having fierce features,
    Who understands sinister
    schemes.
24 His power shall be mighty, but not
    by his own power;
    He shall destroy fearfully,
    And shall prosper and thrive;
    He shall destroy the mighty, and
    also the holy people.

25 "Through his cunning
    He shall cause deceit to prosper
    under his rule;
    And he shall exalt *himself* in his
    heart.
    He shall destroy many in *their*
    prosperity.

---

i Literally *king,* representing his kingdom (compare 7.17, 23)

He shall even rise against the
    Prince of princes;
But he shall be broken without
    human means.

26 "And the vision of the evenings and
    mornings
Which was told is true;
Therefore seal up the vision,
For *it refers* to many days *in the
    future.*"

27And I, Daniel, fainted and was sick
for days; afterward I arose and went
about the king's business. I was astonished by the vision, but no one understood it.

Daniel's Prayer for the People

9 In the first year of Darius the son
of Ahasuerus, of the lineage of the
Medes, who was made king over the
realm of the Chaldeans—2in the first
year of his reign I, Daniel, understood
by the books the number of the years
specified by the word of the LORD
through Jeremiah the prophet, that He
would accomplish seventy years in the
desolations of Jerusalem.

3Then I set my face toward the Lord
God to make request by prayer and supplications, with fasting, sackcloth, and
ashes. 4And I prayed to the LORD my
God, and made confession, and said, "O
Lord, great and awesome God, who
keeps His covenant and mercy with
those who love Him, and with those
who keep His commandments, 5we
have sinned and committed iniquity,
we have done wickedly and rebelled, even by departing from Your
precepts and Your judgments. 6Neither
have we heeded Your servants the
prophets, who spoke in Your name to
our kings and our princes, to our fathers and all the people of the land.
7O Lord, righteousness *belongs* to You,
but to us shame of face, as *it is* this
day—to the men of Judah, to the inhabitants of Jerusalem and all Israel, those
near and those far off in all the countries to which You have driven them,
because of the unfaithfulness which
they have committed against You.
8"O Lord, to us *belongs* shame of
face, to our kings, our princes, and our
fathers, because we have sinned
against You. 9To the Lord our God be-

long mercy and forgiveness, though we
have rebelled against Him. 10We have
not obeyed the voice of the LORD our
God, to walk in His laws, which He set
before us by His servants the prophets.
11Yes, all Israel has transgressed Your
law, and has departed so as not to obey
Your voice; therefore the curse and the
oath written in the Law of Moses the
servant of God have been poured out
on us, because we have sinned against
Him. 12And He has confirmed His
words, which He spoke against us and
against our judges who judged us, by
bringing upon us a great disaster; for
under the whole heaven such has never
been done as what has been done to
Jerusalem.

13"As *it is* written in the Law of
Moses, all this disaster has come upon
us; yet we have not made our prayer before the LORD our God, that we might
turn from our iniquities and understand
Your truth. 14Therefore the LORD has
kept the disaster in mind, and brought
it upon us; for the LORD our God *is*
righteous in all the works which He
does, though we have not obeyed His
voice. 15And now, O Lord our God,
who brought Your people out of the
land of Egypt with a mighty hand,
and made Yourself a name, as *it is* this
day—we have sinned, we have done
wickedly!

16"O Lord, according to all Your
righteousness, I pray, let Your anger
and Your fury be turned away from
Your city Jerusalem, Your holy mountain; because for our sins, and for the
iniquities of our fathers, Jerusalem and
Your people *are* a reproach to all *those*
around us. 17Now therefore, our God,
hear the prayer of Your servant, and
his supplications, and for the Lord's
sake cause Your face to shine on Your
sanctuary, which is desolate. 18O my
God, incline Your ear and hear; open
Your eyes and see our desolations, and
the city which is called by Your name;
for we do not present our supplications
before You because of our righteous
deeds, but because of Your great mercies. 19O Lord, hear! O Lord, forgive!
O Lord, listen and act! Do not delay for
Your own sake, my God, for Your city
and Your people are called by Your
name."

The Seventy-Weeks Prophecy

20Now while I *was* speaking, praying, and confessing my sin and the sin of my people Israel, and presenting my supplication before the Lord my God for the holy mountain of my God, 21yes, while I *was* speaking in prayer, the man Gabriel, whom I had seen in the vision at the beginning, being caused to fly swiftly, reached me about the time of the evening offering. 22And he informed *me,* and talked with me, and said, "O Daniel, I have now come forth to give you skill to understand. 23At the beginning of your supplications the command went out, and I have come to tell y*ou,* for you *are* greatly beloved; therefore consider the matter, and understand the vision:

24 "Seventy weeks are determined
   For your people and for your holy
     city,
   To finish the transgression,
   To make an end of sins,
   To make reconciliation for iniquity,
   To bring in everlasting
     righteousness,
   To seal up vision and prophecy,
   And to anoint the Most Holy.

25 "Know therefore and understand,
   That from the going forth of the
     command
   To restore and build Jerusalem
   Until Messiah the Prince,
   There shall be seven weeks and
     sixty-two weeks;
   The street shall be built again, and
     the wall,
   Even in troublesome times.

26 "And after the sixty-two weeks
   Messiah shall be cut off, but not for
     Himself;
   And the people of the prince who
     is to come
   Shall destroy the city and the
     sanctuary.
   The end of it *shall be* with a flood,
   And till the end of the war
     desolations are determined.

27   Then he shall confirm a covenant
     with many for one week;
   But in the middle of the week
   He shall bring an end to sacrifice
     and offering.

   And on the wing of abominations
     shall be one who makes desolate,
   Even until the consummation,
     which is determined,
   Is poured out on the desolate.''

Vision of the Glorious Man

10 In the third year of Cyrus king of Persia a message was revealed to Daniel, whose name was called Belteshazzar. The message *was* true, but the appointed time *was* long; and he understood the message, and had understanding of the vision. 2In those days I, Daniel, was mourning three full weeks. 3I ate no pleasant food, no meat or wine came into my mouth, nor did I anoint myself at all, till three whole weeks were fulfilled.

4Now on the twenty-fourth day of the first month, as I was by the side of the great river, that *is,* the Tigris, 5I lifted my eyes and looked, and behold, a certain man clothed in linen, whose waist *was* girded with gold of Uphaz! 6His body *was* like beryl, his face like the appearance of lightning, his eyes like torches of fire, his arms and feet like burnished bronze in color, and the sound of his words like the voice of a multitude.

7And I, Daniel, alone saw the vision, for the men who were with me did not see the vision; but a great terror fell upon them, so that they fled to hide themselves. 8Therefore I was left alone when I saw this great vision, and no strength remained in me; for my vigor was turned to frailty in me, and I retained no strength. 9Yet I heard the sound of his words; and while I heard the sound of his words I was in a deep sleep on my face, with my face to the ground.

Prophecies Concerning Persia and Greece

10Suddenly, a hand touched me, which made me tremble on my knees and on the palms of my hands. 11And he said to me, "O Daniel, man greatly beloved, understand the words that I speak to you, and stand upright, for I have now been sent to you." While he was speaking this word to me, I stood trembling.

12Then he said to me, "Do not fear,

Daniel, for from the first day that you set your heart to understand, and to humble yourself before your God, your words were heard; and I have come because of your words. 13But the prince of the kingdom of Persia withstood me twenty-one days; and behold, Michael, one of the chief princes, came to help me, for I had been left alone there with the kings of Persia. 14Now I have come to make you understand what will happen to your people in the latter days, for the vision *refers* to *many* days yet *to come.*"

15When he had spoken such words to me, I turned my face toward the ground and became speechless. 16And suddenly, *one* having the likeness of the sons of men touched my lips; then I opened my mouth and spoke, saying to him who stood before me, "My lord, because of the vision my sorrows have overwhelmed me, and I have retained no strength. 17For how can this servant of my lord talk with you, my lord? As for me, no strength remains in me now, nor is any breath left in me."

18Then again, *the one* having the likeness of a man touched me and strengthened me. 19And he said, "O man greatly beloved, fear not! Peace *be* to you; be strong, yes, be strong!"

So when he spoke to me I was strengthened, and said, "Let my lord speak, for you have strengthened me."

20Then he said, "Do you know why I have come to you? And now I must return to fight with the prince of Persia; and when I have gone forth, indeed the prince of Greece will come. 21But I will tell you what is noted in the Scripture of Truth. (No one upholds me against these, except Michael your prince.

11 "Also in the first year of Darius the Mede, I, *even* I, stood up to confirm and strengthen him.) 2And now I will tell you the truth: Behold, three more kings will arise in Persia, and the fourth shall be far richer than *them* all; by his strength, through his riches, he shall stir up all against the realm of Greece. 3Then a mighty king shall arise, who shall rule with great dominion, and do according to his will. 4And when he has arisen, his kingdom shall be broken up and divided toward the four winds

of heaven, but not among his posterity nor according to his dominion with which he ruled; for his kingdom shall be uprooted, even for others besides these.

Warring Kings of North and South

5"Also the king of the South shall become strong, as well as *one* of his princes; and he shall gain power over him and have dominion. His dominion *shall be* a great dominion. 6And at the end of *some* years they shall join forces, for the daughter of the king of the South shall go to the king of the North to make an agreement; but she shall not retain the power of her authority, and neither he nor his authority shall stand; but she shall be given up, with those who brought her, and with him who begot her, and with him who strengthened her in *those* times. 7But from a branch of her roots *one* shall arise in his place, who shall come with an army, enter the fortress of the king of the North, and deal with them and prevail. 8And he shall also carry their gods captive to Egypt, with their princes *and* their precious articles of silver and gold; and he shall continue *more* years than the king of the North.

9"Also *the king of the North* shall come to the kingdom of the king of the South, but shall return to his own land. 10However his sons shall stir up strife, and assemble a multitude of great forces; and *one* shall certainly come and overwhelm and pass through; then he shall return to his fortress and stir up strife.

11"And the king of the South shall be moved with rage, and go out and fight with him, with the king of the North, who shall muster a great multitude; but the multitude shall be given into the hand of his *enemy.* 12When he has taken away the multitude, his heart will be lifted up; and he will cast down tens of thousands, but he will not prevail. 13For the king of the North will return and muster a multitude greater than the former, and shall certainly come at the end of some years with a great army and much equipment.

14"Now in those times many shall rise up against the king of the South. Also, violent men of your people shall exalt themselves in fulfillment of the vision, but they shall fall. 15So the king of the North shall come and build a siege mound, and take a fortified city; and the forces of the South shall not withstand *him.* Even his choice troops *shall have* no strength to resist. 16But he who comes against him shall do according to his own will, and no one shall stand against him. He shall stand in the Glorious Land with destruction in his power.

17"He shall also set his face to enter with the strength of his whole kingdom, and upright ones with him; thus shall he do. And he shall give him the daughter of women to destroy it; but she shall not stand *with him,* or be for him. 18After this he shall turn his face to the coastlands, and shall take many. But a ruler shall bring the reproach against them to an end; and with the reproach removed, he shall turn back on him. 19Then he shall turn his face toward the fortress of his own land; but he shall stumble and fall, and not be found.

20"There shall arise in his place one who imposes taxes *on* the glorious kingdom; but within a few days he shall be destroyed, but not in anger or in battle. 21And in his place shall arise a vile person, to whom they will not give the honor of royalty; but he shall come in peaceably, and seize the kingdom by intrigue. 22With the force of a flood they shall be swept away from before him and be broken, and also the prince of the covenant. 23And after the league *is made* with him he shall act deceitfully, for he shall come up and become strong with a small *number of* people. 24He shall enter peaceably, even into the richest places of the province; and he shall do *what* his fathers have not done, nor his forefathers: he shall disperse among them the plunder, spoil, and riches; and he shall devise his plans against the strongholds, but *only* for a time.

25"He shall stir up his power and his courage against the king of the South with a great army. And the king of the South shall be stirred up to battle with a very great and mighty army; but he shall not stand, for they shall devise plans against him. 26Yes, those who eat

of the portion of his delicacies shall destroy him; his army shall be swept away, and many shall fall down slain. 27Both these kings' hearts *shall be* bent on evil, and they shall speak lies at the same table; but it shall not prosper, for the end *will* still *be* at the appointed time. 28While returning to his land with great riches, his heart shall be *moved* against the holy covenant; so he shall do *damage* and return to his own land.

The Northern King's Blasphemies

29"At the appointed time he shall return and go toward the south; but it shall not be like the former or the latter. 30For ships from Cyprus*k* shall come against him; therefore he shall be grieved, and return in rage against the holy covenant, and do *damage.*

"So he shall return and show regard for those who forsake the holy covenant. 31And forces shall be mustered by him, and they shall defile the sanctuary fortress; then they shall take away the daily *sacrifices,* and place *there* the abomination of desolation. 32Those who do wickedly against the covenant he shall corrupt with flattery; but the people who know their God shall be strong, and carry out *great exploits.* 33And those of the people who understand shall instruct many; yet *for many* days they shall fall by sword and flame, by captivity and plundering. 34Now when they fall, they shall be aided with a little help; but many shall join with them by intrigue. 35And *some* of those of understanding shall fall, to refine them, purify *them,* and make *them* white, *until* the time of the end; because *it is* still for the appointed time.

36"Then the king shall do according to his own will: he shall exalt and magnify himself above every god, shall speak blasphemies against the God of gods, and shall prosper till the wrath has been accomplished; for what has been determined shall be done. 37He shall regard neither the God*l* of his fathers nor the desire of women, nor regard any god; for he shall exalt himself above *them* all. 38But in their place he shall honor a god of fortresses; and a god which his fathers did not know

k Western lands, especially Cyprus   *l* Or *gods*

he shall honor with gold and silver, with precious stones and pleasant things. 39Thus he shall act against the strongest fortresses with a foreign god, which he shall acknowledge, *and* advance *its* glory; and he shall cause them to rule over many, and divide the land for gain.

The Northern King's Conquests

40"At the time of the end the king of the South shall attack him; and the king of the North shall come against him like a whirlwind, with chariots, horsemen, and with many ships; and he shall enter the countries, overwhelm *them*, and pass through. 41He shall also enter the Glorious Land, and many *countries* shall be overthrown; but these shall escape from his hand: Edom, Moab, and the prominent people of Ammon. 42He shall stretch out his hand against the countries, and the land of Egypt shall not escape. 43He shall have power over the treasures of gold and silver, and over all the precious things of Egypt; also the Libyans and Ethiopians *shall follow* at his heels. 44But news from the east and the north shall trouble him; therefore he shall go out with great fury to destroy and annihilate many. 45And he shall plant the tents of his palace between the seas and the glorious holy mountain; yet he shall come to his end, and no one will help him.

Prophecy of the End Time

12 "At that time Michael shall stand up,
The great prince who stands *watch* over the sons of your people;
And there shall be a time of trouble,
Such as never was since there was a nation,
Even to that time.
And at that time your people shall be delivered,
Every one who is found written in the book.
2   And many of those who sleep in the dust of the earth shall awake,

Some to everlasting life,
Some to shame *and* everlasting contempt.
3   Those who are wise shall shine
Like the brightness of the firmament,
And those who turn many to righteousness
Like the stars forever and ever.
4"But you, Daniel, shut up the words, and seal the book until the time of the end; many shall run to and fro, and knowledge shall increase."

5Then I, Daniel, looked; and there stood two others, one on this riverbank and the other on that riverbank. 6And *one* said to the man clothed in linen, who *was* above the waters of the river, "How long shall the fulfillment of these wonders *be*?"

7Then I heard the man clothed in linen, who *was* above the waters of the river, when he held up his right hand and his left hand to heaven, and swore by Him who lives forever, that *it shall be* for a time, times, and half *a time*; and when the power of the holy people has been completely shattered, all these *things* shall be finished.

8Although I heard, I did not understand. Then I said, "My lord, what *shall be* the end of these *things*?"

9And he said, "Go *your way*, Daniel, for the words *are* closed up and sealed till the time of the end. 10Many shall be purified, made white, and refined, but the wicked shall do wickedly; and none of the wicked shall understand, but the wise shall understand.

11"And from the time *that* the daily *sacrifice* is taken away, and the abomination of desolation is set up, *there shall be* one thousand two hundred and ninety days. 12Blessed *is* he who waits, and comes to the one thousand three hundred and thirty-five days.

13"But you, go *your way* till the end; for you shall rest, and will arise to your inheritance at the end of the days."

HOSEA

1 The word of the LORD that came to Hosea the son of Beeri, in the days of Uzziah, Jotham, Ahaz, *and* Hezekiah, kings of Judah, and in the days of Jeroboam the son of Joash, king of Israel.

The Family of Hosea

2When the LORD began to speak by Hosea, the LORD said to Hosea:

"Go, take yourself a wife of harlotry
And children of harlotry,
For the land has committed great
    harlotry
By departing from the LORD."

3So he went and took Gomer the daughter of Diblaim, and she conceived and bore him a son. 4Then the LORD said to him:

"Call his name Jezreel,
For in a little *while*
I will avenge the bloodshed of
    Jezreel on the house of Jehu,
And bring an end to the kingdom
    of the house of Israel.

5   It shall come to pass in that day
That I will break the bow of Israel
    in the Valley of Jezreel."

6And she conceived again and bore a daughter. Then *God* said to him:

"Call her name Lo-Ruhamah,[a]
For I will no longer have mercy on
    the house of Israel,
But I will utterly take them away.[b]

7   Yet I will have mercy on the house
    of Judah,
Will save them by the LORD
    their God,
And will not save them by bow,
Nor by sword or battle,
By horses or horsemen.''

8Now when she had weaned Lo-Ruhamah, she conceived and bore a son. 9Then *God* said:

"Call his name Lo-Ammi,[c]
For you *are* not My people,
And I will not be your *God.*

The Restoration of Israel

10 "Yet the number of the children of
    Israel
Shall be as the sand of the sea,
Which cannot be measured or
    numbered.
And it shall come to pass
In the place where it was said to
    them,
'You *are* not My people,'
There it shall be said to them,
'*You are* sons of the living God.'

11   Then the children of Judah and the
    children of Israel
Shall be gathered together,
And appoint for themselves one
    head;
And they shall come up out of the
    land,
For great *will be* the day of Jezreel!

2 Say to your brethren, 'My people,'
And to your sisters, 'Mercy *is
    shown.*'

God's Unfaithful People

2   "Bring charges against your mother,
    bring charges;
For she *is* not My wife, nor *am* I
    her Husband!
Let her put away her harlotries
    from her sight,
And her adulteries from between
    her breasts;

3   Lest I strip her naked
And expose her, as in the day she
    was born,
And make her like a wilderness,
And set her like a dry land,
And slay her with thirst.

4   "I will not have mercy on her
    children,
For they *are* the children of
    harlotry.

5   For their mother has played the
    harlot;
She who conceived them has
    behaved shamefully.
For she said, 'I will go after my
    lovers,
Who give *me* my bread and my
    water,

---

a Literally *No-Mercy*   b Or *That I may forgive them at all*   c Literally *Not-My-People*

My wool and my linen,
My oil and my drink.'

6 "Therefore, behold,
I will hedge up your way with
thorns,
And wall her in,
So that she cannot find her paths.
7 She will chase her lovers,
But not overtake them;
Yes, she will seek them, but not find
them.
Then she will say,
'I will go and return to my first
husband,
For then *it was* better for me
than now.'
8 For she did not know
That I gave her grain, new wine,
and oil,
And multiplied her silver and
gold—
Which they prepared for Baal.

9 "Therefore I will return and take
away
My grain in its time
And My new wine in its season,
And will take back My wool and
My linen,
Given to cover her nakedness.
10 Now I will uncover her lewdness
in the sight of her lovers,
And no one shall deliver her from
My hand.
11 I will also cause all her mirth to
cease,
Her feast days,
Her New Moons,
Her Sabbaths—
All her appointed feasts.

12 "And I will destroy her vines and her
fig trees,
Of which she has said,
'These *are* my wages that my lovers
have given me.'
So I will make them a forest,
And the beasts of the field shall eat
them.
13 I will punish her
For the days of the Baals to which
she burned incense.
She decked herself with her
earrings and jewelry,

And went after her lovers;
But Me she forgot," says the
LORD.

God's Mercy on His People

14 "Therefore, behold, I will allure her,
Will bring her into the wilderness,
And speak comfort to her.
15 I will give her her vineyards from
there,
And the Valley of Achor as a door
of hope;
She shall sing there,
As in the days of her youth,
As in the day when she came up
from the land of Egypt.

16 "And it shall be, in that day,"
Says the LORD,
"*That* you will call Me 'My
Husband,'
And no longer call Me 'My Master,'
17 For I will take from her mouth the
names of the Baals,
And they shall be remembered by
their name no more.
18 In that day I will make a covenant
for them
With the beasts of the field,
With the birds of the air,
And *with* the creeping things of the
ground.
Bow and sword of battle I will
shatter from the earth,
To make them lie down safely.

19 "I will betroth you to Me forever;
Yes, I will betroth you to Me
In righteousness and justice,
In lovingkindness and mercy;
20 I will betroth you to Me in
faithfulness,
And you shall know the LORD.

21 "It shall come to pass in that day
That I will answer," says the LORD;
"I will answer the heavens,
And they shall answer the earth.
22 The earth shall answer
With grain,
With new wine,
And with oil;
They shall answer Jezreel.[d]
23 Then I will sow her for Myself in
the earth,

[d] Literally *God Will Sow*

And I will have mercy on *her who
had* not obtained mercy;
Then I will say to *those who were*
not My people,
'You *are* My people!'
And they shall say, '*You are*
my God!' "

Israel Will Return to God

3 Then the LORD said to me, "Go
again, love a woman *who is* loved
by a lover and is committing adultery,
just like the love of the LORD for the
children of Israel, who look to other
gods and love *the* raisin cakes *of the
pagans.*"

2So I bought her for myself for fifteen
shekels of silver, and one and one-half
homers of barley. 3And I said to her,
"You shall stay with me many days;
you shall not play the harlot, nor shall
you have a man—so, too, *will* I *be* toward you."

4For the children of Israel shall abide
many days without king or prince, without sacrifice or sacred pillar, without
ephod or teraphim. 5Afterward the children of Israel shall return and seek the
LORD their God and David their king.
They shall fear the LORD and His goodness in the latter days.

God's Charge Against Israel

4 Hear the word of the LORD,
You children of Israel,
For the LORD *brings* a charge
against the inhabitants of
the land:

"There is no truth or mercy
Or knowledge of God in the land.
2 *By* swearing and lying,
Killing and stealing and
committing adultery,
They break all restraint,
With bloodshed upon bloodshed.
3 Therefore the land will mourn;
And everyone who dwells there
will waste away
With the beasts of the field
And the birds of the air;
Even the fish of the sea will be
taken away.

4 "Now let no man contend, or rebuke
another;

For your people *are* like those who
contend with the priest.
5 Therefore you shall stumble in
the day;
The prophet also shall stumble with
you in the night;
And I will destroy your mother.
6 My people are destroyed for lack
of knowledge.
Because you have rejected
knowledge,
I also will reject you from being
priest for Me;
Because you have forgotten the law
of your God,
I also will forget your children.

7 "The more they increased,
The more they sinned against Me;
I will change their glory into
shame.
8 They eat up the sin of My
people;
They set their heart on their
iniquity.
9 And it shall be: like people, like
priest.
So I will punish them for their
ways,
And reward them for their deeds.
10 For they shall eat, but not have
enough;
They shall commit harlotry, but not
increase;
Because they have ceased obeying
the LORD.

The Idolatry of Israel

11 "Harlotry, wine, and new wine
enslave the heart.
12 My people ask counsel from their
wooden *idols,*
And their staff informs them.
For the spirit of harlotry has caused
them to stray,
And they have played the harlot
against their God.
13 They offer sacrifices on the
mountaintops,
And burn incense on the hills,
Under oaks, poplars, and
terebinths,
Because their shade *is* good.
Therefore your daughters commit
harlotry,
And your brides commit
adultery.

14 "I will not punish your daughters
    when they commit harlotry,
  Nor your brides when they commit
    adultery;
  For *the men* themselves go apart
    with harlots,
  And offer sacrifices with a ritual
    harlot.*ᵉ*
  Therefore people *who* do not
    understand will be trampled.

15 "Though you, Israel, play the harlot,
  Let not Judah offend.
  Do not come up to Gilgal,
  Nor go up to Beth Aven,
  Nor swear an oath, *saying,* 'As the
    LORD lives'—

16 "For Israel is stubborn
  Like a stubborn calf;
  Now the LORD will let them forage
  Like a lamb in open country.

17 "Ephraim *is* joined to idols,
  Let him alone.
18 Their drink is rebellion,
  They commit harlotry continually.
  Her rulers dearly love dishonor.
19 The wind has wrapped her up in
    its wings,
  And they shall be ashamed because
    of their sacrifices.

Impending Judgment on Israel and Judah

5 "Hear this, O priests!
  Take heed, O house of Israel!
  Give ear, O house of the king!
  For yours *is* the judgment,
  Because you have been a snare to
    Mizpah
  And a net spread on Tabor.
2 The revolters are deeply involved
    in slaughter,
  Though I rebuke them all.
3 I know Ephraim,
  And Israel is not hidden from Me;
  For now, O Ephraim, you commit
    harlotry;
  Israel is defiled.

4 "They do not direct their deeds
  Toward turning to their God,
  For the spirit of harlotry is in their
    midst,

And they do not know the LORD.
5 The pride of Israel testifies to his
    face;
  Therefore Israel and Ephraim
    stumble in their iniquity;
  Judah also stumbles with them.

6 "With their flocks and herds
  They shall go to seek the LORD,
  But they will not find *Him;*
  He has withdrawn Himself from
    them.
7 They have dealt treacherously with
    the LORD,
  For they have begotten pagan
    children.
  Now a New Moon shall devour
    them and their heritage.

8 "Blow the ram's horn in Gibeah,
  The trumpet in Ramah!
  Cry aloud *at* Beth Aven,
  '*Look* behind you, O Benjamin!'
9 Ephraim shall be desolate in the
    day of rebuke;
  Among the tribes of Israel I make
    known what is sure.

10 "The princes of Judah are like those
    who remove a landmark;
  I will pour out my wrath on them
    like water.
11 Ephraim is oppressed *and* broken
    in judgment,
  Because he willingly walked by
    human precept.
12 Therefore I *will be* to Ephraim like
    a moth,
  And to the house of Judah like
    rottenness.

13 "When Ephraim saw his sickness,
  And Judah *saw* his wound,
  Then Ephraim went to Assyria
  And sent to King Jareb;
  Yet he cannot cure you,
  Nor heal you of your wound.
14 For I *will be* like a lion to
    Ephraim,
  And like a young lion to the house
    of Judah.
  I, *even* I, will tear *them* and go
    away;
  I will take *them* away, and no one
    shall rescue.
15 I will return again to My place

ᵉ Compare Deuteronomy 23.18

Till they acknowledge their offense.
Then they will seek My face;
In their affliction they will earnestly
  seek Me."

A Call to Repentance

6 Come, and let us return to the
  LORD;
For He has torn, but He will
  heal us;
He has stricken, but He will bind
  us up.
2 After two days He will revive us;
On the third day He will raise
  us up,
That we may live in His sight.
3 Let us know,
Let us pursue the knowledge of the
  LORD.
His going forth is established as the
  morning;
He will come to us like the rain,
Like the latter *and* former rain to
  the earth.

Impenitence of Israel and Judah

4 "O Ephraim, what shall I do to you?
O Judah, what shall I do to you?
For your faithfulness is like a
  morning cloud,
And like the early dew it goes
  away.
5 Therefore I have hewn *them* by the
  prophets,
I have slain them by the words of
  My mouth;
And your judgments *are like* light
  that goes forth.
6 For I desire mercy and not sacrifice,
And the knowledge of God more
  than burnt offerings.
7 "But like men they transgressed the
  covenant;
There they dealt treacherously
  with Me.
8 Gilead *is* a city of evildoers
And defiled with blood.
9 As bands of robbers lie in wait for
  a man,
So the company of priests murder
  on the way to Shechem;
Surely they commit lewdness.
10 I have seen a horrible thing in the
  house of Israel:
There *is* the harlotry of Ephraim;
Israel is defiled.

11 Also, O Judah, a harvest is
  appointed for you,
When I return the captives of My
  people.

7 "When I would have healed Israel,
Then the iniquity of Ephraim was
  uncovered,
And the wickedness of Samaria.
For they have committed fraud;
A thief comes in;
A band of robbers takes spoil
  outside.
2 They do not consider in their hearts
That I remember all their
  wickedness;
Now their own deeds have
  surrounded them;
They are before My face.
3 They make a king glad with their
  wickedness,
And princes with their lies.

4 "They *are* all adulterers.
Like an oven heated by a baker—
He ceases stirring *the fire* after
  kneading the dough,
Until it is leavened.
5 In the day of our king
Princes have made *him* sick,
  inflamed with wine;
He stretched out his hand with
  scoffers.
6 They prepare their heart like an
  oven,
While they lie in wait;
Their baker sleeps all night;
In the morning it burns like a
  flaming fire.
7 They are all hot, like an oven,
And have devoured their judges;
All their kings have fallen.
None among them calls upon Me.

8 "Ephraim has mixed himself among
  the peoples;
Ephraim is a cake unturned.
9 Aliens have devoured his strength,
But he does not know *it;*
Yes, gray hairs are here and there
  on him,
Yet he does not know *it*.
10 And the pride of Israel testifies to
  his face,
But they do not return to the LORD
  their God,
Nor seek Him for all this.

Futile Reliance on the Nations

11 "Ephraim also is like a silly dove,
     without sense—
   They call to Egypt,
   They go to Assyria.
12 Wherever they go, I will spread My
     net on them;
   I will bring them down like birds
     of the air;
   I will chastise them
   According to what their
     congregation has heard.

13 "Woe to them, for they have fled
     from Me!
   Destruction to them,
   Because they have transgressed
     against Me!
   Though I redeemed them,
   Yet they have spoken lies
     against Me.
14 They did not cry out to Me with
     their heart
   When they wailed upon their beds.

   "They assemble together for grain
     and new wine,
   They rebel against Me;
15 Though I disciplined *and*
     strengthened their arms,
   Yet they devise evil against Me;
16 They return, *but* not to the
     Most High;[f]
   They are like a treacherous bow.
   Their princes shall fall by the
     sword
   For the cursings of their tongue.
   This *shall be* their derision in the
     land of Egypt.

The Apostasy of Israel

8 "*Set* the trumpet[g] to your mouth!
   He shall come like an eagle
     against the house of the LORD,
   Because they have transgressed My
     covenant
   And rebelled against My law.
2 Israel will cry to Me,
   'My God, we know You!'
3 Israel has rejected the good;
   The enemy will pursue him.

4 "They set up kings, but not by Me;
   They made princes, but I did not
     acknowledge *them*.

   From their silver and gold
   They made idols for themselves—
   That they might be cut off.
5 Your calf is rejected, O Samaria!
   My anger is aroused against
     them—
   How long until they attain to
     innocence?
6 For from Israel *is* even this:
   A workman made it, and it *is*
     not God;
   But the calf of Samaria shall be
     broken to pieces.

7 "They sow the wind,
   And reap the whirlwind.
   The stalk has no bud;
   It shall never produce meal.
   If it should produce,
   Aliens would swallow it up.
8 Israel is swallowed up;
   Now they are among the Gentiles
   Like a vessel in which *is* no
     pleasure.
9 For they have gone up to Assyria,
   Like a wild donkey alone by itself;
   Ephraim has hired lovers.
10 Yes, though they have hired among
     the nations,
   Now I will gather them;
   And they shall sorrow a little,
   Because of the burden of the king
     of princes.

11 "Because Ephraim has made many
     altars for sin,
   They have become for him altars
     for sinning.
12 I have written for him the great
     things of My law,
   But they were considered a strange
     thing.
13 *For* the sacrifices of My offerings
     they sacrifice flesh and eat *it*,
   But the LORD does not accept them.
   Now He will remember their
     iniquity and punish their sins.
   They shall return to Egypt.

14 "For Israel has forgotten his Maker,
   And has built temples;
   Judah also has multiplied fortified
     cities;
   But I will send fire upon his cities,
   And it shall devour his palaces."

f Or *upward*   g Ram's horn

Judgment of Israel's Sin

9 Do not rejoice, O Israel, with joy
like *other* peoples,
For you have played the harlot
against your God.
You have made love *for* hire on
every threshing floor.
2 The threshing floor and the
winepress
Shall not feed them,
And the new wine shall fail in her.

3 They shall not dwell in the LORD's
land,
But Ephraim shall return to Egypt,
And shall eat unclean *things* in
Assyria.
4 They shall not offer wine *offerings*
to the LORD,
Nor shall their sacrifices be
pleasing to Him.
It shall be like bread of mourners
to them;
All who eat it shall be defiled.
For their bread *shall be* for their
own life;
It shall not come into the house of
the LORD.

5 What will you do in the
appointed day,
And in the day of the feast of the
LORD?
6 For indeed they are gone because
of destruction.
Egypt shall gather them up;
Memphis shall bury them.
Nettles shall possess their
valuables of silver;
Thorns *shall be* in their tents.

7 The days of punishment have
come;
The days of recompense have
come.
Israel knows!
The prophet *is* a fool,
The spiritual man *is* insane,
Because of the greatness of your
iniquity and great enmity.
8 The watchman of Ephraim *is* with
my God;
But the prophet *is* a fowler's snare
in all his ways—
Enmity in the house of his God.
9 They are deeply corrupted,
As in the days of Gibeah.
He will remember their iniquity;
He will punish their sins.

10 "I found Israel
Like grapes in the wilderness;
I saw your fathers
As the firstfruits on the fig tree in
its first season.
But they went to Baal Peor,
And separated themselves *to that*
shame;
They became an abomination like
the thing they loved.
11 *As for* Ephraim, their glory shall fly
away like a bird—
No birth, no pregnancy, and no
conception!
12 Though they bring up their
children,
Yet I will bereave them to the
last man.
Yes, woe to them when I depart
from them!
13 Just as I saw Ephraim like Tyre,
planted in a pleasant place,
So Ephraim will bring out his
children to the murderer."

14 Give them, O LORD—
What will You give?
Give them a miscarrying womb
And dry breasts!

15 "All their wickedness *is* in Gilgal,
For there I hated them.
Because of the evil of their deeds
I will drive them from My house;
I will love them no more.
All their princes *are* rebellious.
16 Ephraim is stricken,
Their root is dried up;
They shall bear no fruit.
Yes, were they to bear children,
I would kill the darlings of their
womb."

17 My God will cast them away,
Because they did not obey Him;
And they shall be wanderers
among the nations.

Israel's Sin and Captivity

10 Israel empties *his* vine;
He brings forth fruit for himself.
According to the multitude of his
fruit

He has increased the altars;
According to the bounty of his land
They have embellished *his* sacred
    pillars.
2 Their heart is divided;
Now they are held guilty.
He will break down their altars;
He will ruin their sacred pillars.

3 For now they say,
    "We have no king,
Because we did not fear the LORD.
And as for a king, what would he
    do for us?"
4 They have spoken words,
Swearing falsely in making a
    covenant.
Thus judgment springs up like
    hemlock in the furrows of the
    field.

5 The inhabitants of Samaria fear
Because of the calf of Beth Aven.
For its people mourn for it,
And its priests shriek for it—
Because its glory has departed
    from it.
6 *The idol* also shall be carried to
    Assyria
As a present for King Jareb.
Ephraim shall receive shame,
And Israel shall be ashamed of his
    own counsel.

7 *As for* Samaria, her king is cut off
Like a twig on the water.
8 Also the high places of Aven, the
    sin of Israel,
Shall be destroyed.
The thorn and thistle shall grow on
    their altars;
They shall say to the mountains,
    "Cover us!"
And to the hills, "Fall on us!"

9 "O Israel, you have sinned from the
    days of Gibeah;
There they stood.
The battle in Gibeah against the
    children of iniquity
Did not overtake them.
10 When *it is* My desire, I will chasten
    them.
Peoples shall be gathered against
    them
When I bind them for their two
    transgressions.

11 Ephraim *is* a trained heifer
That loves to thresh *grain;*
But I harnessed her fair neck,
I will make Ephraim pull *a plow.*
Judah shall plow;
Jacob shall break his clods."

12 Sow for yourselves righteousness;
Reap in mercy;
Break up your fallow ground,
For *it is* time to seek the LORD,
Till He comes and rains
    righteousness on you.

13 You have plowed wickedness;
You have reaped iniquity.
You have eaten the fruit of lies,
Because you trusted in your
    own way,
In the multitude of your
    mighty men.
14 Therefore tumult shall arise among
    your people,
And all your fortresses shall be
    plundered
As Shalman plundered Beth Arbel
    in the day of battle—
A mother dashed in pieces upon *her*
    children.
15 Thus it shall be done to you,
    O Bethel,
Because of your great wickedness.
At dawn the king of Israel
Shall be cut off utterly.

God's Continuing Love for Israel

11 "When Israel *was* a child, I
        loved him,
And out of Egypt I called My son.
2 *As* they called them,
So they went from them;
They sacrificed to the Baals,
And burned incense to carved
    images.

3 "I taught Ephraim to walk,
Taking them by their arms;
But they did not know that I healed
    them.
4 I drew them with gentle cords,
With bands of love,
And I was to them as those who
    take the yoke from their neck.
I stooped *and* fed them.

5 "He shall not return to the land of
    Egypt;

But the Assyrian shall be his king,
Because they refused to repent.
6 And the sword shall slash in his
   cities,
   Devour his districts,
   And consume *them*,
   Because of their own counsels.
7 My people are bent on backsliding
   from Me.
   Though they call to the Most High,*h*
   None at all exalt *Him*.

8 "How can I give you up, Ephraim?
   How can I hand you over, Israel?
   How can I make you like Admah?
   How can I set you like Zeboiim?
   My heart churns within Me;
   My sympathy is stirred.
9 I will not execute the fierceness of
   My anger;
   I will not again destroy Ephraim.
   For I *am* God, and not man,
   The Holy One in your midst;
   And I will not come with terror.

10 "They shall walk after the LORD.
   He will roar like a lion.
   When He roars,
   Then *His* sons shall come trembling
   from the west;
11 They shall come trembling like a
   bird from Egypt,
   Like a dove from the land of
   Assyria.
   And I will let them dwell in their
   houses,"
   Says the LORD.

God's Charge Against Ephraim

12 "Ephraim has encircled Me with lies,
   And the house of Israel with deceit;
   But Judah still walks with God,
   Even with the Holy One*i* *who is*
   faithful.

12 "Ephraim feeds on the wind,
      And pursues the east wind;
   He daily increases lies and
   desolation.
   Also they make a covenant with the
   Assyrians,
   And oil is carried to Egypt.

2 "The LORD also *brings* a charge
   against Judah,

And will punish Jacob according to
   his ways;
   According to his deeds He will
   recompense him.
3 He took his brother by the heel in
   the womb,
   And in his strength he struggled
   with God.*j*
4 Yes, he struggled with the Angel
   and prevailed;
   He wept, and sought favor
   from Him.
   He found Him *in* Bethel,
   And there He spoke to us—
5 That is, the LORD God of hosts.
   The LORD *is* His memorable name.
6 So you, by *the help of* your God,
   return;
   Observe mercy and justice,
   And wait on your God continually.

7 "A cunning Canaanite!
   Deceitful scales *are* in his hand;
   He loves to oppress.
8 And Ephraim said,
   'Surely I have become rich,
   I have found wealth for myself;
   In all my labors
   They shall find in me no iniquity
   that *is* sin.'

9 "But I *am* the LORD your God,
   Ever since the land of Egypt;
   I will again make you dwell in
   tents,
   As in the days of the appointed
   feast.
10 I have also spoken by the prophets,
   And have multiplied visions;
   I have given symbols through the
   witness of the prophets."

11 Though Gilead *has* idols—
   Surely they are vanity—
   Though they sacrifice bulls in
   Gilgal,
   Indeed their altars *shall be* heaps
   in the furrows of the field.

12 Jacob fled to the country of Syria;
   Israel served for a spouse,
   And for a wife he tended *sheep*.
13 By a prophet the LORD brought
   Israel out of Egypt,

---

h Or *upward*   *i* Or *holy ones*   *j* Compare Genesis 32.28

And by a prophet he was
preserved.
14 Ephraim provoked *Him* to anger
most bitterly;
Therefore his Lord will leave the
guilt of his bloodshed upon him,
And return his reproach upon him.

Relentless Judgment on Israel

13 When Ephraim spoke, trembling,
He exalted *himself* in Israel;
But when he offended through Baal
worship, he died.
2 Now they sin more and more,
And have made for themselves
molded images,
Idols of their silver, according to
their skill;
All of it *is* the work of craftsmen.
They say of them,
"Let the men who sacrifice kiss the
calves!"
3 Therefore they shall be like the
morning cloud
And like the early dew that passes
away,
Like chaff blown off from a
threshing floor
And like smoke from a chimney.

4 "Yet I *am* the LORD your God
Ever since the land of Egypt,
And you shall know no God
but Me;
For *there is* no savior besides Me.
5 I knew you in the wilderness,
In the land of great drought.
6 When they had pasture, they were
filled;
They were filled and their heart
was exalted;
Therefore they forgot Me.

7 "So I will be to them like a lion;
Like a leopard by the road I will
lurk;
8 I will meet them like a bear
deprived *of her cubs;*
I will tear open their rib cage,
And there I will devour them like
a lion.
The wild beast shall tear them.

9 "O Israel, you are destroyed,
But your help *is* from Me.
10 I will be your King;
Where *is any other*,

That he may save you in all your
cities?
And your judges to whom you said,
'Give me a king and princes'?
11 I gave you a king in My anger,
And took *him* away in My wrath.

12 "The iniquity of Ephraim *is*
bound up;
His sin *is* stored up.
13 The sorrows of a woman in
childbirth shall come upon him.
He *is* an unwise son,
For he should not stay long where
children are born.

14 "I will ransom them from the power
of the grave;
I will redeem them from death.
O Death, I will be your plagues!
O Grave, I will be your destruction!
Pity is hidden from My eyes."

15 Though he is fruitful among *his*
brethren,
An east wind shall come;
The wind of the LORD shall come
up from the wilderness.
Then his spring shall become dry,
And his fountain shall be dried up.
He shall plunder the treasury of
every desirable prize.
16 Samaria is held guilty,
For she has rebelled against
her God.
They shall fall by the sword,
Their infants shall be dashed in
pieces,
And their women with child ripped
open.

Israel Restored at Last

14 O Israel, return to the LORD your
God,
For you have stumbled because of
your iniquity;
2 Take words with you,
And return to the LORD.
Say to Him,
"Take away all iniquity;
Receive *us* graciously,
For we will offer the sacrifices of
our lips.
3 Assyria shall not save us,
We will not ride on horses,
Nor will we say anymore to the

work of our hands, 'You are our
gods.'
For in You the fatherless finds
mercy."

4 "I will heal their backsliding,
I will love them freely,
For My anger has turned away
from him.
5 I will be like the dew to Israel;
He shall grow like the lily,
And lengthen his roots like
Lebanon.
6 His branches shall spread;
His beauty shall be like an olive
tree,
And his fragrance like Lebanon.
7 Those who dwell under his shadow
shall return;

They shall be revived like grain,
And grow like a vine.
Their scent shall be like the wine
of Lebanon.

8 "Ephraim shall say, 'What have I to
do anymore with idols?'
I have heard and observed him.
I am like a green cypress tree;
Your fruit is found in Me."

9 Who is wise?
Let him understand these things.
Who is prudent?
Let him know them.
For the ways of the LORD are right;
The righteous walk in them,
But transgressors stumble in
them.

The Book of
JOEL

1 The word of the LORD that came to
Joel the son of Pethuel.

The Land Laid Waste

2 Hear this, you elders,
And give ear, all you inhabitants of
the land!
Has anything like this happened in
your days,
Or even in the days of your fathers?
3 Tell your children about it,
Let your children tell their
children,
And their children another
generation.

4 What the chewing locust[a] left, the
swarming locust has eaten;
What the swarming locust left, the
crawling locust has eaten;
And what the crawling locust left,
the consuming locust has eaten.

5 Awake, you drunkards, and weep;
And wail, all you drinkers of wine,
Because of the new wine,
For it has been cut off from your
mouth.
6 For a nation has come up against
My land,
Strong, and without number;
His teeth are the teeth of a lion,
And he has the fangs of a fierce
lion.
7 He has laid waste My vine,
And ruined My fig tree;
He has stripped it bare and thrown
it away;
Its branches are made white.

8 Lament like a virgin girded with
sackcloth
For the husband of her youth.
9 The grain offering and the drink
offering

---

a Exact identity of these locusts is unknown.

Have been cut off from the house
 of the LORD;
The priests mourn, who minister to
 the LORD.
10 The field is wasted,
 The land mourns;
 For the grain is ruined,
 The new wine is dried up,
 The oil fails.

11 Be ashamed, you farmers,
 Wail, you vinedressers,
 For the wheat and the barley;
 Because the harvest of the field has
  perished.
12 The vine has dried up,
 And the fig tree has withered;
 The pomegranate tree,
 The palm tree also,
 And the apple tree—
 All the trees of the field are
  withered;
 Surely joy has withered away from
  the sons of men.

Mourning for the Land

13 Gird yourselves and lament, you
  priests;
 Wail, you who minister before the
  altar;
 Come, lie all night in sackcloth,
 You who minister to my God;
 For the grain offering and the drink
  offering
 Are withheld from the house of
  your God.
14 Consecrate a fast,
 Call a sacred assembly;
 Gather the elders
 And all the inhabitants of the land
 Into the house of the LORD
  your God,
 And cry out to the LORD.

15 Alas for the day!
 For the day of the LORD *is* at hand;
 It shall come as destruction from
  the Almighty.
16 Is not the food cut off before our
  eyes,
 Joy and gladness from the house
  of our God?
17 The seed shrivels under the clods,
 Storehouses are in shambles;
 Barns are broken down,
 For the grain has withered.
18 How the animals groan!

The herds of cattle are restless,
 Because they have no pasture;
 Even the flocks of sheep suffer
  punishment.

19 O LORD, to You I cry out;
 For fire has devoured the open
  pastures,
 And a flame has burned all the
  trees of the field.
20 The beasts of the field also cry out
  to You,
 For the water brooks are dried up,
 And fire has devoured the open
  pastures.

The Day of the LORD

2 Blow the trumpet in Zion,
 And sound an alarm in My holy
  mountain!
 Let all the inhabitants of the land
  tremble;
 For the day of the LORD is coming,
 For it is at hand:
2 A day of darkness and gloominess,
 A day of clouds and thick darkness,
 Like the morning *clouds* spread
  over the mountains.
 A people *come*, great and strong,
 The like of whom has never been;
 Nor will there ever be any *such*
  after them,
 Even for many successive
  generations.

3 A fire devours before them,
 And behind them a flame burns;
 The land *is* like the Garden of Eden
  before them,
 And behind them a desolate
  wilderness;
 Surely nothing shall escape them.
4 Their appearance is like the
  appearance of horses;
 And like swift steeds, so they run.
5 With a noise like chariots
 Over mountaintops they leap,
 Like the noise of a flaming fire that
  devours the stubble,
 Like a strong people set in battle
  array.

6 Before them the people writhe in
  pain;
 All faces are drained of color.
7 They run like mighty men,

They climb the wall like men
of war;
Every one marches in formation,
And they do not break ranks.
8   They do not push one another;
Every one marches in his own
column.
Though they lunge between the
weapons,
They are not cut down.[b]
9   They run to and fro in the city,
They run on the wall;
They climb into the houses,
They enter at the windows like a
thief.

10 The earth quakes before them,
The heavens tremble;
The sun and moon grow dark,
And the stars diminish their
brightness.
11 The LORD gives voice before His
army,
For His camp is very great;
For strong *is the One* who executes
His word.
For the day of the LORD *is* great and
very terrible;
Who can endure it?

A Call to Repentance

12 "Now, therefore," says the LORD,
"Turn to Me with all your heart,
With fasting, with weeping, and
with mourning."
13 So rend your heart, and not your
garments;
Return to the LORD your God,
For He *is* gracious and merciful,
Slow to anger, and of great
kindness;
And He relents from doing harm.
14 Who knows *if* He will turn and
relent,
And leave a blessing behind Him—
A grain offering and a drink
offering
For the LORD your God?

15 Blow the trumpet in Zion,
Consecrate a fast,
Call a sacred assembly;
16 Gather the people,
Sanctify the congregation,
Assemble the elders,

Gather the children and nursing
babes;
Let the bridegroom go out from his
chamber,
And the bride from her dressing
room.
17 Let the priests, who minister to the
LORD,
Weep between the porch and the
altar;
Let them say, "Spare Your people,
O LORD,
And do not give Your heritage to
reproach,
That the nations should rule over
them.
Why should they say among the
peoples,
'Where *is* their God?' "

The Land Refreshed

18 Then the LORD will be zealous for
His land,
And pity His people.
19 The LORD will answer and say to
His people,
"Behold, I will send you grain and
new wine and oil,
And you will be satisfied by them;
I will no longer make you a
reproach among the nations.

20 "But I will remove far from you the
northern *army*,
And will drive him away into a
barren and desolate land,
With his face toward the
eastern sea
And his back toward the
western sea;
His stench will come up,
And his foul odor will rise,
Because he has done monstrous
things."

21 Fear not, O land;
Be glad and rejoice,
For the LORD has done marvelous
things!
22 Do not be afraid, you beasts of the
field;
For the open pastures are
springing up,
And the tree bears its fruit;
The fig tree and the vine yield their
strength.

[b] That is, they are not halted by losses

23 Be glad then, you children of Zion,
    And rejoice in the LORD your God;
    For He has given you the former
      rain faithfully,
    And He will cause the rain to come
      down for you—
    The former rain,
    And the latter rain in the first
      month.
24 The threshing floors shall be full of
      wheat,
    And the vats shall overflow with
      new wine and oil.

25 "So I will restore to you the years
      that the swarming locust has
      eaten,
    The crawling locust,
    The consuming locust,
    And the chewing locust,[c]
    My great army which I sent
      among you.
26 You shall eat in plenty and be
      satisfied,
    And praise the name of the LORD
      your God,
    Who has dealt wondrously
      with you;
    And My people shall never be put
      to shame.
27 Then you shall know that I *am* in
      the midst of Israel:
    I *am* the LORD your God
    And there is no other.
    My people shall never be put to
      shame.

God's Spirit Poured Out

28 "And it shall come to pass afterward
    That I will pour out My Spirit on
      all flesh;
    Your sons and your daughters shall
      prophesy,
    Your old men shall dream dreams,
    Your young men shall see visions.
29 And also on *My* menservants and
      on *My* maidservants
    I will pour out My Spirit in those
      days.

30 "And I will show wonders in the
      heavens and in the earth:
    Blood and fire and pillars of smoke.
31 The sun shall be turned into
      darkness,
    And the moon into blood,

Before the coming of the great and
  awesome day of the LORD.
32 And it shall come to pass
    That whoever calls on the name of
      the LORD
    Shall be saved.
    For in Mount Zion and in Jerusalem
      there shall be deliverance,
    As the LORD has said,
    Among the remnant whom the
      LORD calls.

God Judges the Nations

3 "For behold, in those days and at
      that time,
    When I bring back the captives of
      Judah and Jerusalem,
2   I will also gather all nations,
    And bring them down to the Valley
      of Jehoshaphat;
    And I will enter into judgment with
      them there
    On account of My people, My
      heritage Israel,
    Whom they have scattered among
      the nations;
    They have also divided up My land.
3   They have cast lots for My people,
    Have given a boy *as payment* for
      a harlot,
    And sold a girl for wine, that they
      may drink.

4   "Indeed, what have you to do
      with Me,
    O Tyre and Sidon, and all the
      coasts of Philistia?
    Will you retaliate against Me?
    But if you retaliate against Me,
    Swiftly and speedily I will return
      your retaliation upon your own
      head;
5   Because you have taken My silver
      and My gold,
    And have carried into your temples
      My prized possessions.
6   Also the people of Judah and the
      people of Jerusalem
    You have sold to the Greeks,
    That you may remove them far
      from their borders.

7   "Behold, I will raise them
    Out of the place to which you have
      sold them,

c Compare 1.4

And will return your retaliation
upon your own head.

8 I will sell your sons and your
daughters
Into the hand of the people of
Judah,
And they will sell them to the
Sabeans,
To a people far off;
For the Lord has spoken."

9 Proclaim this among the nations:
"Prepare for war!
Wake up the mighty men,
Let all the men of war draw near,
Let them come up.

10 Beat your plowshares into swords
And your pruning hooks into
spears;
Let the weak say, 'I *am* strong.' "

11 Assemble and come, all you
nations,
And gather together all around.
Cause Your mighty ones to go
down there, O Lord.

12 "Let the nations be wakened, and
come up to the Valley of
Jehoshaphat;
For there I will sit to judge all the
surrounding nations.

13 Put in the sickle, for the harvest is
ripe.
Come, go down;
For the winepress is full,
The vats overflow—
For their wickedness *is* great."

14 Multitudes, multitudes in the valley
of decision!
For the day of the Lord *is* near in
the valley of decision.

15 The sun and moon will grow dark,

And the stars will diminish their
brightness.

16 The Lord also will roar from Zion,
And utter His voice from
Jerusalem;
The heavens and earth will shake;
But the Lord will be a shelter for
His people,
And the strength of the children of
Israel.

17 "So you shall know that I *am* the
Lord your God,
Dwelling in Zion My holy
mountain.
Then Jerusalem shall be holy,
And no aliens shall ever pass
through her again."

God Blesses His People

18 And it will come to pass in that day
That the mountains shall drip with
new wine,
The hills shall flow with milk,
And all the brooks of Judah shall
be flooded with water;
A fountain shall flow from the
house of the Lord
And water the Valley of Acacias.

19 "Egypt shall be a desolation,
And Edom a desolate wilderness,
Because of violence *against* the
people of Judah,
For they have shed innocent blood
in their land.

20 But Judah shall abide forever,
And Jerusalem from generation to
generation.

21 For I will acquit them of the guilt
of bloodshed, whom I had not
acquitted;
For the Lord dwells in Zion."

The Book of

AMOS

1 The words of Amos, who was among the sheepbreeders of Tekoa, which he saw concerning Israel in the days of Uzziah king of Judah, and in the days of Jeroboam the son of Joash, king of Israel, two years before the earthquake.

2And he said:

"The LORD roars from Zion,
And utters His voice from
Jerusalem;
The pastures of the shepherds
mourn,
And the top of Carmel withers."

Judgment on the Nations

3Thus says the LORD:

"For three transgressions of
Damascus, and for four,
I will not turn away its *punishment*,
Because they have threshed Gilead
with implements of iron.

4 But I will send a fire into the house
of Hazael,
Which shall devour the palaces of
Ben-Hadad.

5 I will also break the *gate* bar of
Damascus,
And cut off the inhabitant from the
Valley of Aven,
And the one who holds the scepter
from Beth Eden.
The people of Syria shall go captive
to Kir,"
Says the LORD.

6Thus says the LORD:

"For three transgressions of Gaza,
and for four,
I will not turn away its *punishment*,
Because they took captive the
whole captivity
To deliver *them* up to Edom.

7 But I will send a fire upon the wall
of Gaza,
Which shall devour its palaces.

8 I will cut off the inhabitant from
Ashdod,
And the one who holds the scepter
from Ashkelon;
I will turn My hand against Ekron,
And the remnant of the Philistines
shall perish,"
Says the Lord GOD.

9Thus says the LORD:

"For three transgressions of Tyre,
and for four,
I will not turn away its *punishment*,
Because they delivered up the
whole captivity to Edom,
And did not remember the
covenant of brotherhood.

10 But I will send a fire upon the wall
of Tyre,
Which shall devour its palaces."

11Thus says the LORD:

"For three transgressions of Edom,
and for four,
I will not turn away its *punishment*,
Because he pursued his brother
with the sword,
And cast off all pity;
His anger tore perpetually,
And he kept his wrath forever.

12 But I will send a fire upon Teman,
Which shall devour the palaces of
Bozrah."

13Thus says the LORD:

"For three transgressions of the
people of Ammon, and for four,
I will not turn away its *punishment*,
Because they ripped open the
women with child in Gilead,
That they might enlarge their
territory.

14 But I will kindle a fire in the wall
of Rabbah,
And it shall devour its palaces,
Amid shouting in the day of battle,
And a tempest in the day of the
whirlwind.

15 Their king shall go into captivity,
He and his princes together,"
Says the LORD.

2 Thus says the LORD:

"For three transgressions of Moab,
and for four,
I will not turn away its *punishment*,
Because he burned the bones of the
king of Edom to lime.

2 But I will send a fire upon Moab,
And it shall devour the palaces of
Kerioth;
Moab shall die with tumult,
With shouting *and* trumpet sound.

3   And I will cut off the judge from
        its midst,
     And slay all its princes with him,"
     Says the LORD.

Judgment on Judah

4Thus says the LORD:
     "For three transgressions of Judah,
        and for four,
     I will not turn away its *punishment*,
     Because they have despised the law
        of the LORD,
     And have not kept His
        commandments.
     Their lies lead them astray,
     Lies which their fathers followed.
5   But I will send a fire upon Judah,
     And it shall devour the palaces of
        Jerusalem."

Judgment on Israel

6Thus says the LORD:
     "For three transgressions of Israel,
        and for four,
     I will not turn away its *punishment*,
     Because they sell the righteous for
        silver,
     And the poor for a pair of sandals.
7   They pant after the dust of the earth
        which is on the head of the poor,
     And pervert the way of the humble.
     A man and his father go in to the
        same girl,
     To defile My holy name.
8   They lie down by every altar on
        clothes taken in pledge,
     And drink the wine of the
        condemned *in* the house of
        their god.

9   "Yet *it was* I *who* destroyed the
        Amorite before them,
     Whose height *was* like the height
        of the cedars,
     And he *was as* strong as the oaks;
     Yet I destroyed his fruit above
     And his roots beneath.
10   Also *it was* I *who* brought you up
        from the land of Egypt,
     And led you forty years through the
        wilderness,
     To possess the land of the Amorite.
11   I raised up some of your sons as
        prophets,
     And some of your young men as
        Nazirites.

     Is it not so, O you children of
        Israel?"
     Says the LORD.
12   "But you gave the Nazirites wine to
        drink,
     And commanded the prophets
        saying,
     'Do not prophesy!'

13   "Behold, I am weighed down by you,
     As a cart full of sheaves is weighed
        down.
14   Therefore flight shall perish from
        the swift,
     The strong shall not strengthen his
        power,
     Nor shall the mighty deliver
        himself;
15   He shall not stand who handles
        the bow,
     The swift of foot shall not escape,
     Nor shall he who rides a horse
        deliver himself.
16   The most courageous men of might
     Shall flee naked in that day,"
     Says the LORD.

Authority of the Prophet's Message

3 Hear this word that the LORD has
     spoken against you, O children of
Israel, against the whole family which
I brought up from the land of Egypt,
saying:

2   "You only have I known of all the
        families of the earth;
     Therefore I will punish you for all
        your iniquities."

3   Can two walk together, unless they
        are agreed?
4   Will a lion roar in the forest, when
        he has no prey?
     Will a young lion cry out of his den,
        if he has caught nothing?
5   Will a bird fall into a snare on the
        earth, where there is no trap
        for it?
     Will a snare spring up from the
        earth, if it has caught nothing
        at all?
6   If a trumpet is blown in a city, will
        not the people be afraid?
     If there is calamity in a city, will
        not the LORD have done *it*?

7 Surely the Lord God does
       nothing,
   Unless He reveals His secret to His
       servants the prophets.
8 A lion has roared!
   Who will not fear?
   The Lord God has spoken!
   Who can but prophesy?

Punishment of Israel's Sins

9 "Proclaim in the palaces at Ashdod,
   And in the palaces in the land of
       Egypt, and say:
   'Assemble on the mountains of
       Samaria;
   See great tumults in her midst,
   And the oppressed within her.
10 For they do not know to do right,'
   Says the Lord,
   'Who store up violence and robbery
       in their palaces.'"
   11Therefore thus says the Lord God:
   "An adversary *shall be* all around
       the land;
   He shall sap your strength
       from you,
   And your palaces shall be
       plundered."
   12Thus says the Lord:
   "As a shepherd takes from the
       mouth of a lion
   Two legs or a piece of an ear,
   So shall the children of Israel be
       taken out
   Who dwell in Samaria—
   In the corner of a bed and on the
       edge*a* of a couch!
13 Hear and testify against the house
       of Jacob,"
   Says the Lord God, the God of
       hosts,
14 "That in the day I punish Israel for
       their transgressions,
   I will also visit *destruction* on the
       altars of Bethel;
   And the horns of the altar shall be
       cut off
   And fall to the ground.
15 I will destroy the winter house
       along with the summer house;
   The houses of ivory shall perish,
   And the great houses shall have
       an end,"
   Says the Lord.

4 Hear this word, you cows of
       Bashan, who *are* on the mountain
       of Samaria,
   Who oppress the poor,
   Who crush the needy,
   Who say to your husbands, "Bring
       wine, let us drink!"
2 The Lord God has sworn by His
       holiness:
   "Behold, the days shall come
       upon you
   When He will take you away with
       fishhooks,
   And your posterity with fishhooks.
3 You will go out *through* broken
       walls,
   Each one straight ahead of her,
   And you will be cast into Harmon,"
   Says the Lord.

4 "Come to Bethel and transgress,
   At Gilgal multiply transgression;
   Bring your sacrifices every
       morning,
   Your tithes every three days.*b*
5 Offer a sacrifice of thanksgiving
       with leaven,
   Proclaim *and* announce the freewill
       offerings;
   For this you love,
   You children of Israel!"
   Says the Lord God.

Israel Did Not Accept Correction

6 "Also I gave you cleanness of teeth
       in all your cities.
   And lack of bread in all your
       places;
   Yet you have not returned to Me,"
   Says the Lord.

7 "I also withheld rain from you,
   When *there were* still three months
       to the harvest.
   I made it rain on one city,
   I withheld rain from another city.
   One part was rained upon,
   And where it did not rain the part
       withered.
8 So two *or* three cities wandered to
       another city to drink water,
   But they were not satisfied;
   Yet you have not returned to Me,"
   Says the Lord.

---

a Hebrew is uncertain.   *b* Or *years* (compare Deuteronomy 14.28)

9 "I blasted you with blight and
    mildew.
  When your gardens increased,
  Your vineyards,
  Your fig trees,
  And your olive trees,
  The locust devoured *them*;
  Yet you have not returned to Me,"
  Says the LORD.

10 "I sent among you a plague after the
    manner of Egypt;
  Your young men I killed with a
    sword,
  Along with your captive horses;
  I made the stench of your camps
    come up into your nostrils;
  Yet you have not returned to Me,"
  Says the LORD.

11 "I overthrew *some* of you,
  As God overthrew Sodom and
    Gomorrah,
  And you were like a firebrand
    plucked from the burning;
  Yet you have not returned to Me,"
  Says the LORD.

12 "Therefore thus will I do to you,
    O Israel;
  Because I will do this to you,
  Prepare to meet your God,
    O Israel!"

13 For behold,
  He who forms mountains,
  And creates the wind,
  Who declares to man what his[c]
    thought *is*,
  And makes the morning darkness,
  Who treads the high places of the
    earth—
  The LORD God of hosts *is* His
    name.

A Lament for Israel

5 Hear this word which I take up
against you, a lamentation, O house
of Israel:
2   The virgin of Israel has fallen;
  She will rise no more.
  She lies forsaken on her land;
  There is no one to raise her up.

3 For thus says the Lord GOD:
  "The city that goes out by a
    thousand
  Shall have a hundred left,
  And that which goes out by a
    hundred
  Shall have ten left to the house of
    Israel."

A Call to Repentance

4 For thus says the LORD to the house
of Israel:
  "Seek Me and live;
5   But do not seek Bethel,
  Nor enter Gilgal,
  Nor pass over to Beersheba;
  For Gilgal shall surely go into
    captivity,
  And Bethel shall come to nothing.
6   Seek the LORD and live,
  Lest He break out like fire *in* the
    house of Joseph,
  And devour *it*,
  With no one to quench *it* in
    Bethel—
7   You who turn justice to wormwood,
  And lay righteousness to rest in the
    earth!"

8   He made the Pleiades and Orion;
  He turns the shadow of death into
    morning
  And makes the day dark as night;
  He calls for the waters of the sea
  And pours them out on the face of
    the earth;
  The LORD *is* His name.
9   He rains ruin upon the strong,
  So that fury comes upon the
    fortress.
10   They hate the one who rebukes in
    the gate,
  And they abhor the one who speaks
    uprightly.
11   Therefore, because you tread down
    the poor
  And take grain taxes from him,
  Though you have built houses of
    hewn stone,
  Yet you shall not dwell in them;
  You have planted pleasant
    vineyards,
  But you shall not drink wine from
    them.

[c] Or *His*

12 For I know your manifold
transgressions
And your mighty sins:
Afflicting the just *and* taking
bribes;
Diverting the poor *from justice* at
the gate.

13 Therefore the prudent keep silent
at that time,
For it *is* an evil time.

14 Seek good and not evil,
That you may live;
So the LORD God of hosts will be
with you,
As you have spoken.

15 Hate evil, love good;
Establish justice in the gate.
It may be that the LORD God of
hosts
Will be gracious to the remnant of
Joseph.

The Day of the LORD

16Therefore the LORD God of hosts,
the Lord, says this:
"*There shall be* wailing in all streets,
And they shall say in all the
highways,
'Alas! Alas!'
They shall call the farmer to
mourning,
And skillful lamenters to
wailing.

17 In all vineyards *there shall be*
wailing,
For I will pass through you,"
Says the LORD.

18 Woe to you who desire the day of
the LORD!
For what good *is* the day of the
LORD to you?
It *will be* darkness, and not light.

19 It *will be* as though a man fled from
a lion,
And a bear met him!
Or *as though* he went into the
house,
Leaned his hand on the wall,
And a serpent bit him!

20 *Is* not the day of the LORD darkness,
and not light?
Is it not very dark, with no
brightness in it?

21 "I hate, I despise your feast days,
And I do not savor your sacred
assemblies.

22 Though you offer Me burnt
offerings and your grain
offerings,
I will not accept *them,*
Nor will I regard your fattened
peace offerings.

23 Take away from Me the noise of
your songs,
For I will not hear the melody of
your stringed instruments.

24 But let justice run down like water,
And righteousness like a mighty
stream.

25 "Did you offer Me sacrifices and
offerings
In the wilderness forty years,
O house of Israel?

26 You also carried Sikkuth[d] your
king
And Chiun,[d] your idols,
The star of your gods,
Which you made for yourselves.

27 Therefore I will send you into
captivity beyond Damascus,"
Says the LORD, whose name *is* the
God of hosts.

Warnings to Zion and Samaria

6 Woe to you *who are* at ease in Zion,
And trust in Mount Samaria,
Notable persons in the chief nation,
To whom the house of Israel comes!

2 Go over to Calneh and see;
And from there go to Hamath the
great;
Then go down to Gath of the
Philistines.
Are you better than these
kingdoms?
Or is their territory greater than
your territory?

3 *Woe to* you who put far off the day
of doom,
Who cause the seat of violence to
come near;

4 Who lie on beds of ivory,
Stretch out on your couches,
Eat lambs from the flock
And calves from the midst of the
stall;

---

d A pagan deity

5   Who sing idly to the sound of
      stringed instruments,
      And invent for yourselves musical
      instruments like David;
6   Who drink wine from bowls,
      And anoint yourselves with the
      best ointments,
      But are not grieved for the affliction
      of Joseph.
7   Therefore they shall now go captive
      as the first of the captives,
      And those who recline at banquets
      shall be removed.

8   The Lord GOD has sworn by
      Himself,
      The LORD God of hosts says:
   "I abhor the pride of Jacob,
      And hate his palaces;
      Therefore I will deliver up *the*
      city
      And all that is in it."
9Then it shall come to pass, that if
ten men remain in one house, they shall
die. 10And when a relative *of the dead*,
with one who will burn *the bodies*,
picks up the bodies to take them out
of the house, he will say to one inside the house, "*Are there* any more
with you?"
   Then someone will say, "None."
   And he will say, "Hold your tongue!
For we dare not mention the name of
the LORD."
11   For behold, the LORD gives a
      command:
      He will break the great house into
      bits,
      And the little house into pieces.

12   Do horses run on rocks?
      Does *one* plow *there* with oxen?
      Yet you have turned justice into
      gall,
      And the fruit of righteousness into
      wormwood,
13   You who rejoice over Lo Debar,
      Who say, "Have we not taken
      Karnaim for ourselves
      By our own strength?"

14 "But, behold, I will raise up a nation
      against you,
      O house of Israel,"
      Says the LORD God of hosts;
   "And they will afflict you from the
      entrance of Hamath
      To the Valley of the Arabah."

Vision of the Locusts

7 Thus the Lord GOD showed me: Behold, He formed locust swarms at
the beginning of the late crop; indeed
it was the late crop after the king's
mowings. 2And so it was, when they
had finished eating the grass of the
land, that I said:
   "O Lord GOD, forgive, I pray!
      Oh, that Jacob may stand,
      For he *is* small!"
3   *So* the LORD relented concerning
      this.
   "It shall not be," said the LORD.

Vision of the Fire

4Thus the Lord GOD showed me: Behold, the Lord GOD called for conflict
by fire, and it consumed the great deep
and devoured the territory. 5Then I
said:
   "O Lord GOD, cease, I pray!
      Oh, that Jacob may stand,
      For he *is* small!"
6   *So* the LORD relented concerning
      this.
   "This also shall not be," said the
      Lord GOD.

Vision of the Plumb Line

7Thus He showed me: Behold, the
Lord stood on a wall *made* with a plumb
line, with a plumb line in His hand.
8And the LORD said to me, "Amos, what
do you see?"
   And I said, "A plumb line."
   Then the Lord said:
   "Behold, I am setting a plumb
      line
      In the midst of My people Israel;
      I will not pass by them anymore.
9   The high places of Isaac shall be
      desolate,
      And the sanctuaries of Israel shall
      be laid waste.
      I will rise with the sword against
      the house of Jeroboam."

Amaziah's Complaint

10Then Amaziah the priest of Bethel
sent to Jeroboam king of Israel, saying,
"Amos has conspired against you in the
midst of the house of Israel. The land
is not able to bear all his words.
11For thus Amos has said:
   'Jeroboam shall die by the sword,

And Israel shall surely be led away
  captive
From their own land.' "
12Then Amaziah said to Amos:
"Go, you seer!
Flee to the land of Judah.
There eat bread,
And there prophesy.
13 But never again prophesy at
    Bethel,
For it *is* the king's sanctuary,
And it *is* the royal residence."
14Then Amos answered, and said to
Amaziah:
"I *was* no prophet,
Nor *was* I a son of a prophet,
But I *was* a sheepbreeder
And a tender of sycamore fruit.
15 Then the LORD took me as I
    followed the flock,
And the LORD said to me,
'Go, prophesy to My people Israel.'
16 Now therefore, hear the word of the
    LORD:
You say, 'Do not prophesy against
  Israel,
And do not spout against the house
  of Isaac.'
17"Therefore thus says the LORD:
'Your wife shall be a harlot in the
  city;
Your sons and daughters shall fall
  by the sword;
Your land shall be divided by
  survey line;
You shall die in a defiled land;
And Israel shall surely be led away
  captive
From his own land.' "

Vision of the Summer Fruit

8 Thus the Lord GOD showed me:
Behold, a basket of summer fruit.
2And He said, "Amos, what do you see?"
So I said, "A basket of summer fruit."
Then the LORD said to me:
"The end has come upon My people
  Israel;
I will not pass by them anymore.
3 And the songs of the temple
Shall be wailing in that day,"
Says the Lord GOD—
"Many dead bodies everywhere,
  They shall be thrown out in
    silence."

4 Hear this, you who swallow up the
    needy,
And make the poor of the land
  fail,
5Saying:
"When will the New Moon be past,
That we may sell grain?
And the Sabbath,
That we may trade wheat?
Making the ephah small and the
  shekel large,
Falsifying the scales by deceit,
6 That we may buy the poor for
    silver,
And the needy for a pair of
  sandals—
Even sell the bad wheat?"

7 The LORD has sworn by the pride
    of Jacob:
"Surely I will never forget any of
  their works.
8 Shall the land not tremble for this,
And everyone mourn who dwells
  in it?
All of it shall swell like the River,*e*
Heave and subside
Like the River of Egypt.

9 "And it shall come to pass in that
    day," says the Lord GOD,
"That I will make the sun go down
  at noon,
And I will darken the earth in broad
  daylight;
10 I will turn your feasts into
    mourning,
And all your songs into
  lamentation;
I will bring sackcloth on every
  waist,
And baldness on every head;
I will make it like mourning for an
  only *son,*
And its end like a bitter day.

11 "Behold, the days are coming," says
    the Lord GOD,
"That I will send a famine on the
  land,
Not a famine of bread,
Nor a thirst for water,
But of hearing the words of the
  LORD.

e That is, the Nile

12 They shall wander from sea to sea,
   And from north to east;
   They shall run to and fro, seeking
      the word of the LORD,
   But shall not find *it*.

13 "In that day the fair virgins
   And strong young men
   Shall faint from thirst.
14 Those who swear by the sin*ᶠ* of
      Samaria,
   Who say,
   'As your god lives, O Dan!'
   And, 'As the way of Beersheba
      lives!'
   They shall fall and never rise
      again."

The Destruction of Israel

9 I saw the Lord standing by the altar,
   and He said:
   "Strike the doorposts, that the
      thresholds may shake,
   And break them on the heads of
      them all.
   I will slay the last of them with the
      sword.
   He who flees from them shall not
      get away,
   And he who escapes from them
      shall not be delivered.

2 "Though they dig into hell,
   From there My hand shall take
      them;
   Though they climb up to heaven,
   From there I will bring them down;
3 And though they hide themselves
      on top of Carmel,
   From there I will search and take
      them;
   Though they hide from My sight at
      the bottom of the sea,
   From there I will command the
      serpent, and it shall bite them;
4 Though they go into captivity
      before their enemies,
   From there I will command the
      sword,
   And it shall slay them.
   I will set My eyes on them for harm
      and not for good."

5 The Lord GOD of hosts,

   He who touches the earth and it
      melts,
   And all who dwell there mourn;
   All of it shall swell like the River,*ᵍ*
   And subside like the River of
      Egypt.
6 He who builds His layers in the sky,
   And has founded His strata in the
      earth;
   Who calls for the waters of the sea,
   And pours them out on the face of
      the earth—
   The LORD *is* His name.

7 "*Are* you not like the people of
      Ethiopia to Me,
   O children of Israel?" says the
      LORD.
   "Did I not bring up Israel from the
      land of Egypt,
   The Philistines from Caphtor,
   And the Syrians from Kir?

8 "Behold, the eyes of the Lord GOD
      are on the sinful kingdom,
   And I will destroy it from the face
      of the earth;
   Yet I will not utterly destroy the
      house of Jacob,"
   Says the LORD.

9 "For surely I will command,
   And will sift the house of Israel
      among all nations,
   As *grain* is sifted in a sieve;
   Yet not the smallest grain shall fall
      to the ground.
10 All the sinners of My people shall
      die by the sword,
   Who say, 'The calamity shall not
      overtake nor confront us.'

Israel Will Be Restored

11 "On that day I will raise up
   The tabernacle*ʰ* of David, which
      has fallen down,
   And repair its damages;
   I will raise up its ruins,
   And rebuild it as in the days of old;
12 That they may possess the remnant
      of Edom,
   And all the Gentiles who are called
      by My name,"
   Says the LORD who does this thing.

ᶠ Or *Ashima,* a Syrian goddess   *ᵍ* That is, the Nile   *ʰ* Literally *booth,* figure of a deposed
dynasty

13 "Behold, the days are coming," says
     the LORD,
   "When the plowman shall overtake
      the reaper,
   And the treader of grapes him who
      sows seed;
   The mountains shall drip with
      sweet wine,
   And all the hills shall flow *with it.*
14 I will bring back the captives of My
     people Israel;

They shall build the waste cities
   and inhabit *them;*
They shall plant vineyards and
   drink wine from them;
They shall also make gardens and
   eat fruit from them.
15 I will plant them in their land,
   And no longer shall they be
      pulled up
   From the land I have given them,"
   Says the LORD your God.

The Book of

OBADIAH

The Coming Judgment on Edom

1 The vision of Obadiah.

   Thus says the Lord GOD concerning
      Edom
   (We have heard a report from the
      LORD,
   And a messenger has been sent
      among the nations, *saying,*
   "Arise, and let us rise up against her
      for battle"):

2 "Behold, I will make you small
     among the nations;
   You shall be greatly despised.
3 The pride of your heart has
     deceived you,
   You who dwell in the clefts of the
      rock,
   Whose habitation is high;
   You who say in your heart, 'Who
      will bring me down to the
      ground?'
4 Though you ascend *as* high as the
     eagle,
   And though you set your nest
      among the stars,
   From there I will bring you down,"
      says the LORD.

5 "If thieves had come to you,
   If robbers by night—

Oh, how you will be cut off!—
Would they not have stolen till they
   had enough?
If grape-gatherers had come to you,
Would they not have left *some*
   gleanings?

6 "Oh, how Esau shall be
     searched out!
   How his hidden treasures shall be
      sought after!
7 All the men in your confederacy
   Shall force you to the border;
   The men at peace with you
   Shall deceive you *and* prevail
      against you.
   Those who eat your bread shall lay
      a trap for you.
   No one is aware of it.

8 "Will I not in that day," says the
     LORD,
   "Even destroy the wise *men* from
      Edom,
   And understanding from the
      mountains of Esau?
9 Then your mighty men, O Teman,
     shall be dismayed,
   To the end that everyone from the
      mountains of Esau
   May be cut off by slaughter.

Edom Mistreated His Brother

10 "For violence against your brother
   Jacob,
   Shame shall cover you,
   And you shall be cut off forever.

11 In the day that you stood on the
   other side—
   In the day that strangers carried
   captive his forces,
   When foreigners entered his
   gates
   And cast lots for Jerusalem—
   Even you *were* as one of them.

12 "But you should not have gazed on
   the day of your brother
   In the day of his captivity;
   Nor should you have rejoiced over
   the children of Judah
   In the day of their destruction;
   Nor should you have spoken
   proudly
   In the day of distress.

13 You should not have entered the
   gate of My people
   In the day of their calamity.
   Indeed, you should not have gazed
   on their affliction
   In the day of their calamity,
   Nor laid *hands* on their substance
   In the day of their calamity.

14 You should not have stood at the
   crossroads
   To cut off those among them who
   escaped;
   Nor should you have delivered up
   those among them who remained
   In the day of distress.

15 "For the day of the LORD upon all
   the nations *is* near;
   As you have done, it shall be done
   to you;
   Your reprisal shall return upon
   your own head.

16 For as you drank on My holy
   mountain,
   So shall all the nations drink
   continually;
   Yes, they shall drink, and swallow,
   And they shall be as though they
   had never been.

Israel's Final Triumph

17 "But on Mount Zion there shall be
   deliverance,
   And there shall be holiness;
   The house of Jacob shall possess
   their possessions.

18 The house of Jacob shall be a fire,
   And the house of Joseph a flame;
   But the house of Esau *shall be*
   stubble;
   They shall kindle them and devour
   them,
   And no survivor shall *remain* of the
   house of Esau,"
   For the LORD has spoken.

19 The South shall possess the
   mountains of Esau,
   And the Lowland shall possess
   Philistia.
   They shall possess the fields of
   Ephraim
   And the fields of Samaria.
   Benjamin *shall possess* Gilead.

20 And the captives of this host of the
   children of Israel
   Shall possess the land of the
   Canaanites
   As far as Zarephath.
   The captives of Jerusalem who are
   in Sepharad
   Shall possess the cities of the
   South.

21 Then saviors[a] shall come to Mount
   Zion
   To judge the mountains of Esau,
   And the kingdom shall be the
   LORD's.

a Or *deliverers*

The Book of

JONAH

Jonah's Disobedience

1 Now the word of the LORD came to Jonah the son of Amittai, saying, 2"Arise, go to Nineveh, that great city, and cry out against it; for their wickedness has come up before Me." 3But Jonah arose to flee to Tarshish from the presence of the LORD. He went down to Joppa, and found a ship going to Tarshish; so he paid the fare, and went down into it, to go with them to Tarshish from the presence of the LORD.

The Storm at Sea

4But the LORD sent out a great wind on the sea, and there was a mighty tempest on the sea, so that the ship was about to be broken up.

5Then the mariners were afraid; and every man cried out to his god, and threw the cargo that *was* in the ship into the sea, to lighten the load. But Jonah had gone down into the lowest parts of the ship, had lain down, and was fast asleep.

6So the captain came to him, and said to him, "What do you mean, sleeper? Arise, call on your God; perhaps your God will consider us, so that we may not perish."

7And they said to one another, "Come, let us cast lots, that we may know for whose cause this trouble *has come* upon us." So they cast lots, and the lot fell on Jonah. 8Then they said to him, "Please tell us! For whose cause *is* this trouble upon us? What *is* your occupation? And where do you come from? What *is* your country? And of what people are you?"

9So he said to them, "I *am* a Hebrew; and I fear the LORD, the God of heaven, who made the sea and the dry *land*."

Jonah Thrown into the Sea

10Then the men were exceedingly afraid, and said to him, "Why have you done this?" For the men knew that he fled from the presence of the LORD, because he had told them. 11Then they said to him, "What shall we do to you that the sea may be calm for us?"—for the sea was growing more tempestuous.

12And he said to them, "Pick me up and throw me into the sea; then the sea will become calm for you. For I know that this great tempest *is* because of me."

13Nevertheless the men rowed hard to return to land, but they could not, for the sea continued to grow more tempestuous against them. 14Therefore they cried out to the LORD and said, "We pray, O LORD, please do not let us perish for this man's life, and do not charge us with innocent blood; for You, O LORD, have done as it pleased You." 15So they picked up Jonah and threw him into the sea, and the sea ceased from its raging. 16Then the men feared the LORD exceedingly, and offered a sacrifice to the LORD and took vows.

Jonah's Prayer and Deliverance

17Now the LORD had prepared a great fish to swallow Jonah. And Jonah was in the belly of the fish three days and three nights.

2 Then Jonah prayed to the LORD his God from the fish's belly. 2And he said:

"I cried out to the LORD because of
    my affliction,
    And He answered me.

"Out of the belly of Sheol I cried,
    And You heard my voice.
3   For You cast me into the deep,
    Into the heart of the seas,
    And the floods surrounded me;
    All Your billows and Your waves
        passed over me.
4   Then I said, 'I have been cast out
        of Your sight;
    Yet I will look again toward Your
        holy temple.'
5   The waters surrounded me, *even* to
        my soul;
    The deep closed around me;
    Weeds were wrapped around my
        head.
6   I went down to the moorings of the
        mountains;

The earth with its bars *closed*
   behind me forever;
Yet You have brought up my life
   from the pit,
O LORD, my God.

7 "When my soul fainted within me,
   I remembered the LORD;
   And my prayer went *up* to You,
   Into Your holy temple.

8 "Those who regard worthless
    idols
   Forsake their own Mercy.
9 But I will sacrifice to You
   With the voice of thanksgiving;
   I will pay what I have vowed.
   Salvation *is* of the LORD."

10So the LORD spoke to the fish, and it vomited Jonah onto dry *land.*

Jonah Preaches at Nineveh

3 Now the word of the LORD came to Jonah the second time, saying, 2"Arise, go to Nineveh, that great city, and preach to it the message that I tell you." 3So Jonah arose and went to Nineveh, according to the word of the LORD. Now Nineveh was an exceedingly great city, a three-day journey*a* *in extent.* 4And Jonah began to enter the city on the first day's walk. Then he cried out and said, "Yet forty days, and Nineveh shall be overthrown!"

The People of Nineveh Believe

5So the people of Nineveh believed God, proclaimed a fast, and put on sackcloth, from the greatest to the least of them. 6Then word came to the king of Nineveh; and he arose from his throne and laid aside his robe, covered *himself* with sackcloth and sat in ashes. 7And he caused *it* to be proclaimed and published throughout Nineveh by the decree of the king and his nobles, saying,

Let neither man nor beast, herd nor flock, taste anything; do not let them eat, or drink water. 8But let man and beast be covered with sackcloth, and cry mightily to God; yes, let every one turn from his evil way and from the violence that is in his hands. 9Who can tell *if* God will turn and relent, and turn away

from His fierce anger, so that we may not perish?

10Then God saw their works, that they turned from their evil way; and God relented from the disaster that He had said He would bring upon them, and He did not do it.

Jonah's Anger and God's Kindness

4 But it displeased Jonah exceedingly, and he became angry. 2So he prayed to the LORD, and said, "Ah, LORD, was not this what I said when I was still in my country? Therefore I fled previously to Tarshish; for I know that You *are* a gracious and merciful God, slow to anger and abundant in lovingkindness, One who relents from doing harm. 3Therefore now, O LORD, please take my life from me, for *it is* better for me to die than to live!"

4Then the LORD said, "*Is it* right for you to be angry?"

5So Jonah went out of the city and sat on the east side of the city. There he made himself a shelter and sat under it in the shade, till he might see what would become of the city. 6And the LORD God prepared a plant and made it come up over Jonah, that it might be shade for his head to deliver him from his misery. So Jonah was very grateful for the plant. 7But as morning dawned the next day God prepared a worm, and it *so* damaged the plant that it withered. 8And it happened, when the sun arose, that God prepared a vehement east wind; and the sun beat on Jonah's head, so that he grew faint. Then he wished death for himself, and said, "*It is* better for me to die than to live."

9Then God said to Jonah, "*Is it* right for you to be angry about the plant?"

And he said, "*It is* right for me to be angry, even to death!"

10But the LORD said, "You have had pity on the plant for which you have not labored, nor made it grow, which came up in a night and perished in a night. 11And should I not pity Nineveh, that great city, in which are more than one hundred and twenty thousand persons who cannot discern between their right hand and their left—and much livestock?"

a Exact meaning unknown

The Book of

MICAH

1 The word of the LORD that came to
Micah of Moresheth in the days of
Jotham, Ahaz, *and* Hezekiah, kings of
Judah, which he saw concerning Sa-
maria and Jerusalem.

The Coming Judgment on Israel

2 Hear, all you peoples!
Listen, O earth, and all that is
in it!
Let the Lord GOD be a witness
against you,
The Lord from His holy temple.

3 For behold, the LORD is coming out
of His place;
He will come down
And tread on the high places of the
earth.

4 The mountains will melt
under Him,
And the valleys will split
Like wax before the fire,
Like waters poured down a steep
place.

5 All this is for the transgression of
Jacob
And for the sins of the house of
Israel.
What *is* the transgression of Jacob?
Is it not Samaria?
And what *are* the high places of
Judah?
Are they not Jerusalem?

6 "Therefore I will make Samaria a
heap of ruins in the field,
Places for planting a vineyard;
I will pour down her stones into the
valley,
And I will uncover her foundations.

7 All her carved images shall be
beaten to pieces,
And all her pay as a harlot shall
be burned with the fire;
All her idols I will lay desolate,
For she gathered *it* from the pay
of a harlot,
And they shall return to the pay of
a harlot."

Mourning for Israel and Judah

8 Therefore I will wail and howl,
I will go stripped and naked;
I will make a wailing like the
jackals
And a mourning like the ostriches,

9 For her wounds *are* incurable.
For it has come to Judah;
It has come to the gate of My
people—
To Jerusalem.

10 Tell *it* not in Gath,
Weep not at all;
In Beth Aphrah[a]
Roll yourself in the dust.

11 Pass by in naked shame, you
inhabitant of Shaphir;
The inhabitant of Zaanan[b] does not
go out.
Beth Ezel mourns;
Its place to stand is taken away
from you.

12 For the inhabitant of Maroth pined
for good,
But disaster came down from the
LORD
To the gate of Jerusalem.

13 O inhabitant of Lachish,
Harness the chariot to the swift
steeds
(She *was* the beginning of sin to the
daughter of Zion),
For the transgressions of Israel
were found in you.

14 Therefore you shall give presents
to Moresheth Gath;
The houses of Achzib[c] *shall be* a
lie to the kings of Israel.

15 I will yet bring an heir to you,
O inhabitant of Mareshah;[d]
The glory of Israel shall come to
Adullam.

16 Make yourself bald and cut off your
hair,
Because of your precious children;
Enlarge your baldness like an
eagle,

---

a Literally *House of Dust*   *b* Literally *Going Out*   *c* Literally *Lie*   *d* Literally *Inheritance*

For they shall go from you into
captivity.

Woe to Evildoers

2 Woe to those who devise iniquity,
And work out evil on their beds!
At morning light they practice it,
Because it is in the power of their
hand.

2 They covet fields and take *them* by
violence,
Also houses, and seize *them.*
So they oppress a man and his
house,
A man and his inheritance.

3 Therefore thus says the LORD:
"Behold, against this family I am
devising disaster,
From which you cannot remove
your necks;
Nor shall you walk haughtily,
For this *is* an evil time.

4 In that day *one* shall take up a
proverb against you,
And lament with a bitter
lamentation, saying:
'We are utterly destroyed!
He has changed the heritage of my
people;
How He has removed *it* from me!
To a turncoat He has divided our
fields.' "

5 Therefore you will have no one to
determine boundaries by lot
In the assembly of the LORD.

Lying Prophets

6 "Do not prattle," *you say to those*
who prophesy.
So they shall not prophesy to you;
They shall not return insult for
insult.

7 *You who are* named the house of
Jacob:
"Is the Spirit of the LORD restricted?
Are these His doings?
Do not My words do good
To him who walks uprightly?

8 "Lately My people have risen up as
an enemy—
You pull off the robe with the
garment
From those who trust *you,* as they
pass by,
Like men returned from war.

9 The women of My people you
cast out
From their pleasant houses;
From their children
You have taken away My glory
forever.

10 "Arise and depart,
For this *is* not *your* rest;
Because it is defiled, it shall
destroy,
Yes, with utter destruction.

11 If a man should walk in a false
spirit
And speak a lie, *saying,*
'I will prophesy to you of wine and
drink,'
Even he would be the prattler of
this people.

Israel Restored

12 "I will surely assemble all of you,
O Jacob,
I will surely gather the remnant of
Israel;
I will put them together like sheep
of the fold,
Like a flock in the midst of their
pasture;
They shall make a loud noise
because of *so many* people.

13 The one who breaks open will come
up before them;
They will break out,
Pass through the gate,
And go out by it;
Their king will pass before them,
With the LORD at their head."

Wicked Rulers and Prophets

3 And I said:

"Hear now, O heads of Jacob,
And you rulers of the house of
Israel:
Is it not for you to know justice?

2 You who hate good and love evil;
Who strip the skin from My people,
And the flesh from their bones;

3 Who also eat the flesh of My
people,
Flay their skin from them,
Break their bones,
And chop *them* in pieces
Like *meat* for the pot,
Like flesh in the caldron."

4 Then they will cry to the LORD,
But He will not hear them;
He will even hide His face from
them at that time,
Because they have been evil in their
deeds.

5 Thus says the LORD concerning the
prophets
Who make my people stray;
Who chant "Peace"
While they chew with their teeth,
But who prepare war against him
Who puts nothing into their
mouths:
6 "Therefore you shall have night
without vision,
And you shall have darkness
without divination;
The sun shall go down on the
prophets,
And the day shall be dark for
them.
7 So the seers shall be ashamed,
And the diviners abashed;
Indeed they shall all cover their
lips;
For *there is* no answer from God."

8 But truly I am full of power by the
Spirit of the LORD,
And of justice and might,
To declare to Jacob his
transgression
And to Israel his sin.
9 Now hear this,
You heads of the house of Jacob
And rulers of the house of Israel,
Who abhor justice
And pervert all equity,
10 Who build up Zion with bloodshed
And Jerusalem with iniquity:
11 Her heads judge for a bribe,
Her priests teach for pay,
And her prophets divine for money.
Yet they lean on the LORD, and say,
"Is not the LORD among us?
No harm can come upon us."
12 Therefore because of you
Zion shall be plowed *like* a field,
Jerusalem shall become heaps of
ruins,
And the mountain of the temple
Like the bare hills of the forest.

The LORD's Reign in Zion

4 Now it shall come to pass in the
latter days
That the mountain of the LORD's
house
Shall be established on the top of
the mountains,
And shall be exalted above the
hills;
And peoples shall flow to it.
2 Many nations shall come and say,
"Come, and let us go up to the
mountain of the LORD,
To the house of the God of Jacob;
He will teach us His ways,
And we shall walk in His paths."
For out of Zion the law shall go
forth,
And the word of the LORD from
Jerusalem.
3 He shall judge between many
peoples,
And rebuke strong nations afar off;
They shall beat their swords into
plowshares,
And their spears into pruning
hooks;
Nation shall not lift up sword
against nation,
Neither shall they learn war
anymore.ᵉ

4 But everyone shall sit under his
vine and under his fig tree,
And no one shall make *them*
afraid;
For the mouth of the LORD of hosts
has spoken.
5 For all people walk each in the
name of his god,
But we will walk in the name of the
LORD our God
Forever and ever.

Zion's Future Triumph

6 "In that day," says the LORD,
"I will assemble the lame,
I will gather the outcast
And those whom I have afflicted;
7 I will make the lame a remnant,
And the outcast a strong nation;
So the LORD will reign over them
in Mount Zion
From now on, even forever.

ᵉ Compare Isaiah 2.2-4

8 And you, O tower of the flock,
The stronghold of the daughter of
Zion,
To you shall it come,
Even the former dominion shall
come,
The kingdom of the daughter of
Jerusalem."

9 Now why do you cry aloud?
Is there no king in your midst?
Has your counselor perished?
For pangs have seized you like a
woman in labor.

10 Be in pain, and labor to bring forth,
O daughter of Zion,
Like a woman in birth pangs.
For now you shall go forth from the
city,
You shall dwell in the field,
And to Babylon you shall go.
There you shall be delivered;
There the LORD will redeem you
From the hand of your enemies.

11 Now also many nations have
gathered against you,
Who say, "Let her be defiled,
And let our eye look upon Zion."

12 But they do not know the thoughts
of the LORD,
Nor do they understand His
counsel;
For He will gather them like
sheaves to the threshing floor.

13 "Arise and thresh, O daughter of
Zion;
For I will make your horn iron,
And I will make your hooves
bronze;
You shall beat in pieces many
peoples;
I will consecrate their gain to the
LORD,
And their substance to the Lord of
the whole earth."

5 Now gather yourself in troops,
O daughter of troops;
He has laid siege against us;
They will strike the judge of Israel
with a rod on the cheek.

The Coming Messiah

2 "But you, Bethlehem Ephrathah,
Though you are little among the
thousands of Judah,

Yet out of you shall come forth
to Me
The One to be Ruler in Israel,
Whose goings forth *are* from of old,
From everlasting."

3 Therefore He shall give them up,
Until the time *that* she who is in
labor has given birth;
Then the remnant of His brethren
Shall return to the children of
Israel.

4 And He shall stand and feed *His
flock*
In the strength of the LORD,
In the majesty of the name of the
LORD His God;
And they shall abide,
For now He shall be great
To the ends of the earth;

5 And this *One* shall be peace.

Judgment on Israel's Enemies

When the Assyrian comes into our
land,
And when he treads in our palaces,
Then we will raise against him
Seven shepherds and eight
princely men.

6 They shall waste with the sword the
land of Assyria,
And the land of Nimrod at its
entrances;
Thus He shall deliver *us* from the
Assyrian,
When he comes into our land
And when he treads within our
borders.

7 Then the remnant of Jacob
Shall be in the midst of many
peoples,
Like dew from the LORD,
Like showers on the grass,
That tarry for no man
Nor wait for the sons of men.

8 And the remnant of Jacob
Shall be among the Gentiles,
In the midst of many peoples,
Like a lion among the beasts of the
forest,
Like a young lion among flocks of
sheep,
Who, if he passes through,
Both treads down and tears in
pieces,
And none can deliver.

9   Your hand shall be lifted against
    your adversaries,
    And all your enemies shall be
    cut off.

10 "And it shall be in that day," says
    the LORD,
    "That I will cut off your horses from
    your midst
    And destroy your chariots.
11 I will cut off the cities of your land
    And throw down all your
    strongholds.
12 I will cut off sorceries from your
    hand,
    And you shall have no soothsayers.
13 Your carved images I will also
    cut off,
    And your sacred pillars from your
    midst;
    You shall no more worship the
    work of your hands;
14 I will pluck your wooden images[f]
    from your midst;
    Thus I will destroy your cities.
15 And I will execute vengeance in
    anger and fury
    On the nations that have not
    heard."[g]

God Pleads with Israel

6 Hear now what the LORD says:

    "Arise, plead your case before the
    mountains,
    And let the hills hear your voice.
2   Hear, O you mountains, the LORD's
    complaint,
    And you strong foundations of the
    earth;
    For the LORD has a complaint
    against His people,
    And He will contend with Israel.

3   "O My people, what have I done
    to you?
    And how have I wearied you?
    Testify against Me.
4   For I brought you up from the land
    of Egypt,
    I redeemed you from the house of
    bondage;
    And I sent before you Moses,
    Aaron, and Miriam.
5   O My people, remember now

    What Balak king of Moab
    counseled,
    And what Balaam the son of Beor
    answered him,
    From Acacia Grove to Gilgal,
    That you may know the
    righteousness of the LORD."

6   With what shall I come before the
    LORD,
    And bow myself before the High
    God?
    Shall I come before Him with burnt
    offerings,
    With calves a year old?
7   Will the LORD be pleased with
    thousands of rams,
    Ten thousand rivers of oil?
    Shall I give my firstborn *for* my
    transgression,
    The fruit of my body *for* the sin of
    my soul?

8   He has shown you, O man, what *is*
    good;
    And what does the LORD require
    of you
    But to do justly,
    To love mercy,
    And to walk humbly with
    your God?

Punishment of Israel's Injustice

9   The LORD's voice cries to the city—
    Wisdom shall see Your name:

    "Hear the rod!
    Who has appointed it?
10 Are there yet the treasures of
    wickedness
    In the house of the wicked,
    And the short measure *that is* an
    abomination?
11 Shall I count pure *those* with the
    wicked scales,
    And with the bag of deceitful
    weights?
12 For her rich men are full of
    violence,
    Her inhabitants have spoken lies,
    And their tongue is deceitful in
    their mouth.

13 "Therefore I will also make *you* sick
    by striking you,

By making *you* desolate because of
your sins.

14 You shall eat, but not be satisfied;
Hunger *shall be* in your midst.
You may carry *some* away, but
shall not save *them;*
And what you do rescue I will give
over to the sword.

15 "You shall sow, but not reap;
You shall tread the olives, but not
anoint yourselves with oil;
And *make* sweet wine, but not
drink wine.

16 For the statutes of Omri are kept;
All the works of Ahab's house *are
done;*
And you walk in their counsels,
That I may make you a desolation,
And your inhabitants a hissing.
Therefore you shall bear the
reproach of My people."

Sorrow for Israel's Sins

7 Woe is me!
For I am like those who gather
summer fruits,
Like those who glean vintage
grapes;
There is no cluster to eat
Of the first-ripe fruit *which* my soul
desires.

2 The faithful *man* has perished from
the earth,
And *there is* no one upright
among men.
They all lie in wait for blood;
Every man hunts his brother with
a net.

3 That they may successfully do evil
with both hands—
The prince asks *for gifts,*
The judge *seeks* a bribe,
And the great *man* utters his evil
desire;
So they scheme together.

4 The best of them *is* like a brier;
The most upright *is sharper* than a
thorn hedge;
The day of your watchman and
your punishment comes;
Now shall be their perplexity.

5 Do not trust in a friend;
Do not put your confidence in a
companion;
Guard the doors of your mouth
From her who lies in your bosom.

6 For son dishonors father,
Daughter rises against her mother,
Daughter-in-law against her
mother-in-law;
A man's enemies *are* the men of his
own household.

7 Therefore I will look to the LORD;
I will wait for the God of my
salvation;
My God will hear me.

Israel's Confession and Comfort

8 Do not rejoice over me, my enemy;
When I fall, I will arise;
When I sit in darkness,
The LORD *will be* a light to me.

9 I will bear the indignation of the
LORD,
Because I have sinned against Him,
Until He pleads my case
And executes justice for me.
He will bring me forth to the light;
I will see His righteousness.

10 Then *she who is* my enemy will see,
And shame will cover her who said
to me,
"Where is the LORD your God?"
My eyes will see her;
Now she will be trampled down
Like mud in the streets.

11 *In* the day when your walls are to
be built,
In that day the decree shall go far
and wide.

12 *In* that day they shall come to you
From Assyria and the fortified
cities,[h]
From the fortress[i] to the River,[j]
From sea to sea,
And mountain *to* mountain.

13 Yet the land shall be desolate
Because of those who dwell in it,
And for the fruit of their deeds.

God Will Forgive Israel

14 Shepherd Your people with Your
staff,

---

[h] Possibly *cities of Egypt*   [i] Possibly *Egypt*   [j] That is, the Euphrates

The flock of Your heritage,
Who dwell solitarily *in* a woodland,
In the midst of Carmel;
Let them feed *in* Bashan and
    Gilead,
As in days of old.

15 "As in the days when you came out
    of the land of Egypt,
I will show them wonders."

16 The nations shall see and be
    ashamed of all their might;
They shall put *their* hand over *their*
    mouth;
Their ears shall be deaf.
17 They shall lick the dust like a
    serpent;
They shall crawl from their holes
    like snakes of the earth.

They shall be afraid of the LORD
    our God,
And shall fear because of You.
18 Who *is* a God like You,
Pardoning iniquity
And passing over the transgression
    of the remnant of His heritage?

He does not retain His anger
    forever,
Because He delights *in* mercy.
19 He will again have compassion
    on us,
And will subdue our iniquities.

You will cast all our sins
Into the depths of the sea.
20 You will give truth to Jacob
And mercy to Abraham,
Which You have sworn to our
    fathers
From days of old.

The Book of
NAHUM

1 The burden against Nineveh. The book of the vision of Nahum the El-koshite.

God's Wrath on His Enemies

2 God *is* jealous, and the LORD avenges;
The LORD avenges and *is* furious.
The LORD will take vengeance on His adversaries,
And He reserves *wrath* for His enemies;

3 The LORD *is* slow to anger and great in power,
And will not at all acquit *the wicked*.

The LORD has His way
In the whirlwind and in the storm,
And the clouds *are* the dust of His feet.

4 He rebukes the sea and makes it dry,
And dries up all the rivers.
Bashan and Carmel wither,
And the flower of Lebanon wilts.

5 The mountains quake before Him,
The hills melt,
And the earth heaves at His presence,
Yes, the world and all who dwell in it.

6 Who can stand before His indignation?
And who can endure the fierceness of His anger?
His fury is poured out like fire,
And the rocks are thrown down by Him.

7 The LORD *is* good,
A stronghold in the day of trouble;
And He knows those who trust in Him.

8 But with an overflowing flood
He will make an utter end of its place,
And darkness will pursue His enemies.

9 What do you conspire against the LORD?
He will make an utter end *of it*.
Affliction will not rise up a second time.

10 For while tangled *like* thorns,
And while drunken *like* drunkards,
They shall be devoured like stubble fully dried.

11 From you comes forth *one*
Who plots evil against the LORD,
A wicked counselor.

12 Thus says the LORD:
"Though *they are* safe, and likewise many,
Yet in this manner they will be cut down
When he passes through.
Though I have afflicted you,
I will afflict you no more;

13 For now I will break off his yoke from you,
And burst your bonds apart."

14 The LORD has given a command concerning you:
"Your name shall be perpetuated no longer.
Out of the house of your gods
I will cut off the carved image and the molded image.
I will dig your grave,
For you are vile."

15 Behold, on the mountains
The feet of him who brings good tidings,
Who proclaims peace!
O Judah, keep your appointed feasts,
Perform your vows.
For the wicked one shall no more pass through you;
He is utterly cut off.

The Destruction of Nineveh

2 He who scatters has come up before your face.
Man the fort!
Watch the road!
Strengthen *your* flanks!
Fortify *your* power mightily.

2 For the LORD will restore the excellence of Jacob
Like the excellence of Israel,

For the emptiers have emptied
   them out
And ruined their vine branches.

3   The shields of his mighty men *are*
      made red,
   The valiant men *are* in scarlet.
   The chariots *come* with flaming
      torches
   In the day of his preparation,
   And the spears are brandished.
4   The chariots rage in the streets,
   They jostle one another in the
      broad roads;
   They seem like torches,
   They run like lightning.

5   He remembers his nobles;
   They stumble in their walk;
   They make haste to her walls,
   And the defense is prepared.
6   The gates of the rivers are opened,
   And the palace is dissolved.
7   It is decreed:
   She shall be led away captive,
   She shall be brought up;
   And her maidservants shall lead
      her as with the voice of doves,
   Beating their breasts.

8   Though Nineveh of old *was* like a
      pool of water,
   Now they flee away.
   "Halt! Halt!" *they cry;*
   But no one turns back.
9   Take spoil of silver!
   Take spoil of gold!
   There is no end of treasure,
   Or wealth of every desirable prize.
10 She is empty, desolate, and waste!
   The heart melts, and the knees
      shake;
   Much pain *is* in every side,
   And all their faces are drained of
      color.[a]

11 Where *is* the dwelling of the lions,
   And the feeding place of the young
      lions,
   Where the lion walked, the lioness
      and lion's cub,
   And no one made *them* afraid?
12 The lion tore in pieces enough for
      his cubs,

Killed for his lionesses,
Filled his caves with prey,
And his dens with flesh.
13"Behold, I *am* against you," says
the Lord of hosts, "I will burn your
chariots in smoke, and the sword shall
devour your young lions; I will cut off
your prey from the earth, and the voice
of your messengers shall be heard no
more."

The Woe of Nineveh

3 Woe to the bloody city!
   It *is* all full of lies *and* robbery.
   Its victim never departs.
2   The noise of a whip
   And the noise of rattling wheels,
   Of galloping horses,
   Of clattering chariots!
3   Horsemen charge with bright
      sword and glittering spear.
   There is a multitude of slain,
   A great number of bodies,
   Countless corpses—
   They stumble over the corpses—
4   Because of the multitude of
      harlotries of the seductive harlot,
   The mistress of sorceries,
   Who sells nations through her
      harlotries,
   And families through her sorceries.

5   "Behold, I *am* against you," says the
      Lord of hosts;
   "I will lift your skirts over your face,
   I will show the nations your
      nakedness,
   And the kingdoms your shame.
6   I will cast abominable filth
      upon you,
   Make you vile,
   And make you a spectacle.
7   It shall come to pass *that* all who
      look upon you
   Will flee from you, and say,
   'Nineveh is laid waste!
   Who will bemoan her?'
   Where shall I seek comforters
      for you?"

8   Are you better than No Amon[b]
   That was situated by the River,[c]
   That had the waters around her,
   Whose rampart *was* the sea,

[a] Compare Joel 2.6   [b] That is, ancient Thebes
surrounding canals   [c] Literally *rivers*, that is, the Nile and the

Whose wall *was* the sea?
9 Ethiopia and Egypt *were* her
strength,
And *it was* boundless;
Put and Lubim were your helpers.
10 Yet she *was* carried away,
She went into captivity;
Her young children also were
dashed to pieces
At the head of every street;
They cast lots for her
honorable men,
And all her great men were bound
in chains.
11 You also will be drunk;
You will be hidden;
You also will seek refuge from the
enemy.

12 All your strongholds *are* fig trees
with ripened figs:
If they are shaken,
They fall into the mouth of the
eater.
13 Surely, your people in your midst
are women!
The gates of your land are wide
open for your enemies;
Fire shall devour the bars of your
gates.

14 Draw your water for the siege!
Fortify your strongholds!
Go into the clay and tread the
mortar!

Make strong the brick kiln!
15 There the fire will devour you,
The sword will cut you off;
It will eat you up like a locust.

Make yourself many—like the
locust!
Make yourself many— like the
swarming locusts!
16 You have multiplied your
merchants more than the stars of
heaven.
The locust plunders and flies away.
17 Your commanders *are* like
swarming locusts,
And your generals like great
grasshoppers,
Which camp in the hedges on a
cold day;
When the sun rises they flee away,
And the place where they *are* is not
known.

18 Your shepherds slumber, O king of
Assyria;
Your nobles rest *in the dust*.
Your people are scattered on the
mountains,
And no one gathers them.
19 Your injury *has* no healing,
Your wound is severe.
All who hear news of you
Will clap *their* hands over you,
For upon whom has not your
wickedness passed continually?

The Book of
HABAKKUK

1 The burden which the prophet Habakkuk saw.

The Prophet's Question

2 O Lord, how long shall I cry,
  And You will not hear?
  Even cry out to You, "Violence!"
  And You will not save.
3 Why do You show me iniquity,
  And cause *me* to see trouble?
  For plundering and violence *are*
    before me;
  There is strife, and contention
    arises.
4 Therefore the law is powerless,
  And justice never goes forth.
  For the wicked surround the
    righteous;
  Therefore perverse judgment
    proceeds.

The Lord's Reply

5 "Look among the nations and
    watch—
  Be utterly astounded!
  For *I will* work a work in your days
  Which you would not believe,
    though it were told *you*.
6 For indeed I am raising up the
    Chaldeans,
  A bitter and hasty nation
  Which marches through the
    breadth of the earth,
  To possess dwelling places *that are*
    not theirs.
7 They are terrible and dreadful;
  Their judgment and their dignity
    proceed from themselves.
8 Their horses also are swifter than
    leopards,
  And more fierce than evening
    wolves.
  Their chargers charge ahead;
  Their cavalry comes from afar;
  They fly as the eagle *that* hastens
    to eat.

9 "They all come for violence;
  Their faces are set *like* the east
    wind.
  They gather captives like sand.
10 They scoff at kings,

And princes are scorned by them.
  They deride every stronghold,
  For they heap up earthen *mounds*
    and seize it.
11 Then *his* mind changes, and he
    transgresses;
  He commits offense,
  Ascribing this power to his god."

The Prophet's Second Question

12 Are You not from everlasting,
  O Lord my God, my Holy One?
  We shall not die.
  O Lord, You have appointed them
    for judgment;
  O Rock, You have marked them for
    correction.
13 *You are* of purer eyes than to
    behold evil,
  And cannot look on wickedness.
  Why do You look on those who
    deal treacherously,
  And hold Your tongue when the
    wicked devours
  A *person* more righteous than he?
14 *Why* do You make men like fish of
    the sea,
  Like creeping things *that have* no
    ruler over them?

15 They take up all of them with a
    hook,
  They catch them in their net,
  And gather them in their dragnet.
  Therefore they rejoice and are glad.
16 Therefore they sacrifice to
    their net,
  And burn incense to their dragnet;
  Because by them their share *is*
    sumptuous
  And their food plentiful.
17 Shall they therefore empty
    their net,
  And continue to slay nations
    without pity?

2 I will stand my watch
  And set myself on the rampart,
  And watch to see what He will say
    to me,
  And what I will answer when I am
    corrected.

The Just Live by Faith

2Then the LORD answered me and said:
"Write the vision
And make *it* plain on tablets,
That he may run who reads it.
3 For the vision *is* yet for an
appointed time;
But at the end it will speak, and it
will not lie.
Though it tarries, wait for it;
Because it will surely come,
It will not tarry.

4 "Behold the proud,
His soul is not upright in him;
But the just shall live by his faith.

Woe to the Wicked

5 "Indeed, because he transgresses by
wine,
He is a proud man,
And he does not stay at home.
Because he enlarges his desire as
hell,
And he *is* like death, and cannot be
satisfied,
He gathers to himself all nations
And heaps up for himself all
peoples.

6 "Will not all these take up a proverb
against him,
And a taunting riddle against him,
and say,
'Woe to him who increases
What is not his—how long?
And to him who loads himself with
many pledges'?
7 Will not your creditors rise up
suddenly?
Will they not awaken who oppress
you?
And you will become their booty.
8 Because you have plundered many
nations,
All the remnant of the people shall
plunder you,
Because of men's blood
And the violence of the land *and*
the city,
And of all who dwell in it.

9 "Woe to him who covets evil gain
for his house,
That he may set his nest on high,

That he may be delivered from the
power of disaster!
10 You give shameful counsel to your
house,
Cutting off many peoples,
And sin *against* your soul.
11 For the stone will cry out from the
wall,
And the beam from the timbers will
answer it.

12 "Woe to him who builds a town with
bloodshed,
Who establishes a city by iniquity!
13 Behold, *is it* not of the LORD of hosts
That the peoples labor to feed the
fire,
And nations weary themselves in
vain?
14 For the earth will be filled
With the knowledge of the glory of
the LORD,
As the waters cover the sea.

15 "Woe to him who gives drink to his
neighbor,
Pressing *him to* your bottle,
Even to make *him* drunk,
That you may look on his
nakedness!
16 You are filled with shame instead
of glory.
You also—drink!
And be exposed as uncircumcised!
The cup of the LORD's right hand
will be turned against you,
And utter shame will be on your
glory.
17 For the violence *done to* Lebanon
will cover you,
And the plunder of beasts *which*
made them afraid,
Because of men's blood
And the violence of the land *and*
the city,
And of all who dwell in it.

18 "What profit is the image, that its
maker should carve it,
The molded image, a teacher of lies,
That the maker of its mold should
trust in it,
To make mute idols?
19 Woe to him who says to wood,
'Awake!'
To silent stone, 'Arise! It shall
teach!'

Behold, it is overlaid with gold and
    silver,
Yet in it there is no breath at all.

20 "But the LORD is in His holy temple.
Let all the earth keep silence before
    Him."

The Prophet's Prayer

3 A prayer of Habakkuk the prophet,
on Shigionoth.*ᵃ*

2   O LORD, I have heard Your speech
    and was afraid;
  O LORD, revive Your work in the
    midst of the years!
  In the midst of the years make *it*
    known;
  In wrath remember mercy.

3   God came from Teman,
  The Holy One from Mount Paran.
               Selah

  His glory covered the heavens,
  And the earth was full of His praise.
4   *His* brightness was like the light;
  He had rays *flashing* from His
    hand,
  And there His power *was* hidden.
5   Before Him went pestilence,
  And fever followed at His feet.

6   He stood and measured the earth;
  He looked and startled the nations.
  And the everlasting mountains
    were scattered,
  The perpetual hills bowed.
  His ways *are* everlasting.
7,   I saw the tents of Cushan in
    affliction;
  The curtains of the land of Midian
    trembled.

8   O LORD, were *You* displeased with
    the rivers,
  Was Your anger against the rivers,
  Was Your wrath against the sea,
  That You rode on Your horses,
  Your chariots of salvation?
9   Your bow was made quite ready;
  Oaths were sworn over *Your*
    arrows.   Selah

  You divided the earth with rivers.
10   The mountains saw You *and*
    trembled;
  The overflowing of the water
    passed by.
  The deep uttered its voice,
  And lifted its hands on high.
11   The sun and moon stood still in
    their habitation;
  At the light of Your arrows they
    went,
  At the shining of Your glittering
    spear.

12   You marched through the land in
    indignation;
  You trampled the nations in anger.
13   You went forth for the salvation of
    Your people,
  For salvation with Your Anointed.
  You struck the head from the house
    of the wicked,
  By laying bare from foundation to
    neck.   Selah

14   You thrust through with his own
    arrows
  The head of his villages.
  They came out like a whirlwind to
    scatter me;
  Their rejoicing was like feasting on
    the poor in secret.
15   You walked through the sea with
    Your horses,
  Through the heap of great waters.

16   When I heard, my body trembled;
  My lips quivered at *the* voice;
  Rottenness entered my bones;
  And I trembled in myself,
  That I might rest in the day of
    trouble.
  When he comes up to the people,
  He will invade them with his
    troops.

A Hymn of Faith

17   Though the fig tree may not
    blossom,
  Nor fruit be on the vines;
  Though the labor of the olive may
    fail,

ᵃ Exact meaning unknown

And the fields yield no food;
Though the flock may be cut off
  from the fold,
And there be no herd in the
  stalls—
18 Yet I will rejoice in the LORD,
I will joy in the God of my
  salvation.

19 The LORD God is my strength;
He will make my feet like deer's
  feet,
And He will make me walk on my
  high hills.

To the Chief Musician. With my stringed instruments.

The Book of
ZEPHANIAH

1 The word of the LORD which came to Zephaniah the son of Cushi, the son of Gedaliah, the son of Amariah, the son of Hezekiah, in the days of Josiah the son of Amon, king of Judah.

The Great Day of the LORD

2 "I will utterly consume everything
From the face of the land,"
Says the LORD;
3 "I will consume man and beast;
I will consume the birds of the
  heavens,
The fish of the sea,
And the stumbling blocks*a* along
  with the wicked.
I will cut off man from the face of
  the land,"
Says the LORD.

4 "I will stretch out My hand against
  Judah,
And against all the inhabitants of
  Jerusalem.
I will cut off every trace of Baal
  from this place,
The names of the idolatrous priests
  with the *pagan* priests—
5 Those who worship the host of
  heaven on the housetops;
Those who worship and swear
  oaths by the LORD,

But who *also* swear by Milcom;*b*
6 Those who have turned back from
  following the LORD,
And have not sought the LORD, nor
  inquired of Him."

7 Be silent in the presence of the
  Lord GOD;
For the day of the LORD *is* at hand,
For the LORD has prepared a
  sacrifice;
He has invited His guests.

8 "And it shall be,
In the day of the LORD's sacrifice,
That I will punish the princes and
  the king's children,
And all such as are clothed with
  foreign apparel.
9 In the same day I will punish
All those who leap over the
  threshold,*c*
Who fill their masters' houses with
  violence and deceit.

10 "And there shall be on that day,"
  says the LORD,
"The sound of a mournful cry from
  the Fish Gate,
A wailing from the Second Quarter,
And a loud crashing from the hills.
11 Wail, you inhabitants of Maktesh!*d*

---

a Figurative of idols   *b* Or *Malcam,* an Ammonite god, also called *Molech* (compare Leviticus 18.21)   *c* Compare 1 Samuel 5.5   *d* Literally *Mortar,* a market district of Jerusalem

For all the merchant people are cut
  down;
All those who handle money are
  cut off.

12 "And it shall come to pass at that
    time
    That I will search Jerusalem with
    lamps,
    And punish the men
    Who are settled in complacency,
    Who say in their heart,
    'The LORD will not do good,
    Nor will He do evil.'
13 Therefore their goods shall become
    booty,
    And their houses a desolation;
    They shall build houses, but not
    inhabit *them;*
    They shall plant vineyards, but not
    drink their wine."

14 The great day of the LORD *is* near;
    It is near and hastens quickly.
    The noise of the day of the LORD
    is bitter;
    There the mighty men shall
    cry out.
15 That day *is* a day of wrath,
    A day of trouble and distress,
    A day of devastation and
    desolation,
    A day of darkness and gloominess,
    A day of clouds and thick darkness,
16 A day of trumpet and alarm
    Against the fortified cities
    And against the high towers.

17 "I will bring distress upon men,
    And they shall walk like blind men,
    Because they have sinned against
    the LORD;
    Their blood shall be poured out like
    dust,
    And their flesh like refuse."

18 Neither their silver nor their gold
    Shall be able to deliver them
    In the day of the LORD's wrath;
    But the whole land shall be
    devoured
    By the fire of His jealousy,
    For He will make speedy riddance
    Of all those who dwell in the land.

e Or *shameless*

A Call to Repentance

2 Gather yourselves together, yes,
    gather together,
    O undesirable*e* nation,
2 Before the decree is issued,
    Or the day passes like chaff,
    Before the LORD's fierce anger
    comes upon you,
    Before the day of the LORD's anger
    comes upon you!
3 Seek the LORD, all you meek of the
    earth,
    Who have upheld His justice.
    Seek righteousness, seek humility.
    It may be that you will be hidden
    In the day of the LORD's anger.

Judgment on Nations

4 For Gaza shall be forsaken,
    And Ashkelon desolate;
    They shall drive out Ashdod at
    noonday,
    And Ekron shall be uprooted.
5 Woe to the inhabitants of the
    seacoast,
    The nation of the Cherethites!
    The word of the LORD *is*
    against you,
    O Canaan, land of the Philistines:
    "I will destroy you;
    So there shall be no inhabitant."

6 The seacoast shall be pastures,
    With shelters for shepherds and
    folds for flocks.
7 The coast shall be for the remnant
    of the house of Judah;
    They shall feed *their* flocks there;
    In the houses of Ashkelon they
    shall lie down at evening.
    For the LORD their God will
    intervene for them,
    And return their captives.

8 "I have heard the reproach of Moab,
    And the insults of the people of
    Ammon,
    With which they have reproached
    My people,
    And made arrogant threats against
    their borders.
9 Therefore, as I live,"
    Says the LORD of hosts, the God of
    Israel,

"Surely Moab shall be like Sodom,
And the people of Ammon like
    Gomorrah—
Overrun with weeds and saltpits,
And a perpetual desolation.
The residue of My people shall
    plunder them,
And the remnant of My people shall
    possess them."

10 This they shall have for their pride,
Because they have reproached and
    made arrogant threats
Against the people of the LORD of
    hosts.
11 The LORD *will be* awesome to them,
For He will reduce to nothing all
    the gods of the earth;
People shall worship Him,
Each one from his place,
Indeed all the shores of the nations.

12 "You Ethiopians also,
You shall be slain by My sword."

13 And He will stretch out His hand
    against the north,
Destroy Assyria,
And make Nineveh a desolation,
As dry as the wilderness.
14 The herds shall lie down in her
    midst,
Every beast of the nation.
Both the pelican and the bittern
Shall lodge on the capitals *of* her
    pillars;
Their voice shall sing in the
    windows;
Desolation *shall be* at the
    threshold;
For He will lay bare the cedar work.
15 This is the rejoicing city
That dwelt securely,
That said in her heart,
"I *am it,* and *there is* none
    besides me."
How has she become a desolation,
A place for beasts to lie down!
Everyone who passes by her
Shall hiss and shake his fist.

The Wickedness of Jerusalem

3 Woe to her who is rebellious and
    polluted,
To the oppressing city!
2 She has not obeyed *His* voice,
She has not received correction;

She has not trusted in the LORD,
She has not drawn near to her God.
3 Her princes in her midst *are*
    roaring lions;
Her judges *are* evening wolves
That leave not a bone till morning.
4 Her prophets are insolent,
    treacherous people;
Her priests have polluted the
    sanctuary,
They have done violence to the law.
5 The LORD *is* righteous in her midst,
He will do no unrighteousness.
Every morning He brings His
    justice to light;
He never fails,
But the unjust knows no shame.

6 "I have cut off nations,
Their fortresses are devastated;
I have made their streets desolate,
With none passing by.
Their cities are destroyed;
There is no one, no inhabitant.
7 I said, 'Surely you will fear Me,
You will receive instruction'—
So that her dwelling would not be
    cut off,
Despite everything for which I
    punished her.
But they rose early and corrupted
    all their deeds.

A Faithful Remnant

8 "Therefore wait for Me," says the
    LORD,
"Until the day I rise up for plunder;
My determination *is* to gather the
    nations
To My assembly of kingdoms,
To pour on them My indignation,
All My fierce anger;
All the earth shall be devoured
With the fire of My jealousy.

9 "For then I will restore to the peoples
    a pure language,
That they all may call on the name
    of the LORD,
To serve Him with one accord.
10 From beyond the rivers of Ethiopia
My worshipers,
The daughter of My dispersed ones,
Shall bring My offering.
11 In that day you shall not be shamed
    for any of your deeds

In which you transgress
    against Me;
For then I will take away from your
    midst
Those who rejoice in your pride,
And you shall no longer be haughty
In My holy mountain.
12 I will leave in your midst
    A meek and humble people,
    And they shall trust in the name of
        the LORD.
13 The remnant of Israel shall do no
        unrighteousness
    And speak no lies,
    Nor shall a deceitful tongue be
        found in their mouth;
    For they shall feed *their* flocks and
        lie down,
    And no one shall make *them*
        afraid."

Joy in God's Faithfulness

14 Sing, O daughter of Zion!
    Shout, O Israel!
    Be glad and rejoice with all *your*
        heart,
    O daughter of Jerusalem!
15 The LORD has taken away your
        judgments,
    He has cast out your enemy.
    The King of Israel, the LORD, *is* in
        your midst;
    You shall see disaster no more.

16 In that day it shall be said to
        Jerusalem:
    "Do not fear;
    Zion, let not your hands be weak.
17 The LORD your God in your midst,
    The Mighty One, will save;
    He will rejoice over you with
        gladness,
    He will quiet *you* with His love,
    He will rejoice over you with
        singing."

18 "I will gather those who sorrow over
        the appointed assembly,
    Who are among you,
    To whom its reproach *is* a burden.
19 Behold, at that time
    I will deal with all who afflict you;
    I will save the lame,
    And gather those who were
        driven out;
    I will appoint them for praise and
        fame
    In every land where they were put
        to shame.
20 At that time I will bring you back,
    Even at the time I gather you;
    For I will give you fame and praise
    Among all the peoples of the earth,
    When I return your captives before
        your eyes,"
    Says the LORD.

The Book of
HAGGAI

The Command to Build God's House

1 In the second year of King Darius, in the sixth month, on the first day of the month, the word of the LORD came by Haggai the prophet to Zerubbabel the son of Shealtiel, governor of Judah, and to Joshua the son of Jehozadak, the high priest, saying, 2"Thus speaks the LORD of hosts, saying: 'This people says, "The time has not come, the time that the LORD's house should be built." ' "

3Then the word of the LORD came by Haggai the prophet, saying, 4"*Is it* time for you yourselves to dwell in your paneled houses, and this temple *to lie* in ruins?" 5Now therefore, thus says the LORD of hosts: "Consider your ways!
6 "You have sown much, and bring in
    little;
You eat, but do not have enough;
You drink, but you are not filled
    with drink;
You clothe yourselves, but no one
    is warm;
And he who earns wages,
Earns wages *to put* into a bag with
    holes."

7Thus says the LORD of hosts: "Consider your ways! 8Go up to the mountains and bring wood and build the temple, that I may take pleasure in it and be glorified," says the LORD. 9"*You* looked for much, but indeed *it came to* little; and when you brought it home, I blew it away. Why?" says the LORD of hosts. "Because of My house that *is in* ruins, while every one of you runs to his own house. 10Therefore the heavens above you withhold the dew, and the earth withholds its fruit. 11For I called for a drought on the land and the mountains, on the grain and the new wine and the oil, on whatever the ground brings forth, on men and livestock, and on all the labor of *your* hands."

The People's Obedience

12Then Zerubbabel the son of Shealtiel, and Joshua the son of Jehozadak,

the high priest, with all the remnant of the people, obeyed the voice of the LORD their God, and the words of Haggai the prophet, as the LORD their God had sent him; and the people feared the presence of the LORD. 13Then Haggai, the LORD's messenger, spoke the LORD's message to the people, saying, "I *am* with you, says the LORD." 14So the LORD stirred up the spirit of Zerubbabel the son of Shealtiel, governor of Judah, and the spirit of Joshua the son of Jehozadak, the high priest, and the spirit of all the remnant of the people; and they came and worked on the house of the LORD of hosts, their God, 15on the twenty-fourth day of the sixth month, in the second year of King Darius.

The Coming Glory of God's House

2 In the seventh *month*, on the twenty-first of the month, the word of the LORD came by Haggai the prophet, saying: 2"Speak now to Zerubbabel the son of Shealtiel, governor of Judah, and to Joshua the son of Jehozadak, the high priest, and to the remnant of the people, saying: 3'Who is left among you who saw this temple in its former glory? And how do you see it now? In comparison with it, *is this* not in your eyes as nothing? 4Yet now be strong, Zerubbabel,' says the LORD; 'and be strong, Joshua, son of Jehozadak, the high priest; and be strong, all you people of the land,' says the LORD, 'and work; for I *am* with you,' says the LORD of hosts. 5'*According to* the word that I covenanted with you when you came out of Egypt, so My Spirit remains among you; do not fear!'

6"For thus says the LORD of hosts: 'Once more (it *is* a little while) I will shake heaven and earth, the sea and dry land; 7and I will shake all nations, and they shall come to the Desire of All Nations,*a* and I will fill this temple with glory,' says the LORD of hosts. 8'The silver *is* Mine, and the gold *is* Mine,' says the LORD of hosts. 9'The glory of this

a Or *the desire of all nations*

latter temple shall be greater than the former,' says the LORD of hosts. 'And in this place I will give peace,' says the LORD of hosts.''

The People Are Defiled

10On the twenty-fourth *day* of the ninth *month*, in the second year of Darius, the word of the LORD came by Haggai the prophet, saying, 11"Thus says the LORD of hosts: 'Now, ask the priests *concerning the* law, saying, 12"If one carries holy meat in the fold of his garment, and with the edge he touches bread or stew, wine or oil, or any food, will it become holy?" ' ''

Then the priests answered and said, "No."

13And Haggai said, "If *one who is* unclean *because* of a dead body touches any of these, will it be unclean?"

So the priests answered and said, "It shall be unclean."

14Then Haggai answered and said, " 'So is this people, and so is this nation before Me,' says the LORD, 'and so is every work of their hands; and what they offer there is unclean.

Promised Blessing

15'And now, carefully consider from this day forward: from before stone was laid upon stone in the temple of the LORD—16since those *days,* when *one* came to a heap of twenty ephahs, there were *but* ten; when *one* came to the wine vat to draw out fifty baths from the press, there were *but* twenty. 17I struck you with blight and mildew and hail in all the labors of your hands; yet you did not *turn* to Me,' says the LORD. 18'Consider now from this day forward, from the twenty-fourth day of the ninth month, from the day that the foundation of the LORD's temple was laid—consider it: 19Is the seed still in the barn? As yet the vine, the fig tree, the pomegranate, and the olive tree have not yielded *fruit. But* from this day I will bless *you.*' ''

Zerubbabel Chosen as a Signet

20And again the word of the LORD came to Haggai on the twenty-fourth day of the month, saying, 21"Speak to Zerubbabel, governor of Judah, saying:
'I will shake heaven and earth.
22 I will overthrow the throne of
			kingdoms;
	I will destroy the strength of the
			Gentile kingdoms.
	I will overthrow the chariots
	And those who ride in them;
	The horses and their riders shall
			come down,
	Every one by the sword of his
			brother.
23'In that day,' says the LORD of hosts, 'I will take you, Zerubbabel My servant, the son of Shealtiel,' says the LORD, 'and will make you like a signet *ring;* for I have chosen you,' says the LORD of hosts."

The Book of
ZECHARIAH

A Call to Repentance

1 In the eighth month of the second year of Darius, the word of the LORD came to Zechariah the son of Berechiah, the son of Iddo the prophet, saying, 2"The LORD has been very angry with your fathers. 3Therefore say to them, 'Thus says the LORD of hosts: "Return to Me," says the LORD of hosts, "and I will return to you," says the LORD of hosts. 4"Do not be like your fathers, to whom the former prophets preached, saying, 'Thus says the LORD of hosts: "Turn now from your evil ways and your evil deeds." ' But they did not hear nor heed Me," says the LORD.

5 "Your fathers, where *are* they?
   And the prophets, do they live
      forever?
6   Yet surely My words and My
         statutes,
   Which I commanded My servants
      the prophets,
   Did they not overtake your fathers?
"So they returned and said:
   'Just as the LORD of hosts
      determined to do to us,
   According to our ways and
      according to our deeds,
   So He has dealt with us." ' "

Vision of the Horses

7On the twenty-fourth day of the eleventh month, which is the month Shebat, in the second year of Darius, the word of the LORD came to Zechariah the son of Berechiah, the son of Iddo the prophet: 8I saw by night, and behold, a man riding on a red horse, and it stood among the myrtle trees in the hollow; and behind him *were* horses: red, sorrel, and white. 9Then I said, "My lord, what *are* these?" So the angel who talked with me said to me, "I will show you what they *are.*"

10And the man who stood among the myrtle trees answered and said, "These *are the ones* whom the LORD has sent to walk to and fro throughout the earth."

11So they answered the Angel of the LORD, who stood among the myrtle trees, and said, "We have walked to and fro throughout the earth, and behold, all the earth is resting quietly."

The LORD Will Comfort Zion

12Then the Angel of the LORD answered and said, "O LORD of hosts, how long will You not have mercy on Jerusalem and on the cities of Judah, against which You were angry these seventy years?"

13And the LORD answered the angel who talked to me, *with* good *and* comforting words. 14So the angel who spoke with me said to me, "Proclaim, saying, 'Thus says the LORD of hosts:

   "I am zealous for Jerusalem
      And for Zion with great zeal.
15   I am exceedingly angry with the
         nations at ease;
      For I was a little angry,
      And they helped—*but* with evil
         intent."
16'Therefore thus says the LORD:
   "I am returning to Jerusalem with
         mercy;
      My house shall be built in it," says
         the LORD of hosts,
   "And a *surveyor's* line shall be
         stretched out over Jerusalem." '
17"Again proclaim, saying, 'Thus says the LORD of hosts:
   "My cities shall again spread out
         through prosperity;
      The LORD will again comfort Zion,
      And will again choose
         Jerusalem." ' "

Vision of the Horns

18Then I raised my eyes and looked, and there *were* four horns. 19And I said to the angel who talked with me, "What *are* these?"

So he answered me, "These *are* the horns that have scattered Judah, Israel, and Jerusalem."

20Then the LORD showed me four craftsmen. 21And I said, "What are these coming to do?"

So he said, "These *are* the horns that

scattered Judah, so that no one could lift up his head; but the craftsmen are coming to terrify them, to cast out the horns of the nations that lifted up *their* horn against the land of Judah to scatter it."

Vision of the Measuring Line

2 Then I raised my eyes and looked, and behold, a man with a measuring line in his hand. 2So I said, "Where are you going?"

And he said to me, "To measure Jerusalem, to see what *is* its width and what *is* its length."

3And there *was* the angel who talked with me, going out; and another angel was coming out to meet him, 4who said to him, "Run, speak to this young man, saying: 'Jerusalem shall be inhabited *as* towns without walls, because of the multitude of men and livestock in it. 5For I,' says the LORD, 'will be a wall of fire all around her, and I will be the glory in her midst.' "

Future Joy of Zion and Many Nations

6"Up, up! Flee from the land of the north," says the LORD; "for I have spread you abroad like the four winds of heaven," says the LORD. 7Up, Zion! Escape, you who dwell with the daughter of Babylon."

8For thus says the LORD of hosts: "He sent Me after glory, to the nations which plunder you; for he who touches you touches the apple of His eye. 9For surely I will shake My hand against them, and they shall become spoil for their servants. Then you will know that the LORD of hosts has sent Me.

10"Sing and rejoice, O daughter of Zion! For behold, I am coming and I will dwell in your midst," says the LORD. 11"Many nations shall be joined to the LORD in that day, and they shall become My people. And I will dwell in your midst. Then you will know that the LORD of hosts has sent Me to you. 12And the LORD will take possession of Judah as His inheritance in the Holy Land, and will again choose Jerusalem. 13Be silent, all flesh, before the LORD, for He is aroused from His holy habitation!"

Vision of the High Priest

3 Then he showed me Joshua the high priest standing before the Angel of the LORD, and Satan standing at his right hand to oppose him. 2And the LORD said to Satan, "The LORD rebuke you, Satan! The LORD who has chosen Jerusalem rebuke you! *Is* this not a brand plucked from the fire?"

3Now Joshua was clothed with filthy garments, and was standing before the Angel.

4Then He answered and spoke to those who stood before Him, saying, "Take away the filthy garments from him." And to him He said, "See, I have removed your iniquity from you, and I will clothe you with rich robes."

5And I said, "Let them put a clean turban on his head."

So they put a clean turban on his head, and they put the clothes on him. And the Angel of the LORD stood by.

The Coming Branch

6Then the Angel of the LORD admonished Joshua, saying, 7"Thus says the LORD of hosts:

'If you will walk in My ways,
    And if you will keep My command,
    Then you shall also judge My
        house,
    And likewise have charge of My
        courts;
    I will give you places to walk
    Among these who stand here.

8   'Hear, O Joshua, the high priest,
    You and your companions who sit
        before you,
    For they are a wondrous sign;
    For behold, I am bringing forth My
        Servant the BRANCH.
9   For behold, the stone
    That I have laid before Joshua:
    Upon the stone *are* seven eyes.
    Behold, I will engrave its
        inscription,'
    Says the LORD of hosts,
    'And I will remove the iniquity of
        that land in one day.
10   In that day,' says the LORD of hosts,
    'Everyone will invite his neighbor
    Under his vine and under his fig
        tree.' "

Vision of the Lampstand and Olive Trees

4 Now the angel who talked with me came back and wakened me, as a man who is wakened out of his sleep. 2And he said to me, "What do you see?"

So I said, "I am looking, and there *is* a lampstand of solid gold with a bowl on top of it, and on the *stand* seven lamps with seven pipes to the seven lamps. 3Two olive trees *are* by it, one at the right of the bowl and the other at its left." 4So I answered and spoke to the angel who talked with me, saying, "What *are* these, my lord?"

5Then the angel who talked with me answered and said to me, "Do you not know what these are?"

And I said, "No, my lord."

6So he answered and said to me:

"This *is* the word of the Lord to
Zerubbabel:
'Not by might nor by power, but by
My Spirit,'
Says the Lord of hosts.
7   'Who *are* you, O great mountain?
Before Zerubbabel *you shall
become* a plain!
And he shall bring forth the
capstone
With shouts of "Grace, grace
to it!" ' "

8Moreover the word of the Lord came to me, saying:
9   "The hands of Zerubbabel
Have laid the foundation of this
temple;
His hands shall also finish *it*.
Then you will know
That the Lord of hosts has sent Me
to you.
10   For who has despised the day of
small things?
For these seven rejoice to see
The plumb line in the hand of
Zerubbabel.
They are the eyes of the Lord,
Which scan to and fro throughout
the whole earth."

11Then I answered and said to him, "What *are* these two olive trees—at the right of the lampstand and at its left?" 12And I further answered and said to him, "What *are these* two olive branches that *drip* into the receptacles of the two gold pipes from which the golden *oil* drains?"

13Then he answered me and said, "Do you not know what these *are*?"

And I said, "No, my lord."

14So he said, "These *are* the two anointed ones, who stand beside the Lord of the whole earth."

Vision of the Flying Scroll

5 Then I turned and raised my eyes, and saw there a flying scroll.

2And he said to me, "What do you see?"

So I answered, "I see a flying scroll. Its length *is* twenty cubits and its width ten cubits."

3Then he said to me, "This *is* the curse that goes out over the face of the whole earth: 'Every thief shall be expelled,' according *to* this side of *the scroll*; and, 'Every perjurer shall be expelled,' according *to* that side of it."

4   "I will send out *the curse*," says the
Lord of hosts;
"It shall enter the house of the thief
And the house of the one who
swears falsely by My name.
It shall remain in the midst of his
house
And consume it, with its timber and
stones."

Vision of the Woman in a Basket

5Then the angel who talked with me came out and said to me, "Lift your eyes now, and see what this *is* that goes forth."

6So I asked, "What *is* it?" And he said, "It *is* a basket[a] that is going forth."

He also said, "This *is* their resemblance throughout the earth: 7Here *is* a lead disc lifted up, and this *is* a woman sitting inside the basket"; 8then he said, "This *is* Wickedness!" And he thrust her down into the basket, and threw the lead cover over its mouth. 9Then I raised my eyes and looked, and there *were* two women, coming with the wind in their wings; for they had wings like the wings of a stork, and they lifted up the basket between earth and heaven.

10So I said to the angel who talked

---

a A measuring container, and so elsewhere

with me, "Where are they carrying the basket?"

11And he said to me, "To build a house for it in the land of Shinar;*b* when it is ready, *the basket* will be set there on its base."

Vision of the Four Chariots

6 Then I turned and raised my eyes and looked, and behold, four chariots *were* coming from between two mountains, and the mountains *were* mountains of bronze. 2With the first chariot *were* red horses, with the second chariot black horses, 3with the third chariot white horses, and with the fourth chariot dappled horses—strong *steeds.* 4Then I answered and said to the angel who talked with me, "What *are* these, my lord?"

5And the angel answered and said to me, "These *are* four spirits of heaven, who go out from *their* station before the Lord of all the earth. 6The one with the black horses is going to the north country, the white are going after them, and the dappled are going toward the south country. 7Then the strong *steeds* went out, eager to go, that they might walk to and fro throughout the earth. And He said, "Go, walk to and fro throughout the earth." So they walked to and fro throughout the earth. 8And He called to me, and spoke to me, saying, "See, those who go toward the north country have given rest to My Spirit in the north country."

The Command to Crown Joshua

9Then the word of the Lord came to me, saying: 10"Receive *the gift* from the captives—from Heldai, Tobijah, and Jedaiah, who have come from Babylon—and go the same day and enter the house of Josiah the son of Zephaniah. 11Take the silver and gold, make an elaborate crown, and set *it* on the head of Joshua the son of Jehozadak, the high priest. 12Then speak to him, saying, 'Thus says the Lord of hosts, saying:

"Behold, the Man whose name *is* the BRANCH!
From His place He shall branch out,

And He shall build the temple of the Lord;
13 Yes, He shall build the temple of the Lord.
He shall bear the glory,
And shall sit and rule on His throne;
So He shall be a priest on His throne,
And the counsel of peace shall be between them both." '

14"Now the elaborate crown shall be for a memorial in the temple of the Lord for Helem, Tobijah, Jedaiah, and Hen the son of Zephaniah. 15Even those from afar shall come and build the temple of the Lord. Then you shall know that the Lord of hosts has sent Me to you. And *this* shall come to pass if you diligently obey the voice of the Lord your God."

Obedience Better than Fasting

7 Now in the fourth year of King Darius it came to pass *that* the word of the Lord came to Zechariah, on the fourth day of the ninth month, Chislev, 2when *the people* sent Sherezer, with Regem-Melech and his men, *to* the house of God, to pray before the Lord, 3*and* to ask the priests who *were* in the house of the Lord of hosts, and the prophets, saying, "Should I weep in the fifth month and fast as I have done for so many years?"

4Then the word of the Lord of hosts came to me, saying, 5"Say to all the people of the land, and to the priests: 'When you fasted and mourned in the fifth and seventh *months* during those seventy years, did you really fast for Me—for Me? 6When you eat and when you drink, do you not eat and drink *for yourselves?* 7Should *you* not *have obeyed* the words which the Lord proclaimed through the former prophets when Jerusalem and the cities around it were inhabited and prosperous, and the South and the Lowland were inhabited?' "

Disobedience Resulted in Captivity

8Then the word of the Lord came to Zechariah, saying, 9"Thus says the Lord of hosts:

b That is, Babylon

'Execute true justice,
Show mercy and compassion
Everyone to his brother.
10 Do not oppress the widow or the
    fatherless,
    The alien or the poor.
    Let none of you plan evil in his
    heart
    Against his brother.'
11But they refused to heed, shrugged
their shoulders, and stopped their ears
so that they could not hear. 12Yes, they
made their hearts like flint, refusing to
hear the law and the words which the
LORD of hosts had sent by His Spirit
through the former prophets. Thus
great wrath came from the LORD of
hosts. 13Therefore it happened, *that*
just as He proclaimed and they would
not hear, so they called out and I would
not listen," says the LORD of hosts.
14"But I scattered them with a whirlwind among all the nations which they
had not known. Thus the land became
desolate after them, so that no one
passed through or returned; for they
made the pleasant land desolate."

Jerusalem, Holy City of the Future

8 Again the word of the LORD of hosts
came, saying, 2"Thus says the LORD
of hosts:
    'I am zealous for Zion with great
    zeal;
    With great fervor I am zealous
    for her.'
3"Thus says the LORD:
    'I will return to Zion,
    And dwell in the midst of
    Jerusalem.
    Jerusalem shall be called the City
    of Truth,
    The Mountain of the LORD of hosts,
    The Holy Mountain.'
4"Thus says the LORD of hosts:
    'Old men and old women shall
    again sit
    In the streets of Jerusalem,
    Each one with his staff in his
    hand
    Because of great age.
5   The streets of the city
    Shall be full of boys and girls
    Playing in its streets.'
6"Thus says the LORD of hosts:
    'If it is marvelous in the eyes of the

remnant of this people in these
    days,
    Will it also be marvelous in My
    eyes?'
    Says the LORD of hosts.
7"Thus says the LORD of hosts:
    'Behold, I will save My people from
    the land of the east
    And from the land of the west;
8   I will bring them *back*,
    And they shall dwell in the midst
    of Jerusalem.
    They shall be My people
    And I will be their God,
    In truth and righteousness.'
9"Thus says the LORD of hosts:
    'Let your hands be strong,
    You who have been hearing in
    these days
    These words by the mouth of the
    prophets,
    Who *spoke* in the day the
    foundation was laid
    For the house of the LORD of hosts,
    That the temple might be built.
10 For before these days
    There were no wages for man nor
    any hire for beast;
    There was no peace from the
    enemy for whoever went out
    or came in;
    For I set all men, everyone, against
    his neighbor.
11But now I *will* not *treat* the remnant
of this people as in the former days,'
says the LORD of hosts.
12 'For the seed *shall be* prosperous,
    The vine shall give its fruit,
    The ground shall give her increase,
    And the heavens shall give
    their dew—
    I will cause the remnant of this
    people
    To possess all these.
13 And it shall come to pass
    That just as you were a curse
    among the nations,
    O house of Judah and house of
    Israel,
    So I will save you, and you shall
    be a blessing.
    Do not fear,
    Let your hands be strong.'
14"For thus says the LORD of hosts:
    'Just as I determined to punish you
    When your fathers provoked Me to
    wrath,'

Says the LORD of hosts,
'And I would not relent,
15 So again in these days
I am determined to do good
To Jerusalem and to the house of
Judah.
Do not fear.
16 These *are* the things you shall do:
Speak each man the truth to his
neighbor;
Give judgment in your gates for
truth, justice, and peace;
17 Let none of you think evil in your
heart against your neighbor;
And do not love a false oath.
For all these *are things* that I hate,'
Says the LORD."
18Then the word of the LORD of hosts
came to me, saying, 19"Thus says the
LORD of hosts:
'The fast of the fourth *month*,
The fast of the fifth,
The fast of the seventh,
And the fast of the tenth,
Shall be joy and gladness and
cheerful feasts
For the house of Judah.
Therefore love truth and peace.'
20"Thus says the LORD of hosts:
'Peoples shall yet come,
Inhabitants of many cities;
21 The inhabitants of one *city* shall go
to another, saying,
"Let us continue to go and pray
before the LORD,
And seek the LORD of hosts.
I myself will go also."
22 Yes, many peoples and strong
nations
Shall come to seek the LORD of
hosts in Jerusalem,
And to pray before the LORD.'
23"Thus says the LORD of hosts: 'In
those days ten men from every language of the nations shall grasp the
sleeve of a Jewish man, saying, "Let us
go with you, for we have heard *that*
God *is* with you." ' "

Israel Defended Against Enemies

9 The burden of the word of the LORD
Against the land of Hadrach,
And Damascus its resting place
(For the eyes of men
And all the tribes of Israel
Are on the LORD);

2 Also *against* Hamath, *which*
borders on it,
And *against* Tyre and Sidon,
though they are very wise.

3 For Tyre built herself a tower,
Heaped up silver like the dust,
And gold like the mire of the
streets.
4 Behold, the LORD will cast her out;
He will destroy her power in
the sea,
And she will be devoured by fire.

5 Ashkelon shall see *it* and fear;
Gaza also shall be very sorrowful;
And Ekron, for He dried up her
expectation.
The king shall perish from Gaza,
And Ashkelon shall not be
inhabited.

6 "A mixed race shall settle in
Ashdod,
And I will cut off the pride of the
Philistines.
7 I will take away the blood from his
mouth,
And the abominations from
between his teeth.
But he who remains, even he *shall
be* for our God,
And shall be like a leader in Judah,
And Ekron like a Jebusite.
8 I will camp around My house
Because of the army,
Because of him who passes by and
him who returns.
No more shall an oppressor pass
through them,
For now I have seen with My eyes.

The Coming King

9 "Rejoice greatly, O daughter of
Zion!
Shout, O daughter of Jerusalem!
Behold, your King is coming to you;
He *is* just and having salvation,
Lowly and riding on a donkey,
A colt, the foal of a donkey.
10 I will cut off the chariot from
Ephraim
And the horse from Jerusalem;
The battle bow shall be cut off.
He shall speak peace to the nations;
His dominion *shall be* 'from sea
to sea,

God Will Save His People

11 "As for you also,
Because of the blood of your
covenant,
I will set your prisoners free from
the waterless pit.

12 Return to the stronghold,
You prisoners of hope.
Even today I declare
That I will restore double to you.

13 For I have bent Judah, My *bow*,
Fitted the bow with Ephraim,
And raised up your sons, O Zion,
Against your sons, O Greece,
And made you like the sword of a
mighty man."

14 Then the Lord will be seen over
them,
And His arrow will go forth like
lightning.
The Lord God will blow the
trumpet,
And go with whirlwinds from the
south.

15 The Lord of hosts will defend them;
They shall devour and subdue with
slingstones.
They shall drink *and* roar as if with
wine;
They shall be filled *with blood* like
basins,
Like the corners of the altar.

16 The Lord their God will save them
in that day,
As the flock of His people.
For they *shall be like* the jewels of
a crown,
Lifted like a banner over His land—

17 For how great is its goodness
And how great its beauty!
Grain shall make the young men
thrive,
And new wine the young women.

Restoration of Judah and Israel

10 Ask the Lord for rain
In the time of the latter rain.[d]
The Lord will make flashing
clouds;

He will give them showers of rain,
Grass in the field for everyone.

2 For the idols speak delusion;
The diviners envision lies,
And tell false dreams;
They comfort in vain.
Therefore *the people* wend their
way like sheep;
They are in trouble because *there
is* no shepherd.

3 "My anger is kindled against the
shepherds,
And I will punish the goatherds.
For the Lord of hosts will visit His
flock,
The house of Judah,
And will make them as His royal
horse in the battle.

4 From him comes the cornerstone,
From him the tent peg,
From him the battle bow,
From him every ruler[e] together.

5 They shall be like mighty men,
Who tread down *their enemies*
In the mire of the streets in the
battle.
They shall fight because the Lord
is with them,
And the riders on horses shall be
put to shame.

6 "I will strengthen the house of
Judah,
And I will save the house of Joseph.
I will bring them back,
Because I have mercy on them.
They shall be as though I had not
cast them aside;
For I *am* the Lord their God,
And I will hear them.

7 *Those of* Ephraim shall be like a
mighty man,
And their heart shall rejoice as if
with wine.
Yes, their children shall see *it* and
be glad;
Their heart shall rejoice in the
Lord.

8 I will whistle for them and gather
them,
For I will redeem them;
And they shall increase as they
once increased.

c Compare Psalm 72.8   d That is, spring rain   e Or *despot*

9 "I will sow them among the peoples,
  And they shall remember Me in far
    countries;
  They shall live, together with their
    children,
  And they shall return.
10 I will also bring them back from the
    land of Egypt,
  And gather them from Assyria.
  I will bring them into the land of
    Gilead and Lebanon,
  Until no *more room* is found for
    them.
11 He shall pass through the sea with
    affliction,
  And strike the waves of the sea:
  All the depths of the River*f* shall
    dry up.
  Then the pride of Assyria shall be
    brought down,
  And the scepter of Egypt shall
    depart.

12 "So I will strengthen them in the
    LORD,
  And they shall walk up and down
    in His name,"
  Says the LORD.

Desolation of Israel

11 Open your doors, O Lebanon,
  That fire may devour your
    cedars.
2 Wail, O cypress, for the cedar has
    fallen,
  Because the mighty *trees* are
    ruined.
  Wail, O oaks of Bashan,
  For the thick forest has come down.
3 *There is* the sound of wailing
    shepherds!
  For their glory is in ruins.
  There is the sound of roaring lions!
  For the pride of the Jordan is in
    ruins.

Prophecy of the Shepherds

4Thus says the LORD my God, "Feed
the flock for slaughter, 5whose owners
slaughter them and feel no guilt; those
who sell them say, 'Blessed be the LORD,
for I am rich'; and their shepherds do
not pity them. 6For I will no longer pity
the inhabitants of the land," says the
LORD. "But indeed I will give everyone

into his neighbor's hand and into the
hand of his king. They shall attack the
land, and I will not deliver *them* from
their hand."

7So I fed the flock for slaughter, in
particular the poor of the flock. I took
for myself two staffs: the one I called
Beauty, and the other I called Bonds;
and I fed the flock. 8I dismissed the
three shepherds in one month. My soul
loathed them, and their soul also abhorred me. 9Then I said, "I will not feed
you. Let what is dying die, and what is
perishing perish. Let those that are left
eat each other's flesh." 10And I took my
staff, Beauty, and cut it in two, that I
might break the covenant which I had
made with all the peoples. 11So it was
broken on that day. Thus the poor of
the flock, who were watching me, knew
that it *was* the word of the LORD.
12Then I said to them, "If it is agreeable
to you, give *me* my wages; and if not,
refrain." So they weighed out for my
wages thirty *pieces* of silver.

13And the LORD said to me, "Throw
it to the potter"—that princely price
they set on me. So I took the thirty
pieces of silver and threw them into the
house of the LORD for the potter.
14Then I cut in two my other staff,
Bonds, that I might break the brotherhood between Judah and Israel.

15And the LORD said to me, "Next,
take for yourself the implements of a
foolish shepherd. 16For indeed I will
raise up a shepherd in the land *who* will
not care for those who are cut off, nor
seek the young, nor heal those that are
broken, nor feed those that still stand.
But he will eat the flesh of the fat and
tear their hooves in pieces.
17 "Woe to the worthless shepherd,
  Who leaves the flock!
  A sword *shall be* against his arm
  And against his right eye;
  His arm shall completely wither,
  And his right eye shall be totally
    blinded."

The Coming Deliverance of Judah

12 The burden of the word of the
  LORD against Israel. Thus says the
LORD, who stretches out the heavens,
lays the foundation of the earth, and

f That is, the Nile

forms the spirit of man within him: 2"Behold, I will make Jerusalem a cup of drunkenness to all the surrounding peoples, when they lay siege against Judah and Jerusalem. 3And it shall happen in that day that I will make Jerusalem a very heavy stone for all peoples; all who would heave it away will surely be cut in pieces, though all nations of the earth are gathered against it. 4In that day," says the LORD, "I will strike every horse with confusion, and its rider with madness; I will open My eyes on the house of Judah, and will strike every horse of the peoples with blindness. 5And the governors of Judah shall say in their heart, 'The inhabitants of Jerusalem *are* my strength in the LORD of hosts, their God.' 6In that day I will make the governors of Judah like a firepan in the woodpile, and like a fiery torch in the sheaves; they shall devour all the surrounding peoples on the right hand and on the left, but Jerusalem shall be inhabited again in her own place—Jerusalem.

7"The LORD will save the tents of Judah first, so that the glory of the house of David and the glory of the inhabitants of Jerusalem shall not become greater than that of Judah. 8In that day the LORD will defend the inhabitants of Jerusalem; the one who is feeble among them in that day shall be like David, and the house of David *shall be* like God, like the Angel of the LORD before them. 9It shall be in that day *that* I will seek to destroy all the nations that come against Jerusalem.

Mourning for the Pierced One

10"And I will pour on the house of David and on the inhabitants of Jerusalem the Spirit of grace and supplication; then they will look on Me whom they pierced. Yes, they will mourn for Him as one mourns for *his* only *son,* and grieve for Him as one grieves for a firstborn. 11In that day there shall be a great mourning in Jerusalem, like the mourning at Hadad Rimmon in the plain of Megiddo. 12And the land shall mourn, every family by itself: the family of the house of David by itself, and their wives by themselves; the family of the house of Nathan by itself, and their wives by themselves; 13the family of the house

of Levi by itself, and their wives by themselves; the family of Shimei by itself, and their wives by themselves; 14all the families that remain, every family by itself, and their wives by themselves.

Idolatry Cut Off

13 "In that day a fountain shall be opened for the house of David and for the inhabitants of Jerusalem, for sin and for uncleanness.

2"It shall be in that day," says the LORD of hosts, "*that* I will cut off the names of the idols from the land, and they shall no longer be remembered. I will also cause the prophets and the unclean spirit to depart from the land. 3It shall come to pass *that* if anyone still prophesies, then his father and mother who begot him will say to him, 'You shall not live, because you have spoken lies in the name of the LORD.' And his father and mother who begot him shall thrust him through when he prophesies.

4"And it shall be in that day *that* every prophet will be ashamed of his vision when he prophesies; they will not wear a robe of coarse hair to deceive. 5But he will say, 'I *am* no prophet, I *am* a farmer; for a man taught me to keep cattle from my youth.' 6And *one* will say to him, 'What are these wounds between your arms?' Then he will answer, '*Those* with which I was wounded in the house of my friends.'

The Shepherd Savior

7 "Awake, O sword, against My
      Shepherd,
   Against the Man who is My
      Companion,"
   Says the LORD of hosts.
   "Strike the Shepherd,
   And the sheep will be scattered;
   Then I will turn My hand against
      the little ones.
8 And it shall come to pass in all the
      land,"
   Says the LORD,
   "*That* two-thirds in it shall be cut off
      and die,
   But *one*-third shall be left in it:
9 I will bring the *one*-third through
      the fire,
   Will refine them as silver is refined,

And test them as gold is tested.
They will call on My name,
And I will answer them.
I will say, 'This *is* My people';
And each one will say, 'The LORD
   is my God.'"

The Day of the LORD

14 Behold, the day of the LORD is
   coming,
And your spoil will be divided in
   your midst.
2 For I will gather all the nations to
      battle against Jerusalem;
The city shall be taken,
The houses rifled,
And the women ravished.
Half of the city shall go into
   captivity,
But the remnant of the people shall
   not be cut off from the city.

3 Then the LORD will go forth
And fight against those nations,
As He fights in the day of battle.
4 And in that day His feet will stand
      on the Mount of Olives,
Which faces Jerusalem on the east.
And the Mount of Olives shall be
   split in two,
From east to west,
Making a very large valley;
Half of the mountain shall move
   toward the north
And half of it toward the south.

5 Then you shall flee *through* My
      mountain valley,
For the mountain valley shall reach
   to Azal.
Yes, you shall flee
As you fled from the earthquake
In the days of Uzziah king of Judah.

Thus the LORD my God will come,
And all the saints with You.

6 It shall come to pass in that day
That there will be no light;
The lights will diminish.
7 It shall be one day
Which is known to the LORD—
Neither day nor night.
But at evening time it shall happen
That it will be light.

8 And in that day it shall be
That living waters shall flow from
   Jerusalem,
Half of them toward the
   eastern sea
And half of them toward the
   western sea;
In both summer and winter it shall
   occur.
9 And the LORD shall be King over
      all the earth.
In that day it shall be—
"The LORD *is* one,"[g]
And His name one.
10All the land shall be turned into a
plain from Geba to Rimmon south of
Jerusalem. *Jerusalem* shall be raised up
and inhabited in her place from Benjamin's Gate to the place of the First Gate
and the Corner Gate, and *from* the
Tower of Hananel to the king's winepresses.
11 *The people* shall dwell in it;
And no longer shall there be utter
   destruction,
But Jerusalem shall be safely
   inhabited.
12And this shall be the plague with
which the LORD will strike all the people
who fought against Jerusalem:
Their flesh shall dissolve while they
   stand on their feet,
Their eyes shall dissolve in their
   sockets,
And their tongues shall dissolve in
   their mouths.

13 It shall come to pass in that day
That a great panic from the LORD
   will be among them.
Everyone will seize the hand of his
   neighbor,
And raise his hand against his
   neighbor's hand;
14 Judah also will fight at Jerusalem.
And the wealth of all the
   surrounding nations
Shall be gathered together:
Gold, silver, and apparel in great
   abundance.

15 Such also shall be the plague
On the horse *and* the mule,
On the camel and the donkey,

g Compare Deuteronomy 6.4

And on all the cattle that will be
in those camps.
So *shall* this plague *be*.

The Nations Worship the King

16And it shall come to pass *that*
everyone who is left of all the nations
which came against Jerusalem shall go
up from year to year to worship the
King, the LORD of hosts, and to keep
the Feast of Tabernacles. 17And it shall
be *that* whichever of the families of the
earth do not come up to Jerusalem to
worship the King, the LORD of hosts, on
them there will be no rain. 18If the family of Egypt will not come up and enter
in, they *shall have* no *rain;* they shall
receive the plague with which the LORD
strikes the nations who do not come up
to keep the Feast of Tabernacles.
19This shall be the punishment of Egypt
and the punishment of all the nations
that do not come up to keep the Feast
of Tabernacles.

20In that day "HOLINESS TO THE
LORD" shall be *engraved* on the bells
of the horses. The pots in the LORD's
house shall be like the bowls before the
altar. 21Yes, every pot in Jerusalem and
Judah shall be holiness to the LORD of
hosts. Everyone who sacrifices shall
come and take them and cook in them.
In that day there shall no longer be a
Canaanite in the house of the LORD of
hosts.

The Book of
MALACHI

1 The burden of the word of the LORD
to Israel by Malachi.

Israel Beloved of God

2 "I have loved you," says the LORD.
"Yet you say, 'In what way have You
loved us?'
Was not Esau Jacob's brother?"
Says the LORD.
"Yet Jacob I have loved;
3 But Esau I have hated,
And laid waste his mountains and
his heritage
For the jackals of the wilderness."

4 Even though Edom has said,
"We have been impoverished,
But we will return and build the
desolate places,"
Thus says the LORD of hosts:
"They may build, but I will throw
down;
They shall be called the Territory
of Wickedness,
And the people against whom the
LORD will have indignation
forever.
5 Your eyes shall see,
And you shall say,
'The LORD is magnified beyond the
border of Israel.'

Polluted Offerings

6 "A son honors *his* father,
And a servant *his* master.
If then I am the Father,
Where *is* My honor?
And if I *am* a Master,
Where *is* My reverence?
Says the LORD of hosts
To you priests who despise My
name.
Yet you say, 'In what way have we
despised Your name?'

7 "You offer defiled food on My altar,
But say,
'In what way have we defiled You?'
By saying,

'The table of the LORD is
contemptible.'
8   And when you offer the blind as a
sacrifice,
Is it not evil?
And when you offer the lame and
sick,
Is it not evil?
Offer it then to your governor!
Would he be pleased with you?
Would he accept you favorably?"
Says the LORD of hosts.

9   "But now entreat God's favor,
That He may be gracious to us.
While this is being *done* by your
hands,
Will He accept you favorably?"
Says the LORD of hosts.
10 "Who *is there* even among you who
would shut the doors,
So that you would not kindle fire
on My altar in vain?
I have no pleasure in you,"
Says the LORD of hosts,
"Nor will I accept an offering from
your hands.
11 For from the rising of the sun, even
to its going down,
My name *shall be* great among the
Gentiles;
In every place incense *shall be*
offered to My name,
And a pure offering;
For My name shall be great among
the nations,"
Says the LORD of hosts.

12 "But you profane it,
In that you say,
'The table of the LORD is defiled;
And its fruit, its food, *is*
contemptible.'
13 You also say,
'Oh, what a weariness!'
And you sneer at it,"
Says the LORD of hosts.
"And you bring the stolen, the lame,
and the sick;
Thus you bring an offering!
Should I accept this from your
hand?"
Says the LORD.
14 "But cursed *be* the deceiver
Who has in his flock a male,
And takes a vow,

But sacrifices to the Lord what is
blemished—
For I *am* a great King,"
Says the LORD of hosts,
"And My name *is to be* feared
among the nations.

Corrupt Priests

2   "And now, O priests, this
commandment is for you.
2   If you will not hear,
And if you will not take *it* to heart,
To give glory to My name,"
Says the LORD of hosts,
"I will send a curse upon you,
And I will curse your blessings.
Yes, I have cursed them already,
Because you do not take *it* to heart.

3   "Behold, I will rebuke your
descendants
And spread refuse on your faces,
The refuse of your solemn feasts;
And *one* will take you away
with it.
4   Then you shall know that I have
sent this commandment to you,
That My covenant with Levi may
continue,"
Says the LORD of hosts.
5   "My covenant was with him, *one* of
life and peace,
And I gave them to him *that he
might* fear *Me*;
So he feared Me
And was reverent before My name.
6   The law of truth was in his mouth,
And injustice was not found on his
lips.
He walked with Me in peace and
equity,
And turned many away from
iniquity.

7   "For the lips of a priest should keep
knowledge,
And *people* should seek the law
from his mouth;
For he is the messenger of the LORD
of hosts.
8   But you have departed from
the way;
You have caused many to stumble
at the law.
You have corrupted the covenant
of Levi,"
Says the LORD of hosts.

9 "Therefore I also have made you
     contemptible and base
     Before all the people,
     Because you have not kept My
      ways
     But have shown partiality in
      the law."

Treachery of Infidelity

10 Have we not all one Father?
     Has not one God created us?
     Why do we deal treacherously with
      one another
     By profaning the covenant of the
      fathers?
11 Judah has dealt treacherously,
     And an abomination has been
      committed in Israel and in
      Jerusalem,
     For Judah has profaned
     The LORD's holy *institution* which
      He loves:
     He has married the daughter of a
      foreign god.
12 May the LORD cut off from the tents
      of Jacob
     The man who does this, being
      awake and aware,
     Yet who brings an offering to the
      LORD of hosts!

13 And this is the second thing you do:
     You cover the altar of the LORD
      with tears,
     With weeping and crying;
     So He does not regard the offering
      anymore,
     Nor receive *it* with goodwill from
      your hands.
14 Yet you say, "For what reason?"
     Because the LORD has been witness
     Between you and the wife of your
      youth,
     With whom you have dealt
      treacherously;
     Yet she is your companion
     And your wife by covenant.
15 But did He not make *them* one,
     Having a remnant of the Spirit?
     And why one?
     He seeks godly offspring.
     Therefore take heed to your spirit,
     And let none deal treacherously
      with the wife of his youth.

16 "For the LORD God of Israel says
     That He hates divorce,

     For it covers one's garment with
      violence,"
     Says the LORD of hosts.
    "Therefore take heed to your spirit,
     That you do not deal
      treacherously."

17 You have wearied the LORD with
      your words;
     Yet you say,
    "In what way have we
      wearied *Him*?"
     In that you say,
    "Everyone who does evil
     Is good in the sight of the LORD,
     And He delights in them,"
     Or, "Where *is* the God of justice?"

The Coming Messenger

3 "Behold, I send My messenger,
     And he will prepare the way
      before Me.
     And the Lord, whom you seek,
     Will suddenly come to His temple,
     Even the Messenger of the
      covenant,
     In whom you delight.
     Behold, He is coming,"
     Says the LORD of hosts.

2 "But who can endure the day of His
      coming?
     And who can stand when He
      appears?
     For He *is* like a refiner's fire
     And like launderers' soap.
3 He will sit as a refiner and a purifier
      of silver;
     He will purify the sons of Levi,
     And purge them as gold and silver,
     That they may offer to the LORD
     An offering in righteousness.

4 "Then the offering of Judah and
      Jerusalem
     Will be pleasant to the LORD,
     As in the days of old,
     As in former years.
5 And I will come near you for
      judgment;
     I will be a swift witness
     Against sorcerers,
     Against adulterers,
     Against perjurers,
     Against those who exploit wage
      earners and widows and
      orphans,

And against those who turn away
an alien—
Because they do not fear Me,"
Says the LORD of hosts.

6 "For I *am* the LORD, I do not change;
Therefore you are not consumed,
O sons of Jacob.
7 Yet from the days of your fathers
You have gone away from My
ordinances
And have not kept *them*.
Return to Me, and I will return
to you,"
Says the LORD of hosts.
"But you said,
'In what way shall we return?'

Do Not Rob God

8 "Will a man rob God?
Yet you have robbed Me!
But you say,
'In what way have we robbed You?'
In tithes and offerings.
9 You are cursed with a curse,
For you have robbed Me,
Even this whole nation.
10 Bring all the tithes into the
storehouse,
That there may be food in My
house,
And try Me now in this,"
Says the LORD of hosts,
"If I will not open for you the
windows of heaven
And pour out for you *such* blessing
That *there will* not *be room* enough
to receive it.

11 "And I will rebuke the devourer for
your sakes,
So that he will not destroy the fruit
of your ground,
Nor shall the vine fail to bear fruit
for you in the field,"
Says the LORD of hosts;
12 And all nations will call you
blessed,
For you will be a delightful land,"
Says the LORD of hosts.

The People Complain Harshly

13 "Your words have been harsh
against Me,"
Says the LORD,
"Yet you say,

'What have we spoken
against You?'
14 You have said,
'It is useless to serve God;
What profit *is it* that we have kept
His ordinance,
And *that* we have walked as
mourners
Before the LORD of hosts?
15 So now we call the proud
blessed,
For those who do wickedness are
raised up;
They even tempt God and go
free.' "

A Book of Remembrance

16 Then those who feared the LORD
spoke to one another,
And the LORD listened and heard
them;
So a book of remembrance was
written before Him
For those who fear the LORD
And who meditate on His name.

17 "They shall be Mine," says the LORD
of hosts,
"On the day that I make them My
jewels.
And I will spare them
As a man spares his own son who
serves him."
18 Then you shall again discern
Between the righteous and the
wicked,
Between one who serves God
And one who does not serve Him.

The Great Day of God

4 "For behold, the day is coming,
Burning like an oven,
And all the proud, yes, all who do
wickedly will be stubble.
And the day which is coming shall
burn them up,"
Says the LORD of hosts,
"That will leave them neither root
nor branch.
2 But to you who fear My name
The Sun of Righteousness shall
arise
With healing in His wings;
And you shall go out
And grow fat like stall-fed
calves.

3 You shall trample the wicked,
For they shall be ashes under the
soles of your feet
On the day that I do *this*,"
Says the Lord of hosts.

4 "Remember the Law of Moses, My
servant,
Which I commanded him in Horeb
for all Israel,
With the statutes and judgments.

5 Behold, I will send you Elijah the
prophet
Before the coming of the great and
dreadful day of the Lord.
6 And he will turn
The hearts of the fathers to the
children,
And the hearts of the children to
their fathers,
Lest I come and strike the earth
with a curse."

MATTHEW

The Genealogy of Jesus Christ

1 The book of the genealogy of Jesus Christ, the Son of David, the Son of Abraham:

2Abraham begot Isaac, Isaac begot Jacob, and Jacob begot Judah and his brothers. 3Judah begot Perez and Zerah by Tamar, Perez begot Hezron, and Hezron begot Ram. 4Ram begot Amminadab, Amminadab begot Nahshon, and Nahshon begot Salmon. 5Salmon begot Boaz by Rahab, Boaz begot Obed by Ruth, Obed begot Jesse, 6and Jesse begot David the king.

David the king begot Solomon by her *who had been the wife* of Uriah. 7Solomon begot Rehoboam, Rehoboam begot Abijah, and Abijah begot Asa. 8Asa begot Jehoshaphat, Jehoshaphat begot Joram, and Joram begot Uzziah. 9Uzziah begot Jotham, Jotham begot Ahaz, and Ahaz begot Hezekiah. 10Hezekiah begot Manasseh, Manasseh begot Amon, and Amon begot Josiah. 11Josiah begot Jeconiah and his brothers about the time they were carried away to Babylon.

12And after they were brought to Babylon, Jeconiah begot Shealtiel, and Shealtiel begot Zerubbabel. 13Zerubbabel begot Abiud, Abiud begot Eliakim, and Eliakim begot Azor. 14Azor begot Zadok, Zadok begot Achim, and Achim begot Eliud. 15Eliud begot Eleazar, Eleazar begot Matthan, and Matthan begot Jacob. 16And Jacob begot Joseph the husband of Mary, of whom was born Jesus who is called Christ.

17So all the generations from Abraham to David *are* fourteen generations, from David until the captivity in Babylon *are* fourteen generations, and from the captivity in Babylon until the Christ *are* fourteen generations.

Christ Born of Mary

18Now the birth of Jesus Christ was as follows: After His mother Mary was betrothed to Joseph, before they came together, she was found with child of

a Isaiah 7.14

the Holy Spirit. 19Then Joseph her husband, being a just *man,* and not wanting to make her a public example, was minded to put her away secretly. 20But while he thought about these things, behold, an angel of the Lord appeared to him in a dream, saying, "Joseph, son of David, do not be afraid to take to you Mary your wife, for that which is conceived in her is of the Holy Spirit. 21And she will bring forth a Son, and you shall call His name JESUS, for He will save His people from their sins."

22So all this was done that it might be fulfilled which was spoken by the Lord through the prophet, saying: 23"Behold, the virgin shall be with child, and bear a Son, and they shall call His name Immanuel,"*a* which is translated, "God with us."

24Then Joseph, being aroused from sleep, did as the angel of the Lord commanded him and took to him his wife, 25and did not know her till she had brought forth her firstborn Son. And he called His name JESUS.

Wise Men from the East

2 Now after Jesus was born in Bethlehem of Judea in the days of Herod the king, behold, wise men from the East came to Jerusalem, 2saying, "Where is He who has been born King of the Jews? For we have seen His star in the East and have come to worship Him."

3When Herod the king heard *this,* he was troubled, and all Jerusalem with him. 4And when he had gathered all the chief priests and scribes of the people together, he inquired of them where the Christ was to be born.

5So they said to him, "In Bethlehem of Judea, for thus it is written by the prophet:

6 'But you, Bethlehem, *in* the land of Judah,

Are not the least among the rulers of Judah;

For out of you shall come a Ruler
Who will shepherd My people
     Israel.' "[b]

7Then Herod, when he had secretly called the wise men, determined from them what time the star appeared. 8And he sent them to Bethlehem and said, "Go and search carefully for the young Child, and when you have found *Him*, bring back word to me, that I may come and worship Him also."

9When they heard the king, they departed; and behold, the star which they had seen in the East went before them, till it came and stood over where the young Child was. 10When they saw the star, they rejoiced with exceedingly great joy. 11And when they had come into the house, they saw the young Child with Mary His mother, and fell down and worshiped Him. And when they had opened their treasures, they presented gifts to Him: gold, frankincense, and myrrh.

12Then, being divinely warned in a dream that they should not return to Herod, they departed for their own country another way.

The Flight into Egypt

13Now when they had departed, behold, an angel of the Lord appeared to Joseph in a dream, saying, "Arise, take the young Child and His mother, flee to Egypt, and stay there until I bring you word; for Herod will seek the young Child to destroy Him."

14When he arose, he took the young Child and His mother by night and departed for Egypt, 15and was there until the death of Herod, that it might be fulfilled which was spoken by the Lord through the prophet, saying, "Out of Egypt I called My Son."[c]

Massacre of the Innocents

16Then Herod, when he saw that he was deceived by the wise men, was exceedingly angry; and he sent forth and put to death all the male children who were in Bethlehem and in all its districts, from two years old and under, according to the time which he had determined from the wise men. 17Then was fulfilled what was spoken by Jeremiah the prophet, saying:

18 "A voice was heard in Ramah,
     Lamentation, weeping, and great
       mourning,
     Rachel weeping *for* her children,
     Refusing to be comforted,
     Because they are no more."[d]

The Home in Nazareth

19Now when Herod was dead, behold, an angel of the Lord appeared in a dream to Joseph in Egypt, 20saying, "Arise, take the young Child and His mother, and go to the land of Israel, for those who sought the young Child's life are dead." 21Then he arose, took the young Child and His mother, and came into the land of Israel.

22But when he heard that Archelaus was reigning over Judea instead of his father Herod, he was afraid to go there. And being warned by God in a dream, he turned aside into the region of Galilee. 23And he came and dwelt in a city called Nazareth, that it might be fulfilled which was spoken by the prophets, "He shall be called a Nazarene."

John the Baptist Prepares the Way

3 In those days John the Baptist came preaching in the wilderness of Judea, 2and saying, "Repent, for the kingdom of heaven is at hand!" 3For this is he who was spoken of by the prophet Isaiah, saying:

"The voice of one crying in the
     wilderness:
'Prepare the way of the LORD;
     Make His paths straight.' "[e]

4Now John himself was clothed in camel's hair, with a leather belt around his waist; and his food was locusts and wild honey. 5Then Jerusalem, all Judea, and all the region around the Jordan went out to him 6and were baptized by him in the Jordan, confessing their sins.

7But when he saw many of the Pharisees and Sadducees coming to his baptism, he said to them, "Brood of vipers! Who warned you to flee from the wrath to come? 8Therefore bear fruits worthy of repentance, 9and do not think to say to yourselves, 'We have Abraham as

b Micah 5.2   *c* Hosea 11.1   *d* Jeremiah 31.15   *e* Isaiah 40.3

our father.' For I say to you that God is able to raise up children to Abraham from these stones. 10And even now the ax is laid to the root of the trees. Therefore every tree which does not bear good fruit is cut down and thrown into the fire. 11I indeed baptize you with water unto repentance, but He who is coming after me is mightier than I, whose sandals I am not worthy to carry. He will baptize you with the Holy Spirit and fire. 12His winnowing fan *is* in His hand, and He will thoroughly clean out His threshing floor, and gather His wheat into the barn; but He will burn up the chaff with unquenchable fire.''

John Baptizes Jesus

13Then Jesus came from Galilee to John at the Jordan to be baptized by him. 14And John *tried to* prevent Him, saying, "I need to be baptized by You, and are You coming to me?''

15But Jesus answered and said to him, "Permit *it to be so* now, for thus it is fitting for us to fulfill all righteousness.'' Then he allowed Him.

16When He had been baptized, Jesus came up immediately from the water; and behold, the heavens were opened to Him, and He saw the Spirit of God descending like a dove and alighting upon Him. 17And suddenly a voice *came* from heaven, saying, "This is My beloved Son, in whom I am well pleased.''

Satan Tempts Jesus

4 Then Jesus was led up by the Spirit into the wilderness to be tempted by the devil. 2And when He had fasted forty days and forty nights, afterward He was hungry. 3Now when the tempter came to Him, he said, "If You are the Son of God, command that these stones become bread.''

4But He answered and said, "It is written, 'Man shall not live by bread alone, but by every word that proceeds from the mouth of God.' ''[f]

5Then the devil took Him up into the holy city, set Him on the pinnacle of the temple, 6and said to Him, "If You are the Son of God, throw Yourself down. For it is written:

'He shall give His angels charge
    over you,'

and,

'In *their* hands they shall bear you
    up,
Lest you dash your foot against a
    stone.' ''[g]

7Jesus said to him, "It is written again, 'You shall not tempt the LORD your God.' ''[h]

8Again, the devil took Him up on an exceedingly high mountain, and showed Him all the kingdoms of the world and their glory. 9And he said to Him, "All these things I will give You if You will fall down and worship me.''

10Then Jesus said to him, "Away with you, Satan! For it is written, 'You shall worship the LORD your God, and Him only you shall serve.' ''[i]

11Then the devil left Him, and behold, angels came and ministered to Him.

Jesus Begins His Galilean Ministry

12Now when Jesus heard that John had been put in prison, He departed to Galilee. 13And leaving Nazareth, He came and dwelt in Capernaum, which is by the sea, in the regions of Zebulun and Naphtali, 14that it might be fulfilled which was spoken by Isaiah the prophet, saying:

15 "The land of Zebulun and the land
    of Naphtali,
  By the way of the sea, beyond the
    Jordan,
  Galilee of the Gentiles:
16 The people who sat in darkness
    have seen a great light,
  And upon those who sat in the
    region and shadow of death
  Light has dawned.''[j]

17From that time Jesus began to preach and to say, "Repent, for the kingdom of heaven is at hand.''

Four Fishermen Called as Disciples

18And Jesus, walking by the Sea of Galilee, saw two brothers, Simon called Peter, and Andrew his brother, casting a net into the sea; for they were fishermen. 19Then He said to them, "Follow

f Deuteronomy 8.3   *g* Psalm 91.11, 12   *h* Deuteronomy 6.16   *i* Deuteronomy 6.13
j Isaiah 9.1, 2

Me, and I will make you fishers of men." 20They immediately left *their* nets and followed Him.

21Going on from there, He saw two other brothers, James *the son* of Zebedee, and John his brother, in the boat with Zebedee their father, mending their nets. He called them, 22and immediately they left the boat and their father, and followed Him.

Jesus Heals a Great Multitude

23And Jesus went about all Galilee, teaching in their synagogues, preaching the gospel of the kingdom, and healing all kinds of sickness and all kinds of disease among the people. 24Then His fame went throughout all Syria; and they brought to Him all sick people who were afflicted with various diseases and torments, and those who were demon-possessed, epileptics, and paralytics; and He healed them. 25Great multitudes followed Him—from Galilee, and *from* Decapolis, Jerusalem, Judea, and beyond the Jordan.

The Beatitudes

5 And seeing the multitudes, He went up on a mountain, and when He was seated His disciples came to Him. 2Then He opened His mouth and taught them, saying:

3   "Blessed *are* the poor in spirit,
       For theirs is the kingdom of
          heaven.
4   Blessed *are* those who mourn,
       For they shall be comforted.
5   Blessed *are* the meek,
       For they shall inherit the earth.
6   Blessed *are* those who hunger and
          thirst for righteousness,
       For they shall be filled.
7   Blessed *are* the merciful,
       For they shall obtain mercy.
8   Blessed *are* the pure in heart,
       For they shall see God.
9   Blessed *are* the peacemakers,
       For they shall be called sons of
          God.
10   Blessed are those who are
          persecuted for righteousness'
          sake,

For theirs is the kingdom of
          heaven.

11"Blessed are you when they revile and persecute you, and say all kinds of evil against you falsely for My sake. 12Rejoice and be exceedingly glad, for great *is* your reward in heaven, for so they persecuted the prophets who were before you.

Believers Are Salt and Light

13"You are the salt of the earth; but if the salt loses its flavor, how shall it be seasoned? It is then good for nothing but to be thrown out and trampled underfoot by men.

14"You are the light of the world. A city that is set on a hill cannot be hidden. 15Nor do they light a lamp and put it under a basket, but on a lampstand, and it gives light to all *who are* in the house. 16Let your light so shine before men, that they may see your good works and glorify your Father in heaven.

Christ Fulfills the Law

17"Do not think that I came to destroy the Law or the Prophets. I did not come to destroy but to fulfill. 18For assuredly, I say to you, till heaven and earth pass away, one jot or one tittle will by no means pass from the law till all is fulfilled. 19Whoever therefore breaks one of the least of these commandments, and teaches men so, shall be called least in the kingdom of heaven; but whoever does and teaches *them*, he shall be called great in the kingdom of heaven. 20For I say to you, that unless your righteousness exceeds *the righteousness* of the scribes and Pharisees, you will by no means enter the kingdom of heaven.

Murder Begins in the Heart

21"You have heard that it was said to those of old, 'You shall not murder,*k* and whoever murders will be in danger of the judgment.' 22But I say to you that whoever is angry with his brother without a cause shall be in danger of the judgment. And whoever says to his brother, 'Raca!' shall be in danger of

k Exodus 20.13; Deuteronomy 5.17

the council. But whoever says, 'You fool!' shall be in danger of hell fire. 23Therefore if you bring your gift to the altar, and there remember that your brother has something against you, 24leave your gift there before the altar, and go your way. First be reconciled to your brother, and then come and offer your gift. 25Agree with your adversary quickly, while you are on the way with him, lest your adversary deliver you to the judge, the judge hand you over to the officer, and you be thrown into prison. 26Assuredly, I say to you, you will by no means get out of there till you have paid the last penny.

Adultery in the Heart

27"You have heard that it was said to those of old, 'You shall not commit adultery.'*l* 28But I say to you that whoever looks at a woman to lust for her has already committed adultery with her in his heart. 29If your right eye causes you to sin, pluck it out and cast *it* from you; for it is more profitable for you that one of your members perish, than for your whole body to be cast into hell. 30And if your right hand causes you to sin, cut it off and cast *it* from you; for it is more profitable for you that one of your members perish, than for your whole body to be cast into hell.

Marriage Is Sacred and Binding

31"Furthermore it has been said, 'Whoever divorces his wife, let him give her a certificate of divorce.'*m* 32But I say to you that whoever divorces his wife for any reason except sexual immorality causes her to commit adultery; and whoever marries a woman who is divorced commits adultery.

Jesus Forbids Oaths

33"Again you have heard that it was said to those of old, 'You shall not swear falsely, but shall perform your oaths to the Lord.' 34But I say to you, do not swear at all: neither by heaven, for it is God's throne; 35nor by the earth, for it is His footstool; nor by Jerusalem, for it is the city of the great King. 36Nor shall you swear by your head, be-

cause you cannot make one hair white or black. 37But let your 'Yes' be 'Yes,' and your 'No,' 'No.' For whatever is more than these is from the evil one.

Go the Second Mile

38"You have heard that it was said, 'An eye for an eye and a tooth for a tooth.'*n* 39But I tell you not to resist an evil person. But whoever slaps you on your right cheek, turn the other to him also. 40If anyone wants to sue you and take away your tunic, let him have *your* cloak also. 41And whoever compels you to go one mile, go with him two. 42Give to him who asks you, and from him who wants to borrow from you do not turn away.

Love Your Enemies

43"You have heard that it was said, 'You shall love your neighbor*o* and hate your enemy.' 44But I say to you, love your enemies, bless those who curse you, do good to those who hate you, and pray for those who spitefully use you and persecute you, 45that you may be sons of your Father in heaven; for He makes His sun rise on the evil and on the good, and sends rain on the just and on the unjust. 46For if you love those who love you, what reward have you? Do not even the tax collectors do the same? 47And if you greet your brethren only, what do you do more *than others?* Do not even the tax collectors do so? 48Therefore you shall be perfect, just as your Father in heaven is perfect.

Do Good to Please God

6 "Take heed that you do not do your charitable deeds before men, to be seen by them. Otherwise you have no reward from your Father in heaven. 2Therefore, when you do a charitable deed, do not sound a trumpet before you as the hypocrites do in the synagogues and in the streets, that they may have glory from men. Assuredly, I say to you, they have their reward. 3But when you do a charitable deed, do not let your left hand know what your right hand is doing, 4that your charitable

l Exodus 20.14; Deuteronomy 5.18   *m* Deuteronomy 24.1   *n* Exodus 21.24; Leviticus 24.20; Deuteronomy 19.21   *o* Leviticus 19.18

deed may be in secret; and your Father who sees in secret will Himself reward you openly.

The Model Prayer

5"And when you pray, you shall not be like the hypocrites. For they love to pray standing in the synagogues and on the corners of the streets, that they may be seen by men. Assuredly, I say to you, they have their reward. 6But you, when you pray, go into your room, and when you have shut your door, pray to your Father who *is* in the secret *place;* and your Father who sees in secret will reward you openly. 7And when you pray, do not use vain repetitions as the heathen *do.* For they think that they will be heard for their many words.

8"Therefore do not be like them. For your Father knows the things you have need of before you ask Him. 9In this manner, therefore, pray:

Our Father in heaven,
Hallowed be Your name.
10 Your kingdom come.
Your will be done
On earth as *it is* in heaven.
11 Give us this day our daily bread.
12 And forgive us our debts,
As we forgive our debtors.
13 And do not lead us into temptation,
But deliver us from the evil one.
For Yours is the kingdom and the power and the glory forever.
Amen.

14"For if you forgive men their trespasses, your heavenly Father will also forgive you. 15But if you do not forgive men their trespasses, neither will your Father forgive your trespasses.

Fasting to Be Seen Only by God

16"Moreover, when you fast, do not be like the hypocrites, with a sad countenance. For they disfigure their faces that they may appear to men to be fasting. Assuredly, I say to you, they have their reward. 17But you, when you fast, anoint your head and wash your face, 18so that you do not appear to men to be fasting, but to your Father who *is* in the secret *place;* and your Father who sees in secret will reward you openly.

Lay Up Treasures in Heaven

19"Do not lay up for yourselves treasures on earth, where moth and rust destroy and where thieves break in and steal; 20but lay up for yourselves treasures in heaven, where neither moth nor rust destroys and where thieves do not break in and steal. 21For where your treasure is, there your heart will be also.

The Lamp of the Body

22"The lamp of the body is the eye. If therefore your eye is good, your whole body will be full of light. 23But if your eye is bad, your whole body will be full of darkness. If therefore the light that is in you is darkness, how great *is* that darkness!

You Cannot Serve God and Riches

24"No one can serve two masters; for either he will hate the one and love the other, or else he will be loyal to the one and despise the other. You cannot serve God and mammon.

Do Not Worry

25"Therefore I say to you, do not worry about your life, what you will eat or what you will drink; nor about your body, what you will put on. Is not life more than food and the body more than clothing? 26Look at the birds of the air, for they neither sow nor reap nor gather into barns; yet your heavenly Father feeds them. Are you not of more value than they? 27Which of you by worrying can add one cubit to his stature?

28"So why do you worry about clothing? Consider the lilies of the field, how they grow: they neither toil nor spin; 29and yet I say to you that even Solomon in all his glory was not arrayed like one of these. 30Now if God so clothes the grass of the field, which today is, and tomorrow is thrown into the oven, *will He* not much more *clothe* you, O you of little faith?

31"Therefore do not worry, saying, 'What shall we eat?' or 'What shall we drink?' or 'What shall we wear?' 32For after all these things the Gentiles seek. For your heavenly Father knows that you need all these things. 33But seek first the kingdom of God and His righteousness, and all these things shall be added to you. 34Therefore do not worry about tomorrow, for tomorrow will worry about its own things. Sufficient for the day is its own trouble.

Do Not Judge

7 "Judge not, that you be not judged. 2For with what judgment you judge, you will be judged; and with the measure you use, it will be measured back to you. 3And why do you look at the speck in your brother's eye, but do not consider the plank in your own eye? 4Or how can you say to your brother, 'Let me remove the speck from your eye'; and look, a plank is in your own eye? 5Hypocrite! First remove the plank from your own eye, and then you will see clearly to remove the speck from your brother's eye.

6"Do not give what is holy to the dogs; nor cast your pearls before swine, lest they trample them under their feet, and turn and tear you in pieces.

Keep Asking, Seeking, Knocking

7"Ask, and it will be given to you; seek, and you will find; knock, and it will be opened to you. 8For everyone who asks receives, and he who seeks finds, and to him who knocks it will be opened. 9Or what man is there among you who, if his son asks for bread, will give him a stone? 10Or if he asks for a fish, will he give him a serpent? 11If you then, being evil, know how to give good gifts to your children, how much more will your Father who is in heaven give good things to those who ask Him! 12Therefore, whatever you want men to do to you, do also to them, for this is the Law and the Prophets.

The Narrow Way

13"Enter by the narrow gate; for wide is the gate and broad is the way that leads to destruction, and there are many who go in by it. 14Because narrow is the gate and difficult is the way which leads to life, and there are few who find it.

You Will Know Them by Their Fruits

15"Beware of false prophets, who come to you in sheep's clothing, but inwardly they are ravenous wolves. 16You will know them by their fruits. Do men gather grapes from thornbushes or figs from thistles? 17Even so,

every good tree bears good fruit, but a bad tree bears bad fruit. 18A good tree cannot bear bad fruit, nor can a bad tree bear good fruit. 19Every tree that does not bear good fruit is cut down and thrown into the fire. 20Therefore by their fruits you will know them.

I Never Knew You

21"Not everyone who says to Me, 'Lord, Lord,' shall enter the kingdom of heaven, but he who does the will of My Father in heaven. 22Many will say to Me in that day, 'Lord, Lord, have we not prophesied in Your name, cast out demons in Your name, and done many wonders in Your name?' 23And then I will declare to them, 'I never knew you; depart from Me, you who practice lawlessness!'

Build on the Rock

24"Therefore whoever hears these sayings of Mine, and does them, I will liken him to a wise man who built his house on the rock: 25and the rain descended, the floods came, and the winds blew and beat on that house; and it did not fall, for it was founded on the rock. 26"But everyone who hears these sayings of Mine, and does not do them, will be like a foolish man who built his house on the sand: 27and the rain descended, the floods came, and the winds blew and beat on that house; and it fell. And great was its fall."

28And so it was, when Jesus had ended these sayings, that the people were astonished at His teaching, 29for He taught them as one having authority, and not as the scribes.

Jesus Cleanses a Leper

8 When He had come down from the mountain, great multitudes followed Him. 2And behold, a leper came and worshiped Him, saying, "Lord, if You are willing, You can make me clean."

3Then Jesus put out His hand and touched him, saying, "I am willing; be cleansed." Immediately his leprosy was cleansed.

4And Jesus said to him, "See that you tell no one; but go your way, show yourself to the priest, and offer the gift that Moses commanded, as a testimony to them."

Jesus Heals a Centurion's Servant

5Now when Jesus had entered Capernaum, a centurion came to Him, pleading with Him, 6saying, "Lord, my servant is lying at home paralyzed, dreadfully tormented."

7And Jesus said to him, "I will come and heal him."

8The centurion answered and said, "Lord, I am not worthy that You should come under my roof. But only speak a word, and my servant will be healed. 9For I also am a man under authority, having soldiers under me. And I say to this *one,* 'Go,' and he goes; and to another, 'Come,' and he comes; and to my servant, 'Do this,' and he does *it.*"

10When Jesus heard *it,* He marveled, and said to those who followed, "Assuredly, I say to you, I have not found such great faith, not even in Israel! 11And I say to you that many will come from east and west, and sit down with Abraham, Isaac, and Jacob in the kingdom of heaven. 12But the sons of the kingdom will be cast out into outer darkness. There will be weeping and gnashing of teeth." 13Then Jesus said to the centurion, "Go your way; and as you have believed, *so* let it be done for you." And his servant was healed that same hour.

Peter's Mother-in-Law Healed

14Now when Jesus had come into Peter's house, He saw his wife's mother lying sick with a fever. 15So He touched her hand, and the fever left her. And she arose and served them.

Many Healed After Sabbath Sunset

16When evening had come, they brought to Him many who were demon-possessed. And He cast out the spirits with a word, and healed all who were sick, 17that it might be fulfilled which was spoken by Isaiah the prophet, saying:

"He Himself took our infirmities
And bore *our* sicknesses."[p]

The Cost of Discipleship

18And when Jesus saw great multitudes about Him, He gave a command to depart to the other side. 19Then a certain scribe came and said to Him, "Teacher, I will follow You wherever You go."

20And Jesus said to him, "Foxes have holes and birds of the air *have* nests, but the Son of Man has nowhere to lay *His* head."

21Then another of His disciples said to Him, "Lord, let me first go and bury my father."

22But Jesus said to him, "Follow Me, and let the dead bury their own dead."

Wind and Wave Obey Jesus

23Now when He got into a boat, His disciples followed Him. 24And suddenly a great tempest arose on the sea, so that the boat was covered with the waves. But He was asleep. 25Then His disciples came to *Him* and awoke Him, saying, "Lord, save us! We are perishing!"

26But He said to them, "Why are you fearful, O you of little faith?" Then He arose and rebuked the winds and the sea, and there was a great calm. 27So the men marveled, saying, "Who can this be, that even the winds and the sea obey Him?"

Two Demon-Possessed Men Healed

28When He had come to the other side, to the country of the Gergesenes, there met Him two demon-possessed *men,* coming out of the tombs, exceedingly fierce, so that no one could pass that way. 29And suddenly they cried out, saying, "What have we to do with You, Jesus, You Son of God? Have You come here to torment us before the time?"

30Now a good way off from them there was a herd of many swine feeding. 31So the demons begged Him, saying, "If You cast us out, permit us to go away into the herd of swine."

32And He said to them, "Go." So when they had come out, they went into the herd of swine. And suddenly the whole herd of swine ran violently down the steep place into the sea, and perished in the water.

33Then those who kept *them* fled; and they went away into the city and told everything, including what *had happened* to the demon-possessed *men.*

p Isaiah 53.4

34And behold, the whole city came out to meet Jesus. And when they saw Him, they begged *Him* to depart from their region.

Jesus Forgives and Heals a Paralytic

9 So He got into a boat, crossed over, and came to His own city. 2Then behold, they brought to Him a paralytic lying on a bed. When Jesus saw their faith, He said to the paralytic, "Son, be of good cheer; your sins are forgiven you."

3And at once some of the scribes said within themselves, "This Man blasphemes!"

4But Jesus, knowing their thoughts, said, "Why do you think evil in your hearts? 5For which is easier, to say, '*Your* sins are forgiven you,' or to say, 'Arise and walk'? 6But that you may know that the Son of Man has power on earth to forgive sins"—then He said to the paralytic, "Arise, take up your bed, and go to your house." 7And he arose and departed to his house.

8Now when the multitudes saw *it*, they marveled and glorified God, who had given such power to men.

Matthew the Tax Collector

9As Jesus passed on from there, He saw a man named Matthew sitting at the tax office. And He said to him, "Follow Me." So he arose and followed Him.

10Now it happened, as Jesus sat at the table in the house, *that* behold, many tax collectors and sinners came and sat down with Him and His disciples. 11And when the Pharisees saw *it*, they said to His disciples, "Why does your Teacher eat with tax collectors and sinners?"

12When Jesus heard *that*, He said to them, "Those who are well have no need of a physician, but those who are sick. 13But go and learn what *this* means: 'I desire mercy and not sacrifice.'q For I did not come to call the righteous, but sinners, to repentance."

Jesus Is Questioned About Fasting

14Then the disciples of John came to Him, saying, "Why do we and the Phar-

isees fast often, but Your disciples do not fast?"

15And Jesus said to them, "Can the friends of the bridegroom mourn as long as the bridegroom is with them? But the days will come when the bridegroom will be taken away from them, and then they will fast. 16No one puts a piece of unshrunk cloth on an old garment; for the patch pulls away from the garment, and the tear is made worse. 17Nor do they put new wine into old wineskins, or else the wineskins break, the wine is spilled, and the wineskins are ruined. But they put new wine into new wineskins, and both are preserved."

A Girl Restored to Life and a Woman Healed

18While He spoke these things to them, behold, a ruler came and worshiped Him, saying, "My daughter has just died, but come and lay Your hand on her and she will live." 19So Jesus arose and followed him, and so *did* His disciples.

20And suddenly, a woman who had a flow of blood for twelve years came from behind and touched the hem of His garment. 21For she said to herself, "If only I may touch His garment, I shall be made well." 22But Jesus turned around, and when He saw her He said, "Be of good cheer, daughter; your faith has made you well." And the woman was made well from that hour.

23When Jesus came into the ruler's house, and saw the flute players and the noisy crowd wailing, 24He said to them, "Make room, for the girl is not dead, but sleeping." And they ridiculed Him. 25But when the crowd was put outside, He went in and took her by the hand, and the girl arose. 26And the report of this went out into all that land.

Two Blind Men Healed

27When Jesus departed from there, two blind men followed Him, crying out and saying, "Son of David, have mercy on us!"

28And when He had come into the house, the blind men came to Him. And

q Hosea 6.6

Jesus said to them, "Do you believe that I am able to do this?"

They said to Him, "Yes, Lord."

29Then He touched their eyes, saying, "According to your faith let it be to you." 30And their eyes were opened. And Jesus sternly warned them, saying, "See *that* no one knows *it.*" 31But when they had departed, they spread the news about Him in all that country.

A Mute Man Speaks

32As they went out, behold, they brought to Him a man, mute and demon-possessed. 33And when the demon was cast out, the mute spoke. And the multitudes marveled, saying, "It was never seen like this in Israel!" 34But the Pharisees said, "He casts out demons by the ruler of the demons."

The Compassion of Jesus

35Then Jesus went about all the cities and villages, teaching in their synagogues, preaching the gospel of the kingdom, and healing every sickness and every disease among the people. 36But when He saw the multitudes, He was moved with compassion for them, because they were weary and scattered, like sheep having no shepherd. 37Then He said to His disciples, "The harvest truly *is* plentiful, but the laborers *are* few. 38Therefore pray the Lord of the harvest to send out laborers into His harvest."

The Twelve Apostles

10 And when He had called His twelve disciples to *Him*, He gave them power *over* unclean spirits, to cast them out, and to heal all kinds of sickness and all kinds of disease. 2Now the names of the twelve apostles are these: first, Simon, who is called Peter, and Andrew his brother; James the *son* of Zebedee, and John his brother; 3Philip and Bartholomew; Thomas and Matthew the tax collector; James the *son* of Alphaeus, and Lebbaeus, whose surname was Thaddaeus; 4Simon the Cananite, and Judas Iscariot, who also betrayed Him.

Sending Out the Twelve

5These twelve Jesus sent out and commanded them, saying: "Do not go into the way of the Gentiles, and do not enter a city of the Samaritans. 6But go rather to the lost sheep of the house of Israel. 7And as you go, preach, saying, 'The kingdom of heaven is at hand.' 8Heal the sick, cleanse the lepers, raise the dead, cast out demons. Freely you have received, freely give. 9Provide neither gold nor silver nor copper in your money belts, 10nor bag for *your* journey, nor two tunics, nor sandals, nor staffs; for a worker is worthy of his food.

11"Now whatever city or town you enter, inquire who in it is worthy, and stay there till you go out. 12And when you go into a household, greet it. 13If the household is worthy, let your peace come upon it. But if it is not worthy, let your peace return to you. 14And whoever will not receive you nor hear your words, when you depart from that house or city, shake off the dust from your feet. 15Assuredly, I say to you, it will be more tolerable for the land of Sodom and Gomorrah in the day of judgment than for that city!

Persecutions Are Coming

16"Behold, I send you out as sheep in the midst of wolves. Therefore be wise as serpents and harmless as doves. 17But beware of men, for they will deliver you up to councils and scourge you in their synagogues. 18You will be brought before governors and kings for My sake, as a testimony to them and to the Gentiles. 19But when they deliver you up, do not worry about how or what you should speak. For it will be given to you in that hour what you should speak; 20for it is not you who speak, but the Spirit of your Father who speaks in you.

21"Now brother will deliver up brother to death, and a father *his* child; and children will rise up against parents and cause them to be put to death. 22And you will be hated by all for My name's sake. But he who endures to the end will be saved. 23When they persecute you in this city, flee to another. For assuredly, I say to you, you will not have gone through the cities of Israel before the Son of Man comes.

24"A disciple is not above *his* teacher, nor a servant above his master.

25It is enough for a disciple that he be like his teacher, and a servant like his master. If they have called the master of the house Beelzebub, how much more *will they call* those of his household! 26Therefore do not fear them. For there is nothing covered that will not be revealed, and hidden that will not be known.

Jesus Teaches the Fear of God

27"Whatever I tell you in the dark, speak in the light; and what you hear in the ear, preach on the housetops. 28And do not fear those who kill the body but cannot kill the soul. But rather fear Him who is able to destroy both soul and body in hell. 29Are not two sparrows sold for a copper coin? And not one of them falls to the ground apart from your Father's will. 30But the very hairs of your head are all numbered. 31Do not fear therefore; you are of more value than many sparrows.

Confess Christ Before Men

32"Therefore whoever confesses Me before men, him I will also confess before My Father who is in heaven. 33But whoever denies Me before men, him I will also deny before My Father who is in heaven.

Christ Brings Division

34"Do not think that I came to bring peace on earth. I did not come to bring peace but a sword. 35For I have come to 'set a man against his father, a daughter against her mother, and a daughter-in-law against her mother-in-law'; 36and 'a man's enemies will be those of his *own* household.'r 37He who loves father or mother more than Me is not worthy of Me. And he who loves son or daughter more than Me is not worthy of Me. 38And he who does not take his cross and follow after Me is not worthy of Me. 39He who finds his life will lose it, and he who loses his life for My sake will find it.

A Cup of Cold Water

40"He who receives you receives Me, and he who receives Me receives Him who sent Me. 41He who receives a prophet in the name of a prophet shall receive a prophet's reward. And he who receives a righteous man in the name of a righteous man shall receive a righteous man's reward. 42And whoever gives one of these little ones only a cup of cold *water* in the name of a disciple, assuredly, I say to you, he shall by no means lose his reward."

John the Baptist Sends Messengers to Jesus

11 Now it came to pass, when Jesus finished commanding His twelve disciples, that He departed from there to teach and to preach in their cities.

2And when John had heard in prison about the works of Christ, he sent two of his disciples 3and said to Him, "Are You the Coming One, or do we look for another?"

4Jesus answered and said to them, "Go and tell John the things which you hear and see: 5*The* blind see and *the* lame walk; *the* lepers are cleansed and *the* deaf hear; *the* dead are raised up and *the* poor have the gospel preached to them. 6And blessed is he who is not offended because of Me."

7As they departed, Jesus began to say to the multitudes concerning John: "What did you go out into the wilderness to see? A reed shaken by the wind? 8But what did you go out to see? A man clothed in soft garments? Indeed, those who wear soft *clothing* are in kings' houses. 9But what did you go out to see? A prophet? Yes, I say to you, and more than a prophet. 10For this is *he* of whom it is written:

'Behold, I send My messenger
    before Your face,
Who will prepare Your way
    before You.'s

11"Assuredly, I say to you, among those born of women there has not risen one greater than John the Baptist; but he who is least in the kingdom of heaven is greater than he. 12And from the days of John the Baptist until now the kingdom of heaven suffers violence, and the violent take it by force. 13For all the prophets and the law prophesied until John. 14And if you are willing to receive *it*, he is Elijah who

r Micah 7.6   s Malachi 3.1

is to come. 15He who has ears to hear, let him hear!

16"But to what shall I liken this generation? It is like children sitting in the marketplaces and calling to their companions, 17and saying:

'We played the flute for you,
    And you did not dance;
We mourned to you,
    And you did not lament.'

18For John came neither eating nor drinking, and they say, 'He has a demon.' 19The Son of Man came eating and drinking, and they say, 'Look, a glutton and a winebibber, a friend of tax collectors and sinners!' But wisdom is justified by her children."

Woe to the Impenitent Cities

20Then He began to rebuke the cities in which most of His mighty works had been done, because they did not repent: 21"Woe to you, Chorazin! Woe to you, Bethsaida! For if the mighty works which were done in you had been done in Tyre and Sidon, they would have repented long ago in sackcloth and ashes. 22But I say to you, it will be more tolerable for Tyre and Sidon in the day of judgment than for you. 23And you, Capernaum, who are exalted to heaven, will be brought down to Hades; for if the mighty works which were done in you had been done in Sodom, it would have remained until this day. 24But I say to you that it shall be more tolerable for the land of Sodom in the day of judgment than for you."

Jesus Gives True Rest

25At that time Jesus answered and said, "I thank You, Father, Lord of heaven and earth, that You have hidden these things from the wise and prudent and have revealed them to babes. 26Even so, Father, for so it seemed good in Your sight. 27All things have been delivered to Me by My Father, and no one knows the Son except the Father. Nor does anyone know the Father except the Son, and the one to whom the Son wills to reveal Him. 28Come to Me, all you who labor and are heavy laden, and I will give you rest. 29Take My yoke upon you and learn from Me, for I am gentle and lowly in heart, and you will find rest for your souls. 30For My yoke is easy and My burden is light."

Jesus Is Lord of the Sabbath

12 At that time Jesus went through the grainfields on the Sabbath. And His disciples were hungry, and began to pluck heads of grain and to eat. 2And when the Pharisees saw it, they said to Him, "Look, Your disciples are doing what is not lawful to do on the Sabbath!"

3But He said to them, "Have you not read what David did when he was hungry, he and those who were with him: 4how he entered the house of God and ate the showbread which was not lawful for him to eat, nor for those who were with him, but only for the priests? 5Or have you not read in the law that on the Sabbath the priests in the temple profane the Sabbath, and are blameless? 6Yet I say to you that in this place there is One greater than the temple. 7But if you had known what this means, 'I desire mercy and not sacrifice,'t you would not have condemned the guiltless. 8For the Son of Man is Lord even of the Sabbath."

Healing on the Sabbath

9Now when He had departed from there, He went into their synagogue. 10And behold, there was a man who had a withered hand. And they asked Him, saying, "Is it lawful to heal on the Sabbath?"—that they might accuse Him.

11Then He said to them, "What man is there among you who has one sheep, and if it falls into a pit on the Sabbath, will not lay hold of it and lift it out? 12Of how much more value then is a man than a sheep? Therefore it is lawful to do good on the Sabbath." 13Then He said to the man, "Stretch out your hand." And he stretched it out, and it was restored as whole as the other. 14Then the Pharisees went out and plotted against Him, how they might destroy Him.

Behold, My Servant

15But when Jesus knew it, He withdrew from there. And great multitudes

---

t Hosea 6.6

followed Him, and He healed them all. 16Yet He warned them not to make Him known, 17that it might be fulfilled which was spoken by Isaiah the prophet, saying:

18 "Behold! My Servant whom I have chosen,
    My Beloved in whom My soul is well pleased!
    I will put My Spirit upon Him,
    And He will declare justice to the Gentiles.
19 He will not quarrel nor cry out,
    Nor will anyone hear His voice in the streets.
20 A bruised reed He will not break,
    And smoking flax He will not quench,
    Till He sends forth justice to victory;
21 And in His name Gentiles will trust."u

A House Divided Cannot Stand

22Then one was brought to Him who was demon-possessed, blind and mute; and He healed him, so that the blind and mute man both spoke and saw. 23And all the multitudes were amazed and said, "Could this be the Son of David?"

24Now when the Pharisees heard it they said, "This fellow does not cast out demons except by Beelzebub, the ruler of the demons."

25But Jesus knew their thoughts, and said to them: "Every kingdom divided against itself is brought to desolation, and every city or house divided against itself will not stand. 26If Satan casts out Satan, he is divided against himself. How then will his kingdom stand? 27And if I cast out demons by Beelzebub, by whom do your sons cast them out? Therefore they shall be your judges. 28But if I cast out demons by the Spirit of God, surely the kingdom of God has come upon you. 29Or how can one enter a strong man's house and plunder his goods, unless he first binds the strong man? And then he will plunder his house. 30He who is not with Me is against Me, and he who does not gather with Me scatters abroad.

The Unpardonable Sin

31"Therefore I say to you, every sin and blasphemy will be forgiven men, but the blasphemy against the Spirit will not be forgiven men. 32Anyone who speaks a word against the Son of Man, it will be forgiven him; but whoever speaks against the Holy Spirit, it will not be forgiven him, either in this age or in the age to come.

A Tree Known by Its Fruit

33"Either make the tree good and its fruit good, or else make the tree bad and its fruit bad; for a tree is known by its fruit. 34Brood of vipers! How can you, being evil, speak good things? For out of the abundance of the heart the mouth speaks. 35A good man out of the good treasure of his heart brings forth good things, and an evil man out of the evil treasure brings forth evil things. 36But I say to you that for every idle word men may speak, they will give account of it in the day of judgment. 37For by your words you will be justified, and by your words you will be condemned."

The Scribes and Pharisees Ask for a Sign

38Then some of the scribes and Pharisees answered, saying, "Teacher, we want to see a sign from You."

39But He answered and said to them, "An evil and adulterous generation seeks after a sign, and no sign will be given to it except the sign of the prophet Jonah. 40For as Jonah was three days and three nights in the belly of the great fish, so will the Son of Man be three days and three nights in the heart of the earth. 41The men of Nineveh will rise up in the judgment with this generation and condemn it, because they repented at the preaching of Jonah; and indeed a greater than Jonah is here. 42The queen of the South will rise up in the judgment with this generation and condemn it, for she came from the ends of the earth to hear the wisdom of Solomon; and indeed a greater than Solomon is here.

u Isaiah 42.1-4

An Unclean Spirit Returns

43"When an unclean spirit goes out of a man, he goes through dry places, seeking rest, and finds none. 44Then he says, 'I will return to my house from which I came.' And when he comes, he finds *it* empty, swept, and put in order. 45Then he goes and takes with him seven other spirits more wicked than himself, and they enter and dwell there; and the last *state* of that man is worse than the first. So shall it also be with this wicked generation."

Jesus' Mother and Brothers Send for Him

46While He was still talking to the multitudes, behold, His mother and brothers stood outside, seeking to speak with Him. 47Then one said to Him, "Look, Your mother and Your brothers are standing outside, seeking to speak with You."

48But He answered and said to the one who told Him, "Who is My mother and who are My brothers?" 49And He stretched out His hand toward His disciples and said, "Here are My mother and My brothers! 50For whoever does the will of My Father in heaven is My brother and sister and mother."

The Parable of the Sower

13 On the same day Jesus went out of the house and sat by the sea. 2And great multitudes were gathered together to Him, so that He got into a boat and sat; and the whole multitude stood on the shore.

3Then He spoke many things to them in parables, saying: "Behold, a sower went out to sow. 4And as he sowed, some *seed* fell by the wayside; and the birds came and devoured them. 5Some fell on stony places, where they did not have much earth; and they immediately sprang up because they had no depth of earth. 6But when the sun was up they were scorched, and because they had no root they withered away. 7And some fell among thorns, and the thorns sprang up and choked them. 8But others fell on good ground and yielded a crop: some a hundred-fold, some sixty, some thirty. 9He who has ears to hear, let him hear!"

The Purpose of Parables

10And the disciples came and said to Him, "Why do You speak to them in parables?"

11He answered and said to them, "Because it has been given to you to know the mysteries of the kingdom of heaven, but to them it has not been given. 12For whoever has, to him more will be given, and he will have abundance; but whoever does not have, even what he has will be taken away from him. 13Therefore I speak to them in parables, because seeing they do not see, and hearing they do not hear, nor do they understand. 14And in them the prophecy of Isaiah is fulfilled, which says:

'Hearing you will hear and shall not understand,
And seeing you will see and not perceive;
15 For the hearts of this people have grown dull.
Their ears are hard of hearing,
And their eyes they have closed,
Lest they should see with *their* eyes and hear with *their* ears,
Lest they should understand with *their* hearts and turn,
So that I should heal them.'v

16But blessed *are* your eyes for they see, and your ears for they hear; 17for assuredly, I say to you that many prophets and righteous *men* desired to see what you see, and did not see *it*, and to hear what you hear, and did not hear *it*.

The Parable of the Sower Explained

18"Therefore hear the parable of the sower: 19When anyone hears the word of the kingdom, and does not understand *it*, then the wicked *one* comes and snatches away what was sown in his heart. This is he who received seed by the wayside. 20But he who received the seed on stony places, this is he who hears the word and immediately receives it with joy; 21yet he has no root in himself, but endures only for a while. For when tribulation or persecution arises because of the word, immedi-

v Isaiah 6.9, 10

ately he stumbles. 22Now he who received seed among the thorns is he who hears the word, and the cares of this world and the deceitfulness of riches choke the word, and he becomes unfruitful. 23But he who received seed on the good ground is he who hears the word and understands *it,* who indeed bears fruit and produces: some a hundredfold, some sixty, some thirty."

The Parable of the Wheat and the Tares

24Another parable He put forth to them, saying: "The kingdom of heaven is like a man who sowed good seed in his field; 25but while men slept, his enemy came and sowed tares among the wheat and went his way. 26But when the grain had sprouted and produced a crop, then the tares also appeared. 27So the servants of the owner came and said to him, 'Sir, did you not sow good seed in your field? How then does it have tares?' 28He said to them, 'An enemy has done this.' The servants said to him, 'Do you want us then to go and gather them up?' 29But he said, 'No, lest while you gather up the tares you also uproot the wheat with them. 30Let both grow together until the harvest, and at the time of harvest I will say to the reapers, "First gather together the tares and bind them in bundles to burn them, but gather the wheat into my barn." ' "

The Parable of the Mustard Seed

31Another parable He put forth to them, saying: "The kingdom of heaven is like a mustard seed, which a man took and sowed in his field, 32which indeed is the least of all the seeds; but when it is grown it is greater than the herbs and becomes a tree, so that the birds of the air come and nest in its branches."

The Parable of the Leaven

33Another parable He spoke to them: "The kingdom of heaven is like leaven, which a woman took and hid in three measures[w] of meal till it was all leavened."

Prophecy and the Parables

34All these things Jesus spoke to the multitude in parables; and without a parable He did not speak to them, 35that it might be fulfilled which was spoken by the prophet, saying:

"I will open My mouth in parables;
I will utter things kept secret from the foundation of the world."[x]

The Parable of the Tares Explained

36Then Jesus sent the multitude away and went into the house. And His disciples came to Him, saying, "Explain to us the parable of the tares of the field." 37He answered and said to them: "He who sows the good seed is the Son of Man. 38The field is the world, the good seeds are the sons of the kingdom, but the tares are the sons of the wicked *one.* 39The enemy who sowed them is the devil, the harvest is the end of the age, and the reapers are the angels. 40Therefore as the tares are gathered and burned in the fire, so it will be at the end of this age. 41The Son of Man will send out His angels, and they will gather out of His kingdom all things that offend, and those who practice lawlessness, 42and will cast them into the furnace of fire. There will be wailing and gnashing of teeth. 43Then the righteous will shine forth as the sun in the kingdom of their Father. He who has ears to hear, let him hear!

The Parable of the Hidden Treasure

44"Again, the kingdom of heaven is like treasure hidden in a field, which a man found and hid; and for joy over it he goes and sells all that he has and buys that field.

The Parable of the Pearl of Great Price

45"Again, the kingdom of heaven is like a merchant seeking beautiful pearls, 46who, when he had found one pearl of great price, went and sold all that he had and bought it.

The Parable of the Dragnet

47"Again, the kingdom of heaven is like a dragnet that was cast into the sea

---

[w] Approximately two pecks   [x] Psalm 78.2

and gathered some of every kind, 48which, when it was full, they drew to shore; and they sat down and gathered the good into vessels, but threw the bad away. 49So it will be at the end of the age. The angels will come forth, separate the wicked from among the just, 50and cast them into the furnace of fire. There will be wailing and gnashing of teeth."

51Jesus said to them, "Have you understood all these things?"

They said to Him, "Yes, Lord."

52Then He said to them, "Therefore every scribe instructed concerning the kingdom of heaven is like a householder who brings out of his treasure *things* new and old."

Jesus Rejected at Nazareth

53Now it came to pass, when Jesus had finished these parables, that He departed from there. 54When He had come to His own country, He taught them in their synagogue, so that they were astonished and said, "Where did this *Man* get this wisdom and *these* mighty works? 55Is this not the carpenter's son? Is not His mother called Mary? And His brothers James, Joses, Simon, and Judas? 56And His sisters, are they not all with us? Where then did this *Man* get all these things?" 57So they were offended at Him.

But Jesus said to them, "A prophet is not without honor except in his own country and in his own house." 58Now He did not do many mighty works there because of their unbelief.

John the Baptist Beheaded

14 At that time Herod the tetrarch heard the report about Jesus 2and said to his servants, "This is John the Baptist; he is risen from the dead, and therefore these powers are at work in him." 3For Herod had laid hold of John and bound him, and put *him* in prison for the sake of Herodias, his brother Philip's wife. 4Because John had said to him, "It is not lawful for you to have her." 5And although he wanted to put him to death, he feared the multitude, because they counted him as a prophet.

6But when Herod's birthday was celebrated, the daughter of Herodias

danced before them and pleased Herod. 7Therefore he promised with an oath to give her whatever she might ask.

8So she, having been prompted by her mother, said, "Give me John the Baptist's head here on a platter."

9And the king was sorry; nevertheless, because of the oaths and because of those who sat with him, he commanded *it* to be given to *her*. 10So he sent and had John beheaded in prison. 11And his head was brought on a platter and given to the girl, and she brought *it* to her mother. 12Then his disciples came and took away the body and buried it, and went and told Jesus.

Feeding the Five Thousand

13When Jesus heard *it*, He departed from there by boat to a deserted place by Himself. But when the multitudes heard it, they followed Him on foot from the cities. 14And when Jesus went out He saw a great multitude; and He was moved with compassion for them, and healed their sick. 15When it was evening, His disciples came to Him, saying, "This is a deserted place, and the hour is already late. Send the multitudes away, that they may go into the villages and buy themselves food."

16But Jesus said to them, "They do not need to go away. You give them something to eat."

17And they said to Him, "We have here only five loaves and two fish."

18He said, "Bring them here to Me." 19Then He commanded the multitudes to sit down on the grass. And He took the five loaves and the two fish, and looking up to heaven, He blessed and broke and gave the loaves to the disciples; and the disciples gave to the multitudes. 20So they all ate and were filled, and they took up twelve baskets full of the fragments that remained. 21Now those who had eaten were about five thousand men, besides women and children.

Jesus Walks on the Sea

22Immediately Jesus made His disciples get into the boat and go before Him to the other side, while He sent the multitudes away. 23And when He had sent the multitudes away, He went up on the mountain by Himself to pray. Now when evening came, He was alone there. 24But the boat was now in the middle of the sea, tossed by the waves, for the wind was contrary.

25Now in the fourth watch of the night Jesus went to them, walking on the sea. 26And when the disciples saw Him walking on the sea, they were troubled, saying, "It is a ghost!" And they cried out for fear.

27But immediately Jesus spoke to them, saying, "Be of good cheer! It is I; do not be afraid."

28And Peter answered Him and said, "Lord, if it is You, command me to come to You on the water."

29So He said, "Come." And when Peter had come down out of the boat, he walked on the water to go to Jesus. 30But when he saw that the wind was boisterous, he was afraid; and beginning to sink he cried out, saying, "Lord, save me!"

31And immediately Jesus stretched out His hand and caught him, and said to him, "O you of little faith, why did you doubt?" 32And when they got into the boat, the wind ceased.

33Then those who were in the boat came and worshiped Him, saying, "Truly You are the Son of God."

Many Touch Him and Are Made Well

34When they had crossed over, they came to the land of Gennesaret. 35And when the men of that place recognized Him, they sent out into all that surrounding region, brought to Him all who were sick, 36and begged Him that they might only touch the hem of His garment. And as many as touched it were made perfectly well.

Defilement Comes from Within

15 Then the scribes and Pharisees who were from Jerusalem came to Jesus, saying, 2"Why do Your disciples transgress the tradition of the elders? For they do not wash their hands when they eat bread."

3He answered and said to them, "Why do you also transgress the commandment of God because of your tradition? 4For God commanded, saying, 'Honor your father and your mother';*y* and, 'He who curses father or mother, let him be put to death.'*z* 5But you say, 'Whoever says to his father or mother, "Whatever profit you might have received from me is a gift to God"— 6then he need not honor his father or mother.' Thus you have made the commandment of God of no effect by your tradition. 7Hypocrites! Well did Isaiah prophesy about you, saying:

8 'These people draw near to Me with
      their mouth,
    And honor Me with *their* lips,
    But their heart is far from Me.
9 And in vain they worship Me,
    Teaching as doctrines the
      commandments of men.' "*a*

10When He had called the multitude to Himself, He said to them, "Hear and understand: 11Not what goes into the mouth defiles a man; but what comes out of the mouth, this defiles a man."

12Then His disciples came and said to Him, "Do You know that the Pharisees were offended when they heard this saying?"

13But He answered and said, "Every plant which My heavenly Father has not planted will be uprooted. 14Let them alone. They are blind leaders of the blind. And if the blind leads the blind, both will fall into a ditch."

15Then Peter answered and said to Him, "Explain this parable to us."

16So Jesus said, "Are you also still without understanding? 17Do you not yet understand that whatever enters the mouth goes into the stomach and is eliminated? 18But those things which proceed out of the mouth come from the heart, and they defile a man. 19For out of the heart proceed evil thoughts, murders, adulteries, fornications, thefts, false witness, blasphemies. 20These are the things which defile a man, but to eat with unwashed hands does not defile a man."

A Gentile Shows Her Faith

21Then Jesus went out from there and departed to the region of Tyre and Sidon. 22And behold, a woman of Canaan came from that region and cried out to

y Exodus 20.12; Deuteronomy 5.16   z Exodus 21.17   a Isaiah 29.13

Him, saying, "Have mercy on me, O Lord, Son of David! My daughter is severely demon-possessed."

23But He answered her not a word. And His disciples came and urged Him, saying, "Send her away, for she cries out after us."

24But He answered and said, "I was not sent except to the lost sheep of the house of Israel."

25Then she came and worshiped Him, saying, "Lord, help me!"

26But He answered and said, "It is not good to take the children's bread and throw *it* to the little dogs."

27And she said, "Yes, Lord, yet even the little dogs eat the crumbs which fall from their masters' table."

28Then Jesus answered and said to her, "O woman, great *is* your faith! Let it be to you as you desire." And her daughter was healed from that very hour.

Jesus Heals Great Multitudes

29Jesus departed from there, skirted the Sea of Galilee, and went up on the mountain and sat down there. 30Then great multitudes came to Him, having with them *the* lame, blind, mute, maimed, and many others; and they laid them down at Jesus' feet, and He healed them. 31So the multitude marveled when they saw *the* mute speaking, *the* maimed made whole, *the* lame walking, and *the* blind seeing; and they glorified the God of Israel.

Feeding the Four Thousand

32Now Jesus called His disciples to *Himself* and said, "I have compassion on the multitude, because they have now continued with Me three days and have nothing to eat. And I do not want to send them away hungry, lest they faint on the way."

33Then His disciples said to Him, "Where could we get enough bread in the wilderness to fill such a great multitude?"

34Jesus said to them, "How many loaves do you have?"

And they said, "Seven, and a few little fish."

35So He commanded the multitude to sit down on the ground. 36And He took the seven loaves and the fish and gave

thanks, broke *them* and gave *them* to His disciples; and the disciples *gave* to the multitude. 37So they all ate and were filled, and they took up seven large baskets full of the fragments that were left. 38Now those who ate were four thousand men, besides women and children. 39And He sent away the multitude, got into the boat, and came to the region of Magdala.

The Pharisees and Sadducees Seek a Sign

16 Then the Pharisees and Sadducees came, and testing Him asked that He would show them a sign from heaven. 2He answered and said to them, "When it is evening you say, '*It will be* fair weather, for the sky is red'; 3and in the morning, '*It will be* foul weather today, for the sky is red and threatening.' Hypocrites! You know how to discern the face of the sky, but you cannot *discern* the signs of the times. 4A wicked and adulterous generation seeks after a sign, and no sign shall be given to it except the sign of the prophet Jonah." And He left them and departed.

The Leaven of the Pharisees and Sadducees

5Now when His disciples had come to the other side, they had forgotten to take bread. 6Then Jesus said to them, "Take heed and beware of the leaven of the Pharisees and the Sadducees."

7And they reasoned among themselves, saying, "*It is* because we have taken no bread."

8But Jesus, being aware of *it,* said to them, "O you of little faith, why do you reason among yourselves because you have brought no bread? 9Do you not yet understand, or remember the five loaves of the five thousand and how many baskets you took up? 10Nor the seven loaves of the four thousand and how many large baskets you took up? 11How is it you do not understand that I did not speak to you concerning bread?—but to beware of the leaven of the Pharisees and Sadducees."
12Then they understood that He did not tell *them* to beware of the leaven of bread, but of the doctrine of the Pharisees and Sadducees.

Peter Confesses Jesus as the Christ

13When Jesus came into the region of Caesarea Philippi, He asked His disciples, saying, "Who do men say that I, the Son of Man, am?"

14So they said, "Some *say* John the Baptist, some Elijah, and others Jeremiah or one of the prophets."

15He said to them, "But who do you say that I am?"

16Simon Peter answered and said, "You are the Christ, the Son of the living God."

17Jesus answered and said to him, "Blessed are you, Simon Bar-Jonah, for flesh and blood has not revealed *this* to you, but My Father who is in heaven. 18And I also say to you that you are Peter, and on this rock I will build My church, and the gates of Hades shall not prevail against it. 19And I will give you the keys of the kingdom of heaven, and whatever you bind on earth will be bound in heaven, and whatever you loose on earth will be loosed in heaven."

20Then He commanded His disciples that they should tell no one that He was Jesus the Christ.

Jesus Predicts His Death and Resurrection

21From that time Jesus began to show to His disciples that He must go to Jerusalem, and suffer many things from the elders and chief priests and scribes, and be killed, and be raised the third day.

22Then Peter took Him aside and began to rebuke Him, saying, "Far be it from You, Lord; this shall not happen to You!"

23But He turned and said to Peter, "Get behind Me, Satan! You are an offense to Me, for you are not mindful of the things of God, but the things of men."

Take Up the Cross and Follow Him

24Then Jesus said to His disciples, "If anyone desires to come after Me, let him deny himself, and take up his cross, and follow Me. 25For whoever desires to save his life will lose it, but whoever loses his life for My sake will find it. 26For what profit is it to a man if he gains the whole world, and loses his own soul? Or what will a man give in exchange for his soul? 27For the Son of Man will come in the glory of His Father with His angels, and then He will reward each according to his works.

Jesus Transfigured on the Mount

28Assuredly, I say to you, there are some standing here who shall not taste death till they see the Son of Man coming in His kingdom."

17 Now after six days Jesus took Peter, James, and John his brother, led them up on a high mountain by themselves; 2and He was transfigured before them. His face shone like the sun, and His clothes became as white as the light. 3And behold, Moses and Elijah appeared to them, talking with Him. 4Then Peter answered and said to Jesus, "Lord, it is good for us to be here; if You wish, let us make here three tabernacles: one for You, one for Moses, and one for Elijah."

5While he was still speaking, behold, a bright cloud overshadowed them; and suddenly a voice came out of the cloud, saying, "This is My beloved Son, in whom I am well pleased. Hear Him!" 6And when the disciples heard *it*, they fell on their faces and were greatly afraid. 7But Jesus came and touched them and said, "Arise, and do not be afraid." 8When they had lifted up their eyes, they saw no one but Jesus only.

9Now as they came down from the mountain, Jesus commanded them, saying, "Tell the vision to no one until the Son of Man is risen from the dead."

10And His disciples asked Him, saying, "Why then do the scribes say that Elijah must come first?"

11Jesus answered and said to them, "Indeed, Elijah is coming first and will restore all things. 12But I say to you that Elijah has come already, and they did not know him but did to him whatever they wished. Likewise the Son of Man is also about to suffer at their hands." 13Then the disciples understood that He spoke to them of John the Baptist.

A Boy Is Healed

14And when they had come to the multitude, a man came to Him, kneeling down to Him and saying, 15"Lord, have mercy on my son, for he is an epileptic and suffers severely; for he often falls into the fire and often into the water. 16So I brought him to Your disciples, but they could not cure him."

17Then Jesus answered and said, "O faithless and perverse generation, how long shall I be with you? How long shall I bear with you? Bring him here to Me." 18And Jesus rebuked the demon, and it came out of him; and the child was cured from that very hour.

19Then the disciples came to Jesus privately and said, "Why could we not cast it out?"

20So Jesus said to them, "Because of your unbelief; for assuredly, I say to you, if you have faith as a mustard seed, you will say to this mountain, 'Move from here to there,' and it will move; and nothing will be impossible for you. 21However, this kind does not go out except by prayer and fasting."

Jesus Again Predicts His Death and Resurrection

22Now while they were staying in Galilee, Jesus said to them, "The Son of Man is about to be betrayed into the hands of men, 23and they will kill Him, and the third day He will be raised up." And they were exceedingly sorrowful.

Peter and His Master Pay Their Taxes

24When they had come to Capernaum, those who received the *temple* tax came to Peter and said, "Does your Teacher not pay the *temple* tax?"

25He said, "Yes."

And when he had come into the house, Jesus anticipated him, saying, "What do you think, Simon? From whom do the kings of the earth take customs or taxes, from their sons or from strangers?"

26Peter said to Him, "From strangers."

Jesus said to him, "Then the sons are free. 27Nevertheless, lest we offend them, go to the sea, cast in a hook, and take the fish that comes up first. And when you have opened its mouth, you will find a piece of money; take that and give it to them for Me and you."

Who Is the Greatest?

18 At that time the disciples came to Jesus, saying, "Who then is greatest in the kingdom of heaven?"

2Then Jesus called a little child to Him, set him in the midst of them, 3and said, "Assuredly, I say to you, unless you are converted and become as little children, you will by no means enter the kingdom of heaven. 4Therefore whoever humbles himself as this little child is the greatest in the kingdom of heaven. 5Whoever receives one little child like this in My name receives Me.

Jesus Warns of Offenses

6"Whoever causes one of these little ones who believe in Me to sin, it would be better for him if a millstone were hung around his neck, and he were drowned in the depth of the sea. 7Woe to the world because of offenses! For offenses must come, but woe to that man by whom the offense comes! 8If your hand or foot causes you to sin, cut it off and cast *it* from you. It is better for you to enter into life lame or maimed, rather than having two hands or two feet, to be cast into the everlasting fire. 9And if your eye causes you to sin, pluck it out and cast *it* from you. It is better for you to enter into life with one eye, rather than having two eyes, to be cast into hell fire.

The Parable of the Lost Sheep

10"Take heed that you do not despise one of these little ones, for I say to you that in heaven their angels always see the face of My Father who is in heaven. 11For the Son of Man has come to save that which was lost.

12"What do you think? If a man has a hundred sheep, and one of them goes astray, does he not leave the ninety-nine and go to the mountains to seek the one that is straying? 13And if he should find it, assuredly, I say to you, he rejoices more over that *sheep* than over the ninety-nine that did not go astray. 14Even so it is not the will of your Father who is in heaven that one of these little ones should perish.

Dealing with a Sinning Brother

15"Moreover if your brother sins against you, go and tell him his fault between you and him alone. If he hears you, you have gained your brother. 16But if he will not hear, take with you one or two more, that 'by the mouth of two or three witnesses every word may be established.'b 17And if he refuses to hear them, tell *it* to the church. But if he refuses even to hear the church, let him be to you like a heathen and a tax collector.

18"Assuredly, I say to you, whatever you bind on earth will be bound in heaven, and whatever you loose on earth will be loosed in heaven.

19"Again I say to you that if two of you agree on earth concerning anything that they ask, it will be done for them by My Father in heaven. 20For where two or three are gathered together in My name, I am there in the midst of them."

The Parable of the Unforgiving Servant

21Then Peter came to Him and said, "Lord, how often shall my brother sin against me, and I forgive him? Up to seven times?"

22Jesus said to him, "I do not say to you, up to seven times, but up to seventy times seven. 23Therefore the kingdom of heaven is like a certain king who wanted to settle accounts with his servants. 24And when he had begun to settle accounts, one was brought to him who owed him ten thousand talents. 25But as he was not able to pay, his master commanded that he be sold, with his wife and children and all that he had, and that payment be made. 26The servant therefore fell down before him, saying, 'Master, have patience with me, and I will pay you all.' 27Then the master of that servant was moved with compassion, released him, and forgave him the debt.

28"But that servant went out and found one of his fellow servants who owed him a hundred denarii; and he laid hands on him and took *him* by the throat, saying, 'Pay me what you owe!' 29So his fellow servant fell down at his feet and begged him, saying, 'Have patience with me, and I will pay you all.' 30And he would not, but went and threw him into prison till he should pay the debt. 31So when his fellow servants saw what had been done, they were very grieved, and came and told their master all that had been done. 32Then

his master, after he had called him, said to him, 'You wicked servant! I forgave you all that debt because you begged me. 33Should you not also have had compassion on your fellow servant, just as I had pity on you?' 34And his master was angry, and delivered him to the torturers until he should pay all that was due to him.

35"So My heavenly Father also will do to you if each of you, from his heart, does not forgive his brother his trespasses."

Marriage and Divorce

19 Now it came to pass, when Jesus had finished these sayings, *that* He departed from Galilee and came to the region of Judea beyond the Jordan. 2And great multitudes followed Him, and He healed them there.

3The Pharisees also came to Him, testing Him, and saying to Him, "Is it lawful for a man to divorce his wife for *just* any reason?"

4And He answered and said to them, "Have you not read that He who made *them* at the beginning 'made them male and female,'c 5and said, 'For this reason a man shall leave his father and mother and be joined to his wife, and the two shall become one flesh'?d 6So then, they are no longer two but one flesh. Therefore what God has joined together, let not man separate."

7They said to Him, "Why then did Moses command to give a certificate of divorce, and to put her away?"

8He said to them, "Moses, because of the hardness of your hearts, permitted you to divorce your wives, but from the beginning it was not so. 9And I say to you, whoever divorces his wife, except for sexual immorality, and marries another, commits adultery; and whoever marries her who is divorced commits adultery."

10His disciples said to Him, "If such is the case of the man with *his* wife, it is better not to marry."

Jesus Teaches on Celibacy

11But He said to them, "All cannot accept this saying, but only *those* to whom it has been given: 12For there are

---

b Deuteronomy 19.15   c Genesis 1.27; 5.2   d Genesis 2.24

eunuchs who were born thus from *their* mother's womb, and there are eunuchs who were made eunuchs by men, and there are eunuchs who have made themselves eunuchs for the kingdom of heaven's sake. He who is able to accept *it*, let him accept *it*."

Jesus Blesses Little Children

13Then little children were brought to Him that He might put *His* hands on them and pray, but the disciples rebuked them. 14But Jesus said, "Let the little children come to Me, and do not forbid them; for of such is the kingdom of heaven." 15And He laid *His* hands on them and departed from there.

Jesus Counsels the Rich Young Ruler

16Now behold, one came and said to Him, "Good Teacher, what good thing shall I do that I may have eternal life?"

17So He said to him, "Why do you call Me good? No one *is* good but One, *that is*, God. But if you want to enter into life, keep the commandments."

18He said to Him, "Which ones?" Jesus said, " 'You shall not murder,' 'You shall not commit adultery,' 'You shall not steal,' 'You shall not bear false witness,' 19'Honor your father and *your* mother,'*e* and, 'You shall love your neighbor as yourself.' "*f*

20The young man said to Him, "All these things I have kept from my youth. What do I still lack?"

21Jesus said to him, "If you want to be perfect, go, sell what you have and give to the poor, and you will have treasure in heaven; and come, follow Me."

22But when the young man heard that saying, he went away sorrowful, for he had great possessions.

With God All Things Are Possible

23Then Jesus said to His disciples, "Assuredly, I say to you that it is hard for a rich man to enter the kingdom of heaven. 24And again I say to you, it is easier for a camel to go through the eye of a needle than for a rich man to enter the kingdom of God."

25When His disciples heard *it*, they were greatly astonished, saying, "Who then can be saved?"

26But Jesus looked at *them* and said to them, "With men this is impossible, but with God all things are possible."

27Then Peter answered and said to Him, "See, we have left all and followed You. Therefore what shall we have?"

28So Jesus said to them, "Assuredly I say to you, that in the regeneration, when the Son of Man sits on the throne of His glory, you who have followed Me will also sit on twelve thrones, judging the twelve tribes of Israel. 29And everyone who has left houses or brothers or sisters or father or mother or wife or children or lands, for My name's sake, shall receive a hundredfold, and inherit eternal life. 30But many *who are* first will be last, and the last first.

The Parable of the Workers in the Vineyard

20 "For the kingdom of heaven is like a landowner who went out early in the morning to hire laborers for his vineyard. 2Now when he had agreed with the laborers for a denarius a day, he sent them into his vineyard. 3And he went out about the third hour and saw others standing idle in the marketplace, 4and said to them, 'You also go into the vineyard, and whatever is right I will give you.' So they went. 5Again he went out about the sixth and the ninth hour, and did likewise. 6And about the eleventh hour he went out and found others standing idle, and said to them, 'Why have you been standing here idle all day?' 7They said to him, 'Because no one hired us.' He said to them, 'You also go into the vineyard, and whatever is right you will receive.'

8"So when evening had come, the owner of the vineyard said to his steward, 'Call the laborers and give them *their* wages, beginning with the last to the first.' 9And when those came who *were hired* about the eleventh hour, they each received a denarius. 10But when the first came, they supposed that they would receive more; and they likewise received each a denarius.

e Exodus 20.12-16; Deuteronomy 5.16-20   *f* Leviticus 19:18

11And when they had received *it*, they complained against the landowner, 12saying, 'These last *men* have worked *only* one hour, and you made them equal to us who have borne the burden and the heat of the day.' 13But he answered one of them and said, 'Friend, I am doing you no wrong. Did you not agree with me for a denarius? 14Take *what is* yours and go your way. I wish to give to this last man *the same* as to you. 15Is it not lawful for me to do what I wish with my own things? Or is your eye evil because I am good?' 16So the last will be first, and the first last. For many are called, but few chosen."

Jesus a Third Time Predicts His Death and Resurrection

17Now Jesus, going up to Jerusalem, took the twelve disciples aside on the road and said to them, 18"Behold, we are going up to Jerusalem, and the Son of Man will be betrayed to the chief priests and to the scribes; and they will condemn Him to death, 19and deliver Him to the Gentiles to mock and to scourge and to crucify. And the third day He will rise again."

Greatness Is Serving

20Then the mother of Zebedee's sons came to Him with her sons, kneeling down and asking something from Him. 21And He said to her, "What do you wish?"

She said to Him, "Grant that these two sons of mine may sit, one on Your right hand and the other on the left, in Your kingdom."

22But Jesus answered and said, "You do not know what you ask. Are you able to drink the cup that I am about to drink, and be baptized with the baptism that I am baptized with?"

They said to Him, "We are able."

23So He said to them, "You will indeed drink My cup, and be baptized with the baptism that I am baptized with; but to sit on My right hand and on My left is not Mine to give, but *it is for those* for whom it is prepared by My Father."

24And when the ten heard *it*, they were greatly displeased with the two brothers. 25But Jesus called them to *Himself* and said, "You know that the rulers of the Gentiles lord it over them, and those who are great exercise authority over them. 26Yet it shall not be so among you; but whoever desires to become great among you, let him be your servant. 27And whoever desires to be first among you, let him be your slave—28just as the Son of Man did not come to be served, but to serve, and to give His life a ransom for many."

Two Blind Men Receive Their Sight

29Now as they went out of Jericho, a great multitude followed Him. 30And behold, two blind men sitting by the road, when they heard that Jesus was passing by, cried out, saying, "Have mercy on us, O Lord, Son of David!"

31Then the multitude warned them that they should be quiet; but they cried out all the more, saying, "Have mercy on us, O Lord, Son of David!"

32So Jesus stood still and called them, and said, "What do you want Me to do for you?"

33They said to Him, "Lord, that our eyes may be opened." 34So Jesus had compassion and touched their eyes. And immediately their eyes received sight, and they followed Him.

The Triumphal Entry

21 Now when they drew near Jerusalem, and came to Bethphage, at the Mount of Olives, then Jesus sent two disciples, 2saying to them, "Go into the village opposite you, and immediately you will find a donkey tied, and a colt with her. Loose *them* and bring *them* to Me. 3And if anyone says anything to you, you shall say, 'The Lord has need of them,' and immediately he will send them."

4All this was done that it might be fulfilled which was spoken by the prophet, saying:
5   "Tell the daughter of Zion,
      'Behold, your King is coming to you,
      Lowly, and sitting on a donkey,
      A colt, the foal of a donkey.' "g

6So the disciples went and did as Jesus commanded them. 7They brought the donkey and the colt, laid their

g Zechariah 9.9

clothes on them, and set *Him* on them. 8And a very great multitude spread their clothes on the road; others cut down branches from the trees and spread *them* on the road. 9Then the multitudes who went before and those who followed cried out, saying:

"Hosanna to the Son of David!
'Blessed *is* He who comes in the
     name of the LORD!'*h*
Hosanna in the highest!"

10And when He had come into Jerusalem, all the city was moved, saying, "Who is this?"

11So the multitudes said, "This is Jesus, the prophet from Nazareth of Galilee."

Jesus Cleanses the Temple

12Then Jesus went into the temple of God and drove out all those who bought and sold in the temple, and overturned the tables of the money changers and the seats of those who sold doves. 13And He said to them, "It is written, 'My house shall be called a house of prayer,'*i* but you have made it a 'den of thieves.' "*j*

14Then *the* blind and *the* lame came to Him in the temple, and He healed them. 15But when the chief priests and scribes saw the wonderful things that He did, and the children crying out in the temple and saying, "Hosanna to the Son of David!" they were indignant 16and said to Him, "Do You hear what these are saying?"

And Jesus said to them, "Yes. Have you never read,

'Out of the mouth of babes and
     nursing infants
You have perfected praise'? "*k*

17Then He left them and went out of the city to Bethany, and He lodged there.

The Fig Tree Withered

18Now in the morning, as He returned to the city, He was hungry. 19And seeing a fig tree by the road, He came to it and found nothing on it but leaves, and said to it, "Let no fruit grow on you ever again." Immediately the fig tree withered away.

The Lesson of the Withered Fig Tree

20And when the disciples saw *it*, they marveled, saying, "How did the fig tree wither away so soon?"

21So Jesus answered and said to them, "Assuredly, I say to you, if you have faith and do not doubt, you will not only do what was done to the fig tree, but also if you say to this mountain, 'Be removed and be cast into the sea,' it will be done. 22And whatever things you ask in prayer, believing, you will receive."

Jesus' Authority Questioned

23Now when He came into the temple, the chief priests and the elders of the people confronted Him as He was teaching, and said, "By what authority are You doing these things? And who gave You this authority?"

24But Jesus answered and said to them, "I also will ask you one thing, which if you tell Me, I likewise will tell you by what authority I do these things: 25The baptism of John—where was it from? From heaven or from men?"

And they reasoned among themselves, saying, "If we say, 'From heaven,' He will say to us, 'Why then did you not believe him?' 26But if we say, 'From men,' we fear the multitude, for all count John as a prophet." 27So they answered Jesus and said, "We do not know."

And He said to them, "Neither will I tell you by what authority I do these things.

The Parable of the Two Sons

28"But what do you think? A man had two sons, and he came to the first and said, 'Son, go, work today in my vineyard.' 29He answered and said, 'I will not,' but afterward he regretted it and went. 30Then he came to the second and said likewise. And he answered and said, 'I *go*, sir,' but he did not go. 31Which of the two did the will of *his* father?"

They said to Him, "The first."

Jesus said to them, "Assuredly, I say to you that tax collectors and harlots enter the kingdom of God before you.

h Psalm 118.26   *i* Isaiah 56.7   *j* Jeremiah 7.11   *k* Psalm 8.2

32For John came to you in the way of righteousness, and you did not believe him; but tax collectors and harlots believed him; and when you saw *it*, you did not afterward relent and believe him.

The Parable of the Wicked Vinedressers

33"Hear another parable: There was a certain landowner who planted a vineyard and set a hedge around it, dug a winepress in it and built a tower. And he leased it to vinedressers and went into a far country. 34Now when vintage-time drew near, he sent his servants to the vinedressers, that they might receive its fruit. 35And the vinedressers took his servants, beat one, killed one, and stoned another. 36Again he sent other servants, more than the first, and they did likewise to them. 37Then last of all he sent his son to them, saying, 'They will respect my son.' 38But when the vinedressers saw the son, they said among themselves, 'This is the heir. Come, let us kill him and seize his inheritance.' 39So they took him and cast *him* out of the vineyard and killed *him*.

40"Therefore, when the owner of the vineyard comes, what will he do to those vinedressers?"

41They said to Him, "He will destroy those wicked men miserably, and lease *his* vineyard to other vinedressers who will render to him the fruits in their seasons."

42Jesus said to them, "Have you never read in the Scriptures:

'The stone which the builders rejected
Has become the chief cornerstone.
This was the LORD's doing,
And it is marvelous in our eyes' ?[l]

43"Therefore I say to you, the kingdom of God will be taken from you and given to a nation bearing the fruits of it. 44And whoever falls on this stone will be broken; but on whomever it falls, it will grind him to powder."

45Now when the chief priests and Pharisees heard His parables, they perceived that He was speaking of them. 46But when they sought to lay hands on Him, they feared the multitudes, because they took Him for a prophet.

The Parable of the Wedding Feast

22 And Jesus answered and spoke to them again by parables and said: 2"The kingdom of heaven is like a certain king who arranged a marriage for his son, 3and sent out his servants to call those who were invited to the wedding; and they were not willing to come. 4Again, he sent out other servants, saying, 'Tell those who are invited, "See, I have prepared my dinner; my oxen and fatted cattle *are* killed, and all things *are* ready. Come to the wedding."' 5But they made light of it and went their ways, one to his own farm, another to his business. 6And the rest seized his servants, treated *them* spitefully, and killed *them*. 7But when the king heard *about it*, he was furious. And he sent out his armies, destroyed those murderers, and burned up their city. 8Then he said to his servants, 'The wedding is ready, but those who were invited were not worthy. 9Therefore go into the highways, and as many as you find, invite to the wedding.' 10So those servants went out into the highways and gathered together all whom they found, both bad and good. And the wedding *hall* was filled with guests.

11"But when the king came in to see the guests, he saw a man there who did not have on a wedding garment. 12So he said to him, 'Friend, how did you come in here without a wedding garment?' And he was speechless. 13Then the king said to the servants, 'Bind him hand and foot, take him away, and cast *him* into outer darkness; there will be weeping and gnashing of teeth.'

14"For many are called, but few *are* chosen."

The Pharisees: Is It Lawful to Pay Taxes to Caesar?

15Then the Pharisees went and plotted how they might entangle Him in *His* talk. 16And they sent to Him their disciples with the Herodians, saying, "Teacher, we know that You are true, and teach the way of God in truth; nor

---

l Psalm 118.22, 23

do You care about anyone, for You do not regard the person of men. 17Tell us, therefore, what do You think? Is it lawful to pay taxes to Caesar, or not?"

18But Jesus perceived their wickedness, and said, "Why do you test Me, you hypocrites? 19Show Me the tax money."

So they brought Him a denarius.

20And He said to them, "Whose image and inscription is this?"

21They said to Him, "Caesar's."

And He said to them, "Render therefore to Caesar the things that are Caesar's, and to God the things that are God's." 22When they had heard these words, they marveled, and left Him and went their way.

The Sadducees: What About the Resurrection?

23The same day the Sadducees, who say there is no resurrection, came to Him and asked Him, 24saying: "Teacher, Moses said that if a man dies, having no children, his brother shall marry his wife and raise up offspring for his brother. 25Now there were with us seven brothers. The first died after he had married, and having no offspring, left his wife to his brother. 26Likewise the second also, and the third, even to the seventh. 27Last of all the woman died also. 28Therefore, in the resurrection, whose wife of the seven will she be? For they all had her."

29Jesus answered and said to them, "You are mistaken, not knowing the Scriptures nor the power of God. 30For in the resurrection they neither marry nor are given in marriage, but are like angels of God in heaven. 31But concerning the resurrection of the dead, have you not read what was spoken to you by God, saying, 32'I am the God of Abraham, the God of Isaac, and the God of Jacob'?m God is not the God of the dead, but of the living." 33And when the multitudes heard this, they were astonished at His teaching.

The Scribes: Which Is the First Commandment of All?

34But when the Pharisees heard that He had silenced the Sadducees, they gathered together. 35Then one of them, a lawyer, asked Him a question, testing Him, and saying, 36"Teacher, which is the great commandment in the law?"

37Jesus said to him, " 'You shall love the LORD your God with all your heart, with all your soul, and with all your mind.'n 38This is the first and great commandment. 39And the second is like it: 'You shall love your neighbor as yourself.'o 40On these two commandments hang all the Law and the Prophets."

Jesus: How Can David Call His Descendant Lord?

41While the Pharisees were gathered together, Jesus asked them, 42saying, "What do you think about the Christ? Whose Son is He?"

They said to Him, "The Son of David."

43He said to them, "How then does David in the Spirit call Him 'Lord,' saying:

44 'The LORD said to my Lord,
   "Sit at My right hand,
   Till I make Your enemies Your
      footstool" ' ?p

45If David then calls Him 'Lord,' how is He his Son?" 46And no one was able to answer Him a word, nor from that day on did anyone dare question Him anymore.

Woe to the Scribes and Pharisees

23 Then Jesus spoke to the multitudes and to His disciples, 2saying: "The scribes and the Pharisees sit in Moses' seat. 3Therefore whatever they tell you to observe, that observe and do, but do not do according to their works; for they say, and do not do. 4For they bind heavy burdens, hard to bear, and lay them on men's shoulders; but they themselves will not move them with one of their fingers. 5But all their works they do to be seen by men. They make their phylacteries broad and enlarge the borders of their garments. 6They love the best places at feasts, the best seats in the synagogues, 7greetings in the marketplaces, and to be called by men, 'Rabbi, Rabbi.' 8But you, do not be called 'Rabbi'; for One is your

---

m Exodus 3.6, 15   n Deuteronomy 6.5   o Leviticus 19.18   p Psalm 110.1

Teacher, the Christ, and you are all brethren. 9Do not call anyone on earth your father; for One is your Father, He who is in heaven. 10And do not be called teachers; for One is your Teacher, the Christ. 11But he who is greatest among you shall be your servant. 12And whoever exalts himself will be humbled, and he who humbles himself will be exalted.

13"But woe to you, scribes and Pharisees, hypocrites! For you shut up the kingdom of heaven against men; for you neither go in *yourselves*, nor do you allow those who are entering to go in. 14Woe to you, scribes and Pharisees, hypocrites! For you devour widows' houses, and for a pretense make long prayers. Therefore you will receive greater condemnation.

15"Woe to you, scribes and Pharisees, hypocrites! For you travel land and sea to win one proselyte, and when he is won, you make him twice as much a son of hell as yourselves.

16"Woe to you, blind guides, who say, 'Whoever swears by the temple, it is nothing; but whoever swears by the gold of the temple, he is obliged *to perform it.*' 17Fools and blind! For which is greater, the gold or the temple that sanctifies the gold? 18And, 'Whoever swears by the altar, it is nothing; but whoever swears by the gift that is on it, he is obliged *to perform it.*' 19Fools and blind! For which is greater, the gift or the altar that sanctifies the gift? 20Therefore he who swears by the altar, swears by it and by all things on it. 21He who swears by the temple, swears by it and by Him who dwells in it. 22And he who swears by heaven, swears by the throne of God and by Him who sits on it.

23"Woe to you, scribes and Pharisees, hypocrites! For you pay tithe of mint and anise and cummin, and have neglected the weightier *matters* of the law: justice and mercy and faith. These you ought to have done, without leaving the others undone. 24Blind guides, who strain out a gnat and swallow a camel!

25"Woe to you, scribes and Pharisees, hypocrites! For you cleanse the outside of the cup and dish, but inside they are full of extortion and self-indulgence. 26Blind Pharisee, first cleanse the inside of the cup and dish, that the outside of them may be clean also.

27"Woe to you, scribes and Pharisees, hypocrites! For you are like whitewashed tombs which indeed appear beautiful outwardly, but inside are full of dead *men's* bones and all uncleanness. 28Even so you also outwardly appear righteous to men, but inside you are full of hypocrisy and lawlessness.

29"Woe to you, scribes and Pharisees, hypocrites! Because you build the tombs of the prophets and adorn the monuments of the righteous, 30and say, 'If we had lived in the days of our fathers, we would not have been partakers with them in the blood of the prophets.'

31"Therefore you are witnesses against yourselves that you are sons of those who murdered the prophets. 32Fill up, then, the measure of your fathers' *guilt.* 33Serpents, brood of vipers! How can you escape the condemnation of hell? 34Therefore, indeed, I send you prophets, wise men, and scribes: *some* of them you will kill and crucify, and *some* of them you will scourge in your synagogues and persecute from city to city, 35that on you may come all the righteous blood shed on the earth, from the blood of righteous Abel to the blood of Zechariah, son of Berechiah, whom you murdered between the temple and the altar. 36Assuredly, I say to you, all these things will come upon this generation.

Jesus Laments over Jerusalem

37"O Jerusalem, Jerusalem, the one who kills the prophets and stones those who are sent to her! How often I wanted to gather your children together, as a hen gathers her chicks under *her* wings, but you were not willing! 38See! Your house is left to you desolate; 39for I say to you, you shall see Me no more till you say, 'Blessed *is* He who comes in the name of the Lord!' "*q*

Jesus Predicts the Destruction of the Temple

24 Then Jesus went out and departed from the temple, and His disciples came up to show Him the buildings of the temple. 2And Jesus said to them, "Do you not see all these things? Assuredly, I say to you, not *one* stone shall be left here upon another, that shall not be thrown down."

The Signs of the Times and the End of the Age

3Now as He sat on the Mount of Olives, the disciples came to Him privately, saying, "Tell us, when will these things be? And what *will be* the sign of Your coming, and of the end of the age?"

4And Jesus answered and said to them: "Take heed that no one deceives you. 5For many will come in My name, saying, 'I am the Christ,' and will deceive many. 6And you will hear of wars and rumors of wars. See that you are not troubled; for all *these things* must come to pass, but the end is not yet. 7For nation will rise against nation, and kingdom against kingdom. And there will be famines, pestilences, and earthquakes in various places. 8All these *are* the beginning of sorrows.

9"Then they will deliver you up to tribulation and kill you, and you will be hated by all nations for My name's sake. 10And then many will be offended, will betray one another, and will hate one another. 11Then many false prophets will rise up and deceive many. 12And because lawlessness will abound, the love of many will grow cold. 13But he who endures to the end shall be saved. 14And this gospel of the kingdom will be preached in all the world as a witness to all the nations, and then the end will come.

The Great Tribulation

15"Therefore when you see the 'abomination of desolation,'ʳ spoken of by Daniel the prophet, standing in the holy place" (whoever reads, let him understand), 16"then let those who are in Judea flee to the mountains. 17Let him

who is on the housetop not go down to take anything out of his house. 18And let him who is in the field not go back to get his clothes. 19But woe to those who are pregnant and to those who are nursing babies in those days! 20And pray that your flight may not be in winter or on the Sabbath. 21For then there will be great tribulation, such as has not been since the beginning of the world until this time, no, nor ever shall be. 22And unless those days were shortened, no flesh would be saved; but for the elect's sake those days will be shortened.

23"Then if anyone says to you, 'Look, here *is* the Christ!' or 'There!' do not believe *it*. 24For false christs and false prophets will rise and show great signs and wonders to deceive, if possible, even the elect. 25See, I have told you beforehand.

26"Therefore if they say to you, 'Look, He is in the desert!' do not go out; *or* 'Look, *He is* in the inner rooms!' do not believe *it*. 27For as the lightning comes from the east and flashes to the west, so also will the coming of the Son of Man be. 28For wherever the carcass is, there the eagles will be gathered together.

The Coming of the Son of Man

29"Immediately after the tribulation of those days the sun will be darkened, and the moon will not give its light; the stars will fall from heaven, and the powers of the heavens will be shaken. 30Then the sign of the Son of Man will appear in heaven, and then all the tribes of the earth will mourn, and they will see the Son of Man coming on the clouds of heaven with power and great glory. 31And He will send His angels with a great sound of a trumpet, and they will gather together His elect from the four winds, from one end of heaven to the other.

The Parable of the Fig Tree

32"Now learn this parable from the fig tree: When its branch has already become tender and puts forth leaves, you know that summer *is* near. 33So you also, when you see all these

ʳ Daniel 11.31; 12.11

things, know that it[s] is near—at the doors! 34Assuredly, I say to you, this generation will by no means pass away till all these things take place. 35Heaven and earth will pass away, but My words will by no means pass away.

No One Knows the Day or Hour

36"But of that day and hour no one knows, not even the angels of heaven, but My Father only. 37But as the days of Noah *were*, so also will the coming of the Son of Man be. 38For as in the days before the flood, they were eating and drinking, marrying and giving in marriage, until the day that Noah entered the ark, 39and did not know until the flood came and took them all away, so also will the coming of the Son of Man be. 40Then two *men* will be in the field: one will be taken and the other left. 41Two *women will be* grinding at the mill: one will be taken and the other left. 42Watch therefore, for you do not know what hour your Lord is coming. 43But know this, that if the master of the house had known what hour the thief would come, he would have watched and not allowed his house to be broken into. 44Therefore you also be ready, for the Son of Man is coming at an hour you do not expect.

The Faithful Servant and the Evil Servant

45"Who then is a faithful and wise servant, whom his master made ruler over his household, to give them food in due season? 46Blessed *is* that servant whom his master, when he comes, will find so doing. 47Assuredly, I say to you that he will make him ruler over all his goods. 48But if that evil servant says in his heart, 'My master is delaying his coming,' 49and begins to beat *his* fellow servants, and to eat and drink with the drunkards, 50the master of that servant will come on a day when he is not looking for *him* and at an hour that he is not aware of, 51and will cut him in two and appoint *him* his portion with the hypocrites. There shall be weeping and gnashing of teeth.

The Parable of the Wise and Foolish Virgins

25 "Then the kingdom of heaven shall be likened to ten virgins who took their lamps and went out to meet the bridegroom. 2Now five of them were wise, and five *were* foolish. 3Those who *were* foolish took their lamps and took no oil with them, 4but the wise took oil in their vessels with their lamps. 5But while the bridegroom was delayed, they all slumbered and slept.

6"And at midnight a cry was *heard*: 'Behold, the bridegroom is coming; go out to meet him!' 7Then all those virgins arose and trimmed their lamps. 8And the foolish said to the wise, 'Give us *some* of your oil, for our lamps are going out.' 9But the wise answered, saying, '*No*, lest there should not be enough for us and you; but go rather to those who sell, and buy for yourselves.' 10And while they went to buy, the bridegroom came, and those who were ready went in with him to the wedding; and the door was shut.

11"Afterward the other virgins came also, saying, 'Lord, Lord, open to us!' 12But he answered and said, 'Assuredly, I say to you, I do not know you.'

13"Watch therefore, for you know neither the day nor the hour in which the Son of Man is coming.

The Parable of the Talents

14"For *the kingdom of heaven is* like a man traveling to a far country, *who* called his own servants and delivered his goods to them. 15And to one he gave five talents, to another two, and to another one, to each according to his own ability; and immediately he went on a journey. 16Then he who had received the five talents went and traded with them, and made another five talents. 17And likewise he who *had received* two gained two more also. 18But he who had received one went and dug in the ground, and hid his lord's money. 19After a long time the lord of those servants came and settled accounts with them.

[s] Or *He*

20"So he who had received five talents came and brought five other talents, saying, 'Lord, you delivered to me five talents; look, I have gained five more talents besides them.' 21His lord said to him, 'Well *done,* good and faithful servant; you were faithful over a few things, I will make you ruler over many things. Enter into the joy of your lord.' 22He also who had received two talents came and said, 'Lord, you delivered to me two talents; look, I have gained two more talents besides them.' 23His lord said to him, 'Well *done,* good and faithful servant; you have been faithful over a few things, I will make you ruler over many things. Enter into the joy of your lord.'

24"Then he who had received the one talent came and said, 'Lord, I knew you to be a hard man, reaping where you have not sown, and gathering where you have not scattered seed. 25And I was afraid, and went and hid your talent in the ground. Look, *there* you have *what is* yours.'

26"But his lord answered and said to him, 'You wicked and lazy servant, you knew that I reap where I have not sown, and gather where I have not scattered seed. 27So you ought to have deposited my money with the bankers, and at my coming I would have received back my own with interest. 28So take the talent from him, and give *it* to him who has ten talents.

29'For to everyone who has, more will be given, and he will have abundance; but from him who does not have, even what he has will be taken away. 30And cast the unprofitable servant into the outer darkness. There will be weeping and gnashing of teeth.'

The Son of Man Will Judge the Nations

31"When the Son of Man comes in His glory, and all the holy angels with Him, then He will sit on the throne of His glory. 32All the nations will be gathered before Him, and He will separate them one from another, as a shepherd divides *his* sheep from the goats. 33And He will set the sheep on His right hand, but the goats on the left. 34Then the King will say to those on His right hand, 'Come, you blessed of My Father, inherit the kingdom pre-

pared for you from the foundation of the world: 35for I was hungry and you gave Me food; I was thirsty and you gave Me drink; I was a stranger and you took Me in; 36I *was* naked and you clothed Me; I was sick and you visited Me; I was in prison and you came to Me.'

37"Then the righteous will answer Him, saying, 'Lord, when did we see You hungry and feed *You,* or thirsty and give *You* drink? 38When did we see You a stranger and take *You* in, or naked and clothe *You?* 39Or when did we see You sick, or in prison, and come to You?' 40And the King will answer and say to them, 'Assuredly, I say to you, inasmuch as you did *it* to one of the least of these My brethren, you did *it* to Me.'

41"Then He will also say to those on the left hand, 'Depart from Me, you cursed, into the everlasting fire prepared for the devil and his angels: 42for I was hungry and you gave Me no food; I was thirsty and you gave Me no drink; 43I was a stranger and you did not take Me in, naked and you did not clothe Me, sick and in prison and you did not visit Me.'

44"Then they also will answer Him, saying, 'Lord, when did we see You hungry or thirsty or a stranger or naked or sick or in prison, and did not minister to You?' 45Then He will answer them, saying, 'Assuredly, I say to you, inasmuch as you did not do *it* to one of the least of these, you did not do *it* to Me.' 46And these will go away into everlasting punishment, but the righteous into eternal life.''

The Plot to Kill Jesus

26 Now it came to pass, when Jesus had finished all these sayings, *that* He said to His disciples, 2"You know that after two days is the Passover, and the Son of Man will be delivered up to be crucified."

3Then the chief priests, the scribes, and the elders of the people assembled at the palace of the high priest, who was called Caiaphas, 4and plotted to take Jesus by trickery and kill *Him.* 5But they said, "Not during the feast, lest there be an uproar among the people."

The Anointing at Bethany

6And when Jesus was in Bethany at the house of Simon the leper, 7a woman came to Him having an alabaster flask of very costly fragrant oil, and she poured it on His head as He sat *at the table.* 8But when His disciples saw *it,* they were indignant, saying, "Why this waste? 9For this fragrant oil might have been sold for much and given to *the* poor."

10But when Jesus was aware of *it,* He said to them, "Why do you trouble the woman? For she has done a good work for Me. 11For you have the poor with you always, but Me you do not have always. 12For in pouring this fragrant oil on My body, she did *it* for My burial. 13Assuredly, I say to you, wherever this gospel is preached in the whole world, what this woman has done will also be told as a memorial to her."

Judas Agrees to Betray Jesus

14Then one of the twelve, called Judas Iscariot, went to the chief priests 15and said, "What are you willing to give me if I deliver Him to you?" And they counted out to him thirty pieces of silver. 16So from that time he sought opportunity to betray Him.

Jesus Celebrates Passover with His Disciples

17Now on the first *day of the Feast* of the Unleavened Bread the disciples came to Jesus, saying to Him, "Where do You want us to prepare for You to eat the Passover?"

18And He said, "Go into the city to a certain man, and say to him, 'The Teacher says, "My time is at hand; I will keep the Passover at your house with My disciples." ' "

19So the disciples did as Jesus had directed them; and they prepared the Passover.

20When evening had come, He sat down with the twelve. 21Now as they were eating, He said, "Assuredly, I say to you, one of you will betray Me."

22And they were exceedingly sorrowful, and each of them began to say to Him, "Lord, is it I?"

23He answered and said, "He who dipped *his* hand with Me in the dish will betray Me. 24The Son of Man indeed goes just as it is written of Him, but woe to that man by whom the Son of Man is betrayed! It would have been good for that man if he had not been born."

25Then Judas, who was betraying Him, answered and said, "Rabbi, is it I?"

He said to him, "You have said it."

Jesus Institutes the Lord's Supper

26And as they were eating, Jesus took bread, blessed and broke *it,* and gave *it* to the disciples and said, "Take, eat; this is My body."

27Then He took the cup, and gave thanks, and gave *it* to them, saying, "Drink from it, all of you. 28For this is My blood of the new covenant, which is shed for many for the remission of sins. 29But I say to you, I will not drink of this fruit of the vine from now on until that day when I drink it new with you in My Father's kingdom."

30And when they had sung a hymn, they went out to the Mount of Olives.

Jesus Predicts Peter's Denial

31Then Jesus said to them, "All of you will be made to stumble because of Me this night, for it is written:

'I will strike the Shepherd,
And the sheep of the flock will be scattered.'*t*

32But after I have been raised, I will go before you to Galilee."

33Peter answered and said to Him, "Even if all are made to stumble because of You, I will never be made to stumble."

34Jesus said to him, "Assuredly, I say to you that this night, before the rooster crows, you will deny Me three times."

35Peter said to Him, "Even if I have to die with You, I will not deny You!" And so said all the disciples.

The Prayer in the Garden

36Then Jesus came with them to a place called Gethsemane, and said to the disciples, "Sit here while I go and pray over there." 37And He took with Him Peter and the two sons of Zebedee,

t Zechariah 13.7

and He began to be sorrowful and deeply distressed. 38Then He said to them, "My soul is exceedingly sorrowful, even to death. Stay here and watch with Me."

39He went a little farther and fell on His face, and prayed, saying, "O My Father, if it is possible, let this cup pass from Me; nevertheless, not as I will, but as You *will*."

40Then He came to the disciples and found them sleeping, and said to Peter, "What! Could you not watch with Me one hour? 41Watch and pray, lest you enter into temptation. The spirit indeed *is* willing, but the flesh *is* weak."

42Again, a second time, He went away and prayed, saying, "O My Father, if this cup cannot pass away from Me unless I drink it, Your will be done." 43And He came and found them asleep again, for their eyes were heavy.

44So He left them, went away again, and prayed the third time, saying the same words. 45Then He came to His disciples and said to them, "Are *you* still sleeping and resting? Behold, the hour is at hand, and the Son of Man is being betrayed into the hands of sinners. 46Rise, let us be going. See, My betrayer is at hand."

Betrayal and Arrest in Gethsemane

47And while He was still speaking, behold, Judas, one of the twelve, with a great multitude with swords and clubs, came from the chief priests and elders of the people. 48Now His betrayer had given them a sign, saying, "Whomever I kiss, He is the One; seize Him." 49Immediately he went up to Jesus and said, "Greetings, Rabbi!" and kissed Him.

50But Jesus said to him, "Friend, why have you come?"

Then they came and laid hands on Jesus and took Him. 51And suddenly, one of those *who were* with Jesus stretched out *his* hand and drew his sword, struck the servant of the high priest, and cut off his ear.

52But Jesus said to him, "Put your sword in its place, for all who take the sword will perish by the sword. 53Or do you think that I cannot now pray to My Father, and He will provide Me with more than twelve legions of angels? 54How then could the Scriptures be fulfilled, that it must happen thus?"

55In that hour Jesus said to the multitudes, "Have you come out, as against a robber, with swords and clubs to take Me? I sat daily with you, teaching in the temple, and you did not seize Me. 56But all this was done that the Scriptures of the prophets might be fulfilled."

Then all the disciples forsook Him and fled.

Jesus Faces the Sanhedrin

57And those who had laid hold of Jesus led *Him* away to Caiaphas the high priest, where the scribes and the elders were assembled. 58But Peter followed Him at a distance to the high priest's courtyard. And he went in and sat with the servants to see the end.

59Now the chief priests, the elders, and all the council sought false testimony against Jesus to put Him to death, 60but found none. Even though many false witnesses came forward, they found none. But at last two false witnesses came forward 61and said, "This *fellow* said, 'I am able to destroy the temple of God and to build it in three days.' "

62And the high priest arose and said to Him, "Do You answer nothing? What *is it* these men testify against You?" 63But Jesus kept silent. And the high priest answered and said to Him, "I put You under oath by the living God: Tell us if You are the Christ, the Son of God!"

64Jesus said to him, "*It is as* you said. Nevertheless, I say to you, hereafter you will see the Son of Man sitting at the right hand of the Power, and coming on the clouds of heaven."

65Then the high priest tore his clothes, saying, "He has spoken blasphemy! What further need do we have of witnesses? Look, now you have heard His blasphemy! 66What do you think?"

They answered and said, "He is deserving of death."

67Then they spat in His face and beat Him; and others struck *Him* with the palms of their hands, 68saying, "Prophesy to us, Christ! Who is the one who struck You?"

Peter Denies Jesus, and Weeps Bitterly

69Now Peter sat outside in the courtyard. And a servant girl came to him, saying, "You also were with Jesus of Galilee."

70But he denied it before *them* all, saying, "I do not know what you are saying."

71And when he had gone out to the gateway, another *girl* saw him and said to those *who were* there, "This *fellow* also was with Jesus of Nazareth."

72But again he denied with an oath, "I do not know the Man!"

73And a little later those who stood by came up and said to Peter, "Surely you also are *one* of them, for your speech betrays you."

74Then he began to curse and swear, *saying,* "I do not know the Man!"

Immediately a rooster crowed. 75And Peter remembered the word of Jesus who had said to him, "Before the rooster crows, you will deny Me three times." So he went out and wept bitterly.

Jesus Handed Over to Pontius Pilate

27 When morning came, all the chief priests and elders of the people plotted against Jesus to put Him to death. 2And when they had bound Him, they led Him away and delivered Him to Pontius Pilate the governor.

Judas Hangs Himself

3Then Judas, His betrayer, seeing that He had been condemned, was remorseful and brought back the thirty pieces of silver to the chief priests and elders, 4saying, "I have sinned by betraying innocent blood."

And they said, "What *is that* to us? You see *to it!*"

5Then he threw down the pieces of silver in the temple and departed, and went and hanged himself.

6But the chief priests took the silver pieces and said, "It is not lawful to put them into the treasury, because they are the price of blood." 7And they consulted together and bought with them the potter's field, to bury strangers in. 8Therefore that field has been called the Field of Blood to this day.

9Then was fulfilled what was spoken by Jeremiah the prophet, saying, "And they took the thirty pieces of silver, the value of Him who was priced, whom they of the children of Israel priced, 10and gave them for the potter's field, as the LORD directed me."*u*

Jesus Faces Pilate

11Now Jesus stood before the governor. And the governor asked Him, saying, "Are You the King of the Jews?"

Jesus said to him, "*It is as* you say." 12And while He was being accused by the chief priests and elders, He answered nothing.

13Then Pilate said to Him, "Do You not hear how many things they testify against You?" 14But He answered him not one word, so that the governor marveled greatly.

Taking the Place of Barabbas

15Now at the feast the governor was accustomed to releasing to the multitude one prisoner whom they wished. 16And at that time they had a notorious prisoner called Barabbas. 17Therefore, when they had gathered together, Pilate said to them, "Whom do you want me to release to you? Barabbas, or Jesus who is called Christ?" 18For he knew that they had handed Him over because of envy.

19While he was sitting on the judgment seat, his wife sent to him, saying, "Have nothing to do with that just Man, for I have suffered many things today in a dream because of Him."

20But the chief priests and elders persuaded the multitudes that they should ask for Barabbas and destroy Jesus. 21The governor answered and said to them, "Which of the two do you want me to release to you?"

They said, "Barabbas!"

22Pilate said to them, "What then shall I do with Jesus who is called Christ?"

They all said to him, "Let Him be crucified!"

23Then the governor said, "Why, what evil has He done?"

u Jeremiah 32.6-9

But they cried out all the more, saying, "Let Him be crucified!"

24When Pilate saw that he could not prevail at all, but rather *that* a tumult was rising, he took water and washed *his* hands before the multitude, saying, "I am innocent of the blood of this just Person. You see *to it.*"

25And all the people answered and said, "His blood *be* on us and on our children."

26Then he released Barabbas to them; and when he had scourged Jesus, he delivered *Him* to be crucified.

The Soldiers Mock Jesus

27Then the soldiers of the governor took Jesus into the Praetorium and gathered the whole garrison around Him. 28And they stripped Him and put a scarlet robe on Him. 29When they had twisted a crown of thorns, they put *it* on His head, and a reed in His right hand. And they bowed the knee before Him and mocked Him, saying, "Hail, King of the Jews!" 30Then they spat on Him, and took the reed and struck Him on the head. 31And when they had mocked Him, they took the robe off Him, put His *own* clothes on Him, and led Him away to be crucified.

The King on a Cross

32Now as they came out, they found a man of Cyrene, Simon by name. Him they compelled to bear His cross. 33And when they had come to a place called Golgotha, that is to say, Place of a Skull, 34they gave Him sour wine mingled with gall to drink. But when He had tasted *it,* He would not drink.

35Then they crucified Him, and divided His garments, casting lots, that it might be fulfilled which was spoken by the prophet:

"They divided My garments among
    them,
And for My clothing they cast
    lots."*v*

36Sitting down, they kept watch over Him there. 37And they put up over His head the accusation written against Him:

THIS IS JESUS
THE KING OF THE JEWS.

38Then two robbers were crucified with Him, one on the right and another on the left.

39And those who passed by blasphemed Him, wagging their heads 40and saying, "You who destroy the temple and build *it* in three days, save Yourself! If You are the Son of God, come down from the cross."

41Likewise the chief priests also, mocking with the scribes and elders, said, 42"He saved others; Himself He cannot save. If He is the King of Israel, let Him now come down from the cross, and we will believe Him. 43He trusted in God; let Him deliver Him now if He will have Him; for He said, 'I am the Son of God.' "

44Even the robbers who were crucified with Him reviled Him with the same thing.

Jesus Dies on the Cross

45Now from the sixth hour until the ninth hour there was darkness over all the land. 46And about the ninth hour Jesus cried out with a loud voice, saying, "Eli, Eli, lama sabachthani?" that is, "My God, My God, why have You forsaken Me?"*w*

47Some of those who stood there, when they heard *that,* said, "This Man is calling for Elijah!" 48Immediately one of them ran and took a sponge, filled *it* with sour wine and put *it* on a reed, and offered it to Him to drink.

49The rest said, "Let Him alone; let us see if Elijah will come to save Him."

50And Jesus cried out again with a loud voice, and yielded up His spirit.

51Then, behold, the veil of the temple was torn in two from top to bottom; and the earth quaked, and the rocks were split, 52and the graves were opened; and many bodies of the saints who had fallen asleep were raised; 53and coming out of the graves after His resurrection, they went into the holy city and appeared to many.

54So when the centurion and those with him, who were guarding Jesus, saw the earthquake and the things that

v Psalm 22.18   *w* Psalm 22.1

had happened, they feared greatly, saying, "Truly this was the Son of God!"

55And many women who followed Jesus from Galilee, ministering to Him, were there looking on from afar, 56among whom were Mary Magdalene, Mary the mother of James and Joses, and the mother of Zebedee's sons.

Jesus Buried in Joseph's Tomb

57Now when evening had come, there came a rich man from Arimathea, named Joseph, who himself had also become a disciple of Jesus. 58This man went to Pilate and asked for the body of Jesus. Then Pilate commanded the body to be given to him. 59When Joseph had taken the body, he wrapped it in a clean linen cloth, 60and laid it in his new tomb which he had hewn out of the rock; and he rolled a large stone against the door of the tomb, and departed. 61And Mary Magdalene was there, and the other Mary, sitting opposite the tomb.

Pilate Sets a Guard

62On the next day, which followed the Day of Preparation, the chief priests and Pharisees gathered together to Pilate, 63saying, "Sir, we remember, while He was still alive, how that deceiver said, 'After three days I will rise.' 64Therefore command that the tomb be made secure until the third day, lest His disciples come by night and steal Him away, and say to the people, 'He has risen from the dead.' So the last deception will be worse than the first."

65Pilate said to them, "You have a guard; go your way, make it as secure as you know how." 66So they went and made the tomb secure, sealing the stone and setting the guard.

He Is Risen

28 Now after the Sabbath, as the first day of the week began to dawn, Mary Magdalene and the other Mary came to see the tomb. 2And behold, there was a great earthquake; for an angel of the Lord descended from heaven, and came and rolled back the stone from the door, and sat on it. 3His countenance was like lightning, and his clothing as white as snow. 4And the guards shook for fear of him, and became like dead men.

5But the angel answered and said to the women, "Do not be afraid, for I know that you seek Jesus who was crucified. 6He is not here; for He is risen, as He said. Come, see the place where the Lord lay. 7And go quickly and tell His disciples that He is risen from the dead, and indeed He is going before you into Galilee; there you will see Him. Behold, I have told you."

8So they went out quickly from the tomb with fear and great joy, and ran to bring His disciples word.

The Women Worship the Risen Lord

9And as they went to tell His disciples, behold, Jesus met them, saying, "Rejoice!" So they came and held Him by the feet and worshiped Him. 10Then Jesus said to them, "Do not be afraid. Go and tell My brethren to go to Galilee, and there they will see Me."

The Soldiers Are Bribed

11Now while they were going, behold, some of the guard came into the city and reported to the chief priests all the things that had happened. 12When they had assembled with the elders and consulted together, they gave a large sum of money to the soldiers, 13saying, "Tell them, 'His disciples came at night and stole Him away while we slept.' 14And if this comes to the governor's ears, we will appease him and make you secure." 15So they took the money and did as they were instructed; and this saying is commonly reported among the Jews until this day.

The Great Commission

16Then the eleven disciples went away into Galilee, to the mountain which Jesus had appointed for them. 17When they saw Him, they worshiped Him; but some doubted.

18And Jesus came and spoke to them, saying, "All authority has been given to Me in heaven and on earth. 19Go therefore and make disciples of all the nations, baptizing them in the name of the Father and of the Son and of the Holy Spirit, 20teaching them to observe all things that I have commanded you; and lo, I am with you always, even to the end of the age." Amen.

MARK

John the Baptist Prepares the Way

1 The beginning of the gospel of Jesus Christ, the Son of God. 2As it is written in the Prophets:

"Behold, I send My messenger
before Your face,
Who will prepare Your way before
You." *a*

3 "The voice of one crying in the
wilderness:
'Prepare the way of the LORD;
Make His paths straight.' "*b*

4John came baptizing in the wilderness and preaching a baptism of repentance for the remission of sins. 5Then all the land of Judea, and those from Jerusalem, went out to him and were all baptized by him in the Jordan River, confessing their sins.

6Now John was clothed with camel's hair and with a leather belt around his waist, and he ate locusts and wild honey. 7And he preached, saying, "There comes One after me who is mightier than I, whose sandal strap I am not worthy to stoop down and loose. 8I indeed baptized you with water, but He will baptize you with the Holy Spirit."

John Baptizes Jesus

9It came to pass in those days *that* Jesus came from Nazareth of Galilee, and was baptized by John in the Jordan. 10And immediately, coming up from the water, He saw the heavens parting and the Spirit descending upon Him like a dove. 11Then a voice came from heaven, "You are My beloved Son, in whom I am well pleased."

Satan Tempts Jesus

12Immediately the Spirit drove Him into the wilderness. 13And He was there in the wilderness forty days, tempted by Satan, and was with the wild beasts; and the angels ministered to Him.

Jesus Begins His Galilean Ministry

14Now after John was put in prison, Jesus came to Galilee, preaching the gospel of the kingdom of God, 15and saying, "The time is fulfilled, and the kingdom of God is at hand. Repent, and believe in the gospel."

Four Fishermen Called as Disciples

16And as He walked by the Sea of Galilee, He saw Simon and Andrew his brother casting a net into the sea; for they were fishermen. 17Then Jesus said to them, "Follow Me, and I will make you become fishers of men." 18They immediately left their nets and followed Him.

19When He had gone a little farther from there, He saw James the *son* of Zebedee, and John his brother, who also *were* in the boat mending their nets. 20And immediately He called them, and they left their father Zebedee in the boat with the hired servants, and went after Him.

Jesus Casts Out an Unclean Spirit

21Then they went into Capernaum, and immediately on the Sabbath He entered the synagogue and taught. 22And they were astonished at His teaching, for He taught them as one having authority, and not as the scribes.

23Now there was a man in their synagogue with an unclean spirit. And he cried out, 24saying, "Let *us* alone! What have we to do with You, Jesus of Nazareth? Did You come to destroy us? I know who You are—the Holy One of God!"

25But Jesus rebuked him, saying, "Be quiet, and come out of him!" 26And when the unclean spirit had convulsed him and cried out with a loud voice, he came out of him. 27Then they were all amazed, so that they questioned among themselves, saying, "What is this? What new doctrine *is* this? For with authority He commands even the unclean spirits, and they obey Him." 28And immediately His fame spread throughout all the region around Galilee.

a Malachi 3.1   *b* Isaiah 40.3

Peter's Mother-in-Law Healed

29Now as soon as they had come out of the synagogue, they entered the house of Simon and Andrew, with James and John. 30But Simon's wife's mother lay sick with a fever, and they told Him about her at once. 31So He came and took her by the hand and lifted her up, and immediately the fever left her. And she served them.

Many Healed After Sabbath Sunset

32At evening, when the sun had set, they brought to Him all who were sick and those who were demon-possessed. 33And the whole city was gathered together at the door. 34Then He healed many who were sick with various diseases, and cast out many demons; and He did not allow the demons to speak, because they knew Him.

Preaching in Galilee

35Now in the morning, having risen a long while before daylight, He went out and departed to a solitary place; and there He prayed. 36And Simon and those *who were* with Him searched for Him. 37When they found Him, they said to Him, "Everyone is looking for You."

38But He said to them, "Let us go into the next towns, that I may preach there also, because for this purpose I have come forth."

39And He was preaching in their synagogues throughout all Galilee, and casting out demons.

Jesus Cleanses a Leper

40Now a leper came to Him, imploring Him, kneeling down to Him and saying to Him, "If You are willing, You can make me clean."

41Then Jesus, moved with compassion, stretched out *His* hand and touched him, and said to him, "I am willing; be cleansed." 42As soon as He had spoken, immediately the leprosy left him, and he was cleansed. 43And He strictly warned him and sent him away at once, 44and said to him, "See that you say nothing to anyone; but go your way, show yourself to the priest, and offer for your cleansing those things which Moses commanded, as a testimony to them."

45However, he went out and began to proclaim *it* freely, and to spread the matter, so that Jesus could no longer openly enter the city, but was outside in deserted places; and they came to Him from every direction.

Jesus Forgives and Heals a Paralytic

2 And again He entered Capernaum after *some* days, and it was heard that He was in the house. 2Immediately many gathered together, so that there was no longer room to receive *them*, not even near the door. And He preached the word to them. 3Then they came to Him, bringing a paralytic who was carried by four *men.* 4And when they could not come near Him because of the crowd, they uncovered the roof where He was. So when they had broken through, they let down the bed on which the paralytic was lying.

5When Jesus saw their faith, He said to the paralytic, "Son, your sins are forgiven you."

6And some of the scribes were sitting there and reasoning in their hearts, 7"Why does this *Man* speak blasphemies like this? Who can forgive sins but God alone?"

8But immediately, when Jesus perceived in His spirit that they reasoned thus within themselves, He said to them, "Why do you reason about these things in your hearts? 9Which is easier, to say to the paralytic, 'Your sins are forgiven you,' or to say, 'Arise, take up your bed and walk'? 10But that you may know that the Son of Man has power on earth to forgive sins"—He said to the paralytic, 11"I say to you, arise, take up your bed, and go to your house." 12Immediately he arose, took up the bed, and went out in the presence of them all, so that all were amazed and glorified God, saying, "We never saw *anything* like this!"

Matthew the Tax Collector

13Then He went out again by the sea; and all the multitude came to Him, and He taught them. 14As He passed by, He saw Levi the *son* of Alphaeus sitting at the tax office. And He said to him, "Follow Me." So he arose and followed Him.

15Now it happened, as He was dining

in *Levi's* house, that many tax collectors and sinners also sat together with Jesus and His disciples; for there were many, and they followed Him. 16And when the scribes and Pharisees saw Him eating with the tax collectors and sinners, they said to His disciples, "How *is it* that He eats and drinks with tax collectors and sinners?"

17When Jesus heard *it,* He said to them, "Those who are well have no need of a physician, but those who are sick. I did not come to call *the* righteous, but sinners, to repentance."

Jesus Is Questioned About Fasting

18The disciples of John and of the Pharisees were fasting. Then they came and said to Him, "Why do the disciples of John and of the Pharisees fast, but Your disciples do not fast?"

19And Jesus said to them, "Can the friends of the bridegroom fast while the bridegroom is with them? As long as they have the bridegroom with them they cannot fast. 20But the days will come when the bridegroom will be taken away from them, and then they will fast in those days. 21No one sews a piece of unshrunk cloth on an old garment; or else the new piece pulls away from the old, and the tear is made worse. 22And no one puts new wine into old wineskins; or else the new wine bursts the wineskins, the wine is spilled, and the wineskins are ruined. But new wine must be put into new wineskins."

Jesus Is Lord of the Sabbath

23Now it happened that He went through the grainfields on the Sabbath; and as they went His disciples began to pluck the heads of grain. 24And the Pharisees said to Him, "Look, why do they do what is not lawful on the Sabbath?"

25But He said to them, "Have you never read what David did when he was in need and hungry, he and those with him: 26how he went into the house of God *in the days* of Abiathar the high priest, and ate the showbread, which is not lawful to eat except for the priests, and also gave some to those who were with him?"

27And He said to them, "The Sabbath was made for man, and not man for the Sabbath. 28Therefore the Son of Man is also Lord of the Sabbath."

Healing on the Sabbath

3 And He entered the synagogue again, and a man was there who had a withered hand. 2So they watched Him closely, whether He would heal him on the Sabbath, so that they might accuse Him. 3And He said to the man who had the withered hand, "Step forward." 4Then He said to them, "Is it lawful on the Sabbath to do good or to do evil, to save life or to kill?" But they kept silent. 5And when He had looked around at them with anger, being grieved by the hardness of their hearts, He said to the man, "Stretch out your hand." And he stretched *it* out, and his hand was restored as whole as the other. 6Then the Pharisees went out and immediately plotted with the Herodians against Him, how they might destroy Him.

A Great Multitude Follows Jesus

7But Jesus withdrew with His disciples to the sea. And a great multitude from Galilee followed Him, and from Judea 8and Jerusalem and Idumea and beyond the Jordan; and those from Tyre and Sidon, a great multitude, when they heard how many things He was doing, came to Him. 9So He told His disciples that a small boat should be kept ready for Him because of the multitude, lest they should crush Him. 10For He healed many, so that as many as had afflictions pressed about Him to touch Him. 11And the unclean spirits, whenever they saw Him, fell down before Him and cried out, saying, "You are the Son of God." 12But He sternly warned them that they should not make Him known.

The Twelve Apostles

13And He went up on the mountain and called to *Him* those He Himself wanted. And they came to Him. 14Then He appointed twelve, that they might be with Him and that He might send them out to preach, 15and to have power to heal sicknesses and to cast out demons: 16Simon, to whom He gave the name Peter; 17James the *son* of

Zebedee and John the brother of James, to whom He gave the name Boanerges, that is, "Sons of Thunder"; 18Andrew, Philip, Bartholomew, Matthew, Thomas, James the *son* of Alphaeus, Thaddaeus, Simon the Cananite; 19and Judas Iscariot, who also betrayed Him. And they went into a house.

A House Divided Cannot Stand

20Then the multitude came together again, so that they could not so much as eat bread. 21But when His own people heard *about this*, they went out to lay hold of Him, for they said, "He is out of His mind."

22And the scribes who came down from Jerusalem said, "He has Beelzebub," and, "By the ruler of the demons He casts out demons."

23So He called them to *Himself* and said to them in parables: "How can Satan cast out Satan? 24If a kingdom is divided against itself, that kingdom cannot stand. 25And if a house is divided against itself, that house cannot stand. 26And if Satan has risen up against himself, and is divided, he cannot stand, but has an end. 27No one can enter a strong man's house and plunder his goods, unless he first binds the strong man. And then he will plunder his house.

The Unpardonable Sin

28"Assuredly, I say to you, all sins will be forgiven the sons of men, and whatever blasphemies they may utter; 29but he who blasphemes against the Holy Spirit never has forgiveness, but is subject to eternal condemnation"— 30because they said, "He has an unclean spirit."

Jesus' Mother and Brothers Send for Him

31Then His brothers and His mother came, and standing outside they sent to Him, calling Him. 32And a multitude was sitting around Him; and they said to Him, "Look, Your mother and Your brothers are outside seeking You." 33But He answered them, saying, "Who is My mother, or My brothers?" 34And He looked around in a circle at those who sat about Him, and said, "Here are My mother and My brothers! 35For whoever does the will of God is My brother and My sister and mother."

The Parable of the Sower

4 And again He began to teach by the sea. And a great multitude was gathered to Him, so that He got into a boat and sat *in it* on the sea; and the whole multitude was on the land facing the sea. 2Then He taught them many things by parables, and said to them in His teaching:

3"Listen! Behold, a sower went out to sow. 4And it happened, as he sowed, *that* some *seed* fell by the wayside; and the birds of the air came and devoured it. 5Some fell on stony ground, where it did not have much earth; and immediately it sprang up because it had no depth of earth. 6But when the sun was up it was scorched, and because it had no root it withered away. 7And some *seed* fell among thorns; and the thorns grew up and choked it, and it yielded no crop. 8But other *seed* fell on good ground and yielded a crop that sprang up, increased and produced: some thirtyfold, some sixty, and some a hundred."

9And He said to them, "He who has ears to hear, let him hear!"

The Purpose of Parables

10But when He was alone, those around Him with the twelve asked Him about the parable. 11And He said to them, "To you it has been given to know the mystery of the kingdom of God; but to those who are outside, all things come in parables, 12so that

'Seeing they may see and not perceive,
And hearing they may hear and not understand;
Lest they should turn,
And *their* sins be forgiven them.' "c

The Parable of the Sower Explained

13And He said to them, "Do you not understand this parable? How then will you understand all the parables? 14The sower sows the word. 15And these are the ones by the wayside

c Isaiah 6.9, 10

where the word is sown. When they hear, Satan comes immediately and takes away the word that was sown in their hearts. 16These likewise are the ones sown on stony ground who, when they hear the word, immediately receive it with gladness; 17and they have no root in themselves, and so endure only for a time. Afterward, when tribulation or persecution arises for the word's sake, immediately they stumble. 18Now these are the ones sown among thorns; *they are* the ones who hear the word, 19and the cares of this world, the deceitfulness of riches, and the desires for other things entering in choke the word, and it becomes unfruitful. 20But these are the ones sown on good ground, those who hear the word, accept *it*, and bear fruit: some thirtyfold, some sixty, and some a hundred."

Light Under a Basket

21Also He said to them, "Is a lamp brought to be put under a basket or under a bed? Is it not to be set on a lampstand? 22For there is nothing hidden which will not be revealed, nor has anything been kept secret but that it should come to light. 23If anyone has ears to hear, let him hear."

24Then He said to them, "Take heed what you hear. With the same measure you use, it will be measured to you; and to you who hear, more will be given. 25For whoever has, to him more will be given; but whoever does not have, even what he has will be taken away from him."

The Parable of the Growing Seed

26And He said, "The kingdom of God is as if a man should scatter seed on the ground, 27and should sleep by night and rise by day, and the seed should sprout and grow, he himself does not know how. 28For the earth yields crops by itself: first the blade, then the head, after that the full grain in the head. 29But when the grain ripens, immediately he puts in the sickle, because the harvest has come."

The Parable of the Mustard Seed

30Then He said, "To what shall we liken the kingdom of God? Or with what parable shall we picture it?

31*It is* like a mustard seed which, when it is sown on the ground, is smaller than all the seeds on earth; 32but when it is sown, it grows up and becomes greater than all herbs, and shoots out large branches, so that the birds of the air may nest under its shade."

Jesus' Use of Parables

33And with many such parables He spoke the word to them as they were able to hear *it*. 34But without a parable He did not speak to them. And when they were alone, He explained all things to His disciples.

Wind and Wave Obey Jesus

35On the same day, when evening had come, He said to them, "Let us cross over to the other side." 36Now when they had left the multitude, they took Him along in the boat as He was. And other little boats were also with Him. 37And a great windstorm arose, and the waves beat into the boat, so that it was already filling. 38But He was in the stern, asleep on a pillow. And they awoke Him and said to Him, "Teacher, do You not care that we are perishing?" 39Then He arose and rebuked the wind, and said to the sea, "Peace, be still!" And the wind ceased and there was a great calm. 40But He said to them, "Why are you so fearful? How *is it* that you have no faith?" 41And they feared exceedingly, and said to one another, "Who can this be, that even the wind and the sea obey Him!"

A Demon-Possessed Man Healed

5 Then they came to the other side of the sea, to the country of the Gadarenes. 2And when He had come out of the boat, immediately there met Him out of the tombs a man with an unclean spirit, 3who had *his* dwelling among the tombs; and no one could bind him, not even with chains, 4because he had often been bound with shackles and chains. And the chains had been pulled apart by him, and the shackles broken in pieces; neither could anyone tame him. 5And always, night and day, he was in the mountains and in the tombs, crying out and cutting himself with stones.

6When he saw Jesus from afar, he ran and worshiped Him. 7And he cried out with a loud voice and said, "What have I to do with You, Jesus, Son of the Most High God? I implore You by God that You do not torment me."

8For He said to him, "Come out of the man, unclean spirit!" 9Then He asked him, "What *is* your name?"

And he answered, saying, "My name is Legion; for we are many." 10Also he begged Him earnestly that He would not send them out of the country.

11Now a large herd of swine was feeding there near the mountains. 12So all the demons begged Him, saying, "Send us to the swine, that we may enter them." 13And at once Jesus gave them permission. Then the unclean spirits went out and entered the swine (there were about two thousand); and the herd ran violently down the steep place into the sea, and drowned in the sea.

14So those who fed the swine fled, and they told *it* in the city and in the country. And they went out to see what it was that had happened. 15Then they came to Jesus, and saw the one *who had been* demon-possessed and had the legion, sitting and clothed and in his right mind. And they were afraid. 16And those who saw it told them how it happened to him *who had been* demon-possessed, and about the swine. 17Then they began to plead with Him to depart from their region.

18And when He got into the boat, he who had been demon-possessed begged Him that he might be with Him. 19However, Jesus did not permit him, but said to him, "Go home to your friends, and tell them what great things the Lord has done for you, and how He has had compassion on you." 20And he departed and began to proclaim in Decapolis all that Jesus had done for him; and all marveled.

A Girl Restored to Life and a Woman Healed

21Now when Jesus had crossed over again by boat to the other side, a great multitude gathered to Him; and He was by the sea. 22And behold, one of the rulers of the synagogue came, Jairus by name. And when he saw Him, he fell at His feet 23and begged Him earnestly, saying, "My little daughter lies at the point of death. Come and lay Your hands on her, that she may be healed, and she will live." 24So *Jesus* went with him, and a great multitude followed Him and thronged Him.

25Now a certain woman had a flow of blood for twelve years, 26and had suffered many things from many physicians. She had spent all that she had and was no better, but rather grew worse. 27When she heard about Jesus, she came behind *Him* in the crowd and touched His garment. 28For she said, "If only I may touch His clothes, I shall be made well."

29Immediately the fountain of her blood was dried up, and she felt in *her* body that she was healed of the affliction. 30And Jesus, immediately knowing in Himself that power had gone out of Him, turned around in the crowd and said, "Who touched My clothes?"

31But His disciples said to Him, "You see the multitude thronging You, and You say, 'Who touched Me?' "

32And He looked around to see her who had done this thing. 33But the woman, fearing and trembling, knowing what had happened to her, came and fell down before Him and told Him the whole truth. 34And He said to her, "Daughter, your faith has made you well. Go in peace, and be healed of your affliction."

35While He was still speaking, *some* came from the ruler of the synagogue's *house* who said, "Your daughter is dead. Why trouble the Teacher any further?"

36As soon as Jesus heard the word that was spoken, He said to the ruler of the synagogue, "Do not be afraid; only believe." 37And He permitted no one to follow Him except Peter, James, and John the brother of James. 38Then He came to the house of the ruler of the synagogue, and saw a tumult and those who wept and wailed loudly. 39When He came in, He said to them, "Why make this commotion and weep? The child is not dead, but sleeping."

40And they ridiculed Him. But when He had put them all outside, He took the father and the mother of the child, and those *who were* with Him, and entered where the child was lying. 41Then He took the child by the hand, and said to her, "Talitha, cumi," which is translated, "Little girl, I say to you, arise." 42Immediately the girl arose and walked, for she was twelve years *of age.* And they were overcome with great amazement. 43But He commanded them strictly that no one should know it, and said that *something* should be given her to eat.

Jesus Rejected at Nazareth

6 Then He went out from there and came to His own country, and His disciples followed Him. 2And when the Sabbath had come, He began to teach in the synagogue. And many hearing *Him* were astonished, saying, "Where *did* this Man *get* these things? And what wisdom *is* this which is given to Him, that such mighty works are performed by His hands! 3Is this not the carpenter, the Son of Mary, and brother of James, Joses, Judas, and Simon? And are not His sisters here with us?" So they were offended at Him.

4But Jesus said to them, "A prophet is not without honor except in his own country, among his own relatives, and in his own house." 5Now He could do no mighty work there, except that He laid His hands on a few sick people and healed *them.* 6And He marveled because of their unbelief. Then He went about the villages in a circuit, teaching.

Sending Out the Twelve

7And He called the twelve to *Himself,* and began to send them out two *by* two, and gave them power over unclean spirits. 8He commanded them to take nothing for the journey except a staff— no bag, no bread, no copper in *their* money belts— 9but to wear sandals, and not to put on two tunics.

10Also He said to them, "In whatever place you enter a house, stay there till you depart from that place. 11And whoever will not receive you nor hear you, when you depart from there, shake off the dust under your feet as a testimony against them. Assuredly, I say to you, it will be more tolerable for Sodom and Gomorrah in the day of judgment than for that city!"

12So they went out and preached that *people* should repent. 13And they cast out many demons, and anointed with oil many who were sick, and healed *them.*

John the Baptist Beheaded

14Now King Herod heard *of Him,* for His name had become well known. And he said, "John the Baptist is risen from the dead, and therefore these powers are at work in him."

15Others said, "It is Elijah."

And others said, "It is the Prophet, or like one of the prophets."

16But when Herod heard, he said, "This is John, whom I beheaded; he has been raised from the dead!" 17For Herod himself had sent and laid hold of John, and bound him in prison for the sake of Herodias, his brother Philip's wife; for he had married her. 18Because John had said to Herod, "It is not lawful for you to have your brother's wife."

19Therefore Herodias held it against him and wanted to kill him, but she could not; 20for Herod feared John, knowing that he *was* a just and holy man, and he protected him. And when he heard him, he did many things, and heard him gladly.

21Then an opportune day came when Herod on his birthday gave a feast for his nobles, the high officers, and the chief *men* of Galilee. 22And when Herodias' daughter herself came in and danced, and pleased Herod and those who sat with him, the king said to the girl, "Ask me whatever you want, and I will give *it* to you." 23He also swore to her, "Whatever you ask me, I will give you, up to half my kingdom."

24So she went out and said to her mother, "What shall I ask?"

And she said, "The head of John the Baptist!"

25Immediately she came in with haste to the king and asked, saying, "I want you to give me at once the head of John the Baptist on a platter."

26And the king was exceedingly sorry; *yet,* because of the oaths and because of those who sat with him, he did not want to refuse her. 27Immediately the king sent an executioner and commanded his head to be brought. And he went and beheaded him in prison,

28brought his head on a platter, and gave it to the girl; and the girl gave it to her mother. 29When his disciples heard *of it*, they came and took away his corpse and laid it in a tomb.

Feeding the Five Thousand

30Then the apostles gathered to Jesus and told Him all things, both what they had done and what they had taught. 31And He said to them, "Come aside by yourselves to a deserted place and rest a while." For there were many coming and going, and they did not even have time to eat. 32So they departed to a deserted place in the boat by themselves.

33But the multitudes saw them departing, and many knew Him and ran there on foot from all the cities. They arrived before them and came together to Him. 34And Jesus, when He came out, saw a great multitude and was moved with compassion for them, because they were like sheep not having a shepherd. So He began to teach them many things. 35When the day was now far spent, His disciples came to Him and said, "This is a deserted place, and already the hour *is* late. 36Send them away, that they may go into the surrounding country and villages and buy themselves bread; for they have nothing to eat."

37But He answered and said to them, "You give them something to eat."

And they said to Him, "Shall we go and buy two hundred denarii worth of bread and give them *something* to eat?"

38But He said to them, "How many loaves do you have? Go and see."

And when they found out they said, "Five, and two fish."

39Then He commanded them to make them all sit down in groups on the green grass. 40So they sat down in ranks, in hundreds and in fifties. 41And when He had taken the five loaves and the two fish, He looked up to heaven, blessed and broke the loaves, and gave *them* to His disciples to set before them; and the two fish He divided among *them* all. 42So they all ate and were filled. 43And they took up twelve baskets full of fragments and of the fish. 44Now those who had eaten the loaves were about five thousand men.

Jesus Walks on the Sea

45Immediately He made His disciples get into the boat and go before Him to the other side, to Bethsaida, while He sent the multitude away. 46And when He had sent them away, He departed to the mountain to pray. 47Now when evening came, the boat was in the middle of the sea; and He *was* alone on the land. 48Then He saw them straining at rowing, for the wind was against them. Now about the fourth watch of the night He came to them, walking on the sea, and would have passed them by. 49And when they saw Him walking on the sea, they supposed it was a ghost, and cried out; 50for they all saw Him and were troubled. But immediately He talked with them and said to them, "Be of good cheer! It is I; do not be afraid." 51Then He went up into the boat to them, and the wind ceased. And they were greatly amazed in themselves beyond measure, and marveled. 52For they had not understood about the loaves, because their heart was hardened.

Many Touch Him and Are Made Well

53When they had crossed over, they came to the land of Gennesaret and anchored there. 54And when they came out of the boat, immediately the people recognized Him, 55ran through that whole surrounding region, and began to carry about on beds those who were sick to wherever they heard He was. 56Wherever He entered, into villages, cities, or the country, they laid the sick in the marketplaces, and begged Him that they might just touch the hem of His garment. And as many as touched Him were made well.

Defilement Comes from Within

7 Then the Pharisees and some of the scribes came together to Him, having come from Jerusalem. 2Now when they saw some of His disciples eat bread with defiled, that is, with unwashed hands, they found fault. 3For the Pharisees and all the Jews do not eat unless they wash *their* hands in a special way, holding the tradition of the elders. 4*When they come* from the marketplace, they do not eat unless

they wash. And there are many other things which they have received and hold, *like* the washing of cups, pitchers, copper vessels, and couches.

5Then the Pharisees and scribes asked Him, "Why do Your disciples not walk according to the tradition of the elders, but eat bread with unwashed hands?"

6He answered and said to them, "Well did Isaiah prophesy of you hypocrites, as it is written:

'This people honors Me with *their* lips,
But their heart is far from Me.
7   And in vain they worship Me,
Teaching *as* doctrines the commandments of men.'d

8For laying aside the commandment of God, you hold the tradition of men—the washing of pitchers and cups, and many other such things you do."

9He said to them, "*All too* well you reject the commandment of God, that you may keep your tradition. 10For Moses said, 'Honor your father and your mother';e and, 'He who curses father or mother, let him be put to death.'f 11But you say, 'If a man says to his father or mother, "Whatever profit you might have received from me *is* Corban"—' (that is, a gift *to* God), 12then you no longer let him do anything for his father or his mother, 13making the word of God of no effect through your tradition which you have handed down. And many such things you do."

14When He had called all the multitude to *Himself*, He said to them, "Hear Me, everyone, and understand: 15There is nothing that enters a man from outside which can defile him; but the things which come out of him, those are the things that defile a man. 16If anyone has ears to hear, let him hear!"

17When He had entered a house away from the crowd, His disciples asked Him concerning the parable. 18So He said to them, "Are you thus without understanding also? Do you not perceive that whatever enters a man from outside cannot defile him, 19because it does not enter his heart but his stomach, and is eliminated, *thus* purifying all foods?" 20And He said, "What comes out of a man, that defiles a man. 21For from within, out of the heart of men, proceed evil thoughts, adulteries, fornications, murders 22thefts, covetousness, wickedness, deceit, lewdness, an evil eye, blasphemy, pride, foolishness. 23All these evil things come from within and defile a man."

A Gentile Shows Her Faith

24From there He arose and went to the region of Tyre and Sidon. And He entered a house and wanted no one to know *it*, but He could not be hidden. 25For a woman whose young daughter had an unclean spirit heard about Him, and she came and fell at His feet. 26The woman was a Greek, a Syro-Phoenician by birth, and she kept asking Him to cast the demon out of her daughter. 27But Jesus said to her, "Let the children be filled first, for it is not good to take the children's bread and throw *it* to the little dogs."

28And she answered and said to Him, "Yes, Lord, yet even the little dogs under the table eat from the children's crumbs."

29Then He said to her, "For this saying go your way; the demon has gone out of your daughter."

30And when she had come to her house, she found the demon gone out, and her daughter lying on the bed.

Jesus Heals a Deaf-Mute

31Again, departing from the region of Tyre and Sidon, He came through the midst of the region of Decapolis to the Sea of Galilee. 32Then they brought to Him one who was deaf and had an impediment in his speech, and they begged Him to put His hand on him. 33And He took him aside from the multitude, and put His fingers in his ears, and He spat and touched his tongue. 34Then, looking up to heaven, He sighed, and said to him, "Ephphatha," that is, "Be opened."

35Immediately his ears were opened, and the impediment of his tongue was loosed, and he spoke plainly. 36Then He commanded them that they should tell no one; but the more He commanded

d Isaiah 29.13   e Exodus 20.12; Deuteronomy 5.16   f Exodus 21.17

them, the more widely they proclaimed *it*. 37And they were astonished beyond measure, saying, "He has done all things well. He makes both the deaf to hear and the mute to speak."

Feeding the Four Thousand

8 In those days, the multitude being very great and having nothing to eat, Jesus called His disciples *to Him* and said to them, 2"I have compassion on the multitude, because they have now continued with Me three days and have nothing to eat. 3And if I send them away hungry to their own houses, they will faint on the way; for some of them have come from afar."

4Then His disciples answered Him, "How can one satisfy these people with bread here in the wilderness?"

5He asked them, "How many loaves do you have?"

And they said, "Seven."

6So He commanded the multitude to sit down on the ground. And He took the seven loaves and gave thanks, broke *them* and gave *them* to His disciples to set before *them;* and they set *them* before the multitude. 7They also had a few small fish; and having blessed them, He said to set them also before *them.* 8So they ate and were filled, and they took up seven large baskets of leftover fragments. 9Now those who had eaten were about four thousand. And He sent them away, 10immediately got into the boat with His disciples, and came to the region of Dalmanutha.

The Pharisees Seek a Sign

11Then the Pharisees came out and began to dispute with Him, seeking from Him a sign from heaven, testing Him. 12But He sighed deeply in His spirit, and said, "Why does this generation seek a sign? Assuredly, I say to you, no sign shall be given to this generation."

Beware of the Leaven of the Pharisees and Herod

13And He left them, and getting into the boat again, departed to the other side. 14Now the disciples had forgotten to take bread, and they did not have more than one loaf with them in the boat. 15Then He charged them, saying, "Take heed, beware of the leaven of the Pharisees and the leaven of Herod."

16And they reasoned among themselves, saying, "It is because we have no bread."

17But Jesus, being aware of *it,* said to them, "Why do you reason because you have no bread? Do you not yet perceive nor understand? Is your heart still hardened? 18Having eyes, do you not see? And having ears, do you not hear? And do you not remember? 19When I broke the five loaves for the five thousand, how many baskets full of fragments did you take up?"

They said to Him, "Twelve."

20"Also, when I broke the seven for the four thousand, how many large baskets full of fragments did you take up?"

And they said, "Seven."

21So He said to them, "How *is it* you do not understand?"

A Blind Man Healed at Bethsaida

22Then He came to Bethsaida; and they brought a blind man to Him, and begged Him to touch him. 23So He took the blind man by the hand and led him out of the town. And when He had spit on his eyes and put His hands on him, He asked him if he saw anything.

24And he looked up and said, "I see men like trees, walking."

25Then He put *His* hands on his eyes again and made him look up. And he was restored and saw everyone clearly. 26Then He sent him away to his house, saying, "Neither go into the town, nor tell anyone in the town."

Peter Confesses Jesus as the Christ

27Now Jesus and His disciples went out to the towns of Caesarea Philippi; and on the road He asked His disciples, saying to them, "Who do men say that I am?"

28So they answered, "John the Baptist; but some *say,* Elijah; and others, one of the prophets."

29He said to them, "But who do you say that I am?"

Peter answered and said to Him, "You are the Christ."

30Then He strictly warned them that they should tell no one about Him.

Jesus Predicts His Death and Resurrection

31And He began to teach them that the Son of Man must suffer many things, and be rejected by the elders and chief priests and scribes, and be killed, and after three days rise again. 32He spoke this word openly. Then Peter took Him aside and began to rebuke Him. 33But when He had turned around and looked at His disciples, He rebuked Peter, saying, "Get behind Me, Satan! For you are not mindful of the things of God, but the things of men."

Take Up the Cross and Follow Him

34When He had called the people to *Himself*, with His disciples also, He said to them, "Whoever desires to come after Me, let him deny himself, and take up his cross, and follow Me. 35For whoever desires to save his life will lose it, but whoever loses his life for My sake and the gospel's will save it. 36For what will it profit a man if he gains the whole world, and loses his own soul? 37Or what will a man give in exchange for his soul? 38For whoever is ashamed of Me and My words in this adulterous and sinful generation, of him the Son of Man also will be ashamed when He comes in the glory of His Father with the holy angels."

Jesus Transfigured on the Mount

9 And He said to them, "Assuredly, I say to you that there are some standing here who will not taste death till they see the kingdom of God present with power."

2Now after six days Jesus took Peter, James, and John, and led them up on a high mountain apart by themselves; and He was transfigured before them. 3His clothes became shining, exceedingly white, like snow, such as no launderer on earth can whiten them. 4And Elijah appeared to them with Moses, and they were talking with Jesus. 5Then Peter answered and said to Jesus, "Rabbi, it is good for us to be here; and let us make three tabernacles: one for You, one for Moses, and one for Elijah"—6because he did not know what to say, for they were greatly afraid.

7And a cloud came and overshad-owed them; and a voice came out of the cloud, saying, "This is My beloved Son. Hear Him!" 8Suddenly, when they had looked around, they saw no one anymore, but only Jesus with themselves.

9Now as they came down from the mountain, He commanded them that they should tell no one the things they had seen, till the Son of Man had risen from the dead. 10So they kept this word to themselves, questioning what the rising from the dead meant.

11And they asked Him, saying, "Why do the scribes say that Elijah must come first?"

12Then He answered and told them, "Indeed, Elijah is coming first and restores all things. And how is it written concerning the Son of Man, that He must suffer many things and be treated with contempt? 13But I say to you that Elijah has also come, and they did to him whatever they wished, as it is written of him."

A Boy Is Healed

14And when He came to the disciples, He saw a great multitude around them, and scribes disputing with them. 15Immediately, when they saw Him, all the people were greatly amazed, and running to *Him*, greeted Him. 16And He asked the scribes, "What are you discussing with them?"

17Then one of the crowd answered and said, "Teacher, I brought You my son, who has a mute spirit. 18And wherever it seizes him, it throws him down; he foams at the mouth, gnashes his teeth, and becomes rigid. So I spoke to Your disciples, that they should cast it out, but they could not."

19He answered him and said, "O faithless generation, how long shall I be with you? How long shall I bear with you? Bring him to Me." 20Then they brought him to Him. And when he saw Him, immediately the spirit convulsed him, and he fell on the ground and wallowed, foaming at the mouth.

21So He asked his father, "How long has this been happening to him?"

And he said, "From childhood. 22And often he has thrown him both into the fire and into the water to destroy him. But if You can do anything, have compassion on us and help us."

23Jesus said to him, "If you can believe, all things *are* possible to him who believes."

24Immediately the father of the child cried out and said with tears, "Lord, I believe; help my unbelief!"

25When Jesus saw that the people came running together, He rebuked the unclean spirit, saying to it, "Deaf and dumb spirit, I command you, come out of him and enter him no more!" 26Then *the spirit* cried out, convulsed him greatly, and came out of him. And he became as one dead, so that many said, "He is dead." 27But Jesus took him by the hand and lifted him up, and he arose.

28And when He had come into the house, His disciples asked Him privately, "Why could we not cast it out?"

29So He said to them, "This kind can come out by nothing but prayer and fasting."

Jesus Again Predicts His Death and Resurrection

30Then they departed from there and passed through Galilee, and He did not want anyone to know *it*. 31For He taught His disciples and said to them, "The Son of Man is being betrayed into the hands of men, and they will kill Him. And after He is killed, He will rise the third day." 32But they did not understand this saying, and were afraid to ask Him.

Who Is the Greatest?

33Then He came to Capernaum. And when He was in the house He asked them, "What was it you disputed among yourselves on the road?" 34But they kept silent, for on the road they had disputed among themselves who *would be the* greatest. 35And He sat down, called the twelve, and said to them, "If anyone desires to be first, he shall be last of all and servant of all." 36Then He took a little child and set him in the midst of them. And when He had taken him in His arms, He said to them, 37"Whoever receives one of these little children in My name receives Me; and whoever receives Me, receives not Me but Him who sent Me."

Jesus Forbids Sectarianism

38Now John answered Him, saying, "Teacher, we saw someone who does not follow us casting out demons in Your name, and we forbade him because he does not follow us."

39But Jesus said, "Do not forbid him, for no one who works a miracle in My name can soon afterward speak evil of Me. 40For he who is not against us is on our side. 41For whoever gives you a cup of water to drink in My name, because you belong to Christ, assuredly, I say to you, he will by no means lose his reward.

Jesus Warns of Offenses

42"But whoever causes one of these little ones who believe in Me to stumble, it would be better for him if a millstone were hung around his neck, and he were thrown into the sea. 43If your hand causes you to sin, cut it off. It is better for you to enter into life maimed, rather than having two hands, to go to hell, into the fire that shall never be quenched—44where

'Their worm does not die
    And the fire is not quenched.'
45And if your foot causes you to sin, cut it off. It is better for you to enter life lame, rather than having two feet, to be cast into hell, into the fire that shall never be quenched—46where

'Their worm does not die
    And the fire is not quenched.'
47And if your eye causes you to sin, pluck it out. It is better for you to enter the kingdom of God with one eye, rather than having two eyes, to be cast into hell fire—48where

'Their worm does not die
    And the fire is not quenched.'g

Tasteless Salt Is Worthless

49"For everyone will be seasoned with fire, and every sacrifice will be seasoned with salt. 50Salt *is* good, but if the salt loses its flavor, how will you season it? Have salt in yourselves, and have peace with one another."

Marriage and Divorce

10 Then He arose from there and came to the region of Judea by

g Isaiah 66.24

the other side of the Jordan. And multitudes gathered to Him again, and as He was accustomed, He taught them again.

2The Pharisees came and asked Him, "Is it lawful for a man to divorce *his* wife?" testing Him.

3And He answered and said to them, "What did Moses command you?"

4They said, "Moses permitted *a man* to write a certificate of divorce, and to dismiss *her*."

5And Jesus answered and said to them, "Because of the hardness of your heart he wrote you this precept. 6But from the beginning of the creation, God 'made them male and female.'*h* 7'For this reason a man shall leave his father and mother and be joined to his wife, 8and the two shall become one flesh';*i* so then they are no longer two, but one flesh. 9Therefore what God has joined together, let not man separate."

10In the house His disciples also asked Him again about the same *matter.* 11So He said to them, "Whoever divorces his wife and marries another commits adultery against her. 12And if a woman divorces her husband and marries another, she commits adultery."

Jesus Blesses Little Children

13Then they brought little children to Him, that He might touch them; but the disciples rebuked those who brought *them.* 14But when Jesus saw *it,* He was greatly displeased and said to them, "Let the little children come to Me, and do not forbid them; for of such is the kingdom of God. 15Assuredly, I say to you, whoever does not receive the kingdom of God as a little child will by no means enter it." 16And He took them up in His arms, laid *His* hands on them, and blessed them.

Jesus Counsels the Rich Young Ruler

17Now as He was going out on the road, one came running, knelt before Him, and asked Him, "Good Teacher, what shall I do that I may inherit eternal life?"

18So Jesus said to him, "Why do you call Me good? No one *is* good but One, *that is,* God. 19You know the commandments: 'Do not commit adultery,' 'Do not murder,' 'Do not steal,' 'Do not bear false witness,' 'Do not defraud,' 'Honor your father and your mother.' "*j*

20And he answered and said to Him, "Teacher, all these things I have kept from my youth."

21Then Jesus, looking at him, loved him, and said to him, "One thing you lack: Go your way, sell whatever you have and give to the poor, and you will have treasure in heaven; and come, take up the cross, and follow Me."

22But he was sad at this word, and went away sorrowful, for he had great possessions.

With God All Things Are Possible

23Then Jesus looked around and said to His disciples, "How hard it is for those who have riches to enter the kingdom of God!" 24And the disciples were astonished at His words. But Jesus answered again and said to them, "Children, how hard it is for those who trust in riches to enter the kingdom of God! 25It is easier for a camel to go through the eye of a needle than for a rich man to enter the kingdom of God."

26And they were greatly astonished, saying among themselves, "Who then can be saved?"

27But Jesus looked at them and said, "With men *it is* impossible, but not with God; for with God all things are possible."

28Then Peter began to say to Him, "See, we have left all and followed You."

29So Jesus answered and said, "Assuredly, I say to you, there is no one who has left house or brothers or sisters or father or mother or wife or children or lands, for My sake and the gospel's, 30who shall not receive a hundredfold now in this time—houses and brothers and sisters and mothers and children and lands, with persecutions—and in the age to come, eternal life. 31But many *who are* first will be last, and the last first."

h Genesis 1.27; 5.2   *i* Genesis 2.24   *j* Exodus 20.12-16; Deuteronomy 5.16-20

Jesus a Third Time Predicts His Death and Resurrection

32Now they were on the road, going up to Jerusalem, and Jesus was going before them; and they were amazed. And as they followed they were afraid. Then He took the twelve aside again and began to tell them the things that would happen to Him: 33"Behold, we are going up to Jerusalem, and the Son of Man will be betrayed to the chief priests and to the scribes; and they will condemn Him to death and deliver Him to the Gentiles; 34and they will mock Him, and scourge Him, and spit on Him, and kill Him. And the third day He will rise again."

Greatness Is Serving

35Then James and John, the sons of Zebedee, came to Him, saying, "Teacher, we want You to do for us whatever we ask."

36And He said to them, "What do you want Me to do for you?"

37They said to Him, "Grant us that we may sit, one on Your right hand and the other on Your left, in Your glory."

38But Jesus said to them, "You do not know what you ask. Are you able to drink the cup that I drink, and be baptized with the baptism that I am baptized with?"

39They said to Him, "We are able."

So Jesus said to them, "You will indeed drink the cup that I drink, and with the baptism I am baptized with you will be baptized; 40but to sit on My right hand and on My left is not Mine to give, but it is for those for whom it is prepared."

41And when the ten heard it, they began to be greatly displeased with James and John. 42But Jesus called them to Himself and said to them, "You know that those who are considered rulers over the Gentiles lord it over them, and their great ones exercise authority over them. 43Yet it shall not be so among you; but whoever desires to become great among you shall be your servant. 44And whoever of you desires to be first shall be slave of all. 45For even the Son of Man did not come to be served, but to serve, and to give His life a ransom for many."

Jesus Heals Blind Bartimaeus

46Now they came to Jericho. As He went out of Jericho with His disciples and a great multitude, blind Bartimaeus, the son of Timaeus, sat by the road begging. 47And when he heard that it was Jesus of Nazareth, he began to cry out and say, "Jesus, Son of David, have mercy on me!"

48Then many warned him to be quiet; but he cried out all the more, "Son of David, have mercy on me!"

49So Jesus stood still and commanded him to be called.

Then they called the blind man, saying to him, "Be of good cheer. Rise, He is calling you."

50And throwing aside his garment, he rose and came to Jesus.

51So Jesus answered and said to him, "What do you want Me to do for you?"

The blind man said to Him, "Rabboni, that I may receive my sight."

52Then Jesus said to him, "Go your way; your faith has made you well." And immediately he received his sight and followed Jesus on the road.

The Triumphal Entry

11 Now when they drew near Jerusalem, to Bethphage and Bethany, at the Mount of Olives, He sent two of His disciples; 2and He said to them, "Go into the village opposite you; and as soon as you have entered it you will find a colt tied, on which no one has sat. Loose it and bring it. 3And if anyone says to you, 'Why are you doing this?' say, 'The Lord has need of it,' and immediately he will send it here."

4So they went their way, and found the colt tied by the door outside on the street, and they loosed it. 5But some of those who stood there said to them, "What are you doing, loosing the colt?"

6And they spoke to them just as Jesus had commanded. So they let them go. 7Then they brought the colt to Jesus and threw their clothes on it, and He sat on it. 8And many spread their clothes on the road, and others cut down leafy branches from the trees and spread them on the road. 9Then those who went before and those who followed cried out, saying:

"Hosanna!

'Blessed *is* He who comes in the
name of the LORD!'[k]
10 Blessed *is* the kingdom of our
father David
That comes in the name of the
Lord!
Hosanna in the highest!"
11And Jesus went into Jerusalem and
into the temple. So when He had looked
around at all things, as the hour was
already late, He went out to Bethany
with the twelve.

The Fig Tree Withered

12Now the next day, when they had
come out from Bethany, He was hungry. 13And seeing from afar a fig tree
having leaves, He went to see if perhaps
He would find something on it. When
He came to it, He found nothing but
leaves, for it was not the season for figs.
14In response Jesus said to it, "Let no
one eat fruit from you ever again."

And His disciples heard *it.*

Jesus Cleanses the Temple

15So they came to Jerusalem. Then
Jesus went into the temple and began
to drive out those who bought and sold
in the temple, and overturned the tables
of the money changers and the seats
of those who sold doves. 16And He
would not allow anyone to carry wares
through the temple. 17Then He taught,
saying to them, "Is it not written, 'My
house shall be called a house of prayer
for all nations' ?[l] But you have made it
a 'den of thieves.' "[m]

18And the scribes and chief priests
heard it and sought how they might destroy Him; for they feared Him, because
all the people were astonished at His
teaching. 19When evening had come,
He went out of the city.

The Lesson of the Withered Fig Tree

20Now in the morning, as they passed
by, they saw the fig tree dried up from
the roots. 21And Peter, remembering,
said to Him, "Rabbi, look! The fig tree
which You cursed has withered away."
22So Jesus answered and said to
them, "Have faith in God. 23For assuredly, I say to you, whoever says to
this mountain, 'Be removed and be cast

into the sea,' and does not doubt in his
heart, but believes that those things he
says will be done, he will have whatever
he says. 24Therefore I say to you, whatever things you ask when you pray, believe that you receive *them*, and you
will have *them*.

Forgiveness and Prayer

25"And whenever you stand praying,
if you have anything against anyone,
forgive him, that your Father in heaven
may also forgive you your trespasses.
26But if you do not forgive, neither will
your Father in heaven forgive your trespasses."

Jesus' Authority Questioned

27Then they came again to Jerusalem.
And as He was walking in the temple,
the chief priests, the scribes, and the
elders came to Him. 28And they said to
Him, "By what authority are You doing
these things? And who gave You this
authority to do these things?"
29But Jesus answered and said to
them, "I also will ask you one question;
then answer Me, and I will tell you by
what authority I do these things:
30The baptism of John—was it from
heaven or from men? Answer Me."
31And they reasoned among themselves, saying, "If we say, 'From
heaven,' He will say, 'Why then did you
not believe him?' 32But if we say, 'From
men' "—they feared the people, for all
counted John to have been a prophet
indeed. 33So they answered and said to
Jesus, "We do not know."

And Jesus answered and said to
them, "Neither will I tell you by what
authority I do these things."

The Parable of the Wicked Vinedressers

12 Then He began to speak to them
in parables: "A man planted a
vineyard and set a hedge around *it*, dug
a place for the wine vat and built a
tower. And he leased it to vinedressers
and went into a far country. 2Now at
vintage-time he sent a servant to the
vinedressers, that he might receive some
of the fruit of the vineyard from the
vinedressers. 3And they took *him* and

k Psalm 118.26   l Isaiah 56.7   m Jeremiah 7.11

beat him and sent *him* away empty-handed. 4Again he sent them another servant, and at him they threw stones, wounded *him* in the head, and sent *him* away shamefully treated. 5And again he sent another, and him they killed; and many others, beating some and killing some. 6Therefore still having one son, his beloved, he also sent him to them last, saying, 'They will respect my son.' 7But those vinedressers said among themselves, 'This is the heir. Come, let us kill him, and the inheritance will be ours.' 8So they took him and killed *him* and cast *him* out of the vineyard.

9"Therefore what will the owner of the vineyard do? He will come and destroy the vinedressers, and give the vineyard to others. 10Have you not even read this Scripture:

'The stone which the builders
    rejected
    Has become the chief cornerstone.
11   This was the LORD's doing,
    And it is marvelous in our eyes'? "n

12And they sought to lay hands on Him, but feared the multitude, for they knew He had spoken the parable against them. So they left Him and went away.

The Pharisees: Is It Lawful to Pay Taxes to Caesar?

13Then they sent to Him some of the Pharisees and the Herodians, to catch Him in *His* words. 14When they had come, they said to Him, "Teacher, we know that You are true, and care about no one; for You do not regard the person of men, but teach the way of God in truth. Is it lawful to pay taxes to Caesar, or not? 15Shall we pay, or shall we not pay?"

But He, knowing their hypocrisy, said to them, "Why do you test Me? Bring Me a denarius that I may see *it*." 16So they brought *it*.

And He said to them, "Whose image and inscription *is* this?" They said to Him, "Caesar's."

17And Jesus answered and said to them, "Render to Caesar the things that are Caesar's, and to God the things that are God's."

And they marveled at Him.

The Sadducees: What About the Resurrection?

18Then *some* Sadducees, who say there is no resurrection, came to Him; and they asked Him, saying: 19"Teacher, Moses wrote to us that if a man's brother dies, and leaves *his* wife behind, and leaves no children, his brother should take his wife and raise up offspring for his brother. 20Now there were seven brothers. The first took a wife; and dying, he left no offspring. 21And the second took her, and he died; nor did he leave any offspring. And the third likewise. 22So the seven had her and left no offspring. Last of all the woman died also. 23Therefore, in the resurrection, when they rise, whose wife will she be? For all seven had her as wife."

24Jesus answered and said to them, "Are you not therefore mistaken, because you do not know the Scriptures nor the power of God? 25For when they rise from the dead, they neither marry nor are given in marriage, but are like angels in heaven. 26But concerning the dead, that they rise, have you not read in the book of Moses, in the *burning* bush *passage*, how God spoke to him, saying, 'I *am* the God of Abraham, the God of Isaac, and the God of Jacob'?o 27He is not the God of the dead, but the God of the living. You are therefore greatly mistaken."

The Scribes: Which Is the First Commandment of All?

28Then one of the scribes came, and having heard them reasoning together, perceiving that He had answered them well, asked Him, "Which is the first commandment of all?"

29Jesus answered him, "The first of all the commandments *is:* 'Hear, O Israel, the LORD our God, the LORD is one. 30And you shall love the LORD your God with all your heart, with all your soul, with all your mind, and with all your strength.'p This *is* the first commandment. 31And the second, like *it,* is this: 'You shall love your neighbor as yourself.'q .There is no other commandment greater than these."

---

n Psalm 118.22, 23   o Exodus 3.6, 15   p Deuteronomy 6.4, 5   q Leviticus 19.18

32So the scribe said to Him, "Well *said*, Teacher. You have spoken the truth, for there is one God, and there is no other but He. 33And to love Him with all the heart, with all the understanding, with all the soul, and with all the strength, and to love one's neighbor as oneself, is more than all the whole burnt offerings and sacrifices."

34Now when Jesus saw that he answered wisely, He said to him, "You are not far from the kingdom of God."

But after that no one dared question Him.

Jesus: How Can David Call His Descendant Lord?

35Then Jesus answered and said, while He taught in the temple, "How *is it* that the scribes say that the Christ is the Son of David? 36For David himself said by the Holy Spirit:

'The LORD said to my Lord,

"Sit at My right hand,

Till I make Your enemies Your footstool." '*r*

37Therefore David himself calls Him 'Lord'; how is He *then* his Son?"

And the common people heard Him gladly.

Beware of the Scribes

38Then He said to them in His teaching, "Beware of the scribes, who desire to go around in long robes, *love* greetings in the marketplaces, 39the best seats in the synagogues, and the best places at feasts, 40who devour widows' houses, and for a pretense make long prayers. These will receive greater condemnation."

The Widow's Two Mites

41Now Jesus sat opposite the treasury and saw how the people put money into the treasury. And many *who were* rich put in much. 42Then one poor widow came and threw in two mites,*s* which make a quadrans. 43So He called His disciples to *Himself* and said to them, "Assuredly, I say to you that this poor widow has put in more than all those who have given to the treasury; 44for they all put in out of their abun-

dance, but she out of her poverty put in all that she had, her whole livelihood."

Jesus Predicts the Destruction of the Temple

13 Then as He went out of the temple, one of His disciples said to Him, "Teacher, see what manner of stones and what buildings *are here!*"

2And Jesus answered and said to him, "Do you see these great buildings? Not *one* stone shall be left upon another, that shall not be thrown down."

The Signs of the Times and the End of the Age

3Now as He sat on the Mount of Olives opposite the temple, Peter, James, John, and Andrew asked Him privately, 4"Tell us, when will these things be? And what *will be* the sign when all these things will be fulfilled?"

5And Jesus, answering them, began to say: "Take heed that no one deceives you. 6For many will come in My name, saying, 'I am *He*,' and will deceive many. 7But when you hear of wars and rumors of wars, do not be troubled; for *such things* must happen, but the end *is* not yet. 8For nation will rise against nation, and kingdom against kingdom. And there will be earthquakes in various places, and there will be famines and troubles. These *are* the beginnings of sorrows.

9"But watch out for yourselves, for they will deliver you up to councils, and you will be beaten in the synagogues. You will be brought before rulers and kings for My sake, for a testimony to them. 10And the gospel must first be preached to all the nations. 11But when they arrest *you* and deliver you up, do not worry beforehand, or premeditate what you will speak. But whatever is given you in that hour, speak that; for it is not you who speak, but the Holy Spirit. 12Now brother will betray brother to death, and a father *his* child; and children will rise up against parents and cause them to be put to death. 13And you will be hated by all for My name's sake. But he who endures to the end shall be saved.

r Psalm 110.1   *s* Very small copper coins worth a fraction of a penny

The Great Tribulation

14"So when you see the 'abomination of desolation,'ᵗ spoken of by Daniel the prophet, standing where it ought not" (let the reader understand), "then let those who are in Judea flee to the mountains. 15Let him who is on the housetop not go down into the house, nor enter to take anything out of his house. 16And let him who is in the field not go back to get his clothes. 17But woe to those who are pregnant and to those who are nursing babies in those days! 18And pray that your flight may not be in winter. 19For *in* those days there will be tribulation, such as has not been since the beginning of the creation which God created until this time, nor ever shall be. 20And unless the Lord had shortened those days, no flesh would be saved; but for the elect's sake, whom He chose, He shortened the days.

21"Then if anyone says to you, 'Look, here *is* the Christ!' or, 'Look, *He is* there!' do not believe it. 22For false christs and false prophets will rise and show signs and wonders to deceive, if possible, even the elect. 23But take heed; see, I have told you all things beforehand.

The Coming of the Son of Man

24"But in those days, after that tribulation, the sun will be darkened, and the moon will not give its light; 25the stars of heaven will fall, and the powers in the heavens will be shaken. 26Then they will see the Son of Man coming in the clouds with great power and glory. 27And then He will send His angels, and gather together His elect from the four winds, from the farthest part of earth to the farthest part of heaven.

The Parable of the Fig Tree

28"Now learn this parable from the fig tree: When its branch has already become tender, and puts forth leaves, you know that summer is near. 29So you also, when you see these things happening, know that itᵘ is near—at the doors! 30Assuredly, I say to you, this generation will by no means

pass away till all these things take place. 31Heaven and earth will pass away, but My words will by no means pass away.

No One Knows the Day or Hour

32"But of that day and hour no one knows, not even the angels in heaven, nor the Son, but only the Father. 33Take heed, watch and pray; for you do not know when the time is. 34*It is* like a man going to a far country, who left his house and gave authority to his servants, and to each his work, and commanded the doorkeeper to watch. 35Watch therefore, for you do not know when the master of the house is coming—in the evening, at midnight, at the crowing of the rooster, or in the morning—36lest, coming suddenly, he find you sleeping. 37And what I say to you, I say to all: Watch!"

The Plot to Kill Jesus

14 After two days it was the Passover and *the Feast* of Unleavened Bread. And the chief priests and the scribes sought how they might take Him by trickery and put *Him* to death. 2But they said, "Not during the feast, lest there be an uproar of the people."

The Anointing at Bethany

3And being in Bethany at the house of Simon the leper, as He sat at the table, a woman came having an alabaster flask of very costly oil of spikenard. Then she broke the flask and poured *it* on His head. 4But there were some who were indignant among themselves, and said, "Why was this fragrant oil wasted? 5For it might have been sold for more than three hundred denarii and given to the poor." And they criticized her sharply.

6But Jesus said, "Let her alone. Why do you trouble her? She has done a good work for Me. 7For you have the poor with you always, and whenever you wish you may do them good; but Me you do not have always. 8She has done what she could. She has come beforehand to anoint My body for burial. 9Assuredly, I say to you, wherever this gospel is preached in the whole world,

ᵗ Daniel 11.31; 12.11   ᵘ Or *He*

what this woman has done will also be told as a memorial to her."

Judas Agrees to Betray Jesus

10Then Judas Iscariot, one of the twelve, went to the chief priests to betray Him to them. 11And when they heard *it*, they were glad, and promised to give him money. So he sought how he might conveniently betray Him.

Jesus Celebrates the Passover with His Disciples

12Now on the first day of Unleavened Bread, when they killed the Passover *lamb*, His disciples said to Him, "Where do You want us to go and prepare, that You may eat the Passover?"

13And He sent out two of His disciples and said to them, "Go into the city, and a man will meet you carrying a pitcher of water; follow him. 14Wherever he goes in, say to the master of the house, 'The Teacher says, "Where is the guest room in which I may eat the Passover with My disciples?"' 15Then he will show you a large upper room, furnished *and* prepared; there make ready for us."

16So His disciples went out, and came into the city, and found it just as He had said to them; and they prepared the Passover.

17In the evening He came with the twelve. 18Now as they sat and ate, Jesus said, "Assuredly, I say to you, one of you who eats with Me will betray Me."

19And they began to be sorrowful, and to say to Him one by one, "*Is it* I?" And another *said*, "*Is it* I?"

20He answered and said to them, "*It is* one of the twelve, who dips with Me in the dish. 21The Son of Man indeed goes just as it is written of Him, but woe to that man by whom the Son of Man is betrayed! It would have been good for that man if he had never been born."

Jesus Institutes the Lord's Supper

22And as they were eating, Jesus took bread, blessed and broke *it*, and gave *it* to them and said, "Take, eat; this is My body."

23Then He took the cup, and when He had given thanks He gave *it* to them,

and they all drank from it. 24And He said to them, "This is My blood of the new covenant, which is shed for many. 25Assuredly, I say to you, I will no longer drink of the fruit of the vine until that day when I drink it new in the kingdom of God."

26And when they had sung a hymn, they went out to the Mount of Olives.

Jesus Predicts Peter's Denial

27Then Jesus said to them, "All of you will be made to stumble because of Me this night, for it is written:

'I will strike the Shepherd,
   And the sheep will be scattered.'ᵛ

28"But after I have been raised, I will go before you to Galilee."

29Peter said to Him, "Even if all are made to stumble, yet I *will* not *be*."

30Jesus said to him, "Assuredly, I say to you that today, *even* this night, before the rooster crows twice, you will deny Me three times."

31But he spoke more vehemently, "If I have to die with You, I will not deny You!"

And they all said likewise.

The Prayer in the Garden

32Then they came to a place which was named Gethsemane; and He said to His disciples, "Sit here while I pray." 33And He took Peter, James, and John with Him, and He began to be troubled and deeply distressed. 34Then He said to them, "My soul is exceedingly sorrowful, *even* to death. Stay here and watch."

35He went a little farther, and fell on the ground, and prayed that if it were possible, the hour might pass from Him. 36And He said, "Abba, Father, all things *are* possible for You. Take this cup away from Me; nevertheless, not what I will, but what You *will*."

37Then He came and found them sleeping, and said to Peter, "Simon, are you sleeping? Could you not watch one hour? 38Watch and pray, lest you enter into temptation. The spirit indeed *is* willing, but the flesh *is* weak."

39Again He went away and prayed, and spoke the same words. 40And when He returned, He found them asleep

ᵛ Zechariah 13.7

again, for their eyes were heavy; and
they did not know what to answer Him.
41Then He came the third time and
said to them, "Are you still sleeping and
resting? It is enough! The hour has
come; behold, the Son of Man is being
betrayed into the hands of sinners.
42Rise, let us be going. See, My betrayer
is at hand."

Betrayal and Arrest in Gethsemane

43And immediately, while He was
still speaking, Judas, one of the twelve,
with a great multitude with swords and
clubs, came from the chief priests and
the scribes and the elders. 44Now His
betrayer had given them a signal, saying, "Whomever I kiss, He is the One;
seize Him and lead *Him* away safely."
45As soon as he had come, immediately he went up to Him and said to
Him, "Rabbi, Rabbi!" and kissed Him.
46Then they laid their hands on Him
and took Him. 47And one of those who
stood by drew his sword and struck the
servant of the high priest, and cut off
his ear.
48Then Jesus answered and said to
them, "Have you come out, as against
a robber, with swords and clubs to take
Me? 49I was daily with you in the temple teaching, and you did not seize Me.
But the Scriptures must be fulfilled."
50Then they all forsook Him and fled.

A Young Man Flees Naked

51Now a certain young man followed
Him, having a linen cloth thrown
around *his* naked *body*. And the young
men laid hold of him, 52and he left the
linen cloth and fled from them naked.

Jesus Faces the Sanhedrin

53And they led Jesus away to the high
priest; and with him were assembled all
the chief priests, the elders, and the
scribes. 54But Peter followed Him at a
distance, right into the courtyard of the
high priest. And he sat with the servants and warmed himself at the fire.
55Now the chief priests and all the
council sought testimony against Jesus
to put Him to death, but found none.
56For many bore false witness against
Him, but their testimonies did not
agree.
57Then some rose up and bore false
witness against Him, saying, 58"We
heard Him say, 'I will destroy this temple made with hands, and within three
days I will build another made without
hands.' " 59But not even then did their
testimony agree.
60And the high priest stood up in the
midst and asked Jesus, saying, "Do You
answer nothing? What *is it* these men
testify against You?" 61But He kept silent and answered nothing.

Again the high priest asked Him, saying to Him, "Are You the Christ, the
Son of the Blessed?"
62Jesus said, "I am. And you will see
the Son of Man sitting at the right hand
of the Power, and coming with the
clouds of heaven."
63Then the high priest tore his clothes
and said, "What further need do we
have of witnesses? 64You have heard
the blasphemy! What do you think?"

And they all condemned Him to be
deserving of death.
65Then some began to spit on Him,
and to blindfold Him, and to beat Him,
and to say to Him, "Prophesy!" And the
officers struck Him with the palms of
their hands.

Peter Denies Jesus, and Weeps

66Now as Peter was below in the
courtyard, one of the servant girls of
the high priest came. 67And when she
saw Peter warming himself, she looked
at him and said, "You also were with
Jesus of Nazareth."
68But he denied it, saying, "I neither
know nor understand what you are saying." And he went out on the porch, and
a rooster crowed.
69And the servant girl saw him again,
and began to say to those who stood
by, "This is one of them." 70But he denied it again.

And a little later those who stood by
said to Peter again, "Surely you are *one*
of them; for you are a Galilean, and
your speech shows *it*."
71Then he began to curse and swear,
"I do not know this Man of whom you
speak!"
72A second time *the* rooster crowed.
Then Peter called to mind the word that
Jesus had said to him, "Before the
rooster crows twice, you will deny Me

three times." And when he thought about it, he wept.

Jesus Faces Pilate

15 Immediately, in the morning, the chief priests held a consultation with the elders and scribes and the whole council; and they bound Jesus, led *Him* away, and delivered *Him* to Pilate. 2Then Pilate asked Him, "Are You the King of the Jews?"

He answered and said to him, "*It is as* you say."

3And the chief priests accused Him of many things, but He answered nothing. 4Then Pilate asked Him again, saying, "Do You answer nothing? See how many things they testify against You!" 5But Jesus still answered nothing, so that Pilate marveled.

Taking the Place of Barabbas

6Now at the feast he was accustomed to releasing one prisoner to them, whomever they requested. 7And there was one named Barabbas, *who was* chained with his fellow rebels; they had committed murder in the rebellion. 8Then the multitude, crying aloud, began to ask *him to do* just as he had always done for them. 9But Pilate answered them, saying, "Do you want me to release to you the King of the Jews?" 10For he knew that the chief priests had handed Him over because of envy. 11But the chief priests stirred up the crowd, so that he should rather release Barabbas to them. 12Pilate answered and said to them again, "What then do you want me to do *with Him* whom you call the King of the Jews?"

13So they cried out again, "Crucify Him!"

14Then Pilate said to them, "Why, what evil has He done?"

But they cried out all the more, "Crucify Him!"

15So Pilate, wanting to gratify the crowd, released Barabbas to them; and he delivered Jesus, after he had scourged *Him*, to be crucified.

The Soldiers Mock Jesus

16Then the soldiers led Him away into the hall called Praetorium, and they called together the whole garrison. 17And they clothed Him with purple; and they twisted a crown of thorns, put it on His *head*, 18and began to salute Him, "Hail, King of the Jews!" 19Then they struck Him on the head with a reed and spat on Him; and bowing the knee, they worshiped Him. 20And when they had mocked Him, they took the purple off Him, put His own clothes on Him, and led Him out to crucify Him.

The King on a Cross

21Then they compelled a certain man, Simon a Cyrenian, the father of Alexander and Rufus, as he was coming out of the country and passing by, to bear His cross. 22And they brought Him to the place Golgotha, which is translated, Place of a Skull. 23Then they gave Him wine mingled with myrrh to drink, but He did not take *it*. 24And when they crucified Him, they divided His garments, casting lots for them to determine what every man should take.

25Now it was the third hour, and they crucified Him. 26And the inscription of His accusation was written above:

THE KING OF THE JEWS.

27With Him they also crucified two robbers, one on His right and the other on His left. 28So the Scripture was fulfilled[w] which says, "And He was numbered with the transgressors."

29And those who passed by blasphemed Him, wagging their heads and saying, "Aha! *You* who destroy the temple and build *it* in three days, 30save Yourself, and come down from the cross!"

31Likewise the chief priests also, mocking among themselves with the scribes, said, "He saved others; Himself He cannot save. 32Let the Christ, the King of Israel, descend now from the cross, that we may see and believe."

Even those who were crucified with Him reviled Him.

Jesus Dies on the Cross

33Now when the sixth hour had come, there was darkness over the whole land until the ninth hour. 34And at the ninth

w Isaiah 53.12

hour Jesus cried out with a loud voice, saying, "Eloi, Eloi, lama sabachthani?" which is translated, "My God, My God, why have You forsaken Me?"[x]

35Some of those who stood by, when they heard *that*, said, "Look, He is calling for Elijah!" **36**Then someone ran and filled a sponge full of sour wine, put *it* on a reed, and offered *it* to Him to drink, saying, "Let Him alone; let us see if Elijah will come to take Him down."

37And Jesus cried out with a loud voice, and breathed His last.

38Then the veil of the temple was torn in two from top to bottom. **39**So when the centurion, who stood opposite Him, saw that He cried out like this and breathed His last, he said, "Truly this Man was the Son of God!"

40There were also women looking on from afar, among whom were Mary Magdalene, Mary the mother of James the Less and of Joses, and Salome, **41**who also followed Him and ministered to Him when He was in Galilee, and many other women who came up with Him to Jerusalem.

Jesus Buried in Joseph's Tomb

42Now when evening had come, because it was the Preparation Day, that is, the day before the Sabbath, **43**Joseph of Arimathea, a prominent council member, who was himself waiting for the kingdom of God, coming and taking courage, went in to Pilate and asked for the body of Jesus. **44**Pilate marveled that He was already dead; and summoning the centurion, he asked him if He had been dead for some time. **45**So when he found out from the centurion, he granted the body to Joseph. **46**Then he bought fine linen, took Him down, and wrapped Him in the linen. And he laid Him in a tomb which had been hewn out of the rock, and rolled a stone against the door of the tomb. **47**And Mary Magdalene and Mary the mother of Joses observed where He was laid.

He Is Risen

16 Now when the Sabbath was past, Mary Magdalene, Mary the mother of James, and Salome bought spices, that they might come and anoint Him. **2**Very early in the morning, on the first *day* of the week, they came to the tomb when the sun had risen. **3**And they said among themselves, "Who will roll away the stone from the door of the tomb for us?" **4**But when they looked up, they saw that the stone had been rolled away—for it was very large. **5**And entering the tomb, they saw a young man clothed in a long white robe sitting on the right side; and they were alarmed.

6But he said to them, "Do not be alarmed. You seek Jesus of Nazareth, who was crucified. He is risen! He is not here. See the place where they laid Him. **7**But go, tell His disciples—and Peter—that He is going before you into Galilee; there you will see Him, as He said to you."

8So they went out quickly and fled from the tomb, for they trembled and were amazed. And they said nothing to anyone, for they were afraid.

Mary Magdalene Sees the Risen Lord

9Now when *He* rose early on the first *day* of the week, He appeared first to Mary Magdalene, out of whom He had cast seven demons. **10**She went and told those who had been with Him, as they mourned and wept. **11**And when they heard that He was alive and had been seen by her, they did not believe.

Jesus Appears to Two Disciples

12After that, He appeared in another form to two of them as they walked and went into the country. **13**And they went and told *it* to the rest, *but* they did not believe them either.

The Great Commission

14Later He appeared to the eleven as they sat at the table; and He rebuked their unbelief and hardness of heart, because they did not believe those who had seen Him after He had risen. **15**And He said to them, "Go into all the world and preach the gospel to every creature. **16**He who believes and is baptized will be saved; but he who does not believe will be condemned. 17And these signs will follow those who believe: In My name they will cast out demons; they will speak with new tongues; 18they will take up serpents; and if they drink anything deadly, it will by no means hurt them; they will lay hands on the sick, and they will recover."

Christ Ascends to God's Right Hand

19So then, after the Lord had spoken to them, He was received up into heaven, and sat down at the right hand of God. 20And they went out and preached everywhere, the Lord working with *them* and confirming the word through the accompanying signs. Amen.

The Gospel According to
LUKE

Dedication to Theophilus

1 Inasmuch as many have taken in hand to set in order a narrative of those things which have been fulfilled among us, 2just as those who from the beginning were eyewitnesses and ministers of the word delivered them to us, 3it seemed good to me also, having had perfect understanding of all things from the very first, to write to you an orderly account, most excellent Theophilus, 4that you may know the certainty of those things in which you were instructed.

John's Birth Announced to Zacharias

5There was in the days of Herod, the king of Judea, a certain priest named Zacharias, of the division of Abijah. His wife *was* of the daughters of Aaron, and her name *was* Elizabeth. 6And they were both righteous before God, walking in all the commandments and ordinances of the Lord blameless. 7But they had no child, because Elizabeth was barren, and they were both well advanced in years.

8So it was, that while he was serving as priest before God in the order of his division, 9according to the custom of the priesthood, his lot fell to burn incense when he went into the temple of the Lord. 10And the whole multitude of the people was praying outside at the hour of incense. 11Then an angel of the Lord appeared to him, standing on the right side of the altar of incense. 12And when Zacharias saw *him*, he was troubled, and fear fell upon him.

13But the angel said to him, "Do not be afraid, Zacharias, for your prayer is heard; and your wife Elizabeth will bear you a son, and you shall call his name John. 14And you will have joy and gladness, and many will rejoice at his birth. 15For he will be great in the sight of the Lord, and shall drink neither wine nor strong drink. He will also be filled with the Holy Spirit, even from his mother's womb. 16And he will turn many of the children of Israel to the Lord their God. 17He will also go before Him in the spirit and power of Elijah, 'to turn the hearts of the fathers to the children,'*a* and the disobedient to the wisdom of the just, to make ready a people prepared for the Lord."

18And Zacharias said to the angel, "How shall I know this? For I am an old man, and my wife is well advanced in years."

19And the angel answered and said to him, "I am Gabriel, who stands in the presence of God, and was sent to speak to you and bring you these glad tidings. 20But behold, you will be mute and not able to speak until the day these things take place, because you did not believe my words which will be fulfilled in their own time."

21And the people waited for Zacharias, and marveled that he lingered so long in the temple. 22But when he came out, he could not speak to them; and they perceived that he had seen a vision in the temple, for he beckoned to them and remained speechless.

23So it was, as soon as the days of his service were completed, that he departed to his own house. 24Now after those days his wife Elizabeth conceived; and she hid herself five months, saying, 25"Thus the Lord has dealt with me, in the days when He looked on *me*, to take away my reproach among people."

Christ's Birth Announced to Mary

26Now in the sixth month the angel Gabriel was sent by God to a city of Galilee named Nazareth, 27to a virgin betrothed to a man whose name was Joseph, of the house of David. The virgin's name *was* Mary. 28And having come in, the angel said to her, "Rejoice, highly favored *one*, the Lord *is* with you; blessed *are* you among women!"

29But when she saw *him*, she was troubled at his saying, and considered what manner of greeting this was. 30Then the angel said to her, "Do not

a Malachi 4.5, 6

be afraid, Mary, for you have found favor with God. 31And behold, you will conceive in your womb and bring forth a Son, and shall call His name Jesus. 32He will be great, and will be called the Son of the Highest; and the Lord God will give Him the throne of His father David. 33And He will reign over the house of Jacob forever, and of His kingdom there will be no end."

34Then Mary said to the angel, "How can this be, since I do not know a man?"

35And the angel answered and said to her, "The Holy Spirit will come upon you, and the power of the Highest will overshadow you; therefore, also, that Holy One who is to be born will be called the Son of God. 36Now indeed, Elizabeth your relative has also conceived a son in her old age; and this is now the sixth month for her who was called barren. 37For with God nothing will be impossible."

38Then Mary said, "Behold the maidservant of the Lord! Let it be to me according to your word." And the angel departed from her.

Mary Visits Elizabeth

39Now Mary arose in those days and went into the hill country with haste, to a city of Judah, 40and entered the house of Zacharias and greeted Elizabeth. 41And it happened, when Elizabeth heard the greeting of Mary, that the babe leaped in her womb; and Elizabeth was filled with the Holy Spirit. 42Then she spoke out with a loud voice and said, "Blessed are you among women, and blessed is the fruit of your womb! 43But why is this granted to me, that the mother of my Lord should come to me? 44For indeed, as soon as the voice of your greeting sounded in my ears, the babe leaped in my womb for joy. 45Blessed is she who believed, for there will be a fulfillment of those things which were told her from the Lord."

The Song of Mary

46And Mary said:

"My soul magnifies the Lord,
47 And my spirit has rejoiced in God my Savior.
48 For He has regarded the lowly state of His maidservant;

For behold, henceforth all generations will call me blessed.
49 For He who is mighty has done great things for me,
And holy is His name.
50 And His mercy is on those who fear Him
From generation to generation.
51 He has shown strength with His arm;
He has scattered the proud in the imagination of their hearts.
52 He has put down the mighty from their thrones,
And exalted the lowly.
53 He has filled the hungry with good things,
And the rich He has sent away empty.
54 He has helped His servant Israel,
In remembrance of His mercy,
55 As He spoke to our fathers,
To Abraham and to his seed forever."

56And Mary remained with her about three months, and returned to her house.

Birth of John the Baptist

57Now Elizabeth's full time came for her to be delivered, and she brought forth a son. 58When her neighbors and relatives heard how the Lord had shown great mercy to her, they rejoiced with her.

Circumcision of John the Baptist

59So it was, on the eighth day, that they came to circumcise the child; and they would have called him by the name of his father, Zacharias. 60His mother answered and said, "No; he shall be called John."

61But they said to her, "There is no one among your relatives who is called by this name." 62So they made signs to his father—what he would have him called.

63And he asked for a writing tablet, and wrote, saying, "His name is John." So they all marveled. 64Immediately his mouth was opened and his tongue loosed, and he spoke, praising God. 65Then fear came on all who dwelt around them; and all these sayings were discussed throughout all the hill country of Judea. 66And all those who heard *them* kept *them* in their hearts, saying, "What kind of child will this be?" And the hand of the Lord was with him.

Zacharias's Prophecy

67Now his father Zacharias was filled with the Holy Spirit, and prophesied, saying:

68 "Blessed *is* the Lord God of Israel,
   For He has visited and redeemed
      His people,
69 And has raised up a horn of
      salvation for us
   In the house of His servant David,
70 As He spoke by the mouth of His
      holy prophets,
   Who *have been* since the world
      began,
71 That we should be saved from our
      enemies
   And from the hand of all who
      hate us,
72 To perform the mercy *promised* to
      our fathers
   And to remember His holy
      covenant,
73 The oath which He swore to our
      father Abraham:
74 To grant us that we,
   Being delivered from the hand of
      our enemies,
   Might serve Him without fear,
75 In holiness and righteousness
      before Him all the days of our
      life.

76 "And you, child, will be called the
      prophet of the Highest;
   For you will go before the face of
      the Lord to prepare His ways,
77 To give knowledge of salvation to
      His people
   By the remission of their sins,
78 Through the tender mercy of
      our God,
   With which the Dayspring from on
      high has visited us;
79 To give light to those who sit in
      darkness and the shadow of
      death,
   To guide our feet into the way of
      peace."

80So the child grew and became strong in spirit, and was in the deserts till the day of his manifestation to Israel.

Christ Born of Mary

2 And it came to pass in those days *that* a decree went out from Caesar Augustus that all the world should be registered. 2This census first took place while Quirinius was governing Syria. 3So all went to be registered, everyone to his own city.

4Joseph also went up from Galilee, out of the city of Nazareth, into Judea, to the city of David, which is called Bethlehem, because he was of the house and lineage of David, 5to be registered with Mary, his betrothed wife, who was with child. 6So it was, that while they were there, the days were completed for her to be delivered. 7And she brought forth her firstborn Son, and wrapped Him in swaddling cloths, and laid Him in a manger, because there was no room for them in the inn.

Glory in the Highest

8Now there were in the same country shepherds living out in the fields, keeping watch over their flock by night. 9And behold, an angel of the Lord stood before them, and the glory of the Lord shone around them, and they were greatly afraid. 10Then the angel said to them, "Do not be afraid, for behold, I bring you good tidings of great joy which will be to all people. 11For there is born to you this day in the city of David a Savior, who is Christ the Lord. 12And this *will be* the sign to you: You will find a Babe wrapped in swaddling cloths, lying in a manger."

13And suddenly there was with the angel a multitude of the heavenly host praising God and saying:
14 "Glory to God in the highest,
      And on earth peace, goodwill
         toward men!"

15So it was, when the angels had gone away from them into heaven, that the shepherds said to one another, "Let us now go to Bethlehem and see this thing that has come to pass, which the Lord has made known to us." 16And they came with haste and found Mary and Joseph, and the Babe lying in a manger. 17Now when they had seen *Him*, they made widely known the saying which was told them concerning this Child. 18And all those who heard *it* marveled at those things which were told them by the shepherds. 19But Mary kept all these things and pondered *them* in her heart. 20Then the shepherds returned, glorifying and praising God for all the things that they had heard and seen, as it was told them.

Circumcision of Jesus

21And when eight days were completed for the circumcision of the Child, His name was called JESUS, the name given by the angel before He was conceived in the womb.

Jesus Presented in the Temple

22Now when the days of her purification according to the law of Moses were completed, they brought Him to Jerusalem to present *Him* to the Lord 23(as it is written in the law of the Lord, "Every male who opens the womb shall be called holy to the LORD"),*b* 24and to offer a sacrifice according to what is said in the law of the Lord, "A pair of turtledoves or two young pigeons."*c*

Simeon Sees God's Salvation

25And behold, there was a man in Jerusalem whose name was Simeon, and this man was just and devout, waiting for the Consolation of Israel, and the Holy Spirit was upon him. 26And it had been revealed to him by the Holy Spirit that he would not see death before he had seen the Lord's Christ. 27So he came by the Spirit into the temple. And when the parents brought in the Child Jesus, to do for Him according to the custom of the law, 28he took Him up in his arms and blessed God and said:
29 "Lord, now You are letting Your
      servant depart in peace,
      According to Your word;
30 For my eyes have seen Your
      salvation
31 Which You have prepared before
      the face of all peoples,
32 A light to *bring* revelation to the
      Gentiles,
      And the glory of Your people
      Israel."

33And Joseph and His mother marveled at those things which were spoken of Him. 34Then Simeon blessed them, and said to Mary His mother, "Behold, this *Child* is destined for the fall and rising of many in Israel, and for a sign which will be spoken against 35(yes, a sword will pierce through your own soul also), that the thoughts of many hearts may be revealed."

Anna Bears Witness to the Redeemer

36Now there was one, Anna, a prophetess, the daughter of Phanuel, of the tribe of Asher. She was of a great age, and had lived with a husband seven years from her virginity; 37and this woman *was* a widow of about eighty-four years, who did not depart from the temple, but served God with fastings and prayers night and day. 38And coming in that instant she gave thanks to the Lord, and spoke of Him to all those who looked for redemption in Jerusalem.

The Family Returns to Nazareth

39So when they had performed all things according to the law of the Lord, they returned to Galilee, to their *own* city, Nazareth. 40And the Child grew and became strong in spirit, filled with wisdom; and the grace of God was upon Him.

The Boy Jesus Amazes the Scholars

41His parents went to Jerusalem every year at the Feast of the Passover. 42And when He was twelve years old, they went up to Jerusalem according to the custom of the feast. 43When they had finished the days, as they returned, the Boy Jesus lingered behind in Jerusalem. And Joseph and His mother did not know *it;* 44but supposing Him to have been in the company, they went a day's journey, and sought Him among *their* relatives and acquaintances. 45So when they did not find Him, they returned to Jerusalem, seeking Him. 46Now so it was *that* after three days they found Him in the temple, sitting in the midst of the teachers, both listening to them and asking them questions. 47And all who heard Him were aston-

b Exodus 13.2, 12, 15   *c* Leviticus 12.8

ished at His understanding and answers. 48So when they saw Him, they were amazed; and His mother said to Him, "Son, why have You done this to us? Look, Your father and I have sought You anxiously."

49And He said to them, "Why did you seek Me? Did you not know that I must be about My Father's business?" 50But they did not understand the statement which He spoke to them.

Jesus Advances in Wisdom and Favor

51Then He went down with them and came to Nazareth, and was subject to them, but His mother kept all these things in her heart. 52And Jesus increased in wisdom and stature, and in favor with God and men.

John the Baptist Prepares the Way

3 Now in the fifteenth year of the reign of Tiberius Caesar, Pontius Pilate being governor of Judea, Herod being tetrarch of Galilee, his brother Philip tetrarch of Iturea and the region of Trachonitis, and Lysanias tetrarch of Abilene, 2while Annas and Caiaphas were high priests, the word of God came to John the son of Zacharias in the wilderness. 3And he went into all the region around the Jordan, preaching a baptism of repentance for the remission of sins, 4as it is written in the book of the words of Isaiah the prophet, saying:

"The voice of one crying in the
    wilderness:
'Prepare the way of the LORD;
Make His paths straight.
5   Every valley shall be filled
And every mountain and hill
    brought low;
The crooked places shall be made
    straight
And the rough ways smooth;
6   And all flesh shall see the salvation
    of God.' "d

John Preaches to the People

7Then he said to the multitudes that came out to be baptized by him, "Brood of vipers! Who warned you to flee from the wrath to come? 8Therefore bear fruits worthy of repentance, and do not

begin to say to yourselves, 'We have Abraham as our father.' For I say to you that God is able to raise up children to Abraham from these stones. 9And even now the ax is laid to the root of the trees. Therefore every tree which does not bear good fruit is cut down and thrown into the fire."

10So the people asked him, saying, "What shall we do then?"

11He answered and said to them, "He who has two tunics, let him give to him who has none; and he who has food, let him do likewise."

12Then tax collectors also came to be baptized, and said to him, "Teacher, what shall we do?"

13And he said to them, "Collect no more than what is appointed for you."

14Likewise the soldiers asked him, saying, "And what shall we do?"

So he said to them, "Do not intimidate anyone or accuse falsely, and be content with your wages."

15Now as the people were in expectation, and all reasoned in their hearts about John, whether he was the Christ or not, 16John answered, saying to all, "I indeed baptize you with water; but One mightier than I is coming, whose sandal strap I am not worthy to loose. He will baptize you with the Holy Spirit and fire. 17His winnowing fan is in His hand, and He will thoroughly clean out His threshing floor, and gather the wheat into His barn; but the chaff He will burn with unquenchable fire."

18And with many other exhortations he preached to the people. 19But Herod the tetrarch, being rebuked by him concerning Herodias, his brother Philip's wife, and for all the evils which Herod had done, 20also added this, above all, that he shut John up in prison.

John Baptizes Jesus

21When all the people were baptized, it came to pass that Jesus also was baptized; and while He prayed, the heaven was opened. 22And the Holy Spirit descended in bodily form like a dove upon Him, and a voice came from heaven which said, "You are My beloved Son; in You I am well pleased."

d Isaiah 40.3-5

The Genealogy of Jesus Christ

23Now Jesus Himself began *His ministry at* about thirty years of age, being (as was supposed) *the* son of Joseph, *the son* of Heli, 24*the son* of Matthat, *the son* of Levi, *the son* of Melchi, *the son* of Janna, *the son* of Joseph, 25*the son* of Mattathiah, *the son* of Amos, *the son* of Nahum, *the son* of Esli, *the son* of Naggai, 26*the son* of Maath, *the son* of Mattathiah, *the son* of Semei, *the son* of Joseph, *the son* of Judah, 27*the son* of Joannas, *the son* of Rhesa, *the son* of Zerubbabel, *the son* of Shealtiel, *the son* of Neri, 28*the son* of Melchi, *the son* of Addi, *the son* of Cosam, *the son* of Elmodam, *the son* of Er, 29*the son* of Jose, *the son* of Eliezer, *the son* of Jorim, *the son* of Matthat, *the son* of Levi, 30*the son* of Simeon, *the son* of Judah, *the son* of Joseph, *the son* of Jonan, *the son* of Eliakim, 31*the son* of Melea, *the son* of Menan, *the son* of Mattathah, *the son* of Nathan, *the son* of David, 32*the son* of Jesse, *the son* of Obed, *the son* of Boaz, *the son* of Salmon, *the son* of Nahshon, 33*the son* of Amminadab, *the son* of Ram, *the son* of Hezron, *the son* of Perez, *the son* of Judah, 34*the son* of Jacob, *the son* of Isaac, *the son* of Abraham, *the son* of Terah, *the son* of Nahor, 35*the son* of Serug, *the son* of Reu, *the son* of Peleg, *the son* of Eber, *the son* of Shelah, 36*the son* of Cainan, *the son* of Arphaxad, *the son* of Shem, *the son* of Noah, *the son* of Lamech, 37*the son* of Methuselah, *the son* of Enoch, *the son* of Jared, *the son* of Mahalalel, *the son* of Cainan, 38*the son* of Enosh, *the son* of Seth, *the son* of Adam, *the son* of God.

Satan Tempts Jesus

4 Then Jesus, being filled with the Holy Spirit, returned from the Jordan and was led by the Spirit into the wilderness, 2being tempted for forty days by the devil. And in those days He ate nothing, and afterward, when they had ended, He was hungry.

3And the devil said to Him, "If You are the Son of God, command this stone to become bread."

4But Jesus answered him, saying,*e* "It is written, 'Man shall not live by bread alone, but by every word of God.' "

5Then the devil, taking Him up on a high mountain, showed Him all the kingdoms of the world in a moment of time. 6And the devil said to Him, "All this authority I will give You, and their glory; for *this* has been delivered to me, and I give it to whomever I wish. 7Therefore, if You will worship before me, all will be Yours."

8And Jesus answered and said to him, "Get behind Me, Satan! For it is written, 'You shall worship the LORD your God, and Him only you shall serve.' "*f*

9Then he brought Him to Jerusalem, set Him on the pinnacle of the temple, and said to Him, "If You are the Son of God, throw Yourself down from here. 10For it is written:

'He shall give His angels charge
over you,
To keep you,'

11and,

'In *their* hands they shall bear
you up,
Lest you dash your foot against a
stone.' "*g*

12And Jesus answered and said to him, "It has been said, 'You shall not tempt the LORD your God.' "*h*

13Now when the devil had ended every temptation, he departed from Him until an opportune time.

Jesus Begins His Galilean Ministry

14Then Jesus returned in the power of the Spirit to Galilee, and news of Him went out through all the surrounding region. 15And He taught in their synagogues, being glorified by all.

Jesus Rejected at Nazareth

16So He came to Nazareth, where He had been brought up. And as His custom was, He went into the synagogue on the Sabbath day, and stood up to read. 17And He was handed the book of the prophet Isaiah. And when He had opened the book, He found the place where it was written:

18 "The Spirit of the LORD *is* upon Me,
Because He has anointed Me
To preach the gospel to *the* poor;

---

e Deuteronomy 8.3   *f* Deuteronomy 6.13   *g* Psalm 91.11, 12   *h* Deuteronomy 6.16

He has sent Me to heal the
    brokenhearted,
To proclaim liberty to *the* captives
And recovery of sight to *the* blind,
To set at liberty those who are
    oppressed;
19   To proclaim the acceptable year of
    the LORD."[i]
20Then He closed the book, and gave
it back to the attendant and sat down.
And the eyes of all who were in the synagogue were fixed on Him. 21And He
began to say to them, "Today this Scripture is fulfilled in your hearing."
22So all bore witness to Him, and marveled at the gracious words which proceeded out of His mouth. And they said,
"Is this not Joseph's son?"

23He said to them, "You will surely
say this proverb to Me, 'Physician, heal
yourself! Whatever we have heard done
in Capernaum, do also here in Your
country.' " 24Then He said, "Assuredly,
I say to you, no prophet is accepted in
his own country. 25But I tell you truly,
many widows were in Israel in the days
of Elijah, when the heaven was shut up
three years and six months, and there
was a great famine throughout all the
land; 26but to none of them was Elijah
sent except to Zarephath, *in the region*
of Sidon, to a woman *who was* a widow.
27And many lepers were in Israel in the
time of Elisha the prophet, and none of
them was cleansed except Naaman the
Syrian."

28So all those in the synagogue, when
they heard these things, were filled with
wrath, 29and rose up and thrust Him
out of the city; and they led Him to the
brow of the hill on which their city was
built, that they might throw Him down
over the cliff. 30Then passing through
the midst of them, He went His way.

Jesus Casts Out an Unclean Spirit

31Then He went down to Capernaum,
a city of Galilee, and was teaching them
on the Sabbaths. 32And they were astonished at His teaching, for His word
was with authority. 33Now in the synagogue there was a man who had a spirit
of an unclean demon. And he cried out
with a loud voice, 34saying, "Let *us*
alone! What have we to do with You,

Jesus of Nazareth? Did You come to destroy us? I know who You are—the
Holy One of God!"

35But Jesus rebuked him, saying, "Be
quiet, and come out of him!" And when
the demon had thrown him in *their*
midst, it came out of him and did not
hurt him. 36Then they were all amazed
and spoke among themselves, saying,
"What a word this *is!* For with authority
and power He commands the unclean
spirits, and they come out." 37And the
report about Him went out into every
place in the surrounding region.

Peter's Mother-in-Law Healed

38Now He arose from the synagogue
and entered Simon's house. But Simon's wife's mother was sick with a
high fever, and they made request of
Him concerning her. 39So He stood over
her and rebuked the fever, and it left
her. And immediately she arose and
served them.

Many Healed After Sabbath Sunset

40When the sun was setting, all those
who had any that were sick with various diseases brought them to Him; and
He laid His hands on every one of them
and healed them. 41And demons also
came out of many, crying out and
saying, "You are the Christ, the Son
of God!"

And He, rebuking *them,* did not allow
them to speak, for they knew that He
was the Christ.

Jesus Preaches in Galilee

42Now when it was day, He departed
and went into a deserted place. And the
crowd sought Him and came to Him,
and tried to keep Him from leaving
them; 43but He said to them, "I must
preach the kingdom of God to the other
cities also, because for this purpose I
have been sent." 44And He was preaching in the synagogues of Galilee.

Four Fishermen Called as Disciples

5 So it was, as the multitude pressed
about Him to hear the word of God,
that He stood by the Lake of Gennesaret, 2and saw two boats standing by
the lake; but the fishermen had gone

i Isaiah 61.1, 2

from them and were washing *their* nets. 3Then He got into one of the boats, which was Simon's, and asked him to put out a little from the land. And He sat down and taught the multitudes from the boat.

4When He had stopped speaking, He said to Simon, "Launch out into the deep and let down your nets for a catch."

5But Simon answered and said to Him, "Master, we have toiled all night and caught nothing; nevertheless at Your word I will let down the net." 6And when they had done this, they caught a great number of fish, and their net was breaking. 7So they signaled to *their* partners in the other boat to come and help them. And they came and filled both the boats, so that they began to sink. 8When Simon Peter saw *it*, he fell down at Jesus' knees, saying, "Depart from me, for I am a sinful man, O Lord!"

9For he and all who were with him were astonished at the catch of fish which they had taken; 10and so also *were* James and John, the sons of Zebedee, who were partners with Simon. And Jesus said to Simon, "Do not be afraid. From now on you will catch men." 11So when they had brought their boats to land, they forsook all and followed Him.

Jesus Cleanses a Leper

12And it happened when He was in a certain city, that behold, a man who was full of leprosy saw Jesus; and he fell on *his* face and implored Him, saying, "Lord, if You are willing, You can make me clean."

13Then He put out *His* hand and touched him, saying, "I am willing; be cleansed." Immediately the leprosy left him. 14And He charged him to tell no one, "But go and show yourself to the priest, and make an offering for your cleansing, as a testimony to them, just as Moses commanded."

15However, the report went around concerning Him all the more; and great multitudes came together to hear, and to be healed by Him of their infirmities. 16So He Himself *often* withdrew into the wilderness and prayed.

Jesus Forgives and Heals a Paralytic

17Now it happened on a certain day, as He was teaching, that there were Pharisees and teachers of the law sitting by, who had come out of every town of Galilee, Judea, and Jerusalem. And the power of the Lord was *present* to heal them. 18Then behold, men brought on a bed a man who was paralyzed, whom they sought to bring in and lay before Him. 19And when they could not find how they might bring him in, because of the crowd, they went up on the housetop and let him down with *his* bed through the tiling into the midst before Jesus.

20When He saw their faith, He said to him, "Man, your sins are forgiven you."

21And the scribes and the Pharisees began to reason, saying, "Who is this who speaks blasphemies? Who can forgive sins but God alone?"

22But when Jesus perceived their thoughts, He answered and said to them, "Why are you reasoning in your hearts? 23Which is easier, to say, 'Your sins are forgiven you,' or to say, 'Rise up and walk'? 24But that you may know that the Son of Man has power on earth to forgive sins"—He said to the man who was paralyzed, "I say to you, arise, take up your bed, and go to your house."

25Immediately he rose up before them, took up what he had been lying on, and departed to his own house, glorifying God. 26And they were all amazed, and they glorified God and were filled with fear, saying, "We have seen strange things today!"

Matthew the Tax Collector

27After these things He went out and saw a tax collector named Levi, sitting at the tax office. And He said to him, "Follow Me." 28So he left all, rose up, and followed Him.

29Then Levi gave Him a great feast in his own house. And there were a great number of tax collectors and others who sat down with them. 30And their scribes and the Pharisees complained against His disciples, saying, "Why do You eat and drink with tax collectors and sinners?"

31Jesus answered and said to them, "Those who are well have no need of a physician, but those who are sick. 32I have not come to call *the* righteous, but sinners, to repentance."

Jesus Is Questioned About Fasting

33Then they said to Him, "Why do the disciples of John fast often and make prayers, and likewise those of the Pharisees, but Yours eat and drink?"

34And He said to them, "Can you make the friends of the bridegroom fast while the bridegroom is with them? 35But the days will come when the bridegroom will be taken away from them; then they will fast in those days."

36Then He spoke a parable to them: "No one puts a piece from a new garment on an old one; otherwise the new makes a tear, and also the piece that was *taken* out of the new does not match the old. 37And no one puts new wine into old wineskins; or else the new wine will burst the wineskins and be spilled, and the wineskins will be ruined. 38But new wine must be put into new wineskins, and both are preserved. 39And no one, having drunk old *wine*, immediately desires new; for he says, 'The old is better.'"

Jesus Is Lord of the Sabbath

6 Now it happened on the second Sabbath after the first that He went through the grainfields. And His disciples plucked the heads of grain and ate *them*, rubbing *them* in *their* hands. 2And some of the Pharisees said to them, "Why are you doing what is not lawful to do on the Sabbath?"

3But Jesus answering them said, "Have you not even read this, what David did when he was hungry, he and those who were with him: 4how he went into the house of God, took and ate the showbread, and also gave some to those with him, which is not lawful for any but the priests to eat?" 5And He said to them, "The Son of Man is also Lord of the Sabbath."

Healing on the Sabbath

6Now it happened on another Sabbath, also, that He entered the synagogue and taught. And a man was there whose right hand was withered.

7So the scribes and Pharisees watched Him closely, whether He would heal on the Sabbath, that they might find an accusation against Him. 8But He knew their thoughts, and said to the man who had the withered hand, "Arise and stand here." And he arose and stood. 9Then Jesus said to them, "I will ask you one thing: Is it lawful on the Sabbath to do good or to do evil, to save life or to destroy?" 10And when He had looked around at them all, He said to the man, "Stretch out your hand." And he did so, and his hand was restored as whole as the other. 11But they were filled with rage, and discussed with one another what they might do to Jesus.

The Twelve Apostles

12Now it came to pass in those days that He went out to the mountain to pray, and continued all night in prayer to God. 13And when it was day, He called His disciples to *Himself;* and from them He chose twelve whom He also named apostles: 14Simon, whom He also named Peter, and Andrew his brother; James and John; Philip and Bartholomew; 15Matthew and Thomas; James the *son* of Alphaeus, and Simon called the Zealot; 16Judas *the son* of James, and Judas Iscariot who also became a traitor.

Jesus Heals a Great Multitude

17And He came down with them and stood on a level place with a crowd of His disciples and a great multitude of people from all Judea and Jerusalem, and from the seacoast of Tyre and Sidon, who came to hear Him and be healed of their diseases, 18as well as those who were tormented with unclean spirits. And they were healed. 19And the whole multitude sought to touch Him, for power went out from Him and healed *them* all.

The Beatitudes

20Then He lifted up His eyes toward His disciples, and said:
"Blessed *are you* poor,
   For yours is the kingdom of God.
2Blessed *are you* who hunger now,
   For you shall be filled.
Blessed *are you* who weep now,
   For you shall laugh.

22 Blessed are you when men
  hate you,
  And when they exclude you,
  And revile *you*, and cast out your
  name as evil,
  For the Son of Man's sake.
23 Rejoice in that day and leap for joy!
  For indeed your reward *is* great
  in heaven,
  For in like manner their fathers
  did to the prophets.

Jesus Pronounces Woes

24 "But woe to you who are rich,
  For you have received your
  consolation.
25 Woe to you who are full,
  For you shall hunger.
  Woe to you who laugh now,
  For you shall mourn and weep.
26 Woe to you when all men speak
  well of you,
  For so did their fathers to the
  false prophets.

Love Your Enemies

27"But I say to you who hear: Love your enemies, do good to those who hate you, 28bless those who curse you, and pray for those who spitefully use you. 29To him who strikes you on the *one* cheek, offer the other also. And from him who takes away your cloak, do not withhold *your* tunic either. 30Give to everyone who asks of you. And from him who takes away your goods do not ask *them* back. 31And just as you want men to do to you, you also do to them likewise.

32"But if you love those who love you, what credit is that to you? For even sinners love those who love them. 33And if you do good to those who do good to you, what credit is that to you? For even sinners do the same. 34And if you lend *to those* from whom you hope to receive back, what credit is that to you? For even sinners lend to sinners to receive as much back. 35But love your enemies, do good, and lend, hoping for nothing in return; and your reward will be great, and you will be sons of the Most High. For He is kind to the unthankful and evil. 36Therefore be merciful, just as your Father also is merciful.

Do Not Judge

37"Judge not, and you shall not be judged. Condemn not, and you shall not be condemned. Forgive, and you will be forgiven. 38Give, and it will be given to you: good measure, pressed down, shaken together, and running over will be put into your bosom. For with the same measure that you use, it will be measured back to you."

39And He spoke a parable to them: "Can the blind lead the blind? Will they not both fall into the ditch? 40A disciple is not above his teacher, but everyone who is perfectly trained will be like his teacher. 41And why do you look at the speck in your brother's eye, but do not perceive the plank in your own eye? 42Or how can you say to your brother, 'Brother, let me remove the speck that *is* in your eye,' when you yourself do not see the plank that *is* in your own eye? Hypocrite! First remove the plank from your own eye, and then you will see clearly to remove the speck that is in your brother's eye.

A Tree Is Known by Its Fruit

43"For a good tree does not bear bad fruit, nor does a bad tree bear good fruit. 44For every tree is known by its own fruit. For *men* do not gather figs from thorns, nor do they gather grapes from a bramble bush. 45A good man out of the good treasure of his heart brings forth good; and an evil man out of the evil treasure of his heart brings forth evil. For out of the abundance of the heart his mouth speaks.

Build on the Rock

46"But why do you call Me 'Lord, Lord,' and not do the things which I say? 47Whoever comes to Me, and hears My sayings and does them, I will show you whom he is like: 48He is like a man building a house, who dug deep and laid the foundation on the rock. And when the flood arose, the stream beat vehemently against that house, and could not shake it, for it was founded on the rock. 49But he who heard and did nothing is like a man who built a house on the earth without a foundation, against which the stream beat vehemently; and immediately it fell. And the ruin of that house was great."

Jesus Heals a Centurion's Servant

7 Now when He concluded all His sayings in the hearing of the people, He entered Capernaum. 2And a certain centurion's servant, who was dear to him, was sick and ready to die. 3So when he heard about Jesus, he sent elders of the Jews to Him, pleading with Him to come and heal his servant. 4And when they came to Jesus, they begged Him earnestly, saying that the one for whom He should do this was deserving, 5"for he loves our nation, and has built us a synagogue."

6Then Jesus went with them. And when He was already not far from the house, the centurion sent friends to Him, saying to Him, "Lord, do not trouble Yourself, for I am not worthy that You should enter under my roof. 7Therefore I did not even think myself worthy to come to You. But say the word, and my servant will be healed. 8For I also am a man placed under authority, having soldiers under me. And I say to one, 'Go,' and he goes; and to another, 'Come,' and he comes; and to my servant, 'Do this,' and he does it."

9When Jesus heard these things, He marveled at him, and turned around and said to the crowd that followed Him, "I say to you, I have not found such great faith, not even in Israel!" 10And those who were sent, returning to the house, found the servant well who had been sick.

Jesus Raises the Son of the Widow of Nain

11Now it happened, the day after, that He went into a city called Nain; and many of His disciples went with Him, and a large crowd. 12And when He came near the gate of the city, behold, a dead man was being carried out, the only son of his mother; and she was a widow. And a large crowd from the city was with her. 13When the Lord saw her, He had compassion on her and said to her, "Do not weep." 14Then He came and touched the open coffin, and those who carried him stood still. And He

said, "Young man, I say to you, arise." 15So he who was dead sat up and began to speak. And He presented him to his mother.

16Then fear came upon all, and they glorified God, saying, "A great prophet has risen up among us"; and, "God has visited His people." 17And this report about Him went throughout all Judea and all the surrounding region.

John the Baptist Sends Messengers to Jesus

18Then the disciples of John reported to him concerning all these things. 19And John, calling two of his disciples to *him*, sent *them* to Jesus, saying, "Are You the Coming One, or do we look for another?"

20When the men had come to Him, they said, "John the Baptist has sent us to You, saying, 'Are You the Coming One, or do we look for another?' " 21And that very hour He cured many of infirmities, afflictions, and evil spirits; and to many blind He gave sight.

22Jesus answered and said to them, "Go and tell John the things you have seen and heard: that *the* blind see, *the* lame walk, *the* lepers are cleansed, *the* deaf hear, *the* dead are raised, *the* poor have the gospel preached to them. 23And blessed is *he* who is not offended because of Me."

24When the messengers of John had departed, He began to speak to the multitudes concerning John: "What did you go out into the wilderness to see? A reed shaken by the wind? 25But what did you go out to see? A man clothed in soft garments? Indeed those who are gorgeously appareled and live in luxury are in kings' courts. 26But what did you go out to see? A prophet? Yes, I say to you, and more than a prophet. 27This is *he* of whom it is written:

'Behold, I send My messenger
    before Your face,
 Who will prepare Your way
    before You.'*j*

28For I say to you, among those born of women there is not a greater prophet than John the Baptist; but he who is least in the kingdom of God is greater than he."

j Malachi 3.1

29And when all the people heard *Him,* even the tax collectors justified God, having been baptized with the baptism of John. 30But the Pharisees and lawyers rejected the will of God for themselves, not having been baptized by him.

31And the Lord said, "To what then shall I liken the men of this generation, and what are they like? 32They are like children sitting in the marketplace and calling to one another, saying:

'We played the flute for you,
    And you did not dance;
We mourned to you,
    And you did not weep.'

33For John the Baptist came neither eating bread nor drinking wine, and you say, 'He has a demon.' 34The Son of Man has come eating and drinking, and you say, 'Look, a glutton and a winebibber, a friend of tax collectors and sinners!' 35But wisdom is justified by all her children."

A Sinful Woman Forgiven

36Then one of the Pharisees asked Him to eat with him. And He went to the Pharisee's house, and sat down to eat. 37And behold, a woman in the city who was a sinner, when she knew that *Jesus* sat at the table in the Pharisee's house, brought an alabaster flask of fragrant oil, 38and stood at His feet behind *Him* weeping; and she began to wash His feet with her tears, and wiped *them* with the hair of her head; and she kissed His feet and anointed *them* with the fragrant oil. 39Now when the Pharisee who had invited Him saw *this,* he spoke to himself, saying, "This Man, if He were a prophet, would know who and what manner of woman *this is* who is touching Him, for she is a sinner."

40And Jesus answered and said to him, "Simon, I have something to say to you."

So he said, "Teacher, say it."

41"There was a certain creditor who had two debtors. One owed five hundred denarii, and the other fifty. 42And when they had nothing with which to repay, he freely forgave them both. Tell Me, therefore, which of them will love him more?"

43Simon answered and said, "I suppose the *one* whom he forgave more."

And He said to him, "You have rightly judged." 44Then He turned to the woman and said to Simon, "Do you see this woman? I entered your house; you gave Me no water for My feet, but she has washed My feet with her tears and wiped *them* with the hair of her head. 45You gave Me no kiss, but this woman has not ceased to kiss My feet since the time I came in. 46You did not anoint My head with oil, but this woman has anointed My feet with fragrant oil. 47Therefore I say to you, her sins, *which are* many, are forgiven, for she loved much. But to whom little is forgiven, *the same* loves little."

48Then He said to her, "Your sins are forgiven."

49And those who sat at the table with Him began to say to themselves, "Who is this who even forgives sins?"

50Then He said to the woman, "Your faith has saved you. Go in peace."

Many Women Minister to Jesus

8 Now it came to pass, afterward, that He went through every city and village, preaching and bringing the glad tidings of the kingdom of God. And the twelve *were* with Him, 2and certain women who had been healed of evil spirits and infirmities—Mary called Magdalene, out of whom had come seven demons, 3and Joanna the wife of Chuza, Herod's steward, and Susanna, and many others who provided for Him from their substance.

The Parable of the Sower

4And when a great multitude had gathered, and they had come to Him from every city, He spoke by a parable: 5"A sower went out to sow his seed. And as he sowed, some fell by the wayside; and it was trampled down, and the birds of the air devoured it. 6Some fell on rock; and as soon as it sprang up, it withered away because it lacked moisture. 7And some fell among thorns, and the thorns sprang up with it and choked it. 8But others fell on good ground, sprang up, and yielded a crop a hundredfold." When He had said these things He cried, "He who has ears to hear, let him hear!"

The Purpose of Parables

9Then His disciples asked Him, saying, "What does this parable mean?"

10And He said, "To you it has been given to know the mysteries of the kingdom of God, but to the rest *it is given* in parables, that

'Seeing they may not see,
   And hearing they may not
      understand.'*k*

The Parable of the Sower Explained

11"Now the parable is this: The seed is the word of God. 12Those by the wayside are the ones who hear; then the devil comes and takes away the word out of their hearts, lest they should believe and be saved. 13But the ones on the rock *are those* who, when they hear, receive the word with joy; and these have no root, who believe for a while and in time of temptation fall away. 14Now the ones *that* fell among thorns are those who, when they have heard, go out and are choked with cares, riches, and pleasures of life, and bring no fruit to maturity. 15But the ones *that* fell on the good ground are those who, having heard the word with a noble and good heart, keep *it* and bear fruit with patience.

The Parable of the Revealed Light

16"No one, when he has lit a lamp, covers it with a vessel or puts *it* under a bed, but sets *it* on a lampstand, that those who enter may see the light. 17For nothing is secret that will not be revealed, nor *anything* hidden that will not be known and come to light. 18Therefore take heed how you hear. For whoever has, to him *more* will be given; and whoever does not have, even what he seems to have will be taken from him."

Jesus' Mother and Brothers Come to Him

19Then His mother and brothers came to Him, and could not approach Him because of the crowd. 20And it was told Him *by some*, who said, "Your mother and Your brothers are standing outside, desiring to see You."

21But He answered and said to them, "My mother and My brothers are these who hear the word of God and do it."

Wind and Wave Obey Jesus

22Now it happened, on a certain day, that He got into a boat with His disciples. And He said to them, "Let us cross over to the other side of the lake." And they launched out. 23But as they sailed He fell asleep. And a windstorm came down on the lake, and they were filling *with water*, and were in jeopardy. 24And they came to Him and awoke Him, saying, "Master, Master, we are perishing!"

Then He arose and rebuked the wind and the raging of the water. And they ceased, and there was a calm. 25But He said to them, "Where is your faith?"

And they were afraid, and marveled, saying to one another, "Who can this be? For He commands even the winds and water, and they obey Him!"

A Demon-Possessed Man Healed

26Then they sailed to the country of the Gadarenes, which is opposite Galilee. 27And when He stepped out on the land, there met Him a certain man from the city who had demons for a long time. And he wore no clothes, nor did he live in a house but in the tombs. 28When he saw Jesus, he cried out, fell down before Him, and with a loud voice said, "What have I to do with You, Jesus, Son of the Most High God? I beg You, do not torment me!" 29For He had commanded the unclean spirit to come out of the man. For it had often seized him, and he was kept under guard, bound with chains and shackles; and he broke the bonds and was driven by the demon into the wilderness.

30Jesus asked him, saying, "What is your name?"

And he said, "Legion," because many demons had entered him. 31And they begged Him that He would not command them to go out into the abyss.

32Now a herd of many swine was feeding there on the mountain. So they begged Him that He would permit them to enter them. And He permitted them. 33Then the demons went out of the man

k Isaiah 6.9

and entered the swine, and the herd ran violently down the steep place into the lake and drowned.

34When those who fed *them* saw what had happened, they fled and told *it* in the city and in the country. 35Then they went out to see what had happened, and came to Jesus, and found the man from whom the demons had departed, sitting at the feet of Jesus, clothed and in his right mind. And they were afraid. 36They also who had seen *it* told them by what means he who had been demon-possessed was healed. 37Then the whole multitude of the surrounding region of the Gadarenes asked Him to depart from them, for they were seized with great fear. And He got into the boat and returned.

38Now the man from whom the demons had departed begged Him that he might be with Him. But Jesus sent him away, saying, 39"Return to your own house, and tell what great things God has done for you." And he went his way and proclaimed throughout the whole city what great things Jesus had done for him.

A Girl Restored to Life and a Woman Healed

40So it was, when Jesus returned, that the multitude welcomed Him, for they were all waiting for Him. 41And behold, there came a man named Jairus, and he was a ruler of the synagogue. And he fell down at Jesus' feet and begged Him to come to his house, 42for he had an only daughter about twelve years of age, and she was dying.

But as He went, the multitudes thronged Him. 43Now a woman, having a flow of blood for twelve years, who had spent all her livelihood on physicians and could not be healed by any, 44came from behind and touched the border of His garment. And immediately her flow of blood stopped.

45And Jesus said, "Who touched Me?"

When all denied it, Peter and those with him said, "Master, the multitudes throng and press You, and You say, 'Who touched Me?'"

46But Jesus said, "Somebody touched Me, for I perceived power going out from Me." 47Now when the woman saw

that she was not hidden, she came trembling; and falling down before Him, she declared to Him in the presence of all the people the reason she had touched Him and how she was healed immediately.

48And He said to her, "Daughter, be of good cheer; your faith has made you well. Go in peace."

49While He was still speaking, someone came from the ruler of the synagogue's *house,* saying to him, "Your daughter is dead. Do not trouble the Teacher."

50But when Jesus heard *it,* He answered him, saying, "Do not be afraid; only believe, and she will be made well." 51When He came into the house, He permitted no one to go in except Peter, James, and John, and the father and mother of the girl. 52Now all wept and mourned for her; but He said, "Do not weep; she is not dead, but sleeping." 53And they ridiculed Him, knowing that she was dead.

54But He put them all outside, took her by the hand and called, saying, "Little girl, arise." 55Then her spirit returned, and she arose immediately. And He commanded that she be given *something* to eat. 56And her parents were astonished, but He charged them to tell no one what had happened.

Sending Out the Twelve

9 Then He called His twelve disciples together and gave them power and authority over all demons, and to cure diseases. 2He sent them to preach the kingdom of God and to heal the sick. 3And He said to them, "Take nothing for the journey, neither staffs nor bag nor bread nor money; and do not have two tunics apiece.

4"Whatever house you enter, stay there, and from there depart. 5And whoever will not receive you, when you go out of that city, shake off the very dust from your feet as a testimony against them."

6So they departed and went through the towns, preaching the gospel and healing everywhere.

Herod Seeks to See Jesus

7Now Herod the tetrarch heard of all that was done by Him; and he was perplexed, because it was said by some that John had risen from the dead, 8and by some that Elijah had appeared, and by others that one of the old prophets had risen again. 9Herod said, "John I have beheaded, but who is this of whom I hear such things?" So he sought to see Him.

Feeding the Five Thousand

10And the apostles, when they had returned, told Him all that they had done. Then He took them and went aside privately into a deserted place belonging to the city called Bethsaida. 11But when the multitudes knew *it*, they followed Him; and He received them and spoke to them about the kingdom of God, and healed those who had need of healing. 12When the day began to wear away, the twelve came and said to Him, "Send the multitude away, that they may go into the surrounding towns and country, and lodge and get provisions; for we are in a deserted place here."

13But He said to them, "You give them something to eat."

And they said, "We have no more than five loaves and two fish, unless we go and buy food for all these people." 14For there were about five thousand men.

Then He said to His disciples, "Make them sit down in groups of fifty."

15And they did so, and made them all sit down.

16Then He took the five loaves and the two fish, and looking up to heaven, He blessed and broke *them*, and gave *them* to the disciples to set before the multitude. 17So they all ate and were filled, and twelve baskets of the leftover fragments were taken up by them.

Peter Confesses Jesus as the Christ

18And it happened, as He was alone praying, *that* His disciples joined Him, and He asked them, saying, "Who do the crowds say that I am?"

19So they answered and said, "John the Baptist, but some *say* Elijah; and others *say* that one of the old prophets has risen again."

20He said to them, "But who do you say that I am?"

Peter answered and said, "The Christ of God."

Jesus Predicts His Death and Resurrection

21And He strictly warned and commanded them to tell this to no one, 22saying, "The Son of Man must suffer many things, and be rejected by the elders and chief priests and scribes, and be killed, and be raised the third day."

Take Up the Cross and Follow Him

23Then He said to *them* all, "If anyone desires to come after Me, let him deny himself, and take up his cross daily, and follow Me. 24For whoever desires to save his life will lose it, but whoever loses his life for My sake will save it. 25For what profit is it to a man if he gains the whole world, and is himself destroyed or lost? 26For whoever is ashamed of Me and My words, of him the Son of Man will be ashamed when He comes in His *own* glory, and *in His* Father's, and of the holy angels.

Jesus Transfigured on the Mount

27But I tell you truly, there are some standing here who shall not taste death till they see the kingdom of God."

28Now it came to pass, about eight days after these sayings, that He took Peter, John, and James and went up on the mountain to pray. 29As He prayed, the appearance of His face was altered, and His robe *became* white *and* glistening. 30And behold, two men talked with Him, who were Moses and Elijah, 31who appeared in glory and spoke of His decease which He was about to accomplish at Jerusalem. 32But Peter and those with him were heavy with sleep; and when they were fully awake, they saw His glory and the two men who stood with Him. 33Then it happened, as they were parting from Him, *that* Peter said to Jesus, "Master, it is good for us to be here; and let us make three tabernacles: one for You, one for Moses, and one for Elijah"—not knowing what he said.

34While he was saying this, a cloud came and overshadowed them; and they were fearful as they entered the cloud. 35And a voice came out of the cloud, saying, "This is My beloved Son. Hear Him!" 36When the voice had ceased, Jesus was found alone. But they kept quiet, and told no one in those days any of the things they had seen.

A Boy Is Healed

37Now it happened on the next day, when they had come down from the mountain, that a great multitude met Him. 38Suddenly a man from the multitude cried out, saying, "Teacher, I implore You, look on my son, for he is my only child. 39And behold, a spirit seizes him, and he suddenly cries out; it convulses him so that he foams *at the mouth;* and it departs from him with great difficulty, bruising him. 40So I implored Your disciples to cast it out, but they could not."

41Then Jesus answered and said, "O faithless and perverse generation, how long shall I be with you and bear with you? Bring your son here." 42And as he was still coming, the demon threw him down and convulsed *him.* Then Jesus rebuked the unclean spirit, healed the child, and gave him back to his father.

Jesus Again Predicts His Death

43And they were all amazed at the majesty of God.

But while everyone marveled at all the things which Jesus did, He said to His disciples, 44"Let these words sink down into your ears, for the Son of Man is about to be betrayed into the hands of men." 45But they did not understand this saying, and it was hidden from them so that they did not perceive it; and they were afraid to ask Him about this saying.

Who Is the Greatest?

46Then a dispute arose among them as to which of them would be greatest. 47And Jesus, perceiving the thought of their heart, took a little child and set him by Him, 48and said to them, "Whoever receives this little child in My name receives Me; and whoever receives Me receives Him who sent Me. For he who is least among you all will be great."

Jesus Forbids Sectarianism

49Now John answered and said, "Master, we saw someone casting out demons in Your name, and we for-bade him because he does not follow with us."

50But Jesus said to him, "Do not forbid *him,* for he who is not against us is on our side."

A Samaritan Village Rejects the Savior

51Now it came to pass, when the time had come for Him to be received up, that He steadfastly set His face to go to Jerusalem, 52and sent messengers before His face. And as they went, they entered a village of the Samaritans, to prepare for Him. 53But they did not receive Him, because His face was *set* for the journey to Jerusalem. 54And when His disciples James and John saw *this,* they said, "Lord, do You want us to command fire to come down from heaven and consume them, just as Elijah did?"

55But He turned and rebuked them, and said, "You do not know what manner of spirit you are of. 56For the Son of Man did not come to destroy men's lives but to save *them.*" And they went to another village.

The Cost of Discipleship

57Now it happened as they journeyed on the road, *that* someone said to Him, "Lord, I will follow You wherever You go."

58And Jesus said to him, "Foxes have holes and birds of the air *have* nests, but the Son of Man has nowhere to lay *His* head."

59Then He said to another, "Follow Me."

But he said, "Lord, let me first go and bury my father."

60Jesus said to him, "Let the dead bury their own dead, but you go and preach the kingdom of God."

61And another also said, "Lord, I will follow You, but let me first go *and* bid them farewell who are at my house."

62But Jesus said to him, "No one, having put his hand to the plow, and looking back, is fit for the kingdom of God."

The Seventy Sent Out

10 After these things the Lord appointed seventy others also, and sent them two by two before His face into every city and place where He Himself was about to go. 2Then He said to them, "The harvest truly *is* great, but the laborers *are* few; therefore pray the Lord of the harvest to send out laborers into His harvest. 3Go your way; behold, I send you out as lambs among wolves. 4Carry neither money bag, knapsack, nor sandals; and greet no one along the road. 5But whatever house you enter, first say, 'Peace to this house.' 6And if a son of peace is there, your peace will rest on it; if not, it will return to you. 7And remain in the same house, eating and drinking such things as they give, for the laborer is worthy of his wages. Do not go from house to house. 8Whatever city you enter, and they receive you, eat such things as are set before you. 9And heal the sick there, and say to them, 'The kingdom of God has come near to you.' 10But whatever city you enter, and they do not receive you, go out into its streets and say, 11'The very dust of your city which clings to us we wipe off against you. Nevertheless know this, that the kingdom of God has come near you.' 12But I say to you that it will be more tolerable in that Day for Sodom than for that city.

Woe to the Impenitent Cities

13"Woe to you, Chorazin! Woe to you, Bethsaida! For if the mighty works which were done in you had been done in Tyre and Sidon, they would have repented long ago, sitting in sackcloth and ashes. 14But it will be more tolerable for Tyre and Sidon at the judgment than for you. 15And you, Capernaum, who are exalted to heaven, will be brought down to Hades. 16He who hears you hears Me, he who rejects you rejects Me, and he who rejects Me rejects Him who sent Me."

The Seventy Return with Joy

17Then the seventy returned with joy, saying, "Lord, even the demons are subject to us in Your name."
18And He said to them, "I saw Satan fall like lightning from heaven. 19Behold, I give you the authority to trample on serpents and scorpions, and over all the power of the enemy, and nothing shall by any means hurt you. 20Nevertheless do not rejoice in this,

that the spirits are subject to you, but rather rejoice because your names are written in heaven."

Jesus Rejoices in the Spirit

21In that hour Jesus rejoiced in the Spirit and said, "I thank You, Father, Lord of heaven and earth, that You have hidden these things from *the* wise and prudent and revealed them to babes. Even so, Father, for so it seemed good in Your sight. 22All things have been delivered to Me by My Father, and no one knows who the Son is except the Father, and who the Father is except the Son, and *the one* to whom the Son wills to reveal *Him*."
23Then He turned to *His* disciples and said privately, "Blessed *are* the eyes which see the things you see; 24for I tell you that many prophets and kings have desired to see what you see, and have not seen *it*, and to hear what you hear, and have not heard *it*."

The Parable of the Good Samaritan

25And behold, a certain lawyer stood up and tested Him, saying, "Teacher, what shall I do to inherit eternal life?"
26He said to him, "What is written in the law? What is your reading *of it*?"
27So he answered and said, "'You shall love the LORD your God with all your heart, with all your soul, with all your strength, and with all your mind,'*l* and 'your neighbor as yourself.' "*m*
28And He said to him, "You have answered rightly; do this and you will live."
29But he, wanting to justify himself, said to Jesus, "And who is my neighbor?"
30Then Jesus answered and said: "A certain *man* went down from Jerusalem to Jericho, and fell among thieves, who stripped him of his clothing, wounded *him*, and departed, leaving *him* half dead. 31Now by chance a certain priest came down that road. And when he saw him, he passed by on the other side. 32Likewise a Levite, when he arrived at the place, came and looked, and passed by on the other side. 33But a certain Samaritan, as he journeyed, came where he was. And when he saw him,

l Deuteronomy 6.5   *m* Leviticus 19.18

he had compassion. 34So he went to *him* and bandaged his wounds, pouring on oil and wine; and he set him on his own animal, brought him to an inn, and took care of him. 35On the next day, when he departed, he took out two denarii, gave *them* to the innkeeper, and said to him, 'Take care of him; and whatever more you spend, when I come again, I will repay you.' 36So which of these three do you think was neighbor to him who fell among the thieves?"

37And he said, "He who showed mercy on him."

Then Jesus said to him, "Go and do likewise."

Mary and Martha Worship and Serve

38Now it happened as they went that He entered a certain village; and a certain woman named Martha welcomed Him into her house. 39And she had a sister called Mary, who also sat at Jesus' feet and heard His word. 40But Martha was distracted with much serving, and she approached Him and said, "Lord, do You not care that my sister has left me to serve alone? Therefore tell her to help me."

41And Jesus answered and said to her, "Martha, Martha, you are worried and troubled about many things. 42But one thing is needed, and Mary has chosen that good part, which will not be taken away from her."

The Model Prayer

11 Now it came to pass, as He was praying in a certain place, when He ceased, *that* one of His disciples said to Him, "Lord, teach us to pray, as John also taught his disciples."

2So He said to them, "When you pray, say:

Our Father in heaven,
Hallowed be Your name.
Your kingdom come.
Your will be done
On earth as *it is* in heaven.
3 Give us day by day our daily bread.
4 And forgive us our sins,
For we also forgive everyone who is indebted to us.
And do not lead us into temptation,
But deliver us from the evil one."

A Friend Comes at Midnight

5And He said to them, "Which of you shall have a friend, and go to him at midnight and say to him, 'Friend, lend me three loaves; 6for a friend of mine has come to me on his journey, and I have nothing to set before him'; 7and he will answer from within and say, 'Do not trouble me; the door is now shut, and my children are with me in bed; I cannot rise and give to you'? 8I say to you, though he will not rise and give to him because he is his friend, yet because of his persistence he will rise and give him as many as he needs.

Keep Asking, Seeking, Knocking

9"So I say to you, ask, and it will be given to you; seek, and you will find; knock, and it will be opened to you. 10For everyone who asks receives, and he who seeks finds, and to him who knocks it will be opened. 11If a son asks for bread from any father among you, will he give him a stone? Or if *he asks* for a fish, will he give him a serpent instead of a fish? 12Or if he asks for an egg, will he offer him a scorpion? 13If you then, being evil, know how to give good gifts to your children, how much more will *your* heavenly Father give the Holy Spirit to those who ask Him!"

A House Divided Cannot Stand

14And He was casting out a demon, and it was mute. So it was, when the demon had gone out, that the mute spoke; and the multitudes marveled. 15But some of them said, "He casts out demons by Beelzebub, the ruler of the demons."

16Others, testing *Him*, sought from Him a sign from heaven. 17But He, knowing their thoughts, said to them: "Every kingdom divided against itself is brought to desolation, and a house *divided* against a house falls. 18If Satan also is divided against himself, how will his kingdom stand? Because you say I cast out demons by Beelzebub. 19And if I cast out demons by Beelzebub, by whom do your sons cast *them* out? Therefore they will be your judges. 20But if I cast out demons with the finger of God, surely the kingdom of God has come upon you. 21When a strong man, fully armed, guards his own palace, his goods are in peace. 22But when a stronger than he comes upon him and overcomes him, he takes from him all his armor in which he trusted, and divides his spoils. 23He who is not with Me is against Me, and he who does not gather with Me scatters.

An Unclean Spirit Returns

24"When an unclean spirit goes out of a man, he goes through dry places, seeking rest; and finding none, he says, 'I will return to my house from which I came.' 25And when he comes, he finds it swept and put in order. 26Then he goes and takes with him seven other spirits more wicked than himself, and they enter and dwell there; and the last state of that man is worse than the first."

Keeping the Word

27And it happened, as He spoke these things, that a certain woman from the crowd raised her voice and said to Him, "Blessed is the womb that bore You, and the breasts which nursed You!"

28But He said, "More than that, blessed are those who hear the word of God and keep it!"

Seeking a Sign

29And while the crowds were thickly gathered together, He began to say, "This is an evil generation. It seeks a sign, and no sign will be given to it except the sign of Jonah the prophet. 30For as Jonah became a sign to the Ninevites, so also the Son of Man will be to this generation. 31The queen of the South will rise up in the judgment with the men of this generation and condemn them, for she came from the ends of the earth to hear the wisdom of Solomon; and indeed a greater than Solomon is here. 32The men of Nineveh will rise up in the judgment with this generation and condemn it, for they repented at the preaching of Jonah; and indeed a greater than Jonah is here.

The Lamp of the Body

33"No one, when he has lit a lamp, puts it in a secret place or under a basket, but on a lampstand, that those who come in may see the light. 34The lamp of the body is the eye. Therefore, when your eye is good, your whole body also is full of light. But when your eye is bad, your body also is full of darkness. 35Therefore take heed that the light which is in you is not darkness. 36If then your whole body is full of light, having no part dark, the whole body will be full of light, as when the bright shining of a lamp gives you light."

Woe to the Pharisees and Lawyers

37And as He spoke, a certain Pharisee asked Him to dine with him. So He went in and sat down to eat. 38When the Pharisee saw it, he marveled that He had not first washed before dinner.

39Then the Lord said to him, "Now you Pharisees make the outside of the cup and dish clean, but your inward part is full of greed and wickedness. 40Foolish ones! Did not He who made the outside make the inside also? 41But rather give alms of such things as you have; then indeed all things are clean to you.

42"But woe to you Pharisees! For you tithe mint and rue and all manner of herbs, and pass by justice and the love of God. These you ought to have done, without leaving the others undone. 43Woe to you Pharisees! For you love the best seats in the synagogues and greetings in the marketplaces. 44Woe to you, scribes and Pharisees, hypocrites! For you are like graves which are not seen, and the men who walk over them are not aware of them."

45Then one of the lawyers answered and said to Him, "Teacher, by saying these things You reproach us also."

46And He said, "Woe to you also, lawyers! For you load men with burdens hard to bear, and you yourselves do not touch the burdens with one of your fingers. 47Woe to you! For you build the tombs of the prophets, and your fathers killed them. 48In fact, you bear witness that you approve the deeds of your fathers; for they indeed killed them, and you build their tombs. 49Therefore the wisdom of God also said, 'I will send them prophets and apostles, and some of them they will kill and persecute,' 50that the blood of all the prophets which was shed from the foundation of the world may be required of this generation, 51from the blood of Abel to the blood of Zechariah who perished between the altar and the temple. Yes, I say to you, it shall be required of this generation.

52"Woe to you lawyers! For you have taken away the key of knowledge. You did not enter in yourselves, and those who were entering in you hindered."

53And as He said these things to them, the scribes and the Pharisees began to assail *Him* vehemently, and to cross-examine Him about many things, 54lying in wait for Him, and seeking to catch Him in something He might say, that they might accuse Him.

Beware of Hypocrisy

12 In the meantime, when an innumerable multitude of people had gathered together, so that they trampled one another, He began to say to His disciples first *of all*, "Beware of the leaven of the Pharisees, which is hypocrisy. 2For there is nothing covered that will not be revealed, nor hidden that will not be known. 3Therefore whatever you have spoken in the dark will be heard in the light, and what you have spoken in the ear in inner rooms will be proclaimed on the housetops.

Jesus Teaches the Fear of God

4"And I say to you, My friends, do not be afraid of those who kill the body, and after that have no more that they can do. 5But I will show you whom you should fear: Fear Him who, after He has killed, has power to cast into hell; yes, I say to you, fear Him!

6"Are not five sparrows sold for two copper coins?[n] And not one of them is forgotten before God. 7But the very hairs of your head are all numbered. Do not fear therefore; you are of more value than many sparrows.

Confess Christ Before Men

8"Also I say to you, whoever confesses Me before men, him the Son of Man also will confess before the angels of God. 9But he who denies Me before men will be denied before the angels of God.

10"And anyone who speaks a word

against the Son of Man, it will be forgiven him; but to him who blasphemes against the Holy Spirit, it will not be forgiven.

11"Now when they bring you to the synagogues and magistrates and authorities, do not worry about how or what you should answer, or what you should say. 12For the Holy Spirit will teach you in that very hour what you ought to say."

The Parable of the Rich Fool

13Then one from the crowd said to Him, "Teacher, tell my brother to divide the inheritance with me."

14But He said to him, "Man, who made Me a judge or an arbitrator over you?" 15And He said to them, "Take heed and beware of covetousness, for one's life does not consist in the abundance of the things he possesses."

16Then He spoke a parable to them, saying: "The ground of a certain rich man yielded plentifully. 17And he thought within himself, saying, 'What shall I do, since I have no room to store my crops?' 18So he said, 'I will do this: I will pull down my barns and build greater, and there I will store all my crops and my goods. 19And I will say to my soul, "Soul, you have many goods laid up for many years; take your ease; eat, drink, *and* be merry." ' 20But God said to him, 'Fool! This night your soul will be required of you; then whose will those things be which you have provided?'

21"So *is* he who lays up treasure for himself, and is not rich toward God."

Do Not Worry

22Then He said to His disciples, "Therefore I say to you, do not worry about your life, what you will eat; nor about the body, what you will put on. 23Life is more than food, and the body *is more* than clothing. 24Consider the ravens, for they neither sow nor reap, which have neither storehouse nor barn; and God feeds them. Of how much more value are you than the birds? 25And which of you by worrying can add one cubit to his stature? 26If you then are not able to do *the* least,

---

[n] Coins of very small value

why are you anxious for the rest? 27Consider the lilies, how they grow: they neither toil nor spin; and yet I say to you, even Solomon in all his glory was not arrayed like one of these. 28If then God so clothes the grass, which today is in the field and tomorrow is thrown into the oven, how much more *will He clothe* you, O *you* of little faith?

29"And do not seek what you should eat or what you should drink, nor have an anxious mind. 30For all these things the nations of the world seek after, and your Father knows that you need these things. 31But seek the kingdom of God, and all these things shall be added to you.

32"Do not fear, little flock, for it is your Father's good pleasure to give you the kingdom. 33Sell what you have and give alms; provide yourselves money bags which do not grow old, a treasure in the heavens that does not fail, where no thief approaches nor moth destroys. 34For where your treasure is, there your heart will be also.

The Faithful Servant and the Evil Servant

35"Let your waist be girded and *your* lamps burning; 36and you yourselves be like men who wait for their master, when he will return from the wedding, that when he comes and knocks they may open to him immediately. 37Blessed *are* those servants whom the master, when he comes, will find watching. Assuredly, I say to you that he will gird himself and have them sit down *to eat,* and will come and serve them. 38And if he should come in the second watch, or come in the third watch, and find *them* so, blessed are those servants. 39But know this, that if the master of the house had known what hour the thief would come, he would have watched and not allowed his house to be broken into. 40Therefore you also be ready, for the Son of Man is coming at an hour you do not expect."

41Then Peter said to Him, "Lord, do You speak this parable *only* to us, or to all *people?*"

42And the Lord said, "Who then is that faithful and wise steward, whom

his master will make ruler over his household, to give *them their* portion of food in due season? 43Blessed *is* that servant whom his master will find so doing when he comes. 44Truly, I say to you that he will make him ruler over all that he has. 45But if that servant says in his heart, 'My master is delaying his coming,' and begins to beat the male and female servants, and to eat and drink and be drunk, 46the master of that servant will come on a day when he is not looking for *him,* and at an hour when he is not aware, and will cut him in two and appoint *him* his portion with the unbelievers. 47And that servant who knew his master's will, and did not prepare *himself* or do according to his will, shall be beaten with many *stripes.* 48But he who did not know, yet committed things deserving of stripes, shall be beaten with few. For everyone to whom much is given, from him much will be required; and to whom much has been committed, of him they will ask the more.

Christ Brings Division

49"I came to send fire on the earth, and how I wish it were already kindled! 50But I have a baptism to be baptized with, and how distressed I am till it is accomplished! 51Do *you* suppose that I came to give peace on earth? I tell you, not at all, but rather division. 52For from now on five in one house will be divided: three against two, and two against three. 53Father will be divided against son and son against father, mother against daughter and daughter against mother, mother-in-law against her daughter-in-law and daughter-in-law against her mother-in-law."

Discern the Time

54Then He also said to the multitudes, "Whenever *you see* a cloud rising out of the west, immediately you say, 'A shower is coming'; and so it is. 55And when you see the south wind blow, you say, 'There will be hot weather'; and there is. 56Hypocrites! You can discern the face of the sky and of the earth, but how *is it* you do not discern this time?

Make Peace with Your Adversary

57"Yes, and why, even of yourselves, do you not judge what is right? 58When you go with your adversary to the magistrate, make every effort along the way to settle with him, lest he drag you to the judge, the judge deliver you to the officer, and the officer throw you into prison. 59I tell you, you shall not depart from there till you have paid the very last mite."

Repent or Perish

13 There were present at that season some who told Him about the Galileans whose blood Pilate had mingled with their sacrifices. 2And Jesus answered and said to them, "Do you suppose that these Galileans were worse sinners than all *other* Galileans, because they suffered such things? 3I tell you, no; but unless you repent you will all likewise perish. 4Or those eighteen on whom the tower in Siloam fell and killed them, do you think that they were worse sinners than all *other* men who dwelt in Jerusalem? 5I tell you, no; but unless you repent you will all likewise perish."

The Parable of the Barren Fig Tree

6He also spoke this parable: "A certain *man* had a fig tree planted in his vineyard, and he came seeking fruit on it and found none. 7Then he said to the keeper of his vineyard, 'Look, for three years I have come seeking fruit on this fig tree and find none. Cut it down; why does it use up the ground?' 8But he answered and said to him, 'Sir, let it alone this year also, until I dig around it and fertilize *it*. 9And if it bears fruit, *well*. But if not, after that you can cut it down.' "

A Spirit of Infirmity

10Now He was teaching in one of the synagogues on the Sabbath. 11And behold, there was a woman who had a spirit of infirmity eighteen years, and was bent over and could in no way raise *herself* up. 12But when Jesus saw her, He called *her* to *Him* and said to her, "Woman, you are loosed from your in-

firmity." 13And He laid *His* hands on her, and immediately she was made straight, and glorified God.

14But the ruler of the synagogue answered with indignation, because Jesus had healed on the Sabbath; and he said to the crowd, "There are six days on which men ought to work; therefore come and be healed on them, and not on the Sabbath day."

15The Lord then answered him and said, "Hypocrite! Does not each one of you on the Sabbath loose his ox or donkey from the stall, and lead *it* away to water it? 16So ought not this woman, being a daughter of Abraham, whom Satan has bound—think of it—for eighteen years, be loosed from this bond on the Sabbath?" 17And when He said these things, all His adversaries were put to shame; and all the multitude rejoiced for all the glorious things that were done by Him.

The Parable of the Mustard Seed

18Then He said, "What is the kingdom of God like? And to what shall I compare it? 19It is like a mustard seed, which a man took and put in his garden; and it grew and became a large tree, and the birds of the air nested in its branches."

The Parable of the Leaven

20And again He said, "To what shall I liken the kingdom of God? 21It is like leaven, which a woman took and hid in three measures° of meal till it was all leavened."

The Narrow Way

22And He went through the cities and villages, teaching, and journeying toward Jerusalem. 23Then one said to Him, "Lord, are there few who are saved?"

And He said to them, 24"Strive to enter through the narrow gate, for many, I say to you, will seek to enter and will not be able. 25When once the Master of the house has risen up and shut the door, and you begin to stand outside and knock at the door, saying, 'Lord, Lord, open for us,' and He will answer and say to you, 'I do not know you,

---

° Approximately two pecks

where you are from,' 26then you will begin to say, 'We ate and drank in Your presence, and You taught in our streets.' 27But He will say, 'I tell you I do not know you, where you are from. Depart from Me, all you workers of iniquity.' 28There will be weeping and gnashing of teeth, when you see Abraham and Isaac and Jacob and all the prophets in the kingdom of God, and yourselves thrust out. 29They will come from the east and the west, from the north and the south, and sit down in the kingdom of God. 30And indeed there are last who will be first, and there are first who will be last."

31On that very day some Pharisees came, saying to Him, "Get out and depart from here, for Herod wants to kill You."

32And He said to them, "Go, tell that fox, 'Behold, I cast out demons and perform cures today and tomorrow, and the third *day* I shall be perfected.' 33Nevertheless I must journey today, tomorrow, and the *day* following; for it cannot be that a prophet should perish outside of Jerusalem.

Jesus Laments over Jerusalem

34"O Jerusalem, Jerusalem, the one who kills the prophets and stones those who are sent to her! How often I wanted to gather your children together, as a hen *gathers* her brood under *her* wings, but you were not willing! 35See! Your house is left to you desolate; and assuredly, I say to you, you shall not see Me until *the time* comes when you say, 'Blessed is He who comes in the name of the Lord!' "p

A Man with Dropsy Healed on the Sabbath

14 Now it happened, as He went into the house of one of the rulers of the Pharisees to eat bread on the Sabbath, that they watched Him closely. 2And behold, there was a certain man before Him who had dropsy. 3And Jesus, answering, spoke to the lawyers and Pharisees, saying, "Is it lawful to heal on the Sabbath?"

4But they kept silent. And He took *him* and healed him, and let him go.

5Then He answered them, saying, "Which of you, having a donkey or an ox that has fallen into a pit, will not immediately pull him out on the Sabbath day?" 6And they could not answer Him regarding these things.

Take the Lowly Place

7So He told a parable to those who were invited, when He noted how they chose the best places, saying to them: 8"When you are invited by anyone to a wedding feast, do not sit down in the best place, lest one more honorable than you be invited by him; 9and he who invited you and him come and say to you, 'Give place to this man,' and then you begin with shame to take the lowest place. 10But when you are invited, go and sit down in the lowest place, so that when he who invited you comes he may say to you, 'Friend, go up higher.' Then you will have glory in the presence of those who sit at the table with you. 11For whoever exalts himself will be humbled, and he who humbles himself will be exalted."

12Then He also said to him who invited Him, "When you give a dinner or a supper, do not ask your friends, your brothers, your relatives, nor rich neighbors, lest they also invite you back, and you be repaid. 13But when you give a feast, invite *the* poor, *the* maimed, *the* lame, *the* blind. 14And you will be blessed, because they cannot repay you; for you shall be repaid at the resurrection of the just."

The Parable of the Great Supper

15Now when one of those who sat at the table with Him heard these things, he said to Him, "Blessed *is* he who shall eat bread in the kingdom of God!"

16Then He said to him, "A certain man gave a great supper and invited many, 17and sent his servant at supper time to say to those who were invited, 'Come, for all things are now ready.' 18But they all with one *accord* began to make excuses. The first said to him, 'I have bought a piece of ground, and I must go and see it. I ask you to have me excused.' 19And another said, 'I have bought five yoke of oxen, and I am going to test them. I ask you to have me excused.' 20Still another said, 'I have married a wife, and therefore I cannot come.' 21So that servant came and reported these things to his master. Then the master of the house, being angry, said to his servant, 'Go out quickly into the streets and lanes of the city, and bring in here *the* poor and *the* maimed and *the* lame and *the* blind.' 22And the servant said, 'Master, it is done as you commanded, and still there is room.' 23Then the master said to the servant, 'Go out into the highways and hedges, and compel *them* to come in, that my house may be filled. 24For I say to you that none of those men who were invited shall taste my supper.' "

Leaving All to Follow Christ

25Now great multitudes went with Him. And He turned and said to them, 26"If anyone comes to Me and does not hate his father and mother, wife and children, brothers and sisters, yes, and his own life also, he cannot be My disciple. 27And whoever does not bear his cross and come after Me cannot be My disciple. 28For which of you, intending to build a tower, does not sit down first and count the cost, whether he has *enough* to finish *it*—29lest, after he has laid the foundation, and is not able to finish, all who see *it* begin to mock him, 30saying, 'This man began to build and was not able to finish.' 31Or what king, going to make war against another king, does not sit down first and consider whether he is able with ten thousand to meet him who comes against him with twenty thousand? 32Or else, while the other is still a great way off, he sends a delegation and asks conditions of peace. 33So likewise, whoever of you does not forsake all that he has cannot be My disciple.

Tasteless Salt Is Worthless

34"Salt *is* good; but if the salt has lost its flavor, how shall it be seasoned? 35It is neither fit for the land nor for the dunghill, *but* men throw it out. He who has ears to hear, let him hear!"

The Parable of the Lost Sheep

15 Then all the tax collectors and the sinners drew near to Him to hear Him. 2And the Pharisees and scribes complained, saying, "This Man receives sinners and eats with them." 3So He spoke this parable to them, saying:

4"What man of you, having a hundred sheep, if he loses one of them, does not leave the ninety-nine in the wilderness, and go after the one which is lost until he finds it? 5And when he has found *it*, he lays *it* on his shoulders, rejoicing. 6And when he comes home, he calls together *his* friends and neighbors, saying to them, 'Rejoice with me, for I have found my sheep which was lost!' 7I say to you that likewise there will be more joy in heaven over one sinner who repents than over ninety-nine just persons who need no repentance.

The Parable of the Lost Coin

8"Or what woman, having ten silver coins,q if she loses one coin, does not light a lamp, sweep the house, and search carefully until she finds *it*? 9And when she has found *it*, she calls *her* friends and neighbors together, saying, 'Rejoice with me, for I have found the piece which I lost!' 10Likewise, I say to you, there is joy in the presence of the angels of God over one sinner who repents."

The Parable of the Lost Son

11Then He said: "A certain man had two sons. 12And the younger of them said to *his* father, 'Father, give me the portion of goods that falls *to me*.' So he divided to them *his* livelihood. 13And not many days after, the younger son gathered all together, journeyed to a far country, and there wasted his possessions with prodigal living. 14But when he had spent all, there arose a severe famine in that land, and he began to be in want. 15Then he went and joined himself to a citizen of that country, and he sent him into his fields to feed swine. 16And he would gladly have filled his stomach with the pods that the

q Valuable coins often worn in a ten-piece garland by married women swine ate, and no one gave him *anything*.

17"But when he came to himself, he said, 'How many of my father's hired servants have bread enough and to spare, and I perish with hunger! 18I will arise and go to my father, and will say to him, "Father, I have sinned against heaven and before you, 19and I am no longer worthy to be called your son. Make me like one of your hired servants." '

20"And he arose and came to his father. But when he was still a great way off, his father saw him and had compassion, and ran and fell on his neck and kissed him. 21And the son said to him, 'Father, I have sinned against heaven and in your sight, and am no longer worthy to be called your son.'

22"But the father said to his servants, 'Bring out the best robe and put *it* on him, and put a ring on his hand and sandals on *his* feet. 23And bring the fatted calf here and kill *it*, and let us eat and be merry; 24for this my son was dead and is alive again; he was lost and is found.' And they began to be merry.

25"Now his older son was in the field. And as he came and drew near to the house, he heard music and dancing. 26So he called one of the servants and asked what these things meant. 27And he said to him, 'Your brother has come, and because he has received him safe and sound, your father has killed the fatted calf.'

28"But he was angry and would not go in. Therefore his father came out and pleaded with him. 29So he answered and said to *his* father, 'Lo, these many years I have been serving you; I never transgressed your commandment at any time; and yet you never gave me a young goat, that I might make merry with my friends. 30But as soon as this son of yours came, who has devoured your livelihood with harlots, you killed the fatted calf for him.'

31"And he said to him, 'Son, you are always with me, and all that I have is yours. 32It was right that we should make merry and be glad, for your brother was dead and is alive again, and was lost and is found.' "

The Parable of the Unjust Steward

16 He also said to His disciples: "There was a certain rich man who had a steward, and an accusation was brought to him that this man was wasting his goods. 2So he called him and said to him, 'What is this I hear about you? Give an account of your stewardship, for you can no longer be steward.'

3"Then the steward said within himself, 'What shall I do? For my master is taking the stewardship away from me. I cannot dig; I am ashamed to beg. 4I have resolved what to do, that when I am put out of the stewardship, they may receive me into their houses.'

5"So he called every one of his master's debtors to *him*, and said to the first, 'How much do you owe my master?' 6And he said, 'A hundred measures' of oil.' So he said to him, 'Take your bill, and sit down quickly and write fifty.' 7Then he said to another, 'And how much do you owe?' So he said, 'A hundred measures of wheat.' And he said to him, 'Take your bill, and write eighty.' 8So the master commended the unjust steward because he had dealt shrewdly. For the sons of this world are more shrewd in their generation than the sons of light.

9"And I say to you, make friends for yourselves by unrighteous mammon, that when you fail, they may receive you into an everlasting home. 10He who *is* faithful in *what is* least is faithful also in much; and he who is unjust in *what is* least is unjust also in much. 11Therefore if you have not been faithful in the unrighteous mammon, who will commit to your trust the true *riches*? 12And if you have not been faithful in what is another man's, who will give you what is your own?

13"No servant can serve two masters; for either he will hate the one and love the other, or else he will be loyal to the one and despise the other. You cannot serve God and mammon."

---

r Eight or nine gallons each (Old Testament *bath*) Testament *kor*)

s Ten or twelve bushels each (Old

The Law, the Prophets, and the Kingdom

14Now the Pharisees, who were lovers of money, also heard all these things, and they derided Him. 15And He said to them, "You are those who justify yourselves before men, but God knows your hearts. For what is highly esteemed among men is an abomination in the sight of God.

16"The law and the prophets *were* until John. Since that time the kingdom of God has been preached, and everyone is pressing into it. 17And it is easier for heaven and earth to pass away than for one tittle of the law to fail.

18"Whoever divorces his wife and marries another commits adultery; and whoever marries her who is divorced from *her* husband commits adultery.

The Rich Man and Lazarus

19"There was a certain rich man who was clothed in purple and fine linen and fared sumptuously every day. 20But there was a certain beggar named Lazarus, full of sores, who was laid at his gate, 21desiring to be fed with the crumbs which fell from the rich man's table. Moreover the dogs came and licked his sores. 22So it was that the beggar died, and was carried by the angels to Abraham's bosom. The rich man also died and was buried. 23And being in torments in Hades, he lifted up his eyes and saw Abraham afar off, and Lazarus in his bosom.

24"Then he cried and said, 'Father Abraham, have mercy on me, and send Lazarus that he may dip the tip of his finger in water and cool my tongue; for I am tormented in this flame.' 25But Abraham said, 'Son, remember that in your lifetime you received your good things, and likewise Lazarus evil things; but now he is comforted and you are tormented. 26And besides all this, between us and you there is a great gulf fixed, so that those who want to pass from here to you cannot, nor can those from there pass to us.'

27"Then he said, 'I beg you therefore, father, that you would send him to my father's house, 28for I have five brothers, that he may testify to them, lest they also come to this place of torment.'

29Abraham said to him, 'They have Moses and the prophets; let them hear them.' 30And he said, 'No, father Abraham; but if one goes to them from the dead, they will repent.' 31But he said to him, 'If they do not hear Moses and the prophets, neither will they be persuaded though one rise from the dead.' "

Jesus Warns of Offenses

17 Then He said to the disciples, "It is impossible that no offenses should come, but woe *to him* through whom they do come! 2It would be better for him if a millstone were hung around his neck, and he were thrown into the sea, than that he should offend one of these little ones. 3Take heed to yourselves. If your brother sins against you, rebuke him; and if he repents, forgive him. 4And if he sins against you seven times in a day, and seven times in a day returns to you, saying, 'I repent,' you shall forgive him."

Faith and Duty

5And the apostles said to the Lord, "Increase our faith."

6So the Lord said, "If you have faith as a mustard seed, you can say to this mulberry tree, 'Be pulled up by the roots and be planted in the sea,' and it would obey you. 7And which of you, having a servant plowing or tending sheep, will say to him when he has come in from the field, 'Come at once and sit down to eat'? 8But will he not rather say to him, 'Prepare something for my supper, and gird yourself and serve me till I have eaten and drunk, and afterward you will eat and drink'? 9Does he thank that servant because he did the things that were commanded him? I think not. 10So likewise you, when you have done all those things which you are commanded, say, 'We are unprofitable servants. We have done what was our duty to do.' "

Ten Lepers Cleansed

11Now it happened as He went to Jerusalem that He passed through the midst of Samaria and Galilee. 12Then as He entered a certain village, there met Him ten men who were lepers, who stood afar off. 13And they lifted up *their* voices and said, "Jesus, Master, have mercy on us!"

14So when He saw *them*, He said to them, "Go, show yourselves to the priests." And so it was that as they went, they were cleansed.

15And one of them, when he saw that he was healed, returned, and with a loud voice glorified God, 16and fell down on *his* face at His feet, giving Him thanks. And he was a Samaritan.

17So Jesus answered and said, "Were there not ten cleansed? But where *are* the nine? 18Were there not any found who returned to give glory to God except this foreigner?" 19And He said to him, "Arise, go your way. Your faith has made you well."

The Coming of the Kingdom

20Now when He was asked by the Pharisees when the kingdom of God would come, He answered them and said, "The kingdom of God does not come with observation; 21nor will they say, 'See here!' or 'See there!' For indeed, the kingdom of God is within you."

22Then He said to the disciples, "The days will come when you will desire to see one of the days of the Son of Man, and you will not see *it*. 23And they will say to you, 'Look here!' or 'Look there!' Do not go after *them* or follow *them*. 24For as the lightning that flashes out of one *part* under heaven shines to the other *part* under heaven, so also the Son of Man will be in His day. 25But first He must suffer many things and be rejected by this generation. 26And as it was in the days of Noah, so it will be also in the days of the Son of Man: 27They ate, they drank, they married wives, they were given in marriage, until the day that Noah entered the ark, and the flood came and destroyed them all. 28Likewise as it was also in the days of Lot: They ate, they drank, they bought, they sold, they planted, they built; 29but on the day that Lot went out of Sodom it rained fire and brimstone from heaven and destroyed *them* all. 30Even so will it be in the day when the Son of Man is revealed.

31"In that day, he who is on the housetop, and his goods *are* in the house, let him not come down to take them away. And likewise the one who is in the field, let him not turn back. 32Remember Lot's wife. 33Whoever seeks to save his life will lose it, and whoever loses his life will preserve it. 34I tell you, in that night there will be two *men* in one bed: the one will be taken and the other will be left. 35Two *women* will be grinding together: the one will be taken and the other left. 36Two *men* will be in the field: the one will be taken and the other left."

37And they answered and said to Him, "Where, Lord?"

So He said to them, "Wherever the body is, there the eagles will be gathered together."

The Parable of the Persistent Widow

18 Then He spoke a parable to them, that men always ought to pray and not lose heart, 2saying: "There was in a certain city a judge who did not fear God nor regard man. 3Now there was a widow in that city; and she came to him, saying, 'Get justice for me from my adversary.' 4And he would not for a while; but afterward he said within himself, 'Though I do not fear God nor regard man, 5yet because this widow troubles me I will avenge her, lest by her continual coming she weary me.'"

6Then the Lord said, "Hear what the unjust judge said. 7And shall God not avenge His own elect who cry out day and night to Him, though He bears long with them? 8I tell you that He will avenge them speedily. Nevertheless, when the Son of Man comes, will He really find faith on the earth?"

The Parable of the Pharisee and the Tax Collector

9Also He spoke this parable to some who trusted in themselves that they were righteous, and despised others: 10"Two men went up to the temple to pray, one a Pharisee and the other a tax collector. 11The Pharisee stood and prayed thus with himself, 'God, I thank You that I am not like other men—extortioners, unjust, adulterers, or even as this tax collector. 12I fast twice a week; I give tithes of all that I possess.' 13And the tax collector, standing afar off, would not so much as raise *his* eyes to heaven, but beat his breast, saying, 'God, be merciful to me a sinner!' 14I tell you, this man went down to his house justified *rather* than the other; for everyone who exalts himself will be humbled, and he who humbles himself will be exalted.''

Jesus Blesses Little Children

15Then they also brought infants to Him that He might touch them; but when the disciples saw *it*, they rebuked them. 16But Jesus called them to *Him* and said, "Let the little children come to Me, and do not forbid them; for of such is the kingdom of God. 17Assuredly, I say to you, whoever does not receive the kingdom of God as a little child will by no means enter it.''

Jesus Counsels the Rich Young Ruler

18Now a certain ruler asked Him, saying, "Good Teacher, what shall I do to inherit eternal life?''
19So Jesus said to him, "Why do you call Me good? No one *is* good but One, *that is,* God. 20You know the commandments: 'Do not commit adultery,' 'Do not murder,' 'Do not steal,' 'Do not bear false witness,' 'Honor your father and your mother.' ''*t*
21And he said, "All these things I have kept from my youth.''
22So when Jesus heard these things, He said to him, "You still lack one thing. Sell all that you have and distribute to the poor, and you will have treasure in heaven; and come, follow Me.''
23But when he heard this, he became very sorrowful, for he was very rich.

With God All Things Are Possible

24And when Jesus saw that he became very sorrowful, He said, "How hard it is for those who have riches to enter the kingdom of God! 25For it is easier for a camel to go through the eye of a needle than for a rich man to enter the kingdom of God.''
26And those who heard it said, "Who then can be saved?''
27But He said, "The things which are impossible with men are possible with God.''

28Then Peter said, "See, we have left all and followed You.''
29So He said to them, "Assuredly, I say to you, there is no one who has left house or parents or brothers or wife or children, for the sake of the kingdom of God, 30who shall not receive many times more in this present time, and in the age to come eternal life.''

Jesus a Third Time Predicts His Death and Resurrection

31Then He took the twelve aside and said to them, "Behold, we are going up to Jerusalem, and all things that are written by the prophets concerning the Son of Man will be accomplished. 32For He will be delivered to the Gentiles and will be mocked and insulted and spit upon. 33They will scourge *Him* and kill Him. And the third day He will rise again.''
34But they understood none of these things; this saying was hidden from them, and they did not know the things which were spoken.

A Blind Man Receives His Sight

35Then it happened, as He was coming near Jericho, that a certain blind man sat by the road begging. 36And hearing a multitude passing by, he asked what it meant. 37So they told him that Jesus of Nazareth was passing by. 38And he cried out, saying, "Jesus, Son of David, have mercy on me!''
39Then those who went before warned him that he should be quiet; but he cried out all the more, "Son of David, have mercy on me!''
40So Jesus stood still and commanded him to be brought to Him. And when he had come near, He asked him, 41saying, "What do you want Me to do for you?''
He said, "Lord, that I may receive my sight.''
42Then Jesus said to him, "Receive your sight; your faith has made you well.'' 43And immediately he received his sight, and followed Him, glorifying God. And all the people, when they saw *it,* gave praise to God.

---

t Exodus 20.12-16; Deuteronomy 5.16-20

Jesus Comes to Zacchaeus's House

19 Then *Jesus* entered and passed through Jericho. 2Now behold, *there was* a man named Zacchaeus who was a chief tax collector, and he was rich. 3And he sought to see who Jesus was, but could not because of the crowd, for he was of short stature. 4So he ran ahead and climbed up into a sycamore tree to see Him, for He was going to pass that *way*. 5And when Jesus came to the place, He looked up and saw him, and said to him, "Zacchaeus, make haste and come down, for today I must stay at your house." 6So he made haste and came down, and received Him joyfully. 7But when they saw *it*, they all complained, saying, "He has gone to be a guest with a man who is a sinner."

8Then Zacchaeus stood and said to the Lord, "Look, Lord, I give half of my goods to the poor; and if I have taken anything from anyone by false accusation, I restore fourfold."

9And Jesus said to him, "Today salvation has come to this house, because he also is a son of Abraham; 10for the Son of Man has come to seek and to save that which was lost."

The Parable of the Minas

11Now as they heard these things, He spoke another parable, because He was near Jerusalem and because they thought the kingdom of God would appear immediately. 12Therefore He said: "A certain nobleman went into a far country to receive for himself a kingdom and to return. 13So he called ten of his servants, delivered to them ten minas,u and said to them, 'Do business till I come.' 14But his citizens hated him, and sent a delegation after him, saying, 'We will not have this *man* to reign over us.'

15"And so it was that when he returned, having received the kingdom, he then commanded these servants, to whom he had given the money, to be called to him, that he might know how much every man had gained by trading. 16Then came the first, saying, 'Master, your mina has earned ten minas.'

17And he said to him, 'Well *done*, good servant; because you were faithful in a very little, have authority over ten cities.' 18And the second came, saying, 'Master, your mina has earned five minas.' 19Likewise he said to him, 'You also be over five cities.'

20"Then another came, saying, 'Master, here is your mina, which I have kept put away in a handkerchief. 21For I feared you, because you are an austere man. You collect what you did not deposit, and reap what you did not sow.' 22And he said to him, 'Out of your own mouth I will judge you; *you* wicked servant. You knew that I was an austere man, collecting what I did not deposit and reaping what I did not sow. 23Why then did you not put my money in the bank, that at my coming I might have collected it with interest?'

24"And he said to those who stood by, 'Take the mina from him, and give *it* to him who has ten minas.' 25(But they said to him, 'Master, he has ten minas.') 26'For I say to you, that to everyone who has will be given; and from him who does not have, even what he has will be taken away from him. 27But bring here those enemies of mine, who did not want me to reign over them, and slay *them* before me.' "

The Triumphal Entry

28When He had said this, He went on ahead, going up to Jerusalem. 29And it came to pass, when He drew near to Bethphage and Bethany, at the mountain called Olivet, *that* He sent two of His disciples, 30saying, "Go into the village opposite *you*, where as you enter you will find a colt tied, on which no one has ever sat. Loose it and bring *it* here. 31And if anyone asks you, 'Why are you loosing *it*?' thus you shall say to him, 'Because the Lord has need of it.' "

32So those who were sent went their way and found *it* just as He had said to them. 33But as they were loosing the colt, the owners of it said to them, "Why are you loosing the colt?"

34And they said, "The Lord has need of him." 35Then they brought him to Jesus. And they threw their own clothes

---

u The *mina* was worth about three months' salary.

on the colt, and they set Jesus on him.
36And as He went, *many* spread their clothes on the road.

37Then, as He was now drawing near the descent of the Mount of Olives, the whole multitude of the disciples began to rejoice and praise God with a loud voice for all the mighty works they had seen, 38saying:

" 'Blessed *is* the King who comes in the name of the LORD!'*v*
Peace in heaven and glory in the highest!"

39And some of the Pharisees called to Him from the crowd, "Teacher, rebuke Your disciples."

40But He answered and said to them, "I tell you that if these should keep silent, the stones would immediately cry out."

Jesus Weeps over Jerusalem

41Now as He drew near, He saw the city and wept over it, 42saying, "If you had known, even you, especially in this your day, the things *that make* for your peace! But now they are hidden from your eyes. 43For days will come upon you when your enemies will build an embankment around you, surround you and close you in on every side, 44and level you, and your children within you, to the ground; and they will not leave in you one stone upon another, because you did not know the time of your visitation."

Jesus Cleanses the Temple

45Then He went into the temple and began to drive out those who bought and sold in it, 46saying to them, "It is written, 'My house is a house of prayer,'*w* but you have made it a 'den of thieves.' "*x*

47And He was teaching daily in the temple. But the chief priests, the scribes, and the leaders of the people sought to destroy Him, 48and were unable to do anything; for all the people were very attentive to hear Him.

Jesus' Authority Questioned

20 Now it happened on one of those days, as He taught the people in the temple and preached the gospel, *that* the chief priests and the scribes, together with the elders, confronted Him 2and spoke to Him, saying, "Tell us, by what authority are You doing these things? Or who is he who gave You this authority?"

3But He answered and said to them, "I also will ask you one thing, and answer Me: 4The baptism of John—was it from heaven or from men?"

5And they reasoned among themselves, saying, "If we say, 'From heaven,' He will say, 'Why then did you not believe him?' 6But if we say, 'From men,' all the people will stone us, for they are persuaded that John was a prophet." 7So they answered that they did not know where *it was* from.

8And Jesus said to them, "Neither will I tell you by what authority I do these things."

The Parable of the Wicked Vinedressers

9Then He began to tell the people this parable: "A certain man planted a vineyard, leased it to vinedressers, and went into a far country for a long time. 10Now at vintage-time he sent a servant to the vinedressers, that they might give him some of the fruit of the vineyard. But the vinedressers beat him and sent *him* away empty-handed. 11Again he sent another servant; and they beat him also, treated *him* shamefully, and sent *him* away empty-handed. 12And again he sent a third; and they wounded him also and cast *him* out.

13"Then the owner of the vineyard said, 'What shall I do? I will send my beloved son. Probably they will respect *him* when they see him.' 14But when the vinedressers saw him, they reasoned among themselves, saying, 'This is the heir. Come, let us kill him, that the inheritance may be ours.' 15So they cast him out of the vineyard and killed *him*. Therefore what will the owner of the vineyard do to them? 16He will come and destroy those vinedressers and give the vineyard to others."

And when they heard *it* they said, "Certainly not!"

17Then He looked at them and said, "What then is this that is written:

v Psalm 118.26   *w* Isaiah 56.7   *x* Jeremiah 7.11

'The stone which the builders
  rejected
 Has become the chief
  cornerstone' ?*y*

18Whoever falls on that stone will be broken; but on whomever it falls, it will grind him to powder."

19And the chief priests and the scribes that very hour sought to lay hands on Him, but they feared the people—for they knew He had spoken this parable against them.

The Pharisees: Is It Lawful to Pay Taxes to Caesar?

20So they watched *Him*, and sent spies who pretended to be righteous, that they might seize on His words, in order to deliver Him to the power and the authority of the governor. 21Then they asked Him, saying, "Teacher, we know that You say and teach rightly, and You do not show personal favoritism, but teach the way of God in truth: 22Is it lawful for us to pay taxes to Caesar or not?"

23But He perceived their craftiness, and said to them, "Why do you test Me? 24Show Me a denarius. Whose image and inscription does it have?"

They answered and said, "Caesar's."

25And He said to them, "Render therefore to Caesar the things that are Caesar's, and to God the things that are God's."

26But they could not catch Him in His words in the presence of the people. And they marveled at His answer and kept silent.

The Sadducees: What About the Resurrection?

27Then some of the Sadducees, who deny that there is a resurrection, came to *Him* and asked Him, 28saying: "Teacher, Moses wrote to us *that* if a man's brother dies, having a wife, and he dies without children, his brother should take his wife and raise up offspring for his brother. 29Now there were seven brothers. And the first took a wife, and died without children. 30And the second took her as wife, and he died childless. 31Then the third took her, and in like manner the seven also;

and they left no children, and died. 32Last of all the woman died also. 33Therefore, in the resurrection, whose wife does she become? For all seven had her as wife."

34Jesus answered and said to them, "The sons of this age marry and are given in marriage. 35But those who are counted worthy to attain that age, and the resurrection from the dead, neither marry nor are given in marriage; 36nor can they die anymore, for they are equal to the angels and are sons of God, being sons of the resurrection. 37But even Moses showed in the *burning* bush *passage* that the dead are raised, when he called the Lord 'the God of Abraham, the God of Isaac, and the God of Jacob.'*z* 38For He is not the God of the dead but of the living, for all live to Him."

39Then some of the scribes answered and said, "Teacher, You have spoken well." 40But after that they dared not question Him anymore.

Jesus: How Can David Call His Descendant Lord?

41And He said to them, "How can they say that the Christ is the Son of David? 42Now David himself said in the Book of Psalms:

'The LORD said to my Lord,
 "Sit at My right hand,
43   Till I make Your enemies Your
       footstool." '*a*

44Therefore David calls Him 'Lord'; how is He then his Son?"

Beware of the Scribes

45Then, in the hearing of all the people, He said to His disciples, 46"Beware of the scribes, who desire to go around in long robes, love greetings in the marketplaces, the best seats in the synagogues, and the best places at feasts, 47who devour widows' houses, and for a pretense make long prayers. These will receive greater condemnation."

The Widow's Two Mites

21 And He looked up and saw the rich putting their gifts into the treasury, 2and He saw also a certain poor widow putting in two mites.

---

y Psalm 118.22   *z* Exodus 3.6, 15   *a* Psalm 110.1

3So He said, "Truly I say to you that this poor widow has put in more than all; 4for all these out of their abundance have put in offerings for God, but she out of her poverty put in all the livelihood that she had."

Jesus Predicts the Destruction of the Temple

5Then, as some spoke of the temple, how it was adorned with beautiful stones and donations, He said, 6"These things which you see—the days will come in which not *one* stone shall be left upon another that shall not be thrown down."

The Signs of the Times and the End of the Age

7So they asked Him, saying, "Teacher, but when will these things be? And what sign *will there be* when these things are about to take place?"

8And He said: "Take heed that you not be deceived. For many will come in My name, saying, 'I am *He,*' and, 'The time has drawn near.' Therefore do not go after them. 9But when you hear of wars and commotions, do not be terrified; for these things must come to pass first, but the end *will not come* immediately."

10Then He said to them, "Nation will rise against nation, and kingdom against kingdom. 11And there will be great earthquakes in various places, and famines and pestilences; and there will be fearful sights and great signs from heaven. 12But before all these things, they will lay their hands on you and persecute *you,* delivering *you* up to the synagogues and prisons. You will be brought before kings and rulers for My name's sake. 13But it will turn out for you as an occasion for testimony. 14Therefore settle *it* in your hearts not to meditate beforehand on what you will answer; 15for I will give you a mouth and wisdom which all your adversaries will not be able to contradict or resist. 16You will be betrayed even by parents and brothers, relatives and friends; and they will put *some* of you to death. 17And you will be hated by all for My name's sake. 18But not a hair of your head shall be lost. 19By your patience possess your souls.

The Destruction of Jerusalem

20"But when you see Jerusalem surrounded by armies, then know that its desolation is near. 21Then let those who are in Judea flee to the mountains, let those who are in the midst of her depart, and let not those who are in the country enter her. 22For these are the days of vengeance, that all things which are written may be fulfilled. 23But woe to those who are pregnant and to those who are nursing babies in those days! For there will be great distress in the land and wrath upon this people. 24And they will fall by the edge of the sword, and be led away captive into all nations. And Jerusalem will be trampled by Gentiles until the times of the Gentiles are fulfilled.

The Coming of the Son of Man

25"And there will be signs in the sun, in the moon, and in the stars; and on the earth distress of nations, with perplexity, the sea and the waves roaring; 26men's hearts failing them from fear and the expectation of those things which are coming on the earth, for the powers of the heavens will be shaken. 27Then they will see the Son of Man coming in a cloud with power and great glory. 28Now when these things begin to happen, look up and lift up your heads, because your redemption draws near."

The Parable of the Fig Tree

29Then He spoke to them a parable: "Look at the fig tree, and all the trees. 30When they are already budding, you see and know for yourselves that summer is now near. 31So you also, when you see these things happening, know that the kingdom of God is near. 32Assuredly, I say to you, this generation will by no means pass away till all things take place. 33Heaven and earth will pass away, but My words will by no means pass away.

The Importance of Watching

34"But take heed to yourselves, lest your hearts be weighed down with carousing, drunkenness, and cares of this life, and that Day come on you unexpectedly. 35For it will come as a snare on all those who dwell on the face of the whole earth. 36Watch therefore, and pray always that you may be counted worthy to escape all these things that will come to pass, and to stand before the Son of Man."

37And in the daytime He was teaching in the temple, but at night He went out and stayed on the mountain called Olivet. 38Then early in the morning all the people came to Him in the temple to hear Him.

The Plot to Kill Jesus

22 Now the Feast of Unleavened Bread drew near, which is called Passover. 2And the chief priests and the scribes sought how they might kill Him, for they feared the people.

3Then Satan entered Judas, surnamed Iscariot, who was numbered among the twelve. 4So he went his way and conferred with the chief priests and captains, how he might betray Him to them. 5And they were glad, and agreed to give him money. 6So he promised and sought opportunity to betray Him to them in the absence of the multitude.

Jesus and His Disciples Prepare the Passover

7Then came the Day of Unleavened Bread, when the Passover must be killed. 8And He sent Peter and John, saying, "Go and prepare the Passover for us, that we may eat."

9So they said to Him, "Where do You want us to prepare?"

10And He said to them, "Behold, when you have entered the city, a man will meet you carrying a pitcher of water; follow him into the house which he enters. 11Then you shall say to the master of the house, 'The Teacher says to you, "Where is the guest room where I may eat the Passover with My disciples?"' 12Then he will show you a large, furnished upper room; there make ready."

13So they went and found it just as He had said to them, and they prepared the Passover.

Jesus Institutes the Lord's Supper

14When the hour had come, He sat down, and the twelve apostles with Him. 15Then He said to them, "With *fervent* desire I have desired to eat this Passover with you before I suffer; 16for I say to you, I will no longer eat of it until it is fulfilled in the kingdom of God."

17Then He took the cup, and gave thanks, and said, "Take this and divide *it* among yourselves; 18for I say to you, I will not drink of the fruit of the vine until the kingdom of God comes."

19And He took bread, gave thanks and broke *it*, and gave *it* to them, saying, "This is My body which is given for you; do this in remembrance of Me."

20Likewise He also *took* the cup after supper, saying, "This cup *is* the new covenant in My blood, which is shed for you. 21But behold, the hand of My betrayer *is* with Me on the table. 22And truly the Son of Man goes as it has been determined, but woe to that man by whom He is betrayed!"

23Then they began to question among themselves, which of them it was who would do this thing.

The Disciples Argue About Greatness

24Now there was also a dispute among them, as to which of them should be considered the greatest. 25And He said to them, "The kings of the Gentiles exercise lordship over them, and those who exercise authority over them are called 'benefactors.' 26But not so *among* you; on the contrary, he who is greatest among you, let him be as the younger, and he who governs as he who serves. 27For who *is* greater, he who sits at the table, or he who serves? *Is* it not he who sits at the table? Yet I am among you as the One who serves.

28"But you are those who have continued with Me in My trials. 29And I bestow upon you a kingdom, just as My Father bestowed *one* upon Me, 30that you may eat and drink at My table in My kingdom, and sit on thrones judging the twelve tribes of Israel."

Jesus Predicts Peter's Denial

31And the Lord said, "Simon, Simon! Indeed, Satan has asked for you, that he may sift *you* as wheat. 32But I have prayed for you, that your faith should not fail; and when you have returned to *Me*, strengthen your brethren."

33But he said to Him, "Lord, I am

ready to go with You, both to prison and to death."

34Then He said, "I tell you, Peter, the rooster shall not crow this day before you will deny three times that you know Me."

Supplies for the Road

35And He said to them, "When I sent you without money bag, knapsack, and sandals, did you lack anything?"

So they said, "Nothing."

36Then He said to them, "But now, he who has a money bag, let him take *it*, and likewise a knapsack; and he who has no sword, let him sell his garment and buy one. **37**For I say to you that this which is written must still be accomplished in Me: 'And He was numbered with the transgressors.'*b* For the things concerning Me have an end."

38So they said, "Lord, look, here *are* two swords."

And He said to them, "It is enough."

The Prayer in the Garden

39Coming out, He went to the Mount of Olives, as He was accustomed, and His disciples also followed Him. **40**When He came to the place, He said to them, "Pray that you may not enter into temptation."

41And He was withdrawn from them about a stone's throw, and He knelt down and prayed, **42**saying, "Father, if it is Your will, take this cup away from Me; nevertheless not My will, but Yours, be done." **43**Then an angel appeared to Him from heaven, strengthening Him. **44**And being in agony, He prayed more earnestly. Then His sweat became like great drops of blood falling down to the ground.

45When He rose up from prayer, and had come to His disciples, He found them sleeping from sorrow. **46**Then He said to them, "Why do you sleep? Rise and pray, lest you enter into temptation."

Betrayal and Arrest in Gethsemane

47And while He was still speaking, behold, a multitude; and he who was called Judas, one of the twelve, went before them and drew near to Jesus to kiss Him. **48**But Jesus said to him, "Judas, are you betraying the Son of Man with a kiss?"

49When those around Him saw what was going to happen, they said to Him, "Lord, shall we strike with the sword?" **50**And one of them struck the servant of the high priest and cut off his right ear.

51But Jesus answered and said, "Permit even this." And He touched his ear and healed him.

52Then Jesus said to the chief priests, captains of the temple, and the elders who had come to Him, "Have you come out, as against a robber, with swords and clubs? **53**When I was with you daily in the temple, you did not try to seize Me. But this is your hour, and the power of darkness."

Peter Denies Jesus, and Weeps Bitterly

54Having arrested Him, they led *Him* and brought Him into the high priest's house. But Peter followed at a distance. **55**Now when they had kindled a fire in the midst of the courtyard and sat down together, Peter sat among them. **56**And a certain servant girl, seeing him as he sat by the fire, looked intently at him and said, "This man was also with Him."

57But he denied Him, saying, "Woman, I do not know Him."

58And after a little while another saw him and said, "You also are of them."

But Peter said, "Man, I am not!"

59Then after about an hour had passed, another confidently affirmed, saying, "Surely this *fellow* also was with Him, for he is a Galilean."

60But Peter said, "Man, I do not know what you are saying!"

Immediately, while he was still speaking, the rooster crowed. **61**And the Lord turned and looked at Peter. Then Peter remembered the word of the Lord, how He had said to him, "Before the rooster crows, you will deny Me three times." **62**So Peter went out and wept bitterly.

Jesus Mocked and Beaten

63Now the men who held Jesus mocked Him and beat Him. **64**And having blindfolded Him, they struck Him

b Isaiah 53.12

on the face and asked Him, saying, "Prophesy! Who is the one who struck You?" 65And many other things they blasphemously spoke against Him.

Jesus Faces the Sanhedrin

66As soon as it was day, the elders of the people, both chief priests and scribes, came together and led Him into their council, saying, 67"If You are the Christ, tell us."

But He said to them, "If I tell you, you will by no means believe. 68And if I also ask *you*, you will by no means answer Me or let *Me* go. 69Hereafter the Son of Man will sit on the right hand of the power of God."

70Then they all said, "Are You then the Son of God?"

So He said to them, "You *rightly* say that I am."

71And they said, "What further testimony do we need? For we have heard it ourselves from His own mouth."

Jesus Handed Over to Pontius Pilate

23 Then the whole multitude of them arose and led Him to Pilate. 2And they began to accuse Him, saying, "We found this *fellow* perverting the nation, and forbidding to pay taxes to Caesar, saying that He Himself is Christ, a King."

3Then Pilate asked Him, saying, "Are You the King of the Jews?"

He answered him and said, "*It is as* you say."

4So Pilate said to the chief priests and the crowd, "I find no fault in this Man."

5But they were the more fierce, saying, "He stirs up the people, teaching throughout all Judea, beginning from Galilee to this place."

Jesus Faces Herod

6When Pilate heard of Galilee, he asked if the Man were a Galilean. 7And as soon as he knew that He belonged to Herod's jurisdiction, he sent Him to Herod, who was also in Jerusalem at that time. 8Now when Herod saw Jesus, he was exceedingly glad; for he had desired for a long *time* to see Him, because he had heard many things about Him, and he hoped to see some miracle done by Him. 9Then he questioned Him with many words, but He answered him nothing. 10And the chief priests and scribes stood and vehemently accused Him. 11Then Herod, with his men of war, treated Him with contempt and mocked *Him,* arrayed Him in a gorgeous robe, and sent Him back to Pilate. 12That very day Pilate and Herod became friends with each other, for previously they had been at enmity with each other.

Taking the Place of Barabbas

13Then Pilate, when he had called together the chief priests, the rulers, and the people, 14said to them, "You have brought this Man to me, as one who misleads the people. And indeed, having examined *Him* in your presence, I have found no fault in this Man concerning those things of which you accuse Him; 15no, neither did Herod, for I sent you back to him; and indeed nothing deserving of death has been done by Him. 16I will therefore chastise Him and release *Him*" 17(for it was necessary for him to release one to them at the feast).

18And they all cried out at once, saying, "Away with this *Man,* and release to us Barabbas"—19who had been thrown into prison for a certain rebellion made in the city, and for murder.

20Pilate, therefore, wishing to release Jesus, again called out to them. 21But they shouted, saying, "Crucify *Him,* crucify Him!"

22Then he said to them the third time, "Why, what evil has He done? I have found no reason for death in Him. I will therefore chastise Him and let *Him* go."

23But they were insistent, demanding with loud voices that He be crucified. And the voices of these men and of the chief priests prevailed. 24So Pilate gave sentence that it should be as they requested. 25And he released to them the one they requested, who for rebellion and murder had been thrown into prison; but he delivered Jesus to their will.

The King on a Cross

26Now as they led Him away, they laid hold of a certain man, Simon a Cyrenian, who was coming from the country, and on him they laid the cross that he might bear *it* after Jesus.

27And a great multitude of the people followed Him, and women who also mourned and lamented Him. 28But Jesus, turning to them, said, "Daughters of Jerusalem, do not weep for Me, but weep for yourselves and for your children. 29For indeed the days are coming in which they will say, 'Blessed *are* the barren, wombs that never bore, and breasts which never nursed!' 30Then they will begin 'to say to the mountains, "Fall on us!" and to the hills, "Cover us!" '*c* 31For if they do these things in the green wood, what will be done in the dry?"

32There were also two others, criminals, led with Him to be put to death. 33And when they had come to the place called Calvary, there they crucified Him, and the criminals, one on the right hand and the other on the left. 34Then Jesus said, "Father, forgive them, for they do not know what they do."

And they divided His garments and cast lots. 35And the people stood looking on. But even the rulers with them sneered, saying, "He saved others; let Him save Himself if He is the Christ, the chosen of God."

36The soldiers also mocked Him, coming and offering Him sour wine, 37and saying, "If You are the King of the Jews, save Yourself."

38And an inscription also was written over Him in letters of Greek, Latin, and Hebrew:

THIS IS THE KING OF THE JEWS.

39Then one of the criminals who were hanged blasphemed Him, saying, "If You are the Christ, save Yourself and us."

40But the other, answering, rebuked him, saying, "Do you not even fear God, seeing you are under the same condemnation? 41And we indeed justly, for we receive the due reward of our deeds; but this Man has done nothing wrong." 42Then he said to Jesus, "Lord, remember me when You come into Your kingdom."

43And Jesus said to him, "Assuredly, I say to you, today you will be with Me in Paradise."

Jesus Dies on the Cross

44Now it was about the sixth hour, and there was darkness over all the earth until the ninth hour. 45Then the sun was darkened, and the veil of the temple was torn in two. 46And when Jesus had cried out with a loud voice, He said, "Father, 'into Your hands I commit My spirit.' "*d* Having said this, He breathed His last.

47So when the centurion saw what had happened, he glorified God, saying, "Certainly this was a righteous Man!"

48And the whole crowd who came together to that sight, seeing what had been done, beat their breasts and returned. 49But all His acquaintances, and the women who followed Him from Galilee, stood at a distance, watching these things.

Jesus Buried in Joseph's Tomb

50Now behold, *there was* a man named Joseph, a council member, a good and just man. 51He had not consented to their decision and deed. *He was* from Arimathea, a city of the Jews, who himself was also waiting for the kingdom of God. 52This man went to Pilate and asked for the body of Jesus. 53Then he took it down, wrapped it in linen, and laid it in a tomb *that was* hewn out of the rock, where no one had ever lain before. 54That day was the Preparation, and the Sabbath drew near.

55And the women who had come with Him from Galilee followed after, and they observed the tomb and how His body was laid. 56Then they returned and prepared spices and fragrant oils. And they rested on the Sabbath according to the commandment.

He Is Risen

24 Now on the first *day* of the week, very early in the morning, they, and certain *other women* with them, came to the tomb bringing the spices which they had prepared. 2But they found the stone rolled away from the tomb. 3Then they went in and did not find the body of the Lord Jesus. 4And it happened, as they were greatly

c Hosea 10.8   *d* Psalm 31.5

perplexed about this, that behold, two men stood by them in shining garments. 5Then, as they were afraid and bowed *their* faces to the earth, they said to them, "Why do you seek the living among the dead? 6He is not here, but is risen! Remember how He spoke to you when He was still in Galilee, 7saying, 'The Son of Man must be delivered into the hands of sinful men, and be crucified, and the third day rise again.' "

8And they remembered His words. 9Then they returned from the tomb and told all these things to the eleven and to all the rest. 10It was Mary Magdalene, Joanna, Mary *the mother* of James, and the other *women* with them, who told these things to the apostles. 11And their words seemed to them like idle tales, and they did not believe them. 12But Peter arose and ran to the tomb; and stooping down, he saw the linen cloths lying by themselves; and he departed, marveling to himself at what had happened.

The Road to Emmaus

13Now behold, two of them were traveling that same day to a village called Emmaus, which was seven miles from Jerusalem. 14And they talked together of all these things which had happened. 15So it was, while they conversed and reasoned, that Jesus Himself drew near and went with them. 16But their eyes were restrained, so that they did not know Him.

17And He said to them, "What kind of conversation *is* this that you have with one another as you walk and are sad?"

18Then the one whose name was Cleopas answered and said to Him, "Are You the only stranger in Jerusalem, and have You not known the things which happened there in these days?"

19And He said to them, "What things?"

So they said to Him, "The things concerning Jesus of Nazareth, who was a Prophet mighty in deed and word before God and all the people, 20and how the chief priests and our rulers delivered Him to be condemned to death, and crucified Him. 21But we were hoping that it was He who was going to redeem Israel. Indeed, besides all this, today is the third day since these things happened. 22Yes, and certain women of our company, who arrived at the tomb early, astonished us. 23When they did not find His body, they came saying that they had also seen a vision of angels who said He was alive. 24And certain of those *who were* with us went to the tomb and found *it* just as the women had said; but Him they did not see."

25Then He said to them, "O foolish ones, and slow of heart to believe in all that the prophets have spoken! 26Ought not the Christ to have suffered these things and to enter into His glory?" 27And beginning at Moses and all the Prophets, He expounded to them in all the Scriptures the things concerning Himself.

The Disciples' Eyes Opened

28Then they drew near to the village where they were going, and He indicated that He would have gone farther. 29But they constrained Him, saying, "Abide with us, for it is toward evening, and the day is far spent." And He went in to stay with them.

30Now it came to pass, as He sat at the table with them, that He took bread, blessed and broke *it*, and gave it to them. 31Then their eyes were opened and they knew Him; and He vanished from their sight.

32And they said to one another, "Did not our heart burn within us while He talked with us on the road, and while He opened the Scriptures to us?" 33So they rose up that very hour and returned to Jerusalem, and found the eleven and those *who were* with them gathered together, 34saying, "The Lord is risen indeed, and has appeared to Simon!" 35And they told about the things *that had happened* on the road, and how He was known to them in the breaking of bread.

Jesus Appears to His Disciples

36Now as they said these things, Jesus Himself stood in the midst of them, and said to them, "Peace to you." 37But they were terrified and frightened, and supposed they had seen a spirit. 38And He said to them, "Why are you troubled? And why do doubts arise in your hearts? 39Behold My hands and My feet, that it is I Myself. Handle Me and see, for a spirit does not have flesh and bones as you see I have."

40When He had said this, He showed them His hands and His feet. 41But while they still did not believe for joy, and marveled, He said to them, "Have you any food here?" 42So they gave Him a piece of a broiled fish and some honeycomb. 43And He took it and ate in their presence.

The Scriptures Opened

44Then He said to them, "These are the words which I spoke to you while I was still with you, that all things must be fulfilled which were written in the Law of Moses and the Prophets and the Psalms concerning Me." 45And He opened their understanding, that they might comprehend the Scriptures.

46Then He said to them, "Thus it is written, and thus it was necessary for the Christ to suffer and to rise from the dead the third day, 47and that repentance and remission of sins should be preached in His name to all nations, beginning at Jerusalem. 48And you are witnesses of these things. 49Behold, I send the Promise of My Father upon you; but tarry in the city of Jerusalem until you are endued with power from on high."

The Ascension

50And He led them out as far as Bethany, and He lifted up His hands and blessed them. 51Now it came to pass, while He blessed them, that He was parted from them and carried up into heaven. 52And they worshiped Him, and returned to Jerusalem with great joy, 53and were continually in the temple praising and blessing God. Amen.

The Gospel According to

JOHN

The Eternal Word

1 In the beginning was the Word, and the Word was with God, and the Word was God. 2He was in the beginning with God. 3All things were made through Him, and without Him nothing was made that was made. 4In Him was life, and the life was the light of men. 5And the light shines in the darkness, and the darkness did not comprehend it.

John's Witness: The True Light

6There was a man sent from God, whose name *was* John. 7This man came for a witness, to bear witness of the Light, that all through him might believe. 8He was not that Light, but *was sent* to bear witness of that Light. 9That was the true Light which gives light to every man coming into the world.

10He was in the world, and the world was made through Him, and the world did not know Him. 11He came to His own, and His own did not receive Him. 12But as many as received Him, to them He gave the right to become children of God, to those who believe in His name: 13who were born, not of blood, nor of the will of the flesh, nor of the will of man, but of God.

The Word Becomes Flesh

14And the Word became flesh and dwelt among us, and we beheld His glory, the glory as of the only begotten of the Father, full of grace and truth.

15John bore witness of Him and cried out, saying, "This was He of whom I said, 'He who comes after me is preferred before me, for He was before me.' "

16And of His fullness we have all received, and grace for grace. 17For the law was given through Moses, *but* grace and truth came through Jesus Christ. 18No one has seen God at any time. The only begotten Son, who is in the bosom of the Father, He has declared *Him*.

A Voice in the Wilderness

19Now this is the testimony of John, when the Jews sent priests and Levites from Jerusalem to ask him, "Who are you?"

20He confessed, and did not deny, but confessed, "I am not the Christ."

21And they asked him, "What then? Are you Elijah?"

He said, "I am not."

"Are you the Prophet?"

And he answered, "No."

22Then they said to him, "Who are you, that we may give an answer to those who sent us? What do you say about yourself?"

23He said: "I *am*

'The voice of one crying in the wilderness:

"Make straight the way of the LORD," '*a*

as the prophet Isaiah said."

24Now those who were sent were from the Pharisees. 25And they asked him, saying, "Why then do you baptize if you are not the Christ, nor Elijah, nor the Prophet?"

26John answered them, saying, "I baptize with water, but there stands One among you whom you do not know. 27It is He who, coming after me, is preferred before me, whose sandal strap I am not worthy to loose."

28These things were done in Bethabara beyond the Jordan, where John was baptizing.

The Lamb of God

29The next day John saw Jesus coming toward him, and said, "Behold! The Lamb of God who takes away the sin of the world! 30This is He of whom I said, 'After me comes a Man who is preferred before me, for He was before me.' 31I did not know Him; but that He should be revealed to Israel, therefore I came baptizing with water."

32And John bore witness, saying, "I saw the Spirit descending from heaven like a dove, and He remained upon

a Isaiah 40.3

1041

Him. 33I did not know Him, but He who sent me to baptize with water said to me, 'Upon whom you see the Spirit descending, and remaining on Him, this is He who baptizes with the Holy Spirit.' 34And I have seen and testified that this is the Son of God."

The First Disciples

35Again, the next day, John stood with two of his disciples. 36And looking at Jesus as He walked, he said, "Behold the Lamb of God!"

37The two disciples heard him speak, and they followed Jesus. 38Then Jesus turned, and seeing them following, said to them, "What do you seek?"

They said to Him, "Rabbi" (which is to say, when translated, Teacher), "where are You staying?"

39He said to them, "Come and see." They came and saw where He was staying, and remained with Him that day (now it was about the tenth hour).

40One of the two who heard John *speak*, and followed Him, was Andrew, Simon Peter's brother. 41He first found his own brother Simon, and said to him, "We have found the Messiah" (which is translated, the Christ). 42And he brought him to Jesus.

Now when Jesus looked at him, He said, "You are Simon the son of Jonah. You shall be called Cephas" (which is translated, A Stone).

Philip and Nathanael

43The following day Jesus wanted to go to Galilee, and He found Philip and said to him, "Follow Me." 44Now Philip was from Bethsaida, the city of Andrew and Peter. 45Philip found Nathanael and said to him, "We have found Him of whom Moses in the law, and also the prophets, wrote—Jesus of Nazareth, the son of Joseph."

46And Nathanael said to him, "Can anything good come out of Nazareth?" Philip said to him, "Come and see."

47Jesus saw Nathanael coming toward Him, and said of him, "Behold, an Israelite indeed, in whom is no deceit!"

48Nathanael said to Him, "How do You know me?"

Jesus answered and said to him, "Be-fore Philip called you, when you were under the fig tree, I saw you."

49Nathanael answered and said to Him, "Rabbi, You are the Son of God! You are the King of Israel!"

50Jesus answered and said to him, "Because I said to you, 'I saw you under the fig tree,' do you believe? You will see greater things than these." 51And He said to him, "Most assuredly, I say to you, hereafter you shall see heaven open, and the angels of God ascending and descending upon the Son of Man."

Water Turned to Wine

2 On the third day there was a wedding in Cana of Galilee, and the mother of Jesus was there. 2Now both Jesus and His disciples were invited to the wedding. 3And when they ran out of wine, the mother of Jesus said to Him, "They have no wine."

4Jesus said to her, "Woman, what does your concern have to do with Me? My hour has not yet come."

5His mother said to the servants, "Whatever He says to you, do *it*."

6Now there were set there six waterpots of stone, according to the manner of purification of the Jews, containing twenty or thirty gallons apiece. 7Jesus said to them, "Fill the waterpots with water." And they filled them up to the brim. 8And He said to them, "Draw *some* out now, and take *it* to the master of the feast." And they took *it*. 9When the master of the feast had tasted the water that was made wine, and did not know where it came from (but the servants who had drawn the water knew), the master of the feast called the bridegroom. 10And he said to him, "Every man at the beginning sets out the good wine, and when the *guests* have well drunk, then the inferior. You have kept the good wine until now!"

11This beginning of signs Jesus did in Cana of Galilee, and manifested His glory; and His disciples believed in Him.

12After this He went down to Capernaum, He, His mother, His brothers, and His disciples; and they did not stay there many days.

Jesus Cleanses the Temple

13Now the Passover of the Jews was at hand, and Jesus went up to Jerusalem. 14And He found in the temple those who sold oxen and sheep and doves, and the money changers doing business. 15When He had made a whip of cords, He drove them all out of the temple, with the sheep and the oxen, and poured out the changers' money and overturned the tables. 16And He said to those who sold doves, "Take these things away! Do not make My Father's house a house of merchandise!" 17Then His disciples remembered that it was written, "Zeal for Your house has eaten Me up."*b*

18So the Jews answered and said to Him, "What sign do You show to us, since You do these things?"

19Jesus answered and said to them, "Destroy this temple, and in three days I will raise it up."

20Then the Jews said, "It has taken forty-six years to build this temple, and will You raise it up in three days?"

21But He was speaking of the temple of His body. 22Therefore, when He had risen from the dead, His disciples remembered that He had said this to them; and they believed the Scripture and the word which Jesus had said.

The Discerner of Hearts

23Now when He was in Jerusalem at the Passover, during the feast, many believed in His name when they saw the signs which He did. 24But Jesus did not commit Himself to them, because He knew all *men*, 25and had no need that anyone should testify of man, for He knew what was in man.

The New Birth

3 There was a man of the Pharisees named Nicodemus, a ruler of the Jews. 2This man came to Jesus by night and said to Him, "Rabbi, we know that You are a teacher come from God; for no one can do these signs that You do unless God is with him."

3Jesus answered and said to him, "Most assuredly, I say to you, unless one is born again, he cannot see the kingdom of God."

4Nicodemus said to Him, "How can a man be born when he is old? Can he enter a second time into his mother's womb and be born?"

5Jesus answered, "Most assuredly, I say to you, unless one is born of water and the Spirit, he cannot enter the kingdom of God. 6That which is born of the flesh is flesh, and that which is born of the Spirit is spirit. 7Do not marvel that I said to you, 'You must be born again.' 8The wind blows where it wishes, and you hear the sound of it, but cannot tell where it comes from and where it goes. So is everyone who is born of the Spirit."

9Nicodemus answered and said to Him, "How can these things be?"

10Jesus answered and said to him, "Are you the teacher of Israel, and do not know these things? 11Most assuredly, I say to you, We speak what We know and testify what We have seen, and you do not receive Our witness. 12If I have told you earthly things and you do not believe, how will you believe if I tell you heavenly things? 13No one has ascended to heaven but He who came down from heaven, *that is,* the Son of Man who is in heaven. 14And as Moses lifted up the serpent in the wilderness, even so must the Son of Man be lifted up, 15that whoever believes in Him should not perish but have eternal life. 16For God so loved the world that He gave His only begotten Son, that whoever believes in Him should not perish but have everlasting life. 17For God did not send His Son into the world to condemn the world, but that the world through Him might be saved.

18"He who believes in Him is not condemned; but he who does not believe is condemned already, because he has not believed in the name of the only begotten Son of God. 19And this is the condemnation, that the light has come into the world, and men loved darkness rather than light, because their deeds were evil. 20For everyone practicing evil hates the light and does not come to the light, lest his deeds should be exposed. 21But he who does the truth comes to the light, that his deeds may

b Psalm 69.9

be clearly seen, that they have been done in God."

John the Baptist Exalts Christ

22After these things Jesus and His disciples came into the land of Judea, and there He remained with them and baptized. 23Now John also was baptizing in Aenon near Salim, because there was much water there. And they came and were baptized. 24For John had not yet been thrown into prison.

25Then there arose a dispute between some of John's disciples and the Jews about purification. 26And they came to John and said to him, "Rabbi, He who was with you beyond the Jordan, to whom you have testified—behold, He is baptizing, and all are coming to Him!"

27John answered and said, "A man can receive nothing unless it has been given to him from heaven. 28You yourselves bear me witness, that I said, 'I am not the Christ,' but, 'I have been sent before Him.' 29He who has the bride is the bridegroom; but the friend of the bridegroom, who stands and hears him, rejoices greatly because of the bridegroom's voice. Therefore this joy of mine is fulfilled. 30He must increase, but I must decrease. 31He who comes from above is above all; he who is of the earth is earthly and speaks of the earth. He who comes from heaven is above all. 32And what He has seen and heard, that He testifies; and no one receives His testimony. 33He who has received His testimony has certified that God is true. 34For He whom God has sent speaks the words of God, for God does not give the Spirit by measure. 35The Father loves the Son, and has given all things into His hand. 36He who believes in the Son has everlasting life; and he who does not believe the Son shall not see life, but the wrath of God abides on him."

A Samaritan Woman Meets Her Messiah

4 Therefore, when the Lord knew that the Pharisees had heard that Jesus made and baptized more disciples than John 2(though Jesus Himself did not baptize, but His disciples), 3He left Judea and departed again to Galilee.

4But He needed to go through Samaria. 5So He came to a city of Samaria which is called Sychar, near the plot of ground that Jacob gave to his son Joseph. 6Now Jacob's well was there. Jesus therefore, being wearied from His journey, sat thus by the well. It was about the sixth hour.

7A woman of Samaria came to draw water. Jesus said to her, "Give Me a drink." 8For His disciples had gone away into the city to buy food.

9Then the woman of Samaria said to Him, "How is it that You, being a Jew, ask a drink from me, a Samaritan woman?" For Jews have no dealings with Samaritans.

10Jesus answered and said to her, "If you knew the gift of God, and who it is who says to you, 'Give Me a drink,' you would have asked Him, and He would have given you living water."

11The woman said to Him, "Sir, You have nothing to draw with, and the well is deep. Where then do You get that living water? 12Are You greater than our father Jacob, who gave us the well, and drank from it himself, as well as his sons and his livestock?"

13Jesus answered and said to her, "Whoever drinks of this water will thirst again, 14but whoever drinks of the water that I shall give him will never thirst. But the water that I shall give him will become in him a fountain of water springing up into everlasting life."

15The woman said to Him, "Sir, give me this water, that I may not thirst, nor come here to draw."

16Jesus said to her, "Go, call your husband, and come here."

17The woman answered and said, "I have no husband."

Jesus said to her, "You have well said, 'I have no husband,' 18for you have had five husbands, and the one whom you now have is not your husband; in that you spoke truly."

19The woman said to Him, "Sir, I perceive that You are a prophet. 20Our fathers worshiped on this mountain, and you Jews say that in Jerusalem is the place where one ought to worship."

21Jesus said to her, "Woman, believe Me, the hour is coming when you will neither on this mountain, nor in Jerusalem, worship the Father. 22You worship what you do not know; we know what we worship, for salvation is of the Jews. 23But the hour is coming, and now is, when the true worshipers will worship the Father in spirit and truth; for the Father is seeking such to worship Him. 24God *is* Spirit, and those who worship Him must worship in spirit and truth."

25The woman said to Him, "I know that Messiah is coming" (who is called Christ). "When He comes, He will tell us all things."

26Jesus said to her, "I who speak to you am *He.*"

The Whitened Harvest

27And at this *point* His disciples came, and they marveled that He talked with a woman; yet no one said, "What do You seek?" or, "Why are You talking with her?"

28The woman then left her waterpot, went her way into the city, and said to the men, 29"Come, see a Man who told me all things that I ever did. Could this be the Christ?" 30Then they went out of the city and came to Him.

31In the meantime His disciples urged Him, saying, "Rabbi, eat."

32But He said to them, "I have food to eat of which you do not know."

33Therefore the disciples said to one another, "Has anyone brought Him *anything* to eat?"

34Jesus said to them, "My food is to do the will of Him who sent Me, and to finish His work. 35Do you not say, 'There are still four months and *then* comes the harvest'? Behold, I say to you, lift up your eyes and look at the fields, for they are already white for harvest! 36And he who reaps receives wages, and gathers fruit for eternal life, that both he who sows and he who reaps may rejoice together. 37For in this the saying is true: 'One sows and another reaps.' 38I sent you to reap that for which you have not labored; others have labored, and you have entered into their labors."

The Savior of the World

39And many of the Samaritans of that city believed in Him because of the word of the woman who testified, "He told me all that I *ever* did." 40So when

the Samaritans had come to Him, they urged Him to stay with them; and He stayed there two days. 41And many more believed because of His own word.

42Then they said to the woman, "Now we believe, not because of what you said, for we ourselves have heard *Him* and we know that this is indeed the Christ, the Savior of the world."

Welcome at Galilee

43Now after the two days He departed from there and went to Galilee. 44For Jesus Himself testified that a prophet has no honor in his own country. 45So when He came to Galilee, the Galileans received Him, having seen all the things He did in Jerusalem at the feast; for they also had gone to the feast.

A Nobleman's Son Healed

46So Jesus came again to Cana of Galilee where He had made the water wine. And there was a certain nobleman whose son was sick at Capernaum. 47When he heard that Jesus had come out of Judea into Galilee, he went to Him and implored Him to come down and heal his son, for he was at the point of death. 48Then Jesus said to him, "Unless you *people* see signs and wonders, you will by no means believe."

49The nobleman said to Him, "Sir, come down before my child dies!"

50Jesus said to him, "Go your way; your son lives." So the man believed the word that Jesus spoke to him, and he went his way. 51And as he was now going down, his servants met him and told *him,* saying, "Your son lives!"

52Then he inquired of them the hour when he got better. And they said to him, "Yesterday at the seventh hour the fever left him." 53So the father knew that *it was* at the same hour in which Jesus said to him, "Your son lives." And he himself believed, and his whole household.

54This again *is* the second sign Jesus did when He had come out of Judea into Galilee.

A Man Healed at the Pool of Bethesda

5 After this there was a feast of the Jews, and Jesus went up to

Jerusalem. 2Now there is in Jerusalem by the Sheep *Gate* a pool, which is called in Hebrew, Bethesda, having five porches. 3In these lay a great multitude of sick people, blind, lame, paralyzed, waiting for the moving of the water. 4For an angel went down at a certain time into the pool and stirred up the water; then whoever stepped in first, after the stirring of the water, was made well of whatever disease he had. 5Now a certain man was there who had an infirmity thirty-eight years. 6When Jesus saw him lying there, and knew that he already had been *in that condition* a long time, He said to him, "Do you want to be made well?"

7The sick man answered Him, "Sir, I have no man to put me into the pool when the water is stirred up; but while I am coming, another steps down before me."

8Jesus said to him, "Rise, take up your bed and walk." 9And immediately the man was made well, took up his bed, and walked.

And that day was the Sabbath. 10The Jews therefore said to him who was cured, "It is the Sabbath; it is not lawful for you to carry your bed."

11He answered them, "He who made me well said to me, 'Take up your bed and walk.' "

12Then they asked him, "Who is the Man who said to you, 'Take up your bed and walk'?" 13But the one who was healed did not know who it was, for Jesus had withdrawn, a multitude being in *that* place. 14Afterward Jesus found him in the temple, and said to him, "See, you have been made well. Sin no more, lest a worse thing come upon you."

15The man departed and told the Jews that it was Jesus who had made him well.

Honor the Father and the Son

16For this reason the Jews persecuted Jesus, and sought to kill Him, because He had done these things on the Sabbath. 17But Jesus answered them, "My Father has been working until now, and I have been working."

18Therefore the Jews sought all the more to kill Him, because He not only broke the Sabbath, but also said that God was His Father, making Himself equal with God. 19Then Jesus answered and said to them, "Most assuredly, I say to you, the Son can do nothing of Himself, but what He sees the Father do; for whatever He does, the Son also does in like manner. 20For the Father loves the Son, and shows Him all things that He Himself does; and He will show Him greater works than these, that you may marvel. 21For as the Father raises the dead and gives life to *them*, even so the Son gives life to whom He will. 22For the Father judges no one, but has committed all judgment to the Son, 23that all should honor the Son just as they honor the Father. He who does not honor the Son does not honor the Father who sent Him.

Life and Judgment Are Through the Son

24"Most assuredly, I say to you, he who hears My word and believes in Him who sent Me has everlasting life, and shall not come into judgment, but has passed from death into life. 25Most assuredly, I say to you, the hour is coming, and now is, when the dead will hear the voice of the Son of God; and those who hear will live. 26For as the Father has life in Himself, so He has granted the Son to have life in Himself, 27and has given Him authority to execute judgment also, because He is the Son of Man. 28Do not marvel at this; for the hour is coming in which all who are in the graves will hear His voice 29and come forth—those who have done good, to the resurrection of life, and those who have done evil, to the resurrection of condemnation. 30I can of Myself do nothing. As I hear, I judge; and My judgment is righteous, because I do not seek My own will but the will of the Father who sent Me.

The Fourfold Witness

31"If I bear witness of Myself, My witness is not true. 32There is another who bears witness of Me, and I know that the witness which He witnesses of Me is true. 33You have sent to John, and he has borne witness to the truth. 34Yet I do not receive testimony from man, but I say these things that you may be saved. 35He was the burning and shining lamp, and you were willing for a time to rejoice in his light. 36But I have a greater witness than John's; for the works which the Father has given Me to finish—the very works that I do—bear witness of Me, that the Father has sent Me. 37And the Father Himself, who sent Me, has testified of Me. You have neither heard His voice at any time, nor seen His form. 38But you do not have His word abiding in you, because whom He sent, Him you do not believe. 39You search the Scriptures, for in them you think you have eternal life; and these are they which testify of Me. 40But you are not willing to come to Me that you may have life.

41"I do not receive honor from men. 42But I know you, that you do not have the love of God in you. 43I have come in My Father's name, and you do not receive Me; if another comes in his own name, him you will receive. 44How can you believe, who receive honor from one another, and do not seek the honor that *comes* from the only God? 45Do not think that I shall accuse you to the Father; there is *one* who accuses you—Moses, in whom you trust. 46For if you believed Moses, you would believe Me; for he wrote about Me. 47But if you do not believe his writings, how will you believe My words?''

Feeding the Five Thousand

6 After these things Jesus went over the Sea of Galilee, which is *the Sea* of Tiberias. 2Then a great multitude followed Him, because they saw His signs which He performed on those who were diseased. 3And Jesus went up on the mountain, and there He sat with His disciples.

4Now the Passover, a feast of the Jews, was near. 5Then Jesus lifted up *His* eyes, and seeing a great multitude coming toward Him, He said to Philip, "Where shall we buy bread, that these may eat?'' 6But this He said to test him, for He Himself knew what He would do.

7Philip answered Him, "Two hundred denarii worth of bread is not sufficient for them, that every one of them may have a little.''

8One of His disciples, Andrew, Simon Peter's brother, said to Him, 9"There is a lad here who has five barley loaves and two small fish, but what are they among so many?''

10Then Jesus said, "Make the people sit down.'' Now there was much grass in the place. So the men sat down, in number about five thousand. 11And Jesus took the loaves, and when He had given thanks He distributed *them* to the disciples, and the disciples to those sitting down; and likewise of the fish, as much as they wanted. 12So when they were filled, He said to His disciples, "Gather up the fragments that remain, so that nothing is lost.'' 13Therefore they gathered *them* up, and filled twelve baskets with the fragments of the five barley loaves which were left over by those who had eaten. 14Then those men, when they had seen the sign that Jesus did, said, "This is truly the Prophet who is to come into the world.''

Jesus Walks on the Sea

15Therefore when Jesus perceived that they were about to come and take Him by force to make Him king, He departed again to the mountain by Himself alone.

16Now when evening came, His disciples went down to the sea, 17got into the boat, and went over the sea toward Capernaum. And it was already dark, and Jesus had not come to them. 18Then the sea arose because a great wind was blowing. 19So when they had rowed about three or four miles, they saw Jesus walking on the sea and drawing near the boat; and they were afraid. 20But He said to them, "It is I; do not be afraid.'' 21Then they willingly received Him into the boat, and immediately the boat was at the land where they were going.

The Bread from Heaven

22On the following day, when the people who were standing on the other side of the sea saw that there was no other boat there, except that one which His disciples had entered, and that Jesus had not entered the boat with His disciples, but His disciples had gone away alone—23however, other boats came from Tiberias, near the place where they ate bread after the Lord had given thanks—24when the people therefore saw that Jesus was not there, nor His disciples, they also got into boats and came to Capernaum, seeking Jesus. 25And when they found Him on the other side of the sea, they said to Him, "Rabbi, when did You come here?"

26Jesus answered them and said, "Most assuredly, I say to you, you seek Me, not because you saw the signs, but because you ate of the loaves and were filled. 27Do not labor for the food which perishes, but for the food which endures to everlasting life, which the Son of Man will give you, because God the Father has set His seal on Him."

28Then they said to Him, "What shall we do, that we may work the works of God?"

29Jesus answered and said to them, "This is the work of God, that you believe in Him whom He sent."

30Therefore they said to Him, "What sign will You perform then, that we may see it and believe You? What work will You do? 31Our fathers ate the manna in the desert; as it is written, 'He gave them bread from heaven to eat.'"c

32Then Jesus said to them, "Most assuredly, I say to you, Moses did not give you the bread from heaven, but My Father gives you the true bread from heaven. 33For the bread of God is He who comes down from heaven and gives life to the world."

34Then they said to Him, "Lord, give us this bread always."

35And Jesus said to them, "I am the bread of life. He who comes to Me shall never hunger, and he who believes in Me shall never thirst. 36But I said to you that you have seen Me and yet do not believe. 37All that the Father gives Me will come to Me, and the one who comes to Me I will by no means cast out. 38For I have come down from heaven, not to do My own will, but the will of Him who sent Me. 39This is the will of the Father who sent Me, that of all He has given Me I should lose nothing, but should raise it up at the last day. 40And this is the will of Him who sent Me, that everyone who sees the Son and believes in Him may have ever-

lasting life; and I will raise him up at the last day."

Rejected by His Own

41The Jews then complained about Him, because He said, "I am the bread which came down from heaven." 42And they said, "Is not this Jesus, the son of Joseph, whose father and mother we know? How is it then that He says, 'I have come down from heaven'?"

43Jesus therefore answered and said to them, "Do not murmur among yourselves. 44No one can come to Me unless the Father who sent Me draws him; and I will raise him up at the last day. 45It is written in the prophets, 'And they shall all be taught by God.'d Therefore everyone who has heard and learned from the Father comes to Me. 46Not that anyone has seen the Father, except He who is from God; He has seen the Father. 47Most assuredly, I say to you, he who believes in Me has everlasting life. 48I am the bread of life. 49Your fathers ate the manna in the wilderness, and are dead. 50This is the bread which comes down from heaven, that one may eat of it and not die. 51I am the living bread which came down from heaven. If anyone eats of this bread, he will live forever; and the bread that I shall give is My flesh, which I shall give for the life of the world."

52The Jews therefore quarreled among themselves, saying, "How can this Man give us His flesh to eat?"

53Then Jesus said to them, "Most assuredly, I say to you, unless you eat the flesh of the Son of Man and drink His blood, you have no life in you. 54Whoever eats My flesh and drinks My blood has eternal life, and I will raise him up at the last day. 55For My flesh is food indeed, and My blood is drink indeed. 56He who eats My flesh and drinks My blood abides in Me, and I in him. 57As the living Father sent Me, and I live because of the Father, so he who feeds on Me will live because of Me. 58This is the bread which came down from heaven—not as your fathers ate the manna, and are dead. He

c Exodus 16.4; Nehemiah 9.15; Psalm 78.24   d Isaiah 54.13

who eats this bread will live forever."
59These things He said in the synagogue as He taught in Capernaum.

Many Disciples Turn Away

60Therefore many of His disciples, when they heard *this*, said, "This is a hard saying; who can understand it?" 61When Jesus knew in Himself that His disciples complained about this, He said to them, "Does this offend you? 62*What* then if you should see the Son of Man ascend where He was before? 63It is the Spirit who gives life; the flesh profits nothing. The words that I speak to you are spirit, and *they* are life. 64But there are some of you who do not believe." For Jesus knew from the beginning who they were who did not believe, and who would betray Him. 65And He said, "Therefore I have said to you that no one can come to Me unless it has been granted to him by My Father."

66From that *time* many of His disciples went back and walked with Him no more. 67Then Jesus said to the twelve, "Do you also want to go away?" 68But Simon Peter answered Him, "Lord, to whom shall we go? You have the words of eternal life. 69Also we have come to believe and know that You are the Christ, the Son of the living God." 70Jesus answered them, "Did I not choose you, the twelve, and one of you is a devil?" 71He spoke of Judas Iscariot, *the son* of Simon, for it was he who would betray Him, being one of the twelve.

Jesus' Brothers Disbelieve

7 After these things Jesus walked in Galilee; for He did not want to walk in Judea, because the Jews sought to kill Him. 2Now the Jews' Feast of Tabernacles was at hand. 3His brothers therefore said to Him, "Depart from here and go into Judea, that Your disciples also may see the works that You are doing. 4For no one does anything in secret while he himself seeks to be known openly. If You do these things, show Yourself to the world." 5For even His brothers did not believe in Him.

6Then Jesus said to them, "My time has not yet come, but your time is always ready. 7The world cannot hate you, but it hates Me because I testify of it that its works are evil. 8You go up to this feast. I am not yet going up to this feast, for My time has not yet fully come." 9When He had said these things to them, He remained in Galilee.

The Heavenly Scholar

10But when His brothers had gone up, then He also went up to the feast, not openly, but as it were in secret. 11Then the Jews sought Him at the feast, and said, "Where is He?" 12And there was much complaining among the people concerning Him. Some said, "He is good"; others said, "No, on the contrary, He deceives the people." 13However, no one spoke openly of Him for fear of the Jews.

14Now about the middle of the feast Jesus went up into the temple and taught. 15And the Jews marveled, saying, "How does this Man know letters, having never studied?"

16Jesus answered them and said, "My doctrine is not Mine, but His who sent Me. 17If anyone wills to do His will, he shall know concerning the doctrine, whether it is from God or *whether* I speak on My own *authority*. 18He who speaks from himself seeks his own glory; but He who seeks the glory of the One who sent Him is true, and no unrighteousness is in Him. 19Did not Moses give you the law, yet none of you keeps the law? Why do you seek to kill Me?"

20The people answered and said, "You have a demon. Who is seeking to kill You?"

21Jesus answered and said to them, "I did one work, and you all marvel. 22Moses therefore gave you circumcision (not that it is from Moses, but from the fathers), and you circumcise a man on the Sabbath. 23If a man receives circumcision on the Sabbath, so that the law of Moses should not be broken, are you angry with Me because I made a man completely well on the Sabbath? 24Do not judge according to appearance, but judge with righteous judgment."

Could This Be the Christ?

25Now some of them from Jerusalem said, "Is this not He whom they seek to kill? 26But look! He speaks boldly, and they say nothing to Him. Do the rulers know indeed that this is truly the Christ? 27However, we know where this Man is from; but when the Christ comes, no one knows where He is from."

28Then Jesus cried out, as He taught in the temple, saying, "You both know Me, and you know where I am from; and I have not come of Myself, but He who sent Me is true, whom you do not know. 29But I know Him, for I am from Him, and He sent Me."

30Therefore they sought to take Him; but no one laid a hand on Him, because His hour had not yet come. 31And many of the people believed in Him, and said, "When the Christ comes, will He do more signs than these which this *Man* has done?"

Jesus and the Religious Leaders

32The Pharisees heard the crowd murmuring these things concerning Him, and the Pharisees and the chief priests sent officers to take Him. 33Then Jesus said to them, "I shall be with you a little while longer, and *then* I go to Him who sent Me. 34You will seek Me and not find *Me*, and where I am you cannot come."

35Then the Jews said among themselves, "Where does He intend to go that we shall not find Him? Does He intend to go to the Dispersion among the Greeks and teach the Greeks? 36What is this thing that He said, 'You will seek Me and not find Me, and where I am you cannot come'?"

The Promise of the Holy Spirit

37On the last day, that great *day* of the feast, Jesus stood and cried out, saying, "If anyone thirsts, let him come to Me and drink. 38He who believes in Me, as the Scripture has said, out of his heart will flow rivers of living water." 39But this He spoke concerning the Spirit, whom those believing in Him would receive; for the Holy Spirit was not yet *given*, because Jesus was not yet glorified.

Who Is He?

40Therefore many from the crowd, when they heard this saying, said,

"Truly this is the Prophet." 41Others said, "This is the Christ."

But some said, "Will the Christ come out of Galilee? 42Has not the Scripture said that the Christ comes from the seed of David and from the town of Bethlehem, where David was?" 43So there was a division among the people because of Him. 44Now some of them wanted to take Him, but no one laid hands on Him.

Rejected by the Authorities

45Then the officers came to the chief priests and Pharisees, who said to them, "Why have you not brought Him?"

46The officers answered, "No man ever spoke like this Man!"

47Then the Pharisees answered them, "Are you also deceived? 48Have any of the rulers or the Pharisees believed in Him? 49But this crowd that does not know the law is accursed."

50Nicodemus (he who came to Jesus by night, being one of them) said to them, 51"Does our law judge a man before it hears him and knows what he is doing?"

52They answered and said to him, "Are you also from Galilee? Search and look, for no prophet has arisen out of Galilee."

An Adulteress Faces the Light of the World

53And everyone went to his *own* house.

8 But Jesus went to the Mount of Olives.

2Now early in the morning He came again into the temple, and all the people came to Him; and He sat down and taught them. 3Then the scribes and Pharisees brought to Him a woman caught in adultery. And when they had set her in the midst, 4they said to Him, "Teacher, this woman was caught in adultery, in the very act. 5Now Moses, in the law, commanded us that such should be stoned. But what do You say?" 6This they said, testing Him, that they might have *something* of which to accuse Him. But Jesus stooped down and wrote on the ground with *His* finger, as though He did not hear.

7So when they continued asking Him,

He raised Himself up and said to them, "He who is without sin among you, let him throw a stone at her first." 8And again He stooped down and wrote on the ground. 9Then those who heard *it*, being convicted by *their* conscience, went out one by one, beginning with the oldest *even* to the last. And Jesus was left alone, and the woman standing in the midst. 10When Jesus had raised Himself up and saw no one but the woman, He said to her, "Woman, where are those accusers of yours? Has no one condemned you?"

11She said, "No one, Lord."

And Jesus said to her, "Neither do I condemn you; go and sin no more."

12Then Jesus spoke to them again, saying, "I am the light of the world. He who follows Me shall not walk in darkness, but have the light of life."

Jesus Defends His Self-Witness

13The Pharisees therefore said to Him, "You bear witness of Yourself; Your witness is not true."

14Jesus answered and said to them, "Even if I bear witness of Myself, My witness is true, for I know where I came from and where I am going; but you do not know where I come from and where I am going. 15You judge according to the flesh; I judge no one. 16And yet if I do judge, My judgment is true; for I am not alone, but I *am* with the Father who sent Me. 17It is also written in your law that the testimony of two men is true. 18I am One who bears witness of Myself, and the Father who sent Me bears witness of Me."

19Then they said to Him, "Where is Your Father?"

Jesus answered, "You know neither Me nor My Father. If you had known Me, you would have known My Father also."

20These words Jesus spoke in the treasury, as He taught in the temple; and no one laid hands on Him, for His hour had not yet come.

Jesus Predicts His Departure

21Then Jesus said to them again, "I am going away, and you will seek Me, and will die in your sin. Where I go you cannot come."

22So the Jews said, "Will He kill Him-self, because He says, 'Where I go you cannot come'?"

23And He said to them, "You are from beneath; I am from above. You are of this world; I am not of this world. 24Therefore I said to you that you will die in your sins; for if you do not believe that I am *He*, you will die in your sins."

25Then they said to Him, "Who are You?"

And Jesus said to them, "Just what I have been saying to you from the beginning. 26I have many things to say and to judge concerning you, but He who sent Me is true; and I speak to the world those things which I heard from Him."

27They did not understand that He spoke to them of the Father.

28Then Jesus said to them, "When you lift up the Son of Man, then you will know that I am *He*, and *that* I do nothing of Myself; but as My Father taught Me, I speak these things. 29And He who sent Me is with Me. The Father has not left Me alone, for I always do those things that please Him." 30As He spoke these words, many believed in Him.

The Truth Shall Make You Free

31Then Jesus said to those Jews who believed Him, "If you abide in My word, you are My disciples indeed. 32And you shall know the truth, and the truth shall make you free."

33They answered Him, "We are Abraham's descendants, and have never been in bondage to anyone. How *can* You say, 'You will be made free'?"

34Jesus answered them, "Most assuredly, I say to you, whoever commits sin is a slave of sin. 35And a slave does not abide in the house forever, *but* a son abides forever. 36Therefore if the Son makes you free, you shall be free indeed.

Abraham's Seed and Satan's

37"I know that you are Abraham's descendants, but you seek to kill Me, because My word has no place in you. 38I speak what I have seen with My Father, and you do what you have seen with your father."

39They answered and said to Him, "Abraham is our father."

Jesus said to them, "If you were

Abraham's children, you would do the works of Abraham. 40But now you seek to kill Me, a Man who has told you the truth which I heard from God. Abraham did not do this. 41You do the deeds of your father."

Then they said to Him, "We were not born of fornication; we have one Father—God."

42Jesus said to them, "If God were your Father, you would love Me, for I proceeded forth and came from God; nor have I come of Myself, but He sent Me. 43Why do you not understand My speech? Because you are not able to listen to My word. 44You are of *your* father the devil, and the desires of your father you want to do. He was a murderer from the beginning, and does not stand in the truth, because there is no truth in him. When he speaks a lie, he speaks from his own *resources*, for he is a liar and the father of it. 45But because I tell the truth, you do not believe Me. 46Which of you convicts Me of sin? And if I tell the truth, why do you not believe Me? 47He who is of God hears God's words; therefore you do not hear, because you are not of God."

Before Abraham Was, I AM

48Then the Jews answered and said to Him, "Do we not say rightly that You are a Samaritan and have a demon?"

49Jesus answered, "I do not have a demon; but I honor My Father, and you dishonor Me. 50And I do not seek My *own* glory; there is One who seeks and judges. 51Most assuredly, I say to you, if anyone keeps My word he shall never see death."

52Then the Jews said to Him, "Now we know that You have a demon! Abraham is dead, and the prophets; and You say, 'If anyone keeps My word he shall never taste death.' 53Are You greater than our father Abraham, who is dead? And the prophets are dead. Who do You make Yourself out to be?"

54Jesus answered, "If I honor Myself, My honor is nothing. It is My Father who honors Me, of whom you say that He is your God. 55Yet you have not known Him, but I know Him. And if I say, 'I do not know Him,' I shall be a liar like you; but I do know Him and keep His word. 56Your father Abraham rejoiced to see My day, and he saw *it* and was glad."

57Then the Jews said to Him, "You are not yet fifty years old, and have You seen Abraham?"

58Jesus said to them, "Most assuredly, I say to you, before Abraham was, I AM."

59Then they took up stones to throw at Him; but Jesus hid Himself and went out of the temple, going through the midst of them, and so passed by.

A Man Born Blind Receives Sight

9 Now as *Jesus* passed by, He saw a man who was blind from birth. 2And His disciples asked Him, saying, "Rabbi, who sinned, this man or his parents, that he was born blind?"

3Jesus answered, "Neither this man nor his parents sinned, but that the works of God should be revealed in him. 4I must work the works of Him who sent Me while it is day; *the* night is coming when no one can work. 5As long as I am in the world, I am the light of the world."

6When He had said these things, He spat on the ground and made clay with the saliva; and He anointed the eyes of the blind man with the clay. 7And He said to him, "Go, wash in the pool of Siloam" (which is translated, Sent). So he went and washed, and came back seeing.

8Therefore the neighbors and those who previously had seen that he was blind said, "Is not this he who sat and begged?"

9Some said, "This is he." Others *said*, "He is like him."

He said, "I am *he*."

10Therefore they said to him, "How were your eyes opened?"

11He answered and said, "A Man called Jesus made clay and anointed my eyes and said to me, 'Go to the pool of Siloam and wash.' So I went and washed, and I received sight."

12Then they said to him, "Where is He?"

He said, "I do not know."

The Pharisees Excommunicate the Healed Man

13They brought him who formerly was blind to the Pharisees. 14Now it was a Sabbath when Jesus made the clay and opened his eyes. 15Then the Pharisees also asked him again how he had received his sight. He said to them, "He put clay on my eyes, and I washed, and I see."

16Therefore some of the Pharisees said, "This Man is not from God, because He does not keep the Sabbath." Others said, "How can a man who is a sinner do such signs?" And there was a division among them.

17They said to the blind man again, "What do you say about Him because He opened your eyes?"

He said, "He is a prophet."

18But the Jews did not believe concerning him, that he had been blind and received his sight, until they called the parents of him who had received his sight. 19And they asked them, saying, "Is this your son, who you say was born blind? How then does he now see?"

20His parents answered them and said, "We know that this is our son, and that he was born blind; 21but by what means he now sees we do not know, or who opened his eyes we do not know. He is of age; ask him. He will speak for himself." 22His parents said these *things* because they feared the Jews, for the Jews had agreed already that if anyone confessed *that* He *was* Christ, he would be put out of the synagogue. 23Therefore his parents said, "He is of age; ask him."

24So they again called the man who was blind, and said to him, "Give God the glory! We know that this Man is a sinner."

25He answered and said, "Whether He is a sinner *or not* I do not know. One thing I know: that though I was blind, now I see."

26Then they said to him again, "What did He do to you? How did He open your eyes?"

27He answered them, "I told you already, and you did not listen. Why do you want to hear *it* again? Do you also want to become His disciples?"

28Then they reviled him and said, "You are His disciple, but we are Moses' disciples. 29We know that God spoke to Moses; *as for* this *fellow*, we do not know where He is from."

30The man answered and said to them, "Why, this is a marvelous thing, that you do not know where He is from; yet He has opened my eyes! 31Now we know that God does not hear sinners; but if anyone is a worshiper of God and does His will, He hears him. 32Since the world began it has been unheard of that anyone opened the eyes of one who was born blind. 33If this Man were not from God, He could do nothing."

34They answered and said to him, "You were completely born in sins, and are you teaching us?" And they cast him out.

True Vision and True Blindness

35Jesus heard that they had cast him out; and when He had found him, He said to him, "Do you believe in the Son of God?"

36He answered and said, "Who is He, Lord, that I may believe in Him?"

37And Jesus said to him, "You have both seen Him and it is He who is talking with you."

38Then he said, "Lord, I believe!" And he worshiped Him.

39And Jesus said, "For judgment I have come into this world, that those who do not see may see, and that those who see may be made blind."

40Then *some* of the Pharisees who were with Him heard these words, and said to Him, "Are we blind also?"

41Jesus said to them, "If you were blind, you would have no sin; but now you say, 'We see.' Therefore your sin remains.

Jesus the True Shepherd

10 "Most assuredly, I say to you, he who does not enter the sheepfold by the door, but climbs up some other way, the same is a thief and a robber. 2But he who enters by the door is the shepherd of the sheep. 3To him the doorkeeper opens, and the sheep hear his voice; and he calls his own sheep by name and leads them out. 4And when he brings out his own sheep, he goes before them; and the sheep follow him, for they know his voice. 5Yet they will by no means follow a stranger, but will flee from him, for they do not know the voice of strangers." 6Jesus used this illustration, but they did not understand the things which He spoke to them.

Jesus the Good Shepherd

7Then Jesus said to them again, "Most assuredly, I say to you, I am the door of the sheep. 8All who *ever* came before Me are thieves and robbers, but the sheep did not hear them. 9I am the door. If anyone enters by Me, he will be saved, and will go in and out and find pasture. 10The thief does not come except to steal, and to kill, and to destroy. I have come that they may have life, and that they may have *it* more abundantly.

11"I am the good shepherd. The good shepherd gives His life for the sheep. 12But a hireling, *he who is* not the shepherd, one who does not own the sheep, sees the wolf coming and leaves the sheep and flees; and the wolf catches the sheep and scatters them. 13The hireling flees because he is a hireling and does not care about the sheep. 14I am the good shepherd; and I know My *sheep*, and am known by My own. 15As the Father knows Me, even so I know the Father; and I lay down My life for the sheep. 16And other sheep I have which are not of this fold; them also I must bring, and they will hear My voice; and there will be one flock *and* one shepherd.

17"Therefore My Father loves Me, because I lay down My life that I may take it again. 18No one takes it from Me, but I lay it down of Myself. I have power to lay it down, and I have power to take it again. This command I have received from My Father."

19Therefore there was a division again among the Jews because of these sayings. 20And many of them said, "He has a demon and is mad. Why do you listen to Him?" 21Others said, "These are not the words of one who has a demon. Can a demon open the eyes of the blind?"

The Shepherd Knows His Sheep

22Now it was the Feast of Dedication in Jerusalem, and it was winter. 23And Jesus walked in the temple, in Solomon's porch. 24Then the Jews surrounded Him and said to Him, "How long do You keep us in doubt? If You are the Christ, tell us plainly."

25Jesus answered them, "I told you, and you do not believe. The works that I do in My Father's name, they bear witness of Me. 26But you do not believe, because you are not of My sheep, as I said to you. 27My sheep hear My voice, and I know them, and they follow Me. 28And I give them eternal life, and they shall never perish; neither shall anyone snatch them out of My hand. 29My Father, who has given *them* to Me, is greater than all; and no one is able to snatch *them* out of My Father's hand. 30I and *My* Father are one."

Renewed Efforts to Stone Jesus

31Then the Jews took up stones again to stone Him. 32Jesus answered them, "Many good works I have shown you from My Father. For which of those works do you stone Me?"

33The Jews answered Him, saying, "For a good work we do not stone You, but for blasphemy, and because You, being a Man, make Yourself God."

34Jesus answered them, "Is it not written in your law, 'I said, "You are gods" '?e 35If He called them gods, to whom the word of God came (and the Scripture cannot be broken), 36do you say of Him whom the Father sanctified and sent into the world, 'You are blaspheming,' because I said, 'I am the Son of God'? 37If I do not do the works of My Father, do not believe Me; 38but if I do, though you do not believe Me, believe the works, that you may know and believe that the Father *is* in Me, and I in Him." 39Therefore they sought again to seize Him, but He escaped out of their hand.

The Believers Beyond Jordan

40And He went away again beyond the Jordan to the place where John was baptizing at first, and there He stayed. 41Then many came to Him and said, "John performed no sign, but all the things that John spoke about this Man were true." 42And many believed in Him there.

The Death of Lazarus

11 Now a certain *man* was sick, Lazarus of Bethany, the town of

e Psalm 82.6

Mary and her sister Martha. 2It was *that* Mary who anointed the Lord with fragrant oil and wiped His feet with her hair, whose brother Lazarus was sick. 3Therefore the sisters sent to Him, saying, "Lord, behold, he whom You love is sick."

4When Jesus heard *that,* He said, "This sickness is not unto death, but for the glory of God, that the Son of God may be glorified through it."

5Now Jesus loved Martha and her sister and Lazarus. 6So, when He heard that he was sick, He stayed two more days in the place where He was. 7Then after this He said to *the* disciples, "Let us go to Judea again."

8*The* disciples said to Him, "Rabbi, lately the Jews sought to stone You, and are You going there again?"

9Jesus answered, "Are there not twelve hours in the day? If anyone walks in the day, he does not stumble, because he sees the light of this world. 10But if one walks in the night, he stumbles, because the light is not in him." 11These things He said, and after that He said to them, "Our friend Lazarus sleeps, but I go that I may wake him up."

12Then His disciples said, "Lord, if he sleeps he will get well." 13However, Jesus spoke of his death, but they thought that He was speaking about taking rest in sleep.

14Then Jesus said to them plainly, "Lazarus is dead. 15And I am glad for your sakes that I was not there, that you may believe. Nevertheless let us go to him."

16Then Thomas, who is called the Twin, said to his fellow disciples, "Let us also go, that we may die with Him."

I Am the Resurrection and the Life

17So when Jesus came, He found that he had already been in the tomb four days. 18Now Bethany was near Jerusalem, about two miles away. 19And many of the Jews had joined the women around Martha and Mary, to comfort them concerning their brother.

20Now Martha, as soon as she heard that Jesus was coming, went and met Him, but Mary was sitting in the house. 21Now Martha said to Jesus, "Lord, if You had been here, my brother would

not have died. 22But even now I know that whatever You ask of God, God will give You."

23Jesus said to her, "Your brother will rise again."

24Martha said to Him, "I know that he will rise again in the resurrection at the last day."

25Jesus said to her, "I am the resurrection and the life. He who believes in Me, though he may die, he shall live. 26And whoever lives and believes in Me shall never die. Do you believe this?"

27She said to Him, "Yes, Lord, I believe that You are the Christ, the Son of God, who is to come into the world."

Jesus and Death, the Last Enemy

28And when she had said these things, she went her way and secretly called Mary her sister, saying, "The Teacher has come and is calling for you." 29As soon as she heard *that,* she arose quickly and came to Him. 30Now Jesus had not yet come into the town, but was in the place where Martha met Him. 31Then the Jews who were with her in the house, and comforting her, when they saw that Mary rose up quickly and went out, followed her, saying, "She is going to the tomb to weep there."

32Then, when Mary came where Jesus was, and saw Him, she fell down at His feet, saying to Him, "Lord, if You had been here, my brother would not have died."

33Therefore, when Jesus saw her weeping, and the Jews who came with her weeping, He groaned in the spirit and was troubled. 34And He said, "Where have you laid him?"

They said to Him, "Lord, come and see."

35Jesus wept. 36Then the Jews said, "See how He loved him!"

37And some of them said, "Could not this Man, who opened the eyes of the blind, also have kept this man from dying?"

Lazarus Raised from the Dead

38Then Jesus, again groaning in Himself, came to the tomb. It was a cave, and a stone lay against it. 39Jesus said, "Take away the stone."

Martha, the sister of him who was

dead, said to Him, "Lord, by this time there is a stench, for he has been *dead* four days."

40Jesus said to her, "Did I not say to you that if you would believe you would see the glory of God?" 41Then they took away the stone *from the place* where the dead man was lying. And Jesus lifted up *His* eyes and said, "Father, I thank You that You have heard Me. 42And I know that You always hear Me, but because of the people who are standing by I said *this*, that they may believe that You sent Me." 43Now when He had said these things, He cried with a loud voice, "Lazarus, come forth!" 44And he who had died came out bound hand and foot with graveclothes, and his face was wrapped with a cloth. Jesus said to them, "Loose him, and let him go."

The Plot to Kill Jesus

45Then many of the Jews who had come to Mary, and had seen the things Jesus did, believed in Him. 46But some of them went away to the Pharisees and told them the things Jesus did. 47Then the chief priests and the Pharisees gathered a council and said, "What shall we do? For this Man works many signs. 48If we let Him alone like this, everyone will believe in Him, and the Romans will come and take away both our place and nation."

49And one of them, Caiaphas, being high priest that year, said to them, "You know nothing at all, 50nor do you consider that it is expedient for us that one man should die for the people, and not that the whole nation should perish." 51Now this he did not say on his own *authority*; but being high priest that year he prophesied that Jesus would die for the nation, 52and not for that nation only, but also that He would gather together in one the children of God who were scattered abroad.

53Then, from that day on, they plotted to put Him to death. 54Therefore Jesus no longer walked openly among the Jews, but went from there into the country near the wilderness, to a city called Ephraim, and there remained with His disciples.

55And the Passover of the Jews was near, and many went from the country up to Jerusalem before the Passover, to purify themselves. 56Then they sought Jesus, and spoke among themselves as they stood in the temple, "What do you think—that He will not come to the feast?" 57Now both the chief priests and the Pharisees had given a command, that if anyone knew where He was, he should report *it*, that they might seize Him.

The Anointing at Bethany

12 Then, six days before the Passover, Jesus came to Bethany, where Lazarus was who had been dead, whom He had raised from the dead. 2There they made Him a supper; and Martha served, but Lazarus was one of those who sat at the table with Him. 3Then Mary took a pound of very costly oil of spikenard, anointed the feet of Jesus, and wiped His feet with her hair. And the house was filled with the fragrance of the oil.

4But one of His disciples, Judas Iscariot, Simon's *son*, who would betray Him, said, 5"Why was this fragrant oil not sold for three hundred denarii*f* and given to the poor?" 6This he said, not that he cared for the poor, but because he was a thief, and had the money box; and he used to take what was put in it.

7But Jesus said, "Let her alone; she has kept this for the day of My burial. 8For the poor you have with you always, but Me you do not have always."

The Plot to Kill Lazarus

9Now a great many of the Jews knew that He was there; and they came, not for Jesus' sake only, but that they might also see Lazarus, whom He had raised from the dead. 10But the chief priests plotted to put Lazarus to death also, 11because on account of him many of the Jews went away and believed in Jesus.

The Triumphal Entry

12The next day a great multitude that had come to the feast, when they heard that Jesus was coming to Jerusalem,

f About one year's wages for a worker

13took branches of palm trees and went out to meet Him, and cried out:

"Hosanna!
'Blessed *is* He who comes in the name of the LORD!'*g*
The King of Israel!"

14Then Jesus, when He had found a young donkey, sat on it; as it is written:

15 "Fear not, daughter of Zion;
Behold, your King is coming,
Sitting on a donkey's colt."*h*

16His disciples did not understand these things at first; but when Jesus was glorified, then they remembered that these things were written about Him and *that* they had done these things to Him.

17Therefore the people, who were with Him when He called Lazarus out of his tomb and raised him from the dead, bore witness. 18For this reason the people also met Him, because they heard that He had done this sign. 19The Pharisees therefore said among themselves, "You see that you are accomplishing nothing. Look, the world has gone after Him!"

The Fruitful Grain of Wheat

20Now there were certain Greeks among those who came up to worship at the feast. 21Then they came to Philip, who was from Bethsaida of Galilee, and asked him, saying, "Sir, we wish to see Jesus."

22Philip came and told Andrew, and in turn Andrew and Philip told Jesus. 23But Jesus answered them, saying, "The hour has come that the Son of Man should be glorified. 24Most assuredly, I say to you, unless a grain of wheat falls into the ground and dies, it remains alone; but if it dies, it produces much grain. 25He who loves his life will lose it, and he who hates his life in this world will keep it for eternal life. 26If anyone serves Me, let him follow Me; and where I am, there My servant will be also. If anyone serves Me, him *My* Father will honor.

Jesus Predicts His Death on the Cross

27"Now My soul is troubled, and what shall I say? 'Father, save Me from this hour'? But for this purpose I came to this hour. 28Father, glorify Your name."

Then a voice came from heaven, *saying,* "I have both glorified *it* and will glorify *it* again."

29Therefore the people who stood by and heard *it* said that it had thundered. Others said, "An angel has spoken to Him."

30Jesus answered and said, "This voice did not come because of Me, but for your sake. 31Now is the judgment of this world; now the ruler of this world will be cast out. 32And I, if I am lifted up from the earth, will draw all *peoples* to Myself." 33This He said, signifying by what death He would die.

34The people answered Him, "We have heard from the law that the Christ remains forever; and how *can* You say, 'The Son of Man must be lifted up'? Who is this Son of Man?"

35Then Jesus said to them, "A little while longer the light is with you. Walk while you have the light, lest darkness overtake you; he who walks in darkness does not know where he is going. 36While you have the light, believe in the light, that you may become sons of light." These things Jesus spoke, and departed, and was hidden from them.

Who Has Believed Our Report?

37But although He had done so many signs before them, they did not believe in Him, 38that the word of Isaiah the prophet might be fulfilled, which he spoke:

"Lord, who has believed our report?
And to whom has the arm of the LORD been revealed?"*i*

39Therefore they could not believe, because Isaiah said again:

40 "He has blinded their eyes and hardened their hearts,
Lest they should see with *their* eyes,
Lest they should understand with *their* hearts and turn,
So that I should heal them." *j*

41These things Isaiah said when he saw His glory and spoke of Him.

g Psalm 118.26   *h* Zechariah 9.9   *i* Isaiah 53.1   *j* Isaiah 6.10

Walk in the Light

42Nevertheless even among the rulers many believed in Him, but because of the Pharisees they did not confess *Him*, lest they should be put out of the synagogue; **43**for they loved the praise of men more than the praise of God.

44Then Jesus cried out and said, "He who believes in Me, believes not in Me but in Him who sent Me. **45**And he who sees Me sees Him who sent Me. **46**I have come *as* a light into the world, that whoever believes in Me should not abide in darkness. **47**And if anyone hears My words and does not believe, I do not judge him; for I did not come to judge the world but to save the world. **48**He who rejects Me, and does not receive My words, has that which judges him—the word that I have spoken will judge him in the last day. **49**For I have not spoken on My own *authority*; but the Father who sent Me gave Me a command, what I should say and what I should speak. **50**And I know that His command is everlasting life. Therefore, whatever I speak, just as the Father has told Me, so I speak."

Jesus Washes the Disciples' Feet

13 Now before the Feast of the Passover, when Jesus knew that His hour had come that He should depart from this world to the Father, having loved His own who were in the world, He loved them to the end.

2And supper being ended, the devil having already put it into the heart of Judas Iscariot, Simon's *son*, to betray Him, **3**Jesus, knowing that the Father had given all things into His hands, and that He had come from God and was going to God, **4**rose from supper and laid aside His garments, took a towel and girded Himself. **5**After that, He poured water into a basin and began to wash the disciples' feet, and to wipe *them* with the towel with which He was girded. **6**Then He came to Simon Peter. And *Peter* said to Him, "Lord, are You washing my feet?"

7Jesus answered and said to him, "What I am doing you do not understand now, but you will know after this."

8Peter said to Him, "You shall never wash my feet!"

Jesus answered him, "If I do not wash you, you have no part with Me."

9Simon Peter said to Him, "Lord, not my feet only, but also *my* hands and *my* head!"

10Jesus said to him, "He who is bathed needs only to wash *his* feet, but is completely clean; and you are clean, but not all of you." **11**For He knew who would betray Him; therefore He said, "You are not all clean."

12So when He had washed their feet, taken His garments, and sat down again, He said to them, "Do you know what I have done to you? **13**You call Me Teacher and Lord, and you say well, for *so* I am. **14**If I then, *your* Lord and Teacher, have washed your feet, you also ought to wash one another's feet. **15**For I have given you an example, that you should do as I have done to you. **16**Most assuredly, I say to you, a servant is not greater than his master; nor is he who is sent greater than he who sent him. **17**If you know these things, blessed are you if you do them.

Jesus Identifies His Betrayer

18"I do not speak concerning all of you. I know whom I have chosen; but that the Scripture may be fulfilled, 'He who eats bread with Me has lifted up his heel against Me.'[k] **19**Now I tell you before it comes, that when it does come to pass, you may believe that I am *He*. **20**Most assuredly, I say to you, he who receives whomever I send receives Me; and he who receives Me receives Him who sent Me."

21When Jesus had said these things, He was troubled in spirit, and testified and said, "Most assuredly, I say to you, one of you will betray Me." **22**Then the disciples looked at one another, perplexed about whom He spoke.

23Now there was leaning on Jesus' bosom one of His disciples, whom Jesus loved. **24**Simon Peter therefore motioned to him to ask who it was of whom He spoke.

25Then, leaning back on Jesus' breast, he said to Him, "Lord, who is it?"

k Psalm 41.9

26Jesus answered, "It is he to whom I shall give a piece of bread when I have dipped *it*." And having dipped the bread, He gave *it* to Judas Iscariot, *the son* of Simon. 27Now after the piece of bread, Satan entered him. Then Jesus said to him, "What you do, do quickly." 28But no one at the table knew for what reason He said this to him. 29For some thought, because Judas had the money box, that Jesus had said to him, "Buy *those things* we need for the feast," or that he should give something to the poor.

30Having received the piece of bread, he then went out immediately. And it was night.

The New Commandment

31So, when he had gone out, Jesus said, "Now the Son of Man is glorified, and God is glorified in Him. 32If God is glorified in Him, God will also glorify Him in Himself, and glorify Him immediately. 33Little children, I shall be with you a little while longer. You will seek Me; and as I said to the Jews, 'Where I am going, you cannot come,' so now I say to you. 34A new commandment I give to you, that you love one another; as I have loved you, that you also love one another. 35By this all will know that you are My disciples, if you have love for one another."

Jesus Predicts Peter's Denial

36Simon Peter said to Him, "Lord, where are You going?"

Jesus answered him, "Where I am going you cannot follow Me now, but you shall follow Me afterward."

37Peter said to Him, "Lord, why can I not follow You now? I will lay down my life for Your sake."

38Jesus answered him, "Will you lay down your life for My sake? Most assuredly, I say to you, the rooster shall not crow till you have denied Me three times.

The Way, the Truth, and the Life

14 "Let not your heart be troubled; you believe in God, believe also in Me. 2In My Father's house are many mansions; if *it were* not *so*, I would have told you. I go to prepare a place for you. 3And if I go and prepare a place

for you, I will come again and receive you to Myself; that where I am, *there* you may be also. 4And where I go you know, and the way you know."

5Thomas said to Him, "Lord, we do not know where You are going, and how can we know the way?"

6Jesus said to him, "I am the way, the truth, and the life. No one comes to the Father except through Me.

The Father Revealed

7"If you had known Me, you would have known My Father also; and from now on you know Him and have seen Him."

8Philip said to Him, "Lord, show us the Father, and it is sufficient for us."

9Jesus said to him, "Have I been with you so long, and yet you have not known Me, Philip? He who has seen Me has seen the Father; so how can you say, 'Show us the Father'? 10Do you not believe that I am in the Father, and the Father in Me? The words that I speak to you I do not speak on My own *authority;* but the Father who dwells in Me does the works. 11Believe Me that I *am* in the Father and the Father in Me, or else believe Me for the sake of the works themselves.

The Answered Prayer

12"Most assuredly, I say to you, he who believes in Me, the works that I do he will do also; and greater *works* than these he will do, because I go to My Father. 13And whatever you ask in My name, that I will do, that the Father may be glorified in the Son. 14If you ask anything in My name, I will do *it*.

Jesus Promises Another Helper

15"If you love Me, keep My commandments. 16And I will pray the Father, and He will give you another Helper, that He may abide with you forever—17the Spirit of truth, whom the world cannot receive, because it neither sees Him nor knows Him; but you know Him, for He dwells with you and will be in you. 18I will not leave you orphans; I will come to you.

Indwelling of the Father and the Son

19"A little while longer and the world will see Me no more, but you will see

Me. Because I live, you will live also. [20]At that day you will know that I *am* in My Father, and you in Me, and I in you. [21]He who has My commandments and keeps them, it is he who loves Me. And he who loves Me will be loved by My Father, and I will love him and manifest Myself to him.''

[22]Judas (not Iscariot) said to Him, ''Lord, how is it that You will manifest Yourself to us, and not to the world?''

[23]Jesus answered and said to him, ''If anyone loves Me, he will keep My word; and My Father will love him, and We will come to him and make Our home with him. [24]He who does not love Me does not keep My words; and the word which you hear is not Mine but the Father's who sent Me.

The Gift of His Peace

[25]''These things I have spoken to you while being present with you. [26]But the Helper, the Holy Spirit, whom the Father will send in My name, He will teach you all things, and bring to your remembrance all things that I said to you. [27]Peace I leave with you, My peace I give to you; not as the world gives do I give to you. Let not your heart be troubled, neither let it be afraid. [28]You have heard Me say to you, 'I am going away and coming *back* to you.' If you loved Me, you would rejoice because I said, 'I am going to the Father,' for My Father is greater than I.

[29]''And now I have told you before it comes, that when it does come to pass, you may believe. [30]I will no longer talk much with you, for the ruler of this world is coming, and he has nothing in Me. [31]But that the world may know that I love the Father, and as the Father gave Me commandment, so I do. Arise, let us go from here.

The True Vine

15 ''I am the true vine, and My Father is the vinedresser. [2]Every branch in Me that does not bear fruit He takes away; and every *branch* that bears fruit He prunes, that it may bear more fruit. [3]You are already clean because of the word which I have spoken to you. [4]Abide in Me, and I in you. As the branch cannot bear fruit of itself,

unless it abides in the vine, neither can you, unless you abide in Me.

[5]''I am the vine, you *are* the branches. He who abides in Me, and I in him, bears much fruit; for without Me you can do nothing. [6]If anyone does not abide in Me, he is cast out as a branch and is withered; and they gather them and throw *them* into the fire, and they are burned. [7]If you abide in Me, and My words abide in you, you will ask what you desire, and it shall be done for you. [8]By this My Father is glorified, that you bear much fruit; so you will be My disciples.

Love and Joy Perfected

[9]''As the Father loved Me, I also have loved you; abide in My love. [10]If you keep My commandments, you will abide in My love, just as I have kept My Father's commandments and abide in His love.

[11]''These things I have spoken to you, that My joy may remain in you, and *that* your joy may be full. [12]This is My commandment, that you love one another as I have loved you. [13]Greater love has no one than this, than to lay down one's life for his friends. [14]You are My friends if you do whatever I command you. [15]No longer do I call you servants, for a servant does not know what his master is doing; but I have called you friends, for all things that I heard from My Father I have made known to you. [16]You did not choose Me, but I chose you and appointed you that you should go and bear fruit, and *that* your fruit should remain, that whatever you ask the Father in My name He may give you. [17]These things I command you, that you love one another.

The World's Hatred

[18]''If the world hates you, you know that it hated Me before *it hated* you. [19]If you were of the world, the world would love its own. Yet because you are not of the world, but I chose you out of the world, therefore the world hates you. [20]Remember the word that I said to you, 'A servant is not greater than his master.' If they persecuted Me, they will also persecute you. If they kept My word, they will keep yours also.

21But all these things they will do to you for My name's sake, because they do not know Him who sent Me. 22If I had not come and spoken to them, they would have no sin, but now they have no excuse for their sin. 23He who hates Me hates My Father also. 24If I had not done among them the works which no one else did, they would have no sin; but now they have seen and also hated both Me and My Father. 25But *this happened* that the word might be fulfilled which is written in their law, 'They hated Me without a cause.'[l]

The Coming Rejection

26"But when the Helper comes, whom I shall send to you from the Father, the Spirit of truth who proceeds from the Father, He will testify of Me. 27And you also will bear witness, because you have been with Me from the beginning.

16 "These things I have spoken to you, that you should not be made to stumble. 2They will put you out of the synagogues; yes, the time is coming that whoever kills you will think that he offers God service. 3And these things they will do to you because they have not known the Father nor Me. 4But these things I have told you, that when the time comes, you may remember that I told you of them.

"And these things I did not say to you at the beginning, because I was with you.

The Work of the Holy Spirit

5"But now I go away to Him who sent Me, and none of you asks Me, 'Where are You going?' 6But because I have said these things to you, sorrow has filled your heart. 7Nevertheless I tell you the truth. It is to your advantage that I go away; for if I do not go away, the Helper will not come to you; but if I depart, I will send Him to you. 8And when He has come, He will convict the world of sin, and of righteousness, and of judgment: 9of sin, because they do not believe in Me; 10of righteousness, because I go to My Father and you see Me no more; 11of judgment,

because the ruler of this world is judged.

12"I still have many things to say to you, but you cannot bear *them* now. 13However, when He, the Spirit of truth, has come, He will guide you into all truth; for He will not speak on His own *authority*, but whatever He hears He will speak; and He will tell you things to come. 14He will glorify Me, for He will take of what is Mine and declare *it* to you. 15All things that the Father has are Mine. Therefore I said that He will take of Mine and declare *it* to you.

Sorrow Will Turn to Joy

16"A little while, and you will not see Me; and again a little while, and you will see Me, because I go to the Father."

17Then *some* of His disciples said among themselves, "What is this that He says to us, 'A little while, and you will not see Me; and again a little while, and you will see Me'; and, 'because I go to the Father'?" 18They said therefore, "What is this that He says, 'A little while'? We do not know what He is saying."

19Now Jesus knew that they desired to ask Him, and He said to them, "Are you inquiring among yourselves about what I said, 'A little while, and you will not see Me; and again a little while, and you will see Me'? 20Most assuredly, I say to you that you will weep and lament, but the world will rejoice; and you will be sorrowful, but your sorrow will be turned into joy. 21A woman, when she is in labor, has sorrow because her hour has come; but as soon as she has given birth to the child, she no longer remembers the anguish, for joy that a human being has been born into the world. 22Therefore you now have sorrow; but I will see you again and your heart will rejoice, and your joy no one will take from you.

23"And in that day you will ask Me nothing. Most assuredly, I say to you, whatever you ask the Father in My name He will give you. 24Until now you have asked nothing in My name. Ask, and you will receive, that your joy may be full.

l Psalm 69.4

Jesus Christ Has Overcome the World

25"These things I have spoken to you in figurative language; but the time is coming when I will no longer speak to you in figurative language, but I will tell you plainly about the Father. 26In that day you will ask in My name, and I do not say to you that I shall pray the Father for you; 27for the Father Himself loves you, because you have loved Me, and have believed that I came forth from God. 28I came forth from the Father and have come into the world. Again, I leave the world and go to the Father."

29His disciples said to Him, "See, now You are speaking plainly, and using no figure of speech! 30Now we are sure that You know all things, and have no need that anyone should question You. By this we believe that You came forth from God."

31Jesus answered them, "Do you now believe? 32Indeed the hour is coming, yes, has now come, that you will be scattered, each to his own, and will leave Me alone. And yet I am not alone, because the Father is with Me. 33These things I have spoken to you, that in Me you may have peace. In the world you will have tribulation; but be of good cheer, I have overcome the world."

Jesus Prays for Himself

17 Jesus spoke these words, lifted up His eyes to heaven, and said: "Father, the hour has come. Glorify Your Son, that Your Son also may glorify You, 2as You have given Him authority over all flesh, that He should give eternal life to as many as You have given Him. 3And this is eternal life, that they may know You, the only true God, and Jesus Christ whom You have sent. 4I have glorified You on the earth. I have finished the work which You have given Me to do. 5And now, O Father, glorify Me together with Yourself, with the glory which I had with You before the world was.

Jesus Prays for His Disciples

6"I have manifested Your name to the men whom You have given Me out of the world. They were Yours, You gave them to Me, and they have kept Your word. 7Now they have known that all things which You have given Me are from You. 8For I have given to them the words which You have given Me; and they have received them, and have known surely that I came forth from You; and they have believed that You sent Me.

9"I pray for them. I do not pray for the world but for those whom You have given Me, for they are Yours. 10And all Mine are Yours, and Yours are Mine, and I am glorified in them. 11Now I am no longer in the world, but these are in the world, and I come to You. Holy Father, keep through Your name those whom You have given Me, that they may be one as We are. 12While I was with them in the world, I kept them in Your name. Those whom You gave Me I have kept; and none of them is lost except the son of perdition, that the Scripture might be fulfilled. 13But now I come to You, and these things I speak in the world, that they may have My joy fulfilled in themselves. 14I have given them Your word; and the world has hated them because they are not of the world, just as I am not of the world. 15I do not pray that You should take them out of the world, but that You should keep them from the evil one. 16They are not of the world, just as I am not of the world. 17Sanctify them by Your truth. Your word is truth. 18As You sent Me into the world, I also have sent them into the world. 19And for their sakes I sanctify Myself, that they also may be sanctified by the truth.

Jesus Prays for All Believers

20"I do not pray for these alone, but also for those who will believe in Me through their word; 21that they all may be one, as You, Father, are in Me, and I in You; that they also may be one in Us, that the world may believe that You sent Me. 22And the glory which You gave Me I have given them, that they may be one just as We are one: 23I in them, and You in Me; that they may be made perfect in one, and that the world may know that You have sent Me, and have loved them as You have loved Me.

24"Father, I desire that they also whom You gave Me may be with Me where I am, that they may behold My glory which You have given Me; for You loved Me before the foundation of the world. 25O righteous Father! The world has not known You, but I have known You; and these have known that You sent Me. 26And I have declared to them Your name, and will declare *it*, that the love with which You loved Me may be in them, and I in them."

Betrayal and Arrest in Gethsemane

18 When Jesus had spoken these words, He went out with His disciples over the Brook Kidron, where there was a garden, which He and His disciples entered. 2And Judas, who betrayed Him, also knew the place; for Jesus often met there with His disciples. 3Then Judas, having received a detachment *of troops*, and officers from the chief priests and Pharisees, came there with lanterns, torches, and weapons. 4Jesus therefore, knowing all things that would come upon Him, went forward and said to them, "Whom are you seeking?"

5They answered Him, "Jesus of Nazareth."

Jesus said to them, "I am *He*." And Judas, who betrayed Him, also stood with them. 6Now when He said to them, "I am *He*," they drew back and fell to the ground.

7Then He asked them again, "Whom are you seeking?"

And they said, "Jesus of Nazareth." 8Jesus answered, "I have told you that I am *He*. Therefore, if you seek Me, let these go their way," 9that the saying might be fulfilled which He spoke, "Of those whom You gave Me I have lost none."

10Then Simon Peter, having a sword, drew it and struck the high priest's servant, and cut off his right ear. The servant's name was Malchus.

11So Jesus said to Peter, "Put your sword into the sheath. Shall I not drink the cup which My Father has given Me?"

Before the High Priest

12Then the detachment *of troops* and the captain and the officers of the Jews arrested Jesus and bound Him. 13And they led Him away to Annas first, for he was the father-in-law of Caiaphas who was high priest that year. 14Now it was Caiaphas who advised the Jews that it was expedient that one man should die for the people.

Peter Denies Jesus

15And Simon Peter followed Jesus, and so *did* another disciple. Now that disciple was known to the high priest, and went with Jesus into the courtyard of the high priest. 16But Peter stood at the door outside. Then the other disciple, who was known to the high priest, went out and spoke to her who kept the door, and brought Peter in. 17Then the servant girl who kept the door said to Peter, "You are not also *one* of this Man's disciples, are you?"

He said, "I am not."

18Now the servants and officers who had made a fire of coals stood there, for it was cold, and they warmed themselves. And Peter stood with them and warmed himself.

Jesus Questioned by the High Priest

19The high priest then asked Jesus about His disciples and His doctrine. 20Jesus answered him, "I spoke openly to the world. I always taught in synagogues and in the temple, where the Jews always meet, and in secret I have said nothing. 21Why do you ask Me? Ask those who have heard Me what I said to them. Indeed they know what I said."

22And when He had said these things, one of the officers who stood by struck Jesus with the palm of his hand, saying, "Do You answer the high priest like that?"

23Jesus answered him, "If I have spoken evil, bear witness of the evil; but if well, why do you strike Me?"

24Then Annas sent Him bound to Caiaphas the high priest.

Peter Denies Twice More

25Now Simon Peter stood and warmed himself. Therefore they said to him, "You are not also *one* of His disciples, are you?"

He denied *it* and said, "I am not!"

26One of the servants of the high priest, a relative *of him* whose ear Peter cut off, said, "Did I not see you in the garden with Him?" 27Peter then denied again; and immediately a rooster crowed.

In Pilate's Court

28Then they led Jesus from Caiaphas to the Praetorium, and it was early morning. But they themselves did not go into the Praetorium, lest they should be defiled, but that they might eat the Passover. 29Pilate then went out to them and said, "What accusation do you bring against this Man?"

30They answered and said to him, "If He were not an evildoer, we would not have delivered Him up to you."

31Then Pilate said to them, "You take Him and judge Him according to your law."

Therefore the Jews said to him, "It is not lawful for us to put anyone to death," 32that the saying of Jesus might be fulfilled which He spoke, signifying by what death He would die.

33Then Pilate entered the Praetorium again, called Jesus, and said to Him, "Are You the King of the Jews?"

34Jesus answered him, "Are you speaking for yourself about this, or did others tell you this concerning Me?"

35Pilate answered, "Am I a Jew? Your own nation and the chief priests have delivered You to me. What have You done?"

36Jesus answered, "My kingdom is not of this world. If My kingdom were of this world, My servants would fight, so that I should not be delivered to the Jews; but now My kingdom is not from here."

37Pilate therefore said to Him, "Are You a king then?"

Jesus answered, "You say rightly that I am a king. For this cause I was born, and for this cause I have come into the world, that I should bear witness to the truth. Everyone who is of the truth hears My voice."

38Pilate said to Him, "What is truth?" And when he had said this, he went out again to the Jews, and said to them, "I find no fault in Him at all.

Taking the Place of Barabbas

39"But you have a custom that I should release someone to you at the Passover. Do you therefore want me to release to you the King of the Jews?"

40Then they all cried again, saying, "Not this Man, but Barabbas!" Now Barabbas was a robber.

The Soldiers Mock Jesus

19 So then Pilate took Jesus and scourged Him. 2And the soldiers twisted a crown of thorns and put it on His head, and they put on Him a purple robe. 3Then they said, "Hail, King of the Jews!" And they struck Him with their hands.

4Pilate then went out again, and said to them, "Behold, I am bringing Him out to you, that you may know that I find no fault in Him."

Pilate's Decision

5Then Jesus came out, wearing the crown of thorns and the purple robe. And Pilate said to them, "Behold the Man!"

6Therefore, when the chief priests and officers saw Him, they cried out, saying, "Crucify Him, crucify Him!"

Pilate said to them, "You take Him and crucify Him, for I find no fault in Him."

7The Jews answered him, "We have a law, and according to our law He ought to die, because He made Himself the Son of God."

8Therefore, when Pilate heard that saying, he was the more afraid, 9and went again into the Praetorium, and said to Jesus, "Where are You from?" But Jesus gave him no answer.

10Then Pilate said to Him, "Are You not speaking to me? Do You not know that I have power to crucify You, and power to release You?"

11Jesus answered, "You could have no power at all against Me unless it had been given you from above. Therefore the one who delivered Me to you has the greater sin."

12From then on Pilate sought to release Him, but the Jews cried out, saying, "If you let this Man go, you are not Caesar's friend. Whoever makes himself a king speaks against Caesar."

13When Pilate therefore heard that saying, he brought Jesus out and sat down in the judgment seat in a place that is called The Pavement, but in Hebrew, Gabbatha. 14Now it was the Preparation Day of the Passover, and about the sixth hour. And he said to the Jews, "Behold your King!"

15But they cried out, "Away with *Him,* away with *Him!* Crucify Him!"

Pilate said to them, "Shall I crucify your King?"

The chief priests answered, "We have no king but Caesar!"

16Then he delivered Him to them to be crucified. Then they took Jesus and led *Him* away.

The King on a Cross

17And He, bearing His cross, went out to a place called *the Place* of a Skull, which is called in Hebrew, Golgotha, 18where they crucified Him, and two others with Him, one on either side, and Jesus in the center. 19Now Pilate wrote a title and put *it* on the cross. And the writing was:

JESUS OF NAZARETH,
THE KING OF THE JEWS.

20Then many of the Jews read this title, for the place where Jesus was crucified was near the city; and it was written in Hebrew, Greek, *and* Latin.

21Therefore the chief priests of the Jews said to Pilate, "Do not write, 'The King of the Jews,' but, 'He said, "I am the King of the Jews." ' "

22Pilate answered, "What I have written, I have written."

23Then the soldiers, when they had crucified Jesus, took His garments and made four parts, to each soldier a part, and also the tunic. Now the tunic was without seam, woven from the top in one piece. 24They said therefore among themselves, "Let us not tear it, but cast lots for it, whose it shall be," that the Scripture might be fulfilled which says:

"They divided My garments among them,
And for My clothing they cast lots."*m*

Therefore the soldiers did these things.

Behold Your Mother

25Now there stood by the cross of Jesus His mother, and His mother's sister, Mary the *wife* of Clopas, and Mary Magdalene. 26When Jesus therefore saw His mother, and the disciple whom He loved standing by, He said to His mother, "Woman, behold your son!" 27Then He said to the disciple, "Behold your mother!" And from that hour that disciple took her to his own *home.*

It Is Finished

28After this, Jesus, knowing that all things were now accomplished, that the Scripture might be fulfilled, said, "I thirst!" 29Now a vessel full of sour wine was sitting there; and they filled a sponge with sour wine, put *it* on hyssop, and put *it* to His mouth. 30So when Jesus had received the sour wine, He said, "It is finished!" And bowing His head, He gave up His spirit.

Jesus' Side Is Pierced

31Therefore, because it was the Preparation *Day,* that the bodies should not remain on the cross on the Sabbath (for that Sabbath was a high day), the Jews asked Pilate that their legs might be broken, and *that* they might be taken away. 32Then the soldiers came and broke the legs of the first and of the other who was crucified with Him. 33But when they came to Jesus and saw that He was already dead, they did not break His legs. 34But one of the soldiers pierced His side with a spear, and immediately blood and water came out. 35And he who has seen has testified, and his testimony is true; and he knows that he is telling the truth, so that you may believe. 36For these things were done that the Scripture should be fulfilled, "Not *one* of His bones shall be broken."*n* 37And again another Scripture says, "They shall look on Him whom they pierced."*o*

Jesus Buried in Joseph's Tomb

38After this, Joseph of Arimathea, being a disciple of Jesus, but secretly, for fear of the Jews, asked Pilate that he might take away the body of Jesus; and Pilate gave *him* permission. So he came and took the body of Jesus. 39And Nicodemus, who at first came to Jesus by night, also came, bringing a mixture of myrrh and aloes, about a hundred

m Psalm 22.18   *n* Exodus 12.46; Numbers 9.12; Psalm 34.20   *o* Zechariah 12.10

pounds. 40Then they took the body of Jesus, and bound it in strips of linen with the spices, as the custom of the Jews is to bury. 41Now in the place where He was crucified there was a garden, and in the garden a new tomb in which no one had yet been laid. 42So there they laid Jesus, because of the Jews' Preparation *Day*, for the tomb was nearby.

The Empty Tomb

20 Now the first *day* of the week Mary Magdalene went to the tomb early, while it was still dark, and saw *that* the stone had been taken away from the tomb. 2Then she ran and came to Simon Peter, and to the other disciple, whom Jesus loved, and said to them, "They have taken away the Lord out of the tomb, and we do not know where they have laid Him."

3Peter therefore went out, and the other disciple, and were going to the tomb. 4So they both ran together, and the other disciple outran Peter and came to the tomb first. 5And he, stooping down and looking in, saw the linen cloths lying *there;* yet he did not go in. 6Then Simon Peter came, following him, and went into the tomb; and he saw the linen cloths lying *there,* 7and the handkerchief that had been around His head, not lying with the linen cloths, but folded together in a place by itself. 8Then the other disciple, who came to the tomb first, went in also; and he saw and believed. 9For as yet they did not know the Scripture, that He must rise again from the dead. 10Then the disciples went away again to their own homes.

Mary Magdalene Sees the Risen Lord

11But Mary stood outside by the tomb weeping, and as she wept she stooped down *and looked* into the tomb. 12And she saw two angels in white sitting, one at the head and the other at the feet, where the body of Jesus had lain. 13Then they said to her, "Woman, why are you weeping?"

She said to them, "Because they have taken away my Lord, and I do not know where they have laid Him."

14Now when she had said this, she turned around and saw Jesus standing

there, and did not know that it was Jesus. 15Jesus said to her, "Woman, why are you weeping? Whom are you seeking?"

She, supposing Him to be the gardener, said to Him, "Sir, if You have carried Him away, tell me where You have laid Him, and I will take Him away."

16Jesus said to her, "Mary!"

She turned and said to Him, "Rabboni!" (which is to say, Teacher).

17Jesus said to her, "Do not cling to Me, for I have not yet ascended to My Father; but go to My brethren and say to them, 'I am ascending to My Father and your Father, and *to* My God and your God.' "

18Mary Magdalene came and told the disciples that she had seen the Lord, and *that* He had spoken these things to her.

The Apostles Commissioned

19Then, the same day at evening, being the first *day* of the week, when the doors were shut where the disciples were assembled, for fear of the Jews, Jesus came and stood in the midst, and said to them, "Peace *be* with you." 20When He had said this, He showed them *His* hands and His side. Then the disciples were glad when they saw the Lord.

21So Jesus said to them again, "Peace to you! As the Father has sent Me, I also send you." 22And when He had said this, He breathed on *them,* and said to them, "Receive the Holy Spirit. 23If you forgive the sins of any, they are forgiven them; if you retain the *sins* of any, they are retained."

Seeing and Believing

24Now Thomas, called the Twin, one of the twelve, was not with them when Jesus came. 25The other disciples therefore said to him, "We have seen the Lord."

So he said to them, "Unless I see in His hands the print of the nails, and put my finger into the print of the nails, and put my hand into His side, I will not believe."

26And after eight days His disciples were again inside, and Thomas with them. Jesus came, the doors being shut, and stood in the midst, and said, "Peace to you!" 27Then He said to Thomas, "Reach your finger here, and look at My hands; and reach your hand *here*, and put *it* into My side. Do not be unbelieving, but believing."

28And Thomas answered and said to Him, "My Lord and my God!"

29Jesus said to him, "Thomas, because you have seen Me, you have believed. Blessed *are* those who have not seen and *yet* have believed."

That You May Believe

30And truly Jesus did many other signs in the presence of His disciples, which are not written in this book; 31but these are written that you may believe that Jesus is the Christ, the Son of God, and that believing you may have life in His name.

Breakfast by the Sea

21 After these things Jesus showed Himself again to the disciples at the Sea of Tiberias, and in this way He showed *Himself:* 2Simon Peter, Thomas called the Twin, Nathanael of Cana in Galilee, the *sons* of Zebedee, and two others of His disciples were together. 3Simon Peter said to them, "I am going fishing."

They said to him, "We are going with you also." They went out and immediately got into the boat, and that night they caught nothing. 4But when the morning had now come, Jesus stood on the shore; yet the disciples did not know that it was Jesus. 5Then Jesus said to them, "Children, have you any food?"

They answered Him, "No."

6And He said to them, "Cast the net on the right side of the boat, and you will find *some*." So they cast, and now they were not able to draw it in because of the multitude of fish.

7Therefore that disciple whom Jesus loved said to Peter, "It is the Lord!" Now when Simon Peter heard that it was the Lord, he put on *his* outer garment (for he had removed it), and plunged into the sea. 8But the other disciples came in the little boat (for they were not far from land, but about two hundred cubits), dragging the net with fish. 9Then, as soon as they had come

to land, they saw a fire of coals there, and fish laid on it, and bread. 10Jesus said to them, "Bring some of the fish which you have just caught."

11Simon Peter went up and dragged the net to land, full of large fish, one hundred and fifty-three; and although there were so many, the net was not broken. 12Jesus said to them, "Come *and* eat breakfast." Yet none of the disciples dared ask Him, "Who are You?"—knowing that it was the Lord. 13Jesus then came and took the bread and gave it to them, and likewise the fish.

14This *is* now the third time Jesus showed Himself to His disciples after He was raised from the dead.

Jesus Restores Peter

15So when they had eaten breakfast, Jesus said to Simon Peter, "Simon, *son* of Jonah, do you love Me more than these?"

He said to Him, "Yes, Lord; You know that I love You."

He said to him, "Feed My lambs."

16He said to him again a second time, "Simon, *son* of Jonah, do you love Me?"

He said to Him, "Yes, Lord; You know that I love You."

He said to him, "Tend My sheep."

17He said to him the third time, "Simon, *son* of Jonah, do you love Me?" Peter was grieved because He said to him the third time, "Do you love Me?"

And he said to Him, "Lord, You know all things; You know that I love You."

Jesus said to him, "Feed My sheep. 18Most assuredly, I say to you, when you were younger, you girded yourself and walked where you wished; but when you are old, you will stretch out your hands, and another will gird you and carry *you* where you do not wish." 19This He spoke, signifying by what death he would glorify God. And when He had spoken this, He said to him, "Follow Me."

The Beloved Disciple and His Book

20Then Peter, turning around, saw the disciple whom Jesus loved following, who also had leaned on His breast at the supper, and said, "Lord, who is the one who betrays You?" 21Peter, seeing him, said to Jesus, "But Lord, what *about* this man?"

22Jesus said to him, "If I will that he remain till I come, what *is that* to you? You follow Me."

23Then this saying went out among the brethren that this disciple would not die. Yet Jesus did not say to him that he would not die, but, "If I will that he remain till I come, what *is that* to you?"

24This is the disciple who testifies of these things, and wrote these things; and we know that his testimony is true.

25And there are also many other things that Jesus did, which if they were written one by one, I suppose that even the world itself could not contain the books that would be written. Amen.

THE ACTS

of the Apostles

Prologue

1 The former account I made, O Theophilus, of all that Jesus began both to do and teach, 2until the day in which He was taken up, after He through the Holy Spirit had given commandments to the apostles whom He had chosen, 3to whom He also presented Himself alive after His suffering by many infallible proofs, being seen by them during forty days and speaking of the things pertaining to the kingdom of God.

The Holy Spirit Promised

4And being assembled together with *them*, He commanded them not to depart from Jerusalem, but to wait for the Promise of the Father, "which," *He said*, "you have heard from Me; 5for John truly baptized with water, but you shall be baptized with the Holy Spirit not many days from now."
6Therefore, when they had come together, they asked Him, saying, "Lord, will You at this time restore the kingdom to Israel?" 7And He said to them, "It is not for you to know times or seasons which the Father has put in His own authority. 8But you shall receive power when the Holy Spirit has come upon you; and you shall be witnesses to Me in Jerusalem, and in all Judea and Samaria, and to the end of the earth."

Jesus Ascends to Heaven

9Now when He had spoken these things, while they watched, He was taken up, and a cloud received Him out of their sight. 10And while they looked steadfastly toward heaven as He went up, behold, two men stood by them in white apparel, 11who also said, "Men of Galilee, why do you stand gazing up into heaven? This *same* Jesus, who was taken up from you into heaven, will so come in like manner as you saw Him go into heaven."

The Upper Room Prayer Meeting

12Then they returned to Jerusalem from the mount called Olivet, which is near Jerusalem, a Sabbath day's journey. 13And when they had entered, they went up into the upper room where they were staying: Peter, James, John, and Andrew; Philip and Thomas; Bartholomew and Matthew; James *the son* of Alphaeus and Simon the Zealot; and Judas *the son* of James. 14These all continued with one accord in prayer and supplication, with the women and Mary the mother of Jesus, and with His brothers.

Matthias Chosen

15And in those days Peter stood up in the midst of the disciples (altogether the number of names was about a hundred and twenty), and said, 16"Men *and* brethren, this Scripture had to be fulfilled, which the Holy Spirit spoke before by the mouth of David concerning Judas, who became a guide to those who arrested Jesus; 17for he was numbered with us and obtained a part in this ministry."
18(Now this man purchased a field with the wages of iniquity; and falling headlong, he burst open in the middle and all his entrails gushed out. 19And it became known to all those dwelling in Jerusalem; so that field is called in their own language, Akel Dama, that is, Field of Blood.)
20"For it is written in the Book of Psalms:

'Let his dwelling place be desolate,
    And let no one live in it';[a]
and,
    'Let[b] another take his office.'
21"Therefore, of these men who have accompanied us all the time that the Lord Jesus went in and out among us, 22beginning from the baptism of John to that day when He was taken up from us, one of these must become a witness with us of His resurrection."

---

a Psalm 69.25   *b* Psalm 109.8

23And they proposed two: Joseph called Barsabas, who was surnamed Justus, and Matthias. 24And they prayed and said, "You, O Lord, who know the hearts of all, show which of these two You have chosen 25to take part in this ministry and apostleship from which Judas by transgression fell, that he might go to his own place." 26And they cast their lots, and the lot fell on Matthias. And he was numbered with the eleven apostles.

Coming of the Holy Spirit

2 When the Day of Pentecost had fully come, they were all with one accord in one place. 2And suddenly there came a sound from heaven, as of a rushing mighty wind, and it filled the whole house where they were sitting. 3Then there appeared to them divided tongues, as of fire, and *one* sat upon each of them. 4And they were all filled with the Holy Spirit and began to speak with other tongues, as the Spirit gave them utterance.

The Crowd's Response

5And there were dwelling in Jerusalem Jews, devout men, from every nation under heaven. 6And when this sound occurred, the multitude came together, and were confused, because everyone heard them speak in his own language. 7Then they were all amazed and marveled, saying to one another, "Look, are not all these who speak Galileans? 8And how *is it that* we hear, each in our own language in which we were born? 9Parthians and Medes and Elamites, those dwelling in Mesopotamia, Judea and Cappadocia, Pontus and Asia, 10Phrygia and Pamphylia, Egypt and the parts of Libya adjoining Cyrene, visitors from Rome, both Jews and proselytes, 11Cretans and Arabs— we hear them speaking in our own tongues the wonderful works of God." 12So they were all amazed and perplexed, saying to one another, "Whatever could this mean?"

13Others mocking said, "They are full of new wine."

Peter's Sermon

14But Peter, standing up with the eleven, raised his voice and said to them, "Men of Judea and all who dwell in Jerusalem, let this be known to you, and heed my words. 15For these are not drunk, as you suppose, since it is *only* the third hour of the day. 16But this is what was spoken by the prophet Joel:

17   'And it shall come to pass in the last
          days, says God,
      That I will pour out of My Spirit
          on all flesh;
      Your sons and your daughters shall
          prophesy,
      Your young men shall see visions,
      Your old men shall dream dreams.
18   And on My menservants and on My
          maidservants
      I will pour out My Spirit in those
          days;
      And they shall prophesy.
19   I will show wonders in heaven
          above
      And signs in the earth beneath:
      Blood and fire and vapor of smoke.
20   The sun shall be turned into
          darkness,
      And the moon into blood,
      Before the coming of the great and
          awesome day of the LORD.
21   And it shall come to pass
      That whoever calls on the name of
          the LORD
      Shall be saved.'*c*

22"Men of Israel, hear these words: Jesus of Nazareth, a Man attested by God to you by miracles, wonders, and signs which God did through Him in your midst, as you yourselves also know—23Him, being delivered by the determined purpose and foreknowledge of God, you have taken by lawless hands, have crucified, and put to death; 24whom God raised up, having loosed the pains of death, because it was not possible that He should be held by it. 25For David says concerning Him:

      'I foresaw the LORD always before
          my face,
      For He is at my right hand, that I
          may not be shaken.
26   Therefore my heart rejoiced, and
          my tongue was glad;

c Joel 2.28-32

Moreover my flesh also will rest in hope.
27 For You will not leave my soul in Hades,
Nor will You allow Your Holy One to see corruption.
28 You have made known to me the ways of life;
You will make me full of joy in Your presence.'d

29"Men *and* brethren, let *me* speak freely to you of the patriarch David, that he is both dead and buried, and his tomb is with us to this day. 30Therefore, being a prophet, and knowing that God had sworn with an oath to him that of the fruit of his body, according to the flesh, He would raise up the Christ to sit on his throne, 31he, foreseeing this, spoke concerning the resurrection of the Christ, that His soul was not left in Hades, nor did His flesh see corruption. 32This Jesus God has raised up, of which we are all witnesses. 33Therefore being exalted to the right hand of God, and having received from the Father the promise of the Holy Spirit, He poured out this which you now see and hear.

34"For David did not ascend into the heavens, but he says himself:
'The LORD said to my Lord,
"Sit at My right hand,
35 Till I make Your enemies Your footstool." 'e

36"Therefore let all the house of Israel know assuredly that God has made this Jesus, whom you crucified, both Lord and Christ."

37Now when they heard *this*, they were cut to the heart, and said to Peter and the rest of the apostles, "Men *and* brethren, what shall we do?"

38Then Peter said to them, "Repent, and let every one of you be baptized in the name of Jesus Christ for the remission of sins; and you shall receive the gift of the Holy Spirit. 39For the promise is to you and to your children, and to all who are afar off, as many as the Lord our God will call."

A Vital Church Grows

40And with many other words he testified and exhorted them, saying, "Be

saved from this perverse generation." 41Then those who gladly received his word were baptized; and that day about three thousand souls were added *to them*. 42And they continued steadfastly in the apostles' doctrine and fellowship, in the breaking of bread, and in prayers. 43Then fear came upon every soul, and many wonders and signs were done through the apostles. 44Now all who believed were together, and had all things in common, 45and sold their possessions and goods, and divided them among all, as anyone had need.

46So continuing daily with one accord in the temple, and breaking bread from house to house, they ate their food with gladness and simplicity of heart, 47praising God and having favor with all the people. And the Lord added to the church daily those who were being saved.

A Lame Man Healed

3 Now Peter and John went up together to the temple at the hour of prayer, the ninth *hour.* 2And a certain man lame from his mother's womb was carried, whom they laid daily at the gate of the temple which is called Beautiful, to ask alms from those who entered the temple; 3who, seeing Peter and John about to go into the temple, asked for alms. 4And fixing his eyes on him, with John, Peter said, "Look at us." 5So he gave them his attention, expecting to receive something from them. 6Then Peter said, "Silver and gold I do not have, but what I do have I give you: In the name of Jesus Christ of Nazareth, rise up and walk." 7And he took him by the right hand and lifted *him* up; and immediately his feet and ankle bones received strength. 8So he, leaping up, stood and walked and entered the temple with them— walking, leaping, and praising God. 9And all the people saw him walking and praising God. 10Then they knew that it was he who sat begging alms at the Beautiful Gate of the temple; and they were filled with wonder and amazement at what had happened to him.

Preaching in Solomon's Portico

11Now as the lame man who was healed held on to Peter and John, all the people ran together to them in the porch which is called Solomon's, greatly amazed. 12So when Peter saw *it,* he responded to the people: "Men of Israel, why do you marvel at this? Or why look so intently at us, as though by our own power or godliness we had made this man walk? 13The God of Abraham, Isaac, and Jacob, the God of our fathers, glorified His Servant Jesus, whom you delivered up and denied in the presence of Pilate, when he was determined to let *Him* go. 14But you denied the Holy One and the Just, and asked for a murderer to be granted to you, 15and killed the Prince of life, whom God raised from the dead, of which we are witnesses. 16And His name, through faith in His name, has made this man strong, whom you see and know. Yes, the faith which *comes* through Him has given him this perfect soundness in the presence of you all.

17"Yet now, brethren, I know that you did *it* in ignorance, as *did* also your rulers. 18But those things which God foretold by the mouth of all His prophets, that the Christ would suffer, He has thus fulfilled. 19Repent therefore and be converted, that your sins may be blotted out, so that times of refreshing may come from the presence of the Lord, 20and that He may send Jesus Christ, who was preached to you before, 21whom heaven must receive until the times of restoration of all things, which God has spoken by the mouth of all His holy prophets since the world began. 22For Moses truly said to the fathers, 'The Lord your God will raise up for you a Prophet like me from your brethren. Him you shall hear in all things, whatever He says to you. 23And it shall be *that* every soul who will not hear that Prophet shall be utterly destroyed from among the people.'*f* 24Yes, and all the prophets, from Samuel and those who follow, as many as have spoken, have also foretold these days. 25You are sons of the prophets, and of the covenant which God made with our fathers,

saying to Abraham, 'And in your seed all the families of the earth shall be blessed.'*g* 26To you first, God, having raised up His Servant Jesus, sent Him to bless you, in turning away every one *of you* from your iniquities."

Peter and John Arrested

4 Now as they spoke to the people, the priests, the captain of the temple, and the Sadducees came upon them, 2being greatly disturbed that they taught the people and preached in Jesus the resurrection from the dead. 3And they laid hands on them, and put *them* in custody until the next day, for it was already evening. 4However, many of those who heard the word believed; and the number of the men came to be about five thousand.

Addressing the Sanhedrin

5And it came to pass, on the next day, that their rulers, elders, and scribes, 6as well as Annas the high priest, Caiaphas, John, and Alexander, and as many as were of the family of the high priest, were gathered together at Jerusalem. 7And when they had set them in the midst, they asked, "By what power or by what name have you done this?"

8Then Peter, filled with the Holy Spirit, said to them, "Rulers of the people and elders of Israel: 9If we this day are judged for a good deed *done* to a helpless man, by what means he has been made well, 10let it be known to you all, and to all the people of Israel, that by the name of Jesus Christ of Nazareth, whom you crucified, whom God raised from the dead, by Him this man stands here before you whole. 11This is the 'stone which was rejected by you builders, which has become the chief cornerstone.'*h* 12Nor is there salvation in any other, for there is no other name under heaven given among men by which we must be saved."

The Name of Jesus Forbidden

13Now when they saw the boldness of Peter and John, and perceived that they were uneducated and untrained

f Deuteronomy 18.15, 18, 19   *g* Genesis 22.18; 26.4; 28.14   *h* Psalm 118.22

men, they marveled. And they realized that they had been with Jesus. 14And seeing the man who had been healed standing with them, they could say nothing against it. 15But when they had commanded them to go aside out of the council, they conferred among themselves, 16saying, "What shall we do to these men? For, indeed, that a notable miracle has been done through them *is* evident to all who dwell in Jerusalem, and we cannot deny *it*. 17But so that it spreads no further among the people, let us severely threaten them, that from now on they speak to no man in this name."

18So they called them and commanded them not to speak at all nor teach in the name of Jesus. 19But Peter and John answered and said to them, "Whether it is right in the sight of God to listen to you more than to God, you judge. 20For we cannot but speak the things which we have seen and heard." 21So when they had further threatened them, they let them go, finding no way of punishing them, because of the people, since they all glorified God for what had been done. 22For the man was over forty years old on whom this miracle of healing had been performed.

Prayer for Boldness

23And being let go, they went to their own *companions* and reported all that the chief priests and elders had said to them. 24So when they heard that, they raised their voice to God with one accord and said: "Lord, You *are* God, who made heaven and earth and the sea, and all that is in them, 25who by the mouth of Your servant David have said:

'Why did the nations rage,
    And the people plot vain things?
26   The kings of the earth took their stand,
    And the rulers were gathered together
    Against the LORD and against His Christ.'*i*

27"For truly against Your holy Servant Jesus, whom You anointed, both Herod and Pontius Pilate, with the Gentiles and the people of Israel, were gath-

ered together 28to do whatever Your hand and Your purpose determined before to be done. 29Now, Lord, look on their threats, and grant to Your servants that with all boldness they may speak Your word, 30by stretching out Your hand to heal, and that signs and wonders may be done through the name of Your holy Servant Jesus."

31And when they had prayed, the place where they were assembled together was shaken; and they were all filled with the Holy Spirit, and they spoke the word of God with boldness.

Sharing in All Things

32Now the multitude of those who believed were of one heart and one soul; neither did anyone say that any of the things he possessed was his own, but they had all things in common. 33And with great power the apostles gave witness to the resurrection of the Lord Jesus. And great grace was upon them all. 34Nor was there anyone among them who lacked; for all who were possessors of lands or houses sold them, and brought the proceeds of the things that were sold, 35and laid *them* at the apostles' feet; and they distributed to each as anyone had need.

36And Joses, who was also named Barnabas by the apostles (which is translated Son of Encouragement), a Levite of the country of Cyprus, 37having land, sold *it*, and brought the money and laid *it* at the apostles' feet.

Lying to the Holy Spirit

5 But a certain man named Ananias, with Sapphira his wife, sold a possession. 2And he kept back *part* of the proceeds, his wife also being aware *of it*, and brought a certain part and laid *it* at the apostles' feet. 3But Peter said, "Ananias, why has Satan filled your heart to lie to the Holy Spirit and keep back *part* of the price of the land for yourself? 4While it remained, was it not your own? And after it was sold, was it not in your own control? Why have you conceived this thing in your heart? You have not lied to men but to God."

5Then Ananias, hearing these words,

i Psalm 2.1, 2

fell down and breathed his last. So great fear came upon all those who heard these things. 6And the young men arose and wrapped him up, carried *him* out, and buried *him*.

7Now it was about three hours later when his wife came in, not knowing what had happened. 8And Peter answered her, "Tell me whether you sold the land for so much?"

She said, "Yes, for so much."

9Then Peter said to her, "How is it that you have agreed together to test the Spirit of the Lord? Look, the feet of those who have buried your husband *are* at the door, and they will carry you out." 10Then immediately she fell down at his feet and breathed her last. And the young men came in and found her dead, and carrying *her* out, buried *her* by her husband. 11So great fear came upon all the church and upon all who heard these things.

Continuing Power in the Church

12And through the hands of the apostles many signs and wonders were done among the people. And they were all with one accord in Solomon's Porch. 13Yet none of the rest dared join them, but the people esteemed them highly. 14And believers were increasingly added to the Lord, multitudes of both men and women, 15so that they brought the sick out into the streets and laid *them* on beds and couches, that at least the shadow of Peter passing by might fall on some of them. 16Also a multitude gathered from the surrounding cities to Jerusalem, bringing sick people and those who were tormented by unclean spirits, and they were all healed.

Imprisoned Apostles Freed

17Then the high priest rose up, and all those who *were* with him (which is the sect of the Sadducees), and they were filled with indignation, 18and laid their hands on the apostles and put them in the common prison. 19But at night an angel of the Lord opened the prison doors and brought them out, and said, 20"Go, stand in the temple and speak to the people all the words of this life."

21And when they heard *that*, they entered the temple early in the morning

and taught. But the high priest and those with him came and called the council together, with all the elders of the children of Israel, and sent to the prison to have them brought.

Apostles on Trial Again

22But when the officers came and did not find them in the prison, they returned and reported, 23saying, "Indeed we found the prison shut securely, and the guards standing outside before the doors; but when we opened them, we found no one inside!" 24Now when the high priest, the captain of the temple, and the chief priests heard these things, they wondered what the outcome would be. 25So one came and told them, saying, "Look, the men whom you put in prison are standing in the temple and teaching the people!"

26Then the captain went with the officers and brought them without violence, for they feared the people, lest they should be stoned. 27And when they had brought them, they set *them* before the council. And the high priest asked them, 28saying, "Did we not strictly command you not to teach in this name? And look, you have filled Jerusalem with your doctrine, and intend to bring this Man's blood on us!"

29But Peter and the *other* apostles answered and said: "We ought to obey God rather than men. 30The God of our fathers raised up Jesus whom you murdered by hanging on a tree. 31Him God has exalted to His right hand *to be* Prince and Savior, to give repentance to Israel and forgiveness of sins. 32And we are His witnesses to these things, and *so* also *is* the Holy Spirit whom God has given to those who obey Him."

Gamaliel's Advice

33When they heard *this*, they were furious and plotted to kill them. 34Then one in the council stood up, a Pharisee named Gamaliel, a teacher of the law held in respect by all the people, and commanded them to put the apostles outside for a little while. 35And he said to them: "Men of Israel, take heed to yourselves what you intend to do regarding these men. 36For some time ago Theudas rose up, claiming to be somebody. A number of men, about four hundred, joined him. He was slain, and all who obeyed him were scattered and came to nothing. 37After this man, Judas of Galilee rose up in the days of the census, and drew away many people after him. He also perished, and all who obeyed him were dispersed. 38And now I say to you, keep away from these men and let them alone; for if this plan or this work is of men, it will come to nothing; 39but if it is of God, you cannot overthrow it—lest you even be found to fight against God."

40And they agreed with him, and when they had called for the apostles and beaten *them*, they commanded that they should not speak in the name of Jesus, and let them go. 41So they departed from the presence of the council, rejoicing that they were counted worthy to suffer shame for His name. 42And daily in the temple, and in every house, they did not cease teaching and preaching Jesus *as* the Christ.

Seven Chosen to Serve

6 Now in those days, when *the number of* the disciples was multiplying, there arose a complaint against the Hebrews by the Hellenists, because their widows were neglected in the daily distribution. 2Then the twelve summoned the multitude of the disciples and said, "It is not desirable that we should leave the word of God and serve tables. 3Therefore, brethren, seek out from among you seven men of *good* reputation, full of the Holy Spirit and wisdom, whom we may appoint over this business; 4but we will give ourselves continually to prayer and to the ministry of the word."

5And the saying pleased the whole multitude. And they chose Stephen, a man full of faith and the Holy Spirit, and Philip, Prochorus, Nicanor, Timon, Parmenas, and Nicolas, a proselyte from Antioch, 6whom they set before the apostles; and when they had prayed, they laid hands on them.

7Then the word of God spread, and the number of the disciples multiplied greatly in Jerusalem, and a great many of the priests were obedient to the faith.

Stephen Accused of Blasphemy

8And Stephen, full of faith and power, did great wonders and signs among the people. 9Then there arose some from what is called the Synagogue of the Freedmen (Cyrenians, Alexandrians, and those from Cilicia and Asia), disputing with Stephen. 10And they were not able to resist the wisdom and the Spirit by which he spoke. 11Then they secretly induced men to say, "We have heard him speak blasphemous words against Moses and God." 12And they stirred up the people, the elders, and the scribes; and they came upon *him*, seized him, and brought *him* to the council. 13They also set up false witnesses who said, "This man does not cease to speak blasphemous words against this holy place and the law; 14for we have heard him say that this Jesus of Nazareth will destroy this place and change the customs which Moses delivered to us." 15And all who sat in the council, looking steadfastly at him, saw his face as the face of an angel.

Stephen's Address: The Call of Abraham

7 Then the high priest said, "Are these things so?"

2And he said, "Brethren and fathers, listen: The God of glory appeared to our father Abraham when he was in Mesopotamia, before he dwelt in Haran, 3and said to him, 'Get out of your country and from your relatives, and come to a land that I will show you.'*ʲ* 4Then he came out of the land of the Chaldeans and dwelt in Haran. And from there, when his father was dead, He moved him to this land in which you now dwell. 5And *God* gave him no inheritance in it, not even *enough* to set his foot on. But even when *Abraham* had no child, He promised to give it to him for a possession, and to his descendants after him. 6But God spoke in this way: that his descendants would dwell in a foreign land, and that they would bring them into bondage and oppress *them* four hundred years. 7'And the nation to whom they will be in bondage I will judge,'*ᵏ* said God, 'and

---

ʲ Genesis 12.1   *ᵏ* Genesis 15.14

after that they shall come out and serve Me in this place.'[l] 8Then He gave him the covenant of circumcision; and so *Abraham* begot Isaac and circumcised him on the eighth day; and Isaac *begot* Jacob, and Jacob *begot* the twelve patriarchs.

The Patriarchs in Egypt

9"And the patriarchs, becoming envious, sold Joseph into Egypt. But God was with him 10and delivered him out of all his troubles, and gave him favor and wisdom in the presence of Pharaoh, king of Egypt; and he made him governor over Egypt and all his house. 11Now a famine and great trouble came over all the land of Egypt and Canaan, and our fathers found no sustenance. 12But when Jacob heard that there was grain in Egypt, he sent out our fathers first. 13And the second *time* Joseph was made known to his brothers, and Joseph's family became known to the Pharaoh. 14Then Joseph sent and called his father Jacob and all his relatives to *him*, seventy-five people. 15So Jacob went down to Egypt; and he died, he and our fathers. 16And they were carried back to Shechem and laid in the tomb that Abraham bought for a sum of money from the sons of Hamor, *the father* of Shechem.

God Delivers Israel by Moses

17"But when the time of the promise drew near which God had sworn to Abraham, the people grew and multiplied in Egypt 18till another king arose who did not know Joseph. 19This man dealt treacherously with our people, and oppressed our forefathers, making them expose their babies, so that they might not live. 20At this time Moses was born, and was well pleasing to God; and he was brought up in his father's house for three months. 21But when he was set out, Pharaoh's daughter took him away and brought him up as her own son. 22And Moses was learned in all the wisdom of the Egyptians, and was mighty in words and deeds.

23"Now when he was forty years old, it came into his heart to visit his brethren, the children of Israel. 24And seeing one of *them* suffer wrong, he defended and avenged him who was oppressed, and struck down the Egyptian. 25For he supposed that his brethren would have understood that God would deliver them by his hand, but they did not understand. 26And the next day he appeared to two of them as they were fighting, and *tried to* reconcile them, saying, 'Men, you are brethren; why do you wrong one another?' 27But he who did his neighbor wrong pushed him away, saying, 'Who made you a ruler and a judge over us? 28Do you want to kill me as you did the Egyptian yesterday?'[m] 29Then, at this saying, Moses fled and became a dweller in the land of Midian, where he had two sons.

30"And when forty years had passed, an Angel of the Lord appeared to him in a flame of fire in a bush, in the wilderness of Mount Sinai. 31When Moses saw *it*, he marveled at the sight; and as he drew near to observe, the voice of the Lord came to him, 32saying, 'I *am* the God of your fathers—the God of Abraham, the God of Isaac, and the God of Jacob.'[n] And Moses trembled and dared not look. 33Then the LORD said to him, "Take your sandals off your feet, for the place where you stand is holy ground. 34I have surely seen the oppression of My people who are in Egypt; I have heard their groaning and have come down to deliver them. And now come, I will send you to Egypt." '[o]

35"This Moses whom they rejected, saying, 'Who made you a ruler and a judge?'[p] is the one God sent *to be* a ruler and a deliverer by the hand of the Angel who appeared to him in the bush. 36He brought them out, after he had shown wonders and signs in the land of Egypt, and in the Red Sea, and in the wilderness forty years.

Israel Rebels Against God

37"This is that Moses who said to the children of Israel,[q] 'The LORD your God will raise up for you a Prophet like me from your brethren. Him you shall hear.'

---

[l] Exodus 3.12   [m] Exodus 2.14   [n] Exodus 3.6, 15   [o] Exodus 3.5, 7, 8, 10
[p] Exodus 2.14   [q] Deuteronomy 18.15

38"This is he who was in the congregation in the wilderness with the Angel who spoke to him on Mount Sinai, and *with* our fathers, the one who received the living oracles to give to us, 39whom our fathers would not obey, but rejected. And in their hearts they turned back to Egypt, 40saying to Aaron, 'Make us gods to go before us; *as for* this Moses who brought us out of the land of Egypt, we do not know what has become of him.'[r] 41And they made a calf in those days, offered sacrifices to the idol, and rejoiced in the works of their own hands. 42Then God turned and gave them up to worship the host of heaven, as it is written in the book of the Prophets:

'Did you offer Me slaughtered
   animals and sacrifices *during*
   forty years in the wilderness,
   O house of Israel?
43 You also took up the tabernacle of
   Moloch,
   And the star of your god Remphan,
   Images which you made to
   worship;
   And I will carry you away beyond
   Babylon.'[s]

God's True Tabernacle

44"Our fathers had the tabernacle of witness in the wilderness, as He appointed, instructing Moses to make it according to the pattern that he had seen, 45which our fathers, having received it in turn, also brought with Joshua into the land possessed by the Gentiles, whom God drove out before the face of our fathers until the days of David, 46who found favor before God and asked to find a dwelling for the God of Jacob. 47But Solomon built Him a house.

48"However, the Most High does not dwell in temples made with hands, as the prophet says:

49 'Heaven *is* My throne,
   And earth *is* My footstool.
   What house will you build for Me?
      says the LORD,
   Or what *is* the place of My rest?
50 Has My hand not made all these
   things?'[t]

Israel Resists the Holy Spirit

51"*You* stiff-necked and uncircumcised in heart and ears! You always resist the Holy Spirit; as your fathers *did*, so *do* you. 52Which of the prophets did your fathers not persecute? And they killed those who foretold the coming of the Just One, of whom you now have become the betrayers and murderers, 53who have received the law by the direction of angels and have not kept *it*."

Stephen the Martyr

54When they heard these things they were cut to the heart, and they gnashed at him with *their* teeth. 55But he, being full of the Holy Spirit, gazed into heaven and saw the glory of God, and Jesus standing at the right hand of God, 56and said, "Look! I see the heavens opened and the Son of Man standing at the right hand of God!"

57Then they cried out with a loud voice, stopped their ears, and ran at him with one accord; 58and they cast *him* out of the city and stoned *him*. And the witnesses laid down their clothes at the feet of a young man named Saul. 59And they stoned Stephen as he was calling on God and saying, "Lord Jesus, receive my spirit." 60Then he knelt down and cried out with a loud voice, "Lord, do not charge them with this sin." And when he had said this, he fell asleep.

Saul Persecutes the Church

8 Now Saul was consenting to his death.

At that time a great persecution arose against the church which was at Jerusalem; and they were all scattered throughout the regions of Judea and Samaria, except the apostles. 2And devout men carried Stephen *to his burial*, and made great lamentation over him.

3As for Saul, he made havoc of the church, entering every house, and dragging off men and women, committing *them* to prison.

Christ Is Preached in Samaria

4Therefore those who were scattered went everywhere preaching the word.

---

[r] Exodus 32.1; 23   [s] Amos 5.25-27   [t] Isaiah 66.1, 2

5Then Philip went down to the[u] city of Samaria and preached Christ to them. 6And the multitudes with one accord heeded the things spoken by Philip, hearing and seeing the miracles which he did. 7For unclean spirits, crying with a loud voice, came out of many who were possessed; and many who were paralyzed and lame were healed. 8And there was great joy in that city.

The Sorcerer's Profession of Faith

9But there was a certain man called Simon, who previously practiced sorcery in the city and astonished the people of Samaria, claiming that he was someone great, 10to whom they all gave heed, from the least to the greatest, saying, "This man is the great power of God." 11And they heeded him because he had astonished them with his sorceries for a long time. 12But when they believed Philip as he preached the things concerning the kingdom of God and the name of Jesus Christ, both men and women were baptized. 13Then Simon himself also believed; and when he was baptized he continued with Philip, and was amazed, seeing the miracles and signs which were done.

The Sorcerer's Sin

14Now when the apostles who were at Jerusalem heard that Samaria had received the word of God, they sent Peter and John to them, 15who, when they had come down, prayed for them that they might receive the Holy Spirit. 16For as yet He had fallen upon none of them. They had only been baptized in the name of the Lord Jesus. 17Then they laid hands on them, and they received the Holy Spirit.

18And when Simon saw that through the laying on of the apostles' hands the Holy Spirit was given, he offered them money, 19saying, "Give me this power also, that anyone on whom I lay hands may receive the Holy Spirit."

20But Peter said to him, "Your money perish with you, because you thought that the gift of God could be purchased with money! 21You have neither part nor portion in this matter, for your heart is not right in the sight of God. 22Repent therefore of this your wickedness, and pray God if perhaps the thought of your heart may be forgiven you. 23For I see that you are poisoned by bitterness and bound by iniquity."

24Then Simon answered and said, "Pray to the Lord for me, that none of the things which you have spoken may come upon me."

25So when they had testified and preached the word of the Lord, they returned to Jerusalem, preaching the gospel in many villages of the Samaritans.

Christ Is Preached to an Ethiopian

26Now an angel of the Lord spoke to Philip, saying, "Arise and go toward the south along the road which goes down from Jerusalem to Gaza." This is desert. 27So he arose and went. And behold, a man of Ethiopia, a eunuch of great authority under Candace the queen of the Ethiopians, who had charge of all her treasury, and had come to Jerusalem to worship, 28was returning. And sitting in his chariot, he was reading Isaiah the prophet. 29Then the Spirit said to Philip, "Go near and overtake this chariot."

30So Philip ran to him, and heard him reading the prophet Isaiah, and said, "Do you understand what you are reading?"

31And he said, "How can I, unless someone guides me?" And he asked Philip to come up and sit with him. 32The place in the Scripture which he read was this:

"He was led as a sheep to the
    slaughter;
And as a lamb before its shearer
    is silent,
So He opened not His mouth.
33 In His humiliation His justice was
    taken away,
And who will declare His
    generation?
For His life is taken from the
    earth."[v]

34So the eunuch answered Philip and said, "I ask you, of whom does the prophet say this, of himself or of some other man?" 35Then Philip opened his

[u] Or *a*   [v] Isaiah 53:7, 8

mouth, and beginning at this Scripture, preached Jesus to him. 36Now as they went down the road, they came to some water. And the eunuch said, "See, *here is* water. What hinders me from being baptized?"

37Then Philip said, "If you believe with all your heart, you may."

And he answered and said, "I believe that Jesus Christ is the Son of God."

38So he commanded the chariot to stand still. And both Philip and the eunuch went down into the water, and he baptized him. 39Now when they came up out of the water, the Spirit of the Lord caught Philip away, so that the eunuch saw him no more; and he went on his way rejoicing. 40But Philip was found at Azotus. And passing through, he preached in all the cities till he came to Caesarea.

The Damascus Road: Saul Converted

9 Then Saul, still breathing threats and murder against the disciples of the Lord, went to the high priest 2and asked letters from him to the synagogues of Damascus, so that if he found any who were of the Way, whether men or women, he might bring them bound to Jerusalem.

3As he journeyed he came near Damascus, and suddenly a light shone around him from heaven. 4Then he fell to the ground, and heard a voice saying to him, "Saul, Saul, why are you persecuting Me?"

5And he said, "Who are You, Lord?"

Then the Lord said, "I am Jesus, whom you are persecuting. It *is* hard for you to kick against the goads."

6So he, trembling and astonished, said, "Lord, what do You want me to do?"

Then the Lord *said* to him, "Arise and go into the city, and you will be told what you must do."

7And the men who journeyed with him stood speechless, hearing a voice but seeing no one. 8Then Saul arose from the ground, and when his eyes were opened he saw no one. But they led him by the hand and brought *him* into Damascus. 9And he was three days without sight, and neither ate nor drank.

Ananias Baptizes Saul

10Now there was a certain disciple at Damascus named Ananias; and to him the Lord said in a vision, "Ananias."

And he said, "Here I am, Lord."

11So the Lord *said* to him, "Arise and go to the street called Straight, and inquire at the house of Judas for *one* called Saul of Tarsus, for behold, he is praying. 12And in a vision he has seen a man named Ananias coming in and putting *his* hand on him, so that he might receive his sight."

13Then Ananias answered, "Lord, I have heard from many about this man, how much harm he has done to Your saints in Jerusalem. 14And here he has authority from the chief priests to bind all who call on Your name."

15But the Lord said to him, "Go, for he is a chosen vessel of Mine to bear My name before Gentiles, kings, and the children of Israel. 16For I will show him how many things he must suffer for My name's sake."

17And Ananias went his way and entered the house; and laying his hands on him he said, "Brother Saul, the Lord Jesus, who appeared to you on the road as you came, has sent me that you may receive your sight and be filled with the Holy Spirit." 18Immediately there fell from his eyes *something* like scales, and he received his sight at once; and he arose and was baptized.

19So when he had received food, he was strengthened. Then Saul spent some days with the disciples at Damascus.

Saul Preaches Christ

20Immediately he preached the Christ in the synagogues, that He is the Son of God.

21Then all who heard were amazed, and said, "Is this not he who destroyed those who called on this name in Jerusalem, and has come here for that purpose, so that he might bring them bound to the chief priests?"

22But Saul increased all the more in strength, and confounded the Jews who dwelt in Damascus, proving that this *Jesus* is the Christ.

Saul Escapes Death

23Now after many days were past, the Jews plotted to kill him. 24But their plot became known to Saul. And they watched the gates day and night, to kill him. 25Then the disciples took him by night and let *him* down through the wall in a large basket.

Saul at Jerusalem

26And when Saul had come to Jerusalem, he tried to join the disciples; but they were all afraid of him, and did not believe that he was a disciple. 27But Barnabas took him and brought *him* to the apostles. And he declared to them how he had seen the Lord on the road, and that He had spoken to him, and how he had preached boldly at Damascus in the name of Jesus. 28So he was with them at Jerusalem, coming in and going out. 29And he spoke boldly in the name of the Lord Jesus and disputed against the Hellenists, but they attempted to kill him. 30When the brethren found out, they brought him down to Caesarea and sent him out to Tarsus.

The Church Prospers

31Then the churches throughout all Judea, Galilee, and Samaria had peace and were edified. And walking in the fear of the Lord and in the comfort of the Holy Spirit, they were multiplied.

Aeneas Healed

32Now it came to pass, as Peter went through all *parts of the country*, that he also came down to the saints who dwelt in Lydda. 33There he found a certain man named Aeneas, who had been bedridden eight years and was paralyzed. 34And Peter said to him, "Aeneas, Jesus the Christ heals you. Arise and make your bed." Then he arose immediately. 35So all who dwelt at Lydda and Sharon saw him and turned to the Lord.

Dorcas Restored to Life

36At Joppa there was a certain disciple named Tabitha, which is translated Dorcas. This woman was full of good works and charitable deeds which she did. 37But it happened in those days that she became sick and died. When they had washed her, they laid *her* in an upper room. 38And since Lydda was near Joppa, and the disciples had heard that Peter was there, they sent two men to him, imploring *him* not to delay in coming to them. 39Then Peter arose and went with them. When he had come, they brought *him* to the upper room. And all the widows stood by him weeping, showing the tunics and garments which Dorcas had made while she was with them. 40But Peter put them all out, and knelt down and prayed. And turning to the body he said, "Tabitha, arise." And she opened her eyes, and when she saw Peter she sat up. 41Then he gave her *his* hand and lifted her up; and when he had called the saints and widows, he presented her alive. 42And it became known throughout all Joppa, and many believed on the Lord. 43So it was that he stayed many days in Joppa with Simon, a tanner.

Cornelius Sends a Delegation

10 There was a certain man in Caesarea called Cornelius, a centurion of what was called the Italian Regiment, 2a devout *man* and one who feared God with all his household, who gave alms generously to the people, and prayed to God always. 3About the ninth hour of the day he saw clearly in a vision an angel of God coming in and saying to him, "Cornelius!"

4And when he observed him, he was afraid, and said, "What is it, lord?"

So he said to him, "Your prayers and your alms have come up for a memorial before God. 5Now send men to Joppa, and send for Simon whose surname is Peter. 6He is lodging with Simon, a tanner, whose house is by the sea. He will tell you what you must do." 7And when the angel who spoke to him had departed, Cornelius called two of his household servants and a devout soldier from among those who waited on him continually. 8So when he had explained all *these* things to them, he sent them to Joppa.

Peter's Vision

9The next day, as they went on their journey and drew near the city, Peter went up on the housetop to pray, about the sixth hour. 10Then he became very hungry and wanted to eat; but while they made ready, he fell into a trance 11and saw heaven opened and an object like a great sheet bound at the four corners, descending to him and let down to the earth. 12In it were all kinds of four-footed animals of the earth, wild beasts, creeping things, and birds of the air. 13And a voice came to him, "Rise, Peter; kill and eat."

14But Peter said, "Not so, Lord! For I have never eaten anything common or unclean."

15And a voice *spoke* to him again the second time, "What God has cleansed you must not call common." 16This was done three times. And the object was taken up into heaven again.

Summoned to Caesarea

17Now while Peter wondered within himself what this vision which he had seen meant, behold, the men who had been sent from Cornelius had made inquiry for Simon's house, and stood before the gate. 18And they called and asked whether Simon, whose surname was Peter, was lodging there.

19While Peter thought about the vision, the Spirit said to him, "Behold, three men are seeking you. 20Arise therefore, go down and go with them, doubting nothing; for I have sent them."

21Then Peter went down to the men who had been sent to him from Cornelius, and said, "Yes, I am he whom you seek. For what reason have you come?"

22And they said, "Cornelius *the* centurion, a just man, one who fears God and has a good reputation among all the nation of the Jews, was divinely instructed by a holy angel to summon you to his house, and to hear words from you." 23Then he invited them in and lodged *them.*

On the next day Peter went away with them, and some brethren from Joppa accompanied him.

Peter Meets Cornelius

24And the following day they entered Caesarea. Now Cornelius was waiting for them, and had called together his relatives and close friends. 25As Peter was coming in, Cornelius met him and fell down at his feet and worshiped *him.*

26But Peter lifted him up, saying, "Stand up; I myself am also a man." 27And as he talked with him, he went in and found many who had come together. 28Then he said to them, "You know how unlawful it is for a Jewish man to keep company with or go to one of another nation. But God has shown me that I should not call any man common or unclean. 29Therefore I came without objection as soon as I was sent for. I ask, then, for what reason have you sent for me?"

30So Cornelius said, "Four days ago I was fasting until this hour; and at the ninth hour I prayed in my house, and behold, a man stood before me in bright clothing, 31and said, 'Cornelius, your prayer has been heard, and your alms are remembered in the sight of God. 32Send therefore to Joppa and call Simon here, whose surname is Peter. He is lodging in the house of Simon, a tanner, by the sea. When he comes, he will speak to you.' 33So I sent to you immediately, and you have done well to come. Now therefore, we are all present before God, to hear all the things commanded you by God."

Preaching to Cornelius's Household

34Then Peter opened *his* mouth and said: "In truth I perceive that God shows no partiality. 35But in every nation whoever fears Him and works righteousness is accepted by Him. 36The word which *God* sent to the children of Israel, preaching peace through Jesus Christ—He is Lord of all—37that word you know, which was proclaimed throughout all Judea, and began from Galilee after the baptism which John preached: 38how God anointed Jesus of Nazareth with the Holy Spirit and with power, who went about doing good and healing all who were oppressed by the devil, for God was with Him. 39And we are witnesses of all things which He did both in the land of the Jews and in Jerusalem, whom they killed by hanging on a tree. 40Him God raised up on the third day, and showed Him openly, 41not to all the people, but to witnesses chosen before by God, *even* to us who ate and drank with Him after He arose from the dead. 42And He commanded us to preach to the people, and to testify that it is He who was ordained by God *to be* Judge of the living and the dead. 43To Him all the prophets witness that, through His name, whoever believes in Him will receive remission of sins."

The Holy Spirit Falls on the Gentiles

44While Peter was still speaking these words, the Holy Spirit fell upon all those who heard the word. 45And those of the circumcision who believed were astonished, as many as came with Peter, because the gift of the Holy Spirit had been poured out on the Gentiles also. 46For they heard them speak with tongues and magnify God.

Then Peter answered, 47"Can anyone forbid water, that these should not be baptized who have received the Holy Spirit just as we *have?*" 48And he commanded them to be baptized in the name of the Lord. Then they asked him to stay a few days.

Peter Defends God's Grace

11 Now the apostles and brethren who were in Judea heard that the Gentiles had also received the word of God. 2And when Peter came up to Jerusalem, those of the circumcision contended with him, 3saying, "You went in to uncircumcised men and ate with them!"

4But Peter explained *it* to them in order from the beginning, saying: 5"I was in the city of Joppa praying; and in a trance I saw a vision, an object descending like a great sheet, let down from heaven by four corners; and it came to me. 6When I observed it intently and considered, I saw four-footed animals of the earth, wild beasts, creeping things, and birds of the air. 7And I heard a voice saying to me, 'Rise, Peter; kill and eat.' 8But I said, 'Not so, Lord! For nothing common or unclean has at any time entered my mouth.' 9But the voice answered me again from heaven, 'What God has cleansed you must not call common.' 10Now this was done three times, and all were drawn up again into heaven. 11At that very moment, three men stood before the house where I was, having been sent to me from Caesarea. 12Then the Spirit told me to go with

them, doubting nothing. Moreover these six brethren accompanied me, and we entered the man's house. 13And he told us how he had seen an angel standing in his house, who said to him, 'Send men to Joppa, and call for Simon whose surname is Peter, 14who will tell you words by which you and all your household will be saved.' 15And as I began to speak, the Holy Spirit fell upon them, as upon us at the beginning. 16Then I remembered the word of the Lord, how He said, 'John indeed baptized with water, but you shall be baptized with the Holy Spirit.' 17If therefore God gave them the same gift as *He gave* us when we believed on the Lord Jesus Christ, who was I that I could withstand God?"

18When they heard these things they became silent; and they glorified God, saying, "Then God has also granted to the Gentiles repentance to life."

Barnabas and Saul at Antioch

19Now those who were scattered after the persecution that arose over Stephen traveled as far as Phoenicia, Cyprus, and Antioch, preaching the word to no one but the Jews only. 20But some of them were men from Cyprus and Cyrene, who, when they had come to Antioch, spoke to the Hellenists, preaching the Lord Jesus. 21And the hand of the Lord was with them, and a great number believed and turned to the Lord.

22Then news of these things came to the ears of the church in Jerusalem, and they sent out Barnabas to go as far as Antioch. 23When he came and had seen the grace of God, he was glad, and encouraged them all that with purpose of heart they should continue with the Lord. 24For he was a good man, full of the Holy Spirit and of faith. And a great many people were added to the Lord.

25Then Barnabas departed for Tarsus to seek Saul. 26And when he had found him, he brought him to Antioch. So it was that for a whole year they assembled with the church and taught a great many people. And the disciples were first called Christians in Antioch.

Relief to Judea

27And in these days prophets came from Jerusalem to Antioch. 28Then one of them, named Agabus, stood up and showed by the Spirit that there was going to be a great famine throughout all the world, which also happened in the days of Claudius Caesar. 29Then the disciples, each according to his ability, determined to send relief to the brethren dwelling in Judea. 30This they also did, and sent it to the elders by the hands of Barnabas and Saul.

Herod's Violence to the Church

12 Now about that time Herod the king stretched out *his* hand to harass some from the church. 2Then he killed James the brother of John with the sword. 3And because he saw that it pleased the Jews, he proceeded further to seize Peter also. Now it was *during* the Days of Unleavened Bread. 4So when he had arrested him, he put *him* in prison, and delivered *him* to four squads of soldiers to keep him, intending to bring him before the people after Passover.

Peter Freed from Prison

5Peter was therefore kept in prison, but constant prayer was offered to God for him by the church. 6And when Herod was about to bring him out, that night Peter was sleeping, bound with two chains between two soldiers; and the guards before the door were keeping the prison. 7Now behold, an angel of the Lord stood by *him*, and a light shone in the prison; and he struck Peter on the side and raised him up, saying, "Arise quickly!" And his chains fell off *his* hands. 8Then the angel said to him, "Gird yourself and tie on your sandals"; and so he did. And he said to him, "Put on your garment and follow me." 9So he went out and followed him, and did not know that what was done by the angel was real, but thought he was seeing a vision. 10When they were past the first and the second guard posts, they came to the iron gate that leads to the city, which opened to them of its own accord; and they went out and went down one street , and immediately the angel departed from him.

11And when Peter had come to himself, he said, "Now I know for certain that the Lord has sent His angel, and has delivered me from the hand of Herod and *from* all the expectation of the Jewish people."

12So, when he had considered *this*, he came to the house of Mary, the mother of John whose surname was Mark, where many were gathered together praying. 13And as Peter knocked at the door of the gate, a girl named Rhoda came to answer. 14When she recognized Peter's voice, because of *her* gladness she did not open the gate, but ran in and announced that Peter stood before the gate. 15But they said to her, "You are beside yourself!" Yet she kept insisting that it was so. So they said, "It is his angel."

16Now Peter continued knocking; and when they opened *the door* and saw him, they were astonished. 17But motioning to them with his hand to keep silent, he declared to them how the Lord had brought him out of the prison. And he said, "Go, tell these things to James and to the brethren." And he departed and went to another place.

18Then, as soon as it was day, there was no small stir among the soldiers about what had become of Peter. 19But when Herod had searched for him and not found him, he examined the guards and commanded that *they* should be put to death.

And he went down from Judea to Caesarea, and stayed *there*.

Herod's Violent Death

20Now Herod had been very angry with the people of Tyre and Sidon; but they came to him with one accord, and having made Blastus the king's personal aide their friend, they asked for peace, because their country was supplied with food by the king's *country*. 21So on a set day Herod, arrayed in royal apparel, sat on his throne and gave an oration to them. 22And the people kept shouting, "The voice of a god and not of a man!" 23Then immediately an angel of the Lord struck him, because he did not give glory to God. And he was eaten by worms and died. 24But the word of God grew and multiplied.

Barnabas and Saul Appointed

25And Barnabas and Saul returned from Jerusalem when they had fulfilled *their* ministry, and they also took with them John whose surname was Mark.

13 Now in the church that was at Antioch there were certain prophets and teachers: Barnabas, Simeon who was called Niger, Lucius of Cyrene, Manaen who had been brought up with Herod the tetrarch, and Saul. 2As they ministered to the Lord and fasted, the Holy Spirit said, "Now separate to Me Barnabas and Saul for the work to which I have called them." 3Then, having fasted and prayed, and laid hands on them, they sent *them* away.

Preaching in Cyprus

4So, being sent out by the Holy Spirit, they went down to Seleucia, and from there they sailed to Cyprus. 5And when they arrived in Salamis, they preached the word of God in the synagogues of the Jews. They also had John as *their* assistant.

6Now when they had gone through the island to Paphos, they found a certain sorcerer, a false prophet, a Jew whose name *was* Bar-Jesus, 7who was with the proconsul, Sergius Paulus, an intelligent man. This man called for Barnabas and Saul and sought to hear the word of God. 8But Elymas the sorcerer (for so his name is translated) withstood them, seeking to turn the proconsul away from the faith. 9Then Saul, who also *is called* Paul, filled with the Holy Spirit, looked intently at him 10and said, "O full of all deceit and all fraud, *you* son of the devil, *you* enemy of all righteousness, will you not cease perverting the straight ways of the Lord? 11And now, indeed, the hand of the Lord *is* upon you, and you shall be blind, not seeing the sun for a time."

And immediately a dark mist fell on him, and he went around seeking someone to lead him by the hand. 12Then the proconsul believed, when he saw what had been done, being astonished at the teaching of the Lord.

At Antioch in Pisidia

13Now when Paul and his party set sail from Paphos, they came to Perga in Pamphylia; and John, departing from them, returned to Jerusalem. 14But when they departed from Perga, they came to Antioch in Pisidia, and went into the synagogue on the Sabbath day and sat down. 15And after the reading of the Law and the Prophets, the rulers of the synagogue sent to them, saying, "Men *and* brethren, if you have any word of exhortation for the people, say on."

16Then Paul stood up, and motioning with *his* hand said, "Men of Israel, and you who fear God, listen: 17The God of this people Israel chose our fathers, and exalted the people when they dwelt as strangers in the land of Egypt, and with an uplifted arm He brought them out of it. 18Now for a time of about forty years He put up with their ways in the wilderness. 19And when He had destroyed seven nations in the land of Canaan, He distributed their land to them by allotment.

20"After that He gave *them* judges for about four hundred and fifty years, until Samuel the prophet. 21And afterward they asked for a king; so God gave them Saul the son of Kish, a man of the tribe of Benjamin, for forty years. 22And when He had removed him, He raised up for them David as king, to whom also He gave testimony and said, 'I have found David[w] the *son* of Jesse, a man after My *own* heart, who will do all My will.'[x] 23From this man's seed, according to *the* promise, God raised up for Israel a Savior—Jesus—24after John had first preached, before His coming, the baptism of repentance to all the people of Israel. 25And as John was finishing his course, he said, 'Who do you think I am? I am not *He*. But behold, there comes One after me, the sandals of whose feet I am not worthy to loose.'

26"Men *and* brethren, sons of the family of Abraham, and those among you who fear God, to you the word of this salvation has been sent. 27For those who dwell in Jerusalem, and their rulers, because they did not know Him,

---

w Psalm 89.20   x 1 Samuel 13.14

nor even the voices of the Prophets which are read every Sabbath, have fulfilled *them* in condemning *Him.* 28And though they found no cause for death *in Him,* they asked Pilate that He should be put to death. 29Now when they had fulfilled all that was written concerning Him, they took *Him* down from the tree and laid *Him* in a tomb. 30But God raised Him from the dead. 31He was seen for many days by those who came up with Him from Galilee to Jerusalem, who are His witnesses to the people. 32And we declare to you glad tidings—that promise which was made to the fathers. 33God has fulfilled this for us their children, in that He has raised up Jesus. As it is also written in the second Psalm:

'You are My Son,
  Today I have begotten You.'[y]

34And that He raised Him from the dead, no more to return to corruption, He has spoken thus:

'I will give you the sure mercies of David.'[z]

35Therefore He also says in another *Psalm:*

'You will not allow Your Holy One to see corruption.'[a]

36"For David, after he had served his own generation by the will of God, fell asleep, was buried with his fathers, and saw corruption; 37but He whom God raised up saw no corruption. 38Therefore let it be known to you, brethren, that through this Man is preached to you the forgiveness of sins; 39and by Him everyone who believes is justified from all things from which you could not be justified by the law of Moses. 40Beware therefore, lest what has been spoken in the prophets come upon you:

41 'Behold, you despisers,
  Marvel and perish!
  For I work a work in your days,
  A work which you will by no means believe,
  Though one were to declare it to you.'"[b]

Blessing and Conflict at Antioch

42So when the Jews went out of the synagogue, the Gentiles begged that these words might be preached to them the next Sabbath. 43Now when the congregation had broken up, many of the Jews and devout proselytes followed Paul and Barnabas, who, speaking to them, persuaded them to continue in the grace of God.

44On the next Sabbath almost the whole city came together to hear the word of God. 45But when the Jews saw the multitudes, they were filled with envy; and contradicting and blaspheming, they opposed the things spoken by Paul. 46Then Paul and Barnabas grew bold and said, "It was necessary that the word of God should be spoken to you first; but since you reject it, and judge yourselves unworthy of everlasting life, behold, we turn to the Gentiles. 47For so the Lord has commanded us:

'I have set you as a light to the Gentiles,
  That you should be for salvation to the ends of the earth.'"[c]

48Now when the Gentiles heard this, they were glad and glorified the word of the Lord. And as many as had been appointed to eternal life believed. 49And the word of the Lord was being spread throughout all the region. 50But the Jews stirred up the devout and prominent women and the chief men of the city, raised up persecution against Paul and Barnabas, and expelled them from their region. 51But they shook off the dust from their feet against them, and came to Iconium. 52And the disciples were filled with joy and with the Holy Spirit.

At Iconium

14 Now it happened in Iconium that they went together to the synagogue of the Jews, and so spoke that a great multitude both of the Jews and of the Greeks believed. 2But the unbelieving Jews stirred up the Gentiles and poisoned their minds against the brethren. 3Therefore they stayed there a long time, speaking boldly in the Lord, who was bearing witness to the word of His grace, granting signs and wonders to be done by their hands.

4But the multitude of the city was

y Psalm 2.7   z Isaiah 55.3   a Psalm 16.10   b Habakkuk 1.5   c Isaiah 49.6

divided: part sided with the Jews, and part with the apostles. 5And when a violent attempt was made by both the Gentiles and Jews, with their rulers, to abuse and stone them, 6they became aware of it and fled to Lystra and Derbe, cities of Lycaonia, and to the surrounding region. 7And they were preaching the gospel there.

Idolatry at Lystra

8And in Lystra a certain man without strength in his feet was sitting, a cripple from his mother's womb, who had never walked. 9This man heard Paul speaking. Paul, observing him intently and seeing that he had faith to be healed, 10said with a loud voice, "Stand up straight on your feet!" And he leaped and walked. 11Now when the people saw what Paul had done, they raised their voices, saying in the Lycaonian *language*, "The gods have come down to us in the likeness of men!" 12And Barnabas they called Zeus, and Paul, Hermes, because he was the chief speaker. 13Then the priest of Zeus, whose temple was in front of their city, brought oxen and garlands to the gates, intending to sacrifice with the multitudes.

14But when the apostles Barnabas and Paul heard this, they tore their clothes and ran in among the multitude, crying out 15and saying, "Men, why are you doing these things? We also are men with the same nature as you, and preach to you that you should turn from these useless things to the living God, who made the heaven, the earth, the sea, and all things that are in them, 16who in bygone generations allowed all nations to walk in their own ways. 17Nevertheless He did not leave Himself without witness, in that He did good, gave us rain from heaven and fruitful seasons, filling our hearts with food and gladness." 18And with these sayings they could scarcely restrain the multitudes from sacrificing to them.

Stoning, Escape to Derbe

19Then Jews from Antioch and Iconium came there; and having persuaded the multitudes, they stoned Paul *and* dragged *him* out of the city, supposing him to be dead. 20However, when

the disciples gathered around him, he rose up and went into the city. And the next day he departed with Barnabas to Derbe.

Strengthening the Converts

21And when they had preached the gospel to that city and made many disciples, they returned to Lystra, Iconium, and Antioch, 22strengthening the souls of the disciples, exhorting *them* to continue in the faith, and *saying*, "We must through many tribulations enter the kingdom of God." 23So when they had appointed elders in every church, and prayed with fasting, they commended them to the Lord in whom they had believed. 24And after they had passed through Pisidia, they came to Pamphylia. 25Now when they had preached the word in Perga, they went down to Attalia. 26From there they sailed to Antioch, where they had been commended to the grace of God for the work which they had completed.

27Now when they had come and gathered the church together, they reported all that God had done with them, and that He had opened the door of faith to the Gentiles. 28So they stayed there a long time with the disciples.

Conflict over Circumcision

15 And certain *men* came down from Judea and taught the brethren, "Unless you are circumcised according to the custom of Moses, you cannot be saved." 2Therefore, when Paul and Barnabas had no small dissension and dispute with them, they determined that Paul and Barnabas and certain others of them should go up to Jerusalem, to the apostles and elders, about this question.

3So, being sent on their way by the church, they passed through Phoenicia and Samaria, describing the conversion of the Gentiles; and they caused great joy to all the brethren. 4And when they had come to Jerusalem, they were received by the church and the apostles and the elders; and they reported all things that God had done with them. 5But some of the sect of the Pharisees who believed rose up, saying, "It is necessary to circumcise them, and to command *them* to keep the law of Moses."

The Jerusalem Council

6Now the apostles and elders came together to consider this matter. **7**And when there had been much dispute, Peter rose up and said to them: "Men and brethren, you know that a good while ago God chose among us, that by my mouth the Gentiles should hear the word of the gospel and believe. **8**So God, who knows the heart, acknowledged them by giving them the Holy Spirit, just as *He did* to us, **9**and made no distinction between us and them, purifying their hearts by faith. **10**Now therefore, why do you test God by putting a yoke on the neck of the disciples which neither our fathers nor we were able to bear? **11**But we believe that through the grace of the Lord Jesus Christ we shall be saved in the same manner as they."

12Then all the multitude kept silent and listened to Barnabas and Paul declaring how many miracles and wonders God had worked through them among the Gentiles. **13**And after they had become silent, James answered, saying, "Men *and* brethren, listen to me: **14**Simon has declared how God at the first visited the Gentiles to take out of them a people for His name. **15**And with this the words of the prophets agree, just as it is written:

16 'After this I will return
    And will rebuild the tabernacle of
        David, which has fallen down;
    I will rebuild its ruins,
    And I will set it up;
17 So that the rest of mankind may
        seek the LORD,
    Even all the Gentiles who are called
        by My name,
    Says the LORD who does all these
        things.'*d*

18"Known to God from eternity are all His works. **19**Therefore I judge that we should not trouble those from among the Gentiles who are turning to God, **20**but that we write to them to abstain from things polluted by idols, *from* sexual immorality, *from* things strangled, and *from* blood. **21**For Moses has had throughout many generations those who preach him in every city, being read in the synagogues every Sabbath."

The Jerusalem Decree

22Then it pleased the apostles and elders, with the whole church, to send chosen men of their own company to Antioch with Paul and Barnabas, *namely*, Judas who was also named Barsabas, and Silas, leading men among the brethren.

23They wrote this, *letter* by them:

The apostles, the elders, and the brethren,

To the brethren who are of the Gentiles in Antioch, Syria, and Cilicia:

Greetings.

24   Since we have heard that some who went out from us have troubled you with words, unsettling your souls, saying, "*You must* be circumcised and keep the law"—to whom we gave no *such* commandment— **25**it seemed good to us, being assembled with one accord, to send chosen men to you with our beloved Barnabas and Paul, **26**men who have risked their lives for the name of our Lord Jesus Christ. **27**We have therefore sent Judas and Silas, who will also report the same things by word of mouth. **28**For it seemed good to the Holy Spirit, and to us, to lay upon you no greater burden than these necessary things: **29**that you abstain from things offered to idols, from blood, from things strangled, and from sexual immorality. If you keep yourselves from these, you will do well.

Farewell.

Continuing Ministry in Syria

30So when they were sent off, they came to Antioch; and when they had gathered the multitude together, they delivered the letter. **31**When they had

d Amos 9.11, 12

read it, they rejoiced over its encouragement. 32Now Judas and Silas, themselves being prophets also, exhorted and strengthened the brethren with many words. 33And after they had stayed *there* for a time, they were sent back with greetings from the brethren to the apostles.

34However, it seemed good to Silas to remain there. 35Paul and Barnabas also remained in Antioch, teaching and preaching the word of the Lord, with many others also.

Division over John Mark

36Then after some days Paul said to Barnabas, "Let us now go back and visit our brethren in every city where we have preached the word of the Lord, *and see* how they are doing." 37Now Barnabas was determined to take with them John called Mark. 38But Paul insisted that they should not take with them the one who had departed from them in Pamphylia, and had not gone with them to the work. 39Then the contention became so sharp that they parted from one another. And so Barnabas took Mark and sailed to Cyprus; 40but Paul chose Silas and departed, being commended by the brethren to the grace of God. 41And he went through Syria and Cilicia, strengthening the churches.

Timothy Joins Paul and Silas

16 Then he came to Derbe and Lystra. And behold, a certain disciple was there, named Timothy, *the* son of a certain Jewish woman who believed, but his father *was* Greek. 2He was well spoken of by the brethren who were at Lystra and Iconium. 3Paul wanted to have him go on with him. And he took *him* and circumcised him because of the Jews who were in that region, for they all knew that his father was Greek. 4And as they went through the cities, they delivered to them the decrees to keep, which were determined by the apostles and elders at Jerusalem. 5So the churches were strengthened in the faith, and increased in number daily.

The Macedonian Call

6Now when they had gone through Phrygia and the region of Galatia, they were forbidden by the Holy Spirit to preach the word in Asia. 7After they had come to Mysia, they tried to go into Bithynia, but the Spirit did not permit them. 8So passing by Mysia, they came down to Troas. 9And a vision appeared to Paul in the night. A man of Macedonia stood and pleaded with him, saying, "Come over to Macedonia and help us." 10Now after he had seen the vision, immediately we sought to go to Macedonia, concluding that the Lord had called us to preach the gospel to them.

Lydia Baptized at Philippi

11Therefore, sailing from Troas, we ran a straight course to Samothrace, and the next *day* came to Neapolis, 12and from there to Philippi, which is the foremost city of that part of Macedonia, a colony. And we were staying in that city for some days. 13And on the Sabbath day we went out of the city to the riverside, where prayer was customarily made; and we sat down and spoke to the women who met *there*. 14Now a certain woman named Lydia heard *us*. She was a seller of purple from the city of Thyatira, who worshiped God. The Lord opened her heart to heed the things spoken by Paul. 15And when she and her household were baptized, she begged *us*, saying, "If you have judged me to be faithful to the Lord, come to my house and stay." So she persuaded us.

Paul and Silas Imprisoned

16Now it happened, as we went to prayer, that a certain slave girl possessed with a spirit of divination met us, who brought her masters much profit by fortune-telling. 17This girl followed Paul and us, and cried out, saying, "These men are the servants of the Most High God, who proclaim to us the way of salvation." 18And this she did for many days.

But Paul, greatly annoyed, turned and said to the spirit, "I command you in the name of Jesus Christ to come out of her." And he came out that very hour. 19But when her masters saw that their hope of profit was gone, they seized Paul and Silas and dragged *them* into the marketplace to the authorities. 20And they brought them to the magistrates, and said, "These men, being Jews, exceedingly trouble our city; 21and they teach customs which are not lawful for us, being Romans, to receive or observe." 22Then the multitude rose up together against them; and the magistrates tore off their clothes and commanded *them* to be beaten with rods. 23And when they had laid many stripes on them, they threw *them* into prison, commanding the jailer to keep them securely. 24Having received such a charge, he put them into the inner prison and fastened their feet in the stocks.

The Philippian Jailer Saved

25But at midnight Paul and Silas were praying and singing hymns to God, and the prisoners were listening to them. 26Suddenly there was a great earthquake, so that the foundations of the prison were shaken; and immediately all the doors were opened and everyone's chains were loosed. 27And the keeper of the prison, awaking from sleep and seeing the prison doors open, supposing the prisoners had fled, drew his sword and was about to kill himself. 28But Paul called with a loud voice, saying, "Do yourself no harm, for we are all here."

29Then he called for a light, ran in, and fell down trembling before Paul and Silas. 30And he brought them out and said, "Sirs, what must I do to be saved?"

31So they said, "Believe on the Lord Jesus Christ, and you will be saved, you and your household." 32Then they spoke the word of the Lord to him and to all who were in his house. 33And he took them the same hour of the night and washed *their* stripes. And immediately he and all his family were baptized. 34Now when he had brought them into his house, he set food before them; and he rejoiced, having believed in God with all his household.

Paul Refuses to Depart Secretly

35And when it was day, the magistrates sent the officers, saying, "Let those men go."

36So the keeper of the prison reported these words to Paul, saying, "The mag-

istrates have sent to let you go. Now therefore depart, and go in peace."

37But Paul said to them, "They have beaten us openly, uncondemned Romans, *and* have thrown *us* into prison. And now do they put us out secretly? No indeed! Let them come themselves and get us out."

38And the officers told these words to the magistrates, and they were afraid when they heard that they were Romans. 39Then they came and pleaded with them and brought *them* out, and asked *them* to depart from the city. 40So they went out of the prison and entered *the house of* Lydia; and when they had seen the brethren, they encouraged them and departed.

Preaching Christ at Thessalonica

17 Now when they had passed through Amphipolis and Apollonia, they came to Thessalonica, where there was a synagogue of the Jews. 2Then Paul, as his custom was, went in to them, and for three Sabbaths reasoned with them from the Scriptures, 3explaining and demonstrating that the Christ had to suffer and rise again from the dead, and *saying*, "This Jesus whom I preach to you is the Christ." 4And some of them were persuaded; and a great multitude of the devout Greeks, and not a few of the leading women, joined Paul and Silas.

Assault on Jason's House

5But the Jews who were not persuaded, becoming envious, took some of the evil men from the marketplace, and gathering a mob, set all the city in an uproar and attacked the house of Jason, and sought to bring them out to the people. 6But when they did not find them, they dragged Jason and some brethren to the rulers of the city, crying out, "These who have turned the world upside down have come here too. 7Jason has harbored them, and these are all acting contrary to the decrees of Caesar, saying there is another king—Jesus." 8And they troubled the crowd and the rulers of the city when they heard these things. 9So when they had taken security from Jason and the rest, they let them go.

Ministering at Berea

10Then the brethren immediately sent Paul and Silas away by night to Berea. When they arrived, they went into the synagogue of the Jews. 11These were more fair-minded than those in Thessalonica, in that they received the word with all readiness, and searched the Scriptures daily *to find out* whether these things were so. 12Therefore many of them believed, and also not a few of the Greeks, prominent women as well as men. 13But when the Jews from Thessalonica learned that the word of God was preached by Paul at Berea, they came there also and stirred up the crowds. 14Then immediately the brethren sent Paul away, to go to the sea; but both Silas and Timothy remained there. 15So those who conducted Paul brought him to Athens; and receiving a command for Silas and Timothy to come to him with all speed, they departed.

The Philosophers at Athens

16Now while Paul waited for them at Athens, his spirit was provoked within him when he saw that the city was given over to idols. 17Therefore he reasoned in the synagogue with the Jews and with the *Gentile* worshipers, and in the marketplace daily with those who happened to be there. 18Then certain Epicurean and Stoic philosophers encountered him. And some said, "What does this babbler want to say?"

Others said, "He seems to be a proclaimer of foreign gods," because he preached to them Jesus and the resurrection.

19And they took him and brought him to the Areopagus, saying, "May we know what this new doctrine *is* of which you speak? 20For you are bringing some strange things to our ears. Therefore we want to know what these things mean." 21For all the Athenians and the foreigners who were there spent their time in nothing else but either to tell or to hear some new thing.

Addressing the Areopagus

22Then Paul stood in the midst of the Areopagus and said, "Men of Athens, I perceive that in all things you are very religious; 23for as I was passing through and considering the objects of your worship, I even found an altar with this inscription:

TO THE UNKNOWN GOD.

Therefore, the One whom you worship without knowing, Him I proclaim to you: 24God, who made the world and everything in it, since He is Lord of heaven and earth, does not dwell in temples made with hands. 25Nor is He worshiped with men's hands, as though He needed anything, since He gives to all life, breath, and all things. 26And He has made from one blood every nation of men to dwell on all the face of the earth, and has determined their preappointed times and the boundaries of their dwellings, 27so that they should seek the Lord, in the hope that they might grope for Him and find Him, though He is not far from each one of us; 28for in Him we live and move and have our being, as also some of your own poets have said, 'For we are also His offspring.' 29Therefore, since we are the offspring of God, we ought not to think that the Divine Nature is like gold or silver or stone, something shaped by art and man's devising. 30Truly, these times of ignorance God overlooked, but now commands all men everywhere to repent, 31because He has appointed a day on which He will judge the world in righteousness by the Man whom He has ordained. He has given assurance of this to all by raising Him from the dead."

32And when they heard of the resurrection of the dead, some mocked, while others said, "We will hear you again on this *matter.*" 33So Paul departed from among them. 34However, some men joined him and believed, among them Dionysius the Areopagite, a woman named Damaris, and others with them.

Ministering at Corinth

18 After these things Paul departed from Athens and went to Corinth. 2And he found a certain Jew named Aquila, born in Pontus, who had recently come from Italy with his wife Priscilla (because Claudius had commanded all the Jews to depart from

Rome); and he came to them. 3So, because he was of the same trade, he stayed with them and worked; for by occupation they were tentmakers. 4And he reasoned in the synagogue every Sabbath, and persuaded both Jews and Greeks.

5When Silas and Timothy had come from Macedonia, Paul was compelled by the Spirit, and testified to the Jews *that* Jesus *is* the Christ. 6But when they opposed him and blasphemed, he shook *his* garments and said to them, "Your blood *be* upon your *own* heads; I *am* clean. From now on I will go to the Gentiles." 7And he departed from there and entered the house of a certain *man* named Justus, *one* who worshiped God, whose house was next door to the synagogue. 8Then Crispus, the ruler of the synagogue, believed on the Lord with all his household. And many of the Corinthians, hearing, believed and were baptized.

9Now the Lord spoke to Paul in the night by a vision, "Do not be afraid, but speak, and do not keep silent; 10for I am with you, and no one will attack you to hurt you; for I have many people in this city." 11And he continued *there* a year and six months, teaching the word of God among them.

12When Gallio was proconsul of Achaia, the Jews with one accord rose up against Paul and brought him to the judgment seat, 13saying, "This *fellow* persuades men to worship God contrary to the law."

14And when Paul was about to open *his* mouth, Gallio said to the Jews, "If it were a matter of wrongdoing or wicked crimes, O Jews, there would be reason why I should bear with you. 15But if it *is* a question of words and names and your own law, look *to it* yourselves; for I do not want to be a judge of such *matters*." 16And he drove them from the judgment seat. 17Then all the Greeks took Sosthenes, the ruler of the synagogue, and beat *him* before the judgment seat. But Gallio took no notice of these things.

Paul Returns to Antioch

18So Paul still remained a good while. Then he took leave of the brethren and sailed for Syria, and Priscilla and

Aquila *were* with him. He had *his* hair cut off at Cenchrea, for he had taken a vow. 19And he came to Ephesus, and left them there; but he himself entered the synagogue and reasoned with the Jews. 20When they asked *him* to stay a longer time with them, he did not consent, 21but took leave of them, saying, "I must by all means keep this coming feast in Jerusalem; but I will return again to you, God willing." And he sailed from Ephesus.

22And when he had landed at Caesarea, and gone up and greeted the church, he went down to Antioch. 23After he had spent some time *there*, he departed and went over the region of Galatia and Phrygia in order, strengthening all the disciples.

Ministry of Apollos

24Now a certain Jew named Apollos, born at Alexandria, an eloquent man *and* mighty in the Scriptures, came to Ephesus. 25This man had been instructed in the way of the Lord; and being fervent in spirit, he spoke and taught accurately the things of the Lord, though he knew only the baptism of John. 26So he began to speak boldly in the synagogue. When Aquila and Priscilla heard him, they took him aside and explained to him the way of God more accurately. 27And when he desired to cross to Achaia, the brethren wrote, exhorting the disciples to receive him; and when he arrived, he greatly helped those who had believed through grace; 28for he vigorously refuted the Jews publicly, showing from the Scriptures that Jesus is the Christ.

Paul at Ephesus

19 And it happened, while Apollos was at Corinth, that Paul, having passed through the upper regions, came to Ephesus. And finding some disciples 2he said to them, "Did you receive the Holy Spirit when you believed?"

So they said to him, "We have not so much as heard whether there is a Holy Spirit."

3And he said to them, "Into what then were you baptized?"

So they said, "Into John's baptism."

4Then Paul said, "John indeed baptized with a baptism of repentance, saying to the people that they should believe on Him who would come after him, that is, on Christ Jesus."

5When they heard *this*, they were baptized in the name of the Lord Jesus. 6And when Paul had laid hands on them, the Holy Spirit came upon them, and they spoke with tongues and prophesied. 7Now the men were about twelve in all.

8And he went into the synagogue and spoke boldly for three months, reasoning and persuading concerning the things of the kingdom of God. 9But when some were hardened and did not believe, but spoke evil of the Way before the multitude, he departed from them and withdrew the disciples, reasoning daily in the school of Tyrannus. 10And this continued for two years, so that all who dwelt in Asia heard the word of the Lord Jesus, both Jews and Greeks.

Miracles Glorify Christ

11Now God worked unusual miracles by the hands of Paul, 12so that even handkerchiefs or aprons were brought from his body to the sick, and the diseases left them and the evil spirits went out of them. 13Then some of the itinerant Jewish exorcists took it upon themselves to call the name of the Lord Jesus over those who had evil spirits, saying, "We exorcise you by the Jesus whom Paul preaches." 14Also there were seven sons of Sceva, a Jewish chief priest, who did so.

15And the evil spirit answered and said, "Jesus I know, and Paul I know; but who are you?"

16Then the man in whom the evil spirit was leaped on them, overpowered them, and prevailed against them, so that they fled out of that house naked and wounded. 17This became known both to all Jews and Greeks dwelling in Ephesus; and fear fell on them all, and the name of the Lord Jesus was magnified. 18And many who had believed came confessing and telling their deeds. 19Also, many of those who had practiced magic brought their books together and burned *them* in the sight of all. And they counted up the value of them, and *it* totaled fifty thousand

pieces of silver. 20So the word of the Lord grew mightily and prevailed.

The Riot at Ephesus

21When these things were accomplished, Paul purposed in the Spirit, when he had passed through Macedonia and Achaia, to go to Jerusalem, saying, "After I have been there, I must also see Rome." 22So he sent into Macedonia two of those who ministered to him, Timothy and Erastus, but he himself stayed in Asia for a time.

23And about that time there arose a great commotion about the Way. 24For a certain man named Demetrius, a silversmith, who made silver shrines of Diana, brought no small profit to the craftsmen. 25He called them together with the workers of similar occupation, and said: "Men, you know that we have our prosperity by this trade. 26Moreover you see and hear that not only at Ephesus, but throughout almost all Asia, this Paul has persuaded and turned away many people, saying that they are not gods which are made with hands. 27So not only is this trade of ours in danger of falling into disrepute, but also the temple of the great goddess Diana may be despised and her magnificence destroyed, whom all Asia and the world worship."

28Now when they heard *this*, they were full of wrath and cried out, saying, "Great *is* Diana of the Ephesians!" 29So the whole city was filled with confusion, and rushed into the theater with one accord, having seized Gaius and Aristarchus, Macedonians, Paul's travel companions. 30And when Paul wanted to go in to the people, the disciples would not allow him. 31Then some of the officials of Asia, who were his friends, sent to him pleading that he would not venture into the theater. 32Some therefore cried one thing and some another, for the assembly was confused, and most of them did not know why they had come together. 33And they drew Alexander out of the multitude, the Jews putting him forward. And Alexander motioned with his hand, and wanted to make his defense to the people. 34But when they found out that he was a Jew, all with one voice cried out for about two hours, "Great *is* Diana of the Ephesians!"

35And when the city clerk had quieted the crowd, he said: "Men of Ephesus, what man is there who does not know that the city of the Ephesians is temple guardian of the great goddess Diana, and of the *image* which fell down from Zeus? 36Therefore, since these things cannot be denied, you ought to be quiet and do nothing rashly. 37For you have brought these men here who are neither robbers of temples nor blasphemers of your goddess. 38Therefore, if Demetrius and his fellow craftsmen have a case against anyone, the courts are open and there are proconsuls. Let them bring charges against one another. 39But if you have any other inquiry to make, it shall be determined in the lawful assembly. 40For we are in danger of being called in question for today's uproar, there being no reason which we may give to account for this disorderly gathering." 41And when he had said these things, he dismissed the assembly.

Journeys in Greece

20 After the uproar had ceased, Paul called the disciples to *himself*, embraced *them*, and departed to go to Macedonia. 2Now when he had gone over that region and encouraged them with many words, he came to Greece 3and stayed three months. And when the Jews plotted against him as he was about to sail to Syria, he decided to return through Macedonia. 4And Sopater of Berea accompanied him to Asia— also Aristarchus and Secundus of the Thessalonians, and Gaius of Derbe, and Timothy, and Tychicus and Trophimus of Asia. 5These men, going ahead, waited for us at Troas. 6But we sailed away from Philippi after the Days of Unleavened Bread, and in five days joined them at Troas, where we stayed seven days.

Ministering at Troas

7Now on the first *day* of the week, when the disciples came together to break bread, Paul, ready to depart the next day, spoke to them and continued his message until midnight. 8There were many lamps in the upper room where they were gathered together. 9And in a window sat a certain young man named Eutychus, who was sinking into a deep sleep. He was overcome by sleep; and as Paul continued speaking, he fell down from the third story and was taken up dead. 10But Paul went down, fell on him, and embracing *him* said, "Do not trouble yourselves, for his life is in him." 11Now when he had come up, had broken bread and eaten, and talked a long while, even till daybreak, he departed. 12And they brought the young man in alive, and they were not a little comforted.

From Troas to Miletus

13Then we went ahead to the ship and sailed to Assos, there intending to take Paul on board; for so he had given orders, intending himself to go on foot. 14And when he met us at Assos, we took him on board and came to Mitylene. 15We sailed from there, and the next *day* came opposite Chios. The following *day* we arrived at Samos and stayed at Trogyllium. The next *day* we came to Miletus. 16For Paul had decided to sail past Ephesus, so that he would not have to spend time in Asia; for he was hurrying to be at Jerusalem, if possible, on the Day of Pentecost.

The Ephesian Elders Exhorted

17From Miletus he sent to Ephesus and called for the elders of the church. 18And when they had come to him, he said to them: "You know, from the first day that I came to Asia, in what manner I always lived among you, 19serving the Lord with all humility, with many tears and trials which happened to me by the plotting of the Jews; 20how I kept back nothing that was helpful, but proclaimed it to you, and taught you publicly and from house to house, 21testifying to Jews, and also to Greeks, repentance toward God and faith toward our Lord Jesus Christ. 22And see, now I go bound in the spirit to Jerusalem, not knowing the things that will happen to me there, 23except that the Holy Spirit testifies in every city, saying that chains and tribulations await me. 24But none of these things move me; nor do I count my life dear to myself, so that I may finish my race with joy, and the ministry which I received from the Lord Jesus, to testify to the gospel of the grace of God.

25"And indeed, now I know that you all, among whom I have gone preaching the kingdom of God, will see my face no more. 26Therefore I testify to you this day that I *am* innocent of the blood of all *men.* 27For I have not shunned to declare to you the whole counsel of God. 28Therefore take heed to yourselves and to all the flock, among which the Holy Spirit has made you overseers, to shepherd the church of God which He purchased with His own blood. 29For I know this, that after my departure savage wolves will come in among you, not sparing the flock. 30Also from among yourselves men will rise up, speaking perverse things, to draw away the disciples after themselves. 31Therefore watch, and remember that for three years I did not cease to warn everyone night and day with tears.

32"So now, brethren, I commend you to God and to the word of His grace, which is able to build you up and give you an inheritance among all those who are sanctified. 33I have coveted no one's silver or gold or apparel. 34Yes, you yourselves know that these hands have provided for my necessities, and for those who were with me. 35I have shown you in every way, by laboring like this, that you must support the weak. And remember the words of the Lord Jesus, that He said, 'It is more blessed to give than to receive.' "

36And when he had said these things, he knelt down and prayed with them all. 37Then they all wept freely, and fell on Paul's neck and kissed him, 38sorrowing most of all for the words which he spoke, that they would see his face no more. And they accompanied him to the ship.

Warnings on the Journey to Jerusalem

21 Now it came to pass, that when we had departed from them and set sail, running a straight course we came to Cos, the following *day* to Rhodes, and from there to Patara. 2And finding a ship sailing over to Phoenicia, we went aboard and set sail. 3When we had sighted Cyprus, we passed it on the left, sailed to Syria, and landed at Tyre;

for there the ship was to unload her cargo. 4And finding disciples, we stayed there seven days. They told Paul through the Spirit not to go up to Jerusalem. 5When we had come to the end of those days, we departed and went on our way; and they all accompanied us, with wives and children, till *we were* out of the city. And we knelt down on the shore and prayed. 6When we had taken our leave of one another, we boarded the ship, and they returned home.

7And when we had finished *our* voyage from Tyre, we came to Ptolemais, greeted the brethren, and stayed with them one day. 8On the next *day* we who were Paul's companions departed and came to Caesarea, and entered the house of Philip the evangelist, who was *one* of the seven, and stayed with him. 9Now this man had four virgin daughters who prophesied. 10And as we stayed many days, a certain prophet named Agabus came down from Judea. 11When he had come to us, he took Paul's belt, bound his *own* hands and feet, and said, "Thus says the Holy Spirit, 'So shall the Jews at Jerusalem bind the man who owns this belt, and deliver *him* into the hands of the Gentiles.' "

12Now when we heard these things, both we and those from that place pleaded with him not to go up to Jerusalem. 13Then Paul answered, "What do you mean by weeping and breaking my heart? For I am ready not only to be bound, but also to die at Jerusalem for the name of the Lord Jesus."

14So when he would not be persuaded, we ceased, saying, "The will of the Lord be done."

Paul Urged to Make Peace

15And after those days we packed and went up to Jerusalem. 16Also some of the disciples from Caesarea went with us and brought with them a certain Mnason of Cyprus, an early disciple, with whom we were to lodge.

17And when we had come to Jerusalem, the brethren received us gladly. 18On the following *day* Paul went in with us to James, and all the elders were present. 19When he had greeted them, he told in detail those things which God had done among the Gentiles through his ministry. 20And when they heard *it*, they glorified the Lord. And they said to him, "You see, brother, how many myriads of Jews there are who have believed, and they are all zealous for the law; 21but they have been informed about you that you teach all the Jews who are among the Gentiles to forsake Moses, saying that they ought not to circumcise *their* children nor to walk according to the customs. 22What then? The assembly must certainly meet, for they will hear that you have come. 23Therefore do what we tell you: We have four men who have taken a vow. 24Take them and be purified with them, and pay their expenses so that they may shave *their* heads, and that all may know that those things of which they were informed concerning you are nothing, but *that* you yourself also walk orderly and keep the law. 25But concerning the Gentiles who believe, we have written *and* decided that they should observe no such thing, except that they should keep themselves from *things* offered to idols, from blood, from things strangled, and from sexual immorality."

Arrested in the Temple

26Then Paul took the men, and the next day, having been purified with them, entered the temple to announce the expiration of the days of purification, at which time an offering should be made for each one of them.

27Now when the seven days were almost ended, the Jews from Asia, seeing him in the temple, stirred up the whole crowd and laid hands on him, 28crying out, "Men of Israel, help! This is the man who teaches all *men* everywhere against the people, the law, and this place; and furthermore he also brought Greeks into the temple and has defiled this holy place." 29(For they had previously seen Trophimus the Ephesian with him in the city, whom they supposed that Paul had brought into the temple.)

30And all the city was disturbed; and the people ran together, seized Paul, and dragged him out of the temple; and immediately the doors were shut. 31Now as they were seeking to kill him,

news came to the commander of the garrison that all Jerusalem was in an uproar. 32He immediately took soldiers and centurions, and ran down to them. And when they saw the commander and the soldiers, they stopped beating Paul. 33Then the commander came near and took him, and commanded *him* to be bound with two chains; and he asked who he was and what he had done. 34And some among the multitude cried one thing and some another.

So when he could not ascertain the truth because of the tumult, he commanded him to be taken into the barracks. 35When he reached the stairs, he had to be carried by the soldiers because of the violence of the mob. 36For the multitude of the people followed after, crying out, "Away with him!"

Addressing the Jerusalem Mob

37Then as Paul was about to be led into the barracks, he said to the commander, "May I speak to you?"

He replied, "Can you speak Greek? 38Are you not the Egyptian who some time ago stirred up a rebellion and led the four thousand assassins out into the wilderness?"

39But Paul said, "I am a Jew from Tarsus, in Cilicia, a citizen of no mean city; and I implore you, permit me to speak to the people."

40So when he had given him permission, Paul stood on the stairs and motioned with his hand to the people. And when there was a great silence, he spoke to *them* in the Hebrew language, saying,

22 "Brethren and fathers, hear my defense before you now." 2And when they heard that he spoke to them in the Hebrew language, they kept all the more silent.

Then he said: 3"I am indeed a Jew, born in Tarsus of Cilicia, but brought up in this city at the feet of Gamaliel, taught according to the strictness of our fathers' law, and was zealous toward God as you all are today. 4I persecuted this Way to the death, binding and delivering into prisons both men and women, 5as also the high priest bears me witness, and all the council of the elders, from whom I also received letters to the brethren, and went to Damascus to bring in chains even those who were there to Jerusalem to be punished.

6"Now it happened, as I journeyed and came near Damascus at about noon, suddenly a great light from heaven shone around me. 7And I fell to the ground and heard a voice saying to me, 'Saul, Saul, why are you persecuting Me?' 8So I answered, 'Who are You, Lord?' And He said to me, 'I am Jesus of Nazareth, whom you are persecuting.'

9"And those who were with me indeed saw the light and were afraid, but they did not hear the voice of Him who spoke to me. 10So I said, 'What shall I do, Lord?' And the Lord said to me, 'Arise and go into Damascus, and there you will be told all things which are appointed for you to do.' 11And since I could not see for the glory of that light, being led by the hand of those who were with me, I came into Damascus.

12"Then a certain Ananias, a devout man according to the law, having a good testimony with all the Jews who dwelt there, 13came to me; and he stood and said to me, 'Brother Saul, receive your sight.' And at that same hour I looked up at him. 14Then he said, 'The God of our fathers has chosen you that you should know His will, and see the Just One, and hear the voice of His mouth. 15For you will be His witness to all men of what you have seen and heard. 16And now why are you waiting? Arise and be baptized, and wash away your sins, calling on the name of the Lord.'

17"Now it happened, when I returned to Jerusalem and was praying in the temple, that I was in a trance 18and saw Him saying to me, 'Make haste and get out of Jerusalem quickly, for they will not receive your testimony concerning Me.' 19So I said, 'Lord, they know that in every synagogue I imprisoned and beat those who believe on You. 20And when the blood of Your martyr Stephen was shed, I also was standing by consenting to his death, and guarding the clothes of those who were killing him.' 21Then He said to me, 'Depart, for I will send you far from here to the Gentiles.' "

Paul's Roman Citizenship

22And they listened to him until this word, and *then* they raised their voices and said, "Away with such a *fellow* from the earth, for he is not fit to live!" 23Then, as they cried out and tore off *their* clothes and threw dust into the air, 24the commander ordered him to be brought into the barracks, and said that he should be examined under scourging, so that he might know why they shouted so against him. 25And as they bound him with thongs, Paul said to the centurion who stood by, "Is it lawful for you to scourge a man who is a Roman, and uncondemned?"

26When the centurion heard *that,* he went and told the commander, saying, "Take care what you do, for this man is a Roman."

27Then the commander came and said to him, "Tell me, are you a Roman?"

He said, "Yes."

28The commander answered, "With a large sum I obtained this citizenship."

And Paul said, "But I was born *a citizen.*"

29Then immediately those who were about to examine him withdrew from him; and the commander was also afraid after he found out that he was a Roman, and because he had bound him.

The Sanhedrin Divided

30The next day, because he wanted to know for certain why he was accused by the Jews, he released him from *his* bonds, and commanded the chief priests and all their council to appear, and brought Paul down and set him before them.

23 Then Paul, looking earnestly at the council, said, "Men *and* brethren, I have lived in all good conscience before God until this day." 2And the high priest Ananias commanded those who stood by him to strike him on the mouth. 3Then Paul said to him, "God will strike you, *you* whitewashed wall! For you sit to judge me according to the law, and do you command me to be struck contrary to the law?"

4And those who stood by said, "Do you revile God's high priest?"

5Then Paul said, "I did not know, brethren, that he was the high priest; for it is written, 'You shall not speak evil of a ruler of your people.' "*e*

6But when Paul perceived that one part were Sadducees and the other Pharisees, he cried out in the council, "Men *and* brethren, I am a Pharisee, the son of a Pharisee; concerning the hope and resurrection of the dead I am being judged!"

7And when he had said this, a dissension arose between the Pharisees and the Sadducees; and the assembly was divided. 8For Sadducees say that there is no resurrection—and no angel or spirit; but the Pharisees confess both. 9Then there arose a loud outcry. And the scribes of the Pharisees' party arose and protested, saying, "We find no evil in this man; but if a spirit or an angel has spoken to him, let us not fight against God."

10Now when there arose a great dissension, the commander, fearing lest Paul might be pulled to pieces by them, commanded the soldiers to go down and take him by force from among them, and bring *him* into the barracks.

The Plot Against Paul

11But the following night the Lord stood by him and said, "Be of good cheer, Paul; for as you have testified for Me in Jerusalem, so you must also bear witness at Rome."

12And when it was day, some of the Jews banded together and bound themselves under an oath, saying that they would neither eat nor drink till they had killed Paul. 13Now there were more than forty who had formed this conspiracy. 14They came to the chief priests and elders, and said, "We have bound ourselves under a great oath that we will eat nothing until we have killed Paul. 15Now you, therefore, together with the council, suggest to the commander that he be brought down to you tomorrow, as though you were going to make further inquiries concerning him; but we are ready to kill him before he comes near."

16So when Paul's sister's son heard of their ambush, he went and entered the barracks and told Paul. 17Then Paul called one of the centurions to *him* and said, "Take this young man to the commander, for he has something to tell him." 18So he took him and brought *him* to the commander and said, "Paul the prisoner called me to *him* and asked *me* to bring this young man to you. He has something to say to you."

19Then the commander took him by the hand, went aside, and asked privately, "What is it that you have to tell me?"

20And he said, "The Jews have agreed to ask that you bring Paul down to the council tomorrow, as though they were going to inquire more fully about him. 21But do not yield to them, for more than forty of them lie in wait for him, men who have bound themselves by an oath that they will neither eat nor drink till they have killed him; and now they are ready, waiting for the promise from you."

22So the commander let the young man depart, and commanded *him*, "Tell no one that you have revealed these things to me."

Sent to Felix

23And he called for two centurions, saying, "Prepare two hundred soldiers, seventy horsemen, and two hundred spearmen to go to Caesarea at the third hour of the night; 24and provide mounts to set Paul on, and bring *him* safely to Felix the governor." 25He wrote a letter in the following manner:

26 Claudius Lysias,

To the most excellent governor Felix:

Greetings.

27 This man was seized by the Jews and was about to be killed by them. Coming with the troops I rescued him, having learned that he was a Roman. 28And when I wanted to know the reason they accused him, I brought him before their council. 29I found out that he was accused concerning questions of their law, but had nothing charged against him deserving of death or chains.

e Exodus 22.28

30And when it was told me that the Jews lay in wait for the man, I sent him immediately to you, and also commanded his accusers to state before you the charges against him.

Farewell.

31Then the soldiers, as they were commanded, took Paul and brought *him* by night to Antipatris. 32The next day they left the horsemen to go on with him, and returned to the barracks. 33When they came to Caesarea and had delivered the letter to the governor, they also presented Paul to him. 34And when the governor had read *it*, he asked what province he was from. And when he understood that *he was* from Cilicia, 35he said, "I will hear you when your accusers also have come." And he commanded him to be kept in Herod's Praetorium.

Accused of Sedition

24 Now after five days Ananias the high priest came down with the elders and a certain orator *named* Tertullus. These gave evidence to the governor against Paul.

2And when he was called upon, Tertullus began his accusation, saying: "Seeing that through you we enjoy great peace, and prosperity is being brought to this nation by your foresight, 3we accept *it* always and in all places, most noble Felix, with all thankfulness. 4Nevertheless, not to be tedious to you any further, I beg you to hear, by your courtesy, a few words from us. 5For we have found this man a plague, a creator of dissension among all the Jews throughout the world, and a ringleader of the sect of the Nazarenes. 6He even tried to profane the temple, and we seized him, and wanted to judge him according to our law. 7But the commander Lysias came by and with great violence took *him* out of our hands, 8commanding his accusers to come to you. By examining him yourself you may ascertain all these things of which we accuse him." 9And the Jews also assented, maintaining that these things were so.

The Defense Before Felix

10Then Paul, after the governor had nodded to him to speak, answered: "Inasmuch as I know that you have been for many years a judge of this nation, I do the more cheerfully answer for myself, 11because you may ascertain that it is no more than twelve days since I went up to Jerusalem to worship. 12And they neither found me in the temple disputing with anyone nor inciting the crowd, either in the synagogues or in the city. 13Nor can they prove the things of which they now accuse me. 14But this I confess to you, that according to the Way which they call a sect, so I worship the God of my fathers, believing all things which are written in the Law and in the Prophets. 15I have hope in God, which they themselves also accept, that there will be a resurrection of *the* dead, both of *the* just and *the* unjust. 16This *being* so, I myself always strive to have a conscience without offense toward God and men.

17"Now after many years I came to bring alms and offerings to my nation, 18in the midst of which some Jews from Asia found me purified in the temple, neither with a mob nor with tumult. 19They ought to have been here before you to object if they had anything against me. 20Or else let those who are *here* themselves say if they found any wrongdoing in me while I stood before the council, 21unless *it is* for this one statement which I cried out, standing among them, 'Concerning the resurrection of the dead I am being judged by you this day.'"

Felix Procrastinates

22But when Felix heard these things, having more accurate knowledge of *the* Way, he adjourned the proceedings and said, "When Lysias the commander comes down, I will make a decision on your case." 23So he commanded the centurion to keep Paul and to let *him* have liberty, and told him not to forbid any of his friends to provide for or visit him.

24And after some days, when Felix came with his wife Drusilla, who was Jewish, he sent for Paul and heard him concerning the faith in Christ. 25Now as he reasoned about righteousness, self-control, and the judgment to come, Felix was afraid and answered, "Go away for now; when I have a convenient time I will call for you." 26Meanwhile he also hoped that money would be given him by Paul, that he might release him. Therefore he sent for him more often and conversed with him.

27But after two years Porcius Festus succeeded Felix; and Felix, wanting to do the Jews a favor, left Paul bound.

Paul Appeals to Caesar

25 Now when Festus had come to the province, after three days he went up from Caesarea to Jerusalem. 2Then the high priest and the chief men of the Jews informed him against Paul; and they petitioned him, 3asking a favor against him, that he would summon him to Jerusalem—while *they* lay in ambush along the road to kill him. 4But Festus answered that Paul should be kept at Caesarea, and that he himself was going *there* shortly. 5"Therefore," he said, "let those who have authority among you go down with *me* and accuse this man, to see if there is any fault in him."

6And when he had remained among them more than ten days, he went down to Caesarea. And the next day, sitting on the judgment seat, he commanded Paul to be brought. 7When he had come, the Jews who had come down from Jerusalem stood about and laid many serious complaints against Paul, which they could not prove, 8while he answered for himself, "Neither against the law of the Jews, nor against the temple, nor against Caesar have I offended in anything at all."

9But Festus, wanting to do the Jews a favor, answered Paul and said, "Are you willing to go up to Jerusalem and there be judged before me concerning these things?"

10So Paul said, "I stand at Caesar's judgment seat, where I ought to be judged. To the Jews I have done no wrong, as you very well know. 11For if I am an offender, or have committed anything deserving of death, I do not object to dying; but if there is nothing in these things of which these men accuse me, no one can deliver me to them. I appeal to Caesar."

12Then Festus, when he had conferred with the council, answered, "You have appealed to Caesar? To Caesar you shall go!"

Paul Before Agrippa

13And after some days King Agrippa and Bernice came to Caesarea to greet Festus. 14When they had been there many days, Festus laid Paul's case before the king, saying: "There is a certain man left a prisoner by Felix, 15about whom the chief priests and the elders of the Jews informed *me*, when I was in Jerusalem, asking for a judgment against him. 16To them I answered, 'It is not the custom of the Romans to deliver any man to destruction before the accused meets the accusers face to face, and has opportunity to answer for himself concerning the charge against him.' 17Therefore when they had come together, without any delay, the next day I sat on the judgment seat and commanded the man to be brought in. 18When the accusers stood up, they brought no accusation against him of such things as I supposed, 19but had some questions against him about their own religion and about a certain Jesus, who had died, whom Paul affirmed to be alive. 20And because I was uncertain of such questions, I asked whether he was willing to go to Jerusalem and there be judged concerning these matters. 21But when Paul appealed to be reserved for the decision of Augustus, I commanded him to be kept till I could send him to Caesar."

22Then Agrippa said to Festus, "I also would like to hear the man myself."

"Tomorrow," he said, "you shall hear him."

23So the next day, when Agrippa and Bernice had come with great pomp, and had entered the auditorium with the commanders and the prominent men of the city, at Festus' command Paul was brought in. 24And Festus said: "King Agrippa and all the men who are here present with us, you see this man about whom the whole assembly of the Jews petitioned me, both at Jerusalem and here, crying out that he was not fit to live any longer. 25But when I found that he had committed nothing deserving of death, and that he himself had appealed to Augustus, I decided to send him. 26I have nothing certain to write to my lord concerning him. Therefore I have brought him out before you, and especially before you, King Agrippa, so that after the examination has taken place I may have something to write. 27For it seems to me unreasonable to send a prisoner and not to specify the charges against him."

Paul's Early Life

26 Then Agrippa said to Paul, "You are permitted to speak for yourself."

So Paul stretched out his hand and answered for himself: 2"I think myself happy, King Agrippa, because today I shall answer for myself before you concerning all the things of which I am accused by the Jews, 3especially because you are expert in all customs and questions which have to do with the Jews. Therefore I beg you to hear me patiently.

4"My manner of life from my youth, which was spent from the beginning among my own nation at Jerusalem, all the Jews know. 5They knew me from the first, if they were willing to testify, that according to the strictest sect of our religion I lived a Pharisee. 6And now I stand and am judged for the hope of the promise made by God to our fathers. 7To this *promise* our twelve tribes, earnestly serving *God* night and day, hope to attain. For this hope's sake, King Agrippa, I am accused by the Jews. 8Why should it be thought incredible by you that God raises the dead?

9"Indeed, I myself thought I must do many things contrary to the name of Jesus of Nazareth. 10This I also did in Jerusalem, and many of the saints I shut up in prison, having received authority from the chief priests; and when they were put to death, I cast my vote against *them*. 11And I punished them often in every synagogue and compelled *them* to blaspheme; and being exceedingly enraged against them, I persecuted *them* even to foreign cities.

Paul Recounts His Conversion

12"While thus occupied, as I journeyed to Damascus with authority and commission from the chief priests, 13at midday, O king, along the road I saw a light from heaven, brighter than the sun, shining around me and those who journeyed with me. 14And when we all had fallen to the ground, I heard a voice speaking to me and saying in the Hebrew language, 'Saul, Saul, why are you persecuting Me? *It is* hard for you to kick against the goads.' 15So I said, 'Who are You, Lord?' And He said, 'I am Jesus, whom you are persecuting. 16But rise and stand on your feet; for I have appeared to you for this purpose, to make you a minister and a witness both of the things which you have seen and of the things which I will yet reveal to you. 17I will deliver you from the *Jewish* people, as well as *from* the Gentiles, to whom I now send you, 18to open their eyes, *in order* to turn *them* from darkness to light, and *from* the power of Satan to God, that they may receive forgiveness of sins and an inheritance among those who are sanctified by faith in Me.'

Paul's Post-Conversion Life

19"Therefore, King Agrippa, I was not disobedient to the heavenly vision, 20but declared first to those in Damascus and in Jerusalem, and throughout all the region of Judea, and *then* to the Gentiles, that they should repent, turn to God, and do works befitting repentance. 21For these reasons the Jews seized me in the temple and tried to kill *me*. 22Therefore, having obtained help from God, to this day I stand, witnessing both to small and great, saying no other things than those which the prophets and Moses said would come— 23that the Christ would suffer, that He would be the first to rise from the dead, and would proclaim light to the *Jewish* people and to the Gentiles."

Agrippa Parries Paul's Challenge

24Now as he thus made his defense, Festus said with a loud voice, "Paul, you are beside yourself! Much learning is driving you mad!"

25But he said, "I am not mad, most

noble Festus, but speak the words of truth and reason. 26For the king, before whom I also speak freely, knows these things; for I am convinced that none of these things escapes his attention, since this thing was not done in a corner. 27King Agrippa, do you believe the prophets? I know that you do believe."

28Then Agrippa said to Paul, "You almost persuade me to become a Christian."

29And Paul said, "I would to God that not only you, but also all who hear me today, might become both almost and altogether such as I am, except for these chains."

30When he had said these things, the king stood up, as well as the governor and Bernice and those who sat with them; 31and when they had gone aside, they talked among themselves, saying, "This man is doing nothing deserving of death or chains."

32Then Agrippa said to Festus, "This man might have been set free if he had not appealed to Caesar."

The Voyage to Rome Begins

27 And when it was decided that we should sail to Italy, they delivered Paul and some other prisoners to *one* named Julius, a centurion of the Augustan Regiment. 2So, entering a ship of Adramyttium, we put to sea, meaning to sail along the coasts of Asia. Aristarchus, a Macedonian of Thessalonica, was with us. 3And the next *day* we landed at Sidon. And Julius treated Paul kindly and gave *him* liberty to go to his friends and receive care. 4When we had put to sea from there, we sailed under *the shelter of* Cyprus, because the winds were contrary. 5And when we had sailed over the sea which is off Cilicia and Pamphylia, we came to Myra, *a city* of Lycia. 6There the centurion found an Alexandrian ship sailing to Italy, and he put us on board.

7When we had sailed slowly many days, and arrived with difficulty off Cnidus, the wind not permitting us to proceed, we sailed under *the shelter of* Crete off Salmone. 8Passing it with difficulty, we came to a place called Fair Havens, near the city *of* Lasea.

Paul's Warning Ignored

9Now when much time had been spent, and sailing was now dangerous because the Fast was already over, Paul advised them, 10saying, "Men, I perceive that this voyage will end with disaster and much loss, not only of the cargo and ship, but also our lives." 11Nevertheless the centurion was more persuaded by the helmsman and the owner of the ship than by the things spoken by Paul. 12And because the harbor was not suitable to winter in, the majority advised to set sail from there also, if by any means they could reach Phoenix, a harbor of Crete opening toward the southwest and northwest, *and* winter *there.*

In the Tempest

13When the south wind blew softly, supposing that they had obtained *their* desire, putting out to sea, they sailed close by Crete. 14But not long after, a tempestuous head wind arose, called Euroclydon. 15So when the ship was caught, and could not head into the wind, we let *her* drive. 16And running under *the shelter of* an island called Clauda, we secured the skiff with difficulty. 17When they had taken it on board, they used cables to undergird the ship; and fearing lest they should run aground on the Syrtis *Sands,* they struck sail and so were driven. 18And because we were exceedingly tempest-tossed, the next *day* they lightened the ship. 19On the third *day* we threw the ship's tackle overboard with our own hands. 20Now when neither sun nor stars appeared for many days, and no small tempest beat on *us,* all hope that we would be saved was finally given up.

21But after long abstinence from food, then Paul stood in the midst of them and said, "Men, you should have listened to me, and not have sailed from Crete and incurred this disaster and loss. 22And now I urge you to take heart, for there will be no loss of life among you, but only of the ship. 23For there stood by me this night an angel of the God to whom I belong and whom I serve, 24saying, 'Do not be afraid, Paul; you must be brought before Caesar; and indeed God has granted you all those who sail with you.' 25Therefore take heart, men, for I believe God that it will be just as it was told me. 26However, we must run aground on a certain island."

27Now when the fourteenth night had come, as we were driven up and down in the Adriatic *Sea,* about midnight the sailors sensed that they were drawing near some land. 28And they took soundings and found *it* to be twenty fathoms; and when they had gone a little farther, they took soundings again and found *it* to be fifteen fathoms. 29Then, fearing lest we should run aground on the rocks, they dropped four anchors from the stern, and prayed for day to come. 30And as the sailors were seeking to escape from the ship, when they had let down the skiff into the sea, under pretense of putting out anchors from the prow, 31Paul said to the centurion and the soldiers, "Unless these men stay in the ship, you cannot be saved." 32Then the soldiers cut away the ropes of the skiff and let it fall off.

33And as day was about to dawn, Paul implored *them* all to take food, saying, "Today is the fourteenth day you have waited and continued without food, and eaten nothing. 34Therefore I urge you to take nourishment, for this is for your survival, since not a hair will fall from the head of any of you." 35And when he had said these things, he took bread and gave thanks to God in the presence of them all; and when he had broken *it* he began to eat. 36Then they were all encouraged, and also took food themselves. 37And in all we were two hundred and seventy-six persons on the ship. 38So when they had eaten enough, they lightened the ship and threw out the wheat into the sea.

Shipwrecked on Malta

39When it was day, they did not recognize the land; but they observed a bay with a beach, onto which they planned to run the ship if possible. 40And they let go the anchors and left *them* in the sea, meanwhile loosing the rudder ropes; and they hoisted the mainsail to the wind and made for shore. 41But striking a place where two seas met, they ran the ship aground; and the prow stuck fast and remained immovable, but the stern was being broken up by the violence of the waves.

42And the soldiers' plan was to kill the prisoners, lest any of them should swim away and escape. 43But the centurion, wanting to save Paul, kept them from *their* purpose, and commanded that those who could swim should jump *overboard* first and get to land, 44and the rest, some on boards and some on *parts* of the ship. And so it was that they all escaped safely to land.

Paul's Ministry on Malta

28 Now when they had escaped, they then found out that the island was called Malta. 2And the natives showed us unusual kindness; for they kindled a fire and made us all welcome, because of the rain that was falling and because of the cold. 3But when Paul had gathered a bundle of sticks and laid *them* on the fire, a viper came out because of the heat, and fastened on his hand. 4So when the natives saw the creature hanging from his hand, they said to one another, "No doubt this man is a murderer, whom, though he has escaped the sea, yet justice does not allow to live." 5But he shook off the creature into the fire and suffered no harm. 6However, they were expecting that he would swell up or suddenly fall down dead. But after they had looked for a long time and saw no harm come to him, they changed their minds and said that he was a god.

7In that region there was an estate of the leading citizen of the island, whose name was Publius, who received us and entertained us courteously for three days. 8And it happened that the father of Publius lay sick of a fever and dysentery. Paul went in to him and prayed, and he laid his hands on him and healed him. 9So when this was done, the rest of those on the island who had diseases also came and were healed. 10They also honored us in many ways; and when we departed, they provided such things as were necessary.

Arrival at Rome

11After three months we sailed in an Alexandrian ship whose figurehead was the Twin Brothers, which had wintered at the island. 12And landing at Syracuse, we stayed three days. 13From there we circled round and reached Rhegium. And after one day the south wind blew; and the next day we came to Puteoli, 14where we found brethren, and were invited to stay with them seven days. And so we went toward Rome. 15And from there, when the brethren heard about us, they came to meet us as far as Appii Forum and Three Inns. When Paul saw them, he thanked God and took courage.

16Now when we came to Rome, the centurion delivered the prisoners to the captain of the guard; but Paul was permitted to dwell by himself with the soldier who guarded him.

Paul's Ministry at Rome

17And it came to pass after three days that Paul called the leaders of the Jews together. So when they had come together, he said to them: "Men *and* brethren, though I have done nothing against our people or the customs of our fathers, yet I was delivered as a prisoner from Jerusalem into the hands of the Romans, 18who, when they had examined me, wanted to let *me* go, because there was no cause for putting me to death. 19But when the Jews spoke against *it*, I was compelled to appeal to Caesar, not that I had anything of which to accuse my nation. 20For this reason therefore I have called for you, to see *you* and speak with *you,* because for the hope of Israel I am bound with this chain."

21Then they said to him, "We neither received letters from Judea concerning you, nor have any of the brethren who came reported or spoken any evil of

you. 22But we desire to hear from you what you think; for concerning this sect, we know that it is spoken against everywhere."

23So when they had appointed him a day, many came to him at *his* lodging, to whom he explained and solemnly testified of the kingdom of God, persuading them concerning Jesus from both the Law of Moses and the Prophets, from morning till evening. 24And some were persuaded by the things which were spoken, and some disbelieved. 25So when they did not agree among themselves, they departed after Paul had said one word: "The Holy Spirit spoke rightly through Isaiah the prophet to our fathers, 26saying,

'Go to this people and say:
"Hearing you will hear, and shall not
    understand;
And seeing you will see, and not
    perceive;
27   For the hearts of this people have
        grown dull.
    Their ears are hard of hearing,
    And their eyes they have closed,
    Lest they should see with *their* eyes
        and hear with *their* ears,
    Lest they should understand with
        their hearts and turn,
    So that I should heal them." 'f

28"Therefore let it be known to you that the salvation of God has been sent to the Gentiles, and they will hear it!" 29And when he had said these words, the Jews departed and had a great dispute among themselves.

30Then Paul dwelt two whole years in his own rented house, and received all who came to him, 31preaching the kingdom of God and teaching the things which concern the Lord Jesus Christ with all confidence, no one forbidding him.

f Isaiah 6.9, 10

ROMANS

Greeting

1 Paul, a bondservant of Jesus Christ, called *to be* an apostle, separated to the gospel of God 2which He promised before through His prophets in the Holy Scriptures, 3concerning His Son Jesus Christ our Lord, who was born of the seed of David according to the flesh, 4*and* declared *to be* the Son of God with power according to the Spirit of holiness, by the resurrection from the dead. 5Through Him we have received grace and apostleship for obedience to the faith among all nations for His name, 6among whom you also are the called of Jesus Christ;

7To all who are in Rome, beloved of God, called *to be* saints:

Grace to you and peace from God our Father and the Lord Jesus Christ.

Desire to Visit Rome

8First, I thank my God through Jesus Christ for you all, that your faith is spoken of throughout the whole world. 9For God is my witness, whom I serve with my spirit in the gospel of His Son, that without ceasing I make mention of you always in my prayers, 10making request if, by some means, now at last I may find a way in the will of God to come to you. 11For I long to see you, that I may impart to you some spiritual gift, so that you may be established— 12that is, that I may be encouraged together with you by the mutual faith both of you and me.

13Now I do not want you to be unaware, brethren, that I often planned to come to you (but was hindered until now), that I might have some fruit among you also, just as among the other Gentiles. 14I am a debtor both to Greeks and to barbarians, both to wise and to unwise. 15So, as much as is in me, *I am* ready to preach the gospel to you who are in Rome also.

The Just Live by Faith

16For I am not ashamed of the gospel of Christ, for it is the power of God to salvation for everyone who believes, for the Jew first and also for the Greek. 17For in it the righteousness of God is revealed from faith to faith; as it is written, "The just shall live by faith."*a*

God's Wrath on Unrighteousness

18For the wrath of God is revealed from heaven against all ungodliness and unrighteousness of men, who suppress the truth in unrighteousness, 19because what may be known of God is manifest in them, for God has shown *it* to them. 20For since the creation of the world His invisible *attributes* are clearly seen, being understood by the things that are made, *even* His eternal power and Godhead, so that they are without excuse, 21because, although they knew God, they did not glorify *Him* as God, nor were thankful, but became futile in their thoughts, and their foolish hearts were darkened. 22Professing to be wise, they became fools, 23and changed the glory of the incorruptible God into an image made like corruptible man—and birds and four-footed animals and creeping things.

24Therefore God also gave them up to uncleanness, in the lusts of their hearts, to dishonor their bodies among themselves, 25who exchanged the truth of God for the lie, and worshiped and served the creature rather than the Creator, who is blessed forever. Amen.

26For this reason God gave them up to vile passions. For even their women exchanged the natural use for what is against nature. 27Likewise also the men, leaving the natural use of the woman, burned in their lust for one another, men with men committing what is shameful, and receiving in themselves the penalty of their error which was due.

28And even as they did not like to retain God in *their* knowledge, God gave

a Habakkuk 2.4

them over to a debased mind, to do those things which are not fitting; 29being filled with all unrighteousness, sexual immorality, wickedness, covetousness, maliciousness; full of envy, murder, strife, deceit, evil-mindedness; *they are* whisperers, 30backbiters, haters of God, violent, proud, boasters, inventors of evil things, disobedient to parents, 31undiscerning, untrustworthy, unloving, unforgiving, unmerciful; 32who, knowing the righteous judgment of God, that those who practice such things are deserving of death, not only do the same but also approve of those who practice them.

God's Righteous Judgment

2 Therefore you are inexcusable, O man, whoever you are who judge, for in whatever you judge another you condemn yourself; for you who judge practice the same things. 2But we know that the judgment of God is according to truth against those who practice such things. 3And do you think this, O man, you who judge those practicing such things, and doing the same, that you will escape the judgment of God? 4Or do you despise the riches of His goodness, forbearance, and longsuffering, not knowing that the goodness of God leads you to repentance? 5But in accordance with your hardness and your impenitent heart you are treasuring up for yourself wrath in the day of wrath and revelation of the righteous judgment of God, 6who "will render to each one according to his deeds":*b* 7eternal life to those who by patient continuance in doing good seek for glory, honor, and immortality; 8but to those who are self-seeking and do not obey the truth, but obey unrighteousness—indignation and wrath, 9tribulation and anguish, on every soul of man who does evil, of the Jew first and also of the Greek; 10but glory, honor, and peace to everyone who works what is good, to the Jew first and also to the Greek. 11For there is no partiality with God.

12For as many as have sinned without law will also perish without law, and as many as have sinned in the law will be judged by the law 13(for not the hearers of the law *are* just in the sight of God, but the doers of the law will be justified; 14for when Gentiles, who do not have the law, by nature do the things in the law, these, although not having the law, are a law to themselves, 15who show the work of the law written in their hearts, their conscience also bearing witness, and between themselves *their* thoughts accusing or else excusing *them*) 16in the day when God will judge the secrets of men by Jesus Christ, according to my gospel.

The Jews Guilty as the Gentiles

17Indeed you are called a Jew, and rest on the law, and make your boast in God, 18and know *His* will, and approve the things that are excellent, being instructed out of the law, 19and are confident that you yourself are a guide to the blind, a light to those who are in darkness, 20an instructor of the foolish, a teacher of babes, having the form of knowledge and truth in the law. 21You, therefore, who teach another, do you not teach yourself? You who preach that a man should not steal, do you steal? 22You who say, "Do not commit adultery," do you commit adultery? You who abhor idols, do you rob temples? 23You who make your boast in the law, do you dishonor God through breaking the law? 24For "the name of God is blasphemed among the Gentiles because of you,"*c* as it is written.

Circumcision of No Avail

25For circumcision is indeed profitable if you keep the law; but if you are a breaker of the law, your circumcision has become uncircumcision. 26Therefore, if an uncircumcised man keeps the righteous requirements of the law, will not his uncircumcision be counted as circumcision? 27And will not the physically uncircumcised, if he fulfills the law, judge you who, *even* with *your* written *code* and circumcision, *are* a transgressor of the law? 28For he is not a Jew who *is one* outwardly, nor *is* circumcision that which *is* outward in the flesh; 29but *he is* a Jew who *is one* inwardly; and circumcision *is that* of

b Psalm 62.12; Proverbs 24.12   *c* Isaiah 52.5; Ezekiel 36.22

the heart, in the Spirit, not in the letter; whose praise *is* not from men but from God.

God's Judgment Defended

3 What advantage then has the Jew, or what *is* the profit of circumcision? 2Much in every way! Chiefly because to them were committed the oracles of God. 3For what if some did not believe? Will their unbelief make the faithfulness of God without effect? 4Certainly not! Indeed, let God be true but every man a liar. As it is written:

"That You may be justified in Your words,
And may overcome when You are judged."*d*

5But if our unrighteousness demonstrates the righteousness of God, what shall we say? *Is* God unjust who inflicts wrath? (I speak as a man.) 6Certainly not! For then how will God judge the world?

7For if the truth of God has increased through my lie to His glory, why am I also still judged as a sinner? 8And *why* not *say,* "Let us do evil that good may come"?—as we are slanderously reported and as some affirm that we say. Their condemnation is just.

All Have Sinned

9What then? Are we better *than they?* Not at all. For we have previously charged both Jews and Greeks that they are all under sin.

10As it is written:
"There is none righteous, no, not one;
11 There is none who understands;
There is none who seeks after God.
12 They have all turned aside;
They have together become unprofitable;
There is none who does good, no, not one."*e*
13 "Their throat *is* an open tomb;
With their tongues they have practiced deceit";*f*
"The poison of asps *is* under their lips";*g*

14 "Whose mouth *is* full of cursing and bitterness."*h*
15 "Their feet *are* swift to shed blood;
16 Destruction and misery *are* in their ways;
17 And the way of peace they have not known."*i*
18 "There is no fear of God before their eyes."*j*

19Now we know that whatever the law says, it says to those who are under the law, that every mouth may be stopped, and all the world may become guilty before God. 20Therefore by the deeds of the law no flesh will be justified in His sight, for by the law *is* the knowledge of sin.

God's Righteousness Through Faith

21But now the righteousness of God apart from the law is revealed, being witnessed by the Law and the Prophets, 22even the righteousness of God, through faith in Jesus Christ, to all and on all who believe. For there is no difference; 23for all have sinned and fall short of the glory of God, 24being justified freely by His grace through the redemption that is in Christ Jesus, 25whom God set forth *as* a propitiation by His blood, through faith, to demonstrate His righteousness, because in His forbearance God had passed over the sins that were previously committed, 26to demonstrate at the present time His righteousness, that He might be just and the justifier of the one who has faith in Jesus.

Boasting Excluded

27Where *is* boasting then? It is excluded. By what law? Of works? No, but by the law of faith. 28Therefore we conclude that a man is justified by faith apart from the deeds of the law. 29Or *is He* the God of the Jews only? *Is He* not also the God of the Gentiles? Yes, of the Gentiles also, 30since *there is* one God who will justify the circumcised by faith and the uncircumcised through faith. 31Do we then make void the law through faith? Certainly not! On the contrary, we establish the law.

---

d Psalm 51.4   *e* Psalms 14.1-3; 53.1-3; Ecclesiastes 7.20   *f* Psalm 5.9   *g* Psalm 140.3
h Psalm 10.7   *i* Isaiah 59.7, 8   *j* Psalm 36.1

Abraham Justified by Faith

4 What then shall we say that Abraham our father has found according to the flesh? 2For if Abraham was justified by works, he has *something* to boast about, but not before God. 3For what does the Scripture say? "Abraham believed God, and it was accounted to him for righteousness."*k* 4Now to him who works, the wages are not counted as grace but as debt.

David Celebrates the Same Truth

5But to him who does not work but believes on Him who justifies the ungodly, his faith is accounted for righteousness, 6just as David also describes the blessedness of the man to whom God imputes righteousness apart from works:

7 "Blessed *are those* whose lawless deeds are forgiven,
    And whose sins are covered;
8 Blessed *is the man to whom the* LORD *shall not impute sin."*l*

Abraham Justified Before Circumcision

9*Does* this blessedness then *come* upon the circumcised *only*, or upon the uncircumcised also? For we say that faith was accounted to Abraham for righteousness. 10How then was it accounted? While he was circumcised, or uncircumcised? Not while circumcised, but while uncircumcised. 11And he received the sign of circumcision, a seal of the righteousness of the faith which *he had while still* uncircumcised, that he might be the father of all those who believe, though they are uncircumcised, that righteousness might be imputed to them also, 12and the father of circumcision to those who not only *are* of the circumcision, but who also walk in the steps of the faith which our father Abraham *had while still* uncircumcised.

The Promise Granted Through Faith

13For the promise that he would be the heir of the world *was* not to Abraham or to his seed through the law, but through the righteousness of faith.

14For if those who are of the law *are* heirs, faith is made void and the promise made of no effect, 15because the law brings about wrath; for where there is no law *there is* no transgression.

16Therefore *it is* of faith that *it might be* according to grace, so that the promise might be sure to all the seed, not only to those who are of the law, but also to those who are of the faith of Abraham, who is the father of us all 17(as it is written, "I have made you a father of many nations"*m*) in the presence of Him whom he believed—God, who gives life to the dead and calls those things which do not exist as though they did; 18who, contrary to hope, in hope believed, so that he became the father of many nations, according to what was spoken, "So shall your descendants be."*n* 19And not being weak in faith, he did not consider his own body, already dead (since he was about a hundred years old), and the deadness of Sarah's womb. 20He did not waver at the promise of God through unbelief, but was strengthened in faith, giving glory to God, 21and being fully convinced that what He had promised He was also able to perform. 22And therefore "it was accounted to him for righteousness."*o*

23Now it was not written for his sake alone that it was imputed to him, 24but also for us. It shall be imputed to us who believe in Him who raised up Jesus our Lord from the dead, 25who was delivered up because of our offenses, and was raised because of our justification.

Faith Triumphs in Trouble

5 Therefore, having been justified by faith, we have peace with God through our Lord Jesus Christ, 2through whom also we have access by faith into this grace in which we stand, and rejoice in hope of the glory of God. 3And not only *that*, but we also glory in tribulations, knowing that tribulation produces perseverance; 4and perseverance, character; and character, hope. 5Now hope does not disappoint, because the love of God has been poured

---

k Genesis 15.6   *l* Psalm 32.1, 2   *m* Genesis 17.5   *n* Genesis 15.5   *o* Genesis 15.6

out in our hearts by the Holy Spirit who was given to us.

Christ in Our Place

6For when we were still without strength, in due time Christ died for the ungodly. 7For scarcely for a righteous man will one die; yet perhaps for a good man someone would even dare to die. 8But God demonstrates His own love toward us, in that while we were still sinners, Christ died for us. 9Much more then, having now been justified by His blood, we shall be saved from wrath through Him. 10For if when we were enemies we were reconciled to God through the death of His Son, much more, having been reconciled, we shall be saved by His life. 11And not only *that*, but we also rejoice in God through our Lord Jesus Christ, through whom we have now received the reconciliation.

Death in Adam, Life in Christ

12Therefore, just as through one man sin entered the world, and death through sin, and thus death spread to all men, because all sinned—13(For until the law sin was in the world, but sin is not imputed when there is no law. 14Nevertheless death reigned from Adam to Moses, even over those who had not sinned according to the likeness of the transgression of Adam, who is a type of Him who was to come. 15But the free gift *is* not like the offense. For if by the one man's offense many died, much more the grace of God and the gift by the grace of the one Man, Jesus Christ, abounded to many. 16And the gift *is* not like *that which came* through the one who sinned. For the judgment *which came* from one *offense resulted* in condemnation, but the free gift *which came* from many offenses *resulted* in justification. 17For if by the one man's offense death reigned through the one, much more those who receive abundance of grace and of the gift of righteousness will reign in life through the One, Jesus Christ.) 18Therefore, as through one man's offense *judgment* came to all men, resulting in condemnation, even so through one Man's righteous act *the free gift came* to all men, resulting in justification of life. 19For as by one man's disobedience many were made sinners, so also by one Man's obedience many will be made righteous.

20Moreover the law entered that the offense might abound. But where sin abounded, grace abounded much more, 21so that as sin reigned in death, even so grace might reign through righteousness to eternal life through Jesus Christ our Lord.

Dead to Sin, Alive to God

6 What shall we say then? Shall we continue in sin that grace may abound? 2Certainly not! How shall we who died to sin live any longer in it? 3Or do you not know that as many of us as were baptized into Christ Jesus were baptized into His death? 4Therefore we were buried with Him through baptism into death, that just as Christ was raised from the dead by the glory of the Father, even so we also should walk in newness of life.

5For if we have been united together in the likeness of His death, certainly we also shall be *in the likeness* of *His* resurrection, 6knowing this, that our old man was crucified with *Him*, that the body of sin might be done away with, that we should no longer be slaves of sin. 7For he who has died has been freed from sin. 8Now if we died with Christ, we believe that we shall also live with Him, 9knowing that Christ, having been raised from the dead, dies no more. Death no longer has dominion over Him. 10For *the death* that He died, He died to sin once for all; but *the life* that He lives, He lives to God. 11Likewise you also, reckon yourselves to be dead indeed to sin, but alive to God in Christ Jesus our Lord.

12Therefore do not let sin reign in your mortal body, that you should obey it in its lusts. 13And do not present your members *as* instruments of unrighteousness to sin, but present yourselves to God as being alive from the dead, and your members *as* instruments of righteousness to God. 14For sin shall not have dominion over you, for you are not under law but under grace.

From Slaves of Sin to Slaves of God

15What then? Shall we sin because we are not under law but under grace? Certainly not! 16Do you not know that to whom you present yourselves slaves to obey, you are that one's slaves whom you obey, whether of sin *leading* to death, or of obedience *leading* to righteousness? 17But God be thanked that *though* you were slaves of sin, yet you obeyed from the heart that form of doctrine to which you were delivered. 18And having been set free from sin, you became slaves of righteousness. 19I speak in human *terms* because of the weakness of your flesh. For just as you presented your members *as* slaves of uncleanness, and of lawlessness *leading* to *more* lawlessness, so now present your members *as* slaves *of* righteousness for holiness.

20For when you were slaves of sin, you were free in regard to righteousness. 21What fruit did you have then in the things of which you are now ashamed? For the end of those things *is* death. 22But now having been set free from sin, and having become slaves of God, you have your fruit to holiness, and the end, everlasting life. 23For the wages of sin *is* death, but the gift of God *is* eternal life in Christ Jesus our Lord.

Freed from the Law

7 Or do you not know, brethren (for I speak to those who know the law), that the law has dominion over a man as long as he lives? 2For the woman who has a husband is bound by the law to *her* husband as long as he lives. But if the husband dies, she is released from the law of *her* husband. 3So then if, while *her* husband lives, she marries another man, she will be called an adulteress; but if her husband dies, she is free from that law, so that she is no adulteress, though she has married another man. 4Therefore, my brethren, you also have become dead to the law through the body of Christ, that you may be married to another—to Him who was raised from the dead, that we should bear fruit to God. 5For when we were in the flesh, the sinful passions which were aroused by the law were at work in our members to bear fruit to death. 6But now we have been delivered from the law, having died to what we were held by, so that we should serve in the newness of the Spirit and not *in* the oldness of the letter.

Sin's Advantage in the Law

7What shall we say then? *Is* the law sin? Certainly not! On the contrary, I would not have known sin except through the law. For I would not have known covetousness unless the law had said, "You shall not covet."*p* 8But sin, taking opportunity by the commandment, produced in me all *manner of evil* desire. For apart from the law sin *was* dead. 9I was alive once without the law, but when the commandment came, sin revived and I died. 10And the commandment, which *was* to *bring* life, I found to *bring* death. 11For sin, taking occasion by the commandment, deceived me, and by it killed *me*. 12Therefore the law *is* holy, and the commandment holy and just and good.

Law Cannot Save from Sin

13Has then what is good become death to me? Certainly not! But sin, that it might appear sin, was producing death in me through what is good, so that sin through the commandment might become exceedingly sinful. 14For we know that the law is spiritual, but I am carnal, sold under sin. 15For what I am doing, I do not understand. For what I will to do, that I do not practice; but what I hate, that I do. 16If, then, I do what I will not to do, I agree with the law that *it is* good. 17But now, *it is* no longer I who do it, but sin that dwells in me. 18For I know that in me (that is, in my flesh) nothing good dwells; for to will is present with me, but *how* to perform what is good I do not find. 19For the good that I will *to do*, I do not do; but the evil I will not *to do*, that I practice. 20Now if I do what I will not *to do*, it is no longer I who do it, but sin that dwells in me.

21I find then a law, that evil is present with me, the one who wills to do good.

p Exodus 20.17; Deuteronomy 5.21

22For I delight in the law of God according to the inward man. 23But I see another law in my members, warring against the law of my mind, and bringing me into captivity to the law of sin which is in my members. 24O wretched man that I am! Who will deliver me from this body of death? 25I thank God—through Jesus Christ our Lord!

So then, with the mind I myself serve the law of God, but with the flesh the law of sin.

Free from Indwelling Sin

8 There is therefore now no condemnation to those who are in Christ Jesus, who do not walk according to the flesh, but according to the Spirit. 2For the law of the Spirit of life in Christ Jesus has made me free from the law of sin and death. 3For what the law could not do in that it was weak through the flesh, God did by sending His own Son in the likeness of sinful flesh, on account of sin: He condemned sin in the flesh, 4that the righteous requirement of the law might be fulfilled in us who do not walk according to the flesh but according to the Spirit. 5For those who live according to the flesh set their minds on the things of the flesh, but those who live according to the Spirit, the things of the Spirit. 6For to be carnally minded is death, but to be spiritually minded is life and peace. 7Because the carnal mind is enmity against God; for it is not subject to the law of God, nor indeed can be. 8So then, those who are in the flesh cannot please God.

9But you are not in the flesh but in the Spirit, if indeed the Spirit of God dwells in you. Now if anyone does not have the Spirit of Christ, he is not His. 10And if Christ is in you, the body is dead because of sin, but the Spirit is life because of righteousness. 11But if the Spirit of Him who raised Jesus from the dead dwells in you, He who raised Christ from the dead will also give life to your mortal bodies through His Spirit who dwells in you.

Sonship Through the Spirit

12Therefore, brethren, we are debtors—not to the flesh, to live according to the flesh. 13For if you live according to the flesh you will die; but if by the Spirit you put to death the deeds of the body, you will live. 14For as many as are led by the Spirit of God, these are sons of God. 15For you did not receive the spirit of bondage again to fear, but you received the Spirit of adoption by whom we cry out, "Abba, Father." 16The Spirit Himself bears witness with our spirit that we are children of God, 17and if children, then heirs—heirs of God and joint heirs with Christ, if indeed we suffer with Him, that we may also be glorified together.

From Suffering to Glory

18For I consider that the sufferings of this present time are not worthy to be compared with the glory which shall be revealed in us. 19For the earnest expectation of the creation eagerly waits for the revealing of the sons of God. 20For the creation was subjected to futility, not willingly, but because of Him who subjected it in hope; 21because the creation itself also will be delivered from the bondage of corruption into the glorious liberty of the children of God. 22For we know that the whole creation groans and labors with birth pangs together until now. 23Not only that, but we also who have the firstfruits of the Spirit, even we ourselves groan within ourselves, eagerly waiting for the adoption, the redemption of our body. 24For we were saved in this hope, but hope that is seen is not hope; for why does one still hope for what he sees? 25But if we hope for what we do not see, we eagerly wait for it with perseverance.

26Likewise the Spirit also helps in our weaknesses. For we do not know what we should pray for as we ought, but the Spirit Himself makes intercession for us with groanings which cannot be uttered. 27Now He who searches the hearts knows what the mind of the Spirit is, because He makes intercession for the saints according to the will of God.

28And we know that all things work together for good to those who love God, to those who are the called according to His purpose. 29For whom He foreknew, He also predestined to be conformed to the image of His Son, that He might be the firstborn among many brethren. 30Moreover whom He predestined, these He also called; whom He called, these He also justified; and whom He justified, these He also glorified.

God's Everlasting Love

31What then shall we say to these things? If God is for us, who can be against us? 32He who did not spare His own Son, but delivered Him up for us all, how shall He not with Him also freely give us all things? 33Who shall bring a charge against God's elect? It is God who justifies. 34Who is he who condemns? It is Christ who died, and furthermore is also risen, who is even at the right hand of God, who also makes intercession for us. 35Who shall separate us from the love of Christ? Shall tribulation, or distress, or persecution, or famine, or nakedness, or peril, or sword? 36As it is written:

"For Your sake we are killed all day
  long;
We are accounted as sheep for the
  slaughter."q

37Yet in all these things we are more than conquerors through Him who loved us. 38For I am persuaded that neither death nor life, nor angels nor principalities nor powers, nor things present nor things to come, 39nor height nor depth, nor any other created thing, shall be able to separate us from the love of God which is in Christ Jesus our Lord.

Israel's Rejection of Christ

9 I tell the truth in Christ, I am not lying, my conscience also bearing me witness in the Holy Spirit, 2that I have great sorrow and continual grief in my heart. 3For I could wish that I myself were accursed from Christ for my brethren, my countrymen according to the flesh, 4who are Israelites, to whom pertain the adoption, the glory, the covenants, the giving of the law, the service of God, and the promises; 5of whom are the fathers and from whom, according to the flesh, Christ came, who is over all, the eternally blessed God. Amen.

Israel's Rejection and God's Purpose

6But it is not that the word of God has taken no effect. For they are not all Israel who are of Israel, 7nor are they all children because they are the seed of Abraham; but, "In Isaac your seed shall be called."r 8That is, those who are the children of the flesh, these are not the children of God; but the children of the promise are counted as the seed. 9For this is the word of promise: "At this time I will come and Sarah shall have a son."s

10And not only this, but when Rebecca also had conceived by one man, even by our father Isaac 11(for the children not yet being born, nor having done any good or evil, that the purpose of God according to election might stand, not of works but of Him who calls), 12it was said to her, "The older shall serve the younger."t 13As it is written, "Jacob I have loved, but Esau I have hated."u

Israel's Rejection and God's Justice

14What shall we say then? Is there unrighteousness with God? Certainly not! 15For He says to Moses, "I will have mercy on whomever I will have mercy, and I will have compassion on whomever I will have compassion."v 16So then it is not of him who wills, nor of him who runs, but of God who shows mercy. 17For the Scripture says to the Pharaoh, "For this very purpose I have raised you up, that I may show My power in you, and that My name may be declared in all the earth."w 18Therefore He has mercy on whom He wills, and whom He wills He hardens.

19You will say to me then, "Why does He still find fault? For who has resisted His will?" 20But indeed, O man, who are you to reply against God? Will the thing formed say to him who formed it, "Why have you made me like this?" 21Does not the potter have power over the clay, from the same lump to make one vessel for honor and another for dishonor?

22What if God, wanting to show His wrath and to make His power known, endured with much longsuffering the

q Psalm 44.22   r Genesis 21.12   s Genesis 18.10, 14   t Genesis 25.23
u Malachi 1.2, 3   v Exodus 33.19   w Exodus 9.16

vessels of wrath prepared for destruction, 23and that He might make known the riches of His glory on the vessels of mercy, which He had prepared beforehand for glory, 24*even* us whom He called, not of the Jews only, but also of the Gentiles?

25As He says also in Hosea:

"I will call them My people, who
    were not My people,
And her beloved, who was not
    beloved."*x*

26 "And it shall come to pass in the
    place where it was said to them,
    '*You are* not My people,'
There they shall be called sons of
    the living God."*y*

27Isaiah also cries out concerning Israel:*z*

"Though the number of the children
    of Israel be as the sand of the sea,
The remnant will be saved.

28 For He will finish the work and cut
    it short in righteousness,
Because the LORD will make a short
    work upon the earth."

29And as Isaiah said before:

"Unless the LORD of Sabaoth had left
    us a seed,
We would have become like
    Sodom,
And we would have been made like
    Gomorrah."*a*

Present Condition of Israel

30What shall we say then? That Gentiles, who did not pursue righteousness, have attained to righteousness, even the righteousness of faith; 31but Israel, pursuing the law of righteousness, has not attained to the law of righteousness. 32Why? Because *they did* not *seek it* by faith, but as it were, by the works of the law. For they stumbled at that stumbling stone. 33As it is written:

"Behold, I lay in Zion a stumbling
    stone and rock of offense,
And whoever believes on Him will
    not be put to shame."*b*

Israel Needs the Gospel

10 Brethren, my heart's desire and prayer to God for Israel is that

they may be saved. 2For I bear them witness that they have a zeal for God, but not according to knowledge. 3For they being ignorant of God's righteousness, and seeking to establish their own righteousness, have not submitted to the righteousness of God. 4For Christ *is* the end of the law for righteousness to everyone who believes.

5For Moses writes about the righteousness which is of the law, "The man who does those things shall live by them."*c* 6But the righteousness of faith speaks in this way, "Do not say in your heart, 'Who will ascend into heaven?' "*d* (that is, to bring Christ down *from above*) 7or, " 'Who will descend into the abyss?' "*e* (that is, to bring Christ up from the dead). 8But what does it say? "The word is near you, in your mouth and in your heart"*f* (that is, the word of faith which we preach): 9that if you confess with your mouth the Lord Jesus and believe in your heart that God has raised Him from the dead, you will be saved. 10For with the heart one believes unto righteousness, and with the mouth confession is made unto salvation. 11For the Scripture says, "Whoever believes on Him will not be put to shame."*g* 12For there is no distinction between Jew and Greek, for the same Lord over all is rich to all who call upon Him. 13For "whoever calls on the name of the LORD shall be saved."*h*

Israel Rejects the Gospel

14How then shall they call on Him in whom they have not believed? And how shall they believe in Him of whom they have not heard? And how shall they hear without a preacher? 15And how shall they preach unless they are sent? As it is written:

"How beautiful are the feet of those
    who preach the gospel of peace,
Who bring glad tidings of good
    things!"*i*

16But they have not all obeyed the gospel. For Isaiah says, "LORD, who has believed our report?"*j* 17So then faith *comes* by hearing, and hearing by the word of God.

---

x Hosea 2.23   *y* Hosea 1.10   *z* Isaiah 10.22, 23   *a* Isaiah 1.9   *b* Isaiah 8.14; 28.16
c Leviticus 18.5   *d* Deuteronomy 30.12   *e* Deuteronomy 30.13   *f* Deuteronomy 30.14
g Isaiah 28.16   *h* Joel 2.32   *i* Isaiah 52.7; Nahum 1.15   *j* Isaiah 53.1

18But I say, have they not heard? Yes indeed:

"Their sound has gone out to all the earth,
And their words to the ends of the world."[k]

19But I say, did Israel not know? First Moses says:

"I will provoke you to jealousy by *those who are* not a nation,
I will move you to anger by a foolish nation."[l]

20But Isaiah is very bold and says:

"I was found by those who did not seek Me;
I was made manifest to those who did not ask for Me."[m]

21But to Israel he says:

"All day long I have stretched out My hands
To a disobedient and contrary people."[n]

Israel's Rejection Not Total

11 I say then, has God cast away His people? Certainly not! For I also am an Israelite, of the seed of Abraham, of the tribe of Benjamin. 2God has not cast away His people whom He foreknew. Or do you not know what the Scripture says of Elijah, how he pleads with God against Israel, saying, 3"LORD, they have killed Your prophets and torn down Your altars, and I alone am left, and they seek my life"?[o] 4But what does the divine response say to him? "I have reserved for Myself seven thousand men who have not bowed the knee to Baal."[p] 5Even so then, at this present time there is a remnant according to the election of grace. 6And if by grace, then *it is* no longer of works; otherwise grace is no longer grace. But if *it is* of works, it is no longer grace; otherwise work is no longer work.

7What then? Israel has not obtained what it seeks; but the elect have obtained it, and the rest were blinded. 8Just as it is written:

"God has given them a spirit of stupor,
Eyes that they should not see

And ears that they should not hear,
To this very day."[q]

9And David says:

"Let their table become a snare and a trap,
A stumbling block and a recompense to them.

10 Let their eyes be darkened, so that they do not see,
And bow down their back always."[r]

Israel's Rejection Not Final

11I say then, have they stumbled that they should fall? Certainly not! But through their fall, to provoke them to jealousy, salvation *has come* to the Gentiles. 12Now if their fall *is* riches for the world, and their failure riches for the Gentiles, how much more their fullness!

13For I speak to you Gentiles; inasmuch as I am an apostle to the Gentiles, I magnify my ministry, 14if by any means I may provoke to jealousy *those who are* my flesh and save some of them. 15For if their being cast away *is* the reconciling of the world, what *will* their acceptance *be* but life from the dead?

16For if the firstfruit *is* holy, the lump *is* also *holy*; and if the root *is* holy, so *are* the branches. 17And if some of the branches were broken off, and you, being a wild olive tree, were grafted in among them, and with them became a partaker of the root and fatness of the olive tree, 18do not boast against the branches. But if you do boast, *remember that* you do not support the root, but the root supports you.

19You will say then, "Branches were broken off that I might be grafted in." 20Well *said*. Because of unbelief they were broken off, and you stand by faith. Do not be haughty, but fear. 21For if God did not spare the natural branches, He may not spare you either. 22Therefore consider the goodness and severity of God: on those who fell, severity; but toward you, goodness, if you continue in *His* goodness. Otherwise you also will be cut off. 23And they also, if they

k Psalm 19.4   l Deuteronomy 32.21   m Isaiah 65.1   n Isaiah 65.2   o 1 Kings 19.10, 14
p 1 Kings 19.18   q Deuteronomy 29.4; Isaiah 29.10   r Psalm 69.22, 23

do not continue in unbelief, will be grafted in, for God is able to graft them in again. 24For if you were cut out of the olive tree which is wild by nature, and were grafted contrary to nature into a cultivated olive tree, how much more will these, who *are* natural *branches*, be grafted into their own olive tree?

25For I do not desire, brethren, that you should be ignorant of this mystery, lest you should be wise in your own opinion, that blindness in part has happened to Israel until the fullness of the Gentiles has come in. 26And so all Israel will be saved, as it is written:

"The Deliverer will come out of Zion,
And He will turn away ungodliness from Jacob;
27 For this *is* My covenant with them, When I take away their sins."*s*

28Concerning the gospel *they are* enemies for your sake, but concerning the election *they are* beloved for the sake of the fathers. 29For the gifts and the calling of God *are* irrevocable. 30For as you were once disobedient to God, yet have now obtained mercy through their disobedience, 31even so these also have now been disobedient, that through the mercy shown you they also may obtain mercy. 32For God has committed them all to disobedience, that He might have mercy on all.

33Oh, the depth of the riches both of the wisdom and knowledge of God! How unsearchable *are* His judgments and His ways past finding out!
34 "For who has known the mind of the LORD?
Or who has become His counselor?"*t*
35 "Or who has first given to Him And it shall be repaid to him?"*u*

36For of Him and through Him and to Him *are* all things, to whom *be* glory forever. Amen.

Living Sacrifices to God

12 I beseech you therefore, brethren, by the mercies of God, that you present your bodies a living sacrifice, holy, acceptable to God, *which is*

your reasonable service. 2And do not be conformed to this world, but be transformed by the renewing of your mind, that you may prove what *is* that good and acceptable and perfect will of God.

Serve God with Spiritual Gifts

3For I say, through the grace given to me, to everyone who is among you, not to think *of himself* more highly than he ought to think, but to think soberly, as God has dealt to each one a measure of faith. 4For as we have many members in one body, but all the members do not have the same function, 5so we, *being* many, are one body in Christ, and individually members of one another. 6Having then gifts differing according to the grace that is given to us, *let us use them*: if prophecy, *let us prophesy* in proportion to our faith; 7or ministry, *let us use it* in *our* ministering; he who teaches, in teaching; 8he who exhorts, in exhortation; he who gives, with liberality; he who leads, with diligence; he who shows mercy, with cheerfulness.

Behave Like a Christian

9*Let* love *be* without hypocrisy. Abhor what is evil. Cling to what is good. 10*Be* kindly affectionate to one another with brotherly love, in honor giving preference to one another; 11not lagging in diligence, fervent in spirit, serving the Lord; 12rejoicing in hope, patient in tribulation, continuing steadfastly in prayer; 13distributing to the needs of the saints, given to hospitality.

14Bless those who persecute you; bless and do not curse. 15Rejoice with those who rejoice, and weep with those who weep. 16Be of the same mind toward one another. Do not set your mind on high things, but associate with the humble. Do not be wise in your own opinion.

17Repay no one evil for evil. Have regard for good things in the sight of all men. 18If it is possible, as much as depends on you, live peaceably with all men. 19Beloved, do not avenge your-

---

s Isaiah 59.20, 21 *t* Isaiah 40.13; Jeremiah 23.18 *u* Job 41.11

selves, but *rather* give place to wrath; for it is written, "Vengeance *is* Mine, I will repay,"ᵛ says the Lord. 20Therefore

"If your enemy is hungry, feed him;
If he is thirsty, give him a drink;
For in so doing you will heap coals
of fire on his head."ʷ

21Do not be overcome by evil, but overcome evil with good.

Submit to Government

13 Let every soul be subject to the governing authorities. For there is no authority except from God, and the authorities that exist are appointed by God. 2Therefore whoever resists the authority resists the ordinance of God, and those who resist will bring judgment on themselves. 3For rulers are not a terror to good works, but to evil. Do you want to be unafraid of the authority? Do what is good, and you will have praise from the same. 4For he is God's minister to you for good. But if you do evil, be afraid; for he does not bear the sword in vain; for he is God's minister, an avenger to *execute* wrath on him who practices evil. 5Therefore *you* must be subject, not only because of wrath but also for conscience' sake. 6For because of this you also pay taxes, for they are God's ministers attending continually to this very thing. 7Render therefore to all their due: taxes to whom taxes *are due*, customs to whom customs, fear to whom fear, honor to whom honor.

Love Your Neighbor

8Owe no one anything except to love one another, for he who loves another has fulfilled the law. 9For the commandments, "You shall not commit adultery," "You shall not murder," "You shall not steal," "You shall not bear false witness," "You shall not covet,"ˣ and if *there is* any other commandment, are *all* summed up in this saying, namely, "You shall love your neighbor as yourself."ʸ 10Love does no harm to a neighbor; therefore love *is* the fulfillment of the law.

Put on Christ

11And *do* this, knowing the time, that now *it is* high time to awake out of sleep; for now our salvation *is* nearer than when we *first* believed. 12The night is far spent, the day is at hand. Therefore let us cast off the works of darkness, and let us put on the armor of light. 13Let us walk properly, as in the day, not in revelry and drunkenness, not in lewdness and lust, not in strife and envy. 14But put on the Lord Jesus Christ, and make no provision for the flesh, to *fulfill its* lusts.

The Law of Liberty

14 Receive one who is weak in the faith, *but* not to disputes over doubtful things. 2For one believes he may eat all things, but he who is weak eats *only* vegetables. 3Let not him who eats despise him who does not eat, and let not him who does not eat judge him who eats; for God has received him. 4Who are you to judge another's servant? To his own master he stands or falls. Indeed, he will be made to stand, for God is able to make him stand.

5One person esteems *one* day above another; another esteems every day *alike.* Let each be fully convinced in his own mind. 6He who observes the day, observes *it* to the Lord; and he who does not observe the day, to the Lord he does not observe *it.* He who eats, eats to the Lord, for he gives God thanks; and he who does not eat, to the Lord he does not eat, and gives God thanks. 7For none of us lives to himself, and no one dies to himself. 8For if we live, we live to the Lord; and if we die, we die to the Lord. Therefore, whether we live or die, we are the Lord's. 9For to this end Christ died and rose and lived again, that He might be Lord of both the dead and the living. 10But why do you judge your brother? Or why do you show contempt for your brother? For we shall all stand before the judgment seat of Christ. 11For it is written:

"*As* I live, says the LORD,
Every knee shall bow to Me,

ᵛ Deuteronomy 32.35   ʷ Proverbs 25.21, 22   ˣ Exodus 20.13-15, 17;
Deuteronomy 5.17-19, 21   ʸ Leviticus 19.18

And every tongue shall confess
    to God."z

12So then each of us shall give account of himself to God. 13Therefore let us not judge one another anymore, but rather resolve this, not to put a stumbling block or a cause to fall in our brother's way.

The Law of Love

14I know and am convinced by the Lord Jesus that there is nothing unclean of itself; but to him who considers anything to be unclean, to him it is unclean. 15Yet if your brother is grieved because of your food, you are no longer walking in love. Do not destroy with your food the one for whom Christ died. 16Therefore do not let your good be spoken of as evil; 17for the kingdom of God is not eating and drinking, but righteousness and peace and joy in the Holy Spirit. 18For he who serves Christ in these things is acceptable to God and approved by men.

19Therefore let us pursue the things which make for peace and the things by which one may edify another. 20Do not destroy the work of God for the sake of food. All things indeed are pure, but it is evil for the man who eats with offense. 21It is good neither to eat meat nor drink wine nor do anything by which your brother stumbles or is offended or is made weak. 22Do you have faith? Have it to yourself before God. Happy is he who does not condemn himself in what he approves. 23But he who doubts is condemned if he eats, because he does not eat from faith; for whatever is not from faith is sin.

Bearing Others' Burdens

15 We then who are strong ought to bear with the scruples of the weak, and not to please ourselves. 2Let each of us please his neighbor for his good, leading to edification. 3For even Christ did not please Himself; but as it is written, "The reproaches of those who reproached You fell on Me."a 4For whatever things were written before were written for our learn-

ing, that we through the patience and comfort of the Scriptures might have hope. 5Now may the God of patience and comfort grant you to be like-minded toward one another, according to Christ Jesus, 6that you may with one mind and one mouth glorify the God and Father of our Lord Jesus Christ.

Glorify God Together

7Therefore receive one another, just as Christ also received us, to the glory of God. 8Now I say that Jesus Christ has become a servant to the circumcision for the truth of God, to confirm the promises made to the fathers, 9and that the Gentiles might glorify God for His mercy, as it is written:
    "For this reason I will confess to You
      among the Gentiles,
    And sing to Your name."b
10And again he says:
    "Rejoice, O Gentiles, with His
      people!"c
11And again:
    "Praise the LORD, all you Gentiles!
    Laud Him, all you peoples!"d
12And again, Isaiah says:
    "There shall be a root of Jesse;
    And He who shall rise to reign over
      the Gentiles,
    In Him the Gentiles shall hope."e
13Now may the God of hope fill you with all joy and peace in believing, that you may abound in hope by the power of the Holy Spirit.

From Jerusalem to Illyricum

14Now I myself am confident concerning you, my brethren, that you also are full of goodness, filled with all knowledge, able also to admonish one another. 15Nevertheless, brethren, I have written more boldly to you on some points, as reminding you, because of the grace given to me by God, 16that I might be a minister of Jesus Christ to the Gentiles, ministering the gospel of God, that the offering of the Gentiles might be acceptable, sanctified by the Holy Spirit. 17Therefore I have reason to glory in Christ Jesus in the things which pertain to God. 18For I will not dare to speak of any of those things

---

z Isaiah 45.23   a Psalm 69.9   b 2 Samuel 22.50; Psalm 18.49   c Deuteronomy 32.43
d Psalm 117.1   e Isaiah 11.10

which Christ has not accomplished through me, in word and deed, to make the Gentiles obedient—19in mighty signs and wonders, by the power of the Spirit of God, so that from Jerusalem and round about to Illyricum I have fully preached the gospel of Christ. 20And so I have made it my aim to preach the gospel, not where Christ was named, lest I should build on another man's foundation, 21but as it is written:

"To whom He was not announced,
    they shall see;
And those who have not heard shall
    understand."ᶠ

Plan to Visit Rome

22For this reason I also have been much hindered from coming to you. 23But now no longer having a place in these parts, and having a great desire these many years to come to you, 24whenever I journey to Spain, I shall come to you. For I hope to see you on my journey, and to be helped on my way there by you, if first I may enjoy your *company* for a while. 25But now I am going to Jerusalem to minister to the saints. 26For it pleased those from Macedonia and Achaia to make a certain contribution for the poor among the saints who are in Jerusalem. 27It pleased them indeed, and they are their debtors. For if the Gentiles have been partakers of their spiritual things, their duty is also to minister to them in material things. 28Therefore, when I have performed this and have sealed to them this fruit, I shall go by way of you to Spain. 29But I know that when I come to you, I shall come in the fullness of the blessing of the gospel of Christ.

30Now I beg you, brethren, through the Lord Jesus Christ, and through the love of the Spirit, that you strive together with me in prayers to God for me, 31that I may be delivered from those in Judea who do not believe, and that my service for Jerusalem may be acceptable to the saints, 32that I may come to you with joy by the will of God, and may be refreshed together with you. 33Now the God of peace *be* with you all. Amen.

Sister Phoebe Commended

16 I commend to you Phoebe our sister, who is a servant of the church in Cenchrea, 2that you may receive her in the Lord in a manner worthy of the saints, and assist her in whatever business she has need of you; for indeed she has been a helper of many and of myself also.

Greeting Roman Saints

3Greet Priscilla and Aquila, my fellow workers in Christ Jesus, 4who risked their own necks for my life, to whom not only I give thanks, but also all the churches of the Gentiles. 5Likewise *greet* the church that is in his house.

Greet my beloved Epaenetus, who is the firstfruits of Achaia to Christ. 6Greet Mary, who labored much for us. 7Greet Andronicus and Junia, my countrymen and my fellow prisoners, who are of note among the apostles, who also were in Christ before me.

8Greet Amplias, my beloved in the Lord. 9Greet Urbanus, our fellow worker in Christ, and Stachys, my beloved. 10Greet Apelles, approved in Christ. Greet those who are of the *household* of Aristobulus. 11Greet Herodion, my countryman. Greet those who are of the *household* of Narcissus who are in the Lord.

12Greet Tryphena and Tryphosa, who have labored in the Lord. Greet the beloved Persis, who labored much in the Lord. 13Greet Rufus, chosen in the Lord, and his mother and mine. 14Greet Asyncritus, Phlegon, Hermas, Patrobas, Hermes, and the brethren who are with them. 15Greet Philologus and Julia, Nereus and his sister, and Olympas, and all the saints who are with them.

16Greet one another with a holy kiss. The churches of Christ greet you.

Avoid Divisive Persons

17Now I urge you, brethren, note those who cause divisions and offenses, contrary to the doctrine which you learned, and avoid them. 18For those who are such do not serve our Lord Jesus Christ, but their own belly, and

ᶠ Isaiah 52.15

by smooth words and flattering speech deceive the hearts of the simple. 19For your obedience has become known to all. Therefore I am glad on your behalf; but I want you to be wise in what is good, and simple concerning evil. 20And the God of peace will crush Satan under your feet shortly.

The grace of our Lord Jesus Christ be with you. Amen.

Greetings from Paul's Friends

21Timothy, my fellow worker, and Lucius, Jason, and Sosipater, my countrymen, greet you.

22I, Tertius, who wrote this epistle, greet you in the Lord.

23Gaius, my host and the host of the whole church, greets you. Erastus, the treasurer of the city, greets you, and Quartus, a brother. 24The grace of our Lord Jesus Christ be with you all. Amen.

Benediction

25Now to Him who is able to establish you according to my gospel and the preaching of Jesus Christ, according to the revelation of the mystery kept secret since the world began 26but now made manifest, and by the prophetic Scriptures made known to all nations, according to the commandment of the everlasting God, for obedience to the faith—27to God, alone wise, be glory through Jesus Christ forever. Amen.

The First Epistle of Paul to the

CORINTHIANS

Greeting

1 Paul, called to be an apostle of Jesus Christ through the will of God, and Sosthenes our brother,

2To the church of God which is at Corinth, to those who are sanctified in Christ Jesus, called to be saints, with all who in every place call on the name of Jesus Christ our Lord, both theirs and ours:

3Grace to you and peace from God our Father and the Lord Jesus Christ.

Spiritual Gifts at Corinth

4I thank my God always concerning you for the grace of God which was given to you by Christ Jesus, 5that you were enriched in everything by Him in all utterance and all knowledge, 6even as the testimony of Christ was confirmed in you, 7so that you come short in no gift, eagerly waiting for the revelation of our Lord Jesus Christ, 8who will also confirm you to the end, that you may be blameless in the day of our Lord Jesus Christ. 9God is faithful, by whom you were called into the fellowship of His Son, Jesus Christ our Lord.

Sectarianism Is Sin

10Now I plead with you, brethren, by the name of our Lord Jesus Christ, that you all speak the same thing, and that there be no divisions among you, but that you be perfectly joined together in the same mind and in the same judgment. 11For it has been declared to me concerning you, my brethren, by those of Chloe's household, that there are contentions among you. 12Now I say this, that each of you says, "I am of Paul," or "I am of Apollos," or "I am of Cephas," or "I am of Christ."

13Is Christ divided? Was Paul crucified for you? Or were you baptized in the name of Paul?

14I thank God that I baptized none of you except Crispus and Gaius, 15lest anyone should say that I had baptized in my own name. 16Yes, I also baptized the household of Stephanas. Besides, I do not know whether I baptized any other. 17For Christ did not send me to baptize, but to preach the gospel, not with wisdom of words, lest the cross of Christ should be made of no effect.

Christ the Power and Wisdom of God

18For the message of the cross is foolishness to those who are perishing, but to us who are being saved it is the power of God. 19For it is written:

"I will destroy the wisdom of the wise,
And bring to nothing the understanding of the prudent."[a]

20Where *is* the wise? Where *is* the scribe? Where *is* the disputer of this age? Has not God made foolish the wisdom of this world? 21For since, in the wisdom of God, the world through wisdom did not know God, it pleased God through the foolishness of the message preached to save those who believe. 22For Jews request a sign, and Greeks seek after wisdom; 23but we preach Christ crucified, to the Jews a stumbling block and to the Greeks foolishness, 24but to those who are called, both Jews and Greeks, Christ the power of God and the wisdom of God. 25Because the foolishness of God is wiser than men, and the weakness of God is stronger than men.

Glory Only in the Lord

26For you see your calling, brethren, that not many wise according to the flesh, not many mighty, not many noble, *are called*. 27But God has chosen the foolish things of the world to put to shame the wise, and God has chosen the weak things of the world to put to shame the things which are mighty; 28and the base things of the world and the things which are despised God has

chosen, and the things which are not, to bring to nothing the things that are, 29that no flesh should glory in His presence. 30But of Him you are in Christ Jesus, who became for us wisdom from God—and righteousness and sanctification and redemption—31that, as it is written, "He who glories, let him glory in the LORD."[b]

Christ Crucified

2 And I, brethren, when I came to you, did not come with excellence of speech or of wisdom declaring to you the testimony of God. 2For I determined not to know anything among you except Jesus Christ and Him crucified. 3I was with you in weakness, in fear, and in much trembling. 4And my speech and my preaching *were* not with persuasive words of human wisdom, but in demonstration of the Spirit and of power, 5that your faith should not be in the wisdom of men but in the power of God.

Spiritual Wisdom

6However, we speak wisdom among those who are mature, yet not the wisdom of this age, nor of the rulers of this age, who are coming to nothing. 7But we speak the wisdom of God in a mystery, the hidden *wisdom* which God ordained before the ages for our glory, 8which none of the rulers of this age knew; for had they known, they would not have crucified the Lord of glory.

9But as it is written:

"Eye has not seen, nor ear heard,
Nor have entered into the heart of man
The things which God has prepared for those who love Him."[c]

10But God has revealed *them* to us through His Spirit. For the Spirit searches all things, yes, the deep things of God. 11For what man knows the things of a man except the spirit of the man which is in him? Even so no one knows the things of God except the Spirit of God. 12Now we have received, not the spirit of the world, but the Spirit who is from God, that we might know

a Isaiah 29.14   *b* Jeremiah 9.24   *c* Isaiah 64.4

the things that have been freely given to us by God.

13These things we also speak, not in words which man's wisdom teaches but which the Holy Spirit teaches, comparing spiritual things with spiritual. 14But the natural man does not receive the things of the Spirit of God, for they are foolishness to him; nor can he know *them*, because they are spiritually discerned. 15But he who is spiritual judges all things, yet he himself is *rightly* judged by no one. 16For "who has known the mind of the LORD that he may instruct Him?"*d* But we have the mind of Christ.

Sectarianism Is Carnal

3 And I, brethren, could not speak to you as to spiritual *people* but as to carnal, as to babes in Christ. 2I fed you with milk and not with solid food; for until now you were not able *to receive it*, and even now you are still not able; 3for you are still carnal. For where *there are* envy, strife, and divisions among you, are you not carnal and behaving like *mere* men? 4For when one says, "I am of Paul," and another, "I *am* of Apollos," are you not carnal?

Watering, Working, Warning

5Who then is Paul, and who *is* Apollos, but ministers through whom you believed, as the Lord gave to each one? 6I planted, Apollos watered, but God gave the increase. 7So then neither he who plants is anything, nor he who waters, but God who gives the increase. 8Now he who plants and he who waters are one, and each one will receive his own reward according to his own labor.

9For we are God's fellow workers; you are God's field, *you are* God's building. 10According to the grace of God which was given to me, as a wise master builder I have laid the foundation, and another builds on it. But let each one take heed how he builds on it. 11For no other foundation can anyone lay than that which is laid, which is Jesus Christ. 12Now if anyone builds on this foundation *with* gold, silver, precious stones, wood, hay, straw, 13each one's work will become clear;

for the Day will declare it, because it will be revealed by fire; and the fire will test each one's work, of what sort it is. 14If anyone's work which he has built on *it* endures, he will receive a reward. 15If anyone's work is burned, he will suffer loss; but he himself will be saved, yet so as through fire.

16Do you not know that you are the temple of God and *that* the Spirit of God dwells in you? 17If anyone defiles the temple of God, God will destroy him. For the temple of God is holy, which *temple* you are.

Avoid Worldly Wisdom

18Let no one deceive himself. If anyone among you seems to be wise in this age, let him become a fool that he may become wise. 19For the wisdom of this world is foolishness with God. For it is written, "He catches the wise in their *own* craftiness";*e* 20and again, "The LORD knows the thoughts of the wise, that they are futile."*f* 21Therefore let no one boast in men. For all things are yours: 22whether Paul or Apollos or Cephas, or the world or life or death, or things present or things to come—all are yours. 23And you *are* Christ's, and Christ *is* God's.

Stewards of the Mysteries of God

4 Let a man so consider us, as servants of Christ and stewards of the mysteries of God. 2Moreover it is required in stewards that one be found faithful. 3But with me it is a very small thing that I should be judged by you or by a human court. In fact, I do not even judge myself. 4For I know of nothing against myself, yet I am not justified by this; but He who judges me is the Lord. 5Therefore judge nothing before the time, until the Lord comes, who will both bring to light the hidden things of darkness and reveal the counsels of the hearts. Then each one's praise will come from God.

Fools for Christ's Sake

6Now these things, brethren, I have figuratively transferred to myself and Apollos for your sakes, that you may learn in us not to think beyond what is

d Isaiah 40.13   e Job 5.13   f Psalm 94.11

written, that none of you may be puffed up on behalf of one against the other. 7For who makes you differ *from another*? And what do you have that you did not receive? Now if you did indeed receive *it*, why do you boast as if you had not received *it*?

8You are already full! You are already rich! You have reigned as kings without us—and indeed I could wish you did reign, that we also might reign with you! 9For I think that God has displayed us, the apostles, last, as men condemned to death; for we have been made a spectacle to the world, both to angels and to men. 10We *are* fools for Christ's sake, but you *are* wise in Christ! We *are* weak, but you *are* strong! You *are* distinguished, but we *are* dishonored! 11To the present hour we both hunger and thirst, and we are poorly clothed, and beaten, and homeless. 12And we labor, working with our own hands. Being reviled, we bless; being persecuted, we endure; 13being defamed, we entreat. We have been made as the filth of the world, the offscouring of all things until now.

Paul's Paternal Care

14I do not write these things to shame you, but as my beloved children I warn you. 15For though you might have ten thousand instructors in Christ, yet *you do not have* many fathers; for in Christ Jesus I have begotten you through the gospel. 16Therefore I urge you, imitate me. 17For this reason I have sent Timothy to you, who is my beloved and faithful son in the Lord, who will remind you of my ways in Christ, as I teach everywhere in every church.

18Now some are puffed up, as though I were not coming to you. 19But I will come to you shortly, if the Lord wills, and I will know, not the word of those who are puffed up, but the power. 20For the kingdom of God *is* not in word but in power. 21What do you want? Shall I come to you with a rod, or in love and a spirit of gentleness?

Immorality Defiles the Church

5 It is actually reported *that there is* sexual immorality among you, and such sexual immorality as is not even named among the Gentiles—that a man has his father's wife! 2And you are puffed up, and have not rather mourned, that he who has done this deed might be taken away from among you. 3For I indeed, as absent in body but present in spirit, have already judged (as though I were present) him who has so done this deed. 4In the name of our Lord Jesus Christ, when you are gathered together, along with my spirit, with the power of our Lord Jesus Christ, 5deliver such a one to Satan for the destruction of the flesh, that his spirit may be saved in the day of the Lord Jesus.

6Your glorying *is* not good. Do you not know that a little leaven leavens the whole lump? 7Therefore purge out the old leaven, that you may be a new lump, since you truly are unleavened. For indeed Christ, our Passover, was sacrificed for us. 8Therefore let us keep the feast, not with old leaven, nor with the leaven of malice and wickedness, but with the unleavened *bread* of sincerity and truth.

Immorality Must Be Judged

9I wrote to you in my epistle not to keep company with sexually immoral people. 10Yet *I* certainly *did* not *mean* with the sexually immoral people of this world, or with the covetous, or extortioners, or idolaters, since then you would need to go out of the world. 11But now I have written to you not to keep company with anyone named a brother, who is sexually immoral, or covetous, or an idolater, or a reviler, or a drunkard, or an extortioner—not even to eat with such a person.

12For what *have* I *to do* with judging those also who are outside? Do you not judge those who are inside? 13But those who are outside God judges. Therefore "put away from yourselves the evil person."[g]

Do Not Sue the Brethren

6 Dare any of you, having a matter against another, go to law before the unrighteous, and not before the saints? 2Do you not know that the saints will

g Deuteronomy 17.7; 19.19; 22.21, 24; 24.7

judge the world? And if the world will be judged by you, are you unworthy to judge the smallest matters? 3Do you not know that we shall judge angels? How much more, things that pertain to this life? 4If then you have judgments concerning things pertaining to this life, do you appoint those who are least esteemed by the church to judge? 5I say this to your shame. Is it so, that there is not a wise man among you, not even one, who will be able to judge between his brethren? 6But brother goes to law against brother, and that before unbelievers!

7Now therefore, it is already an utter failure for you that you go to law against one another. Why do you not rather accept wrong? Why do you not rather *let yourselves* be cheated? 8No, you yourselves do wrong and cheat, and *you do* these things *to your* brethren! 9Do you not know that the unrighteous will not inherit the kingdom of God? Do not be deceived. Neither fornicators, nor idolaters, nor adulterers, nor homosexuals,*h* nor sodomites, 10nor thieves, nor covetous, nor drunkards, nor revilers, nor extortioners will inherit the kingdom of God. 11And such were some of you. But you were washed, but you were sanctified, but you were justified in the name of the Lord Jesus and by the Spirit of our God.

Glorify God in Body and Spirit

12All things are lawful for me, but all things are not helpful. All things are lawful for me, but I will not be brought under the power of any. 13Foods for the stomach and the stomach for foods, but God will destroy both it and them. Now the body *is* not for sexual immorality but for the Lord, and the Lord for the body. 14And God both raised up the Lord and will also raise us up by His power.

15Do you not know that your bodies are members of Christ? Shall I then take the members of Christ and make *them* members of a harlot? Certainly not! 16Or do you not know that he who is joined to a harlot is one body *with her?* For "the two," He says, "shall become one flesh."*i* 17But he who is joined to the Lord is one spirit *with Him.*

18Flee sexual immorality. Every sin that a man does is outside the body, but he who commits sexual immorality sins against his own body. 19Or do you not know that your body is the temple of the Holy Spirit *who is* in you, whom you have from God, and you are not your own? 20For you were bought at a price; therefore glorify God in your body and in your spirit, which are God's.

Principles of Marriage

7 Now concerning the things of which you wrote to me:

It is good for a man not to touch a woman. 2Nevertheless, because of sexual immorality, let each man have his own wife, and let each woman have her own husband. 3Let the husband render to his wife the affection due her, and likewise also the wife to her husband. 4The wife does not have authority over her own body, but the husband *does.* And likewise the husband does not have authority over his own body, but the wife *does.* 5Do not deprive one another except with consent for a time, that you may give yourselves to fasting and prayer; and come together again so that Satan does not tempt you because of your lack of self-control. 6But I say this as a concession, not as a commandment. 7For I wish that all men were even as I myself. But each one has his own gift from God, one in this manner and another in that.

8But I say to the unmarried and to the widows: It is good for them if they remain even as I am; 9but if they cannot exercise self-control, let them marry. For it is better to marry than to burn *with passion.*

Keep Your Marriage Vows

10Now to the married I command, *yet* not I but the Lord: A wife is not to depart from *her* husband. 11But even if she does depart, let her remain unmarried or be reconciled to *her* husband. And a husband is not to divorce *his* wife.

12But to the rest I, not the Lord, say:

h That is, catamites   *i* Genesis 2.24

If any brother has a wife who does not believe, and she is willing to live with him, let him not divorce her. 13And a woman who has a husband who does not believe, if he is willing to live with her, let her not divorce him. 14For the unbelieving husband is sanctified by the wife, and the unbelieving wife is sanctified by the husband; otherwise your children would be unclean, but now they are holy. 15But if the unbeliever departs, let him depart; a brother or a sister is not under bondage in such *cases*. But God has called us to peace. 16For how do you know, O wife, whether you will save *your* husband? Or how do you know, O husband, whether you will save *your* wife?

Live as You Are Called

17But as God has distributed to each one, as the Lord has called each one, so let him walk. And so I ordain in all the churches. 18Was anyone called while circumcised? Let him not become uncircumcised. Was anyone called while uncircumcised? Let him not be circumcised. 19Circumcision is nothing and uncircumcision is nothing, but keeping the commandments of God *is what matters*. 20Let each one remain in the same calling in which he was called. 21Were you called *while* a slave? Do not be concerned about it; but if you can be made free, rather use *it*. 22For he who is called in the Lord *while* a slave is the Lord's freedman. Likewise he who is called *while* free is Christ's slave. 23You were bought at a price; do not become slaves of men. 24Brethren, let each one remain with God in that *state* in which he was called.

To the Unmarried and Widows

25Now concerning virgins: I have no commandment from the Lord; yet I give judgment as one whom the Lord in His mercy *has made* trustworthy. 26I suppose therefore that this is good because of the present distress—that *it is* good for a man to remain as he is: 27Are you bound to a wife? Do not seek to be loosed. Are you loosed from a wife? Do not seek a wife. 28But even if you do marry, you have not sinned; and if a virgin marries, she has not sinned. Nevertheless such will have trouble in the flesh, but I would spare you.

29But this I say, brethren, the time *is* short, so that from now on even those who have wives should be as though they had none, 30those who weep as though they did not weep, those who rejoice as though they did not rejoice, those who buy as though they did not possess, 31and those who use this world as not misusing *it*. For the form of this world is passing away.

32But I want you to be without care. He who is unmarried cares for the things of the Lord—how he may please the Lord. 33But he who is married cares about the things of the world—how he may please *his* wife. 34There is a difference between a wife and a virgin. The unmarried woman cares about the things of the Lord, that she may be holy both in body and in spirit. But she who is married cares about the things of the world—how she may please *her* husband. 35And this I say for your own profit, not that I may put a leash on you, but for what is proper, and that you may serve the Lord without distraction.

36But if any man thinks he is behaving improperly toward his virgin, if she is past the flower of youth, and thus it must be, let him do what he wishes. He does not sin; let them marry. 37Nevertheless he who stands steadfast in his heart, having no necessity, but has power over his own will, and has so determined in his heart that he will keep his virgin,*j* does well. 38So then he who gives *her* in marriage does well, but he who does not give *her* in marriage does better.

39A wife is bound by law as long as her husband lives; but if her husband dies, she is at liberty to be married to whom she wishes, only in the Lord. 40But she is happier if she remains as she is, according to my judgment—and I think I also have the Spirit of God.

Be Sensitive to Conscience

8 Now concerning things offered to idols: We know that we all have knowledge. Knowledge puffs up, but love edifies. 2And if anyone thinks that

j Or *virgin daughter*

he knows anything, he knows nothing yet as he ought to know. 3But if anyone loves God, this one is known by Him.

4Therefore concerning the eating of things offered to idols, we know that an idol *is* nothing in the world, and that *there is* no other God but one. 5For even if there are so-called gods, whether in heaven or on earth (as there are many gods and many lords), 6yet for us *there is* one God, the Father, of whom *are* all things, and we for Him; and one Lord Jesus Christ, through whom *are* all things, and through whom we *live.*

7However, *there is* not in everyone that knowledge; for some, with consciousness of the idol, until now eat *it* as a thing offered to an idol; and their conscience, being weak, is defiled. 8But food does not commend us to God; for neither if we eat are we the better, nor if we do not eat are we the worse.

9But beware lest somehow this liberty of yours become a stumbling block to those who are weak. 10For if anyone sees you who have knowledge eating in an idol's temple, will not the conscience of him who is weak be emboldened to eat those things offered to idols? 11And because of your knowledge shall the weak brother perish, for whom Christ died? 12But when you thus sin against the brethren, and wound their weak conscience, you sin against Christ. 13Therefore, if food makes my brother stumble, I will never again eat meat, lest I make my brother stumble.

A Pattern of Self-Denial

9 Am I not an apostle? Am I not free? Have I not seen Jesus Christ our Lord? Are you not my work in the Lord? 2If I am not an apostle to others, yet doubtless I am to you. For you are the seal of my apostleship in the Lord.

3My defense to those who examine me is this: 4Do we have no right to eat and drink? 5Do we have no right to take along a believing wife, as *do* also the other apostles, the brothers of the Lord, and Cephas? 6Or *is it* only Barnabas and I *who* have no right to refrain from working? 7Who ever goes to war at his own expense? Who plants a vineyard and does not eat of its fruit? Or who

tends a flock and does not drink of the milk of the flock?

8Do I say these things as a *mere* man? Or does not the law say the same also? 9For it is written in the law of Moses, "You shall not muzzle an ox while it treads out the grain."*k* Is it oxen God is concerned about? 10Or does He say *it* altogether for our sakes? For our sakes, no doubt, *this* is written, that he who plows should plow in hope, and he who threshes in hope should be partaker of his hope. 11If we have sown spiritual things for you, *is it* a great thing if we reap your material things? 12If others are partakers of *this* right over you, *are* we not even more?

Nevertheless we have not used this right, but endure all things lest we hinder the gospel of Christ. 13Do you not know that those who minister the holy things eat *of the things* of the temple, and those who serve at the altar partake of *the offerings of* the altar? 14Even so the Lord has commanded that those who preach the gospel should live from the gospel.

15But I have used none of these things, nor have I written these things that it should be done so to me; for it *would be* better for me to die than that anyone should make my boasting void. 16For if I preach the gospel, I have nothing to boast of, for necessity is laid upon me; yes, woe is me if I do not preach the gospel! 17For if I do this willingly, I have a reward; but if against my will, I have been entrusted with a stewardship. 18What is my reward then? That when I preach the gospel, I may present the gospel of Christ without charge, that I may not abuse my authority in the gospel.

Serving All Men

19For though I am free from all *men,* I have made myself a servant to all, that I might win the more; 20and to the Jews I became as a Jew, that I might win Jews; to those *who are* under the law, as under the law, that I might win those *who are* under the law; 21to those *who are* without law, as without law (not being without law toward God, but under law toward Christ), that I might win

k Deuteronomy 25.4

those *who are* without law; 22to the weak I became as weak, that I might win the weak. I have become all things to all *men*, that I might by all means save some. 23Now this I do for the gospel's sake, that I may be partaker of it with *you.*

Striving for a Crown

24Do you not know that those who run in a race all run, but one receives the prize? Run in such a way that you may obtain *it.* 25And everyone who competes *for the prize* is temperate in all things. Now they *do it* to obtain a perishable crown, but we *for* an imperishable *crown.* 26Therefore I run thus: not with uncertainty. Thus I fight: not as *one who* beats the air. 27But I discipline my body and bring *it* into subjection, lest, when I have preached to others, I myself should become disqualified.

Old Testament Examples

10 Moreover, brethren, I do not want you to be unaware that all our fathers were under the cloud, all passed through the sea, 2all were baptized into Moses in the cloud and in the sea, 3all ate the same spiritual food, 4and all drank the same spiritual drink. For they drank of that spiritual Rock that followed them, and that Rock was Christ. 5But with most of them God was not well pleased, for *their bodies* were scattered in the wilderness.

6Now these things became our examples, to the intent that we should not lust after evil things as they also lusted. 7And do not become idolaters as *were* some of them. As it is written, "The people sat down to eat and drink, and rose up to play."[l] 8Nor let us commit sexual immorality, as some of them did, and in one day twenty-three thousand fell; 9nor let us tempt Christ, as some of them also tempted, and were destroyed by serpents; 10nor complain, as some of them also complained, and were destroyed by the destroyer. 11Now all these things happened to them as examples, and they were written for our admonition, upon whom the ends of the ages have come.

12Therefore let him who thinks he stands take heed lest he fall. 13No temptation has overtaken you except such as is common to man; but God *is* faithful, who will not allow you to be tempted beyond what you are able, but with the temptation will also make the way of escape, that you may be able to bear *it.*

Flee from Idolatry

14Therefore, my beloved, flee from idolatry. 15I speak as to wise men; judge for yourselves what I say. 16The cup of blessing which we bless, is it not the communion of the blood of Christ? The bread which we break, is it not the communion of the body of Christ? 17For we, *though* many, are one bread *and* one body; for we all partake of that one bread.

18Observe Israel after the flesh: Are not those who eat of the sacrifices partakers of the altar? 19What am I saying then? That an idol is anything, or what is offered to idols is anything? 20Rather, that the things which the Gentiles sacrifice they sacrifice to demons and not to God, and I do not want you to have fellowship with demons. 21You cannot drink the cup of the Lord and the cup of demons; you cannot partake of the Lord's table and of the table of demons. 22Or do we provoke the Lord to jealousy? Are we stronger than He?

All to the Glory of God

23All things are lawful for me, but not all things are helpful; all things are lawful for me, but not all things edify. 24Let no one seek his own, but each one the other's *well-being.*

25Eat whatever is sold in the meat market, asking no questions for conscience' sake; 26for "the earth *is* the LORD's, and all its fullness."[m]

27If any of those who do not believe invites you *to dinner*, and you desire to go, eat whatever is set before you, asking no question for conscience' sake. 28But if anyone says to you, "This was offered to idols," do not eat it for the sake of the one who told you, and for conscience' sake; for "the earth *is* the LORD's, and all its fullness."[m]

---

l Exodus 32.6   m Psalm 24.1

29"Conscience," I say, not your own, but that of the other. For why is my liberty judged by another man's conscience? 30But if I partake with thanks, why am I evil spoken of for the food over which I give thanks?

31Therefore, whether you eat or drink, or whatever you do, do all to the glory of God. 32Give no offense, either to the Jews or to the Greeks or to the church of God, 33just as I also please all men in all things, not seeking my own profit, but the profit of many, that they may be saved.

11 Imitate me, just as I also imitate Christ.

Head Coverings

2Now I praise you, brethren, that you remember me in all things and keep the traditions just as I delivered them to you. 3But I want you to know that the head of every man is Christ, the head of woman is man, and the head of Christ is God. 4Every man praying or prophesying, having his head covered, dishonors his head. 5But every woman who prays or prophesies with her head uncovered dishonors her head, for that is one and the same as if her head were shaved. 6For if a woman is not covered, let her also be shorn. But if it is shameful for a woman to be shorn or shaved, let her be covered. 7For a man indeed ought not to cover his head, since he is the image and glory of God; but woman is the glory of man. 8For man is not from woman, but woman from man. 9Nor was man created for the woman, but woman for the man. 10For this reason the woman ought to have a symbol of authority on her head, because of the angels. 11Nevertheless, neither is man independent of woman, nor woman independent of man, in the Lord. 12For as woman came from man, even so man also comes through woman; but all things are from God.

13Judge among yourselves. Is it proper for a woman to pray to God with her head uncovered? 14Does not even nature itself teach you that if a man has long hair, it is a dishonor to him? 15But if a woman has long hair, it is a glory to her; for her hair is given to her for a covering. 16But if anyone seems to be contentious, we have no such custom, nor do the churches of God.

Conduct at the Lord's Supper

17Now in giving these instructions I do not praise you, since you come together not for the better but for the worse. 18For first of all, when you come together as a church, I hear that there are divisions among you, and in part I believe it. 19For there must also be factions among you, that those who are approved may be recognized among you. 20Therefore when you come together in one place, it is not to eat the Lord's Supper. 21For in eating, each one takes his own supper ahead of others; and one is hungry and another is drunk. 22What! Do you not have houses to eat and drink in? Or do you despise the church of God and shame those who have nothing? What shall I say to you? Shall I praise you in this? I do not praise you.

Institution of the Lord's Supper

23For I received from the Lord that which I also delivered to you: that the Lord Jesus on the same night in which He was betrayed took bread; 24and when He had given thanks, He broke it and said, "Take, eat; this is My body which is broken for you; do this in remembrance of Me." 25In the same manner He also took the cup after supper, saying, "This cup is the new covenant in My blood. This do, as often as you drink it, in remembrance of Me."

26For as often as you eat this bread and drink this cup, you proclaim the Lord's death till He comes.

Examine Yourself

27Therefore whoever eats this bread or drinks this cup of the Lord in an unworthy manner will be guilty of the body and blood of the Lord. 28But let a man examine himself, and so let him eat of the bread and drink of the cup. 29For he who eats and drinks in an unworthy manner eats and drinks judgment to himself, not discerning the Lord's body. 30For this reason many are weak and sick among you, and many sleep. 31For if we would judge ourselves, we would not be judged. 32But when we are judged, we are chastened by the Lord, that we may not be condemned with the world.

33Therefore, my brethren, when you come together to eat, wait for one another. 34But if anyone is hungry, let him eat at home, lest you come together for judgment. And the rest I will set in order when I come.

Spiritual Gifts: Unity in Diversity

12 Now concerning spiritual *gifts,* brethren, I do not want you to be ignorant: 2You know that you were Gentiles, carried away to these dumb idols, however you were led. 3Therefore I make known to you that no one speaking by the Spirit of God calls Jesus accursed, and no one can say that Jesus is Lord except by the Holy Spirit.

4There are diversities of gifts, but the same Spirit. 5There are differences of ministries, but the same Lord. 6And there are diversities of activities, but it is the same God who works all in all. 7But the manifestation of the Spirit is given to each one for the profit *of all:* 8for to one is given the word of wisdom through the Spirit, to another the word of knowledge through the same Spirit, 9to another faith by the same Spirit, to another gifts of healings by the same Spirit, 10to another the working of miracles, to another prophecy, to another discerning of spirits, to another *different* kinds of tongues, to another the interpretation of tongues. 11But one and the same Spirit works all these things, distributing to each one individually as He wills.

Unity and Diversity in One Body

12For as the body is one and has many members, but all the members of that one body, being many, are one body, so also *is* Christ. 13For by one Spirit we were all baptized into one body—whether Jews or Greeks, whether slaves or free—and have all been made to drink into one Spirit. 14For in fact the body is not one member but many.

15If the foot should say, "Because I am not a hand, I am not of the body," is it therefore not of the body? 16And if the ear should say, "Because I am not an eye, I am not of the body," is it therefore not of the body? 17If the whole

body *were* an eye, where *would be* the hearing? If the whole *were* hearing, where *would be* the smelling? 18But now God has set the members, each one of them, in the body just as He pleased. 19And if they *were* all one member, where *would* the body *be?*

20But now indeed *there are* many members, yet one body. 21And the eye cannot say to the hand, "I have no need of you"; nor again the head to the feet, "I have no need of you." 22No, much rather, those members of the body which seem to be weaker are necessary. 23And those *members* of the body which we think to be less honorable, on these we bestow greater honor; and our unpresentable *parts* have greater modesty, 24but our presentable *parts* have no need. But God composed the body, having given greater honor to that *part* which lacks it, 25that there should be no schism in the body, but *that* the members should have the same care for one another. 26And if one member suffers, all the members suffer with *it;* or if one member is honored, all the members rejoice with *it.*

27Now you are the body of Christ, and members individually. 28And God has appointed these in the church: first apostles, second prophets, third teachers, after that miracles, then gifts of healings, helps, administrations, varieties of tongues. 29*Are* all apostles? *Are* all prophets? *Are* all teachers? *Are* all workers of miracles? 30Do all have gifts of healings? Do all speak with tongues? Do all interpret? 31But earnestly desire the best gifts. And yet I show you a more excellent way.

The Greatest Gift

13 Though I speak with the tongues of men and of angels, but have not love, I have become sounding brass or a clanging cymbal. 2And though I have *the gift of* prophecy, and understand all mysteries and all knowledge, and though I have all faith, so that I could remove mountains, but have not love, I am nothing. 3And though I bestow all my goods to feed *the poor,* and though I give my body to be burned, but have not love, it profits me nothing.

4Love suffers long *and* is kind; love does not envy; love does not parade itself, is not puffed up; 5does not behave rudely, does not seek its own, is not provoked, thinks no evil; 6does not rejoice in iniquity, but rejoices in the truth; 7bears all things, believes all things, hopes all things, endures all things.

8Love never fails. But whether *there are* prophecies, they will fail; whether *there are* tongues, they will cease; whether *there is* knowledge, it will vanish away. 9For we know in part and we prophesy in part. 10But when that which is perfect has come, then that which is in part will be done away.

11When I was a child, I spoke as a child, I understood as a child, I thought as a child; but when I became a man, I put away childish things. 12For now we see in a mirror, dimly, but then face to face. Now I know in part, but then I shall know just as I also am known.

13And now abide faith, hope, love, these three; but the greatest of these *is* love.

Prophecy and Tongues

14 Pursue love, and desire spiritual *gifts*, but especially that you may prophesy. 2For he who speaks in a tongue does not speak to men but to God, for no one understands *him;* however, in the spirit he speaks mysteries. 3But he who prophesies speaks edification and exhortation and comfort to men. 4He who speaks in a tongue edifies himself, but he who prophesies edifies the church. 5I wish you all spoke with tongues, but even more that you prophesied; for he who prophesies *is* greater than he who speaks with tongues, unless indeed he interprets, that the church may receive edification.

Tongues Must Be Interpreted

6But now, brethren, if I come to you speaking with tongues, what shall I profit you unless I speak to you either by revelation, by knowledge, by prophesying, or by teaching? 7Even things without life, whether flute or harp, when they make a sound, unless they make a distinction in the sounds, how will it be known what is piped or played? 8For if the trumpet makes an uncertain sound, who will prepare for

battle? 9So likewise you, unless you utter by the tongue words easy to understand, how will it be known what is spoken? For you will be speaking into the air. 10There are, it may be, so many kinds of languages in the world, and none of them *is* without significance. 11Therefore, if I do not know the meaning of the language, I shall be a foreigner to him who speaks, and he who speaks *will be* a foreigner to me. 12Even so you, since you are zealous for spiritual *gifts, let it be* for the edification of the church *that* you seek to excel.

13Therefore let him who speaks in a tongue pray that he may interpret. 14For if I pray in a tongue, my spirit prays, but my understanding is unfruitful. 15What is *the conclusion* then? I will pray with the spirit, and I will also pray with the understanding. I will sing with the spirit, and I will also sing with the understanding. 16Otherwise, if you bless with the spirit, how will he who occupies the place of the uninformed say "Amen" at your giving of thanks, since he does not understand what you say? 17For you indeed give thanks well, but the other is not edified.

18I thank my God I speak with tongues more than you all; 19yet in the church I would rather speak five words with my understanding, that I may teach others also, than ten thousand words in a tongue.

Tongues a Sign to Unbelievers

20Brethren, do not be children in understanding; however, in malice be babes, but in understanding be mature. 21In the law it is written:

"With *men of* other tongues and other lips
I will speak to this people;
And yet, for all that, they will not hear Me,"[n]

says the Lord. 22Therefore tongues are for a sign, not to those who believe but to unbelievers; but prophesying is not for unbelievers but for those who believe. 23Therefore if the whole church comes together in one place, and all speak with tongues, and there come in *those*

n Isaiah 28.11, 12

who are uninformed or unbelievers, will they not say that you are out of your mind? 24But if all prophesy, and an unbeliever or an uninformed person comes in, he is convinced by all, he is convicted by all. 25And thus the secrets of his heart are revealed; and so, falling down on *his* face, he will worship God and report that God is truly among you.

Order in Church Meetings

26How is it then, brethren? Whenever you come together, each of you has a psalm, has a teaching, has a tongue, has a revelation, has an interpretation. Let all things be done for edification. 27If anyone speaks in a tongue, *let there be* two or at the most three, *each* in turn, and let one interpret. 28But if there is no interpreter, let him keep silent in church, and let him speak to himself and to God. 29Let two or three prophets speak, and let the others judge. 30But if *anything* is revealed to another who sits by, let the first keep silent. 31For you can all prophesy one by one, that all may learn and all may be encouraged. 32And the spirits of the prophets are subject to the prophets. 33For God is not *the author* of confusion but of peace, as in all the churches of the saints.

34Let your women keep silent in the churches, for they are not permitted to speak; but *they are* to be submissive, as the law also says. 35And if they want to learn something, let them ask their own husbands at home; for it is shameful for women to speak in church.

36Or did the word of God come *originally* from you? Or *was it* you only that it reached? 37If anyone thinks himself to be a prophet or spiritual, let him acknowledge that the things which I write to you are the commandments of the Lord. 38But if anyone is ignorant, let him be ignorant.

39Therefore, brethren, desire earnestly to prophesy, and do not forbid to speak with tongues. 40Let all things be done decently and in order.

The Risen Christ, Faith's Reality

15 Moreover, brethren, I declare to you the gospel which I preached to you, which also you received and in which you stand, 2by which also you are saved, if you hold fast that word which I preached to you—unless you believed in vain.

3For I delivered to you first of all that which I also received: that Christ died for our sins according to the Scriptures, 4and that He was buried, and that He rose again the third day according to the Scriptures, 5and that He was seen by Cephas, then by the twelve. 6After that He was seen by over five hundred brethren at once, of whom the greater part remain to the present, but some have fallen asleep. 7After that He was seen by James, then by all the apostles. 8Then last of all He was seen by me also, as by one born out of due time.

9For I am the least of the apostles, who am not worthy to be called an apostle, because I persecuted the church of God. 10But by the grace of God I am what I am, and His grace toward me was not in vain; but I labored more abundantly than they all, yet not I, but the grace of God *which was* with me. 11Therefore, whether *it was* I or they, so we preach and so you believed.

The Risen Christ, Our Hope

12Now if Christ is preached that He has been raised from the dead, how do some among you say that there is no resurrection of the dead? 13But if there is no resurrection of the dead, then Christ is not risen. 14And if Christ is not risen, then our preaching *is* empty and your faith *is* also empty. 15Yes, and we are found false witnesses of God, because we have testified of God that He raised up Christ, whom He did not raise up—if in fact the dead do not rise. 16For if *the* dead do not rise, then Christ is not risen. 17And if Christ is not risen, your faith *is* futile; you are still in your sins! 18Then also those who have fallen asleep in Christ have perished. 19If in this life only we have hope in Christ, we are of all men the most pitiable.

The Last Enemy Destroyed

20But now Christ is risen from the dead, *and* has become the firstfruits of those who have fallen asleep. 21For since by man *came* death, by Man also *came* the resurrection of the dead.

22For as in Adam all die, even so in Christ all shall be made alive. 23But each one in his own order: Christ the firstfruits, afterward those *who are* Christ's at His coming. 24Then *comes* the end, when He delivers the kingdom to God the Father, when He puts an end to all rule and all authority and power. 25For He must reign till He has put all enemies under His feet. 26The last enemy *that* will be destroyed *is* death. 27For "He has put all things under His feet."*o* But when He says "all things are put under *Him*," *it is* evident that He who put all things under Him is excepted. 28Now when all things are made subject to Him, then the Son Himself will also be subject to Him who put all things under Him, that God may be all in all.

Effects of Denying the Resurrection

29Otherwise, what will they do who are baptized for the dead, if the dead do not rise at all? Why then are they baptized for the dead? 30And why do we stand in jeopardy every hour? 31I affirm, by the boasting in you which I have in Christ Jesus our Lord, I die daily. 32If, in the manner of men, I have fought with beasts at Ephesus, what advantage *is it* to me? If *the* dead do not rise, "Let us eat and drink, for tomorrow we die!"*p*

33Do not be deceived: "Evil company corrupts good habits." 34Awake to righteousness, and do not sin; for some do not have the knowledge of God. I speak *this* to your shame.

A Glorious Body

35But someone will say, "How are the dead raised up? And with what body do they come?" 36Foolish one, what you sow is not made alive unless it dies. 37And what you sow, you do not sow that body that shall be, but mere grain—perhaps wheat or some other *grain.* 38But God gives it a body as He pleases, and to each seed its own body.

39All flesh *is* not the same flesh, but *there is* one *kind of* flesh of men, another flesh of animals, another of fish, *and* another of birds.

40*There are* also celestial bodies and terrestrial bodies; but the glory of the celestial *is* one, and the *glory* of the terrestrial *is* another. 41*There is* one glory of the sun, another glory of the moon, and another glory of the stars; for *one* star differs from *another* star in glory.

42So also *is* the resurrection of the dead. *The body* is sown in corruption, it is raised in incorruption. 43It is sown in dishonor, it is raised in glory. It is sown in weakness, it is raised in power. 44It is sown a natural body, it is raised a spiritual body. There is a natural body, and there is a spiritual body. 45And so it is written, "The first man Adam became a living being."*q* The last Adam *became* a life-giving spirit.

46However, the spiritual is not first, but the natural, and afterward the spiritual. 47The first man *was* of the earth, *made* of dust; the second Man *is* the Lord from heaven. 48As *was* the *man* of dust, so also *are* those *who are made* of dust; and as *is* the heavenly *Man,* so also *are* those *who are* heavenly. 49And as we have borne the image of the *man* of dust, we shall also bear the image of the heavenly *Man.*

Our Final Victory

50Now this I say, brethren, that flesh and blood cannot inherit the kingdom of God; nor does corruption inherit incorruption. 51Behold, I tell you a mystery: We shall not all sleep, but we shall all be changed— 52in a moment, in the twinkling of an eye, at the last trumpet. For the trumpet will sound, and the dead will be raised incorruptible, and we shall be changed. 53For this corruptible must put on incorruption, and this mortal *must* put on immortality. 54So when this corruptible has put on incorruption, and this mortal has put on immortality, then shall be brought to pass the saying that is written: "Death is swallowed up in victory."*r*

55 "O Death, where *is* your sting?

O Hades, where *is* your victory?"*s*

56The sting of death *is* sin, and the strength of sin *is* the law. 57But thanks *be* to God, who gives us the victory through our Lord Jesus Christ.

58Therefore, my beloved brethren, be steadfast, immovable, always abound-

o Psalm 8.6   *p* Isaiah 22.13   *q* Genesis 2.7   *r* Isaiah 25.8   *s* Hosea 13.14

ing in the work of the Lord, knowing that your labor is not in vain in the Lord.

Collection for the Saints

16 Now concerning the collection for the saints, as I have given orders to the churches of Galatia, so you must do also: 2On the first *day* of the week let each one of you lay something aside, storing up as he may prosper, that there be no collections when I come. 3And when I come, whomever you approve by *your* letters I will send to bear your gift to Jerusalem. 4But if it is fitting that I go also, they will go with me.

Personal Plans

5Now I will come to you when I pass through Macedonia (for I am passing through Macedonia). 6And it may be that I will remain, or even spend the winter with you, that you may send me on my journey, wherever I go. 7For I do not wish to see you now on the way; but I hope to stay a while with you, if the Lord permits.

8But I will tarry in Ephesus until Pentecost. 9For a great and effective door has opened to me, and *there are* many adversaries.

10And if Timothy comes, see that he may be with you without fear; for he does the work of the Lord, as I also *do*. 11Therefore let no one despise him. But send him on his journey in peace, that he may come to me; for I am waiting for him with the brethren.

12Now concerning *our* brother Apol-los, I strongly urged him to come to you with the brethren, but he was quite unwilling to come at this time; however, he will come when he has a convenient time.

Final Exhortations

13Watch, stand fast in the faith, be brave, be strong. 14Let all *that* you *do* be done with love.

15I urge you, brethren—you know the household of Stephanas, that it is the firstfruits of Achaia, and *that* they have devoted themselves to the ministry of the saints—16that you also submit to such, and to everyone who works and labors with *us*.

17I am glad about the coming of Stephanas, Fortunatus, and Achaicus, for what was lacking on your part they supplied. 18For they refreshed my spirit and yours. Therefore acknowledge such men.

Greetings and a Solemn Farewell

19The churches of Asia greet you. Aquila and Priscilla greet you heartily in the Lord, with the church that is in their house. 20All the brethren greet you.

Greet one another with a holy kiss. 21The salutation with my own hand—Paul's.

22If anyone does not love the Lord Jesus Christ, let him be accursed. O Lord, come!

23The grace of our Lord Jesus Christ *be* with you. 24My love *be* with you all in Christ Jesus. Amen.

The Second Epistle of Paul to the

CORINTHIANS

Greeting

1 Paul, an apostle of Jesus Christ by the will of God, and Timothy *our* brother,

To the church of God which is at Corinth, with all the saints who are in all Achaia:

2Grace to you and peace from God our Father and the Lord Jesus Christ.

Comfort in Suffering

3Blessed *be* the God and Father of our Lord Jesus Christ, the Father of mercies and God of all comfort, 4who comforts us in all our tribulation, that we may be able to comfort those who are in any trouble, with the comfort with which we ourselves are comforted by God. 5For as the sufferings of Christ abound in us, so our consolation also abounds through Christ. 6Now if we are afflicted, *it is* for your consolation and salvation, which is effective for enduring the same sufferings which we also suffer. Or if we are comforted, *it is* for your consolation and salvation. 7And our hope for you *is* steadfast, because we know that as you are partakers of the sufferings, so also *you will partake* of the consolation.

Delivered from Suffering

8For we do not want you to be ignorant, brethren, of our trouble which came to us in Asia: that we were burdened beyond measure, above strength, so that we despaired even of life. 9Yes, we had the sentence of death in ourselves, that we should not trust in ourselves but in God who raises the dead, 10who delivered us from so great a death, and does deliver us; in whom we trust that He will still deliver *us,* 11you also helping together in prayer for us, that thanks may be given by many persons on our behalf for the gift *granted* to us through many.

Paul's Sincerity

12For our boasting is this: the testimony of our conscience that we conducted ourselves in the world in simplicity and godly sincerity, not with fleshly wisdom but by the grace of God, and more abundantly toward you. 13For we are not writing any other things to you than what you read or understand. Now I trust you will understand, even to the end 14(as also you have understood us in part), that we are your boast as you also *are* ours, in the day of the Lord Jesus.

Sparing the Church

15And in this confidence I intended to come to you before, that you might have a second benefit—16to pass by way of you to Macedonia, to come again from Macedonia to you, and be helped by you on my way to Judea. 17Therefore, when I was planning this, did I do it lightly? Or the things I plan, do I plan according to the flesh, that with me there should be Yes, Yes, and No, No? 18But *as* God *is* faithful, our word to you was not Yes and No. 19For the Son of God, Jesus Christ, who was preached among you by us—by me, Silvanus, and Timothy—was not Yes and No, but in Him was Yes. 20For all the promises of God in Him *are* Yes, and in Him Amen, to the glory of God through us. 21Now He who establishes us with you in Christ and has anointed us *is* God, 22who also has sealed us and given us the Spirit in our hearts as a guarantee.

23Moreover I call God as witness against my soul, that to spare you I came no more to Corinth. 24Not that we have dominion over your faith, but are fellow workers for your joy; for by faith you stand.

2 But I determined this within myself, that I would not come again to you in sorrow. 2For if I make you sorrowful, then who is he who makes me glad but the one who is made sorrowful by me?

Forgive the Offender

3And I wrote this very thing to you, lest, when I came, I should have sorrow over those from whom I ought to have joy, having confidence in you all that my joy is *the joy* of you all. 4For out of much affliction and anguish of heart I wrote to you, with many tears, not that you should be grieved, but that you might know the love which I have so abundantly for you.

5But if anyone has caused grief, he has not grieved me, but all of you to some extent—not to be too severe. 6This punishment which *was inflicted* by the majority *is* sufficient for such a man, 7so that, on the contrary, you *ought* rather to forgive and comfort *him*, lest perhaps such a one be swallowed up with too much sorrow. 8Therefore I urge you to reaffirm *your* love to him. 9For to this end I also wrote, that I might put you to the test, whether you are obedient in all things. 10Now whom you forgive anything, I also *forgive*. For if indeed I have forgiven anything, I have forgiven that one for your sakes in the presence of Christ, 11lest Satan should take advantage of us; for we are not ignorant of his devices.

Triumph in Christ

12Furthermore, when I came to Troas to *preach* Christ's gospel, and a door was opened to me by the Lord, 13I had no rest in my spirit, because I did not find Titus my brother; but taking my leave of them, I departed for Macedonia.

14Now thanks *be* to God who always leads us in triumph in Christ, and through us diffuses the fragrance of His knowledge in every place. 15For we are to God the fragrance of Christ among those who are being saved and among those who are perishing. 16To the one *we are* the aroma of death *leading* to death, and to the other the aroma of life *leading* to life. And who *is* sufficient for these things? 17For we are not, as so many, peddling the word of God; but as of sincerity, but as from God, we speak in the sight of God in Christ.

Christ's Epistle

3 Do we begin again to commend ourselves? Or do we need, as some *others*, epistles of commendation to you or *letters* of commendation from you? 2You are our epistle written in our hearts, known and read by all men; 3clearly *you are* an epistle of Christ, ministered by us, written not with ink but by the Spirit of the living God, not on tablets of stone but on tablets of flesh, *that is*, of the heart.

The Spirit, Not the Letter

4And we have such trust through Christ toward God. 5Not that we are sufficient of ourselves to think of anything as *being* from ourselves, but our sufficiency *is* from God, 6who also made us sufficient as ministers of the new covenant, not of the letter but of the Spirit;[a] for the letter kills, but the Spirit gives life.

Glory of the New Covenant

7But if the ministry of death, written *and* engraved on stones, was glorious, so that the children of Israel could not look steadily at the face of Moses because of the glory of his countenance, which *glory* was passing away, 8how will the ministry of the Spirit not be more glorious? 9For if the ministry of condemnation *had* glory, the ministry of righteousness exceeds much more in glory. 10For even what was made glorious had no glory in this respect, because of the glory that excels. 11For if what is passing away *was* glorious, what remains *is* much more glorious.

12Therefore, since we have such hope, we use great boldness of speech— 13unlike Moses, *who* put a veil over his face so that the children of Israel could not look steadily at the end of what was passing away. 14But their minds were blinded. For until this day the same veil remains unlifted in the reading of the Old Testament, because the *veil* is taken away in Christ. 15But even to this day, when Moses is read, a veil lies on their heart. 16Nevertheless when one turns to the Lord, the veil is taken away. 17Now the Lord is the Spirit; and where the Spirit of the Lord *is*, there *is* liberty. 18But we all, with unveiled face, beholding as in a mirror the glory of the Lord,

a Or *spirit*

are being transformed into the same image from glory to glory, just as by the Spirit of the Lord.

The Light of Christ's Gospel

4 Therefore, since we have this ministry, as we have received mercy, we do not lose heart. 2But we have renounced the hidden things of shame, not walking in craftiness nor handling the word of God deceitfully, but by manifestation of the truth commending ourselves to every man's conscience in the sight of God. 3But even if our gospel is veiled, it is veiled to those who are perishing, 4whose minds the god of this age has blinded, who do not believe, lest the light of the gospel of the glory of Christ, who is the image of God, should shine on them. 5For we do not preach ourselves, but Christ Jesus the Lord, and ourselves your bondservants for Jesus' sake. 6For it is the God who commanded light to shine out of darkness, who has shone in our hearts to *give* the light of the knowledge of the glory of God in the face of Jesus Christ.

Cast Down but Unconquered

7But we have this treasure in earthen vessels, that the excellence of the power may be of God and not of us. 8*We are* hard-pressed on every side, yet not crushed; *we are* perplexed, but not in despair; 9persecuted, but not forsaken; struck down, but not destroyed— 10always carrying about in the body the dying of the Lord Jesus, that the life of Jesus also may be manifested in our body. 11For we who live are always delivered to death for Jesus' sake, that the life of Jesus also may be manifested in our mortal flesh. 12So then death is working in us, but life in you.

13And since we have the same spirit of faith, according to what is written, "I believed and therefore I spoke,"*b* we also believe and therefore speak, 14knowing that He who raised us up with the Lord Jesus will also raise us up with Jesus, and will present *us* with you. 15For all things *are* for your sakes, that grace, having spread through the many, may cause thanksgiving to abound to the glory of God.

Seeing the Invisible

16Therefore we do not lose heart. Even though our outward man is perishing, yet the inward *man* is being renewed day by day. 17For our light affliction, which is but for a moment, is working for us a far more exceeding *and* eternal weight of glory, 18while we do not look at the things which are seen, but at the things which are not seen. For the things which are seen *are* temporary, but the things which are not seen *are* eternal.

Assurance of the Resurrection

5 For we know that if our earthly house, *this* tent, is destroyed, we have a building from God, a house not made with hands, eternal in the heavens. 2For in this we groan, earnestly desiring to be clothed with our habitation which is from heaven, 3if indeed, having been clothed, we shall not be found naked. 4For we who are in *this* tent groan, being burdened, not because we want to be unclothed, but further clothed, that mortality may be swallowed up by life. 5Now He who has prepared us for this very thing *is* God, who also has given us the Spirit as a guarantee.

6So *we are* always confident, knowing that while we are at home in the body we are absent from the Lord. 7For we walk by faith, not by sight. 8We are confident, yes, well pleased rather to be absent from the body and to be present with the Lord.

The Judgment Seat of Christ

9Therefore we make it our aim, whether present or absent, to be well pleasing to Him. 10For we must all appear before the judgment seat of Christ, that each one may receive the things *done* in the body, according to what he has done, whether good or bad. 11Knowing, therefore, the terror of the Lord, we persuade men; but we are well known to God, and I also trust are well known in your consciences.

Be Reconciled to God

12For we do not commend ourselves again to you, but give you opportunity

b Psalm 116.10

to boast on our behalf, that you may have *an answer* for those who boast in appearance and not in heart. 13For if we are beside ourselves, *it is* for God; or if we are of sound mind, *it is* for you. 14For the love of Christ compels us, because we judge thus: that if One died for all, then all died; 15and He died for all, that those who live should live no longer for themselves, but for Him who died for them and rose again.

16Therefore, from now on, we regard no one according to the flesh. Even though we have known Christ according to the flesh, yet now we know *Him* thus no longer. 17Therefore, if anyone *is* in Christ, *he is* a new creation; old things have passed away; behold, all things have become new. 18Now all things *are* of God, who has reconciled us to Himself through Jesus Christ, and has given us the ministry of reconciliation, 19that is, that God was in Christ reconciling the world to Himself, not imputing their trespasses to them, and has committed to us the word of reconciliation.

20Now then, we are ambassadors for Christ, as though God were pleading through us: we implore *you* on Christ's behalf, be reconciled to God. 21For He made Him who knew no sin *to be* sin for us, that we might become the righteousness of God in Him.

Marks of the Ministry

6 We then, *as* workers together *with* Him also plead with *you* not to receive the grace of God in vain. 2For He says:

"In an acceptable time I have
    heard you,
  And in the day of salvation I have
    helped you."c

Behold, now *is* the accepted time; behold, now *is* the day of salvation.

3We give no offense in anything, that our ministry may not be blamed. 4But in all *things* we commend ourselves as ministers of God: in much patience, in tribulations, in needs, in distresses, 5in stripes, in imprisonments, in tumults, in labors, in sleeplessness, in fastings; 6by purity, by knowledge, by longsuffering, by kindness, by the Holy Spirit, by sincere love, 7by the word of truth, by the power of God, by the armor of righteousness on the right hand and on the left, 8by honor and dishonor, by evil report and good report; as deceivers, and *yet* true; 9as unknown, and *yet* well known; as dying, and behold we live; as chastened, and *yet* not killed; 10as sorrowful, yet always rejoicing; as poor, yet making many rich; as having nothing, and *yet* possessing all things.

Be Holy

11O Corinthians! We have spoken openly to you, our heart is wide open. 12You are not restricted by us, but you are restricted by your *own* affections. 13Now in return for the same (I speak as to children), you also be open.

14Do not be unequally yoked together with unbelievers. For what fellowship has righteousness with lawlessness? And what communion has light with darkness? 15And what accord has Christ with Belial? Or what part has a believer with an unbeliever? 16And what agreement has the temple of God with idols? For you are the temple of the living God. As God has said:

"I will dwell in them
  And walk among *them*.
I will be their God,
  And they shall be My people."d

17Therefore

"Come out from among them
  And be separate, says the Lord.
Do not touch what is unclean,
  And I will receive you."e

18 "I will be a Father to you,
  And you shall be My sons and
    daughters,
  Says the LORD Almighty."f

7 Therefore, having these promises, beloved, let us cleanse ourselves from all filthiness of the flesh and spirit, perfecting holiness in the fear of God.

The Corinthians' Repentance

2Open *your hearts* to us. We have wronged no one, we have corrupted no one, we have cheated no one. 3I do not

c Isaiah 49.8   d Leviticus 26.12; Jeremiah 32.38; Ezekiel 37.27   e Isaiah 52.11;
Ezekiel 20.34, 41   f 2 Samuel 7.14

say *this* to condemn; for I have said before that you are in our hearts, to die together and to live together. 4Great *is* my boldness of speech toward you, great *is* my boasting on your behalf. I am filled with comfort. I am exceedingly joyful in all our tribulation.

5For indeed, when we came to Macedonia, our bodies had no rest, but we were troubled on every side. Outside *were* conflicts, inside *were* fears. 6Nevertheless God, who comforts the downcast, comforted us by the coming of Titus, 7and not only by his coming, but also by the consolation with which he was comforted in you, when he told us of your earnest desire, your mourning, your zeal for me, so that I rejoiced even more.

8For even if I made you sorry with my letter, I do not regret it; though I did regret it. For I perceive that the same epistle made you sorry, though only for a while. 9Now I rejoice, not that you were made sorry, but that your sorrow led to repentance. For you were made sorry in a godly manner, that you might suffer loss from us in nothing. 10For godly sorrow produces repentance *leading* to salvation, not to be regretted; but the sorrow of the world produces death. 11For observe this very thing, that you sorrowed in a godly manner: What diligence it produced in you, *what* clearing *of yourselves*, *what* indignation, *what* fear, *what* vehement desire, *what* zeal, *what* vindication! In all *things* you proved yourselves to be clear in this matter. 12Therefore, although I wrote to you, *I did* not *do it* for the sake of him who had done the wrong, nor for the sake of him who suffered wrong, but that our care for you in the sight of God might appear to you.

The Joy of Titus

13Therefore we have been comforted in your comfort. And we rejoiced exceedingly more for the joy of Titus, because his spirit has been refreshed by you all. 14For if in anything I have boasted to him about you, I am not ashamed. But as we spoke all things to you in truth, even so our boasting to Titus was found true. 15And his affections are greater for you as he remembers the obedience of you all, how with fear and trembling you received him. 16Therefore I rejoice that I have confidence in you in everything.

Excel in Giving

8 Moreover, brethren, we make known to you the grace of God bestowed on the churches of Macedonia: 2that in a great trial of affliction the abundance of their joy and their deep poverty abounded in the riches of their liberality. 3For I bear witness that according to *their* ability, yes, and beyond *their* ability, *they were* freely willing, 4imploring us with much urgency that we would receive the gift and the fellowship of the ministering to the saints. 5And not *only* as we had hoped, but they first gave themselves to the Lord, and *then* to us by the will of God. 6So we urged Titus, that as he had begun, so he would also complete this grace in you as well. 7But as you abound in everything—in faith, in speech, in knowledge, in all diligence, and in your love for us—*see* that you abound in this grace also.

Christ Our Pattern

8I speak not by commandment, but I am testing the sincerity of your love by the diligence of others. 9For you know the grace of our Lord Jesus Christ, that though He was rich, yet for your sakes He became poor, that you through His poverty might become rich.

10And in this I give advice: It is to your advantage not only to be doing what you began and were desiring to do a year ago; 11but now you also must complete the doing *of it;* that as *there was* a readiness to desire *it,* so *there* also *may be* a completion out of what *you* have. 12For if there is first a willing mind, *it is* accepted according to what one has, *and* not according to what he does not have.

13For *I do* not *mean* that others should be eased and you burdened; 14but by an equality, *that* now at this time your abundance *may supply* their lack, that their abundance also may supply your lack—that there may be equality. 15As it is written, "He who *gathered* much had nothing left over, and he who *gathered* little had no lack."*g*

Collection for the Judean Saints

16But thanks *be* to God who puts the same earnest care for you into the heart of Titus. 17For he not only accepted the exhortation, but being more diligent, he went to you of his own accord. 18And we have sent with him the brother whose praise *is* in the gospel throughout all the churches, 19and not only *that,* but who was also chosen by the churches to travel with us with this gift, which is administered by us to the glory of the Lord Himself and *to show* your ready mind, 20avoiding this: that anyone should blame us in this lavish gift which is administered by us— 21providing honorable things, not only in the sight of the Lord, but also in the sight of men.

22And we have sent with them our brother whom we have often proved diligent in many things, but now much more diligent, because of the great confidence which *we have* in you. 23If *any-one inquires* about Titus, *he is* my part-ner and fellow worker concerning you. Or if our brethren *are inquired about, they are* messengers of the churches, the glory of Christ. 24Therefore show to them, and before the churches the proof of your love and of our boasting on your behalf.

Administering the Gift

9 Now concerning the ministering to the saints, it is superfluous for me to write to you; 2for I know your will-ingness, about which I boast of you to the Macedonians, that Achaia was ready a year ago; and your zeal has stirred up the majority. 3Yet I have sent the brethren, lest our boasting of you should be in vain in this respect, that, as I said, you may be ready; 4lest if *some* Macedonians come with me and find you unprepared, we (not to men-tion you!) should be ashamed of this confident boasting. 5Therefore I thought it necessary to exhort the brethren to go to you ahead of time, and prepare your generous gift beforehand, which *you had* previously promised,

that it may be ready as *a matter of* gen-erosity and not as a grudging obliga-tion.

The Cheerful Giver

6But this I *say:* He who sows spar-ingly will also reap sparingly, and he who sows bountifully will also reap bountifully. 7*So let* each one *give* as he purposes in his heart, not grudgingly or of necessity; for God loves a cheerful giver. 8And God *is* able to make all grace abound toward you, that you, al-ways having all sufficiency in all *things,* may have an abundance for every good work. 9As it is written:

"He has dispersed abroad,
    He has given to the poor;
    His righteousness endures
        forever."*h*

10Now may He who supplies seed to the sower, and bread for food, supply and multiply the seed you have *sown* and increase the fruits of your right-eousness, 11while *you are* enriched in everything for all liberality, which causes thanksgiving through us to God. 12For the administration of this service not only supplies the needs of the saints, but also is abounding through many thanksgivings to God, 13while, through the proof of this ministry, they glorify God for the obedience of your confession to the gospel of Christ, and for *your* liberal sharing with them and all *men,* 14and by their prayer for you, who long for you because of the exceeding grace of God in you. 15Thanks *be* to God for His indescrib-able gift!

The Spiritual War

10 Now I, Paul, myself am pleading with you by the meekness and gentleness of Christ—who in presence *am* lowly among you, but being absent am bold toward you. 2But I beg *you* that when I am present I may not be bold with that confidence by which I intend to be bold against some, who think of us as if we walked according to the flesh. 3For though we walk in the flesh, we do not war according to the flesh. 4For the weapons of our warfare *are* not carnal but mighty in God for pull-

g Exodus 16.18   *h* Psalm 112.9

ing down strongholds, 5casting down arguments and every high thing that exalts itself against the knowledge of God, bringing every thought into captivity to the obedience of Christ, 6and being ready to punish all disobedience when your obedience is fulfilled.

Reality of Paul's Authority

7Do you look at things according to the outward appearance? If anyone is convinced in himself that he is Christ's, let him again consider this in himself, that just as he *is* Christ's, even so we *are* Christ's. 8For even if I should boast somewhat more about our authority, which the Lord gave us for edification and not for your destruction, I shall not be ashamed—9lest I seem to terrify you by letters. 10"For *his* letters," they say, "*are* weighty and powerful, but *his* bodily presence *is* weak, and *his* speech contemptible." 11Let such a person consider this, that what we are in word by letters when we are absent, such *we will* also *be* in deed when we are present.

Limits of Paul's Authority

12For we dare not class ourselves or compare ourselves with those who commend themselves. But they, measuring themselves by themselves, and comparing themselves among themselves, are not wise. 13We, however, will not boast beyond measure, but within the limits of the sphere which God appointed us—a sphere which especially includes you. 14For we are not overextending ourselves (as though *our authority* did not extend to you), for it was to you that we came with the gospel of Christ; 15not boasting of things beyond measure, *that is*, in other men's labors, but having hope, *that* as your faith is increased, we shall be greatly enlarged by you in our sphere, 16to preach the gospel in the *regions* beyond you, *and* not to boast in another man's sphere of accomplishment.

17But "he who glories, let him glory in the LORD."[i] 18For not he who commends himself is approved, but whom the Lord commends.

Concern for Their Faithfulness

11 Oh, that you would bear with me in a little folly—and indeed you do bear with me. 2For I am jealous for you with godly jealousy. For I have betrothed you to one husband, that I may present *you as* a chaste virgin to Christ. 3But I fear, lest somehow, as the serpent deceived Eve by his craftiness, so your minds may be corrupted from the simplicity that is in Christ. 4For if he who comes preaches another Jesus whom we have not preached, or *if* you receive a different spirit which you have not received, or a different gospel which you have not accepted—you may well put up with it!

Paul and False Apostles

5For I consider that I am not at all inferior to the most eminent apostles. 6Even though *I am* untrained in speech, yet *I am* not in knowledge. But we have been thoroughly manifested among you in all things.

7Did I commit sin in humbling myself that you might be exalted, because I preached the gospel of God to you free of charge? 8I robbed other churches, taking wages *from them* to minister to you. 9And when I was present with you, and in need, I was a burden to no one, for what I lacked the brethren who came from Macedonia supplied. And in everything I kept myself from being burdensome to you, and so I will keep *myself*. 10As the truth of Christ is in me, no one shall stop me from this boasting in the regions of Achaia. 11Why? Because I do not love you? God knows!

12But what I do, I will also continue to do, that I may cut off the opportunity from those who desire an opportunity to be regarded just as we are in the things of which they boast. 13For such *are* false apostles, deceitful workers, transforming themselves into apostles of Christ. 14And no wonder! For Satan himself transforms himself into an angel of light. 15Therefore *it is* no great thing if his ministers also transform themselves into ministers of righteousness, whose end will be according to their works.

i Jeremiah 9.24

Reluctant Boasting

16I say again, let no one think me a fool. If otherwise, at least receive me as a fool, that I also may boast a little. 17What I speak, I speak not according to the Lord, but as it were, foolishly, in this confidence of boasting. 18Seeing that many boast according to the flesh, I also will boast. 19For you put up with fools gladly, since you *yourselves* are wise! 20For you put up with it if one brings you into bondage, if one devours *you*, if one takes *from you*, if one exalts himself, if one strikes you on the face. 21To *our* shame I say that we were too weak for that! But in whatever anyone is bold—I speak foolishly—I am bold also.

Suffering for Christ

22Are they Hebrews? So *am* I. Are they Israelites? So *am* I. Are they the seed of Abraham? So *am* I. 23Are they ministers of Christ?—I speak as a fool—I *am* more: in labors more abundant, in stripes above measure, in prisons more frequently, in deaths often. 24From the Jews five times I received forty *stripes* minus one. 25Three times I was beaten with rods; once I was stoned; three times I was shipwrecked; a night and a day I have been in the deep; 26*in* journeys often, *in* perils of waters, *in* perils of robbers, *in* perils of *my own* countrymen, *in* perils of the Gentiles, *in* perils in the city, *in* perils in the wilderness, *in* perils in the sea, *in* perils among false brethren; 27in weariness and toil, in sleeplessness often, in hunger and thirst, in fastings often, in cold and nakedness— 28besides the other things, what comes upon me daily: my deep concern for all the churches. 29Who is weak, and I am not weak? Who is made to stumble, and I do not burn *with indignation*?

30If I must boast, I will boast in the things which concern my infirmity. 31The God and Father of our Lord Jesus Christ, who is blessed forever, knows that I am not lying. 32In Damascus the governor, under Aretas the king, was guarding the city of the Damascenes with a garrison, desiring to arrest me; 33but I was let down in a basket through a window in the wall, and escaped from his hands.

The Vision of Paradise

12 It is doubtless not profitable for me to boast. I will come to visions and revelations of the Lord: 2I know a man in Christ who fourteen years ago—whether in the body I do not know, or whether out of the body I do not know, God knows—such a one was caught up to the third heaven. 3And I know such a man—whether in the body or out of the body I do not know, God knows— 4how he was caught up into Paradise and heard inexpressible words, which it is not lawful for a man to utter. 5Of such a one I will boast; yet of myself I will not boast, except in my infirmities. 6For though I might desire to boast, I will not be a fool; for I will speak the truth. But I refrain, lest anyone should think of me above what he sees me *to be* or hears from me.

The Thorn in the Flesh

7And lest I should be exalted above measure by the abundance of the revelations, a thorn in the flesh was given to me, a messenger of Satan to buffet me, lest I be exalted above measure. 8Concerning this thing I pleaded with the Lord three times that it might depart from me. 9And He said to me, "My grace is sufficient for you, for My strength is made perfect in weakness." Therefore most gladly I will rather boast in my infirmities, that the power of Christ may rest upon me. 10Therefore I take pleasure in infirmities, in reproaches, in needs, in persecutions, in distresses, for Christ's sake. For when I am weak, then I am strong.

Signs of an Apostle

11I have become a fool in boasting; you have compelled me. For I ought to have been commended by you; for in nothing was I behind the most eminent apostles, though I am nothing. 12Truly the signs of an apostle were accomplished among you with all perseverance, in signs and wonders and mighty deeds. 13For what is it in which you were inferior to other churches, except that I myself was not burdensome to you? Forgive me this wrong!

Love for the Church

14Now *for* the third time I am ready to come to you. And I will not be burdensome to you; for I do not seek yours, but you. For the children ought not to lay up for the parents, but the parents for the children. 15And I will very gladly spend and be spent for your souls; though the more abundantly I love you, the less I am loved.

16But be that *as it may*, I did not burden you. Nevertheless, being crafty, I caught you by cunning! 17Did I take advantage of you by any of those whom I sent to you? 18I urged Titus, and sent our brother with *him*. Did Titus take advantage of you? Did we not walk in the same spirit? Did *we* not *walk* in the same steps?

19Again, do you think that we excuse ourselves to you? We speak before God in Christ. But *we do* all things, beloved, for your edification. 20For I fear lest, when I come, I shall not find you such as I wish, and *that* I shall be found by you such as you do not wish; lest *there be* contentions, jealousies, outbursts of wrath, selfish ambitions, backbitings, whisperings, conceits, tumults; 21lest, when I come again, my God will humble me among you, and I shall mourn for many who have sinned before and have not repented of the uncleanness, fornication, and lewdness which they have practiced.

Coming with Authority

13 This *will be* the third *time* I am coming to you. "By the mouth of two or three witnesses every word shall be established."*ʲ* 2I have told you before, and foretell as if I were present the second time, and now being absent I write to those who have sinned before, and to all the rest, that if I come again I will not spare—3since you seek a proof of Christ speaking in me, who is not weak toward you, but mighty in you. 4For though He was crucified in weakness, yet He lives by the power of God. For we also are weak in Him, but we shall live with Him by the power of God toward you.

5Examine yourselves *as to* whether you are in the faith. Test yourselves. Do you not know yourselves, that Jesus Christ is in you?—unless indeed you are disqualified. 6But I trust that you will know that we are not disqualified.

Paul Prefers Gentleness

7Now I pray to God that you do no evil, not that we should appear approved, but that you should do what is honorable, though we may seem disqualified. 8For we can do nothing against the truth, but for the truth. 9For we are glad when we are weak and you are strong. And this also we pray, that you may be made complete. 10Therefore I write these things being absent, lest being present I should use sharpness, according to the authority which the Lord has given me for edification and not for destruction.

Greetings and Benediction

11Finally, brethren, farewell. Become complete. Be of good comfort, be of one mind, live in peace; and the God of love and peace will be with you.

12Greet one another with a holy kiss. 13All the saints greet you.

14The grace of the Lord Jesus Christ, and the love of God, and the communion of the Holy Spirit *be* with you all. Amen.

ʲ Deuteronomy 19.15

GALATIANS

Greeting

1 Paul, an apostle (not from men nor through man, but through Jesus Christ and God the Father who raised Him from the dead), 2and all the brethren who are with me,

To the churches of Galatia:

3Grace to you and peace from God the Father and our Lord Jesus Christ, 4who gave Himself for our sins, that He might deliver us from this present evil age, according to the will of our God and Father, 5to whom be glory forever and ever. Amen.

Only One Gospel

6I marvel that you are turning away so soon from Him who called you in the grace of Christ, to a different gospel, 7which is not another; but there are some who trouble you and want to pervert the gospel of Christ. 8But even if we, or an angel from heaven, preach any other gospel to you than what we have preached to you, let him be accursed. 9As we have said before, so now I say again, if anyone preaches any other gospel to you than what you have received, let him be accursed.

10For do I now persuade men, or God? Or do I seek to please men? For if I still pleased men, I would not be a bondservant of Christ.

Call to Apostleship

11But I make known to you, brethren, that the gospel which was preached by me is not according to man. 12For I neither received it from man, nor was I taught it, but it came through the revelation of Jesus Christ.

13For you have heard of my former conduct in Judaism, how I persecuted the church of God beyond measure and tried to destroy it. 14And I advanced in Judaism beyond many of my contemporaries in my own nation, being more exceedingly zealous for the traditions of my fathers.

15But when it pleased God, who separated me from my mother's womb and called me through His grace, 16to reveal His Son in me, that I might preach Him among the Gentiles, I did not immediately confer with flesh and blood, 17nor did I go up to Jerusalem to those who were apostles before me; but I went to Arabia, and returned again to Damascus.

Contacts at Jerusalem

18Then after three years I went up to Jerusalem to see Peter, and remained with him fifteen days. 19But I saw none of the other apostles except James, the Lord's brother. 20(Now concerning the things which I write to you, indeed, before God, I do not lie.)

21Afterward I went into the regions of Syria and Cilicia. 22And I was unknown by face to the churches of Judea which were in Christ. 23But they were hearing only, "He who formerly persecuted us now preaches the faith which he once tried to destroy." 24And they glorified God in me.

Defending the Gospel

2 Then after fourteen years I went up again to Jerusalem with Barnabas, and also took Titus with me. 2And I went up by revelation, and communicated to them that gospel which I preach among the Gentiles, but privately to those who were of reputation, lest by any means I might run, or had run, in vain. 3Yet not even Titus who was with me, being a Greek, was compelled to be circumcised. 4And this occurred because of false brethren secretly brought in (who came in by stealth to spy out our liberty which we have in Christ Jesus, that they might bring us into bondage), 5to whom we did not yield submission even for an hour, that the truth of the gospel might continue with you.

6But from those who seemed to be something—whatever they were, it makes no difference to me; God shows personal favoritism to no man—for those who seemed to be something added nothing to me. 7But on the contrary, when they saw that the gospel for the uncircumcised had been committed to me, as *the gospel* for the circumcised *was* to Peter 8(for He who worked effectively in Peter for the apostleship to the circumcised also worked effectively in me toward the Gentiles), 9and when James, Cephas, and John, who seemed to be pillars, perceived the grace that had been given to me, they gave me and Barnabas the right hand of fellowship, that we *should go* to the Gentiles and they to the circumcised. 10*They desired* only that we should remember the poor, the very thing which I also was eager to do.

No Return to the Law

11Now when Peter had come to Antioch, I withstood him to his face, because he was to be blamed; 12for before certain men came from James, he would eat with the Gentiles; but when they came, he withdrew and separated himself, fearing those who were of the circumcision. 13And the rest of the Jews also played the hypocrite with him, so that even Barnabas was carried away with their hypocrisy.

14But when I saw that they were not straightforward about the truth of the gospel, I said to Peter before *them* all, "If you, being a Jew, live in the manner of Gentiles and not as the Jews, why do you compel Gentiles to live as Jews? 15We *who are* Jews by nature, and not sinners of the Gentiles, 16knowing that a man is not justified by the works of the law but by faith in Jesus Christ, even we have believed in Christ Jesus, that we might be justified by faith in Christ and not by the works of the law; for by the works of the law no flesh shall be justified.

17"But if, while we seek to be justified by Christ, we ourselves also are found sinners, *is* Christ therefore a minister of sin? Certainly not! 18For if I build again those things which I destroyed, I make myself a transgressor. 19For I through the law died to the law that I might live to God. 20I have been crucified with Christ; it is no longer I who

live, but Christ lives in me; and the *life* which I now live in the flesh I live by faith in the Son of God, who loved me and gave Himself for me. 21I do not set aside the grace of God; for if righteousness *comes* through the law, then Christ died in vain."

Justification by Faith

3 O foolish Galatians! Who has bewitched you that you should not obey the truth, before whose eyes Jesus Christ was clearly portrayed among you as crucified? 2This only I want to learn from you: Did you receive the Spirit by the works of the law, or by the hearing of faith? 3Are you so foolish? Having begun in the Spirit, are you now being made perfect by the flesh? 4Have you suffered so many things in vain—if indeed *it was* in vain?

5Therefore He who supplies the Spirit to you and works miracles among you, *does He do it* by the works of the law, or by the hearing of faith?—6just as Abraham "believed God, and it was accounted to him for righteousness."[a] 7Therefore know that *only* those who are of faith are sons of Abraham. 8And the Scripture, foreseeing that God would justify the Gentiles by faith, preached the gospel to Abraham beforehand, *saying*, "In you all the nations shall be blessed."[b] 9So then those who *are* of faith are blessed with believing Abraham.

The Law Brings a Curse

10For as many as are of the works of the law are under the curse; for it is written, "Cursed *is* everyone who does not continue in all things which are written in the book of the law, to do them."[c] 11But that no one is justified by the law in the sight of God *is* evident, for "the just shall live by faith."[d] 12Yet the law is not of faith, but "the man who does them shall live by them."[e]

13Christ has redeemed us from the curse of the law, having become a curse for us (for it is written, "Cursed *is* everyone who hangs on a tree"[f]), 14that the blessing of Abraham might come

---

[a] Genesis 15.6   [b] Genesis 12.3; 18.18; 22.18; 26.4; 28.14   [c] Deuteronomy 27.26
[d] Habakkuk 2.4   [e] Leviticus 18.5   [f] Deuteronomy 21.23

upon the Gentiles in Christ Jesus, that we might receive the promise of the Spirit through faith.

The Changeless Promise

15Brethren, I speak in the manner of men: Though *it is* only a man's covenant, yet *if it is* confirmed, no one annuls or adds to it. 16Now to Abraham and his Seed were the promises made. He does not say, "And to seeds," as of many, but as of one, "And to your Seed,"*g* who is Christ. 17And this I say, *that* the law, which was four hundred and thirty years later, cannot annul the covenant that was confirmed before by God in Christ, that it should make the promise of no effect. 18For if the inheritance *is* of the law, *it is* no longer of promise; but God gave *it* to Abraham by promise.

Purpose of the Law

19What purpose then *does* the law serve? It was added because of transgressions, till the Seed should come to whom the promise was made; *and it was* appointed through angels by the hand of a mediator. 20Now a mediator does not *mediate* for one *only*, but God is one.

21*Is* the law then against the promises of God? Certainly not! For if there had been a law given which could have given life, truly righteousness would have been by the law. 22But the Scripture has confined all under sin, that the promise by faith in Jesus Christ might be given to those who believe. 23But before faith came, we were kept under guard by the law, kept for the faith which would afterward be revealed. 24Therefore the law was our tutor *to bring us* to Christ, that we might be justified by faith. 25But after faith has come, we are no longer under a tutor.

Sons and Heirs

26For you are all sons of God through faith in Christ Jesus. 27For as many of you as were baptized into Christ have put on Christ. 28There is neither Jew nor Greek, there is neither slave nor free, there is neither male nor female; for you are all one in Christ Jesus.

29And if you *are* Christ's, then you are Abraham's seed, and heirs according to the promise.

4 Now I say *that* the heir, as long as he is a child, does not differ at all from a slave, though he is master of all, 2but is under guardians and stewards until the time appointed by the father. 3Even so we, when we were children, were in bondage under the elements of the world. 4But when the fullness of the time had come, God sent forth His Son, born of a woman, born under the law, 5to redeem those who were under the law, that we might receive the adoption as sons.

6And because you are sons, God has sent forth the Spirit of His Son into your hearts, crying out, "Abba, Father!" 7Therefore you are no longer a slave but a son, and if a son, then an heir of God through Christ.

Fears for the Church

8But then, indeed, when you did not know God, you served those which by nature are not gods. 9But now after you have known God, or rather are known by God, how *is it that* you turn again to the weak and beggarly elements, to which you desire again to be in bondage? 10You observe days and months and seasons and years. 11I am afraid for you, lest I have labored for you in vain.

12Brethren, I urge you to become like me, for I *became* like you. You have not injured me at all. 13You know that because of physical infirmity I preached the gospel to you at the first. 14And my trial which was in my flesh you did not despise or reject, but you received me as an angel of God, *even* as Christ Jesus. 15What then was the blessing you *enjoyed*? For I bear you witness that, if possible, you would have plucked out your own eyes and given them to me. 16Have I therefore become your enemy because I tell you the truth?

17They zealously court you, *but* for no good; yes, they want to exclude you, that you may be zealous for them. 18But it is good to be zealous in a good thing always, and not only when I am

g Genesis 12.7; 13.15; 24.7

present with you. 19My little children, for whom I labor in birth again until Christ is formed in you, 20I would like to be present with you now and to change my tone; for I have doubts about you.

Two Covenants

21Tell me, you who desire to be under the law, do you not hear the law? 22For it is written that Abraham had two sons: the one by a bondwoman, the other by a freewoman. 23But he *who was* of the bondwoman was born according to the flesh, and he of the freewoman through promise, 24which things are symbolic. For these are the two covenants: the one from Mount Sinai which gives birth to bondage, which is Hagar—25for this Hagar is Mount Sinai in Arabia, and corresponds to Jerusalem which now is, and is in bondage with her children—26but the Jerusalem above is free, which is the mother of us all. 27For it is written:

"Rejoice, O barren,
   You who do not bear!
Break forth and shout,
You who are not in labor!
For the desolate has many more
   children
Than she who has a husband."[h]

28Now we, brethren, as Isaac *was,* are children of promise. 29But, as he who was born according to the flesh then persecuted him *who was born* according to the Spirit, even so *it is* now. 30Nevertheless what does the Scripture say? "Cast out the bondwoman and her son, for the son of the bondwoman shall not be heir with the son of the freewoman."[i] 31So then, brethren, we are not children of the bondwoman but of the free.

Christian Liberty

5 Stand fast therefore in the liberty by which Christ has made us free, and do not be entangled again with a yoke of bondage. 2Indeed I, Paul, say to you that if you become circumcised, Christ will profit you nothing. 3And I testify again to every man who becomes circumcised that he is a debtor to keep the whole law. 4You have become estranged from Christ, you who *attempt to* be justified by law; you have fallen from grace. 5For we through the Spirit eagerly wait for the hope of righteousness by faith. 6For in Christ Jesus neither circumcision nor uncircumcision avails anything, but faith working through love.

Love Fulfills the Law

7You ran well. Who hindered you from obeying the truth? 8This persuasion does not *come* from Him who calls you. 9A little leaven leavens the whole lump. 10I have confidence in you, in the Lord, that you will have no other mind; but he who troubles you shall bear his judgment, whoever he is.

11And I, brethren, if I still preach circumcision, why do I still suffer persecution? Then the offense of the cross has ceased. 12I could wish that those who trouble you would even cut themselves off!

13For you, brethren, have been called to liberty; only do not *use* liberty as an opportunity for the flesh, but through love serve one another. 14For all the law is fulfilled in one word, *even* in this: "You shall love your neighbor as yourself."[j] 15But if you bite and devour one another, beware lest you be consumed by one another!

Walking in the Spirit

16I say then: Walk in the Spirit, and you shall not fulfill the lust of the flesh. 17For the flesh lusts against the Spirit, and the Spirit against the flesh; and these are contrary to one another, so that you do not do the things that you wish. 18But if you are led by the Spirit, you are not under the law.

19Now the works of the flesh are evident, which are: adultery, fornication, uncleanness, lewdness, 20idolatry, sorcery, hatred, contentions, jealousies, outbursts of wrath, selfish ambitions, dissensions, heresies, 21envy, murders, drunkenness, revelries, and the like; of which I tell you beforehand, just as I also told *you* in time past, that those who practice such things will not inherit the kingdom of God.

22But the fruit of the Spirit is love,

---

[h] Isaiah 54.1   [i] Genesis 21.10   [j] Leviticus 19.18

joy, peace, longsuffering, kindness, goodness, faithfulness, 23gentleness, self-control. Against such there is no law. 24And those *who are* Christ's have crucified the flesh with its passions and desires. 25If we live in the Spirit, let us also walk in the Spirit. 26Let us not become conceited, provoking one another, envying one another.

Bear and Share the Burdens

6 Brethren, if a man is overtaken in any trespass, you who *are* spiritual restore such a one in a spirit of gentleness, considering yourself lest you also be tempted. 2Bear one another's burdens, and so fulfill the law of Christ. 3For if anyone thinks himself to be something, when he is nothing, he deceives himself. 4But let each one examine his own work, and then he will have rejoicing in himself alone, and not in another. 5For each one shall bear his own load.

Be Generous and Do Good

6Let him who is taught the word share in all good things with him who teaches.

7Do not be deceived, God is not mocked; for whatever a man sows, that he will also reap. 8For he who sows to his flesh will of the flesh reap corruption, but he who sows to the Spirit will of the Spirit reap everlasting life.

9And let us not grow weary while doing good, for in due season we shall reap if we do not lose heart. 10Therefore, as we have opportunity, let us do good to all, especially to those who are of the household of faith.

Glory Only in the Cross

11See with what large letters I have written to you with my own hand! 12As many as desire to make a good showing in the flesh, these *would* compel you to be circumcised, only that they may not suffer persecution for the cross of Christ. 13For not even those who are circumcised keep the law, but they desire to have you circumcised that they may boast in your flesh. 14But God forbid that I should boast except in the cross of our Lord Jesus Christ, by whom[k] the world has been crucified to me, and I to the world. 15For in Christ Jesus neither circumcision nor uncircumcision avails anything, but a new creation.

Blessing and a Plea

16And as many as walk according to this rule, peace and mercy *be* upon them, and upon the Israel of God.

17From now on let no one trouble me, for I bear in my body the marks of the Lord Jesus.

18Brethren, the grace of our Lord Jesus Christ *be* with your spirit. Amen.

---

[k] Or *by which* (the cross)

Greeting

1 Paul, an apostle of Jesus Christ by the will of God,

To the saints who are in Ephesus, and faithful in Christ Jesus:

2Grace to you and peace from God our Father and the Lord Jesus Christ.

Redemption in Christ

3Blessed *be* the God and Father of our Lord Jesus Christ, who has blessed us with every spiritual blessing in the heavenly *places* in Christ, 4just as He chose us in Him before the foundation of the world, that we should be holy and without blame before Him in love, 5having predestined us to adoption as sons by Jesus Christ to Himself, according to the good pleasure of His will, 6to the praise of the glory of His grace, by which He made us accepted in the Beloved.

7In Him we have redemption through His blood, the forgiveness of sins, according to the riches of His grace 8which He made to abound toward us in all wisdom and prudence, 9having made known to us the mystery of His will, according to His good pleasure which He purposed in Himself, 10that in the dispensation of the fullness of the times He might gather together in one all things in Christ, both which are in heaven and which are on earth—in Him. 11In Him also we have obtained an inheritance, being predestined according to the purpose of Him who works all things according to the counsel of His will, 12that we who first trusted in Christ should be to the praise of His glory.

13In Him you also *trusted*, after you heard the word of truth, the gospel of your salvation; in whom also, having believed, you were sealed with the Holy Spirit of promise, 14who is the guarantee of our inheritance until the redemption of the purchased possession, to the praise of His glory.

Prayer for Spiritual Wisdom

15Therefore I also, after I heard of your faith in the Lord Jesus and your love for all the saints, 16do not cease to give thanks for you, making mention of you in my prayers: 17that the God of our Lord Jesus Christ, the Father of glory, may give to you the spirit of wisdom and revelation in the knowledge of Him, 18the eyes of your understanding being enlightened; that you may know what is the hope of His calling, what are the riches of the glory of His inheritance in the saints, 19and what *is* the exceeding greatness of His power toward us who believe, according to the working of His mighty power 20which He worked in Christ when He raised Him from the dead and seated *Him* at His right hand in the heavenly *places*, 21far above all principality and power and might and dominion, and every name that is named, not only in this age but also in that which is to come.

22And He put all *things* under His feet, and gave Him *to be* head over all *things* to the church, 23which is His body, the fullness of Him who fills all in all.

By Grace Through Faith

2 And you *He made alive*, who were dead in trespasses and sins, 2in which you once walked according to the course of this world, according to the prince of the power of the air, the spirit who now works in the sons of disobedience, 3among whom also we all once conducted ourselves in the lusts of our flesh, fulfilling the desires of the flesh and of the mind, and were by nature children of wrath, just as the others.

4But God, who is rich in mercy, because of His great love with which He loved us, 5even when we were dead in trespasses, made us alive together with Christ (by grace you have been saved), 6and raised *us* up together, and made *us* sit together in the heavenly *places* in Christ Jesus, 7that in the ages to come He might show the exceeding riches of His grace in *His* kindness toward us in Christ Jesus. 8For by grace you have been saved through faith, and that not of yourselves; *it is* the gift of God, 9not of works, lest anyone should boast. 10For we are His workmanship, created in Christ Jesus for good works, which God prepared beforehand that we should walk in them.

Brought Near by His Blood

11Therefore remember that you, once Gentiles in the flesh—who are called Uncircumcision by what is called the Circumcision made in the flesh by hands—12that at that time you were without Christ, being aliens from the commonwealth of Israel and strangers from the covenants of promise, having no hope and without God in the world. 13But now in Christ Jesus you who once were far off have been brought near by the blood of Christ.

Christ Our Peace

14For He Himself is our peace, who has made both one, and has broken down the middle wall of separation, 15having abolished in His flesh the enmity, *that is*, the law of commandments *contained* in ordinances, so as to create in Himself one new man *from* the two, *thus* making peace, 16and that He might reconcile them both to God in one body through the cross, thereby putting to death the enmity. 17And He came and preached peace to you who were afar off and to those who were near. 18For through Him we both have access by one Spirit to the Father.

Christ Our Cornerstone

19Now, therefore, you are no longer strangers and foreigners, but fellow citizens with the saints and members of the household of God, 20having been built on the foundation of the apostles and prophets, Jesus Christ Himself being the chief corner*stone*, 21in whom the whole building, being fitted together, grows into a holy temple in the Lord, 22in whom you also are being built together for a dwelling place of God in the Spirit.

The Mystery Revealed

3 For this reason I, Paul, the prisoner of Christ Jesus for you Gentiles— 2if indeed you have heard of the dispensation of the grace of God which was given to me for you, 3how that by revelation He made known to me the mystery (as I have briefly written already, 4by which, when you read, you may understand my knowledge in the mystery of Christ), 5which in other ages was not made known to the sons of men, as it has now been revealed by the Spirit to His holy apostles and prophets: 6that the Gentiles should be fellow heirs, of the same body, and partakers of His promise in Christ through the gospel, 7of which I became a minister according to the gift of the grace of God given to me by the effective working of His power.

Purpose of the Mystery

8To me, who am less than the least of all the saints, this grace was given, that I should preach among the Gentiles the unsearchable riches of Christ, 9and to make all see what *is* the fellowship of the mystery, which from the beginning of the ages has been hidden in God who created all things through Jesus Christ; 10to the intent that now the manifold wisdom of God might be made known by the church to the principalities and powers in the heavenly *places*, 11according to the eternal purpose which He accomplished in Christ Jesus our Lord, 12in whom we have boldness and access with confidence through faith in Him. 13Therefore I ask that you do not lose heart at my tribulations for you, which is your glory.

Appreciation of the Mystery

14For this reason I bow my knees to the Father of our Lord Jesus Christ, 15from whom the whole family in heaven and earth is named, 16that He would grant you, according to the riches of His glory, to be strengthened with might through His Spirit in the inner man, 17that Christ may dwell in your hearts through faith; that you, being rooted and grounded in love, 18may be able to comprehend with all the saints what *is* the width and length and depth and height—19to know the love of Christ which passes knowledge; that you may be filled with all the fullness of God.

20Now to Him who is able to do exceedingly abundantly above all that we ask or think, according to the power that works in us, 21to Him *be* glory in the church by Christ Jesus to all generations, forever and ever. Amen.

Walk in Unity

4 I, therefore, the prisoner of the Lord, beseech you to walk worthy of the calling with which you were called, 2with all lowliness and gentleness, with longsuffering, bearing with one another in love, 3endeavoring to keep the unity of the Spirit in the bond of peace. 4*There is* one body and one Spirit, just as you were called in one hope of your calling; 5one Lord, one faith, one baptism; 6one God and Father of all, who *is* above all, and through all, and in you all.

Spiritual Gifts

7But to each one of us grace was given according to the measure of Christ's gift. 8Therefore He says:

"When He ascended on high,
 He led captivity captive,
 And gave gifts to men."*a*

9(Now this, "He ascended"—what does it mean but that He also first descended into the lower parts of the earth? 10He who descended is also the One who ascended far above all the heavens, that He might fill all things.)

11And He Himself gave some *to be* apostles, some prophets, some evangelists, and some pastors and teachers, 12for the equipping of the saints for the work of ministry, for the edifying of the body of Christ, 13till we all come to the unity of the faith and of the knowledge of the Son of God, to a perfect man, to the measure of the stature of the fullness of Christ; 14that we should no longer be children, tossed to and fro and carried about with every wind of doctrine, by the trickery of men, in the cunning craftiness of deceitful plotting, 15but, speaking the truth in love, may grow up in all things into Him who is

the head—Christ—16from whom the whole body, joined and knit together by what every joint supplies, according to the effective working by which every part does its share, causes growth of the body for the edifying of itself in love.

The New Man

17This I say, therefore, and testify in the Lord, that you should no longer walk as the rest of the Gentiles walk, in the futility of their mind, 18having their understanding darkened, being alienated from the life of God, because of the ignorance that is in them, because of the blindness of their heart; 19who, being past feeling, have given themselves over to lewdness, to work all uncleanness with greediness.

20But you have not so learned Christ, 21if indeed you have heard Him and have been taught by Him, as the truth is in Jesus: 22that you put off, concerning your former conduct, the old man which grows corrupt according to the deceitful lusts, 23and be renewed in the spirit of your mind, 24and that you put on the new man which was created according to God, in true righteousness and holiness.

Do Not Grieve the Spirit

25Therefore, putting away lying, "Let each one *of you* speak truth with his neighbor,"*b* for we are members of one another. 26"Be angry, and do not sin":*c* do not let the sun go down on your wrath, 27nor give place to the devil. 28Let him who stole steal no longer, but rather let him labor, working with *his* hands what is good, that he may have something to give him who has need. 29Let no corrupt word proceed out of your mouth, but what is good for necessary edification, that it may impart grace to the hearers. 30And do not grieve the Holy Spirit of God, by whom you were sealed for the day of redemption. 31Let all bitterness, wrath, anger, clamor, and evil speaking be put away from you, with all malice. 32And be kind to one another, tenderhearted, forgiving one another, even as God in Christ forgave you.

---

a Psalm 68.18   *b* Zechariah 8.16   *c* Psalm 4.4

Walk in Love

5 Therefore be imitators of God as dear children. 2And walk in love, as Christ also has loved us and given Himself for us, an offering and a sacrifice to God for a sweet-smelling aroma.

3But fornication and all uncleanness or covetousness, let it not even be named among you, as is fitting for saints; 4neither filthiness, nor foolish talking, nor coarse jesting, which are not fitting, but rather giving of thanks. 5For this you know, that no fornicator, unclean person, nor covetous man, who is an idolater, has any inheritance in the kingdom of Christ and God. 6Let no one deceive you with empty words, for because of these things the wrath of God comes upon the sons of disobedience. 7Therefore do not be partakers with them.

Walk in Light

8For you were once darkness, but now *you are* light in the Lord. Walk as children of light 9(for the fruit of the Spirit *is* in all goodness, righteousness, and truth), 10finding out what is acceptable to the Lord. 11And have no fellowship with the unfruitful works of darkness, but rather expose *them*. 12For it is shameful even to speak of those things which are done by them in secret. 13But all things that are exposed are made manifest by the light, for whatever makes manifest is light. 14Therefore He says:

"Awake, you who sleep,
Arise from the dead,
And Christ will give you light."

Walk in Wisdom

15See then that you walk circumspectly, not as fools but as wise, 16redeeming the time, because the days are evil.

17Therefore do not be unwise, but understand what the will of the Lord *is*. 18And do not be drunk with wine, in which is dissipation; but be filled with the Spirit, 19speaking to one another in psalms and hymns and spiritual songs, singing and making melody in your heart to the Lord, 20giving thanks always for all things to God the Father in the name of our Lord Jesus Christ, 21submitting to one another in the fear of God.

Marriage—Christ and the Church

22Wives, submit to your own husbands, as to the Lord. 23For the husband is head of the wife, as also Christ is head of the church; and He is the Savior of the body. 24Therefore, just as the church is subject to Christ, so *let* the wives *be* to their own husbands in everything.

25Husbands, love your wives, just as Christ also loved the church and gave Himself for her, 26that He might sanctify and cleanse her with the washing of water by the word, 27that He might present her to Himself a glorious church, not having spot or wrinkle or any such thing, but that she should be holy and without blemish. 28So husbands ought to love their own wives as their own bodies; he who loves his wife loves himself. 29For no one ever hated his own flesh, but nourishes and cherishes it, just as the Lord *does* the church. 30For we are members of His body, of His flesh and of His bones. 31"For this reason a man shall leave his father and mother and be joined to his wife, and the two shall become one flesh."*d* 32This is a great mystery, but I speak concerning Christ and the church. 33Nevertheless let each one of you in particular so love his own wife as himself, and let the wife *see* that she respects *her* husband.

Children and Parents

6 Children, obey your parents in the Lord, for this is right. 2"Honor your father and mother," which is the first commandment with promise: 3"that it may be well with you and you may live long on the earth."*e*

4And you, fathers, do not provoke your children to wrath, but bring them up in the training and admonition of the Lord.

Bondservants and Masters

5Bondservants, be obedient to those who are your masters according to the

d Genesis 2.24   *e* Deuteronomy 5.16

flesh, with fear and trembling, in sincerity of heart, as to Christ; 6not with eye service, as men-pleasers, but as bond servants of Christ, doing the will of God from the heart, 7with goodwill doing service, as to the Lord, and not to men, 8knowing that whatever good anyone does, he will receive the same from the Lord, whether *he is* a slave or free.

9And you, masters, do the same things to them, giving up threatening, knowing that your own Master also is in heaven, and there is no partiality with Him.

The Whole Armor of God

10Finally, my brethren, be strong in the Lord and in the power of His might. 11Put on the whole armor of God, that you may be able to stand against the wiles of the devil. 12For we do not wrestle against flesh and blood, but against principalities, against powers, against the rulers of the darkness of this age, against spiritual *hosts* of wickedness in the heavenly *places*. 13Therefore take up the whole armor of God, that you may be able to withstand in the evil day, and having done all, to stand.

14Stand therefore, having girded your waist with truth, having put on the breastplate of righteousness, 15and having shod your feet with the preparation of the gospel of peace; 16above all, taking the shield of faith with which you will be able to quench all the fiery darts of the wicked one. 17And take the helmet of salvation, and the sword of the Spirit, which is the word of God; 18praying always with all prayer and supplication in the Spirit, being watchful to this end with all perseverance and supplication for all the saints— 19and for me, that utterance may be given to me, that I may open my mouth boldly to make known the mystery of the gospel, 20for which I am an ambassador in chains; that in it I may speak boldly, as I ought to speak.

A Gracious Greeting

21But that you also may know my affairs *and* how I am doing, Tychicus, a beloved brother and faithful minister in the Lord, will make all things known to you; 22whom I have sent to you for this very purpose, that you may know our affairs, and *that* he may comfort your hearts.

23Peace to the brethren, and love with faith, from God the Father and the Lord Jesus Christ. 24Grace *be* with all those who love our Lord Jesus Christ in sincerity. Amen.

PHILIPPIANS

Greeting

1 Paul and Timothy, bondservants of Jesus Christ,

To all the saints in Christ Jesus who are in Philippi, with the bishops and deacons:

2Grace to you and peace from God our Father and the Lord Jesus Christ.

Thankfulness and Prayer

3I thank my God upon every remembrance of you, 4always in every prayer of mine making request for you all with joy, 5for your fellowship in the gospel from the first day until now, 6being confident of this very thing, that He who has begun a good work in you will complete *it* until the day of Jesus Christ; 7just as it is right for me to think this of you all, because I have you in my heart, inasmuch as both in my chains and in the defense and confirmation of the gospel, you all are partakers with me of grace. 8For God is my witness, how greatly I long for you all with the affection of Jesus Christ.

9And this I pray, that your love may abound still more and more in knowledge and all discernment, 10that you may approve the things that are excellent, that you may be sincere and without offense till the day of Christ, 11being filled with the fruits of righteousness which *are* by Jesus Christ, to the glory and praise of God.

Christ Is Preached

12But I want you to know, brethren, that the things *which happened* to me have actually turned out for the furtherance of the gospel, 13so that it has become evident to the whole palace guard, and to all the rest, that my chains are in Christ; 14and most of the brethren in the Lord, having become confident by my chains, are much more bold to speak the word without fear.

15Some indeed preach Christ even from envy and strife, and some also from goodwill: 16The former preach Christ from selfish ambition, not sincerely, supposing to add affliction to my chains; 17but the latter out of love, knowing that I am appointed for the defense of the gospel. 18What then? Only *that* in every way, whether in pretense or in truth, Christ is preached; and in this I rejoice, yes, and will rejoice.

To Live Is Christ

19For I know that this will turn out for my deliverance through your prayer and the supply of the Spirit of Jesus Christ, 20according to my earnest expectation and hope that in nothing I shall be ashamed, but with all boldness, as always, so now also Christ will be magnified in my body, whether by life or by death. 21For to me, to live *is* Christ, and to die *is* gain. 22But if *I* live on in the flesh, this *will mean* fruit from *my* labor; yet what I shall choose I cannot tell. 23For I am hard-pressed between the two, having a desire to depart and be with Christ, *which is* far better. 24Nevertheless to remain in the flesh *is* more needful for you. 25And being confident of this, I know that I shall remain and continue with you all for your progress and joy of faith, 26that your rejoicing for me may be more abundant in Jesus Christ by my coming to you again.

Striving and Suffering for Christ

27Only let your conduct be worthy of the gospel of Christ, so that whether I come and see you or am absent, I may hear of your affairs, that you stand fast in one spirit, with one mind striving together for the faith of the gospel, 28and not in any way terrified by your adversaries, which is to them a proof of perdition, but to you of salvation, and that from God. 29For to you it has been granted on behalf of Christ, not only to believe in Him, but also to suffer for His sake, 30having the same conflict which you saw in me and now hear *is* in me.

Unity Through Humility

2 Therefore if *there is* any consolation in Christ, if any comfort of love, if any fellowship of the Spirit, if any affection and mercy, 2fulfill my joy by being like-minded, having the same love, *being* of one accord, of one mind. 3*Let* nothing *be done* through selfish ambition or conceit, but in lowliness of mind let each esteem others better than himself. 4Let each of you look out not only for his own interests, but also for the interests of others.

The Humbled and Exalted Christ

5Let this mind be in you which was also in Christ Jesus, 6who, being in the form of God, did not consider it robbery to be equal with God, 7but made Himself of no reputation, taking the form of a bondservant, *and* coming in the likeness of men. 8And being found in appearance as a man, He humbled Himself and became obedient to *the point of* death, even the death of the cross. 9Therefore God also has highly exalted Him and given Him the name which is above every name, 10that at the name of Jesus every knee should bow, of those in heaven, and of those on earth, and of those under the earth, 11and *that* every tongue should confess that Jesus Christ *is* Lord, to the glory of God the Father.

Light Bearers

12Therefore, my beloved, as you have always obeyed, not as in my presence only, but now much more in my absence, work out your own salvation with fear and trembling; 13for it is God who works in you both to will and to do for *His* good pleasure.

14Do all things without complaining and disputing, 15that you may become blameless and harmless, children of God without fault in the midst of a crooked and perverse generation, among whom you shine as lights in the world, 16holding fast the word of life, so that I may rejoice in the day of Christ that I have not run in vain or labored in vain.

17Yes, and if I am being poured out *as a drink offering* on the sacrifice and service of your faith, I am glad and rejoice with you all. 18For the same reason you also be glad and rejoice with me.

Timothy Commended

19But I trust in the Lord Jesus to send Timothy to you shortly, that I also may be encouraged when I know your state. 20For I have no one like-minded, who will sincerely care for your state. 21For all seek their own, not the things which are of Christ Jesus. 22But you know his proven character, that as a son with *his* father he served with me in the gospel. 23Therefore I hope to send him at once, as soon as I see how it goes with me. 24But I trust in the Lord that I myself shall also come shortly.

Epaphroditus Praised

25Yet I considered it necessary to send to you Epaphroditus, my brother, fellow worker, and fellow soldier, but your messenger and the one who ministered to my need; 26since he was longing for you all, and was distressed because you had heard that he was sick. 27For indeed he was sick almost unto death; but God had mercy on him, and not only on him but on me also, lest I should have sorrow upon sorrow. 28Therefore I sent him the more eagerly, that when you see him again you may rejoice, and I may be less sorrowful. 29Receive him therefore in the Lord with all gladness, and hold such men in esteem; 30because for the work of Christ he came close to death, not regarding his life, to supply what was lacking in your service toward me.

All for Christ

3 Finally, my brethren, rejoice in the Lord. For me to write the same things to you *is* not tedious, but for you *it is* safe.

2Beware of dogs, beware of evil workers, beware of the mutilation! 3For we are the circumcision, who worship God in the Spirit, rejoice in Christ Jesus, and have no confidence in the flesh, 4though I also might have confidence in the flesh. If anyone else thinks he may have confidence in the flesh, I more so: 5circumcised the eighth day, of the stock of Israel, *of* the tribe of Benjamin, a Hebrew of the Hebrews; concerning the law, a Pharisee; 6concerning zeal, persecuting the church; concerning the righteousness which is in the law, blameless.

7But what things were gain to me, these I have counted loss for Christ. 8Yet indeed I also count all things loss for the excellence of the knowledge of Christ Jesus my Lord, for whom I have suffered the loss of all things, and count them as rubbish, that I may gain Christ 9and be found in Him, not having my own righteousness, which *is* from the law, but that which *is* through faith in Christ, the righteousness which is from God by faith; 10that I may know Him and the power of His resurrection, and the fellowship of His sufferings, being conformed to His death, 11if, by any means, I may attain to the resurrection from the dead.

Pressing Toward the Goal

12Not that I have already attained, or am already perfected; but I press on, that I may lay hold of that for which Christ Jesus has also laid hold of me. 13Brethren, I do not count myself to have apprehended; but one thing *I do*, forgetting those things which are behind and reaching forward to those things which are ahead, 14I press toward the goal for the prize of the upward call of God in Christ Jesus.

15Therefore let us, as many as are mature, have this mind; and if in anything you think otherwise, God will reveal even this to you. 16Nevertheless, to *the degree* that we have already attained, let us walk by the same rule, let us be of the same mind.

Our Citizenship in Heaven

17Brethren, join in following my example, and note those who so walk, as you have us for a pattern. 18For many walk, of whom I have told you often, and now tell you even weeping, *that they are* the enemies of the cross of Christ: 19whose end *is* destruction, whose god *is their* belly, and *whose* glory *is* in their shame—who set their mind on earthly things. 20For our citizenship is in heaven, from which we also eagerly wait for the Savior, the Lord Jesus Christ, 21who will transform our lowly body that it may be conformed to His glorious body, according to the working by which He is able even to subdue all things to Himself.

4 Therefore, my beloved and longed-for brethren, my joy and crown, so stand fast in the Lord, beloved.

Be United, Joyful, and in Prayer

2I implore Euodia and I implore Syntyche to be of the same mind in the Lord. 3And I urge you also, true companion, help these women who labored with me in the gospel, with Clement also, and the rest of my fellow workers, whose names *are* in the Book of Life.

4Rejoice in the Lord always. Again I will say, rejoice!

5Let your gentleness be known to all men. The Lord *is* at hand.

6Be anxious for nothing, but in everything by prayer and supplication, with thanksgiving, let your requests be made known to God; 7and the peace of God, which surpasses all understanding, will guard your hearts and minds through Christ Jesus.

Meditate on These Things

8Finally, brethren, whatever things are true, whatever things *are* noble, whatever things *are* just, whatever things *are* pure, whatever things *are* lovely, whatever things *are* of good report, if *there is* any virtue and if *there is* anything praiseworthy—meditate on these things. 9The things which you learned and received and heard and saw in me, these do, and the God of peace will be with you.

Philippian Generosity

10But I rejoiced in the Lord greatly that now at last your care for me has flourished again; though you surely did care, but you lacked opportunity. 11Not that I speak in regard to need, for I have learned in whatever state I am, to be content: 12I know how to be abased, and I know how to abound. Everywhere and in all things I have learned both to be full and to be hungry, both to abound and to suffer need. 13I can do all things through Christ who strengthens me.

14Nevertheless you have done well

that you shared in my distress. 15Now you Philippians know also that in the beginning of the gospel, when I departed from Macedonia, no church shared with me concerning giving and receiving but you only. 16For even in Thessalonica you sent *aid* once and again for my necessities. 17Not that I seek the gift, but I seek the fruit that abounds to your account. 18Indeed I have all and abound. I am full, having received from Epaphroditus the things *sent* from you, a sweet-smelling aroma, an acceptable sacrifice, well pleasing to God. 19And my God shall supply all your need according to His riches in glory by Christ Jesus. 20Now to our God and Father *be* glory forever and ever. Amen.

Greeting and Blessing

21Greet every saint in Christ Jesus. The brethren who are with me greet you. 22All the saints greet you, but especially those who are of Caesar's household.

23The grace of our Lord Jesus Christ be with you all. Amen.

The Epistle of Paul to the

COLOSSIANS

Greeting

1 Paul, an apostle of Jesus Christ by the will of God, and Timothy our brother,

2To the saints and faithful brethren in Christ *who are* in Colosse:

Grace to you and peace from God our Father and the Lord Jesus Christ.

Their Faith in Christ

3We give thanks to the God and Father of our Lord Jesus Christ, praying always for you, 4since we heard of your faith in Christ Jesus and of your love for all the saints; 5because of the hope which is laid up for you in heaven, of which you heard before in the word of the truth of the gospel, 6which has come to you, as *it has* also in all the world, and is bringing forth fruit, as *it is* also among you since the day you heard and knew the grace of God in truth; 7as you also learned from Epaphras, our dear fellow servant, who is a faithful minister of Christ on your behalf, 8who also declared to us your love in the Spirit.

Preeminence of Christ

9For this reason we also, since the day we heard it, do not cease to pray for you, and to ask that you may be filled with the knowledge of His will in all wisdom and spiritual understanding; 10that you may walk worthy of the Lord, fully pleasing *Him*, being fruitful in every good work and increasing in the knowledge of God; 11strengthened with all might, according to His glorious power, for all patience and longsuffering with joy; 12giving thanks to the Father who has qualified us to be partakers of the inheritance of the saints in the light. 13He has delivered us from the power of darkness and conveyed *us* into the kingdom of the Son of His love, 14in whom we have redemption through His blood, the forgiveness of sins.

15He is the image of the invisible God, the firstborn over all creation. 16For by Him all things were created that are in heaven and that are on earth, visible and invisible, whether thrones or dominions or principalities or powers. All things were created through Him and for Him. 17And He is before all things, and in Him all things consist. 18And He is the head of the body, the church, who is the beginning, the firstborn from the dead, that in all things He may have the preeminence.

Reconciled in Christ

19For it pleased *the Father that* in Him all the fullness should dwell, 20and by Him to reconcile all things to Himself, by Him, whether things on earth or things in heaven, having made peace through the blood of His cross. 21And you, who once were alienated and enemies in your mind by wicked works, yet now He has reconciled 22in the body of His flesh through death, to present you holy, and blameless, and above reproach in His sight— 23if indeed you continue in the faith, grounded and steadfast, and are not moved away from the hope of the gospel which you heard, which was preached to every creature under heaven, of which I, Paul, became a minister.

Sacrificial Service for Christ

24I now rejoice in my sufferings for you, and fill up in my flesh what is lacking in the afflictions of Christ, for the sake of His body, which is the church, 25of which I became a minister according to the stewardship from God which was given to me for you, to fulfill the word of God, 26the mystery which has been hidden from ages and from generations, but now has been revealed to His saints. 27To them God willed to make known what are the riches of the glory of this mystery among the Gentiles: which is Christ in you, the hope of glory. 28Him we preach, warning every man and teaching every man in all wisdom, that we may present every man perfect in Christ Jesus. 29To this *end* I also labor, striving according to His working which works in me mightily.

Not Philosophy but Christ

2 For I want you to know what a great conflict I have for you and those in Laodicea, and *for* as many as have not seen my face in the flesh, 2that their hearts may be encouraged, being knit together in love, and *attaining* to all

riches of the full assurance of understanding, to the knowledge of the mystery of God, both of the Father and of Christ, 3in whom are hidden all the treasures of wisdom and knowledge.

4Now this I say lest anyone should deceive you with persuasive words. 5For though I am absent in the flesh, yet I am with you in spirit, rejoicing to see your *good* order and the steadfastness of your faith in Christ.

6As you therefore have received Christ Jesus the Lord, so walk in Him, 7rooted and built up in Him and established in the faith, as you have been taught, abounding in it with thanksgiving.

8Beware lest anyone cheat you through philosophy and empty deceit, according to the tradition of men, according to the basic principles of the world, and not according to Christ. 9For in Him dwells all the fullness of the Godhead bodily; 10and you are complete in Him, who is the head of all principality and power.

Not Legalism but Christ

11In Him you were also circumcised with the circumcision made without hands, by putting off the body of the sins of the flesh, by the circumcision of Christ, 12buried with Him in baptism, in which you also were raised with *Him* through faith in the working of God, who raised Him from the dead. 13And you, being dead in your trespasses and the uncircumcision of your flesh, He has made alive together with Him, having forgiven you all trespasses, 14having wiped out the handwriting of requirements that was against us, which was contrary to us. And He has taken it out of the way, having nailed it to the cross. 15Having disarmed principalities and powers, He made a public spectacle of them, triumphing over them in it.

16So let no one judge you in food or in drink, or regarding a festival or a new moon or sabbaths, 17which are a shadow of things to come, but the substance is of Christ. 18Let no one cheat you of your reward, taking delight in *false* humility and worship of angels, intruding into those things which he has not seen, vainly puffed up by his fleshly mind, 19and not holding fast to the Head, from whom all the body, nourished and knit together by joints and ligaments, grows with the increase *that is* from God.

20Therefore, if you died with Christ from the basic principles of the world, why, as *though* living in the world, do you subject yourselves to regulations— 21"Do not touch, do not taste, do not handle," 22which all concern things which perish with the using—according to the commandments and doctrines of men? 23These things indeed have an appearance of wisdom in self-imposed religion, *false* humility, and neglect of the body, *but are* of no value against the indulgence of the flesh.

Not Carnality but Christ

3 If then you were raised with Christ, seek those things which are above, where Christ is, sitting at the right hand of God. 2Set your mind on things above, not on things on the earth. 3For you died, and your life is hidden with Christ in God. 4When Christ *who is* our life appears, then you also will appear with Him in glory.

5Therefore put to death your members which are on the earth: fornication, uncleanness, passion, evil desire, and covetousness, which is idolatry. 6Because of these things the wrath of God is coming upon the sons of disobedience, 7in which you yourselves once walked when you lived in them.

8But now you yourselves are to put off all these: anger, wrath, malice, blasphemy, filthy language out of your mouth. 9Do not lie to one another, since you have put off the old man with his deeds, 10and have put on the new *man* who is renewed in knowledge according to the image of Him who created him, 11where there is neither Greek nor Jew, circumcised nor uncircumcised, barbarian, Scythian, slave *nor* free, but Christ *is* all and in all.

Character of the New Man

12Therefore, as *the* elect of God, holy and beloved, put on tender mercies, kindness, humility, meekness, longsuffering; 13bearing with one another, and forgiving one another, if anyone has a complaint against another; even as Christ forgave you, so you also *must do*. 14But above all these things put on love, which is the bond of perfection. 15And let the peace of God rule in your hearts, to which also you were called in one body; and be thankful. 16Let the word of Christ dwell in you richly in all wisdom, teaching and admonishing one another in psalms and hymns and spiritual songs, singing with grace in your hearts to the Lord. 17And *whatever* you do in word or deed, *do* all in the name of the Lord Jesus, giving thanks to God the Father through Him.

The Christian Home

18Wives, submit to your own husbands, as is fitting in the Lord. 19Husbands, love your wives and do not be bitter toward them. 20Children, obey your parents in all things, for this is well pleasing to the Lord. 21Fathers, do not provoke your children, lest they become discouraged. 22Bondservants, obey in all things your masters according to the flesh, not with eyeservice, as men-pleasers, but in sincerity of heart, fearing God. 23And whatever you do, do it heartily, as to the Lord and not to men, 24knowing that from the Lord you will receive the reward of the inheritance; for you serve the Lord Christ. 25But he who does wrong will be repaid for what he has done, and there is no partiality.

4 Masters, give your bondservants what is just and fair, knowing that you also have a Master in heaven.

Christian Graces

2Continue earnestly in prayer, being vigilant in it with thanksgiving; 3meanwhile praying also for us, that God would open to us a door for the word, to speak the mystery of Christ, for which I am also in chains, 4that I may make it manifest, as I ought to speak. 5Walk in wisdom toward those *who are* outside, redeeming the time. 6Let your speech always *be* with grace, seasoned with salt, that you may know how you ought to answer each one.

Final Greetings

7Tychicus, a beloved brother, faithful minister, and fellow servant in the Lord, will tell you all the news about me. 8I am sending him to you for this very purpose, that he may know your circumstances and comfort your hearts, 9with Onesimus, a faithful and beloved brother, who is *one* of you. They will make known to you all things which *are happening* here.

10Aristarchus my fellow prisoner greets you, with Mark the cousin of Barnabas (about whom you received instructions: if he comes to you, welcome him), 11and Jesus who is called Justus. These *are my* only fellow workers for the kingdom of God who are of the circumcision; they have proved to be a comfort to me.

12Epaphras, who is *one* of you, a bondservant of Christ, greets you, always laboring fervently for you in prayers, that you may stand perfect and complete in all the will of God. 13For I bear him witness that he has a great zeal for you, and those who are in Laodicea, and those in Hierapolis. 14Luke the beloved physician and Demas greet you. 15Greet the brethren who are in Laodicea, and Nymphas and the church that *is* in his house.

Closing Exhortations and Blessing

16Now when this epistle is read among you, see that it is read also in the church of the Laodiceans, and that you likewise read the epistle from Laodicea. 17And say to Archippus, "Take heed to the ministry which you have received in the Lord, that you may fulfill it."

18This salutation by my own hand— Paul. Remember my chains. Grace *be* with you. Amen.

THESSALONIANS

Greeting

1 Paul, Silvanus, and Timothy,

To the church of the Thessalonians in God the Father and the Lord Jesus Christ:

Grace to you and peace from God our Father and the Lord Jesus Christ.

Their Good Example

2We give thanks to God always for you all, making mention of you in our prayers, 3remembering without ceasing your work of faith, labor of love, and patience of hope in our Lord Jesus Christ in the sight of our God and Father, 4knowing, beloved brethren, your election by God. 5For our gospel did not come to you in word only, but also in power, and in the Holy Spirit and in much assurance, as you know what kind of men we were among you for your sake.

6And you became followers of us and of the Lord, having received the word in much affliction, with joy of the Holy Spirit, 7so that you became examples to all in Macedonia and Achaia who believe. 8For from you the word of the Lord has sounded forth, not only in Macedonia and Achaia, but also in every place. Your faith toward God has gone out, so that we do not need to say anything. 9For they themselves declare concerning us what manner of entry we had to you, and how you turned to God from idols to serve the living and true God, 10and to wait for His Son from heaven, whom He raised from the dead, *even* Jesus who delivers us from the wrath to come.

Paul's Conduct

2 For you yourselves know, brethren, that our coming to you was not in vain. 2But even after we had suffered before and were spitefully treated at Philippi, as you know, we were bold in our God to speak to you the gospel of God in much conflict. 3For our exhortation *did* not *come* from error or uncleanness, nor *was it* in deceit.

4But as we have been approved by God to be entrusted with the gospel, even so we speak, not as pleasing men, but God who tests our hearts. 5For neither at any time did we use flattering words, as you know, nor a cloak for covetousness—God *is* witness. 6Nor did we seek glory from men, either from you or from others, when we might have made demands as apostles of Christ. 7But we were gentle among you, just as a nursing *mother* cherishes her own children. 8So, affectionately longing for you, we were well pleased to impart to you not only the gospel of God, but also our own lives, because you had become dear to us. 9For you remember, brethren, our labor and toil; for laboring night and day, that we might not be a burden to any of you, we preached to you the gospel of God.

10You *are* witnesses, and God *also*, how devoutly and justly and blamelessly we behaved ourselves among you who believe; 11as you know how we exhorted, and comforted, and charged every one of you, as a father *does* his own children, 12that you would walk worthy of God who calls you into His own kingdom and glory.

Their Conversion

13For this reason we also thank God without ceasing, because when you received the word of God which you heard from us, you welcomed *it* not *as* the word of men, but as it is in truth, the word of God, which also effectively works in you who believe. 14For you, brethren, became imitators of the churches of God which are in Judea in Christ Jesus. For you also suffered the same things from your own countrymen, just as they *did* from the Judeans, 15who killed both the Lord Jesus and their own prophets, and have persecuted us; and they do not please God and are contrary to all men, 16forbidding us to speak to the Gentiles that they may be saved, so as always to fill up *the measure of* their sins; but wrath has come upon them to the uttermost.

Longing to See Them

17But we, brethren, having been taken away from you for a short time in presence, not in heart, endeavored more eagerly to see your face with great desire. **18**Therefore we wanted to come to you—even I, Paul, time and again—but Satan hindered us. **19**For what *is* our hope, or joy, or crown of rejoicing? *Is it* not even you in the presence of our Lord Jesus Christ at His coming? **20**For you are our glory and joy.

Concern for Their Faith

3 Therefore, when we could no longer endure it, we thought it good to be left in Athens alone, **2**and sent Timothy, our brother and minister of God, and our fellow laborer in the gospel of Christ, to establish you and encourage you concerning your faith, **3**that no one should be shaken by these afflictions; for you yourselves know that we are appointed to this. **4**For, in fact, we told you before when we were with you that we would suffer tribulation, just as it happened, and you know. **5**For this reason, when I could no longer endure it, I sent to know your faith, lest by some means the tempter had tempted you, and our labor might be in vain.

Encouraged by Timothy

6But now that Timothy has come to us from you, and brought us good news of your faith and love, and that you always have good remembrance of us, greatly desiring to see us, as we also *to see* you—**7**therefore, brethren, in all our affliction and distress we were comforted concerning you by your faith. **8**For now we live, if you stand fast in the Lord.

9For what thanks can we render to God for you, for all the joy with which we rejoice for your sake before our God, **10**night and day praying exceedingly that we may see your face and perfect what is lacking in your faith?

Prayer for the Church

11Now may our God and Father Himself, and our Lord Jesus Christ, direct our way to you. **12**And may the Lord make you increase and abound in love to one another and to all, just as we *do* to you, **13**so that He may establish your hearts blameless in holiness before our God and Father at the coming of our Lord Jesus Christ with all His saints.

Plea for Purity

4 Finally then, brethren, we urge and exhort in the Lord Jesus that you should abound more and more, just as you received from us how you ought to walk and to please God; **2**for you know what commandments we gave you through the Lord Jesus.

3For this is the will of God, your sanctification: that you should abstain from sexual immorality; **4**that each of you should know how to possess his own vessel in sanctification and honor, **5**not in passion of lust, like the Gentiles who do not know God; **6**that no one should take advantage of and defraud his brother in this matter, because the Lord *is* the avenger of all such, as we also forewarned you and testified. **7**For God did not call us to uncleanness, but in holiness. **8**Therefore he who rejects *this* does not reject man, but God, who has also given us His Holy Spirit.

A Brotherly and Orderly Life

9But concerning brotherly love you have no need that I should write to you, for you yourselves are taught by God to love one another; **10**and indeed you do so toward all the brethren who are in all Macedonia. But we urge you, brethren, that you increase more and more; **11**that you also aspire to lead a quiet life, to mind your own business, and to work with your own hands, as we commanded you, **12**that you may walk properly toward those who are outside, and *that* you may lack nothing.

The Comfort of Christ's Coming

13But I do not want you to be ignorant, brethren, concerning those who have fallen asleep, lest you sorrow as others who have no hope. **14**For if we believe that Jesus died and rose again, even so God will bring with Him those who sleep in Jesus.*a*

15For this we say to you by the word

---

a Or *those who through Jesus sleep*

of the Lord, that we who are alive *and* remain until the coming of the Lord will by no means precede those who are asleep. 16For the Lord Himself will descend from heaven with a shout, with the voice of an archangel, and with the trumpet of God. And the dead in Christ will rise first. 17Then we who are alive *and* remain shall be caught up together with them in the clouds to meet the Lord in the air. And thus we shall always be with the Lord. 18Therefore comfort one another with these words.

The Day of the Lord

5 But concerning the times and the seasons, brethren, you have no need that I should write to you. 2For you yourselves know perfectly that the day of the Lord so comes as a thief in the night. 3For when they say, "Peace and safety!" then sudden destruction comes upon them, as labor pains upon a pregnant woman. And they shall not escape. 4But you, brethren, are not in darkness, so that this Day should overtake you as a thief. 5You are all sons of light and sons of the day. We are not of the night nor of darkness. 6Therefore let us not sleep, as others *do*, but let us watch and be sober. 7For those who sleep, sleep at night, and those who get drunk are drunk at night. 8But let us who are of the day be sober, putting on the breastplate of faith and love, and *as* a helmet the hope of salvation. 9For God did not appoint us to wrath, but to obtain salvation through our Lord Jesus Christ, 10who died for us, that whether we wake or sleep, we should live together with Him.

11Therefore comfort each other and edify one another, just as you also are doing.

Various Exhortations

12And we urge you, brethren, to recognize those who labor among you, and are over you in the Lord and admonish you, 13and to esteem them very highly in love for their work's sake. Be at peace among yourselves.

14Now we exhort you, brethren, warn those who are unruly, comfort the fainthearted, uphold the weak, be patient with all. 15See that no one renders evil for evil to anyone, but always pursue what is good both for yourselves and for all.

16Rejoice always, 17pray without ceasing, 18in everything give thanks; for this is the will of God in Christ Jesus for you.

19Do not quench the Spirit. 20Do not despise prophecies. 21Test all things; hold fast what is good. 22Abstain from every form of evil.

Blessing and Admonition

23Now may the God of peace Himself sanctify you completely; and may your whole spirit, soul, and body be preserved blameless at the coming of our Lord Jesus Christ. 24He who calls you *is* faithful, who also will do *it*.

25Brethren, pray for us.

26Greet all the brethren with a holy kiss.

27I charge you by the Lord that this epistle be read to all the holy brethren.

28The grace of our Lord Jesus Christ *be* with you. Amen.

THESSALONIANS

Greeting

1 Paul, Silvanus, and Timothy,

To the church of the Thessalonians in God our Father and the Lord Jesus Christ:

2Grace to you and peace from God our Father and the Lord Jesus Christ.

God's Final Judgment and Glory

3We are bound to thank God always for you, brethren, as it is fitting, because your faith grows exceedingly, and the love of every one of you all abounds toward each other, 4so that we ourselves boast of you among the churches of God for your patience and faith in all your persecutions and tribulations that you endure, 5*which is* manifest evidence of the righteous judgment of God, that you may be counted worthy of the kingdom of God, for which you also suffer; 6since *it is* a righteous thing with God to repay with tribulation those who trouble you, 7and to *give* you who are troubled rest with us when the Lord Jesus is revealed from heaven with His mighty angels, 8in flaming fire taking vengeance on those who do not know God, and on those who do not obey the gospel of our Lord Jesus Christ. 9These shall be punished with everlasting destruction from the presence of the Lord and from the glory of His power, 10when He comes, in that Day, to be glorified in His saints and to be admired among all those who believe, because our testimony among you was believed.

11Therefore we also pray always for you that our God would count you worthy of *this* calling, and fulfill all the good pleasure of *His* goodness and the work of faith with power, 12that the name of our Lord Jesus Christ may be glorified in you, and you in Him, according to the grace of our God and the Lord Jesus Christ.

The Great Apostasy

2 Now, brethren, concerning the coming of our Lord Jesus Christ and our gathering together to Him, we ask you, 2not to be soon shaken in mind or troubled, either by spirit or by word or by letter, as if from us, as though the day of Christ had come. 3Let no one deceive you by any means; for *that Day will not come* unless the falling away comes first, and the man of sin is revealed, the son of perdition, 4who opposes and exalts himself above all that is called God or that is worshiped, so that he sits as God in the temple of God, showing himself that he is God.

5Do you not remember that when I was still with you I told you these things? 6And now you know what is restraining, that he may be revealed in his own time. 7For the mystery of lawlessness is already at work; only He[a] who now restrains *will do so* until He[a] is taken out of the way. 8And then the lawless one will be revealed, whom the Lord will consume with the breath of His mouth and destroy with the brightness of His coming. 9The coming of the *lawless one* is according to the working of Satan, with all power, signs, and lying wonders, 10and with all unrighteous deception among those who perish, because they did not receive the love of the truth, that they might be saved. 11And for this reason God will send them strong delusion, that they should believe the lie, 12that they all may be condemned who did not believe the truth but had pleasure in unrighteousness.

Stand Fast

13But we are bound to give thanks to God always for you, brethren beloved by the Lord, because God from the beginning chose you for salvation through sanctification by the Spirit and belief in the truth, 14to which He called you by our gospel, for the obtaining of the glory of our Lord Jesus Christ.

a Or *he*

15Therefore, brethren, stand fast and hold the traditions which you were taught, whether by word or our epistle.

16Now may our Lord Jesus Christ Himself, and our God and Father, who has loved us and given *us* everlasting consolation and good hope by grace, 17comfort your hearts and establish you in every good word and work.

Pray for Us

3 Finally, brethren, pray for us, that the word of the Lord may run *swiftly* and be glorified, just as *it is* with you, 2and that we may be delivered from unreasonable and wicked men; for not all have faith.

3But the Lord is faithful, who will establish you and guard *you* from the evil one. 4And we have confidence in the Lord concerning you, both that you do and will do the things we command you.

5Now may the Lord direct your hearts into the love of God and into the patience of Christ.

Warning Against Idleness

6But we command you, brethren, in the name of our Lord Jesus Christ, that you withdraw from every brother who walks disorderly and not according to the tradition which he received from us. 7For you yourselves know how you ought to follow us, for we were not disorderly among you; 8nor did we eat anyone's bread free of charge, but worked with labor and toil night and day, that we might not be a burden to any of you, 9not because we do not have authority, but to make ourselves an example of how you should follow us.

10For even when we were with you, we commanded you this: If anyone will not work, neither shall he eat. 11For we hear that there are some who walk among you in a disorderly manner, not working at all, but are busybodies. 12Now those who are such we command and exhort through our Lord Jesus Christ that they work in quietness and eat their own bread.

13But *as for* you, brethren, do not grow weary *in* doing good. 14And if anyone does not obey our word in this epistle, note that person and do not keep company with him, that he may be ashamed. 15Yet do not count *him* as an enemy, but admonish *him* as a brother.

Benediction

16Now may the Lord of peace Himself give you peace always in every way. The Lord *be* with you all.

17The salutation of Paul with my own hand, which is a sign in every epistle; so I write.

18The grace of our Lord Jesus Christ *be* with you all. Amen.

Greeting

1 Paul, an apostle of Jesus Christ, by the commandment of God our Savior and the Lord Jesus Christ, our hope,

2To Timothy, a true son in the faith:

Grace, mercy, *and* peace from God our Father and Jesus Christ our Lord.

No Other Doctrine

3As I urged you when I went into Macedonia—remain in Ephesus that you may charge some that they teach no other doctrine, 4nor give heed to fables and endless genealogies, which cause disputes rather than godly edification which is in faith. 5Now the purpose of the commandment is love from a pure heart, *from* a good conscience, and *from* sincere faith, 6from which some, having strayed, have turned aside to idle talk, 7desiring to be teachers of the law, understanding neither what they say nor the things which they affirm.

8But we know that the law *is* good if one uses it lawfully, 9knowing this: that the law is not made for a righteous person, but for *the* lawless and insubordinate, for *the* ungodly and for sinners, for *the* unholy and profane, for murderers of fathers and murderers of mothers, for manslayers, 10for fornicators, for sodomites, for kidnappers, for liars, for perjurers, and if there is any other thing that is contrary to sound doctrine, 11according to the glorious gospel of the blessed God which was committed to my trust.

Glory to God for His Grace

12And I thank Christ Jesus our Lord who has enabled me, because He counted me faithful, putting *me* into the ministry, 13although I was formerly a blasphemer, a persecutor, and an insolent man; but I obtained mercy because I did *it* ignorantly in unbelief. 14And the grace of our Lord was exceedingly abundant, with faith and love which are in Christ Jesus. 15This *is* a faithful saying and worthy of all acceptance, that Christ Jesus came into the world to save sinners, of whom I am chief. 16However, for this reason I obtained mercy, that in me first Jesus Christ might show all longsuffering, as a pattern to those who are going to believe on Him for everlasting life. 17Now to the King eternal, immortal, invisible, to God who alone is wise, *be* honor and glory forever and ever. Amen.

Fight the Good Fight

18This charge I commit to you, son Timothy, according to the prophecies previously made concerning you, that by them you may wage the good warfare, 19having faith and a good conscience, which some having rejected, concerning the faith have suffered shipwreck, 20of whom are Hymenaeus and Alexander, whom I delivered to Satan that they may learn not to blaspheme.

Pray for All Men

2 Therefore I exhort first of all that supplications, prayers, intercessions, *and* giving of thanks be made for all men, 2for kings and all who are in authority, that we may lead a quiet and peaceable life in all godliness and reverence. 3For this *is* good and acceptable in the sight of God our Savior, 4who desires all men to be saved and to come to the knowledge of the truth. 5For *there is* one God and one Mediator between God and men, *the* Man Christ Jesus, 6who gave Himself a ransom for all, to be testified in due time, 7for which I was appointed a preacher and an apostle—I am speaking the truth in Christ *and* not lying—a teacher of the Gentiles in faith and truth.

Men and Women in the Church

8I desire therefore that the men pray everywhere, lifting up holy hands, without wrath and doubting; 9in like manner also, that the women adorn themselves in modest apparel, with propriety and moderation, not with braided hair or gold or pearls or costly clothing, 10but, which is proper for women professing godliness, with good works. 11Let a woman learn in silence with all submission. 12And I do not permit a woman to teach or to have authority over a man, but to be in silence. 13For Adam was formed first, then Eve. 14And Adam was not deceived, but the woman being deceived, fell into transgression. 15Nevertheless she will be saved in childbearing if they continue in faith, love, and holiness, with self-control.

Qualifications of Overseers

3 This *is* a faithful saying: If a man desires the position of a bishop, he desires a good work. 2A bishop then must be blameless, the husband of one wife, temperate, sober-minded, of good behavior, hospitable, able to teach; 3not given to wine, not violent, not greedy for money, but gentle, not quarrelsome, not covetous; 4one who rules his own house well, having *his* children in submission with all reverence 5(for if a man does not know how to rule his own house, how will he take care of the church of God?); 6not a novice, lest being puffed up with pride he fall into the *same* condemnation as the devil. 7Moreover he must have a good testimony among those who are outside, lest he fall into reproach and the snare of the devil.

Qualifications of Deacons

8Likewise deacons *must be* reverent, not double-tongued, not given to much wine, not greedy for money, 9holding the mystery of the faith with a pure conscience. 10But let these also first be tested; then let them serve as deacons, being *found* blameless. 11Likewise, *their* wives *must be* reverent, not slanderers, temperate, faithful in all things. 12Let deacons be the husbands of one wife, ruling *their* children and their own houses well. 13For those who have served well as deacons obtain for themselves a good standing and great boldness in the faith which is in Christ Jesus.

The Great Mystery

14These things I write to you, though I hope to come to you shortly; 15but if I am delayed, *I write* so that you may

know how you ought to conduct yourself in the house of God, which is the church of the living God, the pillar and ground of the truth. 16And without controversy great is the mystery of godliness:

> God was manifested in the flesh,
> Justified in the Spirit,
> Seen by angels,
> Preached among the Gentiles,
> Believed on in the world,
> Received up in glory.

The Great Apostasy

4 Now the Spirit expressly says that in latter times some will depart from the faith, giving heed to deceiving spirits and doctrines of demons, 2speaking lies in hypocrisy, having their own conscience seared with a hot iron, 3forbidding to marry, *and commanding* to abstain from foods which God created to be received with thanksgiving by those who believe and know the truth. 4For every creature of God *is* good, and nothing is to be refused if it is received with thanksgiving; 5for it is sanctified by the word of God and prayer.

A Good Servant of Jesus Christ

6If you instruct the brethren in these things, you will be a good minister of Jesus Christ, nourished in the words of faith and of the good doctrine which you have carefully followed. 7But reject profane and old wives' fables, and exercise yourself toward godliness. 8For bodily exercise profits a little, but godliness is profitable for all things, having promise of the life that now is and of that which is to come. 9This *is* a faithful saying and worthy of all acceptance. 10For to this *end* we both labor and suffer reproach, because we trust in the living God, who is *the* Savior of all men, especially of those who believe. 11These things command and teach.

Take Heed to Your Ministry

12Let no one despise your youth, but be an example to the believers in word, in conduct, in love, in spirit, in faith, in purity. 13Till I come, give attention to reading, to exhortation, to doctrine. 14Do not neglect the gift that is in you, which was given to you by prophecy with the laying on of the hands of the eldership. 15Meditate on these things; give yourself entirely to them, that your progress may be evident to all. 16Take heed to yourself and to the doctrine. Continue in them, for in doing this you will save both yourself and those who hear you.

Treatment of Church Members

5 Do not rebuke an older man, but exhort *him* as a father, younger men as brothers, 2older women as mothers, younger women as sisters, with all purity.

Honor True Widows

3Honor widows who are really widows. 4But if any widow has children or grandchildren, let them first learn to show piety at home and to repay their parents; for this is good and acceptable before God. 5Now she who is really a widow, and left alone, trusts in God and continues in supplications and prayers night and day. 6But she who lives in pleasure is dead while she lives. 7And these things command, that they may be blameless. 8But if anyone does not provide for his own, and especially for those of his household, he has denied the faith and is worse than an unbeliever.

9Do not let a widow under sixty years old be taken into the number, *and not unless* she has been the wife of one man, 10well reported for good works: if she has brought up children, if she has lodged strangers, if she has washed the saints' feet, if she has relieved the afflicted, if she has diligently followed every good work.

11But refuse *the* younger widows; for when they have begun to grow wanton against Christ, they desire to marry, 12having condemnation because they have cast off their first faith. 13And besides they learn *to be* idle, wandering about from house to house, and not only idle but also gossips and busybodies, saying things which they ought not. 14Therefore I desire that *the* younger *widows* marry, bear children, manage the house, give no opportunity to the adversary to speak re-

proachfully. 15For some have already turned aside after Satan. 16If any believing man or woman has widows, let them relieve them, and do not let the church be burdened, that it may relieve those who are really widows.

Honor the Elders

17Let the elders who rule well be counted worthy of double honor, especially those who labor in the word and doctrine. 18For the Scripture says, "You shall not muzzle an ox while it treads out the grain,"*a* and, "The laborer *is* worthy of his wages."*b* 19Do not receive an accusation against an elder except from two or three witnesses. 20Those who are sinning rebuke in the presence of all, that the rest also may fear.

21I charge *you* before God and the Lord Jesus Christ and the elect angels that you observe these things without prejudice, doing nothing with partiality. 22Do not lay hands on anyone hastily, nor share in other people's sins; keep yourself pure.

23No longer drink only water, but use a little wine for your stomach's sake and your frequent infirmities.

24Some men's sins are clearly evident, preceding *them* to judgment, but those of some *men* follow later. 25Likewise, the good works *of some* are clearly evident, and those that are otherwise cannot be hidden.

Honor Masters

6 Let as many bondservants as are under the yoke count their own masters worthy of all honor, so that the name of God and *His* doctrine may not be blasphemed. 2And those who have believing masters, let them not despise *them* because they are brethren, but rather serve *them* because those who are benefited are believers and beloved. Teach and exhort these things.

Error and Greed

3If anyone teaches otherwise and does not consent to wholesome words, *even* the words of our Lord Jesus Christ, and to the doctrine which accords with godliness, 4he is proud, knowing nothing, but is obsessed with

a Deuteronomy 25.4   *b* Luke 10.7

disputes and arguments over words, from which come envy, strife, reviling, evil suspicions, 5useless wranglings of men of corrupt minds and destitute of the truth, who suppose that godliness is a *means of* gain. From such withdraw yourself.

6Now godliness with contentment is great gain. 7For we brought nothing into *this* world, *and it is* certain we can carry nothing out. 8And having food and clothing, with these we shall be content. 9But those who desire to be rich fall into temptation and a snare, and *into* many foolish and harmful lusts which drown men in destruction and perdition. 10For the love of money is a root of all *kinds of* evil, for which some have strayed from the faith in their greediness, and pierced themselves through with many sorrows.

The Good Confession

11But you, O man of God, flee these things and pursue righteousness, godliness, faith, love, patience, gentleness. 12Fight the good fight of faith, lay hold on eternal life, to which you were also called and have confessed the good confession in the presence of many witnesses. 13I urge you in the sight of God who gives life to all things, and *before* Christ Jesus who witnessed the good

confession before Pontius Pilate, 14that you keep *this* commandment without spot, blameless until our Lord Jesus Christ's appearing, 15which He will manifest in His own time, *He who is* the blessed and only Potentate, the King of kings and Lord of lords, 16who alone has immortality, dwelling in unapproachable light, whom no man has seen or can see, to whom *be* honor and everlasting power. Amen.

Instructions to the Rich

17Command those who are rich in this present age not to be haughty, nor to trust in uncertain riches but in the living God, who gives us richly all things to enjoy. 18Let *them* do good, that they be rich in good works, ready to give, willing to share, 19storing up for themselves a good foundation for the time to come, that they may lay hold on eternal life.

Guard the Faith

20O Timothy! Guard what was committed to your trust, avoiding the profane *and* idle babblings and contradictions of what is falsely called knowledge—21by professing it some have strayed concerning the faith.

Grace *be* with you. Amen.

TIMOTHY

Greeting

1 Paul, an apostle of Jesus Christ by the will of God, according to the promise of life which is in Christ Jesus,

2To Timothy, a beloved son:

Grace, mercy, *and* peace from God the Father and Christ Jesus our Lord.

Timothy's Faith and Heritage

3I thank God, whom I serve with a pure conscience, as *my* forefathers *did*, as without ceasing I remember you in my prayers night and day, 4greatly desiring to see you, being mindful of your tears, that I may be filled with joy, 5when I call to remembrance the genuine faith that is in you, which dwelt first in your grandmother Lois and your mother Eunice, and I am persuaded is in you also. 6Therefore I remind you to stir up the gift of God which is in you through the laying on of my hands. 7For God has not given us a spirit of fear, but of power and of love and of a sound mind.

Not Ashamed of the Gospel

8Therefore do not be ashamed of the testimony of our Lord, nor of me His prisoner, but share with me in the sufferings for the gospel according to the power of God, 9who has saved us and called *us* with a holy calling, not according to our works, but according to His own purpose and grace which was given to us in Christ Jesus before time began, 10but has now been revealed by the appearing of our Savior Jesus Christ, *who* has abolished death and brought life and immortality to light through the gospel, 11to which I was appointed a preacher, an apostle, and a teacher of the Gentiles. 12For this reason I also suffer these things; nevertheless I am not ashamed, for I know whom I have believed and am persuaded that He is able to keep what I have committed to Him until that Day.

Be Loyal to the Faith

13Hold fast the pattern of sound words which you have heard from me, in faith and love which are in Christ Jesus. 14That good thing which was committed to you, keep by the Holy Spirit who dwells in us.

15This you know, that all those in Asia have turned away from me, among whom are Phygellus and Hermogenes. 16The Lord grant mercy to the household of Onesiphorus, for he often refreshed me, and was not ashamed of my chain; 17but when he arrived in Rome, he sought me out very zealously and found *me*. 18The Lord grant to him that he may find mercy from the Lord in that Day—and you know very well how many ways he ministered *to me* at Ephesus.

Be Strong in Grace

2 You therefore, my son, be strong in the grace that is in Christ Jesus. 2And the things that you have heard from me among many witnesses, commit these to faithful men who will be able to teach others also. 3You therefore must endure hardship as a good soldier of Jesus Christ. 4No one engaged in warfare entangles himself with the affairs of *this* life, that he may please him who enlisted him as a soldier. 5And also if anyone competes in athletics, he is not crowned unless he competes according to the rules. 6The hardworking farmer must be first to partake of the crops. 7Consider what I say, and may the Lord give you understanding in all things.

8Remember that Jesus Christ, of the seed of David, was raised from the dead according to my gospel, 9for which I suffer trouble as an evildoer, *even* to the point of chains; but the word of God is not chained. 10Therefore I endure all things for the sake of the elect, that they also may obtain the salvation which is in Christ Jesus with eternal glory.

11*This is* a faithful saying:
　For if we died with *Him*,
　　We shall also live with *Him*.

12 If we endure,
   We shall also reign with *Him*.
   If we deny *Him*,
   He also will deny us.
13 If we are faithless,
   He remains faithful;
   He cannot deny Himself.

Approved and Disapproved Workers

14Remind *them* of these things, charging *them* before the Lord not to strive about words to no profit, to the ruin of the hearers. 15Be diligent to present yourself approved to God, a worker who does not need to be ashamed, rightly dividing the word of truth. 16But shun profane *and* idle babblings, for they will increase to more ungodliness. 17And their message will spread like cancer. Hymenaeus and Philetus are of this sort, 18who have strayed concerning the truth, saying that the resurrection is already past; and they overthrow the faith of some. 19Nevertheless the solid foundation of God stands, having this seal: "The Lord knows those who are His," and, "Let everyone who names the name of Christ depart from iniquity."

20But in a great house there are not only vessels of gold and silver, but also of wood and clay, some for honor and some for dishonor. 21Therefore if anyone cleanses himself from the latter, he will be a vessel for honor, sanctified and useful for the Master, prepared for every good work. 22Flee also youthful lusts; but pursue righteousness, faith, love, peace with those who call on the Lord out of a pure heart. 23But avoid foolish and ignorant disputes, knowing that they generate strife. 24And a servant of the Lord must not quarrel but be gentle to all, able to teach, patient, 25in humility correcting those who are in opposition, if God perhaps will grant them repentance, so that they may know the truth, 26and *that* they may come to their senses *and escape* the snare of the devil, having been taken captive by him to *do* his will.

Perilous Times and Perilous Men

3 But know this, that in the last days perilous times will come: 2For men will be lovers of themselves, lovers of money, boasters, proud, blasphemers, disobedient to parents, unthankful, unholy, 3unloving, unforgiving, slanderers, without self-control, brutal, despisers of good, 4traitors, headstrong, haughty, lovers of pleasure rather than lovers of God, 5having a form of godliness but denying its power. And from such people turn away! 6For of this sort are those who creep into households and make captives of gullible women loaded down with sins, led away by various lusts, 7always learning and never able to come to the knowledge of the truth. 8Now as Jannes and Jambres resisted Moses, so do these also resist the truth: men of corrupt minds, disapproved concerning the faith; 9but they will progress no further, for their folly will be manifest to all, as theirs also was.

The Man of God and the Word of God

10But you have carefully followed my doctrine, manner of life, purpose, faith, longsuffering, love, perseverance, 11persecutions, afflictions, which happened to me at Antioch, at Iconium, at Lystra—what persecutions I endured. And out of *them* all the Lord delivered me. 12Yes, and all who desire to live godly in Christ Jesus will suffer persecution. 13But evil men and impostors will grow worse and worse, deceiving and being deceived. 14But you must continue in the things which you have learned and been assured of, knowing from whom you have learned *them*, 15and that from childhood you have known the Holy Scriptures, which are able to make you wise for salvation through faith which is in Christ Jesus. 16All Scripture *is* given by inspiration of God, and *is* profitable for doctrine, for reproof, for correction, for instruction in righteousness, 17that the man of God may be complete, thoroughly equipped for every good work.

Preach the Word

4 I charge *you* therefore before God and the Lord Jesus Christ, who will judge the living and the dead at His appearing and His kingdom: 2Preach the word! Be ready in season *and* out of season. Convince, rebuke, exhort, with all longsuffering and teaching. 3For the time will come when they will not en-

dure sound doctrine, but according to their own desires, *because* they have itching ears, they will heap up for themselves teachers; 4and they will turn *their* ears away from the truth, and be turned aside to fables. 5But you be watchful in all things, endure afflictions, do the work of an evangelist, fulfill your ministry.

Paul's Valedictory

6For I am already being poured out as a drink offering, and the time of my departure is at hand. 7I have fought the good fight, I have finished the race, I have kept the faith. 8Finally, there is laid up for me the crown of righteousness, which the Lord, the righteous Judge, will give to me on that Day, and not to me only but also to all who have loved His appearing.

The Abandoned Apostle

9Be diligent to come to me quickly; 10for Demas has forsaken me, having loved this present world, and has departed for Thessalonica—Crescens for Galatia, Titus for Dalmatia. 11Only Luke is with me. Get Mark and bring him with you, for he is useful to me for ministry. 12And Tychicus I have sent to Ephesus. 13Bring the cloak that I left with Carpus at Troas when you come— and the books, especially the parchments.

14Alexander the coppersmith did me much harm. May the Lord repay him according to his works. 15You also must beware of him, for he has greatly resisted our words.

16At my first defense no one stood with me, but all forsook me. May it not be charged against them.

The Lord Is Faithful

17But the Lord stood with me and strengthened me, so that the message might be preached fully through me, and *that* all the Gentiles might hear. Also I was delivered out of the mouth of the lion. 18And the Lord will deliver me from every evil work and preserve *me* for His heavenly kingdom. To Him *be* glory forever and ever. Amen!

Come Before Winter

19Greet Prisca and Aquila, and the household of Onesiphorus. 20Erastus stayed in Corinth, but Trophimus I have left in Miletus sick.

21Do your utmost to come before winter.

Eubulus greets you, as well as Pudens, Linus, Claudia, and all the brethren.

Farewell

22The Lord Jesus Christ be with your spirit. Grace be with you. Amen.

Greeting

1 Paul, a bondservant of God and an apostle of Jesus Christ, according to the faith of God's elect and the acknowledgment of the truth which accords with godliness, 2in hope of eternal life which God, who cannot lie, promised before time began, 3but has in due time manifested His word through preaching, which was committed to me according to the commandment of God our Savior;

4To Titus, a true son in *our* common faith:

Grace, mercy, *and* peace from God the Father and the Lord Jesus Christ our Savior.

Qualified Elders

5For this reason I left you in Crete, that you should set in order the things that are lacking, and appoint elders in every city as I commanded you—6if a man is blameless, the husband of one wife, having faithful children not accused of dissipation or insubordination. 7For a bishop must be blameless, as a steward of God, not self-willed, not quick-tempered, not given to wine, not violent, not greedy for money, 8but hospitable, a lover of what is good, sober-minded, just, holy, self-controlled, 9holding fast the faithful word as he has been taught, that he may be able, by sound doctrine, both to exhort and convict those who contradict.

The Elders' Task

10For there are many insubordinate, both idle talkers and deceivers, especially those of the circumcision, 11whose mouths must be stopped, who subvert whole households, teaching things which they ought not, for the sake of dishonest gain. 12One of them, a prophet of their own, said, "Cretans *are* always liars, evil beasts, lazy gluttons." 13This testimony is true. Therefore rebuke them sharply, that they may be sound in the faith, 14not giving heed to Jewish fables and commandments of men who turn from the truth. 15To the pure all things are pure, but to those who are defiled and unbelieving nothing is pure; but even their mind and conscience are defiled. 16They profess to know God, but in works they deny Him, being abominable, disobedient, and disqualified for every good work.

Qualities of a Sound Church

2 But as for you, speak the things which are proper for sound doctrine: 2that the older men be sober, reverent, temperate, sound in faith, in love, in patience; 3the older women likewise, that they be reverent in behavior, not slanderers, not given to much wine, teachers of good things—4that they admonish the young women to love their husbands, to love their children, 5to be discreet, chaste, homemakers, good, obedient to their own husbands, that the word of God may not be blasphemed.

6Likewise, exhort the young men to be sober-minded, 7in all things showing yourself *to be* a pattern of good works; in doctrine *showing* integrity, reverence, incorruptibility, 8sound speech that cannot be condemned, that one who is an opponent may be ashamed, having nothing evil to say of you.

9*Exhort* bondservants to be obedient to their own masters, to be well pleasing in all *things*, not answering back, 10not pilfering, but showing all good fidelity, that they may adorn the doctrine of God our Savior in all things.

Trained by Saving Grace

11For the grace of God that brings salvation has appeared to all men, 12teaching us that, denying ungodliness and worldly lusts, we should live soberly, righteously, and godly in the present age, 13looking for the blessed hope and glorious appearing of our great God and Savior Jesus Christ, 14who gave Himself for us, that He might redeem us from every lawless deed and purify for Himself *His* own special people, zealous for good works.

15Speak these things, exhort, and rebuke with all authority. Let no one despise you.

Graces of the Heirs of Grace

3 Remind them to be subject to rulers and authorities, to obey, to be ready for every good work, 2to speak evil of no one, to be peaceable, gentle, showing all humility to all men. 3For we ourselves were also once foolish, disobedient, deceived, serving various lusts and pleasures, living in malice and envy, hateful and hating one another. 4But when the kindness and the love of God our Savior toward man appeared, 5not by works of righteousness which we have done, but according to His mercy He saved us, through the washing of regeneration and renewing of the Holy Spirit, 6whom He poured out on us abundantly through Jesus Christ our Savior, 7that having been justified by His grace we should become heirs according to the hope of eternal life.

8This is a faithful saying, and these things I want you to affirm constantly, that those who have believed in God should be careful to maintain good works. These things are good and profitable to men.

Avoid Dissension

9But avoid foolish disputes, genealogies, contentions, and strivings about the law; for they are unprofitable and useless. 10Reject a divisive man after the first and second admonition, 11knowing that such a person is warped and sinning, being self-condemned.

Final Messages

12When I send Artemas to you, or Tychicus, be diligent to come to me at Nicopolis, for I have decided to spend the winter there. 13Send Zenas the lawyer and Apollos on their journey with haste, that they may lack nothing. 14And let our *people* also learn to maintain good works, to *meet* urgent needs, that they may not be unfruitful.

Farewell

15All who *are* with me greet you. Greet those who love us in the faith.

Grace *be* with you all. Amen.

The Epistle of Paul to
PHILEMON

Greeting

1 Paul, a prisoner of Christ Jesus, and Timothy *our* brother,

To Philemon our beloved *friend* and fellow laborer, 2to the beloved Apphia, Archippus our fellow soldier, and to the church in your house:

3Grace to you and peace from God our Father and the Lord Jesus Christ.

Philemon's Love and Faith

4I thank my God, making mention of you always in my prayers, 5hearing of your love and faith which you have toward the Lord Jesus and toward all the saints, 6that the sharing of your faith may become effective by the acknowledgment of every good thing which is in you in Christ Jesus. 7For we have great joy and consolation in your love, because the hearts of the saints have been refreshed by you, brother.

The Plea for Onesimus

8Therefore, though I might be very bold in Christ to command you what is fitting, 9yet for love's sake I rather appeal *to* you—being such a one as Paul, the aged, and now also a prisoner of Jesus Christ—10I appeal to you for my son Onesimus, whom I have begotten *while* in my chains, 11who once was unprofitable to you, but now is profitable to you and to me.

12I am sending him back. You therefore receive him, that is, my own heart, 13whom I wished to keep with me, that on your behalf he might minister to me in my chains for the gospel. 14But without your consent I wanted to do nothing, that your good deed might not be by compulsion, as it were, but voluntary.

15For perhaps he departed for a while for this *purpose*, that you might receive him forever, 16no longer as a slave but more than a slave—a beloved brother, especially to me but how much more to you, both in the flesh and in the Lord.

Philemon's Obedience Encouraged

17If then you count me as a partner, receive him as *you would* me. 18But if he has wronged you or owes anything, put that on my account. 19I, Paul, am writing with my own hand. I will repay—not to mention to you that you owe me even your own self besides. 20Yes, brother, let me have joy from you in the Lord; refresh my heart in the Lord.

21Having confidence in your obedience, I write to you, knowing that you will do even more than I say. 22But, meanwhile, also prepare a guest room for me, for I trust that through your prayers I shall be granted to you.

Farewell

23Epaphras, my fellow prisoner in Christ Jesus, greets you, 24*as do* Mark, Aristarchus, Demas, Luke, my fellow laborers.

25The grace of our Lord Jesus Christ *be* with your spirit. Amen.

The Epistle to the
HEBREWS

God's Supreme Revelation

1 God, who at various times and in various ways spoke in time past to the fathers by the prophets, 2has in these last days spoken to us by *His* Son, whom He has appointed heir of all things, through whom also He made the worlds; 3who being the brightness of *His* glory and the express image of His person, and upholding all things by the word of His power, when He had by Himself purged our sins, sat down at the right hand of the Majesty on high, 4having become so much better than the angels, as He has by inheritance obtained a more excellent name than they.

The Son Exalted Above Angels

5For to which of the angels did He ever say:
"You are My Son,
Today I have begotten You"?*a*
And again:
"I will be to Him a Father,
And He shall be to Me a Son"?*b*
6But when He again brings the firstborn into the world, He says:
"Let all the angels of God
worship Him."*c*
7And of the angels He says:
"Who makes His angels spirits
And His ministers a flame of fire."*d*
8But to the Son *He says:*
"Your throne, O God, *is* forever and
ever;
A scepter of righteousness *is* the
scepter of Your kingdom.
9 You have loved righteousness and
hated lawlessness;
Therefore God, Your God, has
anointed You
With the oil of gladness more than
Your companions."*e*
10And:
"You, LORD, in the beginning laid the
foundation of the earth,
And the heavens are the work of
Your hands.
11 They will perish, but You remain;
And they will all grow old like a
garment;
12 Like a cloak You will fold them up,
And they will be changed.
But You are the same,
And Your years will not fail."*f*
13But to which of the angels has He ever said:
"Sit at My right hand,
Till I make Your enemies Your
footstool"?*g*
14Are they not all ministering spirits sent forth to minister for those who will inherit salvation?

Do Not Neglect Salvation

2 Therefore we must give the more earnest heed to the things we have heard, lest we drift away. 2For if the word spoken through angels proved steadfast, and every transgression and disobedience received a just reward, 3how shall we escape if we neglect so great a salvation, which at the first began to be spoken by the Lord, and was confirmed to us by those who heard *Him,* 4God also bearing witness both with signs and wonders, with various miracles, and gifts of the Holy Spirit, according to His own will?

The Son Made Lower than Angels

5For He has not put the world to come, of which we speak, in subjection to angels. 6But one testified in a certain place, saying:
"What is man that You are mindful
of him,
Or the son of man that You take
care of him?
7 You have made him a little lower
than the angels;
You have crowned him with glory
and honor,
And set him over the works of Your
hands.
8 You have put all things in
subjection under his feet."*h*
For in that He put all in subjection

---

a Psalm 2.7   *b* 2 Samuel 7.14   *c* Deuteronomy 32.43; Psalm 97.7   *d* Psalm 104.4
e Psalm 45.6, 7   *f* Psalm 102.25-27   *g* Psalm 110.1   *h* Psalm 8.4-6

under him, He left nothing *that is* not put under him. But now we do not yet see all things put under him. 9But we see Jesus, who was made a little lower than the angels, for the suffering of death crowned with glory and honor, that He, by the grace of God, might taste death for everyone.

Bringing Many Sons to Glory

10For it was fitting for Him, for whom *are* all things and by whom *are* all things, in bringing many sons to glory, to make the captain of their salvation perfect through sufferings. 11For both He who sanctifies and those who are being sanctified *are* all of one, for which reason He is not ashamed to call them brethren, 12saying:

"I will declare Your name to My
    brethren;
  In the midst of the assembly I will
    sing praise to You."*i*
13And again:

"I will put My trust in Him."*j*
And again:

"Here am I and the children whom
    God has given Me."*k*

14Inasmuch then as the children have partaken of flesh and blood, He Himself likewise shared in the same, that through death He might destroy him who had the power of death, that is, the devil, 15and release those who through fear of death were all their lifetime subject to bondage. 16For indeed He does not give aid to angels, but He does give aid to the seed of Abraham. 17Therefore, in all things He had to be made like *His* brethren, that He might be a merciful and faithful High Priest in things *pertaining* to God, to make propitiation for the sins of the people. 18For in that He Himself has suffered, being tempted, He is able to aid those who are tempted.

The Son Was Faithful

3 Therefore, holy brethren, partakers of the heavenly calling, consider the Apostle and High Priest of our confession, Christ Jesus, 2who was faithful to Him who appointed Him, as Moses also *was faithful* in all His house. 3For this

One has been counted worthy of more glory than Moses, inasmuch as He who built the house has more honor than the house. 4For every house is built by someone, but He who built all things *is* God. 5And Moses indeed *was* faithful in all His house as a servant, for a testimony of those things which would be spoken *afterward,* 6but Christ as a Son over His own house, whose house we are if we hold fast the confidence and the rejoicing of the hope firm to the end.

Be Faithful

7Therefore, as the Holy Spirit says:
  "Today, if you will hear His voice,
8   Do not harden your hearts as in the
      rebellion,
  In the day of trial in the wilderness,
9   Where your fathers tested Me,
      tried Me,
  And saw My works forty years.
10 Therefore I was angry with that
      generation,
  And said, 'They always go astray
    in *their* heart,
  And they have not known My
    ways.'
11 So I swore in My wrath,
    'They shall not enter My rest.' "*l*
12Beware, brethren, lest there be in any of you an evil heart of unbelief in departing from the living God; 13but exhort one another daily, while it is called "Today," lest any of you be hardened through the deceitfulness of sin. 14For we have become partakers of Christ if we hold the beginning of our confidence steadfast to the end, 15while it is said:

"Today, if you will hear His voice,
  Do not harden your hearts as in the
    rebellion."*m*

Failure of the Wilderness Wanderers

16For who, having heard, rebelled? Indeed, *was it* not all who came out of Egypt, *led* by Moses? 17Now with whom was He angry forty years? *Was it* not with those who sinned, whose corpses fell in the wilderness? 18And to whom did He swear that they would not enter His rest, but to those who did not obey?

i Psalm 22.22   *j* 2 Samuel 22.3; Isaiah 8.17   *k* Isaiah 8.18   *l* Psalm 95.7-11
m Psalm 95.7, 8

19So we see that they could not enter in because of unbelief.

The Promise of Rest

4 Therefore, since a promise remains of entering His rest, let us fear lest any of you seem to have come short of it. 2For indeed the gospel was preached to us as well as to them; but the word which they heard did not profit them, not being mixed with faith in those who heard it. 3For we who have believed do enter that rest, as He has said:

"So I swore in My wrath,
'They shall not enter My rest,' "n

although the works were finished from the foundation of the world. 4For He has spoken in a certain place of the seventh day in this way: "And God rested on the seventh day from all His works";o 5and again in this place: "They shall not enter My rest."p

6Since therefore it remains that some must enter it, and those to whom it was first preached did not enter because of disobedience, 7again He designates a certain day, saying in David, "Today," after such a long time, as it has been said:

"Today, if you will hear His voice,
    Do not harden your hearts."q

8For if Joshua had given them rest, then He would not afterward have spoken of another day. 9There remains therefore a rest for the people of God. 10For he who has entered His rest has himself also ceased from his works as God did from His.

The Word Discovers Our Condition

11Let us therefore be diligent to enter that rest, lest anyone fall according to the same example of disobedience. 12For the word of God is living and powerful, and sharper than any two-edged sword, piercing even to the division of soul and spirit, and of joints and marrow, and is a discerner of the thoughts and intents of the heart. 13And there is no creature hidden from His sight, but all things are naked and open to the eyes of Him to whom we must give account.

Our Compassionate High Priest

14Seeing then that we have a great High Priest who has passed through the heavens, Jesus the Son of God, let us hold fast our confession. 15For we do not have a High Priest who cannot sympathize with our weaknesses, but was in all points tempted as we are, yet without sin. 16Let us therefore come boldly to the throne of grace, that we may obtain mercy and find grace to help in time of need.

Qualifications for High Priesthood

5 For every high priest taken from among men is appointed for men in things pertaining to God, that he may offer both gifts and sacrifices for sins. 2He can have compassion on those who are ignorant and going astray, since he himself is also subject to weakness. 3Because of this he is required as for the people, so also for himself, to offer sacrifices for sins. 4And no man takes this honor to himself, but he who is called by God, just as Aaron was.

A Priest Forever

5So also Christ did not glorify Himself to become High Priest, but it was He who said to Him:

"You are My Son,
    Today I have begotten You."r

6As He also says in another place:

"You are a priest forever
    According to the order of
    Melchizedek";s

7who, in the days of His flesh, when He had offered up prayers and supplications, with vehement cries and tears to Him who was able to save Him from death, and was heard because of His godly fear, 8though He was a Son, yet He learned obedience by the things which He suffered. 9And having been perfected, He became the author of eternal salvation to all who obey Him, 10called by God as High Priest "according to the order of Melchizedek," 11of whom we have much to say, and hard to explain, since you have become dull of hearing.

n Psalm 95.11   o Genesis 2.2   p Psalm 95.11   q Psalm 95.7, 8   r Psalm 2.7
s Psalm 110.4

Spiritual Immaturity

12For though by this time you ought to be teachers, you need *someone* to teach you again the first principles of the oracles of God; and you have come to need milk and not solid food. 13For everyone who partakes *only* of milk *is* unskilled in the word of righteousness, for he is a babe. 14But solid food belongs to those who are of full age, *that is,* those who by reason of use have their senses exercised to discern both good and evil.

The Peril of Not Progressing

6 Therefore, leaving the discussion of the elementary *principles* of Christ, let us go on to perfection, not laying again the foundation of repentance from dead works and of faith toward God, 2of the doctrine of baptisms, of laying on of hands, of resurrection of the dead, and of eternal judgment. 3And this we will do if God permits.

4For *it is* impossible for those who were once enlightened, and have tasted the heavenly gift, and have become partakers of the Holy Spirit, 5and have tasted the good word of God and the powers of the age to come, 6if they fall away, to renew them again to repentance, since they crucify again for themselves the Son of God, and put *Him* to an open shame.

7For the earth which drinks in the rain that often comes upon it, and bears herbs useful for those by whom it is cultivated, receives blessing from God; 8but if it bears thorns and briers, *it is* rejected and near to being cursed, whose end *is* to be burned.

A Better Estimate

9But, beloved, we are confident of better things concerning you, yes, things that accompany salvation, though we speak in this manner. 10For God *is* not unjust to forget your work and labor of love which you have shown toward His name, *in that* you have ministered to the saints, and do minister. 11And we desire that each one of you show the same diligence to the full assurance of hope until the end,

that you do not become sluggish, but imitate those who through faith and patience inherit the promises.

God's Infallible Purpose in Christ

13For when God made a promise to Abraham, because He could swear by no one greater, He swore by Himself, 14saying, "Surely blessing I will bless you, and multiplying I will multiply you."*t* 15And so, after he had patiently endured, he obtained the promise. 16For men indeed swear by the greater, and an oath for confirmation *is* for them an end of all dispute. 17Thus God, determining to show more abundantly to the heirs of promise the immutability of His counsel, confirmed *it* by an oath, 18that by two immutable things, in which it *is* impossible for God to lie, we might have strong consolation, who have fled for refuge to lay hold of the hope set before *us*. 19This *hope* we have as an anchor of the soul, both sure and steadfast, and which enters the Presence *behind* the veil, 20where the forerunner has entered for us, *even* Jesus, having become High Priest forever according to the order of Melchizedek.

The King of Righteousness

7 For this Melchizedek, king of Salem, priest of the Most High God, who met Abraham returning from the slaughter of the kings and blessed him, 2to whom also Abraham gave a tenth part of all, first being translated "king of righteousness," and then also king of Salem, meaning "king of peace," 3without father, without mother, without genealogy, having neither beginning of days nor end of life, but made like the Son of God, remains a priest continually.

4Now consider how great this man *was*, to whom even the patriarch Abraham gave a tenth of the spoils. 5And indeed those who are of the sons of Levi, who receive the priesthood, have a commandment to receive tithes from the people according to the law, that is, from their brethren, though they have come from the loins of Abraham; 6but he whose genealogy is not derived

---

t Genesis 22.17

from them received tithes from Abraham and blessed him who had the promises. 7Now beyond all contradiction the lesser is blessed by the better. 8Here mortal men receive tithes, but there he *receives them*, of whom it is witnessed that he lives. 9Even Levi, who receives tithes, paid tithes through Abraham, so to speak, 10for he was still in the loins of his father when Melchizedek met him.

Need for a New Priesthood

11Therefore, if perfection were through the Levitical priesthood (for under it the people received the law), what further need *was there* that another priest should rise according to the order of Melchizedek, and not be called according to the order of Aaron? 12For the priesthood being changed, of necessity there is also a change of the law. 13For He of whom these things are spoken belongs to another tribe, from which no man has officiated at the altar.

14For *it is* evident that our Lord arose from Judah, of which tribe Moses spoke nothing concerning priesthood. 15And it is yet far more evident if, in the likeness of Melchizedek, there arises another priest 16who has come, not according to the law of a fleshly commandment, but according to the power of an endless life. 17For He testifies:

"You *are* a priest forever
According to the order of
Melchizedek.""*u*

18For on the one hand there is an annulling of the former commandment because of its weakness and unprofitableness, 19for the law made nothing perfect; on the other hand, *there is the* bringing in of a better hope, through which we draw near to God.

Greatness of the New Priest

20And inasmuch as *He was* not *made priest* without an oath 21(for they have become priests without an oath, but He with an oath by Him who said to Him:

"The Lord has sworn
And will not relent,
'You *are* a priest forever

According to the order of
Melchizedek' "),*v*

22by so much more Jesus has become a surety of a better covenant.

23Also there were many priests, because they were prevented by death from continuing. 24But He, because He continues forever, has an unchangeable priesthood. 25Therefore He is also able to save to the uttermost those who come to God through Him, since He always lives to make intercession for them.

26For such a High Priest was fitting for us, *who is* holy, harmless, undefiled, separate from sinners, and has become higher than the heavens; 27who does not need daily, as those high priests, to offer up sacrifices, first for His own sins and then for the people's, for this He did once for all when He offered up Himself. 28For the law appoints as high priests men who have weakness, but the word of the oath, which came after the law, *appoints* the Son who has been perfected forever.

The New Priestly Service

8 Now *this is* the main point of the things we are saying: We have such a High Priest, who is seated at the right hand of the throne of the Majesty in the heavens, 2a Minister of the sanctuary and of the true tabernacle which the Lord erected, and not man.

3For every high priest is appointed to offer up gifts and sacrifices. Therefore *it is* necessary that this One also have something to offer. 4For if He were on earth, He would not be a priest, since there are priests who offer the gifts according to the law; 5who serve the copy and shadow of the heavenly things, as Moses was divinely instructed when he was about to make the tabernacle. For He said, "See *that* you make all things according to the pattern shown you on the mountain."*v* 6But now He has obtained a more excellent ministry, inasmuch as He is also Mediator of a better covenant, which was established on better promises.

A New Covenant

7For if that first *covenant* had been faultless, then no place would have

u Psalm 110.4   *v* Exodus 25.40

been sought for a second. 8Because finding fault with them, He says: "Behold, the days are coming, says the LORD, when I will make a new covenant with the house of Israel and with the house of Judah—9not according to the covenant that I made with their fathers in the day when I took them by the hand to lead them out of the land of Egypt; because they did not continue in My covenant, and I disregarded them, says the LORD. 10For this is the covenant that I will make with the house of Israel after those days, says the LORD: I will put My laws in their mind and write them on their hearts; and I will be their God, and they shall be My people. 11None of them shall teach his neighbor, and none his brother, saying, 'Know the LORD,' for all shall know Me, from the least of them to the greatest of them. 12 For I will be merciful to their unrighteousness, and their sins and their lawless deeds I will remember no more."w

13In that He says, "A new covenant," He has made the first obsolete. Now what is becoming obsolete and growing old is ready to vanish away.

The Earthly Sanctuary

9 Then indeed, even the first covenant had ordinances of divine service and the earthly sanctuary. 2For a tabernacle was prepared: the first part, in which was the lampstand, the table, and the showbread, which is called the sanctuary; 3and behind the second veil, the part of the tabernacle which is called the Holiest of All, 4which had the golden censer and the ark of the covenant overlaid on all sides with gold, in which were the golden pot that had the manna, Aaron's rod that budded, and the tablets of the covenant; 5and above it were the cherubim of glory overshadowing the mercy seat. Of these things we cannot now speak in detail.

Limitations of the Earthly Service

6Now when these things had been thus prepared, the priests always went into the first part of the tabernacle, performing the services. 7But into the second part the high priest went alone

once a year, not without blood, which he offered for himself and for the people's sins committed in ignorance; 8the Holy Spirit indicating this, that the way into the Holiest of All was not yet made manifest while the first tabernacle was still standing. 9It was symbolic for the present time in which both gifts and sacrifices are offered which cannot make him who performed the service perfect in regard to the conscience—10concerned only with foods and drinks, various washings, and fleshly ordinances imposed until the time of reformation.

The Heavenly Sanctuary

11But Christ came as High Priest of the good things to come, with the greater and more perfect tabernacle not made with hands, that is, not of this creation. 12Not with the blood of goats and calves, but with His own blood He entered the Most Holy Place once for all, having obtained eternal redemption. 13For if the blood of bulls and goats and the ashes of a heifer, sprinkling the unclean, sanctifies for the purifying of the flesh, 14how much more shall the blood of Christ, who through the eternal Spirit offered Himself without spot to God, cleanse your conscience from dead works to serve the living God? 15And for this reason He is the Mediator of the new covenant, by means of death, for the redemption of the transgressions under the first covenant, that those who are called may receive the promise of the eternal inheritance.

The Mediator's Death Necessary

16For where there is a testament, there must also of necessity be the death of the testator. 17For a testament is in force after men are dead, since it has no power at all while the testator lives. 18Therefore not even the first covenant was dedicated without blood. 19For when Moses had spoken every precept to all the people according to the law, he took the blood of calves and goats, with water, scarlet wool, and hyssop, and sprinkled both the book itself and all the people, 20saying, "This is the blood of the covenant which God

w Jeremiah 31.31-34

has commanded you."[x] 21Then likewise he sprinkled with blood both the tabernacle and all the vessels of the ministry. 22And according to the law almost all things are purified with blood, and without shedding of blood there is no remission.

Greatness of Christ's Sacrifice

23Therefore *it was* necessary that the copies of the things in the heavens should be purified with these, but the heavenly things themselves with better sacrifices than these. 24For Christ has not entered the holy places made with hands, *which are* copies of the true, but into heaven itself, now to appear in the presence of God for us; 25not that He should offer Himself often, as the high priest enters the Most Holy Place every year with blood of another—26He then would have had to suffer often since the foundation of the world; but now, once at the end of the ages, He has appeared to put away sin by the sacrifice of Himself. 27And as it is appointed for men to die once, but after this the judgment, 28so Christ was offered once to bear the sins of many. To those who eagerly wait for Him He will appear a second time, apart from sin, for salvation.

Animal Sacrifices Insufficient

10 For the law, having a shadow of the good things to come, *and* not the very image of the things, can never with these same sacrifices, which they offer continually year by year, make those who approach perfect. 2For then would they not have ceased to be offered? For the worshipers, once purified, would have had no more consciousness of sins. 3But in those *sacrifices there is* a reminder of sins every year. 4For *it is* not possible that the blood of bulls and goats could take away sins.

Christ's Death Fulfills God's Will

5Therefore, when He came into the world, He said:

"Sacrifice and offering You did not desire,
But a body You have prepared for Me.

6 In burnt offerings and *sacrifices* for sin
You had no pleasure.
7 Then I said, 'Behold, I have come—
In the volume of the book it is written of Me—
To do Your will, O God.' "[y]

8Previously saying, "Sacrifice and offering, burnt offerings, and *offerings* for sin You did not desire, nor had pleasure *in them*" (which are offered according to the law), 9then He said, "Behold, I have come to do Your will, O God." He takes away the first that He may establish the second. 10By that will we have been sanctified through the offering of the body of Jesus Christ once *for all*.

Christ's Death Perfects the Sanctified

11And every priest stands ministering daily and offering repeatedly the same sacrifices, which can never take away sins. 12But this Man, after He had offered one sacrifice for sins forever, sat down at the right hand of God, 13from that time waiting till His enemies are made His footstool. 14For by one offering He has perfected forever those who are being sanctified.

15But the Holy Spirit also witnesses to us; for after He had said before,

16"This *is* the covenant that I will make with them after those days, says the LORD: I will put My laws into their hearts, and in their minds I will write them,"[z] 17then He adds, "Their sins and their lawless deeds I will remember no more."[a] 18Now where there is remission of these, *there is* no longer an offering for sin.

Hold Fast Your Confession

19Therefore, brethren, having boldness to enter the Holiest by the blood of Jesus, 20by a new and living way which He consecrated for us, through the veil, that is, His flesh, 21and *having* a High Priest over the house of God, 22let us draw near with a true heart in full assurance of faith, having our hearts sprinkled from an evil conscience and our bodies washed with pure water. 23Let us hold fast the confession of *our* hope without wavering, for He who promised *is* faithful.

---

[x] Exodus 24.8　　　[y] Psalm 40.6-8　　　[z] Jeremiah 31.33　　　[a] Jeremiah 31.34

24And let us consider one another in order to stir up love and good works, 25not forsaking the assembling of ourselves together, as *is* the manner of some, but exhorting *one another*, and so much the more as you see the Day approaching.

The Just Live by Faith

26For if we sin willfully after we have received the knowledge of the truth, there no longer remains a sacrifice for sins, 27but a certain fearful expectation of judgment, and fiery indignation which will devour the adversaries. 28Anyone who has rejected Moses' law dies without mercy on the testimony of two or three witnesses. 29Of how much worse punishment, do you suppose, will he be thought worthy who has trampled the Son of God underfoot, counted the blood of the covenant by which he was sanctified a common thing, and insulted the Spirit of grace? 30For we know Him who said, "Vengeance is Mine, I will repay,"*b* says the Lord. And again, "The LORD will judge His people."*c* 31It is a fearful thing to fall into the hands of the living God.

32But recall the former days in which, after you were illuminated, you endured a great struggle with sufferings: 33partly while you were made a spectacle both by reproaches and tribulations, and partly while you became companions of those who were so treated; 34for you had compassion on me in my chains, and joyfully accepted the plundering of your goods, knowing that you have a better and an enduring possession for yourselves in heaven. 35Therefore do not cast away your confidence, which has great reward. 36For you have need of endurance, so that after you have done the will of God, you may receive the promise:

37 "For yet a little while,
　　And He who is coming will come
　　　　and will not tarry.
38 　Now the just shall live by faith;
　　But if *anyone* draws back,
　　My soul has no pleasure in him."*d*

39But we are not of those who draw back to perdition, but of those who believe to the saving of the soul.

By Faith We Understand

11 Now faith is the substance of things hoped for, the evidence of things not seen. 2For by it the elders obtained a *good* testimony.

3By faith we understand that the worlds were framed by the word of God, so that the things which are seen were not made of things which are visible.

Faith at the Dawn of History

4By faith Abel offered to God a more excellent sacrifice than Cain, through which he obtained witness that he was righteous, God testifying of his gifts; and through it he being dead still speaks.

5By faith Enoch was taken away so that he did not see death, "and was not found, because God had taken him";*e* for before he was taken he had this testimony, that he pleased God. 6But without faith *it is* impossible to please *Him*, for he who comes to God must believe that He is, and *that* He is a rewarder of those who diligently seek Him.

7By faith Noah, being divinely warned of things not yet seen, moved with godly fear, prepared an ark for the saving of his household, by which he condemned the world and became heir of the righteousness which is according to faith.

Faithful Abraham

8By faith Abraham obeyed when he was called to go out to the place which he would receive as an inheritance. And he went out, not knowing where he was going. 9By faith he dwelt in the land of promise as *in* a foreign country, dwelling in tents with Isaac and Jacob, the heirs with him of the same promise; 10for he waited for the city which has foundations, whose builder and maker *is* God.

11By faith Sarah herself also received strength to conceive seed, and she bore a child when she was past the age, because she judged Him faithful who had promised. 12Therefore from one man, and him as good as dead, were born *as many* as the stars of the sky in multi-

b Deuteronomy 32.35   *c* Deuteronomy 32.36   *d* Habakkuk 2.3, 4   *e* Genesis 5.24

tude—innumerable as the sand which is by the seashore.

The Heavenly Hope

13These all died in faith, not having received the promises, but having seen them afar off were assured of them, embraced *them* and confessed that they were strangers and pilgrims on the earth. 14For those who say such things declare plainly that they seek a homeland. 15And truly if they had called to mind that *country* from which they had come out, they would have had opportunity to return. 16But now they desire a better, that is, a heavenly *country*. Therefore God is not ashamed to be called their God, for He has prepared a city for them.

The Faith of the Patriarchs

17By faith Abraham, when he was tested, offered up Isaac, and he who had received the promises offered up his only begotten *son*, 18of whom it was said, "In Isaac your seed shall be called,"*f* 19concluding that God *was* able to raise *him* up, even from the dead, from which he also received him in a figurative sense.

20By faith Isaac blessed Jacob and Esau concerning things to come.

21By faith Jacob, when he was dying, blessed each of the sons of Joseph, and worshiped, *leaning* on the top of his staff.

22By faith Joseph, when he was dying, made mention of the departure of the children of Israel, and gave instructions concerning his bones.

The Faith of Moses

23By faith Moses, when he was born, was hidden three months by his parents, because they saw *he was* a beautiful child; and they were not afraid of the king's command.

24By faith Moses, when he became of age, refused to be called the son of Pharaoh's daughter, 25choosing rather to suffer affliction with the people of God than to enjoy the passing pleasures of sin, 26esteeming the reproach of Christ greater riches than the treasures in Egypt; for he looked to the reward.

27By faith he forsook Egypt, not fearing the wrath of the king; for he endured as seeing Him who is invisible. 28By faith he kept the Passover and the sprinkling of blood, lest he who destroyed the firstborn should touch them.

29By faith they passed through the Red Sea as by dry *land, whereas* the Egyptians, attempting *to do* so, were drowned.

By Faith They Overcame

30By faith the walls of Jericho fell down after they were encircled for seven days. 31By faith the harlot Rahab did not perish with those who did not believe, when she had received the spies with peace.

32And what more shall I say? For the time would fail me to tell of Gideon and Barak and Samson and Jephthah, also *of* David and Samuel and the prophets: 33who through faith subdued kingdoms, worked righteousness, obtained promises, stopped the mouths of lions, 34quenched the violence of fire, escaped the edge of the sword, out of weakness were made strong, became valiant in battle, turned to flight the armies of the aliens. 35Women received their dead raised to life again.

Others were tortured, not accepting deliverance, that they might obtain a better resurrection. 36Still others had trial of mockings and scourgings, yes, and of chains and imprisonment. 37They were stoned, they were sawn in two, were tempted, were slain with the sword. They wandered about in sheepskins and goatskins, being destitute, afflicted, tormented—38of whom the world was not worthy. They wandered in deserts and mountains, *in* dens and caves of the earth.

39And all these, having obtained a good testimony through faith, did not receive the promise, 40God having provided something better for us, that they should not be made perfect apart from us.

The Race of Faith

12 Therefore we also, since we are surrounded by so great a cloud

f Genesis 21.12

of witnesses, let us lay aside every weight, and the sin which so easily ensnares *us*, and let us run with endurance the race that is set before us, 2looking unto Jesus, the author and finisher of *our* faith, who for the joy that was set before Him endured the cross, despising the shame, and has sat down at the right hand of the throne of God.

The Discipline of God

3For consider Him who endured such hostility from sinners against Himself, lest you become weary and discouraged in your souls. 4You have not yet resisted to bloodshed, striving against sin. 5And you have forgotten the exhortation which speaks to you as to sons:

"My son, do not despise the
  chastening of the LORD,
  Nor be discouraged when you are
  rebuked by Him;
6   For whom the LORD loves He
  chastens,
  And scourges every son whom He
  receives."*g*

7If you endure chastening, God deals with you as with sons; for what son is there whom a father does not chasten? 8But if you are without chastening, of which all have become partakers, then you are illegitimate and not sons. 9Furthermore, we have had human fathers who corrected *us*, and we paid *them* respect. Shall we not much more readily be in subjection to the Father of spirits and live? 10For they indeed for a few days chastened *us* as seemed *best* to them, but He for *our* profit, that *we* may be partakers of His holiness. 11Now no chastening seems to be joyful for the present, but painful; nevertheless, afterward it yields the peaceable fruit of righteousness to those who have been trained by it.

Renew Your Spiritual Vitality

12Therefore strengthen the hands which hang down, and the feeble knees, 13and make straight paths for your feet, so that what is lame may not be *dislocated*, but rather be healed.

14Pursue peace with all *people*, and holiness, without which no one will see the Lord: 15looking carefully lest any

one fall short of the grace of God; lest any root of bitterness springing up cause trouble, and by this many become defiled; 16lest there *be* any fornicator or profane person like Esau, who for one morsel of food sold his birthright. 17For you know that afterward, when he wanted to inherit the blessing, he was rejected, for he found no place for repentance, though he sought it diligently with tears.

The Glorious Company

18For you have not come to the mountain that may be touched and that burned with fire, and to blackness and darkness and tempest, 19and the sound of a trumpet and the voice of words, so that those who heard *it* begged that the word should not be spoken to them anymore. 20(For they could not endure what was commanded: "And if so much as a beast touches the mountain, it shall be stoned or shot with an arrow."*h* 21And so terrifying was the sight *that* Moses said, "I am exceedingly afraid and trembling."*i*)

22But you have come to Mount Zion and to the city of the living God, the heavenly Jerusalem, to an innumerable company of angels, 23to the general assembly and church of the firstborn *who are* registered in heaven, to God the Judge of all, to the spirits of just men made perfect, 24to Jesus the Mediator of the new covenant, and to the blood of sprinkling that speaks better things than *that of* Abel.

Hear the Heavenly Voice

25See that you do not refuse Him who speaks. For if they did not escape who refused Him who spoke on earth, much more *shall we not escape* if we turn away from Him who *speaks* from heaven, 26whose voice then shook the earth; but now He has promised, saying, "Yet once more I shake not only the earth, but also heaven."*j* 27Now this, "Yet once more," indicates the removal of those things that are being shaken, as of things that are made, that the things which cannot be shaken may remain.

28Therefore, since we are receiving a

---

g Proverbs 3.11, 12   *h* Exodus 19.12, 13   *i* Deuteronomy 9.19   *j* Haggai 2.6

kingdom which cannot be shaken, let us have grace, by which we may serve God acceptably with reverence and godly fear. 29For our God *is* a consuming fire.

Concluding Moral Directions

13 Let brotherly love continue. 2Do not forget to entertain strangers, for by so *doing* some have unwittingly entertained angels. 3Remember the prisoners as if chained with them—those who are mistreated—since you yourselves are in the body also.

4Marriage *is* honorable among all, and the bed undefiled; but fornicators and adulterers God will judge.

5*Let your* conduct *be* without covetousness; *be* content with such things as you have. For He Himself has said, "I will never leave you nor forsake you."*k* 6So we may boldly say:

"The LORD *is* my helper;
I will not fear.
What can man do to me?"*l*

Concluding Religious Directions

7Remember those who rule over you, who have spoken the word of God to you, whose faith follow, considering the outcome of *their* conduct. 8Jesus Christ *is* the same yesterday, today, and forever. 9Do not be carried about with various and strange doctrines. For *it is* good that the heart be established by grace, not with foods which have not profited those who have been occupied with them.

10We have an altar from which those who serve the tabernacle have no right to eat. 11For the bodies of those animals, whose blood is brought into the sanctuary by the high priest for sin, are burned outside the camp. 12Therefore Jesus also, that He might sanctify the people with His own blood, suffered outside the gate. 13Therefore let us go forth to Him, outside the camp, bearing His reproach. 14For here we have no continuing city, but we seek the one to come. 15Therefore by Him let us continually offer the sacrifice of praise to God, that is, the fruit of *our* lips, giving thanks to His name. 16But do not forget to do good and to share, for with such sacrifices God is well pleased.

17Obey those who rule over you, and be submissive, for they watch out for your souls, as those who must give account. Let them do so with joy and not with grief, for that would be unprofitable for you.

Prayer Requested

18Pray for us; for we are confident that we have a good conscience, in all things desiring to live honorably. 19But I especially urge *you* to do this, that I may be restored to you the sooner.

Benediction, Final Exhortation, Farewell

20Now may the God of peace who brought up our Lord Jesus from the dead, that great Shepherd of the sheep, through the blood of the everlasting covenant, 21make you complete in every good work to do His will, working in you what is well pleasing in His sight, through Jesus Christ, to whom *be* glory forever and ever. Amen.

22And I appeal to you, brethren, bear with the word of exhortation, for I have written to you in few words. 23Know that *our* brother Timothy has been set free, with whom I shall see you if he comes shortly.

24Greet all those who rule over you, and all the saints. Those from Italy greet you.

25Grace *be* with you all. Amen.

k Deuteronomy 31.6, 8; Joshua 1.5   *l* Psalm 118.6

JAMES

Greeting to the Twelve Tribes

1 James, a bondservant of God and of the Lord Jesus Christ,

To the twelve tribes which are scattered abroad:

Greetings.

Profiting from Trials

2My brethren, count it all joy when you fall into various trials, 3knowing that the testing of your faith produces patience. 4But let patience have *its* perfect work, that you may be perfect and complete, lacking nothing. 5If any of you lacks wisdom, let him ask of God, who gives to all liberally and without reproach, and it will be given to him. 6But let him ask in faith, with no doubting, for he who doubts is like a wave of the sea driven and tossed by the wind. 7For let not that man suppose that he will receive anything from the Lord; 8*he is* a double-minded man, unstable in all his ways.

The Perspective of Rich and Poor

9Let the lowly brother glory in his exaltation, 10but the rich in his humiliation, because as a flower of the field he will pass away. 11For no sooner has the sun risen with a burning heat than it withers the grass; its flower falls, and its beautiful appearance perishes. So the rich man also will fade away in his pursuits.

Loving God Under Trials

12Blessed *is* the man who endures temptation; for when he has been approved, he will receive the crown of life which the Lord has promised to those who love Him. 13Let no one say when he is tempted, "I am tempted by God"; for God cannot be tempted by evil, nor does He Himself tempt anyone. 14But each one is tempted when he is drawn away by his own desires and enticed. 15Then, when desire has conceived, it gives birth to sin; and sin, when it is full-grown, brings forth death.

16Do not be deceived, my beloved brethren. 17Every good gift and every perfect gift is from above, and comes down from the Father of lights, with whom there is no variation or shadow of turning. 18Of His own will He brought us forth by the word of truth, that we might be a kind of firstfruits of His creatures.

Qualities Needed in Trials

19So then, my beloved brethren, let every man be swift to hear, slow to speak, slow to wrath; 20for the wrath of man does not produce the righteousness of God.

Doers—Not Hearers Only

21Therefore lay aside all filthiness and overflow of wickedness, and receive with meekness the implanted word, which is able to save your souls.

22But be doers of the word, and not hearers only, deceiving yourselves. 23For if anyone is a hearer of the word and not a doer, he is like a man observing his natural face in a mirror; 24for he observes himself, goes away, and immediately forgets what kind of man he was. 25But he who looks into the perfect law of liberty and continues *in it*, and is not a forgetful hearer but a doer of the work, this one will be blessed in what he does.

26If anyone among you thinks he is religious, and does not bridle his tongue but deceives his own heart, this one's religion *is* useless. 27Pure and undefiled religion before God and the Father is this: to visit orphans and widows in their trouble, *and* to keep oneself unspotted from the world.

Beware of Personal Favoritism

2 My brethren, do not hold the faith of our Lord Jesus Christ, *the Lord* of glory, with partiality. 2For if there should come into your assembly a man with gold rings, in fine apparel, and there should also come in a poor man in filthy clothes, 3and you pay attention to the one wearing the fine clothes and say to him, "You sit here in a good place," and say to the poor man, "You stand there," or, "Sit here at my footstool," 4have you not shown partiality among yourselves, and become judges with evil thoughts?

5Listen, my beloved brethren: Has God not chosen the poor of this world *to be* rich in faith and heirs of the kingdom which He promised to those who love Him? 6But you have dishonored the poor man. Do not the rich oppress you and drag you into the courts? 7Do they not blaspheme that noble name by which you are called?

8If you really fulfill *the* royal law according to the Scripture, "You shall love your neighbor as yourself,"*a* you do well; 9but if you show partiality, you commit sin, and are convicted by the law as transgressors. 10For whoever shall keep the whole law, and yet stumble in one *point*, he is guilty of all. 11For He who said, "Do not commit adultery,"*b* also said, "Do not murder."*c* Now if you do not commit adultery, but you do murder, you have become a transgressor of the law. 12So speak and so do as those who will be judged by the law of liberty. 13For judgment is without mercy to the one who has shown no mercy. Mercy triumphs over judgment.

Faith Without Works Is Dead

14What *does it* profit, my brethren, if someone says he has faith but does not have works? Can faith save him? 15If a brother or sister is naked and destitute of daily food, 16and one of you says to them, "Depart in peace, be warmed and filled," but you do not give them the things which are needed for the body, what *does it* profit? 17Thus also faith by itself, if it does not have works, is dead.

18But someone will say, "You have faith, and I have works." Show me your faith without your works, and I will show you my faith by my works. 19You believe that there is one God. You do well. Even the demons believe— and tremble! 20But do you want to know, O foolish man, that faith without works is dead? 21Was not Abraham our

father justified by works when he offered Isaac his son on the altar? 22Do you see that faith was working together with his works, and by works faith was made perfect? 23And the Scripture was fulfilled which says, "Abraham believed God, and it was accounted to him for righteousness."*d* And he was called the friend of God. 24You see then that a man is justified by works, and not by faith only.

25Likewise, was not Rahab the harlot also justified by works when she received the messengers and sent *them* out another way?

26For as the body without the spirit is dead, so faith without works is dead also.

The Untamable Tongue

3 My brethren, let not many of you become teachers, knowing that we shall receive a stricter judgment. 2For we all stumble in many things. If anyone does not stumble in word, he *is* a perfect man, able also to bridle the whole body. 3Indeed, we put bits in horses' mouths that they may obey us, and we turn their whole body. 4Look also at ships: although they are so large and are driven by fierce winds, they are turned by a very small rudder wherever the pilot desires. 5Even so the tongue is a little member and boasts great things.

See how great a forest a little fire kindles! 6And the tongue *is* a fire, a world of iniquity. The tongue is so set among our members that it defiles the whole body, and sets on fire the course of nature; and it is set on fire by hell. 7For every kind of beast and bird, of reptile and creature of the sea, is tamed and has been tamed by mankind. 8But no man can tame the tongue. *It is* an unruly evil, full of deadly poison. 9With it we bless our God and Father, and with it we curse men, who have been made in the similitude of God. 10Out of the same mouth proceed blessing and cursing. My brethren, these things ought not to be so. 11Does a spring send forth fresh *water* and bitter from the same opening? 12Can a fig tree, my

a Leviticus 19.18   *b* Exodus 20.14; Deuteronomy 5.18   *c* Exodus 20.13; Deuteronomy 5.17
d Genesis 15.6

brethren, bear olives, or a grapevine bear figs? Thus no spring yields both salt water and fresh.

Heavenly Versus Demonic Wisdom

13Who *is* wise and understanding among you? Let him show by good conduct *that* his works *are done* in the meekness of wisdom. 14But if you have bitter envy and self-seeking in your hearts, do not boast and lie against the truth. 15This wisdom does not descend from above, but *is* earthly, sensual, demonic. 16For where envy and self-seeking *exist*, confusion and every evil thing *are* there. 17But the wisdom that is from above is first pure, then peaceable, gentle, willing to yield, full of mercy and good fruits, without partiality and without hypocrisy. 18Now the fruit of righteousness is sown in peace by those who make peace.

Pride Promotes Strife

4 Where do wars and fights *come* from among you? Do *they* not *come* from your *desires for* pleasure that war in your members? 2You lust and do not have. You murder and covet and cannot obtain. You fight and war. Yet you do not have because you do not ask. 3You ask and do not receive, because you ask amiss, that you may spend *it* on your pleasures. 4Adulterers and adulteresses! Do you not know that friendship with the world is enmity with God? Whoever therefore wants to be a friend of the world makes himself an enemy of God. 5Or do you think that the Scripture says in vain, "The Spirit who dwells in us yearns jealously"?

6But He gives more grace. Therefore He says:

"God resists the proud,
  But gives grace to the humble."*e*

Humility Cures Worldliness

7Therefore submit to God. Resist the devil and he will flee from you. 8Draw near to God and He will draw near to you. Cleanse *your* hands, *you* sinners; and purify *your* hearts, *you* double-minded. 9Lament and mourn and weep! Let your laughter be turned to mourning and *your* joy to gloom. 10Humble yourselves in the sight of the Lord, and He will lift you up.

Do Not Judge a Brother

11Do not speak evil of one another, brethren. He who speaks evil of a brother and judges his brother, speaks evil of the law and judges the law. But if you judge the law, you are not a doer of the law but a judge. 12There is one Lawgiver, who is able to save and to destroy. Who are you to judge another?

Do Not Boast About Tomorrow

13Come now, you who say, "Today or tomorrow we will go to such and such a city, spend a year there, buy and sell, and make a profit"; 14whereas you do not know what *will happen* tomorrow. For what *is* your life? It is even a vapor that appears for a little time and then vanishes away. 15Instead you *ought* to say, "If the Lord wills, we shall live and do this or that." 16But now you boast in your arrogance. All such boasting is evil.

17Therefore, to him who knows to do good and does not do *it*, to him it is sin.

Rich Oppressors Will Be Judged

5 Come now, *you* rich, weep and howl for your miseries that are coming upon *you!* 2Your riches are corrupted, and your garments are moth-eaten. 3Your gold and silver are corroded, and their corrosion will be a witness against you and will eat your flesh like fire. You have heaped up treasure in the last days. 4Indeed the wages of the laborers who mowed your fields, which you kept back by fraud, cry out; and the cries of the reapers have reached the ears of the Lord of Sabaoth. 5You have lived on the earth in pleasure and luxury; you have fattened your hearts as in a day of slaughter. 6You have condemned, you have murdered the just; he does not resist you.

Be Patient and Persevering

7Therefore be patient, brethren, until the coming of the Lord. See *how* the

e Proverbs 3.34

farmer waits for the precious fruit of the earth, waiting patiently for it until it receives the early and latter rain. 8You also be patient. Establish your hearts, for the coming of the Lord is at hand.

9Do not grumble against one another, brethren, lest you be condemned. Behold, the Judge is standing at the door! 10My brethren, take the prophets, who spoke in the name of the Lord, as an example of suffering and patience. 11Indeed we count them blessed who endure. You have heard of the perseverance of Job and seen the end *intended by* the Lord—that the Lord is very compassionate and merciful.

12But above all, my brethren, do not swear, either by heaven or by earth or with any other oath. But let your "Yes" be "Yes," and *your* "No," "No," lest you fall into judgment.

Meeting Specific Needs

13Is anyone among you suffering? Let him pray. Is anyone cheerful? Let him sing psalms. 14Is anyone among you sick? Let him call for the elders of the church, and let them pray over him, anointing him with oil in the name of the Lord. 15And the prayer of faith will save the sick, and the Lord will raise him up. And if he has committed sins, he will be forgiven. 16Confess *your* trespasses to one another, and pray for one another, that you may be healed. The effective, fervent prayer of a righteous man avails much. 17Elijah was a man with a nature like ours, and he prayed earnestly that it would not rain; and it did not rain on the land for three years and six months. 18And he prayed again, and the heaven gave rain, and the earth produced its fruit.

Bring Back the Erring One

19Brethren, if anyone among you wanders from the truth, and someone turns him back, 20let him know that he who turns a sinner from the error of his way will save a soul from death and cover a multitude of sins.

The First Epistle of

PETER

Greeting to the Elect Pilgrims

1 Peter, an apostle of Jesus Christ,

To the pilgrims of the Dispersion in Pontus, Galatia, Cappadocia, Asia, and Bithynia, 2elect according to the foreknowledge of God the Father, in sanctification of the Spirit, for obedience and sprinkling of the blood of Jesus Christ:

Grace to you and peace be multiplied.

A Heavenly Inheritance

3Blessed *be* the God and Father of our Lord Jesus Christ, who according to His abundant mercy has begotten us again to a living hope through the resurrection of Jesus Christ from the dead, 4to an inheritance incorruptible and undefiled and that does not fade away, reserved in heaven for you, 5who are kept by the power of God through faith for salvation ready to be revealed in the last time.

6In this you greatly rejoice, though now for a little while, if need be, you have been grieved by various trials, 7that the genuineness of your faith, *being* much more precious than gold that perishes, though it is tested by fire, may be found to praise, honor, and glory at the revelation of Jesus Christ, 8whom having not seen you love. Though now you do not see *Him,* yet believing, you rejoice with joy inexpressible and full of glory, 9receiving the end of your faith—the salvation of *your* souls.

10Of this salvation the prophets have inquired and searched carefully, who prophesied of the grace *that would come* to you, 11searching what, or what manner of time, the Spirit of Christ who was in them was indicating when He testified beforehand the sufferings of Christ and the glories that would follow. 12To them it was revealed that, not to themselves, but to us they were ministering the things which now have been reported to you through those who have preached the gospel to you by the Holy Spirit sent from heaven—things which angels desire to look into.

Living Before God Our Father

13Therefore gird up the loins of your mind, be sober, and rest *your* hope fully upon the grace that is to be brought to you at the revelation of Jesus Christ; 14as obedient children, not conforming yourselves to the former lusts, *as* in your ignorance; 15but as He who called you *is* holy, you also be holy in all *your* conduct, 16because it is written, "Be holy, for I am holy."[a]

17And if you call on the Father, who without partiality judges according to each one's work, conduct yourselves throughout the time of your stay *here* in fear; 18knowing that you were not redeemed with corruptible things, *like* silver or gold, from your aimless conduct *received* by tradition from your fathers, 19but with the precious blood of Christ, as of a lamb without blemish and without spot. 20He indeed was foreordained before the foundation of the world, but was manifest in these last times for you 21who through Him believe in God, who raised Him from the dead and gave Him glory, so that your faith and hope are in God.

The Enduring Word

22Since you have purified your souls in obeying the truth through the Spirit in sincere love of the brethren, love one another fervently with a pure heart, 23having been born again, not of corruptible seed but incorruptible, through the word of God which lives and abides forever, 24because

"All flesh *is* as grass,
　And all the glory of man as the
　　flower of the grass.
The grass withers,
　And its flower falls away,
25　But the word of the LORD endures
　　forever."[b]

---

a Leviticus 11.44, 45; 19.2; 20.7　　b Isaiah 40.6-8

Now this is the word which by the gospel was preached to you.

2 Therefore, laying aside all malice, all deceit, hypocrisy, envy, and all evil speaking, 2as newborn babes, desire the pure milk of the word, that you may grow thereby, 3if indeed you have tasted that the Lord *is* gracious.

The Chosen Stone and His Chosen People

4Coming to Him *as to* a living stone, rejected indeed by men, but chosen by God *and* precious, 5you also, as living stones, are being built up a spiritual house, a holy priesthood, to offer up spiritual sacrifices acceptable to God through Jesus Christ. 6Therefore it is also contained in the Scripture,

"Behold, I lay in Zion
    A chief cornerstone, elect, precious,
    And he who believes on Him will
        by no means be put to shame."*c*

7Therefore, to you who believe, *He is* precious; but to those who are disobedient,

"The stone which the builders
    rejected
Has become the chief
    cornerstone,"*d*

8and

"A stone of stumbling
    And a rock of offense."*e*

They stumble, being disobedient to the word, to which they also were appointed.

9But you *are* a chosen generation, a royal priesthood, a holy nation, His own special people, that you may proclaim the praises of Him who called you out of darkness into His marvelous light; 10who once *were* not a people but *are* now the people of God, who had not obtained mercy but now have obtained mercy.

Living Before the World

11Beloved, I beg *you* as sojourners and pilgrims, abstain from fleshly lusts which war against the soul, 12having your conduct honorable among the Gentiles, that when they speak against you as evildoers, they may, by *your*

good works which they observe, glorify God in the day of visitation.

Submission to Government

13Therefore submit yourselves to every ordinance of man for the Lord's sake, whether to the king as supreme, 14or to governors, as to those who are sent by him for the punishment of evildoers and *for the* praise of those who do good. 15For this is the will of God, that by doing good you may put to silence the ignorance of foolish men— 16as free, yet not using liberty as a cloak for vice, but as bondservants of God. 17Honor all *people*. Love the brotherhood. Fear God. Honor the king.

Submission to Masters

18Servants, *be* submissive to *your* masters with all fear, not only to the good and gentle, but also to the harsh. 19For this *is* commendable, if because of conscience toward God one endures grief, suffering wrongfully. 20For what credit *is it* if, when you are beaten for your faults, you take it patiently? But when you do good and suffer, if you take it patiently, this *is* commendable before God. 21For to this you were called, because Christ also suffered for us, leaving us an example, that you should follow His steps:

22 "Who committed no sin,
    Nor was deceit found in His
        mouth";*f*

23who, when He was reviled, did not revile in return; when He suffered, He did not threaten, but committed *Himself* to Him who judges righteously; 24who Himself bore our sins in His own body on the tree, that we, having died to sins, might live for righteousness— by whose stripes you were healed. 25For you were like sheep going astray, but have now returned to the Shepherd and Overseer of your souls.

Submission to Husbands

3 Wives, likewise, *be* submissive to your own husbands, that even if some do not obey the word, they, without a word, may be won by the conduct of their wives, 2when they observe your

---

c Isaiah 28.16   *d* Psalm 118.22   *e* Isaiah 8.14   *f* Isaiah 53.9

chaste conduct *accompanied* by fear. 3Do not let your adornment be *merely* outward—arranging the hair, wearing gold, or putting on *fine* apparel— 4rather *let it be* the hidden person of the heart, with the incorruptible *beauty* of a gentle and quiet spirit, which is very precious in the sight of God. 5For in this manner, in former times, the holy women who trusted in God also adorned themselves, being submissive to their own husbands, 6as Sarah obeyed Abraham, calling him lord, whose daughters you are if you do good and are not afraid with any terror.

A Word to Husbands

7Husbands, likewise, dwell with *them* with understanding, giving honor to the wife, as to the weaker vessel, and as *being* heirs together of the grace of life, that your prayers may not be hindered.

Called to Blessing

8Finally, all *of you be* of one mind, having compassion for one another; love as brothers, *be* tenderhearted, *be* courteous; 9not returning evil for evil or reviling for reviling, but on the contrary blessing, knowing that you were called to this, that you may inherit a blessing. 10For

"He who would love life
And see good days,
Let him refrain his tongue from
   evil,
And his lips from speaking
   deceit.
11   Let him turn away from evil and
   do good;
Let him seek peace and pursue it.
12   For the eyes of the LORD *are* on the
   righteous,
And His ears *are* open to their
   prayers;
But the face of the LORD *is* against
   those who do evil."g

Suffering for Right and Wrong

13And who *is* he who will harm you if you become followers of what is good? 14But even if you should suffer for righteousness' sake, *you are* blessed. "And do not be afraid of their

threats, nor be troubled."h 15But sanctify the Lord God in your hearts, and always *be* ready to *give* a defense to everyone who asks you a reason for the hope that is in you, with meekness and fear; 16having a good conscience, that when they defame you as evildoers, those who revile your good conduct in Christ may be ashamed. 17For *it is* better, if it is the will of God, to suffer for doing good than for doing evil.

Christ's Suffering and Ours

18For Christ also suffered once for sins, the just for the unjust, that He might bring us to God, being put to death in the flesh but made alive by the Spirit, 19by whom also He went and preached to the spirits in prison, 20who formerly were disobedient, when once the Divine longsuffering waited in the days of Noah, while *the* ark was being prepared, in which a few, that is, eight souls, were saved through water. 21There is also an antitype which now saves us—baptism (not the removal of the filth of the flesh, but the answer of a good conscience toward God), through the resurrection of Jesus Christ, 22who has gone into heaven and is at the right hand of God, angels and authorities and powers having been made subject to Him.

4 Therefore, since Christ suffered for us in the flesh, arm yourselves also with the same mind, for he who has suffered in the flesh has ceased from sin, 2that he no longer should live the rest of *his* time in the flesh for the lusts of men, but for the will of God. 3For we *have spent* enough of our past lifetime in doing the will of the Gentiles—when we walked in lewdness, lusts, drunkenness, revelries, drinking parties, and abominable idolatries. 4In regard to these, they think it strange that you do not run with *them* in the same flood of dissipation, speaking evil of *you*. 5They will give an account to Him who is ready to judge the living and the dead. 6For this reason the gospel was preached also to those who are dead, that they might be judged according to

g Psalm 34.12-16   h Isaiah 8.12

men in the flesh, but live according to God in the spirit.

Serving for God's Glory

7But the end of all things is at hand; therefore be serious and watchful in your prayers. 8And above all things have fervent love for one another, for "love will cover a multitude of sins."*i* 9*Be* hospitable to one another without grumbling. 10As each one has received a gift, minister it to one another, as good stewards of the manifold grace of God. 11If anyone speaks, *let him speak* as the oracles of God. If anyone ministers, *let him do it* as with the ability which God supplies, that in all things God may be glorified through Jesus Christ, to whom belong the glory and the dominion forever and ever. Amen.

Suffering for God's Glory

12Beloved, do not think it strange concerning the fiery trial which is to try you, as though some strange thing happened to you; 13but rejoice to the extent that you partake of Christ's sufferings, that when His glory is revealed, you may also be glad with exceeding joy. 14If you are reproached for the name of Christ, blessed *are you*, for the Spirit of glory and of God rests upon you. On their part He is blasphemed, but on your part He is glorified. 15But let none of you suffer as a murderer, a thief, an evildoer, or as a busybody in other people's matters. 16Yet if *anyone suffers* as a Christian, let him not be ashamed, but let him glorify God in this matter.

17For the time *has come* for judgment to begin at the house of God; and if *it begins* with us first, what will *be* the end of those who do not obey the gospel of God? 18Now

"If the righteous one is scarcely saved,
    Where will the ungodly and the sinner appear?"*j*

19Therefore let those who suffer according to the will of God commit their souls *to Him* in doing good, as to a faithful Creator.

Shepherd the Flock

5 The elders who are among you I exhort, I who am a fellow elder and a witness of the sufferings of Christ, and also a partaker of the glory that will be revealed: 2Shepherd the flock of God which is among you, serving as overseers, not by compulsion but willingly, not for dishonest gain but eagerly; 3nor as being lords over those entrusted to you, but being examples to the flock; 4and when the Chief Shepherd appears, you will receive the crown of glory that does not fade away.

Submit to God, Resist the Devil

5Likewise you younger people, submit yourselves to *your* elders. Yes, all of *you* be submissive to one another, and be clothed with humility, for

"God resists the proud,
    But gives grace to the humble."*k*

6Therefore humble yourselves under the mighty hand of God, that He may exalt you in due time, 7casting all your care upon Him, for He cares for you.

8Be sober, be vigilant; because your adversary the devil walks about like a roaring lion, seeking whom he may devour. 9Resist him, steadfast in the faith, knowing that the same sufferings are experienced by your brotherhood in the world. 10But may the God of all grace, who called us to His eternal glory by Christ Jesus, after you have suffered a while, perfect, establish, strengthen, and settle *you*. 11To Him *be* the glory and the dominion forever and ever. Amen.

Farewell and Peace

12By Silvanus, our faithful brother as I consider him, I have written to you briefly, exhorting and testifying that this is the true grace of God in which you stand.

13She who is in Babylon, elect together with *you*, greets you; and *so does* Mark my son. 14Greet one another with a kiss of love.

Peace to you all who are in Christ Jesus. Amen.

---

i Proverbs 10.12   *j* Proverbs 11.31   *k* Proverbs 3.34

The Second Epistle of

PETER

Greeting the Faithful

1 Simon Peter, a bondservant and apostle of Jesus Christ,

To those who have obtained like precious faith with us by the righteousness of our God and Savior Jesus Christ:

2Grace and peace be multiplied to you in the knowledge of God and of Jesus our Lord, 3as His divine power has given to us all things that *pertain* to life and godliness, through the knowledge of Him who called us by glory and virtue, 4by which have been given to us exceedingly great and precious promises, that through these you may be partakers of the divine nature, having escaped the corruption *that is* in the world through lust.

Fruitful Growth in the Faith

5But also for this very reason, giving all diligence, add to your faith virtue, to virtue knowledge, 6to knowledge self-control, to self-control perseverance, to perseverance godliness, 7to godliness brotherly kindness, and to brotherly kindness love. 8For if these things are yours and abound, *you will be* neither barren nor unfruitful in the knowledge of our Lord Jesus Christ. 9For he who lacks these things is shortsighted, even to blindness, and has forgotten that he was cleansed from his old sins. 10Therefore, brethren, be even more diligent to make your call and election sure, for if you do these things you will never stumble; 11for so an entrance will be supplied to you abundantly into the everlasting kingdom of our Lord and Savior Jesus Christ.

Peter's Approaching Death

12For this reason I will not be negligent to remind you always of these things, though you know and are established in the present truth. 13Yes, I think it is right, as long as I am in this tent, to stir you up by reminding *you,* 14knowing that shortly I *must* put off my tent, just as our Lord Jesus Christ showed me. 15Moreover I will be careful to ensure that you always have a reminder of these things after my decease.

The Trustworthy Prophetic Word

16For we did not follow cunningly devised fables when we made known to you the power and coming of our Lord Jesus Christ, but were eyewitnesses of His majesty. 17For He received from God the Father honor and glory when such a voice came to Him from the Excellent Glory: "This is My beloved Son, in whom I am well pleased." 18And we heard this voice which came from heaven when we were with Him on the holy mountain.

19And so we have the prophetic word confirmed, which you do well to heed as a light that shines in a dark place, until the day dawns and the morning star rises in your hearts; 20knowing this first, that no prophecy of Scripture is of any private interpretation,*a* 21for prophecy never came by the will of man, but holy men of God spoke *as they were* moved by the Holy Spirit.

Destructive Doctrines

2 But there were also false prophets among the people, even as there will be false teachers among you, who will secretly bring in destructive heresies, even denying the Lord who bought them, *and* bring on themselves swift destruction. 2And many will follow their destructive ways, because of whom the way of truth will be blasphemed. 3By covetousness they will exploit you with deceptive words; for a long time their judgment has not been idle, and their destruction does not slumber.

Doom of False Teachers

4For if God did not spare the angels who sinned, but cast *them* down to hell

a Or origin

and delivered *them* into chains of darkness, to be reserved for judgment; 5and did not spare the ancient world, but saved Noah, *one of* eight *people,* a preacher of righteousness, bringing in the flood on the world of the ungodly; 6and turning the cities of Sodom and Gomorrah into ashes, condemned *them* to destruction, making *them* an example to those who afterward would live ungodly; 7and delivered righteous Lot, *who was* oppressed by the filthy conduct of the wicked 8(for that righteous man, dwelling among them, tormented *his* righteous soul from day to day by seeing and hearing *their* lawless deeds)—9*then* the Lord knows how to deliver the godly out of temptations and to reserve the unjust under punishment for the day of judgment, 10and especially those who walk according to the flesh in the lust of uncleanness and despise authority. *They are* presumptuous, self-willed. They are not afraid to speak evil of dignitaries, 11whereas angels, who are greater in power and might, do not bring a reviling accusation against them before the Lord.

Depravity of False Teachers

12But these, like natural brute beasts made to be caught and destroyed, speak evil of the things they do not understand, and will utterly perish in their own corruption, 13*and* will receive the wages of unrighteousness, *as* those who count it pleasure to carouse in the daytime. *They are* spots and blemishes, carousing in their own deceptions while they feast with you, 14having eyes full of adultery and that cannot cease from sin, enticing unstable souls. *They have* a heart trained in covetous practices, *and are* accursed children. 15They have forsaken the right way and gone astray, following the way of Balaam the *son* of Beor, who loved the wages of unrighteousness; 16but he was rebuked for his iniquity: a dumb donkey speaking with a man's voice restrained the madness of the prophet.

17These are wells without water, clouds carried by a tempest, for whom is reserved the blackness of darkness forever.

Deceptions of False Teachers

18For when they speak great swelling *words* of emptiness, they allure through the lusts of the flesh, through lewdness, the ones who have actually escaped from those who live in error. 19While they promise them liberty, they themselves are slaves of corruption; for by whom a person is overcome, by him also he is brought into bondage. 20For if, after they have escaped the pollutions of the world through the knowledge of the Lord and Savior Jesus Christ, they are again entangled in them and overcome, the latter end is worse for them than the beginning. 21For it would have been better for them not to have known the way of righteousness, than having known *it,* to turn from the holy commandment delivered to them. 22But it has happened to them according to the true proverb: "A dog returns to his own vomit,"[b] and, "a sow, having washed, to her wallowing in the mire."

God's Promise Is Not Slack

3 Beloved, I now write to you this second epistle (in *both of* which I stir up your pure minds by way of reminder), 2that you may be mindful of the words which were spoken before by the holy prophets, and of the commandment of us, the apostles of the Lord and Savior, 3knowing this first: that scoffers will come in the last days, walking according to their own lusts, 4and saying, "Where is the promise of His coming? For since the fathers fell asleep, all things continue as *they were* from the beginning of creation." 5For this they willfully forget: that by the word of God the heavens were of old, and the earth standing out of water and in the water, 6by which the world *that* then existed perished, being flooded with water. 7But the heavens and the earth *which* are now preserved by the same word, are reserved for fire until the day of judgment and perdition of ungodly men.

8But, beloved, do not forget this one thing, that with the Lord one day *is* as a thousand years, and a thousand years

b Proverbs 26.11

as one day. 9The Lord is not slack concerning *His* promise, as some count slackness, but is longsuffering toward us, not willing that any should perish but that all should come to repentance.

The Day of the Lord

10But the day of the Lord will come as a thief in the night, in which the heavens will pass away with a great noise, and the elements will melt with fervent heat; both the earth and the works that are in it will be burned up. 11Therefore, since all these things will be dissolved, what manner *of persons* ought you to be in holy conduct and godliness, 12looking for and hastening the coming of the day of God, because of which the heavens will be dissolved, being on fire, and the elements will melt with fervent heat? 13Nevertheless we, according to His promise, look for new heavens and a new earth in which righteousness dwells.

Be Steadfast

14Therefore, beloved, looking forward to these things, be diligent to be found by Him in peace, without spot and blameless; 15and consider *that* the longsuffering of our Lord *is* salvation— as also our beloved brother Paul, according to the wisdom given to him, has written to you, 16as also in all his epistles, speaking in them of these things, in which are some things hard to understand, which untaught and unstable *people* twist to their own destruction, as *they do* also the rest of the Scriptures.

17You therefore, beloved, since you know *this* beforehand, beware lest you also fall from your own steadfastness, being led away with the error of the wicked; 18but grow in the grace and knowledge of our Lord and Savior Jesus Christ.

To Him *be* the glory both now and forever. Amen.

What Was Heard, Seen, and Touched

1 That which was from the beginning, which we have heard, which we have seen with our eyes, which we have looked upon, and our hands have handled, concerning the Word of life— 2the life was manifested, and we have seen, and bear witness, and declare to you that eternal life which was with the Father and was manifested to us— 3that which we have seen and heard we declare to you, that you also may have fellowship with us; and truly our fellowship *is* with the Father and with His Son Jesus Christ. 4And these things we write to you that your joy may be full.

Fellowship with Him and One Another

5This is the message which we have heard from Him and declare to you, that God is light and in Him is no darkness at all. 6If we say that we have fellowship with Him, and walk in darkness, we lie and do not practice the truth. 7But if we walk in the light as He is in the light, we have fellowship with one another, and the blood of Jesus Christ His Son cleanses us from all sin.

8If we say that we have no sin, we deceive ourselves, and the truth is not in us. 9If we confess our sins, He is faithful and just to forgive us *our* sins and to cleanse us from all unrighteousness. 10If we say that we have not sinned, we make Him a liar, and His word is not in us.

2 My little children, these things I write to you, so that you may not sin. And if anyone sins, we have an Advocate with the Father, Jesus Christ the righteous. 2And He Himself is the propitiation for our sins, and not for ours only but also for the whole world.

The Test of Knowing Him

3Now by this we know that we know Him, if we keep His commandments. 4He who says, "I know Him," and does not keep His commandments, is a liar, and the truth is not in him. 5But whoever keeps His word, truly the love of God is perfected in him. By this we know that we are in Him. 6He who says he abides in Him ought himself also to walk just as He walked.

7Brethren, I write no new commandment to you, but an old commandment which you have had from the beginning. The old commandment is the word which you heard from the beginning. 8Again, a new commandment I write to you, which thing is true in Him and in you, because the darkness is passing away, and the true light is already shining.

9He who says he is in the light, and hates his brother, is in darkness until now. 10He who loves his brother abides in the light, and there is no cause for stumbling in him. 11But he who hates his brother is in darkness and walks in darkness, and does not know where he is going, because the darkness has blinded his eyes.

Their Spiritual State

12　I write to you, little children,
　　Because your sins are forgiven
　　　you for His name's sake.
13　I write to you, fathers,
　　Because you have known Him
　　　who is from the beginning.
　　I write to you, young men,
　　Because you have overcome the
　　　wicked one.
　　I write to you, little children,
　　Because you have known the
　　　Father.
14　I have written to you, fathers,
　　Because you have known Him
　　　who is from the beginning.
　　I have written to you, young men,
　　Because you are strong, and the
　　　word of God abides in you,
　　And you have overcome the
　　　wicked one.

Do Not Love the World

15Do not love the world or the things in the world. If anyone loves the world, the love of the Father is not in him. 16For all that *is* in the world—the lust of the flesh, the lust of the eyes, and the pride of life—is not of the Father but is of the world. 17And the world is passing away, and the lust of it; but he who does the will of God abides forever.

Deceptions of the Last Hour

18Little children, it is the last hour; and as you have heard that the Antichrist is coming, even now many antichrists have come, by which we know that it is the last hour. 19They went out from us, but they were not of us; for if they had been of us, they would have continued with us; but *they went out* that they might be made manifest, that none of them were of us.

20But you have an anointing from the Holy One, and you know all things. 21I have not written to you because you do not know the truth, but because you know it, and that no lie is of the truth. 22Who is a liar but he who denies that Jesus is the Christ? He is antichrist who denies the Father and the Son. 23Whoever denies the Son does not have the Father either; he who acknowledges the Son has the Father also.

Let Truth Abide in You

24Therefore let that abide in you which you heard from the beginning. If what you heard from the beginning abides in you, you also will abide in the Son and in the Father. 25And this is the promise that He has promised us—eternal life.

26These things I have written to you concerning those who *try to* deceive you. 27But the anointing which you have received from Him abides in you, and you do not need that anyone teach you; but as the same anointing teaches you concerning all things, and is true, and is not a lie, and just as it has taught you, you will abide in Him.

The Children of God

28And now, little children, abide in Him, that when He appears, we may have confidence and not be ashamed before Him at His coming. 29If you know that He is righteous, you know that everyone who practices righteousness is born of Him.

3 Behold what manner of love the Father has bestowed on us, that we should be called children of God!

Therefore the world does not know us, because it did not know Him. 2Beloved, now we are children of God; and it has not yet been revealed what we shall be, but we know that when He is revealed, we shall be like Him, for we shall see Him as He is. 3And everyone who has this hope in Him purifies himself, just as He is pure.

Sin and the Child of God

4Whoever commits sin also commits lawlessness, and sin is lawlessness. 5And you know that He was manifested to take away our sins, and in Him there is no sin. 6Whoever abides in Him does not sin. Whoever sins has neither seen Him nor known Him.

7Little children, let no one deceive you. He who practices righteousness is righteous, just as He is righteous. 8He who sins is of the devil, for the devil has sinned from the beginning. For this purpose the Son of God was manifested, that He might destroy the works of the devil. 9Whoever has been born of God does not sin, for His seed remains in him; and he cannot sin, because he has been born of God.

The Imperative of Love

10In this the children of God and the children of the devil are manifest: Whoever does not practice righteousness is not of God, nor *is* he who does not love his brother. 11For this is the message that you heard from the beginning, that we should love one another, 12not as Cain *who* was of the wicked one and murdered his brother. And why did he murder him? Because his works were evil and his brother's righteous.

13Do not marvel, my brethren, if the world hates you. 14We know that we have passed from death to life, because we love the brethren. He who does not love *his* brother abides in death. 15Whoever hates his brother is a murderer, and you know that no murderer has eternal life abiding in him.

The Outworking of Love

16By this we know love, because He laid down His life for us. And we also ought to lay down *our* lives for the brethren. 17But whoever has this world's goods, and sees his brother in need, and shuts up his heart from him, how does the love of God abide in him?

18My little children, let us not love in word or in tongue, but in deed and in truth. 19And by this we know that we are of the truth, and shall assure our hearts before Him. 20For if our heart condemns us, God is greater than our heart, and knows all things. 21Beloved, if our heart does not condemn us, we have confidence toward God. 22And whatever we ask we receive from Him, because we keep His commandments and do those things that are pleasing in His sight. 23And this is His commandment: that we should believe on the name of His Son Jesus Christ and love one another, as He gave us commandment.

The Spirit of Truth and the Spirit of Error

24Now he who keeps His commandments abides in Him, and He in him. And by this we know that He abides in us, by the Spirit whom He has given us.

4 Beloved, do not believe every spirit, but test the spirits, whether they are of God; because many false prophets have gone out into the world. 2By this you know the Spirit of God: Every spirit that confesses that Jesus Christ has come in the flesh is of God, 3and every spirit that does not confess that Jesus Christ has come in the flesh is not of God. And this is the *spirit* of the Antichrist, which you have heard was coming, and is now already in the world.

4You are of God, little children, and have overcome them, because He who is in you is greater than he who is in the world. 5They are of the world. Therefore they speak *as* of the world, and the world hears them. 6We are of God. He who knows God hears us; he who is not of God does not hear us. By this we know the spirit of truth and the spirit of error.

Knowing God Through Love

7Beloved, let us love one another, for love is of God; and everyone who loves is born of God and knows God. 8He who does not love does not know

God, for God is love. 9In this the love of God was manifested toward us, that God has sent His only begotten Son into the world, that we might live through Him. 10In this is love, not that we loved God, but that He loved us and sent His Son *to be* the propitiation for our sins. 11Beloved, if God so loved us, we also ought to love one another.

Seeing God Through Love

12No one has seen God at any time. If we love one another, God abides in us, and His love has been perfected in us. 13By this we know that we abide in Him, and He in us, because He has given us of His Spirit. 14And we have seen and testify that the Father has sent the Son *as* Savior of the world. 15Whoever confesses that Jesus is the Son of God, God abides in him, and he in God. 16And we have known and believed the love that God has for us. God is love, and he who abides in love abides in God, and God in him.

The Consummation of Love

17Love has been perfected among us in this: that we may have boldness in the day of judgment; because as He is, so are we in this world. 18There is no fear in love; but perfect love casts out fear, because fear involves torment. But he who fears has not been made perfect in love. 19We love Him because He first loved us.

Obedience by Faith

20If someone says, "I love God," and hates his brother, he is a liar; for he who does not love his brother whom he has seen, how can he love God whom he has not seen? 21And this commandment we have from Him: that he who loves God *must* love his brother also.

5 Whoever believes that Jesus is the Christ is born of God, and everyone who loves Him who begot also loves him who is begotten of Him. 2By this we know that we love the children of God, when we love God and keep His commandments. 3For this is the love of God, that we keep His commandments. And His commandments are not burdensome. 4For whatever is born of God

overcomes the world. And this is the victory that has overcome the world—our faith. 5Who is he who overcomes the world, but he who believes that Jesus is the Son of God?

The Certainty of God's Witness

6This is He who came by water and blood—Jesus Christ; not only by water, but by water and blood. And it is the Spirit who bears witness, because the Spirit is truth. 7For there are three that bear witness in heaven: the Father, the Word, and the Holy Spirit; and these three are one. 8And there are three that bear witness on earth: the Spirit, the water, and the blood; and these three agree as one.

9If we receive the witness of men, the witness of God is greater; for this is the witness of God which He has testified of His Son. 10He who believes in the Son of God has the witness in himself; he who does not believe God has made Him a liar, because he has not believed the testimony that God has given of His Son. 11And this is the testimony: that God has given us eternal life, and this life is in His Son. 12He who has the Son has life; he who does not have the Son of God does not have life. 13These things I have written to you who believe in the name of the Son of God, that you may know that you have eternal life, and that you may *continue to* believe in the name of the Son of God.

Confidence and Compassion in Prayer

14Now this is the confidence that we have in Him, that if we ask anything according to His will, He hears us. 15And if we know that He hears us, whatever we ask, we know that we have the petitions that we have asked of Him.

16If anyone sees his brother sinning a sin *which does* not *lead* to death, he will ask, and He will give him life for those who commit sin not *leading* to death. There is sin *leading* to death. I do not say that he should pray about that. 17All unrighteousness is sin, and there is sin not *leading* to death.

Knowing the True—Rejecting the False

18We know that whoever is born of God does not sin; but he who has been born of God keeps himself, and the wicked one does not touch him.

19We know that we are of God, and the whole world lies *under the sway of* the wicked one.

20And we know that the Son of God has come and has given us an understanding, that we may know Him who is true; and we are in Him who is true, in His Son Jesus Christ. This is the true God and eternal life.

21Little children, keep yourselves from idols. Amen.

The Second Epistle of
JOHN

Greeting the Elect Lady

1 The Elder,

To the elect lady and her children, whom I love in truth, and not only I, but also all those who have known the truth, 2because of the truth which abides in us and will be with us forever:

3Grace, mercy, *and* peace will be with you from God the Father and from the Lord Jesus Christ, the Son of the Father, in truth and love.

Walk in Christ's Commandments

4I rejoiced greatly that I have found *some* of your children walking in truth, as we received commandment from the Father. 5And now I plead with you, lady, not as though I wrote a new commandment to you, but that which we have had from the beginning: that we love one another. 6This is love, that we walk according to His commandments. This is the commandment, that as you have heard from the beginning, you should walk in it.

Beware of Antichrist Deceivers

7For many deceivers have gone out into the world who do not confess Jesus Christ *as* coming in the flesh. This is a deceiver and an antichrist. 8Look to yourselves, that we do not lose those things we worked for, but *that* we may receive a full reward.

9Whoever transgresses and does not abide in the doctrine of Christ does not have God. He who abides in the doctrine of Christ has both the Father and the Son. 10If anyone comes to you and does not bring this doctrine, do not receive him into your house nor greet him; 11for he who greets him shares in his evil deeds.

John's Farewell Greeting

12Having many things to write to you, I did not wish *to do so* with paper and ink; but I hope to come to you and speak face to face, that our joy may be full.

13The children of your elect sister greet you. Amen.

The Third Epistle of

JOHN

Greeting to Gaius

1 The Elder,

To the beloved Gaius, whom I love in truth:

2Beloved, I pray that you may prosper in all things and be in health, just as your soul prospers. **3**For I rejoiced greatly when brethren came and testified of the truth *that is* in you, just as you walk in the truth. **4**I have no greater joy than to hear that my children walk in truth.

Gaius Commended for Generosity

5Beloved, you do faithfully whatever you do for the brethren and for strangers, **6**who have borne witness of your love before the church. *If* you send them forward on their journey in a manner worthy of God, you will do well, **7**because they went forth for His name's sake, taking nothing from the Gentiles. **8**We therefore ought to receive such, that we may become fellow workers for the truth.

Diotrephes and Demetrius

9I wrote to the church, but Diotrephes, who loves to have the preeminence among them, does not receive us. **10**Therefore, if I come, I will call to mind his deeds which he does, prating against us with malicious words. And not content with that, he himself does not receive the brethren, and forbids those who wish to, putting *them* out of the church.

11Beloved, do not imitate what is evil, but what is good. He who does good is of God, but he who does evil has not seen God.

12Demetrius has a *good* testimony from all, and from the truth itself. And we also bear witness, and you know that our testimony is true.

Farewell Greeting

13I had many things to write, but I do not wish to write to you with pen and ink; **14**but I hope to see you shortly, and we shall speak face to face.

Peace to you. Our friends greet you. Greet the friends by name.

JUDE

Greeting to the Called

1 Jude, a bondservant of Jesus Christ, and brother of James,

To those who are called, sanctified by God the Father, and preserved in Jesus Christ:

2Mercy, peace, and love be multiplied to you.

Contend for the Faith

3Beloved, while I was very diligent to write to you concerning our common salvation, I found it necessary to write to you exhorting you to contend earnestly for the faith which was once for all delivered to the saints. 4For certain men have crept in unnoticed, who long ago were marked out for this condemnation, ungodly men, who turn the grace of our God into lewdness and deny the only Lord God and our Lord Jesus Christ.

Old and New Apostates

5But I want to remind you, though you once knew this, that the Lord, having saved the people out of the land of Egypt, afterward destroyed those who did not believe. 6And the angels who did not keep their proper domain, but left their own abode, He has reserved in everlasting chains under darkness for the judgment of the great day; 7as Sodom and Gomorrah, and the cities around them in a similar manner to these, having given themselves over to sexual immorality and gone after strange flesh, are set forth as an example, suffering the vengeance of eternal fire.

8Likewise also these dreamers defile the flesh, reject authority, and speak evil of dignitaries. 9Yet Michael the archangel, in contending with the devil, when he disputed about the body of Moses, dared not bring against him a reviling accusation, but said, "The Lord rebuke you!" 10But these speak evil of whatever they do not know; and whatever they know naturally, like brute beasts, in these things they corrupt themselves. 11Woe to them! For they have gone in the way of Cain, have run greedily in the error of Balaam for profit, and perished in the rebellion of Korah.

Apostates Depraved and Doomed

12These are spots in your love feasts, while they feast with you without fear, serving *only* themselves. *They are* clouds without water, carried about by the winds; late autumn trees without fruit, twice dead, pulled up by the roots; 13raging waves of the sea, foaming up their own shame; wandering stars for whom is reserved the blackness of darkness forever.

14Now Enoch, the seventh from Adam, prophesied about these men also, saying, "Behold, the Lord comes with ten thousands of His saints, 15to execute judgment on all, to convict all who are ungodly among them of all their ungodly deeds which they have committed in an ungodly way, and of all the harsh things which ungodly sinners have spoken against Him."

Apostates Predicted

16These are grumblers, complainers, walking according to their own lusts; and they mouth great swelling *words*, flattering people to gain advantage. 17But you, beloved, remember the words which were spoken before by the apostles of our Lord Jesus Christ: 18how they told you that there would be mockers in the last time who would walk according to their own ungodly lusts. 19These are sensual persons, who cause divisions, not having the Spirit.

Maintain Your Life with God

20But you, beloved, building yourselves up on your most holy faith, praying in the Holy Spirit, 21keep yourselves in the love of God, looking for the mercy of our Lord Jesus Christ unto eternal life.

22And on some have compassion, making a distinction; 23but others save

with fear, pulling *them* out of the fire,
hating even the garment defiled by the
flesh.

Glory to God

24 Now to Him who is able to keep
    you from stumbling,
    And to present *you* faultless

Before the presence of His glory
    with exceeding joy,
25 To God our Savior,
Who alone is wise,
Be glory and majesty,
Dominion and power,
Both now and forever.
Amen.

THE REVELATION

of Jesus Christ

Introduction and Benediction

1 The Revelation of Jesus Christ, which God gave Him to show His servants—things which must shortly take place. And He sent and signified *it* by His angel to His servant John, 2who bore witness to the word of God, and to the testimony of Jesus Christ, to all things that he saw. 3Blessed *is* he who reads and those who hear the words of this prophecy, and keep those things which are written in it; for the time *is* near.

Greeting the Seven Churches

4John, to the seven churches which are in Asia:

Grace to you and peace from Him who is and who was and who is to come, and from the seven Spirits who are before His throne, 5and from Jesus Christ, the faithful witness, the first-born from the dead, and the ruler over the kings of the earth.

To Him who loved us and washed us from our sins in His own blood, 6and has made us kings and priests to His God and Father, to Him *be* glory and dominion forever and ever. Amen.

7Behold, He is coming with clouds, and every eye will see Him, even they who pierced Him. And all the tribes of the earth will mourn because of Him. Even so, Amen.

8"I am the Alpha and the Omega, *the* Beginning and *the* End," says the Lord, "who is and who was and who is to come, the Almighty."

Vision of the Son of Man

9I, John, both your brother and companion in the tribulation and kingdom and patience of Jesus Christ, was on the island that is called Patmos for the word of God and for the testimony of Jesus Christ. 10I was in the Spirit on the Lord's Day, and I heard behind me a loud voice, as of a trumpet, 11saying, "I am the Alpha and the Omega, the First and the Last," and, "What you see, write in a book and send *it* to the seven churches which are in Asia: to Ephesus, to Smyrna, to Pergamos, to Thyatira, to Sardis, to Philadelphia, and to Laodicea."

12Then I turned to see the voice that spoke with me. And having turned I saw seven golden lampstands, 13and in the midst of the seven lampstands *One* like the Son of Man, clothed with a garment down to the feet and girded about the chest with a golden band. 14His head and hair *were* white like wool, as white as snow, and His eyes like a flame of fire; 15His feet *were* like fine brass, as if refined in a furnace, and His voice as the sound of many waters; 16He had in His right hand seven stars, out of His mouth went a sharp two-edged sword, and His countenance *was* like the sun shining in its strength. 17And when I saw Him, I fell at His feet as dead. But He laid His right hand on me, saying to me, "Do not be afraid; I am the First and the Last. 18I *am* He who lives, and was dead, and behold, I am alive forevermore. Amen. And I have the keys of Hades and of Death. 19Write the things which you have seen, and the things which are, and the things which will take place after this. 20The mystery of the seven stars which you saw in My right hand, and the seven golden lampstands: The seven stars are the angels of the seven churches, and the seven lampstands which you saw are the seven churches.

The Loveless Church

2 "To the angel of the church of Ephesus write,

'These things says He who holds the seven stars in His right hand, who walks in the midst of the seven golden lampstands: 2"I know your works, your labor, your patience, and that you cannot bear those who are evil. And you have tested those who say they are apostles and are not, and have found them liars; 3and you have persevered and have patience, and have labored for My name's sake and have not become weary. 4Nevertheless I have *this* against you, that you have left your first love. 5Remember therefore from where you have fallen; repent and do the first works, or else I will come to you quickly and remove your lampstand from its place—unless you repent. 6But this you have, that you hate the deeds of the Nicolaitans, which I also hate.

7"He who has an ear, let him hear what the Spirit says to the churches. To him who overcomes I will give to eat from the tree of life, which is in the midst of the Paradise of God." '

The Persecuted Church

8"And to the angel of the church in Smyrna write,

'These things says the First and the Last, who was dead, and came to life: 9"I know your works, tribulation, and poverty (but you are rich); and *I know* the blasphemy of those who say they are Jews and are not, but *are* a synagogue of Satan. 10Do not fear any of those things which you are about to suffer. Indeed, the devil is about to throw *some* of you into prison, that you may be tested, and you will have tribulation ten days. Be faithful until death, and I will give you the crown of life.

11"He who has an ear, let him hear what the Spirit says to the churches. He who overcomes shall not be hurt by the second death." '

The Compromising Church

12"And to the angel of the church in Pergamos write,

'These things says He who has the sharp two-edged sword: 13"I know your works, and where you dwell, where Satan's throne *is*. And you hold fast to My name, and did not deny My faith even in the days in which Antipas *was* My faithful martyr, who was killed among you, where Satan dwells. 14But I have a few things against you, because you have there those who hold the doctrine of Balaam, who taught Balak to put a stumbling block before the children of Israel, to eat things sacrificed to idols, and to commit sexual immorality. 15Thus you also have those who hold the doctrine of the Nicolaitans, which thing I hate. 16Repent, or else I will come to you quickly and will fight against them with the sword of My mouth.

17"He who has an ear, let him hear what the Spirit says to the churches. To him who overcomes I will give some of the hidden manna to eat. And I will give him a white stone, and on the stone a new name written which no one knows except him who receives *it*." '

The Corrupt Church

18"And to the angel of the church in Thyatira write,

'These things says the Son of God, who has eyes like a flame of fire, and His feet like fine brass: 19"I know your works, love, service, faith, and your patience; and *as* for your works, the last *are* more than the first. 20Nevertheless I have a few things against you, because you allow that woman Jezebel, who calls herself a prophetess, to teach and seduce My servants to commit sexual immorality and eat things sacrificed to idols. 21And I gave her time to repent of her sexual immorality, and she did not repent. 22Indeed I will cast her into a sickbed, and those who commit adultery with her into great tribulation, unless they repent of their deeds. 23I will kill her children with death, and all the churches shall know that I am He who searches the minds and hearts. And I will give to each one of you according to your works.

24"Now to you I say, and to the rest in Thyatira, as many as do not have this doctrine, who have not known the depths of Satan, as they say, I will put on you no other burden. 25But hold fast what you have till I come. 26And he who overcomes, and keeps My works until the end, to him I will give power over the nations—

27 'He shall rule them with a rod of
      iron;
    They shall be dashed to pieces like
      the potter's vessels'a—

as I also have received from My Father; 28and I will give him the morning star.

29"He who has an ear, let him hear what the Spirit says to the churches." '

a Psalm 2.9

The Dead Church

3 "And to the angel of the church in Sardis write,

'These things says He who has the seven Spirits of God and the seven stars: "I know your works, that you have a name that you are alive, but you are dead. 2Be watchful, and strengthen the things which remain, that are ready to die, for I have not found your works perfect before God. 3Remember therefore how you have received and heard; hold fast and repent. Therefore if you will not watch, I will come upon you as a thief, and you will not know what hour I will come upon you. 4You have a few names even in Sardis who have not defiled their garments; and they shall walk with Me in white, for they are worthy. 5He who overcomes shall be clothed in white garments, and I will not blot out his name from the Book of Life; but I will confess his name before My Father and before His angels.

6"He who has an ear, let him hear what the Spirit says to the churches." '

The Faithful Church

7"And to the angel of the church in Philadelphia write,

'These things says He who is holy, He who is true, "He who has the key of David, He who opens and no one shuts, and shuts and no one opens":[b] 8"I know your works. See, I have set before you an open door, and no one can shut it; for you have a little strength, have kept My word, and have not denied My name. 9Indeed I will make *those* of the synagogue of Satan, who say they are Jews and are not, but lie—indeed I will make them come and worship before your feet, and to know that I have loved you. 10Because you have kept My command to persevere, I also will keep you from the hour of trial which shall come upon the whole world, to test those who dwell on the earth. 11Behold, I am coming quickly! Hold fast what you have, that no one may take your crown. 12He who overcomes, I will make him a pillar in the temple of My God, and he shall go out no more. I will write on him the name

of My God and the name of the city of My God, the New Jerusalem, which comes down out of heaven from My God. And *I will write on him* My new name.

13"He who has an ear, let him hear what the Spirit says to the churches." '

The Lukewarm Church

14"And to the angel of the church of the Laodiceans write,

'These things says the Amen, the Faithful and True Witness, the Beginning of the creation of God: 15"I know your works, that you are neither cold nor hot. I could wish you were cold or hot. 16So then, because you are lukewarm, and neither cold nor hot, I will vomit you out of My mouth. 17Because you say, 'I am rich, have become wealthy, and have need of nothing'—and do not know that you are wretched, miserable, poor, blind, and naked—18I counsel you to buy from Me gold refined in the fire, that you may be rich; and white garments, that you may be clothed, *that* the shame of your nakedness may not be revealed; and anoint your eyes with eye salve, that you may see. 19As many as I love, I rebuke and chasten. Therefore be zealous and repent. 20Behold, I stand at the door and knock. If anyone hears My voice and opens the door, I will come in to him and dine with him, and he with Me. 21To him who overcomes I will grant to sit with Me on My throne, as I also overcame and sat down with My Father on His throne.

22"He who has an ear, let him hear what the Spirit says to the churches." ' "

The Throne Room of Heaven

4 After these things I looked, and behold, a door *standing* open in heaven. And the first voice which I heard *was* like a trumpet speaking with me, saying, "Come up here, and I will show you things which must take place after this."

2Immediately I was in the Spirit; and behold, a throne set in heaven, and *One* sat on the throne. 3And He who sat there was like a jasper and a sardius

b Isaiah 22.22

stone in appearance; and *there was* a rainbow around the throne, in appearance like an emerald. 4Around the throne *were* twenty-four thrones, and on the thrones I saw twenty-four elders sitting, clothed in white robes; and they had crowns of gold on their heads. 5And from the throne proceeded lightnings, thunderings, and voices. Seven lamps of fire *were* burning before the throne, which are the seven Spirits of God.

6Before the throne *there was* a sea of glass, like crystal. And in the midst of the throne, and around the throne, *were* four living creatures full of eyes in front and in back. 7The first living creature *was* like a lion, the second living creature like a calf, the third living creature had a face like a man, and the fourth living creature *was* like a flying eagle. 8*The* four living creatures, each having six wings, were full of eyes around and within. And they do not rest day or night, saying:

"Holy, holy, holy,
   Lord God Almighty,
   Who was and is and is to come!"

9Whenever the living creatures give glory and honor and thanks to Him who sits on the throne, who lives forever and ever, 10the twenty-four elders fall down before Him who sits on the throne and worship Him who lives forever and ever, and cast their crowns before the throne, saying:

11 "You are worthy, O Lord,
   To receive glory and honor and
      power;
   For You created all things,
   And by Your will they exist and
      were created."

The Lamb Takes the Scroll

5 And I saw in the right *hand* of Him who sat on the throne a scroll written inside and on the back, sealed with seven seals. 2Then I saw a strong angel proclaiming with a loud voice, "Who is worthy to open the scroll and to loose its seals?" 3And no one in heaven or on the earth or under the earth was able to open the scroll, or to look at it. 4So I wept much, because no one was found worthy to open and read the scroll, or to look at it. 5But one of the elders said to me, "Do not weep. Behold, the Lion of the tribe of Judah, the Root of David, has prevailed to open the scroll and to loose its seven seals."

6And I looked, and behold, in the midst of the throne and of the four living creatures, and in the midst of the elders, stood a Lamb as though it had been slain, having seven horns and seven eyes, which are the seven Spirits of God sent out into all the earth. 7Then He came and took the scroll out of the right hand of Him who sat on the throne.

Worthy Is the Lamb

8Now when He had taken the scroll, the four living creatures and the twenty-four elders fell down before the Lamb, each having a harp, and golden bowls full of incense, which are the prayers of the saints. 9And they sang a new song, saying:

"You are worthy to take the scroll,
   And to open its seals;
   For You were slain,
   And have redeemed us to God by
      Your blood
   Out of every tribe and tongue and
      people and nation,
10   And have made us kings and
      priests to our God;
   And we shall reign on the earth."

11Then I looked, and I heard the voice of many angels around the throne, the living creatures, and the elders; and the number of them was ten thousand times ten thousand, and thousands of thousands, 12saying with a loud voice:

"Worthy is the Lamb who was slain
   To receive power and riches and
      wisdom,
   And strength and honor and glory
      and blessing!"

13And every creature which is in heaven and on the earth and under the earth and such as are in the sea, and all that are in them, I heard saying:

"Blessing and honor and glory and
      power
   Be to Him who sits on the throne,
   And to the Lamb, forever and
      ever!"

14Then the four living creatures said, "Amen!" And the twenty-four elders fell down and worshiped Him who lives forever and ever.

First Seal: The Conqueror

6 Now I saw when the Lamb opened one of the seals; and I heard one of the four living creatures saying with a voice like thunder, "Come and see." 2And I looked, and behold, a white horse. He who sat on it had a bow; and a crown was given to him, and he went out conquering and to conquer.

Second Seal: Conflict on Earth

3When He opened the second seal, I heard the second living creature saying, "Come and see." 4Another horse, fiery red, went out. And it was granted to the one who sat on it to take peace from the earth, and that *people* should kill one another; and there was given to him a great sword.

Third Seal: Scarcity on Earth

5When He opened the third seal, I heard the third living creature say, "Come and see." So I looked, and behold, a black horse, and he who sat on it had a pair of scales in his hand. 6And I heard a voice in the midst of the four living creatures saying, "A quart[c] of wheat for a denarius,[d] and three quarts of barley for a denarius; and do not harm the oil and the wine."

Fourth Seal: Widespread Death on Earth

7When He opened the fourth seal, I heard the voice of the fourth living creature saying, "Come and see." 8So I looked, and behold, a pale horse. And the name of him who sat on it was Death, and Hades followed with him. And power was given to them over a fourth of the earth, to kill with sword, with hunger, with death, and by the beasts of the earth.

Fifth Seal: The Cry of the Martyrs

9When He opened the fifth seal, I saw under the altar the souls of those who had been slain for the word of God and for the testimony which they held. 10And they cried with a loud voice, saying, "How long, O Lord, holy and true, until You judge and avenge our blood on those who dwell on the earth?"

11Then a white robe was given to each of them; and it was said to them that they should rest a little while longer, until both *the number of* their fellow servants and their brethren, who would be killed as they *were*, was completed.

Sixth Seal: Cosmic Disturbances

12I looked when He opened the sixth seal, and behold, there was a great earthquake; and the sun became black as sackcloth of hair, and the moon became like blood. 13And the stars of heaven fell to the earth, as a fig tree drops its late figs when it is shaken by a mighty wind. 14Then the sky receded as a scroll when it is rolled up, and every mountain and island was moved out of its place. 15And the kings of the earth, the great men, the rich men, the commanders, the mighty men, every slave and every free man, hid themselves in the caves and in the rocks of the mountains, 16and said to the mountains and rocks, "Fall on us and hide us from the face of Him who sits on the throne and from the wrath of the Lamb! 17For the great day of His wrath has come, and who is able to stand?"

The Sealed of Israel

7 After these things I saw four angels standing at the four corners of the earth, holding the four winds of the earth, that the wind should not blow on the earth, on the sea, or on any tree. 2Then I saw another angel ascending from the east, having the seal of the living God. And he cried with a loud voice to the four angels to whom it was granted to harm the earth and the sea, 3saying, "Do not harm the earth, the sea, or the trees till we have sealed the servants of our God on their foreheads." 4And I heard the number of those who were sealed. One hundred *and* forty-four thousand of all the tribes of the children of Israel *were* sealed:

5   of the tribe of Judah twelve
          thousand *were* sealed;
        of the tribe of Reuben twelve
          thousand *were* sealed;
        of the tribe of Gad twelve thousand
          were sealed;

---

c That is, approximately one quart   d This was approximately one day's wage for a worker.

6 of the tribe of Asher twelve
   thousand *were* sealed;
   of the tribe of Naphtali twelve
   thousand *were* sealed;
   of the tribe of Manasseh twelve
   thousand *were* sealed;
7 of the tribe of Simeon twelve
   thousand *were* sealed;
   of the tribe of Levi twelve thousand
   were sealed;
   of the tribe of Issachar twelve
   thousand *were* sealed;
8 of the tribe of Zebulun twelve
   thousand *were* sealed;
   of the tribe of Joseph twelve
   thousand *were* sealed;
   of the tribe of Benjamin twelve
   thousand *were* sealed.

A Multitude from the Great Tribulation

9After these things I looked, and behold, a great multitude which no one could number, of all nations, tribes, peoples, and tongues, standing before the throne and before the Lamb, clothed with white robes, with palm branches in their hands, 10and crying out with a loud voice, saying, "Salvation *belongs* to our God who sits on the throne, and to the Lamb!" 11All the angels stood around the throne and the elders and the four living creatures, and fell on their faces before the throne and worshiped God, 12saying:

"Amen! Blessing and glory and
   wisdom,
Thanksgiving and honor and
   power and might,
Be to our God forever and ever.
   Amen."

13Then one of the elders answered, saying to me, "Who are these arrayed in white robes, and where did they come from?"

14And I said to him, "Sir, you know."

So he said to me, "These are the ones who come out of the great tribulation, and washed their robes and made them white in the blood of the Lamb. 15Therefore they are before the throne of God, and serve Him day and night in His temple. And He who sits on the throne will dwell among them. 16They shall neither hunger anymore nor thirst anymore; the sun shall not strike them, nor any heat; 17for the Lamb who is in the midst of the throne will shepherd them and lead them to living fountains of waters. And God will wipe away every tear from their eyes."

Seventh Seal: Prelude to the Seven Trumpets

8 When He opened the seventh seal, there was silence in heaven for about half an hour. 2And I saw the seven angels who stand before God, and to them were given seven trumpets. 3Then another angel, having a golden censer, came and stood at the altar. He was given much incense, that he should offer *it* with the prayers of all the saints upon the golden altar which was before the throne. 4And the smoke of the incense, with the prayers of the saints, ascended before God from the angel's hand. 5Then the angel took the censer, filled it with fire from the altar, and threw *it* to the earth. And there were noises, thunderings, lightnings, and an earthquake.

6So the seven angels who had the seven trumpets prepared themselves to sound.

First Trumpet: Vegetation Struck

7The first angel sounded: And hail and fire followed, mingled with blood, and they were thrown to the earth. And a third of the trees were burned up, and all green grass was burned up.

Second Trumpet: The Seas Struck

8Then the second angel sounded: And *something* like a great mountain burning with fire was thrown into the sea, and a third of the sea became blood. 9And a third of the living creatures in the sea died, and a third of the ships were destroyed.

Third Trumpet: The Waters Struck

10Then the third angel sounded: And a great star fell from heaven, burning like a torch, and it fell on a third of the rivers and on the springs of water. 11The name of the star is Wormwood. A third of the waters became wormwood, and many men died from the water, because it was made bitter.

Fourth Trumpet: The Heavens Struck

12Then the fourth angel sounded: And a third of the sun was struck, a third of the moon, and a third of the stars, so that a third of them were darkened. A third of the day did not shine, and likewise the night.

13And I looked, and I heard an angel flying through the midst of heaven, saying with a loud voice, "Woe, woe, woe to the inhabitants of the earth, because of the remaining blasts of the trumpet of the three angels who are about to sound!"

Fifth Trumpet: The Locusts from the Bottomless Pit

9 Then the fifth angel sounded: And I saw a star fallen from heaven to the earth. To him was given the key to the bottomless pit. 2And he opened the bottomless pit, and smoke arose out of the pit like the smoke of a great furnace. So the sun and the air were darkened because of the smoke of the pit. 3Then out of the smoke locusts came upon the earth. And to them was given power, as the scorpions of the earth have power. 4They were commanded not to harm the grass of the earth, or any green thing, or any tree, but only those men who do not have the seal of God on their foreheads. 5And they were not given *authority* to kill them, but to torment them *for* five months. Their torment *was* like the torment of a scorpion when it strikes a man. 6In those days men will seek death and will not find it; they will desire to die, and death will flee from them.

7The shape of the locusts was like horses prepared for battle. On their heads were crowns of something like gold, and their faces *were* like the faces of men. 8They had hair like women's hair, and their teeth were like lions' *teeth*. 9And they had breastplates like breastplates of iron, and the sound of their wings *was* like the sound of chariots with many horses running into battle. 10They had tails like scorpions, and there were stings in their tails. Their power *was* to hurt men five months. 11And they had as king over them the angel of the bottomless pit, whose name in Hebrew *is* Abaddon, but in Greek he has the name Apollyon.

12One woe is past. Behold, still two more woes are coming after these things.

Sixth Trumpet: The Angels from the Euphrates

13Then the sixth angel sounded: And I heard a voice from the four horns of the golden altar which is before God, 14saying to the sixth angel who had the trumpet, "Release the four angels who are bound at the great river Euphrates." 15So the four angels, who had been prepared for the hour and day and month and year, were released to kill a third of mankind. 16Now the number of the army of the horsemen *was* two hundred million; I heard the number of them. 17And thus I saw the horses in the vision: those who sat on them had breastplates of fiery red, hyacinth blue, and sulfur yellow; and the heads of the horses *were* like the heads of lions; and out of their mouths came fire, smoke, and brimstone. 18By these three *plagues* a third of mankind was killed— by the fire and the smoke and the brimstone which came out of their mouths. 19For their power is in their mouth and in their tails; for their tails *are* like serpents, having heads; and with them they do harm.

20But the rest of mankind, who were not killed by these plagues, did not repent of the works of their hands, that they should not worship demons, and idols of gold, silver, brass, stone, and wood, which can neither see nor hear nor walk. 21And they did not repent of their murders or their sorceries or their sexual immorality or their thefts.

The Mighty Angel with the Little Book

10 I saw still another mighty angel coming down from heaven, clothed with a cloud. And a rainbow *was* on his head, his face *was* like the sun, and his feet like pillars of fire. 2He had a little book open in his hand. And he set his right foot on the sea and *his* left *foot* on the land, 3and cried with a loud voice, as *when* a lion roars. When he cried out, seven thunders uttered their voices. 4Now when the seven thunders uttered their voices, I was about to write; but I heard a voice from heaven saying to me, "Seal up the things which the seven thunders uttered, and do not write them."

5The angel whom I saw standing on

the sea and on the land raised up his hand to heaven 6and swore by Him who lives forever and ever, who created heaven and the things that are in it, the earth and the things that are in it, and the sea and the things that are in it, that there should be delay no longer, 7but in the days of the sounding of the seventh angel, when he is about to sound, the mystery of God would be finished, as He declared to His servants the prophets."

John Eats the Little Book

8Then the voice which I heard from heaven spoke to me again and said, "Go, take the little book which is open in the hand of the angel who stands on the sea and on the earth."

9So I went to the angel and said to him, "Give me the little book."

And he said to me, "Take and eat it; and it will make your stomach bitter, but it will be as sweet as honey in your mouth."

10Then I took the little book out of the angel's hand and ate it, and it was as sweet as honey in my mouth. But when I had eaten it, my stomach became bitter. 11And he said to me, "You must prophesy again about many peoples, nations, tongues, and kings."

The Two Witnesses

11 Then I was given a reed like a measuring rod. And the angel stood, saying, "Rise and measure the temple of God, the altar, and those who worship there. 2But leave out the court which is outside the temple, and do not measure it, for it has been given to the Gentiles. And they will tread the holy city underfoot *for* forty-two months. 3And I will give *power* to my two witnesses, and they will prophesy one thousand two hundred and sixty days, clothed in sackcloth."

4These are the two olive trees and the two lampstands standing before the God of the earth. 5And if anyone wants to harm them, fire proceeds from their mouth and devours their enemies. And if anyone wants to harm them, he must be killed in this manner. 6These have power to shut heaven, so that no rain falls in the days of their prophecy; and they have power over waters to turn

them to blood, and to strike the earth with all plagues, as often as they desire.

The Witnesses Killed

7When they finish their testimony, the beast that ascends out of the bottomless pit will make war against them, overcome them, and kill them. 8And their dead bodies *will lie* in the street of the great city which spiritually is called Sodom and Egypt, where also our Lord was crucified. 9Then *those* from the peoples, tribes, tongues, and nations will see their dead bodies three-and-a-half days, and not allow their dead bodies to be put into graves. 10And those who dwell on the earth will rejoice over them, make merry, and send gifts to one another, because these two prophets tormented those who dwell on the earth.

The Witnesses Resurrected

11Now after the three-and-a-half days the breath of life from God entered them, and they stood on their feet, and great fear fell on those who saw them. 12And they heard a loud voice from heaven saying to them, "Come up here." And they ascended to heaven in a cloud, and their enemies saw them. 13In the same hour there was a great earthquake, and a tenth of the city fell. In the earthquake seven thousand people were killed, and the rest were afraid and gave glory to the God of heaven.

14The second woe is past. Behold, the third woe is coming quickly.

Seventh Trumpet: The Kingdom Proclaimed

15Then the seventh angel sounded: And there were loud voices in heaven, saying, "The kingdoms of this world have become *the kingdoms* of our Lord and of His Christ, and He shall reign forever and ever!" 16And the twenty-four elders who sat before God on their thrones fell on their faces and worshiped God, 17saying:

"We give You thanks, O Lord God
　　Almighty,
The One who is and who was and
　　who is to come,
Because You have taken Your
　　great power and reigned.

18 The nations were angry, and Your
  wrath has come,
  And the time of the dead, that they
  should be judged,
  And that You should reward Your
  servants the prophets and the
  saints,
  And those who fear Your name,
  small and great,
  And should destroy those who
  destroy the earth."

19Then the temple of God was opened in heaven, and the ark of His covenant was seen in His temple. And there were lightnings, noises, thunderings, an earthquake, and great hail.

The Woman, the Child, and the Dragon

12 Now a great sign appeared in heaven: a woman clothed with the sun, with the moon under her feet, and on her head a garland of twelve stars. 2Then being with child, she cried out in labor and in pain to give birth.

3And another sign appeared in heaven: behold, a great, fiery red dragon having seven heads and ten horns, and seven diadems on his heads. 4His tail drew a third of the stars of heaven and threw them to the earth. And the dragon stood before the woman who was ready to give birth, to devour her Child as soon as it was born. 5She bore a male Child who was to rule all nations with a rod of iron. And her Child was caught up to God and His throne. 6Then the woman fled into the wilderness, where she has a place prepared by God, that they should feed her there one thousand two hundred and sixty days.

Satan Thrown Out of Heaven

7And war broke out in heaven: Michael and his angels fought with the dragon; and the dragon and his angels fought, 8but they did not prevail, nor was a place found for them in heaven any longer. 9So the great dragon was cast out, that serpent of old, called the Devil and Satan, who deceives the whole world; he was cast to the earth, and his angels were cast out with him.

10Then I heard a loud voice saying in heaven, "Now salvation, and strength, and the kingdom of our God, and the power of His Christ have come,

for the accuser of our brethren, who accused them before our God day and night, has been cast down. 11And they overcame him by the blood of the Lamb and by the word of their testimony, and they did not love their lives to the death. 12Therefore rejoice, O heavens, and you who dwell in them! Woe to the inhabitants of the earth and the sea! For the devil has come down to you, having great wrath, because he knows that he has a short time."

The Woman Persecuted

13Now when the dragon saw that he had been cast to the earth, he persecuted the woman who gave birth to the male *Child*. 14But the woman was given two wings of a great eagle, that she might fly into the wilderness to her place, where she is nourished for a time and times and half a time, from the presence of the serpent. 15So the serpent spewed water out of his mouth like a flood after the woman, that he might cause her to be carried away by the flood. 16But the earth helped the woman, and the earth opened its mouth and swallowed up the flood which the dragon had spewed out of his mouth. 17And the dragon was enraged with the woman, and he went to make war with the rest of her offspring, who keep the commandments of God and have the testimony of Jesus Christ.

The Beast from the Sea

13 Then I stood on the sand of the sea. And I saw a beast rising up out of the sea, having seven heads and ten horns, and on his horns ten crowns, and on his heads a blasphemous name. 2Now the beast which I saw was like a leopard, his feet were like *the feet of* a bear, and his mouth like the mouth of a lion. The dragon gave him his power, his throne, and great authority. 3And *I saw* one of his heads as if it had been mortally wounded, and his deadly wound was healed. And all the world marveled and followed the beast. 4So they worshiped the dragon who gave authority to the beast; and they worshiped the beast, saying, "Who *is* like the beast? Who is able to make war with him?"

5And he was given a mouth speaking

great things and blasphemies, and he was given authority to continue for forty-two months. 6Then he opened his mouth in blasphemy against God, to blaspheme His name, His tabernacle, and those who dwell in heaven. 7It was granted to him to make war with the saints and to overcome them. And authority was given him over every tribe, tongue, and nation. 8All who dwell on the earth will worship him, whose names have not been written in the Book of Life of the Lamb slain from the foundation of the world.

9If anyone has an ear, let him hear. 10He who leads into captivity shall go into captivity; he who kills with the sword must be killed with the sword. Here is the patience and the faith of the saints.

The Beast from the Earth

11Then I saw another beast coming up out of the earth, and he had two horns like a lamb and spoke like a dragon. 12And he exercises all the authority of the first beast in his presence, and causes the earth and those who dwell in it to worship the first beast, whose deadly wound was healed. 13He performs great signs, so that he even makes fire come down from heaven on the earth in the sight of men. 14And he deceives those who dwell on the earth by those signs which he was granted to do in the sight of the beast, telling those who dwell on the earth to make an image to the beast who was wounded by the sword and lived. 15He was granted *power* to give breath to the image of the beast, that the image of the beast should both speak and cause as many as would not worship the image of the beast to be killed. 16He causes all, both small and great, rich and poor, free and slave, to receive a mark on their right hand or on their foreheads, 17and that no one may buy or sell except one who has the mark or the name of the beast, or the number of his name.

18Here is wisdom. Let him who has understanding calculate the number of the beast, for it is the number of a man: His number *is* 666.

The Lamb and the 144,000

14 Then I looked, and behold, a Lamb standing on Mount Zion, and with Him one hundred *and* forty-four thousand, having His Father's name written on their foreheads. 2And I heard a voice from heaven, like the voice of many waters, and like the voice of loud thunder. And I heard the sound of harpists playing their harps. 3They sang as it were a new song before the throne, before the four living creatures, and the elders; and no one could learn that song except the hundred *and* forty-four thousand who were redeemed from the earth. 4These are the ones who were not defiled with women, for they are virgins. These are the ones who follow the Lamb wherever He goes. These were redeemed from *among* men, *being* firstfruits to God and to the Lamb. 5And in their mouth was found no deceit, for they are without fault before the throne of God.

The Proclamations of Three Angels

6Then I saw another angel flying in the midst of heaven, having the everlasting gospel to preach to those who dwell on the earth—to every nation, tribe, tongue, and people—7saying with a loud voice, "Fear God and give glory to Him, for the hour of His judgment has come; and worship Him who made heaven and earth, the sea and springs of water."

8And another angel followed, saying, "Babylon is fallen, is fallen, that great city, because she has made all nations drink of the wine of the wrath of her fornication."

9Then a third angel followed them, saying with a loud voice, "If anyone worships the beast and his image, and receives *his* mark on his forehead or on his hand, 10he himself shall also drink of the wine of the wrath of God, which is poured out full strength into the cup of His indignation. He shall be tormented with fire and brimstone in the presence of the holy angels and in the presence of the Lamb. 11And the smoke of their torment ascends forever and ever; and they have no rest day or night, who worship the beast and his image, and whoever receives the mark of his name."

12Here is the patience of the saints; here *are* those who keep the commandments of God and the faith of Jesus.

13Then I heard a voice from heaven saying to me, "Write: 'Blessed *are* the dead who die in the Lord from now on.'"

"Yes," says the Spirit, "that they may rest from their labors, and their works follow them."

Reaping the Earth's Harvest

14Then I looked, and behold, a white cloud, and on the cloud sat *One* like the Son of Man, having on His head a golden crown, and in His hand a sharp sickle. 15And another angel came out of the temple, crying with a loud voice to Him who sat on the cloud, "Thrust in Your sickle and reap, for the time has come for You to reap, for the harvest of the earth is ripe." 16So He who sat on the cloud thrust in His sickle on the earth, and the earth was reaped.

Reaping the Grapes of Wrath

17Then another angel came out of the temple which is in heaven, he also having a sharp sickle.

18And another angel came out from the altar, who had power over fire, and he cried with a loud cry to him who had the sharp sickle, saying, "Thrust in your sharp sickle and gather the clusters of the vine of the earth, for her grapes are fully ripe." 19So the angel thrust his sickle into the earth and gathered the vine of the earth, and threw *it* into the great winepress of the wrath of God. 20And the winepress was trampled outside the city, and blood came out of the winepress, up to the horses' bridles, for one thousand six hundred furlongs.

Prelude to the Bowl Judgments

15 Then I saw another sign in heaven, great and marvelous: seven angels having the seven last plagues, for in them the wrath of God is complete.

2And I saw *something* like a sea of glass mingled with fire, and those who have the victory over the beast, over his image and over his mark *and* over the

number of his name, standing on the sea of glass, having harps of God. 3They sing the song of Moses, the servant of God, and the song of the Lamb, saying:

"Great and marvelous *are* Your
　works,
Lord God Almighty!
Just and true *are* Your ways,
O King of the saints!
4　Who shall not fear You, O Lord,
　and glorify Your name?
For *You* alone *are* holy.
For all nations shall come and
　worship before You,
For Your judgments have been
　manifested."

5After these things I looked, and behold, the temple of the tabernacle of the testimony in heaven was opened. 6And out of the temple came the seven angels having the seven plagues, clothed in pure bright linen, and having their chests girded with golden bands. 7Then one of the four living creatures gave to the seven angels seven golden bowls full of the wrath of God who lives forever and ever. 8The temple was filled with smoke from the glory of God and from His power, and no one was able to enter the temple till the seven plagues of the seven angels were completed.

16 Then I heard a loud voice from the temple saying to the seven angels, "Go and pour out the bowls of the wrath of God on the earth."

First Bowl: Loathsome Sores

2So the first went and poured out his bowl upon the earth, and a foul and loathsome sore came upon the men who had the mark of the beast and those who worshiped his image.

Second Bowl: The Sea Turns to Blood

3Then the second angel poured out his bowl on the sea, and it became blood as of a dead *man;* and every living creature in the sea died.

Third Bowl: The Waters Turn to Blood

4Then the third angel poured out his bowl on the rivers and springs of water, and they became blood. 5And I heard the angel of the waters saying:

"You are righteous, O Lord,

The One who is and who was and
who is to be,
Because You have judged these
things.
6 For they have shed the blood of
saints and prophets,
And You have given them blood to
drink.
For it is their just due."

7And I heard another from the altar
saying, "Even so, Lord God Almighty,
true and righteous *are* Your judgments."

Fourth Bowl: Men Are Scorched

8Then the fourth angel poured out his
bowl on the sun, and power was given
to him to scorch men with fire.
9And men were scorched with great
heat, and they blasphemed the name of
God who has power over these plagues;
and they did not repent and give Him
glory.

Fifth Bowl: Darkness and Pain

10Then the fifth angel poured out his
bowl on the throne of the beast, and
his kingdom became full of darkness;
and they gnawed their tongues because
of the pain. 11They blasphemed the God
of heaven because of their pains and
their sores, and did not repent of their
deeds.

Sixth Bowl: Euphrates Dried Up

12Then the sixth angel poured out his
bowl on the great river Euphrates, and
its water was dried up, so that the way
of the kings from the east might be prepared. 13And I saw three unclean spirits
like frogs *coming* out of the mouth of
the dragon, out of the mouth of the
beast, and out of the mouth of the false
prophet. 14For they are spirits of demons, performing signs, *which* go out
to the kings of the earth and of the
whole world, to gather them to the battle of that great day of God Almighty.

15"Behold, I am coming as a thief.
Blessed *is* he who watches, and keeps
his garments, lest he walk naked and
they see his shame."

16And they gathered them together
to the place called in Hebrew, Arma-
geddon.

Seventh Bowl: The Earth Utterly Shaken

17Then the seventh angel poured out
his bowl into the air, and a loud voice
came out of the temple of heaven, from
the throne, saying, "It is done!"
18And there were noises and thunderings and lightnings; and there was a
great earthquake, such a mighty and
great earthquake as had not occurred
since men were on the earth. 19Now the
great city was divided into three parts,
and the cities of the nations fell. And
great Babylon was remembered before
God, to give her the cup of the wine of
the fierceness of His wrath. 20Then
every island fled away, and the mountains were not found. 21And great hail
from heaven fell upon men, *each hail-
stone* about the weight of a talent. Men
blasphemed God because of the plague
of the hail, since that plague was exceedingly great.

The Scarlet Woman and the Scarlet Beast

17 Then one of the seven angels who
had the seven bowls came and
talked with me, saying to me, "Come,
I will show you the judgment of the
great harlot who sits on many waters,
2with whom the kings of the earth committed fornication, and the inhabitants
of the earth were made drunk with the
wine of her fornication."

3So he carried me away in the Spirit
into the wilderness. And I saw a woman
sitting on a scarlet beast *which was* full
of names of blasphemy, having seven
heads and ten horns. 4The woman was
arrayed in purple and scarlet, and
adorned with gold and precious stones
and pearls, having in her hand a golden
cup full of abominations and the filthiness of her fornication. 5And on her
forehead a name *was* written:

MYSTERY,
BABYLON THE GREAT,
THE MOTHER OF HARLOTS
AND OF THE ABOMINATIONS
OF THE EARTH.

6I saw the woman, drunk with the blood
of the saints and with the blood of the
martyrs of Jesus. And when I saw her,
I marveled with great amazement.

The Meaning of the Woman and the Beast

7But the angel said to me, "Why did you marvel? I will tell you the mystery of the woman and of the beast that carries her, which has the seven heads and the ten horns. 8The beast that you saw was, and is not, and will ascend out of the bottomless pit and go to perdition. And those who dwell on the earth will marvel, whose names are not written in the Book of Life from the foundation of the world, when they see the beast that was, and is not, and yet is.

9"Here is the mind which has wisdom: The seven heads are seven mountains on which the woman sits. 10There are also seven kings. Five have fallen, one is, and the other has not yet come. And when he comes, he must continue a short time. 11The beast that was, and is not, is himself also the eighth, and is of the seven, and is going to perdition.

12"The ten horns which you saw are ten kings who have received no kingdom as yet, but they receive authority for one hour as kings with the beast. 13These are of one mind, and they will give their power and authority to the beast. 14These will make war with the Lamb, and the Lamb will overcome them, for He is Lord of lords and King of kings; and those who are with Him are called, chosen, and faithful."

15Then he said to me, "The waters which you saw, where the harlot sits, are peoples, multitudes, nations, and tongues. 16And the ten horns which you saw on the beast, these will hate the harlot, make her desolate and naked, eat her flesh and burn her with fire. 17For God has put it into their hearts to fulfill His purpose, to be of one mind, and to give their kingdom to the beast, until the words of God are fulfilled. 18And the woman whom you saw is that great city which reigns over the kings of the earth."

The Fall of Babylon the Great

18 After these things I saw another angel coming down from heaven, having great authority, and the earth was illuminated with his glory. 2And he cried mightily with a loud voice, saying, "Babylon the great is fallen, is fallen, and has become a dwelling place of demons, a prison for every foul spirit, and a cage for every unclean and hated bird! 3For all the nations have drunk of the wine of the wrath of her fornication, the kings of the earth have committed fornication with her, and the merchants of the earth have become rich through the abundance of her luxury."

4And I heard another voice from heaven saying, "Come out of her, my people, lest you share in her sins, and lest you receive of her plagues. 5For her sins have reached to heaven, and God has remembered her iniquities. 6Render to her just as she rendered to you, and repay her double according to her works; in the cup which she has mixed, mix double for her. 7In the measure that she glorified herself and lived luxuriously, in the same measure give her torment and sorrow; for she says in her heart, 'I sit as queen, and am no widow, and will not see sorrow.' 8Therefore her plagues will come in one day—death and mourning and famine. And she will be utterly burned with fire, for strong is the Lord God who judges her.

The World Mourns Babylon's Fall

9"The kings of the earth who committed fornication and lived luxuriously with her will weep and lament for her, when they see the smoke of her burning, 10standing at a distance for fear of her torment, saying, 'Alas, alas, that great city Babylon, that mighty city! For in one hour your judgment has come.'

11"And the merchants of the earth will weep and mourn over her, for no one buys their merchandise anymore: 12merchandise of gold and silver, precious stones and pearls, fine linen and purple, silk and scarlet, every kind of citron wood, every kind of object of ivory, every kind of object of most precious wood, bronze, iron, and marble; 13and cinnamon and incense, fragrant oil and frankincense, wine and oil, fine flour and wheat, cattle and sheep, horses and chariots, and bodies and souls of men. 14The fruit that your soul longed for has gone from you, and all the things which are rich and splendid have gone from you, and you shall find them no more at all. 15The merchants of these things, who became rich by her, will stand at a distance for fear of her torment, weeping and wailing, 16and saying, 'Alas, alas, that great city that was clothed in fine linen, purple, and scarlet, and adorned with gold and precious stones and pearls! 17For in one hour such great riches came to nothing.' Every shipmaster, all who travel by ship, sailors, and as many as trade on the sea, stood at a distance 18and cried out when they saw the smoke of her burning, saying, 'What *is* like this great city?'

19"They threw dust on their heads and cried out, weeping and wailing, and saying, 'Alas, alas, that great city, in which all who had ships on the sea became rich by her wealth! For in one hour she is made desolate.'

20"Rejoice over her, O heaven, and *you* holy apostles and prophets, for God has avenged you on her!"

Finality of Babylon's Fall

21Then a mighty angel took up a stone like a great millstone and threw *it* into the sea, saying, "Thus with violence the great city Babylon shall be thrown down, and shall not be found anymore. 22The sound of harpists, musicians, flutists, and trumpeters shall not be heard in you anymore. No craftsman of any craft shall be found in you anymore, and the sound of a millstone shall not be heard in you anymore. 23The light of a lamp shall not shine in you anymore, and the voice of bridegroom and bride shall not be heard in you anymore. For your merchants were the great men of the earth, for by your sorcery all the nations were deceived. 24And in her was found the blood of prophets and saints, and of all who were slain on the earth."

Heaven Exults over Babylon

19 After these things I heard a loud voice of a great multitude in heaven, saying, "Alleluia! Salvation and glory and honor and power *belong* to the Lord our God! 2For true and righteous *are* His judgments, because He has judged the great harlot who corrupted the earth with her fornication;

and He has avenged on her the blood of His servants *shed* by her." 3Again they said, "Alleluia! Her smoke rises up forever and ever!" 4And the twenty-four elders and the four living creatures fell down and worshiped God who sat on the throne, saying, "Amen! Alleluia!" 5Then a voice came from the throne, saying, "Praise our God, all you His servants and those who fear Him, both small and great!"

6And I heard, as it were, the voice of a great multitude, as the sound of many waters and as the sound of mighty thunderings, saying, "Alleluia! For the Lord God Omnipotent reigns! 7Let us be glad and rejoice and give Him glory, for the marriage of the Lamb has come, and His wife has made herself ready." 8And to her it was granted to be arrayed in fine linen, clean and bright, for the fine linen is the righteous acts of the saints.

9Then he said to me, "Write: 'Blessed *are* those who are called to the marriage supper of the Lamb!' " And he said to me, "These are the true sayings of God." 10And I fell at his feet to worship him. But he said to me, "See *that you do* not *do that!* I am your fellow servant, and of your brethren who have the testimony of Jesus. Worship God! For the testimony of Jesus is the spirit of prophecy."

Christ on a White Horse

11Now I saw heaven opened, and behold, a white horse. And He who sat on him *was* called Faithful and True, and in righteousness He judges and makes war. 12His eyes *were* like a flame of fire, and on His head *were* many crowns. He had a name written that no one knew except Himself. 13He *was* clothed with a robe dipped in blood, and His name is called The Word of God. 14And the armies in heaven, clothed in fine linen, white and clean, followed Him on white horses. 15Now out of His mouth goes a sharp sword, that with it He should strike the nations. And He Himself will rule them with a rod of iron. He Himself treads the winepress of the fierceness and wrath of Almighty God. 16And He has on *His* robe and on His thigh a name written:

KING OF KINGS
AND LORD OF LORDS.

The Beast and His Armies Defeated

17Then I saw an angel standing in the sun; and he cried with a loud voice, saying to all the birds that fly in the midst of heaven, "Come and gather together for the supper of the great God, 18that you may eat the flesh of kings, the flesh of captains, the flesh of mighty men, the flesh of horses and of those who sit on them, and the flesh of all *people*, free and slave, both small and great."

19And I saw the beast, the kings of the earth, and their armies, gathered together to make war against Him who sat on the horse and against His army. 20Then the beast was captured, and with him the false prophet who worked signs in his presence, by which he deceived those who received the mark of the beast and those who worshiped his image. These two were cast alive into the lake of fire burning with brimstone. 21And the rest were killed with the sword which proceeded from the mouth of Him who sat on the horse. And all the birds were filled with their flesh.

Satan Bound 1,000 Years

20 Then I saw an angel coming down from heaven, having the key to the bottomless pit and a great chain in his hand. 2He laid hold of the dragon, that serpent of old, who is *the* Devil and Satan, and bound him for a thousand years; 3and he cast him into the bottomless pit, and shut him up, and set a seal on him, so that he should deceive the nations no more till the thousand years were finished. But after these things he must be released for a little while.

The Saints Reign with Christ 1,000 Years

4And I saw thrones, and they sat on them, and judgment was committed to them. Then *I saw* the souls of those who had been beheaded for their witness to Jesus and for the word of God, who had not worshiped the beast or his image, and had not received *his* mark on their foreheads or on their hands. And they lived and reigned with Christ for a thousand years. 5But the rest of the dead

did not live again until the thousand years were finished. This *is* the first resurrection. 6Blessed and holy *is* he who has part in the first resurrection. Over such the second death has no power, but they shall be priests of God and of Christ, and shall reign with Him a thousand years.

Satanic Rebellion Crushed

7Now when the thousand years have expired, Satan will be released from his prison 8and will go out to deceive the nations which are in the four corners of the earth, Gog and Magog, to gather them together to battle, whose number *is* as the sand of the sea. 9They went up on the breadth of the earth and surrounded the camp of the saints and the beloved city. And fire came down from God out of heaven and devoured them. 10The devil, who deceived them, was cast into the lake of fire and brimstone where the beast and the false prophet *are*. And they will be tormented day and night forever and ever.

The Great White Throne Judgment

11Then I saw a great white throne and Him who sat on it, from whose face the earth and the heaven fled away. And there was found no place for them. 12And I saw the dead, small and great, standing before God, and books were opened. And another book was opened, which is *the Book* of Life. And the dead were judged according to their works, by the things which were written in the books. 13The sea gave up the dead who were in it, and Death and Hades delivered up the dead who were in them. And they were judged, each one according to his works. 14Then Death and Hades were cast into the lake of fire. This is the second death. 15And anyone not found written in the Book of Life was cast into the lake of fire.

All Things Made New

21 Now I saw a new heaven and a new earth, for the first heaven and the first earth had passed away. Also there was no more sea. 2Then I, John, saw the holy city, New Jerusalem, coming down out of heaven from God, prepared as a bride adorned for her husband. 3And I heard a loud voice

from heaven saying, "Behold, the tabernacle of God *is* with men, and He will dwell with them, and they shall be His people. God Himself will be with them *and be* their God. 4And God will wipe away every tear from their eyes; there shall be no more death, nor sorrow, nor crying. There shall be no more pain, for the former things have passed away."

5Then He who sat on the throne said, "Behold, I make all things new." And He said to me, "Write, for these words are true and faithful."

6And He said to me, "It is done! I am the Alpha and the Omega, the Beginning and the End. I will give of the fountain of the water of life freely to him who thirsts. 7He who overcomes shall inherit all things, and I will be his God and he shall be My son. 8But the cowardly, unbelieving, abominable, murderers, sexually immoral, sorcerers, idolaters, and all liars shall have their part in the lake which burns with fire and brimstone, which is the second death."

The New Jerusalem

9Then one of the seven angels who had the seven bowls filled with the seven last plagues came to me and talked with me, saying, "Come, I will show you the bride, the Lamb's wife." 10And he carried me away in the Spirit to a great and high mountain, and showed me the great city, the holy Jerusalem, descending out of heaven from God, 11having the glory of God. Her light *was* like a most precious stone, like a jasper stone, clear as crystal. 12Also she had a great and high wall with twelve gates, and twelve angels at the gates, and names written on them, which are *the names* of the twelve tribes of the children of Israel: 13three gates on the east, three gates on the north, three gates on the south, and three gates on the west.

14Now the wall of the city had twelve foundations, and on them were the names of the twelve apostles of the Lamb. 15And he who talked with me had a gold reed to measure the city, its gates, and its wall. 16The city is laid out as a square; its length is as great as its breadth. And he measured the city with the reed: twelve thousand furlongs. Its

length, breadth, and height are equal. 17Then he measured its wall: one hundred *and* forty-four cubits, *according* to the measure of a man, that is, of an angel. 18The construction of its wall was *of* jasper; and the city *was* pure gold, like clear glass. 19The foundations of the wall of the city *were* adorned with all kinds of precious stones: the first foundation *was* jasper, the second sapphire, the third chalcedony, the fourth emerald, 20the fifth sardonyx, the sixth sardius, the seventh chrysolite, the eighth beryl, the ninth topaz, the tenth chrysoprase, the eleventh jacinth, and the twelfth amethyst. 21The twelve gates *were* twelve pearls: each individual gate was of one pearl. And the street of the city *was* pure gold, like transparent glass.

The Glory of the New Jerusalem

22But I saw no temple in it, for the Lord God Almighty and the Lamb are its temple. 23The city had no need of the sun or of the moon to shine in it, for the glory of God illuminated it. The Lamb *is* its light. 24And the nations of those who are saved shall walk in its light, and the kings of the earth bring their glory and honor into it. 25Its gates shall not be shut at all by day (there shall be no night there). 26And they shall bring the glory and the honor of the nations into it. 27But there shall by no means enter it anything that defiles, or causes an abomination or a lie, but only those who are written in the Lamb's Book of Life.

The River of Life

22 And he showed me a pure river of water of life, clear as crystal, proceeding from the throne of God and of the Lamb. 2In the middle of its street, and on either side of the river, *was* the tree of life, which bore twelve fruits, each *tree* yielding its fruit every month. The leaves of the tree *were* for the healing of the nations. 3And there shall be no more curse, but the throne of God and of the Lamb shall be in it, and His servants shall serve Him. 4They shall see His face, and His name *shall be* on their foreheads. 5There shall be no night there: They need no lamp nor light of the sun, for the Lord God gives them light. And they shall reign forever and ever.

The Time Is Near

6Then he said to me, "These words *are* faithful and true." And the Lord God of the holy prophets sent His angel to show His servants the things which must shortly take place.

7"Behold, I am coming quickly! Blessed *is* he who keeps the words of the prophecy of this book."

8Now I, John, saw and heard these things. And when I heard and saw, I fell down to worship before the feet of the angel who showed me these things.

9Then he said to me, "See *that you do* not *do that.* For I am your fellow servant, and of your brethren the prophets, and of those who keep the words of this book. Worship God."

10And he said to me, "Do not seal the words of the prophecy of this book, for the time is at hand. **11**He who is unjust, let him be unjust still; he who is filthy, let him be filthy still; he who is righteous, let him be righteous still; he who is holy, let him be holy still."

Jesus Testifies to the Churches

12"And behold, I am coming quickly, and My reward *is* with Me, to give to every one according to his work. **13**I am the Alpha and the Omega, *the* Beginning and *the* End, the First and the Last."

14Blessed *are* those who do His commandments, that they may have the right to the tree of life, and may enter through the gates into the city. **15**But outside *are* dogs and sorcerers and sexually immoral and murderers and idolaters, and whoever loves and practices a lie.

16"I, Jesus, have sent My angel to testify to you these things in the churches. I am the Root and the Offspring of David, the Bright and Morning Star."

17And the Spirit and the bride say, "Come!" And let him who hears say, "Come!" And let him who thirsts come. Whoever desires, let him take the water of life freely.

A Warning

18For I testify to everyone who hears the words of the prophecy of this book: If anyone adds to these things, God will add to him the plagues that are written in this book; **19**and if anyone takes away from the words of the book of this prophecy, God shall take away his part from the Book of Life, from the holy city, and *from* the things which are written in this book.

I Am Coming Quickly

20He who testifies to these things says, "Surely I am coming quickly."

Amen. Even so, come, Lord Jesus!

21The grace of our Lord Jesus Christ *be* with you all. Amen.

Congratulations!

You have in your hands one of the most precious books the world has ever seen. It is a book full of profound wisdom and insight about human nature and the character and purpose of the God who created all things. Throughout the centuries people from many lands have opened this book and read from it in their own languages. Here they have learned about God's love and justice. Great leaders and thinkers have searched its pages and explored its truths, looking for the answers to life's problems and challenges.

You are invited to make that same exploration. The following section of special helps is provided to help you begin this rewarding journey.

- *What's in the Bible* gives you a brief summary of every book in the Bible and a handy chart giving an overview of all the books that make up the Bible.
- *How to Read the Bible* provides simple suggestions on how to read the Bible devotionally and to keep notes on the many lessons you'll learn.
- *Read through the Bible in a Year* is a reading plan that is easy to follow and guides you through the entire Old and New Testaments in exactly one year.
- *Some Readings for Special Days* guides you to passages you may want to read on special days like Christmas, Easter, Mother's Day—and even your own birthday.
- *Famous Passages of the Bible* helps you locate those famous Bible stories you've heard time and again, but may never have read for yourself.
- *Finding Help in the Bible* leads you to those passages that can help you when you're facing a difficult problem or special challenge.
- *What the Bible Says about God's Forgiveness* will lead you to places in the Bible where you can learn how much God loves each one of us and what he has done to put us right with himself.

It really doesn't matter where you begin, but it does matter *that* you begin. Use any one of these special reader's helps to get you started on a daily habit of reading the Bible. Discover for yourself the help and hope it has to offer.

The Bible

The word "Bible" comes from the Greek word *biblia*, which means "books." So the Bible is really a collection or library of many books. These books are divided into two main parts, the Old Testament and the New Testament.

Old Testament

The Old Testament tells the history of the people of Israel. This history is based on their faith in the God of Israel and on their religious life as the people of God. The authors of these books wrote about what God had done for them as a people and how they were to worship and obey God in return. The following chart shows the different groups of books that make up the Old Testament.

The Law
Genesis, Exodus, Leviticus, Numbers, Deuteronomy

History
Joshua, Judges, Ruth, 1 Samuel, 2 Samuel, 1 Kings, 2 Kings, 1 Chronicles, 2 Chronicles, Ezra, Nehemiah, Esther

Poetry and Wisdom
Job, Psalms, Proverbs, Ecclesiastes, Song of Songs

Major Prophets
Isaiah, Jeremiah, Lamentations, Ezekiel, Daniel

Minor Prophets
Hosea, Joel, Amos, Obadiah, Jonah, Micah, Nahum, Habakkuk, Zephaniah, Haggai, Zechariah, Malachi

New Testament

The books of the New Testament were written by the followers of Jesus Christ. These followers wanted others to know the Good News about Jesus Christ and the possibility of a "new" life available to them through his death and resurrection. The following chart shows the different groups of books that make up the New Testament. Although scholarly opinion has varied, Paul has traditionally been identified as the author of the letters indicated below.

The Gospels
Matthew, Mark, Luke, John

Paul's Letters
Romans, 1 Corinthians, 2 Corinthians, Galatians, Ephesians, Philippians, Colossians, 1 Thessalonians, 2 Thessalonians, 1 Timothy, 2 Timothy, Titus, Philemon

History
Acts

General Letters
Hebrews, James, 1 Peter, 2 Peter, 1 John, 2 John, 3 John, Jude

Prophecy
Revelation

What's in the Bible

The following are summary capsules for each book of the Bible. It will be obvious from how brief the descriptions are that they are not complete. They should, however, serve as a quick and handy guide to the content of the whole Bible.

Old Testament

GENESIS: In this book of beginnings the stories are about creation, early relationships between God and people, and God's promise to bless Abraham and his descendants.

EXODUS: The name Exodus means "departure" and this book tells about how God led the Israelites out of a life of hardship and slavery in Egypt. God made a covenant with them and gave them the Law to order their lives.

LEVITICUS: This book is named for the priestly tribe of Levi and is made up of laws concerning rituals and ceremonies.

NUMBERS: The Israelites wandered in the wilderness for 40 years before entering Canaan, the promised land. The name of the book comes from two censuses taken during the journey.

DEUTERONOMY: Moses gave three farewell speeches shortly before he died. In them he reviewed the laws of God for the Israelites. This book gets its name—"second law"—from this review.

JOSHUA: Joshua led the Israelite armies into victory over the Canaanites. The book ends with the division of the land among the tribes of Israel.

JUDGES: The Israelites often fell away from God and into the hands of oppressors. God sent "judges" to lead and deliver them.

RUTH: Love and dedication between Ruth and her mother-in-law, Naomi, are the focus of this story.

1 SAMUEL: Samuel was the leader of Israel between the time of Judges and the time of Saul, the first King of Israel. When Saul's leadership failed, David was anointed by Samuel to be king.

2 SAMUEL: Under David's rule, the new nation was strong and unified. But after David committed adultery and murder, his family and nation suffered.

1 KINGS: This book starts with stories about Solomon's reign over Israel. After the death of Solomon, the kingdom went to war with itself, north against south. The result was two nations, Israel in the north and Judah in the south.

2 KINGS: Israel was conquered by Assyria in 721 B.C. Judah was defeated by Babylon in 586 B.C. These events were seen as judgment upon the people because they did not follow the laws of God.

1 CHRONICLES: This book begins with genealogies from Adam to David and then recounts the incidents of David's reign.

2 CHRONICLES: This book covers the same period as 2 Kings but the emphasis is on Judah, the southern kingdom, and its rulers.

EZRA: God's people returned to Jerusalem after being held captive in Babylon for several decades. One of the leaders was Ezra. This book contains his charge to the people to be true to the law of God.

NEHEMIAH: After the Temple was rebuilt, the protective wall around Jerusalem was restored. Nehemiah brought this effort to completion. He also worked with Ezra to restore religious fervor among the people.

ESTHER: This book tells the story of the Jewish queen of Persia who exposed a plot to destroy her people and thus saved all the Jews in that country from destruction.

JOB: The question, "Why do innocent people suffer?" is addressed in the story of Job.

PSALMS: These 150 prayers and hymns were used by the Hebrew people to express their relationship with God. They cover the whole range of human emotions from joy to anger, from hope to despair.

PROVERBS: This is a book of wise sayings and ethical and common sense teachings on how to live a godly life.

ECCLESIASTES: In a quest for happiness and the meaning of life, this writer, known as "the Philosopher," asks many questions that are still raised in today's society.

SONG OF SONGS: This poem describes the joy and ecstasy of love. It has been understood both as a picture of God's love for Israel and of Christ's love for the Church.

ISAIAH: The prophet Isaiah brought the message of God's judgment on the nations, pointed to a future king like David, and promised a time of comfort and peace.

JEREMIAH: Before Babylon destroyed Judah, Jeremiah foretold God's judgment. While his message was largely of destruction, he also pointed toward a new covenant with God.

LAMENTATIONS: As Jeremiah had warned, Jerusalem fell to the Babylonians. This book records five "laments" for the fallen city.

EZEKIEL: Ezekiel's message was given to the Jews held captive in Babylon. He used stories and parables to speak about judgment, hope and restoration.

DANIEL: Daniel remained faithful to God while facing many pressures as a captive in Babylon. This book includes Daniel's prophetic visions.

HOSEA: Hosea used his commitment to his wife in the face of her unfaithfulness to illustrate the "adultery" Israel had committed against God, whose faithful love never ceased.

JOEL: After a locust plague in Judah, Joel urged the people to repent.

AMOS: During an era of prosperity, this Judean prophet preached judgment on the rich leaders of Israel. Amos urged them to consider the poor and oppressed rather than their own self-satisfaction.

OBADIAH: Obadiah prophesied judgment on Edom, a neighboring country.

JONAH: Jonah did not want to preach to the Ninevites, an enemy people. When he finally brought God's message to them, they repented.

MICAH: Micah's message to Judah was a prophecy of judgment as well as forgiveness and hope for restoration. Especially notable is his single verse summary of what God requires of us (6.8).

NAHUM: Nahum announced that God would destroy the people of Nineveh because of their cruelty in war.

HABAKKUK: Habakkuk's book features a dialogue between Habakkuk and God about suffering and justice.

ZEPHANIAH: Zephaniah announced the day of the Lord, which would bring judgment on Judah and other surrounding nations. This coming day would be one of doom for many, but a humble and faithful remnant will survive to bless the whole world.

HAGGAI: After the people return from exile, Haggai reminded them to give God their highest priority and to rebuild the Temple before working on their own homes.

ZECHARIAH: Like Haggai, Zechariah urged the people to rebuild the Temple, assuring them of God's help and blessings. His visions point to a glorious future.

MALACHI: After the exiles returned, they became complacent about their religious life. Malachi tried to stir them up by preaching about the day of the Lord.

New Testament

MATTHEW: This Gospel includes many Old Testament quotations, thus appealing to a Jewish audience and presenting Jesus as the Messiah promised in the Hebrew Scriptures. Matthew told the story of Jesus from birth to resurrection and placed emphasis on his teaching.

MARK: Mark wrote a short, action-packed Gospel. He emphasized Jesus' miracles and his life of suffering. His aim was to deepen the faith and commitment of the believers in the community to which he wrote.

LUKE: In this Gospel, the availability of salvation for all people is emphasized. Luke proclaimed this message by showing Jesus' involvement with people who are poor, needy, and on the fringes of society.

JOHN: The Gospel of John stands apart from the others. John organized his message around seven signs that point to Jesus as the Son of God. His writing style is reflective and filled with striking images.

ACTS: When Jesus left his disciples, the Holy Spirit came to abide with them. Written by Luke as the sequel to his Gospel, Acts records key events in the history of the work of the early Christian Church to spread the Gospel throughout the Mediterranean world.

ROMANS: In this important letter, Paul wrote to the Romans about life in the Spirit, which is given to believers in Christ through faith. The apostle tells them about God's great kindness and declares that because of Jesus Christ, God accepts us and sets us free from our sins.

1 CORINTHIANS: This letter deals with the problems the church in Corinth was experiencing: dissension, immorality, public worship, and confusion about spiritual gifts.

2 CORINTHIANS: In this letter, Paul wrote about his relationship with the church of Corinth and the effects of certain false apostles on his ministry.

GALATIANS: This letter addresses freedom from the law through Christ. Paul declares that it is by faith that all who believe are put right with God.

EPHESIANS: A central theme to this letter is that God's eternal purpose is to bring together from many nations and peoples the universal Church of Jesus Christ.

PHILIPPIANS: This letter emphasizes the joy found in any situation when a person believes in Christ. Paul wrote it while in prison.

COLOSSIANS: In this letter Paul tells the people of Colossae to make Christ the center of their faith and to put aside their superstitions.

1 THESSALONIANS: In this letter Paul gives advice to the people of Thessalonica concerning Christ's return.

2 THESSALONIANS: This letter discusses the same topics as the first. Paul teaches the people a way to be ready for the Lord.

1 TIMOTHY: This letter served as a guide for Timothy, a young leader in the church. It contains advice about worship, ministry, and relationships within the church.

2 TIMOTHY: This is Paul's last letter. In it he offers a final challenge to his co-worker.

TITUS: Titus was ministering in Crete. In this letter, Paul gave him advice on how to help Christians follow Christ.

PHILEMON: In this letter, Philemon is urged to forgive his runaway slave, Onesimus, and accept him as a friend in Christ.

HEBREWS: The letter to the Hebrews challenges new Christians to move beyond their traditional rituals and ceremonies and believe that Christ has fulfilled them all.

JAMES: James advises putting beliefs into practice and offers practical ways for Christians to live out their faith.

1 PETER: This letter was written to comfort early Christians who were being persecuted for their faith.

2 PETER: In this letter Peter warns against false teachers and urges Christians to stay loyal to God.

1 JOHN: This letter explains basic truths about the Christian life, with emphasis on the command to love one another.

2 JOHN: This letter, addressed to "the dear Lady and to her children," warns against false teachers.

3 JOHN: In contrast to 2 John, this letter states the need to welcome people who preach Christ.

JUDE: Jude warns against the influence of evil ones outside the fellowship of believers.

REVELATION: This book was written to encourage persecuted believers and affirm their faith that God will care for them. Using visions and symbols, the writer illustrates the triumph of good over evil and the creation of a new heaven and new earth.

How to Read the Bible

Set aside time each day to read from your Bible. Try to make it the same time each day. Be realistic. Commit yourself only to as much time as you honestly feel that you can stick to on an ongoing basis. Before you begin reading ask for God's guidance and blessing. Some people have found that keeping a daily notebook is helpful. Use the following steps to get the most out of your daily Bible reading:

1. Select a passage (perhaps one from the *Read through the Bible in a Year* section that follows).

2. Examine its context:

   a. What kind of book is it drawn from? A biographical book such as one of the Gospel accounts of Jesus' life; a long historical book, such as *The Second Book of Samuel*, which tells of the reign of King David; a brief letter to a person (*The Letters of Paul to Timothy*) or to a specific church (*The Letters of Paul to the Corinthians*)?

   b. What is the overall purpose/intent of this book? (Do not do lengthy research, but feel free to read the opening and closing paragraphs as well as section headings and introductions if your Bible has them.)

   c. What occurs or is discussed in the passages immediately preceding and following the passage you chose?

3. Read the passage quickly for sense.

4. Identify key words or phrases. Are there words or thoughts that are repeated throughout the passage? Are any cause and effect relationships established? (These are often signaled by words like *if* and *then, therefore, because, since,* and *so*.) Are any comparisons made or similarities pointed out? Are any two people, things or concepts contrasted?

5. Read the passage again and ask yourself what is the intent or purpose of the passage. Try to find out what the author is saying. Be honest; don't just look for what you want to hear. The Bible has many strong messages that can change lives!

6. What do you learn about God from this passage? What do you learn about human nature? Ask yourself how this message applies to you. Is there anything you need to change in your life in order to be a more faithful child of God or more loving to your neighbor? Ask for God's help in making this change.

7. Re-read the passage one more time. Is there one verse you would like to commit to memory? Why not write it on an index card and carry it with you throughout the day as a study aid?

8. Thank God for what he has shown you, and ask for his help as you seek to apply this lesson in your life.

9. Share what you have learned with someone else.

Read through the Bible in a Year

Have you ever read the entire Bible all the way through? By committing just twenty or thirty minutes a day you can use the following daily reading plan to help you do just that in one year. The abbreviations used here are explained in the front of the Bible. For help in finding the passages refer to the *How to Look Up a Bible Reference* box. Begin today and discover the riches of God's Word!

JANUARY

1 ☐ Lk 5.27-39 ☐ Gn 1-2 ☐ Ps 1
2 ☐ Lk 6.1-26 ☐ Gn 3-5 ☐ Ps 2
3 ☐ Lk 6.27-49 ☐ Gn 6-7 ☐ Ps 3
4 ☐ Lk 7.1-17 ☐ Gn 8-10 ☐ Ps 4
5 ☐ Lk 7.18-50 ☐ Gn 11 ☐ Ps 5
6 ☐ Lk 8.1-25 ☐ Gn 12 ☐ Ps 6
7 ☐ Lk 8.26-56 ☐ Gn 13-14 ☐ Ps 7
8 ☐ Lk 9.1-27 ☐ Gn 15 ☐ Ps 8
9 ☐ Lk 9.28-62 ☐ Gn 16 ☐ Ps 9
10 ☐ Lk 10.1-20 ☐ Gn 17 ☐ Ps 10
11 ☐ Lk 10.21-42 ☐ Gn 18 ☐ Ps 11
12 ☐ Lk 11.1-28 ☐ Gn 19 ☐ Ps 12
13 ☐ Lk 11.29-54 ☐ Gn 20 ☐ Ps 13
14 ☐ Lk 12.1-31 ☐ Gn 21 ☐ Ps 14
15 ☐ Lk 12.32-59 ☐ Gn 22 ☐ Ps 15
16 ☐ Lk 13.1-17 ☐ Gn 23 ☐ Ps 16
17 ☐ Lk 13.18-35 ☐ Gn 24 ☐ Ps 17
18 ☐ Lk 14.1-24 ☐ Gn 25 ☐ Ps 18
19 ☐ Lk 14.25-35 ☐ Gn 26 ☐ Ps 19
20 ☐ Lk 15 ☐ Gn 27.1-45 ☐ Ps 20
21 ☐ Lk 16 ☐ Gn 27.46-28.22 ☐ Ps 21
22 ☐ Lk 17 ☐ Gn 29.1-30 ☐ Ps 22
23 ☐ Lk 18.1-17 ☐ Gn 29.31-30.43 ☐ Ps 23
24 ☐ Lk 18.18-43 ☐ Gn 31 ☐ Ps 24
25 ☐ Lk 19.1-27 ☐ Gn 32-33 ☐ Ps 25
26 ☐ Lk 19.28-48 ☐ Gn 34 ☐ Ps 26
27 ☐ Lk 20.1-26 ☐ Gn 35-36 ☐ Ps 27
28 ☐ Lk 20.27-47 ☐ Gn 37 ☐ Ps 28
29 ☐ Lk 21 ☐ Gn 38 ☐ Ps 29
30 ☐ Lk 22.1-38 ☐ Gn 39 ☐ Ps 30
31 ☐ Lk 22.39-71 ☐ Gn 40 ☐ Ps 31

FEBRUARY

1 ☐ Lk 23.1-25 ☐ Gn 41 ☐ Ps 32
2 ☐ Lk 23.26-56 ☐ Gn 42 ☐ Ps 33
3 ☐ Lk 24.1-12 ☐ Gn 43 ☐ Ps 34
4 ☐ Lk 24.13-53 ☐ Gn 44 ☐ Ps 35

5 ☐ He 1 ☐ Gn 45.1-46.27 ☐ Ps 36
6 ☐ He 2 ☐ Gn 46.28-47.31 ☐ Ps 37
7 ☐ He 3.1-4.13 ☐ Gn 48 ☐ Ps 38
8 ☐ He 4.14-6.12 ☐ Gn 49-50 ☐ Ps 39
9 ☐ He 6.13-20 ☐ Ex 1-2 ☐ Ps 40
10 ☐ He 7 ☐ Ex 3-4 ☐ Ps 41
11 ☐ He 8 ☐ Ex 5.1-6.27 ☐ Pr 1
12 ☐ He 9.1-22 ☐ Ex 6.28-8.32 ☐ Pr 2
13 ☐ He 9.23-10.18 ☐ Ex 9-10 ☐ Pr 3
14 ☐ He 10.19-39 ☐ Ex 11-12 ☐ Pr 4
15 ☐ He 11.1-21 ☐ Ex 13-14 ☐ Pr 5
16 ☐ He 11.22-40 ☐ Ex 15 ☐ Pr 6.1-7.5
17 ☐ He 12 ☐ Ex 16-17 ☐ Pr 7.6-27
18 ☐ He 13 ☐ Ex 18-19 ☐ Pr 8
19 ☐ Mt 1 ☐ Ex 20-21 ☐ Pr 9
20 ☐ Mt 2 ☐ Ex 22-23 ☐ Pr 10
21 ☐ Mt 3 ☐ Ex 24 ☐ Pr 11
22 ☐ Mt 4 ☐ Ex 25-27 ☐ Pr 12
23 ☐ Mt 5.1-20 ☐ Ex 28-29 ☐ Pr 13
24 ☐ Mt 5.21-48 ☐ Ex 30-32 ☐ Pr 14
25 ☐ Mt 6.1-18 ☐ Ex 33-34 ☐ Pr 15
26 ☐ Mt 6.19-34 ☐ Ex 35-36 ☐ Pr 16
27 ☐ Mt 7 ☐ Ex 37-38 ☐ Pr 17
28 ☐ Mt 8.1-13 ☐ Ex 39-40 ☐ Pr 18

MARCH

1 ☐ Mt 8.14-34 ☐ Lv 1-2 ☐ Pr 19
2 ☐ Mt 9.1-17 ☐ Lv 3-4 ☐ Pr 20
3 ☐ Mt 9.18-38 ☐ Lv 5-6 ☐ Pr 21
4 ☐ Mt 10.1-25 ☐ Lv 7-8 ☐ Pr 22
5 ☐ Mt 10.26-42 ☐ Lv 9-10 ☐ Pr 23
6 ☐ Mt 11.1-19 ☐ Lv 11-12 ☐ Pr 24
7 ☐ Mt 11.20-30 ☐ Lv 13 ☐ Pr 25
8 ☐ Mt 12.1-21 ☐ Lv 14 ☐ Pr 26
9 ☐ Mt 12.22-50 ☐ Lv 15-16 ☐ Pr 27
10 ☐ Mt 13.1-23 ☐ Lv 17-18 ☐ Pr 28
11 ☐ Mt 13.24-58 ☐ Lv 19 ☐ Pr 29
12 ☐ Mt 14.1-21 ☐ Lv 20-21 ☐ Pr 30

How to look up a Bible reference.

Every verse in this Bible is marked by its own *verse number*. To find any one of the passages listed in these reader's helps, you need to find the book, the chapter in the book, and the verse or verses within that chapter. The chapter number immediately follows the name of the book. This is followed by a period (.) which is followed by the number or range of numbers for the verses you seek. For example: 1 Corinthians 12.1-11 is the First Letter of Paul to the Corinthians, chapter twelve, verses one through eleven.

13 ☐ Mt 14.22-36 ☐ Lv 22-23 ☐ Pr 31
14 ☐ Mt 15.1-20 ☐ Lv 24-25 ☐ Ec 1.1-11
15 ☐ Mt 15.21-39 ☐ Lv 26-27 ☐ Ec 1.12-2.26
16 ☐ Mt 16 ☐ Nu 1-2 ☐ Ec 3.1-15
17 ☐ Mt 17 ☐ Nu 3-4 ☐ Ec 3.16-4.16
18 ☐ Mt 18.1-17 ☐ Nu 5-6 ☐ Ec 5
19 ☐ Mt 18.18-35 ☐ Nu 7-8 ☐ Ec 6
20 ☐ Mt 19.1-15 ☐ Nu 9-10 ☐ Ec 7
21 ☐ Mt 19.16-30 ☐ Nu 11-12 ☐ Ec 8
22 ☐ Mt 20.1-16 ☐ Nu 13-14 ☐ Ec 9.1-12
23 ☐ Mt 20.17-34 ☐ Nu 15-16 ☐ Ec 9.13-10.20
24 ☐ Mt 21.1-27 ☐ Nu 17-18 ☐ Ec 11.1-8
25 ☐ Mt 21.28-46 ☐ Nu 19-20 ☐ Ec 11.9-12.14
26 ☐ Mt 22.1-22 ☐ Nu 21 ☐ Sgs 1.1-2.7
27 ☐ Mt 22.23-46 ☐ Nu 22.1-40 ☐ Sgs 2.8-3.5
28 ☐ Mt 23.1-12 ☐ Nu 22.41-23.26 ☐ Sgs 3.6-5.1
29 ☐ Mt 23.13-39 ☐ Nu 23.27-24.25 ☐ Sgs 5.2-6.3
30 ☐ Mt 24.1-31 ☐ Nu 25-27 ☐ Sgs 6.4-8.4
31 ☐ Mt 24.32-51 ☐ Nu 28-29 ☐ Sgs 8.5-14

APRIL

1 ☐ Mt 25.1-30 ☐ Nu 30-31 ☐ Job 1
2 ☐ Mt 25.31-46 ☐ Nu 32-34 ☐ Job 2
3 ☐ Mt 26.1-25 ☐ Nu 35-36 ☐ Job 3
4 ☐ Mt 26.26-46 ☐ Dt 1-2 ☐ Job 4
5 ☐ Mt 26.47-75 ☐ Dt 3-4 ☐ Job 5
6 ☐ Mt 27.1-31 ☐ Dt 5-6 ☐ Job 6
7 ☐ Mt 27.32-66 ☐ Dt 7-8 ☐ Job 7
8 ☐ Mt 28 ☐ Dt 9-10 ☐ Job 8
9 ☐ Ac 1 ☐ Dt 11-12 ☐ Job 9
10 ☐ Ac 2.1-13 ☐ Dt 13-14 ☐ Job 10
11 ☐ Ac 2.14-47 ☐ Dt 15-16 ☐ Job 11
12 ☐ Ac 3 ☐ Dt 17-18 ☐ Job 12
13 ☐ Ac 4.1-22 ☐ Dt 19-20 ☐ Job 13
14 ☐ Ac 4.23-37 ☐ Dt 21-22 ☐ Job 14
15 ☐ Ac 5.1-16 ☐ Dt 23-24 ☐ Job 15
16 ☐ Ac 5.17-42 ☐ Dt 25-27 ☐ Job 16
17 ☐ Ac 6 ☐ Dt 28 ☐ Job 17
18 ☐ Ac 7.1-22 ☐ Dt 29-30 ☐ Job 18
19 ☐ Ac 7.23-8.1 ☐ Dt 31-32 ☐ Job 19
20 ☐ Ac 8.1-25 ☐ Dt 33-34 ☐ Job 20
21 ☐ Ac 8.26-40 ☐ Js 1-2 ☐ Job 21
22 ☐ Ac 9.1-25 ☐ Js 3.1-5.1 ☐ Job 22
23 ☐ Ac 9.26-43 ☐ Js 5.2-6.27 ☐ Job 23
24 ☐ Ac 10.1-33 ☐ Js 7-8 ☐ Job 24
25 ☐ Ac 10.34-48 ☐ Js 9-10 ☐ Job 25
26 ☐ Ac 11.1-18 ☐ Js 11-12 ☐ Job 26
27 ☐ Ac 11.19-30 ☐ Js 13-14 ☐ Job 27
28 ☐ Ac 12 ☐ Js 15-17 ☐ Job 28
29 ☐ Ac 13.1-25 ☐ Js 18-19 ☐ Job 29
30 ☐ Ac 13.26-52 ☐ Js 20-21 ☐ Job 30

MAY

1 ☐ Ac 14 ☐ Js 22 ☐ Job 31
2 ☐ Ac 15.1-21 ☐ Js 23-24 ☐ Job 32
3 ☐ Ac 15.22-41 ☐ Jg 1 ☐ Job 33
4 ☐ Ac 16.1-15 ☐ Jg 2-3 ☐ Job 34
5 ☐ Ac 16.16-40 ☐ Jg 4-5 ☐ Job 35

6 ☐ Ac 17.1-15 ☐ Jg 6 ☐ Job 36
7 ☐ Ac 17.16-34 ☐ Jg 7-8 ☐ Job 37
8 ☐ Ac 18 ☐ Jg 9 ☐ Job 38
9 ☐ Ac 19.1-20 ☐ Jg 10.1-11.33 ☐ Job 39
10 ☐ Ac 19.21-41 ☐ Jg 11.34-12.15 ☐ Job 40
11 ☐ Ac 20.1-16 ☐ Jg 13 ☐ Job 41
12 ☐ Ac 20.17-38 ☐ Jg 14-15 ☐ Job 42
13 ☐ Ac 21.1-36 ☐ Jg 16 ☐ Ps 42
14 ☐ Ac 21.37-22.29 ☐ Jg 17-18 ☐ Ps 43
15 ☐ Ac 22.30-23.22 ☐ Jg 19 ☐ Ps 44
16 ☐ Ac 23.23-24.9 ☐ Jg 20 ☐ Ps 45
17 ☐ Ac 24.10-27 ☐ Jg 21 ☐ Ps 46
18 ☐ Ac 25 ☐ Ru 1-2 ☐ Ps 47
19 ☐ Ac 26.1-18 ☐ Ru 3-4 ☐ Ps 48
20 ☐ Ac 26.19-32 ☐ 1 S 1.1-2.11 ☐ Ps 49
21 ☐ Ac 27.1-12 ☐ 1 S 2.12-36 ☐ Ps 50
22 ☐ Ac 27.13-44 ☐ 1 S 3 ☐ Ps 51
23 ☐ Ac 28.1-15 ☐ 1 S 4-5 ☐ Ps 52
24 ☐ Ac 28.16-31 ☐ 1 S 6-7 ☐ Ps 53
25 ☐ Ro 1.1-15 ☐ 1 S 8 ☐ Ps 54
26 ☐ Ro 1.16-32 ☐ 1 S 9.1-10.16 ☐ Ps 55
27 ☐ Ro 2.1-3.8 ☐ 1 S 10.17-11.15 ☐ Ps 56
28 ☐ Ro 3.9-31 ☐ 1 S 12 ☐ Ps 57
29 ☐ Ro 4 ☐ 1 S 13 ☐ Ps 58
30 ☐ Ro 5 ☐ 1 S 14 ☐ Ps 59
31 ☐ Ro 6 ☐ 1 S 15 ☐ Ps 60

JUNE

1 ☐ Ro 7 ☐ 1 S 16 ☐ Ps 61
2 ☐ Ro 8 ☐ 1 S 17.1-54 ☐ Ps 62
3 ☐ Ro 9.1-29 ☐ 1 S 17.55-18.30 ☐ Ps 63
4 ☐ Ro 9.30-10.21 ☐ 1 S 19 ☐ Ps 64
5 ☐ Ro 11.1-24 ☐ 1 S 20 ☐ Ps 65
6 ☐ Ro 11.25-36 ☐ 1 S 21-22 ☐ Ps 66
7 ☐ Ro 12 ☐ 1 S 23-24 ☐ Ps 67
8 ☐ Ro 13 ☐ 1 S 25 ☐ Ps 68
9 ☐ Ro 14 ☐ 1 S 26 ☐ Ps 69
10 ☐ Ro 15.1-13 ☐ 1 S 27-28 ☐ Ps 70
11 ☐ Ro 15.14-33 ☐ 1 S 29-31 ☐ Ps 71
12 ☐ Ro 16 ☐ 2 S 1 ☐ Ps 72
13 ☐ Mk 1.1-20 ☐ 2 S 2.1-3.1 ☐ Dn 1
14 ☐ Mk 1.21-45 ☐ 2 S 3.2-39 ☐ Dn 2.1-23
15 ☐ Mk 2 ☐ 2 S 4-5 ☐ Dn 2.24-49
16 ☐ Mk 3.1-19 ☐ 2 S 6 ☐ Dn 3
17 ☐ Mk 3.20-35 ☐ 2 S 7-8 ☐ Dn 4
18 ☐ Mk 4.1-20 ☐ 2 S 9-10 ☐ Dn 5
19 ☐ Mk 4.21-41 ☐ 2 S 11-12 ☐ Dn 6
20 ☐ Mk 5.1-20 ☐ 2 S 13 ☐ Dn 7
21 ☐ Mk 5.21-43 ☐ 2 S 14 ☐ Dn 8
22 ☐ Mk 6.1-29 ☐ 2 S 15 ☐ Dn 9
23 ☐ Mk 6.30-56 ☐ 2 S 16 ☐ Dn 10.1-11.2
24 ☐ Mk 7.1-13 ☐ 2 S 17 ☐ Dn 11.2-20
25 ☐ Mk 7.14-37 ☐ 2 S 18 ☐ Dn 11.21-45
26 ☐ Mk 8.1-21 ☐ 2 S 19 ☐ Dn 12
27 ☐ Mk 8.22-9.1 ☐ 2 S 20-21 ☐ Ho 1.1-2.1
28 ☐ Mk 9.2-50 ☐ 2 S 22 ☐ Ho 2.2-23
29 ☐ Mk 10.1-31 ☐ 2 S 23 ☐ Ho 3
30 ☐ Mk 10.32-52 ☐ 2 S 24 ☐ Ho 4.1-10

JULY

1 ☐ Mk 11.1-14 ☐ 1 K 1 ☐ Ho 4.11-5.3
2 ☐ Mk 11.15-33 ☐ 1 K 2 ☐ Ho 5.4-15
3 ☐ Mk 12.1-27 ☐ 1 K 3 ☐ Ho 6.1-7.2
4 ☐ Mk 12.28-44 ☐ 1 K 4-5 ☐ Ho 7.3-16
5 ☐ Mk 13.1-13 ☐ 1 K 6 ☐ Ho 8
6 ☐ Mk 13.14-37 ☐ 1 K 7 ☐ Ho 9.1-16
7 ☐ Mk 14.1-31 ☐ 1 K 8 ☐ Ho 9.17-10.15
8 ☐ Mk 14.32-72 ☐ 1 K 9 ☐ Ho 11.1-11
9 ☐ Mk 15.1-20 ☐ 1 K 10 ☐ Ho 11.12-12.14
10 ☐ Mk 15.21-47 ☐ 1 K 11 ☐ Ho 13
11 ☐ Mk 16 ☐ 1 K 12.1-31 ☐ Ho 14
12 ☐ 1 Co 1.1-17 ☐ 1 K 12.32-13.34 ☐ Jl 1
13 ☐ 1 Co 1.18-31 ☐ 1 K 14 ☐ Jl 2.1-11
14 ☐ 1 Co 2 ☐ 1 K 15.1-32 ☐ Jl 2.12-23
15 ☐ 1 Co 3 ☐ 1 K 15.33-16.34 ☐ Jl 3
16 ☐ 1 Co 4 ☐ 1 K 17 ☐ Am 1
17 ☐ 1 Co 5 ☐ 1 K 18 ☐ Am 2.1-3.2
18 ☐ 1 Co 6 ☐ 1 K 19 ☐ Am 3.3-4.3
19 ☐ 1 Co 7.1-24 ☐ 1 K 20 ☐ Am 4.4-13
20 ☐ 1 Co 7.25-40 ☐ 1 K 21 ☐ Am 5
21 ☐ 1 Co 8 ☐ 1 K 22 ☐ Am 6
22 ☐ 1 Co 9 ☐ 2 K 1-2 ☐ Am 7
23 ☐ 1 Co 10 ☐ 2 K 3 ☐ Am 8
24 ☐ 1 Co 11.1-16 ☐ 2 K 4 ☐ Am 9
25 ☐ 1 Co 11.17-34 ☐ 2 K 5 ☐ Ob
26 ☐ 1 Co 12 ☐ 2 K 6.1-7.2 ☐ Jon 1
27 ☐ 1 Co 13 ☐ 2 K 7.3-20 ☐ Jon 2
28 ☐ 1 Co 14.1-25 ☐ 2 K 8 ☐ Jon 3
29 ☐ 1 Co 14.26-40 ☐ 2 K 9 ☐ Jon 4
30 ☐ 1 Co 15.1-34 ☐ 2 K 10 ☐ Mic 1
31 ☐ 1 Co 15.35-58 ☐ 2 K 11 ☐ Mic 2

AUGUST

1 ☐ 1 Co 16 ☐ 2 K 12-13 ☐ Mic 3
2 ☐ 2 Co 1.1-2.4 ☐ 2 K 14 ☐ Mic 4.1-5.1
3 ☐ 2 Co 2.5-3.18 ☐ 2 K 15-16 ☐ Mic 5.2-15
4 ☐ 2 Co 4.1-5.10 ☐ 2 K 17 ☐ Mic 6
5 ☐ 2 Co 5.11-6.13 ☐ 2 K 18 ☐ Mic 7
6 ☐ 2 Co 6.14-7.16 ☐ 2 K 19 ☐ Nh 1
7 ☐ 2 Co 8 ☐ 2 K 20-21 ☐ Nh 2
8 ☐ 2 Co 9 ☐ 2 K 22.1-23.34 ☐ Nh 3
9 ☐ 2 Co 10 ☐ 2 K 23.35-24.20 ☐ Hb 1
10 ☐ 2 Co 11 ☐ 2 K 25 ☐ Hb 2
11 ☐ 2 Co 12 ☐ 1 Ch 1-2 ☐ Hb 3
12 ☐ 2 Co 13 ☐ 1 Ch 3-4 ☐ Zep 1
13 ☐ Jn 1.1-18 ☐ 1 Ch 5-6 ☐ Zep 2
14 ☐ Jn 1.19-34 ☐ 1 Ch 7-8 ☐ Zep 3
15 ☐ Jn 1.35-51 ☐ 1 Ch 9 ☐ Hg 1-2
16 ☐ Jn 2 ☐ 1 Ch 10-11 ☐ Zec 1
17 ☐ Jn 3.1-21 ☐ 1 Ch 12 ☐ Zec 2
18 ☐ Jn 3.22-36 ☐ 1 Ch 13-14 ☐ Zec 3
19 ☐ Jn 4.1-26 ☐ 1 Ch 15.1-16.7 ☐ Zec 4
20 ☐ Jn 4.27-42 ☐ 1 Ch 16.8-43 ☐ Zec 5
21 ☐ Jn 4.43-54 ☐ 1 Ch 17 ☐ Zec 6
22 ☐ Jn 5.1-18 ☐ 1 Ch 18-19 ☐ Zec 7
23 ☐ Jn 5.19-47 ☐ 1 Ch 20.1-22.1 ☐ Zec 8
24 ☐ Jn 6.1-24 ☐ 1 Ch 22.2-23.32 ☐ Zec 9
25 ☐ Jn 6.25-59 ☐ 1 Ch 24 ☐ Zec 10
26 ☐ Jn 6.60-71 ☐ 1 Ch 25-26 ☐ Zec 11

27 ☐ Jn 7.1-24 ☐ 1 Ch 27-28 ☐ Zec 12
28 ☐ Jn 7.25-52 ☐ 1 Ch 29 ☐ Zec 13
29 ☐ Jn 8.1-20 ☐ 2 Ch 1.1-2.16 ☐ Zec 14
30 ☐ Jn 8.21-47 ☐ 2 Ch 2.17-5.1 ☐ Ml 1.1-2.9
31 ☐ Jn 8.48-59 ☐ 2 Ch 5.2-14 ☐ Ml 2.10-16

SEPTEMBER

1 ☐ Jn 9.1-23 ☐ 2 Ch 6 ☐ Ml 2.17-3.18
2 ☐ Jn 9.24-41 ☐ 2 Ch 7 ☐ Ml 4
3 ☐ Jn 10.1-21 ☐ 2 Ch 8 ☐ Ps 73
4 ☐ Jn 10.22-42 ☐ 2 Ch 9 ☐ Ps 74
5 ☐ Jn 11.1-27 ☐ 2 Ch 10-11 ☐ Ps 75
6 ☐ Jn 11.28-57 ☐ 2 Ch 12-13 ☐ Ps 76
7 ☐ Jn 12.1-26 ☐ 2 Ch 14-15 ☐ Ps 77
8 ☐ Jn 12.27-50 ☐ 2 Ch 16-17 ☐ Ps 78.1-20
9 ☐ Jn 13.1-20 ☐ 2 Ch 18 ☐ Ps 78.21-37
10 ☐ Jn 13.21-38 ☐ 2 Ch 19 ☐ Ps 78.38-55
11 ☐ Jn 14.1-14 ☐ 2 Ch 20.1-21.1 ☐ Ps 78.56-72
12 ☐ Jn 14.15-31 ☐ 2 Ch 21.2-22.12 ☐ Ps 79
13 ☐ Jn 15.1-16.4 ☐ 2 Ch 23 ☐ Ps 80
14 ☐ Jn 16.4-33 ☐ 2 Ch 24 ☐ Ps 81
15 ☐ Jn 17 ☐ 2 Ch 25 ☐ Ps 82
16 ☐ Jn 18.1-18 ☐ 2 Ch 26 ☐ Ps 83
17 ☐ Jn 18.19-38 ☐ 2 Ch 27-28 ☐ Ps 84
18 ☐ Jn 18.38-19.16 ☐ 2 Ch 29 ☐ Ps 85
19 ☐ Jn 19.16-42 ☐ 2 Ch 30 ☐ Ps 86
20 ☐ Jn 20.1-18 ☐ 2 Ch 31 ☐ Ps 87
21 ☐ Jn 20.19-31 ☐ 2 Ch 32 ☐ Ps 88
22 ☐ Jn 21 ☐ 2 Ch 33 ☐ Ps 89.1-18
23 ☐ 1 Jn 1 ☐ 2 Ch 34 ☐ Ps 89.19-37
24 ☐ 1 Jn 2 ☐ 2 Ch 35 ☐ Ps 89.38-52
25 ☐ 1 Jn 3 ☐ 2 Ch 36 ☐ Ps 90
26 ☐ 1 Jn 4 ☐ Ezra 1-2 ☐ Ps 91
27 ☐ 1 Jn 5 ☐ Ezra 3-4 ☐ Ps 92
28 ☐ 2 Jn ☐ Ezra 5-6 ☐ Ps 93
29 ☐ 3 Jn ☐ Ezra 7-8 ☐ Ps 94
30 ☐ Jd ☐ Ezra 9-10 ☐ Ps 95

OCTOBER

1 ☐ Rev 1 ☐ Ne 1-2 ☐ Ps 96
2 ☐ Rev 2 ☐ Ne 3 ☐ Ps 97
3 ☐ Rev 3 ☐ Ne 4 ☐ Ps 98
4 ☐ Rev 4 ☐ Ne 5.1-7.3 ☐ Ps 99
5 ☐ Rev 5 ☐ Ne 7.4-8.12 ☐ Ps 100
6 ☐ Rev 6 ☐ Ne 8.13-9.37 ☐ Ps 101
7 ☐ Rev 7 ☐ Ne 9.38-10.39 ☐ Ps 102
8 ☐ Rev 8 ☐ Ne 11 ☐ Ps 103
9 ☐ Rev 9 ☐ Ne 12 ☐ Ps 104.1-23
10 ☐ Rev 10 ☐ Ne 13 ☐ Ps 104.24-35
11 ☐ Rev 11 ☐ Es 1 ☐ Ps 105.1-25
12 ☐ Rev 12 ☐ Es 2 ☐ Ps 105.26-45
13 ☐ Rev 13 ☐ Es 3-4 ☐ Ps 106.1-23
14 ☐ Rev 14 ☐ Es 5.1-6.13 ☐ Ps 106.24-48
15 ☐ Rev 15 ☐ Es 6.14-8.17 ☐ Ps 107.1-22
16 ☐ Rev 16 ☐ Es 9-10 ☐ Ps 107.23-43
17 ☐ Rev 17 ☐ Is 1-2 ☐ Ps 108
18 ☐ Rev 18 ☐ Is 3-4 ☐ Ps 109.1-19
19 ☐ Rev 19 ☐ Is 5-6 ☐ Ps 109.20-31
20 ☐ Rev 20 ☐ Is 7-8 ☐ Ps 110
21 ☐ Rev 21-22 ☐ Is 9-10 ☐ Ps 111

22 ☐ 1 Th 1 ☐ Is 11-13 ☐ Ps 112
23 ☐ 1 Th 2.1-16 ☐ Is 14-16 ☐ Ps 113
24 ☐ 1 Th 2.17-3.13 ☐ Is 17-19 ☐ Ps 114
25 ☐ 1 Th 4 ☐ Is 20-22 ☐ Ps 115
26 ☐ 1 Th 5 ☐ Is 23-24 ☐ Ps 116
27 ☐ 2 Th 1 ☐ Is 25-26 ☐ Ps 117
28 ☐ 2 Th 2 ☐ Is 27-28 ☐ Ps 118
29 ☐ 2 Th 3 ☐ Is 29-30 ☐ Ps 119.1-32
30 ☐ 1 Ti 1 ☐ Is 31-33 ☐ Ps 119.33-64
31 ☐ 1 Ti 2 ☐ Is 34-35 ☐ Ps 119.65-96

NOVEMBER

1 ☐ 1 Ti 3 ☐ Is 36-37 ☐ Ps 119.97-120
2 ☐ 1 Ti 4 ☐ Is 38-39 ☐ Ps 119.121-144
3 ☐ 1 Ti 5.1-20 ☐ Jr 1-2 ☐ Ps 119.145-176
4 ☐ 1 Ti 5.21-6.21 ☐ Jr 3-4 ☐ Ps 120
5 ☐ 2 Ti 1 ☐ Jr 5-6 ☐ Ps 121
6 ☐ 2 Ti 2 ☐ Jr 7-8 ☐ Ps 122
7 ☐ 2 Ti 3 ☐ Jr 9-10 ☐ Ps 123
8 ☐ 2 Ti 4 ☐ Jr 11-12 ☐ Ps 124
9 ☐ Titus 1 ☐ Jr 13-14 ☐ Ps 125
10 ☐ Titus 2 ☐ Jr 15-16 ☐ Ps 126
11 ☐ Titus 3 ☐ Jr 17-18 ☐ Ps 127
12 ☐ Phm ☐ Jr 19-20 ☐ Ps 128
13 ☐ Jas 1 ☐ Jr 21-22 ☐ Ps 129
14 ☐ Jas 2 ☐ Jr 23-24 ☐ Ps 130
15 ☐ Jas 3 ☐ Jr 25-26 ☐ Ps 131
16 ☐ Jas 4 ☐ Jr 27-28 ☐ Ps 132
17 ☐ Jas 5 ☐ Jr 29-30 ☐ Ps 133
18 ☐ 1 Pet 1 ☐ Jr 31-32 ☐ Ps 134
19 ☐ 1 Pet 2 ☐ Jr 33-34 ☐ Ps 135
20 ☐ 1 Pet 3 ☐ Jr 35-36 ☐ Ps 136
21 ☐ 1 Pet 4 ☐ Jr 37-38 ☐ Ps 137
22 ☐ 1 Pet 5 ☐ Jr 39-40 ☐ Ps 138
23 ☐ 2 Pet 1 ☐ Jr 41-42 ☐ Ps 139
24 ☐ 2 Pet 2 ☐ Jr 43-44 ☐ Ps 140
25 ☐ 2 Pet 3 ☐ Jr 45-46 ☐ Ps 141
26 ☐ Ga 1 ☐ Jr 47-48 ☐ Ps 142

27 ☐ Ga 2 ☐ Jr 49-50 ☐ Ps 143
28 ☐ Ga 3.1-20 ☐ Jr 51-52 ☐ Ps 144
29 ☐ Ga 3.21-4.20 ☐ Lm 1-2 ☐ Ps 145
30 ☐ Ga 4.21-31 ☐ Lm 3-4 ☐ Ps 146

DECEMBER

1 ☐ Ga 5.1-15 ☐ Lm 5 ☐ Ps 147
2 ☐ Ga 5.16-26 ☐ Ez 1 ☐ Ps 148
3 ☐ Ga 6 ☐ Ez 2-3 ☐ Ps 149
4 ☐ Eph 1 ☐ Ez 4-5 ☐ Ps 150
5 ☐ Eph 2 ☐ Ez 6-7 ☐ Is 40
6 ☐ Eph 3 ☐ Ez 8-9 ☐ Is 41
7 ☐ Eph 4.1-16 ☐ Ez 10-11 ☐ Is 42
8 ☐ Eph 4.17-32 ☐ Ez 12-13 ☐ Is 43
9 ☐ Eph 5.1-20 ☐ Ez 14-15 ☐ Is 44
10 ☐ Eph 5.21-33 ☐ Ez 16 ☐ Is 45
11 ☐ Eph 6 ☐ Ez 17 ☐ Is 46
12 ☐ Phil 1.1-11 ☐ Ez 18 ☐ Is 47
13 ☐ Phil 1.12-30 ☐ Ez 19 ☐ Is 48
14 ☐ Phil 2.1-11 ☐ Ez 20 ☐ Is 49
15 ☐ Phil 2.12-30 ☐ Ez 21-22 ☐ Is 50
16 ☐ Phil 3 ☐ Ez 23 ☐ Is 51
17 ☐ Phil 4 ☐ Ez 24 ☐ Is 52
18 ☐ Col 1.1-23 ☐ Ez 25-26 ☐ Is 53
19 ☐ Col 1.24-2.19 ☐ Ez 27-28 ☐ Is 54
20 ☐ Col 2.20-3.17 ☐ Ez 29-30 ☐ Is 55
21 ☐ Col 3.18-4.18 ☐ Ez 31-32 ☐ Is 56
22 ☐ Lk 1.1-25 ☐ Ez 33 ☐ Is 57
23 ☐ Lk 1.26-56 ☐ Ez 34 ☐ Is 58
24 ☐ Lk 1.57-80 ☐ Ez 35-36 ☐ Is 59
25 ☐ Lk 2.1-20 ☐ Ez 37 ☐ Is 60
26 ☐ Lk 2.21-52 ☐ Ez 38-39 ☐ Is 61
27 ☐ Lk 3.1-20 ☐ Ez 40-41 ☐ Is 62
28 ☐ Lk 3.21-38 ☐ Ez 42-43 ☐ Is 63
29 ☐ Lk 4.1-30 ☐ Ez 44-45 ☐ Is 64
30 ☐ Lk 4.31-44 ☐ Ez 46-47 ☐ Is 65
31 ☐ Lk 5.1-26 ☐ Ez 48 ☐ Is 66

How to look up a Bible reference.

Every verse in this Bible is marked by its own *verse number*. To find any one of the passages listed in these reader's helps, you need to find the book, the chapter in the book, and the verse or verses within that chapter. The chapter number immediately follows the name of the book. This is followed by a period (.) which is followed by the number or range of numbers for the verses you seek. For example: 1 Corinthians 12.1-11 is the First Letter of Paul to the Corinthians, chapter twelve, verses one through eleven.

Some Readings for Special Days

New Year's Day
Colossians 3.5-17
Epiphany
Matthew 2.1-12
Martin Luther King, Jr. Day
Exodus 3.1-22
Christian Unity Sunday
John 17
Valentine's Day
1 Corinthians 13; 1 John 4.7-21
Presidents' Day
Isaiah 32.1-8
Ash Wednesday
Psalm 51; Joel 2.12-19;
Matthew 6.1-6; James 1.12-18
St. Patrick's Day
Isaiah 52.7-12
Palm Sunday
Mark 11.1-11; John 12.12-19;
Philippians 2.5-11
Holy (Maundy) Thursday
Matthew 26.26-30;
John 13.1-35; Psalm 116
Good Friday
John 18.1 – 19.42; Psalm 22;
Isaiah 52.13-53.12
Easter
Matthew 28; Luke 24; John 20;
Acts 10.34-43; Psalm 33
Passover
Exodus 12
Mother's Day
1 Samuel 1.1-28; Proverbs 23.22-25;
Proverbs 31.10-31; Luke 1.26-56
Memorial Day
Isaiah 26.1-19
Pentecost
Acts 2.1-11
Father's Day
Proverbs 4; Proverbs 20.7; Luke 15.11-32

Independence Day
Psalm 33
Labor Day
Genesis 1.26 – 2.4
Yom Kippur
Jeremiah 31.31-34
Grandparent's Day
Psalm 128
World Communion Sunday
1 Corinthians 11.23-34
All Saints Day
Hebrews 11
Stewardship Day
Matthew 25.14-29; 2 Corinthians 9.1-15
Election Day
1 Peter 2.13-17
Veterans Day
Isaiah 2.1-5
Bible Sunday
2 Timothy 3.10-17
Thanksgiving
Deuteronomy 8.1-10; Psalms 65; 67
First Sunday in Advent
Isaiah 63.15 – 64.12; Matthew 24.36-44;
Luke 21.25-36; Psalm 25
Second Sunday in Advent
Malachi 3.1-5; Matthew 3.1-12; Psalm 85
Third Sunday in Advent
Isaiah 12.1-6; Matthew 11.2-19;
Luke 3.7-18; Philippians 4.4-9
Fourth Sunday in Advent
Isaiah 7.10-17; Micah 5.2-5; Luke 1.26-56;
Psalm 89.1-18
Christmas
Luke 2.1-20; Matthew 1.18-25;
John 1.1-18; Titus 3.4-7
Personal Birthday
Psalm 145

Famous Passages of the Bible

Stories from the Old Testament

EARLY BEGINNINGS

Creation and Sin
Genesis 2.4-3.24
The First Murder
Genesis 4.1-15
Noah and the Flood
Genesis 6.1-9.17

The Tower of Babylon (Babel)
Genesis 11.1-9
The Call of Abraham
Genesis 12.1-9
**The Destruction of Sodom
and Gomorrah**
Genesis 19.1-28

PEOPLE OF GREAT FAITH IN THE OLD TESTAMENT

Stories from the New Testament

THE LIFE OF JESUS

JESUS' DEATH AND RESURRECTION

MIRACLES AND HEALINGS OF JESUS

Jesus Turns Water into Wine
John 2.1-11
Jesus Feeds Many People
Matthew 14.13-21; Mark 6.30-44;
Luke 9.10-17; John 6.1-15;
Matthew 15.32-39; Mark 8.1-10
Jesus Calms a Storm
Matthew 8.23-27;
Mark 4.35-41; Luke 8.22-25
The Great Catch of Fish
Luke 5.1-11
Jesus Walks on Water
Matthew 14.22-33;
Mark 6.45-52; John 6.16-21
Jesus Heals People with
Skin Diseases
Matthew 8.1-4; Mark 1.40-45;
Luke 5.12-16; Luke 17.11-19
Jesus Casts Out Demons
Matthew 8.28-34;
Mark 5.1-20; Luke 8.26-39;
Matthew 12.22-37;
Mark 3.20-30; Luke 11.14-23;
Matthew 17.14-21;
Mark 9.14-29; Luke 9.37-43;
Mark 1.21-28; Luke 4.31-37
Jesus Heals the Blind
Matthew 9.27-31; Matthew 20.29-34;
Mark 10.46-52; Luke 18.35-43
Jesus Heals a Deaf Man
Mark 7.31-37
Jesus Heals the Paralyzed and Crippled
Matthew 12.9-14; Mark 3.1-6;
Luke 6.6-11; John 5.1-9;
Luke 14.1-6; Matthew 9.1-8;
Mark 2.1-12; Luke 5.17-26
Jesus Heals Many Women
Matthew 9.18-26;
Mark 5.21-43; Luke 8.1-3;
Luke 8.40-56; Luke 13.10-17;
Matthew 15.21-28; Mark 7.24-30
Jesus Heals the Centurion's Servant
Matthew 8.5-13; Luke 7.1-10
Jesus Heals Peter's Mother-in-law
Matthew 8.14, 15; Mark 1.29-31;
Luke 4.38, 39
Jesus Heals an Official's Son
John 4.46-54
Jesus Revives an Official's Daughter
Matthew 9.18,19,23-26;
Mark 5.21-24,35-42;
Luke 8.40-42,49-56

Jesus Raises the Dead
Luke 7.11-17; John 11.1-44

THE TEACHINGS AND PARABLES OF JESUS

The Sermon on the Mount
Matthew 5-7; Luke 6.20-49
The Beatitudes
Matthew 5.3-11; Luke 6.20-26
The Great Commandment
Matthew 22.37-39; Mark 12.29-31;
Luke 10.27
The Golden Rule
Matthew 7.12; Luke 6.31
The Grain of Mustard Seed
Matthew 13.31, 32; Mark 4.30-32;
Luke 13.18, 19
The Parable of the Sower
Matthew 13.1-23; Mark 4.1-20
The Parable of the Growing Seed
Mark 4.26-29
Some Parables About the
Kingdom of Heaven
Matthew 13.24-52
The Parable of the Unforgiving Servant
Matthew 18.23-35
The Parable of the Workers
in the Vineyard
Matthew 20.1-16
The Parable of the Tenants
in the Vineyard
Matthew 21.33-46; Mark 12.1-11;
Luke 20.9-18
The Parable of the Wedding Feast
Matthew 22.1-14; Luke 14.15-24
The Parable of the Ten Young
Women (Virgins)
Matthew 25.1-13
The Parable of the Three
Servants and Their Coins
Matthew 25.14-30; Luke 19.11-27
The Parable of the Sheep
and the Goats
Matthew 25.31-46

What is a parable?

Parables are stories that use typical, everyday situations in order to teach important truths. Jesus used many parables to teach his followers about the Kingdom of God.